GERMANY AND THE SECOND WORLD WAR

IV

The Attack on the Soviet Union

Germany
and the
Second World War

Edited by the
Militärgeschichtliches
Forschungsamt (Research
Institute for Military History),
Potsdam, Germany

VOLUME IV
The Attack
on the Soviet Union

HORST BOOG
JÜRGEN FÖRSTER
JOACHIM HOFFMANN
ERNST KLINK
ROLF-DIETER MÜLLER
GERD R. UEBERSCHÄR

Translated by
DEAN S. McMURRY
EWALD OSERS
LOUISE WILLMOT

Translation editor
EWALD OSERS

CLARENDON PRESS · OXFORD
1998

Oxford University Press, Walton Street, Oxford OX2 6DP

Oxford New York
Athens Auckland Bangkok Bombay
Calcutta Cape Town Dar es Salaam Delhi
Florence Hong Kong Istanbul Karachi
Kuala Lumpur Madras Madrid Melbourne
Mexico City Nairobi Paris Singapore
Taipei Tokyo Toronto
and associated companies in
Berlin Ibadan

Oxford is a trade mark of Oxford University Press

Published in the United States
by Oxford University Press Inc., New York

British Library Cataloguing in Publication Data
Data available

Library of Congress Cataloging in Publication Data
Data applied for

ISBN 0–19–822886–4

1 3 5 7 9 10 8 6 4 2

Typeset by Best-set Typesetter Ltd., Hong Kong
Printed in Great Britain
on acid-free paper by
Bookcraft Ltd., Midsomer Norton,
Nr. Bath, Avon

Contents

LIST OF ILLUSTRATIONS   xiii

LIST OF TABLES   xv

NOTES ON THE AUTHORS   xvii

NOTE ON THE TRANSLATION   xix

ABBREVIATIONS   xx

GLOSSARY OF FOREIGN TERMS   xxxii

INTRODUCTION   I

PART I

German War Policy and the Soviet Union 1940–1941

I. HITLER'S DECISION IN FAVOUR OF WAR AGAINST
   THE SOVIET UNION
   BY JÜRGEN FÖRSTER   13

   1. The Situation after the War in the West   13

   2. The Turn to the East: Hitler's Decision of 31 July 1940 and
      its Consequences   25

   3. Programmatic Objectives *vis-à-vis* the Soviet Union and their
      Acceptance among the German Officer Corps   30

   4. Euro-Asian Continental Bloc and Maritime Strategy: Alternatives
      to the Turn to the East?   38

   5. German–Soviet Relations from Molotov's Visit to the Beginning
      of the War   42

II. THE SOVIET UNION UP TO THE EVE OF
    THE GERMAN ATTACK
    BY JOACHIM HOFFMANN   52

   1. Origin and Development of the Red Army   52

   2. The Red Army until the Beginning of the German–Soviet War 72

   3. Soviet Aid to Germany   94

III. FROM ECONOMIC ALLIANCE TO A WAR OF
     COLONIAL EXPLOITATION
     BY ROLF-DIETER MÜLLER   118

   1. War-economy Aspects and Consequences of the Alliance with
      the Soviet Union 1939–1940   118

(*a*) German–Soviet Trade Exchange and Hitler's War Policy up to the Summer of 1940   120

(*b*) The Concept of Large-space Economy and the Russian Problem   128

2. Economic Preparations for the War against the Soviet Union   136

(*a*) Economic Aspects of the Operational Plan   136

(*b*) First Preparatory Steps by the War Economy and Armaments Department   142

(*c*) The Thomas Memorandum and its Consequences   150

(*d*) The Establishment of the Economic Organization East   154

(*e*) The Involvement of Private Enterprise   161

(*f*) Economic Objectives of the Campaign   170

3. Economic Framework for Military Planning   187

(*a*) The German War Economy until the Spring of 1941   187

(*b*) Intensification of German–Soviet Trade   191

4. The Equipment of the Eastern Army   199

IV. THE MILITARY CONCEPT OF THE WAR AGAINST THE SOVIET UNION   225

1. Land Warfare
BY ERNST KLINK   225

(*a*) The Red Army in the Judgement of the Army High Command after September 1939   226

(*b*) Early Phases in Planning within the Army High Commmand up to July 1940   240

(*c*) Army Group B as 'Security against the East'   255

(*d*) The Operational Studies by Marcks and Loßberg   257

(*e*) Planning by the Army General Staff and Directive No. 21   275

(*f*) The Deployment Directive for the Army   285

(*g*) The Preparations of the Quartermaster-General   292

(*h*) The Structure of the Army in the East and Deployment   305

(*i*) The Assessment of the Red Army before the Attack   320

2. The German Air Force
BY HORST BOOG   326

(*a*) The Luftwaffe between the Battle of Britain and Barbarossa   326

(*b*) Assessment of the Soviet Air Forces 1939–1941   336

(*c*) Preparations for Deployment   353

3. The German Navy
BY ERNST KLINK   376

V. GERMANY'S ACQUISITION OF ALLIES IN SOUTH-EAST EUROPE
BY JÜRGEN FÖRSTER   386

1. Romania in the Political and Economic Field of Force of the Great Powers   386

2. The Vienna Arbitration Award of August 1940 and the Dispatch of a German Military Mission   393

3. Military Aspects of Romania's Inclusion in the Barbarossa Plan   398

4. The Position of Hungary and Slovakia in the Preparatory Phase of Barbarossa   409

   (*a*) Hungary   409

   (*b*) Slovakia   424

VI. THE INVOLVEMENT OF SCANDINAVIA IN THE PLANS FOR BARBAROSSA

BY GERD R. UEBERSCHÄR   429

1. Finland's Place in Hitler's Calculations at the Time of the Resumption of his 'Eastern Programme' in the Summer of 1940   429

2. Finland as a Political and Economic Sphere of Interest between Stalin and Hitler   436

3. Military Aspects of Finland's Inclusion in the Plans for Barbarossa   443

4. German–Finnish Arrangements and Measures for Finland's Participation in the War against the Soviet Union   455

5. Sweden's Position during the Preparatory Phase of the War against the Soviet Union   471

VII. OPERATION BARBAROSSA AS A WAR OF CONQUEST AND ANNIHILATION

BY JÜRGEN FÖRSTER   481

1. Plans and Preparations for Securing 'Living-space'   481

2. Hitler's Ideological Intentions Translated into Orders   491

   (*a*) The Regulation of SS Activity in the Operations Area of the Army   491

   (*b*) The Limitation of Military Jurisdiction   496

   (*c*) The 'Commissar Order'   507

3. Propaganda Preparations for the War of Annihilation and the Attitude of the Military Leaders   513

PART II

The War against the Soviet Union until the Turn of 1941/1942

I. THE CONDUCT OF OPERATIONS   525

1. The Army and Navy

BY ERNST KLINK   525

   (*a*) The Opening of the Campaign   525

     (i) The offensive of Army Group Centre until the capture of the 'land-bridge' between Vitebsk and Smolensk   525

     (ii) The offensive of Army Group North   537

(iii) The battles at the frontier in the sector of Army Group
South and the German advance into the Ukraine 546
(b) Disputes about the Further Conduct of Operations 569
  (i) The question of the deployment of forces for the second
phase of the campaign 569
  (ii) Vacillation in the directives for the conduct of the war
from 19 July until the end of the month 572
  (iii) The assessment of the enemy at the beginning of August 581
  (iv) Hitler's acceptance of the need to eliminate Moscow 588
(c) The Battle of the Ukraine and the Crimea 594
  (i) The advance to the Crimea 611
  (ii) The advance to the Don 613
  (iii) The conquest of the Crimea 627
(d) The Attack on Leningrad 631
(e) The Actions of German Naval Forces in the Baltic until the
End of 1941 654
(f) The Attack on Moscow 664
  (i) The double battle of Bryansk and Vyazma 672
  (ii) Plans for the resumption of the offensive 684
  (iii) The failure of the second offensive 693
(g) The Repulse of the Winter Offensive of the Red Army 702
  (i) Assessment of the situation and directives for the
winter war 702
  (ii) The crises in Army Group Centre and their effects on the
command of the army 707
  (iii) The fighting retreat of Army Group Centre until the
stabilization of the front 725
  (iv) Winter fighting in the area of Army Group North until the
re-establishment of a solid front 734
  (v) The defensive battles of Army Group South 751

2. The Luftwaffe
BY HORST BOOG 763

(a) The Surprise Attack against the Soviet Air Force 763
(b) Ground Support 768
  (i) II and VIII Air Corps and the battles of encirclement of
encirclement of Białystok and Minsk 768
  (ii) The battle of encirclement at Smolensk 770
  (iii) II Air Corps in the area of Gomel, Bryansk, and Roslavl 773
  (iv) The use of the anti-aircraft units 774
  (v) The conduct of the air war in the Baltic until the
beginning of August 775
  (vi) The thrust towards Leningrad 776
  (vii) V Air Corps support for Armoured Group 1 and
Sixth Army to the Stalin line 778
  (viii) The breakthrough of the Stalin line 778
  (ix) IV Air Corps on the right wing of Army Group South 779
  (x) The Luftwaffe in the battle of encirclement at Uman 780

(xi) The repulse of the Soviet thrust at Boguslav and
      Kanev   781
(xii) Mopping-up operations in the southern Dnieper bend   781
(xiii) Anti-aircraft units in the south   783
(xiv) The battle of encirclement at Kiev (28 August–
      26 September)   783
(xv) Support for the advance of Seventeenth and Sixth
      Armies by V Air Corps   785
(xvi) IV Air Corps and the conquest of the Crimea   786
(xvii) The setback at Rostov   787
(xviii) The Luftwaffe on the Volkhov and at Tikhvin   789
(xix) Air Fleet 2 and preparations for the attack on Moscow   790
(xx) The double battle of Bryansk and Vyazma   793
(xxi) The crisis west of Moscow   794

(c) The Air War at Sea   799
(d) Attempts at an Independent Strategic Air War against the
      Sources of Soviet Strength   802
(e) The Situation of the Luftwaffe at the Turn of 1941–1942   814

II. THE CONDUCT OF THE WAR THROUGH
SOVIET EYES
BY JOACHIM HOFFMANN   833

  1. The Beginning of the War   833
  2. The Reorganization of the Supreme Command   836
  3. The 'Fatherland War': Fight against Disintegration. Mobilization
      of Material and Manpower Reserves   840
  4. The Struggle for Leningrad   858
  5. The Battle of Smolensk   865
  6. The Fighting for the Ukraine   870
  7. The Partisan War   876
  8. The Repulse of the German Autumn Offensive at Leningrad
      and Rostov   882
  9. The Repulse of the German Attack on Moscow   885
  10. The Red Army's Counter-offensive at Moscow, December 1941   896
  11. The Red Army's Counter-attacks at Leningrad and in the Crimea 903
  12. Methods of a War of Annihilation   906
  13. The Red Army's General Offensive in the Winter of 1942   919
  14. The Establishment of the Anti-Hitler Coalition   928

III. STRATEGY AND POLICY IN NORTHERN EUROPE
BY GERD R. UEBERSCHÄR   941

  1. German Operations in the 'Finland Theatre'   941
      (a) Operation Platinum Fox ('Platinfuchs') against Murmansk   941
      (b) Operation Arctic Fox ('Polarfuchs') against the
          Murmansk Railway   945

    (c) Problems of German Naval and Air Operations in the Far
        North   953
    (d) Balance Sheet of Military Operations in Northern Finland to
        1941–1942   960
    (e) New Strategic Deliberations after the Turn of 1941–1942   966

  2. Finnish Army Operations   972
    (a) Recovery of the Former Finnish Territories in Ladoga–Karelia
        and on the Karelian Isthmus   972
    (b) Conquest of East Karelia and Advance to the River Svir   976
    (c) Military Result of Operations in Southern Finland and the
        Problem of Joint Military Planning   980

  3. Political Balance Sheet of German–Finnish 'Brotherhood-in-arms'
    to the Winter of 1941–1942   983

  4. The Attitude of Sweden Following the German Invasion of the
    Soviet Union   993

  5. The Reaction of Occupied Denmark and Norway to Hitler's
    Attack on the Soviet Union   1003

IV. THE DECISIONS OF THE TRIPARTITE PACT STATES
    BY JÜRGEN FÖRSTER   1021
  1. The Committed Allies   1021
    (a) Romania   1021
    (b) Hungary   1028
    (c) Slovakia   1034
    (d) Italy   1037
  2. The Reluctant Allies   1041
    (a) Bulgaria   1041
    (b) Japan   1043

V. VOLUNTEERS FOR THE 'EUROPEAN CRUSADE
  AGAINST BOLSHEVISM'   1049
  1. The 'Crusade' Aspect
    BY JÜRGEN FÖRSTER   1049
  2. Volunteers from Western and Southern Europe
    BY JÜRGEN FÖRSTER   1053
  3. Volunteers from Northern Europe at the Beginning of the War
    against the Soviet Union
    BY GERD R. UEBERSCHÄR   1070

VI. THE FAILURE OF THE ECONOMIC 'BLITZKRIEG
  STRATEGY'
    BY ROLF-DIETER MÜLLER   1081
  1. Economic Policy in Anticipation of Victory   1081
  2. First Modifications   1096
  3. The Supply of the Army in the East until the Failure
    before Moscow   1107

(*a*) Army Group North   1114
(*b*) Army Group South   1117
(*c*) Army Group Centre   1124

4. The Food-supply Issue: Starvation Strategy or Pragmatism   1141
(*a*) Self-supply by the Wehrmacht   1150
(*b*) Selective Starvation Policy against the Soviet Civilian Population   1157
(*c*) Mass Deaths among Soviet Prisoners of War   1172

5. Economic Causes and Consequences of the Failed Blitzkrieg   1180

VII. SECURING 'LIVING-SPACE'
BY JÜRGEN FÖRSTER   1189
1. Pacification of the Conquered Territories   1189
2. Implementation of the 'Commissar Order'   1225
3. The Organization of 'Living-space'   1235

OPERATION BARBAROSSA IN HISTORICAL PERSPECTIVE
BY JÜRGEN FÖRSTER   1245

BIBLIOGRAPHY   1256
I. Unpublished Sources   1256
II. Service Regulations   1294
III. Published Sources   1296

INDEX OF PERSONS   1353

List of Illustrations

DIAGRAMS

I.III.1. Structure of Economic Staff East in 1941   158

I.III.2. Structure of Economic Organization East (Plan)   159

I.III.3. The Material Equipment of the German Army in the East (incl. Army HQ Norway), 22 June 1941   222–3

I.IV.1. Order of Battle of Eighteenth Army on 22 July 1941   246

I.IV.2. Order of Battle of Army Group B, End of September 1940   258

I.IV.3. Structure of the Quartermaster-general's Department, as on 1 October 1940   295

I.IV.4. Structure of the Department for War Administration, as on 1 May 1941   296

I.IV.5. Luftwaffe Chain of Command in the East, 22 June 1941   363

I.VI.1. German–Finnish Deployment and Disposition of Soviet Forces from North to South, 30 June 1941   465

II.I.1. Order of Battle of Army Group Centre, 1 July 1941   528

II.I.2. Order of Battle of Army Group Centre, 4 July 1941   529

II.I.3. Order of Battle of Army Group South, 27 June 1941   550

II.I.4. Order of Battle of Army Group South, 4 July 1941   551

II.I.5. Order of Battle of Army Group South, 12 July 1941   552–3

II.I.6. Order of Battle of Army Group South, 19 July 1941   554–5

II.I.7. Order of Battle of Army Group Centre, 2 October 1941   668–9

II.I.8. Luftwaffe Operations in the East in 1941   806–8

II.I.9. Command Structure between Luftwaffe and Army in the East at the Beginning of January 1942   820

II.III.1. Total Supply Transports to Norway and Finland April 1941–February 1942   961

II.III.2. Disposition of Forces in Finland (North to South) as of January–February 1942   971

II.VI.1. The Ramifications of Economic Organization East from the Start of the Campaign to the End of 1941   1102

II.VI.2. Effective Strength and Losses of Armoured Fighting Vehicles and Assault-guns, 22 June 1941–31 January 1942   1129

II.VII.1. Structure of the Occupied Territories   1192

MAPS

Europe at the End of November 1940   *front endpaper*

I.III.1. The Planned Boundaries of the Economic Inspectorates   162

I.III.2. Grain Distribution within the Soviet Union (1939)   178

I.IV.1. Disposition and Stationing Areas of Eighteenth Army on
        22 July 1940 and Grouping of Red Army Forces Assumed
        by Army High Command (Excluding Frontier Guard Units)   248

I.IV.2. Operations Draft East (Major-General Marcks), 5 August
        1940   261

I.IV.3. Deployment Directive Barbarossa   289

I.IV.4. Tactical Depth of Penetration by German and Soviet
        Bombers   373

I.IV.5. Initial Position of Naval Operations in the Baltic, 22 June
        1941   384

I.VI.1. German–Finnish Operations Plan (1940–1941) for the Attack
        on the Soviet Union   451

I.VII.1. Rosenberg's Plan for a Civilian Administration in the East,
         May 1941   490

II.I.1. The Situation on the Southern Wing of Army Group South,
        30 November–3 December 1941   623

Europe at the Beginning of December 1941   *back endpaper*

List of Tables

I.II.1. Specifications of German and Soviet Tanks 79

I.III.1. Germany's Trade with the USSR during the First Ten Months of the War 127

I.III.2. Armaments Production by the Great Powers, 1940–1941 217

I.III.3. Armaments Programme B: Production of Weapons, Equipment, and Ammunition for the Army from 1 September 1940 to 31 March 1941 218–9

I.III.4. Armoured Fighting Vehicles 219

I.III.5. Equipment of Divisions with Motor Transport 220

I.IV.1. Ammunition Stockpiled in Supply Districts, 17 February 1941 298

I.IV.2. Stockpiles of Ammunition, 21–25 June 1941 298

I.IV.3. Forces Deployed in the Western Soviet Union up to 20 June 1941 325

I.IV.4. Specifications and Performance of the Principal Aircraft of the Soviet Air Forces, Summer 1941 346–7

I.IV.5. Effective Strength and Combat-readiness of Flying Formations (incl. Replacements) of the Luftwaffe in the East on the Eve of Barbarossa (21 June 1941) 364

I.IV.6. Order of Battle of the Air Fleets Deployed against the Soviet Union on the Eve of Barbarossa 368–70

I.IV.7. Specifications and Performance of the Principal Aircraft Models Employed by the Luftwaffe in the East, Summer 1941 374–5

I.IV.8. Disposition of Anti-aircraft Forces 376

II.I.1. German Estimate of Maximum Potential Soviet Strength, Autumn 1941 587

II.I.2. Order of Battle of the Flying Units of Air Fleets 1, 2, and 4 Employed against the Soviet Union, 3 August 1941 772–3

II.I.3. Order of Battle of the Flying Units of Air Fleets 1, 2, and 4 Employed against the Soviet Union, 10 October 1941 791–2

II.I.4. Order of Battle of the Flying Units in the East (Excluding Air Fleet 5 and Air Transport Units), 20 December 1941 796–7

II.VI.1. Armoured Fighting Vehicles and Assault-guns on the Eastern Front between 22 June 1941 and 31 January 1942 1120–2

II.vi.2. Deliveries of Agricultural Produce 1 September 1941–31 August 1942, as of 31 May 1942   1152

II.vi.3. German Armaments Production before and during the Russian Campaign   1181

II.vi.4. Performance of Economic Staff East over its first Twelve Months   1185

Notes on the Authors

Dr HORST BOOG (b. 1928). Publications: *Verteidigung im Bündnis: Planung. Aufbau und Bewährung der Bundeswehr 1950–1972* (co-author) (Munich, 1975); 'Das Offizierkorps der Luftwaffe 1935–1945', in *Das deutsche Offizierkorps 1860–1960* (Boppard a.Rh. 1980; published jointly with MGFA by Hanns Hubert Hofmann), 269–325; *Die deutsche Luftwaffenführung 1935–1945: Führungsprobleme, Spitzengliederung, Generalstabsausbildung* (Stuttgart, 1982); 'Die Anti-Hitler-Koalition', in *Der globale Krieg: Die Ausweitung zum Weltkrieg und der Wechsel der Initiative 1941–1943* (Stuttgart, 1990) = *Das Deutsche Reich und der Zweite Weltkrieg*, vi. 3–94; editor of *The Conduct of the Air War in the Second World War: An International Comparison* (Oxford, 1992; German edn. Herford and Bonn, 1993). Author of numerous articles in German and foreign specialized journals on the history of the Luftwaffe, the air war, air-force tactics and technology, and secret intelligence services, as well as on twentieth-century diplomatic history.

Dr JÜRGEN FÖRSTER (b. 1940). Publications: *Stalingrad, Risse im Bündnis 1942/43* (Freiburg, 1975); 'The German Army and the Ideological War against the Soviet Union' (co-author), in *The Policies of Genocide*, ed. Gerhard Hirschfeld (London, 1986), 15–29; 'The Dynamics of Volksgemeinschaft: The Effectiveness of the German Military Establishment in the Second World War', in *Military Effectiveness*, ed. Allan Reid Millett and Williamson Murray, vol. iii. *The Second World War* (Boston, London, and Sydney, 1988), 180–220; editor of *Stalingrad: Ereignis, Wirkung, Symbol* (Munich, 1993); 'Zum Rußlandbild der Militärs 1941–1945', in *Das Rußlandbild im Dritten Reich*, ed. Hans-Erich Volkmann (Cologne, 1994), 141–84; 'Hitler Turns to the East', in *Two Roads to Moscow*, ed. Bernd Wegner (Oxford, 1995); 'Germany', in *Companion to the Second World War*, ed. Ian C. B. Dear (Oxford, 1995). Other publications on Second World War problems.

Dr JOACHIM HOFFMANN (b. 1930). Publications: 'Der Volkskrieg in Frankreich in der Sicht von Karl Marx und Friedrich Engels', in *Entscheidung 1870: Der deutsch-französische Krieg* (Stuttgart, 1970), 204–55; *Deutsche und Kalmyken 1942 bis 1945*, 3rd edn. (Freiburg, 1977); *Die Ostlegionen 1941–1943: Turkotataren, Kaukasier und Wolgafinnen im deutschen Heer*, 2nd edn. (Freiburg, 1981); *Die Geschichte der Wlassow-Armee*, 2nd edn. (Freiburg, 1986; Russian edn. Paris, 1990); *Kaukasien 1942/43: Das deutsche Heer und die Orientvölker der Sowjetunion* (Freiburg, 1991); 'Die Angriffsvorbereitungen der Sowjetunion 1941', in *Zwei Wege nach Moskau: Vom Hitler-Stalin-Pakt bis zum 'Unternehmen Barbarossa'*, ed. Bernd Wegner on behalf of MGFA (Munich and Zurich, 1991), 367–88 (Russian translation 'Podgotovka Sovetskogo

Sojuza k nastupitel'noj vojne 1941 goda', in *Otečestvennaja Istorija* [Moscow] 1993, No. 4, pp. 19–31). Other publications on nineteenth-century political, diplomatic, and military history.

Dr ROLF-DIETER MÜLLER (b. 1948). Publications: *Das Tor zur Weltmacht: Die Bedeutung der Sowjetunion für die deutsche Wirtschafts- und Rüstungspolitik zwischen den Weltkriegen* (Boppard a.Rh., 1984); *Wer zurückweicht wird erschossen! Kriegsalltag und Kriegsende in Südwestdeutschland,* jointly with Gerd R. Ueberschär and Wolfram Wette (Freiburg, 1985); editor, with Hans Günter Branch, of *Chemische Kriegführung—Chemische Abrüstung* (Berlin, 1985); *Deutschland am Abgrund: Zusammenbruch und Untergang des Dritten Reiches 1945,* jointly with Gerd R. Ueberschär (Konstanz, 1986); *Geschichtswende? Entsorgungsversuche zur deutschen Geschichte* (co-author) (Freiburg, 1987); *Giftgas gegen Abd el Krim! Deutschland, Spanien und der Gaskrieg in Spanisch-Marokko 1922–1927,* with Rudibert Kunz (Freiburg, 1990); editor of *Die deutsche Wirtschaftspolitik in den besetzten sowjetischen Gebieten 1941–1943* (Boppard a.Rh., 1991); *Hitlers Ostkrieg und die deutsche Siedlungspolitik* (Frankfurt, 1991); *Kriegsende 1945: Die Zerstörung des Deutschen Reiches,* jointly with Gerd R. Ueberschär (Frankfurt, 1994); 'Die Mobilisierung der deutschen Wirtschaft für Hitlers Kriegführung', in *Kriegsverwaltung, Wirtschaft und personelle Ressourcen 1939–1941* (Stuttgart, 1988) = *Das Deutsche Reich und der Zweite Weltkrieg,* v/1. 349–689. Other articles on the history of German–Soviet relations and on the economic and armaments policy of the Third Reich.

Dr GERD R.UEBERSCHÄR (b. 1943). Publications: *Hitler und Finnland 1939–1941: Die deutsch-finnischen Beziehungen während des Hitler-Stalin-Paktes;* (Wiesbaden, 1978); *Bomben und Legenden: Die schrittweise Aufklärung des Luftangriffs auf Freiburg am 10. Mai 1940,* jointly with Wolfram Wette (Freiburg, 1981); editor, with Wolfram Wette, of 'Unternehmen Barbarossa' (Paderborn 1984; new rev. paperback edn. *Der deutsche Überfall auf die Sowjetunion,* 2nd edn. (Frankfurt, 1991)); *Wer zurückweicht wird erschossen! Kriegsalltag und Kriegsende in Südwestdeutschland 1944/45,* jointly with Rolf-Dieter Müller and Wolfram Wette (Freiburg, 1985); *Endlich Frieden! Das Kriegsende in Freiburg 1945,* jointly with Th. Schnabel (Freiburg, 1985); *Deutschland am Abgrund,* jointly with Rolf-Dieter Müller (Konstanz, 1986); *Geschichtswende? Entsorgungsversuche zur deutschen Vergangenheit* (co-author) (Freiburg, 1987); (French edn. *L'Histoire escamotée* (Paris, 1988)); *Das Dilemma der deutschen Militäropposition* (Berlin, 1988); *Freiburg im Luftkrieg 1939–1945* (Freiburg, 1990); *Generaloberst Franz Halder* (Göttingen, 1991); editor, with Wolfram Wette, of *Stalingrad: Mythos und Wirklichkeit einer Schlacht,* 2nd edn. (Frankfurt, 1993); *Kriegsende 1945,* jointly with Rolf-Dieter Müller, 2nd edn. (Frankfurt, 1994); editor of *Der 20. Juli 1944: Bewertung und Rezeption des deutschen Widerstandes gegen das NS-Regime* (Cologne, 1994); *Germany's War against the Soviet Union, 1941–1945,* jointly with Rolf-Dieter Müller (Oxford, 1995).

Note on the Translation

PART I was translated by Ewald Osers, Part II.I by Dean S. McMurray, Part II.II by Ewald Osers, Part II.III–VII, as well as the Conclusion, by Louise Willmot. The translation as a whole was revised and edited by Ewald Osers.

In the Bibliography information has been added concerning English translations of German and other foreign-language works. These translations are cited in the footnotes and have been used whenever possible for quotations occurring in the text.

Personal and geographical names in the text and the maps—except those for which established English names exist (e.g. Warsaw, Moscow, Archangel)—have been given in the form laid down by the British Standard and by *Official Standard Names Approved by the US Board of Geographic Names* (US Department of the Interior, Office of Geography).

In the footnotes and the Bibliography Russian sources are given in accordance with the International System of transliteration.

Abbreviations

Note. This list serves mainly as a key to the many abbreviations found in archival sources, but does not reflect the full range of variation in pointing etc. encountered in the citations given in the footnotes.

AA (1), Ausw. Amt	Auswärtiges Amt: ministry of foreign affairs
AA (2)	anti-aircraft
Abt.	Abteilung: section, department, unit, detail, battalion (armoured forces), battery (artillery)
Abw.	Abwehr: foreign intelligence
ADAP	*Akten zur deutschen auswärtigen Politik*: Documents on German Foreign Policy (cf. *DGFP*)
AEG	Allgemeine Elektrizitäts-Gesellschaft: General Electric Company
AFV	Armoused fighting vehicle(s)
AG	Aktiengesellschaft: joint stock company
AHA	Allgemeines Heeresamt: general army office
AK	Armeekorps: army corps
Amt Ausl./Abw.	Amt Ausland/Abwehr: foreign intelligence department in the High Command of the Armed Forces
Anh.	Anhang: annexe, appendix
Anl.	Anlage: enclosure
AO	Abwehroffizier: security officer
AOK	Armeeoberkommando: army headquarters staff
AO Kraft	Armee-Kraftfahr-Offizier: army motor-transport officer
AR	artillery regiment
Art.	Artillerie: artillery
Art.Kdr.	Artillerie-Kommandeur: artillery commander
Art.Rgt.	Artillerie-Regiment: artillery regiment
ASMZ	*Allgemeine schweizerische Militärzeitschrift*
Ast	Abwehrstelle: military security control centre
Att.Abt.	Attaché-Abteilung im GenStdH: attaché section in the Army General Staff
Aufkl.Abt.	Aufklärungs-Abteilung: reconnaissance unit
Ausb.Abt.	Ausbildungs-Abteilung im GenStdH: training department in the Army General Staff
AWA	Allgemeines Wehrmachtamt: general Wehrmacht office
BA	Bundesarchiv: Federal German archives, Koblenz

B-Abt.	Beobachtungs-Abteilung: artillery survey unit
BA-MA	Bundesarchiv-Militärarchiv (Federal German military archives), Freiburg im Breisgau
Battr.	Batterie: battery
BdE	Befehlshaber des Ersatzheeres: commander of the training army
BdK	Befehlshaber der Kreuzer: commander of cruisers
BdS	Befehlshaber der Schnellboote: commander of motor torpedo-boats
Befh.	Befehlshaber: commander
Befh. rückw. H.Geb.	Befehlshaber des rückwärtigen Heeresgebietes: commander of Army Group L of C District
Bef.St.	Befehlsstelle: command post
Bes. Ostgeb.	Besetzte Ostgebiete: occupied eastern areas
besp.	bespannt: horse-drawn
BG	Bomber Geschwader
Bibl.	Bibliothek: library
Br.B.Nr.	Briefbuchnummer: correspondence log number
Brig.	Brigade: brigade
Brü.Bau-Btl.	Brückenbau-Bataillon: bridge-building battalion
Brüko	Brücken-Kolonne: bridging column
Bv.TO	Bevollmächtigter Transportoffizier: authorized transport officer
ChefdGenSt	Chef des Generalstabes: chief of the general staff
ChefdSt.	Chef des Stabes: chief of staff
ChefHRü u. BdE	Chef der Heeresrüstung und Befehlshaber des Ersatzheeres: head of army equipment and commander of the training army
Chefs.	Chefsache: to be seen by senior officer only
ČK	Črezvyčajnaja Komissija po bor'be s kontrrevoljuciej i sabotažem: Extraordinary Commission for the Struggle against Counterrevolution and Sabotage
CP(B)	Communist Party (Bolsheviks)
CPSU	Communist Party of the Soviet Union
CPSU(B)	Communist Party of the Soviet Union (Bolsheviks) (*earlier name*)
CSIR	Corpo di Spedizione Italiano in Russia: Italian Expeditionary Corps in Russia
DBG	Dive-bomber Geschwader
DEV	División Española de Voluntarios: Spanish Volunteer Division
d.G.	des Generalstabes: of the general staff
DGFP	*Documents on German Foreign Policy* (translation of *ADAP*; see the Bibliography)

DHM	Deutsche Heeresmission: German Army Mission
Div.	Division: division
DLM	Deutsche Luftwaffenmission: German Air Force Mission
DMM	Deutsche Marinemission: German Naval Mission
DNB	Deutsches Nachrichtenbüro: German News Agency
DNSAP	Dansk National Socialistik Arbejderparti: Danish National Socialist Workers' (Nazi) Party
Dt.Ges.	Deutsche Gesandtschaft: German embassy
Dulag	Durchgangslager: transit camp
Dv.	Dienstvorschrift: military manual
DVK	Deutsches Verbindungskommando: German liaison HQ
eb	einsatzbereit: combat-ready
Eisenb.Pz.Züge	Eisenbahn-Panzer-Züge: armoured railway trains
EM	Ereignismeldung: incident report
Entgift.Abt.	Entgiftungsabteilung: decontamination battery
Erg	Ergänzungs-: reserve
(F)	Fernaufklärungs-: long-range reconnaissance
FaBG	Fast Bomber Geschwader
Fallsch.Brig.	Fallschirmbrigade: paratroop brigade
F-Aufklärer	Fernaufklärer: long-range reconnaissance aircraft
FdT	Führer der Torpedoboote: leader of torpedo-boats
Feldkdtr.	Feldkommandantur: field HQ established in rear areas
FG	Fighter Geschwader
FH	Feldhaubitze: field howitzer
FK	Feldkommandantur: field HQ in rear areas
F.Kapt.	Fregattenkapitän: commander (navy)
FlaBtl	Flugabwehr-Bataillon: AA battalion
FlakRgt	Flakregiment: AA regiment
Flamm	Flammenwerfer: flame-thrower
Fl.Korps	Fliegerkorps: air corps
FrdHeere Ost, Fr.H.Ost	Abt. Fremde Heere Ost im GenStdH: department Foreign Armies East in the army general staff
Frhr.	Freiherr (title equivalent to 'baron')
FRUS	*Foreign Relations of the United States* (see the Bibliography)
Fü.Abt.	Führungsabteilung: operations department
G, Geschw.	Geschwader (q.v. in Glossary) 3 Gruppen and a staff unit
GAC	German Africa Corps
Geb.	Gebirgs-: mountain
geh.	geheim: secret

Gen.	General: general
Gen.Adm.	Admiral-General (equivalent to Admiral of the Fleet)
Gen.d.Art.	General der Artillery: artillery general
Gen.d.Fl.	General der Flieger: air force general
Gen.d.Geb.Tr.	General der Gebirgstruppe: mountain troops general
Gen.d.Inf.	General der Infanterie: infantry general
Gen.d.Kav.	General der Kavallerie: cavalry general
Gen.d.Pz.Tr.	General der Panzertruppe: armoured forces general
Gen.Feldm.	Generalfeldmarschall: field marshal
Gen.Kdo	Generalkommando: corps HQ
Gen.Lt.	Generalleutnant: lieutenant-general
Gen.Maj.	Generalmajor: major-general
Gen.Oberst	Generaloberst: colonel-general
GenQu	Generalquartiermeister: quartermaster-general
GenSt	Generalstab: general staff
GenStdH	Generalstab des Heeres: Army General Staff
Gen. z.b.V.b. ObdH	General zur besonderen Verfügung beim Oberbefehlshaber des Heeres: general (special duties) attached to the commander-in-chief of the army
gep.	gepanzert: armoured
GFP	Geheime Feldpolizei: secret field police
GK	Generalkommissar: commissioner-general
g.Kdos., g.K.	Geheime Kommandosache: top secret (military)
GL	Generalluftzeugmeister: director general of air armament
gmsd	gvardejskaja motostrelkovaja divizija: motorized Guards rifle division
GOC	General Officer Commanding
GPU	Gosudarstvennoe Političeskoe Upravlenie: State Political Directorate
Gr.	Gruppe(n) (q.v. in Glossary)
Gr. R.Wes.	Gruppe Rechtswesen: Legal Matters Group
g.Rs.	Geheime Reichssache: top secret (political)
GZ	Zentralabteilung im GenStdH: central department in the Army General Staff
H	Heeres(Nah)aufklärung: army short-range reconnaissance
HaPol.	Handelspolitische Abteilung im Ausw. Amt: trade policy department in the ministry of foreign affairs
Haub.	Haubitze: howitzer
H-Aufklärer	Heeres(Nah)aufklärer: army short-range reconnaissance aircraft
H.Dv.	Heeresdruckvorschrift: army manual
H.Geb.	Heeresgebiet: army area

H.Gr.	Heeresgruppe: army group
H.Küst.Art.Abt.	Heeres-Küsten-Artillerie-Abteilung: army coastal artillery battery
Höh.Art.Kdr.	Höherer Artillerie-Kommandeur: higher artillery commander
Höh. Kdo.	Höheres Kommando: higher command
HSSPF	Höherer SS- und Polizeiführer: senior SS and police leader
HTO	Haupttreuhandstelle Ost: Central Trustee Agency East
HV, H.Vers.	Heeresversorgung: army supply
HVBl.	*Heeresverordnungsblatt*: Army Orders and Gazette
HWesAbt	Heerwesen-Abteilung im GenStdH: army affairs department in the Army General Staff
HZ	*Historische Zeitschrift*
IfZ	Institut für Zeitgeschichte: Institute of Contemporary History
i.G.	im Generalstab: in the general staff
IG, Inf.Gesch.	Infanteriegeschütz: infantry (close support) gun
IKL	Isänmaallinen Kansan Liike: People's Patriotic Movement, Finland
IMT	International Military Tribunal (see *Trial of Major War Criminals* in the Bibliography)
Inf.Div.	Infanteriedivision: infantry division
JCH	*Journal of Contemporary History*
JG	Jagdgeschwader: fighter Geschwader
JGr	Jagdgruppe: fighter Gruppe
JWG	*Jahrbuch für Wirtschaftsgeschichte*
K.Adm.	Konteradmiral: rear-admiral
Kalib.	Kaliber: caliber
Kan.Abt.	Kanonen-Abteilung: gunnery battery
Kav.Div.	Kavalleriedivision: cavalry division
Kdo	Kommando: command, HQ
Kdr.	Kommandeur: commander
Kdt.	Kommandant: commandant
Kfz.	Kraftfahrzeug: motor-vehicle
KG	Kampfgeschwader: bomber Geschwader
Kgf.	Kriegsgefangenen-: prisoner of war
KGzbV	Kampfgruppe zur besonderen Verwendung (Transportfliegergruppe): special duties bomber Gruppe (transport Gruppe)
Koluft, Ko-Luft	Kommandeur der Luftwaffe: Luftwaffe commander with an army group or army
Komandarm	army commander (Soviet general's rank)

Kombrig	brigade commander (Soviet general's rank)
Komdiv	divisional commander (Soviet general's rank)
Komkor	corps commander (Soviet general's rank)
Komm.Gen.	general commanding
KONR	Komitet Osvoboždenija Narodov Rossii: Committee for the Liberation of the People of Russia
Korück	Kommandant des rückwärtigen Armeegebietes: commandant of rear army area
Kp.	Kompanie: company
KP	Kommunistische Partei: Communist Party
KPD	Kommunistische Partei Deutschlands: German Communist Party
KTB	Kriegstagebuch: war diary
KTB OKW	*Kriegstagebuch des Oberkommandos der Wehrmacht* (see the Bibliography)
K.Ver.	Kriegsverwaltung: war administration
Kw.K. (t)	Kampfwagenkanone (tschechisch): tank gun (Czech)
Kzg.	Kraftzug: tractor-drawn
L	Abteilung Landesverteidigung im WFA (WFSt): home defence department in the Wehrmacht operations department (Wehrmacht operations staff)
l., le., lei.	leicht: light
La	Landwirtschaft: agriculture
Ld.Schtz.	Landesschützen: local defence units
L.Dv.	Luftwaffendruckvorschrift: Luftwaffe regulations
Leg.Rat	Legationsrat: legation counsellor
leiFlakAbt	leichte Flakabteilung: light AA battery
l.FH	leichte Feldhaubitze: light field howitzer
Lfl.	Luftflotte: air fleet
LG	Lehrgeschwader: training Geschwader
LGL.	Large Glider
Lkw	Lastkraftwagen: truck
LLG	Luftlandegeschwader: airborne Geschwader
LVF	Légion des Volontaires Français contre le Bolchevisme
Lw	Luftwaffe: air force
Lw.Fü.Stab	Luftwaffe operations staff
Maj.	Major: major
Mann.	Mannschaft: men, other ranks
Mar.Gr.	Marinegruppe: naval group
M.Dv.	Marinedruckvorschrift: naval regulations
MG	Maschinengewehr: machine-gun
MGFA	Militärgeschichtliches Forschungsamt: Research Institute for Military History

MGM	*Militärgeschichtliche Mitteilungen*
M.i.G.	Militärbefehlshaber im Generalgouvernement: military commander in the Government-General
Mil.	Militär: military
Mil.Att.	Militärattaché: military attaché
Mil.Geo.	Militärgeographie: military geography
Min.Dir.	Ministerialdirektor: senior civil service rank
Min.Rat.	Ministerialrat: senior civil service rank
Mörs.Abt.	Mörser-Abteilung: mortar battery
mot.	motorisiert: motorized
mot.mech.	motorisiert-mechanisiert: motorized mechanized
MP-1941	mobilizacionnyj plan 1941: mobilization plan
MR	*Marine-Rundschau*
M.Sg.	Manuskriptsammlung: manuscript collection
MSR	Mouvement Social Révolutionnaire
MTB	motor torpedo-boar
Mun	Amtsgruppe für Industrielle Rüstung—Munition—im Heeres-Waffenamt: section for industrial rearmament—ammunition—in the army ordnance department
N	Nachlaß: papers
Nachr.Rgt.	Nachrichtenregiment: signals regiment
Nbg.Dok.	Nürnberger Dokument: Nuremberg document
Nb.Rgt.	Nebelwerfer-Regiment: smoke regiment
NJG	Nachtjagdgeschwader: night fighter Geschwader
NKGB	Narodnyj Komissariat Gosudarstvennoj Bezopasnosti: People's Commissariat of the State Security
NKVD	Narodnyj Komissariat Vnutrennych Del: People's Commissariat of the Interior
NS	National Socialist
NSDAP	Nationalsozialistische Deutsche Arbeiterpartei: National Socialist German Workers' Party (Nazis)
NSKK	Nationalsozialistisches Kraftfahr-Korps: National Socialist Motor Corps
OB	Oberbefehlshaber: commander-in-chief, GOC,
ObdH	Oberbefehlshaber des Heeres: commander-in-chief of the army
ObdL	Oberbefehlshaber der Luftwaffe: commander-in-chief of the Luftwaffe
ObdM	Oberbefehlshaber der Kriegsmarine: commander-in-chief of the navy
Oberstlt.	Oberstleutnant: lieutenant-colonel
Ob.Kdo	Oberkommando: high command
o.D.	ohne Datum: undated

Offz.	Ofizier: officer
OGPU	Ob'edinennoe Gosudarstvennoe Političeskoe Upravlenie: United State Political Directorate
OK	Ortskommandantur: local commandant's office
OKH	Oberkommando des Heeres: Army High Command
OKL	Oberkommando der Luftwaffe: Luftwaffe High Command
OKM	Oberkommando der Kriegsmarine: Navy High Command
OKW	Oberkommando der Wehrmacht: High Command of the Armed Forces
Op./op	Operations-: operational
Op.Abt.	operations department in the army General Staff
OQu	Oberquartiermeister: deputy chief of the general staff
Org.Abt.	Organisations-Abteilung im GenStdH: organization department in the Army General Staff
Osoaviachim	Obščestvo sodejstvija aviacii i chimičeskoj oborony: Society for the Promotion of Aviation and Chemical Defence
OT	Organisation Todt: Todt Organization
PA	Politisches Archiv des Auswärtigen Amtes (political archives of the foreign ministry), Bonn
Pak	Panzerabwehrkanone: anti-tank gun
Pi.Rgt.	Pionier-Regiment: engineer regiment
Pol.Abt.	Politische Abteilung im Ausw. Amt: political department in the ministry of foreign affairs
PPF	Parti Populaire Français
PRO	Public Record Office, London
Pz.	Panzer: tank
Pz.AOK	Panzerarmeeoberkommando: armoured army HQ
Pz.Div.	Panzerdivision: armoured division
Pz.Gr.	Panzergruppe: armoured group
Pz.Jäg.Abt.	Panzer-Jäger-Abteilung: anti-tank battalion
Pz.Kpf.Wg.	Panzerkampfwagen: armoured fighting vehicle
Pz.Zug	Panzerzug: armoured train
Qu	Quartiermeister: quartermaster
RAD	Reichsarbeitsdienst: Reich Labour Service
Radf.Btl.	Radfahr-Bataillon: cycle battalion
RAM	Reichsaußenminister: Reich minister of foreign affairs
R-boot	Räumboot: motor minesweeper
RdL	Reichsminister der Luftfahrt: Reich minister of aviation
Recce	Reconnaisance
Reg.	Regiment

Reg.Rat	Regierungsrat: senior civil service rank
Revvoensovet	Revoljucionnyj Voennyj Sovet: revolutionary military council
Rgt.	Regiment: regiment
RK	Reichskommissariat: Reich Commissariat
RKKA	Raboče-krestjanskaja krasnaja armija: Workers' and Peasants' Red Army
RKP(b)	Rossijskaja Kommunističeskaja partija (bol'ševikov): Russian Communist Party (Bolsheviks)
RM	Reichsmark (currency)
RMfbO	Reichsminister für die besetzten Ostgebiete: Reich minister for the occupied eastern territories
RMfBuM	Reichsminister für Bewaffnung und Munition: Reich minister for armament and ammunition
RNP	Rassemblement National Populaire
Ro	Rohstoffabteilung im Wehrwirtschafts- und Rüstungsamt: raw-materials section in the war economy and armaments department
ROA	Russkaja Osvoboditel'naja Armija: Russian Liberation Army
RSFSR	Russian Soviet Federation of Socialist Republics (= Russia)
RT	Radio-telegraphy
Rü	Rüstungswirtschaftliche Abteilung im WiRüAmt: armament economy section in the war economy and armament department
RüIn	Rüstungsindustrie: armaments industry, munitions
RWM, RWiM	Reichswirtschaftsminister/ministerium: Reich minister/ministry of economic affairs
s., schw.	schwer(e): heavy
SA	Sturmabteilung: storm troopers
schw.Fl.Feuer	schweres Flachfeuer: heavy flat-trajectory fire
SD	Sicherheitsdients: security service of the SS
s.FH	schwere Feldhaubitze: heavy field howitzer
Sich.Div.	security division
SKG	Schnellkampfgeschwader: fast bomber Geschwader
Skl.	Seekriegsleitung: naval war staff
SS	Schutzstaffel ('guard detachment'): élite Party troops
Stabia	Stabsbildabteilung: staff photographic section
StG	Sturzkampfgeschwader: dive-bomber Geschwader
St.S.	Staatssekretär: state secretary
Stuka	Sturzkampflugzeug: dive-bomber
Sturm-Gesch.Abt.	Sturmgeschützabteilung: assault-gun battery
(t)	tschechisch: Czech (origin)

takt.	taktisch: tactical
TB	Tätigkeitsbericht: activity report
T-boot	Torpedoboot: torpedo-boat
Tel.	Telegramm: telegram
TFG	Twin-engined Fighter (Zerstörer) Geschwader
Tgb. Nr.	Tagebuch-Nummer: diary number
TLR	Technische Luftrüstung: technical air armament
T-Minen	Torpedo-Minen: torpedo-mines
tmot.	teilmotorisiert: partially motorized
Trg G	Training Geschwader
TrSt	Transportstaffel: transport Staffel
U.St.S.	Unterstaatssekretär: under-secretary of state
VAA	Vertreter des Auswärtigen Amtes: representative of the foreign ministry
Verb.Offz., VO	Verbindungsofizier: liaison officer
Verf.	Verfasser: author
Vermess.Abt.	Vermessungs-Abteilung: survey unit
Vers.Bez.	Versorgungsbezirk: supply district
Vers.Führg.	Versorgungsführung: supply management
VfZG	*Vierteljahreshefte für Zeitgeschichte*
VIŽ	*Voenno-istoričeskij žurnal*
VKP(b)	Vsesojuznaja Kommunističeskaja Partija (bol'ševikov): Soviet Communist Party
VLR	Vortragender Legationsrat: senior civil service rank
VP	Vierjahresplan: Four-year Plan
VS	Verschlußsache: secret matter, locked file
WaA	Heeres-Waffenamt: army ordnance department
WaStab	Stab des Heereswaffenamtes: staff of army ordnance department
W.Befh., WB	Wehrmachtbefehlshaber: commander-in-chief of the Wehrmacht
Wekusta	Wettererkundungsstaffel: meteorological reconnaissance Staffel
WFA	Wehrmachtführungsamt: armed forces operations department
WFSt	Wehrmachtführungsstab: armed forces operations staff
Wi	Wirtschaft: economy
WiIn	Wirtschaftsinspektion: economic inspectorate
Wi.Pol.Abt.	Wirtschaftspolitische Abteilung: economic-policy department
WiRüAmt	Wehrwirtschafts- und Rüstungsamt: war-economy and armaments department
WiStabOst	Wirtschaftsstab Ost: economic staff East

WK	Wehrkreis: military district
WO	Wehrwirtschaftsofizier: war economy officer
WPr	Abteilung für Wehrmachtpropaganda im WFA (WFSt): Wehrmacht propaganda department in the armed forces operations department (staff)
WR	Wehrmachtrechtsabteilung im OKW: Wehrmacht legal department in the Wehrmacht High Command
WStb	Wehrwirtschaftsstab im WiRüAmt: war economy staff in the war economy and armaments department
WStK	Waffenstillstandskommission: armistice commission
WuG	Amtsgruppe für Industrielle Rüstung—Waffen und Gerät—im WaA: section for industrial armament—weapons and equipment—in the army ordnance department
WWi	Wehrwirtschaftliche Abteilung im WiRüAmt: war economy section in the war economy and armaments department
WWR	*Wehrwissenschaftliche Rundschau*
z.b.V.	zur besonderen Verwendung (Verfügung): for special duties
ZfG	*Zeitschrift für Geschichtswissenschaft*
ZG	Zerstörergeschwader: Geschwader of 'destroyer' aircraft
ZHO	Zentralhandelsgesellschaft Ost: Central Trading Company East
ZK	Zentralkomitee: Central Committee
z.T.	zum Teil: partly

Short designations for departments in the army's operational staffs

Ia	Führungs-Abteilung: operations department
Ib	Quartiermeister-Abteilung: quartermaster department
Ic	Feindaufklärung und Abwehr; geistige Betreuung: reconnaissance concerning the enemy and counter-intelligence; spiritual care
Id	Ausbildung: training
IIa	1.Adjutant (Ofizier-Personalien): 1st adjutant (officer personnel)
IIb	2.Adjutant (Unterofiziere und Mannschaften): 2nd adjutant (NCOs and men)
III	Gericht: court of law
IVa	Intendant (Rechnungswesen, allgemeine Verwaltung): official in charge of financial matters, general administration

IVb	Arzt: medical officer
IVc	Veterinär: veterinary officer
IVd	Geistlicher (ev.: evangelisch; kath.: katholisch): chaplain (ev.: Protestant; kath.: Roman Catholic)
IV Wi	Wehrwirtschaftsofizier: war economy officer
V	Kraftfahrwesen: motor transport

Glossary of Foreign Terms

Anschluss	The union of Austria with Germany, 1938
Außenpolitisches Amt	Foreign affairs office of the Nazi Party
Gau (pl. *-e*)	Regional administrative division of the Nazi Party
Geschwader (pl. same)	Air-force unit consisting of 3–4 Gruppen (q.v.)
Kette (pl. *-n*)	Formation of 3 aircraft
Komsomol	Communist Youth Organization
Lebensraum	'Living-space' for Germany, with connotation of conquest in the east
Luftwaffe	German air force
politruk	Red Army political officer, subordinate to commissar
Rotte (pl. *-n*)	Formation of 2 aiccraft
Rückwärtiges Armeegebiet	The area behind the sector held by an army [*Armee*], line of communication area
Rückwärtiges Heeeresgebiet	The area behind the individual armies' rear (or line of communication) areas, rear army [*Heer*] area
Schwarm (pl. *Schwärme*)	Formation of (usually) 4 aircraft
Staffel (pl. *-n*)	Unit of 9 aircraft, plus 3 in reserve
Wehrmacht	German armed forces
Wilhelmstrasse, the	Term denoting the German ministry of foreign affairs (from its address in Berlin)

Introduction

In the appraisal of Operation Barbarossa military and historical research has hitherto been marked by two diametrically opposed views. One of these proceeds from the argument that Hitler's programme, as developed in the 1920s in *Mein Kampf* and *Hitler's Secret Book*, has to be taken seriously. In these programmatic books Hitler saw the decisive tasks of future German policy in the conquest of living-space in the east and in the destruction of 'Jewish Bolshevism'. These two objectives had been linked by him in such a way that the concept of a racial-biological basis of his anti-Soviet living-space policy has been developed. Historical studies inclining towards that view regard the Barbarossa plan as intimately connected with such programmatic ideas, without falling into the error of denying that Hitler's decision was, in addition, motivated by foreign-policy and military considerations. This 'programmatic' explanation of Operation Barbarossa finds itself confronted by a view which assigns to Stalin a major role in the development which led to war. According to that school of thought it was Stalin's aggressive policy in eastern central Europe, as well as his vigorous rearmament, that provoked Hitler into reacting. This thesis of a preventive war was first put forward by the German side for propaganda reasons during the war—not only in order to convince Europe of the danger threatening the West from the East, but also for purposes of domestic propaganda. Stiffening of the German people's readiness for war and the creation of a crusading atmosphere in Europe were part of the massive propaganda effort which was, to a large extent, aimed also at the German troops who were to implement Hitler's goals. A third interpretation proceeds primarily from the strategic constraints after Germany's victory over France and defeat in the Battle of Britain.

Among Anglo-American researchers these diverse attempts at explanation first appeared in the 1950s. German authors concurred with Anglo-American historians such as Hugh R. Trevor Roper, Alan Bullock, and Gerhard L. Weinberg on the point that Hitler's policy could only be understood in the light of his programme. Mention should be made here of Andreas Hillgruber and Eberhard Jäckel. However, there have also been attempts in Britain to interpret Hitler's foreign policy as, in the strict sense, an aimless vacillating or a mere response to given situations—a view that could be supported by numerous statements by Hitler at various phases of the war. Historians such as A. J. P. Taylor and F. A. Hinsley adopted this view at an early stage.

Among Anglo-American historians such controversies were argued out like any other scholarly disputes. In the Federal Republic, however, there is often more at issue than mere historical interest: in the case of Barbarossa, judgement on Hitler's objectives inevitably simultaneously implies a judgement on the opinions of the 'conservative élites', on those circles among the generals, the top judiciary, and experts from the business world who had, in the spring of 1940 or shortly afterwards, been informed of what Hitler was aiming at and of what methods he intended to see practised.

So far the differing points of view have not yet been sufficiently assembled within an overall scholarly treatment of the structure and policy of the National Socialist state for a universally accepted explanation of the causes of the war against Russia to be achieved. With regard to Hitler—that much has become obvious—a purely psychological approach or a purely descriptive one would be insufficient. Serious consideration of Hitler's programmatic concept, on the other hand, has been beneficial to research in the fields of military and foreign policy, as has since been proved by numerous studies.

The authors of this volume had before them this briefly outlined plurality of interpretations. Their researches have discovered no basis for the assumption that Hitler had, in a manner of speaking, been manipulated by circumstances. After the victory over France there was no opposition to his decisions on how the war was to be continued. But just because it was he who determined the new objectives the question arose of how his assessment of the strategic situation and his racially motivated concept of living-space combined as factors in his decision to go to war and in his planning of that war.

No doubt the situation following the French campaign and the subsequent defeat in the Battle of Britain confronted Hitler with a strategic dilemma. It would nevertheless be facile and one-sided to regard this as the sole motivation for the attack against the Soviet Union. In fact it can be seen—and the present fourth volume of the account of the Second World War follows this realization—that a whole string of reflections, obsessions, misjudgements, and long-term ideas were factors in Hitler's decision in favour of war. One of these reflections was the strategy, much discussed in the literature, of using a German victory over the Soviet Union to compel Britain to recognize German hegemony on the Continent and to force her out of the war—all that in order to gain a vital breathing-space for the conflict with the United States. This is what Hitler tried to explain to his top generals in the autumn of 1940; by the spring of 1941 his 'programmatic' campaign of persuasion had moved to the centre of his endeavours. For no other of his campaigns had he so consistently explained to the military leaders its significance and its objectives, for no other campaign had he put forward such precise demands concerning the methods of conducting the war. Thus, an overall appreciation of the present volume could scarcely arrive at the conclusion that the war against the Soviet Union represented merely an attempt to escape from a strategic dilemma. That war was Hitler's real war. This judgement agrees with that of those authors who are willing to see a link between 'programme' and realities while, at the same time, conceding that there can be no question of compulsive implementation of a programme. Hitler was still dependent on whatever opportunities the course of the war offered him. In the summer of 1940 he believed the moment had come for preparing 'his' war. Even then he did not tie himself down to a final timetable; by November, however, the separate elements of his estimation of the situation had hardened into a definitive decision.

In view of the material and psychological underestimation of the enemy, including his political stability, both by the German military and by Hitler, the plans which began to be drawn up after July 1940 were based on an operational period of a few weeks. The general staff, while beginning to doubt whether the intended indirect elimination of Britain would work, found a long-cherished hope moving nearer fulfilment—Germany's achievement of immunity to blockade, the precondition for a protracted war, through the occupation of the Ukraine and the industrial regions, as well as through command of the Baltic. Halder's concept and plan for this war envisaged victory by means of rapid and decisive operations towards Moscow. He believed that the success of his strategy would convince Hitler. This subject will be discussed in the operational section of this volume. It goes beyond any subjective problems stemming from the character of the chief of the general staff, who no longer wielded the decision-making military authority which, in the First World War, characterized the Hindenburg–Ludendorff team. Concealed behind the relationship between Halder and Hitler lies the diminution of the position of the general staff in the Prussian-German military state, a position achieved by Moltke and his successors. The dubious construct of the old political-military twin summit of the Reich was, oddly enough, broken asunder in the most highly militarized state edifice, the National Socialist Führer state. Since the victory in the west, if not earlier, Hitler had been 'his own Ludendorff', who let the general staff do the planning work but who alone took the strategic decisions. What Beck had failed to achieve in 1938—a decision-sharing role for the most senior military advisor—his successor was even less able to achieve in 1941. His attempt to gain shared military rule—dominance, at least, in the operational field—failed miserably. He was reduced to resorting to indirect methods, to concealment, and to the hope that the magnificent victory sought by the general staff in the direction of Moscow would eventually also convince Hitler and carry him along. Hitler had never shared the view that a great battle outside or for Moscow could bring about the overall decision. He attached greater importance to gaining control of the major industrial regions, the oilfields, and other economic centres, in order thereby to reduce the enemy's vital strength. Halder failed to convince him with his massive effort against Moscow: this did not give enough weight to the problems on the southern wing of the eastern front, where the objectives of the first phase of the advance were not achieved on time. The eventual failure of his concept outside Moscow was a factor in raising Hitler to the sole commanding position in the army. This process within the command system of the war in the east will be described in detail. During the planning phase and during the first few weeks of the advance the solution envisaged by the general staff seemed to be the right road to a rapid victory. The Wehrmacht now demonstrated on a large scale the mobile warfare it had conducted in Poland, France, Yugoslavia, and Greece. The Luftwaffe, after its sobering experience in strategic aerial warfare against Britain, was once more offered a chance of recording major successes as an ancillary arm of the ground forces. All these efforts, however, were marked by a high degree of attrition of German fighting strength and did not pay off in terms of the war economy. On the contrary, the loss of Russian deliveries, the huge requirements of the Wehrmacht, and the fact that no end was in sight to the enterprise in the east made Germany's strategic, economic, and political position at the end of the year appear less positive than before the start of the Barbarossa war.

The findings in this volume go beyond the first scholarly West German overview by Klaus Reinhardt. Above all they show the very limited value, in many respects, of the 'Studies' produced under Halder's general editorship on behalf of the American army.

Another decisive aspect, indeed one crucial to an overall strategic examination, arose inevitably in the late summer of 1941 with the realization that Operation Barbarossa could possibly fail: the danger, in the near future, of a perceptible American participation in the war. It was then that the compulsions first felt in the summer of 1940 clearly emerged with all their consequences and that it became obvious that the exhausted army was no longer capable of bringing about any military situation which might avert a crushing war on two fronts.

At a time when suggestions of the mood after the battle of the Marne or of Verdun were beginning to be mooted among the German military leadership, it was still believed, in total misjudgement of the overall strategic conditions of German warfare, that in 1942 the balance could be restored by cutting off the Soviet Union from its vital economic bases in the south and from its communications with Persia. At the same time, however, it became clear that there could be no relief in the east and that the army would continue to be tied down there.

As in the First World War, it became obvious that Germany was a central European rather than a world power. Yet that continental power was not even able, because of its incredible overestimation of its own capabilities, to give its army winter protection for a war in the east which was protracting beyond the originally envisaged timetable. With all that thrust towards the east it had also omitted to establish rallying-positions for the forces which had burnt themselves out before Moscow. The turning-point in the war was heaving into view.

Another matter clearly documented in the present volume is concurrence between Hitler and the top military in the OKW (the High Command of the armed forces) and the OKH (the High Command of the army) on the meaning of that war. It was to be, simultaneously, a war of annihilation and of conquest of living-space. These categories were familiar to military thinking.

Even before the First World War, military leaders—and certainly not only on the German side—tended to discount the requirements of international law. Military interests, power politics, and scant regard for international law were the obverse of Wilhelminian assurance of strength and power. The Great General Staff's directive on international law of 1902 contained the statement that humanitarian requirements could only be considered to the extent permitted by the nature and objective of the war: 'A vigorously conducted war cannot be aimed solely against the combatants of the enemy state or its fortifications, but will and must equally seek to destroy the entire moral and material resources of the same.' Such a concept of 'total war' explains the readiness to carry the war, as outlined by Hitler in 1941, to the east, especially as that opponent was the enemy *par excellence*—Bolshevism, on the disastrous influence of which the German defeat in 1918 was blamed. For that reason this war acquired a higher degree of inevitability than the war in the west, as well as a character which suppressed any moral scruples. Thus, the political significance with which Hitler endowed this war also far exceeded military and economic objectives, important though these were in the given situation, with the fight against the Anglo-American powers still lying ahead. It far exceeded the objectives of dominion of ordinary imperialism on a Wilhelminian scale, which Hitler had castigated in his *Secret Book*. Particularly significant evidence of this may be found in the plans for Russia's colonial exploitation, for a racial land consolidation in the east, plans which were grossly disproportionate to the basically inadequate military preparations for an 'ideological war'. The economic exploitation of the Soviet Union was planned not just for supplying the Wehrmacht, but already for the period 'after Barbarossa', when a gigantic rearmament drive, primarily for the air force and the navy, was to be launched against the Western powers. Economic experts and Hitler, as the present volume will show, were already planning 'in anticipation of victory'. This was not a case of a preventive strike against the Red Army. Time and again estimates of the enemy's position and assessments of Stalin's intentions suggested, both to Hitler and to the military planners, that for the time being there was no danger of an attack by the Red Army. At the same time, now that Britain had been driven from the Continent, there seemed once again to be an opportunity of defeating the Soviet Union in—at least as far as land operations were concerned—a *war on a single front*, of ending an increasingly expensive German dependence on Soviet readiness for economic co-operation, of gaining a free hand for a future shift of emphasis in armaments towards the navy and the air force, and simultaneously, by the annihilation of the 'Jewish-Bolshevik' arch-enemy, of gaining elbow-room for a racially and ideologically founded living-space policy.

Hitler had at an early date informed those generals earmarked for the war in the east of his political and ideological objectives, well beyond the 'continental sword' argument. After March 1941 they could no longer have been in any doubt about the background of the imminent operation. Halder, as well as other officers and lawyers in the OKW and OKH, participated at that time, either as authors or by approval, in the formulation of the relevant orders. On this point the present volume furnishes further material both on the planning phase and on the measures implemented in 1941 in the areas of economic warfare, of co-operation with Einsatzgruppen (special-purpose squads), and of the partisan war. The character of the war as a war of annihilation was preplanned. It would be a mistake to attribute the prime responsibility for this to Russian resistance, which, on the other hand, resulted in the Wehrmacht being drawn into a pattern of action and reaction that made the war an ideological struggle for both sides. Stalin, moreover, had immediately assumed it to be just that. There had been nothing comparable in the west, the south, or the north. In the east, action was shaped by a different view of the enemy and by different military circumstances. Important new sources have become available in these areas. It has become clear that political, military, and economic expectations in this war, which outclassed all prior misplannings in German political and military history, had been illusory. Warning voices carried no weight in the German Führer system: they were effortlessly supplanted by optimistic forecasts.

Careful study of the sources has revealed the extent to which military and economic or technological inadequacies mutually conditioned and magnified each other. The main reason for the failure of the Barbarossa plan was undoubtedly the material and structural inferiority of the aggressor in virtually all the essential fields from the very outset; after a few months he was no longer able, even in terms of personnel, to fill the gaps which had been inflicted. This statement may seem paradoxical in view of the initial military superiority of the Wehrmacht in the area of the main thrusts chosen by it, but it becomes comprehensible in a comparison of the war-economy capacities of the two sides. The section on the Red Army enables the reader to make that comparison. Faith in superior German command ability should likewise have been shaken, if not indeed destroyed, with the onset of the Soviet winter offensive.

The present volume further shows, on the basis of extensive new source material, that, even more or less independently of the aspects mentioned above, contributory causes for the grandiose fiasco may be found in inadequate preparation for this war. For a 'campaign' scheduled for a few weeks a thorough preparation in terms of armaments and economics did not seem necessary. The advance was to have been accomplished, by and large, with the forces available. But concealed behind the statistics was often the fact that only a limited number of first-rate divisions was available, certainly of motorized formations. One armoured division was not the same as another armoured division. The Wehrmacht had not really been 'equipped', in the proper sense of the word, for war against the Soviet Union. Frequently the only equipment available was captured weapons and vehicles. This process is here for the first time coherently documented from the sources.

All the decisive aspects of the war ultimately resulted from the fact that the anticipated rapid collapse of the Soviet Union did not take place: there was the attrition of German human and material potential, inability to utilize the country economically on the planned scale, and finally also the mass deaths of Soviet prisoners of war. The Soviet Union's power of resistance, which, at enormous sacrifice and despite serious initial errors by the command, caused the foundering of the German leadership's operational and economic aims towards the end of 1941, dispelled Hitler's illusion of being once more able to conduct a war on one front only. By the end of the year all that was beyond discussion for the top leaders in the OKW and the OKH. This meant basically that—in spite of later partial successes and in spite of subsequent upswings in the war economy—the decision had already gone against Germany. The army of the summer of 1941 no longer existed. Thenceforward Germany's scant manpower reserves were no longer sufficient to meet the requirements of both the economy and the armed forces.

This development is illustrated here also from the Red Army's point of view. It is explained by an account of the development of the Red Army and of Soviet rearmament efforts. For that part, unfortunately, with the exception of a few captured documents, statements could rarely be supported by documents. The subject is nevertheless presented comprehensively, showing that Hitler was confronted by an equally ruthless dictator and generalissimo, capable of organizing the economic power of the Soviet Union, forcing armament production into high gear, accepting an ideological war, and repaying in like coin. In the massive crescendo of the disastrous battles of encirclement Stalin succeeded, at the price of hecatombs of victims, in rallying his vital reserves for a counterstroke at Moscow. Opponent, geographical expanse, and climate brought the Wehrmacht to the brink of disaster, robbing it for the year ahead of the breath for a second comprehensive operational strike.

The present volume not only illustrates the command principles and practices of the antagonists, but also attempts to portray the expenditure and attrition of the forces. For both sides the conflict was a war of attrition and exhaustion on a vast scale. Even in its first year it had called for almost unbelievable efforts and improvisation. By the end of 1941 it was clear that it was in the eastern theatre that the war would be decided and the map of Europe redrawn. Participation by Germany's allies was tied to their expectations of that future reshaping. The war of the German coalition became an anti-Soviet struggle of but loosely linked interests and selfish considerations. The present volume discusses in some detail the positions of Finland, Romania, and Hungary. The interests of the wider Balkan area, together with Italy and Turkey, were presented more fully in Volume III of this account of the Second World War.

There is probably no better point in German political or military history than the turn of 1941–2 to illustrate the fact that the aspirations and capabilities of the German national state were no longer able to be reconciled. By the time the plans for 1942, in the direction of Stalingrad and the Caucasus, were formed with a view to cutting off the Soviet Union from its links with the Anglo-Saxon naval powers in the south, while at the same time securing for Germany the unimpeded utilization of the oil, coal, iron, and agricultural produce of the Soviet south, the failure of Barbarossa had created the pre-requisites for the switch of the initiative to the anti-Hitler coalition, now enlarged by the United States. That turn actually came about at the end of 1942. It became obvious that the pattern of Germany's operational options was insufficient for the huge expansion of the theatre of war. Hitler committed the same mistake as the German political leaders in the First World War by exceeding and exhausting the capabilities and potential of a continental central-European great power in the dimensions of a world war against the superpowers of the future. That effort was possible only within the framework of an ideology of force which suppressed reality, which suggested that the impossible was feasible, and which, to that end, had to employ a ruthless discipline of faith in final victory.

Thus, in the very first year of the war against the Soviet Union, this was not merely a struggle for military victory and economic gain, or for new space for German colonization, but also a last attempt by the immanent drive of the German national state finally to achieve the configuration it believed to be its due. Into that effort it invested its national egotism in boundless over-exaggeration.

The first wave of West German accounts, more especially the military memoirs of the postwar period, failed, with a few exceptions, to bring out the dimensions of that war. In them, Hitler frequently appeared as an amateur who messed up the victory for the military men. Manstein spoke of 'lost victories'. Such an approach is inappropriate in every respect. Since then a broadly based process of detailed research has thrown light on military and political aspects of the war in the east, and occasionally produced shock waves. In addition to evaluating new sources, the present volume also seeks to sum up the latest state of research. It has been found that in many fields there is a need for new foundations to be laid, such as in the presentation of war-economy issues. Even on questions of the strategic conduct of the war and of relations between Hitler and his chief of staff the authors have proceeded from the belief that essential aspects have to be presented in an entirely new way.

This fourth volume of *Germany and the Second World War* is once more no 'official' publication. For that reason also it cannot be compared with the fourth volume of the Soviet 'History of the Second World War 1939–1945', which bears the title 'The Fascist Aggression against the USSR: The Collapse of the Blitzkrieg Strategy'. The internal development of military and economic conditions on the German side has, naturally enough, not been covered as extensively or in such detail in the Soviet publication. It may therefore be assumed that the findings here presented will supply new elements to take into account in assessing the official view of the Barbarossa war as stated by historians of the former Soviet state.

It is my hope, along with the authors and with the head of the project, Wilhelm Deist, who took a major part in the preparation and organization of this volume, that their work will not only stimulate discussion of the war against the Soviet Union, but also encourage future research. This may well happen for the very reason that a variety of approaches have been considered—something which itself afforded considerable difficulty to the team of authors. Whether the co-ordination aimed at has sufficiently succeeded it is up to the reader to judge. The overall project of *Germany and the Second World War* will certainly benefit from the broad range of comment expected.

MANFRED MESSERSCHMIDT

PART I

German War Policy and the Soviet Union 1940–1941

HORST BOOG
JÜRGEN FÖRSTER
JOACHIM HOFFMANN
ERNST KLINK
ROLF-DIETER MÜLLER
GERD R. UEBERSCHÄR

I. Hitler's Decision in Favour of War against the Soviet Union

JÜRGEN FÖRSTER

1. The Situation after the War in the West

NINE months after the beginning of the war Poland, Denmark, Norway, Belgium, Luxemburg, and the Netherlands were occupied, and France was laid low. German hegemony, west of the German–Soviet boundary of interests, thus extended over the major part of Europe, from the North Cape to the Bay of Biscay.[1] The importance which the swift victory over France had for the Reich in psychological, strategic, military, and historical respects should not be underrated. Owing to the triumph of *his* style of warfare Hitler in the summer of 1940 was carried on a wave of enthusiasm; concord between population and regime was assured. To Hitler and to those Germans who had experienced defeat in the First World War, the victory over France represented the expunging of a stain, of the 'disgrace of November 1918'. That 'worst disgrace of all time' had been felt so deeply that it had to be mitigated by the legend of the stab in the back. Now the escutcheon of German honour was once more clean. The security service of the SS observed among the population 'an unprecedented inner unity and close ties between front and homeland'.[2] Hitler not only stood on the pinnacle of his popularity in Germany, but his 'personal rule' in foreign and strategic issues was assured to a degree rarely equalled. Emotionally overcome, Walther von Brauchitsch, the commander-in-chief of the army, in an order of the day praised Hitler as 'the first soldier of the German Reich', around whom everyone was rallying 'in boundless confidence'.[3] The Führer would safeguard Germany's future for all time. The military leadership's earlier reservations 'over Hitler's war policy seemed refuted by its brilliant success; opposition no longer had a leg to stand on. Scarcely anyone felt scruples at a time when services were being rewarded and rich spoils awaited distribution.'[4] German war policy was determined by

---

[1] See Hillgruber, *Strategie*, 65 ff.; Krüger, 'Das Jahr 1941'; *Germany and the Second World War*, ii. 417 ff.; Hildebrand, *Das Dritte Reich*, 60 ff.; Carr, *Poland to Pearl Harbor*, 89 ff.; *Zwei Wege nach Moskau*; *Barbarossa*.

[2] *Meldungen aus dem Reich*, 77 (24 June 1940); see also Pflanz, *Geschichte der 258. Infanterie-Division*, i. 138–9.

[3] OKH/GenStdH/OpAbt (Ia), No. 20483/40 geh., 25 June 1940, BA-MA RH 19 I/50. On Brauchitsch see Bond, *Brauchitsch*.

[4] *Germany and the Second World War*, ii. 418.

Hitler's ideological fixations and political calculations even more forcefully than in 1939.

What was entirely overlooked amid those nationalist noises was the fact that Germany's position on the continent of Europe was by no means secure. It depended, above all, on Britain's readiness to come to terms or on her defeat. While the public cherished the hope that the attack against Britain would start immediately, with the British being defeated in six months at the most,[5] Hitler believed that, in view of its military weakness, London would give in. In the event that Britain decided to continue the war, he suggested that this would be based on the hope of holding out and drawing the Soviet Union and the United States into the conflict.[6] This mood among the German leadership had been summed up as early as the end of May 1940 by Hasso von Etzdorf, the German foreign office representative with the Army High Command, in the sentence 'We are seeking to arrive at an understanding with Britain on the basis of a division of the world.'[7] Ernst von Weizsäcker, secretary of state in the ministry of foreign affairs, had also regarded a British surrender as a certainty: 'The outcome will probably be that we shall offer the British the chance of getting out of the continent of Europe with their skin intact, leaving the Continent to us.'[8] Because Hitler was firmly convinced that an 'arrangement' between Britain, the naval power, and Germany, the continental power, was a historical necessity, no attempt was made to test the readiness for peace of the new British national government headed by Churchill. Instead, in a euphoria of triumph and a sense of unlimited capabilities, not only was an immediate start made with the territorial and political reorganization of Europe, but, as 'the most important building task of the Reich', a number of cities were to be architecturally reshaped by the year 1950 in a manner lending appropriate expression to the 'magnitude of our victory'.[9] Behind this stood the dogmatic idea that Britain's 'true' interests—her imperial and maritime interests—were threatened more by that naval and mercantile power, the United States, as well as by Japan, than by German hegemony over Europe. Hitler expected 'congenial' statesmen in London to come to a worldwide political arrangement with him. This would not only have confined Britain to the preservation and development of her Empire—while Germany would concentrate on 'further development' eastward—but also assign to London the role of a 'junior partner'.

[5] *Meldungen aus dem Reich*, 79 (27 June 1940).

[6] OKW/WFA/Abt. L, No. 33110/40 g.Kdos. Chefs., 24 June 1940, WFA notes on conference between Hitler and C.-in-C. Army on 23 June 1940, BA-MA RW 4/v. 581; cf. also Goebbels, *Diaries*, 123 (25 June 1940).

[7] Halder, *Diaries*, 413 (21 May 1940).

[8] *Weizsäcker-Papiere*, 204 (23 May 1940).

[9] Speer, *Inside the Third Reich*, 198 ff., 225 ff. Although this decree lists only Berlin, Munich, Linz, Hamburg, and the Party Rally buildings in Nuremberg, the cities of Königsberg, Oldenburg, Posen (Poznań), Saarbrücken, as well as the Wewelsburg castle were included in these building projects on 12 July 1940, RGBl. 1940, i. 989 ff.

Although Britain's failure to give in soon resulted in a muting of German euphoria, the triumph over France continued to prevent a rational appraisal of Germany's strategic position between the Anglo-Saxon naval powers and the Soviet Union. On 9 October 1939 Hitler justified his decision in favour of swift action against the Western powers by the argument that, with the United States becoming an enemy in the future and the essentially uncertain attitude of the Soviet Union, it was necessary to take advantage of the moment.[10] He was convinced that time was working for his opponents, who, both in terms of personnel and armaments, were inferior only for the time being. On 21 July 1940 Hitler, addressing the top leaders of the army, navy, and air force, made it the duty of the German leadership 'thoroughly to consider the American and Russian question'.[11] Judging the time factor against the background of the situation in the First World War, he believed it to be more favourable now that the western front had disappeared and Germany was armed in all spheres even for a protracted war. This turn in Hitler's estimation of the situation resulted from Britain's resolve to hold out. On 19 July 1940 Hitler, 'as the victor', had addressed to London one final 'appeal to reason': to put an end to the war.[12] His address to the Reichstag, postponed several times, with its attribution of responsibility for the war to 'Jewish-capitalist warmongers' on the one hand, and on the other its prophecy addressed to 'the so-called statesman' Churchill that Germany was assured of final victory, was planned for its propaganda effect on the German public rather than as a peace offer to Britain. The security service of the SS reported a few days later that the offer of peace to Britain had been received by the public with 'surprise'. The predominant view was that this appeal would be rejected with 'typically English arrogance, so that Britain would after all receive her deserved punishment'.[13] Although Hitler's speech was regarded by the Foreign Office as a serious invitation to a compromise peace,[14] it was uncompromisingly rejected by Lord Halifax, the British foreign secretary, on 22 July. With explicit reference to the programmatic speech made by Franklin D. Roosevelt, the American president, on 19 July he proclaimed, on behalf of the British government, an implacable struggle against the Axis. Hitler's unceasing hope that Britain would yield thus proved to be an illusion, and his assurances that London was already defeated and only failed to realize it proved to be wishful thinking.

For Hitler and the leadership élites in the forces, the administration, and the economy the principal question now was why Britain was continuing the struggle and how the war could be concluded. At his above-mentioned confer-

[10] Memorandum and directives on the conduct of the war in the west, in Jacobsen, *Vorgeschichte*, 5 ff.

[11] 1. Skl, KTB, pt. A, 236 (21 July 1940), BA-MA RM 7/14.

[12] Domarus, *Hitler*, ii. 1540 ff.

[13] *Meldungen aus dem Reich*, 89 (22 July 1940); Goebbels, *Tagebücher*, iv. 251 (24 July 1940; not in trans.)

[14] 'Summary of Principal Peace Feelers, April 1941 to June 1942', 1 July 1942, published in *Das 'Andere Deutschland'*, 187 ff.

ence with the top commanders of the army, navy, and air force on 21 July 1940 Hitler listed these reasons for London's unexpected attitude: '1: hope of a turn-round in America . . . 2: hope of Russia.'[15] Was this analysis of British policy correct? Churchill had indeed been hoping since the middle of May 1940 that the United States would abandon its neutrality in favour of non-belligerency and that it would support Britain 'with everything short of actually engaging armed forces'.[16] The seriousness of Britain's determination was emphasized by Churchill not only in his public speeches but also by his action against the French fleet at Oran.[17] In his uncompromising attitude towards Hitlerite Germany Churchill was in tune with the mood among the British public and the government.[18] Matters in London were by no means 'balanced on a knife-edge'[19] before the 'peace-minded' Foreign Office eventually yielded to Churchill's 'hard line for war'.[20]

Admittedly, the war cabinet had discussed the possibility of concluding the war by negotiation. But the discussion had been 'academic' because no one had thought an offer by Hitler that was acceptable to Britain likely to be forthcoming. Churchill's public pronouncement of 17 June 1940 that he would continue the war until victory over Germany was achieved was no one-man show. Sir Alexander Cadogan, under-secretary of state at the Foreign Office, eloquently reflected the militant mood in his diary: 'Everything is awful, but "Come the three corners of the world and we will fight them". We'll fight like cats—or die rather than submit to Hitler.'[21]

Unlike his military advisers, Roosevelt had believed since June 1940 that Britain was not only willing but also able to stand up to the German challenge.[22] But for the time being he adopted a temporizing attitude towards Britain's wooing for massive support. In view of the prevailing isolationist mood in the Congress and his own candidacy for a third term in the White House he confined himself to the public statement that he would 'extend to the opponents of force the material resources of the nation',[23] and speed up America's defence efforts. This attitude to the war in Europe, clearly pro-British while avoiding open conflict, was in line with the mood of the American public. The problem for Roosevelt and the 'internationalists' was to prepare the country for political confrontation with the Axis and with Japan. With their global understanding of the 'national interests' of the United States they regarded that confrontation as unavoidable. As early as January 1939

[15] Halder, *Diaries*, 515 (22 July 1940); 1. Skl, KTB, pt. A, 236 (21 July 1940), BA-MA RM 7/14.
[16] Woodward, *British Foreign Policy*, i. 337.
[17] See *Germany and the Second World War*, ii. 363 ff.
[18] Woodward, *British Foreign Policy*, i. 195; Ludlow, 'Unwinding of Appeasement', 44 ff.; Kettenacker, 'Die britische Haltung', 54 ff.; Kennedy, *The Realities behind Diplomacy*.
[19] Thus Hillgruber, 'Weltpolitische Lage', 270, basing himself on Martin, *Friedensinitiativen*, 270 ff.
[20] Thus Martin, *Friedensinitiativen*, 250, 274.
[21] *Cadogan Diaries*, 299 (15 June 1940); cf. also Colville, *Downing Street Diaries*.
[22] Matloff and Snell, *Strategic Planning*, 20; cf. Carr, *Poland to Pearl Harbor*, 101 ff.
[23] Bailey and Ryan, *Hitler vs. Roosevelt*, 74–5; Langer and Gleason, *Undeclared War*, 195.

Roosevelt had stated to the Senate military affairs committee that Germany, Italy, and Japan were striving for world domination and that, while the United States' first line of defence was in the Atlantic, it also included the existence of eighteen independent countries from the Baltic across the Balkans to Turkey and Persia.[24] Despite the changes in the European scene, violently brought about by Hitler since March and September 1939, the American government had not ruled out the possibility of negotiated peace between Germany, France, and Britain—as evidenced by the mission of Under-Secretary of State Sumner Welles. The defeat of France and the weakening of Britain brought Roosevelt's policies back to their starting-point. 'Anticipation of the consequences' of the German–Italian and Japanese sphere of power for the spiritual, economic, and military position of the United States was the decisive motive for the president to keep Britain and her Empire in the war—not any selfless interest in the preservation of Britain's position as a world power.[25] Roosevelt relied on a swing of public opinion in favour of intervention in the European war and of the deterrence of Japan. This situation, Roosevelt believed, would arise as soon as it was realized that American interests were being challenged by the political, economic, and military aggression of the Axis in Europe and of Japan in South-East Asia. Following his nomination as the Democratic Party's presidential candidate he declared in a keynote speech on 19 July 1940 that the totalitarian countries were *the* enemy of the United States. His election platform, admittedly, ruled out any American intervention in wars outside the western hemisphere, 'except in the case of attack'.[26] In Berlin Roosevelt's speech was understood as 'a clear challenge' to Germany. His rejection of National Socialism, according to the judgement of Hans Heinrich Dieckhoff, the former German ambassador to Washington, was explained by the 'English ideological' and 'New York Jewish atmosphere'. It had progressively intensified into fanatical hatred. Roosevelt's 'ultimate goal', according to Dieckhoff, was 'to assume the leadership of the democratic forces in the struggle against Germany'.[27]

Hitler had also been correct on 21 July 1940 about British hopes of a change in Soviet policy towards Germany. Although the dispatch of Sir Stafford Cripps as the new ambassador to Moscow in the first half of June 1940 was due to a proposal by Clement Attlee, the leader of the Labour Party and a member of Churchill's war cabinet, it was in line with Churchill's long-standing concept—which had failed in August 1939—of a 'grand alliance' between Britain and the Soviet Union to confront the challenge of Hitlerite Germany. Moreover, the British chiefs of staff in their analysis of the situation after the

[24] Quoted according to Offner, *United States*, 13–14.
[25] Junker, 'Weltmacht', 24. See Dallek, *Franklin D Roosevelt*, 199 ff.; Martin, 'Amerikas Durchbruch' 72 ff.; Junker, 'Deutschland'; Hearden, *Roosevelt*, 155 ff.; *Germany and the Second World War*, vi. 3 ff. (Boog).
[26] Bailey and Ryan, *Hitler vs. Roosevelt*, 100.
[27] *DGFP* D. x, Nos. 199 (21 July 1940), 252 (29 July 1940). See also Compton, *Swastika and Eagle*, 50 ff.

elimination of France on 25 May 1940 had made calculated allowance for Soviet alarm over the possible effect on Soviet interests of Germany's increase in power. Stalin, however, as early as 1 July 1940, had rejected the British government's attempt to drive a wedge into German–Soviet co-operation.[28] He had emphasized to Cripps that the Soviet Union had no interest in the restoration of the old political balance of power in Europe. That reply was not surprising, considering the advantage which the Soviet Union, too, was deriving from the German–Soviet non-aggression pact with its secret protocol. Also, Stalin did not share the British appraisal of the situation following the German victory over France. In his opinion Germany was not strong enough to dominate the whole of Europe, since she lacked the requisite sea power. Stalin had, moreover, immediately informed Hitler of his conversation with Cripps.[29] Although on 21 July Hitler described the rejection of the British ideas as 'welcome', this did not dispel his mistrust of Stalin's intentions. He instructed the commander-in-chief of the army to start work on the 'Russian problem'.[30] The Soviet foreign minister, in a major foreign-policy speech to the Supreme Soviet on 1 August 1940, declared that the 'neighbourly and friendly Soviet–German relations' were based 'not on accidental considerations of temporary advantage, but on fundamental state interests' on both sides.[31] Among the German public, on the other hand, there was a conviction that the Soviet Union 'as a final neighbour on Germany's frontier' was scarcely acceptable to Germany, and there was some doubt that the German–Soviet alliance 'under the present circumstances', i.e. after the German victory in the west, 'could really be of long duration'.[32]

The reports of the security service of the SS were not just propaganda efforts. There was disquiet also among the divisions earmarked for safeguarding Germany's eastern frontier. In mid-July 1940 the commander-in-chief of the army felt compelled to counteract rumours about German–Soviet tensions.[33] Brauchitsch dismissed the rumours as British propaganda. The Soviet Union, he said, had 'loyally' fulfilled its economic obligations and so far also kept to 'political agreements'. 'In so far as German interests had been in danger of being encroached upon within the framework of its policy', for instance by the planned annexation of the whole of the Bukowina, 'the Russians had shown understanding in agreeing to German suggestions.' The move of the Eighteenth Army into occupied Poland should likewise not be seen as a sign of worsening German–Soviet relations nor as a preparation

---

[28] Woodward, *British Foreign Policy*, i. 453 ff.; Hillgruber, *Strategie*, 85 ff.; Allard, *Stalin*, 215 ff.; Gorodetsky, *Cripps' Mission*; Kitchen, 'Churchill'.

[29] German Embassy Moscow, telephone message No. 1364, 13 July 1940, *DGFP*, D x, No. 164.

[30] Halder, *Diaries*, 517 (22 July 1940).

[31] 1. Skl, KTB, pt. A, 1 (1 Aug. 1940), BA-MA RM 7/15, and *Archiv der Gegenwart*, (1940), 4645. See also Pietrow-Ennker, *Stalinismus*, 199–200; Volkogonov, *Stalin*, 493.

[32] *Meldungen aus dem Reich*, No. 105 (15 July 1940), BA-MA, Wi/I F 5.3172.

[33] ObdH, No. 1125/40 geh. (17 July 1940), betr. Das deutsch-russische Verhältnis, ibid. RH 54/101.

for 'active military measures'. The commander-in-chief of the army wished all officers and other ranks to be instructed along those lines. But what did German–Soviet relations really look like? How had they developed since 1939?

As a result of Hitler's readiness to start the war for 'living-space' in spite of the British guarantee to Poland, the Soviet Union because of its strategic position had found itself fulfilling a spectacular role in the early summer of 1939.[34] Though unloved by the Western democracies and painted as the Devil by National Socialist Germany, Stalin had been courted by both sides. 'Totalitarian diplomacy of the purest kind'[35] had resulted in an alliance between two arch-enemies, in the German–Soviet non-aggression treaty of 23 August 1939 with its secret protocol, and in a total reversal of propaganda. Although that treaty had opened the door to a German policy of expansion through war, it had also cleared the road for the Soviet Union towards the territorial and political reorganization of eastern Europe. Hitler had concluded a pact 'with Satan' in order to 'cast out the Devil',[36] i.e. to deter the Western powers from fulfilling their obligations to Poland. When this gamble had failed, Germany found herself in, as it were, 'a reversal of fronts'[37] compared with the jumping-off position envisaged in Hitler's 'programme'. Britain, wooed to the last moment, had declared war on him, placing him in a position of strategic and economic dependence on the state whose annihilation was his central objective, the Soviet Union. Hitler left neither the commanders-in-chief of army, navy, and air force nor the senior line officers in any doubt[38] that he regarded the German–Soviet agreement purely as a short-term necessary 'tactical manœuvre'.[39] Treaties were observed only as long as they served a purpose. Permanent neutrality of the Soviet Union could not be ensured by any agreement but only by a swift demonstration of German strength. Germany could confront the Soviet Union only when she was secure in the west. Hitler was considering a German 'further development' towards the east and described occupied Poland as a future German deployment area.[40] Diplomats and economists, on the other hand, had prepared for long-term co-operation with the Soviet Union, with an informal economic hegemony in mind.[41] The Soviet Union was to function as a willing source of war supplies. That purpose was to be served also by the German–Soviet economic agreement of 11 February 1940. Soviet deliveries were regarded as of decisive importance to the

[34] See *Germany and the Second World War*, i. 698 ff.

[35] Bracher, *Krise Europas*, 187. From the Soviet point of view see Sipols, *Vorgeschichte*.

[36] Halder, *Diaries*, 32 (28 Aug. 1939).   [37] Hillgruber, 'Hitler-Stalin-Pakt', 24.

[38] See his observations on 27 Sept. 1939 (Halder, *KTB* i. 86; not in trans.), his memorandum of 9 Oct. 1939 (Jacobsen, *Vorgeschichte*, 5 ff.), and his speech of 23 Nov. 1939 (id., *1939–45*, 133 ff.).

[39] Below, *Hitlers Adjutant*, 184; Hewel, Tagebuch, 2 June 1941, IfZ, ED 100.

[40] Halder, *Diaries*, 107 (18 Oct. 1939). Col.-Gen. Beck, in his memorandum of 20 Nov. 1939, likewise saw a danger for German policy in the 'Russian colossus setting himself into westward motion' (Groscurth, *Tagebücher*, 487).

[41] See I.III.3(*b*) (Müller).

war. The military triumph in the west was thought to have opened for Berlin the road towards utilizing the Soviet Union as a supplier region. This euphoric assessment was at variance with the fact that Germany was not in a position to counterbalance Soviet deliveries by exports of her own, so that Moscow could call in its advances at any time. But how was the Soviet Union to be coerced into its assigned supplementary role in a unified European large-scale economic region for Germany's benefit, an economic region the creation of which had begun immediately after the conclusion of the French campaign? That question, based as it was on imperialist conceptual categories, had to be left open until the strategic situation in the west was finally settled in favour of the Reich, i.e. until Britain had been forced to her knees. What proposals to solve that problem were being worked out by the military staffs?

Major-General Alfred Jodl, chief of the Wehrmacht operations staff, submitted on 30 June 1940 a memorandum on the continuation of the war.[42] On the assumption that political measures were unable to compel Britain to give in, he proposed a direct military assault on the English mother country. This should open with the 'struggle against the British air force', as German command of the air was the prerequisite of a landing.

On 2 July 1940, therefore, the OKW instructed the three services to make preparations for a landing operation, but pointed out that this was merely a preparation for one possible option. In line with these reflections Field Marshal Hermann Göring, commander-in-chief of the Luftwaffe, declared that attack against enemy air-force formations both in the air and on the ground, by day and by night, was the supreme principle of air warfare against Britain. British supplies to Russia were to be cut off by attacks on supply-ports and port installations, as well as on freighters and warships.[43]

General of Artillery Franz Halder, chief of the army general staff, bluntly observed at the end of June 1940 that in the west there were no more victories to be won by the army for a long time.[44] The main burden of future operations, the defeat of Britain, would for the time being be borne by the air force and the navy. The scope of the army should therefore be cut back to 120 divisions; 35 divisions should be dissolved in favour of the economy or for the rehabilitation and reorganization of the remaining formations.[45] On the other hand, in view of the Red Army's entry into the Baltic States as well as into Bessarabia and the northern Bukowina, Halder saw a need for 'striking-power in the east'.[46] The transfer of the Eighteenth Army to the eastern defence districts and to occupied Poland meant the building up of offensive frontier protection. On 3 July 1940 Halder instructed Colonel (General Staff) Hans von Greiffenberg to examine 'the requirements of a military intervention which will compel Russia

---

[42] Klee, *Dokumente*, 298.   [43] See *Germany and the Second World War*, ii. 378.

[44] AOK 18, Ia, No. 157/40, g.Kdos. (29 June 1940), Besprechung am 28.6. durch den Chef des Generalstabes des Heeres in Versailles, BA-MA, 18. Armee 17562/2. The importance of this record, first quoted by I. Lachnit and F. Klein ('*Operationsentwurf Ost*'), is shown in the section by Ernst Klink, sect. I.IV.I. of the present volume.

[45] See sect. I.IV.I(*h*) (Klink).   [46] Halder, *Diaries*, 484 (25 June 1940).

to recognize Germany's dominant position in Europe'.[47] On these lines the army chief of staff informed Eighteenth Army headquarters on the following day of its newly formulated task in the east: 'to take measures for all eventualities'.[48] This task therefore exceeded offensive frontier protection so as to include a preventive strike against the Soviet Union, designed to reduce it to a second-rate power. Halder thereby set in motion an offensive military plan against the Soviet Union, aimed at a limited campaign for the occupation of the Baltic countries, Belorussia, and parts of the Ukraine. The enlargement of the strategic deployment area of the Red Army was not, on its own, sufficient to explain that decision by the Army High Command, since a direct military threat to Germany was not assumed to exist, only one to Romania. Here some earlier concepts were playing a part. Halder's decision sprang not only from his fundamental anti-Bolshevik attitude but also from the steady growth of the Soviet military potential, as well as from his understanding of the role of chief of the general staff. It is also possible that the army command—in contrast to the patent situation after the Polish campaign—was anxious to prove its efficiency in advance and not once more be left empty-handed. The first instruction to the Eighteenth Army also suggests that Weizsäcker had no real need to inform Halder that, after the defeat of Britain, Hitler was thinking of striking towards the east.[49]

The Army High Command—on this point it agreed with Hitler—could only explain London's rigid attitude by assuming that Britain still reposed some hope in Russia. Any understanding between 'the bear and the whale',[50] however, threatened Germany's hopes of hegemony over Europe. A blow against the Soviet Union would put an end to British hopes of a successful continuation of the war.

The German political and military leadership was determined to control future developments. The reduction of the ground forces, already started, was halted and preparations were put in hand for a landing in Britain. Hitler, too, now believed that an invasion was the most effective means for a quick end to the war. He certainly realized the risks involved. The prerequisites of 'Operation Sea Lion', Hitler declared on 21 July 1940, were total command of the air and completion of preparations by the beginning of September. Unless both conditions could be met 'other plans' would have to be considered. At the end of the conference, presumably after Grand Admiral Raeder, the commander-in-chief of the navy, had left, Hitler instructed the commander-in-chief of the army to start dealing with the 'Russian problem'. Initial studies on this had been carried out by the Army High Command since the end of June. On 21

---

[47] Ibid. 490 (3 July 1940).
[48] BA-MA, 18. Armee, 17562/2. Halder's reflections and his instruction to Eighteenth Army are first comprehensively discussed in the section by Klink, sect. I.IV.I(*b*). Hartmann, *Generalstabschef Halder*, 342 ff., arrives at a different assessment.
[49] Halder, *Diaries*, 487 (30 June 1940). On this see sect. I.IV.I(*b*) n. 65 (Klink).
[50] Halder, *Diaries*, 508 (13 July 1940), 503 (11 July 1940).

July Brauchitsch reported on them to Hitler.[51] The following day he informed Halder of Hitler's instructions and of his own report to him on the feasibility of a campaign against the Soviet Union. 'The various points of Halder's notes on the report of the commander-in-chief of the army make it clear that what Hitler had sketched out was not a "great war" for the defeat of the Soviet Union, but a military concept which seemed to agree with Halder's present ideas as well as with the deployment orders to Eighteenth Army.'[52] Hitler's directive to the Army High Command to start considering such an operation was understood by Halder as an instruction for a comprehensive strategic study. He therefore entrusted Major-General Erich Marcks, chief of the Eighteenth Army general staff, with its execution. On 29 July Jodl informed his closest collaborators in the Wehrmacht operations staff that Hitler had decided 'to eliminate once and for all the danger of Bolshevism by a surprise attack on Soviet Russia at the earliest possible moment'.[53]

The day before the conference called by Hitler for 31 July 1940 to review the overall situation of the war the army commander-in-chief and the chief of the general staff once more co-ordinated their views face to face. The naval operations staff had meanwhile come to the conclusion that it would have to advise against operation 'Sea Lion', at least for 1940.[54] Brauchitsch and Halder both saw the greatest danger in waiting for better conditions for an invasion of Britain, in that the military and political initiative might slip from Germany's hands. Along with the planning for a limited war against the Soviet Union they saw yet another possibility of holding on to the initiative against Britain—in military co-operation with Italy in the Mediterranean area and in a Soviet thrust towards the Persian Gulf. The Army High Command was thus taking up a proposal by Jodl of 30 June 1940. As an alternative to a direct strategy he had suggested an extension of the war against Britain along the periphery, with the help of all those states that might derive advantage from the break-up of the Empire. In order to escape the risk of a war on two fronts, a risk which would arise if London allied itself with Moscow and if Germany were first to attack the Soviet Union, four weeks later the Army High Command came out in favour of a continuation of German–Soviet co-operation worldwide. 'This being so, could deliver the British a decisive blow in the Mediterranean, shoulder them away from Asia, help the Italians in building up their Mediterranean Empire, and, with the aid of Russia, consolidate the Reich which we have created in western and northern Europe. That much accomplished, we could confidently face a war with Britain for many years.'[55]

Prior to an account of that decisive conference at the Obersalzberg it is

[51] Halder, *Diaries*, 515–16 (22 July 1940). On the probability of a report to Brauchitsch see sect. I.iv.1(*b*) n. 66 (Klink). This is also surmised by Fugate, *Operation Barbarossa*, though he overlooks Halder's crucial role.

[52] See sect. I.iv.1(*b*) (Klink). This research has not been assimilated by Robertson, 'Hitler', 373.

[53] Warlimont, *Hauptquartier*, 126.   [54] 1. Skl, KTB, pt. A (30 July 1940), BA-MA RM 7/14

[55] Halder, *Diaries*, 529–30 (30 July 1940).

necessary to deal with the navy's ideas on the strategy of the Reich in the summer of 1940. The great success against France and the prospect of peace with the Western powers had given rise within the naval operations staff to two memoranda, designed, beyond purely naval policy questions, to influence German foreign policy.[56] The reflections 'on the building up of the navy after the war' (4 July 1940) and on 'space extension and naval-base issues' (3 June 1940) went back to a directive by Raeder.[57] The formulation of a peacetime naval construction programme was naturally linked with the prerequisite geographical conditions. 'For the protection of the greater German living-space and for the discharge of its task in protecting maritime communications with a German colonial empire in central Africa' the naval command staked out claims to, among other places, Dakar, Conakry, and Freetown on the west coast of Africa, Zanzibar, Dar es Salaam, and Mombasa–Kilindnii on the east coast of Africa, as well as, in the Atlantic–European sphere, not only Iceland and the Faeroes but also the Azores. Some figures in the naval command rejected the idea of any 'compromise peace' with Britain which would let her keep her navy for the protection of the Empire. The officer in charge of strategic questions in the naval operations staff, Commander (*Fregattenkapitän*) Frank Aschmann, declared himself in favour of a peace through victory, which would deprive Britain of the chance of renewing her 'struggle of annihilation against Germany in the future'. 'The realization that America will be our next opponent must urge us on to achieve Britain's total defeat as quickly as possible. The destiny of her heritage [the Empire] should only be of secondary interest to us.'[58] Here issues were touched upon which subsequently, in September 1940, resulted in the development of a comprehensive naval strategy which would enable Germany also to face the United States in a global confrontation. Admittedly, the naval operations staff was somewhat reluctant to devote itself to the preparations it had been ordered to make for an invasion of Britain. A landing of German troops in England was to Raeder, as it was to Hitler, only the *ultima ratio* of German strategy towards Britain.[59] While the interests of the navy lay in other areas—U-boat and auxiliary-cruiser warfare, as well as questions of bases—Hitler, as an 'offended admirer of the British Empire' (K. D. Bracher), could see no advantage to Germany from the smashing of Britain and the resulting break-up of the Empire. 'German blood would be shed to accomplish something that would benefit only Japan, the United States, and others.'[60] These reservations could be perceived in his 'Directive No. 16' of 16 July, in which he informed the three services of his decision 'to prepare a landing operation against England and, *if necessary*, to carry it out'.[61] Hitler's statement of 21 July 1940 that, along with the American question, the 'Russian question' should also be 'thoroughly

[56] Salewski, *Seekriegsleitung*, i. 234–5; *Germany and the Second World War*, iii. 282 ff.
[57] Salewski, *Seekriegsleitung*, iii, Nos. 4, 5.   [58] Schreiber, 'Kontinuität', No. 6.
[59] Salewski, *Seekriegsleitung*, i. 257 ff.; *Germany and the Second World War*, ii. 369 ff.
[60] Halder, *Diaries*, 506 (13 July 1940).   [61] *Hitler's Directives*, No. 16 (author's italics).

considered'[62] presumably induced Raeder to have a memorandum prepared on it. On 28 July 1940 Rear-Admiral Kurt Fricke, chief of the operations department in the naval staff, submitted his 'Observations on Russia'.[63] He proceeded from the premiss that Germany's opponent 'now and in future' remained Britain and her potential allies, the United States and the Soviet Union. Fricke saw a danger to the Soviet Union's neighbours 'in the spirit of Bolshevism! It is in the interest of Europe that this chronic danger should be eliminated, one way or another, before long.' To him the justification for a war against the Soviet Union stemmed both from Soviet expansionism, especially in the direction of access to the Baltic and from Germany's objectives.

The safety of our homeland, however, also demands in the future the development of spatial unassailability, i.e. an expansion that would prevent any unchecked surprise penetration of vital parts of German soil, a deep forefield . . . which would at the same time provide the necessary living-space for the German nation in the future . . . It moreover demands the greatest possible economic autarky, especially in commodities vital in wartime (e.g. oil, foodstuffs). The further development of Germany requires raw materials and also, to the same extent, markets for her manufactures. For both these purposes Russia is ideally suited . . . The Baltic *must* become Germany's 'Mare nostrum'.

The powerful Soviet fleet in the Baltic and a Red Army capable of any kind of military operation seemed to Fricke to represent a permanent threat to Germany, placing a burden on her 'development at home and overseas'. The German Wehrmacht, in his estimation, was 'vastly superior' to the Soviet forces. Although the memorandum did not support any immediate German offensive action against the Soviet Union, it nevertheless regarded a war in the east as promising once the war against Britain had reached some kind of conclusion. This sentence was thickly underlined by Raeder. The memorandum reflects an increased assurance of power after the victory over France as well as a blending of traditional political ideas with National Socialist thinking. At the same time it shows that initially Hitler's 'programme' did not necessarily meet 'with opposition, and certainly not with incomprehension' by the navy.[64]

How then was Hitler going to react to the strategic situation into which he had manipulated the Reich? What possibilities did he see of eliminating the 'reversed fronts' now that Britain was not yielding? Was Hitler prepared to stake the position of power Germany had gained up to the summer of 1940 and risk war with the Soviet Union, his crucial foreign-policy objective, even though Germany was strategically tied down in the west? It would be a misjudgement of Hitler's dogmatism to believe that he had abandoned his 'programme', his ideas revolving around war, living-space, race, Jewry, economic self-sufficiency, and world-power status, or his grandiose alternative: victory or annihilation. From the beginning he had ruled out capitulation, i.e.

[62] See sect. I.I.   [63] Salewski, *Seekriegsleitung*, iii, No. 6.   [64] Ibid. i. 358.

submission to his opponent's will. His living-space programme contained all the factors which, individually or collectively, figured also in the reflections of military leaders, diplomats, and economists. Expansion of living-space 'towards the east', in Hitler's opinion, not only promised the safeguarding of Germany's economic existence within a blockade-proof greater European economy—because of the foodstuffs and raw materials to be found in the Soviet Union—but would also afford an insuperable defence in depth, absolute political freedom of action, and independence from international ties and obligations. Only the creation of a continental empire which included the 'Russian space' would, he firmly believed, enable him to conduct policy on a global scale. Inseparably linked with these political, military-geographical, and economic motives in Hitler's living-space programme were his racial ideas concerning the necessary annihilation of 'Jewish Bolshevism'.

2. The Turn to the East: Hitler's Decision of 31 July 1940 and its Consequences

The military outcome in the west had failed to yield the expected political success. Britain, considered the principal enemy since the autumn of 1939, was not inclined to conclude a compromise which would have left Hitler with the Continent from the North Cape to the Bay of Biscay. London would have been ready to negotiate only if Hitler surrendered himself and his 'programme'. For London, just as for Berlin, this war, which had long become total war, was now about victory or defeat; initiatives aiming at a compromise peace no longer had any hope of success. 'Britain fought on in the hope of American support and of a change in German–Soviet relations.'[65] What conclusion did Hitler draw in view of the long-term threat to Germany's position from the Anglo-American naval powers and from the Soviet Union? At the end of July 1940 he summoned the top leaders of the OKW, the army, and the navy to the Obersalzberg for a conference on the overall situation of the war. These talks centred, initially, on the planned landing in England.[66] Against his own better judgement and that of the naval operations staff, Raeder did not urge a postponement of Operation Sea Lion. Although the commander-in-chief of the navy listed numerous maritime difficulties, he declared the operation to be feasible after mid-September, provided preparations were not upset in some unexpected way by the weather or by enemy measures. Raeder made a note of Hitler's decision that the base date for a landing in England should be 15 September. Admittedly, Hitler made the decision on whether 'Sea Lion' was to be implemented then or deferred until May 1941 dependent on the effect of the planned air offensive against Britain.[67]

---

[65] *Germany and the Second World War*, ii. 418.

[66] Halder, *Diaries*, 530 ff. (31 July 1940); 'Führer Conferences', 122 ff. (31 July 1940).

[67] 'Führer Conferences', 124 (31 July 1940); *Hitler's Directives*, No. 17. The battle for air superiority over England began on 15 Aug. 1940 and was presently extended into strategic aerial

It appears that Raeder did not participate in the subsequent talks at the Berghof. From Hitler's arguments about a strategy for finishing the war against Britain, which was 'in fact won', by an actual victory the chief of the Army General Staff took down the following notes:

Britain's hope lies in Russia and the United States. If Russia drops out of the picture America, too, is lost for Britain, because elimination of Russia would tremendously increase Japan's power in the Far East. Russia is the Far Eastern sword of Britain and the United States pointed at Japan . . . Russia is the factor on which Britain is relying most. Something must have happened in London! . . . With Russia smashed, Britain's last hope would be shattered. Germany then will be master of Europe and the Balkans. Decision: Russia's destruction must therefore be made a part of this struggle. Spring 1941. The sooner Russia is crushed, the better. Attack achieves its purpose only if Russian state can be shattered to its roots with one blow. Holding part of the country alone will not do. Standing still for the following winter would be perilous . . . Resolute determination to eliminate Russia . . .[68]

Hitler defined his war aim as the 'liquidation of Russia's manpower'[69] and the conquest of the Ukraine, the Baltic States, and Belorussia.

Neither during nor after the conference of 31 July 1940, which marked the turn to the east, was there any 'argument about the basic decision or the operational plan as a whole'[70] that could be compared to the period leading up to the offensive in the west. Even though the Army High Command had on the day before expressed the view that it would be better to 'keep on friendly terms with Russia'[71] in order to eliminate the risk of a war on two fronts, it did not put forward that argument when facing Hitler at the Berghof. It would be too simple to explain Brauchitsch's and Halder's behaviour simply as a lack of moral courage. Instead it has to be assumed that both of them agreed with Hitler's assessment of the situation. Because the German claim to hegemony in Europe appeared to be threatened in the long term by the Soviet Union, the army command concurred with Hitler on the need for offensive action against the Red Army. There was also agreement on the view that there was no direct military threat to the Reich from the Soviet Union in the immediate future, although there was such a threat, to a diminished extent, to Romania and Finland. At the same time, information available to OKH on the Red Army seemed to indicate that this was beginning to develop into a modern army, in

warfare against Britain's industrial potential. Even though the proposed landing in mid-Oct. 1940 had to be postponed until spring 1941, the 'fiction of invasion' was maintained by a war of attrition from the air, by diversionary manœuvres in the Mediterranean area, and by propaganda deceptions. See *Germany and the Second World War*, ii. 374 ff., and sect I.iv.2(a) in the present volume (Boog).

[68] Halder, *Diaries*, 533–4 (31 July 1940).

[69] Although the war aim proclaimed by Hitler resembles his intentions before the campaigns against Poland and France, his programmatic objectives lead one to assume a different significance, one which therefore also differs from Clausewitz's much-quoted war aim: not to reach a certain line on the ground but to pursue the annihilation of the opponent, i.e. of his army.

[70] Hillgruber, *Strategie*, 211.   [71] Halder, *Diaries*, 530 (30 July 1940).

terms of leadership, inner structure, and equipment, one that would later be in a position to conduct major offensive mobile-warfare operations even against the Reich.[72] Hitler's decision to secure his domination in Europe by smashing the Soviet Union was therefore in line with the Army High Command's own views. The German Army High Command's appraisal of the Soviet potential, especially the presumed inferiority of the Soviet leadership, was compounded of an exaggerated belief in Germany's military strength after her rapid victory over France, the 'historical enemy', a sense of cultural superiority *vis-à-vis* the Slav world, and an anti-Bolshevik estimation of the enemy, coloured by a latent anti-Semitism.

How is this turn to the east in the summer of 1940, when Hitler proceeded from a global political appraisal of the situation, to be judged? Was there really, in view of Britain's intransigent attitude and refusal to surrender, no other way than to attack the Soviet Union?[73] Is it a fact that Hitler, while returning to his political axiom, the conquest of 'living-space' in the east, actually put forward strategic justifications to his military leaders?[74] Did Hitler want to destroy the Soviet Union because it might be used by Britain as a continental sword both against Germany and against Japan?[75] Should the decision of 31 July 1940 not be interpreted instead in the sense that war against the Soviet Union was being planned not *because* of the continuation of the conflict but *in spite* of it? Or did annihilation of the Soviet Union, the main goal of his political and racial 'programme', become for Hitler, in the summer of 1940, also a means of forcing Britain to make peace?[76]

In the summer of 1940 Hitler linked the realization of his twenty-year-old living-space programme—which united expansion towards the east, annihilation of Bolshevism, and extermination of Jewry[77]—with the strategic necessity of securing the German sphere of power against the growing challenge by the Anglo-American naval powers. Not least because of Roosevelt's 'clear challenge' of 19 July 1940, the United States now moved into the focus of Hitler's strategy. The American president was unmistakably backing Churchill's course and arming his nation for what he believed to be inevitable conflict with the Axis and Japan. For the time being Berlin could meet only indirectly the danger represented by the United States to the German position. That purpose was served by the 'Tripartite Pact', concluded between Italy, Japan, and Germany on 27 September 1940, which was designed to warn Washington

[72] See sects. I.iv.1 (Klink) and I.ii.2 (Hoffmann).

[73] Thus D. C. Watt in the *Times Literary Supplement*, 3879 (16 July 1976), in his review of Cecil, *Hitler's Decision*.

[74] This is how Haffner, *The Meaning of Hitler*, 115, and Cecil, *Hitler's Decision*, 68 ff., interpret Hitler's remarks.

[75] *Germany and the Second World War*, ii. 29. Schustereit, *Vabanque*, likewise perceives no programmatic aims of Hitler. A similar argument in Koch, 'Hitler's "Programme"'

[76] Thus Hillgruber, *Strategie*, 200, and Hildebrand, *Das Dritte Reich*, 63–4.

[77] Erdmann, *Zeit der Weltkriege*, 337, 522; Carr, *Poland to Pearl Harbor*, 121–2. Mayer, *Why Did the Heavens Not Darken?*, on the other hand, emphasizes the theme of the crusade against 'Jewish Bolshevism'.

against extending the war.[78] If Hitler was to hold on to 'the law of action' and if the Reich was to be able in the long term to stand up to the global challenge of the United States, he had, in view of his war dogma of victory or defeat— 'all or nothing'—no other choice than a further rapid campaign to overthrow the last remaining great power on the Continent, the Soviet Union. The compulsion to swift action sprang from the steadily increasing American potential, even though Hitler did not believe the United States would be ready for war until 1942. Before the increasing co-operation of the Anglo-American naval powers and a heavily armed Soviet Union were able to restrict Germany's external freedom of movement, the conquest of the European regions of the Soviet Union was to enable Germany to gain a strategic and economic position that would convince Britain of the hopelessness of her struggle and make confrontation with the United States seem no great danger. His political interest in successfully coming through the overall war was linked in Hitler's strategy with his programmatic goals *vis-à-vis* the Soviet Union. The global political justification for his decision of 31 July to attack the Soviet Union in the spring of 1941 should not lead us to overlook the links between calculation and dogma, between will to power and ideology, in Hitler's war policy. The turn to the east was neither the final, as it were logical, step on the road towards the creation of an autarkic German colonial empire, nor 'mere compulsion to act in order to escape the waiting-war of the summer of 1940 and to reach a decisive conclusion to it'.[79] Hitler's living-space programme must be seen as an equally substantive basis for his decision to hold on to the military and political initiative by smashing the Soviet Union as it was for his directives of March 1941 to conduct Operation Barbarossa as an uncompromising war of annihilation.[80] As in the summer of 1940, Hitler again fused ends and means. Not only was any potential resistance to German rule in the east to be eliminated by the extermination of 'Jewish Bolshevism', but the Germanic race was to be given the chance of a 'pure' development. Only the symbiosis of rational thought and dogma can be viewed, in Max Weber's sense, as an 'adequate cause' of the decision of 31 July 1940 and of the directives of March 1941.

Even though the turn to the east in the summer of 1940 cannot by any means be regarded as irrevocable, as a 'point of no return', it nevertheless immediately triggered political, military, and armament consequences which presently developed a dynamic of their own. Hitler's decision of 31 July 1940, unlike his instruction to the commander-in-chief of the army ten days earlier, for the first time set in motion the entire apparatus of Wehrmacht operations. In strategic terms it affected only the army. Along with other departmental heads in the Army General Staff, Halder issued new instructions also to Major-General Marcks.[81] For the armaments industry the enlargement of the army field forces to 180 divisions with the corresponding troops gave rise to

---

[78] See sect. I.1.4.   [79] As Broszat, 'Motivation', 408, believes.
[80] See sect. I.VII.   [81] See the sect. I.IV.1(*d*) (Klink).

numerous problems of personnel and equipment. On 2 August 1940 Field Marshal Wilhelm Keitel, the OKW chief of staff, justified Hitler's decision to General of Infantry Georg Tomas, chief of the war economy and armaments department, as due to the fact 'that (1) Britain's collapse in 1940 could, in the circumstances, no longer be counted on, (2) an intervention by America was feasible in 1941, (3) relations with Russia might undergo a change in 1941'.[82] While OKH initially assumed that the framework of the armaments programme of 9 July 1940 would not have to be substantially extended, the manpower problem soon gave rise to the most serious problems for armament planning in the army. An order signed by Keitel on 28 September 1940 for a stepping up of armaments defined the principal task for the army as the provision of armaments for 180 field divisions and appropriate occupation divisions by the spring of 1941. In order to maintain or even increase the performance of armament plants, it was decided to withdraw 300,000 trained workers from the army and make them available to the armaments industry.[83]

A change was perceptible also in the foreign policy of the Reich. The war Hitler envisaged against the Soviet Union demanded the availability of lesser states and nations in northern and south-east Europe, as called for by German strategic and economic interests. These interests had now to be safeguarded in Romania and Finland, i.e. in countries which, in the Soviet interpretaion of the Hitler–Stalin pact, belonged to the Soviet Union's sphere of interest. Renewed Hungarian claims to Transylvania, following the Red Army's invasion of Bessarabia and the Bukowina, were jeopardizing 'tranquillity in the Balkans' and increasing the danger of Soviet intervention. Hitler was therefore anxious to terminate the Hungarian–Romanian conflict as speedily as possible. His initial idea was a bilateral agreement between Budapest and Bucharest. However, on 30 August 1940, when these negotiations had reached an impasse, Hitler, with Mussolini's support, imposed on Hungary and Romania an arbitration, albeit one which provided no more than a superficial resolution of the Hungarian–Romanian quarrel. Romania's newly defined frontiers were guaranteed by Germany and Italy.[84] This second 'by-passing' of the Soviet Union—after the Munich agreement of 1938—was perceived by Moscow as an affront against the spirit of the Hitler–Stalin pact.

This political check on a possible realization of Soviet interests was covered, on the military plane, by the creation of a mobile reserve group in the Vienna area. The XXXXth Army Corps was in readiness to thrust across Hungary within a matter of days in order to occupy the Romanian oilfields ahead of a Soviet coup. Whether that objective could have been achieved in the event of

[82] Minute on the development of the armaments situation in summer 1940, sgd. Thomas, in *KTB OKW* i. 968–9.

[83] See sect. I.III.4 (Müller); *Das Deutsche Reich und der Zweite Weltkrieg*, v/1, sect. III.IV.3; and Kröner, 'Squaring the Circle', 292 ff.

[84] See sects. I.IV.2 I.IV.4(*a*).

an armed conflict between Hungary and Romania must remain in doubt. Hitler at any rate was prepared to throw Germany's political weight into the balance in order to secure Romania's supposedly 'vital' mineral oil.

A similarly clear consequence of the decision of 31 July 1940 may be discerned in German–Finnish relations. Hitler—in contrast to his earlier policy towards Helsinki, which had been entirely in line with the German–Soviet partnership—was now showing interest in political support for Finland and her rearmament. Here too the switch in German foreign policy was accompanied by precautionary military measures. Deployment of a force was prepared in northern Norway, so as to occupy the nickel region of Petsamo in the event of Soviet action.[85]

Although the military leadership was claiming a position of hegemony in Europe for the Reich, and although the military leaders believed they had understood the need for a timely elimination of the Red Army, these rather imperialistic ideas differed from Hitler's programmatic aims *vis-à-vis* the Soviet Union and from the 'constants of his picture of the world'.[86]

3. PROGRAMMATIC OBJECTIVES *VIS-À-VIS* THE SOVIET UNION AND THEIR ACCEPTANCE AMONG THE GERMAN OFFICER CORPS

Concepts such as 'programme' and 'step-by-step plan', and adjectives such as 'programmatical' or 'axiomatic', may suggest a high degree of systematic thinking in Hitler's war policy. Used as heuristic tools, however, they assist in an understanding of Hitler's motivations and goals, which, regardless of any tactical improvisations, represented the permanent basis of his political actions as Reich Chancellor.[87] An interpretation of Hitler's policy as a symbiosis of dogma and rational judgement, of ideology and will to power, counteracts any tendency to dismiss his dogmatic ideas as phantasms and to explain his deeds as acts of aimless opportunism. Hitler's 'programme' slots into the continuity of German history. It should be seen as a subjectively moulded conglomerate of political visions articulated in German society since the end of the nineteenth century, of ideological persuasions, and of lessons learnt from the military defeat of 1918, the German revolution, and the Versailles peace treaty of June 1919. Constants in Hitler's view of the world were the social-Darwinist conviction that the struggle for survival governs not only the life of the individual but also, as a universal principle of life, the development of nations; the belief that this struggle for survival can be won only by a people of superior racial quality under an outstanding leader, as well as a radical anti-Semitism

---

[85] See sect. I.VI.I (Ueberschär).   [86] Fest, *Hitler*, 216.

[87] On Hitler's programme see, in addition to his own programmatic writings (*Mein Kampf*, *Hitler's Secret Book*, and his *Monologe*), Jäckel, *Hitlers Weltanschauung*; Kuhn, *Programm*; Hillgruber, *Germany and the Two World Wars*, 69 ff.; Erdmann, *Zeit der Weltkriege*, 336 ff.; Rich, *War Aims*, i. 3 ff.; *Germany and the Second World War*, i. 543 ff.; Hildebrand, 'Hitlers "Programm"', 63 ff.; id. *Das Dritte Reich*, 168 ff.; Hauner, 'World Dominion'.

'of reason', that would ensure a racially 'pure' flowering of 'Germandom'. His fundamental foreign-policy objective, the conquest of 'living-space' in the east, likewise derived from that ideological basis.

Thereby we National Socialists deliberately draw a line under the foreign-policy development of the pre-war period. We start where an end was made six centuries ago. We stop the eternal Germanic drift to the south and the west of Europe and turn our eyes towards the land in the east. We put a final end to the colonial and trade policy of the pre-war period and switch over to the soil policy of the future. But if in Europe today we speak of new land and soil we are, above all, thinking of Russia and the marginal states subjected to it.[88]

Once the German people understood this far-sighted spatial policy, whose aim was a 'healthy' ratio between population total and land area, German foreign policy—of this Hitler was convinced—would acquire stability and the sterile 'economic and frontier policy' of Wilhelminian Germany would be finally overcome.[89] Only an operation which guaranteed security and land for the German people could justify the sacrifice of blood necessary for war. For that reason Hitler saw no solution to Germany's economic or political problems in a mere revision of the treaty of Versailles. Only the expansionist living-space concept could, in his opinion, ensure for the German people independence and power and their 'daily bread'—not the development of a modern industrial and export economy.[90] The natural leadership role of the 'Germanic-northern race' in the international struggle for survival and the unique 'racial quality' of the German people justified, in Hitler's eyes, the conquest of the necessary 'living-space' at the expense of other, racially inferior, nations, in particular the Slavs, for the establishment of a Greater Reich of all Germans and the racial reshaping of Europe. 'The struggle for world hegemony will be decided for Europe by the possession of Russia's space: this will make Europe the most blockade-proof spot in the world.'[91]

Germany's forcible expansion at the expense of the Soviet Union seemed to him so promising because the 'Jewish-Bolshevik' revolution of 1917, together with 'Slav racial instincts', had exterminated the last remnants of the formerly leading Germanic elements in Russia. Slavdom had since been disintegrated by Jewry, that 'ferment of decomposition'. That was why Hitler believed the 'gigantic empire in the east' to be 'ripe for collapse. And the end of Jewish rule in Russia [will] also be the end of Russia as a state.'[92] In view of this 'racially ideological diagnosis of weakness' (M. Messerschmidt) Hitler declared that it was fortunate for the future of the German nation that such a development had taken place in Russia. As a result the spell had been broken 'which might have prevented us from seeking the goal of German foreign policy where alone and solely it can lie: space in the east.'[93]

---

[88] Hitler, *Mein Kampf*, 950.   [89] Id., *Hitler's Secret Book*, 210.
[90] See Krüger, 'Hitlers Wirtschafterkenntnisse', 269 ff.; Zitelmann, *Hitler*, 272 ff.
[91] Hitler, *Monologe*, 62 (17–18 Sept. 1941).   [92] Id., *Mein Kampf*, 952.
[93] Id., *Hitler's Secret Book*, 139.

From the natural claim of the 'Germanic-northern race' to world hegemony
Hitler also derived the need for a revolutionary struggle against 'Jewry', which
he accused of striving on its part for world domination. To prevent this was to
him a 'mission' of the German people, and he saw himself as the protagonist
against that 'world corrupter': 'By opposing the Jew I am fighting for the work
of the Lord.'[94] Jewry was declared to be everyone's enemy' because, as a
parasite, it was 'corroding' the 'racial quality' of every nation. Jewry's ultimate
aim was the 'denationalization, the inter-bastardization, of the rest of the
nations, the lowering of the racial level of the highest, the extermination of
national intelligentsias, and their replacement by members of their own
people'.[95] Because Bolshevism to Hitler represented the most extreme form
of 'world Jewry', because Jewish rule and Bolshevism were to him identical, he
called the 'decomposition' of a nation by Jewry its 'blood Bolshevization'. So
as not to expose his own nation to any 'decomposition of its blood' he wanted
to exterminate the 'cancer' root and branch.

Hitler's fanatical hatred of Jews is attributed by recent psycho-historical
research to a precisely datable key experience at the army hospital of Pasewalk
in November 1918.[96] Hitler is thought to have transferred his personal hatred
for a particular Jew to Jews in general, and to have blamed them for the
German defeat. That personal trauma, it is thought, was only subsequently
transformed by Hitler into a racial attitude and 'rationalized' as a negative
objective. He now saw his task as preventing the 'Jewish world conspiracy' for
the extermination of all 'Aryans'. This psycho-historical interpretation is not
accepted by all historians. Some of them continue to believe that 'the Siamese
twins of anti-Semitism and anti-Marxism' moulded his ideas from 1919–20
onward, 'without it being possible to determine whence or when Hitler
adopted them'.[97] Although Hitler himself differentiated his own anti-Semitism
of 'reason' and action from that of mere 'sentiment',[98] he later managed to
exploit other forms of anti-Semitism, such as religious anti-Judaism or com-
petition-motivated anti-Semitism, for the satisfaction of his own obsession:
the persecution and extermination of the Jews as the prerequisite of a racially
'pure' development of Germandom in Europe. The postulate of certain laws
of history, e.g. the world-moving principle of the racial idea, in a sense
removed his actions from personal individual responsibility for the planned
extermination of 'Jewish Bolshevism', for the decimating and expulsion of the
Slavs from the territories to be conquered.

In the realization of his 'programme' Hitler attached overriding importance
to relations with Britain,[99] as he was anxious to avoid a war on two fronts. War

---

[94] Id., *Mein Kampf*, 84. On Hitler's anti-Semitism see Hillgruber, 'Ideologisch-dogmatische
Grundlage', and Bacharach, 'Rassenantisemitismus'.

[95] *Hitler's Secret Book*, 213.   [96] Binion, *Hitler*. See Hillgruber, 'Tendenzen', 606 ff.

[97] Thus Albrecht Tyrell in his review of Hitler, *Sämtliche Aufzeichnungen*, in *Das Parlament*, 46,
(14 Nov. 1981).

[98] Hitler, *Sämtliche Aufzeichnugen* (16 Sept. 1919).

[99] On Britain's key role see Henke, 'England-Konzeption'; Hildebrand, *Das Dritte Reich*, 18–19;
and *Germany and the Second World War*, i. 548 ff., 594 ff.

with France, the 'perpetual disturber of world peace', he regarded as indispensable anyway, and this was to precede the struggle in the east. His assessment of Britain's reaction to the establishment of a German continental empire was causing Hitler some difficulty because he allowed himself to be guided by wishful thinking and ideological premisses. On the one hand Hitler firmly believed that an 'arrangement' with Britain was possible, a delimitation of interests between a naval and mercantile power and a continental military power, co-operation on a world scale. On the other hand he saw his policy of German hegemony in Europe threatened by the fact that 'world Jewry' with its 'Bolshevik disintegrating tendencies' might determine British policy and eclipse 'ancient British traditions'. In contrast to Russia, where the decision had already gone in favour of Jewry, it seemed to Hitler that in Britain the struggle for power was still undecided. In his wishful image of Britain her imperial and maritime interests occupied a higher position than her interest in maintaining a balance of power in Europe. The latter, however, was diametrically opposed to his expansionist aims. That was why hypotheses on possible modes of action were brought into Hitler's calculations as if they were political realities. If London did not act as expected, it meant that 'the Jew' had won over 'the Briton'.[100]

The question of the relationship between illusion and reality in Hitler's concept of Britain up to his attack on Poland has already been answered in the sense that this was a process of his wishful thinking gradually giving way to an acknowledgement of facts.[101] This interpretation needs some amplification: even beyond 3 September 1939 Hitler still believed in the possibility of a delimitation of interests between Britain and Germany, so that one has to speak of a 'continuity of error' (F. Fischer). Hitler's belief in an arrangement with Britain had by no means been undermined by the British declaration of war. After the German triumph over France Hitler therefore confidently expected Britain to come to terms. In the summer of 1941 he then believed that victory over the Soviet Union would mark the beginning of a durable friendship with Britain, one that would endure even in a future war against the United States.[102] At the beginning of 1942 Hitler revealed the whole contradiction of his 'policy of alliance' with London when he declared that he did not *know* whether Britain would drop out of the war against Germany, but he *thought* so.[103] It was Hitler's 'most sacred conviction' that after the loss of Singapore to the Japanese the British would at long last come to their senses and depose Churchill, the warmonger.[104] When that too failed to materialize, Hitler—as he had done in 1939—attributed the responsibility to 'world Jewry', which had always fought against German–British understanding.

Ideologically founded convictions made any realistic appraisal of British policy impossible: they must be seen as the reason why Hitler's policy *vis-à-vis* Britain had been ambivalent from the outset. Rational judgement and dogma,

---

[100] *Hitler's Secret Book*, 215.   [101] *Germany and the Second World War*, i. 595–6.
[102] Hitler, *Monologe*, 45, 56 (22–3 July, 8–11 Aug. 1941).   [103] Ibid. 184 (7 Jan. 1942).
[104] Ibid. 93, 195 (18 Oct. 1941, 12–13 Jan. 1942).

racial and world policy, were too closely interwoven.[105] Whereas in the long term Hitler was interested in freedom for his racially based, expansionist military strategy against the Soviet Union, the British had a marked interest in the maintenance of peace in Europe. Although British appeasement policy was primarily a defensive strategy for safeguarding Britain's position as a world power,[106] London also showed itself ready to take on Hitler's challenge in order 'to check and defeat Germany's attempt at world domination'.[107] Britain's refusal to tolerate Germany's expansion towards the east compelled Hitler, on the one hand, to improvise in his foreign policy and, on the other, to engage in a political and military gamble in line with the slogan 'Germany will either be a world power or she will not be at all.'[108] The racial-policy version of that social-Darwinist alternative in the struggle against the 'Jewish-Bolshevik world enemy' was: 'Either victory for the Aryan side or else its annihilation and victory for the Jews.'[109]

These doctrinaire ideas of Hitler should not be underrated, in spite of their often untenable premisses. Nor should they be seen as 'predominantly functional, but primarily and in their own right as political objectives'.[110] They were faith and estimation of the enemy at the same time, they can be traced in Hitler's remarks to the very end, and they should be viewed as the basis of his political decisions. From this ideological basis of social Darwinism, of the racial theory, of anti-Bolshevism, and of anti-Semitism sprang also his principal foreign-policy objective—the conquest of new 'living-space' for the German people in the east, its traditional sphere of expansion. To this Hitler adhered inflexibly, in spite of numerous tactical vacillations.

This axiom of future German policy was not only expounded by him in abstract terms in *Mein Kampf* and *Hitler's Secret Book*, but also aggressively championed by Hitler after his appointment as Chancellor. This is proved not only by his well-known statements of 3 February 1935, 5 November 1937, 23 May, 22 August, and 23 November 1939, by his memoranda on the deployment of the economy of August 1936 and on the continuation of the war of 9 October 1939, but also by a hitherto little-quoted address to the commanding officers of the army on 10 February 1939.[111] With it he intended, in a specific political situation, not only to solicit confidence in his risky expansionist strategy, but also to 'expound the fundamental National Socialist ideas to the Wehrmacht's top leaders in a manner in which, for understandable reasons, this could not be done in public'. A general needed to know the categories of

---

[105] See Hildebrand, 'Rassen- contra Weltpolitik', 210.

[106] See Kettenacker, 'Diplomatie der Ohnmacht', 223 ff.

[107] Remark by Chamberlain on 27 Mar. 1939, Committee on Foreign Policy, PRO CAB 27/624.

[108] Hitler, *Mein Kampf*, 950. On 8 Nov. 1938 Himmler had expressed this alternative as 'either the Greater German empire or nothingness': Himmler, *Geheimreden*, 49.

[109] Hitler's speech on 12 Apr. 1922, quoted according to Thies, *Architekt*, 44.

[110] Hildebrand, *Das Dritte Reich*, 173.

[111] BA NS 11/28, published in *Hitlers Städte*, 289 ff. Attention to this speech was first drawn, though in a different context, by Thies, *Architekt*, 112. For the other speeches see ibid. 106, 110, 120.

his policy, in order to comprehend the further actions of the politician. One could champion with 'special boldness and vigour' only what one had understood. For that reason Hitler expounded his belief that its present living-space was too small for the German nation because its people could not be fed and its industry could not be supplied with the raw materials it needed. The alternative solutions on offer were either to ensure the necessary imports of foodstuffs and raw materials by increased exports or to adjust the living-space to the growing population figures. Hitler openly stated that he proposed to take the latter road only. He had determined to solve the problem of German space, and that idea now dominated his entire existence. Although the Soviet Union was not mentioned by name, this was no more than a repetition of his programme of 3 February 1933: 'Perhaps the capture of new export facilities, perhaps—and probably better—conquest of new living-space in the east and its ruthless Germanization.' Nor did Hitler in February 1939 leave his officers in any doubt over the character of the impending war. Because people were now driven into battle by racial realizations, the next war would be 'a purely ideological war, i.e. consciously a national and racial war'. Hitler demanded that the officers should see in him not only the supreme commander of the Wehrmacht, but also the supreme ideological leader, to whom, as officers, they were likewise pledged for life or death. That conviction was heightened by Hitler into the demand 'that even if, in my struggle for this ideology, I am abandoned by the rest of the nation in its entirety, then, more than ever, every German soldier, the entire officers' corps, man by man, must stand beside me and by me'. The reaction of his listeners was 'in part enthusiastic, in part very sceptical'.[112]

Hitler's concept of the officers as the 'very last guard' in the realization of his ideologically coloured objectives derives its importance for relations between National Socialism and Wehrmacht also from the fact that, a mere fortnight earlier, he had declared in a Reichstag speech: 'If international financial Jewry within and outside Europe were to succeed in once more hurling the nations into a world war, then the result will be not the Bolshevization of the earth and thus the victory of Jewry, but the annihilation of the Jewish race in Europe.'[113] And in his address to the commanders-in-chief of the Wehrmacht services on 23 November 1939 Hitler declared: 'The safeguarding of living-space can be solved only by the sword. A racial struggle has erupted about who is to dominate in Europe and in the world.'[114] Once the preparations for the war in the east were fairly advanced, the self-appointed 'supreme ideological leader' clarified this axiom in March 1941. The 'Jewish-Bolshevik intelligentsia [must] be exterminated';[115] this was a 'war of extermination' against a hostile ideol-

---

[112] Engel, *Heeresadjutant bei Hitler*, 45 (18 Feb. 1939).   [113] Domarus, *Hitler*, ii. 1058.
[114] Groscurth, *Tagebücher*, 414; Jacobsen, *1939–45*, 133 ff.; 'Führer Conferences', 60 ff. Maj.-Gen. Hans Felber noted: 'Führer develops his programme. Reference to victory *or downfall*' (BA-MA N 67/2).
[115] *KTB OKW*, i. 341 (3 Mar. 1941).

ogy, a war in which the officers must overcome their soldierly scruples and be leaders.[116]

The real problem, however, with the declaration of a war of annihilation against the Soviet Union is not 'Hitler's personal psychopathology' (H.-U. Wehler), but the answer to the question 'How was it possible for such a "programme" ever to come within the realm of realizability?' In addition to the frequently mentioned co-operation between the Party, the Wehrmacht, industry, and the state apparatus in the reconquest of great-power status for Germany, in addition to the policy concerning the European countries and the ideal of a 'people's community' [*Volksgemeinschaft*], Hitler's living-space programme has to be understood as an integrating factor for the leadership groups. Not only the economic and military justification for extending German rule towards the east, but also the radical concepts of Bolshevism and Jewry as the enemy, as well as belief in the overriding right of the strong in the struggle for survival—all these contributed to making the National Socialist 'programme' realizable in terms of practical politics. 'Domestic and foreign Bolshevism'[117] was regarded among the military leadership class not only as a threat to the bourgeois national state, but 'was a natural component also of the military concept of the enemy' in 1940–1.[118] The idea which the military leaders, who were planning the attack against the Soviet Union, had of Russia was based on experiences, reports, and assumptions going back, for the most part, to the First World War. 'Bolshevism' was held responsible not only for the German collapse of 1918, but also for the undermining of discipline in both the army and the navy. The councils of soldiers, 'the darling children of Bolshevik-inspired revolution', were seen as the originators of the 'disintegration of the fighting forces'.[119] The Jews in particular were regarded as the 'principal exponents of Bolshevik propaganda'.[120] It was through this combination of different national and ideological views that National Socialism, among the German leadership élites in the Wehrmacht, in industry, and in the diplomatic service, was able to achieve the effect which has been described as a 'partial identity of objectives' (M. Messerschmidt). Thus Colonel-General Werner von Fritsch, the former commander-in-chief of the army, who fell victim to an intrigue of the National Socialist regime, wrote in a private letter a few weeks after the 'night of shattered glass':

Shortly after the war I came to the conclusion that three battles had to be fought and won if Germany was to be powerful again: (1) the battle against organized labour, this Hitler has fought and won; (2) against the Catholic Church, or rather against Ultramontanism; and (3) against the Jews. We are still in the midst of these battles.

---

[116] Halder, *Diaries*, 846–7 (30 Mar. 1941); see sect. I.vii.2(*b*).

[117] Minute by Maj. Frh. von Fritsch, the future Army C.-in-C., dated 28 Mar. 1920, Die Anfänge der Ära Seeckt, document No. 46. See his letter to Lt.-Col. Joachim von Stülpnagel of 16 Nov. 1924: Carsten, *Reichswehr*, 223.

[118] See sect. I.iv.i(*a*) (Klink). See also Hillgruber, 'Rußland-Bild', 301; on the attitude of the German military élite see Förster, 'Dynamics'.

[119] *Rückführung des Ostheeres*, 173, 17–18.   [120] Ibid. 5–6.

And the struggle against the Jews is the most difficult. I hope that the difficulty of that struggle is realized everywhere.'[121]

At the end of July 1940 Rear-Admiral Fricke believed it necessary in the interest of Europe to liquidate the chronic danger of Bolshevism 'one way or another'.[122] And within the staff of the German army mission in Romania, too, an ideological definition of the enemy was issued in October 1940: Germany was at war not only against Britain, but also 'against the world of money and finance, against Freemasonry, and—both in finance and propaganda—against worldwide Jewry, incited by our emigrants, who are adding fuel to the flames everywhere'.[123] Colonel-General Georg von Küchler, commander-in-chief of the Eighteenth Army, defined the purpose of the overall war as 'bringing about a long-term pacification of Europe, in which the German people controls a space that will ensure its food supplies and those of the other European states'. That, however, was not conceivable without a conflict between Germany and the Soviet Union.

We are separated from Russia, ideologically and racially, by a deep abyss. R[ussia] is, if only by the mass of her territory, an Asian state . . . The Führer does not wish to palm off responsibility for Germany's existence on to a later generation; he has decided to force the dispute with R[ussia] before the year is out. If Germany wishes to live in peace for generations, safe from the threatening danger in the east, this cannot be a case of pushing R[ussia] back a little—or even hundreds of kilometres—but the aim must be to annihilate European Russia, to dissolve the Russ[ian] state in Europe.[124]

In a note of July 1941 on Germany's strategic position Major (General Staff) Bernardis, 3rd general staff officer at LIst Army Corps HQ, remarked that the conflict with Britain, conducted 'for political, ideological, and economic reasons (democracy, Jewry, and capitalism)', was now taking second place. Germany was at present fighting against the Soviet Union, fighting

for her existence and future . . . I am convinced that these considerations were in the Führer's mind even before the beginning of the war, and that the war in the west had to be fought in order to gain complete freedom in the rear. The Führer would certainly have been ready at any time for an arrangement with Britain. He had to wage the war against Russia in order to free the German people from that danger once and for all.[125]

Germany's adversary in the struggle for a new order in Europe, for the security of its living-space and of its people's vital strength, was Jewry.[126] Major (General Staff) von Coelln, 1st general staff officer, viewed the Soviet Union

---

[121] Reynolds, 'Fritsch-Brief', 370. See Ludendorff, *The Nation at War*, 16–17, 28 ff., 33–4.

[122] See sect. I.1.1.

[123] Minute of a staff conference on 9 Oct. 1940, sgd. Hauffe, BA-MA RH 31-I/v. 24.

[124] Manuscript notes for a conference with divisional commanders, BA-MA, 18. Armee, 19601/2. See Halder, *Diaries*, 845 ff. (30 Mar. 1941).

[125] Manuscript of report, 11 July 1941, BA-MA, LI. AK, 15290/23. Bernardis was hanged on 20 July 1944 after the attempt on Hitler's life (20 July 1944).

[126] Manuscript of report, 12 July 1941, ibid.

as the 'vanguard of Asia'. It was Germany's enemy because Germany was 'the last shield-bearer of the white race, of European culture'.[127]

The German officers were favourably disposed towards major parts of Hitler's 'programme'. That was why they found the assertion credible that a preventive war was necessary in 1941, and why they had no difficulty in giving their consent. Evidence that Hitler's living-space policy was still able to convince senior commanders in the field at a time when the turning-point of the war had long been passed is provided by Colonel-General Wolfram von Richthofen, chief of staff of Luftflotte 4: 'Rereading the chapter on policy towards Russia and the east in "Kampf". Still very interesting and, even in today's situation, providing the answers to nearly all questions. Shall see to it that these observations are given greater prominence among the forces in the whole area.'[128]

4. EURO-ASIAN CONTINENTAL BLOC AND MARITIME STRATEGY: ALTERNATIVES TO THE TURN TO THE EAST?

After victory over France, was there among the German leadership groups an alternative foreign-policy and/or strategic concept to the 'brute-force solution' (A. Hillgruber) proposed by Hitler on 31 July 1940? An answer in the affirmative would not only prevent a 'Hitler-centred approach' in German historiography, but it would also be indirect proof that Hitler's globally designed racial policy and plan of conquest had a character of their own that 'destroyed any political calculations that might have been usefully open to discussion'.[129] Two concepts are regarded in the literature as fully valid alternatives to Hitler's offensive in the east: (1) the Atlantic–Mediterranean–African strategy proposed by the navy command to defeat Britain, even though this accepted as inevitable the United States' entry into the war;[130] and (2) Ribbentrop's idea of an anti-British Euro-Asian continental bloc which would also neutralize the United States.[131] The peripheral strategy for the war against Britain, considered by the Army High Command at the end of July 1940 but not put forward at the Berghof, cannot be considered as an alternative to the war in the east.

In September 1940, following the postponement of the invasion of Britain, the navy saw a need to establish a comprehensive maritime strategy against Britain because 'the overall problem had long exceeded the framework of military operations and moved into the sphere of European-wide grand policy'.[132] It called not only for the utmost support for Germany's Italian ally,

---

[127] Undated note, probably of 11 July 1941, ibid.
[128] Richthofen, Tagebuch, 6 Jan. 1943. I am indebted to the late Col. Dr Gundelach, Freiburg i.Br., for allowing me to see the diary.
[129] Hildebrand, 'Rassen- contra Weltpolitik', 210.
[130] See Salewski, *Seekriegsleitung*, i. 271 ff..
[131] See Michalka, 'Antikominternpakt', 487; id., *Ribbentrop*, 287 ff.
[132] 1. Skl., KTB, pt. A (25 Sept. 1940), BA-MA RM 7/16.

but was interested also in a Spanish entry into the war and in an arrangement with France. Behind this was the intention to topple Britain's position in the Mediterranean by the seizure of Gibraltar and Suez, and to acquire bases for German naval warfare against British supply-lines in the Atlantic also (Dakar, Casablanca, Atlantic islands). Moreover, German control of Egypt and the creation of a land and sea link with Italian East Africa were to shake the British position in the Indian Ocean too. 'Such a jumping-off situation, however, also reduced the American threat—in the eyes of the navy command—to such an extent that an entry into the war by the United States could be envisaged with equanimity.'[133]

Raeder repeatedly proposed this strategy to Hitler. On only one occasion was the commander-in-chief of the navy able to record Hitler's agreement in principle with his line of argument (26 September 1940). But this did not mean that Hitler was prepared to renounce his intended aggression against the Soviet Union and to make the navy command's strategy his own. He was interested only in cover for his southern flank, which he hoped to achieve by political means through tying Spain and Vichy France more firmly to the Axis. Nevertheless, the Mediterranean area took on a new strategic quality for Hitler after the autumn of 1940, when, in consequence of the Italian military defeats, measures to stabilize the Italian position became necessary. In addition, there was concern that the Romanian oilfields might be bombed by the British air force.[134]

Although the fundamental decision to attack the Soviet Union had just been taken in Directive No. 21, at the end of December Raeder once more registered 'serious doubts' about Operation Barbarossa before Britain had been fought to the ground. But Hitler brushed these aside with the argument that 'it is necessary to eliminate at all costs the last enemy remaining on the Continent before I can collaborate with Britain'.[135] The fact that Hitler's concept of an ideological war of annihilation evidently impressed the navy commander-in-chief less than the planned enlargement of the navy after victory over the Soviet Union,[136] and that the naval staff eventually allowed itself to be convinced of the absolute necessity of a 'preventive war'[137] to eliminate the 'chronic danger' of 'Bolshevism',[138] was probably due to the existence of a basically anti-communist attitude, and to geopolitical ideas, as well as to social-Darwinist and racial beliefs within the navy.

The strategy of the naval staff, based as it was on the continued existence of the German–Sovit alliance, would have easily slotted into Ribbentrop's concept of an anti-British Euro-Asian continental bloc from Madrid to Tokyo. Ever since 1937, the 'year of the turning-point' (K. Hildebrand) in Britain's

---

[133] Salewski, *Seekriegsleitung*, i. 280.
[134] See Schreiber, 'Mittelmeerraum', 87 ff.; id. in *Germany and the Second World War*, iii. 232 ff.
[135] 'Führer Conferences', 162 (27 Dec. 1940).
[136] 1. Skl., KTB, pt. A (31 Mar. 1941), BA-MA RM 7/22.
[137] Assmann, *Schicksalsjahre*, 227.
[138] Memorandum by Fricke, 28 July 1940. See sect. I.I.1.

attitude towards Germany's expansionist ambitions, Foreign Minister Joachim von Ribbentrop had tried to develop the 'anti-Comintern pact', signed by Germany, Japan, and Italy in 1936, into a political alliance that would threaten the British Empire from all sides.[139] Despite his fundamentally anti-communist attitude, Ribbentrop was convinced 'that foreign policy can be conducted without ideological considerations'.[140] That was why in his global concept of an anti-British political triangle Rome–Berlin–Tokyo he had banked on Soviet neutrality and hence regarded the German–Soviet alliance of summer 1939 as his crowning achievement. However, the anti-British orientation and the obvious turning away from the anti-Comintern pact did not then suit Japan's aims. Tokyo had been interested in seeing the anti-Comintern pact developed into a military alliance between Italy, Germany, and Japan, directed against the Soviet Union, and not in its extension against Britain.[141] That was why the Hitler–Stalin pact had come as a shock to Japan and resulted in a reorientation of Japanese policy. Admittedly, the new course of strict neutrality in the European war was abandoned as soon as the German offensive in the west began: Japan now wished to have some say in the fate of the Dutch and French colonies in East Asia. The Yonai government put out feelers in Berlin to discover Germany's attitude towards Japan's political, military, and economic interests in that region.

That about-turn in Japan's foreign policy induced Ribbentrop in the summer of 1940 to dust off his old anti-British plan of a global political triangle. In view of the changes in the international situation, the German foreign minister tried not only to revive the tripartite alliance, but, by the hoped-for inclusion of the Soviet Union, to develop it into a genuine Euro-Asian continental bloc. Moreover, its original purely anti-British character was now to be transformed so as to secure American non-belligerency. 'Proceeding from different motivations and objectives, Hitler and Ribbentrop were thus able to decide in favour of a close military alliance with Japan.'[142] On 8 July 1940 Hitler declared to the former Japanese foreign minister, Naotake Sato: 'In the new world order Japan would call the tune in East Asia, Russia in Asia, Germany and Italy in Europe; and in Africa, too, Germany and Italy, possibly with some other interested parties, would exercise exclusive hegemony.'[143] A week later the Japanese leadership adopted a detailed plan for closer relations with the Axis powers. The ensuing negotiations resulted on 27 September 1940 in the conclusion of the 'Tripartite Pact'. Ribbentrop's prolonged wooing of Japan was at last successful because the elimination of France and Holland, as colonial powers, had opened up unexpected perspectives to Japan's expansionist aims in South-East Asia. The thought that Germany might gain a foothold in the French and Dutch colonies persuaded Tokyo that a renewed

[139] See Michalka, *Ribbentrop*, 149 ff.   [140] Quoted according to ibid. 285.
[141] Miyake, *Lage Japans*, 203 ff., 214 ff. See Krebs, *Japans Deutschlandpolitik*.
[142] Michalka, *Ribbentrop*, 259–60.
[143] Quoted according to Sommer, *Deutschland und Japan*, 352.

rapprochement with Berlin would be advisable. After Ribbentrop's statement that Germany had no interest in any European possessions in the Far East the new Japanese government under Konoye, in an official declaration on 1 August 1940, made the unification of Greater Asia under Japanese leadership its foreign-policy programme.

The purpose of the much-publicized 'Tripartite Pact' was to warn the United States against widening the war.[144] However, the pact had the opposite effect on the Anglo-Saxon powers, a 'crystallizing effect' (Th. Sommer), as evidenced by the American embargo against Japan and the co-ordination of British and United States policy in East Asia. Roosevelt's re-election on 5 November 1940 enabled him lisen to continue his policy of support for Britain and of preparing the United States for war. From November 1940 American military leaders were working on the problem that the Axis powers could ultimately be overthrown only by a British offensive on the ground, and that, to accomplish this, Britain needed the support of American ground forces.[145]

Ribbentrop's and Hitler's strategies converged also on another point: the creation of a political bloc against Britain. Both were trying to win Spain and Vichy France over to the idea of an anti-British 'continental coalition'.[146] Both of them opened a diplomatic offensive designed to create 'Europe's counter-deployment against the Western democracies'.[147] The settlement of the clashing interests between French hopes of preserving their possessions and Spanish territorial ambitions was to be primarily at France's expense. This task, difficult enough as it was, was further complicated by Italian claims to French territories in Europe and Africa. But the talks with the Spanish head of state Franco and the French head of state Pétain in October 1940, planned as a 'gigantic fraud',[148] produced no results.[149] This was due not only to the conflicting interests of the countries earmarked as potential satellites, but also to the fact that Hitler's European programme was almost exclusively based on force. Not even the slogans of anti-Bolshevism, anti-Semitism, or the bogey of Western plutocracy succeeded in disguising the fact of Britain's continuous resistance.

Ribbentrop's and Hitler's strategies, however, differed with regard to their thrust. To Ribbentrop the envisaged arrangement between Spain and Vichy France merely represented the first step towards the creation of a world-encompassing continental bloc—which would include the Soviet Union—against the Anglo-American naval powers. To Hitler the wooing of Franco and Pétain was governed by the 'primacy of his eastern policy'.[150] The creation

---

[144] See *Weizsäcker-Papiere*, 219 (28 Sept. 1940); Sommer, *Deutschland und Japan*, 429–50; Dülffer, 'Tripartite Pact'.

[145] Stoler, *Second Front*, 8.

[146] Hitler to Mussolini, 4 Oct. 1940, *DGFP* D xi, Nos. 149, 252.

[147] *Weizsäcker-Papiere*, 222 (26 Oct. 1940).   [148] Halder, *Diaries*, 609 (3 Oct. 1940).

[149] See *Germany and the Second World War*, ii. 402, and iii. 188 ff.

[150] Bormann to Lammers, 2 Nov. 1940, quoted according to Hildebrand, *Foreign Policy*, 103.

of a political bloc in western Europe was to facilitate the impending military conflict with the Soviet Union. That objective was served also—after the postponement of 'Sea Lion'—by the air war against Britain, which increasingly assumed 'the character of a war of terror and exhaustion'.[151] As, however, Britain's determination to resist was not broken even by ceaseless attacks, especially on the 'disgruntled mass of London's eight millions',[152] the focus of the German air offensive against Britain shifted to operations against her supplies. Priority was no longer given to 'smoking her out', but to 'starving her out by a blockade'.[153] The air war in the west, however, was no longer thought capable of bringing about the decision in the war; it was merely as an aspect of the overall war. The focus of German strategy had shifted to preparations for a rapid campaign against the Soviet Union, which would also decide the overall war in favour of the Reich.

5. German–Soviet Relations from Molotov's Visit to the Beginning of the War

In order to strengthen the thrust of the Tripartite Pact, Ribbentrop hoped to extend it into a 'quadripartite pact' by the inclusion of the Soviet Union. Ribbentrop saw the 'historic mission' of Germany, Italy, Japan, and the USSR as 'to adopt a long-range policy and to direct the future development of their peoples into the right channels by delimitation of their interests for the ages'.[154] Although the living-spaces of the four partners would touch, they need not cut across one another.

The German concept of a 'quadripartite pact' not only met with interest in Japan, for whose planned southward expansion an agreement with the Soviet Union and peace on her northern front were indispensable prerequisites, but also fell on fertile ground in Moscow. The German offer happened to coincide with a renewed attempt by Britain to drive a wedge into German–Soviet co-operation,[155] and Stalin, just as in 1939, now found himself courted from all sides. In pursuit of his basic foreign-policy line the Soviet dictator once more gambled on the German card. Stalin's foreign policy, too, was based on an ideological axiom. He saw the Soviet Union, the 'first socialist state in the world', as encircled by a fundamentally hostile 'capitalist world' which threatened the survival of the communist regime.[156] He regarded a military conflict with the capitalist states as inevitable, and he endeavoured to delay it until the potential of the Soviet Union equalled that of its enemies. This was the objective of the five-year plans launched in 1929. The Soviet planned economy

---

[151] *Germany and the Second World War*, ii. 402. Boog, in the present volume, sect. I.IV.2(*a*), arrives at a somewhat different assessment of German aerial warfare against Britain.

[152] *Weizsäcker-Papiere*, 218 (15 Sept. 1940).   [153] Ibid. 225 (17 Nov. 1940).

[154] Ribbentrop, letter to Stalin, 13 Oct. 1940, *DGFP* D xi, No. 176.

[155] Woodward, *British Foreign Policy*, i. 490 ff.

[156] See Jacobsen, 'Primat der Sicherheit', 213 ff.; Allard, *Stalin*, 7 ff.; Pietrow-Ennker, *Stalinismus*, 19 ff.; Hillgruber, 'Hitler-Stalin-Pakt', 16 ff.; Volkogonov, *Stalin*, 524.

developed into a purely rearmament economy, which fundamentally trans-formed the equipment of the Red Army.[157]

This strengthening of his own military power, however, stemmed not only from defensively understood Soviet security interests,[158] but was determined also by power-political calculations which did not rule out an offensive. In the event of conflict within the capitalist-'imperialist' outside world the Soviet Union should not have to stand idly by. For the purpose of achieving a fundamental shift in the ratio of forces Stalin was entirely prepared to inter-vene in such an 'imperialist war'. As early as 1925 he had stated to his party's central committee that the Soviet Union would move in as the last power, 'in order to throw the decisive weight on to the scales'.[159] His fears, following British, French, and German collusion in 1938–9, that these capitalist powers might jointly act against 'the first socialist state' were dispelled only by the treaty with the Reich and by the outbreak of war in Europe. Now Stalin believed that he could, for some time to come, adopt 'the coveted role of an observer of the self-laceration of capitalism and its "fascist afterbirth"',[160] National Socialism. The booty he had secured since 1939 had not only advanced the Soviet Union's strategic forefield to the west and south-east, but was accompanied also by a growth in armament production and by the full utilization of the military manpower of his own as well as the occupied countries. As Britain was offering no more than recognition of the Soviet Union's *de facto* sovereignty over the territories occupied since 1939 until an agreed postwar settlement, Moscow was willing to continue its profitable co-operation with National Socialist Germany. There was, however, a need to discover whether Berlin still respected the 'security interests of the Soviet Union'[161] in the Baltic area and in the Balkans, which had admittedly been recognized in the summer of 1939 but must now be regarded as threatened by the German engagement in Finland and Romania. The extension of the German–Finnish transit agreement at the end of September and the nickel-for-arms barter agreement of 1 October, as well as the dispatch of a German military mission with army instructors to Romania after 12 October 1940, had all resulted in increased Soviet mistrust of German policy. Just because it was aware of Hitler's anti-Soviet policy, the Soviet leadership was interested in 'a long-term delimitation of mutual interests'.[162]

On 12 November 1940 Vyacheslav Mikhaylovich Molotov, the Soviet for-eign minister, arrived in Berlin. During his three-day visit he had two conver-sations each with Hitler and Ribbentrop. However, these were not discussions aiming at compromise, but in Hitler's case simply monologues, time and again

---

[157] See sects. I.II.1. and I.II.2.

[158] This is the interpretation put forward by Soviet historiography. See Zhukov, 'Origins of the Second World War', 22 ff.

[159] Stalin, *Werke*, vii. 11–12.

[160] Bracher, *Krise Europas*, 187. See also Read and Fisher, *Deadly Embrace*.

[161] *Deutschland im zweiten Weltkrieg*, i. 371.

[162] Stalin, letter to Ribbentrop, 21 Oct. 1940, *DGFP* D xi, No. 211. See Volkogonov, *Stalin*, 500.

interrupted by Molotov's searching questions. These, as well as Hitler's evasive replies, clearly revealed the incompatibility of their points of view.[163] Molotov, for instance, showed less interest in the creation of a new community of interests for sharing out the 'gigantic worldwide bankrupt estate' of the British Empire than in the 'new order in Europe'. Each time Hitler mentioned the creation of a 'worldwide coalition of interested parties' in the British bankruptcy assets Molotov turned the conversation back to specific problems of the spheres of influence agreed in 1939. He stressed Soviet interests in Finland and the Balkans. The Soviet Union was interested in an annexation of Finland and of southern Bukowina, in a revocation of the German–Italian guarantee to Romania, in a treaty of alliance with Bulgaria, and in military bases on the Dardanelles and the Bosporus, and had also given notice of aspirations in the direction the Persian Gulf and northern Sakhalin. The German side, on the other hand, emphasized a considerable economic interest in Finland and Romania; both these countries, moreover, were earmarked as allies in the war against the Soviet Union. Bulgaria was needed as a deployment basis for an operation against Greece. On the issue of the straits Hitler offered only a contractual assurance of free passage for Soviet warships. Beyond his direct demands, Molotov also informed Ribbentrop of Soviet interest in Romania, Hungary, Yugoslavia, Greece, and in the fate of Poland. The issue of passage out of and into the Baltic would also need to be discussed between Germany and the Soviet Union.

What is one to make of this Soviet list of desiderata? Were these actual long-term objectives, whose realization presupposed Germany's defeat by the Western powers,[164] or were they tactical maximum demands for the forthcoming negotiations?[165] In the light of the conditions which Molotov submitted on 25 November to the German leadership for political co-operation between the Soviet Union, Germany, Japan, and Italy[166]—a minimum programme—the listing of much more far-reaching wishes of the Soviet Union ten days earlier must be seen as a tactical manœuvre. The point to remember is that accession to the Tripartite Pact did not seem unacceptable to the Soviet Union, though with the proviso 'that Russia would co-operate as a partner and not be a mere object'. The Soviet minimum programme of 25 November 1940, however, also proves—contrary to present-day interpretations from the Marxist point of view—that Moscow was perfectly ready to 'join a conspiracy' with the 'Fascist aggressors against the interests of other states'. The Soviet Union was in fact not so much conducting a foreign policy of 'rigid principle' designed 'to prevent an extension of the war'[167] as a policy of maintaining a completely free hand and of safeguarding for itself an extensive sphere of influence. In Bul-

---

[163] *DGFP* D xi Nos. 325, 326, 328, 329. The nature of the talks emerges more clearly from the less 'manicured' notes of Etzdorf, PA, Handakten Etzdorf, Vertrauliche Aufzeichnungen, No. III.

[164] Hillgruber, *Strategie*, 306; Hildebrand, 'Krieg im Frieden', 24.

[165] Allard, *Stalin*, 267; Pietrow-Enker, *Stalinismus*, 218 ff.

[166] *DGFP*, D xi, No. 404.   [167] *Deutschland im zweiten Weltkrieg*, i. 371.

garia Moscow tried to create a *fait accompli* by simultaneously submitting to that country a proposal for a Soviet–Bulgarian treaty of assistance.[168]

Nor should the second German–Soviet economic agreement of 10 January 1941 be seen solely against the background of the two parties' economic interests.[169] It too was embedded in the political negotiations between Moscow and Berlin. The Soviet side was trying to reach a more durable delimitation of interests than that of 1939 and, by way of advances favouring the Reich, to induce Berlin to make political concessions. That was why Stalin accepted the uncovered German cheque and was ready to pay the price of British annoyance. A few days after the conclusion of the economic agreement Molotov demanded a German reply to the Soviet conditions for joining a 'quadripartite pact'.[170] But Berlin remained silent. It was probably because of his political refusal that Hitler called for a smooth fulfilment of German economic obligations towards the Soviet Union, even though those deliveries were at the expense of Wehrmacht orders from the armament industry.

In this connection the important question arises of whether Hitler really believed that the Soviet Union would join the continental bloc favoured by Ribbentrop, which would indeed have 'represented a significant alternative to a German attack' on that country.[171] Must not Hitler's readiness to conclude a 'quadripartite pact' in November 1940 be interpreted as a tactical move, considering his 'programme', his aggressive policy towards Finland and Romania—a policy violating the agreement of the summer of 1939—and his anti-Soviet remarks shortly before Molotov's visit? Were calls to respect the Soviet spheres of interest not simply useful demonstrations that Germany and the Soviet Union were standing 'shoulder to shoulder' rather than 'back to back'?[172] On 4 November 1940 Hitler, speaking to OKH and OKW top leaders, observed that the Soviet Union remained the 'great problem of Europe'. Everything had to be done 'to prepare for when the showdown comes'.[173] That was why, even before his first talk with Molotov, he signed Directive No. 18, which stated: 'Political discussions for the purpose of clarifying Russia's attitude in the immediate future have already begun. Regardless of the outcome of these conversations, all preparations for which verbal orders have already been given will be continued. Further directives will follow on this subject as soon as the basic operational plan of the army has been submitted to me and approved.'[174] This was done on 5 December 1940. Against the background of the bloody struggle for hegemony in Europe between National Socialist Germany and the Bolshevik Soviet Union—a struggle already decided upon by Hitler—the German concept of shared rule

[168] *DGFP* D xi, No. 438 (25 Nov. 1940); Hoppe, *Bulgarien*, 104 ff.

[169] *DGFP* D xi, No. 637. See sect. I.III.3(*b*) (Müller).

[170] *DGFP* D xi, No. 669 (17 Jan. 1941).   [171] Allard, *Stalin*, 232.

[172] Thus Hitler to Molotov, 13 Nov. 1940, *DGFP* D xi, No. 328. On the talks see Fabry, *Hitler-Stalin Pakt*, 343 ff.; Hillgruber, *Strategie*, 300 ff.; Allard, *Stalin*, 259 ff.; *Germany and the Second World War*, ii. 26 ff., and I.II.3 of the present volume.

[173] Halder, *Diaries*, 674 (4 Nov. 1940).   [174] *Hitler's Directives*, No. 18.

on a world scale at the expense of the British Empire must be judged as a
tactical manœuvre. Moreover, the Soviet maximum programme was bound to
be seen by the German side as extortionist and as a long-term threat to the
hegemony of the Reich. That threat had to be eliminated. The day after
Molotov's departure Raeder found Hitler '*still* inclined towards a confrontation with Russia'.[175] Hitler had opted from the outset in favour of the campaign
against the Soviet Union, which he saw both as a war aim and as an instrument
of war; he had regarded a political solution to the conflicting German and
Soviet interests in Europe as impossible. A military decision also seemed to be
pressing because the expectations which he and Ribbentrop had placed in the
Tripartite Pact with regard to America's policy had proved illusory.

The quasi-alliance between the United States and Britain had grown ever
closer since the autumn of 1940. The destroyers-for-bases exchange agreement of 2 September 1940[176] marked a turning-point in American foreign
policy. Roosevelt was not intimidated by the threat of a war on two oceans, as
implied by the Tripartite Pact, and agreed to Churchill's proposal for British–
American co-operation in East Asia.[177] A few weeks after his re-election for a
third term Roosevelt, under the slogan of 'Germany first', authorized secret
staff talks with Britain, which, however, only began two months later. At the
end of December, in response to a renewed call for help from Churchill,
Roosevelt declared that the United States represented the arsenal of the
democracies, and a few days later introduced the 'Lend-Lease' Bill in Congress.[178] With this formula Roosevelt no doubt deliberately responded to
Hitler's characterization of the war, in a speech to Berlin armament workers,
as a struggle between the National Socialist and the democratic capitalist
world.[179] Hitler realized that, once all his makeshift constructs ('Tripartite
Pact', 'continental bloc') for improving Germany's strategic situation had
failed, the greater potential of the Anglo-American sea powers, together with
an intensifying American rearmament drive, must in the long run result in
Germany's defeat. That was why Hitler's political reaction was a 'redefining of
the function' of the Tripartite Pact as a 'regional European system of alliances'
directed against the Soviet Union and oriented exclusively along German
interests.[180] With the accession of Hungary, Slovakia, and above all Romania—
which had a German–Italian guarantee against Soviet aspirations, reinforced
by the dispatch of a German army and air-force mission—the end of Novem-

---

[175] 'Führer Conferences', 153 (14 Nov. 1940), emphasis added. It is simply not correct to say
that Hitler's final decision to attack the Soviet Union dated only from 26 Nov. 1940, as stated by
Robertson, 'Hitler', 378.

[176] Bailey and Ryan, *Hitler vs. Roosevelt*, 82 ff. 50 destroyers were supplied in exchange for the
use of 8 naval and air bases. See *Germany and the Second World War*, iii. 560 ff.

[177] Langer and Gleason, *Undeclared War*, 38 ff. The Lend-Lease Act, which came into effect on
11 Mar. 1941, gave the President *de facto* full power to authorize an enormous increase in aid to
Britain.

[178] Thus Roosevelt on 29 Dec. 1940 (Langer and Gleason, *Undeclared War*, 38 ff).

[179] Domarus, *Hitler*, ii. 1627 ff.   [180] Hillgruber, 'Hitler-Koalition', 474.

ber 1940 saw the formation of the 'Hitler coalition', which was subsequently to give rise to the 'anti-Hitler coalition'.

In military terms, on 5 December Hitler opted for the army's operations plan, ready since July 1940;[181] this was to defeat the Soviet Union in a swift campaign. His strategic analysis, designed to justify this fateful step, contained the same arguments as on 31 July 1940: 'The decision on hegemony in Europe' would be made in the struggle against the Soviet Union as this would deprive Britain of her 'continental sword'. The purpose of the operation was the annihilation of 'Russia's manpower'.[182] 'Once the Russians are eliminated, Britain has no hope left of defeating us on the Continent, the more so as any effective intervention by America would be rendered difficult by Japan, who will then have a secure rear.'[183] Finland and Romania were counted on as partners in the alliance.

After a further report by Jodl on Directive No. 21, on 17 December 1940 Hitler summed up his global political estimation of the situation underlying his decision to go to war against the Soviet Union in the remark that 'all continental European problems' would have to be solved in 1941 since 'after 1942 the United States would be in a position to intervene'.[184] Reaching for the east, Hitler's great foreign-policy goal ever since the 1920s, had now become for him also the means of getting Germany out of the impasse in which she found herself because of his axiomatic ideas, his political gambles, the unyielding attitude of the British government, and Roosevelt's consistent global policy. Hitler refused to give up; he was determined to implement his 'programme' despite America's foreseeable entry into the war. After the autumn of 1940, therefore, the alternative was not between a maritime strategy and a military solution in the east, nor between a 'quadripartite pact' and Operation Barbarossa, but between the destruction of the Soviet Union as the prerequisite of a decisive turn in the overall war and Germany's ruin,[185] because for a prolonged war of attrition like that of 1914–18 against the naval powers with their long-term planning the territorial and economic position which Germany had gained by 1940 was too weak. 'The military solution in the east had thus become Hitler's great "chance" to bring about the "turn" and to finish *everything* at one blow.'[186] Smashing Russia, Hitler expounded to the top leaders of OKW, army, navy, and air force at the Berghof on 9 January, 'would represent a great relief to Germany—and to Japan . . . After Russia's destruction Germany would be unassailable. Russia's expanses contained immeasurable wealth. Germany must dominate them economically and politically, but not annex them. Thus she would have all the potential for waging war even against continents in the future.'[187]

On 18 December 1940 Hitler signed 'Directive No. 21: Operation

---

[181] See sect. I.IV.1(*e*) (Klink).   [182] Halder, *KTB* ii. 211–12 (5 Dec. 1940; not in trans.).
[183] Bock, Tagebuch, ii. (3 Dec. 1940), MGFA, P–210.   [184] *KTB OKW* i. 996.
[185] Hillgruber, 'Weltpolitische Lage', 276.   [186] Id., *Strategie*, 391.
[187] *KTB OKW* i. 257 (9 Jan. 1941); 'Führer Conferences', 172.

Barbarossa'. This demanded that the Wehrmacht should 'crush Soviet Russia in a rapid campaign'.[188] While the Army High Command incorporated the changed tasks for Army Groups North and Centre—changed as against the conference of 5 December 1940—with insignificant amendments into its 'Deployment instruction Barbarossa' of 31 January 1941, for Army Group South it adhered to an offensive thrust out of Romania.[189] The diverging operational dispositions for Barbarossa were eliminated by Hitler in a decision towards the end of March 1941.

About the end of January 1941, however, the army command began to have doubts about Hitler's strategic justification for war against the Soviet Union. 'Barbarossa: purpose is not clear. We do not hit the British, That way our economic potential will not be substantially improved. Risk in the west must not be underestimated.'[190] Whether it would be possible to smash the bulk of the Red Army in the west of the Soviet Union and prevent the pull-back of effective formations to the east was another question on which the army command was no longer as optimistic as it had been in the summer and autumn of 1940. Talking to Field Marshal Fedor von Bock, the commander-in-chief-designate of Army Group Centre, Halder had to admit on 31 January 1941 that he was by no means certain that the Red Army would accept combat forward of the Dnieper–Dvina line.[191] But there was no opposition to Hitler's decision, such as there had been before the war in the west. Planning for Operation Barbarossa simply assumed that the enemy would act in the manner hoped for, having denied the Wehrmacht the 'favour'[192] of himself launching an attack. If, however, the intended 'swift campaign' against the Soviet Union were to fail, then not only a battle 'but the whole war would be lost'.[193]

The attempt by Friedrich Werner Graf von der Schulenburg, the German ambassador in Moscow, to persuade Hitler of the advantages of continuing the German–Soviet economic alliance was taken up by Weizsäcker in a memorandum. In it he fully agreed with Schulenburg's line of argument and regarded 'war with Russia as a disaster'.[194] Tempting though it may seem, Weizsäcker argued, to deal the mortal blow to the communist system and, in the logic of things, 'now mobilize the European–Asian continent against the Anglo-Saxons and their followers', the crucial question was solely whether such a war would accelerate Britain's fall. Weizsäcker did not share Ribbentrop's justification of an attack on the Soviet Union. He believed that the German–British conflict could actually be prolonged by Operation Barbarossa instead of being shortened.[195] His arguments, however,

---

[188] *Hitler's Directives*, No. 21.   [189] See sects. I.iv.1(e) (Klink) and I.v.3 (Förster)

[190] Halder, *Diaries*, 765 (28 Jan. 1941).

[191] Bock, Tagebuch, ii (31 Jan. 1941), MGFA, P-210.

[192] This was Maj.-Gen. Marcks's formulation in his 'Operationsentwurf Ost' of 5 Aug. 1940.

[193] Hillgruber, *Strategie*, 392.

[194] *Weizsäcker-Papiere*, 248 (21 Apr. 1941). See also the memorandum of Legation Counsellor Gebhardt von Walther, dated 10 Oct. 1940, in Gibbons, 'Opposition', 336 ff.

[195] *Weizsäcker-Papiere*, 249–50 (28 Apr. 1941); *DGFP* D xii, No. 419.

failed to change the German foreign minister's mind. Instead, at the beginning of May 1941 Ribbentrop fully supported the attack against the Soviet Union, even though it ran counter to the foreign policy he had pursued since 1937.[196]

Contrary to Stalin's assessment of the situation—that Hitler would not dare to attack the Soviet Union while the war against the Anglo-American sea powers continued, and would in consequence continue to be economically dependent on the Soviet Union—Hitler was prepared to open the war on two fronts. Hitler's rejection of the Soviet demands that the provisions of the secret protocol on northern and south-east Europe should be fully applied 'undoubtedly came as a serious disappointment to Stalin'.[197] While Hitler was simply trying to face his ally with *faits accomplis* in northern Europe and the Balkans, Stalin was not prepared to give up Soviet 'security interests' in those regions. The consequence was a Soviet policy of 'pinpricks', designed to induce Hitler to change his mind and agree to a clear delimitation of the several spheres of interest.

Just as the conclusion of a Yugoslav–Soviet friendship and non-aggression treaty on 5 April 1941 merely heightened Hitler's mistrust of Stalin's loyalty as a treaty partner, so the surprisingly rapid conclusion of the Balkan campaign resulted in a tactical switch of Soviet foreign policy.[198] The Soviet Union's attempt to establish its claim to a sphere of interest in south-east Europe had failed. Germany would now have to be placated by a deliberate policy of neutrality and prompt deliveries of raw materials, and the former good relations would have to be restored. Although Stalin tried in a great variety of ways to prevent potential conflicts from even arising, he did not, on the other hand, take the initiative for direct diplomatic negotiations. He felt convinced that such a gesture would be interpreted by Hitler as a sign of Soviet weakness and might lead to increased German demands. Stalin judged the German deployment on the Soviet western frontier to be no more than a means for a 'political purpose'.[199] He adhered to that assessment in the spring of 1941 in the face of every detailed warning he received from the Western powers and from his own intelligence of a German attack. At the same time, an increasing scepticism about his ability to delay much longer the unavaoidable conflict with National Socialist Germany is reflected in two of his remarks. As recently as the end of January 1941 he had told Kirill Afanasevich Meretskov, deputy people's commissar for defence, that it was not impossible 'that we may keep the peace until 1942'.[200] At the beginning of May, one day before he also assumed governmental office, the Party general secretary assured graduates of the military academies that it was necessary to avoid a German–Soviet war in 1941, because it

---

[196] *Weizsäcker-Papiere*, 252 (1 May 1941).   [197] Allard, *Stalin*, 269.
[198] See Hillgruber, *Sowjetische Außenpolitik*, 156 ff.; Allard, *Stalin*, 278 ff.; Fabry, 'Sowjetische Außenpolitik', 71 ff.; Pietrow-Ennker, *Stalinismus*, 230 ff.; Halder, *Diaries*, 904 (5 May 1941).
[199] Lenin (*Clausewitz' Werk*, 34–5) first highlighted Clausewitz's ideas on these lines. See Volkogonov, *Stalin*, 534, 537–8, 556.
[200] Quoted according to *Deutschland im zweiten Weltkrieg*, i. 615–16. See Ziemke and Bauer, *Moscow to Stalingrad*, 18.

could be waged under more favourable conditions for the Soviet Union in 1942.[201]

So as not to provide Hitler with any grounds for an attack Stalin avoided anything that could suggest a British–Soviet *rapprochement*, even though the British government displayed considerable interest along those lines. In particular the flight to Britain by Rudolf Hess, Hitler's deputy, and his correct treatment intensified Stalin's distrust of London's policy. On 2 June 1941, when Anthony Eden, the British foreign secretary, drew the attention of Ivan Mikhaylovich Mayskiy, the Soviet ambassador in London, to the German deployment in the east, Mayskiy dismissed it as part of a 'war of nerves'.[202] The clearest demonstration of Stalin's wish for improved German–Soviet relations was given by him following the signing of a treaty of neutrality with Japan on 13 April 1941. At the farewell ceremony for Yosuke Matsuoka, the Japanese foreign minister, at Moscow's railway station Stalin, in the presence of the entire diplomatic corps, demonstratively assured the German ambassador Schulenburg and the deputy military attaché Colonel (General Staff) Hans Krebs of his friendship for Germany. Even though the Soviet–German treaty could not disguise that fact that Moscow and Tokyo continued to mistrust each other, it nevertheless represented a strengthening of the Soviet Union's position *vis-à-vis* Germany, as Japan had undertaken to preserve her neutrality in the event of a German attack.[203]

Further evidence of Soviet endeavours to placate Germany may be seen in the appointment of an ambassador to the French government in Vichy and of a minister to the *coup- d'état* government in Iraq, as well as the expulsion of the diplomatic representatives of countries occupied by Germany: Norway, Belgium, Yugoslavia, and Greece. Among all the gestures of good will to avoid war Germany benefited most from the fact that the Soviet Union was punctiliously fulfilling its obligations, entered into on 10 January 1941, for the delivery of urgently needed raw materials and foodstuffs.

On 13 June 1941 the official Soviet news agency Tass contradicted rumours of an imminent war between the Soviet Union and Germany in a radio and press statement. Both sides were consistently implementing the conditions of the non-aggression treaty of 23 August 1939; neither was Germany planning an attack against the Soviet Union, nor was the latter preparing for war with Germany.[204] That communiqué was undoubtedly issued in the hope that Germany would confirm this interpretation of the tense situation. But Hitler remained silent. The Tass denial of German troop concentrations on the Soviet frontier was certainly also a factor in the Red Army being surprised by the German attack. Stalin persisted to the very end with his policy of placation, which was served also by the final soundings of Molotov and the Soviet ambassador Vladimir Dekanosov on 21 and 22 June 1941. The Soviet Union

---

[201] See sect. I.ii.2 (Hoffmann); Werth, *Russia at War*, 122–3.
[202] Woodward, *British Foreign Policy*, i. 616. See Volkogonov, *Stalin*, 538.
[203] See Herde, *Pearl Harbor*, 36.   [204] *DGFP* D xii, No. 628.

probably harboured no specific aggressive intentions in the summer of 1941, though the deployment of Soviet troops on the Soviet western frontier suggests that measures had been taken 'for all eventualities'.[205] However, the Soviet deployment worried the German command, even though Halder, at a conference with army group and army chiefs of staff on 4 June 1941, played it down. He judged the Soviet deployment to be defensive and regarded a full-scale offensive by the Red Army as 'rather improbable'.[206] According to the notes of another participant, Halder dismissed an offensive as 'nonsense'. Unlike Hitler, he did not even believe in the likelihood of a partial offensive against the Romanian oil region. Hitler's main worry, just as it had been before the attack on Poland, was that the opposite side might wreck his concept at the last moment by some gesture of concession.[207] He wanted to solve Germany's strategic dilemma, in which she had landed through his policy, by a further warlike action. On 22 June some six and a quarter million soldiers were deployed along both sides of a front from Petsamo to Galati, including, on the German side, just short of six hundred thousand Romanians and Finns.

[205] See Sect. I.II.2 (Hoffmann). On Soviet defence plans see Ziemke and Bauer, *Moscow to Stalingrad*, 18 ff., and Volkogonov, *Stalin*, 546 ff. Not even the renewed argument about responsibility for the German–Soviet war, rekindled by Viktor Suvorov in 1985, added any appreciable impetus to historical research, as no evidence was adduced for offensive *intention* on the Soviet side. The Red Army's *capability* of waging war had long been known. See Pietrow-Ennker, 'Deutschland im Juni 1941', and Gorodetsky, 'Stalin'. It is also unscholarly to draw conclusions about an aggressive foreign policy directed against the Third Reich simply on the grounds of Stalin's brutal domestic policy.

For an interpretation of Operation Barbarossa as a preventive measure we therefore so far lack not only the objective facts on the Soviet side, but also the indispensable prerequisite on the German side: a sense of Germany being directly threatened by the Red Army as a factor in the German supreme leadership's decision to attack the Soviet Union.

[206] Notes of the chiefs of staff of Army Group North, of Eighteenth Army, and of Seventeenth Army on the conference at Zossen on 4 June 1941, BA-MA, 18. Armee, 19601/2, and 17. Armee, 14499/5. See Halder, *Diaries*, 946 (4 June 1941), 980.

[207] *Weizsäcker-Papiere*, 260 (18 June 1941); Hewel, Tagebuch (18 June 1941), IfZ, ED 100; Goebbels, *Diaries*, 413 ff. (16 June 1941).

II. The Soviet Union up to the Eve of the German Attack[1]

Joachim Hoffmann

I. Origin and Development of the Red Army

ON 22 June 1941 the world found itself faced with a war machine about which, generally speaking, only the vaguest ideas existed—the Red Army. Information on the development and organization of the Soviet armed forces was full of gaps, even in military circles. That was hardly surprising, considering that anything connected with their structure, or indeed with questions of Soviet national defence generally, was surrounded by a veil of absolute secrecy, a veil which even the military intelligence services and the military attachés accredited in Moscow only rarely succeeded in lifting.[2] As for the Red Army itself, it had by then shown only sporadic instances of its efficiency. The performance of the Soviet troops during the attack on Poland in 1939 had been completely unimpressive. Its initially not very distinguished operations in the Winter War against Finland had merely confirmed an unfavourable assessment of command and troops. Engagements such as those at Lake Khazan and Khalkhin-Gol in Mongolia in 1939, where the Red Army operated successfully against the Japanese and came out on top, had been in remote regions where non-Soviet observers had no chance of forming a judgement. Although it was realized in the Western countries that this was a mass army of considerable numerical strength, and more or less well equipped with material, its operational efficiency was not rated very high.[3] The reason was, as Colonel-General Halder, chief of the Army General Staff, recorded,[4] that it suffered from serious weaknesses of command and training, and also that its weaponry and equipment were regarded as deficient, if not in quantity then certainly in quality. The German military leadership therefore had no doubts that the Red

---

[1] *Preliminary Note.* The subject-matter of the present section makes it inevitable, as far as the attitude of the USSR is concerned, to rely predominantly—with the exception of a few accidentally discovered records and some published documents—on Soviet secondary literature. This, despite its diversity, reveals some common characteristics: anything of any advantage to the Soviet Union is invariably presented in a favourable light, and anything that might in any way be detrimental to its interests is invariably presented unfavourably. However, the Party-coloured picture of history, as painted by Soviet historiography, has never been 'monolithic', as may also be seen in the continuous use of circumlocutions. Comparative study of the literature published in the Stalin era, the Khrushchev era, and the Brezhnev era actually reveals remarkable differences. In particular, the works published after the Twentieth Party Congress until about the end of the 1960s offer quite a number of interesting insights and also provide a starting-point for critical historiography.

[2] *General Köstring*, 82, 84, 89.   [3] Ibid. 267, 282, 285.

[4] Halder, *KTB* ii. 214 (5 Dec. 1940; not in trans.); id., *Diaries*, 765 (5 May 1941).

Army would not be able to stand up for long against the German Wehrmacht with its experience of war and habit of being victorious. Such views, moreover, were not confined to Germany. Military experts and staffs in Britain and the United State likewise credited the Soviet Union with no more than a slight power of resistance.[5] The British War Office, for instance, proceeded from the assumption that the Soviet Union would be defeated within ten days at the most. Henry L. Stimson, the American defence secretary, Frank Knox, the American secretary for the navy, and General George C. Marshall, the US army chief of staff, expected the war to last no more than a few weeks. In the most favourable circumstances, Western military circles believed, the Soviet Union would be able to continue resisting for six months.

The underrating of the Red Army reflected in such judgements contrasts so strikingly with the ability it eventually demonstrated to accept the most serious defeats and yet offer growing resistance to the aggressors that it is appropriate to examine more closely the real nature of those troops and their strength and potential. Naturally, the real nature of the Red Army at the time of the German attack cannot be explained from that moment alone. An answer to the question of the specific character of the Soviet armed forces requires a survey of the entire period from their birth in revolution and civil war to their emergence as a modern force.

This process was initiated and promoted by the conviction, always held by Vladimir Ilyich Lenin and the leaders of the Bolshevik Party, that their position of power, captured by the Revolution, could not be safeguarded by ideological but solely by military means. Although from the start the greatest attention was devoted to the creation of reliable fighting forces, these efforts met with undreamt-of difficulties under the conditions of 1917–18. Defeats in the war against the central powers and the collapse of the Tsarist empire had shaken the Russian army to its foundations. Endeavours at democratization by the provisional government had further contributed to undermining the discipline and fighting efficiency of the troops. The bulk of the soldiers, drawn from the rural population, readily followed the slogans of the Bolsheviks, who had come to power by proclaiming an immediate conclusion of peace and the distribution of the land belonging to the large estate-owners.[6] From the Bolsheviks' point of view the prime task was the smashing of the old army, which in their eyes had been an army of the 'exploiting class', in order to wrest that important military instrument from the hands of the 'class enemy'. Yet once they had attained power, the immediate destruction of the old army was no longer in their interest, at least not while the state of war against the central powers continued and while the young Soviet republic was threatened with intervention by the *entente* powers. Certain measures were therefore taken to 'neutralize' the army and, simultaneously, gain control of it by infiltrating their

[5] Davies, *Mission to Moscow*, 382; *Istorija Velikoj Otečestvennoj vojny*, ii. 180.
[6] Schapiro, 'Geburt der Roten Armee', 32.

own people into what command posts still existed. This purpose was served by the replacement of General Dukhonin by the Bolshevik cadet Krylenko as supreme commander-in-chief, the establishment of a revolutionary committee, and the dispatch of commissars, as well as by 'democratization' through the abolition of military ranks and the introduction of the election of commanders. But in spite of all efforts by Lenin that dual objective was not achieved. In the winter of 1917–18 the army was drifting towards total disintegration, so that the organization of their own fighting forces soon became a pressing task for the Bolsheviks.

In his endeavours to create a reliable military force Lenin was not in an easy position. On the one hand, the mobilization of the broad masses yearning for peace was scarcely possible, considering that the promise of an immediate conclusion of peace had carried the October Revolution to victory. On the other hand, Lenin, in organizing a 'Red workers' and peasants' army', was bound to run into conflict with certain trends among his own supporters and indeed with his own views. Ever since Karl Marx in his *Civil War in France*, regarded as 'one of the most important works of scientific Communism', had glorified the national guard of the Paris commune of 1871 as a kind of model of a proletarian fighting force,[7] it was an article of faith among his followers that the fighting forces of any future state 'of the revolutionary dictatorship of the proletariat' must be of a similar character. Although the elective principle praised by Marx had substantially contributed to the ignominious collapse of the commune's fighting forces,[8] what Franz Mehring called the 'hideously childish toy of the Revolution',[9] and although Friedrich Engels in particular had long moved away from the idea of a 'people in arms' in the sense of the commune,[10] Lenin initially clung to the commune model.[11] He was confirmed in that attitude by the successes of the Red Guards in the conquest of power for the Bolsheviks in Petrograd on 25 October 1917 and in other parts of the country, which seemed to provide brilliant confirmation of Marxist ideas. However, when the peace talks at Brest ended in failure and the Germans on 18 February 1918 launched an offensive along the entire front, the utter fragility of the revolutionary war-machine was revealed, just as in Paris in 1871. The Soviet forces, including the Red Guards, retreated in panic before the German troops. The victory won in conjunction with some revolutionary army formations against—it has to be admitted—a demoralized opponent inside the country simply could not conceal the fact that the Red Guards were not an organized or trained military force but scarcely more than a workers' militia, which, in spite of occasional enthusiasm, was unable to stand up to a solidly structured army. After the failure of the attempt to use what was left of

[7] Marx, *Civil War in France*, 433 ff.   [8] Hoffmann, 'Volkskrieg in Frankreich', 232 ff.

[9] Mehring, 'Pariser Commune', 66.

[10] Engels, introduction to Marx, *Class Struggles in France*, 17 ff.

[11] Lenin, *Über Krieg, Armee und Militärwissenschaft*, i. 704–5; Fischer, 'Anfänge der Roten Armee', 63 ff.

the old army to secure the Bolsheviks' position of power, and after the failure of endeavours to bring discipline into the workers' militias, Lenin eventually resolved to override the ideas and wishes of most of the Bolshevik military experts and to create a 'Red workers' and peasants' army' on a traditional basis. The successes of the German offensive induced Lenin to abandon his own military ideas and, as he himself formulated it, to return to the principle of discipline and order, so exemplarily demonstrated by the Germans, as the foundation of a regular army.[12]

On 3 March 1918 the peace treaty of Brest-Litovsk was signed on the basis of the German and Austrian conditions. The breathing-space thus gained was used by Lenin, subsequently to be hailed as 'the greatest army leader of all countries, all epochs, and all nations', to proceed at once with the creation of a 'Workers' and Peasants' Red Army' (Raboče-krestjanskaja krasnaja armija: RKKA). The real creator and organizer of this fighting force, entrusted with the task by Lenin, was the man whose existence Soviet military historiography has tried to hush up to this day—Lev Trotsky,[13] since 19 March 1918 chairman of the newly established supreme war council and of the people's commissariat for military affairs, who thenceforth embodied supreme power of command under Lenin. During 1918 central command and administrative levels of the Red Army and Red Fleet were set up in rapid succession, and soon these had at their disposal appropriate bodies at *guberniya* [= provincial], district, and area level, performing all functions connected with recruitment, formation, training, supply, and command of the troops.[14] In enforcing the principle of central leadership of the Red Army on the basis of absolute military and political discipline, Trotsky had to overcome considerable opposition from the ranks of militant Communists, who, in the Red Guards, in local soviets, and in the extensive partisan movement, supported the tradition of 'little' or 'irregular' war and could not accustom themselves to a hierarchical chain of command. These circles within the Party clung to Karl Marx's demand that the regular army had to be replaced by the people in arms, failing to realize that, on the contrary, the people in arms would have to be replaced by a regular army if the still unconsolidated Soviet power were to survive the dangers threatening from within and without. For three years Trotsky, according to his own words, had to wage 'day-in, day-out, a struggle against lack of discipline, dilettantism, and all kinds of anarchy'.[15] Gradually he succeeded in overcoming the resistance of the left-wing military opposition and, with Lenin's support until 1920, in setting up a Red workers' and peasants' army organized into fronts, armies, and divisions, reasonably well equipped and based on obedience to orders; this force was able successfully to stand up to foreign intervention and to domestic counter-revolution. There was no longer any talk of democratization or elections. It was openly admitted that those

---

[12] Ritter, *Kommunemodell*, 88.
[13] Trotsky, *History of the Russian Revolution*, iii. 90 ff.; Erickson, *Soviet High Command*, 28 ff.
[14] *50 let vooružennych sil*, 34–5.   [15] Trotzki, Rote Armee, BA-MA RW 5/v. 462.

principles had been designed only to break up the old army.[16] In defiance of the mood of the broad masses of the people, who wished nothing more fervently than to return to a peaceful life and who were not inclined to take up arms in defence of Bolshevik rule, general conscription was introduced for workers and peasants on 29 May 1918, and soon some 5.5 million men were in uniform. Soviet power, disregarding the profound war-weariness of the people, had transformed the whole country into a 'united armed camp'.[17] All administrative and economic measures during that period of 'war Communism' served solely and exclusively the purpose of strengthening the Red Army and hence the consolidation of Bolshevik rule against domestic and foreign enemies.

In creating a modern mass army, one that was at the same time to be an army of a new type, an army of the dictatorship of the proletariat, Trotsky, chairman since 2 September 1918 of the revolutionary war council (*Revolyutsionnyj voennyj sovet: Revvoensovet*), the supreme command and administrative body of the fighting forces, made use of two elements which initially no doubt interreacted like fire and water, but which, tempered in the storms of the civil war and the war against the interventionists, eventually functioned in unison—the military experts of Tsarist Russia, without whom it would have been impossible to create a modern army, and the war commissars of his own party, without whom it seemed impossible to keep the former Tsarist generals and officers under political control. By August 1920 no fewer than 48,000 generals and officers, 14,000 medical officers, and 10,300 army officials of military rank, as well as 200,000 non-commissioned officers, all of whom, according to Trotsky's own words, had played an enormous role in the civil war, had been enlisted in the service of the Soviet government. The recruitment of these 'military specialists'—that was their official designation—was carried rat under the guidance of the former imperial Russian general Bonch-Bruevich, who had gone over to the Bolshevik side: initially this recruitment was on a more or less voluntary basis, with service be made compulsory for all former officers after 29 July 1918,[18] but constraint was also used against reluctant officers or members of their families.[19] Forced, for the most part, into serving the revolutionary power, these officers began to reconcile themselves to the inevitable and to make a decisive contribution, despite themselves, to the development and victory of the Red Army. It was not the civil-war heroes glorified by Soviet propaganda, such as Budenny or Chapaev, but the organizational and leadership skills of the military specialists that enabled the Soviet power to hold out against the domestic and foreign threat. Although these military specialists were, at best, no more than tolerated, and although their services have never been adequately acknowledged, many outstanding leaders of the Red Army have subsequently come from their ranks,

---

[16] *50 let vooružennych sil*, 37.
[17] *Boevoj put' vooružennych sil*, 64; *50 let vooružennych sil*, 47, 56.
[18] *50 let vooružennych sil*, 566.   [19] Ritter, *Kommunemodell*, 145 ff.

such as the Marshals of the Soviet Union Yegorov, Tukhachevsky, and Shaposhnikov, and a whole string of well-known Second World War generals. The huge success of the experiment of making the military experts of the old army serve the Soviet cause was due primarily to Trotsky, who assured those officers loyally co-operating with the Soviet power of his personal protection, while leaving no doubt that ex-officers not up to expectations would have to face Draconian measures and, in the event of desertion, find that their families would be held liable. For their supervision he made use of the war commissars, whose duty subsequently, in constantly changing situations, was to ensure the political reliability of officers, as well as the Party's dominating influence in the fighting forces.

The establishment in March 1918, simultaneously with the creation of regular units of the Red Army, of an institute of war commissars, based on Party cells likewise set up at that time, provided the bond that was to ensure the political stance of the Red Army with its heterogeneous elements along the lines laid down by the central committee of the Russian Communist Party (Bolsheviks) (RKP [b]). Furnished as they were with full powers as representatives of the Soviet system, the war commissars were entrusted principally with the supervision of the military specialists and the swift curtailment of any counter-revolutionary intentions of hostile officers.[20] Every military order given by a unit commander had to be politically sanctioned by the war commissar's countersignature before it was executed; in the ideal situation the unit commander and the commissar would jointly discuss an order, the commander would issue it, and the commissar would help him put it into effect. At the superior level of fronts and armies revolutionary war councils were set up, which included, alongside the commanding officer, two war commissars; at the lower level of companies, batteries, and squadrons the corresponding functions were performed, after October 1919, by a political guidance officer (*politicheskyj rukovoditel: politruk*). The political importance attached to the commissars was reflected by the fact that, under the merciless conditions of civil and interventionist war, captured commissars were usually shot at once. British interventionist troops under Major-General Malleson also adopted these methods when, in 1918, they killed the celebrated 26 commissars, headed by the commissar-extraordinary of the government of the Russian socialist federative Soviet republic (RSFSR) for Caucasian affairs, Shaumyan, 'in a bestial manner'.[21]

Alongside the large group of military specialists Trotsky made great efforts to train his own stratum of Red commanders and officers from the ranks of reliable young Bolsheviks. A whole network of military academies, schools, and training courses was rapidly created for the raising of leadership personnel. The first classes for the training of new officers were held as early as February 1918. On 8 December 1918 the general-staff academy was inaugu-

---

[20] Petrov, *Stroitel'stvo politorganov*, 35.
[21] *50 let vooruzhennych sil*, 40; Smirnov, 'Delo ob ubijstve bakinskich komissarov'.

rated as the first Soviet military academy.[22] A military-engineering academy, a naval academy, and a military medical academy also started operations. By the end of 1920 the Red Army possessed eight military academies and over 150 military schools and classes. By that time 66 per cent of all Red Army officers had been trained in the Soviet era, and only 34 per cent, admittedly occupying important posts, were former officers of the imperial Russian army.

After 1920, following the victory over the White armies of Admiral Kolchak and Generals Denikin, Yudenich, and Vrangel, once the Poles had concluded peace (1920), and once the *entente* powers had suspended their intervention and Soviet Russia had taken possession of the independent republics of the northern Caucasus, as well as of Azerbaijan, Armenia, and Georgia, and had more or less stabilized its power also in Turkestan, the time had come to place the Red Army on a peacetime footing. Demobilization of the 5.5 million men in the forces and their integration into civilian labour could no longer be delayed in view of the country's utterly wrecked economy after the war and the civil war. What remained unchanged was the importance of the security organizations. The task of the 'interior troops' was 'the struggle against political and economic counter-revolution, espionage, and banditry'; the frontier troops, created in 1924, had to guard the state borders. With their origin in the Extraordinary Commission for the Struggle against Counter-revolution and Sabotage (ČK), they were placed in 1922 under the State Political Administration (GPU) of the People's Commissariat of the Interior (NKVD), and in 1924 under the Amalgamated Political Administration (OGPU) of the NKVD of the Soviet Union. Heading these forces until 1926 was Feliks Dzerzhinsky,[23] one of the strangest figures of the Bolshevik Party, who has been called the 'knight of the revolution'. As for the Red Army's forces, which, in accordance with Lenin's demand, were to lose none of their combat efficiency through their numerical reduction, a relatively undisturbed period of development began in 1920. Admittedly, the peasant revolts in the Ukraine, in the Tambov *guberniya*, and in Siberia, the mutiny of 16,000 Red Fleet personnel of the Kronstadt garrison, demanding the restoration of basic freedoms for the 'workers and peasants' in 1921, as well as continually flaring disorders elsewhere,[24] time and again called for the employment of regular formations.

Demobilization was concluded in 1924 with the adoption of a new military-service law based on a combination of cadre and territorial principles. Only the divisions stationed, predominantly, in the western-frontier districts and the technical formations continued to belong to the active forces, which, like the Red Fleet, were operational at all times. In the territorial divisions only the training personnel were on active duty, while the bulk of the men were in civilian employment and, over a number of years, participated only in military

[22] *Akademija imeni Frunze*, 8.

[23] *Feliks Èdmundovič Dzeržinskij*, 260 ff.; Rauch, *Geschichte des bolschewistischen Rußland*, 95.

[24] Stökl, *Russische Geschichte*, 681; Heller and Nekrič, *Geschichte*, i. 90 ff.

exercises. The whole system was a compromise between military and economic necessities, and dictated by the need to keep defence expenditure as low as possible and to integrate the work-force in the economic process. After the foundation of the Soviet Union in 1924, in addition to the standing and territorial divisions there were also national divisions, in which members of the minority nations did their military service.[25] The territory of the USSR was subdivided into the military districts of Moscow, Leningrad, Belorussia, Ukraine, North Caucasus, Volga, Central Asia, and Siberia; in addition there was an independent army in Transcaucasia.[26] After Trotsky's overthrow in 1925 Mikhail Frunze became people's commissar for army and navy affairs, and after his death the same year the post went to Kliment Voroshilov. The armed forces of the Soviet Union consisted of the Red workers' and peasants' army, the Red workers' and peasants' fleet, the air forces of the Red workers' and peasants' army, the interior and frontier troops under the control of the (O)GPU, and an 'escort guard'. Although in theory, under the 1924 constitution, the defence of the Soviet Union was the duty of every Soviet citizen, service in the armed forces was entrusted only to 'workers and peasants'. The bourgeoisie, or whatever was understood by that term, was to remain disarmed.[27]

The fall of Trotsky, who had extensively backed the activity of former Tsarist officers, resulted in a perceptible lessening of the influence of those military specialists. As members of the educated strata were excluded from service in the forces, and as the officers recruited from the lower popular strata and put through short-term training frequently lacked the intellectual prerequisites, the standard of the command personnel at the middle and lower levels soon left much to be desired. An attempt was made in 1924–5 to remedy that state of affairs by a reorganization of military-training institutions and by an extension of the training period for junior, middle-ranking, and senior officers, as well as for the political personnel.[28] During the years which followed much attention was again given to the development of military-training institutions. By 1927 there were six military academies for the training of senior commanders and the military-political academy for the training of the senior political officers. For the purpose of unifying and modernizing the whole system of military training a start was made on the drafting of new service regulations for the Red Army and the Red Fleet. New active-service regulations provisionally introduced in 1925 were finalized and confirmed in 1929. The different services—infantry, cavalry, the air forces, and the navy—received new battle and service regulations after 1927; these reflected for the first time the specifically Soviet ideas of war under contemporary conditions. The year 1924 also saw the publication of the first issue of the army paper *Krasnaya Zvezda* (Red Star).

---

[25] Berchin, *Voennaja reforma*, 116 ff. [26] Mackintosh, 'Rote Armee 1920–1926', 63.
[27] *50 let vooružennych sil*, 179. [28] Berchin, *Voennaja reforma*, 332 ff.

Under the leadership of Trotsky and of his successors Frunze and Voroshilov, the Red Army had thus, since the civil war and the war against intervention, acquired the appearance and character of a regular army. A first decoration had been instituted, the Order of the Red Banner, and entire units could be awarded this honorary banner. In its hierarchical structure the Red Army had also moved away from the equality principle in outward appearance. Since 1919 members of the junior, middle, and senior 'command staff' had again been wearing distinguishing badges in the shape of small triangles, squares, and diamonds on their collar patches and cuffs.[29] One special characteristic which distinguished the Red workers' and peasants' army from other regular armies and which was a reminder of its revolutionary origins was and remained the institution of war commissars, who continued to enjoy authority, far-reaching or more restricted according to political requirements. Although even the Bolshevik Party leaders realized that the best form of military leadership was the concentration of command in one person, the introduction of such a single-command principle was deliberately avoided for the simple reason that it seemed necessary to practise political supervision over the former Tsarist officers in positions of command. An additional reason was that the Red Army rank and file also needed continuous supervision and guidance, as for the most part the men had little taste for war and were anything but Bolshevik-minded. However, as new officers, reliable from the Communist Point of view, were beginning to move in larger numbers into positions of command, and as the Party apparatus became consolidated among the units, the question of strict Party supervision by the commissars now appeared in a new light. However, the revolutionary war council of the USSR, which examined that question in 1924, was unable to decide in favour of abolishing the system of commissars.[30] The desirability of the principle of single power of command was actually admitted—but only commanding officers who were proven Communists were to be entrusted with both the military-administrative and the political command of their units. Such officers were merely given a deputy in charge of political affairs. In most instances the position of the commanding officers was evidently strengthened in respect of military matters, though the war commissar, who had the support of the party-political apparatus in his work, remained fully responsible for the political reliability and morale of officers and other ranks. A decision of the Party's central committee in 1927 expressly reserved the right to reintroduce the commissar system as an instrument of political supervision for certain eventualities.[31] Such an instance arose in 1937 in connection with the mass persecutions of Red Army and Red Fleet officers.[32] The institute of war commissars, which had meanwhile been largely dissolved, was reactivated at the time of the great purges, but in 1940, when conditions had settled down again and command of

---

[29] Andreev and Bobkov, 'O znakach različija'; Bobkov, 'K istorii voinskich zvanij'.
[30] Petrov, *Stroitel'stvo politorganov*, 159 ff.   [31] Ibid. 238.
[32] Schapiro, 'Große Säuberung'.

the forces was in the hands of officers loyal to Stalin, it was once more abolished. The fact that single command was reintroduced by a decree of the supreme soviet praesidium in 1940 and that commanders now had only a deputy for political affairs at their side[33] was largely due to the disappointing experience of the dual rule of commander and commissar in the campaign against Poland, in the Russo-Finnish Winter War, and during clashes in the Far East. Such considerations, however, were brushed aside when, at the beginning of the German–Soviet war and the crushing defeats at the fronts, Stalin believed he had every reason to doubt the loyalty of his commanders in the field. Only when the German offensive got stuck and when a change in the military situation began to take shape in October was the renewed commissar system loosened up again. The position of the commissars was a good barometer of how the political reliability of the army was assessed.

By the end of the 1920s, at any rate, the organization of the Soviet armed forces had been largely consolidated. A clear chain of command had been established, except that the provision of the Red Army with weapons, technical equipment, and vehicles was still unsatisfactory in the extreme. At that time there were no more than 7,000 worn-out artillery pieces, mostly of light calibre, 200 tanks dating from the First World War, 1,000 out-of-date aircraft, as well as a more 350 trucks, 700 staff cars, and 67 tractors. The newly started five-year plans (1929–32 and 1933–7), implemented with substantial help from foreign technicians, were to achieve a fundamental transformation in the equipment of the Red Army. The process of industrialization, of the establishment of a native heavy industry, stemmed from the wish to enhance the country's defensive capacity and included a rapidly growing armoured fighting vehicle and aircraft industry. In 1932, during the first five-year plan, 5,000 armoured fighting vehicles were built; by the end of the second five-year plan the figure was 15,000. The number of guns rose from 7,000 to nearly 56,000 modern types by the beginning of 1939.[34] During the eight years from 1930 to 1938 alone production of rifles increased from 174,000 to 1,174,000 annually, and that of machine-guns from roughly 41,000 to 74,500.[35] The aircraft industry, virtually created from scratch, which had produced an average of 860 aircraft in 1930–1, produced an annual average of 3,578 military machines in 1935–7.[36] Approximately 50 per cent of these were bombers and ground-attack aircraft, and 38 per cent were fighters. Naval shipbuilding also experienced a major increase during the first two five-year plans.[37] More than 500 vessels were launched during that period. In 1930 the first Soviet submarines went into service. By 1938 the Soviet submarine fleet had received an increasing number of vessels of different types. In the second five-year plan construction

---

[33] Petrov, *Stroitel'stvo politorganov*, 260 ff.; OKH/GenStdH/OQu IV, Abt. Frd Heere Ost, No. 10/40, 5 Jan. 1940, BA-MA RH 19 I/122, fos. 146, 89.

[34] Zacharov, 'Kommmunističeskaja partija', 6. For the sake of greater accuracy, numerical data were checked whenever possible on the basis of several Soviet publications.

[35] Zhukov, *Reminiscences and Reflections*, 167.   [36] *Akademija imeni Frunze*, 111.

[37] *Boevoj put' voenno-morskogo flota*, 165 ff.

also began of cruisers and destroyers of native design. To provide an idea of the magnitude of the Soviet rearmament effort, suffice it to say that whereas over the span of the first five-year plan military expenditure amounted to 4,900m. roubles, the figure during the second five-year plan was already 47,000m.[38]

The process of equipping the Red Army and the Red Fleet with modern weapons and a modern war technology during the first two five-year plans had far-reaching consequences in terms of personnel and leadership: the need now was for officers and other ranks to learn to operate the new weapons and handle them under modern battle conditions. In these circumstances the instructional and training programmes of the Soviet armed forces were further developed. The separate faculties of the military-technical academy, established in 1932, were now developed into specialized academies for the officers of the various service branches. Thus there was soon a military academy for mechanization and motorization, an artillery academy, a military-engineering academy, an academy for military chemistry, a military academy of electrical engineering, a military-transport academy, and an academy for war economy. In the strategic and operational training of the senior commanders the general-staff academy, alongside the Frunze military academy, played an ever bigger role.[39] Towards the end of the second five-year plan there were altogether thirteen military academies and one military institute, as well as five military faculties at civilian universities. Training for young officers was provided by no fewer than 75 officers' colleges, 11 of them for artillery officers, 9 for tank officers, 4 for intelligence officers, 18 for air-force officers, and 7 for naval officers. The increasing respect enjoyed by the Red Army's officer corps was reflected in 1935 by the introduction of personal ranks for officers, with the customary designations from lieutenant up to colonel. Blyukher, Budenny, Voroshilov, Yegorov, and Tukhachevsky were given the rank of Marshal of the Soviet Union. For the remaining general-officer ranks the designations brigade commander (*kombrig*), divisional commander (*komdiv*), corps commander (*komkor*), and army commander (*komandarm*) first and second rank were kept until 1940 and only then replaced by the customary designations for generals.

The need for consistent and intensive training of all Red Army members in the new war techniques had by then become inescapable. Occasional military exercises of Red Army men no longer met requirements; in consequence the territorial principle, which in part still existed, was finally abolished in 1935 and all divisions of the Red Army were established on the cadre principle of a standing army. The Red workers' and peasants' army, whose strength had increased from 885,000 in 1933 to 1,513,000 in 1937, underwent a number of changes also in the structure of its controlling bodies. The revolutionary war council of the USSR was dissolved in 1934, the people's commissariat for

---

[38] Kravčenko, 'Ėkonomičeskaja pobeda', 39.   [39] Štemenko, *General'nyj štab*, i. 6.

military and naval affairs was transformed into a people's commissariat for the defence of the USSR, and in 1937 a separate people's commissariat for the ocean fleet was established. Fundamental questions of national defence were examined by the newly created supreme military council of the RKKA and by the supreme military council of the ocean fleet. In 1935 the former staff of the Red workers' and peasants' army was transformed into a general staff of the Red workers' and peasants' army, and the then Marshal of the Soviet Union Yegorov was appointed its chief.[40]

During the first two five-year plans the armed forces of the Soviet Union not only adjusted their organization to modern requirements and were furnished with up-to-date weapons and equipment on a generous scale, but were also greatly increased numerically. During that period, moreover, a whole number of Soviet officers came to the fore, who systematically studied the character of technological warfare, developed the application of the new weapons, and, from the 1930s onward, laid the foundations of Soviet military theory. These Soviet military theoreticians were often young officers, most of whom had begun their military careers in the Tsarist army and who now regarded their break with outdated military views and attitudes and the development of new principles of armed combat as their revolutionary deed. Among these theoreticians the most outstanding were the former Tsarist lieutenant-colonel and subsequent Marshal of the Soviet Union Yegorov,[41] the former Tsarist second lieutenant and subsequent Corps Commander Eydeman,[42] the RKKA divisional commander and chief of the operations faculty of the Frunze military academy, and subsequent professor of operational skills at the general staff academy, Isserson,[43] the Army Commander (1st rank) Yakir,[44] the former Tsarist colonel and subsequent Army Commander (1st rank) Kamenev,[45] the former Tsarist lieutenant-colonel and subsequent Army Commander (2nd rank) and chief of the Frunze military academy Kork,[46] the former Tsarist lieutenant-colonel and subsequent Marshal of the Soviet Union and chief of the Red Army General Staff Shaposhnikov,[47] the former Tsarist general staff officer and subsequent professor at the general staff academy, Lieutenant-General Shilovsky,[48] the former Tsarist staff captain and subsequent Corps Commander Triandafillov,[49] the former Tsarist lieutenant and subsequent Marshal of the Soviet Union Tukhachevsky,[50] the former Tsarist second lieutenant and subsequent Army Commander (1st rank) Uborevich,[51] and the

[40] *50 let vooružennych sil*, 199.

[41] *Voprosy strategii*, 374–88; Vasilevskij, 'Soldat, polkovodec'.

[42] Gladkov, 'Ejdeman'.   [43] *Voprosy strategii*, 389–438; Isserson, 'Razvitie teorii'.

[44] Šelachov and Geller, 'O polkovodčeskoj dejatel'nosti Jakira'; Dubinskij, 'Obraz komandarma'; Pankov, 'Komandarm Jakir'.

[45] *Voprosy strategii*, 145–65.   [46] 'Komandarm Kork'.

[47] Šapošnikov, *Vospominanija*; *Voprosy strategii*, 190–217.   [48] *Voprosy strategii*, 497–517.

[49] Ibid. 291–345; Golubev, 'Vydajuščijsja teoretik'.

[50] Tuchačevskij, *Izbrannye proizvedenija*; Todorskij, *Maršal Tuchačevskij*; *Voprosy strategii*, 71–144.

[51] *Voprosy strategii*, 166–77; 'Komandarm pervogo ranga', 121–2; Savost'janov, 'Uborevič'.

former Tsarist staff captain and subsequent chief of staff of senior Red Army command authorities Varfolomeev.[52]

What were the special characteristics of Soviet military theory, as developed at that time? In answering this question one has to proceed from the fact that Soviet military science assigned the decisive role in a future war to the army, with naval and air forces playing only a supportive role. The principal characteristic of Soviet military theory was its emphasis on offensive thinking: 'The operations of the Red Army will at all times aim at the annihilation of the enemy,' the new active-service regulations[53] stipulated. 'All combat, in attack and defence, serves the purpose of inflicting a defeat on the enemy, but only resolute attack in the direction of the main thrust, developing into relentless pursuit, leads to the total annihilation of enemy forces and material.' In order to avoid becoming bogged down in positional warfare, as in the First World War,[54] principles of 'in-depth operation' were developed especially by Tukhachevsky, Triandafillov, and Isserson.[55] This term signified an offensive operation with the use of artillery, armour, aircraft, and the parachute air-landing troops[56] first seen in manœuvres in 1935–6, when they deeply impressed foreign military attachés. 'The modern means of overwhelming the enemy—primarily armoured fighting vehicles, artillery, aircraft, and mechanized units—employed on a large scale,' the regulations continued, 'provide the opportunity of simultaneously carrying the attack into the very depth of the enemy's order of battle, with the objective of cutting the enemy off, totally encircling him, and annihilating him.' This aim was to be achieved by directing the combat against the full depth of the opponent's 'tactical defence zone' by means of artillery, air operations against the reserves and the rear areas of the enemy's defences, penetration of the enemy's position by infantry with escorting armour, break-through of the long-distance armour into the depth of the 'tactical defence zone', pulling forward of mechanized and cavalry units into the deep rear of the enemy, and by the extensive use of smoke for purposes of concealment and deception. In the second phase of the attack the tactical success should thus be widened into success on a strategic scale.[57]

The principles of such an offensive operation were laid down in 1933 in an essay entitled 'Principles of in-depth operation' (*Osnovy glubokoy operatsii*); they were further developed in the Red Army's military academies and staffs, and tested in practice in major manœuvres, e.g. in Belorussia under Uborevich, in the Ukraine under Yakir, and in the Far East under Blyukher.[58] The active-service regulations issued in 1936 finally turned the new principles into obligatory training directives for the entire Red workers' and peasants'

---

[52] *Voprosy strategii*, 439–69.

[53] Merkblatt 19/9 OKH/Gen StdH/OQu IV/Abt. Fremde Heere Ost, Vorläufige Felddienstordnung . . . 1936, 9.

[54] *Obščevojskovaja armija*, 9.   [55] Kozlov et al., *O sovetskoj voennoj nauke*, 188 ff.

[56] Kostylev, 'Stanovlenie i razvitie'.   [57] Zacharov, 'O teorii glubokoj operacii', 14.

[58] Isserson, 'Razvitie teorii', 44–5.

army. Soviet military theory had thus received a forward-looking formulation, far outstripping operational and tactical views in western Europe, which were still conditioned by the lessons of the Great War.[59]

Of prime importance, therefore, was the creation of armoured and air formations, capable of widening tactical penetrations into strategic success and of swiftly carrying operations into the enemy's hinterland. For the purpose of massive employment air squadrons had been amalgamated into air brigades, and heavy-bomber corps had been established. According to their designation, the air forces were divided into tactical ground-attack and long-range strategic bomber forces.[60] As for the use of armour, the tanks, in the Red Army too, were originally seen as support for the infantry. Tank battalions depended on co-operation with infantry divisions, and the mechanized regiments were attached to the cavalry divisions. In May 1930, however, an independent mechanized brigade was established and, in line with Tukhachevsky's and Triandafillov's recommendations—and still in peacetime—a start was soon made on the creation of large armoured formations. In 1932 there existed, as an independent operational formation, a mechanized corps consisting of two mechanized brigades and one rifle brigade, as well as of further special units, comprising a total of 490 tanks. This first mechanized corps was soon followed by three others, so that in 1932 the Red Army possessed four mechanized corps, several independent mechanized brigades, and independent armoured brigades, all of strategic significance.[61]

By 1935–6 the Red Army had acquired in every respect the character of a modern fighting force. Major-General Ernst August Köstring, the German military attaché in Moscow and a highly experienced and competent observer, described it as the best and soundest institution still to be found in the Soviet Union.[62] However, the positive development which the Soviet forces were undergoing in that increasingly complex foreign-political situation was to be abruptly cut short and the structure of the Red Army and Red Fleet shaken to its foundations by the mass persecutions of the great 'purge' staged by Stalin. In June 1937 Marshal of the Soviet Union Tukhachevsky and seven other senior officers were arrested on threadbare charges of espionage, sentenced to death in a secret trial, and shot almost at once.[63] The arrests carried out in the Soviet armed forces in 1937 and throughout 1938 assumed a colossal scale.[64] Victims of the purge were three of the five Marshals of the Soviet Union (Blyukher, Yegorov, and Tukhachevsky), thirteen of fifteen officers of the rank of army commanders (Alksnis, Belov, Dubovoy, Dybenko, Fedko, Yakir,

---

[59] *General Köstring*, 149; Erickson, *Soviet High Command*, 351, 459.

[60] Koževnikov, 'Razvitie operativnogo iskusstva', 16; Pljačenko, 'Trudy po teorii', 86–7; Černeckij, 'O nekotorych voprosach', 88 ff.

[61] Krupčenko, 'Razvitie tankovych vojsk', 41–2; Ryžakov, 'K voprosu o stroitel'stve', 107–8.

[62] *General Köstring*, 94, 181.

[63] Conquest, *Great Terror*, 224; Heller and Nekrič, *Geschichte*, i. 291 ff.

[64] Schapiro, 'Große Säuberung', 75–6; Garthoff, *Sowjetarmee*, 257; Rauch, *Geschichte des bolschewistischen Rußland*, 335; Nekrič and Grigorenko, *Genickschuß*, 100 ff.

Khalepsky, Kashirin, Kork, Levandovsky, Loktionov, Sedyakin, Uborevich), and a number of army commissars (Amelin, Bulin, Kozhevnikov, Mezits, Okunev, Osepyan, Shifres, Slavin, and others). The chief of the central political directorate of the Red Army, Gamarnik, allegedly committed suicide when he was arrested. Altogether 62 out of 85 corps commanders,[65] 110 out of 195 divisional commanders, 220 out of 406 brigade commanders, and about half of all regimental commanders were liquidated—a total of nearly 35,000 officers, which was about half of the Red Army's and Red Fleet's officer corps, as well as 20,000 political officers, about two-thirds of the total number.[66] Of 6,000 senior officers arrested, from the rank of colonel upwards, 1,500 were executed, usually after torture, and the rest disappeared in concentration camps. Especially affected was the central command apparatus of the Soviet forces, such as the people's commissariat for the defence of the USSR, the military council, the general staff, and the armed forces political directorate. Victims of liquidation were all the commanders of military districts along with their war councils, in addition to all the commanders of the air forces (with one exception), and all commanders of the novy, such as Dushenov, Kireev, Kozhanov, Muklevich, Orlov, Pantserzhansky, Sivkov, Viktorov, and others, as well as countless members of the teaching staff of the military academies and colleges, and the staff of all other military institutions and of the army's political apparatus. Not even well-known and successful armament designers such as Langemak, the creator of the multiple mortar known as 'Katusha' or 'Stalin's organ-pipes', or the mortar designer Shavyrin,[67] were spared. Indeed, the famous aircraft designer Tupolev only just managed to escape execution.[68]

The decimation of the officer corps of the Soviet armed forces was only part of the purges which, since the assassination of Kirov in 1934, had been spreading throughout the country in ever new waves and which can only be described as 'pathological features', a kind of 'collective dementia'. The whole country was in a state of 'feverish excitement'. The first victims were the leading figures of the Bolshevik Party, the trail-blazers of the Revolution and Lenin's comrades-in-arms, such as Zinovyev, Kamenev, Bukharin, Rykov, as well as Trotsky's followers and former Mensheviks, social-revolutionaries, anarchists, and other members of left-wing groups; but soon the arrests extended to the totality of the Communist Party and to foreign Communists resident in the Soviet Union. Everybody was compelled to denounce everybody else. Officials of the Party and governmental apparatus were affected by the arrests just as much as figures in the economy, scientists, artists, and the leading strata of minority nations, and finally the broad masses of the popu-

---

[65] Among them Bazilevič, Borisenko, Boskanov, Chachan'jan, Efimov, Ejdeman, Fel'dman, Gaj, Gajlit, Gekker, Germanovič, Gorbačev, Gorjačev, Gribov, Grjaznov, Kalmykov, Kovtjuch, Kujbyšev, Kutjakov, Lapin, Longva, Nejman, Petin, Primakov, Pugačev, Putna, Sazontov, Serdič, Urickij, Vajner, Zonberg, and many others.

[66] Conquest, *Great Terror*, 228 ff.; Kuznecov, 'Generaly 1940 goda', 29 ff.

[67] Vannikov, 'Iz zapisok Narkoma', 85.   [68] Majskij, *Vospominanija*, ii. 276.

lation. The victims of these mass persecutions were not only the arrested persons themselves, 'but also their families down to their entirely innocent children, whose lives were wrecked from the start'. On 7 April 1935 the Soviet government, in one of the 'most barbaric laws' of the twentieth century, imposed upon twelve-year-old children the same punishments as adults, including the death penalty. There was a wave of suicides among the now totally abandoned children of persons executed or arrested.[69] According to the investigations of Robert Conquest, who carefully analysed all available data,[70] an average of eight million people were held in Soviet concentration camps under unbearable conditions each year between 1936 and 1950; of these, 10 per cent, or 800,000 people, died annually, making a total of 11 million. During Yezhov's term as people's commissar of the interior, i.e. during the great purge, the 'Yezhovshchina', a million people were liquidated. To these 12 million victims of Stalin one should add the 3.5 million rural inhabitants who perished in the course of forcible collectivization, as well as 3.5 million kulaks who were deported to concentration camps and who likewise, virtually all of them, lost their lives. Conquest arrives at the conclusion that at least 20 million people fell victim to the Soviet extermination measures between 1930 and 1950. This total, however, as he points out, is more likely to be too low than too high, and the number of victims should probably be increased by a further 10 million.

The charges brought against Tukhachevsky and the military and political leaders of espionage, particularly for Germany, of betrayal of military secrets to that power, of secret collaboration with 'Fascist circles', and of preparation of an armed uprising—'fantastic in their incredibility'[71] though they may seem—should be viewed against the background of former co-operation between the Red Army and the Reichswehr. As early as 1919 Trotsky, with Lenin's approval, had approached the German armament industry in order to interest it in producing aircraft, weapons, and ammunition for the Soviet Union. In 1921, moreover, military talks were held in Berlin and Moscow, when the Soviet negotiators allowed it to be understood that they would favour German support in an attack against Poland.[72] These repeated negotiations between representatives of German armament firms and officers in the Reichswehr ministry, on the one side, and representatives of the Soviet government and the Red Army, on the other, produced palpable results soon after the conclusion of the Rapallo treaty in 1922. In line with the ideas of Trotsky, Radek, and the Red Army chief of staff Lebedev, German industrial enterprises, with the support of Reich Chancellor Wirth, set up a number of production centres in Russia—the Junkers plant for aircraft manufacture at

[69] Lewytzkyj, *Die rote Inquisition*, 141, 113; Conquest, *Great Terror*, 302.
[70] Conquest, *Great Terror*, 525 ff.; id., *Harvest of Sorrow*; Zlepko, *Der ukrainische Hunger-Holocaust*.
[71] *General Köstring*, 187; Erickson, *Soviet High Command*, 464; Conquest, *Great Terror*, 207.
[72] Erickson, *Soviet High Command*, 153, 265.

Fili, the Krupp plants in Petrograd, Shlisselburg, Tula, Zlatousk, and else-where, as well as factories for the production of ammunition. In addition, a German–Russian company Bersol set up a factory for the production of poison gas at Trotsk, near Samara.[73] Within the framework of co-operation on arma-ment technology, further intensified by agreement after 1923, the deputy war commissar and chief of Red Army supplies Unshlikht, at a conference at the Reichswehr ministry in 1926, proposed German participation in the manufac-ture of heavy guns and optical instruments in the Soviet Union. Simul-taneously, the chief of the Soviet ocean fleet Zof was negotiating with representatives of the German navy command about the transfer of blueprints for the construction of submarines.[74] During those years Germany received 300,000 artillery shells out of the production of the Soviet Union, a deal cleverly exploited in domestic political propaganda since, as a leaflet from that period put it, those shells could very well have been used for fighting the German proletariat.[75] As late as 1930 negotiations were still being conducted between on the one hand People's Commissar Voroshilov, his deputy Unshlikht, and Army Commander Uborevich, and on the other General Ludwig, head of the Reichswehr armament department, and representatives of German firms such as Krupp and Rheinmetall concerning the further rearmament of the Soviet Union.[76]

Since the beginning of the 1920s there had developed, in addition to co-operation in the armament sector, a purely military type of co-operation, from which both countries benefited equally. The Soviet Union was generously supplied with German military directives, strategic and tactical studies, and similar material because, as Radek put it, the Red Army of 1922 was especially interested in raising the still rather low professional standards of its officers. Germany's gain was more practical. The Reichswehr was given an opportunity in the Soviet Union to test military aircraft and tanks, both prohibited under the treaty of Versailles, as well as war-gas, and to train the appropriate personnel on the spot. After preliminary negotiations with Rozengolts, the chief of the Soviet air forces, in 1924 the air centre of Lipetsk was first put into operation,[77] where altogether 450 German fighter pilots and observers were trained over the years and the tactical and technical characteristics of military aircraft tested in co-operation with Soviet personnel. In 1927–8 there followed the establishment of a school for training and techniques in gas warfare on an extensive territory, from which all inhabitants had been evacuated, near Trotsk; its cover-name was 'Tomka'. Eventually an armoured fighting-vehicle school was established in Kazan on the Volga.[78] By setting up those 'stations' under the control of the Reichswehr ministry and directed by 'Zentrale Moskau' under Colonel Thomsen and Major Dr Ritter von Niedermayer, the

[73] Hilger, *Erinnerungen*, 191; Erickson, *Soviet High Command*, 151–2, 157.
[74] Erickson, *Soviet High Command*, 251 ff.   [75] Speidel, 'Reichswehr und Rote Armee', 11.
[76] Hilger, *Erinnerungen*, 200; Erickson, *Soviet High Command*, 272.
[77] Völker, *Entwicklung*, 131 ff., 140 ff.   [78] Erickson, *Soviet High Command*, 263–4.

Soviet Union contributed, to a degree not to be underrated, to the strengthening of Germany's military potential. In the opinion of competent judges, without the training and development work performed in the Soviet Union it would have been impossible to bring the German armour and the German air force to the state of proficiency they achieved after 1933.[79] To the Soviet Union, in return, the participation of Soviet officers in military-training events, troop inspections, and war-games in Germany was no doubt of equal importance.[80] A number of field commanders of the Red Army, including Army Commanders Yakir and Uborevich, as well as Corps Commanders Eydeman and Uritsky, also participated in secret general-staff training courses in Germany. Altogether it is thought that no fewer than 120 Soviet senior officers were able to complete their training in Germany.

German–Soviet co-operation in the military and armament fields resulted in direct official contacts between Soviet politicians and military men and German officers; despite the reserve shown by the Russians, these had led to better mutual acquaintance and understanding. Not only Trotsky, Radek, Rykov, Krasin, and Krestinsky—to name but a few prominent Bolshevik functionaries—had negotiated with the Germans. A whole string of Soviet senior officers had made contact with them. A particularly vigorous champion of collaboration with the Reichswehr was People's Commissar Voroshilov, who, between 1928 and 1932, was in direct touch with leading figures of the German army command, such as Generals Werner von Blomberg, Kurt Freiherr von Hammerstein-Equord, Wilhelm Heye, and Adam, and who had invariably shown himself 'most obliging'. It was Voroshilov, moreover, who in 1928 specifically proposed to Blomberg a German–Soviet alliance against Poland in the event of either country being attacked.[81] Other Soviet figures involved in negotiations or conversations with German military men were the Soviet air-force chiefs Rozengolts, Baranov, and Alksnis, the ocean-fleet chiefs Zof, Muklevich, and Orlov, the Red Army chiefs of staff Lebedev, Yegorov, and to a lesser degree Shaposhnikov, the field commanders Blyukher, Yakir, Tukhachevsky, and Uborevich, and the chief of Red Army supplies, Unshlikht. Even though co-operation between the Reichswehr and the Red Army came to an end after Hitler's rise to power, many a senior Red Army officer continued to display a friendly, and indeed cordial, attitude towards the highly respected German military attaché in Moscow. General Köstring reports a (possibly authorized) approach made to him by Yegorov, the Red Army chief of staff, who conveyed his gratitude for what Soviet officers had learnt during their stay in Germany.[82] People's Commissar Voroshilov in a conversation with General von Blomberg likewise remarked how 'very valuable' the study of German training methods had been to the Red Army.[83] On

---

[79] *General Köstring*, 47.   [80] Carsten, *Reichswehr*, 257, 306, 309.
[81] Erickson, *Soviet High Command*, 265, 272.
[82] Hilger, *Erinnerungen*, 259; *General Köstring*, 85, 180.
[83] Carsten, *Reichswehr*, 307; Erickson, *Soviet High Command*, 265.

the occasion of the departure of the German ambassador, Herbert von Dirksen, in October 1933 Deputy People's Commissar Tukhachevsky told the chargé d'affaires Fritz von Twardowski 'in all seriousness' that the Reichswehr had been the teacher of the Red Army at a difficult time, that this would never be forgotten, and that the 'Red Army would never, never give up any part of its co-operation with the Reichswehr'.[84] And in January 1934 Voroshilov, speaking to the new German ambassador, Rudolf Nadolny, allowed it to be understood that the Red Army was hoping for a restoration of friendly relations with the Reichswehr.[85]

This basically pro-German attitude of many senior officers in the Red Army, which is unlikely to have remained hidden from Stalin, might seem at first sight to justify a story spread after the war: that forged documents of the Reichssicherheitshauptamt (the SS central intelligence department) concerning secret collaboration between the Red Army leadership and Germany had been passed on to Stalin by way of the Czechoslovak president Beneš.[86] Yet even if the contents of these documents were 'unconditionally regarded as the truth', even if they really represented a 'provocation of the Fascist secret service' in a 'monstrous and diabolical' manner, they could never justify carnage on a scale 'virtually bearing the mark of dementia'.[87] Thus a more convincing explanation—if indeed there can be a rational justification—seems to be that the liquidation of the military leadership stratum of the Soviet armed forces was connected with Stalin's struggle to consolidate his own position of power. To Stalin, however, this meant the liquidation not only of his actual but also all his potential opponents, and ultimately also of those Red Army officers who did not owe their positions exclusively to Stalin or who, looking back to the days of the civil war, might tend to regard him as their equal. Thus it was not so much the former military specialists like Shaposhnikov who were affected by the great purge but the heroes of the civil war and the most gifted unit commanders of the Red Army.

Contrary to the most recent interpretations,[88] Stalin's action against the officers of the Red Army and Red Fleet meant a disastrous weakening of Soviet armed strength. This was admitted by Nikita Khrushchev himself when, at the twentieth congress of the CPSU in 1956, he blamed those mass reprisals for the conditions 'which prevailed at the beginning of the war and which most seriously endangered our country'.[89] That view was shared by a whole string of authoritative Soviet military leaders. Thus Marshal of the

---

[84] Unterredung mit Tuchatschewski [Conference with Tukhachevsky], 6 Nov. 1933, BA-MA RW 5/v. 461.

[85] Hilger, *Erinnerungen*, 259; Erickson, *Soviet High Command*, 379.

[86] *Geschichte des Großen Vaterländischen Krieges*, i. 118 ff. These passages are missing from the original Soviet text: *Istorija Velikoj Otečestvennoj vojny*, i. 100.

[87] Schapiro, 'Große Säuberung', 77.

[88] Also Reinhardt, *Moskau*, 20–1; Halder, *Diaries*, 904 (5 May 1941).

[89] Khrushchev's speech, 25 Feb. 1956, according to Telpuchowski, *Geschichte des Großen Vaterländischen Krieges*, 30 E.

Soviet Union Zakharov described the liquidation of the 'most experienced and, in terms of military theory, best-prepared cadres, of the most gifted researchers and qualified army leaders' as having caused 'enormous damage' to the army and the whole country.[90] A similar formulation was used by Army General Shtemenko: 'a great misfortune for our army and the whole country'.[91] For Marshal of the Soviet Union Bagramyan the liquidation of the best Soviet army leaders was one of the principal reasons for the serious failures in the initial phase of the war.[92] Even Marshal of the Soviet Union Zhukov, who for obvious reasons tried to exculpate Stalin and his own activity, could not but admit that the 'distasteful arrests' had had an extremely negative effect on the development of the Soviet armed forces.[93]

This is an appropriate point at which to list some of the consequences of the purge for the operational readiness of the Soviet forces. The liquidation of 'ten thousands of . . . commanding and political officers' meant, first of all, that all vacated posts had to be filled with officers who for the most part lacked the necessary knowledge and experience, and who, often enough, were careerists and 'incompetent lick-spittles'. These (as they were called) 'bold advances' proved particularly damaging in the senior command staffs and special services. The Frunze military academy, for instance, was compelled to fill the gaps made in its teaching staff by line officers with no scientific or educational experience, which seriously impaired teaching work.[94] As late as the autumn of 1940, of 225 regimental commanders checked at random there was not one who had graduated from the academy; 25 of them had graduated from a military college, while the rest had merely completed courses for lieutenants. The purges, moreover, had resulted in a serious undermining of military discipline, since all Red Army troops had for years been encouraged to unmask their superior officers as secret enemies. Everywhere an atmosphere of 'fear, distrust, and suspicion' was spreading; everywhere 'sabotage and treason' were suspected, so that any personal initiative and any readiness to take responsibility were paralysed.[95] No less disastrous were the effects of the purge on Soviet military theory, which had only recently received a stamp of modernity with the doctrine of in-depth operation by massed armour and air-force units in the enemy's hinterland. The arrest of all officers concerned with the development of these modern command principles meant that the theories of those 'enemies of the people' were also swept away as sabotage. All publications by officers in disgrace were confiscated and a large portion of military literature and official manuals disappeared from the libraries; in consequence there was growing uncertainty about future training programmes. The further development of the principles of in-depth operations came to a halt. Serious study of the problems of modern war was replaced in the Soviet Army by the practice of collecting casual remarks made by Stalin on military issues—even

---

[90] *Voprosy strategii*, 22.   [91] Štemenko, *General'nyj štab*, i. 26.
[92] Nekrič and Grigorenko, *Genickschuß*, 101.   [93] Zhukov, *Reminiscences*, 171.
[94] Kuročkin, 'Sorok pjat' let', 113.   [95] Gapič, 'Nekotorye mysli', 50.

if they were totally untenable—as the 'inspired revelations' of a great general and of basing the training of the armed forces upon these 'most important laws'.[96]

2. THE RED ARMY UNTIL THE BEGINNING OF THE GERMAN–SOVIET WAR

Since 1937–8 the armed forces of the Soviet Union had been in a strangel dichotomy: leadership and morale, the spiritual strength of the army, had suffered grave damage as a consequence of Stalin's purges, while its physical strength had been growing vigorously as a result of the high-volume output of the armament industry. On the issue of operational principles, however, the Red Army was now moving in reverse, since even the general-staff academy had meanwhile retreated from the principles of in-depth operation and of the employment of armour ahead of the army front line.[97] This was happening at the very time when in Germany, under the influence of Guderian and with limited support from Colonel-General Ludwig Beck, chief of the general staff, the concept of independent operations by armoured formations was beginning to prevail over the opposition of conservative views.[98] That erroneous trend in the Soviet Union was further strengthened by the conclusions which it was believed had to be drawn from the fighting against the Japanese at Lake Khazan in July–August 1938 and on the Khalkin-Gol river in May 1939, and in particular from the Spanish civil war, in which well-known Soviet military leaders of the Second World War, such as Pavlov, Malinovsky, Voronov, Meretskov, Batov, and others, had participated as military advisers. In Spain tanks had been used mainly in support of infantry, and it was therefore thought that in future, too, they were primarily designed to ensure the success of conventional attacks. The fact that armour and aircraft were weapons which fundamentally changed the character of an offensive, or that they were of strategic rather than of merely tactical importance, had been completely forgotten. That assessment of experience in the Spanish civil war was to result in the abolition of the mechanized corps, now called armoured corps, an organizational step which necessarily deprived in-depth operations of their material basis.[99] During discussions in a special commission presided over by Marshal of the Soviet Union Kulik, the deputy people's commissar for defence, it was in particular Corps Commander Pavlov, chief of the armoured forces directorate, who argued the view that armoured corps with 560 tanks were too cumbersome to be moved in semi-strategic operations.[100] Admittedly, the majority of the members of this commission of the supreme war council, sitting in August 1939, still came out in favour of keeping the corps formations.

---

[96] Kozlov et al., *O sovetskoj voennoj nauke*, 50–1.   [97] Isserson, 'Razvitie teorii', 54–5.
[98] *Germany and the Second World War*, i. 432–3, 434–5.
[99] Kozlov et al., *O sovetskoj voennoj nauke*, 191; Tel'puchovskij, 'Dejatel'nost' KPSS', 63.
[100] Ryžakov, 'K voprosu o stroitel'stve', 109, also for the following passages.

But when the campaign in Poland in September 1939 revealed considerable difficulties in the handling of the XVth and XXVth Armoured Corps employed there, and when the armoured formations lagged behind even the cavalry, evidence of the unsuitability of large armoured formations seemed conclusive. In view of that bad experience, the supreme military council in November 1939 decreed the disbandment of the armoured corps and their replacement by 15 motorized divisions. Altogether 4 such divisions were established by May 1940, each consisting of 1 tank regiment, 2 motorized rifle regiments, 1 artillery regiment, and 1 reconnaissance, signals, and sapper battalion, as well as special units, and totalling 275 tanks. In addition to the motorized divisions, in May 1940 the Red Army had 35 armoured brigades of 258 tanks each, as well as 4 armoured brigades of 156 tanks each for reinforcement of the rifle corps. In addition, there were 20 independent tank regiments within the framework of the cavalry divisions and 98 independent tank battalions within that of the infantry divisions.

The reorganization of the armoured troops at the beginning of the Second World War, between November 1939 and May 1940—that is, the disbandment of the armoured corps—is judged throughout Soviet military literature to have been a mistaken and damaging measure, as it implied the abandonment of the use of large armoured formations for independent operations.[101] As part of the rehabilitation of Stalin, there have recently been attempts to justify the measure by the argument that motorized divisions and armoured brigades are more mobile and easier to control than large corps formations.[102] However, these authors overlook the fact that the difficulties in controlling the armoured corps were largely due to the inadequacy of communications. And the inadequate provision of the Red Army with communications equipment, the neglect of communications generally, was in turn the direct result of interference by Stalin, who had ordered the chief of the communications directorate of the Red Army, Corps Commander Longva, his deputy, Divisional Engineer Aksenov, and a large number of other communication specialists to be arrested and shot, and who had brusquely rejected all requests to remedy the serious shortcomings in communications technique.[103]

The disbandment of the armoured corps at the very time when the Wehrmacht was so strikingly demonstrating the operational potential of large armoured formations was so much at variance with actual requirements that the measure was far from unanimously welcomed even in the Soviet Union. However, anyone venturing to suggest that there were lessons to be learnt by the Soviet forces had to expect persecution and reprisals. As for the German successes in Poland, the official Soviet line continued to be that the rapid

[101] Kozlov *et al.*, *O sovetskoj voennoj nauke*, 191; Isserson, 'Razvitie teorii', 54–5; *Voprosy strategii*, 22; Malan'in, 'Razvitie organizacionnych form', 29; *50 let vooružennych sil*, 236; Zhukov, *Reminiscences*, 220–1.

[102] Krupčenko, 'Razvitie tankovych vojsk', 43; *Sovetskie tankovye vojska*, 13.

[103] Gapič, 'Nekotorye mysli', 49–50.

collapse of that state and its army was due exclusively to the 'rottenness of the regime' and to the 'disruption of the hinterland by the Fascist fifth column'— not to the superiority of the German forces or the employment of large armoured formations. Divisional Commander Isserson, professor of operational skills at the general-staff academy, who had nevertheless published a piece correctly describing the fighting in Poland as the new form of in-depth operation, was instantly arrested. It was traditional among Soviet authors to try to conceal, or fudge, or—like Marshal of the Soviet Union Zakharov[104]— even deny the fact that it was German successes which induced the Soviet military leadership to reconsider the appropriate organization of armoured troops and the principles of their employment. However, the majority of military historians acknowledge that it was the employment of massive armoured forces by the Wehrmacht in Poland and, even more so, in France which, about the middle of 1940, provided the impetus for the re-establishemnt of mechanized cocps in the Soviet Union.[105] In fact 'the summer interval of 1940' marked 'a turning-point in questions of instruction and training of the army on a new basis, hardened by the experience of the war'.[106]

On the strength of an analysis of the German operations in the war against France, carried out by the people's commissariat for defence, Stalin gave orders on 6 July 1940 for mechanized corps to be set up, consisting of two armoured divisions and one motorized division, now with between 1,000 and 1,200 tanks at their disposal. By the end of 1940 nine mechanized corps had been formed: I Corps in the Leningrad military district, III and VI Corps in the 'Western special military district', IV, VIII, and IX Corps in the Kiev special military district, II Corps in the Odessa military district, V Corps in the Trans-Baykal military district, and VII Corps in the Moscow military district; moreover, one independent armoured division each was stationed in the Transcaucasian and in the central Asian military districts. As part of a further strengthening of the Red Army the establishment was begun in February 1941 of 21 further mechanized corps; however, this met with considerable difficulties because of a shortage of trained personnel and of tanks of modern design.[107]

The question which arises in this context is: What ideas on the course or character of a future war did the Soviet military leadership have on the eve of the German attack, and what principles of command were to be applied in the Red Army? In line with the active-service regulations revised in 1939, Soviet military theory was entirely based on the idea of offence. The Red Army was designed, in the event of war and even in repulsing an attack, to carry an

[104] Zacharov, 'O teorii glubokoj operacii', 19–20.

[105] *Boevoj put' vooruzennych sil*, 243; Malan'in, 'Razvitie organizacionnych form', 29; Ryžakov, 'K voprosu o stroitel'stve', 110.

[106] Befehl des Volkskommissars [Order of the People's Commissar] No. 30 21 Jan. 1941, BA-MA, RH 19 I/123, fo. 92.

[107] *Sovetskie tankovye vojska*, 14–15; Anfilov, *Načalo*, 29.

immediate large-scale offensive into the enemy's territory, totally annihilate him there, and achieve victory with only slight casualties on its own side.[108] In this connection Frunze had first held the view that a future war would trigger off an intensified class struggle within the country of the Soviet Union's adversary. Tukhachevsky and others even regarded the proletariat in the enemy's country as a potential ally of the Red Army, and he therefore denied the need for withholding one's own strategic reserves.[109] As the offensive was to be mounted with the entire might of the Soviet forces, these forces, as will be shown in detail, were mostly concentrated near the state frontiers. Soviet military theory, moreover, proceeded from the assumption that 'wars nowadays are no longer declared',[110] as every attacker was naturally anxious to enjoy the advantage of surprise. 'Surprise has a paralysing effect,' it was stated in the service regulations, 'that is why all combat operations must be carried out with maximum concealment and maximum speed . . . The troops of the Red Army must be prepared at any moment to reply with a lightning-like blow to any surprise by the enemy.' The idea that the 'Red Army will be the most offensive army ever',[111] that in the event of hostilities it would unhesitatingly go over to the offensive against the enemy's territory, had the status of law during the period of the 'Stalin personality cult' and was not subject to theoretical discussion.

However, the course of military operations against Poland, and more particularly Finland, had revealed grave deficiencies in the command and training of the troops, which seriously called in question the offensive role of the Red Army.[112] The people's commissar for the defence of the USSR, Marshal of the Soviet Union Semen Timoshenko, whose 'purposeful determination and great seriousness' had deeply impressed General Köstring, the German military attaché, used the whole weight of his personality in order to remedy those deficiencies and improve the training of officers and men. By Order No. 120 of 16 May 1940 staffs and service branches were instructed to use the summer period to make the military training of the troops as realistic as possible.[113] In consequence, exercises during the summer and autumn of 1940 attached great importance to co-operation of infantry with artillery as well as with tanks and aircraft, live shells frequently being fired in the preparatory bombardment. Because the Red Army had encountered great difficulties during the Soviet–Finnish war in its attempt to break through the fortifications of the 'Mannerheim Line', particular attention was now being paid to the problems of penetrating the enemy's defensive front. The infantry was practising the execution of assaults with tank and air support immediately behind a rolling artillery barrage. The air force, too, began to prepare increasingly for joint

[108] Galickij, *Gody*, 14.   [109] Garthoff, *Sowjetarmee*, 202.   [110] Anfilov, *Načalo*, 32.
[111] Isserson, 'Razvitie teorii', 60.
[112] Erfahrungen aus dem finnisch-russischen Krieg [Experiences of the Finno-Russian war], OKH/GenStdH/OQu IV, Abt. Frd Heere Ost, No. 3535/40 geh. 2 Oct. 1940, BA-MA RH 19 I/122, fo. 71.
[113] *Istorija Velikoj Otečestvennoj vojny*, i. 467 ff.

operations with the ground forces and for low-level attacks against ground targets. A conference of leading officers under Timoshenko's chairmanship, held in December 1940–January 1941 to examine past experience in combat training, came to the conclusion that only the penetration of the enemy's front provided the precondition for operational manœuvring in the depth of his hinterland.[114] Although General Romanenko had pleaded for the detachment of strong operational assault forces reinforced by aircraft and artillery, on the model of the Germans in their campaign against France,[115] it was nevertheless decided to use the armoured formations only for enforcing and developing the breakthrough. Similarly, it was the prime task of the air forces, subdivided into front and army air forces, to concentrate on the enemy's defensive front. In view of the complex conditions of mechanized combat, it was considered necessary to improve the strategic and tactical understanding of senior staffs, and of the command personnel at all levels generally, as these had declined alarmingly after the purges. This end was served by the people's commissar's directive of 25 January 1941, 'On the operational training of senior leadership cadres in formation, army and front staffs', as well as by Order No. 30, issued on 21 January 1941, which called for a further intensification of realistic training and political schooling in 1941.

Of considerable importance were the 'Disciplinary penal regulations of the Red Army', introduced on 12 October 1940 by Order No. 356 of the people's commissar for defence;[116] these suspended the existing 'Preliminary disciplinary penal regulations of the Red Army' of 1925 and made 'a clean sweep of the libertarian achievements of the Revolution'. These 'exceedingly severe' new regulations, 'in the interest of the defence of the socialist state', laid down the 'most severe compulsory measures' in the event of any violation of discipline. The theoretically still valid concept of a 'criminal order' by a superior was now abolished. Any order by an officer or person of superior rank was a law unto the subordinate and had to be implemented without contradiction, accurately and punctually. In the event of disobedience or of wilful violation of discipline or good order any officer, even in peacetime, was now not only entitled but actually obliged to resort to all measures of enforcement, including the use of his weapons. As for the consequences of such actions, he was acquitted in advance. Officers failing to show the necessary hardness or resolution in such cases, or failing to take all necessary measures to enforce compliance with an order, were handed over to military tribunals. The 'Red Army's Soviet discipline' was to differ fundamentally, by the severity and strictness of its demands, from the 'class-structure discipline' of all other armies.

---

[114] Zhukov, *Reminiscences*, 219 ff.   [115] Erickson, *Stalin's War*, i. 42–3.

[116] Disziplinarstrafordnung [Disciplinary penal code] 1941, BA-MA RW 4/v. 328; note for report OKH/OQu IV/GenStdH/Abt. Frd Heere Ost [IIc] No. 3824/40 geh. 12 Nov. 1940, BA-MA RH 19 I/122.

Regardless of Timoshenko's vigorous efforts to ensure the Red Army's combat efficiency, there is no denying the fact that Soviet theory was bogged down between the ideas of mobile and positional warfare. The fundamental emphasis placed by Soviet strategic thinking on offensive operations had led, at the same time, to a neglect of defensive fighting. Strategic and tactical defence, the possibilities of retreat and of combat under conditions of encirclement, were not, of course, totally ignored but were considered admissible only in certain directions and as temporary measures.[117] On no account could defensive considerations call into question the principle that the Soviet armed forces would under all circumstances carry the war into the enemy's territory. Only behind closed doors, in certain circles of the general staff and of the general-staff academy, was the question examined of what would have to be done if the war were to take a different course and if, in the initial phase, the Red Army found itself forced on to the defensive.

If offence, therefore, in line with Soviet theory, represented the 'foundation of warfare', and if it was the task of the Red Army to seek out and destroy the enemy on his own territory, then this presupposed that the Soviet Union was in a position to supply the army with the war material necessary for that purpose. The objective of providing it with its material basis was served by the third five-year plan, which started in 1938 and built upon its predecessors, envisaging a massive strengthening of the Soviet Union's economic and military might. During the preceding years a large number of enterprises of the processing industry had already been set up on the basis of the coal and iron and steel industries in the south of the country, on the Dnieper, Donets, and Don, as well as in the Volga basin, in the regions of Moscow and Gorky (Nizhny Novgorod), and elsewhere. For reasons of dispersal new production facilities of the heavy and chemical industry were now being increasingly set up also in the eastern parts of the country, in the Urals, central Asia, eastern Siberia, and even the Far East, on the basis of the rich raw-material and energy resources located there.[118] The creation of a second industrial base in the eastern parts of the country was of considerable strategic importance, as these plants would be virtually beyond the reach of a potential enemy. In 1940 the coalmines of Kuznetsk, Karaganda, the Pechora region, near Irkutsk, Chita, and Sangar already accounted for 35 per cent of the total Soviet output of coal and for 25 per cent of coke production. During the same year the iron and steel plants established in the eastern parts of the Soviet Union—at Magnitogorsk, Kuznetsk, Novotagil, Chelyabinsk, and Novosibirsk—were supplying 28 per cent of the total output of iron ore, 28 per cent of pig-iron, 37 per cent of steel, and 36 per cent of rolling-mill products. Some 25 per cent of the country's total energy was generated in the east, as was 12 per cent of crude oil. The importance which this second industrial base had attained by 1940 can further

[117] *Istorija Velikoj Otečestvennoj vojny*, i. 519.   [118] Kravčenko, *Voennaja èkonomika*, 50 ff.

be gauged from the fact that over 50 per cent of the 31,649 tractors manufactured in the Soviet Union and 14 per cent of its 58,437 machine-tools were produced there.

Altogether, 1,500 major enterprises were commissioned in the Soviet Union during the first five-year plan, 4,500 during the second, and 3,000 during the first three years of the third five-year plan; all of these could be fully switched over to armament production whenever the need arose.[119] Vast sources of energy were available. Coal production alone rose from 128m. t. in 1937 to 166m. t. in 1940. During that year also the Soviet Union produced 14.9m. t. of pig-iron, 18.3m. t. of steel, 13.1m. t. of rolling-mill products, 31.1m. t. of crude oil, 914 railway engines, 32,000 rail waggons, and 58,437 machine tools. The grain harvest totalled 38m. t. Crude oil and grain excepted, these production totals were lower than those current in Germany, but their rate of growth was disproportionately greater; the objective was to approximately double the total volume of industrial production during the third five-year plan. Simultaneously, large quantities of raw materials and foodstuffs were being stockpiled, predominantly so as to keep the Red Army supplied during the first few months of war.[120] The degree to which the USSR's planned economy was purely a rearmament economy is revealed by the high proportion of openly recorded military expenditure in the country's overall expenditure. Expenditure on the armed forces and on the provision of all kinds of military material rose dramatically during the last few years before the war. In 1938 it amounted to 27,000m. roubles, in 1939 to 34,500m. roubles, in 1940 to 56,900m. roubles, and in the first half of 1941 to as much as 83,000m. roubles, or 43 per cent of all state expenditure. This increase in the military budget of the Soviet Union was accompanied by a corresponding growth of the armament industry in the narrower sense.

Even during the first five-year plan the foundations had been laid for the production of modern technological weapons and war equipment, aircraft, all categories of artillery and new types of ammunition, automatic infantry weapons, etc. in specialized enterprises. The Soviet armament industry developed its capacity at great speed. Thus tank production rose from 740 in 1930 to 3,139 in 1937. Altogether 5,000 tanks were manufactured during the first five-year plan, and by the end of the second five-year plan, in 1937, the Red Army possessed no fewer than 15,000 armoured fighting vehicles, 12,000 of which were modern models.[121] Another 2,270 were produced in 1938, and a further 7,000 between 1 January 1939 and 22 June 1941.[122] Stalin told Harry Hopkins, the adviser to the American president, that the Red Army had 24,000 armoured fighting vehicles at the beginning of the German–Soviet war, a figure confirmed by production statistics.[123] Of these 24,000, 1,861 were medium or heavy tanks of the new T-34 and KV (Klim Voroshilov) models,

[119] Tel′puchovskij, 'Dejatel′nost KPSS', 62.   [120] *Istorija Velikoj Otečestvennoj vojny*, i. 412.
[121] *50 let vooružennych sil*, 202.   [122] *Befreiungsmission*, 28.
[123] Werth, *Russia at War*, 282.

TABLE I.III. *Specifications of German and Soviet Tanks*

Model	Weight (t.)	Year	Cannon (mm.)	Machine-guns (No.)	Armour (mm.)	Horsepower	Speed (km./h.)	Range (km./road)	Crew
German tanks									
P I (B)	6.0	1935	—	2	6–13	100	40	140	2
P II (D–E)	10.0	1937	20.0	1	5–30	140	55	200	3
P 38 (t)	9.7	1938	37.0	2	15–25	125	42	200	4
P III (E)	19.5	1939	37.0–50.0	1	10–30	300	40	175	5
P IV (D)	20.0	1939	75.0	2	10–30	300	40	200	5
Soviet tanks									
T 26	9.5	1935	45.0	1–2	15–25	91	30	200	3
BT 7	13.8	1936	45.0	2–3	13–20	500	73	350–500	3
T 28	31.0	1940	76.2	4	20–80	600	37	220	6
T 35	50.0	1936	1 × 76.2 2 × 45.0	5–6	20–30	500	30	150	11
T 34	26.5	1940	76.2	2–3	45–52	500	55	300	4
KV	47.5	1940	76.2	3–4	40–100	600	35	250	5

Sources: Kravčenko, *Voennaja ėkonomika*, 64–5; Senger und Etterlin, *Die deutschen Panzer*; Polubojarov, *Krepče broni*, 112 ff.; *Sovetskie tankovye vojska*, 8; *Oružie pobedy*, 67 ff.; *Deutschland im zweiten Weltkrieg*, ii. 48 ff.

which surpassed all German types in weight, armour, weaponry, and engine performance.[124] The way in which industry had been switched to the production of these new models is revealed by the fact that 358 T-34 and KV tanks were produced in 1940, whereas 1,503 had already been built in the first six months of 1941. Although at the beginning of the war the armoured formations were still predominantly equipped with the 'older' T-26, BT-7, T-28, and T-35 models, it should be borne in mind that even they were superior in their combat qualities to the German Panzer-I and Panzer-II types, and in some respects superior, or at least equal, even to the Panzer-III and Panzer-IV.[125] An outstanding authority, Marshal of Armoured Forces Poluboyarov, wrote after the war that the Soviet armoured forces 'at the beginning of the Great Fatherland War were superior in technical equipment, organizational aspects, methods of employment, and also numerically, to any other foreign power'.[126]

Production of guns, like production of armour, had grown rapidly since 1930. Whereas in 1930 the number of guns of all calibres produced was 1,911, by 1937 the number was 5,020. In 1938 gun production rose to more than 12,500 pieces. By the end of that year the Red Army possessed some 56,000 guns. During the period from 1 January 1939 to 22 June 1941 Soviet industry produced a further 92,578 guns and mortars,[127] so that at the beginning of the German–Soviet war the Red Army had approximately 148,600 guns and mortars at its disposal. Several models, according to Soviet assessment, had outstanding combat characteristics, such as the 7.6-cm. Model-1939 divisional artillery piece, the 12.2-cm. Model-1938 howitzer, and the 15.2-cm. Model-1937 howitzer gun. In addition there were 8.5-cm. anti-aircraft guns, 21-cm. guns, 28-cm. mortars, and 30.5-cm. howitzers, as well as 8.2-cm. battalion and 12-cm. regimental mortars.[128] Production of the 4.5-cm. anti-tank gun, which possessed outstanding combat characteristics and was said to have pierced the armour of all German tanks, had been halted before the war at Stalin's behest. The Red Army's artillery is altogether presented in Soviet accounts as superior to that of any potential enemy in virtually every respect.[129]

Great efforts were also made to increase production of small arms and automatic infantry weapons. In 1930 some 174,000 rifles and 41,000 machine-guns were manufactured; in 1938 the figures were 1,174,000 rifles and 74,500 machine-guns. Between 1 January 1939 and 22 June 1941 some 105,000 light, heavy, and super-heavy machine-guns were produced, as well as 100,000 submachine-guns.[130] The Red Army was equipped with the Model-1891/1930 infantry rifle, the Model-1938 carbine, and, for automatic weapons, the Simonev Model-1936 and the Tokarev Model-1940 self-loading rifles, the

[124] *Oružie pobedy*, 86 ff.; Jurasov, 'Iz istorii', 110 ff.
[125] Vannikov, 'Iz zapisok Narkoma', 81; Nekrič and Grigorenko, *Genickschuß*, 241.
[126] Polubojarov, 'Krepče broni', 111.   [127] Zhukov, *Reminiscences*, 167, 236.
[128] *Oružie pobedy*, 35 ff.   [129] Kravčenko, *Voennaja èkonomika*, 72.
[130] *50 let vooružennych sil*, 225.

Degtyarev and Shpagin submachine-guns, the Degtyarev light machine-gun, the Maxim and Degtyarev heavy machine-guns, as well as the tank, anti-aircraft, and aircraft machine-guns developed from them.[131] All small arms and automatic infantry weapons, if one accepts the judgement of Soviet sources, were likewise superior to those of foreign armies, or at least in no way inferior.[132]

The aircraft industry underwent a similar rapid development during the period of the three five-year plans. Production of military aircraft was stepped up from 860 machines in 1930 to 3,578 in 1937. In 1938 factories already produced 5,500 aircraft,[133] and between 1 January 1939 and 22 June 1941 the figure was no less than 17,745 military aircraft of all types.[134] Most of the aircraft produced, however, were older models which were inferior to comparable German machines. Nevertheless, even older types, such as the well-known I-16 fighter ('Rata') showed a remarkable performance even according to German assessments, and certainly proved a hazard to German bombers through their manœuvrability. By 1940, however, serial production had also begun of modern fighters, ground-attack aircraft, and long-range bombers; by the beginning of the war 3,719 of these had been manufactured, 2,650 in the first half of 1941 alone. Production was growing by leaps and bounds. It was intended that 3,950 military aircraft of all types should be produced in the first half of 1941, and as many as 9,800 in the second half.[135] As for the new models, these were said by Soviet sources to have been not only not inferior to German models but indeed superior in combat and flight characteristics.[136] Thus the maximum speed of the German Me-109 in 1941 was 510 km.p.h., while that of the Soviet Yak-1 was 572 km.p.h., that of the MiG-3 was 640 km.p.h., and that of the LaGG-3 was 549 km.p.h. The Soviet Pe-2 dive-bomber was said to have been 173 km.p.h. faster than the German Ju-87 dive-bomber (the 'Stuka'), and 171 km.p.h. faster than the German He-111 bomber while carrying half of the latter's bomb load. The Soviet IL-2 ground-attack aircraft was also reported to have had outstanding characteristics. 'The IL-2 aircraft', it was said even in 'Nachrichten über die russische Luftwaffe', published by the German Luftwaffe, 'is an excellent machine, sufficiently fast and highly manœuvrable, so that this aircraft is vulnerable only to fire from directly ahead.'[137]

Naturally enough, the Soviet navy did not command the same importance as the Soviet ground and air forces; nevertheless, the national rearmament effort was clearly perceptible also in that service. During the first two five-year plans more than 500 warships were launched. The third five-year plan envisaged the creation of a 'great sea- and ocean-going fleet, worthy of the country

---

[131] *Oruzie pobedy*, 133 ff.   [132] Kravčenko, *Voennaja ekonomika*, 74.

[133] Zhukov, *Reminiscences*, 168.   [134] Fedorov, *Aviacija*, 12.

[135] Šachurin, 'Aviacionnaja promyšlennost'', 80.

[136] Fedorov, *Aviacija*, 13 ff.; *Oruzie pobedy*, 7 ff.; for more precise information see Tables 1.IV.4 and 1.IV.7 below).

[137] Orientierungsheft U.D.S.S.R., Oberbefehlshaber der Luftwaffe, Führungsstab Ic/IV No. 3500/41 geh., BA-MA Lw 135.

of socialism',[138] after 1939 with the proviso that the construction of large naval units, whose technical requirements and operational advantage were disproportionate to their vulnerability, especially from aerial attack, should gradually be cut back and eventually halted altogether. Between 1 January 1939 and 22 June 1941 the total tonnage of the Red Fleet increased by 108,718 for surface craft and 50,385 for submarines.[139] During eleven months of 1940 a total of 100 torpedo-boats, submarines, minesweepers, and motor torpedo-boats were launched and another 269 warships were under construction.[140] On the eve of war against Germany the naval forces of the Soviet Union consisted of approximately 600 warships of all types, including 3 battleships, 7 cruisers, 49 destroyers, 211 submarines, and 279 torpedo-boats. To these should be added 2,500 naval air-force planes and 1,000 coastal artillery guns of all calibres.[141]

This conspicuous growth of Soviet armament production from the beginning of the Second World War was accompanied by an improvement in the strategic position of the country. As a result of its attacks against Poland and Finland, and its annexation of the Baltic States and the Romanian territories of Bessarabia, northern Bukowina, and northern Moldavia, the Soviet frontiers had been shifted to the west by several hundred kilometres and at the same time considerably shortened, so that a far greater troop density was attainable with the same number of personnel. The manpower and material resources of the annexed territories were immediately put to the service of Soviet war preparations. Thus the former armies of Estonia, Latvia, and Lithuania were subjected to a purge and, at the end of August 1940, reorganized into territorial rifle corps of the Red Army. Each of the three rifle corps consisted of two divisions and corps troops (artillery regiment, signals battalion, sapper battalion, and anti-aircraft battery). The Estonian army became the XXII, the Latvian the XXIV, and the Lithuanian the XXIX Territorial Rifle Corps. On 23 February 1941, the 'day of the Red Army', the personnel of the newly acquired troops took their oath.[142]

Alongside these rearmament efforts and the improvement in the strategic position, efforts were proceeding to utilize the country's defensive potential in terms of manpower as well. That objective was served by the introduction of general conscription on 1 September 1939, the day the Second World War broke out; this broke with the principle in force until then that only proletarians, workers, and peasants could be called upon to serve under arms. Thenceforth every Soviet citizen, regardless of nationality or class, was obliged to do military service. The age limit was lowered from 21 to 19, and in special cases even to 18 years, while the compulsory term of service in the ground and

[138] Telpuchowski, *Geschichte des Großen Vaterländischen Krieges*, 29.
[139] Zacharov, 'Kommunističeskaja partija', 11.
[140] *Istorija Velikoj Otečestvennoj vojny*, i. 455.
[141] Zhukov, *Reminiscences*, 244; on this see Piterskij, *Sowjet-Flotte*, 474 ff.
[142] *Bor'ba za sovetskuju Pribaltiku*, i. 38.

air forces was simultaneously raised to three years, and in the navy to five. Every Soviet citizen had to serve in the reserve up to the age of 50. As a result of the new armed-services law of 1 September 1939 the strength of the Soviet armed forces was increased by a factor of 2.8 by 21 June 1941. The extent of the militarization of life in the Soviet Union was also reflected in the activity of Osoaviakhim (Society for the promotion of aviation and chemical defence), a military-training institution which in 1940 alone trained two million snipers, machine-gunners, telephonists, radio operators, horsemen, drivers, pilots, parachutists, and other military specialists. On 1 January 1941 the society had 13 million members, organized in 3,500 sections, 26,868 command units, and 156,000 groups. The success of the Soviet mobilization efforts was reflected in the growth of the armed forces; from 1,513,000 men in 1937 they increased to 4,207,000 at the beginning of 1941 and, following the call-up of 800,000 reservists in May 1941, they grew to 5,000,000.[143] A large number of rifle, armoured, air, and mechnized divisions were formed, as well as artillery and anti-tank units of the high command reserve. The strength of the air-defence and air-landing troops was increased, care was taken to furnish the new formations with weapons and equipment, and training facilities, especially for officers, were improved.

On 22 June 1941 the territory of the Soviet Union along the European coastline was protected by the naval forces of the Northern Fleet under Rear-Admiral Golovko,[144] the Red-banner-decorated Baltic Fleet under Vice-Admiral Tributs,[145] the Black Sea Fleet under Vice-Admiral Oktyabrsky,[146] as well as by the Pinsk war flotilla under Rear-Admiral Rogachev and the Danube war flotilla under Rear-Admiral Abramov.[147] Posted along the land front in the west were the troops of the Leningrad military district under General Popov (Fourteenth, Seventh, and Twenty-third Armies, I and X Mechanized Corps, and eight air divisions), the troops of the Baltic special military district under General Kuznetsov (Eighth, Eleventh, and Twenty-seventh Armies, XII and III Mechanized Corps, and five air divisions), the troops of the Western special military district under General Pavlov (Third, Tenth, Fourth, and Thirteenth Armies, VI, XI, XIII, XIV, XVII, and XX Mechanized Corps, and six air divisions), the troops of the Kiev special military district under General Kirponos (Fifth, Sixth, Twenty-sixth, and Twelfth Armies, XXII, IV, XV, VIII, XVI, IX, XXIV, and XIX Mechanized Corps, and ten air divisions), and the troops of the Odessa military district under General Cherevichenko (Ninth Army, II and XVIII Mechanized Corps, and three air divisions).[148] Of these formations the second echelon in the Leningrad military district was I Mechanized Corps, in the Baltic special military district the Twenty-seventh

---

[143] Grečko, '25 let', 7.
[144] Kozlov and Šlonim, *Severnyj flot*, 96 ff. [145] *Boevoj put' voenno-morskogo flota*, 287 ff.
[146] Bolgari *et al.*, *Černomorskij flot*, 141 ff. [147] *Boevoj put' voenno-morskogo flota*, 432 ff.
[148] *Geschichte des zweiten Weltkrieges*, iv, map 36; conflicting with this *50 let vooružennych sil*, 251–2.

Army, in the Western special military district the Thirteenth Army together with XVII and XX Mechanized Corps, and in the Kiev special military district IX, XXIV, and XIX Mechanized Corps. The immediate surveillance of the Soviet frontier was the duty of the Frontier Guards of the NKVD under Lieutenant-General Sokolov, with a total strength of 100,000 men, composed of 47 land-frontier and six sea-frontier detachments, nine independent frontier commands, and 11 regiments of strategic NKVD troops.[149] A few weeks before the beginning of the war the general concentration of troops on the western frontier was significantly increased. In strictest secrecy[150] a number of major formations were moved forward after April 1941 from the interior of the country to the western military districts: the Twenty-second Army from the Urals military district into the area of Velikie Luki, the Twenty-first Army from the Volga military district into the Gomel area, the Nineteenth Army from the North Caucasian military district into the area of Belaya Tserkov, the Sixteenth Army from the Trans-Baykal military district into the Shepetovka area, and the XXV Rifle Corps from the Kharkov military district to the western Dvina. Altogether four army HQs, 19 corps HQs, and 28 divisional HQs had received relocation orders from the interior of the country to the western state frontier.[151]

The deployment of the Red Army forces in the extreme west of the country was as follows, according to Soviet sources. Concentrated in the Baltic special military district were 19 rifle divisions, 4 armoured divisions, 2 mechanized divisions, a total of 25 divisions as well as a rifle brigade, including the three territorial rifle corps formed from the armies of the Baltic States. Stationed in the Western special military district were 24 rifle divisions, 12 armoured divisions, 6 mechanized divisions, and 2 cavalry divisions, altogether 44 divisions. The total in the Kiev special military district amounted to 58 divisions: 32 rifle divisions, 16 armoured divisions, 8 mechanized divisions, and 2 cavalry divisions. Facing Romania in the Odessa military district were 13 rifle divisions, 4 armoured divisions, 2 mechanized divisions, and 3 cavalry divisions, altogether 22 divisions. Under the new mobilization plan, 'MP-1941', all the troops in the western frontier military districts were to be brought up to full mobilization readiness in the course of the spring of 1941. The date laid down by order No. 008130 of 26 March, issued by the war council of the Western special military district for all units and institutions of that military district, was 15 June 1941.[152] A similar order is on record for the Baltic special military district. The war councils of the Eighth and Eleventh Armies, the commanding officers of corps, divisions, and brigades, as well as the commanders of independent detachments were instructed by order No. OM/00159 of 31 May/

[149] Grenzschutztruppen, OKH/GenStdH/OQu IV, Abt. Frd Heere Ost, No. 1662/41 geh., 2 May 1941, BA-MA RH 19 I/123, fos. 209–10; *Pograničnye vojska*, 27 ff.
[150] Štemenko, *General'nyj štab*, i. 26.
[151] Moskalenko, *Na Jugo-Zapadnom napravlenii*, 9 ff.
[152] Kriegsrat des Westlichen Besonderen Militärbezirks (War Council of the Western Special Military District), BA-MA RW 4/v. 329.

2 June 1941, issued by the staff of the Baltic special military district, to submit by 20 June 1941, reports on their mobilization readiness in accordance with MP-1941.[153] Mobilization readiness did not yet imply mobilization; the army commander-in-chief, General Korobkov, had let it be clearly understood that mobilization would automatically entail the opening of hostilities.[154] However, mobilization of all units was to be prepared down to 'the smallest detail' in accordance with the dates laid down in the deployment directives.

From the spring of 1941 onward the Soviet formations had been moving closer to the frontier. The then chief of the operations department of the Kiev special military district and future Marshal of the Soviet Union, Bagramyan, records a directive of the people's commissar for defence from the beginning of May, according to which five rifle corps and four mechanized corps were to be moved into a strip 30–5 km. from the state frontier.[155] In the Kiev special military district the deployment plan envisaged a depth of defence of 50 km.; in the Western special defence district, in the area of the Fourth Army, the depth of defence was 60–80 km.[156] However, the moving up of the formations had evidently not been completed by the beginning of hostilities. Comparison of published data shows that of the 170 divisions stationed in the western frontier zone, 48 divisions were positioned 10–50 km., 64 divisions 50–150 km., and 56 divisions 150–500 km. east of the Soviet frontier. Striking, at any rate, was the concentration of Soviet formations in the eastern Polish areas incorporated in the Western and Kiev special military districts. This is true particularly of the salient around Biaystok and Lvov, which projected far into German territory.[157] The bulk of the troops of the Western special military district was concentrated at Białystok; even mobile formations such as armoured, mechanized, and cavalry divisions were in an exposed position. Thus three of the four armies of the Western special military district and three of its six mechanized corps—each of a minimum establishment strength of 1,030 tanks—stood in a semicircle around Byaystok; a further mechanized corps was at the starting-point of the salient between Brest and Kobryn. The commander of this military district and, in the event of war, the commander-in-chief of the western front was in fact the expert on the 'employment of mechanized formations in modern offensive operations', Army General Popov, who, with some exaggeration, has been called the 'Soviet Guderian'.[158] Much the same could be observed in the Lvov salient, where three of the four armies and four of the eight mechanized corps of the Kiev special military district were concentrated. The Fifth Army and a further mechanized corps near Lutsk were likewise standing in forward echelon. Not only were the ground forces, including motorized and mobile formations, being moved up close to the new Soviet

[153] Štab Pribaltijskogo Osobogo Voennogo okruga, orgmobotdel, 2 otdelenie [Staff of the Baltic special military district] 31 May–2 June 1941, ibid.
[154] Erickson, *Stalin's War*, i. 91.   [155] Bagramjan, *Tak načinalas' vojna*, 62.
[156] Sandalov, 'Oboronitel'naja operacija', 21.
[157] Fabry, *Hitler-Stalin-Pakt*, 421–2; Helmdach, *Überfall?*, 55–6.
[158] Zhukov, *Reminiscences*, 220; Erickson, *Stalin's War*, i. 8, 26.

frontier, but so were the air forces. Since the spring of 1941 efforts had therefore been in progress to set up a dense network of operational airfields in the
proximity of the western frontier of the Soviet Union.[159] This project had not
been completed by the beginning of hostilities, with the result that aircraft
were crowding together on those airfields which had been completed, offering
an easy target to the German air force.[160] Not only had the ground and air
forces been moved up close to the new state frontier, but also—in a manner
now described as mistaken—supply-depots, fuel stores, and mobilization supplies; these were nearly all lost at the beginning of the war.[161] Roads, tracks,
bridges, troop accommodation, and so on were massively extended, yet no
attempt was made to establish rearward communication links or to set up the
command centres indispensable for a defensive war.[162] In a similar vein was the
suspension of all work on the strengthening of fortifications along the old state
frontier and the partial disarming of the installations; yet the large-scale fortification work planned along the new state frontier in Lithuania and in the
annexed Polish and Romanian areas was making only slow progress.[163] In the
opinion of Soviet experts the defensive lines and permanent fortifications
(*ukreprayony*) established since 1929 at great expense from the Gulf of Bothnia
to the Black Sea, at Kingisepp, Pskov, Polotsk, Minsk, Mozyrsk, Korosten,
Novograd-Volynsk, Kiev, Letichevsk, Starokonstantinov, Mogilev, Kamenets-
Podolsk, Tiraspol, and elsewhere could have been of great importance and
could have represented a serious obstacle to the advancing enemy armies. 'All
measures', the then chief of the intelligence directorate of the people's commissariat for defence, Major-General Gapich, wrote with the knowledge of an
expert in his field, 'were directed at creating bridgeheads and making preparations for delivering a blow to the enemy and carrying the war into enemy
territory.' Measures and omissions equally suggest that the possible need for
defensive fighting in the depth of one's own country was not even considered.
Was this the result of Soviet strategic thinking, which, even in the repulse of an
enemy attack, allowed only for the option that the Red Army forces would in
a counterstrike immediately burst into enemy territory and there destroy the
adversary,[164] or could these measures be interpreted also as the start of Soviet
offensive planning? In view of the confidentiality of Soviet sources, this
question cannot be answered with complete certainty. To begin with, one
would have to bear in mind the conspicuous concentration of powerful and
motorized forces in the frontier salients of Białystok and Lvov,[165] which are not
readily compatible with defensive intentions. Certainly such a 'strategic configuration' was bound—as even the then chief of the Red Army General Staff,
Marshal Zhukov, admits—in the event of an enemy attack to invite the danger

[159] Anfilov, *Načalo*, 40; Zhukov, *Reminiscences*, 227 ff., 243.   [160] Fedorov, *Aviacija*, 24.
[161] Grečko, '25 let', 9; Zhukov, *Reminiscences*, 241–2.
[162] Gapič, 'Nekotorye mysli', 48; Krikunov, 'Frontoviki otvetili', 68–9.
[163] Čeremuchin, 'Ob odnoj fal'šivoj versii', 121.   [164] Erickson, *Stalin's War*, i. 80–1.
[165] Hillgruber, *Strategie*, 436.

of in-depth outflanking, encirclement, and annihilation of those troops.[166] As Major-General Grigorenko also states, it would have been justified in only one situation, 'that is, if these troops were designed suddenly to go over to the offensive. Otherwise they were instantly half-encircled. All the enemy had to do was perform two thrusts towards each other at the basis of our wedge and the encirclement was complete.'[167]

If even in Zhukov's judgement the disposition of the troops in the exposed frontier sectors of the western and south-western front was 'mistaken' for defence, then this can only mean that there was a different motive behind it. This conclusion is too inescapable to be simply dismissed by the suggestion that the Soviet deployment was no more than a mistaken decision 'dating from 1940 and not corrected by the time the war began'. Such a formulation actually reveals that the Soviet Union's military preparations cannot be interpreted as a reaction to the German deployment, which in 1940 had not even begun,[168] but as a reflection of its own ambitions. Seen thus they are in line with certain indications that the Soviet Union, in connection with its plans in the Balkans between the German campaign in the west and the Balkan campaign, may, 'perhaps in the winter of 1940–1', have briefly considered entering the war. Milan Gavrilović, the Yugoslav minister in Moscow, reported remarks by Andrey Vyshinsky, the deputy people's commissar for foreign affairs, on 8 and 13 February 1941, 'that the Soviet Union would enter the war against Germany as soon as the British opened a Balkan front. Soviet forces would move directly against Bulgaria and the Straits.'[169]

Also fitting into this pattern of offensive intentions is a document captured by the Germans in the Fifth Army staff building in Lutsk: a 'Plan for the political safeguarding of army operations during the attack', which likewise dates from the period preceding the German campaign in the Balkans.[170] In it the chief of Fifth Army political propaganda, Uronov, who was no doubt informed of the political line by his main directorate in Moscow, argued that it was necessary 'to deal the enemy a very powerful lightning-like blow in order to shake the troops' moral resistance, which had been artificially buoyed up by their successful lightning-like operations in the various theatres of war (Poland, Norway, Denmark, Holland, Belgium, France)'. The 'first stage' of the impending operation, according to this plan, was the 'assembly of the army, its move to its jumping-off position, and its preparation for crossing the Bug'. Combat operations, it was thought, would take place on the enemy's

---

[166] Zhukov, *Reminiscences*, 279.

[167] Nekrič and Grigorenko, *Genickschuß*, 272; Fabry, *Hitler-Stalin-Pakt*, 425.

[168] Fabry, *Hitler-Stalin-Pakt*, 397 ff.

[169] Hillgruber, *Strategie*, 436–7, quotation according to n. 54.

[170] Übersetzung zweier Schriftstücke der 5. Roten Armee [Translation of two documents of Soviet Fifth Army], OKW/Amt Aus1./Abw. Abt. III No. 12850.8.41 g., 19 Sept. 1941; Plan für die politische Sicherung der Armee-Operationen beim Angriff [Plan for the political safeguarding of army operations during attack], Ast Krakau 7755/41 geh. 15 Aug. 1941, BA-MA RW 4/v. 329.

territory under conditions favouring the Red Army, firstly because of the support to be expected from the Ukrainian and Jewish population, as well as from a major part of the Polish population, who would 'sooner be Bolsheviks than Germans', and secondly because of a progressive collapse of morale among the Wehrmacht. 'That is why hard work is necessary', a report on service morale by the Fifth Army chief of political propaganda, dated from Rovno on 4 May 1941, stated,[171] 'to ensure a further decline of the enemy's morale and thus the completion of the enemy's annihilation on that basis.' Comprehensive preparations were made for propaganda, in the event of a Red Army attack, among the civilian population of the occupied areas of the Government-General, as well as among the enemy forces.

The belief that with its military preparations the Soviet Union had 'an offensive of its own in view', in other words, that it wished to create the prerequisites of possible intervention,[172] was held also by the 'most prominent of Soviet prisoners of war', Lieutenant-General Vlasov,[173] who at the beginning of the war had commanded the IV Mechanized Corps in the foremost line at Lvov and who must have been reasonably well informed on the intentions of the Soviet command. No one in the Soviet Union, Vlasov stated, had believed in the possibility of a German attack, which was also the reason why defensive measures had been so badly behind schedule. On 7 August 1942 the then commander-in-chief of the Second Assault Army, deputy commander-in-chief of the Volkhov front, and future chairman of the Committee for the Liberation of the Peoples of Russia and commander-in-chief of the Russian Liberation Army, told his interrogator, Embassy Councillor Gustav Hilger, that offensive intentions by Stalin had 'undoubtedly existed' in 1941. 'The troop concentrations in the Lvov district suggested that a strike against Romania, towards the oilfields, was planned. The formations assembled in the Minsk area were intended to contain the inevitable German counter-thrust.' On the same occasion the captured commander of the 41st Rifle Division and future deputy chief of staff of the Russian Liberation Army, Colonel (later Major-General) Boyarsky, likewise observed that 'the Kremlin . . . would have

[171] Stimmung der Bevölkerung im Generalgouvernement [Public mood in the Government-General], Leiter der politischen Propaganda der 5. Armee [Fifth Army propaganda chief] Uronov, 4 May 1941, BA-MA RW 4/v. 329; also Propaganda der Roten Armee gegen Deutschland [Red Army propaganda against Germany], OKH/GenStdH/OQu IV, Frd Heere Ost [Chef], No. 476/40 g.Kdos. 16 Sept. 1940, BA-MA, 18. Armee 17562/9.

[172] Fabry, *Hitler-Stalin-Pakt*, 424.

[173] Minute by Hilger, 8 Aug. 1942 *KTB OKW* ii/2. 1287; Hillgruber, *Strategie*, 437 n. 55. Statements by prisoners of war must of course always be treated with some caution. However, Vlasov invariably expressed his views, even in the presence of the Germans, without reserve or embellishment. Bojarski, for his part, repeatedly faced up to the Germans with quite ruthless frankness. The statements by both officers probably reflected their true conviction. Reference should also be made to the fundamental assessment of PoW statements in Soviet historiography: 'Statements by captured soldiers, officers, and generals, as well as deserters, are of major importance as primary sources' 'Kusnezowa and Selesnjow, "Der politisch-moralische Zustand der faschistischen deutschen Truppen", 600'.

struck no later than in the spring of 1942. The Red Army would then have moved in a "south-westerly direction", i.e. against Romania.'[174]

Against the background of such evidence it is necessary to state once more that, if in 1940–1 the Soviet leadership did for a while have offensive intentions, it certainly abandoned these again, while at the same time, as the troop dispositions along the western frontier unambiguously reveal, keeping its options open 'for all eventualities'.[175] The unfinished state of military preparations in 1941 was alone compelling reason for Stalin to dismiss for the time being any idea of warlike adventures. Soviet historiography, trying from the outset to discredit any such suggestions, firmly points to the fact that on 22 June 1941 the Red Army forces were not ready for war.[176] In support of that point of view a number of entirely plausible arguments are put forward. It is emphasized, for instance, that not only the air formations but in particular the armoured formations, which in the event of an attack would deliver the main thrust, were in the process of transformation and retraining. In February 1941, it is argued, the mistake had been made of trying to establish all the 21 mechanized corps of the second wave at the same time, without the necessary technological weapons being available for them.[177] The armament industry, for instance, had only been able to deliver 5,500 new tanks instead of the 16,000 required. Tractors, motor-vehicles, repair equipment, and other material had likewise not been available on the necessary scale, with the result that the mechanized corps stationed near the frontier had only 50 to 80 per cent of their authorized strength of combat vehicles.[178] Despite intensified efforts by the military academy for mechanization and motorization, as well as by other training institutions, it had not been possible to equip the armoured formations with command and technical personnel on the scale that was desired. In addition to the armoured formations, the rifle formations had been below establishment in personnel. Of the 170 divisions and 2 brigades in the western military districts, 144 divisions had had a numerical strength of 8,000 men, 19 of them between 600 and 5,000, and the 7 cavalry divisions an average of 6,000.[179] How, on the other hand, the order of magnitude calculated from these data, i.e. a maximum of 1,289,000 troops, can be reconciled with the total of 2,900,000 men admitted elsewhere[180] (2,680,000 Red Army and 220,000 Red Fleet) must necessarily remain an open question. Further evidence of the absence of aggressive intentions by the Red Army is said to be provided by the system of decentralized camp exercises then in

[174] See Hitler's remark on 27 July 1942: Picker, *Hitlers Tischgespräche*, 114; Fabry, *Hitler-Stalin-Pakt*, 422, 425–6.

[175] Thus als4o Fabry, *Hitler-Stalin-Pakt*, 424 ff.

[176] *Istorija Velikoj Otečestvennoj vojny*, ii. 14–15; Chor'kov, 'Meroprijatija', 90.

[177] *50 let vooružennych sil*, 236.

[178] Telpuchowski, *Geschichte des Großen* Vaterländischen Krieges, 43; *Sovetskie tankovye vojska*, 14–15.

[179] *50 let vooružennych sil*, 235.   [180] Ibid. 252.

use.[181] During summer exercises the separate service branches had been assembled in special camps often at considerable distance from one another.
Thus the artillery regiments of the divisions and the corps artillery had gone to
special firing ranges, while the infantry regiments conducted their own combat
exercises and the sapper units were busy constructing field fortifications. The
deficient road and rail network in Lithuania and in the annexed Polish territories is further adduced as evidence of the incomplete state of preparations
and the difficulties encountered by the Soviet side.

All these discussions relate to 22 June 1941 and have no bearing, naturally,
on the Red Army's readiness for war at a later date, nor on the subsequent
intentions of the Soviet leadership. Given that the military and political
situation of the Soviet Union did not allow her to enter the war in 1941, was
it not conceivable that, following the consolidation of its war-machine and
given a favourable development of the overall situation, i.e. in the event of a
decisive weakening or pinning-down of Germany, the Soviet government
might have been prepared to intervene militarily, just as it did in 1945 in the
war against Japan? Possible reflections along those lines are suggested by
Stalin's well-known speech to the graduates of Soviet military academies on 5
May 1941.[182] Details of the actual contents of this address of over forty minutes
were obtained not only by the long-term German embassy councillor in
Moscow, Hilger, but also by the British journalist Alexander Werth, who
enjoyed great respect in Moscow and on many issues clearly inclined towards
the Soviet point of view.[183] After the outbreak of the war Hilger interrogated
three senior Soviet officers who had been taken prisoner; they had participated
in that Kremlin event and, as Hilger wrote subsequently, their 'accounts
agreed almost verbatim, although they had had no opportunity to communicate with one another'. Werth for his part, after the outbreak of war, received
'a fairly detailed account of that reception, to which great importance was
attached in Moscow at the time'. The accounts of these very disparate sources
do not differ in content, so that the reliability of their informants cannot be
doubted. According to Hilger, Stalin had responded very dismissively to a
toast proposed by Lieutenant-Colonel Khozin, the chief of the Frunze military
academy, to the Soviet Union's peace policy, declaring that an end had now
to be put to the slogan of defence, because it was outdated and because not a
foot of soil could be won with it. The Red Army would have to accustom itself
to the idea that the era of peace policy was over and that of a forcible extension
of the socialist front had begun. Anyone failing to recognize the need for
offensive action was a philistine and a fool. Werth reproduces Stalin's words
in even greater detail. According to him, Stalin explained that it was necessary
to delay war against Germany until the autumn, because by then it would be
too late for a German attack. War with Germany, however, would 'almost

[181] *Istorija Velikoj Otečestvennoj vojny*, i. 473 ff.
[182] Hillgruber, *Strategie*, 432; Erickson, *Stalin's War*, i. 82.
[183] Hilger, *Erinnerungen*, 307–8; Werth, *Russia at War*, 122–3.

inevitably' take place in 1942, and indeed under much more favourable conditions, because the Red Army would then be better trained and equipped. Werth states expressly that all his information had 'basically' agreed, 'especially on one of the most important points', Stalin's conviction 'that, depending on the international situation, the Red Army would either await a German attack or else seize the initiative, since a permanent hegemony of Nazi Germany in Europe was "not normal"'. In his reflections Stalin proceeded from the assumption that Britain was not yet defeated and that a Japanese attack on the Soviet Union need not be expected, whereas the American war potential, on the other hand, would make itself increasingly felt.

The conviction that there would 'almost inevitably' be a German–Soviet war in 1942 and that the Soviet Union would then have to take the initiative appears, according to Werth, to have been widespread in the Red Army. Thus the former chief of staff of a Soviet rifle corps of the Kiev military district and future chief of the officer college of the Russian Liberation Army, Major-General Meandrov, lists 'numerous arguments' that the Soviet Union had been ready to enter the war after the spring of 1942.[184] 'The government's policy in preparing for a major war was entirely clear to us,' he wrote before he was handed over in 1946; 'what was presented to us as defensive measures proved in reality to be a long-prepared and carefully camouflaged plan for aggression.' Efforts were evidently made on Stalin's instruction to prepare and realign the Red Army's top officers for the new course outlined in his address of 5 May 1941. Colonel Pozdnyakov, in the spring of 1941 chief of the chemical service on the staff of the LXVII Rifle Corps, commanded by Brigade Commander Zhmachenko, subsequently chief of the command section of the Russian Liberation Army staff, records an instructional lecture on the Soviet Union's international position given by a representative of the Party central committee in the first half of May 1941, soon after Stalin's speech, to senior officers of the Poltava garrison.[185] The speaker had rendered the contents of Stalin's speech in roughly these words:

The time has now come when we must and can go over from 'defence' in the tactical sense of the word to 'defence' in the strategic sense. In other words, one cannot wait for an attack by the putative adversary, but one must attack him oneself. This affords indisputable advantages, and this is how the strategic 'defence' of the Soviet Union will be conducted.

According to the speaker it was intended to instruct all garrisons in the USSR along those lines. From the point of view of Soviet military theory such arguments appear merely as the continuation of the thesis that an enemy attack against the Soviet Union would in any case immediately develop into a

---

[184] Tagebuch des Generalmajors Borodin, BA-MA MSg 149/46, fo. 31; Brief des Generalmajor Meandrov Jan. 1946, BA-MA MSg 149/414, fo. 10.

[185] Pozdnjakov, Gotovilsja li SSSR k vojne s Germaniej [Did the USSR prepare for war with Germany?], BA-MA MSg 149/11, fo. 25.

Soviet attack aiming at the total annihilation of the enemy. There was only a short step between defence in the Soviet sense and the idea of a first strike, bearing in mind Lenin's statement that what mattered in a war was its causes, its aims, and the classes waging it, and not who 'attacked first'.[186] Any armed conflict of the Soviet Union could therefore be presented from the outset as a purely defensive, and hence a just, war.

Soviet historiography uses the Red Army's deficient preparation for defence at the time of the German attack on 22 June 1941 as a weighty argument in favour of the Soviet government's peaceful intentions. Also adduced in this context is the allegedly incomplete state of the army's equipment, although on this point the published sources are to this day faced with an unresolved dilemma. On the one hand, to help explain the Soviet defeats in the initial phase of the war, they are compelled to make the Wehrmacht's numerical superiority over the Red Army appear overwhelming. On the other, in order not to undermine confidence in the far-sightedness and solicitude of the Party and government, they are anxious to argue that everything had been done to equip the Red Army and Red Fleet for combat and to make them ready for defence. It is emphasized that the country's armament industry had been fully able to deliver to the rapidly growing forces all the equipment they required, and moreover to stockpile appropriate reserves for the raising of new formations in the event of mobilization and for replacing any losses suffered. Khrushchev opted for the former version when, at the Twentieth Congress of the CPSU on 25 February 1956, he declared that 'our army was poorly equipped' and lacked 'sufficient artillery, armour, and aircraft'. The assertion that the 'German hordes . . . had a numerical superiority especially of tanks and aircraft' is found in many sources. Thus the strength of the Germans and their allies is given by Soviet authors as 5.5 million men, 4,300 tanks and self-propelled assault guns, 47,200 guns and mortars, and 4,980 aircraft. Facing them in the western military districts had been only 170 out of 303 existing divisions of the Red Army, as well as two brigades.[187] The personnel strength of these formations would, as mentioned earlier, amount to a calculated maximum of only 1,289,000 men, though according to other data the figure was 2,900,000, including Fleet personnel. These troop concentrations allegedly had at their disposal 1,800 heavy and medium tanks, 34,695 guns and mortars, and 1,540 aircraft, as well as a 'considerable' amount of outdated tanks and outdated aircraft. The aggressors, therefore, had been superior to the Soviet troops by a factor of 1.8 in personnel, of 1.5 in tanks, of 1.25 in guns and mortars, and of 3.2 in aircraft.

It seems appropriate once more to confront these data, evidently part of a 'cover-up', with the actual ratios. The forces deployed for the attack by the Wehrmacht and its allies numbered approximately 3,600,000 men (3,050,000 Germans, 600,000 Romanians, Finns, and Hungarians). The German aggres-

---

[186] Lenin, *Polnoe sobranie sočinenij*, xxiii. 189.
[187] *Geschichte des zweiten Weltkrieges*, iv. 31, 36.

sors had 3,648 tanks and self-propelled guns, 7,146 guns, and 2,510 combat aircraft of the front-line formations under Luftwaffe command; Germany's allies had no armour worth mentioning, only moderate artillery, and altogether some 900 aircraft, most of them second-rate.[188] They were faced in the western frontier military districts by 2,900,000 Soviet troops, equipped with 14,000–15,000 tanks, at least 34,695 guns, and 8,000–9,000 combat aircraft.[189] This numerical ratio shifts further in favour of the Red Army if one bears in mind that 1,700 of the German tanks were auther the totally outmoded I and II types or else of Czech construction. Only 1,880 German tanks of the main strategic assault forces were able to take on the bulk of even the 'older' models of the 14,000–15,000 Soviet tanks stationed in the frontier military districts.

Contrary to the assertions of Khrushchev and most Soviet authors, the Soviet Union's superiority[190] in tanks, artillery, and aircraft over a Wehrmacht now caught in a war on two fronts seems completely overwhelming if one considers the total of weapons and equipment available. According to production statistics, the Red Army at the beginning of the German–Soviet war possessed no fewer than 24,000 tanks (including 1,862 T-34 and KV models), 148,000 guns of all types (mdudring mortars over 5 cm.), as well as 23,245 aircraft built after 1938 alone, including 3,719 of most recent construction. Even though the production process had been slowed down by Stalin's persecutions, the performance of the Soviet armament industry was reflected by the fact that, in spite of the enormous loss of industrial capacity in the territories conquered by the Germans, its output in the war year 1941 amounted to more than treble the peacetime volume of 1940. 'Mass production' of the most modern tanks and aircraft, however, had only just then started, and a dramatic increase in production figures was envisaged. Soviet industry had attained a level which ensured all the prerequisites of shortly supplying the Red Army with 'quite unimaginable equipment'.[191]

---

[188] Telpuchowski, *Geschichte des Großen Vaterländischen Krieges*, 41, n. 6 of the German editors; Piterskij, *Sowjet-Flotte*, 480, n. 6 of the German editor; see sects. I.IV.1[h] (Klink) and I.IV.2(c) (Boog).

[189] Nekrič and Grigorenko, *Genickschuß*, 254.   [190] Conquest, *Great Terror*, 489.

[191] The sections contributed to this volume by the present author have meanwhile been substantially confirmed by numerous publications, especially in the Soviet Union. In consequence, no correction is required in terms of content. However, the arguments might be continued in the light of newly revealed historical facts and insights. This concerns the criminal nature of Soviet rule under Stalin, as well as his shared responsibility for the unleashing of the Second World War, as for instance the realization that Hitler on 22 June 1941, if one examines conditions on the Soviet side, merely anticipated an intensively prepared attack by Stalin. The results of research gained in this area did not always agree with the political-historical world-image in West Germany: in fact, the present author had to face a certain degree of opposition. If Vjačeslav Dašičev believes that many Soviet historians have indissolubly linked their reputation to the Stalin regime, then the same applies also to a number of West German historians, who, adapting to political trends, refused to accept any critical discussion of Stalinism and eagerly and uncritically accepted Soviet propaganda versions. The Austrian philosopher and sociologist Ernst Topitsch refers in this connection to a downright 'scandal of historians of historic dimension' and to an impending scholarly, moral, and political 'Cannae' for a certain type of contemporary

3. Soviet Aid to Germany

Ever since its establishment, the Soviet state had attached prime importance to the development of its armed might. The Red Army stood at the centre of the Soviet government's care and attention, and from 1917 onward it underwent a continuous upsurge. The admitted sole aim of the entire domestic—i.e. 'socialist'—development of the Soviet state, as reflected in the five-year plans, was the strengthening of the Red Army and hence of the military power of the country.[192] By comparison, foreign relations during the period of supposedly incipient world revolution played no more than a subsidiary role during the first few years.[193] Only gradually was a foreign-political safeguarding of the Soviet state considered necessary as well. The main endeavour of the Moscow government was the prevention of an encirclement of the Soviet state by the capitalist powers. The emergence of an anti-Soviet coalition had to be rendered impossible and conflicts between its partners had to be fomented and intensified towards that end.

In its attempt to conclude bilateral agreements with individual countries, Soviet foreign policy was especially interested in Germany as the loser in the First World War, because Lenin believed that the untenable provisions of the treaty of Versailles were bound, sooner or later, to drive that country into an alliance with Bolshevik Russia. That may explain why he never tired of speaking about what he considered to be the inevitable consequences that that peace treaty would have for Germany. 'Germany had a peace imposed on her,' it is stated at one point,

but it was a peace of usurers and cut-throats, a peace of butchers, for Germany and Austria were looted and chopped up. They were deprived of all means of existence, children were allowed to starve to death. That is a monstrous peace of pillage. What then is the treaty of Versailles? A monstrous peace of pillage, which has turned millions and millions of people, among them the most civilized, into slaves. That is no peace, those are conditions dictated, knife in hand, to a helpless victim of robbers.[194]

That ideological rejection, perceptible in the Soviet Union even after the Second World War, of the treaty of Versailles,[195] which in Moscow's view was

historiography. In evidence a number of sources are here listed from which conclusions may be reached about such studies or their subject-matter: Judgement of the 5th civil bench of the Freiburg Landgericht of 19 June 1984, Ref. 5083/84; Dašičev, 'Pakt der beiden Banditen'; id., 'Stalin hat den Krieg gewollt'; Gillessen, 'Krieg der Diktatoren' (1986) and (1987); id., 'Krieg zweier Aggressoren'; Hoffmann, 'Stalin wollte den Krieg'; id., 'Angriffsvorbereitungen der Sowjetunion 1941'; Hosoya, 'Japanese–Soviet Neutrality Pact'; Magenheimer, 'Sowjetunion'; Pavlenko, 'Stalins Krieg'; Rhode, 'Ende des Schweigens'; 'Schlafende Aggressoren'; Schustereit, *Vabanque*; Stegemann, 'Geschichte und Politik'; Suvorov, Eisbrecher; Topitsch, *Stalins Krieg*; Volkogonov, *Triumf i tragedija*.

[192] *50 let vooružennych sil*, 192, 194, 196.   [193] Stökl, *Russische Geschichte*, 696–7.

[194] Lenin, *Über Krieg, Armee und Militärwissenschaft*, i. 774, also 561, 569, 600, 756, 758, 819. Lenin only expressed, somewhat crudely, what some statesmen in western Europe were also feeling—such as Premier Nitti, who had signed the treaty on behalf of Italy and later declared that 'what was aimed at was not peace but the strangulation and partition of Germany'. 'quoted according to Franz-Willing, *Der Zweite Weltkrieg*, 70'.

[195] *Istorija diplomatii*, iii. 924; also *Pravda* '26 Oct. 1939'.

directed not only against Germany but also against the land of the Soviets,
provided the foundation of the policy which, at Rapallo in 1922, brought
Soviet Russia and Germany together. It was on the basis of common hostility
to Versailles that co-operation between the two powers began to develop, and
indeed initially continued even after Hitler's rise to power, although mutual
relations soon cooled perceptibly. Even when, in the Litvinov era, a *rapprochement* took place between the Soviet Union and France, and when the Soviets
co-operated with the Western powers, a great many leading figures—to name
only Radek, still influential, as well as Molotov, Kaganovich, and, above all,
senior circles in the Red Army—and possibly even Stalin himself continued to
be convinced of the need to maintain good relations with Germany.[196]

In effect, therefore, it was only during a brief span of time, from the signing
of the anti-Comintern pact between Germany and Japan in 1936 to the
Munich agreement in 1938, that an undisguisedly antagonistic policy was
pursued. By October 1938 there were indications that a reorientation was
beginning to take place in Moscow in the direction of a renewal of earlier co-
operation with Germany. The decisive turn occurred in March 1939, when
Stalin at the Eighteenth Congress of the All-Union Communist Party (Bolsheviks) publicly hinted that he was prepared to enter into an arrangement with
Germany, and that he had no intention of allowing his country to be dragged
into a conflict for the benefit of the Western powers.[197] Stalin's offer preceded
the negotiations between the Soviet Union and the Western powers on a
collective security agreement against Germany,[198] which invalidates present-
day assertions that the subsequent conclusion of the 'Soviet–German non-
aggression treaty' was the consequence of the failure of those negotiations,
more particularly the failure of the simultaneous military negotiations, for
which Britain and France had to be held solely responsible.[199] The sluggish
progress of the negotiations with the Western powers, moreover, suggests that
these were by then playing only a secondary role and that the Soviet government was primarily interested in gaining time and raising the ante for a treaty
with Hitler. The Western powers in effect had nothing to offer.[200] All they
could expect of the Soviet government was that it would support, and if
necessary fight for, the maintenance of the Versailles system of states, hated
though this was also in Moscow—in other words, as Stalin put it, 'pull the
chestnuts out of the fire' for them. An arrangement with Hitler, on the other
hand, promised some immediate protection against a German attack and even
opened up the future possibility, without the Soviet Union itself risking

[196] Hilger, *Erinnerungen*, 255 ff.; Allard, *Stalin*, 21–2.

[197] Rossi, *Zwei Jahre*, 21–2; Hilger, *Erinnerungen*, 275; Fabry, *Hitler-Stalin-Pakt*, 13. Sipols,
Diplomatičeskaja bor'ba nakanune, 274 ff., who devotes a whole chapter to the prehistory of the
'Soviet–German non-aggression treaty', passes in silence over Stalin's crucial observations in
order to assert that the urgent desire for understanding had come solely from the German side and
had initially met with total rejection from the Soviet side.

[198] *Istorija Velikoj Otečestvennoj vojny*, i. 164.

[199] Žilin, *Problemy voennoj istorii*, 176–7, 304–5; Sipols, *Diplomatičeskaja bor'ba nakanune*,
279 ff.

[200] Rossi, *Zwei Jahre*, 26–7, 36–7, 46.

involvement in a conflict, of at least a partial restoration of the old western frontiers of the Tsarist empire. Against the background of such prospects Maxim Litvinov's dismissal on 3 May 1939 and Molotov's appointment as people's commissar for foreign affairs marked the opening of a new phase in Soviet foreign policy. There could no longer be any doubt about its direction. The significance of that change of ministers emerges from the words with which Litvinov parted in April from Nahum Goldmann, the president of the World Jewish Congress in Geneva: 'If one of these days you read in the paper that I have resigned from my post as foreign minister, you will know that Stalin has decided to conclude a pact with Hitler . . . that means that a few weeks later there will be war, because Hitler will feel secure in the east.'[201]

The non-aggression treaty concluded between the Soviet Union and Germany on 23 August 1939 was therefore from the start not merely a 'treaty about non-aggression, about renunciation of aggression, or, in other words, about peace between two states', in other words a measure dictated by circumstances for the preservation of peace, which of course changed nothing about the continuing fundamental hostility to 'Hitlerite Fascism'.[202] An integral part of that treaty was the secret protocol 'to which the Russians attached the greatest importance' and which Molotov actually described as a *conditio sine qua non*.[203] Moreover, the non-aggression treaty has to be seen in direct connection with the consequential frontier and friendship treaty of 28 September 1939 and its fateful additional secret protocols, with the agreement between the German Wehrmacht and the Red Army of 20 September 1939, with the two major economic agreements, and with certain other arrangements, all of which are passed over in silence in the Soviet literature, along with the secret protocol of 23 August 1939, as if they did not exist.[204] All these agreements far exceeded mere security arrangements; indeed, they clearly reduced these to a purely secondary status.

At the focus of attention were offensive aspirations. The treaties were a reflection of an 'imperialist partnership',[205] and made it clear that the Soviet

[201] Quoted according to Franz-Willing, *Der Zweite Weltkrieg*, 137. Herwarth von Bittenfeld, legation counsellor at the German embassy in Moscow, knew as early as May 1939 that not Britain and France but Hitler would conclude a treaty with the Soviet Union, because he alone was in a position to deliver the Baltic States to Stalin. Herwarth arranged for hints along those lines to be conveyed to the Italian and US embassies in Moscow: Herwarth von Bittenfeld, *Memoirs of a Diplomat*, 154 ff.

[202] *Istorija diplomatii*, iii. 787 ff.; *Istorija Velikoj Otečestvennoj vojny*, i. 176 ff.; Majskij, *Vospominanija*, ii. 524–5; *Istorija Kommunističeskoj Partii*, v. 72–3; Jur'ev, 'Fakty', 93–4.

[203] Rossi, *Zwei Jahre*, 48; Hilger, *Erinnerungen*, 284, 288.

[204] Characteristically Skšipek, 'Pol'sko-sovetskie diplomatičeskie otnošenija', 176, and Nazarevič, 'Rol' PPR v upročnenii pol'sko-sovetskoj družby', 251. As for the contents of the secret protocol of 23 Aug., the US Ambassador in Moscow, Steinhardt, for one, was fairly accurately informed by 24 Aug.: see Steinhardt to Secretary of State, 24 Aug. 1939, *FRUS* (1939), i. 342–3.

[205] Stökl, *Russische Geschichte*, 746. The Polish government called it 'an illegal act in direct violation of existing treaties and international law': Ambassador Potocki to Secretary of State, 30 Sept. 1939, *FRUS* (1939), i. 462.

Union was not only not doing anything to oppose 'aggression by Fascist Germany', but that it was actually paving the way for it. By allying itself with Germany and taking an active part in her acts of aggression, the Soviet Union succeeded in enlarging its living-space by the acquisition of a strategically vital territory. Between 1939 and 1941 an area of the extent of the Reich in 1919— 426,700 square kilometres, with a population of 23 million—was incorporated in the Soviet state.[206] This meant a fundamental redrawing of the political map of eastern Europe, one that could not be dismissed as a 'mere westward shift of the frontiers of the USSR' but which represented an 'extension of the brotherly family of the Soviet peoples'.[207] Nor can these territorial acquisitions be represented as a contribution to the Soviet Union's security or justified by that argument.[208] Even more questionable is the assertion of official historiography that they constituted a 'contribution . . . to the common cause of all peace-loving nations fighting against aggression by Fascist Germany'.[209] The vast territorial gains of the Soviet Union—the annexation of eastern Karelia, Estonia, Latvia, Lithuania, the greater half of Poland, Bessarabia, northern Bukowina, and a corner of Moldavia (the Herta region)—were unambiguously motivated by war or the threat of war, and were therefore diametrically opposed to the interests of peace-loving nations. 'The German– Soviet non-aggression treaty of 23 August 1939'—this was already beyond doubt to Rossi in 1954—'was a treaty of aggression against Poland.' 'The secret agreement proved . . . on a juridical basis that this crime was committed jointly, i.e. by Germany and Russia . . . The German–Soviet agreements of August and September 1939 were based on the partition of eastern Europe.'[210] In the judgement of the former Romanian foreign minister and ambassador in Moscow, Gafencu, the treaty, which covered Hitler's rear, 'unambiguously' meant war:[211] first of all Germany's war against Poland, which was welcome to the Soviet Union because it provided the prerequisite of its taking possession of substantial portions of the 'sphere of interests' assigned to it; and secondly the great conflict, deliberately included by Stalin in his calculations, of the 'capitalist' or 'imperialist' countries, i.e. Germany and the Western powers against one another.[212] General war in Europe meant, for one thing, the removal of the immediate danger of a united move by the capitalist powers against the Soviet state, a possibility never ruled out in Moscow, especially

---

[206] *Wer ist der Imperialist?* (American AFL-CIO trades union).

[207] *Istorija Velikoj Otečestvennoj vojny*, i. 230; *Istorija Kommunističeskoj Partii*, v. 78.

[208] Žilin, *Problemy voennoj istorii*, 273–4, 304, 307. Even Marx on one occasion resolutely rejected the justification of the annexation of foreign territory by any kind of security requirement: see Hoffmann, 'Volkskrieg in Frankreich', 210.

[209] *Istorija Velikoj Otečestvennoj vojny*, i. 249–50; Sipols, *Diplomatičeskaja bor'ba nakanune*, 292.

[210] Rossi, *Zwei Jahre*, 51, 197; Dašičev, 'Pakt der beiden Banditen', id., 'Stalin hat den Krieg gewollt'.

[211] Gafencu, *Vorspiel*, 399, 430.

[212] Rossi, *Zwei Jahre*, 58; Hilger, *Erinnerungen*, 289; also *Germany and the Second World War*, i. 693. Such interpretations are rejected in a testy fashion by *Istorija Kommunističeskoj Partii*, v. 72–3.

after the Munich agreement—the more so as the prospect of a simultaneous arrangement with Japan provided some security also in east Asia. For another, a conflict in Europe, which Moscow, recalling the First World War, certainly expected to be of long duration, held out the prospect that it would inevitably end with a weakening of all participants and with a fundamental change in the balance of power. In the final result the Soviet Union would be in a position, as Stalin had formulated it as early as 1925, decisively to throw into the balance the undiminished weight of its military might. Having his rear covered by the Soviet Union, which was siding with the presumed weaker of the imperialist powers,[213] Hitler could take the first step into war. The Soviet Union was able to keep in the background, which did not, however, rule out its readiness instantly to resort to force whenever this seemed necessary for the attainment of objectives close at hand without jeopardizing its main interest.

At least on one fundamental issue there was complete identity of interests between the Soviet Union and Germany at the beginning of the Second World War, something that was expressly stressed by Stalin and Molotov on several occasions.[214] What united the two powers was rejection of the system of states created by the treaty of Versailles and its follow-up treaties, a system which had demanded territorial sacrifices of Germany as well as of the Soviet Union. As late as 1 July 1940 Stalin quite openly told Sir Stafford Cripps, the British ambassador, that 'the basis of the German–Soviet non-aggression pact had been a common desire to get rid of the "old equilibrium" in Europe, which, prior to the war, Great Britain and France had sought to preserve'.[215] The Soviet Union had associated itself with Germany's revisionist aspirations when it became anxious to conclude a treaty with Germany. As Chargé d'Affaires Georgy Astakhov, authorized by Stalin to conduct the preliminary negotiations, had indicated to Minister Karl Schurre on 26 July 1939, 'Danzig must return to the Reich one way or another, and the question of the corridor' must also be resolved 'somehow in favour of the Reich'.[216] That in the summer of 1939 this could only be accomplished by war was clearly realized in Moscow. Of particular interest in that respect is a report by Augusto Rosso, the Italian ambassador, of 25 August 1939, quoting a remark of Reich Foreign Minister von Ribbentrop, just then in Moscow, that 'the Soviet Union had taken note of the need for Germany to regulate the Danzig issue, and would not therefore raise any objections to a war by Germany against Poland'.[217] On 21 December 1939, when Poland had long been crushed, the Soviet trade-union paper *Trud*—after *Pravda* and *Izvestiya* the third biggest daily in the Soviet Union— observed that of the unjust stipulations of the Versailles treaty, those were still in force in 1939 which separated East Prussia from Germany by the 'so-called

---

[213] Hillgruber, *Strategie*, 105.
[214] Ribbentrop to Schulenburg, 18 Oct. 1939, *DGFP* D viii, No. 271; Cripps to Eden, 8 Aug. 1940, according to *Stalin und Hitler*, No. 298.
[215] Cripps to Foreign Office, 1 July 1940, *FO Documents* (1940), vol. 24844.
[216] Rossi, *Zwei Jahre*, 39.
[217] Report by Rosso, 25 Aug. 1939, according to *Stalin und Hitler*, No. 71.

Polish corridor' and which compelled 'the German city of Danzig' to remain outside the Reich.[218] And in his famous speech of 6 November 1941, months after the beginning of the German–Soviet war, Stalin still observed that in a certain sense the 'Hitlerites' had been 'nationalists', i.e. something entirely positive in his eyes, so long as they had confined themselves to 'bringing together the German countries and reuniting the Rhineland, Austria, etc. with them'.[219] Only when they attacked the living-space of foreign nations had they revealed their true nature.

If, therefore,the Soviet Union was showing a good deal of understanding for German aspirations to shake off what it interpreted as 'unjust' clauses of the treaty of Versailles, then that benevolent attitude was further enhanced by the fact that the Poland of 1939, in Moscow's eyes, was 'one of the most reactionary states in Europe', a country whose 'economic, political, and military backwardness cried to heaven', a country where 'terror', 'oppression', and 'exploitation' ruled, a country in total 'disintegration' and 'decay', while at the same time indulging in 'great-power chauvinism'.[220] Moscow was not alone in its criticism of the character and condition of a state which, regardless of its internal social and national conflicts, was in dispute not only with its great neighbours in the east and west, i.e. the Soviet Union and Germany, but also with Lithuania and the Czechoslovak Republic. Indeed, even leading figures of the Western powers did not refrain from voicing such views. Thus Sumner Welles, the acting American secretary of state, speaking to President Beneš of Czechoslovakia in 1943, observed that what had become of Poland after the Great War was a 'scandal': 'It was a nonsense that a nation of 20 million would play it big in between 80 million Germans and 200 million Russians.'[221] William Strang, head of the central division in the British Foreign Office, and Gladwyn Jebb, secretary to the permanent under-secretary, who travelled in Poland in an official capacity in June 1939, remarked in their report on the aggressive mood in Poland and on the far-reaching great-power plans of Polish chauvinism. By means of conquest and annexation of foreign territories a Greater Poland was to be created and Warsaw to be made the centre of a 'powerful concentration'.[222] And finally Joseph Davies, the American ambassador in Moscow and foreign-policy adviser to Roosevelt, recorded on 26 August 1939 the 'very definite' remark of a Polish minister that 'his government would never agree to Poland and Germany coming together to settle their difficulties because of the Polish corridor and Danzig . . . His government, he said, would show the world; three weeks after the outbreak of war Polish troops would be in Berlin.'[223]

---

[218] Schulenburg to German foreign ministry, 23 Dec. 1939, according to *Stalin und Hitler*, No. 189.

[219] Stalin, *Großer Vaterländischer Krieg*, 27.

[220] Proëktor, *Vojna*, 121; *Istorija Velikoj Otečestvennoj vojny*, i. 210, 245 ff.; *Istorija Kommunističeskoj Partii*, v. 78 ff.

[221] Mastný, 'Beneš–Stalin–Molotov Conversations', 385.   [222] Schickel, 'Polen 1939'.

[223] Davies, *Mission to Moscow*, 355–6; also Allard, *Stalin*, 180.

In view of the intransigent mood in Warsaw, of which Moscow was very well aware, Soviet propaganda had no difficulty in holding Poland responsible for the outbreak of the war. Soviet sources cling to the thesis first formulated by Molotov, chairman of the council of people's commissars, in his radio address of 17 September 1939 in justification of Soviet intervention in Poland: that the Polish people had been hurled into the 'unfortunate war' and into disaster by its 'unreasonable leaders', and that the Soviet Union was virtually compelled to 'place the lives and property of the population of the western Ukraine and western Belorussia under its protection'.[224] However, the situation developing in Poland in mid-September 1939, with its alleged dangers for the Soviet Union, did not come about by accident but was the consequence of the German–Soviet treaty. Moreover, the Soviet Union had from the very first day directly helped in the destruction of the Polish Republic. Thus on 1 September 1939 it had readily complied with a request from the chief of staff of the German Luftwaffe by broadcasting homing signals over the Minsk transmitter for the benefit of the German bombers operating in Poland.[225] On 8 September 1939 the Soviet government informed Wacław Grzybowski, the Polish ambassador, that its territory would be closed to the transit of Allied war material to Poland. Anyway, the Germans were not greatly interested in a swift advance with strong forces to the Soviet state frontier in order to penetrate into Soviet territory at a suitable opportunity and thereby to open the war against the Soviet Union.[226] On the contrary, the German government attached great importance to as unimpeded an advance as possible by the Red Army against 'Polish fighting forces' and its occupation of the territory assigned to the Soviet Union—if only to be able to transfer its own troops to the still weakly held western front.[227] When on 3 September 1939 it received an invitation from the Reich government to take possession of its 'sphere of interest' up to the line of demarcation agreed in Moscow,[228] the Soviet government was 'unconditionally' in favour, except that it wished to postpone for a while the moment for 'concrete action'.[229] One reason was the need for military and organizational preparations, another was the wish to preserve the semblance of neutrality and to avoid being suddenly seen as an aggressor. But when the German advance made unexpectedly rapid progress, the Soviet government found itself under pressure. On 10 September 1939 Molotov admitted to Graf von der Schulenburg, the German ambassador, that his government found itself in

---

[224] *Rundschau*, 17 Sept. 1939, according to *Stalin und Hitler*, No. 121; Note of the government of the USSR to the Polish ambassador in Moscow, 17 Sept. 1939, *FRUS* (1939), i. 429.

[225] Ambassador's minute, 1 Sept. 1939, *DGFP* D vii, No. 496; Soviet government agreement, 1 Sept. 1939, contained in the documents, according to *Stalin und Hitler*, No. 90; minute, 3 Sept. 1939, ibid., No. 91.

[226] As Proèktor, for instance, believes: *Vojna*, 114–15.

[227] Ribbentrop to Schulenburg, 9 Sept. 1939, *DGFP* D viii, No. 34; Schulenburg to foreign ministry, 18 Sept. 1939, ibid., No. 90.

[228] Ribbentrop to Schulenburg, 3 Sept. 1939, ibid. vii, No. 567.

[229] Schulenburg to foreign ministry, 5 Sept. 1939, ibid. viii, No. 5; see *Germany and the Second World War*, ii. 127 ff.

some embarrassment, having hoped to use the German advance as a pretext for declaring that 'Poland was falling apart and it was necessary for the Soviet Union, in consequence, to come to the aid of the Ukrainians and the Belorussians'. This approach, however, would now be denied to it: if, as he assumed, Germany were to conclude an armistice with Poland, the Soviet Union could not very well 'start a "new war"'.[230] Ribbentrop managed to reassure Molotov by having him informed that there could be no question of an imminent armistice with Poland, so that the Soviet Union would have an opportunity to intervene and to use its special justification for that step.[231]

Even during those first ten days of September there thus existed a German–Soviet agreement that the Soviet Union too would take possession of the 'sphere of interest' assigned to it in the secret protocol of 23 August 1939.[232] Hence the motivation subsequently adduced for its intervention in Poland, that in 'mid-September 1939' an unexpected need arose to protect the allegedly threatened 'Ukrainians and Belorussians',[233] is revealed as a mere pretext. The more so as that argument had been the subject of a German–Soviet exchange of opinion ever since 10 September 1939. Besides, one might ask, who was actually threatening that population? On 10 September 1939 Molotov, talking to Schulenburg, was still hoping to present Germany as the alleged source of the threat, but that version was later somewhat modified in the literature, with Proèktor for instance arguing that the 'Ukrainians and Belorussians' had been in danger of coming under the yoke of 'Poles of the *pan*s [big landowners] under the conditions of a Fascist occupation regime'.[234] When the German ambassador objected to that accusation, Stalin 'with the utmost readiness altered the text' so that the statement to be made to the public on 17 September 1939 was acceptable to the Germans.[235] The intensively accelerated military preparations had meanwhile progressed to a point where Stalin, in the night of 16–17 September 1939, in the presence of Molotov and of the people's commissar for defence, Marshal Voroshilov, was able to inform Schulenburg that the Red Army would cross the Polish frontier along the entire line from Polotsk to Kamenets-Podolsk at 6 o'clock in the morning, and that air-force units would 'begin today to bomb the district east of Lvov.'

Planning and execution of the Soviet operation altogether reveal that this was not some kind of 'liberation campaign' but a war of aggression[236] in breach of the Soviet–Polish non-aggression treaty, a case of 'hostilities' even in the restrained language of the International Red Cross. The troops of the specially

[230] Schulenburg to foreign ministry, 10 Sept. 1939, *DGFP* D viii, No. 46.

[231] Ribbentrop to Schulenburg, 13 Sept. 1939, ibid., No. 59.

[232] Schulenburg to foreign ministry, 9, 14 Sept. 1939, ibid., Nos. 37, 39, 63; Ribbentrop to Schulenburg, 15 Sept. 1939, ibid., No. 70.

[233] *Istorija Kommunističeskoj Partii*, v. 81; Žilin, *Problemy voennoj istorii*, 274.

[234] Proèktor, *Vojna*, 114.

[235] Schulenburg to foreign ministry, 17 Sept. 1939, *DGFP* D viii, No. 80.

[236] Stökl, *Russische Geschichte*, 748.

formed Ukrainian and Belorussian fronts were instructed 'not to get involved in frontal engagements', but to bypass 'enemy groupings' along their flanks and rear and speedily to occupy enemy localities.[237] The Soviet communiqué from the front on 17 September 1939 reported the shooting down of ten Polish aircraft[238] and on 20 September the destruction of three Polish infantry divisions and two cavalry brigades, as well as the capture or destruction of 280 guns and 120 aircraft.[239] On 21 September 1939 Soviet artillery began to bombard Lvov.[240] Air attacks against Polish troops were accompanied by propaganda actions. Thus leaflets signed by Army Commander (1st rank) Timoshenko, the commander-in-chief of the Ukrainian front, invited Polish soldiers to wipe out their officers and generals in the spirit of the class struggle.[241] 'The officers and generals are your enemies,' Army Commander (2nd rank) Kovalevsky, the commander-in-chief of the Belorussian front, similarly proclaimed in his leaflets: 'Soldiers! Destroy your officers and generals . . .'[242] The Polish soldiers were begged not to shed their blood for the 'foreign interests of big landowners and capitalists': 'The ministers and generals have taken their looted gold and fled like cowards, abandoning the army and the entire Polish nation to their fate.' Any resistance to the Red Army would end in total annihilation. In view of the weakened condition of the Polish fighting forces, the troops of both fronts advanced rapidly, though here and there against stiff opposition,[243] so that, as Army Commander (2nd rank) Tyulenev, the commander-in-chief of the Twelfth Army, put it, they were compelled to deal 'crushing blows'.[244] Polish opposition was primarily broken by the use of armoured formations.[245]

By the conclusion of the campaign after twelve days some 230,000 Polish troops had been taken prisoner; their number increased to approximately 250,000 after the annexation of the Baltic States. The fate of these prisoners of war, as well as of the Polish civilians detained in the Soviet-occupied territory, was for the most part to be exceedingly severe. According to Soviet literature, all Polish servicemen were immediately released to their homeland, regardless of whether occupied by German or Soviet troops, or else allowed to go abroad. 'A few, however,' it is stated, 'went to the USSR, where patriotic Polish organizations were being formed.'[246] In fact, of the 250,000 Polish prisoners of war and the 1,230,000 Polish civilians arrested or deported, an extremely high

---

[237] *Istorija Velikoj Otečestvennoj vojny*, i. 246 ff.
[238] Entry of 18 Sept. 1939, BA-MA RW 6 V/v. 98; Werth, *Russia at War*, 58.
[239] Morning report, 22 Sept. 1939, BA-MA RW 6/v. 98, pt. 2.
[240] Entry of 21 Sept. 1939, MGFA P 200.   [241] Zawodny, *Zum Beispiel Katyn*, 107.
[242] Rzolnierze Armii Polskiej! [Soldiers of the Polish Army!], 17 Sept. 1939, BA-MA RH 19 II/15.
[243] Antonow, 'Marsch nach Polen', 81.   [244] Tjulenev, *Čerez tri vojny*, 133.
[245] Werturteil über Rote Armee [Assessment of quality of the Red Army], OQu IV/Frd Heere Ost, No. 1995/39 g. 19 Dec. 1939 BA-MA RH 19 I/122, fo. 157.
[246] *Istorija Velikoj Otečestvennoj vojny*, i. 249.

proportion perished in Soviet detention.[247] The question of the whereabouts of the 15,000 Polish army soldiers, 8,000 officers, and 7,000 NCOs, as well as a number of prominent civilians in the hands of the NKVD in the prison camps of Kozelsk, Ostashkov, and Starobelsk, who vanished without a trace west of Smolensk in the spring of 1940, was answered by the discovery of the mass graves at Katyn in 1943. As Zawodny, in agreement with the results of international investigations, records, they had been 'systematically annihilated by the Soviet security police'.[248] The victims of that Moscow-directed extermination included, along with 300 senior officers, Generals Billewicz, Bohatyrewicz, S. Haller, Kowalewski, Łukowski, Minkiewicz, Plisowski, Smorawinski, F. Sikorski, Skierski, and Skuratowicz, and Admiral Czernicki.[249] General Olszyna-Wilczynski, commanding the Grodno military district, had already been murdered in September 1939, after he had gone to the Soviets to offer to surrender without fighting. In Zawodny's judgement 'the officers shot at Katyn and those recorded as missing represented the flower of Polish society. Thousands had been called up from the reserve. In civilian life they were university professors, doctors, scientists, artists, secondary-school teachers . . . who were doing their duty as officers of the reserve.'

If further proof were needed that the campaign in Poland was conducted by agreement between the two aggressors, this may be found in the military negotiations held in Moscow on 20 September 1939,[250] attended on the Soviet side by Marshal Voroshilov, people's commissar for defence, and by Army Commander (1st rank) Shaposhnikov, chief of the Red Army General Staff, and for the 'German High Command' by Lieutenant-General Köstring, the

---

[247] The Polish ministry of justice in London in 1949 estimated the total number of Polish citizens taken prisoner, arrested, deported, and sent to forced labour at 1,442,000–1,660,000: *Documents on Polish–Soviet Relations*, i. 573–4. Rhode, 'Polen', 1028, speaks of 'about' 1.5m. deportees. According to the Polish Committee for Social Self-Defence (KOR; formerly Committee for Workers' Defence), losses amounted to 148,000 out of 250,000 prisoners of war and 600,000 out of 1.6–1.8m. deported civilians: see 'Polen erinnert Moskau an Völkermord'. One remarkable account states that out of 600,000 Polish Jews deported to the Soviet Union in 1939–40 'about 150,000 returned to Poland at the end of the War. The rest—some 450,000—just vanished': *Documents on Polish–Soviet Relations*, i. 607–8.

[248] Zawodny, *Zum Beispiel Katyn*, 104 ff.; Montfort, *Massacre de Katyn*, 223; Pozdnjakov, 'Novoe o Katyni'. On the entirely different fate of the approximately 18,000 Polish officers in German captivity see Schickel, 'Gefangene Polen in deutschen Offizierslagern'.

[249] As recently as 1977 a reputable Soviet legal scholar, Prof. Dr Minasjan, wrote about the 'blood-bath prepared by the Hitlerite hangmen for the Polish officers in the forest of Katyn', which 'the nations of the world will never forget and for which they will never forgive the Nazi criminals': Minasjan, *Meždunarodnye prestuplenija*, 16, 221. Any comment is superfluous. As in similar instances, the Soviet government had also attributed its mass murder of the Polish officers in the forest of Katyn to the Germans. See the official report of the 'Extraordinary State Commission for Ascertaining and Investigating Crimes Committed by the German-Fascist Invaders and their Associates': *Truth about Katyn* (in private ownership). The Soviet Union admits the massacre of Katyn: Šavoronkov, 'Charkow'.

[250] Secret protocol of 20 Sept. 1939, in *General Köstring*, 176 ff.

military attaché, by Colonel Heinrich Aschenbrenner, the air attaché, and by Lieutenant-Colonel (General Staff) Hans Krebs. A jointly signed protocol laid down the modalities of the two sides moving into their respective 'spheres of interest'. The German Wehrmacht undertook to take all 'necessary measures' for the prevention of 'possible provocations or acts of sabotage by Polish gangs and so on' in the towns and villages to be handed over to the Red Army. The Red Army for its part undertook to make available the 'necessary forces for the annihilation of Polish army units and gangs' along the line of withdrawal of the German troops. There was a partial exchange of liaison officers between the withdrawing German and the advancing Soviet formations. Acts of transfer, such as that of the modern fortress of Osowiec between the German Major-General Brand and the Soviet Colonel Berdnikov, were staged in a solemn manner.[251] Poland had demonstrably succumbed to a combined attack by Germany and the Soviet Union—a fact that can be neither hushed up nor argued away.[252] Even the man responsible for Soviet policy, People's Commissar Molotov, in his speech to the Supreme Soviet on 31 October 1939 unambiguously summed up the situation: 'A single blow against Poland,' he said, 'first by the German and then by the Red Army, and nothing was left of that monstrosity of the treaty of Versailles, which had owed its existence to the oppression of non-Polish nationalities.'[253] At Stalin's express behest no remnants at all of Poland's existence as a state were to survive. The German ambassador reported to Berlin that on 20 September 1939 Molotov had informed him 'that the original inclination entertained by the Soviet government and Stalin personally to permit the existence of a residual Poland had now given way to the inclination to partition Poland along the Pisa–Narev–Vistula–San line.'[254] On 25 September 1939 Stalin proposed a territorial exchange to Schulenburg, under which Germany would renounce Lithuania, assigned to her in the secret procotol of 23 August, and instead would receive the entire Voivodship of Lublin and parts of the Voivodship of Warsaw as far as the Bug.[255] The reason for this was simple: the Soviet Union wished to get rid of Polish provinces which were difficult to assimilate and in which millions of Jews were living, and instead gain a free hand in the three Baltic States. In the event of Germany's agreement the Soviet Union, as Stalin declared, would 'immediately take up the solution of the problem of the Baltic countries in accordance with the protocol of 23 August'. The Reich government did not find it easy to agree, but once that agreement was given and enshrined in the

---

[251] Bericht über die Übereignung der Festung Osowiec [Report on the handing-over of the fortress of Osowiec], Group Brand to AOK 4 25 Sept. 1939, BA-MA RH 19 II/15.

[252] As attempted by Žilin, *Problemy voennoj istorii*, 178 ff.

[253] *Izvestija* (1 Nov. 1939); *Rundschau* (Nov. 1939), according to *Stalin und Hitler*, No. 172; *Istorija Velikoj Otečestvennoj vojny*, i. 249.

[254] Schulenburg to foreign ministry, 20 Sept. 1939, *DGFP* D viii, No. 104; Rauch, *Geschichte des bolschewistischen Rußland*, 381. See, on the other hand, the assertion of Sipols, *Diplomatičeskaja bor'ba nakanune*, 316 n. 196.

[255] Schulenburg to foreign ministry, 25 Sept. 1939, *DGFP* D viii, No. 131; Rossi, *Zwei Jahre*, 73.

secret protocol signed by both parties and attached to the 'frontier and friendship treaty' of 28 September 1939[256] nothing stood in the way of the Soviet intentions. Within a few days the Soviet government began to put massive pressure on the Baltic republics to make them agree to the establishment of bases on their territories, which in practice meant military occupation as a first step towards the planned annexation.[257] As for the Polish Republic, 200,036 square kilometres of its sovereign territory were incorporated in the Soviet Union in accordance with the secret protocol of 28 September 1939, while 188,737 square kilometres were annexed or occupied by Germany. According to Soviet data, the Red Army's losses were 737 men killed and 1,862 wounded in Poland, sufficient reason for Stalin to refer in a telegram to Ribbentrop on 27 December 1939 to the 'friendship of the nations of Germany and the Soviet Union' consolidated 'by blood'.[258] German–Soviet collusion against Poland's national existence was finally sealed when the two powers in a secret additional protocol agreed in their respective territories not to tolerate any political 'agitation which affects the territory of the other party', to suppress any 'such agitation' from the outset, and to inform 'each other concerning the most suitable measures for this purpose'.[259] Any stirring of national resistance by the Poles was to be nipped in the bud.

From the very start the Soviet government had regarded Poland as a problem exclusively concerning her two neighbours, Germany and the Soviet Union. After the 'disintegration of the Polish state', in other words after the destruction of its fighting forces and the occupation of its territory by troops of the Wehrmacht and the Red Army, the Polish problem was, in Soviet eyes, 'settled definitively'. In that spirit on 28 September 1939 Molotov and Ribbentrop signed a joint 'declaration by the government of the German Reich and the government of the USSR', which stated that a 'firm foundation' had been created for 'a lasting peace in eastern Europe'.[260] As the Western powers, Britain and France, were as a matter of principle denied the right to interfere in Polish affairs, these countries' declaration of war against Germany was interpreted in Moscow as an arbitrary extension of a local conflict, not as an obligation arising out of a guarantee. Stalin and the Soviet government did not hesitate to put the entire Soviet propaganda machine as well as all the parties of the Moscow-controlled Communist International into the service of a large-scale campaign designed to brand Britain and France as the originators of the war and to hold these two powers responsible for its continuation and extension.[261] The justification given by these countries for their declaration of

---

[256] Boundary and Friendship Treaty, 28 Sept. 1939, *DGFP* D viii, No. 157; Secret additional protocol, 28 Sept. 1939, ibid., No. 159.

[257] Myllyniemi, *Baltische Krise*, 57 ff.

[258] Stalin to Ribbentrop, *Völkischer Beobachter* (27 Dec. 1939).

[259] Secret additional protocol, 28 Sept. 1939, *DGFP* D. viii, No. 160.

[260] Ibid., No. 161; *Izvestija* (30 Sept. 1939). See also Ambassador Steinhardt to Secretary of State, 30 Oct. 1939, *FRUS* (1939), i. 492–3.

[261] Rossi, *Zwei Jahre*, 85 ff., 90, 102 ff.

war against Germany was thus repeatedly characterized as a mere 'pretext' designed to conceal their true intentions.[262] 'Just as the pistol-shots in Sarajevo were only the pretext and not the cause of the first imperialist war,' a joint peace appeal by the Communist Parties of France, Britain, and Germany of January 1940 stated, 'so the self-appointed defence of Poland by Britain and France is only the pretext for the second imperialist war.'[263] Neither was the Western powers' reason for continuing the war against Germany after the collapse of Poland—the moral necessity of a fight against National Socialism, i.e. against the 'Fascism' opposed in every possible way in the Soviet Union too until 1939 and then again from 1941 onward—accepted as valid in Moscow.[264] On 31 October 1939 Molotov expressly and emphatically rejected that motivation when, in his speech to the Supreme Soviet, he declared that there was 'no justification at all' for that kind of war. The chairman of the council of people's commissars explained that one could accept or reject 'the ideology of Hitlerism'—that was a matter of political attitude—'but every person should understand that an ideology cannot be destroyed by force, that it cannot be removed from the world by a war. It is therefore not only pointless but indeed criminal to wage such a war for the "destruction of Hitlerism", camouflaged as a struggle for "democracy".' *Izvestiya*, the mouthpiece of the council of people's commissars, had already carried similar reflections on 9 October 1939, when it stated that 'no kind of ideology, no kind of philosophy' could be destroyed 'by fire and sword'. 'One may respect or hate Hitlerism, like any other system of political beliefs . . . but to unleash wars for the "destruction of Hitlerism" means to permit a criminal piece of political stupidity . . . a senseless and nonsensical atrocity.'[265]

In addition, attempts were made in the Soviet Union to question Britain's and France's morality in conducting a war which, in Molotov's words, was 'reminiscent of the religious wars of earlier days'. The appeal of the Communist Parties of January 1940 reminded the people of Britain, France, and Germany that those who 'oppressed 300 million Indians' or, as Georgy Dimitrov, chairman of the Comintern, described it, 'practised undivided rule over hundreds of millions of colonial slaves' had no right to speak 'of the freedom of nations' while themselves 'practising the worst Hitlerite methods of brute force and oppression against their own nations'. 'There are', it was stated in allusion to the self-righteousness of those countries, 'concentration camps in France and in British India, just as in Germany.' The war, in the Soviet interpretation, was not about a 'reactionary multinational state', about

[262] Molotov addressing the Supreme Soviet, 29 Mar. 1940, according to *Stalin und Hitler*, No. 222; Dimitrov, *Kommunistische Internationale* (Stockholm) (Nov. 1939), ibid., No. 173; *Izvestija* (26 Feb. 1940).

[263] '*Joint Appeal of the Communist Parties of France, Great Britain and Germany*', *Rundschau* (20 Jan. 1940), according to *Stalin und Hitler*, No. 199.

[264] Pieck, *Kommunistische Internationale* (Stockholm) (Dec. 1939), according to *Stalin und Hitler*, No. 185.

[265] *Izvestija* (9 Oct. 1939). See Ambassador Steinhardt to Secretary of State, 9 Oct. 1939, *FRUS* (1939), i. 509–10.

a 'reactionary Fascist Poland',[266] nor about the liquidation of 'Hitlerism' or 'Fascism', about ideological or philosophical issues, or about 'freedom and democracy'. It was in reality about the maintenance of the old balance of power in Europe, a balance created by Britain and France and benefiting only them; to liquidate that balance had, in Stalin's words, been the real point of the German–Soviet treaty.[267] From the Soviet point of view, therefore, the armed conflict had the character of a preventive war by Britain and France against an increasingly powerful Germany,[268] their most dangerous competitor; Moscow had no doubt that the two world powers were concerned with nothing but their own material and imperial interests. Molotov in this context repeatedly spoke of the inevitability of a clash between Britain and Germany. The cause of the war, in his words, was Germany's natural endeavour 'to break the fetters of the treaty of Versailles, whose authors had been Britain and France with the active participation of the United States'.[269] In his observations of November 1939, which defined the political line of the Communist International, Dimitrov called the war a conflict 'for hegemony in Europe, for colonial possessions in Africa and other continents, for colonies and sources of raw materials, for control of shipping-routes, for the subjection and exploitation of foreign nations . . . but in no respect for the dyence of "Dencocracy", "freedom", and "international law", or for safeguarding the independence of small countries and nations'. And on 26 February 1940 the government paper *Izvestiya* outlined the international situation as follows: 'When Germany was beginning to struggle for the annulment of "Versailles", Britain became aware of . . . the renewal of a threat from a dangerous competitor. Britain began serious preparations for a new war . . . the war, fought in defence of the fundamental position of British imperialism, is intended to weaken or even destroy its most dangerous rival in the world market.'[270] Although Germany too was counted—covertly rather than openly—among the imperialist countries, all direct criticism of her was meticulously avoided; the sympathies of the Soviet Union were clearly on her side. Stalin and Molotov repeatedly emphasized their interest in the existence of a strong Germany as the 'indispensable prerequisite of peace in Europe'.[271] The Soviet Union, Stalin declared on 19 October 1939, 'would not consent to the Western powers' creating conditions which might weaken Germany or place her in a difficult position'. In this context Molotov pilloried Britain's and France's 'criminal' aims: they were trying to destroy and chop up Germany and impose on her an even worse Versailles than in 1918.[272]

---

[266] Comintern to CP of the USA, end of Sept. 1939, according to *Stalin und Hitler*, No. 148a; illegal leaflet of the French Communists, ibid., No. 214.

[267] See n. 215.   [268] *Pravda* (5 July 1940); also Newman, *March 1939*, 218–19.

[269] Molotov addressing the Supreme Soviet, 31 Oct. 1939, 1 Aug. 1940, according to *Stalin und Hitler*, Nos. 172, 296.

[270] *Izvestija* (26 Feb. 1940); *Pravda* (26 Oct. 1939).

[271] Ribbentrop to Schulenburg, 18 Oct. 1939, *DGFP* D viii, No. 271; Schulenburg to foreign ministry, 19 Oct. 1939, ibid., No. 280.

[272] Molotov addressing the Supreme Soviet, 29 Mar. 1940, according to *Stalin und Hitler*, No. 222.

In line with the Soviet view that the obstacle to peace had been removed with the liquidation of Poland, Britain and France alone were being held responsible in the German–Soviet government declaration of 28 September 1939 for the continuation of the war, and consultations between the German and Soviet governments 'concerning the necessary measures' were threatened. On 30 September 1939 the Party daily *Pravda* called the continuation of the war a crime being committed against the nations by '*provocateurs* and dishonourable politicians' without any justification.[273] A peace campaign such as the one launched by Moscow did not of course cost the Soviet Union much: if peace really was achieved, the USSR would, on the strength of its success, be a partner to the negotiations and have a considerable say in Europe.[274] The Soviet Union could no longer be excluded from the concert of powers, as it was in Munich. If, however, as seemed likely, the conflict continued, that eventuality would also be welcome to Moscow—quite apart from the propaganda benefit gained from its display of love of peace. It is against this background that the declaration has to be seen which Stalin, summing up official opinion, ordered to be published in *Pravda* on 29 November 1939 and which therefore deserves special attention.[275] Stalin declared:

(1) It was not Germany which attacked France and Britain, but France and Britain which attacked Germany and therefore took upon themselves the responsibility for the present war. (2) After the outbreak of hostilities Germany made peace proposals to France and Britain, and the Soviet Union publicly supported Germany's peace proposals because it believed, and still believes, that a rapid end to the war would radically alleviate the position of all countries and nations. (3) The ruling circles of France and Britain have rejected both German peace proposals and the efforts of the Soviet Union in an offensive manner. These are the facts.

Stalin's exculpation of Germany and attribution to Britain of sole responsibility for the unleashing of the Second World War could not, in the further course of events, be maintained in this one-sided and narrow form, but neither was it ever entirely abandoned. The way in which the first phase of the war— the imperialist war of the capitalist countries against one another—can be viewed in the Soviet Union to this day may be gleaned from the observations of a figure who was intimately acquainted with the policy of the Western powers, especially of Britain, during the war. 'All accounts so far', Ivan Maysky, the former Soviet ambassador in London, states in his memoirs, 'nevertheless show beyond dispute that the real responsibility for the Second World War is borne by Hitler on the one side, and by Chamberlain and Daladier on the other . . . Chamberlain and Daladier, and the aggressive imperialist forces behind them, deserve no mercy before the great judgement of

[273] *Pravda* (30 Sept. 1939); *Trud* (5 Apr. 1940).

[274] Davies, *Mission to Moscow*, 357–8; Rossi, *Zwei Jahre*, 86.

[275] *Pravda* (29 Nov. 1939, 26 Jan. 1940); Rossi, *Zwei Jahre*, 88. A presentation of the events in Stalin's manner was described, in a different context, as 'mendacious' by Žilin, *Problemy voennoj istorii*, 197.

history.'[276] In the eyes of the well-known Soviet diplomat Britain and France thus stand alongside National Socialist Germany. No mention, on the other hand, is made of the responsibility borne by the Soviet Union for the disaster which befell Europe, a responsibility stemming from the treaties concluded with Hitler, the extensive support given to Germany during the first phase of the war, and the execution of the secret protocols.

In what way did the Soviet Union support Germany's war effort? Its support, first of all, was in the political and propaganda field, and subsequently in the economic sphere. However, Germany also received practical military support. Thus the naval base put at Germany's disposal in Zapadnaya Liza Bay, and subsequently in September 1939 in Yakonga Bay on the Murmansk coast, the 'Base North', was of assistance to German naval operations prior to the occupation of Norway.[277] The Soviet Union allowed the Germans free passage through the 'Siberian Straits', the north-east passage, and thereby enabled the auxiliary cruiser *Komet* to break through into the Pacific, where it engaged in raids against British shipping. On 6 September 1940 the German embassy was instructed to convey to the Soviet government the Reich government's gratitude for that 'valuable support'. Grand Admiral Raeder, the commander-in-chief of the navy, did not omit to send a personal letter of thanks as well to Admiral Kuznetsov, the people's commissar for the ocean fleet.

Since in the Soviet view it was solely the Western powers who desired a continuation of the war, the occupation of Denmark and Norway by German troops in the spring of 1940 was regarded in Moscow as a justified counter move against the alleged intention of Britain and France to extend the war to northern Europe. On 9 April 1940 Molotov formally assured the Reich government of the Soviet government's understanding for what he called the 'defensive measures . . . forced upon' Germany and wished it 'complete success' with them.[278] Comment in the government paper *Izvestiya* and in the Party paper *Pravda* was on the same lines.[279] Britain and France had 'invaded' the neutral waters of the Scandinavian countries in order to undermine Germany's military position. In view of the fact that the Western powers had 'violated the sovereignty of the Scandinavian countries' and 'extended military operations to Scandinavia', *Izvestiya* on 11 April 1940 described any discussion of the legitimacy of the procedure 'forced upon' Germany as 'ludicrous'.[280] And on 12 April 1940 *Trud*, the trade-union daily, observed that Britain and France had 'sown the wind and harvested the whirlwind'; by their intervention they had taken upon themselves 'the whole weight of responsibility for the

---

[276] Maiski, *Memoiren*, 499, 503.
[277] Woermann to embassy, 5 Sept. 1940, *DGFP* D ix, No. 22; Heinsius, 'Deutsch-sowjetischer Nichtangriffspakt', 188–9.
[278] Schulenburg to foreign ministry, 9 Apr. 1940, *DGFP* D ix, No. 73.
[279] *Izvestija* (11 Apr. 1940); *Pravda* (18 Apr. 1940).
[280] Schulenburg to foreign ministry, 11 Apr. 1940, according to *Stalin und Hitler*, No. 233.

extension of war operations to Scandinavia'.[281] This exceedingly understanding attitude on the part of the Soviet Union towards Operation Weserübung is explained by the relief felt in Moscow that with the failure of the attempted Anglo-French invasion of Norway the danger of an armed conflict between the Soviet Union and the Western powers in the northern region had disappeared. That reaction refutes the thesis of an allegedly unselfish attitude to the Nordic nations, and conflicts with the interpretations of Soviet historiography, which speaks of a German 'raid', of an 'attack',[282] indeed 'not a preventive war, but open aggression',[283] and suggests that 'when Norway, at the beginning of April 1940, was occupied by Fascist troops, in that most difficult period in the history of the Norwegian people', the Soviet Union had stood 'by its side'. The Soviet government's real assessment of its role emerges from Molotov's speech to the Supreme Soviet on 31 July 1940, when he declared that, without indirect support from the USSR, Germany would not have been able to extend its sphere of power to Scandinavia and Western Europe.[284]

As the Soviet government was blaming only the Western powers for a policy of extending the war and 'violating the rights of neutral states', it managed to find words of understanding and excuse also for the German attack on Holland and Belgium. Behind those words, however, was the unspoken satisfaction of seeing the forces of Germany and the Western powers locked for an unforeseeable time in a 'war of attrition', which would ultimately bring supremacy to the Soviet Union. Against this background, in May 1940, there took place a repeat performance of the previous month's event, when Molotov, though perhaps a little more curtly, expressed his understanding for the German invasion of the two neutral countries[285] and when a few days later keynote articles, inspired by the highest quarters in the Kremlin—that is, by Stalin personally—appeared in *Izvestiya* and *Pravda*.[286] It was pointed out that it had long been part of the plans of the Anglo-French bloc to 'drag' Holland and Belgium 'into the imperialist war by economic and diplomatic pressure, and by direct threats'. Germany had therefore been confronted with the task of delivering a counterblow against the invasion of the Ruhr planned by the Western powers. Britain and France had thus thrust 'two more small countries into the flames of the imperialist war'.[287] The attitude adopted by the Soviet Union in the conflict between the Western powers and Germany can be gauged in particular from the behaviour of the Moscow-controlled Communist Party of France.[288] Having committed the 'grave error' of voting for the war loans in the Chamber on 2 September 1939, it soon performed a complete about-turn on the lines of the peace campaign launched by the Soviet Union. Maurice Thorez, Jacques Duclos, André Marty, and the other Communist

---

[281] Schulenburg to foreign ministry, 12 Apr. 1940, according to *Stalin und Hitler*, No. 236.
[282] *Istorija Velikoj Otečestvennoj vojny*, i. 218; *Befreiungsmission*, 273.
[283] Proèktor, *Vojna*, 176 ff., 232–3, 238.   [284] Allard, *Stalin*, 235.
[285] Schulenburg to foreign ministry, 10 May 1940, *DGFP* D ix, No. 226.
[286] Schulenburg to foreign ministry, 20 May 1940, according to *Stalin und Hitler*, No. 264.
[287] *Pravda* (16 May, 5 July 1940).   [288] Rossi, *Zwei Jahre*, 106 ff.

leaders were now consistently taking the Soviet policy line of holding the 'Anglo-French imperialists' responsible for the war because they had 'induced Poland to reject an amicable revision of the Danzig statute' and because they were refusing to examine Hitler's peace proposals. Despite strict counter-measures by the French government, the French communists did not confine themselves to a covert propaganda struggle against the 'imperialist war' or the 'criminal policy of the warmongers'. To the applause of the Soviet press they next proceeded to undermine the morale of the French army and to paralyse the troops' will to resist. The Communist Party of France thus contributed its share to the success of the German offensive in the west, which, in contrast to the postwar version, was by no means described in 1940 as an 'invasion of Fascist troops', but as a superbly planned and executed strategic operation. After France was defeated, or, as it is now formulated, had come 'under the yoke of Fascist Germany',[289] Molotov again conveyed to the German ambassador 'the warmest congratulations of the Soviet government on the splendid success of the German Wehrmacht'.[290] According to the chief of the press department of the foreign commissariat, Palgunov, the Soviet Union had throughout the campaign played the role of a 'valuable second' to Germany. The pronouncements of the Soviet press and propaganda machine, as ambassador von der Schulenburg reported from Moscow, certainly left nothing to be desired but came up to the 'highest expectations' of the German side.[291] Molotov repeatedly (e.g. in his speech to the Supreme Soviet on 31 July 1940) and in his conversations with Hitler in November 1940 and rightly pointed out that the German–Soviet agreement had been 'not without effect on the great German victories', if only because it had provided Germany with the 'calm feeling of security in the east' and had allowed her to employ the bulk of the Wehrmacht in the west.[292] As for the Communist Party of France after the surrender, it called on the French to adopt a friendly attitude to the German occupation troops; it further demanded that 'those who had driven France into the war and had lied to the French people' be publicly sentenced.[293] A 'Soviet–French policy of friendship', as a 'complement to the German–Soviet treaty', was to create the conditions for durable peace in western Europe.[294]

The German offensive in the west marked the climax, but simultaneously also a certain turning-point, in political and propaganda co-operation between the Soviet Union and Germany. The increment of power which the Reich, after the occupation of important countries of central and northern Europe, had now also achieved in western Europe was bound to cause concern in the

[289] Proèktor, *Vojna*, 367; *Befreiungsmission*, 25.
[290] Schulenburg to foreign ministry, 18 June 1940, *DGFP* D ix, No. 471.
[291] See above, n. 268.   [292] Rossi, *Zwei Jahre*, 98, 121; Hillgruber, *Strategie*, 105.
[293] Abetz to military commander, 22 June 1940, according to *Stalin und Hitler*, No. 271; application *re* licence for *L'Humanité*, 25 June 1940, ibid., No. 274; appeal by the CP organization of Paris, 26 June 1940, ibid., No. 275; Berlioz to lawcourt at Riom, 4 Aug. 1940, ibid., No. 297.
[294] Proèktor, *Vojna*, 366, attempts to question this fact, proved by Rossi (*Physiologie*, 402–10).

Soviet Union. Its interest would have been served by a protracted conflict in the west, which would have worn down the strength of both sides.[295] But now the campaign had been brought to a conclusion after but a few weeks and the Soviet Union was facing its powerful ally alone on the Continent. In a conversation with Sir Stafford Cripps, the British ambassador, on 1 July 1940 Stalin allowed it to be understood that the Soviet Union would not favour German hegemony in Europe, though at the same time he declared that he did not believe in the realizability of such intentions as the Reich lacked the necessary naval power. Thus a renewed attempt by the British ambassador in the autumn to win the Soviet Union over 'for a common defence policy *vis-à-vis* Germany' in view of the new situation again ended in failure.[296] However, preparations were started in Moscow to take possession without delay of the Baltic States assigned to the Soviet Union in the secret protocol of 28 September 1939 in order to improve the country's strategic position.[297] On 15 and 16 June the Soviet government issued ultimata demanding the formation of pro-Soviet governments in Lithuania, Latvia, and Estonia. The Soviet troops already in those countries were reinforced and strategic locations occupied, while Stalin's special envoys—Dekanosov for Lithuania, Vyshinsky for Latvia, and Zhdanov for Estonia—prepared for their definitive incorporation by so-called plebiscites.

While Germany and the Western powers, which had guaranteed Romania's integrity in April 1939, were tied down by the conflict in western Europe, the Soviet Union attempted, by force of arms where necessary, to incorporate in its state territory the Romanian regions claimed by it.[298] Whereas the Reich government fully recognized the justification of the Soviet claims to Bessarabia, which had been part of the Tsarist empire from 1812 to 1917, it objected to the incorporation of the Bukowina, which, as Ribbentrop on 23 May 1940 instructed Schulenburg to point out, had been an Austrian crown land, in the fate of whose ethnic Germans the Reich was taking a lively interest.[299] In view of the German objection the Soviet government decided to content itself with the annexation of the northern Bukowina and a corner of Moldavia, and on 26 June 1940 had a short-term ultimatum delivered to the Romanian government on those lines.[300] The same day, at 22.00 hours, the supreme command had transmitted to the Soviet Twelfth Army and the Mechanized Cavalry Group in Kolomyya (commander-in-chief Lieutenant-General Cherevichenko; chief of staff Major-General Boldin; member of the war council Divisional Commissar Nikitin) order No. 001 for the

---

[295] Allard, *Stalin*, 208, 219.   [296] Rossi, *Zwei Jahre*, 124; Hillgruber, *Strategie*, 302–3.
[297] Myllyniemi, *Baltische Krise*, 122 ff.
[298] Köstring, Schulenburg to foreign ministry, 21 May 1940, *DGFP* D ix, No. 286; Schulenburg to foreign ministry, 23 June 1940, ibid. x, No. 4.
[299] Ribbentrop to Schulenburg, 25 June 1940, ibid. x, No. 13; Schulenburg to foreign ministry, 26 June 1940, ibid., No. 20; Schulenburg to foreign ministry, 26 June 1940, ibid., No. 25.
[300] Gafencu, *Vorspiel*, 386 ff.

opening of hostilities and for an attack in the general direction of Cernäuti–Jassy.[301]

Germany advised the Romanian government to yield, so that force was avoided in the end. However, the annexation of the northern Bukowina without prior notification was felt in Berlin as an affront and aroused concern about Germany's vital oil supplies from Romania. The Soviet government for its part felt bound to describe the transfer of substantial portions of Transylvania to Hungary—as adjudicated by the Vienna arbitration award of 30 August 1940—and the subsequent recognition of Romania's integrity by Germany and Italy as a violation of article 3 of the non-aggression treaty, which provided for mutual consultation.[302] However, Ribbentrop disputed this by arguing that the secret protocol of 23 August 1939 referred only to Bessarabia as part of the Soviet sphere of interest.[303] The Soviet government protested against Germany's dispatch of a military mission to Romania—sent there primarily with a view to the protection of the oilfields—and to the fact that she was stationing troops in that country and subsequently also in Bulgaria. Fundamental differences of opinion on the maximum demands of the Soviet government, about the free hand claimed by it in Finland, about its aspirations to control the exits from the Baltic and the Black Sea, and about its wish to extend its 'sphere of interest', now called 'security zone', to Bulgaria, all cast a shadow over Molotov's outwardly glamorous stay in Berlin in November 1940 and foiled Ribbentrop's hopes of including the Soviet Union in the continental bloc of the Tripartite Pact.[304] Tensions were further aggravated by the German attack on Greece and Yugoslavia, with whose government the Soviet Union had established diplomatic relations on 25 June 1940 and concluded a friendship and non-aggression treaty on 5 April 1941.[305] Although the Soviet government did not draw any immediate conclusions and did not even risk lodging a formal protest, with Molotov only verbally expressing regrets, there can be no doubt that the occupation of Yugoslavia, unlike that of the countries of northern and Western Europe, was no longer applauded in Moscow and that a different tune was now being played there.[306]

The deterioration of relations perceptible after the summer of 1940 behind a façade of continuing mutual understanding underwent a temporary check when Stalin himself on 6 May 1941, surprisingly, assumed the post of chair-

---

[301] Ganz geheim, Besonders wichtig, 1. Ausfertigung, Angriffsbefehl Nr. 001 [Top secret, especially important, copy No. 1, order for attack No. 001], staff of the mechanized cavalry group Kolomea, 26 June 1940, 22.00 hrs., BA-MA RH 19 I/122, fos. 59–61.

[302] Schulenburg to foreign ministry, 1 Sept. 1940, *DGFP* D xi, No. 1.

[303] Ribbentrop to Schulenburg, 3 Sept. 1940, ibid., No. 7.

[304] Schulenburg to foreign ministry, 26 Nov. 1940, ibid. xi, No. 404; Hillgruber, *Strategie*, 307.

[305] Schulenburg to foreign ministry, 4 Apr. 1941, *DGFP* D xii, No. 265.

[306] Schulenburg to foreign ministry, 6 Apr. 1941, ibid. xii, No. 288; appeal by the Central Committee of the Communist Party of Germany, Apr. 1941, *Kommunistische Internationale* (Stockholm), according to *Stalin und Hitler*, No. 367; Gafencu, *Vorspiel*, 86–7.

man of the council of people's commissars in place of Molotov. The assumption of government business by the general secretary of the Party, who as recently as 13 April 1941 had assured the Japanese foreign minister Matsuoka that he was 'a convinced adherent of the Axis and an opponent of England and America',[307] was interpreted by the German ambassador and by diplomatic circles in Moscow as a clear indication of the wish to improve Soviet–German relations, as a disavowal of Molotov's policy, which had in a sense become bogged down, and ultimately as a wish to avoid a conflict with Germany for the time being.[308] The real reason for this change of course emerged from Stalin's above-mentioned address to military-academy graduates on 5 May 1941, when he explained that it was necessary to delay conflict with Germany until the autumn of 1941 because war at that time of year was unlikely and because the Red Army would be able to conduct it under more favourable conditions in 1942. At any rate, Stalin's very first measures were to confirm German expectations of an improvement in the political climate.

The Soviet Union's anxiety to meet Germany's wishes, an anxiety unhampered by any other considerations, is most clearly revealed by the manner in which Soviet relations with other countries were adapted to the 'facts created by German arms'.[309] In 1939 the Soviet Union had broken off relations with the Polish government, as well as with the government of Czechoslovakia, although it had a mutual-assistance treaty with that country, and instead recognized as legitimate under international law the independence of the Slovak Republic,[310] which has since been described as a mere 'puppet in Hitler's hands'.[311] Then, in May 1941, Stalin also withdrew diplomatic status from the Norwegian and Belgian ministers in Moscow and broke off relations with the exile governments in London on the ground that these no longer exercised sovereignty over their countries. The break with Greece occurred in June. Only a month previously Stalin had solemnly recognized Yugoslavia's integrity and independence, and received Gavrilović, the Yugoslav minister, 'in the Kremlin like a brother'; now he too was dropped in a manner that was bound to astound 'even the most experienced and hardened observers of Soviet methods', moreover 'before the Germans had even opened their mouths'.[312] These events caused profound despondency especially in Britain, whose government had, after the fall of France, intensively though vainly endeavoured to loosen Soviet–German co-operation.[313] In London they were taken as a clear signal 'that nothing more was to be expected of Moscow'.[314] If

[307] Schulenburg to foreign ministry, 13 Apr. 1941, *DGFP* D xii, No. 333; Rossi, *Zwei Jahre*, 185.
[308] Schulenburg to foreign ministry, 7 May 1941, *DGFP* D xii, No. 468; Schulenburg to foreign ministry, 12 May 1941, ibid., No. 505; Schulenburg to foreign ministry, 19 May 1941, according to *Stalin und Hitler*, No. 383; Schulenburg to foreign ministry, 24 May 1941, *DGFP* D xii, No. 547.
[309] Reichsministerium für Volksaufklärung und Propaganda [Reich Ministry for Public Enlightenment and Propaganda], 4 June 1941, BA-MA RW 4/v. 251.
[310] Radio message from Gottwald, 13 Mar. 1940, according to *Stalin und Hitler*, No. 216.
[311] *Befreiungsmission*, 21–2.   [312] Gafencu, *Vorspiel*, 257.   [313] Allard, *Stalin*, 248 ff.
[314] Gafencu, *Vorspiel*, 266–7; Churchill, *Second World War*, ii/1. 120–1; Allard, *Stalin*, 282 ff.

any further proof were needed of the pro-Axis line of Soviet foreign policy during that period, it may be seen in the fact that the Soviet government now also formally recognized the government of Iraq,[315] which, under Rashid Ali al-Gailani, had just taken up the struggle for liberation from British colonial rule. After the beginning of the German–Soviet war Churchill, in September 1941, reproachfully told the Soviet ambassador Maysky that Britain 'a mere four months ago' had not known 'whether you were not going to march against us with Germany. We even considered it quite probable . . . You Russians are the last people with a right to reproach us.'[316]

A fact of crucial importance to Germany prior to 1941 was that the Soviet Union was supplying the Reich, which was poor in raw materials, with a vast volume of commodities in order to enable it to wage a prolonged war of attrition against the Western powers. Economic relations followed a development of their own, even though this depended on the state of political co-operation at any given time, and greatly contributed to 'broadly buttressing . . . mutual political understanding.'[317] But Hitler and Göring, his plenipotentiary for the four-year plan, as well as being Reich minister for foreign affairs and minister for economic affairs, expressed their profound satisfaction at the scope of Soviet deliveries and emphasized their importance 'for the victorious prosecution of the war'. Even the first economic agreement, concluded on 11 February 1940, was regarded by the Soviet government, according to Stalin, not as 'an ordinary trade agreement' but, in a wider sense, as a treaty on mutual assistance between two states.[318] In line with its undertaking to support Germany economically during her war,[319] the Soviet government was making 'considerable' efforts to satisfy Germany's material requirements.[320] Deliveries and services during the first twelve months of the treaty were to represent a total value of RM800m., comprising, among other things, 1m. t. of oil, 1m. t. of grain, 8000,000 t. of iron ore and scrap, 500,000 t. of phosphate, 100,000 t. of cotton, 100,000 t. of chrome ore, 80,000 t. of manganese, 10,800 t. of copper, 1,575 t. of nickel, 985 t. of tin, and 1,300 t. of raw rubber. As the Soviet Union did not have sufficient quantities of some of these raw materials and metals itself, some of its own imports were diverted to Germany[321] in fulfiment of Stalin's promises.[322] In fact as much as a half of the Soviet Union's own imports were, according to Stalin, to be resold to Germany. Another concession of major importance was the right of transit from and into Romania, as well as the countries of the Middle and Far East,

---

[315] Schulenburg to foreign ministry, 12 May 1941, *DGFP* D xii, No. 505; Werth, *Russia at War*, 124.

[316] Churchill, *Second World War*, iii/2. 406–7. [317] Rossi, *Zwei Jahre*, 111.

[318] Minute by Ritter, 31 Dec. 1939, *DGFP* D viii, No. 499.

[319] Ribbentrop to embassy, 3 Feb. 1940, ibid., No. 594; Friedensburg, 'Kriegslieferungen', 332; Schustereit, 'Mineralöllieferungen'.

[320] Minute by Schnurre, 22 July 1940, *DGFP* D x, No. 206.

[321] Ritter, Schulenburg to foreign ministry, 11 Oct. 1939, ibid. viii, No. 237; Schnurre, Schulenburg to foreign ministry, 29 Oct. 1939, ibid., No. 314.

[322] Minute by Schnurre, 30 Jan. 1940, ibid., No. 584.

through the Soviet Union.[323] In the opinion of German experts, the obligations of the Soviet Union even in the first year of the treaty exceeded the extent strictly needed by Germany from a purely economic point of view and considerably mitigated the effects of the British blockade.

Economic relations, though suffering to some extent on account of Germany's failure to keep to her contractual obligations as well as through differences of opinion on material compensation for the Lithuanian strip of territory near Mariampol, occupied by the Soviet Union though actually assigned to Germany, underwent a further boost at about the turn of 1940–1. The second economic agreement, successfully negotiated on 10 January 1941 as a result of exceptional Soviet obligingness,[324] was described as the biggest trade agreement ever concluded by Germany.[325] In the opinion of Special Envoy Karl Ritter that treaty represented 'the final collapse of the English blockade and the English attempt at an economic encirclement of Germany'.[326] Stalin had, for the past year, realized that by the scale of its assistance to Germany the Soviet Union would earn the enmity of the Western powers, but he had pointed out that the Soviet Union would not be deflected from its attitude either by Britain or by France. Indeed on 11 January 1941 *Izvestiya*, the government daily, mocked the United States for evidently believing that 'it could sell Britain everything, including warships, in full conformity with international law and its position as a neutral, while the Soviet Union cannot even sell grain to Germany without violating its peace policy'.[327] Not only were all delivery dates observed during the months to come, but the Soviet Union in some respects even exceeded its obligations and, in the German view, accomplished 'a truly admirable achievement' even in the organization of the transports. Thus Germany received, prior to the beginning of the German–Soviet war, no less than 2,220,000 t. of grain, maize, and legumes, 1m. t. of oil, 100,000 t. of cotton, and numerous other products, in particular strategically important metals. As late as May 1941 the first deputy of the people's commissar for foreign trade, Krutikov, complained to Berlin that the German side was not providing sufficient rail capacity for the transport of goods from the Soviet–German frontier[328] and simultaneously indicated a projected increase in deliveries.[329] For the following year alone (1942) 5m. t. of grain were promised.[330] Goods trains carrying these commodities were rolling towards the Soviet–German frontier literally until the last hour before the opening of the German attack.

Bearing in mind the vast scope of the Soviet Union's support for the German war effort during the period of imperialist partnership between the

---

[323] Minute by Schnurre, 26 Feb. 1940, ibid., No. 636.

[324] Minute, 2 Dec. 1939, ibid. xi, No. 437; Schnurre, Schulenburg to foreign ministry, 20 Dec. 1940, ibid., No. 539.

[325] Schnurre to Ribbentrop, 25 Dec. 1940, ibid., No. 568.

[326] General instruction by Ritter, 11 Jan. 1941, ibid., No. 640.   [327] *Izvestija* (11 Jan. 1941).

[328] Foreign ministry to OKW and ministry of transport, 21 Apr. 1941, *DGFP* D xii, No. 380.

[329] Minute by Schnurre, 15 May 1941, ibid., No. 521.   [330] Rossi, *Zwei Jahre*, 188.

two powers, one cannot dispute the justness of the words with which Molotov on the morning of 22 June 1941 dismissed the German ambassador von der Schulenburg after accepting Germany's declaration of war from him: 'This we did not deserve.'[331]

[331] Hilger, *Erinnerungen*, 313.

III. From Economic Alliance to a War of Colonial Exploitation

Rolf-Dieter Müller

1. War-economy Aspects and Consequences of the Alliance with the Soviet Union 1939–1940

WHEN the German Wehrmacht invaded the Soviet Union on 22 June 1941 the close economic co-operation between the two countries came to an abrupt end. For nearly two decades it had probably been the most important positive aspect in German–Soviet relations from the treaty of Rapallo to the Hitler–Stalin pact, surviving the transformation of the alliance of two losers into mistrust, fear, and open confrontation; eventually, at the beginning of the Second World War, it was about to approach a new culmination.[1] This statement should not of course conceal the fact that in the area of German economic and rearmament policy there existed certain traditional lines which, regardless of any domestic or foreign-policy changes, were ultimately determined by a persistent revisionist idea, aiming at the establishment of a power-base in the east.[2]

After the failure of the military solution in 1918, efforts had centred on the establishment of an economic sphere of influence in eastern Europe. This was to provide the prerequisite of Germany's 'renewed rise'. The goal of a blockade-proof great-power position for Germany, based on Russia's ability to deliver, became a central part of Hitler's living-space programme. That consistent line, leading from Weimar to the Third Reich, rendered possible a partial congruence between the national-conservative leadership élites and National Socialist expansionist policy. Against this background the turning-points in German–Soviet relations, from the Rapallo treaty via Hitler's 'seizure of power' to his pact with Stalin, can also be explained with the consistent aspiration to extend German influence towards the east—economically, politically, and ultimately territorially and 'racially'.

At the beginning of 1939, when the outbreak of a European war for the assertion of Germany's expansionist aims appeared increasingly probable,[3] the

---

[1] See the survey in Krummacher and Lange, *Krieg und Frieden*.

[2] See Müller, *Tor zur Weltmacht*; on the key role of economic aspects in Hitler's living-space programme see Zitelmann, 'Zur Begründung des "Lebensraum"-Motivs'. The thesis of a German preventive war against the USSR, still occasionally put forward, fails to carry conviction if only for this reason. It altogether lacks plausibility and support. When apologia and polemics take the place of debate, all rational scholarly discourse ceases.

[3] See *Germany and the Second World War*, i. 680 ff., and in particular Weinberg, 'Deutschlands Wille zum Krieg'.

Wehrmacht at first had to adapt itself to the possibility of a war on several fronts, rather like the initial situation in the First World War. In these circumstances the war-economy staff of the High Command of the Wehrmacht concluded that Germany's inadequate supplies of mineral oil would necessitate, right at the start of the war, not only the occupation of the Romanian oilfields but also the conquest of the southern Russian and Caucasian deposits.[4] Simultaneously the demand was being raised in leading economic circles that 'in the event of war the Ukraine must be economically utilized'.[5] Studies by civilian Reich authorities confirmed that 'military-economic immunity to a blockade' could 'even with the utmost efforts and the most favourable conditions concerning the northern region's willingness to supply [Germany] be achieved only to a limited extent *without the economic incorporation of Russia*'.[6]

From a strategic point of view this meant that, in the event of an enemy coalition including the USSR, Germany would have to occupy the Ukraine immediately after the onset of hostilities, in order, on the one hand, to weaken the Soviet regime as an opponent in the war and, on the other, to strengthen Germany's war economy by the exploitation of occupied Soviet territories.[7] Hitler, however, in a daring diplomatic game, succeeded in ensuring the conclusion of a non-aggression treaty with the Soviet Union.[8] An interim solution had thus been achieved which, by shelving the anti-Soviet expansion plans for the moment, enabled Germany to conduct her conflict with the Western powers with reliance on the deliveries promised by Stalin.

Cut off from overseas sources of raw materials and suffering from increasing production and supply bottlenecks, the Reich found itself in a long-term contest of strength with the potential of the Western democracies, whose superiority was bound to be felt increasingly the longer the war went on. The newly established German–Soviet 'partnership' therefore had to demonstrate that it was a viable arrangements at least in the short term, mainly as a means of supplementing the German was economy. It is against this background that German expectations at the beginning of the war concerning the value and the future prospects of a German–Soviet economic alliance have to be seen.

[4] OKW/WStb, No. 1010/39 g.K. WWiVId, Apr. 1939, Die Mineralölversorgung Deutschlands im Kriege [Germany's mineral oil supplies in the war], BA-MA Wi/I. 37.

[5] The plenipotentiary-general of Minister President Field Marshal Göring for special questions of chemical production, Dr C. Krauch, Arbeitsbericht vor dem Generalrat des Vierjahresplans [Report to the Four-year Plan general council], 20–1 Apr. 1939, BA R 25/14.

[6] e.g. Reichsamt für Wirtschaftsausbau, Möglichkeiten einer Großraumwehrwirtschaft unter deutscher Führung [Reich Department of Economic Development, Potential of a large-space war economy under German leadership], Aug. 1939, BA R 25/53 (quotation ibid.).

[7] WStb, Vortrag Major Petri, Wehrwirtschaft des Auslandes [Report by Maj. Petri, The military economy of foreign countries], May 1939, BA-MA Wi/I. 216.

[8] For details see Weber, *Entstehungsgeschichte*.

(*a*) *German–Soviet Trade Exchange and Hitler's War Policy up to the*
   Summer of 1940

Hitler himself explained to the leaders of the Wehrmacht that one need no
longer 'have any fear of a blockade' as Russia would supply 'grain, cattle, coal,
lead, and zinc'.[9] This particularly impressed the chief of staff at the quartermaster-general's office, Colonel (General Staff) Eduard Wagner, who regarded the treaty with Stalin as the 'last salvation'.[10] The war-economy staff of
OKW, however, warned against excessive expectations.

At a first assessment of the situation the greatest immediate advantage was
thought to be the elimination of the dangerous threat to the vital iron-ore
imports from Sweden.[11] Any rapidly effective relief for the German war
economy from deliveries of Soviet raw materials and foodstuffs was out of the
question if only because of inadequate communications. To meet the need for
exact data to assist long-term economic planning, efforts were made to obtain
a multitude of expert opinions and items of information from public and
private economic institutions.[12]

What was probably the most comprehensive study was submitted by the
Weltwirtschaftsinstitut in Kiel as early as September 1939.[13] It contained the
conclusion—at first sight surprising—that in the short term Germany had no
vital need for Soviet raw materials or foodstuffs. Even so, however, a considerable indirect advantage might be gained at least in the agricultural sector
if the Soviet Union were to supply the neutral countries within Germany's
sphere of influence (Denmark, Belgium, Holland) with grain. This would
maintain their economic strength, from which Germany hoped to profit.
Moreover, with regard to three strategically important raw materials (manganese ore, petroleum products, and raw phosphates) urgently needed additional deliveries for the Reich were expected from the Soviet Union. Taken
overall, however, Russia's significance for the German war economy emerged
only in the longer term, as Russia's agricultural base could become 'of
crucial importance in a drawn-out war'. This 'important possibility of supplementing the greater German economic bloc' should be borne in mind also
with regard to German war aims, as even after the conclusion of the present
war the Soviet Union would occupy 'a significant key position in the German

---

[9] Hitler's address to the commanders-in-chief, 22 Aug. 1939, Doc. 798-PS, *IMT* xxvi. 338 ff.

[10] Wagner, *Generalquartiermeister*, 90 (22 Aug. 1939).

[11] WStb, No. 7430/39 g.Kdos. VIa Az. 3i/60/24, 25 Aug. 1939, Nachrichtenblatt Wehrwirtschaft
U.d.S.S.R. No. 1, BA-MA Wi/ID 19; for background see Wittmann, *Schweden*, 170 ff., and Riedel,
'Eisenerzversorgung'.

[12] In the former secret archives of the WiRüAmt there are nearly thirty such studies (BA-MA
RW 19 appendix I/ . . .). Compilation of results: WStb, WWi No. 11540/39 g. VIa Az. 3i/34/11, of
27 Oct. 1939, betr. Rohstoffe UdSSR [concerning Soviet raw materials], BA-MA Wi/VI. 160.

[13] Institut für Weltwirtschaft, Sept. 1939, Das russische Wirtschaftspotential und die
Möglichkeit einer Intensivierung der deutsch-russischen Handelsbeziehungen [The Russian
economic potential and feasibility of intensifying German–Russian trade relations], BA-MA RW
19 appendices I/700, 702.

global economic sector (in contrast to the British–American global economic sector)'.

The opinions of Western experts, attentively followed in Berlin, confirmed that estimate. Although the possibility was acknowledged that Germany, given an undecided continuation of the war, might succeed after about two years in stepping up its economic relations with the Soviet Union to such an extent that the defeat of the Western powers would become inevitable, this would presuppose that Germany could survive two years of siege both in terms of domestic politics and materially, and that the Soviet Union would be prepared to subordinate its own economic needs to providing aid for Germany—and that was considered exceedingly uncertain. On the contrary, it was to be expected that Moscow would exact a high price for its supplies—especially hegemony in eastern and south-east Europe—and, in the long term, would make use of Germany's increasing dependence in order to steer the 'brown revolution' into Bolshevik channels.[14]

In Germany it was mainly Grand Admiral Raeder, the commander-in-chief of the navy, who in October 1939 emphasized the economic advantage of the German–Soviet alliance. Stalin's economic assistance, he said, was of 'decisive' importance. His offer was 'so generous that the economic blockade is almost bound to fail'.[15] Equally optimistic was Colonel Ritter von Niedermayer, who was Reichswehr representative in Moscow during the 1920s and was subsequently on the teaching staff of the Military Academy. In *Militärwissenschaftliche Rundschau*, published by the Army General Staff, he published a euphoric article on Russia,[16] commending the Soviet ally's military and economic strength, which, after a further suppression of 'Jewry', would emerge even more clearly. He invoked in that context an 'amalgamation of German organizational talent and the inexhaustible material resources of Russia's soil', which would render the 'Eurasian military front' unassailable.

The German foreign ministry initially saw no reason to expedite the economics talks which had already begun with Moscow or to ask the Russians for immediate massive supplies of war material.[17] Although mobilization had revealed the shortcomings of Germany's rearmament and led to a marked exacerbation of the economic crisis in Germany,[18] the speedy defeat of Poland, hastened by the participation of the Red Army, gave rise on the German side to expectations of an early conclusion to the war. Hitler therefore rejected a greater mobilization of the German economy and even considered it possible to conduct a campaign against France before the end of the year and thereby to end the war. The promises concerning commercial policy made by the

[14] Hopper, 'Russia', 243; cf. also Einzig, *Economic Problems*.
[15] Quoted from Cecil, *Hitler's Decision*, 61.
[16] Cf. Niedermayer, 'Sowjetrußland', and similarly Schwerdtfeger, *Deutschland*.
[17] On the negotiations see Birkenfeld, 'Stalin', 482 ff., and Eichler, *Wirtschaftsbeziehungen*, 59 ff.
[18] On this see Thomas, *Wehr- und Rüstungswirtschaft*, 153 ff.

Soviets in connection with the non-aggression treaty seemed sufficient to provide adequate elbow-room for the German war economy at least for the next few months. The Soviet Union had undertaken to deliver additional raw materials to a value of RM180m. within two years and to open the transit route to the Far East. In addition, following the joint occupation of Poland, agreement was reached on developing mutual trade in such a way that 'the exchange of goods will again reach the highest volume attained in the past'.[19] Thus, when talks for the conclusion of a comprehensive economic treaty began in the autumn of 1939, Berlin believed itself to be in a favourable negotiating position. Even though within his exclusive circle of leaders Hitler left no doubt that he regarded the pact with Moscow as merely a provisional solution,[20] diplomats and industrialists initially prepared for long-term cooperation with the Soviet Union, taking up concepts of an informal German economic hegemony developed in the 1920s.

Interest was focused on the raw-material and agricultural sectors of the Soviet economy.[21] It was assumed that the employment of German experts and technologies would result in an enormous increase in production, especially if key enterprises were to be directly managed by German firms. Such a penetration of the Soviet Union would create a 'political-economic bloc whose development opportunities are only just beginning to dawn on the horizon as vague surmises'.[22] Although the 'Russia Committee of German Trade and Industry', an amalgamation of firms interested in trade with the Soviet Union, in a memorandum for the Reich chancellery[23] pointed out that the 'discussion of plans aiming at a change or a loosening of Soviet economic policy' was attended by risks, as it might give rise to disquiet in the Soviet Union and thus unfavourably affect negotiations for a treaty, the long-term programme 'with the objective of utilizing the Russian economic space' became the official directive for the German negotiators.[24]

Specifically, this comprised a total of raw-material requirements of the Berlin economic departments, which in volume greatly exceeded Soviet export

[19] Ribbentrop to Molotov, *DGFP* D viii, No. 162 (28 Sept. 1939).

[20] See his remarks to Reichstag deputies on 28 Aug. 1939 (Halder, *Diaries*, 32), to Reichleiters and Gauleiters on 21 Oct. 1939 (Groscurth, *Tagebücher*, 385), and to the commanders-in-chief on 23 Nov. 1939 (No. 789-PS, *IMT* xxvi. 327 ff.), as well as his note to Mussolini conveyed by Ley on 5 Dec. 1939 (Ciano, *Diary 1939–1943*, 181).

[21] For the following see an unsigned instruction of the German foreign ministry, *DGFP* D vii, No, 147 (20 Aug. 1939), and the observations of the secretary of the Russia Committee of German Industry: Tschunke, 'Wirtschaftsplanung'.

[22] 'Weltwirtschaft im Kriegszustand', 1196. In its assessment of such objectives this source agrees with Długoborski and Madajczyk, 'Ausbeutungssysteme', 381–2.

[23] Schreiben des Rußland-Ausschusses der Deutschen Wirtschaft an die Reichskanzlei, betr. Programmatisches über das gegenwärtige Rußlandgeschäft und seinen Ausbau [Letter from the Russia Committee of German Trade and Industry to the Reich chancellery, concerning programmatic observations on the present trade with Russia and its development], 9 Sept. 1939, BA R 43/332.

[24] See OKW/WiRüAmt, Inspekteurbesprechung [inspectors' conference], 12 Oct. 1939, BA-MA Wi/I F 5.1179, and *DGFP* D viii, No. 208 (6 Oct. 1939).

capacities. Thus the agricultural authorities demanded a doubling of the grain deliveries already agreed by Moscow, to a total of at least 2m. t., in order to top up Germany's meagre reserves.[25] Altogether these demands amounted to additional deliveries to a value of over RM1,500m., to be implemented by the Soviet Union within a year. By way of compensation the German side offered deliveries of industrial products over a period of five years—on condition that the Russians provided the necessary raw materials in short supply, or alternatively purchased them for Germany in third-party countries, thereby circumventing the Allied blockade.

The head of the German delegation, Ambassador Ritter, therefore proceeded from the belief that the trade exchanges could be based 'not on reciprocal business, but on unilateral deliveries by the Soviet Union, i.e. on a kind of subsidizing treaty', as it was formulated in a presentation to Hitler.[26] Moreover, efforts were to be made to obtain from Moscow an explicit recognition of German hegemony in the Balkans.[27] A mere four weeks earlier Hitler had still been prepared, if necessary, to offer Stalin the whole of eastern Europe as a sphere of influence, in order to achieve the conclusion of the treaty. But now Berlin was evidently hoping to get the economically vital supplementary region of eastern and south-eastern Europe under its own control and similarly to gain the Soviet Union as a willing source of war supplies.

Here and elsewhere the ancient German hegemony claim *vis-à-vis* Russia, the 'urge towards the east', concealed by recent formulas of alliance but given its extreme expression in Hitler's living-space goals, emerged clearly. But whether, in the economic and strategic conditions at the beginning of the war, Germany would be able to achieve Russia's alignment with the requirements of Germany's war economy solely by a policy of economic influence and political and territorial arrangements remained to be seen.

The Soviet leadership at first reacted calmly to the growing German pressure: it had no reason to extend deliveries to a war-waging and blockaded German Reich beyond the limit already conceded and thereby weaken its own rearmament efforts. It seems that Stalin for his part intended to derive the greater advantage from the economic relations and to get the German war economy to work extensively for the Soviet Union. Clearly this was in line with his interest in a protracted war of attrition between the capitalist great powers, which would absorb the industrial strength of the belligerents without one side or the other being capable of a decisive blow. As a neutral power wooed by both sides, the Soviet Union would be able to build up its strength unhampered, in order eventually to emerge as a referee in the struggle for the distribution of power in Europe. Moscow therefore endeavoured, moreover

[25] See the minutes of the meeting of the ministerial council for Reich defence on 16 Oct. 1939, No. 2852-PS, *IMT* xxxi. 235.

[26] *DGFP* D viii, No. 430 (8 Dec. 1939).

[27] Note by Weizsäcker, ibid., No. 137 (26 Sept. 1939).

with some success and under the mistrustful eyes of Berlin,[28] to maintain and extend its trade relations with the Western powers, and particularly with the United States, in order to become less dependent on Germany in the field of valuable technologies needed for speedier rearmament.

In the negotiations with Germany the Soviet representativess made it clear from the start that they rejected any kind of performances in advance. They countered the German maximum demands with such rigorous ideas of their own that the intended deal seemed, from the German point of view, to have been stood on its head.[29] In exchange for raw-material deliveries worth RM420m. over one year Berlin was to undertake to supply industrial goods to a value of over RM1,500m. Particular irritation was caused on the German side by the Soviet list of requirements, which contained almost exclusively the most modern military material. Although originally Hitler had been prepared to hand over only limited quantities of material already in use, he had to yield to Moscow's ultimatum-like demands and permit a large Soviet commission to inspect the most important German armament works.[30]

This obligingness was due to a change in German war policy. In the late autumn of 1939 Hitler found himself compelled to postpone his intended decisive battle against France until the following spring and to use the time thus gained for an intensive rearmament phase.[31] With dismay he now realized the poor performance of Germany's armaments industry, especially in the area of ammunition; this might have been acceptable in expectation of an early conclusion of the war after the Polish campaign, but was inadequate for an armaments race with the Western powers.[32] As total mobilization of the economy had to be avoided for political and ideological reasons, and as the exceptionally hard winter of 1939–40 and setbacks in the economic war for control of the neutral continental markets further increased tensions within the German war economy, with finally the prospect of a 'collapse of food supplies in the course of the second year of the war, as in 1918',[33] it was doubly important to step up imports of raw materials and foodstuffs at all costs.

Thus the German leadership inevitably turned its attention increasingly to short-term opportunities for developing German–Soviet trade. Hitler eventually urged a speedy conclusion of a treaty with Moscow,[34] which, in the given

[28] See the letter of the head of the economic-policy department of the German foreign ministry, Wiehl, to the embassy in Moscow, ibid., No. 273 (18 Oct. 1939).

[29] Minute of Legation Councillor Meyer-Heydenhagen (political dept.), ibid., No. 335 (8 Nov. 1939); for the German reaction see Groscurth, *Tagebücher*, 302.

[30] Gibbons, 'Soviet Industry', 50 ff.

[31] *Das Deutsche Reich und der Zweite Weltkrieg*, v/1. 406 ff.

[32] Thomas, *Wehr- und Rüstungswirtschaft*, 148 ff.

[33] Observations by Secretary of State Backe in the Four-year Plan general council, 14 Feb. 1940, PA, Handakte Ritter, Beih. deutsche Kriegswirtschaft [file Ritter, appendix German war economy]; on the problems of wartime German foreign trade generally see Volkmann, 'NS-Außenhandel'.

[34] Note by Ritter, 10 Jan. 1940, PA, Büro des Staatssekretärs, Rußland [office of the secretary of state, Russia], vol. ii; cf. also *DGFP* D viii, No. 543 [16 Jan. 1940].

circumstances, could be achieved only by shelving the far-reaching German demands and by barter offers which entailed a restriction of Germany's own rearmament programme.

On the other side, Moscow too found itself compelled to be more obliging. The war against Finland was forcing Stalin to modernize his armaments and to move closer to his German ally. After all, he could not entirely rule out a reversal of alliances, i.e. an arrangement between Hitler and the Western powers at the expense of the Soviet Union. It had to be remembered that, on the one hand, the Soviet–Japanese front in the Far East could flare up at any moment or that, on the other, the Western powers might be preparing for action against the Soviet Union while hostilities on the German–French front were slight for the time being.[35]

As a result of a gradual *rapprochement* an economic agreement[36] was signed on 11 February 1940. Although this was magnified by National Socialist propaganda into a brilliant success,[37] it bore the unmistakable character of a compromise. The envisaged volume of RM600–700m. was closer to Moscow's original ideas, while Berlin succeeded in getting accepted at least some of its demands for Soviet advance deliveries. Although not all German wishes had been fulfilled, the outcome of the negotiations was of considerable importance for Germany's future economic planning. Hitler now had sufficient latitude to solve the material problems of his intended campaign in the west. In the Four-year Plan general council, the command centre of the German war economy, there was talk of the 'Russian deliveries' decisive importance for the outcome of the war',[38] and the Reich ministry for economic affairs made it known that 'the Russians have already supplied us with vital commodities, such as grain, oil, and phosphates, and have promised further great quantities of raw materials which are simply irreplaceable to our war economy and national economy. For that reason all misgivings, even those of the greatest domestic importance, must be set aside.'[39] In return the Reich had to agree to extensive deliveries of German armaments to the Soviet Union, which were to prove a perceptible burden on German armament production for years to come—especially in the naval-engineering and machine-tool areas.[40]

---

[35] Martin, 'Friedenskontakte'; Lupke, *Japans Rußlandpolitik*; Kahle, 'Infiltrationsbemühungen'; Lorbeer, *Westmächte*.

[36] *DGFP*, D, viii, No. 607; for the background see also Birkenfeld, 'Stalin', 492 ff.; Eichler, *Wirtschaftsbeziehungen*, 121 ff.

[37] See 'Gesprengter Blockadering'; Rundschreiben des AA [German foreign ministry circular], 18 Jan. 1940, betr. Deutsche Wirtschaftspolitik im Abwehrkampf gegen die Feindblockade [German economic policy in the defensive struggle against the enemy blockade], PA, V.A.A. beim Reichskommissar Ukraine, Runderlasse: Wirtschaft.

[38] V.P. 4018—Minutes of the 7th session of the general council, 28 Feb. 1940, PA, Handakte Ritter, Beiheft deutsche Kriegswirtschaft [file Ritter, appendix German war economy].

[39] W I V 636/40, Minutes of a conference in the RWM, 5 Feb. 1940, PA, HaPol.: Handakten Wiehl, Rußland, Bd. 13.

[40] For an assessment see Birkenfeld, 'Stalin', 492–3.

Under the pressure of economic circumstances Germany thus found herself in a greater measure of dependence on the Soviet Union than had originally been intended, a dependence which was likely to increase the longer the war continued. A declining German export capacity would be faced with growing delivery obligations, while the Soviet Union for its part—given an increasing consumption of its own for rearming the Red Army—would presumably demand a progressively higher price for its deliveries of raw materials to the Reich. Against the background of Hitler's decision to employ all reserves for his planned campaign against France, without any regard to the future,[41] his win-or-bust gambling emerges in this context too. In the event of a failure of the German offensive Germany would be totally dependent on Soviet aid; victory in the west, on the other hand, would clear the way for the conquest of those raw-material resources which were indispensable to the Reich if it wished to attain self-sufficient world-power status, and which, so long as they were available to a foreign autonomous power, would always represent both a threat and a temptation. The symptoms of paralysis in Germany's war economy reinforced that argument.[42] They resulted not only from organizational shortcomings of mobilization and the consequences of a grave crisis in coal supplies, but also from the loss of imports due to the Allied blockade; this amounted to 62 per cent in December 1939. The reduction of Germany's export volume by 84 per cent was an indication of a growing inability to pay for urgently needed imports with hard currency or with goods.[43] Although Moscow had promised a twelvefold increase of its share in Germany's imports—which would have offset approximately half the losses due to the blockade—weather-related transport difficulties and the necessary running-in period set a limit to Soviet deliveries until the spring of 1940.[44]

Thus a general impression was created in Germany that one had passed 'close to the edge of a major crisis'.[45] One consequence was that German firms repeatedly refused to accept Soviet orders if there was doubt that they could be fulfilled punctually. As, however, this meant a negative charge to the German clearing-account, involving the risk of a Soviet suspension of deliveries, Berlin endeavoured to fill its contractual export obligations at least in some areas. In order to send the Russians a signal of willingness to deliver, Germany even borrowed a few thousand tonnes of coal from the Dutch government.[46]

[41] Minute by Thomas of a conversation with Göring on 30 Jan. 1940, No. 606-EC, *IMT* xxxvi. 580–1.

[42] See Minister President Field Marshal Göring, plenipotentiary for the Four-year Plan, V.P. 3891 g., Übersicht über die wirtschaftliche Gesamtlage (zusammengestellt auf Grund der Lageberichte der Oberpräsidenten, Regierungspräsidenten und entsprechenden Behörden (Führungsstäbe Wirtschaft)) [Review of the overall economic situation, compiled on the basis of the situation reports from Oberpräsidenten, Regierungspräsidenten, and the relevant authorities [economic command staffs]] as of 24 Feb. 1940, BA R 26 I/44.

[43] *Das Dentsche Reich und der Zweite Weltkrieg*, v/1, 391 ff.

[44] Disagreeing with the political interpretation of Schustereit, 'Mineralöllieferungen', 340.

[45] Letter by Wagner, 3 Feb. 1940: Wagner, *Generalquartiermeister*, 156.

[46] Memorandum of 5 Feb. 1940 (above n. 39); on the problem of German coal supplies see also Riedel, *Eisen*, 271 ff.

TABLE I.III.I. *Germany's Trade with the USSR during the First Ten Months of the War*[a]

	Imports[b]	Exports[c]
1939		
September	5	—
October	6	4
November	15	3
December	12	5
1940		
January	13	5
February	28	3
March	27	4
April	46	13
May	58	24
June	94	48

[a] Measured against the pre-war peak.
[b] 1930 = 100.
[c] 1931 = 100.

Source: Zahlen zur Entwicklung des deutschen Außenhandels seit Kriegsbeginn [Figures on the development of German foreign trade since the beginning of the war], bearb. vom Schlesischen Institut für Wirtschafts- und Konjunkturforschung Breslau [compiled by the Silesian Institute for Economic and Cyclical Research, Breslau], Aug. 1940, Table 15, BA R7/3413, Archiv RWiM/Hauptabt. V Export. Further data in Friedensburg, 'Kriegslieferungen'.

Unimpressed, the Soviet side energetically insisted on the implementation of promised German coal deliveries[47] and refused to accept German manœuvres to dictate prices.[48] Six weeks before the opening of the offensive in the west the Soviet Union suspended its oil and grain deliveries in order to assert its claims. At a hurriedly summoned meeting of all war-economy leadership bodies Göring thereupon declared that there was no alternative to accepting the Soviet demands:

All German departments must proceed from the fact that the Russian raw materials are absolutely vital to us, that for a prolonged war further contracts would have to be concluded, and that, on this account, it is necessary for the current contracts to be executed promptly and all mistrust on the part of the Russians dispelled. According to an explicit decision by the Führer, where reciprocal deliveries to the Russians are

[47] Memorandum of Ambassador Ritter, *DGFP*, D, viii, No. 677 (15 Mar. 1940).
[48] Telegram No. 482 of the German embassy in Moscow to the foreign ministry on 9 Mar. 1940, PA, Büro des Staatssekretärs, Rußland, Bd. 2 [office of the secretary of state, Russia, vol. ii].

endangered, even German Wehrmacht deliveries must be held back so as to ensure punctual delivery to the Russians.[49]

Moscow, nevertheless, was not prepared to resume deliveries until the envisaged quantities of coal had arrived in the Soviet Union. Only at the opening of the German offensive against the Western powers did the Russians cool the conflict and resume deliveries. After all, Stalin had an interest in supporting an intensification of hostilities and thereby tying Hitler down in the west.

It is significant that the military success in the west induced the Wilhelmstrasse to adopt a considerably tougher line *vis-à-vis* the Soviet Union. The ambassador in Moscow was instructed to reject all Soviet complaints about the implementation of the current deals, simply to dispute any shortfall in Germany's implementation of the treaty, and to criticize the performance of Soviet delivery obligations.[50] Germany had to be able to count on uninterrupted supplies of raw materials from the Soviet Union in future. When Stalin thereupon in a personal letter to Göring endeavoured to settle the delivery squabbles once and for all,[51] German government quarters believed that further concessions to the Russians were now unnecessary and that Moscow could be put under pressure to fulfil its delivery obligations. At least the troublesome problem of the coal and oil agreements could now be regulated 'favourably, in accordance with Germany's wishes'.[52]

(b) The Concept of Large-space Economy and the Russian Problem

The unexpectedly rapid successes of the Wehrmacht created a new situation for German–Soviet relations. Latent mistrust of Soviet willingness to deliver, present not only in military circles, and a sense of growing danger to Germany's policy of expansion[53] temporarily receded entirely into the background. In a euphoria of victory it was confidently expected that the war would be concluded by a compromise peace with Britain on the basis of a global share-out, and that Germany in consequence would have a free hand on the Continent. Towards the end of May the 'Society for European economic planning and large-space economy', which enjoyed the support of high-ranking representatives of industry, the administration, and the Wehrmacht, presented an expert opinion[54] which mapped out a 'continental-European large-scale economy under German leadership', which 'in its ultimate peace aim would embrace all the nations of the Continent from Gibraltar to the Urals and from the North Cape to the island of Cyprus, with natural colonial

[49] *DGFP* D ix, No. 32 (1 Apr. 1940).

[50] Letter from Schnurre to the Moscow embassy, ibid., No. 85 (10 Apr. 1940).

[51] Memorandum by Ambassador Ritter to the Moscow embassy, ibid., No. 109 (13 Apr. 1940).

[52] Wi VIa, Geheime Aufzeichnung über Mineralöllieferungen aus der UdSSR [Secret memorandum on mineral-oil deliveries from the USSR], 1 June 1940, BA-MA Wi/I,262.

[53] See Beck's memorandum of 20 Nov. 1939: Groscurth, *Tagebücher*, 487; and sect. I.IV.1(*a*) (Klink).

[54] Memorandum on the establishment of a Reich commissariat for large-scale economics, 31 May 1940: *Weltherrschaft im Visier*, No. 102.

radiations into the Siberian region and across the Mediterranean into Africa'. In the view of the experts there could be no doubt about Russia being included in the German large-scale economy. In the specific plans for the conclusion of peace in the west, the 'further development of close economic relations with Russia' had therefore been regarded as 'one of the most important tasks' since the end of May 1940. How this was to be achieved, however, remained an open question. While the deputy head of the economic department in the foreign ministry, Clodius, in his memorandum[55] argued that Germany after the end of the war would have a growing productive strength and would therefore be better able to satisfy Russian demands, Ambassador Ritter in his memorandum emphasized the need, on the one hand, for a considerable increase in trade with the Soviet Union and, on the other, for defending Germany's economic hegemony in the Baltic and in south-eastern Europe against competition from Moscow.[56] In an appraisal of the situation by the naval operations command of 2 June 1940 the possibility was not even ruled out that the Soviet Union might boycott economic co-operation in the long term and thus manœuvre Germany into a tight corner.[57]

German trade policy was nevertheless faced with the question whether the impending negotiations for a new economic agreement for 1941 could really be dictated by Germany. Unlike the situation with her allies (Italy, Slovakia), which were in any case dependent on Germany, or with the countries seeking a *rapprochement* either voluntarily (Romania, Hungary, Finland) or under pressure (Sweden, Switzerland), or the European countries occupied or annexed by Germany, where the Reich was ruthlessly able to assert its claims to political and economic domination, Berlin had no reliable instrument of pressure for bringing the Soviet Union into greater dependence. Even though diplomats and military men saw no acute danger threatening from the Soviet Union, they realized that Stalin's great-power policy represented a potential threat to Germany's hegemony in Europe.

The problems of German large-area policy emerged clearly from the detailed plans and calculations initiated by the ministry of economic affairs on Göring's instructions.[58] While, amidst the general euphoria over victory in the west, the European continent including Britain and the African and Middle Eastern spheres were already being regarded as available to German interests, with a full realization of the need to secure Russia's raw materials, the present political and economic 'special situation' of the Soviet Union *vis-à-vis* a German-dominated greater European sphere was regretted. According to the calculations of the Reich department for economic development, even with full utilization of production capacities in Europe, Africa, and the Middle East there would remain a shortfall in Germany's supply balance sheet with regard

[55] Memorandum of Minister Clodius, 30 May 1940: *Anatomie der Aggression*, No. 3.
[56] Memorandum by Karl Ritter, 1 June 1940: ibid., No. 4.
[57] No. 170-C, *IMT* xxxiv. 686.
[58] *Das Dentsche Reich und der Zweite Weltkrieg*, v/1. 491 ff.

to 19 out of 33 vital raw materials.[59] A number of other studies by reputable economic institutions confirmed the realization that the German large-area economy within its existing outlines did not dispose of a sufficient measure of domestic resources either in foodstuffs or in industrial raw-material production.[60] The German metal industry, in an expert opinion for the Reich government, pointed out that, according to its calculations, the production capacities for the most important non-ferrous metals in Europe and Africa were not nearly sufficient to cover Germany's future peacetime requirements, let alone her present war needs.[61] In order to match up to the 'steel block of the USA', the principal secretary of the section for the iron-producing industry stated in a lecture to the naval command on 14 June 1940[62] that the import of Russian ores would have to be absolutely assured. This statement explains why one of the leading economic research institutes launched a new series of publications on the Soviet economy, for in-house use, with a survey of 'export possibilities for the products of the Soviet mining industry'.[63]

While Germany's military successes had undoubtedly resulted in a certain easing of the supply balance of the German war economy, prospects for the more distant future appeared exceedingly doubtful in many areas. Especially serious was Germany's dependence on Soviet grain supplies. In the balancing of accounts in the summer of 1940 the German side already counted on Soviet willingness to deliver in the coming year, in order to meet the most pressing needs of Germany and the occupied territories.[64] The quantity of one million tonnes of grain already promised by Moscow was regarded as unsatisfactory. If the Soviet Union were prepared to employ its vast grain reserves, exports could easily be trebled. 'Actually it would without any doubt be easy for Russia to meet the central-European bloc's import requirements of all agricultural produce, provided her economy in general, and her agriculture in particular, were more productive.'[65] However, any influence on the organization or the alignment of the Soviet economy along German requirements, such as was

[59] Reichsamt für Wirtschaftsausbau, Die Rohstoff-Versorgung Europas bei voller Ausnutzung der Gewinnungsmöglichkeiten in Europa und Afrika (nach Zahlen von 1938) [Europe's raw-material supplies given full utilization of extraction potentials in Europe and Africa, according to data from 1938], BA R 25/40.

[60] See Denkschrift des Instituts für Konjunkturforschung, Die Selbstversorgungsmöglichkeiten des mitteleuropäischen Wirtschaftsblocks mit Lebensmitteln [memorandum of the Institute for Economic Research, Self-supply capacities of the central European bloc with regard to foodstuffs], June 1940, BA-MA RW 19 appendix I/1147.

[61] Expert opinion of the Fachgruppe Metallerzbergbau [specialized group for metal-ore mining], 20 Aug. 1940: Schumann, 'Neuordnung', No. 3; these findings were confirmed also by the extensive expert opinion prepared for OKW by Dr F. Friedensburg, Die deutsche Roh- und Treibstofflage [Germany's raw-material and fuel situation], 1939–40, BA-MA Wi/I F 5.2199.

[62] Memorandum on the lecture by J. W. Reichert, 14 June 1940: Eichholtz, *Kriegswirtschaft*, 296.

[63] Schriften des Instituts für Konjunkturforschung, Die Wirtschaft der UdSSR in Einzeldarstellungen [Publications of the Institute for Economic Research, The economy of the USSR in separate presentations], No. 1, Sept. 1940, BA-MA RW 19 appendix I/1135.

[64] See 'Kann Europa ausgehungert werden?'

[65] Memorandum of the Institute for Economic Research (above n. 60).

already being practised in other European countries, remained illusory in the case of the Soviet Union.

What was at stake was explained by the director of the Statistical Office, Walter Grävell, in the leading National Socialist economic periodical.[66] Germany, he argued, must possess a 'supply region available to her at all times', in which Russia would be playing a greater role in supplying Germany with vital commodities than before the war. He expected the exchange of goods to reach 'a scale of thousands of millions'. By contrast, it was an open secret among experts that Russia most probably would not be willing for much longer to play the part of supplier of raw materials and be a market for industrial manufactures. A contemporary economic doctoral thesis argued: 'Russia's expansionist strength is enormous, and planning enables her increasingly to develop that expansionist strength. Given an appropriate trade policy, Russia could bring the Baltic and the Scandinavian states into full dependence on her and thus achieve a position of hegemony in the Baltic area.'[67] Moscow's economic influence could moreover extend unhampered to the Indian subcontinent and the Far East, thereby cutting Germany off from vital foreign markets. That development was being favoured by the present war situation, 'and if Russia succeeds in staying in this war as a profiting neutral, she will have gained a lead over the other countries'.

It is against this background that the prospects of German–Soviet trade at the time have to be judged. The Russia Committee of German Industry in a position paper for the Reich chancellery on 18 July 1940 drew attention to the fact that Soviet readiness for deliveries depended on the course of the war and demanded a number of changes in German–Russian trade relations, all of which were designed to gain a more advantageous position for Germany *vis-à-vis* the Soviet Union.[68] The doubtful prospects of trade with Russia also emerged four days later in a balance sheet of the foreign ministry.[69] Major difficulties were expected because of the considerable arrears of Germany's clearing obligations. Only about half of the Soviet deliveries already made had been covered by German exports. Fulfilling of the orders made by the Soviet trade representatives in Germany, to a value of RM600m., seemed the more uncertain as they concerned almost exclusively high-value capital goods and war material, which competed with extremely urgent orders for the Wehrmacht and the armament industry.

On the same day Walther Funk, the minister for economic affairs, proposed at a conference with the other departmental heads that, by way of a basis for the Führer's decision, the principles and objectives of a future German large-

---

[66] Grävell, 'Richtungswechsel'.   [67] Soika, *Außenhandel*, 166.

[68] Confidential letter from the Russia Committee of German Trade and Industry, 18 July 1940: *Mißtrauische Nachbarn*, No. 41.

[69] *DGFP* D x, No. 206 (22 July 1940). Similar complaints are found also in a letter from the Reich Group for Industry to Schnurre, 23 July 1940, quoted in Gibbons, 'Soviet Industry', 66.

space economy be summed up.[70] Germany now possessed 'the political power in Europe to enforce a reorganization of the economy in line with her require-ments'. It therefore followed 'that the countries must align themselves along-side ourselves'. In dealing with the separate countries Funk expressly excluded the Soviet Union, as 'Russia's position *vis-à-vis* the territories looked after by Germany is still uncertain'. In the light of his warning, approved by Hitler a few days later, that the 'greater German economic space' must not 'become dependent on forces or powers over which we have no influence'[71] it becomes clear that the top leadership was not prepared to accept that 'uncertain' position of the Soviet Union.

Interest in a clarification of that problem was shown also by German industry. If one views its demand that 'the Reich government will use the consequences of the victorious war to bring about such conditions as will ensure the economic and military freedom of the German people for the longest possible time ahead'[72] against the background of the economic-policy analyses, the complaint about the Soviet Union's 'special position' is under-standable. In the opinion of the IG-Farben concern,[73] this would in the long run lead to an alarming development which, 'given constant political condi-tions, would be apt to affect and disturb the confrontation of the European chemical industry with the other large areas'. This company probably the most powerful enterprise of the private sector, had evidently learnt something during the preceding months that would explain its interest in a reshaping of German–Soviet relations.

In connection with the negotiations for the German–Soviet trade agreement for 1940 the firm had been pressured by the foreign ministry's negotiators to comply with the Soviet request for the delivery of a complete plant for the production of synthetic rubber and motor-fuel.[74] Although such installations were at the top of the priority list of German rearmament, it was to be expected that the execution of this deal would take at least three or four years. Thus, while the actual implementation remained uncertain, the price could be entered immediately in the balance sheet of German–Soviet exchanges and thus converted into Soviet raw-material deliveries.

From the outset the management of the concern was not too pleased at having to hand over to the Russians, for political reasons, its most secret and modern production technology.[75] It found its misgivings confirmed when

---

[70] Secret memorandum of a conference of departmental heads in the Reich ministry for economic affairs, 22 July 1940: *Anatomie der Aggression*, No. 7.

[71] Funk, 'Wirtschaftsordnung'; for Hitler's approval see Volkmann, 'Autarkie', 71.

[72] Letter by the head of the Economic Group for the Metal Industry to the minister for economic affairs, concerning large-scale economy, 15 Aug. 1940: Schumann, 'Neuordnung', No. 1.

[73] Letter from IG-Farbenindustrie AG to the minister for economic affairs, 3 Aug. 1940: Eichholtz, *Kriegswirtschaft*, 248 ff.

[74] See Birkenfeld, 'Stalin', 498.

[75] On the following see the letter from IG-Farbenindustrie AG to OKW/WStb, betr. Hydrierung Rußland [concerning hydrogenation, Russia], 10 Apr. 1940, BA-MA Wi/VI. 13b.

Moscow tried to consolidate its advantage by insisting that Soviet experts should be permitted unimpeded access to all manufacturing secrets even during the project phase. The German concern was to provide training courses of several months for a substantial number of them, so that they could acquaint themselves with all plants under construction or in operation in Germany. The Soviet Union moreover expected the German side to take full responsibility for the subsequent erection and operation of the plant ordered. Of considerable importance was the demand for inspection facilities in all workshops and supply enterprises, where parts of the apparatus were manufactured. This would give the Russians possession of the most important production secrets—the manufacturing methods for special apparatus.

The greatest alarm, however, was caused by the Soviet wish to have handed over to them the IG-Farben process for the production of toluene. In this area of high-quality aviation fuel, work in Germany was still in the development stage. However, the Soviet Union even then demanded a binding agreement that, once IG-Farben had gained full-scale production experience, it would immediately be able to acquire the relevant patents.

When the IG-Farben management thereupon alerted the Wehrmacht High Command, the Reich ministry for economic affairs, and the Luftwaffe command, it was soon realized in Berlin that more was at stake on this issue than the preservation of private-enterprise business interests.[76] Here was the beginning of a dangerous development which fundamentally ran counter to German large-area economic plans. Besides, weighty military interests were involved. The representative of the Luftwaffe pointed out that 'the lead of the German air force is largely due' to the employment of high-aromatic, i.e. higher-grade, aviation fuels, achieved by the use of toluene. The Soviet air force, on the other hand, because of a shortage of that substance and a lack of the relevant manufacturing know-how, predominantly used inferior fuels which reduced the performance of the aircraft engines and were therefore regarded internationally as outdated. Apart from this delicate question the delivery of the Buna (synthetic rubber) and hydrogenation plants ordered by Moscow would, given the tight capacity situation, be at the expense of German development plans and thus of the supply of fuels and rubber to the Wehrmacht. That explains, on the one hand, the breaking off of negotiations on this issue in June 1940 and, on the other, the firm's complaint about the Soviet Union's 'special position' in Germany's greater economic sphere.[77]

By the summer of 1940 two tendencies were thus emerging in the economic field with increasing clarity, both of them—quite apart from Hitler's strategic and ideological aims—jeopardizing German–Soviet co-operation on the basis of the Hitler–Stalin pact. The first of these was the Soviet Union's own

[76] OKW Az. 66 b 3340 WiRüAmt/Ro No. 2710/40 g. Vf, memorandum of a conversation concerning the setting up of a hydrogenation plant for aviation fuels in Russia on 13 and 15 Apr. 1940, dated 22 Apr. 1940, ibid.

[77] Letter to the ministry for economic affairs, 3 Aug. 1940: Eichholtz, *Kriegswirtschaft*, 256.

growing consumption of the raw materials and foodstuffs on the availability
of which the Reich's war-economy plans were based; the second was
Germany's obvious 'inability' to force Russia into the role, originally assigned
to her, of a supply-source for a future large-area German economy. The
massive and unimpeded build-up of Soviet armaments, which profited from
Germany's enforced assistance, as well as the unmistakable policy of autarky
pursued by the Moscow leadership, represented a long-term threat to German
great-power and world-power aspirations, a threat which had to be taken
seriously.

The most important indication, in Berlin's eyes, was the Soviet action
against the Baltic States and in the Balkans.[78] Although Stalin was only moving
into the positions assigned to him in 1939, the German reaction was one of
irritation. Both the Baltic region, important for Germany's food supplies, and
the Balkans—then the most important supplier of oil to the German war
economy[79]—had already been viewed by the economic planners as secure
parts of the large-area economy.

On the assumption of an early compromise peace with Britain, the National
Socialist leadership, right up to the end of 1940, was confident of being able to
conduct the apparently inevitable—and, as far as Germany was concerned,
actually intended—conflict with the Soviet Union with a secure rear in the
west. In the course of July, however, it became increasingly clear that Britain
was continuing the struggle with unremitting determination and, in doing so,
was able to rely on increasing support from the United States. Thus a strategic
dilemma arose, in which the Russian problem increasingly moved to the
centre of attention. Hence the Army High Command's preparations for a
limited military strike against the Soviet Union, designed to consolidate the
German claim to hegemony in eastern and south-eastern Europe and to
occupy the economically valuable western territories of the Soviet Union.[80]
Such a move seemed indicated in view of the latest calculations of the Statistical Office on Germany's raw-material position, which clearly revealed her
serious dependence on raw-material deliveries from Russia and the Balkans.[81]
Parallel reflections by the naval command also kept within the framework of a
limited war of annexation on the model of the First World War. In his
'Observations on Russia' of 28 July 1940[82] the chief of staff of the naval
command, Rear-Admiral Fricke, based his arguments mainly on the economic-policy aspects of a military solution in the east. Germany's security, he
suggested, demanded 'the most self-sufficient economy possible, especially

[78] See Volkmann, 'Ökonomie und Machtpolitik'; Myllyniemi, *Krise*.

[79] See sect. I.v at nn. 17 ff. (Förster).   [80] See sect I.iv.1(*b*) (Klink).

[81] Statistisches Reichsamt, Abt. VIII, Rohstoffversorgung des mitteleuropäisch-großdeutschen
Wirtschaftsraumes nach dem Krieg [Supplies of raw material for the central European–Greater
German economic area after the war], July 1940, 103, BA R 24/24.

[82] Chief of staff of the naval command, Rear-Adm. Fricke, Betrachtungen über Rußland, 28
July 1940: Salewski, *Seekriegsleitung*, iii. 137 ff.; for an assessment see Schreiber, 'Mittelmeerraum',
74–5.

with regard to commodities vital in war (e.g. oil, foodstuffs)'. This necessitated raw materials and market opportunities. For both roles Russia was 'ideally suited'. With respect to the planned development of a European large-area economy under German leadership the 'naturally given possibilities of supplementation between German and Russia in nearly all areas of economic life' inevitably leapt to the eye time and again. Fricke believed that economic co-operation as such could be continued also by political means, provided that Russia was weak both politically and militarily, and would bow to German hegemony. Of that, however, he saw no sign. On the contrary, the 'strong economic pressure emanating from a giant empire such as Russia on its neighbour states', the strengthening of the Soviet position on the Baltic, and finally the 'spirit of Bolshevism' which was threatening Europe compelled Germany to liquidate 'this chronic danger one way or another'. From this Fricke derived a number of military reflections, based on the assumption that the political leadership intended 'to clean up matters in the east', with the objective of consolidating the German position on the Baltic and in the Balkans, of annexing the Baltic region as well as part of the Ukraine, 'in order to lay down its peace conditions on the basis of that possession'.

It is impossible to say whether Hitler was informed of these ideas. The economic problems, at any rate, were presented to him once more on 30 July 1940 by the minister for economic affairs.[83] The following day he met the top military leaders and informed them of his firm resolve 'to eliminate Russia'.[84] The war aims formulated by him on that occasion differed substantially in their spatial dimension from those of the general staff: Hitler, in view of the by then obvious necessity to continue the war against Britain for an uncertain period of time and to prepare for an American entry into the war, did not aim merely at 'gaining space' but at smashing the Russian state at a single blow. The operation envisaged for May 1941 would make Germany master of Europe and the Balkans. On these lines Göring a few days later issued instructions that the economic 'new order' plans were to assume that Germany would extend her economic sphere of power 'in Europe and in the rest of the world as far as possible'.[85]

This meant the conclusion of the first phase of the definition of Germany's plans of aggression against the Soviet Union. The decision-making process, proceeding simultaneously with the extension of the German sphere of domination in northern and western Europe, was certainly not initiated solely by Hitler's still vague remarks that he was in principle prepared for conflict with the USSR. Nor can it be understood solely as a reaction to the developing war situation or, more particularly, to Soviet foreign policy. Additional factors were economic considerations and interests which, after Germany's successful expansion on the Continent, veered towards a stronger incorporation of Russia in the German sphere of power. Two levels can be distinguished here,

[83] See *DGFP* D x, No. 261 (30 July 1940).   [84] Halder, *Diaries*, 534 (31 July 1940).
[85] Letter from Göring to Funk, 17 Aug. 1940: Freymond, *Le IIIᵉ Reich*, 245–6.

whose link-up in the summer of 1940 decisively promoted the final decision to attack the Soviet Union. The first of these was the traditional German 'urge towards the east', i.e. economic and hegemony objectives *vis-à-vis* Russia, which during the First World War had first given rise to the plan of a continental empire from the Atlantic to the Urals and which can be found in the eastern policy of the German Reich in the period between the two wars, as well as in Hitler's radical living-space programme. With all necessary grada-tions, a broad band of agreement—viewed thus—can be discerned between the traditional élites and the National Socialist leadership. Secondly, ever since the spring of 1940 there had been a growing realization among the leading circles of Wehrmacht, ministerial bureaucracy, and industry that, in the given circumstances, the German–Soviet economic alliance could guaran-tee neither the required supplies of vital raw materials and foodstuffs nor an undisturbed build-up of German hegemony in Europe. Which factors eventu-ally proved decisive in Hitler's reflections and decisions cannot be stated with complete certainty. Significant, however, is the fact that his decision not only caused no surprise among military men, economists, or ministerial officials, but actually met with broad understanding.

2. ECONOMIC PREPARATIONS FOR THE WAR AGAINST THE SOVIET UNION

(a) Economic Aspects of the Operational Plan

Hitler's decision to strike at the Soviet Union in May 1941 induced the Army General Staff to extend and systematize its preparations for the attack. In this work a special role was played by the pre-existing incipient connection of strategic and economic considerations. A complete occupation of the enemy's territory was ruled out from the start, if only because of the enormous geographical dimensions. The seizure of the Soviet Union's economically vital regions therefore acquired decisive importance in the intended smashing of the Russian empire. Compelling parameters for the planning of the operations stemmed also from Germany's existing economic bottlenecks and from the economic and political objective of a self-sufficient large-area economy.

One of the most important bases was a military-geographical study of European Russia completed at the beginning of August 1940.[86] This pointed out the importance of Moscow and Leningrad as industrial centres and that of the Ukraine as the agriculturally and industrially most valuable part of the Soviet Union. Occupation of those regions would 'pay off particularly'. The underlying thought was not so much the weakening of the enemy's military strength as the profit which Germany would derive in the longer term from

---

[86] First draft of a military-geographical study of European Russia, completed 9 Aug. 1940 (Bibl. MGFA). Location lists of the Soviet armament industry and appropriate material were obtained from the 9th dept. [Mil. geogr.] of the Army General Staff by OKW/WiRüAmt as early as 31 July 1940: cf. KTB WiRüAmt/Wi 1940, 203, BA-MA RW 19/244.

having the agricultural produce and the raw materials of that region at her disposal. Further operational objectives—despite the great distance—were Baku and the industrial region of the Urals. A geographical framework was thus mapped out which, in some respects, exceeded that of 1917–18. The warning contained in the study that even the occupation of all these regions would not necessarily put an end to the war, as—in contrast to the situation in the First World War—a vital and significant economic force existed in the Asian part of the Soviet Union, provided further food for thought.

The operational studies were bound to ask and answer the question of a rational matching of war aims and the means of war. It was here that the experts in the Army High Command would eventually fail.[87]

Marcks's study had first replaced a necessary sober assessment of the situation by a string of speculative assumptions, e.g. that the capture of the western border territories of the Soviet Union would result in a complete collapse of the Soviet war economy.[88] In order to avoid such a collapse the Red Army would stand and fight the decisive battle near the frontier. This would provide the Wehrmacht with an opportunity to annihilate the bulk of the enemy army within a very short time. After that a regeneration of Soviet fighting power could be ruled out, and the German forces would then, in a general chaos as in 1918 and with but little effort, be able to push ahead far to the east in a 'railway advance'. The military geographers' warnings concerning the potential of the Asian part of the Soviet Union and concerning the real principal enemies, climate and vastness of space, received scant attention in such speculations. The question whether the Soviet government might not after all succeed in weakening Germany's fighting strength by stubborn resistance in the European part of the USSR and thus in gaining time for a relocation of its armaments industry, in order, on the basis of Siberia's raw-material and energy resources, to mobilize the country's vast human potential, was left out of consideration from the outset.[89]

Judgement on this issue depended crucially on how one assessed the organizational ability of the Soviet regime and its inner stability. It was here that the general staff was the victim of prejudices which, for more than two decades, had been moulded not only by the National Socialists but also by conservative and bourgeois-liberal circles.[90] Assessment of the industrial development of Siberia was not just a problem of the difficulties (acknowledged to exist) in obtaining information. On the Kuznetsk industrial region, for instance, there

[87] See also the section by Klink, I.iv.1(*d*) of the present volume.

[88] See 'Operations draft East'. The above statement may need qualification in the light of Marcks's subsequent correspondence, but his occasional misgivings did not influence further operational planning. For a full account see sect. I.iv.1(*d*) at nn. 103–17 (Klink)

[89] For the USSR's war-economy capacities see the survey in *Sovetskaja èkonomika*. Information on this point was nevertheless being sought in the general staff: cf. Lt.-Col. Kinzel's lecture on 'The bases of Soviet military strength' on 11 Oct. 1940 (Halder, *Diaries*, 618) and relevant enquiries by Army Grp. B from WiRüAmt on 4 and 15 Oct. 1940 (KTB WiRüAmt/Wi 1940, 281, 296, BA-MA RW 19/244).

[90] Cf. Müller, *Tor zur Weltmacht*; Hillgruber, 'Rußland-Bild'.

had long been excellent studies in the specialized literature.[91] The Wehrmacht High Command, however, unhesitatingly used the outdated Soviet industrial atlas of 1934.[92] There was a widespread inability to evaluate available data and information without prejudice. This explains, for instance, the claim by *Militärwochenblatt* a few weeks before the attack on the Soviet Union that the relocation of the Soviet industry to the interior of the country had remained only a project and existed only on paper.[93]

Such traditional patterns of thinking about the Soviet Union were at no time seriously questioned during the Army General Staff's operational planning, even though there would have been repeated opportunities. A memorandum from the legation councillor at the German embassy in Moscow, Gebhardt von Walther, of October 1940, a memorandum intended for Halder, contained emphatic warnings of the far-reaching economic consequences of a German campaign against the Soviet Union.[94] Hopes of a rapid internal collapse of the Soviet system, it stated, were totally misplaced. Economically, the Soviet armaments industry could not be hit decisively by a German attack at all, and even if large territories were successfully occupied, this would yield no appreciable advantage to Germany. From the Ukraine, for instance, the principal surplus region, there was even less to be gained than in the First World War because of its over-population and its unfavourable structure of agricultural production. There could be no question of taking over its industrial plants as these would certainly be destroyed on Moscow's orders, and anyway German forces would be insufficient to set up a new native administration from scratch.

A further reason for re-examination of prior assumptions could have been provided by the continuous extension of the planned operational limits and main efforts. Halder reacted to this by endeavouring to preserve the principle of a concentric attack against Moscow and to assert the 'predominance of strategic and tactical points of view'[95] over economic considerations. If at times he had doubts about the sense of the whole operation, whether a decision in the war against Britain could really be achieved in that way, or whether Germany's economic basis would be greatly improved,[96] then these confirmed him in his belief that 'operational plans cannot be tailored to suit economic planners'.[97] That eventually a campaign was envisaged with three army groups, each aiming at different economically important targets, was due mainly to Hitler.[98] With an evidently better sense of the importance of

---

[91] See the study by Rosenberg, *Schwerindustrie*.

[92] Collection of maps for Operation Barbarossa (BA-MA Wi/I D. 1740) and the Wehrgeographischer Atlas [military geographical atlas] likewise officially commissioned.

[93] 'Rüstungspotential der Sowjets'.   [94] Gibbons, 'Opposition'.

[95] C. H. Hermann in the preface to Rosinski, *Armee*, 12. Other instances in the section by Klink, I.IV.1 of the present volume.

[96] Halder, *Diaries*, 765 (28 Jan. 1941).   [97] Ibid. 957 (13 June 1941).

[98] See sect. I.IV.1(*e*) (Klink) of the present volume; for the part played by economic considerations in Hitler's conduct of the war in the east generally, also from an economic point of view, see Dworok, *Konventionelle Kriegsführung*. The interpretation of Schustereit, *Vabanque*, is unconvincing.

military-economic aspects he urged that greater attention be given to the marginal zones (Baltic, Black Sea), and that distant regions (Caucasus, Urals) be included in operational plans. Thus at his conference with the top military leaders on 5 December 1940 he once again stated that it was necessary to 'crush Russian manpower'.[99] No bodies capable of regeneration must be left.

On 9 January 1941 Hitler explained to the commanders-in-chief that economic considerations had made him certain of victory also in his past campaigns.[100] For Germany

the shattering of Russia will mean a great relief. Only 40 to 50 divisions would then have to remain in the east, the army could be reduced, and the entire armaments industry could be employed for the air force and the navy. A fully sufficient anti-aircraft defence would then have to be built up and the most important industries relocated to unthreatened regions. Germany would then be unassailable. Russia's space contains immeasurable wealth. Germany must dominate it economically and politically, but not annex it. With that she would possess all the possibilities of waging war even against continents in the future, and she could not then be defeated by anyone.

From this exposé it emerges that Hitler saw the principal justification of his intended attack against the Soviet Union in the need 'to occupy the Ukraine'.[101] Hitler evidently regarded the reference to economic constraints and economic war aims as so convincing that he called with increasing emphasis for an appropriate alignment of operational plans.[102] In this connection he demanded from the Wehrmacht High Command a set of maps on the economic capacity of the Soviet Union.[103] In addition, calculations were to be made of the importance of the various industrial centres of the Soviet Union, first on the assumption of an operations line from the Crimea to Leningrad, which corresponded roughly to the original plan of the Army High Command, and second for the Astrakhan–Archangel line already ordered by him.

The problem of the interdependence of strategic and economic aspects, however, did not only affect the assessment of the enemy's military potential and the definition of German operational objectives, but also the question of material preparations for and the execution of the planned war of conquest. In that respect the general underestimation of economic factors in German military planning had particularly serious consequences. Instead of operational planning being governed by one's own available strength and by logistical possibilities—which would have been sensible if only for geographical reasons—the military objectives of the campaign were laid down in accordance with superior strategic and economic considerations. The question of the material equipment and supply of the eastern army remained, by comparison,

---

[99] Halder, *Diaries*, 723 (5 Dec. 1940).   [100] *KTB OKW* i. 253 ff. (9 Jan. 1941).

[101] Hassell, *Tagebücher*, 183 (2 Mar. 1941).

[102] See Engel, *Heeresadjutant bei Hitler*, 93, for the report of a conference of army leaders with Hitler on 17 Jan. 1941.

[103] Mentioned in Maj. von Petri's account of the examination of the material military strength of the major European and extra-European states (presumably 1944), 22, BA-MA Wi/VI. 397.

a secondary problem. In view of the pre-set premises of the operational plans, preparations for equipping the army were pursued with little urgency, because it was assumed that, given the expected short duration of the campaign, the existing strength would be sufficient. Supply issues were dealt with similarly in the Army High Command.[104]

After initial reflections in October 1940 the new quartermaster-general, Major-General Wagner, presented his thoughts on supplies in November.[105] New large-area solutions of the transport problem were, naturally enough, at the centre of attention, but the most important issue was the calculation of expenditure and its dependence on the factors of time and space. After all, more than three million troops, 500,000 motor-vehicles, and 300,000 horses had to be kept supplied, and the supplies had to be organized from Reich territory into the vast expanses of Russia. Calculations showed that available motor-fuel was sufficient for a rapid advance of some 700–800 kilometres, and ammunition and foodstuffs for twenty days in all. This meant a possible depth of operations of 500 kilometres. With that one would reach neither Leningrad nor Moscow, nor the Donets region. The eastern army, having crossed that logistical boundary, would either have to put in a rest period of several weeks and prepare for a war of presumably two years, or one would have to rely on a rapid collapse of the Red Army and the possibility of a German 'railway advance' during the second phase of the war. As this very assumption was envisaged in the operational plan, the quartermaster-general had little reason, initially, to make provision for a supply operation extended both in time and in space. Just that, however, was becoming increasingly pressing as the envisaged limits of occupation were being shifted ever further to the east. Thus yet another range of tasks was arising for the quartermaster-general: the establishment of a military administration designed to make the hinterland secure and available for the purposes of Germany's war effort.[106] The ideas developed in that context within the Army High Command were apparently all based on the First World War. An occupation policy such as Hitler—at least in his hints to the Army Command—seemed to support until the spring of 1941 did not, however, hold out much advantage in terms of material support for the eastern army. On the strength of the experience of 1917–18 a traditional military administration, which showed consideration for the local population, even making concessions to it and promoting general economic reconstruction, could not at the same time mobilize a maximum of resources to provide the fighting forces and the homeland with urgently needed raw materials and foodstuffs.[107]

Idealistic concepts, such as those championed in the 1920s by the former

---

[104] See sect. I.IV.1(*g*) (Klink); also Krumpelt, *Material*, 140 ff.

[105] Halder, *Diaries*, 685, 690 (12, 15 Nov. 1940).

[106] On the political aspects of military administration see the section by Förster, I.VII.1 of the present volume; on the military aspects in the narrow sense see sect. I.IV.1(*g*) at nn. 171 ff. (Klink).

[107] See the assessment of such experience in Banse, *Wehrwissenschaft*, 23 ff.

chief of the general staff under the commander-in-chief East, General Max Hoffmann, in a model operational plan for the 'liberation' of Russia from Bolshevism,[108] were totally unrealistic in the conditions of 1940. Hoffmann had called for the establishment of an expeditionary force, capable, by the employment of the most up-to-date means of transport and with strong protection for rearward communications, of not only supplying itself but also, instead of living off the land, of bringing considerable quantities of foodstuffs and goods into the country in order to win the co-operation of the Russians. Such a procedure was totally unthinkable for the military leadership in 1940–1. In view of the expected exacerbation of shortages in the Reich in the autumn of 1941 the Wehrmacht would instead have to occupy the Ukrainian wheat-fields and the Caucasian oil wells as fast as possible, and maintain operations by largely living off the land.

Realization of these objectives, however, was called into question from the outset in two respects. First, Halder endeavoured to employ the bulk of the army for a concentric thrust at Moscow, regardless of the fact that scarcely any provisioning facilities existed in the sparse landscape of central Russia; second, the extension, under pressure from Hitler, of both the disposition and the objectives of the operation greatly exceeded the Wehrmacht's logistical potential. The quartermaster-general's preparations inevitably fell victim to the unsettled conflict between Halder and Hitler. No convincing solutions were reached either with regard to supply and provisioning possibilities or with regard to the necessary exploitation of the territory to be occupied. Thus the envisaged military administration was to be assigned no more than a narrowly circumscribed sphere of duties, chiefly the 'collection and utilization of important supply commodities for the fighting forces with a view to relieving supplies from the homeland'.[109] In order to win the co-operation of the population it was suggested 'granting them certain freedoms and material advantages'. Prisoners of war were categorized as 'valuable manpower', to be employed, with observance of the international law of war, for the purposes of the fighting forces and of the German war economy. Up to this point the concept was still in line with Hoffmann's ideas. On the other hand, however, it also contained the basis for more radical procedures. Thus the Army High Command was determined to nip in the bud any active or passive resistance of the population by Draconian punitive measures. This appeared to be

---

[108] See Max Hoffmann, *Aufzeichnungen*, ii. 339 ff., and id., 'Intervention in Rußland'.

[109] OKH/GenStdH/GenQu 1/IIa No. I/050/41 g.Kdos., Anordnungen über militärische Hoheitsrechte, Sicherung und Verwaltung im rückwärtigen Gebiet und Kriegsgefangenenwesen [Regulations concerning military sovereign rights, security, and administration in the rearward area, and prisoner-of-war matters], Feb. 1941 (appendix 15), BA-MA RH 3/v. 132. The concept of military administration and its already discernible tendency towards an opportunistic application of the international law of war met with fierce criticism from Count Helmuth James von Moltke, an international law expert in Canaris's Abwehr (Counter-intelligence) department and a future leading figure in the anti-Hitler resistance movement. His efforts to tie down OKH and the quartermaster-general to a strict observance of international regulations by the military administration failed in the spring of 1941; on this see Müller, 'Kriegsrecht'.

necessary because the lack of German administrative and law-and-order forces ruled out the establishment of a close-knit administrative network as in western Europe, and because native administrative institutions would have to be created from scratch, as in the First World War, in what would presumably be a protracted process. It would therefore be necessary to concentrate one's own forces on the economic surplus areas in order thereby to achieve a maximum yield.

It was therefore envisaged that the Ukraine and Bessarabia would be 'placed under ordered administration', with public life and the economy being re-started and encouraged so that 'their production can strengthen the German war economy as soon as possible'. From that strategy it followed that economically weak regions would be neglected and would 'ruthlessly' be made 'useful to the purposes of the operation'. Such a concept, coming close to the limits of the Hague land-war regulations, seemed justified by the assumption of a short campaign. At the same time it was obvious that any extension of the war in time or space was bound to intensify exploitation and oppression if the military administration hoped to meet the growing demands of the fighting forces. When at the beginning of March 1941 the Army High Command issued orders for a military administration to be set up in Russia,[110] the signals for occupation policy were already pointing in a different direction. In this a key role was to be played by the Wehrwirtschafts- und Rüstungsamt (War Economy and Armaments Department).

(b) First Preparatory Steps by the War Economy and Armaments Department

After Hitler's decision in July 1940 the problem of executing an economic plan that would match up to the military and operational preparations then in progress remained initially unresolved. The main reason was the lack of a central control authority which would have been capable of clarifying the economic prerequisites and objectives of such an enterprise and of orientating Germany's war economy accordingly. Göring, who had only recently, in June 1940, assumed the co-ordinated planning of the economy in the western territories, thus concentrating in his person the principal authority in the field of war economy, was focusing his entire attention on the air war against Britain and was therefore not available as a driving force in economic planning. The staff of experts available to him in the Four-year Plan authority was fully engaged in organizing the 'new order' of the European economy, alongside the industrial-development projects within the Reich. The Army High Command saw no reason to develop any initiative of its own, as it believed firmly in a separation between superior economic-policy planning and the practical handling of day-to-day issues which, in the occupied territories and in those yet to be occupied, were to be the sole responsibility of the military administration.[111] In the case of Russia, therefore, the army command re-

---

[110] Reproduced in *Deutsche Besatzungspolitik*, Nos. 1, 2.
[111] See Halder, *Diaries*, 493 (4 July 1940).

garded the 'systematic administration and exploitation of the country' as a 'worry in the future'.[112]

The Armed Forces High Command, on the other hand, viewed the War Economy and Armaments Department as an institution which, under the leadership of Infantry General Thomas, had long been trying to seize the unified control of the German war economy in competition against the weapons departments of the Wehrmacht services and the civilian economic departments.[113] In the spring of 1940 Hitler, by appointing Fritz Todt Reich minister for armaments and ammunition, had made it clear that he did not believe in military guidance of private industry, placing more trust in the 'subterfuges' of industrialists as a stimulus for war production.[114] However, General Thomas pursued his endeavours to preserve and strengthen OKW influence in the sphere of economic policy. It was natural, therefore, for Field Marshal Keitel, as OKW chief of staff, to inform Thomas of the intentions of the supreme leadership immediately after Hitler's fundamental decision in favour of a campaign in the east,[115] thereby tying the War Economy and Armaments Department into the planning process, in parallel with the Wehrmacht operations staff, which tried to influence operational procedures. Along with armament planning it was predominantly the assessment of the Soviet economic potential that offered itself as an area of activity for becoming involved in the preparations of the army.

Thus the Russian desk of the war-economy section first of all made itself available to the general staff as a supplier of information.[116] The principal activity was the preparation of economic maps and town plans showing the location of Soviet armaments enterprises. General Thomas moreover succeeded in winning the co-operation of a number of economic institutions.[117] Research contracts concerning the Soviet economy were assigned to the Reichsamt für wehrwirtschaftliche Planung (Reich office for war-economy planning), the Studiengesellschaft für bäuerliche Rechts- und Wirtschaftsordnung (Study group for rural law and economy), the Ernährungssicherungsstelle (office for the assurance of food supply), and to the Generalbevollmächtigter für Sonderfragen der chemischen Erzeugung (General plenipotentiary for special questions of chemical production), Carl Krauch. In Paris representatives of OKW inspected captured French material. Arrangements were made with the Reich Statistical Office for a mutual ex-

[112] OKH, Anordnungen über militärische Hoheitsrechte . . . (above, n. 109).

[113] See Die Probleme der deutschen Rüstungswirtschaft im Kriege [The problems of the German armament industry in war], official in charge: Reg.Rat Dr Tomberg (OKW/WiRüAmt/Stab), completed towards the end of Sept. 1940, BA-MA Wi/I F 5.662, pp. 49 ff.

[114] Manuscript minute by Col. Jansen, 29 Mar. 1940: Thomas, *Wehr- und Rüstungswirtschaft*, 509–11; on the rise of Todt see Milward, *German Economy*, 57 ff., and *Das Deutsche Reich und der Zweite weltkrieg*, v./1. 453 ff.

[115] See Thomas, *Wehr- und Rüstungswirtschaft*, 234.

[116] See KTB WiRüAmt/Wi 1940, 230 (28 Aug. 1940), BA-MA RW 19/244.

[117] See relevant references ibid. 249 ff.

change of information. The office of the Reich Peasant Leader made available its entire material on agriculture, food supplies, and the foodstuffs industry in the Soviet Union. Further information was obtained from the specialized economic press. The Institute for Foreign and Colonial Forestry was instructed to produce as soon as possible a study, from a war-economy point of view, of the timber industry and forestry in the Soviet Union.

Careful preparatory work seemed called for if only because in the summer of 1940 General Thomas had got into difficulties with setting up his apparatus in connection with the establishment of a military administration in the west. During the occupation of Poland the armaments inspection authority set up by Thomas had been able to operate as it pleased—because there was no solidly structured military administration. For the west, however, OKH had designed a new type of administration in an attempt, successful up to a point, to curtail the strivings for autonomy by the war-economy apparatus.[118] Armaments inspection bodies were tied closely to the military commanders and infiltrated by a large number of representatives of the weapons department. While OKH was anxious, in this rivalry, to ensure the uniformity of military administration and occupation policy, Thomas was trying to extend the armaments apparatus of OKW and, in the interest of unified armaments control, to make himself independent of the three Wehrmacht services.

In the regulation of organizational problems in France a vital role was played by Lieutenant-General Stud, head of the department for industrial armaments in the Heereswaffenamt (Army weapons department). When, in early October 1940, he was transferred to the OKH senior officers' reserve, it seemed natural for Thomas to entrust him with drawing up an armament organization for Russia. Stud, who in the 1920s had been involved in the secret co-operation between the Reichswehr and the Red Army, immediately got in touch with the Russian desk of the war-economy section and with the armaments-economy department.[119] At a joint conference on 1 November he announced that he envisaged the establishment of a War Economy and Armaments Staff with four inspectorates of three armaments control squads each.[120] This required the location of personnel familiar with the country[121] and the preparation of accurate maps of the principal industrial and raw-material regions of the USSR. Alongside the teams of experts for the armaments industry, Stud also intended to set up a few units for the securing of raw materials.

[118] See Thomas, *Wehr- und Rüstungswirtschaft*, 219–20.
[119] KTB WiRüAmt/Wi 1940, 281, 296 (4, 15 Oct. 1940), BA-MA RW 19/244. The 1944 history of WiStabOst quotes an instruction by Thomas along these lines, 30 Oct. 1940, allegedly based on a directive from the Reich Marshal; see *Deutsche Wirtschaftspolitik*, 27 ff. However, there is no documentary evidence of such an early instruction by Göring, nor is it mentioned by Thomas himself in his own 'history'.
[120] Rü (Ic), minute of 1 Nov. 1940, BA-MA Wi/VIII. 411: *Fall Barbarossa*, No. 107.
[121] See WiRüAmt/Rü (VIc), concerning personnel with foreign experience, 11 Nov. 1940, BA-MA Wi/VIII. 411.

This draft, based on the model of the armaments organization in occupied France, enlarged only by a fourth armaments inspectorate, was based on the idea of localized employment at the armaments centres of Leningrad, Moscow, the Ukraine, and the Caucasus. Numerically small teams of armaments experts, in which the representatives of the weapons departments would no doubt call the tune, were to ensure qualified consultation of the military administration and the implementation of its instructions in the technological field. A draft of the 'tasks of the chief of staff of the War Economy Organization East'[122] therefore envisaged a 'report' to the quartermaster-general in order to clarify the question of integration in the military administration. A handwritten gloss by Thomas, to the effect that such a report should only by made after consultation with him, suggests that he was not willing to let his organization be totally absorbed by OKH.

Another indication of Thomas's striving for autonomy is his early contact not only with civilian economic departments but also with the leading German industrial concerns. This will be discussed later. In view of the Army High Command's efforts to separate planning from execution in the economic sector, the War Economy and Armaments Department was anxious to establish a foothold in both areas and thereby to enhance the influence of OKW. After Hitler on 4 November 1940—with an eye to the impending visit of the Soviet foreign minister Molotov—had affirmed to the top military leaders his determination to have a 'great showdown' with Russia whatever happened,[123] Göring took this opportunity to inform the top officials of the Four-year Plan authority, as well as General Thomas as the OKW representative, of the intentions of the political leadership.[124] As a result of Göring's general instruction to base armament and raw-material planning on the assumption of a 'longish war', Thomas felt encouraged to intensify his department's Russian studies.[125]

The war-economy section was instructed (1) to produce a comprehensive picture of the Soviet armament industry; (2) to establish the state of the power and transport network; (3) to investigate raw-material and oil deposits; and (4) to provide an overview of the USSR's civilian economy. In addition, a card index of all major enterprises and a Russian-language economic dictionary were to be created.[126] The department, mainly thanks to its preparatory work, was able to discharge some of these tasks within a few days.[127] The prerequi-

---

[122] Undated minute, presumably of Nov. 1940, ibid.

[123] Halder, *Diaries*, 674 (4 Nov. 1940).

[124] See Thomas, *Wehr- und Rüstungswirtschaft*, 261, and minutes of the conference with the Reich Marshal at Beauvais on 6 Nov. 1940, BA-MA Wi/I F 5.2151.

[125] Thomas, *Wehr- und Rüstungswirtschaft*, 267; as Thomas dates the for commencement of the Russia studies in retrospect, the accusation of a cover-up cannot be lightly dismissed; see Wagner, 'Vorbereitung', 296.

[126] Thomas, *Wehr- und Rüstungswirtschaft*, 261. A copy of the German–Russian language guide was handed over by a German printer to the Soviet consulate in Berlin in mid-Feb. 1941. It was immediately passed on to Moscow, but met with no interest there; see Bereshkow, *Jahre*, 67.

[127] See KTB WiRüAmt/Wi 1940, 337 (22 Nov. 1940), BA-MA RW 19/244.

sites had thus been created—as indeed in earlier campaigns—of establishing support and guidance for the general staff.[128]

Organizational planning developed in striking contrast to this broadly planned research. The study-group 'War Economy Organization East' was dominated by the representatives of the armaments-industry section, which, because of its close contacts with the weapons departments, led a kind of separate existence within OKW. In agreement with OKH, whose interest was focused on the Soviet armaments industry, they succeeded, against the opposition of the war-economy section, in having the number of armaments inspectorates envisaged for Russia reduced from the original four to two (Ukraine and Moscow), with a total of thirteen squads.[129] Only three 'War Economy Officers' were to be employed in the Baltic provinces as advisers to the military administration. The 'War Economy Staff Russia' was envisaged as a small-scale co-ordination staff.

When Lieutenant-General Stud submitted this organization plan on 7 December 1940, Thomas could not of course withhold his fundamental approval. However, he ruled that, seeing that three inspectorates were employed in France, a third inspectorate should at least be held in readiness for the vastly larger Russian territory.[130] A few days later, when Directive No. 21, 'Barbarossa', laid down the operations plan, Stud had essentially completed his preparations for the organization of armaments. In addition to a study on the Soviet economy, there was a revised organization plan, together with lists of names of specialists familiar with the country.[131] Three induction courses of fourteen days' duration each—starting on 15 February 1941—were to prepare the core staff for their tasks. At the beginning of January the organization tree was eventually further reduced on the initiative of the armaments-industry section.[132] Not only the central departments suffered staff cuts, but also the armaments groups, because 'utilization of the enemy's armaments industry would, if at all, become topical only at a later stage'.

The Economic Organization Russia was thus left only with the task, in cooperation with the agencies of the quartermaster-general, of collecting captured stocks of raw materials and mineral oil and directing them to the army supply organizations. When the section heads submitted this plan, code-

---

[128] A thousand copies of the paper were sent out on 9 Apr. 1940 to the military commands; see OKW/WiRüAmt/Wi (VI) No. 2758/41 g., Az 3i/34/25, Die Wehrwirtschaft der Union der Sozialistischen Sowjet-Republiken (UdSSR), Teil I, Kurze Charakteristik und Gesamtbeurteilung der wehrwirtschaftlichen Lage, Stand März 1941 [The war economy of the Union of Socialist Soviet Republics (USSR), part I, Brief outline and overall assessment of the war-economy situation, as of Mar. 1941], BA-MA W 01-8/296: *Fall Barbarossa*, No. 20. The most important findings had already been communicated to the army general staff in Dec. 1940: see Heusinger's report, in Halder, *Diaries*, 741 (17 Dec. 1940).

[129] Minute Rü I, 5 Dec. 1940, BA-MA Wi/VIII. 411.

[130] Minute Rü Ic, concerning War Economy Organization East, 19 Dec. 1940, ibid.

[131] Minute by Stud, 21 Dec. 1940, ibid.

[132] Minute Rü, Ic, concerning provision of personnel for War Economy Organization East, 9 Jan. 1941, ibid.

named 'Oldenburg', to the departmental head on 27 January 1941, it became
obvious that the War Economy and Armaments Department was seeking the
closest possible integration with the command structure of the army.[133] As the
question of establishing a war-economy staff was regarded in OKH as still
wide open, Thomas presumably, by submitting a new employment procedure,
hoped to gain greater prominence for his organization. It was envisaged that,
at the very start of operations, the forward elements of armaments control
squads, especially the recovery and mineral-oil squads, would be placed under
the liaison officer of the War Economy and Armaments Department at each
army HQ. In this manner the often complained-of belated arrival of the
economic personnel was to be avoided and looting or destruction of stocks of
booty prevented. The armaments commander with his staff would follow on
the heels of the army commands, and with the establishment of a military
administration the forward and rearward elements of the armaments control
squads would eventually link up and establish themselves locally. This procedure, it was intended, would result in the occupation of the conquered
territories in successive leaps by the relevant armaments agencies. The War
Economy Staff Russia was to be attached to the quartermaster-general in the
operations staff of the army in the east.[134]

On 28 January 1941 General Thomas put forward these ideas at a conference of all armaments departments in the Army High Command.[135] Halder
was not yet ready to comment on the problems and assumptions considered,
noting merely that 'entirely new ideas' were involved.[136] After consultation
about conditions within the military administration in France the quartermaster-general proposed a greater measure of centralization of military administration. The military commander, thus strengthened, should have under him
economists and administration experts as 'advisers for special fields'.[137] In a
letter to Thomas, Wagner informed him that no more war-economy organizations were to be set up in future operations.[138] OKW interests were to be
safeguarded by an appropriate enlargement of the staff of Thomas's liaison
officer with the quartermaster-general. This model immediately entered into
the plans for operation 'Marita', the campaign against Greece.[139]

It seemed therefore that by the beginning of February 1941 the Armed
Forces High Command's prospects of establishing a field organization of the
War Economy and Armaments Department for Russia, even one furnished

[133] WiRüAmt/Wi No. 230 g.Kdos., Neue große Ausarbeitung Rußland [New great study
Russia], 29 Jan. 1941, ibid.; the code-name 'Oldenburg' had already been decided on at the
conference on 9 Jan. 1941. The information in Eichholtz, *Kriegswirtschaft*, 233, is therefore
incorrect.

[134] KTB WiRüAmt/Stab 1939/41, 155 (27 Jan. 1941), BA-MA RW 19/164.

[135] See Halder, *KTB* ii. 256 ff. (28 Jan. 1941; not in trans.).

[136] See his handwritten gloss on the minutes of the conference at the office of the head of the
department on 27 Jan. 1941, p. 2, BA-MA Wi/VIII. 411.

[137] Halder, *Diaries*, 779 (11 Feb. 1941).

[138] See minute for the head of department, 6 Feb. 1941, BA-MA Wi/VIII.411.

[139] See KTB WiRüAmt/Stab 1939/41, 160 (30 Jan. 1941), BA-MA RW 19/164.

with few powers, were vanishing. Simultaneously Thomas, even in the area of armaments control within Germany, had to accept substantial curtailments of his authority in favour of Todt. For one thing, Keitel undertook to keep Todt informed in advance about any proposals by Thomas intended for Hitler,[140] and for another Todt announced the creation of 'bottleneck commissions', which would aim at a further extension of 'industrial self-management' in the armaments field at the expense of military direction.[141] Moreover, if one considers the quartermaster-general's intention of no longer involving OKW in future military administrations but using individual industrialists instead, then the fiasco of General Thomas's far-reaching ambitions becomes evident. Although he issued instructions that there should be no opposition to the bottleneck commissions—there was reason to fear that, if there was, Todt would denounce Thomas to Hitler[142]—he tried at the same time to consolidate his position with the help of the weapons departments of the Wehrmacht services. In a circular dated 6 February 1941 he offered them 'the creation, for future large-scale operations, of a *unified* economic organization of the Wehrmacht High Command, one which would take full account of the war-economy interests of the Wehrmacht services and especially of the supply departments', thereby preventing the parallel activities of different economic authorities.[143] The war-economy sections could be 'so extensively staffed with specially selected individuals from the supply departments of the Wehrmacht services that these would feel confident that their interests are sufficiently safeguarded'. However, this proposal for concentrating the armaments interests in the territories to be occupied under the umbrella of OKW did not meet with a response. It seemed, therefore, that General Thomas was giving up his efforts when he appointed the 'working staff Oldenburg', consisting of three officers of his department, for the further study of Russian questions, at the same time relieving Stud of his task.[144]

The expert opinions produced in his department at that time seemed to justify such a retreat.[145] Essentially they confirmed the prognoses of the

---

[140] See Keitel's letter to Todt, 26 Jan. 1941, BA-MA Wi/I F 5.2151.

[141] See Milward, *German Economy at War*, 61–2.

[142] KTB WiRüAmt/Stab 1939/41, 181 (11 Feb. 1941), BA-MA RW 19/164.

[143] OKW Az. 11 WiRüAmt/Rü (Ic) No. 864/41 g., Schreiben an die Waffenämter der Wehrmachtteile, betr. Aufbau der Wehrwirtschaftorganisation für künftige Unternehmungen [Letter to the weapons departments of the Wehrmacht services, concerning creation of a war-economy organization for future operations], 6 Feb. 1941, BA-MA Wi/I F 5.3662.

[144] OKW/WiRüAmt/Rü (Ic) Az 11, betr. Arbeitsstab Oldenburg, 22 Feb. 1941, BA-MA Wi/ VIII. 411.

[145] See Rittmeister Dr Varain (OKW/WiRüAmt/Stab, Oberst Jansen), Die landwirtschaftliche Produktion der Ukraine vor und im Weltkrieg 1914–18 [Agricultural production of the Ukraine before and during the world war 1914–18]. Warum das Wirtschaftsabkommen vom 23.4.1918 zur Lieferung von Agrarprodukten an die Mittelmächte nicht voll zur Ausführung kam [Why the economic agreement of 23 Apr. 1918 on deliveries of agricultural produce to the Central Powers was not fully implemented], 13 Feb. 1941, BA-MA Wi/I D 38, as well as Col. Jansen's collection of papers, Die Lebensmittellieferungen der Ukraine im Jahr 1918 [Ukrainian food supply deliveries in 1918], BA-MA Wi/I D 1658.

Walther memorandum[146] about the insignificant economic advantage of a campaign against the USSR; it was probably this that had induced Halder to work for a strengthening of military administration and the confinement of its activities to supplying the troops. On the basis of First World War experience by the German civilian economic administration in the occupied Russian territories, OKW was aware of the meagre results of all measures then taken for the collection and removal of foodstuffs and raw materials. Along with obstacles due to the war, such as the disorganization of the native economy and the black market, in 1918 it had largely been the mistakes of the occupation authorities which had impaired the result of the collection drive. Because there was then not enough time for a more effective exploitation of the country's economic resources in favour of the needs of the German war economy, it had been necessary to resort to ruthless requisitioning and to neglect the long-term reconstruction of the country. That procedure had curtailed the political scope of the native authorities upon whom German occupation was largely relying. The Ukrainian puppet regime, in particular, had proved incapable of supplying the delivery quotas laid down. A further factor was the German failure to keep promises concerning deliveries of coal and industrial goods; this had resulted in a silent boycott by the Ukrainian authorities.

Especially disastrous, in the view of the experts in the War Economy and Armaments Department, had been the precipitate (because politically motivated) agrarian reform. The break-up of predominantly Russian-owned big estates and the transfer of the land to Ukrainian small peasants had resulted in chaotic conditions and in a rapid decline of agricultural output. Even the most drastic intervention of the military administration had then been unable to improve the utilization of an a priori favourable production situation in the Ukraine.

Typical of the dilemma of German occupation policy had been the unresolved conflict between the military authorities, which demanded ruthless exploitation of the country—if need be by coercive measures—and the civilian economic authorities, which were looking ahead to economic reconstruction and which, for political reasons, wished to see the Ukrainians treated with consideration.[147] Halder's concept of a military administration and its concentration for the purpose of supplying the fighting forces did not, however, meet all the problems raised in the study-papers of the War Economy and Armaments Department. These pointed out, above everything else, that in the present circumstances there was not even any certainty that the meagre results of 1918 could be reached.[148] Ukrainian stocks and the prospects of autumn and spring cultivation, as well as the fertility of the soil, had to be judged even more

---

[146] Gibbons, 'Opposition'.

[147] See Baumgart, 'General Groener'; on the overall issue of the policy of economic exploitation in the Ukraine in 1918 see Borowsky, *Ukrainepolitik*.

[148] Paper by Varain (above, n. 145).

unfavourable, so that 'surpluses for export to and the supply of central Europe' could certainly not be expected.

Further reason for concern was provided by calculations by the War Economy and Armaments Department of the consequences for the German supply situation of even a short-term interruption of raw-material deliveries from the Soviet Union.[149] Thus at least temporary serious dislocations of German war production would occur in the area of certain steel alloys and rubber. When Thomas thereupon warned the supreme leadership that in the event of an eastern campaign motor-fuel and rubber supplies would be sufficient only until the autumn of 1941, and therefore demanded additional authority for the War Economy and Armaments Department *vis-à-vis* civilian- and military-user departments, Hitler had him informed that he would not allow himself to be diverted from his decisions by such pessimistic forecasts.[150] It is conceivable that Thomas, after this rebuff and against the background of OKH's restrictive attitude, reviewed his attitude to the Russian problem and thereby triggered a development which gave a new direction to preparations for the attack on the Soviet Union.

(c) The Thomas Memorandum and its Consequences

On 22 January 1941 Thomas was summoned by Keitel to report to him. On that occasion Thomas disclosed that he intended to have a memorandum prepared on some misgivings, from the war-economy point of view, about the planned operations in the east.[151] Keitel's reaction is not known, but it may be assumed that his own opinion was based on Hitler's expectation that the conquest of Russia would result in a gigantic gain and in relief from all war-economy worries. In consequence, OKW stood to gain nothing from the fact that it supported OKH's cautious assessment of economic aspects by pessimistic forecasts of its own. It seemed advisable, however, to approach the top leadership with a 'sober' profit-and-loss account, which would make it clear 'what is to be gained and what to be lost (past supplies and transit rights) (*a*) from the execution of the enterprise itself, and (*b*) after its successful execution'—as Thomas put it in his instruction to the War Economy Department that same day.[152]

During the next few days Thomas had occasion, in conversations with Keitel, Todt, and Göring, to sound out the expectations of the top leadership.[153] Göring had shortly before been briefed by his experts in the Four-year

---

[149] See KTB WiRüAmt/Stab 1939/41, 148 (21 Jan. 1941), BA-MA RW 19/164.

[150] See Thomas's minute of a report to Keitel and Jodl on 8 Feb. 1941, and a minute of a consultation between the departmental head and State Secretary Landfried concerning the rubber-supply situation, 12 Feb. 1941, No. 1456-PS, Staatsarchiv Nürnberg.

[151] KTB WiRüAmt/Stab 1939/41, 145 (22 Jan. 1941), BA-MA RW 19/164.

[152] Ibid. 142–3.

[153] The minutes of these conversations were removed from the appendix of the KTB at a later date (presumably in connection with the 'History' written by Thomas in 1943–4) and exist only in parts in BA-MA Wi/I F 5.3662. On the following passages see Gibbons, 'Soviet Industry', 101–2, and n. 262 below.

Plan authority on the consequences of an attack on the Soviet Union. With the exception of Herbert Backe, the state secretary in the ministry of food and agriculture, all of them had spoken against it. Backe, who had been interested in the state of Soviet agriculture as early as the 1920s, had believed, from the outbreak of the war, that because of the precarious situation of German food supplies a large volume had to be obtained from Russia. As General Thomas now learnt, Backe had assured Hitler 'that possession of the Ukraine will mean the end of all our economic worries'.[154] Thomas therefore knew what Hitler wished to hear confirmed, and that he was following those questions with keen interest. In this connection it might be recalled that, shortly before the outbreak of the war, Hitler had stated to Carl J. Burckhardt, the League of Nations High Commissioner for Danzig: 'I need the Ukraine, so that we cannot be starved out again as in the last war.'[155] It is significant that Thomas instructed the editor of the Russia memorandum to co-operate with Backe.[156]

After a conference with the Army High Command on 3 February 1941 had once more revealed its doubts,[157] Hitler on 11 February demanded that the Russia memorandum, which Keitel had informed him was being prepared, should be accompanied by a clear map.[158] The study, dated 13 February, was in fact completed and sent to Hitler only on 20 February, following repeated personal intervention by Thomas.[159] Presumably it crossed with a study-paper produced by the Four-year Plan authority, which was based on extensive statistical material.

In contrast to the latter, the Thomas memorandum generally confirmed Hitler's expectations and thus conflicted perceptibly with earlier OKW research as well as with the Walther memorandum. Instead of discussing in detail the economic risks which would stem from the execution of the operation, as the Walther paper did, Thomas devoted much space to long-term economic gain. In spite of all warnings, he believed it possible to extract from the European part of the Soviet Union sufficient agricultural surpluses to cover German import requirements for 1941 and 1942, and subsequently even to improve the German foodstuff situation to a marked degree. He never questioned the prerequisites of this. On the strength of experience from the First World War he proposed that the Russian agrarian order should not at first be changed. His recommendation for achieving the greatest possible yield in the shortest possible time was in line with German practice in other

[154] KTB WiRüAmt/Stab 1939/41, 160 (30 Jan. 1941), BA-MA RW 19/164. On Backe's role in the Third Reich see Lehmann, 'Agrarpolitik'.

[155] Burckhardt, *Danziger Mission*, 348.   [156] See above, n. 154.

[157] No. 872-PS, *IMT* xxvi. 630–1.

[158] KTB WiRüAmt/Stab 1939/41, 182 (11 Feb. 1941), BA-MA RW 19/164. This map became the basis of Hitler's operational decisions until the end of 1941; see Müller, 'Unternehmen Barbarossa', 188.

[159] WiRüAmt No. 10/41 g.Kdos./Chefs., Die wehrwirtschaftlichen Auswirkungen einer Operation im Osten [The war-economy consequences of an operation in the east], 13 Mar. 1941: Thomas, *Wehr- und Rüstungswirtschaft*, 515 ff.

occupied territories: a reduction of domestic consumption by 10 per cent would, in the case of Russia, yield 4m. t. of grain, which would be sufficient to cover the import requirement of the entire German sphere of power.[160] These arguments are likely to have come from Backe.

Even during the preparation of the memorandum Thomas had attached great importance to the need for a rapid strike to seize not only the Ukraine, but also the oilfields of the Caucasus and—because of the transport of rubber—a connection to the Far East. An adequate economic gain could be expected only if the operational objectives were pegged out as far to the east as possible. This supported Hitler's line of argument *vis-à-vis* the Army High Command. As for the operational and, more especially, logistical prerequisites of such an operation, Thomas of course had nothing to say. Instead, without concerning himself with the questionable value of his sources, and in clear conflict with the conclusions of the military geographers of the Army High Command, he declared that the campaign would give Germany possession of 75 per cent of the Soviet armaments industry. The Asian part of the Soviet Union could not represent a serious threat to German dominion in the foreseeable future, so long as Germany succeeded in destroying the industry in the Urals. Germany's economic war aims were defined by him as the seizure and removal of all raw materials and foodstuffs within reach, as well as the utilization of the Russian armaments industry.

In his deliberately factual exposé General Thomas based himself on the same data as were also used by the Army High Command. The crucial difference was that Thomas in his memorandum created the impression that the economic resources and, more particularly, the armaments industry in the European part of the Soviet Union could be captured intact, and within a short period of time put to the use of the German war effort. In doing so he disregarded the real central problem of the whole operation, i.e. the question whether the Soviet regime would in fact rapidly collapse under the German assault, so that the expenditure of time, personnel, and material on the campaign could be kept within limits. Had Thomas wished to 'dissuade Hitler from his decision with all means at his disposal'[161] he could easily, with the information available to his department, have confirmed the objections to such an assumption, the objections contained, for instance, in the Walther memorandum. Furthermore, he could have factually refuted Hitler's expectations of rapid and vast economic gain in the east. He did not do so, and the charge that he was an 'opportunist and a double-dealer'[162] was perhaps not

---

[160] Thomas, *Wehr- und Rüstungswirtschaft*, 517, and KTB WiRüAmt/Stab 1939/41, 184 (12 Feb. 1941), BA-MA RW 19/164.

[161] Birkenfeld in his introduction to Thomas, *Wehr- und Rüstungswirtschaft*, 17–18, basing himself on the interpretation given by Thomas while in American captivity, that his action was an act of resistance: see Thomas, 'Gedanken', 547. Critical attitudes towards the memorandum, on the other hand, in Hillgruber, 'Rußland-Bild', 309, and Streit, *Keine Kameraden*, 62–3.

[162] Thus Keitel's defending counsel in his plea before the Nuremberg tribunal on 8 July 1946, *IMT* xvii. 712.

unjustified. Whatever objective Thomas may have pursued with his memorandum, to Hitler it certainly came as a confirmation of his own views.

Together with the simultaneously submitted draft 'Guidelines on special issues in connection with Directive No. 21' the Thomas memorandum induced Hitler to take a fundamental decision on future occupation policy. Having spent nearly three weeks recuperating at the Berghof, he presumably met Göring, Reich Leader of the SS Heinrich Himmler, and Alfred Rosenberg, the head of the foreign-policy department of the NSDAP, in Munich on 24 February, on the occasion of his speech to celebrate the anniversary of the Party.[163] It cannot be ruled out that—along with the ideas of the generals—conversations in that circle may have influenced his decision from the outset to wage the campaign against the Soviet Union differently from all others. Even before he had clarified the details in his mind he instructed Göring to assume, with the involvement of General Thomas, the administration and exploitation of the eastern territories to be conquered.[164] In order to pacify the rear areas and to safeguard maximum exploitation, Communism had to be 'exterminated' through the liquidation of all political leaders.

This decision was conveyed to General Thomas by Göring on 26 February, when Thomas once more submitted his memorandum to him personally.[165] The two men quickly agreed on economic war aims, so that the question of the potential risks of the operation was relegated to the background from the start. Göring instead announced with 'special emphasis' that the employment of the war-economy organization was to be carried out in a different framework from the past. He demanded a separation from OKH and the creation of an entirely new and independent organization under his own command. Hitler, he explained, had already agreed that Thomas should undertake the preparatory work for it.

The head of the War Economy and Armaments Department thus found himself faced with a totally changed situation. Here at last was an opportunity to set up an economic organization comprising all spheres, an organization of the kind that was in line with his age-old demand that the control of the German war economy should be in the hands of a single man who held 'all full powers', who was familiar with the 'plans of the supreme leadership and who could argue his views to the Führer himself'.[166] Effectively fronted by Göring, he might now expect to achieve such a position and thus decide in his own favour the energy-consuming struggle for the control of the war economy, a struggle he had waged for many years against usually more influential rivals. Understandably enough, he seized the opportunity offered him by Göring and

[163] See Below, *Hitlers Adjutant*, 262–3.
[164] See Göring's notification to Thomas, 26 Feb. 1941, KTB WiRüAmt/Stab 1939/41, 214, BA-MA RW 19/164.
[165] Minute by Thomas on his report to the Reich Marshal, 26 Feb. 1941, BA-MA Wi/I D 1716.
[166] Thomas, *Wehr- und Rüstungswirtschaft*, 300.

'reported' spontaneously, if not quite truthfully, 'that preparatory work on those lines' was 'already in progress'. He promised to submit a draft organizational outline soon. The level of expectation from which Thomas proceeded after his conversation with Göring emerges from the war diary entry[167] which states that the Reich Marshal 'hands over to the department chief the preparations for the entire administration. He emphasizes that the department chief will have a completely free hand; he does not intend to let any other departments or authorities exercise any influence.' Only the food-supply area was to be taken over by Backe.

In order to secure his presumed triumph, Thomas immediately ordered a draft decree[168] to be prepared for Göring, the burden of which was to be the 'concentration of command authority in all questions of the economy'. In all future operations the organization of the OKW would take charge of the 'entire utilization of occupied territories' and perform the 'annexation of the economy of those territories to that of the Greater German economic sphere with a view to the greatest possible enhancement of German armament'. Thomas's ambitions evidently aimed at breaking the autonomy of the separate Wehrmacht services in armaments matters and at making OKW, under Göring's 'patronage', the command centre for the war economy. The future would show whether such hopes were realistic. But there can be no doubt that his model suited the demands of a modern war far better than the procedures practised in the past.

(d) The Establishment of the Economic Organization East

From the end of February 1941 work proceeded feverishly in the War Economy and Armaments Department on the organizational and conceptual foundations of an Economic Organization East.[169] The Russia staff was instructed by Thomas to prepare a new organizational draft for Göring within eight days.[170] It was, among other things, to contain the unequivocal statement that the Organization was independent of any kind of military or civilian administration, receiving its instructions directly from General Thomas. It also contained explicit mention of the taking over of certain areas of responsibility from the Reich ministry of economic affairs, and the demand addressed to the Wehrmacht services to dispense with armaments offices of their own in the occupied territories. Even the take-over and securing of captured military installations was to come within the authority of the war-economy officers. To

---

[167] KTB WiRüAmt/Stab 1939/41, 214 (26 Feb. 1941), BA-MA RW 19/164.

[168] Der Reichsmarschall des Großdeutschen Reiches, draft, Feb. 1941, BA-MA Wi/VIII. 411.

[169] The account by Thomas, *Wehr- und Rüstungswirtschaft*, 266 ff., is not reliable, although the secondary literature is largely based on it—e.g. Gibbons, 'Soviet Industry', 121 ff. Birkenfeld tries to explain the conflict between Thomas's zeal in preparing for the Russian campaign and his alleged resistance by a kind of 'schizophrenia, so typical of men of the Resistance on active service. Duty compels them to devote their entire effort to the preparation of something which passionate volition is trying to prevent': introduction to Thomas, *Wehr- und Rüstungswirtschaft*, 17–18.

[170] See minute dated 28 Feb. 1941, No. 1317-PS, *IMT* xxvii. 169–71.

support the Economic Organization, a 'military administration' was envisaged, which would concern itself mainly with 'looking after the population' and 'safeguarding nutrition in the occupied territories'.[171] The task of the war-economy officers, on the other hand, would be to accompany the army's advance, safeguard captured stocks, and administer the conquered industrial areas. In view of the bottlenecks of the German war economy the collection of raw materials in Russia was a particularly important task.

In order to guarantee staffing of the 'Oldenburg' working team by the necessary personnel, Thomas called a conference of all officers involved in the preparatory work for the beginning of March.[172] He also summoned to it Luftwaffe Lieutenant-General Schubert, the armaments inspector in Paris, who seemed to have the ideal qualifications for a future head of Economic Organization East. As a former military attaché in Moscow and Reichswehr representative during the first few years of secret co-operation with the Red Army, he was familiar with conditions in the Soviet armaments industry,[173] he had experience of managing large armaments organizations, and as a Luftwaffe general he had the necessary 'direct line' to Göring.

To enable the initially modest organization to cope with its new tasks the 'Economic Staff East' was considerably enhanced and enlarged as a directing body. It was to be headed by an 'Economic Control Staff East' as its steering body, headed by State Secretary Paul Körner representing Göring; this was to render possible the participation of other civilian and military agencies. Thomas reserved the 'central responsibility' to himself. On 19 March Göring approved this organization plan[174] and on 29 April Thomas informed the Wehrmacht services.[175] The order establishing the organization, dated 6 May, envisaged five economic inspectorates with a total of 23 economic squads (Wirtschaftskommandos) and 12 field agencies (Außenstellen), with a staff totalling 6,485.[176] The real problem, however, was the relationship of this economic authority with the military administration and the delimitation of its tasks as against the military administration—in other words, its role in the future occupation policy in Russia. A mere week after the commissioning of Thomas with this task, further directives were issued by Hitler: these made it

[171] Draft WiRüAm directive for Göring, Feb. 1941, BA-MA Wi/VIII. 411.

[172] OKW/WiRüAmt/Rü (Ic) No. 574/41 g.Kdos., concerning war-economy staff (special duties) Oldenburg, 26 Feb. 1941, ibid.

[173] On Schubert's role in the 1920s see Müller, *Tor zur Weltmacht*, 99. As late as his account of the early 1960s it is evident how closely he agreed with Göring's and Rosenberg's political ideas: version of 20 July 1965, BA-MA MSg 2/2558. In contrast to the sober businesslike attitude of Thomas, whom he mistrusted, Schubert felt inspired by his task, which he likened 'to the Varingian campaign a thousand years ago'; see Lt.-Gen. Schubert, No. 93/41 g.Kdos., Oldenburg study, 9 Mar. 1941, BA-MA RW 31/80.

[174] Chef WiRüAmt, g.Kdos., report to Reich Marshal Göring on 19 Mar. 1941, minute dated 20 Mar. 1941, BA-MA Wi/VIII. 411.

[175] Minute of the conference on 29 Apr. 1941, No. 1157-PS, *IMT* xxvii. 32 ff.

[176] OKW/WiRüAmt/Rü (Ic) No. 1405/41 g.Kdos., betr. Wirtschaftsorganisation z.b.V. Oldenburg [concerning economic organization, special duties Oldenburg], 6 May 1941, BA-MA Wi/VIII. 347.

clear that what he had in mind was not simply a reorganization in the economic sphere, but generally an integration of political, ideological, economic, and military objectives into an overall strategy.[177]

Hitler ruled that the military administration of the Army High Command was to be confined to the operational areas, while the rear areas were to be handed over to civilian Reich commissars. These were to be assisted by Wehrmacht commanders in the handling of military and war-economy tasks in the hinterland. Overlapping authority, i.e. for the area of the military administration and for the Reich commissariats, was assigned to Himmler for the police sector and to Göring (or, acting on his behalf, General Thomas) for the economic sphere.[178] The idea, therefore, was that the optimal collection of booty, needed on war-economy and on logistical grounds, was to be ensured by the co-operation of the 'four pillars': the Wehrmacht, Himmler's special-action squads, Rosenberg's Reich commissars, and Göring's economic organization. Hitler did not accurately delineate the tasks of each of these. That he left to the rivalry of the different officials. Hence the structural and delimitation issues became the most pressing problem of the new economic organization. To achieve his far-reaching ambitions Thomas had to assert his 'central responsibility' vis-à-vis Göring's civilian economic managers and, at the same time, find a modus vivendi with OKH that took account both of the executive power of the army in the theatre of operations and of the overall economic concerns of OKW.

Although the first drafts and instructions assumed a general directive-issuing authority by the War Economy and Armaments Department, Göring soon made it clear that he had no intention of leaving Thomas an entirely free hand. The draft of a letter by Thomas,[179] designed to get the Reich Marshal to inform the commander-in-chief of the army that he, Thomas, would have full authority to deal with economic matters, was altered by Göring at the crucial passage. Its revised version ran: 'For the preparation and implementation of the organization necessary for this purpose I have set up a control staff answerable to me directly and headed, on my behalf, by State Secretary Körner. It includes, among others, Infantry General Thomas, head of the War Economy and Armaments Department in the Wehrmacht High Command.'[180] On another occasion Göring had given instructions that the economic organization should be staffed by 'the best forces from industry', chosen not by OKW but by the Four-year Plan authority.[181] Moreover, he delegated the top officials of his Four-year Plan authority into the Economic Control Staff East,

[177] See KTB OKW i. 341 (3 Mar. 1941), and sect. I.VII.2(a) (Förster).

[178] See OKW/WFSt/Abt. L (IV Qu) No. 44125/41 g.Kdos., Richtlinien auf Sondergebieten zur Weisung No. 21 [Guidelines on special areas supplementing Directive No. 21], 13 Mar. 1941, No. 447-PS, IMT xxvi. 53 ff.

[179] BA-MA Wi/VIII.323.

[180] VO Wi/RüAmt bei OKH/Gen.Qu., betr. Wirtschaftsorganisation Barbarossa [concerning economic organization Barbarossa], minute dated 14 May 1941, BA-MA Wi/I D. 45

[181] Chef WiRüAmt, minute dated 20 Mar. 1941 (see above, n. 174).

so that Thomas's idea of a loosely constituted advisory body under his 'central responsibility' soon proved to be an illusion.

Although the Economic Staff East and its subordinate agencies were assured of a military channel of control issuing from OKW, the work to be done by the specialized civilian departments was largely controlled by the various Reich authorities. The most important Main Group (Chefgruppe) for Agriculture in the Economic Staff East was headed by Ministerialdirektor Hans Joachim Riecke of the Reich ministry of food, a Party member since 1925 and an SA Gruppenführer. The Main Group Economic Affairs was headed by Ministerialdirektor Gustav Schlotterer, one of Funk's principal assistants. He had been a Party member since 1923 and a leading National Socialist economic journalist. After 1933 he had been in charge of the Department for Export Promotion in the Reich ministry of economic affairs and in that post had been concerned also with trade with the east. The head of his Russian desk, Ministerialrat Wilhelm Ter-Nedden, had been employed since 1939–40 on 'German–Russian economic planning' and was now assigned to the two principal departments in Main Group 'W' of the Economic Staff East. It should also be mentioned that in the summer of 1940 Schlotterer had been in charge, on Göring's instructions, of postwar economic planning. After the beginning of the German–Soviet war he additionally took charge of the newly established Main Department VI (Economic problems of the newly occupied eastern territories) in the Reich ministry of economic affairs as well as Main Group III Wi (Economic-policy co-operation) in the Reich ministry for the occupied eastern territories. (For the structure of the Economic Staff East in 1941 and for the planned chain of command in the Economic Organization East see Diagrams I.III.1 and I.III.2.)

These ministerial representatives, enjoying the confidence of the Party and experienced in the planning and implementation of large-area economic policy, brought with them their own teams of experts into the Economic Organization East, so that OKW was eventually left with only the narrow field of armaments economy. Initial expectations that Göring's concept would not remain a one-off decision but that the organization for the east would rather become a model for all future operations were soon disappointed. On 3 April 1941 Consul-General Franz Neuhausen paid a surprise call on Thomas and informed him that Göring had appointed him 'economic dictator' for Yugoslavia.[182] OKW's organization, which was then being built up for the Balkan campaign, had to be placed under Neuhausen and a complicated harmonization had to be carried out with his own apparatus.

As the Army High Command had been somewhat relieved at the news that it would be spared the 'burden' of administration in Russia, arrangements with Thomas proceeded without any conflict. Both sides considered it necessary for the forward economic agencies to be closely integrated in the

---

[182] See KTB WiRüAmt/Stab 1941, p. 4 (3 Apr. 1941), BA-MA RW 19/165.

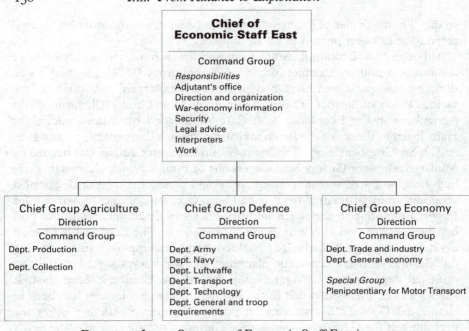

DIAGRAM I.III.I. Structure of Economic Staff East in 1941

command structure of the ground forces. It was therefore agreed that while operations were in progress the Economic Staff East should be located in the immediate proximity of the quartermaster-general, to ensure smooth co-operation.[183] In the rear army areas the subordination of one economic inspectorate each to the commanding officers and the establishment of one or several economic control squads under the security divisions were envisaged, together with one Group IV Wi economist at each field headquarters in the rear areas. In the army area the higher commands were to have a Group IV Wi economic expert assigned to them, who would at the same time be OKW's liaison officer. According to need, these economic agencies would have attached to them collecting and scouting units for manufacturing industry and for agricultural produce and machinery, as well as technical battalions for the restoration of supply enterprises, mineral-oil units, and mining companies.

It was the task of these economic agencies to make themselves available to the Wehrmacht commands to meet the immediate needs of the fighting forces. Although this task enjoyed priority while operations were in progress, preparations were to be made at the same time for the utilization of the country for the German war effort. In the event this meant that the economic officers had

---

[183] On the following passages see Wirtschafts-Führungsstab Ost, Richtlinien für die Führung der Wirtschaft in den neubesetzten Ostgebieten [Economic Control Staff East, Guidelines for the control of the economy in the newly occupied eastern territories], June 1941, pp. 5–6, BA-MA RW 31/128 D: *Fall Barbarossa*, No. 112.

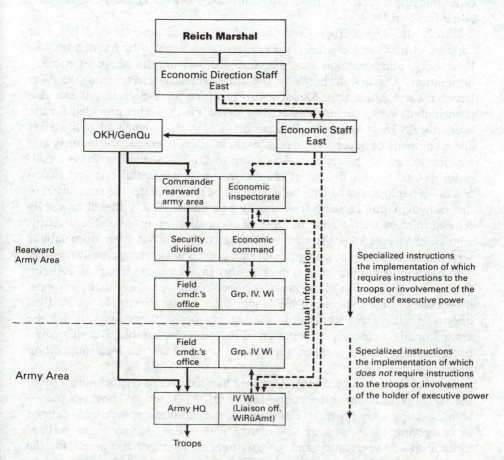

Diagram I.III.2. Structure of Economic Organization East (Plan)

Source: Green Folder, pt. 1, June 1941, BA-MA RW 31/128 D.

to direct supplies simultaneously forward and back, which soon turned out to be highly problematical in practice. The procedure was further impeded by the complicated regulation of authority to issue commands and instructions. Thus while the military and economic apparatuses were leaning upon one another, any clear subordination was avoided. The quartermaster-general found himself compelled to sacrifice the principle of uniform administration in the area of operations to the economic organization's striving for independence.

A question that remained entirely unresolved was that of the relationship between the military administration and economic agencies on the one hand and the envisaged civilian administration on the other. As Göring had been entrusted by Hitler with the unified control of the economy in the occupied eastern territories, Thomas saw no reason for aligning the boundaries of his economic inspectorates along the separation-line between military and civilian administration.

Within the Army High Command there was likewise at first no clear concept of how, or for what purpose, territories were to be handed over to Rosenberg, and attention was therefore focused on the phase of military occupation. Discussion between the quartermaster-general and the War Economy and Armaments Department, in which State-Secretary Backe also participated, led to the drafting of the 'Rayon Plan'.[184] This provided for the economically most important Russian districts to be assigned a headquarters and a company of occupation troops each, in order to ensure the security and exploitation of the hinterland. According to OKW calculations such a procedure would require the use of 360,000 men with 4,000 staff cars and 10,000 trucks—a deployment which might perhaps be possible after the conclusion of the campaign but certainly not during operations. OKH therefore solidly refused to make such a large number of occupation troops available. Eventually Thomas asked for the provision of at least 100,000 men from labour service and replacement units;[185] even that proved to be only partially feasible. Thomas found support from Backe, who in an urgent letter to Keitel[186] demanded the creation of the greatest possible number of occupation troops, if necessary at the expense of the labour force in the Reich. He justified his demand by the grave situation in Germany's foodstuff economy, which, he argued, made a ruthless exploitation of Russia indispensable. But this could not be accomplished without appropriate pressure on the local population there.

As soon as the occupied territories were handed over to civil administration, the Wehrmacht commander appointed by OKW—this was Thomas's plan—would occupy a key position. His duties in the economic sphere were defined as 'supplying the troops in accordance with OKH demands', as well as 'utilization of the country and safeguarding of its economic assets for the purposes of the German economy'.[187] The state secretaries and, more particularly, Rosenberg were informed of this at the beginning of May.[188] Rosenberg was moreover notified that the Wehrmacht commanders would, in these matters, be placed above the civilian administration. Rosenberg objected at once, claiming for himself unrestricted responsibility in all spheres, including the economy. Hitler settled the conflict with his typical 'reluctance to commit himself'.[189] Once the territories had been handed over to civilian administra-

---

[184] See the letter of Arbeitsstab z.b.V. to Gen. Thomas, 13 May 1941, BA-MA Wi/I D. 45.

[185] Chef WiRüAmt, g.Kdos., Fragen, die durch den Herrn Reichsmarschall noch befohlen, bzw. beim Führer geklärt werden müssen [Questions on which orders are still to be issued by the Reich Marshal or which must be approved by the Führer], 5 May 1941, ibid. (partially published in Müller, 'Interessenpolitik', No. 4).

[186] G.Kdos., copy of La B. No. 39/41 g.Kdos., letter by Backe to OKW chief of staff, 14 May 1941, ibid.

[187] See above, n. 178.

[188] OKW/WFSt/L IV, g.Kdos., conference at Reich Leader Rosenberg's office, 1 May 1941, BA-MA RW 4/v. 759.

[189] Haffner, The Meaning of Hitler, 112.

tion, the economic agencies were formally to become part of their apparatus, while in their specialized activities they would continue to come under Göring and his Economic Control Staff. As for the Wehrmacht commanders, Hitler assigned to them only military-security functions and responsibility for supplies to the troops.[190] It was this very point which set the seal on the failure of General Thomas's concept—of his hopes that, once OKH had been successfully squeezed out of responsibility for the occupied territories, he would establish military domination and unified economic control by OKW. The road was open to future chaos in German occupation policy in Russia.[191] (For the proposed boundaries of the economic inspectorates see Map I.III.1.)

To sum up, it may be said that in the spring of 1941 the head of the War Economy and Armaments Department had allowed himself to be induced by Hitler and Göring to act as a wedge within the top military leadership, and, in pursuit of his boundless ambition, to follow an eventually disastrous policy of estrangement from the Army High Command. The separation of the economy from overall occupation policy on the one hand encouraged the inclination of the Army High Command to prepare and execute operations solely according to military and strategic considerations—which made collision with Hitler inevitable since for him the war-economy aspect occupied a higher priority. And on the other hand, it gave free rein to the economic agencies' eagerness for booty, which was now able to run untrammelled by any other considerations. That development was largely also encouraged by German private industry, whose interests it met.

(e) The Involvement of Private Enterprise

The majority of German big business had decided, certainly no later than the early 1930s, to support those political forces which stood for an expansion of the German political and economic sphere towards the east.[192] This general agreement with the eastward expansionist aims of National Socialism also determined attitudes during the phase of immediate war preparations by the Third Reich. Admittedly there were a few industrialists who, at moments of international tension, believed they had to remind the political leadership of that consensus and call for a strict observation of an anti-Soviet expansionist policy,[193] but these were the exception rather than the rule. After all, the fact that Hitler's war policy never lost sight of the creation of an economic 'living-space in the east' was known not only to his closest political and military

---

[190] Hitler's decree of 25 June 1941: *Deutsche Besatzungspolitik*, No. 8.

[191] On this see the extensive treatment in Dallin, *German Rule in Russia*. The factual justification of independence for the economic organization, formulated retrospectively in the history of WiStabOst, is certainly not to be dismissed lightly; see *Deutsche Wirtschaftspolitik*, 27 ff. However, as has been shown above, such considerations were not at the centre of the fundamental decisions made in the spring of 1941.

[192] See Müller, *Tor zur Weltmacht*, 235 ff., and *Germany and the Second World War*, i. 189 ff.

[193] Mention should be made here of Krauch's remarks in Apr. 1939 and of the memoranda by Rechberg and Röchling in 1938 and 1936 respectively, published in *Anatomie des Krieges*, Nos. 47, 80, 82, 93.

Source: Map OKW WiRüAmt/Wi, 1 Mar. 1941, BA-MA Wi/VIII 266

MAP I.III.I. The Planned Boundaries of the Economic Inspectorates

Source: Map OKW WiRüAmt/Wi, 1 Mar. 1941, BA-MA Wi/VIII 266.

circle.[194] The question of exerting direct influence, or of bringing about a change of course, did not therefore arise at all for the top industrialists or bankers. So long as the National Socialist leadership—whose powers of decision had been greatly strengthened after the depression of 1936 in the area of economic policy as well—ensured, or even promised, the satisfaction of basic economic interests with its foreign-policy or military operations, it could

[194] See Müller, *Tor zur Weltmacht*, 245 ff., and for Hitler's military circle the evidence of Below, *Hitlers Adjutant*, 185.

maintain the primacy of politics without opposition. Timing and sequence of individual expansionist steps might be determined by Hitler unopposed. Thus a form of co-operation developed, in which 'on the one hand, the state was guaranteed the pursuance of its political objectives, while, on the other, the effectiveness of free entrepreneurial initiative and the freedom of private capital were not impaired'.[195]

The approval of Hitler's war policy by big business undoubtedly reached its peak in the summer of 1940. The hegemony which had been achieved in Europe assured it of undreamt-of opportunities of expansion and profit, especially as the administration was offering every possible support and encouragement for the achievement of close integration with the European national economies, and thus for the goal of a strong self-sufficient large-area economy under German leadership. Although the resulting tasks required all the strength of the German economy, and although their accomplishment was still far from being in sight, there was unanimity in top economic circles after the campaign in France that the economic 'reorganization' of Europe was no more than the jumping-off base for a global struggle with the Anglo-American bloc for control of the world market, and that German control and freedom to dispose over Russian resources had to be viewed as an indispensable prerequisite.[196] And in that context there could scarcely be any doubt that the solution of the problem through trade policy was totally unsatisfactory in the long term and could represent no more than a provisional solution.

It is, of course, conceivable that prior to taking important decisions Hitler might have conferred also with leading industrialists, and consulted with them, without such contacts necessarily being mentioned in those records that have come down to us.[197] Even so, it may be assumed with some justification that in the decision-making in the spring of 1941 there was no direct impulse from big business towards a realization of anti-Soviet aggressive aims. Indirect influence, on the other hand, may be detected along the fringes of the political decision-making centre, as reflected by the discussion of the problem of large-area economics; and that influence should be seen as operating in parallel with the views of diplomats and military figures outlined above.

When, therefore, Governor-General Hans Frank at an economic conference at the beginning of June 1940 hinted at the possibility of a military conflict with the USSR,[198] he could expect to meet with understanding on the part of the representatives of trade and industry. By July, within the Wehrmacht High

---

[195] Quotation from *Der Wirtschaftsring*, 14 (14 Apr. 1941), 379. See also Volkmann, 'Verhältnis'.

[196] For the contemporary discussion see, among others, the arguments of the well-known economist Brinkmann, 'Die wirtschaftliche Gestaltung'.

[197] See Volkmann, 'Verhältnis', 88. Some particularly striking instances are provided by Dipl.Ing. Erich Schneider, Lt.-Gen. (retd.): Einige Erfahrungen des Heeres-Waffenamtes mit der Industrie, besonders in der Entwicklung und Prüfung von Waffen, Munition und Gerät [Some experiences of the army weapons department in dealing with industry, especially in the development and testing of weapons, ammunition, and equipment], 25 June 1952, BA-MA Bw 9/138.

[198] No. 2233-PS, *IMT* xxix. 419.

Command preparations for a military 'eastern solution' were a secret which, despite all attempts at concealment, was leaking out.[199] The Wehrmacht High Command order 'Aufbau Ost' (Build-up East), resulting in the withdrawal of labour even from vital armaments enterprises, Germany's defeat in the Battle of Britain, as well as the strengthening of the German position in Romania and Finland—all these were indications which, by August 1940, were correctly interpreted by attentive observers on the management floors of the German armaments industry. Detailed preparations for the attack on the USSR were by no means confined, in the initial phase, to the political and military planes. The realignment of armaments inevitably involved numerous enterprises of Germany's privately owned armaments industry, as well as their suppliers. German business in general, in so far as it was able—encouraged by surmises or indiscretions[200]—to adapt to the political leadership's war plans, was anxious at that stage to ensure its influence on the decision-making process of official bodies with regard to the issue of economic policy in the occupied Soviet territories. Until the responsibilities of the different authorities were clearly defined, it was natural for firms to keep to those authorities which in earlier campaigns had been the control centres for the distribution of captured stocks, machinery, enterprises, and other economic assets. Individual firms which made themselves indispensable at an early stage by providing expert opinions and other information, or by making available appropriate expert staff, thus found the field wide open for the pursuit of their own selfish interests.

This meant, primarily, the military economic organization. In contrast to OKH, where the excesses of private enrichment through officially gained information and influence were viewed with mistrust,[201] matters were handled in a comparatively generous way by the War Economy and Armaments Department. The close links and co-operation with private enterprise resulted in a tolerant attitude towards specialized staff called up for army duties, who, in armaments control squads or technical units, or as temporary managers of plants, often pursued the interests of their firms.[202] In the case of planning against Russia the Wehrmacht High Command's position was further strengthened by the fact that the quartermaster-general was focusing his main interest on the Soviet armaments industry, which he believed could, on past evidence, already be regarded as Wehrmacht booty, to be run under the auspices of the weapons departments.

The intensified gathering of intelligence about the Soviet Union, practised since August 1940 by the war-economy section, provided a promising field for

---

[199] See Bräutigam, *So hat es sich zugetragen*, 275.

[200] See e.g. the relevant diary entries in Hassell, *Tagebücher*, 162, 165 (22 Sept., 8 Oct. 1940)

[201] Thus the commander of German forces in Denmark reported that 'all sorts of dubious characters are arriving from Thomas's office (black marketeers)': Halder, *Diaries*, 344 (6 May 1940).

[202] On the close ties between the War Economy and Armaments Department and industry see also the account in Thomas, *Wehr- und Rüstungswirtschaft*, 108 ff.

industrial influence. Thus the Siemens concern offered information on Soviet energy supplies, and IG-Farben provided data on the production of aviation fuel in the USSR.[203] In mid-October OKW decided to commission the concern to compile a major study of the Soviet Union's chemical industry; this provided the basis of the department's war-economy studies and plans. The AEG concern similarly supplied data on the Soviet electrical industry, and in early November, while Molotov was in Berlin, an IG-Farben representative examined and updated the entire material available on Russia at the War Economy and Armaments Department.

When Lieutenant-General Stud, during his initial conversations about an economic organization, gave instructions that not only should experts on Russia be tracked down within the department but in addition contacts should be made with civilian circles, he was thinking predominantly, perhaps a little naïvely, of haulage firms active in east–west trade.[204] The armaments section, however, instructed the officers concerned to go for the big firms which had done business with Russia in the past.[205] The first person proposed was a Siemens engineer,[206] which was hardly surprising considering existing close contacts. During the following period the enlistment of specialists continued to be governed by personal relations and applications from firms.[207] Although the actual preparations for the establishment of the War Economy and Armaments Department, prior to January 1941, concerned only a limited number of technical units, contacts were even then being established on a wide scale in order to collect details of experts on Russia in the business world.

As preparations for the economic aspect of the Russian campaign within the Wehrmacht High Command were petering out at the beginning of 1941—an outward sign was the cancellation of the induction courses originally planned for February—business circles found themselves confronted with a new situation in that there was now no contact person available on the government side. Admittedly Halder intended to include 'advisers' from the world of business in his model of military administration,[208] but these ideas could not be implemented so long as no final decision had been arrived at on the fundamentals of future German occupation policy in Russia.

In consequence, managerial circles increasingly turned their attention to the German–Soviet economic agreement of 10 January 1941, which held out the prospect of new and exceedingly favourable business opportunities. An IG-Farben board meeting on 5 February welcomed the 'relatively favourable

[203] KTB WiRüAmt/Wi 1940, 281 (2 Oct. 1940), BA-MA RW 19/244; this also supports the data which follow.

[204] Rü (Ic), minute dated 1 Nov. 1940, BA-MA Wi/VIII. 411.

[205] Rü (Ib) 15552/40, minute for Col. Dietrich (Wi VI), dated 5 Nov. 1940, ibid.   [206] Ibid.

[207] See e.g. a recommendation from IG-Farben by way of the foreign ministry, letter Großkopf, 22 May 1941, PA, Pol. XIII. 25, p. 198848, and the personal recommendation of Col. Nagel, the War Economy and Armaments Department's liaison officer with Göring, 20 Nov. 1941, BA-MA RW 31/195.

[208] Halder, *Diaries*, 779 (11 Feb. 1941).

success of export business' with the USSR.[209] The Hoesch concern's official in charge of business with Russia expressed himself 'very optimistic' about the development of bilateral economic relations and was favourably impressed by the fact that the Russians were already anxious to discuss business for 1942, which suggested that Moscow was clearly thinking of 'long-term planning'.[210] The firm of Thüringische Zellwolle AG opened negotiations about setting up a complete factory in the Volga region; these were successfully concluded in June 1941.[211] The then first secretary at the Soviet embassy in Berlin, Valentin Berezhkov, in his memoirs records the frequent visits by leading representatives of German big business, who expressed the view 'that the Soviet Union and Germany complement one another in many respects and that the development of trade relations benefits both our countries'.[212] There were even deliberate warnings of Hitler's aggressive intentions, which induced the Army High Command and the foreign ministry to launch counter-measures.[213] However, the interest in exports, which in the 1920s and still in the 1930s had perceptibly marked German industry's attitude towards the USSR, had long died down and had no effective political weight any more. The main interest now was in securing and further stepping up Soviet deliveries of raw materials and foodstuffs, as these had become vital to Germany. General Thomas undoubtedly summed up this attitude correctly when he said that trade exchanges were of course necessary and useful, but if 'the military leadership is in a position to make good the deficiencies in our raw-material resources by way of conquest, then this would be particularly welcomed by our captains of industry'.[214]

In any case, there was no doubt in industrial circles about the seriousness of the military preparations for aggression.[215] The Russia Committee of German Trade and Industry therefore felt it necessary to warn firms engaged in deals with Russia to have themselves briefed by the Committee before engaging in business negotiations.[216]

When Göring, with his instructions to Thomas on 26 February 1941, inaugurated the turn-about in war-economy preparations, he proceeded from the belief that, for the purpose of taking over all important enterprises, it would be 'appropriate from the start to involve reliable figures from German business concerns, as only with their experience will it be possible to do

---

[209] Minute of the 24th board meeting on 5 Feb. 1941, No. 8079-NI, Staatsarchiv Nürnberg.

[210] Confidential report by Leibbrandt, 10 Jan. 1941, PA, Dienststelle Ribbentrop, UdSSR.

[211] Kehrl, *Krisenmanager*, 222; for an extensive survey of the numerous contracts concluded by German firms with Soviet trade representatives in the spring of 1941 see Eichler, *Wirtschaftsbeziehungen*, 185–6.

[212] Bereshkow, *Jahre*, 64.   [213] Ibid. 65, and *DGFP* D xii, No. 260 (3 Apr. 1941).

[214] Thomas, *Wehr- und Rüstungswirtschaft*, 301—in its interpretation conflicting with Gibbons, 'Soviet Industry', 110–11.

[215] See Hassel, *Tagebücher*, 178, 183 (19 Jan., 2 Mar. 1941).

[216] Rußland-Ausschuß der Deutschen Wirtschaft, Tgb. No. 1369/R.D./C., circular letter dated 21 Mar. 1941, BA R 7/4699, RWM, Ländererlasse, xxxvii; on the same lines also a memorandum of the Krupp concern dated 10 Apr. 1941: Gibbons, 'Soviet Industry', 111.

successful work from the outset'.[217] Even in the military section of the economic organization, the key positions, in his opinion, were to be filled by 'the best figures from the business world'.[218]

Following that political decision private industry was involved to a greatly increased degree in the plans and preparations for the economic organization. Admittedly the Wehrmacht High Command was no longer the agency for that. The co-ordinators of state and private-enterprise interests were now the representatives of the civilian economic sector, primarily the ministry for economic affairs and the Four-year Plan authority; German big business preferred to deal with them rather than with the military. This development suited private business: its increasingly close ties with the Party and state apparatus made it easier for business to exploit rivalries between authorities in order to gain decisive influence and strengthen the autonomy of private enterprise against state control.[219]

On 27 March 1941 the 'Kontinentale Öl AG' was founded as the model for the new form of co-operation between state and private economy.[220] This umbrella organization, supported jointly by industry, banking, the military, and the economic bureaucracy, was to ensure for German mineral-oil interests 'the position which Germany as a great power needs and to which it is entitled'.[221] For the German war economy to be dependent on the 'good will' of foreign governments was 'as dangerous as it is intolerable'. In future any oil policy relevant to German supplies was to be made in Germany alone. This referred not only to the Balkans.

Two days prior to the first conference about the establishment of the company Halder had had himself briefed on 'Oil deposits and their importance for the European economy: Baku'.[222] Simultaneously, within the Wehrmacht High Command, 'material for the examination of action against the Caucasian oil region' was being collected, and General Thomas, who was a member of the company's board, never tired of pointing out that the conquest of the Caucasus must absolutely be included in operational plans.[223] A minute by Deutsche Bank correctly described the development of Kontinentale Öl AG as depending 'on the future course of the war'.[224]

On the basis of such close ties between political, military, and industrial expansionist goals, preparations began in March 1941 at the Reich ministry for economic affairs for the attack on the USSR. The names of the administrative experts needed for the direction of the Economic Organization East were

---

[217] Minute by Thomas (above, n. 165).

[218] Minute by Thomas of his report to Göring on 19 Mar. 1941, BA-MA Wi/VIII. 138.

[219] See Müller, 'Interessenpolitik', 108 ff.

[220] For the background see Eichholtz, *Kriegswirtschaft*, 235 ff., and Czollek and Eichholtz, 'Monopole', 66 ff.

[221] Hellmer, 'Neue deutsche Ölpolitik'.   [222] Halder, *Diaries*, 759 (22 Jan. 1941).

[223] See the minute by Thomas (above, n. 165) and annexe to OKW/WFSt/Abt. L (I Op) No. 44565/4/g.Kdos., 4 May 1941: *Fall Barbarossa*, No. 47.

[224] Minute by Hermann J. Abs, 23 Jan. 1941: Czollek and Eichholtz, 'Monopole', 67.

given to the War Economy and Armaments Department by the end of April. To facilitate the recruitment of the large number of experts for the technical units and the forward economic agencies, preliminary discussions were held in certain important fields, such as the iron and metallurgical industry, with those private firms which had already earmarked experts for the take-over of Soviet enterprises.[225] For reasons of security, however, these arrangements were not extended until immediately after the launch of the attack.[226]

Parallel to such questions of personnel, efforts were also being made to ensure an exchange of views and information on the Soviet economy and on the economic objectives of the military operation. To that end the ministry for economic affairs approached the economic self-administration bodies, the industrial and specialized groups, which in turn approached individual firms.[227] Under the heading of 'large-area economy' information was thus exchanged on the prospects of expansion into Russia, and requests and demands were put forward in advance. Thus, weeks before the actual attack, 'lists of booty' were already circulating in entrepreneurial circles; these had either been compiled in industrial archives[228] or made available by governmental agencies.[229] The ministry for economic affairs expected firms to go in for 'forward planning', to make sure they were 'ready for take-off' at the end of the war.[230] On much the same lines were the remarks by Paul Heinrichs, manager of the Zeiss concern, at the beginning of May 1941: 'Meanwhile the Balkans have been cleaned up, and we can now get down to planning for whatever comes next.'[231] What would 'come next' emerged clearly from the principal agenda of the economic research institutions and the economic departments of big business firms; ever since spring that year—and increasingly so after the attack on the USSR—they had been producing expert opinions on Russia's economy and making them available to the state authorities.[232] Interest ranged from sheep-keeping through the leather and footwear industry to cement manufacture.

Competitive pressures and the urge for expansion caused many entrepreneurs to place their hopes in the opening up of new marketing and profit

---

[225] See minute by Hans Reichard, head of the foreign department of the Otto Wolff concern, 25 June 1941: Czollek and Eichholtz, 'Monopole', 73.

[226] See minutes of the IG-Farben board meeting on 10 July 1941, published in part in *Anatomie des Krieges*, No. 170.

[227] See Eichholtz, *Kriegswirtschaft*, 203.

[228] See e.g. Wirtschaftsgruppe Chemische Industrie, Die Chemische Industrie der Sowjet-Union [Economic group for the chemical industry, The Chemical Industry of the Soviet Union], second enlarged version, June 1941, BA-MA RW 19 annexe I/1510, as well as the collection of material on Lagerstätten, eisenschaffende und eisenverarbeitende Industrie im europäischen Gebiet der UdSSR [Location of the iron-producing and iron-processing industry in the European territory of the USSR], which the Reichswerke concern was able to distribute in a third version by July 1941, ibid. 1515.

[229] See the reference-paper of WiRüAmt, Die Lage und Ausrüstungen der Eisenindustrie der Sowjet-Union [The situation and equipment of the ferrous industry of the Soviet Union], Mar. 1941, BA-MA RW 19 annexe I/176; see also Eichholtz, *Kriegswirtschaft*, 203.

[230] Kehrl, *Aufgaben*, 22–3.

[231] Personal letter from Heinrichs, quoted in Schumann, 'Kriegsprogramm', 722.

[232] The papers are in the former secret archive OKW/WiRüAmt, BA-MA RW 19 annexe I.

opportunities in European Russia. In the field of mining it was mainly the semi-state-owned Reichswerke concern, directed by Göring's economic manager Paul Pleiger, which was anxious to expand the empire it had created in central and eastern Europe by the acquisition of the valuable south Russian coal and ore deposits.[233] Relying on favours from Göring, the management of the concern was determined to gain for itself an advantage in Russia over its Rhineland-Westphalian competitors, who based their claims largely on the period of the First World War.

The German textile industry also went into action as early as the spring of 1941. Its representative, the textile industrialist Hans Kehrl, responsible for German textile supplies in the ministry for economic affairs as well as in the Four-year Plan authority, sought assurances from State Secretary Backe that the agricultural leaders would not erect any obstacles to the exploitation of Russian cultivation areas or production capacities.[234] In March the Institute for Economic Research in a study confirmed Russia's surplus potential in textile raw materials of 'particular importance to German textile circles'.[235] Although Europe possessed the world's biggest textile production capacity, it was nevertheless dependent on substantial Soviet deliveries of hemp, flax, raw wool, and linseed.[236] Russia moreover represented a still largely undeveloped gigantic market which, as the result of a Soviet industrialization policy favouring a one-sided development of heavy industry, was characterized by a hitherto unsatisfied backlog of demand. It should also be borne in mind that the further development of cellulose production—as a substitute for the lacking raw materials within the framework of the Four-year Plan—had reached its limits, set by an insufficiency of investments, building capacities, manpower, and finally even timber as its feedstock.

The IG-Farben concern, as the largest and most influential enterprise of the chemical industry, was interested primarily in eliminating any burgeoning competition in Russia and in making sure that the existing capacities there did not fall into state hands, or indeed other private hands.[237] In the boardroom that danger was seen as particularly great in the sphere of Buna. A list was therefore compiled of 'gentlemen suitable for employment in Russia for the purpose of taking over any enterprises for the production of synthetic rubber' and submitted to the Economic Organization East.[238] The issue of Soviet oil deposits had already been settled in the interest of the concern in March by the foundation of Kontinentale Öl AG. Unresolved, on the other hand, was the

---

[233] See Müller, 'Gen Ostland wollen wir reiten', and the comprehensive account in Riedel, *Eisen*, 300 ff.

[234] See Kehrl, *Krisenmanager*, 227 ff.

[235] Institute for Economic Research, Die Wirtschaft der UdSSR in Einzeldarstellungen [The economy of the USSR in separate presentations], issue 2, Mar. 1941, Die Textilwirtschaft der Sowjetunion [The textile industry of the Soviet Union], BA-MA RW 19 annexe I/1134.

[236] See Kiesewetter, 'Rohstoffprobleme', 49 ff.

[237] See affidavit by Max Ilgner (10 July 1947), member of the IG-Farben board and managing director of the Buna Werk GmbH Schkopau, No. NI-6348, published in *Fall 6*, 161–2, and the evidence given by his deputy Otto Ambros, published in *Trials*, viii. 292–3.

[238] Letter from Ambros to Krauch, 28 June 1941: Czollek and Eichholtz, 'Monopole', 74 ff.

problem of nitrogen production, which represented a dangerous bottleneck both for agriculture and for the production of explosives within the German sphere of power. On 26 April 1941 the chairman of the board, Professor Carl Krauch, once more briefed the general council of the Four-year Plan authority on the situation and prospects of European nitrogen supplies.[239] In May the nitrogen syndicate, which was dominated by IG-Farben, therefore prepared a comprehensive study of the Ukraine—rightly regarded as the most important nitrogen-producing and -consuming region of the future German empire in the east—and passed it on to the Wehrmacht High Command as a basis for its planning.[240]

Influential representatives of German big business therefore not only supported the political and military leadership's decision to conquer European Russia in 1941, at the cost of a war on two fronts, but extensively promoted it by their active participation in the organizational preparations. This identification of private enterprise with the National Socialist war for living-space cannot be fully explained by firm-specific expansionist interests. There was also a clear continuity of an eastward-directed imperialist economic policy which went back to the First World War. However, these inclinations were able to turn aggressive in the spring of 1941 only because the political leadership was clearly determined to conduct the planned campaign in the east as a war of pillage and destruction. The resultant abandonment of traditional practices of military occupation and administration allowed business a greater measure of collaboration and of influence even on political and military planning than had been the case in earlier campaigns of conquest. This emerged most conspicuously in the definition of economic war aims.

(f) Economic Objectives of the Campaign

During the first phase of the political and military decision-making process, until the end of 1940, economic war aims had been mainly defined in territorial terms. At the centre of interest was the capture of economically important regions, in order to weaken the enemy and bolster the German war economy. Although the quartermaster-general in his plans had envisaged at least a partial rehabilitation of the eastern territories to be occupied,[241] there existed a variety of ideas among the military leaders concerning future economic policy *vis-à-vis* Russia.

The Navyl High Command, in particular, being more accustomed than the army generals to thinking in global economic terms, regarded the objective of the campaign as the extension of Germany's 'living-space in the east' and hence her definitive immunity against blockade.[242] From that point of view it

---

[239] Notes for the report in the Karinhall Plan file, BA R 25/94, Reichsamt für Wirtschaftsausbau.

[240] Stickstoff-Syndikat, Wiss. Abt., Ukraine, May 1941, BA-MA RW 19 annexe I/1229.

[241] See sect. 2(a) of the present chapter.

[242] In addition to the above-mentioned observations by Fricke on 28 June 1940 see the retrospective observations by Grand Adm. Doenitz at the naval commanders' conference on 17 Dec. 1943, No. 443-D, *IMT* xxxv. 106-7.

was not enough to liquidate the Soviet system or partition the Soviet Union. 'Not until the newly created heavy and armaments industry has been destroyed and once more become dilapidated, and Russia has become a patriarchal authoritarian state with exclusively agricultural and raw-material production, will the threat from the east be lifted from Europe,'[243] noted the German naval attaché in Moscow, Captain Norbert von Baumbach, on 14 September 1940. That kind of picture of a 'new economic order' in the east was in line with the large-area economic plans pursued in Germany since the 1920s and was getting close to Hitler's living-space programme.

Such long-term plans, however, were of no interest initially to the Army High Command and, even less, the Wehrmacht High Command. Their plans were concerned primarily with a possible utilization of the Soviet armaments industry. The question of a specific economic gain from the eastern campaign began to move into the centre of attention with Hitler's Directive No. 21, during the second phase of decision-making. This may have been due partly to the exacerbation of war-economy problems in the Reich about the turn of 1940–1. Increasing importance was certainly being attached to the occupation of the Caucasian oilfields, in order to safeguard German fuel supplies, and of the 'grain-basket' of the Ukraine, in order to relieve the food situation throughout the German sphere of power.

In that assessment of economic war aims Hitler was supported mainly by Backe and Thomas. A possible indirect factor was the alarming memoranda sent by the IG-Farben director Krauch to Göring and Hitler, demanding a greater allocation of manpower and raw materials for the development of the hydrogenation plants; OKW had not been able to grant him such an allocation because of the tight situation in armaments.[244] Hitler himself, in his talk with the Italian top leaders on 20 January 1941, touched on this issue when he spoke of the possibility of freeing manpower for the armaments industry by eliminating the 'danger from the east'.[245] Four weeks later, in his conversations with his Japanese ally, interest was focused on a new share-out of global economic power. On that occasion Hitler claimed the European part of the Soviet Union for himself, while displaying less interest in its Asian territories.[246]

Belief in an economic profit to be gained in the east was not unreservedly shared throughout German leadership circles. There were sporadic critical voices, but these had no effect on the decision-making process. The state secretary in the foreign ministry, Freiherr von Weizsäcker, openly expressed his doubts in a position paper.[247] He was concerned primarily about the risks

---

[243] Notes dated 14 Sept. for the chief of staff of the naval command, BA-MA RM 8/K 10-2/10.
[244] See KTB WiRüAmt/Stab 1939/41, p. 112 (22 Jan. 1941), BA-MA RW 19/164. Against this background Hitler's remark of 20 June 1941 about the economic necessity of a war of conquest is readily understood; see Thomas, *Wehr- und Rüstungswirtschaft*, 300–1.
[245] *KTB OKW* i. 275 (22 Jan. 1941).
[246] Hillgruber, *Strategie*, 484 ff.; id., 'Japan'; Lehmann, 'Leitmotive'.
[247] See *DGFP* D xii, No. 419 (28 Apr. 1941); Hilger, *Erinnerungen*, 305–6; also Weizsäcker, *Erinnerungen*, 314–15.

of a war on two fronts. If Britain were really on the point of collapse, he argued, then

the thought might suggest itself that by the use of force we must feed ourselves from Soviet territory . . . If every Russian city reduced to ashes were as valuable to us as a sunken British warship, I should advocate the German–Russian war for this summer; but I believe that we would be victors over Russia only in a military sense, and would, on the other hand, lose in an economic sense.

He justified his view by the argument that it would not be possible, against the expected passive resistance of the Russians, to exploit the conquered land effectively or fast enough, while on the other hand one would have to assume that the Stalin regime would continue to exist in Siberia and the war in the east would be protracted indefinitely.

On the other hand, of course, there were figures in the foreign ministry who identified more strongly with Hitler's living-space programme and therefore welcomed the war preparations against the Soviet Union.[248] They emphasized the need to provide settlement space for an overpopulated Germany, and, as things stood, such space could be found only in the Ukraine. From there some 10–20 million Slavs would have to be evacuated to Soviet Asia to make room for the Germans. The reservations thus created in Siberia would have to be strictly controlled by the Reich to prevent any flare-up of Slav resistance.

Especially critical comment on the idea of rapid economic gain in the east came from the Reich minister of finance, Lutz Graf Schwerin von Krosigk.[249] When he learnt about the preparations for the campaign in the east he feared an over-extension of German strength and thought it wiser first of all to consolidate what had been accomplished. After Göring had told him that the 'reconstruction of Europe' would be enormously complicated by the continued existence of the Soviet regime and that a change of that state of affairs was therefore indispensable, he sent an extensive memorandum to the Reich Marshal in April 1941, based primarily on economic arguments.[250] In particular he rejected the assumption that the German supply situation could be substantially improved by the conquest of southern Russia. There would be no perceptible relief in the area of foodstuffs. On the contrary, he argued, as the Russians would burn down their barns and fields, less grain would be collected from Russia that year than the Reich would receive on the basis of current delivery contracts. And even if yields could be increased in the long term, there still remained the enormous transport difficulties. Even the greatest gain that could be achieved would never offset the loss which was bound to arise from the inevitable decline of domestic production in the event of a prolongation of the war.

---

[248] Vertraulich, Persönlich, Russische Skizzen [Confidential, personal, Russian sketches], Feb. 1941, estate of Niedermayer (BA-MA N 122/9), who records remarks presumably made by Consul Eisenlohr during his stay in Moscow for the purpose of discussing resettlement issues.

[249] See Schwerin von Krosigk, *Erinnerungen*, ii. 237–8.

[250] Letter from Schwerin von Krosigk to Göring, 19 Apr. 1941, BA R 2/24243.

Significant, however, is his reservation that matters would look different 'if the Russians did not keep their pact with us, failed to make the promised deliveries, etc. So far, however, there are no indications of such an attitude. On the contrary, I believe that, out of understandable fear, the Russians would strip off their own shirts in order to satisfy our delivery requests, even if we stepped them up further.'[251]

Similar views were held also by the spokesman for industry within the circle of the bourgeois opposition movement, Ulrich von Hassell. He foresaw a 'greatly increasing danger to food supplies' in the event of a German attack on the USSR, and expected three consequences: '(1) deliveries from Russia being cut off, whereas the Ukraine can become utilizable only after a long time; (2) new exceedingly heavy burdens on all war material and human resources; (3) deliberately triggered complete encirclement.'[252]

This essentially marginal criticism, therefore, was aimed primarily at the expectation of instant economic gain in the sense of a short-term cost-effectiveness analysis. However, as a result of Backe's and Thomas's contrasting statements both the military leadership and Hitler had long made up their minds. In a third phase of the decision-making process the overall economic profit of the campaign was to them beyond any question. The problem which instead moved to the fore was the methods to be used in order to achieve the maximum profit. Hitler's decision in favour of a new procedure moreover implied exploitational aims which reached further than in his past campaigns.

Göring's instruction to General Thomas to set up an Economic Organization East enabled the Wehrmacht High Command to lay down some initial specific war aims in the economic sphere with binding validity. The basics of this had already been outlined by Thomas in his memorandum to Hitler.[253] The goal was the collection of raw materials and foodstuffs to relieve the German war economy. The question of industrial rehabilitation, however, was left open. Reference to the high level of performance by the Soviet armaments industry suggested that its utilization was at least being considered in the Wehrmacht High Command. That, as well as the development of transport and the production and processing of raw materials, would admittedly require some measure of industrial activity in the occupied territory. And there was always the additional task—in line with Hitler's instructions—of supporting the army in the east.

The new economic organization eventually combined within itself both

---

[251] Göring in his reply did not take up the economic arguments. This is not surprising, as he had meanwhile received different predictions from Thomas.

[252] Hassell, *Tagebücher*, 183 (2 Mar. 1941). On this point Hassell's opposition was not one of principle, as his views were largely in line with the plans for a large-area economy, in the implementation of which in south-eastern Europe he was then taking an active part. His concept for Europe was based also on the involvement of Russia as a supplementary region; see Asendorf, 'Hassell', 395.

[253] Memorandum of 13 Feb. 1941: Thomas, *Wehr- und Rüstungswirtschaft*, 515 ff.

military and civilian obligations—i.e. it had to send supplies both forwards to the fighting forces and backwards to relieve the German war economy.[254] In addition, it was to get the Soviet economy going again—at least in certain sectors—and thereby create the prerequisites of its integration in the German large-area economy. Although supplies for the troops had priority in OKW preparations, the three categories of duties were not clearly delineated. Assuming a campaign of short duration, such a separation of tasks was not perhaps indispensable; but the longer the campaign went on, the greater the problems which a parallelism of different tasks was bound to create. In the spring of 1941, however, such imponderables were disregarded, and not only in the Wehrmacht High Command. The drafts of economic war aims worked out jointly by Thomas's department and the civilian economic authorities, however, reveal another significant feature. The principle, first contained in the quartermaster-general's reflections of February 1941, that not the entire occupied territory but only its economically important parts should be placed under 'orderly administration',[255] had been further developed and defined by Thomas. It was now laid down that territories which 'are of no economic importance for the conduct of operations, or for the greater German war economy, or for the creation of new states' were to be 'economically neglected after the most extensive exploitation'.[256] Moreover, the form of management was to be so chosen 'that the greatest possible benefit is achieved in terms of the overall war effort'. Special importance was to be attached to the 'attainment of a great surplus of agricultural and mineral-oil products'.

Although this concept, in spite of repeated approaches, had not been explicitly approved either by Hitler or by Göring prior to the German attack on the USSR, General Thomas on 29 April 1941 briefed the three Wehrmacht services along these lines on the tasks and structure of his Organization East.[257] Three days later his directives were accepted as a binding outline for future work at a conference of state secretaries.[258] They contained the following statements:

1. The war can be continued only if the entire armed forces are fed from Russia in the third year of the war.

2. Tens of millions of people will undoubtedly starve to death if that which we require is taken out of the country.

3. Of greatest importance is the securing and removal of oil crops, oil-cake, with grain occupying a lower priority. Available fat and meat will presumably be consumed by the troops.

---

[254] See Entwurf [draft] OKW/WiRüAmt, Apr. 1941, and Gen. Thomas's minute dated 5 May 1941: Müller, 'Interessenpolitik', Nos. 3 and 4.
[255] Paper exercise of the quartermaster-general, Feb. 1941, annexe 15, BA-MA RH 3/v. 132.
[256] Entwurf [draft] OKW/WiRüAmt, Apr. 1941: Müller, 'Interessenpolitik', No. 3.
[257] WiRü/Ic, minute dated 29 Apr. 1941, No. 1157-PS, *IMT* xxvii. 32 ff.; in a list of points to be discussed at the subsequent conference of state secretaries it was again pointed out that the submitted draft should at last be signed by the Führer or the Reich Marshal: see Stab Ia, Besprechung Staatssekretäre [conference of state secretaries], 2 May 1941, BA-MA Wi/I D 45.
[258] Minute dated 2 May 1941, No. 2718-PS, *IMT* xxxi. 84.

4. Industry must be restarted only in areas of deficiency, such as:

factories for means of transport
factories for general supply plant (iron)
textile mills
armaments enterprises only in areas where there are bottlenecks in Germany.

Repair workshops for the troops to be, of course, opened on an increased scale.

This programme was absorbed, during the weeks that followed, into a number of papers prepared in the Wehrmacht High Command and containing directives for the exploitation of the eastern territories to be occupied. With a few modifications they continued to be valid for the officers and administrative officials of the Economic Organization East until the collapse of the eastern front in 1944. The relevant decrees by Göring and Hitler shortly after the beginning of the German–Soviet war likewise merely confirmed Thomas's drafts.[259] The most important document was 'Guidelines for the direction of the economy in the newly occupied eastern territories', also known as the 'Grüne Mappe' (green folder) from the colour of its cover.[260] In addition to organizational regulations it contained a detailed presentation of the principles laid down by the state secretaries on 2 May 1941. Again, the problem of agricultural policy played the main part. This was the responsibility of State Secretary Backe of the ministry of food. His decisions were accepted by the Wehrmacht High Command without comment and incorporated in the military directives.

Backe, as mentioned above, had assured Hitler that possession of the Ukraine would relieve him of all economic worries. While this was in line with the ancient German dream of the 'Ukrainian bread-basket', it soon acquired special topicality as a result of the growing crisis in food supplies within the German sphere of power. Indeed, Backe's continual warnings of a collapse of food supplies had contributed to that development.[261] However, the investigations and calculations made at the beginning of 1941 within the Wehrmacht High Command and in the staff of the Reich Peasant Leader about the potential gain arising from an occupation of European Russia gave little ground for optimistic expectations.[262] According to that study 'the world's greatest contiguous economic region' scarcely produced any agricultural surpluses. Even the Ukraine recorded a surplus only in its southern part, while its central and northern areas, because of their high population density and their industrialization, had to be regarded as areas dependent on imports. It was

[259] Führer Decree, 29 June 1941, *KTB OKW* i, document annexe No. 63, and Ordinance by Göring, 27 July 1941: *Deutsche Besatzungspolitik*, No. 76.

[260] The folder was distributed in a thousand copies, BA-MA RW 31/128 D.

[261] See sect. 3(*a*) of the present chapter.

[262] See Erzeugung und Verbrauch von Nahrungs- und Futtermitteln in der UdSSR, bearb. im Stabsamt des Reichsbauernführers [Production and consumption of foodstuffs and feeding-stock in the USSR, compiled by the staff of the Reich Peasant Leader], 28 Mar. 1941, BA-MA Wi/I D 1645. Similar warnings of a deterioration of the situation came also from within the Four-year Plan authority itself, as later reported by Dr Friedrich Richter, in charge of eastern affairs; see excerpt from his field-post letter dated 26 May 1943, BA R 6/60a; also sect. I.III.2(*b*) at n. 144.

necessary, moreover, to remember that, because of the high level of mechanization of Soviet agriculture, wartime effects and internal upheavals must instantly result in substantial losses of yield.

These losses can only be made good over several years and are likely to reach their peak in the second year, when cultivation can no longer be adequately performed. For that reason no surpluses should be expected under the given circumstances for several years to come; even immediate requirements for human and animal consumption will probably scarcely be met for some time.

On the other hand, there were no reliable data on harvest yields. Because of fluctuations in consumption and during the harvest, and of losses in collection and transport etc., virtually any desired surplus or deficit could be calculated for Russia. Estimates of a 'normal' gross harvest varied between 80m. and 120m. t. of grain. What realistic booty targets could be based on that kind of data? The Berlin agricultural experts dodged the question. They proceeded solely from German requirements. The most important basis of calculation was the amount of grain which Moscow was prepared to supply under the trade agreement. These 2.5m. t. were already firmly incorporated in the German balance sheet for food. If one added the supply of the army in the east with its more than three million men, as well as the exceedingly tight food situation in the rest of the German sphere of power, then requirements quickly rose to 8–10m. t. of grain which had to be collected from Russia. Because a 'normal' surplus of scarcely more than 1m. t. could at best be expected from European Russia, the economic leadership had to find new ways of redeeming Backe's promise. The agricultural experts found a way out, with the aid of the geographical conditions on the one hand and, on the other, the introduction of a radical hunger strategy. In an expert opinion the Berlin agro-geographer Waldemar von Poletika had pointed to the familiar disparate distribution of agricultural production in the different climatic zones of the USSR.[263] In the office of the Reich Peasant Leader it had also been realized that, notwithstanding all fluctuations, 'the relative ratio of the individual Russian provinces remained constant'.[264] The idea therefore suggested itself of restoring a condition that had existed in Russia before the First World War—diverting the surpluses of the south across the Black Sea, to be exported to central Europe. The areas of deficiency in central and northern Russia, however, especially the big industrial regions, would thereby be cut off from their foodstuff basis.[265]

In this way the Berlin agricultural experts were hoping to achieve a grain surplus of the order of 8.7m. t. for the purposes of the Reich. This entailed an

---

[263] Prof. Dr W. von Poletika, Naturverhältnisse und Agrargeographie der Sowjetunion [Natural conditions and agro-geography of the Soviet Union], BA-MA RW 19 annexe I/1550.

[264] Study, 28 Mar. 1941 (above, n. 262); see also the presentation in Backe, *Getreidewirtschaft.*

[265] See Poletika's study (above, n. 263); a few months later the author held key positions in the Main Group Agriculture of the Economy Staff East; after the war he was director of the Agricultural Research Centre for the Eastern States in Bonn. For the Soviet judgement on the concept of agricultural exploitation in the Third Reich see Sinicyna and Tomin, 'Proval agrarnoj politiki', 32 ff.

overall reduction of local consumption by some 12 per cent; this would most painfully affect the population in the deficit areas. How was such a forcible intervention in the organically grown structures of the Soviet agrarian and food economy to be accomplished? Quite apart from the enormous transport difficulties, there were the problems of actually getting hold of all the stocks, of ensuring harvesting measures, and of collecting the harvest yield as completely as possible. This ruled out any interference with the existing collective-farm system. In order to attain the collection target, the option of material incentives to win the co-operation of the local population was not available. Backe and Thomas had from the outset relied on a different method—the use of the most brutal coercive measures to compel the Russians to hand over their stocks. That, in their opinion, was necessary especially in the deficit areas, seeing that the German forces had to be fed off the land there too. This meant a double burden for the affected local population. Not only would the usual food supplies not be arriving from the areas of agricultural surplus in the south, but their own already inadequate supplies would be further depleted in order to feed the German troops. The consequences of such a procedure were spelt out clearly at the conference of state secretaries on 2 May 1941. The predictable death by starvation of many millions of Soviet citizens did not particularly worry either the Wehrmacht High Command or the German agricultural leaders. On the contrary, this prediction led, if anything, to a further radicalization of measures, as the people condemned to death by starvation would have to be prevented from becoming a security problem or a threat to economic management. (For the distribution of grain within the USSR see Map I.III.2.)

Quite apart from such apparent constraints, the ideological intoxication of the leaders of the Third Reich was hardly likely to tolerate scruples about the starvation strategy. After all, had not National Socialist propaganda been pillorying the Soviet regime's 'starvation policy' for years, thereby cultivating the age-old prejudice of the Slav people's capacity for suffering? Why then should the German occupiers act more humanely than Stalin had done during his collectivization drive in the early 1930s? Backe's instructions to the German agricultural controllers to be appointed in occupied Russia therefore stated: 'Poverty, hunger, and frugality have been borne by the Russian individual for centuries. His stomach is elastic—therefore no false pity!'[266] The directives for agricultural policy[267] with their undisguised diction and their would-be technocratic arguments clearly revealed the economic war aims of the Third Reich. In connection with the establishment of a self-sufficient German large-area economy the Soviet Union was to be exploited as a colonial

[266] 12 Gebote für Landwirtschaftsführer [12 rules for agricultural controllers], 1 June 1941, No. USSR-089, *IMT* xxxix. 366 ff.; a copy of the 'Kreislandwirtschaftsführer-Mappe' [district agricultural controller's folder], relating to those 12 rules, is kept in BA-MA RW 31/135.

[267] Wirtschaftspolitische Richtlinien für Wirtschaftsorganisation Ost, Gruppe Landwirtschaft [Economic-policy directives for Economic Organization East, Group Agriculture], 23 May 1941, No. EC-126, *IMT* xxxvi. 135 ff.

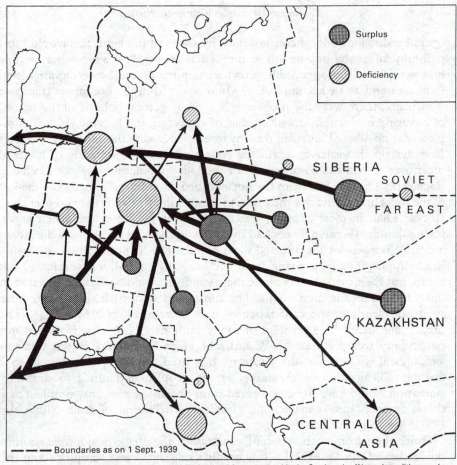

Surplus

Deficiency

Boundaries as on 1 Sept. 1939

SIBERIA

SOVIET

FAR EAST

KAZAKHSTAN

CENTRAL ASIA

Source: Prof. Dr. W. v. Poletika, Berlin: *Naturverhältnisse und Agrargeographie der Sowjetunion* [Natural conditions and agricultural geography of the Soviet Union], BA-MA RW 19 annexe I/1550

MAP I.III.2. Grain Distribution within the Soviet Union (1939)

Source: Prof. Dr W. v. Poletika, Berlin: Naturverhältnisse und Agrargeographie der Sowjetunion [Natural conditions and agricultural geography of the Soviet Union], BA-MA RW 19 annexe I/1550.

hinterland. The aim was not 'to convert the population to National Socialism but to turn it into our tool'. Above all the question must be: 'How does this help Germany?'[268] From that point of view the 'destruction of the Russian processing industry in the forest zone' was 'also an absolute necessity for Germany's future'—a statement reminiscent of the above-quoted navy memorandum of September 1940 (see I.III n. 82) and typical of the continuity of economic-policy attitudes towards the Soviet Union. The consequences of such a programme were discussed in detail. They culminated in the statement

[268] 12 Gebote, No. USSR-089, *IMT* xxxix. 369.

that the 'gradual death both of the industry and of a large portion of the population in the former deficit areas' was indispensable.[269]

Many tens of millions of people will become superfluous in those areas and will have to die or to emigrate to Siberia. Any attempts to save the local population from death by starvation through the importation of surpluses from the black-earth zone can only be at the expense of food supplies for Europe. They would undermine Germany's and Europe's immunity to blockade.

The agricultural leadership wished to see all economic activity subordinated to that one single objective. The immediate task was to ensure 'the supply of the fighting forces with foodstuffs and fodder and the feeding of Greater Germany for years ahead'.[270] The War Economy and Armaments Department, which was in charge of the preparation of the 'Green Folder', concurred with that view in general terms, though its radical deindustrialization plans were not unanimously accepted there. In the short term, at least, OKW did not wish to do without a certain measure of industrial activity. An important starting-point was thought to be the area of the armaments industry, for which the Wehrmacht High Command declared itself to be 'solely competent and responsible'.[271]

The heavy strain on armaments capacities in Germany and the gigantic plans of the Wehrmacht services for the future inevitably focused attention on the extremely modern and highly effective Soviet armaments industry. Even in April 1941 a Luftwaffe commission had been able to inspect enterprises of the Soviet aviation armaments industry and had been surprised by its volume.[272] In January 1941 the war-economy section had assumed that it could not be expected that the Soviet armaments plants would be captured intact. In February General Thomas in his memorandum then predicted the capture of 75 per cent of the Soviet armaments capacity. A certain euphoria seems thereupon to have arisen in the Wehrmacht High Command. The realization that 'in the great unified continental European armaments region, extending from the North Cape to the Mediterranean and backed by the vast Russian economic sphere, no insuperable war-economy problems' would arise 'any longer'[273] was bound to be attractive. Steps were therefore taken in the War Economy and Armaments Department for transferring manufacturing bottle-necks in the armaments area to Soviet enterprises.[274] The prerequisite no doubt was a higher degree of industrial activity than envisaged by the agricultural leadership or than was compatible with the long-term economic-policy objectives of the Third Reich. Even if the Soviet armaments factories really

---

[269] Wirtschaftspolitische Richtlinien (above, n. 267), 138, 156.

[270] Dienstanweisung [official instruction] No. 1 for the Kreislandwirtschaftsführer [district agricultural controller], 1 June 1941, BA-MA RW 31/135.

[271] Green Folder, pt. 1, 21, BA-MA RW 31/128 D.

[272] See sect. I.iv.2(*b*) at n. 313 (Boog).   [273] Schneider, 'Kampf der Giganten'.

[274] OKW/WiRüAmt/Rü IIc, Verfügungsentwurf betr. Ausnutzung, Erkundung, Zuweisung und Verwaltung der russischen Rüstungsindustrie [Draft instruction concerning utilization, exploration, assignment, and administration of the Russian armament industry], May 1941, BA-MA RW 31/162.

were captured intact, there was still the crucial question whether the raw materials, energy, and deliveries necessary for recommissioning them could be made available. As, moreover, these enterprises were predominantly located in the agricultural deficit areas, food supplies for the necessary manpower were, on the Germans' own plans, exceedingly doubtful. This objective of exploiting the Russian territory for armaments production was not in fact pursued with particular urgency in the Wehrmacht High Command. Nevertheless it was included in the list of tasks and objectives in the 'Green Folder',[275] without the conflict between these goals and the premises of the agricultural policy being resolved in any detail.

The inability of the military and civilian agencies to work out between them a realistic and well-thought-out overall economic strategy was revealed also in other areas. Thus, according to all official directives, priority was to be given to raw materials in order to underpin the German war economy. Along with oil, other vital raw materials in short supply were platinum, magnesium, and rubber; these were to be collected immediately and shipped to Reich territory. Raw-material production was generally to be restarted, which would no doubt require a large native workforce. Yet the starvation strategy made it impossible from the outset to feed them properly.

There was yet another regulation, presumably initiated by the ministry for economic affairs, to the effect that there was no point in controlling consumption in the east because no organized economic structure existed there. Instead, all 'raw materials, semi-finished and finished goods of any use to us' were to be withdrawn from trade, and all business with third countries was to be cut off. Any surpluses of goods were, as a matter of principle, earmarked solely for German needs. This meant that the needs of the forces had to be satisfied first of all—especially their immediate requirements of foodstuffs and fodder, motor-fuel, tyres, clothing, sapper and construction materials, workshop equipment, and medical needs. As for matching the short-term demands of the troops and the homeland with the objective of a longer-term economic reconstruction, at least in certain areas—to that question the forward economic control squads found no answer in their documents or instructions.

Another example was the statement in the 'Green Folder' that 520,000 tractors and 180,000 combine harvesters would be available to Soviet agriculture in 1941. These figures had simply been taken over from Soviet statistics, without anyone questioning whether these machines could really still be counted on when military operations died down. Without that fleet of machines, as well as the provision of at least 200,000 trucks together with the necessary fuel—moreover of an order of magnitude that exceeded total German consumption—it would be impossible to bring the harvest in or plant for the next season. Whether Backe's foresight in holding German farm machinery and equipment ready for possible employment in the east[276] rep-

---

[275] On the following passages see Green Folder, pt. 1, June 1941, BA-MA RW 31/128 D.
[276] Evidence in KTB WiStab Ost/Chefgr. La 1941/42, BA-MA RW 31/42.

resented an adequate preparation was exceedingly doubtful. Against that background, General Thomas's summing up is bound to seem more than a little boastful:

The theoretical groundwork, i.e. the equipment of the economic organization to be employed and of the troops moving into Russia with the necessary war-economy material, had been carried out in model fashion; it may be stated that never before had an army been so well furnished with war-economy data about the enemy country as the German army in Russia.[277]

The mere idea that an occupying power might 'take over' the conquered economy without appreciable losses and that it might remould it to its own requirements within a very short period of time, or that, without regard for the subjected population, it could extract a maximum profit, solely on the basis of an open threat of force and terror—that idea seems unrealistic in retrospect, even though to contemporaries and to the actual executants it might have seemed no more than compliance with economic constraints. To restrict economic activity to only a few sectors while the rest were being neglected— that was an economic strategy which might have worked against underdeveloped nations. In the case of the Soviet Union, however, of a great power developing into an industrialized society, it was surely doomed to failure from the outset. It took a whole year before the realization gained ground in German circles that success, even if only in the key areas of army supplies, agriculture, and oil extraction, was not possible in the east except on the basis of a functioning overall economy. The change of direction, however, came too late to have any effect on the course of the war.[278]

The 'eastern experts' of the NSDAP had been busy since 1933, under Rosenberg's leadership, with detailed plans for a political and racial 'new order' for Russia under German rule.[279] In the summer of 1940 they intensified their instructional and research work.[280] In July 1940 the foreign-policy department of the NSDAP prepared a study for Hitler on Moscow's activities in eastern and south-eastern Europe.[281] In September Rosenberg made a comprehensive report to Hitler on his department's research work to date.[282] In April 1941 he submitted a memorandum on objectives and methods of future German occupation policy in the east,[283] and shortly afterwards he was officially appointed 'Plenipotentiary for the central handling of matters relating to the east European region'.[284] The party officials were thus ready to assume

[277] Thomas, *Wehr- und Rüstungswirtschaft*, 266.   [278] *Deutsche Wirtschaftspolitik*, 187.
[279] See the survey in Müller, *Tor zur Weltmacht*, 262 ff.
[280] See e.g. 'Mitteilungen über die Sowjetunion' [Information on the Soviet Union], published twice monthly from Sept. 1940 by the Hauptstelle Ostland des Gauschulungsamtes Danzig-Westpreußen [Central office Eastland of the regional Party schooling department Danzig-West Prussia], BA NS 22/1026.   [281] See Gibbons, 'Soviet Industry', 78.
[282] See Mitteilung Rosenbergs in einem Schreiben an Göring [Report by Rosenberg in a letter to Göring], 5 Oct. 1940, BA NS 43/3.
[283] Memorandum No. 1, 2 Apr. 1941, No. 1017-PS, *IMT* xxvi. 547 ff.
[284] Hitler's Decree, 20 Apr. 1941, No. 965-PS, ibid. 383–4.

their duties in Hitler's living-space programme. The question at this point is not so much Rosenberg's political and ideological disruption plans *vis-à-vis* the Soviet Union as his economic-policy ideas resulting from them, and the influence he had on the formulation of the economic war aims for Operation Barbarossa.

In his very first memorandum of April 1941 he made it clear that the political objectives 'naturally become valid only after the important war-related deliveries from the territories to be occupied—the deliveries necessary to the Greater German Reich for the continuation of the war—have been secured'.[285] And two days before the opening of the attack he declared again:

The feeding of the German people undoubtedly holds the top place now on the list of German demands in the east, and there the southern regions and the northern Caucasus will have to assist the feeding of the German people. We certainly do not see that we have any duty to feed the Russian people from these surplus areas as well. We know that this is a tough necessity, beyond all emotion. Undoubtedly a very extensive evacuation will be necessary and the Russian nation will certainly have to face very difficult years. To what extent industries are to be preserved there (rolling-stock factories etc.) will have to be decided at a later date.[286]

The 'tough necessities', as formulated by the military and business leaders, evidently met with his approval.

The reason for this approval was that the short-term economic objectives coincided, at least in part, with Rosenberg's long-term plans for a 'new order'. This was true especially for the area of 'Old Russia' around Moscow, which had been classified by General Thomas and his experts as a foodstuff deficit area and had therefore been earmarked for ruthless 'exploitation'.[287] Rosenberg accepted the directive of Economic Organization East and demanded 'very extensive economic utilization, such as removal of all expendable stocks, machinery, and equipment, especially of available transport stock, river barges, etc.'[288] Rosenberg justified such a procedure not only on economic grounds but also by National Socialist racial policy: German rule was to be made safe 'by the total annihilation of the Bolshevik-Jewish state administration' and 'Muscovite Russia' used 'on a major scale as a dumping-area for undesirable population elements'. These, in Rosenberg's view, included the native intelligentsia of the Baltic States, whose removal would make room for German settlement. In a similar manner he intended to make the Caucasus and the Ukraine 'racially pure'; as a first stage he envisaged the confinement of Soviet Jews in ghettos.

Even on the question of preserving the collectivization of agriculture—subsequently to become the most contentious issue in occupation policy

---

[285] Memorandum No. 1 (above, n. 283), 548.
[286] Rosenberg's speech on 20 June 1941, No. 1058-PS, *IMT* xxvi. 622.
[287] Minute by Gen. Thomas, 5 May 1941: Müller, 'Interessenpolitik', No. 4.
[288] Memorandum No. 1 (above, n. 283), 549.

during the German–Soviet war—Rosenberg initially showed great understanding for the attitude of the economic departments.[289] There was no doubt
that during the first phase an effective exploitation of the country would only
be possible with the help of the collective farms. The expected shortage of
draught animals, dairy cattle, and general livestock, as well as the necessary
equipment for cultivation, harvesting, and transport, ruled out any immediate
establishment of individual peasant farmsteads, even though decollectivization
occupied a key position in Rosenberg's concept for the east, in order to win the
'willing co-operation' of the rural population.[290] Expecting as they did a short
campaign, the economic departments believed they could dispense with such
co-operation. Even the suggestion of the foreign ministry that the peasants
should at least be promised the reprivatization of farm land at the start of the
German invasion, and that livestock already in private ownership or the
produce of so-called private plots should on no account be requisitioned, was
not acceptable to the military leaders or to the agrarian politicians in Economic Organization East, since any consideration for the native population
must ultimately be at the expense of the hoped-for volume of booty.[291]

There were a number of other contentious issues. In the discussion of the
currency problem, for instance, economic exploitation goals clashed with
Rosenberg's 'new order' ideas. As early as mid-May 1941 the Reichsbank had
submitted a position paper for the Green Folder section on money and
credits.[292] It took account of the exceptional importance of monetary policy
especially in the case of Russia. As the German occupying power would not be
willing or able to offer any real equivalent to the population for services or
local material goods, the success of the economic exploitation policy would
depend largely on the confidence shown by the local population in the currency of the occupying power. The collection of grain in the Ukraine in 1918
had failed primarily because the German authorities did not have enough
roubles and because the parallel use of the rouble and the newly introduced
karbovanec had caused a lot of difficulties.[293] In line with its past practice, the
Reichsbank in 1941 intended to set up in the occupied countries of Europe
fifteen Reich Credit Banks, as well as an issuing-house in the Soviet Union,
and issue uncovered payment vouchers to the troops as well as to the econ-

[289] See Allgemeine Instruktion für alle Reichskommissare in den besetzten Ostgebieten [Gen-
eral instruction to all Reich commissars in the occupied eastern territories], 8 May 1941, No. 1030-
PS, *IMT* xxvi. 578.

[290] See part i of Arbeitsrichtlinien des Reichsministers für die besetzten Ostgebiete für die
Zivilverwaltung (Braune Mappe) [Working directives issued by the Reich minister for the occu-
pied eastern territories for the civilian administration (Brown Folder)], published in Green
Folder, pt. ii, 2nd edn., Aug. 1942, BA-MA RW 31/131.

[291] The representative of the foreign minister complained 'that by our efforts and slogans to
preserve collective and state farms (for sound reasons) in their present form we are giving up the
most effective means of propaganda': Ref. Großkopf e.o.D. IX 3 g. Rs., minute of a conference
at the foreign ministry on 29 May 1941 concerning eastern issues, PA, Pol. XIII. 25.

[292] Reichsbank position paper, 15 May 1941, BA R 2/30921.

[293] Borowsky, *Ukrainepolitik*, 92 ff., 200 ff.

omic administration to meet initial needs. Their redemption was later to be set off against occupation-cost payments and reparations from the occupied territory.[294]

Rosenberg's staff vigorously protested against such manipulation.[295] On 23 May 1941 Rosenberg actually appeared in person, along with his top officials, at the ministry for economic affairs so that, in conversation with Funk, Schlotterer, and a Reichsbank representative, he might get the directive changed.[296] He insisted that the currency problem could not be dealt with from a economic point of view alone, as conditions in the east differed from those in the west. Because of the 'very low standard of education of the Russian people' they would not even be able to read the Reich Credit Bank vouchers envisaged. It would therefore be preferable to introduce the Reichsmark in the Baltic countries at once, while retaining the rouble for the moment in the Ukraine and the Caucasus—until such time as local national banks had been set up—and moreover, in order to avoid a shortage of money, start printing roubles in Germany without delay. Now the Reichsbank objected to the suggestion that it should counterfeit money and doubted that the German army command would agree to pay its troops in forged roubles. Funk, on the other hand, was impressed by Rosenberg's political arguments and instructed Schlotterer 'to negotiate with the military men at once, to find out if they would accept the proposals which had emerged in the course of the meeting'.

The Wehrmacht High Command came out unambiguously against Rosenberg. The introduction of Reich Credit Bank vouchers was ordered in the Green Folder, and explained as follows:

The purpose of the Reich Credit Bank vouchers is, on the one hand, to keep the industry of the occupied country going—in so far as it is of importance to us and is desirable for the preservation of quiet and order—and, on the other, to satisfy and balance the German forces' requirements of money. The former aim is achieved by the granting of credits to industrial and other enterprises, as well as to financial institutions or central or local administration bodies, when the granting of such credits is in the German interest.[297]

Payment of army pay in valid roubles was envisaged as an exception; as a rule Reich Credit Bank vouchers were to be used, and, if necessary, their acceptance by the local population was to be ensured by the threat of force.

Rosenberg's primarily political and ideological ideas were overruled also on the issue in which he was most involved, the special status of the Ukraine. In

---

[294] See Oertel, 'Beteiligung der Deutschen Reichsbank' Boelcke, 'Kriegsfinanzierung', 57–8, and comprehensively Blumhoff, *Einfluß*.

[295] RMfbO, Hauptabt. Wirtschaft, Aktennotiz betr. die politischen Auswirkungen der Währung in den neu zu besetzenden Ostgebieten [Minute concerning the political effects of currency in the eastern territories about to be occupied], 23 May 1941, BA R 6/408.

[296] Minute of the conference with Reich Minister Funk, 28 May 1941, No. 1031-PS, *IMT* xxvi. 581.

[297] Green Folder, pt. I, 24–5, BA-MA RW 31/128 D.

Rosenberg's plans for the disintegration of the Soviet Union the Ukraine held a key position. From that point of view, considerate treatment of the population seemed called for. To the economists, however, the Ukraine was the most important surplus area of all, so that any cut-back in the intended exploitation measures in favour of the native population was out of the question. Rosenberg's staff, on the other hand, believed that the economic targets would more effectively be achieved by means of a political strategy.

Long-term secure deliveries of raw materials and foodstuffs to the German Reich could be achieved with fewer forcible means through a sympathetic treatment of the nationalities concerned than if the accomplishment of those tasks were enforced solely by means of military or police strength through disregard of this ethnic and political situation.[298]

The 'strengthening of Ukrainian awareness' was a means not only of 'securing German production with military force, but of promoting the voluntary collaboration of the Ukrainians in the course of time'.[299] Rosenberg in fact did not question the global economic objectives as such, though he objected to the publication of the OKW draft of a Führer Decree on the economy in the eastern territories to be occupied, 'because it states unequivocally that the occupied eastern territories are of interest to Germany only as objects of extreme economic exploitation. If that became known it would have a fatal political effect in those territories.'[300] Rosenberg's chief concern was to see his political and propaganda objectives taken into account in the handling of the overriding economic issues. As he was claiming chief responsibility for future eastern policy, he was naturally also anxious to bring the area of economic policy into his sphere of power. He therefore rejected the planned organization of the Wehrmacht High Command and the Four-year Plan authority, because to his mind it was structured on 'purely economic points of view'.[301] He explained his attitude by arguing that 'such a central agency would be compelled to carry out a similar treatment in all territories, governed solely by economic considerations, which would render the implementation of the *political* task more difficult or, with a purely bureaucratic concentration, perhaps even impossible'. Rosenberg buttressed his claim to leadership by pointing out that his team of experts had been studying these questions for many years and could field several thousand Russia specialists.[302]

Göring and General Thomas, however, saw no reason for conceding to Rosenberg any influence whatever on the formulation of economic war

[298] Rosenberg's memorandum on the general structure and tasks of an agency for the centralized handling of questions of the east European region, presumably Apr. 1941, No. 1024-PS, *IMT* xxvi. 562.
[299] Instruction to a Reich commissar in the Ukraine, 7 May 1941, No. 1028-PS, ibid. 567–8.
[300] Letter from head of the Reich chancellery to OKW chief of staff concerning administration of east European territories in the event of their occupation, 20 May 1941, BA-MA RW 4/v. 759.
[301] Memorandum No. 1, 2 Apr. 1941, No. 1017-PS, *IMT* xxvi. 554.
[302] Annexe to memorandum No. 2, 7 Apr. 1941, No. 1019-PS, ibid. 558.

aims.[303] The Wehrmacht High Command on the contrary assumed that Economic Organization East would later be maintained also in the areas under civilian administration. Besides, Dr Georg Leibbrandt, the designated political director of Rosenberg's envisaged ministry, had not so long before, in May 1941, described the duties of the eastern ministry as pure propaganda work.[304] Hitler himself never admitted any doubt that war-economy tasks had absolute priority in the east, even though he was reluctant to commit himself for the time being on the organizational and personnel questions of the civilian administration.[305]

The primacy of the economy, to which Rosenberg now had to submit, emerged from the official guidelines for his employees.[306] All he was able to promise them in the event of conflict was to 'bring about an amicable settlement in consultation with the superior military agency'.[307] When two days before the opening of the attack on the USSR Rosenberg once more set out his ideas to the top leaders of the Reich, the Wehrmacht High Command's sober comment was: 'Can only be done by soldiers.'[308]

To sum up: the economic war aims were laid down in a fully autonomous manner by the military and the economic bureaucracy, in agreement with the top representatives of German trade and industry, and put into effect even against political and propaganda interests such as those championed by Rosenberg. These war aims were a summation of private business interests in the acquisition of Russian raw-material sources and processing installations, of long-term economic-policy ideas, and of actual economic constraints. Jointly they represented an unbridled strategy of pillage and plunder. The need for tough action and ruthless exploitation, repeatedly emphasized by economists and officers, was undoubtedly in line with Hitler's ideological premises. It should, however, be remembered that, beyond the general framework, Hitler took no part in the detailed definition of economic war aims. Nor was that necessary, seeing that the plans of the military leaders and economists largely confirmed Hitler's expectations of the economic profit to be derived from the east. In a letter to Mussolini on 21 June 1941 Hitler outlined them as follows:

[303] Backe had received a specific assurance from Göring that he would be able to carry out his agrarian policy without regard to Party ideologists; see Kehrl, *Krisenmanager*, 223–4.

[304] Ref. Großkopf (above, n. 291); such an interpretation of Rosenberg's task is still perceptible in Thomas, *Wehr- und Rüstungswirtschaft*, 272, where he observes that the object had been 'to bring propaganda influence to bear on the conquered territory as soon as possible through the organization of the Party and to carry out the liquidation of unreliable elements by the agencies of the security service and the police'.

[305] See sect. I.VII.1 at n. 29 (Förster).

[306] Undated memorandum on the organization of the administration in the occupied eastern territories and the guidelines to be observed by it, No. 1056-PS, *IMT* xxvi. 592 ff. On the validity of that instruction see Rosenberg's evidence before the Nuremberg Tribunal, *IMT* xi. 529, 540.

[307] No. 1056-PS, *IMT* xxvi. 600.   [308] *KTB OKW* i. 407 (21 June 1941).

I hope above all that it will then be possible for us to secure a common food supply in the Ukraine for some time to come, which will furnish us with such additional supplies as we may need in the future . . . Whatever may now come, Duce, our situation cannot become worse as a result of this step, it can only become better.[309]

Even though it may be assumed that Hitler with his more agriculturally orientated living-space programme may have harboured different ideas from his pragmatic generals on the question of a possible industrial policy in the east, more specifically on the utilization of Soviet armaments capacities, this did not affect agreement between the political and military leadership on the economic objectives of Operation Barbarossa. This emerged clearly on 20 June 1941, when Hitler stated to Todt and Keitel: 'The objective therefore must be to secure for ourselves by conquest all the areas which are of particular interest to us from a war-economy point of view.' General Thomas commented on this in a minute: 'If the military leadership is in a position to secure the lacking raw-material deposits by conquest, then the economic leadership would most warmly welcome that.'[310] This concurrence of views was due largely to the development of Germany's economic position on the eve of the German–Soviet war.

3. Economic Framework for Military Planning

(a) *The German War Economy until the Spring of 1941*

Once the euphoria of the early summer of 1940 had evaporated, it became obvious that Germany, while dominating large parts of the European continent, had not in fact achieved any abundance of material assets as a result. The performance of the German war economy was still considerably below the pre-war level,[311] and since Hitler's future war plans did not allow for a diminution of armaments production, it was unlikely that existing bottlenecks would be overcome in the near future or that the economy would undergo an upswing.[312] Although a further decline was initially prevented by the booty captured in the victorious campaigns, and even although a slight increase in production was recorded, this meant no more—given the danger of long-term exhaustion—than a short-term postponement of Germany's problems. The main difficulties arose from the shortage of manpower, more especially of skilled workers.[313] The Wehrmacht's manpower requirements deprived the economy of the younger age-groups, with the result that not only was the size of the workforce available for the production process greatly reduced by

[309] *DGFP* D xii, No. 660 (21 June 1941).

[310] Thomas, *Wehr- und Rüstungswirtschaft*, 300–1.

[311] See *Das Dentsche Reich und der Zweite Weltkrieg*, v/1. 523 ff.

[312] See Tomberg, Probleme der deutschen Rüstungswirtschaft im Kriege (above, n. 113).

[313] On this see Thomas, *Wehr- und Rüstungswirtschaft*, 236 ff.; Petzina, 'Mobilisierung', 451–2; and, by way of comparison, Milward, 'Arbeitspolitik'.

comparison with the outbreak of the war, but also its work performance. Unlike the Anglo-Saxon countries, Germany was unable to draw on any additional manpower reserves. Repeated demands from military quarters that greater use should be made of female labour were rejected by the political leadership.[314] Any more intensive exploitation of the manpower potential was prevented not only by ideological and administrative obstacles, but also by a lack of enthusiasm for the war among broad circles of the population.[315] There was even some concern in conservative circles that the National Socialist regime, out of fear of a dissatisfied working class, might adopt a 'red course'.[316] Introduction of a second or even third shift, which would have been necessary for the utilization of such labour reserves as existed, therefore remained an unrealistic idea.

Transition to industrial mass production, of the kind most advanced in the United States, continued to meet with obstacles in Germany.[317] One of these was the equipment of German industry, consisting as it did mainly of multi-purpose machines unsuitable for mass production; moreover, due to the direction of investments before the war, these had not been sufficiently updated, especially in the field of consumer products. Even in the metal-processing industry more than half of the machines were over ten years old in 1941.[318] Machine-tool manufacturers were unable to meet the steadily rising demand for capital items. For the past few years the development of the machine-tool industry had been neglected in favour of armaments production, and its technical level generally had in some respects declined by international standards. Additional burdens resulted from export obligations, mainly the Soviet trade, from the erratic and uncoordinated orders of the Wehrmacht services, and from shortage of skilled labour. Delivery delays of several years were not unusual, and all measures for the rationalization and stimulation of production yielded only minimal improvements. The same was true of the one-off relief provided by the employment of over 4,000 'machine-tools captured in Poland',[319] some of which were of the latest American design.

An increase in German war production was further being hampered by the shortage of raw materials. Although production of basic commodities continued to rise in the Reich, thanks to the measures taken by the Four-year Plan authority, self-sufficiency was out of the question except in a few areas.[320] The situation was slightly relieved by booty captured, principally in the west. By the end of 1940, however, the Wehrmacht High Command and the Four-year

---

[314] See minutes by Gen. Thomas, 22 Aug. 1940 and 9 Jan. 1941, BA-MA Wi/I F 5.2232.

[315] See Thomas, *Wehr- und Rüstungswirtschaft*, 236. For an illustration of the sullen mood among workers see the monthly report of the counter-intelligence officer 'Grubengebiet' (mining district) of the Reichswerke plant in Salzgitter for Feb. 1941, Salzgitter AG Konzern-Archiv 14/9/2. On this see also Steinert, *Hitlers Krieg*, 183, and generally Wette, 'Hitlerfaschismus'.

[316] Hassel, *Tagebücher*, 174 (23 Dec. 1940).

[317] Thomas, *Wehr- und Rüstungswirtschaft*, 240 ff.; Milward, *Der Zweite Weltkrieg*, 189–90.

[318] See Wagenführ, *Industrie*, 162, table 7.　　　[319] Thomas, *Wehr- und Rüstungswirtschaft*, 242.

[320] See Wagenführ, *Industrie*, 166.

Plan authority pointed out that 'starting in the summer of 1941 a considerable worsening of the supply situation' would have to be expected.[321] That judgement was confirmed in May 1941.[322] Even coal, though available in Germany in sufficient quantities, increasingly became a commodity in short supply.

The food situation was also developing unfavourably.[323] The shortage of animal feeding-stuffs resulted in a marked drop in meat production. It proved impossible to offset the harvest losses of the first year of the war—over three million tonnes of grain—and the shortfall of oilcake and fodder cereals in spite of higher imports, chiefly from the Soviet Union. The state of the crops promised no more than an average harvest in 1941. In cousequence, once all stocks were consumed by 1 August 1941, the country, for better or worse, would be dependent on the harvest results.[324] By the end of 1940 the army command assumed that food supplies were 'reasonably assured for 1941, but not beyond that. We'll swindle ourselves through 1941.'[325] In view of this outlook rations in Germany had to be drastically cut some weeks before the start of Operation Barbarossa. The army leadership's reaction was irritation: the generals saw the danger of the kind of situation which had existed at the end of the First World War.[326] The effect that this would have on the mood of the population was obvious.[327] Considering that General Thomas and State Secretary Backe were assuring him that possession of the Ukraine would relieve him of all such worries,[328] it is easy to understand why Hitler was so anxious to carry out Barbarossa at all costs before 1941 was out and why he was attaching greater importance to war-economy objectives than to operational considerations.

The threatening decline in German production was partially offset by the exploitation of the occupied and dependent countries within the German sphere of power. It emerged, however, that the economic peacetime plans and large-area projections of the summer of 1940 had painted a false picture of the potential of the Continent.[329] The true conditions were outlined by Göring's state secretary, Erich Neumann, on 29 April 1941 as follows.[330] Germany's

[321] See WiRüAmt/Stab Ia No. 2384/40g.Kdos. I, Voraussichtliche Entwicklung der Wehrwirtschaftslage [Forecast of development of the armaments-industry situation] until 1 May 1941, dated 14 Dec. 1940, BA-MA Wi/I F 5.3662, and a similar observation by Lt.-Gen. von Hannecken at the meeting of the general council of the Four-year Plan authority on 18 Nov. 1940, KTB WiRüAmt/Stab 1939/41, 122, BA-MA RW 19/164.

[322] See OKW WiRüAmt/Stab Ib 5 No. 1943/41g.Kdos., Kriegswirtschaftlicher Lagebericht [Report on the state of the war economy] No. 21 for May 1941, dated 10 June 1941, BA-MA RW 4/v. 308.

[323] See overall view, ibid. 7.

[324] See the information in Hassell, *Tagebücher*, 172 (23 Nov. 1940).

[325] Conference between Halder and Chef H Rüst und BdE, 23 Nov. 1940: Halder, *Diaries*, 747 (23 Dec. 1940).

[326] See Halder, *Diaries*, 914–15, 940 (12, 28 May 1941).

[327] See Steinert, *Hitlers Krieg*, 197–8.   [328] See sect. 2(c) of the present chapter.

[329] On the problematic nature of these calculations see Eichholtz, *Kriegswirtschaft*, 221 ff.

[330] 'Der Vierjahresplan', Vortrag vor der Verwaltungsakademie Berlin ['The Four-year Plan', lecture to the Administration Academy, Berlin], 29 Apr. 1941, Doc. NID-13844, Staatsarchiv Nürnberg.

raw-material and food situation was becoming increasingly difficult as certain industrial raw materials could not be obtained from the occupied or dependent countries either, or only in insignificant quantities, while on the other hand the maintenance of order and of production for the war effort made it necessary partially to supply those countries, once their own stocks were exhausted, with the necessary raw materials from Germany. As, moreover, agricultural production in the countries newly incorporated into the German supply region was largely based on feeding-stuff imports from overseas, from which they were now cut off, those countries were compelled to adopt an extensive form of farming; with the exception of Denmark they were therefore bound, if the war continued for any length of time, to turn from surplus areas into deficiency areas. In addition, there were the obligations Germany had undertaken to make deliveries to her allies.

Although the increase in war-economy potential resulting from the accretion of German power was substantial, it proved possible to make only slight use of it for the German war effort in the second year of the war. Only in the area of armaments production did the reallocation of orders reach significant dimensions; however, it encountered a variety of obstacles and, moreover, had to be paid for by the need to 'feed to a large extent' the territories occupied by Germany.[331] This applied also to the three million foreigners and prisoners of war employed as labour in the Reich in May 1941. With their help it was possible to maintain the manpower total of the previous year, although that was three million below the pre-war level.[332] At the same time, in May 1941, some 50,000 miners went on strike in Belgium, in protest against the bad food-supply situation, thereby endangering coal supplies in the German sphere of power.[333] Altogether the pattern of German imports showed that, even in the second year of the war, the loss of roughly 50 per cent of the pre-war import volume, due to the blockade, could not be made good.[334] With German exports, on the other hand, declining further, so that delivery offers had to be cut back and delivery times extended, the National Socialist leadership was increasingly forced to apply political and military pressure in order to maintain vital supplies from the dependent and occupied countries of Europe, and in order to compel them to accept a trebling of Germany's clearing-debt in 1941.[335] Thus about a half (in value) of German imports were obtained by extortion without collateral. One of the most important suppliers of the German war economy was Stalin.

[331] Kriegswirtschaftlicher Lagebericht [Report on the state of the war economy] No. 21 (above, n. 322).

[332] See *Das Dentsche Reich und der Zweite Weltkrieg*, v/1. 807 ff. For an assessment of foreign labour see Herbert, *Fremdarbeiter*.

[333] See Weber, *Die innere Sicherheit*, 55–6. The strike affected as much as 26% of coal production in the German sphere of power.

[334] See the data in OKW WiRüAmt/Stab Z/SR No. 329/42 g.Kdos., Kriegswirtschaftlicher Lagebericht [Report on the state of the war economy] No. 29 for Jan. 1942, dated 10 Feb. 1942, 9, BA-MA RW 4/v. 308.

[335] See Volkmann, 'NS-Außenhandel', 123–4.

(b) Intensification of German–Soviet Trade

Soviet war deliveries represented a considerable strengthening of the German war potential not only during the first year of the war.[336] Even during the preparatory phase of Operation Barbarossa Hitler could not manage without them. Indeed, they acquired increased importance in view of the small extent of the production increase in the Reich and the continuing tight supply situation. Whether German diplomacy would succeed in inducing Stalin to continue and step up his supplies while, simultaneously, the German military deployment was being carried out in the east—that was a crucial question, political as well as economic, in the summer of 1940.

German trade policy found itself confronted by two principal tasks: (1) to ensure the execution of the deliveries arranged under the trade agreement of 11 February 1940, thereby resolving the problem of the steadily growing backlog of German deliveries to the Soviet Union; and (2) to negotiate a new trade agreement for 1941, in order to ensure a continuous, and if possible increased, inflow of Soviet raw materials up to the very opening of the German attack, bearing in mind that, the Soviet advance deliveries having been ful-filled, German reciprocal deliveries of war material and industrial equipment, to be completed by 11 May 1942, would have to start to their full extent at the beginning of 1941. There was no denying the fact that Moscow was in a more favourable position: for one thing, Germany found it very difficult to make up the backlog of deliveries accumulated by the summer of 1940 and thus to meet her delivery obligations, and for another, the greater interest in a continuation of German–Soviet trade was undoubtedly on the German side—at least while the war against Britain lasted.

The foreign ministry's expectation that after the German victory in the west the Soviet Union might be prepared to give up the exploitation of its favour-able situation in bilateral trade and to accept an increasing German debt[337] soon proved to be an illusion. At a meeting of the inter-ministerial Committee for Trade with Russia on 8 August it was even suggested[338] that the growing German backlog in deliveries suited the Soviet Union very well, as by making excessive demands with its own orders it would be in a position to make the implementation of delivery obligations even more difficult for Germany, which meant in turn that the Soviets would not have to fulfil their own delivery obligations. The committee was divided on how Germany should react to such tactics. The demand by State Secretary Friedrich Landfried of the ministry for economic affairs that deliveries to the USSR should be given top priority was rejected by General Thomas on behalf of the Wehrmacht, because that would be feasible only at the expense of German armaments production. Göring, asked for a decision a few days later, was unwilling to commit

---

[336] On the following see also Birkenfeld, 'Stalin', 500 ff., and Eichler, *Wirtschaftsbeziehungen*, 108 ff.

[337] Minute by Ritter: see *DGFP* D ix, No. 300 (22 May 1940).

[338] KTB WiRüAmt/Wi 1940, 210 (8 Aug. 1940), BA-MA RW 19/244.

himself.[339] Although he rejected Landfried's proposal on the grounds that 'real rearmament was only just starting', he nevertheless asked Thomas to work towards systematic deliveries for the Soviet Union until the spring of 1941. After that, there would no longer be any interest in 'fully satisfying the Russian requests'.

Shortly afterwards Moscow responded to Berlin's dilatory attitude with the threat of an immediate stoppage of Soviet raw-material deliveries,[340] which actually led the Wehrmacht High Command hurriedly to examine the possibility of dispatching 300 trucks to the USSR as an immediate step to defuse the critical situation.[341] The foreign ministry's negotiator, who had gone to Moscow at the Soviet request in order to draw up a balance sheet of reciprocal deliveries, produced a sober assessment for headquarters in Berlin.[342] According to this, the German backlog already amounted to RM73m., with further deliveries to a value of RM234m. due by 11 May 1941.

The territorial changes in eastern Europe gave rise to additional burdens. Although the Russians had taken over the existing delivery contracts of Bessarabia and the Baltic States, they showed no inclination to grant Germany any credit, as the former 'bourgeois' negotiators from those countries used to do. They demanded, moreover, that the German reciprocal deliveries now due were not to be made up of consumer goods, as had previously been the case. Instead, Germany was supply the Soviet Union with greater quantities of armaments, since surely—as Moscow pointedly observed—there must be increased capacities for exports to the Soviet Union after the campaign in France.[343]

The Soviets' intransigent attitude was clearly also due to the fact that, immediately after Hitler's decision of 31 July 1940, measures had been put in hand to broaden the deployment basis against the Soviet Union. Stalin cannot have failed to notice that German influence in both Romania and Finland—which until then had been part of the Soviet sphere of influence—was being built up by means of massive arms deliveries. In the case of Finland this gave rise to a violent quarrel about control of the strategically important nickel deposits of Petsamo,[344] which defied settlement by agreement until the spring of 1941 and which more than once put a heavy strain on German–Soviet economic negotiations.

These had to be temporarily suspended in September 1940, when the head of the German delegation in Moscow, Minister Schnurre, saw no way of

---

[339] Chef WiRüAmt, minute of conference at Reich Marshal Göring's office on 14 Aug. 1940: Thomas, *Wehr- und Rüstungswirtschaft*, 512–13.

[340] Letter telegram No. 1828 from the German ambassador in Moscow to the foreign ministry, 3 Sept. 1940, PA, Büro des Staatssekretärs, Rußland, vol. ii.

[341] KTB WiRüAmt/Wi 1940, 250 (9 Sept. 1940), BA-MA RW 19/244.

[342] Minute by Schnurre, *DGFP* D xi, No. 128. (28 Sept. 1940).

[343] Telegram No. 1890 from the German ambassador in Moscow to the foreign ministry, 10 Sept. 1940, PA, Büro des Staatssekretärs, Rußland, vol. ii.

[344] See sect. I.VI.2 at nn. 23 ff. (Ueberschär).

meeting Soviet demands for intensified German arms deliveries.[345] In Berlin he called for an urgent decision by Hitler, as otherwise the 'massive deliveries of raw materials, especially grain, mineral oil, cotton, precious and non-ferrous metals, and phosphates would cease, at least temporarily, and could at best be resumed at a later date at a much lower level and with heavy sacrifices of German deliveries'. He referred to the statement of the Reich ministry of food, according to which German grain stocks would be exhausted in the course of the current year, with Russia being the only country capable of continuing to make major deliveries in the future. Basically this represented 'very substantial support for the German war economy', and also in particular for the vital route to the Middle and Far East.

When the Soviet Union thereupon heightened the conflict by cancelling all long-term orders for industrial plant (e.g. the negotiations about the construction of hydrogenation plant, which had produced no results since the spring of 1940, and by switching the bulk of its orders to the areas of machine-tools and rolling-mill products, this had a major effect on German armaments production. Göring therefore called an emergency meeting of all departments involved, in the hope that a solution might be found.[346] The foreign ministry and the ministry for economic affairs once more demanded that 'Russian orders' be placed on an equal footing, in the category of top priority, with orders for the Wehrmacht, and indeed even given precedence in specific instances. General Thomas, while acknowledging that the Soviet Union, after south-eastern Europe, had become the 'most important supplier' for Germany, declined to take responsibility for having the Wehrmacht's rearmament drive impaired by an upgrading of Soviet orders and insisted that Hitler be informed. Göring, who was clearly anxious to avoid such a step, tried to achieve a compromise. He ruled that, on the one hand, it should be investigated 'to what extent Russian imports are to be restricted', while, on the other hand, Soviet orders due for delivery by 11 May 1940 were to be accorded top priority. All other Soviet orders, however, were to be ignored.

This decision, of course, produced only a slight relaxation in German–Soviet trade relations. As for the new round of negotiations about another trade agreement, it was impossible to make any further trade-policy concessions with regard to short-term German delivery obligations. So how was Stalin to be induced to continue his raw-material deliveries in the spring of 1940? Territorial concessions in eastern Europe as the price of Soviet advance deliveries—a solution in 1939—had to be ruled out towards the end of 1940 in view of the German deployment in the east. Neutral countries were expecting, if anything, an intensification of German–Soviet trade, as Soviet grain deliver-

---

[345] See *DGFP* D xi, No. 128 (28 Sept. 1940).

[346] Chef WiRüAmt, Notiz über die Besprechung bei Reichsmarschall Göring über die Russenlieferungen [Minute of the conference at Reich Marshal Göring's office concerning Russian deliveries], 4 Oct. 1940, BA-MA RW 19/176. See also a complaint of the firm of Krupp about the burden placed on it by long-term Soviet orders: letter to the ministry for economic affairs, quoted in Gibbons, 'Soviet Industry', 66.

ies to Germany, given the disastrous grain harvest in the Balkans, would no longer be sufficient in their present quantities to supply the German sphere of power.[347]

The invitation to the Soviet foreign minister Molotov to visit Berlin at the beginning of November 1940 to negotiate about a possible Soviet adherence to the Tripartite Pact[348] represented an attempt by the German side to bamboozle Stalin with the transparent offer of territorial expansion towards the Indian Ocean and thereby to gain a basis for negotiations on trade-policy problems. The foreign ministry's estimate in advance of Molotov's visit suggested that Moscow was evidently interested in a meeting.[349] For the following year a delivery of 1.2m. t. of grain had already been firmly promised and a further million tonnes held out as a possibility. In return, Germany offered long-term deliveries of heavy armaments, railway rolling-stock, merchant vessels, and other industrial goods.[350]

In his conversations with Molotov Hitler pointed out that 'peaceful co-operation' between the two countries presupposed respect for Germany's vital economic interests and for her hegemony in eastern Europe.[351] The Soviet Union had to guarantee 'under all circumstances' to deliver the raw materials indispensable to Germany. The Soviet foreign minister, however, rejected Hitler's share-out of spheres of interests and emphasized the specific conflicts existing with regard to Finland and the Balkans. Göring thereupon made one more attempt to persuade Molotov to favour 'large-scale planning of economic relations' and to overlook 'trifling matters'; Molotov retorted that surely Germany had acquired sufficient additional resources in the occupied territories to make it possible for her to meet Soviet orders. After the failure of the political talks about the Soviet Union's adherence to the Tripartite Pact the Soviet leadership was endeavouring once more to strengthen bilateral relations by making concessions in the economic field. During the trade talks in Moscow, shortly after Molotov's return from Berlin, the Russians submitted a proposal which, in its scope, went a long way to meet German ideas.[352] Moscow promised deliveries to a value of RM1,600m. by 11 May 1942, including 2.5m. t. of grain, 970,000 t. of mineral oil, and 200,000 t. of manganese ore. In return, Germany was to ensure the smooth fulfilment of orders already placed, and additionally supply further armaments to a value of RM110m. Top priorty among Soviet requests was again held by machine-tools, which Moscow was now also demanding in payment for transit freight

---

[347] Telegram No. 912 from the German embassy in Ankara to the foreign ministry, 11 Nov. 1940, PA, Büro des Staatssekretärs, Rußland, vol. ii.

[348] See sect. I.1.5 (Förstor).   [349] See *DGFP* D xi/1, Nos. 317, 318 (11 Nov. 1940).

[350] As the Soviet Union was particularly interested in deliveries of tank-turrets and armour plating, Schnurre had recommended an obliging response on these items, so as not to put the conclusion of the agreement in jeopardy. See telegram No. 2310 of the German embassy in Moscow to the foreign ministry, 2 Nov. 1940, PA, Büro des Staatssekretärs, Rußland, vol. ii.

[351] See sect. I.1.5 at n. 16 (Förster).

[352] See *DGFP* D xi, Nos. 409 (27 Nov. 1940), 412 (28 Nov. 1940), 437 (2 Dec. 1940).

to the Far East. This demand, considering Germany's lack of rubber, touched upon a critical bottleneck in the National Socialist war economy. Despite its generous offer, the Soviet Union therefore wished to ensure its own advantage. So far, however, the negotiations had been blocked by the German side because of the issue of additional armaments orders. The representatives of the Four-year Plan authority and of the Wehrmacht High Command, who had been briefed by Göring in November 1940 on the final decision to launch a campaign in the east, had openly boycotted the talks about Soviet armaments requests.[353] Although it was realized that new orders from the USSR would no longer be filled before the date planned for the attack, even the conclusion of any deal and the start of manufacture were bound to compel the German armaments firms to switch manpower resources, which would in consequence be lacking for the implementation of top-priority orders for the Wehrmacht. The foreign ministry's head of delegation was worried that the negotiations would not be concluded successfully owing to a lack of flexibility, and therefore tried to persuade Thomas and Halder to intervene in their own military interest. He induced the foreign ministry to use its influence on the board of the Rheinmetall armaments firm, because that firm had refused to accept Soviet armaments orders on the grounds of being weighed down by orders for the Wehrmacht.[354]

Any concessions from the German side on the issue of armaments deliveries were being impeded by the difficult situation which emerged ever more clearly in the war-economy preparations for Operation Barbarossa. Upon the emphatic urgings of the men responsible for armaments, Hitler had only just agreed to delay manufactures for the war against the Soviet Union.[355] A measure of relief was provided by the negotiations—which were running parallel to the economic talks—on compensation to meet the claims of ethnic German resettlers from the former Baltic States.[356] Molotov's offer of RM150m. again exceeded the expectations of the German delegation.

Another positive element was provided by the territorial requests in connection with the conclusion of a frontier treaty. For the cession of the Lithuanian 'corner' the German side demanded raw-material deliveries to the value of 13m. gold dollars, while the USSR was ready to pay only about a third of that sum. At the beginning of January, however, Molotov revised his offer and came fairly close to the German proposal.[357] When the German foreign minister thereupon asked for immediate payment,[358] not surprisingly in view of the preparations for the attack on the Soviet Union, by then in top gear, the German embassy in Moscow found that demand excessive and requested

[353] See *DGFP* D xi, No. 425 (29 Nov. 1940).

[354] Telegram No. 2613 from the German embassy in Moscow to Ambassador Ritter, 30 Nov. 1940, PA, Büro des Staatssekretärs, Rußland, vol. ii.

[355] Reports by Keitel, Todt, and Fromm, Rü IIa, contribution to KTB, concerning Derzeitiger Stand der Rüstung [Present state of armaments], 17 Dec. 1940, BA-MA Wi. I F 5.120, pt. 2.

[356] See *DGFP* D xi, No. 437 (2 Dec. 1940).

[357] Ibid., No. 591 (2 Jan. 1941).   [358] Ibid., Nos. 598, 605 (3, 4 Jan. 1941).

more latitude for negotiations. However, Stalin's interest in settling the frontier problem was such that eventually he gave way as well on the timing of payments. It was agreed in a secret protocol that the purchasing price of RM32.4m. would be paid within a period of three months, in gold and in non-ferrous metals of importance to the war effort.[359]

Otto Felix Bräutigam, the German consul-general in Batumi, came up with yet another variant of this kind of deal, which undoubtedly was more profitable to the German side. Just before the end of 1940 he urgently proposed that the German population in Russia should be repatriated.[360] Bräutigam had learnt of the German offensive plans in the Wehrmacht High Command at the beginning of July[361]—even before he assumed his new duties—and presumably was at first concerned about the protection of that ethnic group. However, on the model of the German resettlers from the Baltic States, these repatriates from Russia might also have been traded in for additional urgently needed raw materials. As it happened, there was no time to realize that project.

In the end, negotiations about a new trade agreement were successfully concluded only because Germany decided to make concessions in the armaments sector. A short-term release of Luftwaffe equipment to a value of RM7m. and promises to supply over 30,000t. of aluminium and 150t. of cobalt[362] were accepted by the Soviets as tokens of good will. The head of the German delegation regarded the outcome as decisive for Germany's future conduct of the war.[363] This was the most important trade agreement ever concluded by Germany: it placed the Russians under an obligation to supply the very raw materials 'of which we have a shortage that we cannot meet in any other way'. By the time the agreement was eventually signed on 10 January 1940,[364] German trade policy *vis-à-vis* the Soviet Union had not only achieved the objectives stemming from Hitler's decision in the summer of 1940 to an astonishing degree, but had considerably surpassed them. Stalin had undertaken to make substantial deliveries by the summer of 1941, while Germany was allowed to start by making good her delivery backlog from 1940; she would not, therefore, have to embark on her new deliveries to the Soviet Union until a date when the attack would have long been launched.

The foreign ministry was thus justified in drawing attention, in an instruction to all its agencies, to the inestimable value of that agreement.[365] If it were not for the Soviet deliveries, some 'very harsh' economies would be necessary in certain areas, whereas now Germany would have 'abundant supplies'. It

---

[359] Ibid., No. 638 (10 Jan. 1941).

[360] Letter from Bräutigam to Leibbrandt, 30 Dec. 1940, BA-NS 43/37; Bräutigam here made use of his long connection with the Eastern Agency of the Foreign Policy Department of the NSDAP. In Apr. 1941 he was appointed officer in charge of liaison between Rosenberg's staff and the Army High Command; subsequently, under Leibbrandt, he became head of the Basic Department (Grundsatzabteilung) in the ministry for the eastern territories.

[361] Bräutigam, *So hat es sich zugetragen*, 275.

[362] *DGFP* D xi, Nos. 539, 568 (20, 25 Dec. 1940).   [363] Ibid., No. 568 (25 Dec. 1940).

[364] Ibid., No. 637 (10 Jan. 1941).   [365] Ibid., No. 640 (11 Jan. 1941).

may be assumed that the Soviet delivery promises were taken by Hitler as confirmation of the economic motives for his aggressive plans, and that General Thomas was therefore able, shortly afterwards, to show himself in the right light by his memorandum. The exuberant reaction of the German economic press to the conclusion of the agreement with Moscow did much to stimulate German business interest in the resources of the Soviet Union.[366] Thus Hans Jonas, the director of the German Eastern Fair, who had taken an important part in the negotiations and who, at the same time, was involved in the Wehrmacht High Command's economic preparations—moreover, six months later he was put in charge of the economic department of the Reich Commissariat Ukraine—in a reputable economic journal[367] elaborated on the bridging function of East Prussia, for which 'a hinterland extending far south into the Government-General and into the rich southern Russian provinces' had been opened up. East Prussia, in consequence, now had a foreign-trade radius extending 'from the Baltic to the Pacific'. An unpublished economic analysis[368] likewise recalled such traditional economic objectives with regard to the Soviet Union by stating that only the solid integration of Russia into the German large-area economy could ensure German immunity to blockade. The author, not privy to 'grand politics', believed that a trade-policy solution was bound eventually to remain unsatisfactory. Problems resulting from the 'interreaction of the creation of a German large-area economy and Soviet strivings for autarky' could, he believed, be resolved only in the mode of the First World War, i.e. by military means.

Once Hitler had decided that the 'Russian agreement must be implemented at all costs',[369] the departments represented on the Trade Policy Committee agreed to meet German delivery obligations during the next few months whatever happened—even at the expense of Wehrmacht orders—so as not to provoke any further upsets in the urgently needed raw-material shipments from the USSR.[370] Firms were instructed to accept Soviet orders in every case. But whereas Soviet deliveries, after some weather-related transport difficulties, once more rose dramatically after March 1941—so much so that Moscow complained of insufficient rolling-stock being made available by Germany, thus preventing the Soviet Union from filling her orders as promised[371]—Berlin naturally enough endeavoured to delay her deliveries of war material during the final few weeks before the offensive.

The Soviets, however, took no countermeasures. On the contrary, the

---

[366] See e.g. Weiterer Ausbau [Further expansion], which referred to 'vast new possibilities of importing commodities vital to our life and to the war for a long time ahead'.

[367] Jonas, 'Ostpreußen und Königsberg'; Jonas here also mentions the infrastructural plans of the East Prussia Gauleiter Erich Koch, dating from 1933–4, which extended into Russian territory; reported also in Rauschning, *Hitler Speaks*, 132–4.

[368] Wolf, *Handelsbeziehungen*.

[369] KTB WiRüAmt/Stab 1939/41, 130 (5 Feb. 1941), BA-MA RW 19/164; in response to Schnurre's report concerning the granting of priority to Soviet orders, Hitler declined to commit himself in general terms; the departments should arrange matters among themselves.

[370] *DGFP* D xii, No. 13 (4 Feb. 1941).   [371] See Birkenfeld, 'Stalin', 503.

Soviet Union made every effort to meet its delivery obligations punctually and at times even at the expense of its own national stockpiles. Stalin was evidently determined, even aganist his own interests, not to offer Hitler any reason for a military conflict and to prove the value to the Reich of the German–Soviet economic alliance. On the German side, on the other hand, the impression was gaining ground, ever since Hitler's decision in July 1940, that Moscow's solid adherence to the principle of mutually profitable relations was placing an increasing strain on Germany's war economy. This in turn seemed to justify Hitler's decision to go to war. The SS security service's *Meldungen aus dem Reich* (Reports from the Reich) of 12 April 1941 reflected a widespread mood:

It is being said that in return for her deliveries Russia was receiving not foreign currency but top-quality machines, but that Germany would soon be unable to do without those machines and would put a stop to the deliveries. Russia would then refuse to deliver oil and grain. As, however, Germany would have to feed almost the whole of Europe during the coming winter, she was obliged to secure the Ukraine and the Russian oilfields.'[372]

Simultaneously, rumours were making the round in Berlin government cirles that Moscow might, under certain conditions, be prepared to cede those territories voluntarily. Such suppositions were being spread by those who regarded Operation Barbarossa as 'lunacy' and would have preferred instead to operate with the mere threat that the Bolsheviks would 'all have their heads cut off unless they did what Hitler wanted'. In that way they were to be 'made to comply without fighting'.[373] These persons presumably included the German ambassador in Moscow, who on 28 April 1941 made one last attempt to convince Hitler of the advantages of a continued economic alliance.[374] In a conversation with him he suggested that substantially greater concessions could surely still be obtained from Stalin through negotiation. Perhaps Moscow would supply up to five million tonnes of grain in the following year. Hitler, who did not place much faith in his diplomats' reports anyway and who—this was the impression of the foreign minister—appeared to be better briefed from other sources, revealed himself well informed on the problems of German–Soviet trade and rejected such speculations, if only on the grounds of existing transport difficulties.

[372] *Meldungen aus dem Reich*, 143–4.
[373] Hassell, *Tagebücher*, 199 (4 May 1941). American journalists in Berlin regarded such rumours as credible, as the USSR would not stand a chance in a military conflict; see report dated 19 May 1941, PA, Dienststelle Ribbentrop, UdSSR. The Hungarian minister in Berlin spread the speculation that Stalin was ready to concede to the Germans the control of the production and transportation of Soviet raw materials, thereby submitting to the German large-area economy: see St. S. No. 357, minute by Weizsäcker, 22 May 1941, PA, Büro des Staatssekretärs, Rußland, vol. v. In senior SA leadership circles there was a conviction that Molotov would soon come to Berlin to sign a new trade agreement: see Watzdorf, 'Lehren', 15. The military attaché in Moscow, on the other hand, was more cautious: 'Russia will do anything to avoid war and yield on every issue short of making territorial concessions': Halder, *Diaries*, 904 (5 May 1941).
[374] *DGFP* D xii, No. 423 (28 Apr. 1941).

The general approval which Hitler's intention to seize the vital raw materials and foodstuffs by force met with among the top echelons of the armed forces, big business, and economic administration was probably due in no small measure to the fear that the German war economy might become increasingly dependent on Soviet deliveries. Those fears, however, should not be over-rated. Once preparations for the attack on the Soviet Union had entered a concrete phase, a certain relaxed mood began to spread at least among the top leadership of the Reich. This was most perceptible in the armaments area, even though the stresses of German–Soviet trade were particularly marked in that field. In June 1941, at any rate, some RM600m.'s worth of Soviet orders were in process of being manufactured, thereby blocking a considerable pro-portion of German armaments capacities.[375] Why was Hitler prepared, as late as the spring of 1941, to accept that reduction in his own armaments? The answer that he was evidently interested in a smooth functioning of German–Soviet trade is surely insufficient. That paradoxical situation can be explained only by the armaments policy which had been initiated by Hitler's decision of July 1940.

4. THE EQUIPMENT OF THE EASTERN ARMY

At the peak of the campaign in France government circles in Berlin initially believed that the danger of 'over-exertion' through a continuous increase in armaments had, for the moment, been exorcized.[376] It was hoped that arma-ments production would now decline, contributing to a general easing of Germany's economic situation.[377] Hitler, on the other hand, argued that, although the planned creation of 20 divisions could now be abandoned in view of the termination of hostilities in France, and the size of the army reduced to 120 divisions,[378] this new peacetime army should nevertheless be adapted in its material equipment to the lessons learnt in the war and be brought to a peak of quality. He also issued instructions that the armaments programmes of the Luftwaffe and navy were to proceed unchanged. The necessary raw materials, means of production, and manpower were to be made available by a cut-back in armaments for the ground forces. He further directed that the older age-groups be released from the army in order to restimulate civilian production.[379] There was certainly no intention to reduce overall armaments production.

[375] See Bericht VO WiRüAmt zum RWM [Report of War Economy and Armaments Depart-ment officer liaising with the minister for economic affairs], 2 July 1941, BA-MA Wi/VI. 326.

[376] See minute of Gen. Thomas on the development of the armaments situation in the summer of 1940, 20 Aug. 1940, *KTB OKW* i, No. 23.

[377] See WiRüAmt minute of a conference with Gen. Jodl on 18 June 1940, dated 21 June 1940, BA-MA Wi/I A. 13.

[378] See OKW WFA, Abt. L (Chef) No. 00349/40 g.K., Erlaß über die Umsteuerung der Rüstung [Decree on the redirection of armaments production], 14 June 1940: Thomas, *Wehr- und Rüstungswirtschaft*, 406–7.

[379] Chef OKW WFA/L II No. 1270/40 g.Kdos., Erlaß betr. Umsteuerung der Rüstung [Decree concerning redirection of armaments production], 9 July 1940: ibid. 408–12.

Instead, Hitler stuck to his plan of promoting the development of the Wehrmacht to the point where it was equal to the sum total of all potential enemy armies.[380]

The Army High Command was primarily interested in creating the pre-requisites for the reorganization of the army. Re-equipment and replenishment of units were possible not only from existing stocks of weapons, equipment, and ammunition, but also by drawing on new production, which was continuing, albeit on a reduced scale. In addition there was the captured war material of approximately 180 enemy divisions, including almost 5,000 armoured fighting vehicles. The booty collected in France alone was enormous.[381] Its utilization enabled the Army High Command to exceed the envisaged total of 120 divisions from the outset and to raise additional units for limited operations in the east and for preparing the invasion of England. This had no bearing on the problem of new production, as existing material seemed to be entirely sufficient even for the deployment in the east as planned by the Army High Command. The envisaged occupation of the western regions of the Soviet Union would be feasible, according to the estimate of the Army High Command, with 80–100 divisions.[382]

Hitler's decision of 31 July 1940 in favour of an extended operational disposition in the east justified Halder's misgivings over the planned reduction in the size of the army. However, neither Hitler nor the Army High Command believed that the now essential enlargement of the army to 180 field divisions necessitated a complete reorganization of armaments production, let alone total mobilization. The assumption that the campaign against the USSR would take no longer than a couple of months, together with the time still available until the date of the attack in the spring of 1941, made any drastic interference with armaments production appear unnecessary. For the Luftwaffe and navy Hitler's decision was of no great consequence, as they were still primarily concerned with the war against Britain and as the decree for the redirection of armaments gave them priority anyway.

Colonel-General Fritz Fromm, chief of land-force armaments and commander-in-chief of the reserve army, saw no reason for precipitate action, even though he was faced with the task of promoting the qualitative reshaping of the army and, simultaneously, making provision for a further extension. Compared with the army's strength in the campaign against France, the new target of 180 divisions represented an increase of about 20 per cent. Quite apart from personnel problems, the equipment of these formations would have called for

[380] According to information from Todt, 6 July 1940, *KTB OKW* i. 74E (6 July 1940).
[381] See the relevant data in the 10–day report of OKH/GenStdH/Gen.Qu./Qu 1/Ia, 12 July 1940, BA-MA III W 805/2, pt. 2, and Hitler's directives of 23 June 1940 concerning captured weapons, Abt. Landesverteidigung No. 33110/40 Chefs., Notizen WFA über Besprechung Führer-ObdH [Minutes Wehrmacht operations department on conference of 23 June 1940 between Führer and C.-in-C. Army], dated 24 June 1940, BA-MA RW 4/v. 581.
[382] See Halder, *Diaries*, 517 (22 July 1940).

considerable efforts. For these the collection and re-allocation of existing stocks as well as of captured material were certainly not sufficient.

Major claims on new production were therefore inevitable. However, General Thomas immediately pointed out that complete equipment and arming of 180 divisions, plus an additional amount for the reserve army and current supplies, could not be achieved. 'In that case everything else would have to take second place to the army.'[383] The task in hand, therefore, was not so much a general increase in the army's equipment as a definition of new priority areas. In any case, production capacities were already fully taken up with the manufacture of heavy weapons and tanks. To create new capacities in this field would not produce any results before the spring of 1941, as the time needed for the manufacture of certain heavy weapons exceeded that interval. There was, however, thanks to an accumulated stockpile in certain areas, some latitude in light weapons, ammunition, and army equipment, so that production efforts could be focused on areas of deficiency. Because the Army High Command did not consider a major effort necessary for the campaign in the east, the chief of ground-force armaments accepted the new armaments programme, labelled 'B', which only slightly exceeded the programme of 9 July 1940, now named 'A'. In his deliberations, therefore, he did not proceed, from an ideal target for equipping the 1941 field army; instead, the army weapons department examined manufacturing facilities to determine what production could be accomplished by 31 March 1941. Next, the army's general department was to examine 'to what extent the shortfall can be made good by drawing on booty or by a cut in equipment'.[384]

Calculating the expected volume of new production proved exceedingly difficult: on the one hand, manufacturing capacities had to be assessed and, on the other, the question had to be settled whether the manpower, raw materials, and means of production necessary for a full utilization of these capacities would be available. Allocation of raw materials was in the hands of the Wehrmacht High Command; for the army an increase of no more than 10 per cent was scheduled over the next two quarters. The greatest problem was manpower. General Thomas, who briefed the Todt ministry, which was responsible for the finishing stage of armaments production, on the new situation, called for rigorous measures, mainly at the expense of the civilian sector.[385] He realized that such an appeal had little chance of success 'in view of the reluctance of the world of business'.[386] As the army was likewise unable to release any substantial amount of manpower, Hitler's expectation that

---

[383] Rü (II) g.Kdos., minute of conference of OKW chief of staff, 17 Aug. 1940: *Fall Barbarossa*, No. 56.

[384] OKH/Chef HRüst u. BdE/Stab II/Rüst No. 1494/40 g.Kdos., Schreiben an WaA und AHA betr. Programm B und C [Letter to army weapons department and army general department concerning programmes B and C], 19 Aug. 1940, BA-MA Wi/I F 5.120, pt. 1.

[385] Conference on 19 Aug. 1940, KTB Rüstungswirt. Abt., *KTB OKW* i. 75Ef.

[386] That was his judgement on 29 July 1940; see KTB Rüstungswirt. Abt., ibid. 75E.

armaments production would now move into top gear was unrealistic. Thomas and Keitel certainly arrived at that conclusion.[387]

Nor did Hitler, as it seems, close his eyes to those facts when, on 26 August 1940, he was briefed on the army's armaments plans and on the drastic consequences these would have for the equipment of the troops.[388] He approved the proposal of the Army High Command that only the 10 motorized divisions should be brought up to a full state of equipment; the fact would have to be accepted that the 20 armoured divisions would temporarily be equipped with only one tank regiment, and that some of the infantry divisions to be newly set up, as well as the motorized units, would be equipped largely with captured material. This would inevitably reduce the rearward services and the mobility of those units. Hitler's particular wish, the reinforcement of divisional artillery throughout the field army, had to be set aside for the time being because of the bottlenecks in the production of artillery pieces. Only his suggestion that the field divisions be equipped with light anti-aircraft units was still fitted into armaments programme B.

Particularly obscure was the situation in the ammunitions sector. Despite substantial stockpiles and modest consumption, production had to be re-started on a major scale. In a conversation with Keitel at the beginning of September Todt referred to the difficulties of precisely determining the army's ammunition needs for their increased weapons requirements.[389] It would first have to be reliably established what weapons would be available on 1 April 1941, in order, after deduction of existing ammunition stocks, to determine the scale of new production required. The demands for ammunition submitted by the chief of land-force armaments were not in accord with such calculations.

In the War Economy and Armaments Department the developments in the field of armaments for the land force were followed with some concern. One comment of 11 September 1940[390] was that production targets for individual firms under programme A had only recently been laid down, and appropriate readjustments made with regard to manufacture, so that the new programme B had now caused total chaos. The army's stepped-up demands could not be fully met because of existing shortages of manpower and raw materials, the less so as the Führer had just called for a drastic increase in the manufacture of 88-mm. anti-aircraft guns and appropriate ammunition.

[387] Conference between Keitel and Thomas on 20 Aug. 1940, KTB Rüstungswirt. Abt., ibid. 76E.

[388] See, as a result, the ruling of OKW No. 1555/40 g.Kdos. WFSt/Abt. L (II) betr. Ausbau des Kriegsheeres [concerning the further development of the wartime army], 5 Sept. 1940, BA-MA Wi/I F 5.120, pt. 1: *Fall Barbarossa*, No. 59.

[389] See Reich minister Dr. Ing. Fritz Todt, Adjutant, No. 370-455 g.Rs., minute referring to Führer's programme B, dated 6 Sept. 1940, ibid.

[390] Rü IIw, Beitrag zum Vortrag Chef WiRüAmt [Notes for the report by chief of the War Economy and Armaments Department], 13 Sept. 1940, betr. Steigerung der Rüstung und ihre Folgerungen [concerning intensification of armaments production and its consequences], 11 Sept. 1940, ibid.

The existing priority system was clearly no longer adequate for regulating the different armaments programmes of the Wehrmacht services. The Wehrmacht High Command therefore worked out a further subdivision of categories, designed to shorten the list of top-priority items which had to have full chain on available resources. The special category of top-priority items for the three services (for the army this was mainly the construction of the Mark III and Mark IV tank, as well as the latest 50-mm. anti-tank gun) was followed by category I, now subdivided into Ia and Ib, and finally by category II.[391] Other possible ways of relieving the situation were measures in regard to manpower and the utilization of industrial capacities in the occupied territories.

The chief of land-force armaments therefore saw no reason for antagonizing the other Wehrmacht services, even though the production programme worked out by him[392] was based on the optimistic assumption that production capacities would be fully taken up and that an appropriate allocation of raw materials and manpower was possible. Provided the army asserted itself more forcibly in the valid system of priorities, and provided no major capacities were lost as a result of enemy air raids, he estimated that the material prerequisites for the wartime army demanded by Hitler could be 'essentially' fulfilled by 1 May 1941. A few gaps would admittedly have to be expected in meeting the targets for weapons and equipment, but these might be offset by a reduced level of equipment of the units. The ammunition situation also seemed to him to present no problems. Even if the twelve-months' stockpile on top of the initial issue was not achieved by the stipulated date, there would at least be sufficient stocks to bridge such time as it took for current production to catch up with expected consumption.

From this assessment the Wehrmacht High Command concluded that, apart from a production increase in respect of a few weapons in short supply, the demands of the chief of land-force armaments were roughly within the framework laid down for overall armaments production in July 1940.[393] Keitel, however, exposed as he was to Hitler's continual calling for armaments manufacture to move into top gear, insisted that provision be made for an increase in production for the army even after 1 April 1941. One should not, he explained to General Thomas, make a virtue of the present necessity and juggle with fluctuating output figures. It was necessary to extend capacities in the long term: the present situation whereby, for example, production of 88-mm. anti-aircraft ammunition could be increased only if production of ammu-

[391] Der Vorsitzende des Reichsverteidigungsrates [Chairman of the Reich Defence Council], Anordnung betr. Dringlichkeit der Fertigungsprogramme [Ordinance on priorities of manufacturing programmes], 20 Sept. 1940: Thomas, *Wehr- und Rüstungswirtschaft*, 422–9.

[392] OKH/Chef HRüst u. BdE/Stab II (Rüst) No. 1851/40g.Kdos., Schreiben an OKW/WiRüAmt betr. Rüstungsprogramm B [Letter to OKW/WiRüAmt concerning armaments programme B], 16 Sept. 1940, BA-MA Wi/I F 5.120, pt. 1: *Fall Barbarossa*, No. 60.

[393] Rü IIw, minute of a report to Wehrmacht High Command chief of staff, on 17 Sept. 1940, concerning intensification of armaments production, ibid.

nition for the light field howitzer were cut back at the same time, must not become a permanent feature. The objective must be to produce both types of ammunition 'alongside one another at maximum volume'.

A conference on 19 September 1940 of representatives of land-force armaments and the Reich ministry for arms and ammunition soon revealed that the calculations of the authorities concerned still did not agree and that an accurate prescription of production targets in individual cases was not possible at the time.[394] In consequence the participants once more confirmed the principle that only such demands should be made as could in fact be implemented within the seven months still available. The balance was to be taken care of later.

This left two important problems open. One concerned the precise determination of expected figures for tank construction. These figures had to be known so that appropriate production targets could be laid down for tank-guns and ammunition. The 'mobile troops' project ordered by Hitler called for the widest possible replacement of the light Mark I and Mark II types with the medium Mark III and Mark IV types. Production programme A had envisaged an increase in monthly production to 380 tanks, with a view to satisfying the army's overall requirement of 26,700 battle tanks by the end of 1944.[395] The tank-delivery programme of the Todt ministry, dated 23 August 1940,[396] on the other hand, had envisaged delivery of 1,500 battle tanks and 300 self-propelled guns by 1 May 1941; this presupposed an average monthly production of approximately 200 vehicles, which was more or less in line with Hitler's ideas. If one compares the actual production figures for April 1940 (127) and September 1940 (121),[397] then one realizes the additional effort that had to be made with regard to tanks. The fact that at the conference on 14 September substantially higher figures were mentioned by the Todt ministry—the delivery of 2,000 Panzer III and 800 Panzer IV by 1 April 1941—reveals the dilemma of a land-force armaments department which, with such frequently fanciful number-games, was increasingly losing touch with reality.

The second major problem concerned the further extension of production capacities, primarily in the ammunitions field. Existing limited resources were insufficient to increase output and simultaneously extend manufacturing facilities, i.e. set up new places of production. Expansion of the gunpowder and

---

[394] Rü IIw, Aktennotiz über die Besprechung beim Munitionsminister am 19.9. mit Chef HRüst und den WaA-Amtsgruppenleitern Mun und WuG betr. Steigerung der Rüstung [Minute of conference at the ammunitions ministry on 19 Sept. 1940 with the chief of land-force armaments and the army weapons department's section heads for ammunition and weapons and equipment, concerning intensification of armaments production], 20 Sept. 1940, ibid.

[395] See annexe 4 to OKW/WiRüAmt/Rü IIa No. 1350/40 g.K., Aufstellung Waffen und Gerät Heer [Table of weapons and equipment, army], 9 July 1940, BA-MA Wi/I A. 13.

[396] Oberländer and Rohland, Kampfwagen-Liefer-Programm [Programme for the delivery of armoured fighting vehicles], 1 Aug. 1940–1 May 1941, 23 Aug. 1940, BA-MA Wi/I F 5.120, pt. 1.

[397] Rü IIw, minute of 10 Sept. 1940 (above, n. 394).

explosives base was already lagging badly behind schedule. The chief of land-force armaments naturally pleaded for priority for armaments production; he believed that final expansion targets for a long-term programme 'C' could not be firmly laid down so long as the necessary decisions on the structure and equipment of the future army—after the conclusion of the campaign in the east—remained to be made. The Army High Command thereby concurred with the postponement of a long-term armaments programme; this was to prove an important decision affecting the material fighting strength of the army in 1941.

When Keitel and Todt jointly reported to him, Hitler basically approved the production proposals on which the departments had agreed.[398] However, he made some important additions to certain items. He was primarily anxious to increase the number of armour-piercing weapons and the principal types of artillery pieces, and to achieve a greater density of light anti-aircraft weapons. In these areas the figures submitted were to be regarded as minimum targets; wherever possible, higher output figures were to be aimed at as a supplementary programme. Hitler also gave orders that 300,000 metal-workers were to be released from the army and made available to the armaments industry on factory leave until the spring of 1941.

Moreover, Hitler's decree, published on 28 September 1940, on the intensification of armaments production listed a number of additional tasks for the navy (the unlimited continuation of the U-boat programme) and for the Luftwaffe (increase in the production of anti-aircraft guns and suitable ammunition).[399] Whether this list of tasks could be accomplished merely by an appeal for the prescribed system of priorities to be observed, or through the shelving of all non-urgent tasks in the civilian sector—along with some minor measures in the labour market—must have seemed exceedingly doubtful.

Hitler's armaments instructions again upset the equilibrium between requirements and resources, so laboriously balanced by the different departments. On the number of men to be granted army leave for work in industry his ideas likewise diverged greatly from those of the Army High Command; the latter needed all its personnel for the planned enlargement of the army in the field.[400] In addition, the manufacturing programme 'Axis', for the support of Germany's Italian ally, had to be set up.[401] This was placed at the head of the priority scale, even above 'special category' manufacture. Then there was

---

[398] See Reich Minister Dr. Ing. Fritz Todt, G. I. No. 3986/40, Schreiben an den Chef des OKW mit einer Niederschrift über den Vortrag beim Führer über das Winter-Rüstungsprogramm [Letter to Wehrmacht High Command chief of staff with minutes of the report to the Führer on the winter armaments programme], 27 Sept. 1940, BA-MA Wi/I F 5.120, pt. 1.

[399] Führer-Erlaß betr. Steigerung der Rüstung [Führer decree on intensification of armaments production], 28 Sept. 1940: Thomas, *Wehr- und Rüstungswirtschaft*, 432–6.

[400] See sect I.iv.1(*h*) (Klink).

[401] See Chef OKW/WiRüAmt Rü Ia No. 7429/40 g., Anordnung betr. Dringlichkeit der Fertigungsprogramme der Wehrmacht [Instruction concerning priorities in the Wehrmacht's production programmes], 27 Sept. 1940: Thomas, *Wehr- und Rüstungswirtschaft*, 430–1.

the decision to include Soviet armaments orders in priority class Ia.[402] It was obvious that by then the framework of overall armaments production laid down in July 1940 was finally quite destroyed. Implementation of the various programmes was moreover threatened by the multiplicity of overlapping responsibilities of different clients and by the military agencies' lack of supervisory and directing powers *vis-à-vis* private industry. Additional friction arose through the far from smooth operation of an ineffective military bureaucracy.

In the field of armoured fighting vehicles it was therefore agreed that 1,490 new vehicles could presumably be manufactured by 31 March 1941.[403] Although Todt's enormous figures had thus been quietly discarded, it was by no means certain that even the new targets could in fact be reached, considering the serious bottlenecks in all fields. Even a reliable determination of the existing total of armoured fighting vehicles proved extraordinarily difficult. Military leaders were operating with figures (as of 1 September 1940) which fluctuated between 4,833 and 3,563.[404] These divergences presumably arose from double counting of tanks, many of which were undergoing rearming. When even the current total was uncertain, determination of overall requirements became rather difficult.

Hitler's new instructions compelled the chief of land-force armaments to check his calculations in other areas as well. Thus an additional requirement of 1,469 light field howitzers 18, the principal divisional artillery weapon, was initially established; an examination of production capacities, however, revealed that probably only about 60 per cent of this target could be met (i.e. 840 artillery pieces).[405] The balance was to be delivered later, by August 1941. Hitler's demand that a further 800 pieces be manufactured was therefore unrealizable from the start, especially as manufacture of the 88-mm. anti-aircraft gun was to be stepped up at the same time. Indeed, this would have been possible only at the expense of the light field howitzer 18. According to the calculations of the chief of land-force armaments, an additional 900 machine-tools would have to be provided to ensure the ordered production increase. Yet the army could only count on the delivery of, at best, 350 machines-tools by the spring of 1941,[406] and even these would only begin

---

[402] See Der Reichsmarschall des Großdeutschen Reiches, Beauftragter für den Vierjahresplan [Reich Marshal of the Greater German Reich, plenipotentiary for the Four-year Plan], V.P. 16741, ordinance of 15 Oct. 1940 (copy), BA-MA Wi/I F 5.120, pt. 2.

[403] See annexe 4, Fertigung Waffen Heer für die Zeit vom 1.9.1940–1.4.1941, zum Führer-Erlaß vom 28.9.1940 betr. die Steigerung der Rüstung [Production of weapons for the army for the period 1 Sept. 1940 to 1 Apr. 1941, with reference to the Führer's decree of 28 Sept. 1940 concerning intensification of armaments production], ibid.

[404] See ibid., and OKW/WiRüAmt, Dekaden-Übersichten [Ten-year tables], fo. 1, BA-MA Wi/I F 5.366.

[405] Annexe 4 to Fertigung Heer (above, n. 403).

[406] See OKH/Chef HRüst und RMfBuM betr. Steigerung der Rüstung—Durchführungsbestimmungen (Intensification of armaments production—implementation regulations), 18 Oct. 1940, BA-MA Wi/I F 5.120, pt. 1.

to affect output of artillery pieces in the late summer of 1941. In consequence, there was no one who could reliably predict what production targets could in fact be attained over the next few months. The effect such a situation was bound to have on the calculation of ammunition requirements is obvious.

The relief which the Wehrmacht High Command had expected as a result of the use of captured weapons often proved illusory. Although large numbers of the standard weapon of the French field artillery, the field gun M-97, had been captured,[407] of the 860 pieces captured in Czechoslovakia and Poland, 80 had been sold to Romania, 410 had gone to the navy, and 371 had gone to the Luftwaffe. Of the booty taken in the western campaign, 2,440 artillery pieces in all, the navy had by the beginning of October taken over 44 pieces, and the Luftwaffe nearly half of the stocks in order to employ them in barrage-fire batteries for aerial defence. Göring had made sure that all usable M-97 guns were placed at the disposal of the Luftwaffe for that purpose. Attempts by the army's general department to have this decision revoked in order to offset the increasing shortage in the army therefore met with very little success.

It appears that none of these contradictions and imponderables in the armaments situation was felt to be alarming by the Army High Command in the autumn of 1940. The army's weapons department passed on its manufacturing orders to industry. Harmonization with the orders from other services and provision of appropriate resources were then essentially the task of the Wehrmacht High Command.

Fromm held the dual post of chief of land-force armaments and commander-in-chief of the reserve army. It was the second of these functions which increasingly occupied him and his staff after October 1940, when the reconstruction and expansion of the army were gaining momentum. Organizational and personnel measures in this context occupied his entire attention.[408]

Initially there was a sufficient stock of weapons and equipment for refurbishing the units. By September, current production had virtually made good the losses from the campaign in France,[409] so that some support was available for the most urgent armaments projects. Further relief was expected from the transfer—by then massive—of Wehrmacht orders to the occupied territories, more especially to France. Despite considerable political opposition and administrative friction, orders for the delivery of spare parts, as well as for subcontracted deliveries of military equipment, were placed to a total value of RM1,800m.[410] However, the relief felt by armaments manufacturers within

---

[407] On the following see AHA No. 3041/40g.Kdos. AHA Ib, 2. Vortragsnotiz über die Feldkanone M 97 (franz.) aus Beute t, p, b, u. f [Minute of report on the French M-97 fieldcannon from Czech, Polish, Belgian, and French spoils], 8 Oct. 1940, BA-MA RH 8/v. 1022.

[408] See sect. I.IV.1(*h*) at nn. 194ff. (Klink).

[409] See OKW/WiRüAmt, Dekaden-Übersichten [Ten-year tables], BA-MA Wi/I F 5.366.

[410] See KTB Rüstungswirtschaftliche Abteilung, fos. 250ff. (30 Nov. 1940), BA-MA RW 19/257.

Germany was limited, since the raw materials needed to complete an order had, as a rule, to be provided by the German side.

It is a matter of record that in contrast to the Wehrmacht High Command, where the problem of overall control of armaments production and excessive requirements was viewed with increasing concern,[411] the Army High Command reacted calmly. It is, however, significant that Lieutenant-General Stud, previously responsible for industrial production as a group leader in the army's weapons department, addressed the problem of the take-over of the Soviet armaments industry as soon as he was transferred to the War Economy and Armaments Department. That was presumably due to a realization among top military leaders that the overtaxing of Germany's economic capacity had clearly reached a peak and that other solutions had to be found if armaments targets were to be reached. When Göring called for an assessment of the war-economy situation by 1 May 1941, the armaments economy department of the Wehrmacht High Command came to the conclusion that a postponement of target dates was inevitable.[412] 'On the whole' the material equipment of the '1941 wartime army' was ensured, with the exception of a few types of weapons and their ammunition still in short supply; the shortage in stocks, on the other hand, would not be made good until early 1942. By contrast, the tank-construction programme was proceeding smoothly: monthly output figures of 375 armoured vehicles could be expected from April 1941. The army's weapons department was judging the situation sceptically, admitting that, as a result of the new priority system and the resulting switch of man-power, any overall idea of manufacturing capacities had been 'totally lost'.[413] Added to this was the very late allocation of raw materials by the Wehrmacht High Command, which resulted in numerous orders having to be given to industry without the necessary resources being made available. The forecast for tank production had already been reduced by 10 per cent by the army's weapons department because of inevitable delivery problems, with a monthly output of 337 vehicles being laid down for April 1941.[414] There was good reason, therefore, for returning to the idea of planning armaments for the army on a longer-term basis. The first question to be settled was what capacities could additionally be made available within the army in order to carry the tank programme, and possibly also programme B, beyond 1 April 1941.[415]

---

[411] See ibid., fos. 230 ff. (4 Nov. 1940), also published in *KTB OKW* i. 78E ff.

[412] Rüstungswirtschaftliche Abteilung/Rü I 2427/40 g.Kdos., Voraussichtliche Entwicklung und Stand der wehrwirtschaftlichen Lage für den Zeitraum bis 1.5.41 [Projection of the development and state of the war economy during the period up to 1 May 1941], 6 Dec. 1940, BA-MA Wi/F 5.120, pt. 2: *Fall Barbarossa*, No. 62.

[413] Rü IIa, Minute of the conference at Chef Rü with the responsible officers of the procurement departments of the Wehrmacht services on 21 Nov. 1940, dated 22 Nov. 1940, BA-MA Wi/I F 5.120, pt. 1.

[414] See WaA/WaStab Ia³, Vortragsnotiz für den Herrn Ob.d.H. über die Pz.Kpf.Wg.-Fertigung [Note for a report for the C.-in-C. Army on manufacture of armoured fighting vehicles], 1 Nov. 1940, BA-MA RH 8/v. 1068.

[415] See WaA No. 2196/40 g.Kdos. Wa Stab Ia, Interne Verfügung betr. Planung der Kapazitäten [Internal instruction concerning planning of capacities], 18 Nov. 1940, BA-MA Wi/I F 5.120, pt. 1.

Immediately following the conclusion of Molotov's visit Hitler summoned those responsible for land-force armaments to report to him. He wanted to get an idea of the present state and the prospects of armaments production. By then there was no question that drastic intervention was necessary.[416] Although he took note of the fact that only about half of the 300,000 servicemen he had ordered to be released had in fact been made available by the army for the armaments industry, Hitler did not wish to make any changes to the scale of the programme. He merely gave orders that, wherever stocks and consumption permitted, the target dates were to be postponed. Hitler also believed that by switching more civilian production to the occupied territories he could free an additional 100,000 workers for munitions.

At the same time he once more called for the production of specific weapons to be increased, such as the 88-mm. anti-aircraft gun. In addition, construction of air-raid shelters was to be accelerated in the major cities of Germany. The result of this was that the Wehrmacht's quota of raw materials—an increase in which for the first quarter of 1941 had already been rejected—was to be cut into even further as greater quantities of raw materials had to be diverted towards indirect Wehrmacht requirements.[417] A similar need arose for the development of supply facilities, the transport network, and raw-materials enterprises, so that a smaller quota of raw materials was available for armaments manufacture proper than before.

A new system of priorities was therefore being worked out in the Wehrmacht High Command for directing munitions manufacture with a view to concentrating what meagre resources were available on the most important programmes.[418] Since the backlog in the army's equipment for the eastern campaign was not regarded either by Hitler or by the Army High Command as sufficiently serious to warrant special steps for the preparation and execution of that campaign, the Wehrmacht High Command encountered no opposition when it demanded priority for Luftwaffe and naval armaments at the expense of the land forces. Top priority was to be given, in Jodl's view, to anything needed for the 'siege of Britain: U-boats, torpedoes, mines, and light naval forces, bombers, and air-dropped ammunition'; next came the strengthening of air defences in Germany, while the army's requirements came only in third place.[419] In Jodl's opinion the operations in the east could be 'easily conducted' with the material strength available. If it were not possible to bring the envisaged twenty armoured divisions to full strength by the following

---

[416] See Rü IIa, Aktennotiz über die Besprechung bei Reichsminister Dr. Todt am 22.11.1940 (Minute of conference at Reich Minister Dr Todt's office on 22 Nov. 1940], ibid.; Todt gave a briefing on a conference with Hitler on 21 Nov. 1940, at which, apart from himself, Keitel and Fromm had been present.

[417] See KTB WiRüAmt/Stab 1939/41, 92–3 (25–30 Nov. 1940), BA-MA RW 19/164.

[418] Ibid. 96 (2 Dec. 1940).

[419] Wehrmachtführungsstab, Stellungnahme zur Vortragsnotiz des Wi und RüAmtes vom 30.11. betr. Überprüfung der Rüstungsprogramme [Wehrmacht operations department, comment on note for report by the War Economy and Armaments Department of 30 Nov. 1940 concerning examination of armaments programmes], 3 Dec. 1940: Thomas, *Wehr- und Rüstungswirtschaft*, 436–7.

spring, then this was, if anything, an advantage because it would save 'an enormous amount of auxiliary weapons and rearward services'. It was therefore correct, he argued, to reduce new production for the army and instead to maintain full production for the Luftwaffe and naval programmes. Indeed, Jodl went even further. He did not rule out the possibility that, 'if the armaments situation forces us to do so', the campaign in the east may have to be postponed as it was 'not a compelling necessity for victory over Britain'. There are indications that the Army High Command similarly judged the armaments situation and the conclusions to be drawn from it. At any rate, Hitler—parallel to his directive No. 21 for Barbarossa—had submitted to him for signature instructions for manpower support for the armaments industry, designed primarily to benefit the navy and the air force.[420]

The consequences of that decision, needless to say, also affected the army's main programmes, even though they were included in the top priority class. Thus, tank production alone was short of over 6,000 skilled workers in January 1941,[421] so that Todt—who was focusing increasingly on that sector because ammunition manufacture, his real responsibility, was running at only half speed—requested from Hitler the provision of additional labour.[422] This was to be released from the rest of armaments production for the army, as well as from the army's personnel planning. Hitler approved Todt's request, and although Göring thereupon asked for additional manpower for the Luftwaffe, which Hitler granted, Hitler nevertheless appeared to be proceeding from the assumption that munitions for the army would enjoy priority until the summer of 1941, with the Luftwaffe not being 'served' until after that date.[423]

The Wehrmacht High Command, on the other hand, continued its efforts to mobilize all forces primarily for Luftwaffe and naval armaments. In a letter to the chief of land-force armaments, dated 15 January 1941, Keitel referred to 'binding instructions from the Führer' which prevented any greater consideration of the army.[424] Hitler, having 'considered all operational intentions and given full weight to all military misgivings' had 'taken responsibility'. The Wehrmacht High Command continued that line also in its new priority regulation of 7 February 1941.[425] A new special category was established,

---

[420] Der Führer und Oberste Befehlshaber der Wehrmacht [The Führer and Supreme Commander of the Wehrmacht], WFSt/Abt. L II No. 2295/40 g.K., Anordnung betr. personelle Maßnahmen für Rüstungsindustrie und Bergbau [Instruction concerning personnel measures for the armaments industry and mining], 20 Dec. 1940, BA-MA Wi/I F 5.120, pt. 1.

[421] Chef Rü, Aktenvermerk über die Besprechung beim Reichsminister Dr. Todt am 9.1.1941 [Minute of a conference at Reich Minister Dr. Todt's office on 9 Jan. 1941], dated 10 Jan. 1941, BA-MA Wi/I A. 84.

[422] See KTB WiRüAmt/Stab 1939/41, 167–8, 170 (18, 19 Feb. 1941), BA-MA RW 19/164.

[423] See Below, *Hitlers Adjutant*, 254–5.

[424] Der Chef des OKW/WFSt/Abt. L II No. 33468/41 g.Kdos. Chefs., Schreiben an Chef HRüst u. BdE (Letter to chief of land-force armaments and C.-in-C. of the reserve army), 15 Jan. 1941, BA-MA RH 2/v. 427.

[425] OKW WiRüAmt/Rü Ia No. 801/41 geh., Anordnung betr. Dringlichkeit der Fertigungsprogramme der Wehrmacht [Instruction concerning priorities for manufacturing programmes of the Wehrmacht], 7 Feb. 1941: Thomas, *Wehr- und Rüstungswirtschaft*, 438–47.

designated 'SS' and ranking above all other categories. It included the principal armaments programmes of the navy and Luftwaffe, and, as far as the army
was concerned, at least the tank programme and a few areas of deficiency. The
next category down, 'S', covered equipment for the mobile forces, especially
light armoured vehicles, as well as provision of spare parts and workshops for
all armoured fighting vehicles. The programme for trucks was in a lower
category still, even though output was lagging nearly 30 per cent below the
target.[426] This was bound to have grave effects on the army's motorization and
mobility. Nevertheless, the Army High Command saw no reason to call for
greater weight to be given to it in overall armaments production.

This attitude begins to make sense when one considers that, following
negotiations of the armistice commission in the spring of 1941, the bulk of the
French war material from the unoccupied part of France was now also being
transferred to the Wehrmacht. This comprised no less than 341 trains, as well
as 13,000 lorries,[427] the take-over of which made it possible to eliminate at least
some of the bottlenecks in the motorization of the army.

The Army High Command therefore confined itself to releasing some
manpower and raw materials through rearrangements within programme B—
mainly through cut-backs in the production of ammunition and artillery
pieces.[428] They were to fill existing gaps in weapons and equipment for initial
issue, for supplies, for re-equipment, and for export to Germany's allies and
neutral countries. Since just at that time the bulk of the men given labour leave
by the army were returning to their units and a major call-up wave was in
progress, considerable shortages of manpower arose, and these had a detrimental effect chiefly on munitions for the army. Neither Göring's appeal of 18
February 1941 that all non-vital manufacture should be cut back or ruthlessly
halted nor the creation of bottleneck commissions constituted more than a
temporary expedient.[429] Colonel-General Ernst Udet, the Luftwaffe's quartermaster-general, therefore warned that a cut-back in aerial armaments was out
of the question.[430]

Although over 80 per cent of the Luftwaffe equipment programme came

[426] See Chef HRüst u. BdE/Stab IIc (Rüst), Vermerk betr. LKW-Ausstoß [Note concerning
output of trucks], 25 Jan. 1941, BA-MA RH 8/v. 1068.

[427] See Halder, *Diaries*, 834 (18 Mar. 1941). The project goes back to a conference of civilian
and military claimants on 28 Jan. 1941; see Halder, *Diaries*, 764–5.

[428] See OKH/Chef HRüst u. BdE/Stab II (Rüst) a No. 268/41 g.Kdos., Schreiben an OKW betr.
Rüstungsprogramm B [Letter to OKW concerning armaments programme B], 8 Feb. 1941, BA-
MA Wi/I F 5.120, pt. 2.

[429] Der Reichsmarschall des Großdeutschen Reiches, Beauftragter für den Vierjahresplan [The
Reich Marshall of the Greater German Reich and plenipotentiary for the Four-year Plan], V.P.
2703/41 g, instruction of 18 Feb. 1941, ibid.

[430] Der Reichsminister der Luftfahrt u. Oberbefehlshaber der Luftwaffe. Der Generalluftzeug-
meister GL 1 [The Reich Minister of Aviation and C.-in-C. of the Luftwaffe. The Luftwaffe
quartermaster-general GL 1] No. 2794/4.41 (I) geh., Schreiben an OKW/WiRüAmt betr.
Einschränkung der Wehrmachtfertigung zur Entlastung der Arbeitseinsatzlage [Letter to OKW
War Economy and Armaments Department concerning restriction of production for the
Wehrmacht with a view to relieving the manpower situation], 1 Apr. 1941, ibid.

under the two special categories, delivery targets had still not been reached. If anything, he argued, additional manpower, raw materials, and machines were needed. In its preparations for the eastern campaign, which had been in progress since the end of 1940, the Luftwaffe command had proceeded from the assumption that current aircraft production could at best maintain its present strength.[431] It was natural, therefore, that attempts should be made to make full use of existing manufacturing capacities and to search for possi- bilities of extending production. The intended war against the Soviet Union played no particular part in these considerations, even though the Luftwaffe command expected a Soviet superiority of a factor of three or four. Like the army command, it was convinced that the war could be won with the forces available. Additional production efforts were regarded as superfluous and, in view of the short time available, also pointless. Instead, Göring's Luftwaffe was focusing entirely on the period after Barbarossa and on the armaments race with the Anglo-Saxon powers, whose output of aircraft already exceeded that of Germany. The Luftwaffe was therefore aiming at doubling the ca- pacities in aircraft production, which of course could be achieved only at the expense of munitions for the army.

As the navy likewise rejected any further cut-backs in its armaments pro- gramme, and indeed made additional demands for manpower and re- sources,[432] the Army High Command launched a new drive for longer-term armaments planning, to avoid being left even further behind by the other two services.[433] The intention was that, when programme B came to an end, the change-over in land-force armaments, already under way, should be kept going by new projections, thereby preventing any further reduction of the army's share in overall armaments. The army's weapons department expected that, as a result of a further concentration of land-force armaments as well as of the amounts already passed on to the other services, there would be a marked decline in the course of 1941 in the manufacture of many types of weapons, equipment, and ammunition. This was considered acceptable, as the remaining capacities, together with stockpiles, would be sufficient to meet 'all conceivable future requirements of the war'. Any further increase, though desirable, would not become effective, as far as military operations were concerned, before the end of 1941. 'On the assumption of a *development of the war* in line with the intentions of the high command (which rules out any serious continental adversary on the ground in future), a substantial *reduction of the army*, with the exception of the mobile troops, was envisaged.' The resources freed as a result, mainly from the 75 per cent reduction in supply

---

[431] On the following see also sect. I.IV.2(c) at nn. 353 ff. (Boog).

[432] Der Oberbefehlshaber der Kriegsmarine [C.-in-C. of the navy], M Wa Wi III 6364/41 geh., Schreiben an Chef OKW betr. Einschränkung der Wehrmachtfertigung zur Entlastung der Arbeitseinsatzlage [Letter to OKW chief of staff concerning restriction of production for the Wehrmacht with a view to relieving the manpower situation], 12 Apr. 1941, ibid.

[433] See WaA No. 12345/41 g. Wa Stab Ia, Stellungnahme betr. Planung der Kapazitäten [Com- ment on planning of capacities), 7 Apr. 1941 (draft), BA-MA RH 8/v. 1068.

requirements, were to be used for the further promotion of the tank programme.

In a letter to the Wehrmacht High Command, dated 10 April, the chief of land-force armaments therefore pointed out that, despite certain cut-backs in production, the army could not release any further manpower.[434] In parallel to the Luftwaffe, which under its 'Göring Plan' was aiming at quadrupling its aircraft strength, and to the navy, which was planning a gigantic enlargement of the fleet over the next twelve to fifteen years,[435] the army now likewise drafted a megalomaniacal armaments programme which, both in its scale and in its structural weaknesses, revealed the contradictions and limitations of the planning capabilities of the military leadership. This was the 'armour programme 41',[436] which was based on the original target (June 1940) of the establishment and equipment of twenty armoured and ten motorized divisions. The following calculations therefore indicate the dimension which armaments programme B would have had to assume for these formations to be fully equipped for the campaign in the east. The army's general department proceeded from a complete initial equipment of those formations, as well as the provision of their annual requirements for replacements and spares; it concluded that 34,661 armoured fighting vehicles would have to be produced for these purposes.[437] If one added the needs of the reserve army and supplies, that figure increased to 39,759. Further to be added were 126,379 tractor trucks. In order to achieve that target by 31 December 1944, current manufacturing capacities would have to be increased roughly fivefold. That would require 11,500 so-called bottleneck machines by 1 October 1943. In actual fact only 472 of these could be delivered by that date. The conclusion which the army's weapons department drew from this striking disproportion was that either the entire machine-tool capacities of the country should be placed at the army's disposal at once—which would necessitate the shelving of all programmes for other claimants—or else, if drastic changes were to be avoided, manufacture of armoured fighting vehicles and anti-aircraft guns could only be considered in the long term, with no perceptible growth until the years after 1943.

---

[434] OKH/Chef HRüst u. BdE/Stab Rüst IIa No. 1357/41 geh., Schreiben an OKW/WiRüAmt betr. Veränderungen im Arbeitskräftebedarf durch Fertigungsplan Heer 1941 [Letter to OKW War Economy and Armaments Department concerning changes in manpower requirements as a result of army manufacturing plan 1941], 10 Apr. 1941, BA-MA Wi/I F 5.120, pt. 2.

[435] See SKL memorandum 'Betrachtungen über die Grundlagen des Flottenaufbaus' [Reflections on the basis of the development of the fleet], Aug. 1941: Schreiber, 'Kontinuität', 147–8.

[436] See WaA, No. 1100/41 g.Kdos. Wa Stab Ia, Die Schwerpunktprogramme des Heeres, Panzerprogramm 41, Heeresflakprogramm (unter besonderer Berücksichtigung der Werkzeugmaschinen-Lage) [The army's main areas of effort, armour programme 41, army anti-aircraft programme (with special reference to the machine-tool situation)], May 1941, BA-MA RH 8/v. 1130.

[437] Ibid., annexe 4; the armaments plan of 9 July 1940 had envisaged 26,700 tanks by the end of 1944; see Erlaß betr. Umsteuerung der Rüstung [Decree on the redirection of armaments production], 9 July 1940, annexe 4, BA-MA Wi/I F 5.378.

In its memorandum of May 1941 the army weapons department pleaded for the latter alternative. One reason was probably that conveyor-belt production with special-purpose machines was rejected on grounds of principle, although it was obvious that a rapid growth in production figures could only be achieved that way. The army officers instead preferred short manufacturing series with multi-purpose machines. These plans were controversial also in another respect: the 'armour programme 41' unquestioningly projected the existing equipment target into the future, without regard for any modernization or technical advances. Thus a continuous increase in deliveries of the Mark II light tank was envisaged, even though this was regarded as outdated among the troops and was due for gradual replacement by the Mark III and IV medium tanks. As recently as 18 February Hitler himself, at a conference with the men responsible for tank development,[438] had again come out in favour of heavier armament. Yet the plan of the army weapons department stipulated that nearly half the calculated tank fleet as of 1 April 1941 was to consist of the light Mark II.[439]

In contrast to the military armaments programmes of the first year of the war, when an attempt was made to establish what was feasible and to use that as the basis of production demands, the plans of the three services on the eve of Operation Barbarossa were strikingly out of proportion to Germany's economic capacity, even if the German-dominated European territory was included. It would have made sense to set up a central planning agency at the Wehrmacht High Command, to harmonize armaments targets with each other, as well as with actual resources. But although the weapons departments of the three services considered the idea,[440] nothing came of it.[441] The separate services evidently preferred to pursue their ambitious programmes independently and, if necessary, to seek new ways of doing so.

On the one hand, they tried, to a greater measure than in the past, to gain support and co-operation from industry. Thus an industrial council was set up under Göring for aerial armaments, and a tank commission was established for the army under the Reich minister for armaments and ammunition.[442] Both

[438] See the account in Rohland, Bewegte Zeiten, 73.

[439] See Die Schwerpunktprogramme des Heeres (above, n. 436), annexe 4.

[440] See OKW WiRüAmt/Rü IIa No. 20968/41 g., Aktennotiz betr. Zusammenfassung und Steuerung der seitens der Wehrmachtteile vorgesehenen Gesamt-Planung auf dem Rüstungsgebiet [Minute concerning concentration and control of the overall planning in the armaments sector, as envisaged by the Wehrmacht services], 4 Apr. 1941, BA-MA Wi/I F 5.120, pt. 2. Efforts along those lines had first failed during the rearmament phase before the outbreak of the war: see Germany and the Second World War, i. 505 ff.

[441] At the urgent request of WiRüAmt such a planning agency was set up on 9 Oct. 1940 at the Armaments Industry Department, headed by a Luftwaffe general staff officer; its effectiveness, however, was limited. See Thomas, Wehr- und Rüstungswirtschaft, 290.

[442] See Vereinbarung zwischen dem RMfBuM sowie dem Chef der Heeresrüstung betr. Panzerprogramm [Agreement between the Reich Minister for Armaments and Ammunition and the chief of land-force rearmament concerning tank programme], 21 June 1941, and Mitteilung des Generalluftzeugmeisters (Notification of the Luftwaffe quartermaster-general] No. 8308/41 (GL I V) betr. Industrierat des Reichsmarschalls für die Fertigung von Luftwaffengerät [concerning the Reich Marshal's industrial council for the manufacture of Luftwaffe equipment], 22 May 1941, BA-MA Wi/I F 5.120, pt. 2.

these bodies were dominated by the representatives of industry, while the weapons departments had to surrender their influence on the direction of armaments production. On the other hand, the Wehrmacht High Command was increasingly bypassed on these matters and direct access to Hitler sought instead. The Luftwaffe no doubt had an excellent 'direct line' in the person of Göring, but the army—as shown by the establishment of the tank commission —similarly found a champion in Todt, who, as an old Party member, was able to gain Hitler's confidence more readily than the conservative generals.

But as the top military bodies themselves lacked a clear idea of the state and future prospects of German armaments production, and as the diverging interests of the three services could no longer be tied into a common concept, Hitler was in no position to form a realistic picture for himself. At any rate, his own interest was mainly in technical details and output figures. Otherwise he confined himself to the role of a driving force, leaving it to the rival departments to implement in practice his continual demands for higher production. In these circumstances the Wehrmacht High Command chief of staff evinced scepticism about a proposal by the War Economy and Armaments Department that a central planning body should be set up. In view of Hitler's ceaseless personal intervention, he argued, such an agency would forever be trailing behind so-called orders from the Führer.[443]

The final weeks before the attack on the Soviet Union most clearly revealed Hitler's lack of an overall view. Thus on 18 May 1941 he criticized the production and stockpile figures submitted to him concerning land-force armaments, in particular the substantial decline in ammunition and weapons manufacture.[444] He called for the quickest possible switch-over to mass production as well as—here conflicting with the army weapons department—a 'return to more primitive robust types'.[445] Yet a fortnight later he signed Directive No. 32, submitted to him by the Wehrmacht High Command, which, with a view to the post-Barbarossa period, already called for a switch of priorities to Luftwaffe and naval armaments.[446] Accordingly, after consultation with Todt he ordered the Army High Command to cut back radically on land-force armaments in order to free production capacities and manpower for an extended Luftwaffe armaments programme.[447] He even offered the

---

[443] Marginal gloss by Keitel to the WiRüAmt report on performance data in the field of material armaments for the Wehrmacht, 10 July 1941, ibid.

[444] OKW WiRüAmt/Rü (IIa) No. 1714/41 g.K., Aktennotiz über die Besprechung bei Chef OKW, Reichskanzlei Berchtesgaden [Minute of conference at OKW chief of staff, Reich chancellery, Berchtesgaden] on 19 May 1941, ibid.

[445] Abt. Landesverteidigung Gruppe II, Vortragsnotiz betr. materielle Ausstattung der Truppe [Minute for report concerning material equipment of the troops], 29 May 1941, ibid.

[446] Der Führer und Oberste Befehlshaber der Wehrmacht [The Führer and Supreme Commander of the Wehrmacht], OKW/WFSt/Abt. L (I Op.) No. 44886/41 g.K. Chefsache II Ang., Weisung No. 32: Vorbereitungen für die Zeit nach Barbarossa [Directive No. 32: Preparations for the period after Barbarossa], 11 June 1941: *Hitler's Directives*, 78–82.

[447] Der Chef HRüst u. BdE No. 1641/41 g.K., Fernschreiben Atlas, z. Hd. Gen. Maj. Warlimont [Teletype message Atlas, for Maj.-Gen. Warlimont], 23 June 1941 (copy), BA-MA Wi/I F 5.120, pt. 2; this contains the text of Hitler's order of 20 June 1941 and the comment of Chef HRüst und BdE.

Luftwaffe the immediate disbanding of three eastern divisions in order to relieve the manpower sector.[448] Colonel-General Fromm was totally taken aback by this development and declined to implement the Führer's order in that form.[449] Hitler was first to specify the exact scale of the cut-backs, he informed OKW. He was hoping that at least the 'tank programme, urgently commended' to the minister for armaments and ammunition, would escape unscathed.

With the expiry of armaments programme B, therefore, the weight of problems was by no means eased; if anything it had become more pressing. The balance sheet prepared by the War Economy and Armaments Department of Wehrmacht armaments production from 1 September 1940 to 1 April 1941[450] in order to meet Hitler's criticism of the state reached scarcely succeeded in concealing the shortages in German armaments manufacture. The programmes of all three services showed often considerable gaps. These were to be explained not only by the difficulties of controlling manpower employment, transport, and coal supplies, or by the shortage of specialized machine-tools and raw materials; they were also rooted in insuperable organizational problems. In spite of all efforts, as OKW pointed out, that targets demanded by the 'supreme leadership'—targets which had been raised all the time—were never fully achieved 'because even the manufacturing capacities available in the enlarged Greater German territory' were not sufficient. The observation, made in the same breath, that a 'huge increase in the material equipment of the Wehrmacht' had been accomplished and that the programmes had 'by and large been fulfilled despite great difficulties', suggests that the Wehrmacht High Command was here concealing the true state of affairs.

The questionable nature of that balance sheet emerges clearly if one remembers that Germany's overall armaments production in the second year of the war had scarcely increased, whereas in the United States, Britain, and the USSR it had almost doubled over the same period. The armaments output of these great powers was by then three times the German volume (see Table I.III.2).

Germany's increase in weapons production had been achieved mainly at the expense of ammunition; moreover, it was concentrated on a small number of priority areas. Even the army's programme B, the target figures of which had been based on presumed manufacturing capacities, had been only partially implemented. Alarming shortfalls existed mainly in armour-piercing weapons, field artillery, and infantry artillery pieces; this impaired the fire-power of the

---

[448] See Chef des Stabes No. 134/41 g.Kdos., Ch.S. Besprechung Staatssekretär Milch [Conference State Secretary Milch], 26 June 1941: Thomas, *Wehr- und Rüstungswirtschaft*, 448–51, here 450.

[449] Teletype Atlas, 23 June 1941 (above, n. 447).

[450] OKW WiRüAmt/Rü (IIa) No. 1233/41 g.K., Bericht über die Leistungen auf dem Gebiet der materiellen Wehrmachtrüstung in der Zeit vom 1.9.40 bis 1.4.41 [Report on performances in the field of material Wehrmacht armaments during the period 1 Sept. 1940 to 1 Apr. 1941] (draft), BA-MA Wi/I F 5.120, pt. 2: *Fall Barbarossa*, No. 63 (excerpt).

TABLE I.III.2. *Armaments Production by the Great Powers, 1940–1941*

	Cost[a]	
	1940	1941
USA	1.5	4.5
Britain	3.5	6.5
USSR	5.0	8.5
Germany	6.0	6.0
Japan	1.0	2.0

[a] ×$1,000m. in 1944 prices.

Source: Wagenführ, *Industrie*, 34.

infantry units. Similarly, only 30 per cent of the production target for naval guns had been achieved (primarily as a result of Soviet orders), 78 per cent of that for Luftwaffe ammunition (with the exception of ammunition for the 37-mm. anti-aircraft guns), and 60 per cent of that for anti-aircraft weapons and equipment.

Although the number of armoured fighting vehicles and track-mounted assault-guns had gone up by about a third, the bulk of the vehicles were still of light or medium type, including 281 Mark Is and 157 captured Czechoslovak light 35 t types, which were no longer really battle-worthy. Numerical ratios were similar in the artillery. The total of artillery pieces at the beginning of the French campaign was 7,184; against the Soviet Union 7,146 were available.[451] As for fighting aircraft, 3,530 were available in May 1940, compared with 2,510 against the Soviet Union; of that figure only 1,945 could be regarded as operational front-line planes.[452] Approximately 142 divisions were involved in the campaign in the west;[453] against the Soviet Union initially no more than 150 German divisions were deployed. (For details of programme B see Table I.III.3.)

Table I.III.4 shows the state of equipment of the army compared with its strength before the opening of the offensive in the west.[454]

[451] Data from Engelmann and Scheibert, *Deutsche Artillerie*, 237, and Liss, *Westfront*, 126.
[452] See sect. I.IV.2(c) at n. 393 (Boog).   [453] *Germany and the Second World War*, ii. 249.
[454] Data taken from Müller-Hillebrand, *Heer*, ii. 106, partially amended according to Überblick über den Rüstungsstand des Heeres 'Waffen und Gerät', Stand 1.6.1941 [Tables on the state of armaments of the army, 'Weapons and Equipment', as of 1 June 1941], BA-MA RH 8/v. 1090, and OKH/GenStdH/Org.Abt (I) No. 702/41 g.Kdos., betr. Panzer-Nachschub Ost [concerning armour, supplies, east], 15 Sept. 1941, BA-MA RH 2/v. 1326. The figure of 3,350 tanks (not counting assault-guns recorded in the last line of the table] given in the report of GenQu/Abt. Heeresversorgung of 20 June 1941 (ibid.) presumably refers to operational vehicles. The discrepancy of 48 is therefore explained by vehicles undergoing repair at the beginning of the attack.

TABLE I.III.3. *Armaments Programme B: Production of Weapons, Equipment, and Ammunition for the Army from 1 September 1940 to 31 March 1941*

Weapons and equipment	% production[a]	Stocks on 1 Apr. 1941	Appropriate ammunition types[b]	
			% production[a]	Stocks on 1 Apr. 1941
Pistols	95	716,300 }	115	302,800,000
Submachine-guns	163	144,460 }		
Firearms 98	106	4,198,800 }		9,552,000,000
Machine-guns	123	192,600 }		
Anti-tank rifle 38/39	86	18,101	22	2,043,700
Heavy anti-tank rifle 41	9	130	16	188,500
20-mm. AA guns	100	1,933 }		32,778,000
20-mm. four-barrelled AA guns	75	69 }		
20-mm. AFV guns	188	2,711		14,300,900
37-mm. AFV guns	—c	1,459		2,778,600
50-mm. AFV guns	80	1,138	46	663,800
75-mm. AFV guns and assault-guns	10	1,151	83	2,219,400
37-mm. anti-tank guns }	80	14,838		18,680,800
50-mm. anti-tank guns }		719	51	713,100
Light trench mortars 36	110	14,913		31,982,200
Heavy trench mortars 34	114	10,549	104	12,436,000
100-mm. smoke-shell mortars	96	459		1,523,000
Smoke-shell mortars d	77	411	50	199,500
Light infantry guns 18	84	3,951		7,953,600
Heavy infantry guns 33	91	797	79	1,153,300
Mountain guns 36	169	96		858,400
Light field-guns 18	29	106		151,500
Light field howitzer 18	94	6,854	139	25,051,000
Heavy 100-mm. gun 18	98	730	97	2,323,600
Heavy field howitzer 18	110	2,750	82	5,540,700
210-mm. mortar 18	95	346	64	433,100
T-mines			230	1,258,600

TABLE I.III.3 *(cont.)*

Weapons and equipment	% production[a]	Stocks on 1 Apr. 1941	Appropriate ammunition types[b]	
			%	Stocks on production[a]
1 Apr. 1941				
37-mm. AFV guns (t)			78	2,542,100
Heavy field howitzer 25 (5)			72	187,400
Heavy 240-mm. guns (t)			65	941
240-mm. howitzer 39			22	2,148

[a] Actual production compared with target figures.
[b] Gaps indicate ammunition types whose manufacture had earlier been suspended since stokpiles were sufficient.
[c] Manufacture halted since only Model III tanks were now being produced, with 50-mm. guns.

Sources: Report OKW WiRüAmt, 10 July 1941 (see n. 450); supplemented from: Überblick, Munition, Apr. 1941, BA-MA RH 8/v. 1071b.

TABLE I.III.4. *Armoured Fighting Vehicles*

	Strength on 1 Apr. 1940	With the army in the west on 10 May 1940	Strength on 1 June 1941	With the army in the east 22 June 1941
Tanks, I (machine-guns)	1,062	523	877	281
Tanks II (20-mm. gun and flame-thrower)	1,086	955	1,157	743
Tanks, 35 t (37-mm. gun)	143	106	187	157
Tanks, 38 t (37-mm. gun)	238	228	754	651
Tanks, III (37-mm. and 50-mm. L 42 gun)	329	349	1,440	979
Tanks, IV (75-mm. L 24 gun)	280	278	572	444
Armoured staff cars	243	135	330	143
Assault-guns III (75-mm. L 24 gun)	6	6	377	250
TOTAL	3,387	2,580	5,695	3,648

TABLE I.III.5. *Equipment of Divisions with Motor Transport*

No. of Divisions	Wave	Divisions equipped with captured vehicles	Major parts using horse-drawn transport?
26	1	(German material, standard strength)	
16	2	2	no
15	3	12	yes
14	4	2	no
5	5	5	yes
4	6	4	yes
14	7	2	yes
10	8	0	yes
10	11	10	no
6	12	6	yes
9	13	9	yes
8	14	8	yes
15	15	15	no
9 sec. divs.		9	yes

Source: Müller-Hillebrand, *Heer*, annexe 22.

One is therefore forced to conclude that the Wehrmacht's strength in men and materials for the campaign against the Soviet Union was substantially the same as in the western campaign against France and Britain in the spring of 1940. There were, admittedly, some qualitative improvements, such as the partial modernization of the fleet of armoured fighting vehicles. Although the wartime army had been enlarged by about 20 per cent compared with 1940, this was largely offset by additional tasks in the war against Britain. From the North Cape to Crete large numbers of occupation troops and security formations and of coastal-defence and anti-aircraft batteries had to be employed. Added to all that were the operations in North Africa. Anything that could be spared, anything that could be made mobile and battle-worthy, had been deployed by Hitler in the east; the rest was scarcely operational.[455] But for the use of captured material, the Wehrmacht, given the meagre extant of new production of weapons, ammunition, and equipment, would scarcely have been in a position to take on such a variety of tasks. The infantry divisions of the field army, reorganized into so-called waves or newly established, presented a rather disparate picture in regard to their equipment with motor-vehicles (see Table I.III.5).

[455] See GenStdH/Org.Abt (I), No. 652/41 g.Kdos., Beurteilung des Kampfwertes der Divisionen nach dem Stande vom 20.6.1941 [Assessment of the operational value of the divisions as on 20 June 1941], BA-MA RH 2/v. 427.

In addition to 84 infantry divisions, 3 of the 10 motorized divisions as well as 21st Armoured Division were equipped with foreign vehicles. Captured material was moreover used for furbishing the anti-tank units. Some of these were re-equipped with the French 47-mm. anti-tank gun.[456] Because of a lack of appropriate tractors, French armoured vehicles were employed for that purpose in the divisions of the 11th and 12th waves; they were used also as transport vehicles for the infantry of the light divisions. Panhard scout cars and Hotchkiss and Somua armoured vehicles were used in armoured reconnaissance units. The 5,000 armoured vehicles available for such purposes from captured French material were also used for equipping security and occupation divisions in the west. Captured tanks were moreover used in large numbers in the reserve army and on army training grounds, as well as for arming armoured trains. Although the armoured formations of the eastern army operated predominantly with tanks of German manufacture, there were five armoured divisions which were uniformly equipped with Model 38 tanks from former Czech factories. These vehicles in particular, just like other captured material, were by no means inferior to German standards. Even so their employment is significant. For one thing, it confirmed the weaknesses of the German rearmament drive; for another, it confirmed the assumption of the army command in the summer of 1940 that captured material would be a vital prerequisite for the planned deployment of the eastern army. And thirdly, their employment further increased the multiplicity of types in the German army, with all the consequences for supplies of spares and ammunition. This was an additional strain on supply management from the outset. A study of the order of battle of the eastern army on 22 June 1941 (see Diagram I.III.3) shows that the divisions with the best equipment were deployed around the armoured groups, while the gaps and the flanks were held largely by divisions of reduced fighting power and mobility. Altogether, then, the eastern army presented the aspect of a patchwork rug rather than the impression, often propagated in the postwar literature, that Hitler, by means of a skilful blitzkrieg economy and the exploitation of the occupied territories, had succeeded in fielding a huge, uniformly equipped military force against the Soviet Union.[457] This astonishing result was due not only to material limitations of the German war effort at the time, but largely also to the fact that the decision to attack the Soviet Union failed to give rise to any appropriate efforts in the armaments sector. At no time was a maximum effort even considered—an effort commensurate with the enemy's potential—because the German leadership assumed that available forces were sufficient to smash the Soviet military potential within a few weeks. It seems that this evaluation of the situation was largely responsible for the fact that plans for a complete utilization of the German and captured potential were executed only half-heartedly. Neverthe-

---

[456] See OKH/Chef HRüst u. BdE No. 843/41 geh., betr. Umbewaffnung auf 47 mm. Pak (f) [concerning rearming with French 47-mm. anti-tank guns], 7 Mar. 1941, BA-MA RH 19 III/144.

[457] See e.g. *Deutschland im zweiten Weltkrieg*, i. 531 ff.

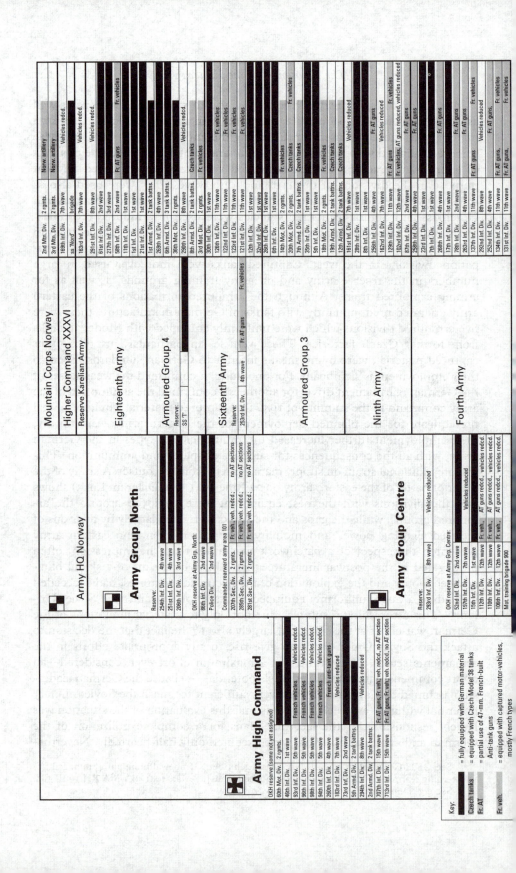

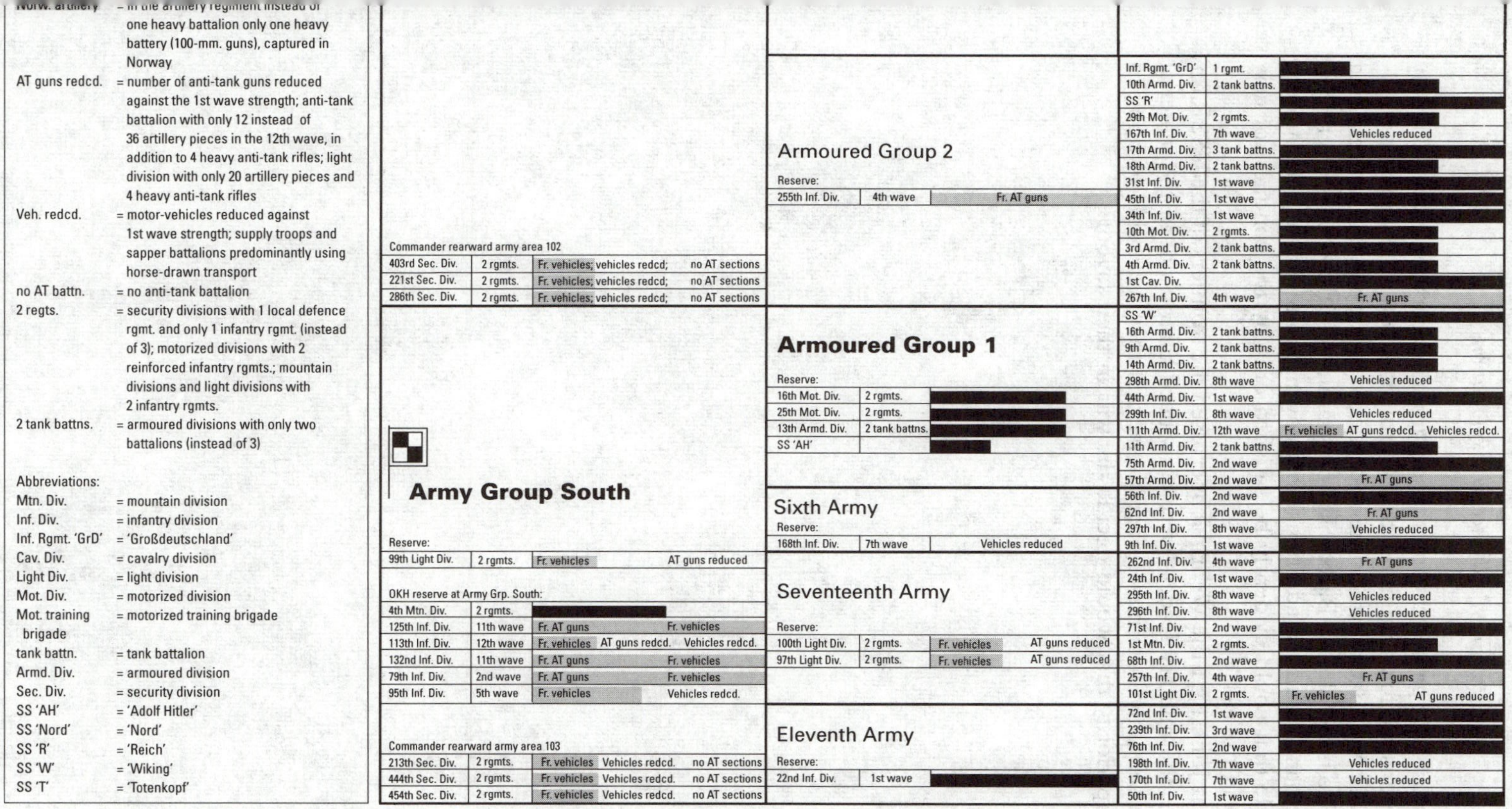

Legend (left margin):

Norw. artillery = ... one heavy artillery regiment instead of one heavy battalion only one heavy battery (100-mm. guns), captured in Norway

AT guns redcd. = number of anti-tank guns reduced against the 1st wave strength; anti-tank battalion with only 12 instead of 36 artillery pieces in the 12th wave, in addition to 4 heavy anti-tank rifles; light division with only 20 artillery pieces and 4 heavy anti-tank rifles

Veh. redcd. = motor-vehicles reduced against 1st wave strength; supply troops and sapper battalions predominantly using horse-drawn transport

no AT battn. = no anti-tank battalion

2 regts. = security divisions with 1 local defence rgmt. and only 1 infantry rgmt. (instead of 3); motorized divisions with 2 reinforced infantry rgmts.; mountain divisions and light divisions with 2 infantry rgmts.

2 tank battns. = armoured divisions with only two battalions (instead of 3)

Abbreviations:
Mtn. Div. = mountain division
Inf. Div. = infantry division
Inf. Rgmt. 'GrD' = 'Großdeutschland'
Cav. Div. = cavalry division
Light Div. = light division
Mot. Div. = motorized division
Mot. training brigade = motorized training brigade
tank battn. = tank battalion
Armd. Div. = armoured division
Sec. Div. = security division
SS 'AH' = 'Adolf Hitler'
SS Nord' = 'Nord'
SS 'R' = 'Reich'
SS 'W' = 'Wiking'
SS 'T' = 'Totenkopf'

Norway

Commander rearward army area 102
403rd Sec. Div.	2 rgmts.	Fr. vehicles; vehicles redcd;	no AT sections
221st Sec. Div.	2 rgmts.	Fr. vehicles; vehicles redcd;	no AT sections
286th Sec. Div.	2 rgmts.	Fr. vehicles; vehicles redcd;	no AT sections

Armoured Group 2

Reserve:
| 255th Inf. Div. | 4th wave | Fr. AT guns |

Inf. Rgmt. 'GrD'	1 rgmt.	
10th Armd. Div.	2 tank battns.	
SS 'R'		
29th Mot. Div.	2 rgmts.	
167th Inf. Div.	7th wave	Vehicles reduced
17th Armd. Div.	3 tank battns.	
18th Armd. Div.	2 tank battns.	
31st Inf. Div.	1st wave	
45th Inf. Div.	1st wave	
34th Inf. Div.	1st wave	
10th Mot. Div.	2 rgmts.	
3rd Armd. Div.	2 tank battns.	
4th Armd. Div.	2 tank battns.	
267th Inf. Div.	4th wave	Fr. AT guns

Armoured Group 1

Reserve:
16th Mot. Div.	2 rgmts.	
25th Mot. Div.	2 rgmts.	
13th Armd. Div.	2 tank battns.	
SS 'AH'		

SS 'W'		
16th Armd. Div.	2 tank battns.	
9th Armd. Div.	2 tank battns.	
14th Armd. Div.	2 tank battns.	
298th Armd. Div.	8th wave	Vehicles reduced
44th Armd. Div.	1st wave	
299th Inf. Div.	8th wave	Vehicles reduced
111th Armd. Div.	12th wave	Fr. vehicles; AT guns redcd. Vehicles redcd.
11th Armd. Div.	2 tank battns.	
75th Armd. Div.	2nd wave	
57th Armd. Div.	2nd wave	Fr. AT guns

Sixth Army

Reserve:
| 168th Inf. Div. | 7th wave | Vehicles reduced |

56th Inf. Div.	2nd wave	
62nd Inf. Div.	2nd wave	Fr. AT guns
297th Inf. Div.	8th wave	Vehicles reduced
9th Inf. Div.	1st wave	
262nd Inf. Div.	4th wave	Fr. AT guns
24th Inf. Div.	1st wave	
295th Inf. Div.	8th wave	Vehicles reduced
296th Inf. Div.	8th wave	Vehicles reduced
71st Inf. Div.	2nd wave	

Seventeenth Army

Reserve:
| 100th Light Div. | 2 rgmts. | Fr. vehicles | AT guns reduced |
| 97th Light Div. | 2 rgmts. | Fr. vehicles | AT guns reduced |

1st Mtn. Div.	2 rgmts.	
68th Inf. Div.	2nd wave	
257th Inf. Div.	4th wave	Fr. AT guns
101st Light Div.	2 rgmts.	

Army Group South

Reserve:
| 99th Light Div. | 2 rgmts. | Fr. vehicles | AT guns reduced |

OKH reserve at Army Grp. South:
4th Mtn. Div.	2 rgmts.	
125th Inf. Div.	11th wave	Fr. AT guns	Fr. vehicles
113th Inf. Div.	12th wave	Fr. vehicles	AT guns redcd. Vehicles redcd.
132nd Inf. Div.	11th wave	Fr. AT guns	Fr. vehicles
79th Inf. Div.	2nd wave	Fr. vehicles
95th Inf. Div.	5th wave	Vehicles redcd.

Commander rearward army area 103
213th Sec. Div.	2 rgmts.	Fr. vehicles	Vehicles redcd.	no AT sections
444th Sec. Div.	2 rgmts.	Fr. vehicles	Vehicles redcd.	no AT sections
454th Sec. Div.	2 rgmts.	Fr. vehicles	Vehicles redcd.	no AT sections

Eleventh Army

Reserve:
| 22nd Inf. Div. | 1st wave | |

72nd Inf. Div.	2nd wave	
239th Inf. Div.	3rd wave	
76th Inf. Div.	2nd wave	AT guns reduced
198th Inf. Div.	7th wave	Vehicles reduced
170th Inf. Div.	7th wave	Vehicles reduced
50th Inf. Div.	1st wave	

DIAGRAM I.III.3. The Material Equipment of the German Army in the East (incl. Army HQ Norway), 22 June 1941

Note: Data on equipment make allowance for captured material used.

Source: Müller-Hillebrand, Heer, ii. 157 ff.

less, Hitler must have gained the impression, from information given to him by the men responsible for munitions, that Germany's potential was being utilized to the limit and that a further intensification was not possible with existing resources. The hopeful post-Barbarossa programmes of the separate services, on the other hand, required additional manpower and raw materials, moreover on a scale that could evidently be satisfied only by the conquest of new 'living-space in the east'.

When on 22 June 1941 the Wehrmacht crossed the frontiers of the USSR for that purpose, the military leaders were convinced that, if not in the material sphere, then certainly in terms of operational skill they were able to bring to the task a superiority that would decide the war in their favour.

IV. The Military Concept of the War against the Soviet Union

1. Land Warfare

Ernst Klink

ANY account of the military objectives, the Wehrmacht's plans, and the preparations for war against the Soviet Union is such a widely ramified undertaking that, within the present framework, clarity can only be achieved by limitation to the central, decisive, and more or less definable processes within the top leadership. Principal attention must go to the assessment of the military situation after the conclusion of the campaign in the west and the lessons derived from it by Hitler and the military command staffs for the further conduct of the war. This does not, of course, exclude earlier historical processes from being considered along with the vital factors in decision-making.

Central to these reflections is the interaction of the expectations and intentions of Hitler on the one hand and of the Wehrmacht High Command on the other. Of particular importance is the judgement of Colonel-General Franz Halder, the chief of the Army General Staff; by comparison, the commander-in-chief of the army, Field Marshal von Brauchitsch, played a distinctly lesser role in the operational field, as indeed had emerged earlier in the planning and execution of all the campaigns since 1939. The reconstruction and presentation of the decisions of Hitler and the Army High Command, to be attempted in the following section, proceed from the belief that these sources have to be understood, unambiguously, in their literal sense. As military orders and instructions had to be obeyed promptly—even against moral reluctance—and as a rule were so obeyed, they generally escape the kind of latitude of interpretation customary, for instance, in the case of political or diplomatic sources. This fundamental state of affairs, which determined military action and has therefore to be taken into methodological account, is in no way invalidated by the circumstance that, as will be shown in the course of the present study, certain military leaders, faced with Hitler's particular style of leadership, in some exceptional cases interpreted his orders rather elastically. Basic acceptance of the text and meaning of instructions, orders, and reports may also help to avoid anachronistic interpretations.[1] The controversial question

---

[1] Hans Buchheim (preface to *Anatomie des SS-Staates*) in 1965 made this demand of contemporary research: 'That is why in Germany, in our intellectual confrontation with National Socialism and its era, we need not emotions or moral reawakening, but sober work with intellect and reason.' His demand was based on the still valid critical observation that there was a growing tendency not to reflect too much on Hitler's dictatorship, since it was 'to be assessed negatively

of what weight should be attributed in the conduct of the war to evaluations of the military situation and decisions stemming from them on the one hand, and to the well-known political, economic, and ideological 'perspectives' on the other, is one to which this kind of study of the sources may offer new answers.

(a) The Red Army in the Judgement of the Army High Command after September 1939

The German–Soviet non-aggression treaty of 23 August 1939 with its secret supplementary protocols resulted, far beyond the partition of Poland, in a massive shift of political power-structures in eastern central Europe. The division of this territory into 'spheres of interest' surrendered the Baltic region as far as the northern frontier of Lithuania and Finland to seizure by the Red Army, while in south-eastern Europe Hitler had declared his lack of interest in the redrawing of Romania's frontiers—which meant the return of Bessarabia to the Soviet Union—provided this preserved peace and protected vital German economic interests.[2] For the German army leadership, more especially its chief of general staff, Artillery General Halder, the territorial 'delimitations of interests' envisaged in the secret supplementary protocols were to be judged primarily from the strategic point of view.[3] The obvious disadvantages of a military presence of the Red Army and Navy in Latvia and Estonia were mitigated by the maintenance of German influence in Lithuania, i.e. the glacis of the East Prussian fortification system. To Halder the military victory over Poland meant, as a matter of course, that Germany could expect preferential treatment for her strategic interests when the frontiers would be drawn in the future. However, he had no influence on this matter and was only informed at second hand about the stipulations of the treaty.

The Red Army's entry into Poland on 17 September 1939 and the cession to it of the Lvov area dealt the first blow to Halder's expectations. Outraged, he described 20 September as a 'day of disgrace for German political leadership'.[4] The surrender of Galicia meant not only the surrender of the oilfields

in every respect', and therefore to move from a historical-rational to a moral-emotional way of looking at things. The present study, which seeks to discover the essential aspects of our subject, endeavours to comply with Buchheim's demand.

   [2] See sect. I.v.1 on Romania in the present volume, as well as sect. I.ii.2 at nn. 150 ff. (Hoffmann).

   [3] The most comprehensive study of the period here under review—Hillgruber, *Strategie*—will be narrowed down in the present chapter to the military sector. An extension of the range of sources, on the other hand, at the same time provides new aspects which may compensate for the loss of an overall view. On the problems of the non-aggression treaty of 23 Aug. 1939—only touched upon here—see *Germany and the Second World War*, i. 696–7, ii. 75–6; Fabry, *Hitler-Stalin-Pakt*, goes furthest in examining the military aspects of the frontier delineation. For a summary see Myllyniemi, *Baltische Krise*. See also OKH/GenStdH/Frd Heere Ost, Lagebericht Baltische Staaten und Finnland [Situation report Baltic countries and Finland], 15 Oct. 1939, as well as Lagebericht Sowjetunion-Finnland [Situation report Soviet Union–Finland], Nos. 1–14 (1 Dec. 1939–25 Jan. 1940), BA-MA RH 19 III/380, and Nos. 15–22 (3 Feb. 1940–18 Mar. 1940), BA-MA RH 19 III/381; BA-MA H 12/135.   [4] Halder, *Diaries*, 86 (20 Sept. 1939).

of Drogobych but also that of direct communications between the Silesian industrial area and the Romanian oil wells. Instead of the Polish army, it was now the Red Army which was standing at the flank of an area important to the German war effort. Although compensation by way of the 'Suwalki' corner represented a strategic improvement of the new frontier in the north-east, the 'frontier and friendship treaty' of 28 September 1939 ceded Lithuania, and hence important stretches of the Dvina and the Niemen, to the Soviet Union. Concentration of a force to invade Lithuania, still envisaged in Hitler's directive of 25 September, was revoked.[5]

The basic reason for that decision was the intention to initiate a military offensive in the west that same year and to safeguard for that purpose the Soviet Union's urgently needed economic assistance. A further consideration of Hitler's related to the presumed longer-term attitude of the Soviet leadership. At a conference with Brauchitsch and Halder on 27 September 1939 he emphasized that 'even treaties' did not represent 'a secure basis for an assessment' of future developments. 'Treaties' were overridden by 'state interest'. 'Eternally valid' were 'success, power' alone.[6] That was why he was so anxious to convince a hesitant Army High Command of the need for a rapid settlement of the war in the west.[7] In his memorandum to the Wehrmacht High Command chief of staff and to the three commanders-in-chief of the Wehrmacht services, dated 9 October, Hitler similarly declared that no treaty and no agreement could guarantee the permament neutrality of the Soviet Union. The best insurance against Russian intervention was a clear display of German superiority or a swift demonstration of German strength.[8] The stubborn struggle for the strategically valuable southern tip of Lithuania, the Mariampol area, which under the treaty of 28 September 1939 was to be open to German military intervention the moment the Red Army initiated 'special measures' in Lithuania, i.e. the establishment of bases, demonstrates the determination with which the generals on both sides were trying to maintain their positions. That agreement was held to be valid in law by the Soviet Union as late as the summer of 1940, for it paid over a sum of 7.5m. gold dollars in compensation for Germany's renunciation of it.[9]

On 20 October the army commander-in-chief within the area of the 'commander-in-chief East' ordered the establishment and consolidation of an outpost line of resistance capable of repulsing a possible enemy attack with the forces then available and of covering the deployment of reinforcements. To ensure rapid transportation of troops, the principal railway, road, and com-

---

[5] Directive No. 4 of 25 Sept. 1939, point 4, and No. 5 of 30 Sept. 1939, point 3: *Hitler's Directives*, 8–10. See also Bleyer and Czollek, 'Die Vereitelung', 422 ff., who conceal the connection with the secret supplementary protocol of 23 Aug. 1939, which had left Lithuania within the German sphere of influence.

[6] Halder, *KTB* i. 86 (27 Sept. 1939; not in trans.).

[7] See *Germany and the Second World War*, ii. 232–3.   [8] Jacobsen, *Vorgeschichte*, 7.

[9] Fabry, *Hitler-Stalin-Pakt*, 158–9, 241; see also *DGFP* D viii, No. 200; ibid. ii., No. 319; and sect. I.III.6. at n. 354 (Müller).

munication lines were to be developed and protected. An instruction along these lines also went out on 26 October to the 'frontier sector North' in East Prussia (Defence District I).[10] The drastic reduction in army formations, and in particular of construction units, which began shortly afterwards, set strict limits to such intentions. An additional major strain on all transport routes and accommodation facilities was caused by the repatriation of Germans from Soviet territory in line with the resettlement agreement.[11]

These security measures were not merely standard military practice, but also reflected Hitler's mistrust of Stalin's political intentions with regard to the future course of the war. That mistrust was shared by the top generals and emerged also in the military arguments against Hitler's intention of going on the offensive in the west.[12] Altogether it may be assumed that Hitler's liaison with Stalin, that utterly surprising reconcilement of two regimes regarded as totally irreconcilable, met with scarcely any genuine approval among the nationally conservative generals or among the middle class sharing that attitude. The *rapprochement* had created the prerequisite of the aggressive war against Poland, but once this war was concluded efforts were being made to keep the 'sacrifices' made for that alliance as slight as possible. The initiation of offensive plans in the west meant that Germany's—as yet limited—dependence on Soviet good will was bound to assume immeasurable dimensions, the more so as the Wehrmacht's prospects of success were not being viewed with a great deal of confidence.

Colonel-General Ludwig Beck, Halder's predecessor in the post of chief of the Army General Staff, expressed these reflections in a number of memoranda after September 1939.[13] Beck believed that the future actions of the Soviet Union, now it had been drawn into European affairs by Hitler, might give rise to serious, possibly even mortal, danger to Germany. About the middle of November 1939 he spoke of the German military success against Poland as being halfed by the 'Russian colossus having been set into motion' westwards.[14] The support received by the German war effort from the Soviet

[10] BA-MA RH 2/v. 390. The transportation of reinforcements into and beyond the outpost line of resistance and the establishment of bridgeheads were to be ensured in the event of defence becoming necessary. The OKH guideline was based on Hitler's directive of 30 Sept. 1939: see *Hitler's Directives*, No. 5. Notes compiled by Keitel on a conference with Hitler on 17 Oct. 1939 sum up German military interests in Poland under point 6: 'to ensure that the territory, in the role of a forward glacis, is of military importance to us and can be utilized for deployment.' In the present context this measure was unequivocally concerned with security, and not with deployment-planning against the Soviet Union. Indeed the latter would scarcely be plausible at a moment when preparations for an offensive in the west were still in dispute. Text in Wagner, *Generalquartiermeister*, 145.

[11] On this see, *Diktierte Option*, ed. Loeber.

[12] Leeb's and Rundstedt's memoranda in Jacobsen, *Vorgeschichte*, 83, 121. On the struggle over the preparations of the campaign in the west see *Germany and the Second World War*, ii. 232 ff.

[13] Beck's memoranda in Groscurth, *Tagebücher*, annexe II, Nos. 64–74, pp. 474 ff. Of interest, with a bearing on Halder's degree of confidence *vis-à-vis* Tippelskirch and Beck, is Maj.-Gen. von Tippelskirch's (OQu IV) comment on No. 64.

[14] Beck's memorandum of 20 Nov. 1939, ibid. 487.

Union, he argued, would never be sufficient for a protracted war; it was questionable, and it was leading to a partnership in which Germany was the donor and the Soviet Union the recipient.

These observations, along with the fundamental attitude to the 'Russian question for Germany', were in line with Halder's views. Beck believed that Soviet objectives lay in the Baltic region and in the Dardanelles.[15] Thus the old Balkan problem was reopened once more. By occupying former territories of the Austro-Hungarian monarchy, the Soviet Union had gained access to Romania and substantially improved its strategic position in the Balkans compared with 1914. The Soviet Union would always pursue only Russian objectives. It was now able at any time to exert strong pressure on 'our eastern front'.

The same question agitated the general staff of the army, especially as the strengthening of the Soviet position in its newly gained territories was proceeding simultaneously with an almost complete withdrawal of combat-ready German forces from the eastern front and with preparations for a campaign in the west.

On 28 November 1939 Halder instructed Major-General Karl Adolf Hollidt, the chief of staff of the commander-in-chief East ('Oberost'), to prepare a study of 'Security in the east against Russia while the war in the west continues'. At the same time he demanded from the Department for Foreign Armies East a study of possible developments of Germany's relations with the Soviet Union.[16] The conclusion of this study was that the disposition of the Soviet formations in Poland was compatible both with the idea of defence and of an operation into Germany. It pointed out that the Soviet Union must be assumed to have 150 fully effective rifle divisions, of which 100 were active and 50 were reserve divisions. Raising another 50 divisions was possible without any personnel problems. As, however, these would have a lower degree of efficiency because of a shortage of weapons, calculations were, for the time being, based on 150 divisions. Of these, a total of 70 were regarded as tied down elsewhere:[17] 10 against Finland, 18 against the Baltic States, 6 against Romania, 30 rifle divisions on the Transcaucasian frontier, in Central Asia, and in the Far East, and a further 6 divisions in the interior of the Soviet

[15] Beck's memorandum of autumn 1939, ibid. 490 ff. Beck's military and political foresight is no less astonishing than his apparently total severance from the information and thinking of the army general staff after his departure from office.

[16] Studie Oberost, 11 Jan. 1940; Studie Fremde Heere Ost, Dec. 1939; both in excerpt in BA-MA RH 2/v. 390. At the same time the Abteilung Frd Heere Ost (Dept. Foreign Armies East) prepared a 'Werturteil über die Rote Armee nach den Berichten über den Einmarsch in Polen, im Baltikum und in Finnland' [Assessment of the Red Army's performance according to reports on its invasion of Poland, the Baltic, and Finland], which was submitted on 19 Dec. 1939: BA-MA H 3/1726. Its basic tenor reflected the impression gained from captured Polish documents; excerpts in BA-MA H 3/675.

[17] It was on the basis of this calculation that Brauchitsch, in his report to Hitler on 21 July 1940, spoke of '50–75 good divisions' in the Red Army: see sect. I.IV.1(b) at n. 67. Besymenski, *Sonderakte 'Barbarossa'* (1968), 248, gives a figure of 4.2m. Red Army men in the field as early as 1939.

Union. It was assumed that the operational objective of an attack on Germany would initially be western Poland and eastern Germany, but such an attack was described as probable only in the event of the German army having been smashed on other fronts. A further prerequisite of such an attack, it was thought, was the clarification of the situation *vis-à-vis* Japan and a consolidation of conditions within the Soviet Union, especially in the border regions and in the Baltic States. Moreover, the military development of an operational basis in Poland would have to be completed first; this required primarily an improvement in rail and road conditions. Finally, it was also to be expected that the 'Red leadership' included in its considerations the question of how far Germany's 'home front' might be weakened by Communist uprisings.

Hollidt's study proceeded from the assumption that the objective of a Soviet attack would be the destruction of Germany's military instruments of power and her economic production potential, the restoration of the old frontier in the Baltic region, domination of the Baltic Sea, and the revival of pan-Slavism in the Balkans, Czechoslovakia, and Poland. A military attack by the Red Army would seek to gain the San–Vistula–Narev line as quickly as possible, in order to thrust deep into German territory: along the lower Vistula, to the Upper Silesian industrial area, and to the Odra line above Breslau (now Wrócław). The study finally concluded that the Red Army, because of its inadequate operational training, would prefer a simple operation, relying on massive superiority, with two groups deployed in the two directions of Warsaw–East Prussia and the Sandak–Sandomierz line. However, both military studies assumed that an attack by the Red Army was not impending.

The conclusion of the Soviet–Finnish war on 12 March 1940 and the resulting Soviet demands on the Baltic States to secure the cession of military bases induced the Army High Command to assess the situation anew. At the same time the Amt Ausland/Abwehr (Foreign Intelligence Department) produced a study on possible further developments in the Near East. Our main concern here is the evaluation by the Army High Command, whose principal interest continued to be focused on the growing strength of the Red Army. The situation report of the Department for Foreign Armies East, dated 29 April 1940, pointed out that, although the troop movements did not reveal any clear intentions, the Soviet Union was nevertheless taking military measures to support its policy in the Near East and in south-eastern Europe. 'Whether or not Russia undertakes an offensive operation against Romania in the foreseeable future therefore depends solely on political conditions. Militarily it is capable of doing so.'[18]

After the opening of the campaign in the west a new phase of Soviet military 'glacis security' measures began. First the units in Lithuania were reinforced;

[18] Studie OKW/WFA Abt. L-Ausl/Abw No. 494/40, 'Die militärpolitische Lage im Nahen Orient' [The military-political situation in the Near East], 21 Mar. 1940, BA-MA RW 4/v. 35 (copy); Lagebericht OKH/Frd Heere Ost: BA-MA H 3/1726.

on 15 June strategic locations were occupied. The governments of the three Baltic States were invited, in the form of ultimatums on 15 and 16 June, to form pro-Soviet governments and to allow the Red Army access to the bases 'in sufficient strength'. This marked the beginning of the end of their sovereignty. The process was concluded at the beginning of August when they were declared to be Soviet republics.

The ultimatum to Romania, demanding the cession of Bessarabia and Bukovina, marked the end of that phase of the Soviet Union's political and military safeguarding of its western forefield.

These developments triggered new reflections in the Army General Staff on what forces from the western army could most speedily be transferred to the east. In addition, a reliable assessment of the Red Army acquired overall importance. Given the continuation of the war against Britain, the question which now arose—beyond the above-mentioned doubts on the viability of German agreements with the Soviet Union—was that of a possible enemy coalition. These reflections concerned, above all, the United States and the Soviet Union.

All intelligence on military conditions in the Soviet Union was collected and evaluated by the Oberquartiermeister IV in the Army General Staff (Lieutenant-General Kurt von Tippelskirch), who was informed on the development of the military situation by Abteilung Ausland/Abwehr (foreign intelligence) in the Wehrmacht High Command as well as by the attachés.[19] Captured Polish army documents proved a valuable source in this respect.[20] Information on foreign-policy developments came from the foreign ministry's representative (Hasso von Etzdorf) to the commander-in-chief of the army.[21] Decisive importance for opinion-forming within the Army General Staff on the Soviet Union and the Red Army, especially in Halder's case, attached to the reports of the military attaché in Moscow, General Köstring. Köstring—who had been reporting on the Soviet Union continually since the autumn of 1935, had a good command of Russian, and, in spite of all obstacles, basically trusted his own judgement—believed that an evolutionary process was under way in the Soviet Union which made an aggressive policy unlikely. He emphasized this view of the foreseeable future even more strongly after having been briefed on

---

[19] In addition to their reports through the normal diplomatic channels, the military attachés also reported their observations and judgements 'semi-officially' direct to OQu IV, who, according to their importance, passed them on to Halder. These private letters are very much instances of personal opinions and no substitute for the reports proper. This needs to be borne in mind especially with regard to Köstring's letters published by Teske. His reports on the Red Army are not extant in their original text, but in evaluations by Abteilung Frd Heere Ost and in H. von Etzdorf, Handakten (PA). Critically on Köstring: Besymenski, *Sonderakte 'Barbarossa'* (1968), 243, and Hillgruber, *Strategie*, 228–9, 'Rußland-Bild', 296. The following quotations of Köstring are from Teske's edition, without individual references. Reports by the intelligence agencies: BA-MA H 3/673.

[20] Polish assessment of the Red Army: BA-MA H 3/675.

[21] This group of sources also includes Weizsäcker's reports to a small circle in OKH; these are referred to by Halder (*Diaries*) on 26 and 30 June 1940.

Germany's intentions *vis-à-vis* the Soviet Union by the chief of the general staff on 3 September 1940.[22] Thus in October 1940 he described the trends to be observed in all fields as a 'peaceful revolution' linking up with 'earlier developments'. 'The political *system* will not undergo any change, but may perhaps receive minor improvements.'[23] And at the time of Molotov's visit to Berlin he remarked: 'I *keep repeating*: the great Soviet Union has no use for war, now less than ever, because the army and the country are undergoing a restructuring and reconstruction' of which 'the results will not come to fruition for some years'. He added: 'But also, time and again, my old sermon: come out of the war strong! That is the only way for an as yet unorganized Europe to set limits to the future plans of an expansionist drive that calls itself "world revolution", "liberation from the capitalist yoke", "protection against capitalist encirclement", or something similar.'[24] If one tries to reduce Köstring's observations to a common denominator, in so far as they are reflected in his military-political reports to Tippelskirch, one is left with the impression that the military attaché in Moscow believed a war against the Soviet Union to be pointless, as all economic and even political concessions could be obtained from Stalin by other means so long as the German armed forces were undefeated and strong.

Halder, however, did not accept this assessment of Soviet interests with its conclusions. His own judgement of the situation was different. What to Köstring seemed a tendency towards a more bourgeois Soviet Union and a renunciation of its claim to world revolution in favour of domestic development was seen by the chief of the general staff as a symptom of the Red Army's enhanced fighting strength.

Reports on the Red Army's performance in Poland, Finland, and Bessarabia suggested a gigantic war-machine which was about to remedy any shortcomings revealed during those operations.[25] Its greatest weakness was thought to be the lack of a trained middle-ranking and senior leader class, which had been lost as a result of the purges of 1937–8 and had not yet been replaced. Its armament, on the other hand, was judged to be modern, even though outdated weapons had not yet been replaced in every unit.

It was impossible to gain any clear idea of the intention behind the troop movements to the frontier areas. The Red Army, it was pointed out, should not be underestimated; emphasis on and exaggeration of its mistakes were hostile propaganda by the Western powers. Neither should the lessons learnt from its advances in Poland and Romania be overestimated; after all, the Red Army had not been seriously challenged there. The Red Army's poor outward

[22] Halder, *Diaries*, 572 (3 Sept. 1940).   [23] *General Köstring*, ed. Teske, 281 (17 Oct. 1940).
[24] Ibid. 286 (14 Nov. 1940).
[25] See the sources listed in n. 3 above; also BA-MA RH 19 III/380, 391; OKH/Frd Heere Ost, Vortragsnotiz: Sowjettruppen in den drei baltischen Staaten [Notes for a report: Soviet troops in the three Baltic States], 3 Aug. 1940, ibid. H 3/1726; Vortragsnotiz Bericht Militärattaché Moskau [Notes on report by military attaché Moscow], 17 Oct. 1940, betr. Werturteil über die Rote Armee [Assessment of performance of the Red Army], PA, Handakten Etzdorf, No. 26.

appearance was weighed up against its marching performance and the functioning of its deployment. Köstring emphasized that the 'generally tough, undemanding, willing, and brave soldier' was no longer the 'good moujik' familiar from the First World War; there had been a cultural improvement and a rise in intelligence. The quality of equipment, however, was not up to the standard of a Western army. For the time being the Red Army was not capable of the large-scale operations of a war of movement, and at a numerical ratio of 1 to 2 or 3 it was 'not superior to us'.

The experience of the Finnish Winter War seemed to be of more topical importance: there the Red Army—in contrast to its advance into eastern Poland, the Romanian territories, and the Baltic countries—had demonstrated its battle-worthiness. Intelligence on this was being evaluated by the Department for Foreign Armies East of the Army General Staff.[26] This then was the overall impression:

- Lack of initiative and stereotyped operation resulted in losses at the beginning of the war.
- Accumulation of large numbers of troops on the Karelian isthmus led to supply difficulties.
- In an attempt to achieve success primarily by mass employment, the Red Army failed to assess correctly the effect and applicability of the different branches; in particular it attached excessive expectations to the performance of armour.
- There was a lack of co-operation between the various branches, especially in artillery support for advancing infantry and in artillery barrages.
- Attacks in deep waves resulted in heavy losses which only failed to result in reverses owing to the numerical inferiority of the Finns and the ample supply of new attacking divisions.

It was found that the course of that war had indicated that the Red Army was not fully equal to modern requirements, but had recognized its shortcomings and drawn conclusions from the many lessons it had learnt. These included above all the restoration of officers' undivided power of command, new directives for the training of senior leaders, and intensification of troop-training.

Special attention was stimulated by Köstring's reports on the evaluation of the lessons of the Finno-Soviet war in the area of Red Army leadership and training. Criticism of the activity of the political commissars on the part of the political directorate was the first signal, in January 1940, that the command structure would be transformed in favour of the sole command authority of the military commanders.[27]

---

[26] 'Erfahrungen aus dem finnisch-russischen Kriege' [Experience of the Finno-Russian war], 2 Oct. 1940, with annexe: BA-MA RH 20-20/124. Abwehr documents are preserved in BA-MA RW 4/v. 325, 325 d, 328 (OKW/WPr). See also BA-MA, 18. Armee, 17562/2.

[27] *General Köstring*, ed. Teske, 281; OKH/GenStdH, OQu IV, Abt. Frd Heere Ost (IIId), 2 Oct. 1940–19 Feb. 1942, BA-MA RH 20-20/124. Kahn, *Hitler's Spies*, 95 ff., 115 ff., summarizes Ger-

The introduction of generals' ranks was regarded as a sign of the tightening of command and as an unambiguous shift of responsibility to the superior in the chain of command. The exercises held under the supervision of People's Commissar Marshal Timoshenko in August 1940 on the basis of experience of the Winter War and the regulations subsequently issued were given a good deal of attention, more especially the marshal's call for greater discipline and intensified manœuvres under warlike conditions. The repeal, by a decree of 5 August 1940, of the decree of August 1937 on the reintroduction of military commissars in the Red Army and Navy and the adoption of new disciplinary penal regulations for the Red Army on 12 October 1940 were interpreted as evidence of a profound reshaping of the forces. In the opinion of the German officers, the Red Army seemed to be making a huge effort to transform itself into a first-rate modern force, equipped with up-to-date military technology. Above all, a superior's duty to implement an order by the use of Draconian full powers aroused attention. Under that regulation a superior officer could not be called to account if, 'for enforcing obedience and the maintenance of discipline and order', he resorted to his weapon.

All measures for the strengthening of the internal structure of the Red Army and the advancement of its state of training were summed up in Timoshenko's order No. 30, dated 21 January 1941, on 'combat and political training in the training year 1941'.[28] Timoshenko demanded that officers and men should thenceforward be trained solely in accordance with the requirements of war and that substantial results were to be achieved by the autumn of 1941. He made it the duty of all military commanders, down to platoon leader, 'fully to identify' with that order.

Assuming the maintenance of the rate and scope of the development and modernization of the Red Army, of its training, and of the tightening of its command structure, it could well reach a state within the foreseeable future when its offensive strength and the determination of its commanders made it capable of any military action. To bridge that period in peace and without conflict had to be, in the German judgement, the most important aspect of Stalin's policy. At the same time, however, the question arose whether that process of irresistible strengthening could still be interpreted as purely defensive.

man intelligence sources and their value. Of interest here is intelligence in the Soviet Union, Finland, Romania, and Hungary. Within the limit of their reach, the Soviet Union was under surveillance by two permanent listening-posts (Königsberg—now Kaliningrad—and Warsaw), as well as by two listening companies (Lyck and Lancut), which transmitted their reports direct to Amt Ausland/Abwehr. Additional intelligence was provided by aerial surveillance of the frontier and by the frontier surveillance service. See BA-MA, 18. Armee, 17562/1, diary entry of 22 July 1940; also BA-MA H 3/675. On findings concerning the Red Army's air forces see the section by Boog, I.iv.2b of the present volume; BA-MA RH 19 I/119, 123, 125 (situation reports of Abt. Frd Heere Ost). Halder, Diaries, 549 (14 Aug. 1940), viewed the changed position of the commissars as an improvement of the Red Army's structure. On this see sect. I.ii.2 at n. 115 (Hoffmann).

[28] Given in translation in BA-MA RH 19 I/123; ibid. for Disziplinarstrafordnung [disciplinary penal regulations], 12 Oct. 1940.

Considerable attention was aroused also by efforts towards a general enhancement of the Soviet population's willingness to fight. Appeals for 'military discipline and bearing', introduction of an eight-hour working day and a six-day working week, a ban on the free movement of labour, introduction of compulsory vocational education and four years' obligatory labour service for juveniles, combined with an arousal of national sentiment—all these suggested a tightening of the performance potential of the Soviet Union. This tremendous transformation seemed, in the field of foreign policy, to demand maintenance of neutrality and avoidance of conflict with a powerful adversary. Domestically this process, described as an 'evolutionary transformation of all-embracing scale', required a number of years, if not decades, before it would come to fruition.

The information gathered on the Soviet Union in the course of 1940 was presented in an official publication, 'The wartime armed forces of the Union of Socialist Soviet Republics', issued on 15 January 1941.[29] The influence of the reports of the military attaché in Moscow is clearly perceptible, as in the statement that 'Communism of doctrinaire type' had been abandoned 'in favour of an authoritarian despotically guided class state'. The stages of reorientation of the Red Army's command structure and organization on the basis of the lessons of the Finno-Soviet war were traced. On the subject of the armaments industry it was stated that it was entirely modern in its equipment and capable of producing serviceable war material and, in the event of war, laying in certain amounts of stockpiles. Adequate supplies could be expected for the first few months of the war; after that bottlenecks would appear due to a shortage of skilled workers and machine-tools. The relocation of the main enterprises of the armaments industry to the regions east of the Urals had been fully realized since 1928. The army of the Soviet Union was described as follows.[30] Subordinated to the people's commissariat for defence were 16 military districts and 2 military commissariats. The structure of the army was unclear; all that was known was that at least eleven armies had been formed in the west. It was to be assumed that the senior staffs for the army groups ('fronts'), armies, and operational groups were provided from the commands of the military districts and armies. On paper 11–12 million men were available for the wartime army (as a basis for mobilization), but there was doubt whether that figure could be reached in view of the resulting labour shortages and the shortage of commanders and material.

The total strength of the Red Army was assumed (in January 1941) to be as follows:

---

[29] OKH/GenStdH/OQu IV, Abt. Frd Heere Ost (II), No. 100/41, pts. 1 and 2. The figures in Besymenski, *Sonderakte 'Barbarossa'* (1968), 248, with which researchers still operate, are not reproduced any more correctly than some sections of the text. This results in regrettable misjudgements by users. The official publication was issued in 2,000 copies and may be seen in BA-MA.

[30] See also sect. I.II.2 at nn. 135 ff. (Hoffmann).

at least 20 armies
20 rifle corps
150 rifle divisions
9 cavalry corps
32–6 cavalry divisions
6 mechanized corps
at least 36 motorized-mechanized brigades.

The number of rifle divisions located in Europe was assumed to be at least 121 at the end of 1940. There was no clear idea, however, on how these forces were disposed.

In all the Department for Foreign Armies East reckoned, in the event of mobilization, on

107 rifle divisions of the first wave
77 rifle divisions of the second wave
25 rifle divisions of the third wave

i.e. altogether 209 rifle divisions.

An increase in the approximately 32 cavalry divisions or the 2 independent brigades (which in the event of war could be brought up to division strength) was not expected.

The number of armoured fighting vehicle regiments among the army troops, or the number of special artillery units, was not known. At least 40 artillery regiments were thought to be at the disposal of the supreme army command. In addition, allowance had to be made for an unspecified number of very heavy batteries, a few independent artillery regiments, 'fortified zones', anti-aircraft units, 20–30 battalions of sappers, 25 railway regiments, motor-vehicle transport battalions, gas-warfare battalions, 9 airship detachments, 1 independent airship group, as well as searchlight battalions.

After the raising of the wartime army, assuming roughly 200 rifle divisions and corresponding numbers of other units, the following manpower strength was assumed:

army in the field approximately	4.0m.
rearward services approximately	0.6m.
home defence units approximately	1.6m.
TOTAL	6.2m.

Added to these were the frontier guard units, which came under the people's commissar of the interior. In the event of war the duty of the frontier guard corps was to provide cover for the army's deployment; after that it was to be integrated into the army in the field.

The Red Army's armour was regarded as an élite force. Nevertheless, it was believed that, because of inadequate combat training and training in co-operation with other branches, it was incapable of conducting a modern war of movement with far-ranging operations by compact formations. Technically, too, the tanks that were known seemed outdated, for the most part copies or developments of foreign models.

The observed troop movements were not interpreted as a deployment for an offensive but attributed to the difficulties of moving major formations under wartime conditions. Of the assumed large formations, 15 divisions, according to the calculations of the Department for Foreign Armies East, were tied down in Finland or engaged in the protection of Leningrad, and 7 were in the Caucasus; 29 rifle divisions, 7 cavalry divisions, and 5 motorized and mechanized brigades were in the Far East and Central Asia. It was expected that, if necessary, 4 divisions could be brought up from Siberia. Added to these were the reserves of the supreme command, among which the 8 artillery divisions of 4 regiments each deserved attention, as well as the corps artillery.

As for Soviet operational intentions, it was assumed that the bulk of the forces were deploying either north or south of the Pripet marshes in order to halt any German attack by striking at its flanks. However, whether the Red Army 'consider[ed] itself capable of such an operation in view of its commanders and training, and also in terms of transport facilities, seem[ed] doubtful'.

The Department for Foreign Armies East concluded that the strength of the Red Army rested upon its bulk and the quantity of its weapons, and upon the frugality, toughness, and bravery of its individual soldiers. That was why special achievements could be expected of the Red Army in defence. 'The ability to hold out, even in defeat and under heavy pressure, is particularly in line with the Russian character.'

These assumptions and a brief account of Soviet combat instructions for attack, defence, and ambush warfare were laid down in a 'Leaflet on the peculiarity of Russian warfare', completed on 25 January 1941.[31] This also made the point that the Soviet soldier, in contrast to his operations in the Finnish Winter War, when he had fought with a lack of enthusiasm, would be inspired by the idea of defending his proletarian fatherland. In conclusion it stated: 'All in all the Russian is better in defence than in attack. In defence he is tough and gallant, and usually allows himself to be killed at the spot where his leader has placed him.'

An attempt at presenting a comprehensive idea of the picture the Wehrmacht leadership and Army High Command had formed of the strength of the Red Army and the abilities of its leaders cannot confine itself to the military information here reproduced. The recipients of that information viewed the Soviet Union not merely as a state with whose forces a clash of arms had to be considered for reasons of rivalry or the assertion of territorial claims; for them Lenin's and Stalin's state was an exceedingly multilayered and incalculable structure. Memories of the effect of political agitation organized from Moscow during the years following the First World War were just as

[31] OKH/GenStdH/OQu IV, Frd Heere Ost, Merkblätter, BA-MA library.

lively as the impression left behind by the Red Brigades in the Spanish civil war. Communism as a threat to the bourgeois national state was a natural constituent also of the image of the enemy in the minds of the generals. Another part of it was the traditional image of the giant empire in the east, whose encroachment on Germany had been prevented by the battle of Tannenberg in 1914. The generation which made the military decisions in 1940 based its picture of Russia on experiences, reports, and assumptions the value of which as objective information was only partially verifiable. The 'Bolsheviks' were seen as the authors of the collapse in 1918, they stood for the demoralization of the army and the home front, they were ultimately held responsible for the upheavals in postwar Germany. Quite apart from political propaganda, which until August 1939 had ceaselessly proclaimed the peril of Bolshevism, and more particularly of 'Jewish Bolshevism', military propaganda too—for instance in the 'Accounts of the postwar operations of German troops and Free Corps', published in 1936 by the Research Institute for War and Army History—had helped to create the image of a politically indoctrinated fanatical population of the Soviet Union.[32]

Yet another component of the traditional image of Russia was the expectation of the internal collapse of the giant empire, from which the Wehrmacht High Command was hoping to profit.[33] However, in Moscow on 10 October 1940 Embassy Counsellor von Walther expressly opposed any inclusion of rebellions by national, ethnic, or religious groups as a calculable positive factor in military plans. Having learnt of such plans in the Wehrmacht High Command—presumably through Embassy Counsellor Hans Heinrich Herwarth von Bittenfeld, a cousin of Lieutenant-Colonel Bernhard von Loßberg on the Wehrmacht operations staff—he approached the foreign ministry's representative in the Army High Command, Hasso von Etzdorf, and uttered an explicit warning:[34] in the event of a defensive war the Soviet government would have the whole population behind it; there would be no break-up into nationalities, and uprisings should not be expected. In the event of a German attack there would undoubtedly be severe setbacks, but not a collapse of the USSR. Like Köstring, Walther also believed that the Soviet Union would not risk an attack and would seek its objectives in areas which did not infringe German interests. He further pointed out that the western territories of the Soviet Union would merely be a burden to the German conquerors, seeing that the

---

[32] On the problem of the long-term effects of the experiences of the German eastern army after the armistice of Brest-Litovsk see *Rückführung des Ostheeres*, 5–6. There the cause of the disintegration is given—along with the condition of the troops—as 'Bolshevik propaganda', whose principal exponents were the Jews. See also *Der Weltkrieg 1914–1918*, xiii. 387, 397; on this also Frantz, 'Rückführung des deutschen Besatzungsheeres'; Fischer, *Deutsche Truppen und Entente-Intervention*, also discusses the actual role of soldiers' councils and their falsified presentation. On the judgement of the German officer corps on Russian warfare see *Der Weltkrieg 1914–1918*, ii. 45, 52, 314, 317, but see also pp. 324 ff.

[33] See the 'Loßberg-Studie', Besymenski, *Sonderakte 'Barbarossa'* (1968), 311.

[34] Herwarth, *Against Two Evils*, 193; Walther's letter to Etzdorf: Gibbons, 'Opposition'.

entire agriculture was mechanized and that the necessary fuel could be obtained only from Soviet-controlled areas. This meant that the expected relief from the 'Ukrainian bread-basket' would not materialize. After the war Köstring repeatedly emphasized that he had warned Halder against war with the Soviet Union. The majority of the Moscow embassy staff believed that Stalin was willing to make sacrifices in order to preserve peace, and that Germany could not expect to derive any advantage from a war.[35] In consequence they saw no point in a war in 1941 and—in Köstring's case this is a matter of record—regarded the Soviet Union, which they believed was on the way to becoming a 'national state' and was increasingly deviating from the principles of the Communist International, as a future partner, at least as long as the Wehrmacht was undefeated and strong. This implied a successful and definitive conclusion of hostilities against Britain.

Despite the very incomplete information on the military potential and combat strength of the Soviet Union, the Army High Command believed that it had grasped the essential elements of the 'gigantic war-machine' of the Red Army. In the balance of its strengths and weaknesses, there appeared to be a preponderance of those problems which could be solved only in the long term—such as the lack of a competent senior officer corps, backwardness in troop training in line with the requirements of a modern war of movement, and insufficient modern war material for *all* units.

In the summer of 1940 both Hitler and the military high commands proceeded from the assumption that a direct threat to Reich territory need not be expected from the Red Army. Considerable misgivings, however, persisted with regard to tranquillity in the Balkans. All measures taken, especially those for the training of leaders at all levels, were seen as endeavours to turn the Red Army into a highly modern fighting force. Quality was now being added to sheer bulk. At the end of that development there could well stand an army capable of any attack, and certainly able to lend support from its forward positions to any far-reaching demands of the political leadership. Certainly, in the event of dissonance in the political arrangements between Hitler and Stalin, as was indeed the case on the occasion of Molotov's visit to Berlin in November 1940, the Red Army was a fighting force to be taken seriously.

During the second phase of the campaign in the west Halder had reason to feel uneasy in view of the parallel changes occurring along Germany's eastern frontier. He had to consider what new tasks might have to be assigned to the army there.

[35] *General Köstring*, ed. Teske, 249, 264, 304 ff. Köstring's deputy, Col. (Gen. Staff) Hans Krebs, as late as 9 Apr. 1941 reported that he could see no indications of an enhanced preparedness for war on the part of the Red Army and on 22 Apr. 1941 confirmed Soviet anxieties about confrontation with Germany after the rapid course of the Balkan campaign; see *General Köstring*, ed. Teske, 302 ff.

(b) Early Phases in Planning within the Army High Command up to July 1940

In expectation of an early end to hostilities in the west and of the conclusion of peace in the foreseeable future, both Hitler and the Army High Command were examining the question of what sections of the army should be kept on an operational footing in the event—still considered a possibility—of a continuation of the war against Britain. As a final stage a 'peacetime army' of approximately 70 divisions was envisaged, including roughly 30 motorized and armoured formations. As an intermediate solution, while the war continued, an army reduced to 120 divisions was decided on, with armour and motorized formations maintained at the planned strength.[36] The prerequisite of this far-reaching measure, with the war still continuing, was, according to the chief of the Army General Staff on 15 June 1940, 'that with the imminent final collapse of the enemy the task of the army has been discharged and inside enemy territory we shall be able to carry out undisturbed this restructuring as the basis of our peacetime organization'.[37] The main effort in the war against Britain was to be made by the Luftwaffe and the navy, whose material and personnel requirements, including armaments, now enjoyed priority. As part of the reduction of the existing approximately 155 major formations to the size of the transitional army, the Army High Command envisaged the transfer of 15 battle-worthy divisions to the east, to protect the frontier; simultaneously the formations of the commander-in-chief East were to be dissolved.[38]

Although the transfer of divisions after the conclusion of a campaign was a perfectly normal procedure, it was then acquiring special importance in view of the major upheavals in the political scene in the Baltic countries and in Romania. On 18 June Halder discussed with Major (General Staff) Reinhard Gehlen (then still in the Home Fortification Department but shortly afterwards assigned to the 'Eastern Group' of the Army General Staff) what he expected of those divisions. Halder's diary notes make it perfectly clear that he envisaged an offensive type of defence; further strengthening of fortifications was therefore to be continued only on a reduced scale. This is what he noted:

Basic policy: Only the minimum! Everything we have should be used for offensive action
Defence:
(*a*) A system of tank obstacles laid out along river lines.
(*b*) Organization permitting instant employment of all forces.
(*c*) First-class net of roads and railways to move these forces.

---

[36] Halder, *Diaries*, 429–30 (28 May 1940); 'Führer Conferences', 108–9 (Hitler on 4 June 1940); Müller-Hillebrand, *Heer*, ii. 62 ff. On the restructuring of the army see sect. I.IV.1(*h*) at n. 187.
[37] Halder's conference in Versailles on 28 June 1940, BA-MA RH 19 III/141; Halder, *Diaries*, 490 (3 July 1940).
[38] See Müller-Hillebrand, *Heer*, ii. 52 ff., and Map. I.IV.1. The 155 formations do not include the brigades or the units of the Waffen-SS which are listed in the army's order of battle.

(*d*) Strategic placing of special defence groups which would canalize enemy invasion *operationally* (not tactically!).

(*e*) Maximum use of minefields.[39]

These cues cover the core of the instructions to Eighteenth Army HQ, which was to be in charge in the eastern part of Reich territory and in the occupied part of Poland. They constituted the guidelines for the work of the Eastern Group of the operations department during the following weeks. The consequences considered by Halder for the restructuring of the army in the event of its being engaged in the east will be referred to at a later stage.

To start with, Hitler on 23 June 1940 approved the envisaged reduction and restructuring of the army.[40] He expected Britain to give in; in case she continued to fight her only hope of success was to draw the United States or the Soviet Union into the war. The main concentration of the new disposition of forces, as envisaged by him and the commander-in-chief of the army, would clearly continue to be in the newly occupied western territories, where 67 divisions and mobile formations would be stationed, as against only 17 divisions in the east, and with the defence of Norway being reinforced by a total of 7 divisions. There was no mention of employing armoured formations with the army in the east, nor was there any mention of mobile troops in connection with Eighteenth Army HQ.

The transfer of Eighteenth Army was to be explained to the Soviet Union as representing a 'return to the homeland'.

The minutes of that conference show that it was concerned solely with matters relating to the securing of the conquered territories in the west. A thrust by armoured formations towards the Mediterranean was considered in the event that the armistice did not materialize as expected.

Halder made the restructuring and reorganization of the army the subject of a conference with the heads of the principal departments of the Army General Staff on 25 June. By then, following the conclusion of the armistice with France and his own previous briefing on the military situation beyond the eastern frontier, he added a new point of view to his considerations: the creation of 'Striking power in the East'.[41] This appears to be the first development of his ideas on the operational channelling of enemy penetrations by 'special defence groups'.

Several motives can be identified for this fundamental change in the planning ideas of the chief of the Army General Staff. The first of these may well have been the rapidly changing strategic situation east of Germany's frontiers. The speed with which the Soviet leadership was transforming its territorial holdings in the Baltic States during the final phase of the war in the west, the

[39] Halder, *Diaries*, 473 (18 June 1940). On this section see Leach, *German Strategy*, 52 ff.

[40] Halder, *Diaries*, 48–1 (23 June 1940), and Loßberg's minute, OKW/Abt. Landesverteidigung No. 33110/40 Chefs., 24 June 1940, BA-MA RW 4/v. 581; Irving, *Hitler's War*, 137–8. For the organizational aspects see sect. I.IV.1(*h*).

[41] Halder, *Diaries*, 484 (25 June 1940).

renewed Soviet claims to Bessarabia, and most of all the concentration of massive forces along the Romanian frontier, aroused increased attention in the Army High Command.[42] Halder does not seem to have expected that the Soviet leadership, disregarding German interests and applying ultimatum-style pressure, would carry out the occupation of Bessarabia and, in addition, claim Bukovina. There was, in addition, a growing danger that the unstable situation in the Balkans, marked as it was by the Hungarian–Romanian conflict, the vacillation of Turkey, and the ambitions of Italy, might deteriorate dramatically. If the Soviet leadership were to favour one of the rival groupings, the situation in the Balkans might get out of hand.[43]

Unlike Hitler, however, Halder at the end of June 1940 did not believe that the use of the army against Britain could be entirely ruled out. Britain remained the main enemy, and in order to overthrow that enemy—given the fact that all of Europe was under blockade—certain prerequisites would have to be created in the east. The following measures should therefore be seen from this overall strategic aspect.

Halder was doubtful, to say the least, whether Britain would 'do the reasonable thing' and put an end to the war. If Britain were to opt for continuing the war, then, Halder believed, the war would be protracted,[44] with all the consequences of a long war. Halder double whether the navy and the Luftwaffe were able to deliver the decisive blow to defeat Britain. The first discussions with representatives responsible for those services soon confirmed that profound differences existed both on the direction and on the operational and technical execution of a landing operation.[45] The view was certainly held in the Army High Command that a rapid decision in the war against Britain was not to be expected. So what could be done in the meantime? The possibility that at some time in the war the Soviet Union might have to be considered as an adversary, despite the conclusion of the treaty of 23 August 1939, had never been ruled out. The question now arose of what role the Soviet Union's attitude could play in Britain's decision to continue the struggle. In the background, moreover, there was the even more alarming threat of the enemy

---

[42] See sect. I.iv.1 at n. 17. On this see Myllyniemi, *Baltische Krise*, 122 ff., also Tippelskirch, diary notes of 12, 19, 20, 24, and 25 June 1940, BA-MA RH 2/v. 1478. Köstring's reports are also relevant in a general way.

[43] Halder's connections with the Hungarian and Romanian general staffs testify to the fact that he was far from relying on the political skill of the foreign ministry, but used his own information in order to form a judgement. See Tippelskirch, diary note of 8 Apr. 1940 (approach by the chief of the Hungarian general staff), 28 Apr.–6 May 1940 (journey to Bucharest, Sofia, Belgrade), BA-MA RH 2/v. 1478. Intensive observation of all military developments in the Balkans was reflected in 'situation reports East', which in turn formed part of the materials presented by Tippelskirch; see BA-MA RH 19 I/119. Hitler too saw this region as the real potential danger-point and commented accordingly. See Stegemann, 'Hitlers Ziele', 97.

[44] Halder, *Diaries*, 480 (22 June 1940); see also Hillgruber, *Strategie*, 144 ff.

[45] On 'Sea Lion' see Klee, *Seelöwe*, and id., *Dokumente*. The controversies between the high commands of the Luftwaffe, the navy, and the army are reflected in the diaries of Halder (e.g. the entry for 30 July 1940) and of the Wehrmacht operations staff in OKW, and in the navy C.-in-C.'s reports to Hitler.

coalition of 1917 if the United States were left enough time to prepare her entry into the war and if Japan's passive attitude in the Pacific permitted America to focus its attention wholly on the European theatre. In that case a situation would arise which the Army High Command saw as the worst possible scenario: a war of attrition on several fronts, of unpredictable duration, but bound to lead to the same end result as in 1918.

Regardless of whether in this situation Hitler decided to concentrate all efforts against the British mother country or on the war in the Mediterranean area, Germany's dependence on Soviet good will and material deliveries would inevitably increase. That the Soviet Union was quick to seize any advantage as it arose had been proved by events of the past few months. Thus a sober assessment of the real power situation beyond Germany's eastern frontier was bound to lead the chief of the Army General Staff to record a disturbing deterioration of Germany's strategic position. Along with the threat to the irreplaceable ore deliveries from Sweden, a threat which increased with the strengthened position of the Soviet Baltic Fleet in the Gulf of Finland, the main source of worry was the Soviet military presence in the vicinity of the Romanian oilfields, which were indispensable to any motorized warfare by Germany. Calculations of the range of Soviet bombers, moreover, revealed that the Silesian armaments and industrial centres could at any time be exposed to attack from the air.[46]

A further motivation for Halder's reflections and decisions stemmed from his understanding of the duties and responsibilities of the chief of the Army General Staff. On 24 June 1940 he instructed the OQu IV, Lieutenant-General von Tippelskirch, to direct the military attaché in Moscow to brief Marshal Voroshilov on the troop movements in the east of the Reich; these were not to be seen as a threat to the Soviet Union.[47] The fact that he saw this as coming within the duties of the chief of the general staff makes it a lot easier to understand the development which began on 25 June. After the war Halder himself repeatedly confirmed the autonomy of that preliminary decision by claiming for the 'military leader' the right to 'protect his country against enemy violation by moving to the attack himself, provided the politician can give him the chance of succeeding' while observing the principles and forms of international law.[48] In this context it should be recalled what role his predecessor Beck, then assisted by Manstein and Halder, had tried to achieve for a

---

[46] BA-MA RH 20-2/139 (notes of Lt.-Col. (Gen. Staff) Feyerabend, who served in the army general staff operations department from 21 July 1940). Halder's reflections are contained in Halder, *Diaries*, 490 (3 July 1940), and Heusinger and Henrici, Feldzug in Rußland, MGFA, T-6b, 1, 18 ff. For an assessment of the situation in the east and of the Red Army in July 1940 see the enemy-situation section of the deployment instruction for Eighteenth Army HQ, BA-MA, 18. Armee, 17562/2.

[47] Tippelskirch, diary notes of 24 June 1940, BA-MA RH 2/v. 1478.

[48] Halder, *Hitler as War Lord*, 39; even more drastically in Bor, *Gespräche*, 195, 201, where the 'war lord' positively becomes the 'thought leader' of the politician. 'War lord' here refers to the all-embracing role of Ludendorff in the First World War.

'Reich chief of general staff' as a director of all Wehrmacht operations in the war.[49]

Halder's diary frequently shows how close he seemed to be to that objective, especially at the height of the war in the west. He suffered what he regarded as the utter ignorance of Hitler and the Wehrmacht High Command on all operational issues in the secure knowledge that his own thinking and the training of his general-staff officers would lay the foundation of victory.[50] *Vis-à-vis* Colonel-General von Brauchitsch, the commander-in-chief of the army, he also clearly insisted on recognition of his extensively understood range of responsibilities and his post.[51] From this point of view it is entirely in line with the logic of military thought that measures should be initiated in good time which would result in the occupation of foreign territories and the seizure of a 'forfeit' for the further development of the war.[52]

The order for the transfer of Eighteenth Army HQ to the east of the Reich territory and for the formation of a new army from 15 infantry divisions to be likewise transferred there was issued on 26 June 1940.[53] The task of that army was defined on 29 June as securing the frontier against Lithuania and the Soviet Union. Preparations were to be made to halt any enemy forces on the San–Vistula line, if not before, and on the East Prussian frontier, so that a counter-attack could be mounted as soon as reinforcements had arrived. For that event the 'Group Guderian' with two corps commands (mot.), 4 armoured divisions, and 2 infantry divisions (mot.) was placed under the army command. These divisions were to be moved to the areas around Berlin and Breslau (now Wrócław). The existing duties of frontier security under 'Oberost' remained unchanged so long as his units were not dismissed. The change of name to 'Military commander in the Government-General' (MiG) inaugurated its transformation into a territorial quartermaster staff.

On 3 July Halder recorded in his diary the opening of talks with the chief of the operations department, Colonel Hans von Greiffenberg. Both men proceeded from the belief that a blow against the Soviet Union would mean the

---

[49] Müller, *Beck*, 103 ff., 133–4; *Keitel*, ed. Görlitz, 123 ff. (memoranda).

[50] Typical are the following entries in 1940: Halder, *Diaries*, 414–15 (22 May), 424 (25 May), 428–9 (28 May), 431–2 (30 May), 443–4 (6 June), and 449–50 (8 June). Some of his criticism is aimed at the army C.-in-C. and at the C.-in-C.s of the army groups; essentially, however, it is clearly directed at Hitler and the Wehrmacht High Command.

[51] Halder, *Diaries*, 95 (1 Oct. 1939); *KTB OKW* i. 135–6 more outspokenly still in Schall-Riaucour, *Aufstand*, 127—otherwise this work should be treated with caution with regard to sources.

[52] Heusinger and Henrici, Feldzug in Rußland, MGFA, T-6b, 41–2, confirm the independent character of Halder's reflections and thus also the thesis that his way of thinking was essentially presented to Hitler on 21 July 1940: 'It seems that Hitler learnt of these reflections on 21 July 1940, when Halder in a report spoke of the uncertain attitude of the Soviet Union.' The territories earmarked by Halder for conquest 'could prove very useful as forfeits in connection with the intention to achieve an early peace after the scoring of successes in the east'.

[53] OKH/GenStdH/OpAbt No. 375/40, 26 June 1940 (order for the regrouping of the army), and 'Instruction to Eighteenth Army HQ', 29 June 1940, BA-MA, 18. Armee, 17562/2; the latter document is reproduced in *Fall Barbarossa*, No. 64.

end of Britain's hopes of successfully continuing the war.[54] Further ideas emerged on 4 July in an oral briefing of the commander of Eighteenth Army, Artillery General Georg von Küchler, and his chief of staff, Major-General Erich Marcks.[55] Halder pointed to the Soviet troop concentrations in the area east of Lvov and south of the Lithuanian frontier. There was no 'political reason' for any hurry. The army HQ was instructed to work out a proposal for the conduct of operations. This was submitted on 9 July and, following examination and approval by Halder, became part of the 'Deployment Instruction for Eighteenth Army', dated 22 July 1940 and signed by von Küchler.[56] The instruction was based on the idea that, in the event of a conflict with Russia, substantial German forces would be employed in the east; until they arrived there Eighteenth Army HQ would need to secure the eastern frontier. In organizing defence on the upper San and in East Prussia the bulk of the forces was to be disposed in such a way that Soviet preparations for attack could be broken up by a German attack. For that purpose the divisions of the military commander in the Government-General and of 'Group Guderian' would be available in addition to the divisions of the army. Two attacking forces were to be formed: one to strike in a south-easterly direction (Lvov–Tarnopol) and the other in a north-easterly direction (Bialystok). All plans and measures of the Army High Command were designed to create the prerequisites for offensive action. This applied not only to the sphere of operational planning, to the training of the new formations—which was anyway proceeding according to the directives for the restructuring of the army— or to the accelerated bringing up of the troops, but above all to the building and improvement of roads, troops' quarters, and communication links. Accordingly, on 13 July Marcks declined to take over the defensive construction work of 'Oberost' on the grounds that the army HQ intended to solve its task offensively.

In the area of construction, above all in the provision of militarily useful traffic routes and quarters, difficulties arose immediately on account of the ill-defined command structure. Outside operational areas it was normally a military commander or the commander of the reserve army who would issue directives and orders on behalf of the army commander-in-chief. But now— under 'peacetime conditions' as it were—an army HQ was acting in the Government-General and in Military District I (East Prussia) as a command staff, claiming the status of a field command authority and demanding the performance of services.

Halder had first addressed this problem as early as 4 July, but was unable to

[54] Halder, *Diaries*, 490–1 (3 July 1940).

[55] Ibid. 492 (4 July 1940); BA-MA, 18. Armee, 17562/2 (note by Marcks).

[56] BA-MA, 18. Armee, 17562/2. Its preparation in the general staff was in the hands of Feyerabend (see above, n. 46). He had to gather information on the Soviet Union, calculate the range of its air forces, and assess the presumable attitudes of Finland and Romania, as a basis both for map exercises and for deployment instructions for Eighteenth Army: notes by Feyerband, BA-MA RH 20-2/139.

DIAGRAM I.IV.1. Order of Battle of Eighteenth Army on 22 July 1940 (Excluding Rearward Services)

Eighteenth Army HQ Armd. trains 21, 22	**XXVI Army Corps** Armd. trains 6, 24 Art. cmdr. 113	217th Inf. Div.
Luftwaffe 4 Long-rge Recce Staffel Gp. 11 Army Recce Staffel (p. mot.) Courier Staffel 12	Hvy. Art. Bn. (mot.) 61 Observer Bn. 554	161st Inf. Div.
	XXX Army Corps Art. cmdr. 19	258th Inf. Div.
Air Cmd. Staff photo interpr. Bn. 18 Met. stn. 18 291st Inf. Div.	Art. Regt. 622 staff Hvy. Art. Bn. (mot.) II/40 Hvy. Art. Bn. (mot.) II/70 Observer Bn. 1 (without balloon)	76th Inf. Div.
XXXXIV Army Corps Anti-tank Bn. 654 (37-mm.) Art. cmdr. 112	**Higher Cmd. XXXV** Armd. train 2 Art. cmdr. 135	292nd Inf. Div.
Hvy. Art. Bn. (mot.) II/54 Hvy. Art. Bn. (mot.) I/108 Observer Bn. 556 Met. Platoon 503 252nd Inf. Div. 168th Inf. Div.	Art. Regt. 511 staff Hvy. Art. Bn. (mot.) II/71 Hvy. Art. Bn. (mot.) I/106 Observer Bn. 555	162nd Inf. Div.
Dep. I Army Corps cmd. ⌐ 395th Home Defence 399th Home Defence	**III Army Corps** Armd. train 25 Art. cmdr. 3	75th Inf. Div.
M.i.G. 209th Inf. Div. 365th Inf. Div. 372nd Inf. Div 379th Inf. Div. 393rd Inf. Div. ⌐	Art. Regt. 501 staff Hvy. Art. Bn. (mot.) II/65 Hvy. Art. Bn. (mot.) 602 Observer Bn. 52 Bridging Bn. 699	62nd Inf. Div.
Only for tact. ops. under army cmd.:	**XVII Army Corps** Art. cmdr. 44	
Armd. Gp. Guderian (XIX Army Corps mot.) XXXX Army Corps (mot.) 9th Armd. Div. 5th Armd. Div. 2nd Armd. Div.	Art. Regt. 787 staff Hvy. art. Bn. (mot.) II/51 Hvy. Art. Bn. (mot.) II/52 Observer Bn. 57 Engineer Regt. 604 staff Engineer Bn. 666 Bridging Bn. 560	298th Inf. Div. 297th Inf. Div.
XVI Army Corps (mot.) 13th Inf. Div. 2nd Inf. Div. (mot.) 3rd Armd. Div.	**Higher Cmd. XXXIV** Art. cmdr. 134 Hvy. Art. Bn. (mot.) IV/109 Observer Bn. 557	257th Inf. Div. 68th Inf. Div.

Note on bracketed column: "subordinated for tactical operations (within corps area)"

Source: BA-MA, 18. Armee, 17562/2.

offer any solution in terms of chain of command, as he was unable to refer to a directive by Hitler. And without such a directive neither the Military District commander nor the civilian authority could be made to accept instructions from an army HQ. A formal change was brought about only when, after a report by the army commander-in-chief and following new directives from Hitler, dated 31 July 1940, for preparation for war against the Soviet Union, the Wehrmacht High Command on 7 August issued a quasi-ministerial instruction—the guidelines 'on build-up East'—addressed principally to the civilian authorities. This was not, therefore, a fundamental war-preparation measure by the Wehrmacht High Command, but rather a ruling in the administrative sense.[57] However, the difference between the Army High Command directive of 29 June and the 'deployment instruction' of 22 July is significant for the way Halder's thinking developed after 18 June. Whereas the earlier document envisaged only the repulse of a Soviet attack with subsequent German counter-attack, the ruling now was that a German attack was to be mounted as soon as offensive intentions were observed on the enemy side. Both documents provided for the moving up of reinforcements: the earlier version after the opening of the enemy attack, the later version in the rather elastic 'event of conflict with Russia'—which meant, most probably, according to the actual state of the feared incursions in the Balkans or on the Romanian frontier. No matter how the connection between the 'deployment instruction' and the independent idea of seizing a 'forfeit' is interpreted, i.e. in connection with a resumption of the struggle against Britain or a serious blockade, their offensive character, given the potential consequences, cannot be denied.[58] In the final analysis this was not a case of offensive defence within the framework of a war already in progress, but an act which represented the opening of a war. The further development of these plans during the next few days—after an anything but precise instruction by the army commander-in-chief following a conversation with Hitler—suggests that Halder was fully aware of those consequences.

Halder's reflections were based primarily on the Red Army's presumed intentions and on its ability to mount a military operation in line with its identifiable disposition and strength in the area near the frontier. This showed a considerable concentration of forces in two areas of main effort, interspersed with mechanized units (see Map I.IV.1). In spite of that deployment and concentration, the Army General Staff did not believe that the Soviet political

---

[57] On the meaning of those guidelines there is some uncertainty in the literature, going back to Jodl's and Warlimont's evidence before the Nuremberg tribunal; see Warlimont, *Hauptquartier*, 127. But the guidelines were neither a fundamental order nor a camouflage order. It is highly probable that they were based on a request by the army C.-in-C.; this is confirmed by Müller-Hillebrand, *Heer*, i. 66. For the text of the 'Guidelines on build-up East' of 7 Aug. 1940 see BA-MA, 18. Armee, 17562/3. Halder's notes of 31 July 1940 defined Hitler's instructions more clearly than *KTB OKW* i. 5 (1 Aug. 1940). The contents of the guidelines are given in Greiner, *Oberste Wehrmachtführung*, 293–4, closest to the original.

[58] See above, n. 52; Halder, *Diaries*, 516–17 (22 July 1940).

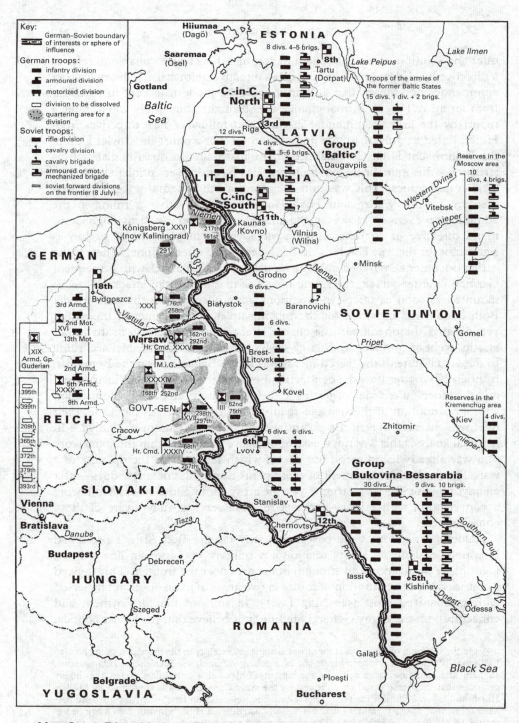

Map I.iv.i. Disposition and Stationing Areas of Eighteenth Army on 22 July 1940 and Grouping of Red Army Forces Assumed by Army High Command (Excluding Frontier Guard Units)

leadership was planning to use those troops offensively against Germany;[59] it would, however, be able with those massed troops to mount an offensive towards the south-west 'at any time or in the event of a change in the political situation'.

Halder's precautionary measures were therefore entirely justified. It may be assumed that by issuing the deployment instructions to Eighteenth Army he had gone to the very limit of what he could set in motion without orders from Hitler, and that he wanted to prepare for a situation which he believed would inevitably be facing the German Wehrmacht.

The inconsistent character of the 'deployment instruction'—in terms of clear military objectives—was criticized on 29 August by Colonel Fritz Bayerlein, the first general staff officer of 'Group Guderian'.[60] He proposed that the areas of operation be substantially extended in line with the mobility and combat strength of the divisions. He also listed the objectives which arose logically from Halder's plans: in the south, thrusts towards Chernovtsy, an operation along the Dnestr with a view to encircling the forces deployed on the Romanian frontier, and an operation in the direction of Kiev, followed by an advance of the left wing down the Dnieper to the south. In case the group was to be used in the north, Bayerlein likewise rejected the loosely phrased directive and proposed the launching of an offensive from East Prussia to both sides of Tilsit towards Vilnius and Minsk. The seizure of Minsk would mean the severance of all links with Leningrad and Moscow. Both proposals were in line with the subsequent disposition of the armoured groups, as was his call for joint operation with the infantry and for keeping supply-routes clear for the exclusive use of the armoured units. Marcks's reaction was that a clear definition of objectives was not possible until the 'event' materialized; he therefore notified the general staff officer that 'Group Guderian' was to confine itself to the tasks set out for it in the 'deployment instructions'.

Simultaneously with the 'deployment instructions', on 22 July the commander of Eighteenth Army, Colonel-General von Küchler, passed on a ruling from the Army High Command designed to scotch rumours about German–Soviet relations.[61] Such rumours were bound to arise with the arrival

[59] Evaluation of enemy situation, 22 July 1940, in the deployment instruction to Eighteenth Army; it was thought that there might be a Soviet offensive against Romania, i.e. the oil wells: BA-MA, 18. Armee, 17562/2.

[60] BA-MA, 18. Armee, 17562/3. Walde, *Guderian*, 113, more or less passes over this 'critical' period in silence. It should be remembered, however, that 'Group Guderian' at the time was a corps staff without troops under its command and that the whole business was probably viewed as a map exercise within the framework of training.

[61] Weisung ObdH über das deutsch-russische Verhältnis [Directive of the C.-in-C. of the army concerning German–Russian relations], 17 July 1940, BA-MA RH 19 I/122. See also *General Köstring*, ed. Teske, 264–5 (1 Aug. 1940). Weinberg ('Entschluß', 302) connected the text of the order of the commander of Eighteenth Army, dated 22 July 1940, which he found in the documents of the Nuremberg trials, with the defensive instructions given to Eighteenth Army on 29 June 1940. Acceptance of Küchler's statement that Eighteenth Army HQ had been moved to East Prussia and that the troops had not arrived until September has blurred the picture; see Hillgruber, *Strategie*, 231. In fact, Eighteenth Army HQ assumed command at Bydgoszcz on 4 July

of the formations in the east. The troops were to be told that this was an operation to protect newly won living-space, to put on a show of strength for the Poles, and to prepare for the future peacetime accommodation of the army. Inside the general staff of Eighteenth Army, however, the connection between a possible future operation and the overall war situation was clearly understood. On 25 July the first general staff officer and the enemy-situation analyst recorded in the army's war diary that a Soviet deployment would be identified in good time and that surprises from the north could be ruled out.[62] A conflict could conceivably arise from the fact that, in the event of a 'crisis in the German–British war', the Soviet Union might occupy further parts of Romania, which Germany would not tolerate. If, following a favourable development of the German–British war, Germany demanded the surrender of Bukovina, the following situations could arise:

(1) under pressure of the German deployment the Soviet Union would yield;

(2) it would yield only after German occupation, i.e. after a war with limited objectives and means; and finally

(3) a last possibility would be the acceptance of war by the Soviet Union along the entire front, 'i.e. march on Moscow'.

To those officers war with the Soviet Union was clearly only a matter of time. This view was possibly reinforced by a request on 23 July 1940 from Colonel von Greiffenberg, head of the Army General Staff's operations department, that Marcks should hold himself ready during the next few days to go to the High Command at Fontainebleau for a week or so[63]—a consequence of the conference Hitler had with the commanders-in-chief of the Wehrmacht services on 21 July 1940. (That conference will be dealt with later.)

The above measures of the Army High Command were at the same strategic level as the reflections on the continuation of the war against Britain, summarized by Major-General Jodl, chief of the Wehrmacht operations department, in a memorandum on 30 June 1940.[64] Haldehad turned his attention to what he considered the more dangerous land-war enemy and, on his own

---

1940 and the bulk of the formations had arrived by the end of July: Weinberg, 'Entschluß', 302 n. 11.

[62] AOK 18/Ia, diary entry of 25 July 1940, BA-MA, 18. Armee, 17562/1.

[63] AOK 18/Ia, diary entry of 23 July 1940, ibid.

[64] Hillgruber, *Strategie*, 157 ff. The main idea behind Jodl's memorandum, however, seems to have been an attempt to ensure, for the further conduct of the war, an effective joint leadership of the Wehrmacht. This is suggested also by the fact that a 1937 memorandum on the top structure of the Wehrmacht in war, by the then C.-in-C. of the army, Col.-Gen. Freiherr von Fritsch, was brought up on 17 May 1941: see *Keitel*, ed. Görlitz, 123 ff. (See also Müller, *Heer*, 293–4, memorandum OKW chief of staff of 19 Apr. 1938: *IMT* xxxviii. 35–50, No. 211-L). All the services insisted on their traditional rights and usages. Even in the areas of administration and law there was no unified joint direction. On 4 Nov. 1940, admittedly, a Wehrmacht quartermaster staff was set up, which, however, 'with full preservation of the quartermaster arrangements of the separate Wehrmacht services', was summoned only occasionally and did not become effective: BA-MA RW 4/v. 145.

responsibility, had initiated measures which were well ahead of the decisions of the supreme commander. Towards the end of June, though, he was perhaps able to find his strategic thinking confirmed in a remark by State Secretary von Weizsäcker of the foreign ministry, who reported that Hitler was keeping 'a steady eye on the East'; he believed that 'Britain probably still needs one more demonstration of our military might before she gives in and leaves us a free hand in the East'.[65] Halder's instruction to Colonel von Greiffenberg, head of the general staff's operations department, to examine the possibilities of a campaign against the Soviet Union as a means of forcing that country to acknowledge Germany's dominating role in Europe, shows that Halder on his own initiative made political objectives part of his military reflections and plans. The instruction to Eighteenth Army, formulated in the course of his conference with Küchler and Marcks on 4 July, fits into the same framework. At that point of planning and preparations by the Army General Staff, by Eighteenth Army HQ, and, up to a point, by the chiefs of staff of Eighteenth Army's corps, Hitler summoned the commanders-in-chief of the army and navy for a discussion of the further military development of the war.[66] On 21 July 1940, two days after Hitler's Reichstag speech in which his unsuccessful attempts to reach an 'arrangement with Britain' were reflected only in meaningless 'peace offers', the central question was what made the British continue the struggle. Hitler saw the answer in British hopes of help from the United States and of an entry into the war by the Soviet Union—as indeed he had remarked on 23 June. He realized that an invasion of Britain would involve very great risks; he therefore wanted to consider a landing only in the event that there was no other way to 'finish off England'. In the discussion of a possible British–Soviet combination the principal aspects were the threat to

[65] Halder, *Diaries*, 487 (30 June 1940). There is some room for doubting the reliability of the attribution of that remark to Hitler, knowing as one does Halder's planning. This was more probably an exchange of identical views between Halder and Weizsäcker. If one bears in mind the anxieties then felt about a Red Army intervention in the Balkans, the limitations of any intended 'turning towards the east' become obvious. There seems to be no doubt that the main topic of that conversation was a speedy armistice with Britain, not any far-reaching 'eastern plans'. That Hitler, just like the entire Wehrmacht High Command, the foreign ministry, and all other political agencies, was carefully watching developments in Romania is obvious. In addition, Soviet attempts with regard to Yugoslavia were being realized, and the Baltic States had not been forgotten either.

[66] Halder, *Diaries*, 515 ff. (22 July 1940), and 'Führer Conferences', 119–20 (21 July 1940). This conference was concerned with questions of the continuation of the war against Britain; the Soviet Union and the United States had to be borne in mind as possible allies of Britain. The combat strength of the Red Army, what German forces would have to be put up against it, and what objectives might be attained by a German attack—these were only secondary issues at the conference. Since the arguments are entirely in line with Halder's intentions as reflected by the measures already taken, it seems clear that the figures, objectives, and directions of the operations were presented by Brauchitsch. Halder's notes, in the form of cues, do not allow for a reliable attribution of the statements to individual participants. Halder himself abandoned his subsequent (handwritten) attribution of the report to Hitler (in his working copy of the transcript of his war diary): 'Actually by his staff (Jodl)'; in the published work it appears as 'can no longer be reliably ascertained'. See Halder, *KTB* ii. 32 n. 9 (not in trans.), and BA-MA N 220/42, 114. Deletion by the editor is also a possibility.

German oil supplies from Romania and the possibility of Soviet air attacks on the German hydrogenation plants in Upper Silesia. Although Hitler did not believe in an imminent British–Soviet coalition, he noted that Stalin was flirting with Britain in order to keep her in the war. This would tie the Wehrmacht down and he, Stalin, would be able to snatch what he wanted. Nevertheless, this clear hint of an extension of the Soviet sphere of power in recent weeks was not equated with any indications of Soviet offensive preparations against the Reich. Hitler eventually ordered that preliminary thought should be given to the solution of the 'Russian problem'. In general terms he emphasized his interest in a speedy conclusion of the war, even though there was no cogent need for this now that the situation was far more favourable than in the First World War.

This was followed by a brief report by the commander-in-chief of the army on planning work and calculations performed within the general staff of the army. This report corresponds so closely with the measures ordered by the Army High Command for the restructuring of formations and the dates by which this was to be completed, including the instructions to Eighteenth Army, that it is difficult to reconstruct any participation by Hitler in that exchange of ideas, except for commonplace observations. The creation of a Ukrainian state and of a Baltic league of states, the separation of Belorussia, and the creation of a strong Finland entirely matched military concepts which had been ever since the First World War. The information that 50–75 'good' divisions would have to be expected came from the Department for Foreign Armies East; against them 80–100 German divisions would be needed.[67] There was some concern about whether the Luftwaffe would be able to cope with operations in the east as well as against Britain, assuming a simultaneous opening of the attacks in the autumn of 1940. The operational routes of the Baltic area and the Ukraine were also contained in Halder's concept. The role to be played by Finland, on the other hand, was not clear; the most plausible assumption was that co-operation was envisaged in a thrust beyond Leningrad and in protecting German domination of the Baltic Sea. Perhaps this was a cue of Hitler's.

The various points of Halder's notes on the report of the commander-in-chief of the army make it clear that what Hitler had sketched out was not a 'great war' aiming at the defeat of the Soviet Union, but a military concept which seemed to agree with Halder's present ideas as well as with the deployment orders to Eighteenth Army. Opposition within the Wehrmacht High Command to a date of attack as early as the autumn of 1940 seems not therefore to have been directed against Hitler's precipitate demand[68] but to have been a reaction against the timetable contained in Halder's concept.

As indicated above, Halder must have been aware of the 'grand solution' which seemed to follow from his assessment of the situation. It seems logical,

---

[67] This calculation is based on the enemy assessment reported in n. 17 above.
[68] Hillgruber, *Strategie*, 222.

therefore, that, having been informed by the army commander-in-chief of Hitler's remarks, he immediately embarked on working out new planning approaches. On that very same 22 July he briefed the heads of the operations department and the Department for Foreign Armies East; on 24 July he briefed the military geography department and assigned the first tasks.[69] On 26 and 27 July Foreign Armies East and the operations department submitted their first reports.[70] At the focus of attention was the initial disposition for the operation. Colonel von Greiffenberg, the head of the operations department, proposed the creation of a strong southern group. Halder, on the other hand, was considering a more powerful northern group, to be employed against Moscow, in order subsequently to compel the strong enemy forces in the Ukraine to do battle with reversed fronts.

Regardless of all this, preparations for an invasion of Britain were still the main concern of the Army General Staff. Halder, moreover, was even thinking about the raising of colonial troops for the future.[71] In consequence, it was not possible for him, or for the head of the operations department, who had at that tune also assumed the duties of OQu I, to work out quietly the basis of a new major campaign. Thus on 23 July 1940, the day after his briefing by Brauchitsch, Halder ordered the chief of staff of Eighteenth Army to hold himself ready for this task and to come to his headquarters.

No matter how far independent thinking, planning, and issuing of instructions within the realm of the army had advanced, Hitler's decision alone was crucial for their development and conversion into actual preparations for an aggressive war. It was on 29 July that he informed Artillery General Jodl, the head of the Wehrmacht operations department, that he had decided to attack the Soviet Union in May 1941. Preparations should be put in hand.[72] Given the structure of Germany's top military leadership, what this new directive meant for Wehrmacht High Command was initially no more than co-ordination of the requirements arising from the army's tasks with the other two services and their adjustment to the capacities of the war economy; it did not imply any operational planning comparable to that of the Army General Staff, let alone authority to issue orders.

The great conference on the overall war situation at Hitler's Berghof on 31 July[73] was opened with a report by Grand Admiral Raeder, the commander-in-

[69] Halder, *Diaries*, 518 ff. (under the dates given).

[70] Ibid. 521 ff.; Feyerabend, notes of 28 July 1940, BA-MA RH 20-2/139. The decisive consideration for Halder was the need to reach Moscow by the fastest route and there to smash the bulk of the Red Army. This he regarded as the prerequisite of a political collapse of the Soviet Union.

[71] Halder, *Diaries*, 474 (19 June 1940). Although there was no order from Hitler on this subject, the activities of the colonial-policy department of the NSDAP had spread over to the Wehrmacht and given rise to numerous enquiries about service in the colonial army: OKW/AuswAmt/Abw. Koloniale Unterrichtungen Nos. V and VI (6 Sept. and 5 Oct. 1940), BA-MA RW 4/v. 145.

[72] Hillgruber, *Strategie*, 222–3.

[73] At the conference on 31 July 1940 the C.-in-C. of the navy remained present only until he had concluded his own report; the Luftwaffe was represented by Jeschonnek. Hitler's 'discussion

chief of the navy, on the state of preparations for a landing in England.[74] That operation for the defeat of Britain, until then unquestionably at the centre of planning, was now being queried both by Hitler and by the Army High Command. Hitler realized its dependence on weather conditions and technical prerequisites, as well as on the success of the Luftwaffe, and therefore, given that mid-September was the latest possible date, asked what might be done to bring Britain to her knees if the landing had to be either abandoned or postponed until the following May, the date regarded as most favourable by the navy. He proceeded from the belief that the war 'as such' had 'been won'. Britain's determination to hold out was based on hopes of the Soviet Union and the United States. If the Soviet Union was eliminated, the United States need no longer be expected to join the war because Japan would then have undergone an 'enormous strengthening' in the Pacific region. Once the Soviet Union was smashed, Britain's last hope would be crushed. Germany would then be 'master of Europe and the Balkans'.

His decision, therefore, was to eliminate the Soviet Union militarily as quickly as possible. To do that it was not enough to occupy a specific territory: the entire state would have to be shattered at a single blow.[75] Preparations would take until the following spring; that was why he was laying down May 1941 as a provisional date. After that, there would be five months left for the execution of the operations. Hitler also commented on operational problems. He spoke of attack by way of two thrusts, one towards Kiev and the other via the Baltic States towards Moscow. Eventually the two thrusts were to link up, presumably beyond Moscow. A partial operation against the oilfields of Baku might be contemplated later. Romania and Finland could be considered in the role of allies, but not so Hungary. The territorial gains from this war, as he saw it, would be the Ukraine, Belorussia, and the Baltic States. Finland was to expand as far as the White Sea. Altogether Hitler calculated that 180 divisions were needed, 120 of them for the east. This meant that, with an existing strength of 120 divisions plus 18 'furlough divisions', 40 divisions would have to be newly raised. This should be done in areas free from air raids, i.e. beyond the reach of the British Air Force.

---

partners' on the 'eastern question' were therefore Keitel, Jodl, Brauchitsch, and Halder. In reply to Hitler's question about what could be done against Britain during the winter, Brauchitsch recommended German support for the Italian attack towards the Suez Canal by the provision of two armoured divisions. This was based on Jodl's memorandum of 30 June 1940; see Warlimont, *Hauptquartier*, 124. Hitler himself suggested the seizure of Gibraltar: 'Führer Conferences', 125 (31 July 1940). On the 'peripheral war' see Hillgruber, *Strategie*, 178 ff.

[74] Halder, *Diaries*, 530 ff. (31 July 1940); *KTB OKW* i. 3 ff. (1 Aug. 1940); Hillgruber, *Strategie*, 222 ff.; Warlimont, *Hauptquartier*, 126 ff. Brauchitsch and Halder, prior to that conference, had been briefed on the Red Army and, in assessing the overall war situation, were agreed that it was wiser to maintain 'friendship with the Russians'; admittedly they did not argue this point of view with Hitler on 31 July 1940: Halder, *Diaries*, 530 (30 July 1940); Tippelskirch, diary note of 29 July 1940, BA-MA, RH 2/v. 1478.

[75] This has to be understood as a direct reference to the limited objectives presented by Brauchitsch on 21 July 1940.

Hitler's remark on the new units in the 'eastern region' was the occasion for the guidelines of the Wehrmacht High Command 'on build-up East' of 7 August 1940. The first operational reflections came from Lieutenant-Colonel (General Staff) von Loßberg, chief of the 'Group Army' in the Wehrmacht operations department.[76]

On 1 August Halder briefed the departmental heads in the Army General Staff and instructed them to examine what questions concerning command tasks had been raised by Hitler's decision. Lieutenant-General Rudolf Bogatsch, the Luftwaffe general attached to the army commander-in-chief, was also informed on that day of the outcome of the conference in so far as it concerned support for the ground troops. The requirements arising in all fields from the raising of 40 divisions were discussed by Halder with the heads of the organization department and the operations department. Another subject discussed was the armaments basis of the future mobile army. That same day, moreover, Halder gare attention to the training of new general-staff officers for the army of 180 divisions.[77] It may be worth mentioning that Halder not only performed this transition smoothly, but that he did not, either to his closest colleagues or to his old intimates of the resistance circle, or even to his no doubt carefully locked-up diary, confide the profound shock which, according to later testimonies, Hitler's sudden decision caused him.

(c) Army Group B as 'Security against the East'

The planning work initiated in August in the Army High Command, as well as in the Wehrmacht High Command, was now based on Hitler's explicit decision of 31 July. According to the fluctuations of the overall strategic situation, the staffs were examining ever new projects to eliminate Britain. Diversions were caused by Hungary's mobilization against Romania, by Italian ambitions in the Balkans, and by Finland's inclusion in the general strategic concept. These aspects will be dealt with elsewhere.[78] They are mentioned here merely as irritants to which the main work of building up the army was subjected. Within the Army General Staff, planning for the war in the east proceeded as ordered by Halder. Thus Major-General Wagner, the quarter-master-general of the staff, submitted initial ideas on the organization of supplies on 9 August,[79] and Lieutenant-Colonel Feyerabend dealt with matters concerning the army's deployment and order of battle[80] that had to be solved in connection with the envisaged restructuring of the army and

---

[76] Loßberg embarked on his work 'end of June–beginning of July'. According to his report, Jodl, at the very first briefing on Hitler's intention to attack the Soviet Union, had added as its strategic concept that it was important to form points of main effort on the flanks; see Heusinger and Henrici, Feldzug in Rußland, MGFA, T-6b, 39. Loßberg had given his plans the code-name 'Fritz' and later proposed to Jodl that it should be changed to 'Barbarossa'; see letter from Loßberg to W.-E. Paulus, 7 Sept. 1956, IfZ ZS 97, and Paulus, *Entwicklung*, 175 ff.

[77] Halder, *Diaries*, 530 (30 July 1940), 536 (1 Aug. 1940). For Halder's independent ideas in the organizational field prior to Hitler's directive see sect. I.IV.1(*a*) at n. 39.

[78] See sect. I.IV.2 (Förster) and I.VI (Ueberschär).   [79] Halder, *Diaries*, 544 (9 Aug. 1940).

[80] Memorandum by Feyerabend, 8 Aug. 1940, BA-MA RH 20-2/139.

the creation of 40 new divisions. Halder in his diary noted that the reorganization was to be carried out 'next fall', followed by a 'gradual transfer to the East'.[81]

This planning work, however, was substantially affected by Hitler's reactions to Soviet activities against Finland and Romania. On 21 August he expressed the wish for 196th Infantry Division to be reorganized into a mountain division in response to Soviet pressure, and for the SS brigade stationed in northern Norway to be reinforced. He also asked for an immediate transfer of an armoured division to East Prussia. The Red Army had occupied the Mariampol corner of Lithuania in violation of the agreement; this gave rise to difficulties which, in the already tense atmosphere created by the foreshadowed ultimatum to Romania, aroused extreme mistrust in Hitler.[82] On 26 August, finally, Hitler demanded the reinforcement of the army in the east.[83] As a first step ten infantry divisions and one armoured division were to be transferred. By 30 August the commander-in-chief of the army proposed the transfer of Army Group B headquarters as well as of Fourth and Twelfth Army HQs; orders for this were given on 12 September.[84]

Army Group B command, under Field Marshal Fedor von Bock, was to hand over its area of command immediately to Army Group C (Leeb) and to transfer Fourth Army HQ, 2 corps HQs, and 4 divisions from its own command area to the east. From the command area of Army Group A (Rundstedt) 2 infantry divisions were to be transferred to the east, and from that of Army Group C Twelfth Army HQ with 2 corps HQs and 4 infantry divisions, as well as 1st Armoured Division. On 7 September the following forces were transferred east from the command area of the director-general of training: 1 corps HQ, 3 armoured divisions, and 2 motorized infantry divisions; 9 infantry divisions were to be transferred into Reich territory from the west for reorganization. According to the directive of the army commander-in-chief, dated 9 September 1940,[85] Bock's army group would be responsible for cover-

---

[81] Halder, *Diaries*, 555 (19 Aug. 1940).

[82] Hitler's instruction for reinforcements in East Prussia and northern Norway, for the fortification of the Baltic coast with artillery batteries: *KTB OKW* i. 46; Eztdorf's report: Halder, *Diaries*, 560–1 (23 Aug. 1940). On Mariampol: Halder, *Diaries*, 559 (23 Aug. 1940); Fabry, *Hitler-Stalin-Pakt*, 241 ff.; Hillgruber, *Strategie*, 231. Etzdorf's report is recorded, much more fully than by Halder, in Tippelskirch's diary entries of 22 Aug. 1940, BA-MA RH 2/v. 1479.

[83] on 27 Aug. 1940 Halder complained about Hitler's 'pipedreams' and his irresolution in making decisions. Hillgruber, *Strategie*, 240 ff., sees this in connection with the 'continental bloc' concept. Study of Hitler's military monologues of that time conveys the impression of volatility as a permanent state unless there was an external compulsion to make a firm decision.

[84] Halder, *Diaries*, 564 ff. (26, 27 Aug. 1940). Tippelskirch records in his diary entries that the situation was being regarded as extremely critical (BA-MA RH 2/v. 1479); likewise Feyerabend (BA-MA RH 20-2/139). The intention was to provide adequate forces for a landing in England, for the occupation of the 'rest' of France, and for an offensive against the Soviet Union. On the transfer to the east see Halder, *Diaries*, 566 (30 Aug. 1940). Order of the C.-in-C. Army: BA-MA RH 2/v. 522, as well as BA-MA, 18. Armee, 17562/2; Müller-Hillebrand, *Heer*, ii. 150, annexe 18.

[85] BA-MA, 18. Armee, 17562/2; Halder, *Diaries*, 574 ff. (5, 6 Sept. 1940). On 2 Sept. 1940 the C.-in-C. Army asked the chief of the army operations staff to issue instructions for measures to camouflage the transfer; on 6 Sept. 1940 Jodl passed these on to Amt Ausl./Abwehr: *KTB OKW* i. 973, annexe 29; Hillgruber, *Strategie*, 236 ff.

ing Germany's eastern frontier from (but excluding) Slovakia to the Baltic. Its task was to repulse any attack, thereby providing the prerequisite for German offensive operations. The army group was, moreover, to continue strengthening ground fortifications, although such work would have to yield priority to road- and bridge-building and to the development of the communications network. In addition, the army group was to make sure that the arrival of the forces now placed under its command—by then no fewer that 35 divisions[86]— or any other measures did not suggest an offensive threat to the Soviet Union. On 20 September Army Group B HQ took over command from Eighteenth Army HQ, which until then had been responsible for 'security against the east'. Fourth and Twelfth Army HQs assumed their new tasks on 23 September 1940. The main effort of Army Group B during the autumn months was focused on reorganization and training, as well as on the speediest possible construction of overland communications and provision of troop accommodation and catering.

(d) The Operational Studies by Marcks and Loßberg

Hitler's decision of 31 July to crush Russia was formulated, in operational terms, as a directive to bring down that state in a *single* blow; conquest of territory was not enough, and remaining stationary in the winter was dangerous.[87] In line with his remarks of 21 July[88] he depicted the outlines of the planned operations as follows: 'First thrust: Kiev and securing flank protection on Dnieper. Air force will destroy river crossings Odessa. Second thrust: Baltic States and drive on Moscow. Finally: Link-up of northern and southern prongs. Thereafter: Limited drive on Baku oilfields.'

These, then, were the main elements of the plans to be worked out by the Army General Staff—the swiftest possible seizure of the bulk of the Red Army and a limitation of the period of operations to the summer and autumn of 1941. The two main operational directions ranked equal.

The chief of the Army General Staff, as mentioned above, had issued his first instructions on the conduct of operations and on organization as early as 22 July. On 23 July Major-General Marcks, the Eighteenth Army chief of staff, was given advance notice to hold himself ready for a briefing by Halder at Army High Command headquarters in Fontainebleau.

Major-General Marcks's study gained fundamental importance for the further planning in the Army General Staff, and therefore, despite having been repeatedly published, deserves somewhat more extensive discussion here. Another study, providing some insight into the ideas of the Wehrmacht High Command leadership, though not necessarily those of Hitler, was prepared by Lieutenant-Colonel (General Staff) von Loßberg. This will be discussed here only to the extent that it diverges from Halder's and Marcks's basic views.

---

[86] See *KTB OKW* i. 65 (5 Sept. 1940), and Diagram I.IV.2.
[87] Halder, *Diaries*, 533–4 (31 July 1940); see above, n. 75.   [88] Ibid. 514 (22 July 1940).

DIAGRAM I.iv.2. Order of Battle of Army Group B, End of September 1940

Army Group B XIX Army Corps (mot.) = 'Group Guderian' (Berlin)	Eighteenth Army HQ (Königsberg [=Kaliningrad])	XXVI Army Corps	291st. Inf. Div. 217th Inf. Div. 161st Inf. Div.
		XVI Army Corps (mot.)	1st Armd. Div. 6th Armd. Div.
		I Army Corps	1st Inf. Div. 21st Inf. Div. 32nd Inf. Div.
	Fourth Army HQ (Warsaw)	XXX Army Corps	76th Inf. Div. 258th Inf. Div.
		Higher Cmd. XXXV	162nd Inf. Div. 292nd Inf. Div.
		XXXXIV Army Corps	268th Inf. Div. 1st Cav. Div. 252nd Inf. Div.
		XII Army Corps	23rd Inf. Div. 31st Inf. Div. 50th Inf. Div.
	Twelfth Army HQ (Cracow)	III Army Corps	62nd Inf. Div. 75th Inf. Div.
		XVII Army Corps	298th Inf. Div. 297th Inf. Div. 168th Inf. Div.
		Higher Cmd. XXXIV	68th Inf. Div. 257th Inf. Div.
		IX Army Corps	56th Inf. Div. 299th Inf. Div. 262nd Inf. Div.
		XIV Army Corps (mot.)	5th Armd. Div. 2nd Mot. Div.
		XXXX Army Corps (mot.)	13th Mot. Div. 2nd Armd. Div. 9th Armd. Div.

Source: OKH/GenStdH, Schematische Kriegsgliederungen [order of battle diagrams], BA-MA.

Marcks arrived in Fontainebleau on 29 July and was at once briefed by Halder on the now more comprehensive tasks ahead. In agreement with the head of the general staff's operations department, Marcks initially regarded the creation of a point of main effort on the southern sector of the front—the operational group Kiev—as the most obvious solution. Halder, on the other hand, believed that the basis indispensable for that plan, Romania, was politically rather uncertain, and that the existence of the river barriers of Dnestr and Dnieper argued in favour of a shift of the point of main effort of the attack. His decisive argument, however, was his belief that the capture of Moscow would mean the end of the campaign and that, in consequence, the shortest approach to Moscow should be chosen.[89] In accordance with Halder's preliminary considerations, as well as with Hitler's directives of 31 July, Marcks therefore prepared a draft for the conduct of operations with the main effort concentrated on the central sector, the principal objective being the capture of Moscow by way of the 'land-bridge' of Smolensk. After two more reports to Halder on 5 and 6 August, Marcks submitted his 'Operations Outline East'.[90] What data were available to him at the time can no longer be established. But he certainly had access to the estimate of the enemy position by the Department for Foreign Armies East and presumably also to the draft study on the Soviet Union by the Military Geography Department of the Army General Staff.[91] He also used an excerpt from Tukhachevsky's book *Advance over the Vistula*.[92] This described the terrain where the main effort of the German operation was to be made. Tukhachevsky had come to the conclusion that the terrain south of the lower Berezina was totally unsuitable for operations by major formations. The most favourable terrain for military movements, he had argued—with regard to both road and rail communications—was north of that region, between Lepel and Dvina.

All operational ideas, both of Halder and Hitler, proceeded from the belief that the eastern army had to be deployed in two groups, south and north of the Pripet marshes. In view of the importance of terrain conditions, which would favour the enemy, it is worth recording briefly how these factors were being assessed by the Army General Staff.

The Military Geography Department had been working since July 1940 on consultative documents for the operations department and for equipping the troops with maps.[93] The 'First draft of a military-geographical study of Euro-

[89] Ibid. 535–6 (1 Aug. 1940).

[90] Ibid. 540–1 (5, 6 Aug. 1940). A contribution also came from Lt.-Col. Feyerabend, until then Ia of XXXX Army Corps, who asked how the troops were to be prepared for the operation in terms of training and organization: Feyerabend's notes, BA-MA RH 20-2/139.

[91] See 'Operationsentwurf Ost'. Jacobsen, *Marcks*, 88, overlooks his preliminary work since 4 July 1940.

[92] M. Tuchačevskij, *Pochod za Vislu: Lekcii, pročitannye na dopolnitel'nom kurse Voennoj akademii RKKA 7–10 fevralja 1923 g.* [The March beyond the Vistula: Lectures Given at the Adranced Training Course of the Red Army Military Academy, 7–10 Feb. 1923] republished in Tuchačevskij, *Izbrannye proizvedenija*, vol. i, here p. 115.

[93] For Halder's instruction to the Mil. Geo. Dept. see *Diaries*, 519 (24 July 1940). GenStdH/Abt. für Kriegskarten und Vermessungswesen [Dept. for war maps and geodesy] (IV. Mil. Geo.): Erster Entwurf zu einer militärgeographischen Studie über das Europäische Rußland [First draft of a military geographical study of European Russia], No. 10a, just like the assessment of the Red Army, probably goes back to Köstring. But see also Hillgruber, *Strategie*, 228 n. 93. Ritter von Niedermayer's article 'Sowjetrußland: Ein wehrpolitisches Bild' conforms with Köstring. The basic elements of the findings are contained in the *Wehrgeographischer Atlas der UdSSR* [Military geographical atlas of the USSR], edited by Niedermayer in 1941.

pean Russia' was completed by 10 August and was available in printed form. What should be emphasized, however, is not so much the speedy and extensive geographical description and assessment of the terrain as the very unusual form of a military evaluation under point 10a, probably included at the last moment. This stated: 'Centres to be considered as especially rewarding for occupation are the Ukraine, Moscow, and Leningrad.' The Ukraine, it continued, was the most valuable part of the Soviet Union because of its industrial and agricultural wealth. The Caucasus with its oil wells was probably too far removed from the German sphere of power. But even if all these territories were conquered the war would not necessarily be concluded, as beyond the Urals and the Caspian Sea there was the vast Asian Russia, which was no longer a wilderness. It had 40 million inhabitants, agricultural and industrial resources, and, in its western part, rail links to the Urals and Orenburg. The 'chief enemies in any attack' were space and climate; the utmost importance attached to the colossal extent of the territory.

This and the succeeding study of the Military Geography Department were based on the latest available data, along with older reports, maps, and other material. It was not possible, however, to obtain accurate information on road conditions or other transport facilities beyond what was to be found in the literature.

It was believed that the principal obstacle on what would be the central sector of a future eastern front was the Polesye region, the Pripet or Rokytno marshes.[94] This was regarded as not negotiable by major military formations, a belief based also on Soviet and Polish judgements. The account of the 1918–20 war between the Soviet Union and Poland, published by the Army General Staff (War History Department) in 1940, relied largely on reports from those countries and represented the experience of a war of movement in that terrain.

The few days available ruled out any more detailed examination of the question of mobility in that territory. Nevertheless, Hitler and—on his instructions—the Army General Staff continued to concern themselves with that problem.[95] Other natural barriers, such as the tributaries of the Dnieper and the Dvina running north to south, or these rivers themselves, were expected to be lines of major enemy opposition. A general assessment of the soil structure and vegetation of the area to be covered was put in hand, as from the outset adequate road and rail networks were not expected. The infantry in particular would have to resort to improvised methods of advance. The route most favourable to Moscow in terms of terrain and transport, indeed the only one promising success to armoured forces, was by way of the 'Smolensk gap', the land-bridge Minsk–Orsha–Smolensk. Geographical constraints governing the opening of operations as well as the structure of the attacking forces obviously

[94] Philippi, *Das Pripjetproblem*, 19 ff.; Furlani, 'Pripjet-Problem und Barbarossa-Planung', 286 ff. The author overlooks both the data of the Mil. Geo. Dept. and the extract from Tuchačevskij used by Marcks.

[95] See sect. I.iv.7(*f*) at n. 152.

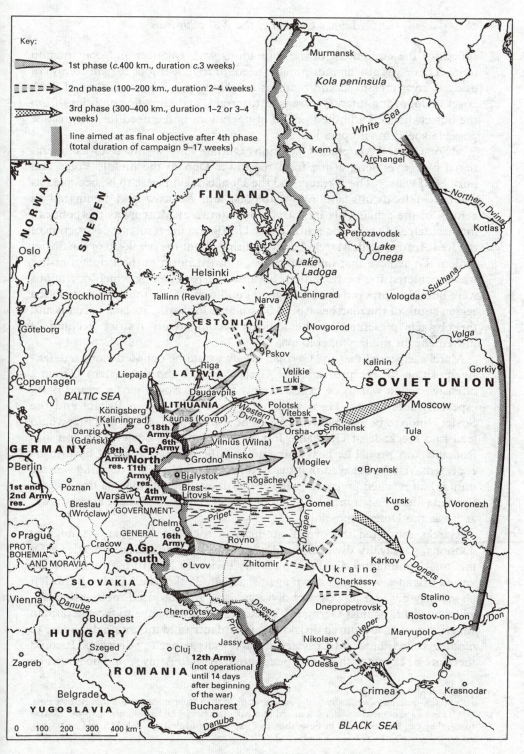

1st phase (c.400 km., duration c.3 weeks)

2nd phase (100–200 km., duration 2–4 weeks)

3rd phase (300–400 km., duration 1–2 or 3–4 weeks)

line aimed at as final objective after 4th phase (total duration of campaign 9–17 weeks)

Murmansk

Kola peninsula

White Sea

Kem

Archangel

Northern Dvina

Kotlas

NORWAY

SWEDEN

FINLAND

Oslo

Petrozavodsk

Lake Onega

Vologda

Sukhana

Helsinki

Stockholm

Tallinn (Reval)

Narva

Leningrad

Novgorod

Volga

Göteborg

ESTONIA

Pskov

Kalinin

Gorkiy

Copenhagen

BALTIC SEA

Liepaja

Riga

LATVIA

Daugavpils

Velikie Luki

SOVIET UNION

Königsberg (Kaliningrad)

LITHUANIA

Kaunas (Kovno)

Western Dvina

Polotsk

Vitebsk

Moscow

Danzig (Gdańsk)

18th Army

Vilnius (Wilna)

Orsha

Smolensk

Tula

GERMANY

9th Army res.

A.Gp. North

6th Army

Grodno

Minsk

Mogilev

Bryansk

Berlin

11th Army res.

Bialystok

Rogachev

Kursk

Voronezh

Poznan

Warsaw

4th Army

Brest-Litovsk

Gomel

Breslau (Wrócław)

GOVERNMENT

Pripet

Dnieper

Prague

Chelm

GENERAL

16th Army

Rovno

Kiev

Karkov

Don

Donets

PROT. BOHEMIA AND MORAVIA

Cracow

A.Gp. South

Lvov

Zhitomir

Ukraine

Stalino

Rostov-on-Don

Vienna

SLOVAKIA

Danube

Chernóvtsy

Dnestr

Cherkassy

Dnepropetrovsk

Maryupol

Don

Budapest

Prut

Jassy

Nikolaev

Dnieper

HUNGARY

Szeged

Cluj

12th Army (not operational until 14 days after beginning of the war)

Odessa

Zagreb

ROMANIA

Bucharest

Crimea

Krasnodar

Belgrade

YUGOSLAVIA

0 100 200 300 400 km

Danube

BLACK SEA

MAP I.IV.2. Operations Draft East (Major-General Marcks), 5 August 1940

called for the equipment of the formations with engineer and construction units. There was also an indisputable need for mobile troops to gain control of bridges, river crossings, and roads as quickly as possible, regardless of flank cover or following infantry. Transport, terrain, and climatic conditions from the outset dictated a limited period of operations and a need for the greatest possible speed in all operations.

Major-General Marcks's 'Operations Outline East' assumed a final operational objective along a line from the lower Don to the middle Volga and northern Dvina.[96] The Ukraine and the Donets region were to be occupied as sources of foodstuffs and raw materials, and Moscow and Leningrad as centres of the armaments industry. The capture of Moscow as the political, intellectual, and economic centre of the USSR and the resultant destruction of the Red Army would, Marcks believed, bring about the break-up of the Soviet Union. To achieve that main objective, a thrust north of the Pripet marshes was considered the best solution, because the roads along which operations were bound to proceed were in a good condition. While the sparsely wooded region south of the marshes would be suitable for battle, its lack of roads and the obstacle presented by the Dnieper would greatly restrict freedom of movement for military operations.

Marcks expected that the German attack would be opposed along a defensive position for the protection of Greater Russia and the eastern Ukraine; offensive action was to be expected only from the Soviet air force and navy, especially submarines. He considered a coalition between Britain and the Soviet Union to be a certainty in the event of a German attack, and that would lead to a blockade of Germany. For its completion, a Soviet incursion into Romania was probable; heavy air raids on the oil region would have to be expected. Marcks believed that the Red Army would opt for delaying warfare until it had reached prepared defensive positions roughly along a line Dvina–Berezina–deep Pripet marshes–Prut or Dnestr. He even thought a withdrawal as far as the Dnieper possible.

Marcks estimated the overall strength of the Red Army at 151 infantry divisions, 32 cavalry divisions, and 38 motorized-mechanized brigades.[97] Of this total, 55 infantry divisions, 9 cavalry divisions, and 10 motorized-mechanized brigades were tied down against Japan, Turkey, and Finland; this left 96 infantry divisions, 23 cavalry divisions, and 28 motorized-mechanized brigades available against Germany. These forces would have to face a German superiority of 24 armoured divisions,[98] 110 infantry and mountain divisions, 12 motorized divisions, and 1 cavalry division—altogether 147 divisions. It could therefore be expected that, once penetrated, the Red Army would no longer be

---

[96] See above, n. 91.

[97] Marcks referred specifically to the assumptions of the Department for Foreign Armies East.

[98] These 24 armoured divisions come from a calculation by Halder: *Diaries*, 429–30 (28 May 1940); they can be found also in Feyerabend's diary notes of July 1940, BA-MA RH 20-2/139.

able to rally its forces, spread out as these would be over a long front, for concerted counteractions and, after some fighting, would soon succumb to the superiority of the German troops and their officers. The Red Army's air force, on the other hand, was regarded by Marcks as an opponent to be taken seriously; its defeat would take some time. The Soviet navy, with its superiority of surface units and submarines, was probably capable of interfering with ore transports from Sweden and with traffic in the Baltic. It certainly ruled out any German landings on Soviet or Finnish territory as well as any regular supply shipments through the Baltic. Only after the capture of the Baltic ports would the Soviet navy find itself in a hopeless position. In that event the only remaining link between Britain and Russia would be through the Arctic Ocean and the White Sea; this route should be threatened at a later stage by Finland's entry into the war.

In agreement with Halder,[99] Marcks intended the main thrust of the German army to be towards Moscow. The guiding idea in this was to defeat and annihilate the bulk of the Soviet northern group to the west of, within, and east of the upper Volga area; once Moscow and northern Russia were in German hands the army would turn south, in order, through co-operation with the German southern group, to conquer the Ukraine and eventually gain the objective of securing the line Rostov–Gorkiy–Archangel. This operation was to be covered on its nothern flank by a force to be deployed across the lower Dvina in the direction of Pskov and Leningrad. Its task would be to seize the Baltic ports and Leningrad. A possible later southward turn, in order to co-operate with the main group, might be considered.

The breakthrough from East Prussia to Moscow was considered difficult, leading as it did across the forest and lakeland belt between Dvina and Dnieper. It was expected that the main battles would be along the six main high roads; these were to be captured by swift action. As the few existing roads had to be reserved for the armoured and heavy formations, Marcks demanded that special preparations be made for the advance of the infantry with regard to organization, equipment, training, and leadership. No doubt Marcks would have liked to assign the main role to the army's southern group in view of the importance of conquering the Ukraine. In his view an attack from Romania, with additional forces from northern Hungary, Galicia, and south-eastern Poland, could become a major offensive capable of deciding the outcome of the war, aiming across the Dnieper at Moscow. Such an attack, as Halder explained on 1 August, was prevented by political conditions in the Balkans, such as the still uncertain participation of Hungary and Romania, as well as by transport conditions in those countries. In consequence, only a massive attack from Galicia and southern Poland was to be launched against Kiev and the middle Dnieper. Having crossed that river, these forces, in close co-operation

---

[99] See sect. I.IV.I(*d*) at n. 103.

with the main operation north of the Pripet marshes, were to advance either on Kharkov or towards the north-east.

As an attack out of Romania could not be dispensed with, an army was to be held ready on Reich territory, to move into Romania across Hungary as soon as the war began and there to undertake the protection of Romania and cover for further deployment. After that, the Romanian army could be expected to mobilize and deploy on the Prut. About two weeks into the war that army could be expected to cross the Prut with the bulk of its forces—i.e. at a time when, according to Marcks's expectations, the army advancing from Galicia would already be engaged near Zhitomir. Both armies were then to advance jointly towards the middle Dnieper.

The most important condition for success, according to Marcks, was surprise and the speed of the offensive movement. To that end, mobile troops in all the armies had to break through the Soviet forces at the first encounter, west of the river and forest positions, in order, with Luftwaffe support, to gain control of the forest zones and the river crossings. The infantry, following close behind, was to cut off and destroy the penetrated enemy forces. Some infantry units were to attach themselves to the mobile forces and extend their gains. Because of the small number of through roads the armoured and motorized formations had to be gathered together extremely tightly, which would result in considerable in-depth echelonment. With the steadily increasing breadth of the area of operations the insertion of massive army reserves would be required, rendering the establishment of new army commands, and probably also a new army group command, necessary in the northern sector. Because of the distance of the chosen objectives, the natural obstacles, and the consolidated defensive positions of the enemy, and also because of the urgent need for a rehabilitation of the units and the enlargement of the entire supply system, Marcks essentially envisaged three phases of the conduct of operations, as follows.

In the first phase the enemy, fighting a delaying action, was to be thrown back to his defensive position. That defensive position was assumed to be on the Dnieper–Dvina line, i.e. some 400 km. from the starting-line. For this operation Marcks allowed approximately three weeks for the bulk of the infantry divisions. If the advance of the armoured divisions succeeded so rapidly that major enemy formations were encircled and the establishment of a coherent defensive front was prevented, the outcome of the campaign could conceivably be decided in this early phase.

The second phase amounted to a struggle for the forest areas and river courses adjacent to the Soviet line of defence. For the penetration of that zone, between 100 and 200 km. deep, Marcks allowed two to four weeks. Here either the decisive breakthrough had to succeed or else the scattered sections of the Red Army would have to be defeated one by one.

The third phase was to result in the capture of Moscow and Leningrad and in a penetration of the eastern Ukraine. This involved covering 400 and

300 km. respectively. Whether this third phase could be directly linked up to the second would depend on the extension of railway tracks and on the state of the army's motor-vehicles. Another crucial factor was whether the defeated Red Army would need only to be pursued or whether it would still be offering resistance with battle-worthy units. In the latter event replenishment of tanks and motor-vehicles would, according to Marcks, require a period of three to six weeks.

Eventually, a fourth phase was to see the pursuit to the Don, the middle Volga, and the northern Dvina. Marcks assumed that following the capture of Kharkov, Moscow, and Leningrad there would be no cohesive Soviet armed forces left in existence. Total occupation of the territory up to the Rostov–Gorkiy–Archangel line, he argued, was neither possible nor necessary. This final phase could be accomplished by mobile troops and infantry divisions in a 'railway advance' within three or four weeks.[100] Marcks calculated that the overall time required for the campaign was between nine and seventeen weeks. In the event that the Soviet government did not fall or sue for peace by then, a pursuit all the way to the Urals might become necessary. Even though Russia, with her forces crushed and her most valuable European territories lost, would no longer be capable of active military operations, she might yet, from an Asian base, remain in an indefinite state of war.

Marcks thus took up the idea of point 10a of the 'First draft' of the Military Geography Department, but without drawing any conclusions from it at this time.[101] Halder did not accept this formulation of Marcks's; he clearly believed that it must be possible so to prepare the army that a decision would be forcibly brought about at Moscow.

Marcks's study had benefited from the fact that its author had intensively concerned himself, ever since Halder's first reflections of 4 July on an offensively handled defence, with questions of the conduct of operations against the Soviet Union. He was guided by Halder's directives and by consideration of the time available for mobile warfare.

Examination of the organizational, training, and equipment aspects demanded by Marcks was in the hands of Lieutenant-Colonel (General Staff) Feyerabend, who, ever since mid-July, had studied questions of the army's order of battle for deployment in the east.[102] In an appendix of his own to the Operations Outline East he demonstrated the connections between these problems and the tactical employment of the troops. Proceeding from the geographical conditions and the transport networks of the individual areas of advance, he called for a renewed examination of experience from the Polish campaign. As all effective roads had to be kept for the exclusive use of the

---

[100] The concept of a 'railway advance' was evidently taken over by Marcks from accounts of the advance of the German troops in the Ukraine in 1918.

[101] This realization probably goes back to Köstring, or to the first draft of Mil. Geo. (above, n. 93). Marcks returns to it: see sect. I.IV.1(*d*) at n. 90.

[102] Feyerabend's diary notes, BA-MA RH 20-2/139.

mobile units, foot troops were to be directed to secondary tracks and open country. Structure and equipment of those units therefore had to be in accordance with that need. Feyerabend's conclusions provided the basis for the directives for the build-up of the army in the east.

Major-General Marcks's operations proposal, formulated within a few days, closely followed the instructions given him by the chief of the Army General Staff. These did not include either observations on the overall war situation or an examination of political developments that might lead to the opening of hostilities in the east.

Marcks had been working most energetically on the execution of his task since 4 July, and had evidently asked himself a number of questions which he could not or did not wish to put to Halder. Having submitted his study, he clearly realized which way the war would develop; he therefore summed up his reflections in a kind of balance sheet. These culminated in the question whether the presumed attitude of a future enemy coalition could be said to have a probability bordering on certainty.

Approximately four weeks after submitting his Operations Outline he sent a memorandum to Lieutenant-General von Tippelskirch, senior quartermaster IV, which attempted to predict the conduct of the war and of operations by an enemy coalition, or just by the Soviet Union, as a reaction to a German attack.[103] This 'Evaluation of Situation Red', dated 10 September 1940, went to an officer who was a close personal friend; Marcks was presumably hoping that he would either give him a reliable answer or else pass his paper on to the chief of the Army General Staff.

Marcks assumed that the intended short campaign against the Soviet Union would instantly give rise to an enemy coalition, in due course to be joined by the United States, which was in any case already involved economically. Turkey would follow suit, thus realizing an 'old English war plan', a blockade designed to exhaust German–Italian military resources. That was a precondition for going over to the offensive. In its initial phase the strategy demanded total strangulation by sea; this, in Marcks's view, was guaranteed. Just as in his Operations Outline, Marcks proceeded from the assumption that, during the first phase of the war, the 'Red side' could rely on German transports across the Baltic being paralysed by Russian and British forces; in consequence, the need for the Russians to attack Sweden with a view to cutting off Swedish ore supplies to Germany would be eliminated. An Allied attack on Romania might be a possibility, provided it could be fitted into the framework of the Red Army's overall operations. Marcks expected air raids on the western half of Germany—the British, he believed, would be capable of such attacks in the winter of 1941–2—and these would be supplemented by Soviet air attacks on the eastern part of the Reich. The enemy coalition would probably assume

---

[103] Letter from Marcks to Tippelskirch, 10 Sept. 1940; see Tippelskirch's reply, 3 Oct. 1940, as well as a letter from Lt.-Col. Kinzel (head of the Department for Foreign Armies East), 3 Oct. 1940, BA-MA, 18. Armee, 17562/9.

that a German invasion of Britain had been postponed and that the Soviet Union would be attacked first. The Soviet Union would have to bear that attack until such time as a general offensive could be launched simultaneously by the Red Army in the east and by a broadly planned landing of British–American troops in the west. In the event of a speedy exhaustion of the German forces in the east, such an offensive was possible in the course of 1941, but it was more probable in 1942. The task of the Red Army, therefore, would be to stand up to the German attack while preparing its own offensive. For that the armaments centres around Leningrad and Moscow, control of the naval bases in the Baltic, and holding on to the raw-material bases in the Ukraine were the prerequisites.

The crucial question in Marcks's operational reflections was how the Red Army command could ensure the protection of these vital regions while simultaneously pulling out major forces for the encirclement and annihilation of the German army. In order to achieve this, the Red Army would have to use its mobile units, taking advantage of the difficult terrain in the sector of the main German attack against Moscow, to fight a delaying action. If the Red Army were to engage only in rearguard action, the German armies would advance too fast. If it engaged major forces well forward, it would be running the risk of premature defeat. The German attack would have to be finally halted at a prepared position, such as along the general line Riga–Polotsk–Berezina–Pripet–Dnieper down to its estuary, to ensure that the bases for a counter-offensive were defended and the bulk of Soviet forces preserved. In the event of a further retreat the Red Army would risk being torn asunder. It was incapable of set battles by separate groups and would have to be pulled back to the Volga. In that case it would become dependent on the industrial centres in Siberia and the Urals, as well as on American supplies. These could be cut off by Japan, though Marcks did not expect Japan to enter the war on the German side. Crucial for the German conduct of the war, in Marcks's opinion, was the conquest of the Ukraine and control over communications in the Baltic. After that, there was no need to fear a blockade; the principal prerequisite of victory for the 'Red coalition' would have disappeared.

By emphasizing the importance of control over Baltic maritime communications and over the Ukraine, Marcks reverted to his first operational reflections, which, in his Outline, had been reduced to the assertion that an attack from Romania was 'necessary in any case'.

In assessing the likely response of the enemy, Marcks assumed that the Soviet military command would probably act systematically; he thought that the construction of several defensive zones by the Red Army was conceivable. This revealed the risks of a German attack much more clearly than the operational study did, since the entire German timetable, including the pauses for rehabilitation and replacement, might be called into question.

Marcks assumed that the massive concentrations in the west of the Soviet Union were not preparations for an attack but were designed to secure the newly acquired territories. The Red Army, he thought, would act defensively 'because that is in line with the situation and also with its character'. He expected that it would defend itself along the line envisaged by him. Delaying resistance, combined with counter-thrusts costly for the attacker, might then enable the Red Army to prepare for the 'second act'. The German armies would then be in danger of being pinned down for the winter at the last Soviet line without having fought the decisive battle. Marcks therefore concluded that the greater the element of surprise in the outbreak of war, the greater the chance of defeating major forces near the frontier. This to him was an indispensable condition of the success of the campaign, and hence of a decisive victory before the 'Red coalition' would come into effect. He therefore concluded: 'Any serious operation by major Russian forces west of the large forest zone and the large rivers can only be welcome to us', emphasizing once more that such a form of engagement would be a positive 'good turn'.

The answers which Marcks received from Lieutenant-General von Tippelskirch, the senior quartermaster IV, and from Lieutenant-Colonel Kinzel, head of the Department for Foreign Armies East, certainly did not do full justice to his arguments. Tippelskirch rejected the idea of a British–American landing on the European continent; instead he expected an offensive in North Africa for the gradual conquest of Libya. Its objective, after the expulsion of the Italians, would be the creation of air-bases for the struggle against Italy. However, the consequences of such an operation, though undoubtedly unpleasant for the conduct of the war by the Axis, would not include the tying down of German forces to an extent that would substantially improve the Soviet Union's prospects of launching an attack or even of mounting a defence. Japan, Tippelskirch believed, would enter the war. Generally he thought that 'a war between Germany and Russia [would] not be triggered off by the *Russian* side during the next year'.

Tippelskirch's letter with its superficial theses offered no answer to Marcks's central question of what would happen if the war were protracted by the 'Red coalition'. Lieutenant-Colonel Kinzel proceeded from the belief that the fortified defensive line assumed by Marcks was unsuitable for the Soviet defence; while the industrial areas around Leningrad and Moscow were admittedly beyond the range of the Luftwaffe, the eastern Ukrainian industrial region, which was important to the Red Army, would be within German range. Kinzel therefore concluded that the bulk of the Red Army would stand and fight west of that line, or else would fall back, in delaying action, across the Dnieper eastward to the Volga, and on to the Urals. But that was a task which the Soviet command would scarcely be able to tackle, among other things with regard to supplies. In reply to Marcks's question concerning what form of combat the Red Army would choose if it accepted battle in western Russia, Kinzel declared with assurance: 'Its regulations and its megalomania demand attack, but its fear of the German army paralyses its resolution.' As for the

Soviet thrust into Romania, also assumed by Marcks, Kinzel thought that that was the least pleasant possibility. If it succeeded, Germany would be reduced to what oil she still had in her containers. But as the Russians would not themselves start a war, that bold decision could be discounted.

Running like a red thread through Marcks's questions about the strategic and operational response of the enemy, and equally through the highly unsatisfactory answers he received, was the concern that the campaign might take longer than envisaged and might expand into a world war. Alongside the lessons learnt on the battlefields of the First World War, which had resulted in a well-thought-out training and re-equipment of the entire Wehrmacht as well as in the operational concept of mechanized, 'lightning-like' co-operation of all service branches, which had brought victory in Poland and in the west, different lessons were also being remembered. These included consideration of geo-strategic conditions and, more especially, the dependence of the war economy and food supplies on the resources of German-dominated western Europe. The economic aspect of that situation has been discussed elsewhere; at this point mention should merely be made of the underlying fear of a blockade. Blockade did not only mean being cut off from overseas imports in wartime; it also meant hunger, continuing for years after the conclusion of a peace treaty. The blockade had not only made the First World War army dependent on substitute materials of all kinds, but it had also brought Germany's ally Austro-Hungary to the verge of collapse in 1917; it had exposed the hereditary lands of the Habsburg crown to political extortion by Hungary, and suggested military intervention in the Ukraine as the only solution in 1918. This, then, was the area with which operational plans—though under totally different conditions both in western Europe and in the Balkans—were now again concerned.

Halder made that point as early as 28 June, when he explained to his assembled general-staff officers the need for a military administration outside the authority of the army on the grounds that all efforts must now be concentrated; it was no longer a case of a blockade of Germany but of a blockade of the whole of Europe. This was said by Halder at a moment when Germany had control of all the wealth of agricultural France, of Denmark and the Netherlands, of the ore deposits of Belgium and—expected soon—the regions of surplus production in Hungary, Romania, and western Poland, not to mention the contractual wheat deliveries from the Soviet Union.

It was this mental hangover from the blockade complex of the First World War, and remembrance of the dependence of an entire national economy on barter trade with sympathetic partners because of a shortage of foreign currency well into the 1920s, that explains the arguments not only of military men but also of Hitler, who would feel blockade-proof and armed against entire continents only after the acquisition of the Ukrainian bread-basket, that reputed El Dorado. Against that belief neither the calculations of agricultural

experts nor the warnings from the embassy in Moscow, nor even the experience of the interventionist army of 1918–19, cut any ice at all.

The question why Tippelskirch did not pass on Marcks's important and far-
sighted study to the chief of the Army General Staff, where it could have
provided the basis for an examination of the problem of space and time within
the overall planning, cannot be readily answered.

The other operational outline to be considered here, the 'study' by Lieutenant-Colonel von Loßberg, was produced over a much longer period of research and under different working conditions. Whereas the chief of the Army
General Staff had at his disposal a fully trained staff of officers, as well as all
the departments of the Army High Command, Loßberg essentially depended
on the people immediately around him and on information from the operations department of the Army General Staff. As there was no such thing as a
joint staff for the direction of the Wehrmacht in war—the name 'Wehrmacht
operations staff' introduced on 8 August 1940 instead of 'Wehrmacht operations department' resulted in no significant change—it may be assumed that
Loßberg's initial work was designed primarily to keep his chief, Artillery
General Jodl, informed and to examine Hitler's intentions as to their military
feasibility.[104] Jodl, as a former general-staff officer, was in an exceedingly
difficult position *vis-à-vis* Halder, who was incomparably better and more
directly informed on the army's problems.[105] As recently as in his memorandum of 30 June Jodl, after the victory over France, had not even considered
a military attack on the Soviet Union as a means of weakening and defeating
Britain.[106] During the exchange of ideas between Hitler and Brauchitsch on 21
July, if not before, Jodl must have learnt that a war in the east was being
considered. He commented on this project in a memorandum explaining that
an attack as early as the late summer of 1940, the date initially suggested by
Hitler, was impossible for military reasons.[107] Hitler abandoned that timetable,
which was presumably based on a misleading reproduction of Brauchitsch's
'report' on 21 July. On 29 July Jodl informed the general-staff officers of his
department that Hitler intended to open the war against the Soviet Union in
May 1941.[108]

---

[104] *KTB OKW* i. 111E ff.; Klink, 'Organization'.   [105] *KTB OKW* i. 185E.

[106] Hillgruber, *Strategie*, 157 ff. It is, however, quite inconceivable that Jodl should not have
followed the (surely much-discussed) developments in the Baltic region and on the Romanian
frontier. Certainly there was no instruction from Jodl to Loßberg to concern himself with 'eastern
questions'. Loßberg began certain preliminary studies 'on (his) own inititative' in July, according
to another version 'about the turn of June–July', including the provision of maps of the Soviet
Union. (See above, n. 76.)

[107] This memorandum has not yet been found. If the assumption made above (sect. I.IV.1(*b*) at
n. 66) about a report by Brauchitsch on Halder's preliminary work is correct, it would not have
taken much convincing to dissuade Hitler from his timetable. That, during the western campaign,
he resolved 'to come to grips with that danger as soon as our military position makes it at all
possible' was confirmed by Jodl on 7 Nov. 1943, though without any indication of a date: Jodl's
note in Jacobsen, *1939–1945*, 315. For publication of the whole report, with notes for the annexes,
see *IMT* xxxvii. 360 ff.; *KTB OKW* iv/1. 1534 ff.

[108] *KTB OKW* i. 3 ff.; Warlimont, *Hauptquartier*, 126–7.

The decisive signal for the start of preliminary work was given to the Wehrmacht operations department by Hitler's conference with the Army commander-in-chief and the chief of the Army General Staff in the presence of Keitel and Jodl on 31 July 1940.[109]

Jodl thereupon instructed the Home Defence Department to compile the material for a draft order and to make preparations both for the transfer of units to the east and for the raising of new units in those areas by issuing guidelines to the high commands of the three Wehrmacht services as well as to the appropriate supreme Reich authorities. It would seem that the point of departure for the strategic reflections in the Wehrmacht operations department was the problem, touched upon by Hitler at his conference on 31 July, of involving Finland and Turkey. Similarly, the settlement of the disputes between Hungary and Romania and the subsequent involvement of Romanian territory called for military-political preparations falling within the responsibility of the Wehrmacht High Command. In order to clarify the operational consequences Jodl issued instructions for the preparation of an appropriate study.

Loßberg's 'Operational Study East' was not completed until 15 September 1940; it was therefore able to include not only Hitler's above-mentioned directives and Jodl's guidelines, but also material supplied by the Army General Staff.[110] For that reason extensive parallels to Marcks's study are inescapable. Here, however, attention will be focused on the points diverging from Marcks.

Loßberg proceeded from the view that the Red Army was already in a state of mobilization and that, in consequence, no substantial increase in the number of its formations was to be expected before the spring of 1941. He also accepted that Soviet forces were tied down against Finland, on the Romanian frontier, in the Caucasus, and in the Far East.[111] As for the Red Army's combat procedure, he assumed three options:

(1) an attack into the incipient German deployment;
(2) acceptance of the German attack in the deployment areas near the forntier, with Soviet positions on the two flanks—the Baltic and the Black Sea—being held;
(3) withdrawal into the depth of Russian territory in order to saddle the attacking German army with the difficulties of extended communications and hence of supplies, with a counterstrike to be launched at a later date.

---

[109] See the previous n.; also Halder, *Diaries*, 530 ff. (31 July 1940).

[110] 'Operationsstudie Ost', published in Besymenski, *Sonderakte 'Barbarossa'* (1968), 307 ff., unfortunately without the appendices; republished in *Fall Barbarossa*, 126 ff.

[111] These 'tied-down' formations, whose appearance at the front in the west of the Soviet Union was ruled out, were considered unavailable in the calculation of German superiority, although there was no firm basis for that assumption in terms of foreign policy. The only doubts on that point were voiced by Marcks in his 'Assessment of Situation Red' (see above, n. 103).

The first option, in Loßberg's opinion, was unlikely because of the inability of the Red Army's command and personnel to mount an attack on a grand scale against, for instance, East Prussia or northern Poland. There might indeed be minor actions against Finland or Romania, but in the case of Finland these would not improve the Soviet position but, on the contrary, in the event of a German attack towards Leningrad would result in a threat to those forces.[112] An attack against the Romanian oilfields, aimed at smashing Germany's supply-base, possibly performed only by Soviet flying formations, would have to be repelled by the German 'instructor' units and by organizing Romania's defence. Thus the future German military mission in Romania became something like an 'advance party' of the German southern flank.[113]

The most probable variant, Loßberg believed, would be that of the Red Army meeting the German attack in the western areas of the Soviet Union because it could not surrender the most valuable parts of its territory without a fight. For the same reasons as those stated by Marcks, he would welcome the Red Army's decision to stand and fight in strength at an early stage.

The most unfavourable variant, in his opinion, would be that of the Red Army meeting a German attack with only minor units while the bulk of its forces were setting up defensive positions along the great river barriers of the Dvina and Dnieper. Major-General Marcks had described this very situation as the prime objective to be aimed at by the Soviet military leadership; conquest of this defensive zone represented the second move of his proposal for the conduct of operations.

For the German strategic effort Loßberg likewise distinguished two operational areas, separated from one another by the Pripet marshes. In favour of a main effort in the north—just as in Marcks's study—were better communications and the German interest in gaining swift control of the Baltic region as well as in a possible co-operation with XXI Group to be launched across Finland, and finally the chance of reaching Leningrad and Moscow.[114]

In favour of a main effort in the south were the threat to Romania, easier supplies from the Romanian oilfields, and finally the importance of the Ukraine. Unlike Marcks, Loßberg from the outset proposed the establishment of two army group commands to conduct the envisaged main effort in the north. The principal direction of attack was to be with the more southerly army group, whose task it would be to encircle the Soviet forces in the Minsk area and then to thrust on in the general direction of Moscow. Here strong motorized formations would have to employed, based on the Minsk–Moscow highway. The more northerly army group was to attack from East Prussia

[112] The assumption of a possible new Soviet attack on Finland, i.e. primarily against the coastal area in the south and against Åland, was bound to result in priority being given to the securing of the Baltic ports for German purposes.

[113] See sect. I.v.3 (Förster).

[114] 'XXI Group' was transformed into Army Command Norway; the German formations employed in Finland later became Twentieth (Monntain) Army.

against and across the lower Dvina. According to how the situation developed, the group engaged in the main effort was to be temporarily wheeled towards the north in order to cut off the Red Army formations facing the German northern flank. Loßberg's proposal of an attack with partial forces from northern Norway towards Murmansk is likely to have been related to soundings in Finland, initiated at Hitler's command in August. The bulk of the German and Finnish formations was to be deployed in southern Finland: initially they were to tie down the Russian forces and subsequently, as soon as Army Group North approached Leningrad, thrust forward to meet it.

The operation south of the Pripet marshes was to be conducted, according to Loßberg's draft, with about two-thirds of the army's total strength, with the objective of enveloping the enemy forces between the marshes and the Black Sea from both sides and annihilating them. The main effort of that operation, according to him, would be the thrust of a major force from southern Poland, in an east-south-easterly direction, covered by a strong left flank. In the course of the operation this was to close up against the Pripet marshes and later against the Dnieper. Another force, to be brought up at the start of the operation, was to strike northwards from the area north of the Danube estuary—covered by the Romanians, now to be regarded as allies, and by the German forces in Romania—and thus to cut off the eastward retreat of any Soviet forces fighting south of the Pripet marshes.[115]

The two groups of the eastern army were then to co-operate east of the Pripet marshes to attack the final military objective, only then to be defined. The choice of that objective would depend on whether the Soviet Union was still capable of action once it had lost its western territories and its link to the Baltic Sea. As a very distant objective Loßberg named the general line from Archangel via Gorkiy and the Volga to the Don. An advantage for the German conduct of operations, Loßberg believed, would be the difficulties which the Soviet government would presumably encounter in the Ukraine; these should be manipulated by agents of the foreign-intelligence department. As for the Soviet air force, he did not, in spite of its numerical strength, credit it with the ability to mount a centrally controlled major operation.

Loßberg, much like Marcks, saw the task of the Luftwaffe as supporting German ground operations at their points of main effort, disrupting the railway network, and securing key points by the employment of paratroops and air-landed units. In his assessment of the operational opportunities of the navy Loßberg, again much like Marcks, proceeded from an assumption of Soviet naval superiority; the prime tasks therefore were securing the German coastal forefield and blocking the exits from the Baltic against attempted break-outs by enemy naval units. Not until Soviet naval bases, including

---

[115] Such a thrust from Romania was in line with Marcks's original intentions, which, however, he did not pursue after Halder's directive of 1 Aug. 1940.

Leningrad, had been eliminated by the army's operations could secure maritime communications between the Baltic region and Finland be expected;
only then could supplies for the northern wing of the army be brought in by
sea.[116]

After the bringing-up of the formations of Army Group B (35 divisions) by
the end of October Loßberg did not believe that any further reinforcement of
the army in the east was necessary; otherwise the Soviet Union might feel
threatened and might take appropriate countermeasures.

The main outlines given here of the drafts for the operational planning of
the Army General Staff and the Wehrmacht operations department character-
ize the assumptions on which the two staffs based the preparation of the final
operational plan and the deployment directive. Both Marcks and Loßberg
regarded the Soviet adversary as neither ready nor willing to attack Germany.
His principal advantage was the vastness of the territory and the large number
of formations that could be fielded. This advantage, however, seemed offset by
the assumed inability of the Red Army command to withdraw major formations from rapid seizure by the swiftly advancing German spearheads of attack.
It was assumed, therefore, that it would be possible to smash the bulk of the
Red Army as soon as the Dnieper–Dvina line was reached, or overcome, and
that a decision could be brought about even in this initial phase of the
campaign. If that was not achieved, a pause would have to be called in
operations in order to rehabilitate the army and reorganize it in accordance
with new main efforts of attack. Both drafts assigned the main effort to the
army group advancing on Moscow north of the Pripet marshes; the reasons
were predominantly those of transport geography, i.e. operational reasons,
even though political considerations probably played a part. The assumed
clear superiority of the German forces led both authors to assign additional
tasks to the army group engaged in the main effort. Loßberg believed a
northward wheeling of some formations of that group to be possible and
necessary, while Marcks called for a southward wheeling in support of the
neighbouring army group. This idea was to affect both the further planning of
operations and the course of operations themselves.[117]

---

[116] It is not clear whether Loßberg had approached the navy for an opinion on these questions;
this would emerge from the (so far still missing) appendices.

[117] In yet another operations study by Inf. Gen. Georg von Sodenstern, the chief of staff of
Army Group A (renamed Army Group South on 1 Apr. 1941), the idea of full concentration of
forces on the principal objective, Moscow, is developed in exemplary form. However, it is
uncertain to what extent this study, dated 7 Dec. 1940, influenced decisions within OKH.
Proceeding from the vastness of the territory and the extent of the front line, as well as from the
enemy's presumed line of resistance along the river courses, he described a large encirclement by
the inner flanks of the army groups north and south of the Pripet region as the only chance of
reaching the principal objective of Moscow within the time available. The two army groups,
'South' and 'North', were to be covered against diversionary attacks from the Pripet marshes by
a weaker army group to be deployed against the marshes. This central army group would also
drive the strong enemy forces—assumed by Sodenstern to be located there—into the developing
pincers of the two neighbouring army groups. The outer flanks of Army Groups North and South
would only need securing. The objective of the operation was neither the Baltic Sea as far as

(e) Planning by the Army General Staff and Directive No. 21

On 3 September 1940 Lieutenant-General Friedrich Paulus, newly appointed Oberquartiermeister I (senior quartermaster I), assumed the co-ordination of all preparatory planning work of the Army General Staff.[118] Basing himself on the preliminary studies by Marcks and Feyerabend, as well as on the more detailed directives of Halder, he concentrated on the operational starting-situation and on the army's order of battle. In all his personnel calculations he still had to take into account the retention of strong formations and headquarter staffs for the attack against Britain. On 29 October Paulus reported to Halder.[119]

Italy's attack on Greece on 28 October 1940, however, turning the spotlight once more on the Balkans, rapidly changed the political and military starting-position for planning the attack on the Soviet Union. On 4 November Hitler decided to abandon his plan of dispatching an armoured formation to Libya and instead to consider a thrust across Bulgaria to the Aegean Sea.[120] This was to prevent the British from establishing air-bases in Greece for raids on the Romanian oilfields, and generally to thwart the creation of an anti-German front in the Balkan region, including Turkey. At the same time, preparations for the capture of Gibraltar, the occupation of the Cape Verde and Canary Islands, and the invasion of Britain were to be speeded up. The struggle against Britain clearly enjoyed priority, and Directive No. 18 of 12 November, which incorporated all the above ideas, seemed to assign no more than subordinate significance to planning for the eastern campaign.[121] Moreover, a decision was to be made only after the submission of the army's plans.[122]

During the first few days of December Paulus staged a map exercise which, proceeding from Hitler's strategic objectives and from Halder's operational

Leningrad, nor the Black Sea. In view of the subsequent difficulties suffered at the hands of an enemy in the Pripet area by Army Group South, whose chief of staff Sodenstern was, it is significant that Sodenstern did not insist on this initial plan. See 'Sodenstern-Studie', reproduced in abridged form in Philippi, *Das Pripjetproblem*, 13 ff. This study is not identical with the preliminary work of Army Group A (later South) command, as reflected in 'Map exercise Otto' (BA-MA RH 19 I/70). A remark by Sodenstern of Jan. (*recte* 5 Feb.) 1941, reported by the future Inf. Gen. Walter Buhle, that the outcome of the map exercise showed the war to be lost, is not compatible with the impression actually gained from the exercise and must therefore be doubted. On this see Uhlig, 'Das Einwirken Hitlers', 210, and, more especially, Hillgruber, 'Rußland-Bild', 308.

[118] Halder, *Diaries*, 540–1 (6 Aug. 1940); Philippi and Heim, *Feldzug*, 30 ff.; Paulus, '*Ich stehe hier auf Befehl!*', 40 ff.

[119] Halder, *Diaries*, 642. Paulus's memorandum has not so far been found.

[120] Halder, *Diaries*, 673–4 (4 Nov. 1940).

[121] That 'programme' was so far-reaching that Halder began to doubt whether planning for the war in the east still played the decisive part. He intended to confront Hitler with all his projects and call for a clear decision: Halder, *Diaries*, 673–4 (4 Nov. 1940); see also above, n. 83. On Directive No. 18 see *Hitler's Directives*, 39 ff.

[122] On Molotov's simultaneous visit see Halder, *Diaries*, 689 ff. (14–16 Nov. 1940), 719 (3 Dec. 1940); *KTB OKW* i. 174; Hillgruber, *Strategie*, 300–1 (which also gives a list of the extensive literature'. Tippelskirch, diary entries for 11, 14, 16 Nov. 1940, based on briefing by Etzdorf, BA-MA RH 2/v. 1479; *DGFP* D x, Nos. 325, 326, 328, 329.

directives, was designed to yield information on the German strength that would be required, on the most favourable conduct of operations and on the presumed reaction of the enemy. In the presence of the departmental heads in the Army General Staff and a few other officers, as well as the Luftwaffe general attached to the commander-in-chief of the army, the appropriateness of the preparations made so far was examined on 2, 3, and 7 December.[123] The results of the first two sections of the exercise—the conduct of operations up to the achievement of the first objectives along the Kiev–Minsk line—were included immediately in the version of the plan presented by Halder to Hitler. This applied, in one instance, to the launch of Army Group South from Romania and southern Poland, where the map exercise had shown that, because of the difficulties of deployment in Romania, the forces available, and command problems, the main effort had to be clearly assigned to the group advancing from Poland. In another it emerged that, in order to destroy the bulk of the enemy forces in the central sector, strong infantry forces would have to be added to the armoured groups for the great battle of encirclement envisaged in the Minsk area, to ensure that the envelopment was rapidly completed by the infantry, with the armoured forces being freed for the further advance. For Army Group North it emerged that its task of occupying the Baltic States would result in a lagging-behind of its right wing and hence in a threat to the flank of Army Group Centre. Generally the most important finding of the exercise was that a swift decision of the campaign by the encirclement and capture of Moscow could be achieved only if Army Groups South and North both saw their main task as providing flank cover for the rapidly advancing Army Group Centre. After the achievement of the first objective, a line along the middle Dnieper south of Kiev, thence Rogachev–Orsha–Vitebsk–Velikie Luki–Pskov–Pjarnu (a line regarded as the base for the decisive attack on Moscow), a pause of about three weeks would have to be called for developing supply-lines (rail and road), and for rehabilitation and resupply. After that, on the fortieth day from the start of the war in the east the offensive was to be resumed.

The assumption was that the Red Army, having by then suffered great losses, would not stand and fight the decisive battle on that line, but would wish to exploit the space around Moscow to gain time for reinforcement. For that reason Army Group Centre would have to resume its offensive as soon as possible, even if the other two army groups were unable to go into action at the same time.

For the resumption of its operations Army Group South demanded the temporary provision of armoured forces on its northern wing to enable it to strike from the area south of Kiev and south of Gomel across the Dnieper and

---

[123] Halder had himself briefed by Paulus on 2 Dec. 1940; on 3 Dec. he took part in the discussions on the second part of the conduct of operations: Halder, *Diaries*, 715–16 (2, 3 Dec. 1940); Paulus, '*Ich stehe hier auf Befehl!*', 107 ff. The data contain a few mistakes on the structure of the army in the east; these are due to lapses of memory.

Desna, with the aim of cutting off the enemy group east of Kiev. Army Group North likewise demanded armoured forces from the centre of the front in order to support its right wing and reach the line from Velikie Luki to Lake Ilmen. While conceding the need for such support, all the commanding officers ultimately refused to have the main thrust towards Moscow thus weakened. Halder eventually ruled that Army Group South, echeloned to the right, with a strong northern wing close against Army Group Centre, must open the attack. Army Group North was to advance with a strong right wing. In the direction of Leningrad the enemy was at first to be tied down; in the Baltic region he was to be contained. The timing of the attack on Leningrad would hinge on the progress of the offensive against Moscow.

The report on the Army High Command's operational intentions was made to Hitler on 1 December 1940.[124] In very typical manner Hitler seized that opportunity to indulge in a rambling monologue—a wearying one for the army officers, who were working under great pressure—on general strategic problems with only marginal relevance to the task in hand.

He opened the conference with a survey of the war situation. Having explained his view on the situation of the Italians in Albania and Libya, and having assured his listeners that no German army units would be transferred to North Africa, he reaffirmed his interest in eliminating the British and French from North Africa. The seizure of Gibraltar formed part of that area of planning. In the Balkans he saw success of the threats against Greece in the fact that the British would be prevented from attacking Romanian sovereign territory with 'auxiliary forces'. He believed that the Turks were also working in that direction, from fear of seeing a new theatre of war emerging in the Balkans. Such a theatre, however, would arise if the Greeks continued to tolerate the presence of British troops; in that case a German attack through Bulgaria would become necessary. Preparations for that eventuality ('Marita') were to be put in hand. Such a campaign against Greece would not affect other plans; Romania would certainly fight alongside Germany against the Soviet Union; the future fate of Finland was likewise linked to a German victory. This general survey of the options touched upon in Directive No. 18, supplemented by the lessons of Molotov's visit, now culminated in the unequivocal statement that the decision on hegemony in Europe would be made in *the struggle against Russia*. This observation by Hitler was addressed to the commander-in-chief of the navy, even though at the same time he conceded the importance of the Mediterranean strategy. The army commanders were once more confirmed in their impression that Hitler's Directive No. 18 showed that he had not yet finally decided in favour of an absolute priority for the campaign in the east. This impression was further strengthened by the announcement that Gibraltar was to be seized and the Balkan campaign to be fought before the campaign against Russia. If a Balkan campaign turned out

---

[124] Halder, *Diaries*, 721 ff. (4, 5 Dec. 1940); *KTB OKW* i. 203 ff. (5 Dec. 1940), 981–2 (appendix 41).

to be unnecessary, the units there would be ready to move against the Soviet Union. Following the capture of Gibraltar, two divisions were to be earmarked for North Africa. All this implied an unpredictable length of time during which offensive forces would be tied down.

Hitler further explained that success in a war against the Soviet Union depended on the choice of the most favourable moment. This applied not only to weather conditions but also to the state of armament and combat-readiness. Whereas the Red Army was inferior in both those respects, the Wehrmacht by the following spring would be at a peak in terms of officers, men, and material. This was a clear hint of the date of attack to be aimed at, but it was not an order to concentrate all available efforts on the project. Hitler emphasized that the Red Army was to be split up in major encirclement operations and 'strangled in parcels'.[125]

It was then Halder's turn, evidently also at some length, to report on the state of his planning activities. After an exposé of the geographical conditions, Halder stated that the Dnieper–Dvina line was the most easterly position from which the Red Army could protect the core of its industrial region. The German intention, therefore, must be to prevent the enemy from establishing any cohesive resistance west of the two rivers. An especially strong assault group (Army Group Centre) was to thrust towards Moscow from the Warsaw area. As for the two neighbouring army groups, Army Group North was to push towards Leningrad and Army Group South with a main effort towards Kiev. For the sector of Army Group South he envisaged three armies, one of which was to advance from the Lublin area, the second from the Lvov area, and the third from Romania. The ultimate objective of the operation was a line roughly along the Volga and the area of Archangel. As for forces, Halder envisaged 105 infantry divisions and 32 armoured and motorized divisisons; major portions of these, divided among two army commands, were to follow up as a second line. Eleventh and Second Army commands were earmarked for that role.

Hitler declared his overall agreement with the operational intentions submitted to him. He emphasized the importance of preventing the Red Army from establishing a cohesive defensive line. He left unresolved the question of whether the advance should aim at Moscow or east of it and he did not comment on Halder's overall operational objective, the Volga–Archangel line.

What was important, he stressed instead, was to make Army Group Centre strong enough to wheel considerable portions of its forces, northwards in order to encircle the enemy forces in the Baltic region. Thus the fundamental principle of Halder's plan, priority for the seizure of Moscow, was called into question. On the southern wing Hitler unambiguously assigned the main effort to the northern group: it was to thrust beyond Kiev and, coming from

---

[125] This was Halder's diction; comparison of the entries in his diaries with those in *KTB OKW* offers insights, beyond factual complementation, into Halder's spontaneous reactions and his assessment of Hitler and OKW—as well as into his own self-assessment.

the north, accomplish the encirclement of the enemy forces in the Ukraine. A later advance, 'with units, possibly, from Romania', was by no means in line with Halder's proposed concept of a large-scale envelopment starting from the areas of Lublin, Lvov, and Romania.

In point of fact this concept, as will be shown elsewhere in this volume, was to have provided for two encircling moves, the inner one of which, aiming from Lvov towards the south-east, required a second prong coming across the Carpathians. This would have called for Hungarian forces, or at least for the Hungarian government's consent to a transfer of German troops to the Carpathian front. Hitler, however, firmly rejected any arrangements with Hungary: neither did he see any war aim for Hungary in the Soviet Union, nor was he prepared to pay for Hungary's participation by concessions at the expense of Romania or Yugoslavia. It was therefore quite impossible for Halder to name the real objective envisaged by him for some of the forces advancing from Lvov, let alone to disclose his Hungarian contacts.[126]

It was typical of the atmosphere of the conference, and indeed of Halder's relationship with Hitler, that these very substantial differences in attitude were never discussed, and that Hitler proceeded from the assumption that his roughly outlined basic concept had to be accepted by Halder, while Halder in turn was confident that developments up to the moment of decision would prove him right and that Hitler would then have to yield to his, Halder's, judgement.[127] Conflict during the campaign was thus assured from the start.

On 13 and 14 December Halder assembled the chiefs of staff of the army groups and armies.[128] He outlined the whole spectrum of Hitler's exposé and repeated his fear, first recorded by Marcks, that Britain would try, with the aid of Turkey and the USSR, to strangulate the German oil basis in the Balkans; that had to be forestalled. The decision on hegemony in Europe would be made in Russia, that was why preparations had to be made for the campaign. For the army this meant a single-front war, for which 130–40 divisions would have to be made available; the Luftwaffe and the navy, on the other hand, would have to fight on several fronts. These statements not only reflect the purely operational approach intended for the audience in question, but also leave no doubt about Halder's belief that the campaign could be concluded successfully in the time envisaged. The main effort of future work would be in the areas of raising and training the formations and of creating all the prerequisites of deployment.

On 14 December the floor was given to the departmental chiefs in the Army General Staff; in addition, Colonel Erich Buschenhagen, chief of staff of the army in Norway, spoke of plans for operations in northern Finland. There was no discussion of the points in Hitler's directives which differed from Halder's

---

[126] See sect. I.v.4 (Förster).

[127] On Halder's attempt to pin Hitler down see sect. I.iv.1(*e*) at n. 138.

[128] Halder, *Diaries*, 735 ff. (13, 14 Dec. 1940); for the time schedule and participants see Halder, *KTB* ii. 462–3 (not in trans.).

concept. Again Halder evidently believed that his plans would prevail and that Hitler would eventually approve them, as he had done in the west.

Within the Wehrmacht's operations department Hitler's guidelines were now being transformed into a formal directive. Put down in black and white, the above-mentioned differences were bound to emerge clearly. Thus Jodl on 6 December pointed out to the Home Defence Department (which was working on the text) that, whatever happened, Hitler intended to continue the advance in the Balkans ('Marita') as far as Athens, whereas Halder's calculations of the forces required were based on an occupation only as far as Salonika.[129] Hitler moreover considered the possibility, in the event of offensive action against Turkey, of employing a further six divisions beyond the six envisaged for security duties. However, the planners of the deployment instructions for the war in the east were subject also to external influences. On 8 December the head of the Ausland/Abwehr (foreign counter-intelligence) department, Admiral Wilhelm Canaris, reported that Franco was no longer willing to enter the war alongside Germany.[130] Dino Alfieri, the Italian ambassador, painted the situation of the Italian troops in Albania 'in the blackest colours'. More reports on the unreliable attitude of the 'Weygand Army' in Syria and North Africa were coming in, inducing Hitler to order preparations for the immediate occupation of 'residual' France. With the abandonment of the plans concerning Gibraltar the struggle in the eastern Mediterranean was bound to gain in importance. This situation was reflected in Directive No. 20, Operation Marita, where the occupation of all of Greece was stated to be the objective. The connection with the operation in the east was provided by item 6, which stated that, following the conclusion of Operation Marita the bulk of the forces would be withdrawn for employment elsewhere.[131]

The requirements resulting from all these operational reflections seemed to the Wehrmacht operations department to exceed the scope of what was possible to such an extent that, during the drafting of its plans for the war against the Soviet Union, it felt that comment had first to be invited from the separate Wehrmacht services.[132] A request was therefore addressed to the naval operations command for comment on the issue of a war on two fronts from its point of view. The response was a clear rejection. Following Hitler's exceedingly optimistic expectations for the spring of 1941, voiced on 5 December, the Luftwaffe was asked what forces it considered necessary for the maintenance of the air war against Britain and for the indispensable protection of German territory—in other words, what forces could realistically be employed in the war against Russia. Lieutant-Colonel von Loßberg was asked for an opinion on the situation in the Mediterranean as seen by the army. Initial calculations

[129] *KTB OKW* i. 210 ff. (6 Dec. 1940).   [130] Ibid. 219 ff.

[131] *Hitler's Directives*, No. 20, pp. 46 ff.

[132] *KTB OKW* i. 228 (12 Dec. 1940), 230 (14 Dec. 1940). The results are not recorded in the KTB. Kriegsmarine: Vortragsnotiz, Lagebeurteilung für einen Zweifrontenkrieg [Navy: report memorandum, estimate of situation for a war on two fronts], 11 Dec. 1940, BA-MA PG 31025.

were also put in hand of fuel requirements, allowing for the loss of Soviet deliveries. In addition, General Thomas, head of the War Economy and Armaments Department, produced a study of the economic consequences of a war against the Soviet Union.[133]

On 12 December 1940 Lieutenant-Colonel von Loßberg submitted the first draft of Directive No. 21.[134] That text underwent revision by Jodl; the occupation of Petsamo and protection of the Arctic Ocean route were included. Moreover, according to a note by Major Deyhle, Jodl's adjutant, a 'later move out of Romania' was envisaged. Whether this addition was in line with the result of the conference of 5 December as seen by Jodl, or whether it was based on a 'recollection' by Halder, who was being kept informed on the progress of work on the directive, remains an open question. It is conceivable that Jodl, in line with Halder's known views, initially envisaged no more than the creation of a point of main effort at the northern wing of Army Group South, together with a halting of the formations released from the Balkan operation, possibly for the envelopment operation from the north. On 14 December the text was returned to Loßberg for further revision. On 16 December the revised draft was submitted to Jodl, with a note that the Luftwaffe's comment on a war on two fronts and the fuel issue was still expected. On 17 December Jodl reported to Hitler. Now followed the written finalization of Hitler's intentions, which, as had been discernible as early as 5 December, diverged from Halder's report;[135] the text had evidently been personally dictated by Hitler. The concept of the main effort in the sector of Army Group Centre remained unchanged, except that the thrust, once the enemy west of the Dnieper–Dvina line was smashed, was to be redirected to the north with strong mobile forces in order first of all to defeat the enemy there in co-operation with Army Group North. As a result, possession was to be taken of the Baltic States with the Baltic coastline. Only when this more urgent task (as Hitler saw it) was 'settled' were offensive operations to be resumed for the seizure of 'the most important transport and armament centre, Moscow'. Only an unexpectedly rapid collapse of Soviet resistance would justify going for the two objectives simultaneously. It proved possible, evidently through Halder's efforts, to replace the word 'settled' by 'made safe', which meant that there was no firm assignment of units.[136] The idea of wheeling round strong forces even before Moscow was reached is already found in Loßberg's study; he regarded the

---

[133] On Thomas's memorandum see sect. I.III.2(c) (Müller).

[134] *KTB OKW* i. 226. On the following see the KTB entries under the dates concerned.

[135] *Hitler's Directives*, No. 21, pp. 49 ff., according to the second copy (the copy of the Naval High Command). The working copy of the Wehrmacht operations staff is the fourth copy; it is initialled by Loßberg, Jodl, Warlimont, and Keitel, and signed (in full) Adolf Hitler. Warlimont's initials are dated 16 Dec. A film copy of the fourth copy, final version with corrections, was the source of *IMT* xxvi. 47, and Jacobsen, *1939–1945*, 180 ff.; BA-MA RW 4/v. 522.

[136] Halder's attempts to tie Hitler down are attested in Heusinger and Henrici, Feldzug in Rußland, MGFA, T-6b, 70. This was not, therefore, simply a stylistic 'improvement' but a substantial amendment.

securing of the Baltic sea communications as an important issue. It may be assumed that, in deference to Halder's arguments, he put that idea aside until such time as Hitler, on 17 December, directly demanded its inclusion in the text of the directive.

Jodl's exact role in Hitler's decision to make what Halder had proposed as a secondary operation into the main purpose of the second phase of the campaign—whether he actually suggested it or merely consented to it—can no longer be reliably established.[137] The minute of the conversation between them on 17 December records that, following the elimination of Soviet forces in the Baltic region, Hitler expected the final suspension of fighting on that sector of the front. That would also ensure the safety of ore deliveries.[138] A mere security task, performed in conjunction with the Finns, would scarcely bind any forces, but on the contrary release the bulk of the army group for the attack towards the south, i.e. for the encirclement of Moscow.

The plan for Army Group South was also finalized in a form which eliminated earlier uncertainties. The Romanian formations were now to support the German southern wing, at least initially, tying down the enemy where no German forces were stationed, and generally to provide auxiliary services in the rearward area. The idea of the main effort of the army group's attack from the Lublin area in the general direction of Kiev was kept, while the forces in Romania were to advance across the Prut, forming a long-range encircling prong. There was no longer any mention of an envelopment operation from the Lvov area.

After the conclusion of the battles north and south of the Pripet marshes efforts were to be made, 'within the framework of a pursuit', to gain rapid control of the economically important Donets basin on the one hand, and of Moscow on the other. Although the capture of this city would be a 'decisive success', politically and economically, there was no suggestion of an operational move that would, as Halder saw it, decide the war.

Halder must surely have immediately realized the consequences which might arise from such a divergence of opinions on the conduct of operations. In order to commit Hitler after all to his own view, he arranged for the inclusion of one clause in Directive No. 21, just before the section on the conduct of army operations. It now read: 'Approving the intentions reported to me.' This made sure, at least, that any divergent decisions by Hitler would be seen as such and would provide justification for counter-arguments.

As an overall operational intention, it was laid down that the bulk of the Soviet army was to be annihilated in the west of the Soviet Union and that the

---

[137] Loßberg informed Halder on 8 Jan. 1952 that Jodl had agreed with Hitler's decisions against the objection of the Home Defence Department (Army), i.e. himself: Heusinger and Henrici, Feldzug in Rußland, MGFA, T-6b, 68. Hence Hitler's changes on 17 Dec. to Loßberg's formulations (probably inspired by Halder) in the first version of the directive, *KTB OKW* i. 233 (17 Dec. 1940).

[138] *KTB OKW* i. 996 (annexe 45).

withdrawal of combat-ready forces was to be prevented. Next, a line was to be reached from which the Soviet air force could no longer strike at Reich territory. The ultimate objective of the operation was to be a Volga–Archangel line, from which, 'if necessary', the last remaining Soviet industrial region in the Urals could be eliminated by the Luftwaffe.

The task of the units stationed in northern Norway continued to be the protection of Norway and the securing of the nickel-ore mines of the Petsamo area and of the Arctic Ocean route. As an offensive operation jointly with Finnish forces the capture of the Murmansk railway was envisaged. The principal task of the bulk of the Finnish army was to be the tying-down of as many Soviet forces as possible by means of attacks west of, or on both side of, Lake Ladoga as well as the capture of Hanko (Hangö). The army was to employ all available units for these operations, while maintaining the security of territories gained so far. Luftwaffe operations were restricted by the instruction to protect the air-space over the Reich and to continue offensive operations against Britain, in particular against her seaborne supplies. The main effort of the German navy, even during the war in the east, was to continue to be unequivocally aimed against Britain. After the elimination of the Soviet fleet in the Baltic the German navy's task would be to ensure supplies to the northern wing of the army. Finally Hitler ordered that 15 May 1941 was to be the date for readiness to attack. Proceeding from the directives for the Wehrmacht services, the commanders-in-chief now had to make their own preparations and report to Hitler, with intentions and timetable, through the Armed Forces High Command.

The weeks to follow also revealed differences between the army command and Hitler in another, even more fundamental, respect. On 9 January 1941 Hitler took the opportunity of a conference on the overall war situation, attended by the Wehrmacht chief of staff, the army commander-in-chief, the chief of the Wehrmacht operations staff, the chief of the Luftwaffe General Staff, and the chief of the operations department of the naval operations staff, to explain once more, in the presence of the Reich minister of foreign affairs, his political and strategic reasons for Operation Barbarossa.[139] The British enemy, he argued, was being propped up by her 'hope of the United States and Russia'. 'Stalin, the master of Russia, is a clever fellow; he will not act against Germany openly, but it has to be expected that, in situations difficult for Germany, he will increasingly create difficulties.' The economic negotiations with the Soviet Union had proved the justification of Hitler's view.[140] Hitler by then realized that his war-economy, and hence also his power-political, elbow-room was shrinking all the time. However, control of the 'immeasurable wealth' of the Soviet Union following a successful campaign would, as he saw it, enable Germany in the future to wage a 'struggle against continents'. While he described the Red Army as a 'clay colossus without a

[139] *KTB OKW* i. 996 (annexe 45) 253 ff.   [140] See sect. I.III.1(*b*) at n. 66 (Müller).

head', he also warned against underestimation of the enemy. That was why the attack was to be made with the strongest possible forces. Once more he emphasized that the most important task was the 'severance of the Baltic region'. In a typical, well-thought-out sequence he listed the following operational objectives: 'annihilation of the Russian army, seizure of the most important industrial regions, and destruction of the remaining industrial regions.' He stuck to these priorities also at the extended conference of 3 February on the deployment directive for Barbarossa. If, however, the Red Army succeeded in a large-scale withdrawal, priority would have to be given to the capture of the Baltic region and Leningrad in order to 'gain the most favourable supply basis for further operations'. In that case the centre of the front would have to hold back to allow the flanks to outmanoeuvre the enemy.[141] Hitler's arguments therefore remained unchanged throughout. Conquest of war-economy bases, both to supply the German troops and to force the enemy to his knees, remained his main objective. Halder, on the other hand, saw the dangers of such a large-scale operation and of a dissipation of forces which would then be lacking for the main attack on Moscow. He believed that with the success of that decisive battle the ecocnomic conquests were bound to fall into Germany's lap unaided.

The above-mentioned far-ranging expansiveness of Hitler's observations on the future points of main effort in the war led the army commander-in-chief to doubt, even when Directive No. 21 was issued, whether Hitler was really serious or merely bluffing.[142] As the outcome of a conference with Brauchitsch on 28 January 1941 Halder noted in his diary: 'Barbarossa: Purpose not clear. We do not hit the British that way. Our economic potential will not be substantially improved.'[143] Added to this were misgivings about a possible 'southern front'. If Brauchitsch and Halder were not convinced of the strategic necessity of an attack on the Soviet Union, and indeed foresaw risks in the event of a war on two fronts, they would have had an opportunity a few days later, on 3 February, of urgently voicing them to Hitler, just as Field Marshal von Bock had earlier done *vis-à-vis* Hitler and Halder.[144] Yet both of them remained silent, and Halder used his own means to fight for *his* operational plan. He made a note for his report to Hitler[145] to the effect that the basic concept was laid down by Directive No. 21 so that its execution alone could be the subject of his report. That report, therefore, no longer constituted an exchange of information on intentions and forces to be employed; basically it was confined to essentials, Halder being well aware of what detail he could go

---

[141] Halder, *KTB* ii. 266 ff. (2, 3 Feb. 1941; not in trans.). Whether Halder raised the points he had jotted down for his report to Hitler is uncertain. On the diverging points, neither did Hitler vigorously react to the starting move of Army Gp. South, which was not in line with his directive, nor did Halder with regard to the switching of the main effort to the Baltic countries. He did not include in his diary Hitler's observation that the operational plans should once more be gone through: *KTB OKW* i. 297 ff. (3 Feb. 1941), 1000 (annexe 48).

[142] Hillgruber, *Strategie*, 369, quoting Engel.   [143] Halder, *Diaries*, 765 (28 Jan. 1941).

[144] Hillgruber, *Strategie*, 373.   [145] Halder, *Diaries*, 770 (2 Feb. 1941).

into without provoking Hitler's interference. After Halder's report on the deployment plan Hitler called for Halder's map material and concerned himself with it for some time to come. Halder used the occasion to ask for Hitler's agreement to the involvement of Hungary in his plans, but Hitler disregaded his request. This meant the loss of another corner-stone of Halder's operations plan for Army Group South; clearly, therefore, he could not inform Hitler about it. This aspect will be examined elsewhere in the present volume.

(f) The Deployment Directive for the Army

Once the basic ideas and guidelines for the conduct of the war against the Soviet Union had been laid down in Directive No. 21, the Army General Staff for its part needed to finalize intentions and timetables, and thereby to issue instructions to army group and army commands. Following the command report to Hitler, these instructions were signed as Deployment Directive Barbarossa by the commander-in-chief of the army and thus became binding orders for the army.[146]

A first draft of that directive was before the chief of the general staff on 22 January. Its first version, dated 31 January 1941, provided the basis for Halder's report to Hitler on 3 February.[147] In view of subsequent interference by Hitler and the resulting amendments, it will be necessary to examine that report more closely, in terms of both content and form.[148] According to the record in the war diary of the Wehrmacht High Command (*KTB OKW*), Halder at first concerned himself in great detail with the Red Army; next he mapped out the German operational approach and the instructions to the separate army groups, without, however, essentially going beyond the data laid down in Directive No. 21. The record shows that Halder dealt in greater detail with the conduct of operations north of the Pripet marshes. On the tasks of Army Group South the record contains only a single sentence: 'A.Gp. South will advance south of the Pripet marshes and across the Dnieper.'

The major part of his report was concerned with questions of detail.[149] Halder had good reasons for reporting with great reserve on the conduct of operations by Army Group South; on a number of points the deployment directive (in the version of 31 January 1941) far exceeded Directive No. 21. Thus the task of the army group was laid down as to thrust forward from the

---

[146] 'Reports by the commanders-in-chief' on envisaged measures were mentioned already in Directive No. 18 of 12 Nov. 1940, where a further directive was foreshadowed 'as soon as the basic outlines of the army's operational plans' were submitted and approved; see *Hitler's Directives*, No. 18.

[147] Aufmarschanweisung 'Barbarossa' [Deployment directive Barbarossa], published in its final version: Halder, *KTB* ii. 463 ff. (not in trans.); draft of 22 Jan. 1941 and first version with all amendments: BA-MA RH 19 I/67. The final version with all amendments published in Halder, *KTB*, but under the date of 31 Jan. 1941, is misleading.

[148] Halder, *KTB* ii. 266 ff. (2 Feb. 1941; not in trans.); *KTB OKW* i. 297 ff. (3 Feb. 1941).

[149] *KTB OKW* i. 303 (demand for Halder's map material), 306 (3 Feb. 1941).

Lublin area with strong armoured forces and, once Kiev was reached, to push southwards along the Dnieper in order to create a pincer movement with the army advancing from Romania for the encirclement of the enemy's forces. After that, the Dnieper crossings were to be secured, providing freedom of movement either for subsequent operational co-operation with the forces operating in northern Russia or for new tasks in southern Russia. Exceeding the provisions of Directive No. 21, the task assigned to Twelfth Army operating out of Romania, in addition to a rapid northward advance towards Seventeenth Army and Armoured Group 1, already envisaged Odessa as an objective, provided an opportunity arose for its surprise capture. The armoured wedge of the army group, Armoured Group 1, was to advance rapidly towards Kiev, along with Sixth Army and with units of Seventeenth Army; thence, with the bulk of Seventeenth Army, it was to thrust towards Twelfth Army, whose mobile formations were *subsequently* to be switched to Armoued Group 1 as quickly as possible. Sixth Army on the left wing, supported by units of the armoured group and providing cover towards the Pripet region, was to advance towards Zhitomir. Completely absent from Hitler's directive was the employment of part of Seventeenth Army with a group to advance from the Carpathians, from Hungary.[150] That employment of Army Group South, however, depended on two conditions: first, the units of Twelfth Army employed on Marita had to be returned to the army and rehabilitated; second, Romania, Hungary, and Slovakia would have to be prepared for the deployment and would have to support it. On 12 February the army group requested the employment of military forces of those states. This applied primarily to Romanian units: their three 'core divisions' and the motorized brigade were to be engaged in the offensive moves of Twelfth Army. Another six or seven divisions, the entire cavalry, and the Romanian army troops were to follow the German forces to the Dnestr and there take over the protection of the front. A further six to eight divisions were to be made available for occupation and security tasks. The main purpose of employing the Romanians was the freeing of German units for the attack.

Halder evidently had not met with opposition from Hitler when he reported to him on the conduct of operations on 3 February. Even his proviso that, if Twelfth Army was not available, the offensive in the form it was planned should be abandoned, caused no changes in the deployment directive.[151] On 7

---

[150] Plans of Army Group South; map exercise 'Otto' of 5 Feb. 1941, BA-MA RH 19 I/70 and 67a. On 24 Feb. The operations department approved the initial move and intentions of the army group. The use of airborne troops and naval units for the capture of Odessa was to be examined. This plan, like the involvement of Hungary, went far beyond the scope envisaged by Hitler: Forstmeier, *Odessa 1941*, 19–20.

[151] This is probably due to the fact that Halder did not go into his measures concerning operational leadership, or at least not to an extent that might arouse Hitler's opposition. This is suggested also by Halder's careful formulation of how to notify the Hungarians: *KTB OKW* i. 299. Halder's provisos are in the notes for his report, Halder, *KTB* ii. 266 ff. (2 Feb. 1941; not in trans.).

March, however, Hitler, having examined the Army High Command's materials and considered developments in the Balkans and Greece, decided that
the offensive from Moldavia was to be scrapped; first of all the Marita attack,
extended down to the Peloponnese, would swiftly eliminate all danger-spots in
the Balkans once and for all. This would require the entire Twelfth Army. As
a consequence he ordered that only the units necessary for security were to be
left at Romania's eastern frontier and that the attack by Army Group South
was to concentrate wholly on an envelopment thrust with its northern wing.[152]
This presupposed that Sixth Army and Armoured Group 1 would quickly
reach Kiev and Zhitomir, and that the bulk of the armoured forces would then
be moved south along the Dnieper. Thus the problem of securing Sixth
Army's left flank against enemy action from the Pripet region acquired increased significance—possibly a decisive significance for the success of the
operation.

The draft of the study of the Pripet marshes, which Hitler had called for,
was completed by the Foreign Armies East department on 12 February.[153] It
contained little more than a compilation of readily available sources, with
quotations on the set of problems. The military assessment was based primarily on difficulties of terrain, through routes, and railway lines. On 18 February
Halder heard about the study and ordered it to be processed. This paper
differed from the original on only one point, but one that seems vital. While
the draft had contained the observation that the only military operations
feasible in that terrain were guerrilla actions, and that the principal significance of the region lay in the fact that it represented a massive obstacle to the
attacker, it nevertheless made the point that an army in control of the railway
would be able to move its troops in all directions of the compass. Its final
conclusion ran: 'It seems therefore that a threat from the Polesye to the flank
and the rear of the armies advancing towards Moscow or Kiev is very much
within the realm of possibilities.' This sentence was deleted from the final
version of the study, dated 21 February, the version submitted to Hitler.
Instead, the study now arrived at the conclusion which Halder had reported to
Hitler as early as 3 February—that it had to be assumed that individual mobile
Russian units, especially cavalry, would operate against the flanks of the

---

[152] *KTB OKW* i. 347 ff.; the order to the chief of the Wehrmacht operations staff was not passed
on to Halder until 17 Mar. 1941. See ibid. 360 ff.; Halder, *Diaries*, 831 ff. (17 Mar. 1941).

[153] This problem is discussed here because it gave rise to particular difficulties for the flanks of
Army Groups Centre and South in the initial phase of the offensive, difficulties which went far
beyond the tactical scope and which it proved impossible to eliminate throughout the period of
occupation. For bibliography see above, n. 94; also Entwurf der Abteilung Frd Heere Ost [Draft
of the Foreign Armies East Dept.], Capt. (Gen. Staff) von Brunn, 12 Feb. 1941, BA-MA RH 2/
v. 1923; 'Studie über das Prijet-Gebiet' [Study of the Pripet region], 21 Feb. 1941, BA-MA RH
2/v. 1928. The discrepancy discussed below must have been noticed by the official responsible:
because of it and because of the conclusion from it the study was classified as 'Chefsache' on 25
Feb. 1941 and it was forbidden to pass it on to subordinate command authorities (BA-MA H 3/
1, fo. 2047/216); Halder, *Diaries*, 832 (17 Mar. 1941); Philippi, *Das Pripjetproblem*, 5.

assault groups. In addition, minor actions (up to regimental strength) were possible at any time. The Russians, fighting on their own ground, were used to difficult conditions and would be able to count on the willing support of the population. In the end, continuous aerial surveillance was recommended as the best way of establishing the whereabouts of major formations and their movements. Hitler's instruction in early March that the points of passage through the marshes should be covered by mines at any rate represented a clear decision;[154] even after submission of the Army High Command study he remained unconvinced that the marshy region was free from danger. On 17 March he told Halder that 'allegedly whole armies could be moved there'.[155]

Halder's particular method of dealing with Hitler in order to make his views—which represented those of the Army General Staff—prevail was to lead in the future to considerable friction, to a nerve-racking tactic of the chief of the general staff, and eventually to his capitulation. On the other hand, Hitler had from the very beginning left no doubt about his determination that he would not leave the conduct of the war in the east in the hands of the Army High Command. And he enforced that decision.

The decision, which formed in Hitler's mind on 8 March,[156] also called for new decisions on the part of the army command. Pressed by the chief of the Wehrmacht operations department, Hitler on 17 March ordered the abandonment of the Twelfth Army's attack as part of the envelopment move of Army Group South; instead he ordered all mobile forces becoming available from the Greek operation to be switched to reinforce Armoured Group 1. He justified this major intervention in Halder's operational planning by misgivings about the weakness of the Hungarian and Romanian armies. There was no sense, he argued, in basing operations on forces whose availability could not be counted on. This decision therefore finally put an end to Halder's second, closer offensive move by the inner wing of Seventeenth Army and the group of forces that was to have come from the Carpathians, pinned down the enemy, encircled him, and prevented him from withdrawing.

Accordingly, on 8 April the operations department amended the deployment directive for Barbarossa and at the same time made new dispositions about Army High Command reserves. The reserves, which were to have been kept ready for the northern sector in the Warsaw area, were now reduced in favour of reinforced reserves in the Rzeszów area, the objective being the provision of additional forces for the long-range one-sided thrust of Army

---

[154] *KTB OKW* i. 350 (8 Mar. 1941).

[155] Halder, *Diaries*, 832 (17 Mar. 1941). 'Allegedly' is probably a mistake by Halder.

[156] *KTB OKW* i. 350; Halder, *Diaries*, 831–2 (17 Mar. 1941). Halder fought in vain for his project, also using the argument that any halt in Moldavia would enable major enemy forces to withdraw to the Dnieper. Because of Hitler's decision, at the same time, 'in no way' to involve Hungary in Barbarossa and to draw upon Slovakia only for deployment and supplies, the planned attack by a group from the Carpathians had to be abandoned. On 27 Mar. 1941, admittedly, the situation changed again as a result of the preparations for an attack on Yugoslavia.

MAP I.IV.3. Deployment Directive Barbarossa

Group South. Instead of Twelfth Army HQ, Eleventh Army HQ from the army reserve was now assigned to command the German, and subsequently also the Romanian, formations.

With the definitive version of the deployment directive for Barbarossa, dated 8 June 1941, the army groups and armies were assigned the following tasks. Within the framework of Army Group South, Eleventh Army had to protect the Romanian region, which was vital to the German war effort. By feigning deployment it was to tie down major enemy forces and prevent any orderly retreat by them by striking into their movements.

The prime task of Armoured Group 1 was, in conjunction with Sixth and Seventeenth Armies, to break through the enemy lines between Rawa Ruska and Kowel and, by way of Berdichev and Zhitomir, to gain the Dnieper at and below Kiev. Thereupon, without losing time, it was to continue its attack in a south-easterly direction along the Dnieper, prevent the enemy from withdrawing behind the river, and destroy his forces by attacking them in the rear.

Seventeenth Army, having successfully broken through enemy positions north-west of Lvov, was to dislodge the enemy in a south-easterly direction by a vigorous advance of its left wing. It was to gain the Berdichev–Vinnitsa area at an early date in order to continue its attack, according to the situation, in a south-easterly or easterly direction. Sixth Army was to attack on both sides of Lutsk and, while providing cover for the northern flank of the army group, push ahead towards Zhitomir with the strongest possible forces. Thereupon it was to be ready to wheel south-eastwards to the west of the Dnieper in order to prevent the enemy from withdrawing, and to defeat him.

The task of Army Group Centre remained essentially as formulated in Directive No. 21. Its objective was to scatter the enemy forces in Belorussia and to concentrate the mobile forces advancing north and south of Minsk, as a prerequisite of co-operation of major forces with Army Group North for the annihilation of enemy forces in the Baltic region and around Leningrad.

Within that framework Armoured Group 2 was instructed, in co-operation with Fourth Army, to break through at and north of Kobrymin and to advance towards Slutsk and Minsk. There it was to link up with Armoured Group 3 attacking north of Minsk and with Ninth Army. The two armoured groups were then to prevent the enemy from establishing a solid line of resistance along the upper Dnieper and the upper Dvina. The two infantry armies were to complete the encirclement and annihilation, prepared by the armoured groups, in the Białystok–Minsk area. Fourth Army was then to force a crossing of the Berezina and gain the Dnieper at Mogilev; Ninth Army, having annihilated the enemy at Minsk, was to reach the Dvina at Polotsk.

Instructions to Army Group North likewise, apart from minor amendments, followed Directive No. 21. Its task was to destroy the enemy forces in the Baltic region, occupy the Baltic ports, and eventually, by the capture of Kronshtadt and Leningrad, deprive the Soviet naval forces of their bases. For that purpose mobile forces were to be brought up from Army Group Centre.

Armoured Group 4, in conjunction with Sixteenth and Eighteenth Armies, was to push towards the Dvina at Daugavpils (Dvinsk) and establish bridge-heads. In addition, it was to reach the area north of Opochka as rapidly as possible and from there, according to the situation, advance further in a northerly or north-easterly direction.

Sixteenth Army, after breaking through enemy forces on both sides of the Ebenrode–Kaunas (Kovno) road, was to occupy the northern bank of the Dvina at Daugavpils and then follow Armoured Group 4.

Eighteenth Army was to thrust forward along the Tilsit–Riga road and cut off the enemy south-west of Riga. Next it was to advance swiftly towards the Ostrov–Pskov line to prevent the enemy forces south of Lake Peipus from escaping. In addition, Estonia was to be cleared of the enemy and preparations were to be made for the occupation of the Baltic ports and of the islands of Saaremaa (Ösel), Hiiumaa (Dagö), and Munu to ensure a surprise capture as soon as the situation allowed.

The task of Army Command Norway, which was directly subordinated to the Wehrmacht High Command, remained unchanged: it was primarily the security of Norway and of the ore-mines of the Petsamo area. The version of 31 January had made an offensive against the Murmansk region, involving units of the Finnish army, dependent on the Swedish railways being made available. If this was not the case, an attack could be launched with two or three divisions from the Rovaniemi area and north of it, aimed at Kandalaksha Bay, with the objective of cutting off the Soviet forces to the north. In the event of the railway being available only for supply transports, direct attack was envisaged from northern Lapland via Petsamo against the ports of Murmansk and Polyarnyy. An amendment of 31 May 1941 emphasized the need to defend the Norwegian coast; the forces employed to that end were not to be substantially weakened by Barbarossa, but on the contrary reinforced. The attack on Murmansk, initially to be morely hemmed in, was now made dependent on the provision of additional forces; the operation against Kandalaksha was no longer mentioned at all. The objectives initially envisaged for the army in the south of Finland were, in the final version, exclusively assigned to Finnish units. They were to eliminate Hanko at an early stage, cover the deployment of German forces in the north, and immediately after-wards, in step with the advance of Army Group North, attack the Soviet forces at their south-eastern front.

With the issuing of the directive at the end of January 1941 the army group and army commands were enlisted in the detailed preparation of the deploy-ment movements.[157] The army groups had to submit their demands and drafts

---

[157] Halder, *Diaries*, 832 (15 Dec. 1940). On that day he envisaged the processing of the deployment directive by the army group chiefs of staff. Army Group B passed on the instructions to Seventeenth Army HQ for processing (for Army Group South), to Fourth Army HQ (for Army Group Centre), and to Eighteenth Army HQ (for Army Group North). Armd. Group Guderian was to process the employment of all the armoured groups. See BA-MA, 18. Armee,

by the middle of February, and the armies—involving corps HQs and, as far as necessary, divisional staffs—had to process their instructions by the middle of March. To that end all command authorities not yet situated within the sphere of Army Group B had to transfer working staffs to the army group. The camouflaged take-over of command was to be accomplished by the army HQs between 3 April and the beginning of May.

The documentation customary in connection with military deployment directives—on the enemy, one's own forces, communications, supplies, and air support—was frequently, following the issuing of the first version of the directive, not studied or updated until weeks or months later. Time and again Halder intervened to co-ordinate or correct, not always in agreement with his commander-in-chief, whose occasional encroachments into his sphere of authority—which, in Halder's eyes, was the whole army—he instantly rejected.

Specialized aspects of the further preparation of the army's operations will be discussed elsewhere in this volume in so far as its scope permits. Closely related to operational plans were the issues of supplies for the army and of the force to be raised for that particular sector of the war. A brief outline of the quartermaster-general's service and of the organizational structure of the army is therefore indispensable.

(g) The Preparations of the Quartermaster-General

It was the duty of the quartermaster-general in the Army General Staff 'to supply the army with everything necessary for its striking power' and 'to shield it from anything that could impair its employability'.[158] This definition, first laid down in 1935, provided the foundation for the preparations that had to be made by the quartermaster-general for the war against the Soviet Union, although the changes which had occurred since the beginning of the war were taken into consideration.[159]

On 1 August 1940 Halder informed Major-General Wagner, the chief of the quartermaster-general's staff, of Hitler's intention to have preparations put in hand for war against the Soviet Union.[160] Wagner immediately began his

17562/8. Marcks, as early as 19 Nov. 1940, had prepared a first draft of 'Considerations of an Offensive out of East Prussia' for the initial move of Army Group North. The map exercise of Armd. Group Guderian, which, after the reflections of July–August, can hardly have found itself faced with an entirely new situation (see above, n. 60), concluded that 11 days were needed for an advance to the Dnieper: Halder, Diaries, 814 (28 Feb. 1941); Bericht Pz.Gr. 3/Ic, BA-MA RH 21-3/v. 423; on Fourth Army HQ see Meier-Welcker, Aufzeichnungen, 95 ff.

[158] H.Dv. 90, Versorgung des Feldheeres [Supplies for the army in the field], pts. 1 and 2, 1 Apr. 1935. This regulation was further developed, especially pt. 2 with its numerical data. The 'Handbuch für den Generalstabsdienst im Kriege' [Manual for general-staff service in war] (H.Dv. g. 92) refers to this.

[159] On the development of military administration in war see Umbreit, Militärverwaltungen, 13, 85 ff. (Poland), and Germany and the Second World War, ii. 138 ff., 260 ff.

[160] Halder, Diaries, 535 (1 Aug. 1940). Wagner, as chief of staff, had been de facto in charge of the department since 1935, but did not become quartermaster-general until 1 Aug. 1940. The previous quartermaster-general, Lt.-Gen. Eugen Müller, became general (special duties) with the C.-in-C. of the army; see sect. I.iv.1(g) at n. 173. On Wagner's personality and work see Wagner, Generalquartiermeister, with contributions by officers close to him.

planning work in the areas of organization and infrastructure, proceeding from the general principle that the vastness of the future theatre of operations, the speed of the German advance, the length of supply-lines, and the poor transport facilities would demand the most economical use of supplies and means of transport.

On 12 and 15 November 1940 Halder had himself briefed on the 'basic aspects of supplies in the event of an operation in the east'.[161] On the assumption of an army of about 3 million men, 300,000 horses, and 500,000 motor-vehicles, the central questions were those of the location of materials required, installation of repair workshops for motor-vehicles in and immediately behind the zone of operations, and the establishment of supply districts within the areas of the army groups and of the army in Romania. These supply districts were to be replenished by the chief of transport from supply assembly-points in Reich territory. This arrangement provided the basis of guidelines for the development of the railway network, of unloading and transloading stations, and of bridge-building and communication links. Halder in this context described supplying the army in the field as a *leadership task* which could not be tackled by organizational means alone.

Along with the planning of the army's material supplies and the replenishment of stores, Wagner devoted himself to training the officers in his service branch for the tasks awaiting them.[162] The emphasis was on preparations for quartermaster service at corps and division level. To this end, allowing for the far-ranging movements to be expected, exercises were staged for quick adaptation of supplies to the intentions of the command and for the calculation of supplies and transport facilities needed. Attention was paid to the differences in the supplies of mobile forces on the one hand and infantry formations on the other, and the quartermaster officers earmarked for armoured and motorized units were specially trained for the problems of large-scale and engagement-determined attacks. In addition they had to concern themselves with the problems of military administration, i.e. the utilization of occupied territory.

Once the 'Deployment Directive Barbarossa' had been issued, all the preparations of the quartermaster-general were formulated as its appendix 6 and summarized in the 'Directions for Supplies', which were updated and issued in stages.[163]

In his general guidelines for supplies to the troops (part A) the quartermaster-general applied the lessons of the campaign in the west, which had shown that direct supplies from Germany via the quartermaster services of the armies were no longer possible. He therefore created command authorities at the level

---

[161] Halder, *Diaries*, 685, 690. Halder concerned himself intensively with the transport problem as the basis of supplies. See Rohde, *Wehrmachttransportwesen*, 173 ff.; Pottgießer, *Deutsche Reichsbahn*, 21 ff.

[162] Richtlinien für die Ausbildung der Generalstabsoffiziere im Quartiermeisterdienst [Guidelines for the training of general-staff officers in the quartermaster service], 13 Nov. 1940, BA-MA RH 2/v. 155.

[163] BA-MA, Pz.Gr. 4/Qu, 22,392/41.

of army groups; these were directly answerable to him and thus able to organize supplies from an expert point of view, independently of the orders of army group HQs.[164] They were responsible for the supply districts, which in turn controlled supply sections within the area of each army. It was there that supply-depots were to be established; these would make it possible, before the opening of an operation, to bridge a fourteen-day suspension of supply transports. In addition, the following stores were to be set up: 2 sets of ammunition for all weapons, 8 consumption quotas of fuel in barrels, 2 further consumption quotas in non-movable tank stores, and 20 sets of daily food rations.

Part B of the instructions contained the regulations for the individual army group areas. These laid down the further route of supply-channels to the armies and assigned supply- and service-units. For Army Group North use of the sea route was envisaged as soon as the war at sea and the progress of land operations permitted.

The entire supply plan after the opening of operations was based on the assumption that during the whole operation, estimated to take four or five months, the army would essentially live off the land and provide itself with everything that could be manufactured within the country or was found there. The dependence of supply management on the transport system constituted a major problem. It was assumed that limited railway capacity would not be available until two weeks after the start of operations. As, moreover, it was not to be expected that any rolling-stock would be seized intact, it was decided to convert the railway network to the German gauge; this necessitated the provision of appropriate construction units and the speediest possible organization of work-teams from prisoners of war and the native population.[165] As for German transport capacity, the quartermaster-general, in addition to the army's transport units, had at his disposal a 'Großtransportraum' (large-scale transport pool), made up of vehicles of the German Reich railway, industry, and other truck fleets; these were brought together under the control of the 'Nationalsozialistisches Kraftfahr-Korps' (NSKK: National Socialist motor transport corps). This transport capacity could be made available only shortly before the start of operations; it was to be integrated in the supply services of the armoured formations in such a way that requirements of ammunition and fuel were punctually available in the form of 'hand baggage'. Supply districts were enjoined to exercise the strictest control over the use of this valuable transport capacity in order to make sure that it did not 'seep away' in the units.[166] The importance Halder attached to road-borne supplies, including

---

[164] Orders affecting the conduct of operations had to be signed by the chiefs of staff; on this see Wagner, *Generalquartiermeister*; Fähndrich, 'Aufgaben und Arbeit' (MS MGFA T-8-2); also Weinknecht, '*Ostfeldzug*', 261 ff.; Rücker, 'Vorbereitungen', 313; Eckstein, 'Tätigkeit', 272 ff.

[165] For the movement of the bulk of the infantry divisions 15,000 *panie* peasant carts, complete with drivers and horses, were hired in Poland and subsequently also in the Ukraine: Halder, *Diaries*, 892 (28 Apr. 1941).

[166] Order of the quartermaster-general of 29 Apr. 1941, BA-MA, Pz.Gr. 4, 22,392/41. 'Hand

DIAGRAM I.IV.3. Structure of the Quartermaster-general's Department, as on 1 October 1940

Quartermaster-general

Chief Group

Subj.: I   Planning
Subj.: II   Personnel matters, officers
Subj.: III Personnel matters, non-commissioned officers and other ranks, orderly officer, central bureau and records

Group Army Supply Commander
Group Army Administrative Officer (IV a)
Group Army Medical Officer (IV b)
Group Army Veterinary Officer (IV c)
Group Army Field Postmaster

Dept. Army Provisions

Subj.:
Provisions for the field army, orders to armies, co-operation with agencies, chief of army provisions, and inspector-general of training.
Liaison with C.-in-C. Luftwaffe/Luftwaffe quartermaster-general

Group Qu 1
Subj.:
Deployment study concerning provision, studies, lessons, and troop structure

Group Qu 2
Subj.:
Rearward services, orders of battle and provision strengths, field-post supervision

Group Qu 3
Subj.:
Ammunition, motor-vehicles, motor-fuel, weapons and equipment

Group Technology
Engineering equipment, road-building, field railways, building materials and equipment

Group Field Gendarmerie
Organization, personnel matters, traffic control, evaluation of experience

Command control centre

Dept. Was Administration

Subj.:
Political matters, co-operation with supreme Reich authorities and Party departments

Group Qu 4
Subj.:
Organization of military administration, executive power, employment of occupation troops and field gendarmerie, captured weapons and equipment

Group Qu 5
Subj.:
Counter-intelligence within the framework of executive power, frontier control, special squads, travel documents and passes

Group Secret Field Police
Direction of the organization and engagement, as well as security-police matters

Under civilian heads:

Group V
Organization, staffing, and control of military administration

Group W
Co-opertiown with the supreme Reich authorities on economic issues, handling of all economic matters incl. those of the military administrations, decrees and laws of an economic character

Source: BA-MA, RH 3/v. 136.

DIAGRAM I.IV.4. Structure of the Department for War Administration, as on 1 May 1941

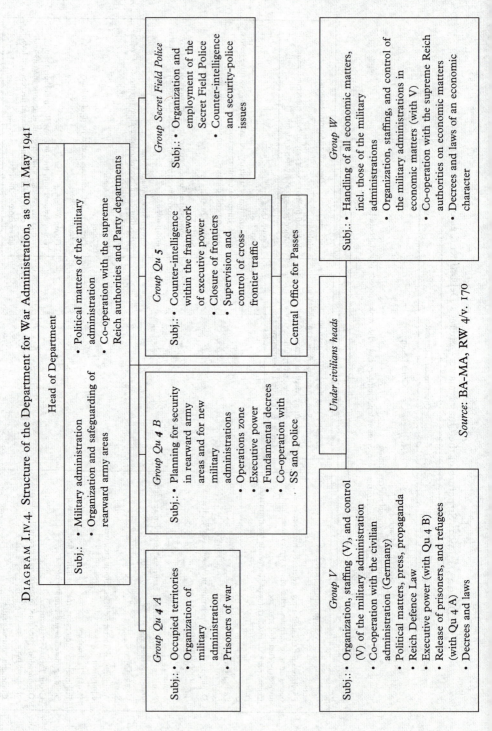

Head of Department

Subj.: • Political matters of the military administration
       • Co-operation with the supreme Reich authorities and Party departments

Group Qu 4 A

Subj.: • Occupied territories
       • Organization of military administration
       • Prisoners of war

Group Qu 4 B

Subj.: • Planning for security in rearward army areas and for new military administrations
       • Operations zone
       • Executive power
       • Fundamental decrees
       • Co-operation with SS and police

Group Qu 5

Subj.: • Counter-intelligence within the framework of executive power
       • Closure of frontiers
       • Supervision and control of cross-frontier traffic

Group Secret Field Police

Subj.: • Organization and employment of the Secret Field Police
       • Counter-intelligence and security-police issues

Central Office for Passes

Under civilians heads

Group V

Subj.: • Organization, staffing (V), and control (V) of the military administration
       • Co-operation with the civilian administration (Germany)
       • Political matters, press, propaganda
       • Reich Defence Law
       • Executive power (with Qu 4 B)
       • Release of prisoners, and refugees (with Qu 4 A)
       • Decrees and laws

Group W

Subj.: • Handling of all economic matters, incl. those of the military administrations
       • Organization, staffing, and control of the military administrations in economic matters (with V)
       • Co-operation with the supreme Reich authorities on economic matters
       • Decrees and laws of an economic character

Source: BA-MA, RW 4/v. 170

their effect on operations, emerges from his note for his report to Hitler on 3 February 1941: '*Motor vehicle* must accomplish everything.'[167]

The field branches of the quartermaster-general were staffed by the end of March 1941 and thus assumed supervision of the replenishment of depots. The idea was that the troops would go into action with 1 set of ammunition, 5 consumption quotas of fuel, and 4 days' rations. Supplies for the mobile units, especially of motor-fuel, were to be ensured for the initial period by stocks carried in the 'large-area transport pool'; beyond that, intermediate stores were to be set up about 100–200 kilometres behind the front, so as to keep transport lines short. The infantry formations were not expected to make such rapid progress and would therefore, at least initially, be supplied from stationary depots. A pause for rehabilitation once the first objectives were reached—some 300–400 kilometres beyond the jumping-off line—would be necessary for reasons of supplies; this had been taken into account by the operational planners.

The quantities of ammunition to be stockpiled in the supply districts were laid down on 17 February 1941 as shown in Table I.iv.4. Approximate figures for resences of ammunition stockpiled on 20 June 1941, including quantities added up to 25 June 1941, are given in Table I.iv.5. In addition there were 20 trainloads of mobile Army High Command stores and 80 trains available for loading.

The preparatory planning described above was in line with past supply practice, allowing for the necessary adjustments called for by the vastness of the space and its peculiarities. Planning was based on military necessities and was exclusively within the control of the chief of the Army General Staff and the quartermaster-general.

The situation was rather different in the area of instructions on the subject of military sovereignty, security, and administration in the rearward army areas, and prisoners of war.[168] Regulation of these questions depended primarily on the intentions which Hitler developed with regard to the future political conditions in the territory of the Soviet Union. On 18 December 1940 the Wehrmacht operations department, as a supplement to Directive No. 21, had issued a draft of 'Guidelines in special areas', which presumably dealt with the purely military treatment of the issue of occupation administration; the contents of this may be surmised from the new regulation. On 3 March Hitler rejected the draft and instead ordered a set of regulations going far beyond the military aspects of security and administration in a war-zone.[169] This contained

baggage' was the requirement to be provided to the mobile units by the 'large-scale transport pool'.

[167] Halder, *KTB* ii. 269 (2 Feb. 1941; not in trans.); *KTB OKW* i. 299 (3 Feb. 1941).

[168] Part c of the quartermaster-general's instructions of 3 Apr. 1941 and appendix 6, pt c, annexe 2, of 14 May 1941 on economic organizations, BA-MA, Pz.Gr. 4, 22,392/41; guidelines on booty, confiscations, and exaction of services, 20 May 1941, BA-MA H 3/1; *Hitlers Weisungen*, 88–9 (not in trans.).

[169] *KTB OKW* i. 340 ff. (3 Mar. 1941).

TABLE I.iv.1. *Ammunition Stockpiled in Supply Districts, 17 February 1941*

District	Quantity (t.)	Subtotals
North 2	20,500	
North 1	22,060	42,560
Centre 3	29,540	
Centre 2	12,030	
Centre 1	45,890	87,460
South 2	21,800	
South 1	20,500	42,300
TOTAL		172,320

Source: Annexe to OKH/GenStdH/GenQu Abt. KrVerw. No. I/750/41, 17 Feb. 1941, order to command authorities, BA-MA RH 17/191.

TABLE I.iv.2. *Stockpiles of Ammunition, 21–25 June 1941* (t.)

	Supply district		
	North	Centre	South
1st set (excl. troops)	19,000	38,000	24,000
Stock 20 June	35,000	62,000	42,000
Issued to army commands	14,000	27,000	18,000
SUBTOTAL	68,000	127,000	84,000
Additions up to 25 June 1941	6,000	8,000	6,000
TOTAL	74,000	135,000	90,000

Source: Note for report by GenQu/Qu3/I, 21 June 1941, BA-MA RH 17/191.

elements of a future permanent domination, a task outside the traditional scope of any armed forces. Once again Hitler revealed to the generals his objective of creating a number of dependent territories, comparable in status to colonies, in the Soviet regions to be conquered. Their basis should be a form of 'socialism', which, by excluding both the bourgeois intelligentsia with its aim of a Greater Russia and the existing 'Jewish-Bolshevik intelligentsia, would eliminate any future threat to the Reich'. The political administration and the forcible securing of those territories was outside the responsibilities of the Army High Command. Having accomplished its operational tasks at the front, the army was to be reduced to a minimum—an idea from which the Army High Command also proceeded in its operational plans.

As an intermediate solution, until the formation of their own 'governments', Hitler envisaged that these territories would be run by 'Reich Commissariats', supported by the military forces of Wehrmacht commanders. These forces, moreover, had to be available to the army for whatever tasks the security of operations at the front demanded. In order to prevent a 'settling down' of the army in the entire zone of operations, the sphere of responsibility of the army commander-in-chief was from the outset to be confined to as narrow an operational area as possible.

Another provision of this concept was that not only would the military opposition at the front have to be broken as quickly as possible, but any sign of resistance to the occupying forces would have to be nipped in the bud. To that end the employment of the Security Service of the SS was envisaged, alongside the Secret Field Police, which had in the past been charged with such tasks as the executive of both the Abwehr (military counter-intelligence) and the army in the field. The task of the SS in the operational zone was, above all, instantly 'to render harmless Bolshevik chieftains and commissars'.[170] Three months later, at the beginning of the war against the Soviet Union, a series of guidelines, ordinances, and orders had been issued on this set of problems; these have since become the subject of extensive discussion. As, however, the origin, meaning, and application of these instructions can be adequately judged only with a knowledge of organizational competences, and because the responsibility of individuals for their consequences can only then be truly established, it is necessary to examine the instructions briefly at this point.

Proceeding from Hitler's above-mentioned fundamental decision, on 5 March the Wehrmacht High Command notified the Army High Command that further regulations were due to be issued in good time prior to the beginning of the offensive. In line with existing practice, the legal departments of the two high commands were involved in the drafting, with assistance from the Army and Luftwaffe General Staffs and from the quartermaster depart-ments concerned. For the Army High Command the officers responsible were Lieutenant-General Eugen Müller, general (special duties) attached to the commander-in-chief of the army, and the quartermaster-general. Müller,

---

[170] Ibid. 341. Wagner's report to Hitler on 13 Mar. 1941 was concerned with policing matters, i.e. the employment of the police in the rearward army areas and questions of entry to the operational area. On 17 Mar. 1941 Wagner reported on the OKW guidelines: see Halder, *Diaries*, 828 (13 Mar. 1941), 834 (18 Mar. 1941).

whose service designation assigned him to the commander-in-chief of the army, came under the 'Legal Affairs Group in the Army High Command'. In line with his service instructions, however, this group dealt only to a minor extent with matters assigned to it by the commander-in-chief; these were procedures reserved to him as the senior legal officer, regulation of powers relating to the confirmation of verdicts, the right of pardon, and the quashing of verdicts.[171]

In all other matters the general (special duties) attached to the commander-in-chief of the army, and hence the Legal Affairs Group, acted according to the directive of the chief of the Army General Staff. These were predominantly:

- control and supervision of the practice of criminal law in the army in the field and *vis-à-vis* the population of the occupied territory: in this area provision was made for co-operation between the Legal Affairs Group and the general (special duties) on the one hand and the Army Affairs Department of the Army General Staff on the other, whenever matters of discipline and criminal jurisdiction converged; further, co-operation with the Army Personnel Department in criminal cases involving officers, and with the quartermaster-general with regard to the application of criminal law relating to the local population;
- co-operation with the War Administration Department of the quartermaster-general with regard to questions of martial law, criminal jurisdiction in the occupied territories, and the law relating to prisoners of war;
- co-operation with the senior quartermaster IV on matters of international law.

This meant that the formal severance of the Legal Affairs Group from the quartermaster-general's sphere, i.e. the Army General Staff, was *de facto* rescinded for all matters relating to the army in the field and the zone of operations by virtue of Halder's right to issue instructions to the 'general (special duties) attached to the commander-in-chief of the army'.

Hitler's directive on the 'practice of jurisdiction in the Barbarossa zone of operations and on special measures by army personnel' of 5 March, together with his ordinance of 13 May 1941, meant that military administration was to confine itself to securing the material assets needed by the German forces, their transportation and storage, and their protection and distribution.[172] In addition, they were obliged to co-operate with 'the agencies of the Reich Leader SS'. These, however, were already engaged in security and reconnaissance tasks, with the further intention of establishing permanent domination.[173]

---

[171] Der ObdH/GenStdH/GZ (I²) 1. Staffel No. 2182/40 geh., 29 Sept. 1941, signed p.p. Halder, BA-MA RH 19 III/146.

[172] See Diagram I.IV.4. This concerns administration by the army, not the military administration authorities. Ordinance on jurisdiction: OKW/WFSt/L (IV/Qu) No. 44178/41 g.Kdos. Chefs., 14 May 1941, BA-MA RW 4/v. 577.

[173] 'Regelung des Einsatzes der Sicherheitspolizei und des SD im Verband des Heeres' [Regu-

The ordinance on the practice of jurisdiction contained four sections. The first of these dealt with the treatment of criminal actions committed by enemy civilians in the rearward areas and by irregulars. The ruling that collective punishment could be ordered by an officer not below the rank of battalion commander reflected Halder's anxiety, on the one hand, to ensure the safety of the troops and, on the other, to prevent arbitrary action or violence by individuals. The second section stated that, in the event of criminal actions by members of the German Wehrmacht against the local population there was no obligation to prosecute, except for certain crimes of violence. This was justified by the Bolshevik influence on the 1918 revolution in Germany and during the postwar period. In such cases the senior law officer had to decide whether a juridical penalty was called for or whether disciplinary punishment was sufficient.

Section 3 made it the duty of commanders in the field to brief all their officers on section 1 thoroughly and in good time.

Fourthly, their legal advisers were to be notified of the regulations and of verbal reports to the commanding generals on the subject of the leadership's political intentions. Only verdicts in line with those intentions were to be confirmed.[174]

The commander-in-chief of the army issued these guidelines on 24 May 1941, accompanied by supplementary instructions. To begin with, he emphasized that the measures taken in the area of security and rapid pacification should not be allowed to detract from the principal task of the army, and that the drastic procedure laid down by Hitler applied to serious cases of insurrection. Criminal actions of a lesser kind were to be punished according to the decision of an officer. In accordance with the supplements, which had to be regarded as absolutely mandatory, it was the duty of superior officers to prevent arbitrary acts by individual members of the forces at all costs. The suspension of jurisdiction in the occupied territory was seen as a temporary state of affairs; proposals for its restoration from army HQs up to army groups, and thence to the Army High Command, were expected.

This was Brauchitsch's understanding; during the period which followed it was passed on verbally by the general (special duties), the quartermaster-general, and the competent judges to the command authorities down to division level.[175] As in the ordinance itself, it was now expressly laid down that

---

lation of the employment of the security police and the SS security service within the structure of the army], OKH/GenStdH/GenQu/Abt. Kriegsverwaltung, 28 Apr. 1941, and 'Grundsätze für die Zusammenarbeit zwischen Geheimer Staatspolizei und den Abwehrdiensten der Wehrmacht' [Principles of co-operation between the secret state police (Gestapo) and the counter-intelligence services of the Wehrmacht], 23 Dec. 1936, BA-MA RH 19 III/388, 271. See the regulation during the Balkan campaign, 2 Apr. 1941, OKH/GenStdH/GenQu/Abt. Kriegsverwaltung No. II. 0308/41, BA-MA RH 31-I/v. 23.

[174] A clear ruling was indispensable to Wagner because his instructions required a legal basis and time was running short.

[175] OKH/Gen.z.b.V.b. ObdH/Gr.R.Wes. No. 80/41 g.Kdos. Chefs., 24 May 1941, BA-MA RH 22/155. For the passing on of this ordinance see BA-MA RH 19 III/722, annexes 24, and 37; Pz.Gr. 3/Ic, Tätigkeitsbericht [Activity report] No. 2, Jan.–July 1941, BA-MA RH 21-3/423, reproduced

the second section, relating to criminal proceedings for excesses committed by members of the German forces, was not to be publicized. In all cases where only disciplinary punishments for criminal acts were being considered, it was necessary to examine whether that was sufficient or whether criminal proceedings should be started.

This meant that the legal position should be aimed at which had applied in the past and which was laid down in article 16a of the 'Decree on military criminal proceedings in war and during special operations', as well as in an ordinance of the commander-in-chief of the army on the subject of disciplinary punishment.[176] That legal ordinance of 1938 ruled that no action might be taken without court proceedings against citizens of enemy countries who had committed punishable actions against the occupying power. Admittedly, a proviso was added even then, to the effect that 'the rulings of the present ordinance for proceedings against citizens of enemy countries' might need amending 'if in those countries the procedural rules and their application do not guarantee the same legal security'. This undoubtedly meant that their application could be restricted to those enemy countries which recognized the Hague Land War Convention and the Agreement on Prisoners of War. Neither was recognized by the Soviet Union in 1941.

As for the guidelines on the treatment of political commissars, Brauchitsch likewise curbed arbitrary actions by ordering that the prerequisite of proceedings against that circle of persons must be 'that the individual in question places himself, or intends to place himself, against the German Wehrmacht by a specific identifiable action or attitude'. The 'disposal' of commissars with the fighting forces had to be accomplished discreetly outside the combat zone proper, on the order of an officer, after the commissars had been separated from their men.

That was the legal position which the army commander-in-chief laid down in his ordinances. What divergences occurred in practice, and under what

---

in garbled form in Jacobsen, 'Kommissarbefehl', Docs. 14, 19, according to NOKW 2672. Regrettable in particular is the omission of the justification for severe penal measures (paragraph A) and of paragraph B on the sole decision of the senior law officer in penal measures against German servicemen.

[176] Verordnung über das Sonderstrafrecht im Kriege und bei besonderem Einsatz (KSSVO) [Ordinance on special criminal law in war and during special operations] and Verordnung über das militärische Strafverfahren im Kriege und bei besonderem Einsatz (KStVO) [Ordinance on military penal proceedings in war and during special operations], 17 Aug. 1938, with amendments in H.Dv. 3/13 and analogous service instructions of the Luftwaffe and navy, with evidence of publication and of the amendments in *RGBl.* (1939) and (1940). Based upon its is the ordinance of the C.-in-C. of the army, 12 Nov. 1939, *HVBl.* (1939), pt. c. No. 1071.

Judgements on the attitude of the C.-in-C. of the army have so far failed to take appropriate note of the fact that reference was expressly made to the invocation by the army C.-in-C. of the authority deriving from Article 16a of KStVO. There was certainly a serious effort by Brauchitsch to avoid the tightening of the regulations that was being feared and to maintain the existing legal position. This can be shown even after the commencement of operations (see sect. II.i.1(*b*) at n. 172). It is also obvious that the interpretations of the juridical situation in the press, which fail to take note of the text of the above-mentioned ordinances of 1938–9, miss the point.

conditions they were ordered, tolerated, or punished is another question—one that will arise from case to case. To demote Brauchitsch's ordinance to the status of a non-committal formula, or to view it solely as a measure for the preservation of discipline—even though that is of overriding importance in any army in the world, if only in the interest of orderly combat—does not seem fair.

The regulations in the field of executive power were to have far-reaching consequences on the work of the quartermaster-general. His department's administrative tasks in the Barbarossa zone of operations were determined, and greatly circumscribed, by the guidelines on special areas supplementing Directive No. 21 and the subsequent service instructions for Wehrmacht commanders, as well as by the activity of the Economic Staff East.[177] Wagner in consequence proceeded from the assumption that the systematic administration and utilization of the occupied country was a *cura posterior* and no business of the army's.[178] At the same time, any senseless destruction or wastage of assets of value to the war effort had to be avoided within the area of the fighting forces.

Collection of material of value to the war effort was regulated by guidelines of the economic organization on 14 May 1941; these applied to the entire occupied territory.[179] Although their primary purpose was to keep the army supplied, preparations were to be made at the same time for the utilization of the occupied territory for the Four-year Plan. In consequence, the economic staff with its economic agencies was, even within the army's zone, no longer subordinate to the army's command authorities. The quartermaster-general, however, was exceedingly concerned to achieve the most efficient possible collection and utilization of any material for the army, not only because of supply shortages but also because of foreseeable transport bottlenecks. Thus, in addition to the administrative regulations and the 'Guidelines for booty, confiscation, and exacting of services', which concerned fiscal questions relating to the property of the Red Army and civilian population, he issued an 'Order for the securing of booty during operations'.[180]

Army and corps commands were instructed immediately to secure captured stocks for keeping military operations going—primarily foodstuffs, motor-fuel, motor-vehicles, horses and horse-drawn vehicles, ammunition, weapons and equipment, medical material, and (to some extent) clothing. All unwanted stocks were to be passed on to the command agencies of the quartermaster-general. Each Wehrmacht service was to receive only the portion of booty used by it; specific equipment was to be handed over to the Luftwaffe or the navy. The decision on the final allocation of motor-vehicles

---

[177] On the general issue of economic planning see sect. I.III.2(*a*) (Müller).

[178] Part C of Wagner's instructions (above, n. 168).   [179] See n. 168.

[180] Befehl für die Erfassung der Beute [Order for the securing of booty], BA-MA H 17/28; 'Richtlinien für Beute, Beschlagnahmung und Inanspruchnahme von Dienstleistungen' [Guidelines on booty, confiscation, and exacting of services], with Jodl's comment on misgivings by the Foreign Department, BA-MA RW 4/v. 525 and H 3/1.

was to be made by the Plenipotentiary-General for Motor Transport. An attached list of urgently needed material clearly revealed the gaps in German stockpiles.

The zone between the rearward area of an army ('rückwärtiges Armeegebiet') and Germany, or the Reich commissariats, or Germany's allies, was called 'rearward army area' ('rückwärtiges Heeresgebiet'). For the discharge of the great variety of tasks to be expected, the creation of HQ staffs 'commander rearward army area' for the three army groups was ordered on 15 March 1941. The three staffs, 101, 102, and 103, were set up from the staffs of the general (special duties) attached to the commander in France and in Belgium and Northern France, and the general (special duties) III in the Army High Command. Allocation of troops proceeded gradually in the form of three security divisions.[181]

In view of the expected speedy execution of the campaign the duties of the commander of the rearward army area were to be of a temporary character only. The commander, answering directly to the army group HQ, exercised executive power in accordance with the directives of the general commanding the army group; he was responsible for the security and utilization of the country. Objects to be safeguarded were supply-bases, supply-routes, transport centres and bridges, transport, airfields, railways, and signals communications. Added to these were the guarding of prisoners of war, their employment, and the guarding of stores left behind and of captured stocks.

The commanders of the security divisions were to act in agreement with the command agency of the quartermaster-general, the senior quartermasters of the separate armies, the managers of supply-depots, and the communications commanders. A small number of well-equipped bases for supplies and for controlling the country were to be set up.

Field garrison HQs and local garrison HQs were to be equipped as permanent posts in accordance with directives from army group HQs. With the security and police forces under their command they were to secure strong points against enemy action.

Field gendarmerie and police units were to be employed in traffic control and maintaining order. Intervention groups (one regiment) were to be held available at tactically important points and employed against scattered enemy forces or emerging bands. To that extent these formations came under the command of the army group commander-in-chief.

For technical tasks (electricity, water, gas) and workshops the armies had technical battalions at their disposal; each army group, moreover, had a detachment of the Technische Nothilfe (Technical emergency service). Their tasks were to be co-ordinated by the command authorities.[182]

---

[181] Establishment instruction of 15 Mar. 1941, BA-MA RH 22/1-2. Guidelines for the training of the security divisions and of the forces under the command of the commander of the rearward army area of 21 Mar. 1941, BA-MA RH 21-2/v. 100.

[182] See Hampe and Bradley, *Die unbekannte Armee*, 35 ff.

From the very outset the Army High Command refused to allow the quartermaster-general any additional forces for the discharge of these manifold tasks beyond his nine security divisions. Wagner was referred to the offer of the police to provide forces for that purpose. This represented a first step towards co-operation, which led to the assignment of battalions of regular police to the commanders of the rearward army areas. The other side of the coin was that these forces, in personnel terms, simultaneously came under the command of the 'senior SS and police commanders'. More far-reaching arrangements, relating to the sphere of the security police, granting it the right to arrest 'important individuals (leading *émigrés*, saboteurs, terrorists, etc.)' and to execute civilians on its own responsibility, led, according to a diary entry by Halder on 25 March 1941, to a protest by Brauchitsch, who had evidently not been informed, although his signature stood under the agreement of 28 March. Brauchitsch now insisted that an immediate separation be carried out between the range of duties of the Secret Field Police and the SS Security Service; he authorized army group and army commanders, if they saw fit, to suspend their activities if these were apt to interfere with the progress of operations.[183] This arrangement, proposed by Brauchitsch, became irrelevant the moment the army's own security agencies ceased to be available in sufficient numbers.

The quartermaster-general's range of duties thus overlapped, *inter alia* in the field of military security and administration in the widest sense, with the theoretically entirely separate areas of occupation policy and economic management. The staffing of the garrison HQs, of the security units, and the rest of the rearward services inevitably called for 'helping out' wherever the fighting front, the economic organization, or any other authority required services. But the overriding task remained the provision of supplies to the army in the field; here the quartermaster-general was dependent not only on strategic and operational decisions, but also on the capacity of the transport system and on the work performance of the Todt Organization, the Reich Labour Service, and the prisoners of war. It was these that would decide whether or not the army in the east was viable and whether its operations could be sustained.

(*h*) *The Structure of the Army in the East and Deployment*
(*See Annexe Volume, No. 1*)

Organizational measures normally reflect proposed control of a future development or intended reactions to it. Isolated consideration of the organization of a military force therefore has justification only in terms of pure history of military structures. If, nevertheless, the structure of the army in the summer of 1940 is specifically examined here, then the purpose is to provide a clear overview, one which will make it possible to describe the problems of its

---

[183] This was in line with the regulation first ordered by Halder for the Balkan campaign on 2 Apr. 1941.

technical and material equipment. These in turn were governed by the overall management of personnel and material.

To begin with, it should be made clear that the restructuring and reorganization, as well as the training and equipment, of the army for a combat task against an enemy superior in numbers and material potential, occupying a geo-strategically vast territory, could obviously not merely be a reshaping or restructuring of the existing fighting force; it had to be a new structure from scratch, calling for an infringement of the criteria of personnel selection valid in the past as well as for consideration of the limits of any rearmament. The extent to which personnel and material resources were necessary, or feasible, would depend on strategic objectives and on the anticipated expenditure of forces. Finally, a decision would have to be made on what tasks were to be assigned to the army and which would be performed by war-service labour, the Reich Labour Service, the Todt Organization, and other Wehrmacht auxiliaries. The transport sector at any rate was dependent, both for organization and for the practical implementation of its tasks, on the personnel of the Reich railways and of the railway administrations of occupied Europe operating under Reich railway management.

The assessment of the presumed further development of the war, both by Hitler and by the military high commands, at the height of the campaign in the west was reflected towards the end of May in a reorientation of the disposition of forces. On 28 May 1940 Hitler, expecting an early arrangement with Britain, informed the commander-in-chief of the army of his intention to have the army gradually reduced to a peace footing.[184] The eventual total strength to be aimed at was 24 armoured and 12 motorized divisions, as well as 30–40 other divisions. Along with the intention to modernize the army and keep it available solely for security tasks in the broadest meaning of the term, the reduction of the approximately 160 mobilized major formations was to meet the manpower needs of the economy, especially an intensified rearmament of the Luftwaffe and the navy. First calculations by the organization department of the Army General Staff suggested a useful structure of 22 armoured divisions, 11 motorized, 24 infantry, and 6 mountain divisions; in addition an initial requirement was indicated for a separate airborne army of 6 infantry and 3 mountain divisions.

The prerequisite of a restructuring of the army along these lines was the conclusion of a secure peace. Until such time, a transitional army was to be created, utilizing the experiences of the operations recently concluded and effectively relieving the manpower needs of industry. On 12 June the organization department of the Army General Staff submitted a rough calculation which provided for the disbandment of 40 divisions. On 15 June Hitler endorsed this proposal with a first directive demanding that, even before the conclusion of the campaign in the west, a start should be made on the

---

[184] See sects. 2 and 3 of the present chapter.

doubling of the mobile units and the reduction of the overall strength of the army to 120 divisions.

In spite of a flare-up of the political and military scene in the Baltic countries and along the Romanian frontiers—which was closely watched by the foreign ministry and by the Wehrmacht—Halder on 16 June arranged for the transfer of surprisingly weak army units to the east, as against the disposition of forces elsewhere. A mere 15 divisions were to be moved to the east, compared with a strength of 85 divisions, 20 of them mobile, in the west. For securing Norway and stepping up the pressure on Sweden Halder envisaged a total of 12 divisions and 2–3 armoured formations. However, the reconstitution of 45 major formations by means of material to be held in readiness remained an option under consideration.

On 18 June the organization department's detailed and comprehensive plan was ready to be submitted. Alongside the modernization of the army and its reduction to the size envisaged by Hitler, the plan already contained a first suggestion of Halder's concept for the repulse of a possible attack by the Red Army, which had just then begun to move westwards. On 23 June Hitler approved the views and the structural proposals of the army commander-in-chief.

The very next day the army group commands were given a first briefing on general intentions. On 26 June the 'Order for the Regrouping of the Army' was issued, followed on 30 June by the order relating to the reduction and restructuring of the army. On 28 June Halder in person, at Army Group B headquarters in Versailles, briefed the representatives of the operations and quartermaster departments of the army groups and armies on all the measures planned, proceeding from the assumption that the main weight of the war effort, 'so long as the political situation remains unchanged', would lie with the Luftwaffe and the navy.[185] The head of the operations department emphasized in his report that priority would be given to initiating the transfer of the units earmarked for the east; the mobile units were to set off at once. The staff of 'Group Guderian' were to hold themselves available in Berlin for Eighteenth Army HQ; the mobile divisions and corps commands would initially come under the Director-General of Training for rehabilitation and would then be placed under the tactical command of Eighteenth Army HQ.

In accordance with the order of 30 June, 35 divisions were to be disbanded and dismissed—as it seemed, for good. These were the divisions of the 5th and 6th wave, the local rifle divisions (altogether 18 units), 4 positional divisions, and 13 divisions of the 3rd wave.[186] The older age-groups, including men born in 1908, were to be discharged; the younger men were to be assigned to units which would continue to exist. Generally, there was to be an assimilation of

---

[185] Minutes of the conference and the orders concerned, BA-MA RH 19 III/141.

[186] The subdivision of the army into 'waves' was carried out—proceeding from the peacetime army—in order to identify the units which were equivalent in terms of equipment and combat-readiness. See Müller-Hillebrand, *Heer*, ii. 122–46, 153 ff.; and sect. I.III.4 (Müller).

personnel and equipment to the divisions of the 1st wave. The last third of the 1919 class and the 1920 class were to be called up for the autumn of 1940 and trained.[187]

Disbanding, restructuring, and replenishing the units were the duty of the Director-General of Training. Training and commanding the units, however, remained the duties of the command authorities of the field forces. The divisions were given a new order of battle; this was partly based on recent experience concerning the relationship between the size of a unit and the effectiveness of its command—this applied to the armoured and mobile units, as well as to the light divisions—and also on the limits set by the availability of weapons, equipment, and motor-vehicles. Alongside the divisions, the army troops, which were assigned to army groups and armies for special tasks, on a case-by-case basis, were lifted out of their previous subordinate positions to become the core of mobile formations shortly to be established and of new army troops. Simultaneously, army troops had to be rapidly assigned to Eighteenth Army command. Primarily, however, the 4 armoured and 2 motorized divisions which were grouped together under XXX (mot.) Army Corps and XVI Army Corps and whose engagement-planning was in the hands of XIX (mot.) Army Corps, the 'Group Guderian' in Berlin, had to be transformed to fit into the new structure and rehabilitated.[188] The army commander-in-chief's order of 30 June 1940 took account of Halder's estimate of the situation at the end of June to the extent that, beyond the establishment of a combat-ready army of the above-mentioned size, the Director-General of Training had to make preparations for the raising of 20 'occupation divisions' in such a way that this could be put into effect at any time after 15 September. Moreover, preparations were going ahead for the assembly of captured weapons for the establishment of further divisions. This meant that the framework of the 120-division army was already exceeded.[189] Eventually the general staff declared the reduction of the army to be impossible if its combat-readiness was at the same time to be maintained. The result was that Hitler, following a report by the commander-in-chief of the army, decided on 13 July

---

[187] Befehl ObdH/GenStdH/Org.Abt. No. 969/40, 30 June 1940, BA-MA RH 19 III/141. The 1921 and 1922 classes were called up on 1 Mar. and 1 May 1941; see Müller-Hillebrand, *Heer*, ii. 101.

[188] OKH/Chef HRüst u. BdE betr. Auffüllung und Auffrischung von Pz. und mot. Div. [re replenishment and rehabilitation of armd. and mot. divisions], 18 July 1940, BA-MA RH 19 III/147. That rehabilitation had to be completed by 31 Aug. 1940; after that date elements of units had to be surrendered for the establishment of new units. Even during restructuring of these units, readiness to move off within 72 hours was to be maintained for combat-worthy elements.

[189] It would be difficult to dismiss altogether a connection between this provident intra-army enlargement and Halder's ideas after 15 June 1940. The 10 envisaged motorized infantry divisions of the army were further augmented by 3 divisions of the Waffen-SS and the 'Großdeutschland' and 'Leibstandarte Adolf Hitler' brigades, the Brigade 900, and the Armoured Brigades 100 and 101, equipped with captured tanks and set up in France. Halder moreover envisaged 25 battalions (from the divisions to be disbanded) for the guarding of prisoners: Halder, *Diaries*, 496 (5 July 1940).

1940 to disband only 17 of the 35 divisions. The bulk of the men of the remaining 18 divisions were merely to be granted leave while remaining available to the army. This measure was ordered on 22 July, one day after Hitler's briefing from Brauchitsch.[190] Rearrangement of the call-up classes and replenishment of all units to the level of the 1st wave were postponed; certain priorities now had to be observed.

Hitler's decision of 31 July 1940 to have preparations started for a war against the Soviet Union created a new situation in the areas of army structure, including the planned restructuring, and the assignment of existing material and of material yet to be provided, and in that of training; all these went far beyond the organizational set-up envisaged. Now the army was to be enlarged to 180 divisions, and the reserve army and army troops, originally scheduled at 20 divisions, extended and equipped. This enlargement of the army took place under the difficult circumstances of preparations for a landing in Britain—these preparations had to be maintained—and of the intensified reinforcement of Eighteenth Army with army troops and the provision of construction units, equipment, and all kinds of material of which the Director-General of Training had only a limited supply.

By September the replenishment of existing divisions and their equipment had progressed sufficiently for partial units to be designated as the cores of divisions to be newly established.[191] On 26 September the transformation of infantry divisions into armoured and motorized divisions was initiated. Parts of the 9 divisions which were laying off men were moreover to be used for establishing the 4th and 5th Mountain Divisions, and for re-establishing the 20 infantry divisions of the 11th and 12th waves. Only these two waves, along with the motorized units and army troops, could be regarded as genuinely battle-worthy new units. But here too a restriction had to be accepted, since of the 10 divisions of the 12th wave 4 were being established only as 'light divisions'. These divisions had just 2 instead of the usual 3 infantry regiments; they had fewer weapons and were intended for operations in impassable terrain. Another peculiarity was the 5th Light Infantry Division (mot.), which was earmarked for North Africa and part of whose core personnel had come from 3rd Armoured Division.

Replacement of the releases, which affected nearly all the divisions of the army after September 1940, came initially from the reserve detachments, provided that these included trained personnel. In addition, there were the untrained recruits enlisted in October.

Battle-worthiness could be established only in stages for the separate waves.

---

[190] Ibid. 491 (3 July 1940), 506 (13 July 1940), 523 (19 July 1940); OKH/GenStdH/Org.Abt. No. 1102/40, 22 July 1940 betr. Verringerung und Umgliederung des Feldheeres [re diminution and restructuring of the field forces], BA-MA RH 19 III/141; also Müller-Hillebrand, *Heer*, ii. 63–4.

[191] Müller-Hillebrand, *Heer*, ii. 78 ff., table 19; OKH orders for the establishment of new divisions: BA-MA RH 19 III/147.

The last of the battle-worthy divisions to reach that state of readiness by mid-May 1941 were the armoured and motorized formations.[192] The main reason for this late date for the highly technical formations was the shortage of tanks, vehicles, and equipment. Motor-vehicles were only gradually being provided, and 20th Armoured Division and the motorized infantry divisions were uniformly equipped with French material. This required the setting up of appropriate replacement columns and depots. For the divisions of the 11th and 12th waves French vehicles with caterpillar tracks (*genilettes*) were made available for the creation of anti-tank units. Altogether 4,930 captured armoured vehicles, including ammunition trailers, were used for that purpose. Armoured Brigades 100 and 101 were likewise set up in France on the basis of captured material. This motley equipment, further increased by Czech production and what was left of Polish booty, not only caused difficulties in training and operational use but also created friction in the entire supply process. It must be obvious even from this haphazard selection of instances that the material equipment of the ground forces for the intended war against the Soviet Union was based primarily on existing army material, with captured equipment available as a second string, new production being drawn upon only as a third resort.[193]

The reorganization of the major army formations in September 1940 was based on the assumption that in the west there remained only security tasks, and that the mobile and battle-worthy formations earmarked for the Soviet Union would gradually have to be moved back to Reich territory. These changes, which coincided with the final phase of the deployment of the eastern army, were initiated by the subdivision of areas of command and by the creation of new command authorities.[194] The three existing army group commands were increased by a further one (D); this was intended to remain behind in the occupied western territories. Army Group C HQ was transferred to Dresden on 1 November 1940; there it was given the task of supervising the training and instruction of the divisions stationed on German war territory, and ensuring their combat-readiness. These units, whose material and personnel were supplied by the military districts, thus came under the command of a field-force authority; this, it was intended, would safeguard the Army General Staff's interests with regard to their future employment. To this end, Eleventh Army HQ (Leipzig) and Second Army HQ (Munich) were placed under the Army Group command.

For the command of the mobile formations—armoured divisions and

---

[192] The following data according to Halder, *Diaries*, 588–9 (17 Sept. 1940), 746 (23 Dec, 1940), 852 (3 Apr. 1941). On combat-readiness, however, note the limitation for 'Group Guderian' and for the formations to be employed in the Balkans after Jan. 1941. On 6 June 1941 Halder observed: 'The armoured divisions in the east are not the same as last year in the west' (minute of his report at Zossen, AOK 18/Ia, KTB, BA-MA 19601/2).

[193] See sect. I.iii.4 at n. 434 (Müller).

[194] Müller-Hillebrand, *Heer*, ii. 68 ff., establishment instructions with the new orders of battle: BA-MA RH 19 III/146 and 147.

motorized infantry divisions[195]—the staffs of XXII Army Corps (Armoured Group 1) and XIX Army Corps (Armoured Group 2), set up during the western campaign and there named after their commanding generals von Kleist and Guderian, were increased by two and on 16 November (7 December in the case of Armoured Group 4) renamed Armoured Group 1–4 HQs.[196] These group commands were intended to assume the leadership of a multiplicity of mobile units during operations; outside operations their superior army commands were to regulate their employment. This subordination to an army HQ subsequently resulted in considerable friction, aggravated by personal disagreements. These emerged even at the initial stage of an operation and called for considerable diplomatic skill on the part of Halder and the army commander-in-chief.

The principal task of these command authorities was training based on the lessons of the western campaign and on the combat conditions likely to be encountered in a future theatre of war. By means of regular inspections and submission of up-to-date reports on the state of the divisions an accurate picture of their combat-readiness was obtained.[197] Exempt from that supervision were the divisions of the 13th and 14th waves, which were to be used as occupation troops; they were composed of the 'divisions on leave', to be recalled when released from the armaments industry, mines, and agriculture after January 1941. Altogether 84 divisions were either restructured or newly established by 1 April 1941.[198]

The main effort of the army was in the areas of training and equipment. These activities, however, were disrupted for some of the units by an envisaged employment connected with the dispute between Hungary and Romania, a dispute verging on war itself, and by the assembly of Twelfth Army, later also of Second Army, for the campaign against Greece and Yugoslavia.[199]

Intensive training was also started for the officer corps by the War Academy, and courses were organized for medium-ranking and unit commanders. Of particular importance to Halder was the training of general-staff officers both

[195] The term 'mobile formations' is used here for the formations listed, even though initially only the armoured units and the cavalry division were so designated.

[196] OKH/GenStdH/Org.Abt., 16 Nov. 1940 for Armd. Gps. 1–3, 7 Dec. 1940 for Armd. Group 4. Reorganization to the new wartime strength took place with effect from 13 Dec. 1940: BA-MA RH 19 III/146.

[197] These reports are found, for example, in H.Gr. C, BA-MA RH 19 III/148 and 149. Training of the armoured groups was supervised by Armoured Group 3 HQ. Second Army HQ was placed under Army Group B at the beginning of April and was subsequently employed against Yugoslavia. Eleventh Army HQ ('Command Staff Munich') transferred to Romania at the beginning of May as 'Command of the German Forces' there.

[198] Halder, *Diaries*, 547–8 (12 Aug. 1940).

[199] See sect. I.1.2 at n. 82 (Förster). On the disruptive effects on army development see Müller-Hillebrand, *Heer*, ii. 83 ff. From 28 Mar. 1941 onwards Halder (*Diaries*, 842–3) was calculating the rehabilitation periods for the formations, especially the mobile forces; see also Halder, *Diaries*, 855 (4 Apr. 1941), 861–2 (7 Apr. 1941). Apart from the delay of Barbarossa, Halder was uneasy about the prematurely tied-down OKH reserves.

for existing staffs and for those to be newly set up.[200] The requirement for general-staff officers—beyond those already available and allowing for the existing reserve of 64 officers—amounted to 138. To that end two courses of approximately ten weeks' duration were set up.[201] The number of general-staff posts, however, increased from 982 in November to 1,053 in the spring of 1941 because of the demands of the quartermaster-general for his field agencies attached to the army groups, for the security divisions and the commanders of the rearward army areas, and for liaison staffs. Because of the shortage of qualified officers, eligible for general-staff training on account, of their age, and in view of the great needs of the fighting forces for new posts and for the replacement of over-age front-line officers, it was decided to appoint reserve officers to the posts of third general staff officers (Ic, responsible for enemy situation) at divisions, corps HQs, and the new army HQs; these now had to be trained.[202] On 9 November 1940 Halder issued an order for the training of general-staff officers; this stressed the need for 'instruction in the ideas of combat conditions in the enlarged Greater German territory'.[203]

The guidelines for the training of the troops were issued as early as July 1940.[204] Training of recruits, performed partly in the field army and partly in the reserve army, was reorganized by ordinance of 21 September with regard to the classes to be called up—1919 (remainder) and 1920. The training period was estimated at three months, as against the eight weeks customary until then

[200] These were 1 army group HQ (D), 3 army HQs (Fifteenth, Eleventh, Seventeenth), 14 corps HQs, 2 Higher Commands, and three agencies for the rearward areas. In addition, general-staff officers were needed for 42 divisions, as well as, after Feb.–Mar., for the 'divisions on leave' and for the staffs of the Wehrmacht commanders in the east.

[201] OKH/GenStdH/GZ, 'Die personelle Entwicklung des Generalstabes des Heeres während des Krieges 1939/1942' [Personnel trends in the Army General Staff during the war, 1939–42], BA-MA RH 2/v. 238 and v. 154–7.

[202] These Ic officers came from a great variety of professional groups. Their selection no doubt allowed for the belief that, during tranquil periods, the Ic would largely be concerned with troop care and 'intellectual armament'. Generally speaking, however, this abandonment of a branch of the general staff to reserve officers testifies to its low assessment; it was always regarded only as a short-term appointment. The most prominent exception was Gehlen—which only confirms the thesis.

[203] In his order (BA-MA RH 2/v. 238) Halder especially emphasized instruction in operational thinking on the next higher command level, the conditions of leadership of motorized units, and the prerequisites for an adequate quartermaster service: Halder's note to the chiefs of staff re further training of general-staff officers, 14 May 1941, BA-MA RH 21-2/v. 100; orders and appointments in H.Gr.C/O1, Training of general-staff officers, 10 Sept. 1940–31 Jan. 1941, and 16 Jan. 1941, BA-MA RH 19 III/153, 154; Guidelines for the training of general-staff officers in the quartermaster service, 13 Nov. 1940, BA-MA RH 19 III/153; Map exercise of the quartermaster-general within the framework of Army Group South, Feb. 1941, BA-MA RH 3/v. 132. Note should be taken in this context of the connection with the map exercise 'Otto' of the Army Group South HQ on 5 Feb. 1941.

[204] ObdH/GenStdH/Az 34 GZ, 5 July 1940, 'Guidelines for troop service in the occupied territories after conclusion of operations', BA-MA RH 19 III/152. This order also regulated the responsibilities of the individual command authorities and of the General (special duties) II for the Reich war territory. Otherwise, needless to say, all other army regulations continued in force; they were further modified by the training department in the Army General Staff and enormously multiplied. In addition, there were the training orders of the individual armies with their 'off-shoots' down to company level.

in the reserve army. On 7 October 1940 the commander-in-chief of the army eventually issued guidelines for field service in the winter of 1940–1; the introduction made the point that 'what matters now is that the time available in the winter is used to the full for enhancing the training of the troops in all areas in such a way that by the spring they will be ready for whatever task the Führer assigns to them'.[205] The generals commanding army groups and armies were to ensure that individual experiences of the troops in the western campaign were not generalized; the troops should 'on the whole' be trained 'for fighting an equal opponent'.

Special emphasis was placed on 'spiritual armament', i.e. explanation of the purpose of the war by unit commanders. A list of written sources, including speeches by Hitler and excerpts from *Mein Kampf*, was followed by an elucidation of the concept of 'living-space': Germany's war aim was the safeguarding of 'living-/economic space', not the subjugation of neighbouring peoples. Autarky was defined as independence from imports of vital commodities.

On 21 February the commander-in-chief of the army issued a set of guidelines to which special attention was directed.[206] They emphasized the demand for training 'officers and men in a ruthless spirit of attack, boldness, and resolute action, inspired by confidence in the superiority of the German soldier over any opponent and by unshakable faith in final victory.' This was followed by directives fully tailored to the difficulties of war in the vastness of the Soviet Union, with its sparseness of roads; they stressed the need for a rapid functioning of the command apparatus, for supplies to be viewed as part of tactical leadership, protection of exposed flanks, and security for lengthy supply-lines. Defence against attacks, ambushes, and deceptions was also to be practised; this applied equally to reserves, resting troops, and rearward services, which had to expect action not only by mobile enemy forces but also by paratroops, sabotage teams, and agents. All branches were to be trained in preventive and swift use of their anti-tank weapons. Advancing and attacking spearheads were to be reinforced by high-penetration artillery pieces; armoured units were to practise conflict between tanks. Movement was not to be halted because of tank warnings. Officers and men had to learn to manage with few, bad, and inaccurate maps. Special emphasis was placed on the need for rapid co-operation between different service branches and on speedy contact with the Luftwaffe. The Balkan campaign too left its trace in an instruction from the Training Department on 28 May. Central to success were adaptability and swift action by commanders; frequently it would not be possible to proceed by written orders but instant decisions would have to be taken instead. Instructions on the supervision of movement along roads as-

[205] BA-MA RH 19 III/152; OKH/GenStdH/Ausb.Abt., 20 Nov. 1940, ibid.; Guidelines ObdH/Ausb.Abt., 21 Feb. 1941, and Lessons from the campaign in the south-east, 28 May 1941, BA-MA RH 21-2/v. 100. Training was also based on examples garnered from the Red Army's field-service regulations and from Soviet periodicals illustrating attack and defence by a Soviet rifle division: BA-MA RH 20-20/124.

[206] Guidelines ObdH/Ausb.Abt., BA-MA 21-2/v. 100.

signed for the advance also made allowance for the conditions to be expected in future.[207]

To ensure supervision of the observance of the training guidelines, the schooling of officers and men in the spirit of the guidelines, and fulfilment of the resulting requirements of discipline and good order, the commander-in-chief of the army appointed the former quartermaster-general in the Army General Staff, Lieutenant-General Müller, for 'special duties'.[208]

Transfer of the headquarters staffs and units of the western army to the east was embarked upon towards the end of 1940.[209] After the withdrawal of the mobile units, of the 'Vosges group' already earmarked for Twelfth Army, and of 22nd (Airborne) Division, the Army Groups A and D still had over 52 infantry divisions and 1 police division at their disposal. These were transferred, in several stages starting in February, to Germany and to the armies deploying against the Soviet Union, in such a way that eventually there were only 4 divisions of the 6th wave left in the west as battle-worthy units. All other units to be transferred in exchange, up to a final strength of 38 divisions, were divisions on leave and divisions of the 3rd wave, hence scarcely mobile or combat-ready. Eventually, on 22 June 1941, all that remained to Army Group D HQ in the west was First, Seventh, and Fifteenth Army HQs, 2 corps HQs, and 6 higher commands. Of the 38 divisions, the police division having been transferred as a reserve to Army Group North, 5 were earmarked as army reserves and were due to be moved to the eastern front after 4 July.[210]

The tasks of the troops in the occupied western territories will be briefly outlined here in order to show how little could be withdrawn from the west if a real crisis were to arise. The coasts had to be guarded and made secure, order had to be ensured in the occupied territory, and the demarcation-line with unoccupied France had to be controlled with the help of the customs frontier guards. Alongside these tasks, the occupation of the territory of unoccupied France had to be made possible, a move ('Attila') that might become necessary in the event of a crisis in North Africa. In an emergency the units could only be made mobile by the confiscation of civilian motor-vehicles.[211] To sum up, the diagrams of the order of battle (Annexe Volume, No. 2) and on material equipment (Diagram I.iii.3 above), show clearly that, in terms of numbers and equipment, the reconstruction and enlargement of the army was completed by the beginning of the Barbarossa offensive, and that the

[207] Generally speaking, the training guidelines conformed to the demands made by Lt.-Col. (Gen. Staff) Feyerabend as part of his Operations Study East.

[208] On the general (special duties) attached to the C.-in-C. of the army see above, n. 170, and Müller-Hillebrand, *Heer*, ii. 96.

[209] OKH/GenStdH/Op.Abt. No. 744/40, 23 Dec. 1940, betr. Bewegungen der großen Verbände und Kommandobehörden bis Frühjahr 1941 [re movements of major formations and command authorities by spring 1941], OB West (HGr. A), 31 Dec. 1940, BA-MA RH 19 I/161; reply OKH/Op.Abt., 12 Feb. 1941, BA-MA RH 2/v. 427. Here too only the outline planning can be reproduced; for details see Müller-Hillebrand, *Heer*, ii. 110–11 (tables 28, 29).

[210] Schematic order of battle as of 22 June 1941 (BA-MA).   [211] BA-MA RH 2/v. 427.

fact that forces were tied down in the south-east[212] and in the north of Europe would not greatly impair the eastern army for the *intended short-term* campaign. The organization of the army troops in accordance with the requirements of the main effort of concentration, with the conditions of the terrain, and with the technical command facilities was likewise on the whole satisfactory, allowing for recourse to captured equipment and new acquisitions. Even so, certain shortages were to be expected in the engineering, especially the bridge-building, units, shortages which it was not possible to remedy in advance but which would have to be overcome by the use of captured and makeshift material. Calculations of manpower reserves, like all other plans, were based on operations being completed before the onset of winter.

The first two major transfers of troops and headquarters staffs from west to east in July and September 1940 had, by the end of the year, resulted in the assembly of 34 divisions, including 6 armoured divisions, under the command of Army Group B, divided into three armies.

As a result of the deployment plan for Greece, Twelfth Army HQ was replaced by Seventeenth Army HQ on 1 January 1941. In three stages a total of 1 armoured group HQ, 6 army corps HQs (including 2 motorized and 1 mountain), 17 divisions, 1 brigade, and 1 independent regiment were transferred to the Marita deployment area. These units were taken from all three army-group areas and partially replaced in the west by the 'divisions on leave' recalled after February.[213] The 13th and 16th Armoured Divisions were in Romania as 'instructional staff' under the chief of the army mission there.[214] Hitler's decisions on 17 and 27 March to occupy Greece down to the Peloponnese and all of Yugoslavia meant that a further army HQ, 5 army corps HQs, and 15 divisions were transferred.[215]

The consequence of the transfer of such major formations, as well as of the abandonment of a Twelfth Army attack across the Prut, was a complete transformation of deployment conditions.[216] Instead of the planned movements from the west and from Reich territory, major transfers now had to be carried out, first into the Balkans and subsequently, after the conclusion of

[212] Not even the release of 35,000 Reich Railway clerks and employees, made necessary by the sudden deployment for the extended Balkan campaign, had any serious effects on the deployment in the east. See Halder, *Diaries*, 852 (3 Apr. 1941), 949–50 (7 June 1941). Halder was trying to create reserves, *inter alia* by preparing the establishment of the 16th wave, i.e. local rifle units which might, in an emergency, release battle-worthy troops: Halder, *Diaries*, 919 (14 May 1941), 938 (27 May 1941), 934–5 (22 May 1941). See Müller-Hillebrand, *Heer*, ii. 86.

[213] Schematic order of battle of the army as of 10 Feb. 1941 (BA-MA); Müller-Hillebrand, *Heer*, ii. 83 ff.

[214] See sect. I.v.3 at n. 43 (Förster).

[215] Second Army HQ had been envisaged as an OKH reserve and until then had supervised rehabilitation and training in the south of Germany.

[216] Halder, *Diaries*, 839 (25 Mar. 1941), 848 (31 Mar. 1941). Twelfth Army HQ was replaced for commanding the German units in Romania by Eleventh Army HQ, which had originally been earmarked as an OKH reserve for the northern sector of the eastern front. Thus the command reserves, including those of corps HQs, were essentially used up.

operations there, all the way to the centre and north of the front against the Soviet Union. This concerned all the armoured and motorized units of Armoured Group 1, as well as the bulk of Second and Twelfth Armies.

Prior to the opening of the Balkan campaign, Halder had calculated its duration, the relevant transport times, and the time needed (three weeks) for the rehabilitation of the units employed there. He thus arrived at a possible date for an attack on the Soviet Union, when, with insignificant exceptions, the units could be stationed in the envisaged areas of operation. That date was 22 June and Hitler approved it. While the available time benefited the equipment and training of the troops, the deployment of the motorized units cost large quantities of fuel and resulted in heavy wear and tear of the vehicles, quite apart from the curtailment of the time left for operations before the onset of winter. The expected rapid progress of the initial operations in the Balkans made it possible to suspend the further transfer of units on 12 April.

With the first two deployment echelons having been moved to the eastern front after mid-February, the third echelon—now that the date of the attack had been laid down—could be brought up by 20 May. This comprised 17 divisions and army troops transferred from Germany. A further echelon (4 A) brought 9 divisions and army troops from the west; the final echelon, from 3 to 23 June, consisted of 12 armoured and 12 motorized divisions from the Reich, the west, and the south-east.[217] The final phase also saw the assignment of the heavy rail-borne artillery which was brought up from the Channel coast.[218] This super-heavy artillery was available only for the 'jump-off' and was shared out among the army groups as follows:

South:	4 artillery pieces K5, each with 90 rounds
Centre:	8 artillery pieces K5 and 2 of type 'Karl'
North:	4 artillery pieces 'Bruno' (short) with 30 rounds

Transport of these artillery pieces and construction of the positions demanded a major effort. Stretches of track had to be kept clear and improved. Work on the track alone, it was calculated, would take two engineer battalions two weeks per unit. In view of the prolonged blockage of the railway routes during deployment as well as the impossibility of camouflaging such extensive installations, Seventeenth Army HQ and Army Group North wanted to forgo the use of those batteries altogether. In the end they were employed at the points of the main effort of the breakthrough.

Even before these units arrived at their destinations, the relevant command authorities, army group HQs, army HQs, and armoured group HQs at first took over the operational map exercises and, from April onwards, their commands, though in a camouflaged form and under a variety of designations.[219]

---

[217] Halder, *Diaries*, 894–5 (30 Apr. 1941).

[218] Order relating to the employment of this, the heaviest, artillery and reflection on this since March: BA-MA RH 2/v. 1325; also Lusar, *Secret Weapons*, 17 ff.

[219] OKH/GenStdH/Op.Abt., 14 Feb. 1941, re working staffs for Barbarossa, BA-MA RH 2/v. 1325.

Plans for the replacement of personnel, just like strategic, operational, and economic plans, were based on the assumption of a short campaign. The units of the field army, including replacement battalions, were established by the middle of June; anything still becoming available in the reserve army was earmarked for supplies and replacement.[220] On 20 May 1941 Colonel-General Fromm reported to Halder on the consequences of these plans.[221] The field replacement battalions contained 90,000 men, already being transferred. The reserve army comprised 475,000 men, of whom the Luftwaffe claimed 90,000. Thus a total of 385,000 men were left as replacements for the army. Estimated losses during the first two months in the 'frontier battles' were approximately 275,000 men, with another 200,000 in September. This meant that the army's trained reserves would be exhausted in October. The next class to be called up was that of 1922, though strictly this was not due to be called to the colours until November, when manpower from the eastern army would be released for industry. Of that call-up class two-fifths were with the Labour Service, a considerable portion of them already employed within the framework of the eastern army's construction units and hence virtually available to the field army. If that age-group was not called up earlier there would be the danger of the army entering the winter without trained replacements. Halder believed that that was a risk he could take. If one considers the numerous improvisations in terms of personnel and material during the raising of that army, the lack of material reserves, especially of motor-vehicles and their equipment, and the failure to take manpower and production measures to ensure capacity in the area of equipment replacement for the army, the military leaders had no choice but to rely on a swift campaign. There was no room for serious setbacks, any more than for an extension of the planned duration of operations into the winter. For neither of these contingencies were there any preparations prior to 22 June 1941.

The combat value of all divisions was assessed by the Army High Command as follows.

Divisions capable of any offensive action

21 armoured divisions	of which 2 were undergoing rehabilitation, 1 of these (20th) with shortcomings in training
13 mot. infantry divisions	of these 6 with shortcomings in training
3 mot. brigades	(1 in rehabilitation)
95 infantry divisions	of which 18 were not yet employed as units
4 mountain divisions	
1 cavalry division	

Divisions of somewhat lesser offensive strength

6 infantry divisions
2 mountain divisions

[220] Halder, *Diaries*, 895 (30 Apr. 1941).   [221] Ibid. 929–30 (20 May 1941).

Divisions of reduced offensive strength and mobility

19 infantry divisions

Divisions of little offensive strength and mobility

22 infantry divisions

Divisions for security tasks and locally limited operations

15 infantry divisions
9 security divisions

TOTAL: 210 units[222]

German forces in the east as of 20 June 1941 totalled:

3,050,000 men
625,000 horses
600,000 motor-vehicles (incl. armoured scout cars)
3,350 armoured fighting vehicles (excluding armoured scout cars)

Artillery

4,760 light artillery pieces
104 army AA guns (88 mm.)
2,252 heavy artillery pieces
30 super-heavy high-/low-angle guns[223]

Of the 21 armoured divisions (including 5th Light Division), 2 had to be deducted for Libya and 2 were in Germany for reorganization—these were already to be re-equipped for operations following Barbarossa—which meant that 17 armoured divisions were left for the eastern army. Of the 13 motorized divisions, all were available, including the 3 divisions of the Waffen-SS, as were also the three motorized brigades ('Großdeutschland', 'Leibstandarte Adolf Hitler', and Brigade (mot.) 900).

The position with regard to officers in the field army at the beginning of the offensive on 22 June 1941 was that the numerical establishment was above emergency level, with a reserve of 300 officers available for the army groups. An interesting feature was the increased assignment of active officers to the units to be employed at the point of main effort: in the armoured, motorized, and mountain divisions there was a 50:50 ratio between active and reserve officers; among the divisions of the 1st, 4th, and the newly created 11th and

---

[222] 'Beurteilung des Kampfwertes der Divisionen nach dem Stand vom 20. Juni 1941' [Assessment of the combat value of the divisions as of 20 June 1941], BA-MA RH 2/v. 427; Müller-Hillebrand, *Heer*, ii. 99–100. Observations on the officer situation according to notes by Küchler and his chief of staff on the conference between Halder and the departmental heads in the Army General Staff, 4 June 1941, AOK 18/Ia, KTB, BA-MA, 18. Armee, 19601/2; Halder, *KTB* ii. 440 ff. (4 June 1941; not in trans.).

[223] Reports of the Inspector of Artillery and the quartermaster-general, 20 June 1941, BA-MA RH 2/v. 1326.

12th waves the ratio was 35:65; for the rest of the divisions it was 10:90. The mumbers of young replacements were considered adequate—only just so among battalion commanders, whereas the proportion, among regimental commanders was good.

As for the material equipment, Halder observed that the armoured divisions were not the same as in the west: organizational adjustments and the maximum utilization of makeshift devices were to be dealt with at superior levels. The replacement battalions of the armoured and motorized divisions were not motorized, and were therefore unable to follow the mobile troops. They had to be supplied and moved by the armies until such time as they could be pulled forward by the armoured groups' own means of transport.

The bulk of the formations in the west and south-east was composed of divisions of little offensive strength and mobility, with some suitable only for security tasks. The only possible mobile reserve was available in France: 2 armoured brigades equipped with captured armour. This meant that a supplementation of the eastern army could not, in the short term, be effected from the west. Nor, with the exception of the 2 mountain divisions, could any battle-worthy units be obtained from south-eastern Europe, let alone from Norway. These German forces were joined in Finland on 22 June by 2 infantry divisions under German command and 15 divisions and 2 brigades under the command of Field Marshal Baron Carl Gustav Mannerheim.[224]

On the southern sector of the front the following Romanian forces were available, under the command of Eleventh Army HQ: 4 infantry divisions, 3 cavalry brigades, and 3 mountain brigades, though some of these had to be seen only as blocking and security units. Of the German divisions, 6 were fully capable of attack, 1 to a limited degree only. These German units were earmarked for the thrust across the Prut to the Dnieper, with support from the Romanian armoured brigade (still in training) and the fully mobile units to be supplied after 22 June.[225]

It may therefore be stated that the German army entered the war against the Soviet Union with all the units which, given the material circumstances, it was possible to equip for combat at all. The Romanian allies were considered to be as weak as in fact they were; the Finns could be considered only for a push towards Murmansk and for relieving the thrust of Army Group North. Hungarians and Slovaks, whose participation was confidently expected, were regarded as suitable only for occupation purposes. Regardless of the combat value of their units, Germany's allies represented on the hand an irreplaceable resource from the war-economy point of view, while on the other, having to be supplied with all war materials, they constituted a permanent drain, one that was acceptable only on the assumption of a short war.

---

[224] On Finland see sect. I.vi.4 (Üeberschär). I.vi.4.

[225] See the instructions to Eleventh Army, given at sect. I.iv.1(*f*) at n. 156. The concentration of the German units in the north of the army made it possible to embark on the thrust to the north-east at an early stage.

In addition, the theatres of war in Africa and the Balkans were diverting substantial forces of the Luftwaffe, the army, and the navy from the future principal front, and in particular proved a great strain on fuel supplies.

Once the limited stockpiles were exhausted, German fuel production and Romanian deliveries would have to meet the requirements of the war effort as well as of the entire European industry. The Wehrmacht operations department had borne this aspect in mind from the start and therefore exerted some influence on the planning of operations.[226] On 4 May it submitted data showing that the Axis powers had stockpiles of 1.5m. t. of mineral oil; these would be sufficient until the end of August, after which date only 850,000 t. would remain. For the further conduct of the war it was therefore necessary to occupy the oil region of the Caucasus. Even on the assumption of extensive destruction, it was calculated that that region would be able to supply 300,000 t. of oil for the Wehrmacht, as well as 900,000 t. for the agriculture of the occupied territories in the east. Transportation on the required scale would be possible only by sea, which meant that the routes through the Mediterranean would have to be made safe. Operational lines across the Donets region to Krasnodar and Maykop–Groznyy thus appeared to be pre-determined. In that situation, however, the chief of the Army General Staff rejected a request from the War Economy Staff to Eleventh Army HQ, dated 12 June 1941, that after the opening of operations the oil region of Drogobycz in Galicia should be occupied as soon as possible. That, Halder said, was a political matter; he refused to accept economic demands addressed to the operational branch.[227]

(i) The Assessment of the Red Army before the Attack

From the time of observations made during the Polish campaign, calculations of the strength of the Red Army by the Foreign Armies East department of the Army General Staff had been essentially based on such sources as incomplete long-range reconnaissance, agents and expatriates, reports from military attachés, and information which allied intelligence services were able to supply.[228] With aerial reconnaissance and the development of radio intercepts, the basis of information-gathering was considerably widened, so that, following the issuing of the deployment directive for Barbarossa and preliminary work for the Balkan campaign after mid-March 1941, a substantially more accurate picture was obtained of troop movements, the location of headquarters staffs, and especially the stationing of the mechanized formations.

At the same time, the Army General Staff realized that the German deployment could not be effectively concealed; the question therefore arose which of

[226] OKW/WFSt/L Op, Chefsachen Barbarossa, May 1941, BA-MA RW 4/v. 577 and sect. I.III.2(*f*) at n. 272 (Müller).

[227] Minute, Seventeenth Army HQ to Army Group South chief of staff, 12 June 1941, BA-MA RH 19 I/68; Halder, *Diaries*, 956–7 (13 June 1941).

[228] See sect. I.IV.1 at nn. 16 ff.

the enemy movements were to be interpreted as reactions to German moves and which concentrations of troops near the frontiers, that had been progressing since the early summer of 1940, suggested offensive intentions.[229] The general principle of the above-quoted Red Army field service regulations still applied:

Any attack on the socialist state of workers and peasants will be repulsed with the whole might of the Soviet Union, and military operations carried into the land of the enemy aggressor. The Red Army's combat operations will always be aimed at the annihilation of the enemy. Forcible attainment of a decisive victory and the total smashing of the enemy are the basic aim of any war forced upon the Soviet Union.

Although as recently as September 1940 Lieutenant-Colonel Kinzel, the chief of Foreign Armies East, had dismissed offensive operations by the Red Army as 'megalomania', that assessment was not necessarily valid for ever. Foreign Armies East, in its 'Situation Report No. 1', dated 14 March 1941 and released the following day, summarized the changed picture of the Red Army as follows.[230]

1. Partial mobilization was in progress; probably four classes would be called up. This was difficult to assess numerically, as the Red Army had been partially mobilized for some eighteen months. It was impossible to tell whether the existing units were being brought up to full wartime strength or whether new divisions were being raised.

2. Troops of all branches were being moved from the Moscow military district in the direction of Minsk–Smolensk, and there were westward moves in the Baltic region: Red Army forces were closing up on the western frontier.

3. Trial air-raid alarms und blackout exercises were being conducted in major cities, in addition to orders for total blackout of certain towns.

4. There was a growing 'war psychosis'. The general population—sometimes boastfully, sometimes anxiously—were frequently referring to an imminent war. Officers' families in near-frontier areas were being moved to the interior of the country.

In a further situation report of 20 March the department noted that rail transports had been occurring in the Baltic region since 10 March, carrying infantry and tanks towards Lithuania. According to unconfirmed reports, new army corps commands had appeared at the centre of the Soviet front, with 5 divisions and a motorized-mechanized brigade; on the southern front there

---

[229] The date of the German attack had been almost publicly discussed since March 1941. See the reports of the military attachés to OQu IV from Helsinki, Moscow, Stockholm, and Tokyo, BA-MA III H, 1001/8, 13, 19, 20. See also the Abwehr reports, BA-MA RH 19 I/123. Besides, the opening of the war against Finland had shown how quickly an attack on the Soviet Union could, if necessary, be arranged. Concentrations of Soviet armoured formations facing Army Group North from 7 Mar. 1941 onwards were interpreted as deployment: AOK 18/Ia, KTB, 7 Mar. 1941 and following entries, BA-MA, 18. Armee, 17562/17.

[230] BA-MA RH 19 III/722; report of 20 Mar. 1941, ibid.; see also *Fall Barbarossa*, Doc. 19, pp. 87 ff.

were 4 army corps commands, 7 rifle divisions, and 5 motorized-mechanized brigades. Such a massive concentration of mechanized and armoured units led to the conclusion that local Soviet offensives on the lower Prut could not be ruled out, even though, generally speaking, the Red Army might be expected to display a defensive attitude.

The reports on the Red Army movements induced Hitler on 25 May to warn the Wehrmacht operations staff that Russian preventive measures were possible over the next few weeks and that a reliable defence against these must be ensured.[231] On 4 April Halder observed that the Foreign Armies East department had been obliged to amend its compilations and that a substantially larger number of enemy formations would have to be expected than previously thought.[232]

In early May 1941, according to Colonel (General Staff) Krebs, Köstring's deputy in Moscow, Halder still considered the external appearance of the Soviet officer corps to be 'decidedly bad', and as making a 'depressing impression'—a second-hand assessment of little evidential value with regard to combat-worthiness.[233]

More important was the evaluation of Soviet regulations and of the accessible literature, to be found, alongside a presentation of the Red Army according to the latest data, in the supplement to *Kriegswehrmacht der UdSSR* [Wartime forces of the USSR] of 30 April. After a discussion of the rules of engagement for the troops, special attention was devoted to the armoured forces; it was found that their rules of engagement had not yet been finally discussed.

As a matter of principle, armoured support was to lend the necessary penetration power to any attack. Each body of troops, according to its task and situation, should have an armoured reserve at its disposal, to lend greater efficacy to its own reserves. Large mechanized formations were to break through the enemy's front or strike against its flank or rear. Infantry divisions at the point of main effort of an attack should have two tank battalions; 'tying-down' groups were not given any tanks, or only enough to open breaches in wire obstacles. After that, the remaining armoured units were to form a long-range armoured group; this was to turn as a spearhead against the depth of the enemy positions. A decisive point was that the armoured groups were tied to the infantry's pace of advance. Instances of engagements of cavalry and mechanized troops were excerpted by Foreign Armies East from service regulations and the literature; these allowed for the conclusion that the use of independent armoured or motorized formations for far-ranging operations was not to be expected.

Five weeks before the opening of the attack, Foreign Armies East issued a number of information sheets and other documents on the Red Army.[234] One

---

[231] OKW/WFSt/L, 25 Mar. 1941, BA-MA RW 4/v. 578. On concealment and signalling of a German offensive facing Moscow see BA-MA RH 2/v. 1325.

[232] Halder, *Diaries*, 853 (4 Apr. 1941).   [233] Ibid. 904 (5 May 1941).

[234] BA-MA RH 2/v. 1326; OKH/GenStdH/OQu IV Abt. Frd. Heere Ost: Merkblatt 19/I,

of these information leaflets (19/2) directly took up Hitler's remark of 5 June 1941 about the possible use of 'means of insidious warfare', implying the poisoning of foodstuffs and wells, nocturnal attacks on sentries, and sadistic treatment of prisoners and wounded. The leaflet emphasized the 'special character' of the campaign. Not only was the Red Army expected to offer stubborn resistance, but in the rear areas there might be a flare-up of subversive forms of combat, primarily on the part of political functionaries or, within the Red Army, political commissars. Although, in accordance with the much-quoted provisional field-service regulations of the workers' and peasants' Red Army, a commissar's duties, along with caring for the troops as well as any prisoners, were clearly concerned with political control and supervision in continuous collaboration with the Communist Party of the Soviet Union, this was no justification for denying him combatant status. Hitler's directives on the 'liquidation' of these military and political auxiliaries are discussed elsewhere in the present volume.

Knowledge of the strength and structure of the Red Army, as revealed by reconnaissance work of all kinds, still contained a lot of gaps, at least where formations and installations in the heart of the Soviet Union were concerned. Errors and mistaken attributions of units were therefore inevitable.

On the day of the attack on the Soviet Union, Foreign Armies East summarized its findings as follows.

In the 4 military districts of the western part of the Soviet Union the following formations were expected to be found:

Odessa Military District

11 rifle divisions
1 cavalry division
2 armoured divisions
5 motorized-mechanized brigades

Kiev Special Military District

45 rifle divisions
10 cavalry divisions
3 armoured divisions
10 motorized-mechanized brigades

Western Special Military District

35 rifle divisions
8 cavalry divisions
1 armoured division
10 motorized-mechanized brigades

Taschenbuch Russisches Heer, Merkblatt 19/2 über die Eigenarten der russischen Kriegführung [on the peculiarities of Russian warfare]. Vorläufige Felddienstordnung der Roten Arbeiter- und Bauernarmee [Provisional field-service regulations of the workers' and peasants' Red Army], 1936; Hitler's remark: BA-MA H 3/1, fo. 2047/64.

Baltic Special Military District

29 rifle divisions
2 armoured divisions
7 motorized-mechanized brigades

In addition:

7–8 paratroop brigades

Altogether, the following were identified in Europe:

> 145 rifle divisions
> $25\frac{1}{2}$ cavalry divisions
> 10 armoured divisions
> 37 motorized-mechanized brigades
> 7–8 paratroop brigades

The following were calculated to be in Asia:

> 25 rifle divisions
> 8 cavalry divisions
> 5 armoured or motorized-mechanized brigades

Hence the assumed overall strength of the Red Army was:

> 179 rifle divisions
> $33\frac{1}{2}$ cavalry divisions
> 10 armoured divisions
> 42 armoured or motorized-mechanized brigades
> 7–8 paratroop brigades[235]

Moreover, it was not ruled out that further formations might be in the process of being established in the Asian part of the USSR; however, no information was available on their size or special character.

Developments in the European part of the Soviet Union up to 20 June 1941 are shown in Table I.IV.3. Added to these Red Army troops there were the frontier guard units of the Ministry for Internal Security.[236]

A considerable part of the information on the Soviet Union, and especially its forces, came from radio-intercept data provided by the Ausland/Abwehr (foreign intelligence) department.[237] On 9 June an agreement was concluded

---

[235] (Geb.) AOK 20/Ic, Sammelmappe X, BA-MA, 20. (Geb.) Armee, 25358/8. Reports from the Romanians, BA-MA RH 19 I/123. OKH/Frd. Heere Ost, Die Landesbefestigungen der UdSSR, Stand vom 15.3.1941 [The land fortifications of the USSR, as of 15 Mar. 1941], pts. I–III, and Lage- und Befestigungskarte UdSSR [Situation and fortification map of the USSR], 6 and 22 June 1941 (MGFA library). On the actual state of the deployment see the Annexe Volume, No. 1.

[236] See sect. I.II.2 at nn. 141, 186 (Hoffmann).

[237] The Abwehr can be discussed only briefly at this point. The extensive literature on the subject is only occasionally susceptible to documentary verification: Gunzenhäuser, *Geschichte des geheimen Nachrichtendienstes*; Höhne, *Canaris*; also Kahn, *Hitler's Spies*. On reconnaissance against the Soviet Union see the evidence of Lt.-Gen. (retd.) Piekenbrock (then head of 'Abwehr I' in the

TABLE I.iv.3. *Forces Deployed in the Western Soviet Union up to 20 June 1941*

	Rifle divs.	Cav. divs.	Armd. divs.	Mot.-mech. brigs.	Paratroop brigs.
20 May	145	$25\frac{1}{2}$	5	37	4–5
13 June	150	$25\frac{1}{2}$	7	38	
20 June	154	$25\frac{1}{2}$	10	37	7–8

Source: Situation reports and OKH situation maps (see nn. 230–2).

on closer co-operation between the entire Abwehr and the field army, to avoid loss of time.[238] 'Abwehr I', responsible for reconnaissance of the enemy, was to set up a forward operational staff, 'Walli I', near Warsaw; Abwehr teams of army groups and armies were to be attached to it. These were placed under the enemy-situation analysts (Ic) of the command authorities and had to accept assignments from them. The 'Abwehr II' teams were concerned with sabotage and actions in the enemy's rear. Squads of 25 men were to reconnoitre in a 300-km.-deep zone of enemy territory and protect vital transport centres against destruction. 'Abwehr III', working in conjunction with foreign-ministry representatives ('Künsberg Group'), was to secure the files of Soviet authorities and foreign missions. The focus of 'Abwehr II' operations was in the Baltic States and the former Polish regions of the Soviet Union, and in the direction of the Caucasian oilfields.[239] The tasks assigned to the Abwehr seemed to be realizable because a certain resurgence of national and religious sympathy was expected in the territories concerned. There was no doubt about this in the Baltic countries, where increasing opposition to Soviet domination had been observed for some time. In the Ukraine, too, large portions of the population were expected to side with the Germans, at least passively and, after the arrival of Ukrainians serving with the Wehrmacht, perhaps even actively. The economically most important long-range objectives in the Caucasus were to be explored by an approach to the local people, who were ethnically and in terms of faith not part of the Russian Bolshevik 'nation', and were to be prepared for German occupation. However, the Abwehr had some difficulty in enlisting suitable teams of *émigrés* and other former local inhabitants, and the lack of appropriate staffing meant that the hoped-for success eluded it.

Ausland/Abwehr department), *IMT* vii. 260 ff. On 'Brandenburg': Kriegsheim, *Getarnt— getäuscht*, 300 ff.; Brockdorff, *Geheimkommandos*, 126 ff., id., *Kollaboration oder Widerstand*, 185, 191, 213 ff.

[238] BA-MA RH 20-11/485; OKW/Ausl./Abw., 9 June 1941, BA-MA H 3/1.

[239] See the files of Ic of AOK 11, BA-MA RH 20-11/334–8, and RH 20-11/271, as well as PG 31025 (operation against Baku–Batumi). Literature with critical comment includes: Höhne, *Canaris*, 457 ff.; Reile, *Geheime Ostfront*, 293 ff.; Buchheit, *Geheimdienst*, 106 ff.; Leverkühn, *German Military Intelligence, passim*, all providing a general insight.

2. THE GERMAN AIR FORCE

HORST BOOG

(a) The Luftwaffe between the Battle of Britain and Barbarossa

By the autumn of 1940 the Wehrmacht leadership—Hitler perhaps more clearly than Göring—realized that military victory over Britain was not to be expected in the foreseeable future through the air war alone.[240] While opinions did not always agree as, time and time again, optimistic reports on the effects of Luftwaffe raids on England were coming in,[241] the chief of the Army General Staff was forced to admit that 'the effect on industrial plants' has not 'been critical'. Major-General Otto Hoffmann von Waldau, chief of the operations department of the Luftwaffe General Staff, observed that the German leadership had underestimated the British fighter force by a hundred per cent.[242] He did, however, believe that it would be possible to reinforce the Luftwaffe in the spring of 1941, even though in his opinion a fourfold increase would be necessary to 'bring [England] to her knees'. On the strength of British and other press reports, Hitler doubted the Luftwaffe's reports of successful action against Britain, and on 12 November, the first day of Molotov's visit, issued Directive No. 18, ordering the continuation of the 'already verbally ordered preparations for the east'. Almost at the same time, however, with the gradual reduction of the round-the-clock air offensive against London, carried out with an average of 200 bombers and fighters but ultimately without result, the real German economic air war against Britain began during the night of 14–15 November 1940 with a massed attack on Coventry, the centre of the British aero-engine industry.[243] Thus the Luftwaffe was still primarily engaged against Britain.

Hitler's assessment of the air situation on 5 December 1940 represented a decisive step in the direction of the war in the east.[244] In it he acknowledged that neither the Royal Air Force nor British industry could be greatly weakened by German air attacks. In spite of American aid, Hitler believed, the RAF would be no stronger in the coming spring than before, whereas the Luftwaffe would. A defensive conduct of the air war against Britain would therefore continue even with major portions of the German fighter force and anti-

[240] See Below, *Hitlers Adjutant*, 245; *Germany and the Second World War*, ii. 402 ff. On the hopeless situation regarding Luftwaffe files see Endres, 'Zum Verbleib der Luftwaffeakten', and Boog, *Luftwaffenführung*, 13–14. As most of the Luftwaffe records were destroyed at the end of the war, it is as a rule no longer possible to trace the decision-making processes of Göring, the Luftwaffe General Staff, or the Luftwaffe commands. Nevertheless, it may be confidently assumed that, on the whole, they were in line with the intentions of the army.

[241] See *KTB OKW* i. 123 (23 Oct. 1940), 125 (24 Oct. 1940); Halder, *Diaries*, 789 (20 Feb. 1941), BA-MA OKM, Case GE 969/PG 32969, fos. 98, 104–5, 208 ff.

[242] Halder, *Diaries*, 610 (4 Oct. 1940), 614 (7 Oct. 1940).

[243] See *Germany and the Second World War*, ii. 402 ff.; Collier, *Defence*, 261–92; Weber, *Luftschlacht um England*, 161–74.

[244] *KTB OKW* i. 205 (5 Dec. 1940); Halder, *Diaries*, 722 (5 Dec. 1940); Below, *Hitlers Adjutant*, 255.

aircraft units engaged in the east. As the campaign in the east was expected to be of short duration, major nuisance raids by night would continue to be possible against Britain. This unfounded optimism was reflected in Hitler's Directive No. 21—the Barbarossa directive—which set the signals for a war in the east and for a temporary abandonment of the air war against Britain. 'The air force', it stated,

will have to make available for this eastern campaign forces of such strength that the army will be able to bring land operations to a speedy conclusion and eastern Germany will be as little damaged as possible by enemy air attack. This build-up of a focal point in the east will be limited only by the need to protect from air attack the whole combat and arsenal area which we control, and to ensure that attacks on England, and especially upon her imports, are not allowed to lapse.

This showed that the warning by Major-General Hoffman von Waldau, chief of the operations department of the Luftwaffe operations staff—that the Luftwaffe was too weak for a war on two fronts[245]—was not being taken seriously. Indeed, the transfer (then being initiated) of X Air Corps to the Mediterranean area suggested that, beginning in the summer of 1941, the Luftwaffe would actually be involved in a war on three fronts.

While the operations department of the Luftwaffe General Staff had been engaged since the beginning of January with the three tasks outlined in Directive No. 21—home defence including nocturnal protection and the use of radio-location instruments; development of a navigational basis 'East' for the war in the east; and the regrouping and special training of the air units stationed in the west for the war against British supplies[246]—the night offensive against the British armaments industry continued. The principal targets in December were the great industrial cities in the Midlands, as well as the main ports on the south and west coasts of England, but above all London, which during the night of 29–30 December experienced a heavy attack on the City, enhanced in its effect by the circumstance that this was a Sunday night and the City was virtually deserted, so that the fires quickly gained a hold. As hopes of success in the strategic air offensive were dwindling, the main effort was shifted to operations against British supplies in co-operation with German U-boats.[247] During January 1941 air attacks were intensified on the coastal cities of Cardiff, Bristol, Portsmouth, Plymouth, and Swansea. In February the main targets of the German bombers were the port and dock installations of Swansea on the Bristol Channel, as well as London and Chatham, and armaments factories and troop encampments.

The strategic reorientation of the economic air war against Britain was reflected in Hitler's Directive No. 23, 'Directives for operations against the

---

[245] Halder, *Diaries*, 614 (7 Oct. 1940); LwFüStab Ia (KM) to 1./Skl 1L, 15 Nov. 1940, BA-MA OKM, Case GE 968/PG 32968, fo. 292.

[246] Manuscript notes by Maj.-Gen. Hoffmann von Waldau, Chefs., re chiefs' conference, 10 Jan. 1941, BA-MA RL 2 I/1.

[247] Halder, *Diaries*, 725–6 (6 Dec. 1940).

British war economy', of 6 February 1941.[248] With the acknowledgement that the German air war so far had not weakened the morale of the British people or, despite a presumed major decline in production, substantially affected Britain's industry, and with the realization that Luftwaffe formations would now have to be pulled out from operations against Britain to be employed in other theatres of war, aerial bombing of industrial centres was no longer seen as the way to deliver the strongest blow to Britain's war economy. Luftwaffe operations in the west were now to lend support to naval operations there, especially to the U-boat war, on which high hopes were pinned. Only *alongside* this task was the aerial-armaments industry to be held down. The main targets henceforth were to be the principal British ports with their installations and shipyards, and incoming merchant shipping—not, however, naval units, which were difficult to sink in any case and attacks on which were linked with excessive German losses. Neither terror raids on residential districts nor attacks on coastal fortifications were expected to yield decisive results. Finally, the directive demanded, aerial and naval warfare against Britain was to be intensified, prior to regrouping for Barbarossa, mainly 'in order to feign the appearance of an attack on the British Isles being imminent this year'.

The Luftwaffe therefore supported the war against seaborne supplies by the creation, on 10 March 1941, of an 'Air Leader Atlantic',[249] by U-boat reconnaissance and operations against shipping from bases in western France, by IX Air Corps flying from bases in Holland, employed mainly on the mining of British coastal waters, by the commander of naval air forces operating from Jutland, and by the Air Leaders North and Lofoten (under Air Fleet 5) engaging in reconnaissance and operations against shipping.[250] In line with the reorientation, the air corps operating against Britain were instructed at the beginning of 1941 to reduce their missions in such a way that the formations for Barbarossa would once more become fully combat-ready without the British suspecting the real intentions of the Luftwaffe. In consequence, missions between large-scale attacks—which continued to be launched in good weather conditions—were reduced and attacks were predominantly made against targets where major losses were not expected. Inexperienced crews were generally employed against closer targets around the English coast, especially the south coast.[251]

Meanwhile, the British defence effort had likewise been intensified by the incipient equipment of night fighters and AA batteries with radar. The radio-

---

[248] *Hitler's Directives*, No. 23, 6 Feb. 1941, pp. 56 ff.; *KTB OKW* i. 307 (6 Feb. 1941); Galland, *The First and the Last*, 121 ff.; Weber, *Luftschlacht um England*, 167; *Germany and the Second World War*, ii. 402 ff.

[249] Der R.d.L. u. Ob.d.L./Generalstab, GenQu., 2. Abt. No. 5437/41 g.Kdos. (II A), 5 Mar. 1941, BA-MA OKM, Case GE 972/PG 32972, 12–13. See Kurowski, *Seekrieg aus der Luft*, 198 ff., and Hümmelchen, *Seeflieger*, 126–7.

[250] See *Rise and Fall of the German Air Force*, 103 ff., and Kurowski, *Seekrieg aus der Luft*, 85 ff.

[251] Deichmann, Das II. Fliegerkorps im Einsatz gegen Rußland vom 22.6.–15.11.1941 [II Air Corps in operation against Russia from 22 June to 15 Nov. 1941], BA-MA Lw 107/80.

navigation procedure of the German bombers was increasingly being interfered with by the British—another reason for attacking closer coastal rather than inland targets, because these did not require radio navigation. Thus the situation of the Luftwaffe formations over England because increasingly difficult from January 1941. Its night attacks resulted in heavier losses and therefore diminished in intensity. Towards the end of February the British, responding to the German change of main effort, transferred major portions of their fighter and AA forces to the coastal areas, even though this meant a weakening of the air defences of some industrial centres inland.[252] Whereas prior to February 1941 only about a twelfth of all Fighter Command missions served the protection of British shipping, the proportion after April 1941 was approximately a half.

Following more Luftwaffe raids during March on London and its docks, as well as on other ports, when the big shipyards in the Glasgow area were put out of action for three to six months, Göring at the beginning of April gave orders for an intensification of the air war during the next few weeks in order to camouflage the deployment in the east.[253] Next came numerous heavy and medium-strength night raids on coastal and industrial towns, all the way from the south coast to Scotland and Northern Ireland, but without recognizable focus. The climax and conclusion of the German nocturnal air offensive against the British Isles came during the night of 10–11 May 1941, when a huge raid was carried out on London with over 500 bombers. In its effects this was the heaviest of all air attacks on England: more than 3,000 persons were killed or injured, over 2,000 fires were started, nearly 150 water mains were destroyed, 5 docks and 71 vital installations received major hits, and nearly all the main railway stations were closed for weeks. In addition to the usual targets, numerous Royal Air Force bases were bombed in May. During the next few nights, until the end of June 1941, the number of aircraft launched against Britain each day dropped to a mere 50–60; moreover, most of these were fighters instead of bombers.[254] Meanwhile, the build-up of British night-time air defences had come to some kind of halt. The share of night fighters in the shooting down of German raiders had risen to more than double the score for AA gunners, increasing from 0.2 per cent at the beginning of the air war to 5–7 per cent. There can be no doubt that German bomber losses over Britain at night—increasing as they were, though still rather slight—would have assumed intolerable proportions if the German air offensive had continued on a large scale.

The Luftwaffe's air offensive against Britain by night—especially in the light of Hitler's speech of 4 September 1940, when he announced that he would 'rub out' England's cities—has often been presented in the literature and in propaganda as a model of a war of terror from the air. Certainly it also bore such a character, especially as, just as with other air forces, it was accepted

[252] Collier, *Defence*, 286 ff.   [253] See Weber, *Luftschlacht um England*, 179.
[254] Lageberichte des Ob.d.L., LWFü.Stab Ic, BA-MA RL 2 II/230–48.

that, given the inaccuracy of existing bomb sights, residential areas were bound to suffer. Although, as a bonus, it was initially expected that this would diminish the British will to resist, an air war against civilians was not the primary intention. Even after Hitler's above-mentioned speech, Hitler, Göring, and the air-fleet commanders still endeavoured to aim their attacks on militarily relevant targets, reserving terror raids merely for reprisals within the meaning of international law—i.e. as exceptional actions—even though their main motivation may well have been fear of an intensification of similar attacks by the enemy.[255] British official quarters confirmed after the war: 'Although the plan adopted by the Luftwaffe early in September [1940] had mentioned attacks on the population of large cities, detailed records of the raids-made during the autumn and winter of 1940–1941 do not suggest that indiscriminate bombing of civilians was intended'[256]—a statement that was confirmed by the daily air-situation reports of the Luftwaffe operations staff at the time[257] but one that should also be seen against the background of the British doctrine and practice of carpet bombing.

Because of its impending deployment against the Soviet Union, the Luftwaffe had to suspend the night offensive against the British war industry without having achieved any decisive success—but also without having suffered a decisive defeat. Neither by its daytime attacks from August to October 1940 nor in the eight months of its nightly economic offensive had the British war industry been paralysed, Britain's seaborne supplies permanently severed, or the British people's morale broken. This failure was only partly due to leadership mistakes[258] within the Luftwaffe, such as inadequate concentration on a point of main effort and lack of persistence in attacking vital targets, the premature abandonment of the struggle for air superiority against the British fighter force—including its radar system—and an overestimation of the effectiveness of a bomber and fighter force of inadequate range and bomb-load capacity. Comparison of the total of high-explosive and incendiary bombs dropped on Britain, mostly in night raids, between November 1940 and June 1941—approximately 32,802 t. or up to 53,595 t.[259] if one includes the daytime raids between August and October 1940—with the roughly 2,450,000 t.[260] dropped by the Allies in their strategic air offensive against Germany and the German-occupied European continent during the whole of the Second World

---

[255] Halder, *Diaries*, 585 (14 Sept. 1940); *KTB OKW* i. 76 (14 Sept. 1940); Bekker, *Angriffshöhe*, 69, 107, 397 ff.; BA-MA RL 3/60, p. 5181; Spetzler, *Luftkrieg und Menschlichkeit*, 264; *Germany and the Second World War*, ii. 53 ff.

[256] Collier, *Defence*, 261.

[257] BA-MA RL 2 II/214–45, RL 2 IV/33; *KTB OKW* i. 26 (13 Aug. 1940), 30 (14 Aug. 1940), 307 (6 Feb. 1941); Halder, *Diaries*, 614 (7 Oct. 1940), 725–6 (6 Dec. 1940), 838 (24 Mar. 1941); Spetzler, *Luftkrieg und Menschlichkeit*, 224 ff., 377; L.Dv. No. 16, sect. 186, annexe 1 to Plan Study 1939, BA-MA RL 4 II/77; *IMT* ix. 336 ff., 340–1, 352, 689; Manstein, *Lost Victories*, 264.

[258] See Gropman, 'Battle of Britain'; Feuchter, *Luftkrieg*, 146–51; Bekker, *Angriffshöhe*, 228–9; *Rise and Fall of the German Air Force*, 86 ff.; Weber, *Luftschlacht um England*, 172 ff., 197 ff.

[259] According to *Germany and the Second World War*, ii. 406.

[260] According to *United States Strategic Bombing Survey*, i. *Overall Report (European War)*, 1.

War in order to achieve sizeable results, albeit at a heavy cost in time and material, suggests that, if only for a lack of adequate means, the German air offensive against Britain never had any chance of succeeding. The Luftwaffe command, however—which just like other air forces at the time overestimated the effect of a bombing war—could not have realized that at the beginning of its air offensive. The 'Battle of Britain', which British historiography considers to have been decided in Britain's favour by 15 September 1940 (Battle of Britain Day), was certainly the first attempt in history by an air power to achieve victory in a war solely by an independent strategic bombing campaign. The Luftwaffe still completely lacked experience of that kind of warfare.

German losses of aircraft over the British Isles during the eight months of the night offensive averaged a total of 50–60 each month due to enemy action—a relatively slight figure compared with those suffered during the preceding daylight raids—even though the British had been able to read the Luftwaffe code since 22 May 1940[261] and thus knew at least some of the German targets. Far more serious were the losses suffered by the Luftwaffe on its own territory and without enemy action.[262] From the beginning of August 1940 to June 1941 the Luftwaffe lost a total of about 6,000 aircraft—of which 3,700 were total losses—as well as nearly 3,700 flying crews killed, 3,000 missing, and some 1,500 wounded. This represented some 60 per cent of all material and personnel losses of the flying formations in the war. Nevertheless, the number of available machines and crews, and especially their readiness for action, was far higher in mid-June 1941 than at the beginning of the German air offensive.[263] In no sense was the Luftwaffe so weakened—certainly not by its night offensive—that it could never have recovered, even though many aircrews with peacetime training had been lost. The significance of the abandonment of the air offensive against Britain, in terms of the overall war, emerged fully only when the war in Russia was protracted well beyond expectation and only negligible forces were available for operations against Britain. That country was now able to produce its armaments without interference and thus to lay the basis for the Allies' subsequent strategic air war, which crucially weakened the German armaments industry. In addition, the abandonment of the air offensive and the invasion, together with certain other factors, was regarded in western Europe as a German defeat and encouraged local resistance against the German occupying power.

This was not realized by all of the handful of Luftwaffe leaders who, in July and August 1940, were briefed in confidence on Hitler's aggressive intentions in the east.[264] It seems that Hitler developed his idea in lengthy conversations with Göring, to a point where the Reich Marshal himself no longer appeared to have much faith in the seriousness of the intended Luftwaffe effort against

---

[261] Hinsley, *British Intelligence*, i. 166.
[262] On this problem see Boog, *Luftwaffenführung*, 29.   [263] BA-MA RL 2 III/708, 713.
[264] See Irving, *Hitler's War*, 147–8; Greiner, *Oberste Wehrmachtführung*, 288 ff., 295; Halder, *Diaries*, 561 (22 July 1940); Hillgruber, *Strategie*, 227; Warlimont, *Hauptquartier*, 126–7.

Britain.[265] This suggests that, given the strict secrecy surrounding the Army High Command's planning for the war in the east,[266] the Luftwaffe General Staff was not yet actively participating in Hitler's thinking and was only subsequently involved.[267] This in itself is an indication of the ancillary role envisaged for the Luftwaffe in the war in the east. Göring, as plenipotentiary for the Four-Year plan, was of course concerned with the overall planning for the east and the resulting realignment of armaments production from the requirements of a war against the enemy's overseas supplies to those of a continental war.[268] In the middle of August 1940 he was instructed by Hitler to establish an air-base in northern Norway.[269] In October Halder held conversations with Hoffmann von Waldau on matters of air operations during the winter of 1940–1, especially with regard to a Soviet air force considered poor but numerically strong,[270] as well as with Lieutenant-General Rudolf Bogatsch, the Luftwaffe general attached to the commander-in-chief of the army, who had been informed on 1 August 1940 of the army's require-ments concerning air support, and of the establishment of new reconnaissance and AA units within the framework of the envisaged enlargement of the army.[271]

Hitler's Directive No. 18 of 12 November 1940 was certainly not drafted without the participation of Göring and his general staff. Simultaneously, however, plans were being made which aimed not towards the east but towards the south, at Greece, Spain, the Portuguese Atlantic islands, and southern France; indeed, these represented the burden of the directive. Meas-ures for the establishment or extension of airfields in the east could be explained, and in fact were explained, as connected and with the transfer of Luftwaffe training from vulnerable bases in the west, and with the protection of the Romanian oilfields and of industrial centres in eastern and central Germany against possible Soviet bombing raids;[272] these were then feared especially by Hitler, but were not ruled out by the Luftwaffe either. The air-

---

[265] Below, *Hitlers Adjutant*, 243.   [266] *KTB OKW* i. 199E; Hillgruber, *Strategie*, 222.

[267] As late as 8 Aug. 1940 the Luftwaffe operations staff asked the Army High Command for data on the establishment of a ground organization within the framework of 'Build-up East' (Greiner, *Oberste Wehrmachtführung*, 295), and two weeks later the Luftwaffe group in the Wehrmacht operations staff still lacked detailed information on the 'grand design' behind that build-up: *KTB OKW* i. 43 (21 Aug. 1940).

[268] *IMT* ix. 333; Thomas, *Wehr- und Rüstungswirtschaft*, 234, 432; Uhlig, 'Das Einwirken Hitlers', 167, 169; Irving, *Hitler's War*, 175, 181–2; Hillgruber, *Strategie*, 262–3, 266; Bross, *Gespräche mit Göring*, 78–9; Engel, *Heeresadjutant bei Hitler*, 87; Speer, *Inside the Third Reich*, 261–2.

[269] Greiner, *Oberste Wehrmachtführung*, 297.   [270] Halder, *Diaries*, 614 (7 Oct. 1940).

[271] Ibid. 535–6 (1 Aug. 1940), 614–15 (8 Oct. 1940), 621 (14 Oct. 1940).

[272] See Irving, *Rise and Fall*, 164; *KTB OKW* i. 29 (29 Aug. 1940); Befragungsprotokoll [interrogation record] Col. (retd.) von Below, 25 July 1973, item 4, MGFA; Schreiben Adjutantur der Wehrmacht beim Führer [letter from Wehrmacht adjutant's office], Br.B. No. 465/40 g., 9 Sept. 1940, to R.d.L. u. Ob.d.L. (Göring), Ministeramt, BA-MA RL 2 II/21; Robinson, Ic, 25 Nov. 1940: Sowjetrußland, Beurteilung der Luftwaffe [Soviet Russia, estimate of the air force], BA-MA OKM, Case GE 969/PG 32969.

base in northern Norway was to serve both operations against Britain and the protection of the nickel-mines at Petsamo. Hitler's aggressive intentions *vis-à-vis* the east—which, according to Below, remained unchanged even after the autumn of 1939—were possibly not yet entirely clear to the Luftwaffe command in the summer and early autumn of 1940. This view gains some support from the discussions of long-term air-force rearmament plans in progress about the middle of October 1940.[273] The commander-in-chief of the army, at his conference with Hitler on 4 November 1940, similarly gained the impression that he had not yet taken the final decision on implementing his intentions in the east.[274] On 25 November 1940, when Hoffmann von Waldau submitted to Artillery General Jodl, chief of the Wehrmacht operations staff, some data on the distribution of Luftwaffe forces in a war on two fronts, Jodl indicated to him that such studies should not be pursued any further for the time being;[275] even on 3 December 1940 Jodl still observed that top priority in the armaments effort was held by 'anything necessary for the siege of Britain, which must not let up'. A 'large-scale campaign'—meaning a war against the Soviet Union—could, and indeed had to, be postponed until later if the armaments situation required it. At the time, however, he thought German armaments adequate for such a task. The armaments programme for the navy and Luftwaffe, on the other hand, especially for the air defences of Germany, must not be cut back.[276]

These circumstances might explain, at least in part, why Göring for a long time evidently regarded Hitler's thoughts on a war in the east as non-committal, and why it was only later, after Molotov's visit on 12 and 13 November, that he reacted to them critically.[277] When Göring asked for a postponement of the enterprise he was doing so not on considerations of principle or international law, but for political and military reasons. He feared a war on two or more fronts, which Hitler, to judge from *Mein Kampf*, did not wish to wage either. He was convinced that Soviet rearmament was directed against Germany, because of the ideological differences between communism and National Socialism, but he did not believe that it would be completed before 1942–43, or even 1944. He was hoping that Germany would by then have reached an arrangement with Britain, though not perhaps 'peace through victory'; to that end he wished to continue to employ the Luftwaffe in massed strength, undiluted by any second theatre of war, to ensure that the sacrifices made so far were not in vain and that the British were prevented from rebuilding their aircraft industry undisturbed. Göring's alternative concept envisaged a weakening of Britain by striking at the western and eastern

---

[273] See sect. I.iv.2(*c*) at n. 344.
[274] Halder, *Diaries*, 674 (4 Nov. 1940); see Below, *Hitlers Adjutant*, 247, also 212, 217.
[275] *KTB OKW* i. 188 (25 Nov. 1940).   [276] Thomas, *Wehr- und Rüstungswirtschaft*, 437.
[277] *IMT* ix. 341–7, 427–8, 628–9, 650–1; Heinkel, *Leben*, 425; Bross, *Gespräche mit Göring*, 26, 56, 78 ff.; Suchenwirth, *Göring*, 109–19, MGFA Lw 21/3; Hillgruber, *Strategie*, 211. It is possible that Göring repeatedly voiced his arguments against a war in the east over a period of several weeks.

accesses to the Mediterranean. With this plan he hoped to divert Hitler from Russia, or at least to keep him from attacking in the foreseeable future.

Hitler closed his mind to these arguments and pacified Göring—who had emphasized the detrimental effect on the Luftwaffe of its uninterrupted employment since the beginning of the war[278]—with the promise that he would be able to resume his air war against Britain within six weeks and that, after the speedy conclusion of the eastern campaign, several hundred thousand men would be made available to him for the aircraft industry.[279] These assurances and clearly favourable estimates of the enemy's air situation by the Luftwaffe operations staff/Ic, as well as personal reasons[280]—loyalty as an officer and leading National Socialist *vis-à-vis* Hitler, fear of losing his power, influence, and luxurious life in the event of further opposition—all these eventually led Göring to abandon his objections and, influenced by Hitler, to see the situation through his eyes. Ultimately Göring was convinced that Bolshevism would have to be eradicated some time, and so, despite occasional misgivings about the size of the territory to be conquered and the length of supply-routes, he believed in a swift victory of German arms, in the collapse of the Soviet state within a fortnight, and—still at that time—in the genius of Hitler, whom he regarded as an incomparable leader, one behind whom one might confidently march.[281] Hitler himself, during the weeks prior to the start of the campaign, was far more sceptical.[282] Deep down, however, Göring remained out of sympathy with the 'uncomfortable' war in the east and increasingly lost interest in the conduct of the war generally.[283] Göring's alternative concept[284] to Hitler's plan for the war in the east lacked any substance. It was a one-off reaction, not based on any serious alternative plan by the Luftwaffe General Staff.

Misgivings and divergent views, some of them in line with Göring's, were voiced also by other senior Luftwaffe officers,[285] who showed a more realistic

[278] Ambassador Hewel, diary, entries for 29 and 31 May 1941, in private ownership.

[279] Halder, *Diaries*, 846 (30 Mar. 1941); *KTB OKW* i. 258 (9 Jan. 1941) and 1018; Brauchitsch, Aufgabe der Luftwaffe [Task of the Luftwaffe], MGFA, A-83, items 23, 24; Suchenwirth, Jeschonnek, 79, MGFA Lw 21/5. Mention was made of up to 500,000 men.

[280] See Suchenwirth, Göring, 116 ff., MGFA Lw 21/3; *IMT* ix. 58, 190–1, 372–3, 428.

[281] On his underestimation of Soviet strength see Engel, *Heeresadjutant bei Hitler*, 87 (15 Sept. 1940); also other highly optimistic remarks by Göring on the chances of success against the Soviet Union: Thomas, *Wehr- und Rüstungswirtschaft*, 18–19; Hillgruber, *Strategie*, 266, 396; Galland, *The First and the Last*, 126 ff.; Irving, *Hitler's War*, 267; id., *Rise and Fall*, 183; Speidel, Generalstab, 70, MGFA P-031a, 26. Teil/I; Hammerstein, Mein Leben, 121, IfZ ED 84; see also Kordt, *Wahn und Wirklichkeit*, 293.

[282] Ambassador Hewel, diary, entries for 29 May and 8 June 1941, in private ownership; Irving, *Hitler's War*, 259–60, 267, 271.

[283] See Speer, *Inside the Third Reich*, 261 ff., and Heinkel, *Leben*, 421.

[284] This was confirmed after the war by Gen. (retd.) Kammhuber (questioned on 30 Oct. 1968, MGFA); Gen. (retd.) Bodenschatz (*IMT* ix. 13); Gen. (retd.) von Seidel (information dated 8 Sept. 1954, in Plocher, Krieg im Osten, 32–3, MGFA Lw 4/9); FM Milch (*IMT* ix. 49, 82–3); Col.-Gen. (retd.) Halder (in Halder, *Hitler as War Lord*, 19–20); and State Secretary Paul Körner (in Suchenwirth, Göring, 113–14, MGFA Lw 21/3).

[285] See Boog, *Luftwaffenführung*, 115 ff.

assessment of the excessive demands that would be made on the Luftwaffe by a war on two fronts and by the vastness of an eastern theatre of war. These included State Secretary Erhard Milch, Major-General Hoffmann von Waldau (head of the Luftwaffe operations department), Lieutenant-General Hans-Georg von Seidel (Luftwaffe quartermaster-general), and Colonel-General Alfred Keller,[286] Field Marshal Albert Kesselring,[287] and Colonel-General Alexander Löhr (the commanders-in-chief, respectively, of Air Fleets 1, 2, and 4, earmarked for employment in the east); their doubts, voiced to Göring or Halder, produced no results. Löhr, together with Major-General Günther Korten, his chief of staff, favoured an exploitation of the successes achieved by his air fleet in the Balkans by a strategic strike into the eastern Mediterranean. Kesselring at that time was inclined to think likewise, even though he was unaware of Löhr's ideas. He had a low opinion of the Soviet fighting forces, based on their poor performance in the Finnish–Soviet Winter War, and relied on the superiority of the Luftwaffe with its experience of several victorious campaigns. Keeping communism out of Europe, even by a preventive strike, seemed to him worth any cost. He was thus expressing an anti-communist conviction widespread among Wehrmacht and public, despite concrete reservations about a war against Russia, a conviction which, regardless of divergences of opinion, was a uniting factor among the Luftwaffe leadership.

Another reason why the Luftwaffe leaders fell in line rather smoothly with the intended war in the east can be found in the few remarks known to have been made by Air General Hans Jeschonnek, chief of the Luftwaffe General Staff.[288] In the First World War, in contrast to Milch, he had fought only in the west; in the 1920s he had come to know the Soviet Union as a backward country. In spite of his misgivings that, in the event of an additional war in the east, the Luftwaffe's activity so far would be greatly curtailed, he was 'absolutely for a fight', with a 'positive attitude' to the new tasks. The reason why he did not object, or react more critically, to the idea of a war in the east was probably that he was then receiving daily reports showing that the independent strategic employment of bomber forces against the British armaments industry and morale was not yielding any perceptible results. This finding was in line with similar experience from the First World War and the war in Spain, as well as with the results of studies conducted between the wars. It was, moreover, in line with existing Luftwaffe doctrine, which envisaged an independent long-range bombing war only after a congealment of the front lines on the ground, or else if there was no other way of bringing about a decision

---

[286] Plocher, Krieg im Osten, 39–40, MGFA Lw 4/9.

[287] Kesselring, *Memoirs*, 85–100; *IMT* ix. 183.

[288] On Jeschonnek's misgivings see Minute C/Skl of a conference with Gen. Jeschonnek, chief of the Luftwaffe General Staff, on 4 Jan. 1941, BA-MA OKM, Case GE 970/PG 32970, fo. 33, and Below, *Hitlers Adjutant*, 255; on his positive attitude to the war in the east see Lt.-Gen. (retd.) Schmid, in Suchenwirth, Jeschonnek, 79, MGFA Lw 21/5, Hoffmann von Waldau, Persönl. Tagebuch [personal diary], 120 ff., BA-MA RL 200/17, and evidence by Rear-Adm.(retd.) Mössel, dated 3 Sept. 1954, in Plocher, Krieg im Osten, 36, MGFA Lw 4/9.

in the war, i.e. as a last resort. This belief was based on the realization that operational and strategic bombing generally produced an effect on the land fronts only at a very late stage and at an excessive cost in material. Finally, this view was determined also by the fact that many senior Luftwaffe commanders came from the army and had their thinking moulded by Germany's geo-strategically unfavourable continental situation.[289] What could be more natural in such a situation than to seek success where it had always been attained in the past: in aerial operations in support of the ground troops, as envisaged by the plan of the campaign against a supposedly weak Soviet Union? Was the lack of tangible success in strategic air warfare not further proof of the correctness of co-operative air warfare? The close links postulated by Directive No. 21 between Luftwaffe and army seemed to ensure that, even without long-range bombers, the Luftwaffe would be able to reach the more distant indus-trial centres of the Soviet Union by fighting its way forward, in conjunction with the army, until it had established suitable jumping-off bases. That was a kind of war which met Jeschonnek's ideas and expectations of success. After the disappointments of the air war against Britain he seemed to have positively longed for it, as suggested by his remark at the time: 'At last a proper war again!'

The Luftwaffe therefore had no influence on Hitler's decision to overthrow the Soviet Union in 1941—or only to the extent that by its expectations of success and its underestimation of the Soviet air forces and aerial-armaments industry (to be later discussed) it confirmed him in his decision.

(b) Assessment of the Soviet Air Forces 1939–1941

The order for an intensive reconnaissance of the Soviet Union was not given until, with Hitler's Directive No. 21 (Barbarossa), the political and military-strategic decision to attack that country had been made.[290] On 10 January 1941 Colonel (General Staff) Josef Schmid, chief of the 5th (Foreign Air Forces) department of the Luftwaffe General Staff, was instructed to provide target data up to a general line Archangel–Leningrad–Lake Ilmen–course of the Dnieper, and to reconnoitre the Soviet air forces.[291] The order was received with surprise in the department as the air battle for Britain was not yet concluded.

Although the Luftwaffe, prior to that date, had engaged in routine recon-naissance towards the east, this had not yielded much information.[292] Ways and means of information-gathering were exceedingly limited because of the strict control and prohibition measures customary there. Work by agents was virtually out of the question; attempts to infiltrate them into senior political

[289] See Boog, *Luftwaffenführung*, 164 ff., and id., 'Generalstabsausbildung', 25, 28–30.
[290] See Kahn, *Hitler's Spies*, 445.
[291] Nielsen, Nachrichtenbeschaffung, 148–9, MGFA Lw 17.
[292] Kahn, *Hitler's Spies*, 451 ff.; Nielsen, Nachrichtenbeschaffung, 137, 139–40, MGFA Lw 17; Schwabedissen, Russische Luftwaffe, 12–13, MGFA Lw 22/1; Plocher, Krieg im Osten, 738 ff., MGFA Lw 4/5.

and military positions had failed. The controlled Soviet press and specialized literature contained only general information and did not allow of precise conclusions on the strength, organization, or combat-readiness of the Soviet air forces. Radio monitoring had been able to supply a few valuable tesserae, but these did not add up to a complete mosaic. Not even the occasional high-altitude long-range reconnaissance missions flown since 1934 on behalf of the Wehrmacht High Command by the Special Staffel Rowehl,[293] which was known as Air Staffel (special duties) and, after 1937, as 'Hansa Luftbild-Abteilung B' (Hansa Aerial Photography Department B), were able to cover the huge territory. Apart from a few separate pieces of information on the Russians' ability to build modern types of aircraft or to fly in formation for aerial reviews, General Köstring, the German military attaché in Moscow, had been unable to gain any deeper insight into the Soviet air forces or their armament potential.[294] On the whole, German ideas of the Red Army's air forces were still largely coloured by the impressions gained by German officers and engineers during the period of secret German–Russian collaboration in the early 1930s. But at that time the Soviet air forces and aircraft industry were still in a state of development and learning. Subsequently, Stalin's purges had created the impression of a Soviet power without a military head.[295]

While the German Condor Legion in the Spanish civil war had been impressed by the new Soviet I-16 fighter, they had not been impressed by the performance of the Soviet flying crews. Their operational control seemed cumbersome and lacking in general staff training. At the same time, they managed to offset some weaknesses by skilful improvisation. Operations by the Red flying units were marked by inadequate concentration of forces and insufficient flexibility in attack and defence. The result was that they suffered excessive losses. The aircrews were courageous and eager over their own territory, but timid over that of the enemy. Outstanding pilots were the exception. Training in formation flying was inadequate, especially for fighters. Soviet bomber crews, because of a lack of adequate training, played only a subordinate part in Spain. Their principal form of action was close ground support. Anti-aircraft artillery, especially light and medium gunners, showed some progress. Communications revealed substantial shortcomings.[296]

Because of the scarcity of information on the Soviet Union the Luftwaffe attached particular importance to reports by Russian *émigrés* and German repatriates from the Soviet Union—especially as their derogatory attitude was in line with the strong traditional feeling of German cultural superiority and with the National Socialist thesis of the 'racial' superiority of Germanic

[293] Rowehl, Chronik der Aufklärungsgruppe des Ob.d.L. [Chronicle of the reconnaissance group of the Luftwaffe C.-in-C.], 4, BA-MA Lw 108/16; Kahn, *Hitler's Spies*, 449–50; Eyermann, *Luftspionage*, ii. 131–2.

[294] Kahn, *Hitler's Spies*, 454 ff.

[295] Schwabedissen, Russische Luftwaffe, 6, MGFA Lw 22/1; Reinhardt, *Moskau*, 20.

[296] See Moritz, 'Fehleinschätzung', 176–7; Schwabedissen, Russische Luftwaffe, 74–5, MGFA Lw 22/1.

peoples over Slavs. That thesis, hammered into the Wehrmacht by National Socialist propaganda, played a part in preventing it from forming a realistic judgement of the Soviet Union and its air forces.[297] Thus Major-General Hoffmann von Waldau, the normally cool and objective chief of the operations department of the Luftwaffe General Staff, called the Soviet Union a 'state of most centralized executive power and below-average intelligence'.[298]

The scanty and prejudiced pre-war information of the Luftwaffe General Staff concerning the Soviet air forces had already been reflected in the observations of the 5th department on the air situation in Europe, dated 2 May 1939.[299] This recorded an increasing degree of haphazardness in the direction of the Soviet armaments industry and administration, as well as a lack of tight and unified leadership at the top of the armed forces. Reports to the effect that the Soviet air forces had a strength of 10,000–12,000 aircraft were deliberately dismissed. Instead, the figure assumed was only 6,000, of which 5,000 were front-line aircraft and only 3,300 in the European part of the USSR. The Soviet air forces, together with their ground organization and supply apparatus, as well as the anti-aircraft artillery, were regarded as highly vulnerable from the air because of their dependence on the transport network, which had always been considered the most serious bottleneck of the Soviet war economy;[300] the striking power of the Soviet Union was thought to be slight and the chances of a vigorous Soviet air war against Germany were considered shin. The aircraft industry, it was thought, would at best be able to cover current needs and normal wear and tear. Operational use of the Soviet air force was expected predominantly in conjunction with the army. The idea of an independent long-range air war by heavy bomber formations was evidently not being pursued there. While it was not disputed that the present weaknesses in the Soviet air forces would one day be overcome, this was thought to be possible only at an 'Asian pace' and with inadequate organization. On the other hand, it was considered 'extremely probable' that the Soviet Union would 'collapse under heavy pressure from outside'.

Although information on the Soviet air forces was totally inadequate, and although the encounter with the Soviets during the occupation of eastern Poland in September 1939 provided no significant new insights, Hitler, after the conclusion of the German–Soviet agreements in August–September 1939, issued an instruction prohibiting any information-gathering on the Soviet Union as a matter of principle.[301] Hitler was happy to have his rear clear

---

[297] BA-MA RL 3/63, 7397–8; Kahn *Hitler's Spies*, 445 ff.; Reinhardt, *Moskau*, 19.

[298] Hoffmann von Waldau, Persönl. Tagebuch [personal diary], 54 (3 July 1941, item 4), BA-MA RL 200/17.

[299] Appendix to Der R.d.L. u. Ob.d.L., Chef d. GenSt, No. 700/39 g.Kdos. (5. Abt. I): 'Die Luftlage in Europa, Stand Frühjahr 1939' [The air situation in Europe, as of spring 1939], 59–66, 77–8, 92, BA-MA RL 2 II/446.

[300] See Macht, 'Engpässe'.

[301] Kahn, *Hitler's Spies*, 453; Höhne, *Canaris*, 460–1; Schwabedissen, Russiche Luftwaffe, 13, MGFA Lw 22/1.

towards the west and did not wish to provoke his new partner needlessly. The ban evidently did not affect routine general-staff evaluation of information, but it certainly caused Admiral Canaris, chief of the Ausland/Abwehr department in the Wehrmacht High Command, to forbid any Abwehr operations against the Soviet Union, now Germany's neighbour. It also seems to have resulted in a reduction, or even temporary suspension, of the strategic reconnaissance flights of the Rowehl Group over Russia.[302] Intelligence analysis of the Soviet Union by the Luftwaffe operations staff Ic (5th department) was further greatly reduced by the redistribution of the staff of the 'eastern group' (whose concern the Soviet Union was) to the 'western group' and by a failure of new information to materialize.[303] Typical of the situation were the parting words of General Jeschonnek, chief of the Luftwaffe General Staff, to the new German air attaché, Colonel Heinrich Aschenbrenner: 'Establish the best possible relations with the Soviet Union and do not bother about intelligence-gathering.'[304]

Over the summer of 1940 Germany's relations with the Soviet Union were deteriorating, both because of the increasing importance the Soviet factor was assuming in Hitler's plans for the defeat of Britain and because of the growing scale of Soviet westward expansion. In consequence, eastern intelligence-gathering by the Luftwaffe was reactivated. At the beginning of October Hitler acceded to a request from the army, and personally instructed Lieutenant-Colonel Theodor Rowehl, commanding the reconnaissance group of the commander-in-chief of the Luftwaffe, to deploy suitable forces to reconnoitre the Soviet space to a depth of 300 km., concentrating on airfields, and to do so by 15 May 1941. Immediately afterwards Rowehl was once more, within a single week, to re-examine from the air all the Soviet airfields in the theatre of operations.[305]

The Luftwaffe General Staff was further confirmed in the optimistic picture it had arrived at in the spring of 1939 by what seemed a poor performance by the Soviet army and air forces in the Finnish–Russian Winter War of 1939–40. Even though there were some suggestions of a Soviet bluff, the weaknesses shown by them against Finland found their way into the estimates of more than the 5th department.[306] What was evidently being overlooked was that initially only the forces of the Leningrad military district were engaged against Finland and that, during the previous summer, the Red Army had defeated a

---

[302] Eyermann, *Luftspionage*, ii. 139, dates the more than 500 violations of Soviet air-space by German reconnaissance planes to the year 1939 and the first half of 1941. For the latter period Koževnikov (*Komandovanie*, 28) mentions 324 air-space violations; *Geschichte des Großen Vaterländischen Krieges*, i. 562, lists 152.

[303] Nielsen, Nachrichtenbeschaffung, 142, MGFA Lw 17; Boog, *Luftwaffenführung*, 110.

[304] Nielsen, Nachrichtenbeschaffung, 140–1, MFGA Lw 17.

[305] See Greiner, *Oberste Wehrmachtführung*, 312–13, and Halder, *Diaries*, 605 (1 Oct. 1940); Rowehl, Chronik der Aufklärungsgruppe des Ob.d.L., 7 ff., BA-MA Lw 108/16.

[306] Nielsen, Nachrichtenbeschaffung, 143, MGFA Lw 17; Kesselring, *Memoirs*, 85–100; Kahn, *Hitler's Spies*, 447–8; Reinhardt, *Moskau*, 20.

Japanese army in Mongolia. At the end of November 1940[307] Colonel (General
Staff) Schmid, chief of the Luftwaffe operations staff's intelligence department, still assessed the Russian air force as not very strong and outdated, the
anti-aircraft artillery as 'exceedingly mediocre', and the growth of the Soviet
air forces in European Russia as a 'provisional deployment towards the west'
which, 'in line with Russian conditions, [will] need a long time'.

Systematic air reconnaissance against the Soviet Union therefore did not
start fully until the winter of 1940–1; at times it was greatly impeded by the
weather. Reconnaissance missions were generally flown at an altitude of
approximately 9,000 m. The aircraft used were He-111s, Do-215s, Ju–88Bs,
and JU-86Ps, equipped with pressurized cabins and 'souped-up' engines. In
line with Stalin's placatory policy at the time, the Soviet Union did not protest
very strongly against these reconnaissance flights, of which it was well aware.
Indeed, Soviet fighters were under orders not to fire at German reconnaissance planes. German crews repeatedly reported such—to them surprising—
encounters in the air. After the war Soviet historiography blamed the 'traitor
Beriya', who was then responsible for the frontier troops protecting Soviet air-
space, for having 'practically' opened Soviet air-space to German aerial
espionage by his ban on opening fire.[308]

From the end of 1940 onward the Abwehr department of the Wehrmacht
High Command and the air attachés in Moscow, Ankara, Tokyo, Stockholm,
Helsinki, Washington, and the Balkan States were, within the limitations of
their possibilities, enlisted in eastern intelligence-gathering. The Rowehl
group dropped agents by parachute. The network of radio-intercept posts was
extended. A group of former Tsarist officers assisted in intelligence analysis
and the breaking of the Soviet code. Radio intelligence in particular yielded
valuable information, which then provided the basis for aerial photo-recon-
naissance. In view of the short period of time available and the lack of
preliminary work, the results of Abwehr operations were limited. The attachés
were scarcely able to gain any insight into the Soviet air forces or their
armaments.[309]

The only exception, up to a point, was the air attaché in Moscow. He
managed to obtain the 'Red Commander's Atlas' with extensive data on
railways and industrial enterprises, as well as a telephone directory which
allowed some conclusions as to the extent of the industry in the Urals, but was

---

[307] Robinson Ic, 25 Nov. 1940: Sowjetrußland, Beurteilung der Luftwaffe [Soviet Russia,
assessment of the air force], BA-MA OKM, Case GE 969/PG 32969.

[308] Koževnikov, *Komandovanie*, 27; Plocher, Krieg im Osten, 268–9, MGFA Lw 4/1; Rowehl,
Chronik der Aufklärungsgruppe des Ob.d.L., 9, BA-MA Lw 108/16; BA-MA RL 3/34, p. 1879;
Geschichte des Großen Vaterländischen Krieges, i. 562.

[309] Col. (retd.) Reinhard von Heinemann, Nachrichten über die russische Luftwaffe von 1940
bis etwa 1942 [Information on the Russian air force from 1940 to about 1942], 10, BA-MA Lw 135;
Boog, *Luftwaffenführung*, 109–10; Schwabedissen, Russische Luftwaffe, 14 ff.; MGFA Lw 22/1;
Nielsen, Nachrichtenbeschaffung, 148, MGFA Lw 17.

otherwise an isolated and superficial source.[310] In March 1941, on Göring's instruction, he gained the Soviet government's consent to an inspection of Soviet aircraft-industry armament and research centres by German experts. Along with the air attaché and the Luftwaffe engineers Tschersich and Schwencke (responsible for planning and foreign armaments under the Generalluftzeugmeister), representatives of Daimler-Benz, Henschel, Askania, Mauser, and other firms participated from 7 to 16 April in an inspection of various aircraft-industry establishments in Moscow, Rybinsk, Perm (Molotov), and elsewhere. The commission of experts was 'most impressed' by the size of the plants and the organization and quality of production. The well-known Russian aircraft designer Artem Mikoyan, a brother of the People's Commissar for Economic Affairs, gave the Germans an unmistakable warning on parting: 'We have now shown you everything we have and we are capable of. Anyone attacking us will be smashed by us.' The experts' detailed reports were disbelieved by the Luftwaffe operations staff and dismissed by Göring as exaggerated; the experts were regarded as victims of a Soviet bluff. Obviously that inspection tour could not provide a complete picture of Soviet aerial armaments, but it did convey a substantial partial impression. The report by the engineers that one of the aircraft-engine factories they had visited was larger than six of Germany's principal engine plants put together aroused Göring's anger. He forbade them to talk about it, called them defeatists, and threatened them with a concentration camp. Hitler, on the other hand, was deeply impressed by the reports. His reaction was: 'Now you see how far these people have already got. We must start at once.'[311]

By the end of April 1941[312] the target study of the Soviet Union within the 300-km. zone, and for certain towns even beyond, was completed. Because of the lack of long-range aircraft, however, airfields in the interior of European Russia or industrial enterprises—in the Donets basin, on the middle Volga, but mainly in the Urals—were beyond German reach. Information on these in particular might have had a sobering effect on the Luftwaffe Operations Staff. In the circumstances, the eastern reconnaissance practised by the Luftwaffe Operations Staff Ic and the agencies under its control during the six months prior to the onset of the campaign will have to be seen mainly as tactical and less as strategic.

[310] See Plocher, Krieg im Osten, 256, MGFA Lw 4/1, and Nielsen, Nachrichtenbeschaffung, 142, MGFA Lw 17. According to Rieckhoff, *Trumpf oder Bluff?*, 251–2, and Baumbach, *Broken Swastika*, 154, Col. Aschenbrenner warned against the strength of the Soviet Union. According to the recollections of the former Gauleiter of Halle-Merseburg (Jordan, *Erlebt und Erlitten*, 217–18), Aschenbrenner, as late as the spring of 1941, had a low opinion of Soviet strength.

[311] Report on inspection: BA-MA RL 3/2245. See *IMT* ix. 81–2; Plocher, Krieg im Osten, 257 ff., 264, MGFA Lw 4/1; Nielsen, Nachrichtenbeschaffung, 141–2, MGFA Lw 17; Irving, *Rise and Fall*, 178; id., *Hitler's War*, 205–6, 763; Groehler, *Luftkrieg*, 291; Below, *Hitlers Adjutant*, 267.

[312] Nielsen, Nachrichtenbeschaffung, 149, MGFA Lw 17.

In May 1941 the Luftwaffe Operations Staff Ic published an information brochure on the Soviet air force, anti-aircraft troops, and aircraft industry, as at 1 February 1941.[313] This combined correct and incorrect data—some inspired by a strong sense of superiority—on the Soviet air forces and armaments potential. It concluded that the Soviet air forces, altough they had been detached from the army and navy since 1936, continued to see their main role in direct support for these two services, especially the army. This was true even of heavy bomber formations, which were credited at most with the capacity to execure nocturnal nuisance raids into German territory but not daytime long-range missions; it was true also of the paratroops and air-landing units, which were short of transport aircraft, of the fighter units, except those directly under the Supreme Army Command for home defence, and of the ground-attack units, which were expected, under fighter cover, to work very closely with the ground forces and armoured units and to launch attacks on railways, trans-shipment centres, and columns on the move. More than in earlier campaigns, low-level attacks were expected against German ground forces and airfields near the front.

Information on the organization and command structure of the Soviet air forces was essentially accurate.[314] It was believed that it had been undergoing reorganization since April 1939, that this process was not yet completed, and that air corps and air brigades were being replaced by mixed and pure air divisions. In 1941 38 air divisions and 162 air regiments had been identified. Altogether 50 air divisions were believed to exist. In the event of war, it was thought, pure long-range bomber and fighter divisions would be placed under the command of the individual 'fronts' (army groups), mixed air divisions would be placed under the armies, and light bomber and ground-attack regiments would be temporarily placed under the army corps; in addition, all army staffs would have reconnaissance aircraft attached to them. It was assumed that there would be a reserve of long-range bomber and fighter divisions, as well as of long-range reconnaissance units under the People's Commissar for Defence, and that fighter divisions would be kept back for home defence in the rearward military districts to support the AA artillery there.

---

[313] Der Ob.d.L., Fü.St.Ic/IV No. 3500/41 g., Prüf.No. 226; Orientierungsheft Union der Sozialistischen Sowjetrepubliken (U.d.S.S.R.) unter besonderer Berücksichtigung der Fliegertruppe und Flakartillerie sowie der Flugrüstungsindustrie im Rahmen der allgemeinen Wehrwirtschaftslage. Stand: 1.2.1941 [Orientation brochure USSR with special reference to flying formations and anti-aircraft artillery, as well as the air armaments industry within the framework of the general war-economy situation. As of 1 Feb. 1941], copy, BA-MA Lw 107/67; Schwabedissen, Russische Luftwaffe, 11–83, MGFA Lw 22/1; Plocher, Krieg im Osten, 270–88, MGFA Lw 4/1. See also appendix 1 to AOK 17, Ia, No. 222/41. g.Kdos./Chefs., 14 May 1941, 5–8 (II. Die russische Luftwaffe), BA-MA LII AK 16041/9, and Großer [rumänischer] Generalstab, Sektion Ia, Büro I, Nachrichten: Bericht mit Material für den Nachrichtenaustausch mit dem deutschen Großen [!] Generalstab, Abschnitt III: Nachrichten über die Luftwaffe der U.R.S.S. [Intelligence: Report with data on the exchange of intelligence with the German Great [sic] General Staff, section III: Intelligence on the air force of the USSR], 27 Mar. 1941, 20–43, BA-MA RH 19 I/123.

[314] See the Annexe Volume, No. 3, and sect. I.II.2 at n. 143 (Hoffmann).

In point of fact the Red air forces, according to Soviet postwar publications,[315] consisted of 70 air divisions and 5 air brigades at the beginning of the war. The air forces of the Supreme Command consisted of 13 long-range bomber and 5 fighter divisions and accounted for 13.5 per cent of the air forces. The flying formations of the ground forces, i.e. of the military districts (fronts), armies, and army corps, accounted for 86.5 per cent and consisted of 63 divisions; of these 9 were bomber, 18 fighter, and 34 mixed divisions. A further 25 air divisions were in the process of being set up. Since the beginning of 1939 the number of air regiments had increased by over 80 per cent. Of 118 air regiments in the five western military districts 34 were being refitted with new types of aircraft. In addition, 40 fighter regiments with 1,500 fighter planes were available for air defence. The navy had 1,445 aircraft in European Russia: the Arctic Fleet had 114, the Red Banner Baltic Fleet 707, and the Black Sea Fleet 624. In the five (out of thirteen) western military districts of European Russia the Luftwaffe was faced with at least 5,440 aircraft, concentrated mainly in the Western and the Kiev Special Military Districts. These comprised 1,688 bombers, 2,736 fighters, 336 close-combat aircraft, 252 reconnaissance aircraft, and some 430 machines in the army corps air squadrons. The inland military districts were equipped with outdated machines. (On the composition and disposition of the Soviet air forces see Annexe Volume, No. 3.)

The Luftwaffe Operations Staff Ic estimated the total strength of the Soviet air force at 10,500 combat aircraft belonging to formations, approximately 7,500 in European Russia and 3,000 in the Asian part. Only about 50 per cent of the machines were regarded as modern. The number of front-line aircraft—which did not include transport or liaison machines—was assumed to be 5,700 in the European part of the Soviet Union; only half of that total, i.e. about 1,360 reconnaissance planes and bombers and 1,490 fighters, were considered combat-ready.[316] However, a reinforcement of the fighter formations by 700 machines was expected during the first half of 1941, as well as re-equipment with 200–300 new models. In the bomber formations no substantial reinforcement was expected, but a 50 per cent re-equipment with up-to-date models. The number of fully trained pilots was estimated at 15,000, that of ground personnel at 150,000 men, and that of training machines at 10,000.

The deployment of the Soviet air forces continued to be viewed as a 'provisional westward deployment' by the Luftwaffe Operations Staff Ic and apparently interpreted as offensive.[317]

---

[315] Koževnikov, *Komandovanie*, 15–35; Groehler, *Luftkrieg*, 298–305; see *Geschichte des Großen Vaterländischen Krieges*, i. 522–5, 529–30, 534–5, 537, 558–9.

[316] The army proceeded from similar figures. See the map exercise 'Otto' of Army Group A in St-Germain on 5 Feb. 1941, BA-MA RH 19 I/70; annexe 3a to OKH/GenStdH/OpAbt IN No. 050/41 g.Kdos. Chefs., 31 Jan. 1941, BA-MA RH 19 I/67; Halder, *Diaries*, 805 ff. (22 Feb. 1941), 812–13 (27 Feb. 1941); KoLuft bei Pz.Gr. 4 Ic Br.B. No. 30/41 g.Kdos., 11 Apr. 1941, BA-MA RL 18/9; Moritz, 'Fehleinschätzung', 177.

[317] See Schwabedissen, *Russische Luftwaffe*, 31–2, MGFA Lw 22/1.

On the subject of the composition of the flying formations, their armaments and equipment, the Luftwaffe Operations Staff Ic had come to the following conclusions. An air division consisted of 3–6 air regiments. Air regiments were always 'pure', i.e. either fighter or reconnaissance or ground-attack regiments, etc. They corresponded to a German Gruppe and, in their turn, usually consisted of 4 squadrons (Staffeln). Although the theoretical wartime strength was 60 aircraft, a fighter or ground-attack regiment in fact had only 48, and a bomber or reconnaissance regiment only 36, aircraft. The actual strength of squadrons varied between 9 and 12 machines.

Reconnaissance aircraft were grouped together in reconnaissance air regiments, independent reconnaissance squadrons, and independent long-range reconnaissance squadrons; as a rule they came under the command of the air divisions. There were also independent squadrons for short-range reconnaissance, artillery-spotting, and liaison duties; tactically these came under the army corps but for supplies under the air divisions. The bulk of the reconnaissance forces consisted of the outdated R-5 and R-6 models. The few R-10s and I-16s were more modern. Organization of the fighters and long-range fighters was similar.

The principal fighter model was the I-16 (Rata). Alongside it there was the outdated I-15 with its variants I-151 and I-153. The Rata was considered a modern aircraft and was more manœuvrable, albeit slower, than the Me-109. It was superior to German bomber aircraft, but its older plywood construction made it vulnerable to cannon fire and highly inflammable. This no longer applied to the newer metal version. The pilot was protected by the engine in front of him and 8-mm. armour behind. Its attacking weapons, four fuselage machine-guns, were not considered equal to those of German machines. Little was known about the MiG and LaGG models about to be introduced, and virtually nothing about a new twin-engined 'destroyer' plane.

The bomber force consisted of 'fast bomber' and 'long-range bomber' regiments in the appropriate air divisions. The former were equipped with SB-2s and SB-3s, copies of the American Martin bombers; the latter used DB-3s in addition to some older TB types. With a bomb-load of 1,000 kg. the penetration depth of the SB models was estimated at 600 km. and that of the DB-3s at about 1,200 km. The defensive armament of the SB models was considered poor, that of the DB-3s better. The former were believed to be suitable only for night attack, and only to a limited degree. No details were known of a new twin-engined bomber.

The ground-attack units were equipped with only a handful of the modern SB-1 and Vultee V-11 models; for the rest they relied on the outdated RZ, DI-6, I-15, and I-4 types. The transport units were organized in 'heavy air regiments', equipped predominantly with older models, and earmarked also for the transportation of paratroop and air-landing units. There were, in addition, a small number of ambulance aircraft attached to armies, corps, and divisions. The naval air units, organized in brigades and independent squadrons, did not meet modern requirements. There were no aircraft-carriers. As for aircraft armament, the 7.62-mm. 'Shkas' machine-gun had proved its worth in Spain and Mongolia. No details were known of aircraft cannon. High-explosive bombs of up to 500 kg. were assumed to exist, as well as fragmentation bombs of up to 15 kg., 2-kg. incendiary bombs, 2.5-kg. thermite incendiary bombs, and 10-kg. and 50-kg. oil-filled incendiary bombs. Only the I-16s and the SB-3s had fuel-tank shields. As for the bombing force, it was believed that only the formation leaders' machines were equipped with transmission and receiving equipment; refurbishment with new aircraft types, it was thought, would progress slowly. The fact that during the eighteen months before the beginning of the war 2,739 aircraft[318] of the most modern types had been produced—399 Yak-1, 1,309 MiG-3, and 322 LaGG-3 fighters, 460 twin-engined bombers of the Pe-2 type, and 249 IL-2 ground-attack aircraft, among the best close-combat planes in the world—was not known to the Luftwaffe Operations Staff Ic.

In contrast to 1939, the state of training of the flying personnel was regarded as generally good, though not equal to that of the Luftwaffe. Night- and blind-flying skills were considered inadequate, the ability of crews to act independently underdeveloped because of excessive formation flying, tactical training unsatisfactory, but combat-readiness in daytime and good weather was thought adequate.

Ground organization in the western part of European Russia, especially around Leningrad and Moscow, was found to be close-knit and still being extended, and new airfields completed since 1939 were known to exist in eastern Poland and in the Baltic region. According to the degree of technical equipment, a distinction was made between 'first-degree airfields' (corresponding to German air-bases and furnished with concrete hangars and runways, road connections, fuel-tanks, and bomb-depots), 'second-degree airfields', and 'third-degree airfields' (corresponding to German forward airfields without permanent structures), as well as a large number of airstrips. 'First-degree airfields' were, for the most part, the locations of the staffs of major air formations and their supply staffs. Supplies, coming under the Supreme Administration of Air Troops, were operated in peacetime by the military districts by way of 'main bases', corresponding to the German 'air parks', and movable air-bases under the control of the air divisions. Of some 2,000 identified airfields in western Russia only 200 were regarded as suitable for bomber formations. The remainder, because of a lack of installations, were often too exposed to the effects of weather, so that the whole organization had only limited value for the operational employment of flying formations. The advantage of mobile air-bases was put in question by inadequate transport routes. In point of fact, since the autumn of 1940 the runways of more than 250 airfields in the western frontier regions of the Soviet Union had been ex-

---

[318] Koževnikov, *Komandovanie*, 17.

TABLE I.IV.4. Specifications and Performance of the Principal Aircraft of the Soviet Air Forces, Summer 1941

Type	General data			Performance				Armament			
	In service since	Total flying weight (kg.)	Engines	Crew	Max. speed (km./h.)	Normal range (km.)	Operating ceiling (m.)	Landing speed (km./h.)	MG and cannon	Calib. (mm.)	Bomb-load (kg.)
Bombers											
SB	1935	6,500	2	3	445	1,000	9,000	130	4	7.62	600–1,500
Pe 2	1941	7,700	2	3	540	1,100	9,000	145	4	7.62	600–1,000
DB 3f	1937	8,000	2	3	440	2,700	6,960	125	3	7.62	1,000–2,500
TB 3	1931	19,200	4	8	288	4,000	6,960	116	8	7.62	2,000–4,000
TB 7	1940	27,000	4	10	443	4,700	10,300	116	6	7.62	2,000–4,000
									3	12.70	
									2	20.00	
Fighter bombers											
Il 2	1941	5,340	1	1	412	510	7,500	140	2	20.00	400–600
									2	7.62	

Fighters								8 RS (rockets)	82.00	
I 15 bis	1935	1,650	367	1	770	9,000	100	4	7.62	150
I 16	1934	1,878	462	1	625	10,800	112	4	7.62	100
I 153	1938	1,858	427	1	690	10,700	105	4	7.62	200
Jak 1	1941	2,917	572	1	700	10,500	140	1 / 2	20.00 / 7.62	—
LaGG 3	1941	3,380	549	1	556	9,600	140	1 / 1 / 2	20.00 / 12.70 / 7.62	200
MiG 3	1940	3,299	620	1	1,000	12,000	140	1 / 2	12.70 / 7.62	200
Reconnaissance aircraft										
R 5	1931	3,430	230	2	600	4,600	105	3	7.62	200–400

Source: Annexe to OKH/GenStdH/GenQu Abt. KrVerw. No. I/750/41 of 17 Feb. 1941. Order to command authorities, BA-MA RH 17/191; Koževnikov, *Komandovanie*, 17.

tended, and 164 new airfields were built between 8 April and 15 July 1941, especially in the new frontier districts acquired by the incorporation of eastern Poland and the Baltic States. To ensure a high degree of combat-readiness and mobility, each air regiment had a main airfield, a reserve airfield, and a field airstrip assigned to it. For the same reason a start was made in April 1941 on severing the flying formations from their rearward services and organizing the latter on a territorial basis. In the western frontier military districts there were now 36 base areas, each designed to ensure supplies for between two and four air divisions.[319]

In the opinion of the Luftwaffe Operations Staff Ic an independent communications system in the Soviet air forces did not exist. The controlling authority was the Inspectorate of Red Army Communications, to which the communications officers of the senior air staffs reported. Communications units existed with the air staffs of the military districts, air divisions, and air-bases, but not with the flying formations, which, had only on-board radio-telegraphy operators and other RT personnel. The principal means of communication was radio traffic. In critical situations there was often *en-clair* radio traffic, although this was against regulations. Aerial RT communications were regarded as poorly organized, the network was thought inadequate for a flexible conduct of air operations, and the RT personnel were considered to be lacking in skill.

Anti-aircraft artillery was part of the army and came under the command of army formations or the commanders of homeland air-defence regions, who also controlled the fighter arm and the air observer and air-raid warning services. It was believed that the Soviet army's AA artillery had a strength of 1,200 heavy and 1,200 light guns, in addition to 800 AA machine-guns and 700 searchlights; the home-defence and coastal AA artillery was thought to have 1,600 heavy and 1,800 light guns, as well as a substantial number of AA machine-guns and searchlights. Jointly the two organizations therefore had at their disposal over 700 heavy and 500 light AA batteries and at least 150 AA machine-gun platoons and 100 searchlight batteries. In actual fact, the home-land air defences had 3,659 guns, 1,500 searchlights, and 850 barrage balloons.[320]

The Soviet aircraft industry was estimated to comprise some 50 airframe factories, 15 engine plants, 40 plants for equipment and instruments, and 100 auxiliary enterprises, employing altogether over a million workers—250,000 of them in the airframe and engine works. No more than 50 per cent of production-plan targets were thought to be attained. Engine manufacture in particular was believed to be dependent on foreign models, production of equipment and instruments to be unsatisfactory, and air safety, in consequence, to be greatly diminished. New light-metal alloys had not proved satisfactory, and Stalin's purges had left weaknesses in industrial management. There was a

[319] Koževnikov, *Komandovanie*, 20 ff.   [320] *Geschichte des zweiten Weltkrieges*, iii. 511.

continuing shortage of adequately trained engineers and skilled workers. For that reason improvements in production or technological progress were considered unlikely. The known centres of Soviet aerial armaments were the Moscow and Leningrad areas, and the regions of central Russia, the Ukraine, and the Urals.[321]

Despite the Soviet Union's large oil deposits, especially in the Caucasus and the Urals, its fuel situation was regarded as unsatisfactory because of increasing consumption, great losses in transport, and wastage at processing plants. There was a particular shortage of aviation fuel. Even in peacetime it had been possible to supply the flying formations and the army only by severely cutting back on the requirements of industry and the population. The centre of the Soviet armaments industry and war economy was still believed to be west of the Urals, mainly in the Ukraine and the Donets basin. Soviet intentions to transfer 40–50 per cent of overall industrial production to the Urals and the Kuznetsk basin by the beginning of the 1940s were not believed to be even remotely realizable. There was insufficient knowledge of the development of industries in Asian Russia or in the Far East.

It was further believed that the railways, which handled 90 per cent of freight and passenger traffic, were not adequately developed. Development of inland waterways, which carried only 8 per cent of freight traffic, would still take a long time. The road system seemed to be incomplete, too thin on the ground, and in poor condition; it was certainly unable to relieve the railways to any great extent. Thus only the railways were credited with any military importance. Civil aviation—among other things in view of its intended transformation to military uses in wartime—was regarded as significant for the Soviet Union; technical improvements of the road network, however, and the fleet of aircraft were considered primitive, and the military uses of civilian aviation therefore inadequate.

Summarizing its findings, the Luftwaffe Operations Staff Ic arrived at the conclusion that, in spite of its threefold or fourfold numerical superiority,[322] the Soviet air forces' striking power was substantially less than that of the German Luftwaffe. In view of the vastness of the territory to be covered, the numerical strength of the front-line formations was insufficient. Doubts were expressed whether training and operational leadership were enough to ensure close co-operation with the ground forces. The cumbersome nature of operational command, believed to be hard and ruthless but lacking in training for

---

[321] See Schwabedissen, *Russische Luftwaffe*, 61–2, MGFA Lw 22/1; *Jahrbuch der deutschen Luftwaffe 1939*, 39–40; *Handbuch der neuzeitlichen Wehrwissenschaften*, iii/2. 400. No notice was evidently taken of the highly positive judgements of the French air industrialists Louis Breguet and Henry Potez in 1936 on the great achievements and manufacturing progress of the Soviet aircraft industry. see Col. (retd.) Schuettel, Entwicklung und Beurteilung der russischen Luftwaffe bis zum Kriegsbeginn mit Sowjetrußland [Development and assessment of the Russian air force prior to the beginning of the war with the Soviet Union], 26–7, BA-MA Lw 107/68, or Schwabedissen, *Russische Luftwaffe*, 62–3, MGFA Lw 22/1.

[322] 1. Skl, KTB, pt. A, 275 (22 June 1941), BA-MA RM 7/25.

modern operations, as well as the difficult communications, did not suggest a systematic creation of operational or strategic main efforts in response to the situation. The leadership, moreover, tended towards rigid patterns, was impeded by Party control, and was incapable of standing up to an opponent with modern equipment. Ground organization was backward, supply organization was poor. Russians, finally, had no natural technical gifts. For all these reasons it was estimated that the combat-readiness of the Soviet air forces was only 50 per cent of their actual capacity, and hence inadequate. In a war against a well-equipped modern adversary this figure would soon drop further. The combat-readiness of the entire air force, in view of the poor supply facilities and the dependence of airfields on weather conditions, could be jeopardized in a relatively short time by attacks on airfields and supply installations.[323] Soviet AA artillery was poorly equipped and, apart from a few important cities, provided no adequate protection considering the size of the country and of the Soviet armed forces.

Although the Soviet war economy was regarded as safe well into the future, because of its wealth of raw-material resources, it had been incapable, even under peacetime conditions, of meeting the needs of the armaments industries while at the same time ensuring adequate supplies of foodstuffs, clothes, and consumer goods for the population. The quality of manufactured goods was still unsatisfactory in many areas, with production of rejects extremely high. All industries were suffering from a painful shortage of skilled workers and adequately trained managing staff. In the event of a prolonged war the aircraft industry would not be able to prevent a rapid decline in front-line strength. Disruption at the intersection-points of the east–west and north–south railway lines would have a disastrous effect on transportation and supply facilities. All other shortages, no matter how serious, would seem slight by comparison with such a failure of goods traffic in the event of war. The information brochure, however, also pointed out that, despite the existence of a number of bottle-necks in the war industry, the vast spread of the armaments industry and its concentration in safe areas would ensure that no branch of industry would be so badly interfered with as to disrupt the overall supply of the USSR to any decisive degree.

The Luftwaffe leadership's general picture of the Soviet air forces was entirely correct in many respects in the military field; this was later extensively confirmed not only by German Luftwaffe officers[324] during the first phase of the campaign in the east, but also by postwar publications in Britain,[325] the United States,[326] and above all in the eastern bloc.[327] The Soviet sources,

---

[323] See also annexe 1 to AOK 17 Ia No. 222/41 g.Kdos. Chefs., 14 May 1941, 8, BA-MA LII AK 16041/9.

[324] Schwabedissen, Russische Luftwaffe, ch. 2, pp. 1–130, esp. 128–9, MGFA Lw 22/1.

[325] Lee, Soviet Air Force.

[326] Garthoff, Soviet Military Doctrine. On the development of the Soviet air forces up to 1941 see also Hardesty, Red Phoenix, 11–59; Whiting, 'Soviet Aviation'; Greenwood, 'Great Patriotic War', 69–76.

[327] Koževnikov, Komandovanie, 15–35; Geschichte des Großen Vaterländischen Krieges, i. 522–59.

because of their presumably deliberate concealment of data, do not permit any reliable direct comparisons of strength. They do, however, show that at the beginning of the German attack the Soviet air forces were in a state of reorganization, of retraining on more modern machines, and of unreadiness, albeit in the expectation of a major confrontation—just as the German command had assumed. Also correct, though with certain reservations, were the German assumptions in the tactical-operational area: inability to wage an effective strategic bombing war,[328] the offensive and co-operative[329] character of the rules of engagement of the Soviet air forces, their structure and chain of command, the main effort of their deployment, the quality of the Soviet aircraft types, their armament and equipment, the poor standard of training, of the ground organization, of the supply-system, and of the communications network, the effectiveness of Russian AA artillery, the inactivity of Soviet paratroop and air-landing troops, the operational command's immobility and inadequate concentration of effort, and the poor striking power of the Soviet air force generally.

On the other hand, there was an underestimation of the value of pre-military education in the Soviet Union and of the Russian ability to improvise; this compensated for many shortcomings in ground organization, supplies, and transport routes. There was also the fact that the Russian soldier had been brought up to defend himself against air attacks with every means at his disposal, including camouflage and infantry weapons. There was, on the German side, a failure to realize that the unfavourable ratio of Soviet air strength to the vastness of the territory applied even more so to the numerically far weaker German Luftwaffe.

The biggest mistake was probably in the assumed number of Soviet machines. On 22 June 1941 the Luftwaffe operations staff believed that of 5,800 aircraft in the European part of the Soviet Union only 1,300 bombers and 1,500 fighters were fully combat-ready,[330] although radio intercepts at the beginning of that month had established the presence of 13,000–14,000 front-line machines in western Russia.[331] Not until 19 July 1941 did Luftwaffe estimates approach the real figures. By then a total strength of 8,700 aircraft was believed to exist in the European part of the Soviet Union at the beginning of the campaign, made up of 4,000 fighters, 2,900 bombers, and 1,800 reconnaissance and other front-line machines; in addition there were some 7,500 trainer planes.[332] These figures were more or less in line with later unofficial Soviet data, according to which nearly a half of some 18,000 front-line aircraft

---

[328] The principles of a strategic air war in a major conflict with a powerful enemy had not yet been worked out, because of a lack of appropriate experience. Organization of the air force was based on the lessons of lesser wars, such as that against the Japanese in 1939 and against Finland in 1939–40. The weaknesses of such an order of battle were revealed during the very first few weeks of the war. See Groehler, 'Anfangsperiode', 121.

[329] The draft of the Red Army's field-service order of June 1941 stated: 'The main task of the air forces is to contribute to the success of the ground forces in combat and operation, and to ensure control of the air' (*Geschichte des Großen Vaterländischen Krieges*, i. 322–3).

[330] BA-MA RM 7/25, 275.   [331] Hümmelchen, 'Luftstreitkräfte der UdSSR', 331.

[332] Ob.d.L., Fü.Stab Ic, Lagebericht No. 679, BA-MA RL 2 II/251.

were stationed in the western frontier districts, viz. 5,300 fighters (including 1,762 I-16s and 1,549 I-153s) 2,800 bombers, 450 reconnaissance machines, and 400 ground-attack aircraft.[333] Thus German estimates of the front-line strength of the Soviet air forces prior to the campaign were too low by nearly a half, for those stationed in the European part of the Soviet Union by about 30 per cent, for fighters by a half, and for bombers by about a third—unless one takes as a basis the later German assumption of 28,265 Soviet front-line planes at the beginning of the eastern campaign.[334] It is true that the Luftwaffe Operations Staff Ic had, rather boastfully, expected at least a threefold Soviet superiority in the air, which they optimistically regarded as more than offset by Germany's qualitative lead, but they had proceeded from the low estimates of Soviet combat strength—most probably excluding the home-defence and naval air formations and only counting pure war-planes available in the east, i.e. bombers, fighters, dive-bombers, and twin-engined 'destroyers'. The modern Soviet types, whose existence did not become known until shortly before the campaign, caused no concern because it was assumed that the war would be over before Soviet aircrews had a chance to familiarize themselves with them.[335]

Far more serious, however, was the German underestimation of the overall strategic sphere; this reflected the lack of overall strategic training of the Luftwaffe General Staff. The decisive aspect in a prolonged war of attrition was the Soviet Union's total potential; although such a war was regarded as the worst possible scenario, it appears to have been left out of consideration. What really was important was Soviet morale, economic and air-armaments capacity, and the relations between the civil and armaments sector in the Soviet economy. This last factor, in particular, was seen with western European eyes: civilian requirements were assessed far too high, and Russian determination and ability to restrict civilian needs were misread. Industrial development beyond the Urals and the switch of capacity to those areas were being underrated, as were the military importance of civil aviation and the actual performance and development potential of the transport system, of the Soviet economy in general, and the air-armaments industry in particular. In 1939 the Soviet Union was already producing some 2,000 more aircraft than Germany, viz. an annual total of 10,382,[336] whereas even in February 1941 Colonel-General Ernst Udet, the Generalluftzeugmeister—(the Luftwaffe's Director of Air Armament), reported Soviet production as being only 600 aircraft per month[337] and in May 1941 the Luftwaffe Operations Staff Ic

---

[333] Hümmelchen, 'Luftstreitkräfte der UdSSR', 327, 330; Koževnikov, *Komandovanie*, 16.

[334] Annexe 8 to Lt.-Col. (Gen. Staff) Sorge: Die luftstrategische Lage Mitteleuropas [The aerial-strategy position of central Europe], GenSt 8. Abt., 14 Apr. 1944, BA-MA RL 2 IV/170. The Speer ministry also believed in the autumn of 1943 that the Soviets had entered the war with 28,000 aircraft (Wag-SU-30/43, 27 Aug. 1943, geh. Reichssache, BA-MA Lw 106/13). See sect. I.II.2 at n. 131 (Hoffmann) on Soviet aircraft construction between 1938 and 22 June 1941.

[335] Moritz, 'Fehleinschätzung', 178.   [336] *Soviet Air Force*, 400.

[337] Generalluftzeugmeister's letter to Göring, 5 Feb. 1941, BA-MA RL 3/63,·7210.

assumed an annual production capacity of only 3,500–4,000 front-line machines.[338] In actual fact, in spite of destruction, relocation, and the loss of extensive industrial regions, the Soviet aircraft industry not only kept pace with that of Germany, but by 1941 surpassed it by more than 3,000, producing a total of 15,735 aircraft that year.[339]

(c) Preparations for Deployment

Given the requirement of nine to twelve months[340] for the construction of an aircraft and hence for increasing aircraft production, industrial preparations for the war in the east with such a high-technology service as the German Luftwaffe should have started long before the military preparations: with the opening of the campaign originally laid down for mid-May 1941 they should therefore have begun no later than July 1940. As the war was going to be a land war, it would have been necessary in particular to increase the number of medium bombers, ground-attack, and transport aircraft earmarked for co-operation with the army, and also that of reconnaissance and fighter planes. But nothing of the kind was done. Admittedly, the main effort of the armaments industry was switched to the Luftwaffe and the navy, but that was intended for the struggle against Britain; besides, with an early switch back to production for the ground forces the earlier shift of emphasis was never carried out.[341] The technical department's Aircraft Delivery Plan No. 18 of 1 July 1940 remained in force almost unchanged until November 1940.[342] At that time there were no indications of intensified air-force rearmament against the Soviet Union. The Generalluftzeugmeister Udet had told his ministry of aviation staff after the western campaign that the war was now finished and all those aircraft were no longer needed.[343] New developments in the pipeline, unless completed in 1940 or becoming effective in 1941, had been put on hold since February 1940.[344] Production of the He-177 long-range bomber was postponed by three months and limited to just a handful per month. Not until January 1942 did production pick up with a few machines. Much the same applied to the Me-210, which Jeschonnek wanted as the standard short-range bomber—also to be used later for the eastern campaign—but which was simultaneously being developed as a hit-and-run bomber, destroyer, and reconnaissance machine. Here the lack of firm control by the Generalluftzeugmeister was particularly felt: for instance, he did not stop his friend Willy Messerschmidt from halting the development of the Me-110 (which itself was to go out of production) in order to develop a new machine with all its teething troubles—which in any case began manufacture only in

---

[338] Plocher, Krieg im Osten, 272, MGFA Lw 4/1.

[339] See *Soviet Air Force*, 400, and Lusar, *Secret Weapons*, 114–15; see also sect. I.II.2 at n. 131 (Hoffmann).

[340] Boog, *Luftwaffenführung*, 60.   [341] See ch. I.III (Müller).

[342] LC 2 IA No. 740/40 g.Kdos., BA-MA RL 3/1015.   [343] Ishoven, *Udet*, 418.

[344] So-called 'development stop'; on this and on the He-177 and ME-210 see Boog, *Luftwaffenführung*, 56 ff.

July 1941 and then in very small numbers. Altogether the German aircraft industry was suffering at the time from Hitler's armaments policy, Udet's incompetence,[345] insufficient rationalization,[346] and inadequate use of available capacity.[347]

The decisive reason, however, for the lack of a perceptible increase in aircraft production in the summer and autumn of 1940 seems to be that the Luftwaffe High Command evidently did not then expect a new campaign— either because it was not yet fully privy to Hitler's plans in the east or because it was not yet taking them seriously. At any rate, on 15 October 1940 Generalingenieur Tschersich, the Generalluftzeugmeister's planning chief, in a planning survey up to the year 1950 assumed a state of peace from 1 April 1941 onwards, with monthly aircraft losses of only 1 per cent as against 25 or more per cent in wartime; outdated models were to be replaced by new ones only to the extent of actual losses. Not until 1 April 1947 was a state of war once more assumed.[348]

Even as late as 15 November 1940 the operations department of the Luftwaffe General Staff stated: '[Germany's] own [aircraft] production at best ensures maintenance of the present strength. Expansion is impossible (either in personnel or in material).'[349] This statement is in line with the programmes and programme drafts for aircraft production[350] submitted by the technical department of the Generalluftzeugmeister after November–December 1940, i.e. at a time when the Luftwaffe too had received instructions to prepare for the campaign in the east. Generally speaking, during the period envisaged for the eastern campaign, summer–autumn 1941, these contain production figures for the various aircraft categories no higher (or only slightly higher) than earlier programmes, e.g. Delivery Plan No. 16 of 1 November 1939[351] or No. 18 of 1 July 1940. Only for bombers is a monthly production increment recorded of about 100 to approximately 350; for fighters there is an increment of only about 25–50 up to the end of 1941. Production of reconnaissance planes, dive-bombers, ground-attack aircraft, destroyers, and transport ma-

---

[345] On Udet's personality see the still unsurpassed study by Suchenwirth, Udet, MGFA Lw 21/6; also Ishoven, *Udet*; Herlin, *Udet*; and Irving, *Rise and Fall*, 151–5.

[346] See Harten, Leistungssteigerung, 3, MGFA; Irving, *Rise and Fall*, 208–9.

[347] Fig. I.1, 'Aircraft Division Industry Report (European Report No. 4), in *United States Strategic Bombing Survey*, vol. ii.

[348] Reichsluftfahrtministerium GL 1, GL 1 No. 710/40 g.Kdos., 15 Oct. 1940: 'Industrie-Vorplanung bis 1.4.1945 ("IVP 45")' [Industrial forward planning up to 1 Apr. 1945], explanation to annexe No. 1, graph-sheet 'Gesamtplanungs-Übersicht 1933 bis 1950' [Overall planning survey 1933 to 1950], BA-MA RL 3/1086, 400–1.

[349] Lw.Fü.Stab Ia (KM) to 1L [in the naval operations staff], 15 Nov. 1940, BA-MA OKM, Case GE 968/PG 32968, 292.

[350] The following programmes and drafts are relevant: Lieferplan No. 18/2 (1 Oct. 1940); No. 18/3 (11 Nov. 1940); No. 19/1 (20 Nov. 1940 and 1 Feb. 1941); No. 19/2 (15 Mar. and 1 June 1941); BA-MA RL 3/990, 991, 1016, 993, 994, 1015. The calls for new constructions underlying the 'X-Fall-Studie 1941' [Study Case X 1941] with its substantially higher figures for bombers (480) were obviously not incorporated in the planning work (GL 1 No. 99/41 (ID) g.Kdos., 6 Feb. 1941, BA-MA RL 3/1104).

[351] C-Amts-Programm No. 16, LC 2 IA No. 855/39 g.Kdos., 1 Nov. 1939, BA-MA Lw 103/5.

chines was not increased. Indeed, for destroyer aircraft there was an actual decline in production targets; this was connected with retooling from the Me-110 to the Me-210. The production targets fluctuated at about 70 close-range and 65 long-range reconnaissance machines, 330–60 bombers, 250–300 fighters, 135 declining, to 100 destroyers, 60 dive-bombers, and 45 liaison and 42 transport machines per month. For 1942 the trend towards increased bomber and fighter production continued, with production of other aircraft categories remaining unchanged; however, for the bombers the graph began to flatten out. This, then, was the state of armaments planning in the spring of 1941; the earliest date that this production could have had an effect on operations in the east would have been at the end of what was planned as a short war. One is left with the impression that planning was mainly for the period after what was expected to be a swiftly won war in the east. In view of the fact that at least Göring and Jeschonnek had been aware of Hitler's eastern plans since the summer of 1940, the lack of an armament effort must be attributed also to the strong sense of German military superiority after the campaign in the west, to the feeling that British air raids would have only an insignificant effect on German territory—which it was believed could be handled by minor fighter forces[352]—and to an over-optimistic estimate of the Soviet enemy; this was shared also by Jodl. Belief in the superiority of German arms and the determination to maintain these chiefly against the British and Americans—the Russians were evidently not being considered then—and therefore to produce quality rather than quantity was reflected also in the instruction of the Wehrmacht High Command of 7 February 1941 on the urgency of the production programmes;[353] that instruction governed priorities and the pace of the armaments programme up to the beginning of the eastern campaign.

Actual military preparations by the Luftwaffe for the eastern campaign seem to have begun shortly before Hitler's Directive No. 21 of 18 December 1940. In addition to the above-mentioned general tasks, this directive contained the following instructions for the new campaign: elimination of the Soviet air forces at the very start; next—or, if circumstances required, simultaneously—support for ground operations at Army Group Centre and on the wing of main effort of Army Group South; disruption of Soviet rail communications according to their importance to the operations; finally, the capture of nearby key transport locations such as river crossings by paratroop and air-landing forces. This last task was later abandoned. The most important sentences of the directive were: 'In order to concentrate all forces against the enemy's air force and for direct support of the army, the armaments industry is not to be attacked during the main operation. Only when ground movements have been completed can such air attacks be considered—primarily against the Urals region.' As the objective of the advance had been defined by the general line

[352] See Galland, *The First and the Last*, 114 ff.
[353] Thomas, *Wehr- und Rüstungswirtschaft*, 283.

Volga–Archangel, it was obvious that any operational or strategic employment of the Luftwaffe would start at a later stage and that until then it would be tied to the army as an auxiliary arm. After that, would it still have sufficient strength to operate against the Soviet armaments potential in the depth of the country? The higher production figures envisaged for the second half of 1941, especially for bombers, suggest that German planning may not have been aimed solely against Britain after the achievement of the objectives in the east, but perhaps for the latter contingency as well. It was evidently thought that the ground battle could be accomplished with the Luftwaffe's existing strength, so long as that was maintained.[354] All further directives and orders, including those for the army,[355] emphasized the attachment of the Luftwaffe to the army. Thus Hitler at the end of March 1941 pointed out that 'air operations must be closely co-ordinated with ground operations. The Russians will crumple under the massive impact of our tanks and planes.'[356] It is possible that the Luftwaffe operations staff was not entirely in agreement with such a use of its air strength: in a statement to the navy on the day of the opening of the campaign[357] the Luftwaffe pointed out that it also had the task of destroying the enemy's armaments industry. Nevertheless, out of at total of 30 bomber Gruppen, 8 Ju-88 and Do-17 Gruppen, 4 Me-109 fighter Gruppen, and 3 Ju-87 dive-bomber Gruppen were equipped with bomb-aiming and -release devices for low-level attacks on marching columns and live targets.[358]

The talks in October 1940 had evidently been only preliminary contacts between Luftwaffe and army; in December 1940, however, the Luftwaffe general attached to the army commander-in-chief ordered the creation of new close-range reconnaissance Staffeln from those already in existence.[359] At the end of January he and the chief of the Army General Staff agreed on the distribution of the Luftwaffe close-range and long-range reconnaissance Staffeln which came tactically under army command.[360] Commencing from 15 March, they were to be transferred to the army command authorities already in the east (see Annexe Volume, No. 2). It was decided that the main effort of aerial reconnaissance should be directed towards main railways and trunk roads, as well as assembly areas of major enemy armoured and motorized formations. It was to be co-ordinated with ground reconnaissance and, to economize forces, to be carried out in close co-operation with air-fleet and air-corps staffs. Army groups and armoured groups were given priority in being

---

[354] See Jodl, ibid. 437.
[355] OKH/GenStdH OpAbt (IN) No. 050/41 g.Kdos., 31 Jan. 1941, 12, BA-MA RH 19 I/67; Abt. Landesverteidigung No. 441058/41 g.Kdos. Chefs. (IOp), 21 June 1941 to WPr, betr.: Barbarossa, BA-MA, RW 4/v. 578, 88.
[356] Halder, *Diaries*, 846 (30 Mar. 1941).
[357] 1. Skl. KTB, pt. A, 274, BA-MA RM 7/25; *KTB OKW* i. 346 (6 Mar. 1941).
[358] Deichmann, Unterstützung des Heeres, 73–4, MGFA Lw 10.
[359] Armeeoberkommando 2—Koluft—Abt. Ia/Br.B. No. 530/40 g.Kdos., 14 Dec. 1940, BA-MA, 2. Armee, 41181/94.
[360] Halder, *Diaries*, 762 (27 Jan. 1941), 811–12 (27 Feb 1941); annexes 5a, 5b to OKH GenStdH OpAbt (IN) No. 050/41 g.Kdos. Chefs., 31 Jan. 1941, BA-MA RH 19 I/67, 147 ff.

furnished with reconnaissance Staffeln. Night reconnaissance units were stationed only at points of main effort of the attack. The long-range reconnaissance Staffeln were also to be used for ranging and adjustment of super-heavy artillery. The army, moreover, had several anti-aircraft units tactically placed under its command for the protection of the ground troops. I and II AA Corps, attached to Air Fleets 2 and 4, depended mainly on Armoured Groups 2 and 1, whose attack they were to support. In addition, along with the Luftwaffe's fighter units, they were responsible for the aerial protection of mobile units, airfields, and supply-routes.[361] Operationally, the mixed AA battalions were generally placed under the army corps, the light AA battalions under the armoured divisions. The staff of a Luftwaffe commander (Koluft) included a staff officer of the AA artillery; he regulated the use of AA artillery within the command area of the army in question. In order to improve channels of command, AA regimental staffs were soon set up, to which the AA battalions belonging to the army area were subordinated (see Annexe Volume, No. 2). The short- and long-range reconnaissance units, as well as AA and air-signals units, assigned and tactically subordinated to the army, came under the Luftwaffe commanders attached to army and armoured group HQs, who in turn in every respect came under the Luftwaffe commanders attached to the army group HQs. Heading all the Luftwaffe units subordinated to the army was the Luftwaffe general attached to the army commander-in-chief. In order to maintain close links with the army authorities and to keep the air fleets and air corps informed on the current ground situation and the army's requirements, air liaison commands were detailed to the armies, and air information liaison parties to army corps and armoured divisions.[362] In spite of the vastness of the territory, the army was given only 6 more long-range reconnaissance Staffeln than in the western campaign, in fact 16, including 3 newly established night reconnaissance Staffeln for the army group HQs. As against 30 close-range reconnaissance Staffeln in the western campaign, the army now had a total of 56 Staffeln, of which 20 were armoured-formation and 36 army reconnaissance Staffeln. The actual strength of the close-range reconnaissance Staffeln was generally only seven Hs-126 and FW-189 aircraft. The long-range reconnaissance Staffeln were equipped with Ju-88s and Me-110s, the night reconnaissance Staffeln with Do-17s. Neither in numbers nor in suitability of models were the aerial reconnaissance forces adequate.[363]

[361] See Besondere Anordnungen für die Luftwaffe [Special instructions for the Luftwaffe], annexe 5e to H.Gr. A (Süd) Ia No. 150/41 g.Kdos., 15 Feb. 1941, BA-MA RH 21-1/55.

[362] See Luftflottenkommando 1 Ia No. 189/41 g.Kdos. Chefs., 10 May 1941, betr. Verbindungsoffiziere der Luftflotte 1 und des I. Fliegerkorps zu Kommandostellen des Heeres [re liaison officers of Air Fleet 1 and I Air Corps with command authorities of the army], BA-MA, 18. Armee, 17562/19; Ob.Kdo. der H.Gr. Süd Ia No. 900/41, g.Kdos. Chefs., 20 May 1941, BA-MA, RH 21-1/55; and Maj.-Gen. (retd.) Uebe, Air Fleet 2 liaison officer with Army Group Centre 1941, BA-MA Lw 107/80.

[363] Plocher, Krieg im Osten, 598–604, MGFA Lw 4/4.

On 28 January 1941 the Luftwaffe quartermaster-general, Lieutenant-General von Seidel, participated in a conference in Halder's office on co-ordination of ammunition and food supplies between army and Luftwaffe in the planned war in the east.[364] When the issue of winter clothing for air crews came up, the army representatives objected vigorously: the campaign would be finished by winter.[365] In the negotiations which followed it was decided to set up supply and transport liaison staffs as well as senior column commanders with the air fleets. Together with the army quartermaster agencies they would co-ordinate the transport columns of both services and ensure supplies for the air fleets.[366] Arrangements were also being made for the supply from the air of encircled or isolated army units.[367]

In accordance with Hitler's fundamental Order No. 1 only the chiefs of staff, the Ia and Ic officers, the quartermasters and senior quartermasters, and the communications and senior communications officers—in addition, of course, to the generals commanding the air fleets and their chiefs of staff—were initially permitted to prepare themselves by reflection and study for their specific tasks in the eastern campaign; this they had to do under conditions of strictest secrecy. Generally speaking, the air-fleet staffs were informed in January–February 1941, and the corps staffs a little later, that Hitler had decided to go to war against the Soviet Union because Molotov, on his visit to Berlin, had made demands unacceptable to Germany. Soviet ground forces, it was claimed, had been so reinforced, and construction of airfields along the demarcation-line so intensified, in recent months that offensive intentions on the part of the Soviet Union had to be assumed. These had to be preempted.[368] Quite a few officers interpreted the situation in the same way; to what extent this was a general feeling it is difficult to establish. The lower-ranking commanders were the last to be briefed on their new tasks.

The Luftwaffe command authorities envisaged for the war in the east set up small working staffs to carry out preliminary work for the campaign;[369] thus Air Fleet 2 set up the 'Working Staff Gatow' in Berlin-Gatow in February 1941, in April V Air Corps set up its 'Working Staff P' in Zamość, and I Air Corps its 'Special Staff B' also in Gatow. VIII Air Corps, being tied down in the Balkans and in the battle for Crete, was unable to set up a small working staff in Berlin-

---

[364] Gen. d. Fl. v. Seidel, in Plocher, Krieg im Osten, 38, MGFA Lw 4/9, gives the date as 28 Jan. 1941. See KTB OKW i. 282 (28 Jan. 1941); Halder, KTB ii. 256 ff. (not in trans.).

[365] Questions put to Col. (Gen. Staff) (retd.) Wodarg on 21 Mar. 1972, MGFA. It is possible that Wodarg referred to a different conference about the same time.

[366] The Luftwaffe supply liaison staff with Air Fleet 1 was set up by order of Luftgaukommando Belgien/Nordfrankreich—Quartiermeister/Ib No. 902/41 g.Kdos. of 31 Mar. 1941—and renamed 'Stab Kuttig' on 23 May 1941 (BA-MA RL 7/16); Dienstanweisung durch Luftgaukommando I, Ib (Fl.) No. 559/41 g.Kdos., 12 May 1941 (BA-MA RL 20/48).

[367] Qu 3/I Beiträge zum Befehl an die Befehlsstellen Süd, Mitte und Nord [Contributions to the order to the command authorities South, Centre, and North], 3 Mar. 1941, g.Kdos., nur durch Offizier [by officer only], BA-MA H 17/191.

[368] Kesselring, Memoirs, 85–90; see Plocher, Krieg im Osten, 292–3, MGFA Lw 4/1.

[369] See Kesselring, Memoirs, 85–90; Plocher, Krieg im Osten, 303 ff., MGFA Lw 4/1.

Gatow under the Corps Ia, Major (General Staff) Lothar von Heinemann, until 20 May 1941. These camouflaged staffs were mainly concerned with preparations for transferring their formations and with updating and extending their ground organizations in the deployment areas assigned to them. They supervised the construction of new and the extension of existing airfields, runways and taxiways, troops' quarters, radio navigation and communication facilities, stockpiling of ammunition, fuel, and materials and equipment of all kinds, and the reconnaissance of new airfields, closer to the front line. On the basis of the target data provided by the Luftwaffe operations staff Ic they processed the orders for the first missions of their formations and played them through in war-games, map exercises, and discussions, as well as testing co-operation between flying formations, AA artillery, communications troops, and army formations. The working staffs also organized map exercises with the commanding officers of the air formations and of the Luftwaffe supply agencies to make sure supplies would function; these, however, for reasons of security, were staged only shortly before the opening of the campaign. The need for secrecy occasionally resulted in curious situations.[370] Construction work was camouflaged as extension of the ground organization for flying-schools and replacement units for formations engaged in the west. Key officers from staffs which had not taken part in the western campaign were assigned to Air Fleet 2 and 3 HQs to acquaint themselves with the latest operational experience.

Particular importance was attached to rapid transferability of VIII (Close-combat) Air Corps, which would co-operate very closely with the army. This revealed shortcomings in the supply field. There was a shortfall of 15,000–20,000 t. of necessary transport capacity; even during the subsequent campaign it was not possible to make that capacity available and the forces had to resort to improvisation to overcome this handicap. As fighters and dive-bombers had only a short radius of action, but nevertheless had to advance swiftly with the armoured spearheads, it was necessary to ensure a rapid forward transfer of their jump-off bases and hence a rapid forward transfer of their ground services. To this end priority passes were issued to their commanders, to enable them to take a place in the most forward columns of the armoured formations. Field Marshal Kesselring, commanding Air Fleet 2, succeeded in getting Göring to agree to his additional demands[371] in view of the fact that the forces concentrated in the central sector would have to bear the main brunt of the campaign.

[370] Thus Col. Hermann Plocher, head of Working Staff P, due to prepare the campaign for V Air Corps, and Col. Kurt Zeitzler, chief of staff of Armd. Gp. 1, who had been personally acquainted with Plocher for a long time, repeatedly met in southern Poland, and even stayed at the same hotel, while trying to conceal from each other the true reason for their presence there by resorting to all kinds of white lies. A few weeks later, shortly before the beginning of the war, they discovered that, as staff officers of their formations, they were supposed to work particularly closely together (Plocher, *Krieg im Osten*, 298, MGFA Lw 4/1).

[371] Kesselring, *Memoirs*, 85–9; *IMT* ix. 205; Plocher, *Krieg im Osten*, 307–8, MGFA Lw 4/1.

Of vital importance for the preparation of the deployment in the east was the work of the Luftgaukommandos (air region commands), as they were responsible for the ground organization in the Luftwaffe. A well-thought-out and smoothly functioning ground organization was the prerequisite of successful operation by the flying formations. The eastern Luftgaukommandos co-operated closely with the working staffs mentioned above. With the beginning of the campaign initially fixed for 15 May, work during the ensuing months proceeded under considerable pressure of time, so that improvisation was indispensable, especially as the required personnel and material were arriving only gradually. For reasons of security it was often impossible to employ Polish workers. German labour was in short supply, even though some Reich Labour Service units and a few Luftwaffe construction battalions were available. Motor transport consisted of a variety of types and was not sufficient to cope with all transportation tasks. Nevertheless, 105 airfields were enlarged or newly laid out in Luftgau II alone during the preparatory period or the first phase of the eastern campaign. Special difficulties attended the projects near the demarcation-line. Large-scale supplies of material had to be brought in during the hours of darkness. In daytime work proceeded behind screens. At the beginning of June the formations were informed of the jump-off bases assigned to them. Earlier notification had been ruled out for reasons of completion, command structure, and security. There was a 90 per cent success rate in the timely delivery of supplies for three days, at two missions per day. On 21 June the preparations were completed.[372]

In the course of the preparations an arrangement which had proved its value in earlier campaigns was again resorted to—the Luftgaustäbe z.b.V. (air region staffs for special duties).[373] Two of these were set up in the area of each air fleet. They were the 'extended arm' of the Luftgaukommandos. It was their task to act as supply staffs and keep the formations fully supplied with material and foodstuffs, and immediately to establish a ground organization—i.e. airfield and airstrip HQs—in the newly occupied territories, to restore captured airfields, and to support the flying units in their reconnaissance of new airfields. In general, an 'air region staff for special duties' was instructed to co-operate with an air corps. The material problems of the 'air region staffs for

---

[372] On this see Air Gen. (retd.) Hellmuth Bieneck's paper on the history of Luftgau II, Posen im Zweiten Weltkrieg [Poznań in the Second World War], MGFA, uncatalogued, and Plocher, Krieg im Osten, 324–35, MGFA Lw 4/1. See also the war diaries of the airfield commands 3/I Neuhausen (BA-MA RL 20/69) and Siedlce (BA-MA RL 20/272), as well as Luftgaukommando I, Quartiermeister Qu No. 1031/41 g.Kdos./Qu 1, 23 Apr. 1941, betr.: Besondere Anordnungen für Planung 41, Ausbau der Bodenorganisation bis 15.5.1941 [re Special instructions for planning 41, development of ground organization until 15 May 1941] (BA-MA RL 20/51).

[373] See Air Gen. (retd.) Walter Sommé: Aufstellung und Einsatz eines Luftgaustabes z.b.V. beim Krieg gegen Rußland von Ostpreußen aus [Structure and employment of an air-region staff for special duties in the war against Russia coming from East Prussia] (BA-MA Lw 107/67), and Dienstanweisung für den Kommandeur des Luftgaustabes z.b.V. 1 [Service instruction for the commander of air-region staff for special duties 1], annexe to Luftgaukommando I, Ib (Fl.) No. 1284/41 g.Kdos., 12 Dec. 1941, BA-MA RL 20/48.

special duties' were considerable, as it proved impossible to equip their transport columns and airfield HQs with a sufficient number of motor-vehicles. Attempts were made, however, shortly before the beginning of the campaign, to eliminate these shortcomings by unloading and movement exercises and by the utilization of all workshops within reach.[374] For the rearward areas outside the Reich frontier 'air defence commanders' were appointed. Aerial defence of Romanian territory was the duty of the German Luftwaffe mission in Romania, in the Slovak–Hungarian region it was conducted by Luftgau XVII Vienna, in the southern Government-General by Luftgau VIII Cracow, in the north by Luftgau II, and in East Prussia by Luftgau I.[375]

Gradually and under conditions of strictest secrecy,[376] the Luftwaffe formations, supported by radio deception and other measures, were withdrawn from operations against Britain. The first to be so withdrawn were the fighters, which were not needed for the night air offensive, and last the bombers, as the exponents of that offensive. The actual deployment of the Luftwaffe formations in the east took place during the first three weeks of June 1941 within the timetable approved by Hitler.[377] However, these movements did not remain hidden from British radio intelligence, which was able to read the Luftwaffe code.[378] As far as possible, the flying formations were first transferred to their home bases for a short period of rehabilitation; from there they flew to their deployment areas, avoiding major towns. The flights had to be carried out singly or in small units by way of remote intermediate refuelling bases. The motorized and ground-personnel sections were moved within the framework of the rail-borne overall deployment plan as far as, approximately, the Oder (Odra) line; from there they had to cover the final stretch by road. By noon of 21 June the formations had to be assembled at airfields at an appropriate distance from the front line, on the central sector west of the Vistula, where they were stretched out and camouflaged as far as possible. Attempts were made to transfer about the same number of trainer planes stationed there back to the west. There was total radio silence. Reconnaissance planes kept constant watch on the airfields, looking out for anything that might prematurely betray the Luftwaffe's deployment. Not until evening were the units allowed to fly to their jump-off airfields near the frontier, flying singly or at very low level. Where the airfields could be observed by the enemy, the German planes flew in only on returning from their first operational mission.[379] VIII Air Corps,

[374] Plocher, Krieg im Osten, 335–9, MGFA Lw 4/1.

[375] See Luftgaukommando VIII, Führungsgruppe Ia No. 635/41 g.Kdos., 15 May 1941: Befehl für den Ausbau der Luftverteidigung (Flakartillerie) im Luftgau VIII [Order for the enhancement of air defence—AA artillery—in Luftgau VIII], BA-MA RL 20/281; and Grabmann, Luftverteidigung, 224, MGFA Lw 11b.

[376] IMT xxxiv. 228–39. Whereas the deployment directive for the army is extant, no such directive seems to exist now for the Luftwaffe, although it must have existed then.

[377] See Plocher, Krieg im Osten, 303 ff. and 309–17, MGFA Lw 4/1; also Kesselring, Memoirs, 85 ff.

[378] See Hinsley, British Intelligence, i. 473 ff.

[379] See Festungsstab Blaurock Ia/Koluft Br.B. No. 857/41 g.Kdos., 14 June 1941, BA-MA RH

which at the end of May and the beginning of June was still playing a major part in the capture of Crete, had only 14 days to accomplish its transfer. On 21 June it was still short of 600 motor-vehicles, 40 per cent of its aircraft, and a number of aircraft engines, transport columns, and communications equipment; this was painfully felt during the first few weeks of the attack.[380] Mission orders were all ready at the jump-off bases, complete with maps and target data of future operational zones;[381] these had also been supplied to all Luftwaffe staffs in the east.

The deployment area extended behind an approximately 1,600-km. broad starting-front of the German army and its allies, and was aimed against an enemy front line roughly 2,400 km. in length between Odessa and Leningrad; added to this was the Finnish—German front line of about 1,000 km. The Luftwaffe's deployment was adapted to the operational and strategic objectives of the army, bearing in mind the two principal tasks of the Luftwaffe— elimination of the Soviet air forces by destroying them on the ground and in the air at the beginning of the conflict, followed by support for the army on the battlefield. Each army group had an air fleet assigned to it, and each army or armoured group at the focus of the fighting had one air corps (see Diagram I.IV.5).

In the area of Army Group South, Air Fleet 4 was under the command of Colonel-General Löhr (see Annexe Volume, No. 3). It was divided into IV Air Corps under Lieutenant-General Pflugbeil, stationed in eastern Romania, V Air Corps under Lieutenant-General Robert Ritter von Greim in the Lublin– Zamość area, II AA Corps under Lieutenant-General Otto Deßloch in southern Poland, and the German Luftwaffe mission in Romania under Lieutenant-General Wilhelm Speidel. Air Fleet 4 (see Table I.IV.5) numbered 887 aircraft, of which 694 were operational. Added to these, in the southern sector, there were 239 reconnaissance and courier machines tactically subordinated to the army; of these 208 were operational. In addition, there were a number (no longer accurately determinable) of Romanian aircraft, possibly about 600, of which 350 were front-line machines and 250 reserve or trainer planes[382]—and, after 27 June 1941, 48 Hungarian aircraft.[383]

24-8/44; Oberbaugruppe Süd, Oberst Gramm, Ia-No. 170/41 g.Kdos., 9 June 1941, BA-MA RH 21-1/55; AOK 18 Koluft Ia No. 21/41 g.Kdos. IX.Ang., 11 June 1941, BA-MA, 18. Armee, 17562/ 19, on the manner of transfer of ground personnel and aircraft. See also Plocher, Krieg im Osten, 309–17, MGFA Lw 4/1.

[380] See BA-MA RL 8/239, 58, 64; BA-MA RL 8/47, 1–2; Plocher, Krieg im Osten, 317–21, MGFA Lw 4/1.

[381] Plocher, Krieg im Osten, 43–4, MGFA Lw 4/1.

[382] Data on the strength of the Romanian air forces on the eve of Barbarossa differ greatly. According to BA-MA RL 7/479 and 9/91, the number of aircraft was 399, or 672, or 353; according to Ploetz, *Kriegsmittel*, 327–8, it was 365 plus 235 reserve and trainer planes; according to Koževnikov, *Komandovanie*, 15, it was 623; Groehler, *Luftkrieg*, 294, speaks of 500 (423 of them engaged against the USSR), and *Soviet Air Force*, 30, of 504 aircraft.

[383] Koževnikov, *Komandovanie*, 15, mentions only 48; Ploetz, *Kriegsmittel*, 319, mentions 232, and Csnadi, Nagyváradi, and Winkler, *A Magyar Repülés Története*, 232, report 363.

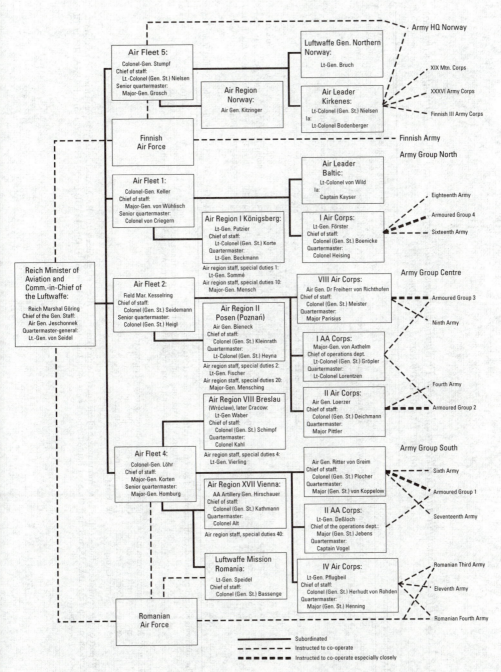

DIAGRAM I.IV.5. Luftwaffe Chain of Command in the East, 22 June 1941
Source: Data of the study-group History of the Air War, Karlsruhe.

TABLE I.IV.5. *Effective Strength and Combat-readiness of Flying Formations (incl. Replacements) of the Luftwaffe in the East on the Eve of Barbarossa (21 June 1941)*

Air Fleet	Under Luftwaffe command									Under tactical army command					Army and Luftwaffe total
	Recce. aircr. ObdL	Sea, F-Wekusta w. Air Fl.	Bombers	Dive-bombers	'Destroyers'	Fighters	Transport aircr. Corps trspt. Staffeln	KGzbV	Total	AOK or A.Gp.	Recce. aircraft long-range	army recce.	Courier aircr. in Courier Staffeln	Total	
	es/cr	es/cr	es/cr	es/cr	es/cr	es/cr	es/cr	es/cr	es/cr	es/cr	es/cr	es/cr	es/cr	es/cr	es/cr
5 (east)	10/7	20/12	22/17	40/37	4/4	12/12			98/82	20		10/9		10/9	108/91
1		56/46	271/211			203/167	14/13	48/9	592/453	north	52/41	87/70	37/32	176/143	768/596
2		46/36	299/222	425/323	98/60	384/284	30/23	85/46	1,367/994	middle	46/33	170/142	28/25	244/200	1,611/1,194
4		46/31	360/307			366/272	30/23	85/61	887/694	south	48/37	149/137	42/34	239/208	1,126/902
ObdL	51/32								51/32						51/32
TOTAL	61/39	168/125	952/757	465/360	102/64	965/735	74/59	218/116	2,995/2,255		146/111	416/358	107/91	669/560	3,664/2,815

Note: The following should be added to the above:

Liaison aircraft in the liaison Staffeln	c.100/100
Liaison aircraft with long-range and close-range reconnaissance units	c.119/98
Transport aircraft with long-range and close-range reconnaissance and other units	c.21/19
	= c.3,904/3,032

Abbreviations:

AOK	Army command	KGzbV	Special-duties group (Transport-Gruppe)
cr	combat-ready	ObdL	C.-in-C. Luftwaffe
es	effective strength	TrSt	Transport Staffel
A.Gp.	Army Group	Wekusta	Meteorological Staffel

Sources: Report on the combat-readiness of the flying formations, 21 June 1941, GenSt GenQu 6. Abt. (1), 24 June 1941, BA-MA, RL 2 III/713; wall-charts of the C.-in-C. Luftwaffe as of 20 June 1941, BA-MA, o.S. 234; Order of Battle Barbarossa as of 16 June 1941, OKH GenStdH/Op Abt (III) (o.D.), Prüf-Nr. 15819, BA-MA, RH 11 III/32; *Soviet Air Force*, 29–30.

The Romanian aircraft and AA guns were of a variety of mostly outdated models of international origin. The flying formations generally came under the Romanian Air Corps. Each of the three Romanian air regions had a Romanian fighter Gruppe and two Romanian AA regiments assigned to it. The Romanian homeland defence AA artillery, like the Romanian flying formations, had been trained by the German Luftwaffe mission in accordance with the latest combat experience. In so far as it was assigned to the defence of Romanian oil production within the German air-defence area[384] it came tactically under that area's commander.[385] The Romanian fighters, however, did not come under his command. Romanian AA artillery was fully integrated in the German air reporting network which, since the spring of 1941, had been built up in Romania and Bulgaria. Civil air defence was a Romanian concern. It was intended that at the beginning of the campaign the duties of the German Luftwaffe mission in Romania—development of air defence and training of Romanian flying and AA formations—would be replaced by the combat duties of a 'field air district', i.e. the further development of a ground organization and an air reporting network, as well as the air defence of the Romanian oilfields.

A curious aspect of the structure of Air Fleet 4 was its lack of close-combat formations, even though a dive-bomber Gruppe had originally been envisaged for IV Air Corps. Instead the air fleet had at its disposal, for direct battlefield support, two Ju-88 bomber Gruppen equipped with dropping-devices for SD-2 anti-personnel fragmentation bombs and a figher Gruppe similarly equipped.

The task of Air Fleet 4 was to help Army Group South, more particularly Armoured Group 1, in its attack towards the Dnieper, to prevent the escape of any sizeable enemy forces eastward across the river, and generally to support the attack of the army group. This task included the paralysation of the Soviet air forces facing it by employing the bulk of its own forces at the start, and the continuous neutralization of its effectiveness against German ground operations by the use of adequate forces in the next phase as well. In addition, there was the elimination of Soviet communication centres and senior HQs. The air fleet's operations were at all times to be based on the grand operational objectives of the army. Intervention in local crises was authorized only if the overall situation permitted it.

IV Air Corps was instructed to co-operate directly with Eleventh Army and with the 'Admiral Romania', but it also had to support the Romanian Third and Fourth Armies. The combat zone of the corps had a width of 600 km. and a depth of 500 km. from Fokşani to the Crimea, and of 1,000 km. from Fokşani to Rostov. Having repulsed Soviet attacks across the Prut and destroyed the

---

[384] See sect. I.v.3 at n. 754 (Förster).

[385] See Air Gen. (retd.) Wilhelm Speidel, Bericht über die Tätigkeit der Deutschen Luftwaffenmission in Rumänien [Report on the work of the German Luftwaffe mission in Romania], BA-MA Lw 107/81.

Soviet air forces, and supply and communications facilities, it was later to support the advance of Eleventh Army. Moreover, in conjunction with the German naval commander Romania, it was to lay mines in the Soviet Black Sea ports and operate against the Soviet Black Sea Fleet and Soviet shipping.

V Air Corps was to co-operate directly with Sixth and Seventeenth Armies and, more particularly, with Armoured Group 1. For that purpose minor forces were to be set aside as a reserve from the start, despite the usual main tasks of the initial days. In the further course of operations, V Air Corps was to support the thrust of Armoured Group 1 and of Sixth Army to the Dnieper as far as Kiev and to prevent their flanks from being threatened by Soviet motorized units. There was a possibility that some of the corps' forces might have to be used temporarily against enemy forces flooding back from Galicia and for supporting Seventeenth Army; there was also a chance of employment in the north-western part of the combat zone of IV Air Corps. The initial front line of V Air Corps had a width of 350 km. and a depth, from Cracow to Rostov, of 1,500 km. The ground organization of Air Fleet 4 came under the Luftgaue (air regions) XVII (Vienna) and VIII (Cracow), as well as under the German Luftwaffe mission in Romania. It was their task to ensure its supplies—with the aid of 'air region staff for special duties' 40 for IV Air Corps and 'air region staff for special duties' 4 for V Air Corps—and to provide it with new bases.[386]

Air Fleet 2 under Field Marshal Kesselring was in the deployment area of Army Group Centre. Its right wing was formed by II Air Corps under Air General Bruno Loerzer in the Warsaw–Brest-Litovsk–Dęblin area. On the left wing of the air fleet, in the Suvalki corner, was VIII Air Corps under Air General Dr Wolfram Freiherr von Richthofen. In addition, Air Fleet 2 had I AA Corps under Major-General Walther von Axthelm under its command.

Air Fleet 2 was the strongest of the air fleets deployed in the east. Of its actual strength of 1,367 front-line and transport machines, 994 were operational. Added to these were 244 reconnaissance and liaison aircraft assigned to Army Group Centre, of which 200 were operational. Nearly all the dive-bombers concentrated in the east were massed under this air fleet—more particularly under VIII Air Corps, with $5\frac{1}{3}$ dive-bomber Gruppen as against 3 with II Air Corps. Moreover, 3 bomber, 1 dive-bomber, 1 destroyer, and 2 fighter Gruppen of VIII Air Corps were equipped with dropping-devices for 2-kg. anti-personnel fragmentation bombs for close combat. The concentration

[386] Ob.Kdo. H.Gr. Süd Ia No. 900/41 g.Kdos., 20 May 1941, betr.: Ergänzung der Aufmarschanweisung Barbarossa [re Supplement to deployment directive Barbarossa], sect. 9 a–g, BA-MA RH 21-1/55; Gen.Kdo. IV. Fliegerkorps Abt. Ia No. 468/41 g.Kdos., 18 June 1941; Korpsbefehl No. 1 für die Kampfführung im Fall 'Barbarossa' [Corps order No. 1 for conduct of operations in case Barbarossa], and (trans.) Great [Rom.] General Aviation Staff, operations department: operational guidelines No. 34 for air-force units, 17 June 1941, both BA-MA RL 8/26; Plocher, Krieg im Osten, 352, 356–7, MGFA Lw 4/1.

of forces, especially of close-combat units, under Air Fleet 2 shows that here was the main effort of the attack and of ground support. This is further confirmed by the fact that the jump-off front line of both air corps between Brest-Litovsk and Suvalki was only about 300 km. wide. The distance from Warsaw to Moscow was about 1,100 km. Air Fleet 2 was to advance towards Moscow with Army Group Centre; in this move II Air Corps was to co-operate with Fourth Army, more especially with Armoured Group 2, and VIII Air Corps with Ninth Army, more especially with Armoured Group 3. I AA Corps was to support Armoured Groups 2 and 3 in their penetration of the frontier fortifications and in their subsequent advance. Food supplies, ammunition, and establishment of a ground organization in the newly occupied territories were the duty of Air Region 2, which for this purpose had the two 'air region staffs for special duties' 2 and 20 available to them.[387]

In the north, with orders to co-operate with Army Group North, was Air Fleet 1[388] under Colonel-General Alfred Keller. The only flying formations he had were I Air Corps under Lieutenant-General Helmuth Förster and the units of Lieutenant-Colonel Wolfgang von Wild, the Air Leader Baltic,[389] derived in late March from the Air Leader East. Air Fleet 1 was to support the operations of Army Group North from East Prussia towards the Dvina and further on to Leningrad. The three bomber Geschwader and the fighter Geschwader of I Air Corps were to assist Armoured Group 4 in its advance along a front of initially 200 km. width and a depth of operational area (to Leningrad) of 850 km. Except for two bomber Gruppen equipped for dropping anti-personnel fragmentation bombs, the corps, in common with the whole air fleet, had not been given any close-combat forces. The Air Leader Baltic had the duty of guarding the coastal flank and keeping it safe from surprise attacks by Soviet surface or submarine naval units; he also had to mine the ports of Kronshtadt and Leningrad, as well as the Neva as far as Shlisselburg, and later the White Sea Canal, and was required to operate against the locks on Lake Onega, protect convoy traffic in the Baltic east of 13° E., and support the army in the seizure of the Baltic islands.

Air Fleet 1 had only 592 front-line and transport aircraft at its disposal; of these 453 were operational. Army Group North had 176 reconnaissance and liaison machines attached to it, of which 143 were operational. The command authority responsible for the ground organization of Air Fleet 1 was Air Region 1 in Königsberg (now Kaliningrad); for the creation of a new ground organiz-

---

[387] Plocher, Krieg im Osten, 352–3, 359–60, MGFA Lw 4/1. See Kesselring, *Memoirs*, 89–90, and id. in *IMT* ix. 205.

[388] On the structure of Air Fleet 1 see Luftflottenkommando 1 OQu No. 1510/41 g.Kdos. Ib, 12 June 1941, BA-MA RL 7/12. This also shows the structure of I Air Corps, of air region 1, and of Air Leader Baltic, including subordinated communications and AA artillery units. On the deployment of Air Fleet 1 see Operationsatlas der Heeresgruppe Nord [Army Group North operations atlas], 11–12, BA-MA RH 19 III/661.

[389] Der R.d.L. u. Ob.d.L. GenSt GenQu 2. Abt. Az. 11b 12.15. No. 5647/41 g.Kdos. (IIA), 29 Mar. 1941, BA-MA OKM, Case GE 972/PG 32972, 162–3. On the duties of Air Leader Baltic see Der Ob.d.L.Fü.Stab Ia No. 6391/41 g.Kdos. Chefs., 4 Apr. 1941, BA-MA RL 2 II/89.

TABLE I.iv.6. *Order of Battle of the Air Fleets Deployed against the Soviet Union on the Eve of Barbarossa*[a]

Air Fleet 5 (East)
   Weather Observation Staffel 5

   Action group special duties (later reinforced and renamed Air Leader Kirkenes)
   1 Kette of Staffel 5, Long-range Recce Gruppe 124
   IV Gruppe (Dive-bombers), Training Geschwader 1
   Staffel 6, Bomber Geschwader 30
   Staffel 1, Fighter Geschwader 77
   Co-operation with Staffel 1, Close-range Recce Gruppe 32

   Luftwaffe General Northern Norway (later Air District Staff Finland)
   'Destroyer' Staffel, Fighter Geschwader 77
   Staffel 1, Long-range Recce Gruppe 124 (reduced by 1 Kette)
   2 Ketten of Coastal Air Gruppe 706

Air Fleet 1
   Long-range Recce Staffel 2, C.-in-C. Luftwaffe, Weather Observation
   Staffel 1, K.Gr.z.b.V. (= Air Transport Gruppe) 106

   I Air Corps
   Staffel 5, Long-range Recce Gruppe 122
   Staff Bomber Geschwader 1 with II, III Gruppen, Bomber Geschwader
      1
   Staff Bomber Geschwader 76 with I, II, III Gruppen, Bomber
      Geschwader 76
   Staff Bomber Geschwader 77 with I, II, III Gruppen, Bomber
      Geschwader 77
   Staff Fighter Geschwader 54 with I, II, III Gruppen, Fighter
      Geschwader 54, II Gruppe, Fighter Geschwader 53 (without Staffel
      6)

   Air Leader Baltic
   Recce Gruppe 125
   Coastal Air Gruppe 806
   Sea Rescue Staffel 9

   Air District I (Königsberg)
   Fighter Training Gruppen 52, 54

Air Fleet 2
   Staff Long-range Recce Gruppe 122 with Staffel 2, Long-range Recce
      Gruppe 122, Weather Observation Staffel 26, Staff Fighter
      Geschwader 53 with I, III Gruppen, Fighter Geschwader 53, Fighter
      Training Gruppe 51

TABLE I.ɪᴠ.6 (*cont.*)

II Air Corps
  Staffel 1, Long-range Recce Gruppe 122, K.Gr.z.b.V. (= Air Transport Gruppe) 102
  Staff Fast Bomber Geschwader 210 with I, II Gruppen, Fast Bomber Geschwader 210
  Staff Bomber Geschwader 3 with I, II, III Gruppen, Bomber Geschwader 3
  Staff Bomber Geschwader 53 with I, II, III Gruppen, Bomber Geschwader 53
  Staff Dive-bomber Geschwader 77 with I, II, III Gruppen, Dive-bomber Geschwader 77
  Staff Fighter Geschwader 51 with I, II, III, IV Gruppen, Fighter Geschwader 51

VIII Air Corps
  Staffel 2, Long-range Recce Gruppe 11, K.Gr.z.b.V. (= Air Transport Gruppe) 1
  Staff Bomber Geschwader 2 with I, II, III Gruppen Bomber Geschwader 2
  Staff Dive-bomber Geschwader 1 with II, III Gruppen, Dive-bomber Geschwader 1
  Staff Dive-bomber Geschwader 2 with I, III Gruppen, Dive-bomber Geschwader 2, II Gruppe Training Geschwader 2, Staffel 10, Training Geschwader 2
  Staff 'Destroyer' Geschwader 26 with I, II Gruppen, 'Destroyer' Geschwader 26, Training Gruppe 26
  Staff Fighter Geschwader 27 with II, III Gruppen, Fighter Geschwader 27, II Gruppe, Fighter Geschwader 52

I Anti-aircraft Corps
  Staff AA Regt. 101 with I Battalion, AA Regt. 12, I Battalion, AA Regt. 22, Light AA Battalion 77
  Staff AA Regt. 104 with I, II Battalions, AA Regt. 11, Light AA Battalion 91

Air District II (Posen)

Air Fleet 4
  Staffel 4, Long-range Recce Gruppe 122, Weather Observation Staffel 76, K.Gr.z.b.V. (= Air Transport Gruppen) 50, 104
  German Luftwaffe Mission Romania
  Staff Fighter Geschwader 52 with III Gruppe, Fighter Geschwader 52
  IV Air Corps
  Staffel 3, Long-range Recce Gruppe 121

TABLE I.iv.6 (*cont.*)

Staff Bomber Geschwader 27 with I, II, III Gruppen, Bomber
   Geschwader 27, and II Gruppe, Bomber Geschwader 4
Staff Fighter Geschwader 77 with II, III Gruppen, Fighter Geschwader
   77, and I Gruppe, Training Geschwader 2

V Air Corps
Staffel 4, Long-range Recce Gruppe 121
Staff Bomber Geschwader 55 with I, II, III Gruppen, Bomber
   Geschwader 55
Staff Bomber Geschwader 54 with I, II Gruppen, Bomber Geschwader
   54
Staff Bomber Geschwader 51 with I, II, III Gruppen, Bomber
   Geschwader 51
Staff Fighter Geschwader 3 with I, II, III Gruppen, Fighter
   Geschwader 3

II Anti-Aircraft Corps
Staff AA Regt. 6 with I Battalion, AA Regt. 7, II Battalion, AA Regt.
   26, Light AA Battalion 93, and I Battalion, AA Regt. 24
Staff Regt. General Göring with I, IV Battalions, Regt. Gen. Göring, II
   Battalion, AA Regt. 43, Light AA Battalions 74, 83, 84

Air District XVII (Vienna)
Fighter Training Gruppe 77

Air District VIII (Cracow)
Fighter Training Gruppen 27, 3

ᵃ The *Flugbereitschaften* (small units of a few liaison and/or transport aircraft for immediate use
by staff members) and liaison and corps-transport Staffeln stationed with Air Fleet, Air Corps,
and operations staffs are not included.

Sources: Tables of C.-in-C. Luftwaffe, Distribution of formations, 27 Oct. 1940–20 Dec. 1941,
BA-MA Lw 106/6; Organization charts in BA-MA RL 7/11 and 12, also 475; Plocher, Krieg im
Osten, MGFA Lw 4/6 and 7; Reports on the combat-readiness of the flying formations,
GenStdLw GenQu 6. Abt. (I), BA-MA RL 2 III/713; *Soviet Air Force*, 31–3.

ation in the conquered territory and for keeping the formations supplied this
had 'air region staffs for special duties' 1 and 10 subordinated to it.[390] The
deployment of the Air Fleet 5 formations aligned against the Soviet Union in
'Action Unit, Special Duties' (subsequently under the Air Leader Kirkenes) is
described in the section by Ueberschär (II.iii.1(*c*)) of the present volume.

Including the flying formations tactically under army command and all
other transport, courier, and liaison machines, the Luftwaffe had a total of

[390] On the deployment of Air Fleet 1 generally see Plocher, Krieg im Osten, 353–4, 360–1,
MGFA Lw 4/1; also OKH GenStdH/GenQuAbtHeeresvers./Qu 1 No. I/0257/41 g.Kdos. Chefs.,
20 Mar. 1941, and other sources, BA-MA RL 7/16 and 20/48.

3,904 aircraft in the east (see Table II.iv.5). Of these, 3,032 were operational. Deducting the transport, courier, and liaison planes, i.e. those not directly engaged in the air war, the Luftwaffe, on the eve of the eastern campaign, had 3,275 aircraft stationed along the German–Soviet frontier; of these, 2,549 were operational reconnaissance, bomber, dive-bomber, destroyer, and fighter aircraft. Of the reconnaissance planes, 562 (469 of them operational) were tactically under army command, so that the Luftwaffe proper began the war in the east with 2,713 real war planes, of which 2,080 were operational.[391] If one further deducts the seven replacement fighter and destroyer Gruppen, some of which were stationed in the deployment area though predominantly used for training, one arrives at a figure of only 2,510, of which 1,945 were operational war planes available for front-line action under Luftwaffe command. A year earlier a few hundred more front-line aircraft had been assembled for the campaign against France.[392]

Even though the Luftwaffe was supported by about 900 aircraft of Germany's allies[393] (including 70 of the Italian expeditionary corps), this was no great reinforcement in view of the Romanians' and Hungarians' lack of combat experience and the vastly greater territory in the east—about ten times that of the western theatre of war. In fact, the overall actual strength of the Luftwaffe front-line formations—5,599 aircraft, not counting courier and liaison machines—had increased only insignificantly, and its numerical combat-readiness had even slightly declined, since the beginning of May 1940.[394]

The effects of a war on several fronts were beginning to be felt; indeed, the Luftwaffe, with its engagement against Britain in the Mediterranean and the west, and with its aerial defence of Reich territory, was already involved in such a war. Of the above-mentioned total of Luftwaffe front-line aircraft on 21

[391] Koževnikov, *Komandovanie*, 15, gives the strength of the Luftwaffe assembled in the east as 4,000; Groehler, *Luftkrieg*, 294, gives 3,055, but more recently (in 'Stärke, Verteilung und Verluste der deutschen Luftwaffe') as at least 3,500. There is no doubt that the following data on the strength of the German air-force formations assembled against the Soviet Union are much too low: Feuchter, *Luftkrieg*, 168, reports only 1,300 operational bombers, dive-bombers, fighters, and destroyer planes; likewise Baumbach, *Broken Swastika*, 120. Bekker, *Angriffshöhe*, 462, speaks of 1,945 aircraft, of which 510 bombers, 290 dive-bombers, 440 fighters, 40 destroyer planes, and 120 long-range reconnaissance planes, i.e. a total of 1,400 aircraft, were operational. Plocher, Krieg im Osten, 203–4, MGFA Lw 4/1, gives the actual strength of the Luftwaffe in the east as 2,000 front-line machines on 20 June 1941, augmented by 230 transport and liaison planes, as well as 700 close-range and long-range reconnaissance aircraft tactically subordinated to the army. Numerical comparisons are meaningful only if command subordination (army or Luftwaffe) is indicated at the same time, as well as the aircraft categories or uses.

[392] According to *Rise and Fall of the German Air Force*, 66, the Luftwaffe began the western campaign with 3,530 front-line machines and 520 transport planes. See *Germany and the Second World War*, ii. 279.

[393] According to Koževnikov, *Komandovanie*, 15, Italy, Finland, Romania, and Hungary together provided 980 aircraft; Groehler, *Luftkrieg*, 294ff., gives the air strength of Germany's satellites, including Croatia and Slovakia, as in excess of 1,000 machines; *Soviet Air Force*, 29–30, estimates the strength of the states fighting against the Soviet Union on the German side at 1,422 aircraft. See also sect. I.ii.2 at n. 186 (Hoffmann).

[394] BA-MA RL 2 III/707 (May 1940) and RL 2 III/713 (June 1941).

June 1941, more than 1,800 (1,200 of them operational) had to be kept back
for other theatres or held in reserve. Their disposition was as follows (number
of operational aircraft in brackets):

Aerial defence of the Reich (Luftwaffe Commander Centre)	282 (227)
Mediterranean/North Africa (X Air Corps)	423 (241)
West (Air Fleet 3)	861 (582)
North (Air Fleet 5)	200 (112)

Thus the Luftwaffe was able to field only about 68 per cent of its total actual
front-line strength against the principal enemy, the Soviet Union. The degree
to which these aircraft were operational can no longer be accurately determined, but the percentage ratio was probably much the same.[395]

Although the Luftwaffe had demanded the so-called Urals bomber as early
as 1933–4, it still had no strategic long-range bomber with which it might have
immediately attacked the industrial centres in the Urals. The average tactical
depth of penetration[396] of the German bombers, under combat conditions and
with only half a bomb-load, amounted to only 900–1,000 km. Destroyers, dive-
bombers, and fighters, unless fitted with extra fuel-tanks, were able to penetrate only about 375, 200, and 180 km. respectively into enemy territory (see
Table I.iv.7 and Map I.iv.4). For bombers the depth of penetration was
further reduced by their distance from the front line—in contrast to the
fighters and dive-bombers, which were stationed well forward. They could
count on fighter escorts for only a short distance. Nevertheless, at night and in
poor weather they were able to cover substantial distances without fighter
escort.

The strength of the AA artillery was continually enhanced and by the end of
February 1941 consisted of 798 heavy and 827 medium and light batteries.[397]
On 30 June 1941, after a further increase, they were distributed among the
different theatres of war as shown in Table I.iv.8. In consequence, 20 per cent
of all heavy AA forces, 15 per cent of all medium and light batteries, and a little
over 10 per cent of all searchlight batteries were stationed in the east.[398]

---

[395] Vortrag über die Einsatzbereitschaft der fliegenden Verbände, Stand: 21.6.1941 [Report on
the combat-readiness of the flying formations, as on 21 June 1941], GenQu 6. Abt. (I), 24 June
1941, BA-MA RL 2 III/713. Because of a shortfall of 800 replacement engines the bomber
formations were thought to have begun the war in the east with only half their front-line strength
(report by the former Luftwaffe quartermaster-general, Air Gen. (retd.) von Seidel, dating from
1949, 49, BA-MA Lw 101/3, pt. 2).

[396] See Lw.Fü.Stab Gruppe T, 1 Apr. 1941, betr. Taktische Eindringtiefen [re Tactical depth
of penetration], BA-MA Lw 106/9. The tactical depth of penetration is half the range—because of
outward and homeward flight—or the greatest theoretical distance from a target, reduced by
technical deductions allowed for in the flight-range tables and by tactical deductions, which for
bombers, fighters, and destroyers amounted to 20% of the technical range as a safety magin
allowing for flight extensions due to opposition or weather conditions, plus half-an-hour's flight
time as a security against bad-weather landings or the need for the maximum permissible
extension of flying time.

[397] Halder, Diaries, 808 (22 Feb. 1941).

[398] See Grabmann, Luftverteidigung, 282, MGFA Lw 11b, and Plocher, Krieg im Osten, 675,
MGFA Lw 4/12.

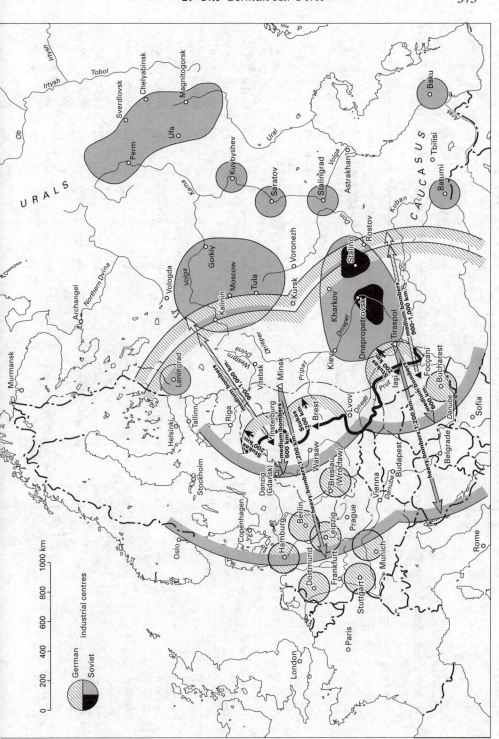

MAP I.IV.4. Tactical Depth of Penetration by German and Soviet Bombers

TABLE I.iv.7. *Specifications and Performance of the Principal Aircraft Models Employed by the Luftwaffe in the East, Summer 1941*

Type	No. of engines	Crew	Empty weight (kg.)	Total flying weight (kg.)	Max. speed at alt. (m.) (km./h.)	Cruising speed (km./h.)	Operating ceiling (m.)	Range (km.)	Tact. depth of penetration (without extra tanks) Min.	Max.	Max. With bomb-load (kg.)	Armament
Long-range recce. aircr.												
Do 17 P	2	3	5,640	7,680	434/4,000	392	9,550	1,700		730	—	3 MG15s
Do 215	2	4	5,800	6,680	485/4,000	460	9,000	2,450				4 MG15s, 3 cameras
Ju 88 D	2	4	8,850	12,350	485/4,800		8,000		720	1,015		1 MG131, 3 MG81s, 1 MG81Z
Close-range (army) recce. aircr.												
Hs 126 A	1	2	2,030	3,090	360/5,000 253/0	320	9,000	710		330	—	1 MG15, 1 Mg17
FW 189	2	3	2,690	3,950	344/2,500	317	7,000	940				2 MG15s, 2 MG17s
Bombers												
Do 17 Z	2	4	5,000	8,000	410/4,000	376	7,000	2,000	320	490	1,000	4 MG15s
Do 217 E	2	4	8,855	16,465	515/4,000	460	7,300	2,300	365	620	2,000	1 MG151, 3 MG15s, 2 MG131s
He 111 H	2	5	7,720	12,030	435/5,200	300	8,400	2,800	770	870 1,000	2,000 1,000	1 MGFF, 6 MG15s

Type												Armament
He 111 P	2	4	410/4,000	11,200	6,020	360	7,400	1,800		960	1,000	1 MGFF, 6 MG15s
Ju 88 A	2	4	472/5,300	12,122	8,620	370	8,000	2,700	435	565	2,000	1 MG131, 3 MG81s, 1 MG81Z
									860	1,165	1,000	
Dive-bombers												
Ju 87 B	1	2	360/5,000	4,250	2,760	320	8,000	800	115	230	500	2 MG17s, 1 MG15
Fighter bombers												
Hs 123	1	1	290/2,000	2,110	1,400	260	6,000			275	200	2 MG17s
Fighters												
Me 109 E	1	1	570/3,750	2,450	2,010		10,450	600	70	150	—	4 MG17s
Me 109 F	1	1	628/6,700	2,970	1,980	500	11,300	710	90	180	—	2 MG17s, 1 MG151
'Destroyers'												
Me 110 C/E	2	2	510/5,000	6,750	5,200	380	10,900	1,200	210	375	—	4 MG17s, 2 MGFFs, 1 MG15
Transport aircraft												
Ju 52	3	3	270/1,000	10,500	5,800	2	10,300	1,280		500	2,000	1 MG131, 2 MG15s

Sources: Luftwaffenführungsstab Gruppe T, 1 Apr. 1941, Taktische Eindringstiefen [Tactical penetration depths] (copy), BA-MA, Lw 106/9; Die Leistungen der deutschen Frontflugzeuge am 1.9.1939 und am 1.9.1944 [Performances of German front-line aircraft on 1 Sept. 1939 and 1 Sept. 1944], compiled from data of Chef TLR of 8. Abt./Chef Genst/1944 (photocopy), MGFA, Sammlung Grabmann, R 849; Kens and Nowarra, *Deutsche Flugzeuge*, 503–37. Figures are approximate because of divergences in the sources.

TABLE I.iv.8. *Disposition of Anti-aircraft Forces*

Theatre of war	Heavy batteries	Medium and light batteries	Searchlight batteries
Reich territory	786	530	163
West	130	172	71
South-east	45	45	6
South	6	5	—
East	239	135	25
TOTAL	1,206	887	265

The opening of the campaign in the east was hardly delayed by the Balkan campaign, and mainly by logistical problems uncommected with it and by unfavourable weather in the eastern territories that spring. The snow melted very late, with the result that muddy ground conditions, affecting airfields and supply-routes, persisted until the end of May. This delayed work on roads, paths, airfields, and communications facilities, and hence the readiness of the jump-off bases to receive the flying formations. The two weeks thus lost to the operation were to be badly missed in the autumn. The Luftwaffe General Staff, however, was confident that by then it would be possible to 'have done with the Soviet Union . . . so that the full weight of the German Luftwaffe can once more be thrown against Britain'.[399] After all, the Russian campaign was planned and prepared in conjunction and in parallel with the Balkan campaign.

3. THE GERMAN NAVY

ERNST KLINK

The strategic reflections of the naval war staff after the conclusion of the campaign in the west proceeded from the assumption that the defeat of Britain, the only remaining enemy, required a switch of the war effort from the army to the navy and air force.[400] In the short term a direct landing in England was seriously considered as an appropriate strategy; however, even preliminary planning revealed that both the navy's own strength and the capability of the

---

[399] Col. Schmid, chief of the Luftwaffe operations staff Ic, to Goebbels, in Tagebuch Joseph Goebbels, 29 Sept. 1942, IfZ ED 83/2. On the relationship between the Balkan and Russian campaigns in 1941 see Boog, *Luftwaffe im Balkanfeldzug*.

[400] The ensuing account is based on Salewski, *Seekriegsleitung*, vols. i and iii; 'Führer Conferences'; Hillgruber, *Strategie*, 144 ff.; Meister, *Seekrieg*; M.Dv. No. 601, Operationen und Taktik, Auswertung wichtiger Erkenntnisse des Seekrieges [Operations and tactics, interpretation of important lessons of the war at sea], vol. 12, Der Ostseekrieg gegen Rußland im Jahr 1941, OKM (Kriegswiss. Abt.), Berlin, Jan. 1944.

Luftwaffe, and indeed the army's requirements, would justify Operation Seelöwe ('Sea Lion') only as a last resort.[401] From July 1940, therefore, the naval war staff concentrated on U-boat and surface-unit actions against British supplies; demands made for allocations of raw materials, armaments capacity, and skilled workers to that end had been approved by Hitler on 30 June 1940.[402] However, the promised enlargement of the fleet was soon restricted again by a lack of co-ordination in the armaments programme of the three Wehrmacht services, the limitation of resources, and more particularly the priority given to the air war against Britain.

The concept of a war against Britain's supplies in the Atlantic—which the navy regarded as the only promising strategy for a quick end to the war before the United States entered it—was now being supplemented by plans for greater activity in the Mediterranean in order to strike at Britain by cutting off her connections to the Middle East and Egypt. Consideration of the consequence of involving the Italian navy, of enlisting Spain and France, or of operations against Gibraltar and some islands off the Moroccan coast resulted in a naval war-staff strategy championed by Raeder as an alternative to Hitler's plans for Sea Lion and Barbarossa. The navy's strategic ideas were thus in open conflict with the 'turning to the east' under preparation by the Army General Staff in accordance with Hitler's intentions.[403] The Soviet Union's benevolent attitude had provided a number of advantages to the navy since the beginning of the war. Peace in the Baltic enabled the navy to withdraw forces needed in the Atlantic and for coastal defence.[404] Any change in that situation was bound to be an additional burden in that it would make operations in the main theatres more difficult. The Soviet occupation of the Baltic States caused Raeder to call attention on 11 July 1940 to the denuding of the German Baltic bases of artillery defences and to request 'prompt information concerning developments in the east'. Although Hitler passed on the navy's request to the Wehrmacht High Command, he also believed that 'rearmament' of the naval bases with captured artillery pieces was necessary.[405]

Some time later, when information from the Wehrmacht operations staff suggested to the naval war staff that Hitler was considering military action against the Soviet Union,[406] new ideas began to be considered. On 28 July

---

[401] On the plans for a landing in England see Klee, *Seelöwe* and *Dokumente*; Hillgruber, *Strategie*, 168 ff.; Salewski, *Seekriegsleitung*, i. 256 ff. See also *Germany and the Second World War*, vol. ii.

[402] Salewski, *Seekriegsleitung*, i. 262.

[403] On the political and military prerequisites and implications, as well as the chances for a realization of that strategy, see *Germany and the Second World War*, ii. 366 ff., and *Das Deutsche Reich und der Zweite Weltkrieg*, vi. 275 ff.

[404] On the co-operation between the German and Soviet navies see Salewski, *Seekriegsleitung*, i. 133 ff., 156 ff., and id., 'Basis Nord'.

[405] 'Führer Conferences', 114 (11 July 1940).

[406] Salewski, *Seekriegsleitung*, i. 65 ff. The naval operations staff did not, any more than the Army General Staff, depend on Hitler's hints about a changed situation due to the occupation of the Baltic States. Interest in Estonian shale was in itself sufficient reason; see Meier-Dörnberg, *Ölversorgung*, 33–4.

Rear-Admiral Kurt Fricke, chief of the operations department of the naval war staff, submitted his 'Reflections on Russia'.[407] Fricke proceeded from the assumption that the Soviet Union and the United States had to be viewed as potential allies of Britain and that Anglo-American warfare would be confined to economic and naval-strategy measures. Germany's security demanded a deep forefield in which, on the one hand, her adversary's forces could be delayed by obstacles and, on the other, the necessary living-space created for the German people. Unreliable small countries had to be eliminated. The economy had to become as self-sufficient as possible. The Soviet Union offered itself for the exchange of raw materials and goods; under normal circumstances the two nations could derive the greatest benefit from it. On the one hand, the Soviet Union was 'an enigma' to Fricke because of the conflicting information about the country; on the other, he considered it so weak politically and militarily that, operating from a position of strength, one would be able to achieve any intended objectives by negotiation. At the same time he viewed the 'spirit of Bolshevism' as a danger and as a destabilizing factor that should be liquidated in the interest of Europe. Fricke mentioned the advantages of economic co-operation, which would also make a political arrangement possible, but he immediately limited that solution by referring to the Soviet Union's striving for territorial power and economic influence. War, he believed, could not remove the natural economic difficulties between great states but only shift them elsewhere by 'giving rise to new economic combinations'. It remains uncertain what Fricke meant by such new combinations.

The military part of the memorandum proposed that the Baltic be turned into a German *mare nostrum*; the dominant position of the Soviet navy was a serious if temporary danger there. Altogether the military strength of the Soviet armed forces was far inferior to that of Germany. In the event of a military conflict, occupation of an area up to the 'Lake Ladoga–Smolensk–Crimea line' was militarily feasible without difficulty. Fricke expected the Russian navy's resistance to collapse with the German seizure of the Baltic coast and Leningrad. 'Whether the capture of Moscow will be necessary will depend on the situation and on the time of the year.' Naval operations against the Soviet Union would have to start as a surprise strike, eliminating both the heavy surface units and the submarine force.

The freedom of movement of the Soviet navy was to be restricted by mines, U-boats, motor torpedo-boats, and destroyers. Luftwaffe strikes against ships and bases would have the greatest effect. Admittedly, Fricke assumed that the air war against Britain would have reached 'a certain conclusion', enabling 'the whole of the Luftwaffe' and a major part of light naval units to be engaged in the east. In conclusion he emphasized that it would not be possible to conduct

---

[407] Published in Salewski, *Seekriegsleitung*, iii. 137 ff., commented on ibid. i. 357 ff. To what extent Hitler's conversation with Raeder in Brauchitsch's presence on 21 July 1940 played any part is uncertain.

Sea Lion and the war in the east simultaneously; an operation against the Soviet Union would clearly place the main burden on the army and Luftwaffe, which meant that armament capacities would be drawn upon at the expense of the navy.

Contrary to the forecasts and intentions of Köstring, the military attaché in Moscow, Captain von Baumbach, the naval attaché, recommended the smashing of the Soviet Union and its heavy industry, and the return of its population into a patriarchal and authoritarian agricultural state.[408] Such ideas may have been designed to arouse sympathy on Fricke's part, but the naval war staff were primarily concerned with the dangers of a war on two fronts and the certainty of the United States entering the war on the enemy side. That was why Raeder, in conversation with Hitler, repeatedly argued his naval-strategy concept of seeking the decision of the war in the Atlantic and the Mediterranean.

At the Führer conferences and in his reports to Hitler after 21 July 1940 the commander-in-chief of the navy of course accepted Hitler's directives, but whenever he thought it necessary also argued against them.[409] Raeder's report on 6 September was concerned with the problem of concentrating his weak naval forces and the date under consideration for an offensive in the east. He thought the most favourable time would be the melting of the ice in the Gulf of Finland, as the enemy would then still be impeded by the ice. Raeder once more emphasized the impossibility of a simultaneous execution of Sea Lion and the eastern operation; no doubt he was hoping that Hitler might yet decide in favour of concentrating the German forces in the Atlantic and Mediterranean. Raeder's arguments on 26 September were along the same lines, stressing once more that the Mediterranean was the strategic centre of the war. The Suez Canal had to be seized, German troops were to advance towards Turkey through Palestine and Syria. Then the 'problem of Russia' would look quite different. If anything, the Soviet Union was afraid of Germany. Hitler declared that he wanted to induce the Soviet Union to seek a way to the ocean by striking south, towards Persia and India.[410] Raeder produced figures on the strength of the Soviet fleet in Leningrad and once more tried to

---

[408] Baumbach's notes for Rear-Adm. Fricke, dated 14 and 19 Sept. 1940, assume the continued pursuit of world revolution by the USSR as a 'law of history'. Hence a clash of the two political systems was inevitable sooner or later. In agreement with other comment from the German embassy in Moscow, however, he too warned against the illusion that the Soviet population would welcome an invading army as liberators: BA-MA RM 8/K 10-2/10.

[409] Raeder was briefed by Hitler on 21 July 1940 but does not seem to have attached much importance to Hitler's observations on the Soviet Union; he certainly did not feel he had been instructed to work out a naval operations plan; see Salewski, *Seekriegsleitung*, i. 275 ff. For the ensuing paragraphs see the entries under the dates in question in 'Führer Conferences' and in the war diary of the naval war staff 1939–45, pt. A, vols. xi ff.

[410] The question of Soviet action in Transcaucasia had been examined by Amt Ausland/Abwehr as early as 21 Mar. 1940 in a study 'The military situation in the Near East'—at that time in reaction to a move by British and French forces towards eastern Turkey, Iraq, and Iran. It had then been described as undesirable because it might jeopardize oil deliveries to Germany: BA-MA RW 4/v. 35, and Leverkühn, *German Military Intelligence*, 155 ff.

dissuade Hitler from his eastern plans. For the same reason Raeder, after Molotov's visit on 14 November, recommended to Hitler a postponement of the Russian operation until after victory over Britain. The Baltic would be lost as a training-ground for German naval forces and the whole U-boat war would suffer. The Soviet Union was building up a navy with German help and was unlikely, for the next few years, to seek conflict.

On 3 December, when he reported to Hitler on Ireland's support and the possibility of landing on that island, he once again emphasized that 'nothing must be allowed to interrupt or weaken' the operations against Britain 'since they will have a deadly effect in the long run, perhaps even this winter. We must carefully avoid any loss of prestige by operations entailing too great a risk, since this would tend to prolong the war and would, above all, create a strong impression in the United States.' Raeder unequivocally regarded the Mediterranean as the next area of operations for overthrowing Britain. Hitler concurred, but evidently 'missed' Raeder's reference to planning for the east and reacted only with a remark on the conditions for an engagement in Ireland.

On 27 December 1940 Raeder again warned against embarking on the operation in the east.[411] Otherwise the hoped-for decision in the Mediterranean could then no longer be brought about with Italian help. France and Spain should be more strongly involved in German measures. Maximum intensification of the U-boat and air war against Britain was called for. Hitler objected that, given the Soviet 'inclination' to interfere in Balkan affairs, the last continental enemy had first to be defeated 'before he can collaborate with Britain'. To that end the army had to be strengthened; after that, capacities would be fully concentrated on the Luftwaffe and the navy. Hitler feared Soviet intervention in Bulgaria and against Turkey, designed to gain control of the Straits. He now explained that Britain's war aim must be to defeat Germany on the continent and to bring the war to a decision there. Only its hopes of Russia and the United States were keeping Britain going. As soon as he perceived Britain's feelers, Stalin would act as an extortionist. The definitive loss of the Soviet Union as Britain's partner would make it possible to continue the war under tolerable conditions. Thus Germany's main enemy, in line with Raeder's concept, was Britain; the Soviet Union was Britain's 'continental sword'.

Viewed thus, the war against the Soviet Union was part of the overall war against Britain, the naval power. Raeder's attempt to ensure for the navy the principal role in the war for a decisive victory over Britain had definitely failed.

The basis of naval operations against the Soviet Union was the 'Combat instruction for the navy' of May 1939, produced after prolonged study within the naval operations staff; in its special instructions for the Naval Group

---

[411] 'Führer Conferences', 162 (31 Dec. 1940). The same reasons were given for a rejection of a war on two fronts on 11 Dec. 1940 in the minutes demanded by OKW/L: see p. 238, BA-MA PG 31025. See *Das Deutsche Reich und der Zweite Weltkrieg*, vi. 276–7.

Commander East it initially envisaged only a defensive role. Not until the supplement issued on 19 August 1939 was an alternative planned which involved an offensive mine war to seal off the Gulf of Finland. The general principle, however, was the most economical use of naval units so as not to jeopardize the main effort in the Atlantic.[412]

According to a Wehrmacht High Command instruction of 21 August 1940, the navy had to ensure the defence-readiness of the German Baltic coast by 1 April 1941.[413] The ports were to be protected by barrages and furnished with supply facilities. The heavy batteries were to be moved as far east as possible in order to protect the naval units operating there and to rule out enemy operations in the Bay of Danzig (Gdańsk). Directive No. 21 (Barbarossa) defined the navy's main task as the continuation of the war against Britain. For the Baltic, its orders were to safeguard sea transports to Finland and the Gulf of Bothnia, and to conduct mine-laying operations to bottle up the Red Fleet in Kronshtadt and Leningrad.

A characteristic aspect of the naval war in the Baltic was the tightness of the theatre; this greatly restricted the use of major units and made the navy dependent on continual co-operation with the Luftwaffe and the army. Reconnaissance and elimination of major enemy naval units were to be left to the Luftwaffe, in addition to its self-evident task of keeping the enemy's air forces in check. The army was to capture the ports from the land side by a rapid advance along the coast.

On 30 January 1941 the naval war staff submitted its operations plan.[414] Its central feature was still the laying of mine barrages in the Gulf of Finland and a limited attack on enemy units. The principal task was the protection of seaborne traffic to Finland, Sweden, and the eastern Baltic ports yet to be captured.

Although assessments of the future enemy referred to the 'relatively large number of ships', the naval war staff emphasized the low level of training and, above all, inadequate command skills: 'The decisive aspect of the performance of the Russian navy will presumably be the fact that its command is rigid and inflexible, that there is no willingness to take responsibility, and that no personal initiative need be expected.' Soviet submarine and mine-laying operations, on the other hand, were expected to represent a serious threat and to cause temporary disruption of German sea communications in the Baltic.

The army's advance along the coast, however, would probably yield considerable number of ships taken as booty for use in the war in the Atlantic. In

---

[412] See 'Kampfanweisungen für die Kriegsmarine (Ausgabe Mai 1939)' [Engagement instructions for the navy—issue May 1939], with the incorporated supplement of 19 Aug. 1939 (1./Skl. Ia 173/39 g.Kdos. Chefs.), BA-MA RM 7/813, fos. 27 ff. and 37–8. See Salewski, *Seekriegsleitung*, i. 77–8 and 365–6.

[413] Salewski, *Seekriegsleitung*, i. 365 ff.

[414] The operations plan was verbally reported to Hitler by Raeder on 4 Feb. 1941: 'Führer Conferences', 176–7. See also war diary of the naval war staff 1939–45, pt. A, vol. xvii (Jan. 1941), 401 ff. (30 Jan. 1941).

polar waters it would be important to weaken the Soviet bases of Murmansk and Polyarnyy by massive air attacks and thereby to render British operational intentions in the Arctic Ocean more difficult.

With the expected capture of these ports from the land side the Soviet naval forces would probably try to move to Britain. According to the situation, an attempt would have to be made at least to cut off the surface units and engage them in battle. In the Black Sea achievement of naval superiority was ruled out from the start. The Soviet fleet was known to be vastly superior to the Romanian and Bulgarian units, and these could not therefore be expected to engage in offensive action.[415]

In the circumstances the navy's only offensive operation within the framework of Barbarossa was naval warfare in the Baltic.

Command was exercised by Naval Group HQ North (General Admiral Carls). The operational commander of the naval war in the Baltic, under Group North, was the Befehlshaber der Kreuzer (B.d.K.: Commander of Cruisers), reinforced for this purpose by some of the staff of the Führer der Torpedoboote (F.d.T.: Leader of Torpedo-boats). To ensure liaison with the Finnish naval forces the Leader of Torpedo-boats, with the rest of his staff, was posted to Helsinki as 'Commander of German naval forces in Finland', where, in conjunction with the German naval liaison staff and the Finnish naval staff, he was to control operations in accordance with instructions from the Commander of Cruisers. There was therefore plenty of opportunity for overlapping of orders and misunderstandings throughout the rest of the war.

For the defence of the bases to be newly established in the east two naval commanders ('C' and 'D') were additionally provided; these were to advance along with the army. The weakness of German forces in the Baltic area was remedied—as a short-term measure, it was hoped—by drawing upon the Leader of Mining Vessels from the North Sea security area; he assumed control of the mine-seeking, mine-sweeping, and patrol services, except in the Gulf of Finland. First consultations between the German naval war staff and the Finnish navy were held on 28 May 1941; they were followed on 6 June by consultations between Group HQ North and the Finns on operational engagement plans. Requests from the Group HQ for the immediate utilization of the Åland Islands and the early occupation of Hanko and Suursari had been rejected by Hitler earlier, on 3 June, because he considered this a Finnish problem and probably wished to rule out additional demands.[416]

On 29 May the formations were moved to the ports of the central and

---

[415] Offensive operations—primarily in mine warfare—were to be 'striven for': see Salewski, *Seekriegsleitung*, iii. 147 ff. See further the directives of the naval war staff of 6 Mar. and 6 May 1941, ibid. i. 370; also M.Dv. No. 601, 6 ff., and Meister, *Seekrieg*, 9 ff. Data on Soviet naval forces and ratios of strength are in M.Dv. No. 601, 3, and Meister, *Seekrieg*, 230 ff.

[416] Salewski, *Seekriegsleitung*, i. 372 ff., and M.Dv. No. 601, 9 ff. On Finland see sect. I.VI.4 (Ueberschär); Jokipii, *Laivasto-yhteistyö*.

eastern Baltic. By 18 June all units had reached their ports, including whose in Finland, without incident. The first mine-barrages were dropped after 18–19 June in order to make sure that, after the start of operations on 22 June, Soviet ships could not leave harbour. After 14 June no German vessel was permitted to make for a Soviet port; Soviet ships were detained. At the western exit of the Gulf of Finland German mining units had been arriving in the skerries around Turku (Åbo) since 14 June; during the night of 21–2 June they laid mines, pursued by Soviet observers and fired on from the air.[417]

On 26 February 1941 Colonel-General Halder and Admiral Otto Schniewind, chief of staff of the naval war staff, discussed the problem of naval support for ground operations. Schniewind made it clear that no active support by the navy was possible; not even the coastal shipping envisaged for carrying supplies to Army Group North could be given protection. On 13 March discussions were held between the operations department and Admiral Karl-Georg Schuster, commanding Naval Group South, and Captain Otto Loycke, naval liaison officer with the commander-in-chief of the army, on the possibilities of sea transportation along the Black Sea coast to Odessa and beyond. However, in view of estimated Soviet superiority in the Black Sea these did not produce any positive results either.[418]

The command agency North of the quartermaster-general envisaged the use of seagoing ships and transport barges to relieve transport capacity by rail and road; their use would depend entirely on the naval-war situation. Initially only the movement of individual small vessels close to the coast ('coastal sneakers') was possible. The following were held in readiness on Day B: 2 ships with food supplies and 4 ships with ammunition at both Memel (Klaipeda) and Königsberg (now Kaliningrad). Another 18 were held ready unladen; these were earmarked for supplies to Eighteenth Army and were to be brought up to Libau (Liepaja) as early as possible. These units were put under the operational command of Naval Commander D in Königsberg. For transportation across the Memel (Niemen) 2,250 t. of river-barge capacity, laden with ammunition, had been readied; a further 1,250 t. were lying unladen at Königsberg.[419] Even these relatively minor aspects of co-operation between the Wehrmacht services depended entirely on amicable agreement at lower level;

---

[417] On engagements prior to 22 June 1941 see 1. Skl to OKW/WFSt/L, 2 June 1941, BA-MA PG 31025.

[418] Halder, *Diaries*, 809 (24 Feb. 1941), 811 (26 Feb. 1941), 828 (13 Mar. 1941). The fundamental limitations on naval support for the army had already been explained to Halder by Capt. Loycke on 14 Aug. 1940: BA-MA PG 32087b. See also Salewski, *Seekriegsleitung*, i. 365 ff. For the result of the conference with Schniewind see Halder, *Diaries*, 811 (26 Feb. 1941).

[419] On 3 Feb. 1941 Halder drew Hitler's attention to the importance of supplies across the Baltic and the Black Sea: see Halder, *KTB* ii. 269 (2 Feb. 1941; not in trans.). Army Group C, command agency North of the quartermaster-general, 'Anordnung über die Ausnutzung der See- und Binnenschiffahrt der Befehlsstelle Nord' [Instruction on the utilization of seagoing and river shipping of command agency North], suppl. 8 to annexe 7 of Besondere Anordnungen während des Aufmarsches [Special instructions during deployment], 2 May 1941, BA-MA 22392/40.

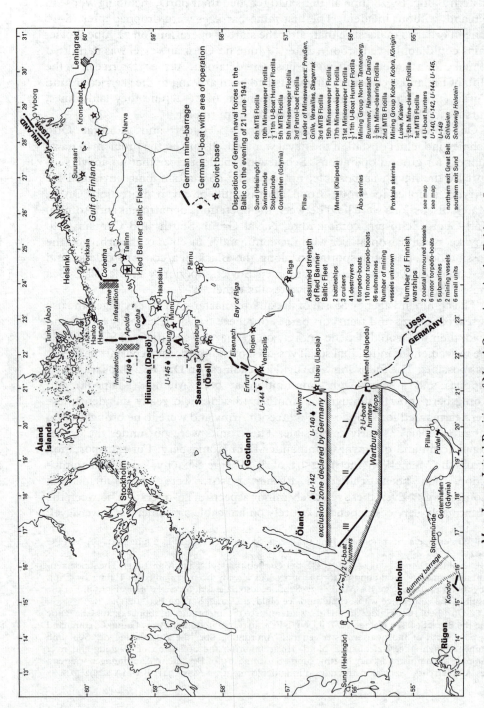

MAP I.iv.5. Initial Position of Naval Operations in the Baltic, 22 June 1941

Source: BA-MA K 10-2/73 and BA-MA RH 19 III/66 I D.

arrangements at senior level, properly the task of the Wehrmacht operations staff, were being avoided.[420]

As can be seen from Map I.IV.5, which shows the initial situation of the sea war in the Baltic, the mine-laying and motor torpedo-boat formations equipped for offensive operations were supported also by five U-boats in the central Baltic in order to prevent evasive action or a breakthrough by Soviet surface units. In addition, German protective barrages had been laid around the ports of Pillau, Kolberg, and Stettin (now Szczecin) to protect them against penetration by enemy naval forces. At the suggestion of the German naval war staff, a further defensive measure was taken by the Swedish navy, which laid a mine-barrage between Stockholm and the boundary of Swedish territorial waters off the Åland archipelago.

[420] Ruge, *Sea Warfare*, 156, and (taking his cue from him) Salewski, *Seekriegsleitung*, i. 373, believe that the Army High Command lacked understanding for a 'supply-route across the Baltic'.

V. Germany's Acquisition of Allies in South-east Europe

Jürgen Förster

1. Romania in the Political and Economic Field of Force of the Great Powers

As a result of Hitler's decision in the summer of 1940 to turn to the east, Romania, along with Finland, came within the range of German strategy. Whereas until then Berlin had emphasized only its economic interest in that country, additional objectives now came to the fore. Romania's inclination towards the Reich, from which sprang her participation in Hitler's war against the Soviet Union, was based on a complex convergence and interplay of historical, political, domestic, ideological, and economic factors. Along with Finland, Romania from 1941 to 1944 became Germany's principal ally against the Red Army, although no formal military alliance had been concluded nor any specific agreements made on common war aims with regard to the Soviet Union. The manner in which the Reich harnessed the forces of its allies to its own cart should not make one overlook the fact that the direction in which they were pulling was not solely up to Hitler, who in turn became dependent on his comrades-in-arms.

German foreign-policy in south-east Europe was favoured by the territorial outcome of the First World War and the consequences of the worldwide depression. The treaties signed in the Paris area in 1919–20 had brought about a political constellation in south-east Europe which was characterized either by support for or by opposition to the 'Versailles system'. While the beneficiaries of the territorial redistribution, Romania, Yugoslavia, and Czechoslovakia, had focused their foreign policy on the maintenance of their possessions, the policy of the losers, Hungary and Bulgaria, was marked by an aspiration for a revision of their frontiers. From the Soviet Union Romania had gained Bessarabia, and from the bankrupt stock of Austria-Hungary she had gained Transylvania, the Bukowina, and the major part of the Banat. As a member of the League of Nations and of the Little Entente, Romania was part of the French system of alliances in south-east Europe and a reliable partner in the 'cordon sanitaire' system against the Bolshevik Soviet Union,[1] which had not recognized the annexation of Bessarabia. Romania's foreign policy was likewise determined by her concern about Hungarian and Bulgarian revisionist intentions; and to defend herself against Soviet claims she had concluded an alliance with Poland in March 1921. While Romania by her gains had doubled

[1] For this section see also Annexe Vol., No. 4. On Romania's history after the First World War see Rhode, 'Südosteuropäische Staaten'; Roman, *Rumänien*; Lungu, *Romania*.

her area as well as her population, becoming the biggest state in south-east Europe, she had also changed from a national into a multinational state. According to the first general census of 1930, Romania had a population of 18.06 million, of which 71.9 per cent were Romanians, 7.9 per cent Hungarians, approximately 4 per cent each Germans, Ukrainians, and Jews, and 1.9 per cent Bulgarians. The main problem of Romanian domestic policy after the First World War was 'the amalgamation of the old kingdom and the newly acquired territories with their diverse social structures, their diverse historical and cultural evolution',[2] and their minorities. The minority problem was aggravated principally by the fact that the Hungarians in Transylvania and the Székler territory, where in some places they formed a majority of over 80 per cent, and the Bulgarians in southern Dobrudja (38 per cent of the population) wished to be reunited with their mother countries.

Romania was a constitutional monarchy, though the Crown was of particular importance in that the formation of the government was entirely in the hands of the king, who could also dissolve parliament at any time. As a result of the electoral system, parliament did not reflect public opinion since the overwhelming majority of seats went to the party which achieved 40 per cent of the vote. Moreover, a pre-war rule was still in force, 'according to which in Romania it was not the elections which determined the government, but the government which determined the elections'.[3]

A particularly pressing problem had been an agrarian reform in the old kingdom, where 60 per cent of the land had been in the hands of 5 per cent of the landowners. Although a strongly ideological land reform, completed in 1928, had eliminated the large estates and strengthened the Romanian peasantry, it had also, because of land fragmentation and high rates of interest on agricultural credits, resulted in 'correspondingly large indebtedness, especially of smallholdings, and in a basic anti-Semitism, as the creditors were often Jews'.[4] In 1930 78 per cent of the population was employed in agriculture and only 7.2 per cent in industry. The petroleum industry, of which up to 75 per cent was foreign-owned, was the most important sector of the Romanian economy. In 1937 exports of oil and oil derivatives accounted for 41 per cent of total exports.

Patent manipulation and corruption in the formation of governments, as well as Romania's unsolved national and social problems, undermined confidence in constitutional monarchy and its representatives. The consequence was the emergence and rapid growth of radical and Fascist organizations. Thus the 'Legion of Archangel Michael', founded by Corneliu Z. Codreanu in 1927, developed within a few years into the fiercest domestic opposition to the monarchy and the established parties.[5] The Legion did not see itself as a party

---

[2] Hillgruber, *Deutsch-rumänische Beziehungen*, 6.
[3] Rhode, 'Südosteuropäische Staaten', 1139.   [4] Ibid. 1141.
[5] See Nagy-Talavera, *Green Shirts*; Fătu and Spălăţelu, *Eiserne Garde*; Thamer and Wippermann, *Faschistische Bewegungen*; Heinen, *Legion 'Erzengel Michael'*.

but as a movement, as a 'form of life'. It was organized as a militant order. In place of a political programme there was belief in the indispensable 'spiritual resurrection of the nation' and in a 'new man'. A fervent mythically Christian nationalism was linked with anti-capitalist and social-revolutionary ideas. Alongside a radical anti-Semitism and anti-Marxism the Legion's members were guided by anti-democratism, irrationalism, a cult of death, and an apologia for war. The Legion saw the 'decisive means for national renewal' in the elimination of the Jews and their influence in politics, the economy, and culture.[6] Corrupt politicians and Communists were also regarded as 'Jews' and reviled as 'foreigners'. In order to escape from its isolation and capture power in the state, 1929–30 Codreanu renamed the Legion the 'Iron Guard'. Its 'mission' was 'to hand out justice to the righteous and death to the wicked'.[7] The successes of the National Socialists in the election of September 1930 in Germany were hailed by Codreanu as a 'victory for the entire Aryan race'.

National Socialist foreign policy after 1933 continued the south-east European policy of the Weimar governments, especially that of Brüning.[8] Foreign-trade policy was not only a vehicle of foreign policy for weakening the French alliance system, but also pursued an objective with regard to Britain.[9] Germany's 'urge towards the south-east' was to signalize her renunciation of colonial claims overseas and thus facilitate German–British understanding. After 1936 German foreign-trade policy acquired a new aspect as the scope and internal dynamics of German rearmament, and Hitler's foreign-policy 'programme', necessitated the country's economic mobilization in the form of the Four-year Plan.[10] In that connection, Romania's mineral-oil products and surplus grain achieved increasing importance for Germany's war economy. However, Bucharest successfully resisted any excessively one-sided economic deals and limited oil deliveries to Germany, effected as clearing transactions, to a quarter of her total trade. Any quantities ordered in excess of that quota could not be exchanged against industrial manufactures but had to be paid for in hard currency.

However, that economic setback was offset by the political success achieved by German diplomacy with the aid of Romania's right-wing parties. In August 1936 King Carol II dismissed his pro-French foreign minister Titulescu, who had intended to safeguard Romania's territorial integrity not only by inclining towards France but also by good relations with the Soviet Union.[11] The parliamentary elections at the end of 1937 failed for the first time to ensure a majority for the government party. It gained only 38 per cent of the vote, whereas the right-wing parties scored a major success. The Iron Guard alone received nearly 16 per cent. In February 1938 King Carol exploited the

---

[6] Broszat, 'Eiserne Garde', 630.   [7] Fǎtu and Spǎlǎţelu, *Eiserne Garde*, 80.
[8] See Schröder, 'Südosteuropapolitik'; Sundhaussen, 'Weltwirtschaftskrise'.
[9] See Wendt, 'Südosteuropa', 417–18.
[10] See *Germany and the Second World War*, i. 232 ff., 437 ff.; Marguerat, *Le IIIe Reich*.
[11] See the political reports of Legation Counsellor von Pochhammer, 17 Mar. 1935 (*DGFP* c iii/2, No. 535) and 1 Jan. 1936 (ibid. iv/2, No. 478).

unstable domestic political situation by staging a *coup d'état*. He dissolved parliament and the political parties, and adopted an authoritarian form of government. To stabilize his dictatorship he not only fought ruthlessly against the Iron Guard but also created a united party, the 'National Regeneration Front'. In his foreign policy, in order to preserve Romania's territory against the revisionist aspirations of her neighbours, Carol performed a balancing act between the Reich and the Western powers.

After the occupation of Austria, Germany launched a renewed economic offensive towards south-east Europe, one which has to be viewed against the background of the German strategy emerging after 1937—one involving conflict with Britain should that be necessary. At the beginning of April 1938 Göring called for the 'economic catchment' of Romania, Hungary, Yugoslavia, and Bulgaria.[12] Whereas Budapest, Belgrade, and Sofia became largely dependent on the German market, Bucharest succeeded in resisting German pressure because of the greater diversity of its trade and because of Germany's lack of hard currency. It was only the next series of power-shifts in the European scene, accomplished by Hitler in 1938–9, as well as British and French economic appeasement, that helped the German economic offensive to succeed also in Romania. On 23 March 1939 a German–Romanian economic agreement was signed, with provisions amounting to Romania's integration within a German-controlled greater economic sphere.[13] Hitler's 'Prague coup', however, resulted not only in the Anglo-French guarantee to Romania, but also in supportive economic activities which neutralized the German–Romanian agreement.[14] The economic and political engagement of the Western powers denied Germany realization of her aspirations towards a monopoly position in Romania's oil industry. As a solution, in April 1939 the economic and armament department of the OKW proposed: 'The only real guarantee for controlling the Romanian oil resources at present is a military solution. Its application should aim at the preservation of the Romanian oil industry's operational capacity.'[15] However, the private interests of Anglo-French capital, which had direct control of 65 per cent of the shares of the major mineral-oil companies in Romania, did not coincide with the Western powers' strategic aims until after the outbreak of the war. In mid-October 1939 the War Cabinet in London set up the 'Hankey committee' in order to prevent Romanian oil from reaching Germany.[16] The Romanian companies supported the boycot policy organized by Lord Hankey by greatly raising prices, by arranging for parent companies to buy up the production of daughter companies, and by an almost watertight embargo against German importers. That policy, however, could work successfully only so long as the Romanian government did not

[12] Quoted according to Volkmann, 'Außenhandel und Aufrüstung', 107–8.
[13] *DGFP* D vi, Nos. 78, 131.   [14] See Barker, *British Policy*, 32.
[15] OKW/WStb/Wi (IVd) No. 1010/39, Apr. 1939, Die Mineralölversorgung Deutschlands im Kriege [Germany's mineral-oil supplies in wartime], BA-MA Wi/I. 37.
[16] Hinsley, *British Intelligence*, i. 103; Marguerat, *Le IIIe Reich*, 168 ff.; Barker, *British Policy*, 30.

intervene in the economy by control measures—and that, in turn, depended on its own political interests.

The turn-about in Romanian policy was triggered by the alliance between Hitler and Stalin, by the resulting fourth partition of Poland, and by the attitude of the Western powers.[17] Carol's foreign-policy tightrope act lost its safety-net as a result of Britain's refusal to extend its guarantee to the contingency of Soviet aggression against Bessarabia. The result was a state of suspension, reflected both in Romania's declaration of neutrality after the German attack against Poland and in her non-recognition of the alliance following the Red Army's advance into Polish territory. In the opinion of Armand Calinescu, the Romanian premier, the German danger was then receding while the Soviet threat was moving to the foreground. Only a few days after discussing with the British and French ministers a plan for the destruction of the Romanian oilfields in the event of a German attempt to seize them,[18] Calinescu on 16 September 1939 proposed to Wilhelm Fabricius, the German minister, an exchange of large quantities of Polish weapons captured by the Germans against long-term deliveries of oil and grain. This barter deal, the political significance of which the Romanian government well realized, was to remain outside the general trade agreements.[19] It offered Germany the opportunity of receiving additional quantities of urgently needed Romanian oil without further overdrawing the clearing account and without having to pay in hard currency. A secret German–Romanian protocol signed on 29 September laid down the directives for the delivery of captured Polish material to a value of RM100m. in exchange for oil and grain.[20] In order to improve the equipment of the Romanian army, Bucharest was above all interested in machine-guns, anti-tank guns, and artillery pieces. The Romanian government obliged Berlin by making a credit of RM40m. available in advance for German purchases of oil. However, owing to domestic, economic, and foreign obstacles, this highly political oil-for-arms deal was deferred until the end of May 1940.

Romania's abandonment of her neutral line was jeopardized domestically by the fact that on 21 September 1939 Premier Calinescu was shot dead by members of the Iron Guard who had slipped in from Germany. The German minister Fabricius's comment on the assassination was: 'Whenever the Romanians in government move closer to us the Iron Guard steps in between, it is as if we were doomed.'[21] On the one hand, Carol's regime reacted to the

---

[17] See Förster, 'Rumäniens Weg', and from the Romanian side Savu, 'Defensive War', 136 ff. Romania in Sept. 1939 mobilized 31 infantry divisions, 3 cavalry divisions, 4 mountain brigades, and 1 fortress brigade.

[18] Campus, 'Anglo-Rumanian Relations', 22 (unpub. manuscript).

[19] DGFP D viii, No. 74.

[20] Ibid., No. 166, and PA Ha. Pol., Rumänien, betr. Kriegsgerät [concerning war equipment], iv.

[21] Letter to Minister Otto von Erdmannsdorff, 27 Sept. 1939, PA, Dt. Ges. Bukarest, Politisch Geheim.

assassination with Draconian measures. The arrested assassins and more than seventy detained members of the Legion were executed by firing-squad and their bodies put on public display. On the other hand, the king had the German minister assured that he would continue his policy towards Germany and, in particular, implement the important oil-for-arms deal. Germany should 'show even greater interest in Romania than in the past and, if necessary, use its influence on Russia'.[22]

Carol's openly declared foreign-policy calculations, which were further nourished by Soviet remarks on the unclarified status of Bessarabia, had been influenced also by Britain's attitude. Britain, in whom Carol II and many of his ministers had originally placed their hopes, not only declined to extend its guarantee to cover Soviet aggression, but was at the same time reluctant, in view of different strategic priorities as well as her own requirements, to supply armaments to Romania.[23] In his hope of German political assistance against the Soviet Union Carol went out of his way to meet Germany's economic requests. In December 1939 his government guaranteed a monthly delivery of 130,000 t. of crude oil—the quantity believed to be necessary by the Reich ministry of economic affairs—devalued the Romanian leu against the Reichsmark in order to counteract the prices driven up by the oil concerns, and employed control measures to intervene in the market. In mid-January 1940 it set up a 'commissariat-general for petroleum' in order to counter the obstructive business policy practised by the mineral-oil companies *vis-à-vis* the German importers.[24] At the end of February the new German negotiator, Hermann Theo Neubacher, accomplished an arms–oil price ratio which was exceedingly favourable to Germany, and on 6 March 1940 a provisional agreement on the oil-for-arms deal was signed.[25] This envisaged the delivery of 360 37-mm. anti-tank guns, 10 20-mm. anti-aircraft guns, 80 75-mm. artillery pieces, and optical equipment of Polish or Czech origin in exchange for 200,000 t. of crude oil during March and April 1940.

The official conclusion of a definitive oil-for-arms agreement was delayed not by any unsettled financial details, but by the Romanian king's political calculations. Carol II was reluctant to abandon his policy of neutrality too readily, or to become dependent on Germany. When, towards the end of March, the Soviet Union publicly confirmed its claim to Bessarabia, Romanian fears increased. Because of Britain's refusal of assistance the Romanian regime found itself in the position of having to choose between Hitler and Stalin. With territorial claims by the Soviet Union, Hungary, and Bulgaria raising the possibility of conflict on three fronts, Carol—against the opposition

[22] German embassy Bucharest, telegram No. 614, 23 Sept. 1939, excerpt, BA-MA Wi/IC 4.34.

[23] Barker, *British Policy*, 22, 29; PRO, Cab 79/1, COS (39) 22nd Meeting, 19 Sept. 1939.

[24] See Förster, 'Rumäniens Weg'.

[25] German embassy Bucharest, Der Sonderbeauftragte für Wirtschaftsfragen [Special Plenipotentiary for Economic Affairs], No. 17744/40, 7 Mar. 1940, PA, Ha. Pol. Rumänien, betr. Kriegsgerät [concerning war equipment], iv; see also *DGFP* D viii, No. 660 (7 Mar. 1940); Kurt von Tippelskirch (OQu IV), minute, 11 Mar. 1940, BA-MA RH 2/v. 1478.

of some of his ministers—decided to align himself with National Socialist Germany. In consequence, the oil-for-arms agreement was eventually signed in Bucharest on 27 May 1940.[26] Its political and military importance was rated so highly by the king that the economic consequences were readily accepted. Carol believed that his economic and domestic concessions with regard to the Iron Guard would earn him Hitler's support for his policy of preserving 'throne and frontiers'.[27] He assumed that, for economic reasons, Hitler would also be interested in Romania's political stability and territorial integrity, and would keep the Soviet Union, Hungary, and Bulgaria in check. As for his obvious turn towards the camp of the Axis powers, Carol tried to conceal this by concluding an economic agreement with Britain as late as 6 June 1940. In Berlin this was seen as evidence of Romania's continuing 'see-saw politics'.

The reasoning behind Carol's oil-for-arms agreement proved an illusion when Stalin, after the surprisingly swift collapse of France, proceeded to take possession of the forefield which Hitler had assigned to him in the secret protocol of summer 1939. In addition to the three Baltic States, Bessarabia and the whole of the Bukowina were to be incorporated in the Soviet Union. The effects of this extension of the Soviet empire upon Finland and the Balkan States were part of the plan. Having harmonized its territorial demands on Romania in negotiations in Berlin and having recognized Germany's economic interests, Moscow transmitted an ultimatum to Bucharest on 26 June 1940.[28] This demanded, within a period of 24 hours, the cession of Bessarabia, the northern Bukowina, and the town of Herţa in the province of Moldavia. While ordering the mobilization of his army and displaying his readiness to fight, Carol simultaneously turned to Germany and Italy for help. But both Axis powers urgently advised him to yield. Hitler and Mussolini feared that in the event of a Soviet–Romanian war the Red Army might penetrate beyond the Pruth and occupy the oil region around Ploieşti. Nor could the use of force by Hungary or Bulgaria be ruled out.

With no foreign support Carol II and his regime had no choice but to swallow this first 'pill of cessions'.[29] On 28 June the Red Army crossed the frontiers and within four days occupied the ceded territories. The order to evacuate Bessarabia, the northern Bukowina, and Herţa without a fight caught the Romanian army and administration by surprise. The sudden abandon-

---

[26] DGFP D ix, No. 338. The direct exchange of oil for war material ended in Oct. 1940. After that date the purchase of mineral oil was again conducted by way of clearing, which led to a big increase in the German debt. In Oct. 1941 this amounted to RM270m. The devaluation of the leu in Dec. 1939 and the concession of pre-war prices resulted in a gain for Germany of RM80m.— without taking into account the fact that weapons captured in Poland and Czechoslovakia entered into the deal.

[27] This was how the German military attaché in Bucharest, Col. Carl Wahle, formulated it in his report on the military and war-economy situation in Romania, No. 137/40, 5 Feb. 1940, BA-MA Wi/IC 4.58.

[28] See Brügel, 'Das sowjetische Ultimatum'.

[29] Semi-official letter of the German military attaché, Col. Wahle, to Lt.-Gen. von Tippelskirch, 28 July 1940, BA-MA III H 1001/7.

ment of the doctrine that Romania's frontiers had to be defended so long as a Romanian soldier held a weapon in his hand resulted in profound demoralization of the Romanian army and in sharp criticism of its supreme command.

2. The Vienna Arbitration Award of August 1940 and the Dispatch of a German Military Mission

The loss of Bessarabia, Herța, and the northern Bukowina confirmed Romania's precarious position. As no help was to be expected from Britain, Carol was feverishly trying to gain German support against the Hungarian and Bulgarian revisionist claims which were now bound to be raised. He saw 'his country's only salvation in a very close alignment with Germany', with which he was willing to co-operate closely in all fields.[30] As a token of her 'new policy', on 1 July 1940 Romania renounced the now worthless Anglo-French guarantee of her frontiers and on 11 July left the League of Nations. Carol, moreover, formed a government of respected pro-German ministers, which included the now rehabilitated commander of the Iron Guard, Horia Sima, and two further Legion members, and initiated the process of depriving Jews of their rights. But despite the proposition that Romania might function as Germany's right wing against the Soviet Union and a request for a German military mission,[31] Hitler insisted that Bucharest must first come to terms with its neighbours before a closer German–Romanian co-operation could be considered.[32] Simultaneously he advised Hungary and Bulgaria to realize their territorial demands through direct negotiations with Romania.

Whereas agreement in principle was soon reached between Bulgaria and Romania on the cession of the southern Dobrudja to Bulgaria,[33] Romanian–Hungarian negotiations got bogged down. When both sides suggested arbitration by the Axis, Hitler assumed the role of arbitrator according to his own judgement. The conflicting national ambitions of Hungary and Romania, as well as the structure of their governmental systems with a basic anti-Communist attitude, made it easy for him, with Italian support, to impose an arbitration award on the two countries.[34]

This was signed by the foreign ministers of Germany, Italy, Hungary, and Romania in Vienna on 30 August 1940.[35] Its aim was to achieve the permanent pacification of the Balkans and to prevent both a British extension of the war to that region and Soviet intervention.

Romania undertook to cede northern Transylvania and the Székler area to

[30] German embassy Bucharest, telegram No. 1056, 30 June 1940, *DGFP* D x, No. 68.

[31] Semi-official letter of the German military attaché, Col. Wahle, to Lt.-Gen. von Tippelskirch, 14 July 1940, BA-MA III H 1001/7, and *DGFP* D x, No. 161 (13 July 1940). Wahle did not think a mere German military mission was much use: 'Just as in the days of the emperor Trajan, when a Roman legion was stationed on the lower Danube, so the future protection of this important colony will have to be taken under our own management.'

[32] Letter from Hitler to King Carol II, 15 July 1940, *DGFP* D x, No. 171.

[33] See Hoppe, *Bulgarien*, 87 ff. The treaty of Craiova was signed on 7 Sept. Bulgaria had 7,695 sq. km. with 319,551 inhabitants returned to her (p. 134).

[34] Broszat, 'Deutschland', 81.   [35] *DGFP* D x, Nos. 408–13.

Hungary. Although Budapest in consequence regained an area of 43,500 square kilometres with 2.5 million inhabitants—over a million of whom were Romanians—this was less than the minimal solution of 50,000 square kilometres specified by the Hungarian side in the autumn of 1939.[36] As a price for that second territorial amputation Romania received a German–Italian guarantee of the remainder of her sovereign territory, clearly designed to prevent any further Soviet ambitions. The Russians must realize, Hitler declared at the annual conference of military attachés on 31 August, 'that Germany attaches vital importance to Romania [and] will shrink from nothing in the protection of German interests'.[37] Romania was inviolable.

The German strategy of confronting the Kremlin in south-east Europe—just as in Finland—was based on Hitler's decision of 31 July 1940 to smash the Soviet Union in the spring of 1941. The risk that Stalin in August 1940 might take advantage of the threat of military conflict between Hungary and Romania by pushing across the Pruth towards Ploieşti was met by Hitler with the creation of a counter-attack reserve in the Vienna region. The XXXX Army Corps (2nd and 9th Armoured Divisions, 13th Infantry Division (motorized), SS-Leibstandarte Adolf Hitler, and the Grossdeutschland Infantry Regiment) was to be held in readiness to secure the Romanian oilfields by occupation.[38] The general commanding the corps was to be advised by a 'war-economy staff for Romania' on the utilization of the country 'for supplying Germany in the area of mineral oil and foodstuffs, as well as for harnessing Romania's economy to the requirements of the German forces employed in Romania'.[39] The XXXX Corps's state of readiness to move off was not countermanded until 19 September, when the situation in Romania had clarified in favour of Germany. A parallel to the urgent military measures for the protection of Romania's oil may be seen in the fact that Hitler ordered 'a deployment for all eventualities' to be prepared in northern Norway for the protection of the nickel-ore region near Petsamo.[40]

The second Vienna award failed to eliminate Hungarian–Romanian rivalry. Instead a paradoxical situation arose compared with the period between the two wars in that Hungary was endeavouring, by complying with German interests, to preserve at least what she had gained, while Romania was pursuing a revisionist policy, recognizing the Vienna award as no more than a provisional decision. This conflict of interests greatly contributed to the fact that both countries participated in Hitler's war against the Soviet Union, while

---

[36] *Allianz Hitler-Horthy-Mussolini*, 66.

[37] Halder, *Diaries*, 569 (31 Aug. 1940); similarly 583 (14 Sept. 1940).

[38] BA-MA XXXX. A.K., 76043/4 and 6. Maj.-Gen. von Tippelskirch had suggested an occupation of the oilfields as early as the beginning of Dec. 1939 because German mineral-oil supplies were then being interfered with by sabotage (minute of 6 Dec. 1939, BA-MA RH 2/v. 1478).

[39] OKW/WiRüAmt/Wi III No. 1846/40, 12 Sept. 1940, BA-MA Wi/IC 4.64. Gen. Thomas was instructed by Keitel at the end of Apr. 1940 to make preparations for 'the Balkan business in terms of war economy' (ibid. RW 19/185).

[40] See sect. I.vi.1 at n. 6 (Ueberschär).

along the still ill-defined Hungarian–Romanian frontier repeated armed clashes occurred which had to be settled by German–Italian commissions.

The transfer of major parts of the country to Hungary unleashed a wave of indignation in Romania, directed predominantly against the king and culminating in an attempted coup by the Iron Guard. Both Britain and Germany tried to take advantage of the domestic crisis. While London championed Juliu Maniu, the leader of the National Peasant Party, Berlin gave its support to General Ion Antonescu, who had fallen into disgrace with Carol. In order to save his regime and to implement the award recognized also by the Iron Guard, the king appointed Antonescu premier with extraordinary powers. The new 'leader of the Romanian state' complied with the Iron Guard's request for Carol's abdication and, with German backing, compelled him to leave the country. On 6 September Antonescu took his oath of allegiance to Michael I, Carol's son. With a realistic assessment of the strength of the Iron Guard after its cruel persecution under Carol, the German leadership had avoided supporting a revolutionary development. Antonescu was regarded as a suitable person to meet Germany's interests. On 7 September Antonescu assured Colonel. Alfred Gerstenberg, the German air attaché and deputy military attaché, that he was determined to co-operate with Germany 'one hundred per cent', to restructure the army and reduce its size, and to shift the focus of defence towards the Soviet Union. He renewed the request for the dispatch of a German military mission.[41] On 11 September 1940 Hitler concurred.

Along with the army and the administration, Antonescu based his regime predominantly on the Legion movement, with which he himself had long sympathized and which, following its recognition as the 'only political force' in Romania, recorded a massive increase in membership. On 14 September 1940 King Michael I signed a decree which proclaimed Romania a 'national Legion state'.[42] Antonescu became leader of the state and chief of the Legion regime; he nominated Horia Sima, the commander of the Legion movement, to the post of vice-premier. The task of the Legion was to be the 'moral and material elevation of the nation'.[43] However, the alliance between the conservative-authoritarian Antonescu and the revolutionary terrorist Sima soon led to conflicts, as the Legion was not content with sharing power but was usurping governmental responsibilities for itself.

In mid-September Lieutenant-General von Tippelskirch, deputy chief of staff (intelligence) in the Army General Staff, flew to Bucharest in order to initiate military collaboration between Germany and Romania, as requested by General Antonescu. He was to establish 'an estimate of instruction teams that would be required and an estimate of the officers required for the training and organization of the new army, and for schools of all descriptions'.[44]

[41] OKH/GenStdH/Att.Abt. No. 3290/40, 8 Sept. 1940, BA-MA H 27/9.
[42] Fătu and Spălăţelu, *Eiserne Garde*, 247.   [43] Nagy-Talavera, *Green Shirts*, 310–11.
[44] Tippelskirch's report on his dicussions in Bucharest, 15–17 Sept. 1940, BA-MA H 27/9, and *DGFP* D xi, No. 75.

However, behind Antonescu's request for a German military mission there was more than the hope of assistance with personnel and material in the development of a numerically reduced but now truly useful Romanian army. He was hoping for a military alliance with Germany and wished to have German troops in the country, as he considered a Soviet attack possible at any moment. On the strength of Tippelskirch's report and the detailed Romanian proposals concerning the purpose, composition, and function of a German military mission, Hitler decided that this should comprise a mission each of the army and of the Luftwaffe, as well as a reinforced division—the 13th Motorized Infantry Division—as an instructional unit. On 20 September 1940 the OKW chief of staff issued a directive defining the 'real tasks' of the military mission:

(a) to protect the oilfields from seizure by a third power and from destruction;

(b) to enable the Romanian army to carry out definite tasks in accordance with an effective plan developed in favour of German interests;

(c) in case a war with Soviet Russia is forced upon us, to prepare for the commitment of German and Romanian forces from the direction of Romania.[45]

Thus two aspirations of the German leadership, which, because of the confused political situation in Romania, had been pursued separately ever since the beginning of July 1940, were now linked together—safeguarding the Romanian petroleum region and tying Romania into the war against the Soviet Union.

Although at his conference with the commander-in-chief of the army on 21 July 1940 Hitler had stressed the need to protect the Romanian oil region, he had not then considered an attack by German troops striking out of Romania or the participation of Romanian units in a war against the Soviet Union.[46] By contrast, Major-General Marcks in his 'draft operations plan East' of 5 August 1940 believed that an attack against Soviet troops in the Ukraine from Romanian territory should not be dispensed with merely because 'political reasons might prevent any deployment there before the beginning of the war'.[47] In the event of a German–Soviet war Marcks expected not only Romania's participation in the conquest of Bessarabia, but demanded that this country effect 'the occupation of Odessa and the Crimea with its important naval bases'. That requirement greatly exceeded Romania's military potential. Lieutenant-Colonel (General Staff) von Loßberg in his 'operational study East' of 15 September 1940 had regarded the instructional troops of the German military mission 'as pre-dispatched personnel of the German southern wing', though they were also intended to diminish the danger of a Soviet 'attempt to seize the

---

[45] These instructions were to be kept secret both from the Romanians and from the German forces: *DGFP* D xi, No. 84. See also ObdH/GenStdH/Org.Abt. II No. 352/40, 24 Sept. 1940, BA-MA RH 27-13/2.

[46] Halder, *Diaries*, 515 ff. (22 July 1940). See sects. I.v.2 at n. 35 (Förster) and I.iv.1(b) at n. 66 (Klink).

[47] 'Operationsentwurf Ost', 118. See sect. I.iv.1(d) after n. 99 (Klink).

Romanian oil region', which Loßberg regarded as probable.[48] Lieutenant-Colonel (General Staff) Kinzel, head of the 'foreign armies East' department, however, did not believe the Soviet command capable of such an operation. A thrust into Romania, designed to destroy the oilfields, would, if successful, be most awkward for the German conduct of the war because it would then have to rely on stockpiles of mineral oil. 'As, however, the Russians in all probability will *not* start a war, and we therefore have the preventive capability, such a bold Russian decision need not be expected.'[49]

In addition to the army and air-force military missions, a military-economics mission was dispatched, even though Romania had not requested it and was therefore surprised by its arrival. Its tasks were identical with those assigned, in the event of the country's occupation, to the 'Military economics staff for Romania': development and utilization for the German war effort of Romania's economic potential.

On 12 October 1940 the advance parties of the German army and air-force missions arrived in Bucharest with their commanding officers, General of Cavalry Erik Hansen und Lieutenant-General Wilhelm Speidel, together with officers of the economic mission.[50] By mid-November the transfer of the instructional unit R I—the reinforced 13th Motorized Infantry Division under Major-General Friedrich-Wilhelm von Rothkirch und Panthen—was completed. The Luftwaffe units—two fighter squadrons, a reconnaissance squadron, and two anti-aircraft batteries—had arrived in Romania earlier. By the end of 1940 the instructional troops had been reinforced by the 16th Armoured Division under Major-General Hans Hube (instructional unit R II) and by further Luftwaffe units.

In line with the 'real tasks' of the German Wehrmacht in Romania, the general training and equipment of the Romanian army—which were the Romanian general staff's principal interest—had the lowest priority among German objectives. Precedence was given to preparatory work for the deployment of German troops to operate against the Soviet Union from Romania, involving preferentially trained Romanian 'model divisions', and to the protection of Romanian petroleum (oil wells, refineries, storage tanks, transshipment locations) by Luftwaffe units and by the 'Brandenburg' instructional regiment of the Abwehr (military intelligence). The Romanian air force was to be trained for that purpose and, 'as far as possible, for later combined operations

[48] Bezymenskij, *Sonderakte 'Barbarossa'* (1968), 308; Halder, *Diaries*, 715 (2 Dec. 1940). See sect. I.iv.1(*d*) at n. 99 (Klink).

[49] Comment dated 27 Sept. 1940, BA-MA, 18. Armee, 17562/9. See ch. I.1 n. 44, and sect. I.iv.1(*d*) at nn. 103 ff. (Klink).

[50] The army and Luftwaffe commanding officers sent to Romania were known from 10 Oct. onward—for political and camouflage reasons—as 'Commander of the German Army/Air Force Mission in Romania'. The senior officer among them (in 1940 this was Cavalry Gen. Hansen) was responsible for all issues concerning both services. In that capacity he bore the designation 'Chief of the German Wehrmacht Mission in Romania'. Under his command came also a number of lesser Wehrmacht establishments for transport, signals, and intelligence tasks, as well as the war-economy mission.

with Romanian army forces'.[51] The catalogue of tasks of the German naval mission, sent to Romania only about mid-February 1941 under Vice-Admiral Friedrich-Wilhelm Fleischer, was likewise divided into 'ostensible tasks' and 'real tasks'. Outwardly it was to advise the Romanian navy in training its units and in coastal defence. But its real task was 'to ensure unified defence of the Romanian–Bulgarian Black Sea coast against attacks by a third power [i.e. the Soviet Union] from the sea' during impending operations against Greece (Operation Marita).[52] Beyond that, 'offensive tasks in the Black Sea' were envisaged, for which the Romanian units were to be prepared 'within the framework of the limited possibilities available'.[53] For reasons of prestige Italy too sent a small number of naval and Alpini officers to Romania as instructors. They had been requested by Antonescu at the Italian government's suggestion.[54] After all, the second Vienna award and the guarantee of Romania's new frontiers had been jointly underwritten by both Axis powers.

The transfer of German troops to Romania created a variety of financial and supply problems. Antonescu had promised that his country would bear the cost of the military mission and the instructional units. The German leadership agreed to his request that he be allowed to pay a lump sum, as it did not wish to jeopardize Antonescu's domestic standing or let the German troops become the object of political squabbles within the country.[55] It therefore accepted a monthly contribution of 100m. lei (approximately RM2m.), even though the budgeted amount was nearly four times that sum.[56] For financial reasons the Romanian leadership declined to make a contribution towards the costs of instructional unit R II.[57] The maintenance costs and the purchases of the Wehrmacht mission led to price increases, shortages, and growing inflation in Romania. This resulted in a decline of the Romanian currency's purchasing power and did not exactly make the German troops popular with the public. Directives and orders of the Wehrmacht mission urging restraint in official and private purchases failed to achieve their purpose.

3. MILITARY ASPECTS OF ROMANIA'S INCLUSION IN THE BARBAROSSA PLAN

On 23 November 1940 Romania joined the Tripartite Pact and fully integrated herself in Hitler's political strategy against the Soviet Union. On that occasion Antonescu assured Hitler and Ribbentrop of his readiness 'with weapon in

---

[51] *DGFP* D xi, No. 84 (21 Sept. 1940).

[52] OKW/WFSt/Abt. L (I op) No. 44123/41, 15 Feb. 1941, PA, Handakte Ritter, No. 26.

[53] 1. Skl I op No. 218/41, 26 Feb. 1941, BA-MA PG 32087 c.

[54] *DGFP* D xi, No. 192 (18 Oct. 1940), and ibid. xi, No. 346 (16 Nov. 1940); minute by Ambassador Ritter, 19 Feb. 1941, PA, Handakte Ritter, No. 26.

[55] Minute by Ambassador Clodius, 14 Nov. 1940: Hegemann, 'Heeresmission', No. 28.

[56] Minute by Ambassador Clodius, 12 Dec. 1940, PA U.St.S., Stromkommission; Militärmission in Rumänien; Bled.

[57] Rum. Gr. Gen. Stab No. 8737/G, 17 Dec. 1940, BA-MA RH 31-I/16.

hand, to fight alongside the Axis powers for the victory of civilization'. Standing behind the regime of Carol II had been the 'dark forces of Bolshevism and Jewry'. He, by contrast, wished to contribute to the victory of the Axis and not merely join the Tripartite Pact.[58] This clearly pro-German avowal was bracketed by Antonescu with an equally clear demand for the revision, in Romania's favour, of the second Vienna award once the war was over. The Romanian leader also emphasized to Keitel the importance of his country as a base for an offensive against the Soviet Union and expressed the conviction that 'with two motorized divisions' he 'could, if necessary, break through the Russian front and advance in the direction of Kiev'.[59] In his conference with the Wehrmacht leaders on 5 December 1940 Hitler therefore proceeded from the assumption that Romania—like Finland—would participate in the war against the Soviet Union, as its future was linked to Germany's victory.[60]

Judging by Antonescu's programmatic statements, Romania's participation was thus no longer a political problem but merely a question of the usefulness of the Romanian army. Hitler's political calculations found themselves under threat from the critical exacerbation of Romanian internal politics after the end of November 1940. The reason was that Horia Sima and the Iron Guard were not satisfied with the sharing of power or with Romania's transformation to date. By their political radicalism and their selective terrorism against hated representatives of the old system, which did not stop even at the army, they had undermined Antonescu's supreme authority in Romania. Since support for the Iron Guard by members of the NSDAP's foreign organization and the SS or SD had become obvious, the army command advised Antonescu 'to shift the focus of his leaning upon Germany to the chief of the Wehrmacht mission'.[61] Although the German commanding officers in Romania had been instructed to keep out of domestic politics, this did not rule out personal sympathies for an Iron Guard Romania. Generals Hansen and Speidel, therefore, did not conceal from their officers that they not only regarded a settlement of the differences between the army and the Guard as useful for political reasons, but also supported it on ideological grounds.

At the beginning of January 1941 Antonescu began his 'flight forward'. He requested permission to visit Hitler in order to discuss with him in person 'questions of defence policy and defence preparedness', as well as of Romanian domestic politics. The Romanian leader wanted to make sure of Hitler's support in his struggle for power in Romania. In a memorandum Antonescu emphasized his readiness for participation in offensive action against the Soviet Union. However, he made that promise conditional on his being recognized in future as the 'sole authority' for Romania's foreign and domestic

---

[58] *DGFP* D xi, Nos. 381, 387; see Förster, 'Rumäniens Weg', 63 ff.

[59] *DGFP* D xi, No. 388; Tippelskirch, minute dated 2 Dec. 1940, BA-MA RH 2/v. 1479.

[60] Halder, *KTB* ii. 213 (5 Dec. 1940; not in trans.); see also sect. I.iv.1(e) at n. 126 (Klink).

[61] Semi-official letter from Col. Emil Just, German military attaché in Bucharest, to Lt.-Gen. von Tippelskirch, 30 Nov. 1940, BA-MA III H 1001/7.

policy. That was an indirect criticism of the multi-track policy pursued by National Socialist Germany towards national-Legionnaire Romania. The Romanian leader's 'soldier-like' procedure was successful. On 14 January 1941 Hitler assured him that he 'was the only man capable of guiding the destiny of Romania'.[62] Hi, However, Hitler advised him to assume at the same time the leadership of the Iron Guard, as it was impossible to govern against it. During the preparatory phase of Barbarossa the only consideration that mattered to the German leadership was the smooth functioning of co-operation in all military and economic fields. Any shared ideology between the NSDAP and the Iron Guard was of secondary importance.

German calculations, however, were threatened when from 20 to 24 January there took place a rebellion of the Iron Guard against Antonescu's rule. Admittedly, his liquidation had long been planned by members of the NSDAP's foreign organization and by the SS or the SD. The precipitate revolt of the Iron Guard was triggered when Antonescu used the assassination of a German officer—probably by a British secret-service agent—as a pretext for a strike against the Guard. Hitler, referring to his own measures against the SA leaders on 30 June 1934, advised him to act ruthlessly. On 21 January 1941 the German troops had received clear orders to 'come out unambiguously in favour of General Antonescu and his leadership in official and unofficial statements' and to advise the Iron Guard to come to terms with him.[63] Thus the Guard's hopes that the Wehrmacht mission would intervene on its side were shattered. With the help of the army Antonescu quashed the revolt. The fact that German quarters enabled Horia Sima and many of his followers to escape to Germany, and subsequent interventions in favour of the 'sound kernel of the Legion' as guarantor of Romania's loyalty to the alliance, reveal the continued multi-track character of German policy vis-à-vis Romania. Horia Sima and his followers were detained in camps in the Reich, 'as a kind of reserve in case of revolution'.[64] Antonescu, whose position after the elimination of the Iron Guard was now unassailable, established a military dictatorship in Romania. In mid-February 1941 he proceeded to abolish the 'national-Legionnaire state' officially and pursued Romania's internal consolidation without the remnants of the compromised Legion movement. In doing so he did not dispense with the 'decorum of a referendum',[65] from which, however, women and Jews were excluded. The plebiscite on his policy of unity and tranquillity, discipline and order, at the beginning of March 1941 produced the expected result of almost a hundred per cent approval.

From the beginning of December 1940 Romania's participation in the war against the Soviet Union was regarded as a certainty by the German leadership, and in two respects: as a deployment base for a German army and as a military ally. Directive No. 21 of 18 December 1940 therefore defined the task of the Romanian army as 'to support the attack of the German southern flank,

---

[62] DGFP D xi, No. 652.   [63] BA-MA RH 31-I/v. 26.
[64] Rhode, 'Südosteuropäische Staaten', 1155.   [65] Ibid.

at least at the outset, with its best troops, to hold down the enemy where German forces are not engaged, and to provide auxiliary services in the rear areas'.[66]

The operations department met that objective by earmarking Romanian units for safeguarding the rearward army areas in the sector of Army Group South.[67] The Army High Command, on the other hand, was in conflict with Directive No. 21 in that, in its deployment order for the offensive of the German southern wing, it also envisaged an offensive thrust by the Twelfth Army out of Romania. What Halder had in mind was the capture of Odessa by way of a coup. Army Group South thereupon demanded the creation of three Romanian task forces of altogether 12–16 infantry divisions, the entire cavalry, the motorized brigade, and the appropriate army troops. In addition, as many units as possible were thought desirable for occupation and security tasks.[68]

In mid-February the chief of staff of the army mission, Colonel (General Staff) Arthur Hauffe, was briefed on the German intentions by the operations department of the Army General Staff and confronted with the military and political requests of Army High Command and of Army Group South:

(a) *Active participation of Romania* under German supreme command by the participation of core divisions within the framework of the attacking forces (about 3 divisions), by the participation of further forces for pinning-down tasks (about 3 divisions), by the provision of occupation forces as the operation progresses (about 4 divisions), by undertaking coastal defence and cover along the *Yugoslav* frontier (about 5 divisions). About 3 divisions would be required as a reserve within the country, bringing the total requirement of Romanian forces to about 18 divisions.

. . .

(c) Establishment of peaceful conditions inside Romania through an arrangement between Antonescu and the Legion and the enlistment of its valuable elements in the state; reorganization measures within the army to produce the necessary foundation for the creation of a useful corps of leaders, of morale and discipline, as required for modern conditions; release of all dispensable forces from the army back into the economy, especially into agriculture, with the objective of raising agricultural production as early as 1941 to the level corresponding to Romania's capability.[69]

Unrealistic military demands made by the operations department, such as the proposed establishment of ethnic German and Legionnaire units, or 'purging the army of Freemason, Jewish, and pro-British elements', were successfully opposed by the army mission. Both it and the intructional staff R I had a very low opinion of the combat efficiency of the Romanian army.

---

[66] *Hitler's Directives*, No. 21.
[67] Op.Abt. (I N) No. 025/40 to GenQu, 15 Jan. 1941, BA-MA RH 2/v. 1325.
[68] H.Gr. A (Süd) Ia No. 151/41, 12 Feb. 1941, BA-MA RH 19 I/67 b.
[69] OKH/GenStdH/Op.Abt. (I), 15 Feb. 1941, Besprechungspunkte für Oberst Hauffe [Points for discussison with Col. Hauffe], BA-MA RH 31-I/v. 40; AOK 12, Ia, No. 0141, 28 Feb. 1941, ibid.

Although there was a perceptible desire on the Romanian side to acquire German 'experience' and utilize it in its training programmes, the fact was that only those units lucky enough 'to be commanded by officers not corrupted by regulations (adapted to French military doctrine) would fully prove their mettle in combat'.[70] The three 'core division' (5th, 6th, and 13th Infantry Divisions) of the first echelon would presumably be fit for use in 'medium-type defensive tasks', and could perhaps even follow the German formations as a second echelon in order to perform 'easy offensive tasks as "nettoyeurs"'.[71] On no account could they be considered for independent offensive tasks. The rest of the first echelon was fit only for security and guard duties. Some of the mountain and cavalry brigades might perhaps be suitable for easy duties. With regard to the overall command and to confidentiality, General Hansen also drew the German leadership's attention to the peculiarities of the German–Romanian alliance.[72]

Until then, only purely defensive measures in the event of a Soviet attack on the province of Moldavia had been discussed with Antonescu. Complete secrecy about the intended participation of Romanian formations in the German attack against the Soviet Union was considered possible by the chief of the army mission only until about 20 March. He therefore thought it necessary to brief 'the leader of the state alone' without delay. In this connection General Hansen also wished to clarify the question of subordination status 'in order to create from the outset a reasonably sound basis for this difficult coalition war'. Hansen's proposal was supported a few days later by the request of General Joanitiu, the chief of the Romanian general staff, who wished to have defined 'anything that was necessary for joint coalition-type action by the German instructional troops and the Romanian units, especially in Moldavia'.[73] However, the chief of the operation department in the Army General Staff, Colonel (General Staff) Adolf Heusinger, instructed the army mission not to make any contact with Antonescu which would exceed the past framework. 'On no account must he be told anything that would allow of any kind of conclusions about our overall intentions.'[74]

On 17 March Hitler, by way of obvious criticism of the Army High Command's operations plan, decided to concentrate the main effort of Army Group South at Lublin and to dispense with any 'attack designed to be decisive or the employment of an armoured division' out of Romania.[75] In-

---

[70] Lehrstab R I/Abt. Ia No. 516/40 to DHM, 20 Dec. 1940, BA-MA RH 27-13/11.

[71] DHM/Abt. Ia No. 104/41 to OKH/GenStdH Op.Abt., 14 Feb. 1941, BA-MA RH 31-I/v. 26. OKH acted upon this assessment and requested Army Group South to regulate the deployment of the Romanian forces in conjunction with the German Army Mission: (OKH) GenStdH/ Op.Abt. (I S) No. 261/41, 24 Feb. 1941, BA-MA RH 19 I/67 b.

[72] DHM/Abt. Ia No. 70/41, 4 Mar. 1941, BA-MA RH 31-I/v. 40. The overall strength of the Romanian army on 22 June 1941 was 22 divisions and 15 brigades.

[73] DHM/Der Chef des Generalstabes No. 90/41, 15 Mar. 1941, ibid.

[74] Letter from Heusinger to Hauffe, 20 Mar. 1941, ibid.

[75] Halder, Diaries, 632 (17 Mar. 1941); OKW/WFSt/Abt. L (I Op) No. 44326/41 (22 Mar. 1941), DGFP D xii, No. 195. See sect. I.IV.1(f) at n. 156.

stead, a defensive front of German and Romanian forces was to be established along the Pruth, so as, on the one hand, to prevent a penetration by Soviet formations and, on the other, to pin them down in Bessarabia. Only as the offensive of Army Group South progressed towards Kiev were the German–Romanian forces, by a follow-up push, to prevent an orderly retreat of the Red Army across the Dniester. Hitler made it clear to Halder and Heusinger that it was a fundamental mistake to attack everywhere. The Pruth and the Dniester were rivers at which any attack would get stuck. An operation must not count on formations which lacked offensive strength. Hitler thus fully accepted Hansen's assessment. On 27 March 1941 Field Marshal von Brauchitsch, the commander-in-chief of the army, bluntly told the commanding officers of the army groups, armies, and armoured groups that the Romanian army was useless.[76]

In the absence of Twelfth Army HQ, still tied up with Operation Marita, the command of the German–Romanian forces in Romania was entrusted to Eleventh Army HQ under Colonel-General Eugen Ritter von Schobert.

As it became progressively more difficult to conceal the German deployment against the Soviet Union, and as Hitler therefore expected Soviet preventive measures, especially against the regions of Petsamo and Ploiesti, the Luftwaffe mission in Romania was repeatedly instructed to ensure at all costs the protection of the Romanian oil region, described as 'vital to the German war effort'.[77] To that end not only were the German air-force units reinforced, but a German infantry division (originally the 22nd, subsequently the 72nd) was transferred to the Ploiesti region in addition to a Romanian division. Locations listed as air-defence zones included not only the centre of oil extraction and refining near Ploiesti—here was the main effort of the anti-aircraft artillery and of III Wing of 52 Fighter Group—but also the transshipment and storage ports of Constanta and Giurgiu, as well as the railway bridge near Cernovada, where the oil pipeline also crossed the Danube.

Subordinate to the Luftwaffe mission, which came tactically under the chief of the Wehrmacht mission, were the commander of fighter aircraft, an AA divisional staff, several AA regiments and additional AA batteries, special fire-fighting units, Luftwaffe construction troops, and signal units, approximately 50,000 men. By mid-June 1941 some 60 fighters, and 348 20-mm. AA guns, 45 37-mm. AA guns, and 144 88-mm. AA guns were employed for the protection of Germany's mineral-oil supplies in Romania.[78] In addition, there were Romanian fighter and anti-aircraft units. On 18 June Lieutenant-General Speidel, the commander of the Luftwaffe mission, was optimistic that 'the superiority of our men and the quality of our weapons' would decide that campaign as well. His parting wish to the AA gunners and the fighters was

[76] Conference notes of C.-in-C. Eighteenth Army, BA-MA 18. Armee, 19601/2.

[77] OKW/WFSt/Abt. L (I Op) No. 44335/41, 26 Mar. 1941, BA-MA RW 4/v. 575.

[78] DLM/Abt. Ia No. 1092/41, 14 June 1941, BA-MA RL 9/53; DLM/Abt. Ia (Op 1) No. 887/41, 20 June 1941, BA-MA RL 9/54.

'Good hunting!' Exceeding the strict combat tasks of the Luftwaffe mission, Speidel also drew the attention of his officers to the ideological character of the eastern campaign. Göring, he said, had given unambiguous orders, concerning Russians taken prisoner, 'that every Bolshevik official [*Hoheitsträger*]' was 'to be instantly shot without any judicial proceedings'. Every officer was entitled to do this.[79]

The German naval mission reported before the opening of Barbarossa that whereas the coastal defences were ready for action, the employment of Romanian naval units was not to be counted on. The reasons given by Vice-Admiral Fleischer were a lack of fighting spirit on the part of the Romanian navy, especially its officers, as well as its extremely low level of training. For the defence of Constanta German heavy naval gunnery units had been deployed and preparations made for the laying of mine-barriers.[80]

The army's deployment preparations in Romania began towards the end of March 1941. The two armoured divisions (the 13th and the 16th), until then used as instructional units, were pulled out and seven infantry divisions (the 22nd, 50th, 72nd, 76th, 170th, 198th, and 239th) brought in instead. These measures, as well as the arrival and establishment of Eleventh Army HQ (AOK 11) and of XI, XXX, and LIV Corps HQs, were to be 'strictly disguised from the Romanians as nothing more than a precautionary measure to meet a possible Russian attack'.[81] For that reason also the training of the Romanian formations earmarked for action was to be continued as long as possible. This order from OKH was thought by Hansen to be naïve. His marginal gloss was: 'Surely this will make the Romanians *laugh*. They are not *that* gullible.'

A few days earlier, Antonescu had sounded out Manfred Freiherr von Killinger, the German minister, about German intentions towards the Soviet Union. He had judged the chances of a German attack to be very favourable 'as long as the support of England by the United States of America was not yet effective'. Such an operation, which, according to Antonescu, offered the advantage of the 'elimination of the Slavic danger . . . and opening up of the routes to the oilfields', could be succesfully accomplished within a month. Killinger, in accordance with his instructions, had been non-committal.[82] The next steps of the German military leadership in Romania *vis-à-vis* the Romanian authorities were discussed in Bucharest in mid-May, four weeks after a working staff of Eleventh Army HQ had been secretly installed in the army mission.[83] Colonel (General Staff) Hauffe and Lieutenant-Colonel (General Staff) Theodor Busse, the first general-staff officer of the army command, agreed on performing the German–Romanian deployment preparations in a

[79] Record of commanding officers' conference, 18 June 1941, BA-MA RL 9/85. See sect. I.vii.2(*c*) (Förster).

[80] KTB DMM, entry of 19 May 1941, BA-MA RM 45/v. 11/698/45605; KTB Admiral Südost, entry of 14 June 1941, BA-MA RM 35 III/5.

[81] OKH/GenStdH/Op.Abt. (I) No. 792/41, 3 May 1941, BA-MA RH 31-I/v. 40.

[82] *DGFP* D xii, No. 416 (28 Apr. 1941).

[83] Minute of a conference on 15 May 1941, BA-MA RH 31-I/v. 40.

three-stage pattern, staggered in terms of time and character. The order for the Barbarossa deployment was to go only to the German corps HQs and to the army mission; an operations directive for the Romanian army concerning the defence of Moldavia and a possible follow-up in the event of an evading movement by the Red Army was to be passed on to the Romanian general staff, and only much later was an army order for the preparation of the attack to go also to the Romanians. On 24 May the commander-in-chief of Eleventh Army, Colonel-General Ritter von Schobert, assumed the protection of the entire Romanian state territory as 'commander-in-chief of German troops in Romania'. The heads of the Wehrmacht and armament missions were placed under his command. As for his report to the Romanian head of state, he had clear instructions from Hitler to explain the deployment of the German army formations as preventive measures against a surprise attack by the Red Army and to be evasive with regard to Antonescu's questions on 'whether Germany expected a war against the Soviet Union or whether Germany, if necessary, would attack Russia'.[84] The game of hide-and-seek with the Romanians therefore continued. On 26 May 1941 the head of the army mission informed the chief of the Romanian general staff of Germany's wish that the formations in the province of Moldavia should be brought up to combat strength, that the defensive line should be manned by 10 June 1941, and that reserves should be moved up. General Hansen had been instructed to avoid the word 'mobilization'.[85] There had been a German suggestion as early as 3 April 1941 that the formations be brought up to two-thirds of their combat strength and that they should 'slowly creep into' their positions.

On 28 May 1941 the German formations received the 'Order for the preparation of the Barbarossa deployment', the first step in the preparations for the German–Romanian operational deployment. This order, which also laid down the tasks of the Romanian forces, was still to be kept secret from the Romanians.[86] General Hansen, the commander-in-chief designate of LIV Army Corps, in a note to Major-General Hauffe, designated his successor as head of the army mission, criticized such treatment of the Romanians. The Romanian general staff, he believed, could not be expected to observe directives from Eleventh Army without prior agreement on a coalition war. While the German troops were now beginning to prepare for an attack across the upper Pruth in the general direction of Vinnitsa (Operation Munich), the German high command on 9 June 1941 issued to the Romanian general staff no more than the general 'Directives for safeguarding and defending Romania's frontiers against Russia'.[87] In this context the German troops would form the mobile striking force of the defence, 'in order to render it active and, if

---

[84] OKW/WFSt/Abt. L (I Op) No. 44780/41, 23 May 1941, ibid.
[85] DHM/Abt. Ia No. 531/41, 27 May 1941, ibid. 29.
[86] Command of German army troops in Romania, Ia No. 0051/41, 28 May 1941, ibid. 41. The instruction was supplemented by order Ia No. 0091/41, 9 June 1941, ibid. 39.
[87] Command of German army troops in Romania, Ia No. 0078/41, 9 June 1941, ibid. 15.

necessary, to attack the enemy with a swift blow and to destroy him'. These directives resembled the then largely outdated instructions to Eleventh Army of 28 May 1941.

German–Romanian co-operation against the Soviet Union in the military-political and operational spheres was eventually defined in a personal conversation between Hitler and Antonescu on 12 June 1941, without, however, any formal military alliance or agreement on common war aims. Whereas Hitler expected Romania to facilitate the prosecution of his war, Antonescu had come to Munich to place Romania's total military, political, and social forces at Hitler's disposal for the repulsion of the 'Slavic menace'. He was ready to join the conflict from the very first day, declaring that 'Romania would never forgive him [Antonescu] for letting the Romanian army remain inactive while the German forces in Romania were marching against the Russians'. Although Hitler had expressly refused to ask Antonescu for support for Operation Barbarossa, he accepted the Romanian offer with the assurance of 'indemnities' which would have 'no territorial limitations'.[88] On the question of the supreme command of the German–Romanian troops, Hitler explained:

An operation extending from the Arctic Ocean to the Black Sea requires unified central control. This is quite naturally in our hands. We must avoid the mistakes of past coalition wars. Every ally shares in the total glory. But I should like you, General Antonescu, to emerge fully, before your nation and before history, as the victorious leader of your armed forces in this historic struggle.[89]

That was why Hitler proposed that the German requirements concerning the Romanian armed forces be personally communicated to Antonescu. Eleventh Army HQ, as his working staff, was then to reformulate them into military orders and issue them over his signature. Antonescu happily agreed to that procedure and to the nominal supreme command over the German–Romanian forces in Romania. He had thus been personally briefed on Germany's actual intentions; not so, as yet, his general staff, the army commanders-in-chief, or the officer commanding the troops earmarked for the operation. In his new capacity of 'commander-in-chief of the army front Romania', Antonescu on 20 June 1941 at last issued the order which briefed the Romanian general staff beyond the defensive task on the concept of 'follow-up' and Operation Munich, i.e. on the attack across the Pruth.[90] An end had to be put, the order argued, to the intolerable threat to Europe represented by the Soviet Union's long-term preparations for attack. The Romanian armed forces would enter the conflict shoulder to shoulder with their German allies 'to redress the wrongs inflicted on us'. Antonescu charged Eleventh Army HQ with the processing of all instructions concerning the common conduct of the

---

[88] *DGFP* D xii, No. 614.

[89] OKW/WFSt/Abt. L (I Op) No. 44981/41, 17 June 1941, BA-MA RH 31-I/v. 40.

[90] Supreme army command. The C.-in-C. of army front Romania, Ia No. 0120/41, 20 June 1941, ibid. 39.

war. Orders of a fundamental nature concerning Romanian units not subordinated to Eleventh Army required Antonescu's signature or approval. On 22 June 1941 the new head of the army mission, Major-General Hauffe, assumed the duties of liaison officer between Eleventh Army and the Romanian army command. He thereby became, in his own estimation, the tactical and strategic adviser of Antonescu and the Romanian general staff 'on all questions of the Romanian and the joint conduct of the war'.[91] The other Romanian command authorities had 'German liaison officers' sent to them, whose duty it was to advise the Romanian commanders on leadership and training, to transmit orders from German command authorities, to supervise the execution of such orders, and to inform the German authorities on the situation.[92]

The Romanian army, which since mid-November 1940 had been drilled by the army mission for an offensively conducted 'forward defence' against a Soviet attack, was faced suddenly, on 20 June, with tasks which it was unable to cope with to the same extent as the German army. As recently as towards the end of May, Hansen, in his capacity of head of the Wehrmacht mission, had described the Romanian army as useless for 'difficult offensive actions'.[93] The only units which could be considered for 'easy attacks'—'alongside German forces and advised by German officers in their direction and verified in execution'—were the 5th, 6th, and 13th Infantry Divisions (the former 'core divisions'), the Frontier and Guards Divisions, the three cavalry brigades, three mountain brigades, and the motorized division (roughly a reinforced tank regiment). Because of the difficult supply situation and the non-motorized supply troops, these formations would be able to advance only as far as the Dniester. Their equipment with anti-tank and anti-aircraft guns was inadequate. It was impossible to apply 'the yardstick of German leadership and performance' to the Romanian command or its troops. Of the senior Romanian officers, apart from Antonescu, only Generals Iosif Iacobici, A. Joaţiu, Nicolae Tataranu, Nikolae Ciuperca, and A. Racoviţa were judged to be good; Petre Dumitrescu was considered insignificant and Eugen Vartejeanu anti-German. Although the divisional and brigade commanders were, generally speaking, up to their jobs, they almost invariably lacked the will to implement the intentions of the higher command. The reason for that state of affairs, according to General Hansen, was not only the prolonged vacillation of the political leadership but also the 'racial foundations'. These, he suggested, resembled those of the Italian army. The men's resistance to rumours and moods of panic was not very strong. Although the officers were well schooled in military theory, they often lacked, 'on racial grounds, hardness and depth', the will to hold out to the end. There

[91] Semi-official letter by Hauffe, 11 Jan. 1942, ibid. 94.

[92] DHM, Ia/Id No. 908/41, 22 May 1941, annexe 3, ibid. 29.

[93] Deutsche Wehrmachtmission in Rumänien, Ia No. 176/41 to OKW/WFSt/Abt. L, 30 May 1941, ibid. 40.

was virtually nothing like a corps of non-commissioned officers. The rank and file were undemanding, tough, and persistent. 'Under good leaders' they would acquit themselves well, especially in the defence of their country. The reconquest of Bessarabia, along with that of Transylvania, was a widely desired war aim.

In almost identical appeals to the unprepared Romanian nation and the troops, on 22 June 1941 Antonescu proclaimed the 'holy war' for the reconquest of the rights inherited from their fathers, and also against the greatest 'enemy of the world, Bolshevism'. Two days later came the official declaration of war against the Soviet Union.[94] Combat operations were at first confined to raiding-patrol forays, artillery duels, and air raids. On 25 June 1941 the Eleventh Army issued the 'Order for the execution of Operation Munich'.[95] The two Romanian armies (Third and Fourth) and the German corps (IX, XXX, and LIV) were to execute their deployment in such a way that the attack could be launched on 2 July. While the Romanian Fourth Army, with eight infantry divisions and one cavalry brigade, in accordance with Antonescu's orders, was initially to defend the Danube delta and part of the Pruth front, the Romanian Third Army, with six infantry divisions, three mountain and three cavalry brigades, and the only armoured brigade, were placed under the German Eleventh Army.[96] This was intended to attack in the general direction of Vinnitsa. On 1 July 1941, in an emphatic letter to Hitler, Antonescu once more confirmed the tasks of the Romanian army. He expressed his conviction that 'final victory' was to be expected very shortly, as the Red Army could already be regarded as smashed.[97]

Thus, from 22 June 1941 onwards Romania, without any formal alliance, participated in Hitler's war against the Soviet Union. While the reconquest of Bessarabia and the northern Bukowina was an aspiration shared by the whole nation, Antonescu was out for more. After the victory over the Soviet Union he expected, in view of Romania's massive contribution to the war, a revision in Romania's favour of the second Vienna award and of the treaty of Craiova. Moreover, immediately after Yugoslavia's occupation Antonescu had given notice of his claims to the rest of the Banat. Common ideological attitudes between authoritarian Romania and National Socialist Germany were to be found not only in the struggle against the 'Slav danger' and Bolshevism, but also in an underlying anti-Semitism. The 'holy war' proclaimed by Antonescu should not therefore be simply equated with the German propaganda slogan of 'Europe's crusade against Bolshevism'. Both motivations, the revisionist and the ideological, were contained in Antonescu's formula of the 'holy war'.

[94] Laeuen, *Antonescu*, 133; *Ursachen und Folgen*, xvii, No. 3146b.

[95] AOK 11, Ia No. 0129/41, 25 June 1941, BA-MA RH 31-I/v. 39; see sect. II.1.1(a) at n. 97 (Klink).

[96] Romanian historians list 12 divisions and 6 brigades. See *Der große Weltbrand*, 171.

[97] Copy in BA-MA RH 31-I/v. 94.

4. The Position of Hungary and Slovakia in the Preparatory Phase of Barbarossa

Unlike Romania and Finland, Hungary and Slovakia in 1940–1 were playing a subordinate role in German strategy. Although both these countries were included in military planning as deployment or transit areas, the political leadership made no attempts, prior to 22 June 1941, to win Hungary or Slovakia as allies in the war against the Soviet Union. For one thing, Hitler did not wish to conduct a coalition war—like the First World War—and for another he expected that both Budapest and Bratislava would, in exchange for appropriate political assurances, agree to whatever German demands were necessary concerning Barbarossa. After 22 June 1941, however, Hitler was ready to accept 'with enthusiasm' offers from other states to take part in Barbarossa.[98] Their participation, as well as that of volunteers, made it easy now for National Socialist propaganda to present its war of conquest and annihilation against the Soviet Union as a 'European crusade against Bolshevism'. An understanding of the historical and domestic- and foreign-policy motivations for the Hungarian and Slovak declarations of war (on 27 and 23 June 1941) requires a short review of the history of the two countries.

(a) Hungary

Hungary was one of the losers of the First World War.[99] Under the treaty of Trianon the kingdom of Hungary under its regent Miklós Horthy von Nagybánya had to cede large territories to Czechoslovakia (Slovakia and Ruthenia), to Yugoslavia (Croatia, Slovenia, Bácska and Baranya, and the western part of the Banat), and to Romania (Transylvania with the Székler territory and the eastern part of the Banat). Its area and population shrank from 282,000 square kilometres (without Croatia) and 18 million inhabitants to 93,000 square kilometres and 7.6 million. Three million Hungarians were now living outside Hungary, half of them in the immediately adjoining areas. Yet even this truncated Hungary remained a multinational state, with only 89.5 per cent of the population claiming Magyar as their language. The largest non-Hungarian ethnic group was the Germans, whose numbers in the course of the revisionist policy had grown to 800,000 by 1941. In its structure Hungary was an agrarian country. In 1930 some 52 per cent of the population were still living by agriculture; the figure in 1940 was approximately 50 per cent.[100] Despite an established parliamentary and pluralist party system, a feudal order continued to exist in Hungary. The 'Uniform Party' under Count István Bethlen succeeded in preventing a fundamental land reform in the twenties.

---

[98] *KTB OKW* i. 409 (24 June 1941).

[99] On the history of Hungary after the First World War see Silagi, 'Ungarn'; Juhász, *Hungarian Foreign Policy*; Hoensch, *Geschichte Ungarns*; Riemenschneider, *Wirtschaftspolitik gegenüber Ungarn*; Gosztony, 'Ungarns militärische Rolle', pt. 1. The author is indebted to Dr Josef Borus of the Hungarian Academy of Sciences, Budapest, for a wealth of verbal and written information.

[100] See Gunst, 'Politisches System', 406.

By 1935, therefore, 1,070 big estates (0.1 per cent of the total number of holdings) still accounted for over 30 per cent of the land. The Uniform Party was controlled by the upper stratum. From 1939 it called itself the 'Movement of Hungarian Life' and after the elections of May 1939 it supplied 70 per cent of all members of parliament. The second strongest political force in Hungary was the Fascist Arrow Cross Party under Ferenc Szálasi; this supported an unconditionally pro-German policy. With massive German support it achieved 20 per cent of all members of parliament in 1939.[101]

Hungarian foreign-policy was characterized by a passionate effort to achieve a revision of the peace treaty of Trianon. Against these revisionist aspirations Yugoslavia, Romania, and Czechoslovakia concluded a military alliance, the Little Entente. The fundamentally antagonistic foreign-policy interests of Hungary and Romania, which, along with a marked growth of extreme right-wing movements in both countries, facilitated National Socialist foreign-policy in south-east Europe, merely reflected the 'fundamental European split between the forces of revisionism and the defenders of the status quo, after 1920.[102] Born out of counter-revolution against Béla Kun's Communist republic of councils, the Horthy regime strove to preserve the existing social order; it was characterized by a militant anti-communism. In August 1936 Horthy, in line with Hitler's propaganda war against Bolshevism, declared that there was no salvation for mankind 'so long as the Soviet remained alive'.[103] Hostility to Bolshevism was the main ideology shared between National Socialist Germany and semi-feudal Hungary.

Premier Gyula Gömbös, the first European head of government to be received by Hitler, had been striving since 1933 for specific political collaboration between Germany and Hungary with the aim of achieving a revision of the First World War peace treaties. He supported his offer by referring to common ideological attitudes and to the German–Hungarian 'common destiny'. Although Hitler was prepared, by secretly granting Budapest preferential status, to facilitate the export of Hungarian agricultural produce to Germany—concessions he denied to Romania because of her close ties with France—he declined in January 1934 to conclude a consultative agreement with Hungary. Although she would give moral support to Hungary's revisionist aspirations, Germany would have to reserve to herself the right of differentiated bilateral relations with the individual members of the Little Entente, as German interest demanded. Hitler had no intention of pulling 'the chestnuts out of the fire' for Hungary.[104] This political slogan, however, did not prevent Colonel-General Beck, the chief of the Army General Staff, from trying, in the summer of 1935, to win over Hungary's military leaders for joint action with

---

[101] See Szöllösi-Janze, *Pfeilkreuzlerbewegung*.   [102] Broszat, 'Deutschland', 46.

[103] Quoted according to ibid. 83.

[104] The German motto in Nov. 1938 was 'to keep both irons in the fire and to shape matters in the German interest according to the way the situation develops': *DGFP* D v, No. 254, Ribbentrop's note.

Germany against Czechoslovakia. Beck succeeded in laying the foundations of German–Hungarian 'secret military diplomacy'.[105] The influence which German hegemony exercised on Budapest and Bucharest increased in line with the extent to which Hitler transformed the political scene of Europe. The occupation of Austria, the Munich agreement, the virtual disintegration of the Little Entente, and the economic appeasement of the Western powers *vis-à-vis* Germany caused the Hungarian–Romanian conflict to enter a new phase. The German attitude of allowing Hungary neither priority nor a free hand in achieving her territorial ambitions resulted in Budapest's readiness to make domestic- and foreign-policy concessions to German wishes. After Premier Kalman Darányi had issued in the spring of 1938 the first anti-Jewish law and banned over four hundred liberal and left-wing periodicals, as well as a dozen dailies,[106] his successor Béla Imrédy, in the autumn of that year, by accepting the first Vienna award of 2 November 1938, recognized Germany's and Italy's hegemony in Europe.[107] He not only did so as a matter of principle, but also contented himself with the acquisition of parts of southern Slovakia (12,400 square kilometres) inhabited by a large number (1.1 million) of Slovaks. Not until March 1939 was Hungary permitted to occupy Ruthenia (the Carpatho-Ukraine). Having officially joined the anti-Comintern pact on 24 February 1939, she left the League of Nations in mid-April. Hungary thus placed herself demonstratively on the side of the Axis at a time when the Western powers, by their guarantees to Poland, Romania, and Greece, were clearly endeavouring to oppose German expansion. In May 1939 the second anti-Jewish law was passed by parliament.

However, the foreign-policy of Count Pál Teleki's government after February 1939 was not one-sidedly aligned with Germany.[108] On the one hand it tried, with Mussolini's support, to balance the growing German pressure by emphasizing the Italian–Hungarian community of interests and, by its declaration of armed neutrality in the event of a German–Polish war, to prevent a break with the Western powers, while on the other Teleki, who himself came from Transylvania, hoped to use the European crisis to assert Hungary's revisionist aspirations *vis-à-vis* Romania. Military preparations for the occupation of Transylvania began in May 1939, deployment along the frontier on 23 August. Romania's offer of a non-aggression treaty was rejected. Teleki, admittedly, did not anticipate a great-power conflict over Poland, but expected another conference like that in Munich in 1938. At such a conference he would raise the Transylvanian problem.[109] If, however, Hungarian territorial demands were not to be satisfied in that way, then, as Teleki wrote to Mussolini on 2 September 1939, he was compelled to state that the Hungarian government would continue its military preparations 'quietly but resolutely' in

[105] See Müller, *Beck*, 153–4.
[106] Pintér, 'Oppositionelle und illegale Propaganda', 4 (unpub. manuscript).
[107] Juhász, *Hungarian Foreign Policy*, 147–8. [108] *Allianz Hitler-Horthy-Mussolini*, 51 ff.
[109] Broszat, 'Deutschland', 77–8.

order 'to put an end now and for a long time to the Romanian–Hungarian territorial question'.[110] Teleki's 'intransigent revisionist policy',[111] however, was blocked for the time being by the Western powers' declaration of war against Germany—a Hungarian attack on Romania might have meant implementation of the British–French guarantees of 13 April—and by German pressure.[112]

If Romania was regarded by Hungary as 'enemy number one', then Slovakia was number two. Hungary took the view that 'discontinuation of German support' would mean 'the end of Slovakia'. In his conversation with Admiral Canaris on 6 July 1939, Colonel István Ujszászy, chief of intelligence in the Hungarian general staff, stated that the British military attaché had promised Hungary the cession of Slovakia in the event of her siding with the Western powers. However, as Ujszászy emphasized Hungarian neutrality in a German–Polish conflict, Canaris regarded the outcome of the conversation as negative: 'Germany is to pull the chestnuts out of the fire for Hungary, while Hungary continues her two-sided policy.'[113]

After the outbreak of the European war Hungarian policy, while maintaining its independence and avoiding an open rupture with the Western powers, was aimed at achieving its revisionist objectives through close alignment with the Axis. A situation that could be made use of in the spirit of *sacro egoismo* arose in the winter and spring at the start of 1940. The German military leadership feared a landing by the Western powers in the Salonika area, aiming at Romania, and was considering a preventive occupation of the Romanian oilfields in order to safeguard its vital mineral-oil supplies. For that purpose the German general staff approached the Hungarian general staff at the beginning of 1940.[114] In mid-January, therefore, Lieutenant-General von Tippelskirch, deputy chief of staff (intelligence), suggested to his Hungarian opposite number, Colonel Ujszászy, that in the event of a major conflict it would be entirely in the German interest if Hungary, with German support, were to attack Romania. This cautious offer of joint action, by means of which the right of transit for German troops was to be gained, met with enormous interest in Hungary. After all, Ujszászy had proposed such 'joint action by Germany and Hungary in the settlement of the minorities issue in Romania' to Admiral Canaris at the beginning of July 1939. By way of justification Ujszászy had argued that Romania was part of 'Germany's living-space' and was Hungary's principal enemy. As Romania could be confidently expected to join the Western powers if war broke out, she had to be considered a common

---

[110] *Allianz Hitler-Horthy-Mussolini*, 58–9.   [111] Broszat, 'Deutschland', 78.

[112] See Tippelskirch, minute of 14 Nov. 1939: 'Werth: It cost the attaché a lot of money to stop things going off on 12 November' (BA-MA RH 2/v. 1478). Werth was the chief of the Hungarian general staff. See Nebelin, *Deutsche Ungarnpolitik*.

[113] Minute by Adm. Canaris of his conversation with Col. Újszászy on 6 July 1939, BA-MA RW 4/v. 334. See also the semi-official letter of the German military attaché in Budapest, Col. Freiherr von Wrede, to Lt.-Gen. von Tippelskirch, 6 May 1939, BA-MA III H 1001/6.

[114] See Förster, 'Rumäniens Weg', 54 ff.

enemy. At the beginning of 1940, therefore, Hungary had a fresh chance of regaining Transylvania. While the Germans were preparing for a contingency, the Hungarians were pressing for an early operation, which they would put off only if Romania succeeded in defending her territory against Soviet and Bulgarian claims.[115] When at the end of March 1940 the Soviet Union confirmed its claim to Bessarabia, the Hungarian command ordered the mobilization of two army corps[116] and made contact with the German general staff. At Hungary's request the German–Hungarian operation was to be under the supreme command of Horthy, who would appear in Transylvania as the liberator of the Hungarians from the Romanian yoke. At the beginning of April 1940 Budapest informed Berlin that it would permit German troops to cross Hungary to Romania. In September 1939 the same government had refused the use of Hungarian territory to the German command to facilitate its operations against Poland. Hungary now suggested that official general-staff consultations be held and that Italy be informed.

Once more, however, Hungarian and German interests in the Balkans were not identical. Hungarian urgings for a tripartite consultation with Germany and Italy about the Transylvanian problem, with emphasis on Hungary's sacrifices so far, met with rejection on Germany's part a few days before the beginning of the war in the west. Germany feared intervention by the Soviet Union and wanted tranquillity in the Balkans in order to use that region as an 'important source of supplies' for the German war effort.[117] The German–Romanian oil-for-arms treaty was about to be signed, provisional agreement having already been reached. Hitler did not rule out the possibility that Britain was behind Hungary's urgings. 'It would serve Britain's interest very well to have the oilfields [in Romania] blazing, and it would not matter who put the match to them. We vitally need the oil deliveries from the Romanian wells, at least until next spring. After that we should be freer.'[118] After agreement with Mussolini, to whom Hitler wished to concede the 'main say' in south-east Europe, the Hungarian government was given to understand that in the event of unilateral action against Romania she could not count on Axis aid. Halder noted in his diary: 'If Hungary does not fall in line, she will be turned into a protectorate.'[119] The great-power status which Germany had meanwhile attained and the relative ratio of strength implied the availability to her of the lesser countries of south-east Europe.

[115] Tippelskirch, minute of 25 Jan. 1940, BA-MA RH 2/v. 1478.
[116] Ibid., minute of 8 Apr. 1940. Col. Újszászy had told the German air attaché as early as the middle of Oct. 1939 that, in the event of the Soviet Union's taking possession of Bessarabia, Hungary would proceed to attack Transylvania (OKW/Ausl. No. 12136/39, BA-MA RW 4/v. 334).
[117] OKW/WFA/Abt. L No. 22004/40, 6 Jan. 1940, *DGFP* D viii, No. 514.
[118] Halder, *Diaries*, 330 (24 Apr. 1940).
[119] Ibid. 426 (26 May 1940). See also Tippelskirch, minute of 26 May 1940, BA-MA RH 2/v. 1478. The Hungarians objected to that kind of treatment, arguing that they had been egged on by Germany to take military measures against Romania. The 'secret military diplomacy' initiated by Beck and continued by Halder had developed a momentum of its own, which was now running counter to German interests.

Hitler rejected the idea of any official general-staff conferences between Germany, Italy, and Hungary about common action against Romania. He merely agreed to contacts 'of the most cautious kind' concerning railway matters with Colonel-General Henrik Werth, chief of the Hungarian general staff, regarded as pro-German. On the one hand, Hitler was anxious to keep the Balkans quiet, viewing the contemplated occupation of the Romanian oilfields as a defensive move in the event of a Soviet or Anglo-French action.[120] On the other, he considered the Hungarians 'unreliable' and referred to them and the British as 'one heart and one soul'.[121] Britain too warned Hungary in June 1940 against enabling Germany to attack Romania from her territory, as Romania held a British guarantee. This diplomatic initiative in Romania's favour offended the Hungarians. With a clear allusion to the Hungarians' different basic attitude towards Poland and Romania, Premier Count Teleki pointed out that there was not a single Hungarian 'who would defend Romania, no matter against whom, with his life'.[122]

The Hungarian–Romanian conflict entered a new phase in the summer of 1940. Hitler's victory over France and Stalin's annexation of the Baltic States and of Bessarabia and the northern Bukowina started a race to Berlin between Bucharest and Budapest. While Carol II was trying to save Romania from a renewed territorial amputation by foreign, domestic, and economic concessions, Hungary's foreign minister, Count István Csáky, emphasized Hungary's title to Transylvania. To achieve that foreign-policy objective, the Hungarian leadership complied with the German economic demands to the limit of the country's capabilities.[123] On 27 June the Hungarian council of ministers declared that Hungary would not this time tolerate any discrimination. If the Romanian government was meeting the Soviet demands, it had to be compelled to meet Hungary's territorial demands as well.[124] That political resolution triggered preparatory military measures along the frontier with Romania. Berlin and Rome were informed, with foreign minister Count Csáky emphasizing that his government would find itself in a difficult position if, on the advice of the Axis powers, it were to continue to practise restraint. Hungary would prefer to reconquer Transylvania in battle. The army was urging that course. It would not tolerate 'another demobilization without prior political victories'.[125] Ribbentrop thereupon promised Hungary a German–Italian examination of 'revisions in the Balkans'. The precondition, however, was that the Hungarian government would follow Germany's advice and not resort to a 'violent solution' of its territorial claims.[126] The German leadership

---

[120] Conference note by Gen. Thomas following his report to the chief of staff of the Wehrmacht High Command, 26 Apr. 1940, BA-MA RW 19/185.

[121] Halder, *Diaries*, 330 (24 Apr. 1940).

[122] Letter to the Hungarian ministers in London and Washington, *Allianz Hitler-Horthy-Mussolini*, No. 93.

[123] Ibid., No. 85; *DGFP* D x, No. 194 (20 July 1940). On the problems besetting German–Hungarian economic relations see Volkmann, 'Außenhandel und Aufrüstung', 114–15.

[124] *Allianz Hitler-Horthy-Mussolini*, 69.   [125] *DGFP* D x, No. 69 (1 July 1940).

[126] Ibid., No. 105 (4 July 1940).

feared that the Soviet Union might use a Hungarian–Romanian conflict to act against Romania in order to cut off Germany's oil imports. Towards the end of August 1940 Germany and Italy imposed an arbitration award on Hungary and Romania, which made Hungary appear as the victor but failed to eliminate Romanian–Hungarian antagonism. Hungary regained less than the 50,000 square kilometres laid down as early as autumn 1939 as the minimal solution, in fact a mere 43,492 square kilometres, although she had originally demanded the whole of Transylvania (78,000 square kilometres) and only reluctantly accepted the award.[127]

Simultaneously with the territorial rearrangement Hungary and Romania had to sign protocols which favoured the German ethnic groups in both countries. They were declared by decree to represent corporations under public law, enjoying autonomous rights. This legal position enabled the 'ethnic German mediation office' of the SS, working through the ethnic organizations in Hungary, to establish National Socialist forms of political life among the Germans there; in this they benefited from the earlier Magyarization efforts of the Hungarian government. Even the pro-German leader of the Fascist Arrow Cross movement, Szálasi, described the ethnic-group agreement as a violation of Hungarian sovereignty,[128] which was later similarly disregarded when the SS reserve office was recruiting ethnic Germans for the Waffen-SS.[129] Outwardly Horthy, in a letter to Hitler, displayed satisfaction at the solution of the Transylvanian problem reached in Vienna. When that letter was presented by the Hungarian minister, Döme Sztójay, Hitler made it clear that Hungary must really now be interested in a 'clear victory of the Axis powers', as in the event of a defeat by Germany and Italy the revisions achieved would certainly become null and void.[130] In his report on his conversation with Hitler, Sztójay outlined a 'programme' which would truly express Hungary's gratitude for the award, and offered proposals for a closer alignment with Germany in foreign and domestic policy. Military relations too were to be deepened 'as far as possible by complete sincerity and co-operation'. Good behaviour towards Germany would be a guarantee of further revisions after the end of the war.[131] The Teleki government readily accepted German political and ideological suggestions. It released Szálasi from prison, permitted the transit of the German military mission and instructional troops through Hungary, enacted the third anti-Jewish laws (after 1938 and 1939), and on 10 October 1940 signed an economic agreement which met Germany's requests.[132] Very soon it also showed its willingness to join the Tripartite Pact, thereby demonstrating that it was prepared to recognize German–Italian hegemony in Europe, as this had enabled it to see the major part of its revisionist hopes fulfilled. But Hitler at first rejected the Hungarian offer. Only

[127] See sect. I.v.2 (Förster), and Annexe Vol., No. 4.
[128] Quoted according to Broszat, 'Deutschland', 49.   [129] See Tilkovszky, 'Waffen-SS'.
[130] Hitler–Stójay conversation, 10 Sept. 1940, *DGFP* D xi, No. 41.
[131] *Allianz Hitler-Horthy-Mussolini*, No. 92.
[132] Juhász, *Hungarian Foreign Policy*, 175–6; Volkmann, 'Außenhandel und Aufrüstung', 114–15.

after the failure of the discussions with Molotov on 12 and 13 November 1940, when the Tripartite Pact was to be refashioned into a regional European treaty system exclusively serving German interests and directed against the Soviet Union, did he allow the south-east European countries to join. Hungary acceded to the pact on 20 November 1940 and thereby definitively fitted herself into Hitler's political strategy. Although Hungary was pressing territorial claims against Yugoslavia as well (the Mur region, the Baranya triangle, Bácska, and the eastern Banat), the two countries concluded a friendship treaty ('treaty of perpetual peace') on 12 December 1940, which Hungary ratified on 27 February 1941. Behind it was the intention, approved by Hitler, to seek a solution by peaceful means. On 25 March 1941, after prolonged hesitation and German pressure, Yugoslavia joined the Tripartite Pact. However, Berlin's euphoria over this political success lasted barely 48 hours. On 27 March 1941 the Cvetkovic government was overthrown by a coup of Serbian officers. 'Tranquillity' in the Balkans, in German eyes, was gone again and the southern flank of the eastern operation now under preparation was threatened. Hitler immediately reacted with the decision to 'make all preparations for smashing Yugoslavia militarily and as a state'. On that same evening, 27 March, Hitler signed Directive No. 25, drafted by the Wehrmacht staff. Even earlier he had tried, through the Hungarian minister Sztójay, to reawaken Hungary's territorial claims, in order to achieve her permission not only for the necessary deployment of German forces in Hungary but also for a military participation of Hungarian formations in his campaign against Yugoslavia.[133] To safeguard German interests in Hungary during the Balkan campaign Major-General Kurt Himer was dispatched to Budapest as 'German general with the high command of the Royal Hungarian army'.

Hopes of a further revision of the treaty of Trianon with German support and of understanding on the part of the Western powers for such a policy helped the Hungarian leadership quickly to overcome any scruples about its treachery *vis-à-vis* Belgrade. With her Third Army (approximately 146,000 men) Hungary participated in the military and political 'smashing' of Yugoslavia. Hungarian losses in that 'campaign' amounted to only 65 killed. At the same time the Hungarian troops perpetrated atrocities in the newly occupied territories, whose victims were predominantly Serbians, Jews, and also Germans.[134] Hungary reacquired Bácska, the Mur territory, and the Baranya triangle, in all 11,475 square kilometres with one million inhabitants. An entry of Hungarian troops into the eastern Banat was described by Berlin, after an intervention by Antonescu, as 'undesirable'.[135] In consequence, Hungary had nearly doubled her territory, compared with her 1920 frontiers, both in area

---

[133] On Hungary's enlistment as an ally see Olshausen, *Zwischenspiel auf dem Balkan*, 64 ff., and *Germany and the Second World War*, iii. 479 ff.

[134] *Allianz Hitler-Horthy-Mussolini*, No. 117 (16 Dec. 1943).

[135] KTB of the German general with the High Command of the Royal Hungarian Armed Forces, entries of 4 and 5 Apr. 1941, BA-MA RH 32-V/1.

and in population: to 172,204 square kilometres with 14.6 million inhabitants. The percentage of ethnic minorities, however, had increased to 25 per cent. In the army it amounted to 20 per cent.

Premier Count Teleki was the only person at the time who realized that the Hungarian leadership was indulging in an illusion if it believed it could utilize the expansion of Hitlerite Germany for its own revisionist aspirations and simultaneously retain the support of the Western powers. On 3 April 1941 he shot himself. On 6 April 1941 Britain broke off diplomatic relations with Hungary. The rupture with London was accepted by Horthy and by the new premier, László von Bárdossy, as the price of Hungary's even closer association with Germany, although they had agreed with Teleki that their principal task was 'to preserve Hungary's military, material, and national strength until the end of the war. . . . The outcome of the war is doubtful. . . . The country, our youth, our army must be risked solely for ourselves and for no one else.'[136]

What was the Hungarian army, the Honvéd, like? In the treaty of Trianon Hungary had been allowed a regular army of 35,000 men. Despite supervision by the Inter-Allied Military Commission (until 1927) and the Little Entente, Hungary succeeded in secretly increasing her peacetime army and in introducing general conscription (1932). By the time the Entente states, in the Bled agreement of the summer of 1938, granted Hungary complete equality in armaments, the Hungarian army comprised 85,252 men. Hungary was now openly stepping up her effort to make good her deficiency in armaments compared with her declared enemy Romania. 'Attainment of the qualitative and, if possible, quantitative level of the Romanian army was defined as the supreme aim of military policy.'[137] Because of her inadequate productive capacity Hungary depended on armament purchases from abroad. Thus nearly a third of the 1939–40 national budget was allocated to the Hungarian army.[138] At the beginning of April 1940 part 1 of the 'Huba' war regulation came into force: this envisaged the establishment of 25 light infantry divisions of 2 infantry regiments each, 1 cavalry division, 2 armoured divisions, 2 mountain brigades, 1 frontier brigade, 1 river brigade, and 2 air groups with 28 tactical and 10 reconnaissance squadrons by the end of 1943. The newly gained territories were immediately taken into account in the realization of this army reform, even though the various mobilizations had interfered with the smooth development and entailed considerable costs. The VIII Army Corps was stationed at Kassa (Kosice) and the IX Corps at Kolozsvár (Cluj). The three army HQs and nine corps HQs were increased by the addition of I Mobile Corps HQ.

The second phase of the army reform came into effect at the beginning of March 1941. It envisaged that the army would have a peacetime establishment

---

[136] Teleki's memorandum, 3 Mar. 1941: *Allianz Hitler-Horthy-Mussolini*, No. 93.

[137] Darnóy, Organisation, fo. 47, MGFA M 2/1–2. See Gosztony, 'Ungarns militärische Rolle', i. 159–60.

[138] Csima, 'Magyarország Katonai', 641.

of 13,574 officers and 174,241 NCOs and other ranks, but this was not in fact achieved. Its wartime strength was to be 24,000 officers and 600,000 other ranks.[139] Hungary's financial constraints, caused by her territorial expansion, and her chronic lack of raw materials rendered cut-backs in the armament programme inescapable. These economies had a particularly detrimental effect on the equipment and armament of the numerically enlarged army. The creation of new units, which was pursued nevertheless, was designed predominantly, by means of existing and trained personnel, to establish the foundations of the Hungarian army's further development into an effective instrument of war. Thus, the Hungarian army was equipped in breadth rather than in depth. Especially inadequate were the air force and anti-aircraft defence, as well as armour and anti-tank defence. Precipitate development and ambitious political aims had prevented a steady build-up of reserves of personnel and material. Ninety per cent of the fighting forces consisted of non-motorized infantry with horse-drawn artillery and horse-drawn supply troops. In spite of its shortcomings, the Mobile Corps with its two motorized infantry brigades and one cavalry brigade was the most modern operational formation of the Hungarian army.[140]

The Hungarian army command endeavoured to compensate for its shortages in equipment and weaponry, and its consequent inferiority to neighbouring armies, by intensive ideological indoctrination. Its ideal was to turn Hungary into 'a modern Sparta or a Hungarian Prussia'.[141] The whole nation was to be fashioned into a single great army. Time and again propaganda glorified the 'eternal military virtues' and praised the Hungarian as 'the best soldier in the world'. The army as an instrument of national interests, i.e. of revisionist policy vis-à-vis its neighbours, was invested with the claim that it stood above class and was non-political. This slogan was to ensure the army's absolute reliability in the hands of the political leadership. Although prior to 1941 the Soviet Union did not represent a specific military target, anti-Communist ideology was, along with education in a warlike and chauvinist spirit, the basis of propaganda work in the army. The ideals of revisionism and anti-Communism also affected the personal composition and replenishment of the officer corps.

In Hitler's plans for a war against the Soviet Union Hungary played an even more subordinate role than she did in those of the German military leadership. Although in Marck's and Loßberg's draft operations plans for Barbarossa Hungary had been earmarked as a transit territory, Hitler on 5 December 1940 rejected any participation by Hungary.[142] That was why in Directive No. 21 she was not mentioned. By contrast, the operations department of the Army

---

[139] On the restructuring of the army see Darnóy, Organisation, fos. 42–53, 66–73, MGFA M 2/1–2; also Csima, 'Magyarország Katonai', 658 ff.
[140] Tóth, 'Ungarns militärische Rolle', 79.
[141] On indoctrination see Tóth, 'Kriegspropaganda' (unpub. manuscript).
[142] Halder, Diaries, 723 (5 Dec. 1940).

General Staff in its plans provided for Hungarian formations as security forces in the rear areas of Army Group South.[143] In the plans of the Army High Command, however, Hungary also played a part as a deployment area. In its 'deployment directive for Barbarossa' it envisaged the attack of an army corps of Seventeenth Army across the Carpathians. That was the reason why Halder on 3 February, at Hitler's conference with the top commanders of the Wehrmacht, again raised the subject of Hungary. 'If she does not take part in the operation itself, she must at least agree to troop detrainment on her territory; Romania was to be declared to be the objective of those troops, and only at the last moment would they wheel towards the Russian frontier.'[144] Hitler did not agree to this proposal; he believed that, 'against appropriate political assurances', Hungary would consent 'to all German demands'. The necessary arrangements, however, were to be made only at the last minute, as Hitler suspected that the British were being kept informed by Hungarian quarters. As Army Group South had not been informed of Hitler's attitude, it requested a few days later that Hungarian forces be moved forward in the wake of XXXXII Army Corps 'as early as possible' in order to clear the rear area of Seventeenth Army of Soviet troops and occupy it.[145] Halder was therefore obliged to rein in the army group. Because of the need to conceal German intentions from Hungary as long as possible, he explained, any employment of 'Hungarian forces will be possible—if at all—only after or at the launch of the operation'.[146] On no account must Hungarian troops come into contact with Romanian ones. In line with Hitler's intentions, the amended Directive No. 21 of 22 March 1941 did not view Hungary as an ally in the preparatory phase of Barbarossa. When army-group and army commanders reported to Hitler on 30 March, Field Marshal von Rundstedt, commander-in-chief of Army Group South, once more, entirely in line with Halder's thinking, called for a Hungarian operation across the Carpathians, as well as for an offensive thrust out of Romania[147]—but in vain.

During the campaign against Yugoslavia, when the Hungarian political leadership feared Soviet intervention, the Hungarian general staff regarded the Soviet measures along the Hungarian eastern frontier as defensive. That assessment by the chief of the Hungarian general staff, Colonel-General Werth, was endorsed by the high command of the German army.[148] Horthy was most anxious that the Hungarian army should not lose 'too much blood'

---

[143] Op.Abt. (I/N) No. 025/40 to GenQu, 15 Jan. 1941, BA-MA RH 2/v. 1325. See sect. I.IV.1(*e*) at n. 126 (Klink).

[144] *KTB OKW* i. 299 (3 Feb. 1941).

[145] H.Gr. A (Süd) Ia No. 151/41, 12 Feb. 1941, BA-MA RH 19 I/67b and RH 20-17/21.

[146] OKH/GenStdH/Op.Abt. (I S) No. 261, 24 Feb. 1941, BA-MA RH 19 I/67b.

[147] Halder, *Diaries*, 847 (30 Mar. 1941). Three days earlier Brauchitsch had informed the commanders-in-chief at Zossen that Hungary would not be involved: BA-MA 18. Armee, 19601/2.

[148] KTB of the German general with the High Command of the Royal Hungarian Armed Forces, 9 Apr. 1941, BA-MA RH 31-V/1. The Hungarian enquiry and the German reply are in BA-MA H 3/1.

in its operation against Yugoslavia, 'as Hungary also has frontiers with Romania and Russia'.[149] The German military attaché in Budapest, Colonel Günther Krappe, after a conversation with Horthy's adjutant, confidently assumed that Horthy had offered 'once more his help in the Russian question', as he had also to Raeder.[150] Despite this and other attempts by Horthy to be made privy to German intentions *vis-à-vis* the Soviet Union, Hitler maintained his negative attitude to Hungary. He continued to believe that, while she was ready to take defensive measures against the Soviet Union, she would not permit a launching of German forces from her territory. In accordance with his instructions the 'German general with the high command of the Royal Hungarian armed forces', Major-General Himer, did not sound the Hungarians on the chances of Hungarian participation in Barbarossa until the end of May 1941. Himer in his conversation with Werth stressed the need for the Hungarian armed forces to be prepared in time for the event 'that the eastern issues would be decided by war'.[151] The Hungarian chief of staff reacted positively and promised to examine the possibility of shortening the Hungarian mobilization period of twenty days. Nothing occurred beyond that sounding, because Hitler forbade Hungary to be officially informed in detail on Germany's intentions before mid-June 1941. For that reason Halder, at his conference with the commanders of the army groups, armies, and armoured groups at Zossen, was able to announce only that participation by Hungarian troops was 'not yet clear'. However, if only by her security measures, Hungary was already tying down Soviet forces. If she were to take an active part in Barbarossa, at least one German division would have to be inserted between Romanians and Hungarians.[152] Within the Hungarian leadership, however, arguments were proceeding about Hungary's attitude even before the date authorized by Hitler for Hungary's notification of the impending German–Soviet conflict.

As early as 6 May Colonel-General Werth had urged Premier Bárdossy in a memorandum to conclude a political agreement with Germany covering the event of German–Hungarian military co-operation. That proposal had been dismissed by Bárdossy with the argument that Germany would not be prepared to conclude such an agreement 'on a reciprocal basis'. On 31 May, following Himer's soundings, Werth requested at least authority 'to make contact on the military plane with the competent German military leaders', but Bárdossy did not react.[153] On 5 June 1941 Colonel Ujszászy informed the head of the political department in the Hungarian foreign ministry, János

---

[149] Himer's report, 10 Apr. 1941, BA-MA H 3/1.

[150] Semi-official letter from Col. Krappe to OQu IV on army general staff, Maj.-Gen. Gerhard Matzky (Tippelskirch's successor), 26 Apr. 1941, BA-MA III H 1001/6.

[151] KTB of the German general with the High Command of the Royal Hungarian Armed Forces, 27–9 May 1941, BA-MA RH 32-V/1; *KTB OKW* i. 399–400, 401 (3 and 5 June 1941).

[152] Minute of Seventeenth Army chief of staff, 6 June 1941, BA-MA 17. Armee, 14499/5.

[153] See the introduction to Werth's memorandum, 14 June 1941: *Allianz Hitler-Horthy-Mussolini*, No. 105.

Vörnle, that a start was being made on the reconnaissance of objects on Soviet territory which would have to be destroyed in the event of a conflict. When Vörnle demurred, Ujszászy remarked that Defence Minister Károly Bartha had given him 'full powers to take whatever measures he considered necessary'. He was merely informing Vörnle of the fact.[154] On 7 June 1941 the Hungarian minister in Berlin urged Bárdossy to offer Hitler as soon as possible 'our firm military participation in a possible operation against the Soviet Union'. Sztójay accompanied his suggestion with the observation that a swift victory by the German army was beyond doubt and that the Hungarian offer was sure to make 'a lasting and favourable impression' on Hitler.[155] In a further memorandum, dated 14 June 1941, Werth again proposed that a formal offer be submitted to Germany of voluntary participation in the war against the Soviet Union; he urged speedy action as the war might break out within ten days. Simultaneously he pointed to Romanian military measures already taken. Werth was firmly convinced that Hungary would have to play an active part in that war, because

(1) this is required for the safeguarding of the territorial integrity of the country and the protection of our social and economic order; (2) a weakening of our Russian neighbour and his removal from our frontiers are of prime national interest for our future; (3) our Christian and nationally based ideology and our fundamental opposition to Bolshevism in the past and present make it our duty; (4) politically we have definitively placed ourselves on the side of the Axis powers; (5) our further territorial enlargement also depends on it.[156]

This was a list of all the motivations which ultimately led Hungary to participate in Operation Barbarossa. Nevertheless, the ministerial council, meeting on the following day, rejected the idea of voluntary participation in order to save the army for future territorial revisions. Bárdossy informed the chief of the general staff that if Germany 'at a later date considers our co-operation necessary and addresses an explicit invitation to us, we shall readily comply with it'.[157] On 15 June 1941, however, Ribbentrop had Bárdossy informed, not officially but in confidence, that by the beginning of July Hitler 'would be compelled to clarify German–Russian relations' and suggested that Hungary take measures to safeguard her frontiers.[158] Just then the study of the Hungarian general staff 'for offensive defence on the Russian front' had been completed and its details passed on by Himer to the operations department of the German general staff. On 19 June 1941 Halder, on a return flight from Bucharest, met Werth at Mátyásfìld for a private conversation. According to Werth's notes for the premier, Halder, while putting the Hungarian chief of staff in the picture, made no demand for participation. If certain military measures—beyond securing the Carpathian line—were to become necessary, Halder would 'specifically request them' from Colonel-General Werth

---

[154] See the introduction to Werth's memorandum, No. 103.   [155] Ibid., No. 104.
[156] Ibid., No. 105.   [157] Ibid., p. 81.   [158] *DGFP* D xii2, No. 631.

through Himer.[159] On 22 June Horthy was officially informed of the German attack in a letter from Hitler, with Ribbentrop simultaneously informing the Hungarian minister. 'As an old crusader against Bolshevism' Horthy was enthusiastic about Hitler's decision for war. 'For twenty-two years he had longed to see this day and now he was happy. Even after centuries mankind would thank the Führer for this deed. 180 million Russians would now be liberated from the yoke imposed on them by two million Bolsheviks.'[160] The Hungarian minister in Berlin, Sztójay, similarly expressed to Ribbentrop Hungary's sympathy for the German decision. Not only his country, 'but the whole of Europe and the world', would be grateful to Hitler when he had defeated Bolshevism.[161]

As Hitler had not invited Hungary to participate in the war against the Soviet Union, but had merely thanked her for intensified frontier security along the Carpathians, thereby tying down Soviet forces, Horthy regarded a declaration of war by Hungary on the Soviet Union as unnecessary. The ministerial council, however, decided on 23 June 1941 to break off diplomatic relations with the USSR. At almost the same hour Molotov, the Soviet foreign minister, informed József Kristóffy, the Hungarian minister in Moscow, that the Soviet government had no claims or aggressive intentions against Hungary. His government would have to know soon 'whether Hungary wished to participate in the war or adopt a neutral attitude'.[162] This Soviet request for clarity on Hungary's position in the German–Soviet war was accompanied by a clear hint that Moscow showed understanding for Hungary's continuing revisionist aspirations with regard to Romania. The telegram from Kristóffy arrived in Budapest on 24 June, but Premier Bárdossy informed neither the regent nor the ministerial council of it.[163]

It was only on the previous day, 22 June, that the head of the operations department in the Hungarian general staff, Major-General Dezsö László—who like Colonel-General Werth was waiting for Halder's invitation to 'join in'—had been informed of Jodl's view: 'Any Hungarian help will always be accepted. We do not want to make any demands, but anything offered voluntarily will be gratefully accepted. There is no question whatever of our not desiring a participation by Hungary.'[164] Vis-à-vis Himer, Halder had amplified Jodl's remark to the effect that it was now important 'for the Hungarian military quarters to set the political ones in motion, so that they themselves should come out with an offer. . . . No demands had been made because they have to be paid for, but any support, especially by mobile troops, would be gratefully accepted. But on no account must German rail transports

---

[159] *Allianz Hitler-Horthy-Mussolini*, No. 106; KTB of the German general with the High Command of the Royal Hungarian Armed Forces, 19 June 1941, BA-MA RH 31-V/1.
[160] *DGFP* D xii, No. 667 (22 June 1941).
[161] *Allianz Hitler-Horthy-Mussolini*, No. 107.   [162] Ibid., No. 108.
[163] Juhász, *Hungarian Foreign Policy*, 189.
[164] KTB of the German general with the High Command of the Royal Hungarian Armed Forces, 22 June 1941, BA-MA RH 31-V/1.

be disrupted.'[165] In a conversation with Werth Himer thereupon once more explained the German leadership's position. Werth for his part had pointed out that unless Hitler invited Hungary to participate in the struggle 'the politicians' would 'hardly go along with it'. At his suggestion an enquiry had been made ten days earlier through political channels concerning Hungary's participation, 'but it seemed that the Führer did not wish Hungary to take part'. Major-General Himer had countered that the military was now speaking. It was not too late for Hungary to participate in the 'crusade against Bolshevism'. Himer's assessment of Werth's hesitation and of his waiting for Horthy's decision on the evening of 23 June was that the Hungarian chief of staff was 'not up to the greatness of the moment'.[166]

Werth informed Defence Minister Bartha and Premier Bárdossy of his conversation with Himer. The premier was annoyed that such an important political decision had been presented to the Hungarian leadership through military channels. To the German minister, Bárdossy emphasized Hungary's interest in not fragmenting her military forces, given the hostility of her Romanian and Slovak neighbours; 'if, however, the German side wished for Hungarian participation in the war against the Soviet Union, then he would pass this on to Horthy'.[167] Even before the desired political invitation had been issued from Berlin, the Hungarian ministerial council decided on the morning of 26 June to mobilize the Mobile Corps and the air-force and anti-aircraft formations.[168] At noon the same day unidentified aircraft bombed Kassa, and Soviet machines—no doubt on a reconnaissance flight—fired cannon at an express near Ráho. Even before the official investigation of the air raid on Kassa had begun, the ministerial council was convened once more in the afternoon of 26 June 1941. Bárdossy announced that, following a report of the defence minister and the chief of the general staff, Horthy had ordered 'reprisal measures' and Hungary's entry into the war against the Soviet Union.[169] Hungary's political and military leaders were convinced that the Soviet Union was behind those air attacks and regarded them as a *casus belli*, even though Moscow issued a denial that same day. On 27 June 1941 the Hungarian air force made 'reprisal raids' on Soviet targets in the Stanislav and Kolomyja area. The regent's decision to make Hungary participate in the war against the Soviet Union was communicated not only to Berlin,[170] but on 27 June also to the Hungarian parliament. As a reason Premier Bárdossy gave the Soviet attack, which violated international law.[171] The Hungarian minister in Berlin, Sztójay, did not regard this rather passive reaction as sufficient to preclude the possibility of preferential treatment for Romania and Slovakia in

---

[165] Ibid., 23 June 1941.
[166] Ibid.; see also *DGFP* D xiii, No. 54.
[167] *DGFP* D xiii, No. 10 (24 June 1941). See Halder, *Diaries*, 976 (25 June 1941).
[168] KTB of the German general with the High Command of the Royal Hungarian Armed Forces, 26 June 1941, BA-MA RH 31-V/1.
[169] Juhász, *Hungarian Foreign Policy*, 190.   [170] *DGFP* D xiii, Nos. 10, 21, 22 (26 June 1941).
[171] *Allianz Hitler-Horthy-Mussolini*, 83; Fenyo, *Hitler, Horthy, and Hungary*, 24 ff.

the 'reorganization of Europe', and therefore once more suggested that Hungary should offer Germany an 'active participation in the war in a broader form'. This might considerably after the 'Hungarian–German balance sheet' in Hungary's favour.[172]

Although the question of who ordered the attack on Kassa, and why, still remains unanswered,[173] it is a fact that the Soviet Union could have had no interest in seeing Hungary join the war. Those air attacks were not the reason for Hungary's declaration of war against the Soviet Union, but they were certainly used as a pretext for Hungary's decision and for its propagandist embellishment. The reasons for the dispatch of Hungarian troops to the eastern front are to be found in Hungary's history since 1919, in the anti-Communist attitude of her leadership, in her intransigent revisionism even after the two Vienna awards, and in the fear that a policy of neutrality might put her at a disadvantage against Romania and Slovakia after the expected swift victory over the Soviet Union, and that Hungary would not have a seat at the table of the victors. Germany had a twofold interest in Hungary's participation in the war against the Soviet Union. On the one hand it strengthened the slogan of 'Europe's crusade against Bolshevism' and on the other it relieved the flanks of Seventeenth Army and Eleventh Army during the initial phase. The Hungarian minister in Berlin, Sztójay, very accurately assessed the German motives at the end of June 1941:

My judgement of the situation is that the Germans do not really need any substantial military support. To protect their northern and southern wings, and their nickel and oil, they have enlisted the Finns and the Romanians. The latter are being coaxed by them, as hitherto, by territorial revisions. Towards other states they are not anxious to enter into obligations, because they like to keep a free hand for themselves; on the other hand, from the propaganda point of view, they find it desirable to have as many countries as possible participate actively in the crusade against Bolshevism. Those who fail to participate will feel it on their own skins some day.[174]

To prevent the Romanians, the Slovaks, and the Croats, who had all entered the war against the Soviet Union before Hungary, from intriguing against Hungary in Berlin, Sztójay suggested to his government that an intensified active participation in Barbarossa be proposed to Germany, so that Hungary's participation should not seem to be merely a passive reaction to a Soviet air attack.

(b) Slovakia

Slovakia was the smallest ally and had been a 'sovereign' state only since mid-March 1939. It comprised a territory of 38,000 square kilometres of predominantly agricultural character and approximately 2.6 million inhabitants, 90 per cent of them of Slovak nationality. Agriculture and forestry occupied 56 per

---

[172] *Allianz Hitler-Horthy-Mussolini*, Nos. 113, 114 (29 June and 2 July 1941).
[173] See Borsányi, *Rätsel.*   [174] *Allianz Hitler-Horthy-Mussolini*, No. 113 (29 June 1941).

cent of the population. Slovakia, as the first satellite state of the Third Reich, was to become 'Germany's visiting-card' for the future new order in Europe.[175] In spite of its limited sovereignty, the new Slovak state was recognized by a total of twenty-seven countries. As a result of the imposed treaty of 18 March 1939, the 'confidential economic protocol' of 23 March 1939, and the 'defence-economy treaty' of January 1940, Slovakia was not only placed under German 'protection', its foreign and military policy greatly limited, with a 'protective zone' conceded to the Wehrmacht in the western part of the state territory, but her economy had been brought in line with German requirements. At the beginning of January 1940 the head of the German army mission, Lieutenant-General Paul Otto, reported to Berlin that the Slovaks were displaying an 'attitude of wanting to be needed' and that their 'employment' for German interests would be possible.[176] Hungary's appetite for further annexations, persisting in spite of a German guarantee and territorial acquisitions already achieved, gave rise to a Slovak national awareness that was continually nourished by the bad treatment the Slovak minority (numbering 600,000) was subjected to in Hungary. At least 70 per cent of the Slovaks had a positive attitude to their state, and 80 per cent were Roman Catholics. The close alliance between the Slovak People's Party, the extreme right-wing Hlinka Guard, and the Catholic clergy resulted in an authoritarian governmental and social system which may be labelled 'clerical Fascism'.[177] Until the middle of 1940 Slovakia remained relatively independent in its domestic policy. After the German victory over France, however, the Slovak leadership was made to understand that Slovakia was situated within the German living-space and that it was Germany's wishes alone that mattered. The Salzburg talks, the dismissal of Ferdinand Ďurčanský, minister of interior and foreign affairs, and the appointment of Killinger as the German minister in Bratislava at the end of July 1940 put an end to Slovakia's relatively independent policy in favour of a more pronounced domestic alignment with Germany.[178] German advisers on police, Jewish, and propaganda affairs and for the organization of the Hlinka Guard were sent to Bratislava. On 28 July 1940 State President Josef Tiso remarked to Hitler that Slovakia was feeling 'happy under the fatherly care of the Führer' and wished to make its modest contribution to the building of a new Europe.[179] Killinger saw his task as 'so guiding Slovakia that in the war it will be 100 per cent at our disposal economically, and ensuring that it is steered politically in a manner that will exclude the least doubt that it might not toe the line in the war'.[180] On 23 November 1940 Slovakia joined the Tripartite Pact. As in Romania, the Guard was initially impatient to achieve unrestricted power by revolutionary means; in the winter

---

[175] On the history of Slovakia see Rhode, 'Tschechoslowakei', 952 ff.; Hoensch, 'Slowakische Republik'; Venohr, *Aufstand*; Jelinek, *Parish Republic*; *Germany and the Second World War*, i. 337 ff.

[176] Tippelskirch, minute of 4 Jan. 1940, BA-MA RH 2/v. 1478.

[177] Venohr, *Aufstand*, 28–9.   [178] Dress, *Slowakei*, 293 ff.

[179] Hitler–Tiso conversation, 28 July 1940, *DGFP* D x, No. 248.

[180] Quoted according to Hoensch, 'Slowakische Republik', 304.

of 1940–1 it was ready—presumably with the backing of members of the German legation and the corps of advisers—to stage a coup against President Tiso. The plan, however, was betrayed by army circles. Hitler meanwhile, just as he did in Romania a few days later, subordinated the ideological aims of National Socialism to the political and economic objectives of the Reich. The new minister in Bratislava, Ludin, assured Tiso that he enjoyed Hitler's confidence and sympathies. Thus the programme of a 'Guardist Slovakia', designed by Premier Vojtech Tuka, had failed.[181]

The establishment of a Slovak national army from the remnants of the Czechoslovak forces was the achievement of the commander-in-chief and defence minister, General Ferdinand Čatloš.[182] The first task was the creation of cadres. Former regiments became battalions, former battalions became companies, and core units were formed with active soldiers of Slovak nationality, replenished with reservists and conscripts. Introduction of the German recruitment and replacement system and the German mobilization procedure was planned for 1 April 1942. In the spring of 1939 Čatloš had only 320 active Slovak officers at his disposal. By drawing on reserve officers and by reactivating retired officers it proved possible to meet the planned requirement of 1,300 officers for the establishment of a peacetime army of two infantry divisions and army troops (approximately 28,000 men). The contractually agreed rearming and refurbishing with German equipment were not to take place until after the war. The year 1940–1 had been earmarked as 'minor training year'. The Slovak army command was advised in its work by a German military mission. Neither it nor the German officers had expected the Slovak army to be used so soon.

Unlike Hitler, who did not wish to see the Slovaks participating in Barbarossa—at least not before victory had been achieved over the Red Army, because he feared fraternization among fellow Slavs[183]—the operations department of the Army General Staff included Slovak units at an early stage in its plans for securing the rear areas in the sector of Army Group South.[184] The army group, having received the Army High Command's 'deployment order for Barbarossa', considered it desirable to move the two Slovak infantry divisions forward, within the framework of Seventeenth Army, to the Sambor and Drogobych area in order to secure the local oilfields.[185] The Army High Command did not meet this request by the army group, because Slovak mobilization, in view of the transport situation, could not begin until the German formations were ready to move off. Slovak forces, the Army High Command suggested, would therefore probably have to be employed only for

[181] Ibid. 305–6.

[182] Venohr, *Aufstand*, 37–8. See the accounts of Otto's activities, of 11 July and 19 Oct. 1940, BA-MA RW 5/v. 443.

[183] Halder, *Diaries*, 832 (17 Mar. 1941).

[184] Op.Abt. (I/N) No. 025/40 to GenQu, 15 Jan. 1941, BA-MA RH 2/v. 1325. See sect. I.iv.1(e) at n. 126 (Klink).

[185] H.Gr. A (Süd) Ia No. 151/41, 12 Feb. 1941, BA-MA RH 19 I/67b.

occupation and security tasks.[186] Slovakia, on the other hand, was included in the plans as a deployment area.[187] On 23 April 1941, therefore, Berlin requested Slovak agreement to the detrainment of three divisions, which would move into occupied Poland. That troop movement was described as a 'purely defensive measure'.[188] The German deployment, however, did not fail to impress the Slovak army command. On 2 May, through Major Becker, the German military attaché, General Čatloš offered Slovak troops in the event of a war against the Soviet Union with Hungarian participation.[189] The Army High Command no doubt replied evasively, because on 6 June 1941 the head of the operations department, Colonel (General Staff) Heusinger, enquired of the Wehrmacht operations staff when it would be possible to discuss Barbarossa with the Slovaks, who were 'anxious to join in'.[190] On 19 June 1941 Halder, *en route* from Budapest, had an incognito meeting with General of Infantry Otto and Lieutenant-Colonel Becker in Bratislava. At Hitler's request the employment was discussed of the two Slovak divisions which had already been included in the army group's plans for the impending campaign. The chief of the German army mission in Slovakia expressed the opinion 'that it may well be possible to employ the Slovak peacetime army raised to a war footing on a quiet front or for security and cover tasks, but that it would not be capable of *dealing with serious battle assignments* or with *long marches*'.[191] Otto informed the German minister Ludin about his conversation with Halder. Ludin on 21 June enquired from State President Tiso and Premier Tuka, in 'an entirely non-committal way', whether Slovakia would participate in a possible operation against the Soviet Union. 'Both gentlemen answered unequivocally in the affirmative.'[192] The next morning, on 22 June 1941, the Slovak minister in Berlin, Matúš Černák, informed State Secretary von Weizsäcker of his government's readiness for military co-operation with Germany and for breaking off diplomatic relations with the Soviet Union. Ribbentrop thereupon instructed Ludin to inform Tuka that Berlin consented to the immediate rupture of diplomatic relations between Slovakia and the Soviet Union, and to the participation of Slovak troops: 'The decisions of the Slovak government on both points are being greatly welcomed by us.'[193] Anti-Bolshevism was the principal common ideological feature between clerical-Fascist Slovakia and National Socialist Germany. On 23 June 1941 Defence

---

[186] OKH/GenStdH/Op.Abt. (I S) No. 261/41, 24 Feb. 1941, ibid. At his conference with the commanders of army groups, armies, and armoured groups on 27 Mar. 1941 Brauchitsch declared that Slovakia would 'not be involved': BA-MA, 18. Armee, 19601/2.

[187] OKW/WFSt/Abt. L (I Op) No. 44326/41, 22 Mar. 1941, *DGFP* D xii, No. 195.

[188] Foreign ministry, telegram No. 428, 23 Apr. 1941, and German Minister Pressburg (Bratislava), telegram No. 428, 24 Apr. 1941, PA, Büro St.S. Slowakei, vol. i.

[189] Jelinek, *Parish Republic*, 74.   [190] *KTB OKW* i. 401 (6 June 1941).

[191] Gen. Otto's situation report, 5 Aug. 1941, BA-MA Wi/IF 3.130.

[192] German Minister Pressburg (Bratislava), telegram No. 620, 21 June 1941, *DGFP* D xii, No. 656. Both Hillgruber, *Strategie*, 500 n. 92, and Dress, *Slowakei*, 331, believe that Otto himself informed the Slovak government and advised it to 'join in immediately'.

[193] *DGFP* D xii, No. 672.

Minister Čatloš issued an order of the day which, while emphasizing the defence of Europe against the 'mortal danger' of Bolshevism, made it clear that the Slovak army was not fighting 'against the great Russian people or against Slavdom'.[194] That was a clear concession to the pan-Slav sentiments of the Slovak people. President Tiso, a Catholic priest, gave his blessing to the Slovak troops employed on the eastern front from 24 June. The papal nuncio in Bratislava commented on Slovakia's participation in the 'crusade against Bolshevism' with the words: 'I am happy to be able to report to the Holy Father only the best from the examplary Slovak state, which is steadily implementing its Christian national programme expressed in the slogan "For God and the nation".'[195]

Operation Barbarossa had not been planned as a coalition war by the German side. The early enlistment of Romania as an ally—along with Finland—did indeed reflect Berlin's strategic interests, but Bucharest was never regarded as an equal partner in the alliance, let alone Budapest or Bratislava. There were no clearly defined or jointly agreed political or military war aims. Although, on Hitler's decision, the south-east European allies were allowed a share in the 'total glory', they had no say in the conduct of the war. Nevertheless, the 'military-action community' against the Soviet Union after 22 June 1941 was in line with the political interests and ideological beliefs of the Romanian, Hungarian, and Slovak state leaderships.

Romania, Hungary, and Slovakia did not participate in Operation Barbarossa because they mistook Hitler's war in the east as a significant crusade against Bolshevism. That was only a welcome side-effect of their military efforts. Germany's mutually hostile allies dispatched their troops to the eastern front and made economic sacrifices because Hitler's enforced new order in Europe and the Balkans had either favoured or severely disadvantaged them. Antonescu believed that by participating in the eastern campaign he might achieve a revision of the second Vienna award of the summer of 1940. Hungary's 'armed assistance' was intended as a gesture of gratitude for her territorial gains since 1938 and as a counterpoise to the massive Romanian contribution. Slovakia's contribution to the German–Soviet war was largely designed to ensure Berlin's support against further territorial demands by Hungary and to build up an effective army. The behaviour of the south-east European allies demonstrated 'that the eagerness to collaborate shown by those who have lost and would like to regain is greater than the zeal of those who already possess'.[196] The correctness of that thesis was again demonstrated in 1941–2. The profound internal conflicts between Romania, Hungary, and Slovakia were barely pasted over by the propaganda effort regarding the alleged 'European crusade against Bolshevism'.

---

[194] Quoted according to Venohr, *Aufstand*, 42.   [195] Ibid. 30.
[196] Broszat, 'Deutschland', 96.

VI. The Involvement of Scandinavia in the Plans for Barbarossa

Gerd R. Ueberschär

1. Finland's Place in Hitler's Calculations at the Time of the Resumption of his 'Eastern Programme' in the Summer of 1940

SCANDINAVIA and northern Europe—like south-east Europe and the Balkans—were gaining greater importance both because of the increasingly emerging differences between Hitler and Stalin and also in German strategy and politics regarding the war against the Soviet Union. Thus, from the summer of 1940 onwards the German government devoted special attention not only to political events in the Balkans but also to foreign-policy, trade, and military developments in Finland and Sweden.

Hitler's decision of 31 July 1940 to initiate military preparations for a war against the Soviet Union, and the resulting reflections concerning a possible participation by Finland in that war, led to a dramatic change in German–Finnish relations and contacts. Even those early formulations of Hitler's military plans in the east raised the question of the extent to which Finland might be induced to participate in some form or other as a potential flank cover in that campaign—the more so as Hitler already regarded Finland as one of the states to be enlarged by conquered regions of the USSR.[1] In this connection Hitler could count on existing political tensions between Finland and the USSR, especially as the Soviet Union by its military attack on Finland in the Winter War of 1939–40 had only partially achieved its political and territorial security objectives. Although by the Moscow peace treaty of 13 March 1940 the Soviet Union imposed on Finland extensive cessions of territory, the Finnish government did not regard the new Finno-Soviet frontier

---

[1] On Hitler's thinking and concept of an enlarged Finland 'up to the White Sea' see Halder, *Diaries*, 517 ff. (22 July 1940), 534 (31 July 1940). On the German–Finnish *rapprochement* see Ueberschär, *Hitler und Finnland*, esp. 166 ff., and Andreen, *Finland i Brännpunkten*, esp. 167 ff.; on Hitler's decision to go to war with the USSR see also *Unternehmen Barbarossa*, and Benz, *Rußlandfeldzug*. On the more recent scholarly discussion of Hitler's decision see Zitelmann, 'Zur Begründung des "Lebensraum"-Motivs'; Ueberschär, 'Pakt mit dem Satan'; Pietrow-Ennker, 'Deutschland im Juni 1941'. Also Wette, 'Wiederbelebung des Antibolschewismus'; Ueberschär, '"Historikerstreit" und "Präventivkriegsthese"'; id., 'Zur Wiederbelebung der "Präventivkriegsthese"'; Benz, 'Präventiver Völkermord?'. Unscholarly assertions to the effect that those historians who do not accept the thesis of a pre-emptive war were yielding to political fashion by following Stalinist versions of history, and that they would suffer a 'Cannae' in 'scholarly, moral, and political respects', are no more than polemics; as expressions of an outsider position they speak for themselves (see Topitsch, *Stalins Krieg*, 1990 edn.).

as definitive. Helsinki's foreign-policy ideas therefore contained a considerable measure of revisionist motives. This was true in particular of the new multi-party government formed in Finland after the conclusion of the peace treaty, even though it did not include the right-wing radical nationalist Patriotic People's Movement. Even under the multi-party government of Premier Risto Ryti, formed during the Winter War in November 1939, there had been a gradual concentration of power within Finland's existing parliamentary system. This process continued after the conclusion of the Winter War under the renewed government of Premier Ryti. The influence of the commander-in-chief of the Finnish armed forces, Field Marshal von Mannerheim, was further enhanced by the appointment of his friend, Major-General Rudolf Walden, to the post of defence minister. The former foreign minister and chairman of the Finnish Social Democrats, Väinö Tanner, remained in the government as minister of national supplies. The bank director Professor Rolf Witting, known for his pro-German sympathies, became foreign minister. Soon after taking office he endeavoured to establish good relations with the German minister in Helsinki, Wipert von Blücher, by informing him comprehensively about the various steps of Finnish foreign policy. While the formation of a coalition government with a large majority in parliament promoted a sense of national unity and an awareness of the country's difficult foreign-policy position after the lost war against the Soviet Union, it also favoured an increasingly perceptible undermining of parliamentary structures. Political decision-making was concentrated in a so-called 'inner circle', consisting of Premier Ryti, Foreign Minister Witting, Defence Minister Walden, and Commander-in-Chief Marshal Mannerheim, with the occasional inclusion of Supply Minister Tanner as chairman of the strongest party. Public discussion of foreign-policy issues—either in parliament or in its foreign-policy committee—was considered inopportune by the government in view of the widespread revisionist ideas about the territories lost to the Soviet Union, and discussion in the press was prevented by the press control which was maintained after the Winter War. With the wartime laws and mobilization measures continuing in force, important decisions were increasingly being taken in secret by the inner cabinet and, as a rule, without parliamentary participation.

After the spring of 1940 the main line of the Ryti government's foreign policy was aimed at utilizing a possible deterioration of German–Soviet relations in order to achieve, with German help, a revision of the territorial terms of the Moscow peace treaty. It thus hoped to regain the ceded regions of Karelia, near Salla, and in the Rybachi peninsula, as well as the base of Hanko handed over to Moscow. Moreover, hopes of also conquering eastern Karelia, White Sea Karelia as far as Lake Onega and the Svir, and the Kola peninsula were not entirely abandoned. Ideas of attachment or association with Sweden in the form of a treaty of union or by way of creating a Scandinavian neutral zone were not, at that time, a deliberately pursued alternative to an orientation and alignment towards Germany. Union with Sweden, moreover, would have presupposed renunciation of revisionist claims against the Soviet Union; it would inevitably have institutionalized Stockholm as the place where political decisions were made, and it would have shifted emphasis to Swedish industrial interests. The Finnish government therefore, soon after the conclusion of the Winter War, staked its hopes on the potential results of a pro-German policy.

In view of Germany's reluctance, during the Winter War, to champion Finland's interests in Moscow, the Finnish government took a certain risk in the spring of 1940 when it placed its hopes in a change of German–Soviet relations in order to make its revisionist and in part revanchist endeavours—e.g. the creation of a Greater Finland—prevail. To begin with, the Finnish government could not be certain that the Reich government would welcome or meet Helsinki's undisguised request for protection and for inclusion in Germany's sphere of interests. On the other hand, it was equally uncertain whether the Soviet Union would not regard the Moscow peace treaty merely as a stage in the eventual attainment of more far-reaching political aims, all the way to a possible occupation of the whole of Finland. Thus in the spring and early summer of 1940 Helsinki found itself under further pressure from Moscow. Several times the Soviet Union made claims which exceeded Finland's contractual obligations under the peace treaty, making it clear that Moscow continued to view Finland as forming part of the Soviet sphere of interests. Finnish efforts to arouse German interest in the country's precarious situation, so as to provide a German counterweight to Moscow's position of strength, initially remained unsuccessful.

As late as 20 May 1940 Hitler—in contrast to the efforts and ideas of the diplomats in the German foreign ministry and of the German firms which were interested in an intensification of German–Finnish trade—maintained his coolly detached, basically anti-Finnish, attitude. In line with his pro-Soviet stand during the Finno-Soviet Winter War he prohibited the resumption of German arms deliveries to Helsinki.[2] Even the Finnish government's readiness, after the German victory over France, to take note of the new power constellation in Europe and to meet German economic wishes, as well as to align its foreign policy alongside Berlin's, failed to produce any change in Hitler's reserve until August 1940. *Rapprochement* between Germany and Finland was not triggered until Hitler's return to his 'programme's' military solution in the east and the resulting strategic considerations concerning the involvement of Scandinavia.

Within the framework of preparations for the intended war against the Soviet Union Finland was now gaining special importance. A large number of intelligence reports received after mid-July 1940 strengthened the belief, in Hitler's mind as well as within the Wehrmacht High Command, that the Soviet leadership was planning a strike against Finland similar to that which it

---

[2] *DGFP* D ix, No. 293, pp. 402–3. Further references in Ueberschär, *Hitler und Finnland*, 178 ff., 191 ff. On Hitler's pro-Soviet attitude during the Winter War, when he banned any kind of assistance to Helsinki, see ibid. 84 ff., 108 ff., 129–30, 134 ff.

had recently made against the Baltic region, when it incorporated Estonia, Latvia, and Lithuania. On the strength of an assessment of the Finnish army produced by the general staff—which did not judge Finland's military position favourably, predicting the early collapse of the country, albeit after fierce initial resistance, in the event of Soviet military action[3]—Hitler at the beginning of August sanctioned the resumption of German arms deliveries to Finland and instructed the foreign ministry to initiate 'indirect and inconspicuous encouragement and support of the Finns (e.g. through Sweden)'.[4]

In order to check an impending occupation of northern Finland in the event of military action by the Soviet Union, Hitler ordered the German forces in northern Norway to be reinforced. One of the main reasons was the great importance attached to the north Finnish Petsamo area; under a recent German–Finnish agreement 60 per cent of Finland's nickel-ore production was to be consigned to Germany.[5] Hitler gave instructions for a force to be concentrated which, in the event of a Soviet attack, could occupy northern Finland and the Petsamo region, preventing any further Soviet move towards the Baltic or Scandinavia and safeguarding German economic interests in the nickel-ore mines at Petsamo–Kolosjoki. Colonel-General Nikolas von Falkenhorst, the Wehrmacht commander in Norway, was ordered to move the 'Mountain Corps Norway' and a new SS brigade into the Kirkenes area (in Finnmark province). The Luftwaffe and the navy were likewise instructed to set up new territorial commands and security forces at the North Cape in order to safeguard 'German interests in the *entire* Scandinavian region'.[6] It was obvious that these measures could only be 'interpreted as directed against Russia'.[7] After Hitler had personally ordered these extensive troop movements and regroupings of forces in Norway, Group XXI—later to be designated Army Command Norway—was instructed to work out an operations plan for the speedy occupation of the Petsamo region and its securing 'against the east'; this operation was explained by the Wehrmacht operations staff as 'merely part of a greater movement'.[8] Mountain Troop General Eduard Dietl was charged with its preparation and execution. The order for Operation Renntier (Reindeer) was issued on 7 September 1940. Anticipating future political developments, the order already envisaged participation by the Finn-

---

[3] 1. Skl, KTB, pt. A, 17 Aug. 1940, BA-MA III M 1000/12; also OKW/Abt. Ausland No. 02947/40, 16 Aug. 1940, and OKH/GenStdH OQ IV Abt. Frd. Heere Ost (II), No. 3379/40, 27 Aug. 1940, both PA, Handakten Etzdorf betr. Nordeuropa.

[4] *DGFP* D x, No. 330, p. 467 (12 Aug. 1940).

[5] On the trade negotiations see Ueberschär, *Hitler und Finnland*, 186 ff.; Krosby, *Petsamo Dispute*, 32 ff.

[6] OKW/WFSt/Abt. L, 16 Aug. 1940, BA-MA, 20. Armee, 20844/1. See also Greiner, *Oberste Wehrmachtführung*, 296–7, and diary entries XIX. A.K., Ia: Die Verlegung des Gebirgskorps nach Nordnorwegen [The transfer of the mountain corps to northern Norway], 15 Aug.–15 Nov. 1940, BA-MA, XIX. A.K., 23450.

[7] Halder, *Diaries*, 554–5 (18 Aug. 1940).

[8] Letter from Maj.-Gen. Warlimont re Renntier ('Reindeer') of 20 Aug. 1940 and Renntier order from Mountain. Trp. Gen. Dietl of 7 Sept. 1940, BA-MA, 20. Armee, 20844/1.

ish army; it may therefore be seen as a precursor of Operation Silberfuchs (Silver Fox), the German–Finnish move from northern Finland the following year, at the time of the German attack on the Soviet Union. Even that early stage of operational planning revealed a problem which was to recur later: the forces available were inadequate for a military enterprise in northern Scandinavia and Finland. For the execution of the operation only the reinforced 2nd Mountain Division was initially envisaged. The poor infrastructure prevented participation by 3rd Mountain Division, stationed in the Narvik area, so long as the political situation ruled out a deployment across Swedish territory. Nor was it possible to calculate the scale of potential Finnish participation. Attempts were therefore made, through local contacts with Finnish frontier troops, to gain more precise and detailed information on the district and port of Petsamo.[9] Field Marshal von Brauchitsch, the army commander-in-chief, and Colonel-General Halder, his chief of the general staff, admittedly criticized such projects as 'pipedreams'.[10]

The close connection between Germany's about-face in her Finnish policy and Hitler's return to his programmatic objective of the conquest of living-space in the east by a war against the Soviet Union was revealed also on the occasion of a reception for the field marshals newly promoted after the western campaign and the conversations which followed it at the Reich chancellery on 14 August 1940. It was then that Hitler explained his thinking on possible developments in the east. According to the extant notes of participants, Hitler stressed his concern about exclusive Soviet domination in the eastern Baltic; this was obstructing German interests there by rendering 'a German attack on Russia more difficult'. He also pointed out that, 'because of the balance of power in the Baltic', he would be 'forced to intervene' in the event of a Soviet attack on Finland.[11] Hitler therefore decided to go beyond indirect support for Helsinki; he gave orders for speedy and extensive supplies of arms and other war material to be sent to Finland.[12]

Contact with Finland was made, on Göring's instructions, by his confidant, Lieutenant-Colonel Joseph Veltjens, as special representative of the German government; neither a Finnish trade delegation in Berlin at that time, nor Ribbentrop and his foreign ministry, were being involved. Veltjens's mission may be seen as one of the most important stages along the road of involving Finland in the war; it would be mistaken, however, to view it as the 'beginning of a military conspiracy' or of 'broad military collaboration between Germany

---

[9] KTB, 15 and 28 Aug. 1940, BA-MA, XIX. A.K., 9269/3; minute Group XXI of 23 Aug. 1940 and Bericht über die Reise des SS-Obersturmbannführers Reitz von dem in Kirkenes stationierten SS-Bataillon [Report on the journey of SS Lt.-Col. Reitz of the SS battalion stationed at Kirkenes], 27 Aug. 1940, BA-MA, XIX. A.K., 26373/2.

[10] Halder, *Diaries*, 563–4 (26 Aug. 1940).

[11] See the diary notes by Leeb, *Tagebuchaufzeichnungen*, 252, and those by FM Milch, reproduced in Irving, *Rise and Fall*, 164, and Bock, Tagebuch I, 77 (14 Aug. 1940), MGFA P-210, vol. i.

[12] *DGFP* D x, No. 330, p. 467 n. 2, and ChefWiRüAmt, 14 Aug. 1940, BA-MA RW 19/185.

and Finland', or indeed to assume that Berlin had been compelled to invent 'alleged aggressive intentions on the part of the USSR against Finland' in order to ensure success for Veltjens's mission.[13] The assumption in Helsinki and Berlin that the Baltic Sea and Finland were the objective of a further military advance by the Soviet Union was virtually inescapable in view of the large-scale exercises of the Red Banner Baltic Fleet then in progress. In Finland, during his conversations on 18 and 19 August 1940 with Field Marshal Mannerheim, Premier Ryti, and ministers Witting and Walden, Veltjens obtained as collateral for the promised German arms deliveries Helsinki's consent to the transit of German troops from the Baltic ports through Finland to Norway, and to regular supply transports across Finnish territory to the German units stationed in northern Norway.

After that 'decisive turn' in German–Finnish relations and the 'change in the Führer's mood vis-à-vis Finland' there were now no obstacles to an 'all-round satisfactory' fulfilment of Finnish requests for arms on a massive scale.[14] Before the month was out the newly established collaboration, following military talks in Berlin, produced the first specific agreements. Finland made some 50,000 t. of shipping capacity available for German supply transports. Supplies were to go through the Finnish ports of Turku, Vaasa, Oulu, and Tornio, thence by rail to Rovaniemi, and by the Arctic Ocean route to Petsamo.

In conversation with German military attachés following their annual conference in Berlin, Hitler expressed the view that his direct and now overt material support for Finland would produce an effect on Moscow: it would prevent Stalin from taking military action against Finland.[15] The first anti-aircraft units started moving through Finland to northern Norway on Göring's orders at the beginning of September. The German–Finnish transit agreement signed on 12 September 1940 already authorized the stationing of German troops for the protection of supply-centres and troop quarters in Vaasa, Oulu, Rovaniemi, and Ivalo along the transit route.[16]

Another indication of Germany's new interests north of the Arctic Circle—interests no longer in conformity with Moscow's—was the abandonment, at the same time, of 'Base North', the base on the Soviet Arctic Ocean coast, placed until then at the German navy's disposal by the Soviet Union. This naval base, of course, had lost much of its operational and strategic import-

[13] For such assertions see Geschichte des zweiten Weltkrieges, ii. 307; Vainu, 'Einbeziehung Finnlands', 59–60. On Veltjens's mission see Upton, Finland 1940–1941, 135 ff.; Korhonen, Barbarossaplanen, 87 ff.; Heinrichs, Mannerheimgestalten, ii. 228 ff.; Ueberschär, Hitler und Finnland, 204 ff.; Andreen, Finland i Brännpunkten, 169 ff.

[14] Blücher, Gesandter, 198; Halder, Diaries, 558 (22 Aug. 1940). The first deliveries included a large consignment of anti-tank mines, some captured Norwegian weapons, and approximately 150 Morane fighter aircraft captured from the French. For Helsinki's political intentions see in general Manninen, 'Political Expedients'.

[15] DGFP D x, No. 366, p. 512 n. 3 (minutes of Göring's conference with Gen. Thomas on 29 Aug. 1940).

[16] See Korhonen, Barbarossaplanen, 109; Andreen, Finland i Brännpunkten, 172–3.

ance after the capture of the Norwegian and French ports. The German naval base, situated west of Murmansk, had held some promise of future German–Soviet collaboration in the area of naval warfare, as well as a blockade-proof ice-free starting-point for long-range German naval warfare in the Atlantic or for naval communications with Japan across the Arctic Ocean north of the USSR. All that was now abandoned.

The change in Hitler's attitude was not primarily due to economic motivations or to diplomatic proposals by the foreign ministry and the German legation in Helsinki. No doubt there had been some initial attempts after the Winter War to bring about a German–Finnish *rapprochement* in the war-economy and commercial areas—but the swift and decisive turn-about in favour of Helsinki was triggered only when Hitler had reverted to his strategic concept, to the conquest of living-space in the east by means of a war against the Soviet Union. The starting-point for Hitler's foreign-policy and strategic decisions with regard to Scandinavia and Finland after the summer of 1940 was his decision to commence preparations for his primarily ideological war. The beginnings of gradually intensifying German–Finnish co-operation in the political, economic, and military spheres were therefore directly linked to Hitler's resumption of his anti-Soviet basic position in the summer of 1940. This new Finnish policy was, so to speak, embedded in Hitler's concept of struggle for living-space in the east, it was 'determined in substance' by his decision to prepare for war in the east, by the 'central goal of his racial and political reflections'.[17] Once he had decided on a military solution in the east, Hitler viewed Finland in terms of northern flank cover for that campaign; the Soviet threat to northern Finland and the Petsamo region thus acquired new significance. Although he did not believe that Finland's participation would be decisive for the outcome of the campaign, he thought that its non-participation as a littoral state on the Baltic would substantially weaken his own starting-position in the war against Moscow. The point about Finland's participation—this was realized at an early stage—was to win its territory as a basis for deployment, supplies, and operations for the war against the Soviet Union. Germany's Finnish policy can thus be seen as an illustration of the increasing importance, owing to Hitler's decisions, of military and strategic considerations in German foreign policy and of the progressive loss of ground by the foreign ministry under Ribbentrop during the Second World War.

During the summer of 1940 several institutions prepared studies and plans for a 'new order in Europe' within the framework of a European large-scale economic sphere under German hegemony; all these were based on German interests and special rights in Finland and demanded that country's economic orientation towards Germany.[18] Whether Hitler, as early as the beginning of

---

[17] Hildebrand, 'Hitlers "Programm"', 184 ff. See also Hillgruber, *Strategie*, 209; Ueberschär, 'Hitlers Entschluß'; likewise Zitelmann, 'Zur Begründung des "Lebensraum"-Motivs'.

[18] See *DGFP* D ix, No. 354, pp. 476 ff. (30 May 1940), No. 367, pp. 496 ff. (1 June 1940); further references and sources in Ueberschär, *Hitler und Finnland*, 214 ff.

September, envisaged Finland's inclusion in his concept of a future Scandinavia as a 'North Germanic union, in which the individual members have a certain sovereignty', while 'they should be both politically and economically closely connected with Germany', must remain an open question, even though Hitler's subsequent plans could support such a supposition.[19] The further development of Finland's position as an interface in the conflict of interests between Moscow and Berlin, with all the consequences resulting from that position, was predetermined the moment Hitler proclaimed his political interests in Romania as his southern and in Finland as his northern flank, deliberately ruling out any retreat from these interests.[20] In both cases he claimed spheres of interest for Germany which only recently, in the German–Soviet agreements, he had renounced or been indifferent to. Hitler's instruction for Operation Renntier and his intention, if necessary, to push into northern Finland were matched, as a southern parallel, by his decision in early September to dispatch a military mission and German instructional troops to Romania to safeguard the oilfields there against seizure by a third party.[21]

2. Finland as a Political and Economic Sphere of Interest between Stalin and Hitler

Once it was clear that a 'lightning campaign' against the Soviet Union in the autumn of 1940 was no longer possible and that Hitler did not intend to realize his military 'eastern solution' until the spring of 1941, Foreign Minister von Ribbentrop succeeded in moving his concept of a European bloc against Britain into the focus of Berlin's diplomatic activity for a short time. It is possible that Germany's then still ambivalent policy *vis-à-vis* Finland in September–October 1940 should be viewed in that connection. While Ribbentrop's policy of a continental bloc 'culminated' at the end of September with the conclusion of the Tripartite Pact,[22] the foreign ministry approached the further development of German–Finnish relations only with great caution. During the Finno-Soviet negotiations on the demilitarization of the Åland Islands and on the concession to the Soviet Union of special control rights over the archipelago, Berlin maintained its disinterested attitude proclaimed in July. Despite the German–Finnish *rapprochement* initiated by Veltjens's visit, Berlin was not prepared to claim any political or military interest for itself in the Åland Islands or to enter into an agreement, offered by Helsinki, that would make it appear as a counterweight to Moscow's special status in the islands. In consequence, on 11 October 1940 Helsinki was compelled to grant the Soviet Union supervisory and control rights over the demilitarization of the archipelago. Hitler also declined to inform the Soviet Union on the exact

[19] See 'Führer Conferences', 135 (6 Sept. 1940).
[20] Halder, *Diaries*, 569 (31 Aug. 1940), 583–4 (14 Sept. 1940). On Romania see sect. I.I.2 at n. 81 (Förster).
[21] See sect. I.v.2 at n. 42 (Förster).   [22] Hildebrand, *Foreign Policy*, 102.

commencement or the scale of German troop transports through Finland, which would have revealed his reaching-out into the Soviet sphere of interests. He also left it to the Finnish government to notify Moscow of the agreement subsequently concluded on 22 September 1940 between Berlin and Helsinki concerning military transports. On 6 September 1940 the Finnish government had also granted the Soviet Union the right to transport troops to its leased area of Hanko. At Helsinki's request, therefore, a retrospective exchange of notes took place between the German and Finnish governments to provide a formal agreement and a political basis for the German troop movements.[23] No matter how much Ribbentrop tried to present the German–Finnish agreement as transportation arrangements 'of no political significance', and directed solely against Britain, Molotov showed his displeasure at not having been notified by Berlin and made it clear that the Soviet government continued to regard Finland as a firm component of its own sphere of interest.

The presence of German troops in Finland—roughly 1,800–2,000 men were stationed as staging and security personnel along the transit route in northern Finland, where during September and October they had to organize the transport of some 5,000 Luftwaffe personnel[24]—was in line with the Finnish government's intention, ever since the unfavourable conclusion of the Winter War, of gaining Germany's understanding for Finnish concerns and fears. The conclusion of the military and political agreements with the Third Reich on 12 and 22 September was therefore regarded by Helsinki as the beginning of a new German policy of interest in the Baltic region and Scandinavia, one that demonstratively included Finland. Finland's population and government welcomed the movement of German troops through the country as a clear token of protection against possible Soviet ambitions. The Finnish general staff co-operated closely with the German authorities in the technical organization of the troop movements. On 1 October the so-called 'Veltjens agreement' was concluded in Helsinki as the basis of the extensive arms deliveries to Finland, which had in fact been in progress ever since Hitler issued his instruction. As a kind of collateral for the German arms consignments Berlin received a blanket 'first option on all concessions of interest to the Greater German Reich in Finland'.[25] Finland hoped that this would provide German 'rear cover' for its continuing negotiations with the Soviet government concerning concessions to the nickel-ore mines at Kolosjoki (near Petsamo).

Control of these mines at Petsamo in northern Finland, the concession to which had been granted to a British–Canadian concern in 1934 on a long-term basis, had become an issue of crucial importance to the German war effort when, at the outbreak of war, the loss of overseas deliveries of nickel and

---

[23] On the Soviet–German transit agreement see also Blücher, *Gesandter*, 199; Upton, *Finland 1940–1941*, 142–3. On the German–Finnish exchange of notes see *DGFP* D xi, No. 86, pp. 148–9; Ueberschär, *Hitler und Finnland*, 221 ff., 231–2; also the following passage.

[24] *DGFP* D xi, No. 197, p. 329 (19 Oct. 1940); see also *KTB OKW* i. 133 (28 Oct. 1940), 140 (30 Oct. 1940).

[25] *DGFP*, D xi, Nos. 139, 140, pp. 232–3, 234 (1 Oct. 1940).

molybdenum, metals important for alloyed steel, had caused a considerable gap in supplies.[26] Agreement on major Finnish deliveries of copper, molybdenum, pyrites, and nickel had therefore been the principal objective of German–Finnish trade negotiations in the spring of 1940. Studies by mining experts of IG-Farbenindustrie AG convinced the Reich ministry of economic affairs that the deliveries of 60 per cent of the total output, agreed in the German–Finnish trade and delivery contracts of 29 June and 23 July 1940, would entirely cover the current German demand for nickel. The nickel-ore deliveries from Petsamo, along with Finnish timber products, were therefore of outstanding importance in German–Finnish trade.

Moscow too had staked a claim to nickel supplies. Helsinki had therefore agreed to supply 40 per cent of the total output to the Soviet Union. At the end of August, however, Molotov made it clear to Juho K. Paasikivi, the Finnish minister in Moscow, that what mattered to the Soviet Union was not merely participation in the ore production, but long-term concessionary rights and, above all, its political interests in the frontier region which, at the end of the Winter War, it had returned to Finland out of consideration for Britain. During the negotiations with the Soviet Union, which dragged on throughout the autumn and winter and into the spring of 1941, Paasikivi continually feared that Moscow might resort to military action to enforce its demands. Helsinki therefore wished to bring up openly the first-option rights granted to the German government, to act as an obstacle to Soviet demands.

However, so long as Ribbentrop was still hoping that the Soviet Union might participate in his concept of a continental bloc, Berlin had to operate cautiously with regard to the Soviet claims. Ribbentrop was anxious to avoid 'the Petsamo question becoming a controversial point with the Russians at the present moment'.[27] Any official support for Helsinki that would have seemed to question the assignment of Finland to the Soviet sphere of interest, representing a breach of existing German–Soviet agreements, had to be avoided for the time being—in fact, until the intended 'delimitation of their interests for the ages' had been agreed with Moscow.[28] For the Finnish government, Berlin's cautious tactical attitude was not enough. It repeatedly, though unsuccessfully, urged Berlin to claim Finland as a German area of interest *vis-à-vis* Moscow. Marshal Mannerheim also warned Colonel Horst Rössing, the German military attaché in Helsinki, more than once of the military risks which might arise from a transfer of the Petsamo concession to the USSR: this could lead to supplies for the German forces in northern Norway coming under Soviet control.[29] Yet Berlin did not communicate to the Soviet Union

---

[26] On the importance of the nickel-ore deposits of Petsamo–Kolosjoki and on the negotiations about concessions and delivery quotas see Krosby, *Petsamo Dispute, passim*, and Ueberschär, *Hitler und Finnland*, 166–79, 186–96, 234–8, 253–66, also *Blauweißbuch*, vol. ii.

[27] *DGFP* D xi, No. 196, p. 328 (19 Oct. 1940).

[28] Thus Ribbentrop's offer in his letter to Stalin, 12 Oct. 1940: see *DGFP* D xi, No. 176, p. 297.

[29] Telegram No. 725, Blücher to foreign ministry, 19 Nov. 1940, PA, Dt.Ges. Helsinki, Erlasse 501–813; also Greiner, *Oberste Wehrmachtführung*, 363 (8 Feb. 1941); *KTB OKW* i. 325 (14 Feb. 1941).

any claim of its own to the concession. However, even without such an openly stated claim to concessionary rights, Hitler's attitude in fact proved to be a guarantee to Finland against the Soviet claims to the Petsamo region. At the beginning of 1941 Hitler told Mussolini and his foreign minister Count Galeazzo Ciano that the reason for Germany's attitude in favour of Helsinki was 'Finland's great importance to Germany because of its nickel deposits', without, however, disclosing to his Italian interlocutors Finland's strategic importance within the (by then commenced) preparations for the intended campaign in the east.[30] The Wehrmacht High Command also made repeated representations to the foreign ministry in order to emphasize its interest in the Soviet Union's exclusion from the Petsamo region.[31]

Nickel-ore deliveries to Germany started even before the end of the year. An additional delivery contract, signed between IG-Farbenindustrie AG and Petsamo-Nikkeli-OY on 19 February 1941, was to ensure the regular arrival of ore from Finland over the next few years. Helsinki showed some skill in keeping both the British and the German governments in play as future customers and in using the rights and interests of both states in its talks with Moscow as an obstacle to any Finno-Soviet arrangements on the issue of ownership. Moreover, by means of delaying tactics and agreed procedures Helsinki and Berlin succeeded in protracting negotiations opened in Moscow on the establishment of a joint Finno-Soviet concessionary company until the summer of 1941, with the result that Moscow's ideas about the alignment of Finland's economy and about direct acquisition of the Petsamo nickel-ore mines were prevented from being implemented before the onset of Operation Barbarossa.

As the finalization of Germany's Finnish policy depended on the development of German–Soviet relations, Molotov's talks in Berlin in November 1940 were of vital importance to the future of German–Finnish relations. Although the Finnish government could not know that its country also possessed considerable military significance for Hitler as a future partner in his eastern plans, the degree of existing collaboration at the diplomatic level, between the two sides' military authorities, on the issue of troop transits, and in the economic co-operation between IG-Farben and Petsamo-Nikkeli clearly suggested that German–Finnish relations had undergone an 'unprecedented improvement'.[32] Even before his talks with Molotov, Ribbentrop had made it clear that Hitler would not surrender his military and economic interests in Finland to Moscow.[33] Prior to Molotov's arrival in Germany the Finnish government reminded Berlin of the advantages of German–Finnish co-operation; Helsinki was anxious to prevent any new German–Soviet settlement of interests at Finland's expense. Blücher, the German minister, and the foreign office in Berlin took up the idea of a further development of German–Finnish

[30] Greiner, *Oberste Wehrmachtführung*, 346–7.
[31] *KTB OKW* i. 327 (16 Feb. 1941), 331–2 (18 Feb. 1941).
[32] Minute by Blücher, 1 Nov. 1940, PA, Büro St.S., Finnland, vol. ii.
[33] See Blücher, *Gesandter*, 204; Ueberschär, *Hitler und Finnland*, 230.

relations. They endeavoured to define the protection of Finland against possible claims and demands by Molotov as a desirable function (that of guarantor) and task of Germany's Finnish policy even before the Soviet foreign
commissar arrived in Berlin.

During Molotov's talks with Hitler and Ribbentrop in Berlin on 12 and 13
November 1940 one of the most contentious issues was the question whether,
in conformity with existing German–Soviet agreements, Finland was to be
viewed 'definitively as an inviolable part of the Soviet sphere of interest' and
whether Hitler would be prepared to tolerate further diplomatic or even
warlike action by Stalin, thereby accepting that country's incorporation into
the Soviet sphere of power.[34] Molotov, who was accurately informed on
Germany's economic interest, the involvement of German firms in the
Petsamo nickel-mines, the extensive German arms deliveries to Helsinki, and
the presence of German troops in Finland, discovered that Hitler was not
prepared to set aside his own interests. Any new military conflict in the Baltic
for the sake of enforcing Soviet interests against Finland would, Hitler declared, place a serious strain on German–Soviet relations.[35] He emphasized
repeatedly that he did not wish to see a new Soviet–Finnish war because he
would regard any Soviet action against Finland as a threat to the status quo in
the Baltic region. Hitler therefore refused to give Stalin a free hand *vis-à-vis*
Helsinki. Ribbentrop's hope of a settlement of interests 'on a scale of centuries' also proved a fiasco, as Molotov did not content himself with the
allocation of areas of interest from Britain's future 'bankrupt assets' but
instead pointed to Soviet 'short- and long-term objectives' in Finland, the
Baltic region, and the Balkans.[36]

The Molotov talks in Berlin revealed the incompatibility of German and
Soviet interests in the Baltic and Finland. Now the stationing of German
troops in Finland proved a useful means of preventing Soviet military action
against Finland and hence the enforcement of Moscow's interests. State
Secretary von Weizsäcker had the impression that Hitler would now regard
any further action by the Soviet Union as a *casus belli*.[37] On 25 November 1940
a catalogue of Stalin's demands in the event of the Soviet Union's accession to
a 'Quadripartite Pact'—offered during the Molotov talks—made it clear that
without a settlement of the German–Soviet clash of interests in Finland in
Moscow's favour the Soviet Union could not be incorporated in Ribbentrop's
continental bloc.[38] Heading the list of proposals was the demand for the

[34] On the Molotov visit see sect. I.1.5 at n. 164 (Förster); Hillgruber, *Strategie*, 304 ff.; Fabry,
Hitler-Stalin-Pakt, 349 ff.; Bereshkow, *Diplomatische Mission*, 25–39; Schmidt, *Statist*, 514 ff.;
DGFP D xi, Nos. 325–9, pp. 533–70. On the Finnish issue see esp. Ueberschär, *Hitler und
Finnland*, 239 ff.; also the following quotation.

[35] Bereshkow, *Diplomatische Mission*, 30, and Halder, *Diaries*, 692–3 (16 Nov. 1940), in
agreement.

[36] On the division of Soviet interests into 'short-term' and 'long-term' objectives see Hillgruber,
Strategie, 305.

[37] Thus von Etzdorf's report to Halder: see Halder, *Diaries*, 691–2 (16 Nov. 1940).

[38] *DGFP* D xi, No. 404, pp. 714–15.

immediate withdrawal of German troops from Finland and the country's reassignment to the Soviet sphere of interest. Hitler left these proposals unanswered, especially as on 4 and 12 November he had given instructions that 'all preparations for which verbal orders have already been given' for the intended military solution in the east were to be continued.[39] Hitler, moreover, is reported to have subsequently remarked that he had not expected anything of Molotov's visit anyway; instead his statements had made it clear that the USSR was pushing towards central Europe and that the Balkans and Finland represented 'dangerous flanks'.[40] The Finnish government was soon informed by von Blücher and by Lieutenant-Colonel Veltjens—who had returned to Finland towards the end of November on a special mission for Göring—that Hitler had not yielded to the Soviet demands but had held on to his own interests in Finland. At the same time Veltjens was able to receive new Finnish requests for arms deliveries. Eventually, on 22 November, after several days of German–Finnish military talks, a further 'Agreement between the German Wehrmacht and the Finnish General Staff' was concluded concerning the transit of extensive and continuous two-way traffic between northern Norway and Finland, consisting of servicemen ṭaking and returning from leave.[41] The agreement contained no time-limit; it envisaged the further development of the German supply organization in northern Finland, with Turku (Åbo) and Rovaniemi as major Wehrmacht control centres. The headquarters of the Wehrmacht commander in Norway, responsible for transit matters, reported that contacts with the Finnish military authorities were marked by a spirit of friendship and trusting co-operation, and that Helsinki was invariably display-ing sympathy for German requests. In view of its strained relations with Moscow, it was in Finland's interest also to win Germany as a military guarantor of northern Finland—so far garrisoned only by insignificant Finnish forces—and to emphasize this situation by an increased presence of German troops.

The insecure and unstable basis of Finnish policy emerged clearly when, in late November and early December, both Moscow and Berlin were exerting their influence on the election of Premier Ryti as Finland's new president. Moreover, Moscow and Berlin both adopted a critical attitude to Finno-Swedish plans for a joint defence treaty between the two Scandinavian coun-tries and actually foiled the realization of such an alliance.[42] The new all-party government under Premier Jukka W. Rangell for the first time included the

---

[39] See 'Führerbesprechung' of 4 Nov. 1940 and Directive No. 18 of 12 Nov. 1940 in Halder, *Diaries*, 674–5 (4 Nov. 1940), and *Hitler's Directives*, No. 18, p. 43.

[40] See Engel, *Heeresadjutant bei Hitler*, 91–2 (15 Nov. and 18 Dec. 1940).

[41] Text of the agreement in BA-MA, 20. Armee, 12564/1; also Ueberschär, *Hitler und Finnland*, 245 ff.

[42] On Moscow's and Berlin's influence on the candidates for the election of a successor to President Kyösti Kallio and on Swedish–Finnish alliance plans see Ueberschär, *Hitler und Finnland*, 248 ff., with a list of sources. According to Andreen, *Finland i Brännpunkten*, 143, the British government also tried to exert pressure on the choice of a president.

Isänmaallinen Kansan Liike (IKL: Patriotic People's Movement), which had to be regarded as belonging to the Fascist camp. The fact that even the Finnish Social Democrats consented to such a widening of the government's basis for the sake of national unity may be seen as evidence of the country's precarious foreign-policy position, but equally as a special gesture towards the National Socialist regime in Germany.[43] After all, co-operation with Germany remained the foreign-policy line under Premier Rangell. There is no doubt that this shift to the right in the government's political position, as a result of the inclusion of the IKL, represented a clear demonstration of its sympathies for the Third Reich. Berlin's powerful military and political status after victory over France, along with a continuing threat from the east, gave an appreciable boost to extreme nationalist tendencies as well as to champions of a revanchist policy and of reorientation towards Germany. At the same time there emerged a readiness for a change of the parliamentary system in the direction of authoritarian government. There was increasing understanding for National Socialist Germany's struggle against Britain. In the autumn of 1940 new nationalist and right-wing radical movements for a 'free' and 'awakening' Finland were being founded, as well as a National Socialist Workers' Movement; none of these, however, grew into mass movements. By the spring of 1941 the democratic parliamentary institutions had been largely excluded from political decision-making. The 'inner circle' which determined policy had been further strengthened in its powers and functions by Ryti's election as president. It was within that circle that all the most important foreign-policy questions were decided, and these decisions conformed with the pro-Berlin course adopted by Finland—especially as enquiries and contacts in Berlin were making a German–Soviet conflict appear an entirely realistic possibility. Unofficial Finnish suggestions that Sweden and Finland might both join the Tripartite Pact should be seen as part of Helsinki's ceaseless endeavours to obtain a firm commitment and demonstrative support from Berlin against Moscow.

After the beginning of 1941 Finland's economic importance to Germany also rapidly increased. The extensive deliveries of nickel and copper ore following the start of production in the Petsamo mines in December 1940 made it clear that Finland had become an indispensable trade partner for the German war economy's requirements of raw materials. The war-economy and armaments department of the Wehrmacht High Command described the nickel-ore deposits of Petsamo as 'the only significant deposits in the central European large-scale sphere' outside the Soviet Union.[44] On the other hand, the deteriorating food situation in Finland after the summer of 1940 led to increased dependence on Germany, which was helping out with grain deliver-

---

[43] Similarly Upton, *Finland 1940–1941*, 201–2. On assessing the IKL as 'Fascist' or 'semi-Fascist' see Nolte, *Faschistische Bewegungen*, 237–8; also Kalela, 'Right-wing Radicalism'; Rintala, *Three Generations*.

[44] Die Wehrwirtschaft Finnlands, kurze Charakteristik und Gesamtbeurteilung, Stand März 1941 [Finland's war economy, a brief characterization and overall assessment, as of Mar. 1941], BA-MA WiIE 4/1; see Milward, *Zweiter Weltkrieg*, 336. On an estimate of the deposits in the USSR see Thomas, *Wehr- und Rüstungswirtschaft*, 521–2.

ies. In June 1941 Britain, because of growing German influence in Finland, refused to renew the 'navicert' system which authorized overseas merchant shipping to pass through the naval war-zone of Petsamo.[45] This increased Finland's dependence on German grain supplies; Keitel and Jodl persuaded Hitler to have these increased 'for military reasons'.[46] The German–Finnish trade agreement, renewed on 31 December 1940, and a supplementary agreement signed on 7 March 1941 made the Finnish economy even more dependent on Germany. Germany's share in Finland's foreign trade in 1941 amounted to roughly 55 per cent for both exports and imports, although Finnish exports in terms of value lagged far behind imports.[47] New German deliveries of war material, in response to Finnish requests, were agreed during the first half of 1941, following talks between General Thomas, head of the war-economy and armaments department, and General Leonhard Grandell, head of the war-economy department in the Finnish ministry of defence. On several occasions either Hitler or Göring received a personal request to decide on the extent and range of military equipment and economic aid—primarily motor-fuel, heavy howitzers, machine-guns, and ammunition.[48]

The state planning committees set up on the German model and a state-of-emergency law enacted in May 1941 resulted in a restructuring of the Finnish economic system and enabled industry to adjust speedily to the requirement of a war economy. Simultaneously, the process of centralization and the weakening of democratic institutions continued at an accelerated pace with a concentration of governmental powers and a massive bypassing of the Finnish parliament. In May and June 1941, when German–Finnish military talks opened, parliament was faced with a *fait accompli*. Despite intensified armaments production, the Finnish economy at the start of Operation Barbarossa was largely dependent on German supplies, in respect of both foodstuffs and armaments. Nevertheless, the war-economy and armaments department of the Wehrmacht High Command believed Finland to be a combat-ready flank partner for the impending war, and one capable of withstanding a certain amount of strain.[49]

3. MILITARY ASPECTS OF FINLAND'S INCLUSION IN THE PLANS FOR BARBAROSSA

Once Hitler had decided in the summer of 1940 to go to war against the Soviet Union, even the first operational ideas and plans of the high commands assumed as a matter of principle—though often still vaguely—that Finland

[45] See also Medlicott, *Economic Blockade*, i. 627–32. On navicerts 'as a commercial passport' see ibid. 94 ff.

[46] See *DGFP* D xii, No. 647, p. 1050 (18 June 1941).

[47] On the development of Finland's commercial dependence on the Third Reich after 1940–1 see Ueberschär, *Hitler und Finnland*, 265 ff.; ibid. 329 ff. for tables and compilations on foreign trade.

[48] See KTB WiRüAmt/Stab, 3, 6, 7, 9, 11, 26 Mar. 1941, BA-MA RW 19/164.

[49] See Die Wehrwirtschaft Finnlands (as above, n. 44).

would participate in it. This general assumption on the part of the senior officers and staffs charged with the studies of operations against the Soviet Union stemmed basically from the good German–Finnish relations which had existed from the time of the First World War until 1939, and on earlier military co-operation in the attainment of Finnish independence. Since then, and more particularly after the Finno-Soviet Winter War, it was natural for the German military leaders to include Finland, as a fundamental adversary of the Soviet Union, in their operational planning.

The 'Operations Draft East', prepared by Major-General Marcks on instructions from the chief of the Army General Staff at the beginning of August 1940, provided for Finland's participation and for a Finnish move against the Murmansk railway 'at a later phase of the war'.[50] The 'Operations Study by the Head of the Land Forces Group (Loßberg Study)', produced in mid-September by the operations staff of the Wehrmacht High Command, accurately envisaged an advance by German formations within the framework 'of Group XXI to be employed by Finland' and co-operation 'with the probably allied Finnish army'.[51] Indeed, as this study proposed a point of main effort in the northern part of the overall front line, exceptional importance attached to an attack by an outer wing, with a thrust towards Murmansk and a joint advance on Leningrad. It is also significant that the 'Reflection on Russia' of 28 July 1940, produced by the naval operations staff, used the slogan of the 'liberation of Finland' as the political objective of military action against the USSR,[52] even though the Naval High Command was otherwise viewing a war against the Soviet Union with a great deal of scepticism. However, the slogan was thought to be an effective propaganda formula in case Hitler intended 'to settle things in the east'. The naval operations staff was likewise convinced that Finland would have to be involved in such a campaign against the Soviet Union.

During the autumn of 1940 Army HQ Norway continued preparations for Operation Renntier.[53] Information was received from the Finnish general staff on the infrastructure and operational facilities in northern Finland. Colonel Rössing, the military attaché in Helsinki, was repeatedly enlisted to discover the disposition and defensive intentions of the Finnish forces. There was not, however, at that time any co-operation between the general staffs or appropriate agreements between Berlin and Helsinki for joint military action against the Soviet Union, although—on the basis of outdated statements during the Nuremberg trials which have since been corrected—this is still occasionally

[50] 'Operationsentwurf Ost', 117.

[51] See 'Loßberg-Studie' in Besymenski, *Sonderakte 'Barbarossa'* (1968), 307–13; *Fall Barbarossa*, No. 32, p. 130.

[52] See Salewski, *Seekriegsleitung*, iii. 137 ff.; 'Betrachtungen über Rußland', 28 July 1940, BA-MA RM 6/66 (also on the following data).

[53] See reference in *KTB OKW* i. 120 (11 Oct. 1940) and Tätigkeitsbericht Gruppe XXI, Ia [Activity report Group XXI, Ia], 1–30 Nov. 1940, BA-MA, 20. Armee, 12564/1; also personal papers of Col.-Gen. von Falkenhorst, 52 ff., BA-MA N 300/4.

asserted.[54] During the reciprocal courtesy calls between the commanders of the respective frontier regions in Finnmark (in Norway) and in Lapland (in Finland), Mountain Troop General Eduard Dietl of the 'Mountain Corps Norway' and Major-General Hjalmar Siilasvuo, strategic and political discussions were expressly excluded.[55] Significantly, there was no prior discussion of the uneven distribution carried out by the Finnish high command or the strong concentration of Finnish forces in the south of the country, with the result that Army HQ Norway was viewing the resulting military vacuum with great concern, considering the Petsamo region to be inadequately protected.[56] There was no direct contact between the two general staffs on the possibility of an early insertion of German units into northern Finland. Even up to January and February 1941 Blücher and Rössing were reporting that, in the event of war with the Soviet Union, Finland intended to evacuate the Petsamo region, with the weak covering forces there offering delaying resistance, and that the entire Petsamo region, including the ore-mines, was not included in the Finnish defence system. The military attaché did not believe that German ideas of a substantial military strengthening of northern Finland would be feasible without the acceptance of contractual obligations by Germany in Finland's favour. However, so long as Hitler was not prepared to enter into such obligations, the military vacuum could be filled only by German preparatory measures.[57]

German–Finnish military contacts in the autumn and winter of 1940–1 were not, however, solely concerned with issues of troop transits or German deliveries of weapons and war material.[58] This was shown during Major-General Paavo Talvela's visit to Berlin in November and December 1940. In August and September, as the officer responsible for the Petsamo traffic, he had headed the discussions on transit traffic and German armaments aid. In his conversations with Göring, Halder, and Vice-Admiral Schniewind, chief of staff of the naval operations staff,[59] he had been instructed by Marshal Mannerheim, for whom he acted as liaison officer with the German military

---

[54] On this thesis of Marxist-Leninist literature see *Geschichte des zweiten Weltkrieges*, iii. 307–8; also *Geschichte der internationalen Beziehungen*, ii. 90; *Deutschland im zweiten Weltkrieg*, i. 528, 433; these date the alleged 'secret negotiations' to the autumn of 1940 and joint general-staff talks to 'December 1940'. The superseded statements are in *IMT* vii. 161, 309–10, 327–8; for a more balanced view see now Menger, *Deutschland und Finnland*, 71 ff.

[55] See Geb.Korps Norwegen, KTB, 7 Nov. 1940, BA-MA, XIX. A.K., 9269/3, and 2. Geb.Div./ Div.Befehl No. 3/1a/5/40 geh., 6 Sept. 1940, BA-MA, XIX. A.K., 9269/4.

[56] Conference with Col. Rössing, 10 Oct. 1940, BA-MA, 20. Armee, E 280/2.

[57] See Rössing's report after his conversation with Maj.-Gen. Airo on 7 Jan. 1941, BA-MA, 20. Armee, 20844/4, and telegram No. 71, von Blücher to foreign ministry, 3 Feb. 1941, PA, Büro St.S., Finnland, vol. ii.

[58] Thus, for instance, the now outdated account in Hölter, 'Probleme des deutsch-finnischen Koalitionskampfes', 17; Erfurth, *Finnischer Krieg*, 26–7; Mannerheim, *Memoirs*, 405.

[59] On Talvela's talks see *DGFP* D xi, No. 439, p. 774, No. 542, pp. 917–18; also minute of the conversation between the chief of staff of the naval operations staff and Gen. Talvela on 19 Nov. 1940, BA-MA, OKM, Case 599/PG 33687, and Talvela's memoirs: Talvela, *Sotilaan elämä*, i. 240–67. See further Hillgruber, *Strategie*, 490–1; Ueberschär, *Hitler und Finnland*, 272–3; Andreen, *Finland i Brännpunkten*, 200 ff.

authorities and Göring—between one military man and another, as it were—
to sound out the possibility of a change in German–Soviet relations. His task
was to obtain definitive information on Germany's position *vis-à-vis* Finland
after the Molotov visit and, at the same time, to allow it to be understood that,
in the event of the adoption of an anti-Soviet policy by Berlin, Finland would
side with Germany. During his conversations in the Army General Staff
Talvela learnt of possible military 'eastern intentions' against the Soviet
Union. In this context Colonel-General Halder enquired about the time
Finland would require for bringing about an 'inconspicuous readiness for
attack towards the south-east' in the direction of Leningrad. General Talvela,
however, was unable to give any detailed information or to conclude any firm
agreements, even though he proposed to Göring 'joint preparations by the two
general staffs' for 'joint tasks in the future'.[60] Whether these talks with Halder
and Göring are to be seen as indirectly connected with the German plans for
Barbarossa[61] must remain an open question. There is no evidence that Talvela,
as the representative of the Finnish general staff, so to speak, or as
Mannerheim's envoy, exerted any direct influence on the planning of what
later became Operation Barbarossa or that he collaborated in the operational
drafts submitted to Hitler on 5 December 1940 at a 'Führer conference'. At
that conference Hitler reiterated that he was counting on the participation of
other states in the war against the Soviet Union. Thus Finland and Romania
would participate, if only because their future existence as states was linked to
a German victory.[62] Both these states were to be enlarged territorially after the
campaign.

Although no negotiations had been opened with the general staffs of the
countries earmarked for participation, these countries, in line with Hitler's
instructions, were being included in future operations or German moves
planned across their territories. Hitler thus envisaged a German operation on
the northern flank, with 'objective: Arctic Ocean', using three divisions, whose
deployment and concentration were to be accomplished by rail transport
through Sweden. Halder's conversations in mid-December with Colonel-
General von Falkenhorst and Colonel Buschenhagen from Army HQ Norway
already assumed an attack by four divisions under the command of General
Dietl, striking from Norway across Finland. Timely concentration of such
major forces at the North Cape would be possible only if three divisions were
transported by rail from Norway through Sweden. The continuing need to
defend and safeguard Norway against British landings, however, compelled
Army HQ Norway for the time being to withhold elements of the divisions
earmarked for the attack and to supply their place by enlisting the motorized

[60] Halder, *Diaries*, 738 (16 Dec. 1940), 741 (17 Dec. 1940); Talvela, *Sotilaan elämä*, i. 250 ff.,
here 259.
[61] Thus Vainu, 'Einbeziehung Finnlands', 62.
[62] Halder, *Diaries*, 722–3 (5 Dec. 1940), id., *KTB* ii. 213 (5 Dec. 1940; not in trans.). See also
Greiner, *Oberste Wehrmachtführung*, 325–6.

SS brigade from central Norway; the transfer of this unit to the frontier region of Kirkenes–northern Norway had been planned in any case.[63]

Hitler's Directive No. 21 for 'Case Barbarossa', issued shortly afterwards, took up Halder's and Buschenhagen's ideas of 14 December 1940 of employing a northern and a central force in Finland, thus assigning to Army HQ Norway two operations which would represent the most northerly attack on the Soviet Union; these would be launched across Finnish territory. Hitler's 'substantial amendment' of the earlier operations plan, which now gave priority to the occupation of Leningrad over the seizure of Moscow, thereby shifting the main effort of strategic intentions to the northern sector of the front, lent increasing importance to the use of Finnish territory by German troops and hence to co-operation with the Finnish army on the northern wing.[64]

According to the directive, the principal task of Army HQ Norway— previously designated Group XXI—even during the war in the east would be the protection and defence of Norway, as well as the safeguarding of the Petsamo region, together with the Arctic Ocean route, once the region was occupied. A thrust towards the Murmansk railway was envisaged jointly with Finnish units. A further operation by two or three divisions from the area around Rovaniemi was, for the time being, made contingent on Sweden's readiness to permit the necessary rail transport. Without prior agreement with Helsinki, Hitler's directive assigned to the Finnish army the task of covering the deployment of Army HQ Norway, of conducting joint operations with it, and, in harmonization with the advance of the German Army Group North, 'the tying down of the strongest possible Russian forces by an attack west, or on both sides, of Lake Ladoga, and of capturing Hanko'. The question of a unified command over German and Finnish troops had not yet been clarified. The Wehrmacht High Command would be responsible for timetables and appropriate joint chains of command. As the directive proceeded from the assumption of rapid success, the actual capture of the city of Murmansk as an important supply-port for the Soviet war economy was, significantly, disregarded. Only later did the city and port of Murmansk move to the foreground of operational considerations; this was in connection with the demands of the navy.[65]

While, at the turn of 1940–1, Hitler's political and military decisions were based on his definitive determination to seek a military solution in the east, tension between Helsinki and Moscow increased as the Soviet government

---

[63] Halder, *Diaries*, 727–8 (7 Dec. 1940), 736–7 (14 Dec. 1940). On the inclusion of Finnish territory in strategic planning see also Ziemke, *German Northern Theater*, 121 ff.

[64] See *KTB OKW* i. 233 (17 Dec. 1940). On the directive see *Hitler's Directives*, 49 ff., also on subsequent details of the directive.

[65] In its 'Lagebetrachtung für einen Ostfeldzug gegen Rußland (Fall "Barbarossa")' [Situation assessment for an eastern campaign against Russia (Case Barbarossa)], 30 Jan. 1941 (Salewski, *Seekriegsleitung*, iii. 145–67), the naval operations staff regretted that 'an operation against this area [Murmansk] from the land side is not at present intended'.

was pressing for an agreement on the Petsamo mines in line with its own wishes. German–Soviet relations, on the other hand, appeared to be outwardly consolidated after the conclusion of a new economic agreement on 19 January 1941. At the 'Führer conference' on 9 January Hitler again made it clear that he rejected new Soviet demands on Finland and that he was ultimately 'persevering unassailably with his programme' of 'smashing' and 'shattering' the Soviet Union.[66] The Foreign Armies East Department of the Army General Staff, in its estimate of the situation in mid-January 1941, observed that substantial parts of the Red Army would be tied down on the Finnish frontier because Finland 'might well exploit the situation for the recovery of its lost territories'.[67] The Army High Command in addition examined the idea of a joint German–Finnish offensive in the Lake Ladoga–Lake Onega area; in conjunction with the elimination of Hanko this was proposed as a kind of southern companion piece to the planned German attack in the Petsamo–Murmansk area.[68]

In order to discuss the problems arising from plans for joint operations against the Soviet Union, Lieutenant-General Erik Heinrichs, chief of the Finnish general staff, was invited to Berlin on 30 January 1941 to report on the Finno-Soviet Winter War of 1939–40.[69] As Hitler had already ruled in Directive No. 21 that all preparations and preliminary work for Barbarossa had to proceed under the guise of 'precautionary measures', the talks with the Finnish general had to be represented as non-committal discussions of potential defence measures in the event of a Soviet attack. From Halder's exposé, however, Heinrichs was able to assume that Hitler was considering war with the Soviet Union and, in this connection, was expecting Finland to participate. Heinrichs assured Halder that within nine days of general mobilization Finland could be ready for battle along the Soviet frontier. Specifically, operational plans were discussed for two Finnish thrusts along both sides of Lake Ladoga. It seems doubtful that Heinrichs would have made a firm commitment to a joint German–Finnish attack on Leningrad, the more so as, for reasons of secrecy, the outbreak of a German–Soviet war was still being presented as a hypothetical case. There were no agreements in writing. Nevertheless, the chief of the Finnish general staff was said to have shown a generally co-operative and open-minded attitude to the German plans, leading Hitler to believe 'in a good comradeship-in-arms'.[70]

---

[66] Halder, *Diaries*, 750–1 (16 Jan. 1941); *KTB OKW* i. 257–8 (9 Jan. 1941); *DGFP*, D xi, No. 630, pp. 1056–60.

[67] Einschätzung der Streitkräfte, der Rüstungsindustrie und des Eisenbahnwesens der Sowjetunion [Assessment of the fighting forces, the armaments industry, and the railway system of the Soviet Union], OKH/GenStdH/Op.Abt. (IN) No. 050/41, 15 Jan. 1941, published in *Fall Barbarossa*, No. 15, pp. 80 ff.

[68] Halder, *Diaries*, 752–3 (16 Jan. 1941).

[69] On Lt.-Gen. Heinrichs's visit see Halder, *Diaries*, 754 (17 Jan. 1941); Heinrichs, *Mannerheimgestalten*, ii. 233; Mannerheim, *Memoirs*, 405; Korhonen, *Barbarossaplanen*, 213 ff.; Ueberschär, *Hitler und Finnland*, 276 ff.; Manninen, 'Beziehungen', 85 ff.; see also Turtola, *Erik Heinrichs*.

[70] Engel, *Heeresadjutant bei Hitler*, 93.

Accordingly, Finland's active participation in the war against the Soviet Union was spelt out in detail in the first version of the Army High Command's 'Deployment Directive Barbarossa'. The Finnish army was assigned the tasks of covering the German deployment in northern Finland, eliminating the Soviet naval base of Hanko, and attacking along both sides of Lake Ladoga.[71] In his report of the deployment directive at the 'Führer conference' on 3 February 1941, Colonel-General Halder additionally pointed out that, according to information from General Heinrichs, one could expect an intensified Finnish deployment in the south of the country, as well as operations against Hanko (with 2 divisions) and in the direction of Leningrad (with 5 divisions) and of Lake Onega (with 3 divisions).[72] Halder emphasized that for these actions the Finns would need strong German support. For Army HQ Norway the most important task would be to secure Norway against potential Allied landing attempts. In addition, in the view of the Army High Command, Army HQ Norway should carry out the occupation of the Petsamo region prior to Finland's entry into the war, and after Finland's entry mount a forceful attack from Rovaniemi towards Kandalaksha, with a view to cutting off the Murmansk region from the south and annihilating the Soviet forces there, or else attack Murmansk and the Murmansk railway directly from Petsamo. The final decision between these variants was left open until an answer was obtained to the crucial question of whether Sweden would permit use of her railways for German troop transports in transit from Norway.

Once the detailed proposals and dispositions had been made for the states earmarked for participation in the attack on the Soviet Union, the problem of co-ordination with the general staffs of Germany's new 'allies' became a priority for the Army High Command. On 3 February 1941, however, Hitler ruled that 'no approaches must be made to Finland, Sweden, Hungary, or Slovakia . . . regarding their participation or indirect help until such time as the German measures can no longer be camouflaged'; the 'deployment in the east' was to be understood 'as long as possible as a grand deception' to cover a presumed imminent landing in England.[73] Similarly, the Wehrmacht High Command in the middle of February once again postponed contacts with those states to a later date and reserved to itself the initiation of such contacts.[74]

The preliminary studies ordered by the Army High Command for the proposed operation in the far north soon revealed that the intentions of Army HQ Norway exceeded the narrow scope of limited flank cover; Army HQ Norway was hoping, with the aid of considerable reinforcements, to achieve a breakthrough towards the White Sea. From there it intended to perform two far-ranging envelopment operations in order to annihilate the Soviet forma-

---

[71] Original version of 'Aufmarschanweisung Barbarossa', OKH/GenStdH/Op.Abt. (I) No. 050/41, g.Kdos., 31 Jan. 1941, as well as draft of 22 Jan. 1941, BA-MA RH 2/v. 1328 and H 28/25.
[72] *KTB OKW* i. 298–9 (3 Feb. 1941).   [73] Ibid. 303 (4 Feb. 1941).
[74] OKW/WFSt/Abt. L (I Op) No. 44141/41 g.Kdos. Chefs., 15 Feb. 1941, BA-MA RW 4/v. 513; see also *KTB OKW* i. 326–7 (15 Feb. 1941).

tions in the Kola peninsula in the north and near Lake Onega in the south (see Map I.vi.1). As there had still been no talks with the Finnish general staff, 'Operational Study Silberfuchs' (Silver Fox) was produced on 27 January 1941 without Finnish participation.[75] For these plans Army HQ Norway regarded 'at least passive participation by Sweden', whose territory must be unconditionally available for deployment and provisioning, as well as 'active participation by Finland', whose army must act offensively in accordance with German directives, as fundamental requirements of the attack. Unless the former prerequisite was met, 'any operation by major forces from northern Norway [would be] impossible'.

Despite a Soviet superiority in ground forces, the unknown strength and combat effectiveness of Soviet naval and air forces, and the difficulties of the terrain and provisioning of German and Finnish troops, the execution of these large-scale operations was thought to be feasible. However, when Army HQ Norway discovered that it could not count on generous reinforcements, so that only some of the divisions stationed in Norway would be available for the operation,[76] and when the Army High Command also suggested a critical re-examination of the operational plan, the objective of Silberfuchs was limited to attacks towards the Murmansk railway and Murmansk itself. For each of these two actions $1\frac{1}{2}$ divisions were earmarked, with OKH approval, including the SS Brigade to be set up in northern Norway.[77] Any co-ordinated action or joint attack with the Finnish army in the Lake Ladoga, Lake Onega, or White Sea area was now outside the plans of Army HQ Norway.

The visit in mid-February of Lieutenant-General von Seidel, the Luftwaffe quartermaster-general, was not so much concerned with operational or political matters as with the enlargement of existing German transit centres into future supply-depots, in much the same way as 'Supply Staff Rovaniemi' had recently been enhanced under German command. At the same time, the information and inspection trip by Colonel Buschenhagen, chief of staff of Army HQ Norway, to Helsinki and northern Finland towards the end of February 1941 showed that for the time being no solid harmonization between the two general staffs on their operational intentions was possible. Talks with Marshal Mannerheim, General Heinrichs, and Aksel F. Airo, the Finnish army's quartermaster-general, were still non-committal, the more so as Buschenhagen had to keep to Hitler's instruction demanding deception and secrecy about the German plans. This was also in line with the intentions of Mannerheim and the Finnish government, who were not prepared to adopt

---

[75] AOK Norwegen No. 3/41 g.Kdos., 27 Jan. 1941, 'Studie über Operationsabsicht "Silberfuchs"' [Study on intended Operation 'Silver Fox'], BA-MA, 20. Armee, 12564/3 (also for the following quotations).

[76] See personal papers of Col.-Gen. von Falkenhorst, 54, BA-MA N 300/4, and Halder's conference with Col. (Gen. Staff) Buschenhagen: Halder, *Diaries*, 769 (1 Feb. 1941).

[77] AOK Norwegen Ia 10/41 g.Kdos. Chefs. to OKH/GenStdH, 13 Feb. 1941, and OKH/ GenStdH/Op.Abt. (IN) No. 188/41 g.Kdos. Chefs. to AOK Norwegen, 2 Mar. 1941, BA-MA, 20. Armee, 20844/4.

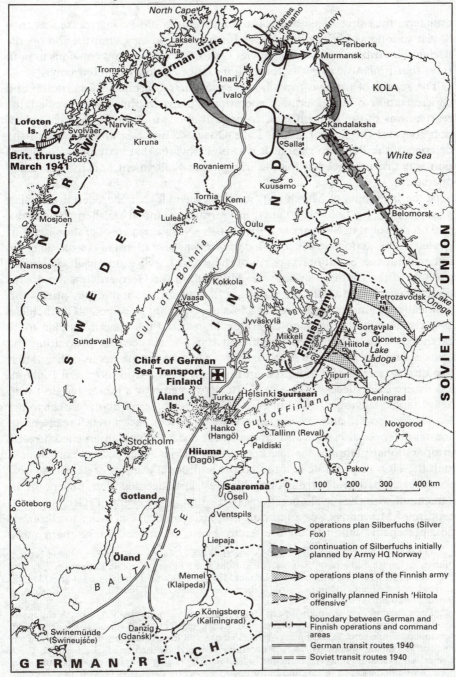

MAP I.VI.1. German–Finnish Operations Plan (1940–1941) for the Attack on the Soviet Union

unilateral measures or embark on a policy that could be interpreted as anti-Soviet so long as Hitler did not give Finland a binding guarantee and openly declare his attitude towards the Soviet Union.[78] Even so, it was obvious to both sides that Finland was ready for military co-operation with Germany.

The results of the two trips, however, facilitated a further finalization and concretization of the German operational plans in that they revealed the reservations of the Finnish high command about unlimited offensive operations beyond the Lake Ladoga–Lake Onega–White Sea line or beyond the defence of the Petsamo region. It was now obvious that systematic co-operation was urgently needed for the impending deployment and the envisaged operations.

At the beginning of March 1941 a British naval force succeeded in effecting a landing on the Lofoten Islands, in German-occupied northern Norway; a raid on the town of Svolvaer and the British–Norwegian co-operation demonstrated in this action clearly revealed the weakness of German coastal defence. In consequence, Scandinavia north of the Arctic Circle found itself even more strongly in the spotlight of the war. Although in the German view the operation had caused no military damage, 'it was an economic pin-prick, and politically undoubtedly resulted in a loss of [German] prestige'.[79] The incident gave rise to a fateful decision by Hitler: he ordered the operations plan to be extended. The Army High Command did not succeed in preventing the transfer of further forces to northern Norway or the simultaneous decision that two attacks were to be mounted on northern Russia from northern Finland. To ensure their success Hitler even intended to employ a motorized unit with heavy tanks. Having stressed in earlier directives[80] the particular threat to the Norwegian coast, and having emphatically demanded a reinforcement of coastal defences at Narvik and on the Arctic coast, he now intervened directly in operational planning for northern Scandinavia. After several conferences with the HQs responsible he ordered the additional transfer of approximately 160 coastal batteries to northern Norway and decided—on this point in agreement with the naval operations staff—that in the event of Barbarossa the capture of Murmansk was an important partial objective in order to eliminate possible enemy landings on the Arctic coast, or at least make them more

---

[78] On Buschenhagen's and Seidel's trip see *DGFP* D xii, No. 69, pp. 122 ff.; telegram No. 93, Blücher to foreign ministry, 14 Feb. 1941, PA, Büro St.S., Finnland, vol. ii; telegram No. 112, 13 Feb. 1941, No. 116, 14 Feb. 1941, PA Dt.Ges. Helsinki, Drahtberichte 1–200, 1941; *IMT* vii. 311–12; Mannerheim, *Memoirs*, 405; Ueberschär, *Hitler und Finnland*, 281–2; Korhonen, *Barbarossaplanen*, 221 ff.

[79] For a summary see the diary reports Geb.Korps Norwegen, Ia, BA-MA, XIX. A.K., 23450. In order to offset the German weakness FM Keitel, chief of the Wehrmacht General Staff, demanded 'most rigorous punishment of the inhabitants of the localities involved' in cases of any succour for enemy operations, and 'if necessary the total destruction of the locality'. Reich Commissar Terboven, however, complied only in part, by having 'the property of the families of persons who had escaped to England burnt down' (report on the period 15 Nov. 1940–15 Mar. 1941, 24–5, ibid.); see also Heß, *Eismeerfront*, 21–4.

[80] See e.g. OKW/WFSt/Abt. L (O Op) No. 44141/41 g.Kdos. Chefs., 15 Feb. 1941, BA-MA RW 4/v. 513.

difficult. Colonel-General Halder failed to persuade Hitler of the Army High Command's view or to achieve a curtailment of operational objectives for the intended 'Falkenhorst army'. As for the occupation of the conquered territories of northern Russia, Hitler expected no difficulties: Finland would take over that task.[81]

Hitler's decisions, following the 'Führer conference', were set out in greater detail in directives to the general commanding the army in Norway: the first, of 26 March 1941, on the defence of Norway,[82] and the second, of 7 April 1941, on the tasks envisaged in the event of Barbarossa.[83] The directives again emphasized that, for the defensive task, the main effort would be in northern Norway, and that Murmansk, as a potential beachhead on the Arctic coast, had to be taken by a thrust through Kandalaksha. As in his 'Guidelines in Special Areas Relating to Directive No. 21 of 13 March 1941', Hitler once more ruled that the decision on contact with the Finnish authorities would not be made until later, and that he reserved for himself the opening of such negotiations.[84] At the conference at the Reich chancellery on 17 May 1941 the commander-in-chief of the army proposed that power of command in that theatre be left to the Wehrmacht High Command, and Hitler agreed. Field Marshal von Brauchitsch declared on his own initiative 'that he would leave all instructions in that territory to the Wehrmacht High Command, in whose hands direction of activities in Norway had been from the outset'.[85] This was undoubtedly an expression of the persistent irritation in the Army High Command at having been bypassed on the Norwegian campaign. Another explanation, however, would be the critical and sceptical attitude of Halder and Brauchitsch towards the proposed operations in the Finnish theatre of war. To what extent Halder 'by all appearances' allegedly disapproved of Brauchitsch's step[86] it is impossible to establish. Finland and the northern wing of the future eastern front thus became an 'OKW theatre of war'. Hitler's intention was to assign regional command over the German and Finnish forces to Marshal Mannerheim. Mannerheim, however, during subsequent discussions declined to accept it, and thus no uniform command structure under supreme OKW control was achieved.[87]

Once planning had reached that stage, the establishment of definite and specific contacts with Helsinki appeared to be the next logical step. In the diplomatic field the Finnish government had been meeting German requests since the beginning of the year: it had lifted existing conditions attaching to

---

[81] See *KTB OKW* i. 348–9 (8 Mar. 1941); Greiner, *Oberste Wehrmachtführung*, 363 ff.; Halder, *Diaries*, 830 ff. (17 Mar. 1941); also Hillgruber, *Strategie*, 502. On the demand of the naval operations staff see Salewski, *Seekriegsleitung*, i. 367, and *IMT* xxxiv, No. 170-C, p. 701.

[82] Published in *KTB OKW* i. 1007–9, Doc. 54.   [83] See ibid. 1011–13, Doc. 57.

[84] See ibid. 352 (11 Mar. 1941), 355 (13 Mar. 1941), 1012, Doc. 57 of 7 Apr. 1941; and *IMT* xxvi, No. 447-PS, p. 57.

[85] See Greiner, *Oberste Wehrmachtführung*, 367–8; Warlimont, *Hauptquartier*, 157–8; *KTB OKW* i. 362–3 (18 Mar. 1941), also on the subsequent passages.

[86] Thus Warlimont, *Hauptquartier*, 158 n. 20.

[87] On the problem of a joint supreme command see Ueberschär, 'Guerre de coalition', 40 ff.

transit traffic, so that Germany, under that cover, was able to conduct a virtually uncontrolled deployment through Finland.[88] Hitler's observation at that 'Führer conference' on 30 March 1941, when he explained to the prospective commanding generals, field officers, and chiefs of staff his ideas of an ideological war of annihilation against Bolshevism, showed that he was very sceptical about the value of an alliance with the countries earmarked for participation in the campaign, and also about their combat value. He warned against illusions about Germany's 'allies' and described the Finnish army as gallant but 'numerically weak and not yet recovered'.[89] For these reasons alone it seemed inopportune to confide in those governments too soon. Moreover, the fact that Finland was maintaining diplomatic relations with Germany's enemies made it seem inadvisable to inform Helsinki too soon about the plans for Barbarossa.

The Soviet leadership did not remain unaware of the German troop movements through Finland into northern Norway; these were becoming increasingly frequent and could scarcely be concealed any longer. It was similarly aware of incipient German–Finnish scout patrols and reconnaissance flights over the Finno-Soviet frontier region. Intercepted Soviet communications made it clear that Moscow was carefully monitoring the troop movements and was bound to realize that such a concentration of forces exceeded the relief of servicemen going on leave from northern Norway.[90] These German measures should have reinforced the warnings passed on to the Soviet leadership by Churchill and the intelligence received from agents,[91] if Stalin—and this is described by Soviet historians as a mistaken assessment of the strategic situation[92]—had not, in his own arbitrary judgement, arrived at a different conclusion for his own future tactics *vis-à-vis* Berlin. Stalin misjudged the importance of those warnings and interpreted Hitler's measures as a purely diplomatic move in a political game of poker between two great powers, a game still related to Molotov's last visit to Berlin. The German military attaché in Moscow therefore reported that, despite continuing call-ups and alerts by the Red Army, the fundamental line of Soviet foreign policy after

[88] See German *aide-mémoire* of 15 Jan. 1941, Blücher's telegram No. 34 to the foreign ministry of 21 Apr. 1941, Finnish *aide-mémoire* of 21 Jan. 1941, PA, Dt.Ges. Helsinki, Berichte 1–250, 1941. On the extensive troop movements after the end of Mar. 1941 see Ueberschär, *Hitler und Finnland*, 286–7.

[89] See Halder, *Diaries*, 845 ff. (30 Mar. 1941); Hillgruber, *Strategie*, 504. On the 'Führer conference' of 30 Mar. 1941 see also sect. I.VII.2(*b*) at n. 53 (Förster).

[90] Leonhard, *Revolution*, 109–10; Zhukov, *Reminiscences*, 216–17. On Moscow radio and *Pravda* reports see *IMT* xxxiv, No. 170-C (compilation by Vice-Adm. Assmann of Aug. 1943 on 'The naval operations staff and the prehistory of the campaign against Russia'), p. 704, and *FRUS* (1941), i. 24 (reports from US Ambassador Steinhardt in Moscow to Secretary of State, Washington, 30 Apr. 1941).

[91] See Churchill, *Second World War*, iii/1. 317 ff.; *FRUS* (1941), i. 712 ff., 723; Deakin and Storry, *Richard Sorge*, 255 ff.; also Hillgruber, *Strategie*, 434; Nekritsch and Grigorenko, *Genickschuß*, 123–36, 217–18, 248 ff., 268; Telpuchowski, *Geschichte des Großen Vaterländischen Krieges*, 28E ff.

[92] *Geschichte der internationalen Beziehungen*, ii. 112; Telpuchowski, *Geschichte des Großen Vaterländischen Krieges*, 42.

mid-April, following Germany's successful campaign in the Balkans, was one of 'appeasement' *vis-à-vis* Hitler. This was observed also with regard to Scandinavia, where Stalin not only avoided an exacerbation of bilateral relations with Finland, but actually, in his policy *vis-à-vis* Hitler, showed particular respect for German interests in that country. Moscow was anxious 'to avoid any incident'.[93] Thus even repeated frontier violations by German reconnaissance flights across the northern Finnish border produced no serious consequences.[94]

4. German–Finnish Arrangements and Measures for Finland's Participation in the War against the Soviet Union

There was now a regular exchange of information between German and Finnish military quarters at local level. German scouting parties repeatedly visited the Finno-Soviet frontier area; divisional staffs exchanged liaison officers, and as a result of contacts between Colonel Rössing, the German military attaché, and the Finnish general staff the first operational talks were held in Helsinki.[95] These military arrangements between individual command authorities, however, still lacked a solid foundation in the form of contractually regulated, mutually harmonized, military co-operation between Berlin and Helsinki, with appropriate agreements, accepted as binding by both parties, on future joint action against the Soviet Union. This basic decision was being demanded with increasing urgency by the German service departments charged with the further planning and execution of operations,[96] whereas Hitler continued to refuse to inform other governments prematurely on Barbarossa, let alone to reveal his proposed date of attack. After mid-April, when Army HQ Norway issued to the corps HQs of its command the relevant instructions for the various offensive operations,[97] it became indispensable for

[93] *IMT* xxxiv, No. 170-C, p. 703 (see above, n. 90).

[94] See telegram No. 233, Blücher to foreign ministry, 9 Apr. 1941, PA, Büro St.S., Finnland, vol. iii; *DGFP* D xii, No. 381, pp. 602–3.

[95] See 2. Geb.Div., Ia, activity report, 30 Mar. 1941, BA-MA RH 28-2/v. 8. On the German scouting actions see the activity reports of the 2nd Mountain Div. for Apr. and May 1941, ibid., also activity report 3. Geb.Div., Ia, 10 June 1941, BA-MA RH 28-3/v. 5, and Bericht über Erkundungsreise vom 9. bis 12.4.1941 mit Gen.Maj. Ernst Schlemmer (2. Geb.Div.) [Report on a scouting tour 9–12 Apr. 1941 with Maj.-Gen. Ernst Schlemmer, 2nd Mountain Div.], BA-MA, XIX. A.K., 15085/33. See also Jägerskiöld, *Fältmarskalken*, 279 ff., and on subsequent military arrangements Jokipii, 'Finland's Entrance'; id., *Jatkosodan synty*.

[96] See data on representations and questions to Hitler by Raeder and Dietl towards the end of Apr. 1941 in 'Führer Conferences', 193 (20 Apr. 1941), and Heß, *Eismeerfront*, 29; also teletype AOK Norwegen Ia No. 52/41 to Geb.Korps Norwegen, 19 Apr. 1941, and Geb.Korps Norwegen Ia No. 146/41 to AOK Norwegen, 18 Apr. 1941, BA-MA, 20. Armee, 20844/4.

[97] See Ueberschär, *Hitler und Finnland*, 288–9; Ziemke, *German Northern Theater*, 129–30. The operations orders covered 'Silver Fox' (the operation mounted from northern and central Finland), 'Reindeer' (the operation to safeguard the Petsamo region), 'Platinum Fox' (the operation against Polyarnyy and Murmansk), and 'Polar Fox' (the thrust from the Rovaniemi area to the White Sea). On the code-names see also Uhlich, 'Decknamen deutscher Unternehmen', 520, 523.

political and military talks to be started at top level—the more so as the ever increasing volume of provisions and material arriving in northern Finland, as well as the stockpiling of supplies and the assembly of the formations, demanded close co-operation with Finnish authorities. The Wehrmacht commander (WB) Norway urgently called for such co-operation:

So that we can move beyond the *non-committal* preliminary military talks that have taken place already and arrive at an urgently needed binding military arrangement with Finland, the political prerequisites will first have to be created by a binding treaty with Finland. Moreover, the operational tasks assigned to the Finnish armed forces *overall* need to be precisely formulated. Not until these preconditions are met can genuinely useful negotiations begin within the scope of WB's duties and produce results. Such talks must open early enough for their outcome to be utilized in good time for the conclusion of preparations in northern and central Finland.[98]

Although Hitler had expressly—'for political reasons'—reserved for himself the approval of further talks with Helsinki, Colonel-General von Falkenhausen repeatedly requested an early decision on when he could expect the conclusion of preliminary political matters with Finland, as important preliminary work and preparations could only be put in effect 'once close military co-operation with Finland has been made possible by a binding political treaty'.[99]

After Hitler had once more postponed the negotiations with the Finnish government and the Finnish high command, originally scheduled for the middle of May 1941, the Wehrmacht High Command on 28 April 1941 eventually confirmed that Hitler, having now fixed the date of Barbarossa for 22 June, had at the same time authorized preparations for official talks with the Finns.[100] Hitler's directive of 1 May 1941 definitively laid down the opening of political talks with the states earmarked for participation in the war—whereby Finland was to be notified before Hungary and Romania—as well as of ensuing military consultations between the German army commands and Finnish headquarters.[101] However, Hitler's intention, on grounds of security, to discuss participation in Barbarossa by the pro-German states under the guise of defensive measures to cover a presumed impending large-scale Ger-

[98] W.B. Norwegen No. 46/41 g.Kdos. Chefs. to OKW/WFSt/Abt. L, 17 Apr. 1941, BA-MA, 20. Armee, 12564/6.

[99] Notification AOK Norwegen Ia No. 51/41 g.Kdos. Chefs. to Mountain Co. Norway, 19 Apr. 1941, and teletype W.B. Norwegen, Ia No. 55/41 g.Kdos. Chefs. to OKW/WFSt/Abt. L, 23 Apr. 1941, BA-MA, 20. Armee, 20844/4.

[100] See the talks in OKW on 22 Apr. 1941, *KTB OKW* i. 384–5, and on 28 Apr. 1941, *IMT* xxvi, No. 873-PS, pp. 399–400, and in Jacobsen, *1939–1945*, 237. Also minute of OKW/WFSt/Abt. L No. 44594/41 g.Kdos. Chefs., 28 Apr. 1941, BA-MA RW 4/575.

[101] OKW/WFSt/Abt. L (I Op) No. 44638/41 g.Kdos. Chefs., 1 May 1941: see *DGFP* D xii, No. 431, pp. 685–6; *Hitlers Weisungen*, No. 21b, pp. 91–2 (not in trans.). The appendices and supplements attached to the directive, governing the scope of military consultations, betr. Besprechung Chef WFSt mit Vertretern Finnlands [re conference of chief of Wehrmacht operations staff with Finnish representatives], are not published there; they are in BA-MA, 20. Armee, 20844/4. See also Halder, *Diaries*, 894–5 (30 Apr. 1941).

man operation in the west (Sea Lion) made it clear from the outset that he did not propose to comply with the wishes of the various commands for properly negotiated treaties with the envisaged participants on their functions in Barbarossa. Hitler was not prepared to subject the military and political decisions he had already made to any discussion within the framework of treaty negotiations. It was clear that, from the very start, he was laying claim to conducting 'his' war against the Soviet Union untrammelled by the possible wishes of his allies.

Hitler's conditions for co-operation with his allies emerge also from his directive of 3 April 1941 for the Balkan campaign. That directive made it clear that the military tasks assigned to participating forces derived from his, Hitler's, political war aims, and that he reserved for himself the unified leadership also in matters of military operations.[102] Even before the beginning of Barbarossa, Hitler in a discussion with General Antonescu made it clear that this principle applied also to the war against the Soviet Union: 'An operation ranging from the Arctic Ocean to the Black Sea requires unified central guidance. That, naturally, is in our hands.'[103] The forthcoming talks with the pro-German states could not therefore be concerned with a carefully harmonized conduct of a coalition war or with consideration of each participant's interests and war aims. Such a procedure was in line with the intentions of the political leadership: there was no question of conceding special interests to the other governments.

Halder and Brauchitsch also criticized the fact that, despite Hitler's directive of 1 May 1941, Army High Command responsibility for the negotiations on the military operations out of northern and south-east Finland continued to be ill-defined, that the Wehrmacht High Command was too anxious to keep the whole of the action in Finland in its own hands, that in consequence the schedule for Barbarossa could not be kept with regard to Finland, and that solution of the 'Finland problem' was not therefore making any headway.[104] Considering the fast that, ever since August 1940, the Army High Command had been viewing the plans for a large-scale offensive mounted from Finland with disapproval and scepticism, and had been anxious to avoid a frittering away of German offensive strength among too many points of main effort, it is hardly surprising that Colonel-General Halder also refused to make additional forces available for supporting a Finnish attack on Hanko or for a surprise strike against the White Sea Canal.[105] There was fierce criticism of the splitting-up of forces called for by the present operations plan and of the failure to form a clear point of main effort for the proposed capture of

[102] See *Hitler's Directives*, No. 26, pp. 63–4.

[103] Discussion with Gen. Antonescu in Munich on 12 June 1941, OKW/WFSt/Abt. L (I Op) No. 44981/41 g.Kdos. Chefs., 17 June 1941, BA-MA RH 31-I/v. 40. On the problems of the conduct of the German–Finnish coalition war see Ueberschär, 'Guerre de coalition', 44 ff., and id., 'Koalitionskriegführung im Zweiten Weltkrieg', 357 ff.

[104] Halder, *Diaries*, 901 (4 May 1941), 918–19 (14 May 1941), 926 (17 May 1941).

[105] See *KTB OKW* i. 317 (11 Feb. 1941); OKH's reply in Halder, *Diaries*, 982–3 (14 Feb. 1941).

Leningrad and for co-operation between Army Group North and the German and Finnish forces operating north of it with a view to staging a far-ranging envelopment of the entire Soviet northern front. It seemed illogical that, on the one hand, major forces were being employed against Murmansk and the Murmansk railway, while on the other General Jodl of the Wehrmacht operations staff should declare that the only attainable objective was 'the safeguarding of the Petsamo region; anything more will be a gift'.[106] Even before the crucial discussions were opened with representatives of the Finnish armed forces, Halder made the highly critical observation that Army High Command utterly rejected any wide-ranging offensive warfare launched from Scandinavia on the northern wing: 'The whole undertaking is an expedition, not an operation. It is a shame to waste the men allocated for this purpose.'[107] This point of view was the more justified as Army High Command's reserves for the proposed eccentric advance on the eastern front were in very short supply; whatever forces were at all available should have been made ready for the decisive operation.

Official political and military contacts between Germany and Finland were inaugurated on 20 May 1941 with a call by Minister Schnurre on President Ryti. As Hitler's personal emissary, Schnurre—whose true reason for making the trip was being kept from the press—was instructed to inform the Finnish government about Molotov's demands in November and about the likelihood of an imminent war with the Soviet Union. He was also to convey an invitation for a military delegation to be sent to Germany with a view to co-ordinating proposed measures. Schnurre confirmed German support for Finland and assured the Finnish president that Hitler would regard a Soviet attack on Finland as a *casus belli*. However, no formal treaty between the two countries, as suggested by the German command authorities, was yet concluded, nor was there any information on, or harmonization of, the two parties' war aims.

Ryti and those members of his cabinet whom he had informed approved the proposal for joint military talks, and negotiations between the German high commands and a Finnish military delegation under the chief of the Finnish general staff, Heinrichs, began on 25 May 1941. In an exchange of views with Keitel, Jodl, Halder, Wehrmacht High Command officers, the high commands of the three services, and Army HQ Norway, the members of the Finnish delegation were briefed in detail on German operational intentions and on the tasks to be assigned to the Finns.[108]

[106] Jodl's letter to Dietl of 15 May 1941, BA-MA, XIX. A.K., 15085/33: Sondertätigkeitsbericht Vorbereitung des Feldzuges gegen Rußland [Special activity report: preparatory work for the campaign against Russia], 7. For general criticism of the overall plan see Uhlig, 'Das Einwirken Hitlers', 204.

[107] Halder, *Diaries*, 919 (14 May 1941); see also ibid. 903–4 (5 May 1941).

[108] On the opening of the talks see Procopé, *Sowjetjustiz*, 145; Mannerheim, *Memoirs*, 407–8; correspondence Mil.Att. Helsinki and Att.Abt. in OKH and Att.Abt. with Op.Abt./OKH, 22 May and 24 May 1941, BA-MA H 27/43. On the course of the talks see Halder, *Diaries*, 937 (26 May 1941); Greiner, *Oberste Wehrmachtführung*, 387; Loßberg, *Im Wehrmachtführungsstab*, 114. The presentation by Wuorinen, *History of Finland*, 367, to the effect that 'the Germans did not mention

These discussions at last, in conjunction with the German troop transits and deployment moves, removed any doubts about an impending armed conflict with the Soviet Union. General Jodl deliberately referred to the participation of other states on the German side as a 'crusade against Bolshevism'. The Finns, however, initially avoided committing themselves or entering into binding agreements, for which in any case they had no full powers. As a result, a number of detailed problems remained unresolved. From the point of view of Army HQ Norway, which depended on appropriate co-operation with the Finns, the talks did not produce a satisfactory outcome.

Divergences in operational intentions emerged especially with regard to Finnish participation or support, as requested by the German side, for operations against Murmansk and Salla–Kandalaksha, and for the attack on Leningrad by means of Finnish thrusts beyond the old Finno-Soviet frontier. Whereas Jodl believed that the Finnish main front in Karelia needed only to hold the frontier defensively, as the Soviet front would 'automatically' collapse with the progressive advance of Army Group North, Halder demanded offensive action by the Finnish army at its front in the south-east.[109] According to the intentions of the Army High Command, co-operation with the main Finnish forces was to take place west or east of Lake Ladoga, according to the progress of operations by the German Army Group North in its attack on Leningrad after the crossing of the Dvina. Lieutenant-General Heinrichs, on the other hand, wished to engage the Finnish attack force only for limited objectives within the framework of the 'Histola offensive', i.e. for the reconquest of former Finnish sovereign territory north-west of Lake Ladoga (see Map I.VI.1).[110] An operation east of Lake Ladoga, he believed, could only, for reasons of supplies, be conducted roughly as far as a line from Olonets to Petrozavodsk. The Finnish reservations show that the intended advance across the Svir, in particular, as part of a wide-ranging envelopment operation against Leningrad, did not meet with the agreement of the Finnish high command. This divergence in the operational concept may be seen also as a symptom of the two countries' different war aims, which had not yet been openly discussed, and of Helsinki's resultant hesitant political attitude. It also emerged that the Finnish army would only be able to assume the tasks assigned to it if it was

---

Operation Barbarossa', can no longer be maintained now that the minutes of the talks have been found. On the minutes of the OKW talks see *DGFP* D xii, No. 554, pp. 879–85, and teletype Col. Buschenhagen to AOK Norwegen No. 105/41 g.Kdos. Chefs., 26 May 1941, BA-MA, 20. Armee, 20844/5. On the OKH talks see OKH/GenStdH-Op.Abt. IN No.991/41 g.Kdos. Chefs., 26 May 1941, BA-MA H 3/1. On the naval talks see Seekriegsleitung B, No. 1, Skl. I Op. 00748/41 g.Kdos. Chefs., 27 May 1941, BA-MA OKM, Case 527/PG 32601. On 'Questions on co-operation of the air forces' see Müller-Hillebrand, *Militärische Zusammenarbeit*, 386, MGFA P-108/II, and personal papers of Col.-Gen. von Falkenhorst, BA-MA N 300/2.

[109] On the divergent intentions of Jodl and Halder see Abt. Ausland No. 183/ 41 g.Kdos. Chefs. Ausl. III Org., 28 May 1941 (letter from Capt. Leopold Bürkner), BA-MA, 20. Armee, 20844/5.

[110] See Upton, *Finland 1940–1941*, 252; Jägerskiöld, *Marskalken av Finland*, 88 ff.

mobilized in good time. But as Hitler, for security reasons, had been anxious to avoid a premature discovery of the German deployment, in case the Soviets took countermeasures, the Finnish mobilization and hence the beginning of operations in Finland had to be scheduled for dates after the German attack. These postponements ran down along the Finno-Soviet frontier from north to south.

There was, however, agreement on the proposed division of command in northern and southern Finland: in the north the Wehrmacht High Command was in charge through Army HQ Norway, while in the south Marshal Mannerheim was in command also of any non-Finnish contingents assigned to that front. Direct harmonization was to be ensured by a German liaison staff in the Finnish HQ. Significantly, the Finnish military delegation repeatedly pointed out that Finland urgently needed extensive German deliveries of weapons and foodstuffs for the impending war. Operations by naval forces in the Baltic, under the unified command of the German Naval Command North (General Admiral Carls), were to be 'offensive operations', such as the laying of extensive minefields and actions by motor torpedo-boats and U-boats. To make it impossible for Soviet Baltic units to exit from the Baltic, the Finnish navy was to seal them off inside the Gulf of Finland. Harmonization of plans and tactical operations by the two independently operating naval forces was to be ensured by the exchange of liaison staffs. Finnish requests for an early German—or at least joint—occupation of Åland (Ahvenanmaa in Finnish), Hanko, and Suursari, on the other hand, proved unrealizable, the more so as Hitler on 2 June expressly ruled that this was an 'exclusively Finnish affair'.[111] In the conversations it also emerged that both German and Finnish leaderships were greatly concerned about possible Soviet preventive measures during the continuing German–Finnish deployment. Hitler therefore gave instructions that the defence of northern Norway and the operations for the occupation of the Petsamo region must be instantly executable at short notice and that they were to be triggered immediately by clearly identified Soviet preventive measures.

The second stage of the military negotiations took place between 3 and 5 June 1941, when Colonel Buschenhagen from Army HQ Norway, representing the Wehrmacht High Command, and Colonel Kinzel from the Foreign Armies East Department, representing the Army High Command, along with Colonel Rössing, the military attaché in Helsinki, called on the Finnish general staff to hear their comment and answers to the German proposals. These talks in Helsinki, with the results they produced, have to be viewed as the definitive basis of military co-operation between the two countries. After their conclusion it was clear to the Army High Command that the Finnish government was prepared 'for full participation' and would tackle the tasks assigned

[111] Teletype B. No. 1 Skl. I Op 00803/41 op Chefs. to Group North, 3 June 1941, BA-MA OKM, Case 527/PG 32601, and teletype OKW/WFSt/Abt. L (I Op) No. 44832/41 g.Kdos. Chefs., 2 June 1941, to W.B. Norwegen, BA-MA, 20. Armee, 20844/5.

to it 'with sails set full'.[112] Colonel-General Halder expected a far-ranging massive participation of the Finnish army in connection with the German operations against Leningrad. A Finnish government memorandum presented to the German officers, taking up the Wehrmacht High Command wording of a 'crusade against Bolshevism', pointed out that Finland's participation and interest in the impending war against the Soviet Union were 'by no means of purely operational or military-technical character', but that Hitler's intention to have this military confrontation with Bolshevism was being seen 'as a historic token of a great era'. The crucial moment for the struggle against Finland's age-old enemy had arrived.[113]

The detailed arrangements envisaged the subordination of Finnish units to German command and their participation in the attack on the Murmansk railway, as well as the handing-over of Finnish airfields to the Luftwaffe. German units were to be employed on the capture of the Soviet military base of Hanko. The line from Oulo to Belomorsk was to divide the German and Finnish operations and command areas in the north and south of the country. Meanwhile the Finnish high command was willing to consider the execution of the main Finnish attack—in line with German wishes—both west and east of Lake Ladoga as far as the Svir. The Finns also agreed to carry out a phased mobilization beginning on 10 June 1941. For domestic and constitutional reasons, however, the Finnish government declined to open hostilities against the Soviet Union on its own initiative. Moscow's measures in response to the German attack would therefore have to be presented as having 'provoked [Finland] into attacking'.[114]

Despite Finland's readiness for military co-operation, Finnish political reservations about National Socialist hegemony and a new order in Europe also emerged clearly during these negotiations. Helsinki did not enter into any firm commitments which would result in Finland's automatic participation in Hitler's war against the Soviet Union. Lieutenant-General Heinrichs also regretted interference by SS agencies in the Finnish reserve army when, with official sanction from both sides, they were recruiting Finnish volunteers for the Waffen-SS. He also warned 'against any attempt to set up a kind of Quisling government; this would be bound to cut short any further collaboration between Finland and Germany'.[115] The persisting problems and conflicts concerning proposed military and political co-operation between the two states were typically revealed by the fact that Berlin did not give Helsinki any

[112] See Ergebnis der deutsch-finnischen Besprechungen in Helsinki [Results of the German–Finnish discussions in Helsinki], 3–5 June 1941, published in Ueberschär, *Hitler und Finnland*, 336–7; also the note in Halder, *Diaries*, 949 (7 June 1941), and abridged version in *DGFP* D xii, No. 592, p. 963.

[113] Finnish 'Pro Memoria', 2 June 1941, published in Ueberschär, *Hitler und Finnland*, 335; further references to the minutes of the talks ibid. 294–5.

[114] OKH/Fremde Heere Ost/Chef No. 74/41 g.Kdos. Chefs., Kinzel's minutes of 10 June 1941, BA-MA H 3/1.

[115] Ibid.; see also Jägerskiöld, *Fältmarskalken*, 290 ff.

precise information on the planned opening of the war or about German war aims, and that Hitler, even after the military talks, clung to his instruction that the Finns were to be briefed on German operational intentions only to the degree absolutely necessary for successful local co-operation. This situation, on the other hand, made it possible for the Finnish government to claim for itself the right to its own free decision on participation in the war—even though, with numerous German troops stationed in Finland, such a claim was of a purely formal character and 'in practice [had] long been pre-empted'.[116]

On 5 June 1941 Hitler approved the 'Schedule for Barbarossa' prepared by the Wehrmacht High Command; this also laid down deployment, assembly, and attack dates for the drives against Murmansk and Kandalaksha.[117] The amended version of 'Deployment Directive Barbarossa' of 8 June 1941[118] laid greater emphasis on the offensive task alongside the defensive one of protecting northern Norway. 'If necessary', Army HQ Norway had to execute 'Reindeer' even before the beginning of operations and, in co-operation with Finnish forces, protect the Petsamo nickel-mines, which were vital to German armaments. Murmansk, the enemy's important base, was to be encircled (Operation Silberfuchs) and, once additional attacking forces had been brought up, captured. The directive further ruled that Army HQ Norway, which already came under the Wehrmacht High Command as the staff of the 'Wehrmacht commander Norway', was also to be 'directly subordinated to the Wehrmacht High Command' for the operations envisaged under Barbarossa. In the final version of the deployment directive the plan for two Finnish directions of attack '*on both sides* of Lake Ladoga' had been abandoned; now, in synchronization with the crossing of the Dvina by Army Group North, only one Finnish attack was laid down 'in accordance with the demands of the Army High Command with its point of main effort *either* east *or* west of Lake Ladoga, as far towards the east as possible' for wide-ranging co-operation across the Svir.

While the talks in Helsinki were still going on, extensive German transports, under the code-name 'Blue Fox', were shipped across the Baltic to the northern Finnish ports on the Gulf of Bothnia. For camouflage reasons these were officially described as relief moves within the transit agreements for the troops stationed in northern Norway; in fact they were a transfer of corps troops of Higher Command XXXVI and 169th Infantry Division with roughly 32,000 men by sea from Germany and Norway, as well as of the SS Combat Group North with about 8,000 men by land to northern Finland.[119] Special

---

[116] Hillgruber, *Strategie*, 493.

[117] 'Zeitplan Barbarossa', OKW/WFSt/Abt. L No. 44842/41 g.Kdos. Chefs., 1 June 1941, *IMT* xxxiv, No. 039-C, pp. 228 ff.

[118] Final version in Greiner, *Oberste Wehrmachtführung*, 353–4, and Halder, *KTB* ii, app. 2, pp. 463–9 (not in trans.), also on the following passage.

[119] See the transport data in 2. Geb.Div., Ia, activity reports 1 Mar–18 June 1941, BA-MA RH 28-2/v. 8, and 3. Geb.Div., Ia, activity reports 1 Mar–18 June 1941, BA-MA RH 28-3/v. 5; also

agreements concerning the by then large number of German troops stationed in Finland were concluded between the Wehrmacht High Command and the Finnish high command on 10 July 1941. These regulated administrative matters and granted the German troops special extraterritorial rights.[120] After 10 June 1941 the Finnish government reinforced its frontier troops. On 11 June 1941 the 'Command Post Finland' was set up as a forward German command authority of Army HQ Norway near Rovaniemi. Infantry General Waldemar Erfurth of the Army High Command arrived in Helsinki as the newly appointed 'Commander of Liaison Staff North'. Only then were the Finnish cabinet and parliament informed by President Ryti of impending co-operation with the Third Reich. The arrangements concluded with the German authorities and the mobilization dates agreed with them were now explicitly approved. But before ordering general total mobilization, the Finnish government demanded a binding assurance from Berlin that the intended armed conflict with the Soviet Union would actually materialize. It may be assumed that a Tass report from Moscow on 14 June 1941, discounting all rumours of war, had irritated the Finnish government. On the strength of a personal authorization by Hitler, Colonel Buschenhagen on 16 June confirmed in Helsinki that the outbreak of war could be confidently expected. After this, Helsinki ordered general mobilization.[121]

Colonel-General von Falkenhorst was one of the military leaders present at Hitler's great 'Führer conference' on 14 June 1941, when Hitler once more rehearsed the prehistory, reasons, and execution of his war against the Soviet Union, trying to attune his listeners to the imminent opening of the war in the east. On 15 June 1941 the Finnish III Corps and the security group in Petsamo were directly subordinated to Army HQ Norway. Several advance elements of Mountain Corps Norway had already been pushed forward into the Petsamo region. In consequence, the whole of northern Finland was now under the command of Colonel-General von Falkenhorst, while in the south Marshal Mannerheim took over command of roughly 16 divisions with some 200,000 men.[122] The Finnish supreme commander, moreover, was given command

AOK Norway Ia No. 98/41 g.Kdos. Chefs., 29 May 1941, BA-MA, 20. Armee, 20844/5, and 1. Skl. KTB, pt. A, BA-MA OKM, III M 1000/20–2. On the seaborne transports see also Meister, *Seekrieg*, 10.

[120] See 'Besondere Anordnungen für die im finnischen Hoheitsgebiet untergebrachten Deutschen Truppen' [Special instructions for the German troops quartered on Finnish sovereign territory], OKW/WFSt/Abt. L IV/Qu No. 44903/41 g.Kdos. Chefs., 10 June 1941, BA-MA H 27/43.

[121] *DGFP* D xii, No. 624, p. 1023, and No. 636, pp. 1038–9. Also teletype No. 751, Col. Buschenhagen to OKW for Gen. Jodl, 14 June 1941, and Hitler's reply by telegram, FM Keitel to Buschenhagen, 15 June 1941, both in BA-MA H 27/43. For the separate mobilization dates see teletype No. 699, Mil.Att. Helsinki to OKH/Att.Abt., 9 June 1941, ibid. See also Halder, *Diaries*, 952 (10 June 1941); Mannerheim, *Memoirs*, 410; Mäkelä, *Im Rücken des Feindes* 79.

[122] See AOK Norwegen-Befehlsstelle Finnland Abt. Ia No. 39/41 g.Kdos. Chefs., Armeebefehl zur Übernahme des Befehls in Nordfinnland [Army order for the assumption of command in northern Finland], 17 June 1941, BA-MA, 20. Armee, 19070/2. On the Finnish strength see Ploetz, *Kriegsmittel*, 329 ff. The total of 650,000 men given in *Geschichte des zweiten Weltkrieges*, iii. 404,

over the German units promised him on the opening of hostilities, for the attack on the Soviet naval base of Hanko. The Finnish air forces, also under Mannerheim's command, consisted of 307 front-line aircraft, of which 243 were operational (see Diagram I.vi.1).[123] Air Fleet 5 under Colonel-General Jergen Stumpf, responsible for German air warfare in Scandinavia, Denmark, and northern Finland, had as its main task the aerial defence and protection of the Norwegian region north of the Arctic Circle, with the forces of the 'Luftwaffe General for Northern Norway', as well as support for operations 'Reindeer' and 'Silver Fox', to be conducted by Army HQ Norway in northern Finland and northern Russia.[124] In addition it was to fly strategic missions against the port installations of Murmansk and Kandalaksha, the Murmansk railway, and the White Sea Canal. For the discharge of these tasks, some of which had been assigned to the Luftwaffe as requirements of the navy, an 'operational group, special duties' had been set up in mid-June 1941 under the 'Air Leader Kirkenes', Lieutenant-Colonel (General Staff) Andreas Nielsen, as a forward command post of Air Fleet 5 in Kirkenes. By comparison with the Soviet 1st Air Division facing him (its HQ staff in Kandalaksha), with its 5–6 air regiments (about 145 aircraft, of which some 80 were bombers), the 'Operations Staff Nielsen' with its total of 80–90 operational aircraft had rather scant forces available for its extensive list of tasks.[125]

Shortly afterwards Major-General Walter Lorenz and Rear-Admiral Reimar von Bonin were appointed chiefs of specific liaison staffs of the Luftwaffe and

results from *Suomen Sota* 1941–1945, i. 352, where all mobilized fighting forces, territorial, frontier-guard, and other auxiliary troops under the Finnish defence ministry were included in the calculation.

[123] Of the 243 operational aircraft 186 were fighters, 26 bombers, and 31 reconnaissance, liaison, and transport machines. According to a report by the German air attaché, in June 1941 the Finnish air force comprised 181 operational aircraft, of which 132 were fighters, 21 bombers, and 28 reconnaissance planes: see telegram No. 444, Blücher to foreign ministry, 16 July 1941, PA, Dt.Ges. Helsinki, Berichte 251–550, 1941. Ploetz, *Kriegsmittel*, 333, reports 222 aircraft; according to *Deutschland im zweiten Weltkrieg*, i. 566, the number was 225.

[124] On the tasks and instructions of Air Fleet 5 see *KTB OKW* i. 1011–13, and W.B. Norwegen Ia No. 66/41 g.Kdos. Chefs. to Air Fleet 5 re 'Silver Fox', 8 May 1941, BA-MA, XIX. A.K., 15085/33; OKW/WFSt/L (I Op) No. 44883/41 g.Kdos. Chefs. to Ob.d.L., Fü.Stab Ia betr. 'Einsatz der Luftwaffe in Finnland' [re 'Luftwaffe employment in Finland'], 4 June 1941, AOK Norwegen Ia No. 145/41 g.Kdos. (Silberfuchs) betr. 'Einsatz der Luftwaffe' [re 'Luftwaffe employment'], 10 June 1941, and Air Fleet 5 HQ Ia No. 88/41 g.Kdos. Chefs. betr. Weisungen für den Kampf im Falle 'Barbarossa' [re Directives for operations in the event of Barbarossa], 12 June 1941, all in BA-MA, 20. Armee, 20844/5.

[125] For the area of the 'operational group, special duties' the following were available: 1 Gruppe dive-bomber units, 1 transport Gruppe, 1 bomber Gruppe, 1 Schwarm 'destroyer' planes, 1 fighter Staffel, 1 close-range reconnaissance Kette, and the 'long-range reconnaissance Kette Lapland'. See Der Chef der Luftflotte 5 Ia/O.Qu. Nr. 1222/41 betr. 'Einsatzgruppe z.b.v.' [re 'operational group. special duties'], 5 June 1941, and Luftflottenkommando 5 Ia/O.Qu. 1223/41 g.Kdos. Ib betr. Vorgeschobener Gefechtsstand des Luftflottenkommandos 5 [re forward command post of Air Fleet 5 HQ], 6 June 1941, both in BA-MA, 20. Armee, 20844/5; also Girbig, *Jagdgeschwader 5*, 12, 20, 23, 278, 333; Knabe, *Auge Dietls*, 47 ff. On the Soviet air forces see Höheres Kommando XXXVI, Abt. Ic 258/41 geh. Nachrichtenblatt No. 2: Truppenverteilung und Befestigungen [Distribution of troops and fortifications], 17 June 1941, BA-MA, XXXVI. Geb.K., 22102/9.

Diagram I.vi.i. German–Finnish Deployment and Disposition of Soviet Forces from North to South, 30 June 1941

GERMANY/FINLAND	SOVIET UNION
Admiral Norway Cmdg. admiral: Adm.-Gen. Boehm └Adm. Polar Coast (Rear-Adm. Schenk)	*Naval forces of the NORTHERN FLEET* C.-in-C.: Rear-Adm. Golovko
Air Fleet 5 Command Cmdg. the Air Fleet: Col.-Gen. Stumpff └Chief of Staff: Lt.-Col. (Gen. Staff) Nielsen 'Special Action Group' with Air Leader Kirkenes (Lt.-Col. (Gen. Staff) Nielsen)	*Air forces of the NORTHERN FRONT*

Army Command Norway/Command Post Finland
C.-in-C. Col.-Gen. von Falkenhorst
Chief of Staff: Col. (Gen Staff) Buschenhagen
├Mtn. Corps Norway (Gen. of Mtn. Troops Dietl)
  ├2nd Mtn. Div. (Maj.-Gen. Schlemmer)
  └3rd Mtn. Div. (Maj.-Gen. Kreysing)
├Higher Cmd. XXXVI (Inf. Gen. Feige)
  ├169th Inf. Div. (Maj.-Gen. Dittmar)
  └SS Combat Group 'North' (SS Maj.-Gen. Demelhuber)
└Finnish III Corps (Maj.-Gen. Siilasvuo)
  ├Finnish 6th Div. (Col. Viikla)
  └Finnish 3rd Div. (Col. Fagernäs)
	NORTHERN FRONT (Leningrad mil. distr.)
	C.-in-C.: Lt.-Gen. Popov
	Chief of Staff: Maj.-Gen. Nikishev
	├Fourteenth Army: Lt.-Gen. Frolov
	  ├14rh Rifle Div.
	  ├52nd Rifle Div.
	  └42nd Rifle Corps (Maj.-Gen. Panin)
	    ├122nd Rifle Div.
	    ├104th Rifle Div.
	    └25th Mech. Rifle Div.
	      (1st Armd. Div.)
	──88th Rifle Div. (as reserve)

Finnish Army
C.-in-C.: FM Mannerheim
Chief of Staff: Lt.-Gen. Hanell
Quartermaster-General: Maj.-Gen. Airo
German Liaison Staff North
Inf. Gen. Dr Erfurth
├14th Div. (Col. Raapana)
─KARELIAN ARMY
  C.-in-C.: Lt.-Gen. Heinrichs
  Chief of Staff: Col. Tapola
	─Seventh Army: Lt.-Gen. Gorelenko

	─54th Rifle Div.

German Liaison Staff North
─Chief Group: Lt.-Gol. Hölter
├Group Oinonen (Maj.-Gen. Oinonen)
  ├Cavalry Brigade (Col. Ehrenrooth)
  ├2nd Chasseurs Brigade (Col. Sundman)
  └1st Chasseurs Brigade as reserve (Col. Lagus)
	─71st Rifle Div.

├VI Corps (Maj.-Gen. Talvela)
  ├5th Div. (Col. Koskimies)
  └11th Div. (Col. Heiskanen)
	─237th Rifle Div.

├VII Corps (Maj.-Gen. Hägglund)
  ├7th Div. (Col. Svensson)
  ├19th Div. (Col. Hannuksela)
  ├1st Div. as army reserve (Col. Paalu)
  └German 163rd Inf. Div. as army reserve
    (Lt.-Col. Engelbrecht)
	└168th Rifle Div.
	
	└Twenty-third Army: Lt.-Gen. Pshennikov

├II Corps (Maj.-Gen. Laatikainen)
  ├2nd Div. (Col. Blick)
  ├15th Div. (Col. Hersalo)
  ├18th Div. (Col. Pajari)
  └10th Div. as reserve (Col Sihvo)
	├19th Rifle Corps
	  ├142nd Rifle Div.
	  └115th Rifle Div.

└IV Corps (Lt.-Gen. Oesch)
  ├12th Div. (Col. Vihma)
  ├4th Div. (Col. Viljanen)
  └8th Div. (Col. Winell)
─17th Div. off Hanko (Col. Snellman)
	└50th Rifle Corps
	  ├43rd Rifle Div.
	  └123rd Rifle Div.
	
	*c.*1 division in Hanko

─*Finnish air forces*: Lt.-Gen. Lundqvist
─*Finnish naval forces*: Lt.-Gen. Valve
  Chief of Staff: Rear-Adm. Sundman
  ├Fleet commander (Rear-Adm. Rahola)
  └Special fleet detachment Gulf of Finland
    (Commodore Enkiö)
German Naval Group Command NORTH
Cmdg. admiral: Adm.-Gen. Carls
├Commander Baltic
  (Commander of Cruisers: Vice-Adm. Schmundt)
├Commander Gulf of Finland
  (Leader of Torpedo-boats: Capt. Bürow)
└Leader of Minesweeper Forces North
  (Capt. Boehmer)
	Red Banner BALTIC FLEET
	C.-in-C.: Vice-Adm. Tributs

Source: *Suomen Sota 1941–1945*, ix. 342–3; *Geschichte des zweiten weltkrieges*, iii. 405.

navy respectively; they ranked equal with General Erfurth's liaison staff, who, strictly speaking, were responsible for the overall co-ordination of German–Finnish operations in the far north. As, in addition, the German military attaché at the Helsinki legation had been charged with various tasks relating to the stationing and employment of German troops in Finland, there was from the outset no clear delineation of responsibilities in the area of co-operation with the Finnish high command—a situation aggravated by the fact that Marshal Mannerheim had dispatched General Harald Oehquist to Germany as his own liaison officer with the Wehrmacht and the Army High Commands.[126]

It was not possible to keep the German deployment movements or the Finnish mobilization measures entirely secret. Just like the US embassy and the Swedish and British governments, so the Soviet leadership was aware of the troop concentrations in Finland. Although Helsinki replied evasively to Soviet enquiries about the reason for the mobilization of Finland's armed forces, Stalin clung to his foreign-policy line.[127] It was this formally correct behaviour of the Soviet Union that seemed to make it difficult for Marshal Mannerheim to find a suitable *casus belli*. The Finnish intelligence service was unable to discover inside the Soviet Union any major responses or reactions to the German and Finnish preparations for attack. Despite a preliminary alert, there were no identifiable indications that the Soviet armed forces or the troops along the Finnish frontier—which had been reinforced since the summer of 1940—were prepared for an imminent German–Finnish attack. Instead, Moscow's Baltic Fleet withdrew to Leningrad and maintained passive positions, with the result that German mine-laying units, some of which had been stationed in Finnish ports since 18 June, were able without any interference, even before the beginning of the war, to lay the minefields not only for the 'Wartburg' barrages in the Baltic between the island of Saaremaa (Ösel) and the coast at Liepaja but also in the Gulf of Finland. Not until 21 June 1941 was the Red Banner Baltic Fleet put on immediate alert; during the night of 21–2 June German mine-laying vessels in the Gulf of Finland came under fire.[128] It seems doubtful, therefore, that the Soviet government had identified

---

[126] On the establishment of a liaison staff see personal papers of Gen. Erfurth, Tagebuch, i. 14 ff., BA-MA N 257/1; Halder, *Diaries*, 822 (7 Mar. 1941), 939 (27 May 1941), 947–8 (6 June 1941), 960–1 (20 June 1941); OKH/GenStdH/Org.Abt. (II) No. 1450/41 g.Kdos. 'Dienstanweisung für den Kommandeur des "Verbindungsstabes Nord"' [Service instruction for the commander of 'Liaison Staff North'], 6 June 1941, BA-MA H 27/43; also Ueberschär, 'Guerre de coalition', 45 ff. On the appointment of the 'Liaison officer of the Luftwaffe commander-in-chief with the operations staff of the Finnish armed forces' see teletype OKW/WFSt/Abt. L (I L Op) No. 44968/41 g.Kdos. Chefs. to AOK Norwegen, 14 June 1941, BA-MA, 20. Armee, 20844/5.

[127] See telegrams (Nos. 439, 443), Minister von Blücher to the foreign ministry, 16 June 1941, also No. 472, 20 June 1941, PA, Büro St.S. Finnland, vol. iii; and *Blauweiß-Buch*, ii. 36.

[128] See M.Dv. No. 601, Operationen und Taktik, Auswertung wichtiger Ereignisse des Seekrieges [Operations and tactics, evaluation of major events in the war at sea], pt. 12, Der Ostseekrieg gegen Rußland im Jahr 1941 [The war in the Baltic against Russia in 1941], OKM (Kriegswiss. Abt.), Berlin, Jan. 1944; also Mäkelä, *Im Rücken des Feindes*, 81–2; Rohwer, 'Minenkrieg', 16–17; Meister, *Seekrieg*, 10; Kuznecow, *Am Vorabend*, 349–50, 354, 374.

the full scale of the Finnish mobilization measures or interpreted them correctly in conjunction with other warnings of an attack by Hitler. It certainly became obvious at the Finno-Soviet frontier that the deployment of German and Finnish troops could not be viewed as a reaction to an allegedly impending Soviet coup against Finland. Here too the National Socialist thesis of a pre-emptive strike against an alleged Bolshevik deployment for war was proved not to agree with the facts.

Right up to the beginning of Barbarossa the Finnish government insisted that the Soviet Union should bear the 'odium of aggressor'. It was therefore careful to avoid taking the first step before Hitler, and indeed would not even more simultaneously with the German main attack. It was important to it to create the impression, before its own public and parliament, that it was being dragged into the war by Soviet offensive actions. As a result, a special situation arose in that Finland on 22 June 1941 did not take part in the attack on the Soviet Union, though it made its territory fully available to the German army, navy, and air force, and indeed had already placed its own troops in northern Finland under German command. Thus, on 22 June 1941 the Mountain Corps Norway was able to move into the Petsamo area according to plan and to deploy for its operation against Murmansk. With Helsinki's approval, reconnaissance and offensive missions against Soviet targets in the Murmansk area were flown by the German Air Fleet 5 from Finnish airfields or were carried out by overflying Finnish territory. Finnish units simultaneously occupied the until then demilitarized Åland Islands, and the Finnish government continued its mobilization measures as agreed with Germany.

In spite of these measures, on the day of the German attack against the Soviet Union Helsinki issued a declaration of neutrality.[129] The value and truthfulness of that 'neutrality' were, however, revealed in Hitler's public 'proclamation to the German people' and his order of the day to the 'soldiers of the eastern front' of 22 June 1941, when he stated that German soldiers 'in alliance with Finnish divisions' were standing along the shores of the Arctic Ocean and in Finland, so as to jointly protect that country.[130] In order to weaken the impression of being an 'ally on Hitler's side' and to correct the idea that, with the German attack, Finland automatically entered the war against the Soviet Union, the Finnish government instructed its diplomatic representatives to explain that it would remain neutral in this new war as long as possible. President Ryti was gratified to receive Hitler's official message regarding the validity and confirmation of the German–Finnish agreements concluded by the military commands of both countries.[131] There was a variety of tactical reasons for Finland's 'neutrality phase'. But when, despite Hel-

[129] See the reports of US Minister Schoenfeld from Helsinki in *FRUS* (1941), i. 40–1.

[130] See Hitler's 'Proclamation to the German People' in Domarus, *Hitler*, ii. 1726 ff., and Hitler's order of the day to the 'soldiers of the eastern front', 22 June 1941, BA-MA RH 22/4, published in *Unternehmen Barbarossa*, 319 ff.

[131] See Hitler's letter to Ryti; 23 June 1941, published in Ueberschär, *Hitler und Finnland*, 387–8.

sinki's protests, Soviet artillery and air-force units from 22 June onwards repeatedly struck at Finnish cities, coastal shipping, and other military targets, the 'hoped-for offensive action by the Russians' had now taken place and on 25 June 1941 Premier Rangell was able to make a government statement in parliament to the effect that these military actions had compelled Finland to declare war on the Soviet Union.[132] The Finnish parliament thereupon unanimously passed a declaration to the effect that Finland had been subjected to attack by the Soviet Union and in consequence had begun 'to defend itself with all military means at its disposal'.[133]

Ever since the summer of 1940 Hitler had counted on Finland's participation in his plans for a war against the Soviet Union. Military co-operation between Berlin and Helsinki had now been achieved, and the Finnish government must have gained a fairly good idea of Hitler's intentions. It could scarcely be in any doubt about the ultimate objective of the planned operations.[134] The Finnish high command, in consequence, allowed it to be understood, even before the country entered the war, that Finland was ready for the struggle 'without attaching any conditions to its alignment with Germany'.[135] This was reflected also in Helsinki's willing agreement in the spring of 1941 to the raising of a Finnish volunteer battalion of about 1,200 men for the Waffen-SS.[136] The bilateral relations developing under the aspect of a German–Finnish *rapprochement* and Finland's enlistment as a military and economic partner against the Soviet Union were unmistakably marked by the political, economic, and military preparations for Barbarossa. Not only were they closely linked with Hitler's axiomatic determination to go to war with the Soviet Union, but they also reflected the absolute dominance of the strategic and military component in German policy *vis-à-vis* Scandinavia and Finland. Co-operation between Germany and Finland was almost exclusively based on military motivations, seeing that Finnish territory was acquiring prime strategic significance in Hitler's war plans. For the German navy's freedom of action, for the Third Reich's foreign trade across the Baltic, and for seaborne supplies for the German advance in the Baltic region it was of vital importance that Finland should be on the German side and that its coast should not serve as a springboard for operations by Germany's opponents.

On the other hand, it is doubtful whether German plans for operations against Murmansk and the Murmansk railway really deserved the importance attached to them by Hitler and the command authorities involved. Hitler

---

[132] Statement by Lt.-Gen. Heinrichs, 22 June 1941, personal papers of Gen. Erfurth, Tagebuch, i. 32, BA-MA N 257/1; *Blauweiß-Buch*, ii. 146–7. See also *DGFP* D xii, No. 669, p. 1079; No. 675, pp. 1083–4; ibid. xiii, No. 15, pp. 19–20.

[133] See communiqué of 26 June 1941 in *Blauweiß-Buch*, ii. 56.

[134] See information given by Ryti to US Minister Schoenfeld, 28 Jan. 1941, *FRUS* (1941), i. 7. There is a similar assessment in Andreen, *Finland i Brännpunkten*, 313, 325, 345.

[135] Personal papers of Gen. Erfurth, Tagebuch, i. 19 (14 June 1941), BA-MA N 257/1.

[136] On the establishment of the Finnish volunteer battalion see Stein and Krosby, 'Das finnische Freiwilligen-Bataillon der Waffen-SS', 413 ff.; Ueberschär, *Hitler und Finnland*, 304 ff.; Jokipii, 'Strohhalm für Finnland'; see also ch. II.v of the present volume.

expected the capture of Murmansk to produce decisive effects on the Soviet conduct of the war, whereas the Army General Staff, on the grounds that climatic and geographical conditions would not allow the employment and provisioning of major motorized forces, rejected the employment of several large formations in that 'unimportant secondary theatre of war' on the coast of the Arctic Ocean as a frittering away of its forces. Its view, however, did not prevail. There was unanimous approval of the employment of the Finnish army along Lake Ladoga as a measure in support of the planned attack on Leningrad.

German economic and financial assistance to Finland, had from an early date served the development of the country's armaments industry as well as the enhancement of the infrastructure of northern Finland as a deployment and supply base for the planned attack against northern Russia. The fact that, despite Finnish hopes of a break-up or gradual dissolution of the German–Soviet alliance, there was no formally based alliance between Berlin and Helsinki clearly reveals the divergent political and military war aims of the two 'brothers-in-arms'. Hitler was not interested in a coalition war in which Finland would be an equal partner; this might have diluted the ideological concept of 'his' war against the Soviet Union. There was no jointly developed strategy in the preparatory phase, nor an institutionalized unified command over the two countries' forces, even though mixed units did go into action.[137]

This circumstance enabled the Finnish government, despite its involvement in Hitler's ideological war of annihilation against the Soviet Union, to choose the moment of its own entry into the war and to declare the war itself to be a 'continuation' of the Winter War of 1939–40, separate from the struggle of the great powers. The resulting 'community of military action' between Berlin and Helsinki was based not on sympathy for Hitler or his 'programme' of conquering living-space in the east, or indeed for the National Socialist regime in Germany. It should be viewed instead as an attempt by the Finnish government, at a moment of German supremacy in Europe, not to be left behind by Hitler's new order in Europe, to regain, as a limited objective, the territories ceded to the Soviet Union under the Moscow peace treaty, and, possibly, to win adjacent parts of eastern Karelia by attaching them to their neighbouring province. For Finland the war was no ideological struggle for the physical destruction of a 'Jewish-Bolshevik leading stratum' or for the smashing and extinction of the USSR as a state for the purpose of gaining ownerless colonial territory. Hitler's war in the east was misunderstood in Finland both as a 'normal' power-political process and as a 'crusade' of the European nations from the Arctic Ocean to the Black Sea 'against Stalinist Bolshevism'; it was not seen as a racially motivated war of annihilation. This misreading, as well as a lack of information, prevented the Finnish government from compre-

---

[137] On this set of problems see Ueberschär, 'Guerre de coalition', 27 ff.; id., 'Koalitionskriegführung im Zweiten Weltkrieg', 355 ff.

hending the complete 'otherness', the racial-ideological core, and the programmatic ultimate goal of Hitler's war of conquest and annihilation at an
early stage.[138] In consequence, no attempt was made by Helsinki at the
beginning of the 'brotherhood-in-arms' to exert any mitigating or corrective
influence on Hitler's 'struggle of two ideologies'. In spite of Finland's special
importance as a strategic partner in Germany's operations plans, the Finnish
government, because of the military and economic ratio of power, was far too
weak to declare its own attitude to Hitler's ideological struggle to any effect.
That was why Army HQ North's command post in Rovaniemi passed on
Hitler's 'criminal orders' for the war in the east[139] to the formations and units
under its command. Both Hitler's 'Decree on the Practice of War Jurisdiction
in the Barbarossa Territory and on Special Measures by the Troops' of 13 May
1941 and his 'Guidelines for the Treatment of Political Commissars' of 6 June
1941, known as the 'commissar order', were passed down and discussed
during the final few days before the beginning of the war. As for the treatment
of political commissars in the Soviet forces, the relevant instructions and
elucidations were, in accordance with orders, passed on only by word of
mouth.[140] On 17 June, in addition, the 'Guidelines for the Behaviour of the
Forces in Russia', available since the middle of May, were passed on by Army
HQ Norway to its subordinate units for notification to the troops.[141] Simultaneously an 'Information Leaflet: Warning against Insidious Soviet Warfare',
produced by Army HQ Norway itself, was distributed among relevant commands and units.[142]

At a conference at the Berghof on 5 June 1941 Hitler thought it necessary for
the Wehrmacht High Command to have that kind of leaflet prepared in order
to draw the attention of the German troops to all eventualities of insidious
warfare by the Red Army.[143] From the outset, and without quoting any such
experience, the leaflet of Army HQ Norway made the following generalization
about the conduct of the war by Soviet troops: 'The Russian . . . [is capable
of] any sadistic bestiality.' It continued:

[138] See Hillgruber, *Strategie*, 516 ff.

[139] On the issue of 'Hitler's criminal orders' see ch. I.VII (Förster); also Messerschmidt,
Wehrmacht, 390 ff.; Uhlig, 'Der verbrecherische Befehl'; Jacobsen, 'Kommissarbefehl'; Krausnick,
'Kommissarbefehl'; Streit, *Keine Kameraden*, 28 ff., 83 ff., with further bibliographical details. On
a general classification of a total, ruthless conduct of war see Bartov, *Eastern Front*. On the
implementation of the 'criminal orders' see also '*Gott mit uns*'; Mayer, *Krieg als Kreuzzug*; Streit,
'Sowjetische Kriegsgefangene'; Schulte, *German Army*.

[140] Geb.Korps Norwegen Ic/Ost, KTB, 19 and 20 June 1941, BA-MA, XIX. A.K., 15085/21.
Briefing on the commissar order by Army HQ Norway to the corps under its command took place
on 17 June 1941: ibid. 15085/33; see sect. I.VII.2(c) (Förster).

[141] See app. 3 to AOK Norwegen 48/41 g.Kdos., 17 June 1941, BA-MA, 20. Armee, RH 20-20/
133. In Mountain Co. Norway the guidelines were issued on 20 June: see Geb.Korps Norwegen
Ic/Ost, KTB, 20 June 1941, BA-MA, XIX. A.K., 15085/21.

[142] On the distribution of this instruction leaflet on 21 June 1941 see Gen.Kdo. Geb.Korps
Norwegen, Abt. Ic, KTB, 21 June 1941, BA-MA, XIX. A.K., 15085/21. For the quotations from
the leaflet see Tätigkeitsbericht AOK Norwegen Ic No. 107/41 g.Kdos. AZ I, 3 July 1941, with the
printed leaflet as app. 20, BA-MA RW 39/20.

[143] Report on the conference at the Berghof on 5 June 1941, appendix to No. 165/41 g.Kdos.
ObdH, 9 June 1941, BA-MA H 3/1.

In contrast to the chivalrous warfare in Norway, every officer and soldier of the Wehrmacht, in the war against Russia, must be prepared for the most insidious, mendacious, and unchivalrous methods of Soviet warfare. The enemy will use unscrupulously any means of deception, cunning, and propaganda; nor will he shrink from criminal actions.

The instruction leaflet, which bore the signature of Colonel-General von Falkenhorst, referred to the possible 'use of chemical and bacteriological weapons', as well as to 'ambushes and tricks'; the forces were therefore enjoined to 'watch out in particular for priests, commissars, and Jews'.

Although military co-operation was in the interest of both countries, there were, at the beginning of the joint war against the Soviet Union, considerable differences of interest; these had not been ironed out by the numerous visits, military discussions, or agreements. Expecting a quick victory for the German arms and the conclusion of the war by the autumn of 1941, the Finnish government undertook the risk of war on the side of the Third Reich, although the country's economy, in terms of both materials and food supplies, was unprepared for a major or prolonged war. The fact that German supplies certainly provided momentary relief for the Finnish food situation cannot obscure the fact that in a number of important sectors of the war economy and armaments industry Finland could not be an equal partner but would continue to be dependent on German deliveries.[144] In this respect too the thesis of Finland's separate war had its limitations.

5. SWEDEN'S POSITION DURING THE PREPARATORY PHASE OF THE WAR AGAINST THE SOVIET UNION

The importance of neutral Sweden to the Third Reich was for a long time viewed too much in terms of Swedish iron-ore deliveries for the German armaments industry and war economy. Not only later historians, but broad circles of the international press, diplomacy, business, and the war economy of the day almost exclusively assessed German–Swedish relations by Swedish iron-ore exports.[145] Since then, historical research has been increasingly focused on general trade relations between Stockholm and Berlin, and on the political concepts of Sweden's and Finland's long-term inclusion in a German-controlled 'large-scale economic sphere', as well as on Sweden's position during the preparations for and the execution of Operation Barbarossa.[146]

[144] See e.g. *DGFP* D xii, No. 250, pp. 433 ff.

[145] On the importance and assessment of Swedish ore deliveries and on the controversy formulated by A. S. Milward, 'Could Sweden Have Stopped the Second World War?', see the data in Fritz, *German Steel*; Milward, *Zweiter Weltkrieg*, 332–5; Wilhelmus, 'Die Bedeutung des schwedischen Eisenerzes'; *Germany and the Second World War*, ii. 185–90. On the other side, more extensively, Wittmann, *Schwedens Wirtschaftsbeziehungen*.

[146] See e.g. Carlgren, *Swedish Foreign Policy*; Wittmann, 'Deutsch-schwedische Wirtschaftsbeziehungen'; Björkman, *Sverige inför Operation Barbarossa*; see the contributions by Sten Carlsson, Carl-Axel Wangel, Martin Fritz, Ulf Brandell, Wilhelm Carlgren, Bengt Åkerrén, Sven Wäsström, and Åke Thulstrup in the collective volume *Schwedische und schweizerische Neutralität*.

At the outbreak of war in September 1939 Sweden was economically strong
and politically united. After the general depression and from the time when
the Social Democrat government under Per Albin Hansson came to power in
the autumn of 1932, Swedish business and industry had been marked by a
continual improvement of performance.[147] By means of a new economic
programme, by financial expansion, and by support from the public purse a
considerable economic upswing had been inaugurated after 1933. Rationalization and state support had similarly led to an increase in agricultural production, so that Sweden at the beginning of the war was largely self-sufficient in
the agricultural sector. The drop in unemployment had strengthened the
domestic position of the Social Democrats, who only just failed to win an
absolute majority in the parliamentary elections in the autumn of 1936. Under
the coalition government formed at that time by Premier Hansson, consisting
of Social Democrats and the Peasant League, the policy of reforms was
steadily continued. National Socialist groupings and tendencies were of no
importance in Swedish domestic politics. The 'Nordic Idea', pushed by Third
Reich propaganda, scarcely met with an echo in Sweden; if anything it resulted
in an occasional strain on relations with Berlin. The Swedish press in particular voiced extreme criticism and dislike of the ideas of a 'Nordic community of
destiny' under German leadership, as championed by Alfred Rosenberg and
the 'Nordic Society', just as it did with regard to the National Socialist
treatment of the Jews. Hitler's march into Austria led the Social Democrat
government to abandon its previous opposition to major rearmament efforts
and expenditure, and instead to approve a strengthening of Sweden's defences. This made it possible to embark on a modernization of the Swedish
armed forces. Despite divergent party-political opinions, there had been until
1939 a domestic equilibrium in the social, political, and cultural spheres. The
Swedish public therefore stood firmly united behind its government's neutral
attitude in foreign politics.

As a reflection of its carefully balanced neutrality in foreign and trade policy,
Sweden on 7 December and 22 December 1939 had signed new wartime trade
agreements with both Britain and Germany.[148] Even after the Soviet attack on
Finland it was the consistent aim of the Swedish government under Premier
Hansson, despite various actions in support of Finland, not to be drawn into
the war against the Soviet Union. In order to buttress that policy by a solid
parliamentary majority, the existing coalition government of Social Democrats
and Peasant League was broadened in December 1939 into a 'government of
national cohesion' under Premier Hansson; this also included representatives
of the right wing and of the liberal People's Party. Foreign Minister Rickard
Sandler, who after the outbreak of the Finno-Soviet Winter War called for

[147] On domestic developments see Andersson, *Schwedische Geschichte*, 484 ff.; on Swedish
foreign policy see Johansson, *Per Albin*; Carlgren, *Swedish Foreign Policy*, also on the following
passage; also Carlsson, 'Schwedische Neutralität'; Wangel, 'Verteidigung'; Fritz, 'Wirtschaftliche
Neutralität'; Carlgren, 'Mediationstätigkeit'.   [148] Hägglöf, *Svensk krigshandelspolitik*, 52 ff.

intervention on Finland's side, was replaced by the diplomat Christian Günther. The new Hansson government was thus able to rely on a massive parliamentary majority. The Swedish government was not prepared to make the country available, as a kind of operational base, for an intended intervention by the Western powers in support of Finland. It repeatedly declined to grant London or Paris permission for the transit of their intervention troops.

With the German operation Weserübung Scandinavia found itself directly involved in the military operations of the belligerent great powers; however, Sweden still refused to take any risks and insisted on remaining aloof from the war. At the same time Sweden, after the German occupation of Denmark and Norway, was no more able than Finland had been to prevent herself from coming under increasing military and economic pressure from Germany. This resulted in a gradual reorientation of Sweden through foreign-policy and trade concessions in favour of Berlin. By the middle of April 1940 the Swedish government deviated from valid rules of neutrality by permitting the German Wehrmacht a 'humanitarian' transit of foodstuffs, medical items, and army medical-corps personnel across Swedish territory to the German troops fighting in northern Norway.[149] The conclusion of the fighting for Narvik and the withdrawal of the Western powers from Norway drastically changed Sweden's situation: while invariably emphasizing the country's observance of 'strictest neutrality' as well as its determination to repel any violation of its frontiers, as King Gustav V Adolf formulated it in his letter to Hitler,[150] Sweden was increasingly ready to comply with German demands. This tendency became even more marked after Hitler's victory over France and Germany's resulting hegemony in Europe. In his conversation with the Swedish Vice-Admiral Fabian Tamm on 16 April 1940 Hitler had made it clear that he expected Sweden, even without direct German occupation, to grow progressively into the German sphere of power, the more so as Sweden and the Reich would complement one another as 'natural business partners' within the framework of his concept of a closed economic system of 'the Baltic as a free inland sea'.[151] There were in fact times when Sweden's trade with Germany accounted for 80 per cent of the former's total foreign trade. The idea of Sweden as a neutral country, but one subjected to German influences and controls due to the military situation, eventually led Berlin to demand from Stockholm its consent to the transit of German troops and war material to Norway. On 8 July 1940 the Swedish government authorized these 'war' transports.[152] As a kind of collateral Hitler, on the recommendation of the

---

[149] See Halder, *Diaries*, 315 (14 Apr. 1940); *Handlingar . . . 'Transiteringsfrågor . . . april–juni 1940*, 49 ff.; Lutzhöft, 'Deutschland und Schweden'; Wilhelmus, 'Das faschistische Deutschland und Schweden'; Brandell, 'Transitfrage'.

[150] See *Handlingar . . . Transiterinsfrågor . . . april–juni 1940*, 66; *DGFP* D ix, No. 142, pp. 208–9 (19 Apr. 1940).

[151] *Staatsmänner*, i. 121 ff.; *Handlingar . . . Transiteringsfrågor . . . april–juni 1940*, 43–4.

[152] *DGFP* D x, Nos. 131–3, pp. 157–9. See also Zetterberg, 'Le transit allemand'.

foreign ministry, authorized the renewal of German deliveries of war material to Sweden; these had been suspended in April 1940 as part of Operation Weserübung and as a means of political pressure to support German transit demands.[153]

The agreements of 8 July 1940 became the contractual basis for continuous Wehrmacht traffic across Sweden, consisting of troops in transit and servicemen going on or returning from leave, which lasted until 1943. Because of their direct effect on the regime of German occupation in neighbouring Norway they soon became a controversial issue in Swedish public opinion.[154]

When it became known in Sweden that the country, along with the other states of northern Europe, was being included in German plans, drawn up in the summer of 1940, for an economic new order in Europe, as an integrated economic partner in a proposed new 'greater economic sphere',[155] public reaction was reserved and mistrustful. Berlin, however, remained unimpressed by the statements of Swedish government ministers or by the reservations voiced in the Swedish press about tutelage exercised by the Axis powers, who would hold a leading position in the large-scale economic sphere.[156] At the end of July Hitler believed that his plan for the establishment of a 'Greater Germanic Empire' which would overcome 'Germanic particularism' was meeting with sympathy in Stockholm.[157] Accordingly, in September 1940 he expounded to Grand Admiral Raeder his ideas on the political future of the Scandinavian countries within his expansionist and economically imperialist concept. Within a 'north Germanic community' envisaged by him, Sweden was to enjoy a certain measure of sovereignty but would otherwise be 'politically and economically most closely tied to Germany'.[158] Proposals by German industrial groups and concerns, made within the planning work ordered by Göring for the economic and financial penetration of the Nordic countries, likewise concerned Sweden.[159] Despite all 'verbal approval', the Swedish government maintained its 'essential reserve' *vis-à-vis* such 'plans for a new order'.[160] This attitude did not change when, in a supplementary agreement of September 1940, Sweden consented to an expansion of troop transits, even though the intensified transports through the country greatly facilitated the construction, as ordered by Hitler, of defensive positions by Army HQ Nor-

[153] *DGFP* D ix, No. 202, pp. 290 ff. (7 May 1940); ibid. x, No. 15, pp. 14–15 (25 June 1940) with n. 2 (5 July 1940), p. 15; Lutzhöft, 'Deutschland und Schweden', 406 ff.; Wilhelmus, 'Das faschistische Deutschland und Schweden', 104 ff., 111 ff.

[154] Carlgren, *Svensk utrikespolitik*, 399.

[155] See *DGFP* D ix, No. 367, pp. 496 ff. (1 June 1940).

[156] On reaction in the Swedish press see e.g. Gustmann, *Schwedische Tagespresse*, 196 ff.; on the statements by Swedish ministers see Wittmann, *Schwedens Wirtschaftsbeziehungen*, 235 ff.; Wilhelmus, 'Schwedisches Echo', 41–2. On Sweden's press policy generally see Thulstrup, 'Schwedische Pressepolitik'.

[157] Halder, *Diaries*, 518 (22 July 1940).

[158] 'Führer Conferences', 135 (notes of 7 Sept. 1940).

[159] See e.g. Eichholtz, *Kriegswirtschaft*, 165; *Anatomie des Krieges*, 261–2, 269–70.

[160] See Wittmann, *Schwedens Wirtschaftsbeziehungen*, 235–6; Wilhelmus, 'Schwedisches Echo'.

way. These defences along the Norwegian coast would make it easier to repel landing attempts by the Western powers. The agreement must be viewed as a further Swedish concession to Germany.

Even though the plans for an attack on the Soviet Union, drafted since July 1940, did not envisage or consider participation by Sweden, the country's strategic importance was nevertheless being transformed by the military preparations for that war. Hitler therefore opposed the idea, voiced by the Helsinki and Stockholm governments during the latter part of 1940, of a political union between Finland and Sweden. Such ideas ran counter not only to his intention to win Finland over as an independent, active partner in his eastern war, but also to his own conception of a 'new order' for northern Europe.[161] The German–Swedish economic agreements on trade exchanges and payments, with their new Swedish concessions, show that Berlin was using the position it had recently gained in Europe and especially in the Baltic Sea as a lever for obtaining appropriate compliance from Stockholm within the concept of the advertised 'community of destiny on the Baltic'. More ambitious economic projects, however—such as the development of an aircraft-engine industry working directly for German armaments—were not realized; Swedish industry declined to be degraded to the status of a mere subcontractor for Germany.[162]

At the 'Führer conference' on 5 December 1940, when the operations plans prepared by the Army High Command were presented to Hitler, and again on 7 December in the conversations between Colonel-General Halder and Colonel-General von Falkenhorst of Army HQ Norway, in charge of directing operations in northern Finland, it became clear that part of the extensive deployment of the units to be launched against the USSR from Finnish territory would have to be effected through Sweden, even though direct participation by Sweden was not envisaged.[163] At the same time the question was being considered in the Army High Command whether Sweden might not make 3–5 divisions of its own army available as 'assistance to Finland' in the event of Barbarossa.[164] In Directive No. 21 of 18 December (the Barbarossa directive) the Wehrmacht High Command pointed out that the possibility had to be taken into account that Sweden's transport network would be available for the deployment of the German northern group not later than at the opening of operations,[165] although there had never been any negotiations on this with the Swedish government. Likewise, without any contact with Stockholm the Wehrmacht leaders blithely included in the directive a major opera-

---

[161] On Hitler's observations to Sven Hedin on 5 Dec. 1940 see *Staatsmänner*, i. 392; also *KTB OKW* i. 299 (3 Feb. 1941); similarly Gruchmann, 'Schweden', 599; Carlgren, *Mellan Hitler och Stalin*.

[162] See Wittmann, 'Deutsch-schwedische Wirtschaftsbeziehungen', 199; Gruchmann, 'Schweden', 594; also Fritz, 'Question of Practical Politics'.

[163] Halder, *Diaries*, 722–3 (5 Dec. 1940), 727 (7 Dec. 1940).

[164] Ibid. 736–7 (14 Dec. 1940), 738 (16 Dec. 1940, talk with the Finnish Maj.-Gen. Talvela).

[165] *Hitler's Directives*, No. 21, p. 50.

tion mounted from Finland against the Soviet Union, although this had to be made expressly dependent on Sweden's willingness to authorize rail transports across its territory.[166] In its 'Deployment Directive Barbarossa' of 31 January the Army High Command pointed out, with some reserve, that it could 'in any case' be expected 'that Sweden [would] itself [ensure] the protection of its own north-eastern frontier with adequate forces'.[167] Active participation in the operations was not envisaged. Army HQ Norway, on the other hand, which was responsible for operations against northern Russia, had in mind a greater measure of involvement of Sweden,[168] causing Halder, at the 'Führer conference' on 3 February 1941, to put the question: 'Is Sweden to be involved?'[169] It was typical of Hitler's plans and his attitude towards states which might become his allies against the Soviet Union that he should now assume, without ever having negotiated with Helsinki or Stockholm, that he could rob Finland of the Åland Islands in order to give them to Sweden as its price and reward for participation in Barbarossa.[170] For the time being, therefore, Sweden, Finland, Hungary, Romania, and Slovakia were included in Wehrmacht and Army High Command considerations as countries earmarked for co-operation or direct participation.[171]

When the deployment for Barbarossa with its troop movements to northern Norway resulted in a substantial increase of troop and material transports through Sweden, the Swedish government in March 1941 pointed out that such an imbalance in the 'equivalence principle' of rail transports could lead to a total suspension of transits. Simultaneously the country's defence efforts were demonstratively intensified by new call-ups. Stockholm also refused a German request for authorization of the transit of two infantry divisions in addition to leave transports of servicemen; this, the Swedes argued, would cause 'domestic difficulties'. Any further concessions were regarded by the Swedish government as incompatible with its policy of neutrality. Germany was permitted only one seaborne transport through Swedish territorial waters northwards along the Norwegian coast.[172] Simultaneously, the Swedish government again conveyed its dislike of the German plans for a 'new order' in Europe. An official comment by the Swedish foreign ministry clearly voiced Stockholm's rejection of such German power-political and economic ideas.[173]

---

[166] Ibid., p. 51.   [167] Halder, *KTB* ii. 468, annexe 2 (not in trans.).

[168] See conversation between Col. Buschenhagen (Army HQ Norway) and Col.-Gen. Halder in Halder, *Diaries*, 769 (1 Feb. 1941).

[169] Halder, *KTB* ii. 269 (2 Feb. 1941) (not in trans.).

[170] *KTB OKW* i. 299 (3 Feb. 1940).

[171] See OKW/WFSt/Abt. L (I Op) No. 44141/41 g.Kdos. Chefs., 13 Feb. 1941 (draft) and 15 Feb. 1941, BA-MA RW 4/v. 513; GenStdH Op.Abt. (Ia) No. 226/41 g.Kdos., 20 Feb. 1941, BA-MA RH 2/v. 1325.

[172] On the negotiations during the 'March crisis' see *DGFP* D xii, Nos. 184–6, pp. 319–23, No. 255, pp. 439–40; Halder, *Diaries*, 820 (5 Mar. 1941), 826 (11 Mar. 1941); West, 'German–Swedish Relations', 282–300; Zetterberg, 'Marskrisen 1941'.

[173] See the official statement of the head of the economic division of the Swedish foreign ministry, Gunnar Hägglöf, and of the chairman of the board of the Swedish National Debt

Since the beginning of 1941 the Swedish government had received indications through intelligence channels of a potentially imminent German–Soviet conflict; it was also informed on the build-up of German forces against the Soviet Union. In the spring of 1941, therefore, it was no longer quite so scrupulous about preserving its own neutrality and was also trying to dissuade Finland from making common cause with Germany. However, the meetings of the two foreign ministers Witting and Günther in Stockholm and Helsinki in mid-March and early May 1941 did not lead to any specific political co-operation between the two countries, as Sweden clung to its neutrality and Finland to its alignment with Berlin.[174] At the same time, however, Witting was unable to give the Swedish foreign ministry any information on the possibility of a German–Soviet conflict.

On 17 March 1941 Hitler therefore revised his earlier assumption about Sweden's participation in the war. He now remarked: 'We cannot expect anything from Sweden because we have nothing to offer it.'[175] Even permission for German troops to move through Sweden into northern Norway and Finland now had to be considered in further planning as most unlikely. That left only the sea route. It was by sea, therefore, that German units and command authorities were moved to northern Finland at the beginning of June 1941. At the same time, however, the German embassy in Stockholm was reporting a growing willingness of military circles around the chief of the Swedish general staff, General Olof Thörnell, to participate in a German–Soviet conflict on the side of Berlin and Helsinki; this they considered to be in Sweden's own vital interest.[176] State Secretary von Weizsäcker continued likewise to be very optimistic about winning Sweden over as a partner in the war against the USSR in the event of a Soviet provocation against Finland.[177] Nevertheless, after March 1941 the German high commands in their further plans for military operations no longer counted on an active participation by Sweden; an attempt might, however, be made to achieve the greatest possible compliance with German wishes regarding commercial and military supply traffic through Swedish territory or territorial waters.[178]

Administration, Dr Karl Hildebrand, reproduced in Bericht D.Ges. Stockholm, C 674, 14 May 1941, with the two statements as annexes, PA, Ha.Pol. Abt. VI, Schweden, Wirtschaft, 6/2, Großraumwirtschaft (No. 23/4).

[174] On the extent of Swedish information on the Barbarossa plan see e.g. *DGFP* D xii, No. 105, p. 191; Björkman, *Sverige inför Operation Barbarossa*, 203 ff., 215 ff.; Gruchmann, 'Schweden', 601; Jägerskiöld, *Fältmarskalken*, 280 ff. On the foreign ministers' meeting see *FRUS* (1941), i. 16, 57; *DGFP* D xii, Nos. 400, 426, 437, 458, 471, pp. 633, 678–9, 690–1, 717–18, 735 ff.; Andreen, *Finland i Brännpunkten*, 62 ff. On the Finnish attitude see Blücher, *Gesandter*, 218–21; *DGFP* D xii, No. 430, p. 684.

[175] Halder, *Diaries*, 826 (17 Mar. 1941), also on the following passage.

[176] See *DGFP* D xii, Nos. 390, 434, pp. 620–1, 687–8; also copy Pol. I M (Att.) 3185 g, telegram from Stockholm, 8 Apr. 1941, PA, Dt.Ges. Helsinki, Schriftwechsel geheim, vol. i.

[177] *DGFP* D xii, No. 397, pp. 629–30.

[178] See e.g. 'Barbarossa'-Planung des Marinegruppenkommandos Nord [Barbarossa-planning of Naval Group Command North], Buchnr. Ra 8/41 g.Kdos. Chefs., 31 Mar. 1941, BA-MA OKM, M/127/34835, KTB of Naval Group Command North.

In view of the Swedish government's continual insistence on its neutrality and Premier Hansson's unequivocal statement that it remained the unalterable aim of Swedish government policy to keep Sweden out of the war,[179] occasional German reflections on whether Sweden and Finland should jointly accede to the Tripartite Pact[180] were pure speculations. This was revealed also when, on instructions from Hitler, Minister Schnurre, on his return trip from a briefing mission in Helsinki, called on Premier Hansson and Foreign Minister Günther in order to discover Sweden's precise attitude to the planned war against the Soviet Union. The Swedish government declined to participate in a German attack on the USSR, but was willing in principle to grant support and assistance to Germany in other areas once a military conflict with the Soviet Union had broken out.[181] This piece of information made it possible to include in the Wehrmacht High Command's 'Timetable for Barbarossa', issued on 5 June 1941, a rail transport of German troops through Sweden after the beginning of operations. This directive therefore envisaged the rail-borne deployment across Sweden of a German division to be employed in the attack on the Soviet base of Hanko on Finland's southern coast.[182] It was, however, expressly pointed out that no contact had taken place with Sweden regarding participation in the attack on the Soviet Union.

At the beginning of June transportation for the German deployment in northern Finland was very largely across the Baltic Sea; these movements were very carefully monitored by Stockholm.[183] Once 163rd Infantry Division, stationed in southern Norway, despite its inadequate equipment with weapons and artillery, had been chosen for the attack on the Soviet-leased military base of Hanko, along with the Finnish 17th Division, the operations staff of the Wehrmacht High Command began to make detailed plans for that unit's transit through Sweden. Together with other ideas about Swedish assistance and support, 'up to the limit of what was possible', these 'wishes' were submitted by Minister Schnurre to the Swedish government at the beginning of the German attack on the Soviet Union on 22 June 1941.[184] Emphasizing

---

[179] Telegram No. 478, German legation Stockholm to foreign ministry, 2 May 1941, betr. Rede Hanssons zur 1. Mai-Kundgebung [re Hansson's speech at a May Day rally], PA, Büro St.S., Schweden, vol. ii.

[180] See *DGFP* D xii, Nos. 250, 449, pp. 433–5, 702.

[181] Letter from Maj.-Gen. Bruno von Uthmann (military attaché in Stockholm) to Maj.-Gen. Matzky, 27 May 1941, BA-MA III H 1001/19. See also Hillgruber, *Strategie*, 495.

[182] See *IMT* xxxiv, No. 039-C, pp. 230–1, also on the following passage.

[183] See the German legation and attaché reports from Stockholm and Helsinki, e.g. telegram No. 404, Blücher to foreign ministry, 10 June 1941, PA, Dt.Ges. Helsinki, Berichte 251–550, 1941, and teletype Mil.Att. Stockholm to Att.Abt., 11 June 1941, BA-MA H 27/43; in general see also Carlgren, *Svensk underrättelsetjänst.*

[184] The first list of 'military requests and others overlapping the military field', as well as proposals 'in the quartermaster field', compiled by the OKW WFSt, 9 June 1941. See Abt. L No. 44885/41 g.Kdos. Chefs. (I Op), 9 June 1941, BA-MA RW 4/v. 578. On 17 June 1941 the list was sent to the foreign ministry: see Weisung OKW/WFSt/Abt. L (I Op) No. 44885/41 g.Kdos. Chefs., 17 June 1941, with annexe 1 (*DGFP* D xii, No. 638, pp. 1040–2). On Schnurre's trip see ibid., No. 668, pp. 1078–9.

that Germany and Finland had a new war 'forced upon them' by the putative Soviet deployment, the German leadership, while not expecting Sweden to participate, nevertheless hoped that the country, 'if only in the interest of Finland, will do everything to co-operate in the elimination of the Bolshevist armed forces threatening the Scandinavian area' and that it would moreover, with a few units of its army, participate in a war apostrophized as a 'crusade against Bolshevism'.[185] Meanwhile, preparations continued for the transportation and employment of 163rd Infantry Division against Hanko. The division's commanding officer, Lieutenant-General Erwin Engelbrecht, together with Infantry General Erfurth of the Liaison Staff North, had visited the Finnish general staff and the Hanko region before the war to gather information on Finnish operation plans and to reconnoitre the terrain.[186]

Schnurre's demand at the beginning of the war for the transit of 163rd Infantry Division (the 'Engelbrecht Division') resulted in a government crisis in Stockholm. Although Foreign Minister Günther had already expressed 'definite understanding' for the German requests, Sweden's parliament and government consented only after the personal intervention of King Gustav V, who supported the German requests and threatened to abdicate if they were not met. On 25 June Sweden eventually authorized the troop transport, but with the proviso that this was a once-only arrangement.[187] The transfer of the German troops from southern Norway began the same day 'under the most favourable conditions imaginable and with the most amicable support of the Swedish military and railway authorities'; on 26 June 1941 the first train ran across Sweden to Finland via Tornio, and on 29 June the first elements of the division detrained in Finland at Joensuu.[188]

The Swedish government moreover authorized supply traffic across its territory to Finland 'on any scale technically feasible'. It was further willing to deliver arms and ammunition to Finland, to grant to the German Luftwaffe courier and transport routes, as well as airfields for emergency landings, to assist the German navy by mine-barrages and other services in its war against the Soviet Union, and to channel German intelligence communications to Finland through Sweden. Germany's requests were therefore being 'met in all essential respects' and Sweden's will 'for businesslike co-operation with Germany in the military field' proved in practice.[189]

[185] *DGFP* D xii, No. 638, pp. 1040 ff.

[186] See 163. Inf.Div., Ia, KTB from 16 June 1941, BA-MA 16260/16; personal papers of Gen. Erfurth, Tagebuch, i. 29, BA-MA N 257/1.

[187] See *DGFP* D xii, No. 668, pp. 1078–9; ibid. xiii, Nos. 8, 9, 16, 17, pp. 11–13, 20–2; Björkman, *Sverige inför Operation Barbarossa*, 337–44; Gruchmann, 'Schweden', 602–3; Carlgren, *Svensk utrikespolitik*, 299 ff.; *KTB OKW* i. 409 (25 June 1941); Nilsson, 'Midsommarkrisen 1941'; Thulstrup, 'Gustav V's roll under midsommarkrisen 1941', 72 ff.; further bibliography on the 'midsummer crisis' of 1941 in West, *German–Swedish Relations*, 322–54.

[188] On the transport of 163rd Inf. Div. see 163. Inf.Div., Ia, KTB from 25 June 1941, BA-MA 16260/16.

[189] On detailed assistance see *DGFP* D xiii, Nos. 28, 41, 42, 43, pp. 30–2, 44–50; see also Halder, *Diaries*, 841 (26 Mar. 1941), 946 (5 June 1941).

Stockholm's new readiness to co-operate with Germany, acknowledged by Ribbentrop with satisfaction and gratitude,[190] was due largely to the fact that meanwhile, on 26 June 1941, Finland had entered the war against the Soviet Union on the German side. There was no doubt that the Swedish government, with its decision to authorize the transit of a German division from Norway to Finland, had reached the uttermost limit of its policy of neutrality, if indeed it had not exceeded it.[191] But even though Sweden's numerous measures of support and assistance were deviations from its officially proclaimed neutrality, Swedish policy generally continued to be governed by a reluctance to be drawn into the war. This fundamental position was unaffected by occasionally voiced views among the Swedish officers' corps, where there was a greater inclination to participate in the German attack on the Soviet Union.[192] The Swedish government, after all, had made it clear that its permission for the transit of the German division did not set a precedent for similar demands in the future.

[190] See Ribbentrop's telegram, *DGFP* D xiii, No. 30, p. 33.

[191] See also the account and assessment in Björkman, *Sverige inför Operation Barbarossa*, 422 ff., 479 ff. Wittmann, *Schwedens Wirtschaftsbeziehungen*, 270 n. 46, suspects, in view of 'the intensity of German endeavours', that the demand for the transit of 163rd Inf. Div. 'was, at least in part, designed to draw Sweden over to the [German] side by making her violate her neutrality'.

[192] See Björkman, *Sverige inför Operation Barbarossa*, 436, 462; Wilhelmus, 'Schweden und das faschistische Deutschland', 801.

VII. Operation Barbarossa as a War of Conquest and Annihilation

JÜRGEN FÖRSTER

1. PLANS AND PREPARATIONS FOR SECURING 'LIVING-SPACE'

THE 'dual face of the eastern campaign'—as a military operation and as an ideological war—is fully revealed only when, in addition to operational plans, acquisition of allies, and preparations for economic exploitation, the measures are outlined for the domination of the 'living-space' in the east and for the annihilation of 'Jewish Bolshevism'.

Reflections on securing, exploiting, and administering the conquered Soviet territories began in OKH and OKW in the summer of 1940, simultaneously with the first draft operations plans. Major-General Marcks in his study of 5 August 1940 proposed that initially a military administration should be set up in the occupied territories. Subsequently, administration of the Ukraine, the Baltic countries, and Belorussia would be transferred to 'native non-Bolshevik governments'.[1] Although on 31 July 1940 Hitler had mentioned that the Ukraine, Estonia, Latvia, Lithuania, and Belorussia were to come to Germany, he had left open the question of their juridical attachment to the Reich. Lieutenant-Colonel (General Staff) von Loßberg in his 'operations study East' of 15 September 1940 similarly envisaged for the Ukraine the establishment of a 'government' in line with German requirements, in order to facilitate security for Army Group South in its extensive rear areas.[2] When the Army High Command on 5 December 1940 submitted its operations plan to Hitler, he envisaged the establishment of three new political entities on Soviet territory, this time described as 'buffer states'.[3] Four weeks later he told the top Wehrmacht leaders that as a result of the conquest of the 'Russian space' the Reich would become unassailable and capable 'of waging war even against continents'. That space contained 'immeasurable wealth'. Germany must dominate it economically and politically, but not incorporate it.[4]

In February 1941 Major-General Wagner, the senior Army General Staff officer in charge of 'war administration', issued instructions on military sovereignty, security, and administration in the rear areas.[5] These envisaged a

---

[1] 'Operationsentwurf Ost', 120.

[2] Bezymenskij, Sonderakte 'Barbarossa' (1968), 311.

[3] KTB OKW i. 205 (5 Dec. 1940).

[4] Ibid. 257 (9 Jan. 1941).

[5] OKH/GenStdH/GenQu/Qu i/IIa No. I/050/41 g. Kdos., Feb. 1941, app. 15 and supplements to the working directives for the military administration, Verhalten der Bevölkerung im

military administration as a non-political instrument of the executive. This was not—as in western Europe in 1940—planned as a close network, because, for one thing, the 'primitive conditions in Russia' did not seem to make that necessary and, for another, the prerequisites in terms of staff and material were lacking. On the principle that preservation of the army's mobility was the supreme law of warfare, security and ruthless utilization of the country were to have precedence initially over an orderly administration in the interest of the Soviet population. The main tasks, in Wagner's view, were: securing of food-supply bases, safeguarding supplies and reinforcements, seizure and utilization of important supply assets for the forces, and relieving supplies from the Reich, as well as the guarding, putting to work, and rearward transportation of prisoners of war. In addition, German forces would have to be quick in ensuring control of the 'assets of the country for the strengthening of the German war economy'.

The decisive planning phase began when on 3 March 1941 Hitler returned the OKW draft of 'Guidelines in special fields concerning Directive No. 21', instructing General of Artillery Jodl, chief of the Wehrmacht operations staff, to revise it:

The impending campaign is more than a clash of arms; it also entails a struggle between two ideologies. To conclude this war it is not enough, given the vastness of the space, to defeat the enemy's forces. The entire territory must be dissolved into states with their own governments. Any revolution of major dimensions creates facts which can no longer be expunged. The socialist idea . . . alone can form the domestic basis for the creation of new states and governments. The Jewish-Bolshevik intelligentsia, as the oppressor in the past, must be liquidated. . . . Our task is to set up, as soon as possible, and with a minimum of military force, socialist state structures which are dependent on us. These tasks are so complex that one cannot expect the army to perform them.[6]

A few days earlier Hitler had remarked that what mattered in the war against the Soviet Union was 'first of all to quickly finish off the Bolshevik leaders'.[7]

In unambiguously defining his target as 'Jewish Bolshevism' Hitler not only proceeded from his dogma, but he also saw the 'Jewish-Bolshevik intelligentsia' as the germ-cell of any resistance to a long-term German occupation of large parts of the Soviet Union. Hitler's idea of a 'socialist . . . republic without

allgemeinen [Behaviour of the population generally] (OKH/GenStdH/GenQu/Ib/Qu 2 No. 098/40, 3 Apr. 1940), BA-MA RH 3/v. 132, and OKH/GenStdH/GenQu/Qu 1/II No. I/059/41, 10 Feb. 1941, BA-MA RH 2/v. 427. See Müller, 'Kriegsrecht', 139 ff., Nos. 2, 3.

[6] *KTB OKW* i. 341 (3 Mar. 1941). Hitler was not the only one to equate Jewry with Bolshevism. As early as the summer of 1918 Maj. Karl Freiherr von Bothmer, the Supreme Army Command's plenipotentiary in Moscow, identified the Bolsheviks with a 'gang of Jews' and wished 'to see a few hundred of those Jewish louts, next to one another . . . hanging on the Kremlin wall. If possible in such a way that death takes place slowly, in order to heighten the effect' (quoted according to Baumgart, *Ostpolitik*, 221 n. 45).

[7] Minute by Inf. Gen. Thomas on his report to Göring, 26 Feb. 1941, g.Kdos., BA-MA RW 19/185.

Stalin' was no doubt that of a Greater Germanic empire in Europe—as it emerged a few months later—an egalitarian 'people's community' under NSDAP rule. Hitler did not wish to see either Russian *émigrés* or Communists play any part in this. The disenfranchised and decimated Slav masses were to eke out the existence of helots.[8]

In accordance with Hitler's directives Jodl instructed his staff on how the draft for the organization of an administration in the occupied territories of the Soviet Union was to be amended: although the army needed a theatre of operations, this should be limited in depth as far as possible. Behind it no military administration was to be set up. Instead, Reich commissars would take over in large regions to be delineated on ethnic grounds; their duty would be the swift political development of new state structures. They would be assisted by 'Wehrmacht commanders' who, for their purely military matters, would come under the commander-in-chief of the army, and in all other matters under the Wehrmacht High Command. Security in the Reich commissariats would be provided by police forces, the bulk of which would come under the Reich commissar, while the rest would remain under the 'Reich leader of the SS and chief of the German police', who would also be represented by other bodies. For the phase of military administration in the theatre of operations Jodl did not envisage any military jurisdiction, either for punishable acts by the civilian population against the Wehrmacht or for disputes of the local inhabitants with each other. 'Military courts... were to concern themselves only with judicial matters within the army.' The question of whether SS authorities should be employed also in the army's theatre of operations, alongside the army's secret field police, was to be examined in consultation with Himmler, although Jodl believed that the 'need to render all Bolshevik bigwigs and commissars instantly harmless'[9] would be an argument in favour. Jodl allowed the Wehrmacht operations staff to make contact with the Army High Command about these questions, but regarded contacts with the ministry of the interior as unnecessary for the time being.

Hitler's directives and Jodl's instructions for the revision of the 'Guidelines in special fields concerning Directive No. 21' triggered the usual activities in the relevant departments of OKW and OKH. Military men and jurists set out to formulate the planned limitation of military jurisdiction in legally valid shape. Hitler's determination to conduct the war against the Soviet Union also as a struggle between two antagonistic ideologies did not encounter any resolute opposition in the Wehrmacht or in the army commands. The revised draft went to the high commands of the Wehrmacht services for comment as early as 5 March.[10] Without having undergone any significant amendments, the 'Guidelines in special fields concerning Directive No. 21' were issued by

---

[8] See *Hitler's Secret Book*, 44–5; Hitler, *Monologe*, 48, 54–5 (27 July and 8–11 Aug. 1941).

[9] *KTB OKW* i. 341 (3 Mar. 1941). See Förster, 'German Army'.

[10] OKW/WFSt/Abt. L (IV/Qu) No. 44125/41 g.Kdos. Chefs., Mar. 1941, BA-MA RW 4/v. 575. See Halder, *Diaries*, 820 (5 Mar. 1941).

the Wehrmacht chief of staff on 13 March.[11] The occupied territory was to be separated from the army's theatre of operations as soon as military operations permitted and 'dissolved' into states with their own governments. By analogy with the three Army Groups North, Centre, and South, the establishment of three Reich commissariats (Baltic, Belorussia, and Ukraine) was initially envisaged. The political executive would be in the hands of each Reich commissar, who would receive his directives from Hitler. The task of military security, both internally and against any external threat, was assigned to a Wehrmacht commander, who would also be responsible for making use of the country in order to supply the fighting forces.[12] The OKW directives assigned to Himmler 'special tasks on the Führer's instructions' in the army's theatre of operations. These tasks, which arose 'from the final struggle between two opposing political systems', were to be performed by SS agencies independently and on their own responsibility. This represented a limitation of the executive power of the commander-in-chief of the army in the theatre of operations. There is no record of the army command having objected to these arrangements. An official of the naval command, on the other hand, commented on the transfer of those 'special tasks' to the SS with the words: 'Now that means something!'[13] Objections on the part of the army might indeed have been expected after its unpleasant experiences with the SS in Poland; after all, in 1941 the Army High Command, in contrast to 1939, could no longer assume that it could control the activity of Himmler's agencies in the rear of the operational zone. It seems therefore that the army command viewed the SS as support for the security divisions, which it believed were too weak for the pacification of the conquered territories. As early as mid-January 1941 the operations staff had recommended the deputy chief of staff 'to take up the offer of police regiments made [at the time] by the police for the west',[14] so that as few army formations as possible were lost to the actual combat operations. The operations staff had moreover envisaged the strengthening of the security forces of Army Group South by the Romanian, Hungarian, and Slovak armies, even though neither Hungary nor Slovakia was then included in Hitler's plans as a potential ally.

While the guidelines of 13 March 1941 announced the issue of special orders relating to the troops' behaviour *vis-à-vis* the Soviet population and to the tasks of Wehrmacht courts, the armed forces high command kept silent about Hitler's demand, also made on 3 March, for the annihilation of the 'Jewish-Bolshevik intelligentsia'. That was to prove of significance later on.

---

[11] *Hitlers Weisungen*, No. 21a (not in trans.). See OKW/WFSt/Abt. L IV/Qu No. 254/41, 22 June 1941, PA, U.St.S., Rußland I.

[12] See also Hitler's decree on the appointment of Wehrmacht commanders in the occupied territories: *Ursachen und Folgen*, xvii, No. 3152a.

[13] Marginal gloss on the copy of the OKW directives intended for OKM, BA-MA RM 7/985.

[14] OKH/GenStdH/Op.Abt. (I/N) No. 025/40 g.Kdos. Chefs., 15 Jan. 1941, signed Gehlen, BA-MA RH 2/v. 1325.

A fortnight later Hitler repeated to the army the guidelines he had given the Wehrmacht command on the character of the war in the east. After a conference on strategic matters with Colonel-General Halder and Colonel (General Staff) Heusinger, chief of the operations department, and after a report by the deputy chief of staff for supplies, he made clear the further objectives of Barbarossa: 'The intelligentsia put in by Stalin must be exterminated. The controlling machinery of the Russian empire must be smashed . . . Force must be used in its most brutal form. The ideological ties holding together the Russian people are not yet strong enough and the nation would break up once the functionaries are eliminated.'[15] This ideologically based assumption of Hitler's was not contradicted by the chief of the general staff, even though since the autumn of 1940 he had been aware of a contrary assessment by the German embassy in Moscow. Embassy Counsellor Gebhardt von Walther had pointed out that in a defensive war the Soviet government would not have to fear 'any kind of signs of disintegration among the population or in the army on social or national grounds'.[16] No doubt Halder, Wagner, and Heusinger believed that Hitler's planned policy of extermination of parts of the civilian population did not concern the army, since its participation was not explicitly required. At least Halder and Wagner then realized, since negotiations had already begun between the army and the SS on the use of Himmler's agencies in the theatre of operations, that special commandos of the security police and the SD would hunt down so-called 'enemies of the state and the Reich' in the occupied regions of the Soviet Union. They evidently accepted the need for radical measures by those units against real and putative opponents in the rear areas. Field Marshal von Brauchitsch, addressing the top commanders of the eastern army at Zossen on 27 March 1941, drew their attention to the special character of the war against the Soviet Union. On the treatment of the enemy he declared, anticipating Hitler's speech on that subject: 'The troops have to realize that this struggle is being waged by one race against another, and proceed with the necessary harshness.'[17]

The OKW guidelines of 13 March, together with its earlier reflections, provided the basis for the 'Special instructions on supplies, part C' by the Generalquartiermeister of 3 April 1941.[18] These also regulated the organization and security in the operations area behind the combat zone. Because of its size the 'operations area' was to be divided up. Within the Armeegebiet ('army area') the army group commanders were to exercise executive power and be responsible for securing and utilizing the country. The provost services em-

---

[15] Halder, *Diaries*, 833 (17 Mar. 1941).

[16] Gibbons, 'Opposition', 337–8.

[17] Minute of 1. GenSt.Offz. des AOK 18 [Eighteenth Army first general-staff officer], BA-MA 18. Armee, 19601/2. See Halder, *Diaries*, 842 (27 Mar. 1941).

[18] OKH/GenStdH/GenQu/Abt. Kriegsverwaltung No. II/0315/41 g.Kdos. Chefs., 3 Apr. 1941, BA-MA RH 22/12; *Fall Barbarossa*, No. 91. See Diagram II.vii.1.

ployed on these tasks were to come under the 'commandant of the rearward army area'. Behind these areas, Heeresgebiete ('rearward landforces areas') were to be set up in the sectors of the army groups, where the 'commander of the rearward land forces area' would exercise military sovereignty in accordance with the directives of the commander-in-chief of the relevant army group. For the discharge of their tasks the commanders in the rearward land forces areas each had assigned to them three mopping-up divisions, to each of which one motorized battalion of uniformed police was in turn subordinated. Field or local HQs were to be set up at important supply-bases and transport centres. In addition to field gendarmerie and secret field police, however, the commander was entitled, in case of need, to draw also on the Waffen-SS and uniformed police units employed in his area for the performance of security tasks, though these came under the command of the 'senior SS and police leader'. As for the treatment of the civilian population, the Army High Command had ruled that any active or passive resistance was to be quashed with rigorous punitive measures. 'Self-assured and ruthless behaviour towards anti-German elements will prove an effective preventive means.' As for prisoners of war, other ranks were to be regarded as valuable labour to be immediately employed by the troops for their purposes. 'Willing work' was to be rewarded by adequate nourishment and good care, while rigorous measures were to be taken against 'disobedience'. The 'leadership personnel (officers, political commissars, and NCOs)', on the other hand, were to be urgently separated out and transported to the organization based in Germany established by OKW. Beyond the statement that captured field kitchens were to be left to the POW detachments, nothing was said about the feeding of prisoners. However, the OKW guidelines on prisoners of war, dated 16 June 1941, foreshadowed a special order on the subject.[19] Until then the existing regulations would remain in force. These (i.e. army instruction 38/2 of 22 October 1939) ruled, in line with the stipulations of the Geneva Convention, that the rations of prisoners of war should be 'equivalent in quantity and quality to those of depot troops'. In the treatment of prisoners of war the troops, according to the directives, should proceed from the realization that Bolshevism was the mortal enemy of National Socialist Germany. In consequence, 'extreme reserve and greatest vigilance' were 'called for towards captured Red Army men. Insidious behaviour has to be expected from prisoners of war, especially those of Asiatic origin. Therefore: ruthless action at the least sign of disobedience, especially towards Bolshevik agitators. Total liquidation of any active or passive resistance!'[20] The OKW guidelines, however, also pointed out that the Geneva Convention of 27 July 1929 on the treatment of prisoners of war, to which the Soviet Union had not acceded, provided the basis of the treatment of prisoners

[19] OKW/AWA/Abt. Kriegsgefangene No. 26/41 g.Kdos., Chefs., 16 June 1941, BA-MA RW 4/v. 578.
[20] Ibid.

of war. 'Leader personnel' (officers and NCOs) were to be separated out and transported back. Directives issued meanwhile on the treatment of political commissars had resulted, through quartermaster channels, in their removal from the list of categories to be transported to Germany. In the organization based in Germany the other ranks were to be sorted according to ethnic criteria. Removal of prisoners of war from the operations area was envisaged as follows: from the collecting-points at division level the prisoners were to be taken to army prisoner collecting-points, and from there to transit camps ('Dulag') in the rearward land-force areas; these camps came under the local district commandant. Only back on Reich territory and in occupied Poland were OR camps ('Stalag') and officers' camps ('Oflag') set up; these came under the prisoner-of-war department of the general Wehrmacht department in OKW. Others were to be established in the Reich commissariats. The camps in Poland, Belorussia, the Ukraine, and the Baltic countries were to be kept filled 'to the utmost limit of capacity' before transports were sent to the Reich, as the camps on Reich territory were ready to take a total of only 790,000 prisoners. Accurate registration and reports on captured Red Army men to the Wehrmacht information centre, which maintained contact with the International Red Cross, were not considered necessary.

Given the strategic deployment of the German army and the assumption that the Red Army would stand and fight west of the Dnieper and Dvina, OKW and OKH were bound to expect large numbers of prisoners. It proved impossible, however, to arrive at any conclusion in precise figures. A supply exercise of the quartermaster-general of Army Group South in February–March 1941, which has been preserved, assumed the taking of 72,000 prisoners over the first four days of the attack, with a further 122,000 over the next six days. Problems of accommodation and food supplies were expected. In order to relieve its supply situation, Armoured Group I in the map exercise urgently requested the removal of 37,000 prisoners as food supplies at Polonnoe were down to one day's prooision.[21] It should be remembered in this connection that the prisoners of war—like the Wehrmacht generally, in fact—were expected to live off the land. Overall responsibility for the economic utilization of the occupied territories was with the specially created 'economic staff East'.[22] Administration of the conquered Soviet territory, according to the OKW guidelines of 13 March 1941, was initially to be in the hands of three Reich commissars. Their authority, however, was circumscribed from the outset by the fact that military sovereignty was to be exercised by the Wehrmacht commander in question, with economic duties being discharged

[21] OKH/GenStdH/GenQu/Qu I/Abt. Kriegsverwaltung (Qu 4) No. I/050/41, VII. Angelegenheit, 4 Mar. 1941, BA-MA RH 3/v.132.

[22] See sect. I.III.2(*d*) at n. 172 (Müller).

by the economic staff East. The Reich commissars were to receive their directives for the political administration from Hitler. On 2 April 1941 he therefore instructed Alfred Rosenberg, Reich leader of the NSDAP, to 'set up a central political office for eastern affairs'.[23] Rosenberg, unaware that approved plans by the armed forces high command were already in existence, demanded in an extensive memorandum responsibility not only for issuing binding instructions concerning occupation, but also concerning security for vital deliveries from the occupied territories to the Reich. In Rosenberg's opinion the 'political shattering of the great empire in the east' was to be along national or geographical lines:

(a) Greater Russia with Moscow as its centre;
(b) Belorussia with Minsk or Smolensk as its capital;
(c) Estonia, Latvia, and Lithuania;
(d) the Ukraine and the Crimea with Kiev as its centre;
(e) the Don region with Rostov as its capital;
(f) the Caucasus region;
(g) Russian Central Asia or Russian Turkestan.[24]

The 'Jewish-Bolshevik state administration' was to be totally annihilated, 'undesirable elements of the population'—these also included the Latvian intelligentsia and 'racially inferior' Lithuanians—were to be resettled in 'Muscovite Russia', while the Baltic was to become a 'German settlement region in the future, with the assimilation of the racially most suitable'.

A few days later Rosenberg made personal recommendations for the appointment of Reich commissars: Gauleiter Hinrich Lohse for the 'Baltic provinces and White Ruthenia [Belorussia]', State Secretary Backe for the 'Caucasus', Stabsleiter Arno Schickedanz for the 'Ukraine', Minister President Dr Dietrich Klagges for the 'Don and Volga region', and Gauleiter Erich Koch for 'greater Russia'. Finally, Rosenberg proposed himself as the head of an 'authoritarian' office, directly subordinated to Hitler and furnished with the necessary full powers, to be called the 'Protectorate-General for the occupied eastern territories'.[25] On 20 April Hitler appointed Rosenberg his 'Delegate for the central examination of questions concerning the east European space'. He was entitled to call on the closest co-operation of the supreme Reich authorities and to bring in their representatives for consultation. These were primarily the armed forces high command, the Four-year Plan authority, and the Reich ministry of economic affairs.[26]

On 2 May Rosenberg had himself briefed by OKW on the instructions already issued by the military command concerning the delimitation of the

---

[23] Memorandum of 2 Apr. 1941 concerning USSR: *Ursachen und Folgen*, xvii, No. 3132b, pp. 116 ff. See Rich, *War Aims*, i. 218 ff.; *Das Dentsche Reich und der Zweite Weltkrieg*, v/1. 85 ff.
[24] Memorandum of 2 Apr. 1941: *Ursachen und Folgen*, xvii, No. 3132b, pp. 116 ff.
[25] Appendix to memorandum No. 2 of 7 Apr. 1941, ibid. 122–3.
[26] Letter from Hanns Lammers, Reich minister and head of the Reich chancellery, 21 Apr. 1941, BA-MA RW 4/v. 759.

area of operations, the arrangements between army and SS, and the duties of the army commander attached to the Reich commissar.[27]

During the time left before the beginning of the war, Rosenberg was anxious to receive the powers he was striving for in order to get his ideas on the structure and tasks of the political administration in the east to prevail. Although special instructions for the Reich commissar for the Ukraine and for the Reich commissar Ostland ('Eastland'),[28] as well as general directives for all the Reich commissars, had been issued by the beginning of May 1941,[29] Hitler had not yet finally decided on the boundaries and administrative centres of the planned four Reich commissariats. The views of the different authorities—the Rosenberg office, the ministry of the interior, and the Reich leader of the SS—on the political reorganization of the occupied territories diverged considerably. No decisions had yet been made on what parts of the Soviet Union were to be annexed by Germany, or administered by her, or given autonomous governments.[30] Although a 'Führer decree on the administration of the newly occupied eastern territories' was available in draft form, Hitler decided on 16 May to leave matters open for the time being and to have separate conversations with the competitors. For the time being, at any rate, he had 'agreed in principle' that there should be four Reich commissariats. Lithuania, Latvia, and Estonia, together with Belorussia and the Smolensk administrative district, were to form the Baltenland (Baltic land); the Ukraine was to be enlarged by the Saratov district and the Crimea; the region of the Caucasus mountains with their foothills as far as the Volga was to form the Reich commissariat 'Caucasia', and the territory inhabited by Russians was to come under the Reich commissar for the 'administrative district Russia' (see Map I.vii.1).

In Rosenberg's view the political objective of Operation Barbarossa was not to conduct a crusade against Bolshevism, but to 'pursue German military policy and make the German Reich secure'.[31] Organic state structures should be carved out of the USSR's territory and built up against Moscow, 'in order to free the German Reich of its eastern nightmare for centuries to come.... Reversing the Russian dynamism towards the east [is] a task [demanding] the strongest characters.' The second 'gigantic task' according to Rosenberg—though this was up to Göring—was to 'safeguard Germany's food supplies and war economy'. There was absolutely no obligation 'to feed the Russian people as well'. A few days earlier Otto Bräutigam, the deputy-chief designate of the political department of the future eastern ministry, had pleaded in an internal memorandum that the war against the Soviet Union

---

[27] Abt. Landesverteidigung [Home-defence department], Besprechung beim Reichsleiter Rosenberg [Conference at Reich Leader Rosenberg's office], 1 May 1941, ibid.

[28] *IMT* xxvi. 567ff., 573ff.

[29] *Ursachen und Folgen*, xvii, Nos. 3132–3, pp. 126ff.

[30] Letter from Lammers, 20 May 1941, with three draft decrees, BA-MA RW 4/v. 759. See also *DGFP* d.xii, Nos. 573, 591.

[31] Speech of 20 June 1941, *IMT* xxvi. 610ff.

MAP I.VII.I. Rosenberg's Plan for a Civil Administration in the East, May 1941
Source: BA-MA RW 4/v. 759.

should be 'a political campaign, not an economic war of pillage'. If the sympathies of the broad masses were to be won, the conquered territory 'as a whole must not be viewed as an object of exploitation'. Moreover, a differentiated treatment was necessary for the different peoples of the USSR.[32] But against the directives worked out by the economic control staff East (the 'Green Folder')[33] this programme stood no chance of realization.

---

[32] Gibbons, 'Richtlinien', 259.   [33] See sect. I.III.2(*f*) (Müller).

2. HITLER'S IDEOLOGICAL INTENTIONS TRANSLATED INTO ORDERS

(a) The Regulation of SS Activity in the Operations Area of the Army

Negotiations between the army and the SS on the employment of special SS commandos began on 13 March 1941. They were conducted—as before the attack on Poland—between Major-General Wagner, the quartermaster-general, and SS-Gruppenführer Reinhard Heydrich, chief of the security police and the SD. In July–August 1939 they had soon reached agreement on the tasks of the security-police action groups: 'Struggle against all anti-Reich and anti-German elements in the enemy country behind the fighting troops.'[34] In his 'Guidelines for the employment of the security police and the SD abroad' Heydrich had defined this formula in the sense that the action commandos were charged, in principle, with all the duties of a state police authority in the Reich. This general statement was subsequently further elucidated. On 19 September 1939 Heydrich had listed to Wagner as the objective of the employment of his agencies in Poland: 'house-cleaning: Jews, intelligentsia, clergy, nobility.'[35] At the beginning of July 1940 the chief of the security police and SD had named the following 'anti-Reich elements': émigrés, Freemasons, Jews, Communists, and political-clerical opponents.[36]

Knowledge of the murders committed by the SS in Poland was evidently no obstacle to the negotiations between Heydrich and Wagner in March 1941, during which the quartermaster-general remained in close touch with the chief of the Army General Staff. On 26 March 1941 Wagner—after agreement with Heydrich in principle—was able to submit a draft order.[37] This provided that the 'special commandos of the security police (SD)' were to discharge their special tasks outside the armed forces 'on their own responsibility' and that they were entitled 'to take executive measures' against the civilian population. They would receive their specialized instructions from Heydrich; only in matters of movement, supplies, and accommodation would they be subordinated to the army commanders-in-chief or commanding officers in the rearward land-force area. Their tasks in the rearward area of individual armies (Armeegebiet) were: 'Securing of defined objects (material, archives of anti-Reich or anti-state organizations, associations, groups, etc.) and of especially important individuals (leading émigrés, saboteurs, terrorists, etc.)' prior to the beginning of operations. In the rearward land-force area their task—much as it had been in Poland—was quite generally to discover and combat all 'anti-state and anti-Reich endeavours, in so far as these were not part of the enemy's armed forces' (sic). The last-named task was presumably the preserve of the secret field police. Its duties, in fact, were to be not only 'counter-intelligence'

---

[34] Umbreit, Militärverwaltungen, 76; Krausnick and Wilhelm, Die Truppe des Weltanschauungskrieges, 36. For the negotiations before the campaign in France see ibid. 107 ff.

[35] Halder, Diaries, 85 (19 Sept. 1939).

[36] Krausnick und Wilhelm, Die Truppe des Weltanschauungskrieges, 19.

[37] OKH/GenStdH/GenQu/Abt. Kriegsverwaltung No. II o.No./41 geh., 26 Mar. 1941, BA-MA RW 4/v. 575; Jacobsen, 'Kommissarbefehl', No. 2.

tasks within the forces but also their direct protection. The secret field police, whose leaders were composed of Gestapo and criminal-investigation officers, functioned in the operations zone as the 'political counter-intelligence executive'[38] of the army, in order to protect and support its operations. The focus of its attention was to be not so much 'spy-catching'—which was the task of Abwehr III—but 'preventive security' for the fighting forces.

The draft order of 26 March further stipulated that in each army sector and in each rearward land-force area a 'delegate' of Heydrich's was to be appointed to provide central control of the special commandos. He was obliged to inform the army commander-in-chief or the commander of the rearward land-force area promptly of the directives received by him from the chief of security police and SD, and was directed to co-operate continuously with their enemy-situation analysts. The Ic (intelligence) officer was to co-ordinate the tasks of the special commandos with military counter-intelligence, with the work of the secret field police, and with operational requirements. The military commanders were entitled to ban the employment of commandos in parts of the operations area to avoid interference with operations. That, however, was the only objection raised in OKH to the activity of Himmler's agencies 'on their own responsibility', with regard both to so-called 'enemies of the state and the Reich' and to the civilian population. The army's bad experience with subordinate special squads in Poland was in 1941 no longer sufficient—as it had been before the western campaign—to make it either completely rule out the employment of the security police or the SD in the operations area altogether or at least insist on stricter control of their employment. Despite the high degree of verbal camouflage in the definition of the tasks of the SS, there could be no doubt among the army command, after Hitler's numerous public and private remarks on the connection between Bolshevism and Jewry, after the measures taken in the Reich, and after the murders in Poland, that along with the Communist leadership stratum the Jews in the occupied Soviet territories were also to be exterminated. Whether the Army High Command had been informed before 22 June of the relevant instructions sent by Hitler to Himmler and Heydrich cannot be proved. It is noteworthy, however, that Halder and Wagner, in emending the draft order of 26 March 1941, extended the tasks of the SS forces employed in the Balkan campaign by adding to '*émigrés*, saboteurs, and terrorists' two further categories of adversaries: 'Communists, Jews.'[39] Did the chief of the Army General Staff and the quartermas-

---

[38] H.Dv. g. 150, 24 July 1939. The GFP's duty was the 'discovery of and fight against all endeavours hostile to the nation and state'. See Gessner, 'Geheime Feldpolizei'; id., *Geheime Feldpolizei*.

[39] OKH/GStdH/GenQu/Abt. Kriegsverwaltung No. II/0308/41 geh., 2 Apr. 1941, concerning Regelung des Einsatzes der Sicherheitspolizei und des SD beim Unternehmen 'Marita' und 'Fünfundzwanzig' [Regulation of the employment of the security police and the SD in Operations 'Marita' and 'Fünfundzwanzig'], BA-MA RH 31-I/v. 23. I am indebted to Detlef Vogel for this reference.

ter-general see the sinister forces of Communism and Jewry behind the Serbian officers who overthrew the pro-German Cvetkovic government in Belgrade on 27 March 1941? At any rate, the assumption of Soviet backing for the new Yugoslav government was voiced in Berlin as early as 2 April.[40] Or did the Army High Command view Jews and Communists generally as potential elements of resistance to Germany's 'smashing of Yugoslavia'?

On another point, too, the order of 2 April 1941 on 'Regulating the employment of the security police and the SD in Operation Marita and Twenty-five'—which Halder signed *'per pro.* the commander-in-chief of the army'—differed from the draft order of 26 March 1941. By analogy with Heydrich's guidelines of August 1939, it simply stated that the special commandos would discharge their tasks *'outside* the fighting forces' within the framework of the duties performed by the security police and the SD 'in the homeland'.

Four weeks after the submission of the draft, on 28 April 1941, the OKH order on the 'Regulation of the employment of the security police and the SD within the framework of the army' was issued for Barbarossa. This time it was signed by the army commander-in-chief and not by Halder.[41] In substance it did not differ from the agreement reached between Wagner and Heydrich, and therefore—in contrast to Halder's order of 2 April—contained no special reference to the 'securing' of Jews and Communists. Two days later the commanders of the rearward land-force area were notified by the quartermaster-general of the impending arrival of one group of secret field police for each security division. They were to be available to the division Ic (intelligence officer) for the prevention of high treason, espionage, and sabotage. Wagner emphasized that the 'main effort' of the field-police employment in the military field would be counter-intelligence police issues and security policy as required for the safety of the fighting forces. In terms of discipline and specialized work these groups of secret field police were subordinated to the division Ic.[42]

The focus of co-operation between the army's Ic service, the Abwehr (counter-intelligence), and the special commandos was with the Ic officers of the armies and armoured groups. They bore the main responsibility for the practical implementation of the directives issued on the subject.[43] This was explained to them at several meetings by the head of the department for 'war

[40] See German embassy Belgrade, telegram No. 278, 27 Mar. 1941, PA, Büro St.S., Jugoslawien, vol. ii, and *KTB OKW* i. 373 (1 Apr. 1941). Towards the end of March the German military attaché reported from Belgrade that the Serbian people were 'indoctrinated and anti-German' (minute by Otto von Grotes, legation secretary in the foreign ministry, 29 Mar. 1941, PA, Büro St.S., Jugoslawien, vol. ii).

[41] OKH/GenStdH/GenQu/Abt. Kriegsverwaltung No. II/2101/41 geh., 28 Apr. 1941, BA-MA RH 22/155; Jacobsen, 'Kommissarbefehl', No. 3.

[42] OKH/GenStdH/GenQu/Abt. Kriegsverwaltung (Qu 4b/Org/GFP) No. II/2161/41 geh., 30 Apr. 1941, BA-MA RH 22/271.

[43] OKH/GenStdH/OQu IV B. No. 200/41 g.Kdos. Chefs., 11 June 1941, BA-MA H 27/43.

administration' on the quartermaster-general's staff, Major (General Staff) Hans-Georg Schmidt von Altenstadt. On 16 May 1941 Wagner's delegate briefed the Ic and Ib officers, senior quartermasters and quartermasters of army groups, armies, and armoured groups, and the commanders of the rearward land-force areas, as well as the Ia officers of the security divisions— all of whom had assembled at the armoured-forces training school at Wünsdorf near Berlin—on the planned exercise of executive power.[44] The executive, he explained, was divided between army and SS. Anything to do with the Red Army and the safety of the forces was the task of the army; the rest was the task of the SS. Within the army area only insignificant 'special commandos' would be employed by the Reich leader of the SS; major actions would take place only in the rearward land-force area, where the main effort would be away from the roads. These units would perform their tasks on their own responsibility. Employment of the special commandos in the army area could be banned by the army commander-in-chief. For combat employment in the rearward land-force area the commanding officer had all police and SS units at his disposal. Any genuine subordination, however, had been declined by the army commander-in-chief because that would have made the army also responsible for the 'execution of political tasks'.[45]

On 4 June 1941 the quartermaster-general briefed the army and army-group commanders on the political intentions connected with Barbarossa. The conquered territory would be 'split up into individual states'. While socialism would remain the basis, neither the Bolsheviks nor the former leading strata were fit for future leadership. Executive power in the area of operations was subdivided into 'four columns': (*a*) commander-in-chief of the army (highest level), (*b*) Reich leader of the SS (politically 'alongside the military posts, *in so far as military requirements permit*'), (*c*) Reich Marshal (economy), (*d*) Rosenberg (political shaping). Because of the 'lateral arrangement' of these four columns the chief of the Army General Staff foresaw difficulties and asked the chiefs 'to work against it'. Major-General Wagner pointed out that the army should not concern itself with the 'political executive' of the special commandos; its task remained the protection of roads and supply-lines.[46] The chief of army administration, Lieutenant-Colonel (General Staff) Radke, announced at the same conference that Brauchitsch and Himmler had arrived at an understanding for finally burying the conflict which had erupted between the army and the SS because of the murders in Poland.

[44] OKH/GenStdH/GenQu, Chefgruppe No. I/2665/41 g.Kdos., 2 May 1941, concerning conference at OKH/GenQu, BA-MA RH 26-454/6.

[45] See the minutes of the Ninth Army's first staff officer in charge of supplies (BA-MA 9. Armee, 13904/3b), of the Ia, 285th Security Division (BA-MA RH 26-285/4), of the Ic, Eleventh Army HQ (BA-MA, Alliierte Prozesse 9, NOKW-486), and of the Ic/AO III, Army Group North (BA-MA RH 19 III/722). See Gersdorff, *Soldat im Untergang*, 84–5.

[46] Minutes of the chiefs of staff of Seventeenth Army (BA-MA, 17. Armee, 14499/5), Eighteenth Army (19601/2), and Army Group North (ibid.). On the report of Chef H Wes Abt see Halder, *KTB* ii. 482, app. 10 (4 June 1941; not in trans.).

Two days later, at an Ic conference, Schmidt von Altenstadt defined the role of the 'fourth delegate' even more clearly: the Wehrmacht, he explained, was concerned with 'fighting the enemy into the ground', while the SS was concerned with the 'political police struggle against the enemy'. If the great tasks were to be accomplished, co-operation was 'of crucial importance'. SS Standartenführer Nockemann specified the duties of the security police and the SD. The political security of the occupied territories demanded the creation of 'the basis for the final liquidation of Bolshevism'. For that purpose it was necessary in the rearward army area to round up not only the enemy's political material but also the 'politically dangerous individuals (Jews, *émigrés*, terrorists, political churchmen, etc.)' and in the rearward land-force area to track down all 'anti-state and anti-Reich efforts'. According to the order he had received, 'extreme hardness and harshness are to be applied'. The forces employed for this would be 2,500 men: 500 for each army group, of whom 80 would operate in the forward area of each army.[47]

The arrangements agreed between OKH and the Reich leader of the SS concerning Barbarossa were amplified on 21 May 1941 by the provision that in each of the three rearward land-force areas one 'senior SS and police leader' would be appointed. He would be in charge not only of the 'action squads of the security police and the SD' in his area, but also of one police regiment and of units of the uniformed police. These units were to support the three security divisions under the commander of the rearward land-force area in the pacification of the country. The police units were to be reinforced by Waffen-SS contingents. The 'senior SS and police leader' was obliged to inform the commander of the tasks assigned to him by Himmler.[48]

The permanent staff of the SS action groups were assembled after May 1941 at the frontier police college at Pretsch-on-Elbe. The command personnel were recruited from officers (or aspirants) of the Gestapo and the criminal police, and from members of the SD. The auxiliary personnel, however, also included non-members of the SS. These had been enlisted for 'long-term emergency service' on the strength of the 'emergency-service regulation' of 15 October 1938. The example of Action Group A in particular shows that the command personnel were composed, for the most part, of fairly young 'SS leaders or criminal-police officers with rather above-average abilities, ambitions, and training qualifications',[49] who had come to National Socialism at an early age. Almost a dozen of the seventeen SS leaders had completed their law studies; the six non-jurists, admittedly, had all failed at school, in their vocational training, or in their chosen occupations.

[47] Record made by Ic/AO III of Army Group North on the Ic (intelligence officers') conference at OKW/Abw and OKH/OQu IV and GenQu, 5–6 June 1941, Berlin (BA-MA RH 19 III/722); and minute of Ic of Army Command Norway, g.Kdos. (BA-MA, 20. Armee, 20844/5).

[48] Reichsführer SS, Tgb. No. 114/41 g.Kdos., 21 May 1941, BA-MA RH 22/156. See OKH/GenStdH/GenQu/Abt. Kriegsverwaltung (Qu 4 B/Org) No. II/807/41 g.Kdos., 14 June 1941, BA-MA RH 22/12. See Birn, *Die Höheren SS- und Polizeiführer*.

[49] Krausnick and Wilhelm, *Die Truppe des Weltanschauungskrieges*, 281.

Four action groups were established: Action Group A (headquarters, special commandos 1a and 1b, action commandos 2 and 3) with Army Group North for the Baltic region; Action Group B (headquarters, special commandos 7a and 7b, action commandos 8 and 9, and forward commando Moscow) with Army Group Centre for Belorussia; Action Group C (headquarters, special commandos 4a and 4b, action commandos 5 and 6) with Army Group South for the northern and central Ukraine; and Action Group D (headquarters, special commandos 10a and 10b, action commandos 11a, 11b, and 12) with Eleventh Army for Bessarabia, the southern Ukraine, and the Crimea. The strength of a fully motorized action group exceeded the figure of 500 originally notified to the army. At the start of Operation Barbarossa Action Group B, for instance, numbered 655 men, including 134 members of the uniformed police.[50]

In June 1941 the leaders of the action groups and action commandos were informed by Heydrich, by word of mouth, of Hitler's order that all Communists, Jews, and 'other radical elements' were to be executed.[51] In that connection, anti-Jewish or anti-Communist Poles, Lithuanians, Latvians, Estonians, Belorussians, and Ukrainians were also to be used for 'self-purging operations'. The 'special duties' of the SS in connection with 'preparations for a political administration', however, went beyond the mere execution of 'enemies of the state and the Reich'. The action groups were also responsible for preliminary administrative tasks of the most varied nature, such as the organization of native 'auxiliary police services' (Ordnungsdienste) and the creation of Jewish ghettos.

(b) The Limitation of Military Jurisdiction

On 3 March 1941 Hitler, in addition to the annihilation of the 'Jewish-Bolshevik intelligentsia', had demanded a limitation of military jurisdiction. This was to concern itself solely with juridical matters within the armed forces. Criminal offences by the civilian population were therefore to be punished in a different manner. Ministerialdirigent Dr Rudolf Lehmann, head of the Wehrmacht's legal department, when consulted by the quartermaster group of the Wehrmacht operations staff, tried to meet Hitler's demand in his second draft of the 'Guidelines in special fields concerning Directive No. 21', dated 5 March, by restricting the competence of Wehrmacht courts in the theatre of operations to criminal offences by Soviet citizens against the Wehrmacht for which the evidence was clear-cut.[52] All other cases were to be passed on to the

---

[50] Befh. rückw. Heeresgebiet 102 [Commander rear army area 102 (i.e. Centre)], Ia Br.B. No. 284/41 geh., 24 June 1941, corps order No. 18, annexe, BA-MA RH 22/224.

[51] This has been convincingly proved by Krausnick (Krausnick and Wilhelm, *Die Truppe des Weltanschauungskrieges*, 150 ff.). Streim, *Die Behandlung sowjetischer Kriegsgefangener*, 82 ff., on the other hand, believes that the order for the liquidation of all Jews was not issued until several weeks after the start of the operation. See *Mord an den Juden*.

[52] OKW/WFSt/Abt. L (IV/Qu) No. 44125/41, draft Mar. 1941, BA-MA RW 4/v. 575. On German military judiciary in the Second World War see Messerschmidt, 'Deutsche Militärgerichtsbarkeit im Zweiten Weltkrieg', and Messerschmidt and Wüllner, *Wehrmachtsjustiz*.

'nearest agency of the Reich leader of the SS'. This meant that suspects were deprived of all legal protection and that responsibility for their presumable execution was shuffled on to the SS. Underlying Lehmann's proposal was perhaps the intention not to overload the Wehrmacht courts with lengthy proceedings which might conceivably even result in acquittal. The OKW guidelines of 13 March merely foreshadowed a special order concerning the tasks of the Wehrmacht courts. This suggests that the supreme leadership wished to exceed Lehmann's draft.

In Berlin on 30 March 1942 Hitler addressed the assembled commanders-in-chief of the army groups, air fleets, and armies, the commanding officers of armoured groups and air corps, and their chiefs of staff, for nearly two and a half hours. The real purpose of the meeting was the discussion of the strategic intentions of Operation Barbarossa and their planned execution. It had to be postponed twice,[53] largely because of the surprising turn of events in Yugoslavia. Hitler used the opportunity for an extensive justification of his decision, skilfully blending political and ideological arguments. Against the background of the coup of Serbian officers and their suspected collusion with both London and Moscow, which had painfully upset the 'peace in the Balkans' necessary for Barbarossa, Hitler had no difficulty in introducing an ideological note to the generals' meeting. Colonel-General Halder made this note for himself:

Clash of two ideologies: Crushing denunciation of Bolshevism, identified with asocial criminality. Communism is an enormous danger for our future. We must forget the concept of comradeship between soldiers. A Communist is no comrade before nor after the battle. This is a war of extermination. If we do not grasp this, we shall still beat the enemy, but 30 years later we shall again have to fight the Communist foe. We do not wage war to preserve the enemy. *War against Russia*: Extermination of the Bolshevik commissars and of the Communist intelligentsia. The new states must be Socialist, but without intellectual classes of their own. Growth of a new intellectual class must be prevented. A primitive Socialist intelligentsia is all that is needed. We must fight against the poison of disintegration. This is no job for military courts. The individual troop commanders must realize the issues at stake. They must be leaders in this fight. The troops must fight back with the methods with which they are attacked. Commisars and GPU men are criminals and must be dealt with as such.

This need not mean that the troops should get out of hand. Rather, the commanders must give orders which express the common feeling of their men . . . Commanders must make the sacrifice of overcoming their personal scruples.[54]

Although Hitler's concept of an ideological war against Bolshevism had presumably long been familiar to the assembled officers from his many public and private remarks, he was now calling for specific measures against the

---

[53] OKH/GenStdH/Op.Abt. (Ia) No. 447/41, 18 Mar., and No. 479/41, 21 Mar. 1941, concerning conference at OKH, BA-MA RH 19 I/67a.

[54] Halder, *Diaries*, 846–7; FM von Bock summed up Hitler's remarks as 'Ruthless action. It is not our business to preserve criminals. Commissars': Bock, Tagebuch, vol. ii (30 Mar. 1941), MGFA P-210. FM Ritter von Leeb, on the other hand, recorded only 'Führer addresses commanders-in-chief on the situation' (Leeb, *Tagebuchaufzeichnungen*, 270).

exponents of the Bolshevik idea, i.e. Soviet state and party officials, as well as political commissars in the Red Army. As for the latter, he denied them military status and wanted to see them 'dealt with' as criminals. Hitler's formula of the 'poison of disintegration' must have evoked among his listeners memories of the disintegration of the eastern army in 1918–19, which in 1936 the official military historians of the general staff had attributed to Bolshevik agitation.[55] The Jews had been highlighted as the 'principal exponents of Bolshevik propaganda'. The establishment of soldiers' councils, the 'favourite children of the Bolshevik-influenced revolution', had been a fatal mistake which had facilitated the 'elimination of the leadership and the disintegration of the fighting forces'. Against the backdrop of this construed explanation of the causes of the collapse of imperial Germany, Hitler's linkage of the internal enemy then and the external enemy now, the Soviet Union—in other words, 'Jewish Bolshevism'—fell on fertile ground. To many officers it seemed reasonable that the war against the 'Jewish-Communist rulers' and their representatives should not be conducted according to the rules of international law or of military traditions. That was why Hitler succeeded in manœuvring the army, beyond its strictly military tasks, into a war of annihilation against an ideology and its followers, for which the action groups in particular were earmarked. Because he regarded military jurisdiction as an obstacle to his intentions, he wanted to neutralize it as far as possible.

It was probably at a joint breakfast of the Army High Command with the senior commanders that the first protests were voiced against Hitler's ideologically motivated conduct of the war. But that protest was primarily directed against the exclusion of the courts martial, which the commanders feared might lead to a slackening of discipline and good order. It is exceedingly doubtful whether the army and field commanders seriously considered compelling Hitler to relinquish his demands by threatening collective resignation.[56] After all, there was agreement on the view that political commissars in the Red Army did not have combatant status. Brauchitsch regarded it as his personal concern to work for the preservation of discipline and good order in this unusual war.

Towards the end of April 1941 the head of the Wehrmacht's legal department submitted a draft of the intended ordinance limiting military jurisdiction in the Barbarossa theatre of operations.[57] In line with Hitler's intentions he envisaged self-help by the troops against attacks by the civilian population: 'Guerrillas are to be ruthlessly finished off by the forces either in combat or while escaping. Other attacks against the Wehrmacht by civilians must be repelled by the troops ruthlessly and with all means, to the point of annihila-

[55] *Rückführung des Ostheeres*, 4 ff., 17–18, 172 ff.

[56] See Krausnick, 'Kommissarbefehl', 712–13; Bock, Tagebuch, vol. ii (4 and 7 June 1941), MGFA P-210; evidence given by Ritter von Leeb (see Leeb, *Tagebuchaufzeichnungen*, 270 n. 17); *Fall Barbarossa*, No. 101.

[57] WR 30/41 g.Kdos. Chefs., 28 Apr. 1941, BA-MA RW 4/v. 575.

tion of the attacker. . . . Only when, exceptionally, this has not been done are they to be prosecuted in the courts.'

Lehmann wished further to see the abolition of *obligatory* prosecution of punishable actions by Wehrmacht members against the civilian population, even when the action was 'at the same time a military felony or offence'. The judicial authority should prosecute such actions by courts martial only if this were demanded for the maintenance of discipline or the security of the troops.

On 6 May 1941, with time pressing—all preparations for Barbarossa requiring a somewhat longer starting-up time were to be completed by 15 May—Lieutenant-General Müller, 'general for special duties with the commander-in-chief of the army', following conversations with Lehmann and Halder, submitted to OKW his own drafts for the regulation of jurisdiction and the treatment of Soviet commissars within and outside the Red Army.[58] Significant about this is not only the fact that the army command saw some inner connection between the two measures—which it justified by the need to safeguard the forces against the 'exponents of the Jewish-Bolshevik ideology'—but that on questions of 'the application of criminal law in the field army and *vis-à-vis* the population of the occupied territories' Lieutenant-General Müller received his instructions not from the commander-in-chief of the army but from the chief of the general staff.[59] Hence it was not the 'general for special duties with the commander-in-chief of the army' who was at the centre of the army command's preparations for the struggle against the ideological enemy, but Halder. On the subject of jurisdiction for Barbarossa Müller asked the homeland defence department of OKW to take note of and expeditiously examine his draft, as the army command wished to issue Hitler's intentions in a juridically unassailable form as an ordinance from the commander-in-chief of the army.

Whereas Lehmann declared himself satisfied that the army's proposal was similar to his own ideas, Major-General Walter Warlimont, head of the homeland defence department, added the marginal gloss: 'Goes beyond WR [Wehrmacht legal department].'[60] The point was that Halder and Müller proposed that even potential guerrillas, saboteurs, or resisters be shot by the troops 'in combat or while escaping'. The draft was prefaced, in line with Hitler's address to the generals, by an ideological explanation designed to justify the ordered abandonment of international conventions on the law of

---

[58] OKH/Gen.z.b.V. b. ObdH No. 75/41, g.Kdos. Chefs., BA-MA RW 4/v. 577; Halder, *Diaries*, 907 (6 May 1941).

[59] ObbdH/GenStdH/GZ (I²) 1.St. No. 2182/40 geh., 29 Sept. 1940, app. 1, Dienstanweisung für die Gruppe 'Rechtswesen im OKH (Hauptquartier)' [Service regulation for group 'Law at OKH (Headquarters)'], BA-MA RH 19 III/146. This is the one that Halder signed *per pro*. the C.-in-C., 9 May 1941: see sect. I.iv.1(*g*) at n. 173 (Klink). Since 1 July 1935 the chief of the general staff had been the permanent deputy of the C.-in-C. of the army 'in ministerial functions': BA-MA RH 2/195.

[60] WR No. 32/41 g.Kdos. Chefs., 9 May 1941, BA-MA RW 4/v. 577.

war. 'This time', i.e. in contrast to past campaigns, the troops would be confronted not only by the usual guerrillas, but also, 'as a particularly danger-ous, disruptive, element from the civilian population, by the exponent of the Jewish-Bolshevik ideology'. On Halder's proposal, therefore, 'collective forc-ible measures' were envisaged against localities if the individual culprit was not quickly identified. 'It is the demand of self-preservation and the duty of all commanders to act with iron severity and without any delay against cowardly attacks by a deluded population.'

As already envisaged in the second part of Lehmann's draft of 28 April, 'punishable actions committed by members of the army *out of indigna-tion over atrocities* or over the *disruptive activity* of exponents of the Jewish-Bolshevik system' were not to be prosecuted 'except where, in the individual case, intervention is demanded for the maintenance of discipline'. In instances where the 'motivation of indignation' emerged only in the course of court hearings, commanders-in-chief and commanding officers should con-firm only those sentences which were in line with the '*military* and *political* aspects' of the war in the east. Halder and Müller of course foresaw the risk of arbitrary excesses by individual members of the forces if they relaxed the obligation of the judiciary authority to prosecute criminal offences. They tried to avert the degeneration of the fighting forces by emphasizing in their draft that, on the one hand, a soldier was in all cases bound by the orders of his superiors, and that, on the other, each chain-of-command superior should make full use of the latitude granted him by the wartime criminal-proceedings regulations of 1938 and by the order of the commander-in-chief of the army of November 1939 for imposing disciplinary punishments in all cases where these would be justified by the offence and the person of the offender.

Warlimont ruled that Lehmann, with all due expedition and after consulta-tion with the army and the Luftwaffe High Commands, should submit a new draft. Lehmann therefore, on the basis of the existing drafts of 28 April and 6 May and after consultation with Lieutenant-General Müller and Air Force General Jeschonnek, as well as with the heads of their legal departments, produced a further draft, which he sent to Jodl and Warlimont on 9 May. Lehmann's covering letter, explaining its origin and contents, is exceedingly revealing. It shows that Halder[61] wanted to retain for the Wehrmacht courts certain rights to concern themselves with criminal offences by civilians. Lehmann, on the other hand, like his professional colleagues in the other legal departments, was quite ready, for the duration of hostilities and during the first pacification phase, to eliminate Wehrmacht jurisdiction over local inhabi-tants completely. But they considered it 'absolutely necessary' to reintroduce Wehrmacht justice 'at the appropriate time'. 'Once we take this step,' Lehmann explained to his superiors,

---

[61] WFSt/Abt. L IV/Verw. g.Kdos. Chefs., note for report, 11 May 1941, ibid.

it must be taken fully. Otherwise there is a danger that the army will pass on to the courts the matters with which it feels uneasy and that in consequence (for these of course will be the doubtful cases) the opposite will happen of what it is intended to achieve . . . After the conclusion of hostilities and in somewhat calmer conditions it will be impossible to get the army to deal with such matters at all.

General Jeschonnek also believed that the army would let quite a lot of people get away 'who in fact would have deserved different treatment'. Lehmann, in line with the OKH draft, thought it necessary for 'elements suspected of an action' to be immediately brought before an officer, who would decide on their execution by firing-squad. Warlimont was in favour of passing on such cases to the SS special commandos, but Lieutenant-Colonel (General Staff) von Tippelskirch, head of the quartermaster group, objected that even the handing-over to a special commando would have to be subject to the decision of an officer, and that the officer's responsibility in both circumstances 'would probably be the same'.[62] At that level in the armed forces high command there was therefore no doubt about what being handed over to a special commando would mean for a Soviet civilian. Tippelskirch prepared a synopsis of the drafts of 28 April and 6 and 9 May as a basis for a decision by OKW. From his memorandum and from Lehmann's covering letter of 9 May it emerges clearly that OKW, OKH, and OKL were fully inclined to restrict Wehrmacht jurisdiction temporarily, i.e. until a sufficient pacification of the country was achieved, but that, at the same time, they were relying on an officer corps which wished to adhere to the existing form of military justice. It was also realized that a burden was being placed on line officers by assigning to them the decision over the life or death of individual Soviet citizens or entire village communities. That was why Lehmann had prefaced his second version with an appeal to the forces' security needs in order to make 'the business', i.e. the executions, 'a little more palatable' to the officers.[63]

On Hitler's behalf Keitel on 13 May issued the 'Decree on the exercise of war jurisdiction in the Barbarossa area and on special measures by the fighting forces'.[64] Its preamble emphasized that Wehrmacht jurisdiction served 'primarily the *maintenance of discipline*'. Given its small staff, however, jurisdiction could confine itself to that principal task only 'if *the troops themselves* ruthlessly oppose any threat from a hostile civilian population'. That hostility was presumed from the outset in view of the 'particular nature of the enemy'. The first part, 'Treatment of criminal offences by enemy civilians', stipulated that these would for the time being be removed from the jurisdiction of courts martial and summary courts. '*Guerrillas* are to be ruthlessly finished off by the troops in combat or while trying to escape.' All other attacks by·the civilian

---

[62] Ibid.; *Fall Barbarossa*, No. 95.

[63] WR No. 32/41 g.Kdos. Chefs., 9 May 1941, BA-MA RW 4/v. 577.

[64] The Führer and Supreme Commander of the Armed Forces, 13 May 1941, passed on to the Wehrmacht services as OKW/WFSt/L (IV/Qu) No. 44 178/41 g.Kdos. Chefs., 14 May 1941 (23 copies), ibid.; Jacobsen, 'Kommissarbefehl', No. 8; *Fall Barbarossa*, No. 97.

population were likewise to be instantly 'crushed with the utmost means, up to and including the annihilation of the attacker'. Where such measures had been omitted, 'elements suspected of an offence' were to be immediately brought before an officer, who would decide on their execution by firing-squad. Against localities from which the Wehrmacht had been 'insidiously or treacherously' attacked, if 'circumstances' prevented the swift identification of individual culprits, 'collective forcible measures' could be put into effect by any officer not below the rank of battalion commander.

The second part, 'Treatment of criminal offences by members of the Wehrmacht and its train against local inhabitants', laid down that there was no obligation to prosecute, 'not even if the offence is simultaneously a military felony or offence'. In judging such actions the judiciary authority should in each case take into account 'that the collapse in 1918, the subsequent sufferings of the German people, and the struggle of National Socialism with the countless blood sacrifices of the movement were primarily due to Bolshevik influence and that no German has forgotten that'. An artificial justification of criminal offences was thus being created in advance, resembling that in Hitler's amnesty decree of 4 October 1939. At that time it was ruled, alluding to the 'Bromberg [Bydgość] bloody Sunday', that there should be no punishment for actions committed 'out of indignation over the atrocities committed by Poles'.[65] The ruling for Barbarossa now was that the judiciary authority should nevertheless start court-martial proceedings if there was a danger of the fighting forces degenerating. Halder's and Müller's proposals for a disciplinary punishment of offences had not been accepted.

The third part held the commanding officers in the field personally responsible for having all officers of the units under their command thoroughly briefed on the principles of part I. Along with their juridical directives, their legal advisers should also be informed of the 'political intentions of the leadership'. The judiciary authority should confirm only those sentences which were in line with those intentions—meaning the intentions voiced by Hitler on 30 March.

The 'Führer decree' of 13 May 1941 was not only an 'example of the systematic projection of National Socialist "legal thinking" on to an ideological enemy'[66] but also reflected to a considerable extent the experience of the First World War, 'the sufferings of East Prussia',[67] after the invasion of Russian troops. Their rigorous behaviour towards the German population had not been forgotten: as early as 1925 it had been pilloried in an official history as the importation of Asiatic customs into German cultural territory.[68] The

---

[65] Quoted according to Krausnick and Wilhelm, *Die Truppe des Weltanschauungskrieges*, 82.

[66] Messerschmidt, *Wehrmacht*, 409.

[67] Thus the heading of a chapter in vol. ii of the archival work 'Der Weltkrieg 1914 bis 1918' (pp. 318 ff.). See Gause, *Russen in Ostpreußen*.

[68] 'Der Weltkrieg 1914 bis 1918', ii. 326.

third general-staff officer of Armoured Group 3, when briefed on the provisions of part I of the jurisdiction decree, felt likewise reminded of the First World War: 'The Russians in Gumbinnen: execution of all villagers living along the Tilsit–Insterburg track in the event of the track being damaged.'[69] However, the point to remember is that by means of the 'Führer decree' the purpose of the law of war—protection of the individuals and society of an occupied country against arbitrary actions—had, with the active help of lawyers, been reinterpreted into a tool of political and military intentions. The shooting of civilians on the mere suspicion of guerrilla activity or sabotage was clearly unlawful. Not even reference to the threatened security of the troops 'can ever serve the liquidation of the most fundamental human rights'.[70] Anxiety about the discipline of the fighting forces was evidently greater than legal scruples about the abolition of obligatory prosecution of criminal actions committed by Wehrmacht members against local inhabitants.

The 'Führer decree' was notified to the army by Brauchitsch on 24 May 1941.[71] He had it distributed in print down to commanders with their own jurisdiction; beyond that the principles were made known by word of mouth. The commander-in-chief of the army, however, extended the decree by two supplements which once more took up the points contained in the OKH draft of 6 May for the maintenance of discipline. With that 'disciplinary decree' Brauchitsch hoped to prevent the threatening degeneration of the troops. Even before—during and after the Polish campaigns—the army commander-in-chief had felt compelled to issue strict orders against indiscipline by officers and other ranks, and to rule that members of the army were forbidden to participate in 'police executions'.[72]

Now, in May 1941, Brauchitsch in his appendix to part I of the 'Führer decree' emphasized that the real task of the forces was to fight the Red Army. Special 'search and purge actions' should therefore 'on the whole' be ruled out by the fighting forces. Hitler's guidelines on the treatment of criminal actions by local inhabitants should apply only to serious cases of rebellion; lesser offences were to be punished by 'improvised measures', such as tying up or setting to work. The commanders-in-chief of the army groups were to seek his approval before reintroducing Wehrmacht jurisdiction in 'pacified regions'. Brauchitsch further announced an impending special regulation on the 'treatment of political figures of authority (*politische Hoheitsträger*)'.

[69] Minute of a conference with the 'general, special duties' in Warsaw, 11 June 1941, BA-MA RH 21-2/v. 423. This passage is missing from Jacobsen, 'Kommissarbefehl', No. 14.

[70] Betz, *Landkriegsvölkerrecht*, 192.

[71] OKH/Gen.z.b.V. b. ObdH/Gr.R. Wes. No. 80/41 g.Kdos., Chefs. (340 copies), BA-MA RH 22/155; Jacobsen, 'Kommissarbefehl', No. 10 (with divergences). Important in this context is an earlier ruling by C.-in-C. Army that death sentences should be implemented at once 'for the maintenance of discipline, for the liquidation of violent crime and criminal saboteurs, and for the expiation of crimes by hostile local inhabitants against the security and reputation of the German Wehrmacht' (ObdH/Az 469 Gen.z.b.V./Gr.R. Wes. No. 450/41, 9 May 1941, BA-MA RH 22/183).

[72] See Umbreit, *Militärverwaltungen*, 169, 189.

In his supplement to part II of the 'Führer decree' on the treatment of criminal actions by Wehrmacht members against local inhabitants Brauchitsch stressed the duty of all superior officers

under all circumstances to prevent arbitrary excesses by *individual* members of the army, so as to be in good time to prevent the degeneration of the troops. The individual soldier must not reach a point where, in dealing with local inhabitants, he does or omits to do whatever seems right to *him*; rather, he is in all instances *bound by the orders of his officers*.

Timely intervention by all officers must '*help*' to maintain 'discipline, the basis of our successes'. Significant incidents under parts I and II were to be reported by the fighting forces to OKH as special occurrences.

This 'disciplinary decree' on the one hand limited the right of an officer to order the shooting of local inhabitants to 'serious cases of rebellion' and, on the other, transferred personal and human responsibility for the choice of means down to company commander level. The army command, however, must surely have realized that by this decree the methods of warfare in the east became dependent on the education, attitude, and ideology of each individual officer. If it had really wished to prevent an undermining of the troops' sense of justice as a result of the ideological precepts of the supreme leadership, then at least it should not have made a contribution of its own towards the bending of international law, and should have more vigorously resisted the limitation of its jurisdiction. Brauchitsch's supplements by no means rescinded the 'Führer decree'.

Even before the 'Führer decree' was passed on with his comments by the army commander-in-chief on 24 May, the fighting forces were briefed on the handling of jurisdiction in the theatre of operations by the head of the 'legal section' on the staff of the 'general with special duties', Oberstkriegsgerichtsrat Dr Erich Lattmann: army jurisdiction was being suspended with regard to local inhabitants. There was no punishment, only military measures and combat. Every guerrilla would be shot. Against localities from which there was any shooting collective forcible measures were necessary: 'No setting on fire, but 30 men to be shot.' Army jurisdiction would not be reintroduced until after the conclusion of operations. Prosecution of punishable actions by soldiers against local inhabitants *might* be dispensed with. 'Prosecution only if discipline demands intervention. (Motivation is decisive, indignation over atrocities).'[73]

That there was a close connection between the limitation of jurisdiction and

---

[73] Minutes of Ic/AO of Eleventh Army of the conference at OKH/GenQu on 16 May, BA-MA, Alliierte Prozesse 9, NOKW-486. See those of Ia of 285th Security Division, BA-MA RH 26-285/4. As early as 9 May 1941 it had been remarked at a conference of Ic (intelligence officers) at the office of the commander of the rear army area North that the 'experience' acquired during the occupation of France had suggested that court-martial sentences on civilians there had been 'very lenient' and had thus merely encouraged further acts of sabotage. That was why 'measures' were needed to have the severest penalities imposed on civilians from the start (BA-MA RH 19 III/722).

the treatment of Soviet commissars emerges also from the fact that Lattmann, beyond his explanations on the treatment of local inhabitants, also made some observations on that of commissars.[74]

An additional significant factor in the development was the elucidations given by Lieutenant-General Müller in person on the 'Führer decree', and on the army commander-in-chief's supplements, before the third general-staff officers and the army judges of army groups, armies, and armoured groups at Allenstein (Olsztyn) (10 June) and in Warsaw (11 June).[75] The 'general with special duties' pointed out that in the war against the Soviet Union a 'sense of justice must, in certain circumstances, yield to the requirements of war'. Until army jurisdiction was reintroduced, self-help by the troops against guerrillas was needed, i.e. 'a return to the ancient usage of war. . . . One of the two adversaries must remain dead on the ground; exponents of the enemy attitude must not be conserved but finished off.' A population's right to defend itself against an attack and to take up arms spontaneously and voluntarily, as laid down in article 2 of the Hague Convention on land warfare of 18 October 1907, was out of the question *vis-à-vis* the Soviet Union. The concept of 'guerrillas', in Müller's view, included 'in an extended sense also agitators, distributors of leaflets, saboteurs', as well as all those not obeying German instructions. Punishment of guerrillas should be instantaneous.

'Criminals' not caught until later were to be brought before an officer, who could take only one of two decisions: 'execution or release, but no summary trial or saving for subsequent court proceedings'. As clear evidence would often prove impossible to produce, suspicion would frequently have to be sufficient in case of doubt. In less serious cases flogging of individuals might sometimes be enough. Collective punitive measures against localities or against a group of local inhabitants should not be acts of revenge: the main consideration should always be the safety of the fighting forces and the speedy pacification of the country. The troops should not be 'needlessly put on a hair-trigger or act under the influence of blood-lust. The principal task of the troops, as well as of the security divisions in the rearward land-force area, is military action, not the liquidation of guerrillas.' Even though a harsh war demanded harsh punishment, officers should meticulously ensure that 'measures against enemy civilians' were taken '*after* a clash and only on the orders of an *officer*'.

In his elucidation of part II of the 'Führer decree', which regulated the treatment of criminal actions by Wehrmacht members against local inhabitants, Müller was supported by his legal adviser, Oberstkriegsgerichtsrat Dr Lattmann. Both of them emphasized that the troops should not be informed of the suspension of obligatory prosecution, but only the judiciary authorities and the army judges. Chain-of-command superiors were to act 'as in the past'

---

[74] See sect. I.VII.2(*c*) at n. 82.

[75] Record of Ic/AO III of Army Group North, 10 June 1941 (BA-MA RH 19 III/722), and of the Ic of Armoured Group 3, BA-MA RH 21-3/v. 423.

and submit a statement of incident. The judiciary authority would then decide whether an obligation to prosecute existed or whether the matter was to be dealt with by disciplinary means. Court proceedings should be instituted in all cases where discipline was threatened and there was a risk of degeneration of the troops, 'especially in the case of sexual offences'.[76] The 'general with special duties' and his legal advisers once more took up their earlier proposal of 6 May 1941 and called on army judges to remind chain-of-command superiors of article 16a of the wartime criminal-proceedings regulations of 17 August 1938.[77] Under that article they were authorized to deal with criminal offences by NCOs and other ranks by disciplinary measures. But were these officers sufficiently informed on the application of the disciplinary code? Probably not, as it was found that in the area of Eleventh Army the younger company commanders in particular, and officers commissioned for the duration in general, had no detailed knowledge of the possible extension of their disciplinary powers to offences committed by their subordinates which in themselves were also liable to prosecution in a court.[78]

Although the army had acted against guerrillas with the utmost rigour even during the Polish campaign, the OKW 'Decree on the execution of army jurisdiction in the Barbarossa territory and on special measures by the fighting forces' of 13 May 1941 nevertheless, despite the army commander-in-chief's supplements, marked the formal beginning of a new road. With it, the Armed Forces and Army High Commands largely accepted Hitler's intentions, while simultaneously, against the background of Polish experience, endeavouring to counteract any possible effects which the ideological war against 'Jewish Bolshevism' might have on discipline and good order among the troops. In spite of the supplements of the commander-in-chief of the army, the commander-in-chief of Army Group Centre, Field Marshal Fedor von Bock, still felt that the jurisdiction decree was virtually giving any soldier the right 'to shoot, from in front or from behind, at any Russian he regards—or pretends to regard—as a guerrilla. The ruling waives any obligation to prosecute any action on such lines, even if a military felony or offence has been committed.'[79] Protest was also voiced in the staff of Fourth Army HQ and in that of LVII

---

[76] Note by the army judge of Eleventh Army HQ for the commanding officers' conference on 18 June 1941 (BA-MA RH 20-11/11), minute by Ic/AO III of Army Group North, 10 June 1941 (BA-MA RH 19 III/722), and of the Ic of Armoured Group 3 (BA-MA RH 21-3/v. 423). On 4 June 1941 the general, special duties, had expounded the 'Führer decree' to the army and army-group chiefs of staff, pointing out that the holder of the jurisdiction (*Gerichtsherr*) was entitled to refer criminal offences against local inhabitants back to disciplinary action. Confirmation and execution of death sentences, however, were in the hands of army C.-in-C.s and no longer with the forces in the field (minute of the chiefs of staff of Eighteenth Army and Army Group North, BA-MA 18. Armee, 19601/2).

[77] H.Dv. 3/13, reprint Jan. 1940, Berlin, 1941. Important in the present context is annexe 6.

[78] Report on activity of Abt. III (Law) Eleventh Army HQ for the period 5 Oct. 1940–31 Oct. 1941, sgd. Dr Weber, BA-MA RH 20-11/386.

[79] Bock, Tagebuch, vol. ii (4 June 1941), MGFA P-210. See Gersdorff, *Soldat im Untergang*, 87 ff.

Armoured Corps. The Fourth Army's Ic, Major (General Staff) Erich Helmdach, enquired about the 'Führer decree' with the army affairs department of OKH and with the Wehrmacht propaganda department in the Wehrmacht operations staff, pointing out that the 'radical measures' ordered would render a sensible businesslike policy in the occupied territories difficult and would 'stun' the local population. Colonel (General Staff) Hasso von Wedel, head of the Wehrmacht propaganda department, promised to inform Jodl along those lines.[80] In mid-June 1941, at a commanding officers' conference of LVII Armoured Corps (which was commanded by Armoured Troops General Adolf Kuntzen), the passing-on of the army commander-in-chief's instruction was forbidden for the time being and further supplements were foreshadowed.[81] On the other hand, the guidelines for the treatment of political commissars, announced at the same time, did not cause any offence either in the Fourth Army staff or in that of LVII Armoured Corps. That such protests against the 'Führer decree' on the limitation of army jurisdiction were primarily motivated by military concerns on the part of commanders emerges, among other things, from an instruction by the commander-in-chief of the rearward land-force area South, Infantry General Karl von Roques. He drew his subordinate commanders' attention to the fact that Brauchitsch's decree had 'increased their responsibility' for discipline among their men. 'Wherever officers do not show themselves up to that task, and wherever the first signs of degeneration might appear, I expect immediate firm action by the next higher-ranking officer.'[82]

(c) The 'Commissar Order'

Closely linked, both ideologically and legally, with the jurisdiction decree were the OKW 'Guidelines on the treatment of political commissars' of 6 June 1941. It would also be extremely unrealistic to assume that the lifting of obligatory prosecution had not deliberately allowed for a radical treatment of Soviet commissars. That was why the 'general with special duties with the commander-in-chief of the army' on 6 May simultaneously submitted to OKW a draft for the limitation of army jurisdiction and a draft of 'Guidelines concerning exponents of political authority . . . '.[83] In both of them the latter group were described as 'exponents of the Jewish-Bolshevik system' and

---

[80] AOK 4, KTB-Einträge (Fourth Army HQ, war-diary entries), 14–16 June 1941, BA-MA RH 20-4/671.

[81] LVII Armoured Corps, commanding officers' conference, 17 June 1941, copy, BA-MA RW 4/v. 578.

[82] Befh. rückw. Heeresgebiet 103 [commander rear army area 103 (i.e. South)], Abt. Ia No. 056/41 g.Kdos., 12 June 1941, betr. Behandlung feindlicher Zivilpersonen und Straftaten Wehrmachtangehöriger gegen feindliche Zivilpersonen [Treatment of enemy civilians and criminal offences by Wehrmacht members against enemy civilians], BA-MA RH 22/155. The officer commanding 45th Inf. Div. likewise on 17 June 1941 drew his unit commanders' attention to the responsibility resulting for them from the 'Führer decree', BA-MA RH 26-45/16.

[83] OKH/Gen.z.b.V. b. ObdH No. 75/41 g.Kdos. Chefs., 6 May 1941, BA-MA RW 4/v. 577.

held responsible for 'atrocities' and 'undermining and disruptive activities in the past'. Against whom or when was not stated, although, given the measure of ideological agreement between Wehrmacht and National Socialism, the answer could be assumed to be known. Halder's comment on the two drafts of Lieutenant-General Müller and his legal adviser Dr Lattmann was: 'Troops must do their share in the ideological struggle of the eastern campaign.'[84] The chief of the Army General Staff regarded the draft for the intended shooting of the commissars as entirely 'along the lines of the last Führer address to the generals' on 30 March 1941. In his initiative of 6 May 1941 Müller referred the OKW to an 'instruction given him as early as 31 March 1941'. This cannot have been an order by Hitler, because when the head of the homeland defence department on the Wehrmacht operations staff received the OKH decree, Warlimont wanted to have examined the question of whether a written decree of that kind was actually necessary. It seems, therefore, that the 'general with special duties', who on legal matters received his instructions from the chief of the Army General Staff, had acted on Halder's direction. The OKH draft of 6 May 1941 envisaged the 'liquidation' of all political functionaries captured by the army. Their execution was to be ordered by an officer with disciplinary powers. Only the execution of 'qualified managers of economic and technical enterprises' was subject to the condition that they had opposed the Wehrmacht. The political instructors (commissars) in the Soviet forces were categorized as political functionaries and not accorded combatant status. 'Special importance attaches to their immediate identification among the prisoners and to their separation, because they in particular are able to continue their propaganda as prisoners of war in the homeland.' Their rearward transportation was forbidden. They were, if possible, to be 'finished off' at the POW collecting-points, or at the latest in the transit camps. In the rearward land-force area civilian officials and commissars were to be handed over to the action commandos of the security police and the SD, whereas 'troop commissars' were to be shot on the spot by the fighting forces themselves. The unlawful killing of captured troop commissars and civilian functionaries was justified by the increased threat they represented to the safety of the troops and to the pacification of the conquered territories. With that draft Halder, Müller, and Lattmann fully and unreservedly accepted Hitler's wish that political commissars were not to be regarded as combatants and thus not granted the protection of the Geneva Convention.

It seems that Lattmann gave an exposé of the principal stipulations of the OKH draft to the officers assembled at the Wünsdorf armoured-troops training-centre on 16 May 1941, because the Eleventh Army Ic/AO (intelligence and security officer) made a note: 'Political commissars to be handed over to

---

[84] Halder, *Diaries*, 907 (6 May 1941).

SS in the rearward land-force area. Instruction follows for army area.'[85] The treatment of Soviet commissars was also the subject of a conference on the assignments of interpreters in the 'foreign armies East' department on 26 May 1941. The commissars were to be handed over to the SD. 'First of all', however, 'these often clever people (often cleverer than officers!)' were to be interrogated by the Ic officers. 'Many of the non-Jewish commissars are no doubt only fellow-travellers and not convinced of the Communist idea.'[86] That judgement may be seen as further proof that Hitler's identification of Jewry and Bolshevism was not unique.

On 12 May 1941 Warlimont presented the OKH draft to Jodl.[87] In doing so he drew his attention to the diverging points of view of OKH and Rosenberg, since 20 April Hitler's 'Delegate for the central processing of questions concerning the east European space', on the treatment of political functionaries. In his third memorandum Rosenberg had proposed that among the municipal and economic functionaries 'only' the senior and top officials should be 'finished off', as he regarded the middle and lower cadres as 'indispensable' to the administration of the occupied territories. In view of these two different concepts Warlimont suggested that a decision be obtained from Hitler. With regard to contents, Warlimont mitigated the OKH draft by proposing that functionaries 'not guilty of any hostile action' should 'for the moment' remain unmolested. Functionaries opposing the forces were to be regarded as 'guerrillas' and 'finished off' in accordance with the jurisdiction decree and the guidelines of 19 May. 'Functionaries within the forces will have to be treated according to the OKH proposal. They will not be recognized as prisoners of war and have to be finished off, at the latest, in the transit camps; on no account are they to be moved to the rear.'

It was realized both at OKH and at OKW that the systematic annihilation of the Red Army's political cadres was an infringement of international law. In his search for a justification Jodl suggested that 'the whole action' be presented 'as retaliation' in advance,[88] but that the shooting of captured commissars should not be made dependent on any alleged precondition. With this in mind he drafted a preamble designed to dispel any human or legal scruples among the officer corps; the argument that commissars threatened the safety of the fighting forces figured only in third place.[89] Although Jodl's inept bending of the right of reprisal was eventually dropped, his ideological justification— smoothed stylistically—nevertheless formed part of the preamble of the OKH

[85] Minute of 19 May 1941, BA-MA, Alliierte Prozesse 9, NOKW-486.

[86] Record of Ic/AO III H.Gr. Nord of a conference at GenStdH/Fr.H. Ost, BA-MA RH 19 III/722.

[87] WFSt/Abt. Landesverteidigung (IV/Qu) g.Kdos. Chefs., 12 May 1941, BA-MA RW 4/v. 577; Jacobsen, 'Kommissarbefehl', No. 7.

[88] Ibid. But 'preventive reprisals' are also infringements of international law.

[89] As n. 87, published in facsimile in Maser, *Nürnberg*, 312.

'Guidelines on the treatment of political commissars' of 6 June 1941.[90] 'In the struggle against Bolshevism the enemy *cannot* be expected to behave in accordance with the principles of humanity or international law. In particular *political commissars of all kinds*, as the real exponents of resistance, can be expected to indulge in a hate-filled, cruel, and inhuman treatment of those of our men they have taken prisoner.' The troops should realize that in this struggle any consideration for 'such elements' on grounds of international law would be a mistake. They were not only the 'originators of barbaric Asiatic fighting methods', but also represented a danger to the safety of the troops and the rapid pacification of the conquered territories. Political commissars, therefore, 'if captured in battle or while resisting, are as a matter of principle to be finished off with the weapon *at once*'. The following rules were to apply. First, in the area of operations political commissars of whatever kind or rank, even if only suspected 'of resistance, sabotage, or instigation of these', were to be 'treated' according to the jurisdiction decree. Second, commissars in the Red Army were not to be regarded as soldiers and were to be 'separated' from prisoners of war on the battlefield itself, and 'finished off'. Non-suspect civilian political commissars should initially not be 'harmed'. Only subsequently should a decision be made about allowing them to continue in their post or handing them over to the special commandos of the security police and the SD. 'In reading a verdict the [officer's] personal impression of the political stance and attitude of the commissar has to be given greater weight than the facts of the case, which may be difficult to prove.' Relevant 'incidents' with commissars were to be reported through Ic channels. None of these measures, however, must be allowed to hold up operations; there should be no 'search and purge actions' by the fighting forces. In the rearward land-force area commissars arrested 'for questionable behaviour' were to be handed over to the action group or the action commandos of the security police and SD.

On 8 June 1941 these guidelines, amplified by two supplements, were notified in writing by Brauchitsch to the army groups, armies, and armoured groups.[91] Commanding officers and commanders-in-chief were to be briefed only verbally. The commander-in-chief of the army ruled, first, that the prerequisite of action against a political commissar must be 'that the person in question opposes, or intends to oppose, the German Wehrmacht by a *specific identifiable action or attitude*'. Secondly, Brauchitsch ordered that 'the finishing off of the political commissars in the forces must take place after their separation, *outside the combat zone proper*, inconspicuously, *on the order of an officer*. Brauchitsch—probably more so than Halder—feared the effects of the fighting forces on the state and wished to tie the ordered measures, as he had done in the jurisdiction decree, to the decision of an officer. However, Brauchitsch's

---

[90] OKW/WFSt/Abt. L (IV/Qu) No. 44822/41 g.Kdos. Chefs., 6 June 1941, BA-MA H 3/1; Jacobsen, 'Kommissarbefehl', No. 12; *Fall Barbarossa*, No. 100.

[91] OKH/Gen.z.b.V. b. ObdH/Gr.R. Wes. No. 91/41 g.Kdos. Chefs., 8 June 1941; Jacobsen, 'Kommissarbefehl', No. 13; *Fall Barbarossa*, No. 102.

supplements cannot be regarded as a genuine restriction of the OKW guidelines.

On 10 and 11 June 1941 the Ic officers and army judges at army and army-group level were personally briefed by Lieutenant-General Müller on the practical application of that decree. Their task in turn was to brief their subordinate commanders-in-chief and commanding officers, as well as their intelligence officers and legal advisers. The 'general with special duties' pointed out that 'here too', as with the jurisdiction decree, there must be 'no massacres'. The safety of the fighting forces was paramount. The ordinary political commissars were to be treated like all other local inhabitants. They were of interest to the army only if guilty of an attack against the Wehrmacht. Political commissars within the fighting forces were to be separated from the other prisoners, moved to the rear, and 'finished off' on the order of an officer. Provided this was possible without loss of time, they should first be taken to the Ic for interrogation. Reports were to be made to OKH every ten days.[92]

Summing up the elucidations of the two decrees of 24 May and 8 June 1941, Oberkriegsgerichtsrat Dr Weber declared at a commanding officers' conference of Eleventh Army on 18 June 1941:

> Every soldier must know that he has to defend himself against all attacks in battle, and that in cases of doubt he has to bring detained persons to the nearest officer. Every officer must know that he can have detained persons shot or released, that political commissars are to be taken aside and finished off. Every battalion commander must know that he can order collective forcible measures.[93]

The following examples illustrate the 'packaged' manner in which the decree on the 'treatment of political commissars' was made known among the fighting forces. At a conference of Ic officers and directors of the secret field police of the rearward land-force area North in Elbing on 16 June 1941 the counter-intelligence officer III with Army Group North, Captain Dr Keune, stated: 'The commissars of the Russians are well known, they are to be rendered harmless.'[94] The commanding officers in LVII Armoured Corps were informed that Hitler had ordered the Russian political commissars to be 'liquidated'. This order was to be passed on by word of mouth.[95] Infantry General Viktor von Schwedler, the general commanding IV Army Corps, informed his divisional commanders on 19 June 1941 that, even though the commissars in the Red Army wore uniform, they were not recognized as soldiers. They were to be separated from the rest of the prisoners and shot 'on

---

[92] Minute Ic/AO III H.Gr. Nord, 10 June 1941 (BA-MA RH 19 III/722), and note for report of the army judge at Eleventh Army HQ for commanding officers' conference on 18 June 1941 (ibid. RH 20-11/11).

[93] BA-MA RH 20-11/11.

[94] Report of activity of Abt. Ic/AO for the period 16–30 June 1941, BA-MA RH 22/253.

[95] LVII Armoured Corps, commanding officers' conference, 17 June 1941, copy, BA-MA RW 4/v. 578

the spot at the order of an officer'. The commissars in the Soviet civilian administration were to be shot only if they participated 'in hostilities, sabotage, etc.'.[96] Following a commanding officers' conference in the 22nd Infantry Division, the Ic briefed the adjutants on the 'treatment of political commissars, Jews, and other prisoners'.[97] What the forces knew about the Red Army's war commissars was based on the official publication *The Wartime Forces of the Union of Socialist Soviet Republics* of 15 January 1941 and on an order by the war commissar for defence of 21 January 1941.[98] The commissars, these explained, were identified by a red star with a gold-embroidered hammer and sickle on the sleeves of their uniform. But there appeared to be uncertainty about the level at which a commissar was employed. Thus it was announced in the 454th Security Division on 20 June 1941 that there was a political commissar with each company, who, after capture, had to be shot outside the combat zone on the order of an officer.[99] That information was incorrect, since at company, battery, and squadron level there was only a political guidance officer, a *politruk*. Not until the end of August 1941 were the guidelines on the treatment of commissars extended to cover *politruks*.[100]

In the discussion on the two unlawful decrees after the war the 'Guidelines on the treatment of political commissars' played a far greater part than the 'Führer decree' on the limitation of army jurisdiction. This was due to the fact that the ordered execution of the commissars within the army was a more conspicuous breach of international law. For a specific group of the Soviet leadership the reinforced obligation of execution no longer depended even on the mere suspicion of 'guerrilla activity' or resistance to the Wehrmacht, but 'solely on the holding of a certain function in the opponent's system of government'.[101] It was quite simply postulated that the field commissar was not a soldier but a party functionary. And the Bolshevik cadres alone were believed capable of organizing resistance in the hinterland. With the additional equation of Bolshevism and Jewry by the Wehrmacht it is not surprising that as early as 1935 the draft of a leaflet defamed the 'gentlemen commissars and party functionaries' as 'mostly filthy Jews'. In it the Red Army men were

---

[96] BA-MA RH 24-4/34. In contrast, the entry of 13 June 1941 in the diary of the general commanding XIII Army Corps, Inf. Gen. Hans Felber, states: 'Map exercise with divisional commanders. Commissar order discussed. Rejected' (ibid. N 67/1).

[97] On 20 June 1941, BA-MA RH 26-22/66; see 22. Div./Abt. Ia No. 437/41 g.Kdos., 20 June 1941, BA-MA RH 26-22/67.

[98] OKH/GenStdH/OQu IV, Abt. Fr.H. Ost (II), No. 100/41, 15 Jan. 1941, BA-MA RHD 18/210, and Kdo.Pz.Gr. 4, Ic No. 360/41, 6 May 1941, annexe 2; Befehl des Volkskommissars für Verteidigung der UdSSR [Order of the People's Commissar for the Defence of the USSR] No. 30, 21 Jan. 1941, concerning military and political preparation of the forces for the training-year 1941, BA-MA RH 21-4/265.

[99] Notes on commanding officers' conference on 20 June 1941, Ziff. 3, BA-MA RH 26-454/6.

[100] See sect. II.vii.2 at n. 208.

[101] Krausnick, 'Kommissarbefehl', 712. On the Institute of Military Commissars in the Red Army see sect. I.ii.1 at nn. 16 and 27 (Hoffmann), and the contemporary account by Reitenbach, *UdSSR*, 88 ff.

invited to fight against the 'accursed Jewish commissars'.[102] Thus, for German propaganda after 22 June 1941 the commissar, along with the Soviet leadership, was 'enemy Number one'.

3. Propaganda Preparations for the War of Annihilation and the Attitude of the Military Leaders

In contrast to the attack against Poland, Hitler before 22 June 1940 was unable to produce a preventive justification for the German public or the armed forces of his planned war of aggression against the Soviet Union. There were no German revisionist claims on Moscow comparable to the Danzig or 'Corridor' issues, nor did hostile 'provocations' or excesses against ethnic Germans supply German propaganda with the necessary material. The 'otherwise desirable preparation of the German soldier and the German people' had to 'take second place'[103] to the strategic plan of letting Britain believe in an impending invasion and striking the USSR by surprise. Their, and the outside world's, 'enlightenment' and 'psychological preparation', were to start 'abruptly' only on the day of the attack. Until then the Wehrmacht had to camouflage Operation Barbarossa. The armed forces high command set in motion 'extensive measures of diversion and deception of friend and foe'.[104] It issued its first directive in mid-February 1941,[105] and a week later the Wehrmacht propaganda department was instructed by Jodl to prepare basic propaganda guidelines for the war against the Soviet Union and for the fighting forces' attitude towards Bolshevism, as well as a proclamation to the troops.[106]

The 'psychological preparation' of the forces for an ideological war against the Soviet Union was, despite the short time available, readily based on foundations laid ever since 1934 by the Reichswehr and the Wehrmacht leadership. The systematic education of the forces in the National Socialist spirit had initially served to safeguard the Reichswehr's, and after 1935 the Wehrmacht's, monopoly as an armed force. In 1936 Reich War Minister von Blomberg had ensured that National Socialist teaching covered all instruc-

---

[102] Psychologisches Laboratorium des Reichskriegsministeriums [Psychology laboratory of the Reich war ministry] No. 241/35, 2 Nov. 1935, Völkerpsychologische Untersuchung 5: Die nationale Zusammensetzung der Bevölkerung der UdSSR und die Möglichkeit für eine propagandistische Bearbeitung [Ethnopsychological study 5: The national composition of the population of the USSR and possibilities of applying propaganda], reprint, p. 7, BA-MA RH 2/v. 981.

[103] OKW/WFSt/Abt. L (I H Op) No. 44646/41 g.Kdos. Chefs., BA-MA RW 4/v. 577.

[104] This was the formulation of the OKW chief of staff in identical letters to the ministers Todt and von Ribbentrop, and to Gov.-Gen. Frank, dated 9 Mar. 1941, BA-MA RW 4/v. 575.

[105] OKW/WFSt/Abt. L (I Op) No. 44142/41 g.Kdos. Chefs., 15 Feb. 1941, Richtlinien für die Feindtäuschung [Directives for enemy deception], BA-MA RM 7/985; *Fall Barbarossa*, No. 72. They were amplified and specified by OKW/WFSt/Abt. L (I Op) No. 44277/41 g.Kdos. Chefs., 12 Mar. 1941 (BA-MA RM 7/985); OKW/WFSt/Abt. L (I Op), No. 44699/41, g.Kdos. Chefs., 12 May 1941 (ibid.); and OKW/WFSt/Abt. L (IV/Qu) No. 44787/41 g.Kdos. Chefs., 22 May 1941 (BA-MA RW 4/v. 578).

[106] *KTB OKW* i. 333 (21 Feb. 1941).

tional institutions, especially those for officers. Immediately before the outbreak of the war Hitler's real main theses came to predominate in the syllabus over the earlier programme, 'which was to demonstrate to the soldier the identity of military and National Socialist attitudes'.[107] Thus it was stated in an article in *Schulungshefte für den Unterricht über nationalsozialistische Weltanschauung und nationalpolitische Zielsetzung* [Instruction pamphlets for the teaching of National Socialist ideology and national political objectives], published since 1939 by OKW/Inland, that the struggle against Jewry would continue even when the last Jew had left Germany: 'the struggle against world Jewry', which 'is trying to incite all the nations of the world against Germany'.[108] This represented a logical restatement of Hitler's 'prophecy' of 30 January 1939.

Although the Wehrmacht propaganda department had been responsible for the armed forces' psychological welfare since April 1939, Rosenberg, as Hitler's delegate for the supervision of the NSDAP's spiritual and ideological education, succeeded towards the end of 1940, in a 'working agreement' with the OKW chief of staff, in securing his influence on the ideological schooling of the Wehrmacht as well.[109] Brauchitsch had already issued guidelines for the ideological education of officers and other ranks at the beginning of October 1940. Among the main points in five subject areas were: racial purity, Führer state, securing German living-space. As teaching and lecture aids the army commander-in-chief recommended Hitler's *Mein Kampf*, the NSDAP's 'instruction circulars', and OKW's 'instruction pamphlets'. Because of the official German–Soviet alliance, no direct mention was made of the danger of 'Jewish Bolshevism'.[110]

The 'Guidelines for the behaviour of the fighting forces in Russia', worked out in agreement with OKH, were ready in mid-May 1941 and went out to the Wehrmacht services.[111] However, they were to be notified to the men only together with Hitler's order of the day. These guidelines were to indoctrinate the troops and ensure the implementation of the jurisdiction decree and the guidelines on the commissars. Their key sentences read:

I. 1. *Bolshevism is the mortal enemy of the National Socialist German people. Germany's struggle is aimed against that disruptive ideology and its exponents.*

   2. That struggle demands ruthless and energetic action against *Bolshevik agitators, guerrillas, saboteurs, Jews* and the complete liquidation of any active or passive resistance.

---

[107] Messerschmidt, 'Politische Erziehung', 273; id., *Wehrmacht*, 232 ff.

[108] 1st year (1939), fasc. 5, quoted according to Messerschmidt, 'Politische Erziehung', 276.

[109] Ibid. 268–9.

[110] ObdH/GenStdH/OQu I No. 500/40, 7 Oct. 1940, annexe 1, BA-MA, 99. le.Inf.Div., 21400/17; *Fall Barbarossa*, No. 71. See Bartov, *Eastern Front*, 82 ff.

[111] OKW/WFSt/Abt. L (IV/Qu) No. 44560/41 g.Kdos. Chefs., 19 May 1941, Besondere Anordnungen No. 1 zur Weisung No. 21 [Special instructions No. 1 on Directive No. 21], annexe 3, BA-MA RH 31-I/v. 40; OKH/GenStdH/GenQu/Abt. Kriegsverwaltung No. II/0514/41 g.Kdos. Chefs., 23 May 1941, BA-MA RH 22/12.

II. 3. Extreme reserve and most alert vigilance are called for towards all members of the *Red Army*—even prisoners—as treacherous methods of fighting are to be expected. The *Asiatic soldiers* of the Red Army in particular are inscrutable, unpredictable, insidious, and unfeeling.

    4. After the capture of units the *leaders* are to be *instantly separated* from the other ranks.

The aspect of a war of annihilation against 'Jewish Bolshevism' was strengthened by the 'Directives on the practice of propaganda in Operation Barbarossa', prepared by Wedel. This was distributed before the opening of the attack to army groups, armies, armoured groups, air fleets and air corps, propaganda companies, and air-force war-reporter companies.[112] These 'directives' contained fundamental organizational and practical propaganda guidelines. The main theme of propaganda was that Germany's enemies were not the 'nations of the Soviet Union, but exclusively the Jewish-Bolshevik Soviet government with its functionaries and the Communist Party', which was 'working for world revolution'. The Wehrmacht was entering the country as a liberator and would 'save' the population 'from the tyranny of the Soviets'. Naturally, any resistance would be mercilessly crushed. The 'planned dismemberment of the Soviet Union' as well as the preservation of collectivized agriculture, made necessary for economic reasons, must be concealed. War reporters were to give special emphasis to 'atrocities and infringements of international law' by the Red Army. The armed forces high command confidently expected that a large-scale active propaganda against the Red Army would be 'even more successful than with all previous adversaries of the Wehrmacht'. To ensure that success, each army or armoured group had attached to it a propaganda company of altogether some 2,250 men.[113] While active propaganda against the Red Army would be mainly by leaflets, the Soviet population was to be influenced by posters and loudspeakers on the lines of the political and ideological directives issued by Berlin. Along with the Soviet leadership, the commissar was 'enemy Number One'. He was therefore the 'centre-piece' of German leaflet propaganda against the Red Army. The commissar was reviled as a Jew, liar, tormentor, murderer, etc. Moreover, an attempt was made to drive a wedge between the commissar and his officers in order to loosen the cohesion of Soviet units. The planned propaganda campaign against 'the commissars' developed the foundations laid as early as 1935 by the 'Psychological laboratory in the Reich war ministry', as revealed by a comparison of leaflets.[114] Anti-Soviet propaganda in 1941 thus reflected not only pragmatic points of view but also much older ideological attitudes.

Hate propaganda was also channelled into the Wehrmacht. In this context not only did the commissar decree have the 'status of a propaganda dogma',[115]

---

[112] OKW/WFSt/WPr No. 144/41 g.Kdos. Chefs., June 1941, BA-MA RW 4/v. 578.
[113] Buchbender, *Das tönende Erz*, 56 ff.
[114] See n. 102 and Buchbender, *Das tönende Erz*, 98 ff.
[115] Buchbender, *Das tönende Erz*, 96.

but the 'information' on the commissar, prepared by the Wehrmacht propaganda department, was to facilitate the implementation of that unlawful decree. In the first June issue of 'Information for the troops', therefore, the definition of Bolshevism contained in the 'Guidelines on the behaviour of the fighting forces' was extended. Not only was the Bolshevik system presented as infiltrated, pervaded, and dominated by Jews; the propaganda formulas were also designed to facilitate a ruthless conduct of the struggle.

Anyone who has ever looked into the face of a Red commissar knows what Bolsheviks are. There is no need here for theoretical reflections. It would be an insult to animals if one were to call the features of these, largely Jewish, tormentors of people bestial. They are the embodiment of the infernal, of personified insane hatred of everything that is noble humanity. In the shape of these commissars we witness the revolt of the subhuman against noble blood. The masses whom they are driving to their deaths with every means of icy terror and lunatic incitement would have brought about the end of all meaningful life, had that incursion not been prevented at the last moment.[116]

Machine-guns and bombs were to speak the decisive word. Adolf Hitler was apostrophized as the 'instrument of providence' for the salvation of Europe from Bolshevism.

Hitler moreover thought it necessary at the beginning of June 1941 to draw the forces' attention, by means of leaflets, to all the possibilities of 'treacherous warfare of which we believe the enemy capable'.[117] These, however, were to be distributed only at the beginning of operations, as their premature publication might suggest these very possibilities to the enemy. Hitler evidently did not regard as sufficient the 'Memo sheet on the particular nature of Russian warfare', distributed by the department 'foreign armies East' on 25 January 1941 down to platoon level; this had not contained the element of 'treachery'.[118] Hitler considered that element to be realistic in that the enemy might poison routes of retreat, food-stores, seed-grain, and wells. As a centralized revision of such leaflets by the department for foreign armies East was no longer possible for technical (printing) reasons, the department asked the army groups, armies, and armoured groups to prepare them locally but not to distribute them before the day of the attack.[119] These leaflets bore headlines such as 'Watch out!' or 'Do you know the enemy?'

Although Hitler had ordered the planning and execution of a war of conquest and annihilation, responsibility for the war was nevertheless to be shuffled on to the enemy. The slogans of a war 'forced on Germany' and of Germany's 'encirclement', first used in 1939, were dished up again on 21 and 22 June 1941. In nearly identical proclamations to the German people and to

---

[116] Quoted according to Messerschmidt, *Wehrmacht*, 326–7.
[117] ObdH/1. GenSt.Offz. No. 165/41 g.Kdos, BA-MA H 3/1.
[118] BA-MA RHD 18/233. It was reissued in Jan. 1942.
[119] OKH/GenStdH/OQu IV/Fr.H. Ost (unnumbered), 13 June 1941, BA-MA H 3/1.

the soldiers on the eastern front, drafted in the Wehrmacht propaganda department and edited by Hitler, 'the Führer and supreme commander of the Wehrmacht' justified the attack against the Soviet Union with predominantly ideological arguments.[120] Propaganda resumed the formula of Germany being threatened by 'Jewish Bolshevism', a formula sunk without a trace since the Hitler–Stalin treaty. Responsibility for the German–Soviet war was attributed in a historical perspective to a conspiracy 'between the Jewish-Anglos-saxon warmongers and the equally Jewish rulers of the Bolshevik Muscovite centre'. The 'familiar plot between Jews and democrats, Bolsheviks, and reactionaries' had tried from the outset to prevent the establishment of the 'new German national state'. 'For more than two decades [i.e. since 1917] the Jewish-Bolshevik rulers in Moscow have endeavoured to set not only Germany but the whole of Europe ablaze.' Ceaselessly they had tried to force their domination upon Germany and the rest of the European states. They had also organized the coup in Belgrade on 27 March 1941. The declared task of the German army in the east was 'the security of Europe and thus the salvation of all'; Hitler, in consequence, operated as the guardian of European culture against 'Jewish Bolshevism'. It was intended to produce in Germany the sense of a 'just' war against the Soviet Union, even though the thesis of a preventive war was not fully developed by German propaganda until after 22 June. Among the German population the news of the beginning of the German–Soviet war caused 'the greatest surprise ... especially the present moment for the offensive in the east'.[121]

The ideological justifications of the German attack clearly eclipsed all other explanations, such as reference to the massive deployment of the Red Army along Germany's eastern frontier. The entirely secondary character of the preventive-war argument at that time, as against the ideological argument, emerges from the fact that, while mention was made of Soviet frontier violations, the version of 'fire being returned' used in 1939 was absent. The Wehrmacht propaganda department was nevertheless instructed the same day that reports from the front should 'exploit' the Soviet concentrations in the frontier areas by pointing out 'that the Russians were deployed "ready to pounce" and that the German action' had therefore been 'an absolute military necessity'.[122]

Because his aggressive intentions were all too clearly governed by other motivations, Hitler had made a further attempt the previous week to convince the generals and admirals, in a 'lengthy political address'[123] at the Reich chancellery, of the need for a war against the Soviet Union—even though the

[120] Domarus, *Hitler*, ii. 1726 ff., and BA-MA RH 22/4; Balfour, *Propaganda*, 227. See Pietrow-Ennker, 'Sowjetunion', 92 ff.
[121] *Meldungen aus dem Reich*, 155.
[122] Abteilung L (I Op) No. 441058/41 g.Kdos. Chefs., 21 June 1941, BA-MA RW 4/v. 578.
[123] Halder, *Diaries*, 958 (14 June 1941).

'Situation Report No. 1' of the department for foreign armies East in the Army General Staff on Soviet intentions, dated 15 March 1941, had assessed the moving up of Soviet troops to the frontier as a 'defensive measure' in response to the identifiable German reinforcements.[124] The expected victory over the Soviet Union would not only secure Germany's foodstuff and raw-material supplies for the foreseeable future,[125] but would also ensure Germany's freedom in the rear. Victory over the Soviet Union would induce Britain to abandon the 'hopeless further struggle'. Realization that American aid, in view of Germany's now unassailable position of power on the Continent and of the successes scored by the Luftwaffe and U-boats against British supplies, would now come too late would promote London's readiness for peace.[126] However, Hitler's optimism, which was widespread also among the officer corps at all levels, was to prove an illusion.

The reason for such a detailed account of the attitude of OKW, OKH, and commanders in the field towards the role assigned to the Wehrmacht by Hitler in his ideological war against the Soviet Union is that it provides additional criteria for the assessment of relations Fbetween the army and Hitler. By transforming Hitler's ideological intentions towards the Soviet enemy into military orders, the Wehrmacht and Army High Commands assisted in turning the Wehrmacht into an instrument in the war of annihilation against 'Jewish Bolshevism'. SS operations and military combat were thus linked into an indissoluble whole in order thus to 'ensure a durable guarantee of the conquered living-space'.[127] The SS's deliberate racial-political operations against the 'Jewish-Bolshevik mortal enemy' were to be supported by the army's display of extreme ruthlessness and the greatest annihilating effect in its operations against the Red Army and its commissars, against Bolshevik functionaries, Jews, guerrillas, and the civilian population. To claim that only the action groups of the security police and SD were envisaged as creating the 'basis for the definitive liquidation of Bolshevism'[128] would be to distort Hitler's intentions. The army too was regarded as a means to that end. The Army High Command in the spring of 1941 showed itself ready to fight the 'ideological struggle' as well.[129] In doing so it proceeded from the belief that, although the international law of war would have to be suspended because of the particular conditions of an ideological war, this would be only for a short time, given the expected swift victory over the Red Army. For Hitler, on the

[124] OKH/GenStdH/OQu IV/Abt. Fr.H. Ost (II) No. 33/41 g.Kdos. Chefs., 15 Mar. 1941, BA-MA RH 19 III/722.

[125] See sect. I.III.2(*f*) at n. 306 (Müller).

[126] Bock, Tagebuch, vol. ii (14 June 1941), MGFA P-210. Below, *Hitlers Adjutant*, 277, on the other hand, believes that Hitler declared on 14 June 1941: 'It isn't the land that we are after; rather, Bolshevism must be destroyed.' On Hitler's motivations see Goebbels, *Diaries*, trans. Taylor, 413 ff. (16 June 1941).

[127] Messerschmidt, *Wehrmacht*, 396; see Hillgruber, 'Endlösung', 143.

[128] Minute of Ic/AO III H.Gr. Nord of the conference at OKW/Abw and OKH on 5–6 June 1941, BA-MA RH 19 III/722.

[129] Halder, *Diaries*, 907 (6 May 1941).

other hand, the guidelines for co-operation between army and SS in the rearward areas, and the execution of commissars and suspect civilians, were of fundamental significance against the background of his living-space policy. To him the annihilation of the 'Jewish-Bolshevik leadership stratum', the extermination of the Jews, and the decimation of the Slav masses in the occupied territories were the most important prerequisite for a racially 'pure' unfolding of Germandom in the newly gained living-space. Along with his 'ideological force',[130] the SS, the army too was to participate in the annihilation of 'Jewish Bolshevism'. Military combat for the conquest of living-space in the east, political and police measures for its security, and its economic exploitation were only different facets of one great war of annihilation against the Soviet Union and its population. 'For mastering the great tasks outlined, the co-operation of all employed bodies' was specifically ordered.[131]

As an explanation of the military leadership's falling into line with Hitler it would be totally inadequate to point to the principle of absolute obedience or to a lack of backbone. Contemporary characterizations of the generals in OKW and OKH as 'military technicians' (H. von Moltke) or as 'hopeless sergeants' (U. von Hassell) are too superficial. Relations between the army and Hitler were determined also by a substantial measure of agreement on ideological questions.[132] Along with anti-Slavism and anti-Semitism there was also a militant anti-Communism. Although a 'genuine blending of traditional and National Socialist elements in the image of Russia'[133] probably existed only for a few officers, a 'partial identity of objectives' (M. Messerschmidt) provided a sufficient basis for collaboration between army and National Socialism in the ideological war against the Soviet Union.

The degree of conformity or affinity with Hitler's ideas achieved by some commanders-in-chief emerges from two examples. Colonel-General Georg von Küchler, commander-in-chief of Eighteenth Army, addressing his divisional commanders on 25 April, observed:

The political commissars and the GPU people are criminals. They are the people who enslave the population. Read or hear the reports by ethnic Germans on the doings and activities of those people. They are to be put before a court martial and sentenced on the strength of the testimony of the inhabitants. There is also the point that these measures should drive a wedge between the political leadership and the probably quite decent Russian soldiers. When it becomes known that we put the political commissars and GPU people straight before a court martial, there is a hope that the Russian troops and the population themselves will free themselves from this servitude. In any case we

[130] See Krausnick and Wilhelm, *Die Truppe des Weltanschauungskrieges*; Wegner, 'Garde des "Führers"', 210 ff.

[131] Minute of Ic of Army Command Norway on Ic conference at OKW on 5–6 June 1941 (g. Kdos.), BA-MA 20. Armee, 20884/5.

[132] This aspect is lacking in Müller, 'Armee und Drittes Reich'.

[133] Hillgruber, 'Rußland-Bild', 302. See Förster, 'New Wine in Old Skins?'

shall apply those measures. It will save us German blood and we shall make headway faster.[134]

Küchler thus characterized the Soviet commissars and NKVD members in the same terms which Halder had jotted down during Hitler's speech of 30 March 1941.

The following operations order of Armoured Group 4 likewise dates from before the first OKH draft on the treatment of the commissars and represents an independent transformation of Hitler's ideological intentions into an order. Colonel-General Erich Hoepner had this to say on the basis of combat against the Red Army:

The war against Russia is an essential phase in the German nation's struggle for existence. It is the ancient struggle of the Germanic peoples against Slavdom, the defence of European culture against the Muscovite-Asiatic tide, the repulse of Jewish Bolshevism. That struggle must have as its aim the shattering of present-day Russia and must therefore be waged with unprecedented hardness. Every combat action must be inspired, in concept and execution, by an iron determination to ensure the merciless, total annihilation of the enemy. In particular, there must be no sparing the exponents of the present Russian Bolshevik system.[135]

Because the view of Lieutenant-Colonel (General Staff) Henning von Tresckow, the first general-staff officer of Army Group Centre—'if international law is to be infringed it should be done by the Russians and not by us'[136]—was not universally shared, Hitler was able to suspend vital norms of the law of war. Many officers quite simply shared his view that the war commissar in the Red Army was not an officer but an extra-combatant political functionary, who supervised the commanding officer and incited the men. That was why the commissar was denied the quality of a soldier and hence combatant status. Since 1933 the army command had supported the principle of sole command responsibility and had repeatedly insisted that political education too should remain in the hands of the officer and not be handed over to the Party. Many officers therefore accepted Hitler's suggestion of 30 March 1941 and regarded themselves as *leaders* in the struggle against a hostile ideology, against 'Jewish Bolshevism'. Thus 'the called-for unity of soldierdom and National Socialism became reality to a high degree'.[137] This made an institution such as the commissars appear unnecessary on the German side. For most officers the Soviet Union, the state of Lenin and Stalin, represented a threat to German hegemony in Europe. They agreed with Hitler

[134] Handwritten notes by Küchler, BA-MA 18. Armee, 19601/2. On his observations on the political intentions *vis-à-vis* the Soviet Union see sect. I.i.3 at n. 122.

[135] Kdr. Pz.Gr. 4, Ia No. 20/41 g.Kdos., 2 May 1941, Aufmarsch- und Kampfanweisung 'Barbarossa' [Deployment and operational instruction Barbarossa], study, annexe 2: Kampf führung [conduct of operations], BA-MA LVI. A.K., 17956/7a. The latest biography of Hoepner (Bücheler, *Hoepner*, 127 ff.) unfortunately fails to mention this at all.

[136] Engel, *Heeresadjutant bei Hitler*, 103 (10 May 1941).

[137] Messerschmidt, 'Verhältnis', 18.

that the future development of the German nation required the attainment of a territorially unassailable and economically self-sufficient great-power status. The slogan of an inevitable preventive war in the east met with unqualified approval among the German officers, not so much because of the modernization of the Red Army, but because of their own—predominantly military and political—concepts of Germany's role in Europe and in the world.

PART II

The War against the Soviet Union until the Turn of 1941/1942

Horst Boog
Jürgen Förster
Joachim Hoffmann
Ernst Klink
Rolf-Dieter Müller
Gerd R. Ueberschär

I. The Conduct of Operations

1. THE ARMY AND NAVY

ERNST KLINK

(a) The Opening of the Campaign

WHEN, on 22 June 1941 between 3.00 and 3.30 a.m., the Wehrmacht, together with Romanian forces, began the German attack on the Soviet Union and crossed the frontier separating the German and Soviet 'spheres of interest',[1] the European war which had begun in September 1939 acquired a new dimension. On the day of the attack neither Hitler nor the responsible officers of the Wehrmacht doubted that their military forces and the time available until autumn would be sufficient to destroy the enemy.

In view of the enormous extent of the operations area, the planning of the Army General Staff, which reached down to division level, envisaged the conduct of operations by army group commands, which were to direct their formations, including the supporting Luftwaffe units, independently until they reached the objectives set in their deployment orders. It therefore seems advisable to follow this division in the account of the fighting.[2]

(i) THE OFFENSIVE OF ARMY GROUP CENTRE UNTIL THE CAPTURE OF THE 'LAND-BRIDGE' BETWEEN VITEBSK AND SMOLENSK
(See the Annexe Volume, No. 5)

The Army General Staff had chosen the central sector of the front as the main area of operations at an early stage in their planning. Army Group Centre thus received a special role, which Halder took into consideration by assigning the chief of his operations department, Major-General von Greiffenberg, to its commander-in-chief, Field Marshal von Bock, as chief of the latter's general staff.[3] Assuming basic agreement between the Army High Command and the army group, this arrangement provided an additional guarantee that direct contact between Hitler and von Bock or similar 'cross-fire from the upper atmosphere' would not lead to serious disagreement with regard to the priority of capturing Moscow.[4] But certain problems in this army group did result

---

[1] The different starting-times were due to the different times of sunrise along the entire front. The code-word 'Dortmund' had been issued on 20 June.

[2] Cf. Annexe Vol., Nos. 2 and 1.

[3] Greiffenberg was chief of the general staff of Twelfth Army Jan.–May 1941.

[4] Halder's description of 25 July 1941, *Kriegstagebuch*, iii. 112 (Halder's 'preliminary notes', from which the quotation comes, are not included in the English translation). The extent to which

from the fact that, in addition to the commander-in-chief, it had a second field marshal, Günther von Kluge (commander-in-chief of Fourth Army), and that its two armoured groups were led by colonel-generals who, however, did not have the rank and authority of the commander-in-chief of an army but were merely 'commanders'.[5]

According to the deployment orders for Barbarossa, Army Group Centre was to advance on both sides of Minsk into the area around and north of Smolensk and destroy enemy forces in Belorussia to prepare the way for further advances to the north-east and east.

The enemy's dispositions were:[6] the bulk of the mobile units under the command of the Soviet Western Front (Army General Pavlov) were organized in three army areas and deployed in a large salient extending far to the west between Brest-Litovsk and the Suvalki area. An additional army, Thirteenth Army, which also included mobile units (mechanized units and armoured brigades), was located around Minsk. Army Group Centre was therefore deployed to form strong, fast pincers on both wings. To capture the river crossings and at the same time co-ordinate the advance of the mobile units and the infantry, Armoured Group 2 under Colonel-General Guderian was assigned to Fourth Army command for the initial operations, and Armoured Group 3 under Colonel-General Hermann Hoth was assigned to Ninth Army command (commander-in-chief Colonel-General Adolf Strauss). Fourth Army was to form an additional group to foil enemy attempts to break through to the west and was then to advance eastward from the middle of the front to close the encirclement ring forming near Białystok, break the resistance of the encircled Soviet units, and eliminate them. 1st Cavalry Division, the only division of its kind the Germany army still had, was to cover the southern flank towards the Pripet marshes.[7] Army reserves consisted of a higher command (*Höheres Kommando*) with four infantry divisions and a corps command with two infantry divisions as well as the motorized Brigade 900.[8]

The offensive on 22 June 1941 surprised the defensive forces of the Red Army.[9] On the right wing Armoured Group 2 crossed the Bug at Brest-Litovsk, bypassing the fortress, which was to be attacked by XII Army Corps. The divisions of the two armoured corps on this front (XXIV and XXXXVII Armoured Corps) advanced rapidly, ignoring the enemy units on their flanks,

the control of C.-in-C.s of army groups and armies by their superiors could be guaranteed in the event of a conflict between Halder's appeals and their local assessments of the situation was yet to emerge.

[5] This led to a personal intervention by the C.-in-C. of the army in the question of the assignment of the armoured groups for the attack on 22 June 1941.

[6] Cf. the Annexe Vol., No. 1. For all movements of the army and objectives reached cf. the daily reports, not cited individually here, of the operations department of the army general staff in *KTB OKW* i. 490–873 (30 Dec. 1941), ii. 181 ff.

[7] 1st Cavalry Div. was reorganized into 24th Armd Div. on 28 Nov. 1941.

[8] This brigade was equipped with tanks captured in France.

[9] Röhricht, *Kesselschlacht*, 21 ff., example III, 'Der Ansatz der Heeresgruppe Mitte bei der Eröffnung des Rußlandfeldzuges im Juni 1941'; for both armoured groups cf. ibid. 48 ff.; Hofmann, Feldzug, pt. II, 2, MGFA P-114b; Geyer, *IX. Armeekorps*, 28.

which were to be eliminated by the infantry later. On the northern wing of the army group Armoured Group 3 captured intact the three bridges over the Neman at Olita and Merkine, the essential prerequisite for the rapid fulfilment of its task. On 24 June the armoured group reached Vilnius and prepared to move on to Vitebsk. Its commander believed this would be in accordance with its objective of preventing the enemy's escape over the Dvina and the Dnieper. Moreover, he did not expect that an advance in this direction would encounter any significant resistance. Accordingly, even after receiving the order to turn his attack in the direction of Borisov and Minsk, Hoth attempted to obtain permission from the chief of the army general staff to continue his advance eastward. But his request was rejected and he was instructed, together with Armoured Group 2, to form an outer ring east of Minsk in order to prevent the escape of enemy forces through the thin encirclement formed by the wing corps of Fourth and Ninth Armies east of Białystok. As on 23 June Halder was still uncertain as to whether the Red Army would stand and fight near the frontier or withdraw eastward,[10] he gave priority to the certain destruction of strong enemy forces and not to deep penetrations behind the front. At the same time, however, he sought to limit the use of mobile units on the encirclement fronts to an unavoidable minimum. Strong advance units were to capture the crossings on the upper Dnieper at Mogilev and Orsha as well as the Dvina crossings at Vitebsk and Polotsk.[11]

The encirclement was not completely successful, and the infantry could not keep up with the advancing armour. Thus those parts of the four Soviet armies which had broken out moved eastward in front of Army Group Centre until the last units were surrounded near Novogrodek on 9 July. But even then numerous Red Army soldiers avoided capture, and their presence as partisans and roaming groups was quickly felt in rear areas. As an undesirable consequence of the protracted resistance in the pockets, mobile units remained tied down there and were delayed in resuming their advance eastward. Not surprisingly, under these circumstances the commanders of the armoured units were suspected of wishing to evade tight control of their movements and, notwithstanding their task of destroying enemy forces, continued to advance as fast as possible.[12] To solve the resulting problems, the main tasks of the army group were given to separate commanders. Field Marshal von Kluge and his staff took over the command of the two armoured groups and two infantry corps, which formed the offensive group as 'Fourth Armoured Army'. The rest of Fourth Army was placed under Second Army command under Colonel-General Maximilian Freiherr von Weichs, which had previously been retained by the Army High Command as a reserve (see Diagrams II.i.1, 2). Its task, together with Ninth Army, was to completely isolate and destroy the encircled enemy units as soon as possible.[13]

[10] Halder, *Diaries*, 968, 971 (23, 24 June 1941).
[11] Hoth, *Panzer-Operationen*, 60 ff.; Halder, *Diaries*, 968 (23 June 1941).
[12] Guderian, *Panzer Leader*, 94, gives an example.
[13] Halder, *Diaries*, 973 (24 June 1941). In these deliberations communications and supply

DIAGRAM II.1.1. Order of Battle of Army Group Centre, 1 July 1941

Army Gp. Centre Cmdr. Rear Army Area 102 102nd Inf. Div. LIII A.Co. 45th Inf. Div. 167th Inf. Div. 52nd Inf. Div. 255th Inf. Div. 267th Inf. Div. Second Army HQ Army High Cmd. reserves Higher Cmd. XXXV 197th Inf. Div. 15th Inf. Div. 112th Inf. Div. 293rd Inf. Div. XXXXII A.Co. 110th Inf. Div. 106th Inf. Div.	Armd. Gp. 3	XXXIX Mot. A.Co.	14th Mot. Div. 20th Mot. Div. 20th Armd. Div. 7th Armd. Div. 12th Armd. Div.
		LVII Mot. A.Co.	18th Mot. Div. 19th. Armd. Div.
	Ninth Army 403rd Sec. Div. 900th Mot. Brig.	VI A.Go.	26th Inf. Div. 6th Inf. Div.
		V A.Co.	35th Inf. Div. 5th Inf. Div. 161st Inf. Div.
		VIII A.Co.	28th Inf. Div. 8th Inf. Div.
		XX A.Co.	87th Inf. Div. 162nd Inf. Div. 256th Inf. Div. 129th Inf. Div.
		XIII A.Co.	252nd Inf. Div. 78th Inf. Div.
		VII A.Co.	258th Inf. Div. 23rd Inf. Div. 7th Inf. Div. 268th Inf. Div.
	Fourth Army 286th Sec. Div. 221st Sec. Div.	IX A.Co.	17th Inf. Div. 263rd Inf. Div. 137th Inf. Div. 292nd Inf. Div.
		XXXXIII A.Co.	134th Inf. Div. 131st Inf. Div.
		XII A.Co.	31st Inf. Div. 34th Inf. Div.
	Armd. Gp. 2 1st Cav. Div. 10th Mot. Div.	XXXXVI Mot. A.Co.	Inf. Reg. 'GD' 10th Armd. Div. SS 'Reich'
		XXXXVII Mot. A.Co.	29th Mot. Div. 17th Armd. Div. 18th Armd. Div.
		XXIV Mot. A.Go.	3rd Armd. Div. 4th Armd. Div.

Diagram II.1.2. Order of Battle of Army Group Centre, 4 July 1941

Army Gp. Centre	Army	Armd. Gp.	Corps	Divisions
Army Gp. Centre	Ninth Army XXIII A.Co. 206th Inf. Div. 86th Inf. Div.		VI A.Co.	26th Inf. Div. 6th Inf. Div.
102nd Inf. Div. Mot. Brig. 900 XXXXIII A.Co. 131st Inf. Div. 134th Inf. Div. 252nd Inf. Div.			V A.Co.	35th Inf. Div. 5th Inf. Div. 161st Inf. Div.
			VIII A.Co.	28th Inf. Div. 8th Inf. Div.
			XX A.Co.	256th Inf. Div. 129th Inf. Div.
Cmdr. Rear Army Area Centre	Second Army		LIII A.Co.	267th Inf. Div. 255th Inf. Div. 52nd Inf. Div. 167th Inf. Div.
162nd Inf. Div. 87th Inf. Div. 403rd Inf. Div. 221st Inf. Div. 286th Inf. Div.			Higher Cmd. XXXV	45th Inf. Div. 293rd Inf. Div.
			XIII A.Co.	17th Inf. Div. 78th Inf. Div.
Army High or Cmd. reserves			VII A.Co.	258th Inf. Div. 23rd Inf. Div. 7th Inf. Div. 268th Inf. Div.
197th Inf. Div. 15th Inf. Div. 260th Inf. Div. 112th Inf. Div.			IX A.Co.	263rd Inf. Div. 137th Inf. Div. 292nd Inf. Div.
XXXXIII A.Co. 110th Inf. Div. 106th Inf. Div. 96th Inf. Div.			XII A.Co.	31st Inf. Div. 34th Inf. Div.
	Fourth Armd. Army Inf. Reg. 'GD'	Armd. Gp. 3, 12th Armd. Div. 14th Mot. Div.	XXXIX Mot. A.Co.	20th Mot. Div. 20th Armd. Div. 7th Armd. Div.
			LVII Mot. A.Co.	18th Mot. Div. 19th Armd. Div.
			XXXXVI Mot. A.Co.	10th Armd. Div. SS 'Reich'
		Armd. Gp. 2, 1st Cav. Div.	XXXVII Mot. A.Co.	29th Mot. Div. 17th Armd. Div. 18th Armd. Div.
			XXIV Mot. A.Co.	10th Mot. Div. 3rd Armd. Div. 4th Armd. Div.

On 28 June the two armoured groups reached the vicinity of Minsk, closing the outer ring. Armoured Group 2 was on the right wing facing Bobruysk; Halder hoped that Guderian would advance further to Rogachev and Mogilev on the Dnieper. He was prevented from issuing a direct order for such an operation by Hitler's belief that the diversion of the entire armoured group would jeopardize the success of the encirclement.[14] As Halder had been convinced since 24 June that the mass of the Red Army was not planning a rapid retreat but intended to stand and fight, he considered a thrust to the Dnieper crossings essential for an envelopment of the enemy forces, the capture of the area between Vitebsk and Smolensk, and the opening of the way to Moscow. On 30 June he issued a corresponding order to the two armoured groups to secure the line Rogachev–Mogilev–Orsha–Vitebsk–Polotsk as quickly as possible.[15]

When the armoured units reached Minsk, discussions began about the best time for their further advance towards Smolensk, already envisaged in their deployment orders. Armoured Group 3 seemed to meet the prerequisites for this—closing the Novogrodek pocket and forming up of the units for the attack—earlier than the units under Guderian, which were more occupied with containing break-out attempts by Soviet forces. Colonel-General Halder had envisaged 5 July as the date for the resumption of the advance by the armoured groups, but in agreement with the army group he decided on 3 July and was able to defend his decision against the doubts of Brauchitsch and Hitler.[16]

Thus on 1 July Army Group Centre ordered the armoured groups to begin their advance on 3 July.[17] Armoured Group 2, after crossing the Dnieper in the Rogachev–Orsha sector, was to advance principally along the Minsk–Moscow highway up to a line running from Yelnya to the high ground east of Yartsevo. Armoured Group 3 was ordered, after crossing the swampy area of the upper Berezina, to attack on both sides of Vitebsk up to the line Berezovo–Velizh and to send some units to advance on Nevel. Second Army was ordered to place most of its strength on its southern wing and continue its advance beyond the line Slutsk–Minsk against and beyond the Dnieper sector from Mogilev to north of Orsha.[18] Ninth Army was to attack the Dvina sector south of the line Vitebsk–Polotsk. The most important objective of both infantry armies was the capture of the land-bridge between Orsha and Vitebsk. To give the attack

---

factors played a role, and the desire to 'tie down' the armoured group commands was also a major factor. Bock too objected to this command structure (Tagebuch (1, 7 July 1941), BA-MA N 22/9); Halder, *Diaries*, 983, 993 (28 June, 1 July 1941); operations order of Army Group Centre, 1 July 1941 (copy), in Hofmann, Feldzug, pt. II, 112, appendix A, MGFA P-114b.

[14] Halder, *Diaries*, 181–2 (29 June 1941).

[15] *KTB OKW* i. 423 (30 June 1941), operations order of Army Group Centre (n. 13 above).

[16] Halder, *Diaries*, 987–8, 991 ff. (29 June, 30 June–2 July 1941).

[17] Hoth, *Panzer-Operationen*, 72–3; Hofmann, Feldzug, pt. II, appendix A (n. 13 above). On Hitler's doubts cf. Bock, Tagebuch, 11 ff., (1, 2 July 1941), BA-MA N 22/9.

[18] Bock, Tagebuch, 11 (1 July 1941), BA-MA N 22/9. Cf. nn. 108–9 below.

the necessary momentum, the army group was provided with Higher Command XXXV (with five infantry divisions) behind Second Army and with XXXXII Army Corps (with two infantry divisions) behind Ninth Army.[19]

Contrary to expectations, it became evident on the first day of the attack that the enemy had had sufficient time to bring up defensive forces and was even able to launch vigorous counter-attacks. At Borisov, Soviet armoured formations with air support attacked the Berezina crossings. And on the flanks, near Polotsk and Gomel, strong enemy forces were detected; there could be no question of taking Vitebsk in a lightning attack.[20] Moreover, movements were hindered by isolated thunder-showers and impassable roads. Armoured Group 3, which was equipped with captured French vehicles, had to report some of its formations incapable of combat. Only 19th Armoured Division was able to cross the Dvina, at Dysna (Verkhnedvinsk), where a bridgehead could be established. Newly brought-up divisions of the Red Army reserve appeared everywhere, equipped with armour and attacking vigorously. Armoured Group 3 still did not have 12th Armoured Division, which had to provide support for the encirclement far to the rear. The encircled Soviet units defended themselves energetically and in places inflicted heavy losses on the attacking German infantry units.[21] At first Armoured Group 2 was able to break out of the Berezina bridgeheads between Bobruysk and Borisov to the Dnieper only on the right wing, near Rogachev, which was reached on 5 July.[22] The following day the right wing of XXIV Armoured Corps had to defend itself against enemy formations attacking south of Rogachev across the Dnieper.

In this situation the effects of the differing importance attached by the various commands to the main objectives of this first phase of the campaign became evident. To carry out the order to advance as rapidly as possible with the armoured forces to the area around Smolensk and stand by for further, 'decisive', attacks required bringing up all mobile forces. On the other hand, the simultaneous order to disarm the encircled Red Army soldiers and prevent them from continuing the fight as partisans tied down precisely these forces. Moreover, between the prongs of the advancing mobile troops large areas remained open in which the infantry could follow up only slowly and not

[19] Organization of Army Group Centre and Army High Command reserves according to operations order of Army Group Centre of 1 July 1941. On orders of the Army High Command a corps had to be transferred to the right wing to eliminate a threat to the inner flanks of Army Groups Centre and South. This was presumably done at Hitler's behest, for Halder considered the relevant reports to be 'horror stories' and believed that, instead of the reported army with three armoured and two infantry corps, at most only two or three divisions were in the Pripet area. Bock feared that he would 'never again' see this corps: Halder, *Diaries*, 999 (3 July 1941); Bock, Tagebuch, 13 (2 July 1941), BA-MA N 22/9.

[20] Hoth, *Panzer-Operationen*, 155–6: Armd. Group 3, Ia, group order No. 10 and enemy intelligence sheet 3 July 1941.

[21] This battle continued for weeks; in the end only the completely exhausted Red Army soldiers who were unable to break out remained in the pocket, which was one of the causes of the large number of deaths.

[22] Guderian, *Panzer Leader*, 149; Bock, Tagebuch, 15 (5 July 1941), BA-MA N 22/9.

without encountering considerable resistance. While Hitler was primarily concerned with capturing as many of the Soviet troops in the pockets as possible and pacifying the rear areas as a prerequisite for their administration and exploitation, Halder in his conduct of operations considered the threat to the flanks and the pockets of enemy troops in rear areas as a secondary problem, to be dealt with by the infantry armies. In his view maintaining forward momentum had absolute priority. However, the wording of orders from the Army High Command did not always clearly convey Halder's intentions and had to take into account Hitler's oral instructions, which sometimes led to uncertainty at middle-command levels.

The army group command and the armoured groups were able to refer to concrete planning concluded months earlier and to the repeatedly confirmed instructions for Operation Barbarossa for Army Group Centre, issued in their final form on 28 April,[23] according to which both armoured groups, after annihilating enemy forces between Białystok and Minsk, were to co-operate closely in rapidly conquering the area near and south of Smolensk and Vitebsk to prevent a concentration of enemy troops on the upper Dnieper and the Dvina, thus giving the army group freedom of action for further tasks.

On 7 July Guderian was confronted with a situation in which his attack on the left wing with 17th Armoured Division stalled and was repulsed in a counter-attack (see the Annexe Volume, No. 6). Armoured Group 3, on the other hand, went on the defensive on its left flank between Drissa and Polotsk and concentrated its attack entirely on Vitebsk in the centre of the front.[24] With the use of four mobile divisions, the attack led to the capture of the city on 9 July. Now, reinforced by 12th Armoured Division, which was no longer needed for encirclements, the two armoured groups were to make a thrust deep into enemy territory. This movement was planned as an envelopment of enemy forces over a large area with a turning inward east of Smolensk and thereafter as an armoured wedge which, together with the inner corps of Armoured Group 3, would have Moscow as its objective. To maintain the contact indispensable for such an operation it would have been necessary to halt the right wing of Armoured Group 2 and join up with Armoured Group 3 on the left. This, however, was not done. On the contrary, on 7 July, except for covering forces, Guderian withdrew 17th Armoured Division, which had been forced to go on the defensive, back across the Dnieper in order to use it in the attack on Orsha. The situation demanded a decision by the superior high command of Fourth Armoured Army. The commander-in-chief of the army group was inclined to strengthen the group under Hoth and its promising operational start and recommended that Field Marshal von Kluge order Guderian to halt and close up to the left.[25] Kluge hesitated to give Guderian

---

[23] Extract of assignment figures in Hofmann, Feldzug, pt. 1, appendix B, MGFA, P-114b.

[24] Hoth, *Panzer-Operationen*, 76 ff., 82.

[25] On 7 July Bock was compelled to renounce his intention to concentrate his main effort on the sector held by Armd. Group 3 and on the northern wing of Armd. Group 2, but he considered

the order that Bock suggested. On the contrary, he ordered that 12th Armoured Division of Armoured Group 3 should be brought up to Guderian's left wing, where the situation was critical.

Since 7 July Guderian had been energetically preparing to cross the Dnieper between Zhlobin, north of the confluence with the Berezina, and Orsha.[26] Thus, when Kluge became aware of the state of Guderian's attack preparations, which were directed away from Armoured Group 3, a dispute inevitably followed. Guderian referred to the still valid directive; he had not received new binding orders.[27] Finally, on 9 July Kluge agreed to the attack.

This decision had serious consequences, for it weakened the plan to concentrate the main effort of the attack in the area north of Smolensk, the most direct route to Moscow. Evidently there was no relevant order for both armoured groups. They still assumed that their areas of main effort were Vitebsk and Smolensk, and moreover were not sufficiently informed of each other's strategic and tactical intentions. This situation was a consequence of the lack of unity in the command of the army group, which itself resulted from the formation of 'Fourth Armoured Army'. It made an energetic advance, as Bock wished, almost impossible.

But Kluge's decision, which could be interpreted as evidence of weak leadership, acquires a different significance if one considers Hitler's intentions at this time. He had informed Halder on 8 July that, after the two armoured groups had reached the areas assigned to them in the deployment order, they should ideally be so used that Armoured Group 3 would be available for an attack against Leningrad *or* against Moscow. Guderian's armoured group, on the other hand, should be employed east of the Dnieper in a southerly or south-easterly direction to co-operate with Army Group South. While Field Marshal von Bock and the commander of Armoured Group 3 evidently agreed on a concentrated thrust of both armoured groups over the Smolensk landbridge against Moscow, Halder was able to accept for the time being Hitler's 'ideal solution' with regard to Guderian's armoured group. For it served the large-scale encirclement of the 'dry gap between the Dnieper and the Dvina', which he had already noted as a plan in his diary on 29 June.[28] As Hitler, and at this point presumably also Halder, assumed that, with the Soviet forces around Smolensk 'finished off', they would be able to simply 'take over' the

Kluge's justification for rejecting his suggestion on grounds of transport conditions to be only a pretext. He believed that Kluge was afraid to stand up to Guderian. Bock again criticized the creation of this level of command as well as the establishment of the new level of Higher Command XXXV on the Pripet flank by the Army High Command: Bock, Tagebuch (7, 9, 11 July 1941), BA-MA N 22/9.

[26] Guderian, *Panzer Leader*, 96 ff. The problem, however, lay not in waiting for the infantry, but in the clear concentration of the main effort on the left wing, together with Armd. Group 3.

[27] Kluge's order to Guderian, mentioned by Halder (*Diaries*, 1020), appears to have been in oral form, which Guderian did not regard as binding. Guderian's actions constituted a threat to the intention of the army group to continue the attack eastward on 11 July after combining the two armoured groups on both sides of Smolensk.

[28] Halder, *Diaries*, 986 (29 June 1941).

area all the way to the upper Volga without serious fighting, Halder was able to put aside for the moment the idea of using the armoured group and thus ignore Hitler's words of 8 July, especially as he believed that the army group enjoyed an 'overwhelming superiority' over the enemy forces facing it.

The offensive with a spearhead consisting of both armoured groups was intended to encircle numerous enemy formations and break the enemy front by capturing the triangle Orsha–Smolensk–Vitebsk.

On the southern wing Armoured Group 2 with its right corps (XXIV Armoured Corps) was to take the Propoysk-Roslavl road. The centre corps (XXXXVI Armoured Corps) was deployed in the direction of Gorkiy–Pochinok–Yelnya; the left (XXXXVII Armoured Corps) was to advance south of the highway between Minsk and Smolensk. The Dnieper was successfully crossed; the fortified town of Mogilev and the evacuated bridgehead at Orsha were bypassed. On 13 July the armoured group was fiercely attacked from the area around Gomel, but Halder was of the opinion that the Soviet forces involved did not deserve serious attention. The attacks were also accompanied by sallies from the enemy bridgeheads at Orsha and Mogilev.[29] This development, however, forced Guderian's right corps to change the direction of its attack, and the 'Moscow Chaussée' between Propoysk and Roslavl could not be taken. To secure the easternmost point reached for the thrust towards Moscow, however, the front salient at Yelnya was held, even though this involved heavy personnel and material losses. Strong attacks on Guderian's right flank and Second Army providing cover in the south slowed the advance of the southern encirclement arm of Halder's envelopment operation considerably.

On the left wing of the attack Armoured Group 3 maintained its direction of advance towards Moscow. Its objective was to reach the line of Berezovka–Velizh–Nevel. The main attack was aimed at the ridge between Smolensk and Nevel. After reaching this objective the armoured group with XXXIX Armoured Corps was to pursue the enemy via Velizh and bring up LVII Armoured Corps via Nevel. The intention of this extensive encirclement via Rzhev and north of Moscow is clear.[30] 12th and 7th Armoured Divisions were to cover the developing encirclement near Smolensk from a distance and stop enemy break-outs in the north and east. On Kluge's orders, however, 12th Armoured Division remained assigned to the Smolensk ring and was thus not available for the pursuit envisaged by Hoth after the breakthrough of the enemy front.[31] The other two divisions of the corps reached Demidov and

[29] Guderian, *Panzer Leader*, 98: order of Army Group Centre for the continuation of operations, 14 July 1941 (copy): Hofmann, Feldzug, pt. II, appendix B, MGFA P-114b.

[30] On 13 July Bock objected strongly to the armoured groups being pulled out in order to encircle enemy forces facing the inner wings of Army Groups South and Centre (Tagebuch, 24 ff.: 13 July 1941), while Halder was already considering complying with Hitler's wish (*Diaries*, 1032: 12 July 1941).

[31] Hoth, *Panzer-Operationen*, 88 ff.

Velizh on 13 July. LVII Armoured Corps advanced on Nevel from the Drissa bridgehead and then marched on Velikie Luki.

On 13 July Hoth had to abandon the attack, which had diverted his forces from the main objective of the army group's attack, and, with XXXIX Armoured Corps, to concentrate on the encirclement north of Smolensk.[32]

Apart from Hoth's own intentions, however, the diverted direction of the attack was actually in line with Hitler's wish to support the attack on Leningrad by reducing the pressure on Sixteenth Army of Army Group North, which was involved in heavy fighting. For this purpose 19th Armoured Division, which was the nearest, could be brought up.[33] As a result of Hitler's constant urging to speed up operations on the wings of the eastern front, Halder seems to have accepted the idea on 12 July of encircling more enemy forces by diverting the armoured groups in the centre from a direct push towards Moscow, provided that they first achieved freedom of movement towards the east. However, the order to the chief of the operations department defined these conditions more precisely: in the north the enemy falling back before the right wing of Army Group North (II Army Corps of Sixteenth Army) was to be cut off with such forces of Armoured Group 3 as were able to advance on Velikie Luki and Kholm 'notwithstanding the order to reach the area north-east of Smolensk'. In the south a group from Armoured Group 2 was to be sent against Roslavl. On 23 July Halder informed the chief of the general staff of Army Group Centre of these plans. His oral report to Hitler the following day[34] showed again his compliance with Hitler's wishes with regard to Army Group North. For Army Group South, however, he first required the crossing of the Dnieper. In particular, he minimized the importance of the Korosten group (Soviet Fifth Army) in order to avoid early use of Guderian's armoured group.

This fragmentation of the armoured groups led to a protest by the commander-in-chief of Army Group Centre. Bock considered the prospects for a thrust towards Moscow to be very favourable, but it would require all available forces. Halder thereupon instructed Greiffenberg not to permit 19th Armoured Division to attack beyond Nevel in the direction of Velikie Luki before Sixteenth Army had been successful there.[35]

Halder's deliberations with the chief of the general staff of Army Group

[32] Halder had in mind a thrust via Nevel to Velikie Luki, considerably further than Bock wanted to go. See n. 30 above and sect. II.1.1(*b*) at n. 146.

[33] Halder, *Diaries*, 1036–7 (13 July 1941).   [34] Ibid.

[35] This was the basis of Hoth's decision to employ stronger forces against Smolensk (*Panzer-Operationen*, 94). 19th Armd. Div. was sent against Velikie Luki on 17 July, captured the town, and then abandoned it on Kluge's orders on 18 July. This represented a concession to Bock, who wanted to avoid tying the division down on the left wing, as an annihilation of the enemy was impossible because Army Group North lacked sufficient forces. On the disputes concerning this question cf. Bock, *Tagebuch*, 31–8 (17–21 July 1941), BA-MA N 22/9. On 21 July Halder expressed his profound regret that the city had been abandoned (*Diaries*, 1066). For Hoth's views cf. Hoth, *Panzer-Operationen*, 99.

Centre, which assumed division of the army group into a 'front group' consisting of Ninth and parts of Second Army with Armoured Group 3 on the northern wing and a 'group for turning movement to the south-east'[36] consisting of Second Army (for an inner ring) and Armoured Group 2 (for an outer ring), were probably less an expression of strategic planning than an acceptance of Hitler's demands, which are presented elsewhere.

The 'expedition' of Armoured Group 3 ended on 19 July with the arrival of 19th Armoured Division in Velizh. Now the entire armoured group was again in a continuous front between Smolensk and Belev. Fierce attacks against the pocket near Smolensk to free the encircled Soviet formations tied down large parts of both armoured groups. Attacks on the southern flank of Second Army and Armoured Group 3 achieved deep local penetrations that had to be eliminated. The basic plan remained, however, not to tie these units down for a long period of time in a direction that would seriously affect the attack on Moscow.

These decisions about the further operations of Army Group Centre[37] were influenced primarily by the delay in the conclusion of current operations. With the capture of Yartsevo north-east of Smolensk by the spearheads of Armoured Group 3, and of Smolensk itself by Armoured Group 2 on 16 July 1941, the second great battle of encirclement approached its end.[38] However, the Germans were not able to prevent the break-out or timely withdrawal of strong enemy forces, especially motorized units. The 'hole' east of Smolensk was not closed until 24 July. When the army group issued the order 'for ending the battle of Smolensk and reaching the starting position for new operations' on 22 July, the territorial objectives mentioned in the deployment order for Barbarossa had been achieved.[39] The double battle of Białystok-Minsk had resulted in the capture of 324,000 prisoners, 3,300 tanks, and 1,800 artillery pieces; after the battle of Smolensk these figures were doubled. But the stubborn resistance of the Red Army became stronger; there were no signs of an exhaustion of the enemy's 'vital fighting strength'. The way to Moscow was still not open. After a visit to the Army Groups Centre and North by Lieutenant-Colonel (General Staff) Reinhard Gehlen, chief of the operations department and group leader North, Halder considered on 21 July how to meet Hitler's demands to speed up operations on the wings and at the same time continue the advance towards Moscow. He planned to attach the southern wing of Army Group North to the left wing of Army Group Centre, Ninth Army, to enable Field Marshal Ritter von Leeb to concentrate entirely on Leningrad without receiving additional armoured formations. The thrust to-

[36] Halder, *Diaries*, 1056–7 (18 July 1941). On the other hand, on 18 July Bock decided that the main task of Second Army was to continue the advance to the north-east and not to turn sharply south. He also considered Guderian's advance on Yelnya, at that time, to be a mistake. He believed that the enemy east of Smolensk should be completely cut off first. Cf. Bock. Tagebuch, 33 ff. (18–20 July 1941), BA-MA N 22/9.

[37] Cf. sect. II.1.1(b) at n. 150.   [38] Halder, *Diaries*, 1048 (16 July 1941).

[39] Army group order in Hofmann, Feldzug, pt. I, appendix E, MGFA P-114b.

wards Moscow was to be carried out in a 'one-armed' fashion—with armour from Armoured Group 3, Ninth Army, and the reinforced Second Army— with the objective of encircling the city. On the right wing Kluge was to advance on Stalingrad with Armoured Group 2 and the southern part of Second Army 'in accordance with Rundstedt's instructions'. But Halder continued to believe that this regrouping of Army Group Centre would generally have to wait until after the objectives set out in the deployment order had been reached, i.e. after Army Group South had crossed the Dnieper. On the whole, with the exception of the southern sector, Halder was satisfied with the progress made on the way to a 'decisive battle before Moscow'.[40] The assumptions made in German campaign-planning about enemy operational decisions seemed to have been confirmed. Halder believed that the German forces still retained their freedom of action.

(ii) THE OFFENSIVE OF ARMY GROUP NORTH

On the basis of its enemy estimate and the largely known fortifications and terrain, the Army High Command had calculated that the German forces in the attack sector of Army Group North would enjoy a superiority over the Soviet forces facing them.[41] In the Baltic Special Military District 29 Soviet infantry divisions, 4 cavalry divisions, 4 armoured divisions, and 7 armoured brigades had been identified, of which 18 infantry divisions, 1 armoured division, and 4 amoured brigades would oppose Army Group North; the rest would face Army Group Centre. The organization of these units under a front staff (in Riga) in two army headquarters (Eighth Army in Jelgava (Mitau) and Eleventh in Kaunas (Kovno)) with one group as an operational and one as a strategic reserve did not permit any conclusions about a point of main effort in the event of a conflict; details of their organization were not known. It was assumed that the population in the countries to be freed from Soviet rule would be friendly.[42] It was uncertain whether the Baltic States would be defended at all. Intelligence indicated that the strong frontier defence forces had been pulled back. It was therefore all the more important to engage the bulk of the enemy forces rapidly while still west of the Dvina.[43]

The organization of the army group and the orders to its units were intended to secure under all circumstances the fastest possible free movement of

[40] Oral reports by Heusinger and Gehlen; Halder's decisions: Halder, *Diaries*, 1066 ff. (21 July 1941). Assessment by operations department cited here as Halder's own opinion: cf. ibid. 1073 (25 July 1941).

[41] Cf. the Annexe Vol., No. 1; Müller-Hillebrand, Nordabschnitt, pt. 1, 9 ff., MGFA P-114a. This study—'Der Feldzug gegen die Sowjetunion im Nordabschnitt der Ostfront 1941–1945', pt. 1, 'Die Offensive des Jahres 1941 bis zum Ladoga-See', and pt. 11, 'Das Ringen um die Behauptung des gewonnen Raumes' (MGFA P-114a), with annexe volumes—in addition to the study by the army group's chief of staff, General Brennecke, *et al.*, 'Die Operationen der Heeresgruppe Nord bis vor Leningrad' (MGFA T-17), has been used here especially because of the copies of orders and reports it contains. See the headnote to the Bibliography.

[42] Müller-Hillebrand, Nordabschnitt, pt. 1, 9 ff., MGFA P-114a.

[43] Chales de Beaulieu, *Panzergruppe 4*, 24.

the armoured divisions.[44] For this reason, unlike the other army groups, Armoured Group 4 under Colonel-General Hoepner was not placed under an infantry army.[45] Sixteenth Army on the right and Eighteenth Army on the left had to adjust their respective wings to the movements of the rapidly advancing armoured group, cover its flanks, and 'round up' remnants of overrun enemy forces. The armoured group had only two armoured corps, LVI Corps under General von Manstein and XXXXI Corps under General Georg-Hans Reinhardt. Manstein's corps had only one armoured, one motorized, and one normal infantry division. XXXXI Armoured Corps, in whose attack sector strong opposition was to be expected and which was able to deploy and advance on a broad front, had two armoured divisions, one motorized, and one normal infantry division. As a reserve the armoured group had only one motorized division (SS Totenkopf: 'Death's Head').[46] The armoured group advanced towards the Dvina with one corps in each of two spearheads, Manstein on the right towards Daugavpils (Dünaburg, Drinsk) and Reinhardt on the left towards Jekabpils (Jakobstadt). After establishing bridgeheads the two were to reach the area of Opochka rapidly and from there turn north or north-east. (See the Annexe Volume, No. 5.)

Under the command of Colonel-General Ernst Busch, Sixteenth Army on the right wing was to break through the enemy positions towards Kaunas, cross the Neman, and secure a crossing-point as early as possible south of Daugavpils. Eighteenth Army under the command of Colonel-General von Küchler was ordered to concentrate its efforts on the right wing to capture Jekabpils and Saungeljava, force a crossing, and cut off the enemy troops remaining west of the Dvina. The ports of Liepaja (Libau) and Ventspils (Windau) were to be taken with minimum forces and, after the crossing of the Dvina, forces were to be made available for an attack on Riga. Estonia, because of its large size, was at first excluded from this order. Air support was to be provided by Air Fleet 1, which, for naval targets, included an 'Air Leader Baltic'.[47]

The role of the navy, especially important for the supplying of Army Group North and for operations against the Baltic islands, was at first limited to the promise of providing transport capacity for logistical purposes and to supporting an attack on the islands with motor torpedo-boats and transport ships. The navy wanted to provide two batteries of coastal artillery and 'additional per-

[44] This meant that the mobile troops were not to wait until the infantry caught up. Cf. deployment and battle orders for Barbarossa of Army Group North, 5 May 1941, in Müller-Hillebrand, Nordabschnitt, pt. I, appendix A3, also for the following account.

[45] Chales de Beaulieu, Panzergruppe 4, 14.

[46] In considering the weakness of the armoured group, however, it should be taken into account that in accordance with Hitler's wishes armoured units of Army Group Centre were to be brought up for the decisive attack on Leningrad. Moreover, the terrain in front of Army Group North was not suited to armoured warfare.

[47] On the planning and mission assignments of the Luftwaffe cf. sect. I.IV.2(c) at nn. 353 ff. (Boog).

sonnel'.[48] After the Dvina line had been reached, Finnish troops were to move in from the north to complete the encirclement of Leningrad and link up with the German army group east of the city.[49]

As on other sectors of the front, the start of the German offensive on 22 June surprised the enemy forces opposite Army Group North. This is all the more astonishing as it had been quite impossible to conceal the masses of German troops crossing the lower course of the Neman to reach their assembly area, not to mention the conspicuous bridge-building activity.[50] The armoured spearheads were able to cross the Neman, the Dubisa, and the Venta, which would have constituted serious and time-consuming obstacles had the bridges there been destroyed.[51] After this initial success LVI Armoured Corps quickly fought its way through to Daugavpils and captured the Dvina bridges intact on 26 June; then it was ordered to wait there until the infantry could catch up. To the right, Sixteenth Army took Kaunas but then found itself threatened on the right flank by the withdrawal of the left wing of Ninth Army of Army Group Centre, which had been sent to complete the encirclement east of Białystok.[52] The left spearhead, XXXXI Armoured Corps, became involved in a battle with a strong enemy armoured force of around 200 tanks at the Dubisa bridgehead near Raseiniai, which, however, it was able to annihilate. It then continued its attack on the Dvina line. To secure as broad a crossing as possible for the German units following, Reinhardt's corps occupied the west bank of the Dvina between Livani (Liwenhof) and Jekabpils. Military bridges and ferries were established, as the enemy defence was concentrated around Daugavpils. Heavy fighting prevented the expansion of the bridgehead, the main crossing-point for Manstein's armoured corps and Sixteenth Army, until 30 June.[53]

On 1 July most of the Dvina was in the hands of Army Group North, Riga was captured, and new bridgeheads were established. 291st Infantry Division, under direct Eighteenth Army command, had taken Liepaja (Libau) and Ventspils (Windau). The stiffening of Soviet resistance after 23 June and the increasing use of armoured formations in Soviet counter-attacks eliminated German doubts about Soviet intentions to conduct a forward defence. But the

[48] On 21 June 1941 the naval commander D decided that no further units could be provided to protect the coasts: AOK 18/Ia, KTB 3b, BA-MA, 18. Armee, 19601/2. On the naval shock-troop battalion placed under the Eighteenth Army command on 1 June (291st Inf. Div.), see ibid., KTB (1 June 1941), BA-MA, 18. Armee, 17562/17.

[49] Cf. sect. II.III.2(*a*) at n. 139 (Ueberschär).

[50] Halder, *Diaries*, 966–7 (22 June 1941); Leeb, *Tagebuchaufzeichnungen*, 275 (22 June 1941). On the question of surprise on the Soviet side cf. sect. II.II.1 (Hoffmann), and Salisbury, *Leningrad*, 67 ff.

[51] Manstein, *Lost Victories*, 175 ff., and criticism: Chales de Beaulieu, *Panzergruppe 4*, 13 ff.; id., *Hoepner*, 136 ff.

[52] Cf. Leeb, *Tagebuchaufzeichnungen*, 275.

[53] To strengthen the right wing, L Army Corps with two infantry divisions was brought up on 27 June. Cf. Leeb, *Tagebuchaufzeichnungen*, 281 (27 June 1941); Halder, *Diaries*, 983 (28 June 1941); sect. II.II.1. at n. 12 (Hoffmann), and sect. II.I.2(*a*) at n. 798 (Boog). Salisbury, *Leningrad*, 158 ff.

Germans remained uncertain as to whether large enemy formations should be expected between the Dvina and the old Russian frontier.[54]

The supply situation in the north proved to be considerably less difficult than on the other fronts as a result of the large quantities of Red Army supplies that were found, and the fact that numerous bridges and railway lines were captured undamaged. The general-staff officer in charge of supply estimated that from Daugavpils, to be built up as a base, Armoured Group 4 could be supplied until it reached Leningrad and the infantry corps until it reached the line between Opochka and Marienburg. On 1 July Army Group North was able to go over to the second operations sector.[55] (See the Annexe Volume, No. 6.)

On 29 June Field Marshal Ritter von Leeb ordered Armoured Group 4 to prepare for a thrust to the area of Opochka–Ostrov. Reconnaissance was then to be extended beyond the line Velikie Luki–Lake Ilmen to the east and beyond the line Lake Ilmen–Lake Peipus to the north. The armoured group reported that it would be ready to move off on 2 July; Sixteenth and Eighteenth Armies were to move off on 4 July. Advancing against the area south of Opochka, Sixteenth Army also had to employ a corps as flanking echelon on the right wing in contact with Ninth Army. For this reason it was not to be expected that the infantry would rapidly follow the armoured group from this army. Army Group North therefore limited the advance of Eighteenth Army towards Estonia to two infantry divisions to take Tallinn (Reval), so that most of the army could closely follow the armoured units after reaching Ostrov and Pskov.[56]

On 3 July the Army High Command ordered the mobile units of Army Group North south of Pskov to be so organized after reaching the line Opochka–Ostrov that they would soon be able to move north with the objective of blocking the land-bridge between Lake Peipus and Narva Bay. Thereafter Leningrad was to be cut off between the Gulf of Finland and Lake Ladoga.[57]

Apart from strong resistance on the right flank, operations after Armoured

[54] Halder, *Diaries*, 973 (25 June 1941); assessment of enemy's situation in army group order of 27 June 1941: Müller-Hillebrand, Nordabschnitt, pt. I, appendix B2, MGFA P-114a.

[55] Halder, *Diaries*, 994 (1 July 1941); H.Gr. Nord/Ia, Heeresgruppenbefehl, 1 July 1941; Müller-Hillebrand, Nordabschnitt, pt. I, appendices C1, C2; Leeb, *Tagebuchaufzeichnungen*, 283 ff. (22 June–1 July 1941)

[56] Halder took a rather grand view of the situation: the infantry divisions were to eliminate enemy resistance in Estonia and secure the coast, advance in as great a strength as possible towards Leningrad and the south shore of Lake Ladoga, and still cover the eastern flank in the direction of Nevel. Cf. Halder, *Diaries*, 997 (2 July 1941). The directive of the Army High Command of 3 July has not been found; cf. however, the directive of 8 July 1941, RH 2/v. 1326, fos. 155–6. At the same time the three divisions of XXIII Army Corps (Army High Command reserve) were to be used to cover the gap between Army Groups North and Centre, and two divisions were to secure the rear areas. Cf. Leeb, *Tagebuchaufzeichnungen*, 285 (2 July 1941).

[57] *KTB OKW* i. 426 (3 July 1941); Leeb, *Tagebuchaufzeichnungen*, 286 (3 July 1941), with the note that Hitler attached importance to an early capture of Tallinn, which agrees with his remarks to Halder of 30 June 1941 (Halder, *Diaries*, 991).

Group 4 moved into battle proceeded with little interference from the enemy. On 4 July both corps reached the old Latvian–Russian frontier. Then the spearhead division of LVI Armoured Corps became bogged down in the swampy forested area; the corps had to shift the main effort of its attack to Porkhov. On 5 July the armoured group took Ostrov and pushed on in the direction of Pskov and Porkhov.

The further conduct of operations was prepared by the guidelines of the Army General Staff, in accordance with a briefing by the commander-in-chief of the army at the headquarters of the army group on 7 July; they were finalized in an army-group order of 8 July.[58] This order assumed that a Finnish offensive between Kronshtadt Bay and Lake Ladoga and an advance of Armoured Group 3 of Army Group Centre via Nevel towards Velizh could be expected after 10 July. These operations would tie down the enemy facing the army group's own right flank.

The object of the new thrust by Armoured Group 4 was to be Leningrad; the city was to be cut off from the south and south-east. Until Sixteenth Army could come up, the armoured group had to defend itself against enemy forces attacking from the area east of Lake Ilmen. At the same time it was to occupy the Narva crossings to prevent a withdrawal of enemy units from Estonia. To protect the eastern flank of this attack and the rear area of the armoured group around Porkhov, Sixteenth Army was to advance on Kholm and send a flanking force against Velikie Luki. Advance units were sent against Kholm, Staraya Russa, and Novgorod. Eighteenth Army was ordered to turn north after reaching the area west of the road between Ostrov and Pskov to follow Armoured Group 4. Its task remained to conquer Estonia and capture Tallinn and Paltiskis.[59]

On 8 July the Army General Staff issued a directive significantly changing the plan of the army group with its concentration on the line between Leningrad and Narva, which would have required Armoured Group 4 to make a new thrust of more than 250 kilometres.[60] This instruction was the result of a discussion of the situation with Hitler on 8 July, at which Halder was primarily concerned with the beginning of the battle of envelopment of Army Group Centre in the triangle Orsha–Smolensk–Vitebsk. At this conference Hitler accepted Halder's plan of concentrating entirely on Moscow in so far as he described as the 'perfect solution' the possibility that Army Group North might carry out its orders with its own resources.[61] This meant that Armoured

---

[58] On 5 July 1941 Jodl informed Brauchitsch of Hitler's thoughts on the future conduct of operations. Guidelines in *KTB OKW* i. 429 (8 July 1941); Leeb, *Tagebuchaufzeichnungen*, 287; army group order of 8 July 1941: Müller-Hillebrand, Nordabschnitt, pt. I, appendix DI, MGFA P-114a; teletype message OKH/GenStdH/Op.Abt. (IN) No. 1345/41 (8 July 1941) to Army Group North, BA-MA RH 2/v. 1326, pp. 155–6.

[59] With the above directive of the Army High Command recipients were informed that Army Group North could not, for the time being, expect to receive the mobile units of Army Group Centre promised in the deployment order. Cf. Halder, *Diaries*, 212 (8 July 1941), and sect. II.1.1(*b*) at n. 145.

[60] Leeb, *Tagebuchaufzeichnungen*, 289–90 (9 July 1941).   [61] Cf. above, n. 59.

Group 3 would not support Army Group North. Moreover, Hitler also wanted Armoured Group 4 with a strong right wing to cut off Leningrad especially in the *east and south-east*. And Halder, who assumed that the army group enjoyed a 'clear' numerical superiority and had always placed special emphasis on giving it a strong right wing, readily agreed to this plan.[62] This shift of the point of main effort of the German attack to the Novgorod–Luga or the Volkhov–Shlisselburg line was also intended as support for the Finnish attack from the north. Moreover, the Army General Staff also ordered strong advance infantry units to be moved towards Leningrad from the south to make the mobile units south and south-west of the city available for other tasks as soon as possible.

Army Group North accepted the order calmly. This can only be explained by its continuing belief that the enemy would withdraw if he were attacked with sufficient ferocity, that the enemy forces south-east of Leningrad were his last units in the area capable of offering serious resistance, and that the German force was clearly superior. It still wanted to prevent the Red Army from withdrawing strong units eastward and welcomed the opportunity to halt and bring up fresh troops.[63] The commander-in-chief of Army Group North doubted that the defenders were determined to hold the area around Leningrad under all circumstances.[64] On the other hand, the experience of Armoured Group 4, which showed that the terrain to the north-east was not suited for a thrust by mobile units in that direction, was not taken into consideration.

The armoured group began its advance on 10 July, with the two corps using different roads: LVI Armoured Corps advancing on the right in the direction of Porkhov–Novgorod–Chudovo; on the left XXXXI Armoured Corps advancing along the road Pskov–Luga–Leningrad. This direction would inevitably lead Manstein's corps very quickly into an almost impassable marsh along the Volkhov, but the armoured group was determined to cover the distance to the starting-position for the encirclement of Leningrad within about four days. This represented a thrust of about 300 kilometres, which could succeed only if the formations involved were stopped neither by the enemy nor by difficult terrain. The six mobile units of the armoured group were not able to protect the 200-kilometre-long eastern flank and the equally long rear of the army group between Novorzhev and Lake Ilmen. SS

---

[62] Halder, *Diaries*, 211–12 (8 July 1941). On the vacillation concerning the use of Armd. Group 3 cf. sect. II.1.1(*b*) at n. 145.

[63] On 10 July 1941 the armoured group command took a similar view of the situation; in spite of all doubts, this seemed to be the only course that promised success (Chales de Beaulieu, *Panzergruppe 4*, 60). The general commanding XXXXI Armd. Corps had serious doubts because of the difficult terrain: report to Armd. Group 4, Müller-Hillebrand, Nordabschnitt, pt. 1, appendix D3, MGFA P-114a, printed in Chales de Beaulieu, *Panzergruppe 4*, 157–8, annexe 8.

[64] Pz.Gr.-Befehl [armd. gp. order] No. 11, 9 July 1941, and directive of the commander of the armoured group, 10 July 1941, BA-MA, Pz.Gr. 4, 18738/2; Chales de Beaulieu, *Panzergruppe 4*, 61—here also the assessment of difficulties involved in the attack. Leeb did not press for a change: cf. Leeb, *Tagebuchaufzeichnungen*, 290 (9 July 1941); cf. also below, n. 78.

Totenkopf Division, located to the right of LVI Armoured Corps and involved in hard fighting in Sebezh since 5 July, was also dependent on their support.[65] The commander of the armoured group therefore decided to skirt the difficult terrain and break strong enemy resistance by employing *all* his forces if he encountered serious difficulties.

As early as the second day of the attack it became evident that enemy resistance was stiffening and that the marshy forested terrain did not permit a rapid advance. Colonel-General Hoepner thereupon decided after reaching Zapole to have XXXXI Armoured Corps turn north about 40 kilometres from Luga to capture the ridge north of the lower Luga for an attack on Leningrad from the south-west. On 12 July the three mobile divisions began their advance in this direction; 269th Infantry Division took over the defence of the position already reached. This change of direction succeeded after two days and the corps advanced on the lower Luga and established bridgeheads across the river.[66] But this meant that direct contact with LVI Armoured Corps, which was pushing through equally difficult terrain towards Leningrad, had been lost. After capturing Porkhov on 11 July, 8th Armoured Division advanced towards the Mzha sector and was subjected to fierce attacks from all sides on 15 July. For a time it was cut off and had to withdraw. With the help of two divisions of I Army Corps of Eighteenth Army, the situation was stabilized.

It has already been pointed out that the order of the Army High Command of 9 July was incompatible with the original intentions and preparations of the army group with regard to the expansion of the operations area to the north-east as well as to the point of maximum effort. The immediate decision of the armoured group command to divert XXXXI Armoured Corps after realizing the difficulties involved in the advance on Luga and Novgorod was presumably also due to the desire to keep at least that corps intact for the attack on Leningrad.[67] The decision to keep back SS Totenkopf Division in spite of the critical difficulties Manstein was encountering supports this assumption. Halder's ready acceptance of the plan to use the armoured corps for a widely fanned-out attack in unsuitable terrain was probably due to the guiding principle of all previous German operations in the Soviet Union, the encirclement of enemy forces from both sides. Halder presumably considered the operation by Manstein's corps not only as the prelude to the creation of an eastern spearhead of an attack on Leningrad, but also as the future northern flank of an attack on Moscow. The constant 'removals' of units from Sixteenth Army, which were quite incompatible with its stated primary task of securing

---

[65] Cf. Manstein's account in *Lost Victories*, 193–4, and the statement of Chales de Beaulieu in *Panzergruppe 4*, 51–2.

[66] Chales de Beaulieu, *Panzergruppe 4*, 64 ff.; note of conversation between Leeb and Reinhardt, 13 July 1941, ibid., annexe 9; Manstein, *Lost Victories*, 196–7; Halder, *Diaries*, 1040–1 (14 July 1941).

[67] Collection of opinions on the continuation of the attack by Armd. Group 4 according to the diary of the armoured group, 15–18 July 1941: Müller-Hillebrand, Nordabschnitt, pt. I, appendix D8, MGFA P-114a; Pz.Gr. 4/Ia, KTB, BA-MA 18738/1.

the attack on Leningrad, can also be understood in this light.[68] On 14 June Hitler noticed that Armoured Group 4 was operating in a way completely contrary to his orders and reacted angrily.[69] He sent his adjutant, Colonel Robert Schmundt, to the army group and the armoured group. In answer to the question why the armoured group had not attacked Novgorod with a stronger right wing, Leeb replied that this situation had been an inevitable result of the fact that XXXXI Armoured Corps had made good progress while LVI Corps had encountered fierce resistance.[70]

In his order to the army group of 15 July Leeb assumed that enemy resistance would now be centrally directed and that the period of surprise thrusts was past.[71] Marshal Voroshilov was recognized as the driving force behind the increasingly stubborn Soviet resistance and counter-attacks along the front of Army Group North. At the same time the army group was tied down by hard fighting against enemy units which had been bypassed during the finger-like advance of the German armoured forces and were now being activated as part of a reorganization of the Red Army's defences. Leeb therefore ordered Armoured Group 4 to secure first the general line Novgorod–Luga–Narva and then to begin cutting the city off with the main effort in the south-east. The start of the attack by the right wing (LVI Armoured Corps) depended on the arrival of I Army Corps from Eighteenth Army to protect the flank. Two-thirds of Sixteenth Army were still tied down on the southern wing, co-operating with Ninth Army in the envelopment of the group of enemy forces around Nevel. Eighteenth Army was first to defeat the enemy in Estonia and then take Tallinn and Paltiski, and occupy the islands Hiiumaa (Dagö) and Saaremaa (Ösel) in the course of Operation Beowulf. It was also to send a corps to the area of Kingisepp subsequently to relieve the west wing of Armoured Group 4.

On 17 July the command of Army Group North summed up its assessment of the situation and future possibilities and came to the conclusion that the operations area, the strength of the German forces, and the stiffened enemy resistance made it advisable to carry out further operations in stages, and not at one stroke.[72] Consequently, Sixteenth Army would have to encircle the enemy forces confronting it or force them to withdraw eastward. The attack

---

[68] Manstein (*Lost Victories*, 197, 202) reports early knowledge of the intention to have Sixteenth Army attack in the direction of Moscow; Halder, *Diaries*, 1032–3 (12 July 1941). Cf. sect. II.1.1(*b*) at n. 145.

[69] Halder, *Diaries*, 1043–4 (14 July 1941).

[70] Leeb, *Tagebuchaufzeichnungen*, 296 (15 July 1941); Chales de Beaulieu, *Panzergruppe 4*, 22–3. On 11 July Hitler had already demanded that the left wing of Army Group Centre should be used to shorten the fighting of II Army Corps of Sixteenth Army; this was contrary to Halder's efforts to hold the forces of the army group together for the attack on Moscow: Halder, *Diaries*, 1032–3 (12 July 1941).

[71] Army group order, 15 July 1941, in Müller-Hillebrand, Nordabschnitt, pt. I, appendix D7, MGFA P-114a; excerpt in Chales de Beaulieu, *Panzergruppe 4*, 160.

[72] Situation assessment of Army Group North, 17 July 1941, in Müller-Hillebrand, Nordabschnitt, pt. I, appendix D9, MGFA P-114a; assessment of 19 July 1941, ibid., appendix D10; Leeb, *Tagebuchaufzeichnungen*, 298–9.

across the line Novgorod–Narva could take place only when I Army Corps had been reinforced with one or two additional corps. Until then it would be the task of Armoured Group 4 to push forward to that line. And for the attack on Estonia available forces were for the moment too small.[73] The army group command believed it could carry out the resupplying and especially the reorganization of its formations in such a way that a new attack in the direction of Leningrad could be started about 25 July.[74]

On 21 July Hitler arrived at Leeb's headquarters.[75] The commander-in-chief of the army group delivered an oral report on the situation and his plans. The armoured group would begin to cut Leningrad off from the rest of the Soviet Union as soon as sufficient infantry forces had been brought up. The capture of Tallinn, Paltiskis, and the islands of Hiiumaa and Saaremaa were secondary objectives. As a third objective Leeb mentioned the advance of Sixteenth Army along both sides of Lake Ilmen to cut the railway line between Moscow and Leningrad. Hitler pointed out the urgent need to capture Leningrad. Because of the uninterrupted flow of iron ore from Sweden the situation in the Gulf of Finland had to be 'taken care of'. The advance on Leningrad also had to result soon in the severing of the railway line to Moscow to prevent the transfer of Soviet forces there to other fronts and to the Soviet capital itself. For this purpose he was considering bringing up Armoured Group 3. Hitler expected stubborn resistance, as Leningrad had a symbolic significance for the Soviet regime.[76] This formulation, which reflected Hitler's basic conviction of the leadership function of the Communist Party as the decisive element in the resistance of the Red Army as well as the mobilizing of the civilian population, cannot, however, be separated from his assessment of the area around Leningrad as a strategic factor of primary importance. Not only did the last bastion of the Red Fleet in the Baltic have to be eliminated and a direct rail link between Germany and Finland established, but in and around Leningrad were located the most modern Soviet facilities for the production of tanks, artillery, and ammunition, which covered a substantial part of the requirements of the Red Army.

Army Group North did not include this possible armoured support in its 'Order for the Continuation of Operations' on 22 July.[77] Presented in the form of an oral report on the group's plans, this order had already been approved by Hitler. Points of friction between Hitler's headquarters and the army group could only concern the use of the forces available, and Hitler had already

---

[73] Chales de Beaulieu, *Panzergruppe 4*, 78–9; Manstein *Lost Victories*, 196–7; Leeb papers according to Leeb, *Tagebuchaufzeichnungen*, 298–9 n. 149; Brauchitsch's report after visit to army group command in Halder, *Diaries*, 1053–4 (17 July 1941).

[74] Halder, *Diaries*, 1054 (17 July 1941).

[75] Leeb, *Tagebuchaufzeichnungen*, 302–3 (21 July 1941); Halder, *Diaries*, 1066–7 (21 July 1941); *KTB OKW*, i. 1029–30, 17 July 1941 (76), 21 July 1941 (77).

[76] Objectives of Armd. Group 4 for the continuation of operations, 22 July 1941, in Chales de Beaulieu, *Panzergruppe 4*, 161–2, annexe 11.

[77] Müller-Hillebrand, Nordabschnitt, pt. I, appendix E2, MGFA P-114a.

explained his ideas in this respect in detail. Leeb sought a workable solution between the two points of main effort demanded for the attack and the single, concentrated thrust of an armoured spearhead demanded by Hoepner. First he placed an army corps under the command of each of the two attack spearheads, XXXXI and LVI Armoured Corps. The main point of the attack was between Lakes Ilmen and Peipus. There LVI Armoured Corps was to make the first thrust, advancing as far as the line Novgorod–Luga. Then XXXXI Armoured Corps with the attached XXXVIII Army Corps was to launch its attack from the west. As the attack progressed, Sixteenth Army headquarters would take over command of the entire right wing, including LVI Armoured Corps. But nothing had been said about the composition of the corps. Through reorganization and assignment of reserves most of the mobile troops could thus, after all, be united under one command, in the group formed by Hoepner.[78] Leeb believed that now, after the heavy casualties suffered by the enemy in the recent fighting, he could afford to keep the right flank relatively weak in favour of giving the group at the point of maximum effort more depth and perhaps employing the forces to the north-east, if that should become necessary.

Leeb's intentions show that at the end of July 1941 the German offensive in the sector for which Army Group North was responsible could be continued beyond the initial objectives but also that the enemy's fighting strength had still not been broken decisively. The main operational objectives would have to be addressed individually after the reorganization of the army group and systematic preparation. It became increasingly evident that the 'ideal solution'—isolating Leningrad while securing the long eastern front and at the same time taking the pressure off the northern flank of Army Group Centre with the forces of Army Group North alone—was unrealistic. Nevertheless, with regard to the near future the strategic results of Wehrmacht operations in the northern sector of the German eastern front were positive. Confining the 'Red Banner Baltic Fleet' to the area of Kronshtadt Bay and the conquest of the Baltic coast to a point west of Narva secured the vital Swedish iron-ore shipments, the sea links with Finland, and the supplying of the army group by sea.

(iii) THE BATTLES AT THE FRONTIER IN THE SECTOR OF ARMY
GROUP SOUTH AND THE GERMAN ADVANCE INTO THE UKRAINE
(See the Annexe Volume, Nos. 1 and 7)

Army Group South was under the command of Field Marshal von Rund-stedt and, according to 'Deployment Order Barbarossa', had the task of 'destroying the Soviet forces in Galicia and the western Ukraine still west of the Dnieper and capturing the Dnieper crossings at and south of Kiev at an

---

[78] Agreement had already been reached between Leeb, Busch, and Hoepner: Müller-Hillebrand, Nordabschnitt, pt. I, appendix E3; Leeb, Tagebuchaufzeichnungen, 303–4 (22 July 1941).

early stage'.[79] Halder's original plan of achieving these objectives with a large envelopment operation from southern Poland and Romania, combined with a pincer operation by German and Hungarian formations in Galicia, had been abandoned for various reasons after Hitler's decision of 17 March 1941.[80] Now the main thrust of the army group was concentrated on the line Lublin–Kiev, with the intention of reaching the same general objectives of this initial phase.

Nevertheless, within the German general staff the idea of a large-scale envelopment continued to form the basis for operational decisions made after the initial German attack.[81] Colonel-General Ritter von Schobert, for example, who had taken command of Eleventh Army in Romania on 24 May, informed the army group of his intention, in addition to defending and securing Romania's frontiers, of preparing the attack across the upper Prut to the north-east.[82] The army group left it to the Army High Command to decide when the rather risky dispersion of defensive forces along the Prut, which such preparations would require, could be carried out. The order for the attack was to be issued at the earliest five days after the reorganization.[83] The attack objective, Vinnitsa or the area north of it, was to be reached in co-operation with the adjacent Seventeenth Army.[84] This represented a return to at least a variant of Halder's draft plan of 5 December 1940,[85] but the delay, the basically different start of the attack, and the lack of the 'Carpathian Group' should not be overlooked.

Army Group South command assumed that after the German forces had broken through the weak Soviet frontier defences enemy resistance would be concentrated along the rivers at right angles to the direction of the attack and along fortified lines. It was believed that a broken line of fortifications existed along the Dniester from the river mouth via Mogilev to Novograd Volynskiy and Petrikov. Further west was the old Austrian and Polish line from Khotin via Ternopol, Brody, Kishinev, Hołowczyce (Golovchitsy), the course of the Rokhod, and Pinsk. Little was known about how well it had been maintained and strengthened. Kiev, Kolomyya, Lvov, Sambor, and Stanislav were

---

[79] Halder, *Kriegstagebuch*, ii. 465, and deployment order for Barbarossa, 31 Jan. 1941 (not in trans.).

[80] Cf. sect. I.IV.1(*f*) at n. 156.

[81] Cf. sect. II.I.1(*a*), at n. 88; H.Gr. Süd/Ia, KTB, 2 May 1941, BA-MA, RH 19 I/6, where, after Hitler's rejection of Halder's solution, in addition to the 'main case' the 'variant' of a double envelopment of the enemy in the area east of Lvov is mentioned as a possibility: Hauck, Südliches Gebiet, pt. I, 207 ff. (appendix 2), 223 ff. (appendix 4), MGFA P-114c.

[82] Schobert, however, considered the prospects for an attack to be, with few exceptions, unfavourable, and in some cases non-existent: AOK 11/Ia, KTB, BA-MA, RH 20-11/4a.

[83] On 3 June 1941 Army Group South had changed the orders for Eleventh Army accordingly. Instead of an incipient attack, only an imminent attack was to be feigned, which did not require a significant transfer of troops. This was the result of an order Halder had issued to Eleventh Army on 28 May 1941: H.Gr. Süd/Ia, KTB, BA-MA, RH 19 I/66.

[84] Order for preparation of deployment for Barbarossa, 28 May 1941, with annexes, BA-MA RH 20-11/4 a K.

[85] Cf. sect. I.IV.1(*e*) at n. 125.

thought to be fortified and would possibly slow the German advance. South-east of the Carpathians the main obstacles were the lowlands with their numerous rivers west of the Dniester, the Dniester itself, and its tributaries. Further east strong resistance was expected along the Dnieper and especially around Kiev.

For the attack Army Group South disposed of thirty-eight divisions, including armoured units, against eighty known enemy divisions. The deployment of the enemy units, especially the strong massing of troops near Lvov, indicated a defence planned close to the frontier. Because of the open right flank of Seventeenth Army (the frontier with Hungary) and the fact that Eleventh Army was not ready to attack, success depended on the mobile forces of Armoured Group 1 in the northern deployment area under Colonel-General von Kleist breaking through Soviet defences at a strategically import-ant point and then operating independently in the enemy's rear area. This basic idea dominated the conduct of operations. Sixth Army under Field Marshal Walter von Reichenau was to force an opening for the armour in enemy positions near the frontier and then follow the armoured units closely to destroy the enemy, provide assistance at river crossings, and cover the northern flank of the army group in the direction of the Pripet marshes. To accomplish the first task the armoured group was placed under the com-mander-in-chief of Sixth Army[86] and itself took over several infantry divisions of Sixth Army to ensure that transport movements could be carried out smoothly. The army group sought to forestall the danger of armoured forma-tions getting tied down in tactical tasks by issuing a directive that they were to be so used only on its orders.

Seventeenth Army under General Carl Heinrich von Stülpnagel was to cut off the area around Lvov and later, under cover provided by Armoured Group 1 and Sixth Army, to advance in the direction of Ternopol and Vinnitsa. Most of the German forces in Romania under Eleventh Army command were concentrated in the area north of Iași for the planned attack across the Prut. After the government of Romania had declared its readiness to participate actively and offensively in the war, the question of the command of Romanian forces and German forces assembled in Romania was solved by Marshal Antonescu being made their nominal commander, while the headquarters staff of Eleventh Army was to plan and supervise the actual execution of operations.[87] After a new agreement between Antonescu and the commander-in-chief of Eleventh Army had been reached on 19 June, the sector of the Romanian Fourth Army, which was entrusted with the security of the coast and the lower Prut, was left under the Romanian army command. The Romanian Third Army command and that of the Romanian IV Army Corps were excluded from controlling their units; they were placed under the direct

---

[86] The same resistance and doubts arose here as in Armd. Groups 2 and 3. It was up to the C.-in-C. of the army to devise a compromise.

[87] Cf. sect. I.v.3 at n. 87 (förster).

command of Eleventh Army. The staff of the Romanian Third Army retained responsibility only for supply operations.

On the first day of the attack the enemy seemed to be completely surprised along the entire front. Neither the tactical leadership nor measures taken by higher commands of the Red Army indicated a readiness for battle on short notice. German and Romanian forces were able to penetrate the enemy's most forward positions.[88] Even the Romanians were able to capture bridgeheads on their section of the Prut front. Halder's view that no enemy attack was to be expected there and his plan to reorganize Eleventh Army for an attack to the north-east as early as 24 June were thus confirmed.[89] But it was not yet possible to obtain a clear picture of Soviet intentions—whether to hold the area near the frontier under all circumstances or to withdraw. After the initial surprise, however, Soviet resistance also stiffened considerably in this sector. Counter-attacks with large forces significantly slowed the progress of the German advance. In contrast to the thrusts by the armoured units of the two army groups further north, the advance by Armoured Group 1 to the Styr between Dubno and Lutsk had to be carried out against frontally defending Soviet units, which also mounted dangerous attacks on the German flanks. The infantry divisions of Seventeenth Army attacking in the direction of Lvov also made only comparatively slow progress.[90]

The army group, however, still assumed that the enemy intended to evacuate the 'Lvov pocket'. On 24 June this assessment of the situation seemed to permit the cancellation of the subordination of Armoured Group 1 to Sixth Army and to enable its free operation east of the Styr. The commander-in-chief of the army group, Field Marshal von Rundstedt, decided, however, to wait until strong units of the two armoured corps involved (XXXXVIII and III) had crossed the river. By the evening of 24 June it was clear that the enemy had no intention of disengaging and that stubborn resistance had to be expected everywhere.[91] On the whole, however, the Army High Command believed that a disengagement in the area of Lvov could be expected. It was to be prevented by a thrust of Eleventh Army, which had to be ready to attack on 2 July.

On 25 June the dangerous extension of the right flank of Armoured Group 1 as a result of the slow progress of Seventeenth Army caused the army group command and the commanders of the two armies to consider whether the strong enemy forces west of Lvov could be cut off and the enemy front made to collapse by sending XIV Armoured Corps and XXXIV Army Corps (1st

[88] Halder, *Diaries*, 966–7 (22 June 1941).

[89] Ibid. 972 (24 June 1941); order to Eleventh Army: H.Gr. Süd/Ia, No. 1588/41, 25 June 1941, BA-MA RH 19 I/71.

[90] Army Group South urged a rapid thrust and, to make German formations available, ordered covering divisions and Slovak units to be brought up to the right wing of Seventeenth Army: H.Gr. Süd/Ia, KTB, 23 June 1941, BA-MA RH 19 I/71. Cf. the development of the organization of Army Group South Diagrams II.1.3–6.

[91] Halder, *Diaries*, 973 (25 June 1941); H.Gr. Süd/Ia, KTB, 24 June 1941, BA-MA RH 19 I/71.

DIAGRAM II.I.3. Order of Battle of Army Group South, 27 June 1941

Army Gp. South 99th Lgt. Div. Assgnd. Army High Cmd. reserves: Higher Cmd. XXXIV 68th Inf. Div. 132nd Inf. Div. (brgt. up from south-east 28 June–4 July) LI 79th Inf. Div. 95th Inf. Div. (transf. from Army Gp. D 27 June–3 July) 113th Inf. Div.	Armd. Gp. 1	XIV Mot.	SS Div. 'W' SS 'A.H.' 9th Armd. Div.
		III. Mot.	14th Armd. Div. 25th Mot. Div. 13th Armd. Div.
		XXXXVIII Mot.	11th Armd. Div. 16th Armd. Div. 16th Mot. Div.
	Sixth Army HQ 168th Inf. Div. 213th Sec. Div.	XXIX	299th Inf. Div. 44th Inf. Div.
		LV	111th Inf. Div. 75th Inf. Div.
		XVII	56th Inf. Div. 62nd Inf. Div. 298th Inf. Div.
		XXXXIV	297th Inf. Div. 57th Inf. Div. 9th Inf. Div. 262nd Inf. Div.
	Seventeenth Army HQ 125th Inf. Div. Slovak mot. unit	IV	296th Inf. Div. 24th Inf. Div. 295th Inf. Div. 71st Inf. Div. 97th Lgt. Div.
		XXXXIX Mtn.	4th Mtn. Div. 1st Mtn. Div. 257th Inf. Div. 100th Lgt. Div.
		LII	101st Lgt. Div.
		Cmdr. Rear Army Area 103	444th Sec. Div. 454th Sec. Div.
	Eleventh Army HQ Rom. Cav. Co. HQ	Military Mission Romania	72nd Inf. Div.
		Rom. Mtn. Co.	Rom. 7th Inf. Div. Rom. 2nd Mtn. Brig. Rom. 4th Mtn. Brig. Rom. 1st Mtn. Brig.
		XI	Rom. 8th Cav. Brig. Rom. 5th Cav. Brig. Rom. Mot. Mech. Brig. Rom. 6th Inf. Div. 22nd Inf. Div. 239th Inf. Div. 76th Inf. Div.
		XXX	Rom. 6th Cav. Brig. Rom. 14th Cav. Brig. Rom. 8th Inf. Div. 198th Inf. Div.
		LIV	170th Inf. Div. 50th Inf. Div.

Diagram II.1.4. Order of Battle of Army Group South, 4 July 1941

Army Group	Army HQ	Corps		Divisions

Army Gp. South
 	
71st Inf. Div.
60th Mot. Div.
 	
Assgnd. Army High Cmd. reserves:
 	
Higher Cmd. XXXIV
  132nd Inf. Div.
  98th Inf. Div.
  (from Army Gp. D UNTIL 8 July)
 	
LI
  79th Inf. Div.
  95th Inf. Div.
  113th Inf. Div.
  168th Inf. Div.
  (Higher Cmd. LXV until 13 July)
XXXX Mot.
	Armd. Gp. 1	XIV Mot.		SS Div. 'W'
				9th Armd. Div.

		III Mot.		SS 'A.H.' 25th Mot. Div. 14th Armd. Div. 13th Armd. Div.
		XXXXVIII Mot.		16th Mot. Div. 16th Armd. Div. 11th Armd. Div.
	Sixth Army HQ Cmdr. Rear Army Area South 213th Sec. Div. 68th Inf. Div.	XVII		99th Lgt. Div. 58th Inf. Div. 62nd Inf. Div.
		XXIX		298th Inf. Div. 299th Inf. Div. 44th Inf. Div.
		LV		111th Inf. Div. 75th Inf. Div. 262nd Inf. Div.
		XXXXIV		57th Inf. Div. 296th Inf. Div. 297th Inf. Div. 9th Inf. Div.
	Seventeenth Army HQ 454th Sec. Div. (at disposal of staff officer in charge of supply & admin.)	IV		125th Inf. Div. 24th Inf. Div. 295th Inf. Div. 97th Lgt. Div.
		XXXXIX Mtn.		4th Mtn. Div. 1st Mtn. Div. 257th Inf. Div.
		LII		Slovak Mot. Brig. 444th Sec. Div. 100th Lgt. Div. 101st Lgt. Div.
		Slovak Army Gp.		Slov. 2nd Inf. Div. Slov. 1st Inf. Div.
	Eleventh Army HQ 239th Inf. Div. 46th Inf. Div. (in transfer)	Rom. Third Army	Rom. Mtn. Corps	Rom. 4th Mtn. Brig. Rom. 1st Mtn. Brig. Rom. 2nd Mtn. Brig.
				Rom. 8th Cav. Brig. Rom. 7th Inf. Div.
		Rom. Cav. Co.		Rom. 6th Cav. Brig. Rom. 5th Cav. Brig.
		Rom. IV. Co.		Rom. 6th Inf. Div.
		XI		22nd Inf. Div. Rom. Armd. Brig. 76th Inf. Div.
		XXX		Rom. 13th Inf. Div. Rom. 14th Inf. Div. Rom. 8th Inf. Div. 198th Inf. Div. 170th Inf. Div.
		LIV		Rom. 5th Inf. Div. 50th Inf. Div.
		Army Mission Romania		72nd Inf. Div.

Armoured Division, SS Leibstandarte Adolf Hitler, and two infantry divisions) east of the city to attack from the rear. The armoured group and the general commanding XIV Armoured Corps, Gustav von Wietersheim, stated, however, that they were able to defend their right flank themselves. In the end Field Marshal von Rundstedt agreed. This averted the splitting of the ar-

DIAGRAM II.1.5. Order of Battle of Army Group South, 12 July 1941

Army Gp. South
 	
Hung. Mob. Co.
with:
  Hung. 1st Mot. Brig.
  Hung. 2nd Mot. Brig.
  Hung. 1st Cav. Brig.
 	
At disposal
of Army High
Cmd. in
Romania:
  Military
  Mission in
  Romania
 	
Assgnd.
Army High
Cmd. reserves:
 	
Hghr. Cmd.
XXXIV (at
Sixth Army HQ)
168th Inf. Div.
132nd Inf. Div.
 	
Li (at Sixyh
Army HQ)
95nd Inf. Div.
113nd Inf. Div.
	Armd. Gp. 1	XIV Mot.	SS Div. 'W'
			9th Armd. Div.

		III. Mot.	14th Armd. Div. 13th Armd. Div.
		XXXXVIII Mot.	16th Mot. Div. 16th Armd. Div. 11th Armd. Div. 60th Mot. Div.
	Sixth Army HQ 25th Mot. Div. 68th Inf. Div. 71st Inf. Div. to Higher Cmd. XXXIV	XVII	299th Inf. Div. 79th Inf. Div. 56th Inf. Div. 62nd Inf. Div.
		XXIX	298th Inf. Div. SS 'A.H.' 44th Inf. Div. 99th Lgt. Div.
		LV	111th Inf. Div. 75th Inf. Div. 296th Inf. Div. 262nd Inf. Div.
		XXXXIV	57th Inf. Div. 9th Inf. Div.
		IV	297th Inf. Div. 24th Inf. Div. 295th Inf. Div.
	Seventeenth Army HQ Slovak Mob. Brig. Pelfouzek	XXXXIX Mtn.	97th Lgt. Div. 4th Mtn. Div. 1st Mtn. Div. 125th Inf. Div.
		LII	257th Inf. Div. 101st Lgt. Div. 100th Lgt. Div.
	Cmdr. Rear Army Area South		454th Sec. Div. 444th Sec. Div. 213th Sec. Div.
		Slovak Army Gp.	Slovak 2nd Inf. Div. Slovak 1st Inf. Div.

DIAGRAM II.I.5. (*cont.*)

	Rom. Third Army	Rom. Mtn. Corps	Rom. 4th Mtn. Brig. Rom. 1st Mtn. Brig. Rom. 2nd Mtn. Brig.
	Rom. Fourth Co.	Rom. XI	Rom. 2nd Fort. Brig. Rom. 1st Fort. Brig.
		Rom. V Co.	Rom. 7th Cav. Brig. Rom. 21st Inf. Div. Rom. Guards Div.
98th Inf. Div. 294th Inf. Div. (unloading until 14 July)	Eleventh Army HQ	Rom. III Co.	Rom. Frontier Div. Rom. 15th Inf. Div. Rom. 11th Inf. Div.
XXXX Mot. (at Seventeenth Army HQ) 2nd Armd. Div. in transfer until 13 July)	46th Inf. Div. 73rd Inf. Div. (unloading until 13 July)	Rom. Cav. Co.	Rom. 6th Cav. Brig. Rom. 5th Cav. Brig. Rom. 8th Cav. Brig.
		XI	239th Inf. Div. 22nd Inf. Div. 76th Inf. Div.
94th Inf. Div. (at Seventeenth Army HQ)		Rom. IV Co.	Rom. 6th Inf. Div.
		XXX	Rom. 13th Inf. Div. Rom. 14th Inf. Div. Rom. 8th Inf. Div. 198th Inf. Div. 170 Inf. Div.
		LIV	Rom. 35th Inf. Div. 50th Inf. Div. Rom. 5th Inf. Div. 72nd Inf. Div. Rom. Armd. Brig.

moured group, for which a third spearhead had been envisaged in the area of Seventeenth Army once the 'armour road South' had been cleared.[92] In this situation the participation of Hungarian forces was of the greatest importance. But the Hungarian government wanted to receive an official German request for assistance. Along its Carpathian frontier only German radio-deception units were attempting to tie down enemy forces. But the attack of the Hungarian units was already being prepared in accordance with operational requirements of the German conduct of the war.[93] On the other hand, on 25 June the addition of three Italian divisions for Eleventh Army was announced, although their combat-readiness was considered limited.[94]

[92] This 'armour road' was to be constructed from Tomaszow to Ternopol and on towards Proskurov; a second was to extend from Sokal towards Berdichev, and a third via Lutsk and Zhitomir towards Kiev.

[93] Cf. sect. I.IV.1(*f*) at n. 150; Halder, *Diaries*, 979 ff. (27 June 1941).

[94] Cf. sect. II.IV.1(*d*) (Förster).

The realization that, in regard to his will to fight, toughness, and leadership, the enemy had to be taken seriously and that the crisis of the frontier battles still had to be faced caused the chief of the general staff of the army group, General Georg von Sodenstern, to consider new operational

DIAGRAM II.1.6. Order of Battle of Army Group South, 19 July 1941

	Armd. Gp. I	III Mot.	SS 'A.H' 14th Armd. Div. 13th Armd. Div. 25th Mot. Div.
		XIV Mot.	60th Mot. Div. SS Div. 'W' 9th Armd. Div.
		XXXXVIII	16th Mot. Div. 16th Armd. Div. 11th Armd. Div.
Army Gp.South At disposal of Army High Cmd. in Romania: Army High Cmd. reserves assigned to Army Mission in Romania: Higher Cmd. XXXIV (at Armd. Gp. I) 132nd Inf. Div. 98th Inf. Div. 294th Inf. Div. XXXX Mot. (at Seventeenth Army HQ) 2nd Armd. Div. 94th Inf. Div. (at Seventeenth Army HQ)	Sixth Army HQ 56th Inf. Div. 44th Inf. Div.	XVII	299th Inf. Div. 79th Inf. Div. 298th Inf. Div. 62nd Inf. Div.
		XXIX	95th Inf. Div. 99th Lgt. Div. 113th Inf. Div.
		LI	71st Inf. Div. 262nd Inf. Div. 296th Inf. Div.
		LV	168th Inf. Div. 111th Inf. Div. 75th Inf. Div.
	Group Schwedler (under Armd. Gp. I)	XXXXIV	68th Inf. Div. 57th Inf. Div. 9th Inf. Div.
		IV	297th Inf. Div. 24th Inf. Div. 295th Inf. Div.
	Seventeenth Army HQ	XXXXIX Mtn.	125th Inf. Div. 99th Lgt. Div. 4th Mtn. Div. 1st Mtn. Div. Slovak Mobile Brig.
		LII	257th Inf. Div. 101st Lgt. Div. 100th Lgt. Div.
		Hung. Mobile Corps	Hung. 1st Cav. Brig. Hung. 2nd Cav. Brig. Hung. 1st Mot. Brig.

DIAGRAM II.1.6. (*cont.*)

		Rom. Third Army	Rom. Mtn. Co.	Rom. 4th Mtn. Brig. / Rom. 1st Mtn. Brig. / Rom. 2nd Mtn. Brig.
			Rom. Cav. Co.	Rom. 6th Cav. Brig. / Rom. 5th Cav. Brig. / Rom. 8th Cav. Brig.
		Rom. IV Co.		Rom. 6th Inf. Div.
		XI		239th Inf. Div. / 22nd Inf. Div. / 76th Inf. Div.
	Eleventh Amry HQ 46th Inf. Div. 73rd Inf. Div. (unloading until 26 July)	XXX		Rom. 13th Inf. Div. / Rom. 14th Inf. Div. / Rom. 8th Inf. Div. / 198th Inf. Div. / 170th Inf. Div.
Cmdr. Rear Army Area South (at Armd. Gp. 1): 454 at disposal of staff officer in charge supply & admin. 444th Sec. Div. 213th Sec. Div. Slovak Army Gp. Slov. 2nd Inf. Div. Slov. 1st Inf. Div.	Ital. Mobile Army Corps (in transfer 13 July– 3 Aug.)	LIV		50th Inf. Div. / Rom. 5th Inf. Div. / 72nd Inf. Div. / Rom. Armd. Brig. / Rom. 15th Inf. Div.
		Rom. Fourth Army	Rom. III Co.	Rom. Frontier Div. / Rom. 11th Inf. Div.
		35th and 7th Inf. Divs. (in transfer)	Rom. V Co.	Rom. 7th Cav. Brig. / Rom. 21st Inf. Div. / Rom. Guards Div.
			Rom. XI	Rom. 2nd Fort. Brig. / Rom. 1st Fort. Brig.

measures.[95] If it was not possible, before the momentum of the German attack and the limited German reserves were exhausted, to defeat the enemy around Lvov and in front of Sixth Army, which was continuously bringing up reinforcements, the army group would not be able to fulfil its task of encircling and destroying Soviet forces west of the Dnieper. Then a considerably more limited attack by Eleventh Army would have to be carried out, not across the Dnieper but to the north against Proskurov, and, moreover, the armoured groups would have to attack considerably earlier towards the south-east in order to encircle the enemy east of Lvov.

This revision of the army group's original operational intentions was expressed in its Directive No. 1 of 26 June.[96] On the one hand the armoured

---

[95] H.Gr. Süd/Ia, KTB, 25 June 1941, BA-MA RH 19 I/71, situation assessment, 26 June 1941, early morning (copy); Hauck, *Südliches Gebiet*, pt. 1, 228 ff., appendix 5, MGFA P-114c.

[96] Copy in Hauck, *Südliches Gebiet*, pt. 1, 233 ff., appendix 6, MGFA P-114c.

group was removed from the command authority of Sixth Army and ordered to thrust eastward as rapidly as possible to encircle the enemy in front of the army group and in the Carpathian bend in co-operation with Eleventh Army. On the other hand, a more limited envelopment was recommended as an alternative. This required the armoured group first to reach the area of Shepetovka and then turn south-east. It also had to adjust to the new situation in so far as it was required to advance with three spearheads on Berdichev–Zhitomir without taking into consideration its long flanks. XIV Armoured Corps, the southern group, was to advance as early as possible and with 'all available forces' against Brody and then cross the Goryn on a broad front. Seventeenth Army was ordered to continue its attacks with the main point of effort north of Lvov. In its deliberations Eleventh Army was to assume that the Italians would arrive about 10 July and that they would be used in the offensive against Kishinev. By then the Romanian forces on the lower Prut were to be brought forward to the Dniester.

This directive of the army group took into account the greatly reduced fighting power of the infantry units, but it also called into question the task of the army group as a whole. Instead of along the Dnieper, enemy forces were to be annihilated solely along the Ukranian Bug. Halder also based his plans now on this more narrow encirclement, for which Eleventh Army would be barely adequate.[97] This attack plan, which seemed to be the most probable at the time, contained the partition of the armoured group into a spearhead turning to the south-east and a second one attacking in the direction of Kiev. In addition to advancing eastward towards Kovel and securing the railway between Khelm, Kovel, and Lutsk, Sixth Army, which felt threatened on its left flank, was now to secure both flanks of the armoured group as long as Seventeenth Army was still fighting west of the area around Grodze and Tsolkeev.

On 27 June, the day after this adjustment of the operational plan of Halder and Army Group South to the changed situation, it became evident around Lvov that the Soviet armies were withdrawing.[98] The Soviet defenders in front of Seventh Army withdrew to the east, covered by strong protecting forces and local counter-attacks, including armoured units. The armoured group succeeded in crossing the Goryn against strong resistance by rearguard units and ambushes by Soviet formations that had been overrun. Sixth Army pushed its northern wing further in the direction of Kovel. Two divisions (168th Infantry Division and 99th Light Division) had to be brought up from the reserves to eliminate strong enemy groups in the rear area between the Bug and the Luga.

An analysis of the situation showed that the enemy intended to establish a new front modelled on older positions in the line from Novograd Volynskiy to

---

[97] Halder, *Diaries*, 979–80 (27 June 1941). This attack had been discussed with Brauchitsch on 26 June at Army Group South command: H.Gr. Süd/Ia, KTB, 26 June 1941, BA-MA RH 19 I/71.
[98] H.Gr. Süd/Ia, KTB, 27 June 1941, BA-MA RH 19 I/71.

Shepetovka and Setsuveni (Dniester). The army group ordered an immediate pursuit by Seventeenth Army to prevent the enemy from occupying positions in the new line. Through his adjutant, Colonel (General Staff) Schmundt, Hitler informed the army group that reaching a set geographical objective was less important than destroying the 'vital strength' of the enemy. Where that was done was not important. Hitler thus agreed to drop the rigid requirement that Kiev should be captured before the army group could turn south. The army group then chose Berdichev, a town behind the line of Soviet fortifications, as the new point at which the armoured group should turn south.

On 28 June the idea of using XIV Armoured Corps, which had not yet seen action, on the right flank of the armoured group to broaden the armoured wedge, an idea first considered on 26 June, was revived. The armoured group command would have preferred to send this corps to the two other armoured corps in order to be able, in deep echelon, to attack and break through the line of fortifications near Novograd Volynskiy. Mainly, however, the armoured group wanted to avoid being tied down in the tactical fighting on the left wing of Seventeenth Army.[99] But Rundstedt ordered the corps to be employed only after the 'armour road south' had been cleared by Seventeenth Army. This also seemed advisable with regard to the decision to be taken as to whether, after the breakthrough had been achieved, one or two armoured spearheads should attack towards Kiev or to the south-east. The Soviet positions in the line of fortifications were to be penetrated 'without engaging in major frontal attacks', which caused Halder to consider how the army group could best be organized for this purpose.[100]

At this time Armoured Group I and Sixth Army were involved in repulsing persistent enemy counter-attacks, which achieved deep penetrations near Dubno and prevented a rapid advance to the east. Directive No. 2 of the army group,[101] issued on 30 June, was, however, based entirely on the idea of pursuing the enemy as quickly as possible and penetrating the fortified line along with him to prevent him from occupying the fortifications there. Only then was the large envelopment movement to be begun that was intended to create the conditions for ending the campaign in the operational area of Army Group South before the onset of winter. Eleventh Army was to advance from the south towards Vinnitsa, break the defence of the fortified line together with Seventeenth Army, and cut off the retreat of the enemy troops to the south-east. The Italian corps would be used on the west wing; the Romanian units would provide flank cover along the Dniester. A new arrival was the Hungar-

---

[99] H.Gr. Süd/Ia, KTB, 28 June 1941. A strong argument against bringing XIV Armd. Corps up behind III Armd. Corps (in the direction of Kiev) was that the 'armour road' to the north would be needed for supply transports of the field office of the General Staff Supply Officer South as soon as supply facilities in Rovno were completed.

[100] H.Gr.-Befehl [army gp. order], 28 June 1941, copy: Hauck, *Südliches Gebiet*, pt. 1, 238, appendix 7, MGFA P-114c; Halder, *Diaries*, 985–6 (29 June 1941).

[101] Hauck, *Südliches Gebiet*, pt. 1, 241, appendix 9, MGFA P-114c; H.Gr. Süd/Ia, KTB, 29 June 1941, BA-MA, RH 19 I/71.

ian VIII Army Corps, which, via Stanislav, was to advance across the
Carpathians towards the Dniester after 2 July. Seventeenth Army would move
towards Proskurov via Ternopol and tie down enemy forces 'with unremitting
attacks'. Sixth Army would thrust towards Berdichev with most of its forces,
while at the same time protecting the northern flank. III Armoured Corps,
advancing towards Zhitomir, was to be given sufficient infantry forces capable
of closely following the corps. After the successful breakthrough towards
Berdichev, this corps was to be employed near Kiev to establish a bridgehead
across the Dnieper. If the armoured divisions were not able to break through,
they were to go on the defensive and wait for the arrival of the infantry of Sixth
Army. If the breakthrough succeeded, most of the armoured group was to turn
south-east. But first the breakthrough had to be achieved. In the sector of
Seventeenth Army, Lvov was taken on this day.[102]

A reorganization of Army Group South was undertaken for the phase of the
attack beginning on 2 July. Except for indispensable covering forces, the seven
German divisions in Romania—another was being transferred there—were
moved forward to the northern wing of Eleventh Army. Two Slovak divisions
replaced the two covering divisions with Seventeenth Army. The Slovak
motorized brigade, on the other hand, was placed under LII Army Corps.[103]
Additional corps commands and divisions as well as artillery from Army
Group Centre were intended to guarantee the success of the group at the
centre of Sixth Army's attack. An armoured corps command with 2nd Armoured Division was envisaged for Seventeenth Army. The total result was a
considerable increase in the number of strong formations, to which it was
planned to add three Italian formations under a corps command and three
Hungarian mobile brigades of the 'Mobile Corps'.[104]

The question of a single command of the infantry and armoured units in the
attack sector of Armoured Group 1 was settled by a compromise. For the time
being, the armoured group was not placed under Sixth Army. But Rundstedt
did order that the army should immediately take over command of the
armoured group if a more massive support of its attack by infantry units
should become necessary and it were not able to operate independently.[105]

The addition of fresh divisions was intended not only to strengthen the
stronger wing of the attack for the planned breakthrough of the Stalin line, but
also to secure the left wing against Soviet units operating from the Pripet area.
Information gathered by signal intelligence indicated that seven divisions were
located there under the command of the Soviet Fifth Army. At the same time
the continuing fighting in the rear operations area required the use of combat

---

[102] H.Gr. Süd/Ia, KTB, 30 June 1941, BA-MA RH 19 I/71.

[103] This international contingent created several problems, as the Italians could not be sent into
action on the Black Sea and the Hungarians and Romanians could not be used in neighbouring
sectors. The Drogobych oilfield had to be protected from seizure by the Hungarians; the Slovak
Army Group was to be used for this purpose. Cf. sect. II.iv.1(c) (Förster).

[104] Cf. the development of the structure of Army Group South, Diagrams II.1.3–6.

[105] H.Gr. Süd/Ia, KTB, 30 June 1941, BA-MA RH 19 I/71.

troops in addition to the security forces there. Although Halder did not see any danger to operations in this situation, he intensely disliked using for such tasks any infantry divisions urgently needed for the attack.[106] Hitler was also worried about the danger of flank attacks; an 'offensive mopping-up' of the area, using troops of both army groups, was ordered.[107]

The attack of Sixth Army was obstructed by vigorous attacks of the Soviet Fifth Army, supported by armoured troops, from the Pripet marshes, attacks which were dangerous primarily because they severed supply-lines.[108] Halder released army reserves on the left wing of the army group to eliminate these disruptions. Sixth Army headquarters ordered XVII Army Corps to use four divisions to comb the forested area. In the north Army Group Centre sent Higher Command XXXV against Pinsk in a move to meet the forces of Sixth Army.[109] By very skilful tactical manœuvring the Soviet Fifth Army was able to avoid a decisive encounter with these groups and concentrated on flank attacks against Sixth Army, which was advancing towards Kiev. After reaching Slutsk on 7 July, Sixth Army abandoned attempts to fight its way through the impassable area, suffering further losses, and continued its advance along the southern edge of the marshes. The resulting uncertainty on the left flank of Army Group South with the constant threat to the vital communications lines to Zhitomir, and the hard and costly fighting with 'nests of Russians' in the rear area, affected not only operations but also the fighting ability of small units and even individuals. Troops who were neither trained nor equipped for combat in the marshy forests were easily ambushed, and the terrain presented almost insurmountable obstacles to the movement of vehicles and heavy weapons. This combination of the individual German soldier's insecurity against the possibility of surprise attack and an extremely hostile natural environment led to the use of the 'most brutal methods' to defeat the enemy, who for his part found ideal conditions in the marshes not only for regular troops but also for partisan groups.

In spite of these difficulties, the offensive of the German forces at the main

---

[106] On the intentions of Army Group South cf. Halder, *Diaries*, 985 ff. (29 June 1941). On 1 July penetrations of the flank of the armoured group by enemy forces from the Pripet area were reported: ibid. 995 (2 July 1941).

[107] Ibid.; H.Gr. Süd/Ia, KTB, 1 July 1941, copy, Hauck, *Südliches Gebiet*, pt. 1, 248, appendix 11, MGFA P-114c.

[108] Halder, *Diaries*, 1008 (6 July 1941). Cf. also the text preceding n. 125 above, and the first passage of sect. II.1.1(b)(ii) below. According to a report of Army Group South of 3 July and the talk between Halder and Sodenstern of 6 July 1941, the army group was to employ strong forces of the Army High Command reserve on the left wing in order to keep the left flank of III Armd. Corps free for the thrust to Kiev. Moreover, the commander of rear army area 103 (south) was to be involved by Eleventh Army headquarters. It should be noted that in his draft plan for the operation Sodenstern wanted to launch an independent army group against the Soviet forces in the Pripet marshes (cf. sect. I.IV.1(d) n. 117); Hitler considered this plan, but Halder rejected it. Cf. Philippi, 'Das Pripjetproblem', 14–15. Philippi does not seem to have had access to the two versions of the Pripet study by Foreign Armies East.

[109] Report by Col. (ret.) Zerbels on the difficulties of this operation in Philippi, 'Das Pripjetproblem', 32–3.

point of attack (Armoured Group I and Sixth Army) achieved a penetration of the Stalin line on 5 July. On 7 July the armoured group reached Berdichev and on 9 July Zhitomir. The right wing of Sixth Army advanced on Ternopol with Seventeenth Army, which was under less pressure because of the advance of the Hungarians from the Carpathians.[110] On the southern wing, however—contrary to the assumed general withdrawal of Soviet armies in front of the army group—Soviet forces slowed the progress of Eleventh Army by staging fierce attacks with motorized formations against the Romanian Fourth Army and the German units remaining there. Heavy rains created additional problems and made the movements of the army group more difficult. In any case, it was clear that Eleventh Army would no longer be able to reach the area around Vinnitsa in time to co-operate tactically with Sixth Army.[111]

To understand the decisions that had to be taken after the capture of Zhitomir, it is necessary to take a closer look at the thinking of Hitler, Halder, and the army group command. When Army Group South resumed its advance and the Białystok pocket was closed in the sector of Army Group Centre, Hitler began to consider the next strategic objectives of the campaign in the east and the required forces.[112] He assumed that after Fourth Armoured Army had reached Smolensk a decision would have to be taken as to whether the main thrust of further operations should be towards Leningrad, Moscow, or the area around the Sea of Azov. Hitler demanded that, if Armoured Group I did not have sufficient forces after reaching Zhitomir to turn the enemy's flank in the south-east, strong armoured forces from Army Group Centre should be brought up, as this would be most in accord with the idea of annihilating the enemy.[113]

Halder intervened early in the deliberations of Army Group South about decisions to be taken after the breakthrough towards Zhitomir and Berdichev had been achieved. From the beginning of the offensive, on 3 July, the army group believed that, after breaking through the fortified line with the bulk of its armoured formations, it would be able to advance to the south-east from the area of Berdichev to link up with Eleventh Army. At the same time Kiev was to be attacked by an armoured corps and infantry.[114] The question of the attack on Kiev was at first closely connected with the question of whether most of the enemy forces would withdraw behind the Dnieper or whether the order to encircle large enemy forces 'west of the Dnieper'—estimated at twenty-

[110] These reached the Dniester near Zaleshchiki and Nizhniev on 6 July. On 7 July Army Group South was informed that the Hungarian army continued fighting and that the mobile brigades, combined under a corps command, would be placed under the army group as of 9 July. The remaining mobile units became occupation troops under the 'Carpathian Corps': H.Gr. Süd/Ia, KTB, 7 July 1941, BA-MA RH 19 I/71.

[111] Hauck, Südliches Gebiet, pt. I, 55, MGFA P-114c; KTB OKW i. 509 ff. (5–11 July 1941).

[112] KTB OKW i. 1020 (66), (67), (68), 3–5 July 1941; Halder, Diaries, 1000 (3 July 1941). Cf. sect. II.I.1(b).

[113] KTB OKW i. 1021 (69), (70), 8 July 1941.

[114] Halder, Diaries, 1002–3 (5–6 July 1941); H.Gr. Süd/Ia, KTB, 3 July 1941, BA-MA RH 19 I/71.

eight divisions—could still be carried out. If the enemy withdrew beyond the Dnieper, the spearhead achieving the breakthrough towards Berdichev and Zhitomir would then advance on Kiev and Cherkassy and Eleventh and Seventeenth Armies would move directly eastward towards the Dnieper, with cover provided by Romanian forces in the south and Hungarian forces in the north. The great battle of annihilation could then take place east of the Dnieper, perhaps in the area of Poltava. These considerations formed the background for the measures of the army group command and were reported to Hitler by his army adjutant, Major Gerhard Engel, who visited the army group on 4–5 July.[115]

Because of supply problems, the attack on Kiev could have as its objective only the establishment of a bridgehead, as the armoured group estimated that it would not be able to conduct a large-scale action until after a pause in operations. The thrust west of the Dnieper towards the south-east was considered the only realistic possibility. The army group command shared the view of the armoured group but insisted, for the operational reasons mentioned above, that III Armoured Corps should attack Kiev. This view was supported by the operations department. For this reason the creation of an 'attack group Kiev' was begun on 7 July. As the Army High Command rejected the creation of a special operations staff because of the shortage of reserves, the command of XVII Army Corps, under General Werner Kienitz, was placed in charge of the attack group ('attack group Kienitz'). The group was to consist of III Armoured Corps and XXIX and XVII Army Corps with the divisions assigned to them. LI Army Corps with four divisions might also be assigned to the group later.

But Halder had still not decided whether the withdrawal of the enemy (to avoid encirclement by Eleventh and Seventeenth Armies) would end far beyond the Dnieper or was mainly intended to make possible the establishment of a strong defence and the creation of reserves.[116] Late in the evening of 7 July he pressed the commander of Army Group South to carry out a close encirclement with the armoured group, as Hitler desired. Afterwards the group was to push on to the Dnieper between Kiev and Cherkassy.[117] This splitting of the armoured group necessitated the definitive abandonment of the breakthrough of the enemy front near Kiev, envisaged in the operations plan.

The successful breakthrough of the armoured group and Sixth Army on 8 July meant that a decision about the course of further operations could not be

---

[115] H.Gr. Süd/Ia, KTB, 4–5 July 1941, BA-MA RH 19 I/71.

[116] Halder, *Diaries*, 1011–12 (7 July 1941).

[117] '. . . as preparation for a new operation to be ordered by the Army High Command beyond the river': H.Gr. Süd/Ia, KTB, 7 July 1941, BA-MA RH 19 I/71; teletype message OKH/GenStdH/Op.Abt. (IS) No. 1347, 8 July 1941, to H.Gr. Süd, BA-MA RH 2/1 326. According to this message, elements of Armd. Group 1, in co-operation with Eleventh Army, were to cut the enemy off west of Vinnitsa; a second group was to be moved against Dnepropetrovsk to attack enemy lines of communication. Other elements and infantry were to establish a bridgehead near Kiev: Halder, *Diaries*, 1021, 1023 (9, 10 July 1941).

postponed. Before the decision could be taken, however, Field Marshal von Reichenau suggested to the army group command that the direction of the attack on Kiev should be entrusted to his command and that IV Army Corps (of Seventeenth Army) should be placed under Sixth Army to form a group named after the general commanding the corps, General Viktor von Schwedler, which, initially also under the command of Sixth Army headquarters and then under Armoured Group 1, was to advance to the south-east. Rundstedt agreed to this proposal.[118] (See the Annexe Volume, No. 6.)

After agreement with the Army General Staff, Army Group South issued its directive for the continuation of operations on 9 July.[119] The main objective of the army group, the annihilation of the encircled enemy forces west of the Dnieper in a co-ordinated effort by all armies in the area of Vinnitsa, was retained. An additional, new objective was, however, the establishment of a deep bridgehead east of the Dnieper near Kiev. In accordance with these plans the armies, or their corps divided into groups, were sent into battle. It was typical of the organization of the German forces that the northern group of Sixth Army, which was to attack Kiev, was additionally to take over command of the armoured corps only when the infantry divisions went into action in the battle to capture the city. The aim of this plan was to prevent the mobile units from being tied to the infantry army. The main task of the bulk of the armoured group remained, however, to annihilate enemy forces near Vinnitsa and advance to the line Gaysin–Uman. At the same time lesser forces were to push on to the south-east to cut the main lines of communication across the Dnieper and thus prevent the removal of important industrial and other equipment by the Red Army. The request to Air Fleet 4 to give most of its tactical support, especially that provided by Stuka (dive-bomber) formations, to the parts of Armoured Group 1 and Sixth Army attacking Kiev, and to concentrate its strategic support on the sector of the enemy front assigned to Armoured Group 1, shows clearly the different priorities given to these two objectives.

The resulting argument about whether to attack Kiev requires a more detailed analysis. It can be assumed that at first Hitler was not primarily interested in occupying the city of Kiev, but rather in destroying all enemy forces west of the Dnieper.[120] This idea was also reflected in Halder's previously mentioned suggestion of 9 July[121] that the army group should not concentrate from the very beginning on forming a large encirclement ring, but

[118] This meant the end of the 'Group Kienitz'. Reichenau wanted to advance against Kiev with III Armd. Corps, XXIX Army Corps, and LI Army Corps under his direct command; 'Group Schwedler' was to be formed from IV, XXXIV, and LV Army Corps: H.Gr. Süd/Ia, KTB, 8 July 1941, BA-MA RH 19 I/71. Cf. structure of Army Group South, Diagrams II.1.3–6.
[119] Cf. teletype message OKH No. 1347 (above, n. 117); army group directive in Hauck, Südliches Gebiet, pt. 1, 249, appendix 12, MGFA P-114c.
[120] For this purpose he wanted to use Armd. Group 2 east of the Dnieper to the south or southeast: Halder, Diaries, 1015–16 (8 July 1941); cf. paragraphs preceding nn. 135 and 146 below.
[121] Cf. n. 117 above.

rather on smashing the enemy in a close encirclement with a direct thrust to the south from the area of Berdichev. The army group, on the other hand, wanted to include the area around Belaya Tserkov in a larger envelopment. On the basis of the experience gained in operations around Białystok, Halder concluded that the enemy could succeed in breaking out of an encirclement if sufficient infantry forces did not closely follow the advancing armoured units.

On the morning of 9 July it became evident that the forces of the army group were perhaps not sufficient for the double task it had been given. The operations department of the Army General Staff informed the army group that Brauchitsch and Halder had doubts about the wisdom of withdrawing XVII Army Corps from covering the northern flank along the Pripet marshes. These doubts were given concrete support by a report from Sixth Army command which arrived at the same time and which stated that both the commander-in-chief and the chief of the general staff were 'very impressed' by the immense expanse of the area. They demanded that XVII Army Corps with at least three divisions be used to cover the northern flank east of Novograd Volynskiy. The army command doubted that XXIX and LI Army Corps alone would be sufficient for an attack on Kiev and suggested that LV Army Corps should be brought from the start. But, excluding reserves, that would leave the army with only two corps for the turn to the south-east. This situation would develop only if III Armoured Corps did not succeed with the first assault in capturing the bridgehead at Kiev, which would therefore necessitate a systematic attack with strong infantry forces.[122]

The army group command agreed with this reasoning but still argued that the attempt had to be made to take Kiev by surprise with III Armoured Corps. Halder approved 'with reservations' the view which Sodenstern expressed with such certainty. But at the same time he repeated the urgent wish of the commander-in-chief of the army that most of the armoured group should not turn south-east but, after reaching Belaya Tserkov, to the south, towards Uman, to form a 'safe' pocket.[123]

The decisive factor was the demand of the army group to place LI Army Corps and the army reserves assigned to Sixth Army under its command to enable Sixth Army if necessary to take Kiev in an infantry attack. Asked by the operations department what forces would then be available to secure the rear area, Sodenstern replied that none were available and that therefore at least two additional divisions would be necessary. But they were not available.[124] After these deliberations became known, Hitler reacted immediately. Early in the morning of 10 June, two hours after Halder's discussion with Sodenstern, he forbade an attack on Kiev with armour but without sufficient infantry support. Sixth Army command was informed immediately and claimed that sufficient infantry forces for an attack on Kiev could not be expected until the

---

[122] H.Gr. Süd/Ia, KTB, 9 July 1941, BA-MA RH 19 I/71, directive No. 3 for the continuation of operations.
[123] Ibid.   [124] Ibid.

end of July, unless the weather and thus the terrain became more favourable and there were no further major battles west of Kiev. Headquarters also pointed out the 'unimaginable difficulties' in penetrating the forest area east of Sarny and the need to bring up new covering forces to free XVII Army Corps on the northern flank.[125]

With Hitler's order and the report from Sixth Army headquarters, the decision against a double offensive by the army group—against Kiev and Belaya Tserkov—had been taken. By comparison the reports of the commander-in-chief of the army during his visit to the command of Army Group South on 10 July had only an interpretative character. Brauchitsch brought Hitler's order that after reaching the line Zhitomir–Berdichev the most forward units of Armoured Group 1 should be turned south immediately to block the Bug at and south of Vinnitsa for the enemy's retreat, and if possible to link up with Eleventh Army. The parts of Armoured Group 1 further to the rear were to provide cover in the direction of Kiev; an attack on the city with insufficient forces was expressly forbidden. But Hitler left the final decision about the future conduct of operations in the hands of the command of Army Group South: 'Should it become apparent that there are no large bodies of enemy forces left to cut off west of the Bug, Armoured Group 1 will be massed for an advance on Kiev and the Dnieper line to the south-east. Investment must be executed in such a way as to bar enemy reinforcements from reaching the city from the north-west.'[126]

Perhaps Rundstedt and Sodenstern, given their roughly comparable responsibility in the decision about the encirclement of the British Expeditionary Force at Dunkirk, would have reached a clear decision on their own. For the army group wanted to take Kiev and saw no chance to destroy the bulk of the enemy forces even in a close encirclement to the south. The slow progress of Eleventh Army as well as of the formations of Sixth Army envisaged for the encirclement were reasons to choose a broader envelopment operation. But the fact that the enemy units west of Kiev would have to withdraw through the city and across the bridges there represented a good reason for capturing the town. Rundstedt was able to point out that Hitler's written order, unlike Halder's telephoned instructions, did not absolutely forbid any attack on Kiev.[127] Brauchitsch favoured postponing the decision on a close or broad encirclement. After the capture of Belaya Tserkov the then available picture of the enemy's position and intentions would determine whether the direction of

---

[125] Ibid. The Slovak army group was envisaged for the southern part of the rear army area and 294th Inf. Div., which was being brought up, for the northern part.

[126] Halder, *Diaries*, 1022 ff. (10 July 1941). The main idea was thus the encirclement of strong enemy forces. Details of this development in war diary of Army Group South, 10 July 1941, BA-MA RH 19 I/71. On the comparison with Dunkirk cf. Jacobsen, *Dünkirchen*, 70 ff., and *KTB OKW* i. 179E.

[127] Halder, *Diaries*, 1022 ff. (10 July 1941). The operations department was represented by two officers accompanying Brauchitsch. Hitler took his decision after Halder's oral report; Halder strongly emphasized the tasks given Army Group South in the deployment directive.

the attack would be south or south-east. Hitler approved this solution and requested that care be taken to draw the armoured group together there and avoid endangering its northern flank.

With regard to Kiev the commander-in-chief of the army was of the opinion that 'an advance on Kiev' would definitely 'be in line with appropriate cover for the northern flank'.[128] If an opportunity presented itself to capture the city, that would be compatible with the army group's orders. This interpretation provided no help. Neither Reichenau, who was at first absolutely certain and whose doubts and demands have already been described, nor the army group command could accept the idea of capturing the city by surprise. The units indispensable for infantry fighting were not available, as the encirclement of the bulk of the enemy forces in co-operation with Eleventh and Seventeenth Armies had priority.[129]

This meant that, for various reasons, the army group had failed in its efforts to carry out both operations at the same time. This fact was taken into account in a supplement to Directive No. 3.[130] But the way Brauchitsch had pointed out was left open. The army group ordered III Armoured Corps to provide flank cover in the area north-east of Zhitomir, but thereafter the corps was to continue the attack against the Kiev bridgehead within the framework of Sixth Army's operations. The armoured group command was informed that a surprise capture of Kiev could be carried out if a favourable opportunity presented itself which the commander on the scene believed he could exploit without exposing himself to the danger of a setback. Thus the decision was finally left to the lowest-ranking commander.

Before this decision to be taken in advance could actually be put into effect, the basis had to be prepared. In the days before 14 July fierce attacks by two Soviet armoured divisions on the armoured spearhead of the German advance brought the attack to a halt. And Sixth Army had to face the attack of the newly refreshed Soviet Fifth Army from the area around Korosten. The Pripet marshes again provided a secure assembly area for the enemy; for this reason Army Group South decided to attack Korosten. But without the assistance of the divisions on the right wing of Army Group Centre, which had just begun an attack on Smolensk, success could not be achieved. On 9 July Eleventh Army and the Romanian Fourth Army had to defend themselves against heavy attacks on their southern flank, which forced Eleventh Army command to turn a corps towards Kishinev to capture the city. The northern group of Eleventh Army with the units of the Romanian Third Army was now between Soroki

---

[128] Cf. Halder's entry of 10 July 1941. According to a quote in the war diary of Army Group South (BA-MA RH 19 I/71, p. 200), Brauchitsch decided to compromise by avoiding a clear yes or no with regard to the attack on Kiev.

[129] On the question of forming an 'inner ring' near Uman against the wishes of Army Group South, compared to which the capture of Kiev was of secondary importance, cf. Halder, *Diaries*, 1013 (7 July 1941, 11.00 p.m.), 1022–3 (9 July 1941).

[130] Amendment of Directive No. 3 in H.Gr. Süd/Ia, KTB, 10 July 1941, BA-MA RH 19 I/71; Hauck, Südliches Gebiet, pt. 1, 256–7, MGFA P-114c.

and Mogilev and was about to cross the Dniester. Halder's general impression was that the arrival of new commanders along the enemy 'Fronts'—in the south Marshal Semën Budënny—had stiffened Soviet resistance and that the general retreat had been replaced by fierce counter-attacks.[131] Only Seventeeth and the north wing of Eleventh Army still viewed the fighting on the Soviet side as mainly rearguard actions. German advances were limited to those by 13th and 14th Armoured Divisions towards Belaya Tserkov.

As a consequence of these defensive battles, the attack date for the armoured group was postponed, as the group would not be ready before 14 July. Because of supply difficulties and operations to protect its southern flank, Eleventh Army reported that it would not be able to attack before 17 July. On 13 July reconnaissance of the fortifications and troop concentrations around and in Kiev showed conclusively that the city could not be occupied in a surprise operation. By 14 July the armoured group had overcome its tactical crises and the attack on Belaya Tserkov was resumed. Seventeenth Army observed the reinforcement of enemy units in the Stalin line but still believed it would be able to carry out its orders to encircle the enemy.[132]

Hitler intervened once again in the orders of the army group. On 13 July he ordered 25th Infantry Division (mot.) and SS Leibstandarte Adolf Hitler, which he himself had ordered to reinforce the protective forces on the northern flank, to be replaced by infantry forces from Sixth Army. The two mobile units were then to be reassigned to the attack group.[133] But until the arrival of the infantry units of Sixth Army, which were still 160 kilometres away, the mobile units were indispensable and thus not available for the thrust to the south-east.

On the northern flank, on the edge of the Pripet marshes, the situation was becoming threatening. Sixth Army command assumed that an advance to the south or against Kiev would only be possible when the forces of the Soviet Fifth Army operating from that area had been destroyed. Beating back the continuing attacks from within the marshes cost considerable casualties. The situation in the area of Novograd Volynskiy and Korosten urgently needed to be brought under control, but that seemed possible only in co-operation with Army Group Centre. As, however, in spite of a request to that effect on 15 July, Army Group Centre was not in a position to help, Reichenau and his northern group had to force the Soviet Fifth Army away from the Dnieper alone. At the same time they were to attempt to reach a crossing north of Kiev. It is understandable that the divisions of III Armoured Corps, which were far ahead of other units—13th Armoured Division was about 200 kilometres in

[131] Halder, Diaries, 1027 (11 July 1941); H.Gr. Süd/Ia, KTB, for the following days, BA-MA RH 19 I/71.
[132] It was therefore not to make a direct attack on the fortified line but to prevent the withdrawal of the enemy with his movable equipment.
[133] H.Gr. Süd/Ia, KTB, 13 July 1941, BA-MA RH 19 I/71.

front of the leading infantry units—and with Kiev before them, should have believed that they were in a position to take the city by surprise. For the commander of Sixth Army, however, the elimination of the danger to the northern flank, which tied down army reserves to protect the highway to the north, had priority for the moment.[134] But this new attempt to eliminate the Soviet Fifth Army by an encirclement from the south and west failed, as the Soviet units attacked were always able to withdraw into impassable terrain and no counter-force could be employed in the north to contain such movements. (See the Annexe Volume, No. 8.)

Armoured Group 1 meanwhile moved the mobile units, 25th Infantry Division (mot.) and SS Leibstandarte Adolf Hitler, towards III Armoured Corps. Subsequently all mobile units near Kiev were replaced by LV Army Corps and XXIX Army Corps of Sixth Army, which cut the city off between Vasilkov on the Dnieper and the lower Irpen sector from the south and west by the beginning of August.

On 18 July the Army General Staff and the army group agreed[135] to start the attack to encircle the enemy with III and XIV Armoured Corps with the main effort towards the south-east, in the direction of Kirovograd. To achieve a closer encirclement XXXXVIII Armoured Corps was to advance towards Uman. This attack was repeatedly disturbed from the east by the Soviet Twenty-Sixth Army, and by 21 July it had been stopped. In the west XXXXVIII Armoured Corps reached the area north of Uman at this time. By 3 August the encirclement there, for which only 11th and 16th Armoured Divisions were available, was completed with the 'Group von Schwedler' in the north and Seventh Army and Hungarian units in the west. Eleventh Army, which had crossed the Dniester near Mogilev-Podolskiy and Soroki, broke through the Stalin line from the south but failed to reach the encirclement area in time. Its role was confined essentially to providing flank protection for Seventeenth Army. The disputes between Hitler, the Army High Command, and the army group between 18 July and the end of the battle of Uman cannot be described here. In view of the enemy forces already cut off, the army group had doubted the wisdom of the encirclement and the commitment of mobile units at Uman. In the end Hitler and Halder had their way; they considered the encirclement around Uman to offer a more certain victory than the attempt to annihilate the enemy at Kirovograd with Seventeenth Army and cut

---

[134] Philippi (*Pripjetproblem*, 36) agrees with Halder on the lack of strategic significance of the Soviet Fifth Army and on Reichenau's excessively tactical thinking. That army, however, had already been reconnoitred on 2 July with the aid of captured documents and information provided by prisoners, and not, as Halder states (*Diaries*, 1036–7: 13 July 1941), only by radio intelligence. It was clearly more than a collection of cut-off troops. Cf. III. Pz.K./Ia, KTB, BA-MA RH 24-3/134.

[135] The war diary of Army Group South from 16 July to 15 August 1941 is missing from BA-MA. It is therefore necessary to base the account of this period on Hauck, Südliches Gebiet, pt. 1. Army high command. directives up to 23 July are also missing from RH 2/v. 1 326. On 18 July 1941 cf. Hauck, Südliches Gebiet, pt. 1, 69–70, MGFA P-114c.

his retreat route with the armoured group, which the army group had outlined in its Directive No. 4 of 21 July.[136]

Hitler evidently regarded the battle of Uman as the achievement of the first objective of the campaign in the sector of Army Group South.[137] About twenty divisions of the Soviet Sixth, Twelfth, and Eighteenth Armies were destroyed, about 103,000 prisoners were taken, and large quantities of equipment and supplies were captured.[138] But the second task—establishing and securing bridgeheads on the eastern bank of the Dnieper[139]—was not fulfilled.

Unlike the situation of the armoured groups of the two northern army groups, the operations of Army Group South were at no point marked by thrusts of armoured spearheads unhindered by enemy resistance on the flanks. Halder described the fighting in the south very vividly when he spoke of the 'weeks of grinding at the Russian front in the Ukraine'.[140] As the operations department of the Army General Staff observed,[141] success was finally achieved in the south more slowly than had been hoped. And in the first phase of operations Army Group South had been even less successful than the other two army groups in achieving the general objective of destroying most of the Soviet armed forces west of the Dnieper and Dvina. Several factors contributed to this development. The poor roads and unfavourable terrain in the south created difficulties for the motorized units that were made considerably worse by rainfall in the decisive operational phase. But the Germans had been aware of these natural conditions, with which both sides had to contend, since the First World War, if not earlier. More important was the fact that the abandoning of Halder's original plan meant the renunciation of the chance to encircle the enemy from both sides. This gave the enemy the opportunity to concentrate his defensive operations against just one thrust of the attacking German units. It was, however, decisive that the Soviet military leaders were able to exploit energetically the chances this situation offered and, together with the Soviet forces still operating in the western Ukraine and the Pripet marshes, either to stop the German attack head-on or repeatedly to endanger its flanks. Thus the main reason why the objectives of Army Group South could not be achieved was the energetic and skilful Soviet defence (which, however, involved high losses). This development was all the more significant

---

[136] Ibid. 259–64 (appendices 14, 15, 16), army group directive No. 4: pp. 265 ff., appendix 17.

[137] Halder, *Diaries*, 1154–5 (5 Aug. 1941), Hitler's directive to cut off enemy forces west of the Bug and to transfer available German forces to the east (towards the Dnieper). He considered this to be a indication of his views. Cf. sect. II.1.1(*b*).

[138] According to *KTB OKW* i. 560 (8 Aug. 1941): 103,054 prisoners, 858 artillery pieces, 317 tanks, 186 anti-tank guns, 5,286 vehicles. The number of Soviet wounded and dead was estimated to be twice as high as the number of prisoners.

[139] Since 20 July, because of the deployment order, Army Group South had always given priority to the fulfilment of this task. Cf. conference between the chief of the Army General Staff and the army group command, 20 July 1941, and the resulting 'ideas on the further conduct of operations' of 21 July and their formulation in army group directive No. 4; cf. n. 136 above; Halder, *Diaries*, 1057–8, 1062 ff., 1065–6 (18, 20, 21 July 1941).

[140] Ibid. 1085 (30 July 1941).　　[141] Halder, *KTB* iii. 112 (25 July 1941; not in trans.).

as the most important objectives of Operation Barbarossa in the Soviet war and armament industry were located in the south.

(b) Disputes about the Further Conduct of Operations

(i) THE QUESTION OF THE DEPLOYMENT OF FORCES FOR THE SECOND PHASE OF THE CAMPAIGN

(See the Annexe Volume, No. 9)

After developments had gone according to plan in the first days of the campaign against the Soviet Union, Hitler on 26 June 1941 began to consider the conduct of the second phase. In addition to plans to accelerate the advance of Army Group South by increasing its air support, especially against the enemy's transport routes to the front, the regrouping he had envisaged of the forces of Army Group Centre was now his main concern. On 27 June he again emphasized that not the capture of Moscow, but the destruction of the fighting strength of the enemy, was the most important objective. Because of the need to eliminate the Soviet Baltic Fleet as a threat to iron-ore imports from Sweden, Leningrad remained the main objective.[142]

On 4 July he realized that this 'most difficult decision of the war' would require a weakening of the central sector of the front, so as to be able to send strong armoured forces against Leningrad and the eastern Ukraine. Only infantry armies were to advance towards Moscow until operations in the north and south had been completed. Hitler thus confirmed again the strategic perspective that had dominated his planning for the campaign in the east from the very beginning.

Numerous statements by Hitler and Halder at this time clearly show that both men considered the military campaign against the Soviet Union to be essentially won. On 3 July Halder noted that the objective of the army, 'to shatter the bulk of the Russian army this side of the Dvina and the Dnieper', had been accomplished.[143] In terms of the operational objectives in the directives, the campaign had been accomplished according to plan within fourteen days. When the great rivers had been crossed, the most important objective would be to prevent the enemy from creating new divisions from his enormous human reserves and equipping them with the help of his remaining production facilities. Achieving this objective would require pursuit of the enemy over a large area and the occupation of considerable territory. Even if one considers the justified optimism and euphoria of the moment, which prevent us from viewing these notes as evidence of rational military judgement and intention in the narrow sense of those terms, they must be seen in the perspective of the demands placed on the army groups and armies. Halder was fully aware that the first objectives of the operations, the complete destruction of the enemy's fighting strength and reaching the Dnieper line all the way to the Black Sea,

[142] *KTB OKW* i. 1019 (61, 62) (26–7 July 1941).
[143] Halder, *Diaries*, 1000–1 (3 July 1941). The deliberate belittling of the enemy forces in the Pripet area was typical; reports on their strength were considered to be 'old wives' tales'.

had not been achieved. And Hitler's remark about 'perhaps the only . . . really important decision in this war'[144] indicates that although there was no doubt as regards the achieving of victory within the period set, the sequence of operations and the corresponding distribution and use of forces were still being rethought. The determining factor in all deliberations was the emerging picture of the condition of the Red Army.

On 8 July the judgement of the German army leaders was based on the assumption that of the previous 164 large enemy units known to be ready for action, 89 could be considered destroyed, while 46 were believed to be still capable of fighting; 18 units on 'secondary fronts' had to be included. No information was available on the location of 11 other units, which were presumably being kept in reserve. An important factor in this picture of the enemy was the assumption that of the 29 Soviet armoured divisions encountered at the front, 20 were completely or partially out of action and only 9 still fully fit for combat. Because of the high losses of officers and technical personnel, it was believed that the Soviet Union would not be able to restore the combat-readiness of the defeated divisions, although it was to be expected that the time gained through the heavy defensive losses at the front would be used to create new units and mount counter-attacks.[145]

On the basis of this assessment of the military situation, the following conclusions were reached on 8 July: the offensive of Army Group Centre was to be continued until the bulk of the enemy forces west of Moscow had been destroyed. Then the two armoured groups were to halt their advance. If necessary, Armoured Group 3 was to provide support for Army Group North—something which, to judge by Hitler's remarks, seemed probable, though he considered the 'desirable ideal solution' to be for Army Group North to fulfil its task with its own forces. But he obviously doubted that these forces would be sufficient. Nevertheless, he had also considered a second possible use for Armoured Group 3, a drive to encircle Moscow from the north. Halder was completely satisfied when he noted that Hitler had approved his conduct of operations. Hitler had also developed the new idea of using a 'strong right wing of Group Hoepner' to isolate Leningrad in the east and south-east. This idea seemed to Halder to be correct, but the discrepancy remains between it and Hitler's remarks of 5 December 1940, when he approved Halder's planning. Hoepner's 'right wing' was part of Armoured Group 4, while Hitler was clearly referring to the left wing of Armoured Group 3.

In Halder's view sending Guderian's armoured group to the south or south-east to co-operate with Army Group South beyond the Dnieper presented fewer difficulties. For the army group still had to cross the Dnieper, and by then Guderian would have conquered enough territory further east to create

---

[144] *KTB OKW* i. 1021 (68) (5 July 1941).
[145] Ibid. 1021 (70); Halder, *Diaries*, 1015 (8 July 1941); cf. text preceding n. 158 below.

a good starting-position for the right wing of the attack on Moscow. Beyond that, the armoured group could be employed merely with partial forces and without significantly weakening the attack group to be directed against Moscow.[146]

The differences between Hitler's and Halder's views concerning the distribution and use of German forces were also evident on 13 July. Unlike Hitler, Halder saw in the area of Army Group North only a 'defence group consisting of forces hastily gathered up and strengthened by improvisations, showing no operational ability'. On the other hand, in the area of Nevel and Velikie Luki he perceived strong, in part fresh, enemy forces which would have to be eliminated by 'a special operation'.[147] He therefore proposed to advance to Velikie Luki and towards Kholm with parts of Armoured Group 3, while Hitler was clearly thinking of an operation with all or part of the armoured group to support Army Group North to isolate Leningrad.

The argument about the use of the mobile units no longer involved in an offensive towards Moscow became more intense. At this point Hitler and Halder were both aware of the need to close the existing pockets and eliminate strong enemy forces before continuing the rapid advance to the east. It is a matter of secondary importance how far Halder's insight in this regard was due to military necessity, i.e. the urgent need of many German units for a rest and replenishment of supplies, while Hitler, on the other hand, wanted to secure the area already conquered for purposes of economic exploitation and to prepare parts of the German army to spend the winter in the east.

In any case, immediately after the plan to halt Armoured Group 3 became known, Army Group Centre objected strenuously.[148] As the group could have received its information only from Halder, it can be assumed that he supported its protest. As the situation was described in the army groups, Hitler did not confine himself to making suggestions for general-staff planning; although he was prepared to change his views, he intervened with directives to the Army High Command and with changes in the target-planning of the Luftwaffe to such an extent that his basic plan, which was diametrically opposed to Halder's views, was preserved. At the conclusion of the first phase of the campaign Halder had to force a decision contrary to Hitler's original intentions, which he prepared in the form of a memorandum. The note on the draft that it was approved by the chief of the general staff on 30 June shows that it was written as a preventive measure.[149] With the start of the final phase of the first part of the campaign, Hitler, on the other hand, realized that the Army General Staff had set a definite course towards Moscow. As he considered that city to be only the third most important objective, he intervened energetically in the planning process.

---

[146] Cf. sect. II.1.1(*c*) at n. 230.   [147] Halder, *Diaries*, 1036 (13 July 1941).
[148] Ibid. 1037–8 (13 July 1941).
[149] *KTB OKW* i. 1031 (79); the fact that the date of the memorandum was left open also indicates that it was written with an eye to a foreseeable crisis in operations.

(ii) VACILLATION IN THE DIRECTIVES FOR THE CONDUCT OF THE
WAR FROM 19 JULY UNTIL THE END OF THE MONTH

The directive of 19 July 1941 for the continuation of the war in the east clearly
reflects Hitler's realization that the large-scale encirclement operations which
had marked the campaign until then had not fulfilled the expectations placed
in them.[150] In spite of the enormous number of prisoners taken—most of the
Soviet forces in the west—and the huge amount of equipment captured, the
fighting strength of the Red Army had by no means been destroyed. Neither
was that to be expected from the elimination of still existing pockets of Soviet
troops. For this reason, the directive confined itself to describing the outcome
of 'the second series of battles' as the breakthrough of the Stalin line and the
thrusts of the armoured groups. But in the sectors of the Army Groups Centre
and South the forward movement had been slowed by the creation of pockets
and by continuing enemy presence in the rear area (the Pripet flank). The aim
of operations in the coming weeks was therefore limited to preventing the
enemy units still within reach from withdrawing further into the vast spaces of
the enormous country and to destroying them. In contrast to the broad,
ambitious plans of the 'grand strategy', the directive prescribed how the Soviet
Twelfth and Sixth Armies were to be encircled at Uman; it laid down that the
Soviet Fifth Army in the Pripet marshes was to be eliminated by the co-
ordinated efforts of the inner wings of Army Groups Centre and South, and
that, in addition to the southward turn of infantry from Army Group Centre,
mobile units were to be sent south-eastward to cut off the enemy who had
crossed over to the east bank of the Dnieper. Having completed their present
task, the encirclement at Smolensk, these mobile units were to be detached
from the centre of the army. This meant the removal of at least strong parts of
Guderian's armoured group. In the total strategy Army Group Centre was to
assume a secondary role by continuing its advance towards Moscow with the
mobile units that had not turned south-eastward (Armoured Group 3), cutting
the lines of communication between Moscow and Leningrad, and thus covering the right flank of Army Group North in its attack on the latter city. Army
Group North was to continue its attack on Leningrad only after its right flank
had been secured and Eighteenth Army had joined up with Armoured Group
4. The main task of the Finnish front remained co-operation with Army
Group North, which required the mountain corps in Lapland to neglect its
objectives there for the time being. The Luftwaffe was to make forces available
from the centre of the army, support the southern front, and carry out 'reprisal
attacks' on Moscow to demoralize the population there. The navy was assigned the task of preventing the escape of the Soviet fleet from the ports of the
eastern Baltic, ensuring the transport of supplies by sea, and disrupting shipments of supplies to the enemy via the Arctic Ocean.

---

[150] *Hitler's War Directives*, No. 33, pp. 85 ff.; 'Führererwägungen am 17. Juli 1941' and note on
Hitler's visit to Army Group North on 21 July 1941 in *KTB OKW* i. 1029 (76, 77).

Using the arguments in his memorandum mentioned above, Halder must have expressed his reservations to the Wehrmacht High Command immediately after the directive was issued, or indeed while it was still being written.[151] The commander-in-chief of the army also sought to induce Hitler to cancel the directive, which in the eyes of the Army High Command was premature and even disastrous, as it required abandoning the plan to concentrate the main effort of the German attack on Moscow. Moreover, the direct issuing of operational and tactical orders to the branches of the Wehrmacht in the form of Führer directives seemed to mark the beginning of a development that could deprive the general staffs of freedom in planning and real command authority in supervising the execution of operations.[152]

Brauchitsch's oral report induced Hitler to issue a 'supplement to Directive No. 33' on 23 July, which sharply restricted the instructions contained in the directive itself.[153] Reflecting Halder's views, the co-operation between Army Groups Centre and South to destroy the Soviet Fifth Army was eliminated. And the planned 'turning' of parts of Army Group Centre to annihilate Soviet forces east of the Dnieper was restricted and defined more precisely. The transfer of armoured units was made dependent on the operational and supply situation. After capturing the industrial area around Kharkov, the armoured army newly created from Armoured Groups 1 and 2 was to cross the Don and push on towards the Caucasus.[154] After the conclusion of other tasks and the elimination of enemy resistence to the south, the central sector, the most affected part of the eastern front, was to defeat the enemy between Smolensk and Moscow with 'sufficiently strong infantry units' and capture Moscow. Armoured Group 3 was to be placed under Army Group North only temporarily. The group was expected to participate in a thrust to the northern Volga, to be accompanied by an 'accelerated advance of the left wing', intended as part of the encirclement of Moscow.

Brauchitsch presumably also pointed out the lack of a long-range objective in the directive. Only in this way can the addition of such objectives in the supplement be explained—which, however, led to Halder's protest and Brauchitsch's lodging a complaint with Keitel, as they would have required troop movements incompatible with the envisaged concentration on Moscow.

[151] Cf. n. 149 above. Because of the new Directive No. 33a and Jodl's alignment of his views with those of Halder, the memorandum was not sent off.

[152] That Brauchitsch appeared personally is clear from the first sentence of the following directive and from Halder's remarks (*Diaries*, 1065: 20 July 1941) about low spirits of the C.-in-C. of the army and the worsened mood 'in the highest leadership'. Halder was of the opinion that there was no reason for this and that it was necessary to await the 'ripening' of the results of the battle to achieve a breakthrough.

[153] *Hitler's War Directives*, 89–90; *KTB OKW* i. 1031 (79). On 21 July 1941 Halder adapted his views to Hitler's ideas. Cf. sect. II.1.1(*c*) at n. 219 and the source given in n. 160 below.

[154] Thus clearly in accord with Halder's views, who wanted to avoid tying Guderian tactically to Sixth Army, e.g. to help during the Dnieper crossing. This had been preceded by a discussion at Army Group South on 20 July, in which Halder assumed that the northern wing of Sixth Army would link up with the southern wing of Higher Command XXXV east of the Pripet marshes by 26 July: Halder, *Diaries*, 1062 ff. (20 July 1941); cf. sect. II.1.1(*c*) at n. 219.

For this reason Brauchitsch urged the head of the Wehrmacht High Command to withdraw the supplement to Directive No. 33, in spite of the changes that had been made, until the battles in progress had been concluded. This new attempt was unsuccessful, although Brauchitsch and Halder were given the opportunity to present their dissenting opinions to Hitler on the evening of 23 July.[155]

Halder began his carefully prepared report with a survey of the assumed strength of the enemy. He estimated that 20 infantry and $3\frac{1}{2}$ armoured divisions were facing Army Group North; 32 infantry and $3\frac{1}{2}$ armoured divisions Army Group Centre, and 26 infantry, 6 armoured, and 2 cavalry divisions Army Group South. Halder's sums, therefore, were quite different from the ones he had presented on 8 July.[156] At that time he had told Hitler that of 164 known Soviet infantry divisions only 46 were considered ready for combat. This picture was intended to persuade Hitler that it was to be expected that most of the enemy's forces would confront Army Group Centre and that the Wehrmacht should also concentrate its strength in that sector.[157] Halder estimated the fighting strength of the German divisions at, on average, 80 per cent for the infantry and 50 per cent for the armoured divisions and motorized infantry.[158] In developing his own operational plans, Halder carefully weighed numerous elements. Supplying his own troops played a central role in his thinking, but he had to assume that not all armies could be adequately supplied with necessities at the same time.[159] Halder concluded that on the whole the enemy had been 'decisively weakened', but not yet 'completely defeated'. Each new operation had to 'achieve its own freedom of movement by breaking anew the enemy's resistance'. The aim of all future operations had to be the 'destruction of the enemy's arms-production plants' (around Moscow), as the human reserves of the Soviet Union were inexhaustible. He assumed that the German troops would reach the Leningrad and Moscow areas as well as the line between Orel and the Crimea around 25 August. It would be possible to reach the Volga by the beginning of October and Baku and Batum by the beginning of November. But Hitler refused to change his directive stipulating that after the conclusion of the battle of Smolensk Armoured Groups 2 and 3 should be withdrawn from the

[155] *KTB OKW* i. 1034–5 (80) (23 July 1941). Halder's plan for his oral report in 'notes for oral reports' (*Vortragsnotizen*), *Kriegstagebuch*, iii. 103 ff. (23 July 1941; not in trans.). It is not possible to determine which ideas in these notes were presented to Hitler.

[156] Oral report on situation of the enemy: *KTB OKW* i. 1030 (78), figures of 8 July. Cf. sect. II.1.1(*b*) at n. 144.

[157] The widths of the sectors of the army groups should be borne in mind, as well as Halder's expectation that the Red Army would withdraw forces from other fronts to defend Moscow.

[158] This rough estimate provides no information on the condition of the units of Army Group Centre and probably also served to justify the bringing up of additional forces later.

[159] This reflected the supply and transport situation, but it was also clearly aimed at securing the release of production held back by Hitler and against an early withdrawal of units, which had been considered since 14 July. Cf. *KTB OKW* i. 1022 ff. ('Führererwägungen und Vortragsnotiz Op.Abt.'). Detailed plans in *Hitler's War Directives*, No. 33a (supplement to Directive No. 33), which Halder rejected for that reason.

central sector of the front to support the other army groups in the north and south.

Nevertheless, at the general-staff level Halder continued his efforts to prevent the realization of Hitler's plans. A comparison of the 'supplement to Directive No. 33' with the working paper which Halder sent to the general staffs of the army groups shows that he quickly mastered the feelings of resignation still noticeable after his report to Hitler on 23 July.[160] In accordance with Hitler's directive, Army Group South combined Armoured Groups 1 and 2 to form Fourth Armoured Army, which was given the task, in co-operation with Army Group South, of advancing via Kharkov to the Don and the Caucasus. Moreover, co-operation between the southern wing of Army Group Centre and Army Group South to annihilate the enemy around Korosten was to be prepared, but in such a way that Armoured Group 2 was to turn south only after crossing the general line between Bryansk and Gomel, i.e. without achieving a close envelopment with forces of Sixth Army south of the Pripet marshes.

More important were Halder's views concerning the sector of Army Group Centre. Hitler intended to use infantry units to defeat the enemy forces defending the road to Moscow after the end of the battle of Smolensk and the elimination of enemy resistance on the southern flank. Armoured Group 3 was to be available on the left wing of the attack, but only after completing its part in the attack on Leningrad. However, Halder believed that, as preparation for a pincer movement, the industrial areas north and south of Moscow could be captured only with armoured troops. While Hitler wanted to use Armoured Group 3 as flank cover and a driving force in the conquest of Leningrad, Halder limited its use essentially to cutting the railway line between Moscow and Leningrad. For him there could no longer be any question of using the group to cover the flank of the attack on Leningrad. Moreover, he expected to use Armoured Group 3 and 'possibly' Armoured Group 4 in Army Group Centre for the attack on Moscow. Hitler had not mentioned assigning the latter group to the central sector.

Hitler wanted to strengthen Army Group North to the point where Leningrad could be taken in the shortest possible time. Halder, on the other hand, considered that to be primarily a problem to be solved by redistributing forces within the army group. In the framework of his plan, strong forces were to capture the northern Valday hills to cover the flank of the main attack group and sever the above-mentioned rail link early.[161] For this purpose Armoured Group 3, as soon as it could be detached from the current operations of Army Group Centre, was 'in addition' (*sic*) to be placed under the tactical command

---

[160] On 23 and 24 July army groups were informed of Hitler's decisions and received new directives. They were required to submit time estimates and operational plans: OKH/GenStdH/Op.Abt. (I) No. 1390/41, BA-MA RH 2/v. 1326.

[161] This interruption of supplies for Leningrad was also intended to prevent the bringing up of reinforcements for the defence of Moscow in the event of a possible evacuation of Leningrad.

of Army Group North. The scheduling of its attack for the middle of August at the earliest and the fact that it was to attack in such a way that 'its use planned for later in the area of Army Group Centre in the general direction of Moscow will still be possible' meant nothing less than that Army Group North was not to use the armoured group in the attack on Leningrad.

Halder's next step in the conflict about the future conduct of operations was to call a meeting of the army-group chiefs of staff on 25 July.[162] More important than the exchange of situation assessments and operational plans, which in any case could be made orally or by teletype on a daily basis, was the 'rallying' of these responsible general-staff officers behind Halder's claim to have the final word in operational matters. He hinted that Hitler and the Wehrmacht High Command had to be borne with patience, but 'checked in good time'. Moreover, the flow of information to Hitler was to be channelled through special 'emissaries', for Hitler was more prepared to believe front officers than those on the general staff. He emphasized that the army-group chiefs of staff were the 'branch representatives' of the Army High Command and requested an exchange of ideas on a long-term basis. Therefore closer control had to be exercised in the armies in this regard. Like the armoured groups, they were not to deviate from the basic operational guidelines they received, for reasons such as tactical difficulties or the behaviour of the enemy. This appeal was clearly aimed at Army Group North.

Halder was able to achieve a consensus on basic principles and thus obviate the danger that the commanders-in-chief would make contrary demands or claims to Hitler. The chief of the general staff of Army Group South, General von Sodenstern, believed that he would essentially be able to complete operations west of the Dnieper by the end of the month and then begin his attack across the river, where it would be possible to combine Armoured Groups 1 and 2 later, perhaps near Kharkov.

The chief of staff of Army Group Centre, Major-General von Greiffenberg, reported that, after some rehabilitation and replenishment, he would be able to start his attack with the two infantry armies on the wings of his army group on about 10 August. Halder had already assigned him the objective of the industrial areas north and south of Moscow on 24 July. Army Group Centre expected to be able to use at least parts of Armoured Group 3 in future on the left wing it was to push forward north of Moscow. And Armoured Group 2, which had not been expected to link up with Armoured Group 1 until it had reached the longitude of Kharkov, had not been written off yet. The almost insoluble supply problems in the area of the Valday hills were an additional reason for not using Armoured Group 3 with Army Group North. The ground was thus prepared for also solving this problem as Halder desired.

On the following day Halder attempted to win the support of Brauchitsch and Field Marshal von Bock for his opposition to a possible withdrawal of

---

[162] Halder, *Diaries*, 1073–4 (25 July 1941).

forces towards Gomel away from the main direction of attack towards Moscow. He rejected an attack, together with the northern wing of Army Group South, against the 'enemy group Gomel' as a change from operational to tactical command. This amounted to a rejection of Hitler's point of view. Halder was able to reach agreement with Bock without difficulty, as both men considered Moscow to be the most important objective.[163]

But on 26 July Hitler returned to his operational and tactical deliberations in Directive No. 33. Although he fully appreciated the importance of the unexpectedly rapid territorial gains,[164] he was disturbed that, as Halder formulated it in the language of a military expert in his memorandum, the Red Army could not be defeated with operational successes, 'because they simply do not know when they are defeated'.[165] Halder did not deny that this argument was in some respects quite valid, but he saw clearly the danger that the 'strategy of imaginative operations' could lose its momentum and doubted that Hitler's tactic of pursuing more limited objectives would be successful.

Hitler, however, emphatically rejected new large-scale envelopment operations and demanded that the operation along the Dnieper be abandoned if it were not completely successful in the immediate future. The group of enemy forces in the triangle between Army Groups Centre and South was to be eliminated immediately; the army group facing Moscow need not hurry. Again Hitler demanded the shift of Armoured Group 3 from the Valday hills to provide support for the attack on Leningrad.[166] On the same day, 26 July, Halder sent Lieutenant-General Paulus to Army Group North. As Halder expected, Paulus reported that between Lake Ilmen and Lake Peipus there was no terrain suitable for mobile units. In that area infantry units, followed by Manstein's corps, should be employed. Halder pointed out the danger that if the idea of a fast attack on Moscow, for which it would be necessary to concentrate all available forces, were abandoned, the enemy might succeed in halting the German offensive before the beginning of winter. This would permit him to regain his strength, and the military objective of the war against the Soviet Union would not be reached.[167]

On 27 July the commander-in-chief of the army had a talk with the commander-in-chief of Army Group Centre, the army group most affected by the directive. Field Marshal von Bock expressed his fears that Hitler's order for an attack by Guderian's armoured group on Roslavl as the first step in an advance on Gomel, and the consequent weakening of the right wing of Army Group Centre in the direction of Moscow, 'the crucial objective', would leave it with inadequate forces. Clearly accepting Halder's arguments, the head of the Wehrmacht operations staff, General Jodl, also supported a continuation of

---

[163] This is evident from the fact that Bock was informed immediately: ibid. 1074–5 (26 July 1941).

[164] *KTB OKW* i. 1041 (29 July 1941).   [165] Halder, *Diaries*, 1076–7 (26 July 1941).

[166] *KTB OKW* i. 1040 (28 July 1941) and Halder, *Diaries*, 1077 (26 July 1941). On Paulus's trip cf. n. 361 below.

[167] *KTB OKW* i. 1031 ff.

the attack on Moscow, but at the same time he accepted Hitler's principle of 'first destroying the vital strength of the enemy wherever it is found'.[168] The convergence Halder had observed between his own views and those of the Wehrmacht operations staff was obvious.

But Halder's attempts to persuade Hitler directly and indirectly of the incorrectness of his basic strategic idea were unsuccessful.[169] On 28 July Hitler issued instructions completely in line with the ideas of Directive No. 33: slowing of the large-scale operations, destruction of the enemy west of the Dnieper, attacks on Leningrad and the group of enemy forces near Gomel.[170] There, after the necessary rehabilitation, Armoured Group 2 was to prevent the escape of the enemy to the east or south-east. To carry out this order, Hitler envisaged the formation of an 'Army Group Guderian' consisting of Armoured Group 2 and parts of Second Army (IX Army Corps with three infantry divisions). Armoured Group 3 was to be placed under Ninth Army and replaced at the front by its formations. These mobile units were to be sent to Army Group North, which was to take Leningrad as rapidly as possible and link up with the Finnish army on the Karelian isthmus. The large-scale operations of Army Group South were all postponed. They were to be carried out only after the annihilation of the enemy west of the Dnieper 'in co-operation with the mobile units and infantry divisions of Army Group Centre'.

All these ideas were diametrically opposed to the planning of the Army General Staff. Halder feared that the German attack would become bogged down in positional warfare and miss the only opportunity to defeat the enemy in the east decisively before dealing with the main enemy, Britain, who was still determined to carry on the war.

The directive of the commander-in-chief of the army of 28 July for the continuation of operations took account of Hitler's unequivocal will.[171] But there was a clear differentiation between the intentions of the 'supreme commander' and those of the Army High Command. The former were based on Hitler's 'security ideas' but took up again the additional objectives mentioned in the supplement to Directive No. 33 that Hitler had left open in his 'considerations and instructions': the Ukraine west of the Volga, Tula and Gorkiy, Rybinskoe, and Moscow. In presenting the plans of the Army High Command, the directive merely listed the tactical operations to destroy enemy forces in the near future and then set further goals: for Army Group South the Donets basin; for Army Group Centre the industrial area around Moscow, for

    [168] Bock, *Tagebuch*, (27 July 1941), BA-MA N 22/9; report of C.-in-C. of the army: Halder, *Diaries*, 1080 (27 July 1941), quote ibid. 1082 (28 July 1941); Jodl's comment in *KTB OKW* i. 1036 (82).

    [169] Halder's negotiating technique was very strenuous. The resulting tension is frequently reflected in his diary.

    [170] 'Erwägungen und Anordnungen des Führers', 28 July 1941, in *KTB OKW* i. 1040–1 (86, 87).

    [171] OKH/GenStdH/Op.Abt. (I) No. 1401/41, BA-MA RH 2/1326, pp. 163–84. For Halder's efforts to bring about a change by sending Paulus to the Wehrmacht High Command cf. Halder, *Diaries*, 1084 (29 July 1941).

which, if necessary, Armoured Group 3 was to be brought in as soon as it could be released from Army Group North. Army Group North was to prepare to transfer its mobile forces (including Armoured Group 4) to Army Group Centre after encircling Leningrad and linking up with the Finns. The objectives and the related organization of the large formations of the army thus seemed set. Again Halder sent Paulus to the Wehrmacht operations staff, primarily because of the order to cut the retreat route to the east of the enemy at Leningrad, for which VIII Air Corps was to be removed from the centre of the front and sent to Leningrad.

The unclear reaction of the Wehrmacht High Command indicated that Hitler had changed his mind. On 30 July he decided to postpone all instructions issued regarding the reorganization and to order the army to complete all encirclements already begun and then to rehabilitate the mobile units.[172]

In the sector of Army Group North the attack on Leningrad was to be continued. The German forces on the central sector of the front would essentially confine themselves to preparing for the next attack and improving their starting-positions.

Army Group South was to complete the encirclement of Uman and then establish bridgeheads near Kiev and south of that city. The Soviet Fifth Army in the Pripet marshes was to be eliminated by Sixth Army alone. Thus the 'July crisis' in the German military leadership was ended for the time being. But it was clear that after the replenishment period of approximately ten days a decision would have to be taken and pushed through. Halder hoped that by then favourable developments at the front would strengthen his position. Then Hitler's restrictions on large-scale tactical operations, which were basically due to tactical considerations, would take care of themselves. The broader objectives Hitler had included in the supplement to Directive No. 33 clearly showed, however, that for him the operational idea 'against Moscow' meant occupying the lines of communication from the city to the north (the route to the Arctic Ocean and other supply-lines), to the interior of Russia (Gorkiy), and along the middle and upper Volga. This idea still played a role in Hitler's thinking at the peak of the crisis at the front in December. The city of Moscow itself, however, remained for him, as it had been since he began planning the campaign against the Soviet Union, merely 'a geographical term'.

The 'supplementary directive' issued by the Army High Command[173] adhered essentially to Hitler's orders, much to the disgust of Halder, who accused the commander-in-chief of the army of having failed to show any trace of a will of his own.[174]

But Directive No. 34 and the 'supplementary directive' were not completely identical. The latter ordered the period of replenishment for Army Group

---

[172] *Hitler's War Directives*, No. 34, pp. 90 ff.

[173] OKH/GenStdH/Op.Abt. (I) No. 1401/41, 'Supplementary directive', 31 July 1941, BA-MA RH 2/v. 1326, p. 185.

[174] For Halder's reaction cf. Halder, *Diaries*, 1089 (31 July 1941).

Centre to be conducted in such a way that 'appropriate forces' would be ready to deal with 'unforeseen local tasks'; orders for later use of this group were still to be issued, but they were to be prepared in such a way that Armoured Group 2 could be sent in the direction of Gomel, while Armoured Group 3 would be sent towards the Valday hills. These orders took into account the weakness of both infantry armies, which were exposed to strong attacks on a rugged and over-extended front. The plan to attack the Valday hills also implied the use of the armoured forces in a northern encirclement of Moscow. Although it took Hitler's directive into account, the attack on Gomel was also intended to prepare a thrust against Moscow from the south.

The attack on Roslavl was the first step in an offensive to be carried out later by Armoured Group 2 to stabilize the situation on the southern flank of the army group. It was to be continued against Rogachev. For that purpose, according to Halder's plans, an armoured division at most would be required.

On the left flank of the army group, where deliberations had already begun on the use of Armoured Group 3, enemy resistance was to be eliminated under the command of Ninth Army with one or two divisions of II Army Corps (of Army Group North) by a thrust to Toropets. Afterwards the left wing of Ninth Army was to advance to the highlands south of the Valday lakes to cover the lines of communication to Army Group North and 'prepare possible further operations of Army Group Centre towards the east'. This instruction prepared the inclusion of the southern area under Army Group North in the attack on Moscow by Army Group Centre. The directive to Army Group North was in accordance with Hitler's wishes, apart from the placing of parts of II Army Corps under Ninth Army. It pushed the left wing of Army Group Centre as far north as necessary to provide flank protection for the right wing of Army Group North, but without transferring to that army group the additional forces Hitler demanded.

Directive No. 34 of 30 July represented a new postponement of the decision about the future conduct of operations, with which Hitler had concerned himself since the end of June. Halder had not succeeded in pushing through his plan to give priority to the attack on Moscow, but he had prevented Hitler from paralysing the centre of the German front by radically weakening the forces there and shifting the main effort of the German offensive to Leningrad and the eastern Ukraine. 'This decision', Halder wrote in his diary, 'frees every thinking soldier of the horrible vision obsessing us these last few days, when the Führer's obstinacy made the final bogging down of the eastern campaign appear imminent.'[175] But Halder was probably aware that his 'solution' only put off a final decision.

It must be remembered that when the directive was issued, neither the fighting in the Smolensk pocket, which tied down most of Ninth Army, nor the encirclement of Uman had been concluded. The stable situation at the

[175] Ibid. 1088 (30 July 1941).

front necessary for replenishing supplies and preparing to start new operations did not exist.

The completion of the operation at Uman, with hard defensive fighting near Kiev and the slow advance of Reichenau's group with the bulk of Sixth Army against Korosten, was accompanied on the southern flank of Army Group Centre by the continuing attack of VII and IX Army Corps against Roslavl.[176] On the left wing of Army Group Centre parts of Ninth Army moved against Velikie Luki. The attack failed, evidently because of errors by the commander in charge, for Halder had placed the forces involved under the command of XXXX Armoured Corps, commanded by General Georg Stumme. The advance on Toropets had to be abandoned for the time being. In this sector of the front, as also in the Yelnya salient, consistently high losses had to be accepted for the sake of the future offensive against Moscow.[177]

(iii) THE ASSESSMENT OF THE ENEMY AT THE BEGINNING OF AUGUST

In view of this development, the assessment of the enemy's strength and options was especially important for the impending decision.[178] It was assumed that the Soviet leaders intended to halt the German advance by ruthlessly throwing their reserves into battle without regard to losses in order to save the industrial centres in the Ukraine, Moscow, and Leningrad as the basis for a reorganization.[179] It was expected that new Soviet defensive positions would be encountered along the line of the Bug, the Desna, the upper Volga, the Valday hills, Lake Ilmen, and Luga. Subtracting the Soviet divisions considered already destroyed, the units in northern Finland, the Caucasus, Central Asia, and the Far East, German military leaders assumed a Soviet strength of 150 infantry divisions, 25 armoured divisions, and 5 cavalry divisions, of which only 6 divisions had little or no combat experience. Because of their high losses, most of the Soviet units were considered exhausted, with an effective fighting strength of fewer than 80 infantry divisions, 13 armoured divisions, and 2 or 3 cavalry divisions. The existence of 23 new divisions had been established, and a large number of others were believed to have been created, but inadequately armed and without sufficient equipment. Soviet defensive forces were believed to be concentrated south of Kiev, west of Moscow, and near Leningrad.

The individual intelligence estimates do not contain any indication of the size of the partisan movement behind the German lines. While in the first days of the offensive partisan attacks may have seemed to be actions of bypassed

---

[176] Ibid. 1140 (2 Aug. 1941); on Bock's doubts cf. ibid. 1145 (3 Aug 1941). Cf. also Bock, *Tagebuch*, 2 Aug. 1941, on the urgency of rehabilitating the armoured division and the nervousness of the senior officers, BA-MA N 22/9.

[177] Cf. sect. II.i.1(b) at n. 206.

[178] Estimate of strength and condition of enemy forces, annexe 1 to directive of Wehrmacht High Command, 28 July 1941, BA-MA RH 2/v. 1326, p. 173.

[179] The convergence of the ideas of Halder and Foreign Armies East with the 'Assessment of Situation Red' by Maj.-Gen. Marcks is clear. Cf. sect. I.iv.1(d) at n. 103.

Soviet units or individuals, the appeal of the Central Committee of the CPSU and Stalin's speech of 3 July clearly showed that an organized military front was being prepared. Stalin's speech contained the specific order to resist the enemy in the areas occupied by German forces and described the individual forms of such resistance. It was hardly possible to view Stalin's words as purely political propaganda, and when the report of the head of the political propaganda directorate on the north-west front, Army Commissar First Class Mekhlis, to the Red Army's Chief Directorate of Political Propaganda became known, there could no longer be any doubt regarding the operational objectives of the resistance.[180] The captured document provided insight into the organization of the partisan movement, the units already organized, and their tasks, methods, and weapons. Political functionaries sent to partisan units, and local party and state organizations, were ordered by the Chief Directorate of Political Propaganda of the army front to promote the expansion of the partisan movement behind German lines.

At first the German Army High Command reacted with a legalistic statement[181] that members of Soviet partisan organizations 'which, as regards respect for the laws of war, uniforms, equipment, or identifiability, do not clearly qualify as a regular military unit, militia, or volunteer corps' were to be treated as guerrillas. Civilians who aided such partisan units thus supported irregular combat operations and, 'in accordance with the customs of war', were also to be regarded as guerrillas. The next step by the Army High Command was a decree on the treatment of enemy civilians and Russian prisoners of war in the rear areas occupied by the German army.[182] This decree proclaimed the maximum degree of security for the German soldier to be the guiding principle of all measures to be taken. For this reason the decree

[180] Cf. sect. II.II.7 (Hoffmann), and sources; Hesse, *Der sowjetrussische Partisanenkrieg*, 51 ff.; Mechlis's order No. 81, BA-MA, 18. Armee, 13767/20.

[181] OKH/Gen. z.b.V. beim ObdH/Gr. Rechtswesen, Az. 454, No. 1260/41, 18 July 1941, BA-MA RH 22/271. This directive referred to the report OKH/GenstdH/Abt. Fr. H. Ost (II) No. 3016, 15 July 1941, which consisted of an analysis of the courier post of an aircraft that had made an emergency landing on 14 July. It contained the report addressed to the 'Chief Political Propaganda Directorate of the Red Army, for Political Commissar 1st Class Gen. Mechlis' on the direction of partisan operations by the head of political propaganda on the north-west front and the organization of partisan detachments (BA-MA RH 22/271). The directive of the general for special tasks at the office of the C.-in-C. of the army, No. 1332, 25 July 1941 (ibid.), referred explicitly to the planned operation against partisans. The numerous reports of murders of prisoners of war since the beginning of the campaign against the Soviet Union confirmed in the eyes of German officers and men the propaganda leaflets about the insidious tactics of Red Army soldiers and thus the first part of the 'jurisdiction decree': cf. Leeb, *Tagebuchaufzeichnungen*, 281 (25 July 1941). In line with OKH/Gen. z.b.V. beim ObdH/Gr. Rechtswesen, No. 1215/41, 9 July 1941, the C.-in-C. of the army ordered German forces to refrain from retaliation. On 17 July 1941 Second Army headquarters issued analogous instructions on the treatment of the civilian population (BA-MA RH 20-2/1090, annexe 242). For the Ukraine: Befehlshaber rückw. Heeresgebiet 103/Ic No. 968/41, 11 July 1941, Besondere Anordnungen für die Behandlung der ukrainischen Frage, BA-MA RW 41/4.

[182] Cf. n. 181, directive of 25 July 1941.

essentially repeated the rules of the decree on jurisdiction.[183] But the Army High Command also realized that pacification of the occupied areas could be most rapidly achieved if it were possible to induce the civilian inhabitants to work. All possibilities to achieve this aim were to be exhausted. Experience with the inadequate guarding of prisoners of war was reflected in a ban on fraternization and in the instruction to resort immediately to the use of arms in the event of insubordination.

The use of partisans behind the German front proved to be tactically effective, as it tied down German forces that would otherwise have been available at the front itself or in other operations. In July 1941, in addition to the security units and Germany's allies, these forces consisted of six divisions. When one considers how difficult it was for Halder to accept that the left flank of Sixth Army was still pinned to the Pripet front, where ambushes played a significant part in tying down large numbers of German troops for long periods of time, the difficulty of the German army leaders in incorporating such unconventional forms of warfare into their operational thinking becomes clear. Depending on local conditions, the task of finding a solution to the partisan problem was at first left to the army headquarters and subordinate commands. The lack of proper training for such a task and the inadequacy of the security forces soon became evident. Certainly at this time the size of the danger represented by partisan units operating behind the German lines was not yet understood. Halder still refused to consider it a serious threat to normal military operations.[184]

A few days after the issuing of Hitler's directive of 30 July, difficulties in moving supplies emerged as an important factor in an extensive exchange of ideas between Halder, the commander-in-chief, and the chief of the general staff of Army Group Centre.[185] The discussion was mainly concerned with preparations for Hitler's visit to Army Group Centre on 4 August, during which the general question of the aims and the distribution of forces for the second phase of operations would once more arise.[186] With the help of the commanders of the armoured groups, Colonel-Generals Guderian and Hoth,

[183] Cf. sect. I.IV.I(*g*) at n. 173; Anordnung OKH/GenQu/Abt. Kr. Verw. (W) No. II/11035/41, 31 July 1941, betr. Arbeitseinsatz von Arbeitslosen [Putting unemployed to work], BA-MA, 18. Armee, 13767/20; ibid., translation of propaganda instruction of the army commissar of the Soviet Eighth Army, 15 July 1941.

[184] In fact, however, considerable reserves were tied down with Army Groups Centre and North.

[185] 'Zustand der schnellen Verbände' gem. Besprechungspunkten für Heeresgruppen Chef-Besprechung ['Status of the Mobile Units': agenda for conference of Army Group chiefs of staff], 25 July 1941, Halder, *KTB* iii. 115–16 (1 Aug. 1941; not in trans.).

[186] Halder, *Diaries*, 1144 ff. (3 Aug. 1941). It is interesting that Greiffenberg was instructed to point out to Bock the differences between the directive of the Wehrmacht High Command and that of the Army High Command and to present the situation at Yelnya as cautiously as possible so as to prevent Hitler from ordering the evacuation of this exposed position, whose defence had proved to be very costly; for Halder wanted not only to hold but also to expand it. For Guderian's doubts, see ibid.

who were brought in for the meeting, Hitler was persuaded to release 400 new tank motors, which were considered essential for any new large-scale operations.[187] But in the decisive question Hitler remained inflexible. The important thing was, he explained, to deprive the enemy of the 'vital areas'. Among these he still considered Leningrad to be the most important. He expected Army Group North to seal off Leningrad by 20 August; after that most of the units and the parts of the relocated Air Fleet 2 would be available to Army Group Centre.[188] The second most important area, in Hitler's view, was the 'south of Russia, especially the Donets region', which he described as the 'basis of the entire Russian economy'.[189] For him, Moscow ranked only third as an objective of the campaign,[190] and he refused to change his views in spite of Field Marshal von Bock's objections. When Hitler visited Army Group South on 6 August, Field Marshal von Rundstedt, the commander-in-chief, was likewise unable to convince him of the importance of an attack on Moscow, as Halder had proposed.[191]

Halder again had to accept that as an objective Moscow ranked behind Leningrad and the Ukraine. He evidently did not believe in the feasibility of this sequence of operations. The hard fighting and the newly created units of the Red Army would inevitably tie down such large German forces that it would not be possible to attack Moscow early enough and with sufficient strength.[192] As late as 4 August he pressed Brauchitsch to take a clear decision: either to attempt to annihilate the enemy in a battle for Moscow, or to conquer the Ukraine and the Caucasus for economic reasons. If the annihilation of the enemy were given priority, everything had to be concentrated on that objective. The following day, Brauchitsch was able to interpret remarks by Hitler in such a way that, in Halder's view, an all-out offensive against Moscow was still possible.[193] After Hitler had again clearly stated his priorities at the headquarters of Army Group South on 6 August, and demanded the annihilation

[187] Using informal contacts, Halder had been able to obtain their immediate delivery by air, which corresponded to the urgency of the situation but not to Hitler's directive. Cf. Halder (*Diaries*, 1151: 4 Aug. 1941), who mentions 350 engines. Hitler's reasons for holding them back (as well as 2nd and 5th Armd. Divs.) were his fear of a British landing and his desire to hold fresh forces in reserve for the occupation of the Caucasus and the Urals industrial region: minute of Hitler's visit to Army Group Centre, 4 Aug. 1941, *KTB OKW* i. 1041 ff. (88), and study for operation across the Caucasus, ibid. 1038 ff. (84).

[188] i.e. VIII Air Corps.

[189] The fundamental discussion of Hitler's intentions between Keitel and Bock, 25 July 1941, *KTB OKW* i. 1035–6 (81).

[190] Cf. sect. II.1.1(*b*) at n. 142.   [191] Halder, *Diaries*, 1151, 1157 (4, 6 Aug. 1941).

[192] Primarily because of the dissipation of fighting strength. Cf. Bock, Tagebuch, 49 (31 July 1941), 52 (4 Aug. 1941), BA-MA N 22/9. It should be mentioned that Bock took advantage of the opportunity to intercede with Hitler on behalf of the 'friendly and co-operative population'. He referred to the labour question. After this conversation he had the intelligence officer of the army group, Maj. Rudolf-Christoph Freiherr von Gersdorff, request the 'senior SS and police officer' (who was not his subordinate) 'to issue instructions that executions in the area of my command should be carried out only when armed bandits or criminals are involved. Gersdorff reports that Nebel has agreed to this request.'

[193] Halder, *Diaries*, 1152, 1154–5 (4, 5 Aug. 1941).

of the Soviet Fifth Army in a joint operation between Army Groups South and Centre,[194] Halder on 7 August called on the head of the Wehrmacht operations staff, General Jodl, in an attempt to use the most direct official way available to him to persuade Hitler to change his mind.[195] Halder convinced Jodl that the choice between Moscow and the Ukraine was an illusion: both had to be taken. After its victory at Uman, Army Group South still had sufficient forces to conquer this last objective,[196] just as Army Group North was entirely strong enough to take Leningrad. Moscow and the Ukraine had to be conquered, 'or else we shall not be able to eliminate this source of the enemy's strength before autumn'. The concentration of Soviet forces east of the Pripet marshes was not an operational objective. They had to be made to 'rot away'.[197] In the end both generals agreed that Hitler had to be persuaded to concentrate all available forces in Army Group Centre. They also agreed to play down the importance of the enemy forces north of Kiev.

Jodl kept his word. He presented Hitler with a summary of the situation in which the bulk of the Red Army was concentrated around Moscow and advocated a concentrated thrust in the central sector of the front towards the Soviet capital. Flank attacks with limited objectives had already been started with the thrust by Second Army and parts of Guderian's group (this was the draft plan Halder had presented at Bock's headquarters).[198] In the north of Army Group Centre, Jodl supported an attack by Armoured Group 3, but without a further advance towards the Valday hills. He thus conceded at the very beginning a grouping of forces against Velikie Luki which Hitler considered necessary. Halder's influence was also reflected in Jodl's concluding proposal to let Army Groups North and South defeat the enemy units confronting them alone in order to be able to support them more effectively after the victory of Army Group Centre over the Soviet forces around Moscow.[199]

Details of Jodl's description of the situation cannot be reconstructed, but situation reports of the department Foreign Armies East of the Army General Staff from this period are available. They permit a rough estimate of the extent of agreement between Jodl and Halder, i.e. the extent to which the two generals were able to influence Hitler's decision.[200] As early as the end of July, when the battles of encirclement at Uman and Smolensk were approaching their conclusion, Foreign Armies East had reported the reorganization of the Soviet defences facing Army Group Centre with the creation of a Soviet Front Staff Centre and a Front Staff Western Front, each with three armies. More-

---

[194] Hauck, Südliches Gebiet, pt. 1, 293, appendix 24, MGFA P-114c.

[195] Halder, *Diaries*, 1158–9 (7 Aug. 1941).   [196] Cf. sect. II.1.1(*c*) at n. 227.

[197] This was a result of Halder's own assessment of the situation. Cf. however, the judgement of Sixth Army headquarters, sect. II.1.1(*c*) at n. 219.

[198] Cf. sect. II.1.1(*a*) at n. 32.

[199] Jodl's oral report, 10 Aug., *KTB OKW* 1043–4 (89); Guderian's view, *Panzer Leader*, 101.

[200] OKH/GenStdH/OQu IV, Abt. Fr. H. Ost, situation reports East under the following dates, beginning with No. 46, 31 July 1941, BA-MA RH 19 I/121.

over, the radio-intercept service reported the deployment of 28 divisions in the wider area of Moscow. Stubborn enemy resistance was expected along the line formed by the Desna, the Uzha, the Dnieper, and the upper Volga after the end of the battle of Smolensk. The divisions around Moscow seemed to be moving towards the west and south-west to be sent into action against, and on the right flank of, Army Group Centre. On 6 August a copy of an order was captured for the creation of a front staff of the Soviet reserve armies to prepare an in-depth defence. This staff, to which Forty-third, Thirty-second, Thirty-first, and Thirty-third Reserve Armies were subordinate, was given the task of constructing a rallying-position near Ochakov north-west of Bryansk and west of Vyazma. Army Group North also reported strong enemy units approaching the front. In the south long columns of enemy troops were sighted moving from Krivoi Rog towards Dnepropetrovsk, which indicated preparations for a defence. The assessment of the enemy's situation of 8 August agreed upon by the generals for the oral report to Hitler presented the following picture.

After the successes of Armoured Group 2 at Roslavl, the enemy forces facing Army Group South were also defeated. Approximately 15 divisions and 5 armoured divisions had been annihilated. The Red Army leaders were confronted with new tasks. It was hardly to be expected that the enemy would evacuate Kharkov, Moscow, and Leningrad. For that would also mean the evacuation of the huge government apparatus, which could hardly be set up again in another location, as well as the isolation of the Red Army from its vital food-growing areas and supply-bases.

Forces available along the entire front to the Red Army for the continuation of the war had a fighting value of 60–5 divisions and, at most, 10 armoured divisions. In rear areas about 40 divisions were being organized, but with inadequate leadership, arms, and equipment.

They did not represent a usable, stable structure. And the limits of Soviet human reserves would also be reached in the foreseeable future. Generally speaking, one million civilians could provide soldiers for two divisions at war strength; therefore the European part of Russia, with 160 million people, could provide 320 large formations, and the Asian part, with 30 million people, could provide a total of only 50.[201] This number had now been reached or exceeded. (For German estimates of the number of Soviet divisions already at the front or in other parts of the country see Table II.1.1.)

The fighting spirit and value of the Red Army were described as declining. Supply problems, inadequate nutrition, news about hardship on the home front, threats against their dependents if they were captured, and a feeling of inferiority against the German Wehrmacht all contributed to the poor morale

---

[201] These figures were provided by Foreign Armies East and yielded a total of 366 divisions at war strength: letter of Capt. Eberhard Graf zu Münster to the intelligence officer of III Armd. Corps, Maj. von Graevenitz, 7 Oct. 1941, BA-MA RH 24-3/136. The 360 divisions mentioned by Halder (*Diaries*, 1170) on 11 Aug. 1941 represent all identified enemy units according to their numbers, rather than combat-ready divisions. Comparison with the rough estimate of 200 enemy divisions at the beginning of the campaign is therefore misleading.

TABLE II.1.1. *German Estimate of Maximum Potential Soviet Strength, Autumn 1941*

At the front:	approx. 260	infantry and motorized divisions
	approx. 50	armoured divisions
	approx. 20	cavalry divisions
Behind the front:	approx. 40	divisions
On other fronts:	approx. 20	divisions
TOTAL	approx. 390	divisions

of the Soviet soldiers. Pressure from commissars and officers seemed to be losing its effect.

Total Soviet forces are no longer sufficient for a large-scale attack or for the establishment of a continuous defensive front. The creation of a front in the rear area along the general line of Lake Ilmen, Rzhev, and Bryansk may have the following aims:

1. defence against a German attack on Moscow;
2. a rallying-position for a withdrawal from the existing front;
3. the formation of a new front to pull out forces for use against Army Group South.

In summary the report observed:

1. The number of new units being organized may have reached its peak. The creation of more new units is hardly to be expected.
2. Available forces are sufficient only to delay the German advance on vital bases of the army and the state, in the hope of protracting the fighting until the arrival of bad weather in winter in order to revive and reorganize Soviet forces with British and American help. Continued fighting and new heavy losses will lead to a further decline of morale in the Red Army.

After the battle of Uman, the enemy forces confronting Army Group South seemed to be defeated. Only isolated cases of heavy fighting were still reported. In the area of Army Group Centre enemy attacks concentrated on Guderian's army group and the eastern front of Ninth Army.

The following seven Soviet reserve armies of the Front Staff of the Reserve Armies were identified facing the Army Groups Centre and North:

Thirty-eighth Army east of Lake Ilmen (4 infantry divisions)
Thirty-fourth Army in the Valday hills (2 infantry divisions)
Thirty-first Army between Rzhev and Ochakov (1 armoured and 2 infantry formations)
Thirty-fifth Army in the area north-west of Gzhatsk (number of divisions unknown)
Thirty-second Army around Vyazma (6 infantry divisions)
Forty-third Army (1 armoured and 3 infantry formations)

    Thirty-third Army around Spas-Demensk (1 armoured and 4 infantry
       formations)
    perhaps 1 additional infantry and armoured formation

Foreign Armies East concluded that these reserve armies had the task of
protecting Moscow and providing personnel and material replacements for the
formations at the front. There were indications that these armies were to send
not only complete formations, but also individual regiments to the front. In
their operations areas they were to construct defensive positions and, in the
event of an enemy breakthrough, receive troops of retreating Soviet forces.

Comparison of the results of reconnaissance and intelligence findings presented here with Jodl's 'agreed' report to Hitler clearly shows Halder's intention to marshal convincing reasons for his operational planning. His task was
to prove that Army Groups North and South were able, with the forces
available to them locally, to overcome the enemy forces opposing them. In
reality, however, he was well aware that the Soviet colossus had been underestimated and, in spite of great losses, would always have enough human
reserves to create new divisions in an emergency.[202] Moreover, with every
kilometre he retreated the enemy approached his arms-production centres and
an extensive transportation network, while every demolished bridge and every
road made impassable by bad weather increased the difficulties facing the
German army.

(iv) HITLER'S ACCEPTANCE OF THE NEED TO ELIMINATE MOSCOW
(See the Annexe Volume, No. 10)

At first the oral situation report to Hitler seemed to have had the desired effect.
With a supplement to Directive No. 34, issued on 12 August, Halder achieved
a certain success.[203] For Hitler now ordered that Moscow, as the enemy's
'government, armament, and traffic centre', must be captured 'before the
coming of winter'.[204]

Hitler thus accepted Halder's thesis of the importance of Moscow, but he
failed to draw all the necessary conclusions. He still assumed that the destruction of enemy divisions and the capture of objectives important for Germany's
war economy must determine the sequence of operations. But now he used
arguments based on the assessment of the enemy's situation: if the bulk of the
Red Army had been massed to defend Moscow, and Soviet forces on other
fronts were really as weak as claimed, German attacks obviously had to be
directed at these points. Jodl and Halder had assumed that in Hitler's eyes the
main objective was to destroy the 'vital strength' of the enemy, but now it

---

[202] Halder, *Diaries*, 1170 (11 Aug. 1941). The intention to tailor a picture of the situation to
Hitler's assumed mental state is evident. The fact that figures on the enemy side were not
recorded until this day is not a result of new intelligence of the enemy's strength, but rather
evidence of German disappointment.

[203] *Hitler's War Directives*, No. 34a, pp. 93 ff.

[204] But not the expected bulk of the Red Army's vital strength, as Halder and Jodl expressed it.

became clear that his primary objectives were securing control over the areas already conquered and capturing the sources of raw materials. Destroying those parts of the Red Army that could still be forced to accept battle before the beginning of winter was of only secondary importance.

Nevertheless, Moscow was now clearly the main objective. But in his directive Hitler had included several significant obstacles. After the battle of annihilation at Uman, Army Group South was now, 'with its own strength' and employing forces of Germany's allies, to fulfil its new tasks—the occupation of the Crimea and the industrial areas of the Donets and around Kharkov.[205] The co-operation between the inner wings of Army Groups Centre and South, eliminated from the directive on 30 July, had been reintroduced and clarified with an order to cut the enemy supply-routes to Ovruch and Mozyr with the objective of annihilating the Soviet Fifth Army. This could easily tie down strong forces, which would inevitably make extremely uncertain the use of parts of Army Group South to provide flank protection for the attack on Moscow.

A second obstacle was Hitler's insistence that the attack on Moscow should be dependent on progress in the attack to encircle Leningrad. The directive no longer placed Armoured Group 3 under Army Group North, but it demanded the use of mobile units to defeat the enemy west of Toropets. The left wing of Army Group Centre was then to be pushed far to the north to enable Army Group North to divert additional infantry divisions to the attack front against Leningrad. Regardless of this, attempts were to be made to transfer 'some division or other' to Army Group North even earlier.

Halder immediately grasped the importance of these conditions and frequently expressed his view that they were obstructive and unnecessary. When, on 9 August, the command of Army Group Centre reported that the elimination of enemy resistance at Velikie Luki did not require the use of armoured forces, Halder deliberately pointed out that a 'combat group strong enough to be launched eastward through Toropets' should be detached for the possible overall attack.[206] He thus excluded an attack in a northerly direction, e.g. as part of an attack on Leningrad, but the transfer to the extreme left wing of Army Group Centre was to be prepared. Finally, Bock and Halder supported the use of Armoured Group 3 against Toropets, but if possible only after 20 August. Then the group could be expected to reach Toropets by 28 August. This meant perhaps an operation of one week (pushed through by Hitler) within the deployment for a northern encirclement of Moscow, which would result in a corresponding postponement of the general attack by Army Group Centre.[207] Halder thus believed that in spite of the 'obstacles' he could still begin the offensive against Moscow in August. But for that it was essential that no demands were made by Army Groups North and South which might

---

[205] The relevant directive of the Army High Command to Army Group South was issued on 12 Aug. 1941. Cf. n. 226 below.

[206] Halder, *Diaries*, 1165 (9 Aug. 1941).   [207] Ibid. 1171 (11 Aug. 1941).

interfere with the reorganization and build-up of supplies at the central point of the envisaged attack on Moscow. In this regard the most vulnerable point in the German front was the southern flank of Army Group Centre.

On 1 August 'Army Group Guderian' had begun its attack on Roslavl with VII Army Corps and XXIV Armoured Corps.[208] By 3 August the enemy forces there, with a strength of four divisions and armoured formations, were encircled. The armoured group had thus reached a point between Krichev and the upper Desna south of the road to Moscow. An expansion of the deployment to secure the southern flank was prepared by Second Army, which was to advance via Rogachev to Gomel in order to eliminate the Soviet Fifth Army for good in co-operation with Army Group South.[209] This operation as a whole met the requirements of the tactical situation of the army group as well as Hitler's conditions for an attack on Moscow. It therefore had to be completed with large forces in the shortest possible time to permit regrouping from the newly captured starting-points to be carried out by 20 August.

But developments of the situation in the sector of Army Group North marked the beginning of a new, seemingly decisive, turn of events against Halder's intentions. On 14 August the army group reported a dangerous concentration of enemy forces on its southern flank, which could further delay the encirclement of Leningrad. This development so alarmed Hitler that he again intervened in the use of the mobile units before the attack on Moscow and ordered the immediate transfer of major elements of Armoured Group 3 to Army Group North.[210]

At first Halder was powerless to take any measures against Hitler's order of 15 August. Not only the transfer of Armoured Group 3, but also the abandoning of operations by Army Group Centre to improve its starting-positions and the withdrawal from exposed positions such as the Yelnya salient were incompatible with his plans.[211] In Halder's opinion the effects of Hitler's directive required a reaction by the commander-in-chief of the army, but he was evidently not prepared to express his views.[212]

It can be assumed that Halder immediately contacted Jodl. At the same time he ordered the operations department to formulate all points of view for the future use of Army Group Centre as 'operational proposals'.[213] The

---

[208] Guderian, *Panzer Leader*, 99 ff.; Halder, *Diaries*, 1144 ff. (3 Aug. 1941). The renaming as an 'army group' (*Armeegruppe*) was for the assignment to capture Gomel (assignment of VIII Army Corps with 7th, 23rd, 78th, and 197th Inf. Divs. as well as IX Army Corps with 263rd, 292nd, and 137th Inf. Divs.). Cf. sect. II.1.1(c) at n. 219. To relieve the mobile units still in the Yelnya salient, XX Army Corps with 15th and 268th Inf. Divs. was also placed under the 'army group'.

[209] Halder, *Diaries*, 1088 (30 July 1941); Guderian, *Panzer Leader*, 100. With the cutting of the Mozyr–Gomel–Bryansk railway line the retreat of the Soviet Fifth Army from the Pripet area became unavoidable.

[210] Cf. sect. II.1.1(d) at n. 362; *KTB OKW* i. 1045 (91).

[211] Halder, *Diaries*, 1176 ff. (14, 17 Aug. 1941).   [212] Ibid. 1181, 1184 (15, 17 Aug. 1941).

[213] Assessment of the situation in the east by OKW/WFSt/Abt. L on 18 Aug. 1941 and 'Proposal for the continuation of the operation of Army Group Centre in connection with the operations of Army Groups South and North' of the C.-in-C. of the army, same date: *KTB OKW* i. 1054 ff. (94, 95).

Wehrmacht High Command's assessment of the situation in the east, signed by Warlimont, expressed in diplomatic form, and with a certain understanding for Hitler's drive to capture the tempting east Ukranian industrial region, the same views as the extensive analysis by Halder's operations department.

From the 'operational proposal' of the commander-in-chief of the army it is clear that Halder believed the decisive moment had arrived to obtain Hitler's final consent to this campaign and was no longer prepared to tolerate 'interference from above'. He did describe the objectives of Army Groups South and North as the conquest of the east Ukranian industrial areas and the Baltic coast, but this constituted at the same time a rejection of all more ambitious objectives. Even the conquest of the Crimea was to be postponed if serious resistance were encountered there. Army Groups North and South had to reach their objectives, for only these successes combined with the conquest of the industrial area around Moscow would deprive the enemy of his last human and material reserves for further resistance. And conversely, without the conquest of Moscow successes in the north and south would not be decisive. To assist in the offensive against Moscow, Army Groups North and South were to advance simultaneously and follow Army Group Centre relatively closely in echelons staggered towards the centre of the front and assume the task of providing cover for the two wings of the attack. It is not necessary to present this operational proposal in detail here. It expressed more clearly than all previous ideas and drafts Halder's strategy during the preparatory and execution phase of Operation Barbarossa, which he now openly tried to realize against Hitler's wishes. The basic assumption of this strategy was that the annihilation of the enemy's 'vital strength' and the conquest of the sources of his strength around Moscow in 1941 had to remain the objective of German military operations. For this purpose it was necessary to keep all forces together and 'set aside other tactical, isolated actions not decisive for operational success'. What in Halder's view, however, were 'tactical successes' were in fact Hitler's main objectives—pushing on to the lower Don and the Caucasus, as well as defeating the Soviet Fifth Army with Guderian's forces. Halder did not have to wait long for an answer. Hitler must have studied exhaustively the ideas and proposals of the general staff, for his answer was impulsive but also very detailed.[214]

Hitler tersely rejected Brauchitsch's (and Halder's) proposal with the explanation that it was not Moscow or the strong Soviet forces there which were important, but the conquest of industrial centres. Moreover, he wanted to be able to put pressure on Iran in the south because of Anglo-Soviet plans there. Similarly, it was necessary to eliminate the Crimea as an air-base against the Romanian oilfields as soon as possible.

In a long letter to the commander-in-chief of the army, Hitler also rejected the operational proposal of the general staff and explained that the most

[214] *KTB OKW* i. 1061 contains two notes, 20 and 21 Aug. 1941 (97, 98); in addition, letter (1062–8) of C.-in-C. of the army, 21 Aug., and Hitler's 'study' of 22 Aug. 1941 (99, 100).

important objectives—the conquest of the Crimea and of the Donets industrial and coal area, cutting off Soviet oil supplies from the Caucasus, and
linking up with the Finns on Lake Ladoga—had to be achieved before the
beginning of winter. He also ordered that strong forces from Army Group
Centre should help Army Group South cross the Dnieper and encircle and
eliminate the enemy facing the boundary between the two groups. Only after
the conclusion of these operations could the necessary forces be made available for an attack on Moscow.

Hitler's 'study' of 22 August was evidently not edited by the Wehrmacht
operations staff, as it contains indications of agitation as well as passages in
which Hitler took direct issue with Halder's arguments for an attack by the
army on the eastern front. Hitler justified his operational priorities in detail
with the well-known political and war-economy arguments, but also with
military arguments. For example, in his view the necessity of crossing the
Dnieper on a broad front south of Kremenchug was a logical step required for
the conquest of the Crimea, itself essential to fulfil the most important task of
protecting the Romanian oilfields against air attack. He also rejected Halder's
argument that a large encirclement movement to the east of Army Group
South would weaken Guderian's army group, as the elimination of the threat
to the southern flank of the attack on Moscow could be achieved only by
destroying the enemy forces there. The impending concentrated attack by
armoured forces should not continue endlessly but, in accordance with his
orders for the conduct of the campaign often repeated in the past weeks,
should consist of short encirclement operations to destroy enemy units as they
were encountered. Hitler's general instructions about the conduct of army
operations undoubtedly seemed quite grotesque to Halder, who had always
refused to consider strictly local requirements and wanted to concentrate
forces for the attack on Moscow in the centre of the German front. Hitler's
reproach that the army stubbornly insisted on an organization based on large
units completely ignored the methods actually practised by the army leaders.
As early as 25 July, Brauchitsch had stressed to the chiefs of the general staffs
of the army groups that neither armies, nor armoured groups, nor corps
formed indivisible units. And the creation of larger combat groups for special
tasks disproved this reproach in practice.[215] For Göring Hitler's comparison of
his tight command of operations of the Luftwaffe with the alleged situation in
the army was undoubtedly a source of satisfaction, but the army leaders found
it offensive. The concluding part of the 'study' was more conciliatory than the
general tendency of Hitler's rather 'explosive' criticism gave reason to expect.
He explained that, for the reasons stated, he could not, 'in general', accept the
draft submitted by the army for the further conduct of operations.

What was in fact decided? Firstly, the disposition of XXXIX Armoured
Corps of Armoured Group 3 within the framework of Army Group North was

[215] Halder, *Kriegstagebuch*, iii. 118 (25 July 1941; not in trans.).

retained, with the objective of advancing the encirclement of Leningrad. Secondly, Hitler decided that Army Group Centre with Guderian's army group should facilitate the Dnieper crossing of Sixth Army and Armoured Group 1 by engaging the enemy on their front and then subsequently annihilating enemy forces east of the Dnieper in a great battle of encirclement. Thirdly, he decided that the subsequent attack on Moscow should be carried out in stages, in which it would be more important to destroy as many enemy units as possible than to capture Moscow quickly. In his orders Hitler assumed that Army Group North would shortly be able to fulfil its task of cutting Leningrad off from the east.

Hitler's rejection of their views caused great dismay among the army leaders, but the officers concerned obeyed him.[216] On 23 August Halder flew to the headquarters of Army Group Centre to discuss the situation with Field Marshal von Bock, whose army group was most affected by Hitler's decisions. Bock explained that he could not halt his advance on the existing front. Guderian was also consulted and criticized the new attack direction, especially because of the road conditions, supply problems, and resulting wear and tear on vehicles it would involve.[217] But Guderian too was unable to persuade Hitler to give up his plan; the decision for a 'battle of Kiev' had been taken. The disputes about the conduct of operations between Hitler and the Army High Command, in which Jodl had generally supported Halder, had come to a 'temporary' conclusion.

Apart from this conflict about operational objectives, which had been smouldering since plans for the war in the east were first considered, the controversy between Hitler and the Army General Staff, which continued for more than a month, was also a result of the growing realization that a number of mistakes had been made in the basic planning for the war against the Soviet Union. The objective stated in the deployment order for Barbarossa—to destroy 'the bulk of the Russian army in western Russia'—had not been achieved to the extent that a withdrawal of strong Soviet forces into the vast expanse of the country further east could be prevented. Contrary to German expectations, the Soviet leaders had been able to organize an effective defence in spite of the catastrophic losses of the first few weeks of the campaign. In contrast, the size of the area to be conquered and the declining strength of their own forces presented increasingly difficult problems for the German leadership. Halder's intention to reach the operational objectives of each of the three army groups within approximately the same period of time had clearly not been realized in the sector of Army Group South. It was no longer possible to maintain the original time plan for this 'rapid campaign'. At the end of August 1941 a survey of the strategic situation by the Wehrmacht High Command, which was approved by Hitler, expressly mentioned the possibility

---

[216] Halder, *Diaries*, 1195 (22 Aug. 1941).

[217] Ibid. 1196–7 (23, 24 Aug. 1941); Bock, Tagebuch, 71 (23, 24 Aug. 1941), BA-MA N 22/9; Guderian, *Panzer Leader*, 101.

that additional operations might be necessary completely to crush Soviet resistance in 1942 and made this consideration the basis of further strategic deliberations.[218] It seems that Halder, more than Hitler, resisted this view and believed that a final effort to capture Moscow would lead to the collapse of Soviet defences. Hitler, on the other hand, drew the correct (in his view) operational conclusions dictated by his priorities. Military-economic necessity was the decisive factor; he never considered a Cannae around Moscow. But the German leaders still hoped—even if they no longer expected with certainty—to conclude the campaign against the Soviet Union satisfactorily in 1941 in so far as they might manage to deprive the enemy of the basis to rehabilitate and redispose his forces and to reduce the German army in the east to the size which they had envisaged and for which alone they had prepared. With these objectives in mind, they concentrated their attention on Leningrad and the industrial area of the Ukraine.

(c) The Battle of the Ukraine and the Crimea
(See the Annexe Volume, No. 11)

On 21 July, even before the conclusion of the battle of Uman, Army Group South command had informed the commanders-in-chief of its armies of the task of destroying enemy forces west of the Dnieper and of the direction of coming operations.[219] The main point of offensive effort was to be on the northern wing, which, possibly in co-operation with parts of Army Group Centre, was to advance on the Donets industrial area. Zaporozhye, Dnepropetrovsk, and Cherkassy were envisaged as possible bridgeheads for crossing the Dnieper, depending on the point of main effort, for Seventeenth Army and Armoured Group 1. After capturing bridgeheads south of Kiev, Sixth Army was also to advance to the south-east. Because of the distant operational objectives, the army group wanted to reach the Dnieper as rapidly as possible and extend its envelopment as far eastward as possible, while the Army High Command insisted on a close encirclement near Uman.[220] While the army group was thus intent upon assembling its mobile units in the Dnieper bend for rehabilitation before the impending operations, Hitler and Halder insisted on pursuing the enemy to the south via Pervomaysk in order to force him to accept battle west of the Bug and to reach the Black Sea as quickly as possible.[221]

Between 4 and 7 August the situation of the army group changed as a result of strong, dangerous enemy thrusts from the area around Kiev and from the direction of Ovruch. The commander-in-chief of Sixth Army believed that the

---

[218] DGFP D xiii, No. 265, p. 431.

[219] H.Gr. Süd/Ia, Directive No. 4, 21 July 1941, in Hauck, Südliches Gebiet, pt. 1, 265 ff., appendix 17, MGFA P-114c.

[220] Army High Command, directive for the continuation of operations, 28 July 1941, and supplementary directive, 31 July 1941, BA-MA RH 2/v. 1326, fos. 163 ff., 185 ff.

[221] Halder, Diaries, 1150 (4 Aug. 1941): Sodenstern's report on this action and Halder's arguments. Cf. also ibid. 1171 (11 Aug. 1941).

Soviet Fifth Army could cause the collapse of his northern wing.[222] He based his judgement on identified transport movements between Chernigov and Ovruch, which, however, Halder correctly interpreted as evacuation measures. Reichenau viewed the exhaustion of his own troops as the main danger and therefore demanded mobile units and an earlier attack by the southern wing of Army Group Centre. This demand again raised the problem of eliminating enemy resistance at the boundary between the two army groups in the Pripet area, still a controversial subject between Hitler and the army leaders. Since Hitler's directive of 19 July,[223] the elimination of that resistance had been assigned primarily to Second Army and Second Armoured Army. On the basis of a directive of the commander-in-chief of the army of 28 July, itself based on Hitler's directive, and the supplementary directive, XXIV Armoured Corps of Armoured Group 2 launched a large-scale attack on 12 August to support and cover the attack of Second Army in the direction of Gomel. The aim of this attack was to cut off the Soviet Fifth Army and support a thrust by Sixth Army north of Kiev. As described above, however, Sixth Army was under heavy attack and thus not able to carry out such an offensive movement.[224]

On the whole the army group command considered the situation in front of Seventeenth Army, Armoured Group 1, and Eleventh Army on 8 August to be favourable. Halder spoke of a complete destruction of the southern wing of the Red Army, now too weak to undertake an offensive operation in the Ukraine, in the battle of Uman. From the number of destroyed and shattered enemy units he concluded that Army Group South was sufficiently strong to fulfil its task; perhaps it would even be able to support Army Group Centre (i.e. by transferring troops).[225]

The intensification of Soviet attacks against Sixth Army completely changed this favourable picture. Now the transfer of mobile units (I Armoured Corps), to be replaced in Armoured Group 1 by Hungarian and Italian mobile units, seemed necessary to support this army, which was to halt its attack on Kiev. Moreover, 'Group Schwedler' had to be strengthened by army group reserves and transfers from Seventeenth Army for a counter-attack against the enemy penetration at Boguslav. This unexpected splitting of the armoured group for thrusts across the two wings of the army group and its involvement in defensive battles was carried out primarily at the expense of preparations for the fast operation beyond the Dnieper, which formed the centre of the German concept.

[222] Ibid. 1167 (10 Aug. 1941); teletype message from Army Group South to ops. dept., Army General Staff, 9 Aug. 1941: Hauck, *Südliches Gebiet*, pt. 1, 294, appendix 25; directive of Army Group South, No. 5, 10 Aug. 1941, ibid. 299, appendix 26, MGFA P-114c.

[223] *Hitler's War Directives*, No. 33, pp. 85 ff.

[224] Cf. n. 220 above; situation conference Army Group Centre, 27 July 1941. Cf. sect. II.1.1(*b*) at n. 167; Guderian, *Panzer Leader*, 98–9; Halder, *Diaries*, 1076–7 (26 July 1941). Bock (Tagebuch, 26 July 1941, BA-MA N 22/9) emphasizes the lack of a clear objective, as the offensive elimination of a threat to a flank had developed into an encirclement attack.

[225] Halder, *Diaries*, 1163–4 (8 Aug. 1941).

On 12 August the use of mobile units Hitler demanded against Nikolaev and the mouth of the Dnieper—about which the army group had serious reservations as the enemy facing Eleventh Army was withdrawing towards Odessa in the south and important enemy units could no longer be encircled—led to a directive of the commander-in-chief of the army to Army Group South intended to take into account its intentions with regard to a continuation of the attack beyond the Dnieper as well as Hitler's desire for the attack to be directed towards the Black Sea.[226] The directive ordered Army Group South to prepare to cross the Dnieper and to establish bridgeheads across the river early where sufficient forces were available. In conjunction with this operation Eleventh Army, together with Armoured Group 1, was to defeat the enemy between the mouth of the river and Zaporozhye and gain bridgeheads for the crossing to the Crimea as well as towards the Sea of Azov. For the fighting in the Crimea, three mountain divisions were to be transferred from Seventeenth Army. The occupation of the coast was to be left to the Romanians.

Reinforced with mobile units of Germany's allies, Armoured Group 1 was to reach the Dnieper between Zaporozhye and Kremenchug and conquer Dnepropetrovsk as a bridgehead as soon as possible; the armoured corps sent to take Nikolaev was, after fulfilling its task, to attack in the general direction of Zaporozhye, to prevent an enemy escape to the south, and gain river crossings for Eleventh Army near Kherson, Berislav, Nikopol, and Zaporozhye. Parts of the group were to reach the Dnieper between Kremenchug and Cherkassy and hold their positions there until the arrival of Seventeenth Army. In contrast, Sixth Army was to wait; instead of III Armoured Corps, as had been planned, only an armoured division was to be brought up, but in accordance with Sixth Army's changed task—to bring about the 'disintegration' of the Soviet Fifth Army—it was to abandon its attack on Kiev. The further tasks east of the Dnieper were outlined as follows: occupation of the Crimea and the industrial area around Kharkov, and later the Donets basin. The point of main effort of the army group thus shifted to Seventeenth Army, which was to advance 'in the general direction of Voroshilovgrad and Stalingrad'. For this purpose Eleventh Army had to provide several of its own units to cover the flanks of the advance, and on the left wing Sixth Army, with cover in the direction of Kiev, was to advance north of Seventeenth Army in echelon to the left. The main task of Armoured Group 1 was to push forward the attack on Kharkov.

The directive clearly shows that at this point the Army High Command was thinking neither of co-operation between Army Group South and 'Guderian's army group' in the form of an encirclement operation nor of a concentration of the main effort around Kiev, as envisaged in the directive. The main objective of the attack was to drive a wedge across the Dnieper towards the

[226] OKH/GenStdH/Op.Abt. (IS) No. 1436/41, 12 Aug. 1941 to H.Gr. Süd, BA-MA RH 2/v. 1326, fos. 192 ff.

east Ukranian industrial area. Eliminating enemy resistance at the boundary between the two army groups was considered to be a tactical problem.

Beyond the operational objective, it is interesting that, with the attack of the Italian and Hungarian mobile units, the detaching of an armoured corps from Armoured Group 1 was already envisaged for the attack on Moscow, and that Halder obviously expected primarily to pursue the defeated enemy beyond the Dnieper and not to encounter organized resistance on a large scale from the Red Army there.

The attack of XXXXVIII Armoured Corps with 16th Armoured Division and the Leibstandarte—i.e. a mobile brigade—succeeded in capturing Nikolaev and Kherson. Halder therefore envisaged an attack on Odessa as early as 16 August and did not exclude an evacuation of the Crimea. Ostashkov was taken by 50th Infantry Division, but the Romanian attack on Kiev came to a halt short of its objective. On 21 August Halder concluded: 'No Odessa, no Crimea.'[227]

While, with the exception of Odessa, the situation in the area of Eleventh Army, Seventeenth Army, and Armoured Group 1 developed largely as expected during August—that is, the Dnieper had been reached and bridgeheads established at Dnepropetrovsk, Kremenchug, and Cherkassy—Sixth Army remained tied down under the pressure of the attacks on Kiev and those from the Pripet marshes. The possibility of an offensive co-operation with Second Army emerged only on 20 August, when Second Army had captured Gomel. Now the Army High Command also urged such action, though pointing to the danger that the right wing of Army Group Centre could be halted 'by highest authority', which would entail a delay of its own plans to have Army Group Centre advance towards Moscow.[228]

While as late as 18 August Sixth Army command did not expect the Soviet Fifth Army to avoid contact, Halder and the army group command pressed for a rapid pursuit of the enemy. In spite of the addition of 11th Armoured Division, Sixth Army hesitated to start this action because of the condition of roads and bridges in the area. The army group command now clearly shifted the point of main effort of future operations, and the bulk of its forces, to Seventeenth Army, to which it also assigned the reorganized 'Group Schwedler'.[229]

This was the situation obtaining at the time of the arrival of Hitler's decision of 21 August on co-operation between Army Groups South and Centre, which was to go far beyond the previously envisaged close co-operation of their inner wings.[230]

Hitler's directive contained no basically new ideas; it was rather an expression of impatience with the long delay in eliminating enemy resistance in the Pripet area, an objective now stipulated in the form of a clear order, taking into

[227] Halder, *Diaries*, 1192 (21 Aug. 1941).
[228] H.Gr. Süd/Ia, KTB, 29 Aug. 1941, BA-MA RH 19 I/72.   [229] Ibid., 18 Aug. 1941.
[230] *KTB OKW* i. 1062–3 (99).

account the situation only in so far as it no longer demanded the encirclement of the enemy in his previous combat area but rather the encirclement and destruction of the Soviet Fifth Army, even if it attempted to avoid contact, by the inner wings of Army Groups Centre and South before it could regroup in a new position along the Desna and the Sula. Army Group Centre was ordered, regardless of later operations, to employ as much force as might be necessary to achieve this objective. Hitler expected only a limited intervention of Army Group South in this encirclement operation, in which Armoured Group 2 was to take a major role, as Sixth Army had to cross the Dnieper and in any case would arrive too late to concentrate significant forces on the right wing. Again making clear the difference between his views and those contained in the Army High Command's memorandum of 18 August,[231] Hitler designated the rapid conquest of the Crimea as the next objective of Army Group South.

In his directive to Army Group Centre, Halder evidently did not assume that Hitler's decision was final and insusceptible of interpretation. For he merely ordered those parts of Gomel and Chernigov that could be reached to be captured in order to intercept the Soviet Fifth Army.[232] He limited the use of Armoured Group 2 to those parts of Guderian's mobile units which were 'not needed for other tasks of the army group and were ready for action or mobile'.[233] Guderian, who was probably scarcely aware of the background of this limitation, argued against this action. He referred to the road and fuel situation and to the need for the mobile troops to be replenished, assuming that they would be needed for the coming advance on Moscow.[234] A conversation between Guderian and Hitler, suggested by Halder and Bock, about the technical difficulties of the operation ordered for the armoured group ended with the confirmation of the new objective. Guderian's proposal there and then to use the entire armoured group[235] led to a dispute with Bock and

---

[231] Ibid. 1055 ff. (95). In his 'study' of 22 Aug. Hitler had already rejected as 'not worth considering' the idea of making an envelopment movement east of Kiev dependent on the participation of Army Group South. Cf. n. 214 above.

[232] OKW/GenStdH/Op.Abt. to H.Gr. Süd, 22 Aug. 1941: Hauck Südliches Gebiet, pt. 1, 332, appendix 31, MGFA P-114c. Amplification and confirmation after conferences on 23 Aug. in directive (Op.Abt. No. 31741/41 to H.Gr. Süd and Mitte, 24 Aug. 1941, BA-MA RH 2/v. 1326, pp. 199 ff.).

[233] Cf. n. 232 above and directive OKH/GenStdH/Op.Abt. (IM), 23 Aug. 1941 to H.Gr. Mitte, BA-MA RH 2/v. 1326, p. 202.

[234] Guderian, *Panzer Leader*, 101. Bock had attempted to 'slow' Guderian as late as 21 Aug.; he sought primarily not to expand the success away from the main direction of attack but to push for rehabilitation. The first papers for the operation eastward were ready on 22 Aug. Cf. Bock, *Tagebuch*, 69 (22 Aug. 1941), BA-MA N 22/9; there also Bock's conversation with Brauchitsch as the basis of the Army High Command directive of 24 Aug. 1941 cited in n. 232 above.

[235] Halder (*Diaries*, 1196: 24 Aug. 1941) severely criticized Guderian's 'caving in'. Guderian resolutely defended himself in *Panzer Leader* (101). It cannot be assumed that Guderian considered it his task to debate with Hitler the war-economy aspects involved in deciding on the point of main effort. He evidently did not bring himself to state simply that his armoured units were no longer mobile or ready for action (as the Army High Command assumed on 24 Aug.). On 22 Aug. he had flatly rejected this operation in a conversation with Bock. Cf. Bock, *Tagebuch*, 22, 23 Aug. 1941, BA-MA N 22/9.

considerable friction in regard to the envisaged operation.[236] No joint command was established for those parts of both army groups that were supposed to co-operate in the new operation.

After Guderian had brought up XXXXVII Armoured Corps from the area around Roslavl, the offensive of Armoured Group 2 made rapid progress. With 17th Armoured Division on the left wing, the armoured group advanced towards the Desna on a broad front on 25 August. XXIV Armoured Corps advanced with 3rd Armoured Division towards Novgorod–Severskiy and was able to capture the local bridge over the Desna intact, an essential condition for a rapid continuation of the advance.[237]

Second Army continued its attack with 7th Infantry Division towards Chernigov but was not able to advance as rapidly as the right wing of the armoured group, which was thus exposed to Soviet counter-attacks and did not reach its first objective, to cross the Desna at Korop. In the following days Armoured Group 2 suffered heavy attacks on its flanks against the Desna bridgehead, which was still being developed, and against the attack spearheads pushing out from it. The threat on the eastern flank proved to be so great that Guderian requested the release of his third armoured corps, of which the SS division 'Das Reich' and the reinforced infantry regiment 'Großdeutschland' were sent to join him.[238]

At the end of August Army Group South had reached its assembly areas for the crossing of the Dnieper by Seventeenth Army and Armoured Group 1. It considered the strong enemy artillery fire as a feint to conceal the basic intention to withraw from the Dnieper after the completion of positions further to the east. The logical conclusion for the German forces was to cross the river rapidly and pursue the enemy to avoid having to attack another deep system of enemy positions. In reality this meant that the army group command had decided to order its exhausted troops to undertake this operation with 'their last remaining strength' and without a rest.[239] Seventeenth Army was to make the main effort of the attack and cross the Dnieper near Kremenchug at as many places as possible. The bridgehead Dnepropetrovsk, which still had to

[236] Bock held XXXXVI Armd. Corps back—Guderian demanded it on 27 Aug.—so as to have at least one mobile unit for Moscow and for crisis situations. Cf. Bock, *Tagebuch*, 75 (27 Aug. 1941), BA-MA N 22/9; Halder, *Diaries*, 1203 (27 Aug. 1941). On that day Hitler wanted to use an additional armoured corps (XXXX) on the left wing of Army Group Centre to envelop the enemy facing Sixteenth Army. Bock on the other hand wanted to have II Corps of Army Group North begin its attack to the south-east in order to keep his own forces together for the attack on Moscow.

[237] For Halder's criticism of Guderian's ambitious reach towards the east see *Diaries*, 1198 (25 Aug. 1941). Cf. also Guderian, *Panzer Leader*, 102–3.

[238] Guderian, *Panzer Leader*, 105; Halder, *Diaries*, 1204–5 (28 Aug.–5 Sept. 1941).

[239] Cf. the directive of Army Group South, No. 7, 28 Aug. 1941: Hauck, *Südliches Gebiet*, pt. I, 348 ff., appendix 36, MGFA P-114c; H.Gr. Süd/Ia, KTB, 28 Aug. 1941, BA-MA RH 19 I/72, with the conclusion that the enemy was beginning to withdraw from large areas. Guidelines of Army High Command, 28 Aug., envisaged placing Guderian's army group under Army Group South once Sixth Army had crossed the Dnieper, in accordance with the closer encirclement ordered by Hitler, while Army Group South considered co-operation with Armd. Group 2 to be probable only in the Kharkov area.

be supplied largely over a captured floating bridge and a footbridge, was to be expanded by the three formations of III Armoured Corps there to eliminate the enemy artillery and make possible the crossing of at least one armoured and one motorized division with their heavy equipment. In fact, however, in the following days it was not possible to reduce enemy activity to an extent that would permit an orderly transfer of units to the east bank of the Dnieper. On the contrary, the three divisions lost a total of about 300 men each day.[240]

On 1 September the chief of the general staff of Army Group South contacted Second Army command to co-ordinate the issuing of orders on the left wing, and immediately made clear that because of the river plains and the lack of river-crossing equipment Sixth Army was dependent on assistance from Second Army.[241] He mentioned the area of Sumy as the objective for Armoured Group 2 and the line between Priluki and Romny for Second Army.[242] He justified this operation again as being in the best interests of Army Group Centre, because the elimination of enemy forces between the Dnieper and Kharkov would secure the southern flank for the great attack on Moscow. The expected 'battle of Poltava', as Sodenstern called it, thus appeared decisive for the campaign. After this battle, Sodenstern expected only 'expeditions' to occupy the country, as the enemy would be completely and definitively eliminated by the operation now beginning.

Sodenstern's remarks were caused by an order from the operations department of the Army General Staff received on 30 August to the effect that Army Group Centre was to make preparations to place the divisions of Second Army under Guderian's armoured group after Second Army had crossed the Desna 'for further operations with Army Group South'. The army headquarters and 'parts of Second Army not needed for further operations south of the Desna' were to be placed at the disposal of Army Group Centre. The number of 'parts needed' therefore depended also on the demands of Army Group South.[243] This decision seemed to recognize that the coming operation would be directed by Army Group South and no longer be merely an intensified effort, for which Army Group Centre would be responsible, to eliminate enemy forces at the boundary between the two groups.[244]

With the conquest and expansion of the bridgeheads across the Dnieper between Berislav (Eleventh Army) and Kremenchug (Seventeenth Army) on

[240] Report III. Pz.K., 7 Sept. 1941, BA-MA RH 24-3/51.

[241] H.Gr. Süd/Ia, KTB, 31 Aug. 1941, BA-MA RH 19 I/74; Hauck, Südliches Gebiet, pt. i, 356, appendix 38, MGFA P-114c.

[242] Copies were sent to the chief of staff of Army Group Centre and the chief of the operations department. Sodenstern believed he would be able to free at least twelve divisions for the attack on Moscow, provided Second Army and Armd. Group 2 pushed on across the Desna: H.Gr. Süd/Ia, KTB, 1 Sept. 1941, BA-MA RH 19 I/72.

[243] OKH/GenStdH/Op.Abt. (I) No. 31754/41, 30 Aug. 1941 to Army Groups Centre and South, BA-MA RH 2/v. 1326.

[244] On the other hand, Halder expected Second Army (of which elements would continue to move eastward) and Armd. Group 2 to be available after the 'intermezzo' as of 10 Sept. (Diaries, 1210 ff.: 31 Aug. 1941).

30–21 August and 2 September, the army group gained starting-positions south of Kiev. The stiffening of enemy resistance and the realization that he was bringing up strong units from other sections of the front and areas further to the east changed the German assessment of his position after the end of August. It became clear that Stalin had ordered the Dnieper line to be held and that large numbers of enemy troops were confronting the army group. On 4 September Army Group South ordered Seventeenth Army to attack from its bridgehead near Kremenchug in the direction of the general line Mirgorod–Lubny in order to encircle the enemy forces on the middle Dnieper and in Kiev. Armoured Group 1 was to cover this movement on its right flank and advance via Krasnograd towards Poltava.[245] (See the Annexe Volume, No. 12.)

On 6 September, in an order largely identical with the plans of the Army General Staff and its directive of 10 September 1941,[246] the Wehrmacht High Command instructed Armoured Group 1, now reinforced with infantry divisions (but without III Armoured Corps), to carry out the encirclement and Seventeenth Army to carry out the attack on Poltava. The purpose of that change was the fastest possible accomplishment of the envelopment. Only two corps of Seventeenth Army were engaged against Poltava and Krasnograd. As a consequence of this distribution of forces strong mobile units were tied down in protracted operations against the pocket east of Kiev, and the army group advanced more slowly than planned after the conclusion of the battle.

Of course Army Group Centre and Guderian pressed for the bringing up of the armoured forces of Army Group South after Armoured Group 2 for its part had several times found itself hard pressed. But the command of Army Group Centre was concentrating its attention only on the operation against Moscow—which, according to Brauchitsch and Halder during a visit to Bock's headquarters on 2 September, would now certainly be carried out—and insisted that all available forces be released soon for that objective.[247]

On 9 September Guderian with his XXIV Armoured Corps crossed the Seym, and on 10 September 3rd Armoured Division reached Romny and thus the objective for the meeting with Armoured Group 1. But this group had not been able to make sufficiently rapid progress because of the difficulty of the Dnieper crossing and the almost impassable muddy roads; Guderian's units therefore proceeded to Lovitsa. On 6 September Second Army attacked towards the Desna and was able to take Chernigov three days later. The first

[245] H.Gr. Süd/Ia, KTB, 4 Sept. 1941: Hauck, *Südliches Gebiet*, pt. i, 359, appendix 39, MGFA P-114c.

[246] *Hitler's War Directives*, No. 35 (6 Sept. 1941), pp 96 ff. On the acceptance of the operational idea 'Moscow' cf. Halder, *Diaries*, 1208–9 (30 Aug. 1941); also sect. II.1.1(*b*) at n. 205. The operation of Army Group South was to be carried out as fast as possible, which explains the employment of 3 armoured and 3 motorized infautry divisions in the direction of Romny. The bulk of Seventeenth Army was to attack in the direction of Poltava and Kharkov, supported by 1 armoured and 1 infantry division (mot.). This confirmed the plan of 12 Aug., H.Gr. Süd/Ia, KTB, 6 Sept. 1941, BA-MA RH 19 I/72.

[247] Bock, *Tagebuch*, 81–2 (2 Sept. 1941), BA-MA N 22/9.

signs of disintegration became apparent in the Soviet units now threatened by envelopment on several sides. From the west, Sixth Army attacked on 3 September and was able to establish the first contact with the spearheads of Second Army seven days later.

Nevertheless, the decisive thrust by Army Group South was delayed. After building up the necessary supplies and constructing a suitable bridge, the spearhead of Armoured Group 1 attacked from the bridgehead at Kremenchug with XXXXVIII Armoured Corps on 12 September.[248] The bridgehead at Dnepropetrovsk, which had been held with heavy losses, was to be opened from the rear by 13th Armoured Division of III Armoured Corps, attacking likewise from Kremenchug along the Dnieper. On 13 September the part of the pincer movement of Armoured Group 1 attacking from the south-west had already reached Lubny, where both armoured spearheads met. The first ring, albeit still weak, was closed near Lokhvitsa on 15 September. In addition to this broad envelopment of the main forces of the Soviet south-west front, the Dnieper crossing by the right wing of Sixth Army at Rechitsa made possible a complete encirclement of Kiev, which fell on 19 September. Protected on the left flank by XIV Armoured Corps, south of Kremenchug beyond the Dnieper, Seventeenth Army attacked Poltava.

In addition to purely operational and tactical questions, the capture of Kiev raised serious problems concerning the safety of the troops in the city.[249] On 13 September Sixth Army command ordered that until the area of the city had been completely cleared of all forms of enemy resistance, German troops would be permitted to remain there only with written permission of the army headquarters. At the same time an order was issued concerning the securing of stocks and the maintaining of order in Kiev. After the fighting in the city came to an end on 19 September, it became evident not only that all important material had been removed and the railway lines destroyed but also that extensive acts of destruction had been prepared for the time after the fighting by the use of numerous explosive charges to be detonated by remote control. As a result of a tip from an anonymous source, on 19 September 99th Light Division learnt of explosive charges planted in large buildings suitable as quarters for staffs and troops. An extensive, partially successful, search was begun, but on 24 September an explosion next to the main post office in a depot for captured equipment and ammunition started a large fire which spread rapidly and could not be extinguished by Fire Brigade Regiment Sachsen. To contain the fire, Sapper Battalion 99 and demolition squads from

---

[248] OKH/GenStdH/Op.Abt. (I) No. 1494/41, 10 Sept. 1941, Weisung für die Fortführung der Operationen [Directive for the continuation of operations], BA-MA RH 2/1326, pp. 209 ff. Hauck (Südliches Gebiet, pt. 1, 128–9, MGFA P-114c) offers a summary of the coming battles from the perspective of the army group, which for reasons of space can be treated here only very briefly. Cf. Röhricht, *Kesselschlacht*, 59 ff.; Haupt, *Kiew*, 109 ff., with literature on the history of numerous units.

[249] Gen.Kdo XXIX. AK/Ia, KTB, 1 July–31 Sept. 1941, annexe 1, BA-MA, XXIX. AK, 15147/3.

99th and 71st Infantry divisions cleared large fire-breaks.[250] The conflagration was finally put out on 29 September, by additional German soldiers, technical emergency units, and city and German fire brigades. Sapper Battalion 99 was proud of having 'rendered in exemplary fashion a great service in saving the city of Kiev through the personal efforts of every individual involved'. The losses in dead and injured in this incident caused Hitler to forbid the taking of such risks again. 'Partisans and Jews' were blamed for the original fire and repeated flare-ups, and were shot on the spot. This marked the beginning of one of the most ghastly massacres of the war. Military Administration Headquarters 195 had to be removed; the commander of 113th Infantry Division was to take over the role of commandant of the city. These incidents of arson with the resulting losses—among others, Colonel Freiherr von Seidlitz und Gohlau of the Army General Staff died in the fire in Kiev—were one of the reasons for the order concerning the behaviour of German troops in the east issued by the commander-in-chief of Sixth Army, Field Marshal von Reichenau, on 10 October 1941.[251] They also confirmed Hitler's view that large fortified cities should not be taken by direct attack, especially not with armoured units, but should be bypassed, encircled, and forced to surrender by means of artillery fire and air attacks. Referring to Kiev, on 7 October 1941 Hitler expanded this principle to include not only Moscow and Leningrad but also other large Soviet cities, and repeated his prohibition against sending troops into these cities, so as not to expose them to losses through enemy explosive devices or other forms of sabotage. The effects of Hitler's often repeated basic order on this procedure will be examined at the appropriate point. It should, however, be noted here that neither Kiev nor Dnepropetrovsk nor Kharkov was destroyed and 'obliterated' by bombing and shelling, as the German forces needed these transportation centres and their buildings for staffs, depots, and other supply installations. Moreover, the common interest of the occupiers and a large part of the native population in maintaining a functioning infrastructure led to relations based to a considerable degree on mutual agreement in this regard.

On 25 September most of the fighting in the pocket east of Kiev ended. The end of the 'battle of Kiev', as this operation was later called, gave rise to the hope among German military leaders that, with relatively slight forces, they would be able to conquer the Crimean peninsula and cross over to the

[250] Report on fire-fighting by Sapper Bn. 99: 99 Lgt. Div., war diary, annexe to vol. v, BA-MA RH 26-99/16; also XXIX Army Corps, war diary, annexe, reports of 20 Sept.–19 Nov. 1941, BA-MA, XXIX. AK, 15192/7. Generally orders were to seek out 'party activists and Jews' as instigators and hostages after acts of sabotage. This was justified by references to existing guidelines and to evidence provided by the population.

[251] Other militarily justified reasons were Soviet atrocities against German prisoners of war and reports of attacks on military hospitals, individual sentries, and similar incidents mentioned in 'Erfahrungen aus den jüngsten Kämpfen' of 28 June 1941. Individual passages of this order can be found in previous instructions from Foreign Armies East as well as from the general for special tasks in the Army High Command. However, the rounding up and subsequent execution of the Jewish population of Kiev cannot be justified by any reference to a military threat.

Caucasus before the beginning of winter. In their view, the enormous losses suffered by the Red Army in the three months of the campaign justified the assumption that the attack on Moscow, 'Operation Typhoon', could still succeed in spite of the advanced season.[252] For the necessary massing of forces, Army Group South was required to transfer two corps commands and ten divisions—among them one armoured division and two motorized infantry divisions—to Army Group Centre immediately after the victory east of Kiev. It thus retained only two armoured corps for operations over the great distances to the Caucasus.

For its new tasks the army group was reorganized; the Romanian units which remained under its command were assigned to Eleventh Army Headquarters, but with the important change that the Romanian Fourth Army was withdrawn completely from the German area of command and placed under the sole command of Antonescu for the siege of Odessa. Along with their corps command, the three Hungarian brigades were placed under the 'Group von Roques', which at the same time exercised command authority in the rear area of the army. In this capacity it also contained two additional Hungarian brigades with a corps staff, the Slovak security division, and three German security divisions. The Italian expeditionary corps, only partially motorized and assigned to III Armoured Corps, was not an adequate replacement for XXXXVIII Armoured Corps, which had been transferred. In accordance with the plans for further operations, Army Group South took III Armoured Corps under its command even before the new attacks in the east in order to have a mobile formation, 'Group Mackensen', ready for use as the situation required.[253] (See the Annexe Volume, No. 13.)

The advance of Eleventh and Seventeenth Armies at first assumed the form of a pursuit. On 17 September this caused Halder and Sodenstern to consider ordering Armoured Group 1 in future to advance not to the east or north-east, but to the south-east on the shortest route to Rostov.[254] Halder estimated that the armoured group could reach the Donets industrial region at approximately the same time as Seventeenth Army, which was advancing rapidly from Kharkov and was supposed to reach the city before the enemy could construct new defensive positions and reorganize his units. With the main task of securing the northern flank of the army group, Sixth Army was to follow Seventeenth Army in echelon. The problem of protecting the flanks of the two army groups in the event of a rapid advance of Seventeenth as well as Second Army towards Kursk was to be solved by having Sixth Army follow after them, moving towards the Donets industrial region. Army Group South, while

[252] According to figures of Army Group South (Ia, KTB, 26 Sept. 1941, BA-MA RH 19 I/73), this battle resulted in the capture of 665,000 Soviet soldiers, 3,018 artillery pieces, 884 tanks, and 418 anti-tank guns. On the question of the expected duration of the war in connection with the late start of Typhoon cf. sect. II.1.1(*b*) at n. 216.

[253] H.Gr. Süd/Ia, KTB, 16 Sept. 1941, BA-MA RH 19 I/73.

[254] Ibid., 17 Sept. 1941, and order No. 2216/41, 20 Sept. 1941. According to this order, Armd. Group 1 was first to open the bridgehead of Dnepropetrovsk and capture the Samara bridges as a precondition for the transport of supplies beyond the river.

recognizing the need to employ a mobile unit along this boundary to provide flexible cover for the area, was not able to detach forces for that purpose from the now reduced Armoured Group 1[255]—except possibly XXXXVIII Armoured Corps, which was to be transferred to Army Group Centre—until Sixth Army arrived. It should be noted that, because of the great success in the 'battle of Kiev', Halder regarded the danger of a Soviet thrust from the southeast and east to be so improbable that he believed the transfer of an additional armoured group to this flank, as had been considered by the Wehrmacht High Command and thus by Hitler, to be unnecessary, and that it was also Halder who planned and approved the eccentric attack by Kleist's armoured group.[256] Indeed, he considered the rapid thrust of Armoured Group 1 to be necessary 'not because of concern that the enemy will organize stronger resistance—for lack of the necessary forces he is no longer able to do that—but because he may withdraw large forces which can then no longer be caught'. Halder did not rule out a Soviet withdrawal as far as the Don.

Army Group South was optimistic but believed that the situation was not without problems and that heavy fighting still lay ahead.[257] Enemy resistance was also stiffening along the Dnieper between Melitopol and Zaporozhye. This development was believed to be connected with a build-up of enemy forces around Kharkov. Although these forces were not considered to have a very high combat value, it was to be expected that Seventeenth Army would experience heavy fighting before reaching the industrial area.[258] At the bridgehead in Dnepropetrovsk, however, enemy pressure began to decline as a result

[255] The idea of transferring Armd. Group 1 to Army Group Centre to provide flank cover for the offensive against Moscow came from the Wehrmacht High Command and was presented to Armd. Group 1 by Warlimont on 21 Sept.: H.Gr. Süd/Ia, KTB, 21 Sept. 1941, BA-MA RH 19 I/ 73. On the other hand, as early as 18 Sept. Halder had discussed with Jodl the use of parts of Armd. Group 1 in co-operation with Eleventh Army to attack Rostov: Halder, *Diaries*, 1244. On 21 Sept. this approach seemed to the army group to offer the only chance, in the event of favourable weather, of occupying the oilfields north of the Caucasus in 1941.

[256] Chief of the operations department to the operations department (Ia) of Army Group South, 20 Sept. 1941, regarding the question of whether the Army High Command intended to issue a directive confirming that 'the approval of the Führer and Supreme Commander has yet to be obtained regarding the intentions of the C.-in-C. of the army, and especially for the use of Armd. Group 1 to reach the Sea of Azov and Rostov on the Don, which has not yet been proposed to him'. Hitler gave his consent: H.Gr. Süd/Ia, KTB, 21 Sept. 1941, BA-MA RH 19 I/73; OKH/ GenStdH/Op.Abt. (IS) No. 1523/41, Weisung für die Fortführung der Operation der Heeresgruppe Süd [Directive for the continuation of the operation by Army Group South], 21 Sept. 1941, ibid. For Halder's assessment of the enemy's situation and quote, 23 Sept. 1941, see ibid., fos. 94 ff.

[257] Situation analysis of Army Group South, 23 Sept. 1941, ibid.: Hauck, Südliches Gebiet, pt. 1, 376 ff., appendix 46, and intelligence (Ic) assessment of enemy's situation, ibid. 379, MGFA P-114c.

[258] On 21 Sept. Heusinger and Sodenstern discussed whether Kharkov or the industrial area further south should be attacked. According to the directive of the Army High Command, both were to be attacked by Seventeenth Army, Kharkov to be taken first, then Voroshilovgrad with the industrial area, and subsequently the Don crossings. This task was similar to that given them on 12 Aug. (cf. n. 226 above). The operations department of the army group and Seventeenth Army headquarters were agreed that the industrial area had priority and that Kharkov possessed more prestige value. The quick capture of Kharkov would depend on the addition of a mobile unit to Seventeenth Army: H.Gr. Süd/Ia, KTB, 21 Sept. 1941, BA-MA RH 19 I/73.

of the withdrawal of the siege forces, which were then transferred to the front facing Seventeenth Army.

The indications of the future line of operations given to the commanders-in-chief of the armies and the commanders of the armoured group and 'Group von Roques' in a preliminary orientation on 21 September were defined more precisely by the Army High Command.[259] Generally, while keeping its northern flank covered, the army group was to occupy the Crimea and the eastern Ukraine and establish positions for advancing into the Caucasus by crossing both the strait of Kerch and the Don. A new element, compared with earlier deliberations, was the planned attack by Armoured Group 1 from the area around Kremenchug, first along the Dnieper to the south in order to turn the flank of the Soviet Dnieper defences, including Cherkassy and Dnepropetrovsk. Subsequently the armoured group was to turn east and concentrate on the industrial area on the north bank of the Don. Eleventh Army was still to occupy the Crimea and advance along the northern coast of the Sea of Azov towards Rostov. Seventeenth Army's orders were expanded to include, in addition to Kharkov, a thrust towards Voroshilovgrad to occupy the Don crossings between the mouth of the Sal and the Tsirskaya, not far from the narrowest point between the Don and the Volga at Stalingrad. Sixth Army was to cover the deep northern flank of Seventeenth Army and to advance via Belgorod and occupy the bank of the Don on both sides of Pavlosk. There was no order to secure the southern flank of Army Group Centre.

The attack by Eleventh Army on the isthmus of Perekop had as its objective the Crimea, but the situation around Odessa had not developed favourably for the Romanians. As without Odessa the urgently needed supply-route via the Black Sea could not be used,[260] the use of German units to capture the city seemed to be the logical solution. The army group suggested transferring two or three units from the west, but the Army High Command immediately rejected this. The vague hope remained that the occupation of the Crimea would induce the enemy to abandon Odessa. In the end the surrounded Soviet troops evacuated the city in the middle of October. As the besiegers failed to notice this action in time, they were unable to interfere effectively with the removal of troops and equipment.[261]

All tentative objectives mentioned here were summarized in a directive of the army group command on 25 September.[262] The 'Group von Roques' was

[259] Sources as in n. 256 above.

[260] Forstmeier, *Odessa*, 125 (strength of Soviet Black Sea Fleet during the fighting for Odessa).

[261] The deliberations of Halder and the army group regarding the capture of the Crimea can be followed in both relevant war diaries after 15 Aug. As early as 20 Aug. the army group doubted that the Romanians alone would be able to take Odessa. Hitler decided to leave the capture of the city to the Romanians under Antonescu's command, but the Army High Command simultaneously alerted the army group that Eleventh Army should be held ready to intervene if necessary: H.Gr. Süd/Ia, KTB, 20 Aug. 1941, BA-MA RH 19/73. Not until 5 Oct., however, did Hitler decide to urge Antonescu to accept German assistance: *KTB OKW* i. 1069–70 (102). On the course of events as a whole cf. Forstmeier, *Odessa*, 33 ff.

[262] H.Gr. Süd, Directive No. 9, 25 Sept. 1941, for the continuation of Operation Barbarossa in

additionally ordered to secure the sector of the Dnieper between Melitopol and Dnepropetrovsk, still held by the Red Army, and to tie down the enemy at the front by feints or real attacks until the attack by Armoured Group 1 began to take effect. The Slovak Mobile Division, 132nd Infantry Division, and, after Kharkov had been reached, a division of Seventeenth Army formed the reserves of the army group. A special instruction was issued concerning allied units; on Hitler's orders, they were to be employed as parts of larger German forces or together with them.

The attack on the isthmus of Perekop began on 24 September with LIV Army Corps and 73rd and 46th Infantry Divisions (see the Annexe Volume, No. 14). Lack of cover and enemy air supremacy led to heavy losses among the German troops. The other two corps of the army were involved in defensive fighting in the east. Within a few days the assessment of the enemy's situation and intentions had changed completely. While Halder had assumed a week earlier that the Crimea could be taken in a surprise attack and the enemy also cut off west of Kerch,[263] Manstein was not able to capture the strongly fortified, narrow isthmus in one attack with only two divisions and all available artillery.[264] The mountain corps, actually intended for the fighting in the Caucasus after the crossing of the Kerch strait, was sent into action immediately on the northern wing of the army.[265] After the southern part of the isthmus had been penetrated near Ishun, the advance came to a halt when a crisis arose in the Romanian Third Army following an attack by the Soviet Ninth Army. The offensive forces had to wait until a thrust by Armoured Group 1 weakened the position of this army and the Soviet Eighteenth Army.

Because one of its armoured divisions was tied to Seventeenth Army, the attack of Armoured Group 1 across the Orel river and from Dnepropetrovsk did not advance as rapidly as expected. Nevertheless, on 1 October Zaporozhye was taken. The following day, the Soviet forces facing Eleventh Army found themselves in danger of being cut off and withdrew to the east. The two inner wings of the attack by Armoured Group 1 and Eleventh Army were able to encircle large elements of the enemy force near Berdyansk, thus opening the way to Mariupol. On 11 October III Armoured Corps reached the

---

the Donets industrial area: Hauck, *Südliches Gebiet*, pt. 1, 386, appendix 49, MGFA P-114c. Deliberations between Halder and Sodenstern after 23 Sept. in war diary of the army group, BA-MA RH 19 I/74; the authority was Hitler's Directive No. 36, 22 Sept. 1941, pp. 154 ff.

[263] Halder, *Diaries*, 1240–1 (17 Sept. 1941); H.Gr. Süd/Ia, KTB, same day; Lehmann, *Leibstandarte*, ii. 155. This was the only mobile unit available for the capture of Perekop. Because of the failure of the breakthrough attempt by 73rd Inf. Div., the division was pulled out and transferred to the defensive battles on the Sea of Azov.

[264] Manstein, *Lost Victories*, 211–12; report AOK 11/Ia, 25 Sept. 1941. On 26 Sept. Eleventh Army demanded XXXXIX Mountain Corps for the Crimea, which left only one German corps for the thrust on the northern shore: H.Gr. Süd/Ia, KTB, 25, 26 Sept. 1941, BA-MA RH 19 I/73.

[265] The heavy artillery and anti-tank battalions of 1st and 4th Mountain Divs. continued to support the Romanian Third Army; moreover, 170th Inf. Div. was added to the army, which since August had been offered to the Romanians attacking Odessa.

Mius north of Taganrog. After 14 October cold weather and rain prevented a further advance.[266]

On the northern wing of the army group, Seventeenth Army, whose units could be withdrawn only gradually from the encirclement front and which began its attack along the line between Krasnograd and Poltava on 23 September, was also unable to reach its objectives in anything approaching the time planned. Accepting heavy losses, the 'motley' forces fiercely resisted the attempt to take the industrial area. The attack on Kharkov as well as against Lozovaya so completely dissipated the strength of the offensive that a division from Armoured Group 1 had to be transferred to the army.[267]

Because of the long period it had remained in the area of Kiev, its numerous transfers to other formations, and the exhaustion of its troops, Sixth Army was not able to afford adequate protection to the left wing of Seventeenth Army. This necessitated a widening of the latter's sector of the front, since in addition Armoured Group 2 on the left was moving further away. On 4 October the head of the operations department observed that in the further course of operations it would no longer be possible to maintain contact between the army groups.[268]

Heavy rain and the onset of cold weather, in addition to the increasing number of counter-attacks, slowed all movements at the end of September and the beginning of October. Hitler had to abandon the rapid thrust to Kharkov. On 1 October he ordered that priority should be given to the attack on the Donets basin. It would be in order for Sixth Army to take Kharkov later.[269] As it was not possible to detach troops from the fighting, it was necessary to wait until Sixth Army arrived. The two corps of Seventeenth Army on the left were placed under Sixth Army, and Seventeenth Army headquarters now concentrated on preparing for the attack in the direction of Izyum. Having begun its attack, Sixth Army forced the enemy back across the Vorskla and reached Akhtyrka and Sumy on 10 October. On that day Seventeenth Army reached Lozovaya. The army group's further advance was halted by mud and exhaustion. Because of the destruction of the Dnieper bridges, supplies were often delayed. Road conditions, a lack of maintenance of vehicles, and general exhaustion forced a halt.[270]

[266] The armoured group was now called First Armd. Army: Pz.Armeebefehl No. 2, 8 Oct. 1941, BA-MA RH 24-3/56. On 2 Oct. 1941 the 'battle of the Sea of Azov' had resulted in the separation of the tasks of occupying the Crimea and pushing on to Mariupol between Eleventh Army and First Armoured Army.

[267] Halder, *Diaries*, 1257 (26 Sept. 1941); H.Gr. Süd/Ia, KTB, 27 Sept. 1941, BA-MA RH 19 I/73. After a tussle with the army group the Army High Command decided on 29 Sept. that 'only weak parts of Armd. Group 1' were to be withdrawn temporarily to eliminate the threat to the flank of Seventeenth Army. The C.-in-C. of that army, Gen. von Stülpnagel, was relieved of his command on 9 Oct. and replaced by Col.-Gen. Hoth. Cf. Halder, *Diaries*, 1268 (2 Oct. 1941), 1263–4 (Stülpnagel).

[268] H.Gr. Süd/Ia, KTB, 29 Sept.–4 Oct. 1941, BA-MA RH 19 I/73.

[269] Halder, *Diaries*, 1267 (1 Oct. 1941); the fact that 13th Armd. Div. was not ready for action played an important role in this decision.

[270] Assessment of the situation by Army Group South, 12 Oct 1941: Hauck, Südliches Gebiet,

From intelligence reports on the enemy's situation, especially around Kharkov and Valki, the army group concluded that the Red Army had probably decided to evacuate the western part of the Donets industrial area and to establish a new line of defence along the river. At the same time, however, it was determined to hold Rostov at all costs, for III Armoured Corps encountered extremely fierce resistance on the Mius.[271]

Because of this assessment, Hitler intervened on 14 October. Again he feared that Soviet forces would escape beyond the Donets, and so ordered Seventeenth Army to send two divisions northward to prevent, in conjunction with the divisions of Sixth Army advancing on Bogodukhov, the Soviet defensive forces west of Kharkov from withdrawing into the city and to encircle them.[272] The army group protested against having to withdraw important parts of Seventeenth Army from the attack to the south-east, as that would prevent it from being able to carry out its orders. The almost immobilized southern sector of the army group was completely dependent on co-operation of the right wing of Seventeenth Army with the left corps of First Armoured Army in its efforts to capture the Donets area. Any change of direction would require an enormous effort and was simply unworkable. The operational aspect of the envisaged later thrust by First Armoured Army towards Maykop, which was dependent on the progress made by Seventeenth Army, was also presented as an argument against weakening the latter. A strong enemy armoured attack against the spearheads of Sixth Army near Bogodukhov confirmed the assumption that Kharkov and the Donets line would require considerable defensive forces. At the same time, because of the great distances, the movement of supplies collapsed in many areas; fuel had to be flown in to maintain the anti-tank defences of Sixth Army.[273]

While the army group and the operations department were marshalling all arguments against the planned new attack, which was repeated as an order from Hitler by the Army High Command on 15 October, Seventeenth Army believed that in view of the weak defences in front of the industrial area it would be able to continue the attack even after some of its units had been diverted to the north. Aerial reconnaissance indicated that the enemy forces west of Kharkov were preparing to withdraw. The army group accepted this view. The left wing of Sixth Army was now to be sent against Belgorod. Although it was pointed out that the enemy movements spotted by aerial

---

pt. I, 395 ff., appendix 50, MGFA P-114c; H.Gr. Süd/Ia, KTB, 12 Oct. 1941: BA-MA RH 19 I/74. Transport problems were aggravated after 1 Oct. by the removal of 30,000 prisoners daily from the battle of Kiev; this required 4,500 German soldiers for a whole fortnight: ibid., 2 Oct. 1941.

[271] Report, H.Gr. Süd/Ia, KTB, 14 Oct. 1941 and following days, BA-MA RH 19 I/74. On 13 Oct. First Armd. Army headquarters had ordered that use must be made of every opportunity to attack, on the assumption that only a few more weeks of fair weather remained before the beginning of winter. On 15 Oct. the army ordered that the objectives remained unchanged in spite of reports that muddy road conditions had rendered them unrealizable: BA-MA RH 24-3/56.

[272] Hitler's wish and report, H.Gr. Süd/Ia, KTB, 14 Oct. 1941, BA-MA RH 19 I/74.

[273] Hitler's wish and report, H.Gr. Süd/Ia, KTB.

reconnaissance might only be transports of replacements, the army group did not change its view that the situation as a whole strongly supported the belief that the enemy was withdrawing beyond the Donets.

The assessment of the situation given to the operations department suggested that Hitler's order had been overtaken by events, as an encirclement of large enemy forces west of Kharkov was no longer possible.[274] The operations department reported Halder's agreement, provided the assessment of the enemy's situation was confirmed, and expected the advance of the outer wings of Sixth and Seventeenth Armies into the area east of Kharkov. The southern group of Seventeenth Army was now to advance to the south-east to link up with First Armoured Army at Stalino.[275] If necessary, the Hungarian Mobile Corps was to move in a northerly direction to provide flank cover, for Hitler's plans required the northern attack group of Seventeenth Army to cross the Donets and attack along the line Kupyansk–Chuguev so as to link up with the right wing of Sixth Army there and cut off the enemy's withdrawal to the east. The army group demanded attacks 'everywhere' and the pursuit of the defeated enemy 'as far as endurance permits'.[276]

The next objective of First Armoured Army was Rostov; Eleventh Army was to conquer the Crimea. Hitler confirmed these orders with the remark that every opportunity should be taken to cut off enemy forces. For this reason the front of First Armoured Army was to be extended to the north to make sure of destroying the enemy forces there by an envelopment from the north, should it not be possible to break out of the bridgehead at Taganrog.[277] In this confirmation Hitler again demanded the destruction of any enemy forces still west of the Donets. The army group pointed to its situation assessment, the supply problems, and the possibility of enveloping the retreating enemy east of the Donets. As, in view of the condition of the troops, it was not to be expected that the enemy could be 'annihilated' even there, the army group proposed that the left wing of Seventeenth Army should attack in the direction of Chuguev to prevent the enemy establishing defensive positions along the Donets.

The directive of the Army High Command of 16 October 1941, based on this exchange of ideas with Army Group South, assumed therefore that a defence of the industrial area in the Donets basin was no longer to be expected.[278] The army group still rejected the idea of having IV and XXXXIV

---

[274] Even if this favourable evaluation of the situation was doctored to avoid the exhausting transfer of the main point of attack, the judgement of Seventeenth Army headquarters of 16 Oct. was still that the enemy facing IV Army Corps 'is fighting without any enthusiasm and running away'. First Armd. Army came to a similar conclusion: H.Gr. Süd/Ia, KTB, BA-MA RH 19 I/74; situation assessment of Army Group South, 19 Oct. 1941 (excerpt), in Hauck, Südliches Gebiet, pt. I, 400, appendix 52, MGFA P-114c.

[275] H.Gr. Süd/Ia, pursuit order, 16 Oct. 1941, BA-MA RH 19 I/74.   [276] Ibid.

[277] Ibid. As after the battle of Smolensk, the main idea here was to dispense with conquest of territory in favour of preventing an escape and regrouping of the Red Army.

[278] OKH/GenStdH/Op.Abt. (I) No. 1588/41, to H.Gr. Nord, Mitte, Süd, 16 Oct. 1941, BA-MA RH 2/1327.

Army Corps of Seventeenth Army turn north-east. The group command pointed out the possibility of enveloping the enemy west of Kharkov with advance units only and, on the evening of 16 October, ordered an attack by mobile forces via Merefa against Kharkov, to be followed by XI Army Corps. Hitler, however, followed every change on the situation map, and on 17 October again demanded the encirclement of the enemy forces still west of Kharkov.

Oddly enough, the army group justified the subsequent order to Seventeenth Army command by the withdrawal of the enemy forces defending Stalino; this would how permit the occupation of the industrial area by weaker German units.[279] On the other hand, it proposed to the operations department a reformulation of the orders for Seventeenth Army so as to take into account this most recent change. The draft submitted on 18 October was not without a certain grim humour, considering the reports on the condition of the troops and the supply situation at this time. It recommended that First Armoured Army should be ordered to occupy a bridgehead near Rostov as well as an area extending to the Don south of the line between Voroshilovgrad and Stalingrad. Seventeenth Army was to conquer the area west of the Don and north of that line, and Sixth Army the area north of the line between Kharkov and Novaya Kalitva and on the Don between the latter town and Voronezh.[280] The impression still prevailed that the enemy would withdraw before the advance of Sixth and Seventeenth Armies. The events of 19 October seemed at first to confirm this assumption. First Armoured Army and Seventeenth Army reached the western edge of the industrial area; in its thrust towards Belgorod Sixth Army reached Borisovka.

(i) THE ADVANCE TO THE CRIMEA

After the battle on the Sea of Azov it would have been possible to restart preparations for the battle for the Crimea.[281] But the new deliberations of the army group concerning the attack of First Armoured Army had also changed the situation of Eleventh Army. Its task was now confined to the conquest of the Crimea. This resulted in a new distribution of forces. Manstein kept LIV and XXX Army corps with a total of six divisions, of which parts of 50th Infantry Division were facing Odessa. To provide cover, the Romanian Mountain Corps with one mountain and one cavalry brigade was also placed under his command.[282] Manstein was also given the rest of the Romanian Third Army with renewed orders to secure the coast to Mariupol. Attention was primarily concentrated on strengthening the units to be used in the attack on Odessa, which was taken by the Romanian Fourth Army on 16 October.

[279] H.Gr. Süd/Ia, KTB, 18 Oct. 1941, BA-MA RH 19 I/74.   [280] Ibid.

[281] Cf. the paragraphs preceding n. 267 above.

[282] H.Gr. Süd/Ia, KTB, 7, 8 Oct. 1941; supplement to Directive No. 9 of army group, BA-MA RH 19 I/74; Manstein, *Lost Victories*, 216 ff. The request to bring up Hungarian units had already been rejected on 4 Aug.

The fall of Odessa made more difficult the attack on the Crimea by Eleventh Army, as Soviet units evacuated from that city were now used in the defence of the peninsula. Manstein therefore requested that all German units now no longer needed against Odessa, as well as the army troops and 132nd Infantry Division, be assigned to his army.[283]

In the attack begun by the divisions of LIV Army Corps on 18 October the strong enemy defences and the complete lack of armoured units quickly led to heavy losses on the German side. Soviet air supremacy had an especially disastrous effect on the German troops. The efforts of fourteen German dive-bombers were unable to substantially change this situation. After urgent requests Fourth Air Corps sent additional air units, which had to be withdrawn from other sectors of the army group's front, to silence enemy batteries in fortified positions, destroy airfields, and disrupt assemblies of enemy troops. The highly respected Colonel Werner Mölders was placed in charge of the fighter escorts.[284] The penetration of the narrow neck of land north of Ishun on 19 October seemed to mark a decisive turn in the attack, but the fighting remained hard and costly until a breakthrough of the enemy's positions had been achieved. The attacking divisions were completely exhausted. Manstein demanded that he be sent a mobile unit, and on 22 October Army Group South reported to the Army High Command that a rapid conquest of the Crimea was not possible with the German forces fighting there.[285] For in addition to the conquest of the peninsula, on 20 October Manstein had been ordered to assemble a corps with three divisions to cross over to Tuapse and Krasnodar, which would require at least one additional corps.[286] The army group at first requested a mobile division, which, as it was well aware, was not available. Explaining the connection between the crossing from the Crimea to the Caucasus via Kerch and the intended operations of First Armoured Army, it therefore suggested that 60th Motorized Infantry Division of III Armoured Corps should be transferred to Eleventh Army, as a three-week break in operations would be indispensable after the Don had been reached.[287]

A decision by Hitler was required as to whether the main German effort should concentrate on conquering the Crimea or on crossing the Don. Hitler agreed to the transfer of the motorized division, but only if the remaining units

---

[283] H.Gr. Süd/Ia, KTB, 17 Oct. 1941, BA-MA RH 19 I/74; Manstein, *Lost Victories*, 220.

[284] Cf. sect. II.1.2(*b*) at n. 848 (Boog).

[285] H.Gr. Süd/Ia, KTB, 22 Oct. 1941, BA-MA RH 19 I/74. Moreover, no Romanian troops were to be used in the Crimea as a matter of principle—but if that should become unavoidable they were not to be used on the west or south coasts. Owing to the lack of sufficient security forces, the Romanian brigades, like the SD, were indispensable for combating partisans and for other tasks in rear areas.

[286] Ibid., 20 Oct. 1941.

[287] Ibid. The request of Army Group South to the Army High Command, 22, 25 Oct. 1941, was due largely to expected supply problems, which, because of the considerable loss of vehicle transport capacity, made the construction of supply-dumps unavoidable. For the detailed report of the army group to the Army High Command on the situation, the urgent need for rehabilitation, and the impossibility of reaching operational objectives in the Crimea and towards the Don at the same time, see H.Gr. Süd/Ia, KTB, 22 Oct. 1941, BA-MA RH 19 I/74.

of III Armoured Corps had sufficient fuel reserves to ensure that they would be able to fulfil their tasks. In view of the fuel situation of First Armoured Army, this condition amounted to a rejection of the transfer request.[288] First Armoured Army also resisted having to transfer its only remaining 'full-strength' unit and argued that it would not be able to reach Rostov if the division were transferred. Thereupon, on 26 October, Hitler decided that Rostov should be given priority.

The promised Luftwaffe reinforcements arrived on 24 October, and of these three fighter and two dive-bomber Gruppen were used to support Eleventh Army. Two fighter Gruppen and one dive-bomber Gruppe were sent to Rostov; one fighter Gruppe and two Italian fighter squadrons were deployed in the combat area of Seventeenth and Six Armies.

After a crisis on 25 October, German forces succeeded in breaking through the Soviet positions into the Crimea. At the same time Manstein repeated his urgent demand for a motorized unit, pointing out that if the attack stalled an armoured corps with at least two armoured divisions and one motorized division would be necessary to resume it. But the army group could promise only to send him an infantry division as of the middle of November. On 28 October the defence of the Crimea collapsed, and the divisions of LIV and XXX Army Corps were able to begin the pursuit of the enemy.

(ii) THE ADVANCE TO THE DON
(See the Annexe Volume, No. 13)

Differences in the evaluation of the situation by the field army commands, the Army High Command, and Hitler delayed agreement in assessing the situation of the enemy and resulted in divergent command decisions. This in turn led to Hitler issuing direct, even tactical, orders far from the front.[289] Because of the absolutely necessary rehabilitation period for First Armoured Army, the army group command proposed to Halder that operations should be confined to eliminating enemy resistance west of the Don before the beginning of winter. But Halder demanded the crossing of the Don to secure a base for future operations. Only if that did not succeed could the turning of the left wing of First Armoured Army to the north be considered. Seventeenth Army was to continue to concentrate the main effort of its advance on reaching Stalingrad, with Sixth Army providing cover to the north (around Kursk) and north-east (towards Voronezh) for this operation. The army group command incorporated these orders into its directive of 20 October 1941.[290]

---

[288] According to a report of First Armd. Army, the following quantities of fuel were available on 25 Oct.: 330 m.³ received, 600 m.³ *en route*, 550 m.³ in the dump at Zaparozhye. Even an increase to 1,000 m.³ would only mean that half the fuel thought necessary for reaching the Don would be available: BA-MA RH 19 I/74, p. 163.

[289] Cf. sect. II.1.1(b) at n. 150.

[290] H.Gr. Süd/Ia, Directive No. 10 for the continuation of the operation; H.Gr. Süd/Ia, KTB, 20 Oct. 1941, with notes on the talk between the army group and the operations department before the directive was written, BA-MA RH 19 I/74, fos. 127 ff.

With the approach to Kharkov, the army group command and Sixth Army were confronted with a problem which, although having nothing to do with operational considerations, was nevertheless of considerable importance. On 20 October the Army High Command informed subordinate commands of Hitler's decision that, after the problems experienced in Kiev, no German soldier was to enter cities in which hidden explosive charges could be expected. Such cities were to be 'worn down' by artillery bombardment and air attacks and the population induced to flee. Because of the danger involved, fire-fighting was forbidden, as was the feeding of the population 'at the expense of the German homeland'.[291] As this order also applied 'in a general sense' to Kharkov, Sixth Army was confronted with a dilemma. It needed the rail connections and quarters the city could provide, and therefore decided to interpret the order with strong emphasis on 'general', even more so as the population would then be more inclined to welcome rather than reject the German occupation.

The problems of lodging and supplies for the coming winter came to play an increasingly important role in German deliberations. In this respect the conversion of the gange of the railway line to Kharkov was essential. On 22 October Sixth Army headquarters reported that weather forecasts indicated that the roads could no longer be expected to dry out, while lasting frost would arrive only in December. This meant that operations had to be halted. The number of vehicles and horses ready for action had sunk to a 'no longer acceptable level'. It was therefore not possible to reach the objectives the army group had set.[292]

As it based its assessment on the same information, the army group agreed with this report.[293] On the Donets, Sixth Army had reached its provisional objective. Thrusts beyond that point would be possible only when the railway between Kharkov and Belgorod had been converted to standard gauge. Because of the transport situation, which was essentially dependent on the typical horse-drawn wagons, this meant in practice that the supply-depots of German units had to be within 50 kilometres of a railhead. In its report to the Army High Command on 22 October the army group command urged that, in view of the situation assessment by Sixth Army, a three-week pause in operations should be ordered.

The commanders of the armies were informed that the objectives set out in Directive No. 10 from the army group were for the long term. After the Donets and the mouth of the Don had been reached, operations would come to a halt at least until the period of hard frost set in around the middle of December. Seventeenth Army was to attempt to capture a bridgehead at Izyum, while Sixth Army would push on towards the area around Belgorod, where it would have usable rail connections.[294] The troops were ordered to lay in supplies

[291] H.Gr. Süd/Ia, KTB, 20 Oct. 1941, BA-MA RH 19 I/74.
[292] Ibid., 22 Oct. 1941.   [293] Ibid.
[294] Ibid., 25 Oct. 1941, report to that effect to operations department, with the rider that the

from the country for the winter. Only after adequate stocks of supplies had been built up would it be possible to advance along the railway lines with mobile units further to the east. Colonel Alfred Baentsch of the general staff, head of the army supply department under the quartermaster-general, confirmed that it was impossible to supply the troops using the normal lines of communication and that they would have to be supplied from the respective army areas. What could not be obtained there would be provided from the western Ukraine.[295] Supply considerations also induced First Armoured Army to reject the offer to have the Romanian Third Army placed under its command to protect the coast, as it had already established various supply-bases near the coast and begun replenishing its stores.[296]

But First Armoured Army still had not reached its objective, the Don. On 19 October III Armoured Corps command sent its subordinate units information on the situation and the plans to take Rostov, in order to explain the importance of the 'last effort'.[297] After emphasizing the political and economic importance of the city, the command described the situation of the enemy and the fortifications that had to be overcome. To cover the operation to the north, XIV Armoured Corps was standing by. Because of the fuel situation, however, only troop movements essential to the carrying out of the operation could be undertaken. Objectives were to be decided according to circumstances and in such a way that they would not place excessive demands on fuel supplies.

On 19 October the armoured army ordered the conquest of the industrial area of Stalino and the capture by surprise attack of the bridges at Rostov. It was also important to capture fuel stores in the city.[298]

Strong counter-attacks forced III Armoured Corps to go on the defensive, while on the left XIV Armoured Corps crossed the Mius. On 28 October First Armoured Army, like Sixth Army, found it necessary to send a memorandum to the Army High Command summarizing all difficulties and shortages in the supply situation.[299] It concluded that, in spite of the firm will to reach the objectives set, it would be irresponsible to continue the attack without adequate supplies. The high command simply had to realize when its demands no longer bore any relation to what the troops could actually achieve. Such a situation had now arisen with the reaching of the Donets. If it were not taken into account, the troops would be condemned to helplessness, their fighting

Don could no longer be reached as supplies were not being received and winter clothing would not arrive until the end of November.

[295] Ibid.

[296] Ibid. An order of III Armd. Corps (23 Oct. 1941) is revealing: units were to prepare to survive on their own for several days with regard to food, ammunition, and fuel. The troops by then were responsible also for road construction. The main form of transport was the horse-drawn wagon. Each team cost 50–70 pfennigs a day. In relays, e.g. between Zaporozhye and Mariupol, 2,500 such wagons transported 60 t. a day: BA-MA RH 24-3/57.

[297] BA-MA RH 24-3/56.   [298] BA-MA RH.

[299] H.Gr. Süd/Ia, KTB, 28 Oct. 1941, BA-MA RH 19 I/74; Hauck, Südliches Gebiet, pt. 1, 406, appendix 56, MGFA P-114c.

ability would decline rapidly, and their combat-readiness even after the return of good weather would be endangered. The chief of the operations department, Colonel Heusinger of the general staff, shared this view of the situation but nevertheless proposed to advance at least to the lower Don and replace the attack on Rostov with a thrust from the north. For this it would be necessary to reinforce First Armoured Army, something which the army group opposed as long as the situation remained 'unclear'—i.e. until the industrial area of Voroshilovgrad had been captured—as it would be at the expense of Seventeenth Army. Heusinger still considered the 'ideal final objective' for the operation to be the line Maykop–Stalingrad–Voronezh, while the head of the army group general staff retorted that one would have to accept the fact that this line could not be reached until spring.[300]

In its analysis of the situation, however, First Armoured Army went even further. It pointed out to the Army High Command that after 10,000–20,000 kilometres army vehicles were no longer fit for service and that their combat-readiness and that of the tanks was rapidly declining. Thorough rehabilitation to full usability in the coming year would be possible only in Germany. For smaller operations during the winter, overhauls and repairs requiring one to two months were possible in the army areas, but these would preclude full usability in the spring.[301] The operational conclusions to be drawn from this report were obvious.

Halder therefore once more intervened directly in the deliberations and expressed his fear that a halt in operations after the Don had been reached, as announced in the army group order of 22 October, would create the wrong impression in midlevel commands and among the troops.[302] They might lose the momentum necessary to make every effort to reach the strategic objectives—if possible Stalingrad—in the event of a snow-free period of frost in the current year. Instead of depicting openly and forcefully the limits of the troops' endurance and the conclusions to be drawn, Sodenstern stated that he was basically of the same opinion and that the army chiefs of staff had been informed accordingly. 'In the opinion of the army group command, however', it could not be ignored that a four-week operations halt for resupply purposes was becoming necessary. Halder accepted this view but stressed clearly that a snow-free period of frost, which was to be expected in December, had to be taken advantage of at all events.

The conference of the chiefs of staff of the army group and the armies on 31 October was conducted in a similar spirit.[303] The participants were in accord concerning the difficulties of shifting forces[304] and the general transport and supply situation. On the question of providing protection for the flanks of the spearhead against the lower Don, the chief of staff of the army group envisaged the need for forces which he did not even have.

---

[300] H.Gr. Süd/Ia, KTB, 29 Oct. 1941, BA-MA RH 19 I/74.   [301] Cf. n. 299 above.
[302] Telephone conversation between Halder and Sodenstern, H.Gr. Süd/Ia, KTB, 30 Oct. 1941, BA-MA RH 19 I/74.
[303] Ibid., 31 Oct. 1941.   [304] Ibid.

The question of the chief of staff of Seventeenth Army, whether it was perhaps the intention of the enemy to draw the pursuers into an even more difficult supply situation in order to destroy them in a counter-attack, was answered in the negative. The explanation was: 'The Army High Command no longer expects the greatly weakened enemy to take active measures. He will try only to withdraw and reorganize his forces undisturbed.'[305] The question can be left open as to how much consolation the probably surprised general-staff officers were able to draw from Sodenstern's assurance that the commander-in-chief of the army group would not permit Halder's demand that they reach the Don in the current year to involve the divisions in an insurmountable crisis.[306]

The lack of suitable vehicles and fuel forced the German commanders to entrust necessary military movements to 'pursuit detachments', which in reality meant that fighting requiring any movement was reduced to a minimum. In the opinion of the Sixth Army chief of staff, even these detachments were to consist of infantry and peasant carts. Only the accompanying anti-aircraft detachments were to be motorized. Skis and other winter equipment still had to be provided. Because of the transport time required, there could be no question of the urgently needed rehabilitation of First Armoured Army being effected in Germany. All still usable equipment was therefore to be collected and repaired and the personnel sent to Germany for re-equipment.[307] In the end a consensus was reached that it would be better to halt operations now and have refreshed troops ready in the spring than to reach distant objectives and permit the fighting value of the German divisions to decline to a point where they would no longer be usable.[308]

The next opportunity for the army group command to present its assessment of the situation to its responsible superiors was the visit of the commander-in-chief of the army on 3 November.[309] Referring to his already

---

[305] This belief originated with Halder (*Diaries*, 1284–5: 3 Nov. 1941). It might be assumed that knowledge of the enemy increased in direct proportion to proximity to the front. Abstract speculation among the general staff, however, evidently flourished most in Army Group South, a level of command that should have had an adequate overall view of the situation.

[306] Sodenstern did not doubt that the demand 'in its present sharp form' had been made not by Hitler, but by Halder, who was mainly interested in separating Soviet forces in the north from those in the south and thus destroying the operational unity of enemy operations: BA-MA RH 19 I/74, 31 Oct. 1941. Hitler's view is in Halder, *Diaries*, 1289 (7 Nov. 1941): 'What is not possible this year, will have to be taken care of next year.'

[307] An armoured division required about 80 trains, while only 30 could be provided on a daily basis. Gen. von Mackensen, commanding III Armd. Corps, considered more powerful anti-tank weapons more important than new tanks. Otherwise, faced with superior Soviet armoured forces, German soldiers would lose confidence in their leaders: Gen.Kdo. (mot.) III. AK/Ia No. 1097/41 geh., 28 Oct. 1941, BA-MA RH 24-3/57.

[308] It evidently did not occur to Sodenstern to try to persuade Halder to accept this view, although he also came to the conclusion that strategic considerations did not play a 'very important role' in the Red Army, as it constantly raised new units, which then had to be defeated. The crisis of confidence which thus became inevitable between the Army High Command and the senior front staffs will be considered below: cf. sect. II.1.1(*c*) at n. 381, sect. II.1.1(*f*) at nn. 515 ff.

[309] H.Gr. Süd/Ia, KTB, 3 Nov. 1941, BA-MA RH 19 I/87. Halder complained on 3 Nov.

submitted memorandums, Rundstedt again explained his decision to halt all operations when the lower Don and the Donets were reached. Brauchitsch, who had obviously been sent by Halder after Sodenstern had cautiously expressed reservations about the latter's strategy, acknowledged all difficulties. He 'believed, however'—and this was another formulation for an order soon to be issued—that it must be possible nevertheless 'to reach parts of the Don in the foreseeable future, at least near and south of Voronezh, with specially organized, relatively small units, if necessary only with raiding parties'. He also had the bright idea of equipping and supplying the detachments carrying out this thrust not with motor-vehicles, but with convoys of peasant carts. He assumed that not even strong resistance, let alone offensive activity, was to be expected from the enemy between the Donets and the Don. Although he expressed 'understanding' for the situation of the army group, he expected a more favourable development of the supply situation than the one which the army group and Sixth Army had used as the basis of their planning. Then he stressed the decisive importance the Army High Command attached to an early capture of a line along the Don and the elimination of the railway line via Stalingrad. The oilfields of Maykop were also to be captured, even if that considerably reduced the combat-readiness of First Armoured Army in the spring.[310]

When Brauchitsch mentioned the possibility of an attack by First Armoured Army via Shakhty to bypass fortified Rostov, he was informed that this was impossible because of the lack of fuel. The subsequent discussion among the three field marshals von Brauchitsch, von Rundstedt, and von Reichenau was evidently rather outspoken. At any rate, Halder noted Brauchitsch's concern about Rundstedt's health, frequently an indication that the commander-in-chief of the army was considering relieving the individual involved of his duties because of differences of opinion on command questions.[311]

Rundstedt reaffirmed his views, expressed in his conversation with Brauchitsch, with a report to the Army High Command, in which he again pointed out the connection between operations, supplies, winter clothing, and the general condition of the troops.[312] The continuation of operations would lead to almost complete immobility of First Armoured Army and most of the

(Diaries, 1285) about the pessimism of Army Group South: 'Some energetic "persuading" would be in order to knock the lead out of them.'

[310] H.Gr. Süd/Ia, KTB, 3 Nov. 1941, BA-MA RH 19 I/87. It is difficult to understand what Brauchitsch meant by the combat-readiness of an armoured division, if it were subjected to more wear and tear in large-scale operations. Cf. n. 524 below.

[311] Halder, Diaries, 1287 (4 Nov. 1941); H.Gr. Süd/Ia, KTB, 3 Nov. 1941, BA-MA RH 19 I/87.

[312] H.Gr. Süd/Ia, KTB, 3 Nov. 1941, BA-MA RH 19 I/87. Cf. also report of III Armd. Corps on the situation and morale, 29 Oct. 1941. According to this report, the soldiers did not want to be preached at; the capture of Kharkov and that of Odessa were matters of indifference to them as long as they did not have enough to eat and could not hear their own artillery. On 3 Nov. 1941 First Armd. Army responded by referring to numerous economic initiatives to improve supplies for the troops, e.g. noodle, margarine, and sock factories. Report and response in BA-MA RH 24-3/57.

infantry divisions in the spring. He again urged that offensive operations on the lower Don and the Donets be stopped, but he failed to receive a positive answer.

The Army High Command did not abandon plans for a thrust to the lower Don and for the occupation of Rostov by First Armoured Army. Seemingly unimpressed by developments, the chief of the army group general staff, to some extent as a result of the discussion with Brauchitsch, informed the chiefs of staff of First Armoured Army and Seventeenth Army of the orders of the commander-in-chief of the army for the near future—the operations against Maykop ('Winter Sport') and Stalingrad.[313]

On 5 November First Armoured Army began its attack on Rostov with XIV Armoured Corps. The attackers succeeded in breaking through and advancing 30 kilometres to the east; then the corps turned south towards the city and established a bridgehead near Atamanovskiy Vlasovo across the Krepkaya. Rain beginning on 7 November paralysed all movement and gave the defenders the opportunity to construct defensive positions at this unlikely spot. The armoured army regrouped and was able to resume its attack only on 17 November after the rain had given way to temperatures as low as $-22\,°C$.[314] This time the main effort of the attack was made by III Armoured Corps, which, coming from the west, at first attacked north of Rostov and then turned towards the Don. The city fell on 20 November. The expected enemy forces, mostly east of the city, were preparing for a counter-attack on 18 November.

On 22 November the attack of the Soviet armies began against Rostov from the south and east and, at the same time, against the rest of the front of First Armoured Army. Army Group South expected an enemy movement with the objective of encircling the army from the north and cutting it off with a thrust towards Taganrog.[315] On 21 November First Armoured Army had pointed out that there could be no question of destroying the identified enemy forces offensively; it planned to hold Rostov but also to fall back to the Tuzlov and, if the enemy pressure there were still too great, to take up positions on the Mius.[316] In accordance with this plan, it first evacuated the area up to the Tuzlov and abandoned Rostov on 28 November. The decision on a further withdrawal had to be taken on 30 November.[317]

---

[313] H.Gr. Süd/Ia, KTB, 3 Nov. 1941, BA-MA RH 19 I/87.

[314] Ibid., 17 Nov. 1941; Lehmann, *Leibstandarte*, ii. 223.

[315] Assessment of enemy's situation by Army Group South, 21 Nov. 1941: Hauck, Südliches Gebiet, pt. I, 424–5, appendix 62, MGFA P-114c. 13th Armd. Div. had to be withdrawn from the front on this day. It was assumed that the following enemy forces (excluding the Crimea and the Caucasus) were facing the army group: 7 armies with approximately 40 infantry divisions, 13 cavalry divisions, 7 armoured brigades, and 1 airborne corps (facing Sixth Army).

[316] Hauck, Südliches Gebiet, pt. I, 426–7, appendix 63, MGFA P-114c; Halder, *Diaries*, 1311 (22 Nov. 1941).

[317] Ibid. 1322–3 (29 Nov. 1941); H.Gr. Süd/Ia, KTB, 21–8 Nov. 1941, BA-MA RH 19 I/87. Order of the day of III Armd. Corps, 21 Nov. 1941; order No. 31 of First Armd. Army, 22 Nov., printed in Lehmann, *Leibstandarte*, ii. 235 ff., according to BA-MA RH 24-3/58.

The army group had little chance of avoiding a withdrawal by providing more troops and material help. Operational assistance was also unavailable. Halder and the army group command attempted several times, unsuccessfully, to induce Reichenau to undertake a thrust with Sixth Army towards Kupyansk. The discussion about this operation continued until 28 November, when Reichenau bluntly stated his own point of view and argued convincingly that such an attack with his exhausted divisions would be irresponsible and in any case could not be supplied.[318] Halder was so angry at Reichenau's behaviour that on 29 November he ordered an investigation to determine possible shortcomings in the functioning of the Army General Staff.[319] A realistic assessment of available troops and equipment and the impossibility of providing significant forces from other sectors of the eastern front or from Germany itself led to the conclusion that a withdrawal from the hard-won Don crossing was inevitable. The situation assessment by First Armoured Army on 21 November made this fact clear to all commands involved.[320] It would therefore have been necessary to prepare a line of retreat for this eventuality. But on 21 November the first general-staff officer of the army group discussed with the operations department the initiation of 'all measures of the army group that would make possible a later offensive solution'.[321] In addition to the bringing up of the light divisions ordered long before, these measures a included the request to the Army High Command for a motorized corps and mobile units. Both officers agreed that there was no prospect whatever that such requests would be granted. Evidently, however, the idea of restraint and the withdrawal of an armoured army was for them unthinkable, even though the tanks of the army were almost immobilized, fuel supplies were inadequate, the army was being supplied largely by starving horses, and one of its commanding generals (Mackensen) considered even a successful defensive action to be a matter of luck. Anyway, the first general-staff officer of the army group explained that, while 'how' the enemy group should be destroyed was still unclear, a crossing of the Kerch strait by Eleventh Army seemed to him to be of great importance in this regard. This meant nothing less than an encirclement of the Caucasus or at least a penetration of that area. Even if the individual operations were to be ordered only when the supply situation permitted, the directive issued by the army group on 21 November 1941 for the occupation of the oilfields around Maykop and of enemy transportation lines along the Volga, as well as for reaching the Don near Svoboda, was so completely unrealistic that in the

---

[318] Halder's urging of Reichenau to attack, *Diaries*, 1315 (26 Nov. 1941); H.Gr. Süd/Ia, report to Army High Command, operations department, 28 Nov. 1941: Hauck, Südliches Gebiet, pt. I, 420–1, appendix 60, MGFA P-114c.

[319] Halder, *Diaries*, 1286–7 (4, 5–29 Nov. 1941). This procedure was abandoned after Reichenau assumed command of the army group. Contrary to Halder's assumption that both armies were ready for action at the beginning of December, the general-staff officer in charge of supply and administration observed on 10 Nov. 1941 that ordering them to go beyond the Donets could not be justified: H.Gr. Süd/Ia, KTB, 10 Nov. 1941, BA-MA RH 19 I/87.

[320] H.Gr. Süd/Ia, KTB, 21 Nov. 1941, BA-MA RH 19 I/87.   [321] Ibid.

actual situation it is difficult to regard it as a piece of serious military planning.[322]

At this time command procedures were still a purely internal matter for the Army General Staff. No binding order had been received from Hitler to attack the Caucasus at all events in the current year, nor were the commanders of the army group and the armies or the chiefs of their general staffs convinced of the feasibility of such an operation. On the contrary, the chiefs of staff seem to have been operating under a double strain in that they believed they had to take into account not only the obvious situation at the front but also Halder's general strategic picture, as he had impressed it upon them again in Orsha on 13 November.[323] It is abundantly clear that Halder considered himself and his chiefs of the army group general staffs to be, in the final analysis, the real pillars of the entire conduct of the war. This conviction also manifested itself in the serious situation in which Army Group South found itself at the end of November 1941 when he—and, as a direct result, the army group command—insisted that Sixth Army should undertake an offensive against Kupyansk and the lower Oskol. Reichenau's personal appearance at the headquarters of the army group on 27 November and his description of the situation of the army and the impossibility of carrying out the envisaged attack eventually persuaded Rundstedt to accept his arguments. Rundstedt then demanded a report to the commander-in-chief of the army.[324] Reichenau's readiness to undertake a temporary offensive with two divisions via Chuguev to the south-east was a concession to Halder's strategic plans made in spite of his awareness of the current situation.

The sobering encounters with reality in the Pripet fighting and in the morass of the black-earth region left little room for the type of general-staff thinking, always confronted with the 'will of the supreme war lord', in which a decision could be won by throwing the very last battalion into battle. In this situation deliberations about whether the Soviet attack of 26 November represented a co-ordinated operation against Rostov, as Foreign Armies East believed, or a concentrated attack to be expected 'in the foreseeable future, perhaps this very day' were rather academic. What was obvious was 'the enemy's unified command'. First Armoured Army had long planned an evacuation of Rostov as soon as the army group recognized the correctness of its assessment of the situation, if enemy pressure became too strong.[325]

Hitler discussed with Brauchitsch troop transfers and countermeasures in the event of possible negative developments; he also demanded a report from Army Group South.[326] The Wehrmacht High Command did not provide

---

[322] H.Gr. Süd/Ia, Directive No. 11, KTB, 21 Nov. 1941.

[323] Cf. sect. II.1.1(*f*) at nn. 526 ff.

[324] Report by Army Group South to Army High Command, operations department; cf. n. 314 above.

[325] H.Gr. Süd/Ia, KTB, 27 Nov. 1941, BA-MA RH 19 I/87.

[326] Ibid., memorandum of telephone conversation between Halder and Sodenstern, 28 Nov. 1941.

sufficient help, nor did the situation require that the city should be held at all costs. On 28 November, when the situation demanded a decision, Hitler explained logically that he was of the same opinion as the army group command: it was the responsibility of the commander of First Armoured Army to decide whether to give the order to abandon Rostov.[327] He thus agreed with Halder that Army Group South no longer had the mobility or the strength to mount attacks.[328]

On the other hand, Hitler considered the location of the defensive positions to be extremely important. On 29 November First Armoured Army reported that it was withdrawing to the Kolmytskaya sector; the army group agreed to this plan. The withdrawal continued under strong enemy pressure on 30 November; it led to feverish activity in the command apparatus above the army-group level and to an intervention by Hitler.

Because the effects of this development, which led to the commander-in-chief of an army group being relieved of his command, were more important than the event itself, not least because of the mistrust it expressed in an erratic leadership, it will be treated at somewhat greater length here.

Hitler objected to an intended line of withdrawal, reported to him by Halder, namely Taganrog–Mchus–Mius–mouth of the Bakhmut, and demanded that the retreat from Rostov should stop further east. This reported line did not, however, truly reflect the intentions of First Armoured Army, which wanted to withdraw 'behind the sector Sambek–Mius–Mchus–Glukhaya'. (The name 'Mchus' was an invention of the cartographer, who misread it for the Mius. This was not without consequences, as on the German situation map the Mius flowed into a *liman* (coastal salt lake) west of Taganrog and into the Sea of Azov. On the army map the same river became the Mchus north of that point.)

Rundstedt approved the decision of First Armoured Army to withdraw III and XIV Armoured Corps to the prepared positions along the line Varenovka–Sambek–Pokrovskoe–Mius and wanted Seventeenth Army to close up to the left wing of First Armoured Army (XXXXIX Mountain Corps) with an attack by IV Army Corps on 3 December, as the armoured army considered the withdrawal of Seventeenth Army to the Bakhmut sector a danger to its left flank.[329] The operations department of the Army High Command was informed of this plan at 5 p.m. Hitler's reaction, through Keitel, was an enquiry at 7.15 p.m. as to whether an enemy penetration had occurred, which the army group answered in the negative. Thereupon Keitel proposed not to withdraw

---

[327] Ibid., 'According to information provided by Maj. (Gen. Staff) Philippi, operations department'.

[328] Halder, *Diaries*, 1323 (29 Nov. 1941).

[329] Line according to Halder, *Diaries*, 1327 (30 Nov. 1941). According to the report of Army Group South to the operations department, the withdrawal of First Armd. Army 'behind the sector of the Mchus [Mius] and the Krynka to the general line between Taganrog and Gorlovka' and of the eastern wing of Seventeenth Army behind the Bakhmut sector' should be considered. For the entire course of events cf. H.Gr. Süd/Ia, KTB, 30 Nov. 1941, BA-MA RH 19 I/87.

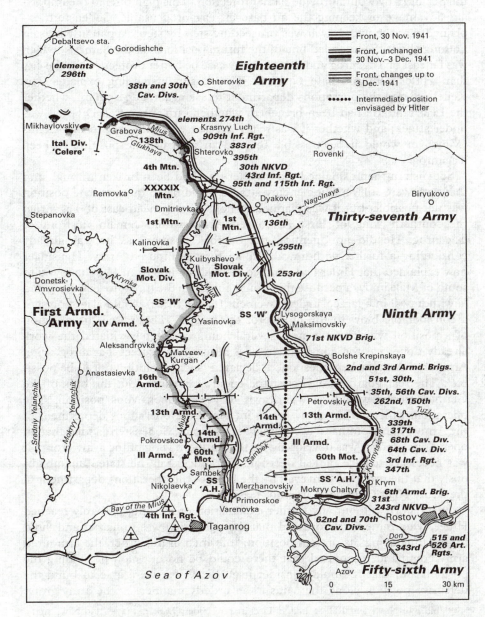

MAP II.I.I. The Situation on the Southern Wing of Army Group South, 30 November–3 December 1941

Note: Soviet units are taken from the situation map of First Armoured Army and are given here in italic.

to the Mius in one movement but to choose an intermediate position where the Sea of Azov would provide flank protection. This plan offered the important advantage of keeping the air-base at Taganrog usable. Sodenstern explained that the withdrawal was proceeding step by step. Apparently he said nothing about the intended line of the future positions on the Sambek, which was far east of Taganrog and would in any case be better protection for the city than Hitler's intermediate position. This misunderstanding explains why Keitel ordered the operations department to ask again, at 7.25 p.m., whether the Leibstandarte had been breached, whether 13th Armoured Division was under attack, and whether it was really necessary to withdraw to the Mchus (Mius), or would it be 'possible to hold an intermediate position to keep Taganrog?'

Sodenstern then explained that neither unit had been broken through and that both were still repelling enemy attacks. Holding an intermediate position was not possible, but it was planned to hold a bridgehead east of Taganrog; the southern wing of First Armoured Army would remain in front of Taganrog. He did not mention the Sambek position, as he was already considering a further withdrawal, unlike First Armoured Army. Heusinger now explained that Hitler had planned to hold the line from Merzhanovski to south of Maksimovka because this would eliminate the threat to Taganrog and 'a withdrawal in a large, single movement (to the Mius) would also represent a considerable blow to the morale of the troops'. This raised the question of a position which in the next several hours completely vitiated the work already done, i.e. the construction of a position to protect Taganrog. First Armoured Army, when questioned, declared 'such a solution not to be possible'. The rear guard would resist the enemy's advance, but the bulk of the German troops would be withdrawn to the Sambek–Mius position. The operations officer of the army group informed the operations department of the Army High Command accordingly at 8.00 p.m. Sodenstern added that an operational danger was developing on the southern wing of the army group; it was necessary to take radical decisions. In conclusion, he stated unambiguously that the proposal conveyed by the head of the operations department of the Army High Command was not feasible.

This report, without any further explanation of the line, probably reached Hitler, who immediately ordered that the right wing was to halt at and 'hold for the time being' its present position. Informed of this order, the armoured army command responded that there could be no question of holding the position and that it would consider itself lucky if it were able to build the defensive position along the Mius in an orderly manner.[330] The army group

[330] Ibid., 30 Nov., and RH 19 I/88, 1 Dec. 1941; Halder, *Diaries*, 1327–8 (30 Nov. 1941). Heusinger reported that Rundstedt had declared that Hitler's order could not be carried out. The nervousness and confusion of the reports and orders are evident in Halder, *Diaries*, 1328 ff. (30 Nov.–2 Dec. 1941). Cf also the account in Lehmann, *Leibstandarte*, ii. 258, according to which Hitler's permission to occupy the Mius position was given as a result of Reichenau's report that the enemy had broken through this unit (Halder's report, *Diaries*, 1327 ff.); Lehmann states that

sent a corresponding report to the operations department of the high command, requesting the rescission of the order. At 11.15 p.m. Heusinger conveyed proposals to the army group, presumably on Hitler's orders, to support First Armoured Army, but these did not change the situation in terms of time or forces available and were therefore not given a positive reception.

Hitler concluded from the rejection of the completely unsuitable 'intermediate position' he had ordered that the commander-in-chief of Army Group South was stubbornly refusing to carry out his orders and, on 1 December at 2.00 a.m., relieved him of his command and replaced him by Field Marshal von Reichenau.[331] In consideration of the condition of his troops, however, Reichenau had been the most articulate critic of any offensive operations, which Halder's strategy would have required. Very soon, at 5.50 a.m., Reichenau received Hitler's order to halt the withdrawal of the two corps of First Armoured Army or to permit it to go no further than the line between Merzhanovska and Maksimovka. Moreover, he was to take all necessary measures, including air-lifts, to bring up the necessary reinforcements in the shortest time possible, as the operations department had already suggested the previous day. Finally, the army group was to make preparations to start an offensive from the areas held by IV Army Corps and XXXXIX Mountain Corps against the Voroshilovgrad area, intended to threaten the flank of any further enemy advance and to secure starting-positions for future attacks. Reichenau ordered the first two points to be carried out immediately but refrained from ordering the execution of the third.[332]

In spite of his personal efforts, Reichenau was unable to carry out Hitler's order to hold the completely open line.[333] The reports from the commanders concerned made it very clear that the units involved would simply have to be 'written off' if they were not withdrawn immediately to the prepared Sambek–Mius line. General von Mackensen, commanding III Armoured Corps, emphasized the same point. Hitler took note of the corresponding reports from Reichenau and wanted to speak to him later about his declared intention to avoid the offensive Hitler himself had demanded.[334] But a short time later Hitler approved Reichenau's order for the southern wing of First Armoured Army to withdraw to the Sambek–Mius line.[335] On 2 December Hitler flew to

---

in reality this report was fabricated for that purpose, as the unit had had no contact with the enemy at the time.

[331] Reichenau was officially appointed on 5 Dec. 1941.

[332] The thought of an offensive against Voroshilovgrad had arisen as a spontaneous idea of Hitler's on 30 Nov. Halder immediately labelled it an 'idea ground out in a vacuum' (*Diaries*, 1327: 30 Nov. 1941). The day before, after being informed of Halder's views, Army Group South had demanded in a memorandum that all operational movements be stopped, which was exactly what Reichenau had already demanded: H.Gr. Süd/Ia, KTB, 30 Nov. 1941, BA-MA RH 19 I/87.

[333] H.Gr. Süd/Ia, KTB, 1 Dec. 1941, BA-MA RH 19 I/88. Cf., however, n. 330 above.

[334] Ibid.

[335] Without attaching too much importance to the report procedures described, it seems reasonable to assume that clearer information about the course of the Sambek–Mius position would have prevented the senseless act of relieving Rundstedt. After being briefed by the C.-in-

the headquarters of First Armoured Army to form an opinion about the situation on the spot. The commander-in-chief of the army group and the chief of staff of Air Fleet 4 also participated in the discussions. The commander of the Leibstandarte, the unit most directly affected, reported on the condition of his troops and the inevitability of a withdrawal. The following day Hitler visited the headquarters of the army group in Poltava to exchange views on the causes of the retreat as well as on future operations. In the course of his visit he stated that he had first heard of the serious crisis near Rostov in the last days of November, otherwise he could have sent reinforcements of 6,000 men (*sic*) in time. The army group was able to point out that it had been sending relevant reports to the Army High Command since 21 November.[336]

Even after Hitler's visit, the operational objectives of Army Group South remained the Caucasus and Stalingrad. But as a next step the front had to be consolidated. The situation on the northern sector of Seventeenth Army's front, held by the Italian expeditionary corps, was critical.[337] Reports from radio intelligence indicated that an attack with airborne troops across the sea against Mariupol and Taganrog had to be expected. To shorten the front, Seventeenth Army attacked with IV Army Corps on 4 December. In view of the weak enemy defence, Sixth Army pushed out of the Chuguev bridgehead with LV Army Corps to the south-east and reached the line Savintsy–Pechenegi, thus consolidating the link-up with Seventeenth Army. Now the army group was to change to basically static defensive tactics to gain time to restore the fighting power of its units.

The chief of the general staff of Army Group South assumed that the Red Army intended to break through to the Dnieper and cut off the entire southern wing of the eastern front in the course of the winter. The army group had to prepare for this development and use a mobile defence to gain time to bring up forces for a counter-attack.[338] Sodenstern even considered withdrawing to the line from Melitopol via Zaporozhye towards Kupyansk if necessary, his guiding principle being that the essential prerequisite for resuming the offensive was to avoid defeat. Probably after being informed of the talk between

---

C. of First Armd. Army, Hitler declared his agreement with Rundstedt's measures and shortly afterwards made him 'Commander-in-Chief, West'. On Rundstedt's dismissal cf. Zeitzler papers, BA-MA N 63/53.

[336] H.Gr. Süd/Ia, KTB, 3 Dec. 1941, BA-MA RH 19 I/88. Sodenstern's direct report to Hitler had no unpleasant consequences for Halder, but he was clearly taken aback by Hitler's failure to consult the Army High Command about his trip (*Diaries*, 1331–2, 1334–5: 2, 3 Dec. 1941). Cf. generally in this regard the observation in sect. II.1.1(*f*) at n. 517. Clearly the internal reporting practice of the general staff with the regular phrase 'measures being taken' gave Hitler the impression that unpleasant news was being played down. Together with similar reports from Army Group Centre, these events caused Hitler to issue an order on honesty in reporting on 26 Dec. 1941. Cf. sect. II.1.1(*g*) at n. 625.

[337] Assessment of situation of Army Group South, 4 Dec. 1941, BA-MA RH 19 I/88; Halder, *Diaries*, 1333 (3 Dec. 1941).

[338] Sodenstern's statement to the head of the operations department, 4 Dec. 1941. Sodenstern submitted this assessment without first making sure of the agreement of Reichenau, who was more inclined not to surrender any terrain: BA-MA RH 19 I/88.

Sodenstern and Heusinger on 6 December, Halder ordered the latter to examine the question of what should be done if First Armoured Army had to be withdrawn even further.[339]

(iii) THE CONQUEST OF THE CRIMEA
(*See the Annexe Volume, No. 14*)

In the extreme south of the army group, Eleventh Army was pursuing the Soviet Fifty-first Army after breaking through the defensive positions at Ishun.[340] Three army corps advanced via Simferopol—one towards Sevastopol, the other towards the south coast, and the third towards the Feodosiya–Kerch line. The Romanian Mountain Corps followed via Simferopol, the capital and most important transportation centre of the Crimea.[341] Eleventh Army Headquarters was confronted with the necessity of deciding whether first to attack Sevastopol as the dominant fortress or Kerch as the crossing-point to the Caucasus. Manstein assumed that the enemy would attempt to escape via Feodosiya and Kerch and that delaying actions west and north of Feodosiya would enable the bulk of the Soviet troops to embark there. He saw no difficulties in mounting a pursuit in this direction, whereas the crossing at Kerch would require long, thorough preparations.[342] He therefore decided to concentrate the bulk of his forces, four infantry divisions, against Sevastopol and to limit the pursuit in the direction of Kerch to three divisions under a corps command. The Romanian Mountain Corps was assigned to providing cover in the Yayla mountains.

The 'western group' against Sevastopol, LIV and XXX Army Corps, quickly encountered increasing enemy resistance and difficult road conditions that delayed its progress. On 8 November Eleventh Army reported that a temporary halt in the advance of LIV Army Corps could not be avoided.

But the enemy on the tongue of land at Kerch seemed to be fighting only a delaying action after Feodosiya was taken on 3 November, and the enemy forces in the Crimea had been split by the German thrust to the south coast. On 16 November the defence of Kerch collapsed. With the exception of the fortress of Sevastopol, the Crimea was now in German hands, although well-organized partisan groups consisting of soldiers from scattered Soviet units continued fighting from their protected and inaccessible hiding-places in the Yayla mountains.

At Sevastopol everything indicated that the enemy was preparing to offer determined resistance. The fortress could clearly not be taken in a running attack; Manstein added 22nd Infantry Division to the right wing of his en-

---

[339] Ibid., 6 Dec. 1941. On 7 Dec. Sodenstern discussed these questions with the chief of staff of First Armd. Army, Col. Zeitzler, who wanted to avoid a further withdrawal even under enemy pressure and to form strong mobile reserves as soon as possible.

[340] Manstein, *Lost Victories*, 220 ff.; H.Gr. Süd/Ia, KTB, BA-MA RH 19 I/64, 87.

[341] H.Gr. Süd/Ia, KTB, BA-MA RH 19 I/64, 87.

[342] Telephone conversation between Manstein and Sodenstern, 1 Nov. 1941, KTB, H.Gr. Süd/Ia, BA-MA RH 19 I/87.

circlement front and prepared to deploy heavy artillery to soften up the defences. The lack of a bridge across the Dnieper and the extremely limited transport capacity greatly slowed the bringing up of the necessary artillery and ammunition. In addition, the rainy period beginning in November further limited all ground movements.[343]

Apart from the need to prevent a possible reinforcement of the enemy, Eleventh Army had no reason to hurry, for the attack on Maykop via Kerch was dependent on First Armoured Army gaining a starting-position between Shakhty and Rostov and on the resting and resupplying of the units intended for the attack.[344] And the front against Sevastopol did not remain quiet. The siege-ring had to be extended through the mountains around the fortress, and sorties by the defenders had to be repulsed.

After 20 November a transfer of forces from the Crimea to replace the losses suffered by other armies of the army group was considered. On 23 November Heusinger suggested to the army group that forces for the crossing at Kerch, which would not take place for the time being, could be released to First Armoured Army. Sodenstern at first rejected this proposal, but added that the army group would initiate the transfer of these divisions with an official announcement that the crossing had been abandoned.[345] This marked the beginning of a long, increasingly bitter, dispute among the commands involved about the withdrawal of units of Eleventh Army.[346] In the end Eleventh Army had to transfer 73rd Infantry Division; however, at the beginning of December there was a danger that a second division, 170th Infantry, might have to be transferred. But Manstein's urgent appeals led to a reversal of this last decision, primarily because of the imminent attack on Sevastopol.

On 13 December Eleventh Army began the bombardment of enemy positions and port facilities in Sevastopol. That evening Reichenau decided to postpone the attack by twenty-four hours, as all dive-bombers of IV Air Corps were needed to halt the enemy penetration on the eastern wing of Seventeenth Army.[347]

Manstein now considered the prospects of success to be favourable only for the first phase, provided that air support and supplies were guaranteed. But on 14 December air support was again refused because of new tasks in the sector facing Seventeeth Army, and the attack on Sevastopol had to be postponed by another twenty-four hours. Manstein was now inclined to start the attack without the dive-bombers, whose use might be ruled out in any case by bad weather. The attack on the fortress finally began on 17 December and, with heavy losses, some penetrations were achieved with the first surprise of the defenders. The weather ruled out any dive-bomber support. To strengthen his

[343] Ibid., report Eleventh Army headquarters, 17 Nov. 1941.
[344] Supplement to Directive No. 10 of Army Group South, 20 Oct. 1941, KTB, H.Gr. Süd/Ia, same day; ibid., intentions of command of Army Group South for 'Winter Sports', 17 Nov. 1941 (also records Manstein's doubts about whether the troops could endure these battles).
[345] Supplement to Directive, 23 Nov. 1941.
[346] Ibid., 25 Nov. 1941, 2 Dec. 1941 (BA-MA RH 19 I/88).   [347] Ibid., 13 Dec. 1941.

attack, Manstein repeatedly requested that 73rd Infantry Division not be taken from him, but the army group refused his request with the pointed remark that holding the eastern front was more important than capturing Sevastopol.[348]

The low combat strength of the infantry and the possibility that the enemy could at any time obtain reinforcements by sea were a cause for concern. Manstein considered it very important to conclude the hard and difficult fighting for Sevastopol at an early date, as landings at other points in the Crimea were to be expected. On 21 December Hitler enquired how much time the attack on the fortress would still require. He was told that that would be known only after some days, but the attackers were hoping for early success.[349]

The attackers were also able to press forward in the northern part of the fortress area and to reach the coast north of Lyubimovka. Manstein hoped to advance further at this point by reorganizing his forces. He assumed that he would be able to repel any landings near Kerch with the forces already there: two batteries and one infantry regiment with artillery.

When, on the morning of 26 December, the enemy landed on a broad front on the Kerch peninsula and rapidly established beachheads there, the attack on Sevastopol had to be halted. Reichenau decided to make available to Eleventh Army one regiment of the disputed 73rd Infantry Division with a light artillery battalion, as the forces of 46th Infantry Division and the two Romanian brigades deployed near Kerch were not sufficient to carry out the order to XXXXII Corps to 'throw the enemy off the Kerch peninsula again'. The army group also ordered the thorough destruction of the port of Kerch in the event of an evacuation.

After the conclusion of its reorganization on 27 December 1941, LIV Army Corps renewed its attack on Sevastopol; the army was hoping to reach the bay within three days. But the situation in the eastern part of the Crimea had been changed completely by a successful enemy landing near Feodosiya carried out under cover of fog. Contrary to instructions from the army, the commander of XXXXII Army Corps, Lieutenant-General Hans Graf von Sponeck, ordered the withdrawal of 46th Infantry Division[350] in order to attack the enemy beachhead and to prevent the division from being cut off at the narrow base of the Kerch peninsula at Parpach. As telephone communications were lacking, the situation on the peninsula remained unclear, but as early as 29 December it became obvious that one division would have to be sent to Feodosiya from the Sevastopol front. This decision meant that the attack on the fortress would have to be abandoned at the very moment when LIV Army Corps believed that 'in the event of a collapse of the enemy counter-attacks' it would be able to break through to the bay of Sevastopol. Hitler, however, ordered the attack to be continued irrespective of the situation on the Kerch peninsula. Sodenstern informed Heusinger, who had passed Hitler's order on,

---

[348] Ibid., 17 Dec. 1941.   [349] Ibid., 21 Dec. 1941.

[350] Einbeck, *Sponeck*, 22 ff.; H.Gr. Süd/Ia, KTB, 29 Dec. 1941, BA-MA RH 19 I/88; Manstein, *Lost Victories*, 225–6.

that it would of course be carried out, but the Crimea and Eleventh Army would then be lost unless the enemy was stopped at the narrow base of the peninsula. The army group could not send any additional forces. In fact, however, parts of a Romanian division were sent, missions by Air Fleet 4 were ordered against Feodosiya and Kerch, and personnel replacements were ordered to be flown in for Eleventh Army. As expected, the Romanians offered only weak resistance against the enemy units landed near Feodosiya. That Eleventh Army's lines of communication were not immediately cut, thus seriously threatening the army, was due only to the extreme caution of the Soviet commanders.

The orders concerning the critical situation in the Crimea were typical of the divergence between the demands made on the troops at this time and the means available to carry them out. Hitler demanded a continuation of the attack on Sevastopol, as he urgently needed a military victory to improve the depressed morale in the army and at home. Manstein's staff was well aware that the attack had to be broken off, but expressed this conclusion as follows: 'The prospects of freeing forces to eliminate the enemy in the eastern part of the Crimea by a quick, decisive victory at Sevastopol have . . . diminished.'[351] Again all necessary steps to reinforce the German units defending the narrow base of the Kerch peninsula were promised, and again the army group commander-in-chief, Reichenau, had to decide between alternatives that were in fact no longer available. For neither could the attack on Sevastopol be continued with any prospect of success, nor could anything be achieved by ordering General Franz Mattenklott, commanding XXXXII Army Corps, to 'attack the enemy group around Feodosiya with available forces and subsequently clear the Kerch peninsula', as Mattenklott's only division, 46th Infantry, had lost all its heavy weapons and equipment at Kerch and was completely exhausted.[352]

As in the evacuation of Rostov, every command could point to memorandums and reports which had explained the futility of the operation from the very beginning unless certain conditions were fulfilled—conditions which everyone involved knew could not be met. 'To remove any doubt, the commander-in-chief of the army group repeated in a teletype order that the task of Eleventh Army was still to take Sevastopol as soon as possible, dislodge the newly landed enemy forces, and hold the Crimea.'[353] On the afternoon of 30 December the operations department explained that it could not send any additional forces. Sodenstern stressed the seriousness of the situation in the Crimea and expressed the opinion that, in view of the strong enemy landing near Feodosiya, Sponeck's decision to withdraw 46th Infantry Division could

---

[351] H.Gr. Süd/Ia, KTB, 29, 30 Dec. 1941, BA-MA RH 19 I/88.

[352] H.Gr. Süd/Ia, KTB, 30 Dec. 1941. By then an operational danger to the entire Eleventh Army was considered possible.

[353] The exact wording of the order in KTB of Army Group South, 30 Dec. 1941, BA-MA RH 19 I/88.

possibly be justified, as without that division the situation could not be saved. That evening Manstein expressed his doubts to Reichenau as to whether the forces of XXXXII Army Corps would be sufficient to hold their positions if the enemy were able to land several divisions. Reichenau's answer, that the Red Army too was facing serious supply problems, is quite incomprehensible in view of Manstein's frequent reports to the effect that Sevastopol could easily be supplied by sea. In the end a report was sent to Hitler indicating that the attack on Sevastopol would be continued and the enemy forces in the eastern Crimea would be dislodged by XXXXII Army Corps. The head of the operations department accepted this report and remarked that it 'agrees with the view of the Führer'.[354] At any rate Reichenau pointed out that issuing the order did not guarantee success. The army group took the harsh reality into account by appointing the commandant of Poltava, Lieutenant-General Karl Spang, 'commander of the Isthmuses of Perekop and Genichesk' and envisaging 'special help for securing and fortifying the isthmuses of the Crimea'.[355]

These measures apparently satisfied the requirements of the ritual described in such detail above. On 31 December the attack on Sevastopol was halted in order to defeat the enemy forces near Feodosiya.

Thus, at the end of 1941 the troops of Army Group South were well over 1,200 kilometres from their starting-point (the air distance from Lvov to Rostov is about 1,300 kilometres), deep in the Soviet Union. Their performance had far exceeded all expectations, but the operational idea that required such efforts had not been realized. The 'vital strength' of the enemy had by no means been 'destroyed'.

(d) The Attack on Leningrad
(See the Amexe Volume, No. 15)

The strategic-operational thinking of the German commanders and the course of the fighting previously described repeatedly reflected the basic problem confronting the Wehrmacht in the east: providing the necessary fighting forces in an expanding theatre of operations from an unchanging and limited number of available soldiers. Examination of the differences of opinion in the German high command reveals different phases in the setting of priorities and the resulting distribution of forces.[356] That these differences were not resolved in Army Group North at a time when success was still possible is the central problem with which this section is concerned. In general it can be said that in spite of all parallels that can be shown in the switching of forces from Army Group Centre to the wings of the eastern front, substantial differences re-

---

[354] Ibid.

[355] Ibid. Manstein expected three or four additional enemy divisions to be landed on the Kerch peninsula and near Feodosiya. This was the reason for his urgent request for additional troops and his reaction to the withdrawal order issued by Lt.-Gen. Graf von Sponeck on his own responsibility.

[356] Cf. sect. II.1.1(b).

mained. Army Group South needed considerably more reserves to reach its first main operational objective, the Dnieper line, as well as the help of the neighbouring Second Army and Armoured Group 2. But the engagement of these units in support of Army Group South undermined the entire strategic plan of the second stage of the campaign. Moreover, the objectives of this army group were so ambitious that they were liable to require a large part of the German army unless conditions were exceptionally favourable. But such conditions could not be expected with objectives which required nothing less than the encirclement of the Caucasus, blocking the Volga at Stalingrad, and securing the flanks as well as the occupied territory. The 'retrieval' of these formations to their original fronts was inevitably bound to cause incalculable difficulties.

Army Group North, on the other hand, had advanced far beyond its first operational objectives by the end of July 1941 and thus had a claim, approved at the very beginning, to an effective mobile unit so as to be able to reach its preliminary final objective, Leningrad.[357] In contrast to the situation in the south, the time and forces required to reach this objective were predictable, and success would release a considerable number of units for other purposes. Moreover, this would decisively improve the strategic situation in the entire northern area, as control of the Baltic and the supply-routes from the Arctic Ocean would make it possible to terminate the fighting in that area. This expectation had been one reason for the use of Finnish forces there.

Hitler had argued from this position ever since the beginning of his operational planning against the Soviet Union, though without drawing the necessary conclusions energetically and in time. Only after it became evident during his visit to Army Group North on 21 July that that army group, because of its over-extended front sector and the tying down of its southern wing, did not have sufficient forces to capture Leningrad rapidly did Hitler agree to send it strong units of Armoured Group 3, while Halder wanted to solve the problem through a new start of the operation and by transferring the task of providing cover for the southern flank to Ninth Army of Army Group Centre.[358] After receiving the suggestions of the army group, the commander-in-chief of the army issued a directive on 23 July[359] in which he pointed out that, with the order to destroy enemy forces in and around Leningrad, the army group had been given a new task.

Halder now called upon Army Group North to sever the railway line between Moscow and Leningrad speedily and for good so as to prevent an enemy withdrawal to the south and south-east. The most important measure he demanded in this regard was concentration of the main effort along both sides of Lake Ilmen in the direction of Lake Ladoga. There the strongest

---

[357] Hitler wished to complete the operation against Leningrad, for which forces of Army Group Centre were to be transferred, before advancing against Moscow. Cf. sect. II.i.i(*b*) at nn. 356 ff.

[358] Halder, *Diaries*, 1066–7, 1069, 1071 (21, 22, 23 July 1941).

[359] OKH/GenStdH/Op.Abt. (I) No. 1390/41, 23 July 1941, BA-MA RH 2/v. 1326.

possible armoured forces were to be used, which ran counter to the entire combat experience of Armoured Group 4. For this new effort Halder envisaged bringing up XXXXI Armoured Corps, i.e. the main combat strength of Armoured Group 4. The army group was to move up sufficiently strong forces to cover this attack on the Valday hills. This greatly limited the use of Armoured Group 3, which had initially also been ordered to participate. On the left wing of the army group, on both sides of Luga, approximately one infantry corps was to be used to cut off Leningrad. The forces to be used for the conquest of Estonia were to be limited to five divisions.

The views of the commander of Armoured Group 4, Colonel-General Hoepner, were decisive in the objections of the army group command to this plan of attack.[360] Hoepner developed a new plan which avoided sending mobile troops into the difficult terrain between Novgorod and Chudovo, which had only recently proved an insurmountable obstacle for Manstein's armoured corps. The exclusive use of infantry forces (six divisions) at the point of main effort, as well as the plan to use Armoured Group 3 together with still unspecified divisions for the attack in a northerly direction east of the chain of lakes (north of Ostashkov), totally conflicted with the plans formulated by Halder, who wanted to spare the last-named unit at all events. Moreover, the attack of the entire Armoured Group 4 and the additional eight infantry divisions from the area between Lake Ilmen and Lake Peipus towards the north would result in a concentration of forces south-west of Leningrad which Halder wanted to avoid. Halder sent his deputy chief of staff (operations), Lieutenant-General Paulus, himself an expert in armoured warfare, to persuade the armoured group and Leeb to change their plans. He also referred to the 'wish of the higher leadership' to have the armoured units advance in the 'operationally correct direction'.[361] After receiving an oral report on the results of Paulus's visits to the army group on 24 and 26 July, in which all four armour commanders insisted that the terrain Halder envisaged for the attack was totally unsuited for armour, Halder accepted a compromise proposed by Leeb. The main effort of the attack was still to be made in the area of Novgorod and Lake Ladoga, but primarily by infantry units. 8th Armoured Division and the SS Totenkopf Division were to be assembled in such a way that, depending on the situation, they could be quickly sent into action.

This meant that an armoured corps (LVI) was, on paper, deployed in the 'operationally correct direction', while Leeb at the same time took into ac-

---

[360] Situation assessment by C.-in-C. of Army Group North, 24 July 1941: Müller-Hillebrand, Nordabschnitt, pt. I, appendix E9, MGFA P-114a; ibid., Pz.Gr. 4, Führungsabsicht, 23 July 1941, appendix E6, and Führungsabsicht, H.Gr. Nord, appendix E5.

[361] Ibid., directive, operations department, 24 July 1941, and memorandum of conference between Halder and Brennecke (chief of staff of Army Group North), 25 July 1941, appendices E8, E10. Paulus's discussion with Army Group North and Armd. Group 4: ibid., H.Gr. Nord/Ia, KTB copy, appendix E11; Halder, *Diaries*, 1077 (26 July 1941); for Hoepner's doubts on 24 July and talk with Paulus at Leeb's headquarters, see Leeb, *Tagebuchaufzeichnungen*, 306–10 (27 July 1941); Manstein, *Lost Victories*, 197–8.

count Hoepner's doubts by reserving the right, 'under certain conditions', to move 8th Armoured Division (the only such division of this corps) up behind XXXXI Armoured Corps once the attack was well under way. The corresponding army group order was written on 27 July.[362] In his directive of 28 July[363] Halder himself took Leeb's arguments into account. What had he achieved in terms of keeping together the attack force to be used against Moscow? He had the views of highly skilled armour generals and an army group commander-in-chief highly valued by Hitler that the terrain in the area of Ninth Army and Armoured Group 3 was totally unsuited for motorized and armoured warfare. From the very beginning Halder had no intention of discussing the use of these units suggested by Hoepner. As early as 25 July the army group command was told that Armoured Group 3 could not be made available before 9 August.[364] A further delay, until 15 August, was announced on 29 July, which ruled out any serious consideration of including the armoured group in the army group's plans.

On 30 July Hitler sent Keitel to Leeb[365] to emphasize again the importance of the attack on Leningrad—even VIII Air Corps was to be transferred to the Leningrad front—but that was only by way of consolation for the delay announced on the same day in the transfer of Armoured Group 3. Moreover, the army group was informed that, instead of receiving additional forces, it had to expect that a second corps would be tied down on its southern wing (Ninth Army).

The order to the army group was reduced. Its task remained the isolation of Leningrad, but it was no longer required to prevent the withdrawal of enemy forces to the east, i.e. to continue the offensive on the long eastern front.

Army Group North was able and obliged to accept the non-availability of Armoured Group 3. But the complete over-extension of the right flank in the direction of Leningrad meant that a withdrawal of units had to be expected from that direction at any time if the enemy attacked on that flank to relieve pressure on the Leningrad front. A covering front of 350 kilometres could not be held with the remaining divisions of Sixteenth Army.[366] Leeb demonstrated to the commander-in-chief of the army that he needed thirty-five divisions for all his tasks, but he had only twenty-six. He had already had to transfer two corps commands with four divisions to Army Group Centre and was expecting a further request for one corps. A case of 'Please return promptly.'

Brauchitsch at least left the decision regarding the use of Armoured Group

---

[362] H.Gr. Nord/Ia No. 1770/41, army group order No. 2, 27 July 1941, copy: Müller-Hillebrand, Nordabschnitt, pt. 1, appendix E14, MGFA P-114a.

[363] OKH/GenStdH/Op.Abt. (I), directive for the continuation of operations, 28 July 1941, BA-MA RH 2/v. 1 326.

[364] Leeb, *Tagebuchaufzeichnungen*, 312 n. 206.

[365] Ibid. 313 ff. (31 July–4 Aug. 1941); statement by chief of staff of Army Group North on new directive from Army High Command (31 July 1941): Müller-Hillebrand, Nordabschnitt, appendix E19, MGFA P-114a.

[366] Assessment of situation by C.-in-C., 3 Aug. 1941, ibid., appendix E20; Leeb, *Tagebuchaufzeichnungen*, 313 ff.

4 to Leeb. The consequences of a new extension of the army group's front and the inevitable halting of the eastern flank were foreseeable if there was only one division to be used along the 150-kilometre line between Toropets and Staraya Russa, and that division also had to reach the area east of Kholm.

The necessary regrouping and supply problems led to the attack by Armoured Group 4 being set for 8 August.[367] In the meantime the defenders around the bridgeheads on the lower Luga had constructed such strong field fortifications, behind which additional troops and material for an attack planned on the same day were assembled, that the attack by XXXXI Armoured Corps was very costly and made little, progress, if any. The fact that LVI Armoured Corps was not able to attack because of the weather enabled the enemy to concentrate his defences in this sector.

The general attack began on 10 August, effectively supported by the formations of VIII Air Corps. From 13 August the attack by XXXXI Armoured Corps penetrated the enemy's defences and broke his resistance. But to sustain the attack the only reserve unit, the SS Totenkopf Division, would have had to be brought up—something which because of the enemy attack on the south-east flank near Dno, Leeb refused to permit.

After 13 August enemy attacks against the southern flank also increased, which caused the army group to fear a penetration via Staraya Russa into the rear of the attack front. On 15 August the army group summed up its knowledge of the enemy's intentions in a report stating that, according to statements by prisoners, the Russians planned to break through the gap between Kholm and Staraya Russa with Thirty-fourth Reserve Army in order to halt the attack on Leningrad. Four Soviet divisions were identified at the front and an additional one near Gorkiy; another four divisions were known to be part of Thirty-fourth Reserve Army. Heusinger reported by telephone that, according to radio intelligence, a Soviet cavalry division had been ordered to advance to Dno and establish contact with partisans there. The German troops were exhausted and, according to a report by the general commanding X Army corps, could not be expected to resist for very long.[368]

This development jeopardized the attack for the encirclement of Leningrad, as reinforcements for the defence of the south-eastern sector of the army group front could be drawn only from those forces around Leningrad.

After the 'draining' of Sixteenth Army in deference to the *idée fixe* of a

---

[367] Because of weather conditions this attack had to be postponed; the corps of Sixteenth Army therefore attacked in echelon up to 10 Aug. 1941: Leeb, *Tagebuchaufzeichnungen*, 319–25 (4–10 Aug. 1941); Chales de Beaulieu, *Panzergruppe 4*, 164 ff.; Müller-Hillebrand, Nordabschnitt, pt. I, appendices E21, F1, MGFA P-114a.

[368] Report of chief of staff Army Group North to chief of operations department, Army High Command, 15 Aug. 1941: Müller-Hillebrand, Nordabschnitt, pt. I, appendix F2, MGFA P-114a. 'The incident is inconsequential even in the view of army group. Nevertheless the Führer had Jodl call up to order commitment of one armoured corps (later reduced to one armoured division) to contain the penetration. This reacting to all pinpricks frustrates any planning on an operational scale and prevents concentration of our forces': Halder, *Diaries*, 1177, 1178–9 (14,·15 Aug. 1941); cf. sect. II.1.1(*b*) at n. 206.

deployment against Moscow, no assistance could be expected from the army high command. Hitler used the report on the tactically difficult situation on the southern wing of Army Group North to push through the concentration of forces against Leningrad, where he had ordered that the main effort should be made in this phase of operations. He ordered the immediate transfer there of as many mobile units from Armoured Group 3 as could be used and supplied. Halder now had to accept the transfer of XXXIX Armoured Corps, but he ordered it to be kept out of the fighting south of Lake Ilmen; it was to be used instead to form the centre of an attack via Novgorod against the southern flank of Leningrad.[369] That was precisely the direction which had been found to be unsuitable on 26 July.

To put in order the situation on its southern wing, the army group immediately withdrew the corps command of LVI Armoured Corps and transferred it to the Lovat, which simultaneously deprived XXXXI Armoured Corps on the Luga–Narva front of the urgently demanded support for the attack. Halder and the army group rejected the obvious solution of bringing up XXXIX Armoured Corps to reinforce the wing of the attack with the explanation that an advance northward via Novgorod was operationally the best direction, the strong enemy defences on the Luga would prevent an effective use of the armoured corps, and supply problems were to be expected. I Army Corps was placed under Armoured Group 4 instead of LVI Armoured Corps. The command of L Army Corps, which had been returned by Army Group Centre, assumed command of the southern front against Leningrad. Halder strongly opposed any further transfers to the army group.[370] The situation on the southern flank was straightened out by LVI Armoured Corps and the three divisions of X Army Corps. Between 19 and 23 August six Soviet divisions were encircled.[371] To the surprise of the army group, the breakthrough to Novgorod was achieved on 15 August. On 20 August Chudovo was reached

---

[369] XXXIX Armd. Corps consisted of 12th Armd. Div., 18th and 12th Inf. Divs. (mot.): Halder, *Diaries*, 1180–1 (15 Aug. 1941), with reaction of Army Group Centre; briefing for operations department by Army Group North, 16 Aug. 1941, and situation assessment by Army High Command, 17 Aug. 1941: Müller-Hillebrand, Nordabschnitt, pt. I, appendices F4, F5, MGFA P-114a. On the withdrawal of LVI Armd. Corps see Chales de Beaulieu, *Panzergruppe 4*, 169 (statement by Armd. Group 4, 15 Aug. 1941), 76 ff. XXXIX Armd. Corps took the place of LIV Armd. Corps, which had been sent south-eastward, a senseless, fuel-consuming movement in the opposite direction.

[370] Halder, *Diaries*, 1178–9 (15 Aug. 1941). He attempted at first to divert only an infantry division (mot.) from the armoured corps to be brought up. The playing down of the alarming reports from Army Group North, which did not take the situation so lightly, could be based on reports from Armd. Group 4; it was, however, primarily due to Halder's disappointment at not being able to rehabilitate the armoured corps for the attack on Moscow. For Leeb's demand, see Müller-Hillebrand, Nordabschnitt, pt. I, appendix F2, MGFA P-114a; Leeb, *Tagebuchaufzeichnungen*, 332 (15 Aug. 1941).

[371] The astonishing result of this 'pinprick' (Halder) was: 18,000 prisoners, 234 artillery pieces, 201 tanks, 243 machine-guns, and 117 mortars captured or destroyed (figures according to Müller-Hillebrand, Nordabschnitt, pt. I, 127, MGFA P-114a). On the transfer and the attack cf. Manstein, *Lost Victories*, 199 ff.

and the railway line between Moscow and Leningrad cut. The units of the approaching XXXIX Armoured Corps followed the infantry corps into the future deployment area of the 'point of main effort East'. On the left, XXXVIII Army Corps advanced through forests and swamps; XXXXI Armoured Corps attacked towards Krasnogvardeysk. On 20 August the road and rail links with Leningrad were also cut at this point. Divisions of Eighteenth Army had already taken Kingisepp and Narva on 17 August. The attacks towards the coast of Estonia were also proceeding according to plan; on 28 August Tallinn fell. This phase of the attack thus developed more favourably than had been expected. Only XXXXI Armoured Corps, which, after very hard initial fighting, had broken through and believed it could break into Leningrad with the help of the two divisions to be brought up from LVI Armoured Corps, was disappointed, a disappointment comparable to that of III Armoured Corps against Kiev. In both cases the troops of the mobile units felt restrained from the rear, not by the enemy.[372]

For the next phase of the operation, Army Group North placed XXXIX Armoured Corps under the command of Sixteenth Army; with the addition of XXVIII Army Corps, the 'Group Schmidt' was formed (named after the general commanding XXXIX Armoured Corps, General Rudolf Schmidt). Because of concern about the vulnerability of the long southern and south-eastern flank, the third mobile unit of the army group, LIV Armoured Corps, remained on the Lovat (with 3rd Infantry Division (mot.) and SS Totenkopf Division; its 8th Armoured Division had been transferred to XXXXI Armoured Corps). Here, however, German deliberations were already based on the idea of an offensive encirclement of the enemy forces confronting II Army Corps by an attack in the direction of Demyansk.[373]

On 21 August the army group issued orders and assigned objectives for the attack front against Leningrad and for offensive flank protection.[374] In the course of this attack, 12th Armoured Division reached the Neva on 30 August and thus also cut Leningrad's most important links to the east. (See the Annexe Volume, No. 16.)

Even now, in the last decisive preparatory phase, elements of Sixteenth Army (II Army Corps) were assigned to co-operate with Ninth Army, which had captured Toropets after its success at Velikie Luki. To shorten the front and reach a favourable starting-position for future participation in the offensive to the east (Moscow), Sixteenth Army was to continue its attack with the

---

[372] Chales de Beaulieu, *Panzergruppe 4*, 136 ff. On III Armd. Corps cf. sect. II.1.1(*a*) at n. 131. In both cases these were subjective impressions at the point of an attack, which cannot be maintained upon examination of other conditions.

[373] Cf. order of battle of Army Group North, 20 Aug. 1941: Müller-Hillebrand, Nordabschnitt, pt. 1, appendix F7, MGFA P-114a.

[374] Army Group North, order No. 5 for the continuation of the attack, 21 Aug. 1941, ibid., appendix F8; order to Sixteenth Army, 25 Aug. 1941, ibid., appendix F9; Leeb, *Tagebuchaufzeichnungen*, 338 (20, 21 Aug. 1941), n. 331.

line between Ostashkov and the Valday hills as its preliminary objective.[375] The boundary between the two army groups was moved north.

On 24 August, Army Group North submitted a first general study of the forces necessary for the encirclement of Leningrad and for flank cover, and of their disposition. On 29 August 'Army group order No. 1 for the encirclement of the city of Leningrad' was issued.[376] Leeb assumed that the Red Army would shift its main defensive effort in the north to the Volkhov sector and consider Leningrad as a position that could not be held in the long term.[377] The task of securing the front on both sides of Lake Ilmen was to be left to Sixteenth Army. Armoured Group 4 was to lead the attack on Leningrad and take over the lower Volkhov sector to relieve Sixteenth Army. Leeb at first planned an advance to a further encirclement front along the line Izhora–Detskoe Selo–Pulkovo–Uritsk, which would establish bridgeheads across the Neva between Shlisselburg and Ivanovskoe. A 'closer' siege-line would be formed later. Every opportunity to advance was to be exploited. If the population played a significant part in the fighting, industrial cities were to be bypassed, captured from the rear, or encircled. Leningrad itself was not to be attacked with infantry, but to be cut off. Military facilities were then to be destroyed and all water and energy supplies cut off. Armoured Group 4 would receive the conditions under which an offer of surrender could be accepted. The situation assessment of the army group was largely based on reports by deserters and civilians leaving Leningrad to the effect that parts of the population, industrial facilities, armaments, and works of art were being evacuated from the city. Like Army Group South at Kiev, Army Group North misinterpreted these actions, including the removal of food and utility installations, as a preparation for the ending of resistance in Leningrad, whereas they were actually intended to strengthen other fronts and save valuable machinery. The Soviet troops remaining in the city and civilians suitable for any kind of military service were to continue fighting under the overall leadership of the political organs. If the city were destroyed and the front collapsed, they were to fight underground.

The optimism of Leeb and the chief of his general staff, Lieutenant-General Kurt Brennecke, can be seen in their situation assessment of 31 August, in which they already considered using the units that would be available after the encirclement of Leningrad for attacks north and south of Lake Ilmen in the direction of Moscow.[378] But to make that possible the siege had to succeed

---

[375] OKH GenStdH/Op.Abt. (I) No. 1 457/41 g.Kdos. Chefs., 24 Aug. 1941, to Army Groups North and Centre, BA-MA RH 2/v. 1326. For the deliberations of Leeb and Army High Command see Leeb, *Tagebuchaufzeichnungen*, 338, 342 (20, 24 Aug. 1941). At this time Halder was very dissatisfied with what he considered to be the slow progress of Army Group North and its excessive flank cover: *Diaries*, 1194 ff. (22 Aug. 1941).

[376] Army Group North, situation assessment to Army High Command, 24 Aug. 1941, and army group order No. 1, 29 Aug. 1941: Müller-Hillebrand, Nordabschnitt, pt. 1, appendices G1, G2, MGFA P-114a; deliberations of Armd. Group 4: Chales de Beaulieu, *Panzergruppe 4*, 109 ff.

[377] Leeb, *Tagebuchaufzeichnungen*, 344 (26 Aug. 1941).

[378] Situation assessment by chief of the general staff and reflections of C.-in-C. on continuation

quickly and the Finns had to make progress in Karelia and reach the Svir between Lakes Ladoga and Onega. A secure boundary would also have to be established with Ninth Army.

However, Armoured Group 4's at first optimistic assessment of the situation had to be adjusted in the first days of September because of increasingly stubborn enemy resistance and rain. The slow progress made by units of Eighteenth Army from Estonia also delayed the start of the attack by XXXXI Armoured Corps. Because of heavy enemy attacks on the Volkhov front, the group responsible for making the main effort on the right wing was increasingly diverted from its objectives from as early as 25 August, when 18th Motorized Infantry Division had to be switched from Chudovo and Lyuban to the north. In its place 12th Armoured Division took over the thrust against Leningrad but was able to advance no further than Izhora. The third division of the corps (20th Motorized Infantry Division) attacked towards the Neva in order to establish bridgeheads. From 3 September all three mobile divisions of the armoured corps were employed in defence, which ruled out the concentration of all armoured units of Armoured Group 4 against Leningrad. XXXVIII Army Corps thus had to begin its attack on Leningrad from the south-east on 7 September without armoured support.[379]

On 4 September the army group command envisaged an attack in three phases.[380] First, 'liquidation of the pocket north of Luga and breaching of the Leningrad defence-line'; next, 'capture of the coastal fortifications' in Estonia; finally, 'a north-eastward thrust to join hands with the Finns'.[381] Final preparations for the attack were discussed at the army group command on 6 September. But no date was set; it was agreed only that the attack should begin as soon as possible.

The advance of the encirclement front against Leningrad and the assumption that the employment of XXXIX Armoured Corps would make it possible to complete the main task of Army Group North in a few days caused Hitler on 5 September to assign entirely new tasks to all forces of the army group within the framework of his directive for the attack on Moscow.[382] The Leningrad area was to be cut off soon in the east by attacks of German and Finnish units from the Neva bridgeheads, but only after the annihilation of enemy forces around the city had been concluded. On the lower Volkhov the encirclement front was to be closed off to the east. In co-operation with the

of operation, 31 Aug. 1941: Müller-Hillebrand, Nordabschnitt, pt. I, appendix G3, MGFA P-114a; Halder, *Diaries*, 1212–13 (1 Sept. 1941); Leeb (*Tagebuchaufzeichnungen*, 346–7: 31 Aug. 1941) presents the basic discussion with Hoepner.

[379] Chales de Beaulieu, *Panzergruppe 4*, 113 ff.; Leeb, *Tagebuchaufzeichnungen*, 346 ff. (1 Aug.–5 Sept. 1942), on the delay of the attack by Armd. Group 4.

[380] Halder, *Diaries*, 1216 (4 Sept. 1941); Leeb, *Tagebuchaufzeichnungen*, 349–50 (5 Sept. 1941).

[381] It was still assumed that the Finns were prepared to advance beyond the Svir and on the Karelian isthmus; Leeb was primarily concerned to see enemy forces tied down. Cf. sect. II.III.2(*b*) at n. 159 (Ueberschär).

[382] Directive No. 35, 6 Sept. 1941, *Hitler's War Directives*, 96 ff.; Halder, *Diaries*, 1217–18 (5 Sept. 1941); Leeb, *Tagebuchaufzeichnungen*, 350–1 (6, 7 Sept. 1941).

Finns, the bay of Kronshtadt was to be blocked by mine-barrages and artillery to prevent a break-out by Soviet naval units into the Baltic. By 15 September the mobile units deployed against Leningrad and VIII Air Corps were to be transferred to Army Group Centre to be available for the attack towards Moscow. Army Group North was to cover this attack by advancing eastward north and south of Lake Ilmen.

The new and now final determination of the main point of effort for the army and Luftwaffe units in the coming attack on Moscow placed Army Group North under great pressure of time if it wanted to make use of their fighting power. The transfer of units and army troops reduced the army group to a point where its strength seemed inadequate even for purely defensive tasks.[383] Immediately after receiving Hitler's new directive, the commander-in-chief of the group informed the Army High Command of his reservations.[384] Considerably stronger enemy resistance was now being encountered on the Leningrad front; at all events the Red Army would attempt to reopen communication lines from the city to the east. A withdrawal of units and army troops by 15 September, as envisaged, would mean that action against Leningrad would have to be limited to the first encirclement line, and the purpose of the operation would not be achieved. The coastal fortifications in the bay of Kronshtadt would not be cut off, and the city—especially the airfields—would avoid being brought within range of German artillery. The encirclement east of the city between the Neva and Lake Ladoga, a joint operation with the Finns, would be endangered; and if it did not succeed, the supply-lines across the lake and from the area in between would remain open.

Leeb pointed out that the defenders of the city would mount a counter-attack when they realized that German troops were being withdrawn. With the arrival of freezing temperatures, the Volkhov and Lake Ilmen could easily be crossed. Abandoning the plan for a close encirclement would in fact lead to a permanent state of crisis and make impossible the release of additional units. He urgently requested that the units scheduled to be transferred be left with Army Group North until the conclusion of the operations envisaged against Leningrad, as otherwise the enemy would be 'let go' at the very moment when his destruction was to be completed. The consequences of the new situation were reflected in a second army group order for the encirclement of Leningrad, issued on 6 September.[385]

---

[383] Message of Army High Command to Army Group North, 11 Sept. 1941: Müller-Hillebrand, Nordabschnitt, pt. 1, appendix G7, MGFA P-114a. The army group was most seriously affected by the transfer of the bulk of its reconnaissance units, sappers, and heavy artillery. The artillery was to be replaced by seven French mortars and twelve field howitzer batteries. The troops for these weapons were to be provided by the remaining artillery units.

[384] Situation assessment and intentions of Army Group North to Army High Command, operations department, 6 Sept. 1941: Müller-Hillebrand, Nordabschnitt, pt. 1, appendix C5, MGFA P-114a; Leeb, *Tagebuchaufzeichnungen*, 350 (6, 7 Sept. 1941).

[385] Army group order No. 2, 7 Sept. 1941: Müller-Hillebrand, Nordabschnitt, pt. 1, appendix G6, MGFA P-114a.

The tasks of Sixteenth Army, primarily concerned with providing offensive cover for the right flank, were redefined. After destroying the enemy west of the Valday plateau, it was to go over to the defensive along the line from Lake Velye via the north shore of Lake Ilmen to the Volkhov. Plans for an expansion of the bridgehead at Novgorod and a thrust towards Ostashkov were temporarily abandoned and were to be revived only after Ninth Army had made satisfactory progress. XXXIX Armoured Corps, which was now left with only one strong artillery group, with 20th Motorized Infantry Division, and with parts of 122nd Infantry Division, was to push on to Lake Ladoga and cover the rear of the Neva front towards the east. A later link-up with the Finns on the Svir was to be prepared. The continuation of the attack across the Neva was postponed.

Now the attack front against Leningrad was concentrated on Armoured Group 4. Under the corps command of XXVIII Army Corps three infantry divisions and 20th Motorized Infantry Division were to be subordinated to it to form the 'main point of effort East'. After sufficient forces had been provided, this reorganized Armoured Group 4 was to attack across Leningrad's outer ring of defences. To the left of the armoured group, Eighteenth Army was to advance via Krasnoe Selo against the city and the coastal fortifications on the bay of Kronshtadt. The take-over of the entire front against Leningrad by Eighteenth Army headquarters was to be prepared.[386]

Air Fleet 1 was again to use VIII Air Corps to support the attack. Realizing that the attack towards Moscow could not begin before the end of September, Halder agreed to permit Leeb the use of the mobile troops until he had reached his objectives.

On 8 September Army Group North was able to report two important successes, the capture of Shlisselburg in the north and Demyansk in the southeast (by II Army Corps and LVII Armoured Corps respectively). But on the whole Leeb was compelled to regroup his forces as a result of counter-attacks and newly identified transports of enemy troops to the front. He regarded such regroupings as a 'poor man's war', as they repeatedly gave the enemy the opportunity to avoid decisive battles. On 11 September he considered the situation in the south-east of his army group, in the area of Demyansk, to be sufficiently settled to enable him to transfer the two mobile units in action there on 15 September.[387] (LVII Armoured Corps of Armoured Group 3 had been placed under Army Group North only for Demyansk.) On the other hand, in view of the progress made in the attack on Leningrad, he requested

---

[386] The remaining units were placed under Sixteenth Army and were 'used up' in defensive actions, ibid.; orders to Army Group North and transfers of Armd. Group 4 and mobile units: OKH/GenStdH/Op.Abt. (II) No. 1494/41, 10 Sept. 1941, Weisung für die Fortführung der Operationen [Directive for the continuation of operations], with annexe 1, BA-MA RH 2/v. 1326.

[387] Situation assessment of Army Group North/Ia, 11 Sept. 1941: Müller-Hillebrand, Nordabschnitt, pt. 1, appendix G8, MGFA P-114a; Halder, *Diaries*, 1224 (11 Sept. 1941).

that XXXXI Armoured Corps remain with Army Group North until Krasnogvardeysk had been captured. Otherwise the battle would have to be broken off at the crucial moment, with the consequences already depicted on 6 September. Halder was sympathetic, but he pressed Leeb if at all possible to transfer Armoured Group 4 on the date set and disputed Leeb's assertion that breaking off the encirclement operation would require pulling back the front.[388]

In the meantime, the fighting in which the two divisions of Eighteenth Army still in Estonia were involved was approaching its conclusion. After the capture of Narva on 17 August 1941 the operations of the parts of Eighteenth Army in Estonia took place separately from those of the eastern wing of the army group and the front against Leningrad.[389] (See the Annexe Volume, No. 16.)

On 9 July the first German convoy left for Riga, which had already been captured on 29 June. This was a daring operation in so far as Riga and its port Dünamünde could be completely dominated by the offshore islands. The Irben strait was not mined, however, and the first convoy arrived without losses. But the incipient resistance of the numerous heavy artillery emplacements, the air units, and the ships of the Soviet Baltic Fleet soon forced a reduction of supply shipments. German heavy army artillery, provisionally placed at appropriate points, was not able to provide adequate protection for the convoys.[390] Together with the navy, 291st Infantry Division prepared to seize the islands. After the capture of Tallinn by XXXXII Army Corps (254th, 61st, and 217th Infantry Divisions) on 28 August, the corps was divided: 254th Division was sent east, 217th was made available for coastal defence, and 61st was made available for the attack on the Baltic islands.[391] With the capture of Tallinn, it became urgently necessary to protect the sea routes against Soviet air units and long-range artillery on the islands of Hiiumaa (Dagö) and Saaremaa (Ösel). On the other hand, the withdrawal of most of the Soviet Baltic Fleet permitted German naval units to operate without great risk. Landings on the island of Vormsi and two smaller islands in the Muhu sound were begun on 8 September to prevent Soviet ships from interfering with the landings on the larger islands. The capture of Saaremma was begun on 14 September with a landing on the island of Muhu accompanied by massive air attacks to suppress enemy artillery fire and feints

[388] Telephone conversation between Halder and Brennecke, 12 Sept. 1941, 12.00 a.m.: Müller-Hillebrand, Nordabschnitt, pt. I, appendix G9, MGFA P-114a; Halder, *Diaries*, 1227 (12 Sept. 1941); Leeb, *Tagebuchaufzeichnungen*, 354. After being briefed by Schmundt on 11 Sept. Keitel granted a postponement of 48 hours: Army group order for pulling out the mobile units of Armd. Group 4, 14 Sept. 1941: BA-MA Pz.Gr. 4, 18738/2. In fact this was not completed until 20 Sept. 1941.

[389] Melzer, *Baltische Inseln*, 21 ff.; Hubatsch, *61. Infantrie-Division*, 60 ff.; M.Dv. No. 601, pp. 21 ff., 35: H.Gr. Nord/Ia, KTB, BA-MA RH 19 III/171.

[390] M.Dv. No. 601, pp. 15 ff.

[391] Melzer, *Baltische Inseln*, 26–7, 134 ff. (assignment of troops for Saaremaa), 138 ff., annexes 5, 6; M.Dv. No. 601, pp. 21 ff. (maps 1–3); cf. n. 385 above.

by German and Finnish naval units.[392] Against strong resistance and with fire support from cruisers and torpedo-boats, the island was captured by 5 October. Hiiumaa fell on 21 October. Thereafter the command of XXXXII Army Corps was withdrawn to be used against Odessa; 61st Infantry Division was transferred to Sixteenth Army against Tikhvin, and 217th Division was used in the attack on Oranienbaum. The last island in the group still in Soviet hands, Odensholm, was occupied without resistance by a naval shock-troop detachment on 5 December.

In the conquered Baltic areas a 'Reich Commissariat Ostland' was established, but the northern sector, with the ports, remained part of the rear area of the army under the responsibility of 207th Security Division.

After transferring numerous units for the attack on Moscow, at the end of September 1941 Army Group North was confronted with the question of how it could use the remaining units at the expected points of main effort without reducing—indeed, if possible increasing—the pressure of the ring around Leningrad while securing its eastern flank and protecting its southern flank, which would inevitably lengthen as Ninth Army advanced towards Moscow. As it was not possible to fulfil all these tasks at the same time, and as the strength of enemy attacks at specific locations could not be predicted, the army group command drew up a list of priorities.[393] Top of the list was the consolidation of the situation of XXXXI Armoured Corps on the Volkhov front, where, in addition to the division already scheduled to be withdrawn from the Leningrad front, it might become necessary to remove a division from the siege of Kronshtadt. Because of the strong fortifications on the island and the presence of the reinvigorated Soviet Eighth Army, as well as the guns of the Soviet Baltic Fleet, the army group expected protracted fighting, which would make it impossible to start operations on the Volkhov front first. But that very situation would be highly desirable, as it would then make forces available for the main objective, Leningrad. The fall of Leningrad would break the back of the defence of Kronshtadt. Rest and replacements were essential for continuation of the fighting. In a long memorandum Eighteenth Army headquarters compared its personnel and material situation with the tasks it had been given and with the situation of the enemy. It came to the conclusion that heavy losses, especially of officers and non-commissioned officers, had significantly reduced the fighting value of the $9^2/_3$ infantry divisions remaining on the Leningrad front and the south coast of the Gulf of Finland, a conclusion that applied to all divisions. In addition to personnel replacements, more

[392] Cf. sect. II.1.1(*e*) at n. 424.

[393] H.Gr. Nord/Ia, situation assessment, 20 Sept. 1941; AOK 18/Ia, ideas on the continuation of the operation, 22 Sept. 1941; H.Gr. Nord to OKH/Op.Abt., 23 Sept. 1941: Müller-Hillebrand, Nordabschnitt, pt. 1, appendices G14, G15, G17, MGFA P-114a. Copy of report H.Gr. Nord/Ia No. 2203/41 (as Op.Abt. IN to OKH), 24 Sept. 1941, and comment by the operations department: BA-MA RH 2/v. 1326, pp. 260 ff.

artillery ammunition and adequate air support were urgently needed. Success could be achieved only if all available forces were concentrated on just one task at a time.[394]

On 22 September the expected enemy attacks began against the southern wing of the army group as well as from the north across the Neva, south of Shlisselburg. Under heavy attack intended to re-establish land communications with Leningrad, XXXIX Armoured Corps soon found itself in a difficult situation; a division had to be withdrawn from the encirclement front at Oranienbaum and brought up to reinforce the corps.

The corps repulsed the attacks but took significant losses. Two days later, however, the army group came to the conclusion that, in view of the constantly growing strength of the enemy south of Lake Ilmen as well as on the front between the Neva and the Volkhov, it was not in a position to mount new attacks. XXXIX Armoured Corps (with 8th and 12th Armoured Divisions and 20th Motorized and 96th Infantry Divisions) had suffered such high casualties that it would probably not be able to hold its present positions. The army group urgently requested replacements; in particular, it wanted to bring up 36th Motorized Infantry Division, which had not yet been transferred, to maintain the encirclement of Leningrad. If the close encirclement was not successful, the city would have to be forced to surrender by bombing and starvation. That outcome could not, however, be expected with certainty, as experience of other large cities had shown. Moreover, Leningrad still had a hinterland extending to the Finnish front and the water route across Lake Ladoga.[395]

In view of the special importance Hitler and Army Group North attached to the capture of Leningrad, but also because of the future fate of its defenders, it is appropriate here to outline several German deliberations at various command levels regarding the city.

As early as 6 September the question arose in Hitler's Directive No. 35 whether the surrender of the city should be accepted and what should be done with the inhabitants. In a memorandum of 21 September the department for home defence of the Wehrmacht High Command presented the following variants:[396]

---

[394] The army reported the following losses as of 15 Sept. 1941: 2,035 officers, 304 replacements; 56,700 non-commissioned officers and men, 25,578 replacements. The shortfall was therefore 1,731 officers and 31,122 men: Müller-Hillebrand, Nordabschnitt, pt. 1, appendix G16, MGFA P-114a.

[395] H.Gr. Nord/Ia, reports to OKH/Op.Abt, as in n. 389 above; Müller-Hillebrand, Nordabschnitt, pt. 1 appendices G19, G21, G22, MGFA P-114a; Leeb, Tagebuchaufzeichnungen, 361 ff. (23–7 Sept. 1941); for the following cf. also Salisbury, Leningrad.

[396] OKW/WFST/Abt. L, Chefsachen 'Barbarossa', 21 Sept. 1941, BA-MA RW 4/v. 578; H.Gr. Nord/Ia, KTB, 21 Sept. 1941, BA-MA RH 19 III/168. The result of these deliberations was that all variations considered were found to be unfeasible and that a decision by Hitler was required: Hitler's decision, 12 Oct. 1941, KTB OKW i. 1070 (103). On these questions cf. Leeb, Tagebuchaufzeichnungen, 373 (12 Oct. 1941) n. 484; KTB, H.Gr. Nord, BA-MA RH 19 III/168. Cf. also the problems in the case of Kharkov, ibid. 466. On 12 Oct. the intention to let the civilian population leave Leningrad resulted, in connection with Hitler's directive, in an addendum by the

1. Occupy the city, which was to be rejected, as the Wehrmacht would then be responsible for feeding the population.

2. Isolate the city, if possible with an electric fence to be guarded with machine-guns. Disadvantages of this solution: weak inhabitants would starve, the strong would take the food available and survive; danger of epidemics, which could spread to the German front. 'Moreover, it is doubtful whether we can expect our soldiers to fire at escaping women and children.'

3. 'Remove women, children, and the elderly through openings in the encirclement; let the rest starve.' Criticism: an expulsion beyond the Volkhov, though theoretically possible, was not feasible in practice. This solution too would involve the danger of epidemics and of some of the strongest inhabitants surviving for a long time.

4. After isolating the city, withdraw behind the Neva and leave the city to the Finns. The 'Finns have stated unofficially that they would like the Neva as their frontier, but Leningrad would have to be removed.' Thus the question of how the population should be treated would remain a German responsibility.

'Conclusion and proposal: there is no completely satisfactory solution. When the time comes, however, Army Group North must receive an order that can actually be carried out.'

The following proposals were submitted:

(*a*) Declare to the world that Leningrad is being defended as a fortress and that therefore the city and its inhabitants must be treated as military targets. Nevertheless, Roosevelt should be permitted, with an assurance of safe conduct, to supply the inhabitants or remove them to his part of the world after a capitulation of the city.[397] Such an offer could not, of course, be accepted and should be treated only as propaganda.

(*b*) 'We first isolate Leningrad hermetically and, as far as possible, pound it to dust with artillery and air attacks (only weak air units available for the time being).'

(*c*) Once the city had been worn down by terror and hunger, a few passages should be opened and defenceless people let out. 'As far as possible, deporta-

---

C.-in-C. of the army to Army Group North with instructions to 'narrow the present encirclement ring around Leningrad only where absolutely necessary for tactical reasons'.

[397] The deliberations concerning an American offer to take responsibility for the population were probably due, among other things, to an intelligence report of a campaign by the American Red Cross and other charity organizations in favour of the USSR. The aim was to organize an unprecedented aid campaign with nurses and doctors. A first group of 120 missionaries was already on its way to Vladivostok; the dispatch of a second group via Iraq and Iran was imminent. It would be accompanied by photographers entrusted with the task of taking 'rather a lot of pictures of the misery of refugees in Russia' in order to 'present Germany as a barbaric country in the USA': OKW/Amt. Ausl./Abw. to WPr., annexe 1, to 'Bremen', 21 Aug. 1941, BA-MA RW 4/v. 329, 6972/41, 28 Aug. 1941. Moreover, FM Mannerheim, who was also president of the Finnish Red Cross, requested help from the International Red Cross to feed prisoners of war. In spite of donations from the USA, Sweden, and Switzerland, almost a third of the approximately 64,000 prisoners died because of earlier exhaustion: Roschmann, *Gutachten*, suppl. 3 to annexe 2.

tion to interior of Russia. The rest will inevitably become scattered across the country.'

(d) 'Rest of "fortress troops" will be left to themselves through the winter. In spring we then force our way into the city (if the Finns do so first, we have no objections), remove all those still alive to the interior of Russia or take them prisoner, level Leningrad with demolition charges, and hand over the area north of the Neva to the Finns.'

These proposals, set out for internal use, were given binding form in an order of the chief of staff of the Wehrmacht High Command of 12 October 1941. After the experiences and 'extreme dangers' for the troops in Kiev—and even worse was to be expected in Leningrad and Moscow—no German soldier was to enter these cities. Small open gaps, which would make it possible for the population to escape into the interior of Russia, could 'therefore only be welcome'. Before their capture these cities were to be worn down and the inhabitants induced to flee by artillery fire and air attacks. Hitler expected that this measure would increase the chaos in Russia and facilitate the administration and exploitation of the occupied areas in the east. But all these ideas of wearing the cities down failed because of a shortage of siege artillery and suitable air units and because, in the case of Leningrad, the Finnish government did not want to extend its attacks on that front.

Even after this general decision by Hitler, deliberations continued within the army group itself about how the inhabitants of Leningrad should be treated after the city had been taken. Many were already fleeing the city. Several thousand were reported already on the way to Krasnogvardeysk and Pskov, and 100–20 Red Army men were reported to be deserting daily.

Army Group North thereupon asked the army high command whether, in the event of a surrender of Leningrad, enemy troops there should be treated as prisoners of war. If they were not, a battle to the bitter end had to be expected, with correspondingly heavy losses.[398] On 17 October the Army High Command replied that an offer to surrender by the troops in Leningrad was to be reported immediately, as 'only at that point will a decision be taken at the highest level regarding the further treatment of this question'. But that situation never arose.

The Army High Command and Army Group North differed widely in their judgements regarding the probability of a withdrawal by the Red Army. The army group saw no sign of an imminent evacuation of large areas, such as the Wehrmacht and Army High Commands, basing their views on reports from the Luftwaffe, expected.

The quiet on the Leningrad front was not interpreted as meaning that the enemy had accepted his fate, although movements in the port on Lake Ladoga might indicate that he wanted to save troops in Leningrad by evacuating them

---

[398] H.Gr. Nord/Ia, KTB, 14–17 Oct. 1941, BA-MA RH 19 III/168, and note mentioned above (p. 644).

to the interior of Russia. 'If this assumption is correct, it can also be assumed that the enemy considers the situation in Leningrad to be hopeless.' The narrow corridor held by Eighteenth Army at Shlisselburg ('the bottleneck') was a constant source of concern. Here the army group saw the possibility that the enemy might withdraw after a German attack on Tikhvin. If this did not happen, an attack would also have to be prepared in that direction. Leeb had to abandon any plans for a direct attack on Kronshtadt; a close encirclement of Leningrad was not possible with the forces at his disposal.

Thus a decisive effect was not to be expected from available artillery, as the airfields and supply facilities in Leningrad remained beyond its range. Neither did the army group, after the experience of London, expect decisive results from the use of the Luftwaffe. The possibility of starving the city into submission also seemed remote, as according to German calculations freighters and barges with a capacity of approximately 23,000 GRT were still available. Assuming personal rations of 400 grammes each, a thousand tons of food would yield 2.5 million rations. An attack was therefore necessary on the (eastern) Schlisselburg front across the lower Volkhov.

Eighteenth Army command, which would be most immediately affected by such developments, began to consider what to do if Leningrad offered to surrender and how German forces should behave towards starving civilians leaving the city. The general impression was that the troops would not be able to stand the nervous strain if required repeatedly to fire on women, children, the elderly, and others trying to escape from Leningrad.[399]

The commander of 58th Infantry Division—on the left wing of Eighteenth Army, outside the envisaged escape route for the population of Leningrad—emphasized that the troops did not fear the strained military situation, but they did fear a confrontation with the civilian population.

Our troops understand very well that we cannot feed the millions of people encircled in Leningrad without having to accept adverse effects on the food situation in our own country. For this reason the German soldier would use his weapons to prevent such break-outs. But that could easily lead to the German soldier losing his inner moral stability, i.e. he would not shrink from such violence even after the war. The command and the troops are trying hard to find another solution to this problem but have not yet found any acceptable way.

Leeb had little sympathy for the proposal of 27 October by the army high command to lay minefields in front of the German lines so as to spare the troops the task of firing on the civilian population. He saw no reason to maintain the encirclement after the surrender of the Red Army troops in Leningrad and Kronshtadt, and concluded that even then a large part of the population would die, 'but at least not before our eyes'. Deportation of parts of the population to the east should also be considered.

Subsequent developments relieved the Wehrmacht High Command as well

[399] H.Gr. Nord/Ia, KTB, 24 Oct. 1941.

as the front commands and the troops of such concerns. First of all, the enemy's relief attacks between the Volkhov and the Neva had to be halted and an encirclement front established for the winter. The army group planned an attack east of the Neva with the reinforcements brought from the Oranienbaum pocket after 12 October, from France (227th and 212th Infantry Divisions), the Spanish 250th Infantry Division, and paratroop regiments.[400]

After an oral report by the commander-in-chief of the army, on 3 October Hitler intervened with an operations proposal of his own: to make Tikhvin the objective of the attack with the mobile units of XXXIX Armoured Corps. He argued that an attack in this direction would keep casualties lower than an operation against the enemy's front across the narrow land-bridge from the west, block the front on both sides of the Volkhov, and enable the encirclement of enemy forces between the present front, the Volkhov sector, and Lake Ladoga.[401]

Leeb's reservations concerning this proposal stemmed mainly from the lack of adequate forces and from the postponement of the attack from 6 to 21 October. Hitler took this objection into account and on 5 October decided to cancel the attack with the mobile units and to use the units to be newly brought up on the existing defensive front of the armoured corps. The corps was to be pulled out of the front for rehabilitation and would, if necessary, advance via Tikhvin after all. The army group interpreted this use of the mobile units as being connected with the abandonment of the close encirclement of Leningrad, and requested permission to carry out the attack as planned, at least as far as Putilovo. On 6 October Hitler decided that the attack was to be carried out with the infantry already at the front and those troops which were yet to be brought up, which would require two weeks for regrouping.

After 2 October the attack by Army Group Centre at first relieved pressure on the northern sector of the eastern front. Hitler and the Army High Command considered it possible that the Red Army would withdraw substantial forces facing Army Group North, falling back to the western edge of the Valday plateau and from there to the Rzhev position in order to shorten the front. It would then be forced to abandon attempts to relieve Leningrad and would have to withdraw beyond the Volkhov. This could then require Army Group North either to advance via Tikhvin or, on the left flank of Ninth Army, to push forward via Borovichi and defeat the withdrawing enemy in the Valday area. For this purpose the pulling out of the mobile units and their rehabilita-

[400] To meet the 'uncovered requirements' of the three weakest divisions alone (11,673 men), Halder initially envisaged the dispatch of 8,500 replacements from convalescent companies, replacement transfer battalions, and Denmark: Halder, *Diaries*, 1254 (29 Sept. 1941).

[401] Army Group North to Sixteenth Army headquarters, 2 Oct. 1941, and reaction of the latter: Müller-Hillebrand, Nordabschnitt, pt. 1 (appendices H1, H2), MGFA P-114a; Halder, *Diaries*, 1268 (1 Oct. 1941): 'Out of this world!'; Leeb, *Tagebuchaufzeichnungen*, 367 (2, 3 Oct. 1941), 369–70 (5, 6 Oct. 1941).

tion and transfer to the area of Chudovo for rest and re-equipping was ordered on 5 October.[402] The attack from the present area of XXXIX Armoured Corps would then have only the function of tying down the withdrawing enemy. The army group issued an order to this effect on 8 October.[403] Both operational directions were to be assigned mobile units. On 13 October the Army High Command was certain that, on the whole, the enemy facing Army Group Centre had been defeated and was now bringing up forces south of Lake Ilmen. On the other hand, his intention to break the encirclement by halting on the Volkhov and Ladoga fronts was confirmed.[404]

Army Group North was ordered to advance with strong forces as soon as possible from the area around Chudovo via Tikhvin and west of that town to the lower Volkhov, in order to cut the way to the east for the enemy forces south of Lake Ladoga and, together with the German forces attacking across the Volkhov from the west, to encircle them. Moreover, contact was to be established with the Finnish Karelian Army via Lodeynoe Pole. The Finns were to be requested to cross the Svir and advance to meet the Germans. The army group set the start of the attack for 16 October.[405] On the first day of the attack 126th Infantry Division established bridgeheads across the Volkhov, from which the mobile units of XXXIX Armoured Corps began their advance. Rain, mud, ice, and snow made the terrain almost impassable. Not until 26 October were Malaya Vishera and Budogoshch reached. Meanwhile the isolated units of the Red Army started counter-attacks south of Lake Ladoga and near Shlisselburg.[406]

The assumption that the enemy was withdrawing quickly proved to be wrong. Fighting everywhere was hard, and only south of Lake Seliger was Sixteenth Army able to establish contact with Ninth Army. Leeb's request to the Army High Command to have Armoured Group 3 and the northern wing of Ninth Army placed under his authority so as to begin the annihilation of the

[402] OKH/GenStdH/Op.Abt. to Army Group North: Müller-Hillebrand, Nordabschnitt, pt. I, appendix H6, MGFA P-114a; Halder, *Diaries*, 1273 (5 Oct. 1941). Cf., however, the new directive OKH/GenStdH/Op.Abt. (IN) No. 41252/41, 8 Oct. 1941, BA-MA RH 2/v. 1327, pp. 23 ff.; Leeb, *Tagebuchaufzeichnungen*, 370 (8 Oct. 1941). The thrust towards Tikhvin was directed against the railway line between the White Sea and Moscow and was also intended to establish contact with the Finns on the Svir front. But Halder was primarily interested in the attack by Sixteenth Army from the area around Chudovo in a south-easterly direction to reduce pressure on the northern wing of the attack against Moscow.

[403] Army Group order and report to Army High Command: H.Gr. Nord/Ia, KTB, 9 Oct. 1941, BA-MA RH 19 III/168.

[404] OKH/GenStdH/Op.Abt. (I) No. 1584/41, directive for the continuation of operations of Army Groups Centre and North, BA-MA RH 2/v.1327, pp. 30 ff.

[405] Army Group Order No. 2 for the continuation of the operation, 14 Oct. 1941: Müller-Hillebrand, Nordabschnitt, pt. I, appendix H12, MGFA P-114a; Leeb, *Tagebuchaufzeichnungen*, 373 (11, 13 Oct. 1941), mentions Paulus's visit, during which the distribution of forces for both offensives was discussed. From 10 Oct. to 3 Nov. 1941 Paulus stood in for Halder, who had suffered a riding accident.

[406] Leeb, *Tagebuchaufzeichnungen*, 376 ff. (16–24 Oct. 1941); Müller-Hillebrand, Nordabschnitt, pt. I, 178 ff., MGFA P-114a; H.Gr. Nord/Ia, KTB, BA-MA RH 19 III/168.

enemy with a unified command was rejected, as the Army General Staff had not yet reached a decision about the further conduct of operations.[407] First the northern wing of Army Group Centre had to close up to Kalinin and Torzhok. II and X Army Corps of Army Group North were to pursue the enemy on towards Vyshniy Volochek and Valday.

The attack on Tikhvin became bogged down in mud on 25 October. Leeb flew to Hitler, who wanted to halt the attack. Leeb proposed that the decision about breaking off the attack be postponed, as it was still making some progress. If the weather forced a halt, a bridgehead across the Volkhov should be maintained and the mobile units gradually withdrawn.[408] Hitler left the decision to Leeb.

At the same time, Hitler refused Leeb's request to attack in the direction of Oranienbaum in order to release German forces tied down there. Hitler believed an attack against the strong coastal fortifications and the guns of the Soviet ships in Kronshtadt would be too costly. Eighteenth Army therefore had to go on the defensive.

On 28 October the commander-in-chief of Sixteenth Army still saw a chance of advancing to meet Ninth Army and thereby eliminating the enemy on his southern front. Leeb pointed out that Ninth Army might not even reach Vyshniy Volochek and dampened the hopes of the army in that direction. On the other hand, he permitted the attack on Tikhvin to continue without any limitations. On 29 October he considered the situation to be still quite promising: 'If we continue to make such good progress, the enemy will have to decide in the next few days whether he wants to stand and fight west of the Volkhov, even if that involves the danger of being cut off, or whether he considers it more advisable to withdraw beyond the Volkhov.'

Leeb believed that the enemy south-east of the Volkhov front was in the same situation. He considered the position of the enemy to be much more favourable to the German forces than did Hitler, and saw no reason to cancel the attack on Tikhvin. He expected more pressure on the enemy in the coming days in the area of Volkhovstroy, which might cause him to abandon his positions west of the river.

The directive of the Army High Command of 30 October for the continuation of operations against the enemy forces between the Volga and Lake Ladoga was intended to defeat the enemy around Moscow by cutting the rail link Yaroslavl–Rybinskoe, depriving him of the possibility of obtaining supplies. Costly direct attacks on the front were to be avoided. Army Group

---

[407] Situation assessment by Leeb and request to Army High Command, 17 Oct. 1941, and its rejection, 19 Oct. 1941, in Müller-Hillebrand, Nordabschnitt, pt. 1, appendices H13–H16, MGFA P-114a. The Army High Command wanted a more spacious thrust around Moscow; Army Group North, on the other hand, wanted to encircle the enemy forces facing its own sector of the front. Cf. sect. II.1.1(f) at n. 493.

[408] Leeb, Tagebuchaufzeichnungen; 381 ff. (26–8 Oct. 1941); Müller-Hillebrand, Nordabschnitt, pt. 1, appendix 19, MGFA P-114a; situation assessment by C.-in-C. of Army Group North, 29 Oct. 1941, ibid., appendix 20. Cf. however, KTB H.Gr. Nord, 25 Oct. 1941, BA-MA RH 19 III/168.

North was to attempt to take Tikhvin and establish contact with the Finns. If the attack on Volkhov did not succeed and Tikhvin could not be held, the bridgehead on the Volkhov was to be held.[409]

Tikhvin was captured on 8 November; the attack on both banks of the Volkhov advanced to within 15 kilometres of the town of that name. But the objective of this double pressure, to force the enemy to evacuate the area south of Lake Ladoga, was not achieved. Tikhvin was to become the starting-point for the final thrust against Volkhov. But that effort could succeed only if the right flank of Sixteenth Army was adequately covered. With the decision to forgo the attack by the northern wing of Army Group Centre against the enemy forces facing Sixteenth Army, as Leeb had proposed, the enemy gained freedom of action and was able at any time to create difficulties for the eastern and southern fronts of the army group.

Army Group North command attempted to acquire reserves and again concluded that the only possibility in this regard was the release of the German forces facing Oranienbaum and Kronstadt after the conquest of that area. On 10 November Leeb visited the commander-in-chief of Eighteenth Army to discuss the possibility of an attack. Colonel-General von Küchler declined to undertake such an operation, as the strength of the army was not sufficient for a concentrated attack, while isolated actions would involve heavy losses. The general commanding XXVI Army Corps and the divisional commanders declined to attack the strong fortifications with the forces at their disposal. Leeb stated that he nevertheless reserved the right to order an attack if the enemy transferred additional forces from Oranienbaum to the front south of Lake Ladoga and near Tikhvin.

On 12 October he reported to the Army High Command that he considered an attack on the area south of Kronstadt to be necessary[410] and referred to Hitler's order forbidding the execution of the already prepared operation in October. But now the situation had developed in such a way that the fortress had to be neutralized. Again he argued that the enemy was withdrawing forces to strengthen the defence of Leningrad and pointed out that it was impossible to build up the necessary reserves for the other front sectors. And again Hitler refused to permit the attack.

Not only did four divisions of Eighteenth Army remain tied down there, as they were still responsible for securing the area between Uritsk and Petergof on the bay of Kronstadt, but heavy artillery and a battalion of self-propelled

[409] Situation assessment by C.-in-C.s of Army Group North and Sixteenth Army, request to Army High Command for continuation of operation, KTB H.Gr. Nord, BA-MA RH 19 III/168, appendices H20–H22; directive, OKH/GenStdH/Op.Abt. No. 1610/41, 30 Oct. 1941, for continuation of operations against enemy forces between the Volga and Lake Ladoga, BA-MA RH 2/v. 1327, fos. 44 ff. This attack was entirely in line with Hitler's views, as it avoided a direct attack on Moscow. After reaching the Selizharovo–Kalinin–Volga reservoir road as a supply-line, Ninth Army was not to advance further northward. Cf. sect. II.1.1(*f*) at n. 500.

[410] Leeb, *Tagebuchaufzeichnungen*, 390 (12, 13 Nov. 1941), 393 (18 Nov. 1941); assessment of chances of success by Sixteenth Army, 19 Nov. 1941: Müller-Hillebrand, Nordabschnitt, pt. 1, appendix H35, MGFA P-114a.

assault-guns were withdrawn. Hitler's frequently evident fear of attacking strongly fortified places unless abundant siege artillery was available thwarted what in Leeb's eyes was the only chance of freeing forces to deal with future crises.

On 19 November Sixteenth Army command still saw a possibility of destroying the enemy forces west of the Volkhov so as to gain the five divisions fighting there as relief for the mobile units and as reinforcements for the northern sector of the front. After two divisions (61st and 215th Infantry Divisions) had been brought up, the defence of Tikhvin seemed secure, but for the defence of the lake area from Ostashkov to Lake Velye and for the securing of the southern shore of Lake Ladoga two additional divisions seemed indispensable. Leeb still hoped to hold Tikhvin.

On 20 November the enemy achieved his first penetration south of Tikhvin in the front sector held by 8th Armoured Division. After the developments of the previous days, Leeb concluded that a continuous front had to be formed. He demanded that he be given four or five divisions in the event that the mobile units of XXXIX Armoured Corps were withdrawn. Abandoning Tikhvin would reduce this requirement by one division.[411]

On 1 December, however, the army group saw that the only chance of establishing reserves was in halting the attacks, going on the defensive, evacuating Tikhvin, and taking up a position south-west of the town. Only the 'bottleneck' at Shlisselburg was to be widened by additional attacks.[412]

The sudden drop in temperature on 5 December 1941 to −35 °C made the situation considerably worse, especially as it immobilized German units near Tikhvin, which the enemy had surrounded. Hitler ordered the town to be held and the planned relief attack south of Lake Ladoga to be postponed until the arrival of additional forces—100 tanks as material replacements, and 24 depot and trained replacement battalions with 22,300 men—on 14 December.[413]

At Leeb's request, however, the Army High Command approved the withdrawal from Tikhvin on 7 December, and Hitler gave his consent the following day. The operation against the lower Volkhov had thus finally failed. Not even the order to at least keep the Leningrad–Moscow railway line under control by artillery fire could be carried out. The inevitable strengthening of Leningrad's defences following the evacuation of Tikhvin had to be accepted, as did the abandonment of the now unrealistie hope of linking up with the Finns. In

---

[411] Situation assessment by Leeb, 22 Nov. 1941, with report to Army High Command: Müller-Hillebrand, *Nordabschnitt*, pt. 1, appendices H37, H38, MGFA P-114a; Leeb, *Tagebuchaufzeichnungen*, 394 ff. (21–4 Nov. 1941).

[412] Army Group North to Sixteenth Army, 1 Dec. 1941 (Müller-Hillebrand, *Nordabschnitt*, pt. 1, appendix 43, MGFA P-114a), ordered Tikhvin to be evacuated in time if necessary, as the army group could not replace losses. The situation in the Schlisselburg area, on the other hand, was to be dealt with offensively, as the enemy could now escape across the frozen Lake Ladoga: Leeb, *Tagebuchaufzeichnungen*, 402 ff. (3–5 Dec. 1941).

[413] Leeb, *Tagebuchaufzeichnungen*, 405 nn. 602–8; Müller-Hillebrand, *Nordabschnitt*, pt. 1, appendices H43–H61, Hitler's order H48, MGFA P-114a; Halder's notes of a conference with Hitler, 6 Dec. 1941: Halder, *Diaries*, 1339.

other words, the complete isolation of Leningrad had become impossible. Leeb hoped to gain new forces for extending the encirclement near Shlisselburg by withdrawing the Tikhvin front to a 'swamp position', if necessary to the Volkhov. On this question a dispute arose between the Wehrmacht and the Army High Commands as well as the army group.[414]

The development of the situation forced a decision to withdraw Sixteenth Army to the 'swamp position' on 9 December and to bring up 8th and 12th Armoured Divisions and place them at the disposal of the army group.[415]

Hitler eventually approved this withdrawal, but only on condition that it was considered as a transition to a final position, and that XXXIX Armoured Corps held a line 30 kilometres in front of this position as long as possible. At the same time, XXVIII Army Corps was to attack south of Lake Ladoga to the line Shum–Lavrovo. On 14 December deep enemy penetrations of the swamp position forced the cancellation of this plan of attack as well as a withdrawal of forces to the Volkhov and the Kirishi–Malukssa railway line.

During his visit to Hitler's headquarters on 16 December, Leeb obtained approval for the withdrawals already begun[416] to the Volkhov, which were successfully completed by 27 December.

The front south of Lake Ilmen had stabilized with the conclusion of the attack operations of Sixteenth Army and remained quiet. Here six infantry divisions covered a sector 240 kilometres wide. Between Lake Ilmen and Shlisselburg thirteen infantry and two armoured divisions were completely exhausted and short of almost all equipment. Nine infantry divisions faced Leningrad on a front of 130 kilometres. Hitler authorized withdrawal to the Volkhov only on condition that the front was defended to the last man and the encirclement of Leningrad maintained.

Hitler's approval of the withdrawal to the Volkhov on 16 December 1941— in the absence of alternatives it can hardly be called a decision—was a move which applied along the entire front in view of the Soviet counter-offensive. In spite of its extended front, at this time Army Group North was nowhere in serious danger of being cut off from its rearward communications.

The evacuation of Tikhvin, however, represented more than the abandonment of the objective of the army group's last partial offensive—namely, the disruption of communications between the Russian interior and Leningrad via Lake Ladoga. An important step towards a link-up with the Finnish Svir front on the way to the 'edge of the tundra', as Halder once described the ultimate

---

[414] Leeb's telephone conversation with Halder, 7 Dec. 1941, and all subsequent important deliberations, as well as Hitler's decision, 9 Dec. 1941, and order to Army Group North, 15 Dec. 1941, in Müller-Hillebrand, Nordabschnitt, pt. 1, appendices H49–H60, MGFA P-114a.

[415] Leeb, *Tagebuchaufzeichnungen*, 411 (9, 10 Dec. 1941).

[416] Ibid. 418 ff. (16–18 Dec. 1941). Hitler made his decision conditional on his talk with Leeb and the views of the C.-in-C. of Sixteenth Army, Col.-Gen. Busch. Keitel, however, had already approved in advance the withdrawal of the armoured units behind the Volkhov: *KTB OKW* i. 1083 (109).

objective of the army group, also had to be retraced. The first objective of the second phase of operations, begun at the end of July—the encirclement of Leningrad—had not been achieved. This was not due solely to the withdrawal of major forces in favour of the offensive against Moscow; the Finnish army's refusal, not yet realized by the Germans, to advance beyond the old frontier was also a contributing factor.

Soviet defensive actions had been able to tie down major parts of Sixteenth Army at the boundary with Army Group Centre in such a way that Army Group North had been unable to transfer its forces for offensive thrusts against Leningrad and Tikhvin. The continuing commitment of divisions of Eighteenth Army to maintain the Oranienbaum pocket also relieved pressure on Leningrad. But the protection provided by the last bastion of the Soviet Baltic Fleet, the naval base and fortress of Kronshtadt in the approaches to Leningrad, was decisive in the Soviet ability to hold this beachhead. It prevented Army Group North and the German navy from achieving their main common objective, eliminating the enemy fleet and protecting the sea routes.

Until the freezing over of the Baltic, however, domination of the sea area was secure and thus the task was fulfilled.

(e) The Actions of German Naval Forces in the Baltic until the End of 1941
(See the Annexe Volume, No. 17)

The strategic and operational guidelines for the conduct of the naval war against the Soviet Union, submitted in the 'Situation Assessment for the Eastern Campaign against Russia (Case Barbarossa)' by the naval war staff on 30 January 1941, underwent no essential changes before the opening of hostilities.[417] According to these guidelines, the main tasks of the navy in the Baltic were protecting Germany's coasts and shipping, including troop transports; moving supplies for Army Group North; and preventing a break-out by Soviet naval forces into the open Baltic.

These tasks determined the extent of the measures to be taken and the distribution of forces. To carry out the defensive part of their task, German naval forces laid an extensive system of mine-barrages between Memel and the southern tip of the Swedish island of Öland ('Wartburg I–III'), beginning on 18 June 1941 with a total of 1,500 mines and 1,800 explosive buoys. This system was completed by a Swedish barrage, laid to meet German demands, in Swedish territorial waters. Subsequently, however, these mine-barrages, like the booms installed at German Baltic ports, caused only German losses.[418]

---

[417] Salewski, Seekriegsleitung, iii, No. 7, pp. 145 ff. Cf. ibid. i. 354 ff. The best overall view of the naval war in the Baltic is in Seemacht, 602–22.

[418] Explosive buoys are devices which destroy or damage enemy mine-sweeping equipment. Meister (Seekrieg, 11) calculates losses up to the end of 1941 as at least 10 merchant ships and 2 minesweepers. Moreover, 3 minelayers were lost in the Swedish barrage on 9 July 1941 because the naval war staff and subordinate command staffs had failed to inform them of the barrage, which had been laid on 28 June 1941.

They did not fulfil their intended function, as Soviet surface units never ventured into the protected areas.

In contrast, the two large mine-barrages at the western entrance to the Gulf of Finland between the northern end of the island Hiiumaa and Finnish Hanko, and between the Estonian Pakerort and Finnish Porkkala ('Apolda' and 'Corbetha'), with a total of 980 mines and 1,373 explosive buoys, had a clearly offensive character. A few hours before the start of hostilities, during the night of 21–2 June 1941, this mining operation was extended to within 3.5 nautical miles of the coast of Hiiumaa. The German units involved were probably sighted by Soviet forces and reconnaissance aircraft, but they were not hindered in their work. In the Gulf of Finland, Finnish submarines and minelayers supplemented the German barrages. Additional barrages were laid at the entrance to the Gulf of Riga (the Irben strait and the Muhu sound) to obstruct enemy shipping until the Soviet bases and ports in the area fell to Eighteenth Army. It was intended at the same time to push the Soviet Baltic Fleet back into the eastern end of the Gulf of Finland. However, to guard the numerous barrages and prevent possible enemy attempts to break through, only a few German and Finnish motor torpedo-boats were available. In view of the weak German naval forces and the narrow confines of the operations area, co-operation with the units under the 'Air Leader Baltic' and Air Fleet 1 was urgently necessary. From the navy's point of view, however, this co-operation remained unsatisfactory, mainly because of the priority given to direct air support for the units of Army Group North as well as the small number of aircraft available for sea patrols. The fact that the operations of Eighteenth Army were not aimed primarily at occupying the Estonian ports delayed the early use of shore-based artillery for the surveillance of the barrages and the control of sea passages, which the navy's plans assumed would be available.

In their operational planning, Soviet naval leaders had obviously assumed that they would face a considerably stronger concentration of German naval forces in this operations area. This miscalculation and the lack of combat-readiness of their own ships and formations caused them to adopt a defensive operational plan limited to a sealing off of the Gulfs of Finland and Riga and a coastal defence based on heavy concentrations of artillery. Only submarines were to undertake offensive sorties from the Baltic naval bases which were protected by mine-barrages. Immediately after the start of hostilities, ships of the Soviet Baltic Fleet began their defensive mining operations according to plan. This defensive plan and an evidently quite inadequate evaluation of reconnaissance carried out in their own coastal area led to Soviet naval forces suffering heavy losses from German and Finnish mine-barrages in the first days of the war. The German side believed that this had such a paralysing effect on the Soviet fleet command that, with the exception of the defensive measures mentioned, it refrained for the time being from initiating further actions. The expectations of the German naval war staff were thus fully confirmed.[419] The Germans considered the passiveness of Soviet surface forces and the ineffectual nature of the few submarine attacks to be a first important success of their own naval warfare. They were now able to concentrate on their second task.

After Eighteenth Army had captured Liepaja, supply shipments by sea, using coastal motor-ships and smaller vessels, were begun as of 3 July 1941. Although German ships bound for ports in western Finland used Swedish territorial waters as far as possible for safety, they were seldom in danger on the open sea. Only after 6 July did light Soviet surface forces and submarines become more active. Destroyers, patrol-boats, and aircraft constantly attacked German supply-ships headed for Dünamünde but did not achieve any decisive successes, although extensive mine-laying resulted in what had until then been the safest route having to be closed for several days. Moreover, a heavy coastal battery placed near Werder to protect shipping there could not be held, which made it necessary for the time being to continue protecting transports with the few available motor torpedo-boats and additional minefields. The Soviet countermeasures necessitated the most unwelcome transfer of two additional modern minesweeper and motor-minesweeper flotillas from the western theatre to the Baltic. At first only mine-free channels for shallow-draught vessels could be cleared close to the coast, which limited the transport capacity for supplying Army Group North. On the other hand, these routes in shallow coastal waters offered the best protection against enemy submarines.

The very limited operational capability of the light German and Finnish surface forces, a result of their small numbers and of obsolescence in some cases, did not permit them to interfere effectively from the sea with supply transports of the Soviet Baltic Fleet along the Estonian coast, to the Baltic islands and to the islands west of Leningrad. Only traffic to the base at Hanko, which was also bombarded by Finnish coastal artillery, was so thoroughly disrupted that the Soviet command was forced to resort to submarines for transport purposes.

Let us now turn to the conduct of offensive operations.

The naval war against the Soviet fleet in the Gulf of Finland was co-ordinated between the Finnish naval command and the German naval war staff or local commanders. But evidently no more than a tactical co-ordination of assessments of the enemy's situation was achieved. While, in spite of its confidence in German superiority, the naval war staff believed it had to take seriously the danger of operations by Soviet submarines and surface forces, and therefore even ordered the laying of mine-barrages near its own ports, the Finnish naval command clearly relied on the Soviet naval command's operational passivity. Accordingly, it expected mine warfare to be focused east of the line Porkkala–Tallinn; from this point of view the German mine-barrages

---

[419] M.Dv. No. 601, p. 14: H.Gr. Nord/Ia, KTB, BA-MA RH 19 III/171; Rohwer, 'Minenkrieg', 16 ff. Losses in Meister, *Seekrieg*, 359, and M.Dv. No. 601, p. 47 (annexe 4a), amplified with Soviet figures published after the war: Matveev and Selyanichev, 'Krasnoznamennyj Baltijskij Flot'; Achkasov and Pavlovich, *Soviet Naval Operations*. Cf. also Salisbury, *Leningrad*, 233 ff.

Apolda and Corbetha represented rather a restriction of German–Finnish naval movements.[420] Logically, the Finns laid their first barrage ('Valkijärvi') in that area only on 29 June, and this was then expanded when Eighteenth Army approached Tallinn.

After 6 August the capture of Kunda permitted a land-based observation and control of the barrage designed to put a stop to the transports of the Soviet navy along the Estonian coast and between Hanko and Kronshtadt. On 8 August, therefore, the minelayer group 'Cobra' began a series of mine-laying operations north of Cape Juminda and was soon joined by additional light surface vessels and Finnish submarines and minelayers. By 31 August the ships had laid a system of thirty-two different barrages with a total of 1,409 mines and 912 explosive buoys in a small area (approximately 24 by 32 nautical miles). This constituted a considerable obstacle to Soviet naval movements in the Gulf of Finland, but in the view of the German navy the air units and coastal artillery assigned to guard these barrages were still inadequate.[421] The 'Juminda' barrage was intended to play an important role when the Red Army had to abandon the Baltic coast with its bases, especially Tallinn, the large islands, and Hanko. For the transfer of the ships and units stationed there to Kronshtadt and Leningrad could be effected in the narrow waters only with heavy losses. When XXXXII Army Corps approached Tallinn on 19 August and the fighting for the city reached its climax on 25–6 August, the first large-scale evacuation by sea began.[422] With support from ships and coastal artillery, the Soviet Tenth Infantry Corps, which had been encircled in Tallinn, was able to disengage and embark on a total of about forty vessels of various sizes during the night of 27–8 August. To cover the operation, the Soviet naval command had assembled a large force: in addition to the cruiser *Kirov*, 18 destroyers, 6 torpedo-boats, 28 minesweepers, 83 patrol-boats, and 6 submarines. Although they were preceded by the minesweepers, the transport and cover formations suffered heavy losses when they broke through the Juminda barrage: 16 warships and 15 transports. Air attacks and artillery fire sank another ten transport vessels or damaged them so heavily that they had to be beached. Luftwaffe attacks had a devastating effect on the ships of the evacuation fleet, closely massed and confined to narrow channels.[423] No Soviet statistics are available on losses suffered in this operation.

[420] M.Dv. No. 601, p. 19; Meister, *Seekrieg*, 14. The commander of torpedo-boats in Helsinki was of the same opinion.

[421] Figures on the mine-barrage north of Cape Juminda: M.Dv. No. 601, map 2. By 26 Aug. 1 destroyer, 7 minesweepers, 14 steamships, and 2 barges had been sunk by the Juminda barrage: Meister, *Seekrieg*, 359 ff.

[422] For the Soviet perspective cf. Piterskij, *Sowjet-Flotte*, 193 ff., with corrective notes by Rohwer; specifically on Tallinn ibid. 201 and note pp. 519–20. Cf. also Ačkasov, 'Durchbruchs-Operation', 26–41, with corrective notes by Rohwer; Rohwer, 'Verluste', 44; Meister, *Seekrieg*, 15–16; more recently also Achkasov and Pavlovich, *Soviet Naval Operations*, 56 ff., although they avoid exact figures for the losses (cf. ibid. 63).

[423] The combat formation of the Luftwaffe (seven aircraft of II Gruppe Bomber Geschwader 77) was actually earmarked for an attack on the locks of the White Sea Canal but could not carry out that operation because of weather conditions. It was therefore available to attack naval targets near the Juminda barrage from 25 to 29 Aug. 1941.

With the capture of Tallinn and the forced withdrawal of most Soviet naval vessels to the bay of Kronshtadt, supporting a landing by army units on the Baltic islands involved considerably fewer risks for the German navy than in the first weeks of the campaign. From the beginning of planning for a landing, the participation of the navy was limited to merely providing assistance in an operation to be carried out by the army. Because of the islands' proximity to the coast and the lack of an adequate number of suitable vessels to carry out a landing independently, a larger role for the navy was neither necessary nor possible. The Erprobungsverband der Ostsee ('Trial Formation Baltic') provided barges and ferries. It also had several coastal motor-boats and ordnance-carriers.[424]

As a first step, the island of Vormsi was captured by the 'Group Cellarius' on 9 September. Before the start of the crossing, 'Operation Beowulf I', minesweepers had to clear a route to Muhu, the next objective. Then the first wave of 61st Infantry Division attacked in assault-craft on 14 September. To deceive the enemy, the navy, with the support of Finnish naval forces, undertook several feints which simulated landing preparations with a comparatively large number of torpedo-boats, fast patrol-boats, and covering vessels which intervened in the fighting with their fire.[425] In one of these actions the Finnish armoured vessel *Ilmarinen* struck a mine and sank.[426] Troops of 61st Infantry Division were able to capture the causeway between Muhu and Saaremaa on 14 September; moreover, the crossing by the 'Trial Formation Baltic' on ferries and other vessels now began. By 21 September all units of the division were on Saaremaa. At the request of XXXXII Army Corps, the navy also participated, with the bombardment by the cruisers *Emden* and *Leipzig* and operations by the boats of 2nd Torpedo Boat Flotilla, in suppressing the stubborn enemy resistance on the Svorbe peninsula (Operation Weststurm).

The second main step in the landing operations, the capture of the island of Hiiumaa, began with a feint intended to make the enemy believe that, as on Saaremaa, this landing would be carried out at the closest point between the two islands with assault-craft.[427] In fact, however, transport capacity now

---

[424] M.Dv. No. 601, pp. 22 ff. H.Gr. Nord/Ia, KTB, BA-MA RH 19 III/17; cf. also Melzer, *Baltische Inseln*, 46 ff.; Hubatsch, *61. Infanterie-Division*; *Seemacht*, 610.

[425] Detailed account of these feints in M.Dv. No. 601. The operations order from Naval Group North to commander of cruisers was issued on 9 Sept. 1941 at the same time as the order to use motor torpedo-boats near the Juminda barrage to prevent a break-out by the Soviet fleet. For this order and subsequent operations cf. BA-MA RM 7/521, fos. 14 ff. An important reason for the order to use motor torpedo-boats was a report from Air Fleet 1 on 8 Sept. of a concentration of twenty-five ships in five lines astern between Leningrad and Kronshtadt (ibid. 38). In the evening of 10 Sept. the port of Leningrad was reported to be almost empty and most of the warships and merchantmen transferred to Kronshtadt (ibid. 57).

[426] Ekman, 'Untergang der "Ilmarinen"'. Total German losses were 3 minesweepers and more than two-thirds of the personnel as a result of explosions in a shipyard in Helsinki, attributed to sabotage: BA-MA RM 7/521, fos. 28, 325.

[427] On 16 Sept. the Luftwaffe General Staff informed the navy that 24 Soviet vessels of 300–5,000 t., which had been standing by to remove Soviet personnel from Saaremaa and Hiiumaa, had been destroyed in Triigi Bay: BA-MA RM 7/522, fo. 57.

available was sufficient to land troops on the east and west coasts of the island. Only the last group crossed the sound in assault-craft. Again the navy supported the army units with a diversionary manœuvre, in which the light cruiser *Köln* with several torpedo-boats and minesweepers bombarded hostile batteries. With the exception of Odensholm, which was abandoned by its Soviet defenders without a fight only in December, the occupation of the Baltic islands was concluded on 21 October.

Even while Tallinn was being evacuated, German and Finnish minelayers began to close the gaps in the Juminda barrage again and to extend the barrage system. At the beginning of September additional mine-barrages were laid in the eastern part of the Gulf of Finland to reduce the freedom of movement of the Soviet Baltic Fleet to the area around Leningrad, but also to prevent a break-out by some of the fleet from that city, which was now coming under increasing pressure from Army Group North.[428] At the same time, the Luftwaffe transferred dive-bombers to that operations area. The naval war staff considered it 'highly improbable that Russian warships and merchant vessels will break out of Kronshtadt Bay' to Sweden and was of the opinion that only isolated light, fast units under determined and ruthless commanders might succeed in doing so. Although Raeder persuasively presented these views to him on 17 September, Hitler ordered all necessary measures to be taken to prevent an attempted break-out.[429]

It was presumably information provided by an intelligence report that was largely responsible for Hitler's order. On 15 September agents in Sofia had recorded an exchange of telegrams between the commander of the Baltic Fleet and the commander of the Soviet Black Sea Fleet.[430] In the telegram from the commander of the Baltic Fleet the situation as assessed by the fleet command was described as desperate. Even with British help, an attempt to break

---

[428] After receipt of the above-mentioned reports from Air Fleet 1 (seen. 425) and the preparations for the bombardment of Leningrad by German army artillery, as well as reports of minesweepers off Kronshtadt, a Soviet decision had been expected ever since 13 Sept. 1941 on whether the Soviet Baltic Fleet would remain at its bases or break out: BA-MA RM 7/521, fos. 258. On 13 Sept. Air Fleet 1 was ordered to support the attack on Leningrad: ibid., fo. 278; cf. Sect. II. 1.2(*c*) at n. 906 (Boog).

[429] *Führer Conferences*, 233; Salewski, *Seekriegsleitung*, i. 422–3; M.Dv. No. 601, pp. 12, 27 ff.: H.Gr. Nord/Ia, KTB, BA-MA RH 19/III/171; Rohwer, 'Minenkrieg, (2)', 97 ff.

[430] Intelligence report from OKW/Ausl. IIIc/O.v.D. No. 03874 to OKW/L, 24 Sept. 1941, No. 7148/41, BA-MA RW 4/v. 329. It may be safely assumed that this report did not remain unread for eleven days and that Hitler was therefore aware of it. On 16 Sept. 1941 Naval Group Command South transmitted a report from the Wehrmacht Commander South-east that the British command would do everything to save the Soviet Black Sea Fleet by having it interned in Turkish ports and placed under British: command: BA-MA RM 7/522, fo. 26. According to reports received at the same time from the German missions in Stockholm and Göteborg, the Norwegian ships being fitted out there were preparing to break out and be given a British escort: BA-MA RM 7/521, fo. 290, RM 7/522, fo. 135; cf. also *Sveriges förhållande till Danmark och Norge*, 74 ff. Already on 13 Sept. Naval Group North had ordered the transfer of 2nd Torpedo-Boat Flotilla, after completion of Operation West Wind, to BSO (Befehlshaber der Sicherung der Ostsee: Commander, Baltic Sea Security with orders to prevent such a break-out: ibid., RM 7/521, fos. 224, 345. Transports of 6th Mountain Div. from Oslo to Finland were suspended until 23 Sept. 1941.

through the Kattegat would not succeed. The Swedish government had therefore been requested through the British and Swedish ambassadors to permit the Soviet Baltic Fleet to enter a Swedish port. This request had not been granted, but a new attempt was to be made. On 20 September Hitler issued a new order to prevent a break-out by the Soviet Baltic Fleet. The commander in charge of cruisers requested more mines, and the naval war staff immediately created a formation of heavy surface forces available in the Baltic,[431] which, as the Baltenflotte ('Baltic Fleet'), was placed under the commander of battleships, who was flown in from Brest for that purpose. The northern group of this force—consisting of the battleship *Tirpitz*, the heavy cruiser *Admiral Scheer*, the light cruisers *Nürnberg* and *Köln*, and 3 destroyers, 5 torpedo-boats, and several fast patrol-boats—operated in the Åland Sea. The weaker southern group, consisting of the light cruisers *Leipzig* and *Emden* with several fast patrol-boats, was transferred to Liepaja. Moreover, all available Ju-88 aircraft in the Group Command North were placed under the command of Air Leader Baltic.[432]

However, this concentration of naval and air forces had no immediate operational significance, as on 21 and 23 September attacks by Dive Bomber Geschwader 2 on the battleships and other vessels anchored at Leningrad and Kronshtadt achieved considerable success, which completely eliminated the danger of a break-out. The presence of the heavy surface forces in the Baltic was therefore no longer necessary. On 23 September the naval war staff recalled the *Tirpitz* and the *Admiral Scheer* to their home ports and released the remaining units of the northern group a few days later. As mentioned above, the southern group participated in the feints and diversionary manœuvres connected with the occupation of the Baltic islands and provided fire support for the army units.

The concentration of heavy German units in the eastern Baltic was evidently misinterpreted by Soviet naval leaders. The Baltic Fleet command feared that the German units would force their way into the Gulf of Finland to support the attack on Leningrad. In view of this danger, Stalin intervened and ordered that no Soviet unit must be allowed to fall into enemy hands. Preparations were to be made to scuttle the units at Kronshtadt and Lenin-

---

[431] Transmission of Führer order by naval war staff to Naval Group North, 20 Sept. 1941, 3.30 p.m. According to this order, the risk of ship losses was to be accepted 'where absolutely unavoidable'. All combat-ready motor torpedo-boats of 1st–3rd flotillas were to be employed: BA-MA RM 7/522, fo. 249. On 22 Sept. the commander of cruisers requested the designation 'Naval Force East': ibid., fo. 356; on 23 Sept. the naval war staff decided on the designation 'Baltenflotte' (Baltic Fleet): ibid., fo. 428.

[432] Sixteen aircraft were involved: F.d.Luft 1, Cb No. 5448/41, evening report, 22 Sept. 1941, BA-MA RM 7/522, fo. 347. Simultaneously the 'Air Leader Baltic' was made responsible for carrying out reconnaissance for naval operations; he was to follow orders of the commander of cruisers and the commander of motor torpedo-boats. At the same time, however, Air Fleet 1 was forbidden to attack any naval forces west of the Juminda barrage, with the exception of submarines. Two coastal flying Gruppen and Reconnaissance Gruppe 125 were placed under Air Fleet 1: ObdL/Fü.Stab/Ia, No. 11883/41, 22 Sept. 1941, BA-MA RM 7/522, fo. 353.

grad if necessary.[433] To deter and damage enemy units, six submarines were to be stationed west of Leningrad and Kronshtadt and additional mines were to be laid.

The broad chronological description of the action in the Gulf of Finland and the geography of these waters could give the impression that the operations of German and Finnish naval forces (on the whole successful) as well as those of the Soviet Baltic Fleet, which involved high losses but not a decisive defeat, should be considered in isolation. This is certainly not the case; the operations of the German navy and German-allied naval forces outside the Baltic are presented elsewhere (Volume VI of the present work).

Here it should merely be noted that the great volume of shipping between Norway, Sweden, Denmark, and Finland, as well as from German ports to these countries, resulted in various convoy and escort tasks for the German navy. In September alone transports for Finland required 59 troop-ships for 20,000 men, 4,278 horses, 2,454 vehicles, and 56,935 t. of equipment. In the same month 16,834.4 t. of supplies were shipped to other Baltic ports from Königsberg and Danzig aboard small vessels; 5,609 t. of captured material were brought back to Germany.[434]

The clearest expression of the close connection between the tasks of the German navy and the progress of the attack by Army Group North on Leningrad was the order to the navy to prevent a break-out by the Soviet Baltic Fleet. At the same time, Hitler's decision to withdraw important forces from Army Group North for the attack on Moscow affected the threat to Leningrad from the north. To increase Finnish pressure on Leningrad, the Army High Command wanted to transfer two heavy artillery battalions (eighteen guns) to a port in the south of Finland. On 19 September Hitler ordered armed vessels to be transferred to Lake Ladoga as soon as possible, as an early link-up between German and Finnish units could not be expected because of the withdrawal of armoured and mobile units from the army group and because the only link still open between Leningrad and the Russian interior crossed this lake. The naval war staff was able to promise vessels for both projects only after the conclusion of Operation Beowulf.

In September 1941 all three Wehrmacht services were abruptly confronted with the fact that in personnel and material terms adequate resources were simply not available to keep fighting, let alone force a decision, on all sectors of the greatly expanded, fan-shaped land front and the increasingly porous air front, as well as against the undeniably effective Anglo-American alliance at sea.

In the Baltic a consequence of this disproportion was that the small units, especially the fast patrol-boats and minesweepers, which in any case had had to remain there longer than originally planned and were urgently needed to

---

[433] Tribuc, 'Die Räumung', 104; Rohwer ('Minenkrieg (2)', 100 n. 8) bases his account on that of Adm. Kuznetsov.

[434] BA-MA RM 7/771, fo. 102.

escort convoys to North Africa and in the Aegean, had to be prepared as of 12 September for transfer to the Mediterranean and the Channel coast.[435]

The forces still assigned to the area of the Gulf of Finland were already allocated. If necessary the mining operation in the Aegean was to be postponed until after the operation against Crete.[436] In view of the known strength of the Soviet Black Sea Fleet—1 battleship, 6 light cruisers, 6 destroyers, 4 torpedo-boats, 6 submarines, and 16 freighters in Sevastopol alone—and the possibility that it would attempt to escape to the Mediterranean, which the naval war staff had expected from the very beginning, this postponement was a difficult decision. On 17 September Hitler ordered the accelerated transfer of fast patrol-boats and minesweepers to the Mediterranean and, at the same time and accepting all risks involved, the use of all available forces in the Gulf of Finland.

Two other reports inevitably had a direct effect on the operational objectives of the army on the southern sector of the eastern front. On 25 September the chief of naval intelligence reported that on 9 September 1941 the British minister of war transport had informed the consul in Basra of preparations to send 168 locomotives and 3,000 wagons for the trans-Iranian railway. The Wehrmacht commander south-east reported that according to information in his possession, Afghanistan had approved the passage of four Polish divisions and Czech units as well as war material on the line Peshawar–Kabul–Termez, i.e. to the Soviet rail system.[437] The navy had only armed merchant raiders and U-boats with which to attempt to frustrate these plans. For the Army High Command, on the other hand, these reports meant that an Anglo-Soviet southern front could become a reality; in Hitler's eyes they confirmed his strategic plan to cut the supply-routes to the interior of Russia even if that meant advancing to the Arctic Ocean and the frontiers of India. In the last weeks before the start of winter the naval war in the Baltic presented the following picture.

The German–Finnish offensive mine war and the more intensive Luftwaffe attacks on the naval bases in Leningrad and Kronshtadt reduced the freedom of movement of the remaining Soviet naval forces to a point where they were unable either to intervene in the fighting around the Baltic islands or to protect shipments of supplies for the naval base at Hanko at the entrance to the Gulf of Finland. Because of the urgent need for troops on the Oranienbaum and Leningrad fronts, the loss of the positions on the Baltic coast across from Hanko, and the supply difficulties, the Soviet command on the Leningrad front decided to evacuate Hanko, especially as no important Finnish forces were tied down there. These forces, though now available, would not increase the threat on the static front north of Leningrad.

---

[435] Cf. the account in Vol. VI of the present work.
[436] In question was the relief of 5th Mountain Div. by an Italian division.
[437] For the Afghanistan report see BA-MA RM 7/772, fo. 24; for Iran, ibid. 410.

Moreover, it was clear that the base would have to be abandoned with the arrival of winter and the freezing over of the surrounding waters.[438] After long deliberations, the decision to evacuate Hanko was taken by the Soviets on 23 October. The island of Suursaari (Hogland) was to be used as a staging-post for supplying the light ships and as a base for the rescue service and the minesweeper units. On 27 October minesweepers removed the first unit, an infantry brigade of about 500 men, from Hanko and brought it to Oranienbaum, where the troops were immediately sent into action. On 3 November an evacuation convoy transported over 4,000 men with weapons and equipment to Kronstadt without serious difficulties. By contrast, the next two convoys, on 3 and 9 November, suffered serious losses in the German and Finnish mine-barrages but were still able to bring some 1,200 men to the Leningrad front. After these losses, the Soviet naval command decided not to use any more large convoys and instead to continue the operation with small vessels and formations. In this way an additional 9,000 men and part of their equipment were gradually removed from Hanko by 28 November. The remaining troops, about 12,000 men, were to be evacuated with all available units in a single operation. The warships and merchantmen ready for action were divided into a fast and a slow group. The danger from mines and the lack of minesweeper units ready for service meant that the Soviet naval leaders accepted a high risk.

While the slow group (1 transport and 11 smaller vessels) lost only one vessel, the fast group strayed into the German Corbetha barrage. The electrical-turbine ship *Iosif Stalin* (7,500 GRT), with between 7,000 and 8,000 men on board, struck four mines. The artillery ammunition in the cargo hold exploded, causing high losses (about 4,000 men). The accompanying minesweepers were able to take 1,830 men on board, but the stricken ship could no longer be steered and ran aground on the Estonian coast. About 2,000 men were taken prisoner.[439]

These movements, and the mine explosions, were observed by German and Finnish forces; individual Soviet ships that came within range of their artillery were fired upon. But storms and the shorter periods of daylight made monitoring such movements increasingly difficult. The uncertain situation was made more complicated by the fact that the storms had torn many mines from their moorings. Only when, after 24 November, strong anti-aircraft fire was repeatedly observed over Hanko, in the absence of air attacks, and large demolition explosions and fires were seen there, was the assumption confirmed that an evacuation was imminent. Because of the weather and the

---

[438] Tribuc, 'Die Räumung', 103–10, 158–84, with comments of *Marine-Rundschau*. The garrison was about 25,000.

[439] Comment of *Marine-Rundschau* on Tribuc, 'Die Räumung', 172; *Seemacht*, 610–11. Achkasov and Pavlovich (*Soviet Naval Operations*, 70) give total losses of the army units in the evacuation of Hanko as 4,987 men, but this figure does not include the heavy losses among the personnel of the warships and merchantmen involved.

inadequate German and Finnish forces in the area, however, it could not be prevented.[440]

Around the end of November 1941, the formation of ice in the Gulf of Finland increasingly paralysed shipping movements. When it became evident that the conquest of Leningrad and thus the definitive elimination of the Soviet Baltic Fleet could not be expected before spring, the German and Finnish navies were forced to prepare for a continuation of the war in the Baltic in 1942. To obtain a favourable starting-position for 1942, Finnish commandos occupied the island of Suursaari on 14 December; at the beginning of January 1942 German troops occupied the island of Tyttärsaari. Neither island could be held; both had to be temporarily abandoned.

(f) The Attack on Moscow
(See the Annexe Volume, No. 18)

Hitler's study of 22 August, in which he defended his rejection of the continuation of operations with the main effort aimed at reaching Moscow, represented the climax and, it seemed, the conclusion of disputes about a 'final battle' to decide the entire campaign in the east.[441] Hitler ruled that the Soviet armies west of Moscow should first be thoroughly defeated one by one before the actual attack on the Soviet capital was launched. This mainly tactical plan, which Hitler had advocated in an earlier phase of the campaign, was incompatible with Halder's ideas of large-scale encirclement, as it would leave the initiative to the enemy.[442]

In addition to an explanation of the ideas contained in his study and the blunt form of his rejection of the campaign plans the army had submitted, Hitler's talk with Brauchitsch on 30 August must have contained a few positive aspects for the Army High Command, for, apart from the limitations placed on the attack by Guderian's armoured group towards the south, the commander-in-chief of the army was generally satisfied.[443] Halder was therefore able to discuss the new offensive with some confidence at Army Group Centre headquarters on 2 September, before receiving a new directive from Hitler.[444]

The operations plan of the Army General Staff of 18 August 1941 envisaged the formation of a southern (Bryansk–Roslavl and Kaluga–Medyn) and a northern wing with two attacks, from the area east of Beloe and from the area

---

[440] After the detachment of the commander of cruisers and the leader of torpedo-boats, operational command was transferred to the naval liaison staff in Helsinki on 22 Oct. 1941: BA-MA RM 7/771, fo. 120.

[441] *KTB OKW* i. 1063 ff. (100). Hitler's remarks to the C.-in-C. of the army and Keitel's interpretation *vis-à-vis* Bock on 25 July 1941 were typical: ibid. 1034 ff. (80, 81); cf. sect. II.1.1(b) at n. 206.

[442] Halder, *Diaries*, 1209 (30 Aug. 1941).

[443] Ibid., but with serious doubts about Hitler's intention really to concentrate all forces against Moscow. This was probably in part the reason for Halder's sharp criticism of the directions of Guderian's (ibid. 1210: 31 Aug. 1941) and Leeb's (ibid. 1214: 1 Sept. 1941) attacks and their conduct of operations. Bock received the news from Kesselring on 31 Aug.

[444] Halder, *Diaries*, 1214 (2 Sept. 1941); Bock, Tagebuch 81–2 (2 Sept. 1941), BA-MA N 22/9.

around Toropets.[445] The northern wing was to advance towards Rzhev and from there generally eastward. The centre of the front was to remain essentially on the defensive and was therefore to consist of only ten infantry divisions. The decision was to be achieved by the strong wings of the attack. Whether, after achieving a breakthrough, the mobile units were to continue their advance eastward and encircle Moscow from the north and south, or turn inward earlier to destroy strong concentrations of enemy troops, would depend on how well the attack developed.

This proposal was based on Halder's basic strategic conviction that a decision to the campaign should be sought only at Moscow by destroying the massed forces of the Red Army there. Basing his plans on the approaching decision on the wings of the operations area as a whole, Hitler in a directive of 6 September ordered the preparation of an operation to seek a decision against the Army Group Timoshenko,[446] which had been committed to attacks along the centre of the German front. The enemy forces facing Army Group South and the southern flank of Army Group Centre still had to be defeated, but as soon as that task had been completed parts of Second and Sixth Armies and of Armoured Group 2, no longer needed in those areas, were to be regrouped for the new operation.

Hitler initially limited the activity of Army Group Centre to the encirclement of 'Army Group Timoshenko' in the 'general direction of Vyazma' with strong, concentrated armoured forces on the wings. On the southern wing these were limited to the 'available forces' of Army Group Centre and 5th and 2nd Armoured Divisions, which had been released for that purpose. The northern wing was to consist of Ninth Army, including units to be transferred from Army Group North. Not until the second phase, after the bulk of 'Army Group Timoshenko' had been destroyed 'in these highly co-ordinated, closely encircling operations of annihilation', was Army Group Centre to start its attack and pursuit in the direction of Moscow. This movement would be limited on the right by the Oka and on the left by the upper Volga; in the south it was to be covered by mobile units available from the area of Army Group South and in the north by an advance along both sides of Lake Ilmen.

On the basis of this directive the Army High Command issued a 'Directive for the continuation of operations' on 10 September 1941.[447] A comparison of the texts of the two directives shows the same pattern as is found in the interpretation of Hitler's other directives. Although the same formulations were used in both, the changes in the assigned tasks made in the directive of the Army High Command went far beyond the decisions normally left to the chief of the general staff, giving Halder, in complete agreement with the views

[445] C.-in-C. of the army, proposal for the continuation of operations of Army Group Centre in connection with operations of Army Groups South and North, *KTB OKW* i. 1055 ff. (95).

[446] *Hitler's War Directives*, No. 35, pp. 96 ff.; draft OKH/GenStdH/Op.Abt. (I): BA-MA RH 2/v. 1326, fos. 218 ff.

[447] OKH/GenStdH/Op.Abt. (I) No. 1494/41, BA-MA RH 2/v. 1326, fos. 209–17.

of the commander of Army Group Centre, abundant latitude.[448] He reduced the priority assigned to defeating and 'annihilating' the 'Army Group Timoshenko': 'Only after the encirclement has been consolidated and the annihilation of the enemy forces surrounded east of Smolensk between the Roslavl–Moscow road and Beloy is assured' was the pursuit in the direction of Moscow to begin. Expanding the scope of Hitler's directive, Halder envisaged the use of mobile units and infantry divisions for a frontal attack on Moscow, which Hitler wanted to avoid at all costs. The 'forces which then become available', which Hitler had not described more precisely, were defined by Halder as Second Army and Armoured Group 2, which were to attack from the area around Romny to the north-east—with the right wing probably capturing Orel—and turn the flank of the enemy forces facing the newly formed Second Army from the south. Halder thus not only removed the bulk of Second Army from the encirclement operation east of Kiev; it was clear that he intended to form a third assault group against Moscow, independent of the encirclement operation against Vyazma. It was therefore obviously in Halder's interest to release the 'forces which then become available' as soon as possible from the operation against Kiev and to make them as strong as possible. For this new grouping of forces Halder did not consider Sixth Army, but he planned to use Armoured Group 1, at first with its main effort clearly directed against the line between Romny and the mouth of the Sula, i.e. in conjunction with Armoured Group 2, while the bulk of Seventeenth Army was to advance in the direction of Poltava and Kharkov to cover the eastern flank of this movement. While according to Hitler's directive the flank of this thrust against Moscow in the second phase was to be protected by mobile units to be made available 'from the area of Army Group South' (most probably Armoured Group 1) advancing in echelon, Halder gave this task to Second Army and Armoured Group 2. He also reduced the armoured support Hitler desired for the advance south of the lower Dnieper against Melitopol as follows: 'The task of Eleventh Army to conquer the Crimea remains unchanged. As far as the situation permits, the attack of individual—if necessary Hungarian and Romanian—mobile units is to create the basis for an early advance by assorted forces towards the north coast of the Sea of Azov.'

The advance planning for the future points of main effort of the German army in the east can be seen clearly in the distribution of forces ordered in annexe 1 to the directive of 10 September. Special importance was attached to

---

[448] There was thus no conflict between the army high command and FM von Bock, whose proposals were included in the directive of the C.-in-C. of the army. Subsequent discussions with Halder (e.g. on 17 Sept.) were based on a common position and marked by the clash between Bock's eagerness to capture Moscow and Halder's difficulty over being too obvious in bringing Hitler round to his own way of thinking. Cf. Bock, Tagebuch (17 Sept. 1941), BA-MA N 22/9, and the agreement about wheeling round near Vyazma (ibid.: 14 Sept. 1941). The plan for giving Armd. Group 2 considerable freedom on the right wing would scarcely have come from Bock, but had been Halder's plan since the first order of battle for the encirclement of Kiev. Cf. Reinhardt, *Moskau*, 50.

the mobile troops: in addition to a corps command and 4 infantry divisions, a further corps command of an armoured corps, 2 armoured divisions, and 2 motorized infantry divisions from Army Group South were to be transferred to Armoured Group 2. Army Group North was to hand over Armoured Group 4 command, 3 corps commands, 5 armoured divisions, and 2 motorized divisions. The 2 armoured divisions *en route* from Germany were also to be assigned to this main point of the attack. (Cf. Diagram II.I.7.)

The commander-in-chief of Army Group Centre considered the encirclement movements contained in both directives, with the envisaged link-up in the Vyazma area, to be too limited and to involve the danger again of tying down mobile troops in operations against pockets. He therefore contacted Halder and reminded him of the agreement of 2 September.[449] Halder very clearly indicated to him that the description of the objective as 'Vyazma' (by Hitler) was not to be taken too seriously and that it would not interfere with the advance on Moscow which both men had planned.

Before describing the further development of preparations for the operation, we shall briefly analyse the personnel and material situation. The creation of the points of main effort for the armour placed an enormous burden on the entire transport system of the German forces in the east, as, in addition to bringing up forces from Germany itself, the transfer back of the distant units of Armoured Groups 1 and 2 and, on the northern wing of the offensive front, the transfer of forces from Army Group North had to be executed. In addition to the poor transport network for movements of forces parallel to the front, the fact that many of the units envisaged for the attack on Moscow were tied down longer than had been expected by the encirclement operations east of Kiev and in the continuation of the attack on Leningrad caused delays, and in the case of 8th Armoured Division (Army Group North) even the cancellation of its planned transfer to Army Group Centre.

At the start of planning for this operation, Halder had himself informed on the combat-readiness of the armoured divisions, which had inevitably declined as a result of continuous action and the lack of rehabilitation. On 4 September 1941 30 per cent of the tanks were completely out of action; 23 per cent were being overhauled. In half of the divisions envisaged for the operation approximately 34 per cent of the tanks were, on average, ready for action. The 125 tanks provided as replacements did not change this figure significantly. Problems in overhauling the tanks, which at this time was still done in Germany, and the continued heavy demands placed on them, gave reason to expect that they would become even more prone to breakdowns in future. Halder attempted to improve the situation and requested the release of a total of 181 tanks, which, together with the 125 already in Orsha and Daugavpils, would raise the combat-readiness, especially of the weakened armoured divisions, by

---

[449] Halder, *Diaries*, 1234 (13 Sept. 1941); Bock, Tagebuch (14 Sept. 1941), BA-MA N 22/9; cf. sect. II.I.I(*f*) at n. 441.

DIAGRAM II.1.7. Order of Battle of Army Group Centre, 2 October 1941

Army Gp. Centre Inf. Reg. 'GD' 19th Armd. Div. Mot. Brig. 900	Ninth Army 161st Inf. Div.	Armd. Gp. 3	XXIII A.Co.	251st Inf. Div. 102nd Inf. Div. 256th Inf. Div. 206th Inf. Div.
			VI A.Co.	110th Inf. Div. 26th Inf. Div.
			XXXXI Mot. A.Co.	36th Mot. Div. 1st Armd. Div. 6th Inf. Div.
			LVI Mot. A.Co.	14th Mot. Div. 6th Armd. Div. 7th Armd. Div. 129th Inf. Div.
			V A.Co.	35th Inf. Div. 5th Inf. Div. 106th Inf. Div.
			VIII A.Co.	28th Inf. Div. 8th Inf. Div. 87th Inf. Div.
			XXVII A.Co.	255th Inf. Div. 162nd Inf. Div. 86th Inf. Div
			IX A.Co.	137th Inf. Div. 263rd Inf. Div. 183rd Inf. Div. 292nd Inf. Div.
			XX A.Co.	268th Inf. Div. 15th Inf. Div. 78th Inf. Div.
			VII A.Co.	267th Inf. Div. 7th Inf. Div. 23rd Inf. Div. 197th Inf. Div.
Cmdr. Rear Army Area Centre 707th Inf. Div. 339th Inf. Div. SS Cav. Brig. 221st Sec. Div. 286th Sec. Div. 403rd Sec. Div. 454th Sec. Div.(in transfer)	Fourth Army	Armd. Gp. 4	LVII Mot. A.Co.	20th Armd. Div. 3rd Mot. Div. SS 'Reich'
			XXXXVI Mot. A.Co.	5th Armd. Div. 11th Armd. Div. 252nd Inf. Div.
			XXXX Mot. A.Co.	2nd Armd. Div. 10th Armd. Div. 258th Inf. Div.
			XII A.Co.	98th Inf. Div. 34th Inf. Div.

DIAGRAM II.1.7 *(cont.)*

		XIII A.Co.	17th Inf. Div. 260th Inf. Div.
	Second Army 112th Inf. Div.	XXXXIII A.Co.	52nd Inf. Div. 131st Inf. Div.
		LIII A.Co.	56th Inf. Div. 31st Inf. Div. 167th Inf. Div.
		XXXXVII Mot. A.Co.	29th Mot. Div. 17th Armd. Div. 18th Armd. Div.
		XXIV Mot. A.Co.	4th Armd. Div. 3rd Armd. Div. 10th Mot. Div.
	Armd. Gp. 2	XXXXVIII Mot. A.Co.	9th Armd. Div. 25th Mot. Div. 16th Mot. Div.
		Higher Cmd. XXXV	95th Inf. Div. 296th Inf. Div. 262nd Inf. Div. 293rd Inf. Div. 1st Cav. Div.
		Higher Cmd. XXXIV	45th Inf. Div. 134th Inf. Div.

10 per cent.[450] In view of the continuing operations and the related heavy losses of equipment, these figures, at a time when the 'decisive' battle of the campaign was being planned, were surprisingly low.

The shortfall of motor-vehicles was estimated at 22 per cent at the beginning of the offensive. Most of those still in use were old vehicles which had undergone makeshift repairs and which would probably suffer a high breakdown rate in future. All calculations by the technical services indicated that, apart from difficulties caused by road conditions, weather, and fighting, a significant reduction of the army's mobility at the decisive moment of pursuit was inevitable. The situation could be improved only if Hitler immediately released vehicles just off the production line for service at the front. Major-General Adolf von Schell, plenipotentiary for motor-vehicles, calculated that enough vehicles would then remain to equip an armoured division for the tropics. Problems resulting from the desired release would be less serious than

---

[450] OKH/GenStdH/Org.Abt (I) No. 702/41, 15 Sept. 1941, re armour supply east before the beginning of operations of Army Group Centre, BA-MA RH 2/v. 1326, fos. 233 ff. Of the 181 tanks only 30 were Mark IVs; the rest were Mark IIIs (95) and Czech P-38s (56). These tanks were stationed in Magdeburg and Vienna and were thus not taken from new production for newly raised units.

those which would be created if the army were largely immobilized 'on a broad front deep in Russia at the start of winter'.[451] But the necessary decision was not taken. The situation with regard to fuel was similar. Reserves at the supply-base were largely exhausted. Even in the sector of Army Group North, which was in a favourable position because of good rail connections and its ability to receive supplies across the Baltic, fuel stocks had dropped to 2.5 units of consumption. Except in Army Group North, and to a limited extent in Army Group Centre, it was not possible to build up stocks, primarily because of the inadequate rail network. For all transfers of units, replenishment of supplies, and reserves for at least four days as a 'buffer', 27 tank-wagon trains were needed in September 1941. As the Wehrmacht High Command was able to promise 22 trains daily by 16 September and 27 by 30 September, fuel supplies for preparing the operation could be guaranteed only to a limited extent. For operations in October requirements were estimated at 29 trains daily, but only 20 could be promised. For November only 3 trains a day were promised, as it was expected that operations would come to a halt and that rail capacity could be used to build up stocks of supplies for the winter and for transports of new equipment.[452]

In the meantime, Army Group Centre began to assemble the operational staffs, formations, and army troops for Operation Taifun ('Typhoon'), the code-name ordered on 19 September for the attack on Moscow.[453] In addition, starting-positions for the attack of the northern wing of Army Group Centre in co-operation with Army Group North were to be improved, as Halder had already ordered on 30 August.[454] The two armoured divisions of Army Group Centre in the area of Toropets and LVI Army Corps were to be used to annihilate the enemy between Lake Volgo and Valday. The plan of Army Group Centre to advance its northern wing to the upper Dvina was approved.

On 17 September the commander-in-chief of Army Group Centre submitted the operation plans to Halder.[455] Bock's main concern was that the units and formations still assigned to the other army groups should be transferred

[451] OKH/GenStdH/GenQu, Abt. Heeresversorgung No. I/01017/41, 11 Sept. 1941, note for an oral report on the situation with regard to fuel and vehicles for new operations, ibid., fos. 226 ff. Cf. the heavy losses of Armd. Group 2 in Halder (*Diaries*, 1235: 14 Sept. 1941), according to whom the combat-readiness of the divisions of the group varied between 20% and 31%.

[452] These figures were only for the requirements of the army. A further decline in the number of trains had catastrophic consequences for the soldiers fighting in the harsh winter.

[453] On the code-names cf. *Hitler's War Directives*, 96. For the amendment of the directive regarding the attack by Armd. Group 1 from Dnepropetrovsk, 7 Sept., see ibid. 97. For an overview of forces available to Army Group Centre for an operation in the east, as annexe to directive for the continuation of the operation from army high command, see OKH/GenStdH/Op.Abt., 10 Sept. 1941 (cf. n. 447 above), BA-MA RH 2/v. 1326, fos. 203 ff.; this also lists the changes in troop distribution carried out in the weeks following.

[454] Teletype message to Army Groups Centre and North, OKH/GenStdH/Op.Abt. (I) No. 31754/41, 30 Aug. 1941, BA-MA RH 2/v. 1326, fo. 205.

[455] Halder, *Diaries*, 1241 (17 Sept. 1941). Bock complained about the slow transfer of the units from Army Group North. Cf. sect II.1.1(*d*) above and Halder, *Diaries*, 1250 (22 Sept. 1941); Reinhardt, *Moskau*, 53 nn. 20, 23–4.

back to his group in good time. Here he could count on help from Halder, who used tactical assignments to avoid a clear order-of-battle commitment of the staffs and troops earmarked for the attack on Moscow, and who strove to transfer them as soon as possible with little regard to the wishes of the local commanders.[456]

The last important conference took place at the headquarters of Army Group Centre in Smolensk on 24 September. Present in addition to the commander-in-chief of the army and Halder were the commanders-in-chief of Army Group Centre and Air Fleet 2, as well as the commanders-in-chief of the armies and armoured groups.[457] The most important outcome of the conference, which departed from previous planning, was the decision that Guderian's armoured group should begin its attack two days earlier than the rest of the army group, in order to reach the surfaced road between Orel and Bryansk as soon as possible. In the meantime the supply situation had been improved to the point where an operation of the planned short duration could be carried out using stocks in the supply-bases and dumps of Supply District Centre and with current deliveries. The army group, which now had approximately 78 large formations and 1.9 million men, did not, however, possess the fighting power these figures suggested. Most of the units, e.g. almost all of the mobile divisions, had been transferred directly from operations in other areas without significant replenishment. Because of heavy losses and often inadequate replacements, in terms of their fighting ability they were no longer the units they had been on 22 June. An essential element in the decision to undertake a hazardous late-autumn offensive was the crisis-tested stamina of the German soldier and the still unshaken belief that the German forces, given adequate equipment and arms, were superior to the Red Army.[458]

On 26 September 1941 Army Group Centre summarized its plans in an order assigning its armies their specific objectives.[459] Fourth Army, with the attached Armoured Group 4, was to concentrate the main effort of its attack

---

[456] The attack groups, on the verge of success, had not yet produced sufficiently concrete results to create the 'basis for launching a decisive operation against the Red Army Group Timoshenko', as had been assumed in the directive of the C.-in-C. of the army of 10 Sept. (see n. 447 above). Nevertheless, on 30 Aug. the units of Second Army were ordered to be made available for Army Group Centre; on 9 Sept. they and Armoured Group 2 were ordered to remain under Army Group Centre: BA-MA RH 2/v. 1326, fos. 207–8. Cf. also Brauchitsch's urgent letter to Reichenau of 29 Sept. 1941, BA-MA RH 20-6/133.

[457] Reports: Halder, *Diaries*, 1254 (24 Sept. 1941); Guderian, *Panzer Leader*, 105–6; Bock, *Tagebuch* (24 Sept. 1941), BA-MA N 22/9.

[458] 2nd and 5th Armd. Divis. were still relatively fresh. On the material and personnel preparations cf. Reinhardt, *Moskau*, 52 ff.; for the order of battle see ibid., annexe 9 (p. 318), and Diagram II.1.7: seven large formations were used to provide security in rear areas alone, which clearly shows the importance of the supply, transport, and administrative systems, but also the scale of partisan warfare behind the front. Halder was aware before June 1941 that trained replacements would be 'used up' by October (cf. sect. I.IV.1(*b*) at n. 221). In addition to replacement units, units in the west, security divisions, and SS brigades were already being drawn upon. More troops from allied countries were also brought up; increasing use was also made of the native population. At the front the Spanish (Blue) Division and other European volunteer units were also sent into battle.

[459] Reinhardt, *Moskau*, 298–9 (annexe 1).

north and south of the road from Roslavl to Moscow. After achieving a breakthrough, the army, with covering forces protecting its eastern flank, was to wheel with strong forces towards the Moscow–Smolensk highway on both sides of Vyazma. The northern arm of the pincer movement, Ninth Army with the attached Armoured Group 3, was to break through enemy positions between the highway and the area of Belyy and push on to the Vyazma–Rzhev railway line. The main thrust was aimed at Kholm, with the mobile units turning east of the upper Dnieper against the highway west of Vyazma. The inner wings of the two armies were to feign systematic attacks and tie down the enemy by isolated thrusts with limited objectives. Apart from the pincer movement, Second Army was to cover the southern flank of Fourth Army and advance in the direction of Sukhinichi and Meshchovsk. If, in addition to the provision of cover for Fourth Army, the opportunity should present itself, the urban and industrial area of Bryansk–Ordzhonikidzegrad—especially the railway yards—was to be taken by a surprise attack. Finally, Armoured Group 2 was to push forward beyond the line between Orel and Bryansk two days before the start of the general attack. Its right wing was to be based on the Svopa and Oka sector, while the left wing was to turn the flank of the Desna position from the south so as to eliminate the enemy forces in the Desna bend in co-operation with Second Army. Ahead of the right flank, Army Group South was to push its northern wing (Sixth Army) forward north of Kharkov; ahead of the left flank Army Group North was to secure the line between Lake Zhdane and Lake Ilmen with Sixteenth Army.

At the start of the offensive Hitler addressed an appeal to the soldiers of the eastern front, in which he proclaimed the concluding phase of the war in the east: enormous stocks of food, fuel, and ammunition were ready for this offensive. During the past three and a half months of the campaign the Wehrmacht had created the conditions to destroy the enemy with a last, mighty blow before the beginning of winter. Hitler announced the start of the last great decisive battle of the year, which would crush the Soviet enemy and thus also Britain, the instigator of the war.[460]

(i) THE DOUBLE BATTLE OF BRYANSK AND VYAZMA
(See the Annexe Volume, No. 19)

On 30 September Armoured Group 2 began its attack between the Seym and the Desna in the direction of Orel and Bryansk with XXIV and XXXXVII Armoured Corps.[461] Its right wing was to break through to Orel, while the left wing, in co-operation with Second Army, was to complete the encirclement of Bryansk. By 2 October, the day for the start of the general attack, the two

---

[460] Domarus, *Hitler*, ii. 1756 ff., read in the night of 1–2 Oct., published in *Völkischer Beobachter*, 10 Oct. 1941.

[461] Guderian, *Panzer Leader*, 109 ff. On Hitler's and Halder's misgivings over the slow progress of Army Group South, Guderian's attack, and the entire army group cf. Halder, *Diaries*, 1261 ff. (28 Sept.–2 Oct. 1941).

armoured corps had reached the line of Sevsk–Dmitrovsk–Golubovka as planned.[462] The German commanders had the impression that the long-prepared attack had surprised the enemy, as in some places he yielded ground without significant organized resistance, and local counter-attacks were reported only in the afternoon. This did not agree with information gathered from observation over the previous days. Increased enemy aerial reconnaissance had undoubtedly detected the German deployment. Soviet bombing raids on lines of communication in rear areas, and troop movements in the area west of Moscow, indicated preparations for defence. Besides, the movements of Armoured Group 2 must have revealed the German intentions to the enemy, for counter-attacks on the Bryansk front were significantly more intense than earlier local reconnaissance thrusts. In fact, communication difficulties seem to have prevented the Soviet command from realizing the objectives of the German attack in time and issuing appropriate instructions to its units at the front.[463] Mistakes obviously due to an erroneous evaluation of intelligence about the German deployment enabled Guderian to achieve a rapid breakthrough. In spite of the surprise, however, it soon became clear that the enemy was mobilizing reserves. There could be no doubt that he was prepared to fight this last battle west of Moscow with all the means at his disposal.

Between 2 and 7 October Armoured Groups 3 and 4 were able to encircle strong Soviet forces near Vyazma.[464] However, owing to the mobile units of Armoured Group 3 being halted by supply problems, the enemy again succeeded, with heavy losses on both sides, in extricating some of his troops from the pincer movement.[465] Nevertheless, after the experience of previous encirclements, the eastern part of the pocket was now better secured. After reaching Orel on 3 October, Second Armoured Army captured Bryansk four days later and thus encircled large parts of the Soviet Third Army. Between the two pockets, the inner wings of Ninth and Fourth Armies advanced on Moscow via Sukhinichi and Yukhnov.

On 7 October Army Group Centre concluded that the destruction of the bulk of the enemy forces was imminent. The fighting in the isolated pockets and on their edges continued, but neither Halder nor the army group commanders considered this a sufficient reason for halting the advance. Halder interpreted the withdrawal of strong enemy forces facing Army Group North to a position along the line between Rzhev and the Valday hills as an attempt to close up from the north to positions defending Moscow. But he believed that the Soviet forces concentrated around Moscow would not be sufficient to repel the strong German attack; with 'reasonably good direction of battle

---

[462] H.Gr. Mitte/Ia, daily reports, 16 Sept.–7 Oct. 1941, BA-MA RH 19 II/132.

[463] *Geschichte des Großen Vaterländischen Krieges*, ii. 282. Cf. sect. II.ii.9 (Hoffmann); evidence: Reinhardt, *Moskau*, 62–3, and daily reports H.Gr. Mitte/Ia, BA-MA RH 19 II/132.

[464] Röhricht, *Kesselschlacht*, example IV, pp. 35 ff.; Halder, *Diaries*, 1268 ff. (2, 6 Oct. 1941).

[465] Reinhardt, *Moskau*, 69–70.

and moderately good weather' the encirclement of Moscow was certain to succeed.[466]

The planned thrust of Second Armoured Army against Tula was, however, incompatible with notice given by Second Army on 7 October that it would be able to close the Bryansk pocket only if parts of the armoured army halted their advance near and north of the city. The army group rejected this request with the explanation that, after a successful thrust by the armoured army and the right wing of Fourth Army, the enemy facing Second Army would no longer be able to escape destruction. Those parts of the armoured army still in action around the pocket were therefore to be released as soon as possible.[467]

After the conclusion of this first phase of the offensive, the commander-in-chief of the army came to the headquarters of Army Group Centre to discuss the situation.[468] According to Brauchitsch, it was Hitler's intention to isolate Moscow in a large ring to 'exert political pressure', but not to enter the city. Brauchitsch also informed the army group that great importance was being attached to the capture of Kursk, the first indication of a new orientation that began shortly thereafter. He agreed with Halder that it was now possible to 'take a risk' and begin the pursuit in the direction of Moscow even before the units surrounding the pockets became available. Developments in the following days showed this to be a gross misjudgement of the situation.

The order to Second Armoured Army to advance on Tula was confirmed; it was also to attack towards the Oka between Serpukhov and further east. The objective was, together with the parts of Fourth Army to be released from the Bryansk pocket, to complete the isolation of Moscow from the south and west. For this reason Fourth Army was to advance first towards the line Kaluga–Gzhadsk. LVII Armoured Corps was to attack via Yukhnov towards Medyn and east of it. But parts of two armoured corps (XXXVI and XXXX) remained tied down for the time being at the Vyazma pocket. After being relieved by infantry, they were to advance eastward in the general direction of Gzhadsk.

On the left wing Ninth Army was ordered to use Armoured Group 3 and 'many infantry divisions' for its advance to the north-east in order to isolate Moscow from the north and north-west. Should the enemy attempt to hold his positions from west of Rzhev to south of Lake Ilmen, parts of Armoured Group 3 and Ninth Army were to turn to attack those formations.

---

[466] Here he clearly states his objective: Halder, *Diaries*, 1281 (8 Oct. 1941); OKH/GenStdH/Op.Abt. (IN) No. 41452/41 to Army Group North, 8 Oct. 1941, expected the enemy forces to withdraw at least to the Volkhov, perhaps even to the lake area 'west of Pestovo–Russkoe', to establish the shortest possible line to the lake area of the Valday hills. No more attacks to break the German siege of Leningrad were expected on this sector, as some of the Soviet forces there were needed to protect Moscow: BA-MA RH 2/v. 1327, pp. 23 ff.

[467] H.Gr. Mitte/Ia, No. 1854/41 to Second Army, 7 Oct. 1941, BA-MA RH 19 II/123; Bock, *Tagebuch*, 104–5 (7 Oct. 1941), with strong criticism, BA-MA N 22/9.

[468] Protocol of 'Conference on 7 Oct. 1941 on the start of the operation against Moscow', H.Gr. Mitte/Ia, KTB, BA-MA RH 19 II/123; Reinhardt, *Moskau*, 71.

Agreement about the favourable situation was general.[469] The army group command had reservations only about the eccentric assault group which was to attack Kursk and suggested detaching two corps to Sixth Army of Army Group South for that purpose. Bock also rejected using Armoured Group 3 to attack in a northerly direction.[470]

After this conference Army Group Centre command issued the 'Order for the continuation of operations in the direction of Moscow' on 7 October.[471] The tasks of the individual armies were precisely defined. In addition to carrying out the attack across the Oka, Second Armoured Army was to hold the industrial area around Bryansk and the transport links between Bryansk and Orel until the approach of units of Second Army. Second Army retained the task of destroying the pockets and quickly clearing the road between Roslavl and Bryansk. The attack in the direction of Tula and Kaluga was described as a task to be completed later. All available forces of Armoured Group 4 were to advance along the highway from Vyazma and Mozhaysk and penetrate the enemy fortifications there.

Immediately after this order had been issued, the Army High Command intervened and directed 'on the basis of a Führer order' that on the left wing Armoured Group 3 was to be replaced by Armoured Group 4 so that it would be able to attack in a general northerly direction. There, in co-operation with the inner wings of Ninth and Sixteenth Armies, it was to destroy enemy forces between Beloe and Ostashkov.[472] The same day Army Group North was informed of the objective of the new attack by Armoured Group 3 and the consequences for the northern sector of the front.[473] On the right wing, Kursk was to be captured rapidly. Bock's attempt to give this task to Army Group South by transferring an army corps to it had failed.

The directive of the Army High Command is the first example of the effects of Operation Typhoon, which was developing in an almost classic[474] fashion, on the planning of the army leaders. Hitler's role in these deliberations cannot be determined precisely.[475] However, the development as a whole leaves no doubt that he was not interested in the city of Moscow, but in eliminating the

[469] Halder, *Diaries*, 1277 ff. (7, 8 Oct. 1941).

[470] The attack in the north is not mentioned in the above protocol, but in Bock (Tagebuch, 104: 7 Oct. 1941, BA-MA N 22/9). Order to Army Group Centre to take Kursk, 8 Oct. 1941: BA-MA RH 2/v. 1327, p. 22. Cf. here Leeb's demand, sect. II.1.1(*d*) at n. 407.

[471] Wording in Reinhardt, *Moskau*, 300–1 (annexe 2). On 8 Oct. the army group passed the order to capture Kursk on to Second Armd. Army: BA-MA RH 19 II/123. To keep the armoured army free for purely offensive purposes, Higher Command XXXV, with 1st Cavalry Div. and 4th Inf. Div., was placed under Second Army.

[472] OKH/GenStdH/Op.Abt. (IM) No. 1569/41, 8 Oct. 1941, to H.Gr. Mitte, BA-MA RH 2/v. 1327, p. 19; Halder, *Diaries*, 1281 (8 Oct. 1941). Hitler's decision was based on his assessment of the behaviour of the enemy facing Army Group North (cf. n. 466 above).

[473] Cf. Halder, *Diaries*, 1281 (8 Oct. 1941).   [474] Halder, *Diaries*, 1272–3 (4 Oct. 1941).

[475] In addition to reports of intelligence and the Luftwaffe, Hitler's decisions were usually based on the assessments of the enemy's situation by the Army High Command department for Foreign Armies East. It should also be noted that Jodl, Warlimont, and Loßberg generally represented Halder's views to Hitler or had suitable formulations ready for him.

bulk of the enemy's remaining armed forces and in reaching a favourable winter position for the campaign in 1942.[476] Hitler's order of 12 October on the treatment of Moscow reflected the view he had been advocating for months.[477]

The belief that, as far as the enemy was concerned, the situation was under control was reflected in the directive of the Army High Command for the continuation of the operations of Army Groups Centre and North on 13 October 1941.[478] Certain that the enemy before Moscow had been largely defeated,[479] the Army High Command was now mainly concerned with smashing once and for all the enemy forces facing the two other army groups. The northern wing of Army Group North was instructed to destroy enemy groups south of Lake Ladoga and to establish contact with the Karelian Army. Army Group Centre was to capture the area around Moscow in a close encirclement and, at the same time, offensively secure its flanks—again an announcement of the thrust towards Kursk. Second Armoured Army was still available to isolate Moscow from the south-east and south. Fourth Army with Armoured Group 4 retained the task, but with the envisaged echeloning of the mobile units on the northern wing, of providing cover in the direction of Yaroslavl and Rybinsk. A later advance in this direction could be 'considered'. From the area of Kalinin–Torzhok–Staritsa a strong force of Ninth Army with Armoured Group 3 was to capture the area around Vyshniy Volochek as soon as possible and destroy the enemy forces facing the northern wing of the army group and the southern wing of Sixteenth Army before they could withdraw to the east.[480] In the view of Field Marshal von Bock that was the end of the concentrated attack on Moscow. (See the Annexe Volume, No, 19.)

After 8 October worsening road conditions made the fighting increasingly difficult. The previously clear dry weather gave way to snow and occasional frost, which impeded troop movements and forced the Luftwaffe to reduce its activities. On 12 October Second Armoured Army complained of unimaginable difficulties: one kilometre per hour was the normal progress made by

[476] Moscow remained for him a 'geographical term'. At this time its operational importance in his eyes was that a large number of enemy units had been assembled to defend the city, which, he believed, was bound to weaken the enemy front facing Army Group North. This misjudgement was due to a failure to identify the new units being brought up from the interior of the Soviet Union.

[477] OKH/GenStdH/Op.Abt. (IM) No. 1571/41, 12 Oct. 1941, to Army Group Centre on Hitler's decision not to accept a surrender of Moscow if it were offered. For an explanation of this decision cf. n. 401 above (regarding Leningrad).

[478] OKH/GenStdH/Op.Abt. (I) No. 1584/41, BA-MA RH 2/v. 1327, pp. 30 ff.

[479] H.Gr. Mitte/Ic, report on prisoner interrogation, 9 Oct. 1941; assessment of enemy situation, 14 Oct. 1941; information from Army Group North on withdrawal movements of enemy forces facing the southern wing of Sixteenth Army, 10 Oct. 1941: BA-MA RH 19 II/123; the clearest expression of this belief is found in directive OKH/GenStdH/Op.Abt. (I) No. 1588, 16 Oct., to army group, completely dominated by the idea that the vastness of the country offered enemy forces endless possibilities of withdrawal and manœuvre: BA-MA RH 2/v. 1327, pp. 35 ff.

[480] It was believed that the enemy units to the west of Moscow were withdrawing to the north and south. This was the reason for the order from Army Group Centre to Armd. Group 3, 12 Oct. 1941, to reach the area around Torzhok soon and capture Kalinin, Vyshniy Volochek, and Ostashkov: BA-MA RH 19 II 123.

motorized units.[481] As a result of their rapid advance after the battle of Kiev, some units of Second Army had become separated from each other by distances of up to 240 kilometres. After 6 October several divisions reported that an orderly distribution of supplies was no longer possible.[482] On the northern wing of the army the Vyazma–Moscow highway was the main supply-line, but it was repeatedly broken by explosive charges with time-fuses planted by the enemy. As a result the supply situation in the area of Ninth Army and Armoured Group 3 rapidly became critical. In this situation the only solution was to capture and secure the railway links between Bryansk and Orel, Orel and Tula, Sukhinichi and Kaluga, Smolensk and Mozhaysk, Velikie Luki and Rzhev, and Vyazma and Rzhev. Even possession of these lines would not remove difficulties involved in the onward distribution of supplies by truck or in maintaining existing communications; the commander of the rearward army area had to prepare the organization of cavalry squadrons of Cossacks and of Ukrainian and Belorussian prisoners of war.[483]

On 12 October XXIV Armoured Corps of Second Armoured Army reached Mtsensk. The army's right wing with 9th Armoured Division advanced towards Kursk, but the left wing, along with the bulk of Second Army, remained pinned down around the Bryansk pocket until 20 October. Fourth Army was in the Mozhaysk fortifications belt near Kaluga. Armoured Group 3 of Ninth Army had reached Kalinin, while most of its infantry was still in the area of Vyazma–Rzhev. But the pocket at Vyazma still pinned down such strong forces that the 'pursuit' in the direction of Moscow became a hard, costly struggle.[484]

Nevertheless, on 14 October the report from Army Group Centre on the situation of the enemy judged that he was no longer able of opposing an attack on Moscow with such strong forces that prolonged resistance was to be feared.[485] In the meantime, the Red Army, largely with the help of the civilian population, continued to strengthen its positions between Orel and Kalinin with Mozhaysk as their cardinal point.

Field Marshal von Bock vainly resisted the eccentric movements ordered for the armies on his wings and the weakening of the attack as a whole, whose effects would be felt at precisely the moment when he wanted to regroup his forces to pursue the enemy.[486] After a preliminary orientation by the officer responsible for Army Group Centre in the operations department of the Army General Staff, Colonel-General Helmuth von Grolman, the chief of the gen-

---

[481] Situation briefing by Second Armoured Army chief of staff, 12 Oct. 1941, ibid.

[482] Reinhardt, *Moskau*, 79.

[483] On the creation of these units cf. Hoffmann, *Ostlegionen*, 11 ff.; commander of rear army area Centre, corps order No. 61 and report for Sept. 1941: BA-MA RH 19/123, pp. 178, 202–11. As of 15 Oct. all construction forces were placed directly under the army group command.

[484] During this reorganization and supply phase there could be no question of a pursuit in the military sense of the term.

[485] Cf. n. 479 above.

[486] Bock, *Tagebuch*, 111 (14 Oct. 1941), BA-MA N 22/9; conversation between Greiffenberg and Grolman, 12 Oct. 1941, BA-MA RH 19 II/123.

eral staff of the army group sought to retain at least unlimited control of Fourth Army as an assault force for the attack on Moscow. In addition to the removal of Armoured Group 3 from the attack on Moscow, Ninth Army had also been seriously weakened by transfers of army troops, artillery, assault-guns, sappers, and construction units.[487] But Bock and Greiffenberg failed in their attempts to change the situation. Finally, on 14 October, the army group issued the order for the continuation of operations, which followed almost word for word the directive issued by the Army High Command the previous day.[488]

On 15 October worsening road conditions caused by the weather were the main problem facing Army Group Centre. Although planned as the pursuit of a defeated enemy, the advance slowed in all sectors. The commander-in-chief of Fourth Army, Field Marshal von Kluge, believed that 'the psychologically most critical moment of the campaign in the east' had arrived.[489] The lack of winter clothing, the impassable terrain, and the stubborn enemy defence, especially of roads and buildings that might serve as quarters, shattered all expectations of a quick end to operations. Fuel and supply problems were the main factors in determining the speed of the advance and the attainability of its objectives.[490]

Near Mtsensk and Bolkhov XXIV Armoured Corps of Second Armoured Army was involved in heavy fighting. Fourth Army gained but little ground in the east; it was delayed by well-aimed tactical attacks on the Medyn–Maloyaroslavets road, on the highway, and in the areas south of Detchino and west of Mozhaysk. Armoured Group 3 held Kalinin and its 1st Armoured Division reached Torzhok. Ninth Army took Rzhev and regrouped for the advance northward via Lukovnikovo, where it was to cut the retreat route of the enemy forces facing Sixteenth Army.[491]

After the Bryansk pocket had been cleared, Second Armoured Army and Second Army began to prepare their further advance on 19 October. Second Armoured Army hoped to begin its attack on Mtsensk on 20 October, if road conditions permitted. Second Army was to take Kursk; the plans regarding Voronezh were postponed.[492] Fourth army continued its costly penetration of the enemy positions protecting Moscow and entered Mozhaysk. Heavy attacks by enemy armour and the extensive system of defensive positions exhausted the troops. On 18 October Ninth Army reported that it hoped to continue its

---

[487] H.Gr. Mitte/Ia No. 1941/41, ibid.   [488] H.Gr. Mitte/Ia No. 1690/41, ibid.

[489] H.Gr. Mitte/Ia, KTB, 15 Oct. 1941, ibid.; Bock, Tagebuch, 112 (15 Oct. 1941), BA-MA N 22/9.

[490] The weather conditions cannot have come as a surprise; on 10 June 1941 a 'brief survey of climatic conditions in European Russia in the months August to October' had been distributed to the armies: text in BA-MA RH 2/v. 1326, pp. 115–26. Cf. also *Wehrgeographischer Atlas der UdSSR* with numerous climate and weather charts and geographical descriptions from a military point of view, which all staffs possessed (MGFA, library).

[491] Cf. n. 478 above.

[492] The regrouping and advance of Second Armoured Army encountered serious transport and march difficulties: Bock, Tagebuch, 116–17 (20, 21 Oct. 1941), specifically: 'The Russians are slowing us down far less than the wetness and the mud', BA-MA N 22/9.

advance until it reached the line Kalinin–Torzhok–Kuvshinovo. Then the supply situation would require a long halt.

The head of the quartermaster-general's field office produced a memorandum on the consequences of the new operational objective, the ordered encirclement (not the conquest) of Moscow. With regard to supplies, conclusions had to be drawn for shipments in the direction of Moscow. Whereas earlier it had been possible to assume that supply transports would be able to move parallel to these lines of communication, the vast inferiority of the lateral roads now had to be taken into account. Because of the greatly increased difficulties caused by the weather and the loss of bulk transport facilities it was now necessary to demand an improvement and defence of railway connections.

Second Army headquarters needed the line between Orel and Bryansk as a basis; supplies for Second Armoured Army would have to be brought at least as far as Tula by rail. For the other armies railways had to be built to Kaluga, between Smolensk and Mozhaysk, in the north between Velikie Luki and Rzhev, and between Vyazma and Rzhev. Even if these lines, which were considered minimum requirements, were completed, serious difficulties were still expected between the railheads and individual units. This meant that the conduct of operations would have to be determined by the supply network if the fighting strength of the troops was to be maintained. In the following weeks the importance of this argument for their bare survival became clear.[493]

But neither operational considerations nor the foreseeable difficulties involved in such a large part of the army spending the winter in the Soviet Union if the fighting continued induced Hitler or the Army High Command to change their plans. In addition to the operations on the wings, the offensive against Moscow was to be continued with the assigned forces *alongside* the operations of the wings. The assessment of the enemy's intentions seems to have played a decisive role: it was feared that the Red Army would withdraw to the east, leaving a 'scorched earth' behind, to regain its strength for fighting in the spring.[494] On 16 October all army groups were urged not only to reach their operational objectives but to attempt to engage the strongest possible enemy forces before they could withdraw. For this purpose pursuit detachments were to be organized. Among the armoured units they were to be provided with abundant supplies of fuel, if the fuel situation permitted, and employed against distant objectives.[495] Army Group North immediately re-

---

[493] Remarks of head of field office of general staff officer in charge of supply and administration of supplies for future operations, annexe 2 to H.Gr. Mitte/Ia No. 1923/41, 12 Oct. 1941, BA-MA RH 19 II/123.

[494] OKH/GenStdH/Op.Abt. No. 1588/41, 16 Oct. 1941, BA-MA RH 2/v. 1327, pp. 35–6.

[495] The style of the above-mentioned directive indicates that it was suggested by Hitler. The idea of surrounding the enemy facing Seventeenth Army by having First Armoured Army turn north in the event that its attack to win a bridgehead across the Don did not succeed was incompatible with Halder's insistence on crossing the Don in 1941. This objective was motivated not only by the desire to capture the oilfields, but also by the intention to cut off the Soviet Union from supply shipments via Persia. Cf. sect. II.1.1(*e*) at n. 434 and sect. II.11.14 at n. 419 (Hoffmann).

ported that no disengagement moves were to be observed in the area of Sixteenth Army and that the enemy was continuing to defend himself in fortified field positions.[496] The army group also referred to the promised attack by Army Group Centre, with the purpose of encircling the enemy. On 19 October the operations department replied that no final decision had been taken as to whether the encirclement was to be carried out in the manner envisaged or whether a much large envelopment from the area of Kalinin via Bezhetsk in the direction of Cherepovets offered better chances of success.[497] The direction of this operation meant that Moscow would be bypassed and enemy lines of communication to northern Russia were to be interrupted instead.[498] On the same day the Army General Staff instructed Army Group Centre to assemble strong, mobile forces in the area of Kalinin and Torzhok for a pincer movement against the enemy group in the Valday hills. There Halder saw another great operational task to be completed before the end of autumn. Its objective, after the destruction of the enemy forces facing Sixteenth Army, was to secure the front over a great distance towards the northeast and east. After the occupation of Rybinsk (the air distance between Kalinin and Rybinsk is about 230 km.), the line from Vologda to the lakes area and the 'western edge of the tundra' was to be reached and the railway line between Archangel and Moscow cut.[499]

While strategic ideas replaced reality in the thinking of the Army General Staff, a rapid thaw and rainy weather set in along the front of the army group and quickly led to a serious supply crisis. In a proposal to the Army High Command on 21 October Field Marshal von Bock attempted to take this development into account: wherever road conditions or lack of fuel were impeding the advance, personnel needed for vehicle maintenance were to be left behind, while all other officers and men were to be formed into infantry combat units and the necessary artillery, heavy weapons, and supply services with motor or local horse-drawn vehicles assigned to them. These extemporized mobile units were to be sent to the front immediately. Where serviceable vehicles were still available, mixed formations were to be formed and attempts made to reach the assigned objectives. This plan was submitted to the commander-in-chief of the army, who, however, refused to issue the necessary order.[500]

On 22 October, unimpressed by the fierce enemy attacks on the positions of

[496] H.Gr. Nord/Ic, 16 Sept. 1941, BA-MA RH 19 II/123.

[497] OKH/GenStdH/Op.Abt. (IN) No. 41562/41, 19 Oct. 1941, to Army Group North, information to Army Group Centre, BA-MA RH 2/v. 1327, p. 40.

[498] Telephone conversation between Halder and Greiffenberg, 19 Oct. 1941; cf. Reinhardt, *Moskau*, 83–4.

[499] This line was the only remaining supply link via the Arctic Ocean. This thrust could only be carried out, however, if the Red Army facing Army Group North withdrew on a broad front.

[500] H.Gr. Mitte/Ia No. 2086/41, 21 Oct. 1941, BA-MA RH 19 II/124; Bock, Tagebuch, 117 (21 Oct. 1941): 'That, however, doesn't change the fact that sensible commanders are doing it this way on their own initiative.' On 16 Oct. the army high command had issued a similar order. Cf. n. 494 and sect. II.1.1(c) at n. 273.

Ninth Army near Kalinin, the Army High Command again demanded an early attack to the north-east. At the same time a reinforcement of the attack in the south against Kursk and Voronezh, with XXXXVIII Armoured Corps, was considered. However, the army group, also bearing in mind the enemy pressure on the right flank of Fourth Army, insisted that all available forces of Second Armoured Army be concentrated for the thrust towards Tula. If the movement was to be continued via Kursk to Voronezh, the army should be divided, with XXXIV Army Corps being placed under Sixth Army and XXXV Army Corps under Second Armoured Army.[501] The Army High Command thereupon ordered mobile units to be assigned to Second Army, which was then to take Voronezh.[502]

On 23 October, mainly because of the difficult situation of Ninth Army, Bock reacted to the Army High Command's demand to strike north-east from the Kalinin area by ordering planning for attacks beyond Kalinin to be postponed, so that the enemy north of the Volga reservoir could first be defeated. That, he hoped, would establish a safe rear area for a further advance by Ninth Army.[503] The more slowly the advance on Moscow proceeded—the bulk of vehicles were stuck in the mud and the troops had suffered serious losses—the more Hitler sought new solutions on the flanks. When it became clear that the enemy facing Army Group North was not withdrawing, that he was offering determined resistance between the Volga and the Volkhov, and that he would probably attempt to recapture Kalinin, Hitler decided to eliminate the enemy forces between the Volga and Lake Ladoga by cutting the railway lines via Yaroslavl and Rybinsk to Bologoe and Khotsay as well as the line via Vologda to Tikhvin. Costly direct attacks would thus be avoided.[504] But the army group command was more alarmed by Hitler's intervention in the operations of its last mobile 'pursuit group', Second Armoured Army.

On 23 October Second Armoured Army had launched an offensive. XXIV Armoured Corps was successful near Mtsensk and was able to penetrate as far as Chern. During this slow and laborious movement a report from the chief of the operations department arrived on the evening of 26 October: Hitler had expressed very specific views about the progress of operations to the commander-in-chief of the army.[505]

Hitler demanded that Second Armoured Army should not advance eastwards beyond Tula but turn towards Voronezh to cut off strong enemy forces.

[501] OB H.Gr. Mitte/Ia, No. 2099/41 to OKH/GenStdH, 22 Oct. 1941, BA-MA RH 19 II/124.

[502] OKH/GenStdH/Op.Abt. (I) No. 31903/41, 23 Oct. 1941 to H.Gr. Süd and Mitte, BA-MA RH 2/v. 1327, p. 41. The army group, thereupon, placed XXXXVIII Armd. Corps with 9th Armd. Div. and 16th Inf. Div. (mot.), as well as the 'higher command', under Second Army on 24 Oct.: BA-MA RH 19 II/124.

[503] Army Group Centre to Ninth Army, 23 Oct. 1941, 79, BA-MA RH 19 II/124.

[504] For this purpose Armd. Groups 3 and 4 and strong infantry units of Army Group Centre were to be moved to the area north of Moscow, if possible before the first heavy snowfall: OKH/GenStdH/Op.Abt. (I) No. 1610/41, 30 Oct. 1941, BA-MA RH 2/v. 1327, fos. 44 ff.

[505] Reinhardt, *Moskau*, 85–6 with sources; H.Gr. Mitte/Ia, KTB, 144 ff., 157–68, BA-MA RH 19 II/124; Guderian, *Panzer Leader*, 114 ff.

He also feared that the armoured army would not have enough bridging material to cross the numerous river stretches it would encounter in its previous direction of attack. In addition, he considered Fourth Army strong enough to take over, with its right wing, the tasks of Second Armoured Army in the encirclement of Moscow. As the thrust by Armoured Group 4 with mobile units towards Bezhevka did not offer good prospects of success because of road conditions, infantry was to be transferred to Kalinin as fast as possible for that task. Armoured Groups 3 and 4 were to be combined to advance in the direction of Rybinsk and Yaroslavl. West of Kalinin Ninth Army was to go on the defensive.

The army group was to present its views on the two proposed wing operatons, allowing for road conditions, supply facilities, and bridging material. On the evening of 27 October, while the the army group's response was being decided, Heusinger informed it that the Wehrmacht High Command had taken a 'firm decision' with regard to Voronezh. Only an hour later the order arrived for Second Armoured Army to halt its advance towards Tula until reconnaissance provided more information on road conditions and a decision could be taken on a possible wheeling towards Voronezh.[506] On 28 October Bock and Halder discussed the measures ordered. Bock stressed that for tactical and psychological reasons he could not halt the advance of Second Army at that moment. Halder was not able to comment, but he completely accepted Bock's view and suggested describing the further advance as a 'reconnaissance in force in the direction of Tula'. Bock replied that he would order Second Armoured Army to create 'a situation that would enable it to turn towards the south-east'. In his view this meant at least reaching the Upa sector near Tula. Subsequently Bock and the command of Second Armoured Army agreed that they both shared this opinion.[507]

On 28 October the opposing views of the Army General Staff finally induced Hitler to rescind the order for Second Armoured Army to halt and change its direction of advance, with 'the proclaimed objective of exploiting some lucky chance to capture a bridge across the Oka intact'.[508] In view of the situation of Fourth Army and the road conditions, Hitler now ordered Second Armoured army to continue its attack in a general north-easterly direction. Its task was the early capture of a bridge across the Oka east of Serpukhov by a surprise thrust and the cutting of the railway line from Moscow to the south.

On 28 October the army group also ordered Ninth Army to suspend its attack to the north and to go on the defensive along the line running from Kalinin to south of Torzhok and on to Bolshaya Kosha.[509] Its main task

---

[506] OKH/GenStdH/Op.Abt. (IM) No. 3191I/41, 27 Oct. 1941, BA-MA RH 2/1327, p. 48.

[507] BA-MA RH 19 II/124; Bock, Tagebuch, 121 ff. (27, 28 Oct. 1941), BA-MA N 22/9. This technical trick to circumvent those of Hitler's directives that were considered impractical had already been used successfully in the campaign in the west.

[508] Telephone call of operations department to Army Group Centre/Ia, 28 Oct. 1941, 3.10 p.m., BA-MA RH 19 II/124; Hitler's order received at OKH/GenStdH/Op.Abt. (IM) No. 1609/41, 29 Oct. 1941, BA-MA RH 2/v. 1327, p. 43.

[509] H.Gr. Mitte/Ia No. 2198/41 to Ninth Army, 28 Oct. 1941, BA-MA RH 19 II/124.

remained the elimination of enemy resistance in the area south and south-west of Kalinin between the Volga and the Volga reservoir, as well as the capture of road- and rail-bridges across the western tip of the reservoir.

These varied orders, in many respects contradictory and issued without regard to their feasibility, were to be replaced by guidelines for the near future. This was accomplished with the directive of the Army High Command of 30 October for the 'Continuation of operations against enemy forces between the Volga and Lake Ladoga'.[510]

This directive contained a number of statements of intent which have been presented here in their various stages. The plan to cut off enemy forces facing the front in the north-east by cutting the railway from Yarslavl to Bologoe and through Vologda to Tikhvin was restated. In view of calculations by the war-economy and armaments office of possible British shipments, which could be transported to the interior of the Soviet Union from ports on the Arctic Ocean, this operation was to become increasingly important.[511] The plan for Armoured Groups 3 and 4 to attack towards Yaroslavl and Rybinsk as part of this operation has been mentioned. A change from previous plans was made for the attack by Ninth Army; its task was limited to capturing and securing the road between the last station on the railway line Selizharovo–Kalinin–Volga reservoir and the supply-points. The task of a joint offensive with the right wing of Army Group North was abandoned. In addition to the encirclement of Leningrad, that army group still had the task of tying down Soviet forces south of Lake Ilmen and 'immediately pursuing them in the event of their withdrawal'.[512]

Not a word was said in the directive about capturing Moscow, the only objective that still prevented Army Group Centre from succumbing to apathy. In formulating its own 'Order for the continuation of operations', Army Group Centre therefore refrained from repeating the illusory objectives in the directive of the Army High Command and strove to present Hitler's and Halder's long-term objectives in a form that would not cause lower commands to shake their heads over them from the outset.[513]

The order stated clearly that the encirclement of Moscow required the defeat of the enemy between the confluence of the Moskva river and Kalinin.

[510] OKH/GenStdH/Op.Abt. (I) No. 1610, BA-MA RH 2/v. 1327, pp. 44 ff.; advance briefing on 27 Oct. regarding further use of Ninth Army and Armd. Group 3, BA-MA RH 19 II/124, fos. 158–9.

[511] Chef WiRüAmt in OKW No. 3409/41, 22 Oct. 1941, BA-MA Wi/I D 73. Although Hitler doubted those figures, his operational thinking aimed at cutting this supply-line. Moreover, reports had been received of its being used for deliveries of British/American supply shipments: OKH/GenStdH/Abt. Fr. Heere Ost No. 142, 4 Nov. 1941, BA-MA H 3/484. Cf. also situation reports of the navy from the Navy High Command and the naval war staff after Sept. 1941, BA-MA RM 7/771 ff., on convoys and British naval units identified in Archangel.

[512] In view of their situation, this hackneyed phrase must have seemed quite inappropriate to the soldiers of the army group. This was indicated in Brauchitsch's order of the day to them, 20 Oct. 1941, which was issued with instructions to make it known to the troops but not to include it in the front newspaper: BA-MA RH 19 II/124, fo. 36.

[513] Reinhardt, *Moskau*, 302–3 (annexe 3). Cf. also Halder's memorandum, 7 Jan. 1941; sect II.1.1(f) at n. 525.

The grand objective was therefore not abandoned, nor was the task of Second Armoured Army to push on across the Oka. The order also 'referred to' the industrial areas of Stalinogorsk and Kashira. Fourth Army remained the main force directed against Moscow. Its attack was to be resumed without delay north and south of the highway once the weather and the ammunition supplies had improved. Its northern wing was to advance towards Klin, i.e. against Moscow's communication to the north. The originally considered thrust by Armoured Groups 3 and 4 to Rybinsk and Vologda was included in the encirclement of Moscow as an operation to be executed later. The task of Ninth Army remained essentially to go on the defensive after reaching the lines mentioned above. Armoured Group 3 was to prepare for a thrust to the north-east.[514]

This order represented the conclusion, for the time being, of the offensive within the framework of Operation Typhoon. In human and material terms Army Group Centre was exhausted. A pause for rehabilitation was necessary. That pause was to serve, above all, the strengthening of the forces' defensive capacity, the construction of defensive positions, and the creation of the logistical prerequisites of survival in winter under extremely unfavourable conditions.

(ii) PLANS FOR THE RESUMPTION OF THE OFFENSIVE
(*See the Annexe Volume, No. 19*)

After the Wehrmacht High Command had come to the conclusion, at the end of August 1941, that the war against the Soviet Union would continue into 1942, the Army General Staff too began by October 1941 to prepare for this development.[515] In regard to operations, assignments for the army groups and armies had previously always aimed at creating favourable jumping-off lines for decisive battles to crush the Red Army. One result of this objective was that regroupings were undertaken while operations were in progress and that the number and length of breaks for resting and re-equipping exhausted units were inadequate. As a consequence of the realization that none of the great battles of encirclement had had any decisive effect on the campaign as a whole, directives of the Army High Command were now intended to establish bases

[514] Report Ninth Army to Army Group Centre, 29 Oct. 1941, on the planned defensive positions, BA-MA RH 19 II/124. The spreading of the army along a 200-km.-wide front meant that it could not be used for offensive purposes; it was therefore requested that Sixteenth Army be ordered to advance towards the Kalinin–Vyshniy Volochek line to make the corps on the northern wing available.

[515] OKH/GenStdH/Op.Abt. (IIb), conference at office of the deputy chief of staff (*Oberquartiermeister*), 24 Oct. 1941, *KTB OKW* i. 1072–3 (105). Here the objective for 1942, the operation across the Caucasus, was discussed. Hitler too was prepared to postpone attack operations with strategic objectives until the following year. Cf. the discussion between Hitler and Brauchitsch according to Halder's notes (Halder, *Diaries*, 1290). This view is also supported by his later acceptance of the evacuation of Rostov and his leaving of the decision about Tikhvin to Leeb. Cf. Map II.1.1 and sect. II.1.1(*e*) at n. 330. To the navy too he expressed his preference for giving priority to the securing of areas already conquered. Cf. Salewski, *Seekriegsleitung*, i. 476, and n. 524 below.

for large-scale conquests in the coming year. But for the moment the army-group and army commands of the field army had to concentrate on quite different problems, such as holding a 'winter-proof' line, ensuring supplies, and maintaining the material and personnel strength of their forces. The chief of the Army General Staff considered these concerns to be problems that would have to be solved by the determination of the leadership and the organizational ability of the general staff.[516]

It was therefore inevitable that opinions differed among the staffs as to how much effort should be devoted to and how many sacrifices should be made for the sake of strategic and operational planning for the future, i.e. primarily how many additional troops and what quantities of supplies would have to be provided.[517] In this respect the role of the commander-in-chief of the army, when he visited the field commands, seems to have been more that of a comforting old comrade than of an energetically helpful superior.[518] In the end, opinions about what the troops were still able to accomplish remained divided. Numerous reports of commanders in the field indicated that on 6 November the actual fighting power of the 136 large units of the German army in the east was considered to be equivalent to that of 83 such units.[519]

By 1 October 1941 total losses of Army Group Centre had reached 229,000 men; by 16 October they had risen to 277,000. Total replacements were 151,000 men.[520] But these figures reveal nothing about the fighting ability of individual units and soldiers or about the morale of the troops as a whole.

For Army Group Centre, as for the other two army groups, the main objectives in planning a further attack were to weaken the enemy to such an extent that he would not be able to recover by the coming spring, while at the same time gaining favourable jumping-off positions for the spring offensive, which by then was clearly recognized as necessary.[521] Hitler and the Army High Command were agreed that this would require more sacrifices from the Wehrmacht.[522] Both believed that the fighting strength of the army would still be sufficient after a pause for rehabilitation.

---

[516] At the beginning of Nov. 1941 Halder elucidated this difference with the alternatives of 'conservation' (*Erhaltungsgedanke*) and 'striking efficiency' (*Wirkungsgedanke*). An acceptable compromise between these two extremes had to be found and made to percolate down to army level through general-staff channels: Halder, *Diaries*, 1288 (5 Nov. 1941).

[517] On the conflict between Halder and the army group cf. Reinhardt, *Moskau*, 135–6.

[518] e.g. his visit to Army Group South on 3 Nov. 1941, when Brauchitsch stated his position regarding the future supply situation. Cf. sect. II.1.1(*c*) at n. 312.

[519] OKH/GenStdH/Org.Abt. (I), *KTB OKW* i. 1074–5 (106), assessment of the fighting power of the units of the army in the east.

[520] Tables in Reinhardt, *Moskau*, 315–17 (annexes 6–8); 'local forces' of the rear-area services, which were difficult to count, are not considered.

[521] This emerged clearly from the personnel measures taken in mid-Dec. Cf. sect. II.1.1(*g*) at n. 575.

[522] This is proved not only by Halder's notes (*Diaries*, 1289: 7 Nov. 1941) but also by the disputes with the army groups and the armies. It is regrettable that because of an accident Halder did not continue his notes. As a result his diaries, an important source for this period of difficult decisions, are silent here.

Like the estimates of the fighting ability of their own troops, evaluations of the position of the enemy varied widely among the senior German operations staffs and field commands, not to mention the lower commands. The Wehrmacht High Command and the Army General Staff repeatedly produced forecasts based on the high numbers of Soviet prisoners, the enormous material losses of the Red Army and its supposedly exhausted fighting strength, and the assumed situation of the Red Army leaders, predicting the imminent collapse of that 'gigantic instrument of war'.[523] To avoid this catastrophe, it was believed, large Soviet units were being withdrawn to escape capture. In contrast, German field commanders reported stubborn defence of fixed positions and offensive counter-thrusts that went beyond mere tactical actions. On the whole, however, belief in German superiority still prevailed; only the material situation had to be improved and difficulties resulting from the weather overcome.

It was intended in the sector of Army Group Centre to end the extremely exhausting and costly fighting forced on the German army by the enemy and the weather by launching a second large-scale offensive. In this decision Hitler's need to demonstrate to the German people before the end of the year his unbroken faith in victory and to restore the optimism of his allies played an important role. Nothing strengthens confidence and readiness to make further sacrifices in a war more than expectations of victory.

After Halder had discussed the possibilities that presented themselves as a 'final balance of the situation' with the head of the operations department of the general staff, Colonel Heusinger, on 5 November, he received a detailed memorandum two days later, intended to serve as the basis for a discussion of these questions by the chiefs of staff of the army groups and armies.[524] Halder was mainly anxious to achieve a consensus of views in this circle of his most important general staff officers. The starting-point for the discussion was an overview of the possibilities left, in Halder's judgement, to the Soviet leaders. In his view their choices had become so few since the end of October or the beginning of November 1941 that, in spite of all efforts to mount a vigorous defence, a coherent front could not be maintained by them. Halder assumed that the Red Army would continue to withdraw in order to gain time for a new build-up and would be able to hold only the area around Moscow ('Vologda, Moscow, Tambov') and the Caucasus region. It would have to abandon the

[523] According to the calculation of the general-staff officer in charge of supply and administration, as of 20 Dec. 1941 3,350,639 prisoners had been taken. This figure includes those who had died, fled, or been released, for whom no reliable figures are available. Cf. sect. II.II.3 at n. 56 (Hoffmann). 25,696 guns of all kinds, 13,935 tanks, and 52,221 motor-vehicles were captured. Cf. *KTB OKW* i. 1106, appendices.

[524] Chef GenStdH/Op.Abt. (Ia)/GZ No. 1630/41, 7 Nov. 1941, BA-MA RH 21-2/879 with map. Hitler gave this consent on 11 Nov. 1941, but with the proviso that the troops must not lose contact with their supply-base. According to a letter of the operations department of 3 Nov. 1941, Hitler referred to Halder's objectives for the winter as being for 'east operations 1942': BA-MA RW 4/v. 578, fos. 162 ff., letter OKH/GenStdH/OQu IV/Fr. Heere Ost, 4 Nov. 1941, with map WiRü, 1 Mar. 1941, BA-MA RH 21-2/v. 879.

area in between, extending to the steppes east of the Volga. He believed that extensive evacuation measures had been detected in the foothills of the Caucasus. In the area of Leningrad too he expected evacuation and withdrawal of Red Army troops as far as Rybinsk so as to concentrate forces in the 'Moscow bridgehead' in order to hold the rail links converging there and, with help from industry in the Urals, create a new army for an attack in 1942, 'or even later'. The Caucasus front could then be held thanks to its naturally strong position and with help from the British and Americans.[525] This view of the situation, which had already emerged from the directive for Army Groups North and Centre of 30 October, formed the basis of the memorandum of 7 November.

The logical conclusions for the conduct of the war in this large strategic framework were obvious: the enemy had to be deprived of railway lines and armaments centres for a new build-up. Assuming that the enemy carried out certain evacuations, the operational objectives of Voroshilovgrad, Ivanov, Yaroslavl, and Rybinsk, as 'minimum objectives', were indeed ambitious, but not totally unattainable, at least if all prerequisites were met in the areas of leadership and transport. But this was simply not possible. Even more unrealistic was the idea of really controlling this enormous area. Halder's recent acceptance of Hitler's strategic plan was evident in his desire to occupy Maykop, Stalingrad, Gorkiy, and Vologda as the 'maximum objective'—which, however, he considered it 'urgently desirable' to reach. Halder's objectives thus included the oilfields of the Caucasus, the transport centres for supplies sent through Iran, numerous armaments and transport centres in the interior of the Soviet Union, and the last link to the Arctic Ocean still in Soviet hands. He was well aware of the risks involved in trying to reach all these widely scattered objectives, which is why he considered it vital for the further course of the war to take up winter positions that could later be used as favourable starting-points for operations to be undertaken in 1942.

In line with his image of the enemy, he saw the main danger in the development of the weather situation, although the effects of this could be reduced by ensuring adequate stocks of supplies. Here he formulated concrete requirements intended to overcome the shortages reported by the staffs of the forces at the front. Although he recognized that the fighting ability of the German troops had been weakened, he maintained that they were clearly superior to the 'still usable Russian forces'. In conclusion, Halder urged the continuation of offensive activity with 'raiding parties' and tank columns even during the period of bad weather.

The objectives contained in the working paper for the conference in Orsha summarized here were based primarily on a draft of 1 October 1941 prepared

---

[525] Halder (*Diaries*, 1284–5, 1287–8, 1289–90: 3, 5, 7 Nov. 1941) provides evidence of Hitler's concurrence with his objectives. But Hitler envisaged the occupation of the oilfields for the following year (cf. n. 515 above). Halder's view was undoubtedly influenced by the successes in the Crimea and against Tikhvin.

by the war-economy and armaments office, which Foreign Armies East passed on to the army groups and armies on 4 November. Although in the covering letter Foreign Armies East stated that it could not agree with the conclusions of the war-economy and armaments office, this seems only to have motivated Halder to push even more energetically for an attack in winter. It is astonishing that the map accompanying Halder's memorandum of 7 November, which contained the first data on the remaining Soviet military potential in the economic sector, was largely identical with that accompanying the analysis of 1 March 1941 by the war-economy and armaments office.

Attempts at co-ordination with the Wehrmacht High Command, more precisely with Hitler, with regard to the winter offensive had by no means produced the agreement suggested in Halder's diary and accepted by much of the literature on this period of the war as a historical fact. While the written report of the operations department of 3 November was accepted in its goals, it was with the reservation that lines of communication must be maintained between the troops and their supply-bases; moreover, no decision about the chain of command in winter was taken. It is clear therefore that Hitler exerted no pressure on Halder. On the contrary, the objectives which, according to Halder, had to be reached even after the onset of winter appeared as operational objectives for 1942 in Jodl's notes on Hitler's comments.

However much importance Halder may have attached to the argument in favour of conquering the centres of the Soviet economy so as to prevent a new build-up of the Red Army, a glance at the maps was sufficient to show the field commands the total lack of realism in the consequent operational aims. They were far more ambitious than anything the field commands had seriously considered. Any agreement between Halder and the general-staff officers mentioned above depended on whether their basic assessments of the enemy's situation were identical. But that was certainly not the case among the army groups and armies at this time.

With regard to the further actions by Army Group Centre to be considered here, it should be noted that the group's commander-in-chief vigorously opposed Halder's unrealistic objectives. Bock's operational aim was no longer a close encirclement of Moscow within the railway line around the city, let alone a thrust into its centre, but at most the attainment of the line Dimitrov–Zagorsk–Orekhovo–Kolomna. However, he considered a line along the Moskva river and the Moskva–Volga canal to be more realistic.[526] He wanted to attack only close objectives, as in his opinion the reduced strength of the army group no longer permitted any strategic envelopment. These views were getting close to Hitler's earlier deliberations, which had induced him to plan the attack on Moscow as a series of individual steps to be concluded only after the Red Army units facing other sections of the front had been destroyed. The

---

[526] Classification of objectives according to Bock: 'long-range, short-range, and interim.' Cf. Halder, *Diaries*, 1294–5 (11 Nov. 1941), and Bock, *Tagebuch*, 133, BA-MA N 22/9; Reinhardt, *Moskau*, 137.

supply situation necessitated a staggered advance of the individual armies in order to make any progress at all before the first heavy snowfall. This meant that those parts of the army group at that time not capable of participating in an offensive because of supply shortages had to remain where they were. At best they could be brought up later. In accordance with his assessment before the offensive in September, Bock did not believe that the front as it then was could be defended, although he did not wish merely to establish more favourable winter positions with a forward movement. Neither could he expect Sixteenth Army of Army Group North or Sixth Army of Army Group South to move closer to his sector of the front, thereby relieving pressure on Army Group Centre. On the contrary, the withdrawal of parts of Second Army had shown that a thrust in the direction of Rostov and Voroshilovgrad entirely ruled out any flank protection from that quarter.

The conference of the chiefs of staff of the army groups and the armies, as ordered by Halder, took place in Orsha near Smolensk on 13 November.[527] From the Army General Staff the chief of supply and administration, the heads of the central department and the organization department, the officers responsible for sectors Centre and North in the operations department, and several accompanying officers were present. The composition of this group shows that internal general-staff matters were also discussed. Halder received a totally negative answer to the most important question in his memorandum: to what extent could next year's offensive be prepared for during the winter by further advances to 'operationally valuable' starting-positions? As was clear from the increasingly urgent demands for personnel and material replacements, the graphic descriptions of the imminent physical and psychological collapse of the troops, and the concern about their sheer survival during the winter, all responsible general-staff officers considered the situation to be extremely serious. As relief clearly could not be provided in time, they rejected any further large-scale offensive. They had learnt from experience in various situations during the campaign the value of such terms as 'measures in hand' and of qualifications such as 'if the supply situation permits'. In most cases it had been necessary to improvise as orders had been issued, orders accompanied by open or implied appeals to make more sacrifices, irrespective of the supply situation or the condition of the troops. In the discussion of Halder's ambitious aims in this circle there was no shortage of sarcastic comment.[528]

The chief of staff of Army Group Centre argued that only a direct thrust on Moscow was possible, without the broad envelopment of the city envisaged by

[527] i.e. the chiefs of staff of the armies envisaged for the attack—Eighteenth and Sixteenth Armies of Army Group North, Sixth and Seventeenth Armies of Army Group South (First Armd. Army was still involved in the attack on Rostov), and the armies of Army Group Centre, except Second Army: Halder, *Diaries*, 1287 (5 Nov. 1941), 1294 ff. (11–19 Nov. 1941). On the conference at Orsha cf. Reinhardt, *Moskau*, 139–42 nn. 91–2. In an assessment of the situation the pulling out of Air Fleet 2 and II Air Corps should be considered. Cf. sect. II.1.2(*a*) at n. 886 (Boog).

[528] Remark by Col. Kurt Freiherr von Liebenstein, chief of staff of Second Armd. Army, quoted in Guderian, *Panzer Leader*, 117.

Halder. In this respect he was only presenting the views of his commander-in-chief. Moreover, his staff was already busy planning an attack as soon as possible. Halder now realized that all available information indicated that a second major offensive against Moscow would not be successful. Yet that was what he demanded. His answer to misgivings about the army group's supplies, voiced by the head of the field office of the general-staff officer in charge of supply and administration, Major Eckstein—that one just had to trust to the soldier's good luck—was hardly an adequate response. He had repeatedly been informed of the supply problems by the responsible general-staff officer; they cannot have been new to him, quite apart from the fact that he also received information through operations-department channels. Why then did the commander-in-chief of the army group and the chief of the Army General Staff advocate and order an attack which, though limited to the western edge of Moscow, was nevertheless, in view of the condition of the German troops, an extremely dangerous undertaking?

Firstly, it is necessary to outline the various positions of those responsible. According to the scant evidence available on Hitler's views on the further conduct of operations in the east,[529] he wanted in the long term an encirclement of Moscow by mobile troops, which would at the same time sever all lines of communication from the Atlantic, the Black Sea, and the trans-Caucasus area to the interior of the Soviet Union. Thereafter the city was to be subjected to an increasingly tight encirclement. Militarily it would be important only in so far as it might influence the flanks and rear area of the main future operation against the Caucasus and the Middle East.

Halder and his chief of the operations department, now chief of staff of Army Group Centre, Major-General von Greiffenberg, had from the very outset of planning looked for a decision at and in Moscow. In his dealings with Hitler Halder had always promoted and defended this operational direction with all his energy. In spite of the Red Army's failure to collapse after the battles of Minsk and Smolensk, he still sought to destroy the bulk of its units, its 'vital fighting strength', at Moscow. Now he had pushed through his plan for making this attack the point of amin effort of all German operations in the east—very late and under conditions completely different from those underlying his planning, but, he believed, still not too late provided several weeks of freezing weather without snow permitted a war of movement.

In this regard he met considerable resistance to his plans in Orsha and agreed to a compromise according to which the large-scale offensive that he and Hitler wanted was to be replaced by a partial offensive adjusted to available forces and directed against the outskirts of the city. At the same time, and in spite of the reservations he expressed to Greiffenberg on 11 November, he accepted Bock's belief that the offensive with limited objectives should be started as soon as possible without the envisaged, time-consuming expansion

---

[529] Halder, *Diaries*, 1290, 1304 (7, 19 Nov. 1941); Jodl, 11 Nov. 1941, BA-MA RW 4/v. 578.

of the supply network. The assessments of relative strength and the conclusions drawn regarding the depth of the attack and its direction were provided by Army Group Centre. Halder accepted these assessments and agreed to Bock's offensive plan.[530] Neither, however, can have seriously believed that an attack on the outskirts of Moscow, under the enormous risks to supply transports and the great sacrifices to be expected, would end up at the Moskva–Volga canal. The armies and armoured groups were well aware that the positions they had reached were not favourable, but it was equally clear that they would find nothing better at the edge of Moscow. Indeed, they would be exposed there to massed air attacks and fire from the defending artillery. The chosen limited offensive could not sever the rail links to the east; the enemy would thus be able constantly to bring up reinforcements. From Bock down to the last private of the army group there could only be one real objective—the capture of the city. Only that objective could justify the disregarding of all warnings and reservations from the leading operational strategists of the army group as well as from the officers responsible for supplies. The fact that the attack was to be executed by stages and its opening delayed did not change this situation. For Halder, and probably also for Bock, more must have been involved in this high-risk operation than the mere conquest of territory, the possible occupation of a shattered, burnt-out human habitation, or a new jumping-off position for future operations. It seems probable that both men hoped that this attack would mark the beginning of the fall of Moscow and thus the end of the war against the Soviet Union.

What role did their image of the enemy play in their deliberations? In the final analysis the success of an attack by exhausted troops, without adequate replacements and dependent on vulnerable supply-lines, could not be based only on the hope of freezing, snow-free weather, for which the troops were not even adequately equipped.

The German commanders realized that the Red Army and the able-bodied inhabitants of Moscow would defend the city. This time there could be no question of strong enemy units escaping. On the other hand, they believed that the heavy Soviet losses in the battles of Kiev, Bryansk, and Vyazma–Smolensk had been a blood-letting of war material and trained soldiers who could not be replaced by hastily organized new units or militia formations. The strength of Soviet air defences and air-force units had been clearly demonstrated. The transfer of trained and fresh Soviet units from the Far East to the defence of Moscow was a known fact and mentioned in intelligence reports as well as in the battle reports of various units. There is evidence that all offices and officers concerned with such questions produced serious and constantly updated assessments of the enemy's situation. It can only be concluded that Halder and the operations department did not attach sufficient importance to these reports. As had been the case since the beginning of operational planning for

---

[530] On Bock's decision, which cannot be seen as uninfluenced by Halder, cf. Reinhardt, *Moskau*, 139; Messerschmidt, *Wehrmacht*, 134; Hofmann, Feldzug, ii. 88 ff., MGFA P-114b.

the war in the east, materials produced by the department Foreign Armies East, however low their information value may be judged now, were evaluated by the 'experts' from the perspective of their own assumed superiority. In addition, the heavy losses of the Red Army led the German leaders to conclude that even the Soviets' enormous human reserves were not sufficient to permit the creation and training of a new, combat-ready army. There remained, however, a large number of Soviet units in the trans-Caucasus and the Far East whose existence was known and which had to be regarded as virtually intact peacetime forces. It was also known that Soviet transport facilities were sufficient to transfer these units to the fighting front. How, under these circumstances, throwing the 'last battalion' into the battle could be expected to tip the balance in favour of the German army will remain the secret of Halder and Bock. They simply placed their hopes in the demonstrated superiority of the German command system and the stamina of their own soldiers.[531] In addition to the enemy, they also in the final analysis ignored the climate, the condition of the terrain, and temperature records—all of them elementary factors about which meteorologists and geographers could have supplied abundant information.

In mid-November 1941 a line extending from Kolomna along the Moskva river to the western suburbs of the capital and from there along the Moskva–Volga canal to the shore of the Volga reservoir was still regarded as an attainable objective. From there the front was to be established via Kalinin as previously ordered—an attack with a limited objective because of the limited means available and the late season.

Thus Second Armoured Army on the right wing of the attack was ordered, while covering its right flank towards the Moscow–Voronezh railway line and with XXIV Armoured Corps forming the spearhead, to advance northward towards Kashira and Kolomna. Ever since the conference in Orsha, when an attack via Ryazan was still under discussion, the chief of the army's general staff, Colonel Kurt Freiherr von Liebenstein, had observed that, with the means available to it, the armoured army would only be able to reach Venev. Since then the supply situation had not improved.

On the left wing of the attack Ninth Army with Armoured Group 3 was ordered to push forward to the Volga reservoir and the Moskva–Volga canal on 15 November; then the armoured group was to turn towards Moscow.

At the centre of the army group Fourth Army, with Armoured Group 4 on its left wing, was to make a direct, frontal attack. In view of the supply situation and the vigorous enemy attacks beginning on 13 November against the right wing of the army, the date of the attack was still undecided.[532] The

---

[531] Halder, *Diaries*, 1294–5 (11 Nov. 1941). On the problem of the evaluation of reconnaissance results by the operations department of the Army High Command cf. Reinhardt, *Moskau*, 203–4.

[532] For this reason FM von Kluge had to accept some criticism as C.-in-C. of Fourth Army. Cf. Reinhardt, *Moskau*, 157–8.

echelon form of the attack left long flanks of the attacking units exposed and gave the enemy command the opportunity to move troops to threatened sectors.[533]

(iii) THE FAILURE OF THE SECOND OFFENSIVE

At first the attack on the two wings of the army group made surprisingly good progress. In the sector of Ninth Army, Armoured Group 3 and the parts of Armoured Group 4 advancing with it achieved a breakthrough south of the Volga reservoir on 18 November, which opened the way for a further attack on Klin and Solnechnogorsk on the Moscow–Kalinin–Leningrad railway line. When three more army corps of Armoured Group 4 began their advance, the prospects for a breakthrough on a broad front north of the Smolensk–Moscow highway seemed good.

On the right wing Second Armoured Army attacked past Tula on the right. XXXXIII Army Corps, abutting Fourth Army, came under vigorous attack by Soviet forces and had to go on the defensive. This produced a 'pocket' with a possible future threat to the left flank of the attacking wedge. The situation on the right wing was similarly difficult. Second Army had to give its full attention to the situation on the northern boundary of Army Group South around Kursk and Tim, and advance on Voronezh. This left Guderian with only XXIV Armoured Corps for the spearhead of his attack on Kashira and Kolomna. Most of XXXXVII Armoured Corps was occupied with maintaining contact with Second Army. The weak LIII Army Corps (two divisions) was to widen the base of the attack and protect the spearhead from threats to its flanks.

At first Second Armoured Army considered that the position of the enemy, though not its own supply situation, favoured an advance.[534] On 19 November Guderian had himself informed of the condition and further expectations of XXIV Armoured Corps. There and in the operations area of LIII Army Corps enemy resistance had begun to stiffen with the arrival of new Soviet divisions, slowing down the German advance. Additional problems were caused by the lack of sufficient ice-studs for the tanks. Such supply problems, which the assistant chief of staff (operations) of the armoured army summarized on 18 November, were the main reason for Guderian's request for an early decision by the commander-in-chief of the army with regard to the indispensable objectives and thus the end of that particular phase of the offensive.[535]

[533] Cf. sect. II.II.13 (Hoffmann); Reinhardt, *Moskau*, 153 ff., with the reaction of the Soviet leaders; Chales de Beaulieu, *Hoepner*, 210 ff., viewed from the perspective of Armd. Group 4.

[534] Situation assessment in war diary of second Armd. Army, 16, 18 Nov. 1941, BA-MA RH 21-2/v. 244. According to this source 317 m.³ of fuel had been arriving daily since 1 Nov., while four times that amount was considered necessary to build up reserves. For the offensive it was therefore possible to create only three or four units of consumption because the motorized divisions received no more allocation. On 18 Nov. Brauchitsch felt that the prospects of reaching Moscow were fading; Halder, however, still considered it a 'question of will-power': Halder, *Diaries*, 1302.

[535] Assessment of the supply situation by staff officer in charge of supply and administration, 19 Nov. 1941, BA-MA RH 21-2/v. 244.

On 20 November Guderian informed Army Group Centre that newly arrived enemy forces, Siberian divisions 'keen for battle and well trained', were being unloaded on the eastern flank of his armoured group. He wanted, in addition to the divisions of LIII Army Corps, to send 18th Armoured Division into action against them, but that division was tied down on the southern flank. Parts of the motorized divisions could not be used because of the lack of fuel. Thus 4th Armoured Division had to be left to attack eastward, which weakened the spearhead of XXIV Armoured Corps. From these facts Guderian concluded that it was doubtful whether he would be able to fulfil his assigned task of gaining a crossing of the Oka at Kashira. He wished to inform Bock personally of this situation. The following day he suggested that Lieutenant-General Paulus or a representative (from the Army High Command) should also be consulted, as he wished to raise the subject of a change of operational objectives. The armoured army was still attacking successfully and was able to destroy the two Siberian divisions. There the enemy was reported to be withdrawing and had abandoned Stalinogorsk in front of 4th Armoured Division; the crossing of the Don near Donskoe was planned for 24 November. However, the losses suffered by 112th and 167th Infantry Divisions were so heavy that their total exhaustion had to be expected.[536] On 21 November XXIV Armoured Corps was able to capture the rail junction of Uzlovaya on the Moscow–Rostov line and, after crossing the Shat, secured its freedom of movement towards Venev.

These reports evidently gave Halder the impression that the offensive was proceeding well and that alarming reports about the condition of the troops need not be taken too seriously. On 21 November, probably after receiving the report from Army Group Centre about Guderian's intention to raise the question of the next objectives and the necessity of reaching them, he suspected that Guderian was preparing to remove the mobile units from the fighting for rehabilitation, which would mean suspending the war of movement.[537] Halder therefore refused Guderian's request, submitted on 24 November through the army group. Nor did Halder change his instructions after hearing the direct oral report of the Army High Command liaison officer with Second Armoured Army, Lieutenant-Colonel von Kahlden.[538] Before taking up winter positions, it was to defeat the enemy facing it.

---

[536] According to a report of LIII Army Corps, 22 Nov. 1941, the two divisions suffered losses of about 200 dead and 500 wounded within three days: BA-MA RH 21-2/v. 244. On 23 Nov. 112th Inf. Div. reported 20 rifles as the average fighting strength of its companies: ibid. 135.

[537] Halder, *Diaries*, 1308 (21 Nov. 1941). Guderian undoubtedly also had this idea, but for him the main danger was that the German forces would 'bleed to death'. This induced him to report the imminent exhaustion of their ability to attack, which at the end of November, with a temperature of −35 °C, was not too soon. Cf. H.Gr. Mitte/Ia, KTB, 21 Nov. 1941, BA-MA RH 19 II/121; Reinhardt, *Moskau*, 156–7; Guderian, *Panzer Leader*, 119–20 (here is the origin of the error that 23 Nov. 1941 was the actual date of the conference, a mistake frequently found in the literature, although in fact it was only the originally scheduled date); Bock, *Tagebuch*, 148 (23 Nov. 1941), BA-MA N 22/9; Halder, *Diaries*, 1312.

[538] Report by Kahlden: Halder, *Diaries*, 1313 (24 Nov. 1941), complete in war diary of Second Armd. Army, 24 Nov. 1941, pp. 138 ff., BA-MA RH 21-2/v. 244.

Halder was receiving numerous complaints about the condition of the troops and the conclusions to be drawn with regard to operations. The general tenor of his decisions and orders—to push the attack forward in any case and under all circumstances—therefore requires an interpretation, which at this point will apply especially to the sector of Army Group Centre and Second Armoured Army.

After the first successes of the offensive on 18 and 19 November on the wings, Hitler, Halder, and the commander-in-chief of Army Group Centre were convinced that, with sufficient vigour, the envisaged objectives could be reached. Bock and Halder were profoundly convinced that one last great effort would destroy the enemy facing them and that 'victory will go to the side that sticks it out longer'. Imbued with this certainty, Halder jotted down the points of his oral report to Hitler on 19 November; he envisaged, as an operational guideline on the southern wing, that Second Army and Second Armoured Army should continue their attack as early as possible, independently of the start of the attack by Fourth Army.[539] In spite of the weakness of the German troops, Halder believed, the enemy could not withstand the attack. Hitler reacted to this judgement by expressing the wish that the operations against Moscow should be conducted in such a way that partial attacks would ensure that individual enemy units were smashed and not just pushed back, a directive already issued after the encirclement at Smolensk, which was an essential part of his 'study' of 22 August, and which had led to 'short' encirclement movements west of the Dnieper in the area of Army Group South. This tactic involved an acceptance of delays. But the more distant objectives of Yaroslavl, Rybinsk, and Vologda would also be kept in sight, the supply situation and the weather permitting. However, Hitler did not insist that these objectives had to be reached; it would be enough, he believed, if Vologda and Gorkiy were reached at the end of May 1942.[540]

As Fourth Army remained behind, the operation which the Army High Command ordered Army Group Centre to carry out on 20 November seemed to be an envelopment in which the wings played the major role.[541] Field Marshal von Bock, who by an extreme effort of will still agreed verbally with Halder in his assessment of the prospects of victory but who clearly realized the position of Fourth Army and the resulting danger to the inner wings of the attacking armies, vigorously protested against this order, as neither the forces of the armoured formations after reaching the envisaged line nor those of Fourth Army were sufficient for such encirclement movements. Meanwhile, on 19 November, Guderian had expressed his doubts as to whether, in view of

[539] Halder, *Diaries*, 1304 (19 Nov. 1941).

[540] Following fierce enemy attacks after 13 Nov., Fourth Army did not begin its advance: cf. sect. II.1.1(*f*) at n. 532. Hitler's wish, passed on as a directive from the Wehrmacht High Command to the Army High Command and then transmitted to Army Group Centre (cf. OKH/GenStdH/Op.Abt. (IM) No. 1652/41, 19 Nov. 1941, BA-MA RH 2/v. 1327, p. 58), mentions only the northern wing and Hitler's request that Army Group Centre should soon express its views on these ideas. On Hitler's timetable cf. Halder, *Diaries*, 1304 (19 Nov. 1941).

[541] Bock, Tagebuch, 144–5 (20 Nov. 1941), BA-MA N 22/9.

the supply situation and the considerable wear and tear to which vehicles had been subjected, Kashira could still be reached. Bock too doubted that on the left wing of the army group the attack could be continued eastward beyond the Istra. The moving up of the only reserve division of the army group to the front on 21 November, together with his comparison of the existing situation to the battle of the Marne in 1914 (the failure of the younger Moltke), testifies to his strange, ambivalent attitude, which reflected a final effort with all remaining reserves rather than optimistic expectations of victory.[542] At the same time he refused to yield to the urgings of Halder, Hoepner, and Guderian to give Fourth Army a clear order to begin the attack with its right wing.[543] Halder's views on the war situation at this time were reflected in a conference of his general-staff officer in charge of supplies and administration with the deputy chiefs of staff of the eastern front on 23 November.[544] He believed that, as a consequence of the German successes against the Soviet Union, Britain had lost her 'sword on the Continent' and had been pushed back to the periphery—the Siberian part of Russia, the Middle East, and North Africa. The Soviet Union had been decisively beaten, but not yet destroyed.[545] He concluded that Germany would never again have an army like that of June 1941, but neither would it be necessary. Army armament programmes would have to yield priority to those of the Luftwaffe and the navy; in the area of personnel, the war would be continued with convalescents and the age-group of 1922. Halder concluded that the main effort of the war was shifting to the maintenance of morale and holding out economically. Again he described the Caucasus, the Volga line, and Vologda (with the railway line to Archangel) as the objectives for 1942. The operational objectives to be reached before the onset of winter depended on the resilience of the troops, but mere gains of territory were not decisive: 'Whether Moscow is encircled or not' would 'not decide the course of the war; the Army High Command does not insist on taking Moscow.'

These views must have greatly surprised the representatives of the eastern front. Halder informed Second Armoured Army that the structure of the Soviet forces was creaking and groaning under the German attack and that it was important not to relent. Strong enemy forces still had to be annihilated by individual blows in 1941. In conclusion he repeated his faith in the words of

[542] Ibid. 145 ff. (21 Nov. 1941); cf. *Der Weltkrieg 1914 bis 1918*, iv. 533 ff. (14 Sept. 1914).

[543] Bock, Tagebuch, 148 ff. (23 Nov. 1941).

[544] Detailed notes of representative of staff officer in charge of supply and administration of Second Armd. Army, 25 Nov. 1941, BA-MA RH 21-2/v. 257; Halder, *Diaries*, 1312 (23 Nov. 1941). The qualification in n. 2 of the latter—concessions to the listeners in the sense of Hitler's 'official view'—refers to his expectation 'that the realization of the fact that the two groups of belligerents cannot annihilate each other will bring about a negotiated peace', ibid. 1305. This remark was not particularly explosive. More important was his statement on 23 Nov. that the enemy had been decisively beaten.

[545] According to the above-mentioned report of the staff officer in charge of supply and administration of Second Armd. Army, Halder used the word 'demolished' (*abserviert*); his reasoning: 'which is likewise not to be expected, as he [the Russian] has all of Asia behind him.'

Field Marshal von Bock: 'We are in a situation like the battle of the Marne.' The battle must be continued until the inner strength of the Red Army was broken. At the same time, however, the German army must recover its own fighting strength. How that should be done was a matter for the commanders-in-chief of the army groups. Combining economical use of remaining forces and executing necessary advances were more difficult than operational decisions. The influence of Hitler's views and guidelines here is unmistakable; a few months earlier Halder would not have voiced such opinions.

In spite of its continued advance eastward, the command of Army Group Centre was well aware that the bulk of its troops would have to spend the coming winter in open country and under constant threat of enemy attack. On 10 November 1941 it had therefore issued 'Guidelines for the conduct of fighting in winter and special characteristics of the winter war in Russia'.[546] It was assumed that the construction of a strong defensive line in a continuous front was not possible. Only at certain strategic points were positions in depth to be established. In other areas the defence would make use of fixed strong points but would otherwise have to be conducted with mobile tactics. Most attacks by the Red Army were expected to be in the form of actions by strong formations along roads and railway lines, probably supported by tanks and armoured trains. Away from roads, attacks by ski-troops using tanks with snow tracks to achieve penetrations of up to 100 kilometres were expected. In addition, partisan operations and air attacks could be expected. Strong groups of German troops were to be kept in reserve for rest and training in the system of strong points, which was still to be constructed. Laying up of supplies and the securing of the rear areas with all transport installations and depots were to be begun immediately.

This order assumed that the military situation in the rear areas would be sufficiently stable to permit the use of at least a considerable part of the construction units and sappers to build emplacements and strong points. But the combat situation in the second phase of the attack on Moscow required the use of everyone capable of bearing arms; units could scarcely be spared for other tasks, quite apart from the shortage of necessary materials, especially timber, which had to be brought up over considerable distances. All commanders realized that construction only now beginning had to be carried out with all available resources if the positions were to be ready before the onset of hard frosts.

The clash between the measures ordered and daily tactical necessity was striking. The latter exhausted the troops, made impossible the laying up of supplies for an effective defence, and forced German commanders to abandon even half-way tenable positions and troop quarters. On the other hand, commanders were able to refer to the measures ordered for the preparation of secure winter quarters, which gave them a certain latitude in their decisions.

---

[546] H.Gr. Mitte/Ia No. 2570/41, 10 Nov. 1941, BA-MA RH 21-2/v. 257.

The commander-in-chief of Fourth Army, Field Marshal von Kluge, has been accused of using the heavy defensive fighting to avoid pushing the two corps on his right wing into attack and of leaving them in their positions, which had been developed over the weeks. The same accusation was made against the commander-in-chief of Sixth Army. Both were subjected to sharp criticism by Halder, and both eventually began their attacks against their own better judgement.[547] Both, however, were appointed commanders-in-chief of army groups at the peak of the crisis, while two generals of armoured forces, Guderian and Hoepner, who, against their pronounced sense of responsibility, had driven their soldiers on to the point of exhaustion, were replaced or relieved of their commands in disgrace.[548]

On 25 November, however, in compliance with the directive received from the army group, Guderian ordered the preparation of a forward line along the Don, Shat, and Upa rivers.[549] The 'objective Kashira', the principle purpose of which was the severing of the railway line between Moscow and Rostov, was downgraded to effective destruction of the line by a demolition party, although this did not in fact succeed. The only operationally important objective remained the capture of Tula, especially because the flanks of the attacking spearheads were becoming exposed as a result of the failure of Fourth Army to advance rapidly and of the diverging direction of Second Army, which was moving primarily towards Kursk and Voronezh. In addition to eliminating the threat to the exposed inner flanks of Second Armoured Army and Fourth Army, the capture of Tula would provide the armoured army not only with a jumping-off point for future attacks but also with a resupply and maintenance base.[550] Having reached the most forward point of the attack by Second Armoured Army just south of Kashira on 25 November, Guderian halted his advance in that direction because of fierce enemy counter-attacks. Again he asked for 296th Infantry Division so that, together with XXXXIII Army Corps and XXIV Armoured Corps, he could encircle Tula. On 27 November he therefore demanded the immediate start of the attack by the right wing of Fourth Army, when it became evident that the attack by XXXXIII Army

---

[547] Halder, *Diaries*, 1307–8, 1315 (21, 26 Nov. 1941); regarding Reichenau, ibid. 1312 (23 Nov. 1941) and, *expressis verbis*, 1325 (29 Nov. 1941). On Kluge: Chales de Beaulieu, *Hoepner*, 210–11. On the problem of the crises between the neighbouring armies cf. Reinhardt, *Moskau*, 156 ff., as well as the observations in this section.

[548] Cf. Chales de Beaulieu, *Hoepner*, 236, and Bücheler, *Hoepner*, 169 ff.; also sect. II.1.1(g) at n. 601.

[549] Pz.AOK 2/Ia No. R 346/41, BA-MA RH 21-2/v. 257. Not until 23 Nov. was the question of the prepared defensive lines to the rear of Army Group Centre presented to Halder by Greiffenberg. Halder left the planning of its course to the army group: Bock, Tagebuch, 148–9 (23 Nov. 194); Halder, *Diaries*, 1312 (23 Nov. 1941).

[550] Guderian, *Panzer Leader*, 122; Walde, *Guderian*, 150 ff.; Reinhardt, *Moskau*, 166–7. On 21 Nov. Second Armd. Army demanded that it be given the army group reserve (296th Inf. Div.) and the right of disposal over 56th Inf. Div. on the left boundary in order to protect the thrust by XXIV Armd. Corps and to be able to advance on Tula and Serpukhovo if the right wing of Fourth Army were forced to halt. The task of the last-mentioned unit was originally in this direction: BA-MA RH 21-2/v. 244; Bock, Tagebuch, 148–9 (23 Nov. 1941), BA-MA N 22/9.

Corps was hardly making any progress. Bock, however, ordered the armoured army to fight the battle of Tula alone and then, renouncing the objectives of reaching the Oka and Kashira, ordered it to cover its position towards the north and east.[551]

Yet even after a regrouping the encirclement of Tula did not succeed, although the city was effectively isolated on 3 December. Meanwhile the temperature had dropped to $-35\,°C$; vehicles and weapons broke down and air support could no longer be provided. Even with a last great effort the city could not be encircled and captured against the resistance of the defenders and the attacks mounted by Zhukov's forces from the north and east. On 5 December Guderian reported that he had had to break off the operation.[552] Three days later he summarized his reasons for this decision in a report to the army group and emphasized that it was more important to preserve his remaining fighting strength than to continue the attempt to capture Tula, which, even if it were captured, would be costly to defend. He received permission to withdraw to the prepared line along the Don, Shat, and Upa, as only there would he have time to regroup for the winter war and to replenish his forces.[553]

The withdrawal of the armoured army in individual sectors, with its equipment, failed because of a lack of towing-vehicles, nor were there any prepared winter positions to which the Germans could withdraw. The men would have to build their own positions, if time permitted. Guderian still assumed that the destruction of enemy supply-lines and buildings which could be used as quarters, in addition to the expulsion of the civilian population to the east, would make it possible to hold the positions. But for that it was essential that adequate supplies were available and that neighbouring sectors of the front would hold.

The decisions of Second Army, to the right of the armoured army, were to a considerable degree dependent on the left wing of Army Group South, Sixth Army under Reichenau.[554] Because of the need to protect Kursk and to capture Voronezh, the weak Second Army could neither provide dependable flank cover for Second Armoured Army nor close the gap between itself and Army Group South. On 1 December, with the consent of the army group

[551] The assignment of 296th Inf. Div. the next day inevitably weakened the right flank of Second Army: Bock, Tagebuch, 151 (27 Nov. 1941), BA-MA N 22/9.

[552] On 25 Nov. XXIV Armd. Corps was already of the opinion that its forces were insufficient; on 30 Nov. it reported a strength of 72 tanks; because of the problems with their vehicles the motorized infantry companies were able to transport a fighting strength of only 70 men: 2. Pz.Armee/Ia, KTB, 5 Dec. 1941, BA-MA RH 21-2/v. 244.

[553] Report Second Armd. Army headquarters, 8 Dec. 1941 (filed under 5 Dec.), ibid.; Bock, Tagebuch, 161 ff. (5–8 Dec. 1941), BA-MA N 22/9; army order No. 24 for occupying winter position, 2. Pz.Armee/Ia, KTB, 6 Dec. 1941, BA-MA RH 21-2/v. 177.

[554] Sixth Army, however, was urged by Rundstedt and First Armd. Army to push southward to support the attack on Rostov (cf. Map II.1.1). These displacements, which also became a permanent condition on the boundary to Army Group South, resulted in arguments about front widths and strengths.

command, it therefore abandoned all further attacks. The day before Bock had warned against advancing too far on Guderian's right flank, where enemy resistance was slight.[555] Thus Second Army halted its advance on 1 December and began to prepare defensive positions.

In the course of the fighting on the northern wing and in the central sector of Army Group Centre since 23 November, when the road between Moscow and Leningrad was cut, the attack by Armoured Groups 3 and 4 had made only slow progress against stubborn enemy resistance. In the end the spearhead of Armoured Group 4 advanced to about 30 kilometres from the Kremlin. In addition to the supply problems already mentioned, the separation from the corps of Fourth Army extended the right flank of the armoured group and deprived it of the necessary strength. Developments on the evening of 27 November were decisive, when Armoured Group 3 had to abandon the bridgehead over the Moskva canal near Yakhroma, which had been captured by 7th Armoured Division, and thus the belief, which had sustained the German forces, that the collapse of the north-western defences of Moscow was imminent, disappeared. On 29 November Field Marshal von Bock reported to Halder that the attack would have to be halted unless a decision was achieved within the next few days. In view of the Red Army's ability to draw on its enormous reserves, which he now recognized, and the possibility that the attack by the northern wing would not achieve a breakthrough, he feared that the situation might become a 'second Verdun', for which he was not prepared to accept the responsibility.[556]

In the sector of Fourth Army, clearly reacting to accusations from neighbouring armies that he was failing to support them and was preventing a successful attack on Moscow, Kluge finally decided to start the attack of the corps on his right wing. In spite of his reservations, Bock agreed and reported that the enemy was withdrawing forces from the central and southern front of Fourth Army. He believed that the high command attached great importance to the attack, 'even if it means risking the last strength of troops completely'. Halder confirmed that 'that is also the view of the Army High Command'.[557]

With the attack by Fourth Army, Hitler again saw the possibility of encircling large enemy formations near Moscow. This shocked Bock, who, like Guderian and other commanders-in-chief, doubted that the Army High Command had properly submitted his reports on the condition of his troops to Hitler. He demanded the immediate bringing up of reserves if the army group was to hold the front through the winter. If no reserves were available and if supply shipments could not be considerably increased, a withdrawal to a shorter front better suited to defence in winter should be ordered immedi-

---

[555] Bock, Tagebuch, 148 ff. (23, 30 Nov. 1941), BA-MA N 22/9; Reinhardt, *Moskau*, 168–9.

[556] Bock, Tagebuch, 153–4 (29 Nov. 1941), BA-MA N 22/9; Halder, *Diaries*, 1323 (29 Nov. 1941, evening situation).

[557] Bock, Tagebuch, 153–4 (29 Nov. 1941), BA-MA N 22/9. On the morning of 29 Nov. Bock still had reservations about this attack. Cf. Halder, *Diaries*, 1325 (29 Nov. 1941).

ately.[558] On 3 December Bock wanted to ascertain whether his reports had reached Hitler, as he was unable to understand enquiries he had received over the past few days about the start of the attack by Fourth Army. Nevertheless, he reported to Jodl that he still hoped, with the help of Armoured Group 3, to keep the flank of V Army Corps sufficiently free to enable it to advance to the south. The order to attack along the whole front was still in force, but the moment was approaching when the strength of the troops would be spent. If the attack were halted then, a switch to defence would be very difficult.[559]

The same day Kluge reported that he would have to break off his attack and pull the troops of LVII Armoured and XX Army Corps back to their starting-positions. On 3 December Armoured Group 4 also reported that it had reached 'the end' of its strength and proposed ordering the establishment of a defensive line along the Istra. The armoured group did this on its own initiative, as Bock was clearly waiting until the Army High Command and Hitler had given their consent. Like Guderian, Hoepner wrote a report in which he justified the change to a defensive strategy and in particular pointed to the repeated misjudgement of the situation of the German forces and that of the enemy.[560]

Army Group Centre believed that with the attack being halted it would have to withdraw in the face of local enemy counter-thrusts but that it would otherwise be able to perform its withdrawal, grounded on tactical and supply considerations, without being exposed to significant pressure from pursuing enemy forces. Physically and psychologically the troops had reached the limit of their endurance; signs of apathy were becoming apparent. The cold weather, inadequate clothing, lack of food, difficulties in caring for the sick and wounded, heavy losses—all these were factors affecting the reliability and combat-readiness of the individual soldier. In addition, serious losses of weapons and equipment and a lack of towing-vehicles and draught-animals also paralysed the German advance.[561] All these factors endangered fighting morale, quite apart from the effects of enemy action.

Now, however, the Red Army began its counter-offensive. Any thought of rest and rehabilitation for the German troops had to be completely abandoned and the soldier's will to survive transformed into a readiness to make sacrifices in situations where the purpose of the sacrifice was not so clear as it had been to many in the early phase of the offensive against Moscow.

Field Marshal von Bock attempted to explain to himself the origins of the 'present crisis' after a vigorous attack by the Red Army had achieved

---

[558] Bock, *Tagebuch*, 156 ff. (1 Dec. 1941), BA-MA N 22/9.

[559] Ibid. 159 ff. (3 Dec. 1941). It is difficult to understand why with this report, which still testifies to his fighting spirit though it had long since been overtaken by events, Bock attempted to give Jodl the impression that this was really 'the eleventh hour'.

[560] Chales de Beaulieu, *Hoepner*, 213; Reinhardt, *Moskau*, 164–5.

[561] Reinhardt, *Moskau*, 164 n. 160, 172 ff.; personnel losses, ibid. 523 (annexe 6). Personnel losses of the German army in the east up to 31 Dec. 1941 are in *KTB OKW* i. 1120 ff; losses of Waffen-SS ibid. 1115–16.

penetrations during the withdrawal movements on 7 December 1941, losses through frostbite had increased, and it had become clear that troops envisaged for the creation of new units in Germany could not be released from the eastern front.[562] Bock concluded that the autumnmud, the failure of the railways, and underestimation of the enemy's stamina had led to the present situation. The mud had prevented the exploitation of the success at Vyazma. Bock concluded that the demands of the military leaders that the attacks be continued were justified as long as they believed that enemy forces were on the verge of collapse. But that assumption had been a mistake, and the army group was now forced to go on the defensive under extremely difficult conditions. In his analysis, however, Bock carefully avoided addressing the question of his own share of the blame for the disaster, and that of the chief of the Army General Staff.

(g) The Repulse of the Winter Offensive of the Red Army

(i) ASSESSMENT OF THE SITUATION AND DIRECTIVES FOR THE WINTER WAR

In mid-November 1941 the Red Army began its first counter-offensives on the outermost wings of the front with very long-range operational objectives. These offensives, which forced First Armoured Army to abandon Rostov in the south and Sixteenth Army to evacuate Tikhvin in the north, where aimed primarily at recapturing strategically important positions. They were not part of a total, co-ordinated offensive by the Red Army to destroy the invading German army.[563] The attacks on the armies of Army Group Centre were intended primarily to relieve pressure on the threatened capital. The counter-offensive that began on the right wing of Fourth Army on 13 November had as its main objective the shattering of the German attack front. The Red Army used the time thereby gained to bring up reserves, which were integrated into the offensive without their deployment being detected by German reconnaissance. As late as 4 December the department Foreign Armies East in the Army General Staff believed that the enemy forces facing Army Group Centre were not in a position to mount a large-scale attack 'at present' without significant reinforcements.[564] On 5 December the expected enemy attacks began in the sector of Ninth Army and those of Armoured Groups 4 and 3. These attacks and the realization that the enemy was bringing up reinforcements made a withdrawal to winter positions, and the resulting reduction of casualties,

---

[562] Bock, *Tagebuch*, 164–5 (7 Dec. 1941), BA-MA N 22/9.

[563] Cf. sects. II.1.1(c) and II.1.1(d) above; sect. II.11.13 (Hoffmann); Reinhardt, *Moskau*, 192–3.

[564] OKH/GenStdH/Abt. Fr. H. Ost, situation report east No. 172, 4 Dec. 1941, BA-MA RH 19 II/127. These daily reports should be read along with the detailed printed assessments of the department, here 'Die Kriegswehrmacht der UdSSR, Stand Dezember 1941 [Wartime fighting forces of the USSR, as of Dec. 1941]', pts. I and II. These reports contain findings on the total military potential of the Soviet Union gained through long observation.

urgently necessary. The decline in fighting strength, the lack of any hope of receiving replacements in time, and the exhaustion of the soldiers, which was approaching apathy in heavily attacked sectors, required immediate decisions.[565]

On 5 December, therefore, the army group command informed Fourth Army and the armoured groups of the envisaged withdrawal line. The withdrawal, which it was estimated would require two nights, should be possible, upon receipt of a special order, as of 6 December. The start of this 'preparatory measure' was made dependent on a new directive from Hitler.[566]

On 5 December Second Armoured Army too received approval from the army group for a withdrawal behind the Don–Shat line. Thus in the sector of Army Group Centre preparations had already been made even before Halder discussed the war situation in detail with Hitler on 6 December 1941.[567]

This conference was held primarily to discuss organizational and personnel questions concerning the preparation of the army for new operations in the spring of 1942. The basis for the discussion was a paper submitted by the Army General Staff, from which Hitler at first discussed only the figures on German and enemy casualties.[568] In his view a comparison of these figures alone did not reflect the real fighting strength of the two armies. He therefore had no intention of taking political steps to end the war, as Dr Fritz Todt, minister for weapons and munitions, had suggested in view of the condition of the army.[569] Hitler observed that Germany did not lack soldiers, but rather workers. Therefore Russian prisoners of war were to be employed in factories, mines, and steel mills to free Germans for military service. Additional reserves for the eastern front could be obtained by replacing divisions in the east with divisions from the west. But this must not lead to a reduction in the number of units in the west or the Balkans. On the contrary, he envisaged one or two armoured divisions for Norway to repel a possible Anglo-American landing. German soldiers might also be needed in Croatia.

With regard to the operational situation, Hitler and Halder seem to have

[565] Situation assessment by army headquarters and armd. group, 3, 4 Dec. 1941, to Army Group Centre, BA-MA RH 19 II/127; report of Second Army headquarters, 5 Dec., on the line still to be reached by attack, ibid. 202.

[566] Ibid. 199. Although Bock had feared 'another Verdun' from 19 Nov. and reported heavy losses on 1 Dec., Halder still maintained that a last effort had to be made to subdue the enemy. If it became absolutely clear that this was not possible, new decisions would have to be taken. On 4 Dec. the chief of staff of the army group still saw no need to halt the attack, except in the case of Fourth Army. Bock intended to report on 4 Dec. on whether a withdrawal would be necessary: Halder, *Diaries*, 1322 ff. (29 Nov. 1941); Bock, Tagebuch on dates given, BA-MA N 22/9.

[567] Halder, *Diaries*, 1339 (6 Dec. 1941).

[568] Ibid. The 'draft' mentioned there was very probably a draft of the Army High Command's 'Weisung für die Aufgaben des Ostheeres im Winter 1941/42' [Directive on the tasks of the army in the east in the winter of 1941–2]. Cf. *KTB OKW* i. 1076 ff. (108). Of the five annexes only the assessment of the enemy's situation of 1 Dec. 1941 is printed there (ibid. 1075). For a complete copy, unfortunately without map, see BA-MA RH 2/v. 1327, pp. 60–88.

[569] Cf. sect. II.vi.5 (Müller).

been in basic agreement; subsequently Halder ensured the vigorous execution of the orders they had decided upon and was if anything even more consistent in this respect than Hitler.

In the sector of Army Group North, the full encirclement of Leningrad was to be completed; in the south the Don was to be crossed near Rostov while the winter weather permitted. In the centre Hitler had no objections to shortening the front, i.e. to a limited withdrawal, after new positions had been prepared.[570]

It is remarkable that, although this conference took place at a time when the most alarming reports were being received from the eastern front, the actual situation and the urgency of taking a decision were not mentioned.[571] But the reports of 6 and 7 December on the situation near Tikhvin, especially those concerning strong enemy penetrations near Moscow, caused Halder to conclude that local commanders should be given freedom of decision: that is, withdrawals should be permitted at threatened points.[572] The commander-in-chief of the army settled disputes in this area with Hitler, who on 8 December issued Directive No. 39 on the conduct of the fighting.[573] This directive began with the observation that the surprisingly early winter and the supply problems it had caused had made it necessary to end the offensive and go on the defensive. The aim of this defence was to retain areas operationally and economically important to the enemy. Moreover, the German troops should be given the opportunity to recover their strength and prepare for offensive operations in the coming year. For this purpose the bulk of the army was to occupy a defensive line to be determined by the commander-in-chief of the army. This line would permit the removal of individual units and troops. In recognition of the impossibility of constructing and holding a rigid defensive line, positions were to be built behind the front, to which the troops were not to be withdrawn until after they had been completed. It was also ordered that withdrawals from individual sectors of the front were to be co-ordinated with the situation as a whole. This meant that, in the event of enemy breakthrough attempts, positions had to be held as long as was necessary to avoid the encirclement and thus the loss of individual units.

The course of the defensive line was to be determined by supply-routes; supply difficulties to be expected in the spring were to be taken into account by stockpiling provisions in well-protected strong points. Lines behind salients and rear positions were to be fortified immediately with the help of all available labour.

---

[570] Halder, *Diaries*, 1339 (6 Dec. 1941).

[571] Soviet camouflage measures and the sending of newly raised and brought-up units into action without prolonged assembly periods prevented the preparations for the attack from being detected in time. The decisive factor was, however, the complete misjudgement of the remaining fighting power of the Red Army and its equipment. Halder did not take into consideration basically correct assessments by Foreign Armies East in the above-mentioned 'Kriegswehrmacht der UdSSR' (see n. 564). Cf. also Reinhardt, *Moskau*, 197 ff. (on Soviet preparations) and 202–3.

[572] Halder, *Diaries*, 1340 (7 Dec. 1941).   [573] *Hitler's War Directives*, No. 39 (8 Dec. 1941).

The detailed directive of the commander-in-chief of the army was in line with this part of the directive of the Wehrmacht High Command.[574] It stated as a basic guideline: 'Reconnaissance and preparation of lines of resistance are precautionary measures to be taken by commanders. They do not affect the determination to accomplish the tasks to be fulfilled after the winter in an offensive manner.'

Already on 6 December, before the extent of the enemy offensive had been realized, Hitler had discussed with Halder attacks to prepare for the coming spring offensive. Army Group South was to occupy Rostov and the Donets bend, conquer Sevastopol in the Crimea, and then transfer the Eleventh Army forces freed by this operation to First Armoured Army.[575]

After receiving additional attack units, Army Group North was to complete the encirclement of Leningrad, establish contact with the Finns, and then go on the defensive in this sector of the front as well.

Both the orders regarding defensive actions and those for limited offensives completely ignored reality. Neither sufficient time nor adequate forces were available to build a fortified line, whose general course had been set out only on 8 December. The plans of attack were far beyond the actual capacity of the army. Under these circumstances there could be no question of thinning out the front to permit parts of the army to rest and resupply in rear areas. The bringing up of replacements and new units was primarily intended to maintain the operational ability of the army in 1942, even in the event of heavy losses. Thus, except for convalescent battalions and battalions in waiting, which were to leave for the front immediately so that all would arrive by 15 January 1942, Hitler at first promised only infantry divisions and an armoured division from the west, which were to be designated after the army had submitted a comprehensive plan for the organization and deployment of forces.[576]

Nor was it possible to promise a radical improvement of the transport system, an essential factor in the conduct of any defence, to relieve pressure on the front. This situation was made more difficult by the fact that security and supply units had already had to send considerable parts of their fighting units to the front, although the efforts of partisan groups to paralyse the transport system would have made a strengthening of these forces necessary.[577]

[574] OKH/GenStdH/Op.Abt. (Ia) BA-MA RH 2/v. 1327, V. Eisenbahnnetz und Widerstandslinien [Railway network and lines of resistance]. Both directives were probably based on preparatory work by the operations department. Cf. n. 567 above and Halder, *Diaries*, 1333 (3 Dec. 1941, Heusinger).

[575] Army Group South expected this; in Directive No. 39 the decision was left open. Cf. sect. II.1.1(*c*) at n. 344.

[576] Questions of personnel replacement had been prepared by Halder; he rejected the call-up of the 1922 age-group in Jan. 1942 and demanded a limitation of deferments and a 'combing-out drive'. On 3 Dec. he expected three or four transports daily (of a total of 100 trains)—'however this may interfere with regular supply movements': Halder, *Diaries*, 1333 (3 Dec. 1941).

[577] The creation of 'local' security units was a result of the personnel shortage, at first at army level and with the commanders of rear areas. This was the beginning of a development that deviated completely from Hitler's orders and even led to such units being taken into the Wehrmacht. Cf. Hofmann, *Ostlegionen*, 11 ff.

As both directives were based on an already outdated assessment of the situation, they were basically illusory when they were issued. The withdrawals on all fronts had been begun under enemy pressure and on orders from army headquarters, and had only subsequently been approved by the army group commands and the Army High Command, or by Hitler.[578]

The measures taken by the individual armies for the winter—e.g. the construction of defensive positions by Fourth Army and the reconnaissance of fall-back positions by Second Armoured Army—had only local effects or could not be carried out because of a lack of construction personnel and engineering equipment.

Realizing that the two main efforts of the Soviet attack were directed against Army Group Centre, the Army High Command directed reserves to be assembled in the area of Ostashkov, which were at the same time intended to protect the long left flank. Behind the front between Belgorod and Orel mobile units due for rehabilitation were to be deployed in such a way that they could check attacks from the direction of Voronezh. The announcement of 'preparatory measures for a transfer of forces in the area of the army group' represented only a vague promise of help for the seriously threatened, weak Second Army.

The task of the Luftwaffe units remained the provision of defensive support for the army. Moreover, they were to use their available forces for attacking the enemy air force, the Soviet armament industry, and transportation lines.

The army groups were to submit their proposals on the planned forward line, the conduct of the fighting as a whole, and the envisaged lines of resistance with blocking-positions and lines behind salients by 15 December. With regard to plans for the coming year, the army group commands were informed that objectives would be determined largely by the extent to which the army in the east, and especially the mobile units, had been rehabilitated.

The army group commands, facing problems of operational and tactical defence which became more serious every day and which relegated any consideration of future offensive operations to the background, can only have understood this directive to mean that their reports about the seriousness of the situation had not received the attention they deserved. In Army Group Centre this attitude was not limited to Field Marshal von Bock's staff; the army commanders too, especially Colonel-General Guderian, openly expressed their doubts that their reports and requests were being presented to the commander-in-chief of the army and to Hitler in the original wording; they therefore demanded a personal appearance by Brauchitsch.[579]

---

[578] e.g. the withdrawals from Tikhvin and Rostov, and the above-mentioned movements of Army Group Centre. A system of pretence of systematic planning developed for what was in reality an attempt to channel forced retreats. This led to doubts about the reliability of reports and, on 26 Dec. 1941, to Hitler's first order about reporting back: BA-MA 16. Armee, 23468/8.

[579] Bock, Tagebuch, 166 (8 Dec. 1941), BA-MA N 22/9.

In view of the weakened condition of the German troops, they would have been able to fight as ordered only if the bulk of the Red Army had halted its advance; that, according to assessments of the enemy's situation, was not to be expected. Foreign Armies East estimated the strength of the Red Army facing the German front at 275 large units, among them 35 cavalry divisions and 40 armoured brigades. In addition, 24 large units were assumed to be on the Finnish front, 34 others in Asia and the Far East, and 22 in the Caucasus. The last-mentioned group was thus readily available for the front in the west. New units of undetermined size were assumed to be in the area of the lower Volga and the military districts of the Urals and Siberia. The organization of a Polish legion of six infantry divisions and an armoured brigade was also known. To these units had to be added the unknown number of army troops at the disposal of the Soviet leadership.[580]

More important than the units of the Red Army, which could not be precisely identified, was the German opinion of the Soviet military leaders, who had shown by their attack from the Rostov area that they were now able to concentrate their actions more effectively and give them additional force by adding heavy weapons, armour, and air units. Foreign Armies East expected only a limited change to positional warfare. On the contrary, the Red Army would continue to launch large-scale attacks during the winter. At the same time, a resumption of operations in the rear areas of the German troops by partisans and sabotage detachments had to be expected.

(ii) THE CRISES IN ARMY GROUP CENTRE AND THEIR EFFECTS ON THE COMMAND OF THE ARMY
(See the Annexe Volume, No. 20)

As mentioned above, the commander-in-chief of Army Group Centre, at the urging of the armies, had ordered the preparation of a line in the rear area on 5 December. Fourth Army had already constructed a winter position before the second phase of Operation Typhoon and, to judge by reproaches from its neighbouring units and from Halder, was reluctant to leave it. Most of the army group, however, had neither the forces nor the material to build winter positions capable of withstanding enemy counter-thrusts, let alone a large-scale attack. Field Marshal von Bock therefore concluded that a withdrawal over a large area was not possible, as it would not enable the troops to improve

---

[580] These figures in the 'enemy situation report', 1 Dec. 1941, *KTB OKW* i. 1075 (107). The expectations regarding the winter fighting of the Red Army were taken from statements by prisoners and the 'Regulation on operations by the troops in the winter', issued by the People's Commissariat for Defence of the USSR on 4 Mar. 1941, which was attached in translation to 'Kriegswehrmacht der UdSSR', a study of the Soviet forces as of Dec. 1941 (see n. 564 above): BA-MA RHD 18/243. The figures from the 'enemy situation report' of 1 Dec. 1941 were rather unreliable, as is evident from the detailed calculations in 'Kriegswehrmacht'. It was assumed that the Polish Legion wanted to 'cross the Caucasus' to fight on a British front, as it consisted of former prisoners (taken during the Red Army's advance into Poland in 1939). Cf. report of 9 Sept. 1941 (see text above at n. 437).

their position. There was thus no alternative to standing fast, but this was feasible only if replacements were provided immediately.[581]

The immediate problem, however, was to prevent a collapse of the front as a result of massive enemy penetrations. As reserves were lacking, all units were to be ordered not to disengage if that would endanger neighbouring units. This order, however, would quickly produce a conflict between the interests of the armies and of the armoured groups. Finding a solution required a strong hand and seemed to be possible only by subordinating some units to others. On 8 December Bock therefore transferred command authority over Armoured Groups 3 and 4 to the commander of Armoured Group 4, Colonel-General Hoepner.[582]

The withdrawal of the armoured groups was to be completed on 10 December. In this regard the transport centre of Klin, through which large numbers of troops would have to pass, was of extreme importance. South of Kalinin Ninth Army had to fight costly defensive battles; on the right wing of the army group, withdrawal battles of Second Army against attacks from the area of Tula and on the northern flank proceeded according to plan.

On 8 December enemy attacks became so strong that Bock had to consider a withdrawal on the left wing and as far as the centre of Fourth Army to a shortened line from Ruza via Volokolamsk to Staritsa, which would involve great losses of material and equipment.

All armies reported that the envisaged positions could not be held with available infantry forces. They—and especially Second Army, whose commander-in-chief, General Schmidt, was aware that his position was the most critical point of the entire front—demanded the immediate bringing up of reserves and replacements.[583] But now the enemy had seized the initiative and proceeded to drive a wedge into the army's thinly held front, which could lead to the encirclement of Army Group Centre and Army Group South. Such a concentrated thrust could not be stopped with seven weakened infantry divisions. If the railway line between Orel and Kursk were lost, the army would be split in two and could no longer be supplied. As a withdrawal of the entire army along the Orel–Bryansk railway was not feasible, Second Army command was of the opinion that, if Second Armoured Army retreated at the same

[581] Bock, Tagebuch, 121 ff. (5, 6 Dec. 1941), BA-MA N 22/9. Here 'holding the original position' meant holding the line ordered on 5 Dec. on the left wing of the army group and the Don–Shat position of Second Armd. Army, as well as consolidation of the positions of Second Army east of Kursk and Orel. Kluge advocated a slow withdrawal to gain time to prepare positions and remove artillery, wounded, and captured equipment properly: BA-MA RH 19 II/122, fos. 39 ff.

[582] H.Gr. Mitte/Ia, 8 Dec. 1941, BA-MA RH 19 II/122. This was very much against Reinhardt's wishes, for such transfers involved considerable inconvenience for the persons affected. Cf. Reinhardt, Moskau, 206–7; Chales de Beaulieu, Hoepner, 216.

[583] H.Gr. Mitte/Ia, KTB, 8–12 Dec. 1941, BA-MA RH 19 II/122, also for the following. Cf. the Annexe Vol., No. 20. The primary task of Second Army was to secure the vital transport routes for supplying the inner wings of Army Groups Centre and South. For an assessment of the situation of Second Army see BA-MA RH 19 II/127, fos. 273 ff. (10 Dec. 1941).

time, the army would have to be divided and the southern part would have to hold on to the railway line between Kursk and Konotop. In that case, however, the front could only be re-established much further west and with fresh forces. In consequence, Schmidt demanded the bringing up of at least four divisions. If the enemy succeeded in breaching the German front between Kursk and Orel, strong forces would be required to close the resulting gap. The breach of the front near Livny, reported the same day, underlined the seriousness of the situation.[584]

In addition to this extremely weak point on the front, the area around Kalinin, where strong penetrations had to be expected, was important for the Luftwaffe because of the large quantity of immobile material and non-air-worthy aircraft there. But even at this point help could be provided only in the form of an *ad hoc* machine-gun battalion of 255th Infantry Division.[585]

Altogether the commander-in-chief of Army Group Centre had to report to Halder that the army group was not able to check large-scale Soviet attacks at any point on its front. He also noted that abandoning large quantities of equipment and heavy weapons was tantamount to a defeat, and demanded that the true situation be reported to the commander-in-chief of the army. On 9 December it became clear that Second Armoured Army would be able to hold the envisaged line between the Don and the Shat for a short time only and that a withdrawal to a line from Korovinka via Dedilovo and Tula to Aleksin would then have to be planned. The focus of the defence in the sector of Fourth Army was Klin, where a counter-attack by 2nd Armoured Division was to bring the situation under control on 11 December.

On 9 December it became clear that the Red Army intended to exploit its penetrations operationally, push on to the rear communications of Second Army and Armoured Group 2, and capture Kalinin in the area of Ninth Army by an encirclement from the south.

This impression seemed to be confirmed by an intercepted radio message from the Soviet military council of the western front demanding the final rout of the 'Fascist rabble' and their merciless annihilation: 'We shall smash the Hitlerite hordes and bury them in snow-covered fields and forests near Moscow.'[586]

In considering the risks of foreseeable great losses of weapons and equipment in a rapid withdrawal or in 'sitting out' the enemy offensive with local containment actions and retreats, Bock and Kluge on 10 December came to the conclusion that the line proposed by the Army High Command was not far enough from the front and that fighting conditions there, compared with the present line, would be worse, as it could not be fortified quickly. The German

---

[584] The only immediately available unit was SS Brigade 1 from the area of the commander of the rear army area Centre. On 11 Dec. the staff of 299th Inf. Div. and two regiments of Army Group South were transferred to this area.

[585] H.Gr. Mitte/Ia, KTB, 8 Dec. 1941, BA-MA RH 19 II/122, pp. 53 ff.

[586] Report Fourth Army headquarters Ic, 9 Dec. 1941, BA-MA RH 19 II/127, fo. 270.

forces would therefore either have to fight where they were or carry out a large-scale withdrawal. Bock fully realized that a large-scale withdrawal might reach a dimension far beyond that for which he could accept military responsibility.[587] The commander-in-chief of the army, briefed orally by Halder, replied that both he and Hitler were aware of the difficult situation and that everything would be done to provide troops and supplies.[588]

In addition to the scant help to be obtained from bringing up weak reserves, the increasingly critical situation of Second Army required the intervention of parts of Second Armoured Army on 11 December. Bock therefore decided to place Second Army temporarily under the command of Second Armoured Army and thus to make Guderian responsible for holding the area.[589] This 'army group' was given the task of halting the enemy along the general line from Kursk to the areas around Novosil and Aleksin, if not sooner. The make shift system of filling gaps with practically immobile and exhausted troops along the entire front was bound to lead to a rapid collapse; moreover, individual units no longer had the mental or physical stamina to offer resistance, let alone counter-attack. On 13 December Field Marshal von Kluge added his support to a withdrawal in a single large movement, and to the abandoning of material if that were necessary to save the troops.[590]

During his visit to Bock's headquarters the same day, Brauchitsch confirmed that he was aware of all reports on the condition of the troops and agreed with Bock in his new view. There was nothing left but to give the order to withdraw; otherwise the army group would go to pieces. The following day Guderian presented his assessment of the situation to Brauchitsch in Roslavl and received permission to withdraw to the line between the Susha and the Oka. He initiated this movement immediately.[591] The result of this conversation, conducted in the absence of Field Marshal von Kluge, was evidently not co-ordinated with the army group command. There an order had been received from Hitler to propose a line which, in the opinion of the army group, could be held. He would then discuss it with Brauchitsch when he returned.[592]

[587] H.Gr. Mitte/Ia, KTB, 10 Dec. 1941, BA-MA RH 19 II/122, fo. 79—there also Bock's letter to the C.-in-C. of the army with the demand for immediate replacements.

[588] Ibid., fo. 87. A total of 7 convalescent battalions of 41 companies and 34 battalions in waiting (staffs) of 154 companies were to be sent to the front immediately, of which the divisions affected, in so far as they received replacements, were to be given one convalescent company and one company in waiting each. Moreover, after the survey of the Army High Command ordered in Directive No. 39 had been submitted, Hitler released three divisions from the west for Army Group Centre. For the organization of replacements for each army see BA-MA RH 19 II/127, fos. 161 ff.

[589] On the basis of experience Bock expected this transfer, as with Armd. Group 4, to make the commander more willing to move forces to threatened sectors. As of 12 Dec., the large formation was referred to as 'Army Group Guderian'. Criticism in Bock, Tagebuch, 171 (12 Dec. 1941), BA-MA N 22/9; H.Gr. Mitte/Ia, KTB, 12 Dec. 1941, fos. 97–8, BA-MA RH 19 II/122; ibid., 13 Dec., fos. 106–7.

[590] Bock, Tagebuch, 173 (13 Dec. 1941), BA-MA N 22/9.

[591] Guderian, Panzer Leader, 125–6.

[592] H.Gr. Mitte/Ia, KTB, 13 Dec. 1941 (as in n. 589 above). During this visit Bock suggested to the C.-in-C. that he seek a replacement for him, as he still had not recovered from his illness: Bock, Tagebuch, 173 (13 Dec. 1941), BA-MA N 22/9.

Brauchitsch himself had come to the conclusion that a withdrawal of the army group to the line from Kursk to the Volga reservoir (via Orel, Medyn, Gzhatsk, and Rzhev) was inevitable. And the central sector of the army group, which had suffered relatively few attacks, would not be able to hold its position if the front on the wings were abandoned.[593]

In his first decision, obtained through his Wehrmacht adjutant, Colonel Schmundt, during Brauchitsch's visit to the front, Hitler agreed to a straightening of the front at Klin and Kalinin and to Guderian's withdrawal. But nothing was to be abandoned and there were to be no withdrawals until the most vital preparations had been made in the new lines in the rear.[594] This order was in complete agreement with the views that Bock and Kluge had been advocating until that day.

Hitler's decision therefore clearly permitted local withdrawals under enemy pressure, but not unless a new line to the rear had been prepared. The line envisaged by Bock was to be fortified and occupied by security troops from the rear to the extent necessary to stop a Soviet attack there if the army group should be overrun. Again a directive from Hitler had been tied to conditions which did not exist and which neither Hitler himself nor the Army High Command could bring about in the short term. On the contrary, it soon became clear that Hitler was not thinking about strengthening a line in the rear by bringing up troops; instead, their task would be to hold the front.

Immediately after Brauchtisch's conversations with Kluge and Guderian had become known and after the order to prepare for the retreat had been received, the commander-in-chief of Second Army, Schmidt, reported to the army group[595] that the line ordered ahead of the railway line between Kursk and Orel could not be held unless the enemy made serious tactical mistakes, and there was no indication of that. Because of the crucial role of the positions held by Second Army for the entire eastern front, the decision must finally be taken to use all available aircraft to bring up sufficient reserves quickly from Germany. Moreover, the armies formerly well equipped for attack should immediately transfer units and army troops to the points of the main defensive effort. Troops from the army in the west and the training army should replace the spent units; all limits on weapons and vehicles should be scrapped. These measures had to be carried out in spite of any consequences for the later conduct of the war as a whole. Schmidt also demanded 'maximum-scale' operations of the Luftwaffe in support of the army. The Red Army, he observed, was making its final efforts with newly created and poorly armed units and had been successful. 'In spite of the urgent situation we are still not making an all-out effort.' In the long term only a counter-attack could restore a secure front for the army. While Hitler and Halder wished to maintain the

---

[593] Teletype message H.Gr. Mitte to Second Army, 9 Dec., BA-MA RH 19 II/127, fo. 269, and order of 15 Dec. 1941, ibid., fos. 337 ff.

[594] H.Gr. Mitte/Ia, KTB, 14 Dec. 1941, BA-MA RH 19 II/122, fos. 110–11; Reinhardt, *Moskau*, 217; for additional decisions by Hitler cf. sect. II.1.1(*g*) at nn. 604 ff., 613.

[595] AOK 2/Ia No. 679/41, 15 Dec. 1941, to C.-in-C. of Army Group Centre, BA-MA RH 19 II/127, fos. 334 ff.

substance of a future offensive army despite all the assistance provided for the armies in the east, Schmidt, no doubt in agreement with all generals of the eastern front, virtually demanded the renunciation of the next summer offensive in order to deal with the present emergency. Moreover, the air war against Britain should be virtually wound down.

The decision promised by Hitler on the withdrawal of the front of Army Group Centre, after he had received Brauchitsch's report on the situation on the eastern front, was to have the character of a binding order with far-reaching consequences for the entire German army in the east. It therefore required further deliberations. First, on 15 December, Army Group Centre received permission to withdraw Armoured Groups 3 and 4 and the right wing of Ninth Army to the position Ruza–Volokolamsk–Staritsa. There was no dispute about this decision, as it had been agreed upon after numerous telephone conversations. But Hitler still had not taken a decision about a further withdrawal to the line from Kursk to Orel, Kaluga, Gzhatsk, and Rzhev.[596]

While the withdrawal of the left wing of the army group had now been definitely decided upon, Hitler did not take a corresponding decision about its right wing until 16 December, as the latter's retreat would significantly affect the position of Army Group South. Nevertheless, Kluge and Bock were agreed that XXXXIII Army Corps should be withdrawn to the west, but in no case beyond the Oka. At 1.10 p.m. on 15 December, however, Guderian reported that the corps had to withdraw to a position west of Aleksin beyond the Oka and then to the line Begatkov–Pastove.

This retreat exposed the right flank of Fourth Army and forced it to withdraw too. At Guderian's urging, Kluge therefore placed 137th Infantry Division at the disposal of XXXXIII Army Corps, but on 16 December, because of an enemy penetration near Serpukhov that led to a crossing of the Protva and the Oka, he had to use those parts that had not yet been transferred (a third) to support XIII Army Corps.

Until this point Army Group Centre command had been able to direct evacuations and withdrawals required by local tactical necessity in such a way that serious losses through encirclement of troops left behind after enemy penetrations had been avoided. This method placed a severe burden on the confidence of the soldiers in their leaders and on their discipline, which was

---

[596] The entry in the war diary of Army Group Centre under 15 Dec., 12.10 p.m., seems doubtful (BA-MA RH 19 II/122, fo. 124). According to this entry, Heusinger informed Greiffenberg that Hitler had approved both movements. The same day, however, Halder made notes at noon of a conversation with Greiffenberg, according to which Jodl had informed him (Greiffenberg) that no withdrawals were to be carried out where the front could be held; 'no retiring before all preparations are completed' (Halder, *Diaries*, 1357). This fact is recorded clearly in Heusinger's report to Halder shortly thereafter. The directive of the army group to the armies, 15 Dec., 10.00 p.m. (No. 3111/41, BA-MA RH 19 II/127, fo. 343), also mentioned that units affected would be informed of the decision on the withdrawal 'of the rest of the front to the line from Kaluga to Gzhatsk and Rzhev envisaged by the army group'. There can be no question that Hitler might have withdrawn approval on 16 Dec. Cf. Reinhardt, *Moskau*, 217.

based on their acceptance of the need to make great sacrifices. The situation could be remedied only by the bringing up of fresh forces, whose assignment would be decided upon by Hitler alone, as the army had long since exhausted its own reserves.

As explained, the directives of 8 December assumed that sufficient time remained to bring up convalescent battalions and battalions in waiting, to transfer several units from the western to the eastern front, and at the same time to construct winter positions there.

After receipt of the earlier alarming reports, on 14 December Hitler had himself briefed by his adjutant, who had accompanied Brauchitsch during the latter's visit to Army Group Centre. Colonel Schmundt informed Hitler that he had the impression that there was no time to lose, and Hitler reacted immediately without waiting for the report of the commander-in-chief of the army or consulting the chief of the general staff. That same night he summoned the commander of the replacement army and demanded a report on units that could be flown to the front immediately. Göring was also included in the consultations so as to speed up the organizational preparations for the entire transport sector. On 16 December the head of the Wehrmacht transport department, Lieutenant-General Rudolf Gercke, who was responsible for rail transport, was ordered together with Göring to initiate immediately the dispatch of the fighting units of the divisions named by Fromm and of the battalions in waiting to the front.[597]

From the replacement army, troops with a strength of four and a half divisions were to be prepared to move—the Walküre divisions. In addition, Hitler ordered the transfer of five divisions from the western front, a measure that had already been envisaged on 8 December.[598] An additional four divisions were to be made available from the forces in the Balkans; the Italians and Bulgarians were to take over the occupation duties there, except in areas of great significance for the war economy.[599]

From Germany itself, additional troops who could 'build, protect, and fight' in some form were to be equipped for winter combat and sent to the eastern front. The Luftwaffe was to make available immediately four combat Gruppen, a Gruppe of Me 110s, and five transport Gruppen for VIII Air

[597] Telephonic briefing of Halder by Brauchitsch on 14 Dec. and immediate organizational preparations of the Army High Command in agreement with the Wehrmacht High Command as the basis for Hitler's decisions: Halder, *Diaries*, 1355, 1357 (14, 15 Dec. 1941). This procedure shows how far Hitler had already taken over the functions of the C.-in-C. of the army, and also that only Halder's apparatus could guarantee the organizational execution of such orders. Brauchitsch's imminent collapse had been obvious for some weeks, so that Halder urged his replacement on 4 Dec.: Halder, *Diaries*, 1381; cf. also sect. II.1.1(*g*) at n. 608.

[598] Hitler's remark on 16 Dec. that he could not send everything out into the winter just because the enemy had achieved a few penetrations in the sector of Army Group Centre referred not to a refusal to send troops but to bringing troops back for 'winter rest'. Cf. conversation between Bock and Schmundt, 16 Dec. 1941, KTB, H.Gr. Mitte, BA-MA RH 19 II/122, fo. 131; Reinhardt, *Moskau*, 218.

[599] Hitler's order, written out as: Chef OKW/WFSt/L. No. 442174/41, 15 Dec. 1941, *KTB OKW* i. 1083 (109).

Corps or for the air transport of the battalions in waiting. The 218th Infantry Division was to be pulled out from Denmark and replaced by local units.

Hitler's operational decisions for the conduct of the fighting of 15 December and the following days were based on the assumption that these orders, intended to provide considerable reinforcements for the eastern front, would be carried out rapidly and unconditionally. At noon on 16 December Halder informed Army Group Centre about Hitler's imminent directive to the effect that the approved withdrawal movements of the left wing, of Armoured Groups 3 and 4, and of Ninth Army were to be carried out only 'if there is no alternative'. Guderian's army group was to employ all available reserves to close the breaches north of Livny and west of Tula and then to hold the line from Livny to Dubna and Aleksin. Fourth Army was not to retreat 'one step'.[600]

At first Field Marshal von Bock could only answer that he had no reserves left; he requested that his answer be reported to Hitler immediately. Quite logically, he passed on to the armies the essential points of Hitler's directive as he had received them from Halder, but maintained the order for the construction of rear-area defensive positions along the line from Orel to Kursk, Gzhatsk, and Rzhev. All preparations for a withdrawal to that line were to be continued. When Colonel Schmundt informed him that night that Hitler, bypassing the Army High Command, would take all decisions personally immediately after hearing Bock's views, Bock replied that he had already reported the relevant developments to the commander-in-chief of the army on 13 December and that Hitler would now have to decide whether the army group was to stand and fight or withdraw. In either case there was the danger that the army group would 'go to pieces', for in the event of a withdrawal to an unprepared and not significantly shorter position (the line ordered by Hitler), the promised reserves would arrive too late to play a decisive role.[601]

Without mentioning the ordered rear-area line, Bock explained why the position stipulated by Hitler was untenable and added that, because of the lack of fuel and the condition of the horses, heavy equipment and artillery would have to be abandoned. Moreover, he was troubled by the thought that the troops would withdraw even further and not obey orders to halt.

This was the main problem for the army group command. Not only among the men themselves had there been signs of panic, a horror of tanks, and a

---

[600] H.Gr. Mitte/Ia, KTB, 16 Dec. 1941, BA-MA RH 19 II/122, fo. 129.

[601] Ibid., 16 Dec. 1941. Schmundt established that the Army High Command had not sent the alarming reports on to Hitler. Bock therefore retransmitted the text and thus created the same situation as in Army Group South and First Armd. Army on 30 Nov. 1941. Cf. sect. II.1.1(c) at n. 329. The question as to the extent to which reports from the army group and the armies went directly to Hitler cannot be answered conclusively. It should be remembered that the Army High Command tried to keep control of the army; at the same time there was proven co-operation between Harder and Jodl, and it was Jodl who selected the reports to be submitted. Hitler also received information from the Luftwaffe operations staff.

collapse of order; even the commanders of armies, corps, and divisions were no longer always 'under control' when it was a case of saving their exhausted troops. On 16 December Colonel-General Guderian had an opportunity to inform Schmundt that the fate of the army would be at stake unless replacements and fresh forces were speedily sent to the front. He requested that this should be reported directly to Hitler.[602]

When the advance briefing on the content of Hitler's expected directive reached Second Army at 1.30 p.m., Guderian observed that that order could not be carried out; the army was no longer capable of mounting more than limited thrusts. He therefore ordered a further withdrawal. The Upa position, reached on the evening of 16 December, could be held for a day or two, but on the whole a withdrawal beyond the Susha–Oka sector was necessary. He informed the commander-in-chief of the army group of his views and the measures he had taken and received from him a confirmation that Hitler insisted on his order being carried out in spite of Schmundt's report. Hitler himself contacted Guderian during the night. He acknowledged the difficulty of Guderian's situation, but the front had to be held under all circumstances. The armoured army should attempt to reach a new position that could be reinforced. He assured Guderian that he would do everything to help the army. Replacements, three twin-engined fighter Gruppen of the Luftwaffe, and fresh divisions from the west would be brought up.[603]

Beyond the measures initiated, however, an immediate success was not to be expected from this direct contact between Guderian and Hitler. On the other hand, only thirty-five minutes later Field Marshal von Bock ordered that in future any withdrawal from division level upward would require his personal approval.[604]

Hitler's decision, of which he informed Brauchitsch and Halder in the night of 16–17 December, was based largely on the same arguments as those exchanged between Bock and Kluge, which Bock had presented to Hitler and which, in Hitler's judgement, justified the 'great gamble' of risking the loss of Army Group Centre. He hoped to overcome this danger with an iron will and by transferring all available fighting forces to the east. On 16 December he ordered that Army Group North could withdraw to the Volkhov, but then this

[602] 2. Pz.Armee/Ia, KTB, 16 Dec. 1941, BA-MA RH 21-2/v. 277, fo. 74; Guderian, *Panzer Leader*, 125–6. In the following days Bock used the term 'Führer psychoses' to Guderian and Hoepner; these had to be overcome: H.Gr. Mitte/Ia, KTB, 18 Dec. 1941, BA-MA RH 19 II/122, fo. 142.

[603] 2. Pz.Armee/Ia, KTB, 16 Dec. 1941, 3.00 a.m., BA-MA RH 21-2/v. 277; Guderian (*Panzer Leader*, 126) is wrong: on 9 Dec. 5 convalescent companies and 5 battalions in waiting of 27 companies were promised; the convalescent battalion was to arrive on 13 Dec.: BA-MA RH 19 II/127, fos. 263–4. The remark can only refer to the telephone conversation with Hitler, given in BA-MA RH 21-2/v. 879.

[604] H.Gr. Mitte/Ia No. 3147/41, BA-MA RH 21-2/v. 879. It should be remembered that in addition to the 'hold-out order' the directive of the army group and the order of Second Armd. Army to fortify rear-area positions were in effect. The same was true in the other armies. The discrepancies between these directives and orders led to constant reports that an order could not be carried out.

new front was to be defended to the last man.[605] Army Group South was to hold its entire front and, after the imminent capture of Sevastopol, provide reserves from the Crimea.

Army Group Centre was to proceed from the realization that large withdrawal movements could not be carried out because of the total loss of heavy weapons they would involve: 'By the personal engagement of commanders-in-chief and all commanders and other officers, the troops are to be forced to defend their positions fanatically, regardless of any enemy breakthroughs on the flanks or in the rear.' The purpose of such resistance was to gain time to bring up reinforcements from the west and from Germany itself. Only when reserves had reached the positions in the rear could a withdrawal to them be considered.

Beyond the measures Hitler had ordered, the commander-in-chief of the army ordered Army Group South on the left wing of Sixth Army to provide forces to take the pressure off Second Army near Kursk.

As of 1 January 1942, five infantry divisions were to be transferred to Army Group Centre at one-week intervals. Moreover, regiments, battalions, and 'raiding parties' consisting of home-defence troops from Germany were also to be sent east. Whatever could be dispensed with elsewhere was to be sent to the front by air.[606]

All these transports were affected by weather conditions and other difficulties which could not be overcome overnight. The army group did not expect help to arrive in time, and Field Marshal von Kluge offered to explain to Hitler the conflict between the order to hold the front and the means left to the army group. His aim was to achieve a more flexible conduct of the defence. Field Marshal von Bock, however, advised against such a trip to Hitler.[607]

Now Hitler returned to Bock's request to be relieved of his duties for reasons of health and, through the commander-in-chief of the army, suggested that he submit a request for leave of absence, which was approved.[608] Kluge assumed command of Army Group Centre.

The following day, 19 December 1941, Hitler also relieved the commander-in-chief of the army of his duties. Field Marshal von Brauchitisch had been seriously ill several times during the past few weeks, but an additional reason

[605] Hitler's 'hold-out order', drawn up as OKW/WFSt/Abt. L (I Op) No. 442182/41, 16 Dec. 1941, BA-MA RW 4/v. 578, according to a draft of operations dept., 15 Dec. 1941, BA-MA RH 2/v. 1327, fos. 90–1. Briefing of Army Group Centre with all envisaged transfers of troops in *KTB OKW* i. 1084–5 (110), copy Army High Command, 18 Dec. 1941.

[606] Police and military guard units, Labour Service, and other rear-area services. See e.g. Winterstein and Jacobs, *General Meindl*, 59 ff. On the use of the Luftwaffe units cf. sect. II.1.2(*b*) at n. 891 (Boog).

[607] Hitler's arguments were also his own, and he could therefore expect that no new decisions in favour of the army group would be taken: H.Gr. Mitte/Ia, KTB, 18 Dec. 1941, fo. 144, BA-MA RH 19 II/122.

[608] Bock, *Tagebuch*, 179–80 (17, 18 Dec. 1941), BA-MA N 22/9. Bock seems not to have meant this very seriously; he was more concerned about securing a statement by Hitler that he had not relieved him because of failure. That was indeed not the case, otherwise Hitler would not have made Bock C.-in-C. of Army Group South a little later.

for his inability to meet the demands of his post was that, besides constant arguments to find compromises between Hitler's directives and the intentions of the general staff, new tensions were arising from the fact that the commanders in the field were increasingly making demands which he did not actually have the power to approve. Though only indirectly connected with the crises of command at the front, Brauchitsch's dismissal marked the conclusion of a conflict that had been smouldering ever since the debate about the senior command structure of the Wehrmacht before the war. To describe that conflict would go beyond the scope of the present study. It should be noted, however, that Hitler's purpose in removing Brauchitsch was quite certainly not to eliminate a possible representative of the internal resistance or to deal with military insubordination, as had to be assumed initially in the case of Rundstedt. In Hitler's eyes Brauchitsch was simply a man who had failed to inform him and to react fast enough in a crisis. That he himself was responsible for this failure and, with his intervention in all matters concerning the field army from the planning of operations down to tactical details, had constantly countermanded Brauchitsch's orders was surely due in the final analysis to his desire to command the army even at the functional level. But neither the commanders-in-chief at the front nor the chief of the Army General Staff, not to mention other advisers, seem to have regarded Brauchitsch as indispensable. Hitler's demands that he be informed directly about developments at the front, and the acceptance of operational directives bypassing the Army High Command, show that the army had begun to adjust to the wishes of its supreme commander.[609]

To Hitler a commander-in-chief of the army must have seemed unnecessary. He took the operational decisions himself; he kept the apparatus of the general staff; and he already communicated directly with front commanders in difficult situations. He had just now 'shown' the army that he alone knew how to overcome all obstacles, mobilize the defence potential of the country, and put the Luftwaffe in the right place. The 'buffer' between the front and Hitler, between Halder and Hitler, and in the final analysis between friction-points in the structure of the army itself, was worn out. In addition to his many other functions, Hitler now took over this one, but not in its entirety.

Formally, the process was accomplished by Hitler's declaration of 19 December 1941 that he had decided to take over direct command of the army himself.[610] He placed the chief of the Army General Staff immediately under

---

[609] This reactivated conservative opposition to Hitler; the military opposition primarily in the staff of Army Group Centre is dealt with in a subsequent volume of the present work.

[610] Hitler's orders in BA-MA RH 2/v. 156; there also the following letters by Keitel and Halder. On 6 Dec. 1940, as a result of an incident, Hitler had demanded the concentration of the conduct of the war as a whole in the Wehrmacht operations staff: *KTB OKW* i. 215. Cf. also Jodl's efforts, evident in the memorandum on the continuation of the war against Britain, ibid. 212. The statement of Hitler's army adjutant, Maj. Engel, that Schmundt had pressed Hitler to take over command of the army himself cannot be considered decisive when compared with Halder's role in this development. Cf. *KTB OKW* i. 189E.

himself and transferred all other powers of the Army High Command as the highest command and administrative authority to the chief of the Wehrmacht High Command, Field Marshal Keitel, who was to exercise them on his behalf. This first directive was overridden as early as 21 December, when Hitler reserved the right to issue direct orders concerning fundamental questions to the chief of army armament programmes and commander of the training army, as well as to the head of the army personnel office. Moreover, Hitler reserved the right to use his adjutants for special tasks, as he had done before; they were to maintain close contact with a newly established office called the 'Army High Command Staff'. This staff was the former adjutant's office of the commander-in-chief of the army. It now served to co-ordinate army matters within the framework of Keitel's overall activities. It was to maintain contact with the chief of the Army General Staff and remained an office of the army which, in economic matters, was attached to the general staff.

Along with all his new burdens, the chief of the Army General Staff, who was the person most strongly affected by these changes, evidently saw an opportunity for himself to bring about decisions immediately that affected the conduct of the war as a whole, a chance of wielding influence in a manner approaching that of a theoretical 'chief of the Reich general staff'. On 31 December, however, Keitel effectively blocked such ambitions by ordering that in official communications between the Army High Command and the Wehrmacht High Command on all questions affecting the Wehrmacht as a whole, in military or non-military areas, all submissions and reports for Hitler were to be channelled exclusively through the relevant office and departmental heads of the Wehrmacht High Command.

An indication of Halder's possible ambition was a letter he wrote on 25 December 1941 to the commanders-in-chief of the army groups, armies, and armoured armies, the commanders of the armoured groups, and the military governors on Brauchitsch's departure. 'To prevent rumours', Halder emphasized that Brauchitsch had been seriously ill, and his physical decline had also affected his mental vigour. For that reason he had requested Hitler to relieve him of his duties and grant him leave of absence. Hitler had also granted furlough to Field Marshals von Bock and von Rundstedt for reasons of health, 'after a personal, cordial exchange of views'. Halder explained that Hitler's assumption of command represented a clear strengthening of the position of the army: 'We can and should be proud that the Führer himself is now at the head of our army.'

Hitler had already taken over *de facto* the most important activity of the commander-in-chief of the army, the selection of personnel to fill the senior military positions, as the relief of the commander-in-chief of Army Group South, without previous consultation with Brauchitsch, had demonstrated. That Hitler would carry out such measures without considering earlier meritorious service became evident on 20 December 1941, when Guderian, whom he greatly valued as a soldier, reported that he was not prepared to transmit Hitler's 'hold-on order' verbatim to his units.[611]

Several factors were involved in this decision. To explain them it is necessary to consider the decision itself more closely. On the one hand, Guderian had a 'direct line' to Hitler, of which he occasionally made use, via Schmundt. On 18 December Halder, through Keitel and Jodl, learnt of conversations between Hitler and Guderian concerning an attack by 3rd and 4th Armoured Divisions designed to dispose of enemy forces near Aleksin and Odoevo.[612] Guderian rejected both actions. At the same time he transferred 4th Armoured Division to the area of Orel and 3rd Armoured Division south of Mtsensk as a reserve. He seems to have reported neither action to the army group, for on 20 December the group ordered that such rest and rehabilitation measures were to be reported in advance.[613] In the further planning of withdrawal movements Guderian, as described, while under the command of Field Marshal von Bock, refused to be deflected from his purpose and, in the face of all Hitler's orders, referred to Brauchitsch's consent of 13 December.

As he agreed with Guderian and also enjoyed Hitler's confidence, Bock had shown generosity and had even managed to cope with the difficulties presented by the team of Guderian and Kluge, without having to resort to hard, direct orders in dealing with either of the two men. The fact that, seeking to understand Guderian, he occasionally exchanged views with Halder about Guderian's 'peculiarities' and his attitude towards military obedience did not affect his high opinion of Guderian's achievements as a military commander. The situation changed with Kluge's appointment as commander-in-chief of the army group.

On 19 December Kluge briefed Halder in detail on the situation, including the threatening penetration on the right wing of Fourth Army, which Kluge had not yet turned over to the general of mountain troops, Ludwig Kübler. There, shortly before in conversation with Hitler, Guderian had rejected an operation by 3rd and 4th Armoured Divisions. Hitler was also aware of Guderian's requests to be permitted to withdraw to the prepared intermediate positions and of their rejection by Halder. Moreover, on this very day Hitler repeatedly ruled that no line was to be abandoned voluntarily until he had been informed that behind that line new positions had been prepared.[614] It is therefore rather astonishing that Hitler should have listened to Guderian's reports and proposals for several hours and have tried to convince him that it

---

[611] H.Gr. Mitte/Ia, KTB, 19 Dec. 1941, fo. 147, BA-MA RH 19 II/122; Guderian, *Panzer Leader*, 126–7; Walde, *Guderian*, 155 ff.; 2. Pz.Armee/Ia, KTB, 19, 20 Dec. 1941, BA-MA RH 21-2/277. Already on 17 Dec. Guderian had flatly refused to obey Bock's order to withdraw units at division level or above only with his approval. Cf. the above-mentioned war diary of Second Armd. Army, 17 Dec. 1941.

[612] Cf. Halder, *Diaries*, 1364 ('Situation at Dubna').

[613] 2. Pz.Armee/Ia, KTB, 18–20 Dec. 1941, BA-MA RH 21-2/v. 277.

[614] Halder, *Diaries*, 1369–70 (20 Dec. 1941).

was absolutely necessary to hold the line that had been reached, in spite of the great losses involved.

The lengthy instructions about details of the conduct of the fighting at the front as well as the basic guidelines for the behaviour, equipment, and supplies of the troops, down to the encirclement of Leningrad and the matter of protective covering for locomotives, clearly show the topics which dominated Hitler's attention that day. His suggestions, instructions, and orders, which, with regard to the solution of technical and personnel problems, came at least six months too late, were transmitted to the Army High Command the following day by teletype in a 'Summary of the tasks of the army for the immediate future'.[615] Again, and not for the last time, Hitler ordered positions to be held and defended to the last man, in order to gain time to improve the transport system and bring up reserves, remove equipment that could be repaired, and strengthen the rear lines by constructing strong points. All forces available in Germany and the west were to be directed to the eastern front, winter clothing for the troops was to be taken off prisoners and local civilians, and possible quarters for the advancing enemy were to be destroyed in areas to be evacuated.[616]

Moreover, in this directive the greater use of allied forces, already suggested in Hitler's directive of 15 December, was taken up again and explained in greater detail. Now Italy, Hungary, and Romania were to be induced 'to provide strong forces for 1942 in good time, so that they can be brought up before the snow melts and can march to the front'.

Problems which arose in the totally unprepared war economy as a result of call-ups and personnel transfers were to be solved by the use of prisoners of war, foreign civilian workers, and not least by forced labour in the concentration camps.[617] This part of the directive was already concerned with preparations for the summer offensive of 1942. Let us return now to the acute crisis of December 1941.

Hitler's order forbidding a withdrawal of the front, even in case of threatening encirclement and the loss of troops and material that this would involve, was repeated not only to Guderian but also to Kluge on 20 December. It especially concerned the further withdrawal of Second Armoured Army on its northern wing to prevent the gap between it and Fourth Army near Likhvin from becoming a danger. Kluge reported that under certain circumstances

---

[615] OKW/WFSt/Abt. L IH Op to OKH/Op.Abt., 21 Dec. 1941, *KTB OKW* i. 1085–6 (III). The version in Halder (*Diaries*, 1369–70) contains a reading mistake by the teletype transmission office.

[616] This destruction had a military purpose in so far as the German troops needed quarters and were concentrated there, with the result that the areas in between could not be guarded. Stalin's destruction orders were based on the same idea. However, thanks to their better preparation and equipment, the Soviet troops were not dependent on permanent structures and frequently exploited the gaps in the German strong-point system. Cf. the regulation on operations in the winter (n. 580 above).

[617] Cf. sect. II.vi.5 at n. 392 (Müller).

events could be stronger than the will to resist them; Hitler should realize the consequences.[618]

During Guderian's absence the chief of staff of Second Armoured Army informed the commander of the army group that the armoured army intended to withdraw to a prepared line and to establish a rallying-position behind the Oka. Moreover, he reported that 3rd and 4th Armoured Divisions had been withdrawn from the front. Field Marshal von Kluge came to the not un-founded conclusion that Second Armoured Army wished to withdraw to a position west of the Oka. Referring to Hitler's order, he ordered the with-drawal of LIII Army Corps and XXXXVII Armoured Corps to be halted at once. When Guderian's deputy, General Schmidt, objected that the corps no longer had sufficient strength to fight, Kluge replied with understanding that in spite of binding orders commanding generals had to act according to the situation and that in the event of a successful enemy breakthrough positions simply could not be held any longer.[619] The two corps were ordered to hold the general line from the upper Susha to east of Chern and Odoev.

All the other armies and corps of the army group reported similar intentions to evacuate positions that could no longer be held, e.g. VII Army Corps, for which Kluge promised 600 replacements and air support in the next few days, in addition to limited assistance from the neighbouring XX Army Corps.

The dispute about the withdrawal of Guderian's army group took place by telephone between Kluge and Halder during the decisive days of Guderian's absence. The new commander-in-chief of Army Group Centre was well aware that there could be no question of rigidly holding the front at any price. The critical question was essentially one of authority, and Kluge was clearly an-gered that Guderian—at first with Brauchitsch's consent, to which he referred, and now having obtained a decision from Hitler—seemed to be thinking only of the fate of the units under his own command. The insinuation that his armoured army wished to withdraw to positions in the rear without fighting was for Guderian a personal insult. Kluge's judgement, in a conversation with Colonel Schmundt, that Guderian was exhausted and too pessimistic to practise his command was clearly aimed at obtaining his removal.

After Guderian had received Hitler's strict order to hold his positions, he briefed the corps under his command on the new situation and the discontinu-ation of the retrograde movement. On the southern wing of Second Army the enemy was mounting a powerful thrust towards the Tim, threatening Kursk and thus the communications with Sixth Army. In the area of Kaluga an unexpected attack began at the same time, forcing XXXXII Army Corps to withdraw—something Hitler and Halder had just rejected.

But Halder still believed that the attacks of the Red Army, whose poor training and equipment he had repeatedly stressed (on the assumption that the Germans were superior and that Soviet successes were due only to sheer

[618] H.Gr. Mitte/Ia, KTB, 20 Dec. 1941, BA-MA RH 19 II/122, fos. 156–7.
[619] Ibid., fos. 156 ff.; 2. Pz.Armee/Ia, KTB, 20 Dec. 1941, BA-MA RH 21-2/v. 277.

numbers), would lose momentum and that it was necessary to hold out for only two weeks or so. He based his view on a tactically vague assessment of the enemy's situation, as aerial reconnaissance provided no clear results and available infantry forces were not able to carry out significant reconnaissance because of the poor weather.[620]

Enemy penetrations during the following days, until the end of the year, repeatedly confronted Army Group Centre with the same situation, in which decimated divisions had to be withdrawn by the corps or were simply lost, and the armies were requesting authorization from the army group for retrograde movements already begun, with Kluge arguing with Halder and Hitler, who finally relented in every instance when operational encirclements seemed inevitable.

These disputes with Hitler's headquarters, the results of which were constantly confronting the commanders in the field with serious conflicts of conscience, even extended to tactical movements, e.g. in the case of Guderian, who refused to obey the order forbidding him to withdraw LIII Army Corps and XXXXVII Armoured Corps behind the Susha–Oka line. That same day General Schmidt evacuated Livny on his own responsibility, which forced XXXXVIII Armoured Corps to withdraw behind the Tim–Sosna line, a move that in turn affected the entire front of Second Armoured Army.

Kluge pointed out to Halder the necessity of a retreat by XXXXVII Armoured Corps and promised the armoured army command that he would obtain Hitler's approval 'provided there is a clear determination to hold the Oka sector'. Guderian emphasized that no interference in his command would change the situation and requested to be relieved of his post, adding that he would have no objection to defending his actions at a court martial. Kluge realized that the basic difference between Guderian's and Hitler's views of the situation was, in the long run, intolerable.[621]

This meant that the break between Hitler and Guderian was final, in spite of their agreement in the operational area about the measures to be taken— measures which Kluge also advocated vis-à-vis Halder and Hitler. The final disputes arose on 25 December on the question of the withdrawal of XXXXVII Armoured Corps and the evacuation of Chern, and because of Guderian's statement that he commanded his army as his conscience dictated. Kluge, who shared this view of a commander's responsibility, saw between it and the duty to carry out orders such a fundamental incompatibility that he informed Halder that 'either he or I [must go]'. Guderian then gave up the struggle and requested to be relieved of his command, which Hitler ordered the same day. General Schmidt took over command of the army group.

---

[620] H.Gr. Mitte/Ia, KTB, 21 Dec. 1941, BA-MA RH 19 II/122, p. 172.

[621] On 25 Dec. Kluge emphasized to Halder that he was basically of the same opinion as Guderian: the German troops could not simply let themselves be slaughtered. The dispute is recorded in detail in the war diaries of Army Group Centre and Second Armd. Army. Cf. also Reinhardt, *Moskau*, 227 ff.; Guderian, *Panzer Leader*, 130 ff.

Although it is indisputable that the removal of a general would not have been effected any differently under Brauchitsch, the dismissal of Guderian highlighted the disappearance of the most important function of the commander-in-chief of the army: to achieve and defend a consensus, especially in difficult situations. This was probably Halder's aim in sending several trusted officers to the commands at the front and in the rear areas on 21 December 1941 so as to 'restore order and confidence'.[622]

The effects of Hitler's assumption of direct command of the army on Halder's position and work soon became evident. Halder's daily oral report to Hitler—together with the head of the Wehrmacht transport department, the head of Wehrmacht communications, and the general-staff officer in charge of supply and administration—was not only extremely time-consuming; in the case of direct orders it left almost no time for consultation or for the collection of the necessary data.[623]

Halder shared his first insights into the new style of leadership with the chiefs of staff of the army groups and armies,[624] who were to pass them on to their commanders-in-chief. In accordance with Hitler's will, the senior commands (high commands of the army, army groups, and armies) were to conduct their operations with stricter discipline. The principle of simply issuing orders to subordinate units and leaving the execution to them, it was argued, had sometimes led to circumstances in which the intentions of the higher command had been jeopardized with serious effects on the situation as a whole. Therefore it was again necessary to issue clear, unequivocal orders. The higher command was to intervene decisively in detailed actions to ensure that the intended objective was reached: 'The soldier's duty to obey leaves no room for the sensibilities of subordinate commands; rather it requires the most rapid and best possible execution of orders as desired by the authority issuing them.' The Army High Command would issue its orders accordingly, and Halder requested that the army groups and armies should do likewise. During the transition to a coherent defensive front, this required that they should concern themselves more with the tactical details of the situation. Only in this way could they ensure that orders were issued promptly and that they did not become dependent on subordinate commands.

This represented the formal confirmation of the end of one of the most basic German military principles, 'mission responsibility'. In effect the principle of providing every commander with all necessary support and equipment needed for him to carry out his mission independently within the framework of the relevant directives and orders, trusting in his sound training, character, and ability, had been abandoned ever since the offensive drive by the German army in the east had come to a halt. In fact, however, this principle of

---

[622] Halder, *Diaries*, 1371 (21 Dec. 1941).   [623] Cf. Erfurth, *Generalstab*, 287 ff.

[624] Chef GenStdH/GZ/Op.Abt. (I) No. 10010/42, 6 Jan. 1942 (copy), BA-MA, 16. Armee, 23468/6. The individual elements of this announcement can be traced in Halder's war diary entries from the beginning of the war, but especially after 14 Dec. 1941.

command had already become a 'pious myth' with the development of modern communications and the increasing dependence of armies on air support.

At the end of his appeal to his closest subordinates in the commands, Halder stressed the will and confidence of the top leadership, which would enable them to master the difficult situation: 'We shall master it if we firmly seize the reins of command without consideration for inappropriate sensibilities, if the commands are entirely frank and truthful in their reports, and if a single will, the will of the Führer, prevails from the highest levels down to the soldier at the front.'

Hitler too had demanded absolute honesty in reports in his first 'basic order' after assuming direct command of the army.[625] There he stated that every report was a contribution to the conduct of operations and thus could provide an impulse for important decisions. It must therefore be inspired by love of truth and conscientiousness, provide the leadership with a clear picture of the situation, or give an unequivocal answer to questions asked. Honest reporting of his own failure to fulfil his tasks and of his own mistakes did credit to a soldier. In conclusion Hitler demanded that all persons in positions of authority should strive to achieve compliance with these principles; on the other hand, subordinates should know that reports would be required only when they were actually necessary.

That was a point at which the rejection of the idea of 'mission responsibility' overlapped with required reporting practice. The demands meant that the various military staffs would have to be able to provide data, position locations, information on troop units, and similar details at any time of the day or night. As the completely shattered larger formations were often not able to provide data on the strength of their smaller units at the moment when a report was demanded and, moreover, requirements with regard to indispensable units behind the front differed depending on their location, and no reporting procedure could prevent 'unclear items' from being concealed, this system inevitably came to resemble more and more a form of harassment, and those who had to carry out its provisions increasingly saw no purpose in the complicated procedure.[626] On the contrary, some commands seem to have taken the opportunity to report to Halder, often in extreme detail and at great length, their losses, shortages of equipment and supplies, and demands,

[625] Der Führer und Oberste Befehlshaber der Wehrmacht: Grundsätzlicher Befehl über Meldewesen [The Führer and Supreme Commander of the Armed Forces: Fundamental Order on Reporting], 26 Dec. 1941 (see n. 578 above).

[626] With some irony the chief of staff of Army Group North transmitted these new demands, justified by 'a certain change' after Hitler's assumption of command of the army, to the chiefs of staff of Sixteenth and Eighteenth Armies on 3 Jan. 1942: BA-MA, 16. Armee, 23468/8; transmission by chief of staff of Sixteenth Army to the corps chiefs of staff on 5 Jan. 1942, BA-MA, 16. Armee, 23468/6. The reports of the armies, supported by maps, were to be submitted three times a month and were truly colourful works of art that had to include details of forward strong points down to platoon level. Changes between the stipulated dates were to be reported daily: H.Gr. Nord/Ia, ibid.

repeatedly raised in vain, of which he was already aware and which often set in motion a time-consuming process of essentially pointless requests, rejections, excuses, and improvisations. The fact that Hitler was now in a position to direct individual battalions and even tanks did not relieve field commands of their responsibilities, but the impression arose that, after the elimination of the 'intermediate level' represented by the commander-in-chief of the army, Hitler himself was now to blame for all grievances. Earlier excuses—best expressed in the phrase 'If the Führer knew . . .', which had almost achieved the status of a slogan—could no longer be put forward.

(iii) THE FIGHTING RETREAT OF ARMY GROUP CENTRE UNTIL THE STABILIZATION OF THE FRONT

The difficulties Guderian had foreseen in bringing up 4th Armoured Division under the command of XXIV Armoured Corps as a result of road conditions—deep snowdrifts which could not be kept cleared for long—prevented this unit from closing the gap in the front east of Likhvin. Other troops that had been brought up had to withdraw to Sukhinichi. By the end of the year LIII Army Corps also had to abandon Belev. This development created a broad opening for a thrust towards Sukhinichi by the attacking Soviet Forty-ninth and Fiftieth Armies. The way seemed to be open for the southern arm of the planned large-scale encirclement operation against Army Group Centre.[627]

On the left wing of the defensive front of Army Group Centre, Ninth Army under Colonel-General Strauss had come to a temporary halt in the Staritsa position. From 25 December, however, the threat became so clear that Kluge considered separating the armoured units from Armoured Groups 3 and 4 to create a mobile reserve.[628] In the area of VI and XXIII Army Corps especially there were increasing indications of an imminent attack. The army command was ordered to halt before reaching the Volga–Gzhatsk line, to which it had requested permission to withdraw. While Kluge considered this request justified, Halder rejected the idea of a 'middle line' between remaining in the old positions and early withdrawal. He still expected a large operational breakthrough which would confront the entire army group with the question of its own survival.[629]

[627] For Soviet operational plans and the organization of units for the deployment cf. sect. II.ii. 10 atn. 292 (Hoffmann).

[628] On 24 Dec. 1941 Hitler had already authorized Kluge to withdraw the centre and the right wing of Fourth Army westwards until the danger of XIII and XII Army Corps being cut off had been eliminated: OKH/GenStdH/Op.Abt. (IM) No. 1755/41, BA-MA RH 2/v. 1327. fo. 95. Moreover, in accordance with this order, air units were to be withdrawn from the war against Britain and prepared for short-term service in the east, depending on the situation of Army Groups Centre or North (OKW/WFSt/Abt. L (IOp) No. 442243/41), in supplement to the directive of 18 Dec. 1941.

[629] H.Gr. Mitte/Ia, KTB, 25 Dec. 1941, BA-MA RH 19 II/122, fos. 208–9; Halder, *Diaries*, 1373 (25 Dec. 1941): 'Ninth Army begins to crumble.'

Starting on 26 December, a major Soviet attack with strong armoured forces was directed against the sector held by V Army Corps. Penetrations were achieved, and Colonel-General Hoepner expressed his doubts as to whether it would be possible to hold the position there. On 26 December Colonel-General Strauss also reported that the enemy was in a position to penetrate his left wing. On 29 December the pressure on XXXXIII and LVII Army Corps became so strong that the army group wanted to withdraw Fourth Army and the corps of Armoured Group 4 on the right wing to a line from Vereya to west of Kaluga in order to shorten the front and create reserves. The bulk of VI Army Corps was wiped out near Staritsa; as of 31 December, here too a wide gap opened in the German front for the enemy's thrust to Rzhev. On 2 January, even in this situation, Hitler insisted that Ninth Army should remain where it was. The front of XX Army Corps near Borovsk had to be held under all circumstances; Fourth Armoured Army had to transfer units for this purpose even if that endangered its own front.[630] Borovsk was lost, and all attempts to close the gap failed.

By this time the enemy had already achieved a breakthrough in the front of Ninth Army north-west of Rzhev and the army was in danger of having its rear lines of communication cut. But that danger was considerably greater for XX Army Corps north of the penetration near Borovsk, which was threatened with encirclement by enemy forces turning north. That would have represented a successful breakthrough on a broad front of a thrust aimed directly at Vyazma; even more serious, an inner arm for the planned great envelopment of Army Group Centre would have been able to achieve the desired objective. On 6 January Colonel-General Hoepner requested permission to withdraw the corps, but in vain. After waiting until 8 January for authorization of the decision, which he considered absolutely essential, he ordered the break-out of his corps, which had been cut off from its supplies, at noon that day on his own responsibility. Neither Kluge nor Halder agreed with this step. That same night Hitler relieved Hoepner of his duties and demanded that he be discharged dishonourably from the army.[631]

Fourth Army Headquarters next requested permission to withdraw in order to gain enough forces to protect the threatened main supply-route from

[630] From 1 Jan. 1942 Armd. Groups 3 and 4 were designated armoured armies; Third Armd. Army was placed under Ninth Army on 3 Jan. Hitler's insistence on holding Borovsk was due to agreement with 'his gentlemen', especially Halder, at least according to the war diary of Army Group Centre, BA-MA RH 19 II/122, fos. 260 ff. On the situation of Ninth Army, AOK 9/ Fü.Abt., KTB, 1 Jan.–31 Mar. 1942, BA-MA 21520/1, indicates that Col.-Gen. Strauß, with the consent of the army group, attempted to evade this directive by the formula 'withdrawals forced by the enemy'.

[631] Hoepner was dishonourably discharged from the army only after 20 July 1944: Chales de Beaulieu, *Hoepner*, 242 ff. Cf. also AOK 4, KTB, BA-MA RH 20-4/281; Pz.AOK 4, KTB, BA-MA RH 21–4/50, both under 8 Jan. 1942. Kluge's report, like Guderian's case, pointed out that the order had been given independently and that it had been issued without notification to the army group. Hoepner's successor was Gen. Richard Ruoff, until then general commanding V Army Corps. The chief of staff of the armoured army, Col. Walter Chales de Beaulieu, was also relieved of his duties. On Hoepner in general cf. Bücheler, *Hoepner*, here 165 ff.

Roslavl to Yukhnov.[632] Hitler approved a withdrawal between Ugra and Luza; along the line Zubovo–Tavarkovo–Medyn a new front was to be established and secured.

Beyond the intended use of the forces of Fourth Army, whose timely arrival he did not expect, Hitler also ordered units to be airlifted from the rear to Yukhnov or another appropriate landing-place along that road. In addition, units becoming available from the area north of Kaluga were to launch an attack in the general direction of Zubovo.[633]

For the moment the situation in Sukhinichi—encircled since 29 December, supplied by air, assigned the role of an 'Alcazar' of the eastern front in Hitler's view of the war and thus forbidden to surrender—remained unclear. As the Soviet Tenth Army did not subject the town to a thoroughly prepared assault but attacked it repeatedly though without success in passing, on the way to the operational objectives of Kirov and Vyazma, the fighting in this area continued until the end of January.

On 11 January Hitler received the commander-in-chief of the army group before issuing a new directive for it on 12 January.[634] The views of both men, like that of Halder, were based on the belief that for every day that stubborn resistance was continued more time would be gained for restoring the situation in the sector of Army Group Centre. The closure of existing gaps in the front was to be achieved by defensive and offensive measures. As in January, Hitler still assumed that sufficient forces could be removed from the less threatened sectors.

Second Army, in whose sector the situation had unexpectedly stabilized— the feared offensives against Orel and Kursk had not taken place—was now once more under the command of Colonel-General Freiherr von Weichs, and was placed under Army Group South. Only the greatly weakened units of Higher Command XXXV remained.

Second Armoured Army was to withdraw the strongest possible forces from its eastern-front sector and attack the flank of the Soviet Tenth Army near Sukhinichi, the objective being to reduce the size of the penetration and relieve pressure on Sukhinichi, whose defenders were to tie down the enemy. The forces of LIII Army Corps south of Belev were also to defend their positions 'till the last possible moment'.

The task of Fourth Army remained to keep the supply-route from Roslavl to Medyn open. But there too the holding of the new position was no longer demanded in the same terms.

After closing the penetration north of Medyn by an attack, Fourth Army

---

[632] Halder, *Diaries*, 1384–5 (8, 9 Jan. 1942); AOK 4/Ia, KTB, 8 Jan. 1942, BA-MA RH 20-4/281.

[633] Führer order, OKH/GenStdH/Op.Abt. (IM) No. 420013/42, 9 Jan. 1942, BA-MA RH 2/1327, fos. 96–7. For the mission of one such unit quickly thrown into battle cf. Winterstein and Jacobs, *General Meindl*, 59 ff.

[634] Halder, *Diaries*, 1386 (11 Jan. 1942); Hitler's directive: OKH/GenStdH/Op.Abt. (I) No. 420020/42, 12 Jan. 1942, BA-MA RH 2/v. 1327, fos. 98 ff.

was free, if necessary, to withdraw to a line between Medyn and Vereya Ruza. Forces were to be placed at the disposal of the army group as rapidly as possible.

Ninth Army was to cut off the penetration west of Rzhev and maintain contact with Army Group North south of Ostashkov.

A demand to hold the respective front sectors unconditionally and inflexibly is no longer found in these orders, with the exception of Sukhinichi. With a concluding sentence Hitler indicated the imminent withdrawal to 'winter positions': to increase the mobility of the 'parts of the army group facing the enemy', all equipment not necessary for the actual fighting was to be withdrawn from the forward area of combat.[635]

Permission for Army Group Centre to commence retrograde movements could no longer be avoided. The reserves from Germany that Hitler had assumed would be available did not reach the front in time or in sufficient strength, and the approved measures to shorten the front did not yield the envisaged units capable of offensive operations. On 15 January, after permission had already been given in isolated cases, Hitler had to order Army Group Centre to withdraw Fourth Army and the two northern armoured armies to a line east of Yukhnov, Gzhatsk, and Zubtsov and north of Rzhev.[636] The road between Yukhnov and Rzhev was to be secured as a lateral connection. This line was to be held against all attacks.[637] This order was due not only to the urging of Army Group Centre and the armies on the left wing; it also took into account Halder's ideas aiming at an 'active solution', i.e. offensive actions to improve the situation at Rzhev.[638] This possibility had also been proposed by the commander-in-chief of Ninth Army, in opposition to Kluge.

As a condition for the withdrawal to this winter line, Hitler accordingly demanded that the gap west of Rzhev should be closed, which would cut off the northern arm of the Soviet encirclement operation against Vyazma. The two other offensive tasks contained in the directive of 12 January, securing the gap north of Medyn and reopening the supply-route between Roslavl and

---

[635] Pz.AOK 2/Ia, KTB, 13 Jan. 1942, BA-MA RH 21-2/v. 876, 877; Der Führer und Oberste Befehlshaber der Wehrmacht, OKH/GenStdH/Op.Abt. (I) No. 420020/42, 12 Jan. 1942, to Army Group Centre, BA-MA RH 2/v. 1327, fos. 98 ff.: 'To increase the mobility of elements of the army facing the enemy, all equipment not needed for combat' was 'to be sent back'. This indicates that a further withdrawal was expected.

[636] Der Führer und Ober-Befehlshaber des Heeres/GenStdH/Op.Abt. (I) No. 420021/42, 15 Jan. 1942, carbon copy in BA-MA RH 2/v. 1327, fos. 101 ff.; printed in KTB OKW ii/2. 1268–9. For the individual shortenings of the front wrested from Hitler cf. Halder, Diaries, 1387–8 (13, 14 Jan. 1942); Reinhardt, Moskau, 246–7, with sources for the armies affected. Strauß requested permission to resign his command on 15 Jan. after the army group had issued a tactical order to XXIII Army Corps over the head of the army command, and not because of Hitler's directive. Reinhardt's interpretation (Moskau, 247) is mistaken.

[637] Halder, Diaries, 1387 (13 Jan. 1942).

[638] 'Active solution', Halder, KTB iii. 384 (not in trans.); Großmann, Rshew, 33 ff.; AOK 9/Ia, KTB, BA-MA 21520/1, and Die Winterschlacht bei Rshew [The Winter Battle of Rzhev], report of Pz.AOK 3, BA-MA RH 21-3/v. 138.

Yukhnov, were not abandoned, nor was the order to Second Armoured Army to relieve Sukhinichi. The withdrawal was to be carried out in easy stages; material losses were to be kept to a minimum and all transport facilities and possible lodging for the enemy destroyed.

Hitler's first order to 'pull back a major sector of the front', as he himself expressed it, was to be carried out in such a way that it would be dominated by 'the feeling of superiority of the troops over the enemy and their fanatical will to inflict as much damage and injury on him as possible'.[639] Halder likewise concerned himself with the psychological effects of the order to withdraw, but he sought to attribute a certain dejection among the troops in the face of the enemy's strong position to the report procedures of the intelligence officers.[640] In a directive to the chiefs of staff of the army groups, armies, and corps on 17 January 1942 he observed that the large number of enemy units reported had a certain paralysing effect which clashed with the sense of superiority of the troops. He continued: 'It is not acceptable that a command should succumb to an obsession with figures which only emphasizes the large number of units on the enemy's side and the present decline of fighting power on our side.' In providing a picture of the situation an exaggeration of the importance of the number of enemy units should be avoided. Intelligence staff were to be trained accordingly. 'Then there will be an end to the situation—which is quite unacceptable to the German general staff, when time and again the fighting spirit and toughness of our troops have put to shame the worried number-worshippers in the staffs.' This remark, made with an eye to Hitler's accusations, seems rather questionable in view of past developments and the many weeks of disputes about authorization of withdrawals which had in any case already been carried out and which were sometimes nothing other than panic-stricken flight. It should also be remembered that not only the commander-in-chief of Army Group South, but also Colonel-Generals Hoepner and Guderian, the commanding generals Graf von Sponeck and Freiherr von Gablenz (XXVII Army Corps), and on 15 January also the commanders-in-chief of Army, Group North and Ninth Army, had either already been removed from their commands or had requested to be relieved of their duties. The last-mentioned officer eventually decided to resign his command because of a dispute with Kluge. In fact this directive did not prevent any command from continuing to quote relevant figures on the enemy's strength in support of its accusations that insufficient forces were being provided to carry out the assigned tasks.

Under the new commander-in-chief of Ninth Army, General Walter Model, Hitler's first demand—that the enemy must be thrown back at Rzhev—was fulfilled after unsuccessful attempts on 21 January. The Soviet Thirty-ninth

---

[639] See n. 636 above.

[640] Directive of Chef GenStdH No. 10/42 regarding assessment of enemy's situation, 17 Jan. 1942, BA-MA RH 20-4/287; remark of chief of staff of Fourth Army for his Ic: 'Poor Helmdach.'

Army was pushed back near Sychevka; on 23 January contact was re-established between XXIII Army Corps in the north and VI Army Corps south of the penetration.[641] The defensive battles of Ninth Army along this front against Soviet attacks on both sides, thinly held at first, became in the end a German encirclement operation towards the south-west.

XXIV Armoured Corps, which had regrouped after receipt of Hitler's order on 13 January, was given the task of breaking the encirclement of Sukhinichi on the southern wing of the army group with forces of Second Armoured Army. The corps now had 18th and 4th Armoured Divisions, 208th Infantry Division, newly arrived parts of 339th Infantry Division, and three 'groups'.[642] After the preparatory attack by the armoured corps caught the enemy by surprise on 18 January, it was instructed to advance rapidly to Sukhinichi. From the very start it was not assumed that the town could be held, but it was necessary to await Hitler's decision. On 21 January Hitler wanted to thrust beyond Sukhinichi to cut off the enemy forces along the supply-route between Roslavl and Yukhnov, and he promised an attack group from Fourth Army from the area around Yukhnov to provide support: however, Fourth Army headquarters indicated that this could be provided only after a delay of at least ten days. Owing to heavy losses and a temperature of $-44\,°C$, the armoured army was by no means certain that it would be able to hold the town or, as ordered on 22 January, decisively defeat the enemy there. Because of heavy counter-attacks on the flanks of the thrust it was possible to advance only with a pointed wedge of two battalions of 216th and 208th Infantry Divisions. On 24 January they and several tanks of 18th Armoured Division were able to link up with the point of the break-out effort by the 'Group von Gilsa'. Losses in securing the narrow corridor to the town, estimated at 200 dead and wounded a day, forced the abandonment of the town on 28 January, after the wounded had been evacuated and demolition, mainly of the railway facilities, had been prepared. Even an order from Hitler to hold the town if at all possible, using artillery if necessary, thereby relieving pressure on Fourth Army, did not change the situation, any more than a later appeal by Halder, who considered that abandoning Sukhinichi after the great moral victory of relieving it would be too great a loss.[643] Field Marshal von Kluge ordered the annihilation of the

---

[641] For the source see n. 638.

[642] 2. Pz.Armee/Ia, KTB, 13 Jan. 1942, BA-MA RH 21-2/v. 876, 877. No formation had all its established units left. Divisions were broken up according to need: this was the origin of the 'groups' named after their commanders. After the arrival of Col.-Gen. Freiherr von Weichs on 15 Jan. 1942 Col.-Gen. Schmidt handed over command of Second Army.

[643] Halder, *Diaries*, 1395 (28 Jan. 1942). Hitler's demand for more pressure on Sukhinichi was repeated in the following days, with the promise of priority in assigning replacements. Second Armd. Army was to receive 1,000 men daily, but they could not be brought up without endangering supply transports; thus only two companies could be created: 2. Pz.Armee/Ia, KTB, 24, 29 Jan. 1942, BA-MA RH 21-2/v. 876, 877. Hitler's decree to the 'Soldaten der Kämpfe um Szuchinitschi' [Soldiers of the Sukhinichi battles], 27 Jan. 1942, is in BA-MA RH 20-4/287m, fo. 241.

enemy forces which had penetrated the area west and north-west of Bolkhov to be given priority over the tying down of forces at Sukhinichi.[644]

On 30 January the army group command saw the approach of catastrophe for Ninth Army, requiring intervention by Second Armoured Army, as the enemy was already 100 kilometres north-west of Smolensk at Velizh and Beloe. For this action 3rd Armoured Division, which had completed the restoration of the situation around Kursk, and parts of 211th Infantry Division along the railway line were available. On the other hand, the chance also presented itself of destroying the Soviet Sixty-first Army south-west of Belev.[645] Neither operation was carried out, in spite of Hitler's repeatedly expressed wishes. On the contrary, the supplying of explosive charges and detonators ordered by the Army High Command for the destruction of the artillery of the German units in the event of a forced withdrawal was continued. On 30 January the army group ordered Second Armoured Army to give priority to tying down strong enemy forces at Sukhinichi, and to subordinate its offensive task to that purpose.[646]

In spite of repeated, fierce enemy attacks, the situation of Second Armoured Army stabilized, and isolated thrusts led to defensive successes against the Soviet Sixty-first Army in the sector of XXXXVII Armoured Corps. On 13 February information was received from spies that the Soviet Third Army was going to suspend its attack. Optimism resulting from the belief that the situation was now under control became so strong that arguments between the commands of the armoured army and the army group on 13 February were no longer concerned with a withdrawal but with an offensive operation against Kirov; however, no clear orders could be obtained as the Army High Command and Hitler reserved the right to make all decisions. Colonel-General Schmidt commented: 'Difficile est, satiram non scribere [It is difficult not to write a satire].' The tactical planning of the army concentrated on closing the gaps in the front. With a total of forty-five combat-ready tanks and an additional forty-four undergoing repairs, and with the troops exhausted and battle-weary, while replacements were often not ready for action, nothing more could be expected. Improving forward positions took second place to the establishment of secure lines of communication against the muddy conditions of spring. Again the remote, complicated command structure restricted initiative, e.g. in the offensive to the north repeatedly demanded by Hitler west of

[644] Order H.Gr .Mitte/Ia No. 750/42, 27 Jan. 1942, BA-MA RH 20-4/287m, fos. 234 ff.; H.Gr. Mitte/Ia No. 813/42, 30 Jan. 1942, to 2. Pz.Armee, ibid. 288, fo. 97.

[645] Cf. enemy intelligence sheet AOK 4/Ic No. 2/42, 27 Jan. 1942, in which Vyazma and Smolensk were mentioned as the enemy's objectives: BA-MA RH 20-4/288, fo. 97; on the strategic effects of the attack on Sukhinichi from a Soviet perspective cf. sect. II.II.13 at n. 398 below (Hoffmann), and Reinhardt, *Moskau*, 250. 3rd Armd. Div. was placed under Army Group South.

[646] Order, 20 Jan. 1942, H.Gr. Mitte Ia betr. Zerstörladungen für Geschütze [re demolition charges for artillery pieces], BA-MA RH 20-4/288, fo. 48. Cf. also n. 638 above.

Sukhinichi, for which 3rd Armoured Division was to be made available. It now consisted of a battalion of eleven tanks, an infantry battalion of two companies, a sapper battalion of two companies, an artillery battalion of six guns, four anti-tank guns (self-propelled), and a motor-cycle rifle battalion. Army headquarters enquired with good reason how a decisive operation was to be carried out with these units.[647]

The uncertainty of the commanders was evident at a conference held on 9 March at the headquarters of Second Armoured Army, at which all commanding generals presented their opinions to the commander-in-chief of the army group. They had reservations about Kluge's demand to pull forces out of the front for rehabilitation. Nevertheless, Kluge insisted that the view that this could not be done was not acceptable. The wishes of the Army High Command had to be met. His personal opinion, however, was that the enemy would force the high command to change their plans.[648] This revealing remark completely confirmed the impression which Second Armoured Army and other headquarters had gained in the past months: that correct command decisions were not being supported with sufficient vigour towards higher levels of authority.

While the danger to the outer wings of the army group had been warded off by the middle of February, threatening situations still developed, especially for Fourth Army. After the penetration by the Soviet Thirty-ninth Army west of Rzhev had been sealed off, that army and XI Cavalry Corps remained in the rear area of Ninth Army and Fourth Armoured Army. Together with increasingly strong partisan groups, now under firm military command, they threatened the rear communication lines of both German armies.

Since the breakthrough at the boundary with Fourth Armoured Army north of Medyn and the simultaneous thrust by the Soviet I Guards Cavalry Corps, Fourth Army had been in danger of being encircled. The vital supply-route between Roslavl and Yukhnov was threatened and the railway line from Bryansk to Vyazma cut. Since 18 January 1942 the thrust into the rear of the 'winter position' of Fourth Army had resulted in the isolation of four army corps in the area of Yukhnov and forced the army constantly to shift its forces to threatened sectors of the front. This led its commander-in-chief—since 20 January General Gotthard Heinrici—to assess the situation very pessimistically.[649] On 1 February he expressed his doubts that it would be possible to lead the army out of its present situation. In contrast, however, the chief of his general staff and his first general-staff officer reported to the army group their conviction that such an effort would succeed. The new chief of staff of Fourth

---

[647] 2. Pz.Armee/Ia, KTB, 13, 19 Feb. 1942, BA-MA RH 21-2/876, 877. For the following, ibid., 9 Mar. 1942.

[648] Ibid., 9 Mar. 1942.

[649] Kluge's successor, Gen. Kübler, had not felt equal to the task and had been relieved: situation assessment Chef AOK4, 1 Feb. 1942, 10.10 a.m., BA-MA RH 20-4/288; Halder, *Diaries*, 1397 (28 Jan.–2 Feb. 1942).

Army—since 17 January Colonel Julius von Bernuth[650]—remarked to Halder that theoretically one could say that Fourth Army was lost, but it still had the will to keep fighting. The important thing was to reduce the salient somewhat but to hold the road between Yukhnov and Gzhatsk at all costs.[651]

On 3 February the situation was improved and a continuous front restored by the closing of the gap between Fourth Army and XX Army Corps of Fourth Armoured Army.

The most prominent feature of this phase of the winter battle of Fourth Army—more than was true of the other armies of Army Group Centre in comparable situations—was the necessity not only to defend itself on pocket-like front sectors in all directions, but, at the same time, also to master new dangers to supply-lines and strong points in its rear area. The first major airborne operation of the Red Army had created a situation that could certainly not be dealt with by the remaining security forces alone.[652]

The enemy forces identified on 12 February behind Fourth Armoured Army in the area of Vyazma, and especially along the railway line from Vyazma westward, may not have been able to mount any major independent operations, but fighting them was difficult. Recruitment from the local population led to strong concentrations, especially in the area of Bryansk. Intelligence indicated, however, that although the regular units concerned themselves with the organization and training of the partisans, in some cases they rejected their attempts to join the Red Army. On 21 January Fourth Army reacted to this situation by ordering the immediate strengthening of the defences of all supply installations and transport centres, and the detention and imprisonment of all male residents between 16 and 50 years of age. They were to be released after the area had been pacified.[653] In addition to fighting units in the rear area, which were combined in March under the commander of Rear Army Area Centre to form a 'Group Schenckendorff' (parts of 10th and 11th Armoured

---

[650] His predecessor, Maj.-Gen. Günther Blumentritt, took over the position of deputy chief of Army General Staff for operations from Lt.-Gen. Paulus.

[651] Heinrici's report can be inferred from the records of the conference between Kluge and Heinrici, 31 Jan. 1942, BA-MA RH 20-4/288, fo. 110. Evidently he wanted to evacuate the entire salient, which would have ruled out any prospect of closing the gap at Medyn and establishing contact with Fourth Armd. Army. The dissenting opinion of a chief of the general staff in a crisis can seldom be documented so clearly: ibid., 1 Feb. 1942, fos. 134–5; conversation between Bernuth and Halder, ibid. fo. 135; Halder, *Diaries*, 1396 (31 Jan. 1942). Heinrici wanted, in agreement with Kluge, to withdraw behind the Ugra. Cf. Reinhardt, *Moskau*, 251–2, with additional sources.

[652] First indications of a Soviet concentration of transport aircraft for airborne and paratroop operations on 13 Jan. 1942: AOK 4/Ia, KTB, 13 Jan. 1942, BA-MA RH 20–4/281, with confirmed annexe ibid. in 286, Reinhardt, 'Luftlandungen'. On similar operations in the sector of Army Group North and at Demyansk cf. sect. II.1.1(*g*) at n. 698.

[653] Report 537th Army Signal Reg., 23 Jan. 1942, BA-MA RH 20-4/287, fo. 108. According to this report, the staff of the partisans in Mitkino called itself the 'staff of the Soviet Twenty-third Army'. Elements of Soviet 6th Inf. Div., 5th Cavalry Div., and 6th Airborne Brg. were identified in the rear area of Fourth Armd. Army. The order of Fourth Army headquarters of 21 Jan. was limited to the combat area up to 10 km. behind the front on 23 Jan. 1941 and to the 'area in and north of the forest of Bogorodiskaya occupied by paratroops and partisans': ibid., fos. 76, 107.

Divisions still in fighting condition, the staff of 221st Division with troops), mounted detachments and the already approved 'native' security forces were organized.[654]

As, in addition to the usually young civilians, escaped prisoners of war were to be found among the recruited partisans, Fourth Army headquarters issued a directive to the troops on the treatment of prisoners taken in the rear area. All 'newly conscripted soldiers and civilians, former Red Army soldiers, and regular soldiers fighting in organized units' were to be treated in principle as prisoners and sent to prisoner collection-points 'in order to neutralize the propaganda of the commissars and politruks and make the fighting easier for our troops'. Persons suspected of being partisans were to be turned over for interrogation to Field Security Police 750, its special unit with XII Army Corps, or Rear Area Command 559. Individual partisans or partisan groups 'caught carrying out acts of sabotage or other hostile actions directed against the German Wehrmacht' and 'Red Army soldiers in German uniforms' were 'to be shot on the command of an officer'.[655]

In spite of the heavy and costly defensive fighting in which Army Group Centre was involved, on 2 February the chief of the Army General Staff believed that with the incipient restoration of a continuous front—the closing of the gaps near Rzhev and Medyn—the most dangerous phase of the winter campaign was coming to an end. He regarded the dispatch of strong Soviet units to the rear area of Ninth Army as a degeneration of the war 'into a sort of slugging bout' that would not produce any military decision.[656]

On 12 February guidelines for a new assignment of missions were issued in the 'Directive for the conduct of the fighting in the east after the end of winter'.[657]

(iv) WINTER FIGHTING IN THE AREA OF ARMY GROUP NORTH
UNTIL THE RE-ESTABLISHMENT OF A SOLID FRONT

After the evacuation of Tikhvin and the withdrawal of the right wing of Eighteenth Army behind the Volkhov—the bridgeheads Grusiny and Kirishi were still held—Army Group North expected that the Red Army would attempt to break the encirclement of Leningrad with an energetic thrust to crush the 'bottleneck' at Shlisselburg. With the establishing of an 'ice road'

---

[654] On 11 Feb. Hitler had forbidden any further creation of Ukrainian or Baltic field combat units (OKH/GenStdH/Org.Abt. (II) No. 736/42, 29 Mar. 1942, BA-MA RH 20-4/302). On 15 Mar. 1942, however, Fourth Army headquarters stated that only 'already initiated recruitments' would be carried out. This amounted to permission for the direct use of prisoners of war and other sections of the native population. Exact figures for the number with the German forces cannot be determined, as they were to be subtracted from reports on combat and supply strength. Cf. Gen.Kdo. XXXXIII. AK/IIa No. 130/42, 26 Jan. 1942, BA-MA RH 20-4/288, fo. 156 and elsewhere in this file. The shooting of exhausted prisoners was expressly forbidden. Cf. ibid., fos. 225–7.

[655] BA-MA RH 20-4/296. This was in line with the regulation of 18 July 1941. Cf. sect. II.1.1(b) at n. 178.

[656] Halder, Diaries, 1397 (2 Feb. 1942).   [657] Cf. sect. II.1.1(g) at n. 738.

across frozen Lake Ladoga the necessary strengthening of Soviet forces in Leningrad seemed quite possible. For this reason, on 23 December 1941 Field Marshal Ritter von Leeb considered abandoning the 'bottleneck' in order to free 227th Infantry Division for the strengthening of other sectors of the front.[658]

However, more likely than a thrust from Leningrad was an attack against the Volkhov front in the area of the boundary between Sixteenth and Eighteenth Armies with Chudovo and then a turn to the north as its objective. A third wedge of the attack was expected to be directed at the area around Staraya Russa south of Lake Ilmen. Another probable attack, between Rzhev and Ostashkov with the objective of cutting off II and X Army Corps, was not assumed to be imminent. The intention of the enemy units identified on the southern boundary of the army group seemed rather to be the encirclement of Ninth Army in the north. The covering forces were accordingly thin in the area around Peno, where, against Leeb's wishes, the Army High Command had sent a regiment of the newly arrived 81st Infantry Division as a reserve.

After the costly battles and heavy losses from frostbite, and in view of the low number of new units brought up—three divisions (81st, 225th, and 218th Infantry Divisions), several regiments and battalions of the army, the Waffen-SS, the Luftwaffe, and the police—the commander-in-chief of Army Group North was certain that his forces would not be able to repel a major Soviet attack.

In the north too the guiding principle of the German defence was the order to hold existing lines and strong points. The order to hold the strong points, regardless of whether or not the defenders believed they had been bypassed, and the ban on any operational evacuation without Hitler's permission were issued with the promise to close the larger gaps in the front with fresh divisions from Germany or western Europe. The strengthening of air support by the Luftwaffe and the declining fighting power of the enemy in the middle of winter would bring his attacks to a standstill. 'Until then hold every village, do not retreat a step, fight to the last bullet and shell—that is what the situation demands now.'[659]

The most important requirement for this form of combat was the bringing up of new units and sufficient replacements. That was all the more necessary as with the arrival of hard frost the swamps, previously almost impassable, had to be included and occupied in any defence. The army group had to resort to shifting individual units, bringing rear-area personnel up to the front, and to the conversion of 8th and 12th Armoured Divisions, already withdrawn for rehabilitation, into three construction battalions each under their divisional

[658] Leeb, *Tagebuchaufzeichnungen*, 422. After the Soviet forces in Oranienbaum had been strengthened by the troops evacuated from Hanko, the command of Army Group North expected the establishment of a link with Leningrad.

[659] Führerbefehl betr. Lage und Kampfführung im Osten [Führer order concerning situation and conduct of operations in the east], 1 Jan. 1942, BA-MA, 16. Armee, 23468/8.

commander. At the same time these battalions were employed as security forces in the rear of I and XXVIII Army Corps. As the last significant 'mobile' unit, the army group placed parts of 20th Motorized Infantry Division behind the army boundary near the mouth of the Tigoda river. At the same time an alternative position was reconnoitred west of the Volkhov.

The bulk of 81st Infantry Division was assembled in the area of Chudovo to counter the expected main effort of the attack at the mouth of the Tigoda. The urgently requested 225th Infantry Division from France was still in Liepaja port. In order to have at least parts of it available in time, the army group demanded that the division should be airlifted to the front via Danzig by the Luftwaffe.

On 1 January the fighting along the salient on the Volkhov between Gruziny and Malukssa reached its first climax. The army group planned to hold the 'Tigoda corner' with all available reserves and strong air support. Because of the extreme cold, −40 °C, counter-attacks were considered futile.[660] On 4 January Leeb concluded that enemy attempts to overrun the defences on the Volkhov had failed, but he expected further large-scale attacks. It remained to be seen whether their objective would be Leningrad or the elimination of the 'bottleneck'. Once the bay of Kronshtadt had frozen over, he did not rule out the possibility of a Soviet attack against the left wing of the German forces besieging Oranienbaum.

On 8 January 1942 the expected strong enemy attack against Staraya Russa began south of Lake Ilmen; at the same time an additional thrust was taking shape south of Ostashkov, which the army group interpreted as an attempt to cut off the two southern corps of Sixteenth Army. The defensive positions around Staraya Russa were regarded as sufficiently strong to protect that important supply-point. On the southern wing, however, the enemy succeeded in penetrating the front of 123rd Infantry Division. Sixteenth Army headquarters thereupon ordered II Army Corps immediately to transfer there all non-essential elements of 12th and 32nd Infantry Divisions, which were west of Lake Velye and had not yet taken part in the fighting.[661]

After this enemy penetration, the army had to expect that supplies from Staraya Russa for II Army Corps would be cut off, and therefore prepared to transfer such operations to Kholm and the railhead of Loknya. From there the corps was to be supplied by motorized transport. Once the enemy had made numerous penetrations of the position of 123rd Infantry Division and cut the supply-route south of Staraya Russa, Field Marshal von Leeb saw no purpose in trying to hold the position. On 10 January he had no choice but to withdraw II and X Corps to the Lovat. This action also offered the best possibility of freeing forces for the Volkhov sector.[662]

[660] H.Gr. Nord/Ia, KTB, *passim*, BA-MA RH 19 III/178; Leeb, *Tagebuchaufzeichnungen*, 427 ff. (1–3 Jan. 1942).

[661] H.Gr. Nord/Ia, KTB, 9 Jan. 1942, BA-MA RH 19 III/178; AOK 16/Ia, situation assessment, 9 Jan. 1942, BA-MA, 16. Armee, 23468/19.

[662] Together with this situation assessment, Leeb considered sending a letter of resignation and presumably discussed it with Halder: Leeb, *Tagebuchaufzeichnungen*, 432 (9, 10 Jan. 1942): H.Gr.

The commander-in-chief of Sixteenth Army, however, still saw no tactical need for a withdrawal, but he conceded that for supply reasons, even after the transfer to Kholm and Loknya, such a decision would have to be taken under certain circumstances, though this would result in a significant loss of fighting power.[663]

On the morning of 12 January Leeb reported this situation to Halder. At the same time he added that it was not to be expected that the front could be held against the imminent enemy attack on the Volkhov and that therefore a phased removal of XXXIX Armoured Corps via Lyuban–Tosno to the west, starting on the right wing, should be prepared.

The report of enemy penetrations between Lake Ilmen and Staraya Russa and the temporary disruption of communications to the south caused Hitler to issue an immediate order to restore the situation by offensive action. X Army Corps was to hold the line to the western shore of Lake Velye.

After this first decision, which was transmitted by Keitel and envisaged the withdrawal of forces from the southern front of Sixteenth Army for the purpose of an attack, the army group ordered the army to prepare to establish a new defensive front east of Molvotitsy, i.e. the withdrawal of II Army Corps on its southern front.

In a lengthy conversation Leeb explained to Hitler the need to withdraw II Army Corps. Staraya Russa could be considered secure. Hitler reminded Leeb of the situation on the front as a whole and stated that he could not accept a wide gap in the direction of Ninth Army. Therefore a second blocking-position was to be established along the railway line. Leeb's feelings were evident from the fact that, shortly after this conversation, he asked the commander-in-chief of Eighteenth Army, Colonel-General von Küchler, to make plans in case 'far-reaching decisions' had to be taken, i.e. a withdrawal of the parts of the army facing Leningrad in the event of an enemy breakthrough on the Volkhov front.[664] Fear of a collapse of the central section of his eastern front dominated Leeb's thoughts far more than the situation on his southern front.

The army group was promised an assault-gun battalion and the reinforcement of Air Fleet 1 with a dive-bomber Gruppe. Moreover, available tanks were ordered to be repaired immediately for use behind the front in the event of enemy breakthroughs. The bringing up of 218th Infantry Division was accelerated.

The basic difference between Hitler's plan, which envisaged the holding of

Nord/Ia, KTB, 10 Jan. 1942, BA-MA RH 19 III/178. Leeb's basic idea was that the Red Army wanted to open the ring around Leningrad from the south and that all defensive forces should therefore be concentrated on the Volkhov.

[663] The differences in the assessment of the situation by the two C.-in-C.s stem from Leeb's above-mentioned report. On 11 Jan. 1942 at 12.50 p.m. the general-staff officer in charge of supply and administration ordered the immediate rerouting of supplies for the southern wing of Sixteenth Army via Kholm: H.Gr. Nord/Ia, KTB, 10, 11 Jan. 1942, BA-MA RH 19 III/178.

[664] Ibid., 12, 13 Jan. 1942; Leeb, *Tagebuchaufzeichnungen*, 432 ff. He probably also suggested a possible successor.

the area around Demyansk as a base for future operations, and Leeb's purely defensive thinking persisted even after their personal conversation on 13 January. Leeb requested to be relieved of his post, and Hitler granted his request on 17 January. The commander-in-chief of Eighteenth Army, Colonel-General von Küchler, became the new commander-in-chief of Army Group North. The chief of staff, Lieutenant-General Brennecke, was also relieved and replaced by Colonel Wilhelm Hasse. The new commander-in-chief of Eighteenth Army was General Georg Lindemann.

The enemy attacks to isolate II Army Corps continued on 15 January. By then the commander-in-chief of Sixteenth Army also came to the conclusion that a withdrawal of the corps behind the Lovat was the only chance of saving it.[665]

On 16 January the chief of the Army General Staff, whose main anxiety at this time was the situation of Army Group Centre, whose left flank he believed would be even more endangered by a withdrawal of II Corps, objected to the 'negative direction' and the 'operations mania' in the staff of Army Group North. The group had been given an explicit order not to withdraw. The top leadership would accept responsibility. Accordingly, Hitler forbade a withdrawal of II Army Corps in an order of 16 January.[666] As a means of stabilizing the situation on the Volkhov he suggested forces from the Leningrad sector, whose withdrawal from that front seemed acceptable, since the enemy was also reducing his forces there.

Thus the decision was taken in the southern sector of Army Group North, and any withdrawal, though called for by tactical and supply reasons, was forbidden. Nevertheless, a number of good reasons can be presented for maintaining the course of the front of Sixteenth Army in this sector. Firstly, the situation on the northern wing of Army Group Centre at this time was so precarious that any action which would have freed significant Soviet forces on the Kalinin front would quickly have made an encirclement inevitable. The intention of Sixteenth Army to retreat slowly and with delaying actions could scarcely have been realized. The German troops occupied more or less fortified positions and still had most of their heavy equipment and artillery. Reports on mobility and starving horses leave no doubt that little more than infantry weapons could have been brought back if the intention of the enemy units in the gap in the direction of Ninth Army was—and Leeb was certain of this—to attack vigorously from the south through the Lovat valley.

For Hitler, and also for Halder, the decisive factor—in addition to the situation of Ninth Army, the simultaneous order to Army Group Centre to hold its front, and operational plans for 1942—was very probably the need to demonstrate 'strong nerves'. On 8 January he had explained that the Soviet

---

[665] H.Gr. Nord/Ia, KTB, 15 Jan. 1942, BA-MA RH 19 III/178. Leeb informed Keitel orally. He was so impressed by the Soviet attack on the Volkhov front that he believed 'great decisions' were imminent.

[666] H.Gr. Nord/Ia, KTB, 16 Jan. 1942; Leeb, *Tagebuchaufzeichnungen*, 439 (16 Jan. 1942).

conduct of the fighting assumed an operational sensitivity on the German side from which the Soviet command was not suffering. The Soviet intention, according to Hitler, was to drive the German troops out of their strong positions and thus deprive them of their immobile heavy weapons. As this attack was not being carried out by units that could be considered of the highest calibre, strong nerves would be decisive.[667] The only possibility for the Germans was therefore 'to resist as strongly as possible—on principle'. A unit was entitled to retreat only when, for lack of ammunition or supplies, it was no longer able to harm the enemy. 'The command of any formation can speak of the necessity of a withdrawal of large units only when it believes that only thus can it avoid certain annihilation.' None of these conditions applied to the southern wing of Sixteenth Army.

The new commander-in-chief of the army group had himself briefed by the commander-in-chief of Sixteenth Army on 18 January and, rejecting the latter's reasons for the necessity of a withdrawal, referred to the fate of Napoleon's army, which had been destroyed by enemy forces attacking from the surrounding countryside during its retreat. But there was no time now for theoretical discussions about a well-prepared withdrawal accompanied by various delaying actions. The same day Küchler ordered the transfer of XXXIX Armoured Corps command to the right wing of the army group with orders to secure the southern flank from Kholm up to the boundary with II Army Corps.[668]

But on 27 January, even before the command arrived there, the city had already fallen. Of the parts of 218th Infantry Division ordered there only the commander, Major-General Theodor Scherer, and his staff had reached Kholm. The troops consisted of four companies of police, three companies of infantry, some smaller parts of 385th Infantry Regiment, the baggage-train, and rear area services, with a total of about 3,500 men. Attempts to provide immediate relief were unsuccessful.

Ever since 14 January General Graf von Brockdorff-Ahlefeldt, commanding general of II Army Corps, whose fronts were extended by the incipient encirclement, had been demanding reinforcements and more supplies.[669] As a first unit a regimental group was airlifted to Demyansk from Riga. On 18

---

[667] Extract from Hitler's order by H.Gr. Nord/Ia No. 2/42 in BA-MA, 16. Armee, 23468/8. The data underlying this order, based on assessments of the enemy's situation by Foreign Armies East, can be easily proved, but a considerable number of C.-in-C.s did not accept Hitler's conclusions, e.g. Guderian, Hoepner, and Leeb. For those commanders who could not escape the conflict between the duties of command and the welfare of their troops by resigning their posts or reporting sick, the situation became tragic. The most obvious example was Gen. Walter Graf von Brockdorff-Ahlefeldt, who urged the withdrawal of his corps and very reluctantly became the 'hero of Demyansk'.

[668] Röhricht, *Kesselschlacht*, example XII, pp. 131 ff.; popular account in Haupt, *Demjansk*, 36 ff.; Müller-Hillebrand, Nordabschnitt, pt. II, 245 ff., MGFA P-114a; order AOK 16/Ia No. 330/42 to Gen.Kdo. XXXIX. Pz.Korps, 22 Jan. 1942: BA-MA, 16. Armee, 23468/6. As late as 20 Jan. 1942 the army headquarters, like Halder, had considered the situation at Kholm not to be dangerous: H.Gr. Nord/Ia, KTB, BA-MA RH 19 III/178.

[669] AOK 16/Ia, KTB, 14 Jan. 1942 and following days, BA-MA, 16. Armee, 23468/11.

January the corps reported that the condition of the troops and the lack of sufficient supplies and fuel made it impossible to hold their position for more than a few days; the report was accompanied by a request that it be forwarded to the Army High Command. Moreover, the following day the corps requested the sending of a more senior general-staff officer of the Army High Command—a sign of its limited confidence in its immediate superior.[670]

On 23 January the commander-in-chief of the army stated clearly that he expected the corps not only to hold the front lines but also to form reserves to halt enemy penetrations. In contrast, the commanding general of the corps was of the opinion that there were only two alternatives: either to eliminate the breakthrough on the right flank by attacks or to pull the entire front back. On 26 January he again pointed out that 190 kilometres of front could not be defended with his available equipment and forces. On 27 January, after acknowledging the problems, Halder expressed his criticism of this attitude to the chief of the general staff of Army Group North. He confirmed the intention, which required the holding of the front of II Corps, to close the gap in the direction of Ninth Army at a later date, starting from there, and demanded obedience from the commanding general of the corps. Agreement between himself, Hasse, and the commander-in-chief of the army group was crucial. Hasse defended the use of the few forces of the corps and Sixteenth Army, which had to defend its eastern front and could not always expose sectors as Halder desired so as to create groups at points of main effort.[671] For Halder the central problem of the situation south of Lake Ilmen was the securing of Staraya Russa as a supply-base; after the solution of this question everything else was to be regarded as settled.[672] The army group itself considered the town to be already adequately secured, and it did in fact remain in German hands. The attacks by the Soviet Eleventh Army were directed towards the south and aimed at encircling the two German corps around Demyansk and at recapturing Kholm.[673]

At the same time the situation north of Lake Ilmen was dominated by the identified grouping of the Soviet Second Assault Army and Fifty-second Army for an attack across the Volkhov against German communications in the direction of Leningrad. On 13 January these units attacked on a narrow front

[670] On 24 Jan. 1942 Halder dispatched Lt.-Col. Graf zu Eulenburg to report on the boundary between Army Groups Centre and North: Halder, *Diaries*, 1394 (27 Jan. 1942).

[671] H.Gr. Nord/Ia, 23, 26, 27 Jan. 1942, BA-MA RH 19 III/178. Halder referred to the report by Eulenburg and Brockdorff-Ahlefeldt as the cause of 'irritation' regarding agreement between himself, Küchler, and Hasse.

[672] On 28 Jan. (ibid.) Halder's clearly perceptible criticism caused Hasse to discuss the matter with Heusinger later and again argue his point that the Soviet Third Assault Army was aiming at Kholm and the Lovat, and that it was therefore necessary to strengthen defences in the sector of II Army Corps. Halder, on the other hand, saw this Soviet army only as a danger to Ninth Army.

[673] The importance of Kholm as a transport centre on the only all-weather north–south road between Staraya Russa and Toropets justified the numerous attacks by the Soviet army as well as its extensive and costly defence. The thrusts under the command of XXXIX Armd. Corps to free the road to Kholm had the character only of an assault party and achieved a single delivery of assault-guns.

after a heavy artillery barrage. Following a successful penetration at Myasnoy Bor, the spearheads of the attack reached the railway line between Novgorod and Chudovo.

To the north, in the area of the Tigoda debouchment into the Volkhov and near Pogostye, enemy offensives began the following day; with the exception of the loss of a front sector near Pogostye, these were repelled.[674] The two thrusts clearly revealed the enemy's intention to encircle the German units west of the Volkhov and, after destroying them, to push on to Leningrad. The thrust Leeb expected from the area of Oranienbaum was limited to an attack with armoured support against 217th Infantry Division on the left wing; the attack was thrown back. In consequence, large parts of three divisions could be taken out of the encirclement front facing Leningrad and moved to the threatened Volkhov front in order to contain the enemy penetration. The Luftwaffe provided regiments and battalions for use as infantry units; army troops, security units, and other armed personnel were sent to the front from the rear area, in addition to the Spanish (250th) Infantry Division, the Dutch Legion, and the Norwegian battalion of the Waffen-SS. Guard-duty and escort battalions were brought in by air. An extremely heterogeneous fighting force was assembled, to which Halder contributed a Walküre division (329th Infantry Division).

At the end of January 1942 Army Group North was under such pressure that it reported it would be able to defend its front only if it received more divisions in the immediate future. Attempts of blockade by Eighteenth Army at the beginning of February succeeded only with considerable effort in limiting the further fanning out of enemy forces west of the Volkhov. More units than the 'combat groups' mentioned were not available.[675]

At the beginning of February the lack of fighting power and differences of opinion about the necessary manning of the front led to serious disputes between the commander-in-chief of the army group and the commander-in-chief of Sixteenth Army; these had to be settled by Hitler himself. They had already arisen in January on the issue of which reserves were to be taken out of the front of the corps in the area around Demyansk so as to repel unexpected enemy penetrations. The strain increased perceptibly, as did signs that 'strong nerves' were necessary not just when facing the enemy.[676]

All attempts west of Demyansk to prevent a link-up of the enemy groups

---

[674] The assessment of the situation of the enemy showed the Soviet Fifty-second Army, Second Assault Army, and XIII Army Corps with a total of 20 units: H.Gr. Nord/Ia, KTB, BA-MA RH 19 III/179, and operations atlas of the army group, ibid. 661D.

[675] AOK 16/Ia, KTB, 1–28 Feb. 1942, BA-MA, 16. Armee, 23 468/3; army group order, 1 Feb. 1942: H.Gr. Nord/Ia, KTB, 2 Feb. 1942, BA-MA RH 19 III/179.

[676] BA-MA RH 19 III/179 and AOK 16/Ia, BA-MA, 16. Armee, 23 468/3; Halder, *Diaries*, 1397–8 (2, 3 Feb. 1942). Küchler demanded that Busch take strong measures with II Army Corps. Busch considered such reproaches 'not acceptable', but ordered the corps immediately to pull a battalion out of the line and place it under its western front ('Group Eicke'). Küchler then demanded that Busch be relieved of his command, but because of Hitler's mediation this was not done. Halder and Keitel unequivocally supported Küchler's point of view.

approaching from the north and south were unsuccessful. After land contact between Staraya Russa and II Army Corps had been cut on 8 February, Sixteenth Army command attempted to re-establish contact with 290th infantry Division on the north-western front of the pocket the following day, using the first regiments of 5th Light Infantry Division to arrive, but this unsuccessful effort produced only heavy losses. The encircled divisions of II and X Army Corps in Demyansk had supplies sufficient to last them until 13 February; thereafter a secure corridor would have to be established or else the corps would have to be supplied by air. The third possibility—to retreat to the Lovat—was no longer open, and not only because of Hitler's orders. The enemy forces there were so strong that 5th Light Division had to be drawn upon to check an attack on Staraya Russa on 15 February. The second thrust envisaged with this division against the western front of the Demyansk pocket was not carried out.[677] The six divisions in this area of about 3,000 square kilometres prepared to defend themselves against attacks from all directions.

In view of the enemy's strength and the heavy losses suffered in the first attempt, the general commanding X Army Corps did not consider a renewed relief effort possible until all parts of 5th Light Division had been assembled. As that was scheduled only for 19 February and as by then the situation of 290th Infantry Division would become increasingly exposed, he requested its withdrawal behind the railway line but did not receive Küchler's agreement.[678] The only assistance immediately available would be intensified Luftwaffe attacks on the Soviet First Assault Army.

Hitler thereupon intervened in the deliberations and advocated a repetition of the attack after the arrival of the entire 5th Light Division.[679] Generally, however, infantry attacks without adequate armoured or air support had no prospects of success. The northern part of the forest zone east of Staraya Russa therefore had to be subjected to several days of concentrated attacks by the Luftwaffe in order to eliminate the threat to the flanks posed by the attack from the north. But such attacks, especially with the limited forces available, could not achieve the effect of days of massed artillery bombardment, as Hitler had perhaps imagined. The army group command was perfectly aware of this and therefore, like Halder, initially interpreted Hitler's 'suggestion' as permission to use Air Fleet 1 as it saw fit. Only gradually did the second, much more alarming, aspect of that suggestion become evident, when it was put in the form of an order on 4 March.[680] All attacks by army units now had to be

---

[677] This division had been reorganized from 5th Inf. Div., which had been pulled out of the front facing Moscow, as had 8th Lgt. Div., which was later brought up. Cf., however, Reinhardt, *Moskau*, 82. There can be no question of these divisions having been pulled out because victory was considered a certainty; they were exhausted.

[678] H.Gr. Nord/Ia, KTB, 10 Feb. 1942, BA-MA RH 19 III/179; reports of X Army Corps to Army Group North: BA-MA, 16. Armee, 23468/11.

[679] H.Gr. Nord/Ia, KTB, 10 Feb. 1942; the commanding general of the corps had demanded that the danger should be reported 'to the highest decision-making authority'.

[680] Message from Halder to Army Group North, 10 Feb. 1942, H.Gr. Nord/Ia, KTB, BA-MA RH 19 III/179; OKH/GenStdH/Op.Abt. (IN) No. 420088/42, 4 Mar. 1942, BA-MA RH 19 III/707; confirmation by Hitler: H.Gr. Nord/Ia No. 1009/42, 22 Mar. 1942, BA-MA 16. Armee, 23468/8,

postponed until the Luftwaffe was able to provide adequate support. This made operationally or tactically necessary measures dependent on weather conditions and technical factors involved in air support, and it encouraged a tendency not to carry out attacks without air support or to shift responsibility for the necessary decisions to the Luftwaffe. The effect this had on the maintenance of schedules for attacks is obvious.

How strongly Hitler again believed that, in spite of the condition of the army, he could take advantage of new 'opportunities' was shown by his reaction to reports from Foreign Armies East that the Red Army was now able to mass strong concentrations of troops on the Volkhov front and at Staraya Russa by withdrawing units from more distant front sectors, e.g. from the Leningrad area. Hitler concluded that the defences of the city could now be overrun by a shock troop assault. Only with some effort was the army group command able to make him understand that neither was sufficient ammunition available for such an assault, nor could a position be established in front of the outer encirclement ring that could be held when the spring thaw set in. Moreover, the army group command pointed out, it was now too late—a clear reminder of the failure to create a point of main effort during the summer.[681]

As late as 11 February the army group command and Sixteenth Army headquarters were uncertain whether the enemy planned to encircle Staraya Russa from the south after penetrating the Lovat valley or intended instead to turn east and encircle the German forces around Demyansk. The chief of staff of the army group considered the second possibility to be 'not so bad' because it would allow the massing of German troops at Staraya Russa to proceed undisturbed. The chief of staff of Sixteenth Army, on the other hand, saw a great danger to 290th Infantry Division, whose supply-dump had burnt out the day before. Hitler, however, rejected a new request to withdraw the division as the Luftwaffe had promised delivery of adequate supplies.[682]

The decision about freeing the two army corps in the pocket had to be based on the assumption that the forces of 5th Light Division so far available were not sufficient, and that 290th Infantry Division in the extreme north-west of the pocket, nearest to a relief thrust from Staraya Russa, had after all to be pulled back. This greatly increased the distance and necessitated a change in the direction of a new thrust—no longer from Staraya Russa eastwards, but

Leeb's comment. Cf. also Bock, *Tagebuch*, 21 Mar. 1942, BA-MA N 22/13; here the fallacy is revealed particularly clearly in the case of the Crimea.

[681] H.Gr. Nord/Ia, KTB, 9–11 Feb. 1942, BA-MA RH 19 III/179, shows that Hitler expected a 'positive foreign-policy effect on Finland'. Halder too seems not to have excluded the possibility that the Soviet Leningrad front could collapse 'like a house of cards'. This view was one reason for the continued recourse to the German units there; by then these would scarcely have been able to withstand a sally by the Soviet troops.

[682] Sixteenth Army learnt of this rejection on 11 Feb. through the chief of staff of the air fleet when he requested data for supply flights: BA-MA, 16. Armee, 23468/3; message on Hitler's rejection by head of operations department to chief of staff of Army Group North according to teletype message H.Gr. Nord/Ia to AOK 16 No. 374/42, BA-MA, 16. Armee, 23468/11; Halder, *Diaries*, 1401–2 (11 Feb. 1942).

southwards in the direction of the 'Group Eicke' on the western edge of the pocket. This last solution ran counter to Halder's intentions; he objected to such a 'makeshift solution' and insisted that 290th Division should hold its positions. On 13 February Hitler accepted this view, which in any case was in line with his basically still valid order.[683]

In order to assemble the relief group and prepare the air strikes, the attack envisaged for 14 February was postponed to the 18th or 19th of the month, which meant that 290th Infantry Division would be forced to hold its positions, although this was no longer possible given its situation as a whole and the enemy pressure to which it was exposed. Hasse remarked to Heusinger: 'There are certain limits. Anything beyond them is against reason and in the final analysis incompatible with discipline.' He had to accept responsibility for the orders he issued, and that required knowing that they could be carried out. He also emphatically defended his point of view to Halder.[684]

Airborne supply deliveries for the two 'fortresses' Demyansk and Kholm now began. On 17 February Hitler expressed his determination to have II Army Corps hold out and promised Army Group North additional forces.[685] The battalions to be flown in immediately were, however, intended to make the SS Police Division and other units from the Leningrad front available for the Volkhov pocket.

On 18 February, at a major oral situation report by the commanders-in-chief of Army Groups North and Centre, in the presence of the chiefs of the Army and Luftwaffe General Staffs, Hitler made new decisions.[686] In his first survey of the situation he assumed that the danger of a panic like that of 1812, which had seemed imminent in November 1941, had been overcome. The situation of Army Group South was stable, and a basis for future operations had even been created there. In the sector of Army Group Centre there was still some uncertainty, but the measures taken there promised to stabilize the situation soon. At Rzhev the encirclement of large enemy forces was preparing the ground for a success. Hitler accepted the judgement of Army Group North that the Soviet operations in that sector had only one great objective—to raise the siege of Leningrad. For military and political reasons that had to be prevented.[687] (See the Annexe Volume, No. 21.)

---

[683] The same view was held by the chief of staff of Army Group North in KTB, 13 Feb. 1942: BA-MA RH 19 III/179; Halder, *Diaries*, 1403 (13 Feb. 1942). But cf. draft AOK 16, 12 Feb. 1942, BA-MA, 16. Armee, 32468/3.

[684] H.Gr. Nord/Ia, KTB, 15 Feb. 1942, BA-MA RH 19 III/179.

[685] For this purpose 337 transport aircraft were to be made available; the additional forces included 5 police battalions, 1 battalion of the Leibstandarte, and the Norwegian Legion of the Waffen-SS. These units, however, because of their short training period, were not envisaged for immediate duty at the front; 8th Lgt. Div. was promised the following day: Halder, *Diaries*, 1405 (17, 18 Feb. 1942); H.Gr. Nord/Ia, KTB, for those days, BA-MA RH 19 III/179.

[686] H.Gr. Nord/Ia, KTB, 18 Feb. 1942, BA-MA RH 19 III/179; Halder, *Diaries*, 1405 (18 Feb. 1942).

[687] Hitler was alluding to the danger of an Anglo-American landing in the far north, which he considered to be very great.

In addition to the need to eliminate the enemy penetration on the Volkhov front, Hitler emphasized his intention to close the gap between Army Groups Centre and North by an attack from the area of Ostashkov. After being promised two additional divisions, Army Group Centre agreed that such an operation was feasible, while the commander-in-chief of Army Group North expressed himself more cautiously: first it was necessary to await the result of the operation south of Lake Ilmen. Hitler agreed with the measures taken there and placed 329th Infantry Division and 8th Light Division at the disposal of the army group.

Küchler obtained approval for a withdrawal of 290th Infantry Division. That this entailed a new direction of attack and would require an increase in the strength of the relief group was, however, not discussed.[688]

The situation in Kholm became especially critical on 19 February. There Major-General Scherer urgently requested replacements and the immediate dispatch of a company of paratroops, as otherwise the position could be held only for a very short time.[689]

The operations department of the Army General Staff now decided to co-ordinate all plans of attack by Army Group North in such a way that the divisions made available from the Leningrad front were to be used first against the Volkhov pocket and subsequently in part against Demyansk. There, on 22 February under enemy pressure, II Army Corps had to carry out a further straightening of its front.[690] Generally speaking, Army Group North was still unable to work out a definitive schedule for the removal of battle-worthy units from the Leningrad front or the time required for the envisaged operations. On 23 February Hitler decided that the attack against the Demyansk pocket should not take place until after the arrival of 8th Light Division, i.e. in the middle of March at the earliest, dangerously close to the beginning of the spring thaw.[691]

On 24 February the commander-in-chief of Army Group North described for Hitler the basic problems of the offensives yet to be launched. He con-cluded that, because of the dependence on good weather, the actions of the enemy, and air support, the forces for the two operations should be completely separated.[692] In specific terms this meant that the two divisions to be removed from the Leningrad front for the Volkhov offensive should be kept ready

[688] In fact only 5th Lgt. Div. was mentioned. Küchler's report was submitted to the Army High Command and sent to the army headquarters: Gedanken über die Lage und die Fortsetzung der Verteidigung [Thoughts on the situation and the continuation of defence], 18 Feb. 1942, BA-MA, 16. Armee, 23468/5.

[689] Army Group North reported this to the Army High Command; Halder learnt that such forces were no longer available: H.Gr. Nord/Ia, KTB, 19 Feb. 1942, BA-MA RH 19 III/179.

[690] Hitler approved all requests, including the transfer of a Luftwaffe battalion to Demyansk: ibid., 22 Feb. 1942.

[691] Hitler demanded a report on envisaged attacks, the forces to be used, the timing, and the schedule for the entire army group area by 24 Feb.: ibid., 23 Feb. 1942.

[692] H.Gr. Nord/Ia, No. 470/42, 24 Feb. 1942, to OKH/GenStdH/Op.Abt., BA-MA, 16. Armee, 23468/5. This conclusion was based on Küchler's report of 18 Feb. 1942 (see n. 688 above).

exclusively for that purpose, and that another group of forces should be assembled from available and expected units for the thrust against Demyansk. Bringing up new forces was a transport problem for whose solution Küchler demanded suitably energetic measures.[693] He removed an additional division from Eighteenth Army on the Leningrad front; it was to be ready for action after 12 March. The two divisions from the Leningrad front for the Volkhov attack were to be ready on 5 and 6 March, after their relief units had arrived.

The attacks on the point where the Soviet armies had penetrated across the Volkhov were to be carried out towards Kretsno by the SS Police Division from the north and 58th Infantry Division from the south.[694] At the same time the German units and combat groups along the fronts of the pocket were to attack the enemy forces facing them.

The northern group had a total of eleven battalions at its disposal, of which seven had an average combat strength of 420 men, the others only 180 men each. There were also fifteen artillery batteries and thirty-three tanks. The southern group had six battalions of an average strength of 320 men and was supported by twelve artillery batteries and eight tanks. As the attack progressed, an additional eight battalions, eighteen batteries, and twenty-six tanks became available. They had been scraped together as a mobile formation of the army group at the end of February 1942 and, apart from the determination of dates demanded by Luftwaffe support, were commanded down to tactical details by the supreme commander of the Wehrmacht, the chief of the Army General Staff, the army group command, and Eighteenth Army command.

The situation of the attack group south of Lake Ilmen was similar. To start the attack, after Luftwaffe units from the Volkhov front became available on about 16 March, Küchler planned to use 329th Infantry Division, 5th and 8th Light Divisions, and the six battalions of 18th Infantry Division (mot.). Parts of 122nd Infantry Division were to be brought up later. To cover the flanks of the thrust the army group was counting on fourteen battalions from the Luftwaffe. Until the start of the relief attack the army group expected daily personnel losses of about 200 men in the divisions involved (5th Light and 18th Motorized). Of the sixteen tanks, 40 per cent might not be fit for action. It was important that no unexpected developments should force an early intervention on the western encirclement front.

---

[693] Demands of this kind are to be found from the very beginning in the war diary of Army Group North, for it possessed the Baltic ports and a more efficient transport network than the two army groups further south. Therefore in the eyes of the army group only the rail system could be blamed for the failure. Cf. Rohde, *Wehrmachttransportwesen*, 290.

[694] H.Gr. Nord/Ia No. 490/42, 26 Feb. 1942; with supplements, 6 Mar. 1942, BA-MA, 16. Armee, 23468/5. Hitler's objections and suggestions, of 25 Feb. 1942 are in KTB, H.Gr. Nord, BA-MA RH 19 III/179. The police division was handed over to the Waffen-SS as of 24 Feb. 1942. Cf. Tessin, *Verbände und Truppen*, xiv. 287.

It was not only the situation at Demyansk that gave cause for concern in the army group order of 26 February 1942; that at Kholm was also repeatedly very serious. All relief thrusts by the 'Group Uckermann' had failed because of snow and stubborn Soviet resistance. The supply situation was made worse by the temporary loss of the airfield.

On 2 March, after approving the proposal of Army Group North, Hitler summoned the commanders-in-chief of the army group, both armies, and the participating army corps.[695] For the Volkhov operation he proposed risking as few losses as possible and starving out the encircled enemy instead of wiping him out in attacks. Demyansk was to be defended 'like a fortress' until it was relieved. Because of the need for Luftwaffe support, the dates for the operations were set for 5 March for Kholm, 7 March for the Volkhov attack, and 15 March for the relief of the Demyansk pocket.

On this occasion Küchler attempted in vain to 'save' a mountain infantry regiment first promised by Hitler for the relief attack against Kholm and then for the operation against Demyansk. In view of this wrangling over a mere regiment, the filling of personnel gaps with 'borrowed' police units, rear-area services of all kinds, army troops, and increasingly with 'native' units, the demand made by Hitler and Halder to provide troops for the occupation of the Finnish islands in the eastern part of the Gulf of Finland seemed to the army group to be 'utter nonsense',[696] as did the Luftwaffe's request a little later for attacks on the Soviet Baltic Fleet in Kronshtadt, at a time when every aircraft was needed for ground support.

The commanders-in-chief of Sixteenth and Eighteenth Armies had requested the creation of separate corps commands to direct the attacks on the Volkhov and against Demyansk, as each would then be able to concentrate on its specific task. After the conference with Hitler, Halder informed Küchler that Hitler had doubts about the commander-in-chief of Sixteenth Army. He had aged and was indecisive. Hitler also considered the commanding general of X Army Corps, General Christian Hansen, to be insufficiently decisive. Halder himself was certain that the demands of his position were physically and psychologically too much for General Graf von Brockdorff-Ahlefeldt. As a solution he proposed to remove no one and to create no new corps commands, but instead to entrust actual command of the attack group of X Army Corps to Lieutenant-General Walter von Seydlitz-Kurzbach and of the breakout group in the pocket, the 'Group Eicke', to Lieutenant-General Hans Zorn,

---

[695] Halder, *Diaries*, 1411 (2 Mar. 1942); H.Gr. Nord/Ia, KTB, 28 Feb., 2 Mar. 1942 (3.30 p.m.), BA-MA RH 19 III/179, 688; Hitler's order, 4 Mar. 1942, ibid. 707.

[696] H.Gr. Nord/Ia, KTB, 3 Mar. 1942, ibid. 688. Küchler diverted two battalions for Kholm from 122nd Inf. Div. In April 'local' troops with the army group were: 4 groups of 100 Ukrainians, Belorussians, German Russians, Finno-Ugrians, Estonians, Russians, Finns (in the armies); in the rear area: Estonians, Lithuanians, Latvians; a cavalry battalion each of Ukrainians, Tatars, Cossacks, Caucasians, Kazakhs, and Belorussians: ibid., 13 Apr. 1942, BA-MA RH 19 III/181. So much for 'race ideology'.

both under the nominal command of the two commanding generals. Hitler attached great importance to a direct role for Küchler, who was to create a forward command post and 'gently push aside the lower commander'.[697]

In addition, Halder placed a general-staff officer and two assistant adjutants at the disposal of each of the commanders of the two attack groups and a major from his circle of advisers at the disposal of the commanding general of II Army Corps and his staff. This, he hoped, would reduce to a minimum any disruptive delays caused by the corps commands and the army commands.

The attempt to relieve Kholm failed. Already during the forming up in temperatures of −40 °C the troops had suffered serious losses. Losses in the course of the fighting could not be replaced, and opportunities offered by the effective air support could not be exploited.

Because of unfavourable flying weather the first of the large-scale attacks by Army Group North to re-establish a workable defensive line, the planned cutting off of the enemy penetration on the Volkhov under the code-name Raubtier ('predatory animal'), was delayed a week. Both the army group command and Eighteenth Army command repeatedly, but in vain, requested permission to begin the attacks, as the assembled units could not be kept waiting indefinitely. Enemy attacks had to be expected at any time on the dangerously exposed sectors of the front, and the date for the breakthrough to the Demyansk pocket depended on the early conclusion of the Volkhov operation.

As a result of their own decisions being dependent on the combat-readiness of the Luftwaffe, the question arose for the army group command as to whether it was still justifiable to wait for air support on the scale Hitler had ordered, especially as much of the blast effect of the bombs, and also of artillery shells, would be neutralized by the deep snow.[698] The attack of the SS Police Division and 58th Infantry Division, begun in extreme cold and heavy snowfall on 15 March, achieved a first link-up of the two divisions and thus the isolation of both of the Soviet armies which had pushed on westward to a point beyond Chudovo. Now the fighting units of Air Fleet 1 were free for the attack by 'Group Seydlitz' to open the Demyansk pocket.

General Graf von Brockdorf-Ahlefeldt reported that the numerous changes to the date of attack had led to symptoms of depression in the pocket. It would be best to give II Army Corps the order to fight its way out, then at least some

---

[697] H.Gr. Nord/Ia, KTB, 3 Mar. 1942, BA-MA RH 19 III/688; Hitler's order according to OKH/GenStdH/Op.Abt. (IN) No. 420088/42, 4 Mar. 1942 (see n. 695 above). On 18 Mar. 1942 Küchler established the command post Seeadler with a small staff; Army High Command order on the appointment of the two generals in H.Gr. Nord/Ia, No. 552/42, 5 Mar. 1942, BA-MA, 16. Armee, 23468/11.

[698] H.Gr. Nord/Ia, KTB, 16 Mar. 1942, BA-MA RH 19 III/688. Hitler had insisted that the Luftwaffe should be used in as concentrated a fashion as possible, while the army group, in order to meet the early attack date, suggested that the bombers should be divided into small groups. Hitler had ordered an additional day of attacks against Kholm: Operationsatlas, H.Gr. Nord, Der Feldzug gegen die Sowjetunion, Kriegsjahr 1942 [The campaign against the Soviet Union, 1942], BA-MA RH 19 III/663.

of the troops in the pocket would escape annihilation.[699] Hitler ordered Operation Brückenschlag ('Bridging') to begin on 21 March. Preparatory air attacks were launched on 20 March.[700]

The attack group under Seydlitz was organized as follows: 5th and 8th Light Divisions formed the spearheads; 329th Infantry Division was to secure the right flank and widen the penetration; on the left wing 18th Infantry Division (mot.) secured Staraya Russa. In the second line 122nd Infantry Division (one infantry regiment and one regiment of 7th Mountain Division) stood ready to support the attack. 81st Infantry Division was to the left of the attack group and had the task of deceiving and pinning down the enemy.[701] At first both spearheads of the attack gained ground. Soon, however, it became evident how justified the urgings to start the attack earlier had been. For the spring thaw, setting in suddenly on 24 March, greatly reduced mobility and created problems in preparing the crossings of the Lovat. Nevertheless, on 24 March Sixteenth Army headquarters believed that it was in a position to 'strike the decisive blow' on 26 March. On the pocket front enemy attacks concentrated on 30th Infantry Division with the aim of pushing it back from the railway line. In the rear area enemy airborne troops, who it was feared would attack the airfields, caused considerable losses. The continuing thaw made it impossible to use the frozen streams as supply-routes. Sleighs had to be replaced with vehicles. Difficulties in penetrating the heavily forested areas brought the attack to a halt, and on 30 March it had to be suspended. Seydlitz suggested shifting the point of main effort to the left wing and reorganizing the entire group accordingly. The reservations of the army group in this regard were due to the presence of strong concentrations of enemy forces on the northern flank and a greater vulnerability of supply-routes there. Nevertheless, Küchler agreed to Seydlitz's proposal and reported this to the Army High Command. By contrast, the commander-in-chief of Sixteenth Army was of the opinion that 'Group Seydlitz' had not exhausted all suggested possibilities, the regrouping would require two days, and the link-up with 'Group Eicke' would be delayed.[702]

Nevertheless, the army group did not change its decision. The attack was resumed on 2 April but did not reach the Lovat from the west until 15 April. 5th Light Division was so exhausted that it was no longer capable of

[699] H.Gr. Nord/Ia, KTB, 16 Mar. 1942, BA-MA RH 19 III/688.

[700] Hitler's decision was announced at the army group on 19 Mar. at 2.00 p.m., ibid. On 21 Mar. 236 aircraft attacked in front of X Army Corps, 34 in front of II Army Corps, 18 on both sides of the encirclement ring on the Volkhov, and 20 at Pogostye; 315 aircraft carried 586 t. of supplies to Demyansk. Cf. sect. II.1.2(*b*) at n. 891 (Boog).

[701] Conference of C.-in-C. Army Group North with Seydlitz, 21 Mar. 1942, 1.00 p.m., on attack procedures: H.Gr. Nord/Ia, KTB, BA-MA RH 19 III/688. Ibid. for Seydlitz's report, 30 Mar. 1942, 5.00 p.m., to Army Group North, to the effect , that the attack was not feasible.

[702] The distance between the spearheads was 15 km. in the south and 20 km. in the north. The direct control of 'Group Seydlitz' by the army group command, bypassing or even in conflict with Sixteenth Army command, became more pronounced in the following weeks. Seydlitz thus confronted both commands with a *fait accompli*.

offensive action. The lead of the spearhead was therefore taken over by 8th Light Division on 14 April.

But on the western edge of the pocket 'Group Eicke' was under heavy attack and had considerable difficulty in eliminating penetrations. For this reason additional forces from the pocket fronts had to be made available for Operation Fallreep ('Gangway'). This attack began on 14 April and, against vigorous enemy resistance, reached the Lovat by 20 April. Both groups were now able to establish a ferry connection across the river. By 28 April the troops were utterly exhausted by the heavy fighting, the problems created by the thaw, and the muddy roads, together with the lack of any prospect of being relieved. The task of securing and holding the 'corridor' now established to supply the two corps in the pocket against flank attacks presented serious problems.[703] The question of what should be done after the link-up with the two corps was discussed extensively between the chief of staff of Army Group North and the head of the operations department on 12 April.[704] The main topics were the lack of sufficient replacements for the army group at a time when losses were being incurred at three points of main effort and the uncertainty about where and when the enemy would establish strong attacking forces on the relatively quiet Leningrad front. It was also quite clear that preparations for the offensive on the southern sector of the eastern front would not permit the bringing up of significant forces for the other army group areas.

To save forces for future operations Heusinger and Hasse considered and advocated withdrawing the divisions of II and X Army Corps during the dry summer period. But this solution was incompatible with the offensive action planned by Hitler and Halder to close the gap in the direction of Army Group Centre, where the Rzhev salient was being held.[705] Both general-staff officers agreed that major top-level decisions would soon have to be taken and that Küchler's report the following day should prepare Hitler for them. The conference on the situation and the difficulties of Army Group North with Hitler on 13 April 1942 convinced the commander-in-chief that there could be no question of additional personnel amounting to two and a half divisions for Eighteenth Army alone. Hitler recommended that the two threatening groups of enemy forces west of the Volkhov—in addition to the large pocket, a second had been created near Pogostye as a result of the breakthrough by the Soviet Fifty-fourth Army on the front of I Army Corps—should not be smashed by

[703] In 'Brückenschlag' and 'Fallreep' losses were 4,000 dead and 13,000 wounded or missing: H.Gr. Nord/Ia, KTB, 15 May 1942, BA-MA RH 19 III/182.

[704] H.Gr. Nord/Ia, KTB, 12 Apr. 1942, BA-MA RH 19 III/181. This conversation was to prepare the situation report of the C.-in-C. of the army group to Hitler on 13 Apr.

[705] Hitler's order, OKH/GenStdH/Op.Abt. (IM) No. 42082/42, 1 Mar. 1942, to Army Group Centre, BA-MA RH 19 III/707. Both salients were to be held with heavy losses until the spring of 1943. Heusinger deliberately suggested the withdrawal of II Army Corps (all units in the Demyansk pocket) as an alternative to Halder's plan. Cf. H.Gr. Nord/Ia, KTB, 12 Apr. 1942, BA-MA RH 19 III/181; the personnel question ibid., 13 Apr. 1942. Between 19 Jan. and 23 Mar. 1942 the ration strength of Ninth Army rose from 151,100 to 221,200; the combat strength from 59,582 to 139,100; the number of operational artillery pieces from 369 to 608, and of tanks from 1 to 83: AOK 9/Ia, KTB, 1 Jan.–31 Mar. 1942, BA-MA, 9. Armee, 21520/1.

an attack but 'smoked out'. If both enemy groups succeeded in linking up near Lyuban, they would not only form a strong attack force to relieve Leningrad on the city's most important communications to the south-east, but the German units between them on the Volkhov would be in direct danger of being encircled. Both pockets were linked with the Soviet hinterland, and in addition were receiving personnel and supplies by air.

The third problem, the solution of which the army group considered a matter of honour, was the liberation of Kholm. On 5 May this bitterly contested base was relieved by an attack group of XXXIX Armoured Corps. The intensity of the fighting on both sides is shown by the fact that the south-eastern part was not captured until 18 May and isolated Soviet groups continued fighting in the north-eastern part until 8 June. This forward bridgehead was also left standing; only in the second half of June was a continuous front to the north established.

The thaw and mud greatly reduced the mobility of both sides and forced a certain halt in the fighting on the Volkhov fronts. Eighteenth Army organized its units as well as it could and prepared to re-establish the encirclement ring. On 22 May the withdrawal of the enemy to the east led to a resumption of the attack, at first in the north-western part of the pocket. On 31 May the old penetration west of the Volkhov in the area of Myasnoy Bor was closed again. In a concentric attack by all formations and 'groups' participating in the encirclement this pocket was eliminated by 29 June. Although Army Group North had suffered considerable losses as a result of the numerous critical situations around Demyansk and on the Volkhov, on the whole it had survived the winter without decisive enemy breakthroughs. The isolation of Leningrad to the south had been maintained. For the summer of 1942 the task of the army group was to secure the lines won and to establish blocking-positions and strong-points in rear areas. These developments will be discussed later.

Remembering the horrors of the past winter, however, the army group command already began to plan for the coming months: 'If we want a quiet situation with no plans for further attacks, and if we want to conserve our forces, we shall have to establish a general line between Staraya Russa and Kholm and thoroughly prepare it for next winter.'[706]

On 4 May 1942, in view of its shortage of personnel and in the expectation that it would not receive sufficient forces to secure its forward line, the army group logically requested permission to withdraw the troops under the command of II Army Corps to a position on the Lovat.

(v) THE DEFENSIVE BATTLES OF ARMY GROUP SOUTH

For the expected large-scale attack by the Red Army on the southern wing of the eastern front the chief of staff of Army Group South had envisaged a mobile conduct of operations with the main objective of gaining time and

---

[706] H.Gr. Nord/Ia, KTB, 29 Apr. 1942, BA-MA RH 19 III/181; order of Army High Command/ Army General Staff on the strengthening of positions, 26 Apr. 1942, and request of Army Group North: BA-MA RH 19 III/707.

launching a counter-attack from a prepared line once the units had been brought up to strength.[707] A line from Melitopol via Zaporozhye and Novomoskovsk in the general direction of Kupyansk was considered a rear limit of what was strategically acceptable for the army group. The improvement of forward positions of Seventeenth and Sixth Armies was concluded by 10 December, as was the transfer of units to the expected main points of attack between Seventh and First Armoured Armies in the sector of the Italian expeditionary corps. After a visit by Hitler additional personnel and small quantities of material replacements had been received.[708] The Crimea was deliberately neglected in favour of the eastern front; if necessary it was to be sacrificed and the Perekop isthmus defended as part of the southern flank of the army group. Because of a lack of personnel the positions, even in the lines held by the troops, had not been significantly strengthened.

A problem now to be faced was that of the largely uncovered flank in the direction of Army Group Centre, which had been deliberately accepted during the pursuit phase in the expectation that, with the advance on Moscow and to the middle Don, the enemy would hardly be able to exploit gaps between the army groups, so that maintaining contact between the inner wings was sufficient. This was all the more important as the army group expected that the main operational effort in 1942 would be made in the southern sector of the eastern front.[709]

Beyond the orders of the commander-in-chief of the army of 8 December 1941, which applied to all army groups, Army Group South was to capture Sevastopol with Eleventh Army as its last offensive action. Thereafter the bulk of that army would be given new tasks.[710] One of the causes of the failure of the operation against Sevastopol was the concern of Army Group South about its eastern front and its resulting refusal to transfer sufficient forces to the Crimea. The second 'special task' of the army group was to improve conditions for a major spring offensive by smaller actions against the lower Don and the Donets during the winter, as soon as the weather permitted.

The army group was therefore to hold the front between the Sea of Azov and the Donets under all circumstances. The area around Kharkov was to be solidly held and communications to the southern wing of Army Group Centre secured, especially road and rail links between Belgorod and Kursk. Army

---

[707] Cf. n. 338 above; Sodenstern to Heusinger, 4 Dec., and Halder's order, 6 Dec. 1941, H.Gr. Süd/Ia, KTB, BA-MA RH 19 I/88.

[708] Between 26 Nov. and 5 Dec. 1941 3,268 men were airlifted to First Armd. Army; 50 assault-guns and 60 2-cm. anti-aircraft guns were allotted to the army group. On 7 Dec. the immediate transfer of 950 replacement personnel from Vinnitsa was ordered: ibid.

[709] Hitler's remark to Reichenau during his visit to Poltava. Cf. H.Gr. Süd/Ia, KTB, 8 Dec. 1941, BA-MA RH 19 I/88; on this see also the conference at the office of the deputy chief of staff in charge of operations, 24 Oct. 1941, KTB OKW i. 1073.

[710] Cf. sect. II.1.1(g) at n. 575. Like Hitler's Directive No. 39, this directive of 8 Dec. had been prepared by Halder through the assignment of tasks to the chiefs of staff of the army group. Cf. also Führervortrag and notes on the Führer conference, 6 Dec. 1941: Halder, Diaries, 1339 (6 Dec. 1941); printed in KTB OKW, i. 1076 ff. (108).

Group South undoubtedly regarded as quite unrealistic the order to retake Rostov and the Donets bend during the winter.

The directive of the army group to its armies reflected these plans.[711] First Armoured Army and Sixth Army were ordered to close up towards each other after achieving slight improvements in the position of the front.

Tactical directives for the preparation of a protracted defence were supplemented by guidelines for securing the rear area. There the troops and staffs were to move closer together and prepare for a 'fortress-like' defence. Stocks were to be laid up for the period when the weather made movement of supplies impossible. The directive of 14 December for the fighting in winter assumed that the enemy's intentions were to keep open his support- and supply-lines between Moscow and the Caucasus, to tie down as many German units as possible by attacks aimed at attrition and harassment, and to destroy German winter quarters and supply-lines.[712] The armies were instructed to secure the Crimea with as few forces as possible, to pull out of the front and rehabilitate the armoured formations of First Armoured Army, and, once again, to secure the most important communications on the boundary between Army Group Centre and Sixth Army. Lines in the rear were to be reconnoitred and prepared to meet an expected large-scale attack. As a last defensive line the army group ordered the 'Wotan' line to be reconnoitred, which was to extend from Melitopol via Zaporozhye, Poltava, and Romny to the upper course of the Desna.

To reinforce the fighting units, as elsewhere, elements of the security and supply troops suitable for combat were sent to the front. The army group planned to meet the problem of a possible uprising by a partial evacuation of Kharkov, but Hitler rejected this proposal as the evacuated civilians would then have to be fed behind the front. Keitel suggested sending them east to areas under Soviet control.[713] Reichenau observed that the population would resist deportation to the east, whereas, in the event that they were moved to the rear area, they would not constitute a drain on German food supplies since they would remain in areas remote from roads, which in any case were insignificant. Deportation of the civilian population to the east could be carried out only by force of arms, something which could not be demanded even of battle-hardened troops. In consequence, the civilian population remained where they were and had to feed themselves.

First Armoured Army headquarters had reservations about the defensive line on the Kalmius, far to the rear, as envisaged by the army group, since that

---

[711] Preliminary order, 9 Dec. 1941, mentioned in H.Gr. Süd/Ia, KTB, 9 Dec. 1941, annexe 216, BA-MA RH 19 I/88; printed in Hauck, Südliches Gebiet, pt. II, appendix 7, MGFA P-114c. Ibid. for the 'Richtlinien für Kampf und Sicherungen im Winter und Frühjahr 1941/42' [Guidelines on operations and security in winter and spring 1941–2] and the 'Weisung für Kampf und Sicherung im Winter 1941/42' [Directive for operations and security in winter 1941–2].

[712] H.Gr. Süd/Ia, KTB, 14 Dec. 1941, copy: Hauck, Südliches Gebiet, pt. II, appendix 8, MGFA P-114c.

[713] H.Gr. Süd/Ia, KTB, 18 Dec. 1941, BA-MA RH 19 I/88.

would involve abandoning Mariupol, an indispensable rehabilitation and technical repair centre for the German forces. Sodenstern reassured the army command by pointing out that this line would be occupied only after every effort had been made to hold the existing front.

Large enemy troop movements from the front facing First Armoured Army to the area facing Seventeenth Army were interpreted as preparations for an attack aiming at a breakthrough near Artemovsk and Stalino in order to attack the armoured army from the rear.[714]

On the northern wing of Sixth Army too, strains were expected as a consequence of the development of the situation of Second Army. For this reason two-thirds of 168th Infantry Division were transferred there and placed under Second Army.[715] In addition, elements of 62nd Infantry Division were removed from anti-partisan operations and also placed under Second Army as the situation on the boundary to it and in its sector became threatening. The expected attack against the northern wing of First Armoured Army began on 25 December. The parts of the army already pulled out of the front and destined for rehabilitation were immediately assembled in the Stalino area as a reserve. Newly arrived tanks were to be combined in a battalion and the army reserves of Seventeenth and Sixth Armies were to be assembled in the areas of Artemovsk and Kharkov.

The fighting which now began also on the northern wing of Sixth Army and the repulsion of a thrust towards Kursk forced the withdrawal of the covering forces of Sixth Army in the Kharkov area. Reports from the intelligence service and information provided by deserters and prisoners, as well as large movements of enemy troops near Lisichansk and Kupyansk, indicated an imminent large-scale offensive aiming at a breakthrough to the middle Dnieper.

In addition, the strain on the southern wing of the army group after the Soviet landing near Kerch and Feodosiya is reflected by the fact that Hitler promised Eleventh Army fifty tanks to restore the situation there. As the tanks could not be brought to the front quickly enough from Germany, they were to be taken from a transport for First Armoured Army.[716]

On 2 January, in addition to an offensive solution of the situation in the Crimea, Hitler demanded that his orders to hold positions should be taken 'literally and seriously' and that all preparations should be made to repulse an attack on Kharkov and to crush an uprising, which, according to foreign news sources, was perhaps to be expected.[717] On 10 January Reichenau reported that he viewed the situation at Kharkov with optimism and that only in the north-eastern sector was the situation of the army group strained. If a secure link

---

[714] KTB H.Gr. Süd, ibid., 22 Dec. 1941.   [715] Ibid., 2 Jan. 1942, BA-MA RH 19 I/89.
[716] KTB H.Gr. Süd.

[717] Ibid., telephone conversation between Halder and Sodenstern. On 8 Jan. Hitler then issued the order for the defence of all positions and defined the cases in which withdrawal was authorized: extracts in KTB OKW ii/2. 1262, BA-MA 16. Armee, 23468/8, Führerbefehle, fos. 31–2. According to this source, this order was to be destroyed after being given orally to the divisional commanders.

could be established with Second Army, that would be an important success for the conduct of the war in winter. With this objective Sixth Army began its attack with XVII Army Corps from the Prokhorovo–Oboyan line across the railway line between Prokhorovo and Solntsevo. As an attack from the Second Army sector was not possible because of a shortage of forces, this success had only a local effect. As a consequence of the difficult situation at the boundary of the army group, Second Army was placed under Army Group South, which did not please Reichenau as he now became responsible for an especially vulnerable sector of the front.[718]

Hitler combined this change with an order to Army Group South to remove forces from First Armoured Army and transfer them to the Kharkov area. According to Hitler, the difficulties of Army Group Centre were only a result of the fact that it had not been possible to pull forces out of sectors with abundant equipment and troops in order to transfer them in good time to weak and threatened sectors. This argument was taken verbatim from remarks by the commander-in-chief of Second Army. Reichenau agreed with the view that an attack on Kharkov was imminent[719] and reported that the situation in the north of the army group had to be restored first. Forces of First Armoured Army could be transferred there. Moreover, he intended to remove motorized units from the front in order to create mobile reserves.[720]

On 13 January Field Marshal Reichenau suffered a stroke. As his replacement Hitler first chose the commander-in-chief of First Armoured Army, Colonel-General von Kleist, and then, the following day, Colonel-General Hoth, till that time commander-in-chief of Seventeenth Army. But Hoth was also unable to take up his duties, as Hitler on the very same day appointed Field Marshal von Bock—who had only a few weeks before been granted furlough—to be the new commander-in-chief of Army Group South. Bock assumed command of the army group on 20 January 1942. At the same time General Paulus became commander-in-chief of Sixth Army, a post which until then had been vacant.[721] The enemy attacks that began at various points along

---

[718] H.Gr. Süd/Ia, KTB, 12 Jan. 1942, BA-MA RH 19 I/89. This move was due to a request from the C.-in-C. Army Group Centre and went into effect on 15 Jan.: Halder, *Diaries*, 1386 (11 Jan. 1942).

[719] This expectation was not supported by a speech by Marshal Timoshenko at the end of November, which was known to the army group command. Timoshenko argued that the main aim should be the destruction of German equipment and supplies so as to render a winter and spring offensive impossible. The fighting west of Moscow offered the most favourable opportunity to do this: H.Gr. Süd/Ia, KTB, 13 Jan. 1942 (Ic, 11 Jan. 1942). Other reconnaissance operations indicated an imminent offensive against Kharkov and beyond to the Dnieper: BA-MA RH 19 I/89.

[720] Sodenstern remarked: 'At present there are no motorized units capable of movement with First Armd. Army. Tactical mobility can be expected only after arrival of new vehicles and rehabilitation' (ibid., 12 Jan. 1942).

[721] Ibid., 15, 16 Jan. 1942. Reichenau died on 17 Jan. 1942; Hitler's order of the day on this occasion, 18 Jan. 1942: BA-MA 16. Armee, 23468/8, fo. 14. Bock was briefed on his duties by Hitler on 18 Jan.: Halder, *Diaries*, 1389 (18 Jan. 1942); Bock Tagebuch, 16, 18 Jan. 1942, BA-MA N 22/13.

the front of the army group on 18 January, especially against Seventeenth Army from the mouth of the Bakhmut to Zaliman, appeared to be essentially aimed at tying down German forces and did not indicate a co-ordinated offensive along the entire front. The situation between Bogorodichnoe and Izyum was considered serious, and 298th Infantry Division was withdrawn behind the Donets.[722]

On 19 January, however, Seventeenth Army reported that, given the strength of the enemy and its own lack of sufficient troops and equipment, a defence with improvisations would not be effective for long.

On 20 January it was realized that this offensive was in fact a large-scale breakthrough attack towards the Dnieper with twelve to fifteen divisions and four armoured brigades identified at the front. The fortified positions, organized like strong points, were scarcely able to offer effective resistance against these latter units. Replacements of men and equipment were brought up, some from Germany and some also from First Armoured Army, as well as a Romanian division.[723] The railway line between Kursk and Orel was threatened on account of a penetration by the Soviet II Cavalry Corps in the sector of Second Army. The last dive-bomber Gruppe from the Crimea was sent into action there. The first enquiry from the chief of staff of Seventeenth Army on 22 January, whether he could authorize the abandonment of isolated strong points, suggested an incipient crisis.[724] The commander-in-chief of Seventeenth Army doubted that the front north-west of Slavyansk could be held until the arrival of a combat group in the area north of Lozovaya. If not, the way to the railway line between Stalino and Dnepropetrovsk would be open to the Red Army.

The army group command refused to approve the evacuation requested by Seventeenth Army and referred to similar situations in Army Group Centre, where such attacks had repeatedly petered out. The army group ordered all available assault-guns of First Armoured Army to be transferred to the left wing and 14th Armoured Division to be held ready for use against an attack expected there. The situation should be restored by offensive action. Together with 'Group Friedrich' of Sixth Army approaching from the north-west, 14th Armoured Division and 100th Light Division were to attack the enemy penetration. Second Army also considered the important rail link between Kursk and Shchigry to be threatened and requested assistance. Hungarian and

---

[722] 'Nach Einholung der Genehmigung durch den Führer' [After the Führer's consent has been received], H.Gr. Süd/Ia, KTB, 19 Jan. 1942, BA-MA RH 19 I/89.

[723] 113th Inf. Div. was sent to Seventeenth Army instead of the Crimea: Report by C.-in-C. of army group to Hitler, 21 Jan. 1942, ibid.

[724] The abandoning of a strong point meant that artillery and other heavy equipment could not be brought back. According to the directive of 1 Jan. 1942, such an action if due to lack of ammunition did not require Hitler's approval. But in the case of Seventeenth Army it meant the abandoning of two other strong points, for which Sodenstern wanted to obtain the approval of the Army High Command. The almost word-for-word adoption of the Polish and Soviet orders for the campaign of 1918–20 shows the continuity of military thinking: *Der polnisch-sowjetrussische Krieg 1918–1920*, i. 261 ff. (annexes II, IV, VIII; for the Soviet side annexe IX).

Romanian troops, as well as security divisions, were brought up and the defence of Novomoskovsk and Dnepropetrovsk was prepared. Poltava was to be got ready for all-round defence.

On 26 January Seventeenth Army command proposed a retreat of the army and the evacuation of Lozovaya, on the grounds that it would be better for the remaining German forces to move back to meet their reinforcements. That evening it wanted to withdraw to the west.[725] In contrast, the army group believed that this would lead to a widening of the enemy penetration and that Soviet cavalry would encircle the wings of Seventeenth and Sixth Armies and make their position untenable with thrusts against their supply-line. The situation was to be restored by a concentrated attack of the reserves being brought up; until then the penetration was to be contained in such a way that the deployment of the attack groups was secured. For these attack forces— essentially 100th Light Division, 14th Armoured Division, and Armoured Battalion 60—a command staff was to be made available. Two-thirds of 113th Infantry Division were to be assembled north-east of Novomoskovsk. To ensure that the attack was carried out with less pessimism about the future, Field Marshal von Bock decided to place Seventeenth Army headquarters tactically under the command of First Armoured Army and to employ the command of III Armoured Corps as 'Group von Mackensen' on the left wing.[726] This attack group consisted of parts of 14th Armoured Division, 100th Light Division, and XI Army Corps with the Romanian 1st, 298th, and elements of 9th Infantry Divisions. From the sector of Sixth Army, 'Corps Group Dostler' attacked with a third each of 57th, 62nd, 294th, and 79th Infantry Divisions.

Field Marshal von Bock briefed Hitler on the situation. Three Soviet cavalry corps of three divisions each and an armoured brigade had broken through the gap near Izyum. One corps had turned north to envelop Sixth Army; two corps had turned south towards the rear area of Seventeenth Army. Two infantry divisions had reached Lozovaya. As the staff of Seventeenth Army seemed 'rather tired' after the heavy fighting of the past few days, he had transferred command to First Armoured Army headquarters, which was 'fresh and eager for action' and promised to provide a strong impulse for the counter-attack. He also reported on the two groups attacking from the north. Hitler approved all his decisions.

The units earmarked for the counter-attack moved to the assembly areas in heavy frost and a snowfall. On 31 January 'Group von Mackensen' began its attack in a snowstorm, as did the two groups from Sixth Army.[727] A completely

---

[725] H.Gr. Süd/Ia, KTB, 26 Jan. 1942, BA-MA RH 19 I/89; Bock, Tagebuch, 26, 27 Jan. 1942, BA-MA N 22/13.

[726] H.Gr. Süd/Ia, KTB (as in n. 725). The entire group was then called 'Army Group von Kleist'. For Hitler's approval and order to the armies to obtain Bock's approval before abandoning strong-points see Bock (as in n. 725).

[727] Army order, 31 Jan. 1942: H.Gr. Süd/Ia, KTB under this date. The corps group XI Army Corps and the 'name groups' consisted of remnants and individual battalions or regiments of

successful attack could not be expected with the units of the attack groups, especially as they had to advance in continuous blizzards. They were, however, able to contain the Soviet penetration and eliminate the immediate danger of a breakthrough to the Dnieper. Throughout the subsequent weeks they were unable to push back the 'sack' near Izyum. The fighting exhausted the troops, and on 3 March the army group had to report that it was not possible at that time to regain the old front.

The army group was able to identify preparations for the feared attack on Kharkov early enough for reinforcements from the sector of Second Army to be transferred in time, even though they consisted only of the remnants of 3rd Armoured Division and a regiment of 88th Infantry Division. The Soviet offensive began on 3 March with the point of main effort between Pechenegi and Volchansk. The attack group, which advanced from the south against the right flank of Sixth Army, quickly succeeded in crossing the Donets. Another penetration of the Donets line, thirty kilometres wide, was achieved east of Kharkov, but the Red Army was not able to take the city itself. The onset of the thaw brought all movements of the Soviet counter-offensive to a halt. Army Group South had succeeded in holding its operationally most important positions, its supply-bases, and its lines of communication. A retreat to the Dnieper had been avoided. The decisive factor in this defensive success was the failure of the Red Army to concentrate its numerically far superior forces on a single point of main effort. This mistake resulted in an early exhaustion of the momentum of the attack and thus in a reduction of the pressure on the German front. This had enabled the army group command to transfer forces repeatedly from sectors less threatened or not threatened at all to points requiring the greatest defensive effort. In view of the virtual immobility of the heavy weapons, the Luftwaffe played a decisive role in the German defensive success.[728]

The special situation of the Crimean peninsula within the defensive operations of Army Group South can now be analysed.

In connection with the southern part of the eastern front as a whole, and especially with regard to the large-scale operations planned for 1942, Hitler at the end of 1941 still attached great importance to holding and securing the Crimea. The Soviet troops who had landed near Feodosiya were therefore to be annihilated and the Kerch peninsula retaken as soon as possible.[729] Like all other major units, the commander-in-chief of Eleventh Army reported serious supply problems and personnel shortages in his divisions. Since, apart from Romanian troops, he did not have sufficient security forces at his disposal, he

divisions, local defence units, and rear-area services. Even units of the Wehrmacht commander for the Ukraine were combed for manpower: ibid., 1 Feb. 1942, BA-MA RH 19 I/90.

[728] e.g. the report of Sixth Army, 21 Jan. 1942, that no reserves were available and the only thing to do was to wait and see where the next main attack would be in order to send reinforcements there from quieter sectors (ibid.).

[729] Halder, *Diaries*, 1380–1 (2, 3 Jan. 1942); AOK 11/Ia, KTB, BA-MA RH 20-11/455; H.Gr. Süd/Ia, KTB, BA-MA RH 19 I/89.

requested and received permission to raise volunteer units from the local Tatar population.[730]

Hitler assumed that 46th Infantry Division was available for operations against Feodosiya and therefore considered the requested use of a second division unnecessary. When Halder explained that this assumption was questionable, Hitler ordered an extensive report on the condition of the infantry division and the circumstances of its retreat. It soon emerged that the division's withdrawal had by no means been 'according to plan' and that at that moment it was not ready for action.[731]

The second Soviet landing, at Evpatoriya on 5 January 1942, was considered to be a 'tester'. However, Manstein reported, if an attack aimed at forcing a decision was now taking shape, his forces would not be in a position to repel it.[732] Sodenstern observed that in that case a decision would have to be taken on whether Eleventh Army or the Crimea was to be sacrificed, as there could be no question of transferring additional forces there. On the contrary, his planning assumed that forces could be taken from the Crimea for operations elsewhere.[733] The recapture of the much more important Feodosiya on 15 January required the use of XXXXII and XXX Army Corps. On 18 January the enemy forces there were defeated, and the eastern group of Eleventh Army began its attack against the Parpach position.[734]

Between 27 February and 3 March Eleventh Army had to repulse a second large-scale attack from Sevastopol as well as from the Parpach front. After this attack was repeated on 15 March the divisions of XXXXII Army Corps (46th and 170th Infantry Divisions) reported that they were no longer ready for action. In addition to the attacks at the front, activities of partisan groups in the rear area of the German forces began to achieve tactical significance. Manstein decided to use the newly arrived 22nd Armoured Division together with the divisions of XXXXII Army Corps for a counter-attack on the Parpach position.[735] The attack failed to achieve the desired success; on the contrary, the new and inexperienced armoured division suffered heavy losses.[736]

---

[730] Manstein, *Verlorene Siege*, 247 (not in trans); H.Gr. Süd/Ia, KTB, 3 Jan. 1942, BA-MA RH 19 I/89. Cf. also Hoffmann, *Ostlegionen*.

[731] H.Gr. Süd/Ia, KTB, 2 Jan. 1942, BA-MA RH 19 I/89. On 4 Jan. Reichenau reported to Hitler that the report about 46th Inf. Div. was 'objectively incorrect': Lt.-Gen. Graf von Sponeck was to blame; there was no doubt that insubordination 'with considerable prejudice and danger to the security of Germany' was involved. Reichenau was especially indignant about the outer form of the retreat: guidelines for the investigation, 10 Jan. 1942, AOK 11/Ia, KTB, BA-MA RH 20-11/456; Einbeck, *Sponeck*, 33 ff.

[732] Manstein's report, 4 Jan. 1942, AOK 11/Ia, KTB, BA-MA RH 20-11/455.

[733] The attack was repulsed on 7 Jan. 1942. As the Romanian 53rd Artillery Regiment had fled, Hitler ordered an investigation of the course of events: Manstein, *Lost Victories*, 228 ff.

[734] AOK 11/Ia, army order, 20 Jan. 1942, and Befehl über den Angriff gegen Parpatsch-Stellung [Order concerning attack against the Parpach position], 21 Jan. 1942, BA-MA RH 20-11/455.

[735] Conference C.-in-C. Eleventh Army with general commanding XXXXII Army Corps and commander of 22nd Armd. Div.: army order, 16 Mar. 1942, BA-MA, RH 20-11/458. Manstein wanted to use the armoured division and the newly arrived 28th Lgt. Div. offensively before they were 'spent' in defensive battles.

[736] Report 22nd Armd. Div., 20 Mar. 1942, ibid. Many officers were still in France. On 30 Mar.

This failure marked the end of operationally effective fighting in the Crimea for the winter of 1941–2. Planning for the new offensives and the bringing up of heavy siege artillery were carried out simultaneously with these defensive battles. On 7 March coastal defence was transferred to the 'Naval Commanding Officer Crimea'.[737]

The conduct of the war in the Crimea in the winter of 1941–2 was governed by two diametrically opposed concepts. On the one hand, German forces there were given the task of conquering the Kerch peninsula for the coming spring offensive, as a jumping-off point for the crossing to the Caucasus. An essential condition for such an operation was the previous capture of Sevastopol. On the other hand, Eleventh Army was to be considered as a personnel reserve for Army Group South whenever the Soviet winter offensive threatened to reach the Dnieper; that would have meant abandoning the whole of the Crimea. In the event the containment of the Soviet penetration west of Izyum made it possible to leave Eleventh Army in place and to recapture Kerch; Sevastopol too was stormed later. Nevertheless, neither the crossing to the Caucasus nor domination of the Black Sea was achieved. Both operations will be discussed in the account of the war in the east in the summer of 1942.

The directive for the conduct of operations after the end of winter, issued on 12 February 1942,[738] not only stated that the crisis had been overcome; the parts of it referring to the future were clearly based on a sober assessment of Germany's potential. As early as November 1941 the effects of the catastrophic vehicle and fuel situation on the build-up of a new operational army were incalculable.[739] Studies and memorandums by the chief of army armament programmes and commander of the replacement army, as well as by the war-economy and armaments office of the Wehrmacht High Command, all pointed in the same direction.[740] Only half a million men, including wounded who had recovered, were available to replace the approximately one million dead, wounded, sick, and missing suffered by the German forces in the east by the end of January 1942.[741]

1942 losses amounted to 42 officers, 1,030 non-commissioned officers and men, 32 tanks (totally destroyed), and numerous other weapons and pieces of equipment: BA-MA RH 20-11/458.

[737] AOK 11/Ia, Dienstanweisung für den Seekommandanten Krim als Kommandanten der Küstenverteidigung [Service instruction to naval commander Crimea as officer commanding coastal defence], ibid.

[738] OKH/GenStdH/Op.Abt. (Ia) No. 420053/42, BA-MA RH 2/v. 1327, printed in KTB OKW i. 1093 (115).

[739] OKH/GenStdH/Org.Abt. (III) No. 3356/42, 18 Nov. 1941; reply by operations dept., 26 Nov. 1941, BA-MA RH 2/v. 428.

[740] Cf. sect. II.vi.5 at n. 398 (Müller).

[741] Casualty figures according to Halder (Diaries, 1393: 25 Jan. 1942). Cf. also KTB OKW i. 1106, D, appendices. On 27 Jan. 1942 Halder promised the army groups and armies in the east additional replacements of 500,000 men to compensate for shortages. These were convalescents and men previously not considered fit for military service; most were inadequately trained and at first only of limited military use. The age-group 1922, then in training, was envisaged as a source of replacements for losses in the summer offensive of 1942: OKH/GenStdH/Org.Abt. (I) No. 488/42, 27 Jan. 1942, BA-MA RH 20-4/288, p. 235.

The conclusions drawn from this personnel and vehicle situation[742] were clearly reflected in operational planning for the summer of 1942. The directive mentioned above therefore envisaged the establishment of a continuous line suitable for prolonged defence in the northern and central sections of the front. The entire offensive strength, for which the bulk of the newly trained age-group of 1922 was available, was to be concentrated on the southern front. The task of the army group, after elimination of the penetration west of Izyum, would be the capture of Sevastopol, and the recapture of Kerch, for an attack on the Caucasian oilfields and the mounting of a second thrust aimed at Stalingrad. In addition to eliminating the centre of arms production on the Volga, the supply-lines from Afghanistan and Iran to the interior of Russia were to be cut. This would deprive the Red Army of the means to restore its full fighting strength. The 'raids' considered as recently as December 1941 to sever transport routes from Moscow to the Russian interior via Gorkiy and to the Arctic ports via Vologda were no longer included in the plan.

The efforts made to realize these plans will be described in the account of the build-up of the operational army for 1942. After the crisis of the winter campaign, however, Hitler's basic standpoint was already clear: he saw the most serious problems not in the mobilization of reserves and replacements for the field army but in providing manpower and the means of production to equip the Wehrmacht. This led to the increasing use of previously exempted categories in Germany itself, and especially of manpower from Germany's allies and from occupied areas, and of prisoners of war. Regardless of their personal readiness to serve, most of the individuals thus taken into the armed forces were not up to the standards of the army that had been trained in peacetime and acquired experience in war. Along with the loss of weapons and technical equipment, it was especially the lack of experienced officers and non-commissioned officers which showed that the army had passed the peak of a force able to fight and conduct offensives on any sector of the front.

In retrospect one might ask when the war against the Soviet Union reached this turning-point. An unequivocal answer is possible if one disregards the problems of the conduct of the war as a whole—i.e. including the non-European theatres—armaments capacity, and the enemy's mobilization of reserves, and thus considers only the military aspect of the campaign. The decisive criterion in this question is the campaign-planning of the Army General Staff. It emerges, on the basis of the course of operations, the complete exhaustion of the units attacking Moscow, and the resulting renunciation of the attempt to achieve a decision there, that the plan for the conduct of the war as a whole had failed. In reality the enforced deviation from the operational plan—and thus the precondition for the turning-point—is to be

---

[742] By the end of 1941 only 660 armoured vehicles had been received to replace losses of 3,770: *KTB OKW* i. 1104, annexe 4 to OKH/GenStdH/GenQu/Abt. I/Qu 2 (III) No. I/58/42, 5 Jan. 1942.

dated much earlier than the stalling of the German attacks on Moscow, Leningrad, and Rostov.

The conquest of Moscow, even with the occupation of a smouldering expanse of rubble, would not have brought 'final victory' any nearer. The capture of Leningrad with German forces alone was not possible because of the skilfully executed Soviet thrusts at the boundary between Army Groups Centre and North, but neither had it been envisaged. The Finnish offensive on the Karelian front came to a halt soon after the old frontier had been reached, which meant that this chance had been lost by the end of September 1941. A glance at the position of the front of Army Groups Centre and South at their inner wings in July and August 1941 clearly reveals the cause of the failure of the offensive: the fact that Sixth Army, envisaged as the driving force of the offensive, remained stuck south of the Pripet area. The tying down of the bulk of its divisions as well as army reserves and parts of First Armoured Army prevented the early wheeling of the German forces to encircle the enemy west of the Dnieper and the establishment of a bridgehead near Kiev. A second reason was the weakness of Eleventh Army and Germany's allies, who, like Seventeenth Army, had to launch frontal attacks against the fortified enemy positions along the tributaries of the Bug and the Dnieper. The inability of Army Group South to move forward as planned necessitated a flanking encirclement of the enemy facing it by Second Army and Second Armoured Army. This in turn made it impossible for the armoured troops to be rehabilitated; the entire movement against Moscow suffered a decisive delay, with further progress being dependent on the increasingly unfavourable weather. The Red Army thus had more time to train new reserves and move them to the front.

All criticism of Guderian's move to encircle Kiev is based on the mistaken assumption that on the southern sector of the eastern front only 'pursuit' was necessary once the Soviet Fifth Army in the Pripet marshes had been 'outmarched' and the crossing of the middle Dnieper achieved. As the fighting in the Donets area was to show, this belief was just as mistaken as the assumption that the Crimea could be overrun. The situation at the front made it essential to capture Kiev before attacking Moscow. Contrary to what Halder expected, the Red Army did not intend to mass all its essential strength to defend Moscow, which would have opened the way to the Don and the Volga. The right flank of the attack on Moscow—the attack Halder and Bock were anxious to carry out—could never be secured with the forces of Army Group Centre alone. If the army on the left wing of Army Group South had been withdrawn for that task, the remaining forces of the group would not have been able to reach the important industrial objectives it had been assigned. Nor could the crossing to the Caucasus, either along the Don or via the Crimea, have been achieved. The success of Halder's military plan was basically in doubt as early as July 1941. The alternative Hitler envisaged from the very beginning—the concentration of the main effort on the wings of the front as a whole—was never carried out, in consequence of Halder's tactical manœuvring and more especially because Hitler himself did not pursue it with absolute consistency.

At the end of 1941 the German military leaders were faced with the consequences of their misjudgement of Soviet military strategy and the 'vital strength' of the Red Army after the planned battles of encirclement. The stage had been reached which Major-General Marcks, by this time seriously wounded as a divisional commander, had raised for consideration on 10 September 1940. It was not the Red Army in the east but the British Army in North Africa which now ushered in the 'second act' on 18 November and, with the counter-offensive of its Eighth Army to raise the siege of Tobruk, finally forced the execution of the long-planned transfer of the command of Air Fleet 2 with II Air Corps from the Moscow front.[743] In addition to economic aid, the alliance with Britain now began to reduce military pressure on the Soviet Union, and the activities of the various partisan groups in Yugoslavia, supported by the Soviet Union as well as Britain, would lead to the creation of a new 'front' in the Balkans.

2. THE LUFTWAFFE[774]

HORST BOOG

(a) The Surprise Attack against the Soviet Air Force

According to Hitler's Directive No. 21, an 'effective intervention by the Russian air force . . .' was to be 'prevented from the very beginning of operations by powerful strikes'. To that end, all Soviet airfields reported operational near the frontier, as well as ground-support organizations and the flying units themselves, were to be subjected to surprise attacks with all available forces. These attacks were to continue until the Soviet air force could be considered eliminated. Because of a lack of precise information on the actual strength of the Soviet air force, the Luftwaffe operations staff had not developed exact estimates of how much time these attacks would require.[745]

Thus the Luftwaffe began the war in the east using the plans and tactics that had proved successful in previous 'Blitz' campaigns. Officers and men entered the conflict with the awareness of being part of a decisive weapon on the battlefield and a feeling of superiority based on previous successes and ex-

---

[743] Cf. sect. 11.1 2(*b*) at n. 891 (Boog) On the war against the Soviet Union see *Das deutsche Reich und der Zweite Weltkrieg*, vi. 701 ff.

[744] Luftwaffe support for the army in the far north is dealt with in sect. II.III.1(*c*) at n. 54 (Ueberschär). On the role of the Luftwaffe as a whole in the east in 1941 cf. Plocher, Krieg im Osten, MGFA Lw 4/2-4/13 (or the English translation, without annexes: Plocher, *German Air Force versus Russia, 1941*), and Kurowski, *Luftkrieg über Rußland*; for the period 22 June–8 Nov. 1941 cf. especially the daily situation reports, Ob.d.L., Fü.Stab Ic, Nos. 653 (23 June 1941)–791 (9 Nov. 1941), BA-MA RL 2 II/246–69.

[745] According to the Ia op of the Luftwaffe operations staff Ia, Col. (ret.) Ernst Kusserow, in a letter of 2 Sept. 1954, BA-MA Lw 107/67.

perience. The operations staffs of the army generally accepted the employment of the Luftwaffe primarily for the destruction of the enemy air force rather than for the provision of direct air support for the ground troops during the first few days of the campaign. After all, achievement of air superiority, or perhaps even supremacy, meant that the army could carry out its operations with fewer losses and without interference from enemy aircraft.

Taking advantage of the favourable weather—generally cloudless with moderate ground haze in the morning hours—German bomber, dive-bomber, and fighter formations crossed the German–Soviet frontier after 3.00 a.m. on 22 June 1941—the bombers, to preserve the advantage of surprise, at operating ceiling even ahead of the army's attack.[746] In waves they struck at their targets in high- and low-level attacks. Depending on the distance of their bases from the front, the bombers each flew four to six sorties a day, the dive-bombers seven to eight, and the fighters five to eight.

The attacks in the early morning of 22 June were directed primarily against thirty-one airfields and against the supposed quarters of senior staffs, barracks, artillery positions, bunkers, and oil-storage facilities. Initially Soviet fighters showed little desire to engage in combat and turned away at considerable range if fire was opened. Soviet anti-aircraft fire was initially weak. On the morning of 22 June the Soviets lost a total of 890 aircraft, 222 of them in aerial combat or to anti-aircraft fire and 668 on the ground. The Luftwaffe, on the other hand, lost only 18 aircraft.[747] By midnight on 22 June Soviet losses had risen to a total of 1,811 aircraft, with 1,489 destroyed on the ground and 322 destroyed mostly in the air. German losses rose to 35 aircraft.[748]

During the first days of the attack aerial reconnaissance discovered many previously unknown airfields with a large number of aircraft, which necessitated continued massed attacks by the Luftwaffe against Soviet air-force units during the following days. Between 23 and 26 June a total of 123 airfields were attacked.[749] By the end of June some 330 German aircraft had been lost, against a total of 4,614 Soviet aircraft reported destroyed, 1,438 in the air and 3,176 on the ground.[750] By the end of the fighting in the frontier area on 12 July, the figures had risen to 6,857 Soviet aircraft destroyed against 550 total losses and 336 damaged aircraft on the German side.[751]

---

[746] Cf. Kesselring, *Memoirs*, 88; Bekker, *Angriffshöhe*, 275.

[747] Situation report No. 652, Ob.d.L./Fü.Stab Ic, 22 June 1942, pp. 8–9, 11–12, BA-MA RL 2 II/246.

[748] Situation report No. 653, Ob.d.L./Fü.Stab Ic, 23 June 1941, 27–8; ibid. According to Koževnikov (*Komandovanie*, 36), the Soviet Union lost 1,200 aircraft on the first day of the war, 800 of them on the ground.

[749] Situation reports Nos. 653–7, Ob.d.L./Fü.Stab Ic, 23–7 June 1941, BA-MA RL 2 II/246, 247. Cf. also Groehler, 'Grenzschlachten', 122.

[750] On Soviet losses cf. situation reports, Ob.d.L./Fü.Stab Ic, Nos. 654–61, 24 June–1 July 1941, BA-MA RL 2 II/246–8; on German losses see the corresponding reports, GenQu der Luftwaffe, 6. Abt., BA-MA RL 2 III/713. Plocher (Krieg im Osten, 13, MGFA Lw 4/2) gives Soviet losses up to the night of 30 June 1941 as 4,900 aircraft.

[751] Report on combat-readiness of flying units as of 12 July 1941, GenQu, 6. Abt., 15 July 1941, BA-MA RL 2 III/713. Cf. also Groehler, 'Verluste der deutschen Luftwaffe', 331.

The first German surprise air attacks, with half of the Luftwaffe units stationed in the east, caught the Soviet air force unprepared and unprotected at their airfields, often with flying and technical personnel asleep in their tents. Evidently Soviet military leaders had not taken any measures to reduce the effectiveness of a concentrated German first strike from the air, although their own reconnaissance[752] as well as the German campaigns in Poland, France, and the Balkans, and finally the political situation, clearly suggested that such an attack was to be expected. Some Soviet aircraft were found uncamouflaged and closely parked on the edges of runways at airfields near the frontier. Many bomber units had not been moved further away from the frontier, and the air-bases as a rule lacked anti-aircraft guns. Soviet historians explain this situation and the resulting heavy losses of aircraft by the fact that the telegram from the people's commissar of defence, intended to inform the commanders of military districts of the time of a possible German surprise attack and ordering a combat alert and dispersal of aircraft at the airfields, reached the frontier military districts only four hours before the start of the German attack. It was therefore no longer possible to warn individual units in time. The mobility of many air units was greatly restricted by construction work at the airfields; camouflage and cover were still inadequate. Soviet historians also emphasize the inexperience of Soviet air commanders in defence against massed air attacks and the inferiority of Soviet aircraft compared with their modern German counterparts.[753]

Although the Soviet pilots, in the opinion of German observers,[754] soon distinguished themselves by attacks marked by 'different ideas of the value or otherwise of human life', such efforts generally achieved little because of 'the lack of a sense of personal responsibility' among mid-level and lower leaders and the 'habit of acting only on command'. Field Marshal Kesselring, then commander of Air Fleet 2, in retrospect considered it to have been 'almost a crime' for Soviet military leaders 'to order their clumsy aircraft to attack in such tactically impossible ways'. For example, 'one squadron after another attacked at regular, predictable intervals and thus offered our fighters easy prey. It was like "a slaughter of innocents".'[755] Fighter Geschwader 3 under Major Günther Lützow shot down twenty-seven attacking Soviet bombers within fifteen minutes without suffering any losses of its own.[756] Entire bomber squadrons with no fighter escort were intercepted and shot down by German fighters. Halder also considered the Soviet air force to be 'completely out of the picture'.[757] Reported Soviet aircraft losses were so heavy that at first even Göring would not believe them.[758]

---

[752] Cf. sect. II.I.I(*a*) at n. 47 (Klink), and sect. II.II.I (Hoffmann).
[753] Koževnikov, *Komandovanie*, 47. Cf. Groehler, 'Beginn des faschistischen Überfalls', 123 ff.
[754] Hoffmann von Waldau, Tagebuch, 53 (3 July 1941), BA-MA RL 200/17.
[755] Kesselring, *Memoirs*, 90.
[756] Situation report No. 669, Ob.d.L./Fü.Stab Ic, 9 July 1941, pp. 25–6, BA-MA RL 2 II/249.
[757] Halder, *Diaries*, 972 (24 June 1941).
[758] Göring believed these reports of successes only after the area had been occupied, and, upon being checked, they turned out to be too low: Kesselring, *Memoirs*, 89 ff.

The Luftwaffe was thus able to fulfil its first task—achieving air supremacy or at least superiority by destroying the Soviet air force in surprise strikes— 'within two days'.[759] Its low opinion of the tactical and operational abilities of Soviet air-force leaders, the level of training of Soviet crews, and the quality of their aircraft in the first months of combat was confirmed. The successful surprise and the lack of preparedness of the Soviet air force in the first days of the German offensive strengthened this impression, which was also supported by the interrogation of captured Soviet air crews.[760] In the first days of the campaign both the army and the Luftwaffe were very optimistic. Major-General Hoffmann von Waldau, head of the operations department of the Luftwaffe General Staff, considered 'complete tactical surprise' to have been achieved and expected 'a brilliant success'.[761] On 1 July 1941 the commanding general of VIII Air Corps, General Freiherr von Richthofen, believed that the bulk of the Red Army's attack forces had been annihilated; on 13 July he believed that there were no more military obstacles on the road to Moscow. German forces could reach the Soviet capital in eight days.[762]

The Soviet bomber fleet had indeed been practically eliminated and hardly made its presence felt during the following months, even though it still undertook sporadic, ineffective, and costly attacks against the German rear area.[763] At this time the Soviet air force was unable to create significant difficulties for the German army in the east. Although the German surprise attacks and their own qualitative inferiority very nearly resulted in a collapse of the Soviet air units, they increasingly began to offer resistance once the element of surprise had worn off; this was reflected by the decline in the number of their aircraft destroyed on the ground and the increase in the number of those destroyed in the air. More and more the Luftwaffe had to assert its superiority in aerial combat, but for the time being remained tacti-cally and technically far superior to its Soviet adversary, which was gradually able to recover thanks to its own efforts and the breathing-space provided by the weather in the autumn of 1941.[764]

The total destruction of the Soviet air force was not achieved because the crews of the numerous aircraft destroyed on the ground generally survived and could be employed afresh, as could also many of the crews of the Soviet

[759] Ibid.

[760] Cf. Ergebnisse aus einer Vernehmung russischer Kriegsgefangener [Results of an interroga-tion of Russian prisoners of war], annexe 5 to situation report No. 655, Ob.d.L./Fü.Stab Ic, 25 June 1941, pp. 2–3, BA-MA RL 2 II/246, where captured Soviet airmen are described as quite unlike British and French officers in their formal education, with a limited horizon, not trained to think or act independently, mentally confused, helpless—because they had still not been informed that war had broken out—and extremely mistrustful because of the danger of being spied on by their fellow officers. For this reason they had deliberately avoided expanding their own knowl-edge, e.g. when acting as observers by talking to the pilot about his tasks. Because of their very limited knowledge they were of little value as sources of operational information. They expected to be tortured and then shot and considered that the right of the victor.

[761] Hoffmann von Waldau, Tagebuch, 49 (22 June 1941), BA-MA RL 200/17.

[762] BA-MA RL 8/47, pp. 12 (1 July 1941), 18 (13 July 1941).   [763] Kesselring, *Memoirs*, 89.

[764] Schwabedissen, Russische Luftwaffe, 34 , MGFA Lw. 22/1.

aircraft shot down over their own territory. Moreover, it was not possible to suppress the resistance of the surviving Soviet flying units indefinitely, as the Luftwaffe also suffered losses in men and machines and as its second major task of direct and indirect support for the army, which was begun with some delay around 25 June, now required most of its resources.[765] The war against the Soviet air force was continued 'as a sideline' without any system and only whenever the reviving activity of enemy air units became a problem for the German ground forces. In such cases support for the army had to be reduced. The Luftwaffe had to divide itself,[766] dealing with one task after the other,[767] as its resources were no longer sufficient to fulfil all at once. Only by costly transfers and exposure of parts of the front was it still able to carry out concentrated attacks like those at the beginning of the campaign. Primarily, however, its strategy was determined, in accordance with Directive No. 21, by the situation on the ground, even though the Luftwaffe operations staff soon realized that the Soviet air force was much stronger than had been expected. In a conversation with Halder on 1 July 1941 Major-General Hoffmann von Waldau, who had taken a sceptical view even before the start of the campaign in the east, admitted that the Luftwaffe had greatly underestimated the Soviets, who had well over 8,000 front-line aircraft, of which only approximately half had been destroyed.[768] On 3 July he noted in his diary:

The complete surprise struck at a gigantic Russian deployment . . . The military means of the Soviet Union are considerably stronger than studies before the start of the war . . . indicated. We had regarded many statistics as propagandist exaggerations. The material quality is better than expected . . . As a result we scored great successes with relatively low losses, but a large number of Soviet aircraft remain to be destroyed . . . The will to resist and the toughness of the masses exceeded all expectations.'[769]

However, euphoria was still the dominant mood among the Luftwaffe leaders.

[765] Plocher, Krieg im Osten, 21, MGFA, Lw 4/2. From the Soviet point of view the Luftwaffe had achieved only a tactical, not a strategic, success, having generally destroyed only obsolete Soviet aircraft that were scheduled in any case to be replaced by new models. Cf. Hardesty, *Red Phoenix*, 59. On the use of Soviet airpower cf. Greenwood, 'Great Patriotic War'.

[766] Groehler, 'Grenzschlachten', 123 ff.

[767] Cf. assessment of the state of the Luftwaffe in the east by the C.-in-C. of the Luftwaffe: teletype message OKH/GenStdH/G/Op.Abt. (Ia) No. 16608/41 g.Kdos., 26 July 1941 (copy), BA-MA. 18. Armee, 17562/91; Richthofen, Tagebuch (privately owned), 1 Aug. 1941: 'If the Luftwaffe is helping the ground troops it cannot also attack targets far behind the front' (this diary used with the kind permission of Dr Gundelach, Col. (ret.) of the general staff; Halder, *KTB* iii. 300 (19 Nov. 1941; not in trans.): 'Air! Probably only in partial actions one after the other . . .'.

[768] Halder, *Diaries*, 994 (1 July 1941).

[769] In view of the huge deployment of the Red Army, Gen. von Richthofen and Maj.-Gen. Hoffmann von Waldau were of the opinion that, after the conclusion of its virtually complete armament programme, it would have attacked Germany: Hoffmann von Waldau, Tagebuch, 50 ff. (3 July 1941), BA-MA RL 200/17; Richthofen, Tagebuch (Privately owned), 2 Aug. 1941; Hassel, *Tagebücher*, 266 (Sept. 1941). This reflected the official German position at the time, e.g. in Hitler's appeal to the German soldiers on the eastern front.

(b) Ground Support

(i) II AND VIII AIR CORPS AND THE BATTLES OF ENCIRCLEMENT
     OF BIAŁYSTOK AND MINSK[770]
             (See the Annexe Volume, Nos. 5 and 6)

After the surprise strikes to achieve air superiority, all air fleets in the east, in accordance with instructions, concentrated on supporting the army as their main task from approximately the third day of the campaign. From the very beginning the dive-bombers of II Air Corps were used to silence the enemy batteries in the area of Brest-Litovsk and on a range of hills extending in an east–west direction north of the city. Because of their commanding position these batteries could have seriously endangered the advance of Armoured Group 2. The armoured group had therefore attached considerable importance to preventing the batteries from firing. Contrary to its usual combat guidelines, which provided for the destruction of targets with concentrated forces, the air corps therefore suppressed their fire by continuous waves of separate flights of dive-bombers.

At the end of June bombers and dive-bombers attacked enemy forces encircled in the area of Białystok, Zelva, and Grodno,[771] which were trying to use the cover of the forests to escape eastwards. Warned by the appearance of reconnaissance aircraft, the Soviet troops were always able to leave the roads, which were completely congested anyway, and withdraw into the forest in time to avoid bombing attacks. The Luftwaffe therefore began armed reconnaissance flights, in which the bombers flew in on a broad front, did their own reconnaissance, and immediately attacked any targets they identified.

Enemy counter-attacks against the German flanks frequently led to crisis situations, in the overcoming of which the Luftwaffe played an important role. Thus on 24 and 25 June bombers and dive-bombers of VIII Air Corps smashed a Soviet tank attack on VIII and XX Army Corps in the area of Kuznitsa, Odelsk, Grodno, and Dombrova in relay attacks.[772] A similar attack on the flank of Armoured Group 3 near Lida was halted by continuous attacks by bombers and close-support aircraft of VIII Air Corps until reinforcements arrived in the form of V Army Corps, which, in co-operation with the air units, was able to repulse the attack. The armoured group then continued its advance without losing its freedom of manœuvre.

By mounting continuous air attacks, both air corps of Air Fleet 2 played an effective part in preventing the break-out of Soviet ground forces from the pocket of Białystok and in the defeat of the four Soviet armies in the pocket near Minsk further east. They thus contributed decisively to the victory in the

---

[770] On the role of Air Fleet 2 cf. Kesselring, *Memoirs*, 85–100; for the period under consideration here, the daily notes on the activity of VIII Air Corps, 19 June–3 Aug. 1941, compiled by Col. (ret.) H. W. Deichmann, BA-MA RL 8/47, and Plocher, *Krieg im Osten*, 117–43, MGFA Lw 4/2; sect. II.1.1(a) (Klink).

[771] Situation report No. 658, Ob.d.L./Fü.Stab Ic, 28 June 1941, p. 20, BA-MA RL 2 II/247.

[772] Richthofen, *Tagebuch* (privately owned), 24 June 1941.

double battle of Białystok and Minsk, which ended on 9 July. In the attempt to seal off the pocket from the air it became evident that, in view of the scattered position and flimsy construction of the houses in villages and towns, air attacks on road intersections did not have the same effect as in western Europe. In the Soviet Union the countryside was too open and obstacles created by rubble too small and too easily circumvented to have the desired effect. Better results were achieved by attacks on bridges over small rivers and streams, especially if they were in flood.

Distinguishing between friend and foe from the air proved very difficult, as German ground forces often refrained from laying out the required ground panels for fear of enemy air attacks. They thus occasionally fell victim to friendly bombing.[773] Some relief was obtained by the increased use of air communications troops and dive-bomber and fighter control units with the most forward ground forces.

The continuous support provided by VIII Air Corps for Armoured Group 3, advancing on the northern wing of Army Group Centre, created no problems, as the corps was specially equipped and organized to provide close support. Matters were different with the heterogeneous II Air Corps supporting Armoured Group 2 on the southern wing of Army Group Centre. There it soon became clear that, because of supply problems, bombers and long-range reconnaissance aircraft could not be based as close to the front as the close-support units and fighters, and that a unified command of the corps was therefore difficult. Thus, after the first few days of the campaign the command of the close-support formations advancing with Armoured Group 3 was placed in the hands of the *ad hoc* Close Support Leader II (Major-General Martin Fiebig) and his improvised staff,[774] operating within the framework of directives from II Air Corps. Fiebig quickly overcame initial difficulties.

In addition to providing direct support for the army, after 25 June Air Fleet 2 attempted to seal off the battle area by attacking the railway lines leading into it at Minsk, Orsha, Molodechno, Zhlobin, and Osipovichi. It also struck at airfields in the area of Smolensk, Bryansk, Polotsk, and, on 2 July, Gomel.

All attacks on bridges were discussed in advance with the army in order to determine which of them were important for its own advance and supplies and should not therefore be destroyed. The destruction of the great railway bridge at Bobruysk was an especially important success for the Luftwaffe. However, it was rebuilt within about thirty-six hours by over a thousand workers under the direction of the people's commissar for transport and served its purpose even though it did not meet Western standards of safety.

The close-support units of Air Fleet 2 accompanied the further advance of Armoured Groups 2 and 3, while its bombers attacked roads, railway lines, and junctions in the hinterland in the area of Mozyr, Gomel, Roslavl,

---

[773] Cf. Guderian, *Erinnerungen*, 168 (not in *Panzer Leader*); Tuchzeichen, supplement to Gen.Kdo. I. Fl.Korps/Ia No. 504/42 g.Kdos., 18 Mar. 1942, BA-MA RH 24-10/116.

[774] Kesselring, *Memoirs*, 90–1.

Smolensk, Vitebsk, Polotsk, and Daugavpils.[775] These attacks on railway lines, however, were rather of a tactical-operational nature and their strategic effect was overestimated.

Not until Guderian's armoured group was crossing the Berezina at Bobruysk and the Dnieper at Mogilev on 11 July did strong Soviet air formations attack the advancing German forces, but they suffered heavy losses at the hands of Fighter Geschwader 51 under Colonel Werner Mölders.[776]

(ii) THE BATTLE OF ENCIRCLEMENT AT SMOLENSK[777]
(See the Annexe Volume, Nos. 6 and 15)

After supporting the envelopment movements[778] of Armoured Groups 2 and 3, the close-support units of Air Fleet 2 attacked the enemy troops in the pocket, their attempts to break out, and attempts to prise open the pocket from outside. Other forces of the air fleet concentrated on roads and railway lines. On 14 July the rail link between Smolensk and Moscow was attacked for the first time; at the end of the month the railway station at Orel was bombed. Near Yartsevo, between 23 and 25 July, VIII Air Corps, together with its 99th Anti-aircraft Regiment,[779] was able, in a quick succession of attacks and using equipment capable of rapidly refuelling nine aircraft simultaneously, to slow the break-out attempt of a group of enemy forces attacking from the area north and around Dorogobyzh across the Vop, a situation which endangered not only the army units but also the command post of the air corps itself east of Dukhovshchina, as well as several of its airfields. German ground forces then arrived in time and intercepted the enemy. The air transport units used here close to the front suffered their first losses. South-east of Smolensk the enemy mounted strong attacks, attempting to break open the pocket. Support provided by II Air Corps contributed considerably to the frustration of efforts by Soviet armoured units to break through in the direction of Shatalovka. Air Fleet 2 also tried to close a gap only a few kilometres wide on the east side of the Smolensk pocket.[780] As sufficient aircraft were not available at that time and paratroops, who could have closed the gap, were no longer dropped from the air after their heavy losses on Crete, the gap could to some extent be closed by day only, not at night. Field Marshal Kesselring estimated that over 100,000 Soviet troops were able to escape through it and could thus serve as cadres for newly created Soviet units. In this respect Smolensk was only a 'vulgar victory', in which it had again been shown that the Luftwaffe alone was not able to seal off gaps in the front.

[775] Halder, *Diaries*, 1027 ff. (11 July 1941).

[776] Situation report No. 661, Ob.d.L./Fü.Stab Ic, 1 July 1941, p. 17, BA-MA RL 2 II/248; Guderian, *Erinnerungen*, 145 (not in *Panzer Leader*), and *Panzer Leader*, 96 ff.

[777] Plocher, Krieg im Osten, 144–63, MGFA Lw 4/2; cf. sect. II.1.1(a) at n. 22 (Klink).

[778] Cf. daily surveys of the fighting of II Air Corps, Gen.Kdo. II. Fl.Korps/Ia No. 1323/41 g.Kdos., 14 July 1941; No. 1328/41 g.Kdos., 15 July 1941; No. 1332/41 g.Kdos., 16 July 1941; and No. 1339/41 g.Kdos., 18 July 1941: BA-MA RH 20-2/165b.

[779] Daily notes on the activity of VIII Air Corps, 23–5 July 1941, pp. 8–10, BA-MA RL 8/47.

[780] Richthofen, Tagebuch (privately owned), 26 July 1941, and daily notes (as in n. 779 above), p. 27 (2 Aug. 1941); *KTB OKW* i. 1036 (25 July 1941); Kesselring, *Memoirs*, 92–3.

Although the Smolensk pocket could not be considered essentially closed until 5 August, the commander-in-chief of the Luftwaffe, acting on the basis of Directive No. 34 of the Wehrmacht High Command of 30 July 1941, had ordered the transfer of VIII Air Corps to the northern sector of the eastern front for an earlier date. On 3 August it was temporarily removed from Air Fleet 2[781] (cf. Table II.1.2). In spite of the bad weather, most of the bomber and dive-bomber formations of II Air Corps were sent into action even earlier to strike at roads and railway lines in the area of Roslavl, Sukhinichi, Bryansk, and Unecha used to bring up fresh Soviet forces to attack the large salient at Yelnya. A secondary task of the corps was the elimination of river monitors, which seriously interfered with the advance of 1st Cavalry Division along the northern edge of the Pripet marshes.

The constant raids by Soviet ground-attack pilots on the German forward line of the southern wing of Army Group Centre abutting Armoured Group 2 were especially unwelcome. Although not very effective, they constituted a considerable psychological stress for the ground forces. They were usually carried out by one or two aircraft flying at low level. German fighters usually arrived too late and, as they were not armoured, could not pursue the low-flying attackers because of strong Soviet opposition with infantry weapons from the ground. Defensive patrol flights were ruled out by the shortage of German fighter forces. The German ground troops therefore had to be constantly reminded to strengthen their own defences against strafing attacks with additional machine-guns, as the Soviet infantry had done from the very beginning. This was true of the entire eastern front.[782]

The need to move the close-support formations forward to keep up with the rapid advance of the armoured units, to supply them, to set up vital communications links quickly, and to protect airfields against Soviet air attacks and attacks by Soviet stragglers, and the increasingly strong partisan groups were among the most important problems facing the ground-support troops of the Luftwaffe in the central sector and other parts of the eastern front. Their training in ground fighting and the fact that they quickly learnt to prepare for immediate all-round defence after occupying an airfield proved to be extremely valuable.[783] Because of the frequently congested roads, the Fieseler Storch was an important and often the only form of transport linking the command staffs of the army and the Luftwaffe.[784] It also provided commanders who appreciated its virtues, such as General von Richthofen, with the means of obtaining an immediate picture of the front. Frequently, however,

[781] Plocher, Krieg im Osten, 152 ff., MGFA Lw 4/2; daily notes (as in n. 779 above), pp. 27–8 (2, 3 Aug. 1941).

[782] Cf., among others, order of 8th Armd. Div./Ia, 9 Oct. 1941, on infantry defences against Soviet aircraft, BA-MA RH 27-8/44; letter: Luftflottenkommando 1/Führungsabteilung/Ia No. 5373/41 g.Kdos., 13 Dec. 1941 to Ob.d.L./Fü.Stab, z.Hd. Gen. Hoffmann v. Waldau, BA-MA, 18. Armee, 17562/233; operation experience report, close-support leader 2/Ia No. 171/42 geh., 25 Jan. 1942, BA-MA RH 20-4/288.

[783] Kesselring, Memoirs, 92.

[784] Richthofen, Tagebuch (privately owned), 23 July 1941.

TABLE II.1.2. *Order of Battle of the Flying Units of Air Fleets 1, 2, and 4 Employed against the Soviet Union, 3 August 1941*

Air Fleet 1   Long-range Recce. Staffel 2, C.-in-C. of the Luftwaffe
Weather Recce. Staffel 1
Air Transport Gruppe 106

I Air Corps
Long-range Recce Staffel 5, Gruppe 122
Staff, Bomber Geschwader BG 1 with Gruppen II and III of BG 1
Staff, BG 76 with Gruppen I, II, and III of BG 76
Staff, BG 77 with Gruppen I, II, and III of BG 77
Staff, TFG 26 with Gruppen I and II of TFG 26
Staff, FG 54 with Gruppen I, II, and III of FG 54 and Gruppe II, FG 53
   without Staffel 6

VIII Air Corps
Long-range Recce. Staffel 2, Gruppe 11; Gruppe IV of Transport
   Geschwader 1 (special duties)
Staff, BG 2 with Gruppe I of BG 2; Gruppe III of BG 3; staff, FaBG
   210, and Gruppe II, FaBG 210
Staff, DBG 2 with Gruppen I and III, DBG 2; Gruppe II, TrgG 2 and
   Staffel 10, TrgG 2
Staff, FG 27 with Gruppe III, FG 27 and Gruppe II, FG 52

Air Leader Baltic
Recce. Gruppe 125
Coastal Gruppe 806
Replacement Fighter Gruppe 54 (1 Staffel)

Air Fleet 2   Long-range Recce. Staffel 2, Gruppe 122
Long-range Recce. Staffel 1, C.-in-C. Luftwaffe
Weather Recce. Staffel 26
Air Transport Gruppe 9

II Air Corps
Long-range Recce. Staffel 1, *Gruppe* 122
Coastal Gruppe 102 (special duties)
Staff, BG 3 with Gruppen I and II of BG 3
Staff, BG 53 with Gruppen I and III of BG 53
Staff, DBG 1 with Gruppe III of DBG 1
Gruppe I, FaBG 210
Staff, FG 51 with Gruppen I, II, III, and IV of FG 51

Air Fleet 4   Long-range Recce. Staffel 4, Gruppe 122
Weather Recce. Staffel 76
Bomber Gruppe 50 (special duties)

TABLE II.I.2 *(cont.)*

V Air Corps
  Long-range Recce. Staffel 4, Gruppe 121; Corps Transport Staffel V
  Staff, BG 55 with Gruppen I, II, and III of BG 55
  Staff, BG 54 with Gruppen I and II of BG 54
  Staff, DBG 77 with Gruppen I, II, and III of DBG 77
  Staff, FG 3 with Gruppen I, II, and III of FG 3
  Staff, FG 53 with Gruppe I of FG 53 and Gruppe III of FG 52

IV Air Corps
  Long-range Recce. Staffel 3, Gruppe 121 and Long-range Recce. Staffel
    3, C.-in-C. of the Luftwaffe
  Corps Transport Staffel IV
  Staff, BG 51 with Gruppen I and II of BG 51
  Staff, BG 27 with Gruppen I, II, and III of BG 27
  Staff, FG 77 with Gruppen II and III of FG 77

German Luftwaffe Mission in Romania
  Staff, FG 52 with Gruppe I of TrgG 2 and Replacement Gruppe of FG
    77

Sources: Tables of the C.-in-C. of the Luftwaffe, distribution of units, 27 Oct. 1940–20 Dec. 1941, BA-MA Lw 106/6; Plocher, Krieg im Osten, MGFA Lw 4/6 and 7; reports on the combat-readiness of the flying units: GenStdLw GenQu 6. Abt. (I), BA-MA RL 2 III/714.

these machines were shot down by enemy stragglers in the broken terrain between the roads used by advancing German troops.

(iii) II AIR CORPS IN THE AREA OF GOMEL, BRYANSK, AND ROSLAVL[785]
(*See the Annexe Volume, Nos. 15 and 16*)

In the first days of August II Air Corps supported the combined forces under the command of Colonel-General Guderian in their defence against a force of the Soviet Twenty-eighth Army attacking from the area of Roslavl; it helped to encircle and destroy them, and thus prevented them from endangering the ring around Smolensk. Between 9 and 24 August close-support forces of the air corps attacked the Soviet Twenty-first Army and parts of the Fifth, which were encircled by Armoured Group 2 and Second Army near Gomel. Simultaneously bomber formations attacked Soviet troop movements in the area of Chernigov, Konotop, and Gomel, as well as railway lines, in order to prevent the withdrawal of forces and the transport of new units to the front facing the southern wing of Army Group Centre.[786] Between 22 and 26 August II Air

[785] Plocher, Krieg im Osten, 163–76, MGFA Lw 4/2; cf. sect. II.I.1(*c*) at n. 233 above (Klink).
[786] Cf. operational orders of II Air Corps, 6–9, 16–25 Aug. 1941, BA-MA RH 20-2/170a, 170b, 172a, 172b, 174, 175.

Corps, in co-operation with VIII Air Corps, wiped out a large part of the Soviet Twenty-second Army near Velikie Luki. Bombers of Air Fleet 2 again attacked Soviet air-bases to reduce enemy pressure on the army. During this fighting on the wings of Army Group Centre the German forces of the most forward positions, in the Yelnya salient, were involved in heavy defensive battles and called for air support. But the German air units in the central sector of the front were no longer sufficient to perform several tasks at the same time, considering that air attacks on Moscow had begun on 21–2 July.[787] Thus Air Fleet 2 decided to use all of II Air Corps to support the southern wing of the army group and help Second Army, which had remained far behind, to advance and eliminate the danger threatening the southern flank of Army Group Centre there. It was assumed that a closing up by Second Army would in itself reduce pressure on the German forces in the Yelnya salient. The army, which in the second half of August was undecided about whether or not to hold this position, openly criticized the 'high-handed' action of the Luftwaffe.[788] Only when Kesselring heard that the salient might have to be abandoned did he agree to provide air support for a few days; this was made available from 30 August until the evacuation of the position on 6 September,[789] though only with parts of II Air Corps, whose bulk remained employed with Second Army[790] and Armoured Group 2. The decision of the Luftwaffe proved to be correct, as no more than a tactical defensive success could be expected in the Yelnya salient, while the main effort near and east of Gomel and south-west of Bryansk helped eliminate the deep Soviet wedge between Army Groups South and Centre and establish the northern starting-position for the encirclement of Budenny's armies east of Kiev, and thus resulted in an operational success.[791]

(iv) THE USE OF THE ANTI-AIRCRAFT UNITS[792]
(See the Annexe Volume, Nos. 5, 6, 15, and 16)

As in the sector of Army Group South, anti-aircraft units were used primarily against ground targets by Army Group Centre,[793] although their task should

---

[787] Cf. Kesselring, Memoirs, 94–5.

[788] Halder, Diaries, 1144–5, 1151–2, 1176–7, 1178, 1192–3, 1214, 1217 (3, 4, 14, 15, 21 Aug., 2, 5 Sept. 1941). Cf. sect. II.1.1(b) at nn. 175, 206 (Klink).

[789] Plocher, Krieg im Osten, 170–1, MGFA Lw 4/2; situation reports, Ob.d.L./Fü.Stab Ic No. 722, 31 Aug. 1941, p. 7; No. 723, 1 Sept. 1941, pp. 13, 29; No. 724, 2 Sept. 1941, pp. 19–20 (BA-MA RL 2 II/257); No. 726, 4 Sept. 1941, pp. 9, 17; No. 729, 7 Sept. 1941, p. 9 (ibid. 258).

[790] On co-operation of II Air Corps with the large army units cf. operational orders, 1, 2, 4–6 Sept. 1941, ibid., RH 20-2/177, RH 20-4/228; AOK 2/Ia, 24 Oct. 1941, report on operations of Second Army from Gomel up to the great battle of Kiev, 20 Aug.–18 Sept. 1941, ibid., RH 20-2/181.

[791] Hoffmann von Waldau, Tagebuch, 70 (27 Aug. 1941), BA-MA RL 200/17.

[792] Plocher, Krieg im Osten, 177–93, MGFA Lw 4/2, distribution of anti-aircraft artillery of Air Fleet 2, as of 9, 27 July, 1, 6, 13, 17, 21, 29 Aug. 1941: BA-MA RH 20-2/164a, 168a–170a, 171b, 172b, 173, 175.

[793] Cf. Ob.d.H./GenStdH/Ausb. Abt. (I) No. 2200/41 g., 22 Sept. 1941, betr. Erfahrungen des Ostfeldzuges [Experience of the campaign in the east], and AOK 4, Koluft/Ia No. 3157/41 g., 12

have been to provide protection against air attacks. The high velocity and flat trajectory of the heavy anti-aircraft guns and their relatively high rate of fire made them a feared and successful weapon against armour and bunkers.[794] A notable success of I Anti-aircraft Corps of Air Fleet 2 was its ability to keep open the road bridge across the Berezina at Borisov for Armoured Group 2 and the defence of that bridge against Soviet air attacks by 101st Anti-aircraft Regiment on 5 and 6 July.[795] The same was true of the surprise capture of the airfield at Bobruysk and the securing of the bridge across the Berezina there by 104th Anti-aircraft Regiment. In the Yelnya salient batteries of I Anti-aircraft Corps formed the main defence of the army units fighting there for more than four weeks. By 30 August I Anti-aircraft Corps[796] had shot down 259 enemy aircraft in the east. On 9 September the anti-aircraft units of Army Group Centre, which were under the Luftwaffe commander with the army group, shot down their 500th enemy aircraft; they had also destroyed 360 Soviet tanks.[797]

(v) THE CONDUCT OF THE AIR WAR IN THE BALTIC UNTIL THE BEGINNING OF AUGUST[798]
(*See the Annexe Volume, Nos. 5, 6, and 15*)

After the initial attacks to destroy the Soviet air force, Air Fleet 1,[799] to which no large anti-aircraft units were directly subordinate, concentrated on supporting the ground forces advancing towards the Dvina, especially Armoured Group 4. In this task, working with the army, I Air Corps[800] destroyed about 200 enemy tanks in smashing a Soviet counter-attack carried out with strong armoured forces near Shyaulyai (Raseinyai).[801] In addition, the air fleet de-

Sept. 1941, betr. Einsatz der Flakartillerie im Erdkampf [Use of AA artillery in ground fighting], both in BA-MA RH 27-11/21; Gen.Kdo. XXXXI. AK/Abt. Ia, 15 Aug. 1941, BA-MA RH 27-8/32; H.Gr.Kdo. Nord/Ia No. 920/41, 12 Aug. 1941, Einsatz der Flak-Verbände [Employment of AA units], BA-MA RH 24-42/12; II./Flakregiment 23, Abt. Ia; operation experience report, 19 July 1941, über den Einsatz der schweren Batterien II./Flak 23 im Osten gegen überschwere Panzer (52 t.) [Use of heavy batteries . . . against super-heavy tanks in the east], BA-MA RH 27-8/28.

[794] Cf. army order 'T' No. 1, Besondere Anordnungen für die dem Heere unterstellten Teile der Luftwaffe [Special instructions for Luftwaffe elements placed under army command], annexe 5 to AOK 4 Ia No. 3333/41 g.Kdos., 23 Sept. 1941, BA-MA RH 20-4/252.

[795] Cf. situation report No. 665, Ob.d.L./Fü.Stab Ic, 5 July 1941, p. 33, BA-MA RL 2 II/248.

[796] Ibid., No. 731, 9 Sept. 1941, p. 34, BA-MA RL 2 II/259. Cf. also use of I Anti-aircraft Corps, 4 June–14 Oct. 1941, according to Col. (ret.) Erich Gröpler of the general staff, 8 Feb. 1956, BA-MA Lw 107/78.

[797] Situation report No. 735, Ob.d.L./Fü.Stab Ic, 13 Sept. 1941, p. 33, BA-MA RL 2 II/259.

[798] Except the activity of Air Leader Baltic, described in sect. II.1.2(*c*) (Boog). Cf. also Plocher, Krieg im Osten, 204–20, MGFA Lw 4/3; sects. II.1.1(*a*) at n. 41, II.1.1(*d*) at nn. 356 ff. (Klink).

[799] On the conduct of operations of Air Fleet 1 cf. H.Gr. Nord, Führungsabteilung, Operationsatlas: Der Feldzug gegen die Soviet Union, Kriegsjahr 1941 [The campaign against the Soviet Union, 1941], BA-MA RH 19 III/661.

[800] On the activity of I Air Corps cf. summary report on operations of I Air Corps, 22 June–1 Nov. 1941 (author unknown, no date), BA-MA Lw 118/5, and radio messages of I Air Corps/Ia on conduct of its own operations to units of Armd. Group 4, 6–31 July 1941, BA-MA RH 27-8/18, 26–9, and RH 27-6/30–3.

[801] Situation report No. 657, Ob.d.L./Fü.Stab Ic, 27 June 1941, p. 9, BA-MA RL 2 II/247.

fended East Prussia so effectively against enemy aircraft that very soon no more significant Soviet bombing attacks were carried out there.[802] After Army Group North had broken through the old frontier fortifications and reached the general line of Opochka–Ostrov–Pskov–Tartu (Dorpat)–Pyarnu at the beginning of July, the units of I Air Corps were moved forward to the area of Daugavpils and Riga. When strong Soviet air formations had been largely destroyed over the bridgehead on the Velikaya at Ostrov on 6 July—out of 72 attacking aircraft 65 were shot down—the Soviets refrained from further large-scale bomber attacks in the sector of I Air Corps. Until the middle of August transport aircraft[803] were temporarily responsible for all supply shipments for Sixteenth Army, as the only road from Pskov via Gdov was controlled by Soviet stragglers and units still fighting from the cover of the forests. To support the advance of the left wing of Army Group North, especially Armoured Group 4, attacks, were mounted against road and rail traffic northeast and east of Pskov, in Estonia, and on the line between Leningrad and Moscow.[804] The rail junction at Bologoe was an especially important target. Operations against the Soviet air force were continued with attacks on airfields at Lake Ilmen and Leningrad. Moreover, remnants of Soviet units in the swampy forests had to be kept in check from the air, a laborious small-scale war which made heavy demands on the sense of orientation of the air crews.

(vi) THE THRUST TOWARDS LENINGRAD[805]
(See the Annexe Volume, Nos. 15–18)

Reinforced by VIII Air Corps (cf. Table II.1.2) at Dno, Air Fleet 2 supported the breakthrough of the fortifications at Luga and the thrust of Eighteenth Army towards Novgorod.[806] Evidently Hitler himself had issued most precise instructions for the use of the corps and the air fleet, in agreement with Göring but without informing the Army High Command.[807] In doing so he intervened directly not only in the operational but also in the tactical direction of the Luftwaffe. On 15 August First Army Corps captured Novgorod with the support of VIII Air Corps.[808] On 21 August Eighteenth Army reached the Gulf

---

[802] Cf. ibid., No. 655, 25 June 1941: No. 699, 8 Aug. 1941; No. 700, 9 Aug. 1941: BA-MA RL 2 II/246, 253, 254.

[803] Ibid., No. 659, 29 June 1941, p. 21, BA-MA RL 2 II/247, and No. 666, 6 July 1941, p. 25, ibid. 248.

[804] Ibid., No. 694, 3 Aug. 1941, p. 24, BA-MA RL 2 II/253.

[805] Plocher, Krieg im Osten, 220–52, MGFA Lw 4/3; sect. II.1.1(*d, f*) (Klink).

[806] Cf. Luftflottenkommando 1, Führungsabteilung Ia, No. 2486/41 g.Kdos., 4 Aug. 1941, directive for the continuation of the attack towards Leningrad, BA-MA RH 21-4/15, pp. 66–7; Gen.Kdo. VIII Air Corps/Ia No. 2155/41 g.Kdos., 5 Aug. 1941, order for the attack on 8 Aug. 1941, BA-MA 16. Armee, 22745/7.

[807] Richthofen, Tagebuch (privately owned), 31 July 1941; Halder, *Diaries*, 1084–5, 1163 (29 July, 8 Aug 1941).

[808] Tätigkeit des VIII. Fliegerkorps bei der Unterstützung des I. A.K. bis zur Eisenbahnlinie Leningrad-Moskau [VIII Air Corps activity in support of I Army Corps as far as the Leningrad–Moscow railway], 10–21 Aug. 1941, annexe to Gen.Kdo. I. AK/Ia No. 545/41 g.Kdos., 16 Sept. 1941, BA-MA RL 8/48; Halder, *Diaries*, 1182 (15 Aug. 1941).

of Finland at Narva, and on 28 August Tallinn was captured with the help of I Air Corps[809] and the Air Leader Baltic, whose formations, however, in spite of the sinking and damaging of numerous war and merchant ships,[810] were not able to prevent the removal of Soviet troops and the withdrawal of the bulk of the Soviet Baltic fleet. Air Fleet 1 also played an important role in the successful defensive battle south of Staraya Russa, which lasted until 24 August.[811] Further attacks by I Air Corps in August were directed against rail traffic south-west of Leningrad and south and east of Lake Ilmen. A revival of Soviet air activity was largely prevented by continuous attacks on air-bases. By 23 August I Air Corps reported the destruction of 2,541 and the probable destruction of 433 Soviet aircraft.[812] From 14 September Air Fleet 1 participated in the conquest of the Baltic islands.[813] In the siege of Leningrad, which began on 26 September, the air fleet, which until then had only supported the penetration of the city's outer ring of fortifications with I and VIII Air Corps, was given the task of attacking important military targets in Leningrad and the Soviet Baltic Fleet in Kronshtadt,[814] supporting the army in the containment of attempts to break out of the city, in the defence of the covering front south of Lake Ladoga, and, especially towards the end of September, by disrupting supply and evacuation traffic across the lake.[815] Not the least important factor in the failure of the attack on Leningrad was the inability of Air Fleet 1 to concentrate its forces on only one task at a time.[816] Although the city had not been captured, VIII Air Corps was transferred back to the sector of Air Fleet 2 at the end of September, over the objections of Army Group North, in order to support the attack on Moscow there.[817]

[809] On the activity of I Air Corps in Aug.–Sept. 1941 cf. Kdo.Pz.Gruppe 4/Ia No. 1566/41 g.Kdos., 29 July 1941, order for the attack on Leningrad; Panzergruppenbefehl No. 19, BA-MA RH 27-8/29; daily radio messages of I Air Corps on its own activities to Armd. Group 4 and subordinate units, 1 Aug.–30 Sept. 1941, BA-MA RH 27-8/30–4, 37–9, RH 27-6/34–40, RH 27-1/48, 50, 51; Gen.Kdo. I. Fl.Korps/Abt. Ia No. 5500/41 g. to Luftflottenkommando 1, 3 Aug. 1941, BA-MA RH 21-4/24; Panzergruppenbefehl No. 21, Kdo.Pz.Gr. 4/Ia No. 1637/41 g.Kdos, 5 Aug. 1941, BA-MA RH 27-8/30.

[810] Situation report No. 721, Ob.d.L./Fü.Stab Ic, 30 Aug. 1941, p. 26, BA-MA RL 2 II/256. Cf. sect. II.1.1(e) at n. 421 (Klink).

[811] Situation report No. 706, Ob.d.L./Fü.Stab Ic, 15 Aug. 1941, p. 28, BA-MA RL 2 II/254; Nos. 709 (18 Aug. 1941, p. 34) and 712 (21 Aug. 1941, p. 20), both ibid. 255.

[812] Ibid., No. 716, 25 Aug. 1941, p. 33, ibid. 256.

[813] Cf. sects. II.1.1(d), at n. 388, II.1.1(e) at nn. 417 ff. (Klink); sect. II.1.2(c) at n. 900 (Boog).

[814] Cf. sect. II.1.2(c) at n. 906 (Boog); cf. Verbindungsoffizier der Luftwaffe beim AOK 18 [Luftwaffe liaison officer with Eighteenth Army], No. 916/41 g., 26 Sept. 1941, No. 982/41 g., 3 Oct. 1941, Auszüge aus der Tätigkeit der Luftflotte 1 [Excerpts from the activity of Air Fleet 1], BA-MA, 18. Armee, 17562/152, 159.

[815] Situation report No. 741, Ob.d.L./Fü.Stab Ic, 19 Sept. 1941, 27, BA-MA RL 2 II/260.

[816] Richthofen, *Tagebuch* (privately owned), 20–6, 28 Sept. 1941. Here Richthofen expresses his displeasure at the futility of the activity of the Luftwaffe at Leningrad, in strong criticism of the supposedly unenergetic leadership of Army Group North, Sixteenth Army, and Air Fleet 1.

[817] Halder, *Diaries*, 1173 (12 Aug. 1941), 1227 (12 Sept. 1941); Richthofen, *Tagebuch* (privately owned), 20, 27 Sept. 1941. Cf. notes on the conference of C.-in-C. Ninth Army with Gen. Rickthofen, commanding VIII Air Corps, 22 Sept. 1941, BA-MA 9. Armee, 14008/15, and the letter of C.-in-C. Sixteenth Army, 28 Sept. 1941, to VIII Air Corps, 142, BA-MA, 16. Armee, 22745/10. Cf. also BA-MA RL 8/50.

(vii) V AIR CORPS SUPPORT FOR ARMOURED GROUP I AND
    SIXTH ARMY TO THE STALIN LINE[818]
            (*See the Annexe Volume, No. 7*)

From 26 June V Air Corps was employed primarily in defensive operations
against Soviet attacks with heavy armoured support on the flanks and in the
rear of Armoured Group I near Toporov and Brody, Klevan, Olyka, and in the
area of Dubno–Rovno–Lutsk. This also helped secure further advances.[819]
When it became clear that the Soviet forces unexpectedly wanted to withdraw
to the Stalin line according to plan and, it seemed, beyond the Dnieper, V Air
Corps attacked roads and railway lines leading eastwards and transport
centres to prevent regrouping, transfers, and removal of troops and equipment.
Destruction of rolling-stock was to be avoided so that it could be used later for
moving German supplies on the Soviet lines. The main targets were the transit
centres Lvov, Brody, Zlotuv, Zhitomir, Berdichev, Starokonstantinov, Belaya
Tserkov, and Kazatin. Attacks on railway lines were at first concentrated west
of the Dnieper in the area of Shepetovka–Kazatin–Kiev–Korosten, and were
conducted by day and night in closed formations as well as by single aircraft
and flights of three. By 9 July rail traffic in that area had been considerably
reduced.[820] Attacks on staff quarters seriously interfered with Soviet operations.
Air attacks on 30 June had a devastating effect on the roads congested with two
or three marching columns east and south-east of Lvov. However, V Air Corps
did not succeed by direct support in helping Armoured Group I, delayed at
Goryn longer than expected, to advance faster, as requests for dive-bomber
formations were rejected by the commander-in-chief of the Luftwaffe.

(viii) THE BREAKTHROUGH OF THE STALIN LINE[821]
        (*See the Annexe Volume, Nos. 7 and 22*)

While the Stalin line was penetrated with relative ease near Polonnoe–
Miropolye in the direction of Berdichev on 6 July, strong bunker fortifications
delayed the breakthrough near Novograd Volynskiy towards Zhitomir until 9
July. The formations of V Air Corps played an important part in repulsing
enemy counter-attacks. In particular, during the armoured battles of Rovno–
Dubno and Zhitomir–Berdichev their close fighter cover prevented any significant action by the enemy air force against the German armoured spearheads,
and eliminated threats to their flanks.[822] To prevent retreat by Soviet troops,

---

[818] On the activity of Air Fleet 4 until the beginning of Oct. 1941 cf. daily reconnaissance reports
June–Oct. 1941, BA-MA RH 19 I/130–15; radio messages, reports, and the daily enemy information sheet (to No. 104, 30 Sept. 1941) of its operations dept. Ic with the air, ground, and sea
situation and the progress survey of the air fleet, BA-MA RL 7/468; 7/471–3. Cf. Plocher, Krieg
im Osten, pp. 29–43, MGFA Lw 4/2, and sect. II.1.1(*a*) at. nn. 77 ff. (Klink).
[819] Hoffmann von Waldau, Tagebuch, 56 (15 July 1941), BA-MA RL 200/17.
[820] Halder, *Diaries*, 1027, 1030–1 (11, 12 July 1941).
[821] Cf. Plocher, Krieg im Osten, 43–52, MGFA Lw 4/2, and sect. II.1.1(*a*) at n. III (Klink).
[822] Hoffmann von Waldau, Tagebuch, 57–8 (15 July 1941), BA-MA RL 200/17.

they subsequently returned to attacks on columns and railway lines and for the first time attacked the Dnieper crossings at Cherkassy, Kanev, Kiev, and Gornostaypol. Because of the lack of very heavy bombs, it was not possible to destroy the bridges completely; attempts were therefore also made to sever railway lines east of the Dnieper to prevent the bringing up of fresh Soviet forces. In this regard the destruction of the rail junction of Bakhmach was especially important.[823] SD-2 fragmentation bombs caused considerable losses among the Soviet troops, who in some places were retreating along the roads in four parallel columns. V Air Corps had a major share in the successes of Armoured Group 1, as well as of Sixth and Seventeenth Armies, and helped create the conditions for the now envisaged encirclement of the Soviet forces in the Ukraine west of the Dnieper.

Because of the lack of roads, the flying units were initially supplied with bombs and fuel by transport aircraft. The speed with which they could be moved forward and supplied depended on how rapidly communications and lateral connections could be constructed, how rapidly new airfields could be reconnoitred and prepared, and how much traffic the roads used for the advance could accommodate. The chief of staff and the quartermaster of V Air Corps therefore often had to fly along the roads in a Fieseler Storch, make a landing, find the fuel columns, and personally ensure that their right of way, confirmed in writing, was respected.

Soviet air-force units that had escaped destruction attempted to delay the German advance by attacks on armoured spearheads and supply-routes. Their high-altitude and low-level attacks were aimed primarily at bridges, such as those at Lutsk, Dubno, Rovno, Ostrog, Polonnoe, Miropolye, Novograd, and Zhitomir. With considerable courage and tenacity they repeatedly attacked targets which, from previous losses to German anti-aircraft fire and fighters, they knew to be heavily defended.

(ix) IV AIR CORPS[824] ON THE RIGHT WING OF ARMY GROUP SOUTH[825]
(*See the Annexe Volume, Nos. 7 and 8*)

This corps began its direct and indirect support of the army with Eleventh Army's attack across the Prut on 2 July. It supported the advance of this army, which, in co-operation with the main forces of Army Group South, was aimed in a north-eastern direction via Balti towards Mogilev Podolskiy on the Dniester and later against Kishinev. Romanian and Hungarian forces were supported in their advance by their own air forces. To isolate the operations area, road and rail traffic, especially bridges, was attacked in the Odessa area, on the lower Dnieper at Zaporozhye and Dnepropetrovsk, and on the Dniester

---

[823] Situation report No. 675, Ob.d.L./Fü.Stab Ic, 15 July 1941, p. 20, BA-MA RL 2 II/250.

[824] On the activity of IV Air Corps; see BA-MA RL 8/26 (Corps order No. 1, 18 June 1941), RL 8/27 (reconnaissance reports 22 June–3 Sept. 1941).

[825] Cf. Plocher, *Krieg im Osten*, 52 ff., MGFA Lw 4/2.

at Mogilev Podolskiy. From mid-July, after the crossing of the Dniester, IV Air Corps provided continuous support for the advancing German and Romanian ground units.

(x) THE LUFTWAFFE IN THE BATTLE OF ENCIRCLEMENT AT UMAN[826]
(*See the Annexe Volume, Nos. 8 and 11*)

V Air Corps was assigned the task of supporting Armoured Group 1 at the point of main effort in the battle. Its mission was not only to make possible a rapid advance but also to support Seventeenth Army and to attack enemy air formations and communications in the enemy's rear. In view of its declining effective strength, these multifarious tasks exceeded the capacity of the corps. The pressure of time resulting from the planned army operations and the speed and mobility of the flying units increasingly made them the most important support of the army in crisis situations and soon restricted their activities almost exclusively to such support. To prevent Soviet troops from escaping to the eastern bank of the Dnieper, railway lines and marching columns west of the river were continually attacked. Soon the attacks were extended to include terrain east of the river in the area of Konotop, Glukhov, Gorodishche, Priluki, and Bakhmach. Although the attacks were carried out even in bad weather and persistent rain, and although thunderstorms reduced the roads to quagmires, it proved impossible to prevent the escape of some of the enemy forces to the east. Stuka dive-bombers were especially important in breaking the resistance of Soviet troops trapped in the pocket near Uman, Golovanevsk, and Novo-Archangelsk. German fighter formations had achieved air superiority there in spite of very serious supply problems.[827]

Because of the shortage of aircraft and the priority given to close support for German forces at the point of main effort in the battle of Uman, V Air Corps had to reject urgent requests for help from Sixth Army, which was seriously threatened on its northern flank by the Soviet Fifth Army. This greatly reduced the army's confidence in the Luftwaffe, but the only available fighter Geschwader in the huge operations area between Korosten, Kiev, Kremenchug, and Zaporozhye—Fighter Geschwader 3—could not possibly provide simultaneous cover for Sixth Army in the area of Korosten and Kiev, for Seventeenth Army near Uman, and for Armoured Group 1 near Zaporozhye. Between 4 and 7 August V Air Corps supported the thrust of XXIX Army Corps of Sixth Army towards Kiev from the south. Soviet aircraft clearly tried to concentrate the main weight of their attacks on the airfield at Belaya Tserkov, forward infantry units, and all bridges in the battle area, but without lasting success.

---

[826] Ibid. 54–60, and sect. II.1.1(*a*) at n. 117 (Klink).

[827] Summary assessment of Luftwaffe activity in the battle of encirclement at Uman, in the daily order of the C.-in-C. of Air Fleet 4 and Cmdr. South-east, 14 Aug. 1941, BA-MA RH 20-11/91.

(xi) THE REPULSE OF THE SOVIET THRUST AT BOGUSLAV
AND KANEV[828]
(See the Annexe Volume, No. 11)

On 7 August, when Army Group South—its northern flank covered by Sixth
Army with Armoured Group 1—was about to launch its thrust against
Dnepropetrovsk and Nikolaev, attempting to establish a bridgehead on the
east bank of the Dnieper and to mop up resistance west of the river with
Eleventh and Seventeenth Armies, Soviet forces, at first in division strength,
attacked across the river near Kanev, broke through the weak German covering units, and overran supply facilities. Parts of Sixth Army (Group von
Schwedler) and 11th Armoured Division of Armoured Group 1 were turned
south and north respectively to cut off this penetration. However, before they
could make contact V Air Corps attacked the enemy armour and cavalry units
which had broken through with all available aircraft. The operation order
caught the corps completely by surprise; there was no time for target reconnaissance or briefing. The bomber, dive-bomber, and fighter crews had to
attack their targets individually or in twos and threes, in difficult weather
conditions, and in relays without overall co-ordination. At the same time they
had to conduct reconnaissance to provide the command with a picture of the
situation. In the first three days 94 tanks and 148 other motor-vehicles were
destroyed. On the fourth day of fighting it became clear that the Soviets had
employed an entire army, Twenty-sixth, for this breakthrough attempt, with
three fresh and two weakened infantry divisions, two cavalry divisions, and
one or two armoured divisions. They were pushed back by Group von
Schwedler with support from dive-bomber formations near Kanev and
prevented from breaking through until eventually they withdrew to the east
bank of the Dnieper on 13 August. On the congested bridges near Kanev the
Soviet forces suffered especially heavy losses from dive-bomber attacks on 15
August. V Air Corps had contained the breakthrough, which had already been
accomplished for two days until the arrival of the first German ground forces
and thereby averted a serious threat to German army operations in the
Ukraine.

(xii) MOPPING-UP OPERATIONS IN THE SOUTHERN DNIEPER BEND[829]
(See the Annexe Volume, Nos. 11 and 12)

From 17 August onwards bomber formations of V Air Corps were employed
by day and night in attacks against the transport centre Dnepropetrovsk to
prevent the withdrawal of major enemy forces and their digging in on the east
bank of the river. On that day alone the remaining 44 operational fighters of
the corps shot down 33 Soviet aircraft, among them 29 bombers, and de-

---

[828] Cf. sect. II.1.1(c) at n. 219 (Klink); Plocher, Krieg im Osten, 60–6, MGFA Lw 4/2.

[829] Cf. sect. II.1.1(c) at nn. 225 ff. (Klink); Plocher, Krieg im Osten, 66–77, MGFA Lw 4/2. On
the activity of Air Fleet 4 in this period cf. also its directives Nos. 3 (18 Aug. 1941) and 4 (29 Aug.
1941), BA-MA RL 7/466; reconnaissance reports, 22 Aug.–12 Sept. 1941, ibid. 467.

stroyed 3 more on the ground.[830] On 30 August Fighter Geschwader 3 under Major Lützov scored its thousandth air victory in the east.[831] German air operations were made increasingly difficult by insufficient supplies of fuel and ammunition, as well as by the extreme distances, which made it necessary to use the poorly supplied airfield at Krivoy Rog as a base for some units. Transport aircraft had to ferry in the most urgent supplies, as supply columns could make little progress on the rain-sodden roads and the railheads were still too far west. In spite of timely warnings from air officers who had been sent to Lipetsk in the Soviet Union in the years 1926–31, the supply columns were equipped with vehicles which were poorly suited to the terrain and road conditions in the east and generally broke down completely in mud. It was necessary to resort to Russian volunteer helpers, who repaired captured Soviet vehicles in their own home-made workshops and set up their own supply columns with them.

To improve direct support of Armoured Group 1, V Air Corps formed a staff of the Close Support Leader South under Lieutenant-Colonel Clemens Graf Schönborn, to whom Gruppe 1 of dive-bomber Geschwader 77, Gruppe 2 of Fighter Geschwader 3, and Gruppe 3 of Fighter Geschwader 52 were made available. In accordance with instructions from the air corps, he attacked enemy preparations for a counter-attack against the German bridgehead at Dnepropetrovsk. Bombers also attacked all roads and railway lines leading to the bridgehead, which was substantially expanded on 28 August as a result of diminishing enemy pressure.

On the northern wing of Army Group South a Close Support Leader North was created for Sixth Army. His task was to prevent the retreat of the Soviet Fifth Army from the area north of Kiev across the Dnieper by attacking transport centres and enemy columns.[832] Major Lützow, with Gruppe 3 of Dive-bomber Geschwader 77 and Gruppe 3 of Fighter Geschwader 3, was made close-support leader. Other forces of V Air Corps were also used for the same purposes.

The weak German fighter forces protecting the wooden bridge across the Dnieper at Gornostaypol, which had been captured in a surprise attack by 111th Infantry Division, were unable to prevent its destruction by strong Soviet air attacks; these considerably delayed the attack of Sixth Army. In contrast, on 8 September German fighter units under the Close Support Leader South effectively assisted Seventeenth Army in establishing a bridgehead on the east bank of the Dnieper at Kremenchug and were able to defend it and its crossings against persistent Soviet air attacks. V Air Corps provided support by bombing Soviet air-bases at Kharkov, Poltava, and Kiev. The employment of the Luftwaffe was also an important factor in the expansion of the bridgehead into the southern jumping-off position for the next large-scale

---

[830] Situation report No. 713, Ob.d.L./Fü.Stab Ic, 22 Aug. 1941, p. 35, BA-MA, RL 2 II/255.
[831] Ibid., No. 728, 5 Sept. 1941, p. 26, ibid. 258.
[832] Cf. Halder, *Diaries*, 1188–9 (19 Aug. 1941).

operation, the encirclement of the armies under Budenny's command in and east of Kiev.

Meanwhile, IV Air Corps supported the advance of Eleventh Army in the south of Army Group South, preventing the withdrawal of enemy troops and equipment from Nikolaev and Odessa, and attacking port facilities at Sevastopol and Novorossiysk. At the beginning of September, most importantly, it supported the crossing of the Dnieper by Eleventh Army and thus helped to establish a jumping-off point for the attack on the Crimea.

(xiii) ANTI-AIRCRAFT UNITS IN THE SOUTH

II Anti-aircraft Corps under Lieutenant-General Otto Dessloch was assigned the tasks of protecting the mobile units of the army, especially Armoured Group 1, of supporting army units in breaking enemy opposition on the ground (fortifications, tanks), and of protecting airfields, especially in so far as they were bases for bombers and dive-bombers. The Luftwaffe commanders attached to the large army formations used their anti-aircraft guns to provide protection against air attacks for the ground troops. Since the beginning of the campaign all units of II Anti-aircraft Corps had been integrated into the armoured and motorized infantry columns to protect the armoured spearheads in particular from enemy aircraft. They also provided valuable assistance in destroying fortifications and were increasingly used in ground fighting as the danger of Soviet air attacks diminished, e.g. against enemy armour in the tank battles of Dubno–Rovno–Lutsk, Zhitomir, and Berdichev, and in the battle of encirclement at Uman.[833]

(xiv) THE BATTLE OF ENCIRCLEMENT AT KIEV (28 AUGUST– 26 SEPTEMBER)[834]
(See the Annexe Volume, Nos. 12, 13, and 23)

Although the chief of Air Fleet 2, Field Marshal Kesselring, considered an advance on Moscow to be correct and feasible after the victory at Smolensk, so that after a short rest he would have preferred such an operation,[835] he like the Luftwaffe leaders, who evidently did so without objection, had to accept Hitler's decision to turn south. In the resulting battle of encirclement east of Kiev the army units were supported in the northern part of the encirclement by Air Fleet 2 with II Air Corps and in the southern part by Air Fleet 4 with

[833] On the activity of II Air Corps cf. Plocher, Krieg im Osten, 81–7, MGFA Lw 4/2, and annexe 77a, MGFA Lw 4/12; Gen.Kdo. II Flakkorps Ic, 9 Apr. 1942, Daten zur Geschichte des II. Flakkorps [Data on the history of II AA Corps] (copy), BA-MA Lw 107/85; extracts from corps orders of II Air Corps, Nos. 1 (28 May 1941)–62 (19 Sept. 1941), ibid.; situation reports, Ob.d.L./ Fü.Stab Ic No. 656, 26 June 1941, p. 29, No. 659, 29 June 1941, p. 32, BA-MA RL 2 II/247; No. 671, 11 July 1941, p. 27, ibid. 249; No. 677, 17 July 1941, p. 27, ibid. 250; No. 682, 22 July 1941, p. 29, ibid. 251; No. 697, 6 Aug. 1941, p. 31, ibid. 253; No. 708, 17 Aug. 1941, p. 34, ibid. 255; No. 714, 23 Aug. 1941, p. 36, ibid. 256.

[834] Cf. sect. II.1.1(c) at nn. 227 ff. (Klink); Plocher, Krieg im Osten, 350–77, MGFA Lw 4/3, and pp. 1–109, ibid., Lw 4/7.

[835] Kesselring, Memoirs, 94, 97–8.

V Air Corps. The flying units provided aerial reconnaissance; they ensured air superiority over the battlefield, its isolation by bombers from enemy actions from outside, and the smashing of the enemy within the pocket, especially by the close-support units. V Air Corps[836] attacked the railway line between Romodan and Poltava, as well as Soviet troops on both sides of the roads east of the line from Khorol to Lokhvitsa, employing strong bomber formations to prevent their retreat and the removal of equipment. At the same time formations of the Close Support Leader of V Air Corps struck at enemy columns and field positions in the area of Lubny, Lokhvitsa, Priluki, and Yagotin, and near Akhtyrka, Gadyach, and Mirgorod. Because of the weakness of the advance detachments of Armoured Group 2 and in view of the continuous flank attacks by the enemy, the situation near Lubny and Lokhvitsa was precarious and could be stabilized only by air attacks. The formation of a new group of enemy forces around Mirgorod, Gadyach, Akhtyrka, and Poltava by elements of enemy units that had escaped from the pocket and been reinforced from the east—which could have carried out dangerous relief attacks against the Sula sector—was prevented by waves of bombing attacks and simultaneous support by V Air Corps for the attack by Seventeenth Army in the direction of Poltava. Fighters cleared the area of enemy aircraft. To suppress the activities of enemy air-force units the airfields at Kharkov and Poltava were repeatedly bombed. The air attacks on the Soviet forces in the pocket prevented their commanders from assembling them to break through the encirclement ring and inflicted heavy losses, which increased as the pocket became smaller. On 16 and 17 September V Air Corps had to seriously restrict its activities because of a shortage of fuel caused by the over-extended supply-lines and the inadequate transport system. From 18 September Gruppe 3 of Dive-bomber *Geschwader* 77 and Gruppe 3 of Fighter Geschwader 52 operating from Belaya Tserkov supported Sixth Army's attack on Kiev. According to an earlier directive from Hitler, they were to reduce the city to 'rubble and ashes' and do 'half the work'[837] for the army by bombing the fortress until it was ripe for attack. This made it possible to take Kiev the next day. Subsequently the dive-bombers were used to crush any resistance within the pocket. Between 12 and 21 September alone V Air Corps flew 1,422 sorties, dropped 567,650 kg. of bombs and 96 Type-36 incendiary bomb clusters, shot down 65 enemy aircraft, destroyed 42 on the ground, wrecked 23 tanks, 2,171 motor-vehicles, 6 anti-aircraft batteries, 52 trains, and 28 locomotives, and damaged 355 motor-vehicles, 41 horse-drawn wagons, and 36 trains; it also destroyed a bridge and severed 18 railway lines. German casualties were only 9 men killed, 5 wounded, and 18 missing, with 17 aircraft lost and 14 damaged.[838]

---

[836] Cf. the relevant parts of situation reports Ob.d.L./Fü.Stab Ic Nos. 724–47, 2–26 Sept. 1941, BA-MA RL 2 II/257–61.

[837] Gen. Fritz Brand in Halder, *Diaries*, 1161 ff. (8 Aug. 1941).

[838] According to a battle report of V Air Corps in Plocher, Krieg im Osten, 358–9, MGFA Lw 4/3.

II Air Corps[839] on the northern front of the encirclement supported Armoured Group 2 and Second Army in crossing the Desna, bombed railway lines to isolate the battlefield,[840] and, with the forces of Close Support Leader II, assisted the advance of Armoured Group 2 towards Konotop and further towards Romny. Bomber Geschwader 3 and 53,[841] Fast Bomber Geschwader 210,[842] and Fighter Geschwader 51[843] under his command contributed significantly to the success of the encirclement operation and to breaking the last resistance of the Soviet armies in the pocket, as army commanders themselves confirmed.[844] On 18 September units of 104th Anti-aircraft Regiment especially distinguished themselves in preventing the break-out of superior enemy forces through a gap in the encirclement ring near Romny.[845] The ruthless use of the two air corps, the speed and force of their attacks, and the cover provided by their fighters and anti-aircraft artillery accelerated the operations of the army units in spite of rain, storms, and mud—an especially valuable gain of time in view of the approaching winter.

(xv) support for the advance of seventeenth and sixth armies by v air corps[846]
(See the Annexe Volume, No. 13)

On 2 October Seventeenth Army began its attack towards the Donets south of Kharkov; the same day Sixth Army attacked towards Kharkov and Kursk. Soon, however, both armies' advance was slowed by the stubborn resistance of the Soviet troops under Marshal Timoshenko. In addition, the soft ground slowed the motorized units more than the infantry, which were equipped with horse-drawn carts. Even before the attack, bombers of V Air Corps sought to disrupt enemy rail movements near and east of Kharkov in order to cut the flow of supplies and prevent the removal of industrial assets, machines, and food from Kharkov and the Donets basin to the east. Between 23 September and 12 October they destroyed 95 trains, including 4 ammunition and 4 fuel trains, and 12 locomotives; they heavily damaged another 288 trains and 10

---

[839] On the activity of II Air Corps cf. operational orders, 8–20, 22–6, 29 Sept. 1941, BA-MA RH 20-2/178, 180, 181, 208–10, and ibid., RH 20-4/232.

[840] On missions of II Air Corps to isolate the battlefield as part of direct support for the army cf. relevant parts of situation reports Ob.d.L./Fü.Stab Ic Nos. 724–48 and 1–26 Sept. 1941, BA-MA RL 2 II/257–61.

[841] Cf. situation report No. 754, Ob.d.L./Fü.Stab Ic, 2 Oct. 1941, 33–4, BA-MA RL 2 II/262.

[842] Ibid., No. 757, 5 Oct. 1941, p. 32, ibid. 263.

[843] Ibid., No. 734, 12 Sept, 1941, p. 34, ibid. 259.

[844] Cf. Guderian, *Erinnerungen*, 185, 192, 194 (not in *Panzer Leader*); Halder, *Diaries*, 1221–2 (10 Sept. 1941).

[845] Cf. Guderian, *Erinnerungen*, 199 (not in *Panzer Leader*); Plocher, Krieg im Osten, 365–70, MGFA Lw 4/3; and situation report No. 732, Ob.d.L./Fü.Stab Ic, 10 Sept. 1941, p. 33, BA-MA RL 2 II/259.

[846] Cf. the organization of Air Fleets 1, 2, and 4, of 10 Sept. 1941, Table II.1.3. On the activity of Air Fleet 4, 10 Sept.–4 Nov. 1941, cf. radio messages and reports in BA-MA RL 7/468–70 and the daily enemy intelligence sheets (with report on its own situation) of the air fleet command, Führungsabteilung Ic, Nos. 105 (1 Oct. 1941)–134, (30 Oct. 1941), BA-MA RL 7/474. Cf. sect. II.1.1(c) at n. 252 (Klink); Plocher, Krieg im Osten, 379–97, MGFA Lw 4/3.

locomotives, and cut railway lines at 64 points.[847] These successes indirectly reduced the strong Soviet pressure on the German troops. The uninterrupted Soviet air attacks from the airfields at Kharkov and Bogodukhov interfered with the movements of the German army. Between 25 and 27 September V Air Corps therefore temporarily concentrated its attacks on those airfields, which quickly led to a decline of enemy air activity. Although the corps had placed the bulk of its fighters at the disposal of Air Fleet 2 and had only Gruppe 3 of Fighter Geschwader 52 for its own use, (which in fact it had to transfer to IV Air Corps in the Crimea on 22 October), it achieved air superiority in the area of Seventeenth Army and over Kharkov, and was thus able to attack enemy columns, troop concentrations, and assemblies of armoured vehicles on the roads west of the city and the city itself, with the exception (as requested by Sixth Army) of its north-eastern part. Kharkov was an important command, transport, and transit centre for Soviet military movements. It was conquered on 24 October. The support provided by V Air Corps for the two armies was largely indirect. Aerial reconnaissance at an early stage discovered a marked increase in rail traffic between Rostov, the Caucasus, Voronezh, and Stalingrad, especially on the line connecting Baku, Rostov, and Voronezh. In spite of supply problems at their base at Taganrog and strong enemy fighter opposition along this main line, German bomber forces were able for weeks to carry out attacks extending to Mineralnye Vody, and to cause considerable damage: 79 trains were destroyed and 148 damaged by direct hits.[848]

(xvi) IV AIR CORPS AND THE CONQUEST OF THE CRIMEA[849]
(See the Annexe Volume, No. 14)

After the capture of Odessa on 16 October, IV Air Corps supported the attack of Eleventh Army to conquer the Crimean peninsula. Not the least important objective of this attack was to eliminate the threat to the Romanian oilfields from Soviet aircraft based there.[850] The task of the corps was to support the infantry advancing across the Perekop isthmus—the only land link between the Crimea and the mainland—which provided little or no cover, and to protect it against the concentrated attacks of several hundred Soviet bombers and fighters, which also operated at night. Command of the German fighter units was placed in the hands of Colonel Mölders,[851] who after his hundredth

---

[847] Plocher, Krieg im Osten, 388, MGFA Lw 4/3.

[848] Plocher, Krieg im Osten, 397, and situation report No. 775, Ob.d.L./Fü.Stab Ic, 24 Oct. 1941, p. 8, BA-MA RL 2 II/267.

[849] On the activity of IV Air Corps in Sept. and Oct. 1941 cf. BA-MA RL 8/28 (reconnaissance reports), 8/32 (situation reports), 8/33–4 (operational plans, orders, and surveys). On its operations against the Crimea cf. sect. II.1.1(c) at n. 278 (Klink); Plocher, Krieg im Osten, 398–412, MGFA Lw 4/3; teletype message Rundstedt, H.Gr. Süd/Ia, No. 2043/41 g.Kdos, 20 Oct. 1941, to chief of staff of Air Fleet 4, Col.-Gen. Löhr, and letter of C.-in-C. Eleventh Army to chief of staff of Army Group South, 20 Oct. 1941, BA-MA RH 19 I/75.

[850] Cf. Hitler's directive to Ob.d.H. Wehrmachtführungsstab/L No. 441412/41 g.Kdos. Chefs., 21 Aug. 1941, KTB OKW i. 1063, and sect. II.1.2(e) at n. 951 (Boog).

[851] Cf. teletype message OKH/GenStdH/Op.Abt. (I) No. 44001/41 g.Kdos. II. Angel., 22 Oct.

victory in the air on 16 July 1941 became the first German flyer to be awarded the Oak Leaves with Swords and Diamonds to the Knight's Cross. The combat formations of IV Air Corps concentrated their attacks on Soviet airfields in the Crimea. The dive-bombers were directed against the strongly fortified positions on the isthmus. Reinforced to a temporary strength of $6^2/_3$ bomber, 3 dive-bomber, 2 ground-attack, and 5 fighter Gruppen, IV Air Corps attacked Soviet field positions, batteries, bunkers, troop concentrations, and assembly areas. On 26 October, after eight days of fighting, a breakthrough was achieved on the isthmus. The fleeing enemy was then attacked from the air. By 16 October the Crimea was occupied, with the exception of Sevastopol, which from 17 December onwards was attacked by Eleventh Army with support from a specially organized close-support formation. The danger to Romania from the Crimea was thus eliminated. Stronger forces now became available for the air war at sea.[852]

As the Soviet navy still dominated the Black Sea and large-scale landings had to be expected at any time, continuous reconnaissance at sea was necessary in addition to attacks on loading and embarkation ports, but, because of a lack of adequate forces and the prevailing unfavourable weather, this was not possible on the desired scale. Unnoticed by German aerial and naval reconnaissance, which discovered neither the preparations in Sevastopol and Novorossiysk nor its approach by sea, the Soviet Fifty-first Army landed near Kerch on 26 December and the Soviet Forty-fourth Army near Fedosiya on 29 December. On 5–6 January 1942 a lesser Soviet force landed at Evpatoriya.[853] All available German air units in the south were employed to attack troops after their landing. The landing at Feodosiya led to the withdrawal of 46th Infantry Division, the loss of the Kerch peninsula, the breaking off of the attack on Sevastopol—which, however, continued to tie down strong German encirclement forces—and, for the Luftwaffe, the tying down of IV Air Corps to Eleventh Army, for which it was now to provide continuous direct and indirect support. Half the staff of V Air Corps, which by then was already in Brussels, had to be returned to the combat sector of Air Fleet 4 as 'Special Staff, Crimea'.

(xvii) THE SETBACK AT ROSTOV[854]
(See the Annexe Volume, No. 13, and Map II.I.I)

V Air Corps was intended to support the attack by First Armoured Army via Shakhty towards Rostov, envisaged for 3 November. Its tactical operations staff was therefore transferred to the operations staff of the armoured army at

---

1941; section of war diary H.Gr. Süd, 23 Oct. 1941, about Luftwaffe operations for carrying out the attack on the Crimea, 174; and teletype message AOK 11/Ia No. 41 760/41 g., Der Oberbefehlshaber, 25 Oct. 1941, to Army Group South, all BA-MA RH 19 I/75; Manstein, *Lost Victories*, 217 ff.; situation report No. 778, Ob.d.L./Fü.Stab Ic, 27 Oct. 1941, pp. 4, 9, BA-MA RL 2 II/267.

[852] Cf. sects. II.1.2(*c*) and II.1.2(*d*).   [853] Cf. sect. II.1.1(*g*) at nn. 727 ff. (Klink).

[854] Cf. Plocher, *Krieg im Osten*, 413–26, MGFA Lw 4/3; sect. II.1.1(*c*) at nn. 289 ff. (Klink).

Mariupol. A fuel shortage and poor ground conditions delayed the start of the attack until 5 November. It was soon partially halted at Dyakova. With considerable assistance from the close-support forces of the air corps the danger to the southern flank of the armoured army was eliminated. Soon, however, the attack became bogged down in the mud. The heavy rail traffic discovered by long-range reconnaissance on the lines north of Rostov, and especially from Valuyki to the east, was continually attacked by bombers of V Air Corps. By 12 November they had destroyed 12 trains and 51 locomotives, and reported 161 trains and 32 locomotives damaged. Fighters in action ahead of the front of First Armoured Army were also successful. But because the cold often made it impossible to start up the engines, their interceptor wings were frequently unable to defend their most important base, at Taganrog, against the numerous Soviet air attacks; in addition, the anti-aircraft units were often unable to fire at enemy aircraft because of the lack of low-temperature lubricant. On 12 November Bomber Geschwader 54 and 55 (except for one Gruppe of the latter), with an average of six to nine combat-ready aircraft, were withdrawn from the front and transferred to Germany. Sabotage and bad weather considerably impaired the supplying of the close-support formations of V Air Corps either by rail or by air. These forces had at their disposal only their aircraft and their best technicians. The vehicles necessary in order to maintain their combat-readiness had to be borrowed from the army, the anti-aircraft units, and Luftwaffe intelligence units. Winter clothing and food had to be brought in by air. In view of the permanent fuel shortage, it was only because of the bad weather—which prevented German and Soviet aircraft alike from taking off—that the fighter and dive-bomber formations of the close-support leader were not totally out of action. 'At Rostov', the head of the operations department of the Luftwaffe operations staff noted, 'we are making no headway, either because of supply problems or on account of difficulties with the weather.'[855] On 20 November, three days after the start of the renewed attack by First Armoured Army, which on that day pushed to within some five kilometres of Rostov, the situation on the army's eastern flank became so threatening that Air Fleet 4 placed Bomber Geschwader 27 of IV Air Corps under V Air Corps. In view of the crisis, the close-support leader, whose activities had been seriously restricted by the weather from 17 to 20 November, now attacked towns strongly held by enemy forces in this area with fighters and dive-bombers in spite of light snowfall and a cloud ceiling of only 150 metres. The bomber formations attacked troop movements, rail traffic, and unloading-points far behind the front facing First Armoured Army. This support made it possible to take Rostov on 21 November, but it had to be abandoned again on 27 November because of strong enemy pressure. The front was re-established behind the Mius. Further north too, hard pressed by a strong Soviet counter-offensive, Seventeenth and Sixth Armies withdrew

---

[855] Hoffmann von Waldau, Tagebuch, 82 (15 Nov. 1941), BA-MA RL 200/17; cf. ibid. 79 (21 Oct. 1941), and Halder, *Diaries*, 1290 (7 Nov. 1941).

behind the Donets. The withdrawals, especially that of First Armoured Army, were supported by V Air Corps, as well as by formations of IV Air Corps.[856] As Army Group South subsequently described the situation, these relay attacks by Air Fleet 4 foiled not only a breakthrough towards Taganrog, but also the destruction of the southern wing of First Armoured Army. An orderly retreat was made possible only by the attrition which the constant air attacks wrought upon the attacking Soviet troops.

Not only was Army Group South too weak to conquer the Crimea, the Donets basin, and the oilfields of the Caucasus all at the same time, but Air Fleet 4 was not strong enough to support simultaneously the advance of four armies, suppress Soviet air activity, attack supply shipments by rail, cut the flow of oil from the Caucasus, and eliminate the Soviet Black Sea Fleet. Its personnel were exhausted by the uninterrupted sorties. 'The campaign in the east won't reach the desired final objective this way,' Major-General Hoffmann von Waldau wrote in his diary. 'Rostov with the bridgeheads east of the Don as the jumping-off point for Maykop force was lost . . . The war is extending and becoming harder and longer.'[857] After the withdrawal of V Air Corps[858] Air Fleet 4 was left with only IV Air Corps to fulfil its many tasks, the most important being continued support of the defensive efforts of Army Group South. Rostov was the first serious setback of the German campaign in the east.

(xviii) THE LUFTWAFFE ON THE VOLKHOV AND AT TIKHVIN[859]
(See the Annexe Volume, Nos. 21, 18, and 19)

In the second half of October Air Fleet 1[860] employed I Air Corps[861] primarily to support the breakthrough by XXXIX Armoured Corps of the Soviet defences on the Volkhov and the subsequent attack on Tikhvin. For this purpose the commander of Bomber Geschwader 77, Colonel Johann Raithel, was appointed *ad hoc* Air Leader Tikhvin.[862] In addition to his Geschwader he commanded Long-range Reconnaissance Staffel 5 (F) of Gruppe 122, a

[856] Cf. Gen.Kdo. IV. Fl.Korps/Abt. Ic, 2 Dec. 1941, Übersicht über Einsätze und Erfolge und Verluste der Verbände des IV. Fliegerkorps [Survey of operations, successes, and losses of units of IV Air Corps], 1–30 Nov. 1941, BA-MA RH 20-11/179.

[857] Hoffmann von Waldau, Tagebuch, 91–2 (3 Dec. 1941), BA-MA RL 200/17; cf. Halder, *Diaries*, 1322–3 (29 Nov. 1941).

[858] Lt.-Gen. Plocher, Zusammenstellung über den Gesamteinsatz des V. Fliegerkorps im Ostfeldzug [Survey of overall operations of V Air Corps in the campaign in the east] vom 22.6.–30.11.1941 , annexe 51, in Plocher, Krieg im Osten, MGFA Lw 4/7.

[859] Cf. sect. II.1.1(e) at n. 373 (Klink); Plocher, Krieg im Osten, 252–64, MGFA Lw 4/3.

[860] Cf. extracts from the reports of the Luftwaffe liaison officer at Eighteenth Army headquarters on the activity of Air Fleet 1 (3, 10, 15–18 Nov., 12, 13 Dec. 1941), BA-MA 18. Armee, 17562/163, 207, 208, 234.

[861] On the conduct of operations of I Air Corps cf. radio messages I. Fl.Korps/Ia, 1–22 Oct. 1941 (with gaps), BA-MA RH 27-8/39, 44–7; Gen.Kdo. I. Fl.Korps/Ia No. 2460/42 geh., 29 Apr. 1942, Erfahrungsbericht über Führung und Einsatz im Herbst und Winter 1941/42 [Report on experience in command and operations during autumn and winter 1941–2], BA-MA 18. Armee, 44911/4.

[862] Cf. corps order No. 33, Gen.Kdo. XXXIX. AK/Abt. Ia, 15 Oct. 1941, BA-MA RH 27-8/46.

Gruppe of Fighter Geschwader 54, a heavy anti-aircraft battalion, and air-signal units. Besides providing direct support for German ground forces, the flying units attacked railway lines leading to the flanks of the advance. The planned torching of the oil lakes—open storage facilities for large quantities of oil—near Rybinsk was not successful. After the capture of Tikhvin on 9 November formations of I Air Corps joined in the defensive battles there, which went on for four weeks. In addition, they mounted continuous attacks against rail traffic east of the Volkhov and Lake Ilmen, as well as against military targets in Leningrad. They were not, however, able to disrupt the flow of supplies to the city by the ice route across Lake Ladoga between 25 November and 3 December,[863] as the holes made in the ice by the bombs quickly froze over. Earlier attempts by the Luftwaffe to disrupt shipping across the lake by using Siebel ferries operated by the Luftwaffe had also been unsuccessful, as they were too slow and also unprotected. Altogether the German and Finnish ships employed proved not to be strong enough for this task. In late autumn and early winter information provided by aerial re-connaissance became increasingly scanty. This was due less to the growing strength of enemy fighter and anti-aircraft defences[864] than to the weather and the smaller number of operational reconnaissance aircraft. Moreover, their effectiveness, was reduced by the freezing of swamps, rivers, and lakes in winter. Reconnaissance along a relatively small number of routes had thus to be replaced by the much more time-consuming reconnaissance of large areas. Transfers of units further reduced the supplemental aerial reconnaissance by fighters and bombers. The severe winter greatly reduced the activities of Air Fleet 1. After the evacuation of Tikhvin on 12 December I Air Corps sup-ported the defensive battles of the troops retreating to positions on the west bank of the Volkhov (the 'swamp positions').

In the general emergency Luftwaffe ground personnel became infantry soldiers with the task of defending airfields[865] and of fighting in the ranks of army units. As their ground-combat training was inadequate, they suffered heavy losses. They remained, however, part of the Luftwaffe and formed the core of the Luftwaffe field divisions created in 1942.[866]

(xix) AIR FLEET 2 AND PREPARATIONS FOR THE ATTACK ON MOSCOW
(*See Table* II.1.3)

In connection with the preparations for the attack by Army Group Centre on Moscow, ordered by Hitler's Directive No. 35 of 6 September 1941, Air Fleet 2, which co-operated with that army group and whose staff was located in a

---

[863] Cf. Halder, *Diaries*, 1336 (4 Dec. 1941).

[864] Cf. ibid. 1259 (27 Sept. 1941): 'Enemy air force has shifted its main concentration northwards.'

[865] Luftflottenkommando 1/Führungsabteilung Ia No. 13051/41 g., 15 Dec. 1941, Befehl für die Sicherung der Flugplätze im Winter [Order on airfield security in winter], BA-MA 18. Armee, 17562/234.

[866] Cf. Denzel, *Luftwaffen-Felddivisionen*; Stumpf, 'Luftwaffe'; and sect. II.1.2(*b*) at n. 891.

TABLE II.1.3. *Order of Battle of the Flying Units of Air Fleets 1, 2, and 4 Employed against the Soviet Union, 10 October 1941*

Air Fleet 1 Weather Recce. Staffel 1
Air Transport Gruppe I, Geschwader 172 (special duties)
Special Staffel LGL. 1 (transport)

I Air Corps
Long-range Recce. Staffel 5, Gruppe 122
Staff, BG 1 with Gruppen II and III of BG 1
Staff, BG 4 with Gruppen I and (personnel only) II of BG 4
Staff, BG 77 with Gruppen I and (personnel only) III of BG 77
Coastal Gruppe 806
Staff, FG 54 with Gruppen I, II, and III of FG 54

Air Leader Baltic
Recce. Gruppe 125
Coastal Gruppe 506
Replacement Fighter Gruppe 54
3 minesweeper aircraft

Air Fleet 2 Staff, Recce. Gruppe 122 with Long-range Recce. Staffel 2 of
Gruppe 122
Long-range Recce Staffel 1, C.-in-C. Luftwffe
Weather Recce. Staffel 26
Special large-glider Staffeln LG 2 and 22 (transport)

VIII Air Corps
Long-range Recce. Staffel 2, Gruppe 11; Tactical Recce. Staffel 7,
Gruppe 21
Gruppe 4, Geschwader 1 (special duties); and 106 (special duties)
(transport Gruppen)
Gruppe I, Airborne Geschwader 1
Staff, BG 2 with Gruppe I of BG 2, Gruppe III of BG 3, and Gurppe III
of BG 4
Staff, BG 76 with Gruppen I and III of BG 76,
Staff, DBG 2 with Gruppen I and III of DBG 2, Gruppe II of TrgG 2,
and Staffel 10 of TrgG 2
Staff, FG 27 with Gruppe III of FG 27, Gruppen I and II of FG 52, and
Staffel 15 of FG 27 (Spanish)
Gruppe II of TFG 26

II Air Corps
Long-range Recce. Staffel 1, Gruppe 122; Tactical Recce. Staffel 5,
Gruppe 23
Transport Gruppen 9, 105, and Grueep II of Transport Geschwader 1
(all special duties)

TABLE II.1.3 (cont.)

Staff, BG 3 with Gruppen I and II of BG 3
Staff, BG 53 with Gruppen I, II, and III of BG 53
Staff, BG 28 with Gruppe I of BG 28, Bomber Gruppe 100, and Gruppe II of BG 26
Staff, FaBG 210, with Gruppe II of FaBG 210
Staff, DBG 1 with Gruppen II and III of DBG 1
Staff, DBG 77 with Gruppen I, II, and III of DBG 77
Staff, FG 51 with Gruppen I, II, III, and IV of FG 51
Staff, FG 3 with Gruppen II and II of FG 3

Air Fleet 4 Long-range Recce. Staffel 4 of Gruppe 122 and Recce.
Gruppe 3, C.-in-C. of the Luftwaffe; one flight of Recce.
Gruppe 125 (3 Arado AR 196)
Staffeln 1 of BG 28 and 6 of BG 26 (aerial torpedo groups)
Weather Recce. Staffel 76
Transport Gruppe 50 and Gruppe I of Transport
Geschwarder 1 (all special duties)
Special large-glider Staffel LG 4 (transport)

V Air Corps
Long-range Recce. Staffel 4, Gruppe 121
Corps Transport Staffel V
Staff, BG 55 with Gruppen II and III OF BG 55
Staff, BG 54 with Gruppen I and III of BG 54
Gruppe III, FG 52 and Staffel 15 of FG 52 (Croatian)

IV Air Corps
Long-range Recce. Staffel 3, Gruppe 121
Corps, Transport Staffel IV
Staff, BG 51 with Gruppen I and III of BG 51
Staff, BG 27 with Gruppen I and II of BG 27
Staff, FG 77 with Gruppen II and III of FG 27; *Staffel* 3, TrgG 2

German Luftwaffe Mission in Romania
BG (special duties) 104 (transport)
Staff, FG 52 with Gruppe I of TrgG 2 (without Staffel 3) and Replacement Fighter Gruppe 77
2 minesweeper aircraft

Sources: Tables of C.-in-C. of the Luftwaffe, distribution of units, 27 Oct. 1940–20 Dec. 1941, BA-MA Lw 106/6; Plocher, Krieg im Osten, MGFA Lw 4/6 and 7; reports on the combat-readiness of the flying units, GenStdLw GenQu 6. Abt. (I), BA-MA RL 2 III/715.

forest camp near Smolensk, was significantly reinforced.[867] At the end of September VIII Air Corps[868] was transferred from the front at Leningrad to the left wing of the army group in the area of Smolensk, where it was assigned the tasks of supporting Ninth Army, more particularly the spearheads of Armoured Groups 3 and 4. The corps had not been rehabilitated after the fighting in the north and was therefore considerably weaker than had been envisaged for the attack. Individual army units considered this to be so serious that they advised against the attack.[869] Armoured Group 4 was also reinforced by II Anti-aircraft Corps,[870] which for this purpose had been transferred from Air Fleet 4 to Air Fleet 2 and moved to Roslavl. II Air Corps[871] at Shatalovka-East was also reinforced by formations from Air Fleet 4 and, together with I Anti-aircraft Corps, which was used as 'reinforcement and assault artillery', deployed on the right wing of Army Group Centre for co-operation with Second and, especially, Fourth Armies and Armoured Group 2.[872] Its close-support forces were combined under a single close-support leader.

(xx) THE DOUBLE BATTLE OF BRYANSK AND VYAZMA[873]
(See the Annexe Volume, Nos. 18 and 19)

With direct and especially indirect support from Air Fleet 2, which therefore had to reduce its attacks on industrial targets in and around Moscow,[874] the attack launched by Army Group Centre on 2 October made rapid progress.[875] Immediately after the capture of Orel the airfield there became a base for dive-bombers and fighters and a supply-centre with the primary task of providing fuel for Second Armoured Army.[876] It became the target of fierce Soviet air

[867] On the attack preparations of Air Fleet 2 cf. Kesselring, *Memoirs*, 94–5.

[868] On the activity of VIII Air Corps, 28 Sept. 1941–12 Apr. 1942, cf. Richthofen's diary and notes of Col. (ret.) Deichmann, VIII. Fliegerkorps, Rußland-Feldzug: Mittelabschnitt II. Teil— 1941 ab 28.9.1941, [Russian campaign . . . from 28 Sept. 1941], BA-MA RL 8/49.

[869] Richthofen, Tagebuch (privately owned), 26 Sept., 1, 2 Oct. 1941.

[870] Cf. Gen.Kdo. II. Flakkorps, Führungsgruppe Ia No. 0753/41 g.Kdos., corps order No. 53, 10 Sept. 1941; ibid., No. 0784/42 g.Kdos., corps order No. 63, 19 Sept. 1941; ibid., No. 0791/41 g.Kdos., preliminary order for Operation Typhoon, 26 Sept. 1941; and ibid., No. 088/41 g.Kdos., corps order No. 67, 29 Sept. 1941: annexes 77 a–d in Plocher, Krieg im Osten, MGFA Lw 4/12.

[871] Gen.Kdo. II. Fl.Korps/Ia op No. 1709/41 g.Kdos. Chefs., 30 Sept. 1941; corps order for Typhoon, BA-MA RH 20-4/252; Kriegsgliederung des II. Fl.Korps für Unternehmung 'T' [Order of battle of II Air Corps for Operation 'T'], annexe to Gen.Kdo. II. Fl.Korps Ia op No. 1709/41 g.Kdos., no date, ibid. 232.

[872] Cf. AOK 4/Ia No. 3333/41 g.Kdos., 23 Sept. 1941, army order 'T', No. 1, for assembly and the first attack, ibid., 252. On I Anti-aircraft Corps, which at that time had destroyed 314 enemy aircraft and more than 3,000 tanks, cf. Kesselring, *Memoirs*, 95–6.

[873] Cf. sect. II.1.1(*f*) at nn. 461 ff. (Klink). Plocher, Krieg im Osten, 427–61, MGFA Lw 4/4.

[874] Cf. Ob.Kdo. der H.Gr. Mitte/Ia No. 1620/41 g.Kdos. Chefs., 26 Sept. 1941, army group order for the attack, p. 4, BA-MA RH 20-4/216, and ibid., No. 1960/41 g.Kdos. Chefs., 14 Oct. 1941, order for continuation of operations, ibid. 218.

[875] Cf. situation report No. 753, Ob.d.L./Fü. Stab Ic, 1 Oct. 1941, pp. 11, 19, BA-MA RL 2 II/262; Halder, *Diaries*, 1268, 1272, 1275 (2, 4, 6, Oct. 1941), and the daily mission plans and success reports of Air Fleet 2 compiled by the liaison officer of Air Fleet 2 with Army Group Centre, 30 Sept.–31 Oct. 1941, BA-MA RH 19 II/123 (p. 21), 126 (pp. 274–340).

[876] For fuel transport by air cf. also Richthofen, Tagebuch, (privately owned), 5, 9, 10, 13 Oct. 1941.

attacks. Around 10 October the two pockets at Bryansk and Vyazma were sealed. General Freiherr von Richthofen had the impression that 'the Russians can now be finished off militarily, if everybody makes an all-out effort'.[877] While the Soviet troops in the northern pocket were all defeated by 13 October, large elements of those in the southern pocket at Bryansk were able to break out to the east, although they were constantly pursued by II Air Corps. On 20 October the Soviet troops in the southern pocket also surrendered. Air Fleet 2 had made a significant contribution to this success.[878]

In the fighting in the Vyazma pocket between 2 and 13 October II Air Corps alone shot down 29 enemy aircraft and destroyed 14 tanks, 17 bunkers, 104 artillery pieces, 18 fortified field positions, 5 pockets of resistance, and 94 machine-gun nests. It also destroyed or captured a goods train and 579 vehicles, broke up a cavalry squadron and 7 columns, fought 23 infantry attacks to a standstill, and captured 3,842 prisoners.[879]

(xxi) THE CRISIS WEST OF MOSCOW[880]
(See the Annexe Volume, Nos. 19 and 20)

After 7 October the weather worsened, and at the end of the month operations and sorties became increasingly difficult as the roads turned to bottomless mud and the forward air strips became sodden. In the Kalinin area the army could be supplied only by air. For some elements of Second Armoured Army food had to be air-dropped.[881] As Major-General Waldau noted in his diary on 16 October 1941, 'The boldest hopes disappear in rain and snow.'[882] Flying was increasingly restricted, especially that of reconnaissance aircraft; on some days only one or two machines in Air Fleet 2 were able to take off. Nevertheless, in addition to providing support for army units, the Luftwaffe had to continue its attacks on Soviet airfields, especially around Moscow, where activity was constantly increasing, and against rail transports. In a bombing and strafing attack lasting one and a half hours close-support forces of II Air Corps prevented the demolition of a bridge across the Snopot until German armoured troops were able to capture this important crossing. The only

[877] Ibid., 11 Oct. 1941.

[878] On the intensity of the fighting in the area of Air Fleet 2 cf. situation reports, Ob.d.L./ Fü.Stab Ic No. 757, 5 Oct. 1941, p. 18; No. 758, 7 Oct. 1941, pp. 9, 25; No. 759, 8 Oct. 1941, p. 10: BA-MA RL 2 II/263; No. 766, 15 Oct. 1941, pp. 4–5; No. 769, 18 Oct. 1941, p. 5: ibid. 265; and No. 772, 21 Oct. 1941, p. 4: ibid. 266. On the role of the air fleet in the fighting cf. teletype message of C.-in-C. Second Army, 13 Oct. 1941, to II Air Corps, BA-MA RH 20-2/217. Cf. also progress report of II Air Corps, 2–9, 11, 12, 14, 16 Oct. 1941; situation report, Gen.Kdo. II. Fl.Korps/Abt. Ic Nos. 97–103, 106, 107, 109, 111, 120 (Oct. 1941); operational orders, 30 Sept., 6, 8, 10 Oct. 1941: order for the reorganization of close-support forces of II Air Corps, 9 Oct. 1941: BA-MA RH 20-2/212–18, RH 20-4/232, 234–6, 239.

[879] Situation report No. 773, Ob.d.L./Fü.Stab Ic, 22 Oct. 1941, p. 12, BA-MA RL 2 II/266.

[880] Cf.sects II.I.1(*f*)–(*g*) (Klink); Plocher, Krieg im Osten, 462–95, MGFA Lw 4/4.

[881] Kesselring, *Memoirs*, 95–6.

[882] Hoffmann von Waldau, Tagebuch, 77, BA-MA RL 200/17; cf. also situation reports, Ob.d.L./Fü.Stab Ic Nos. 772–8, 20–7 Oct. 1941, BA-MA RL 2 II/266, 267.

surfaced road for the advance of Second Armoured Army between Orel and Tula was threatened by an attack carried out by Soviet armoured forces in spite of unfavourable (muddy) ground conditions, and this was only repulsed by the employment of a large number of bombers of II Air Corps operating in very bad weather at extremely low level and with heavy losses. By 13 November the situation had been stabilized after the ground had frozen, which increased the mobility of German tank and infantry units.[883] With this kind of action and under such climatic and ground conditions the combat-readiness of the flying units declined visibly, as did the effectiveness of their attacks on the enemy.

After the mud and period of bad weather the resumption of operations against Moscow was ordered for 17 November in the optimistic expectation of a period of mild frost. After a few days, however, the weather changed to fog and snow, and temperatures dropped to below $-30\,°C$. This development, the intensifying Soviet air attacks from well-equipped airfields in and around Moscow, and the premature and hasty pulling out[884] of the staffs of Air Fleet 2 and II Air Corps[885] with the bulk of their units posted for duty in the Mediterranean—even though the operational objective had not been reached—further weakened the Luftwaffe forces in the central sector of the eastern front. Only VIII Air Corps remained (cf. Table II.1.4), taking over command from Air Fleet 2 on 30 November.[886] In addition to its own forces, it had command of Close Support Leader II, I and II Air Corps, 12th Anti-aircraft Division, and the air district (*Luftgau*) of Moscow. The weakness of the German air units, the almost unusable field airstrips, and the massed Soviet anti-aircraft fire made sustained, effective operations against the strong Soviet air activity in the area of Moscow impossible. All remaining formations had to be used for direct and indirect support of the ground forces, which still made some progress with relatively weak air support until the exhausted troops were no longer able to advance against the stubborn enemy resistance

[883] Guderian, *Panzer Leader*, 116–17.

[884] e.g. Richthofen in his diary (privately owned), 5 Dec. 1941; on planning and return transportation of the units of Air Fleet 2 cf. also ibid., 11, 27–9 Nov. 1941; teletype message Ob.d.L./Fü.St. Ia (Robinson) No. 13003/41 g.Kdos. (op 1), 28 Oct. 1941, to Air Fleets 2, 4, 1 and Luftwaffe Commander Centre, BA-MA RL 2 II/106.

[885] In Gen. Loerzer's order of the day, 13 Nov. 1941, issued on this occasion the achievements of II Air Corps since the beginning of the campaign in the east were listed as follows: more than 40,000 take-offs; over 21,000 t. of bombs dropped; 3,825 aircraft destroyed with certainty, 281 probably; 811 aircraft damaged; 789 tanks, 614 artillery pieces, 14,339 vehicles destroyed; 240 field and other positions and 33 bunkers destroyed; 3,579 attacks on railway lines made and tracks destroyed at 1,736 locations; 159 trains and 304 locomotives destroyed; 1,584 trains and 103 locomotives damaged. The anti-aircraft units of the corps had shot down over 100 aircraft; the air signals units had, under enemy attack, laid and maintained more than 3,000 km. of cables and transmitted 40,000 radio messages and 30,000 teletype messages: Plocher, *Krieg im Osten*, 466 ff., MGFA Lw 4/4.

[886] Cf. Richthofen, *Tagebuch* (privately owned), 3 Dec. 1941, and BA-MA RL 8/49, p. 25; teletype message H.Gr. Mitte/Ia No. 2834/41 g., 4 Dec. 1941, to VIII Air Corps, BA-MA RH 19 II/127, p. 193.

TABLE II.1.4. *Order of Battle of the Flying Units in the East (Excluding Air Fleet 5 and Air Transport Units), 20 December 1941*

Air Fleet 1   Weather Recce. Staffel 1

I Air Corps

Long-range Recce. Staffel 5, Gruppe 122; Long-range Recce. Staffel 3, Gruppe 22; one flight, Night Staffel 1

Staff, BG 1 with Gruppen II and III of BG 1

Staff, BG 4 with Gruppen I of BG 4

Staff, BG 76

Staff, FG 54 with Gruppen I and III of FG 54 and *Gruppe* I of FG 51

Special Missions Staffel, FG 54

VIII Air Corps

Long-range Recce. Staffel 2, Gruppe 11; Long-range Recce. Staffel 4, Gruppe 11; Long-range Recce. Staffel 1, Gruppe 33; Long-range Recce. Staffel 3, Gruppe 33; Long-range Recce. Staffel 4, Gruppe 14; Long-range Recce. Gruppe Gehrken; one flight, Night Staffel 2

1 Staffel, Gruppe III, BG 3

Gruppe II, BG 30, excluding Staffel 4 (in transfer)

Gruppe II, BG 76 (in transfer)

Gruppe III, BG 76

Staff, DBG 2 with Gruppe III of DGB 2, Gruppe II of DBG 1 (excluding Staffel 5); Staffeln 4 and 10 of TrgG 2

Gruppen I and II of Night Fighter Geschwader 4

Staff, FG 52 with Gruppen I and II of FG 52 and Staffel 15 of FG 27 (Spanish)

Close Support Leader 2

Staff, BG 53 with Gruppen II and III of BG 53; Gruppe II, BG 3; Gruppe II, BG 4; Gruppe III, BG 26 (excluding Staffel 7); and Staffel 15, BG 53

Gruppe II, FaBG 210

Staff, FG 51 with Gruppen II, III, and IV of FG 51

Air Fleet 4   Long-range Recce. Staffel 4, Gruppe 122; Long-range Recce. Staffel 2, Gruppe 22; Long-range Recce. Staffel 3, Gruppe 10; Long-range Recce. Staffel 3, Gruppe 11; Long-range Recce. Staffel 7, Long-range Recce. TrgG 2; Night *Staffel* 1; Weather Recce. *Staffel* 76

Air Leader South

Staff, Recce. Gruppe 125

IV Air Corps

Long-range Recce. Staffel 3, Gruppe 121

TABLE II.I.4 (*cont.*)

Staff, BG 27 with Gruppen I and III of BG 27
Staff, BG 51 with Gruppen I, II, and III of BG 51
Staff, DBG 77 with Gruppen I and II of DBG 77
Staff, FG 77 with Gruppe III of FG 77; Gruppe III of FG 52; Staffel 15
    of FG 52 (Croatian)
Gruppe I of TrgG 2

German Luftwaffe Mission in Romania
Special Missions Staffel, FG 77

Sources: Tables of C.-in-C. of the Luftwaffe, distribution of units, 27 Oct. 1940–20 Dec. 1941, BA-MA Lw 106/6; Plocher, Krieg im Osten, MGFA Lw 4/6 and 7; reports on the combat-readiness of the flying units, GenStdLw GenQu 6. Abt (I), BA-MA RL 2 III/716.

and the weather.[887] On 8 December Hitler[888] reluctantly ordered the attack to be halted and positions already taken to be held. As the objectives of the attack had not been reached, Major-General von Waldau consoled himself with the thought of the enormous territory that had been conquered and the heavy Soviet losses.[889] Richthofen, who described the operational objective of 'a totally defeated enemy' as 'an ideal planned in October', could only tell himself: 'The Russians are certainly much worse off.'[890]

Hitler's directive of 8 December 1941 contained operational tasks for the Luftwaffe far behind the enemy front. It was to 'impede the recovery of the Soviet armed forces as far as possible by attacking armament and training centres, specifically Leningrad, Moscow, Rybinsk, Gorkiy, Voronezh, Rostov, Stalingrad, Krasnodar, etc.' The enemy's lines of communication were to be severed. Moreover, the army was to be supported in its defensive battles. Only when the operations of the army had been concluded were units to be pulled out of the front for rehabilitation, as far as the situation permitted. Rehabilitation areas were to be established close to the eastern front. Ground organization should be maintained in such a way that rapid switching of forces was possible. Long-range aerial reconnaissance was to be executed to discover enemy regroupings in good time. Air defences were to be strengthened. Flying units for Army Group South were not to be withdrawn from the Moscow front

[887] Cf. success reports of VIII Air Corps, 30 Nov.–13 Dec. 1941, compiled daily by its liaison officer with Army Group Centre, BA-MA RH 19 II/127, pp. 143–56, and pessimistic entries in Hoffmann von Waldau's Tagebuch, 84, 86, 91–2, 94 (23, 27, 28 Nov., 9 Dec. 1941), BA-MA RL 200/17; Halder, *Diaries*, 1310 (22 Nov. 1941)—'The troops here are finished'—1326–7 (30 Nov. 1941), 1329 ff. (1 Dec. 1941), 1340 (7 Dec. 1941)—'But worst of all, the Supreme Command does not realize the condition our troops are in . . .'

[888] *Hitler's War Directives*, No. 39; cf. *KTB OKW* i. 1081. Preliminary decision taken earlier; cf. Richthofen, Tagebuch (privately owned), 5 Dec. 1941.

[889] Hoffmann von Waldau, Tagebuch, 94 (9 Dec. 1941), BA-MA RL 200/17.

[890] Richthofen, Tagebuch, (privately owned) 5 Dec. 1941.

without Hitler's permission. This directive is interesting in that it attempted to make good past negligence, a result of Directive No. 21, by ordering attacks on Soviet armaments centres. But how were such tasks to be performed with the few remaining air units (cf. Table II.i.4)? First, VIII Air Corps had to support the withdrawal, begun on 13 December, against attacks by fresh Soviet troops, and it became fully occupied with helping to master the resulting crisis. For the first time Luftwaffe ground personnel and persons from anti-aircraft and air-signal units were assembled to form Luftwaffe fighting formations and field regiments and sent into ground actions to support the army.[891] Even pilots for whom aircraft were no longer available or whose aircraft were not ready for action and 'most valuable specialists' were used in ground fighting in accordance with Richthofen's wishes.[892] In view of the long and expensive training these individuals had received, this policy (like his diary entry: 'The men really enjoyed facing the enemy for once, at 150 metres with a carbine'[893]) seems rather irresponsible, even though understandable in view of the crisis confronting the ground troops.

In his new directive of 16 December,[894] which now took into account the real situation on the eastern front, Hitler finally ordered reinforcements for VIII Air Corps: three newly created bomber Gruppen, one bomber Gruppe from the western front, one twin-engine heavy fighter Gruppe from the night fighter strength, and five transport Gruppen, one of them from Air Fleet 4 and the other four obtained by 'taking the last Ju-52 from the chief of training and by the relentless plundering of commands and staffs, except for machines absolutely necessary for courier duty'. As with the army, the directive interfered radically in important basic details of tactical combat operations, organization, and training of the Luftwaffe. Particularly in the last-mentioned area, this led to serious restrictions and problems in the training of bomber crews, for which the Ju-52 was especially important. The transport groups were combined under the command of the air transport leader in Smolensk, Colonel Fritz Morzik, who was responsible to VIII Air Corps. After 18 December entire parts of Army Group Centre were thus supplied by air, the only effective way to ferry in new personnel and equipment.[895] From January–February 1942, when the air transport leader was transferred under the command of Air Fleet 1, transport aircraft were also used in the first great airlift to supply German forces cut off in a pocket with an expanded air transport fleet operating primarily from Pskov. The army units trapped in the pockets of Demyansk and Kholm (95,000 and 5,000 men respectively) were thus able to hold out

---

[891] Cf. above, at n. 866; Richthofen, Tagebuch (privately owned), 19, 20 Dec. 1941; Halder, *Diaries*, 1386 (11 Jan. 1942); cf. Luftgaukommando VIII, Quartiermeister No. 46 (16)/42 g.Kdos. Qu/Ib, 13 Jan. 1942, BA-MA RL 20/282.

[892] Richthofen, Tagebuch (privately owned), 17 Dec. 1941.   [893] Ibid., 15 Dec. 1941.

[894] Der Führer and Oberste Befehlshaber der Wehrmacht No. 442182/41 g.Kdos. Chefs. WFSt/Abt. L (I Op.), 16 Dec. 1941, BA-MA RW 4/v. 578, pp. 172 ff.; Halder, *Diaries*, 1361 (16 Dec. 1941).

[895] Richthofen, Tagebuch (privately owned), 20, 22 Dec. 1941.

until relief forces reached them in the middle of May 1942. These supply flights proved very costly, as they were over enemy territory and, to ensure accurate targeting, passed within range of enemy infantry weapons at the dropping-points. With a total transport volume of 24,303 t.—not counting the 15,446 soldiers who were flown into the pockets and the 22,093 wounded flown out—the supplying of the Demyansk pocket alone cost 262 aircraft and 385 men.[896] Like the bombers, the fundamentally 'strategic' air transport units were again given the role of providing direct support for the army, a role they were to maintain for a long time. For the moment there could be no question of independent operations by the Luftwaffe. On the central sector of the eastern front its activities were now entirely determined by the needs of the army; because of road conditions and the difficult terrain it also became an often decisive factor in tactical and operational ground fighting as 'flying artillery'.

(c) The Air War at Sea[897]

In the east the air war at sea was conducted in three geographically separate areas—the Black Sea and the Sea of Azov, the eastern Baltic, and the Arctic Ocean. Because of its proximity to the coasts, the air war was dependent on the conduct of the land war, which remained at the centre of attention. The air war at sea was therefore fought with relatively weak forces and varying intensity and with little activity or initiative on the Soviet side.

German objectives and targets on the Black Sea were the base of the Soviet Black Sea Fleet at Odessa; the naval base and commercial port of Nikolaev, which was also a centre of shipbuilding and ship repair; the commercial port of Kherson at the Dnieper estuary; the naval base and fortress of Sevastopol; the naval base of Novorossiysk, which was also the terminus of an important Caucasus railway line; and the terminals of the oil pipelines at Tuapse and Batumi. Another target was the Soviet Black Sea Fleet itself, which in 1941 consisted of an ageing battleship, 5 cruisers, 17 destroyers, 43 submarines, 2 patrol vessels, 70 torpedo cutters, 2 minelayers, and 7 minesweepers.[898] German, Romanian, and Bulgarian coastwise shipping and tanker and merchant shipping through the Bosporus also had to be protected. Occupation of the Crimean peninsula was important for the air war at sea, as its position made it an 'aircraft-carrier' for operations over the Black Sea. Soviet fighter units there, in co-operation with the Black Sea Fleet, were able to protect transport ships close to the coast so effectively that they could not be attacked in daytime. This situation changed only after German troops had occupied the Crimea. But the lack of sufficient Luftwaffe forces prevented the full exploi-

---

[896] Cf. Morzik, *Transportflieger*, 121–50, esp. 145; KTB OKW, ii. 43; Suchenwirth, Jeschonnek, 97, MGFA Lw 21/5; id., Wendepunkte, 36–7, MGFA Lw 35. Cf. sect. II.1.1(g) at nn. 657 and ff. (Klink).

[897] Cf. Plocher, Krieg im Osten, 388–444, MGFA Lw 4/10; Kurowski, *Seekrieg aus der Luft*, 94–5, 161 ff., 177, 188–9, 196.

[898] Piterskij, Sowjet-Flotte, 297 and editor's remarks (Rohwer), ibid. 540–1.

tation of the Crimea's favourable position. Some insignificant successes by Soviet submarines against German shipping through the Bosporus had to be accepted. Initially the war against the Soviet battle and merchant fleets and their bases was conducted by IV Air Corps[899] as a secondary activity without co-ordination with naval operations—in 1941 there were only weak Romanian and Bulgarian and no German naval forces in the Black Sea—but always in connection with the operations of Army Group South. After the breakthrough by Eleventh Army on the Perekop isthmus, V Air Corps was also employed against enemy ships in the Black Sea and the Sea of Azov, and for the destruction of the ports of Kerch and Novorossiysk to prevent the embarkation and disembarkation of troops there. But the lack of adequate forces ruled out any systematic operations against the Soviet Black Sea Fleet.

In the Baltic the main targets of German air operations were the ports of Riga and Tallinn, the Soviet base at Hanko on the south coast of Finland, the main base of the Soviet Baltic Fleet at Kronshtadt, the shipyards and repair facilities at Leningrad, and the fleet itself. It consisted of the two battleships *Marat* and *Oktyabrskaya Revolutsiya*, the heavy cruisers *Kirov* and *Maksim Gorkiy*, the mine-laying cruiser *Marti*, 27 destroyers, 100 motor torpedo-boats, and 94 submarines.[900] Other targets for air attacks were the locks of the White Sea canal and the Leningrad sea canal to Kronshtadt. The most important task of the Luftwaffe was constant surveillance of the strong Soviet Baltic Fleet, which, it was feared, was in a position to endanger ore transports from Sweden and shipments of supplies by sea to Finland, northern Norway, and Army Group North. There was virtually no systematic Soviet reconnaissance of German coastal areas or German routes of advance by sea. Only the Gulf of Finland was kept under regular surveillance by Soviet air units. By contrast, their air patrols on the Baltic coast at the start of the war had been very active but were later pushed back by the advance of Army Group North. The Soviet air force carried out no bombing, mining, torpedo or combined sea–air operations. Indeed, no co-operation between the Soviet fleet and air units was observed by the Luftwaffe in the Baltic, although it did take place.[901]

In 1941 German air superiority permitted the use of older types of aircraft with low losses. Luftwaffe operations were conducted primarily by the Air Leader Baltic, whose formations mined sea routes, the port of Kronshtadt, the Neva, and the White Sea canal and were employed in mine-sweeping, convoy, and reconnaissance duties, in attacking Soviet ships at sea and in ports, and in keeping track of shipping in the eastern Baltic.[902] By 31 August 1941 they had flown 1,775 sorties and sunk or damaged numerous Soviet warships and

---

[899] On the mission and success of IV Air Corps against ships in the Black Sea and against the city and port of Odessa, 21 Aug.–20 Oct. 1941, cf. BA-MA RL 8/35.

[900] Lorenz, 'Ostsee-Kriegführung', 96.

[901] Plocher, Krieg im Osten, 409–10, MGFA Lw 4/10.

[902] Cf. also Kurowski, *Seekrieg aus der Luft*, 161 ff.

merchantmen. With a total of 20 aircraft lost they had shot down 46 enemy aircraft and destroyed 12 on the ground.[903]

The units under the Air Leader Baltic provided important assistance in the conquest of the Baltic islands. In this operation the air leader together with the staff of 10th Anti-aircraft Regiment, 10th Air Signals Regiment, an air-signal bottalion for special duties, and an air-reporting leader was placed under the *ad hoc* staff of Air Leader 'B' under Major-General Heinz von Wühlisch, although his tasks were taken over again by Air Leader Baltic after the withdrawal of several flying units in the middle of September.[904] During the operations to seize the Baltic islands (see the Annexe Volume, No. 17) his aircraft flew 1,524 sorties against Saaremaa and Hiiumaa with only light losses and destroyed or damaged several Soviet aircraft, warships, and merchant vessels.[905] On 27 October 1941[906] the post of Air Leader Baltic was abolished after its tasks in that area had been largely achieved with the occupation of the coast, and when its flying units were needed in the Mediterranean (Coastal Air Gruppe 806), in the west with Air Fleet 3 (Coastal Air Gruppe 506), and in the Black Sea or northern Norway (Sea Reconnaissance Gruppe 125). The staff was transferred as 'Air Leader South' to Saki in the Crimea. Its remaining tasks were taken over by I Air Corps. Earlier, this corps, together with units of VIII Air Corps attached to Air Fleet 1 in August and September, had attacked ships in Kronshtadt and Leningrad on Hitler's orders to prevent the feared break-out of the Soviet Baltic Fleet to Sweden. On 21 September the Soviet battleship *Marat* was struck by a 1,000-kg. bomb dropped by aircraft of Dive-bomber Geschwader 2 and settled on the sea bed. The attacks had to be flown in a target area of 10 × 10 km. through the massed fire of approximately 1,000 anti-aircraft guns. But it was not possible to sink the Soviet ships. With their heavy guns, among them those on the stern of the *Marat*, they continued to play an important role in the fighting for Leningrad.[907]

In the area of the Arctic Ocean, the Barents Sea, and the White Sea the railheads of Murmansk and Archangel were attacked—the latter to a lesser extent because of navigational problems involved in entering it from the sea. Other targets were the Soviet naval base of Polyarny, along with Murmansk

[903] Plocher, *Krieg im Osten*, 310 ff., MGFA Lw 4/3.

[904] Cf. orders 'Beowulf', Nos. 1, 2, and 3, Lfl.Kdo. 1, Führungsabteilung Nos. 3044/41, 3321/41, 3322/42 g.Kdos., 20 Aug., 5, 6 Sept. 1941, BA-MA 18. Armee, 17562/128 (No. 8), 17562/134 (Nos. 22, 23); teletype message Fliegerführer B Ia No. 28/41 g., 17 Sept. 1941, BA-MA, RH 24-12/13.

[905] Plocher, *Krieg im Osten*, 265 ff., 287 ff., MGFA Lw 4/3; GenStdLw/8. Abt., Der Einsatz der Luftwaffe bei der Besetzung der Baltischen Inseln [Luftwaffe operations in the seizure of the Baltic islands], BA-MA RL 2 IV/34. Cf. also sect. II.1.1(*e*) at nn. 421 ff. (Klink).

[906] Teletype message Ob.d.L./Führungsstab Ia, Br.B. No. 13 I 42/41 g.Kdos. (op 1), 4 Nov. 1941 (copy), BA-MA RM 6/139.

[907] Cf. Rudel, *Trotzdem*, 32 ff.; Richthofen, Tagebuch (privately owned), 19–24 Sept. 1941; situation reports, Ob.d.L./Fü.Stab Ic Nos. 744 (22 Sept. 1941)–746 (24 Sept. 1941), BA-MA RL 2 II/261; No. 751, 29 Sept. 1941, ibid. 262; No. 760, 9 Oct. 1941, ibid. 263; Steigleder. 'Baltische Rotbannerflotte'; id., 'Eissstoß'; Plocher, *Krieg im Osten*, 234 ff., MGFA LW 4/3. Cf. also sect. II.1.1(*e*) at n. 424 (Klink).

the only port on the north coast of the Soviet Union free from ice throughout the year, and the Soviet Arctic Fleet itself.[908] The 'Air Leader Kirkenes' also had to protect coastal shipping along the north Norwegian coast, especially shipping within the range of Soviet aircraft, and in addition had to mount constant dive-bomber attacks on the heavily fortified Soviet batteries on the west side of the Rybachiy Peninsula. He was responsible for aerial reconnaissance east of Spitsbergen, Bear Island, and the North Cape—tasks which because of frequent sea mist and a lack of sufficient forces and equipment could not be carried out adequately. Finally, he was to attack Soviet supply shipping, which was generally done by armed reconnaissance, and also—though not very effectively—by mining the entrances to Murmansk and to the White Sea.[909]

The activity of Soviet flying units in the far north was at first defensive and limited to escorting convoys and providing fighter protection over naval bases. It was surprising that the Soviet command did not order the nickel-mining area of Petsamo and the long supply-routes to be systematically attacked. Nor were any combined Soviet sea–air operations observed in northern waters. Evidently the Soviet command considered them to be a secondary theatre and for that reason only weak air units were stationed there.

In the periods of 22 June to 31 July and 1 September to 31 October the Luftwaffe estimated that it had sunk 79 merchant ships of 156,000 GRT, 1 cruiser, and several destroyers and submarines, and had damaged 137 merchant ships of 371,000 GRT, 2 battleships, 3 cruisers, and several other warships in the three geographical areas in which the war at sea in the east was fought.[910] In fact, in 1941 the Luftwaffe sank only 1 battleship, 1 cruiser, 7 destroyers, 1 coastal defence ship, 1 submarine, 3 motor torpedo-boats, 1 submarine-chaser, 2 gunboats, 2 ice-breakers, and 1 monitor.[911] Claims of other successes cannot be substantiated. In the war in the east as a whole the air war at sea played only a subordinate role, which the German navy acknowledged with regret and which gave rise to serious questions of authority, even including the demand for a naval air arm.

(d) *Attempts at an Independent Strategic Air War against the Sources of Soviet Strength*

The failure of the Luftwaffe to prevent a recovery of the Soviet air force by destructive strategic attacks against its aircraft factories, sources of industrial strength in rear areas, railway lines, and other transport routes for supplies and replacements from the factories to the front made itself increasingly felt. Any systematic attacks on the armaments industry and sources of strength in the Soviet hinterland from the very beginning would not, however, have been

[908] On the strength of the Soviet Arctic Fleet cf. sect. II.III.1(c) at n. 59 (Ueberschär).

[909] Plocher, Krieg im Osten, 559–69, MGFA Lw 4/4.

[910] Ob.d.L., Fü.Stab Ic, situation reports Nos. 708, 17 Aug. 1941, annexe 5; 740, 18 Sept. 1941; 749, 27 Sept. 1941; 760, 9 Oct. 1941; 767, 16 Oct. 1941; 777, 26 Oct. 1941; 788, 6 Nov. 1941: BA-MA RL 2 II/255, 260, 262, 265, 267, 269.

[911] According to Rohwer, 'Sowjetische Kriegsschiff-Verluste'.

compatible with Directive No. 21, which ruled that the bulk of Luftwaffe formations in the east should support the ground forces for the duration of the mobile operations of the army. It was only after the general line Volga–Archangel–Astrakhan had been reached, so as to shield the conquered European part of the Soviet Union against the Asian part, that 'if necessary, the last industrial area remaining to Russia in the Urals' was to be eliminated by independent strategic attacks by German bomber formations. Actions which had until then been plasmed and indeed rigorously executed as more or less independent or seemingly operational Luftwaffe missions were usually carried out to support the army and were tied to its operations. At most they can be considered indirect support for the army and, less often, for the navy. Among such attacks were the bombing of railway lines to cut off Soviet land forces on the battlefields and to accelerate their destruction; the mining of important ports, canals, and shipping routes; and occasional attacks on ships. Besides, German interest in capturing the Soviet armaments industry, stockpiles of food, and the engineering structures on railway lines intact, west of the line from the Caspian Sea via the Volga and Gorkiy to Archangel, made a strategic bombing war within that area undesirable.[912]

In addition to the general misjudgement of the duration of the campaign to break Soviet resistance and of the support which would be required by the army, it was certainly also a wrong assessment of the Soviet armaments potential which prevented the Luftwaffe leaders from carrying out systematic, centrally directed air attacks on the enemy's aviation and other industries. The Soviet air armaments potential was underestimated; the scale of industrial relocation[913] beyond the Urals and of the new industrial centres in Siberia was not recognized. As late as mid-November 1941 the Luftwaffe operations staff believed that in the period from 1 December 1941 to 1 May 1942 European Russia—excluding the areas of Moscow and Voronezh, which were to be conquered during that period—would be capable of a total production of only 1,240 front-line aircraft and the Asian part of the Soviet Union of only 1,300, without deducting the probable losses in production caused by German air attacks. It was expected that the Red Army would have only 2,000 front-line aircraft in the spring of 1942 and that they would probably only be able to 'support the Soviet army with major forces at points of main effort'.[914] In fact the assumed production figures were far too low: on average the Soviet aircraft

---

[912] Cf. extracts from a draft, 8. Abt., GenStdLw, 11–18: Überlegungen und Entscheidungen vor dem strategischen Luftkrieg im russischen Großraum (copy) [Reflections and decisions before strategic air warfare in Russia],BA-MA Lw 107/79; Plocher, Krieg im Osten, 353–4, MGFA Lw 4/10.

[913] *Geschichte des Großen Vaterländischen Krieges*, ii. 177; sect. II.11.3 at n. 78 (Hoffmann).

[914] Derzeitiger Stand der SU-Fliegertruppe und voraussichtliche Weiterentwicklung bis zum Jahre 1942 [Present state of Soviet air units and presumed development until 1942], Feindnachrichtenblatt No. 1, Ob.d.L./Fü.Stab Ic, No. 42010/41 g. (IIIC/IV), 19 Nov. 1941, BA-MA OKM, Case GE 958/PG 32957, pp. 274 ff. On the assessment of the strength of Soviet flying units in the second half of 1941 cf., in addition to situation reports of Luftwaffe operations staff/Ic (BA-MA RL 2 II/246–69), Halder, *Diaries*, 1201 (26 Aug.), 1219 (7 Sept.), 1228 (12 Sept.), 1237 (15 Sept.), 1280 (8 Oct.), 1350–1 (12 Dec.).

industry was already producing 1,400 aircraft a month by the end of 1941; in March 1942 the figure was 1,647, and for the year as a whole the total was 25,436, an average of 2,000 a month,[915] in spite of the industrial relocations carried out in 1941–2. Pessimistic Soviet assessments of their own situation in captured documents[916] also probably tended to confirm the views of the Luftwaffe leaders, for whom a large-scale strategic bombing campaign was not feasible in any case as some of the Soviet armaments centres were beyond the range of German bombers.

But in spite of the decision of the Luftwaffe leaders not to mount a strategic bombing campaign in the east, for whatever reasons, it would have been necessary, in view of the basic assumption of Directive No. 21 that the war against the Soviet Union could be won in a short, swift campaign and in accordance with the principle supported by the Luftwaffe leaders of advance preparation, especially of independent, long-range air operations,[917] at least to prepare studies for such missions and to determine what targets should be considered, which were the most important, what priorities should accordingly be established within the framework of the conduct of the war as a whole, what forces would be necessary for these operations, and what their probable performance would be in relation to the results to be achieved. But no such forward-looking planning for a systematic, centrally directed, independent strategic bombing campaign against the Soviet war economy after the completion of the war of movement was undertaken by the Luftwaffe. Evidently it was not even envisaged in such an event to combine and train long-range bomber units under a single command. All flying units were and remained under the individual air fleets, which were themselves organized for co-operation with the army, and it was accepted without question that an air fleet should use all available forces to support the army units in the area for which it was responsible, especially as the army was constantly requesting such assistance. A long-range bomber unit under the direct command of the commander-in-chief of the Luftwaffe would have been independent in the choice of its targets, but that would not have excluded its temporary use to support the army. But even this organizational preparatory measure was never taken.[918]

The principle of co-operation with the army could not, however, be maintained without exception as more and more new aircraft and tanks appeared on the Soviet side, and it was logically concluded that these must have been produced somewhere. As early as 4 July 1941 Air Fleet 2 observed that in spite of heavy losses the number of Soviet aircraft had scarcely declined.[919] The army began to point out that here and there the enemy had regained air superiority and that the direction of Soviet air units was increasingly marked

[915] Boog, *Luftwaffenführung*, 113.

[916] Cf. Gen.Kdo. IV. Fl.Korps/Abt. Ic Br.B. No. 1196/41 g., 11 Oct. 1941, BA-MA RL 8/37.

[917] L.Dv. 16, Ziff. 31.

[918] Cf. Plocher, Krieg im Osten, 581 ff., MGFA Lw 4/4, and 354–5, ibid., 10.

[919] KTB Lfl. 2, fasc. 51, quoted in a draft, 8. Abt., GenStdLw (copy and extract), BA-MA Lw 107/82.

by a 'clear-headed and aggressive leadership'.[920] On 17 July the Luftwaffe operations staff intelligence department estimated the total number of Soviet aircraft at approximately 5,000; on 12 August it still assumed 3,800 aircraft of all kinds, although Soviet aircraft losses were put at 10,300.[921] On 9 October Soviet losses were calculated at 12,700 aircraft of all kinds, leaving 2,600 front-line and training aircraft in service.[922] On 21 October the figure was 2,550. The Soviet air force had not been knocked out of the war, although on 11 December Hitler was able to speak publicly of 17,322 aircraft destroyed, a figure which according to the Luftwaffe rose to 20,392 by the end of the year.[923] Clearly the Soviet aircraft industry was producing a steady and sufficient volume of replacements. But the Luftwaffe failed to realize even remotely the real magnitude of this production effort.

In view of the situation described above, the Luftwaffe was occasionally forced to undertake strategic operations. The resulting bombing attacks, however, were not of a strategic nature in the true sense of the term, as they were carried out with inadequate forces, were not sustained, and were not based on an overall plan. They were rather unsystematic isolated actions against strategic operational targets (cf. Diagram II.1.8), while the bulk of the aircraft continued to be used in indirect and increasingly also in direct support of the army. With the exception of the attacks on Moscow, these actions were due to initiatives of individual air fleets or air corps, in whose operations areas the respective targets were located.[924]

The attacks on Moscow[925] represented the only operational-strategic use of the Luftwaffe in 1941 on orders from Hitler or the Wehrmacht High Command. At the end of June and the beginning of July 1941[926] Hitler had stated repeatedly that Moscow had to be attacked early in the war and, like Leningrad, razed to the ground. On 14 July he considered it necessary to strike Moscow as the 'centre of Bolshevik resistance and prevent the orderly evacuation of the Russian governmental apparatus'. He also wanted to counteract enemy propaganda about the exhaustion of the force of the German attack. In

[920] Cf. Halder, *Diaries*, 1050, 1053, 1069 (16, 17 22 July 1941).

[921] Ia/KM (Kapt. z.S. Mössel), Derzeitiger Kampfwert der Russ. Fliegerkräfte [Present combat value of Russian air forces]; report, 12 Aug. 1941, based on materials of LwFüSt Ic/IV, BA-MA OKM, Case GE 958/PG 32957, 60.

[922] BA-MA RM 7/29, p. 158.

[923] Jacobsen, *1939–1945*, 250; Überblick über die deutsche Luftkriegführung 1939–1944 [Survey of German air warfare 1939–44], Studie der 8. Abt. des GenStdLw (copy), 11, BA-MA Lw 106/13. On assessments of the strength of the Soviet air force, 22 June–21 Oct. 1941, by Luftwaffe operations staff Ic cf. annexe 76a, in Plocher, Krieg im Osten, MGFA Lw 4/8, summary based on daily situation reports.

[924] Plocher, Krieg im Osten, 354–5, MGFA Lw 4/10, 355 ff. and 385–597, MGFA Lw 4/4, (summary list of the few strategic actions by the Luftwaffe in the east in 1941).

[925] Cf. *Hitler's War Directives*, No. 33, Plocher, Krieg im Osten, 1–52, MGFA Lw 4/8, 357 ff., MGFA Lw 4/10; situation reports, Ob.d.L./Fü.Stab Ic, Nos. 682–777, BA-MA RL 2 II/251–67; Arenz, *Luftangriffe auf Moskau*, and the relevant works and articles by Groehler in the Bibliography of the present volume.

[926] *KTB OKW* i. 1021, 1022 (8, 14 July 1941).

DIAGRAM II.1.8. Luftwaffe Operations in the East in 1941

Month	Air Fleet 4	Air Fleet 2	Air Fleet 1	Air Fleet 5 (East)
	Surprise attacks to destroy Soviet air forces			
June	Support for army thrust towards Lvov	Support for army near Biatystok and Minsk	Support for army advance to Dvina	Support for army mtn. corps near Salla and west of Liza Bay
	Attacks on Soviet retreat east of Lvov	Attacks on railway lines near Gomel, Bryansk, Smolensk, Mogilev	Attacks on locks of White Sea canal	Mining of Murmansk harbour
	Attacks on aircraft factory in Kiev	Attack on Smolensk	Mining of roadstead at Kronshtadt	Attacks on Murmansk railway and Salla–Kandalaksha railway line
	Mining of ports of Nikolaev and Sevastopol			Attacks on power station and nitrogen plant at Kirovsk
July	Support for Armd. Gp. 1 in thrust to Kiev and advance of Eleventh Army in Bessarabia	Support in battle of Biatystok and Minsk	Support in penetration fortifications on old Soviet frontier	Support for Mtn. Corps Norway
	Attacks on railway lines near Shepetovka, Kasatin, Kiev, Korosten	Attacks on railway lines up to 300 km. from frontier, esp. junction of Orel	Advance to Lake Ilmen	Mining of port of Murmansk and western entrance to White Sea
	Attacks on Dnieper crossings	From 22 July continuous attacks on Moscow	Thrust of Armd. Gp. 4 towards Luga	Attacks on airfields, concentrations of ships in Liza Bay, and on Murmansk railway
	Further mining of port of Sevastopol		Advance in Estonia	
	Attacks on Odessa and shipping between Odessa and Nikolaev		Attacks on railwalinesy Leningrad, Bologoe	
			Mining operations in Baltic	
			Attacks on warships and merchant vessels and locks of White Sea canal	
Aug.	Support for army in battle of Uman	Support for army in battles of Smolensk	Support for army advance on Novgorod	Support for Mtn. Corps Norway. Attacks on airfields, port of
			Defensive	

DIAGRAM II.1.8. (*cont.*)

Month	Air Fleet 4	Air Fleet 2	Air Fleet 1	Air Fleet 5 (East)
	Conquest of Ukraine to Dnieper Attacks on munitions factory at Lozovaya Mining of ports of Sevastapol and Novorossiysk Attacks on ports of Odessa, Nikolaev, Sevastopol, Novorossiysk, and on shipping in Black Sea	and Gomel	fighting south of Staraya Russa Attacks on railway lines near Leningrad and east of Lake Ilmen Attacks on locks of White Sea canal, port of Tallinn, on ships of Soviet evacuation fleet leaving Tallinn, and on ships in Ladoga canal	Murmansk, and Murmansk railway.
Sept.	Support for Eleventh Army crossing of Dnieper Battle of encirclement east of Kiev Attacks on ships in Black Sea Mining of port of Sevastopol	Support for army advance across Desna to Romny Battle of encirclement east of Kiev Attacks on aircraft factory at Voronezh and factories in or near Bryansk, Tula, Aleksin, and Kaluga	Support for encirclement of Leningrad Defensive fighting south of Lake Ladoga Conquest of Muhu and Saaremaa Attacks on industrial targets in Leningrad and Kronshtadt Mining of the Neva Attacks on locks of White Sea canal and on shipping at Kronshtadt	Individual operations in support of Mtn. Corps Norway Attacks on airfields, Murmansk railway, and hydro-power station Nivages at Kandalaksha
Oct.	Support for army in battle north of Sea of Azov Breakthrough to Crimea	Support for army in battle of encirclement near Vyazma and Bryansk	Support for army in conquest of Hiiumaa Breakthrough of Volkhov defences,	Individual operations as in Sept. Harassing attacks on Murmansk and Murmansk

DIAGRAM II.1.8. (cont.)

Month	Air Fleet 4	Air Fleet 2	Air Fleet 1	Air Fleet 5 (East)
	Attacks on tank factories in Rostov and Kramatorsk, aircraft factory in Voronezh, industrial targets in Kharkov Mining of ports of Sevastopol, Novorossiysk Attacks on ports of Sevastopol, Kerch, Anapa, Novorossiysk, and on shipping in Black Sea	Advance on Moscow Attacks on aircraft factory in Voronezh, industrial targets in Aleksin, Kashira, Balabanova, Narafominsk, and chemical plant at Tula	thrust towards Tikhvin Attacks on Leningrad, Kronshtadt, and railway lines at Yaroslavl, Vologda, Archangel, Leningrad, Bologoe	railway
Nov.	Support for army in conquest of Crimea Occupation of Donets basin Attacks on railway lines in Caucasus Attacks on shipping in Black Sea	Support for army at Moscow Attacks on tank factory in Gorkiy	Support for army in defensive fighting around Tikhvin Attacks on supply-lines and important military targets in Leningrad	Individual operations as in Sept. Attacks on Murmansk, Murmansk railway, and hydro-power station at Kandalaksha
Dec.	Support for continued occupation of Donets region Withdrawals near Rostov Defence against Soviet landings on Kerch peninsula Attacks on refineries at Tuapse Attacks on shipping in Black Sea	Support for withdrawal movements west of Moscow Attacks on aircraft factory at Rybinsk and on open oil storage facilities near Rybinsk	Support for withdrawal to Volkhov position Attacks on ice route across Lake Ladoga Attacks on important military targets in Leningrad	Individual operations as in Sept.

Sources: Studie Chef GenSt 8. Abt.: Der Luftkrieg im Osten 1941, BA-MA, RL 2 IV/162; Plocher, Krieg im Osten, MGFA, Lw 4/4, pp. 585–97; ibid., Lw 4/10, pp. 353 ff.

Directive No. 23 of 19 July 1941 on the 'Continuation of the war in the east' it was therefore ordered that 'The attack on Moscow by Air Fleet 2, temporarily reinforced by bomber forces from the west, is to be carried out as soon as possible as "retaliation for Soviet attacks on Bucharest and Helsinki".' Firstly, however, the directive stated that 'For the Luftwaffe it is especially important, if forces in the centre of the front become available, to shift the weight of its support with fighter and anti-aircraft forces to the army's attack on the south-east front, if necessary by speedily bringing up reinforcements or by an appropriate regrouping.' This makes it clear that it was not the air attack on Moscow but support for the army in the south-east that was to be the main aim of the Luftwaffe's efforts. Indeed, as early as the beginning of August Air Fleet 2 was weakened by the loss of 11½ flying Gruppen, i.e. a third of its aircraft (cf. Table II.1.2), as a result of a new shift of the main effort of the overall attack and the related transfer of VIII Air Corps to Air Fleet 1 in the north. This was due primarily to the execution of Hitler's original plan for the campaign.[927] To what extent, in addition to the principal military reasons, his decision was influenced by propaganda and ideological factors, such as his view of Leningrad as the 'exponent of the [Bolshevik] revolution', is difficult to determine. But in Hitler's case these should not be underestimated.[928] This does not mean that the Luftwaffe did not give priority to military targets and aspects in carrying out this mission. Leningrad, after all, was also an important industrial and armaments centre. From September to the end of December 1941, a total of approximately 1,500 t. of high-explosive bombs was dropped on the city, although it was defended by several hundred fighters, 600 anti-aircraft guns, and approximately 300 barrage balloons. The weight of bombs dropped on Leningrad during this period, including incendiary bombs, thus equalled the weight dropped on average on a German city every night during the last year of the war. Air Fleet 1 was far too weak to achieve any strategic effect with such attacks. These four months saw 79 per cent of all air attacks on Leningrad over the entire war.[929]

The first air attack on the Soviet capital, which in addition to being the seat of government and the military commands was also the country's most important transport junction and a major armaments centre, was made in the night of 21–2 July 1941 with good visibility from altitudes of between 2,000 and 4,000 metres by 195 bombers of Geschwader 2, 3, and 53 under the command of II Air Corps and augmented by Pathfinder Bomber Gruppe 100. High-explosive bombs totalling 104 t. in weight and 46,000 incendiary bombs were dropped by the 127 aircraft that reached the target area. These bomber units were later temporarily reinforced with units from Bomber Geschwader 4 of Air

---

[927] Cf. sect. II.1.1(*b*) at nn. 142 ff. (Klink); *KTB OKW* i. 1029–30 (17, 21 July 1941).

[928] Cf. Richthofen, Tagebuch, (privately owned), 12 Sept. 1941, where Schmundt is quoted as repeating a remark by Hitler that Leningrad should be 'ploughed under'.

[929] On details of armament production in Leningrad cf. Salisbury, *Leningrad*, 207, 329, 335–6, 402, 434.

Fleet 1, normally used to lay mines, Bomber Geschwader 54 and 55 of Air Fleet 4, and Bomber Geschwader 28 from IX Air Corps of Air Fleet 3 stationed in the west. Available forces were clearly not sufficient for an effective operation and had to be scraped together from wherever they could be found. The first attacks were made at night, as German fighters could not provide complete protection during the day because they did not have sufficient range. The attacks were aimed at militarily and politically important targets, although under the conditions prevailing other buildings and facilities were also hit. The bombing attacks made in late autumn and the winter of 1941–2 were of an operational rather than a strategic character, not only because the city was then within the operations area of the army, but also because a strategic effect could not be expected from the number of aircraft involved. Moscow's anti-aircraft defences and air-raid protection had been improved steadily and with increasing intensity since the outbreak of the war in the east. The anti-aircraft defences with approximately 1,000 guns were, as German bomber crews reported, stronger than those of London. Moscow was also protected by 585 fighters and numerous barrage balloons and search-lights.[930] The city was attacked a total of 76 times at night and 11 times during the day. By 25 October 1941 59 attacks had been carried out and Gust over 1,000 t. of high-explosive bombs dropped, approximately half of what the Royal Air Force dropped on average in a single night in its strategic attacks on Germany in 1944. The 75th German attack on Moscow took place on 6 December 1941, and the last on 5 April 1942.[931] Only the first 3 attacks were carried out with more than 100 bombers; 6 involved 50 bombers each, 19 involved 15–40, and 59 involved 3–10 aircraft.[932] German losses were especially low in the first three attacks—only one aircraft in each attack—and remained within acceptable limits later. This proves that the failure of the attacks on Moscow to achieve any effect on the war in the east as a whole was due more to the weakness of the attacking German formations than to the strength of the Soviet air defences. In their turn, the long-range Soviet bombing attacks on Berlin, made with heavy losses and inadequately trained crews as a response to the attacks on Moscow, also remained without any significant military effects. They merely provided another demonstration of the performance of Soviet aircraft, as long as the Baltic islands were available to them. According to Soviet figures, 1,088 persons were killed in the air raids on Moscow.[933]

The German air offensive against Moscow was an attempt with inadequate forces and in an inadequate form to demonstrate strength at a moment when

---

[930] On the organization of Moscow's air defences cf. Groehler, 'Luftverteidigung Moskaus', 119–21.

[931] Cassidy, *Moscow Dateline*, 77. Cf. Zur Frage des operativen Luftkrieges im Osten [On the question of operational air war in the east], 3–4, collection of materials of the Studiengruppe Geschichte des Luftkrieges, Karlsruhe, BA-MA Lw 106/13.

[932] Plocher, Krieg im Osten, 359, MGFA Lw 4/10.

[933] Cassidy, *Moscow Dateline*, 77. On Sovier strategic bombing raids or Germany see Grochter, *Bombenkricg*, 160–6.

German expectations of victory were high. It was, as Göring later explained,[934] a series of prestige attacks hastily initiated as an answer to Hitler's sarcastic question whether he, Göring, believed that there was a Geschwader left in the Luftwaffe with enough courage to fly to Moscow. Even though this explanation does not correspond to the facts, it clearly shows the frivolousness and lack of planning with which the attacks were initiated. Not without reason did Kesselring give the order for the first attack on Moscow only half-heartedly.[935] The timing of the start of the attacks was clearly wrong, because in July the main task was still to provide all-out support for the ground troops to help them reach their operational objectives.[936]

Severing the supply-routes from the ice-free ports in the far north of the Soviet Union by means of regular strategic bombing would have been a more worthy objective for the German bombers, especially after the ground forces had failed to reach their objectives Murmansk, Kandalaksha, and the Murmansk railway line, and the front had hardened. The main target should have been the Murmansk railway line, which was serviceable throughout the year, and not the parallel poor road or the White Sea canal, which could not be used in winter because of ice and was in any case suitable only for small ships. The question must, however, be asked whether, in 1941, the Luftwaffe General Staff and the German leadership were fully aware of the potential importance of this supply-route for possible shipments from Britain (in the first place). While a significant strengthening of the Soviet Union through such assistance was still not to be expected at that time, the importance of this supply-line, soon to be heightened by the start of Anglo-American supply shipments,[937] should have been foreseen. As early as 1942 more than half of all supplies sent to the Soviet Union were shipped to Russia via the North Atlantic route, which by then was fiercely challenged.[938]

Even the instructions for the theatre in the far north[939] in Directive No. 21 clearly show that for the German military planners the offensive elimination of the supply-line there was of secondary importance and to be achieved only after northern Norway and the Petsamo area had been secured. They viewed the world largely from a continental European perspective and were not sufficiently aware of the global-strategic potential of a supply-line via the

---

[934] Interrogation of Göring by Americans, 1 June 1945 (copy of proceedings), BA-MA Lw 107/74.

[935] Richthofen, Tagebuch, (privately owned), 21 July 1941 Kesselring: 'leaves matters open'.

[936] Plocher, Krieg im Osten, 368–70, MGFA Lw 4/10.

[937] Huan, 'Marine soviétique', 278.

[938] Plocher, Krieg im Osten, 571 ff., MGFA Lw 4/4; cf. id., *German Air Force versus Russia, 1941*, 200. On total Anglo-American aid deliveries to the Soviet Union in the Second World War cf. Deane, *Strange Alliance*, 87 ff.; Lukas, *Eagles East*, 233 ff. The Soviet Union received, among other equipment, about 14,800 American aircraft and 427,284 trucks (a quarter of the total being delivared via Murmansk), which was equal to two-thirds of the initial truck stock of the German army in the east. These vehicles greatly increased the mobility of the Red Army and were a major factor in its offensive operations in the later years of the war.

[939] On the assessment of the importance of the far north and the use of the Luftwaffe to support the army there in 1941 cf. sects. II.III.1(*c*), and (*d*) at n. 89 (Ueberschär).

Arctic Ocean and the ports of Murmansk, Kandalaksha, and Archangel. Certainly the hope of a short campaign, during which supply questions would not be especially significant, played a role in their thinking. And they probably also believed that the encirclement of Leningrad and linking up with Finnish forces north-east of the city would greatly reduce the importance of the far north. In later directives from the Wehrmacht High Command and Hitler the tasks of securing Norway and the nickel-mines in Petsamo against enemy landings and air attacks were still repeatedly described as the main objectives of the Wehrmacht commander or the army headquarters command in Norway.[940] Air Fleet 5 therefore saw its main task as attacking supply shipments for Britain in and around Scotland, defending Norway against British sea and air forces, and covering the arrivals and departures of German naval forces. It considered support for the advance of the Army Command Norway from Finland to be an incidental additional task.[941] The briefing of the Luftwaffe for Operation Barbarossa similarly described the severing of the Murmansk railway line as a 'secondary task' to be carried out with elements of Air Fleet 5.[942] It is obvious that the far north was treated as a minor theatre of the war from the very beginning.[943] This was also evident in the assignment to that area of only weak and primarily tactical instead of strategic Luftwaffe units, which were not significantly reinforced during the summer of 1941 and were thus in no position to fulfil either their 'secondary task' or their main task of supporting the army, although Murmansk and the Murmansk railway line became regular targets of the Luftwaffe and attacks were occasionally carried out on Archangel.[944] Regardless of whether the strategic importance of occupying Murmansk and cutting all transport lines from the port was taken seriously enough—it was certainly recognized—or whether, as a result of the excessive demands made on the Luftwaffe in all theatres of the war, not enough bomber formations could be made available for that purpose, the failure to take sufficiently strong measures in the far north had serious strategic consequences.[945]

[940] Cf. Weisung an den Wehrmachtbefehlshaber Norwegen über seine Aufgaben im Falle 'Barbarossa' [Instructions to Armed Forces Commander Norway on his tasks in the event of Barbarossa], OKW No. 44355/41 g.Kdos. Chefs. WFSt/Abt. L (I Op), 7 Apr. 1941, BA-MA, 20. Armee, 20844/4; Wehrmachtbefehlshaber in Norwegen/Ia No. 66/41 g.Kdos. Chefs., 8 May 1941 to Lfl. 5 betr. Silberfuchs (ibid.); id., Ia No. 135/41 g.Kdos. Chefs. (Silberfuchs), 8 June 1941 to Chef der Lfl. 5 und Befh. Nord, BA-MA, 20. Armee, 20844/5, and Der Chef des OKW/WFSt/Abt. L No. 441580/41 g.Kdos. Chefs., 22 Sept. 1941 to FM Mannerheim, BA-MA RW 3/v. 639.

[941] Der Chef der Lfl. 5 und Befh. Nord, 5 June 1941, to Wehrmachtbefh. in Norwegen und Lfl. Kdo. 5/Fü.Abt./Ia Br.B. No. 88/41 g.Kdos. Chefs., 12 June 1941, betr. Weisungen für den Kampf im Falle 'Barbarossa' [Combat directives in the event of Barbarossa], BA-MA, 20. Armee, 20844/5.

[942] This directive has not been found. The above statement is based on testimony by the then chief of staff of Air Fleet 5 in Plocher, Krieg im Osten, 373, MGFA Lw 4/10.

[943] Likewise Huan, 'Marine soviétique', 404.

[944] Cf. sect. II.iii.1(e) at n. 54 (Ueberschär), and for Luftwaffe operations in the east in 1941 Diagram II.i. 8 in sect. II.i.2(d) below.

[945] Cf. Plocher, Krieg im Osten, 370–7, MGFA Lw 4/10.

Moreover, carefully planned, sustained attacks on tank and aircraft plants would have been of basic importance. Just as the flow of new aircraft could not be stemmed, the supply of more tanks could not be halted, as Hitler observed with surprise and irritation at the beginning of August 1941.[946] At that time Anglo-American deliveries had not yet started. The importance of the Soviet tank factories was therefore obvious. The same was true of Soviet aircraft plants, whose systematic destruction would have considerably reduced pressure on the German front line. The railway lines to and from Siberia, from the Arctic Ocean and the Caspian Sea to the interior of the country, the oil refineries in Tuapse and the oil pipelines in the Caucasus and from Guryev on the Caspian to Orsk, the cracking-plants for the production of aviation fuel in Ufa and Orsk, and the oilfields of Groznyy and Baku—all these would have been worthwhile targets for an independent strategic air war. In October 1941 demands along these lines from V Air Corps were not listened to at higher levels.[947]

Although in terms of its personnel and technical superiority over the Soviet air force the Luftwaffe would have been in a position to conduct a systematic, independent, long-range air war in the east for a certain time, and although its operational training and knowledge of existing important strategic targets repeatedly raised the question of the need for such a strategic air war for the Luftwaffe leaders, only isolated missions were flown against strategic targets in 1941, and only when bomber forces could be temporarily spared from the ground fighting and the weather for a limited time offered a favourable opportunity for a successful strategic attack.[948] But there was no planned, independent air war against the sources of Soviet military strength in 1941. The reasons were to be found, among other places, in Luftwaffe doctrine, in the tasks assigned to the Luftwaffe by the Wehrmacht High Command and the commander-in-chief of the Luftwaffe, who insisted on continuing the war against supply shipments for Britain. Other reasons were the lack of a strategic bomber fleet large enough for all theatres of the war, the lack of an appropriate strategic plan and an appropriate organization of the strategic bomber forces, the increasing use of bombers for direct support of the army and the resulting heavy attrition, the lack of a suitable large bomber, and last but not least the failure of the German attack on Moscow in December, which required the use of almost all Luftwaffe units in the east for ground fighting. The prerequisite for a large-scale, independent, strategic use of the Luftwaffe envisaged in Directive No. 21—the reaching of the above-mentioned line between the Volga and Astrakhan, and thus the end of the war of movement—was not fulfilled in 1941.

The protection of the Romanian oilfields by units of the German Luftwaffe mission in Romania can be considered strategic in a defensive sense. Repeated attacks by Soviet air forces were successfully repulsed by anti-aircraft and

[946] Cf. Guderian, *Panzer Leader*, 88–9, 101–2.
[947] Plocher, Krieg im Osten, 382, MGFA Lw 4/10.   [948] Sources as n. 912 above.

fighter units belonging to the mission and by suitable Romanian forces. After the conquest of the Crimea these attacks ceased. By December 1941 the Luftwaffe mission had recorded 95 enemy attacks by a total of 336 aircraft. Because of the inadequate night-flying training of Soviet crews, most of the raids were carried out in daylight; 81 of the participating Soviet aircraft were shot down.[949] Much damage was prevented by the use of dummy facilities and staged fires. German and Romanian losses were kept low and the oil installations suffered no significant damage. Oil production and transports were not affected.[950]

(e) The Situation of the Luftwaffe at the Turn of 1941–1942

On 18 September 1941 the state secretary for aviation and inspector-general of the Luftwaffe, Field Marshal Erhard Milch, stated to the industrial council: 'Perhaps we underestimated the Russians earlier, but now they are soft.'[951] On 15 October 1941 he considered some of the bomb and ammunition requirements of the Luftwaffe quartermaster-general to be 'much too high, especially if one considers that the war situation indicates that the great campaign against Russia will be concluded in the near future'.[952] At about the same time, in accordance with instructions from Hitler, the chief of the operations department of the Luftwaffe General Staff was considering the strengthening of the air defences of the Reich territory by bringing back anti-aircraft units from the east as well as the strength of the Luftwaffe units to be left there after the conclusion of military operations. He proposed to the head of the Army General Staff that only 8 bomber Gruppen, 3 dive-bomber Gruppen, 10½ fighter Gruppen, 3 aerial reconnaissance Staffeln, and 5 anti-aircraft regiments under two air fleets should remain in the east.[953] The organization department of the Luftwaffe General Staff ordered a reorganization of the occupied eastern territories in air command districts (*Luftgaue*), to come into effect 'at the conclusion of operations in the east'. The staffs of the three new districts Rostov, Kiev, and Moscow were to be ready to be designated by 15 November 1941.[954] Not only, in addition to the abolition of the post of Air Leader Baltic,

---

[949] Deutsche Luftwaffenmission in Rumänien, Führungsabteilung Ia No. 1841/41 g.Kdos., 14 Dec. 1941, betr. Bericht über Luftverteidigung Ölgebiet Rumänien [Report on air defence of Romania's oil region], BA-MA RL 9/62.

[950] Cf. Plocher, Krieg im Osten, 88–105, MGFA Lw 4/2.

[951] BA-MA RL 3/51, p. 1155. The navy was of a similar opinion (cf. BA-MA RM 7/159, fo. 77).

[952] Letter of the Staatssekretär der Luftfahrt und Generalinspekteur der Luftwaffe, Gst No. 675/41 g.Kdos. to the Generalquartiermeister der Luftwaffe betr. Steigerung der Rüstung [Intensification of armaments], BA-MA RL 3/51, p. 467. Outcome of the conference in 1. Skl/IL, Robinson, 3 Nov. 1941, BA-MA OKM, Case 958/PG 32957, pp. 224–5.

[953] Halder, *Diaries*, 1280 (8 Oct. 1941); teletype message Ob.d.L./Fü.St. Ia (Robinson) No. 12751/41 g.Kdos., 21 Oct. 1941, to General der Luftwaffe beim Ob.d.H., pp. 22–3, BA-MA RH 2/v. 428.

[954] Der Reichsminister der Luftfahrt und Oberbefehlshaber der Luftwaffe, Generalstab/Gen. Qu./2. Abt. Az. 11b14.10 No. 7529/41 g.Kdos. (IIa), 15 Oct. 1941, betr. Einteilung der besetzten Ostgebiete in Luftgaue [Division of occupied eastern territories into *Luftgaue*], BA-MA RL 3/51, pp. 1065–72.

were the staffs of Air Fleet 2 and II Air Corps with their fleets and corps troops (reconnaissance, transport, weather reconnaissance, liaison Staffeln, and air-signal units) and elements of the units which might have been thought indispensable for the capture of Moscow transferred from November 1941 to the Mediterranean, where the British had opened a new offensive, but the staff of V Air Corps, which had been removed from Air Fleet 4 on 30 November 1941, was at the same time transferred with its corps troops to Brussels to organize a new mine-laying air corps.[955] Moreover, as had long been planned, a number of front-line formations were pulled out of the eastern front for rehabilitation in Germany or for new duties in southern and western Europe.[956] All these actions were taken largely on the assumption that a victorious conclusion of operations in the east was imminent, which would reduce the pressure on Luftwaffe units there by the end of 1941. But, as is shown by the withdrawal of VIII Air Corps from Leningrad, in spite of the fact that operations there had not been successfully concluded, it was one more indication of the general lack of sufficient forces and seemed nonsensical not only to later observers.

Hopes of an early end to the fighting in the east were dashed by the Soviet counter-offensive at Moscow in the first days of December 1941, if indeed not before. On 12 December Freiherr von Richthofen, commanding general of VIII Air Corps, which had taken over the tasks of Air Fleet 2, informed the head of the Luftwaffe General Staff, General Jeschonnek, that in the east it was now a question of 'to be or not to be'.[957] On 16 and again on 24 December, after being informed of the situation,[958] Hitler immediately ordered the withdrawal of air units from the west and the creation of new operational and transport formations to reinforce VIII Air Corps and to support Army Groups Centre and North. At the beginning of January 1942 half the staff of V Air Corps under General Robert Ritter von Greim was again transferred to the Crimean peninsula on the eastern front as 'special staff Crimea', which meant that the creation of a special mine-laying air corps operating against Britain was not carried out. The other half, under the chief of staff of the corps, Colonel Hermann Plocher, reached the central sector of the eastern front at the beginning of February 1942 in order to prepare the transfer of VIII Air Corps for duty in the Crimea and the assumption of command by the newly formed 'Luftwaffe command east'.[959] Thus within a few weeks the situation of the Luftwaffe in the east had been unexpectedly reversed and entered an acute crisis. Many of the transfers of Luftwaffe forces to the west for the war against

[955] Plocher, Krieg im Osten, 16, MGFA Lw 4/14.

[956] Cf. teletype message Ob.d.L./Fü.St. Ia (Robinson) No. 13003/41 g.Kdos. (op 1), 28 Oct. 1941, to (*inter alia*) Luftflotten 2, 4, 1, BA-MA RL 2 II/106; Richthofen, Tagebuch (privately owned), 23 Oct., 11 Nov. 1941; Kesselring, *Memoirs*, 103.

[957] Quoted according to Reinhardt, *Moskau*, 213.

[958] Der Führer und Oberste Befehlshaber der Wehrmacht No. 442181/41 g.Kdos. Chefs. WFSt/Abt. L (I Op), 16 Dec. 1941, BA-MA RW 4/v. 578; teletype message OKW/WFSt/Abt. L(I Op) No. 44224/41 g.Kdos. Chefs., 24 Dec. 1941, quoted in Plocher, Krieg im Osten, 485 ff., 493, MGFA Lw 4/4.

[959] Plocher, Krieg im Osten, 16, MGFA Lw 4/14.

Britain, undertaken with some misgivings[960] but in optimistic misjudgement of the situation in the east in the late autumn of 1941, had to be cancelled. As Göring later complained: 'What was once sent east never came back again but remained in the east.' The hope that he too had initially entertained that the struggle against Britain would not have to be halted because of the campaign in the Soviet Union, and that the Geschwader would be needed in the east 'only for the first four days to make a bigger impression', in his own exaggerated phrase, had proved to be illusory.[961]

At that moment, however, as we know from the diary of General von Richthofen, who spent some time at this point with Göring, Jeschonnek, and Hitler, the Luftwaffe leaders at first obviously did not regard the defeat at Moscow as the beginning of the turning-point of the war in the east, any more than did Hitler or the army leaders. Göring, who was hardly interested in that war and, ever since the beginning of the campaign in the east, had largely withdrawn into his private world, was inclined to underestimate the Soviet Union[962] and, unlike his head of the Luftwaffe operations department, Major-General Hoffmann von Waldau, to take a rosy view of the situation. This tendency to ignore unpleasant facts was made easier by Japan's entry into the war on 7 December 1941. Not only Jeschonnek and Richthofen but also the sceptical Hoffmann von Waldau expected this development to lead to a great improvement on the eastern front.[963] The transfer of Soviet troops from Siberia to Moscow would enable the Japanese to 'attack the centres of Soviet strength in the rear of our enemy', which, as Richthofen stated in his order of the day on 10 December 1941, would have a favourable effect on the German conduct of the war.[964] He was inclined to see the defeat at Moscow as a 'local setback' and still hoped to be able to return to Germany with his units in three weeks, if everything went well.[965] But his optimism was not entirely unclouded by forebodings, for on 11 December, as he noted in his diary, he treated his generals to 'fiery words and morale-boosters, not quite honestly, but with success'.[966] Apart from the belief that the Soviet troops were also suffering,[967] Richthofen found consolation in the thought that Soviet forces were not sufficiently mobile to be able to mount attacks against stubborn German resistance for any length of time.[968] On 25 December Hoffmann von Waldau believed that the shock had been overcome.[969] In the end Göring, Jeschonnek,

[960] Cf. Göring's statement on the transfer of flying units to the Mediterranean in Gundelach, *Luftwaffe im Mittelmeer*, i. 331 ff.

[961] BA-MA RL 3/61, p. 5866.

[962] Richthofen, Tagebuch (privately owned), 3, 4 Sept. 1941.

[963] Ibid., 7–10, 16, 28 Dec. 1941; Hoffmann von Waldau, Tagebuch, 95–6 (9 Dec. 1941), BA-MA RL 200/17.

[964] Richthofen, Tagebuch (privately owned), 10 Dec. 1941; BA-MA RL 8/49, p. 31.

[965] Richthofen, Tagebuch (privately owned), 7 Dec. 1941.

[966] Ibid., 11 Dec. 1941.   [967] Cf. text at n. 890 above.

[968] Richthofen, Tagebuch (privately owned), 5, 15, 25, 28 Dec. 1941; Hoffmann von Waldau, Tagebuch, 101 (20 Dec. 1941), BA-MA RL 200/17.

[969] Hoffmann von Waldau, Tagebuch, 103 (25 Dec. 1941), BA-MA RL 200/17.

Richthofen, Goebbels, and Himmler, who were all present at Hitler's head-quarters on 17 December 1941, concluded fatalistically that reverses had to be accepted in a struggle for world domination and that the people had to make sacrifices. 'No doubts at all of victory eventually.'[970]

What then was the general situation of the Luftwaffe? On 27 December 1941, after six months of fighting in the east, it still had 5,167 front-line aircraft, including transporters. Its real strength had declined by 403 aircraft since the beginning of the war in the east and its combat-readiness from 3,812 to only 2,560 (from 69 to 50 per cent of actual strength). In some of the units in the east the figure was far below that, e.g. only 37 per cent of the bombers and 34 per cent of the long-range reconnaissance aircraft. Of a total of approximately 1,900 front-line machines, including transport aircraft, in the east, about 960 were ready for action;[971] by 10 January 1942 the figure was only 775 out of 1,713, including close- and long-range reconnaissance aircraft under army command. Only a third of all Luftwaffe units were still in the east.

There were various reasons for the low state of readiness of the Luftwaffe. To start with, the wear and tear was higher than expected; the strained supply situation impeded maintenance and repairs. The Red Army had systematically destroyed most of the suitable facilities, which often made it necessary to transport heavily damaged aircraft back to Germany, where the aircraft industry was already overburdened because of the shortage of labour. Field airstrips as a rule were primitively equipped and the responsible officers of the field air districts often lacked experience. Finally, adequate preparations had not been made for maintaining aircraft at temperatures far below freezing; in January 1942 only 15 per cent of the Luftwaffe vehicles used for transporting aircraft spares were in operating condition. Instructions for cold-start procedures were not issued until October 1941, and as late as February 1942 the deputy chief of staff in charge of supply and administration had to issue explanations. The Red Army solved the problem of ensuring the combat-readiness of its flying units by establishing two new posts, the chiefs of rear-area services and of technical services, both of them deputies of the commander-in-chief of the air force. This arrangement gave appropriate organizational priority to supply, support, and technical maintenance. New air-base organizations now ensured better maintenance and faster repair of aircraft.[972]

By 27 December 1941 German aircraft losses in the east were 2,505 destroyed, 327 of which were not due to enemy action, and 1,895 damaged. This meant that within six months of the opening of the eastern front 4,400 aircraft were permanently or temporarily out of action. On other fronts during this period an additional 1,330 front-line aircraft were lost, 779 totally. Total losses

---

[970] Richthofen, Tagebuch (privately owned), 17 Dec. 1941; cf. Göring in *IMT* ix. 428.

[971] Report on the combat-readiness of the flying units as of 27 Dec. 1941, Generalquartiermeister der Luftwaffe, 6. Abt., 30 Dec. 1941, and as of 10 Jan. 1942, ibid., 13 Jan. 1942, BA-MA RL 2 III/716, 717.

[972] Overy, *Air War*, 50 ff. Cf. sect. II.II.2 at n. 19 (Hoffmann).

on all fronts since the beginning of the war in the east were therefore 5,730, about three-quarters of them in the east. This figure represented a third of all losses of front-line aircraft in the twenty-eight months since the outbreak of the war.[973]

In comparison, new production (excluding seaplanes, gliders, and courier aircraft) from June until the end of December 1941 was only 5,147,[974] far too low to make up for the losses of the previous six months. Only with the reuse of about 2,000 repaired aircraft over this period would that have been possible. But repaired aircraft as a rule were used for training, and not all of them were suitable for front-line duty. Moreover, many of the new and repaired aircraft were forever being transferred or redirected or in transit, and were thus not yet available to the supply and replacement officer of the Luftwaffe.

Between 22 June and 27 December 1941 personnel losses of the three branches of the Luftwaffe—the flying, anti-aircraft, and signals units—which on 20 May 1941 numbered 1,269,000 men,[975] totalled 6,232 killed (including 732 officers), 2,564 (476) missing or captured, and 11,425 (831) wounded. It can be assumed that the bulk of these losses were suffered in the east. They increased total Luftwaffe personnel losses since 1 September 1939 to 16,525 (2,321) killed, 10,859 (1,677) missing or captured, and 21,290 (1,844) wounded.[976] Crew losses of the flying units in the east were 3,010 (including 664 officers) killed, missing, or captured. This represented a fifth of the flying crews lost in this way since the start of the war in 1939. At the beginning of September 1939 the Luftwaffe had had a little over 4,000 air crews, or 11,000–12,000 men, in its front-line units.[977] Together with wounded, crew personnel losses in the war in the east amounted to 4,404, including 1,008 officers. Personnel losses of front-line crews thus remained within acceptable limits and in comparison were far lower than aircraft losses. Further, as the number of training hours had not been significantly reduced since the start of the war in 1939[978] and the number of crews undergoing flight training had scarcely declined, the Luftwaffe, in terms of quantity and quality of its flying personnel, was still far from exhausting its resources.[979] On 27 December 1941 it had 6,149

---

[973] Cf. Reports on the combat-readiness of the flying units as of 21 June and 27 Dec. 1941. Generalquartiermeister der Luftwaffe, 6. Abt., 24 June, 30 Dec. 1941, BA-MA RL 2 III/713, 716. Inaccurate figures in the original texts prevent precise calculations; however, the figures are sufficient to illustrate the general situation of the Luftwaffe. Somewhat different figures in Groehler, 'Verluste der deutschen Luftwaffe', 330–1.

[974] Table of German aircraft production figures according to month and model by 6. Abt. des Generalquartiermeisters der Luftwaffe, 28 June 1945, BA-MA Lw 103/84, and lists by Studiengruppe-Geschichte des Luftkriegs, Karlsruhe, BA-MA Lw 112/6.

[975] Figures in Groehler, 'Luftwaffe vor dem Überfall', 124.

[976] Report on the combat-readiness of the flying units as of 27 Dec. 1941, Generalquartiermeister der Luftwaffe, 6. Abt., 30 Dec, 1941, BA-MA RL 2 III/716.

[977] Figures from Völker, *Luftwaffe*, 184–5; Kreipe, Köster, and Gundelach, MGFA Lw 15/1, annexes 14 and 15; report of the general-staff officer of the Luftwaffe in charge of supply and administration, 6th dept., on the combat-readiness of the flying units as of 2 Sept. 1941, BA-MA RL 2/III/702.

[978] Cf. *Defeat of the German Air Force*, 3 ff. and fig. 3.

[979] Of course since 1941 the staff officer of the Luftwaffe in charge of supply and administration (*Generalquartiermeister*) had warned about the shortage of bomber crews (cf. Kreipe, Köster, and

front-line crews and an actual strength of only 5,167 front-line aircraft[980]—274 more crews than on 21 June 1941. Much the same was true of their combat-readiness.

Although the Luftwaffe was still a strong, efficient, and combat-ready instrument of war at the end of 1941, the figures nevertheless show that in terms of material and armaments it was declining. In view of the recovery of the Soviet air force and the entry of a powerful new enemy, the United States, into the war, this development was bound to have serious long-term consequences, especially as the already existing armaments gap threatened to become wider as a result of the growing number of tasks the Luftwaffe would have to discharge in the future. In addition, there was a real danger that flight training would have to be curtailed because of high fuel consumption over the past nine months and the dwindling of stocks to only twice the consumption of a combat month. In the second half of 1942 this danger became a reality when the average number of practice flying hours had to be reduced from 240 to 210 hours for each pilot.[981] By the winter of 1941–2 the number of bomber pilots instructed in instrument flying declined sharply when the Ju-52s until then used for training were transferred to air transport units.

In addition to the failure to predict requirements and attrition, as well as the losses suffered by the flying units, especially the bombers, the reasons for the armaments shortfall were to be found in the direct ground support on the eastern front, the widespread optimism about the war situation as a whole and the air situation over Germany, a mood which in some places persisted until the autumn, and the inadequate and poorly managed air armaments programme. Loss and production figures[982] for front-line models reveal that from June to December 1941 new production of night fighters, twin-engine fighters, long-distance reconnaissance aircraft, seaplanes, and transport aircraft exceeded the overall losses, while new production of bombers, fighters, dive-bombers, and close-reconnaissance aircraft—the types primarily used in the east—fell short of these losses. Only 1,660 fighters had been produced over the previous seven months to replace the 1,823 lost over the previous six months. In the case of close-reconnaissance aircraft, new production amounted to only

Gundelach, 187, MGFA Lw 15), but Groehler's statement ('Verluste der deutschen Luftwaffe', 322–3) that in the first 8–9 months 'the élite of the Fascist Luftwaffe trained before the war was killed' is exaggerated for obvious reasons—to emphasize the supposedly decisive role of the Soviet army and the Soviet air force in the defeat of the Luftwaffe—and its inaccuracy is demonstrated by the figures given above. Even assuming (which is improbable) that only the élite suffered the losses, it would have largely perished in other campaigns and other theatres.

[980] Cf. annexe 41 (1)–(9) in Kreipe, Köster, and Gundelach, MGFA Lw. 15/1, and the report on the combat-readiness of the flying units of the Luftwaffe as of 27 Dec. 1941, Generalquartiermeister der Luftwaffe, 6. Abt., BA-MA RL 2 III/716; as of 21 June 1941, ibid. 713. Murray, *Strategy*, 81–102, although essentially right in his general assessment of the situation, takes perhaps too negative a view of Luftwaffe air-crew and aircraft losses and their immediate effects on Luftwaffe operations.

[981] *Defeat of the German Air Force*, fig. 3, and monthly report, Jan. 1942, Ob.d.L., general staff/ Generalquartiermeister 6. Abt. No. 908/42 g.Kdos., 4 Feb. 1941, BA-MA III W 805/8, pt. 1.

[982] Cf. n. 974 above and report on the combat-readiness of the flying units of the Luftwaffe as of 27 Dec. 1941, Generalquartiermeister der Luftwaffe, 6. Abt., BA-MA RL 2 III/716.

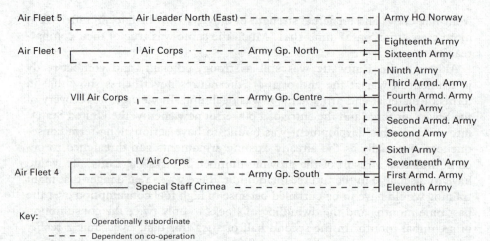

Key:
——— Operationally subordinate
– – – – Dependent on co-operation

DIAGRAM II.1.9. Command Structure between Luftwaffe and Army in the East at the Beginning of January 1942

Source: Plocher, Krieg im Osten, annexe 2, MGFA Lw 4/17.

half the losses. This was primarily the result of the use of the Luftwaffe to provide co-operation with, and subsequently direct support for, the army in the east, a logical consequence of its entire previous theoretical and practical development.[983] When the war against the Soviet Union dragged on longer than initially expected, this kind of co-operation became a 'Verdun' for the Luftwaffe, a constant, heavy drain on its resources with no end in sight (cf. Diagram II.1.9).

Because of the lack of sufficient close-support forces—VIII Air Corps under General von Richthofen was the only close-support corps in the Luftwaffe— the twin-engined bomber, the backbone of the Luftwaffe and better suited to an operational and strategic air war, was increasingly employed in direct support for the army, sometimes under *ad hoc* close-support commanders. This kind of operation, as a rule at low level by medium bombers, which were too large and ponderous for this purpose, resulted in heavy losses and frequent damage, as Soviet ground forces used infantry weapons for unexpectedly strong opposition to such easy targets.[984] It soon became evident that German infantry and armoured units were able to make progress against the generally

[983] Cf. Boog, *Luftwaffenführung*, 151–204; and sects. I.IV.2(*a*), (*b*) at n. 291 (Boog).

[984] Ob.Kdo. der H.Gr. Süd/Ia No. 1736/41 g.Kdos., 28 July 1941, betr. Leistungsfähigkeit der Luftwaffe, Abwehr von Tiefangriffen [Performance of the Luftwaffe, defence against low-level attacks], annexe to Panzergruppe 1, Ia No. 921/41 g.Kdos., 2 Aug. 1941, BA-MA RH 24-14/58; Der Oberbefehlshaber der Luftwaffe, Führungsstab Ia No. 1060/42 g.Kdos. (II), 29 Mar. 1942, betr. Abwehr feindlicher Tiefflieger mit Gewehr usw. [Defence against low-level enemy air attacks by rifle fire etc.], BA-MA RH 20-2/31. Cf. Suchenwirth, Wendepunkte, 79 ff. (Verschleiß der zweimotorigen Bomber in der unmittelbaren Heeresuntestützung) [Wear and tear of twin-engined bombers in direct ground support], MGFA Lw 35.

stubborn and dogged Soviet resistance only when they were supported by the Luftwaffe. On the other hand, the generous granting of air support in all blitzkrieg campaigns led to the army demanding such support not only against enemy forces concentrated for decisive offensive or defensive engagements but also against weak forces too small to justify an air attack, offering too few targets, which could be just as easily destroyed by artillery. Admittedly, numerous tractors for hauling heavy artillery broke down during the winter. As the army was often ignorant of the basic principles for the use of the Luftwaffe,[985] especially the principle of concentrating the main effort of air attacks within the decisive combat area, demands for air support, often unnecessary and incapable of fulfillment, increasingly dissipated the strength of air attacks and rendered them ineffective. Only in the operations of air Fleet 2 at the beginning of the campaign against the Soviet Union, in the army's attack against Leningrad in August and September, and in the attempt to take Moscow in the following months were the Luftwaffe forces used in a genuinely concentrated fashion in the east in 1941. Göring therefore repeatedly emphasized the principle of a maximum concentration of force at the most important point of an attack.[986]

Under growing Soviet pressure, especially after the German army had gone over to the defensive on the entire eastern front in December 1941, the principles of an operational air war, which had been made all the more necessary by the loss of forward momentum, were virtually discarded in favour of direct support for the army.[987] Hitler's assumption of command of the army on 19 December 1941 also contributed to this development.[988] As supreme commander of the Wehrmacht he now not only co-ordinated the requests of the army and the tasks of the Luftwaffe in a general way in the decisive ground battles[989] but also, as commander-in-chief of the army, increasingly directed tactical air support to overcome the crisis. His main military interest, however, had always been in the land war.[990] Soon he ordered that 'planned attacks [by

[985] Cf. directive of chief of staff of Air Fleet 1, Col.-Gen. Keller, on points of main effort: Luftflottenkommando 1, I No. 7039/41 g., 14 Aug. 1941, BA-MA, 18. Armee, 17562/111; AOK 16, hints No. 19, 30 Sept. 1941, BA-MA RH 27-8/39; Richthofen, Tagebuch (privately owned), 6 July 1941.

[986] e.g. teletype message Gen.Kdo. VIII. Fl.Korps Ia No. 3173/42 g.Kdos., 1 Feb. 1942 (copy), BA-MA RH 20-4/288.

[987] GenStdLw/8. Abt.: Die Lage der Reichsverteidigung am 1.9.1944 [The state of Reich defence, 1 Sept. 1944], study of 22 Sept. 1944, BA-MA Lw 107/170, and Auswirkungen und Folgerungen aus dem Einsatz von Teilen der strategischen Luftwaffe zur unmittelbaren Unterstützung des Heeres [Consequences of and conclusions from the employment of elements of the strategic Luftwaffe in direct ground support for the army], GenStdLw/8. Abt., Gruppe 1, 24 Dec. 1943, BA-MA RL 2 IV/42. Cf. also Rieckhoff, *Trumpf oder Bluff*, 258–9.

[988] Cf. sect. II.1.1(g) at n. 610 (Klink).   [989] L.Dv. 16, Ziff. 125.

[990] Cf. Hitler in Jodl, Tagebuch 1937–1939, 27 Jan. 1938 (*IMT* xxviii 345–90): 'For Germany the army is the decisive factor; the other Wehrmacht services have only an auxiliary and complementary role', and in order of the day on the occasion of his taking over direct command of the army on 19 Dec. 1941: 'Among the Wehrmacht services the army, however, carries the burden of the fighting' (Domarus, *Hitler*, ii. 1814). Cf. also Irving, *Hitler's War*, 360; Picker, *Hitler's Table Talk*, 27 (10 Sept. 1941).

the army] are to be postponed unless reliable support by the Luftwaffe is available'.[991] General Hoffmann von Waldau complained that the tone in which the army's demands for air support were presented often disregarded the equal status of the Luftwaffe,[992] which was probably due to the fact that the army was able to refer to orders from Hitler. The use of the Luftwaffe to provide direct support for the army was in agreement not only with the views of many army commanders even before the war[993] but also with those of many Luftwaffe leaders who were former army officers, e.g. the commander-in-chief of Air Fleet 2, Field Marshal Kesselring, who ordered the generals of his flying and anti-aircraft units to 'consider the wishes of the army as my orders'. He prided himself 'on anticipating the wishes of the army and on carrying out any reasonable request based on the development of the situation as quickly and completely' as possible.[994] In this way the Luftwaffe in the east was made completely subordinate to the army. The importance of the air fleets as operational planning and co-ordinating staffs declined. Command of the flying units was increasingly concentrated in the hands of the air corps, which were orientated more towards tactical actions and army operations, or in the hands of *ad hoc* close-support and air leaders created to support army units.[995] The air corps in the east became tactical air corps, the 'operational' air fleets tactical air fleets.

Under the pressure of circumstaces the Luftwaffe in the east became the 'flying artillery' of the army,[996] at first with the approval of the chief of the Luftwaffe General Staff, who was devoted to Hitler but who later realized the absurdity of using bombers in this manner,[997] as did the head of his operations department at the beginning of 1942.[998]

---

[991] Short protocol of conference at Hitler's headquarters, 2 Mar. 1942 (Hitler, Keitel, Jeschonnek, *et al.*), BA-MA, 18. Armee, 36061/212; OKH 420104/42, 12 Mar. 1942, quoted according to Gen.Kdo. X. AK/Ia No. 436/42 g.Kdos., 27 Mar. 1942, in teletype message I. Fliegerkorps/Ia No. 708/42 g.Kdos., 4 Apr. 1942, to Ob.d.L. (Robinson), BA-MA RL 7/8; order repeated in GenStdH/Op.Abt. No. 10328/42 g.Kdos., 22 Mar. 1942, ibid. Cf. also Halder, *KTB* iii. 399 (13 Feb. 1942; not in trans.): 'Attack only with Luftwaffe. Saves morale.' Cf. Deichmann, Unterstützung des Heeres, 211, 267, MGFA Lw 10, and Führerlage 4 Oct. 1943 in *Hitlers Lagebesprechungen*, 394. Hitler had, however, from the very beginning stressed the necessity of a maximum concentration of effort in this support for the army, warned against dispersing Luftwaffe forces, and ordered the army to formulate its requests to the Luftwaffe accordingly: Gen.Kdo. VIII. Fliegerkorps/Ia No. 3173/42 g.Kdos., 1 Feb. 1942 (copy), annexe to AOK 4/Ia No. 259/42, p. 180, BA-MA RH 20-4/288. Cf. sect. II.I.1(*g*) at n. 676 (Klink).
[992] Hoffmann von Waldau, Tagebuch, 117 (24 Jan. 1942), BA-MA RL 200/17.
[993] Cf. GenStdH No. 406/42 g.Kdos. 8. Abt. to General der Luftwaffe beim Ob.d.H., 21 Dec. 1937, BA-MA RL 3/192; Völker, *Luftwaffe*, 88–9; Boog, *Luftwaffenführung*, 174–5.
[994] Kesselring, *Memoirs*, 89.   [995] Cf. Groehler, 'Niederlage vor Moskau', 121 ff.
[996] Deichmann, Unterstützung des Heeres, 205–6, MGFA Lw 10.
[997] Der Chef des Generalstabes der Luftwaffe No. 1150/42 g.Kdos., 24 July 1942, to Generalluftzeugmeister, betr. Forderungen und Vorträge für das Flugzeugbeschaffungs-programm [Requests and reports on the aircraft-provision programme], BA-MA RL 3/865. Cf. also the remark of the general of the bomber units, according to whom the bombers were being used for targets easily within the range of lighter aircraft: L. In 2 No. 80125/42 g.Kdos. (TO), 27 Nov. 1942, betr. Stellungnahme zum derzeitigen Flugzeugprogramm [Comment on current aircraft programme], BA-MA RL 3/51, pp. 754 ff.; Boog, *Luftwaffenführung*, 198–9.
[998] Hoffmann von Waldau, Tagebuch, 116–17 (16 Jan. 1942), BA-MA RL 200/17.

Air transport units, which had an essentially strategic function and had already suffered severe losses—well in excess of 100 aircraft—in the conquest of Crete,[999] were likewise increasingly used for direct ground support. Often as a result of Hitler's personal intervention, they were soon detailed to carry fuel, mines, and even infantry reserves to the front.[1000] The supplying by air of the pockets at Demyansk and Kholm[1001] had far-reaching consequences in two respects: for one thing, the aircraft used had to be taken from instrument flying courses, which seriously interfered with the training of bomber crews, especially as they were often flown by instruction crews and any losses therefore affected the future training of crews. For another, the Luftwaffe, leaders, and Hitler in particular, felt, in spite of the heavy losses of transport aircraft, that the eventual liberation of the encircled ground forces and the holding of the front for future operations had demonstrated the correctness of such costly operations, and were therefore later only too ready to order similar actions at Stalingrad and in North Africa even when there was no longer any hope of freeing the encircled army units by land. Only in conjunction with offensive actions on the ground and over territory held by German forces would a prolonged employment of the expensive transport aircraft and their crews have been justified. After the turn of 1941–2, the ratio between new and lost Ju-52s became negative: in the first six months of 1942 the figures were 235 new aircraft[1002] as against 516 aircraft lost. But at the end of 1941 this danger was not yet apparent to the German leaders.

Direct support for the army was also costly in terms of the number of close-reconnaissance aircraft lost. Of 56 close-reconnaissance Staffeln at the start of the campaign, only 19 were still ready for action at the end of the year. The limited readiness for action of the long-range reconnaissance units since the beginning of the campaign made their losses especially serious. Such losses also demonstrated the wastefulness of the tactical fragmentation of these units between the army and the Luftwaffe and the resulting frequent duplication of effort and omissions in reconnaissance. Oversights resulting from such a lack of reconnaissance aircraft—long-range reconnaissance aircraft were also used as bombers on the battlefield—were an important factor in the German failure to realize in time the scale of the westward transports of fresh Soviet troops from Siberia in the late autumn of 1941.[1003] By the end of March 1942 all close- and long-range reconnaissance, anti-aircraft, and air-signal units assigned to

---

[999] Gundelach, *Luftwaffe im Mittelmeer*, i. 223.

[1000] Cf. Halder, *Diaries*, 1255 (25 Sept. 1941), and notes of VIII Air Corps, 5, 9, 10 Oct., 20, 21, 22 Dec. 1941, BA-MA RL 8/49; Richthofen, Tagebuch (privately owned), 25 June, 25 Sept., 5, 9, 10, 13 Oct. 1941.

[1001] Cf. sect. II.I.2(*b*); and sect. II.I.I(*g*) (Klink).

[1002] Survey, Generalquartiermeister der Luftwaffe, 6. Abt., 28 June 1945, BA-MA Lw 103/84 (photocopy).

[1003] Cf. Koluft beim AOK 4/Ia, 13 Oct. 1941, Wünsche für die Tag- und Nachtaufklärung der Heeresgruppe Mitte [Army Group Centre's requests for day and night reconnaissance], BA-MA RH 20-4/218; Plocher, Krieg im Osten, 846 ff., MGFA Lw 4/5; cf. esp. letter of Lt.-Gen. (ret.) Schmidt to Generals Deichmann and Plocher, 28 Apr. 1955, Führungsakademie der Bundeswehr, Luftwaffen-Archiv 4 (bk. 1); Kesselring, *Memoirs*, 96.

the army were progressively returned to Luftwaffe commands, and the Luftwaffe staffs in the armies disbanded and replaced by Luftwaffe liaison officers with the army staffs.[1004] This reduced the need for staffs and made possible a more economical and more concentrated use of the weakened reconaissance units. The final result of these measures, however, was that the Luftwaffe was bound even more closely to the army, as the air fleets and air corps now had to concern themselves even more with the wishes of the army and found even less time for the operational-strategic tasks of the flying units.[1005]

To be able to devote themselves again to these urgent tasks, as senior Luftwaffe officers in the east reported in retrospect,[1006] or actually demanded at the time,[1007] the Luftwaffe leaders would have had to detach the bomber formations suited to long-range tasks from direct-support actions for the army, as indeed was called for by their losses in such actions. As four-engined bombers were lacking, twin-engined types should have been used for long-range attacks and single-engined aircraft for close-support and air-defence tasks. But this would have required a different order of battle and the availability of adequate replacements to meet the needs of army operations.

The Luftwaffe was organized regionally in air fleets and independent air corps that were generally dependent on co-operation with the corresponding army units. Each of these large units was a 'little Luftwaffe' within its own region and capable of fulfilling the most varied offensive and defensive tasks. But this regional fragmentation prevented them from solving problems on a larger scale, as they existed in the Soviet Union because of the vastness of the area and the strategic objectives to be attacked. The resulting concentration of forces on an *ad hoc* basis by transfers over often considerable distances—as with VIII Air Corps or the bomber formations operating against Moscow—generally required much time and always entailed a significant number of breakdowns and other failures.[1008] Moreover, it was an illusion to believe that bomber crews who had long been flying ground-support missions in ground contact could suddenly be used to attack distant targets calling for considerable navigational skill and experience. The acquisition of such skills again required time.[1009] To reduce bomber losses a functional organization of air units—not only in the east—into long-range bomber, support or close-support, and fighter commands corresponding to the British bomber, fighter, and co-operation commands or the American tactical and strategic air forces

---

[1004] Cf. Boog, *Luftwaffenführung*, 192, 196, 254–5.

[1005] Maj.-Gen. (ret.) Sigismund Freiherr von, Falkenstein, Die Unterstützung des deutschen Heeres durch die deutsche Luftwaffe im Zweiten Weltkrieg, BA-MA Lw 133/1, 35.

[1006] Cf. Plocher, Krieg im Osten, 75–125, MGFA Lw 4/9.

[1007] Cf. Boog, *Luftwaffenführung*, 191.

[1008] Cf. *Rise and Fall of the German Air Force*, 169.

[1009] This became evident in 1943–4 in the preparations of IV Air Corps for strategic long-range bombing. The preparations required so much time that the pull-back of the front carried out in the meantime eventually made such operations impossible. Cf. Herhudt von Rohden, 'Letzter Großeinsatz'.

would have been necessary around the turn of 1941–2 if not before. Hitler's Directive No. 39 of 8 December 1941, in which he demanded attacks on armament and training centres in the Soviet hinterland as well as direct and indirect support for the army, could have provided the impulse for such a step. But there is no record of such deliberations in the Luftwaffe General Staff at this time, probably because the strained situation in the east seemed to leave no time for such a reorganization and because it would have raised the question of creating air units within the army. That would have contradicted one of Göring's most vigorously defended principles: that all aircraft, of whatever kind and function, had to remain under his command.

In contrast, the Red Army was able to put its experience in the war into practice. The Soviet air force recovered and its integration in the total political, military, civilian, and economic war effort was improved. Air armies were created, as well as a strategic reserve consisting of large units of specific types of aircraft (fighters, ground-attack aircraft, etc.), which could be switched from one front to another, a strategic long-range bomber command, and a strategic air-defence command consisting of fighters. These organizational innovations gave the flying units greater strategic mobility, the ability to concentrate attacks more quickly, and the ability to achieve air superiority over the key areas of ground operations at a time when the over-extended and in every respect overtaxed Luftwaffe was scarcely in a position to concentrate on a point of main effort. Moreover, Soviet air strategists continued to develop the idea of attacks to paralyse enemy air units and ground-support organizations, to interfere with supply movements, and above all to support their own ground forces. They reformulated their doctrine accordingly.[1010]

From the intelligence sources, the second influence determining the Luftwaffe's situation assessment at the end of 1941, came reassuring reports as late as the winter of 1941–2. The number of enemy incursions from March to the end of August 1941, Luftwaffe Commander Centre (home air defence) reported, had not risen as sharply as the number of enemy aircraft shot down by German air defences over Germany itself.[1011]

The monthly war-economy situation reports of the Wehrmacht High Command described the effects of the British and the few Soviet raids on Germany until after the turn of the year as 'insignificant'.[1012] The navy evidently viewed the air war with less optimism and, because of its main areas of activity in the Mediterranean and around Britain, was more concerned about the future. As early as 25 July 1941, therefore, the chief of the naval war staff enquired from the intelligence department of the Luftwaffe operations staff what the material

[1010] Cf. sect. II.ii.2 (Hoffmann); Overy, *Air War*, 52 ff.

[1011] General report on enemy activity and defensive successes, 24 Mar.–31 Aug. 1941, Luftwaffenbefehlshaber Mitte, Führungsabteilung I, Gruppe Ic—No. 2945/41 g.Kdos., 9 Sept. 1941, BA-MA RL 7/577.

[1012] Cf. Hoffmann von Waldau, Tagebuch, 78 (16 Oct. 1941), BA-MA RL 200/17, and the war-economy reports of the War Economy and Armament Office of the Army High Command, June–Dec. 1941, BA-MA RW 19/99.

and personnel situation of the Luftwaffe would be 'after the liquidation of the eastern problem', what, in view of the other theatres of war, it thought it could achieve against Britain, when it believed it would be able to reach its former numerical strength in terms of aircraft, and how it assessed the Royal Air Force then and in six months' time.[1013]

Remembering the unsuccessful German air campaign against Britain in the summer of 1940, the operations department of the Luftwaffe operations staff assessed the success of the British daylight attacks in June and July 1941 by concluding that 'the heavy losses suffered in these raids . . . will soon force the enemy to abandon such operations'. German fighter forces in the west were indeed operating under a certain strain, but it was a great advantage that the pilots, if their aircraft were shot down, could 'bail out' over their own territory. The effect achieved by the night attacks on the German war economy was 'quite unimportant' and was 'regarded merely as a nuisance'. In the last two months 'no significant damage to the war economy' had 'been inflicted by air attacks'. It would be possible to 'offset' the expected increased night attacks by 'equipping all night fighters with radar'.[1014] At the end of July 1941 the technical officer of the Luftwaffe operations staff believed that, assuming the envisaged production targets could be achieved and losses in the east in autumn and winter were not excessive, it would be possible, in terms of personnel and equipment, to compensate for losses of fighters in the east by February 1942 and for losses of bombers by May of that year. This forecast was based on an assumed monthly German production of 1,000 aircraft and a British production of 700. This latter figure was 50 per cent short of the level the British aircraft industry had actually achieved.[1015] As late as 1 August 1941 section west of Luftwaffe operations staff intelligence did not expect any significant increase in American aircraft deliveries to Britain, if, as had been the case until then, Britain received only half of all American deliveries.[1016] In the summer of 1941 German officers thus underestimated not only Britain but also the United States. A comparison of air armaments, dated 30 July 1941,[1017] assumed for

[1013] Letter (copy), Generalstabsoffizier der Luftwaffe bei der 1./Skl., 25 July 1941 to Kapt. z.S. Mössel, Verbindungsoffizier der Kriegsmarine beim Luftwaffenführungsstab/Ia, BA-MA OKM, Case GE 958/PG 32957, p. 44.

[1014] Luftwaffenführungsstab Ia (KM) to OKM/IL, 29 July 1941 (copy), BA-MA RM 7/170, pp. 111 ff.

[1015] Luftwaffenführungsstab Ia (KM), 31 July 1941 to OKM/1. Skl, BA-MA OKM, Case GE 958/PG 32957, p. 53. According to Postan (British War Production, 484), Britain produced 1,601 military aircraft in Aug. 1941.

[1016] Ic/III A, 31 July 1941, Kurze Beurteilung der RAF—Stand: 1.8.—als Vortragsunterlage für IM [Brief assessment of the RAF—as of 1 Aug.—for a report to IM], BA-MA OKM, Case GE 958/PG 32957, pp. 55 ff.

[1017] Comparison of air armament Germany–Italy and Britain–USA 1939–1943, as of 1 July 1941, pt. 1, 6–7, Der Generalluftzeugmeister No. 1123/42 g.Kdos., 30 Aug. 1941, BA-MA RL 3/1833. As late as 1942 the head of development in the technical office of the director-general of air armament (Generalluftzeugmeister) stated—quite incomprehensibly—that for a long time he had known nothing about the development of an American four-engine bomber, which had come as a surprise to him (development conference, 30 Oct. 1942, BA-MA RL 3/34, p. 2347). After the war Schmid's successor as head of the Luftwaffe operations staff/Ic, Col. (ret.) Wodarg of the general

1943 an Anglo-American superiority of at most 48 per cent in fighters and 63 per cent in bombers in Europe and of only 50 per cent in aluminium production, as against a German 'Elch' (Elk) programme to double the strength of the Luftwaffe,[1018] implementation of which was doubtful from the start because of the shortage of aluminium. In fact combined Anglo-American aircraft production in 1943 was 34,715 fighters and 37,083 bombers, as compared with only 11,198 fighters and 8,295 bombers and ground-support aircraft in Germany.[1019] In the comparison of 30 August 1941 the four-engined bombers, of which Britain and the United States built 14,100 in 1943, were counted twice, which made the underestimation even more serious.

In June 1941 the head of department 5 of the Luftwaffe operations staff was still of the optimistic opinion that the United States would not be 'able to participate actively in the war in the foreseeable future'.[1020] Yet in October 1940 the German aircraft producer Fritz Siebel had uttered a warning about the enormous American bomber and air-armaments programme.[1021] But, in spite of initial doubts, Göring shared Hitler's purposive optimism, which confidently expected the war in the east to be finished before the United States was ready to intervene, as well as his erroneous belief that Americans were incapable of 'producing anything other than refrigerators'.[1022] As late as 18 September 1941 even Milch estimated probable American aircraft production for 1942 at 16,000.[1023] That year the Americans in fact produced 47,836 aircraft. The underestimation of Soviet aircraft production after the end of 1941 has already been mentioned.[1024]

So far, therefore, no air-armaments measures had been taken that might have had a positive effect on the situation of the Luftwaffe in the east by the beginning of 1942. The 'development stop', Göring's order of 9 February 1940 to pursue only those development plans 'that can be completed in 1940 or will produce results at the latest in 1941',[1025] was in a general sense still in force; it was repeated by the Wehrmacht High Command in October 1941,[1026] and

staff (interview, 18 Apr. 1972, MGFA), stated: 'Compared with the lead we had . . . initially, no one could have imagined that the Western Allies could organize such an armament programme.'

[1018] Cf. *KTB OKW* i. 1016 ff., and GL 1 I, programme draft 'Elch' and Göring programme, 25 and 29 July 1941, BA-MA RL 3/1411; probable delivery plan: 'Elch' programme, LC 2 Ia No. 1569/41, 13 Aug. 1941 (preliminary draft), BA-MA RL 3/1010.

[1019] Cf. Holley, *Buying Aircraft*, 550; Postan, *British War Production*, 484–5; Lusar, *Geheimwaffen*, 171.

[1020] Luftwaffenführungsstab/Ic, 7 June 1941, gez. Schmid, BA-MA RL 3/63, p. 7141.

[1021] Cf. Boog, *Luftwaffenführung*, 119–20.

[1022] Irving, *Hitler's War*, 335; interview protocol Col. (ret.) Hans Wolter of the general staff, 6 June 1972, MGFA.

[1023] BA-MA RL 3/51, p. 1156.   [1024] Cf. sect. II.1.2(*d*).

[1025] Protocol record V.P. [= Four-year Plan] 2699 g. Reichssache, BA-MA RL 3/63, pp. 7281 ff., and Udet's letter to Göring, 7 Feb. 1940, ibid. 7294–5. Cf. Boog, *Luftwaffenführung*, 59 ff.

[1026] Chef OKW/WiRüAmt/Rü (IIa) No. 3080/41 g.Kdos., 10 Oct. 1941, betr. Anpassung und Abgleichung der Beschaffungsnotwendigkeiten der Wehrmacht an die Leistungsfähigkeit der Industrie [Adjustment and harmonization of Wehrmacht supply requirements to industrial capacity] (copy), BA-MA Lw 103/25. There it was stated that 'the demands' were 'to be limited to the most important developments and those absolutely necessary for field use'.

continued to delay promising new developments. The method of telescoping various development phases[1027] so as to accelerate the series production of aircraft, as it had evolved under the enormous time pressure created by Hitler's increasingly ambitious and constantly changing political and strategic aims, continued to be practised and led to design faults whose elimination after series production had started caused additional delays and reduced output even further. Aircraft production still used primitive, inefficient methods[1028] and suffered from a manpower shortage when sufficient workers from the promised demobilized army divisions did not become available. This shortage in turn prevented the introduction of second or third shifts to make full use of existing production capacity. Production of new aircraft was also slowed in part by the lack of enough replacement engines, a result of the emphasis on quantity rather than depth in armament programmes. The replacements needed had to be taken from new aircraft.[1029] The director-general of air ormament, Ernst Udet, could not master the problems of his office, although he was not to blame for all of them. Too much the artist, Bohemian, and test pilot, he was not the organizer and manager he would have needed to be to direct and step up modern mass production of aircraft. As a sensitive person he increasingly felt the burden of responsibility for the failures in aircraft production and his own inability to remedy the situation.

Göring and Jeschonnek were not unaware of Udet's inadequacies. On 14 May 1941 an 'industrial council of the Reich Marshal for the production of aircraft equipment'[1030] was created to assist Udet in the rationalization and improvement of the performance of the aircraft industry. Milch was instructed to support and keep an eye on Udet, which led to considerable friction between the two men. But Udet's 'slipping programmes'—a new aircraft programme, a new draft, or changes in existing programmes were introduced every few weeks without one of them being carried out completely—made these measures necessary. On 20 June 1941, after Hitler, in the expectation of an early victory over the Soviet Union, had ordered arms production in general to be cut back in favour of aircraft production for the intensified war against Britain to be fought after victory in the east,[1031] Göring announced a

---

[1027] Cf. Dipl.-Ing. Robert Lusser, Wehrwirtschaftsführer, Denkschrift über die Entwicklung und Entwicklungsplanung in der deutschen Luftrüstung [Memorandum on developments and development planning in German aerial armament], 15 Jan. 1942, BA-MA RL 3/51, pp. 802–19. Cf. also Boog, Luftwaffenführung, 51 ff.

[1028] Cf. sect. I.IV.2(c) above, n. 346.

[1029] Betrachtungen über den derzeitigen Lieferstand nach Programm 19 (2) für Zellen und Motoren [Present state of deliveries of cells and engines], GL 1 I, 5 June 1941, BA-MA RL 3/887. On Dir.-Gen. of Air Armament Udet cf. sources and sect. I.IV..2(c) above, n. 345; Boog, Luftwaffenführung, 237 ff., and lecture by Gen. v. Seidel, 1949, p. 49, BA-MA Lw 101/3, pt. II.

[1030] Der Generalluftzeugmeister, GL-Befehl No. 373, 22 May 1941, BA-MA RL 3/2102. Cf. also Ludwig, Technik und Ingenieure, 373; Boog, Luftwaffenführung, 253.

[1031] Cf. sect. IV.1 at n. 4 below (Müller); Irving, Rise and Fall, 125; Hitler's grant of authority to Göring, 22 June 1941 (copy), BA-MA RL 3/864.

fourfold increase in the size of the Luftwaffe and gave Milch comprehensive special powers to carry out this task.[1032] Udet remained nominally dirctor-general of air armament but was in practice placed under Milch. Since Göring's programme[1033]—which had been designed specifically for the war against Britain and therefore placed special emphasis on increasing monthly production of bombers, fighters, and twin-engined fighters to 880, 720, and 225 aircraft respectively, with less emphasis on types designed to intervene in ground fighting and on transport aircraft—could not be carried out immedi-ately, a reduced programme, the Elch programme, was worked out. This envisaged only a doubling of the Luftwaffe. Milch, convinced that aircraft production could be substantially increased,[1034] ordered the feasibility of the reduced Göring programme to be examined, and on 10 November 1941 came to the conclusion that 'the "Göring aircraft delivery programme" can be fulfilled, apart from some changes in the output figures'.[1035] Udet, however, continued to maintain that even the delivery figures envisaged in the Elch programme could not be met. On 20 August 1941 he informed the Luftwaffe staff officer in charge of supply and administration that 'in the present material and personnel situation' monthly bomber production would have to decline from 340 to 322 by the end of the year, while fighter production would drop from 221 to 208 by November and not rise again until 1942, as would bomber production. Total monthly output of new military aircraft indeed declined from 1,010 in August 1941 to 734 in November and 780 in December 1941. As Udet observed: 'An increase in deliveries to the figures of the Elch programme cannot be expected unless preference in principle is ordered for the air-armaments programme with regard to allocation of materials and personnel.'[1036]

In the meantime, however, the Wehrmacht High Command[1037] had come to realize that enemy air armament was assuming a threatening character, that operations in the east could not be concluded or army armament strengthened as quickly as had been expected, and that armaments programmes on the whole would have to be simplified. Certainly the Luftwaffe General Staff seems to have become generally less optimistic in its assessment of the air

---

[1032] Irving, *Rise and Fall*, 125.   [1033] Cf. n. 1018 above.

[1034] Address to the Industrial Council, 18 Sept. 1941, BA-MA RL 3/51, p. 1157.

[1035] 'Voraussetzungen für die Durchführung des "Göring-Programms" [Prerequisites of the implementation of the "Göring Programme"]', R.d.L. u. Ob.d.L., GL/A-Pl, 10 Nov. 1941, gez. I.V. Milch, BA-MA III W 803. The reduced 'Göring Programme' is contained in the study of the director-general of air armament, on which this memorandum is based and which has the same title: Amt LAP, 18 Oct. 1941, as fourth draft of the Göring aircraft delivery programme, LC 2 IA No. 2048/41 g.Kdos., BA-MA RL 3/1104.

[1036] Letter, Generalluftzeugmeister GL 1 Az. 89 a-m No. 845/41 g.Kdos., 20 Aug. 1941, to Generalquartiermeister, GenSt 6. Abt. betr. Lieferzahlen bis 1 Apr. 1942 [Deliveries to 1 Apr. 1942], BA-MA RL 3/2142. Cf. also Technisches Amt LC/B 2 No. 2233/41 g.Kdos. IA, 30 Oct. 1941, betr. Lieferzahlen bis 1 May 1942 [Deliveries to 1 May 1942], ibid.

[1037] Cf. Thomas, *Wehr- und Rüstungswirtschaft*, 285, 287.

situation, at least with regard to Britain. Jeschonnek, together with other high-ranking Luftwaffe officers, advocated a strengthening of the fighter units.[1038] In September 1941 an increase of monthly aircraft production to 850 bombers and twin-engined fighters, 485 fighters, 174 dive-bombers and ground-attack aircraft, and 90 transport aircraft was called for.[1039] On 18 September 1941 Milch explained to the industrial council[1040] how this increase could be achieved: 'to put it simply, we are confronted with the question of whether we shall have no aircraft at all in 1943 or whether we shall have a large number of those that have proved their worth.' In 1942–3, therefore, the 'tried and tested old models' were to be 'produced in large numbers . . . At first quantity will be given priority.' Of course, development programmes could not be abandoned completely, 'but we must not forget that what we develop must contribute to winning this war'. Series production of aircraft already developed, which did not have so many 'teething problems' as new types, was therefore still given priority over development, as the latter required too many engineers, who were more urgently needed for the former. The armaments programmes of the individual Wehrmacht services, however, competed with each other. On 11 September 1941 Hitler ordered their co-ordination.[1041] Because of the growing requirements of the war in the east, the expected needs of future theatres, and the defence of Germany against air attacks, army and anti-aircraft equipment again came to the fore. This trend was confirmed in the decree 'Armaments 1942' of 10 January 1942. The air-armaments programme was thus denied the means of production equal to the increasing tasks and losses of the Luftwaffe in the east and its simultaneous involvement in other theatres of the war. Available raw materials were no longer sufficient to carry out all programmes of the Wehrmacht branches at the same time. General Thomas reported that an increase in aircraft production seemed virtually impossible before 1943 and that even previous levels could be maintained only if the anti-aircraft pro-gramme were cut back.[1042]

Udet had realized the inadequacies of German air armament, which were not exclusively his fault but were rooted primarily in German armament policy. In the autumn of 1941, after his friend Fritz Siebel had warned him again about the immense air-armaments potential of the Americans, whose support for the British was becoming increasingly overt,[1043] and considering the demands to increase air armaments to be unfulfillable, he concluded that

---

[1038] Cf. Boog, *Luftwaffenführung*, 142 ff.

[1039] Programmvorschlag IV (Anlehnung an die vom Generalstab geforderten Nachschubzahlen) [Programme proposal IV, based on supply data demanded by the deneral staff] GL 1 No. 923/41 g.Kdos, 10 Sept. 1941, BA-MA RL 3/1104.

[1040] BA-MA RL 3/51, pp. 1159–60, 1168.

[1041] Der Führer und Oberste Befehlshaber der Wehrmacht No. 340/41 g.Kdos. Chef OKW (copy), BA-MA Lw 103/25.

[1042] Cf. Der Chef OKW No. 345/41 g.Kdos., Chef OKW to Chef WiRüAmt, 19 Sept. 1941 (copy), BA-MA RL 3/352; Thomas, *Wehr- und Rüstungswirtschaft*, 288; Reinhardt, *Wende vor Moskau*, 266–7.

[1043] Boog, *Luftwaffenführung*, 119–20.

the war could no longer be won. Tension between Udet and Milch, who still believed in victory, increased, especially as Milch did not shrink from interfering in Udet's area of responsibility (which admittedly was necessary).[1044] Feeling himself squeezed out and persecuted by Milch and abandoned by Göring, desperate about the air-armaments situation, and profoundly depressed, Udet committed suicide on 17 November 1941. Officially his death was explained as the result of an accident during the testing of a new weapon.

This deliberate disinformation by Göring, and the practice, based on Hitler's Order No. 1 on secrecy, of limiting information to the smallest possible number of people even within the top leadership, prevented the true reasons for Udet's death from becoming known to all Luftwaffe leaders at the time and being generally understood as an indication of the futility of continuing the war. The crisis in the east shortly thereafter also helped divert attention from Udet's death. Milch still considered the air-armaments situation to be not so hopeless as Udet had believed.[1045] There were still numerous material and labour reserves that could be exploited by intensive rationalization of production and distribution of weapons and aircraft to the troops, especially in the occupied areas in the west and by the use of prisoners of war, without whom later production increases would not have been possible. The shift of emphasis to greater production of tried and tested aircraft, with much lower priority being given to new developments, helped to avoid or at least delay an admission of the foreseeable total failure of the air war. Contrary to rational insight, even the powerful emotions released by the setback at Moscow were often apt to reinforce this tendency, as when the head of the operations department of the Luftwaffe General Staff—in spite of his admission that the objective of the campaign against the Soviet Union had not been reached (Rostov, Leningrad, and Moscow had not been captured; the war was now becoming 'very serious'; and food supplies and transport were guaranteed 'only to a limited extent')—concluded his reflections at the end of 1941 with the words: 'There is still the hope that spring will bring military successes again . . . to help overcome all depressing thoughts. The nation's readiness for sacrifice has probably never been so great . . . as in this war. The important thing is to maintain that will.'[1046]

The plan to eliminate the Soviet air force and the Soviet Union itself in 1941 had indeed failed. The struggle in the east had to be continued while at the same time a struggle against a powerful new enemy, the United States, began

---

[1044] Cf. Irving, *Rise and Fall*, 119–20, and the report of the head of the Berlin office of the Donau-Flugzeugbau AG, Budapest, Schmid, on the 'over-organization' of the area of the director-general of air armament, 22 Mar. 1943, BA-MA RL 3/859. Cf. also Boog, *Luftwaffenführung*, annexes 3.2a, b.

[1045] In view of his many statements to the contrary, it is doubtful that, at the beginning of 1942, Milch seriously questioned that the war would end in a positive way for Germany, in spite of the remark by Speer (*Third Reich*, 301) that Milch and others believed that the war had to be won with available weapons by the autumn of 1942, otherwise it would be lost.

[1046] Hoffmann von Waldau, Tagebuch, 126–9, BA-MA RL 200/17.

in the west. Largely undisturbed by the Luftwaffe, Germany's third important enemy in the air, Britain, was able to continue recovering and building up her air force. In spite of the unbroken feeling of superiority of the German air crews with regard to their morale and flying ability,[1047] in terms of armaments potential and strength the flying units of the Luftwaffe were soon inferior not only to the Soviet air force but also to each of the other two great air forces in the European war, the Royal Air Force and the United States Army Air Force. Unlike the army, which had had periods of rest between the individual campaigns before 22 June 1941, the Luftwaffe had been involved in almost uninterrupted combat in the most diverse theatres of the war and, as was now most obvious, could not expect to have any time to rehabilitate its personnel or equipment in the future. As a support weapon in the east and in North Africa, it was no longer able to concentrate its forces on objectives of its own choosing, and it was now burdened with a growing number of tasks that it could not fulfil.[1048] To make available the numbers of aircraft necessary on the fronts in the east, south, and west of Europe and to protect Germany itself against the expected attacks by the British and American bomber fleets, it would have been necessary—contrary to the decisions that had actually been taken in this regard—to give air armaments the highest priority within the German armaments programmes as a whole and to rescind the development stop in order to preserve the qualitative superiority of German aircraft. That, however, would have demanded a clear acknowledgement of the situation in which Germany found herself at the end of 1941. All these measures would have required firm, uniform, and forward-looking leadership in every theatre of the war.[1049] But such leadership did not exist. As far as is known, there were no such deliberations among the Luftwaffe leaders at this time. They were too involved in dealing with the most pressing problems at the fronts, especially in the east, and in filling gaps. A remark by the head of the Luftwaffe General Staff at the beginning of 1942 was typical of this situation and of the attitude of the senior Luftwaffe officers: first Russia would have to be defeated; then it would be possible to concentrate on training.[1050] This marked the beginning of the end of the Luftwaffe.

[1047] Operation experience report of Fighter Geschwader 54, BA-MA RL 10/476, p. 20, and 10/477, pp. 7–8.
[1048] Cf. Plocher, Krieg im Osten, 841, MGFA Lw 4/5.
[1049] Ibid. 75–129, MGFA Lw 4/9; 382 ff., MGFA Lw 4/10; 803 ff., MGFA Lw 4/12.
[1050] Gen. (ret.) von Seidel, lecture, 1949, p. 52, BA-MA Lw 101/3, pt. II. Cf. Galland, *Die Ersten und die Letzten*, 151–2; also Jeschonnek's proposal at the conference with Göring, 6 Mar. 1942 (BA-MA RL 3/60, p. 5172), of thoroughly 'combing through' the training system of the Luftwaffe for Ju-87 and Me-109 aircraft to cover the missions of the Me-210 Gruppen.

II. The Conduct of the War through Soviet Eyes

Joachim Hoffmann

1. The Beginning of the War

In the early hours of 22 June 1941 the German and German-allied armies crossed the Soviet frontier and penetrated into Lithuania, the Soviet-annexed parts of Poland, and soon afterwards also into Romania. The attack by armoured and motorized formations, supported with massive strikes by the Luftwaffe, gained ground rapidly, even though the Soviet troops offered often stubborn resistance in the frontier area itself, e.g. at Liepaja, Brest, and Przemysl. There was, however, no question of a systematic defence by the Soviet divisions against the German attack. This seems the more astonishing as the Soviet leadership, in a multitude of reports arriving in Moscow through diplomatic channels, espionage, reconnaissance, or in other ways, had been very well informed that aggression was imminent.[1] The argument that the Soviet Union had been taken by surprise by the German attack is totally devoid of foundation. Taken by surprise—according to the judgement of the future Soviet minister of defence, Marshal of the Soviet Union Grechko—were the frontier troops alonec, but not the government or the senior commands of the army.[2] Besides, the element of surprise cannot explain the unprepanedness of defences, since the Soviet theory of war maintained the principle that modern wars began without a declaration of war, with a surprise attack.[3] There has been lively discussion in the Soviet literature on the reasons for such disregard of numerous warnings. The emerging opinion was that Stalin was indulging in illusions about the continuing validity of the non-aggression treaty and anticipated the possibility of a warlike conflict with Germany only in the event that the Soviet Union allowed itself to be taken in by 'provocations' from 'victory-drunk German generals'.[4] As the wish and will of the 'wise and experienced leader of the Soviet Union, the great Stalin'[5] were unassailable law, his attitude was bound to be adopted also by the Red Army command authorities responsible for the country's external security.

Not only did the Red Army leadership simply brush aside all those well-founded warnings, but it actually halted such defensive measures as were being initiated by responsible military leaders—a procedure which, according

---

[1] Khrushchev's speech, 25 Feb. 1956, according to Telpuchowski, *Geschichte des Großen Vaterländischen Krieges*, 28E; Chor'kov, 'Meroprijatija', 88–9.

[2] Grečko, '25 let', 10.   [3] Čeredničenko, 'O načal'nom periode', 34.

[4] Nekritsch and Grigorenko, *Genickschuß*, 138.   [5] Molotov, *28-ja godovščina*, 18–19.

to the future Soviet defence minister, Marshal of the Soviet Union Malinovskiy, bordered on the criminal.[6] Thus, immediately before the war, the commanders of the Baltic and Kiev Special Military Districts had on their own initiative taken a number of measures to enhance the combat-readiness of their troops. These measures, however, had to be suspended and rescinded on orders from the Red Army General Staff.[7] Requests by other commanding officers to be allowed to move their units forward into defensive positions and to man gun emplacements had likewise been rejected. Blackout and air-raid precautions were also prohibited; uncamouflaged aircraft were lined up in close order on their airfields; and it was forbidden for anti-aircraft artillery to open fire. Once the Central Directorate of Political Propaganda had labelled warnings of a conflict as 'provocative rumours', the initiative of field commanders was paralysed; no one wished to be accused of having fallen for enemy provocations.[8] Particularly damaging to the combat-readiness of the Soviet forces was the well-known statement issued by the Tass agency on 14 June 1941, which officially and categorically denied the possibility of a German attack on the Soviet Union, describing all rumours to the contrary as 'lies and provocations'. Soviet military historians, compelled to prove that the 'Communist Party, the Soviet government, and the military command' had done an 'enormous job' strengthening the country's defence capability on the eve of the war, endeavoured to escape from the dilemma they find themselves in by concealing the true causes and responsibilities. An attempt was made to explain the heavy defeats suffered by the Red Army in the initial phase of the war by references to a 'series of political, economic, and military factors'[9] which basically were no one's fault. However, the responsibilities cannot be fudged. Apart from Stalin and his close entourage in the Politburo, the Central Committee, and the Soviet government, the Red Army's lack of preparedness for defence was due to omissions by Voroshilov, the People's Commissar for Defence, and his successor Timoshenko, as well as by Zhukov, chief of the Red Army General Staff, and more particularly Golikov, head of the reconnaissance department in the general staff,[10] who is accused of having deliberately doctored all information to suit what he thought Stalin wished to hear.[11]

Under these circumstances the advance of the German army groups, scarcely impeded by uncoordinated opposition in the frontier districts, was bound to produce a dangerous crisis on the Soviet side during the very first days. On 22 June 1941 the commands of the military districts—now renamed North-west Front, Western Front, South-west Front, and, in the case of the Odessa Military District, Soviet Ninth Army—and many of the army staffs

[6] Malinovskij, 'Dvadcatiletie načala', 6.
[7] Anfilov, Načalo, 45–6; Kozlov et al., O sovetskoj voennoj nauke, 192.
[8] Bor'ba za sovetskuju Pribaltiku, i. 46. [9] 50 let vooružennych sil, 261.
[10] Istorija Velikoj Otečestvennoj vojny, ii. 10; Grečko, 25 let, 8.
[11] Zhukov, Reminiscences, 228 ff.; Nekritsch and Grigorenko, Genickschuß, 190, 291–2; Erickson, Stalin's War, i. 88–9.

had already lost an overall view of the situation and contact with their formations. After the many penetrations achieved by the German forces it was
impossible to restore a cohesive front. As a result of German air raids, signs of
disorganization appeared in the hinterland. A situation had thus arisen in
which the only salvation of the Soviet troops would have been a strategy of
flexible defence and withdrawals. Yet the People's Commissariat for Defence
and the Soviet general staff, with no accurate idea of what was really happening and, contrary to the most recent assertions,[12] in a state of total confusion,
clung to the doctrine that the only task of the Red Army was to go over to
counter-attacks and carry the war into the enemy's territory.[13] At a time when
Armoured Groups 3 and 4 had already achieved a deep penetration at the
boundary between the North-west and Western Fronts, when German tanks
on the sector of the Western Front were already at Kobrin, 50 km. east of
Brest, having achieved successes also on the South-west Front, when therefore
the danger of a far-ranging encirclement was beginning to take shape, on that
evening of 22 June 1941 the People's Commissar for Defence ordered the
'fronts' (i.e. army groups) and armies to mount counter-attacks against the
German spearheads and, having annihilated them, to occupy the areas of
Suwalki and Lublin. In consequence, the over-hasty counter-attack of the
Soviet XII and III Mechanized Corps near Siauliai between 23 and 29 June, as
well as the attacks of VI and XI Mechanized Corps near Grodno, and those of
VIII, IX, XV, XIX, and XXII Mechanized Corps for the encirclement of the
German spearhead groups in the Lutsk–Rovno–Brody area, were, in view of
the state of command and troops, doomed to failure from the start,[14] even
though Soviet units achieved a few surprise successes and managed temporarily to delay the advance of Armoured Group 1 in the southern sector.

As, however, the Soviets were unable to halt the German forces completely,
let alone annihilate them, and as an exceedingly threatening situation was
developing especially in the area of the Western Front near Minsk, the Soviet
High Command after 27 June 1941 found itself compelled to change its moves.
The strategic reserves hurriedly brought up from the interior of the country
now had to be employed in the establishment of a defensive line along the
western Dvina and Dnieper; as a result, they were no longer, as originally
planned, available for mounting a counter-offensive. The North-west Front
was now instructed to use its formations to hold the Dvina line from Riga to
Kraslava, while the troops of Twenty-second, Nineteenth, Twentieth, and
Twenty-first Armies were to strengthen and occupy a defensive position
roughly on a line Drissa–Polotsk–Vitebsk–Orsha–Mogilev–Zhlobin all the way
to Gomel–Chernigov–Kremenchug.[15] Simultaneously, troops of Twenty-
fourth and Twenty-eighth Armies were establishing a second line of defence
further east, along the line Nelidovo–Dorogobuzh–Bryansk, to make sure that

---

[12] Šechovcov, 'Sovetskoe strategičeskoe rukovodstvo', 48–9.
[13] Zacharov, *Načal'nyj period*, 9.   [14] Dorofeev, 'O nekotorych pričinach', 32 ff.
[15] Panov and Naumov, 'Vosstanovlenie strategičeskogo fronta', 15 ff.

a breakthrough in the direction of Moscow could be contained in a deeply echeloned defence system. Whereas by the end of June 1941 the Germans had crossed the Dvina and taken Pskov on 9 July, the Dysna–Zhlobin line was in fact partially held until 10 July by units of the Western Front now amalgamated with reserve armies. The former commander of that Front, Army General Pavlov, had been replaced by Marshal of the Soviet Union Timoshenko. In the sector of the South-west Front the Russians also succeeded, until 10 July 1941, in temporarily halting the German thrust towards Kiev with counter-attacks by units of IX, XXII, and XIX Mechanized Corps at Novgorod Volynskiy and with units of XV, IV, and XVI Mechanized Corps at Zhitomir and Berdichev.

Nevertheless, by 10 July the German armies and armoured groups had penetrated Soviet territory to a depth of 450–500 km. in the north-western sector, 450–600 km. in the western sector, and of 300–50 km. in the south-western sector. The Germans had occupied Lithuania, Latvia, the major part of Estonia and Belorussia, substantial areas of the Ukraine, and, after 1 July 1941, also attacked parts of the Moldavian SSR from Romania. Since 29 June 1941 the Soviet armies of the Northern Front had also been compelled to retreat in the face of German and Finnish attacks on Murmansk and into Karelia. Between 22 June and 10 July 1941 the Soviet forces suffered enormous losses of men and material. The extent of these losses is deliberately passed over in silence in the Soviet literature. Marshal Grechko nevertheless conveys an approximate idea when he writes that no fewer than 28 Soviet divisions had been totally annihilated within a span of three weeks, with a further 70 divisions losing more than 50 per cent of their personnel and equipment.

2. The Reorganization of the Supreme Command

The difficult situation in which the Red Army forces found themselves owing to the headlong advance of the Germans and their allies during the first few days of the war called for an immediate reorganization of Soviet strategic leadership.[16] Most important of all was the creation of a unified supreme command authority, capable of checking the signs of disintegration in all sectors of the front and of initiating and co-ordinating the necessary countermeasures. As the People's Commissariat for Defence and the general staff in their existing structure were not up to these tasks, the Politburo of the Central Committee of the VKP(b) on 23 June 1941 approved a proposal of the Council of People's Commissars of the USSR for the establishment of a Headquarters of the High Command of the Armed Forces (Stavka glavnogo komandovanija).[17] Under the chairmanship of the People's Commissar for Defence, Timoshenko, it included Stalin, Molotov, the Marshals of the Soviet Union Voroshilov and Budennyy, and Admiral Kuznetsov. This body, how-

---

[16] Štemenko, *General'nyj štab*, i. 30–1.
[17] Žukov, 'Voenačal'niki vspominajut' in *VIŽ* (1970), No. 5, p. 52.

ever, was unable to operate satisfactorily, since without Stalin's approval Timoshenko could not take any fundamental decisions. For this reason the Headquarters of the High Command, the supreme strategic control body, was transformed on 10 July 1941 into the Headquarters of the High Command (Stavka verchovnogo komandovanija) under the direct control of Stalin,[18] who since 19 July 1941 had additionally held the post of a People's Commissar for Defence, and since 8 August that of Supreme Commander. With his simultaneous chairmanship of the State Defence Committee he therefore held unlimited power. On 8 August 1941 the leading body was officially designated 'Headquarters of the Supreme High Command', more accurately, 'Headquarters of the Command of the Supreme Commander', shortened as 'Supreme Command Headquarters' (Stavka verchovnogo glavnokomandovanija). The body used by these headquarters for the preparation and execution of its plans was the general staff, initially under Army General Zhukov and from 29 July 1941 under Marshal of the Soviet Union Shaposhnikov;[19] this underwent repeated restructuring. The general staff, working on the basis of Headquarters decisions, drafted directives to the troops, assigned operational and strategic tasks to the commanding generals of the 'fronts' and armies, verified the implementation of Headquarters orders, assembled strategic reserves, and ensured that the lessons of war were learnt, that the troops were trained for wartime conditions, and that they were adequately supplied with weapons and equipment. To facilitate strategic control and co-ordinate the activities of the fronts, three higher commands were set up on 10 July 1941 for the principal strategic directions: the North-west Sector (or North-western Direction) Command under Marshal of the Soviet Union Voroshilov (covering the Northern Front, the North-west Front, and the Red Banner Baltic Fleet), the Western Sector Command under Marshal of the Soviet Union Timoshenko (the Western Front), and the South-west Sector Command under Marshal of the Soviet Union Budennyy (the South-west Front, the Southern Front, and the Black Sea Fleet). The establishment of these commands for the strategic sectors, i.e. of command levels between Headquarters and the front commands, did not, however, prove a success: for one thing, they lacked the forces and means for independent action, and, for another, Headquarters continued to issue direct orders to the fronts. In 1942, therefore, the commands of the strategic sectors or directions were again abolished, and co-ordination of operations by different fronts was accomplished by the appointment of Stavka (Headquarters) plenipotentiaries whenever necessary.

The establishment of a Supreme Command Headquarters also entailed a reorganization of the People's Commissariat for Defence, which had acquired a different significance under war conditions. A number of departments, such as the Chief Directorate for Raising and Replenishing Red Army Troops, the Chief Directorate for Defence Construction, and some others, were newly

---

[18] Vasilevskij, *Delo vsej žizni*, 123.   [19] Kulikov, 'Strategičeskoe rukovodstvo', 14.

created, and other departments, already in existence—such as the Directorate of Red Army Intelligence—were raised to the rank of chief directorates. Intelligence was generally in such a desolate state that the People's Commissar for Intelligence, Peresypkin, also assumed the duties of Head of the Chief Directorate of Red Army Intelligence.[20] There was a tendency to appoint to the top positions of the chief directorates of the commissariats, of army services, and of specialized branches persons with an extended decision-making authority. The post of Chief of Red Army Artillery was revived; the Chief Directorate of Artillery in the People's Commissariat came under him. There was a Chief of Engineering Troops and a Chief of Guards Mortar Troops. Guards mortars or rocket mortars were the BM-13 salvo-launchers, also known as 'Katyushas' or 'Stalin organ-pipes'. These first went into action at Orsha on 14 July. Simultaneously the post of Commander of Red Army Air Forces was created, and the air-force staff now detached from the Chief Directorate of Air Forces in the People's Commissariat placed under his command. The troops of the country's air defences were placed under a separate commander and, for this purpose, removed from the direct control of military districts and fronts. The airborne troops were also given an independent commander. The Red Army's rear-area organization was also completely restructured. Lieutenant-General Khrulev of the administrative branch was appointed Chief of Rear Areas and of Rear Services with extensive full powers, and simultaneously placed in charge of the newly created Chief Directorate of Rear Areas.[21] Security in the rear areas against plots by the enemy or by anti-Soviet resistance activists was entrusted to the special troops of the People's Commissariat of the Interior (NKVD).

It was not only the central command apparatus of the Soviet forces that underwent fundamental reorganization. The grave setbacks of the initial phase of the war also called for changes in the organization of the field army. The price was now being paid for the liquidation by Stalin of the most experienced military leaders and his lack of interest in the development of suitable means of communication. The front commands were not up to their tasks; the fronts, therefore, had to be reduced in size and their number increased. In December 1941, instead of the earlier five, there now existed nine active Fronts: Karelian Front, Leningrad Front, Volkhov Front, North-west Front, Kalinin Front, Western Front, South-west Front, Southern Front, and Transcaucasus Front. In July 1941 the lack of senior officers and communications equipment and the heavy losses of artillery pieces and engineering material were major reasons for the abolition of the rifle corps as intermediate command levels between armies and divisions. This, however, did not overcome the difficulties in the communication field.[22] Most of the rifle divisions were thenceforth placed directly

[20] Peresypkin, 'Vojska svjazi', 36 ff.; id., 'Svjaz' General'nogo štaba', 19 ff.

[21] Chrulev, 'Stanovlenie strategičeskogo tyla'; Goluško, 'Tyl Sovetskich vooružennych sil', 33-4.

[22] Malan'in, 'Razvitie organizacionnych form', 30.

under the armies, whose number was simultaneously increased. A beginning was also made in the process of considerably reducing the combat strength of rifle divisions; the personnel and material thereby released served to establish new units. The mechanized corps, set up as recently as July 1940 on the basis of the lessons of the German campaign in France, had similarly to be abolished 'to facilitate command' and also because of a lack of tanks and motor-vehicles. In their place armoured divisions with a reduced number of tanks were established, as well as armoured brigades and tank battalions. To increase the manœuvrability of the Soviet forces a large number of smaller cavalry divisions were set up, even though the disadvantages of cavalry formations in modern war were being fully realized. The rapid advance of the German forces into the interior of the country urgently demanded an intensified construction of fortifications and defensive positions. To this end no fewer than nine independent engineering armies were created by the end of the year under the new Chief Directorate for Defence Construction. In the big cities, such as Moscow, Leningrad, Smolensk, Kiev, Odessa, and Sevastopol, detachments composed of civilians were created under the old title of 'narodnoe opolchenie' [People's Army, used in 1812].

Apart from the reorganization of the Soviet fighting forces, Headquarters turned its particular attention to efforts to replace the enormous losses suffered at the front by raising immediate strategic reserves in the interior of the country. Under the mobilization decree of the Supreme Soviet Praesidium of 22 June 1941 all persons of the 1905–18 classes liable for active service were called to the colours in the military districts—with the exception of the Central Asian, the Trans-Baikal, and the Far Eastern Military Districts. All male Soviet citizens from 16 to 50 who were not yet called up were, under special resolutions of the State Committee for Defence, obliged to undergo premilitary training; this was to ensure a sufficient pool of military manpower.[23] Although there was probably a sufficient supply of men fit for active service, a painful shortage of qualified officers soon emerged. This was only partly mitigated by the call-up of 65,000 reserve officers. In order to meet the vast officer requirements of the Red Army and the Red Fleet, the training period in the military academies and officers' schools had to be cut drastically. The state of training, especially of subalterns, many of whom had only attended three or four months of improvised courses, soon turned out to be inadequate. Even though the establishment of new units was causing great difficulties because of the continuing shortage of officers, it was nevertheless possible, between 22 June and 31 December 1941, to raise no fewer than 286 new rifle divisions (including 24 'People's Army' divisions), 22 further rifle divisions formed from other service branches, 159 rifle brigades, and a large number of artillery regiments, independent armoured brigades, and tank battalions.[24] During that period some of the forces—altogether 97 divisions—

[23] *50 let vooružennych sil*, 266.
[24] Kravcov, 'Krach nemecko-fašistskogo plana "Barbarossa"', 44.

were also withdrawn from heartland military districts, the Far East, Transcaucasia, and Central Asia and transferred to the European theatre of war. The newly established units, and those brought in from the eastern and southern parts of the USSR, were intended primarily to shore up the tottering front lines, build up deeply echeloned defences along the threatened sectors, and create some reserves for counter-attacks (at that time still limited). Simultaneously, Headquarters began, under conditions of greatest secrecy in the interior of the country, to establish reserve armies which, at the right time, would launch a counter-offensive. This was entirely in line with the demands made in the past by Tukhachevskiy and others.[25] The Headquarters reserves also included cannon and howitzer regiments, anti-tank regiments formed to replace the cumbersome anti-tank brigades, guards mortar regiments and battalions, communication troops, and other specialized units and independent detachments. These reserves partly consisted of forces which, like the artillery regiments of the dissolved corps, had been eliminated from the front-line troops. Bomber and fighter units also had their fleets of aircraft reduced, to allow the forces thus freed to be used for independent missions. The immediate formation of extensive strategic reserves[26] regardless of the difficult situation at the fronts certainly testifies to the far-sightedness of Headquarters and was to bear fruit even before the end of the year.

3. The 'Fatherland War': Fight against Disintegration Mobilization of Material and Manpower Reserves

On 22 June 1941 there occurred more than the immediate break-up of cohesion between the Soviet forces deployed on the country's western frontier. The accepted theory of war, according to which the sole task of the forces of the Red Army was to attack a potential aggressor and, after the annihilation of the enemy forces, carry the war into the territory of the opponent, had also been completely discredited. Soon after the opening of the German attack, Red Army officers and headquarter staffs at all levels, up to the command agencies of the general staff and the People's Commissariat for Defence, were in a state of almost total disruption.[27] As for the troops which had to stand up to the assault of the enemy, there were countless instances of stubborn resistance and self-sacrificing gallantry. The Germans soon discovered that they were facing a different adversary from the kind they had met in earlier campaigns. The overwhelming impression during the first few weeks and months of the war, however, was not so much of the combat performance of the individual Soviet soldier as of a determination which acquired colossal scale. For years the main emphasis in the political training of every Red Army man had been on turning him into 'a fighter boundlessly devoted to his socialist homeland', on injecting

---

[25] *Voprosy strategii*, 79, 346 ff.   [26] Zemskov, 'Nekotorye voprosy', 14.
[27] *Istorija Velikoj Otečestvennoj vojny*, ii. 49–50; Nekritsch and Grigorenko, *Genickschuß*, 279.

him with a 'sense of high responsibility . . . for the task entrusted to him in the defence of his socialist homeland', 'Soviet patriotism', 'high morale, outstanding perseverance, valour, and heroism'. Every Soviet soldier had been conditioned, in fulfiment of his 'sacred duty to defend his socialist fatherland', to fight to the last round, to his last drop of blood.[28] He had to be victorious or die, there was no intermediate. Even Red Army men no longer fit for combat were forbidden, by Article 58 of the Criminal Code (*Ugolovnyj kodeks*) of the RSFSR and by other regulations for service within the country, to let themselves be taken prisoner by the enemy.[29] Being taken prisoner always counted as desertion and treason; the Red Army was the only force in the world which had made such action severely punishable. Thus, after the Soviet–Finnish war of 1939–40 all Red Army men who had fallen into enemy hands were, on their return from captivity, deported under strict guard and were never seen again. After the Second World War all Red Army military personnel who had been prisoners of war in Germany were similarly regarded as enemies of the people and traitors to their country, regardless of whether they had gone into captivity of their own free will or, like Major Gavrilov, the defender of the citadel of Brest, fallen into enemy hands severely wounded and incapable of combat. All of them without exception disappeared in concentration camps after the war or underwent serious harassment.[30] As the Soviet state found it impossible to accept that Revolutionary soldiers of the Workers' and Peasants' Red Army would surrender to the class enemy, the Soviet government as early as 1917 no longer regarded itself as a signatory of the Hague Convention on Land Warfare, and in 1929 refused to sign the Geneva Convention for the Protection of Prionsers of War. As a matter of principle it took no interest in the fate of its servicemen in enemy hands; indeed there is evidence that it not only omitted to do anything that might have alleviated the situation of these prisoners, but whenever possible endeavoured, through agents in the POW camps, to make their lot even harder by provoking reprisals by the detaining power.[31]

It is against the background of this fundamental attitude to its prisoners of war that the Soviet government's note of 17 July 1941 should be viewed. In that note it announced that, on condition of reciprocity, it would consider itself bound by the rules of the Hague Convention. But what interest could the Soviet government have had in ensuring the protection and privileges of the 1907 Hague Convention for Soviet servicemen in enemy captivity when, at the same time, it had given orders that they were to be 'annihilated with all means' as 'deserters' and 'traitors'. As Tolstoy correctly observes, 'this "offer"

[28] *Istorija Velikoj Otečestvennoj vojny*, i. 465–6; Nekritsch and Grigorenko, *Genickschuß*, 244.

[29] Text of Article 58 in Fricke, *Politik und Justiz in der DDR*, 106 ff. See Solzhenytsin, *The Gulag Archipelago*, 235; Popel', *Tanki*, 395–6; Hoffmann, *Deutsche und Kalmyken*, 86; id., *Ostlegionen*, 77; id., *Wlassow-Armee*, 129 ff.

[30] Reitlinger, *Haus auf Sand gebaut*, 115–16; Ehrenburg, *People and Life*, vi. 91.

[31] Pozdnjakov, 'Sovetskaja agentura'.

was patently a blind'. This is, further confirmed by the fact that the Soviet government refused to implement the most important provision of that convention and, despite repeated demands both from the International Red Cross and the Axis powers, as well as from the Western powers, never reverted to the issue. Red Cross representatives, who ceaselessly tried to visit Moscow in person to clear up assumed differences of opinion, were, regardless of their distinguished supporters, invariably refused entry.[32]

To judge by official records, the fighting forces of the Soviet Union at the beginning of the German–Soviet war were imbued with self-confidence and regarded themselves as invincible. The myth of the unshakeable morale of the Soviet warriors and their invincibility later continued to be a solid component of Soviet historiography of the 'Great Fatherland War'. 'The forces of the Red Army and Fleet', a history of the armed forces published on their fiftieth anniversary still maintained, 'were tempered like steel in a moral and political respect, and boundlessly devoted to their socialist homeland.'[33] In actual fact, despite all political indoctrination and the threat of punishment, millions of Red Army men, including members of the Communist Party, ceased to resist even during the first few months of the war. The officers, political officials, and troops of the Red Army, manœuvred as they had been by their leaders into a hopeless situation, swept into the vortex of disorganized retreat, and, worn down in battles of encirclement, frequently no longer thought of resistance but surrendered in vast numbers.

That, given the Soviet doctrine, was a monstrous occurrence. It triggered special measures on the part of the Soviet leadership, which—though largely passed over in silence in the Soviet literature—call for discussion in detail. Papers captured by the German troops throw light on the Soviet reaction. An eloquent document in this respect is Order No. 001919, issued on 16 July 1941 by Supreme Command Headquarters and signed by Stalin, as People's Commissar for the Defence of the USSR, and Marshal Shaposhnikov, chief of the Red Army General Staff.[34] This stated: 'On all fronts there are numerous elements which actually run up to meet the enemy, and on the first contact throw down their weapons, drawing others with them . . . while the number of

[32] Tolstoy, *Victims of Yalta*, 33 ff., 438; Hoffmann, *Wlassow-Armee*, 135 ff. The assertion by Streit, *Keine Kameraden*, 225 ff., that the Soviet government had genuinely tried to make the Hague Convention the basis of the treatment of prisoners of war and 'to base the treatment of prisoners on both sides on principles of humanity', and that these efforts had failed solely because of Germany's refusal, reveals ignorance of the true state of affairs and a misreading of the methods of Stalinism. The fact that the Soviet government was never really interested in keeping to the conventions on prisoners of war is unambiguously proved by the *Rapport du Comité International de la Croix-Rouge*, i. 419–53 (esp. pp. 422–3, 436, 440–3, 446–8, 453). See also Dallin, *German Rule*, 420. This fact cannot be expunged by the quotation of German documents which have long been known. For a total misinterpretation of the Soviet Note of 17 July 1941 see also Jacobsen, 'Kommissarbefehl', 192–3, and Streim, *Die Behandlung sowjetischer Kriegsgefangener*, 33–4. See also Harriman to Byrnes, 11 June 1945, *FRUS* (1945), v. 1097.

[33] *50 let vooruzhennych sil*, 246.

[34] Order of Supreme Command Headquarters No. 001919, 16 July 1941, BA-MA RW 4/v. 329.

steadfast commanders and commissars is not very great.' Order No. 0116 of the Political Directorate of the North-west Front, of 20 July 1941,[35] drew attention to a directive issued on 15 July by Stalin and the head of the Political Chief Directorate of the Red Army, Army Commissar (1st rank) Mekhlis, to the effect that 'among the persons called up in the western regions of the Ukraine and Belorussia, as well as among the persons called up in Moldavia, the Bukovina, and the Baltic regions, a large number of traitors has been found to exist.' This was confirmed also by the testimony of General Romanov, the captured commander of 172nd Rifle Division.[36]

Particularly alarming was the fact that the collapse of morale was evident even among political activists or the Communists in the forces. Directive No. 81 of Army Commissar Mekhlis, dated 15 July 1941,[37] contained the following passage

Many members of the political agencies and deputies of commanding officers prefer to lounge about at headquarters, rarely visit their units, scarcely attempt to combat instances of unsatisfactory organization, confusion, panic, and indiscipline, or fight the criminal decline in vigilance. Not infrequently members of the Communist Party and the Komsomol [Communist Youth Organization] fail to provide examples of steadfastness in battle or to take steps against panic-mongers, cowards, or deserters.

Marshal of the Soviet Union Budennyy, GOC Troops of the South-western Direction, similarly stated in his Order No. 5 of 16 July 1941 that it had 'frequently' happened 'that commanding officers and political functionaries are forgetting their sacred duty towards the fatherland and vilely breaking their oath'. The practical effects of the demoralization of the forces is revealed also in documents from the South-west Front, consisting of Fifth, Thirty-seventh, Twenty-sixth, Thirty-eighth, and Fortieth Armies. According to a statement of losses compiled by Major-General Tupikov, Head of the Chief Directorate for the Raising and Replenishment of Red Army Troops,[38] the South-west Front reported 726 soldiers taken prisoner between 22 June and 31 August 1941. A further 80,205, however, were recorded as missing in action—in other words they too had been separated from their units and had, for the most part, fallen into German hands. It is significant that, in addition to those losses and the figures of men killed, wounded, and sick, there were 14,593 men reported missing 'for other reasons'. It would probably be correct to assume that these soldiers had been shot or at least arrested by the blocking units set up in the meantime or by NKVD troops. During the same period the troops of the

[35] Order of the Political Directorate of the North-west Front No. 0116 (Directive of the People's Commissar for War, Stalin), 20 July 1941, ibid.

[36] Interrogation of the Russian Gen. Mikhail Timofeevich Romanov, Army Group Centre, Ic/AO, 6 Oct. 1941, BA-MA RH 19 II/123.

[37] Directive of Army Commissar Mekhlis No. 81, 15 July 1941, BA-MA RW 4/v. 329; Order No. 5 of Marshal Budennyy, GOC South-western Direction, 16 July 1941, BA-MA RH 24-3/134.

[38] Staff of the South-west Front to Head of the Chief Directorate for Replenishment and Raising of the Red Army, BA-MA RH 19 II/123, fos. 214–17.

South-west Front captured only 62 German officers and 626 NCOs and men. The 'Order to the Troops of the South-west Front', No. 41,[39] signed by Colonel-General Kirponos, GOC South-west Front, by Major-General Tupikov, its chief of staff, and by Member of the War Council Burmistenko, complained that officers and commissars did not act with appropriate severity in the 'shameful instances of desertion or absence without leave from their units'. During the period 10–20 August 1941 the 289th Rifle Division alone reported 76.9 per cent of its personnel missing; in 264th Rifle Division the figure was 74.6 per cent, and in 160th Rifle Division 70.2 per cent. 'Even more alarming' was the fact that among those missing from 289th and 227th Rifle Divisions were 189 and 50 officers respectively. According to a report by the commander of the NKVD troops in the rear area of the South-west Front,[40] 18,156 men of Fifth Army, 7,376 men of Twenty-sixth Army (including 31 senior and 224 other officers), 968 men of Thirty-seventh Army (including 36 officers), 796 men of Thirty-eighth Army, and 513 men of Sixth Army (including 1 senior and 21 other officers) were 'detained' between 5 July and 1 September 1941. Report No. 00134 of the War Council of Lieutenant-General Kostenko's Twenty-sixth Army, dated 16 September 1941 and addressed to the War Council of the South-west Front,[41] similarly referred to disproportionate losses 'not justified by combat operations' in its 301st Rifle Division; these were due to 'runaways', 'deserters', and 'traitors to the fatherland'. Among men whose homes were on the western side of the Dnieper there had been a downright 'mass mood imbued with a wish not to fight but . . . to run off home. The same mood was observed also among some . . . of the reserve officers.' Although Colonel Sokolov, the divisional commander, and Regimental Commissar Nikolaev, the divisional commissar, had been given a 'final warning', and although a number of unit commanders, officers, and commissars had been executed by firing-squad or otherwise punished, the War Council found itself compelled to report that, because of the collapse of the men's morale, the division was 'not fit for action at the present moment'.

In order to stem this spreading disintegration, which was threatening to paralyse the striking power of the Red Army, an attempt was made to intensify political propaganda through a reorganization of the party-political apparatus in the forces. As was first done on 8 May 1937, at the time of the great purge, a separation of command was introduced. To this end the military command posts, i.e. the unit commanders at all levels, were stripped of their political duties and the entire party-political guidance of the forces placed in the hands of war commissars, reintroduced into the Red Army on 16 July 1941 and into the Soviet navy on 20 July 1941. In all corps, divisions, regiments, staffs, military training establishments, and other armed-forces institutions the war commissars, abolished as recently as 12 August 1940, were reintroduced, and in all companies, batteries, and squadrons political guides, were reintroduced

[39] Ibid., fo. 220.   [40] Report of the commander of NKVD troops, ibid., fo. 221.
[41] Ibid., fo. 223.

with the same functions. There were war commissars also in the technical sections of tank battalions and artillery battalions, and in the battalions of rifle divisions from December 1941. Although the Soviet interpretation of this reorganization of the Party apparatus describes it as 'an extraordinary measure made necessary by specific and complex circumstances', it firmly disputes that it was due to any kind of 'mistrust of the officers in the forces'.[42] The demand for 'amicable co-operation between unit commander and commissar in strengthening the combat capacity of the troops' did not, however, prevent numerous difficulties from arising—as indeed had been the case between 1937 and 1940.[43] Even though 'any supervision of the unit commanders' activities by the commissars, as practised during the period of foreign military intervention and the civil war, [was to be] totally ruled out', the work of the commissars and politruks [political-guidance officers], in line with Lenin's demands, was bound to amount in practice to supervision. In point of fact, a divisional commander could not, even in operational and tactical matters, make a decision on his own. Orders by a unit commander not countersigned by a commissar—who represented the 'Party and government within the Red Army'—were invalid. Orders by a commissar, on the other hand, were valid even without the counter-signature of the unit commander and had to be obeyed. Alongside the commissar, the head of the Special NKVD Detachment also enjoyed unlimited authority. He was entitled to be present at all official discussions and have access to all files, he had his confidants everywhere, and he could detain any officer—including the divisional commander—or soldier and order him to be shot.[44] 'The NKVD is a terrible body which can destroy any of us at any moment,' declared General Muzychenko, GOC Sixth Army, captured near Uman.[45] This also explains the statement made under interrogation by Lieutenant-General Lukin, the captured GOC Nineteenth Army, who, on the basis of his personal experience, stated than an army commander was no longer capable 'of any independent step. He is surrounded by commissars, narks, and his War Council . . . Even generals are spied upon by narks, the regimental commanders too, etc.' If any proof were needed that the real reason for the reorganization of the Red Army was mistrust, then this is supplied by the text of the orders of the People's Commissar for Defence and

[42] Petrov, *Stroitel'stvo politorganov*, 288.

[43] H.Gr. Nord, Feindnachrichten [A.Gp. North, enemy intelligence], 28 Aug.–7 Oct. 1939, BA-MA RH 19 II/15.

[44] Interrogation of officers (deserters) Ivan Nikitovich Kononov, major commanding 436th Rifle Regt. . . . , AOK 4, Ic/AO No. 549/41 geh., 6 Sept. 1941, BA-MA RH 22/271. The Special Detachments of the NKVD were formed in mid-July 1941 from the agencies of military counterespionage of the People's Commissariat for Defence (organy voennoj kontrrazvedki NKO). The importance of the Special Detachments was reflected also in the ranks of their personnel. Thus a lieutenant of state security (gosbezopasnosti) corresponded to a captain, a senior lieutenant of state security to a major, a captain of state security to a colonel, a major of state security to a major-general, a senior major of state security to a lieutenant-general, and a commissar of state security to a colonel-general: Belousov, *Zapiski armejskogo čekista*, 35.

[45] Interrogation of the commander of the Russian Sixth Army, H.Gr. Süd/Ic, 9 Aug. 1941, 8, BA-MA, H.Gr. Süd, 17664/46.

other senior command authorities, as well as by the fact that it was necessary to take the most severe reprisals against military commanders all the way up to general officers commanding armies.

The re-establishment of the Institute of War Commissars and Political Guides and, on 17 July 1941, the simultaneous reorganization of the former Chief Directorate for Political Propaganda into a Political Chief Directorate of the Workers' and Peasants' Red Army under Mekhlis, the creation of Political Directorates at front level, and of Political Departments at army, corps, and divisional level, gave rise to the development of 'mass political propaganda' by way of talks, lectures, lessons, and 'meetings' in the units. This, however, was only one aspect of the programme for the consolidation of the fighting morale of the Red Army. Another aspect was the Draconian severity, which it was hoped would have a deterrent effect. In his speech of 3 July 1941 Stalin had proclaimed a 'merciless fight' against all 'disorganizers of the hinterland, deserters, panic-mongers, and disseminators of rumours'.[46] This was followed by a whole string of orders and directives implementing his demands. Marshal of the Soviet Union Budennyy, for instance, in his Order No. 5 of 16 July demanded that such elements be 'liquidated on the spot . . . To settle accounts with cowards, panic-mongers, and deserters and to restore discipline is our most sacred duty.'

The directive of Stalin and Mekhlis dated 15 July 1941 (see above at n. 35) ordered that all units should be purged of unreliable elements. Particular distrust was henceforth focused on those Soviet 'officers, political guides, and Red Army men' whose units had been encircled and routed at the front and who, instead of taking advantage of the situation and allowing themselves to be taken prisoner, had fought their way back to their own forces from behind enemy lines, often exposed to hardship and danger. In order to prevent 'spies and White Guardists penetrating into command personnel escaping from some encirclement', these men were subjected to strict checks by the Special Detachments of the NKVD. According to Major-General Grigorenko,[47] these 'encirclees' were 'welcomed with an execution order . . . by way of settling accounts with the traitors who had opened the front to the enemy':

Those shot included soldiers and officers, members of the supply services, infantry-men, airmen who had lost their machines, tank crews who had miraculously saved themselves from their blazing tanks, and gunners who had personally dragged their already useless artillery pieces without ammunition for hundreds of kilometres. And the following day those who shot them dead might find themselves in an enemy pocket and could expect the same fate as the men they executed the day before.

Only the absence of a cohesive front and the collapse of systematic leadership, according to Grigorenko, had saved 'hundreds of thousands' from senseless mass extermination. To support the NKVD troops in the performance of such

---

[46] Stalin, *Großer Vaterländischer Krieg*, 10, 12.
[47] Nekritsch and Grigorenko, *Genickschuß*, 280.

tasks, Order No. 001919 of Supreme Command Headquarters, dated 16 July 1941, envisaged the establishment within each division of so-called blocking detachments of especially reliable officers, political officials, and soldiers in battalion strength.[48] The blocking detachments were employed in the rear of the divisions, roughly along the line of the artillery positions, with orders to prevent by force of arms any unauthorized retreat of front-line troops and to shoot all cowards and deserters trying to escape from the battle. On 14 July 1941 Headquarters had, moreover, notified all generals commanding the fronts, as well as all officers, political officials, and troops, that loss of a weapon on the battlefield represented a serious violation of the military oath and would be punished accodingly.

Mistrust,[49] combined with an attempt to conceal the real reasons and his own responsibility for the collapse of the fronts, had induced Stalin ever since early July 1941 to make an example of the Western Front, encircled at Bialystok and Minsk and by then largely shattered. On his instruction Army General Pavlov, GOC western Front, together with General Klimovskikh, its chief of staff, General Semenov, chief of the operations department, General Grigoryev, commanding the communications troops, General Klich, the artillery commander, and other generals on the staff of the front, were tried by court martial, sentenced to death, and shot.[50] It seems that Zhukov, chief of the Red Army General Staff, who had a share in the responsibility for the desolate situation of the Western Front, was not entirely unconnected with this. Elsewhere too senior field officers were 'accused of treason and physically liquidated'[51] because of alleged mistakes 'which sometimes were not even matters within their power'. This applied Major-General Korobkov, GOC Fourth Army of the Western Front, Major-General Kosobutskiy, commanding the 41st Rifle Corps of the North-west Front, Major-General Selikhov, commanding 60th Mountain Rifle Division of the Southern Front, Major-General Galaktionov, commanding 30th Rifle Division, and other senior officers.[52] Lieutenant-General Rychagov, Head of the Chief Directorate of the Red Army Air Forces, was shot because, quite unjustly he was held solely responsible for the heavy losses of aircraft at the beginning of the war.[53] The reprisals, initially still somewhat arbitrary, were given a solid basis by Order No. 270 of Supreme Command Headquarters, dated 16 August 1941,[54] which was notified down to company level and equivalent units, and read out to all

[48] On the establishment of blocking detachments in the divisions see Order to Nineteenth Army Troops No. 04/00378, 15 Sept. 1941, BA-MA RW 4/v. 329.

[49] Štemenko, *General'nyj štab*, i. 31.   [50] Zhukov, *Reminiscences*, 260.

[51] *Geschichte des Großen Vaterländischen Krieges*, ii. 57. This statement is missing from the original Russian text: *Istorija Velikoj Otečestvennoj vojny*, ii. 50.

[52] Namen und Dienststellung der bis Oktober 1941 gefangenen, gefallenen und erschossenen sowjetischen Generale [Names and posts of Soviet generals captured, killed in action, or executed up to Oct. 1941], OKH/Fremde Heere Ost, BA-MA H 3/152.

[53] Conquest, *Great Terror*, 489.

[54] Order of Supreme Command Headquarters of the Red Army No. 270, 16 Aug. 1941, BA-MA H-3/152; Buchbender, *Das tönende Erz*, 295–6.

Red Army servicemen. This fateful document, signed by Stalin in his capacity of Chairman of the State Defence Committee, by Molotov as his deputy, and by Marshals of the Soviet Union Budennyy, Voroshilov, Timoshenko, Shaposhnikov, and Army General Zhukov deserves special attention as an indication of the thinking and methods of the Soviet leadership. In it Lieutenant-General Kachalov, GOC Twenty-eighth Army of the Western Front, Lieutenant-General Ponedelin, GOC Twelfth Army of the South-west Front, and Major-General Kirillov, commanding the 13th Rifle Corps, were branded cowards, renegades, and criminals for having been encircled by the Germans and, together with some of their troops, taken prisoner. As for Lieutenant-General Kachalov, there was not the slightest doubt in Moscow that he had in fact been killed in action near Roslavl. His memory was merely besmirched for the sake of political capital.[55] The members of the War Council, the political officers, and the members of the Special NKVD Detachments, who had made no attempt to prevent the capture of the commanding officers or their units, were themselves accused of 'despicable cowardice' for 'displaying unallowed dejection'. An end was to be put to such a state of affairs: all 'cowards and deserters' were to be liquidated in future. All members of the Red Army were once more enjoined to 'fight self-sacrificingly to the last possible moment' in all conditions, and especially in encirclement; 'officers and political officials ripping off their insignia of rank in battle and escaping to the rear, or surrendering to the enemy' were to be 'shot on the spot' as 'wicked deserters' and 'traitors to the fatherland'. Henceforward superiors had to watch their subordinates closely, and subordinates their superiors; every one of them was obliged 'to liquidate by every means on the ground or from the air' any Soviet servicemen who preferred going into captivity. There was no shrinking even from the most extreme measures in the struggle against disintegration: this was made clear by Order No. 270, which threatened to hold culprits' families responsible. Accordingly, the families of officers and politicalofficials who had become prisoners of war were to be arrested as 'next-of-kin of deserters'; families of Red Army men in captivity were to lose all state support or assistance. The rigorous manner in which these rules were applied is shown by Order No. 0098 of 5 October 1941, addressed to the troops of the Leningrad Front.[56] Basing itself on Article 58, section 1, of the Penal Code of the RSFSR, it threatened Red Army men that, if they went into enemy captivity, the members of their families would be arrested and handed over to the courts. Application of the principle of family liability emerges also from captured documents of the Chief Military Prosecutor's Office of the USSR.[57]

Despite the Draconian countermeasures, there was no stopping a further growth in the number of prisoners of war. In the encirclement battles of

---

[55] Lewytzkyj, *Die rote Inquisition*, 195–6.   [56] BA-MA H 3/152.
[57] Glavnaja Voennaja Prokuratura (Voennyj jurist 1. ranga Vraskoj) to Voennomu Prokuratoru 54 Armii No. 08683, 15 Dec. 1941, BA-MA RW 2/v. 158, fos. 110 ff.

Bialystok, Minsk, Smolensk, Uman, Kiev, Bryansk, and Vyazma alone, i.e. up to 18 October 1941, some 2,053,000 Soviet soldiers had been taken prisoner. Altogether, some 1.5 million Red Army men had surrendered by mid-August 1941, and over 3 million by mid-October 1941—almost ten times the figure of 378,000 men missing in action admitted by Stalin in his speech on 6 November 1941, on the eve of the twenty-fourth anniversary of the October Revolution.[58] By the end of 1941 some 3.8 million Soviet servicemen had fallen into German hands,[59] and by the end of the war the total was approximately 5.25 million, an order of magnitude indirectly confirmed by the Party daily *Pravda*.[60] Even as late as 1944–45 one in every sixteen Soviet prisoners of war was a deserter, whereas during the same period 4,692 American, British, or French soldiers had to be captured before a single deserter was found. In other words, there were 330 Soviet deserters to every one deserter from the armies of the Western powers. As for the German side, in December 1941 it was an 'extremely rare' event, specially mentioned by Marshal of the Soviet Union Yeremenko,[61] that the German Lieutenant Konrad with remnants of his company laid down his arms in a hopeless situation and let himself be taken prisoner. Even that instance was thought to be a sign of a decline of morale among the German troops. The vast number of Soviet servicemen who, in violation of their military duty *vis-à-vis* the Soviet regime, went into German captivity or deserted to the Germans cannot be explained by any concatenation of accidents. It is equally impossible to label 3.8 million generals, officers, political officials, and Red Army soldiers as criminals and traitors. The sheer order of magnitude suggests that there must have been deeper, undoubtedly political, reasons. That there was widespread irritation and dissatisfaction with the regime at the time of the German attack on the Soviet Union was confirmed by the attitude of the civilian population in the parts of the country occupied by German troops. It was, of course, hardly surprising that the overwhelming majority of the population in the recently annexed Baltic States, as well as in the Polish and Romanian territories, continued to feel bitter hostility towards their new government. In those areas the German troops were generally welcomed, and many inhabitants spontaneously offered them their assistance. According to official German estimates, about 75 per cent of Balts and Ukrainians 'sincerely' welcomed the Wehrmacht 'as liberators'.[62] In the old Soviet regions the mood was admittedly more reserved, and there was also, as a rule, a difference between the friendlier rural inhabitants and the rather more pro-Soviet urban population. On the whole, however, the German forces not infrequently met with a benevolent welcome even in the old areas of the Soviet Union, while by contrast the civilian population—as Major Shabalin, Head of the Special Detachment of the NKVD with Fiftieth Army, confided to his

---

[58] Stalin, *Großer Vaterländischer Krieg* 19.
[59] Dallin, *German Rule*, 69, 410–11; Müller, *Wehrmacht und Okkupation*, 177.
[60] *Pravda*, 24 Mar. 1969; on the following see Hoffmann, *Wlassow-Armee*, 131.
[61] Eremenko, 'Nastuplenie', 69.   [62] Buchbender, *Das tönende Erz*, 264.

diary on 12 October 1941[63]—at times was 'not very friendly' to Russian military personnel: 'This will have to be remembered!' A person familiar with the situation, Herwarth von Bittenfeld—formerly legation secretary at the German embassy in Moscow, adjutant during the war to the General of Volunteer Formations, and later ambassador, state secretary, and head of the office of the Federal President—summed up these phenomena as follows:[64]

At the beginning of the eastern campaign the German troops were hailed as liberators by the majority of the Soviet population. The Soviet citizens were in no way afraid of the Germans. The inhabitants remained in their villages and towns, making no attempt to escape from the German invaders. Efforts by the Soviet administration to evacuate the population from areas threatened by the Germans were disregarded, and they mostly ended in failure . . . Orders by the Soviet government to destroy the harvest and all stores were disobeyed. The peasants did all they could to prevent their cattle being driven away. Stalin's order to leave the occupied territories to the Germans as scorched earth were regarded as an act of desperation which only served to intensify hatred of the dictator.

But even if the local population, as occasionally happened, displayed no more than a passive attitude, this still ran counter to the official doctrine. After all, there was the unassailable principle that Soviet society represented a 'moral and political unity', that the nations of the Soviet Union were linked to one another in 'unbreakable friendship', that every Soviet citizen was inspired by 'self-sacrificing patriotism', and that the 'entire Soviet people' was rallying in 'boundless devotion' to the Communist Party.

This instability of domestic conditions in the Soviet Union, as reflected in the behaviour of a large part of Red Army troops and civilians *vis-à-vis* the German invaders, has its explanation in the public's experience of Soviet rule during the Stalin era. Forcible collectivization of agriculture, with its concomitant features of artificially created famines and reprisals, in the course of which millions of farmers denounced as 'kulaks' [wealthy peasants] were driven into misery or, as Stalin stated to Churchill in 1941, 'beaten to death', ruthless industrialization, the paranoia of the great purge, and the ubiquitous system of the NKVD and the concentration camps—all these had left deep scars on the public's memory. Scarcely a family was left untouched.[65] Given that basic attitude, there was little doubt—even in the sceptical judgement of Dallin[66]—that 'a skilful effort to win over the population, civilian or military, to oppose the Soviet regime, could have yielded substantial, and during the first months of the war perhaps decisive, results'. There is evidence that, at the beginning of the war, Stalin feared nothing more than the establishment of a Russian

---

[63] Diary of NKVD Maj. Shabalin, Head of the Special NKVD Detachment with the Fiftieth Army, BA-MA RH 19 II/125.

[64] Herwarth von Bittenfeld, Russian Volunteers, 1 (privately owned).

[65] Lewytzkyj, *Die rote Inquisition*, 111 ff.

[66] Dallin, *German Rule*, 65; see also on the following passages Chol'mston-Smyslovskij, *Izbrannye stat'i*, 16–40.

counter-government on the German side, and hence an immediate transformation of a defensive war against a foreign enemy into a civil war threatening his
regime. The subsequent leaders of General Vlasov's Russian Liberation
Movement, who were exceedingly well informed on the mood and conditions
inside the Soviet Union, invariably emphasized that in that case the foundations of the Red Army and the Soviet state could have been shaken from
within. That Stalin managed fairly soon to overcome this initial insecurity was
due primarily to the fact that, contrary to propaganda statements about an
alleged campaign of liberation, Hitler from the outset waged his war for the
purpose of territorial expansion, colonial oppression, and exploitation, in
order, as he put it, to turn Russia into a 'German India'.[67] Soon the Soviet
government had convincing arguments available to persuade Russians,
Ukrainians, and Belorussians—less so the minorities on the periphery—of the
need for resolute struggle against the foreign invaders. Even at the time of
Stalingrad, when political co-operation with the Russian population had long
become a requirement for the German forces' self-preservation, all a leading
article in the Party daily *Pravda* had to do—as Goebbels himself complained[68]—was to quote from *Deutsche Ukrainische Zeitung* in order to demonstrate the Germans' intentions of exploitation and enslavement.

Disastrous for the reputation of the Germans, even in the first phase of the
war, were the mass murders of the Jewish section of the population by
the special squads of the Security Police and the SD (the security service of the
SS) and the execution of political commissars, who very often represented the
educated element in the Red Army[69] and whose duties included the welfare of
Red Army men, as well as, more particularly, mitigation of the inhuman
conditions in which Soviet soldiers in German captivity were kept. As early as
21 October and 2 December 1941 the quartermaster-general in the Army
General Staff had laid down, for 'all Russian prisoners of war in the occupied
Russian territory, including the region of Wehrmacht commanders Ukraine
and Ostland, in the Government-General, in Norway, and in Romania', food
rations at an entirely adequate level;[70] it seems, however, that these rations—
if only because of the collapse of the transport system in the east—were not in
fact issued, except in rare cases. There is evidence that they were issued in the
Crimea and the army rear-area North. There is no doubt that the fate of the
prisoners of war was at times exacerbated by political blindness and human
indifference. Certainly the fact that, during autumn and winter 1941–2, an

---

[67] Picker, *Hitler's Table Talk*, 24.   [68] *The Secret Conferences of Dr. Goebbels*, 319.

[69] Interrogation of Maj.-Gen. Sotenskiy, Fifth Army commander of artillery, VAA. beim AOK
2, Lt. Count Bossi-Fedrigotti, Report No. 24, 28 Sept. 1941, BA-MA RH 19 II/123.

[70] The conclusions drawn in Streit's dissertation *Keine Kameraden*, 137 ff., are factually without
foundation and are indeed disproved by the contents of the tables and data in that study. His
attempt to connect the quartermaster-general, just because of his instructions on the food rations
of prisoners of war, with Hitler's 'policy of extermination' in the east is not justified in any way.
The rations approved for Soviet prisoners of war by the quartermaster-general in the Army
General Staff were adequate and in fact higher than those of the German population even years
after the conclusion of the Second World War: see Hoffmann, *Ostlegionen*, 83 ff., 178.

exceedingly large number of Soviet soldiers—those who had not been prepared to fight to the last drop of blood 'for the Soviet homeland, the Party and
government, and for Comrade Stalin', i.e. potential allies of Germany—
perished from starvation, epidemics, or brutality in German captivity[71] soon
became common knowledge on the Soviet side. Regardless of how the individual soldier felt about Stalin, it once more stiffened the Red Army. The
damage thus done to the reputation of the Germans was never entirely
undone, even after the spring of 1942, when conditions in the POW camps
began to improve, or after 1943, when they became tolerable and a start had
long been made on building golden bridges for the political officials of the Red
Army.

The Soviet government showed some skill in filling the political vacuum and
exploiting the Germans' mistakes for their own purposes. A simple but effective mass campaign was launched on a vast scale, designed to make the public
forget their antagonism and rouse the nations of the Soviet Union, and every

---

[71] The frivolous manner in which figures are manipulated in this context is exemplified by
Jacobsen, 'Kommissarbefehl', 197, 279, and Streit, *Keine Kameraden*, 10, 105, who speak of 5.7
million prisoners of war and 3.3 million dead, of whom, according to Streit, about 600,000 had
been shot. By contrast, Streim, deputy head of the Central Office of the Land Justice Administration in Ludwigsburg, in his book *Die Behandlung sowjetischer Kriegsgefangener*, 244 ff., evidently on
the strength of more accurate information, arrives at the conclusion that of roughly 5.3 million 'at
least 2,530,000 Soviet prisoners of war' had died, including 140,000 who lost their lives through
separation measures. A critical analysis of the original documents unknown to these authors, and
of other data and factors, leads one to the result that of exactly 5,245,882 prisoners of war some
2 million had died of starvation and epidemics by the spring of 1942. A few tens of thousands were
probably executed by the SD, but no precise statement is possible on this point. Roschmann
actually mentions only 1,680,000 deaths.

The original document 'Nachweisung des Verbleibs der sowjetischen Kriegsgefangenen nach
dem Stand vom 1.5.1941' [Record of whereabouts of Soviet prisoners of war, as of 1 May 1941],
Kriegsgef. Org. (Id), BA-MA RH 2/v. 2623, is reproduced by Jacobsen, 'Kommissarbefehl', 279,
as document No. 42 with disfiguring changes. A difference of 280,810 between prisoners of war
transferred to the OKW area and those actually arrived there is rendered by Jacobsen as 'perished
in transit camps or disappeared'. The original document explains that difference by 'losses in
transport, counting-errors, and such like'. Indeed, counting-errors probably played a significant
part. Jacobsen explains the loss of '490,441' prisoners of war in the OKH area and '539,716 (of
which 66,694 escapes)' in the OKW area as follows: 'Escapes, transfers, to SD (executed)'. The
original document, however, states for the OKH area 'other losses (e.g. escapes, transfers to SD,
to Lw' and for the OKW area 'other losses (e.g. transfers to SD, Lw, SS)'.

There is no mention here of 'executed'. Neither transfer to the SS, or even to the SD, can be
simply equated with execution—especially as the entire auxiliary police ('protection squads',
'order service', etc.) in the Reich Commissariats Ostland and Ukraine under the sole authority of
the Reich Leader SS were largely recruited from prisoners of war. The security police and the SD
also had their own security squads and auxiliary services, such as the 8,000-man 'Družina'
Brigade, the 20,000-strong Tartar formations in the Crimea, Operation Zeppelin, and others. The
total strength of 'protection squads' under the Reich Leader SS had grown to 300,000 men in
1942, according to Krausnick and Wilhelm, *Die Truppe des Weltanschauungskrieges*, 168 ff.

On the prisoner-of-war problem see also 'Monatliche Meldung über Kriegsge-
fangenenzugang—Februar' [Monthly report on accretion of prisoners of war—February], OKH/
GenStdH/GenQu, Abt. Kriegsverwaltung (Qu 4) No. II/1241/45, 23 Mar. 1945, BA-MA RH 2/v.
2623; 'Kriegsgefangenenlage im Operationsgebiet Ost—Sowjets—Stand 1.2.1945' [Prisoner-
of-war situation in operations area east—Soviets—as of 1 Feb. 1945], OKH/GenStdH/GenQu,
Abt. Kriegsverwaltung (Qu 4) No. II/898/45 geh., 7 Mar. 1945, ibid.; Hoffmann, *Wlassow-Armee*,
142 ff.

single Soviet citizen, to mobilize their efforts in the service of a cause which Stalin, in his speech of 3 July 1941, had for the first time called a 'war for the defence of the fatherland'. This conflict was described by him not as an ordinary war between two armies, but as a just war by the entire 'Soviet people' against the Hitlerites. Stalin appealed to the Soviet citizens to turn their whole country, in alliance with Great Britain, the United States of America, and 'all freedom-loving nations', into one vast war camp. All mental and physical efforts of the Soviet nations were to be placed at the service of the struggle against the enemy, and the entire domestic life of the country was to be subordinated to the interests of the front. That which in Germany was attempted only after the defeat of Stalingrad, and then only half-heartedly— the conduct of a 'total war'—had become reality during the first few days of the war by the proclamation of the people's 'fatherland war'. Henceforth it was no longer a case of attaining the goals of international Communism, but of defending 'our freedom, our honour, our homeland'—in the spirit of Grand Duke Alexander Nevskiy, who in 1240 defeated the Swedes on the Neva and in 1242 the Order of German Knights on Lake Peipus, in the spirit of Grand Duke Dmitriy Donskoy of Moscow, who in 1380 inflicted a crushing defeat on the Tartars under Mamay on the Field of Quails, in the spirit of Kuzma Minin, the mayor of Nizhniy Novgorod, who, along with Prince Dimitriy Pozharskiy, organized a people's force and in 1612 drove the Poles from Moscow, and finally in the spirit of Generals Suvorov and Kutuzov, who had successfully fought against Napoleon's armies. The official slogan 'Workers of all lands, unite!', which until then had adorned every newspaper and every official document, was replaced by the slogan 'Death to the German occupiers!' Even the Orthodox Church became a welcome ally in this struggle. The policy of suppressing it was discontinued, and it began to bless the arms of the Red Army.[72]

In order to unite all efforts in the service of the conduct of the war, the State Defence Committee (Gosudarstvennyj Komitet Oborony) was established on 30 June 1941 under Stalin's direct control.[73] Its decisions had to be unconditionally obeyed by all Party, state, and military authorities, and by all citizens. Simultaneously, new people's commissariats were created, including a separate one for the tank industry and mortar production, as well as numerous new Directorates and Committees for every conceivable area. The State Defence Committee, as the supreme agency of national defence, saw its principal task as the transformation of the Soviet economy to the requirements of the war. Industry, agriculture, and transport had to be entirely reorganized and a redistribution had to be carried out of raw materials and foodstuffs. To that end current economic plans were suspended, and replaced by already prepared economic mobilization plans. These called for an immediate in-

---

[72] Stalin, *Großer Vaterländischer Krieg*, 31; Rauch, *Geschichte des bolschewistischen Rußland*, 440 ff.; Stökl, *Russische Geschichte*, 730 ff.

[73] Belikov, 'Gosudarstvennyj Komitet Oborony'.

crease in the production of war material, and for priority allocation of man-power, raw materials, and energy to the war industry.[74] However, by the time these plans came into force, the transfer of strategic stockpiles to the western frontiers of Belorussia and the Ukraine—as ordered by Stalin, Mekhlis, and Zhukov—had already resulted in the loss of major parts of the mobilization stocks.[75] Simultaneously, by their advance the Germans also gained possession of territories with highly important production facilities, territories where before the war 58 per cent of Soviet steel, 71 per cent of pig-iron, and 57 per cent of rolling-mill items had been produced. German seizure of the Nikopol region soon resulted in the loss to the Soviets of 92 per cent of manganese production. In losing the Donets basin, the Rostov coalfields, and the Moscow coal basin the Russians lost 63 per cent of their coal extraction. Faced with these developments, on 4 July 1941 the State Defence Committee found itself compelled to order a new economic mobilization plan to be prepared, based predominantly on the industrial capacities of the Volga region, the Urals, western Siberia, Kazakhstan, and central Asia. It was intended as a matter of urgency to develop this 'second industrial basis' into the country's real arma-ments centre.[76] But before armaments production could be started there, it was necessary to reorganize and modernize the foundries in the Urals and western Siberia, such as those of Magnitogorsk and Kuznetsk, where high-quality steels, rolling-mill products, and pipes had not preciously been manu-factured. At the same time, new ore deposits had to be opened up and the necessary facilities for the extraction of manganese, molybdenum, nickel, zinc, etc., set up. The fuel and power industry likewise had to be put on a new basis. New power stations had to be built, the capacity of existing ones increased, and the transport network improved in every respect. This process of a fundamental transformation of existing industrial enterprises in the eastern parts of the country, combined with the opening up of new raw-material, fuel, and energy sources, was further complicated by the large-scale evacuation of industrial equipment from the western and central parts of the Soviet Union.

In connection with the rapid advance of the German armies, Stalin, in his radio address of 3 July 1941, had demanded that 'all valuable assets' were to be 'absolutely' destroyed before they fell into enemy hands. Not only were all rolling-stock units, stockpiles of raw materials, and reserves of motor-fuel to be destroyed, but also every kilogramme of grain and every domestic animal—without any regard for the civilian population, who would be left behind and thus doomed to starvation. This was the 'scorched-earth policy' which had been declared to be the programme in an unpublished directive of the Central Committee of the Soviet Communist Party and the Council of People's Commissars addressed to Party and state officials on 29 June 1941.[77] In towns and localities threatened by the enemy destruction on the greatest possible

[74] Kravčenko, *Voennaja èkonomika*, 90.
[75] Chrulev, 'Stanovlenie strategičeskogo tyla', 65–6. [76] Dokučaev, *Sibirskij tyl*, 45.
[77] *Istorija Velikoj Otečestvennoj vojny*, ii. 56.

scale was carried out, provided there was still time to do so. Thus, on orders of the Supreme Command Headquarters, engineering squads were set up in Kharkov under the control of the Chief Directorate for Military Engineering, in co-operation with the South-west Front, with the sole task of blowing up or mining all major buildings and houses in the region.[78] In the subsequent fighting for Moscow the Soviet leadership ordered all inhabited localities in the territory of the enemy forces 'to be totally destroyed' and the forests set on fire in order 'to drive the Germans out into the frost'.

Before the destruction of the buildings, however, every effort was to be made to save all movable chattels, especially industrial equipment, from seizure by the Germans and to transfer them to the eastern regions of the country. This evacuation of production facilities from the western regions and their reassembly in safe areas—described as 'relocation'—is presented in Soviet histories of the Second World War as one of the greatest economic achievements ever, 'as a magnificent victory of the entire Soviet people and its Communist Party'.[79] Under the direction of a special Evacuation Council, headed until mid-July 1941 by Kaganovich and thereafter by Shvernik, between July and November 1941, in accordance with a strict schedule, no fewer than 1,523 industrial enterprises were transported to the east fron the areas of Rostov, Kursk, Voronezh, Tula, Moscow, Kalinin, Leningrad, and Murmansk.[80] Special importance was attached to the speedy relocation of tractor plants, aircraft factories, enterprises for the manufacture of arms and ammunition, plants of non-ferrous and ferrous metallurgy, and installations of the chemical industry.[81] Thus in the Ukraine 283, in Belorussia 109, in the Moscow region 498, and in the Leningrad region 92 industrial plants of economic importance to the Union as a whole were dismantled and transferred. Of the 1,523 enterprises which arrived in the eastern part of the country, 1,360 were major armaments works. Approximately 80 per cent of the evacuated enterprises were directed to the Urals, western Siberia, central Asia, and Kazakhstan; the rest went to the central regions of the Soviet Union: 667 to the Urals, 244 to western Siberia, 78 to eastern Siberia, 308 to central Asia and Kazakhstan, and 226 to the Volga region.[82] The main difficulty about this evacuation was the need to carry it out within a short period of time, often over vast distances, and occasionally under enemy action. It was impeded also by the shortage of transport and the overloading of the railway system; the relocation of the industrial plants required no fewer than 1.9 million railway wagons. It was not therefore surprising that the industrial equipment frequently failed to arrive at its destination on time or complete, or that it arrived damaged.[83] Some evacuated equipment quickly became stuck *en route*, owing to the disorganization of the transport system; thus, the relocation increasingly

[78] Starinov, 'Èto byla tajnoj'.   [79] Kumanev, 'Perebazirovanie'.
[80] Guluško, 'Tyl Sovetskich vooružennych sil', 33.   [81] Čadaev, *Èkonomika SSSR*, 76.
[82] Belikov, 'Tjaželuju promyšlennost'—v glubokij tyl', 47–8.
[83] Kravčenko, *Voennaja èkonomika*, 101.

became a transport problem. Resumption of production at the new locations was initially also impeded by the lack of workshops and the necessary transport connections, inadequate supplies of fuel and power, and not least a shortage of skilled labour. Armaments production, having undergone an increase during the first three months of the war, dropped to a low towards the end of the year.

On the whole, however, the colossal capacity of the Soviet armaments industry was reflected in the fact that a far greater quantity of weapons and war material was produced during the six war months of 1941 than during the first six months of the year. In the first half of 1941 Soviet factories had produced 1,800 modern tanks, 3,950 aircraft, 15,600 artillery pieces and mortars, 11,000 sub-machine-guns and machine-guns, 792,000 rifles and carbines, and 18.8 million shells. During the second half of the year, despite the loss of highly important industrial regions, production amounted to 4,740 tanks, 8,000 aircraft, 55,500 artillery pieces and mortars, 143,000 sub-machine-guns and machine-guns, 1.5 million rifles and carbines, and 40.2 million shells. Anti-tank rifles were first produced in the second half of the year, reaching a total of 18,152.[84] It should be remembered, moerover, that there was not only a quantitative increase in the output of tanks and aircraft, but that in the main new, more efficient types were being produced. The armaments industry's skill in increasing its output so massively is revealed even more clearly by a comparison of its output in 1941 and 1942. When Lieutenant-General Lukin, GOC Nineteenth Army, was taken prisoner by the Germans in December 1941, he pointed out to his captors—who had some very inaccurate ideas of the capacity of Soviet armaments production—that Soviet industry was virtually capable of equipping an armoured brigade with 60, or even more, modern T-34 and KV tanks each day. In actual fact, tank production in 1942 increased from 6,542 to 24,445, that of military aircraft from 12,516 to 21,342, and that of all types of artillery pieces and mortars from 71,100 to 127,092.[85] If one considers that this production came predominantly from the country's second industrial base, one can form an idea of what the Soviet armaments industry would have been like if the capacities of the western parts of the country had been fully available.

No less important to national defence than an increase in armaments output was an increase in agricultural production. By November 1941 the German troops had occupied a territory which, before the war, had produced 38 per cent of the Soviet Union's grain and 84 per cent of its sugar beet. Also within those regions were 38 per cent of all Soviet cattle and 60 per cent of pigs. Although major efforts had been made to evacuate at least the movable chattels of collective and state farms, in particular their grain-stores, livestock, and agricultural equipment such as tractors, from the regions threatened by the enemy, this transfer had only been partially successful.[86] Agricultural

---

[84] *50 let vooružennych sil*, 265.   [85] Nikitin, 'Perestrojka', 16 ff.
[86] Arutjunjan, *Sovetskoe krest'janstvo*, 35 ff.

production in 1941, compared with the preceding year, declined from 36,446,000 to 24,298,000 t. of grain, from 1,500,000 to 478,000 t. of sunflower seeds, from 17,355,000 to 1,670,000 t. of sugar beet, and from 987,000 t. to 826,000 of meat. This drop in production of foodstuffs and agricultural produce continued in a thoroughly alarming manner in 1942. If the nutrition of the Red Army and the Soviet Union generally was to be ensured, then cropping areas in the eastern parts of the country, especially in the Volga region, the Urals, Siberia, central Asia, and Kazakhstan, had to be substantially extended and production increased in every respect. Moreover, this would have to be achieved against the background of a steady diminution of available manpower, farm equipment, tractors, vehicles, and motor-fuel, under wartime conditions and often in climatically unfavourable latitudes.

An indispensable condition for an increase in armaments production and agricultural output was the mobilization of the requisite manpower—a task which had been embarked upon on a major scale immediately after the beginning of the war. A decree of 26 June 1941 by the USSR Supreme Soviet Praesidium introduced a seven-day week for all persons in employment, the daily working hours were increased, and all kinds of leave in the Soviet Union were cancelled in return for financial-compensation. A decree of 26 December 1941 by the USSR Supreme Soviet Praesidium declared all workers and clerical employees in the armaments industry to be 'mobilized persons'.[87] It was now forbidden to change or leave one's place of work without authorization. The application of military categories to the non-military sphere was reflected also in the creation of mobile workers' squads and construction battalions. Measures were simultaneously taken to integrate women, children, and elderly people into the labour process on the greatest possible scale. On 23 February 1942 a decree of the USSR Supreme Soviet Praesidium designated the entire urban population capable of work—men from 16 to 55, women from 16 to 45—as mobilized for the duration of the war.[88] In the countryside, form 17 April 1942 there was compulsory labour for all males from 14 to 55 and all females from 14 to 50. In fact, however, even children from the age of 12 upwards were obliged to reach a standard work norm of at least 50 work-days per annum. It was no longer just a case of making every fit person work, but of extracting from workers as much output as possible. To that end the work targets were raised excessively. Any mobilized person leaving his place of work without authorization was regarded as a 'deserter' to be tried by court martial. Rigorous punitive measures were to ensure fulfilment of the work norms and observance of work discipline.[89] Thus the principle of 'total war' applied in the Soviet Union from 1941 as the supreme guideline of all Soviet life. This was to become one of the reasons for the growing strength of the Red Army and for its superiority over the troops of the Wehrmacht.

---

[87] Lichomanov, *Organizatorskaya rabota*, 125. [88] Čadaev, '*Ėkonomika SSSR*, 106.
[89] Arutjunjan, *Sovetskoe krest'janstvo*, 77 ff.

4. The Struggle for Leningrad

By 10 July 1941 the attack by Army Group North across the Baltic States in a north-easterly direction, with the general objective of Leningrad, had made massive progress. The rapid success of the German troops was largely due to the fact that the command of the Baltic Special Military District under Colonel-General Kuznetsov had, by literally obeying the directives of the Soviet general staff, failed to put its units in a state of defence in good time.[90] After some hasty but unsuccessful counter-attacks by XII Mechanized Corps and elements of III Mechanized Corps near Siauliai and Kaunas, Eighth Army under Lieutenant-General Sobennikov had retreated to Riga and across the Dvina (Daugava), Twenty-seventh Army under Major-General Berzarin via Daugavpils to Opochka, and Eleventh Army under Lieutenant-General Morozov to Polotsk.[91] An attempt by the command of the new North-west Front to establish a stable line of defence along the Dvina, from Riga to Kraslava, had failed from the very start. While Eighth Army was hurriedly withing towards the north and by 10 July 1941 had been forced back to a line from Tartu to Pärnu,[92] preparations were made to build up a new line of defence along the Velikaya south of Pskov with units of Twenty-seventh Army. But this endeavour also failed when the Germans succeeded in capturing the fortified localities of Ostrov and Pskov and in crossing the river on a broad front. Unfulfillable demands by Headquarters, combined with marked shortcomings in the command of the North-west Front[93] and to some extent in that of its subordinate armies, had brought about a situation whereby on 10 July 1941 Eleventh and Twenty-seventh Armies were manning a rather weak delaying-position in the area of the Cherekha river south-east of Lake Peipus.

With the Germans having crossed the boundaries of the Leningrad region and gained favourable jumping-off positions for further attacks in Pskov and Ostrov,[94] for the first time the danger of a strategic breakthrough towards Leningrad began to emerge. Leningrad, the ancient historic St Petersburg, was not only the second largest city of the country (after Moscow), an important industrial centre, and with Kronshtadt the base of the Red Banner Baltic Fleet, but also, as the 'cradle of the Revolution' and 'Lenin's city', of enormous political and ideological, as well as strategic, significance for the whole of the Soviet Union. Vigorous preparations were therefore put in hand to put the city into a state of defence and to secure its more distant and closer approaches by defensive lines. On orders from Supreme Command Headquarters, Lieutenant-General Popov, the GOC Northern Front—which had not so far been involved in the fighting—had to prepare a defensive line along the Luga, from Narva to the south-east as far as Lake Ilmen, and to man it

---

[90] *Bor'ba za sovetskuju Pribaltiku*, i. 46 ff.   [91] Kuročkin, 'My sražalis'', 17.
[92] *Èstonskij narod v bor'be*, 190.   [93] *Istorija Velikoj Otečestvennoj vojny*, ii. 36.
[94] Zacharov, 'Predislovie', 8.

with some of the troops of the Northern Front together with divisions of the newly raised Leningrad People's Army, a kind of civilian militia. Lieutenant-General Pyadyshev, the deputy GOC Northern Front, was appointed to the command of this special 'Luga Tactical Group'.[95] The air forces of the Northern Front, under Major-General Novikov, were instructed to lend the greatest possible support to the operations of this group. With a view to mobilizing Leningrad's manpower and material reserves for the defence of the city, a special commission was formed on 1 July 1941 under the chairmanship of Zhdanov, Secretary of the CPSU Central Committee; other members of this commission were such leading Party and government figures as Kuznetsov, Shtykov, Popkov, and Solovyev.[96] The entire available civilian population, some 500,000 people, were henceforth enlisted for the construction of positions which, extending to 900 kilometres, surrounded Leningrad in multiple echelon.[97] Behind the outer line of defences along the Luga between Petrodvorets (Petergof), Krasnogvardeysk (Gatchina), and Kolpino, a second line was established at the southern approaches to the city. This inner ring of defences extended from Avtovo–Predportovaya–Srednaya Rogatka to the Neva. A double line of fortifications was also established at the Karelian isthmus.[98]

Construction of the defensive sector along the Luga had not yet been completed when Armoured Group 4, its flank covered by Sixteenth Army, which was hanging back slightly, reached Soltsy, established a bridgehead further north near Luga, and, reaching out towards the north, advanced as far as the Kingisepp area. However, on 14 July 1941, as the Germans threatened to advance beyond Soltsy and Shimsk in the direction of Novgorod, they were struck a fierce blow on their flank by the Soviet Eleventh Army. This caused a temporary crisis and necessitated a regrouping and weakening of the attacking units. That thrust into their flank, along with the stubborn resistance on the Luga defensive sector, caused the offensive against Leningrad to be temporarily halted. Nevertheless, the situation in the city remained tense, especially after the Finnish Karelian Army, on 10 July 1941, had gone over to the attack north of Lake Ladoga and pushed back the Soviet Seventh Army under Lieutenant-General Gorelenko almost to Petrozavodsk and Olonets. On 31 July, moreover, the Twenty-third Army under General Pshennikov was involved in heavy fighting as a result of an offensive by the Finnish South-eastern Army from the Karelian isthmus. During the next few weeks the Soviet troops were forced to abandon Vyborg and fall back to Leningrad's outer belt of defences. In the course of July 1941, despite vigorous opposition, the Soviet Twenty-seventh and Eleventh Armies on the left wing of the North-west Front had been forced back beyond Dno as far as the Lovat between Staraya Russa and Kholm. When on 7 August the Germans reached the Gulf of Finland at Kunda, the Soviet Eighth Army on the right wing of the North-west Front was

---

[95] *Bor'ba za sovetskuju Pribaltiku*, i. 108. [96] Zubakov, 'Kniga-dokument', 76.
[97] Popov, in *Oborona Leningrada*, 44. [98] Byčevskij, *V načale vojny*, 64–5.

split in two: 10th Rifle Corps took up defensive positions around Tallinn, while 11th Rifle Corps withdrew to Narva.[99]

After a brief pause, on 8 August 1941 the German northern assault group opened its attack on Kingisepp, advancing from its bridgeheads on the Luga; as a result, the Soviet Eighth Army elements fighting there soon found themselves in a difficult position. In spite of stubborn resistance the Soviet troops had to abandon Kingisepp, and on 21 August Krasnogvardeysk fell. However, Forty-second Army under Major-General Shcherbakov succeeded in foiling a German attempt to break through to Leningrad and, with the assistance of Eighth Army and units of the Baltic Fleet, in delaying the German advance to the coast. Not until the middle of September did the Germans succeed in reaching the Gulf of Finland near Strelna and in surrounding the remnants of Eighth Army in the Oranienbaum pocket. The attack of the southern assault group, which began on 10 August in the direction of Novgorod–Chudovo–Lyuban, at first also gained ground rapidly. Forty-eighth Army under Lieutenant-General Akimov (replaced since the beginning of September by Lieutenant-General Antonyuk) had been forced to abandon Novgorod and to fall back to the Malyy Volkhovets river. A surprise counter-thrust by Thirty-fourth Army under Major-General Kachanov and by elements of Eleventh Army near Staraya Russa indeed succeeded in holding up the German attack for a few days, but not in preventing the capture of Chudovo.[100]

In view of the growing threat from the south-east and south-west, Marshal of the Soviet Union Voroshilov, at a meeting of the Party leaders of the city of Leningrad on 20 August 1941, considered it essential to mobilize the last forces and resources in order to repulse the enemy. Zhdanov demanded an enlistment of workers on the same scale as in 1918–19. 'The enemy is at our gates,' he declared, 'this is a matter of life and death.' A War Council was set up for the defence of Leningrad under Voroshilov and Zhdanov, and a series of drastic defence measures were put in hand.[101] At the same time, on 23 August 1941, Supreme Command Headquarters considered it opportune to split the existing Northern Front into a Leningrad Front under Lieutenant-General Popov (a member of Zhdanov's War Council) and a Karelian Front under Lieutenant-General Frolov. Eighth, Twenty-third, and Forty-eighth Armies came under the new Leningrad Front. The duties of the short-lived War Council for the Defence of Leningrad were assumed on 30 August 1941 by the War Council of the Leningrad Front. As a result of this restructuring, the commander of the Leningrad Front was now able to devote his undivided attention to the defence of the city. Simultaneously, Fifty-fourth Army under Marshal of the Soviet Union Kulik and Fifty-second Army under Lieutenant-General Klykov, both of which continued to be under the direct command of Headquarters, were brought up to the eastern bank of the Volkhov in order to

[99] *Istorija ordena Lenina Leningradskogo Voennogo okruga*, 214.
[100] *Istorija Velikoj Otečestvennoj vojny*, ii. 88–9.
[101] *Istorija ordena Lenina Leningradskogo Voennogo okruga*, 223.

prevent any further advance by the Germans in the direction of Volkhov and Tikhvin.

In spite of all the efforts of the defenders, however, the German attack continued to make progress. The pressure of the German troops, who since 26 August 1941 had been attacking towards the north-east via Chudovo and Lyuban, along the Leningrad–Moscow railway line, was so strong that the Soviet Fifty-fifth Army under Major-General Lazarev could not withstand it. Mga was lost, and on 8 September the Germans had reached Lake Ladoga at Shlisselburg and severed Leningrad from its land communications to the east. As a result, Forty-second, Fifty-fifth, and Twenty-third Armies, as well as units of the Red Banner Baltic Fleet, were encircled in the city. Shortly before, resistance near Tallinn, which had been defended by 10th Rifle Corps under Major-General Nikolaev and naval units under Vice-Admiral Tributs, had come to an end. On 28 August 1941 began the evacuation of the naval units and the remnants of the defenders—but, because of inadequate preparations, that evacuation entailed heavy losses.[102] Of 67 vessels participating in the breakthrough, only 33 reached Kronshtadt or Leningrad; the remainder were caught in the mine-barrages or were lost through air attack, motor torpedo-boat attack, or artillery fire. Of the defenders of Tallinn, 15,000 men were taken prisoner; 3,000 of them were Estonians.

On 8 September 1941 German troops reached Lake Ladoga and a few days later the Gulf of Finland, thus tightening their stranglehold on Leningrad. When, in the Uritsk–Pulkovo Heights sector, they had pushed right up to the outer suburbs from the south, the fate of the city seemed to be sealed. From 4 September 1941 onwards Leningrad had been under German artillery bombardment. In early September the command of the Leningrad Front actually regarded the military situation as so desperate that, just as in Kiev, Kharkov, and elsewhere, preparations were being made for the destruction of the most important buildings in case the Germans penetrated into the city.[103] In this critical situation Supreme Command Headquarters decided on one final attempt to hold the city against the expected assault by the enemy. On 9 September Stalin dispatched Army General Zhukov to Leningrad on a special mission. He was instructed to replace Marshal of the Soviet Union Voroshilov—who had been appointed GOC Leningrad Front only on 5 September—as well as a number of other commanders who were not up to their tasks and had been conducting the city's defence 'with inadequate steadfastness'. Thus the incompetent GOC Fifty-fourth Army, Marshal of the Soviet Union Kulik, was relieved of his command. Forty-second Army, on the particularly threatened southern outskirts of Leningrad, was taken over by Major-General Fedyuninskiy. Lieutenant-General Khozin was appointed chief of staff of the Front. It was not just that some of the commanders of the forces at Leningrad had proved failures and given up hope. Even more

[102] Ačkasov, 'Operacija po proryvu', 29.   [103] Zhukov, *Reminiscences*, 315.

alarming were instances of exhaustion and disintegration among the troops themselves. It was against these that Zhukov, in line with his full powers, was to fight with all means at his disposal. Present-day accounts of the battle before Leningrad abound in instances of heroic resistance and self-sacrifice by Soviet soldiers. 'In the defence of Leningrad the forces and the population displayed an unprecedented mass heroism. Fighting on the approaches to the city was one great heroic deed,' it is stated in the *History of the Great Fatherland War*.[104] What the will to resist was really like in September 1941 is illustrated by Order No. 0098 of 5 October 1941, issued by Zhukov, the GOC Leningrad Front, and members of the War Council Zhdanov, Kuznetsov, and Admiral Isakov, and addressed to the troops of the Leningrad Front. This order was to be passed on to all commanding officers, unit commanders, and political officials down to company level. It dealt with an 'unparalleled incident' in the area of the 289th Independent Machine-gun Battalion stationed in the Slutsk–Kolpino fortification zone, an event which had produced far-reaching consequences. German soldiers had penetrated into the position of the battalion's No. 2 Company, had engaged the Red Army men in conversation, and without obstruction from their superiors had succeeded in persuading them to desert. What most alarmed the Front command was the fact that not only had the immediately concerned military leaders and political officials tolerated this 'criminal fraternization', but the commissars and staff members of the Political Departments and Special NKVD Detachments at battalion level, fortified-zone level, and the level of 168th Rifle Division and Fifty-fifth Army had taken no action, and instead had tried to hush up the incident. Measures now taken included execution by firing-squad and other punishments. The Leningrad Front threatened all traitors and cowards, and all those exhibiting 'criminal inactivity', with merciless liquidation and with arrest and court sentences for their families. Zhukov,[105] here as elsewhere, left no doubt that he would suppress all manifestations of defeatism with 'hardness and ruthlessness', and that he would not shrink from holding family members liable.

That these methods were not entirely successful is shown by the relatively high number of prisoners taken at Leningrad. German monitoring teams operating in this area and intercepting enemy radio traffic collected quite a few indications of persistent demoralization among Soviet formations. As late as August 1941 the officer commanding 191st Rifle Regiment of 198th Rifle Division (Twenty-third Army) was shot dead by a subordinate while trying to go over to the Germans.[106] Twenty-third Army HQ, in a signal to 19th Rifle Corps and six divisions subordinated to it, complained 'that the number of men missing in action is disproportionately high compared to other losses'.[107] Similar observations were made in Fifty-fifth Army, which reported heavy

---

[104] *Istorija Velikoj Otečestvennoj vojny*, ii. 91.   [105] Leeb, *Tagebuchaufzeichnungen*, 66–7.
[106] Radio situation report 5/8, commander of monitoring troops North, 6 Aug. 1941, BA-MA RH 19 III/671.
[107] Ibid. 672, pt. I, 116.

losses of prisoners and deserters: 'Morale among the fighters of 125th Rifle Division is low.'[108] A particular shock to the Soviet leadership was the behaviour of the 2,500 Leningrad University students who had been enlisted and immediately sent to the front; a very large proportion of them—the figure of 2,000 is mentioned—went over to the Germans.

Naturally, the various measures for stabilizing the front, including efforts to base the defence on deeper echelons and to involve the guns of the Baltic Fleet, as well as attempts to mount counter-attacks, could only produce results over several weeks. They certainly had practically no effect on the decisions of the German troops, who, albeit often in heavy fighting, broke through the defensive belt around Leningrad during the first days of September. The German command felt convinced that it would be possible, without great difficulty, to penetrate the city itself and to take possession of it. Hitler, however, preferred to see Leningrad tightly encircled, besieged, and starved into submission rather than have the city captured—because he feared that, as had happened in Kiev and elsewhere, the Germans would suffer heavy losses from mines and time bombs if they forced their way in. On 17 September, when a withdrawal of battle-worthy units finally weakened the German attacking forces, the War Council of the Leningrad Front issued a 'most strict' Order to Forty-second and Fifty-fifth Armies, signed by Zhukov, Zhdanov, Kuznetsov, and Khozin, forbidding them to fall back by as much as a single step from the defensive lines on the southern edge of the city. The defenders actually succeeded in gradually stiffening their resistance and, in certain sectors, e.g. from the Oranienbaum pocket and on the Volkhov, even in improving their positions by counter-attacks.[109] The blockade of Leningrad, which began in the second half of September, is presented in Soviet historiography as one of the 'most frightful atrocities of the German Fascist conquerors' and as a 'systematic murder of the city's peaceful inhabitants'.[110] It is a fact that the civilian population of Leningrad—especially during the first winter of the war, when the city could be but inadequately supplied by a temporary motor road over the ice of Lake Ladoga[111]—suffered a large number of deaths from starvation, bombardment, and disease.[112] Tragic though these events were, there is no case for moral accusations against the German troops: siege and bombardment of a defended city and fortress were still part and

---

[108] Radio situation report 8/10, commander of monitoring troops North, 8 Oct. 1941, ibid. 676.

[109] Lagunov, Loman, and Sot, 'O nekotorych netočnostjach'.

[110] Ščelokov and Komarov, 'Oborona Leningrada', 90. Lev Bezymenskij, a Soviet journalist and political observer of *Novoe Vremja*, a weekly published in nine languages by the USSR foreign ministry in conjunction with the KGB, formerly published attacks in a theatening tone against the present author for his presentation of the blockade of Leningrad, the partisan war, and Stalin's preparations for attack. It would be interesting to discover the political motivation of such action. However, an advertised continuation never appeared: Bezymenskij, 'Kogda polupravda chuže lži'; id., 'Byt' li vtoromu Njurnbergu?'

[111] Šikin, 'Podvigu žit''

[112] Prochorova, in *Oborona Leningrada*, 445 ff.; 'Iz dnevnika Mironovoj Aleksandry Nikolaevny', ibid. 754 ff.

parcel of the most usual and unquestioned methods of warfare. Soviet troops in turn applied the method of siege without scruples during the second half of the war, trying to reduce enemy cities with all the fire-power available to them. One need only cite the instances of Königsberg (present-day Kaliningrad) and Breslau (Wrocław). Indeed, in 1945 Marshal of the Soviet Union Zhukov actually prided himself on having fired no fewer than 1,800,000 artillery shells at Berlin between 21 April and 2 May.[113]

Towards the end of September the German armoured forces were withdrawn and fighting at Leningrad began to subside into a kind of siege warfare. The time had then come for a German attack on the Baltic islands of Saaremaa (Ösel) and Hiiumaa (Dagö), which were still being held by Red Army forces. Although possession of the Moon Sound islands and the Hanko (Hangö) peninsula had lost some of its importance to the Soviet command now that the whole of Estonia was in German hands, these bases, irritatingly, were still interfering with German control of the eastern Baltic and the Gulf of Finland. From Sanremaa, moreover, a few DB-3 long-range bombers of the Red Banner Baltic Fleet under Colonel Preobrazhenskiy had repeatedly, during August and September 1941, carried out nuisance raids as far as Berlin—a point of considerable importance to Soviet war propaganda.[114] This explains the Soviet determination to defend those bases, 400 kilometres behind their front, to the last man. Under the command of General Yeliseev the garrison of Saaremaa resisted until 5 October and that of Hiiumaa until 21 October 1941.[115] The garrison of Hanko, under the command of Lieutenant-General Kabanov, which held out for five months, was evacuated to Kronshtadt and Leningrad in December 1941.[116]

The fact that, despite their great successes on the north-western sector, the German troops failed to attain the real objective of the operation, the capture of the city of Leningrad, was celebrated on the Soviet side as a 'huge political and moral victory of the Soviet people and a magnificent testimony to their courage and inflexible will'. 'The Fascist hordes'—it is stated in the memorial of the Leningrad military district—'having penetrated from the frontier to the suburbs of Leningrad, were unable to overcome the final 2–5 kilometres and enter Leningrad through Pulkovo and Ligovo. The steadfastness, the extraordinary heroism and valour of the city's defenders frustrated the plans of the German command.'[117] Deliberately or otherwise, this statement overlooks the fact that during the critical days of September even Army General Zhukov and the Leningrad Front command did not believe that it would be possible to hold Leningrad. The entry of German troops into the city was at that time expected 'at any moment'.[118]

[113] Zhukov, *Reminiscences*, 612.
[114] Žavoronkov, 'Avgust-sentjabr' 1941'; Cykin, 'Taktika', 68.
[115] Krinicyn, 'Oborona'; Ačkasov, 'Protivodesantnaja oborona'.
[116] Tribuc, 'Èvakuacija'; Kabanov, *Na dal'niych podstupach*.
[117] *Istorija ordena Lenina Leningradskogo Voennogo okruga*, 245.
[118] Zhukov, *Reminiscences*, 317.

5. The Battle of Smolensk

When on 10 July 1941 the Germans mounted their attack on Smolensk with several spearheads between Vitebsk and Mogilev, they came up against the defensive line of the Soviet Western Front. This consisted of seven armies under the overall command of Marshal of the Soviet Union Timoshenko. The defensive forces along the Drissa–Zhlobin–Rechitsa line were composed of Twenty-second Army under General Yershakov, Nineteenth Army (in echelon behind it) under Lieutenant-General Konev, Twentieth Army under Lieutenant-General Kurochkin, Thirteenth Army under Lieutenant-General Filatov, and Twenty-first Army under Lieutenant-General Gerasimenko. Sixteenth Army under Lieutenant-General Lukin, recently arrived in the Smolensk area, formed the reserve in second echelon. Western Front HQ had been instructed to establish a solid defensive front, together with the remnants of broken units. It was to take advantage of the river obstacles of the Western Dvina and the Dnieper, and thus simultaneously cover the arrival and deployment of additional forces from the interior of the country.[119] But in view of the inadequate artillery and armour of the divisions in the foremost line, the Germans, attacking with superior forces at the point of main effort, succeeded during the very first days in achieving deep penetrations north of Vitebsk and on both sides of Mogilev. Despite fierce resistance and repeated counter-attacks, the Soviet Twenty-second Army—except for some lesser units which offered resistance on the Lovat near Velikie Luki—was encircled, and Nineteenth Army forced back towards Smolensk. Simultaneously, the Germans had pierced the front of Twentieth Army north of Mogilev, thrown back that army north-west of Smolensk, and encircled it there along with Sixteenth Army.[120] Thirteenth Army, operating south of Mogilev, was split in two: two of its corps were caught in the Mogilev pocket, while two others, also trapped at first, succeeded in fighting their way through to the south and in establishing a new line of defence with Twenty-first Army on the Sozh. Although on 13 July Twenty-first Army made a locally successful relief attack near Bobruysk, Smolensk eventually fell on 26 July and the Germans struck further east beyond Yelnya.

The loss of the Dnieper–Dvina line and the city of Smolensk conjured up the danger of a German breakthrough to Moscow. Supreme Command Headquarters therefore took vigorous measures to stabilize the front again. Stalin in particular regarded the loss of Smolensk as very serious; he was altogether outraged at developments on the western sector of the front.[121] Fresh forces were brought up without delay and defences were staggered in deep echelon. Twenty-ninth Army along the Ostashkov–Selizharovo–Olenino line, and Thirtieth Army were combined on 12 July 1941 with Twenty-fourth and

[119] Čeremuchin, 'Na smolensko-moskovskom strategičeskom napravlenii', 4.
[120] Panov and Naumov, 'Vosstanovlenie strategičeskogo fronta', 21.
[121] Zhukov, Reminiscences, 274.

Twenty-eighth Armies standing between Nelidovo and Bryansk, and with Thirty-first Army at Torzhok–Rzhev–Kalinin, to form the Front of Reserve Armies under the command of Lieutenant-General Bogdanov. Its task was, in second echelon behind the Western Front, to secure the Ostashkov–Belyy–Yelnya–Bryansk line against a possible German breakthrough in the direction of Moscow. The same purpose was served by the Mozhaysk line of defence created at the approaches to the capital and held by poorly equipped and poorly trained divisions of the People's Guard (Thirty-second and Thirty-third Armies) and by Thirty-fourth Army.[122] Simultaneously with the establishment of deeply echeloned defences, Headquarters in a directive of 20 July 1941 ordered the launching of counter-attacks in order to weaken the enemy's striking power and to consilidate the general position around Smolensk. To this end, divisions were pulled out from the Front of Reserve Armies and formed into several army groups under the command of Generals Khomenko, Kalinin, Kachalov, Rokossovskiy, and Maslennikov. These army groups were instructed, with several spearheads from the Belyy–Yartsevo and Roslavl areas, to attack in the general direction of Smolensk and, in co-operation with forces of Sixteenth and Twentieth Armies, to destroy the enemy forces which had broken through north and south of Smolensk. However, this first major offensive operation by Soviet troops, under overall command of Marshal of the Soviet Union Timoshenko, was for a number of reasons denied success.[123] These reasons included not only the relatively poor equipment of the attacking units as regards artillery, armour, and aircraft, but also the inability of commanders at all levels to execute a grand-scale operation.[124] The attacks, on 23 July 1941 from the Roslavl area and on 24 and 25 July from the areas of Belyy and Yartsevo, were badly co-ordinated and launched at too great a distance from one another. They were checked by the quick-reacting Germans and repulsed. Although some elements of Sixteenth and Twentieth Armies, encircled north of Smolensk, succeeded with the aid of Rokossovskiy's army group[125] in breaking through to the other bank of the Dnieper, Kachalov's army group, attacking south of Smolensk, found itself encircled at Roslavl and was annihilated. The final outcome of the operation was that the Soviet troops had again suffered heavy losses, even though they succeeded in establishing themselves once more in a defensive line along the Desna and to the north of it, and even though some forces of Army Group Centre had been worn down in these battles.

The German gains, especially against the left flank of the Western Front, represented an increasing threat to the South-west Front, which was then engaged in heavy fighting for Kiev. To ward off the danger of a thrust into its flank from the north, Supreme Command Headquarters on 24 July 1941, with

---

[122] Čeremuchin, 'Na smolensko-moskovskom strategičeskom napravlenii', 8.
[123] Radzievskij, 'Proryv oborony', 12–13.
[124] Panov and Naumov, 'Vosstanovlenie strategičeskogo fronta', 22.
[125] Rokossovskij, *Soldatskij dolg*, 25 ff.

quite unusual promptness,[126] established a Central Front along the boundary of the Western and South-west Fronts; this Central Front consisted of Thirteenth Army, Twenty-first Army, and the remnants of Fourth Army. Colonel-General Kuznetsov was placed in command of it.[127] Simultaneously, on 25 July 1941, the Front of Reserve Armies was again dissolved, having scarcely been in existence for ten days. From the units of that, front, with the exception of Twenty-ninth and Thirtieth Armies, which had already been incorporated in the Western Front, Headquarters on 30 July 1941 created a unified Reserve Front under the command of Army General Zhukov. Significantly, State Security Commissar (3rd rank) Kruglov, a close relatve of People's Commissar Beriya, became a member of its War Council. The reinforcement of the Rzhev–Vyazma–Kirov line by the Reserve Front formed from Thirty-fourth, Thirty-first, Twenty-fourth, Forty-third, and Thirty-third Armies and the appointment of Zhukov—who to this end was relieved in his former post of Chief of the Red Army General Staff by Marshal of the Soviet Union Shaposhnikov—were connected with differences of opinion in the supreme command on what were the most urgent measures at the moment. At the end of July 1941 Zhukov and the top generals of the general staff, such as Generals Vasilevskiy and Zlobin, no longer expected an immediate resumption of the German attack on Moscow; they had instead come to the conclusion that the Germans would use the advantages of their position in order to strike at the flank or the rear of the Central Front and the South-west Front.[128] Stalin, on the other hand, continued to believe that the German main forces, albeit with outflanking moves in the north and south, would persist in trying to break through to Moscow.[129] He clung to this view even when Army Group Centre, having in fact gone over to the defence at Smolensk on 30 July 1941, wheeled south on 8 August 1941 with forces of Armoured Group 2 and Second Army to attack the newly formed Soviet Central Front. In order to prevent a breakthrough of German formations in the strategic direction of Moscow—the move Stalin and Shaposhnikov feared—a new front, the Bryansk Front, was created on 16 August 1941 at the boundary between the Central Front and the Reserve Front. This Bryansk Front, under the command of Lieutenant-General Yeremenko, consisted of Major-General Petrov's Fiftieth Army and Major-General Golubev's Thirteenth Army.[130] Its immediate task was to be nothing less than the destruction of the enemy's Armoured Group 2.[131] However, despite Stalin's optimism, further enhanced by Yeremenko, this grouping proved far too weak to block or halt its opponent. On 18 August 1941, when the Germans were approaching Gomel and the Novozybkov–Starodub line, and when they had already driven a deep wedge between the Bryansk and Central Fronts, Zhukov warned Supreme Command Headquarters of the danger of a far-ranging envelopment of the armies of the South-west Front.

[126] Vasilevskij, *Delo vsej žizni*, 142.   [127] *Istorija Velikoj Otečestvennoj vojny*, ii. 71.
[128] Zhukov, *Reminiscences*, 286.   [129] Vasilevskij, *Delo vsej žizni*, 136–7.
[130] Eremenko, *Na zapadnom napravlenii*, 86.   [131] Grigorovič, *Kiev—gorod-geroj*, 70.

Even at that late moment Stalin and his new chief of the general staff were not convinced that the main direction of the thrust had in fact been changed towards the south, or that the South-west Front and substantial parts of the Central Front were threatened. At any rate, they believed that the Bryansk Front would succeed in halting the enemy.[132] They therefore authorized only the withdrawal of the right wing of the South-west Front across the Dnieper to the east. Thirty-seventh Army, under the command of General Vlasov, and the forces of the Kiev fortified zone had to stay put and continue to defend Kiev. Headquarters also expected that, once Twenty-first Army had been pulled back to the Iput, it would be possible to maintain the cohesion between the Central Front and the Bryansk Front. In order to facilitate the defensive operations against the enemy attacking towards Chernigov and Konotop, the forces of the Central Front (Third and Twenty-first Armies) were on 26 August 1941 amalgamated with those of the Bryansk Front. This measure, however, as Yeremenko had to admit, was a mistake, since it was the troops of the Central Front who had to check the main southward thrust of the Germans. Even so, it provides additional evidence that Stalin and Shaposhnikov had failed to realize in time the fundamental change in the thrust of the German operations.

Supreme Command Headquarters judged that the situation in the second half of August was promising enough to warrant an attempt to regain the initiative and recapture Smolensk. It therefore ordered the Western Front to continue its counter-attacks north of Smolensk and set it the task of reaching the Velizh–Demidov–Smolensk line with forces of Thirtieth, Nineteenth, Sixteenth, and Twentieth Armies by 8 September 1941. Simultaneously, the Reserve Front with Twenty-fourth and Forty-third Armies was to liquidate the salient at Yelnya and advance to the area west of Roslavl by the same date. While Armoured Group 2 was thus, during its advance to the south, being threatened from its rear, the Bryansk Front, substantially reinforced by air units from the Headquarters reserve, was to strike at the enemy's flank in the wider neighbourhood of Starodub (at Pochep, Trubchevsk, and Novgorod Severskiy) and, having annihilated him, reach a line approximately from west of Roslavl to Krichev and Klintsy. Headquarters hoped that these co-ordinated operations would destroy substantial elements of Army Group Centre, push the enemy back along his entire front, and thus fundamentally change the position on the western sector.[133] The Soviet forces, however, achieved only one success worth mentioning: Twenty-fourth Army recaptured Yelnya after heavy fighting on 6 September 1941.[134] The attack of the Western Front, on the other hand, made only slight progress in a few places and had to be halted by order of Headquarters on 10 September 1941. The Bryansk Front—whose opportunities had been greatly overrated—likewise failed to

---

[132] Ivanov and Čeremuchin, 'O knige "V načale vojny"', 75–6.

[133] Čeremuchin, 'Na smolensko-moskovskom strategičeskom napravlenii', 16.

[134] Chorošilov and Baženov, 'El'ninskaya nastupatel'naja operacija'.

score any success. Neither was Yeremenko able to check the advance of Armoured Group 2, which was driving ever deeper into the rear of the South-west Front, nor, contrary to Stalin's and Shaposhnikov's expectations, did he himself seize the initiative for destroying the units of the German armoured group.[135] Thus, on 13 September the Bryansk Front was forced to suspend its attacks and go over to the defensive; on 16 September 1941 the Reserve Front had to do likewise.

The battle of Smolensk, the biggest armed clash during the summer campaign of 1941, came to a close after almost two months' fighting without either side having achieved its objectives. The Soviet troops, despite repeated attempts, had failed to destroy the German assault groups, and hence the main forces of Army Group Centre, in the Smolensk area. Instead, the Germans had crossed the Dnieper in its middle reaches on a broad front and had advanced eastwards by, on average, 170–200 km., as they had also done in the sector of the western Dvina.[136] As a result, however, Army Group Centre—having continuously had to repel vigorous, albeit often improvised and poorly conducted, counter-attacks—had been so weakened in its attacking strength that a direct advance on Moscow had to be put off for the moment. The units of Armoured Group 2 and of Second Army wheeled to the south in order to eliminate the latent threat to the southern flank and to bring the raging battle for Kiev to a successful conclusion. This outcome of the fighting near Smolensk is described by Soviet historiography as a great defensive success of the Red Army, which, it is claimed, had managed to divert the German command from its original concept, gaining time for the further mobilization of human and material resources and for preparations for the defence of the Soviet capital. In actual fact some 80 per cent of available strategic reserves had been drawn upon to reinforce the western sector and hence to protect Moscow.[137] The defensive success at Smolensk had been achieved at the cost of exceptionally high losses. The counter-attacks ceaselessly demanded by Supreme Command Headquarters, even though 'neither objective nor subjective prerequisites for them existed', had led to the encirclement and annihilation of valuable major formations. Thus, according to German data, 426,000 Soviet generals, officers, and other ranks were taken prisoner in the battle of Smolensk—evidence of a still shaky fighting morale among the Red Army. That these figures were by no means (as claimed by the Soviet literature) 'false reports of the Fascist intelligence service'[138] is shown by the above-mentioned Order No. 270, issued about the same time, which sought to prevent the disintegration of the army by the application of Draconian measures.

---

[135] Ivanov and Čeremuchin, 'O knige "V načale vojny"', 78; Vasilevskij, *Delo vsej žizni*, 142; Grigorovič, *Kiev—gorod-geroj*, 70.

[136] *Boevoj put' vooružennych sil*, 274.   [137] Zacharov, 'Načal'nyj period', 11.

[138] *Geschichte des Großen Vaterländischen Krieges*, ii. 90. This allegation is not present in the Russian original *Istorija Velikoj Otečestvennoj vojny*, ii. 76–7.

6. The Fighting for the Ukraine

On about 10 July 1941 the Germans also resumed their offensive against Colonel-General Kirponos's South-west Front; his chief of staff was initially General Purkaev and later General Tupikov; the War Council member was Burmistenko. The attacks were opened from the salient in the Sluch sector. Units of Armoured Group 1 and Sixth Army thrust ahead in two directions, via Zhitomir and Berdichev. At the boundary between Major-General Potapov's Fifth Army, which defended the fortified district of Korosten at the old state frontier, and the forces of the Kiev fortified district a spearhead drove ahead as far as the Irpen within a few days, thus posing a direct threat to the Ukrainian capital. With flank cover from the German Sixth Army, Armoured Group 1 simultaneously advanced southwards with a far-ranging envelopment, designed to encircle and annihilate General Muzychenko's Sixth Army and General Ponedelin's Twelfth Army well to the west of the Dnieper. South-west Front command had initially turned its attention to the right wing and mounted a number of counter-attacks from the Korosten fortified district with units of its Fifth Army. Simultaneously it prepared for the defence of Kiev against a presumed German attack,[139] which, however, was not attempted until the end of the month, and then only as a coup without real preliminary deployment. The Germans meanwhile succeeded in driving an ever broader wedge between the Soviet Fifth and Sixth Armies, and in wheeling through Belaya Tserkov in the direction of Uman. As a result, the main forces of the South-west Front, above all Sixth and Twelfth Armies, found themselves in a difficult situation: pinned down since 6 July 1941 by the attack of the German Seventeenth Army and, after that army's breakthrough at Zhmerinka on 16 July 1941, cut off from its southern neighbour, the Soviet Eighteenth Army of the Southern Front, the South-west Front forces were in growing danger of having their eastward retreat cut off by the German armoured group. Eighteenth Army, in its turn, was in danger of being encircled once the German Eleventh Army and the Romanian Third Army had crossed the Dnestr, thereby threatening its left flank. By that time the troops of the South-west Front had suffered enormous losses. Up to 30 per cent of the rifle divisions were reduced to 1,500 men, another 30 per cent had only 3,000–4,000 men, some had no artillery, and most of the armoured formations had no tanks left.[140] In the hope of gaining time for bringing up and assembling reserves on the Dnieper, South-west Front command had at first kept the threatened Sixth and Twelfth Armies in their positions along the old state frontier; only on 16 July 1941 had it, belatedly, ordered them to withdraw to the east.[141] Simultaneously, from 19 July onwards, counter-attacks were made, on orders from Headquarters, by Lieutenant-General Kostenko's Twenty-sixth Army

---

[139] Bagramjan, 'Geroičeskaja oborona'.

[140] Pokrovskij, 'Na Jugo-Zapadnom napravlenii', 66.

[141] Arušanjan, 'Boevye dejstvija', 63–4.

operating south of Kiev against the flank of Armoured Group 1. Although these slowed down the German attack, they came too late to save the two armies from the encirclement threatening them.[142] While the Soviet Twenty-sixth Army was, for its part, under attack, the pocket forming at Uman was assuming ever clearer outlines. From the north, Armoured Group 1 was pushing against the area east of Uman, while from the south Seventeenth Army was attacking towards the same objective. On 2 August 1941 the German forces linked up at Pervomaysk.

The grouping of Sixth and Twelfth Armies—which, because of the belated order for its withdrawal, had slipped out of the control of the South-west Front and since 23 July had been concentrated under the command of General Ponedelin and subordinated to General Tyulenev's Southern Front—now found itself encircled and was annihilated within a few days.[143] According to the history of the Soviet armed forces, some of the encircled troops succeeded in breaking out. 'Thousands, however, lost their lives on the battlefield'[144] because, as Colonel-General Pokrovskiy writes, 'they preferred death to the disgrace of captivity'.[145] An attempt is made to create the impression that there had been no prisoners. The Germans, on the other hand, reported that 'great masses of the enemy' were coming over to them. At the conclusion of the fighting at Uman on 8 August 1941 some 103,000 Soviet officers and men were counted as prisoners of war—including the two army commanders Ponedelin and Muzychenko, as well as General Kirillov, GOC 13th Rifle Corps, and other generals. The number of men killed in action was estimated at double that figure.

In view of the increasingly critical situation in the sector of the South-west Front, on 5 August 1941 Stalin, after unsuccessful attempts to halt the enemy before he reached the Dnieper, instructed the commanding generals of the fronts, as well as Marshal of the Soviet Union Budennyy, GOC South-western Direction, to build up a secure line of defence along the Dnieper from the bridgehead at Kiev to Kremenchug, and thence along a general Krivoy Rog–Kakhovka–Kherson line. The troops of the South-west Direction were given definite orders not on any account to allow the Germans to break through to the eastern bank of the Dnieper.[146] Ninth Army under Lieutenant-General Sofronov, which had been cut off since 10 August and thereupon organized as an Independent Coastal Army, was ordered, in conjunction with the forces of the Black Sea Fleet under Rear-Admiral Zhukov, to defend the port of Odessa to the last breath.[147] Simultaneously, reserves were brought up from the heartland military districts; for the reinforcement of the troops defending the Kiev fortified district these were organized into the Thirty-seventh Army

---

[142] Bagramjan, *Tak načinalas' vojna*, 247.   [143] Tjulenev, *Čerez tri vojny*, 155 ff.
[144] *50 let vooružennych sil*, 284.
[145] Pokrovskij, 'Na Jugo-Zapadnom napravlenii', 68. Differently *Istorija Velikoj Otečestvennoj vojny*, ii. 102, and Zhukov, *Reminiscences*, 279.
[146] Vasilevskij, *Delo vsej žizni*, 133.   [147] Krylov, 'Slovo', 70.

under General Vlasov, and at Cherkassy into the Thirty-eighth Army under Lieutenant-General Ryabyshev (later under Major-General Feklenko); on the sector of the Southern Front a Reserve Army was formed under Major-General Malinovskiy in the Dnepropetrovsk area. The concentration of such strong forces near Kiev and on the Dnieper bend, and the determination of Supreme Command Headquarters and of South-western Direction command not to surrender an inch of Ukrainian soil, were to cost the Soviet troops dear.

The German advance continued to make rapid progress after the conclusion of the battle of Uman. On 5 August 1941, when Stalin rejected Budenny's request for permission to pull back the entire Southern Front to the Ingul,[148] the town of Kirovograd, situated on that river, was already in German hands. The German troops made a defence of the Ukraine west of the Dnieper—as demanded by Headquarters—impossible and by 20 August 1941 had forced the Southern Front back to the river bank between Nikopol and Kherson. Although on 19 August 1941 Supreme Command Headquarters had ordered the fronts of the South-western Direction to hold at all costs the bridgeheads at Kiev, Dnepropetrovsk, Berislav, and Kherson, these were nevertheless reduced. The Germans crossed the Dnieper at Dnepropetrovsk[149] and for their part established bridgeheads there as well as down river at Kakhovka; from these they advanced towards the south and south-east at the beginning of September. The Fifty-first Independent Army only just succeeded in halting the Germans at the approaches to the Crimea. The Southern Front was forced to withdraw to the Dnepropetrovsk–Zaporozhye–Melitopol line. An alarming situation had also arisen at Kremenchug, where the Germans on 2 September 1941 likewise established a bridgehead and where they assembled the main strength of Seventeenth Army and Armoured Group 1. As the Bryansk Front had failed to contain the southward thrust of Armoured Group 2 and Second Army, and as strong German motorized forces had penetrated as far as the Konotop area and crossed the Desna near Chernigov, six Soviet armies of the South-west Front, standing in the salient formed by the Dnieper and Desna, found themselves in danger of large-scale encirclement.[150]

South-west Front command had realized the growing threat to its flanks as early as 4 September 1941.[151] In view of the development of the situation, on 7 September 1941 Colonel-General Kirponos demanded the immediate pulling back of the (already half-encircled) Fifth Army and the right wing of Thirty-seventh Army to the Desna. But not until fully two days later, on 9 September, when the Germans attacking from the north had already reached the river at some points, did Headquarters—albeit reluctantly—authorize the request, which also had Budennyy's support. Headquarters, however, demanded that the Kiev bridgehead be held.[152] As the Germans had simul-

[148] Vasilevskij, *Delo vsej žizni*, 135.   [149] Zamercev, 'V bojach', 80 ff.

[150] Grigorovič, *Kiev—gorod-geroj*, 71.   [151] Bagramjan, *Tak načinalas' vojna*, 309.

[152] Vasilevskij, *Delo vsej žizni*, 144.

taneously achieved a penetration at the boundary between Fortieth and Twenty-first Armies and, from the bridgehead at Kremenchug, were mounting an attack towards the north, disaster was inevitable unless it proved possible to evacuate the troops of the South-west Front from the Kiev salient. At that point serious differences of opinion emerged between the top figures of the Red Army. Colonel-General Kirponos, who on 11 September 1941 demanded the immediate withdrawal of the threatened South-west Front to the Psel, was forbidden, by order of Marshal Shaposhnikov, chief of the Red Army General Staff, to pull out even a single division from the Kiev salient; he was to stand fast along the existing defensive line.[153] When Marshal Budennyy and the War Council of the South-western Direction once more repeated their request—which seemed to have the support also of Army General Zhukov, a member of Headquarters, and of leading general-staff officers, such as General Vasilevskiy—and when Budenny pointed out that any delay in the withdrawal would result in the loss of the troops and of vast quantities of war material,[154] Stalin intervened in person. In a direct telephone conversation with the GOC South-west Front on the evening of 11 September he categorically prohibited any withdrawal and instead demanded, even at that time, that Kiev be held at all costs and that the enemy groupings in the Konotop–Bakhmach area be destroyed in co-operation with the Bryansk Front.[155] Stalin, accusing not only Kirponos but also Marshal of the Soviet Union Budenny of 'forever looking for new lines of retreat' instead of finding opportunities for resistance,[156] now appointed Marshal of the Soviet Union Timoshenko to the command of the South-western Direction. The mood prevailing at Headquarters was clearly revealed in an order of 14 September 1941, in which Marshal Shaposhnikov, chief of the Red Army General Staff, described as panic-mongering the entirely accurate reports from the South-west Front about the certainty of disaster within a few days, thereby (as it were) reminding Colonel-General Kirponos and his chief of staff General Tupikov of the fate of the commander of the Western Front and his staff, and demanding strictest compliance with the directives of Comrade Stalin, in other words, holding out in their present positions.[157] As General Grigorenko put it, the directives of an 'incompetent Supreme Command'[158] prevented 'any sensible measures at the front from averting the approaching catastrophe'.

On 15 September 1941 Armoured Groups 1 and 2 linked up at Lokhvitsa. Lieutenant-General Kuznetsov's Twenty-first Army, Major-General Potapov's Fifth Army, General Vlasov's Thirty-seventh Army, Lieutenant-General Kostenko's Twenty-sixth Army, and units of General Podlas's Fortieth Army and General Feklenko's Thirty-eighth Army were thus encircled. With the

---

[153] *Istorija Velikoj Otečestvennoj vojny*, ii. 107.
[154] Bagramjan, *Tak načinalas' vojna*, 326–7.
[155] Vasilevskij, *Delo vsej žizni*, 145–6; Pokrovskij, 'Na Jugo-Zapadnom napravlenii', 71.
[156] Zhukov, *Reminiscences*, 299–300.   [157] Moskalenko, *Na Jugo-Zapadnom napravlenii*, 89.
[158] Nekritsch and Grigorenko, *Genickschuß*, 247.

first signs of demoralization soon appearing among the trapped troops, in the absence of orders to withdraw from Headquarters, and amid dwindling prospects of an organized break-out, the new GOC South-western Direction, Timoshenko, though initially siding with Shaposhnikov, determined to act on his own responsibility. To destroy the two German armoured groups seemed impossible. But an attempt could be made, with concentrated forces, to achieve a breach in the encircling ring before this was properly consolidated, thus opening a way to the Psel for the trapped formations. Major-General Bagramyan, chief of the operations department of the South-west Front staff, was instructed to fly out to the staff of the South-west Front at once and to convey to Colonel-General Kirponos his verbal order for an immediate evacuation of the Kiev fortified district and for a speedy withdrawal of the front's main forces to the Psel. But when Bagramyan appeared at the front's staff north of Piryatin, the GOC refused to comply with the order—the only possible order left in the existing situation—on the grounds that it ran counter to Headquarters directives and to Marshal Timoshenko's original orders.[159] Kirponos asked to see a 'document'; after prolonged hesitation he eventually, on the evening of 17 September, agreed to enquire from Headquarters direct.[160] Shaposhnikov's barely concealed threats of 14 September had evidently been effective. A reply was received from Moscow in the early morning of 18 September 1941, but further valuable time had been lost. Even then, authorization was given only for the evacuation by Thirty-seventh Army of the Kirov fortified district; there was still no question of a general surrender of the Dnieper–Desna salient.[161] But this time Kirponos did not hestitate. Before communications with his army staffs were cut off he had issued orders for a break-out by the South-west Front in an easterly direction. Under this plan, Twenty-first Army was to strike at Romny, Fifth Army was to cover the withdrawal of Twenty-first Army while simultaneosuly attacking towards Lokhvitsa with some of its forces, Twenty-sixth Army was to withdraw in the direction of Lubny, and Thirty-seventh Army, as the South-west Front's rearguard, was to break through in the direction of Piryatin. Fortieth and Thirty-eighth Armies, some of whose units were outside the pocket, were instructed to support the break-out attempt by attacks on Romny and Lubny. But an orderly withdrawal was no longer possible. Pressed hard by the Germans, weakened by their heavy losses, and often without their commanders, the Soviet troops became increasingly disorganized and were largely involved in individual engagements. An exception amidst the general chaos was General Vlasov's Thirty-seventh Army, which had successfully defended Kiev until 19 September 1941 and which had initially succeeded in evading the German trap. The defence of Kiev is regarded in Soviet military historiography as a 'glorious page in the history of the Soviet

---

[159] 'Pravda o gibeli', 62.   [160] Bagramjan, *Tak načinalas' vojna*, 338.
[161] *Istorija Velikoj Otečestvennoj vojny*, ii. 109.

people',[162] although the fact that the successful defender of the Ukrainian capital was General Vlasov, future commander of the Russian Liberation Army, is deliberately concealed.[163] Like the rest of the formations of the South-west Front, the troops of Thirty-seventh Army were fragmented in the course of the breakthrough battles and some of them destroyed by 26 September 1941. The staff of the South-west Front with its GOC, its chief of staff Major-General Tupikov, and its War Council member Burmistenko, under cover of 289th Rifle Division, had reached Dryukovshchina south-west of Lokhvitsa on the morning of 20 September. There the column, which had been joined also by the staff of Fifth Army, was surrounded by German units and destroyed after two days of fighting. Contrary to reports alleging suicide, Kirponos, Tupikov, and Burmistenko were apparently killed in action,[164] while Bagramyan succeeded in fighting his way through to the Soviet lines. A number of generals, including the GOC Fifth Army, the artillery commander under the GOC Fifth Army, Major-General Sotenskiy, and others, were taken prisoner.[165]

According to the traditional line of Soviet military history, only 'individual detachments' succeeded in breaking free of the encirclement; 'some of the soldiers joined the partisans, many died a hero's death'. Of those who surrendered to the Germans no mention is made, even by the accurately informed former chief of staff of the South-western Direction, General Pokrovskiy.[166] But it was these who represented the bulk of the losses suffered at Kiev. According to German reports, 492,885 prisoners were taken by Army Group South and 172,327 (since Gomel) by Army Group Centre. At least the *History of the Great Fatherland War* reported that a third of the trapped officers and men had become prisoners of war[167]—a figure that is certainly too low, considering that on 22 September 1941 the German Sixth Army alone reported that the number of its prisoners had risen from 15,500 to 141,500 in a single day. At any rate, even Soviet publications confirm that the personnel of the South-west Front had for the most part been either killed in action or taken prisoner, and that this front, in consequence, had ceased to exist. The encirclement and annihilation of the troops of the South-west Front in the Kiev salient were a direct result of the rigid orders to hold out issued by the Supreme Command Headquarters, which were based on its mistaken estimate of the situation. Headquarters, having right up to the end placed unfounded hopes in a successful counter-attack by General Yeremenko's Bryansk Front,

[162] Grigorovič, 'Geroičeskaja stranica', 24–5; Čeremuchin, Kiev—gorod-geroj, BA-MA MSg 149/48.

[163] Bagramjan, *Tak načinalas' vojna*, 350–1.

[164] 'Pravda o gibeli', 67; Molodych, 'O načal'nike štaba JuZF', 125.

[165] Interrogation of Maj.-Gen. Sotenskiy, artillery commander under the GOC Russian Fifth Army, AOK 2/Abt. Stoart, BA-MA RH 19 II/123.

[166] Pokrovskij, 'Na Jugo-Zapadnom napravlenii', 72; *V sraženijach za Pobedu*, 45.

[167] *Istorija Velikoj Otečestvennoj vojny*, ii. 110–11.

was still indulging in the illusion that, in co-operation with the South-west Front, it would be possible to crush the German spearheads, at a time when the actual situation had long called for an evacuation of Kiev. By rejecting, with the aid of scarcely veiled threats, all requests for authorization of a withdrawal, and by refusing to acknowledge the danger of a double envelopment, Stalin and his chief of the general staff Marshal Shaposhnikov in fact created the conditions for the success of the German operations plan. Soviet publications frequently argue that the prolonged resistance in the Kiev salient had been of advantage to the overall course of the war in that it foiled German intentions to complete the campaign speedily and delayed the attack on Moscow.[168] These arguments, however, would be valid only if it had also been possible to save the troops of the South-west Front from annihilation. Instead, as Grigorenko formulates it, Headquarters had itself been reponsible for this 'greatest catastrophe of the Great Fatherland War'. A huge gap had been torn in the southern sector of the front, one which was only laboriously closed by drawing on virtually all the strategic reserves of Headquarters. The units now thrown into the breach had been raised only with great difficulty and were sorely needed in other sectors of the Soviet defensive front. There was now a danger of a German breakthrough to Kharkov and into the Donets basin.

7. The Partisan War

An important factor in the German–Soviet conflict was the partisan war, which flared up in the rear of the German army and gradually assumed considerable scale. A vast number of publications have appeared on the armed struggle of paramilitarily organized civilians in the German-occupied territories of the Soviet Union. Most of these present that form of active resistance as the manifestation of the 'profound love of the Soviet people for their socialist homeland', 'for the Communist Party, for the immortal cause of Lenin'. In this context it is argued by Soviet historiography that, apart from a 'small handful of renegades',[169] all strata of the population had, from the first day, confronted the German occupying troops with 'burning hatred' and had employed all their strength and means against the foreign conquerors. If one compares these versions of a patriotic historiography with the numerous documents testifying to the fact that the population in the occupied territories, if indeed they did not welcome the German troops as liberators, regarded them with curiosity and reserve, and certainly without hatred or hostility, one realizes how difficult it is to describe the beginnings of a struggle which, as a rule, consisted of uncoordinated individual actions.

In portraying partisan warfare in the east European theatre of war one has to remember that the population's participation in a struggle against foreign

---

[168] Moskalenko, *Na Jugo-Zapadnom napravlenii*, 93; Bagramjan, *Tak načinalas' vojna*, 368; Vasilevskij, *Delo vsej žizni*, 148.

[169] *Istorija Velikoj Otečestvennoj vojny*, ii. 120.

invaders has numerous precedents in Russian history. Not only had Napoleon's campaign of 1812 demonstrated the power of irregular detachments, but there are impressive earlier instances from the wars against Swedes, Poles, Tartars, and steppe tribes. From the point of view of Marxist military theoreticians it is a simple matter of course that national independence and liberation wars were not just the business of armies against each other, but the business of the entire nation. Thus Friedrich Engels in his writings outlined the character of a total war which no longer distinguishes between front and hinterland, between combatants and non-combatants, a war in which 'all means are just, and the most effective are the best'.[170] Total insurrection and civil war, extending to all aspects of life, also represented the natural form of struggle of the working masses against their capitalist exploiters; this was doubly true of a conflict in which the world's 'first socialist state', the Soviet Union, had to stand up against its internal and foreign enemies. After the Party of Bolsheviks had come to power through revolution and civil war, Lenin and Trotsky had turned their attention to moulding the Red Army and the partisans, under strict Party control,[171] into a united, though separately operating, instrument of power in the hands of the workers' and peasants' government. As a matter of fact, the partisans developed considerable activity after 1918. In spite of this, and of the fundamental Bolshevik conviction that in a future war too not only the Red Army but the entire nation would be embattled, and that it would have to be prepared for that in peacetime,[172] partisan warfare gradually lost in importance in the theoretical reflections of the next few years. About the middle of the 1930s all preparations for a partisan war were definitively suspended. The stockpiles of weapons, ammunition, technical equipment, and foodstuffs accumulated for such a contingency were dispersed.[173] One reason for this step was the spirit of independence inherent in that form of warfare—a spirit which even Lenin had opposed as being destructive and which Stalin tried to suppress with all means available, including the liquidation of meritorious partisan leaders in the great purge of 1937. Another reason was Soviet military doctrine, based as it was on the idea of offensive defence. According to that doctrine, in the event of a war of 'imperialist aggressors' against the Soviet Union the war would immediately be carried to the enemy's territory; there was no room for the idea that the enemy armies might succeed in penetrating into the territory of the Soviet state.

When precisely that event occurred in 1941, when German troops were rapidly gaining ground towards the east, hasty attempts were made to remedy all omissions. In a directive issued on 29 June 1941 by the Council of People's Commissars and the Central Committee of the CPSU(B), Party and state agencies in the regions close to the fronts were enjoined, in a general way, to

[170] Hoffmann, 'Volkskrieg in Frankreich', 221–2. [171] *Vojna v tylu vraga*, 16.
[172] Cvetkov, 'Vojna v tylu vraga', 109–10.
[173] Ponomarenko, 'Bor'ba sovetskogo naroda', 34.

mobllize all forces of the Soviet population for a struggle against the Germans and to organize an all-embracing people's war in the enemy's rear.[174] Stalin in his broadcast speech of 3 July 1941 addressed a similar appeal to the nations of the Soviet Union. On 18 July 1941 the Central Committee of the Party passed a special resolution 'on the organization of the struggle in the rear of the German troops'. On the basis of these official Party declarations, the Party Central Committees of the Union Republics and their subordinate Party agencies at regional and district level issued a multitude of separate instructions taking account of local conditions. Thus an underground Party apparatus was to be set up speedily in the enemy-occupied areas, and the most experienced and reliable Party activists were to assume command of the partisan detachments and groups to be set up. Even in as yet unoccupied but threatened areas a start was made on the establishment of Party and Komsomol cells; after the arrival of the Germans they were to go underground. At the same time so-called 'destruction battalions' were beginning to be set up;[175] recruited mainly from the local population, they had the task of making the rear of the Red Army secure, fighting against the activity of enemy diversionists (evidently expected on a considerable scale), and destroying economic assets at the approach of the enemy. If necessary, however, they could also take up the struggle in the enemy's rear.

Largely because of past omissions, the development of the partisan movement ran into great difficulties from the start.[176] Neither the material nor the personnel, nor yet the leadership prerequisites, were present. Partisan detachments and groups could not be equipped on an adequate scale[177] because of a failure in the past to set up appropriate stores of weapons, explosives, mines, etc., and because there existed virtually no radio transmitters. Because of a shortage of trained leaders and specialists, and also of manpower, these deficiencies could not be eliminated. A particular disadvantage was the fact that no theoretical instructions for partisan activity in the conditions of a modern war had been worked out in peacetime. The authorities charged with the conduct of the partisan war had no precise ideas either on the tactics to be applied or on the most suitable forms of organization.[178] Initially this resulted in efforts to create the largest possible units and to control them on a strictly centralized pattern. But this deprived the partisans of their initiative. Not only did large units prove too cumbersome to control, but their appearance also made it easier for the enemy to take timely countermeasures. Questions concerning organization, material equipment, and co-operation with Red Army units, as well as the unified application of lessons learnt in combat, would have been best solved by the immediate establishment of an operational central control of the partisan movement. The fact that these matters were left to the Party organizations of the individual Union republics and to their

[174] Byčkov, *Partizanskoe dviženie*, 47.   [175] *Zaroždenie i razvitie*, 60 ff.
[176] Lesnjak, 'Nekotorye voprosy', 30, 38.   [177] *Istorija Velikoj Otečestvennoj vojny*, ii. 130.
[178] Absaljamov and Andrianov, 'Organizacija partizanskich sil', 24.

corresponding administrative bodies resulted in a fragmentation of forces and delayed the unfolding of partisan warfare.[179] Eventually, after a few false starts, a Central Staff of the Partisan Movement in the Supreme Command Headquarters was established on 30 May 1942[180] under the chairmanship of Ponomarenko, Secretary of the Central Committee of the CP(B) of Belorussia, and including one well-known representative each of the People's Commissariat of the Interior (NKVD) and the Red Army General Staff. Under this Central Staff there soon sprang up Staffs of the Partisan Movement at republican, regional, and district level; these were represented on the War Councils of the individual fronts by tactical groups.

While Soviet military historiography on the whole tried to convey the impression that the 'heroic struggle of the Soviet people in the rear of the Fascist armies' had begun spontaneously and on a large scale at the very beginning of the war, some authors were forced to admit that during the first few months of the war the partisans scored only insignificant successes.[181] Thus Colonel Neryanin, chief of the operations department of the Soviet Twentieth Army and future chief of the operations department in the command of the Russian Liberation Army, had been roving about the rear of the German troops for three weeks without observing the slightest evidence of partisan activity. He was later to state to the Germans that the Soviet leadership had been bitterly disappointed at the slight extent of the partisan struggle.[182] However, the ineffectiveness of the partisan war[183] prior to the spring of 1942 was not, as is claimed, due only to poor command and organizational shortcomings. The main reason was that it lacked the prerequisite[184] which Friedrich Engels had described as indispensable for successful guerrilla warfare—reliable support by the local population. This lack is readily understood if one bears in mind the widespread public dissatisfaction with the Soviet regime, as well as the fact that the true aims of the Germans, posturing as liberators, were at first not realized. Wherever partisan groups appeared during the early period—in so far as these were not in fact scattered elements of the Red Army,[185] who were often afraid to return through the lines because of reprisals awaiting them—these usually met with uniform rejection and resistance on the part of the local population, whose main interest was in a return to normal conditions. Only gradually, and scarcely before the spring of 1942, did a favourable climate develop for a partisan war.

This was due largely to disappointment at the failure of the Germans to produce a constructive occupation programme, the preservation of the hated collective-farm system, the hardships of the population in the occupied terri-

---

[179] Lesnjak, 'Nekotorye voprosy', 24.

[180] Ponomarenko, 'Bor'ba sovetskogo naroda', 34–5.

[181] Naumov, 'Taktika belorusskich partizan', 40.

[182] Interrogation of Col. (gen. staff) Neryanin, Andrey Georgevich, Ia of the Russian Twentieth Army, BA R 6/77.

[183] Galai, 'Die Partisanen', 175 ff.   [184] Klokov, *Vsenarodnaja bor'ba*, 67.

[185] Kalinin, 'Učastie sovetskich vojnov', 25.

tories, and some discriminatory measures by the occupying authorities. The inhumane conditions to which Soviet prisoners of war were subjected and the atrocities committed against the Jewish part of the population also left a deeper impression than the Germans suspected. The indiscriminate procedure of the security forces—who often did failed to differentiate between the peaceful population and partisans—reprisal executions, the shooting of hostages, and the burning of homes all helped to drive the population into the arms of the partisans. Initially these saw their main task as provoking further reprisals by repeated but still aimless attacks, in order to make the Germans hated among the local people. Purposeful propaganda,[186] hand in hand with ruthless terror against local officials and police,[187] was to remind the population of the ubiquity of Soviet power. Torn between the occupying power, which threatened Draconian punishment even for failure to report hostile activity, and the partisans, who threatened death for even the slightest support of the Germans, such as the enforced surrender of agricultural produce,[188] the population often saw no alternative to joining whichever side was stronger—which very soon, in some remote regions at least, meant the partisans. Not until 1942, when they had succeeded locally in winning support among the population, did the partisans begin to conduct systematic actions against German military targets.

The partisan war,[189] characterized as a rule by ambushes and raids, rarely by open attacks mounted by armed civilians, is presented in Soviet historiography as the 'justified manifestation of a lawful struggle by the people's masses against the Hitlerites', who had committed 'unheard-of crimes' and 'a serious breach of international law by their war of aggression'.[190] This attempt to justify partisan warfare by reference to the aggression and culpable behaviour of the adversary, however, ignores the fact that the Hague Convention invariably obliges both belligerents, regardless of the question of guilt, to observe the laws and usages of land warfare. In consequence, at least one of the judges of the Nuremberg Military Tribunal could not avoid describing the partisan war as a phenomenon incompatible with the spirit or the letter of international law. In point of fact, the Hague Land Warfare convention of 18 October 1907 requires unequivocally that for irregular fighting forces—'milices' or 'corps de volontaires'—not to come under the heading of irregulars, they have to meet the following conditions:[191]

1. They must be commanded by someone who is responsible for his subordinates.

---

[186] Rudakov, 'Rol' voennych sovetov', 5.   [187] Hoffmann, *Deutsche und Kalmyken*, 109.
[188] *Geschichte des zweiten Weltkrieges*, iv. 428.
[189] Auszugsweise Übersetzung der Kampfanweisung für Partisanen-Gruppen [Translation of excerpts from the operational directive for partisan groups], Army Group North Ic/AO to commander rearward army area North, No. 405/41 geh., 20 Aug. 1941, BA-MA RH 22/271; Absaljamov and Andrianov, 'Taktika sovetskich partizan'.
[190] Byčkov, *Partizanskoe dviženie*, 12–13.   [191] Laun, *Die Haager Landkriegsordnung*, 75.

2. They must wear an identifying badge recognizable from afar.
3. They must carry their weapons openly.
4. In their operations they must observe the laws and usages of war.

The partisans met only the first of these conditions. The manner in which they were accustomed to operating may be gauged from a directive of the Central Committee of the CP(B) of Belorussia, dated 1 July 1941.[192] This directive—which is quoted here as only one of countless instances—instructs the partisans

to destroy all communications in the enemy's rear, blow up or damage bridges and roads, set fire to motor-fuel and food stores, motor-vehicles, and aircraft, arrange for railway disasters, annihilate enemies, giving them no respite day or night. Destroy them wherever they are caught, kill them with anything that comes to hand: axe, scythe, crowbar, pitchfork, knife. Link up with other partisan detachments, make surprise raids on enemy units and annihilate them . . . In annihilating the enemy do not shrink from using any means: strangle, chop up, burn, poison the Fascist scum. Let the enemy feel the ground burning under his feet.

On 1 October 1941 Kozlov, a captured partisan, reported a suggestion of Kazalapov, a member of the Central Committee of the Party from Kholm, that German soldiers or wounded be 'tortured by mutilation before execution'.[193] There is also ample evidence that partisans proceeded mercilessly not only against German servicemen but equally against disliked or even totally uninvolved local inhabitants. Thus members of the 'native' administration (mainly mayors and policemen) were invariably 'mercilessly' beaten to death, usually also the members of their families, including women and children. Another partisan principle was that all witnesses of a raid were to be killed if necessary—men, women, and children—to prevent a possible betrayal to the Germans.[194]

Contrary to Soviet assertions,[195] partisan activity against the German occupying power did not develop on an appreciable scale until 1942, except in the Crimea, where more favourable conditions existed. The ever increasing scale of the partisan war also proves that the German–Soviet conflict was an ideological war of annihilation, in which little room was left for principles enshrined in international agreements. It was the Soviet side that unleashed the partisan war, which ran counter to international law. But the Germans similarly, in opposing the irregulars, did not shrink from the utmost ruthlessness or from employing any means that seemed to them suitable. It was the civilian population that suffered most from the barbaric methods of both belligerents.

---

[192] *Zaroždenie i razvitie*, 53–4.

[193] Supplementary interrogation of Yevgeniy Kozlov, Gruppe Geheime Feldpolizei [Group Secret Field Police] 727, No. 336/41 geh., 1 Oct. 1941, BA-MA RH 22/271; Zayas, *Die Wehrmacht-Untersuchungsstelle*, 133 ff., 427 ff.

[194] Hesse, *Der sowjetrussische Partisanenkrieg*, 109, 61.

[195] *Istorija Velikoj Otečestvennoj vojny*, ii. 134–5.

8. The Repulse of the German Autumn Offensive at Leningrad and Rostov

Once the German command had decided not to capture Leningrad but to besiege it and starve it out, if only to avoid the need 'to feed that city of millions', the Soviet troops gained a breathing-space during which they were able to organize the defence of the city more efficiently. In accordance with the demand of the State Defence Committee that Lenin's city be transformed into an unconquerable fortress, the Leningrad Front, with support from Zhdanov and other Party and government officials, embarked on the development of a deeply echeloned system of defences. Included in the defence measures were the air force (Air Defence Corps and 7th Fighter Corps),[196] as well as the ships, batteries, and aircraft of the Red Banner Baltic Fleet.[197] For an offensive operation against the German siege artillery a special artillery group was formed under Major-General Sviridov and Rear-Admiral Gren.[198] A considerable burden of the defence effort, especially in the construction of positions and barricades, was borne by the civilian population of Leningrad, although they were exposed to increasing hardship owing to the shortage of foodstuffs and fuel. The food shortage became so acute in the course of the autumn that from 20 November 1941 the non-working population, including children, received only 125 g. of bread daily.[199] Soon, therefore, attempts were made to use the Ladoga flotilla to carry vital cargo, such as foodstuffs, weapons, and ammunitions, on at least a modest scale to the city, which by then could be reached only by way of Lake Ladoga, and simultaneously to evacuate such useless consumers as the wounded, women, and children.[200] When Lake Ladoga froze over in November, on 19 November the Leningrad Front resolved to lay a supply-route, the so-called 'lifeline',[201] over the ice. During the winter of 1941–2 no less than 361,106 t. of vital goods reached the city in this way, and 514,000 persons were evacuated from the city to the east.

At the same time, measures were put in hand to burst through the blockade ring and restore free access to Leningrad. On 14 October 1941 Colonel-General Voronov, the Headquarters representative with the Leningrad Front, arrived with a directive from the Supreme Command Headquarters instructing the Neva Group, in conjunction with General Fedyuninskiy's Fifty-fourth Army operating east of the encirclement ring, to crush the enemy forces between Shlisselburg and Sinyavino, in the so-called 'bottleneck', and to open up a corridor to Leningrad. This action,[202] however, which upon Headquarters' urgings started on 20 October, did not succeed because it was anticipated by a rapidly advancing German attack towards Tikhvin and Volkhov, and because of shortcomings in the way it was directed. Although the Soviet Fifty-fourth Army managed to hold Volkhov, and although General Klykov's Fifty-

[196] Novikov, in *Oborona Leningrada*, 75 ff.
[197] Panteleev, ibid. 144 ff.; Kuznecov, ibid. 222 ff.   [198] Odincov, ibid. 102 ff.
[199] Ibid., 771.   [200] Chrulev, 'V bor'be za Leningrad', 28.
[201] Šikin, 'Podvigu žit''.   [202] Voronov, in *Oborona Leningrada*, 217.

second Army contained the German thrust towards Malaya Vishera, the Soviet troops found themselves in difficulties and Tikhvin fell to the Germans on 8 November 1941. This meant the severance of the last railway line by which goods could be brought to the eastern shore of Lake Ladoga for shipping to Leningrad. Moreover, it gave rise to the real danger of a break-through into the rear of Army General Meretskov's Seventh Independent Army, which was facing the Finns on the Svir. Because of the total failure of General Yakovlev's Fourth Army, which retreated in disorganized units in various directions,[203] Meretskov, by order of Headquarters, was temporarily put in command of Fourth Army as well. Meretskov, a former chief of the Red Army General Staff, now in command of all formations between the Svir front and the German penetration area near Tikhvin, began to assemble all available forces and go over to counter-attacks in the main directions.[204] In conse-quence, the projecting German spearhead to the east was increasingly threat-ened from its flanks and, from 19 November 1941, also attacked at its point by the Fourth Army. Under Meretskov's vigorous leadership the initiative on this sector gradually passed to the Soviet troops. The German plan to cut Lenin-grad off completely from the rest of the world and to link up with the Finnish Karelian Army proved impracticable.

On the southern wing of the front too the Soviet forces eventually succeeded in halting the German offensive, which had resumed towards the end of September 1941. Prior to that success, however, they had been forced into extensive withdrawals. The German attack out of the bridgeheads at Dnepropetrovsk and Kakhovka had instantly got the Soviet Twelfth Army into difficulties and resulted in the encirclement and annihilation of elements of Lieutenant-General Smirnov's Eighteenth and Major-General Kharitonov's Ninth Armies. By 11 October 1941 Army Group South had taken 106,000 Soviet prisoners in the 'battle north of the Sea of Azov'. Countless others, including General Smirnov, GOC Eighteenth Army, had been killed in action. In a memorial article in 1968 Colonel-General Anisimov reported that the Germans, who still indulged in that kind of gesture during the initial months of the war, had buried him in a dignified manner in a separate grave. Attempts by Lieutenant-General Cherevichenko, the GOC Southern Front, to halt the enemy along improvised lines were unsuccessful.[205] On 17 October Taganrog was abandoned. By the end of October the forces of the Southern Front had been thrown back as far as the approaches to Rostov. On 25 October the troops of the South-west Front under the command of Marshal Timoshenko (Major-General Tsyganov's Thirty-eighth and Major-General Malinovskiy's Sixth Armies) abandoned Kharkov after extensively mining the city,[206] and manned a defensive line north of Izyum. No less critical was the situation in the Crimea, where on 18 October the German Eleventh Army opened its

[203] Mereckov, 'Na jugo-vostočnych podstupach', 66, 70–1.
[204] Mereckov, *Na službe narodu*, 230 ff.   [205] Anisimov, 'Komandarm 18-j', 117.
[206] *V sraženijach za Pobedu*, 77–8.

attack for the seizure of the peninsula. Even before the start of this offensive, the Russians had begun to evacuate the troops of the Odessa defence district,[207] who, under the command of Rear-Admiral Zhukov and the GOC Independent Coastal Army, Lieutenant-General Sofronov, had been tying down considerable Romanian and German forces over a period of two weeks.[208] On 23 October the forces of the Odessa defence district, now transferred to the Crimea, and the troops of Lieutenant-General Batov's Independent Fifty-first Army were placed under the command of Vice-Admiral Levchenko, the commander of the Crimean troops, who was in charge of coordinating the defence of the land front with the actions of the Black Sea Fleet.[209] Nevertheless, the Germans after a few days broke through the defensive positions near Ishun on the Perekop isthmus. The Independent Fifty-first Army was forced to retreat to Kerch, and on 16 November the Taman peninsula was evacuated. The Coastal Army withdrew to Sevastopol. At that point all land and air forces, as well as the ships and aircraft of the Black Sea Fleet, were placed under the command of Major-General Petrov, the commander of the Sevastopol defence zone; after 10 November they came under Vice-Admiral Oktyabrskiy, the capable commander of the Black Sea Fleet.[210] By dint of vigorous efforts the Sevastopol area, subdivided into several defence sectors and tightly encircled by the Germans, was, for the time being, held against all attacks.[211]

While Sevastopol was preparing for defence, there arose in the sector of the Southern Front, at and north of Rostov, first a crisis and then a turn for the better. On 5 November 1941 the German First Armoured Army had mounted an attack for the capture of Shakhty; this, however, did not succeed, even though Kharitonov's Ninth Army was pushed back towards the east. After the failure of this envelopment move the Germans on 17 November launched a direct thrust towards Rostov from a north-westerly direction; Rostov was regarded as the gate to the Caucasus and an objective of great strategic importance. After no more than a delaying defence by General Remezov's Independent Fifty-sixth Army, the city fell to the Germans a few days later.[212] By that time, however, preparations had been completed on the Soviet side for a large-scale counter-attack against the flank and the rear of the German forces spearheaded towards Rostov. The idea, proposed by Major-General Bagramyan, won the support of Lieutenant-General Bodin, chief of staff of the South-western Direction, and, after some hesitation, also that of the GOC, Marshal Timoshenko.[213] Headquarters had likewise given its approval, but declared itself unable to provide reinforcements. In consequence, the command of the South-western Direction had to establish an assault group from the forces of the South-west Front and the Southern Front under its com-

---

[207] Chrenov and Aganičev, 'Ėvakuacija vojsk.'   [208] Sofronov, 'Odesskij placdarm'.
[209] Eliseev, 'Pervye dni', 51.   [210] Bolgari *et al.*, *Černomorskij flot*, 176.
[211] Ryži, 'Na Sevastopol'skich rubežach'.   [212] Krajnjukov, 'V bojach za Rostov', 82.
[213] Bagramjan, 'Razgrom 1-j tankovoj armii', *VIŽ* (1969), No. 11, 60 ff.

mand. In accordance with a demand by Marshal Shaposhnikov, chief of the Red Army General Staff, the Southern Front had been reinforced at the expense of the South-west Front, and a new army, Thirty-seventh Army under Major-General Lopatin, had been established as the main attacking force. Simultaneously, some air units were made available from the Headquarters reserve. On 17 November this Thirty-seventh Army, composed of four rifle divisions, four armoured brigades, and several artillery, anti-tank, and mortar regiments, and supported by elements of General Kolpakchi's Eighteenth Army and above all by Ninth Army, opened its offensive in the general direction of Bolshekrepinskaya–Taganrog. Although during the first few days the attack only slowly gained ground,[214] the German First Armoured Army, which had meanwhile broken through to Rostov, was compelled after 23 November to withdraw some forces in order to support its northern flank. The Independent Fifty-sixth Army, which had likewise gone over to the attack, striking from the east, thus saw its chance, in conjunction with the left wing of Ninth Army, to recapture Rostov on 29 November. The fact that the First Armoured Army was compelled, under the combined pressure of the Soviet Thirty-seventh, Ninth, and Fifty-sixth Armies, to withdraw to the Mius at the beginning of December, not only meant a stabilization of the German–Soviet front in this sector for some time to come, but was of major propaganda importance as the 'first great victory of the Red Army'. The Soviet troops had certainly scored a victory, but, contrary to Bagramyan's claims, they had not succeeded in achieving their real objective—the destruction of Kleist's armoured army.

9. The Repulse of the German Attack on Moscow

Since the battle of Smolensk Stalin, Supreme Command Headquarters, and the Red Army General Staff had taken a variety of measures to safeguard the capital against a German assault in the event of a resumption of the German offensive.[215] In order to repel a possible attack from the west, three combined fronts (until 15 September 1941 under the command of Marshal Timoshenko's South-western Direction) had been assembled to face the German Army Group Centre.[216] These were the Western Front (since 12 September under the command of Colonel-General Konev) in the sector between Ostashkov and Yelnya; east of it, as second echelon in the Vyazma defensive line from Ostashkov to Selizharovo, the Reserve Front (commanded by Marshal Budennyy) with Major-General Rakutin's Twenty-fourth Army and Major-General Sobennikov's Forty-third Army west of Spas-Demensk and Kirov, but also in the foremost line; and finally the Bryansk Front (commanded by Colonel-General Yeremenko) with General Yermakov's tactical

[214] Ibid., No. 12, 66 ff.   [215] Vasilevskij, *Delo vsej žizni*, 150–1.
[216] Žukov, 'V bitve za stolicu', *VIŽ* (1966), No. 8, 54.

group on the left wing, holding the sector from east of Kirov to Glukhov. There are divergent data in the Soviet literature on the actual strength of those three fronts, which, together with Yermakov's tactical group, embraced sixteen armies.[217] The figures range from a maximum of 1,250,000 men, 10,598 artillery pieces and mortars, 990 tanks, and 950 aircraft to a minimum of 800,000 men, 6,800 artillery pieces and mortars, 780 tanks, and 360–527 aircraft. In order to emphasize their own inferiority and to offer some excuse for the subsequent defeats of the Soviet troops,[218] the figures of Soviet effective strength are clearly being kept low, and the level of accuracy of the Soviet figures must inevitably remain in doubt. There is, however, no denying that in the double battle of Vyazma and Bryansk the Germans took 673,000 Red Army prisoners by 20 October, and listed 1,242 tanks and 5,412 artillery pieces as destroyed or captured; this suggests that Soviet strength must have been substantially greater than officially admitted.

Despite the general preparations for defence, the deployment of major forces, and the construction of a deeply echeloned defensive system outside Moscow, the Soviet leadership was nevertheless taken by surprise by the opening of the German offensive against the capital. The Soviet command had failed to identify the preparations in time and to foil German intentions. Not until 26 September 1941 did Stalin and the chief of the Red Army General Staff receive a report from the GOC Western Front, which, on the strength of reconnaissance data, predicted an attack against Moscow along the Vyazma–Moscow highway.[219] Thus, even Konev at that time expected only one operation on the relatively limited sector defended by Nineteenth, Sixteenth, and Twentieth Armies. And Headquarters still did nothing more than issue a belated directive the following day calling in general terms for 'stubborn resistance' and intensified construction of the system of positions. It failed to make any kind of preparations for co-ordinated operations by the three fronts actually involved, and it failed to clarify relations between the Western Front and the Reserve Front, two of whose armies were standing in the foremost line and were thus responsible for the safety of the left wing of the Western Front. It was soon to become obvious how important it would have been, even before the start of the German offensive, to subordinate both fronts to a single operations staff. As the Russians had failed to identify the points of main effort of the German attack,[220] no measures had been taken to reinforce the threatened sectors or to concentrate reserves at those points—an omission which Marshal Zhukov in retrospect blamed not on Headquarters but on the commands of the Western and Reserve Fronts.[221] There is no doubt that the errors and omissions of the Soviet command were the main reason why Army Group

[217] 'Moskovskaja bitva v cifrach: Period oborony', 71; Sokolovskij, 'Velikaja bitva', 20; Fedorov, *Aviacija*, 74; *50 let vooružennych sil*, 290; *Geschichte des zweiten Weltkrieges*, iv. 118.

[218] 'Moskovskaja bitva v cifrach: Period oborony', 69.

[219] Konev, 'Načalo Moskovskoj bitvy', 58–9.   [220] Žukov, 'Bitva pod Moskvoj, 1', 63.

[221] Žukov, 'V bitve za stolicu', *VIŽ* (1966), No. 8, 60.

Centre was able to penetrate the defences at the crucial points so rapidly. This was facilitated also by the fact that, shortly before the opening of the German offensive, Soviet forces, misreading the situation and acting upon express orders from Stalin and Headquarters, had begun to carry out limited offensive operations—with the result that these officers and men were lost to a concentrated defence. The Soviet formations striking into the German attack, such as Major-General Sobennikov's Forty-third Army of the Reserve Front northwest of Roslavl and General Yermakov's tactical group at Glukhov, suffered considerable losses. On the very first day of the attack Armoured Group 2 tore apart the Bryansk Front at the boundary between Major-General Gorodnyanskiy's Thirteenth Army and Yermakov's tactical group, pushed beyond Sevsk in the direction of Orel and Tula, and at the same time wheeled some of its units north towards Karachev and Bryansk, thereby threatening the rear of Thirteenth Army as well as Major-General Kreyzer's Third Army. A counter-attack mounted against the German spearhead by Thirteenth Army from the north and by the Yermakov tactical group from the south was unsuccessful.[222] By 3 October 1941 Orel was lost because the garrison commander, Lieutenant-General Tyurin, had been incapable of organizing the city's defence.

Once Armoured Group 4 had driven a wedge between the Forty-third Army of the Reserve Front and Major-General Petrov's Fiftieth Army, and once Bryansk had been taken by the new Second Armoured Army on 6 October 1941, the bulk of the Bryansk Front was split up and cut off from its rear communications, and Major-General Kreyzer's Third Army, Major-General Gorodnyanskiy's Thirteenth Army, and elements of Major-General Petrov's Fiftieth Army were in the pocket. Colonel-General Yeremenko, who realized the disastrous situation of his troops and was scarcely by this stage in a position of command, had in vain asked Headquarters as far back as 4 October for permission to withdraw the entire front towards the east, in order at least to save its combat strength for the defence of Moscow.[223] Not until 7 October, when the encirclement was complete and nothing but a break-out was possible, did Marshal Shaposhnikov, on behalf of Stalin, concur. He explained the fateful delay by communications trouble. On 8 October the three encircled armies began their attempt to break out; however, in the conditions prevailing until 23 October that attempt was made only in a disjointed manner. Only at the price of exceedingly high losses in personnel and material were the remnants of Fiftieth Army able to man a new defensive line on the Oka near Mtsensk, the remnants of Third Army a line between Zmievka and Ponyri, and those of Thirteenth Army a line between Fatezh and Makarovka.

As the Soviet command had failed to recognize the preparations for a general attack on Moscow and had, since 30 September 1941, been turning its attention to the speedily developing attack towards Orel and Tula, it did not

---

[222] Eremenko, *Na zapadnom napravlenii*, 102.
[223] Id., 'Na jugo-zapadnych podstupach', 79.

realize that the principal danger threatening it was in the sector of the Reserve and Western Fronts. In consequence, the attack of Armoured Groups 3 and 4, directed on 2 October against the centre of the Western Front at the boundary of Lieutenant-General Lukin's Nineteenth Army and Major-General Khomenko's Thirtieth Army, and simultaneously against the positions of Major-General Sobennikov's Forty-third Army of the Reserve Front, made rapid progress without any reaction whatever from Headquarters.[224] The northern spearhead, after the capture of Kholm Zhirkovskiy, was by 3 October threatening Vyazma from the north, while further south the main thrust directed against the Soviet Forty-third Army by Armoured Group 4 and Fourth Army simultaneously reached Spas Demensk and, wheeling north-wards, likewise aimed at Vyazma. What was beginning to take shape during the first few days of October was the danger of an encirclement of the entire Soviet grouping of Western Front and Reserve Front forces in the Vyazma area. The price was now being paid for the lack of co-ordination between the two Fronts, whose armies now both found themselves deeply outflanked without being able to relieve one another.[225] When hastily mounted and uncoordinated counter-attacks, e.g. by the newly established tactical group of Lieutenant-General Boldin at Vyazma, failed to achieve results, on 4 October Colonel-General Konev, GOC Western Front, asked Headquarters and the general staff for permission to withdraw to defensive positions near Gzhatsk, hoping like Yeremenko that the forces of his Front could thus be preserved for further operations in the defence of Moscow. Once more a decision was delayed. On 5 October the Supreme Command Headquarters still refused to believe that Armoured Group 4 had that day reached Yukhnov. Colonel Sbytov, commanding the air forces of the Moscow military district, who had submitted his reconnaissance findings on those lines, was threatened by the NKVD with prosecution for 'spreading panic'.[226] Not until the afternoon of 5 October, when the correctness of his statement happened to be confirmed, was the order given for the withdrawal of Thirtieth, Nineteenth, Sixteenth, and Twentieth Armies. Belatedly, Major-General Dalmatov's Thirty-first Army and Major-General Vishnevskiy's Thirty-second Army were now placed under the Western Front in order to achieve a unified command. However, there was no time to accomplish the withdrawals—which were often associ-ated with complicated regrouping operations—if only because of a total disor-ganization of the senior commands. Major Shabalin, chief of the Special NKVD Detachment of the Fiftieth Army, confided some remarkable impres-sions to his diary.[227] 'The army is not what we have come to believe in the homeland. Enormous shortcomings!', he recorded as early as 6 September. 'We are surrounded!', he wrote on 4 October. 'The entire Front—this means

[224] Konev, 'Načalo moskovskoj bitvy', 62.   [225] Vasilevskij, *Delo vsej žizni*, 151.

[226] This is hushed up by Fedorov, *Aviacija*, 83–4.

[227] Diary of NKVD Maj. Shabalin, chief of the Special NKVD Detachment of Fiftieth Army, BA-MA RH 19 II/125.

three armies—was trapped in the encirclement. And what are our generals doing? They "consider" . . . In our unit everyone, as usual, has lost their heads and is incapable of action.' 'The heads of the front staff lost command throughout the time of the German attack and, it seems, lost their heads,' Shabalin wrote on 6 October 1941. On the following day he noted: 'Such a thing as the defeat of the Bryansk Front has not been witnessed by history . . . The Front command had lost control from the first days of the German attack. It is said the idiots have skedaddled to Moscow.'

When, on the evening of 6 October 1941, Armoured Groups 3 and 4 linked up east of Vyazma, substantial forces of the Western Front west of the city were indeed surrounded.[228] They were Lieutenant-General Lukin's Nineteenth Army, Lieutenant-General Rokossovskiy's Sixteenth Army (which had been absorbed into Lieutenant-General Yershakov's Twentieth Army), Lieutenant-General Boldin's tactical group, as well as Major-General Vishnevskiy's Thirty-second Army and Major-General Rakutin's Twenty-fourth Army, which both belonged to the Reserve Front.[229] The encirclement of major forces of the Bryansk Front, and of the Western and the Reserve Fronts in the Bryansk and Vyazma area during the first few days of October, created great confusion among the Soviet leadership. With the principal task now being the speediest possible establishment of new defences outside Moscow, and with the GOCs of the Front evidently no longer enjoying confidence, plenipotentiaries were dispatched from the Supreme Command Headquarters and the State Defence Committee—Molotov, Mikoyan, Malenkov, Voroshilov, Vasilevskiy, and, independently from that group, Army General Zhukov—with special instructions for the threatened sectors. These representatives of the top leadership discovered disastrous conditions on the Western and Reserve Fronts, whose commands had lost any overall view of the situation and frequently also contact with their subordinate armies.[230] It was essential to put an end at last to the fatal division of command bodies in the sector west of Moscow. On 10 October, in response to the reports from the special representatives, the troops of the Western and Reserve Fronts were amalgamated, Colonel-General Konev and Marshal Budennyy were relieved of their posts, and Army General Zhukov was appointed the new GOC Western Front.[231] Konev, for the time being still the nominal second-in-command to Zhukov, henceforward commanded the forces on the right wing of the Western Front at Kalinin; after the Germans captured the town on 14 October, thereby threatening the rear of the North-west Front as well as that of the Moscow defences, Konev on 17 October became GOC of the newly created Kalinin Front. This consisted of Major-General Vostrukhov's Twenty-second Army, Major-General Maslennikov's Twenty-ninth Army,

[228] Rokossovskij, 'Na volokolamskom napravlenii', 46.
[229] Samsonov, 'Moskvu zaščiščala vsja strana', 54.
[230] Žukov, 'V bitve za stolicu', *VIŽ* (1966), No. 8, 58–9.
[231] Konev, 'Načalo Moskovskoj bitvy', 67.

Major-General Yushkevich's Thirty-first Army, and Major-General Khomenko's Thirtieth Army. Twenty-ninth, Thirty-first, and Thirtieth Armies moved into a defensive line in a semicircle behind Kalinin,[232] while Twenty-second Army succeeded, in violent fighting, in maintaining its positions in the Torzhok area. Just as on the right wing, at Kalinin and Torzhok, the defenders of Moscow succeeded also on the left wing, in the sector of the Bryansk Front, in containing the advance of Second Armoured Army and Second Army in the course of October, albeit after heavy setbacks. Already during the first ten days of October Major-General Lelyushenko's 1st Guards Rifle Corps (directly subordinated to Headquarters) had stubbornly defended the town of Mtsensk and thereby gained time to prepare for the defence of Tula.[233] It was not until 29 October that Second Armoured Army, whose task it was to envelop Moscow in a wide sweep from the south, reached the approaches of Tula. However, Major-General Yermakov's Fiftieth Army, reinforced by People's Guard detachments, repulsed the German attack and at the beginning of November, along with elements of Major-General Kreyzer's Third Army, even mounted counter-attacks against the flank of the German spearhead. At the end of the first phase of the general attack on the Soviet capital the situation at Tula, which, like Kalinin, represented a cornerstone of the defences outside Moscow, appeared temporarily stabilized.

What measures were taken after Zhukov's appointment on 19 October 1941 to reorganize the forces of the Western Front and to halt the German offensive in front of Moscow? Once the first line of defence, the Vyazma line, was pierced, the Soviet command turned its attention to a hurried preparation of a second line of defence, the Mozhaysk line, running from Volokolamsk to Kaluga. Those troops of the former Western and Reserve Fronts who had escaped being trapped in the Vyazma pocket were now assembled in that new, artificially consolidated, line. Headquarters moreover transferred to this defensive line forces from the North-west, Bryansk, and South-west Fronts, and also assembled in it units of the Moscow military district, as well as reinforcements arriving, from mid-October onwards, from the Caucasus, central Asia, and the Far East. By exhausting all capacities it proved possible, within a short time, to concentrate 11 rifle divisions, 16 armoured brigades, and over 40 artillery regiments—approximately 90,000 men—within the Mozhaysk defence line. The GOC Western Front created points of main defensive effort at the approach roads to Moscow, and at these points concentrated all available artillery and anti-tank forces.[234] The Volokolamsk sector was defended by the newly established Sixteenth Army under Lieutenant-General Rokossovskiy; Mozhaysk was covered by Fifth Army under Major-General Lelyushenko; the Maloyaroslavets sector was manned by Forty-third Army under Major-General Golubev; the Kaluga area was defended by Forty-ninth Army under

[232] Rakickij and Presnjakov, 'Boevye dejstvija', 85.

[233] Leljušenko, *Moskva, Stalingrad, Berlin, Praga*, 35 ff.

[234] 'Prikaz komandujuščego Zapadnogo fronta, 30.10.1941', in *Moskva—frontu*, 32–3.

Lieutenant-General Zakharkin. A short time later Thirty-third Army under Lieutenant-General Yefremov was inserted at Naro-Fominsk. To support these formations in preventing a German breakthrough to Moscow at all costs, the following air units were available in addition to the air forces of the Western Front: 6th Fighter Corps of Air Defence under Major-General Klimov, the air forces of the Moscow military district, a few divisions of long-range bombers, and four newly established air regiments.[235] Attempts were going ahead at the same time to improve the shaken morale of the troops and to fight signs of defeatism by every available means.[236] Order No. 0345, dated 13 October 1941 and issued by Zhukov and War Council member Bulganin, appealed to all Soviet servicemen, from top commanders down to the last Red Army private, to make an extreme effort. Cowards and panic-mongers, i.e. soldiers abandoning their positions without authorization, were to be 'shot on the spot' as traitors to the fatherland.

After the war the Marshals of the Soviet Union Zhukov, Konev, and Vasilevskiy,[237] looking back to that period, all wrote that only by the perseverance of the armies encircled at Vyazma had the necessary time been gained for the strengthening of the Mozhaysk defensive line. But this alleged advantage, which is so greatly stressed by Soviet historians, had to be paid for by enormous losses in men and material. When resistance came to an end on 20 October 1941, five armies and Boldin's tactical group had ceased to exist. In this context one cannot without some reservation speak of the 'heroism of the Soviet warriors gallantly fighting at Vyazma' or about their 'undying glory', considering that by 20 October no fewer than 673,000 of them allowed themselves to be taken prisoner by the Germans, contrary to the terms of Soviet military penal law and to the unequivocal orders of the Soviet command. Among the prisoners of war was Lieutenant-General Yershakov (GOC Twentieth Army), Major-General Vishnevskiy (GOC Thirty-second Army), and Lieutenant-General Lukin (GOC Nineteenth Army), who had been charged with the command of the trapped formations. Indeed, Lukin, who was severely wounded, conveyed to the Germans a very negative impression of the morale of the Soviet troops encircled at Vyazma.[238] According to him, the infantry in the pocket 'did not show the necessary will to fight their way out. The men preferred to go into captivity.' That was why they had been 'driven forward' and in the course of vain breakthrough attempts 'time and again' sacrificed in their tens of thousands. Major Kononov, the commander of 436th Rifle Regiment and future Major-General in the Russian Liberation Army, who had come over to the Germans with his units, painted a similar picture during his interrogation: 'A panicky mood is prevalent in the army . . . The

---

[235] Fedorov, *Aviacija*, 97.   [236] *Istorija Velikoj Otečestvennoj vojny*, ii. 243.

[237] Žukov, 'V bitve za stolicu', *VIŽ* (1966), No. 9, 55; Konev, 'Načalo Moskovskoj bitvy', 66; Vasilevskij, *Delo vsej žizni*, 151.

[238] Interrogation of Lt.-Gen. Lukin, Mikhail Feodorovich, GOC Nineteenth Army (most recently in command of the sector of Thirty-second, Twentieth, Twenty-fourth, and Nineteenth Armies), Heeresgruppe Mitte [Army Group Centre] Ic/AO, 14 Dec. 1941, BA R 6/77.

troops attack only under direct compulsion from the political officials.'[239]
Lukin, one-time holder of the responsible position of commandant of the city
of Moscow, lived in the Soviet Union after the war 'as a loyal son of the
Communist Party', a man who 'dedicated his entire conscious life to boundless service to the fatherland, to the cause of the Communist Party'.[240] In
actual fact, Lukin's experiences at Vyazma had caused a deep rift in his
attitude to Stalin. On 12 December 1941 he had spontaneously submitted a
proposal to the Germans—which was brought to Hitler's notice—for the
establishment of a 'Russian counter-government'. 'Peasants had been promised land, workers had been promised a share in industry,' he stated in
justification of his attitude; 'peasants and workers were deceived . . . With
hardships and terror reigning, and above all a joylessness in life, you will
understand that these people must gratefully welcome their liberation from the
Bolshevik yoke.' Realization of such a plan, he believed, would cause a deep
split among the people and prove that one might well fight against Stalin and
the 'hated Bolshevik system' without ceasing to be a Russian patriot. 'There
are Russians on the side of the so-called enemy—hence it is no high treason to
go over to them, but merely a turning away from a system; this will open up
new hopes!' Contrary to the official version, this most prominent of army
commanders in German captivity therefore sympathized with the liberation
movement of his comrade-in-arms at Moscow, Lieutenant-General Vlasov,
GOC Twentieth Army. Other generals too would have been entirely prepared
'to take up arms against Bolshevism', but they demanded 'first an official
declaration by the German Reich government . . . When none was received,
these former Soviet generals declined.'[241] Those who held such views evidently
included Generals Muzychenko and Ponedelin, GOCs Sixth and Twelfth
Armies, taken prisoner at Uman.[242] Lack of confidence in the intentions and
capabilities of the Germans, as well as consideration for his family, eventually
induced General Lukin to remain aloof from any anti-Soviet activity that
might compromise him. On the other hand, Major-General Malyshkin, Nineteenth Army chief of staff, Colonel Bushmanov, Thirty-second Army chief of
staff, and Brigade Commissar Zhilenkov, member of the War Council of
Thirty-second Army, did join the Vlasov movement.[243] Colonel Vanyushin,

---

[239] Interrogation of officers (deserters) Ivan Nikitovich Kononov, Major, commander of 436th
Rifle Regiment . . . , AOK 4, Ic/AO No. 549/41 geh., 6 Sept. 1941, BA-MA RH 22/271. The fact
that Stalin and the Soviet command were conducting all operations 'under the inhuman slogan'
that 'human lives must not be spared' is confirmed also by Gen. Grigorenko, *Erinnerungen*, 279.

[240] 'M. F. Lukin', in *Krasnaja Zvezda*, 28 May 1970; Titov, 'Kljatvoprestupniki', 233–4; Lukin,
'My ne sdaemsja tovarišč general!', newspaper cutting, BA-MA MSg 149/52.

[241] Besuch General Wlassow [Gen. Vlasov's visit], Capt. Knoth, head of Propaganda Department Ostland, BA-MA RL 2/v. 3058 a.

[242] Pozdnjakov, *Roždenie ROA*, 19.

[243] The names of Vlasov and Malyshkin were omitted from the 'List of commanders of fronts,
armies, and corps in the battle of Moscow'; those of Zhilenkov and Bushmanov, on the other
hand, are given—presumably in ignorance of their later activities: 'Moskovskaja bitva v cifrach:
Period kontrnastuplenija', 99–100.

the commander of the air forces of Twentieth Army, also later took up a leading post in the air force of the Russian Liberation Army.

As for the encirclement of the six Soviet armies at Vyazma—for which Supreme Command Headquarters and the general staff bore the main responsibility—this can scarcely have enhanced the defence of Moscow, considering that the Mozhaysk line had been broken at several points as early as 13 October, at a time when resistance inside the pocket was still continuing. On that day Forty-ninth Army abandoned Kaluga; the Germans pushed ahead towards the Protva, threatening Maloyaroslavets from the rear, and by 16 October had reached Naro-Fominsk. Forty-third Army was compelled to retreat behind the Nara. Fifth Army was likewise unable to withstand the pressure of the Germans. Having defended the historic battlefield of Borodino,[244] it had to give up Mozhaysk on 18 October. Matters were somewhat more favourable at Volokolamsk, which was initially held by Rokossovskiy, who made use of a deeply echeloned defence system; however, on 27 October it also fell to the Germans.[245] The German penetration of the Mozhaysk line and, on the Naro-Fominsk sector, also of the third line of the Moscow defence zone, which ran from Klin in a wide arc to Serpukhov, created an immediate threat to the Soviet capital even before the end of the third week of October. Now that it seemed impossible to stem the onslaught of the enemy, alarming signs of demoralization appeared in spite of all propaganda efforts of the Party and in spite of all threats. When on 16 October most of the Party and governmental machine was evacuated to Kuybyshev, panic broke out among the population of Moscow and there were instances of looting. On 19 October the State Defence Committee found itself obliged to declare a state of siege throughout the Moscow region and to decree that any disturbance of public order would be punished by military tribunals. NKVD troops were ordered to 'shoot *provocateurs*, spies, and other agents of the enemy . . . on the spot'.[246] Efforts were made simultaneously to reinforce the sectors of the Moscow defence zone by hurriedly levied People's Guard divisions, in all some 40,000 men, to set up tank obstacles and field fortifications, and to bring up new reserves.[247] By the end of October it had proved possible to integrate into the front west of Moscow at least 13 rifle divisions and 5 armoured brigades from the interior of the country. As a result, the situation in the lines east of Volokolamsk along the Nara and Oka as far as Aleksin was temporarily stabilized. By mid-November 1941 Headquarters had provided the Western Front with a number of further rifle and cavalry divisions, as well as armoured brigades, totalling some 100,000 men, 300 tanks, 2,000 artillery pieces, and additional anti-tank guns,[248] so that on 15 November

[244] Leljušenko, Moskva, Stalingrad, Berlin, Praga, 60 ff.

[245] Rokossovskij, 'Na volokolamskom napravlenii', 52.

[246] 'Postanovlenie Gosudarstvennogo Komiteta Oborony, 19.10.1941', in *Moskva—frontu*, 26–7.

[247] Mironov, 'Rol' Moskovskoj zony oborony', 117.

[248] Žukov, 'Bitva pod Moskvoj, 1', 67.

1941 the Germans were eventually facing 84 divisions and 20 brigades, albeit weakened in their combat strength.[249] From 1 October to 15 November the number of tanks of the Western Front had increased from 450 to 700. In addition, 1,138 aircraft, most of them of new types,[250] were stationed at airfields around Moscow, ready to repulse the German attack. On 10 November the Fiftieth Army of the now dissolved Bryansk Front was placed under the command of the Western Front, while Third and Thirteenth Armies were assigned to the South-west Front.

The Soviet leadership expected the German offensive in the second half of November. Having until then focused its attention on reinforcing the two wings of the Western Front, it now tried to harass the Germans by swift counter-strikes. Against the opposition of Zhukov[251] and the army commanders, who were anxious not to fritter away their forces and to keep their scant reserves in readiness, on 13 November 1941 Stalin and the chief of the general staff insisted on the immediate execution of counter-attacks along the sector of Sixteenth and Forty-ninth Armies. The attack launched by Rokossovskiy against his own conviction and virtually without preparation, needless to say, did not improve the position of the Soviet forces but made it worse.[252] Sixteenth Army suffered considerable losses, and Major-General Dovator's 3rd Cavalry Corps barely escaped encirclement. An attack launched by Lieutenant-General Zakharkin with elements of Forty-ninth Army against Serpukov was repulsed with heavy losses, even though it caused some delay to the opening of the German Fourth Army's attack. On 15 November the Germans, on the right wing outside Moscow, struck at Major-General Khomenko's Thirtieth Army; the following day they struck heavily at the boundary of the Kalinin Front (Thirtieth Army) and the Western Front (Sixteenth Army). The reason why they made such rapid progress towards Klin and Solnechnogorsk was that, on orders from Headquarters, the last reserves had been switched to Volokolamsk to execute a counter-attack. In order to reorganize the confused command conditions among the disarrayed and retreating formations north-west of Moscow, Major-General Khomenko, GOC Thirtieth Army, was relieved of his command and replaced by Major-General Lelyushenko; in addition, on 17 November—by which time it was too late—Thirtieth Army was placed under the command of the Western Front.[253] At this point a serious conflict occurred between Rokossovskiy and Zhukov, who rescinded an order endorsed by Marshal Shaposhnikov, chief of the Red Army General Staff, for a withdrawal to the Istra and instead categorically demanded a struggle 'to the last man',[254] without in the end being able to prevent Klin and Solnechnogorsk from falling to the Germans on 23 November and Istra on 27 November. The

[249] Kazakov, *Sozdanie i ispol'zovanie*, 48.   [250] Fedorov, *Aviacija*, 123.
[251] Žukov, 'V bitve za stolicu', *VIŽ* (1966), No. 9, 61.
[252] Rokossovskij, 'Na volokolamskom napravlenii', 55.
[253] Leljušenko, *Moskva, Stalingrad, Berlin, Praga*, 78.
[254] Rokossovskij, 'Na severnych podstupach', 53.

exceedingly critical situation on the right wing of the Western Front in the sector of Sixteenth and Thirtieth Armies forced the GOC to throw in all available forces, including the anti-aircraft artillery of the Moscow defences, at the threatened points. Headquarters, moreover, during the final days of November reinforced the Western Front with 8 rifle divisions, 7 cavalry divisions, 4 rifle brigades, 1 airborne corps, and independent armoured and other specialized units. But it was only with the intervention of the First Assault Army under Lieutenant-General Kuznetsov and of the Twentieth Army (formed only recently) under Major-General Vlasov, the defender of Kiev (whose name is omitted from Soviet accounts of the fighting for Moscow)—i.e. the intervention of reserve armies assembled in strictest secrecy as the second echelon east of Moscow[255]—that the exhausted German forces were halted at Yakhroma on the Moskva–Volga Canal and at Krasnaya Polyana north-west of Moscow at the beginning of December.

The purpose of the dissolution of the Bryansk Front on 10 November 1941—the subordination of Fiftieth Army to the Western Front and of Third and Thirteenth Armies to the South-west Front—was to simplify command structures for the impending defensive battle on the left wing of the Western Front, in the Tula sector. This step, however, was to prove a mistake,[256] because the South-west Front possessed only an incomplete command apparatus and the two Front staffs were showing an understandable tendency to draw their newly acquired armies closer to their main forces. The result was a weakening of the boundary between the troops of the Western and of the South-west Fronts south of Tula, a boundary that was particularly threatened by the German Second Armoured Army. On 14 November 1941 Marshal Timoshenko, who feared with some justification that a German breakthrough at that spot would complicate the defence of Moscow as well as the situation of his own overstretched front, asked Stalin to create an independent front, the Orlov Front, from the armies of his northern wing and place it under the command of Lieutenant-General Kostenko.[257] The decision, however, was delayed, and proposals by Zhukov along the same lines were not authorized either. As a result of the neglected command structure on the defence sector south of Tula, the German Second Armoured Army quickly succeeded on 18 November in achieving a breakthrough, bypassing Tula on the east and proceeding via Stalinogorsk in the direction of Venev. At first Headquarters had demanded that the widening gap be closed again by a 'concentric attack' of troops of the Western and South-west Fronts; because of the weakness of Fiftieth and Third Armies, however, this was asking for the impossible. Headquarters eventually had to bring up reinforcements as the German attack fanned out northwards towards Kashira and simultaneously eastwards in a general direction of the Oka and Ryazan, and as, in Zhukov's words, an

---

[255] Vasilevskij, *Delo vsej žizni*, 159 ff.   [256] Eremenko, 'Na jugo-zapadnych podstupach', 86.
[257] Bagramjan, *Tak načalas' vojna*, 431–2.

'exceptionally dangerous situation' was developing.[258] Major-General Belov's 2nd Cavalry Corps was therefore hurriedly flung against the German spearhead driving against the rear of the Western Front at Kashira. On 26 November this formation, now renamed I Guards Cavalry Corps, succeeded—in co-operation with Colonel Getman's 112th Armoured Division, a further armoured brigade, and a regiment of multiple rocket mortars, as well as reinforced air units—in forcing the Germans back as far as the area of Mordves. A German attempt to outflank the city of Tula from the north failed in the face of counter-attacks by elements of Lieutenant-General Zakharkin's Forty-ninth Army and Lieutenant-General Boldin's Fiftieth Army. On 1 December 1941 Lieutenant-General Golikov's Tenth Army, assembled at Ryazan, was at Zhukov's request transferred from the Headquarters reserve to the Western Front in order to prevent a further advance of the enemy through Mihkaylov to the Oka.[259]

Faced with stiffening Soviet resistance, the German attack was gradually losing momentum, also in the sector of the South-west Front at the boundary between Major-General Kreyzer's Third Army (after 3 December under Lieutenant-General Pshennikov) and Major-General Gorodnyanskiy's Thirteenth Army west of Yelets. Thus, in the early days of December a threat to Moscow at the two wings of the Western Front had finally ceased to exist—even though this result was achieved only by the employment of Soviet strategic reserves originally assembled for the execution of a counter-offensive. In this situation the Soviet troops had but little difficulty in repulsing the last German breakthrough attempt towards the Soviet capital, made on 1 December 1941 at the centre of the Western Front, on both sides of Naro-Fominsk. Although the German Fourth Army succeeded in accomplishing a breach at the boundary between Lieutenant-General Govorov's Fifth Army and Lieutenant-General Yefremov's Thirty-third Army, and in advancing as far as Golitsyno along the Moscow railway line, this finally exhausted its strength. Reserves brought up to the Western Front and the main forces of the two armies first halted the Germans at Burtsevo and Kuznetsevo, and by 5 December had thrown them back to their starting-positions on the Nara.[260] The German general offensive for the capture of Moscow had definitively failed.

10. THE RED ARMY'S COUNTER-OFFENSIVE AT MOSCOW, DECEMBER 1941

From the very beginning of the German offensive Red Army Supreme Command Headquarters and the general staff had focused their efforts not only on halting the enemy outside Moscow but also on depriving him of the strategic initiative and going over to the counter-attack.[261] At the same time as Army Group Centre seemed to be irresistibly advancing towards the nation's capital,

---

[258] Zhukov, *Reminiscences*, 359.   [259] Golikov, 'Rezervnaja armija vstupaet', 62 ff.
[260] Surčenko, 'Likvidacija proryva'.   [261] Sokolovskij, 'Velikaya bitva', 28.

confronted by poorly trained and ill-equipped People's Army divisions, concentration began, under conditions of strictest secrecy, of a second strategic echelon of reserve armies along the Vytegra–Ryabinsk–Gorkiy–Saratov–Stalingrad–Astrakhan line.[262] By resolution of the State Defence Committee of 5 October 1941 the Tenth, Twenty-sixth, and Fifty-seventh Reserve Armies were formed from the second half of October onwards. The second half of November then witnessed the establishment of the First Assault Army and of the Twentieth, Twenty-eighth, Thirty-ninth, Fifty-eighth, Fifty-ninth, Sixtieth, and Sixty-first Armies.[263] Since the beginning of the war, therefore, 291 divisions and 94 brigades had been incorporated in the field army: 70 divisions had come from military districts of the interior, 27 divisions from the Far East, central Asia, and Transcaucasia, and 194 divisions and 94 brigades had been newly raised. Although great difficulties were encountered in staffing the troops, especially with officers, in furnishing them with weapons, equipment, and transport, and in raising the standard of training to the requisite level,[264] at the beginning of December 1941 Headquarters nevertheless had strong strategic reserves at its disposal. It was therefore possible substantially to reinforce the troops of the Kalinin Front, the Western Front, and the northern wing of the South-west Front; these had been earmarked for the counter-offensive at Moscow. Since the end of November Lieutenant-General Kuznetsov's First Assault Army and Major-General Vlasov's Twentieth Army had been engaged in defensive fighting at the immediate danger spots to the north-east of the capital. Twenty-fourth, Twenty-sixth, and Sixtieth Armies were moved forward into the Moscow area. Lieutenant-General Golikov's Tenth Army took over the sector west of Ryazan, at Mikhaylov; Colonel-General Kuznetsov's Sixty-first Army was concentrated at the boundary between the Western and South-west Fronts, between Ryazhsk and Ranenburg. At the beginning of December 15 armies, 3 cavalry corps, and 1 airborne corps—in all 104 divisions—stood ready for attack. Even though the three actively involved fronts had been additionally reinforced by a large number of independent specialized units, such as artillery regiments, guards rocket-mortar battalions, air regiments, and engineering brigades, Soviet war historians used to describe the Soviet forces as still greatly inferior to the Germans.[265] This assertion clearly ignore's the well-known fact[266] that the German divisions had meanwhile declined to half their normal strength and that their losses of weapons and tanks had been exceptionally high. The German–Soviet ratio of forces in the strategic direction west of Moscow at the opening of the counter-offensive is presented by Soviet authors as follows:[267]

[262] Štemenko, *General'nyj štab*, i. 38.   [263] *Istorija Velikoj Otečestvennoj vojny*, ii. 271.
[264] Golikov, 'Rezervnaja armija gotovitsja k zaščite', 67, 72 ff.
[265] 'Moskovskaja bitva v cifrach: Period kontrnastuplenija', 89; Žukov, 'Bitva pod Moskvoj, 2', 45.
[266] 'Prikaz komandujuščego vojskami Zapadnogo fronta, 6.12.1941', in *Moskva—frontu*, 85–6.
[267] 'Moskovskaja bitva v cifrach: Period kontrnastuplenija', 91–2; *50 let vooruženych sil*, 295; *Geschichte des zweiten Weltkrieges*, iv. 344.

(*maximum*) men 1,708,000 : 1,100,000, artillery pieces, mortars, and rocket mortars 13,500 : 7,652, tanks 1,170 : 774; (*minimum*) men 860,000 : 760,000, artillery pieces 10,400 : 5,615, tanks 1,000 : 670. Only for the air forces is a Soviet superiority conceded. Thus, approximately 600 German aircraft are said to have been confronted by 1,370 Soviet machines (according to some sources the latter figures is 1,000, or even as low as 762).[268]

The plan for the offensive, laid down in outline by Supreme Command Headquarters, or more accurately by the general staff under Marshal Shaposhnikov, since 20 November 1941,[269] then worked out in detail and endorsed by the commands of the three fronts, envisaged simultaneous attacks by the right and left wings of the Western Front, in co-operation with the Kalinin Front and the right wing of the South-west Front. Its first, still limited, objective was the routing of the enemy's assault groupings threatening Moscow from the north and south. According to how the situation developed, an attempt was then to be made to force the enemy back frontally, and eventually to defeat him decisively.[270] Accordingly, Major-General Lelyushenko's Thirtieth Army north of Moscow, Lieutenant-General Kuznetsov's First Assault Army, Major-General Vlasov's Twentieth Army, and Lieutenant-General Rokossovskiy's Sixteenth Army were instructed to attack via Klin and Solnechnogorsk, respectively, in the direction of Teryaeva Sloboda and Volokalamsk. South of Moscow, Lieutenant-General Golikov's Tenth Army, in co-operation with Lieutenant-General Boldin's Fiftieth Army and Major-General Belov's I Guards Cavalry Corps, were to advance from the Tula–Mikhaylov sector via Stalinogorsk and Bogoroditsk, and then wheel towards Kaluga–Belev. The armies of the Western Front—Lieutenant-General Govorov's Fifth Army, Lieutenant-General Yefremov's Thirty-third Army, Major-General Golubev's Forty-third Army, and Lieutenant-General Zakharkin's Forty-ninth Army—were initially to conduct only holding attacks, while preparing for a general offensive.[271] In order to support the attack of the right wing of the Western Front, the Kalinin Front was ordered, with forces of Major-General Yushkevich's Thirty-first Army and Major-General Maslennikov's Twenty-ninth Army, to strike towards Turginovo and into the rear of Armoured Group 3 at Klin and, in co-operation with the First Assault Army of the Western Front, to annihilate the armoured group.[272] Simultaneously, Lieutenant-General Kostenko's mobile group, formed on the right wing of the South-west Front, was to strike at the forces of the German Second Army at Yelets–Livny and, in conjunction with Major-General Gorodnyanskiy's Thirteenth Army (which was attacking further to the north), to encircle and likewise annihilate them.[273]

[268] Fedorov, *Aviacija*, 169.   [269] Vasilevskij, *Delo vsej žizni*, 162.
[270] Žukov, 'Kontrnastuplenie', 70.
[271] 'Prikaz komandujuščego vojskami Zapadnogo fronta, 30.11.1941', in *Moskva—frontu*, 82.
[272] Direktiva Stavki [Supreme Command Headquarters directive], 1 Dec. 1941, ibid. 82–3.
[273] Direktiva Voennogo soveta operativnoj gruppy general-lejtenanta Kostenko [Directive of the War Council of Lt.-Gen. Kostenko's tactical group], 4 Dec. 1941, ibid. 83–4.

During the preparations for the counter-offensive at Moscow a difference of opinion[274] arose on 1 December 1941 between Lieutenant-General Vasilevskiy—who for a short time deputized for Marshal Shaposhnikov, chief of the Red Army General Staff—and Colonel-General Konev, the GOC Kalinin Front. Konev, instead of advancing towards Turginovo, intended an attack with a view to capturing Kalinin. On behalf of Stalin, Vasilevskiy demanded strict observance of the Supreme Command Headquarters directive, transmitted that day, which envisaged the employment of five battle-worthy divisions, one motorized brigade, the bulk of the artillery from the Headquarters reserve, and all rocket-mortars for an attack on Turginovo. Vasilevskiy dismissed Konev's argument that he was too weak; he demanded that the Kalinin Front, too, mobilize absolutely all available forces to support the offensive of the Western Front, which in any case would be launched under difficult conditions, instead of employing its forces on objectives of purely local importance.

The counter-offensive at Moscow was opened on 5 December 1941 by the two armies of the left wing of the Kalinin Front; on the following two days they were joined by the attacking armies of the right and left wings of the Western Front and of the right wing of the South-west Front. Although the Soviet assault formations, massively supported by the wings, succeeded in breaking into the German defences almost everywhere, the development of the attack did not at first fulfil Headquarters' expectations.[275] The pace of the advance was generally slight, and the Soviet commanders still had little experience of executing offensive operations. Thus, until 13 December 1941, when Western Front command expressly prohibited that kind of operation,[276] they would mostly attack frontally along the roads, failing to realize that what mattered was to bypass points of enemy resistance and to drive as deeply as possible into the enemy's flank and rear. Nevertheless, by the middle of the second week of December they had achieved some appreciable success at several points of the 500-kilometre front between Kalinin and Yelets. In the northern sector Thirty-first Army crossed the Kalinin–Turginovo road;[277] on 9 December Thirtieth Army reached Klin;[278] First Assault Army recaptured Yakhroma; Twentieth Army recaptured Krasnaya Polyana and on 10 December reached the approaches of Solnechnogorsk,[279] while Sixteenth Army took Kryukovo.[280] On the southern sector, where preparations for the offensive could not be completed in time,[281] Tenth Army succeeded at the first attempt in capturing Mikhaylov and Serebryanye Prudy, thereby cutting the Kashira–Pavelets rail-

[274] Vasilevskij, *Delo vsej žizni*, 164–5; Konev, 'Na Kalininskom fronte', 71–2.
[275] *Istorija Velikoj Otečestvennoj vojny*, ii. 277.
[276] 'Prikaz komandujuščego vojskami Zapadnogo fronta, 13.12.1941', in *Moskva—frontu*, 89.
[277] Konev, 'Na Kalininskom fronte', 73.
[278] Leljušenko, *Moskva, Stalingrad, Berlin, Praga*, 113–14.
[279] Žukov, 'Bitva pod Moskvoj, 2', 45.
[280] Lobačev, *Trudnymi dorogami*, 264; Rokossovskij *Soldatskij dolg*, 99–100.
[281] Bagramjan, *Tak načinalas' vojna*, 486.

way line; on 8 December I Guards Cavalry Corps[282] took Mordves and Venev; Thirteenth Army, attacking on both sides of Yelets in co-operation with General Kostenko's mobile group, succeeded in encircling the German forces in that area and in capturing Yelets on 9 December.[283]

Stalin and Marshal Shaposhnikov displayed considerable annoyance at the relatively slow advance of the Kalinin Front, more especially of its Twenty-ninth Army, whose leadership had in fact revealed substantial shortcomings. As recently as 1 December, Vasilevskiy, deputizing for the chief of the general staff, had blamed the GOC Kalinin Front for wishing to take Kalinin instead of striking at Turginovo further south. On 12 December he was reproved for not yet having taken Kalinin,[284] which evidently, after all, was of more than mere local importance. Suddenly Colonel-General Konev, who tried in vain to justify himself, received strict orders from Headquarters to take the city as soon as possible. To that end, Major-General Shvetsov was put in command of Twenty-ninth Army, while Major-General Maslennikov took over command of Thirty-ninth Army, which after 22 December 1941 was inserted south-west of Torzhok. In point of fact, the forces of the Kalinin Front, reinforced by individual units, recaptured the city of Kalinin on 16 December 1941. During the final third of December the right wing of the Kalinin Front, with Major-General Vostrukhov's Twenty-second Army and with Thirty-ninth Army, also went over to the offensive, although at first this developed but slowly.[285] By the beginning of the new year, however, the troops of the Kalinin Front had reached Staritsa and the approaches to Rzhev and Zubtsov. The attacking armies, some of whom had gained 150 kilometres of ground, were able by 7 January 1942 to envelop Rzhev from three sides and to threaten the flank of the German Ninth Army on the upper reaches of the Volga. Although the counter-offensive at Moscow was increasingly making progress, it soon became clear that Supreme Command Headquarters, as well as Western Front command, had entertained excessive expectations. Realization of the objective of the offensive, extended beyond the original intentions and since 9 December 1941 including 'the encirclement and annihilation of all enemy armies fighting against the Western Front', was soon put in doubt, largely because of weaknesses in command[286] and because of the stiffening German resistance. Western Front command, which on 13 December 1941 in a categorical order assigned the task formulated on 9 December to its subordinate armies, which had held the army commanders personally responsible for reaching the jumping-off positions, and which in an appeal to the troops on the following day had demanded the 'ruthless liquidation' of all those who 'are slowing down our forward movement',[287] soon found itself compelled to tone down its hopes. The point was that neither did the right wing of the Western

[282] Sazonov, *Nastupaet 1-ja gvardejskaja*.   [283] Bagramjan, 'Èto bylo pod El'com'.
[284] Vasilevskij, *Delo vsej žizni*, 166–7.   [285] *Istorija Velikoj Otečestvennoj vojny*, ii. 298–9.
[286] Semenov, *Kratkij očerk*, 162–3.
[287] 'Prikaz komandujuščego vojskami Zapadnogo fronta, 14.12.1941', in *Moskva—frontu*, 91.

Front, as had been expected, rapidly reach Gzhatsk, nor did the left wing reach the area of Kozelsk.[288] One objective within reach was Klin, enveloped from both sides by units of Major-General Lelyushenko's Thirtieth Army and of Lieutenant-General Kuznetsov's First Assault Army. The town was recaptured on 15 December after an airborne unit dropped in the German rear had vainly tried to cut off the garrison's line of retreat.[289] Simultaneously, Major-General Vlasov's Twentieth Army along with Lieutenant-General Rokossovskiy's Sixteenth Army, covered in the south by Lieutenant-General Govorov's Fifth Army, took the town of Istra, crossed the Istra river, and occupied the area of the Istra reservoir.[290] Teryaeva Sloboda fell on 18 December, and Volokolamsk on 20 December 1941. By 25 December, when the offensive came to a temporary halt, the armies of the right wing of the Western Front had forced back the opposing German troops as far as the Lama and Ruza rivers and inflicted heavy losses on them.[291] As Marshal of the Soviet Union Sokolovskiy, then Western Front chief of staff, observes, the threat to Moscow from the north-west had been eliminated.[292] What had not been accomplished, however, was the annihilation (planned in conjunction with the Kalinin Front) of the German forces confronting them or the development of the right prong into a pincer movement enveloping the main forces of Army Group Centre.

Operations on the left wing of the Western Front also made considerable progress in December, though again without achieving their real strategic objective. On 14 December 1941 Lieutenant-General Golikov's Tenth Army, attacking in a westerly direction together with I Guards Cavalry Corps, had reached the Dedilovo–Uzlovaya–Bogoroditsk line. Only the previous day this army, which indeed had a considerable number of shortcomings,[293] had been accused by Western Front command of preventing the success of the operations plan and the encirclement of the German Second Armoured Army through its 'passivity and non-fulfilment of orders'. Simultaneously, while Lieutenant-General Boldin's Fiftieth Army was attacking in a southerly direction on both sides of Tula, Lieutenant-General Zakharkin's Forty-ninth Army, further to the north, advanced as far as the Oka and took Tarusa and Aleksin. In order to exploit that success and block the German troops' line of retreat, the forces of Fiftieth Army, on orders from Supreme Command Headquarters, now wheeled north and began to launch a frontal assault on the heavily defended transport centre of Shchekino. On 17 December 1941 the town was taken, but the Germans had meanwhile escaped across the Upa. Even though the encirclement of the German Second Armoured Army, which had been under attack from several sides, had not succeeded, the eccentric withdrawal of its units towards Kaluga and Orel nevertheless provided new opportunities. I Guards Cavalry Corps was now ordered to thrust into the gap

---

[288] Žukov, 'Kontrnastuplenie', 73.   [289] Fedorov, *Aviacija*, 175–6.
[290] Rokossovskij, 'Na severnych podstupach', 59–60.   [291] *Sovetskie tankovye vojska*, 49.
[292] Sokolovskij, 'Velikaja bitva', 30.   [293] Golikov, 'Rezervnaja armija vstupaet', 65 ff.

which had opened, to cross the Oka, and then to wheel north-west towards Yukhnov. Fiftieth Army, which for that purpose formed a mobile group under Major-General Popov, and Forty-ninth Army were instructed to capture Kaluga as soon as possible,[294] while Tenth Army was to advance further in the direction of Belev–Kozelsk–Sukhinichi. Whereas I Guards Cavalry Corps had been making good progress since 19 December 1941, Fiftieth Army soon experienced a crisis: although its mobile Popov group managed to reach Kaluga, it found itself cut off from its rear communications and had to fight in a pocket. Not until 30 December, after ten days of fighting, was the city captured by Popov's group in co-operation with Fiftieth and Forty-ninth Armies. By that time the armies of the left wing of the Western Front had advanced as far as a line Aleshkino–Babynino–Meshchovsk–Kozelsk–Belev. At some points they succeeded in gaining even further ground before the operations came to a temporary halt on 7 January 1942, but the speed of their advance had noticeably diminished, and they were unable to capture the important transport junction of Sukhinichi.[295] Thus the left prong of the pincer movement for the encirclement of Army Group Centre had also become bogged down.

As in the case of the left wing of the Western Front, so the right wing of the South-west Front, supporting it with its own attack, was able to score considerable success—at least in a tactical respect. The troops of Major-General Kreyzer's (from 13 December 1941 Lieutenant-General Pshennikov's) Third Army, of Major-General Gorodnyanskiy's Thirteenth Army, and of Major-General Kostenko's mobile group, having taken Yelets, by 16 December advanced to a line Gogol–Verkhnaya Lyubovka–Livny. By an encircling manœuvre in pursuit these formations succeeded in enveloping substantial elements of the German XXXIV Army Corps,[296] but they were unable to annihilate the main forces of Second Army. The fact that the armies of the right wing of the South-west Front lacked an independent command, that they came under an already overstressed front command, now proved a major handicap. More than a month earlier Marshal Timoshenko had proposed just such an independent command, but in vain; now, on 18 December 1941, Supreme Command Headquarters decided to create once more a Bryansk Front from the armies of the right wing, and to place it under the command of Colonel-General Cherevichenko. This reconstituted Bryansk Front was composed of the mobile Kostenko group, of Thirteenth Army, and of the newly formed Sixty-first Army, whose command Lieutenant-General Popov had to take over a few days later from Colonel-General Kuznetsov, who at times was over-fond of alcohol.

The restoration of the Bryansk Front, along with the reinforcement of the Kalinin Front by two armies, was to create favourable conditions for the

[294] *Boevoj put' sovetskich vooružennych sil*, 303.
[295] *Istorija Velikoj Otečestvennoj vojny*, ii. 293–4.
[296] Moskalenko, *Na Jugo-Zapadnom napravlenii*, 119 ff.; Bagramjan, *Tak načinalas'vojna*, 503 ff.

encirclement of the main forces of Army Group Centre by means of a large-scale pincer movement—an objective which, on the strength of the current successes, Headquarters considered feasible.[297] The armies of the Bryansk Front, attacking in a north-westerly direction from 18 December 1941, did in fact manage to gain further ground. However, after reaching the Belev–Mtsensk–Verkhovye line in the first days of January 1942, their strength was spent. The hoped-for routing of the German forces on the southern wing of Army Group Centre, planned in co-operation with the neighbouring Western Front, was not achieved.

Within the framework of the large-scale enveloping manœuvre of the wings of the Western Front, along with the troops of the Kalinin and Bryansk Fronts, the four armies at the centre of the Western Front were now also ordered to go over to the attack in order to tie down and break up the enemy forces. However, Lieutenant-General Yefremov's Thirty-third Army and Major-General Golubev's Forty-third Army, both attacking south of the Moscow–Mozhaysk railway line, had not received the slightest reinforcements of personnel or material, and made only slow progress. Not until 26 December 1941 did Thirty-third Army take Naro-Fominsk, situated near the front line, and not until 2 January 1942 did Forty-third Army take Maloyaroslavets. On 4 January 1942 Thirty-third Army succeeded in breaking into the German defences at Bobruysk. Lieutenant-General Zakharkin's Forty-ninth Army, which had captured Tarusa, also gained ground and by the end of December 1941 advanced to a line from Maloyaroslavets to Kaluga. Altogether, by the beginning of January 1942 Soviet troops had thrown back the Germans along the Moscow front by between 100 and 250 kilometres and inflicted heavy losses on them. Yet despite the tactical breakthroughs at Rzhev and Kaluga they had failed to accomplish the grand strategic encirclement—a fact that has been skilfully concealed by Soviet historiography behind the conspicuous successes of the counter-offensive at Moscow.

11. The Red Army's Counter-attacks at Leningrad and in the Crimea

In much the same way as on the Moscow front, so Stalin, Supreme Command Headquarters, and the general staff also harboured unrealistic expectations concerning the strength and combat performance of the Soviet troops in the area south-east of Leningrad. Admittedly, the Soviet forces in the Tikhvin salient after late November and early December 1941 had definitively seized the initiative and, albeit with heavy losses, had gradually gained ground. Thus, Army General Meretskov's Fourth Army, attacking in two assault groups, occupied Tikhvin on 9 December; Army General Fedyuninskiy's Fifty-fourth Army, assigned to the Leningrad Front, overcame German resistance at

---

[297] Sokolovskij, 'Velikaja bitva', 30–1.

Voybokalo in mid-December—with some delay due to weaknesses in its command and tactical mistakes; and Lieutenant-General Klykov's Fifty-second Army simultaneously reached the area of Bolshaya Vishera.[298] Ignoring the fact that these operations had largely exhausted the attacking strength of the Soviet formations, Supreme Command Headquarters began to initiate a large-scale strategic operation also at Leningrad. Stalin, along with his closest advisers, Marshal Shaposhnikov and Lieutenant-General Vasilevskiy, blinded by the successes achieved so far, now aimed at nothing less than an operation to route the main forces of Army Group North. Urged on by Zhdanov, the Party Secretary of Leningrad, they intended to burst open the blockade of the great city, where conditions during the winter had become catastrophic. To this end Fourth Army (now taken over by Major-General Ivanov), Fifty-second Army, Major-General Galinin's Fifty-ninth Army (still being organized), and Major-General Sokolov's Twenty-sixth Army (after the end of December the Second Assault Army) were on 17 December combined into a Volkhov Front under the command of Army General Meretskov. The formations of this newly established front were ordered to annihilate the German grouping at Tikhvin, then to cross the Volkhov in a north-easterly direction and, in conjunction with the troops of General Khozin's Leningrad Front, now also going over to the attack (Forty-second, Fifty-fifth, Eighth, and Fifty-fourth Armies), to encircle and annihilate the German divisions at Leningrad, and thereby to open up a wide land-bridge into the beleaguered city.[299] Starting not later than 24 December 1941, Eleventh Army of the North-west Front was to advance via Staraya Russa in the direction of Soltsy, in order, jointly with a southward-aiming spearhead of Fifty-second Army, to cut off the retreat of the German forces at Novgorod.

But with this operations plan Supreme Command Headquarters had lost touch with reality. Although Army General Meretskov, having reached the northern Volkhov, believed that a pause was urgently needed for the rehabilitation of his exhausted and battered troops and to allow time for the bringing up of units of Fifty-ninth Army and Second Assault Army,[300] Headquarters persistently called for greater speed and, in a directive of 24 December 1941, categorically demanded the immediate continuation of the operation and the forcing of the Volkhov without a prior halt. However, the massive strategic operation planned south-east of Leningrad did not progress beyond its initial stages. It proved unrealizable. In the final analysis it did not even succeed in annihilating the German forces at Tikhvin,[301] let alone in routing the main forces of Army Group North. A few minor bridgeheads were, in a final effort, established at Gruziny, Kinshi, and elsewhere—but by then even Headquarters had to face realities and order the suspension of the operation.

Within the general framework of its counter-offensive at Moscow, Supreme

---

[298] *Istorija ordena Lenina Leningradskogo Voennogo okruga,* 259 ff.

[299] Mereckov, *Na službe narodu,* 251 ff.   [300] Mereckov, in *Oborona Leningrada,* 189.

[301] Semenov, *Kratkij očerk,* 170.

Command Headquarters had ambitious plans not only on the northern wing, at Leningrad, but also on the southern wing of the front. Towards the end of November 1941, when the troops of the Sevastopol defence zone had, though not without difficulty, repulsed the first organized attack on the naval fortress, Headquarters conceived the idea of a landing on the Kerch peninsula.[302] This was to create the prerequisites for an immediate cleansing of the entire territory of the Crimea.[303] In accordance with the operations plan endorsed on 7 December 1941, the troops of the Transcaucasus Front under Lieutenant-General Kozlov, in co-operation with naval units of the Black Sea Fleet under Vice-Admiral Oktyabrskiy and of the Azov Flotilla under Rear-Admiral Gorshkov, were to land at several points on the northern, eastern, and southern coast in the Kerch area, as well as at Feodosiya, annihilate the German forces in the peninsula, and subsequently thrust westwards into the interior of the Crimea. The main part in the operation was to be played by the Feodosiya landing party, which was part of Major-General Pervushin's Forty-fourth Army, while the landing party attacking on the east coast, formed mainly by part of Lieutenant-General Lvov's Fifty-first Army, was instructed to tie down the enemy forces while they were being encircled. The first serious difficulties arose during the preparations for the invasion, when the resumption of the German attack on Sevastopol on 17 December 1941 resulted in a postponement of the timetable and the transfer of urgently needed ground and naval forces.[304] The landing operation eventually began, under unfavourable weather conditions, on 26 December 1941 at Kerch and on 29 December at Feodosiya; initially it did not proceed according to plan and only began to succeed during the next few days.[305] Again the Germans managed to evade encirclement and were able to establish a solid line of defence at Kiet–Koktebel east of Feodosija, blocking the Crimea. This German success was due to mistakes made by the command of the Transcaucasus Front, above all of Forty-fourth Army, which proved incapable of properly exploiting the success of the landing operation.[306] The Soviet troops had succeeded in occupying the Kerch peninsula, but the annihilation of the German troops fighting there and the breakthrough to Sudak, Simferopol, and Dzhanskoy, into the deep interior of the Crimea[307]—as demanded by Supreme Command Headquarters on 2 January 1942, totally misreading the situation—had proved unrealizable.[308]

In the course of its counter-offensive in December 1941 the Red Army had inflicted a number of serious defeats on the German army in the east—in the approaches to Moscow, at Leningrad, and in the Crimea—and had regained considerable territory. The threat to the capital was definitively eliminated,

[302] Markov, 'Kerčensko-Feodosijskaja desantnaja operacija', 121.
[303] Bolgari *et al.*, *Černomorskij flot*, 186.   [304] Maksimov, *Oborona Sevastopolja*, 67.
[305] Kodola, 'Vnezapnost'', 16 ff.
[306] Mazunin, 'Kerčensko-Feodosijskaja desantnaja operacija', 103.
[307] Bolgari *et al.*, *Černomorskij flot*, 195.   [308] D'jačan, 'Boevye dejstvija', 106 ff.

and the situation of Leningrad eased in the sense that foodstuffs and other commodities could now be carried by the northern railway almost as far as Mga and thence taken into the hard-pressed city on a considerable scale. Finally, the position of Sevastopol had been relieved as German siege forces had to be withdrawn in order to block off the Kerch peninsula. These successes, however, should not conceal the fact that Supreme Command Headquarters, Stalin himself, Marshal Shaposhnikov, chief of the general staff, and Lieutenant-General Vasilevskiy, his first assistant, had in fact set their sights at more far-reaching objectives. After the first Soviet successes they had called for a breakthrough to Vyazma, the encirclement and annihilation of the main forces of Army Group North, the lifting of the blockade of Leningrad, the relief of Sevastopol, and the reconquest of the entire territory of the Crimea. Considering the state of the Soviet troops and the standard of their leadership, these objectives were unrealistic from the outset and, in consequence, were nowhere near achieved. But even in their more limited form the successes of the Soviet armed forces were of considerable military and also political importance in that they greatly enhanced the international prestige of the Soviet Union. The Red Army had inflicted a heavy defeat—the first defeat of the war—on a Wehrmacht that was accustomed to victories. This circumstance provided Soviet war propaganda with effective arguments for a gradual stiffening of the morale of the Soviet troops, which had been gravely shaken by the retreats of the first few months of the war.

12. METHODS OF A WAR OF ANNIHILATION

When in 1941 the troops of the Wehrmacht and its allies invaded the territory of the Soviet Union and rapidly gained ground, the Soviet leadership was exceedingly anxious that all movable and immovable material assets be destroyed before falling into the enemy's hands. Acting in accordance with the directive of the Communist Party Central Committee and the Council of People's Commissars of 29 June, as well as with Stalin's broadcast address of 3 July 1941, Red Army troops, along with the specially created destruction battalions,[309] whenever there was an opportunity during their retreats, had applied the 'tactics of scorched earth' and destroyed 'all valuable chattels' on the greatest possible scale without regard for the needs of the population. As a result of the Soviet counter-offensive in the winter of 1941, this was the first time that the German troops were forced to abandon a vast territory, and there is no reason to doubt that they applied the principle of destruction just as unscrupulously as the Red Army. The Soviet soldiers in the reconquered regions were frequently confronted with scenes which were methodically used by war propaganda to fan hatred against the German occupiers. In the grand framework of the German–Soviet conflict, which for the most part was con-

[309] Bilenko, *Istrebitel'nye batal'ony*; Kirsanov, in *VIŽ'* (1970), No. 12, 94–5.

ducted with disregard of all formalities, individual occurrences probably play a subordinate role, and it may seem almost pointless to view them more closely. However, a few incidents in connection with the fighting for Moscow have acquired a strong symbolical significance and were traditionally quoted in the Soviet and Soviet-subservient literature as special instances of the 'bestialities and destructive fury of the Fascists'. A few explanatory observations are therefore not out of place. The accusation levelled at the German troops of having devastated the Tchaikovsky Museum in Klin was already refuted before the Nuremberg Military Tribunal by defending counsel Dr Laternser through the submission of documentary evidence.[310] The same is true of the alleged looting of Tolstoy's estate at Yasnaya Polyana, which had actually been shown undamaged in a Soviet film made in 1942, after its reoccupation. Colonel-General Guderian, GOC Second Armoured Army, who had established his command post at Yasnaya Polyana, emphatically points out in his memoirs that the German troops had spared this memorial right up to their withdrawal, but that the immediate surroundings of the author's grave had previously been mined by Soviet troops.[311] As for the destruction in Istra of the Novo-Yerusalimskiy monastery, founded in 1654,[312] blame on the part of the German troops can be neither confirmed nor denied. Soviet literature in this context never tires of emphasizing that, in contrast to the barbaric behaviour of the German troops, the Soviet regime had always devoted its particular care to the 'architectural monuments' of Russia's past by 'restoring and solicitously preserving' them. Yet those who accuse the German troops of systematic 'national-cultural genocide'[313] should remember the extent to which monasteries and churches, which once represented Russia's artistic wealth, had been desecrated or destroyed in the Soviet era. One instance of many is the Simonov monastery in Moscow, founded in 1370 and restored after the damage it suffered in the 1812 conflagration; this monastery was destroyed down to the last stone by a Red Army unit on 22 January 1930 in honour of the anniversary of Lenin's death.[314] In the opinion of expert observers[315] there was probably not a single city in the RSFSR, including Siberia, where 'either all or almost all' artistically or historically important buildings had not fallen victim to an ideologically motivated destruction mania.

Among the charges levelled at the 'Fascist criminals', accusations of atrocities committed against the peaceful civilian population occupy a prominent place. No one would deny that atrocities were in fact committed on a large

[310] Minasjan, *Meždunarodnye prestuplenija*, 311; *IMT* xxi. 441.

[311] Minasjan, *Meždunarodnye prestuplenija*, 310; Guderian, *Panzer Leader*, 257.

[312] Minasjan, *Meždunarodnye prestuplenija*, 313; *Istorija Velikoj Otečestvennoj vojny*, ii. 286.

[313] Minasjan, *Meždunarodnye prestuplenija*, 307 ff.

[314] Photo reportage in *Berliner Zeitung* (16 Feb. 1930). On the deliberate destruction by the Red Army of the cathedral of Vitebsk and other 'masterpieces of religious architecture' see Grigorenko, *Erinnerungen*, 136 ff.; Byčkov, 'Blutiges Jahr'.

[315] Dudin and Miller, 'The Russians', 122.

scale by the action squads of the security police and the SS security service. But the claim encountered in the literature on the subject, that the gallows found after the recapture of the town of Volokolamsk were a typical example of the atrocities committed by the German troops,[316] is poorly founded. The fact is that the ten who were hanged were not, as is misleadingly claimed, 'peaceful inhabitants'[317] of the town of Volokolamsk but—as is admitted elsewhere—partisans who had fulfilled an 'operational mission in the rear of the enemy'.[318] 'All eight were guerillas', it was stated in *Soviet War News*, published by the Soviet Embassy in London, on 5 February 1942;[319] 'when the Germans approached the town these individuals went to the forest and began methodical operations against the occupation troops'. But armed civilians participating in the fighting came under the heading of irregulars according to the unambiguous terms of the Hague Convention on Land Warfare, as well as the common usage of war; they enjoyed no protection under international law. This applies also to Zoya Kosmodemyanskaya, executed by German troops on 29 November 1941 for arson; this young woman is presented as a shining example to the youth of the Soviet Union. 'By embarking on the road of partisan warfare'—this is how her activity is characterized—'she took a sacred oath to the fatherland to fight to her last breath against the Fascist conquerors.'[320] Deplorable though the fate of the young Komsomol girl may have been, it should not be overlooked that it was inevitable under the merciless laws of war.

Atrocities of alarming magnitude have been committed in the ideological war of annihilation in eastern Europe—but it should be pointed out that, practically from the first day onward, both belligerents were equally involved in them. It almost seems as if the principles of international law and humanity must inevitably lose their validity in a warlike conflict between two totalitarian dictatorships, even though military leaders on both sides repeatedly tried to curb such excesses—if only in order to maintain discipline among their troops and preserve traditional forms as much as possible. As far as the violation of the norms of international law by the Germans is concerned—above all, the liquidation actions of the special squads of the security police and the SS security service, whose victims were racially or politically undesirable—these are treated very fully in the present volume of this work. Unless, however, the picture is to remain one-sided, there is a need for at least a brief discussion of actions on the Soviet side, actions similarly inspired by the idea of annihilating

---

[316] *Istorija Velikoj Otečestvennoj vojny*, vol. ii, picture following p. 288; *Vojna v tylu vraga*, picture following p. 160; *50 let vooružennych sil*, 296.

[317] *Deutschland im zweiten Weltkrieg*, vol. ii, picture with caption following p. 320.

[318] *Istorija Velikoj Otečestvennoj vojny*, ii. 290–1. Soviet leaflets, according to *Soldaten-Zeitung*, 46 (Aug. 1941), and *Nachrichten von der Front*, openly referred to the actions of the partisans as actions by 'Soviet irregulars': BA-MA RH 24-3/134.

[319] 'The Common Graves', in *Soviet War News*, 177 (London, 5 Feb. 1942), 41.

[320] *Istorija Velikoj Otečestvennoj vojny*, ii. 121, and picture following p. 128. Soviet military tribunals, incidentally, even after the end of the war, ordered German minors to be executed for acts of resistance—e.g. Hans Hösen and Host Schulz, both aged 15; see Fricke, *Politik und Justiz in der DDR*, 114–15.

the 'class enemy', i.e. a national and political opponent. A regime which, as Major-General Grigorenko confirms, even treats its own soldiers according to the 'inhuman slogan' that 'human lives must not be spared', is unlikely to show mercy to real or putative enemies. It should also be remembered from the outset that the Soviet leadership possessed an executive agency which closely corresponded to the special squads of the security police and the SS security service. These were the Special NKVD Detachments which *de facto* came under the People's Commissar of the Interior, Beriya; their duties included the administration of the eighty 'concentration-camp systems' then existing in the Soviet Union with hundreds of individual camps,[321] as well as guarding the political prisoners and the prisoners of war handed over to them by the military. From the first days of the war the NKVD troops had been charged with the execution of liquidation orders on a large scale. At the very start Stalin had ordered the immediate execution by firing-squad of all persons suspected of espionage[322] throughout the territory of the Soviet Union, as well as the speedy arrest of persons politically unreliable.[323] It is thought that some two million people were affected by the latter measure. Political prisoners in the areas threatened by German and German-allied troops—i.e. initially in the Baltic States, eastern Poland, and eastern Romania, and before long also in Belorussia and in the Ukraine—were to be shot on Stalin's special orders[324] before falling into enemy hands. In line with this instruction, mass shooting began in the first few days of the war in the overcrowded prisons and camps of the western regions; their victims were predominantly Baltic nationals, Poles, and Ukrainians. 'In every city in the western Ukraine', as stated by an investigating committee set up in 1954 by the United States Congress under the chairmanship of Representative Charles J. Kersten,[325] 'in the first days of the war the NKVD and its agents shot all the political prisoners except a mere handful who were miraculously saved.' The corpses of those murdered, including women and children, were found in many localities of the western frontier region of the Ukraine, e.g. in Stanislav, Chortkov, Tarnopol, Rovno, Lutsk, Sambor, Dubno, Sarny, Dobromil, and Drogobych. In Belorussia too, and everywhere in the Baltic republics, political prisoners were liquidated before the withdrawal of the NKVD troops. Such murders of prisoners took place in Brest, Minsk, Kaunas (Kovno), Vilnius, and Riga—to name but a few. However, mass shootings also occurred in the remote hinterland—in Smolensk, Berdichev, Uman, Stalino, Dnepropetrovsk, Kiev, Kharkov, Rostov, Odessa, Zaporozhye, Simferopol, Yalta, and elsewhere.[326] According

---

[321] Lewytzkyj, *Die rote Inquisition*, 172.   [322] Ibid. 191.

[323] Galay, 'Political Groups', 226.

[324] Dudin and Miller, 'The Russians', 115; Raschhofer, *Der Fall Oberländer*, 61; Lewytzkyj, *Die rote Inquisition*, 191; Zayas, *Die Wehrmacht-Untersuchungsstelle*, 328.

[325] According to Zayas, *Die Wehrmacht-Untersuchungsstelle*, 348.

[326] Kirimal, 'The Crimean Turks', 24; Dudin and Miller, 'The Russians', 115; Yurchenko, 'The Ukrainians', 144; Glowinskyi, 'The Western Ukrainians', 151; Conquest, *Great Terror*, 491; Zayas, *Die Wehrmacht-Untersuchungsstelle*, 328–9, 350; also Carnes, *General zwischen Hitler und Stalin*, 275.

to the findings of the Congressional committee of inquiry, 80,000–100,000 political prisoners were shot by NKVD agencies in the Ukraine alone before the arrival of the Germans and their allies.

An instructive example of the barbaric procedure of the security troops of both belligerents is provided by events in Lvov immediately after the beginning of the war in June–July 1941. As can be gleaned from the separate investigations of different bodies (the Wehrmacht-Untersuchungsstelle, the defence in the trials before the International Military Tribunal, the Select Committee on Communist Aggression (House of Representatives), the International Commission at The Hague) as well as from the specialized literature, particularly the works of Ukrainians in exile, NKVD agencies during the days up to 30 June 1941 murdered some 4,000 Ukrainian and Polish political prisoners and other civilians regardless of age or sex, as well as individual German prisoners of war, often after severe torture, in the prisons of the city of Lvov (the Brigidki, Zamarstynow, and NKVD prisons).[327] After the occupation of the city the German military authorities at first continued to act against the spontaneous anti-Jewish pogroms; in July, however, there arrived Action Squad C of the security police and the SS security service, which by way of so-called 'reprisal for inhuman atrocities' murdered some 7,000 inhabitants of Lvov and surroundings, mostly of Jewish origin, who had no connection whatever with the earlier events. The behaviour of the two belligerents upon occupying a region scarcely differed at all. Immediately after capture or recapture the region in question was combed through by special detachments for hostile, unpopular, or undesirable persons or entire population groups. In the jargon of the NKVD this was called 'cleansing of the entire territory liberated from the German occupiers and especially of inhabited localities'.[328] The victims of the security police and the SS security service were the Jews, initially also members of non-Russian minorities ('Asiatics'), as well as officials of the Communist Party; the victims of the Special NKVD Detachments were so-called 'agents of the enemy and other hostile elements', 'enemy elements and their helpers'. What such a 'cleansing' meant is revealed sufficiently by the practice of the Soviet security agencies: the shooting of all those Soviet citizens, regardless of age or sex, who had maintained even minimal relations with the German occupying power or their troops. Thus, while Kharkov was temporarily back in Soviet hands, the NKVD frontier troops, according to 'thorough' investigations, liquidated no less than 4 per cent of the remaining population, approximately 4,000 people, 'including girls who had gone with German soldiers'.[329] In all, hundreds of thousands[330] fell victim to the purges

---

[327] Raschhofer, *Der Fall Oberländer*, 40; Zayas, *Die Wehrmacht-Untersuchungsstelle*, 333.

[328] *Pograničnye vojska*, 473, 490.

[329] Stimmungsbericht [Mood report], 31 Mar. 1943, personal file Maj. Müller, vol. ii, BA R 6/52.

[330] Kabysh, 'The Belorussians', 86; Dudin and Miller, 'The Russians', 115; Galay, 'Political Groups', 219; Tolstoy, *Victims of Yalta*, 400.

of the NKVD agencies, which followed hard upon the heels of the regular troops of the Red Army.

Virtually from the first day of the war, Stalin and the Soviet leadership demonstrated by their measures that for them the armed conflict with Germany, compared with earlier 'European national wars', had a totally different character. 'The war with Fascist Germany must not be regarded as an ordinary war,' Stalin declared in his broadcast address on 3 July 1941;[331] 'it is not only a war between two armies. It is, at the same time, the war of the entire Soviet people against the Fascist German troops', a war 'that knows no compassion with the enemy'. The manner in which the leadership of the Soviet Union disregarded the norms of international law and human rights is shown not only by the mass liquidation of political opponents in the enemy-threatened regions, or by the directive of the Council of People's Commissars and the Communist Party Central Committee of 29 June 1941 with its subsequent orders, which unleashed unrestricted partisan warfare—i.e. virtual licence for any Soviet citizen to kill any soldier of the enemy army in any, even the most hideous, way—but also by another measure which proceeded less openly. On 28 August 1941 the USSR Supreme Soviet Praesidium issued a decree abolishing the Volga German Autonomous Republic,[332] the first in a series of similar actions whose subsequent victims were the Kalmyk, Chechen, Ingush, Kabardin, Balkar, and Crimean Tartar nations. Beginning in July 1941, the deportation and dispersal of the 400,000 Volga Germans, along with 140,000 Germans from the Ukraine, the Crimea, and the Caucasus, took place under inhuman conditions and involved the liquidation of their leading strata and the destruction of the highly developed cultural institutions of these ethnic groups. The extinction, on national and political grounds, of the German minority which had been settled in Russia for 200 years unquestionably represents the fact of the international crime of genocide,[333] as defined in the 1948 Convention of the United Nations.

In the ideological war of annihilation in eastern Europe it was, owing to the special nature of their tasks, mainly the NKVD troops and the nascent partisan detachments and units that infringed valid international law and human rights. As for the role of the regular Red Army troops in this context, one has to consider the basic political attitude prevailing in the USSR. Lieutenant-General Vlasov, GOC Russian Liberation Army, who attended a conference in the Kremlin after the battle of Kiev, has conveyed an idea of that

[331] Rundfunkrede des Vorsitzenden des Staatskomitees für Verteidigung J. W. Stalin am 3. Juli 1941 [Broadcast address by I. V. Stalin, Chairman of the State Committee for Defence, 3 July 1941], leaflet, BA-MA RH 24-3/134; Stalin, *Großer Vaterländischer Krieg*, 10, 13.

[332] 'On the Administrative Organization of the Territory of the Former Volga German Republic: Decree of September 7, 1941', in *Genocide in the USSR*, doc. 4, p. 265; Vvedensky, 'The Volga Germans', 49 ff.; Fleischhauer, '"Unternehmen Barbarossa" und die Zwangsumsiedlung der Deutschen'.

[333] Deker, 'The Meaning of Genocide', 1; Minasjan, *Meždunarodnye prestuplenija*, 264.

attitude. He reports that Stalin had called upon People's Commissar Beriya to fan 'hatred, hatred, and again hatred' of all Germans.[334] Along those lines, using the stereotyped slogan 'Death to the German occupiers!', the Soviet propaganda machine began to unleash a mass campaign which proceeded from the premiss that the German attack did not constitute a war in the conventional sense, but a criminal act. The soldiers of the enemy army, therefore, were to be viewed not as regular combatants but as criminals and bandits. Thus Marshal of the Soviet Union Budennyy, GOC Troops of the South-western Direction, in his order No. 5 of 16 July 1941,[335] called the Germans the 'gangs of that man-eater Hitler', 'Fascist beasts'. 'Fascist scum'. 'Fascist carrion', a 'Fascist monster' which one 'crushes like a snake'.

The anti-German agitation which now developed with full force had its spokesman in the writer Ilya Ehrenburg, who published keynote articles in the press every few days from the beginning of the war. It is highly rewarding to cast at least a brief glance at Ehrenburg's propaganda products of 1941–2. His method was that of presenting allegedly real individuals as representative of the totality of Germans. In this way he fanned boundless hatred, not against the political enemy, 'Fascism', but against the German nation as such. Ehrenburg repeatedly expressed the sentiment that to him the Germans had ceased to be human beings. 'There is something terrible about the German himself,' he wrote. Even the ancient Germans had been barbarians, clothing themselves in the skins of wild animals. 'We hate every one of them . . . he fair-haired and the dark-haired.'[336] His defamation of the German soldiers, whom he dehumanized by all conceivable kinds of insults and animal comparisons in order to suggest the need for their extermination,[337] was to have serious consequences. Thus he described the field marshals as 'raging wolves', 'plague-carrying rats', the generals as 'cannibals', the officers as 'two-legged beasts'. Every single enemy soldier was a 'murderer' to him; the German soldiers were 'millions of murderers', and therefore 'undoubtedly like wild beasts', 'worse than wild beasts', 'beasts of prey', 'Aryan beasts', 'monsters', 'dying scorpions', 'starving rats'. 'We do not regard them as human beings.'[338] The Geneva Convention had placed prisoners of war under the protection of the Red Cross—but that did not stop Ehrenburg from publicly insulting even those prisoners as 'beasts of prey', 'lousy curs', 'murderers', and 'bandits' from whom even the dogs turned away.[339] His assertion that the people hated even dead Germans justified the destruction, ordered by Stalin, of the German military cemeteries in the regions reconquered by the Russians. Ehrenburg's pronouncements time and again reveal unmistakable pathological traits—for instance when, with joyous satisfaction, he reports seeing 'thousands and

---

[334] Pozdnjakov, *Andrej Andreevič Vlasov*, 293.   [335] BA-MA RH 24-3/134.
[336] Examples of typical manifestations of racial and national hatred in Ehrenburg, *Russia at War*, 240, 189, 131, xi, 92, 94, 108, 186.
[337] Ibid. 14, 61, 80, 105, 257, 118, 49, 262, 248, 130, 258, 276, 55, 62, 75, 91, 210, 232, 265.
[338] Ibid. 130, 97.   [339] Ibid. 51, 109, 37, 273, 277, 14, 29, 52.

thousands' of mutilated German corpses,[340] 'some shell-torn, some tank-squashed, others resembling waxwork figures', 'lumps of flesh resembling crushed machinery parts'. 'For us there is no sight more cheerful than German corpses,' he wrote in 1942;[341] and elsewhere: 'A colonel shows his old rat's yellow fangs.' The sorrow of the mothers and wives of those killed in action comes in only for sneers and mockery. He advises them: 'If you don't wish to weep, then dance, jest, pipe away.' 'In the spring the snow will melt and you will smell the stench of corpses.'[342]

Inciting articles of this kind did no more than serve the immediate objective of permanently whipping up the Red Army troops. In view of the intensity of political indoctrination in the Soviet forces, it is not surprising that these outpourings of hate affected the attitude of the troops. The feelings of hate fanned in them often resulted not only in an enhancement of their fighting zeal, but also in atrocities committed against enemy soldiers who had, by then helpless, fallen into their hands. A variety of records, of statements by prisoners of war and deserters, of intercepted radio messages, and of captured files of Soviet HQs unequivocally show that prisoners, especially wounded ones, were as a rule shot either immediately upon capture or after an initial interrogation.[343] These instances of shooting or mutilation, which began 'in the same way and at the same time' in the most varied sectors of the front during the first few days, are unlikely to have been spontaneous excesses by Soviet soldiers. There is ample evidence that such actions were committed upon specific orders or with the connivance of unit commanders of various ranks, mainly at the level of company, battalion, or regimental commanders,[344] though at times also involoing senior staffs.[345] Thus on 21 February 1941 a captured Soviet colonel reported the shooting of a German Luftwaffe officer in the presence of the army commander, Lieutenant-General Kuznetsov, and other top officers. An active role in this respect, however, was played by the political departments of the various units. Time and again there is evidence that individual or mass executions were carried out on the orders of the war commissars or political officials.[346] Major incidents during the early phase of the war included the shooting of 180 German soldiers at Broniki on 30 June 1941, the shooting of 300–400 Romanian and a number of German soldiers on orders from Major Savelin, commanding 225th Rifle Regiment, at Storozhinets in the Bukovina on 2–3 July 1941, and the shooting of 80 German soldiers in the area of 26th Rifle Division on 13 July 1941.[347] Altogether 'several

[340] Ibid. xi–xii, 50, 55, 238, 240.

[341] Il'ja Èrenburg, 'Ubej!', in Zayas, *Die Wehrmacht-Untersuchungsstelle*, 434; Buchbender, *Das tönende Erz*, 305.

[342] Ehrenburg, *Russia at War*, 97, 187 ff.

[343] Zayas, *Die Wehrmacht-Untersuchungsstelle*, 304.   [344] Ibid. 282, 295, 300.

[345] Ibid. 277, 284, 283, 293.   [346] Ibid. 283, 292–5, 300–1.

[347] Bericht über die Besichtigung des Tatortes auf der Höhe westlich Broniki, Gericht der 25. Inf.Div. (mot) [Report on the inspection of the scene of the crime on the latitude west of Broniki, Court of 25th (mot.) Inf. Div.], 2 July 1941, BA-MA RH 24-3/134; Zayas, *Die Wehrmacht-Untersuchungsstelle*, 273, 277–8, 282.

thousand reports' of shootings of prisoners of war, especially of wounded men left behind, were collected by the Wehrmacht Investigation Office for Breaches of International Law.[348]

This illegal practice, however, and the inhuman treatment of German prisoners of war, of whom 90–5 per cent perished in 1941–2,[349] do not seem to have been in line with the intentions of the Red Army command. It appears that the People's Commissariat for Defence and the army commands were guided, as far as the treatment of prisoners of war was concerned, by a decree of the USSR Council of People's Commissars on the Position of Prisoners of War of 1 July 1941, which was entirely in line with the regulations of the Hague Convention, though it was not translated into reality[350] any more than the above-mentioned Soviet note of 17 July 1941 (see sect. II.II.3 at n. 31). At least, Lieutenant-General Khrulev, the Red Army's chief administration official—acting in much the same way as his German opposite number, Major-General Wagner, quartermaster-general in the Army General Staff—in his Circular No. 017 of 3 July 1941[351] laid down entirely adequate food rations for prisoners of war. Major-General Utkin and Divisional Medical Officer Smirnov of the Red Army's Chief Military Health Directorate similarly, in a directive to the deputy chiefs of staff of the fronts, military districts, and armies, dated 29 July 1941,[352] recommended appropriate hospital treatment for wounded or sick prisoners of war. Marshal of the Soviet Union Shaposhnikov, chief of the Red Army General Staff, having learnt in August 1941 that 'individual enlisted personnel' in 'detachments and units' were in the habit of taking 'personal valuables, money, and documents' from prisoners of war, once more ordered the chiefs of the staffs of fronts and armies to ensure that prisoners of war were treated in accordance with the decree of the Council of People's Commissars of 1 July 1941.[353] Major-General Gordov, the Twenty-first Army chief of staff, and Brigade Commissar Pogodin, the Twenty-first Army war commissar, likewise reminded their subordinate rifle corps of the government's order that 'prisoners [must not be] treated roughly'.[354] The deplorable practice of looting, which 'disgraced the Red Army', had to be stopped.

The really serious aspect, however, was not so much the 'rough treatment' or even the looting of the prisoners' possessions, but the stark fact that they

---

[348] Zayas, *Die Wehrmacht-Untersuchungsstelle*, 284.　　　[349] Ibid. 277.

[350] Položenie o voennoplennych, Postanovlenie SNK SSSR Nos. 1798-800s, sekretno, utverždeno, 1 July 1941, BA-MA RW 2/v. 158, fo. 127. On this and the following passage see also the misleading presentation in Rževevskij and Ivanickij, 'Pravda i lož'', 77.

[351] Cirkuljar Glavnogo Intendanta Krasnoj Armii No. 017, sekretno, 3 July 1941, BA-MA RW 2/v. 158, fo. 128.

[352] NKO SSSR, Sanitarnoe Upravlenie Krasnoj Armii (General-Major Utkin, Divvrač Smirnov) to Zam. Načalnikov Štabov Frontov, Okrugov i Armij Krasnoj Armii, No. 3/122/451926s, sekretno, 29 July 1941, ibid., fo. 59.

[353] Načal'nik General'nogo Štaba RKKA, Maršal Šapošnikov to Načal'nikam Štabov Frontov i Armij, ibid., fo. 103.

[354] Nač. Štaba 21. Armii, General-Major Gordov, Voennyj Komissar, Brigadnyj Komissar Pogodin to Komandiru '. . .' SK, sročno, sekretno, ibid., fo. 47.

were murdered. German troops captured a number of documents revealing that the command agencies of the Red Army endeavoured to put a halt to that barbaric practice—which merely confirms its existence. Thus Major-General Potapov, GOC Fifth Army, in Order No. 025 of 30 June 1941,[355] also signed by War Council member Divisional Commissar Nikishev, and by Brigade Commissar Kalchenko, head of the political propaganda department, criticized the practice—not only in 'individual cases'—of Red Army men and officers not taking enemy prisoners but shooting them on the spot. Unit commanders and heads of propaganda departments were ordered to draw their subordinates' attention to the damage done by such actions. 'I categorically forbid any shootings without authorization,' Potapov's order concludes. Similarly, Brigade Commissar Ivanchenko, head of the political propaganda department of XXXI Rifle Corps, in his order No. 020 of 14 July 1941[356] described as a downright 'criminal failure, the fact that during operations 'Red Army men and commanders take no soldiers or officers prisoner'. It had become known 'that they strangle prisoners or stab them to death'. Ivanchenko ordered that measures be taken 'with all means of Party-political effort' to put a stop to a 'behaviour towards prisoners of war that is unworthy of the Red Army'. Major-General Alekseev, GOC VI Rifle Corps, in an order of 22 July 1941,[357] also signed by his commissar, Brigade Commissar Shulikov, and by his chief of staff, Colonel Yeremin, similarly complained that 'many units of the corps have so far shot their prisoners'. A 'frankly outrageous case' had been the shooting of a prisoner on 19 July 1941 at the instance of the head of the political propaganda department and the chief of the Special Detachment. Those guilty were reprimanded, and the divisional commander's attention was drawn to such inadmissible treatment of prisoners of war.

Similar instances also became known to the Germans from the area of Fourteenth Army on the Murmansk front. An order issued on 8 September 1941 by Colonel Malitskiy, the deputy of the army's chief of staff, jointly with Battalion Commissar Burylin, the deputy of the army commissar, criticized the fact that, although the units assembled prisoner transports, these were subsequently liquidated '*en route*'.[358] The Soviet commands protested against such acts chiefly for military reasons: interrogation of prisoners was an import-

---

[355] NKO SSSR, Upravlenie Političesk. propagandy 5 armii (Komandujuščij 5 Armii, General-Major Potapov, Člen Voennogo Soveta, Divizionnyj Komissar Nikišev, Načal'nik OPP, Brigadnyj Komissar Kal'čenko' to Komandiram Soedinenij Načal'nikam Otdelov Polit-propagandy, No. 025, 30 June 1941, ibid., fo. 51.

[356] NKO SSSR, Otdel Politpropagandy 31 strelkovogo korpusa (Načal'nik OPP 31 sk, Brigadnyj Komissar Ivančenko) Vsem Načal'nikam OPP [Propaganda unit of xxxi Rifle Corps . . . to all commanders], No. 020, 14 July 1941, ibid., fo. 52.

[357] Befehl an das 6. Schützenkorps, Kommandeur, Generalmajor Alexeew, Kommissar, Brigadekommissar Schulikow, Stabschef, Oberst Jeremin, Geheim [Order to vi Riffle Corps . . .], 22 July 1941, ibid., fo. 123.

[358] Oberst Malitzkij (für den Chef des Stabes der Armee), Bataillonskommissar Burylin (für den Kommissar) an die Leiter der Abteilungen für Aufklärung der Verbände und Einheiten [Col. Malitskij (for Army Chief of Staff) to heads of propaganda units], 8 Sept. 1941, ibid., fos. 157, 161.

ant means of gaining intelligence about the enemy. Occasionally, however, the argument from political propaganda was adduced that this kind of treatment was making it impossible to destroy the enemy's morale. Brigade Commissar Ivanchenko reminded the heads of the political propaganda departments of yet another aspect: 'A German soldier who surrenders ceases to be an enemy.' Along with practical military reasoning, we observe here a humanitarian motivation of the kind that underlies the international conventions.

Efforts by the Red Army leaders to curb such excesses by Soviet troops and to ensure appropriate treatment for prisoners of war were encountering extraordinary difficulties—as is proved by the ceaseless repetition of similar orders. They became totally ineffective the moment they came into conflict with the new propaganda campaign launched towards the end of 1941. On 6 November 1941,[359] at a festive session of the Moscow Soviet and of Party and social organizations, Stalin delivered a programmatic speech in which he stated:

From now on it will be our task, the task of the nations of the Soviet Union, the task of the fighters, the commanders, and the political functionaries of our army and our navy, to annihilate all Germans who have penetrated as occupiers into the territory of our homeland, down to the last man. [*Tumultuous applause, shouts of 'Hear, hear!', shouts of 'Hurray!'*] No mercy for the German occupiers! Death to the German occupiers! [*Tumultuous applause.*]

The contents of this speech, made by Stalin on the occasion of the 24th anniversary of the 'Great Socialist October Revolution', were very effectively brought to the notice of the Red Army by means of war propaganda and through the Army's political machine.[360] Now Ehrenburg at last had an, opportunity, long awaitrd, to put his own case. From November 1941 there is a striking repetition in his articles of turns of phrase in which he undisguisedly calls for the murder of all German soldiers without exception.[361] 'It will be five million . . . corpses that we will bury in our earth,' he observed on 2 December 1941. 'Now we are resolved to kill all Germans who have invaded our country,' he called out to the Red Army soldiers on 3 December 1941. 'We simply want to annihilate them. It has fallen to the lot of our people to carry out this humane mission. We are continuing the work of Pasteur, who discovered the serum against rabies. We are continuing the work of all the scientists who have discovered the means of destroying deadly microbes.' 'The Germans . . . must be driven into the earth. They must be destroyed one after the other,' he wrote on 22 December 1941. On 20 February 1942 it was: 'You've got to kill them—put them underground'; and on 13 March 1942: 'You must squeeze the Germans off the face of the the earth.' Yet some senior commands of the Red

[359] Stalin, *Großer Vaterländischer Krieg*, 31.
[360] Zayas, *Die Wehrmacht-Untersuchungsstelle*, 296 ff.
[361] Ehrenburg, *Russia at War*, 229, 86, 234, 113, 267.

Army in no way lagged behind Ehrenburg. Thus an order issued on 14 December 1941 by Army General Zhukov, GOC the Troops of the Western Front, and by Bulganin, member of the War Council of the Western Front and Deputy Chairman of the USSR Council of People's Commissars,[362] contained this passage: 'Not one Hitlerite bandit who invaded our country shall be allowed to get away alive . . . It is our sacred duty to take cruel revenge . . . and to wipe out all the German occupiers down to the last man.' On 1 January 1942 the War Council of the Leningrad Front[363] addressed an appeal to the population in the German rear not to allow any enemy soldiers, referred to as 'Hitlerite dogs' and 'Fascist cannibals', to escape anywhere, 'except into the ground, into their graves'. In this 'merciless war of annihilation' any means was fair: 'rifle, grenade, axe, scythe, crowbar.' About the same time a leaflet of the Political Directorate of the North-west Front declared: 'Officers and soldiers in green greatcoats are not humans but wild beasts . . . Destroy German officers and soldiers as you would kill rabid dogs.'[364]

According to the findings of the German army high command, Stalin's appeal to the Red Army was universally 'understood and interpreted' in the sense that 'any member of the German Wehrmacht—whether fighting or wounded or taken prisoner—was to be killed'.[365] It therefore represented the prelude to a new wave of murders whose victims during that period, as emerges from captured documents and from the interrogation of deserters and captured Red Army men, were the majority of German and German-allied prisoners of war.[366] A few particularly shocking instances may be quoted here. Between 1 and 6 December 1941 a hundred German prisoners of war were murdered at Naro-Fominsk on orders from the commissar of '1 gmsd' (1st Motorized Guards Rifle Division) and several more by other units, such as 222nd Rifle Division.[367] It has also been established that in January 1942 Brigade Commissar Vasilyev, the army commissar of Second Assault Army, issued an order for the shooting of prisoners of war.[368] One direct result of Stalin's appeal was the murder of all German prisoners who fell into the hands

---

[362] 'Prikaz komandujuščego vojskami Zapadnogo fronta, 14.12.1941', in *Moskva—frontu*, 91.

[363] Der Kriegsrat der Leningrader Front, Leningrader Gebietskomitee der AKP(B), An die Bevölkerung . . . , 1 Jan. 1942, BA-MA RH 22/271.

[364] According to Zayas, *Die Wehrmacht-Untersuchungsstelle*, 285.

[365] General z.b.V. b. ObdH an Heerwesenabteilung, betr. bolschewistische Kriegführung [General (special duties) with the C.-in-C. of the Army to Army Administration Department, re Bolshevik conduct of the war], geh., 18 Jan. 1942, BA-MA, W 01-6/578; Hoffmann, *Deutsche und Kalmyken*, 107; BA-MA RW 2/v. 158, fos. 80, 82, 96, 146, 198, 210, 281 ff.

[366] BA-MA RW 2/v. 158, fos. 80 ff., 88–9, 96, 146, 188, 198, 209, 238, 256, 266, 281, 287, 300; Zayas, *Die Wehrmacht-Untersuchungsstelle*, 296 ff.

[367] Spravka, Načal'nik RO Štarma 33, Kapitan Potapov, 8 Dec. 1941, BA-MA RW 2/v. 158, fo. 172.

[368] Zusätzliche Vernehmung des Überläufers Technik-Intendant II. Ranges Maljuk [Additional interrogation of deserter Malyuk, Technical *Intendant* 2nd rank], Abwehrtrupp I/AOK 18 to Abt. Ic, No. 40/42, g., 9 June 1942; Dienststelle [Office] Maj. Baun to Abw. IHOstN, No. 5866/42, g., 1 July 1942, ibid., fos. 227, 231.

of the Soviet troops during the landing at Feodosiya at the end of December; this had been ordered by the political departments of various units, among them the commissar of IX Rifle Corps[369]—'one of the worst atrocities of this terrible war', in the words of Reginald (later Lord) Paget, the British defence counsel of Field Marshal von Manstein.[370] Some 160 seriously wounded Germans left behind in the military hospitals of Feodosiya were seized by Soviet soldiers or Red Fleet sailors, thrown out of the windows, exposed to death by freezing through having water poured over them or by immersion in the sea, or killed by having their skulls smashed with blunt instruments, or brutally mutilated.

Such a degeneration of warfare was certainly not in the interests of the Red Army either; indeed it began seriously to worry the Soviet command authorities. Army General Zhukov, who on 14 December 1941 had come out entirely in favour of Stalin's appeal, found himself compelled in the winter of 1941–2, jointly with War Council member Khokhlov, to address the following rather revealing order to 'commanders and war council members' of subordinate formations: 'I declare that Comrade Stalin never mentioned the shooting of enemy soldiers once they have laid down their arms or have voluntarily come over to us.' 'The shooting of prisoners' was to be specifically forbidden with immediate effect.[371] Stalin himself virtually countermanded his appeal of 6 November 1941 by stating, in Order No. 55 of 23 February 1942: 'The Red Army takes German soldiers and officers prisoner when they surrender.'[372] As early as 2 December 1941 the staff of the Independent Coastal Army,[373] in Order No. 0086, had, for military and political reasons, objected to the generally observed 'rule' of shooting prisoners of war without interrogation, instead of transferring them to the staffs. Similar orders are also known from other units. Thus Colonel Pankratov, the commander of 168th Cavalry Regiment of 41st Independent Cavalry Division, jointly with Senior Political Guide Kutuzov, complained on 28 December 1941[374] that 'captured German Fascists are not taken to the regimental staff but shot on the spot'. Major Kotik, the chief of staff of a Rifle Division (apparently the 65th), and its commissar, Battalion Commissar Kitsa, likewise criticized 'do-it-yourself justice' meted out to captured soldiers and officers, and, on behalf of the divisional commander, threatened the commander and commissar of 38th Rifle Regiment with severe punishment in the event of a repetition.[375] Finally Major-General

---

[369] Zayas, Die Wehrmacht-Untersuchungsstelle, 308 ff.

[370] Paget, Manstein, 41; Manstein, Verlorene Siege, 246 (not in trans.).

[371] Schukow, Chochlow, Allen Kommandierenden und den Gliedern des Kriegsrats, no date, copy authorized by military court, BA-MA W 01-6/578; Hoffmann, Deutsche und Kalmyken, 107.

[372] Ržeševskij and Ivanickij, 'Pravda i lož'', 77.

[373] Vefügung Nr. 0086 des Stabes der Küstenarmee (Chef des Stabes), 2 Dec. 1941, BA-MA RW 2/v. 158, fo. 312.

[374] Prikaz po 168 Kavallerijskomu polku 41 OKD (Komandir 168 Kp, Polkovnik Pankratov, Voenkom, St. Politruk Kutuzov, Načal'nik Štaba . . .), 28 Dec. 1941, ibid., fo. 150.

[375] Načal'nik Štaba, Major Kotik, Komissar, Bat. Komissar Kica to Komandiram častej. Tol'ko komandiru 311 sp, ibid., fo. 183.

Moskvin, the Sixty-second Army chief of staff, and Regimental Commissar Zaytsev, the war commissar of that army's staff, prohibited 'any shooting, of any number of prisoners whatsoever, on the battlefield'.[376] In the event of infringement the relevant divisional commanders and other accessories were to be held 'seriously responsible'.

The Red Army commanders were well aware that inhuman methods of warfare as a rule only strengthened the enemy's determination to resist. Such documents as chanced to fall into German hands also show that, generally speaking, they were anxious to avoid the murder of prisoners of war and to ensure appropriate treatment for them. Unlike the NKVD troops, who had to carry out the annihilation orders of Stalin and the political leadership, and unlike the partisans who knew no scruples, the Red Army leaders appear only in exceptional cases to have been guilty of outright violations of international law. Yet their clear orders, both during the period here discussed and in the further course of the war, were, for whatever reasons, frequently disregarded. A striking illustration of this dates from the days of the battle of Stalingrad, when in February 1943 Soviet troops at Krasnoarmeyskoe and Grishino, at the behest of various authorities—it has been established that one of them was the political department of 14th Guards Armoured Brigade—shot or otherwise brutally murdered no fewer than 600 German, Italian, Romanian, and Hungarian prisoners of war and wounded, as well as civilian prisoners, including Red Cross nurses and female radio operators.[377] It should also be borne in mind that atrocities such as those of Feodosiya and Krasnoarmeyskoe–Grishino were discovered only when—as happened rarely enough in the further course of the war—German troops happened to reconquer the scene of such massacres of prisoners.

13. The Red Army's General Offensive in the Winter of 1942

On the strength of the successes of December 1941 Stalin believed that the time had come to bring about the collapse of the entire German eastern front and to rout the main forces of the German army in the east by massive offensive operations from Lake Ladoga to the Black Sea. On 5 January 1942 he informed the members of the State Defence Committee, Supreme Command Headquarters, and the general staff of his intention to go over to the offensive simultaneously in all strategic directions, to encircle and annihilate the German Army Groups North and Centre, and to inflict a crushing defeat on Army Group South as well.[378] Objections by Army General Zhukov, the GOC

---

[376] Načal'nik Štaba Armii, General-Major Moskvin, Voennyj komissar, Polkovoj Komissar Zajcev, Načal'nik Razvedotdela, Polkovnik German to Komandiram 57 (87?), 196, 131, 399, 112 SD, 33 Gv sd, 35 SD, 20 MSBR, sekretno, ibid., fo. 277.

[377] Hoffmann, *Deutsche und Kalmyken*, 108; Zayas, *Die Wehrmacht-Untersuchungsstelle*, 318 ff.

[378] Žukov, 'Kontrnastuplenie', 79.

Western Front, who argued in favour of transferring the available reserves—14 divisions and 7 brigades—to the Western Front, and of seeking a decision in that sector alone, rather than dissipating the forces, were rejected, even though Deputy People's Commissar Voznesenskiy supported the creation of such a point of main effort. Stalin, who had earlier consulted with Marshal Timoshenko and who, as usual, was supported by Marshal Shaposhnikov, chief of the general staff, as well as by Malenkov and Beriya, persisted in his decision.[379] The Soviet command, therefore, was about to do what it had always accused its enemy of—pursue an adventurous and totally unrealistic operations plan. The underestimation of the German enemy reflected in that decision is the more striking as, according to data in the Soviet historical literature, the ratio of strength at that time was about equal, with only a slight superiority on the part of the Red Army. The armies of Germany and her allies, which, according to greatly exaggerated Soviet figures, on 1 January 1942 numbered 3,909,000 men, about 35,000 artillery pieces and mortars, and 1,500 tanks, were confronted by Soviet forces of allegedly only 4,199,000 men, 27,700 artillery pieces and mortars, and 1,784 tanks.[380]

The order for the attack of 7 January 1942 assigned to the troops of the Leningrad Front, the Volkhov Front, and the right wing of the North-west Front the task of routing the armies of the German Army Group North and lifting the siege of Leningrad. The formations of the left wing of the North-west Front, the Kalinin Front, the Western Front, and the Bryansk Front—which were to conduct the main strike at the centre—were to encircle and annihilate the bulk of Army Group Centre. The South-west and Southern Fronts, finally, were to rout Army Group South, while the Transcaucasus Front was to annihilate Eleventh Army and occupy the Crimea. A special directive from Headquarters, dated 10 January 1942, applied the lessons of past mistakes in offensive operations and demanded that front staffs in future create powerful assault groups for the purpose of bursting through the enemy's defences, that they employ armour and artillery at the points of main effort, and that they organize the co-operation of the different branches.[381]

In view of the precarious situation of the city of Leningrad, Supreme Commanal Headquarters had fixed 7 January 1942 for the opening of the attack in a north-westerly direction, a date on which, in the opinion of Army General Meretskov—the GOC Volkhov Front, which was to strike the main blow—the troops would not yet be ready for attack. Although the three Soviet fronts on the northern wing had some slight superiority in men, artillery, and armour, the formations still lacked all kinds of personal weapons, transport, supply facilities, and other necessities. The troops, and above all the command staffs, were inadequately trained, and the Second Assault Army (until the end of December the Twenty-sixth Army) and Fifty-ninth Army, brought up for reinforcement, were not yet assembled in the deployment areas. The attack by

---

[379] Zhukov, *Reminiscences*, 353.   [380] *Istorija Velikoj Otečestvennoj vojny*, ii. 317.
[381] Direktivnoe pis'mo Stavki, 10 Jan. 1942, *VIŽ* (1974), No. 1, pp. 70–4.

Fourth and Fifty-second Armies, launched prematurely on 7 January 1942, ended—just as the front staff had predicted—in total failure. The attacking formations were soon thrown back to their jumping-off positions.[382] After a brief pause the two armies resumed their offensive on 13 January 1942; again it produced no results. On the other hand, Major-General Klykov's Second Assault Army, which likewise went over to the offensive, succeeded, in conjunction with the left wing of Major-General Galanin's Fifty-ninth Army, in breaking through the German defences on the Volkhov, albeit on a narrow strip east of Myasnoy Bor, and, in the course of January, in advancing to west of Lyuban. However, the planned encirclement of the German Eighteenth Army, or at least of its forces on the Vokhov, was not accomplished because the simultaneous pincer movement by Major-General Fedyuninskiy's Fifty-fourth Army of the Leningrad Front had got stuck at Podgostye.[383] Even though, after the failure of the envelopment effort, Second Assault Army was now in an exceedingly exposed position, Supreme Command Headquarters clung to its original objective. On 28 February Headquarters issued orders to the Volkhov Front to create an assault force, to be further reinforced with armour, artillery, and air forces; in co-operation with Fifty-fourth Army of the Leningrad Front this was to force a breakthrough to Lyuban and encircle the enemy formations west of the Volkhov.[384] Again the hoped-for success was not achieved, although Fifty-fourth Army managed to overcome the German defences at Kirishi and to work its way forward to within 30 kilometres of Lyuban. The reason for the failure of the encirclement operation was a gross underestimate of the enemy, who had been substantially reinforced in that sector, as well as shortcomings in the preparation and execution of the offensive, such as the lack of any co-ordination between the attacking armies and faulty employment of the air units. Suddenly, from the end of March 1942, Second Assault Army was in its turn threatened with encirclement. It was Supreme Command Headquarters, and by no means the new GOC, Lieutenant-General Vlasov,[385] an experienced army commander who had proved his mettle at Kiev and Moscow, who had manœuvred Second Assault Army into a situation which eventually ended in its annihilation.

In concert with the armies of the Volkhov Front, the troops of the right wing of the North-west Front under Lieutenant-General Kurochkin had gone over to the offensive on 7 January 1942, and those of the left wing on 9 January. The Soviet objectives in the sector south of Lake Ilmen were no less extensive than those in the neighbouring sector to the north, consisting as they did in the encirclement and annihilation of the entire forces of the German Sixteenth Army. Lieutenant-General Morozov's Eleventh Army had the task of penetrating deep into the German rear, via Staraya Russa in the direction of

---

[382] Mereckov, *Na službe narodu*, 258–9. [383] Mereckov, in *Oborona Leningrada*, 192.

[384] *Istorija ordena Lenina Leningradskogo Voennogo okruga*, 280.

[385] Mereckov, *Na službe narodu*, 275, 282 ff.; Vasilevskij, *Delo vsej žizni*, 185–6; Žilin, 'Kak A. Solženycin vospel predatel'stvo vlasovcev'. *Contra*, Hoffmann, *Wlassow-Armee*, 334 ff.

Soltsy–Dno, and, in co-operation with elements of Fifty-second Army of the Volkhov Front, of routing the German grouping at Novgorod. General Berzarin's Thirty-fourth Army, originally earmarked only for pinning down the German forces at Demyansk, was now, under a modified plan, instructed to encircle and annihilate those forces,[386] and subsequently, with the support of the right wing of Lieutenant-General Purkaev's Third Assault Army[387] (until 25 December the Sixtieth Reserve Army), to fight its way through to Kholm. However, the development of the attack after 7 January 1942 did not entirely meet the exaggerated expectations of Supreme Command Headquarters. Because of some friction within its command, Eleventh Army was unable to meet even the minimum objective—demanded by Stalin in the form of an ultimatum—of taking the important transport junction of Staraya Russa by 11 January 1942. Thirty-fourth Army, which had fragmented its forces, initially also made but slight progress.

In view of the only marginal superiority of the Soviet troops, the North-west Front command tried to convince Supreme Command Headquarters that, instead of a deep thrust into the rear of Army Group North, the envisaged objective should be limited to the encirclement of the German forces at Demyansk. However, Stalin and Marshal Shaposhnikov would not hear of such a curtailment,[388] though eventually they agreed to reinforce the North-west Front by transferring to it Lieutenant-General Kuznetsov's First Assault Army, as well as two Guards rifle corps from the Headquarters reserve. Throughout February the attacks on the flanks of the Demyansk grouping continued with undiminished violence; towards the end of the month they ended with Eleventh Army going over to the defence at Staraya Russa and on Lake Ilmen, with First Assault Army[389] on the Kholynya river and Third Assault Army in the Kholm area doing likewise. As might have been predicted, no stunning success in a westerly direction had been achieved. Even so, Major-General Gryaznov's I Guards Rifle Corps, attacking east of the Lovat in a southerly direction, succeeded on 20 February in linking up at Zaluchye with elements of Third Assault Army attacking northwards and—by closing the inner ring—in encircling six German divisions on the Valday hills near Demyansk. Supreme Command Headquarters, hoping to achieve a conspicuous victory, ordered the speedy annihilation of the trapped forces before they had a chance to organize their defence.[390] On the other hand, the attacks carried out on the orders of North-west Front command by elements of Thirty-fourth Army, I Guards Rifle Corps, and the right wing of Third Assault Army produced no results. More than that, in the spring of 1942 German relief forces succeeded at Ramushevo in opening up a narrow corridor to the trapped division, who thus escaped the fate of the Soviet Second Assault Army in a similar position.

[386] Kuročkin, 'My sražalis'', 25–6.   [387] Semenov, 'Iz opyta', 89.
[388] Kuročkin, 'My sražalis'', 36.   [389] Lisicyn, '1-ja Udarnaja nastupaet', 82 ff.
[390] Kuročkin, 'My sražalis'', 39.

The offensive of the left wing of the North-west Front, the Kalinin Front, the Western Front, and the Bryansk Front, which began at the centre on 8 January 1942 and aimed at splitting and routing Army Group Centre, created a precarious situation for some of the German divisions but ultimately failed to attain its strategic objective. Formations of Lieutenant-General Purkaev's Third Assault Army (until then the Sixtieth Reserve Army) and of Lieutenant-General Yeremenko's Fourth Assault Army (until then Twenty-seventh Army), which at the beginning of the offensive still came under the North-west Front but from 22 January 1942, in order to simplify the chains of command, was placed under Colonel-General Konev's Kalinin Front, had been advancing rapidly in a south-westerly direction since 9 January 1942. While elements of Third Assault Army reached Kholm on 20 January and encircled the town, and on 2 February were already fighting at the approaches to Velikie Luki, Fourth Assault Army had taken Andreapol and Toropets and driven its spearheads in a new surge as far as the Usvyaty–Velizh–Demidov line; indeed, Major-General Tarasov's 249th Rifle Division even reached the area north-east of Vitebsk.[391] However, a further advance towards the important transport triangle Vitebsk–Smolensk–Orsha proved impossible because the forward movement of Third Assault Army had got stuck on the right wing and because Major-General Vostrukhov's Twenty-second Army of the Kalinin Front, operating on the left wing, was likewise unable to make any further progress once it had taken Olenino. Yeremenko's Fourth Assault Army, whose flanks were consequently exposed and whose attacking strength was exhausted, proved unable to exploit the success achieved at the boundary between Army Group North and Army Group Centre and was increasingly being forced on to the defensive.[392]

Rapid progress was initially made also by the Kalinin Front, which had been charged by Stalin's directive of 7 January 1942 first with detaching a combat group for the capture of Rzhev and then striking past that city towards the south, in the direction of Sychevka and Vyazma, cutting the vital Gzhatsk–Smolensk supply-line and, in co-operation with troops of the Western Front, 'taking prisoner or annihilating' the entire German grouping in the Mozhaysk–Gzhatsk area. Lieutenant-General Maslennikov's Thirty-ninth Army, which had opened the attack on 8 January, reached Sychevka almost on schedule on 15 January 1942, with support from Major-General Shvetsov's Twenty-ninth Army.[393] Colonel Sokolov's XI Cavalry Corps, brought forward to deepen the penetration, succeeded in pushing further to the south and, on 26 January 1942, in cutting the Gzhatsk–Smolensk railway line west of Vyazma. The situation at the beginning of February 1942 was such that the assault formations of the Kalinin Front in co-operation with Twenty-second Army operating at Belyy had temporarily encircled seven German divisions at Olenino and driven a deep wedge into the rear of Ninth Army and Fourth

[391] Eremenko, 'Nastuplenie'.   [392] Id., *Na zapadnom napravlenii*, 180.
[393] Žukov, 'Bitva pod Moskvoj, 2', 48.

Armoured Army, but, owing to ceaseless and eventually successful German counter-attacks at the penetration point near Rzhev, found its own rearward lines under threat.

While the centre of the Western Front, in co-operation with the troops of the Kalinin Front, was intended to encircle the German forces in the wider neighbourhood of Gzhatsk, the armies of the right and left wings of the Western Front were to break up the enemy by simultaneous local attacks and thereby ensure flank cover for the main forces. The offensive thrusts on the right wing of the Western Front were opened on 10 January 1942[394] by Lieutenant-General Vlasov's Twentieth Army, Lieutenant-General Kuznetsov's First Assault Army, and Major-General Pliev's II Guards Cavalry Corps with a penetration of the German defences at Volokolamsk. Once Lieutenant-General Rokossovskiy's Sixteenth Army and Lieutenant-General Govorov's Fifth Army had also gone over to the attack, these armies were soon rapidly advancing beyond the Shakhovka–Mozhaysk line. Their attacking strength was broken when First Assault Army and the command staff of Sixteenth Army were withdrawn on orders from Supreme Command Headquarters and inserted instead in the sector of the North-west Front and on the left wing.[395] Stalin, grossly underrating the potential of the enemy, rejected all Zhukov's counter-proposals,[396] with the result that it was no longer possible to approach Gzhatsk. After some initial success, the attack of Lieutenant-General Golikov's Tenth Army had also got bogged down on the left wing of the Western Front. Tenth Army, which had advanced its front to Bakhmutovo–Kirov–Zhizdra and whose command proved incapable of creating a point of main effort,[397] was seized at its flanks from the south and was unable to prevent the Germans from once more relieving the encircled town of Sukhinichi. Not until the HQ of Rokossovskiy's Sixteenth Army had assumed command in this sector and Lieutenant-General Popov's Sixty-first Army of the Bryansk Front was subordinated to the Western Front was it possible to stabilize the situation at Sukhinichi to some degree.[398] Golikov was relieved of his command.

The main thrust at the centre of the Western Front was characterized by a combined attack by Lieutenant-General Boldin's Fiftieth Army and Major-General Belov's I Guards Cavalry Corps; these advanced past Yukhnov in the south, while Major-General Golubev's Forty-third Army and Lieutenant-General Zakharkin's Forty-ninth Army bypassed that area in the north. Western Front command shortly expected to be able to smash the German forces at Yukhnov and to link up its armies with the assault formations of the Kalinin Front near Vyazma. Because of the stubborn German resistance, which completely tied down the troops of Fiftieth, Forty-ninth, and Forty-third Armies at Yukhnov, on 20 January 1942 Zhukov was induced to change the direction of thrust of Thirty-third Army (originally aimed at Gzhatsk) and to assign to

---

[394] Žukov, 'Kontrnastuplenie', 81. [395] Istorija Velikoj Otečestvennoj vojny, ii. 325.
[396] Zhukov, Reminiscences, 355. [397] Rokossovskij, Soldatskij dolg, 108.
[398] Lobačev, Trudnymi dorogami, 285 ff.

it the capture of Vyazma in conjunction with I Guards Cavalry Corps, which was wheeling round Yukhnov. However, the grand encirclement operation planned and called for by Supreme Command Headquarters ended in failure. Although XI Cavalry Corps of the Kalinin Front, as well as strong forces of the Western Front—I Guards Cavalry Corps, supported by airborne units hastily dropped at Znamenka,[399] and Thirty-third Army—were approaching Vyazma from various directions, neither the capture of that important linchpin nor the link-up between the two fronts was accomplished. Instead, the advanced Soviet force for its part found itself in difficulties after it had been cut off from its rear communications by a German counter-thrust on both sides of Yukhnov on 2 February and when, simultaneously, Twenty-ninth Army of the Kalinin Front was encircled and both XI Cavalry Corps, and Thirty-ninth Army were more or less separated from the rest of the front. The situation of the exhausted Soviet troops was beginning to be threatening. The fact that Supreme Command Headquarters continued to cling stubbornly to its encirclement and annihilation plans reveals a complete misjudgement of the situation as well as of the real ratio of strength. On 1 February 1942 the Western Direction Command was reconstituted. Its GOC, Army General Zhukov, who simultaneously retained command of the Western Front, was instructed to take vigorous measures 'to solve as speedily as possible the main strategic task—the final routing of Army Group Centre'.[400] On 16 February 1942, disregarding the increasingly complicated situation, Headquarters repeated its demand in a directive. The Kalinin Front was now promised the transfer of seven rifle divisions, and the Western Front of three rifle divisions as well as reinforcements of aircraft and armour from the Headquarters reserve—but these arrived too late. Simultaneously, the Western Front was instructed, in conjunction with the Kalinin Front, to annihilate the German forces in the Rzhev–Vyazma–Yukhnov area—i.e. the German Ninth Army, Fourth Armoured Army, and substantial elements of Fourth Army—and to advance to the Olenino–Dnieper–Yelnaya–Desna line by 5 March. The left wing of the Western Front had to smash the units of Fourth Army and Second Armoured Army east of Bryansk and to take the city itself. Zhukov, though well aware of the gradually waning strength of his troops, issued appropriate orders[401] on the basis of that directive, and thereby contributed to a hopeless dissipation of the Soviet offensive effort.

The final result of the Kalinin Front's offensive for the annihilation of the enemy forces at Olenino was that the last remnants of the encircled Twenty-ninth Army only just managed to fight their way through to Thirty-ninth Army, which in turn was about to be encircled. Although Forty-third, Forty-ninth, and Fiftieth Armies, after heavy fighting at the beginning of March 1942, succeeded in cutting off the Yukhnov salient and taking the town itself, they failed in their attempt to link up with the troops of Thirty-third Army, I

[399] Soldatov and Korol'čenko, 'Znamenskij desant', 72.
[400] *Istorija Velikoj Otečestvennoj vojny*, ii. 327.   [401] Žukov, 'Kontrnastuplenie', 83 ff.

Guards Cavalry Corps, and the airborne units (which had meanwhile been reinforced) trapped south-west of Vyazma. Supreme Command Headquarters, however, was not impressed by the failures of the increasingly weakening Soviet armies. Stalin remained convinced that success was bound to come, if not today then surely tomorrow. As late as 20 March 1942 he categorically demanded that the German armies fighting in the Olenino–Rzhev–Vyazma area be annihilated and the line Belyy–Dorogobuzh–Yelnya–south-west of Bryansk reached by 20 April.[402] Against their own better judgement, Zhukov and the Western Front HQ passed on these demands to the armies under their command and called for ceaseless attacks, which, as was later admitted, 'only cost pointless casualties'. This attitude of the Soviet leadership, however, is not mentioned in more recent publications.[403] Not until 20 April 1942 were the armies of the Kalinin Front and the Western Front authorized to suspend the pointless attacks and to go over to the defensive in the regained sectors.

Whereas the unrealistic extent of the Soviet leadership's expectations was, up to a point, concealed in the northern and central sectors of the front by the considerable gain of ground actually achieved there, the disproportion between wishful thinking and actual capacity was more strikingly revealed in the southern sector, where the front line was shifted to the west only over a relatively narrow strip. Supreme Command Headquarters and the general staff had instructed the GOC South-western Direction, Marshal of the Soviet Union Timoshenko—whose own plans were even more ambitious—to tear open the front of Army Group South by a vigorous blow between Balakleya and Artemovsk, in order subsequently to envelop the German forces north and south of that penetration with two massive prongs and crush them.[404] Next, the left wing of Lieutenant-General Kostenko's South-west Front with Major-General Maslov's Thirty-eighth Army, Major-General Gorodnyanskiy's Sixth Army, and Major-General Bychkovskiy's VI Cavalry Corps (after 12 February under Major-General Moskalenko) was to move via Krasnograd–Bogodukhov and wheel around Kharkov in a wide arc, enveloping substantial elements of the German Sixth Army. The right wing of Lieutenant-General Malinovskiy's Southern Front with Lieutenant-General Ryabyshev's Fifty-seventh Army, Lieutenant-General Lopatin's Thirty-seventh Army, and the newly brought-up I and V Cavalry Corps (the latter under Major-General Grechko), exploiting the expected success of Major-General Kharitonov's newly transferred Ninth Army and of II Cavalry Corps, would attack via Pavlograd in the direction of the Dnieper, gain the crossings at Dnepropetrovsk and Zaporozhye, and reach the Sea of Azov by way of Bolshoy Tokmak, in order to push the German Seventeenth Army and First Armoured Army to the coast.[405] These far-ranging envelopment movements, which were launched despite the fact that, even according to Soviet estimates,

---

[402] Id., *Reminiscences*, 359–60.   [403] *Geschichte des zweiten Weltkrieges*, iv. 378.
[404] Moskalenko, *Na Jugo-Zapadnom napravlenii*, 152.   [405] Ibid. 135.

the strength of the German Army Group South greatly exceeded that of the Soviet South-western Direction not only in men but also in artillery and armour, were doomed to failure from the start and did not proceed beyond some initial successes.

The attack of the left wing of the South-west Front and the right wing of the Southern Front, which opened on 18 January 1942, achieved major penetrations of the German defences only along the attacking sector of the Sixth and Fifty-seventh Armies. Balakleya and Slavyansk on both sides of the penetration were held by the Germans, and Thirty-eighth and Thirty-seventh Armies made only insignificant progress. Time and again the Soviet armies which had broken through to the west were compelled to hive off substantial forces to fight German nests of resistance and to deal with threats to their flanks. Soon they lost their offensive momentum. The cavalry corps, held back for the exploitation of the penetration, and especially Ninth Army, had to be used increasingly for flank cover, with the result that the offensive—after a slight widening of the penetration area and the capture of Lozovaya—ground to a halt. In the final analysis the Soviet Sixth, Ninth, and Fifty-seventh Armies in the 'Barvenkovo salient' west of Izyum were in a threatened position similar to that of the Second Assault Army south of Lyuban, Thirty-ninth Army and XI Cavalry Corps east of Belyy, and Thirty-third Army and I Guards Cavalry Corps at Dorogobuzh south-west of Vyazma. All these Soviet forces—now encircled or half-enveloped because of Headquarters' exaggerated offensive plans—were annihilated by the Germans in the spring of 1942.

The failure on the southern sector emerges even more clearly when one considers that neither the right wing of the South-west Front with the Bryansk Front on its northern side, nor the (Trans)-Caucasus Front, came anywhere near attaining their far-reaching objectives. The task of the Bryansk Front (Third and Thirteenth Armies) under the command of Colonel-General Cherevichenko and of the right wing of the South-west Front (Fortieth and Twenty-first Armies) had been the occupation, by means of two converging thrusts from a northerly and a southerly direction, of the important areas around Orel and Kursk—an enterprise which became bogged down from the start. The Caucasus Front under the command of Lieutenant-General Kozlov, according to an operations plan confirmed by Supreme Command Headquarters on 2 January, was to attack from the Kerch bridgehead in a north-westerly direction towards Perekop, in order to cut off the Germans' retreat from the Crimea. By a simultaneous attack on Simferopol it was, in conjunction with a landing operation of the Black Sea Fleet, to annihilate 'the entire' Eleventh Army and to occupy the Crimea. However, as a result of 'a series of gross mistakes' by the front's staff[406] the Germans pre-empted that offensive and on 15 January 1942 recaptured Feodosiya. Although the Russians' jumping-off position had substantially deteriorated as a result, Head-

---

[406] Semenov, *Kratkij očerk*, 174.

quarters on 28 January 1942 renewed its demands and ordered Kozlov's newly established Crimean Front to execute an attack in the direction of Karasubazar with a view to striking, in conjunction with the Black Sea Fleet, at the rear of the German forces besieging Sevastopol. This offensive, launched belatedly on 27 February 1942 and repeated several times, likewise remained unsuccessful.

With its winter offensive of 1942 the Soviet leadership had set itself the ambitious objective of routing the entire German army in the east. The operations plans of Supreme Command Headquarters and of the general staff lacked nothing in consistency or boldness; their weakness was simply that they were based on fundamentally incorrect assumptions regarding the relative strength of the two sides. An overrating of its own potential and an under-estimate of the strength and capabilities of the Germans induced Headquarters to launch its offensive simultaneously in all directions—a strategy to which the Soviet leadership clung with remarkable obduracy. The result was a hopeless dissipation of the strategic reserves of Headquarters.[407] Of nine armies which, in the course of the winter battle, were for the most part newly raised and moved into action, two went to the Volkhov Front, one to the North-west Front, one to the Kalinin Front, three to the Western Front, and one each to the Bryansk and South-west Fronts. If one considers the precarious situation in which the German Army Group Centre found itself as a result of the attacks, one realizes what opportunities the Soviet leadership had thrown away by its failure to concentrate on specific points of main effort. Even if one bears in mind the many mistakes made by the Soviet side, and generally the 'still maladroit Soviet command' even at the level of fronts, armies, and subordinate formations,[408] the fact remains that genuine chances had been missed. What happened was that the mistakes of Supreme Command Headquarters were copied downward, by unit commanders simultaneously pursuing several objectives, failing to create points of main efforts at the tactical level, or yielding to their inclination to split up their armour and use it in support of infantry. From the beginning, Army General Zhukov had pleaded for the Headquarters reserves to be employed solely on the Western Front, so that a decision could be brought about in the Moscow sector. Stalin and the general staff headed by the ailing Marshal of the Soviet Union Shaposhnikov had dismissed that suggestion. Because of their lack of realism in the field of 'strategic planning and utilization of reserves' they bear the responsibility for the fact that the winter offensive of 1942, while achieving considerable success, failed to produce a decisive triumph. The strategic plans at any rate had failed.

14. THE ESTABLISHMENT OF THE ANTI-HITLER COALITION

For approximately two years the Soviet Union, though of course only from practical considerations, had been a valuable helper in the war effort of the

---

[407] *Istorija Velikoj Otečestvennoj vojny*, ii. 359.   [408] Svetlišin, 'Ot soldata do maršala', 36.

German Reich. The German attack on 22 June 1941 cleared the Soviet Union
of the odium of complicity with Hitler. This event, in which the Soviet Union
itself had no hand and which was seen as 'a real godsend' by Joseph E.
Davies,[409] adviser of the President of the United States and former US
Ambassador in Moscow, from the outset elevated the Soviet Union to the rank
of an equal and valuable ally of Britain, the British Empire, and (though then
still in the background) the United States of America. For the sake of the
struggle against what was now the common enemy, the two sides instantly
agreed to set aside existing differences and conflicts between them and emphasize only that which united them in the new phase of the war. In a spontaneous
speech on 22 June 1941 Churchill declared that no one had been a 'more
unconditional opponent of Communism' than he himself and that he would
not retract any of his words on that subject.[410] Yet all that paled against the
spectacle now unrolling in eastern Europe. The prime minister emphasized
that Britain would stand by the side of the Soviet Union in its struggle against
Germany and lend it all possible assistance. Now that it became vital to
support the new ally, the matters that Britain until then had taken exception
to were regarded as insignificant—'stabbing Poland in the back', a matter
about which there had been 'moaning . . . in the press, the radio, in parliament, and from the pulpits', likewise the Soviet attack on Finland, which
triggered off an outright 'anti-Soviet storm' in England, or the annexation of
the Baltic States, which the foreign secretary, Lord Halifax, had described to
Soviet Ambassador Mayskiy as 'aggression with all the consequences arising
therefrom'.[411] And conversely, where the Soviet Union was concerned, there
was no longer any talk of Britain being responsible for the beginning, the
continuation, or the extension of the war, or of the fact that Moscow had
called a war for the elimination of National Socialism a piece of 'criminal
stupidity', or that it had accused the United States of fanning the flames of war
in Europe under the 'hypocritical flag of neutrality' and of having become the
supplier of arms for Britain and France.[412]

[409] Davies, *Mission to Moscow*, 311.

[410] What Churchill thought of his new ally emerges very strikingly from his book *The Aftermath*
(vol. v of *The World Crisis*; London, 1929). In it, in explanation of his own attitude, he quotes a
statistical study by Prof. Sarolea, according to which the Bolshevik 'dictators' by 1924 alone had
murdered the following persons: '28 bishops, 1,219 priests, 6,000 professors and teachers, 9,000
doctors, 12,950 landowners, 54,000 officers, 70,000 policemen, 193,290 workmen, 260,000 soldiers, 355,250 intellectuals and professional men, and 815,000 peasants.' 'These figures', Churchill added, 'are endorsed by Mr. Hearnshaw, of *Kings College, London, in his brilliant introduction to
"A survey of Socialism"*. They do not, of course, include the vast abridgements of the Russian
population which followed from famine.' As Churchill observes, 'in the cutting off of the lives of
men and women no Asiatic conqueror, not Tamerlane, not Jenghiz Khan can match with
[Lenin]', whom he also called a 'plague bacillus'. For Churchill, 'the frontiers of Asia and the
conditions of the Dark Ages had advanced from the Urals to the Pripet marshes'; Russia was
'frozen in an indefinite winter of sub-human doctrine and superhuman tyranny'. As early as 1919
he had spoken of 'fighting against the foul baboonery of Bolshevism'. 'A dose of Communism',
he says elsewhere, 'induces a desire in any population to welcome any other form—even the
harshest—of civilized authority': Churchill, *Aftermath*, 74–5, 102, 163, 272, 276.

[411] Maiski, *Memoiren*, 531–2, 622.

[412] Molotov to the Supreme Soviet, 1 Aug. 1940, according to *Stalin und Hitler*, No. 296; Order

Measures for a co-ordination of efforts in an anti-Hitler coalition were taken soon after the beginning of the German–Soviet war. Yet regardless of its readiness to form an anti-Hitlerite coalition, the Soviet government never doubted that in this war Britain and the United States were concerned solely with the preservation and extension of their rule over 'colonies and semi-colonies' and with the elimination of their 'most dangerous competitors', Germany, Italy, and Japan.[413] It was generally accepted in Moscow that the Anglo-American powers were supporting the USSR only in order to place upon it the main burden of the struggle, in order thereby to weaken it so that in the end they might throw their own unreduced weight into the scales. This explains the Soviet Union's ever wakeful mistrust of its capitalist allies as well as Stalin's demand, first voiced on 18 July 1941 and repeated continually and with increasing urgency, that they should open a second front in France or Norway with a view to relieving the Soviet Union.[414] Although Britain rejected this demand firmly, and under ever new pretexts,[415] a first British–Soviet agreement was signed in Moscow on 12 July 1941 regarding mutual assistance and the obligation not to conclude an armistice or a peace treaty with Germany except by mutual consent.[416] The assistance provided for in the agreement could, in the prevailing circumstances, consist on the British side only of deliveries of commodities needed by the Soviet Union. As, however, both British and American experts—no different from their German colleagues—had only slight confidence in the USSR's power of resistance, and therefore expected the war to last no more than a few weeks, Britain and the United States initially displayed perceptible reserve in this respect as well. Only after Harry Hopkins, sent to Moscow as the American President's personal adviser gained a more positive impression of the Soviet Union's defence potential were steps taken to turn the offers of assistance into reality.[417]

On 2 August 1941, immediately after Hopkins's return, the United States government, in spite of its formal neutrality, described the Soviet Union's military resistance as being in the interest of America's national defence and assured the Soviet government of all practicable economic support.[418] Deliveries of strategically important commodities and war material to the Soviet Union, at first slow to get into their stride, were based on an exchange of notes between Sumner Welles, the acting American Secretary of State, and Soviet Ambassador Umanskiy; this in turn was based on trade agreements concluded with Britain on 16 August 1941 and on an extended agreement signed on 1

---

of the People's Commissar for the Defence of the USSR, 1 May 1941, BA-MA RH 19 I/123, fo. 226.

[413] Maiski, *Memoiren*, 735; *Geschichte des zweiten Weltkrieges*, iv. 204.
[414] Stalin to Churchill, 18 July 1941, in *Perepiska Predsedatelja Soveta Ministrov*, i, No. 3; *Stalin's Correspondence*, i, No. 3; Gwyer, *Grand Strategy*, iii. 198 ff.
[415] Maiski, *Memoiren*, 638 ff.   [416] *Istorija Kommunisticeskoj Partii*, v. 190.
[417] Motter, *Persian Corridor and Aid to Russia*, 21–2.
[418] Memorandum on the Russian situation, in Davies, *Mission to Moscow*, 356 ff.; Roosevelt and Churchill to Stalin, 15 Aug. 1941, in *Stalin's Correspondence*, ii, No. 2.

October 1941 in Moscow by representatives of Britain, the United States, and the Soviet Union. Under it, Britain and the United States, extending the lend-lease agreement of 6 September and 7 November to the Soviet Union, undertook to supply each month, from October 1941 to June 1942, 400 aircraft (100 bombers and 300 fighters), 500 tanks, a further 5,250 fighting vehicles, 10,000 trucks, 152 anti-aircraft guns, 1,256 anti-tank guns, and vast quantities of vital non-ferrous metals and other valuable commodities; as for foodstuffs, they would supply a total of 1,800,000 t. of wheat and 620,000 t. of sugar.[419] Until the beginning of 1942, however, the amounts actually shipped fell considerably short of the undertakings. Thus, during the months from October to December 1941 the two powers delivered only 750 aircraft, 501 tanks, and 8 anti-aircraft guns.[420] Moreover, the war material supplied was inferior in quality and was by no means appreciated by the men of the Red Army. Thus the British Hurricane fighters were crudely described by Stalin as 'rubbish'.[421] The tanks likewise did not even reach the combat performance of the older Soviet models. However, the slow start of Anglo-American material aid should not be allowed to obscure the fact that in the course of the war it eventually reached colossal proportions. Litvinov, the Soviet ambassador to the United States, by 1943 referred to the decisive effect of the deliveries on the Soviet Union's power of resistance.[422] This, however, applied not primarily to weapons, which Soviet industry was itself producing at a growing rate and, for the most part, of better quality, but rather to transport equipment indispensable to modern warfare. In the course of the war the USSR received 427,284 trucks, 1,966 railway engines, and 10,000 items of rolling-stock. Probably of even greater importance were the deliveries of foodstuffs, which assumed enormous scale, such as 4.5 million t. of tinned meat—sufficient to provide more than half a pound a day for every single Red Army man. Without American supplies of all kinds of food a large proportion of the Soviet population, following the loss of the black-earth regions, would have been doomed to certain starvation.[423]

The difficulties of assembling sufficient shipping space for the long and dangerous sea routes to Archangel, Murmansk, and Vladivostok induced the Soviet government in July 1941 to propose to the British government the establishment of direct transit through Iranian territory.[424] The two powers began to apply massive pressure—the 'strongest possible'—on the Iranian government. On 25 August 1941, ten days after the signing of the Atlantic Charter, which condemned any violation of the sovereign rights of nations or aggressive actions, Soviet and British troops invaded Persia under the pretext of having to suppress the alleged activity by German agents, and occupied the country up to an agreed north–south demarcation-line. The Iranian army had,

---

[419] Gwyer, *Grand Strategy*, iii. 158–9.   [420] *Istorija Velikoj Otečestvennoj vojny*, ii. 189, 365.
[421] Zhukov, *Reminiscences*, 384.
[422] 1. Skl, KTB, pr. A, 223 (Mar. 1943), BA-MA RM 7/46.
[423] Ibid. 500 (Apr. 1943), BA-MA RM 7/46.
[424] Israèljan, *Antigitlerovskaja koalicija*, 37, divergent from *Istorija Velikoj Otečestvenenoj vojny*, ii. 195; see also Gwyer, *Grand Strategy*, iii. 185 ff.

at a few points, offered resistance to the two invaders, but that was halted after a few days. That this rape of a neutral country[425] was simply the liquidation of a 'deployment area of Fascist Germany against the Soviet Union'[426] had been very clearly stated by Churchill as early as 30 August 1941. 'Our objective in invading Persia', he wrote to Stalin, 'was not so much the protection of the oil wells as the establishment of a further line of communication to you, one that cannot be cut.'[427] An agreement was forced upon the Iranian government, under which it had to make all its resources, especially oil, available to the Allies, and not only to tolerate but to promote the transit of military material across its territory by road, rail, or air.

As part of the creation of a coalition of states fighting against Germany, the Soviet government found itself compelled to revoke certain steps which for the sake of its partnership with Hitler it had taken in the past. It had to resume diplomatic relations with the governments of German-occupied countries, which, in the Soviet interpretation, had thereby lost their sovereignty. On 18 July 1941 it had no difficulty in recognizing the Czechoslovak government-in-exile in London or in signing an agreement on mutual aid and the establishment of Czechoslovak military units on Soviet territory. Nor did the resumption of diplomatic relations with the exile governments, all of them in London, of Norway, Belgium, Greece, and Yugoslavia in the summer of 1941 raise any particular problems, even though, in the case of Yugoslavia, the Soviet government by November 1941 refused to subordinate Josip Broz-Tito's Communist partisans, whom it supported—the future National Liberation Movement—to War Minister Draža Mihajlović of the Royal Yugoslav government-in-exile, which it had recognized. The Soviet government, which until 22 June 1941 had maintained diplomatic relations with the French government in Vichy, on 27 September 1941 recognized the 'Free France National Committee' under Brigade-General Charles de Gaulle as representing 'fighting France'. Exceedingly complicated, on the other hand, were the negotiations with the Polish exile government of Premier Władysław Sikorski, who naturally enough demanded restitution of the losses suffered as a result of the Soviet Union's aggression and, above all, recognition of the integrity of the Polish republic within the frontiers of the peace of Riga, frontiers originally delineated in free negotiation with the Soviet state and recognized by the Conference of Ambassadors of the Entente and by the United States.[428] As the Soviet government refused to enter into discussion on these points, the matter was, under British pressure, officially passed over in silence.[429] Premier

---

[425] Churchill, *Second World War*, iii/2. 428.
[426] Štemenko, *General'nyj štab*, i. 45; *Die Befreiungsmission*, 48 ff.
[427] Churchill to Stalin, 30 Aug. 1941, in *Stalin's Correspondence*, i, No. 9; also Israèljan, *Antigitlerovskaja koalicija*, 39.
[428] *Documents on Polish–Soviet Relations*, i, No. 89, pp. 113–14; No. 92, pp. 119–22; No. 93, pp. 122–8; No. 96, pp. 132–4; No. 97, pp. 134–5; No. 100, pp. 136–8; No. 103, p. 139; No. 104, pp. 139–40.
[429] Ibid. 576.

Sikorski, however, immediately made it clear that there must not even be a 'suggestion that the 1939 frontiers of the Polish state could ever be in question' or 'that Poland resigned anything'.[430] The Polish–Soviet agreement concluded, with that reservation, on 30 July 1941 concerning the annulment of the Soviet–German treaties of 1939 and the resumption of diplomatic relations, as well as the military agreement of 14 August 1941 on the establishment of a Polish army on the territory of the USSR[431] only thinly concealed those differences of opinion. The Soviet Union now agreed to declare an 'amnesty' for the Polish prisoners of war in Soviet captivity and for Polish prisoners and deportees. As, however, disregarding Polish protests, it had forced Soviet citizenship upon the entire population of the annexed eastern Polish provinces,[432] it refused to recognize the Polish government's authority over millions of Polish citizens. The release of prisoners of war, detainees, and deportees also progressed unsatisfactorily. Lieutenant-General Anders, commander-in-chief of the Polish army on USSR territory and himself recently released from a Soviet prison, while setting up his army found that the 8,000 officers and 7,000 NCOs in Soviet prison camps, with whom communication had existed until the spring of 1940, had vanished without trace. Efforts by the Polish government to obtain information on the whereabouts of these military personnel—approximately fifty official enquiries were addressed to the Soviet government—were all unsuccessful. On 3 December 1941 in the Kremlin Premier Sikorski, in the presence of Ambassador Kot and General Anders, made this observation to Stalin concerning the missing men:[433] 'It has been proven that not one of them is [in Poland], nor in any of our prisoner-of-war camps in Germany. These people are here. Not one of them has returned.' Stalin replied: 'That is impossible. They have escaped.' To General Anders's question 'Where, then, could they escape?' Stalin replied: 'Well, to Manchuria.' For nearly two years the Soviet government emphatically denied any knowledge of the vanished military personnel. But on 15 April 1943,[434] two days after the Germans had reported the discovery of the mass graves of Katyn, it announced that the former Polish prisoners of war, engaged on construction work west of Smolensk in the summer of 1941, had fallen into the hands of the 'German Fascist hangmen'. When the Polish government decided to demand an investigation of the affair by the International Red Cross,[435] the Soviet government broke off relations with the Polish government on the pretext that it was in secret communication with 'Hitler's government', that it was trying to please

---

[430] Ibid., No. 109, pp. 144–5.

[431] Ibid., No. 106, pp. 141–2; No. 112, pp. 147–8; Dombrovskij, 'Pol'sko-sovetskoe bratstvo po oružiju', 293; Rhode, 'Polen', 1029–30.

[432] *Documents on Polish–Soviet Relations*, i, No. 71, p. 92.

[433] Ibid., No. 159, pp. 231–43, here 233; Beckmann, 'Katyn', 142–3.

[434] *Documents on Polish–Soviet Relations*, i, No. 306, pp. 524–5.

[435] Communiqué issued by the Polish Minister of National Defence concerning the fate of Polish prisoners of war in the camps of Kozielsk, Starobielsk, and Ostashkov and the appeal to the International Red Cross for investigation, 16 Apr. 1943, ibid., No. 307, pp. 525–7.

'Hitler's tyranny', and that it had joined a Fascist campaign of defamation of the USSR.[436]

The general wartime alliance concluded between Britain and the Soviet Union on 12 July 1941 and between the United States and the Soviet Union on 2 August 1941 was given a kind of ideological buttressing on 14 August 1941, when Churchill and Roosevelt proclaimed their war aims in what has become known as the Atlantic Charter.[437] A conference held in London on 24 September 1941 by representatives of Britain, the United States, the Soviet Union, and the governments-in-exile of Belgium, Greece, Yugoslavia, Luxemburg, the Netherlands, Norway, Poland, Czechoslovakia, and the Free France National Committee endorsed the principles of the Atlantic Declaration as the basis of the anti-Hitler coalition; however, the mere fact that the Soviet ambassador Mayskiy felt it necessary to make a supplementary declaration shows that the façade of unity was concealing a diversity of goals. Britain and the United States of America—apart from an extension of trade represented by the principle of the freedom of the high seas—were basically concerned with the restoration of the *status quo ante bellum* in Europe. The necessary prerequisite, the liquidation of National Socialism, was a demand which—contrary to its earlier attitude—the Soviet government now not only regarded as possible but as indispensable, placing it at the top of its own list of war aims. The germ of serious differences of opinion, however, was concealed in the simultaneously proclaimed principle that Britain and the United States would not recognize, or even tolerate, any territorial or other aggrandizements which 'were not in accord with the freely expressed wishes of the people concerned'. All nations 'which had been violently robbed of them' were to have their 'sovereign rights and self-administration returned to them'; and all nations were to be entitled 'themselves to chose the form of government under which they wished to live'. Although the official document and various commentaries, such as Churchill's in the House of Commons, only referred to aggression by the Axis powers, mainly to 'National Socialist tyranny', the principles of the Atlantic Charter might readily be invoked also for the acts of aggression and annexation carried out by the Soviet Union during its partnership with Hitler. The Soviet government, having in its supplementary declaration likewise proclaimed the principle of self-determination of nations, of the right to political independence and territorial integrity, found

[436] Ibid., No. 313, p. 533. See the strange justification in Stečkevič, 'Sovetsko-pol'skie dogovory', 384. The success of that manœuvre was observed even in Western countries, e.g. when W. Brandt, as late as 1945, commenting on 'Katyn', used the circumlocution 'that among the Polish troops and groups abroad Fascist elements were evidently able to cause mischief': Brandt, *Der Zweite Weltkrieg*, 42. Attempts to blame the Soviet–Polish rupture in April 1943 on manipulations by 'pro-Fascist-minded' members of the Polish government, and not on the mass shootings of Polish officers and NCOs 'by NKVD agencies of the USSR', were resumed after the declaration of martial law in Poland in 1982 under the heading 'Against bourgeois falsifiers of history': see Meritorious Scholar of the RSFSR, Prof. Dr of Historical Sciences Maj.-Gen. Monin, 'K istorii "Katynskogo dela"'.

[437] Gwyer, *Grand Strategy*, iii. 118 ff.

itself in a very vulnerable position when it asserted that the incorporation of the eastern Polish and Finnish regions, of the Baltic republics, of the Bukovina, and of Bessarabia had been based on 'the freely expressed will of the people'. After all, everyone knew what so-called plebiscites meant under the stage management of the NKVD.[438] On the other hand, however, the Soviet government had a very convincing argument on its side. It could easily blunt the point of any Western insinuations by reminding them that 'colonial possessions' had been explicitly exempted from the provisions of the Atlantic Charter; thus Britain's title 'to her rule in the colonies of the Empire' was not affected and could not be called in question.[439]

It had been clear ever since the Soviet–Polish negotiations in July 1941 that the foremost obstacle to a consolidation of the anti-Hitlerite coalition would be the Soviet conquests since 1939. Britain had found itself compelled on 30 July 1941 to give an official assurance to the Polish exile government[440] 'that His Majesty's Government do not recognize any territorial changes which have been effected in Poland since 1939'. Putting its faith in Britain, Poland concluded the agreement with the Soviet Union without any explicit recognition of Poland's pre-war frontiers. The British government initially also showed a firm attitude with regard to the Soviet Union's territorial acquisitions in Finland, Romania, and the Baltic. But when Eden, the British foreign secretary, went to Moscow in the second half of December, the envisaged signing of an extended treaty of alliance and of a treaty regulating postwar conditions suffered shipwreck because of Eden's refusal of the Soviet demand that the frontiers existing at the time of the German attack be recognized.[441] Britain was compelled to take that attitude, if only out of consideration for the United States, whose administration adopted a 'fiercely rejecting stand' in the matter of annexations and which would have regarded acceptance of the Soviet demand as a violation of the principles of the Atlantic Charter. But Churchill too voiced very similar sentiments. 'Stalin's demands about Finland, the Baltic states, and Romania', he wrote to the Lord Privy Seal on 20 December 1941, 'are directly contrary to the first, second, and third articles of the Atlantic Charter, to which Stalin has subscribed . . . The mere desire to have an agreement . . . should never lead us into making wrongful promises.'[442] The British government was careful formally to maintain its point of view during the subsequent period as well—which did not, however, prevent it from quietly coming to an arrangement with the Soviet Union at the expense of Poland and other affected countries.[443]

The beginning of such a policy can be traced back to September 1939, when the British government formally fulfilled its obligations as an ally of Poland but

[438] *Documents on Polish–Soviet Relations*, i. 572; No. 160, p. 244.
[439] Israèljan, *Antigitlerovskaja koalicija*, 68–9.
[440] *Documents on Polish–Soviet Relations*, i, No. 107, pp. 142–3.
[441] Churchill, *Second World War*, iv/1. 296; Gwyer, *Grand Strategy*, iii. 320, 324 ff.
[442] Churchill, *Second World War*, iii/2. 559.
[443] *Documents on Polish–Soviet Relations*, i, No. 176, p. 270; p. 594; Maiski, *Memoiren*, 725–6.

in fact left that country to its fate.[444] Britain and France, at any rate, then
replied to the German attack on Poland by declaring war on Germany.
Accordingly, the French foreign ministry on 7 September 1939 informed the
United States ambassador in Paris, William C. Bullitt, that 'France and
Britain would consider an attack of the Soviet Union on Poland an act of war
against France and Britain.'[445] When, however, an open and unprovoked
violation of the non-aggression treaty had in fact been committed by Russia
and when the Polish government 'solemnly' protested[446] 'against the unilateral
violation of the Non-Aggression Pact by Russia and against the invasion of
Polish territory' by Soviet troops, Britain contented herself with a general
declaration and a paper protest.[447] The British government was able to point
out that the stipulations of the Anglo-Polish mutual-aid agreement of 25
August 1939 were, according to the attached secret protocol, to come into
effect only in the event of an attack by Germany but not by the Soviet Union.
In the Polish view, however, Britain was under an obligation, in the event of
a Soviet attack on Poland, to consult with the Polish government on measures
to be taken jointly and, in future treaties of alliance, not to tolerate any
violation of Poland's sovereignty or territorial inviolability.[448] Not only was the
stipulation on consultation disregarded, but, as the future was to show, also
the undertaking to defend the sovereignty and territorial integrity of Poland.
In 1940, when the British government was anxious to prise the Soviet Union
away from Germany and to loosen Soviet–German relations, it proposed—in
a curious interpretation of its obligations *vis-à-vis* Poland—to recognize *de
facto* 'the sovereignty of the USSR in the Baltic, in Bessarabia, in the western
Ukraine, and in western Belorussia', in other words, the annexation of more
than half of Poland's state territory.[449] On 14 December 1940 Poland, albeit in
amicable terms, had objected to any measure by the British government that
could be interpreted as recognition or approval of the annexation of Polish
territory.[450] The degree of importance attached by the British government to
what was to Poland a vital frontier issue also emerged on 30 July 1941, the day
of the signing of the Polish–Soviet agreement: while the British government
officially declared that it would not recognize any territorial changes in Poland
since August 1939, Foreign Secretary Eden immediately made it clear in the
Commons that this did 'not involve any guarantee of frontiers by His Majesty's Government'.[451] As late as January 1942, when the influential British

---

[444] *Istorija Velikoj Otečestvennoj vojny*, i. 206; Ržeševskij, 'Iz istorii odnogo predatel'stva', 27 ff.;
Žilin, *Problemy voennoj istorii*, 178–9.

[445] Ambassador Bullitt to Secretary of State, 7 Sept. 1939, *FRUS* (1939), i. 420.

[446] *Documents on Polish–Soviet Relations*, i, No. 45, p. 47.

[447] Ibid., No. 47, p. 49; Ambassador Kennedy to Secretary of State, 18 Sept. 1939, *FRUS*
(1939), i. 437–8; Ambassador Steinhardt to Secretary of State, 21 Sept. 1939, ibid. 446.

[448] *Documents on Polish–Soviet Relations*, i. 552.

[449] Halifax to Minister Zaleski, 27 Nov. 1940, ibid., No. 80, pp. 97–8; Maiski, *Memoiren* 625;
Allard, *Stalin*, 255.

[450] Minister Zaleski to Halifax, 14 Dec. 1940, *Documents on Polish–Soviet Relations*, i, No. 81, pp.
98 ff.   [451] Ibid., No. 108, pp. 143–4; p. 577.

ambassador in Moscow, Sir Stafford Cripps, 'out of profound conviction' supported recognition of the Soviet conquests in eastern Europe,[452] Premier Churchill grandly declared any surrender of the Baltic nations to be incompatible with Britain's honour. 'The 1941 frontiers of Russia . . . were acquired by acts of aggression in shameful collusion with Hitler,' he wrote to Foreign Secretary Eden on 8 January 1942.[453] 'The transfer of the peoples of the Baltic States to Soviet Russia against their will would be contrary to all principles for which we are fighting this war and would dishonour our cause. This also applies to Bessarabia and to Northern Bukovina, and in a lesser degree to Finland.' At that moment, Churchill felt British 'sincerity to be involved in the maintenance of the principles of the Atlantic Charter'. Yet a few months later, in March 1942, he declared that he 'did not feel that this moral position could be physically maintained'.[454] In a letter to President Roosevelt on 7 March 1942 he opposed an interpretation of the principles of the Atlantic Charter 'so as to deny Russia the frontiers she occupied when Germany attacked her', the more so, as he significantly added, as in his opinion the Russians had 'liquidated in one way or another' the hostile 'personalities and elements' in the Baltic countries,[455] so that opposition by the nations concerned to incorporation in the Soviet Union was no longer to be expected. Within a few days the prime minister no doubt realized that his new policy was bound to meet with determined opposition from his Polish ally. In the presence of Eden and other important figures, Premier General Sikorski observed to Churchill on 11 March 1942[456] that, on moral grounds and in accordance with her centuries-old tradition, Poland would take a stand against any surrender of the Baltic nations. Even though the issue of Poland's eastern frontier had been bracketed out of the British–Soviet negotiations, Poland would never accept the annexation of Lithuania or of the Bukovina and Bessarabia, because that would mean that Poland was encircled by the Soviet Union in the same way as she had been by Germany in the past. Sikorski emphatically told Churchill that he was not in a position 'to cast the Polish nation as a prey to the Soviets'. A British–Soviet agreement on the basis of the conditions and territorial claims of the Soviet Union, he added, would result in 'incalculable consequences on the European continent' and provide the Germans with a 'real foundation for calling a crusade against Russia'. Sikorski followed his statement by a warning which produced a perceptible reaction on the part of Eden and Churchill. He declared that, in the event of the conclusion of a British–Soviet treaty, he would no longer be able to conceal from the world public 'the monstrous barbaric treatment of the Polish population' by the Soviet Union, 'the unbe-

---

[452] Ibid., No. 176, pp. 269 ff.; No. 211, p. 339.

[453] Churchill, *Second World War*, iii/2. 615–16.   [454] Ibid. iv/1. 293.

[455] Ibid. iii/2. 615; Kaelas, *Human Rights and Genocide*; Meissner, 'Die kommunistische Machtübernahme'; Hillgruber, *Strategie*, 436; Myllyniemi, *Baltische Krise*, 144.

[456] Extract from a conversation between Gen. Sikorski and Mr Churchill on the Soviet expansionist territorial claims made in the course of British–Soviet negotiations, 11 Mar. 1942, *Documents on Polish–Soviet Relations*, i, No. 191, pp. 295–9.

lievable brutality and refinement in the tortures inflicted by the Bolsheviks on many Poles', 'the real face of the Russians and their brutal imperialism'. On 24 March 1942[457] Sikorski discussed with President Roosevelt the 'abandonment', evidently intended by the British government, 'of the principles of democracy proclaimed by the West'. Poland's opposition to a British–Soviet treaty on the basis of Soviet territorial demands assumed ever fiercer forms during the weeks to follow. The British government was repeatedly—e.g. on 27 March, 13 April, and 21 April—reminded 'with the utmost earnestness'[458] that negotiations with the Soviet Union were touching directly or indirectly on Poland's 'vital interests' and were therefore not in accordance with the spirit—or, in the case of the annexation of Lithuania with the Polish city of Wilna (Vilnius), even the letter—of the Polish–British alliance of 25 August 1939. It was mainly due to the Polish government's inflexible attitude towards a 'second Munich' and to Sikorski's 'severe and serious words' opposing any 'concessions to Soviet imperialism'[459] that Britain reluctantly exercised restraint in the matter of delineation of frontiers in eastern Europe.[460] Added to this was American support for the Polish attitude. Neither President Roosevelt nor the State Department, especially under Secretary of State Cordell Hull, showed any inclination to take up the question of frontiers before the conclusion of the war, let alone to recognize the territorial claims of the Soviet Union.[461]

The British government, anxious to conclude an early treaty with the Soviet Union, had meanwhile hit on other forms of compliance: on 6 December, in response to Soviet wishes, it declared war not only on Romania and Hungary, but also on democratic Finland, which but a year ago had been cheered and supported[462]—although that country, as Churchill himself admitted, was scarcely doing anything other than recover territory lost the previous year.[463] Eden's resistance to the Soviet claims, at any rate, as Ambassador Mayskiy noted with satisfaction, had been weakening 'from one meeting to the next'.[464] By the time Foreign Commissar Molotov, in response to a British invitation, visited London in May 1942 to discuss some contentious issues of the draft treaty, subsequently travelling to Washington, Britain's attitude on the frontier problem had once more stiffened out of consideration for her Polish ally and for the mood in the United States. But there could now be no doubt about the general trend, even though a text was eventually agreed that passed over the territorial issues in silence. The reassurance of the Poles, in consequence, was

[457] Note on the conversation between Gen. Sikorski and President Roosevelt concerning Soviet territorial claims, 24 Mar. 1942, ibid., No. 194, pp. 310–11.

[458] Ibid., No. 196, pp. 312–17; No. 202, pp. 321–2; No. 209, pp. 332–5. Eden's rejection, ibid., No. 208, pp. 329–32; No. 217, pp. 349–51.

[459] Record made by Minister Raczyński of a conversation between Gen. Sikorski, Mr Churchill, and Sir Stafford Cripps, 26 Apr. 1942, ibid., No. 211, pp. 336–40.

[460] Ibid., No. 225, pp. 364–6; Butler, *Grand Strategy*, iii. 592.

[461] See n. 457; *Documents on Polish–Soviet Relations*, i, No. 206, pp. 327–8.

[462] Maiski, *Memoiren*, 539 ff.; Gwyer, *Grand Strategy*, iii. 212 ff.

[463] Churchill, *Second World War*, iii/2. 467.   [464] Maiski, *Memoiren*, 726.

of short duration.[465] After nearly five months of negotiations, on 26 May 1942 Britain and the Soviet Union signed their agreement on a 'wartime alliance against Hitlerite Germany and its allies in Europe', and on 'co-operation and mutual aid' over the next 20 years. A supplementary agreement between the United States and the Soviet Union on the principles of mutual aid was concluded in Washington on 11 June 1942. As far back as 1 January 1942 a declaration of twenty-six states, the so-called Declaration of the United Nations, had been issued in Washington against the Tripartite Pact. In it the signatories, primarily Britain and the United States, jointly with Stalin's and Beriya's Soviet Union, undertook 'to preserve life, freedom, independence, and justice both in their own and in other countries'. This declaration and the new agreements in which the Western powers pledged political, military, and economic co-operation with the Soviet Union during and after the war were hailed in Moscow as a significant success of Soviet foreign policy. Even though the Soviet Union had not yet been able to obtain an open recognition of its territorial claims, it had become abundantly clear that the incorporation of foreign territories did not, for Britain or the United States, present an obstacle to close co-operation in all fields.

The United States', and even more so Britain's, increasingly compliant attitude towards the Soviet Union was due to the changed strategic situation following Japan's entry into the war on 7 December 1941. The great successes of the Japanese in the Philippines, the Dutch East Indies, and in Oceania, and the capture of Hong Kong and Singapore, had dealt a heavy blow to Anglo-American prestige and threatened British colonialism in India. An increase in the number of ships sunk by German U-boats in the battle of the Atlantic, the German naval squadron's breakthrough through the English Channel, the ground gained by the German–Italian counter-offensive in North Africa—all these had made the position of Britain and the United States seem alarming in the spring of 1942 and virtually produced a cabinet crisis in London.[466] The British public was deeply impressed by the fact that this unfavourable development was taking place at the very time when the Red Army had seized the strategic initiative and gone over to decisive offensive operations in a westerly direction. As early as December Churchill had written the following about the 'magnificent Russian successes at Leningrad, on the Moscow front, at Kursk, and in the south': 'German armies largely on the defensive or in retreat, in addition the most terrible winter conditions and ever more violent Russian counter-attacks'.[467] In a letter to Roosevelt on 1 April 1942 he admitted that 'all now depends upon the vast Russo-German struggle'.[468] The fact that the only

---

[465] Memorandum of Gen. Sikorski to Under-Secretary of State Sumner Welles on the Polish–Russian frontier, 23 Dec. 1942, *Documents on Polish–Soviet Relations*, i, No. 283, pp. 469–72.

[466] Churchill, *Second World War*, iv/1. 352 ff.; Maiski, *Memoiren*, 722 ff.

[467] Gwyer, *Grand Strategy*, iii. 321.

[468] Churchill, *Second World War*, iv/1. 179.

successes at that time were recorded on the Soviet–German front so raised the international reputation of the Soviet Union that it now received moral recognition as well, and soon assumed the leading role in the anti-Hitlerite coalition.

III. Strategy and Policy in Northern Europe

Gerd R. Ueberschär

1. German Operations in the 'Finland Theatre'

On 22 June 1941 Mountain Corps Norway executed Operation Reindeer ('Renntier') and advanced unhindered from Norway into the area round Petsamo.[1] Its subsequent eastward deployment into the new assembly area on the Finnish–Soviet border was also completed without attempts at interference by Soviet forces. On 27 June 1941 Mountain Corps Norway handed over the task of defence and coastal defence in northern Norway to the newly established 'Sector Staff Northern Norway' (renamed Higher Command LXXXI) under Lieutenant-General Emmerich von Nagy, with 199th and 702nd Infantry Divisions being placed under his command.

Meanwhile, the mobilization of the Finnish units attached to Army Command Norway, and of the two divisions of the Finnish III Army Corps, had been completed.[2] The Finnish border units and the Ivalo Battalion had been placed under the command of Mountain Corps Norway on 22 June 1941. On 29 June German and Finnish troops of Mountain Corps Norway launched an attack towards Murmansk 'in closest brotherhood in arms . . . for the protection of Finland and to safeguard European culture'.[3] It was followed on 1 July 1941 by the attack of Higher Command XXXVI (renamed XXXVI Mountain Corps from November 1941) in the central army sector towards Salla–Kandalaksha, and by the advance of the Finnish III Corps in the direction of Louchi-Kemi.[4] (For the following description of operations see the Annexe Volume, Nos. 24 and 25.)

(a) Operation Platinum Fox ('Platinfuchs') against Murmansk

Mountain Corps Norway (Mountain Troop General Dietl), consisting of the strengthened 2nd and 3rd Divisions and subordinated Finnish border troops,

---

[1] On the planning of 'Reindeer' see sect. I.vi.3 at nn. 52 ff.

[2] Upon mobilization on 15 June 1941 the Finnish Fifth Army Corps was renamed Finnish Third Army Corps, consisting of 3rd and 6th Divisions. On the deployment of Army Command Norway see papers of Col.-Gen. von Falkenhorst, vol. iv, BA-MA N 300/4.

[3] Army order of the day from Col.-Gen. von Falkenhorst, 26 June 1941, BA-MA, 20. Armee, 19070/2. See also *KTB OKW* i. 424 (30 June 1941). On the Finnish border units see war diary of the Finnish Ivalo Bn., 22 June 1941–31 Mar. 1942, BA-MA, 20. Armee, 23861.

[4] On the operations of Army Command Norway see the records of Twentieth Army, BA-MA 19070/1–14, 35198/1–7, 20844/1–6, 25353/1–8, 58628/1–2, 35641. See also *General Dietl*, 218 ff.; Hölter, *Armee in der Arktis*, 11 ff.; Hess, *Eismeerfront*, 32 ff.; Ziemke, *German Northern Theater*, 139–87; Erfurth, *Finnischer Krieg*, 47–56; on the operations of Army Command Norway from the Finnish point of view see *Suomen Sota 1941–1945*, v. 81 ff.

planned to implement 'Platinum Fox' by concentrating its main effort in the offensive against Murmansk on Titovka and Zapadnaya Litsa. At the same time, only the relatively weak forces of 2nd Mountain Division (Major-General Ernst Schlemme) could be used to attack the Soviet troops on the flank of the Rybachiy Peninsula.[5] However, it soon became apparent that these forces were not sufficient to capture the strongly fortified peninsula. As a result, at the beginning of July the army command agreed to switch to defence in that sector by taking up a fortified defensive position at the neck of the Rybachiy Peninsula. After an advance by 3rd Mountain Division (Major-General Hans Kreysing)[6] towards Motovka had failed in impassable terrain, units of this division joined with 2nd Mountain Division[7] in the advance across the river Titovka towards Zapadnaya Litsa. Despite initial success, the corps advanced only slowly in the trackless tundra east of the Titovka. Large elements of these forces frequently had to be diverted to tasks of road-building and the transport of supplies. On 6 July 1941, when Hitler's Armed Forces Adjutant, Colonel (General Staff) Schmundt, visited Mountain Corps Norway, its commanding officer General Dietl was already referring to the weakness of his forces and the serious shortage of supplies available to him for the attempt to achieve the operational objective of capturing Murmansk. As the offensive continued, the town of Zapadnaya Litsa was captured only after bitter fighting and heavy casualties. Further attacks were launched from 6 July 1941. However, due to determined Soviet counter-attacks and troop landings on the flank north of Litsa Bay, the corps failed to achieve the hoped-for breakthrough to the deeply echeloned enemy defensive line at the River Litsa. The decisive factor here was the lack of adequate reserves for Mountain Corps Norway, whose mountain divisions, in contrast to the three-unit infantry divisions, consisted of only two regiments.

After the unsuccessful and costly German attacks across the Litsa, the Soviet army launched a series of powerful counter-attacks on 18 July. The army command was forced to order a temporary halt to the offensive of Mountain Corps Norway, and to restructure its formations. The aim was to gain time for a reorganization of supply services and the establishment of lines of communication needed to set up a defensive position. A rapid break-through to the Kola peninsula was no longer considered possible.[8] On 30 July

[5] On the fighting involving Mountain Corps Norway see the records of XIX Mountain Corps (formerly Mountain Corps Norway), BA-MA 15085/1–32, 15085/33, 26373/1, 76,205. See also Hess, *Eismeerfront*, 25 ff.; *General Dietl*, 219–34; Rüf, *Gebirgsjäger*, 18–210; Ziemke, *German Northern Theater*, 140–56; Buchner, *Deutsche Gebirgstruppe*, 118–41; Ruef, *Winterschlacht*. From the Soviet point of view, Rumjancev, *Razgrom*, 29–48.

[6] On the fighting involving 3rd Mountain Div. see the records of 3rd Mountain Div., BA-MA RH 28-3/v. 6–v. 18, RH 28-3/v. 23–6, v. 32. Also Klatt, 3. *Gebirgs-Division*, 71–96; Bessell-Lorch, *Kampf an der Liza*; Ruef, *Odyssee*, 154–219.

[7] On operations involving 2nd Mountain Div. see the records of 2nd Mountain Div., BA-MA RH 28-2/v. 11–21, 26, 29K–30, 48–55, 73–4. Also Wiesbauer, *In Eis und Tundra*, 73–118; Kräutler and Springenschmid, *Edelweiß*, 144–273; Buchner, *Gebirgsjäger an allen Fronten*, 146–66.

[8] Telex Army Command Norway/Headquarters Finland, Ia No. 40/41 g.Kdos. Chefs. to OKW Dept. L on evaluation of the situation, 19 July 1941, and No. 44/41 g.Kdos. Chefs., evaluation of

1941 Hitler finally acceded to the repeated requests of Colonel-General von Falkenhorst and General Dietl for another division to be made available. In his Directives No. 33 of 19 July and No. 34 of 30 July 1941 Hitler continued to demand that the attack on Murmansk and the Murmansk railway be maintained.[9] To strengthen Mountain Corps Norway, the Wehrmacht High Command ordered the transfer of 6th Mountain Division (Major-General Ferdinand Schörner) from Greece. However, the transport of this newly assigned division across the North Sea along the Norwegian coast had to be halted in mid-September, when British naval formations appeared off the coast of northern Norway.[10] Only at the end of September did it prove possible to transport these troops. Moreover, the Wehrmacht High Command suspected that British and Soviet troops might make landings in the rear of the corps at Petsamo or on the Rybachiy Peninsula. This uncertainty, coupled with Hitler's perpetual fear of a possible Allied landing in Norway, prevented the transfer of major formations from northern Norway.[11] Hitler finally agreed that Dietl's mountain corps should also by reinforced by individual infantry units from Norway, but only after Major-General Warlimont of the Wehrmacht Operations Staff had convinced himself of the inadequate strength of the corps during a visit on 11 August 1941.[12] In order to make effective use of the remaining summer period, it was intended that the mountain corps—reinforced by two infantry regiments from Norway—would renew its efforts to break through the Soviet positions on the Litsa even before the bulk of 6th Mountain Division reached Petsamo at the beginning of October. The Chief of the Wehrmacht Operations Staff, Artillery General Jodl, also visited the mountain corps on 5 September 1941 to investigate the possibilities of an advance on Murmansk, and to obtain a personal view of the difficulties being encountered by the corps.[13] In order to strengthen the imminent offensive across the Litsa, a decision was taken to switch the main focus of the attack by Army Command Norway, and the Luftwaffe support, to Mountain Corps Norway. Although the attack across the Litsa from 8 September 1941 led to local territorial gains and the establishment of a bridgehead east of the river,

the situation, 24 July 1941, also Command Mountain Corps Norway to Army Command Norway/ Headquarters Finland No. 70a/41 g.Kdos. Chefs., situation report of 28 July 1941; all BA-MA, 20. Armee, 58628/1. See also Halder, *Diaries*, 1139 (1 Aug. 1941).

[9] *Hitler's Directives*, 88, 92; *DGFP* D xiii, No. 164, pp. 196 ff.

[10] See Ruef, *Zwischen Kreta und Murmansk*, 229 ff.

[11] On the fear of an Allied landing on the Arctic Sea front, and Hitler's consideration of whether to station two armoured divisions in Norway, see telex Army Command Norway, Chef No. 200/ 41 g.Kdos. Chefs to Mountain Corps Norway, 5 July 1941, and telex OKW/WFSt/Abt. L (I Op) No. 441325/41 g.Kdos. Chefs. to Army Command Norway/Headquarters Finland, 5 Aug. 1941, both BA-MA, 20. Armee, 58628/1; Halder, *Diaries*, 1016 (8 July 1941). On the opposing assessment of Army Command Norway see telex Abt. Ia No. 52/41 g.Kdos. to OKW/WFSt, Gen. Jodl, 3 Aug. 1941, BA-MA, 20. Armee, 58628/1.

[12] On the proposal of Maj.-Gen. Warlimont see telex OKW/WFSt/Abt. L (I Op) No. 441375/ 41 g.Kdos. Chefs, to Army Command Norway/Headquarters Finland, 13 Aug. 1941, BA-MA, 20. Armee, 58628/1, and Warlimont, *Hauptquartier*, 209 n. 15.

[13] On the issue of further efforts by the mountain corps, and the discussions with Gens. Jodl and Warlimont, see Rüf, *Gebirgsjäger*, 124–9.

the Soviet defensive lines again remained intact. On the Soviet side, the deployment of a newly arrived division was decisive. In this attack the Germans suffered heavy casualties and faced enormous problems of supply. These factors, combined with the first snowfalls, ensured that 3rd Mountain Division, deployed for a wide encirclement action on the right, had to be pulled back behind the Litsa on 19 September 1941.

The failure of these attacks across the Litsa, along with increasing difficulties of supply caused by the onset of winter and the inability of the German navy to prevent the blockade of supply-routes along the Norwegian Arctic coast, eventually forced the suspension of the offensive against Murmansk. The decision was approved by Hitler in his Directive No. 36 of 22 September 1941.[14] At the same time, he had continued to demand the conquest of the western part of the Rybachiy Peninsula. However, this project had to be abandoned following protests by Army Command Norway and the command of the mountain corps, which regarded an attack as impracticable given the inadequate strength of the mountain divisions. Instead, the two exhausted divisions had sustained such heavy casualties that they were to be relieved as soon as possible by the newly arrived 6th Mountain Division, which was placed under the command of the mountain corps. On 10 October 1941 Hitler ordered that Army Command Norway as a whole should move over to defence and reorganization for the winter war, 'in view of the lateness of the season before the onset of winter'.[15]

Together with Finnish border units, the Mountain Corps adopted a defensive position at the Litsa and the Rybachiy Peninsula for what was now regarded as the 'most urgent task' of securing the nickel region of Petsamo in a shortened front line consisting of individual strong points. From mid-October, during bitter defensive fighting, 6th Mountain Division at last took over the positions held by 3rd Mountain Division on the west bank of the Litsa, and the bridgehead sector of 2nd Mountain Division at Litsa Bay.[16] 3rd Mountain Division was detached from the command of Mountain Corps Norway in November 1941. It was temporarily placed directly under the army command in its new assembly area in southern Lapland, before being transported back to Germany from the middle of December. 2nd Mountain Division was withdrawn as corps reserve for rest and rehabilitation in the region Kirkenes/Northern Norway; its planned exchange with 5th or 7th Mountain

[14] *Hitler's Directives*, 99. See also Halder, *Diaries*, 1252–4 (23 Sept. 1941).

[15] 'Draft for Directive No. 37', 6 Oct. 1941, Dept. Defence No. 441660/61 g.Kdos. Chefs. (I Op), BA-MA RW 4/v. 578. The final version of Directive No. 37 nevertheless referred to 'the favourable developments of the situation in the Eastern Theatre, together with reports from Army Command Norway on the state of the forces there and on the possibilities of further operations in Finland'; see *Hitler's Directives*, 102 (also for the following). See order of Army Command Norway, Headquarters Finland, Abt. Ia, No. 90/41 g.Kdos. Chefs., 18 Oct. 1941, BA-MA, XXXVI. AK, 24307/2.

[16] Ruef, *Zwischen Kreta und Murmansk*, 247 ff. On the deployment of 6th Mountain Div. see Buchner, *Gebirgsjäger an allen Fronten*, 167–90.

Divisions, whose re-equipment and reorganization in Germany were still incomplete, could not be effected on schedule.[17] In its fixed defensive line the corps had to withstand bitter defensive fighting against Soviet Fourteenth Army units (52nd and 14th Rifle Divisions). Nevertheless, the winter positions were held on the Rybachiy Peninsula and on both sides of the Litsa.

Mountain Corps Norway had not succeeded in advancing to Murmansk and capturing the city, despite three attacks lasting from June to the end of October 1941. It had been thwarted by the strength of the enemy troops and their superiority in supplies and artillery. Instead, only half way to Murmansk after an attack about 40 km. east of the border, it had established a bridgehead on the Litsa. The Army General Staff was forced to conclude that further attacks on Murmansk offered 'not much chance of success'.[18] Various reasons can be cited for the failure of the offensive: the insufficient number of German forces; the mistaken estimates of enemy strength and incorrect evaluation of geographical conditions in the battle area; the setting of over-ambitious objectives; the collapse of lines of supply.[19] As a result of these unfavourable circumstances, the two mountain divisions of Mountain Corps Norway suffered the highest losses in percentage terms of any German unit on the entire eastern front up to winter 1941–2.[20]

(b) Operation Arctic Fox ('Polarfuchs') against the Murmansk Railway

XXXVI Army Corps (Infantry General Hans Feige), operating in the centre of the army area, was given the objective of advancing from the region round Kemijärvi via Salla towards the Murmansk railway at Kandalaksha.[21] The attack by 169th Infantry Division, the SS Division 'North', and the Finnish 6th Division—under the corps command—began on 1 July 1941. It rapidly be-

[17] On the reorganizations, reinforcements, and relief movements see 'Implementation instructions No. 1 to Directive 37', OKW No. 441861/g.Kdos. Chefs. WFSt/Abt. L (I Op), 7 Nov. 1941, *Hitlers Weisungen*, 164–7 (not in trans.); also minute of talks and report on trip of Org. Dept. in the Army General Staff: Org.Abt. (I) No. 3214/41 g.Kdos., 'Report on the visit to Army Command Norway/Headquarters Finland and Mountain Corps Norway'; also Op.Abt. (III), 'Reorganization in Army Command Norway', 5 Nov. 1941, and Org.Abt. (I) No. 3374/41 g.Kdos., 19 Nov. 1941, on issues relating to the 'reorganization and relief of the German forces in Finland'; also No. 3573/41 g.Kdos., 'Result of the discussions with Army Command Norway/Headquarters Finland on 30 Nov. and 1 Dec. 1941', 5 Dec. 1941: all BA-MA RH 2/v. 428.

[18] Halder, *Diaries*, 1313 (24 Nov. 1941).

[19] See the reasons given by Gen. Dietl in his discussion with 'Admiral Norway' on 23 July 1941, BA-MA III M 1000/22. See also Rüf, *Gebirgsjäger*, 163; Ziemke, *German Northern Theater*, 155–6; Erfurth, *Finnischer Krieg*, 49.

[20] See diagram showing losses June 1941–Dec. 1944, BA-MA, 20. Armee, 75430; also progress report Abt. IIa with casualty lists of Mountain Corps Norway, BA-MA, XIX. Geb.Korps, 15085/32, and the figures in Rüf, *Gebirgsjäger*, 181; Kräutler and Springenschmid, *Edelweiß*, 257.

[21] Higher Command XXXVI was renamed XXXVI Army Corps on 18 Nov. 1941, XXXVI (Mountain) Army Corps from 24 Nov. 1941. In the following 'XXXVI Army Corps' will be used. On the operations of the corps see files BA-MA, XXXVI. AK, 22102/3–24, 23305, 24307/1–10. especially the individual corps orders from No. 647/41 of 23 June 1941. See also Erfurth, *Finnischer Krieg*, 47 ff.; Ziemke, *German Northern Theater*, 157–67, 170–8. From the Soviet point of view, Rumjancev, *Razgrom*, 48–58.

came apparent that the first frontal assault had been insufficient to drive the opposing Soviet troops from their well-fortified and deeply echeloned border fortifications. Since the ceding of the Salla region to the USSR in the Finnish–Soviet peace treaty of March 1940, the Soviets had constructed strong fortifications to protect the Murmansk railway and the new branch terminal line to the border at Salla.[22] Although the stretch of line on the Finnish side, from Rovaniemi to the border, had not been completed by summer 1941, it still provided an important rear supply-line for XXXVI Army Corps. Supplies could therefore be moved to German troops in this sector more effectively than in the case of Mountain Corps Norway.

After crossing the border, 169th Infantry Division (Major-General Kurt Dittmar)[23] advanced on the northern flank of the corps. However, it did not succeed in taking Salla from the front in the first assault. SS Division North (SS Brigadeführer [Major-General] Karl Demelhuber), deployed to relieve the southern flank, failed in its attack owing to its woefully inadequate level of training and the incompetent leadership of its SS officers.[24] Indeed, after the first battles its troops streamed backwards in virtual headlong flight, and the division was thus unable to provide any support for 169th Infantry Division. In consequence, the attack over the border came to a halt before Salla. Although the commander of SS Division North quickly rallied his troops and regrouped them to secure the front, the failure of the SS division provoked a reaction in Berlin. When the divisional commander called for the replacement and withdrawal of his division from Finland on the grounds that it was 'no longer fully operational', his appeal was rejected by Hitler and Himmler. The request for time to improve the levels of equipment and training in the division, which had formerly been a purely police unit in Norway, was not granted. SS Division North remained at the front in northern Finland without the prospect of replacement, although it was not at first assigned further attacking objectives. Instead, in order to strengthen the offensive capability of the army corps, Hitler approved the request of Army Command Norway for units of 163rd Infantry Division, currently being transported by rail from Sweden to southern Finland, to be redirected to the Salla front and deployed there. This decision led to the fragmentation and weakening of 163rd Infantry Division, which was earmarked for operations on the Karelia front under Field Marshal

---

[22] Rumjancev, *Razgrom*, 24.

[23] On the fighting involving 169th Inf. Div. see the division's files, BA-MA, 169. Inf.Div., 20291/1–2 and 17664/11–52, 20291/4–5; also the reports of the former commander: Dittmar, 'Schlacht um Salla'; id., '"Flüstermarsch" der Kampfgruppe Behle'; id., 'Schlacht um Gora Lyssaja'.

[24] The 'SS Combat Group North' had been formed on 15 Mar. 1941 from two SS regiments in Norway, was renamed SS Division North on 23 June 1941, SS Mountain Division North in Jan. 1942, and 6th SS Mountain Division North from 1943. On the operation of the division as part of XXXVI Army Corps and its initial failure, see BA-MA RS 3-6/2–9, 23–4. The inadequacies of the SS division were recognized by the divisional commander and by XXXVI Army Corps even before it went into action, and had been reported both to the SS leadership and to Army Command Norway. See also Schreiber, *Nordlicht*, 36 ff., 42–59, 70–87; Halder, *Diaries*, 1045 (15 July 1941), 1226 (12 Sept. 1941).

Mannerheim. It was therefore bitterly criticized by the Army High Command. In Colonel-General Halder's view, the decision produced an unnecessary weakening of the German–Finnish attacking force at the critical point against Leningrad in the south. As such, it 'clearly shows up the dubiousness of this entire Murmansk operation, which serves only political ends and is open to the gravest censure from the operational point of view'.[25]

Not until 7 July 1941 were the Soviet fortifications penetrated and the town of Salla captured after heavy fighting and high casualties. To achieve it, the attacking formations had been reorganized to include the Finnish 6th Division (Colonel Viikla), which also turned northwards to Salla, and greater air support from the dive-bomber units of Air Fleet 5. The corps immediately continued the offensive over the Salla massif towards Kandalaksha. However, the retreating Soviet troops succeeded in preventing a rapid advance of the German divisions by the skilful placing of obstructions in the difficult woodland and lakeland terrain. Army Command Norway noted impatiently that 169th Infantry Division and the Finnish 6th Division in the southern sector of the corps were constantly being compelled to make time-consuming and extensive enveloping movements. On the Soviet side, new troops were brought to the front on the Murmansk railway, making a rapid German breakthrough increasingly unlikely. Meanwhile, the Army Commander-in-Chief, Colonel-General von Falkenhorst, pressed the commanding general of XXXVI Army Corps, Infantry General Feige, to push on with the offensive on Kandalaksha 'as soon as possible and ruthlessly, setting aside any misgivings', despite the flagging strength of the corps as an attacking force.[26] However, the army command was unable to provide the forces demanded by the army corps for that purpose. Instead, at the end of July the bulk of SS Division North was placed under the command of the neighbouring Finnish III Army Corps, which appeared to have greater prospects of rapid success. The remnants of the divided SS division remained with Army Corps XXXVI as support group for 169th Infantry Division and the Finnish 6th Division.

At the end of August, after a new attack and the successful advance of Finnish troops, large parts of the opposing Soviet XXXXII Corps were destroyed in a battle of encirclement at Kairala on Lake Kuolo-Apa. The road to Alakurtti near the old Finnish–Soviet border was reached. After the capture of Alakurtti, however, the advance of 169th Infantry Division and the Finnish 6th Division ground to a halt in front of the massif of the Lysaya and Voyta. Meanwhile, the corps had been compelled to hand over the remaining units of SS Division North to support a promising attack by Finnish III Corps in the south, and to reinforce Mountain Corps Norway in the northern army sector.

[25] Halder, *Diaries*, 1007 (5 July 1941).
[26] Army Command Norway, Abt. Ia No. 325/41 g.Kdos. to Higher Command XXXVI, 4 July 1941, BA-MA, XXXVI. AK, 22102/11, and situation report of Army Command Norway Ia No. 46/41 g.Kdos. Chefs., 28 July 1941, BA-MA, 20. Armee, 19070/2. See also Halder, *Diaries*, 1135–40 (1 Aug. 1941).

Adequate combat strength and sufficient reserves were therefore lacking for a further advance along the railway line and the road to Kandalaksha. On 4 September 1941, in discussions with Artillery General Jodl, the army command urgently requested reinforcements for the advance on Kandalaksha. However, Hitler refused to transfer 163rd Infantry Division, now deployed on the Finnish southern front, while continuing to insist on the proposed reinforcement of Mountain Corps Norway. The strongly fortified massif of the Lysaya and Voyta was finally taken in September, only after difficult and exhausing encirclement operations. Once again, many of the Soviet units were able to withdraw and establish a new defensive line. In consequence, the two divisions of the corps were eventually left 'utterly exhausted' and 'battle-weary' in front of newly constructed Soviet defensive positions on the River Verman.[27] On 17 September 1941 the army command informed XXXVI Corps command that its successes could not be exploited because of the unavailability of reserves. The corps was directed to switch over to defence in static winter positions.

However, Hitler's Directive No. 36 of 22 September 1941 was issued shortly afterwards. This ordered XXXVI Army Corps to prepare for a resumption of the attack on Kandalaksha at the beginning of October, with 'the aim of at least cutting Murmansk off from its rail communications by the time winter sets in'. The attacks in the other two army sectors were to be halted for the present.[28] As requested on several occasions, XXXVI Army Corps was to be reinforced for this offensive by 163rd Infantry Division, previously deployed on the Finnish southern front, and by units of SS Division North, formerly attached to the Finnish III Corps. However, it was soon apparent that Hitler's plan to transfer 163rd Infantry Division could not be completed in time because of transport problems, that further reinforcements were unavailable because of Mannerheim's reluctance, and that the moment for tactical pursuit across the Verman sector had already been missed in mid-September during the enemy retreat. In consequence, the projected attack was eventually postponed.[29]

The Wehrmacht High Command now responded to the demands of XXXVI Army Corps and Army Corps Norway. In accordance with Hitler's Directive No. 37 of 10 October 1941,[30] OKW abandoned the plan for a renewed attack on Kandalaksha by XXXVI Army Corps. Instead it proposed the relief of 169th and also 163rd Infantry Division, the main part of which—

---

[27] Higher Command XXXVI, commander, situation on 15 Sept. 1941, BA-MA, XXXVI. AK, 22102/11. The command reported on 16 Sept. 1941 that 169th Inf. Div. was 'no longer combat-ready' and would have to be withdrawn; see ibid., telex Higher Command XXXVI, Ia No. 808/41, and 814/41 g.Kdos., to Army Command Norway, Headquarters Finland, 16 and 17 Sept. 1941.

[28] *Hitler's Directives*, 99. See also the comments on the directive in Halder, *Diaries*, 1253 (23 Sept. 1941).

[29] Erfurth, *Finnischer Krieg*, 73.

[30] *Hitler's Directives*, 101–4.

as before—was to be transferred from the Svir front to Army Command Norway. OKW had concluded that further attacks in the Finnish theatre of operations were unnecessary because of German successes elsewhere on the eastern front. Army command was instructed to switch to defence 'in favourable, easily defended positions' to relieve and rehabilitate the exhausted and decimated units. The intention was to reach the Murmansk railway in the following year.[31]

Within the Wehrmacht High Command and Army Command Norway, plans for a renewed offensive by XXXVI Army Corps with the objective of capturing Kandalaksha were subsequently discussed. However, this proved impracticable because of the inadequate combat strength of the German and Finnish divisions. To enable it to undertake an operation of this kind in winter, the corps command demanded the provision of at least two new divisions, preferably fully mobile in winter conditions. Without them, 'a conclusive success in achieving the operational objective of Kandalaksha [did not appear] possible in any case'.[32] The reinforcement of the corps with 7th Mountain Division, and its conversion to a fully equipped mountain corps, could not be achieved until mid-January 1942 because of the Finnish transport situation. Consequently, Army Command Norway was also forced to agree to Field Marshal Mannerheim's demand for the postponement of the attack until March 1942.[33] As part of the intended reorganization and reduction of the Finnish Army, Mannerheim had repeatedly requested that Finnish divisions should be removed from the control of Army Command Norway and attached to his own high command again. Following German–Finnish discussions in Rovaniemi on 13–14 December 1941,[34] OKW decided on 20 December that the Finnish 6th Division deployed with XXXVI Army Corps should be returned to Finnish control. On the other hand, SS Division North was to remain with the Finnish III Army Corps until the end of January, though the corps itself would be transferred to Finnish command as soon as possible.[35] The proposed attack on Kandalaksha by XXXVI Army Corps was finally abandoned. Instead, an advance by the Finnish Army on Belomorsk (Sorokka), proposed by Mannerheim and planned with German participation, was envisaged for March 1942.

By September 1941 XXXVI Army Corps had advanced approximately 60 km. and had reconquered the former Finnish border region. At the begin-

---

[31] Ibid. 102.

[32] XXXVI Corps Command, Ia No. 39/41 g.Kdos., on 'Proposal for an offensive operation in winter with Kandalaksha as the objective', 21 Oct. 1941, BA-MA, XXXVI. AK, 24307/2.

[33] See 'Implementation instructions No. 2 to Directive 37: Preparation of the attack on Kandalaksha', 21 Nov. 1941, *Hitlers Weisungen*, 167 ff. (not in trans.).

[34] On the exchange of views between FM Mannerheim and Col.-Gen. von Falkenhorst see telex Army Command Norway, Ia No. 138/41 g.Kdos. Chefs. to OKW/WFSt Abt. L, 15 Dec. 1941, memorandum of discussions, 13 Dec. 1941, and telex from Inf. Gen. Erfurth No. 121/41 to OKW/WFSt, Abt. L, 16 Dec. 1941, BA-MA, 20. Armee, 58628/1.

[35] Telex OKW/WFSt/Abt. L (I Op) No. 442214/41 g.Kdos. to Army Command Norway, Headquarters Finland, 20 Dec. 1941, ibid. See also Erfurth, *Finnischer Krieg*, 89.

ning of winter, reduced in strength, the corps went over to defence in a reinforced 'permanent winter position' in the Verman sector, roughly on the latitude of the old Finnish–Soviet border.[36] This sector of the front remained largely unchanged until autumn 1944. It became apparent that XXXVI Army Corps did not possess sufficient strength to achieve its objective of severing the Murmansk railway at Kandalaksha.

Finnish III Corps, under the command of the Finnish Major-General Siilvarsuo,[37] was deployed in the southern army sector between Kuusamo and Suomussalmi. After it had handed over the Finnish 6th Division (Colonel Viikla) to XXXVI Army Corps, its remaining Finnish 3rd Division (Colonel Fagernäs) had been divided into two divisional groups—'J' (Lieutenant-Colonel Turtola) and 'F' (Colonel Fagernäs)—for the attack of 1 July 1941. The objective of the advance on Uhtua (Ukhta) and Kiestinki (Kestenga) was to reach the Murmansk railway and capture the towns of Louchi and Kem (Kemi) on the White Sea and on the railway.[38] Against weak resistance from the opposing Soviet 54th Rifle Division, the Finnish troops were able to exploit their experience in woodland fighting and make swift progress by means of repeated pincer movements. Both Army Command Norway and Hitler, in his directive of 30 July 1944, considered that further attacks by Finnish III Army Corps might offer the best prospect for a rapid breakthrough to the Murmansk railway.[39] The southern divisional group, 'F', advanced on Uhtua. At the end of July Army Command Norway transferred elements of SS Division North, previously deployed with XXXVI Army Corps by Army Command Norway, to Division J for the attack towards Louchi.[40] On 8 August Finnish and German units captured the transport junction of Kiestinki on the terminal branch line to the Murmansk railway.

However, stiffening enemy resisance quickly brought the advance towards Louchi to a standstill. After the Soviets brought up 88th Rifle Division from Archangel to establish a new line of defence, General Siilvasuo reported on 25 August 1941 that his forces were insufficient to achieve the breakthrough to the Murmansk railway; he urgently needed a new division, equipped and prepared for fighting in almost primeval forest conditions.[41] All that Army

---

[36] See XXXVI Army Corps, Ia No. 936/41 g.Kdos., corps order, 19 Nov. 1941, BA-MA, XXXVI. AK, 24307/2, and Erfurth, *Finnischer Krieg*, 88.

[37] On the operations of Finnish III Corps see the files BA-MA, III. finn. AK, 19654/1–4; also Ziemke, *German Northern Theater*, 158, 167–70, 179–82; Erfurth, *Finnischer Krieg*, 53–4; from the Finnish point of view, Kuussaari and Niitemaa, *Finlands Krig*, 88–94, and *Suomen Sota* 1941–1945, v. 163 ff.

[38] See Army Command Norway Ia No. 148/41 geh., chief (Silver Fox), operational directive for Finnish V Army Corps, 10 June 1941, BA-MA, 20. Armee, 13386/1. The corps was renamed III Army Corps on mobilization.

[39] See Army Command Norway Ia No. 46/41 g.Kdos. Chefs., situation report, 28 July 1941, BA-MA, 20. Armee, 58628/1, and on Hitler's directive of 30 July 1941 see *Hitler's Directives*, 91–3.

[40] On the operations of SS Division North with Finnish III Corps see BA-MA RS 3-6/2–9. Also Schreiber, *Nordlicht*, 88–170; Erfurth, *Finnischer Krieg*, 53–4.

[41] Operational HQ III Army Corps No. 1024 a/III geh., 'To commander of Army command Norway', 25 Aug. 1941, BA-MA, 20. Armee, 19070/2.

Command Norway could offer as reinforcement in this sector was the concentration of all SS units with Finnish III Army Corps, as demanded on several occasions by SS Division North. In addition, extensive air support by Air Fleet 5 was promised. As soon as conditions within XXXVI Army Corps allowed, part of the Finnish 6th Division would also be attached to Finnish III Army Corps. No other units were available. Although the corps went on the attack again on the southern flank before Uhtua, strong Soviet counter-attacks soon endangered its position at Kiestinki, where the exhausted Finnish formations and SS units were able to repulse enemy counter-thrusts only at the cost of heavy casualties.[42] Army Command Norway then requested additional Finnish units as reinforcements for Finnish III Corps. However, Infantry General Erfurth, chief of liaison staff North at Finnish headquarters, considered the request inappropriate for political reasons.[43] Consequently, during Colonel-General von Falkenhorst's visit of 14 September 1941, Hitler eventually agreed to call a halt to the attack by Finnish III Army Corps and ordered a switch to the defensive.

At the end of the month, however, Army Command Norway advocated a fresh attack by Finnish III Army Corps towards Louchi. It was forced to rescind the order to attack when, on 8 October 1941, Wehrmacht High Command ordered a halt to all operations and their postponement 'for the winter'; the intended attack of Finnish III Army Corps was expressly forbidden.[44] When opposing Soviet formations withdrew to a newly constructed rear defensive position, Finnish III Army Corps nevertheless went back on the offensive at the beginning of November 1941, on the order of Army Command Norway. It succeeded in encircling and destroying part of the Soviet 88th Rifle Division. However, on 12 November 1941 Major-General Siilvasuo ordered a switch to a defensive position and explained that continued attacks would have no prospect of success given the enemy reserves and the insufficiency of the forces available to him. Yet Colonel-General von Falkenhorst, who still thought the operational objective of the Murmansk railway could be achieved in the sector occupied by Finnish III Army Corps, insisted that the attack be continued.

The divergent views of German and Finnish headquarters were the subject of discussions in Helsinki on 15 November 1941. The participants were Major-General Warlimont of the Wehrmacht Operations Staff, Major-General Buschenhagen, chief of the general staff of Army Command Norway, and Infantry General Erfurth of liaison staff North at Mannerheim's headquarters.[45] On the insistence of Mannerheim, Army Command Norway was forced to drop its plans for further offensive operations by Finnish III Army

---

[42] Halder, *Diaries*, 1240–2 (17 Sept. 1941).

[43] See Erfurth, *Finnischer Krieg*, 72–3, and papers of Gen. Erfurth, diary, i. 111, 130, BA-MA N 257/1.

[44] Telex OKW/WFSt/Abt. L (I Op) No. 441679/41 g.Kdos Chefs., to Army Command Norway, Headquarters Finland, 19 Nov. 1941, BA-MA, 20. Armee, 58628/1.

[45] Erfurth, *Finnischer Krieg*, 84 ff.

Corps. The Wehrmacht High Command also declared its readiness to grant the requests of Field Marshal Mannerheim and return III Corps to the Finnish national high command for inclusion in the forthcoming reorganization and reduction of the Finnish army.[46] On 17 November 1941 Major-General Siilvasuo finally brought the operations of both Division J and SS Division North to an end, although both divisional commanders estimated that further offensive operations towards Louchi had some prospects of success.[47] Colonel-General von Falkenhorst finally accepted the halting of the attack, although he suspected that the conduct of Major-General Siilvasuo was due less to the military situation than to the diplomatic efforts to achieve a separate peace between Helsinki and Moscow, which had been initiated by the United States at that time.[48]

Recently, the United States had warned the Finnish government of serious consequences if American deliveries of war materials to the USSR were disrupted by the advance of Finnish troops to the Murmansk railway. Helsinki was therefore unlikely to want the troops of Finnish III Army Corps, fighting under German command, to advance so far and so successfully that they posed the only serious threat to the Allied delivery of supplies to the Soviet Union along the Murmansk railway.[49] In the view of Army Command Norway and the German commanders, it was likely that Major-General Siilvasuo had been 'tipped off' by Helsinki and was no longer interested in continuing the attack.

The exchange of SS Division North with the Finnish 6th Division[50]—previously deployed with XXXVI Army Corps—was ordered by Hitler on 10 October 1941 at the request of Mannerheim. However, it had not taken place by the end of 1941 because of powerful Soviet counter-attacks in the sector. Moreover, though the Wehrmacht High Command had intended the newly arrived XVIII Army Corps to take over the whole sector of the front occupied by Finnish Army Corps at the turn of the year, the plan could not be carried out because of the lack of German troops. Only in summer 1942 did new units of XVIII Army Corps (Mountain Troop General Franz Boehme) and 7th

---

[46] See telex OKW/WFSt/Abt. L (I Op) No. 002743/41 g.Kdos. Chefs., to Army Command Norway, Headquarters Finland, 19 Nov. 1941, BA-MA, 20. Armee, 58628/1.

[47] III Army Corps HQ No. 652/III/3b/sa to 'commander of Army Norway', 18 Nov. 1941, BA-MA, 20. Armee, 20844/2. On the assessment of the prospects of success for further attacks by the German and Finnish divisional commanders see ibid., German Liaison Officer Group J, 'Memo to war diary', 26 Nov. 1941, and ibid., RS 3-6/2, pt. 2, 6th SS Mountain Div. North, war diary, 15 and 16 Nov. 1941.

[48] See army orders of Army Command Norway No. 115/41 and 2337/41 g.Kdos., 18 Nov. 1941, BA-MA, Finn. III. AK, and German liaison officer with Finnish III Army Corps, 'Report on the suspension of the attack of (Finn.) III A.Co. mid-November 1931', 21 Nov. 1941 with the glosses of Col.-Gen. von Falkenhorst, BA-MA, 20. Armee, 20844/2. See also papers of Col.-Gen. von Falkenhorst, iv. 61–2, BA-MA N 300/4, and Schreiber, *Nordlicht*, 126–7; also Jägerskiöld, *Marskalken av Finland*, 178–9. On the interventions of the USA on 27 and 30 Oct. 1941 see *FRUS* (1941), i. 81–98.

[49] See also Ziemke, *German Northern Theater*, 182; Schreiber, *Nordlicht*, 126–7.

[50] See Directive No. 37, *Hitler's Directives*, 101–4.

Mountain Division take over the Kiestinki sector. In consequence, and in accordance with Mannerheim's wishes, there was a 'clean separation' into purely German and purely Finnish sectors of the front. This restored the Finnish commander's 'full freedom to make his own decisions'.[51]

During the positional battles of the winter, Army Command Norway and SS headquarters in Berlin discussed plans to withdraw SS Division North, which was no longer combat-ready,[52] and to transport it home for rest and rehabilitation. However, 'the development of the situation in Norway' meant that this could not be achieved either.[53] The division was instead reorganized at the beginning of 1942 into the mobile SS Mountain Division North, and remained in the Kiestinki sector.

The attack by Finnish III Army Corps in the Kiestinki sector, advancing to within 30 km. of Louchi, had come closest to the Murmansk railway. The railway line itself, however, was not reached. After the bitter fighting of autumn 1941, this sector of the front also rigidified into trench warfare from November of that year. During the winter of 1941 Finnish III Army Corps mounted a successful defence of its often makeshift defensive positions against sporadic enemy attacks at Kiestinki and on the southern flank at Uhtua. There were no further major offensive and defensive operations.

(c) Problems of German Naval and Air Operations in the Far North

As a result of the operational direction of Army Command Norway, with its changing and simultaneous points of main effort, the Luftwaffe formations gathered within Air Fleet 5 under the 'special duty squad' were also fragmented. From 24 June 1941, even before the start of land operations, Murmansk and the Murmansk railway were subjected to several air raids by Luftwaffe formations operating from Finnish airfields.[54] Enemy air-bases within the range of German forces were attacked with some success in the first few days. Particularly after its attacks on the Soviet airfields in the Murmansk region, the Luftwaffe had achieved air superiority at the outset. However, the Soviet air forces could not be eliminated entirely, because the 'Air Leader Kirkenes' was quickly forced to divide his 'special duty squad' among several

---

[51] Hillgruber, 'Einbau', 674.

[52] See the reports of the divisional commander, SS Brigadeführer Demelhuber, Sept.–Nov. 1941, his visit to Berlin on 12 Oct. 1941, and the entry in the divisional war diary on 24 Nov. 1941—the companies now had only 'a combat strength of 15–20 men.; BA-MA RS 3-6/7 and 2, pt. 2.

[53] See Schreiber, *Nordlicht*, 165; Halder, *Diaries*, 1343–5 (9 Dec. 1941). On the intended reorganization of the SS formations see also Org.Abt. (I) No. 3374/41 g.Kdos., memorandum on discussion in OKW, 19 Nov. 1941, BA-MA RH 2/v. 428.

[54] On Luftwaffe operations see Der Einsatz der Teilverbände der Luftflotte 5; Horst von Riesen; II./K.G. 30 vom Apr. bis Sept. 1941; Andreas L. Nielsen, Einsatz der deutschen Luftwaffe im finnischen Raum: all in BA-MA Lw 118/5; Hans-Jürgen Stumpff, Gedanken zum Kampf der deutschen Luftwaffe im Gebiet nördlich des Polarkreises, BA-MA Lw 127/1; papers of Gen. Erfurth, diary, vol. i, BA-MA N 257/1; also Rüf, *Gebirgsjäger*, 15; Hess, *Eismeerfront*, 37; Girbig, *Jagdgeschwader 5*, 23 ff., 278 ff. For the Soviet side see e.g. Rumjancev, *Razgrom*, 18.

sectors in support of the ground fighting. In July 1941 the main focus of Luftwaffe operations lay in supporting the advances of Mountain Corps Norway and XXXVI Army Corps. German Stuka formations played an important role in this process by destroying the Soviet fortifications in the battle for Salla. The dive-bomber Gruppe was also successfully deployed during the further advances of XXXVI Army Corps towards Kajrala–Alakurrti, and of Finnish III Corps towards Louchi.

In accordance with the objectives of Air Fleet 5,[55] a number of air raids were also carried out on the ports and important railway stations of Murmansk and Archangel, regarded as the main bases of the Soviet Arctic Fleet. Though these attacks achieved some success, Murmansk remained the most important place of transhipment for supply traffic with the Western powers. In addition, the Luftwaffe flew repeated missions against the Murmansk railway and the line from Kandalaksha to Salla. Here too success was limited. There were insufficient forces to achieve either disruption over a longer period or the complete destruction of this vital Soviet supply-line.

With the onset of winter conditions, the Soviet air forces recovered rapidly from their early reverses in summer 1941. In places they regained local air superiority. This development can be attributed to three major factors: the deliveries of the Western Allies[56] and the Soviet success in transferring replacements to the front in the north; the rapid construction of field airstrips along the Murmansk railway; and an intensified defence by flak and fighters along the Murmansk railway. In contrast, the German formations received no significant reinforcement. Instead there was a perceptible reduction of Luftwaffe activity in the northern sector of operations, since the Luftwaffe forces available proved completely insufficient to achieve the extensive objectives they had been set.

When the onset of winter severely restricted Luftwaffe activity from September 1941 onwards, Air Fleet 5 indicated that it was 'no longer in a position to provide effective support for army operations'.[57] In view of temperatures as low as −50°C, the Air Fleet held that 'climatological conditions for flying' had made operations much more difficult, if not completely 'impossible'. On the other hand, Army Command Norway considered that continued attacks on the Murmansk railway were necessary to disrupt this enemy supply-line. In his directive of 10 October 1941 Hitler maintained that the Luftwaffe's role lay in providing air defence for northern Norway and northern Finland, air reconnaissance, and air attacks on Murmansk and the Murmansk railway. He also demanded measures 'in order to simplify the co-operation' of

---

[55] On these tasks see sect. I.VI. 4. at n. 121.

[56] From the middle of September 81st and 134th RAF Squadrons were stationed in the Murmansk region to protect the British convoys. The aircraft were later taken over by the Soviet air force. Seen Girbig, *Jagdgeschwader 5*, 25.

[57] Telex Army High Command Norway, Headquarters Finland, Abt. Ia No. 1173/41 g.Kdos. to OKW/WFSt/Abt. L (Wolfsschanze), 27 Aug. 1941, BA-MA, 20. Armee, 19070/2 (also for the following).

the three branches of the Wehrmacht. In consequence, at the end of October 1941 an attempt was made to create a more effective control of the Luftwaffe in the far north. This was to be achieved by uniting the formations operating from northern Norway and northern Finland under the newly established 'Air Leader North (East)' in Rovaniemi.[58] At the same time, the fighter formations were amalgamated in a 'fighter Gruppe for special duties' in Kirkenes/ Petsamo. The 'General of Luftwaffe Northern Norway' also transferred his command staff to Kirkenes, with the aim of co-ordinating the attacks on enemy air and naval forces and on transport movements off the Finnish–north Norwegian coast and the Kola peninsula. Finally, from the beginning of 1942 the 'Air Leader North (West)', newly based in Bardufoss, was to be involved in reconnaissance and attacks on British convoys to Murmansk.

Depite these changes, the Luftwaffe achieved no significant successes in the winter of 1941–2. Due to a shortage of resources, the air formations were also unable to provide air transport for the vital supply of the army during the winter months.

The difficulties encountered in mounting Luftwaffe operations in the far north were due in part to the lack of adequate resources. However, a role was also played by the limited supply of war materials and provisions owing to the shortage of transport capacity and the inadequate development of communications. This situation was scarcely improved in autumn 1941 by the transfer of the Air Fleet 5 forward command staff to Kemi on the Gulf of Bothnia. Limited supplies, inadequate means of communication, and serious leadership problems continued to hamper the operational prospects of the Luftwaffe even when the weather began to improve in the spring of 1942.

Similarly, the German naval forces concentrated in northern Norway were too weak and inadequately armed to undertake major operations against the Soviet forces in the Arctic Ocean and the Barents Sea, either independently or in co-operation with the army and Luftwaffe. With good reason, the naval leadership had advised against war on more than one front as long as the 'main front' against Britain in the west continued to exist. From the point of view of the chiefs of naval operations, the war against the Soviet Union was therefore a secondary task. It soon became clear, however, that the forces available were scarcely sufficient even for 'secondary tasks'.

Problems had become apparent even on 6 June 1941, during discussions with the Finnish Commodore Sundman in Kiel on the question of joint German–Finnish naval operations. Naval Group Commander North, Admiral-General Carls, had complained that the submarines promised to him for the Arctic Ocean had been withdrawn after a protest from the Commander of U-boats, Admiral Dönitz. These were now earmarked for use in operations against Britain without Carls having rights of direction over these forces in the

---

[58] *Hitler's Directives*, 101–4, and *DGFP* D xiii, No. 395. Also Air Fleet 5 HQ, Ops., Ia No. 91/ 41 g.Kdos. Chefs., 'Directives for operations of the formations of Air Fleet 5 in winter 1941–2', 22 Oct. 1941, BA-MA, 20. Armee, 58638/1.

North Atlantic should the need arise for a co-ordinated naval war effort in the Arctic Ocean.[59] No Finnish forces were stationed in the Arctic Ocean apart from the Petsamo naval detachment with three small patrol steamers. In consequence, the German navy faced the Soviet Arctic Fleet with only a minesweeper flotilla and approximately 15 captured and converted Norwegian torpedo-boats and outpost- and coastal-protection boats. Soviet naval forces comprised 8 destroyers, 7 coastal-protection ships, 2 minesweepers, 14 coastal-protection cutters, and 15 submarines; the navy air force had 116 aircraft.[60] The German naval command assumed that German troops would quickly capture Polyarnyy and Murmansk by land, thus depriving the Soviet Arctic Fleet of its bases; Soviet naval forces could then be eliminated indirectly. Early in July 1941 Naval Group Command North in Kiel had considered a major attack by German destroyers against Murmansk. In contrast, the Naval War Staff assigned German naval forces in the Arctic Ocean a much more limited tactical function of providing support to the army. It described this objective as 'Support of Group Dietl, attack on enemy, and protection of own sea routes'.[61] On the order of the Naval War Staff, there were therefore no offensive operations against the Soviet Northern Fleet in the form of minelaying or destroyer attacks, as envisaged by Naval Group Command North at the beginning of Operation Barbarossa. The Naval War Staff saw no pressing need for a major deployment of the navy against the Soviet Union.[62]

This decision allowed the Soviet Northern Fleet to mount minor landing operations and thereby intervene in the fighting involving Mountain Corps Norway. In addition, the Soviet fleet was able to inflict considerable damage on German supply transports off the Norwegian and Finnish coasts by deploying submarines and laying mine-barriers. To counteract such activity by the superior Soviet forces and to secure some protection—however limited—against possible operations by British naval forces off the Arctic coast, Hitler, in his directives of 19 and 23 July 1941, ordered five destroyers of the 6th destroyer flotilla to be transferred to Kirkenes and a number of U-boats to be dispatched to northern Norway. These were given several objectives: to oppose and damage the Soviet Northern Fleet by making attacks along the Norwegian coast towards Kola Bay; to provide tactical support for the land operations of Army Command Norway; and to safeguard German supplies and disrupt enemy transports of supplies and reinforcements. The aim was to

[59] On the German–Finnish discussions and Adm. Carl's criticism see war diary of Naval Group Command North, 6–7 June 1941, BA-MA OKM M/127/34835, app. 8.

[60] On strength see the figures in Piterskij, *Sowjet-Flotte*, 109; *Seemacht*, 643; Hess, *Eismeerfront*, 78; Seaton, *Der russisch-deutsche Krieg*, 383–4.

[61] War diary Naval Group Command North, 1 July 1941, 261, with subsequent handwritten addition by Adm. Schniewind, BA-MA OKM M/127/34835.

[62] On the navy's operations in the Arctic Sea and the Baltic see Salewski, *Seekriegsleitung*, i. 354–75, 418–25; Hess, *Eismeerfront*, 77–91; Rohwer, 'Seekrieg im Nordmeer 1941–1945', 642 ff.; on the individual events and dates see the compilation of Rohwer and Hümmelchen, *Chronik*, 133 ff.

'reduce the temptation for England to intervene in the fighting along the Arctic coast'.[63] However, the destroyers' field of action was restricted by inadequate fuel supplies, allowing very few wide-ranging offensive operations to be undertaken against enemy targets. Combat activity therefore remained infrequent.

From August 1941 British naval forces—aircraft-carriers, cruisers, and destroyers—appeared off the north Norwegian coast; this was regarded as a serious threat. At the urging of the Soviets, London had launched an attack on Kirkenes on 30 July 1941 using an aircraft-carrier formation (two carriers, two heavy cruisers, and seven destroyers). However, the attack of the carrier aircraft was successfully beaten off and only minor damage was sustained. Nevertheless, the appearance off the north Norwegian coast of superior British naval forces and several British and Soviet submarines posed a serious threat to the small German naval forces and the supply-routes along the coast to northern Norway and northern Finland. British submarines, which were also operating from Murmansk, managed to inflict considerable damage on German supply-routes on several occasions and, from August 1941, to sink several German supply-ships. The German navy had insufficient anti-submarine forces at their disposal to combat these attacks effectively. At the same time, approximately eight Soviet submarines were operating off the Norwegian Arctic coast. Under these circumstances, Naval Group Command North had begun to consider that it would be a positive achievement if the German navy in the area of northern Norway at least 'succeeds in securing supplies for Norway to some degree'.[64] Equally, there could be no question of German naval forces off the Murmansk coast offering offensive support for the operations of Army Command Norway. The situation at sea would be improved only if Mountain Corps Norway succeeded in capturing the Soviet naval base of Murmansk. During the planning of Operation Barbarossa from the beginning of 1941, the Commander-in-Chief of the Navy, Grand Admiral Raeder, had confirmed that the occupation of Murmansk and Polyarnyy was a major demand. At the beginning of 1942 the navy continued to insist that the capture of Murmansk by land forces was essential.[65]

From the end of September 1941 the first British convoys were able to transport their war material to Murmansk and Archangel largely unmolested. The Soviet leadership had urgently pressed the Allies to use this shorter and quicker transport route for delivering supplies to Murmansk in preference to routes via east Siberia or the Persian Gulf. The British convoys PQ1 to PQ6 completed their journeys in the second half of 1941, with QP1 to QP4 making the return to Britain/Iceland. At the outset these convoys were assembled

---

[63] *Hitler's Directives*, 89–90 (Directive No. 33 of 19 July 1941), and war diary Naval Group Command North, 2 and 6 July 1941, 45, BA-MA M/127/34835.

[64] War diary Naval Group Command North, 31 July 1941, 90, BA-MA M/127/34835.

[65] On the navy's demand for the occupation of Murmansk see sect. I.VI.3 with nn. 65 and 386, also Salewski, *Seekriegsleitung*, i. 367.

every four weeks, and later at intervals of ten days.[66] The powerful British escort ships returning from Murmansk also posed a considerable danger to the ill-defended German supply transports along the north Norwegian coast. Hitler's directive of 10 October 1941 thus ordered the navy 'to attack enemy supplies going by sea to Murmansk and to protect our own traffic in the Arctic Ocean within the limits of its forces'.[67] To achieve this, more U-boats, motor torpedo-boats, minesweepers, and outpost formations were transferred to northern Norway. Then, in December 1941, the destroyers of 6th Detroyer Flotilla were replaced by vessels of 8th Destroyer Flotilla. Only in that month did the navy command resolve to use the U-boats which had been transferred to northern Norway to attack the Allied convoys. At the end of the year German destroyers made a successful foray into the sea east of Murmansk. Early in 1942 the attempt was also made to lay mine-barriers in the straits to the White Sea in order to restrict the activity of the Soviet Northern Fleet. Nevertheless, even in 1942 the inadequate German naval forces were unable to achieve any decisive success against increasing Allied deliveries of supplies for the Soviet war effort. Enemy supplies on the convoy route through the Arctic Ocean were not halted. This objective could not be attained by a reorganization of the command structure as ordered by Hitler in his Directive No. 37 of 10 October 1941, although the establishment of the command area 'Admiral Arctic Ocean' (Vice-Admiral Hubert Schmund) in Kirkenes (which was also intended as an emergency naval base) promised better co-operation with the new 'Air Leader North (East)'.[68] Extra forces were desperately required to improve German prospects of success, but could not be supplied to the new navy commander in the Arctic Ocean.

Despite German operational discussions, the Soviet Fourteenth Army was able to rely on naval and air superiority during its defence of the area round Murmansk. It received effective support from the other Soviet services. Enemy naval and air superiority in the Arctic Ocean was expressed in several ways: by Soviet submarine operations; by the operations of British naval forces against Spitsbergen and to cut off German supply transports in the Arctic Ocean; and by the raids of British carrier aircraft on Kirkenes, Petsamo, and Liinahamari. In his Directive No. 36 of 22 September 1941 Hitler was forced to admit that enemy disruption of German sea communications along the polar coast had 'still further reduced the likelihood' that the mountain corps could 'reach Murmansk this year'.[69] Repeated Soviet landings on the Rybachiy peninsula greatly endangered the supply-route for Mountain Corps Norway, so that individual army units had to be withdrawn from the front on numerous occasions to secure the open sea flank and the long supply-lines. At the end of

---

[66] See the overall details in Bidlingmaier, *Seegeltung*, 247; Schofield, *Russian Convoys*, 31–53; see also *Das Deutsche Reich und der Zweite Weltkrieg*, vi. 407.

[67] *Hitler's Directives*, 101–4 (Directive No. 37 of 10 Oct. 1941).

[68] Ibid., item 8.

[69] Ibid. 99–101 (Directive No. 36 of 22 Sept. 1941).

1941 the struggle on the Arctic front was increasingly being determined by problems of supply.

Supplies had to be brought in for approximately 200,000 men in the German army in northern Finland, for units of the Finnish III Army Corps promised to the Finns by the Wehrmacht High Command,[70] and for 163rd Infantry Division operating on the Svir front in the south. In each case the exceptional geographical and climatic features of the theatre of operations meant that supplies were largely dependent on the transport situation. The problem proved remarkably difficult to solve, due to the shortage of technical equipment and winter-proof supply-lines in Lapland, and the refusal of Sweden to accede to German transport requests.[71]

'Home Staff Overseas' in Berlin thus faced serious problems with land and sea transport from Germany to Finland.[72] These were intensified, and had more direct effects on the conduct of operations by the army command at the front, from the middle of September 1941, when British and Soviet naval operations in the Arctic made it impossible to bring in supplies from depots in Norway by sea. Additional transports were organized through the southern Finnish railway network to bring about some relief in the supply of ammunition, provisions, clothing, and replacement parts. This temporary solution was made possible by the co-operation of the German transport officer with the military attaché in Helsinki. However, the capacity of the railway network was already over-stretched because of domestic transport needs, and could hardly be increased without German assistance.[73]

Schemes for the building of a railway line parallel to the Arctic Ocean road from Rovaniemi to Petsamo, involving the 'ruthless employment of Russian prisoners of war' by the Todt Organization, had been mooted at the end of September 1941 and taken up by Hitler in his Directive No. 36 of 22 September 1941. However, a local inspection by Reich Minister Todt revealed the scheme to be impracticable due to a shortage of material and time.[74] The project was

[70] See e.g. Halder, *Diaries*, 1140–4 (30 July 1941); telex Army Command Norway, Headquarters Finland, Abt. Ia No. 1173/41 g.Kdos. to OKW/WFSt/Abt. L (Wolfsschanze), 27 Aug. 1941, BA-MA, 20. Armee, 19070/2, and army order of Army Command Norway, Headquarters Finland, Abt. Ia No. 79/41 g.Kdos. Chefs., 6 Oct. 1941, BA-MA, XXXVI. AK, 24307/2.

[71] On the supply problems see Hess, *Eismeerfront*.

[72] The 'Home Staff Overseas' had been created in summer 1941 from the 'Home Staff North' of the 'Wehrmacht Commander Norway' based in Berlin, to provide unified direction of the transport preparations; it was subordinate to OKW and was instructed to co-operate with 'Wehrmacht Transport Control Berlin' of BdE. It was also responsible for supply to the Mediterranean and North Africa. See *Hitler's Directives*, 80.

[73] See Home Staff Overseas of OKW, Abt. Ia B. No. 161/41 g.Kdos. Chefs., on transport planning on the basis of Directive No. 37, to OKW/WFSt, 11 Nov. 1941, BA-MA, 20. Armee, 58628/1. See also Halder, *Diaries*, 1322–4 (29 Nov. 1941), and the account of the former German transport officer in Helsinki: Erfurth, 'Transportdienststellen', 13–16, 17–19.

[74] *Hitler's Directives*, 100. See also Erfurth, *Finnischer Krieg*, 72 ff. In his letter to Mannerheim of 22 Sept. 1941 Keitel on Hitler's behalf requested the Finnish government's agreement to this railway building, commenting that 'it is a matter of course that this railway will later pass into Finnish ownership'; chief of OKW, WFSt/Abt. L No. 441580/41 g.Kdos. Chefs. to C.-in-C. of the Finnish armed forces, FM Mannerheim, 22 Sept. 1941, BA-MA, 20. Armee, 58628/2.

abandoned after a report by Todt to Hitler. As a substitute, Hitler ordered the extension of the road from northern Norway through Karasjoki–Inari to Ivalo.[75]

In the winter of 1941–2 the Gulfs of Bothnia and Finland were frozen for months on end; sea transport along the north Norwegian coast to the North Cape was subjected to a virtual blockade by British naval operations after October 1941 and brought to a total standstill for a time. At this stage the army in Lapland faced a critical supply situation (see Diagram II.III.1.)[76] It could only be alleviated by increased recourse to the material reserves in the north Norwegian depots. Thereafter, from the beginning of 1942, the Wehrmacht High Command ordered advanced planning and stockpiling of the entire supply requirements of the German troops in Finland for almost a full year, in order to make them independent of supplies from home for longer periods.[77] At the same time the 'Finland Branch of Home Staff Overseas' and the post of 'German Transport Plenipotentiary in Finland' were established in Helsinki to ensure better co-ordination of the entire supply and transport needs of the Wehrmacht.[78] In autumn 1941 the Luftwaffe had already set up the 'Air Region Staff Finland' to make better use of the limited supply capacity. In general, the problem of supply and communications was severely restricting German operations in northern Finland.[79]

(d) Balance Sheet of Military Operations in Northern Finland to 1941–1942

By the end of 1941, six months after the launching of German–Finnish operations in northern Finland, the units of High Command Norway had advanced between 30 and 75 km. into Soviet territory. In none of the three corps sectors, however, had they achieved the operational objective of capturing the Murmansk railway; nor had they managed to make a decisive breakthrough which would have improved prospects for its capture. By the end of July 1941 the heavy fighting and casualties of the first few weeks had already led the Wehrmacht High Command to discuss halting the attack on the front controlled by Army Command Norway 'until the progress of operations on the main front, with Army Group North, affects the situation in Finland'.[80] It

[75] Chief of OKW, WFSt/Abt. L No. 441707/41 g.Kdos. Chefs. to C.-in-C. of Finnish armed forces, FM Baron Mannerheim, 13 Oct. 1941, BA-MA, 20. Armee, 58628/2.

[76] See the 'memorandum on the supply situation' of Army Command Norway, OQu/Qu 1 Br. No. 334/41 g.Kdos., 26 Nov. 1941, BA-MA RH 2/v. 428, and Falkenhorst's visit to Gen. Erfurth on 10 Nov. 1941, papers of Gen. Erfurth, diary, i. 228 ff., BA-MA N 257/1.

[77] In autumn 1940 Hitler had ordered that the German troops in northern Norway be supplied 'with provisions for 1 year, with ammunition for 6 equipments', but this had been possible only for three months. See Report on the transfer of the Mountain Corps to Northern Norway, 15 Aug.–15 Nov. 1940, 8, BA-MA, XIX. Geb.K., 23450, and ibid. RW 4/v. 769.

[78] See OKW Home Staff Overseas, Abt. Ia No. 280/42 g.Kdos. on 'provisional service regulations for Field Agency Finland of Home Staff Overseas', 20 Jan. 1942, BA-MA Wi/VI. 119; also Erfurth, 'Transportdienststellen', 19, and papers of Gen. Erfurth, diary, i. 268, BA-MA N 257/1.

[79] See Andreas Nielsen, Einsatz der deutschen Luftwaffe im finnischen Raum, BA-MA Lw 118/5.

[80] Telex OKW/WFSt No. 001524/41 g.Kdos. to Army Command Norway/Headquarters Finland, 20 July 1941, BA-MA, 20. Armee, 58628/1.

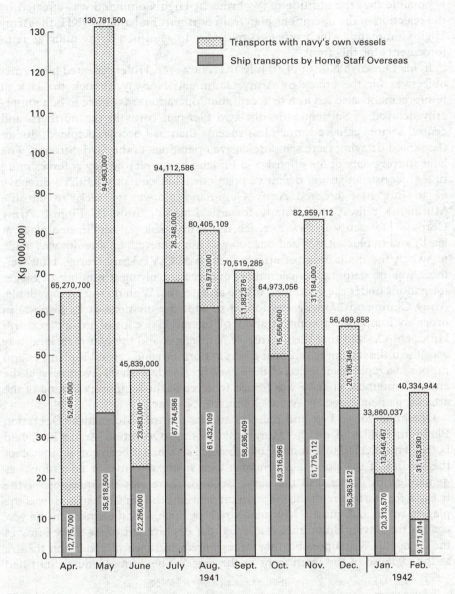

DIAGRAM II.III.1. Total Supply Transports to Norway and Finland April 1941
February 1942

Source: Individual reports in BA-MA RW 4/v. 769.

is possible that the attitude of Wehrmacht High Command was affected by the rejection of the operations plan from northern Finland by OKH, the Army High Command, which was also reluctant to send new army units as reinforcements for this front.

In his Directive No. 33 of 19 July 1941, however, Hitler repeated his former objectives for the attack by Army Command Norway, though the lack of reinforcements also led him to accept that 'operations may have to be temporarily delayed'.[81] Subsequently, the two German corps in the northern and central sectors achieved much less success than had been anticipated, due to the skilled delaying tactics and defensive operations of the Soviet troops. The later starting-date of the offensive in Finland had given the Soviet forces more time to construct strong defensive positions. Consequently, Hitler's directive of 30 July 1941 ordered Army Command Norway to seek 'to cut the Murmansk railway, particularly towards Louchi', using III Finnish Army Corps.[82] The aim was now to reach the Murmansk railway 'in one place at least', and to block it.[83] When this too was not achieved, an attempt was made to switch the main point of attack back to XXXVI Army Corps. However, there was no genuine concentration of forces involving a number of bigger formations under the command of one army corps. With no reserves available, Army Command Norway was forced to split the divisions at its disposal in order to improvise a concentration of operational control in one sector.[84] Hitler emphasized that the capture of Murmansk and the Murmansk railway was 'the ultimate aim of our operations in northern and central Finland',[85] and proposed a rapid resumption of the attack on Kandalaksha. Neverthless, at the end of September 1941 he was forced to agree to the temporary halting of the attacks, as demanded by Army Command Norway.

Operation Silver Fox and the two attacks towards Murmansk (Operation Platinum Fox) and on the Murmansk railway (Operation Arctic Fox) had failed. This fact led to a number of debates. First, had it been correct to accept the seizure of the port of Murmansk as a main objective of operations, as demanded by Hitler and the navy? Second, there was the question of the reasons for the failure of the German offensive from Finnish Lapland: was the plan to reach and cut the Murmansk railway such a vital element in the war against the Soviet Union that it justified the deployment of an entire army in the far north? Was it possible that forces were being squandered in this theatre at the expense of the main front in the east?[86] The Army General Staff had

---

[81] *Hitler's Directives*, 88.   [82] Ibid. 92, and *DGFP* D xiii, No. 164.

[83] Army order Army Command Norway No. 43/41 g.Kdos. Chefs., 23 July 1941, BA-MA, III. finn. AK, 19654/2.

[84] See telex of Col.-Gen. von Falkenhorst No. 63/41 g.Kdos. Chefs. to OKW, Gen. Jodl, 12 Sept. 1941, BA-MA, 20. Armee, 58628/1.

[85] *Hitler's Directives*, 99–101.

[86] On criticism of OKW operational planning for Army Command Norway and the reasons for its failures see papers of Col.-Gen. von Falkenhorst, iv. 55, BA-MA N 300/4; Hess, *Eismeerfront*, 111–18; Hölter, *Armee in der Arktis*, 17 ff.; Erfurth, 'Murman-Bahn', 281–95; also Seaton, *Der russisch-deutsche Krieg*, 118–19.

from the start been severely critical of the German attack from northern Finland because 'the whole undertaking is an expedition, not an operation'.[87] However, the Wehrmacht High Command took the view that the Murmansk railway was of such strategic significance as a supply-line for the delivery of vital war materials from the Western Allies that it was essential to deploy the German army in Norway on this most northerly front.[88] In addition, there were political reasons for this choice of operational objective. Hitler believed that the severance of the supply-line would have a powerful psychological effect in both London and Moscow, particularly since it had been extended in 1941 by the construction of a connecting line from Sorokka–Obozerskaya to the Archangel railway.[89] As a result, the prevailing opinion was that it was more important to cut off the Murmansk railway than to capture Murmansk, despite the demands of the navy. It is possible that, after a successful assault on Kandalaksha, an attack on Murmansk along the railway line from the south might have had more chance of success than a direct advance from Petsamo through pathless tundra to the east.[90] Further criticism was levelled at the decision to allow Mountain Corps Norway to launch a frontal attack through the broken tundra towards Murmansk without providing adequate reserves or strength in depth.[91]

It seems that Army Command Norway already faced an almost impossible task in trying to provide sufficient forces to attack both Murmansk and the Murmansk railway. A third operational objective, one of equal importance, the attack of Finnish III Corps through Kiestinki towards Louchi, was then added. This development tends to support the view that the attacking forces, already relatively small, were being needlessly dispersed. In these circumstances it is difficult to discount criticism both of the thinking of the supreme leadership and of the operational planning and objectives assigned to Army Command Norway. In retrospect, it is easy to 'blame' the Finnish High Command for its failure to concentrate its forces and provide them with sufficient strength. However, it is exceedingly doubtful that the Finns should have claimed that it was impossible to deploy and supply more than two divisions per sector at any one time, even given the low supply capacity available to them.[92] An energetic advance by XXXVI Army Corps on

[87] On the assessment of the Army General Staff see Halder, *Diaries*, 919 (14 May 1941), and letter Asst. Chief of Staff IV, Maj.-Gen. Matzky, to Military Attaché Stockholm, Maj.-Gen. von Uthmann, 21 Sept. 1941, BA-MA III H 1001/19.

[88] See esp. Hölter, *Armee in der Arktis*, 19 ff., 79–80. The Murmansk railway, built during the First World War as a single-track line, was electrified along the Kandalaksha–Murmansk sector in 1941–2. Between 10 and 15 pairs of trains travelled along it each day in both directions.

[89] Halder, *Diaries*, 1005–8 (5 July 1941); also Polvinen, *Finland i stormaktspolitiken*, 30.

[90] See *General Dietl*, 228–9.

[91] See letter from the former commander of 6th Mountain Div, Maj.-Gen. Schörner, to Maj.-Gen. Buschenhagen of Army Command Norway, parts of which are published in Ruef, *Odyssee*, 156.

[92] Ruef, *Zwischen Kreta und Murmansk*, 216. See also Hölter, *Armee in der Arktis*, 17, 19, which repeats the comments of Buschenhagen regarding the consultation by the Finnish side during operational planning.

Kandalaksha involving several divisions—as envisaged during the operational planning of 'Silver Fox'—would undoubtedly have provided the main thrust of the offensive and a starting-point for subsequent operations against Murmansk.[93] However, the failure of SS Division North, along with the decision to leave 163rd Infantry Division in the Finnish sector of the front in the south, reduced the attacking forces in this army sector by half. Concentration of forces could be achieved only by a repeated splitting of the divisions. On 23 September 1941 General Dietl had complained to the Wehrmacht Operations Staff about the lack of adequate concentration.[94] The reply of General Jodl, Chief of the Wehrmacht Operations Staff, reveals that the Wehrmacht High Command was well aware that the forces deployed on this 'secondary front' on the Arctic Ocean were insufficient to achieve major success. Army Command Norway and General Dietl's mountain corps had already noted that the artillery provision was inadequate. It appears that these failings were the result of the opinion of the supreme leadership that the German divisions in northern Finland were fighting in a less significant 'secondary theatre of operations', despite being assigned the strategic objectives of Murmansk and the Murmansk railway.[95]

From July 1941, depending on local reports of success from Mountain Corps Norway, XXXVI Army Corps, and Finnish III Corps, the Wehrmacht High Command and Hitler repeatedly changed their minds about the future main focus of operations in the region. Finally, on 10 October 1941, Hitler ordered a halt to the offensive along the entire army front due to the failure of all three attacking thrusts.[96] At the end of October the reorganization and amalgamation of several German divisions were announced and demands were made for Finnish participation in yet another large-scale winter offensive on Kandalaksha. However, an operation of this type proved impracticable in winter 1941–2 due to the inadequate winter training of the German divisions and the need for additional Finnish reinforcements. Furthermore, it became apparent that army command's assessment of Finnish military and political war aims had been incorrect in assuming that the cutting of the Murmansk railway link was 'also of decisive significance for Finnish political and military objectives'. This led to the mistaken assumption that the Germans could always rely on the availability of Finnish divisions for an assault on Kandalaksha.[97]

The fact was that the German offensive had nowhere achieved its objectives, while the Finns had achieved at least some successes. This not only created a sense of disappointment in Finland and an attitude of resignation and pessi-

---

[93] Ziemke, *German Northern Theater*, 185.

[94] Dietl's letter to Gen. Jodl and his reply are printed in *General Dietl*, 231–3 (also for the following).

[95] Ruef, *Odyssee*, 162.

[96] *Hitler's Directives*, 101–4, and *DGFP* D xiii, No. 395.

[97] See telex Army Command Norway, Headquarters Finland, Abt. Ia No. 78/41 g.Kdos. Chefs. to Liaison Staff North Inf. Gen. Erfurth, 3 Oct. 1941, BA-MA, 20. Armee, 58628/1.

mism among the German troops, but also led to German–Finnish ill feeling as a result of the persistent requests for Finnish reinforcements.[98] Differences of opinion over the prospects for the subsequent conduct of the war in the north could not be eliminated altogether. Personal talks involving Major-General Warlimont, Colonel-General von Falkenhorst, Infantry General Erfurth, and Field Marshal Mannerheim were held on 15–16 November and 13–14 December 1941 in Helsinki and Rovaniemi. Even then, there was no real agreement on a genuine coalition to wage the war.[99] Mannerheim in fact established a link between the conquest of Leningrad by the German army and a new offensive in northern Finland. He was thereby making Finnish participation in a further assault on Murmansk and the Murmansk railway conditional on the link-up of the German and Finnish armies on the Svir front and at Leningrad.[100]

Apart from the failure to establish a focal point of attack and the resulting inadequacy of forces in all three army sectors, a number of other reasons played a part in the failure of Operation Silver Fox. These involved difficulties in obtaining supplies to satisfy the enormous requirements of the troops; exceptional climatic and geographical conditions in the theatre of operations; the perfunctory provision and inadequate allocation of reserves; the lack of a joint German–Finnish war effort under a unified command; inadequate air and naval support; inaccurate assessment of the forces and potential of the enemy and his familiarity with climatic and geographical conditions.[101] Purely political factors also played a part in the failure of Army Command Norway. At the very beginning of the operation the staffs of the future port commanders of Murmansk and Archangel were set up prematurely in Norway—clear evidence that the Germans greatly underestimated the difficulty of the attacks on Murmansk and the Murmansk railway.[102]

In his Directive No. 39 of 8 December 1941 Hitler called a halt to all major attacking operations. The decision was publicly confirmed in his proclamation to the soldiers of the army and the Waffen-SS on 19 December 1944. This directive, and the switch to defensive operations in manpower-saving positions, also affected the operations of Army Command Norway in northern

---

[98] Halder, *Diaries*, 1152 (4 Aug. 1941), 1226 (12 Sept. 1941); also papers of Col.-Gen. von Falkenhorst, iv. 58, BA-MA N 300/4; letter from Military Attaché Helsinki to Asst. Chief of Staff IV, 31 July 1941, BA-MA III H 1001/8. On the attitude of the troops see order of Army Command Norway No. 1634/41 g.Kdos., 29 Sept. 1941, BA-MA, 20. Armee, 58628/1; Halder, *Diaries*, 1297 (5 Nov. 1941). On the 'rather cool' rejection of German wishes by FM Mannerheim see Erfurth, *Finnischer Krieg*, 84 ff.

[99] See memorandum on the discussions in BA-MA, 20. Armee, 58628/1 and 19070/3; also Erfurth, *Finnischer Krieg*, 84 ff.

[100] Erfurth, *Finnischer Krieg*, 86 ff.

[101] On the 'lack of a concrete conception of the enemy' and the resulting 'hybrid sense of superiority' see esp. Hillgruber, 'Rußland-Bild', 305 ff., 309–10. On the tendency to ignore and underestimate information on the strength of the USSR provided by the Finnish intelligence service see Mäkelä, *Im Rücken des Feindes*, 74.

[102] Rüf, *Gebirgsjäger*, 17.

Finland.[103] In view of the serious position along the entire eastern front, in December 1940 the Army High Command even considered a withdrawal of troops from Finland to meet the manpower needs of the main front.[104] Ultimately, Hitler's plan for the 'resumption of the offensive struggle'[105] had to be postponed until spring 1942, in northern Finland as elsewhere. The projected winter offensive against Kandalaksha was abandoned. When Mannerheim proposed to launch an offensive against Sorokka in spring 1942, the Wehrmacht High Command agreed all the more readily because this was to be undertaken mainly by the Finnish Army.[106] Though it is doubtful that the attack on the Murmansk railway was 'dictated by strategic reasons', the unsuccessful course of the German–Finnish attack on Murmansk and the White Sea can certainly be described as 'one of the missed opportunities in the Second World War'.[107]

(e) New Strategic Deliberations after the Turn of 1941–1942

At the turn of 1941–2, after German failure in the northernmost sector of operations against the Soviet Union, the United States entered the war. This event helped to provoke a fundamental change in the assessment of the position and tasks of German troops on the 'northern flank of the European eastern front' in northern Finland and northern Norway.[108] Even in autumn 1941, fears of a possible British landing near Murmansk or in northern Norway—exacerbated by the American occupation of Iceland in July—had led to Hitler's demand for the northern flank to be secured by strong naval forces and for further reinforcement of the Wehrmacht Commander in Norway by one or two highly mobile or armoured divisions.[109] These deliberations were given new impetus by the entry of the United States into the war on 7 December 1941, and by surprise British naval and landing operations at Vestvågøy (Vestfjord, Lofoten) and Måløy (north of Bergen on North Fjord). The new office of 'Admiral Arctic Ocean' (Admiral Schmund), established in mid-October 1941, took command of all naval operations in the Arctic Ocean. By taking control of the office of 'Admiral Polar Coast' in Tromsö, this office also became responsible for coastal defence. At the turn of the year 'Admiral Norway', Admiral-General Boehm, drew attention to the great danger of a

[103] *Hitler's Directives*, 107–10, and *DGFP* D xiii, No. 564; also the 'Proclamation by the Führer' after Hitler took supreme command over the army, 19 Dec. 1941, BA-MA RS 3-6/7.
[104] Halder, *Diaries*, 1356 (14 Dec. 1941).
[105] 'Proclamation by the Führer' (as n. 103 above).
[106] Erfurth, *Finnischer Krieg*, 89.
[107] Hölter, *Armee in der Arktis*, 80.
[108] On the fundamental change in the military and political situation see Wehrmacht Commander Norway, Ia No. 5129/41 g.Kdos. Chefs. on 'Assessment of the military situation in Norway', and telex of von Falkenhorst No. 2853/41 g.Kdos., to OKW, WFSt, Abt. L, 25 and 26 Dec. 1941, BA-MA, 20. Armee, 19070/4; also the position adopted by Abt. L in WFSt No. 442262/41 g.Kdos. Chefs. II. Ang., 27 Dec. 1941, and by WFSt/Op (H) No. 55013/42 g.Kdos. Chefs. as 'memorandum to Chef WFSt', 2 Jan. 1942; both in BA-MA RW 4/v. 639; also Ziemke, *German Northern Theater*, 213 ff.; Salewski, *Seekriegsleitung*, ii. 1–52.
[109] Halder, *Diaries*, 1290–1 (8 Nov. 1941), 1338–9 (6 Dec. 1941).

British attack on Norway.[110] Hitler was now convinced that the entire theatre in the north had become 'more significant'; he even regarded the defence of northern Norway as 'of decisive importance for the war'.[111] However, Army Command Norway reported that an Anglo-American landing operation on the north Norwegian coast could not be prevented with the defensive forces available. The need, therefore, was to reinforce coastal defences and to improve fuel supplies; such steps were essential to safeguard northern Finland and northern Norway against Soviet attacks on the Gulf of Bothnia and northern Scandinavia, and against Allied landings and attacks on the north Swedish ore regions at Kiruna–Gällivare. New priority was to be given to overall 'protection of the front to the west . . . from Kirkenes to the Spanish border'. The position of Norway was deemed to be particularly exposed following American entry into the war: British–American action against the Norwegian and Finnish Arctic coasts was now considered possible and even 'likely' in co-ordination with Soviet land operations.[112] Such developments appeared more feasible since the attitude of Sweden was deemed to be uncertain.

Hitler and the Wehrmacht High Command calculated that a major Allied landing was possible in northern Norway in spring 1942.[113] From the beginning of that year there were renewed efforts to improve Norway's defensive capability. In a discussion at his headquarters on 22 January 1942 Hitler ordered 'considerable reinforcement of army personnel and material' for units in Norway, the 'zone of destiny of this war'.[114] As far as possible, the Luftwaffe was also to scrape some units together.[115] The new basic 'operations directive for the defence of Norway' was issued by the Wehrmacht High Command on 18 January 1942.[116] Accordingly, various reinforcements including fortification battalions were sent to the Wehrmacht Commander Norway to be assigned to Higher Commands LXX (under Mountain Troop General Valentin Feuerstein in southern Norway) and XXXIII (under Cavalry General Georg Brandt in central Norway), and to the sector staff (with Lieutenant-General Nagy as commander in the polar region). However, the army and Luftwaffe

[110] Admiral Norway, B. No. g.Kdos., 295 A I Chefs., 'The military situation of Norway: Tasks and conclusions for the Navy', 8 Jan. 1942, BA-MA, 20. Armee, 35641.

[111] See report of Asst. Chief of Staff I, Lt.-Gen. Paulus, 'to Chief of Operations Dept.', 15 Dec. 1941, BA-MA RH 2/v. 428, and 'Führer Conferences', 243 ff. See also Salewski, *Seekriegsleitung*, i. 458 ff.

[112] See Hitler's proclamation of 19 Dec. 1941 (n. 103 above); letter of Maj.-Gen. Buschenhagen to Maj.-Gen. Warlimont, 19 Dec. 1941, BA-MA, 20. Armee, 19070/4, and Army Command Norway, Headquarters Finland, Ia No. 147/41 g.Kdos. Chefs., army order of 21 Dec. 1941, ibid., XXXVI. AK, 24,307/2. See also Warlimont, *Hauptquartier*, 209, 250–1.

[113] See notes of Wehrmacht Commander Norway for discussions on 28 Jan. 1942, 24 Jan. 1942, BA-MA, 20 Armee, 35641; 'Führer Conferences', 246 ff. In contrast, the Finnish government considered this 'not very probable': see *ADAP* E i. 349.

[114] 'Führer Conferences', 246–9.

[115] Ibid. 260 (7 Feb. 1942).

[116] OKW No. 00226/42 g.Kdos. WFSt/Op., 'Battle instructions for the defence of Norway', 18 Jan. 1942, BA-MA, 20. Armee, 35641.

found it impossible to assemble substantial defensive forces. In order to achieve at least a deterrent effect against possible Allied landings, while also facilitating the disruption of Allied convoys from Scotland to Murmansk and Archangel, Hitler ordered the transfer to Norway of the battleships *Tirpitz*, *Scharnhorst*, and *Gneisenau*, the heavy cruisers *Prinz Eugen* and *Admiral Scheer*, and additional destroyers, U-boats, and naval vessels.[117] To that end, Hitler demanded that the *Scharnhorst*, *Gneisenau*, and *Prinz Eugen* should return from the Atlantic port of Brest and break through the Channel into home waters. This was achieved on 11–12 February 1942 as Operation Cerberus. By mid-May 1942 the heavy cruisers *Admiral Hipper* and *Lützow* had also entered the waters of northern Norway. In the same way, the Luftwaffe was instructed to concentrate torpedo Staffeln in the northern Arctic in order to launch effective and 'successful' attacks on enemy convoys and ports on the Murmansk coast. Hitler and the Wehrmacht Operations Staff were well aware that 'to strengthen the forces in the Arctic Ocean . . . it is necessary to accept a weakening of the deployment in other areas'. To this end, Hitler held that 'in particular, ocean reconnaissance over the Atlantic, the range of which was no longer sufficient for the U-boat operations there, [could] be considerably reduced'.[118]

Norway itself was therefore regarded by the German leaders as 'the key point of European defence in 1942' and a possible 'main theatre of war'. As such, it had to be defended by providing replacement formations and units from all branches of the armed forces in the west.[119] Consequently, there was no prospect that new formations from Norway would be dispatched to the German forces operating in northern Finland or northern Russia. Instead, the army command in northern Finland was additionally instructed 'always to have sufficient reserves on the Arctic coast to deal with a major attack on the coast'.[120]

Hitler frequently referred to the possibility and even likelihood of American–British action in Norway. These fears and prophecies clearly demonstrate that, within the framework of his overall continental strategy, he regarded an enemy invasion of Norway as potentially decisive for the entire course of the war. Given this background, it is no surprise that all three Wehrmacht services were ordered to transfer forces to the Norwegian region, despite the fact that

[117] 'Memorandum' OKW/WFSt/Op. (M) No. 55598/42 g.Kdos Chefs., 1 Apr. 1942, BA-MA RW 4/v. 639, and 'Führer Conferences', 260, 261, 246–9; Bidlingmaier, *Seegeltung*, 246–7; *Sea Power*, 555.

[118] Directive of 'the Führer and Supreme Commander of the Wehrmacht—OKW/WFSt/Op. (M) No. 55493 g.Kdos. Chefs., 14 Mar. 1942', KR telex to C.-in-C.s of the navy and Luftwaffe, to Wehrmacht Commander Norway, Army Command Lapland, and C.-in-C. of the army, BA-MA RW 4/v. 639.

[119] This was the assessment in Wehrmacht Commander in Norway, Ia No. 12/42 g.Kdos. Chefs., 'Directive for the defence of Norway', 27 Jan. 1942, and minutes of discussion with the commanding generals and divisional commanders on 28 Jan. 1942 in Oslo: both in BA-MA, 20. Armee, 35641.

[120] 'Führer directive' No. 55493 g.Kdos.Chefs., 14 Mar. 1942 (see n. 118 above).

they could scarcely be dispensed with on the other fronts. The navy was most affected by this development. In this case, the switch to Hitler's assessment of the situation and the creation of a strategic concentration in Norway also suggested that the Atlantic battleship strategy of the Commander-in-Chief of the Navy, Grand Admiral Raeder, had to be regarded as having failed.[121]

At this stage a proposal emanating from Air Fleet 5, and based on earlier discussions within Army Command Norway in May 1941, was revived. This suggested that Spitsbergen should be occupied in spring 1942 in order to improve the prospects for destroying enemy naval transports and to enable early weather forecasts to be made for attacks on the convoys by air and sea. The proposal was opposed by the Wehrmacht Operations Staff on the grounds that it would involve 'considerable new burdens in a wide variety of areas when conditions are already difficult in the Arctic'.[122] In particular, there seemed no prospect of providing stocks of supplies adequate to cope with the extensive requirements of a Luftwaffe base. The Wehrmacht Operations Staff reported:

According to the proposal, the occupation of Spitsbergen is designed to improve our *attacking* potential. However, it is highly probable that a situation would be created in which we could not exploit the new position due to the lack of secure sea routes, and would instead be forced to commit valuable transport capacity and fighting forces at sea and in the air, which could otherwise have been used to attack from Norway, to the *defence* of the base [Spitsbergen].

Since the value of a base on Spitsbergen 'would bear no relation to the expense necessary to acquire and maintain it', Hitler decided on 22 March 1942 'that an occupation of Spitsbergen should not be undertaken'.[123] The decision not to attempt the capture of Spitsbergen demonstrates that German forces and potential were inadequate to establish the air and sea superiority necessary for the conduct of the war in this region. Wehrmacht High Command regarded the military situation, especially at sea, as so greatly strained 'even now' that any improvement of the German strategic position had to be abandoned in favour of the 'scraping together' of forces to repel an expected Allied landing on the Norwegian coast. On the other hand, the proposals reflected the positively Utopian wishful thinking of the operations staffs of the army and Luftwaffe. In reality, the navy was unable to mount any offensive operations against Allied convoy vessels in the Arctic Ocean because of a lack of air support. In spring 1942, according to information from Naval Group Com-

---

[121] Salewski, *Seekriegsleitung*, ii. 16, refers to a '180-degree about-face'.

[122] OKW/WFSt/Op. No. 55518/42 g.Kdos. Chefs., 'Memorandum on Spitsbergen', 18 Mar. 1942, BA-MA RW 4/v. 639, and telex Mountain Corps Norway, Ia No. 37/41 g.Kdos. Chefs. to Army Command Norway, 28 May 1941, BA-MA XIX. Geb.Korps, 15085/33 (also for the following quote).

[123] OKW/WFSt/Op. (M) No. 555377/42 g.Kdos. Chefs., 'Subject: Spitsbergen', 22 Mar. 1942, BA-MA RW 4/v. 639.

mand North, the 'grotesque picture' had developed in which the enemy 'is chasing [the German navy] out of the coastal approaches while he himself puts to sea there unmolested'.[124]

The changed assessment of the military situation in Norway also influenced Hitler's decision of 7 November 1941 to divide the command of German troops in Norway and northern Finland. The plan was to establish a new army command for the Finnish theatre—first projected as 'Army Northland'.[125] On 27 December 1941 Colonel-General von Falkenhorst was recalled to Oslo in his function as 'Wehrmacht Commander Norway'. In place of the former 'Headquarters Finland' of Army Command Norway, an 'Army Command Lapland' was established and took over the sector of the front in northern Finland on 14 January 1942. Despite Falkenhorst's plea that the defence of the whole of Norway should be kept under unified command,[126] the new 'Army Command Lapland' also became involved in the task of defending Norway when Mountain Corps Norway, under its new commanding general, Lieutenant-General Schörner, was instructed to take over coastal defence in the Varanger area west of Kirkenes as far as Tana Fjord.[127] Moreover, for purposes of political administration the area continued to come under the control of the Reich Commissioner for Norway, Gauleiter Josef Terboven. The change of command demonstrated that the recalled Colonel-General von Falkenhorst was being held responsible for the failure of the offensive. By appointing Dietl, a personal favourite who was also respected in Finland, Hitler was apparently hoping to regain the confidence of Finnish headquarters in the German conduct of the war, and to avoid further differences with Mannerheim concerning the conduct of operations in northern Finland.[128]

Plans for the creation of a joint high command for the German–Finnish front as part of this reorganization also came under discussion for a short time. These schemes, which would have subordinated Dietl and 'Army Command Lapland' to the Finnish commander-in-chief, were not realized.[129] A proposal along those lines by the Wehrmacht High Command to the Finnish High Command, and to Infantry General Heinrichs on his visit to the Führer's headquarters on 6 January 1942, was not accepted. Instead, Wehrmacht

[124] War diary Naval Group Command North, 12 Mar. 1942, taken from Salewski, *Seekriegsleitung*, ii. 28.

[125] See implementation instruction No. 1 to Directive No. 37, *Hitlers Weisungen*, 164 (not in trans.). See also Halder, *Diaries*, 1312 (23 Nov. 1941).

[126] See telex Army Command Norway, Headquarters Finland, Abt. Ia No. 116/41 g.Kdos. Chefs. to OKW/WFSt z. Hd. Maj.-Gen. Warlimont, 18 Nov. 1941, BA-MA, 20. Armee, 58628/1; Org. Abt. (I) No. 3573/41 g.Kdos., minutes 'Result of discussions with Army Command Norway Headquarters Finland on 30 Nov. and 1 Dec. 1941', 5 Dec. 1941, BA-MA RH 2/v. 428.

[127] OKW No. 003043/41 g.Kdos. WFSt/Abt. L (I Op) on 'Assumption of command Army Command Lapland', 21 Dec. 1941, BA-MA, 20. Armee, 19070/4.

[128] See papers of Col.-Gen. von Falkenhorst, iv. 67–8, BA-MA N 300/4; Ziemke, *German Northern Theater*, 183–4.

[129] Papers of Gen. Erfurth, diary, i. 244, BA-MA N 257/1; Erfurth, *Finnischer Krieg*, 86.

DIAGRAM II.III.2. Disposition of Forces in Finland (North to South) as of January–February 1942

GERMANY/FINLAND	SOVIET UNION

Admiral Norway
Cmdg.Adm.: Adm.-Gen. Boehm
└─ Adm. Arctic Ocean
   Vice-Adm. Schmundt
   └─ Adm. Polar Coast
      Rear-Adm. Schenk

Naval forces of ARCTIC FLEET
C.-in-C.: Rear-Adm. Golovko

Air Fleet 5
Chief of Air Fleet: Col.-Gen. Stumpff
Chief of Staff: Col. (Gen. Staff) Nielsen
├─ Luftwaffe Gen. North Norway (Lt.-Gen. Bruch)
└─ Air Leader North (East) (Col. Holle)

Air forces of the KARELIAN FRONT

Army Command Lapland
C.-in-C.: Mtn. Troop Gen. Dietl
Chief of Staff: Maj. -Gen. Jodl
├─ (XIX) Mtn. Corps Norway: (Lt.-Gen. Schörner)
│ ├─ 6th Mtn. Div. (Maj.-Gen. Philipp)
│ └─ 2nd Mtn. Div. (Col. von Hengl)
├─ XXXVI (Mtn.) A.Co.: Inf. Gen. Weisenberger
│ ├─ 169th Inf. Div. (Lt.-Gen. Tittle)
│ ├─ Elements of 163rd Inf. Div. (1 Regt.)
│ └─ Remainder of withdrawn 3rd Mtn. Div.
└─ (Finn.) III Corps (Maj.-Gen. Siilasvuo)
  ├─ Finn. Div. Gp. 'F' (= elements of Finn. 3rd Div.)
  ├─ (Finn.) 6th Div. (Maj.-Gen. Viham)
  ├─ Finn. Div. Gp. 'J' (Col. Palojärvi)
  └─ SS Div. 'Nord' (SS Brigadefübrer Demelhuber)

KARELIAN FRONT
C.-in-C.: Lt.-Gen. Frolov
Chief of Geno Staff: Col. Skvirsky
├─ Fourteenth Armys (Maj.-Gen. Panin)
│ ├─ 14th Rifle Div.
│ ├─ 52nd Rifle Div.
│ └─ 42nd Rifle Corps (Maj.-Gen. Shevchenko)
│   ├─ 104th Rifle Div.
│   └─ 122nd Rifle Div.
└─ Operational Army Group 'Kem'
C.-in-C.: Maj.-Gen. Nikisin
Chief of Staff: Col. Birman
├─ 88th Rifle Div.
└─ 54th Rifle Div.
   Elements of 186th Rifle Div. ('Polar Div.')

Finnish Army
C.-in-C.: FM Mannerheim
Chief of Gen. Staff: Inf. Gen. Heinrichs
Quartermaster Gen.: Maj.-Gen. Airo
German Liaison Staff North: Inf. Gen. *Dr Erfurth*
├─ 14th Div. (Maj.-Gen. Raappana)
├─ Army Gp. 'Maaselka':
├─ GOC: Lt.-Gen. Laatikainen
│ ├─ II Corps
│ │ ├─ 8th Div.
│ │ └─ 3rd Brig.
│ └─ VII Corps (Maj.-Gen. Hägglund)
│   ├─ 4th Div.
│   ├─ 1st Rifle Brig.
│   └─ 2nd Rifle Brig.

   27th Rifle Div.
Operational Gp. 'Masselskaya'
├─ Elements of 186th Rifle Div.
│ ('Polar Div.')
├─ 289th Rifle Div.
├─ 367th Rifle Div.
├─ 263rd Rifle Div.
└─ 61st Brigade
Operational Gp. 'Medvezhyegorsk'
├─ 71st Rifle Div.
├─ 313th Rifle Div.
└─ Elements of 37th Rifle Div.

LENINGRAD FRONT
C.-in-C.: Lt.-Gen. Chozin
Chief of Staff: Col. Gorodetskiy
├─ Seventh Independent Army
C.-in-C.: Lt.-Gen. Gorelenko
Chief of staff:
Maj.-Gen Krutikov
├─ 272nd Rifle Div.
├─ 114th Rifle Div.
├─ 21st Rifle Div.
├─ 314th Rifle Div.
└─ 67th Rifle Div.

├─ Army Gp. 'Olonec' ('Aunus')
GOC: Lt.-Gen. Oesch
│ ├─ V Corps (Maj.-Gen. Mäkinen)
│ │ ├─ 7th Div.
│ │ └─ 11th Div.
│ └─ VI Corps (Maj.-Gen. Blick)
│   ├─ 17th Div.
│   ├─ 5th Div.
│   └─ Elements of German 163rd Inf.-Div. (Lt.-Gen. Engelbrecht)
└─ Army Gp. 'Karelian Isthmus'
GOC: Lt.-Gen. Oehquist
  ├─ 15th Div.
  ├─ 10th Div.
  ├─ 2nd Div.
  └─ 18th Div.

Twenty-third Army
C.-in-C.: Gen. Cherepanov
├─ 142nd Rifle Div.
├─ 43rd Rifle Div.
├─ 123rd Rifle Div.
└─ 291st Rifle Div.

High Command confirmed to the Finnish general that the sector currently held by Finnish III Army Corps would be taken over by German
troops.[130]

2. FINNISH ARMY OPERATIONS

(a) *Recovery of the Former Finnish Territories in Ladoga–Karelia and on the
    Karelian Isthmus*

At the German–Finnish military discussions of June 1941 the Finnish High
Command had agreed to launch an attack more or less where the Germans
requested, either west or east of Lake Ladoga. After Army Group North had
made a successful advance starting on 22 June 1941, the Army High Command demanded 'that Finland must make all preparations for starting offensive operations east of Lake Ladoga' in order to carry out the most
wide-ranging encirclement manœuvre possible. However, the operational objective was not jointly agreed.[131] Field Marshal Mannerheim accepted this
demand in his headquarters in Mikkeli only after long discussions and deliberations with General Erfurth of the 'Liaison Staff North'.[132] On 10 July 1941
Mannerheim opened the main attack on the Soviet Union in the wide-ranging
manner requested by the German general staff. The 'Karelian Army' (6
divisions) under Lieutenant-General Heinrichs was ordered to advance towards Olonec (Aunus)–Lodeynoe Pole (Lotinanpelto) on the Svir, east of
Lake Ladoga.[133] Nevertheless, every one of the Finnish army's objectives was
in Ladoga–Karelia, within the former border of 1939. It appears that
Mannerheim was exercising some caution in his acceptance of the German
proposals.[134] To reinforce the main point of attack east of Lake Ladoga,
elements of the German 163rd Infantry Division, moving on the transport
route through Sweden and originally intended for the attack on Hanko, were
placed directly under the command of the Finnish Commander-in-Chief.
With the agreement of the Army High Command, these were now to act as

---

[130] Telex OKW/WFSt/Op. No. 0087/42 g.Kdos. to Army Command Norway, Headquarters
Finland, 9 Jan. 1942, BA-MA, 20. Armee, 19070/4.

[131] See Halder, *Diaries*, 973 (24 June 1941), 975 (25 June 1941); *KTB OKW* i. 419 (24 June
1941).

[132] On Erfurth's discussions with Mannerheim and Gen. Heinrichs on the question of the main
Finnish attack see papers of Gen. Erfurth, diary, i. 43–9 (25–8 June 1941), BA-MA N 257/1; also
Erfurth, *Finnischer Krieg*, 43; Halder, *Diaries*, 989 (29 June 1941), 1019 (9 July 1941). A survey of
the discussion among Finnish researchers on the question of Mannerheim's plan of operations can
be found in Manninen, 'Syväri vai Kannas', 5–43, and Jägerskiöld, *Marskalken av Finland*, 88 ff.,
also containing parts of the Finnish operational order of 30 June 1941, 838 n. 132; on Finnish
operational leadership in general see Juutilainen, 'Operational Decisions'. On Mannerheim's
position see also Tervasmäki, *Mannerheim*.

[133] See *KTB OKW* i. 431 (10 July 1941), and Halder, *Diaries*, 1022 (10 July 1941); Mannerheim,
Memoirs, 418 ff. On the demand of Army High Command for the Finnish attack to be launched
on 10 July 1941 see papers of Gen. Erfurth, diary, i. 60–1, BA-MA N 257/1.

[134] See most recently Jägerskiöld, *Marskalken av Finland*, 106, and Manninen, 'Syväri vai
Kannas', 38.

reserves for the 'Karelian Army'.[135] In his order of the day on 7 July 1941 Mannerheim referred to the 'ancient and firm brotherhood-in-arms' of Finnish and German soldiers in the common struggle against 'Bolshevism and the Soviet Union'. This, it was claimed, was the guarantee of victory and a successful future for both countries.[136]

Within a few days, 5th and 11th Divisions of VI Corps (Major-General Paavo Talvela) and the mobile rifle brigades of 'Group Oinonen' (Major-General Waldemar Oinonen) had advanced rapidly to the north-east shore of Lake Ladoga at Koirinoja.[137] The Soviet formations at Sortavala were cut off. Here the Finns were helped by the fact that the Soviet command had already transferred its reserves to the German eastern front in the south. The VI Corps advanced further south along the northern shore of Lake Ladoga and, after seizing the town of Mansila on 22 July 1941, came to a halt on the former Finnish–Soviet border. Meanwhile, the advance of the German 163rd Infantry Division[138] and Finnish 1st Division towards Suojärvi (Lake Suo)—Suvilahti, and the independent operations of the Finnish 14th Division, secured the north-eastern flank of the 'Karelian Army' by linking up with Army Command Norway. A first attempt by 163rd Infantry Division to attack Suojärvi, however, had to be broken off.

At the end of July the second phase of the Finnish attack began. The VII Corps (Major-General Waldemar Hägglund), with 19th and 7th Divisions, and II Corps (Major-General Taavetti Laatikainen), based in the northern sector on the Karelian isthmus with 2nd, 15th, and 18th Divisions, advanced on the north-west shore of Lake Ladoga at Sortavala and Hiitola. Hiitola was captured on 11 August 1944. VII Corps was then relieved by the newly established I Corps (Major-General Einar Mäkinen). With 7th, 19th, and 2nd Divisions, I Corps succeeded in driving the Soviet troops from Sortavala in mid-August and taking the town on 16 August 1941. The II Corps took the town of Käkisalmi (Kexholm) on the western shore of Lake Ladoga shortly afterwards. Despite the rapid Finnish advances, which had cut off many Soviet troops to the north-west of Lake Ladoga, the Soviet leadership was still able to bring a large proportion of its troops across the water to safety. Neither the

---

[135] Halder, *Diaries*, 989 (29 June 1941); *KTB OKW* i. 424 (30 June 1941), 431 (10 July 1941). See the corresponding proposal by Gen. Erfurth in telex Liaison Staff North, Ia No. 96/41, g.Kdos. Chefs., to OKW/WFSt/Abt. L, 25 June 1941, BA-MA, 20. Armee, 58628/1, and telex OKH/GenStdH/Op. Abt. I N No. 1294/41, g.Kdos. Chefs. to Army Command Norway, Headquarters Finland, 30 June 1941, ibid. 19070/2.

[136] Order of the day from Finnish C.-in-C. No. 4, 7 July 1941, BA-MA, 20. Armee, 19070/2.

[137] See the account of Finnish operations in Ziemke, *German Northern Theater*, 190–212; Erfurth, *Finnischer Krieg*, 56 ff.; Klink, 'Waffenbrüderschaft', 397 ff.; from the Finnish point of view, Kuussaari and Niitemaa, *Finlands Krig*, 18–87; Mikola, *Finland's Wars*, pp. xxi–xxiv; Mannerheim, *Memoirs*, 415–49; also Jägerskiöld, *Marskalken av Finland*, 119 ff., and *Suomen Sota*, vols. ii–iv.

[138] On 16 July 1941 163rd Inf. Div. had been placed by Mannerheim under the C.-in-C. of the 'Karelian Army', Lt.-Gen. Heinrichs. For the operations involving the division see the divisional records, BA-MA 16260/16–24.

weak Finnish air force nor the German Luftwaffe were able to prevent this development. After the conclusion of operations around Lake Ladoga, Field Marshal Mannerheim considered that the starting-point for an offensive on the Karelian isthmus had been established. In consequence, he initially rejected the demand of Army High Command for a further rapid advance to the River Svir. Instead, on 22 August 1941 Mannerheim launched an attack in the southern sector of the Karelian isthmus towards Viipuri (Viborg) with 4th, 8th, and 12th Divisions of IV Corps (Lieutenant-General Karl Lemart Oesch).[139] Though this offensive offered some prospect of relieving the German troops south of the Gulf of Finland, it carried little threat to the Soviet troops in the rear of Leningrad. Colonel-General Halder of Army High Command regarded this latter objective, to be achieved by an advance to the Svir, as much more important. The attacks of IV Corps were successful in combination with the advance of II Corps in the eastern part of the Karelian Isthmus. On 30 August 1941 the town of Viipuri was captured, and on 2 September 1941 Koivisto fell.[140] At the beginning of September 1941, after a campaign lasting four weeks, the Finns had reached the former Finnish–Soviet border along the entire width of the Karelian isthmus.

After a regrouping operation east of Lake Ladoga, troops of the freshly arrived VII Corps went into action with 'Group Engelbrecht', assembled from the German 163rd Division and 2nd Rifle Brigade. From the middle of August these troops launched an attack on the left flank of the 'Karelian Army' in the region round Lake Suo. Here too the Soviet troops were driven back across the old Finnish–Soviet border as far as Lake Syam (Säämäjärvi). However, the German 163rd Division, which participated in the attack, suffered heavy casualties. It became apparent that the division was not properly equipped for forest fighting, in which it had little experience. Moreover, by transferring a third of its units to XXXVI Army Corps on the Salla Front, it had suffered a significant loss in combat strength.[141] Following these battles, the division was moved again at the end of August; 163rd Division was held in reserve behind the 'Karelian Army' in the Salmi region on the eastern shore of Lake Ladoga. The Finnish 14th Division, maintaining the link with III Finnish Army Corps sector in the north, had captured Repola (Reboly) on 8 July 1941 and then advanced eastwards to Rukajärvi (Rugozero). There, on the orders of Mannerheim, it went over to defence in the middle of September.[142]

At the end of August and beginning of September the successful Finnish offensive tapered off at the old border. It thus became certain—as General Erfurth of 'Liaison Staff North' had realized in mid-July—that Mannerheim's objectives were limited. He was interested neither in a wide-ranging advance

[139] Mannerheim, *Memoirs*, 424 ff.

[140] See Halder, *Diaries*, 1212–15 (1 Sept. 1941).

[141] See the figures in war diary of 163rd Inf. Div., BA-MA, 163. Inf.Div., 16260/16.

[142] On the fighting involving 14th Div. see Erfurth, *Finnischer Krieg*, 54–6; Kuussaari and Niitemaa, *Finlands Krig*, 85–7; *Suomen Sota*, v. 13–79.

east of Lake Ladoga deep into Soviet territory beyond the River Svir, which would have cut Leningrad off from its eastern supply-lines and linked up with German units south of the Svir, nor in an advance on Leningrad from the Karelian isthmus.[143] Although Mannerheim used his liaison officer at Army High Command, Lieutenant-General Oehquist, to offer reassuring explanations of his conduct,[144] he had already promised President Ryti that 'under no circumstances' would he undertake an attack against Leningrad.[145]

In his Directives No. 33 of 19 July 1941 and No. 34 of 30 July 1941, as well as in his supplements to Directive No. 34,[146] Hitler had maintained his commitment to the plan for joint action by the Finnish Army and Army Group North. Consequently, in an exchange of letters with Field Marshal Mannerheim on 22 and 26 August 1941, Field Marshal Keitel sought to clarify Finland's military aims and obtain acceptance of German ideas for the next operational objectives of the Finnish Army.[147] The failure to make any binding agreement about joint conduct of the war before it began was now proving to be a serious disadvantage[148] In his reply Mannerheim made it clear that German requests were going far beyond the content of military discussions before the outbreak of the war.[149] Though he was willing to resume the attack east of Lake Ladoga through Olonec (Aunus) to the River Svir, and to contain Soviet forces by means of Finnish operations on the Karelian isthmus, Mannerheim, in agreement with President Ryti and the Finnish government, rejected the German demands. His decision was based on political reasons as well as the lack of adequate forces and the high level of casualties already sustained by the Finns. Mannerheim did not believe that the Finns could launch two simultaneous attacks, firstly on the Karelian isthmus over the old border towards Leningrad, and secondly east of Lake Ladoga over the Svir in order to link up with German troops south of the lake. He also regarded a Finnish attack on Hanko, requested by OKH, as impracticable without extensive German air and artillery support. This could not be undertaken before the conclusion of operations in the east.[150]

[143] See Erfurth's report to Army High Command: Halder, *Diaries*, 1041 (14 July 1941), and papers of Gen. Erfurth, diary, i. 66 (13 July 1941), BA-MA N 257/1.

[144] Halder, *Diaries*, 1067 (21 July 1941).

[145] Mannerheim, *Memoirs*, 416.

[146] *Hitler's Directives*, 88, 91, 95, and *DGFP* D xiii, No. 164.

[147] The letter from FM Keitel on 22 Aug. 1941 is published in *DGFP* D xviii/1, No. 228. On the accompanying letters and explanations from Gen. Erfurth of 24 Aug. and 27 Aug. 1941, and Mannerheim's reply of 26 Aug. 1941, see PA, Handakten Ritter betr. OKW 1941–1944, No. 56, and BA-MA, 20. Armee, 58628/2. See also the report in papers of Gen. Erfurth, diary, i. 118–26, BA-MA N 257/1; Jägerskiöld, *Marskalken av Finland*, 151–2.

[148] On the probelms of waging a coalition war see Ueberschär, 'Guerre de coalition', 30 ff., and id., 'Koalitionskriegführung im Zweiten Weltkrieg', 374 ff.

[149] Similar views were expressed by Lt.-Gen Heinrichs to Lt.-Gen. Engelbrecht, commander of 163rd Inf. Div.: 'The comments of Lt.-Gen. Heinrichs make it clear that on the Finnish side the German demand for the extension of operations with Finnish forces beyond the Svir was regarded as very far-reaching.' See 163rd Inf. Div., war diary 31 Aug. 1941, BA-MA 16260/16.

[150] On the discussion of the political and military reasons for Mannerheim's hesitation over proceeding with the Finnish attack see Jägerskiöld, *Marskalken av Finland*, 142 ff.

The Chief of the Finnish general staff, Lieutenant-General Edvard Fritjof Hanell, told General Erfurth of 'Liaison Staff North' that Mannerheim's caution was due to a fear that the German Army Group North might 'halt at the Volkhov and leave him with the task of advancing with the Karelian Army to the Volkhov'.[151] Moreover, the government in Helsinki had not given its unanimous consent to major incursions over the old border, and had only agreed to operations east of Lake Ladoga to the River Svir. Not until 1 September 1941 did it also give permission for a limited advance on the Karelian isthmus to straighten the front on the far side of the former border. Even this was to be done only 'to gain tactically favourable and manpower-saving positions'.[152] There was no consent for direct participation in the siege of Leningrad. Despite Jodl's discussions with the Finnish commander-in-chief at the Finnish headquarters at Mikkeli on 4 September 1941, the Finnish decision was not altered.[153]

(b) Conquest of East Karelia and Advance to the River Svir

At the beginning of September, therefore, the decision was taken to accede to German demands and resume the offensive east of Lake Ladoga towards the Svir and Lake Onega. Helsinki's previous thesis of a 'defensive struggle' against Moscow was thus undermined: Finland's war was now revealed as one of conquest. The Finnish government sought to justify the invasion of east Karelia on the grounds that it was necessary to eliminate the enemy's strategic bases of attack and favourable supply-lines in east Karelia on the far side of the old Karelian border.

On 4 September 1941 the 'Karelian Army' east of Lake Ladoga resumed the offensive.[154] On the left flank 'Group Oinonen' advanced with two brigades north of Lake Syam eastwards towards Lake Onega. In the centre VII Army Corps with 1st and 11th Divisions went on the attack between Lake Syam and Lake Vedlo towards Petrozavodsk (Äänislinna), capital of the Karelo-Finnish Soviet Republic. In the southern army sector VI Corps with three divisions (5th, 7th, and 17th) and one brigade attacked along Lake Ladoga and through Olonec towards the River Svir. By 7 September VI Corps had already reached the Svir opposite Lodeynoe Pole. Next day, the Murmansk railway was cut off at the Svir. The great success of the Finnish offensive was crowned with the

---

[151] PA, Handakten Ritter, betr. OKW 1941–1944, No. 56, and BA-MA, 20. Armee, 20844/2: Inf. Gen. Erfurth No. 441452/41, g.Kdos. to OKW/WFSt/Abt. L (Wolfsschanze), 27 Aug. 1941 (also for the following).

[152] See telex from Gen. Erfurth, Liaison Staff North, Ia No. 840/41, g.Kdos. Chefs., to OKW/WFSt/Abt. L, 1 Sept. 1941, PA, Handakten Ritter, betr. OKW 1941–1944, No. 56; telegram No. 871, Blücher to foreign ministry, 2 Sept. 1941, ibid., Büro St.S., Finnland, vol. iii; and war diary of Naval Attaché Helsingfors, ii, 31 Aug. and 1 Sept. 1941, BA-MA PG 48779–84; also Halder, *Diaries*, 1212–14 (1 Sept. 1941); Erfurth, *Finnischer Krieg*, 67; *DGFP* D xiii, No. 264.

[153] Ziemke, *German Northern Theater*, 198–9; Mannerheim, *Memoirs*, 427; Erfurth, *Finnischer Krieg*, 68–9.

[154] Erfurth, *Finnischer Krieg*, 69 ff.; Jägerskiöld, *Marskalken av Finland*, 162 ff.; and especially the memoirs of Talvela, *Sotilaan elämä*, ii. 9 ff.

capture of Petrozavodsk and the western coast of Lake Onega on 1 October 1941. The bulk of the 'Karelian Army'—including the German 163rd Infantry Division—then took up defensive positions along the Svir. However, units of 'Group Oinonen' and the newly arrived II Corps (4th and 8th Divisions, 2nd Rifle Brigade) north of Petrozavodsk advanced along the Murmansk railway to Medvezhyegorsk (Medvez haa Gora, Karhumäki) during October. But with the onset of winter, the advance became increasingly difficult and slow. Nevertheless, the troops of II Corps under Major-General Laatikainen succeeded in capturing the railway station of Medvezhyegorsk on 5 December 1941, and Povenets (Poventsa) on the Stalin Canal on 6 December. Thereafter the units north of the so-called 'Maaselkä ridge' (Mazelskaya), the isthmus between Lake Seg (Seesjärvi) and Lake Onega, went on the defensive.

German troops captured Reval at the end of August and were now approaching the suburbs of Leningrad. In consequence, the issue of a coordinated operation by Finnish and German units, and their linking up at Lake Ladoga, again became acute. Army Group North reached the Neva on 8 September 1941 and took Shlisselburg on Lake Ladoga, largely cutting Leningrad off from its land supply-routes. It seemed that the German forces still had a chance to link up with the Finnish Army. While the Soviet troops made enormous efforts to break through the ring enclosing Leningrad, Hitler decided that the objective of the operation had been achieved; further battles for the city, and the struggle to link up with the Finns, would now form a 'subsidiary theatre' of operations.[155] At the same time, armoured formations essential to its mobile attacking force (Armoured Group 4, LVII Armoured Corps) were detached from Army Group North for the attack on Moscow.

On 6 September 1941, however, Hitler's Directive No. 35 had also demanded that Leningrad should be more tightly encircled in conjunction with the Finnish units on the Karelian isthmus; 'forces of Army Group North will move north across the Neva sector as soon as possible' in order to forge the 'link-up with the Karelian Army on the Svir'.[156]

Army Group North was thus faced with two conflicting demands. It was to transfer several large formations, but was still expected to link up with the Finnish Army. The Wehrmacht High Command hoped to find a way out of this dilemma by involving the Finns more directly in the encirclement of Leningrad and demanding that the Finns should link the two armies by attacking across the Svir. On 13 and 22 September Field Marshal Keitel asked Field Marshal Mannerheim to order the 'Karelian Army' with 163rd Infantry Division to attack across the Svir towards Novaya Ladoga at the mouth of the Volkhov, there to link up with Army Group North. Since the first objective of Army Group North would be to tighten the ring round Leningrad, German troops could not initially carry out any attacks over the Neva to the north or across the lower Volkhov. In addition, Keitel led the Finnish commander-in-

---

[155] Halder, *Diaries*, 1217 (5 Sept. 1941).   [156] *Hitler's Directives*, 98.

chief to understand that the German leadership intended to starve Leningrad out rather than occupy it.[157] It had been decided that the city could 'have no more right to exist in the future reorganization of Europe'; it was consequently doomed to 'total destruction' and would be razed to the ground.[158] The region north of the Neva would then be handed over to Finland.

The Germans were thus asking Mannerheim to establish the link with Army Group North, and to participate directly in the siege of Leningrad. Demands were being made which the Finnish High Command had rejected as impracticable for political reasons since the start of the first German–Finnish discussions. Mannerheim's reply on 25 September 1941[159] was a clear rejection of all the German operational objectives. The Finnish High Command was neither willing to resume the attack on the Karelian isthmus towards Leningrad, nor to advance across the Svir. Equally, it was not prepared to abandon the planned offensive northwards to Medvezhyegorsk on the Murmansk railway as the new 'main objective of the Finnish army'. Furthermore, Mannerheim announced a reduction and reorganization of the Finnish army into brigades. It became clear that 'before winter, no further Finnish operations' would take place. Mannerheim also made it perfectly clear 'that the *German* troops of Army Group North [would have to] seek to link up with the Finns towards Lodeynoe Pole [on the Svir]', and that the capture of Leningrad was a German task.[160] Only then could new and more offensive Finnish operations be contemplated.

Despite this bold and forthright refusal, the Germans maintained their demand for Finnish accommodation. Apparently unaware of Mannerheim's attitude, Colonel-General Halder contacted the Finnish liaison officer, Lieutenant-General Oehquist, with a request 'if possible to attack on the Karelian isthmus' to contain the Soviet forces there.[161] The commander-in-chief of

[157] On the discussion of the attack on Leningrad see Abt. L No. 002099/41 g.Kdos. (I Op.), explanations of situation map for foreign ministry, 19 Sept. 1941, PA Handakten Etzdorf, betr. Rußland, and Abt. L No. 02119/41 g.Kdos. (I Op.), 'Memorandum Leningrad', 21 Sept. 1941, BA-MA RW 4/v. 578; Leeb, *Tagebuchaufzeichnungen*, 358 (17 Sept. 1941), 373–5 (12 Oct. 1941); Engel, *Heeresadjutant bei Hitler*, 108; Irving, *Hitler's War*, 303, 313; Domarus, *Hitler*, ii. 1755–6.

[158] Thus Keitel in his letter to Mannerheim: chief of OKW, WFSt/Abt. L, No. 44580/41, g.Kdos. Chefs. to commander-in-chief of Finnish armed forces, FM Mannerheim, 22 Sept. 1941, BA-MA, 20. Armee, 58628/2. See also 'Memorandum Leningrad', 22 Sept. 1941 (as n. 157 above). At the beginning of October Hitler decided once again 'that a capitulation by Leningrad or later by Moscow [should] not be accepted', according to Gen. Jodl in his letter to the C.-in-C. of the army (Ops. Dept.) on 7 Oct. 1941, No. 123-C, *IMT* xxxiv. 426. See also Army Group North, war diary, 12 Oct. 1941, BA-MA RH 19 III/168. In contrast, Army Group North initially wanted a military occupation of the city; see war diary of 15 and 17 Sept., 24 and 27 Oct. 1941, ibid. RH 19 III/167, 168; also Leeb, *Tagebuchaufzeichnungen*, 349 (5 Sept. 1941). On the economic reasons for Hitler's decision see sect. II.VI. 4 (*b*) at n. 350 (Müller).

[159] C.-in-C. of the Finnish armed forces to FM Keitel, 25 Sept. 1941, BA-MA, 20. Armee, 20844/2. (also for the following).

[160] Gen. Erfurth, Liaison Staff North, Ia No. 83/41, g.Kdos. Chefs. to OKW/WFSt/Abt. L, 25 Sept. 1941, BA-MA, 20. Armee, 58628/2 (author's emphasis). See also Army Group North, war diary, 27 and 28 Sept. 1941, BA-MA RH 19 III/167.

[161] Halder, *Diaries*, 1259 (26 Sept. 1941), 1275 (5 Oct. 1941).

Army Group North, Field Marshal Ritter von Leeb, was permitted to liaise with General Erfurth and Finnish headquarters only on 9 September 1941. Meanwhile, he too had made several requests for the Finnish army to remain 'on the attack' on the Karelian isthmus, and to create a bridgehead on the Svir to draw stronger enemy forces towards it.[162] Leeb argued that Soviet resistance at Leningrad was increasing constantly as more forces were transferred from the Finnish front. Heavy German casualties were the result. He argued:

If the Finnish Army were to continue its attack on Leningrad, the battle of Leningrad would be decided in a few days in favour of the joint armies, and the region round Leningrad, and thus the success of Finn[ish] operations so far, would be safeguarded. A rapid cleaning up at Leningrad would also help the establishment of a link towards the Svir. Only if stronger infantry forces can be released at Leningrad in the near future can the removal of the enemy from the area west of the Volkhov be contemplated and the foundation be laid for an advance towards the Svir.[163]

On the other hand, Army Group North would face a critical situation if the Finnish advance were halted. From 16 October 1941 Army Group North attempted to advance with XXXIX Army Corps through Tikhvin towards Lodeynoe Pole to the River Svir, without any Finnish promise of a simultaneous assault by Finnish troops on the Svir. The attempt failed:[164] Tikhvin was captured on 8 November 1941 but had to be evacuated the next day after heavy fighting. The attack developed into a near catastrophe. Disaster was averted only with great difficulty at the end of December, by means of a timely withdrawal behind the Volkhov. In the meantime, the command of the 'Karelian Army' and German 163rd Infantry Division had become convinced that, owing to a reduction of combat strength, the division and Finnish VI Corps both lacked adequate forces to hold a bridgehead once the Svir had been crossed.[165] Mannerheim therefore refused to undertake a limited 'demonstrative action' on the Svir front to relieve the German advance on Tikhvin. Even an attack solely by 163rd Infantry Division, as requested by the Wehrmacht High Command, was refused.[166] Preparations for such an attack, which had already begun, were dropped at the end of October 1941.[167]

---

[162] Army Group North, war diary, 1, 3, 9, 18, 25 Sept. 1941, BA-MA RH 19 III/167; Leeb, *Tagebuchaufzeichnungen*, 348 (3 Sept. 1941).

[163] Army Group North, war diary, 15 Sept. 1941, BA-MA RH 19 III/167.

[164] On 'Operation Tikhvin' see e.g. the war diary entries of Army Group North in Oct. 1941, BA-MA RH 19 III/168; also Halder, *Diaries*, 1292 (9 Nov. 1941), 1303–5 (19 Nov. 1941), 1312 (28 Nov. 1941), 1341–3 (8 Dec. 1941); Ziemke, *German Northern Theater*, 200 ff.; Erfurth, *Finnischer Krieg*, 79; Philippi and Heim, *Feldzug*, 79 ff.; Leeb, *Tagebuchaufzeichnungen*, 369–412 (5 Oct.–11 Dec. 1941).

[165] See the assessment of the situation by 163rd Inf. Div. in war diary, 16–19 Sept. 1941, Ba-MA 16260/16, and 163rd Inf. Div. Ia No. 623/41, g.Kdos. to Liaison Staff North, 27 Aug. 1941, ibid. 16260/21.

[166] See chief of OKW, WFSt/Abt. L, No. 441707/41, g.Kdos. to C.-in-C. of Finnish armed forces, FM Mannerheim, 13 Oct. 1941, BA-MA, 20. Armee, 58628/2.

[167] 163rd Inf. Div., war diary, 18–27 Oct. 1941, BA-MA 16260/16, and Erfurth, diary, i. 293 (20 Dec. 1941), BA-MA N 257/1.

The Finnish High Command was unsettled by the withdrawal of German troops from Tikhvin and the retreat behind the Volkhov, which had been forced by constant enemy penetrations.[168] Within the framework of Mannerheim's proposed reduction of the Finnish Army, the sectors on the Svir front were reorganized from November 1941 and a defensive position was established. After the beginning of December 1941 no further major operations were launched by the Finns in any sector of the front.

Even the occupation of the port of Hanko on 3 December 1941 was due less to direct German or Finnish operations than to the withdrawal of Soviet troops from the naval base for strategic and supply reasons.[169] Nevertheless, the 'recapture of Hanko' was greatly celebrated by Hitler and Ribbentrop in their message of congratulation, where it was described as 'a further great success in the Finnish people's historic struggle for freedom'.[170]

(c) Military Result of Operations in Southern Finland and the Problem of Joint Military Planning

After the retreat of German troops behind the Volkhov, if not earlier, the Finnish High Command was forced to accept the prospect of a prolonged war. The first doubts about German victory emerged. Field Marshal Mannerheim believed that a 'serious setback' was possible on the Karelian isthmus and the Svir front.[171] At the very least, it was clear that Helsinki and Berlin had been fundamentally mistaken in expecting a lightning war against the Soviet Union; their belief at the outset that the war would be won in a matter of weeks, and by autumn 1941 at the latest, was fatally flawed. When the Germans did recognize that the war was likely to last considerably longer, they conspicuously failed to correct the Finnish assumption that victory would be achieved 'in a few weeks'. Major-General Warlimont had argued that a more realistic corrective view was necessary in the middle of August 1941, after his visit to Finland.[172]

At the beginning of the war, the Finnish government had organized the total exploitation of the economic and manpower resources of the country. For example, no less than 16 per cent of the population had been conscripted. This situation could not long be sustained without serious consequences and disruption of the war economy. Hitler too was convinced that Finland could not

[168] See Mannerheim to Erfurth, papers of Gen. Erfurth, diary, i. 293 (20 Dec. 1941), BA-MA N 257/1.

[169] See Halder, Diaries, 1333–5 (3 Dec. 1941).

[170] See Hitler's and Ribbentrop's messages to President Ryti, FM Mannerheim, and Foreign Minister Witting of 4 Dec. 1941, PA, Büro St.S., Finnland, vol. iv.

[171] Thus in his letter to FM Keitel, 19 Dec. 1941, papers of Gen. Erfurth, diary, i. 299, BA-MA N 257/1.

[172] Report of Liaison Officer/Wehrmacht Dept. Propaganda in Liaison Staff North, 11 Feb. 1942, and Amt Ausland/Abwehr report on public mood in Finland, 20 Apr. 1942, BA-MA RW 4/ v. 325; Paasikivi, Supermacht, 421. On the proposal of Gen. Warlimont see Ritter memorandum of 16 Aug. 1941, PA Büro St.S., Finnland, vol. iii.

'tolerate much blood-letting'.[173] Admittedly, German arms deliveries since summer 1940 had ensured high levels of equipment in some sectors of munitions and the war economy.[174] However, the effects of the Finnish–Soviet Winter War of 1939–40 had not been fully overcome. There was still a serious lack of balanced armaments production capacity and suitable war-economy reserves. Many shortages of ammunition, motor-vehicles, supply equipment, heavy weapons, and air-force equipment were apparent.

After a reorganization in 1940–1, the Finnish air force was able to provide successful support for ground fighting conducted by its own army units. However, it remained dependent on German assistance in questions of supply, air defence against Soviet air raids on Finnish cities, strategic operations against the Murmansk railway, and the movement of enemy shipping on Lake Ladoga, the Stalin Canal, and the White Sea ports.[175] Such support was repeatedly requested by Mannerheim, but it could be provided only infrequently: the formations of Air Fleet 5 were concentrated on northern Finland and the support of Army Command Norway, while Air Fleet 1 in the south was primarily engaged in providing relief for the operations of Army Group North. It was highly unfortunate that Mannerheim's first request for German air support, during the Finnish army's attack of 10 July 1941, had been turned down. The Luftwaffe could provide only a 'psychological effect' in support of the Finnish advance.[176] This led to numerous complaints from the Finnish High Command that the promised assistance had failed to materialize.[177]

In autumn 1941—partly due to German transport demands—a major crisis developed throughout the Finnish transport system. Additional German deliveries of lorries and captured Soviet railway engines and wagons were therefore requested by Mannerheim, in his letter to Keitel on 12 November 1941, and by President Ryti from the German envoy.[178] The request could not be granted until summer 1942. Until the end of 1941 the Finns received only minor deliveries of captured Estonian railway stock.[179] In addition, casualty rates in the Finnish army increased as the war dragged on, leading to a more realistic assessment of Finnish prospects. This new attitude was partly responsible for

---

[173] See e.g. Halder, *Diaries*, 1176–7 (14 Aug. 1941), 1315–16 (26 Nov. 1941), 1365–6 (18 Dec. 1941); Erfurth, *Finnischer Krieg*, 81; Engel, *Heeresadjutant bei Hitler*, 113.

[174] See *Geschichte des zweiten Weltkrieges*, iii. 404–5; Mannerheim, *Memoirs*, 415.

[175] On the operations of the Finnish air force see Erfurth, *Finnischer Krieg*, 92.

[176] See papers of Gen. Erfurth, diary, i. 59–64, 68, BA-MA N 257/1.

[177] Ibid. 116.

[178] Ibid. 237–8; Erfurth, *Finnischer Krieg*, 83; telegram No. 1239, Blücher to foreign ministry, 1 Nov. 1941, PA Büro St.S., Finnland, vol. iii, and *DGFP* D xiii, No. 477 n. 2. Army Command Norway supported the Finnish requests: see telex Army Command Norway, Headquarters Finland, Abt. Ia No. 101/41, g.Kdos. Chefs. to OKW/WFStSt/Abt. L, 4 Nov. 1941, BA-MA, 20. Armee, 58628/1.

[179] See the restrained reply of FM Keitel in his letter to Mannerheim, Chief of OKW No. 441979/41, g.Kdos. Chefs. WFSt/Abt. L (I Op) to HE FM Baron von Mannerheim, 21 Nov. 1941, BA-MA, 20. Armee, 58628/2. The desired railway materials had to have the Russian gauge, and could not therefore be taken from regular German production.

Mannerheim's rejection of the ambitious German operational objectives. From the end of 1941 the Finnish High Command reorganized and regrouped the army from divisions into 16 brigades. By spring 1942 its strength had been reduced from approximately 500,000 to 150,000 men.[180] In December 1941 the Finnish commander-in-chief had made his position crystal clear to the Wehrmacht High Command: it was of 'vital significance' for all future operations on the German–Finnish front that the situation at Leningrad be resolved by German troops, who would also have to effect a link-up with the 'Karelian Army' on the Svir.[181] Only after these two problems were solved would the Finnish Army be able to respond to German requests and deploy the troops thus released for an attack towards Sorokka (Belomorsk) on the Murmansk railway and northern Russia. As a result, at the end of December 1941 Mannerheim rejected Army High Command's proposal for a feinted Finnish attack. He had no wish needlessly to provoke the Soviet troops on the Finnish front into great activity.[182] For the Finns, as General Heinrichs stated on his visit to Wehrmacht High Command on 6 January 1942, a new and successful German attack on Leningrad was the 'key to the entire German–Finnish front'.[183]

By the end of 1941 the underlying military objectives of the two national high commands had become clear. It was sadly apparent that there was no joint conduct of operations, nor any co-ordination of partial and ultimate objectives within the framework of an agreed plan of action. No unified command under a single central high command had emerged. The Finns were now determined not to commit themselves to any new, extensive operational objectives beyond the front line they had already established. Their attitude was the result of several factors: the first doubts about German victory; the heavy losses already sustained; the regime's uncertain political war aims in domestic affairs; and the fear of foreign-policy difficulties with the United States and involvement in the war between the great powers. Accordingly, the strategic decisions of the Finnish High Command were determined by consideration of the country's position in domestic and foreign affairs.[184] The impression of joint Finnish–German conduct of the war was given only in the early stages of the conflict against the Soviet Union, when the military objectives of the two countries appeared to coincide. When victory was not forthcoming and expectations were disappointed, it became clear that Helsinki would not pursue strategic objectives which went beyond its own interests—

---

[180] *DGFP* D xiii, No. 436; Liaison Staff North, Ia No. 112/41, g.Kdos. to Army Command Norway—Headquarters Finland, 22 Nov. 1941, BA-MA, 20. Armee, 58628/1; Erfurth, *Finnischer Krieg*, 82.

[181] See Mannerheim's letters to Keitel on 4 and 19 Dec. 1941, papers of Gen. Erfurth, diary, i. 273 ff., 295 ff., BA-MA N 257/1 (also for the following).

[182] Erfurth, *Finnischer Krieg*, 90.

[183] Papers of Gen. Erfurth, diary, i. 266, BA-MA N 257/1. On Heinrichs's report on his discussions in OKW and with Hitler see also Jägerskiöld, *Marskalken av Finland*, 233 ff.

[184] Papers of Gen. Erfurth, diary, vol. i, *passim*, BA-MA N 257/1.

such as reunification with the former Finnish territories in Ladoga–Karelia and on the Karelian isthmus, and the capture of territory inhabited by the ethnically related population of east Karelia.[185] A further Finnish advance into northern Russia, to the coast of the White Sea, or Finnish participation in the siege of Leningrad, would inevitably have begun a struggle for the very existence of Finland. It would thus have demanded the deployment of all the reserves and resources of the state, and meant an almost total dependence on German deliveries of arms and industrial items.

The two high commands consequently conducted military actions in their areas of operation largely independently and in pursuit of their own plans. There was no effective or extensive co-ordination of German and Finnish operations. In addition, Hitler deliberately attempted to maintain secrecy; his aim was to leave the states involved in the war in the east in the dark about his operational objectives in Operation Barbarossa, and to retain all decision-making in his own hands. These factors further discouraged any discussion of joint military operations in an atmosphere of trust, and may even have made it impossible.[186]

On the other hand, the situation was not without advantages for Helsinki. The Finns were able to conduct their own military operations against the Soviet Union without fear of the military predominance of Berlin, which would have been unavoidable if the war aims had been co-ordinated within the framework of a coalition. The coincidence of Finnish and German military objectives was thus reduced to a common intention and military plan to defeat and destroy the USSR in a lightning war lasting a few weeks. This aim could not be achieved. Subsequently, at the beginning of 1942, State President Ryti and the Finnish commander-in-chief, Field Marshal Mannerheim, both concluded that the entry of the United States into the war had made Germany's military position 'alarming' if not catastrophic.[187] Helsinki was greatly worried about the increasing possibility of a British–American landing to attack German positions in northern Scandinavia.

3. Political Balance Sheet of German–Finnish 'Brotherhood-in-arms' to the Winter of 1941–1942

Even during the first months of war, helped by the lack of a formal wartime alliance with the Third Reich, the Finnish government portrayed its participation in Operation Barbarossa as a specific and independent struggle against the Soviet Union. On 26 June 1941 President Ryti justified Finland's entry into the war by referring to Moscow's 'innermost intention' to destroy the independence of Finland. He described the attack on the Soviet Union as the consequence of a persistent Soviet policy of aggression and as a renewed

---

[185] See Mannerheim, *Memoirs*, 416. [186] Ueberschär, 'Guerre de coalition', 51 ff.
[187] Jägerskiöld, *Marskalken av Finland*, 130–1.

'defensive struggle' following the Finnish–Soviet Winter War of 1939–40.[188] It became clear that Finland intended to pursue a 'separate' war against the Soviet Union, detached from German war aims and the European war of the great powers. This struggle was waged side by side with Hitler's war in the east 'operationally' but not 'genetically'; the Finnish population regarded it as the 'continuation' of the Winter War of 1939–40.[189] The 'separate war' theory also implied that Finland would wage a 'normal European national war' against the neighbouring Soviet Union.[190] As an 'event of pure power politics', it was thus in stark contrast to Hitler's own plans for the conquest of 'living-space'. The Finnish position was determined by considerations of domestic and foreign policy, with the government emphasizing on numerous occasions that the 'separate war' was a form of 'self-defence' against Soviet attacks. The argument was supported by the fact that it had been the Soviet Union that had opened hostilities against Finland.[191]

Shortly after Finland entered the war, Foreign Minister Witting told the German minister von Blücher that 'Finland had entered a new phase of her policy'.[192] Nevertheless, the Finnish government tried to avoid becoming dependent on Germany in foreign policy; it hoped to maintain existing relations with the Western powers and the United States in order to demonstrate its theory of 'separate war'. From June 1941 the British government had stopped trade and begun economic reprisals against Finland because of the German invasion of the Soviet Union and the waging of war from Finnish territory.[193] Nevertheless, Helsinki was reluctant to accede to Ribbentrop's demand for diplomatic relations with Britain to be broken off.[194] The Finnish government also avoided taking any foreign-policy action against the United States on the grounds that this would be 'unpopular among broad circles'.[195]

The Finnish government finally responded to German pressure and broke

---

[188] On Ryti's radio broadcast to the Finnish people see *Blauweß-Buch*, ii. 147–56; Ryti, *Reden*, 79–91, and *Archiv der Gegenwart* (1941), 5092–3.

[189] See *DGFP* D xiii, No. 262, and Blücher, *Gesandter*, 244–5. On this subject see also the report on the Finnish research by Vehviläinen, 'Finnische Kriegsziele'. For the German assessment of the Finnish position see the report by the former German military attaché, Col. Horst Kitschmann, 29 ff., Ba-MA W 02-24/1.

[190] See Hillgruber, 'Endlösung', 139.

[191] See Helsinki's memorandum to the British government on 7 Oct. 1941, in telegram No. 1071, Blücher to foreign office, 7 Oct. 1941, PA, Büro St.S., Finnland, vol. iii. Also Procopé, *Sowjetjustiz*, 32. The Soviet Union did not accept Finland's 'separate war' theory; see statement of the Soviet prosecutor Maj.-Gen. Zorya in *IMT* vii. 344.

[192] *DGFP* D, xiii, No. 29. On the political relations between Berlin and Helsinki see also Polvinen, *Finland i stormaktspolitiken*, 43 ff.

[193] On the British attitude towards Finland see Churchill's statement of 5 July 1941: 'There is no need to declare war, but it seems to me they should have much the same treatment as if they were at war': PRO, Premier 3/170/4, Prime Minister's Personal Minute No. M.704/1.

[194] See *DGFP* D xii, No. 643, and ibid. xiii, Nos. 85, 140; *FRUS* (1941), i. 36, 51. See also Halder, *Diaries*, 1076 (26 July 1941).

[195] Telegram No. 551, Blücher to foreign ministry, 1 July 1941, PA, Büro St.S., Finnland, vol. iii.

off diplomatic relations with Britain, but only after a treaty of alliance had been signed between Britain and the Soviet Union on 12 July 1941, and British carrier aircraft had launched air raids on Kirkenes and Liinahamari in the Petsamo region. Even then, Helsinki was anxious that neither the Germans nor the press should interpret this conduct as signifying Finnish entry into the war against Britain.[196] Helsinki had no desire to aggravate relations with London and Washington during the following months. Two incidents served to make its attitude apparent. The first of these occurred in September 1941, when the British government, at the request of the Soviet Union, warned Helsinki not to continue its attack into 'purely Russian territory' beyond the line of the old Finnish–Soviet border.[197] The second incident came in October–November 1941, when the American government tried to persuade Finland to halt hostilities against the USSR and withdraw to the old Finnish–Soviet border.[198] Though the Finnish government rejected the accusation that it was waging aggressive war, it also slowed its advance and stopped the attack of Finnish III Army Corps on the Murmansk railway.

In August 1941 Reich Foreign Minister von Ribbentrop had opposed a Japanese proposal for Finland to join the anti-Comintern pact or Tripartite Pact.[199] When war broke out Finland therefore had no treaty with Germany which could have offered a platform for the waging of a unified military and political war against the Soviet Union under Hitler's leadership. However, in November 1941 Berlin urged Helsinki to join Denmark, Bulgaria, Croatia, Nanking-China, Romania, and Slovakia in the anti-Comintern pact. With great reluctance, the Finnish government decided to comply. The country was dependent on German support and deliveries of food-stuffs; moreover, the Germans were virtually promising to reward Finnish accession by delivering another 75,000 t. of grain for the six months of winter 1941–2.[200]

In this context the Germans also skilfully exploited Molotov's earlier demands for the inclusion of Finland in the Soviet sphere of influence.[201] Finland declared its entry into the anti-Comintern pact on 25 November 1941, the

[196] See *DGFP* D xiii, Nos. 140, 160; *FRUS* (1941), i. 54; Mannerheim, *Memoirs*, 423; Blücher, *Gesandter*, 236–7. On the question of German pressure see Jägerskiöld, *Marskalken av Finland*, 203 ff.

[197] See the visit of the Soviet ambassador Maisky to Churchill on 4 Sept. 1941, PRO, Premier 3/170/1, and Eden's communication to the Finnish government, *DGFP* D xiii, No. 353. Also Ziemke, *German Northern Theater*, 205 ff.; *FRUS* (1941), i. 71–2, 77 ff.; see also Roosevelt, *Personal Letters*, ii. 1207–8; Hull, *Memoirs*, ii. 978 ff.

[198] Telegram No. 3815, Minister Thomsen (Washington) to foreign ministry, 4 Nov. 1941, PA, Büro St.S., Finnland, vol. iii, and *DGFP* D xiii, No. 461; also *FRUS* (1941), i. 74–5, 82 ff., 91 ff.; Schwartz, *America and the Russo-Finnish War*, 68–9.

[199] *DGFP* D xiii, No. 197 n. 4; Ribbentrop's directive of 1 Aug. 1941, memorandum of State Secretary von Weizsäcker No. 512, 14 Aug. 1941, also Blücher's letter, Tgb. No. 225g to foreign ministry, 21 Aug. 1941, PA, Büro St.S., Finnland, vol. iii.

[200] See *DGFP* D xiii, Nos. 423, 493; also ibid., Nos. 40, 162; and Blücher, *Gesandter*, 259 ff.

[201] See notes of State Secretary von Weizsäcker of 22 and 29 Oct. 1941, PA, Büro St.S., Finnland, vol. iii.

occasion of its fifth aniversary and extension.[202] Nevertheless, the decision was described as an expression of Finland's 'principled anti-Communist attitude' and its readiness to combat Communism in the ideological sphere, and not as the manifestation of a military alliance with Hitler.[203] In his proclamation at the ceremony in Berlin Foreign Minister Witting stressed, in addition to the tasks of military defence, the need for action against the Communist menace 'with the means of the spirit'.[204]

In the spirit of 'separate war', Helsinki informed the Western powers that Finland was pursuing specifically Finnish goals in the struggle against the Soviet Union, and was merely 'a co-belligerent with Germany'.[205] Nevertheless, it soon transpired that Finland's discussions concerning political war aims had been influenced by the country's war on the side of the Third Reich during its early successes in the east. The Finns eventually accepted ideas akin to National Socialism on the 'gaining of new living-space in the east' and on the 'European crusade to destroy Bolshevik rule'.[206]

For the National Socialist leadership, the description of the war in the east as a 'European crusade against Bolshevism' was merely a propaganda device to disguise its real intentions.[207] Yet this notion of an anti-Bolshevik crusade offered the Finnish government an integrating image of the enemy, rooted in the anti-Communism of the Finnish population which had been latent since the war of independence. Helsinki constantly described its participation in Operation Barbarossa as a contribution to the common defence of Western culture against the east; it was clear that the aim was to join Berlin and win the war by destroying the Bolshevik system 'for all time'.[208] In the first weeks of war the orders of the day, appeals, and proclamations of the Finnish High Command and the government repeatedly called for a 'holy war' against the 'eternal threat from the east', for a 'final struggle' against the

[202] On the negotiations for accession and German pressure during them see Grundherr's notes, Pol. VI 7891g of 14 Nov. 1941, PA, Dt. Ges. Helsinki, Schriftwechsel geheim, vol. iii, and DGFP D xiii, Nos. 472, 474, 477, 485. On the 'Memorandum on extending the duration of validity of the agreement against the Communist International' of 25 Nov. 1941 see DGFP D xiii, No. 498.

[203] Telegram No. 1418 to foreign ministry, 30 Nov. 1941, PA, Büro St.S., Finnland, vol. iv.

[204] Statement of Finnish Foreign Minister Witting in Berlin on 25 Nov. 1941, in Monatshefte für auswärtige Politik, 8 (1941), 12/1050.

[205] US Minister Schoenfeld, Helsinki, to Secretary of State, 4 July 1941, FRUS (1941), i. 46–7.

[206] See Ryti's radio broadcast of 26 June 1941; Ryti, Reden, 91.

[207] Clearest on this subject was Rosenberg's speech 'to those most closely concerned with the eastern problem' on 20 June 1941: 'Today however we are not waging a "crusade" against Bolshevism solely to save the "poor Russians" from this Bolshevism for all time, but to pursue German world policy': IMT xxvi. 614–15. On Hitler's motives for the war 'before the eyes of the world . . . according to tactical points of view', see his remarks in the discussion of 16 July 1941, IMT xxxviii, Bormann Aktenvermerk, pp. 86 ff. See also Lang, Bormann, 469–70, and Hillgruber, 'Endlösung', passim. On the question of National Socialist European policy see Kluke, 'Europaideologie', 241–75.

[208] See Mannerheim's order of the day on 7 July 1941, in telegram No. 615 to foreign ministry, 13 July 1941, PA, Büro St.S., Finnland, vol. iii. On Mannerheim's attitude towards Bolshevism see Jägerskiöld, Marskalken av Finland, 70 ff.

'European plague threat', and for a 'crusade' against 'Finland's traditional enemy'.[209] Significantly, Helsinki was interested in the idea of the 'anti-Bolshevik crusade' mainly because of its integrating function in domestic politics. It did not mean that Finland sympathized with Hitler's ideological war of annihilation against the Soviet Union. The Finnish government did not accept the idea of a ruthless 'struggle of two world-views'. Equally, it was not committed to any racial-ideological or anti-Semitic programme, nor to any plan to conquer new 'living-space' in the east by decimating the population of the Soviet Union. Though the Germans laid great emphasis on solidarity in the 'struggle against Bolshevism until its final destruction',[210] the Finnish war against the Soviet Union was different in nature from the war Hitler intended to wage. The two countries had no common ideological foundation for a war based on political and racial theory, nor for anti-Semitic measures and practice in Finland itself. Jews served as soldiers and officers in the Finnish army throughout the war.[211]

At the beginning of the war Finnish war aims had been informal. However, these aims, consisting of the recovery of the territories ceded to the Soviet Union in the Peace of Moscow of 1940, were quickly made official. They were associated with the hope of a revision of the Moscow peace treaty, and the expectation of appropriate reward in Hitler's territorial and economic reorganization of Europe after the war.[212] Desire for an 'increase in territory' also coincided with Hitler's own intention to expand Finnish territory, which he had announced before launching the war in the east. When the initial successes of the German and Finnish armies in the summer of 1941 made a rapid victory seem within reach, Finnish territorial expectations grew. There was also an increase in the small number of advocates of a 'Greater Finland'.[213] Demands for a 'secure border' were thus expanded to include plans to regain east Karelia and shift the border well to the east in order to guarantee the 'security of the country'. Such schemes played an increasing part in discus-

---

[209] See Mannerheim's order of the day on 28 June 1941, in Lundin, *Finland*, 127; papers of Gen. Erfurth, diary, vol. i, BA-MA N 257/1; Mannerheim's order of the day to the German 163rd Inf. Div. of 7 July 1941 and to the divisional commander, Gen. Engelbrecht, on 10 July 1941, both in BA-MA, 163. Inf. Div., 16260/18; Ryti's radio broadcast of 26 June 1941, in Ryti, *Reden*, 91; Ryti's letter to Hitler, 1 July 1941, *DGFP* D xiii, No. 52; Ryti's statement to the US Minister, Schoenfeld, *FRUS* (1941), i. 47.

[210] Thus Keitel in his letter to Mannerheim; see Chief of OKW WFSt/Abt. L No. 441707 g.Kdos. Chefs. to C.-in-C of the Finnish armed forces, FM Mannerheim, 13 Oct. 1941, BA-MA, 20. Armee, 58628/2.

[211] On German pressure for the adoption of anti-Jewish measures in Finland see Lipscher, 'Verwirklichung der antijüdischen Maßnahmen', 140; Ueberschär, *Hitler und Finnland*, 317; Kersten, *Totenkopf*, 178 ff.; on the attitude of the Finnish government concerning German policy towards the Jews see Laqueur, *Terrible Secret*, 35–7, 86–7, 216–17. See also Bassin, 'Les Juifs en Finlande', 45.

[212] See President Ryti and Foreign Minister Witting to US Minister Schoenfeld, 4 and 16 July 1941, *FRUS* (1941), i. 47, 49, and *DGFP* D xiii, No. 262; Vehviläinen, 'Finnische Kriegsziele', 36.

[213] On the first 'Greater Finland' speeches in parliament on the occasion of the declaration of war on 25 June 1941 see Lundin, *Finland* 134–5, and Upton, *Finland 1940–1941*, 292.

sions within Finland itself.[214] Field Marshal Mannerheim, in his order of the day on 10 July 1941, called for the 'fulfilment' of an ealier promise to 'liberate' east Karelia and create a 'Greater Finland'.[215] The issue of territorial claims and 'political' war aims was given particular impetus in September 1941, when the government yielded to German pressure and ordered the Finnish army to cross the 1939 border.[216] Even the Finnish government was apparently becoming convinced of the 'need for a Greater Finland'.[217]

In September 1941, as the British and American governments waged a diplomatic campaign to persuade the Finnish goverment to announce a cease-fire with the Soviet Union, numerous newspaper articles made the claim that Finland was 'war-weary'. The Finnish government felt compelled to inform the Germans publicly that such speculations were groundless. The minister of commerce and chairman of the Social Democratic Party, Väinö Tanner, made it clear in a speech in Vaasa on 14 September 1941 that Finland was determined to continue the war.[218] Tanner also revealed that the Finnish government preferred not to be forced into a public discussion of the country's war aims at present. He stressed:

Finland is still the same democratic, freedom-loving people, defending its independence, that it was during the Winter War . . . If events have made us loyal brothers-in-arms with Germany, there is still no doubt that our war is with Russia and Russia alone. We have no part in the current war between the great powers, and we have no desire to be drawn into the competition of the great powers . . . For us this is no more than a defensive war to create secure borders and a durable peace for ourselves.

Tanner was realistic enough to acknowledge that no one could say 'where the war will end and where anything at all will end'. Significantly, however, he also felt bound to make concessions to the triumphalist mood by responding to the demand for territorial conquest. He therefore argued that the recovery of the former Finnish lands had achieved Finland's war aims 'to a certain extent' only; by crossing the former border of 1913, Finland had done no more than 'regain the extra interest belonging to it'. It seems unlikely that this 'interest' was intended to be returned voluntarily to the Soviet Union at a later date. As the Finnish Social Democrats were unwilling to associate themselves publicly

---

[214] See e.g. the speech by the president of the Finnish parliament, Väinö Hakkila, on 20 July 1941, in war diary of Naval Attaché Helsingfors, vol. ii, 20 and 21 July 1941, BA-MA PG 48779–84.

[215] Heinrichs, *Mannerheimgestalten*, ii. 279ff., and Jägerskiöld, *Marskalken av Finland*, 112ff., who does not see it as announcing a programme of political annexation. See also Lundin, *Finland*, 127, 285.

[216] See Blücher, *Gesandter*, 249.

[217] See the observation in war diary of Naval Attaché Helsingfors, vol. ii, 24 Oct. 1941, BA-MA PG 48779–84.

[218] Speech by the chairman of the Finnish Social Democrats and Finnish Minister of Trade Tanner in Vaasa, 19 Sept. 1941, in *Monatshefte für auswärtige Politik*, 8 (1941), 10867–72 (also for the following quotations); on the German assessment of the speech see ibid. 851–2, and telegram No. 953, Minister von Blücher to foreign ministry, 15 Sept. 1941, PA, Büro St.S., Finnland, vol. iii; also *FRUS* (1941), i. 66ff.

with proposals for conquest, the 'Greater Finland' plans did not become a programme supported by all the political parties. Nevertheless, they acquired a quasi-official character in September and October 1941, when President Ryti told Berlin that the line Neva–Lake Ladoga–Svir–Lake Onega–White Sea 'with glacis' would become the Finnish border. The Finns also demanded the 'disappearance' of Leningrad as a great industrial city.[219] These territorial demands involved not only 'White Sea Karelia' or 'Far Karelia' situated beyond east Karelia, 'but also the Kola peninsula'.[220] Additionally, the Finnish government hoped that Germany would annex the region round Archangel and the northern Dvina to the east as a 'forest colonial area', since it would be better for Finland not to border on Russia in future.[221]

Berlin agreed to these plans, except for the claim to the Kola peninsula. Hitler, who intended to seize this area for Germany, had already made Gauleiter Terboven responsible for its exploitation.[222] It was clear that ambitious Finnish schemes would tie the country more closely to Germany. Moreover, political war aims of this kind would turn the war between Finland and the Soviet Union into a life-and-death struggle for both sides, a development which Field Marshal Mannerheim had previously tried to avoid. Finnish commitment to an expansionist programme ruled out a political solution in the form of a separate peace between Finland and the Soviet Union. Hitler was willing 'to be generous [to Helsinki] in regard to territorial questions'. However, he wanted to discuss the 'special case' of the Kola peninsula with a Finnish plenipotentiary.[223] Foreign Minister von Ribbentrop was especially pleased that Finnish demands 'now also extend to former Russian territory'.[224] By making extensive plans for the conquest of territory, and demanding a border 'that guarantees its people security against a new Russian attack for generations to come',[225] the Finns were close to adopting German notions of conquest. Not surprisingly, plans were made for the resettlement of several

[219] *DGFP* D xiii, Nos. 301, 436. See also 'Memorandum of report Leningrad', OKW/WFSt/Abt. L, 21 Sept. 1941, BA-MA RW 4/v. 578: 'Finns have unofficially declared they would like to have Neva as national border, but Leningrad must go'; and *IMT* vii. 183: 'Finland has also declared clearly that she is not interested in the further existence of the city in the immediate vicinity of her new boundary.' See also the statement in Engel, *Heeresadjutant bei Hitler*, 113. This is denied by Mannerheim, *Memoirs*, 427–8, and Jägerskiöld, *Marskalken av Finland*, 153.

[220] *DGFP* D xiii, No. 301 (11 Sept. 1941) (also for the following). On the attitude of Finnish military circles and their desire in all circumstances to go beyond the old border in making territorial claims see Talvela, *Muistelmat*, ii. 124.

[221] *DGFP* D xiii, No. 436, pp. 719–20.

[222] See 'Bormann minute' on the discussions of 16 July 1941, No. 221-L, *IMT* xxxviii. 90–2. In Aug. 1941 a staff of the war economy and armaments department had already been set up in Rovaniemi (later in Helsinki) under Commander Bartholdi to deal with 'war-economy needs on the Kola peninsula for Gen. Thomas or State Secretary Körner (Economic Operations Staff East)'; see letter, diary, No. 215g to foreign ministry, 13 Aug. 1941, PA, Bonn, Dt. Ges. Helsinki, correspondence, vol. ii, and T No. 326g, 2 Dec. 1941, ibid., vol. iii.

[223] Hewel's diary entry of 13 Sept. 1941, *DGFP* D xiii, No. 301 n. 3.

[224] Ibid. xiii, No. 331.

[225] Thus the declaration by Minister Tanner during his visit to Berlin in Oct. 1941; see *Monatshefte für auswärtige Politik*, 8 (1941), 852.

million people of related origin from other parts of Russia in the 'settlement area' of 'Western culture' in east and White Sea Karelia and the region round Archangel. The Finns also showed an interest in the ethnically related populations of occupied Estonia and Ingermanland, and in the political future of these regions.[226] Significantly, Finnish propaganda now began to claim that the Finnish people had Nordic racial characteristics. This literature demanded the extension of living-space through the acquisition of Finland's 'natural eastern marches' with the Kola peninsula and east and White Sea Karelia, plus the 'removal of the Russians settled there'.[227]

After November 1941 military developments produced a more sober Finnish assessment both of the prospects for victory and of appropriate political objectives.[228] In these circumstances it was Hitler, on the occasion of Witting's signing of the anti-Comintern pact in Berlin on 25 November 1941, who spoke of Finland's desire for territorial conquests as far as the White Sea. He was now prepared to give the Kola peninsula to Finland. Hitler emphasized that Finland's resolution of its problems with the Soviet Union must be of 'truly historical dimensions'.[229] Expansionist war aims of this kind, however, far exceeded anything the Finns could hope to justify as a 'guarantee of territorial security' against the Soviet Union.[230]

On 6 December 1941 Finland unilaterally nullified the Peace of Moscow and proclaimed the reincorporation of the reconquered regions of Karelia, Salla, and Hanko.[231] Simultaneously, the British government declared war on Finland in response to pressure from the Soviet Union. The British view that Finland was supporting Hitler's policy was also shared by the Dominions and the United States. It became obvious that Helsinki could not completely separate itself from German conduct of the war, nor wage a national struggle independent of the European conflict as a whole and without regard for the

[226] See telegram No. 1045, Blücher to foreign ministry, 2 Oct. 1941, telegram Pol.V 4340 to German Minister, Helsinki, Oct. 1941, and memorandum State Secretary von Weizsäcker No. 743, 10 Nov. 1941, PA, Büro St.S., Finnland, vol. iii; also telegram No. 45, Ribbentrop to German Minister Helsinki, 21 Jan. 1942, ibid., vol. iv, and memorandum State Secretary von Weizsäcker No. 739, 10 Nov. 1941, ibid., Handakten Ritter, Rußland (No. 29); and Blücher, *Gesandter*, 272.

[227] Auer *et al.*, *Finnlands Lebensraum*, 36; Jaakkola, *Ostfrage Finnlands*, 67 ff., 77.

[228] See the report on Finnish 'doubts about the economic profitability of east Karelian territories', in war diary Naval Attaché Helsingfors, vol. ii, 13 Nov. 1941, BA-MA PG 48779–84.

[229] *DGFP* D xiii, No. 507; also *Staatsmänner*, i. 638–47.

[230] Regarding the conflict between the limited goal of a guarantee of territorial security and the political war aim of the conquest of a new 'settlement area', see the speech in parliament by Premier Rangell on 29 Nov. 1941, quoted in telegram No. 1418, Blücher to foreign ministry, 30 Nov. 1944, PA, Büro St.S., Finnland, vol. iv, and papers of Gen. Erfurth, diary, i. 267–8, BA-MA N 257/1. The striving for territorial expansion out of 'national-romantic motives' is also reported by Polvinen, *Finland i stormaktspolitiken*, 49.

[231] On the correspondence between Churchill and Mannerheim, and the British ultimatum to Helsinki on 27 Nov. 1941 as a result of Soviet pressure, see PRO, Premier 3/170/1: Prime Minister's Personal Telegram to FM Mannerheim No. T 892, 28–9 Nov. 1941, and Mannerheim to Prime Minister Churchill, No. T 920, 2 Dec. 1941 (contact was via the US legation); also Jägerskiöld, *Marskalken av Finland*, 211–12; Polvinen, *Finland i stormaktspolitiken*, 80 ff.; Mannerheim, *Memoirs*, 435–8; *DGFP* D xiii, Nos. 533, 540; *FRUS* (1941), i. 85, 113 ff.

policy of the Third Reich. Japan's attack on Pearl Harbor on 7 December 1941, and Hitler's declaration of war on the United States four days later, led the Finns to fear that the Americans would follow the British example, inevitably drawing Finland into the global conflict between the great powers. The Finns therefore began to respond to political reactions in Washington. From the beginning of 1942 these new considerations undoubtedly had a major effect on the military operations of the Finnish army against the Murmansk railway; the Finns had no wish to give the United States grounds for a deterioration in political relations.

At the turn of 1941–2 Berlin and Helsinki had still failed to reach clear agreement on the political objectives of the war against the Soviet Union. Their long-term ideas regarding the Soviet Union coincided only to a limited extent. The two countries differed fundamentally about aims and objectives. There was no unity of political interest which might have encouraged military co-operation and led to the creation of a genuine wartime coalition.[232] On one hand, its determination to sustain the theory of a 'separate war' made Helsinki anxious to avoid supporting many German political requests and demands, and to prevent a joint conduct of the war. On the other hand, Hitler's desire for a free hand after the war made him unwilling to enter into political agreements or hold discussions about his war aims. In making such an analysis, the sheer megalomaniac extent of Hitler's political goals must never be forgotten. According to a minute from Bormann dated 16 July 1941, these even included the 'annexation of Finland as a federal state' at some later date.[233] Given these underlying attitudes, Hitler was not prepared to keep the Finns fully informed either of his political ideas for a New Order in the east or of his operational and strategic views.

Genuine partnership was not the aim of German policy. This fact is also demonstrated by German economic plans for the extension of German–Finnish trade relations, and by the ideas of German firms regarding Finland. Owing to the serious decline in its industrial and agricultural production, Finland had become greatly dependent on Germany in the economic sphere and in the munitions sector. Even after the recovery of the former Karelian territories, economic resources were scarcely any greater than before the war because the region had been largely destroyed and there was no prospect of rapid reconstruction. Helsinki therefore hoped to obtain economic deliveries from the western territories of the Soviet Union which had been conquered by German troops.[234] The collapse of the Finnish economy in the second half of

---

[232] See also Hillgruber, 'Einbau', 681. On this aspect of a German–Finnish coalition see Hölter, 'Probleme des deutsch-finnischen Koalitionskampfes'; Ueberschär, 'Guerre de coalition', 55 ff., and id., 'Koalitionskriegführung im Zweiten Weltkrieg', 374 ff.

[233] See No. 221-L, *IMT* xxxviii. 86 ff.

[234] See OKW Az 3120 WiRüAmt/WiVIe No. 12863/41g, 'War-economy guidelines of the Finnish front No. 1: The reincorporated old Finnish territories', 9 Dec. 1941, BA-MA OKW/Abt. Wehrmachtpropaganda, RW 4/v. 325; and letter from the Finnish minister, Kivmäki, 26 Aug. 1941, PA, Büro St.S., Finnland, vol. iii.

1941 was avoided only by large-scale deliveries of German foodstuffs, raw materials, and military equipment.[235] Hitler and Göring themselves intervened to promise the Finnish government supplies of foodstuffs which could only be achieved 'at the expense of the supply situation of the German people'.[236] A 'German War Economy Officer in Finland' was appointed in mid-December 1941 'to unify all the war-economic work of the German Wehrmacht that is necessary in Finland', and to organize the extensive German deliveries to that country. This office also liaised with the war-economy and armaments office in Helsinki.[237] Almost inevitably, Helsinki became vulnerable to German pressure in establishing its claim to hegemony and leadership in 'reorganizing' raw-material distribution in northern Europe. This process was also regarded as one of Germany's 'main points of economic penetration and political influence'.[238]

Almost immediately, Berlin and IG-Farben repeated the demands for rights to the nickel-ore deposits at Petsamo that they had previously addressed to Moscow. During the German–Finnish economic discussions of October–November 1941 an attempt was made to persuade the Finns to expropriate the British–Canadian concession-holders in favour of a German–Finnish society dominated by German firms.[239] Following its entry into the war, the Finnish government had already taken over the custodianship of the concession through the Petsamo Nikkeli OY company, and had agreed to increase German supplies to 90 per cent of the development. However, the Finns refused to regulate the concession rights and conditions of ownership while hostilities lasted.[240] For the time being, German plans could not be put into practice.

[235] See e.g. Halder, *Diaries*, 1039 (13 July 1941). On Finland's catastrophic economic position see the 'special report on the Finnish armaments industry' and the 'memorandum of the Finnish ministry of national supply on the food situation', in liaison officer Liaison Staff North No. 576/41g, situation report of 7 Nov. 1941 with appendices, BA-MA Wi/F 5.655. For Helsinki's request for weapons and war equipment, and the discussions of the head of the Finnish war economy department, Gen. Grandell, with Gen. Thomas of the war economy and armaments department, see the notes in war diary WiRüAmt 1 Apr. 1941–31 Mar. 1942, BA-MA RW 19/165, 166. On deliveries of foodstuffs see the discussions in the foreign ministry, memorandum HaPol 732gRs, 1 Nov. 1941, PA, Büro St.S., Finnland, vol. iii; also memorandum Schnurre, 18 Nov. 1941, ibid., vol. iv.

[236] See Schnurre memorandum HaPol No. 7709/41g, 27 Nov. 1941, PA, Büro St.S., Finnland, vol. iv.

[237] OKW Az 11 WiRüAmt/Stab/I/O No. 6569/41g on the establishment of a department of the 'German war-economy officer in Finland' (WO Finland), 19 Dec. 1941, PA Dt. Ges. Helsinki, Schriftwechsel geheim, vol. iv, and Auswärtiges Amt Pol I M (Att) 491g, 22 Jan. 1942, ibid. See also 'The war-economy officer and his tasks, based on the example of Finland', BA-MA Wi/I F 5.2294, Commander Henry Koch became WO Finland.

[238] Eichholz, 'Expansionsrichtung Nordeuropa', 18.

[239] On the negotiations over the nickel agreement at Petsamo see report of the liaison officer to the Reich ministry of economic affairs, 15 Oct. 1941, BA-MA RW 45/15; letter of IG Farben, 5 Sept. 1941, PA, Dt. Ges. Helsinki, Schriftwechsel geheim, vol. ii; *DGFP* D xiii, No. 429. Also Krosby, *Petsamo Dispute*, 186 ff., 197 ff.; Jäger, *Wirtschaftliche Abhängigkeit*, 230–1; and Ueberschär, *Hitler und Finnland*, 315.

[240] See *DGFP* D xiii, No. 469; Blücher, *Gesandter*, 258, and BA-MA RW 45/16 (report of 26 Feb. 1942). The opposition stemmed largely from the attitude of Minister of Trade Tanner: see letter

In view of Berlin's plans for hegemony, the prospects for genuine coalition with the Third Reich, or for co-determination on the part of its allies or co-belligerents, were non-existent. This was true on economic and commercial as well as political grounds. Close military and political co-operation was out of the question. It was made impossible by Hitler's leadership claims, as well as his desire to take sole responsibility for the war in the east in order to fulfil 'his' mission.[241] Even after the entry of Finland into the war, Hitler was not interested in forging a stable and enduring political alliance as the foundation for long-term trusting co-operation. It was hoped that the difficulty of co-ordinating such different political ideas could be overcome by the achievement of a 'blitzkrieg' victory. In consequence, the two states' conduct of the war against the Soviet Union was based on a momentary understanding between their political leaders, and on occasional military discussions at high-command level and among local commanders.[242] Unified leadership was lacking, a situation which was partly responsible for the inadequacies of the war waged by Berlin and Helsinki. In the last analysis, there was only a limited community of interest in the German–Finish 'brotherhood-in-arms', to use Helsinki's description of the war against the Soviet Union.[243] This community of interest was based on a common anti-Soviet attitude, and on a struggle which was fought simultaneously but independently in both military and political terms. It was not the result of any military or political interests uniting Berlin and Helsinki in the pursuit of identical objectives. To this extent, the basis of the common struggle against the Soviet Union was a loose political relationship held together largely by the common enemy. In consequence, the war waged by Germany and Finland in the northernmost theatre is a paradigm for the entire conduct of the Second World War by the Axis powers and the governments which were allied with or friendly to them.

4. THE ATTITUDE OF SWEDEN FOLLOWING THE GERMAN INVASION OF THE SOVIET UNION

After the launching of Operation Barbarossa, Berlin expected Sweden to support the German war effort against the Soviet Union, in line with the declarations of intent made at the end of June 1941. However, these hopes for active participation in the 'anti-Bolshevik crusade' against Moscow were quickly disappointed. By the end of the year the Germans had been forced into a more sober assessment. As a Baltic state, Sweden naturally followed German

---

of Wehrmacht commander in Norway, Col.-Gen. von Falkenhorst, to FM Keitel, 6 Nov. 1941, PA, Dt. Ges. Helsinki, Schriftwechsel geheim, vol. iii, and telegram No. 1285, German legation Helsinki to foreign ministry, 10 Nov. 1941, ibid., Büro St.S., Finnland, vol. iii.

[241] See Hillgruber, *Strategie*, 484.

[242] On this issue see Ueberschär, 'Guerre de coalition', 40 ff., and id., 'Koalitionskriegführung im Zweiten Weltkrieg', 380 ff.

[243] Blücher, *Gesandter*, 246.

intentions and political measures in east central Europe with great interest. This attention was even more essential after the outbreak of war, when Sweden assumed the role of Poland's diplomatic protecting power in Berlin; in the summer of 1941 it took on the same role for the Soviet Union.[244]

It was in this capacity that on 19 July 1941 Stockholm informed the German foreign ministry of the Soviet offer to apply the regulations of the Hague Land Warfare Convention of 1907 'on condition of reciprocity' in dealing with each other's prisoners of war.[245] This note undoubtedly occasioned considerable irritation and insecurity on the German side. Until then the Soviet Union had not been party to the Geneva convention of 1929 regarding prisoners of war; there was also some doubt whether, as the successor to the Tsarist state, it had regarded itself as committed to the less detailed agreements of the Hague Land Warfare Convention. In its message via the Swedes Moscow was announcing its recognition of the simple rules of the Land Warfare Convention and attempting to force the hand of the German government. However, Hitler and the Wehrmacht High Command were not interested in any agreement. The issuing of Hitler's 'criminal orders' had already created situations wholly incompatible with these regulations. Moreover, in those first weeks after the outbreak of war Hitler's attitude was based on a certainty of victory and the desire for a free hand to achieve his racial and ideological objectives in the east. In September 1941 he decided 'that no legal agreement may be reached with the Soviet Union on the question of the treatment of prisoners of war'. Hitler even intervened personally to stiffen the German reply to the Swedish government, making it virtually impossible for the Soviet government to use this method for further initiatives. His over-confident assessment of the German position appears to have led him to squander an opportunity which had been created with Swedish help, and which offered 'the most important and promising chance to base the treatment of each other's prisoners on the principles of humanity'.

It was very difficult for Sweden, as protecting power for the Soviet Union, to participate either covertly or indirectly in Germany's self-proclaimed struggle of European culture against 'Bolshevik barbarism'. In the first weeks

[244] Åkerrén, 'Schweden als Schutzmacht'.
[245] On this subject see the study by Streit, *Keine Kameraden*, 224 ff., and Streim, *Die Behandlung sowjetischer Kriegsgefangener*, 33–4; also the documents from military sources in BA-MA RW 5/v. 506 and 6/v. 279 (also for the following quotations). On the other hand, Roschmann, *Gutachten*, 3–4, is not to the point. In view of the published documents in *DGFP* D xiii, Nos. 173, 389 (also *ADAP* E i, No. 51: Ribbentrop memorandum for Hitler, 22 Dec. 1941), attempts have been made (as in this volume, sect. II.11.3 at n. 31 (Hoffmann)) to cast doubt on Streit's arguments and documentary evidence by arguing that they are not wholly in accordance with the facts and are the result of misinterpretation and a denial of actual events. As regards Hitler's basic attitude, and his fear that an agreement with the USSR might create the impression on the eastern front that German prisoners would be treated according to the convention by the Russians, while the list of names which the Germans would have to hand over to the Soviet government would enable it to discover 'that not all Russian soldiers fallen into German hands are alive', see *ADAP* E i, No. 106.

after the attack on the USSR the early successes of the Wehrmacht led the Germans to expect a swift victory. Their hopes for Swedish accommodation were correspondingly great. For example, Berlin expected Stockholm to provide the Germans with detailed intelligence information through the Swedish legation in Moscow. These optimistic expectations were soon modified, however. In July 1941 it became clear that there was no chance of Sweden joining the Tripartite Pact. Ribbentrop also regarded the creation of a special bilateral alliance as out of the question.[246] In consequence, he noted, 'we shall ignore her in the future'.[247]

Nevertheless, in June 1941 military circles round the Swedish commander-in-chief, General Thörnell, did provide some arguments in favour of action to support Germany in its struggle with the Soviet Union. Admittedly, the action under consideration was relatively minor, involving the occupation of the Finnish Åland islands by Swedish troops, for example. This would offer indirect support to Germany and make the task of the German navy in the Baltic easier. Such attitudes were strengthened after Finland entered the war on the German side. A sense of solidarity with Finland made the defeat of the Soviet Union and of Communism appear very desirable, particularly as it would result in a shift of the Finnish–Soviet border to the east, further from the border with Sweden. These circles also believed that Sweden would be treated with greater respect in the subsequent peace negotiations if it had participated actively in the victory over the Soviet Union, and that it might then have a part to play in the reorganization of Europe by the Third Reich.

However, the official view of the Swedish government differed from that being discussed in pro-German military circles. The government's primary interest lay in ending its commercial and political isolation in the Baltic. From July 1941, with the permission of Berlin and London, Sweden resumed its maritime trade between Göteborg and abroad, which had been halted in March of that year.[248] The 'Göteborg trade' was subjected to British and German control in each country's areas of naval operations. Nevertheless, its resumption was significant as a symbol of Swedish attempts to preserve free foreign trade. Virtually as a quid pro quo, the Third Reich expected the Swedes to agree to the transit of another German division through Swedish territory (6th Mountain Division, envisaged as reinforcement for the Arctic Front). However, Stockholm turned down this request on 1 August 1941. On the other hand, transports of material to Norway and Finland, and the overflying of Swedish territory for German hospital and courier aircraft, continued as they had before the war in the east. These were restricted only by the limitations of Swedish capacity.

---

[246] See *DGFP* D xiii, Nos. 77, 79; Halder, *Diaries*, 1020 (9 July 1941); Carlgren, *Svensk utrikespolitik*, 315; also Wilhelmus, 'Beziehungen zwischen dem faschistischen Deutschland und Schweden', 687–99.

[247] Halder, *Diaries*, 1076 (26 July 1941).

[248] See *DGFP* D xiii, No. 91; also Rockberger, *Göteborgstrafiken*.

At the begining of November and again in mid-December, however, Stockholm refused to accept Wehrmacht troop requests exceeding the level previously agreed. In this case, the Swedish government under Premier Hansson referred to the country's policy of strict neutrality and to the availability of other options—sea routes, land routes through Finland, and the use of Swedish territorial waters along the Baltic coast to the north.[249] At the end of February Minister Schnurre, special emissary of the German foreign ministry, reported that Stockholm was still adhering 'stubbornly and rigidly' to this position.[250]

German bitterness at the various refusals was intensified by increasing dissatisfaction with the general attitude of Sweden. In particular, its co-operation with 'the struggle of Europe against Bolshevism' was regarded as inadequate.[251] In the first weeks after the launching of Operation Barbarossa, circles within the Swedish army had viewed the destruction of Bolshevism in Russia as highly desirable not only for military and foreign-policy reasons, but also because of its effect on internal conflicts with the Swedish Communists. In general, these elements hoped that the removal of the Soviet Union from the Baltic Sea area would have positive effects on domestic affairs within Sweden. On several occasions the leadership of the Swedish forces supported demands for a ban on Communist activity and for effective government measures against Communism in Sweden. They were even prepared to accept a deterioration in relations with the Western powers, if favourable and positive relations with a victorious Germany and Finland could be attained. However, this initial enthusiasm for the German 'struggle against Bolshevism' had 'completely subsided' by the middle of August; by this stage the Swedish press was openly reporting the 'purely imperialistic plans of Hitler'.[252] This encouraged the general line of the Swedish government to 'keep all possibilities open',[253] and to stay out of the conflict. Berlin reproached the Swedish government for continuing to tolerate the actions of the Communist Party and refusing to ban it.[254] In addition, Berlin had not been able to persuade Sweden to join the anti-Comintern pact with Finland and Denmark in November 1941. King Gustav V Adolf's confidential message to Hitler on 28 October

[249] Telegram No. 746, Ribbentrop to German legation Helsinki, 29 July 1941, No. 745, Ritter to German legation Stockholm, 29 July 1941, both in PA, Büro St.S., Schweden, vol. ii; telegram No. 782, Ribbentrop to German legation Stockholm, 3 Aug. 1941, ibid., vol. iii; *DGFP* D xiii, Nos. 172, 176, 178; memorandum from Swedish 'Royal Ministry of the Exterior', 4 Nov. 1941, BA-MA Wi/I E 3.30b. See also Gruchmann, 'Schweden', 603; Wilhelmus, 'Schweden und das faschistische Deutschland', 804.

[250] Telegram No. 395, German legation Stockholm to foreign ministry, 19 Feb. 1942, and No. 453, 24 Feb. 1942, both in PA, Büro St.S., Schweden, vol. iii.

[251] See telegram No. 782, Ribbentrop to German legation Stockholm, 3 Apr. 1941, ibid.

[252] Report of liaison officer war economy and armaments department Stockholm, Col. Drews, No. 691/41 Mil.Att.: assessment of public mood in Sweden, 14 Aug. 1941, BA-MA Wi/E 3.30b; on the attitude of the Swedish press see also Marandi, *Med grannens ögon*.

[253] Halder, *Diaries*, 1222 (10 Sept. 1941).

[254] See *ADAP* E i, No. 151.

1941, congratulating him on the triumphs of the Wehrmacht and thanking him for averting the danger of Bolshevism in Europe, was scant consolation.[255] In his reply of 7 December 1941 Hitler referred to the anti-German sentiments of certain circles in Sweden and demanded greater interest in the 'unique historic action' being undertaken by Germany.[256] Nevertheless, Sweden rejected new demands from Berlin in December.

At the outset, the Germans had hoped that Sweden might serve as a 'war-economy reservoir' and a 'supply hinterland for the Finnish theatre of war'.[257] In reality, Swedish support for Germany and Finland in their conduct of war in the far north fell far below the economic and financial expectations of Berlin.[258] The Swedish government did approve deliveries of supplies for the German troops in Finland and Norway; however, despite repeated German requests it refused to sell larger amounts of urgently needed winter equipment to German formations deployed in northern Finland.[259] After Sweden had delivered 500 lorries to Finland in July 1941, both the Finnish and German sides made further requests for the delivery of lorries and personnel-carriers, hutments, and tents in September. Stockholm granted these requests only in part, as a 'once and for all' measure, by offering to sell another 800 motor-vehicles, without rubber tyres, against extra deliveries of nickel from Petsamo. The Stockholm government cleverly justified its decision by pointing out that German deliveries of coal and coke had been incomplete, and that Sweden therefore needed adequate means of transport to guarantee fuel supplies in the form of increased domestic deliveries of wood.[260] Berlin was unable to refute this argument, in view of the fact that it had broken its agreement on coal exports. Finnish requests for credit, war material, and foodstuffs were generally treated more sympathetically by the Swedes. However, even these were fulfilled only if they evoked no protests from and commercial difficulties with Britain.[261]

Tension in German–Swedish relations was also created by the rivalry between Berlin and London over the Norwegian merchant ships which had been impounded in the Swedish port of Göteborg. Initially the Swedes had proposed to deliver these to England according to the demands of the Norwegian

---

[255] *DGFP* D xiii, No. 430.

[256] Ibid., Nos. 554, 574.

[257] Memorandum of 17 Nov. 1941, BA-MA RW 45/15; Wittmann, 'Deutsch-schwedische Wirtschaftsbeziehungen', 210–11, 217–18.

[258] Report on the Swedish economy in Dec. 1941, BA-MA Wi/I E 3.30b. On the Swedish deliveries see memorandum of the Swedish government, 18 Nov. 1941, *DGFP* D xiii, No. 530, and the 'confidential memorandum' of 20 Jan. 1942, copy of translation, Pol.VI 5209g, PA, Ha.Pol., Handakten Wiehl, Schweden, vol. vi.

[259] See *DGFP* D xiii, No. 418, and telegram No. 1956, German legation Stockholm to foreign ministry, 20 Nov. 1941, PA, Büro St.S., Schweden, vol. iii.

[260] See telegrams Nos. 1541, 1558, German legation Stockholm to foreign ministry, 25 and 26 Sept. 1941, PA, Büro St.S., Schweden, vol. iii.

[261] See telegram No. 961 to foreign ministry, 16 July 1941, PA, Büro St.S., Schweden, vol. ii, and report of liaison officer, Col. Drews, at the German legation Stockholm to OKW/WiRüAmt: Swedish deliveries for Finland, 11 Sept. 1941, BA-MA Wi/E 3.30b.

government-in-exile in London. However, on 26 September 1941 Ribbentrop told the Swedish chargé d'affaires in Berlin that Sweden would be committing 'an unfriendly act' towards Germany if it allowed a single Norwegian ship to leave Göteborg.[262] During his conversation with the Swedish diplomat the German foreign minister complained bitterly about the Swedish attitude during the 'gigantic struggle' against Bolshevism. Ribbentrop also criticized the refusal of the Swedish government to allow Swedish volunteers to take part in the war against the Soviet Union on the German side. (They were permitted only to serve as volunteers in the Finnish Army.[263]) Instead of active participation in the struggle, the Swedes were offering only 'ever new instances of unfriendliness and insults'. On several occasions the foreign minister expressed his regret that Sweden 'had excluded herself from co-operation in the battle against Bolshevism'. As regards the release of the Norwegian ships, the country was taking a position 'which not only did not help Germany and her allies, but practically amounted to a stab in the back'. His words had the desired effect. Though the Swedish government strongly repudiated Ribbentrop's criticism,[264] it then decided—despite angry protests from London—to detain the Norwegian merchant ships in Göteborg for the time being.

For the Swedish government, the nature of German occupation policy in Norway was also a crucial factor in determining its approach to Berlin. The Swedish foreign minister, Günther, repeatedly emphasized in parliament that Sweden took a special interest in political developments there. The Swedish government publicly opposed any permanent German occupation of Norway. On 29 October 1941 Günther made an important declaration on his country's foreign policy: Sweden, he noted, 'could not remotely contemplate a future of the north which does not involve this region regaining its freedom in its entirety'.[265] Swedish declarations about German occupation measures in Norway eventually led to considerable ill feeling in Berlin. In May 1942 Ribbentrop instructed the German legation in Stockholm 'from now on, to ignore any communications from the Swedish side relating to the situation and events in Norway'.[266] The German foreign minister angrily denied that the

---

[262] On the German position see *DGFP* D xiii, Nos. 335, 364; for the following quotation see No. 364. On Swedish readiness to let the Norwegian ships put to sea see telegram No. 1486, German legation Stockholm to foreign ministry, 20 Sept. 1941, PA, Büro St.S., Schweden, vol. iii, also Rockberger, *Göteborgstrafiken*.

[263] On the issue of the participation of Swedish volunteers in the war in the east see sect. II.v.3.

[264] Memorandum of State Secretary, St.S. No. 673, 7 Oct. 1941, PA, Ha.Pol., Handakten Wiehl, Schweden, vol. vi.

[265] Telegram No. 1818, German legation Stockholm to foreign ministry, 29 Oct. 1941, PA, Büro St.S., Schweden, vol. iii.

[266] Telegram No. 586, special train Ribbentrop to German legation Stockholm, 27 May 1942, ibid., vol. iv (also for the following). On the contacts of the Swedish government with the Norwegian government-in-exile see the published documents *Handlingar: fragor i samband med norska regeringens 1940–1943*.

Swedish government had any 'active right' to 'make Norwegian affairs the subject of communications to the German legation'.

Sweden remained an important trading partner of the Third Reich. During German–Swedish economic negotiations in Sepember 1941, the German foreign ministry's trade department reported that economic relations with Sweden had developed 'satisfactorily'. In comparison with the period before the war, Sweden had 'maintained increased deliveries to Germany', even though Germany had 'delivered only part' of the coal supplies it was due to provide in both 1940 and 1941.[267] In particular, the Germans considered that deliveries of timber and iron ore were being maintained 'at a very significant level'. Sweden was also forced to make commercial concessions to Germany in the second half of 1941, reflecting the fact that the country had become commercially dependent on the Third Reich after its invasion of the Soviet Union and Swedish isolation on the Baltic. In December 1941 Sweden joined the German–Scandinavian 'forestry agreement' alongside Denmark and Finland and was forced to adapt to German economic plans for forestry and timber.[268] On 19 December 1941 the existing German–Swedish economic agreements were renewed for 1942. Owing largely to German difficulties over deliveries and payment, and to rising Wehrmacht transport costs, Germany had become increasingly indebted to Sweden by the end of 1941. The consequence was a gradual decline in Swedish deliveries of iron ore to Germany. In order to guarantee the export of iron ore at its previous levels, Stockholm therefore granted a bigger state export credit for deliveries to Germany as part of the new economic agreement. An attempt was made to settle the balance of payment and trade by arranging new Swedish purchases of war equipment in Germany.[269] Berlin also wanted German firms to gain a decisive influence over Swedish companies by means of the export of capital or supply contracts. These last plans, however, could not be fully implemented.[270]

The Germans, convinced that Britain would be eliminated from the Continent after the defeat of the Soviet Union, also revived general ideas for the 'economic reorganization of Europe' at this time. Following the German attack on the USSR, these plans included schemes for the incorporation of northern Europe in the new economic order. The German foreign ministry informed the Swedish legation in Berlin that it expected Swedish participation in the 'work of reconstruction in the east'.[271] It is important to remember the

---

[267] Memorandum of the trade department, 18 Sept. 1941, PA Ha.Pol., Handakten Wiehl, Schweden, vol. vi (also for the following).

[268] See Wittmann, *Schwedens Wirtschaftsbeziehungen*, 227; Wilhelmus, 'Schwedisches Echo', 44 ff.

[269] See *ADAP* E i, No. 11. Also Wittmann, 'Deutsch-schwedische Wirtschaftsbeziehungen', 212; Wilhelmus, 'Die Bedeutung des schwedischen Eisenerzes', 44–5.

[270] On individual cases of Germans exerting influence see Eichholtz, 'Expansionsrichtung Nordeuropa', 23.

[271] See Lutzhöft, 'Schwedische Reaktionen', 74–5. On German plans for the participation of other states in the economic exploitation of the occupied territories of the USSR see also Eichholtz, 'European Greater Economic Sphere'.

constraints on the states of northern Europe at this time. As regards their own future trade with Germany, they had to assume that in future Germany would satisfy many of her economic needs from the conquered territories of the USSR rather than from them. There was clearly some justification for their fears. In one of his 'table talks' at the end of 1941 Hitler remarked that he intended to supply Europe with iron from the conquered eastern territories. He added: 'If one day Sweden declines to supply any more iron, that's all right. We'll get it from Russia.'[272]

Apart from the ease and rapidity of their adjustment, it is therefore scarcely surprising that Swedish industrial and agricultural circles showed great interest in German ideas for the participation of the north European economy in the exploitation of the economic potential of the occupied eastern territories. These schemes appeared almost as a replacement for the expected shift of trade policy from central Europe to the east. In autumn 1941 the foreign ministry and Reich ministry for economic affairs held their first discussions about the participation and involvement of other states in the proposed economic development of the occupied Soviet territories. At this stage the governments of several allied, friendly, and neutral countries had expressed an interest in German plans. Sweden was one of the governments to make an enquiry. It had expressed an interest in 'obtaining raw materials from the eastern territories by supplying industrial products';[273] in addition, it showed 'direct interest in an active co-operation in the solution of economic tasks in the new eastern territories, for example by taking over businesses, obtaining concessions, and also by settlement'.

On 21 November 1941 a discussion was held in the Reich ministry for economic affairs 'on the participation of foreign countries in the economic development of the eastern territories'. Here the representatives of the various German authorities concluded 'that the development of the eastern territories is not a purely German matter but a European affair, Europe should therefore be engaged in the eastern territories'.[274] Such an involvement of other states was to be recommended on principle, since Germany 'alone [could] not, in the near future, supply the necessary workforce and investments for the economic utilization of the occupied territories'.[275] In addition, the native population was 'in part unsuited, in part unwanted' for the task.

Despite this apparent willingness to co-operate with other states, there was no change to the principle of undiminished German economic dominance in

[272] Hitler, *Monologe*, 59 (19–20 Aug. 1941).

[273] Minute V.Ld. 9777/41g: Participation of foreign countries in the economic development of the eastern territory, 24 Nov. 1941, BA R2/30921 (also for the following).

[274] Minute on today's discussion in the Reich ministry of economic affairs on the participation of foreign countries in the economic development of the eastern territory, No. 3057a/41g., 21 Nov. 1941 (signed Dr Worbs), ibid.

[275] On the discussion in the ministry of economic affairs on 21 Nov. 1941 see also the memorandum in PA, Pol.Abt. XIII, No. 17: Allgemeine Akte betr. Lage in den besetzten Ostgebieten [situation in the occupied eastern territories] (also for the following), see also Groehler and Schumann, 'Bündnisbeziehungen', 636 ff.

these territories. German interests were not to be damaged under any circumstances. Various possibilities for the involvement of other states were considered: (1) conclusion of merchandise compensation agreements with the interested states; (2) involvement of individual foreigners as managers and workers in specific branches of the economy and industry; (3) granting of economic concessions to foreign groups of firms; and (4) settlement of foreigners in the occupied Soviet territories. The 'guiding' economic-political objective in the occupied territories was 'in the first instance, to gain agricultural surpluses and obtain sources of raw materials'.[276] The German ministries and departments saw 'no room' for a further 'policy of construction' in the industrial sphere, similar to that in western Europe.

Sweden was among the countries regarded by Berlin as most suitable for this task. This was made clear by a 'memorandum on the current state of preparations to involve the European states in the economic development of the occupied Russian territories', produced by the trade department of the foreign ministry on 23 November 1941.[277] It indicated that Berlin was particularly interested in Swedish co-operation in the reconstruction of the Soviet ferrous industry, in the expansion of water power and electricity, and in forestry and agriculture. However, Swedish requests for the return of former possessions, and particularly of former investments in the Baltic States, were rejected.

The Swedes evaded demands for direct participation in the 'Germanization of the east' planned by Berlin. None the less, in February 1942 the German special emissary, Schnurre, continued to discuss 'the new agrarian order created by Germany in the Ukraine' with members of the Swedish government. These discussions reveal that the Swedes were showing considerable interest in such proposals and plans for participation.[278] Significantly, the ministry for the east under Rosenberg advocated an immediate transformation of Swedish interest in this economic branch into an active 'Swedish co-operation in the exploitation of the occupied eastern territories'. Yet this was a step which the Swedish government had no desire to take in the spring of 1942, when there was considerable friction and even a deterioration in relations between Stockholm and Berlin over the Swedish refusal to make additional military concessions. Besides, after the entry of the United States into the war and the failure of the German 'blitzkrieg' strategy in the fighting near Moscow, the Swedes too were becoming increasingly doubtful that German

[276] Minute V.Ld. 9777/41g, 24 Nov. 1941 (see n. 273 above) (also for the following quotation).

[277] Deutsches Zentralarchiv Potsdam, Auswärtiges Amt, No. 68701: Handakten Clodius, Aufbauausschuß 'Ost'. The author is grateful to Prof. W. Schumann, Berlin, and Dr G. Schreiber, Freiburg, for permitting him to see this document. See also Groehler and Schumann, 'Bündnisbeziehungen', 637.

[278] See the interdepartmental discussion in the foreign ministry on 14 Jan. 1942 in response to Swedish and Danish enquiries, PA, Pol.Abt. XIII, No. 17, Allg. Akten betr. Lage in den besetzten Ostgebieten [situation in the occupied eastern territories]; also Lutzhöft, 'Schwedische Reaktionen', 75 (and for the following).

plans for a New Order in Europe could ever be realized. The wisdom of Swedish economic dependence on Germany was being assessed more cautiously at the beginning of 1942, and in places was already being rejected. From early 1942 German irritation at repeated Swedish refusals to co-operate led to a deterioration in relations between the two countries and to increasing tension.[279]

After Britain declared war on Finland on 6 December 1941, Swedish neutrality appeared even more gravely threatened by possible British military intervention in northern Scandinavia and a preventive strike by Berlin. In late 1941 and early 1942 the Swedish government was alarmed by rumours of a possible military move against Sweden by the Third Reich. The government in Stockholm was aware of the reinforcement of the German troops in Norway which Hitler had ordered from the beginning of 1942. Although the Germans had not planned any action against Sweden, the Swedes thought that British–American landings or new German military action might be undertaken with the aim of occupying Sweden in the spring of 1942.[280] Preparatory mobilization measures were implemented to increase the strength of the Swedish army to around 300,000 men. At the same time the king of Sweden sent Hitler official reassurance from the government 'that Sweden would never tolerate Anglo-American designs on northern Scandinavia involving a march through Sweden. He was absolutely determined to prevent the penetration of Anglo-American troops into Sweden by force of arms.'[281] Hitler himself wanted to stabilize the political situation in Scandinavia; he was anxious to avoid new conflicts to the rear of the planned German spring offensive in the east and the westward-facing defensive line in Norway. On 13 March 1942 he therefore informed Sweden's king and government that 'for its part Germany would take no step which would violate the neutrality of Sweden'.[282] As a result, political relations between the two countries became less strained.

In many areas Sweden did help to supply the German and Finnish troops in Norway and in the Finnish theatre. However, it never deployed its military forces directly against the Soviet Union, as Berlin had wanted, and did not participate militarily in the war in the east. Despite ensuring 'important relief' at certain points, Swedish deliveries were not of decisive significance to the German war effort in the far north.[283]

Goebbels's diary entries typify the irritation within the National Socialist leadership over the attitude of Sweden in the spring of 1942, particularly regarding the German demand for greater support or involvement in the war

[279] See *DGFP* D xiii, No. 336.

[280] See ibid., No. 561. On the 'February crisis' between Germany and Sweden from 12 Feb. see *ADAP* E i; Uhlin, *Februarkrisen* 1942; Wilhelmus, 'Vorbereitungen', 1035.

[281] *ADAP* E i, No. 282.

[282] Ibid. n. 4, and Ribbentrop's telegram No. 721 to German legation in Stockholm, 13 Mar. 1942, PA, Büro St.S., Schweden, vol. iv.

[283] According to Wittman, 'Deutsch-schwedische Wirtschaftsbeziehungen', 210–11, and id., *Schwedens Wirtschaftsbeziehungen*, 262; also Carlgren, 'Sweden and the Great Powers'.

against the Soviet Union. In January 1942 the Reich minister of propaganda still thought that Sweden 'had done more for the German war effort than is generally assumed';[284] in particular, the Swedes had provided 'considerable support' in the war against the Soviet Union. Though the country was guarding its neutrality, it was interpreting it very much to the benefit of Berlin. However, as regards the German–Finnish war effort against the USSR in the north, Goebbels regarded Swedish support as 'meagre'. He was especially critical of the lack of support by the Swedish press, whose attitude was more 'provocative and insolent'. For the time being, however, the Germans would have to be satisfied with what they had.

By 15 April 1942 Goebbels had changed his mind, maintaining that the Swedish attitude towards Germany had deteriorated. He now argued that it would 'have been better if we had broken Sweden too' when Norway was occupied in the spring of 1940, since Sweden 'has no right to national existence anyway'. Advocates of the 'idea of the greater Germanic empire', or the 'north Germanic community of destiny on the Baltic', were bound to be disappointed by Sweden's sober attitude towards German propaganda for the 'struggle of Europe against barbarism'. However, this did not lead to a more realistic German policy towards Sweden; there was little attempt to give due weight to practical political possibilities in foreign policy or to the country's democratic political system. Political and military thinking regarding Sweden remained thoroughly unrealistic at the beginning of 1942; there was still a strong assumption that, whatever its reluctance, Sweden would allow itself to be drawn into the German sphere of influence within the framework of a 'greater economic area' controlled by Berlin. In fact, the aim of Swedish foreign policy was to keep out of the war of the great powers and to protect the independence of the country. The Swedish government was therefore anxious to strengthen its own defensive power with all the means at its disposal. Potential aggressors were to be deterred by the prospect of sustaining heavy casualities and making huge sacrifices. The foreign ministry in Berlin described the Swedish attitude at the beginning of 1942 as a 'line of armed neutrality'.[285] With the political climate greatly changed by the entry of the United States into the war against the Axis, Berlin had no chance of drawing Sweden into the war on the side of Germany.

5. THE REACTION OF OCCUPIED DENMARK AND NORWAY TO HITLER'S ATTACK ON THE SOVIET UNION

It is clear from previous descriptions of military and political events that northern Europe was profoundly affected by the preparations for Operation

---

[284] Goebbels, *Diaries*, 19–20 (28 Jan. 1941), 122 (15 Apr. 1941) (also for the following quotations).

[285] See the text prepared by the foreign ministry for Ribbentrop No. e.o.Pol. VI 5225g, 3 Feb. 1942, Handakten Wiehl, Schweden, vol. vi.

Barbarossa, and by the military operations against northern Russia after the German invasion of the Soviet Union. Alongside Sweden and Finland, the other north European countries of Denmark and Norway also had a specific role to play in the German war effort against the Soviet Union. The nature and implications of this role extended beyond purely military factors and, in different ways, affected the diplomatic, ideological, and economic spheres. With the German invasion of the Soviet Union on 22 June 1941 these factors—together with German expectations concerning the conduct of occupied Denmark and Norway—had a deep impact on domestic affairs in the states concerned.

After the German invasion of the Soviet Union, discussions immediately began in Berlin over the form in which occupied Denmark should and could be involved in the war.[286] Almost as a matter of course, the Germans expected police measures to be taken against the Soviet legation and its staff in Denmark. They also demanded that the Danish police arrest former Tsarist Russian citizens and foreign Communists. The Danish government, under Premier Thorvald Stauning, acceded to this unequivocal demand: approximately 300 people were arrested. As the German plenipotentiary, Cecil von Renthe-Fink, reported with satisfaction to Berlin on 22 June 1941, these measures had been ordered 'without delay' on that day.[287] Only two days later the Danish foreign minister, Scavenius, told the German minister that Copenhagen was recalling its minister from Moscow and breaking off diplomatic relations with the USSR as an expression of 'solidarity with Germany and Finland in the struggle against the Soviet Union'.[288] In its declaration of 26 June 1941[289] the Danish government welcomed the war of Germany and Finland against the Soviet Union as decisive for the whole of Europe. Copenhagen's official announcement emphasized the 'common European interest' in this conflict, but maintained the country's status as a non-belligerent state. Nevertheless, the Germans welcomed the Danish decision to enter 'morally into the European front against the Soviet Union'. It was noted that, with the consent of the Danish government departments, Danish volunteers could be recruited for the Waffen-SS as well as the Finnish army.[290] Communist activity was stopped on 22 June. Finally, after repeated German requests and demands from the Danish National Socialists under their leader Frits Clausen, the

---

[286] On the occupation and subsequent occupation policy in Denmark see *Germany and the Second World War*, ii. 206 ff. (Stegemann); Kirchhoff, *Kamp*; and esp. Thomsen, *Besatzungspolitik* (for the following ibid. 80 ff.).

[287] Telegram No. 803, Minister von Renthe-Fink to foreign ministry, 22 June 1941, PA, Büro St.S., Dänemark, vol. ii.

[288] Telegram No. 814, minister to foreign ministry, 24 June 1941, ibid.

[289] See telegram No. 827, Minister von Renthe-Fink to foreign ministry, 26 June 1941 (also for the following); Thomsen, *Besatzungspolitik*, 81.

[290] On the participation of Danish volunteers in the war in the east see sect.II.v.3 at n. 120.

Danish Communist Party was banned by law on 22 August 1941.[291] The law was passed unanimously in the Folketing.

At this stage, however, Danish public opinion was largely preoccupied with the issue of Iceland. The island, which belonged to Denmark, was occupied by the United States on 7 July 1941 in response to the fact that British troops, who had landed there in May 1940, were now urgently needed in other theatres. On 17 May 1941 the Icelandic parliament decided unilaterally to dissolve the treaty of union with Denmark and declare Iceland a republic. For Danish citizens and politicians the loss of constitutional sovereignty over the North Atlantic island was a bigger talking-point in the summer of 1941 than the German invasion of the Soviet Union.

The German foreign ministry was anxious to avoid open interference in the domestic political and ideological affairs of Denmark. It therefore refused to support the illegal attempts of the Dansk National Socialistik Arbejderparti (DNSAP: Danish National Socialist Workers' Party) to secure a share in government. Consequently, despite individual financial contributions from Germany, the Danish National Socialists received little German support for their efforts to force greater Danish participation in the war against Bolshevism. In order to obtain voluntary co-operation and participation from the Danish government, and to prevent internal unrest, the Germans had ruled out the use of force. The unique nature of occupation rule in Denmark, presented as the 'showcase' of a just and restrained 'supervisory administration' by the foreign ministry, was not to be threatened. With the New Order in Europe in mind, the aim was to retain the legal appearance of the German presence in Denmark for as long as possible. At the beginning of November 1941 the situation was summarized by the foreign ministry in a detailed political report for Ribbentrop on 'Denmark's attitude towards Germany'. Given that the Danish government and people were unsympathetic to the ideology of National Socialist Germany, the report emphasized the political achievement of ensuring that none of the countries occupied by Germany 'is as peaceful and offers such close and virtually trouble-free co-operation as Denmark'.[292] In its requests and demands for Danish agreement and co-operation the German leadership therefore concentrated on actual areas of practical political activity rather than on issues of the political future. The government in Copenhagen adopted a very cautious approach to the question of Danish participation in the 'construction of the new Europe'; ultimately this would involve tasks intended for the Danish people, which would have to be

---

[291] See the exchange of telegrams between the Reich plenipotentiary, Minister von Renthe-Fink, and the foreign ministry in July and Aug. 1941, PA, Büro St.S., Dänemark, vol. ii. On the DNSAP in general see Poulsen, *Besættelsesmagten*.

[292] Memorandum by Minister von Grundherr for Ribbentrop: Denmark's attitude towards Germany, 4 Nov. 1941, *DGFP* D xiii, No. 447; an amended version can be found in PA, Büro St.S., Dänemark, vol. ii (also for the following quotations). On 'showpiece Denmark' see Rings, *Leben*, 48 ff.

carried out 'according to Danish custom'. The attitude of the Danish people towards the DNSAP and its leader Clausen was overwhelmingly negative: the DNSAP had about 30,000 members. The Germans were aware that 'a real inner conversion of the Danish people . . . [could] only be expected after the final German victory'.

Guided by this assessment of the political situation, in mid-November 1941 Ribbentrop obtained Hitler's agreement to the maintenance of existing policy for the future development of German–Danish relations.[293] Of decisive importance here was the fact that 'only a small number of German military forces [were required] to secure calm in the country' as a result of the close co-operation of German and Danish governmental and administrative authorities in Denmark. It was also very significant that the production of Danish industry was being largely turned over to German armaments purposes. Such developments could be regarded as an important Danish contribution to the war against the Soviet Union. Hitler therefore agreed that there should be no 'acceleration of the tempo by means of an increased activation of the National Socialist movement in this country', and that the foreign ministry should 'cautiously' maintain its previous line.

On the issue of Danish entry into the anti-Comintern pact, however, such 'caution' clearly had its limits. On 20 November 1941, with renewal of the treaty imminent, the German minister in Denmark made a demand for Danish accession to the pact. The demand was rejected by the Danish cabinet due to 'fear of English reprisals, and of a demand for a military contribution in the struggle against the Soviet Union'.[294] The Danes offered to make a unilateral declaration of sympathy with the terms of the anti-Comintern pact, but the proposal was rejected as inadequate by the Germans. The government in Berlin offered reassurances of its own: joining the pact would not commit Denmark outside its borders, and did not imply any military contribution to the war in the east. However, Danish doubts and hesitations were not allayed. At this stage Ribbentrop intervened to put direct and massive pressure on the Danish government. On 23 November he issued an ultimatum. If Denmark was not prepared to join the anti-Comintern pact, the government would be 'placing itself in the Bolsheviks' camp and ruling itself out of European co-operation'; moreover, Germany would no longer feel bound by the constitutional promises of 9 April 1940 regarding the sovereignty of Denmark.[295] This was nothing other than a naked threat to change the status of the occupation. In these circumstances the government and King Christian X agreed that same day to join the anti-Comintern pact. On the next day the Danish delegation under Foreign Minister Scavenius was

[293] 'Memorandum for the Führer' from Ribbentrop, 11 Nov. 1941, and report from the Reich foreign minister's office to State Secretary von Weizsäcker, 17 Nov. 1941, both in PA, Büro St.S., Dänemark, vol. ii.

[294] Thomsen, *Besatzungspolitik*, 83 ff. (also for the following).

[295] Memorandum from von Renthe-Fink, 23 Nov. 1941, given ibid. 85.

forced to travel to Berlin to complete the formalities of entry on 25 November 1941.

The Danish government tried to qualify its position in a special minute containing its continuing reservations. Nevertheless, Berlin had achieved its political objective of obtaining the accession of more European states in order to inflate the value of the pact in propaganda and political terms. Ribbentrop exploited the opportunity in his speech to celebrate the signing of the pact in Berlin on 26 November 1941. He described the voluntary enlistment of men from many European countries 'for the struggle against the common Bolshevik enemy', and the inclusion of the 'majority of European states' in the treaty, as a 'significant development' and a 'milestone on the road to the amalgamation and shaping of the new Europe'. Europe was now moving to combat the threat of the 'Jewish-Bolshevik steel roller', and uniting to fight against 'perpetual enslavement by Jewish Bolshevism'.[296] In similar vein, in his reception of Foreign Minister Scavenius on 27 November 1941 Hitler judged the entry of several more states to the anti-Comintern pact to be 'the demonstration of a new Europe slowly taking form'.[297] Ribbentrop promised his co-signatories that German triumphs in the east meant that the economic resources of occupied European Russia would now be available to satisfy fully the economic needs of all Europe. Soviet war industries seized there would be 'utilized for the war economy of Germany and her allies'.[298] The 'organization of this gigantic expanse' was already 'fully under way'. These promises were not merely propaganda announcements for public consumption. Behind the words of the German foreign minister lay the unspoken intention of the National Socialist leadership to involve other, mainly 'Germanic', states in the exploitation of the occupied eastern territories. Hitler had already made this intention clear to his inner circle in August 1941. There he argued that the greatest future task of National Socialism, within the framework of a planned racial policy, was not to 'allow any more Germans to emigrate to America'.[299] The Norwegians, Swedes, Danes, and Dutch would all have to be 'attracted' into the newly conquered eastern territories, there to become 'members of the German Reich'. On 11 September 1941 Hitler expressed similar views to the new Danish minister, Mohr, when he referred to the need for other states to participate in the economic exploitation of the new territories in the east.[300] He was somewhat more restrained in his conversation with Scavenius. On that occasion Hitler stressed that the conquered east must be mobilized with the co-operation of the European states not *against* but *for* Europe, in order 'to make Europe autarkic'. Hitler was glad that Denmark would 'be there' when it

[296] Ribbentrop speech given in Ribbentrop, *Freiheitskampf Europas*, 6–7, 21–2, 38–9.
[297] *Staatsmänner*, i. 654.
[298] Ribbentrop, *Freiheitskampf Europas*, 22 (also for the following).
[299] Hitler, *Monologe*, 55 (8, 9, 10 Aug. 1941), also 63 (17, 18 Sept. 1941) and 78–9 (13 Oct. 1941).
[300] *Staatsmänner*, i. 656.

was done.[301] He intended 'calling together' various senior economic figures from the states whose co-operation was being envisaged—including the specialists at the head of Danish industry—in order to provide central information and tours of inspection in the east. These tours would give them an overall view of the great economic possibilities, and win them over for the work of construction in the conquered eastern territories.[302]

German proposals and ideas evoked a positive response from the government in Copenhagen. In view of the great military successes of the German Reich, the Danes saw the prospect of resuming their former economic interests and connections in the Baltic territories of the new Reich Commissariat Ostland. By the end of October 1941 Reich Plenipotentiary von Renthe-Fink was reporting that Danish economic circles and businessmen were showing a 'growing interest' in the east. He was also able to report the imminent creation of a working committee of 'financially powerful', 'substantial Danish economists'. This came together at the suggestion of the minister for public works, Gunnar Larsen, and was intended 'to operate in accordance with the Führer's wishes in Russia'.[303] The Stauning government informed Berlin that it would follow Hitler's proposals 'willingly'. During the visit of Gauleiter Lohse to Denmark (he was also leader of the Nordic Society) Danish circles also expressed interest in the Reich Commissariat Ostland, of which Lohse had been appointed Reich commissioner. This 'area of operations' would accommodate Danish agricultural circles. After winning concessions in forestry and agriculture and obtaining mineral rights, these men were developing the first plans for economic co-operation with the former Baltic States, with the aim of obtaining extra animal feed there. Minister Larsen confirmed Danish ideas for the country's participation in the economic utilization of the conquered eastern territories during his visit to Reich Minister Rosenberg at the end of October 1941. Rosenberg's ministry for the east then expanded its own activity. He saw this task as a new field of activity for the Nordic Society of which he was patron,[304] and which he hoped to use as a link between the various Danish and German departments. On 21 November 1941 an important discussion was held at the Reich ministry for economic affairs on the issue of participation by foreign countries in the economic exploitation of the eastern territories. The meeting, attended by representatives of various ministries and national authorities, concluded that Danish involvement was desirable and should be encouraged.[305] There was particular interest in the work of

---

[301] On this issue see the description in Thomsen, *Besatzungspolitik*, 88 ff. (also for the following); also Eichholtz, 'Expansionsrichtung Nordeuropa', 29.

[302] Hitler, *Monologe*, 79 (13 Oct. 1941).

[303] Telegram from Minister von Renthe-Fink to foreign ministry No. 1389, 27 Oct. 1941, and memorandum from von Weizsäcker, St.S. No. 732, 6 Nov. 1941, about the visit of the Danish minister: both in PA, Büro St.S., Dänemark, vol. ii; similarly the foreign ministry minute (Minister von Grundherr) for Ribbentrop: Denmark's attitude towards Germany, *DGFP* D xiii, No. 447.

[304] Here see Myllyniemi, *Neuordnung*, 169 ff. (also for the following quotation).

[305] On this subject see the references and evidence concerning Sweden in this chapter (sect. II.III.4 at n. 271) and nn. 272–7 (also for the following).

the Danish cement-machine industry, in structural and civil engineering, and in the recruitment of agricultural specialists in animal husbandry. Negotiations for commercial and economic agreements were to take place through the relevant government agencies.

These earlier proposals gained a new impetus with the comments made by Hitler and Ribbentrop when Denmark joined the anti-Comintern pact. Under discussion was the co-operation of 'Germanic' experts for tasks of economic leadership in the east, and the founding of new factories by foreign industry. However, there were also plans for the settlement of the east by 'Germanic people', particularly Danes and Dutchmen, as Hitler had proposed in his table talks months before. At the beginning of December 1941 the first meeting of the 'working committee to promote Danish initiative in east and south-east Europe' took place in Copenhagen under the Danish economic director, Juncker. This body had been founded beforehand on a private basis, though with government participation.[306] At this stage the material interests of those Danish firms which had previously been active in the east came blatantly to the fore.

By mid-January 1942 the co-operation of other countries in the economic reconstruction of the conquered Soviet territories had not progressed beyond the stage of plans and preliminary discussions. According to information from the foreign ministry, these were currently limited 'to the deployment of a number of specialists, in particular Dutch farmers',[307] despite the fact that requests had been received from Sweden and the Danish 'working committee' for involvement in the work of economic construction in the east. Progress was hindered partly by the struggle for power among the German authorities (for example, over who should lead the negotiations—the ministry for the east, the Nordic Society, the Reich Commissariat Ostland, or the foreign ministry). However, other interests of the German participants also proved to be serious obstacles to the development of a large-scale planned participation of foreign business circles and capital in the economic exploitation of the occupied Soviet territories. Some preliminary activity did take place: there was a tour of inspection by a commission composed of representatives of the German ministry for the east and the ministry for economic affairs in March 1942, and a visit by Minister Larsen and the chairman of the Danish committee for the east, Juncker, to Reich Commissioner Lohse in April and May 1942.[308] However, during these tours it became clear that the German economic agencies

---

[306] See memorandum by von Weizsäcker, St.S. No. 772, 19 Nov. 1941, PA, Büro St.S., Dänemark, vol. ii; also Thomsen, *Besatzungspolitik*, 89.

[307] Foreign ministry circular to a number of German embassies and legations, 13 Jan. 1942, PA, Ha.Pol.Abt., Va Ostgebiet, Wirtschaft 6: Beteiligung des Auslandes am wirtschaftlichen Aufbau der besetzten Gebiete [Participation of foreign countries in the economic development of the occupied territories].

[308] Telegram No. 114 from von Renthe-Fink to foreign ministry, 12 May 1942, and press communiqué: 'Discussions with Denmark on co-operation in the eastern territories', published in *Völkischer Beobachter* (13 May 1942); memorandum from von Weizsäcker, St.S. No. 323 for Ribbentrop, 13 May 1942: all in PA, Büro St.S., Dänemark, vol. ii. See also Eichholtz, 'Expansionsrichtung Nordeuropa', 29; Thomsen, *Besatzungspolitik*, 91–2.

and businessmen in the Ostland were not interested in an independent participation by Denmark in the economic exploitation of the east. The Danish
economic experts were forced to realize that, as private individuals, they
would be given few opportunities. Subsequently, at the beginning of June
1942, the government in Copenhagen appointed an official 'office for the east'
within the Danish foreign ministry. Despite this official commitment by
the government, Danish plans and ideas met with scant success, particularly
as new financial problems had begun to hamper plans for activity in the
east. Apart from the construction of a cement factory, Denmark did not
participate in the exploitation of the occupied Soviet territories before early
summer 1942.

Schemes to involve other countries in the east had been particularly encouraged by Alfred Rosenberg. He had certainly hoped to increase his own political power and prestige on the basis of new commercial and business ties, and
even to establish his claims in the domain of the foreign ministry. However, in
two discussions with Hitler in February and May 1942 Rosenberg discovered
that the Führer would allow other countries only limited tasks and rights in the
east for as long as the war continued.[309] To that extent, the failure of the
'blitzkrieg concept' in the battle for Moscow acted as a significant brake on
developments. Only after final victory, in the position of sole victor, was Hitler
prepared to allocate particular tasks to the other European countries in the
economic exploitation of the east. It is possible that, in the first half of 1942,
the Danes were disappointed by the obvious lack of interest that had followed
the generous offers of autumn 1941, or at least by the delaying tactics adopted
by German agencies in implementing them.[310] German conduct involved the
virtual withdrawal of the offer of equal partnership that had already been
made. Of course, there is some doubt whether Danish willingness to co-
operate in the east reflected genuine interest in the opportunities there. It may
have been little more than a non-committal promise which could be made at
little cost as a concession to meet the wishes of the occupying power.

Danish government agencies and entrepreneurs thus attempted to gain
acceptance as economic partners of Germany. At the same time, in another
aspect of foreign policy, the Danish government was being confronted with the
evidence of its status as an occupied country and of the restrictions on its
sovereignty. A few days after Germany declared war on the United States, the
German foreign ministry demanded that the American legation be expelled
from Copenhagen. The precise form of this move was generously left to the
Danes. However, the Germans made it clear that this was regarded as an
opportunity for Denmark 'to demonstrate its support for the new Europe'.[311]

[309] See Myllyniemi, *Neuordnung*, 173.

[310] Thomsen, *Besatzungspolitik*, 92.

[311] See telegram No. 1549, Weizsäcker (foreign ministry) to German legation Copenhagen, 16
Dec. 1941; No. 1627, Minister von Renthe-Fink to foreign ministry, 17 Dec. 1941; No. 1561,
Weizsäcker (foreign ministry) to German legation Copenhagen, 19 Dec. 1941; all in PA, Büro
St.S., Dänemark, vol. ii, parts of which are published in *ADAP* E i, No. 21, p. 26 and n. 5.

Foreign Minister Scavenius hastened to confirm that the Danes would 'of course make sure that the US legation leaves Denmark'; he was 'thankful that the choice of form has been left to the Danish government'.[312] On 24 January 1942 the United States was forced to close its legation and withdraw its diplomats from Copenhagen.

The Danish and foreign press—and the Danish public—now began to express their fears, either openly or indirectly, about the possible extent of collaboration with the Germans. It seemed that the government might be only too willing to collaborate with the occupying power in other areas, even to the extent of making a direct military contribution to the war against the Soviet Union. In his talks with the German plenipotentiary, Foreign Minister Scavenius tried to rebut such rumours. He explained that if the Germans broached the Jewish question by pressing or forcing Denmark to introduce anti-Semitic laws, any chance of maintaining the 'policy of Danish orientation towards Germany' would be 'destroyed'.[313] The Germans decided not to press the point at that stage. Nevertheless, they were convinced that Denmark would eventually have to agree 'to a European settlement of the Jewish question by the end of the war if not sooner'. The occupying power could not extend its political pressure on Copenhagen without endangering the fiction of Danish sovereignty. This fact was clearly revealed in the diplomatic arena. After the German occupation in April 1940, and in some instances very soon after, the Danish ministers in the United States, Great Britain, Argentina (simultaneously accredited in Chile, Bolivia, and Uruguay), Mexico (simultaneously accredited in seven other Central and South American countries), Iran, and Iraq had renounced their obligations to the existing Danish government. They accused it of being too accommodating to the Germans and later, when Denmark joined the anti-Comintern pact, of collaborating too closely with the occupying power.[314] Attempts by the Danish government to counteract such claims met with little success. For example, when Denmark acceded to the pact on 25 November 1941 Foreign Minister Scavenius declared publicly in Berlin that his country was not one of the belligerent states despite its commitment to the 'common fight against Bolshevism'.[315] The Danish government subsequently claimed that accession to the anti-Comintern pact was merely 'a confirmation of the government's policy with regard to

[312] Telegram No. 1640, Minister von Renthe-Fink to foreign ministry, 21 Dec. 1941, *ADAP* E i, No. 44, pp. 69–70.

[313] Telegram No. 18, Minister von Renthe-Fink to foreign ministry, 6 Jan. 1942, PA, Büro St.S., Dänemark, vol. ii (also for the following quotation). On the rumours and fears see also telegram No. 11, 4 Jan. 1942, and memorandum in foreign ministry (Grundherr) Pol. VI 5033g for Ribbentrop, 6 Jan. 1942, ibid.

[314] See here the individual telegrams and reports of Minister von Renthe-Fink to the foreign ministry in PA, Büro St.S., Dänemark, vol. ii. See the summing up by von Renthe-Fink in his report, *ADAP* E i, No. 52, pp. 91 ff.

[315] The statement by Scavenius is published in *Monatshefte für auswärtige Politik*, 8 (1941), 121049–50.

Communism', and was 'actually nothing new'.[316] However, rumours that Denmark might soon be compelled to take an active part in the war against the Soviet Union continued to circulate.

The Stauning government recognized that the country's forced membership of the anti-Comintern pact had produced 'severe stress' in domestic affairs.[317] This fact led the German foreign ministry to reject demands by the DNSAP leader Frits Clausen for the dismissal of some Danish ministers and the transformation of the former Stauning government to satisfy the wishes of the Danish National Socialists. It was thought that such an intervention would lead to 'serious excitement in the country', and to domestic unrest. Berlin also recognized that the Danish government had tried hard to satisfy German military, domestic, and foreign-policy demands since 9 April 1940. This was particularly apparent in the war against the Soviet Union, where Denmark had supplied large quantities of war material and essential foodstuffs to the German and Finnish troops in Scandinavia.[318]

Looking back at the beginning of 1942, the German agencies were satisfied that 'the optimum had been obtained from Denmark' for the German war effort and food economy, without the need for additional military forces to be stationed there.[319] In foreign affairs the Danish government had 'joined the European front led by Germany as far as was possible under the current circumstances and given its tenacious efforts to stay out of the war'. On the other hand, in August 1941, at a time when the Danish government wanted to increase the size of its army, it had refused German demands for a regular Danish infantry regiment to fight against the Soviet Union. The Danish ministry of war had preferred instead to abandon the plan to strengthen its armed forces.[320]

Even after the death of Premier Stauning on 3 May 1942 and the appointment by King Christian X of a new government a few days later, the Germans could safely assume that Denmark would maintain continuity in policy; it would continue to show a loyal attitude towards the German occupying power and co-operate with the Third Reich. Such co-operation included, in addition to 'the protection of German military interests', the 'common European interest in the struggle against Bolshevism' and Denmark's continued adherence to the anti-Comintern pact. In response to a specific German request, Premier Buhl emphasized this approach in his official government procla-

[316] Telegram No. 1573, Minister von Renthe-Fink to foreign ministry, 3 Dec. 1941, PA, Büro St.S., Dänemark, vol. ii.

[317] Thus the assessment by Renthe-Fink in telegram No. 173 to the foreign ministry, 5–6 Feb. 1942, *ADAP* E 1, No. 212, pp. 383 ff. (also for the following quotation).

[318] See the detailed 'Summary of the important requests in the military, foreign, and domestic area fulfilled by the Danish government since 9 Apr. 1940' produced by the German legation, diary No. 57/42 II, 11 May 1942, as copy Pol VI 6175g, PA, Büro St.S., Dänemark, vol. ii; also Halder, *Diaries*, 1140–4 (2 Aug. 1941).

[319] Thus the report by von Renthe-Fink, 4 Jan. 1942, *ADAP* E, i, No. 90, pp. 167–8 (also for the following quotation).

[320] *DGFP* D xiii, Nos. 142, 198 (12 Aug. 1941); Thomsen, *Besatzungspolitik*, 53.

mation.[321] Buhl also promised 'to do the optimum for Germany in the economic sphere', and stressed his government's interest 'in reconstruction in the east'. From the beginning of 1942, however, anti-German opinion was hardening among the Danish population; the threat of a permanent German occupation appeared much more real than the danger of becoming 'the spoils of Bolshevism'. The Germans attributed the increase in such sentiments to the stalemate in the east and the entry of the United States into the war. They were therefore confident that fresh military triumphs on the eastern front, which they expected from the offensives in spring and early summer 1942, would improve Danish attitudes towards the struggle against Bolshevism and strengthen the promised moral solidarity of June 1941.

In international law, the government in Copenhagen was a valid partner of Germany in its efforts to wage the 'common European struggle against Bolshevism'. The German government could therefore hope to win over the Danes to some form of indirect participation by exerting appropriate political pressure. In Norway the situation was different. After the flight into exile in Britain of King Haakon VII and the legal Nygaardsvold government, and the establishment of the provisional 'Administration Council' on 16 April 1940, there was no legally valid negotiating partner[322] for the Germans in their efforts to encourage Norwegian participation in the war against the Soviet Union. Significantly, on 10 July 1940 Reich Foreign Minister von Ribbentrop ordered the withdrawal of the diplomatic representation of friendly states from Oslo. In agreement with the occupying power, the Supreme Court in Oslo had called the 'Administration Council' into being. Though this could not be regarded solely as the executive authority of the German war effort and German interests, neither was it an equal and legally valid partner. Even after Gauleiter Terboven took office as 'Reich commissioner for the occupied Norwegian territories', the council at first remained in existence. In the summer of 1940, in order to permit the establishment of a functioning government, Gauleiter Terboven entered into negotiations with Norwegian representatives of various political committees and parties. The subject of these talks was the deposition of King Haakon VII and the replacement of the government-in-exile in London, which was finding it difficult to gain acceptance as the recognized partner of the Western powers.

However, after his meeting with Vidkun Quisling on 17 August 1940, Hitler ordered the abandonment of discussions concerning the appointment of a new legal Norwegian government in the form of a 'National Council'. He had again decided to support the *fører* of the Norwegian National Socialist Party,

[321] Report by von Renthe-Fink in telegram No. 636 to foreign ministry, 5 May 1942, PA, Nachlaß Renthe-Fink, No. 2/6; similarly *ADAP* E ii, No. 181, pp. 303–4, No. 218, pp. 374–5, No. 235, pp. 401 ff. (also for the following quotation).

[322] For this section see the description in Loock, 'Zeitgeschichte Norwegens', 91 ff.; id., *Quisling*; *Germany and the Second World War*, ii, 220 ff. (Stegemann); the Norwegian report *Undersøkelseskommisjonen av 1945*; Petrick, 'Okkupationsregime'; Hoidal, *Quisling*; *Norge i Krig*.

the Nasjonal Samling, as the protagonist of National Socialist development and renewal in Norway. By now it was apparent that the war would last longer than had been anticipated. In these circumstances the anti-Bolshevik 'leader' of the Norwegian National Socialists had again become a useful tool of German policy in Scandinavia and had thus regained the favour of the German dictator. In part this development was a response to Reichsleiter Rosenberg's intervention on behalf of the Norwegian party leader, and to Hitler's memory of Quisling's loyalty during the occupation of Norway. However, it was undoubtedly also connected with Hitler's recent decision to prepare for war against the Soviet Union. Reich Commissioner Terboven nevertheless rejected Quisling's request to be appointed head of a new Norwegian government of ministers chosen from his Nasjonal Samling. Terboven, who needed to bear in mind the opposition of the Norwegian population to such a solution, also wanted to retain control over decisions about the composition of any 'National Council'. He also saw Quisling as his rival for political power in occupied Norway. It was Hitler who eventually decided that Quisling's supporters should be included in a new government. On 25 September 1940, when the Norwegian Storting refused to bow to German demands, Reich Commissioner Terboven appointed 'provisional state councillors' to carry out government business. There were thirteen of them, including eight members of Quisling's party. The Nasjonal Samling was declared to be the sole party of state; the others were banned. Quisling delivered a speech celebrating this measure as the end of the party-political system in Norway, and as a 'liberation from the yoke of capitalism'.[323]

During the implementation of German occupation decrees by the 'provisional government' there were numerous conflicts with the Supreme Court and other Norwegian institutions and associations. Despite his personal sense of mission for Norway, Quisling failed to win the support of the Norwegian population either for himself or for a mass National Socialist party. His plans to regain the sovereignty and integrity of the country within the framework of a conditional independence from Germany were clearly unrealistic.[324] After the entry of members of the Nasjonal Samling into the 'provisional government', Quisling attempted to achieve a preferential position for Norway as a 'Nordic land' within the German sphere of influence; at the very least, he was anxious to ensure that the country was not reduced to 'protectorate' status in any future New Order in Europe. Quisling aimed to achieve independence for a Norway led by himself within a 'Greater Germanic empire'.[325] In a memorandum of 25 October 1940 he advocated the creation of a 'Greater Germanic confederation of states' within which Norway would occupy a special position by virtue of its relations with the German Reich. For himself he laid claim to

[323] *Quisling ruft Norwegen*, 108–9.
[324] Hayes, 'Quislings politische Ideen', 202 ff., 205. On Quisling see also the controversial biography by Hewins, *Quisling*, 316 ff.
[325] From Loock, *Quisling*, 588 (also for the following).

the position of a 'regent' of Norway. In this plan a German command would act as the supreme federal body in the 'Greater Nordic confederation of states', while a Norwegian national army would take over the defence of Norway as part of the overall organization of the confederation's fighting forces.[326] When Quisling visited him in December 1940, however, Hitler would not commit himself to plans of this kind.

For Quisling, the opportunity to control Norwegian military forces played an important part in his efforts to regain Norwegian autonomy and demonstrate it to the outside world. In order to approach this objective, he had already suggested in August 1940 that volunteers should be recruited in Norway to fight on the German side.[327] On 13 January 1941 he made a public appeal to his countrymen to volunteer for service in the SS-Standarte 'Nordland'. The response was minimal. Six months later only about 300 Norwegian volunteers were serving in the Waffen-SS instead of the 3,000 hoped for.[328] Quisling's objectives could not be achieved in this way.

As the first Norwegian volunteers were reporting to the Waffen-SS, the government-in-exile in London reached an agreement with the British government for the establishment of Free Norwegian forces on the basis of obligatory military service for Norwegians living outside the country. The government-in-exile thereby regained its freedom of manœuvre in foreign policy. By achieving this diplomatic success, and with the help of British radio broadcasts, it was able to provide effective support for the establishment of secret resistance organizations within Norway. The Nasjonal Samling's appeal for volunteers to serve the occupying power was thus bound to discredit Quisling's party in Norwegian eyes, and did much to isolate it in the country. The events of spring 1941, when many Norwegians welcomed the British landings at Svolvaer on the Lofoten Islands and a partial state of siege had to be imposed in northern Norway, were also a defeat for the efforts of the Nasjonal Samling.[329] Most of the Norwegian population was hostile towards the German occupying power and towards National Socialism in general, whether of German or Norwegian stamp.[330]

Quisling's hopes of being appointed by Hitler as head of an autonomous government were further disappointed in the first half of 1941. Thereafter, the war against the Soviet Union gave him the chance to remind Hitler of his old role as an anti-Communist follower, and to assure him of his co-operation in the new 'struggle against Bolshevism'. After 22 June 1941 participation in the

---

[326] On Quisling's memorandum see also Hewins, *Quisling*, 347–8.

[327] See the account ibid. 344.

[328] On the Norwegian volunteers see sect. II.v.3 at nn. 111 ff. On Quisling's appeal of 13 Jan. 1941 see *Nordland-Echo*, 2/3 (19 Jan. 1941).

[329] See the press survey of the foreign ministry's press department, 'Swedish information from Norway', 1 Apr. 1941, PA, Abt. Inland IIg, Waffen-SS: Finland, vol. 303.

[330] See 'Report on the internal situation of Norway, as of 15 June 1941', appendix 24 to progress report Ic/Army Command Norway, 16 June 1941, BA-MA RW 39/20; Loock, 'Zeitgeschichte Norwegens', 97; also Gordon, *Norwegian Resistance*; Andenæs et al., *Norway and the Second World War*, 80 ff., 93 ff.

war in the east at Hitler's side could only help him to achieve his main objective. For the Norwegian National Socialists, the development assisted their efforts to persuade the population that the Soviet Union rather than Britain was now the main enemy of Germany. When Reich Commissioner Terboven announced the establishment of a volunteer 'Norwegian Legion' on 29 June 1941, this shift in emphasis was manifest: 'From now on the question is no longer first and foremost: England or Germany, but it is, beyond all domestic variations of opinion and differences, simply, clearly, and imperiously: European Nordic culture or Asiatic Bolshevism.'[331] He emphasized that Norway must and would 'take part' in 'this conflict of unique historical significance'. However, German observers noted that the Norwegian population was not enthusiastic. As before, only a minority could be described as pro-German or pro-Nazi. Hostility towards the Nasjonal Samling had 'scarcely altered'.[332] National Socialist propaganda about the imminent threat of a Soviet 'assault against the Nordic states and their culture' was not accepted. Much of the population wanted 'an end to the war at any price'.

With this 'development of the foreign-policy situation', the German attack on the Soviet Union ensured that the war had 'entered a decisive phase' for Norway. It also had implications for Norwegian domestic affairs. Reich Commissioner Terboven issued a new decree imposing a civil state of emergency over the entire country, to prevent any 'occurrences of an exceptional kind which touch on the public life of Norway'.[333] This decree gave the higher SS and police leader in Norway the 'extraordinary authority to depart from legal regulations that are in force' and to impose martial law, including the death penalty. In an effort to counter British radio propaganda, all radio receivers in much of western Norway had to be handed over to the authorities; the manufacture, purchase, and sale of radio equipment were forbidden. For the Norwegian population, the new war against the Soviet Union brought further restrictions to everyday life under occupation. In consequence, virtually no new groups could be persuaded to support the German war effort in the east.

The German occupation authorities intended to make use of the Norwegian economy and industry to meet Germany's war-economy and armaments needs. Thus in the summer of 1940 the share capital of Norway's biggest industrial enterprise, the 'Norsk-Hydro-Elektrisk-Kvaelstof A/S', was increased; the aim was to allow the German company IG-Farben to increase its influence and to eliminate the French majority interest. A few weeks later

[331] Radio announcement by Terboven, 29 June 1941, published according to DNB report in *Monatshefte für auswärtige Politik*, 8 (1941), 3/675–6; see also PA, Büro St.S., Norwegen No. 12/65 (also for the following quotation).

[332] 'Report on the internal situation of Norway, as of 30 June 1941', appendix 25 to progress report Ic/Army Command Norway, BA-MA RW 39/20 (also for the following quotation).

[333] The decree is reproduced in DNB—Uncensored press material No. 214, 2 Aug. 1941, 20–1, Büro St.S., Norwegen No. 12/65 (also for the following material).

Reich Commissioner Terboven founded a 'working group for the development of electricity in Norway' in order to achieve greater utilization of Norwegian energy output by encouraging German capital participation. Like the extensive investment projects in the Norwegian aluminium industry, these measures should be seen in the larger context of German plans for a 'New Order' in northern Europe. IG-Farben, for example, produced its 'Norway proposals' for peacetime planning on 15 September 1941; these called for an increased use of Norwegian industrial capacity for the 'establishment of a New Order of the continental European economic space' under German leadership.[334] With the German invasion of the Soviet Union, the whole of Norway was regarded more or less as a powerful rear supply area for the German front in northern Russia and on the Arctic Circle. Its economic capacity was to be exploited to the full on behalf of the German war effort.[335] Earlier deliberations on the long-term integration of the Norwegian economy into the coming 'reorganization of the greater economic sphere' now receded into the background. They were superseded by demands for a direct Norwegian economic contribution to the German war effort, particularly in view of the increased military difficulties that would be encountered in carrying out the blitzkrieg concept in the east.[336]

With the deterioration of the military situation after the battle of Moscow in December 1941, the ambitious investment plans for the industry and economy of Norway were scaled down. Norwegian industry and its workers began to be exploited for the benefit of German armaments production. Exploitation of Norwegian energy sources was now an important task of German occupation rule under Reich Commissioner Terboven. However, this also led to occasional friction with Quisling and his supporters.[337] Confronted by the hostile mood of the Norwegian population, and aware of the danger to Norway's own economic supplies by the end of 1941, not even Quisling's men were always eager to meet German demands.[338]

As the Germans grew more determined to use and operate Norwegian economic capacity, Norwegian industrial firms and entrepreneurs were also considered as possible participants in the economic exploitation of the occupied territories of the Soviet Union. As in the case of Sweden and Denmark, Hitler's first comments on the participation of other countries and allied states

[334] See Eichholtz, 'Norwegen-Denkschrift', 4 ff., here 51; *Deutschland im zweiten Weltkrieg*, ii. 470; Milward, *Fascist Economy in Norway*, 67 ff., 171 ff.

[335] On the general question of how far 'new elements of the economic "New Order" policy towards northern Europe after 22 June 1941 [can be] clearly recognized', see Eichholtz, 'Expansionsrichtung Nordeuropa', 18 ff.

[336] Milward, *Fascist Economy in Norway*, 70 ff.

[337] See e.g. Eichholtz, 'Expansionsrichtung Nordeuropa', 23–4.

[338] 'Secret reports on the internal situation of Norway, as of 14 Dec. 1941 and as of 31 Dec. 1941', appendix 20 to progress report Ic/Army Command Norway No. 3374/41, and appendix 21 to progress report Ic/Army Command Norway No. 39/42, BA-MA RW 39/26.

in the 'new task' in the east were followed by the attempt of German economic agencies to develop plans for Norwegian involvement.[339] Norwegian co-operation in the occupied Soviet territories appeared most desirable in the case of the metallurgical industry; a memorandum from the foreign ministry noted its potential use for smelting Soviet ores. However, the lack of a Norwegian government was a significant obstacle, since no genuine partner was available. The administrative executive of provisional state councillors under Reich Commissioner Terboven could play only a limited role as a link with Norwegian businessmen. Reich Commissioner Terboven was prematurely appointed representative for the exploitation of the Kola peninsula by Hitler and Göring on 16 July (when it had yet to be conquered), thus signalling apparent acceptance of the aim of Norwegian participation in the exploitation of the occupied Soviet territories.[340] However, it soon became clear that this would also 'boost' Norwegian claims to northern Finnish territory and to the Kola peninsula itself, which Hitler planned to offer to the Finns. The decision was therefore changed. Similar reasoning underpinned the refusal of Colonel-General von Falkenhorst, commander-in-chief of Army Command Norway in northern Finland, to send the Norwegian Volunteer Legion into action in the region.[341]

On 1 February 1942 Quisling's long struggle to have himself appointed Norwegian head of government was at last rewarded. Hitler appointed the *fører* of the Nasjonal Samling as Norwegian 'premier'. As the ostensible 'responsible head of government business', Quisling would take over the functions of the Storting and the king. Ministers were appointed to replace the provisional state councillors, whose role was now belatedly described as a 'constitutional interim phase'.[342] However, Quisling was still subordinate to Reich Commissioner Terboven as the 'representative of the Führer', and to his directives. His cabinet was a puppet government from the outset. Quisling's hopes for a separate peace treaty were also dashed. During his 'state visit' to Berlin on 13 February, he attempted once again to win Hitler's support for this political objective, but the German dictator rejected it. His request to set up his own Norwegian fighting forces was also refused. Hitler and Goebbels regarded Quisling's ideas as 'naïve' and 'somewhat grotesque', while the Reich propaganda minister doubted that he possessed any statesmanlike qualities.[343] The foreign ministry also rejected the detailed

[339] Compare in detail Hitler, *Monologe*, 49 (27 July 1941), 64 (17–18 Sept. 1941), and 79 (13 Oct. 1941); also the references and data on Sweden and Denmark in this chapter, sects. II.III.4 with nn. 272–7 and II.III.5 with n. 305 (also for the following).

[340] 'Bormann minute' on the discussion of 16 July 1941, No. 221-L, *IMT* xxxviii. 90–2.

[341] Telegram No. 4, German legation Helsinki to foreign ministry, 19 July 1941, PA, Büro St.S., Norwegen No. 12/65; also Milward, *Fascist Economy in Norway*, 92.

[342] See press survey 'Clarity in the relationship between Germany and Norway', *Aftenposten*, 83/ 56 (3 Feb. 1942), in PA, Büro St.S., Norwegen, No. 12/65. On Goebbels's ban on the use of the German word *Führer* for Quisling's Norwegian title of *fører*, and his intention to make 'favourable publicity' for Quisling in the German press see Goebbels, *Diaries*, 30 (3 Feb. 1942).

[343] Goebbels, *Diaries*, 32 (4 Feb. 1942), 46 (13 Feb. 1942).

memorandum[344] Quisling had handed to Hitler in Berlin, in which he outlined proposals for an immediate peace treaty and the 're-establishment of the independence of Norway' within the framework of a 'Greater Germanic confederation'. The foreign ministry was not convinced by Quisling's arguments for a 'Norwegian national army' and the enlargement of the Norwegian Volunteer Legion. State Secretary von Weizsäcker felt it reasonable to wonder at whom these troops would actually fire. Quisling's promise to join both the anti-Comintern pact and the Tripartite Pact after the conclusion of a peace treaty was more welcome to the Germans. For the time being, however, his wishes were dismissed as 'premature'; Hitler did not intend to conclude a peace treaty in the form suggested by Quisling. His appointment as premier was not accompanied by any concrete or new proposals for a Norwegian contribution to the war. In general terms, Norway was expected to be ready for 'active co-operation in the execution of joint tasks', including those involved in the 'struggle against Bolshevism'.[345] The German occupation authorities reported that the Norwegians remained 'unchanged in their rejection' of the German war effort; real improvements in the internal situation would be brought about mainly by German military victories in the east.[346] However, the domestic political atmosphere was clearly being damaged by the Quisling government's decision to take hostages and pass death sentences under the state of emergency. In the spring of 1942 these measures were an additional burden on Berlin's relations both with the Norwegian population and with the governments and peoples of Sweden and Denmark.[347]

There was no uniform reaction in northern Europe to Hitler's war against the Soviet Union. Despite his almost unchallenged power in Europe in the summer of 1941, Hitler was compelled to treat the Scandinavian states differently in an attempt to persuade them to fall into line or even take part on his side. Their differences remained apparent even during the extension and renewal of the anti-Comintern pact in Berlin in November 1941, which was the most effective German propaganda device proclaiming the united struggle of Europe against Bolshevism. Even then, the states of northern Europe expressed their reservations about the German war effort. Berlin could neither brush these aside nor leave them out of account in shaping its political and economic relations with Finland, Sweden, Denmark, and Norway. During these months, Hitler and Ribbentrop received several European politicians

[344] See Quisling's memorandum, *ADAP* E i, No. 248, pp. 465 ff., and No. 262, pp. 494–5 (also for the following); see also Quisling's ideas for the creation of a 'new Norway' on 'Germanic foundations' and its 'venture outside in the world', in *Quisling ruft Norwegen!*, 136 ff.

[345] See the references in n. 342.

[346] 'Secret report on the internal situation of Norway, as of 15 February 1942', appendix 9 to progress report Ic/Army Command Norway No. 663/42g, BA-MA RW 39/30.

[347] See e.g. *ADAP* E ii, No. 237, pp. 406–7; see the clear rise in the number of executions according to figures in Gerhardt, *Norwegische Geschichte*, 290: 1 execution in 1940, 34 in 1941, 105 in 1942.

and statesmen at state receptions in Berlin. Yet there was no discussion of any concept which might have served to transform Fascist ideas on Europe and to act as a European counterpart to the Atlantic Charter of the Allies.

By December 1941 it was apparent that the German Wehrmacht could not defeat the Soviet Union in the first assault. Berlin had misjudged the military potential of the Soviet Union, and the United States had entered the struggle against National Socialist Germany after the Japanese attack on Pearl Harbor and Hitler's declaration of war against the Americans. In consequence, by the beginning of 1942 German prospects of final victory were already being viewed with scepticism by the countries of northern Europe. A growing political restraint was gradually becoming perceptible in the unoccupied states of Finland and Sweden, alongside a decline in willingness to collaborate among the Danes and Norwegians under German occupation. Furthermore, Hitler had no interest in finding a genuine political solution to encourage closer co-operation with the countries of northern Europe during the war.

IV. The Decisions of the Tripartite Pact States

JÜRGEN FÖRSTER

1. THE COMMITTED ALLIES

(a) Romania

Although Romania took an active part in Hitler's war on the Soviet Union from 22 June 1941, the two armies involved (Third and Fourth) did not join the major offensive with the German Eleventh Army until 2 July. General Ion Antonescu, the head of state, had assumed nominal command over 'Army Front Romania' and transferred the business of government to his deputy in the council of ministers, Mihai Antonescu. The deputy chief of the general staff, Brigadier Tătăranu, was appointed as liaison officer to Eleventh Army HQ. The head of the German Army Mission, Major-General Hauff, acted as liaison officer between the commander-in-chief of Eleventh Army, Colonel-General Ritter von Schobert, and Romanian headquarters. Hauffe and the German officers seconded to the lower Romanian commands and formations became an important element in the German–Romanian war effort on the southern flank of the eastern front. The dual tasks of the German liaison officers—advisers to the Romanian leadership and representatives of the German leaders[1]—inevitably led to friction during tactical crises, when the Romanian commanders felt that they were being supervised and tended to perceive German advice as instruction. The Army Mission regarded the 'German liaison command' as a 'valuable means of leadership for the implementation of orders given, and for objective reporting';[2] they expected the liaison officers to conduct themselves as 'representatives of the Greater German Reich and as representatives of the best of German soldiering'.[3] Though Major-General Hauffe succeeded in gaining the confidence of Antonescu and becoming his 'tactical and operational adviser in all questions of the Romanian as well as the joint war effort',[4] it was apparent that Romanian sensibilities could easily be offended.

The delay before the launch of a general offensive had created some nervousness in the Romanian Army and in the high command. In part, this was

[1] German Army Mission, Ia/Id No. 908/41, 22 May 1941, General Directive No. 1 for German Liaison Command, BA-MA RH 31-I/v. 94.

[2] German Army Mission, Ia No. 32/41, 18 Jan. 1942, 'Development and employment of the Romanian army since the existence of the German Army Mission', 7, ibid. v. 98.

[3] See n. 1 above.

[4] Comment by Head of German Army Mission on the military problems in Romania, 11 Jan. 1942, ibid. v. 94.

because some units had sustained heavy casualties even in the first days of the war, during the establishment of bridgeheads across the Pruth. While the Romanian Third Army advanced alongside German Eleventh Army, the Romanian Fourth Army was forced to make the Pruth crossing alone. Even this limited tactical objective was undertaken against the judgement of the German Army Mission, which had advised against the allocation of independent attacking objectives to Romanian formations, and had warned that 'the standard of German leadership' should not be applied to them.[5] Major-General Hauffe felt that his assessment of the fighting strength of the Romanian Army had been confirmed when General Antonescu was forced to request a German corps to support Fourth Army for the recapture of Kishinev. The decision of Eleventh Army HQ on 22 July 1942 to ask Antonescu to undertake 'the seizure of Odessa' is thus all the more astonishing.[6] The Romanian Fourth Army was given this objective because of the operational restrictions placed on Eleventh Army by the battle of Uman, the underestimation of the Soviet forces' will to resist at Odessa, and Antonescu's declared aim of seizing the territory between the Dnestr and Bug for Romania. For that reason the Romanian head of state did not object to this new goal. He may even have thought, as the Red Army retreated, that the operation would be more akin to a surprise occupation than a difficult offensive operation. However, his optimistic belief that he could capture the naval fortress without German help was supported by the head of the German Army Mission.

On 27 July 1941 Hitler used the reconquest of Bessarabia and the northern Bukovina as an opportunity to thank Antonescu for choosing 'to fight this struggle at the side of the German Reich to the bitter end'.[7] His praise for the achievements of the Romanian Army was combined with a highly political request for Antonescu 'to advance in the region south-west of the Bug and thus to take over security tasks in this territory also'. The Romanian head of state responded effusively to his ally's praise for the Romanian soldiers. Antonescu was aware that Romania owed the recapture of Bessarabia and the northern Bukovina '80 or even 90 per cent to the Führer and the German Army'.[8] In his reply to Hitler he confirmed his desire to share in the campaign against 'Russian Bolshevism, the arch-enemy of European civilization and of my country . . . to the final goal'.[9] For that reason he agreed to fulfil the tasks allotted to Romania. In so doing he was hoping not merely to extend Romania 'beyond the Dnestr', but also to 'satisfy the requirements of civilization'. On 7 August 1941 Hitler recognized Antonescu's important role in ensuring the

---

[5] German Wehrmacht Mission, Ia No. 176/41, 30 May 1941, 'Further summary assessment of the Rom. army (as of end of May 1941)', ibid. v. 40.

[6] German Army Mission, Ia No. 32/41, 18 Jan. 1942, ibid. v. 98. See Förstmeier, *Odessa*, 19, 22–3, 35–6.

[7] *DGFP* D xiii, No. 159.

[8] Thus Antonescu to Minister Clodius at the beginning of Aug. 1941, memorandum from Clodius, 16 Aug. 1941, PA, Büro St.S., Rumänien, vol. 7.

[9] Letter from Antonescu to Hitler, 30 July 1941, *DGFP* D xiii, No. 167.

Romanian contribution to the war effort by awarding him the Knight's Cross and the Iron Cross first and second class.[10] On this occasion Antonescu explained that he wanted his army group 'to occupy not just Odessa but also Sevastopol and the Crimea, in order to gain control of the Russian air-bases'. Since 23 June 1941 the Soviet air force had launched repeated attacks on Ploeşti, Giurgiu, and Consanţa in an attempt to disrupt the oil production which was 'vital' to the German war effort.[11]

Antonescu's anti-Bolshevik sentiments were not the only reason for his decision to order the Romanian Army to advance even beyond Bessarabia, a decision which was controversial in Romania itself. He was also pursuing solid interests in the sphere of power politics. On the one hand, as mentioned above, he wanted to seize the territory east of the Dnestr as far as the old border of the former Russian republic of Moldavia. In order to gain Hitler's agreement to this, he was anxious to discover what territorial claims Germany's other main ally, Finland, was making against the Soviet Union.[12] On the other hand, the Romanian government had informed Berlin that it was anxious to see a 'new ordering' of the USSR; Mihai Antonescu had advocated an incorporation of Galicia into the Government-General and a reduction in the territory of the Ukraine. Behind these schemes lay Romania's interest in achieving a common border with the Third Reich, and its fear of the emergence of a 'greater Slavic empire', free of Bolshevism, in the north.[13] Romanian wishes ran parallel with similar German ideas, which were put into practice at the beginning of August.[14]

Antonescu's decision to deploy Romanian troops over the Dnestr was determined by a second, even more important, motive. He was striving for a revision in Romania's favour of the second Vienna Award of 30 August 1940. For that reason, in his verbal reply to Hitler's letter of 27 July Antonescu emphasized that he, 'the general', would march to the end, without making conditions, because he had 'every confidence in the justice of the Führer'.[15] A few days later he told Minister Clodius in blunt terms that he had resolved 'to march against Hungary when the next opportunity offers itself'.[16] Given the German desire to guarantee the Balkan status quo until the end of the war, this comment may be regarded as an empty threat. Nevertheless, it is symptomatic of the relationship between Hungary and Romania, who were allies against

[10] Ibid., No. 188. See Hitler, *Monologe*, 75 (27–8 Sept., 9 Oct. 1941): 'By race certainly not Romanian, but Germanic, Antonescu is a born soldier. His misfortune that he has Romanians under him!'

[11] See German Luftwaffe Mission report on 'Air defence of the Romanian oil region', 4 Dec. 1941 (German Luftwaffe Mission Ia No. 1841, BA-MA RL 9/85), and that by the German consul in Ploesti, 19 July 1941 (PA, Dt. Kons. Ploesti, 1/5).

[12] German legation Helsinki, telegram No. 759, 10 Aug. 1941, PA, Büro St.S., Finnland, vol. 3.

[13] Memorandum Under-Secretary of State Woermann, 24 July 1941, *DGFP* D xiii, No. 147.

[14] See sect. II.vii.3 at n. 281.

[15] *DGFP* D xiii, No. 159 n. 3.

[16] Memorandum from Clodius, 16 Aug. 1941, PA, Büro St.S., Rumänien, vol. 7.

Bolshevism but still deeply hostile to one another. According to the German–Italian commission of investigation, it was precisely at that time—late July and early August 1941—that Hungarian units were provoking serious incidents on the disputed border in Transylvania.[17]

With Odessa only just surrounded on the landward side by the Romanian Fourth Army, and Third Army still engaged in occupying the territory between the Dnestr and the Bug, Hitler asked Antonescu to take over security responsibilities in the territory between Bug and Dnieper. He even requested Romanian troops for the operations of Army Group South east of the Dnieper.[18]

Antonescu, appointed Marshal of Romania by King Michael I on 23 August 1941, again announced that he was 'happy to be able to contribute with Romanian troops to the consummation of the victory beyond the Dnieper and to the saving of civilization, justice, and liberty among the nations'.[19] However, he insisted on a directive from Hitler formally transferring to Romania the 'rights and responsibilities with regard to the administration and economic exploitation between the Dnestr and the Bug', as well as the tasks of security in the whole region between the Dnestr and the Dnieper. Convinced that the Red Army would soon be destroyed along the entire line, Antonescu was ready to accommodate German military wishes as much as possible. However, his prestige as head of state and commander-in-chief was threatened when the attack on Odessa by Fourth Army was unsuccessful. Despite the arrival of Romanian reinforcements, Antonescu was forced to accept German assistance.[20] Shortly before a final German–Romanian attack, the Soviet Union voluntarily surrendered Odessa. With the expected political repercussions, Romanian propaganda interpreted the evacuation as a victory.[21] However, the battle for this well-fortified naval base had been fought at the cost of much Romanian blood. Fourth Army had lost 106,561 men, a fifth of whom had been killed.[22]

After the seizure of Odessa, the Romanian Army was reorganized and new formations established. The two army commands (Third and Fourth) were withdrawn from the front. Under German command, a number of formations took part in the continued advance, or were employed on security tasks in the rear of Army Sector South or in the Reich Commissariat Ukraine. These were the mountain corps with three brigades, the cavalry corps with three brigades, and VI Army Corps with three infantry divisions and two motorized regi-

---

[17] German legation Bucharest, telegram Nos. 2457, 4 Aug. 1941, 2452, 9 Aug. 1941, ibid. Hungarian liaison officers with Eleventh Army refused to allow Col.-Gen. Ritter von Schobert to present them to the C.-in-C., Antonescu. For his part, Antonescu refused to allow Hungarian troops to enter the Bukovina.

[18] Letter from Hitler, 14 Aug. 1941, *DGFP* D xiii, No. 204.

[19] Letter from Antonescu, 17 Aug. 1941, ibid., No. 210.

[20] Army Group South, war diary, 29 Sept. 1941, BA-MA RH 19 I/73.

[21] Förstmeier, *Odessa*, 88.

[22] German Army Mission, Ia No. 32/42, 18 Jan. 1942, 6, BA-MA RH 31-I/v. 98.

ments. From autumn 1941 the German Army Mission was again dispatched to train the home-based forces in Romania, which also formed the reservoir of recruits for security and operational troops. In two detailed reports on the deployment of the Romanian army in the middle of January 1942, Major-General Hauffe concluded that the Romanian formations had 'fulfilled the—sometimes difficult—tasks allotted to them, though with many difficulties and a great deal of friction'.[23] The Third Army, Hauffe stated, had received preferential treatment in terms of men and equipment. The level of supply had consistently been inadequate for the requirements of 'the troops, in themselves undemanding'; this fact should be seen as the reason for much 'unpermitted requisitioning'. Hauffe stressed his belief that 'all available means' must be used 'to leave responsibility to the Romanians or to force them to assume it, but that they must still—skilfully and inconspicuously—be supervised'.[24] The issue was first to lead, only then to manage.

The Romanian goal of extending the state territory beyond the recapture of Bessarabia and the northern Bukovina was achieved on 30 August 1941, exactly a year after the signing of the 'Vienna diktat'. In the treaty of Tighina the territory between the Dnestr and the Bug (Transnistria) was relinquished to Romania 'for purposes of security, administration, and economic utilization'.[25] In the Bug–Dnieper region, however, executive authority was divided: while Bucharest was to be responsible for security, the 'administration and economic utilization' of the area remained in German hands. Romanian control of the iron-ore deposits of Krivoy Rog and the manganese deposits of Nikopol, much feared by the war economy and armaments office, was thus averted.[26] In addition, Germany had ensured her share of Transnistrian resources in the interests of supplying Army Group South.

Even before this region was fully conquered, Antonescu appointed the university professor Georg Alexianu as governor of the new province on 19 August 1941.[27] In October Alexianu transferred the seat of office from Tiraspol to Odessa. He was assigned a senior German military administration official 'for advice and support'.

Romania made it clear to both Berlin and Washington that it did not regard the conquest of this territory as compensation for the loss of northern Transylvania. At the beginning of September 1941, in discussions with the

---

[23] Ibid.

[24] Comment by the head of the German Army Mission, 11 Jan. 1942, 2, ibid. v. 94.

[25] Agreements on the security, administration, and economic utilization of the territories between Dnestr and Bug (Transnistria) and Bug and Dnieper (Bug–Dnieper territory), 30 Aug. 1941, signed Tătăranu and Hauffe, PA, U.St.S., Rußland, vol. 42. See also OKW/WFSt/Abt. L (IV/Verw.) No. 001848/41, 24 Aug. 1941, and letter from German Army Mission, Operations Detachment, Ib to the Romanian general staff, 24 Aug. 1941 (BA-MA RH 31-I/v. 93). See the Annexe Vol., No. 4.

[26] OKW/WiRüAmt/Stab Ia, No. 3320/41, 23 Aug. 1941, BA-MA Wi/I F 5.2748. In the middle of November the Bug–Dnieper territory was added to Reich Commissariat Ukraine.

[27] Copy of Antonescu decree, Eleventh Army Command, OQu/Qu 2 Br. B. No. 560/41, 28 Aug. 1941, app. 2, BA-MA RH 20-11/381.

American secretary of state, the Romanian chargé d'affaires used the argument of the 'Red menace' to justify his country's participation in Hitler's war against the Soviet Union. Secretary Hull agreed that the spread of the Communist system was a genuine problem; his government, however, regarded 'Hitlerism' as the greatest enemy at the current time.[28]

Antonescu's political position had become closely linked with German victory over the Soviet Union. His personal prestige was therefore weakened by the continued resistance of the Red Army, the deployment of Romanian troops east of the Dnestr, the high casualties sustained thereby, and the economic effects of the war on the population. Serious domestic political tensions began to re-emerge in Romania, and the smouldering conflict with the 'Legion of the Archangel Michael' (see sect. I.v.1 at n. 5) broke out anew. In July 1941, despite the intervention of the German minister, Antonescu had eight Iron Guard members shot. After declaring that every sacrifice must be made for the army since it was vital for the existence of the Romanian nation, the Marshal, in early November 1941, again resorted to a plebiscite to confirm his dictatorship. Germany's representatives in Romania were well aware that Antonescu's position was unstable. However, they regarded him as the protagonist of German interests and sought to strengthen his position. Both the minister, von Killinger, and Hauffe repeatedly pressed for a halt to the uncontrolled bulk buying of goods by the German armed forces, since this was undermining the price structure, currency, and even economy of Romania. Neubacher proposed that, as a 'friendly gesture' towards the Antonescu regime, Berlin should present Romania with 300 tractors worth RM1m.; after all, the oil-for-weapons pact had brought Germany a profit of RM80m.[29] The minister and the head of the Army Mission warned against Germany being led, 'by misunderstanding our own interests, to do the work of our enemies';[30] Germany must take care to avoid becoming the cause of Romania's 'financial and economic collapse'.[31] It was in the German interest to strengthen the country's potential 'in order to have a valuable ally rather than a lead weight'.[32] When the Romanian central bank refused to make more money available to the Wehrmacht because German debts were undermining the currency, their Romanian suppliers faced bankruptcy.[33] The German leadership considered that a reduction in the number of German troops in Romania—in mid-November there were around 63,000 men, including 45,000 in the Luftwaffe—offered a first step towards improving the economic situation.[34] Despite this

[28] On 4 Sept. 1941; *FRUS* (1941), i. 326–7.
[29] German legation Bucharest, telegram No. 3152, 2 Oct. 1941, BA-MA Wi/I C 4.2a.
[30] Report by Killinger, 17 Oct. 1941, *DGFP* D xiii, No. 406.
[31] Comment by chief of German Army Mission, 11 Jan. 1941, 4, BA-MA RH 31-I/v. 94.
[32] Ibid.
[33] WiRüAmt, Stab, war diary, 11 Dec. 1941, BA-MA RW 19/166.
[34] See memoranda on visit to Romania by OKW Chief of Staff, 10 Nov. 1941, and OKW/WFSt/ Abt. L (IV/Qu) No. 003051/41, 16 Dec. 1941, BA-MA Wi/I 345. At the end of Jan. 1942 the strength of the Wehrmacht in Romania was reduced to approximately 40,000 men. From the

development, Berlin pressed for an increase in oil production and a reduction in Romanian consumption in order to satisfy the growing requirements of the Axis. However, Bucharest was not inclined to accommodate these unbacked German demands to the extent deemed necessary by the German economic authorities. Minister Neubacher proposed the appointment of a Romanian general as 'oil dictator' to supervise the central direction of the Romanian petroleum industry.[35] In the middle of November 1941 the war economy and armaments office was even arguing that matters were in such an appalling state that 'one day we will have to take everything into our own hands'.[36] On the other hand, the Reich ministry for economic affairs advocated political concessions at Hungary's expense in order to persuade Antonescu to curb Romanian domestic oil consumption.[37] In a discussion with the deputy premier, Mihai Antonescu, on 26 November 1941 Göring explained bluntly that, 'after the blood of its soldiers, the most valuable contribution Romania could make to the common cause was its petroleum'.[38] Though Hitler had vaguely promised not to 'pump Romania completely dry' in the two years which was the longest he expected the war to last,[39] Antonescu had only an agreement promising to involve Romania in the exploitation of the oilfields in the Caucasus.[40] But these regions had not even been conquered! Yet in 1941 Romania more than doubled its 1940 deliveries of mineral oil to Germany (3,055,094 t. as against 1,374,447).[41] Though there were repeated attacks by the Soviet air force on Ploeşti, Constanţa and Giurgiu until mid-October 1941, these achieved 'no significant disruption or destruction of the oil production which is vital for the German leadership'. This fact, along with the shooting down of 81 Soviet aircraft, was claimed as a major success by the German Luftwaffe Mission.[42]

In 1942 the German leadership was forced to demand an increased military contribution from its ally, because of the enormous losses of men and machines sustained by the Wehrmacht in 1941, and in the light of Hitler's eccentric operational objectives for 1942. Hitler was insistent on continuing the war of annihilation against the Soviet Union which, in the view of the Wehrmacht High Command, involved 'not only the fate of Germany, but also

---

middle of May the highest total was 26,700, including 6,500 from the army: OKW/WFSt/Qu (I) No. 001276, 21 Apr. 1942, ibid., and GenStdH/Org.Abt, war diary, 8–14 Apr. 1942, ibid. RH 2/ v. 821.

[35] WiRüAmt, Stab, war diary, 1 Nov. 1941, BA-MA RW 19/166.

[36] Ibid., 17 Nov. 1941.

[37] Ibid., 25 Nov. 1941.

[38] Discussion between Göring and Mihai Antonescu, *DGFP* D xiii, No. 505.

[39] Discussion between Hitler and Mihai Antonescu, 28 Nov. 1941, *Staatsmänner*, i, No. 94, p. 671.

[40] Protocol of 17 Jan. 1942, *ADAP* E i, No. 144.

[41] Ibid., No. 93: Neubacher to foreign ministry, 5 Jan. 1942.

[42] German Luftwaffe Mission, Ia No. 1841/41, 14 Dec. 1941, BA-MA RL 9/85. See also the report by the German consul in Ploeşti, Count Adelmann, 19 July 1941, PA, Dt. Kons. Ploesti, 1/5.

the existence or non-existence of the other European nations'.[43] On 29 December 1941 he therefore pressed for increased Romanian participation in the summer campaign of 1942.[44] Antonescu was convinced that victory over the Red Army was 'a 100 per cent certainty',[45] and therefore agreed to a massive reinforcement of the Romanian formations on the eastern front. However, this commitment to the 'final reckoning with the Slavs'[46] was to depend on the fulfilment of two basic conditions: first, that Hungary should also make an increased military contribution; and second, that neither Hungary nor Bulgaria would attack Romania after the war. Hitler agreed to both conditions.[47] Marshal Antonescu's decision was not universally welcomed in Romania. The chief of the general staff, General Iacobici, resigned, and the chairmen of the National Peasants' Party, Juliu Maniu, and the National Liberal Party, C. I. C. Brătianu, sent memorandums protesting against the obligations entered into by their head of state. They were unable to make Antonescu change his mind. His own calculations, and the political ambitions of his allies, did not allow for a Romanian return to non-belligerence.[48] On 12 December 1941, after the European war became a world war, Marshal Antonescu described his policy as follows: 'I am the ally of the Reich against Russia. I am neutral between Great Britain and Germany. I am for the Americans against the Japanese.'[49] But was there any real hope that Britain and the United States would understand the Romanian position? Was not all hope destroyed once Britain, under pressure from the Soviet Union, declared war on Romania on 7 December 1941, and Romania, under pressure from Germany, declared war on the United States five days later?

(b) Hungary

Hungary had declared war on the Soviet Union on 27 June 1941. The first hostilities consisted of an air raid against the city of Stanislav east of the Carpathians, which was declared to be a 'reprisal measure'. Next day, Horthy wrote to tell Hitler that his army would fight 'shoulder to shoulder with the famed and victorious German army in the crusade for the elimination of the Communist menace, and for the protection of our culture'.[50] On 1 July 1941 Hitler thanked the Hungarian regent for Hungarian participation in the war against the Soviet Union, which had been decided 'on [Horthy's] own initiative'.[51] The other co-belligerents had also made their decision of their own free

[43] OKW contribution to Ribbentrop's discussion with Horthy, 4 Jan. 1942, *ADAP* E, i, No. 92.
[44] Letter to Antonescu, 29 Dec. 1941, ibid., No. 63. Hitler had first mentioned the increased use of Germany's allies to Halder on 20 Dec. 1941: Halder, *Diaries*, 1369–70.
[45] Discussion between Göring and Antonescu, 13 Feb. 1942, *ADAP* E i, No. 241, p. 437.
[46] Ibid.
[47] Discussion between Hitler and Antonescu, 11 Feb. 1942, ibid., Nos. 244, 245.
[48] See also Mihai Antonescu's arguments to the American minister in Bucharest on 3 Oct. 1941: *FRUS* (1941), i. 332–3.
[49] Quoted in Hillgruber, *Hitler, König Carol und Marsohall Antonescu*, 144.
[50] Letter of 28 June 1941, quoted in Hillgruber, 'Deutschland und Ungarn', 666.
[51] Copy for Seventeenth Army commander, BA-MA, 17. Armee, 14499/5.

will. Now the aim was for Hungarian forces to advance towards and beyond the Kolomyya–Stanislav line as soon as possible. In this way, the Soviet troops retreating on both sides of Lvov to the east and south-east would be prevented from making an orderly withdrawal.

From 1 July 1941 the 'Carpathian group' under Lieutenant-General Ferenc Szombathelyi, the general commanding VIII Army Corps, took part in the campaign against the Soviet Union. It also included corps troops from the 'Mobile Corps' under Major-General Béla von Miklós with two motorized infantry brigades and one cavalry brigade, one mountain brigade and one border-patrol brigade. The Hungarian army group had a strength of approximately 45,000 men; it was not placed under the command of Army Group South. Tactical requests for the deployment of Hungarian troops, which were sent directly to the 'Carpathian Group', were regarded as having been approved by Hitler. Horthy gave instructions that these requests should be granted 'in the interests of a united and streamlined leadership'. In the coordination of the movements of Seventeenth and Eleventh Army, the German leadership was anxious to avoid 'at all costs' any contact between the Romanian, Hungarian, and Slovak troops under the command of the two armies.[52] What Martin Brozsat has called the 'inner paradox' of the 'Hitler coalition' thus exerted its effect on the operational leadership of Army Group South. Moreover, the German leadership was also eager to ensure that the petroleum region round Drogobych was not occupied first by Hungarian troops.[53]

Only a few days after the appearance of the 'Carpathian Group', it was disbanded as a big formation. The 'mobile corps', the most modern operational formation in the Hungarian Army (24,000 men),[54] was placed directly under the command of Army Group South from 9 July, and took part in the continuing advance. The two less mobile brigades initially remained in Galicia. There they were assigned to security tasks and, in response to a special request by the Hungarians, to bringing in the harvest.[55] After Galicia had been incorporated into the Government-General, the reduced 'Carpathian Group' was placed under the command of the commander of Rear Army Area South on 13 August 1941, and was moved to the east. After the creation of the Reich Commissariat Ukraine, it was subordinated to the appropriate Wehrmacht commander.

The beginning of August 1941 saw the revival of tensions within the Hungarian leadership, and between government and opposition, over Hungary's participation in the war against the Soviet Union. The chief of the general staff, Colonel-General Werth, was ready to offer the Germans more troops for offensive operations or for security tasks.[56] In contrast, the chairman of the

[52] Army Group South, war diary, 30 June 1941, BA-MA RH 19 I/71.
[53] Seventeenth Army, Ia No. 092/41, 30 June 1941, appendix, BA-MA RH 22/5.
[54] See Tóth, 'Ungarns militärische Rolle', 79.
[55] Foreign ministry, telegram No. 787, 4 Aug. 1941, PA, Büro St.S., Ungarn, vol. 4.
[56] Report of the German military attaché in Budapest, Toussaint, 5 Aug. 1941, ibid.

small Farmers' Party, Endre Bajczy-Zsilinszky, wrote a letter to Premier Bárdossy advocating an end to military co-operation with Hitler in the east,[57] which he believed was based '50 per cent on the situation and 50 per cent on crude coercion'. Even the crusade for Europe and civilization was no more than a 'cheap phrase'. Since Hitler would be unable to create a New Order in Europe, the Hungarians should 'extricate themselves in good time from this débâcle, which would occur as certainly as 2×2 makes 4'. Every day that passed without the Hungarian government acting 'to strengthen inner resistance and effect our withdrawal from the Russian war' involved 'terrible dangers' for the Hungarian nation. No record of Bárdossy's answer has survived. Colonel-General Werth, however, took the opposite approach. In a lengthy memorandum to the head of government, the chief of the general staff argued that the Hungarian troops on the eastern front should be strengthened immediately by at least four or five army corps, on a voluntary basis. Werth claimed that despite its traditional anti-Bolshevik stance, the government had provided only weak forces to join the German attack on the Soviet Union. Increased participation in the war should be offered to Berlin at the political level and linked with four demands: the recovery of Hungary's thousand-year-old frontiers, the resettlement of the Slav and Romanian minorities, the expulsion of the Jews, and participation in the exploitation of Soviet raw materials.[58] Bárdossy submitted Werth's memorandum to Horthy a week later and linked it with a vote of confidence in himself. He argued that it was better to wait for a request from Germany before offering any reinforcement of Hungarian troops on the eastern front. A contribution of the kind proposed by Werth would, Bárdossy thought, weaken the existing political system as well as the army and the economy.[59]

On 6 September 1941 Horthy decided to support Bárdossy in the argument over Hungary's attitude in the war against the Soviet Union. Werth was dismissed. The new chief of the general staff was the former commanding general of the 'Carpathian Group', Lieutenant-General Szombathelyi. Major-General László, chief of the operations department, remained in office.

Szombathelyi may have been appointed because of a situation report he had been allowed to submit to the regent on the recommendation of Horthy's son. Here Szombathelyi had concluded that hopes for a rapid victory over the Soviet Union would be disappointed: 'The war will last for a long time, we must prepare for that and not for a lightning war. Great-power politics and the waging of war, those we must leave to the great powers, we must keep under cover close to the wall.'[60]

The change of military command did not bring any radical turn in

[57] *Allianz Hitler-Horthy-Mussolini*, No. 115.
[58] Quoted in Juhász, *Hungarian Foreign Policy*, 199.
[59] See ibid. 200, and Fenyo, *Hitler, Horthy, and Hungary*, 30–1.
[60] Quoted in Tóth, Kriegspropaganda [privately owned manuscript], 14; also Gosztony, 'Ungarns militärische Rolle', 2. 154.

Hungarian policy. A few days after his appointment, it was Szombathelyi who told Jodl of Hungarian designs on Galician territory. Although the territory claimed by Budapest had already been assigned to the Government-General, Berlin did not reject Hungarian designs out of hand.[61] Budapest advocated the withdrawal of the 'mobile corps' from the beginning of September. However, this request did not signify any change of policy; the aim was only to replace it and provide for its rehabilitation in Hungary. Both 1st Armoured Group, then in command of the Hungarian formation, and Army Group South emphasized their interest in keeping the 'Mobile Corps', especially as it could scarcely be replaced by better forces. It had proved itself able to offer 'efficient assistance', and was actually in a better condition than the German mobile formations.[62]

On 7 September 1941, at Hitler's invitation, Horthy travelled to 'Führer headquarters' at Vinnits with his new chief of the general staff, Szombathelyi, and Premier Bárdossy. During the ensuing discussions, the Hungarian leaders pressed strongly for the rapid withdrawal of the Mobile Corps, which had sustained heavy casualties. In the opinion of the German chief of the Army General Staff, the request concealed a 'self-centred' desire[63] to use this modern and battle-hardened formation as the nucleus for the creation of an armoured division equipped with German war material. Hitler rejected the request, but promised to provide German equipment to make the corps 'capable of mobility' for further operations, and to supply the equipment for an armoured division.[64] Understandably, the Hungarian side hoped for a more rapid delivery of the promised equipment than was envisaged by the German agencies.

The Hungarians linked a new appeal for the relief of the Mobile Corps and the two brigades of the 'Carpathian Group' with an offer to replace them with four brigades for occupation purposes.[65] Berlin turned down the first part of the Hungarian proposal, but immediately accepted the second. At the beginning of October 1941, when the chief of the Hungarian general staff asked the German military attaché 'what is expected of Hungary in the next year',[66] the Wehrmacht High Command passed on a request for another two security brigades for the rear area.[67] Szombathelyi had already been assuming 'that

[61] See Juhász, *Hungarian Foreign Policy*, 201.

[62] Army Group South, war diary, 30, 31 Aug., 1 Sept. 1941, BA-MA RH 19 I/72.

[63] Halder, *Diaries*, 1221 (9 Sept. 1941).

[64] Memorandum from Operations Dept. of the Hungarian general staff, No. 6466/1, 14 Oct. 1941, for the minister of war, initialled by László and Szombathelyi, Military Archive Budapest, file 257. The author is grateful to Dr Josef Borus, Hungarian Academy of Science, for providing a translation of this hitherto unknown source.

[65] Telephone conversation between Col. (Gen. Stoff) Ernst-Anton von Krosigk [chief of General Staff Rear Army Area South] and Army Group South, Ib [Col. (Gen. Stoff) G. Schall], 24 Sept. 1941 (BA-MA RH 22/7), and OKH/GenStdH/GenQu, Abt. K Verw. (Qu 4/A) No. II/7544/41, 31 Oct. 1941 (ibid. RH 22/9).

[66] Foreign ministry, telegram No. 1159, 24 Oct. 1941, PA, Büro St.S., Ungarn, vol. 5.

[67] Foreign ministry, telegram No. 1234, 9 Nov. 1941, ibid.

Hungary would gradually have to fight the war with all its forces at the side of Germany'.[68] At the beginning of November 1941 the Hungarian government agreed to provide the two brigades for security tasks, and OKW assented to the Hungarian request for the relief of the Mobile Corps. Though the latter left Seventeenth Army's area of command on 20 November 1941, it was not finally moved until the end of December because of transport problems. By that time Hungarian casualties amounted to approximately 4,500 men in total.[69] At the end of 1941 the reinforcement of the security brigades was also completed (the 102nd, 105th, 108th, 121st, and 124th, and two bicycle battalions), amalgamated under the command of the 'Hungarian Occupation Group' (around 38,000 men). This group was divided at the end of January 1942, with the Dnieper as the dividing-line. Hungary had finally been permitted to withdraw the Mobile Corps, but had been forced to find replacements for it. In purely numerical terms, the Hungarian contribution to the war against the Soviet Union was only marginally smaller in the winter of 1941–2 than in the summer of 1941, although the type of formations being deployed had changed.

The war against the Red Army had aroused no enthusiasm among the Hungarian soldiers. On 23 August 1941 the war diary of the Mobile Corps noted that the men of 12th Bicycle Battalion were all wondering when they would be able to return home. 'In this context, the officer corps cannot find any tangible arguments to influence the people in the opposite direction.'[70] Though the majority of active officers and some reserve officers supported the war against the Soviet Union for political and even ideological reasons, an assessment made at the end of 1941 argued that most conscripted soldiers and many of the reserve officers lacked any 'awareness that the adjacency of the Soviet Union [presents] an offensive threat to the country'.[71] In contrast, the infantry brigades deployed for security tasks in the rear area showed few scruples in their actions against partisans.[72]

On 29 December 1941 Hitler informed Horthy as well as Antonescu of his decision to continue the war of annihilation against the Soviet Union.[73] He requested an intensified and timely participation by Hungary in a conflict which would decide 'the existence or non-existence of all of us'. Unlike Antonescu, Horthy was not deliberately flattered by a proposal to place the Hungarian formations under their own Army High Command. However,

---

[68] Foreign ministry, telegram No. 1159, 24 Oct. 1941, ibid.

[69] Gosztony, 'Ungarns militärische Rolle', 2. 154; Darnóy, Organisation, 68 and apps. E–X, MGFA M 2/1–2, by contrast gives 4,000 men.

[70] Quoted in Tóth, *Kriegspropaganda*, 13.

[71] Ibid. 12.

[72] For example, members of 105th Inf. Brig. shot a '90-strong Jewish gang' for supplying food to partisans; for the period from the beginning of Nov. 1941 to the middle of Jan. 1942, the division reported that approximately 1,800 partisans had been rendered 'harmless': extract from the operations diary (22 Dec. 1941 and 10 Jan. 1942), BA-MA RH 22/182.

[73] *ADAP* E i, No. 64.

Hitler did promise material support for the equipment of the Hungarian formations which would participate in the summer offensive.

The aim of the Wehrmacht High Command was 'to deploy at least half the Hungarian and half the Romanian army' in the east.[74] Account was taken of Hungarian–Romanian hostility over the question of persuading Germany's allies to make increased military and economic commitments. At the beginning of January 1942 Ribbentrop travelled to Budapest. As 'tactics' for the discussions with Horthy and Bárdossy, the Wehrmacht High Command had urged him to press for the full deployment of Hungary's military strength in the approaching decisive battle in the east.[75] He was to indicate that Romania would 'likewise' be sending an army. Within his intimate circle, Hitler commented that the Hungarians would be useful 'as padding'.[76]

The Hungarian political leaders promised to take part in the summer offensive to a much greater extent than in 1941. Nevertheless, they refused to make the Hungarian army available '100 per cent for the campaign in the east', indicating that the revisionist policy of Romania made this impossible. Ribbentrop did manage to obtain a promise from Horthy 'that Hungary would not undertake anything against Romania'.[77] In addition, the Hungarian government agreed to make 20,000 'ethnic Germans' available for the Armed SS.[78] The details of Hungarian military participation in 1942 were to be worked out between the Wehrmacht High Command chief of staff and Szombathelyi.

In his answer to Hitler in mid-January, Horthy claimed that Hungary was eager 'to take part in the decisive struggle with enthusiasm, not only because of our traditional, loyal brotherhood-in-arms, but also out of egoism'.[79] Yet there were other factors which Hungary could not afford to ignore. His country, Horthy argued, lived 'with gates open to the Balkans, surrounded by those peoples whose hatred is directed first and foremost against us'. Besides, if the Balkans were overrun by Bolshevism, only Hungary would be left as a 'factor of order'. Hungary could provide troops for the spring offensive only to the extent permitted by 'armaments, time, and the enemies surrounding us'.

In view of this attitude, it is not surprising that Keitel's discussions with Defence Minister Bartha and Chief of the General Staff Szombathelyi, from 20 to 22 January 1942, were 'not very smooth'.[80] Since the declared aim of the Wehrmacht High Command was to deploy half the Hungarian army on the

---

[74] Ibid., No. 14 (16 Dec. 1941).

[75] Ibid., No. 92.

[76] Hitler, *Monologe*, 178 (4–5 Jan. 1942).

[77] *ADAP* E i, No. 137. On the simultaneous negotiations on the armaments economy see WiRüAmt/Stab, war diary, 7 Jan. 1942, BA-MA, RW 19/66.

[78] See Tilkovszky, 'Waffen-SS', 141–2.

[79] *ADAP* E i, No. 130. On the amendments to the draft by Horthy, see Horthy, *Confidential Papers*, 356 ff.

[80] German legation Budapest, telegram No. 100, 22 Jan. 1942, *ADAP* E i, No. 256.

eastern front, they could scarcely be otherwise. Keitel's demand for the sending of the Mobile Corps, fifteen infantry divisions, and seven occupying brigades was rejected as impracticable by the Hungarian military leadership. The Hungarian leadership shifted its position only after the Wehrmacht High Command chief of staff promised extensive German material support to Hungarian formations in order to bring their levels up to that of German units. The Hungarians subsequently declared themselves willing to provide an army with three corps commands, nine light infantry divisions, and one armoured division for the 'struggle against Bolshevism'.[81] In addition, the Hungarian 'Occupation Group' was to be strengthened to seven brigades. Hungary was thus making a good third of its land forces available for the campaign in the east.

An important motive for the Hungarian promise to provide an entire army for the war against the Soviet Union was the fear 'that if Hungary stood aside in the campaign in 1942, this would cause Germany to give complete support to Romania in the clash over Transylvania'.[82] After all, Antonescu had declared his willingness to send two armies to the eastern front. But there were also domestic political reasons for the Hungarian decision. Horthy and Bárdossy hoped that this increased military contribution would appease the right-wing opposition under Imrédy and the Fascist 'Iron Cross' movement under Szálasi, which was advocating the absolute co-ordination of Hungarian with German interests in the struggle against Bolshevism.

(c) Slovakia

Unlike Hungary, Slovakia had announced its readiness for military co-operation with Germany on 22 June 1941, and had broken off diplomatic relations with the Soviet Union. In fact, on mobilization the Slovak military leadership went further than had been proposed by the German Army Mission under Infantry General Otto. According to the old mobilization plan, based on Czech foundations, around 90,000 men were called up by the beginning of July. This was many more than were needed to bring the peacetime army from two divisions including army troops (around 28,000 men) to war strength. In the view of the Army Mission, this excessive zeal was due to an 'inappropriate craving for prestige and an overestimation of strength'.[83] Continuing tension with Hungary had also played a part. Slovakia provided an army group under the command of General Čatloš for deployment on the eastern front. This consisted of two infantry divisions, an advance party, and army troops (around 41,000 men). The advance party, an almost fully motorized formation, con-

---

[81] Report of the conduct of Hungarian Second Army in the war against Bolshevism, 5 May 1943, signed Szombathelyi, in Darnóy Organisation, annexe D/IV-C, MGFA M 2/1–2, and GenStdH/Org.Abt., war diary, 21–5 Jan. 1942, BA-MA RH 2/v. 821. See Gosztony, 'Ungarns militärische Rolle', I. 154, referring, in contrast to Szombathelyi's report, to oral agreements only.
[82] Hillgruber, 'Einbau', 671.
[83] German Army Mission Slovakia, Ia No. 244/41, 10 Oct. 1941, BA-MA Wi/I F 3.130.

tained two anti-tank companies, two self-propelled anti-tank gun companies, an artillery battery, an infantry battalion, and a bicycle squadron. It was composed predominantly of regular soldiers. General Otto had advised the establishment of this mobile formation for political reasons, since he wanted to give the Slovaks the opportunity to fight in the front line. It was placed under the command of Colonel Pilfousek, and had a strength of around 4,800 men. The advance party was ready for action by 24 June 1941, and took part in the advance of Seventeenth Army. However, Army Group South warned Seventeenth Army 'not to expose [the Slovak unit] to individual beatings'.[84] The remainder of the Army Group under General Čatloš was also placed under the command of Seventeenth Army on 1 July 1941. This Slovak formation consisted of some 36,000 men, 60 per cent of whom were inadequately trained and poorly equipped reservists, and was assigned by Seventeenth Army to covering and security tasks. In the judgement of the Army Mission, the structure of the Army Group had to be consolidated before it could be brought into action, perhaps behind the right flank of Seventeenth Army. Ten days later the Army Group was placed under the commander of the Rear Army Area South. General von Roques ensured that it was given only security tasks 'capable of being fulfilled', such as military security and pacification of the oilfield area round Drogobych. At the same time, he gave it the opportunity for further training.[85] The military value of the Army Group had now fallen below that of the peacetime army. In the view of the Army Mission and the German military attaché, it was not 'fully fit for duty', and would even be 'a danger' in the event of deployment at the front line.[86] Nevertheless, General Čatloš urged that his two infantry divisions should be moved to the front as soon as possible.[87] In contrast, the Slovak government argued that the burdens imposed by the war should be kept to a minimum. At the beginning of July 1941 they obtained leave for 15,000 agricultural workers from the replacement formations so that the harvest could be brought in.[88] Moreover, it soon became clear that the Slovak army group, apart from the 'Mobile Brigade Pilfousek', was not capable of carrying out the tasks assigned to it. At the end of July 1941 the Slovak government also realized that deployment in self-contained formations was not feasible because of the inadequate levels of Slovak training and equipment. To give the Slovaks the opportunity to improve their fighting skills, and to relieve the strains on the Slovak economy, the army group was reorganized.[89]

[84] Army Group South, war diary, 26 June 1941, ibid. RH 19 I/71; Gosztony, *Hitlers fremde Heere*, 128–9, 173 ff. The Slovak air force provided an air regiment and five anti-aircraft units for the eastern front. See the report by the German Luftwaffe Mission, 30 Oct. 1941, ibid. RW 5/v. 445.

[85] Commander Rear Army Area South, war diary, 11 July 1941 (BA-MA RH 22/3); Commander Rear Army Area 103, Abt. Ia No. 964/41, 11 July 1941: Slovak army force (ibid. RH 22/5).

[86] Intelligence office in Military District VII, No. 10491/41, 9 July 1941, ibid. Wi/I F 3.143.

[87] German legation Bratislava, military attaché, No. 322/41, 10 July 1941, ibid.

[88] German legation Bratislava, military attaché, No. 315/41, 9 July 1941, ibid.

[89] See High Command of Slovak Armed Forces, III Dept. No. 107278, 25 July 1941 (BA-MA RH 31-IV/v. 15); Halder, *Diaries*, 1078 (27 July 1941); German Army Mission Slovakia, Abt. Z

The majority of reservists were released; a mobile division was created from the regular troops, with the brigade under Colonel Pilfousek at its heart; the remainder of the regular soldiers were amalgamated into a security division. The strength of the Slovak armed forces was fixed at around 32,000 men. General Čatloš transferred command of the Slovak troops on the eastern front to Colonel Pulanich. Colonel Turanec took over the Mobile Division (8,500 men), and Colonel Malar was appointed commander of the security division (8,000 men). In addition, the Slovak air force deployed two reconnaissance Staffeln, two fighter Staffeln, and flak units—1,500 men in all.

At Lipovets, near Vinnitsa, the Mobile Division was involved in clashes with Soviet units for the first time while participating in the advance of the German XXXXIX Army Corps on 22 June 1941. It was unable to achieve the objectives assigned by the corps command, which the German liaison officers had also regarded as too difficult. The Germans described the conduct of the artillery detachment and the anti-tank company as good. However, the infantry officers were regarded as 'impossible'; they had such a 'bad spirit' that they had no influence over their troops.[90] The German liaison officer was highly critical of the inappropriate use of the term 'mobile brigade' and of the 'completely impossible' working methods of the Slovak staff. He also expressed profound gratitude that he had not been wounded, since the medical facilities dated back to the era of the empress Maria Theresa.[91] By the middle of August Slovak casualties numbered 320 men, a third of whom had been killed.

In a report of early October 1941, the German Army Mission in Slovakia concluded that the Mobile Division was not equal to a German division despite the training it had been given. Instead it was suitable 'for military objectives of a not too difficult character'. This was also revealed by its deployment at Kiev. General Otto praised the 'willing acceptance' of German proposals by the Slovak officers and NCOs.[92] The German leadership also gave a positive assessment of the security division. The tasks laid down had been carried out willingly and with care. In general the 'human material' was good. 'The young unit is particularly suitable for patrol duty and for action against partisans.'[93] The Slovak soldiers had generally behaved bravely, though

No. 66/41, 5 Aug. 1941 (BA-MA Wi/I F 3.130); commander Rear Army Area South, Ia, report of 12 Aug. 1941 (BA-MA RH 22/6); OKH/GenStdH/GenQu/Abt. Heeresversorgung/Qu 1/I No. I/20171/41, 6 Sept. 1941 (BA-MA RH 22/7). This reorganization is wrongly interpreted by Dress, *Slowakei*, 334, as evidence that the Slovak government had been forced to withdraw 35,623 men because of opposition, passive resistance, and unreliability. The German military sources present a completely different picture, though they too state that there was no enthusiasm for the war in Slovakia.

[90] See the reports and situation reports of Maj. von Lengerke and Lt.-Col. Schwarzhaupt, 24, 25, 27 July 1941, BA-MA RH 31-IV/v. 15.

[91] Report of Lengerke, 2 Aug. 1941, ibid.

[92] German Army Mission Slovakia, Ia No. 244/41, 10 Oct. 1941, BA-MA Wi/I F 3.130, and signal from First Armoured Army, 22 Oct. 1941, ibid. RH 19 I/75.

[93] Wehrmacht Commander Ukraine, Abt. Ia No. 570/41, 26 Oct. 1941, ibid. RH 19 I/75.

the mass of the officer corps could be given 'no good report'.[94] General Otto expected the older officers' spirit to be stiffened by action and by German example in the field. The Germans had long ceased to worry about possible Slovak unwillingness to fight Soviet soldiers on grounds of ethnic solidarity.

At the beginning of 1942 the Slovak government requested the withdrawal of the two Slovak divisions from the eastern front. The Wehrmacht High Command refused, but yielded to pressure from Bratislava for the units to be better equipped, as Hitler had promised at the end of November.[95] On the invitation of the Slovak premier Tuka, the Wehrmacht High Command chief of staff discussed this matter personally with the Slovak political and military leadership. President Tiso made it clear that, 'after the disposal of the Bolsheviks', the Slovak army would have to be equipped with modern, i.e. German, material, because Slovakia had no 'friends, but [only] neighbours' who could not be trusted. Field Marshal Keitel renewed Germany's full guarantee of the Slovak frontiers against Hungarian demands. In response, Premier Tuka observed that Slovakia 'valued the protection promised by Germany, but the protection [should] not be that of the sheepdog for a flock of sheep'.[96] In view of the German defeats in the east and Berlin's desire to leave both Slovak divisions in the area of operations, the Slovak leadership was able to demonstrate a degree of self-confidence. In the spring of 1942, on its own initiative, it offered to establish another regiment in order to reorganize the Slovak security division into a combat unit. Its massive need for security forces persuaded the Army High Command to accept this 'assistance'.

(d) Italy

Italy and Japan, Hitler's actual partners in the Tripartite Pact, were officially informed of his decision to attack the Soviet Union only on 22 June 1941. The global political triangle of Berlin, Tokyo, and Rome was again revealed to be an empty geometric design, despite the fact that the struggle against Bolshevism had been the original *raison d'être* of the pact.[97] In the war against the Soviet Union, consequently, a shift in alliances took place. Though Hitler thought he could do without Italy and Japan, Romania and Finland became welcome comrades-in-arms.

Hitler told Mussolini about the 'hardest decision' of his life only at the last moment, hoping to present him with a *fait accompli*. Although this conduct contradicted both the letter and the spirit of the 'Pact of Steel' of May

---

[94] Report by Otto, 10 Oct. 1941 (see n. 92 above). See also the report by the German military attaché on the visit by Tiso, Tuka, and Čatloš to Hitler, Ribbentrop, Keitel, Brauchitsch, and Göring on 20–1 Oct. 1941, BA-MA RW 5/v. 445. Gen. Čatloš was awarded the Grand Cross of the Order of Merit of the German Eagle with swords.

[95] Foreign ministry, telegram No. 120, 27 Jan. 1942; legation Bratislava, telegram No. 178, 1 Feb. 1942, PA, Büro St.S., Slowakei, vol. 2.

[96] Minutes of the discussion on 23 Feb. 1942 (PA E 362867–70). I am grateful to Dr Gosztony, Berne, for his kindness in providing a photocopy.

[97] See Hillgruber, 'Hitler-Koalition', 474–5.

1939,[98] Italy was far from surprised by the German attack on the Soviet Union. Since the beginning of 1941, Hitler and Ribbentrop had frequently referred to the deterioration in German–Soviet relations; moreover, the Italian military attachés in Berlin, Moscow, and Bucharest had reported the military build-up by both sides. Mussolini had concluded that he must prepare for active Italian participation in a German–Soviet conflict, which now appeared inevitable.[99] On 30 May 1941 he instructed the chief of the Italian general staff, General Ugo Cavallero, to set up a special army corps in the Lubljana–Zagreb region.[100] Mussolini justified his decision on the grounds that he was calculating on the possibility of a conflict between Germany and the Soviet Union, and that Italy could not stand aside in this case 'because it would be a matter of the struggle against Communism'. On 3 January 1940, influenced by German policy during the Soviet–Finnish War, Mussolini had already told Hitler that the struggle against Bolshevism must be given priority over the war against the Western democracies.[101] In his discussion with Hitler on 2 June 1941 he urged a 'final solution of the Russian question'.[102] When Hitler ruled out the possibility of a military alliance with the Soviet Union, and explained that the outbreak of war was only a question of time, Mussolini pushed ahead with preparations for Italian involvement in the war. It appears that after a discussion with Cavallero on 15 June 1941, he instructed his military attaché in Berlin, Efisio Marras, to offer the Wehrmacht High Command an army corps for action on the eastern front. By 19 June 1941 it was clear that the 'Corpo d'Armata Autotrasportabile' under General Francesco Zingales would consist of two motorized infantry divisions and one mobile division, with corps troops and air-force formations.[103] Hitler accepted the Italian offer of military assistance for the campaign in the east 'with a heart filled with gratitude' on 21 June 1941. However, he also informed Mussolini that there was no need for the immediate dispatch of an army corps.[104] He emphasized instead, 'in a burst of malice and realism',[105] that the best help that Italy could provide for the common war effort lay in reinforcing the Italian army in North Africa and intensifying the air and submarine war in the Mediterranean. State Secretary von Weizsäcker regarded the plan to send an Italian contingent to the eastern front as an 'acte de présence',[106] the Romanian general staff as a 'symbol, nothing more'.[107] In contrast, in his reply on 23 June 1941 Mussolini offered thanks for the acceptance of Italy's offer and stressed the ideological dimen-

---

[98] *DGFP* D xii, No. 660; Halder, *Diaries*, 975–6 (25 June 1941).
[99] *Le operazioni al fronte russo*, Nos. 1–3.
[100] Cavallero, *Comando Supremo*, entry of 30 May 1941; *DGFP* D xii, 924, editors' note.
[101] *DGFP* D viii, No. 504.
[102] Ibid. vii, No. 584.
[103] See *Le operazioni al fronte russo*, 71 ff.
[104] *DGFP* D xii, No. 660.
[105] Collotti, 'L'alleanza italo-tedesca', 24.
[106] *Weizsäcker-Papiere*, 261 (23 June 1941).
[107] Memorandum of Legation Councillor Hans Kramarz, Pol I M No. 48/g, 3 July 1941, PA, Büro St.S., Rumänien, vol. 7.

sion to his decision. Italy could not stand aside in such a war. The German attack on the Soviet Union had met with 'enthusiastic approval . . . especially among the old guard of the Party'.[108] The Italian press was instructed to portray Italian participation as an 'anti-Bolshevik crusade', with emphasis laid on European solidarity in the struggle against Communism.[109] Alongside ideological considerations, Italy's claim to be recognized as a great power also played a part. Mussolini wanted to be involved in the defeat of the Soviet Union, even though Italian war aims lay in the Mediterranean and the Balkans rather than in the east. Furthermore, he regarded Britain as the main enemy, and the destruction of British positions in the Mediterranean as the key to Axis victory.[110]

On 30 June 1941 Hitler thanked Mussolini for his offer. Echoing Mussolini's letter of 3 January 1940, he claimed that their march together against the 'Bolshevik world enemy' would be 'a symbol of the war of liberation' being waged by them.[111] This bombastic profession of a mutual anti-Bolshevism only revealed once again its 'opportunistic usefulness'.[112] On the one hand, it accommodated Mussolini's craving for prestige and also disguised the fact that Hitler regarded his ally as of very little value since the Italian military catastrophe of the winter of 1940–1. On the other hand, Mussolini was anxious not to lag behind Germany's other allies or to lose the claim to a say in the New Order in Europe. 'We cannot allow ourselves to be put in the shadows by Slovakia, we owe it to our German ally.'[113] For that reason, on 14 July 1941 he instructed Cavallero to prepare a second army corps for the eastern front. In addition, the use of anti-Bolshevik terminology, particularly by the Italian government, was designed to gain the moral support of the Pope.[114] However, Mussolini's calculations proved to be based on illusion. Hitler had already made disparaging references about Italy's role in the Europe of the future at the end of May. He regarded the fate of the Latin race as sealed, and did not intend to have any regard for Italy once the Soviet Union was defeated.[115] Privately, Hitler even regarded the imminent appearance of Italian troops on the eastern front with mistrust. Experience of the war in the west had convinced him that they were no more than 'harvest hands', who 'must in no case be allowed in the Crimea',[116] which was to be incorporated into the German

---

[108] *DGFP* D xiii, No. 7; telegram No. 15004 from German military attaché in Rome, 23 June 1941, BA-MA, H 27/43.

[109] Quoted from Collotti, 'L'alleanza italo-tedesca', 23. See Ragionieri, 'Italien', 761 ff.

[110] Deakin, *Brutal Friendship*, 16; *Germany and the Second World War*, iii. 99–126.

[111] *DGFP* D xiii, No. 50.

[112] Funke, 'Deutsch-italienische Beziehungen', 844.

[113] Operative memorandum from Mussolini for Comando Supremo, 21 July 1941, quoted in Messe, *Krieg im Osten*, 37.

[114] See Collotti, 'L'alleanza italo-tedesca', 24.

[115] Hewel diary, entry of 30 May 1941, quoted in Thies, *Architekt*, 175. See *Weizsäcker-Papiere*, 251–2 (1 May 1941), where he reproduces a memorandum by Hewel on Hitler's remarks about France and the 'Latin race'.

[116] Halder, *Diaries*, 971 (24 June 1941).

empire. The Eleventh Army was instructed to deploy the Italian corps on its left flank rather than near the Black Sea.[117]

On 9 July 1941 the Italian formation was renamed the 'Corpo di Spedizione Italiano in Russia' (CSIR: Italian Expeditionary Corps in Russia). A few days later, Corps General Giovanni Messe took command in place of Zingales, who had fallen ill.[118] The Italian leaders considered it essential that the army corps should be well equipped in both men and material, not only on grounds of operational effectiveness, but also to enable it to stand comparison with the other non-German formations. The transporting of the CSIR from Italy to Romania took almost a month. At the end of August 1941 the Expeditionary Corps was placed under the command of Army Group South. The corps consisted of 2 infantry divisions (Pasubio, Torino), each with 2 infantry and 1 artillery regiment, and the 3rd Mobile Division (PADA). This latter contained 1 Bersaglieri regiment, 2 cavalry regiments, 1 artillery regiment, and 1 armoured batallion with 40 light tanks. Directly attached to the corps, alongside the usual corps troops, were big engineer and supply units, 1 reconnaissance and 1 fighter group of the air force (83 aircraft), 3 battalions of the Fascist militia ('Blackshirts'), and 12 detachments of Carabinieri. In total, the CSIR numbered 62,000 men. Since the expeditionary corps had only enough vehicles to transport one division, and only the three Bersaglieri battalions were motorized, the formation was unsuitable for rapid and wide-ranging operations. In mid-September 1941 the Italian ambassador in Berlin, Dino Alfieri, contacted Ribbentrop as a 'private person' to make an 'absolutely confidential and strictly personal' suggestion that Mussolini be awarded the Knight's Cross.[119]

On several occasions Mussolini informed the German leadership that he was ready to strengthen the CSIR by at least one army corps. Under the slogan 'Fewer workers, more soldiers' he wanted to increase Italian participation in the German military operations against the Soviet Union.[120] Although Hitler informed the Italian head of government at the end of October 1941 that he regarded the campaign in the east as 'in the main brought to a decisive conclusion',[121] Mussolini intensified his efforts. The time for 'partial, semi-symbolical participation' was over.[122] Italy had the duty and the right to increase its operational efforts during 1942. Mussolini saw this offer as the best way to combat speculation about possible Italian willingness to conclude a

[117] Army Group South, war diary, 12 July 1941, BA-MA RH 19 I/71. At the end of June 1941 Eleventh Army was instructed to insert the Italian formations between the Hungarian and Romanian troops.

[118] *Le operazioni al fronte russo*, 71 ff.; Cruccu, 'Operazioni italiane in Russia'.

[119] *DGFP* D xiii, No. 308 (12 Sept. 1941). Alfieri referred specifically to the awards to Antonescu (8 Aug. 1941) and Horthy. The latter, however, was not honoured until 10 Sept. 1941. Alfieri was confusing him with Mannerheim, who received the Knight's Cross on 18 Aug.

[120] *DGFP* D xiii, No. 424.

[121] Letter from Hilter, 29 Oct. 1941, ibid., No. 433.

[122] Letter from Mussolini, 6 Nov. 1941 (ibid., No. 454), and discussion between Ribbentrop and Ciano, 25 Nov. 1941 (ibid., No. 501).

separate peace with the Soviet Union. The idea of reinforcing the CSIR to compensate for the transfer of German forces to Sicily may also have played a part. The commanding general of the CSIR, General Messe, was not alone in his opposition to the sending of further troops to the eastern front. At the end of November 1941 Hitler told Ciano, the Italian foreign minister, that Italy should concentrate on holding North Africa.[123] However, he thought that Italy might make a 'useful contribution' to the coming summer offensive by providing 'Alpine troops' for the conquest of the Caucasus and further advance into the Middle East. Mussolini received this request 'with pleasure', and was eager to send an army corps of Alpini and mountain troops.[124] At the end of 1941, however, the German leadership changed its policy towards Italy. In view of the enormous losses suffered by the German army, the value of the Italian formations increased. In a personal letter to Mussolini on 29 November, Hitler justified the need for increased and timely participation by Italy in the summer offensive of 1942.[125] He accommodated Mussolini's craving for prestige by suggesting the subordination of all Italian troops under one Italian Army Command. In negotiations between the Comando Supremo and the Wehrmacht High Command it was decided that the expeditionary corps should be reinforced by a corps command with three infantry divisions and a corps command with three Alpini divisions.[126] The CSIR had lost approximately 8,700 men by the end of 1941, roughly one in twelve of whom had been killed.[127]

2. The Reluctant Allies

(a) Bulgaria

Among the European states allied with Germany, Bulgaria occupied a special position.[128] Even after 22 June 1941, Sofia maintained diplomatic relations with Moscow and acted as representative of German, Hungarian, and Romanian interests there. At the end of July 1941 the German foreign ministry requested that Bulgarian–Soviet relations be broken off, but hoped that this step could be linked with the fall of Leningrad and Moscow.[129] The problem dragged on until the summer of 1944: Moscow refused to accept Bulgaria's declaration of neutrality on 23 August 1944 and declared war on Bulgaria on 5 September.

Bulgarian sympathy for Russia had deep roots, dating back to 1878. Hitler's

[123] Discussion between Hitler and Ciano, 29 Nov. 1941, *Staatsmänner*, i, No. 97, p. 678.
[124] Report of German military attaché in Rome, No. 150114/41, 2 Dec. 1941, BA-MA H 27/43.
[125] *ADAP* E i, No. 62.
[126] See Förster, *Stalingrad*, 14, *Le operazioni al fronte russo*, 186 ff.
[127] German Liaison Command to Italian Expeditionary Corps No. 594/42, 9 June 1942, BA-MA RH 31-IX/22. See also *Le operazioni al fronte russo*, 487.
[128] See Miller, *Bulgaria*; Hoppe, 'Balkanstaaten', and id., *Bulgarien*.
[129] Hoppe, *Bulgarien*, 129.

war against the Soviet Union was therefore unpopular among the Bulgarian population. The authoritarian regime of Emperor Boris III did not offer troops for the eastern front, and volunteers failed to come forward. In fact, the German leadership itself opposed the involvement of Bulgarian troops in Operation Barbarossa for two reasons. First, the Germans hoped that the Bulgarian army would secure the south-eastern flank of Europe against Turkey, thereby providing relief for the German war effort by taking over police functions in the Balkans. Second, Hitler and the Wehrmacht High Command feared that any operations by Bulgarian troops on the eastern front might lead to 'fraternization between Bolshevik and Slav'.[130] Only in mid-December 1942, under the impact of the unexpected successes of the Red Army, did the foreign ministry discuss the creation of a Bulgarian legion within the Waffen-SS. The German minister opposed this plan, since the volunteers would be drawn from opposition circles and this would inevitably arouse distrust of German intentions within the Bulgarian government.[131] In mid-July 1941, however, the Bulgarian minister of war, Teodori Daskalov, agreed with Field Marshal Keitel that the Bulgarian army should be expanded to enable it to deal with its functions in the Balkans.[132] Bulgaria's involvement in the German–Soviet war was limited to providing a complete military hospital and 2,000 beds for the recuperation of German soldiers in Bulgarian health resorts. Not even Soviet air raids on several Bulgarian cities on 23 July and 11 August 1941, and open Soviet support of the partisans in Bulgaria, could persuade the government in Sofia to change its attitude. For tactical reasons, the pro-German premier, Bogdan Filov, wanted the Soviet Union to be the one to break off diplomatic relations.[133] Under German pressure, however, Bulgaria joined the anti-Comintern pact on 25 November 1941. Hitler took this opportunity to inform the Bulgarian king that nobody could change the course of the war, 'neither England nor America, nor any other coalition'.[134] Sofia declared war on these two states on 13 December 1941. In March 1942 Boris III opposed a new request from Hitler for the severing of diplomatic relations with Moscow.[135]

The Bulgarian king sought to maintain a degree of national sovereignty by making domestic political concessions to National Socialist Germany 'so as not to lag behind Romania in proclaiming loyalty to Hitler'.[136] The passing of the first anti-Jewish laws in January 1941 was followed by the introduction of further professional restrictions for Bulgarian Jews in October.[137] Yet though

---

[130] Ambassador Ritter's enquiry to Ribbentrop, 11 Feb. 1942, *ADAP* E i, No. 229.

[131] Foreign ministry, telegram No. 2181, 14 Dec. 1942, *DGFP* E iv, No. 286 and n. 1.

[132] See Hoppe, *Bulgarien*, 133–4.

[133] Ibid. 129.

[134] Discussion between Hitler and Popov (Bulgarian foreign minister), 27 Nov. 1941, *Staatsmänner*, i, No. 90.

[135] Memorandum from Under-Secretary of State Woermann on Bulgaria, Pol IV 1262g, 29 Mar. 1942, *ADAP* E ii, No. 77.

[136] Kazasov, *Burni godini*, 660, quoted in Hoppe, *Bulgarien*, 92.

[137] Hoppe, *Bulgarien*, 138 ff.

the withdrawal of Jewish rights was accelerated by the 'Wannsee conference', widespread protests among the population ensured that less severe supplementary regulations were introduced. In trade affairs too, Bulgaria was ready to accommodate German wishes. The original German credit balance of RM17m. at the beginning of 1941 had become a German debt of RM105m. by 31 December.[138] In order to reduce the labour shortage in the German armaments industry, the Bulgarian government had supplied 12,500 Bulgarian workers by the end of 1941, a move which also served to reduce unemployment in Bulgaria. After 22 June 1941 the government in Sofia made efforts to deflect German reproaches about its misguided tolerance of the Communists; these criticisms had been made for some years, but had been encouraged by Bulgarian government policy since the German–Soviet agreement of summer 1939. A total of 3,000 Communists were interned, and a screening process weeded out others from the reservists who had been called up. On 22 November 1941 Bulgaria also agreed to align her propaganda and base it on the German model.[139] The intention was to counter the prevailing pro-Russian sympathies of the Bulgarian public, and to counteract the expression of sentiments friendly to the West.

With Turkey remaining neutral despite German pressure and Turkish enthusiasm for German successes against the Red Army, Bulgaria remained Germany's only ally in the Balkans.

(b) Japan

Outside Europe the Third Reich had one more ally, Japan. Tokyo was officially informed of the German attack on the Soviet Union only on 21 June 1941.[140] Some weeks before, however, Hitler and Ribbentrop had disclosed to the Japanese ambassador in Berlin, General Hiroshi Oshima, that a German–Soviet war could be expected in the near future. They had left the Japanese to decide whether to join Germany, but had made it clear that they hoped for the co-operation of the Japanese army to bring about the defeat of the Soviet Union. In the report of his discussions with Hitler and Ribbentrop on 3 and 4 June 1941, Oshima had emphasized German strategic calculations: it was believed 'that an overwhelming German victory over the Soviet Union might lead America to abandon any idea of entering the war in favour of Britain' and persuade it to restrict itself to the American continent.[141] The Germans were thus claiming that a German–Soviet war would provide Japan with the freedom it needed to achieve its aims in South-East Asia. The outcome had been a new discussion of strategy within the Japanese leadership. By 22 June 1941 this, however, had not been completed.

Hitler had hoped for German–Japanese military co-operation since the

[138] Ibid. 131 ff.
[139] *DGFP* D xiii, No. 490.
[140] Ibid., N. 1058.
[141] Hillgruber, 'Japan', 329 ff. On Hitler's expectations see *KTB OKW* i. 258 (9 Jan. 1941).

beginning of 1941. His aim was to persuade Japan to seek expansion towards the south at the earliest possible moment:

The earlier Japan attacks, the easier will be the military conditions it will find. It must get possession of Singapore and all the raw-material territories it requires to continue the war, especially if America intervenes. The longer Japan delays, the stronger America will become and the weaker Japan's position will be . . . All those military operations which Germany wants to see in the interests of its struggle against Britain, and perhaps against America, should be defined.[142]

The Germans wanted a Japanese drive for expansion which would threaten the United States from the Pacific flank, thereby preventing American intervention in the European war by creating the spectre of a potential war in two oceans. It was hoped that the Japanese task would be made easier by the German offer of a dual guarantee against the Soviet Union and the United States. On 4 April Hitler had spoken to Matsuoka, the Japanese foreign minister: 'If Japan is drawn into a conflict with the United States, Germany would accept the consequences . . . It would not hesitate for a moment to reply immediately to any extension of the war, whether by Russia or by America.'[143] Grandiose over-optimism regarding his own prospects had persuaded Hitler to sign this blank cheque, even though the coincidence of German and Japanese interests was limited to South-East Asia. Both Japan and Germany were pursuing a policy of 'sacro egoismo'; each regarded its ally as an instrument with a specific function within its own overall strategy. Germany thus hoped to use Japan as a political counterweight against the United States, taking account of the effects of Operation Barbarossa on Japanese expansion southwards against the British position in East Asia. For its part, despite its endeavours to establish a 'Greater East Asian Co-Prosperity Sphere', Japan was interested in securing peace in the Pacific and sought secret negotiations to reach a settlement with the United States. To achieve this objective, the Japanese government was prepared to accept a *de facto* annulment of the 'preventive defensive' Tripartite Pact of 27 September 1940, which was directed against the United States.[144]

After 22 June 1941, Ribbentrop was the main protagonist of attempts to encourage Japanese military action against the Soviet Union. In an instruction to the German ambassador in Tokyo, Major-General (ret.) Eugen Ott, he pointed out that the German–Soviet war 'would have as its consequence the final solution of the Russian question as a whole'. Referring to the anticipated rapidity of the operations, he urged Japan to 'reach its decision for military

---

[142] *KTB OKW* i. 328–9 (17 Feb. 1941).

[143] *Staatsmänner*, i, No. 73.

[144] On Japanese policy see Sommer, *Deutschland und Japan*; Martin, *Deutschland und Japan*; Libal, *Japans Weg in den Krieg*; Nish, *Japanese Foreign Policy*; Martin, 'Japans Weg in den Krieg'; Herde, *Pearl Harbor*; Toyama, 'Japanische Planungen'; Krebs, *Japans Deutschlandpolitik*; Carr, *Poland to Pearl Harbor*, 144 ff.; Wetzler, 'Hirohito'; and *Das Deutsche Reich und der Zweite Weltkrieg*, vi. 192 ff. (Rahn).

action against Soviet Russia without hesitation'.[145] Ott was instructed to persuade the Japanese government to opt for 'active intervention against the Soviet Union' as quickly as possible.[146] A few days later, Ribbentrop made a personal appeal to the Japanese foreign minister, Matsuoka. In his view, the 'need of the hour' was for the Japanese army to occupy Vladivostok 'as soon as possible', and to advance westwards as far as it was able. The German and Japanese troops would 'meet half-way'. Japan would then be able to direct all its power towards expansion to the south. The political weight of Germany and Japan after victory over the Soviet Union would deter the United States from entering the war.[147] German hopes for Japanese participation in the German–Soviet war were boosted by Germany's recognition of the Chinese government of Wang Tzing-wei, a Japanese puppet, in Nanking.

These efforts ended in failure, because they were supported in Japan only by Matsuoka. At the liaison conference of civilian and military leaders on 30 June, he withdrew his agreement to a Japanese move against South-East Asia and proposed an immediate attack on the Soviet Union. However, Matsuoka was vigorously opposed by the chiefs of staffs of the army and navy, supported by Premier Konoye, who advocated the conquest of southern Indo-China and then the Dutch East Indies in order to satisfy Japan's urgent need for raw materials. They were prepared to accept the danger of a war against the Anglo-Saxon maritime powers in order to achieve this objective.[148] On 2 July 1941, at the imperial conference chaired by Emperor Hirohito in Tokyo, the die was cast. The Japanese decided to realize the 'Greater East Asian Co-Prosperity Sphere' which had been proclaimed a year before. In other words, they committed themselves to the attempt to create an autarkic, heavily armed Japan, prepared for war-against all comers and surrounded by a chain of satellite states and dependent raw-material areas, without taking account of the interests of Germany or the Anglo-Saxon naval powers. Japan thus abandoned 'any chance of evading the aggressive counter-pressure of the United States after July 1941 other than by flight into war'.[149] Specifically, on 2 July 1941 the Japanese regime decided not to enter the German–Soviet war for the present; the alliance with Germany was to be maintained, but Japanese efforts were to be directed at establishing control over the whole of Indo-China. Priority was thus given to expansion towards the south. Expansion to the north was not completely ruled out, but was made conditional on the successful development of Operation Barbarossa. On 19 July, therefore, the order was given for the Japanese advance into French Indo-China. Though the army in Manchuria was reinforced to bring it to a strength of 700,000 men, it was withdrawn from the Japanese–Soviet border. After the imperial conference,

[145] *DGFP* D xiii, No. 35 (28 June 1941).
[146] Ibid., No. 36 (28 June 1941).
[147] Ibid., No. 53.
[148] See Herde, *Pearl Harbor*, 76 ff.; Toyama, 'Japanische Planungen'.
[149] Libal, *Japans Weg in den Krieg*, 240.

the army concentrated on the conquest of Malaya, Java, Borneo, New Guinea, the Philippines, and the Bismarck Islands, while the navy planned its surprise attack on the American fleet at Pearl Harbor.

From the point of view of the Germans, the Japanese leadership had taken the wrong decision.[150] Nevertheless, Hitler and Ribbentrop did not change their calculations regarding Japan. In mid-July 1941, with victory over the Soviet Union apparently assured, Hitler took the initiative. In a conversation with General Oshima, he defined the 'destruction of Russia' as the 'political life's work of Germany and Japan'. It would 'be our eternal enemy'.[151] Though Hitler did not wish to give the impression that he needed the Japanese army, he pressed for joint military action against the Soviet Union. Moreover, the dictator turned his previous defensive strategy against the United States into an offensive one, offering Japan a comprehensive alliance for its 'destruction'. Italy was not mentioned at all.

The United States and Britain', Hitler declared,

will always be our opponents. This realization must become the foundation of our state policy. After long consideration, this has become my holy conviction, the basis of our political understanding. America and Britain will always turn against whomever they believe to be isolated. Today there are only two states which have no possibility of conflict with one another, these being Germany and Japan. In its new imperialistic spirit, America presses sometimes against the European living-space, sometimes against the Asiatic. From our point of view, Russia threatens in the east and America in the west; for Japan, Russia threatens in the west and America in the east. I am therefore of the opinion that we must destroy them together. There are tasks in the lives of peoples that are hard. One cannot solve these tasks by ignoring them or leaving them to a later date.'

Hitler did not tell Oshima of his speculation that the victorious campaign in the east would bring about a political upheaval in Britain and lead to the fall of Churchill. In that case, he expected the new British government to join 'Europe's struggle against America' as a 'junior partner' of Germany.[152]

Hitler had still hoped to persuade Japan that 'its great moment against Russia had come'.[153] In this he was disappointed. But because he had scarcely expected a rapid Japanese attack in Manchuria (i.e. before the end of 1941), by the end of July 1941 he was already expressing concern that Japan's inactivity might call into doubt the 'collapse of the Soviet system'. Yet this, in his view, was necessary, 'since Russia could not be conquered'.[154] Hitler believed that a

---

[150] *DGFP* D xiii, No. 63.

[151] *Staatsmänner*, ii. 548 ff. (14 July 1941).

[152] Hewel diary, entry of 10 July 1941, quoted in Hillgruber, *Zenit*, 11–12. See Hitler, *Monologe*, 44 ff. (22–3 July 1941), 56 (8–11 July 1941). This speculation was resolutely repudiated by the naval war staff (Salewski, *Seekriegsleitung*, i. 406).

[153] Bock, *Tagebuch*, ii (25 July 1941), MGFA P-210. At this time Keitel was at Army Group Centre HQ and informed Bock of Hitler's opinion.

[154] Ibid. See discussion between Ribbentrop and Oshima, 23 Aug. 1941, *DGFP* D xiii, annexe IV.

double onslaught from Germany and Japan would precipitate the collapse of the Stalinist system. The air raids on Moscow, which were carried out at this time, were also undertaken with this objective in mind. At the beginning of August the secretary of state in the foreign ministry, Ernst von Weizsäcker, also wished 'that the Japanese too would lend a hand with the Russians in the east'.[155] At the same time, the Japanese general staff informed the Germans that the army and government were determined to intervene in the war against the Soviet Union at the earliest possible moment.[156] However, the German side failed to understand Japan's view of the obstacles to such an operation.[157] At the end of August 1941 Hitler was convinced that Japan would attack Vladivostok as soon as the assembly of forces was completed.[158] The wish was father to the thought. Despite German recognition that the stubborn resistance of the Red Army had made 'aid from Japan more necessary than previously thought',[159] the Japanese had long since abandoned any plan to solve the 'northern problem' during 1941.

The trade embargo imposed by the United States, Britain, and the Dutch East Indies, in anticipation of the planned Japanese occupation of south Indo-China, had also produced a change in Japan's attitude towards the United States.[160] Japan had to choose between giving way or making war. The Japanese government did not decide at once, although the rapid decline in its stocks of oil and bauxite, and the increasing rate of American armament, called for a rapid decision. Readiness for war was now increasing in the navy; at a conference with the army leadership the decision was taken to intensify preparations for a conflict. Though Premier Konoye sought a meeting with Roosevelt, his initiative for a Japanese–American summit collapsed owing to reluctance in Washington. Independently of this, on 3 September the Japanese authorities took the decision 'to open hostilities against the United States, Great Britain, and The Netherlands' if Japanese demands—an end to the war with China without hindrance from the United States and Britain, and the lifting of the economic boycott—were not achieved by mid-October in the coming diplomatic negotiations.[161] This decision was confirmed by the imperial conference on 7 September 1941. At the same time, Hitler decided not to intensify the pressure on Japan to join the war against the Soviet Union in case this was regarded as a sign of weakness.[162] Subsequently the initial successes of Operation 'Typhoon' revived Hitler's hopes of defeating the Soviet Union unaided. Indeed,

[155] *Weizsäcker-Papiere*, 263 (10 Aug. 1941).

[156] Etzdorf memorandum, 5 Aug. 1941, as photocopy in *Deutschland im zweiten Weltkrieg*, ii. 169.

[157] See Halder, *Diaries*, 1152 (4 Aug. 1941).

[158] 'Führer Conferences', 229 (22 Aug. 1941).

[159] *Weizsäcker-Papiere*, 265 (31 Aug. 1941).

[160] See Herde, *Pearl Harbor*, 109–10; Toyama, 'Japanische Planungen'.

[161] See Herde, *Pearl Harbor*, 134; Toyama, 'Japanische Planungen'.

[162] *DGFP* D xiii, No. 291 (8 Sept. 1941).

Japanese intervention would be an obstacle to a subsequent 'settlement peace' with Britain.[163]

Just as Hitler had left Tokyo in the dark about his plans to attack in the east, Tokyo kept the surprise attack on Pearl Harbor secret from the Germans. The plan was approved by the chief of staff of the navy on 3 November. Only days before Operation Hawaii, which Emperor Hirohito approved on 1 December, Tokyo made sure that Germany (and Italy) would join Japan in the event of war against the United States according to the terms of the Tripartite Pact. Hitler's attitude to the Japanese attack on the United States was ambivalent. On one hand, he saw it as a 'turning-point of unimaginable proportions',[164] because the United States would now be tied up in the Pacific and its defeat would be 'no more than a question of iron endurance' by the Reich.[165] Hitler also thought that Japan's entry into the war would have positive effects on the war against Britain, which would now be fearful for the existence of its Empire, especially India. This assessment was shared by Luftwaffe General von Richthofen: 'With Japan, all British, American, and Russian hopes swim away for the coming years. Would be a hell of a coup! Then local setbacks (as long as they remain local) can be accepted here or in Africa.'[166] On the other hand, Hitler regretted that 'the white race would disappear from this area' as a consequence of the Japanese action: 'I did not want that!'[167] He then returned to the hopes expressed in July 1941 for a possible German–British partnership at world-power level after the elimination of the Soviet Union: 'East Asia could have been held, if all the white states had built a coalition. Japan would not have been able to move against it!'[168] If Britain changed course now, it could save at least some of its Empire. It was Hitler's 'most sacred conviction'[169] that the conquest of Singapore by Japanese troops would lead to the dismissal of Churchill and a British change of course in favour of Germany. It was soon apparent that this belief was an illusion. In December 1941 the German and Japanese strategies against the Anglo-Saxon maritime powers converged, with both resolved to fight jointly until victory and not to conclude a separate armistice or peace. Yet in the months before, Tokyo and Berlin had been marching separately. 'Four years later they were defeated separately.'[170]

---

[163] *Weizsäcker-Papiere*, 274 (21 Oct. 1941); PA, Handakten Etzdorf, Vertrauliche Aufzeichnungen, No. 3, 3 Nov. 1941.

[164] Hitler, *Monologe*, 179 (5 Jan. 1942).

[165] Ibid. 193 (10 Jan. 1942).

[166] Richthofen, Tagebuch (entries of 7 Dec. 1941) (privately owned). I am grateful to Col. (ret.) Dr Gundelach, Freiburg, for allowing me to see the document.

[167] Hitler, *Monologe*, 156 (18 Dec. 1941).

[168] Ibid. 163 (31 Dec. 1941–1 Jan. 1942).

[169] Ibid. 195 (12–13 Jan. 1942).

[170] Sommer, *Deutschland und Japan*, 492.

V. Volunteers for the 'European Crusade against Bolshevism'

1. The 'Crusade' Aspect

Jürgen Förster

EVEN today, the brutal war of conquest and annihilation waged against the Soviet Union is sometimes misinterpreted as a crusade by the civilized Christian West against Bolshevism. After 22 June 1941 National Socialist propaganda certainly presented Operation Barbarossa as a 'European crusade against Bolshevism' and as a 'pan-European war of liberation',[1] in the hope of gaining sympathy in Europe for the German action against the Soviet Union. Hitler himself ordered that every offer from foreign states to participate in this crusade was to be accepted with 'enthusiasm'.[2] Behind this decision lay the intention to involve other states in his own attack against the Soviet Union, and thereby to give his war of annihilation a European legitimacy. Propaganda for joint European action against the 'world enemy' was designed to manipulate opinion by dividing Europe into two groups—people of culture and the opponents of all civilization. To a large extent, the propaganda attempted to exploit feelings of being under threat, the desire for revenge, ethnic prejudices, and ideological resentments; its aim was to rouse Europe into emotional and military action against the Soviet Union. Yet as early as 1927 the German foreign minister, Stresemann, had told his Belgian, British, French, Italian, and Japanese colleagues that the current idea of a 'crusade against Russia' was foolish and insane. It would only weld Russia together and weaken Europe.[3] In 1941 the German press, following the line taken by Hitler when the war began, was instructed to revert to the image of 'Jewish Bolshevism' it had used before the German–Soviet pact. Wehrmacht propagandists were instructed to concentrate on the 'Jewish-Bolshevik Soviet government with its functionaries' and the CPSU as the enemies of Germany.[4] The aim of National Socialist propaganda efforts, based solely on the 'anti' complex of anti-Bolshevism and anti-Semitism, was to disguise the real objective of 'breaking the Soviet Union apart' and conquering 'living-space'. At the end of May 1941 Artillery General

---

[1] See 'Deutsche diplomatisch-politische Informationen', 27 June 1941 (*Ursachen und Folgen*, xvii. 253 ff., and the journal *Signal* (1941–2; repr. 1977), 32, 36); Kluke, 'Europaideologie', 258 ff.; Förster, 'Croisade'. See in this context the title of the German edition of the book by Arno J. Mayer: *Krieg als Kreuzzug* [War as crusade].

[2] *KTB OKW* i. 109 (24 June 1941).

[3] On 14 June 1941 in Geneva: *DGFP* B v, No. 236.

[4] OKW/WFST/WPr No. 144/41, June 1941, BA-MA RW 4/v. 578. See Buchbender, *Das tönende Erz*, 54 ff.

Jodl had realized that the concept of a 'crusade against Bolshevism'—as expressed to the Finns—was no more than a figure of speech.[5] Similarly Alfred Rosenberg, in a speech to his closest colleagues on 20 June 1941, declared that Germany was not waging a 'crusade' against Bolshevism in order to save 'the poor Russians', but 'to pursue German world policy and to safeguard the German Reich'.[6] After the start of operations, the secretary of state in the foreign ministry, Ernst von Weizsäcker, commented that those who expected to witness the certain 'death of Bolshevism' would almost all be mistaken. 'For our plan is not to re-establish former conditions in the territory to be conquered. The scheme is instead to put these lands and their mineral resources into service for us fully and promptly.'[7] When Hitler thought the war in the east was won, he made it clear that the propaganda thesis of a 'pan-European war of liberation' did not mean that Germany was waging war on behalf of Europe. The beneficiaries of this war were to 'be the Germans alone'.[8]

How well Hitler used the propaganda weapon can be seen from his many comments from those days. 'The happy thing in an unhappy time', he told the Croatian deputy head of state, Slavko Kvaternik, on 21 July 1941, 'is that the struggle against Bolshevism has united all Europe. There are things which do more than anything else to lead nations to a common goal.'[9] In his opinion, the unity of the European nations was now prevented only by the Jews still living there, whom he described to Kvaternik as the 'focus of bacilli for new decomposition'. In his order of the day at the start of Operation 'Typhoon' on 2 October 1941, Hitler again glorified the war against the Soviet Union as a pan-European act. The struggle against 'Jewish Bolshevism' was 'regarded by all the nations of Europe—perhaps for the first time—as a common action to save the most valuable continent of culture'.[10] For Hitler, however, Europe was 'not a geographical, but a blood-conditioned term'.[11] For that reason he believed that German rule over the European continent was most threatened by its racial enemy, the Jews. After the failure of the 'rapid campaign', and once the real nature of German objectives became glaringly apparent, German propaganda declarations acquired an imploring character. In February 1942 Hitler explained to the Croatian minister in Berlin, Mile Budak, that it was Germany's great task to 'organize' the occupied Soviet territories 'not as previously against Europe, but for it'. The struggle against Bolshevism, 'the bestial degeneration of humanity . . . is a crusade such as previously took place only against the Huns and against the Turks. This struggle must bring to-

[5] OKW/WFSt/Abt. L (I Op) No. 44794/41, 25 May 1941, DGFP D xii, No. 554.
[6] IMT xxvi. 610 ff.
[7] Weizsäcker-Papiere, 261–2 (29 June 1941).
[8] Bormann memorandum, 16 July 1941, IMT xxxviii. 86. See Sect. II.vii.3 at n. 243.
[9] Staatsmänner, ii. 553.
[10] Domarus, Hitler, ii. 1757.
[11] Hitler, Monologe, 55 (8–11 Aug. 1941).

gether and unite the European peoples.'[12] Yet even at the start of the war against the Soviet Union, clear-sighted allies regarded the German slogan of a 'European crusade against Bolshevism' as an 'empty phrase' or mere propaganda.[13] At the end of October 1941 Weizsäcker too was sceptical that anything like a 'European solidarity' could emerge 'so long as we regard the occupied European territories simply as tools to prolong our powers of resistance'.[14]

The Germans had certainly hoped for the response that 22 June 1941 and its propaganda justifications evoked among the anti-Communist forces in Europe. Nevertheless, the offers of service and the applications from volunteers found the foreign ministry, its representatives abroad, and the Wehrmacht leadership unprepared. The associated political, legal, and organizational problems had not been clarified. Not until 30 June 1941 was a discussion held between the foreign ministry, Wehrmacht High Command's foreign department, SS main office, and the NSDAP foreign political department to work out general guidelines for the treatment of 'volunteer registrations in foreign countries for the struggle against the Soviet Union'.[15] Ambassador Ritter demanded a positive approach to the volunteer question, 'both for the current struggle against Soviet Russia and with regard to the future political development of Europe'. Among the initiated, of course, there was no talk of a crusade.

At this discussion it was decided that only self-contained volunteer units would be accepted into the Wehrmacht or the Waffen-SS. The volunteers would wear German uniforms with nationality badges in order to identify them as regular combatants, but naturalization would not be necessary. The issue of the oath of allegiance and of payments remained unresolved. It was also decided that Czech and Russian *émigré* volunteers would not be accepted. A few days later, Wehrmacht High Command issued its 'Guidelines for the employment of foreign volunteers in the struggle against the Soviet Union'.[16] Significantly, they were to take the oath to Adolf Hitler for the 'fight against Bolshevism'. Like German soldiers, they were to receive service pay, front-line allowance, and incidental expenses.

National Socialist racial policy led to the classification of the volunteers as 'Germanic' or 'non-Germanic'. While 'Germanic' volunteers—Danes, Finns (*sic*), Flemings, Dutchmen, Norwegians, and Swedes—were incorporated

---

[12] Discussion between Hitler and Budak, 14 Feb. 1942, *Staatsmänner*, ii. 62 ff. See Hitler's remarks to the Finnish foreign minister, Witting, on 27 Nov. 1941: *DGFP* D xiii, No. 507.

[13] This, for example, was the view of the chairman of the Hungarian 'Smallholders' Party', Endre Bajczy-Zsilinszky, on 5 Aug. 1941 (*Allianz Hitler–Horthy–Mussolini*, No. 115), and the Hungarian minister in Berlin, Sztójay, on 28 and 29 June 1941 (ibid., Nos. 112, 113).

[14] *Weizsäcker-Papiere*, 274 (29 Oct. 1941).

[15] PA, Handakten Ritter, No. 55. The foreign ministry's representative at Army High Command, von Etzdorf, described these efforts as 'crusade foreign legion-gathering' (1 July 1941).

[16] OKW/WFSt/Abt. L (II Org.) No. 001331/41, 6 July 1941, BA-MA Wi/I. 345. See *DGFP* D xiii, No. 96. This decree was revised at the beginning of 1942: OKW/WFSt/Org I No. 19/42, 10 Jan. 1942, BA-MA RL2 II/106.

into the Waffen-SS, the 'non-Germanics'—Frenchmen, Croats, Spaniards, and Walloons—fought in Wehrmacht units. However, SS propaganda appeals for foreign volunteers were not based on the war against the Soviet Union. Their roots lay in the ideology of the SS and its rivalry with the Wehrmacht in the recruitment of able-bodied men for replacement formations and new units.[17] As early as the beginning of November 1938, Himmler had announced his intention of 'getting Germanic blood from the whole world, robbing and stealing it' wherever he could.[18] The SS Standarte 'Germania' did not bear its name 'in vain'. In less than two years, he claimed, it would be filled with 'non-German Germanics' (*nichtdeutsche Germanen*). The occupation of Denmark, Norway, the Netherlands, and Belgium subsequently opened the way for the activities of the SS. Though the newly established Standarte 'Nordland' and 'Westland' had attracted only a few hundred Danish, Norwegian, Dutch, and Belgian volunteers in 1940–1,[19] from 22 June 1941 the SS was able to use propaganda of a 'European crusade against Bolshevism' as an additional aid to mobilization. Its ideological framework was not the German national state, but the racial community, the 'Greater Germanic empire'.

At the end of 1941 12,000 'Germanic volunteers of non-German nationality' were fighting in the Waffen-SS: 2,399 Danes, 1,180 Finns, 1,571 Flemings 4,814 Dutchmen, 1,883 Norwegians, 39 Swedes, 135 Swiss and Liechtensteiners. There were also 6,200 'ethnic German' volunteers from Alsace, Lorraine, Luxemburg, Romania, Serbia, Slovakia, and Hungary. In addition, 24,000 Frenchmen, Croats, Spaniards, and Walloons were serving in the Wehrmacht.[20] Overall, therefore, some 43,000 'foreign volunteers' were wearing German uniform in 1941. Alongside the ideological motives and idealism of recruits, a role was also played by opportunism, the lust for adventure, and the desire to escape domestic restrictions or oppressive daily life under occupation. Additionally, some Spaniards had nursed a strong personal desire for revenge since the civil war. For the commanders, some sections of the officer corps, and the political groups and military élites who supported the units, there were important domestic political motives. Within the Walloon battalion and the French regiment, for example, these led to power-struggles which destroyed the internal structures and endangered political calculations. All the volunteers appear to have expected that the Red Army would collapse very quickly, allowing them to return home as celebrated heroes. This belief was an illusion. As a result of the enormous losses of men in the German army by the end of December 1941, the German leadership began to value both its allies and the volunteer units much more highly than

---

[17] See Stein, *Geschichte der Waffen-SS*; Buss and Mollo, *Hitler's Germanic Legions*; Wegner, 'Garde des "Führers"'; id., *Hitlers politische Soldaten*.

[18] Himmler, *Geheimreden*, 37–8.

[19] On 30 June 1940 the Standarte Westland contained 382 volunteers, and Standarte Nordland 245; quoted from Wegner, 'Pangermanische Armee', 101–2.

[20] The figures were reported to the foreign ministry on 21 Jan. 1942 by OKW foreign department and SS main office: PA, Handakten Ritter, No. 56.

before. However unsatisfactory the performance of some, it was now considered not merely 'desirable', but 'even necessary', that they be strengthened.[21] Hitler and the Wehrmacht High Command held that the war against the Soviet Union involved 'the existence or non-existence of the other European nations'.[22] Nevertheless, it was much easier to force Romania, Hungary, and Italy to increase their contingents of troops in 1942, and to bring 'ethnic Germans' into the Waffen-SS, than to use defeat in the east to produce large numbers of volunteers for the 'struggle against Bolshevism'.

2. Volunteers from Western and Southern Europe

Jürgen Förster

In 1941 the largest unit was provided by Spain, although as a proportion of the population the biggest contingent came from the Netherlands. On 22 June 1941 Ramón Serrano Suñer, chairman of the Falange's Junta Política and Spanish foreign minister, obtained Francisco Franco's agreement for his offer to the German ambassador, Eberhard von Storrer, that a number of Falange volunteer units should take part in the war against the Soviet Union as a 'gesture of solidarity'.[23] Madrid did not intend to make a formal declaration of war, although that was what the Germans wanted. Hitler accepted the offer because he hoped to tie Spain more closely to Germany. He urged the rapid dispatch of the volunteers. Most of all, Serrano Suñer expected the offer to improve German–Spanish relations, which had been strained since the 'dilatory rejection' of joint conquest of the British rock fortress of Gibraltar. He also hoped to buttress his own position in Spanish domestic politics. The announcement of the offer in Spain, and recruitment among the Falangist youth, led to a power-struggle between supporters and opponents of the Falange Junta chairman. The battle-lines ran between Serrano Suñer, the army, and the old Falangists. For its part, the army wanted to prevent the Falange from becoming the sole beneficiary of the expected increase in power and prestige, actually arguing for the dispatch of a full army corps to Russia. At the same time, many old Falangists—disappointed by the Caudillo's 'new state'—chose to 'emigrate' to the front.[24] The volunteer units offered by the passionately anti-Communist Serrano Suñer were not merely a contribution to the struggle against Communism and a gesture of political gratitude for the deployment of the Condor Legion during the civil war; they also had a domestic political motive. Franco resolved the power-struggle with a compromise which also accommodated Wehrmacht High Command's preference for

---

[21] Thus Gen. Jodl on 14 Dec. 1941: *ADAP* E i, No. 14.

[22] Keitel's letter to Ribbentrop, 4 Jan. 1942, ibid., No. 92. See Hitler's letter to Horthy, 29 Dec. 1941, ibid., No. 64.

[23] See Proctor, *Agonia de un Neutral*; Ruhl, *Spanien im Zweiten Weltkrieg*; Kleinfeld and Tambs, *Spanish Legion*.

[24] Ruhl, *Spanien im Zweiten Weltkrieg*, 29.

a united Spanish volunteer force rather than separate army and Falange units. The infantry division to be dispatched would be a national unit of volunteer regular soldiers and Falangists under good leadership, thus enabling it to fulfil its purpose and be worthy of the Spanish military tradition. From first lieutenant upwards, the officer corps was recruited only from regular officers. Two-thirds of the second lieutenants and NCOs were also drawn from the army, and only a third from the Falangist militia. The ranks were recruited from the civilian population by local branches of the Falange and the army, with preference given to veterans of the civil war. All soldiers were screened for political and social reliability.[25] As commander Franco appointed General Augustin Muñoz Grandes, a battle-hardened officer, acceptable to both the army and the Falange. The Spanish volunteer division, División Española de Voluntarios (DEV), was soon to become known as the 'Blue Division' (División Azul) because of the blue shirts worn by the Falangists. In line with the will of the general staff, it was to be recruited from all eight military regions as well as Morocco. The division was to consist of four infantry regiments and an artillery regiment, with a strength of 640 officers, 2,272 NCOs, and 14,780 men.[26] The decision was followed by a rush to volunteer. Only in Military Region IV (Barcelona) was the target figure not reached. Soldiers there had to be 'persuaded' to volunteer, and some vacant posts were filled by volunteers from Valencia.

The Falangists were convinced anti-Communists who accepted the German justification for the attack. For them, the 'European crusade against Bolshevism' was more than an empty phrase. But they were also convinced that their place in the new Spain, and its weight in the reorganization of Europe, depended on their willingness to risk their lives against the common enemy. Among the officers, these ideological motives were bolstered by concern for their careers. Months spent on the eastern front counted double for promotion, and any decorations brought additional plus-points over colleagues at home.

As the training of the voluteers began in barracks throughout Spain, a commission was sent to Berlin, where it was confronted with German demands for men and material. The commission discovered that the Germans were expecting the strength of the division to be 526 officers, 2,813 NCOs, and 14,397 men with 300 lorries and 400 motor-cycles.[27] This meant that the DEV had an excess of officers and men and a shortage of NCOs. The level of mobility demanded also exceeded Spanish capacity. After the intervention of various agencies, the German demands were dropped for political reasons— not least, out of regard for Spanish domestic politics.

On 13 July 1941 Serrano Suñer bade farewell to the DEV at Madrid's north station at a ceremony attended by the military leadership and the diplomatic

---

[25] Kleinfeld and Tambs, *Spanish Legion*, 6 ff.
[26] Ibid. 9, 355.
[27] Ibid. 20 ff.

corps. Two days previously a corrida in honour of the volunteers had been held in the presence of General José Valera, the minister of war. In his speech Serrano Suñer again stressed the motives which had led him and the soldiers to this step: revenge for the Soviet intervention in the civil war; gratitude for German and Italian assistance during it; defence of civilization against the inhuman, barbaric, and criminal system of Bolshevism; and struggle for the glory of Spain. The Spanish volunteer division, 17,909 men, was transported to the troop training-ground at Grafenwöhr near Nuremberg. There it was to be reorganized according to the German model, re-equipped, and trained. The volunteers took the oath of allegiance on 31 July 1941. The reorganization of the DEV into the 250th Infantry Division, consisting of three infantry regiments and an artillery regiment, facilitated the establishment of a divisional reserve, the 'mobile 250 Reserve Battalion' consisting mainly of veterans and foreign legionaries. Less satisfying was the division's low level of motorization and the switch to drawing the guns by horses. General Muñoz Grandes pressed successfully for a reduction in the training period, which the Germans had set at three months. This decision meant that the men had insufficient practice in handling the horses, which was to have an adverse effect on marching discipline, equipment, and the animals themselves. The Germans doubted the political reliability of the division, partly because of the low proportion of Falangists (about 30 per cent). In contrast to Serrano Suñer, the Spanish army was careful to ensure that the division was not regarded as a Falangist unit. It became clear to the Germans that sympathies for the Falange must inevitably damage the other pillar of the Franco regime, the army.

Even before the departure of 250th Infantry Division to the eastern front, to Army Group Centre's area of operations from 21 August 1941, the German command was told of the Spanish government's request for the division to be sent into action 'at the focal point of the struggle'.[28] A few days before, however, the army group had gone over to the defensive on the order of Hitler. The Spaniards knew nothing of the crisis between him and the general staff. Hitler received a courtesy visit from General Muñoz Grandes on 1 September, while the Spanish soldiers marched from the unloading area at Grodno towards Minsk. The week-long march to their final operations zone brought the division its first encounter with German views of organization and marching discipline, their assessment of their allies, and the treatment of Slavs and Jews in the east. The commander of Fourth Army, Field Marshal von Kluge, refused to deploy the Spaniards in his area of operations, apparently under the impression that they were more like gypsies than soldiers. The reports of the German liaison officer to the Spanish division had a 'refreshing' effect on the commander of Army Group Centre, Field Marshal Fedor von Bock. In his war diary he noted the appearance of the division, 'unfamiliar to German soldiers', the poor condition of the horses, and the fact that the Spaniards

---

[28] Army Group Centre, Ia, war diary, 20 Aug. 1941, BA-MA RH 19 II/119.

regarded all women as fair game and 'held orgies' even with Jewish women in Grodno.[29] On 24 September 1941 Hitler decided that 250th Infantry Division should reinforce Army Group North. At the beginning of September this army group had been forced to hive off troops to Army Group Centre for the attack on Moscow. Instead of attacking, the Spaniards were now expected to march on, from Smolensk to Vitebsk, before completing their journey by train. On 10 October 1941 the division was placed under the command of the von Roques Group in Sixteenth Army's sector, relieving 18th Infantry Division and part of 126th Infantry Division. The position ran through Novgorod north of Lake Ilmen along the Volkhov.

The 250th Infantry Division was assessed as incapable of offensive operations, and the condition of its horses and lorries as alarming.[30] The Germans regarded the troops as rather odd, but General Muñoz Grandes was seen as an energetic commander with a deep interest in German battle experiences. Obvious differences in mentality and conduct at the front led the Germans to underestimate the fighting spirit of the Spaniards. Within a short time the division proved itself well able to hold its sector of the front against fierce attacks by the Red Army. The *élan* and personal courage of the individual soldiers remained unbroken by the rigours of the winter and inadequate levels of equipment. Muñoz Grandes vigorously rejected the hasty judgement of the new corps commander, Infantry General Friedrich-Wilhelm von Chappuis, that the division was the greatest problem facing XXXVIII Army Corps and would be unable to resist increased Soviet pressure. Chappuis stuck to his opinion, urging Sixteenth Army HQ to agree to the relief of the Spaniards. Muñoz Grandes and his division were determined to repel this attack on their military honour, with its possible repercussions on German–Spanish relations, by holding their sector of the front intact. He ordered that the positions were to be defended as if Spain itself was at stake. The fierce fighting that followed, which included atrocities by both sides, led to heavy casualties among the Spaniards. In two and a half months the division lost almost 3,000 men.[31] Since the Spaniards had held their positions, Muñoz Grandes felt able to agree to a shortening of its sector of the front without losing face. At the beginning of January 1942 he was awarded the Iron Cross First Class. Hitler too was under the impression that, as troops, the Spaniards were a 'dilapidated formation' and that the relations between officers and men were 'miserable'. But at the same time he praised the fact that the division had abandoned 'not a metre' of ground. 'One cannot imagine pluckier people. They take no cover, they let themselves be killed. Yes, our men are happy when they have the Spaniards in the adjoining sector of the front.'[32]

[29] Bock, Tagebuch, ii (3, 20 Sept. 1941), MGFA P-210.

[30] Army Group North/Ia, war diary, 10 Oct. 1941, BA-MA RH 19 III/168.

[31] Kleinfeld and Tambs, *Spanish Legion*, 168 ff. In Mar. 1942 the division had a strength of 13,766 men.

[32] Hitler, *Monologe*, 178 (4–5 Jan. 1942).

Disputes between the Spanish and German leadership, and between the Falange and the army, broke out anew over the form of rehabilitation and reorganization of the division. Franco wanted to withdraw the division from the front to enable it to be replenished for the spring offensive; he was proposing a fixed rotation of personnel—2,000–2,500 soldiers every three or four months. Serrano Suñer, on the other hand, wanted an exchange of the Falangists. Both suggestions were rejected by the German leadership. Though they too wanted Spanish losses to be made good, the military difficulties on the Volkhov led them to oppose the transfer of the division to the rear. At the end of 1941 Franco was forced to accept that the unexpected powers of resistance displayed by the Red Army meant that the 'European crusade against Bolshevism' would continue for some time. The spread of the European war into a world war made Spain's entry into the conflict on the side of the Tripartite Pact even less likely. Nevertheless, Franco kept 250th Infantry Division fighting on the eastern front.

The willingness of the Spanish government to establish a volunteer formation for the 'struggle against Bolshevism' led the German minister in Lisbon, Oswald Baron von Hoyningen-Huene, to explore the attitude of Portugal to the war against the Soviet Union. On 1 July 1941 the Portuguese premier and foreign minister, Salazar, emphasized 'Portugal's deathly enmity towards Bolshevism . . . in these days of the decisive struggle' at a public rally of the anti-Bolshevik Legion. Unlike the Spaniards, however, he saw no need to repay any debt of gratitude for German help.[33] The foreign ministry in Berlin welcomed Salazar's attitude, but thought it did not go far enough. The secretary of state informed the minister of Germany's political interest in the participation of a Portuguese unit—however small—in Operation Barbarossa. This would demonstrate the unity of Europe in the struggle against Bolshevism, and would also have a beneficial 'effect on opinion in Brazil'.[34] Huene was not successful. Out of regard for Britain, Salazar would not permit the establishment of a volunteer unit, even though 'pro-German Portuguese officers' had been placed in the ministry of war for that purpose.[35]

In France, news of the German attack on the Soviet Union came through on the first anniversary of the Franco-German armistice. The domestic political situation was very different from that of Spain. Three-fifths of France was occupied by German troops, with the remainder under the authoritarian rule of the Vichy regime; the country was suffering the psychological, personal, and material consequences of defeat and the 'reality of the armistice'.[36] The official German version of a preventive war to safeguard Europe from Bolshevism

[33] *DGFP* D xiii, No. 60.
[34] Weizsäcker to Huene, July 1941, Pol I M 4,822 g., PA, Handakten Ritter, No. 55.
[35] *DGFP* D xiii, No. 60 n. 2.
[36] Jäckel, *Frankreich*, 85.

served to intensify and accentuate several very different trends in France—
resistance, 'wait and see', and willingness to collaborate.[37] After the collapse of
the German–Soviet alliance of 1939, the French Communists were also able to
join the resistance and provoke the occupying power to disastrous over-
reaction by attacking German soldiers. Equally, the events of 22 June 1941
offered the leaders of politically organized collaboration an unexpected political opportunity to unite the policy of total collaboration with Germany with
that of anti-Communism. Participation in the 'European crusade against
Bolshevism' appeared to give them the chance to win German consent to their
struggle for the 'national rebirth' of France. However, the supporters of
collaboration were utterly divided as to the desired political shape of this new
France. They were united only in their rejection of the 'reactionary' Vichy
regime, of parliamentary government, and of Communism. Many of them also
demonstrated a militant anti-Semitism. Jacques Doriot, the leader of the 'Parti
Populaire Français' (PPF), responded to the news of the German attack in the
east with the words: 'If there is a war to which I am sympathetic, it is this.'[38]
He publicly demanded the establishment of a volunteer legion and declared
that he himself would report for service. His domestic political rivals, Marcel
Déat of the 'Rassemblement National Populaire' (RNP) and Eugène Deloncle
of the 'Mouvement Social Revolutionnaire' (MSR), also wanted to participate
in the anti-Bolshevik crusade. The idea of a legion was further encouraged by
the German ambassador, Otto Abetz.[39]

On 1 July 1941 Secretary of State von Weizsäcker informed the German
ambassador that the government was ready to find a place in the Wehrmacht
for Frenchmen who volunteered for 'the struggle against the Soviet Union'.
Only self-contained units wearing German uniform would be considered.
'Berlin had no interest in the prominent appearance of Russian *émigrés*.'[40]
Abetz reported that there were some 3,000 volunteers, including 80 fighter
pilots, and asked for further instructions. Once the Wehrmacht defence department had indicated that it was not considering the use of French and
Walloon volunteers, Minister Ernst Eisenlohr appealed to the foreign minister, Ribbentrop.[41] On 5 July 1941 Ambassador Ritter informed Paris that the
Germans had decided in favour of a French volunteer formation. There were
constraints, however. The number of volunteers was not to exceed 10,000, and
'support for such enrolment on the part of the French government was not
wanted'.[42] The initiative for the founding of the legion was thus to come from
the political groups of occupied France, since Hitler was determined to ensure

[37] Ibid. 180.
[38] Quoted from Wolf, *Doriot-Bewegung*, 253.
[39] Davey, 'Origins of the LVF', 29 ff.
[40] PA, Handakten Ritter, No. 55. Abetz had reported on information from these circles on 23
June.
[41] Telex to Ambassador Ritter, 3 July 1941, ibid.
[42] *DGFP* D xiii, No. 78; Abetz situation report, 23 July 1942, PA, Büro St.S., Frankreich, vol.
9.

that the creation of a French volunteer formation did not leave him with any obligation to Vichy. The Vichy government had broken off diplomatic relations with Moscow on 30 June. Petain, who had consented to the creation of a legion, had to rescind the law forbidding French soldiers to serve outside the French army.

Once permission was received from Berlin, Abetz named Doriot, Déat, and two other representatives of smaller groups, Marcel Bucard of 'Francisme' and Pierre Constantini of the 'Ligue Française', to work from the embassy. The French representatives decided jointly to set up a 'Légion des Volontaires Français contre le Bolchevisme' (LVF). On 8 July a joint appeal appeared in the *Cri du Peuple*. This described the aims of the Legion: participation in the crusade against Bolshevism, French representation on the eastern front, and the defence of European civilization. It also stressed the agreement of Pétain and Hitler.[43] Three other party leaders thereupon declared their willingness to take part in the undertaking: Jean Boissel (Front Franc), Pierre Clémenti (Parti Français National Collectiviste), and Eugène Deloncle (MSR). A central committee was established under the chairmanship of Deloncle and given the task of setting up the Legion. In the unoccupied zone an action committee was to set to work under Simon Sabiani, the PPF representative from Marseilles. The recruitment campaign was opened by Doriot and Déat with separate rallies on 6 July 1941. Appropriately enough, Abetz offered the use of the offices of the 'Intourist' Soviet travel agency to assist the central committee. At this stage important issues such as the oath, the uniform, and payment had still to be clarified. The military commander, Infantry General Otto von Stülpnagel, agreed to a first joint meeting by the pro-German parties on condition that Bastille Day passed off quietly on 14 July. The meeting took place on 18 July 1941 in the 'Vélodrome d'Hiver'. Only after Wehrmacht High Command 'Guidelines for the service of foreign volunteers in the struggle against the Soviet Union' had arrived in Paris, and the military commander's staff had worked out 'Instructions for entry into the French Volunteer Legion for the struggle against Bolshevism', were the necessary questions of organization discussed between the German military and diplomatic authorities.[44] The military commander was represented by Colonel (General Staff) Dr Hans Speidel and Major (General Staff) Hans Crome. They reported the disappointment of the German embassy representatives, Dr Ludger Westrick and Dr Liebe, at the 'excessively narrow' procedure laid down by OKW for the recruitment of volunteers. Though individual issues remained unresolved in July 1941, it was now clear that the French would take their oath to Hitler and would receive pay plus supplements like those of the German troops. Only Frenchmen of Aryan descent aged between 18 and 40 (officers up to 50) were to be accepted as volunteers. The issue of uniform had still to be finalized; the

---

[43] Davey, *La Légion*, 13.
[44] Military commander in France, HQ Staff Ic/VODB, No. 973/41, 15 July 1941, with instructions.

instructions stated that the volunteers would 'probably' wear French uniform with German badges of rank. Uniforms and equipment were to be provided. These regulations were passed to the central committee by the German embassy and published in amended form in the *Cri du Peuple* on 18 July 1941.[45] The recruitment campaign could now begin in earnest. However, it soon became apparent that the numbers volunteering for service were much smaller than the target figures.

There were many reasons for this. They included a general French reluctance to regard participation in the 'crusade against Bolshevism' as an opportunity for the national rebirth of France, as Doriot had hoped; Hitler's decision not to allow French prisoners of war to opt for the Legion; and the inadequate support provided by the German leadership. This last point was linked with Hitler's refusal to make the necessary political concessions to the French government, which he considered tantamount to dissolving the armistice regime. First of all he wanted to solve the 'Russian problem'. Until then, France was to be handled in a dilatory manner.[46]

The formation of the Legion was overshadowed by a political attack. The first official call-up ceremony for the Legion was held on 27 August 1941 at the Borgnis-Desborde barracks in Versailles, and attended by the leading figures of collaboration—Pierre Laval, Count Fernand de Brinon, Doriot, Déat, Deloncle, and Constantini. (Ambassador Abetz and the commander of the Legion, Colonel Roger Labonne, were absent.) During the formalities, one of the legionnaires fired his machine-gun at the assembled dignitaries and wounded Laval and Déat. This episode was the first public manifestation of the political struggle within the pro-German groups, which ultimately brought about the collapse of the LVF.

On 6 September 1941 the first contingent of the Legion, 25 officers and 803 NCOs and men, arrived at Dęba training camp in Poland.[47] It became the basis of 1st Battalion of 638th Infantry Regiment. Already it was apparent that there would be no French formation with its own uniform, fighting with the Wehrmacht in the struggle against Bolshevism; instead, 638th Infantry Regiment would be a German regiment in which French was spoken. The establishment and training of the unit were the responsibility of Military District VIII (Breslau). Major Hammerschmidt was appointed chief of the German training staff. On 17 September Ambassador Abetz arrived for an ostensibly private visit to the camp after the departure of Colonel Labonne for discussions with the military commander in Paris. Abetz, who had come from the Führer's headquarters, had no wish to observe the training of the legionaries; he had come to exchange political views with Doriot. The subject of the

---

[45] Davey, *La Légion*, 21.

[46] PA, Handakten Etzdorf, Vertrauliche Aufzeichnungen, No. 1, 26 July 1941; Jäckel, *Frankreich*, 178–9.

[47] See war diary of training staff of French Legion, 24 Aug. 1941–31 Mar. 1942, BA-MA RH 53-23/49.

conversation was the decline in the number of volunteers registering for service. It was to be counteracted in three ways: by increased German propaganda, by the creation of a French honorary committee of prominent figures, and by the exchange of 2,000 PPF members in North Africa for 2,000 members of the colonial army currently in southern France. The honorary committee, which was designed to make the Legion socially acceptable in France, contained men from the government, academic life, and the press, as well as the rector of the Catholic Institute in Paris, Cardinal Alfred Baudrillart. The visit also revealed to the German officers the influence wielded by Doriot within the LVF, despite his relatively junior rank of lieutenant. On 20 September 1941 a second contingent of 127 officers and 659 NCOs and men arrived in Dęba, followed by another 11 officers a few days later. Colonel Labonne used the opportunity to make the new arrivals aware of his view of the aims of the LVF. He also wanted to explain why they should wear German uniform, 'as the sign of a loyal, unconditional, and complete reconciliation between France and Germany'. He was striving for co-operation between the two great nations for a healthy Europe, free 'from the yoke of the ghettos, the lodges, Bolshevism, and British gold. We are taking to the field against this vast Bolshevik–capitalist coalition, which dares to give itself ideological airs.' Labonne drew attention to the expansionist tendency of Bolshevism and recalled that many Frenchmen had demanded a crusade against it during the Soviet–Finnish war of 1939–40. Though the legion was small, it—not the men in the pay of the British Foreign Office—represented the true France. On 5 October the legionaries in Dęba were sworn in by Infantry General Hans Halm, commander of Military District VIII. Both he and Labonne used the occasion to stress that Germany was fighting for civilization and a new Europe alongside those who recognized the danger in the east. In fact, this interpretation of the struggle against Bolshevism bore no resemblance to Hitler's own. In mid-July 1941 he had described as insolence the view of one Vichy newspaper that the war against the Soviet Union was Europe's war.[48] Hitler was not prepared to share the fruits of victory with his foreign 'brothers-in-arms', apart from agreeing to some territorial acquisitions for Finland and Romania. The French oath to Hitler for the struggle against Bolshevism was thus based on entirely mistaken assumptions about German intentions.

On 12 October another contingent of 21 officers and 623 NCOs and men arrived in Dęba. Labonne's speech at their swearing-in ceremony revealed that the ideological element had been intensified since his earlier speeches. He described his legionaries as successors of Godfrey de Bouillon, while emphasizing the Asiatic and bestial character of the Red Army and calling Stalin 'Attila, the scourge of God'.[49] On 25 October Brinon came inspect to the Legion in Dęba, where he was welcomed by Labonne as the champion of

[48] 16 July 1941, No. L-221, *IMT* xxxviii. 86.
[49] War diary of training staff, 19 Oct. 1941, BA-MA RH 53-23/49. See also the speech by an MSR representative in Merglen, 'Soldats français', 72.

future German–French co-operation. For his part, Brinon praised the legion's willingness to assist the German struggle to save civilization in Europe. On this occasion Labonne handed over a message for Marshal Pétain, which was published in *Cri du Peuple* on 5 November along with Pétain's positive reply. The Marshal referred here not only to the anti-Bolshevik crusade under German leadership, but also to the Legion's service for France. This, however, was far from being Hitler's intention. On 19 October 1941 the Army High Command informed Army Group North that it should not expect the transfer of the LVF: 'the Führer wants the question of the Legion to be handled in a dilatory manner for political reasons.'[50] Nevertheless, only three days later Army Group Centre was told by Army High Command that (French) 638th Infantry Regiment would be dispatched to Smolensk. The army group was to place the regiment—comprising regimental staff, signals platoon, motor-cycle dispatch platoon, band, two infantry battalions, each with three rifle companies and a machine-gun company, and each with one anti-tank gun company and one infantry gun company—under the command of a suitable division.[51] The regiment was entrained at the end of October. *En route* to the eastern front, Colonel Labonne was received for short discussions by Field Marshal von Brauchitsch and, at his personal request, by Goebbels. On 4 November Labonne and Doriot reported to the commander of Army Group Centre, Field Marshal von Bock. The latter described Labonne as an 'older man, who knows half the world, no old campaigner, also no adventurer, but apparently a great idealist'; as regards Doriot, he remarked only that 'the adjutant is a reserve officer and professional politician'.[52] After the regiment assembled in Smolensk, the march to the front began on 9 November. Since Bock regarded 638th Infantry Regiment as more of a free corps than a disciplined unit, 'initiation personnel' from 7th Infantry Division were attached to it. These were 'first to assist it, and second to ensure that no acts of indiscipline occur which damage our reputation, since the French are wearing German uniforms'.[53] A few days later the German liaison officer, Captain Winneberger, informed the army group that the regiment was already totally exhausted by an average march of 8–10 kilometres per day on good roads. In his view this state of affairs was due to the failings of the officers, inadequate care of the horses, complete ignorance of marching discipline, and inadequate training of the men. It also appeared that the troops had not received regular rations. With the agreement of Labonne, the army group ordered shorter marches and more frequent rest-days, to get the regiment 'at least up to behind the front line'.[54]

[50] Army Group North/Ia, war diary, 19 Oct. 1941, BA-MA RH 19 III/168.
[51] BA-MA RH 19 II/124.
[52] Bock, Tagebuch, ii (4 Nov. 1941), MGFA P-210.
[53] Ibid. (6 Nov. 1941).
[54] Army Group Centre/Ia, war diary, 16 Nov. 1941, BA-MA RH 19 II/121. See Bock, Tagebuch, ii (15 Nov. 1941), MGFA P-210.

On 19 November the French regiment was placed under the command of 7th Infantry Division within VII Army Corps. The 7th Division was then engaged in the fighting to open the isthmus of Kubinka, approximately 100 kilometres west of Moscow. I Battalion 638th Infantry Regiment was sent to the front line on 24 November, and II Battalion on 3 December, where they relieved elements of the division. However, the division assessed 13th and 14th companies as being 'not yet ready to be employed'. The ration strength of the regiment was set at 1,366 men, 605 of them still on the march.

Barely six weeks after the Spanish division, the French division was sent into action on the eastern front. Only a few days later, however, it had to be withdrawn from the line, having suffered casualties of 60 dead and wounded and 150 with frostbite. What reasons were given for the decision to withdraw it? When the intelligence officer of 7th Infantry Division submitted an initial report on the operation of the French Legion (I and II/638), he made all the arguments which were to be repeated in subsequent reports:

In part the Legion had already become separated during the advance. Some units have still not arrived. During moving off, more signs of disintegration became apparent. The men are generally willing but inadequately trained, the NCOs good in part but unable to develop because guidance from above is lacking. The officers are incapable, selected on political grounds. There is a lack of organizational talent, German thoroughness, understanding of the care of weapons, equipment, and horses. Redress can be found only by providing another leadership corps and longer training.[55]

The German liaison officer divided the legionaries into three categories: the 'pure idealists', who recognized Bolshevism as a danger and had volunteered from conviction, were 'unfortunately' in the minority; more strongly represented were the 'adventurers', mainly former Foreign Legionnaires, and (thirdly) those who simply wanted to be looked after.[56] The politicization of the Legion, created by the rivalry between the various groups, the presence of Doriot, his influence on Colonel Labonne, and the latter's promotion practices, contributed to the failure to develop any sense of solidarity. Discipline and combat-readiness among soldiers depend more on their ties to the primary military group (group, platoon, company), and on the conduct of NCOs and officers, than on abstract ideological objectives. The professional incompetence of most of the officers, who had indeed been chosen for their political reliability, also helped to destroy the internal structure of the regiment.

Initially the Legion was transferred to the Rear Army Area Centre. The German leadership was keen to see it reorganized and then given light security tasks. When even this proved impossible, the unit was sent out of the area of operations to Radom in Poland. There the Legion was to be 'completely

---

[55] Combat report on the French Legion, 23 Dec. 1941, BA-MA RH 26-7/19. See two French reports of 28 Oct. and 19 Dec. 1941, in Merglen, 'Soldats français', 73, 74.

[56] Report on the operations of the French Legion and lessons learnt, 14 Feb. 1942, PA, Handakten Etzdorf, Frankreich, vol. 2; report by commander of Rear Army Area Centre, Ia No. 263/42, 24 Jan. 1942, BA-MA RH 22/230.

depoliticized' and moulded into a 'militarily usable instrument'.[57] Hitler decided that it should consist of 15,000 men. The guidelines envisaged the
dismissal of coloured troops, former Foreign Legionnaires, Russian émigrés,
and legionaries who failed either in action or in exercises lasting several days.
(It seems that, despite the regulations, not only 'Aryan Frenchmen' had been
accepted for service.) To avoid hurting the pride of the legionaries and in the
hope of creating a positive attitude among those dismissed (who were regarded
as potential foreign workers for Germany), dismissal was to be on medical
grounds wherever possible.[58] The legionaries also had to commit themselves
'to an unpolitical attitude' during their service. Four officers and eleven men
did not sign the required declaration. To avoid the fiasco of the LVF becoming too obvious, Colonel Labonne and seven other legionaries were awarded
the Iron Cross Second Class. There are varying figures on the size of the
Legion. According to the war diary of the training staff in Dęba, disbanded at
the end of March 1942, 190 officers and 2,902 NCOs and men had arrived at
the camp, of whom 9 officers and 152 men were returned to France, presumably either on medical grounds or because of inability to reach the required
standard. A memorandum for the chief of the Army General Staff of 9 July
1942 refers to 113 officers and 3,528 NCOs and men. In addition, it gives the
strength of the two battalions at the end of January 1942 as 58 officers and
1,038 men.[59]

Hitler himself regarded the French Legion and the groups as valuable
mainly in the context of French domestic politics. The soldiers' task was 'not
to see action on the eastern front, but if necessary to be active in Paris one day
to protect our Party men there (Marcel Déat!) from their own countrymen'.
Hitler expected these 'Party men' to 'bring Paris into opposition to Vichy and
keep it there'.[60]

In occupied Belgium volunteers also came forward to take part in Hitler's war
in the east as members of the 'Walloon Legion'. The most famous legionary,
Léon Degrelle, gave the following motives for himself and his comrades:
defence of the West and the common European fatherland against Bolshevism, and thirst for adventure. He made no mention of his domestic political
motives. In autumn 1940 Degrelle had already developed an ambitious plan
for a Fascist Greater Belgium under the leadership of his Rexist movement;
this would operate within the framework of a 'New Order' in Europe guaranteed by Germany, and be shaped by the 'hard, pure, and revolutionary' idea

[57] Letter from OQu IV in Army General Staff to Abetz, 19 Mar. 1942, PA, Handakten Etzdorf,
Frankreich, vol. 2. On the number see Army General Staff/Org.Abt., war diary, 11–15 Feb. 1942,
BA-MA RH 2/v. 821.

[58] Military commander in Government-General, Abt. Ia/Org. No. 169/42, annexe, BA-MA RH
23-53/v. 95.

[59] PA, Handakten Etzdorf, Frankreich, vol. 2.

[60] PA, Handakten Etzdorf, Vertrauliche Aufzeichnungen, No. 1, 20 Feb. 1942; telegram from
Ambassador Abetz, 23 June 1944, ibid., Inland IIg, vol. 366.

of National Socialism. The idea was directed both against the German military administration and against the 'old democratic, plutocratic, Masonic, and even Jewish cliques' in Belgium which collaborated with it and which must be 'eradicated pitilessly'.[61] Degrelle's scheme had been blocked by the military commander. However, the launching of the supposed 'crusade of Europe against Bolshevism' appeared to offer Degrelle a new opportunity to win influence for himself and his movement in discussions on the future shape of Belgium. He therefore volunteered for service on the eastern front with 'several hundred of his best followers'.[62] Degrelle claimed later that these men were now ruled by 'a new law. The law of existence or non-existence . . . There was no going back, there was only ahead, they had burnt the boats behind them with their own hands.'[63]

The Wehrmacht High Command guidelines of 6 July 1941 made no mention of Walloon volunteers, while Flemings were permitted to join the Waffen-SS. According to Hitler's racially inspired—but never implemented—plan to divide Belgium, devised in the summer of 1941, the Walloon areas of Belgium were to be dealt with in the same way as France. Similar treatment was also to be applied to Walloon volunteers: they were to be registered and sent on their way by the military commander in Belgium.

On 8 August 1941 860 Walloon volunteers left Brussels by train for Meseritz camp in the Warthegau [formerly western Poland]. Measures were taken there to establish and train the '373rd Walloon Infantry Battalion', comprising four companies. Until the end of December 1941 its commander was Captain Jacobs. The battalion was not—as Degrelle later maintained[64]—part of a 'European organization', but was an integral part of the Wehrmacht. At the end of August 1941 it swore an oath of allegiance to Adolf Hitler for the 'struggle against Bolshevism'. The first period of training ended in the middle of October, when the transport of almost 850 Walloon volunteers to the eastern front began. The battalion was to be placed under the command of 97th Light Infantry Division,[65] which it finally reached at the beginning of December 1941. In the interim perod it was apparently used in companies against local partisan groups.

The 97th Light Infantry Division fought as part of Seventeenth Army on the southern flank of the eastern front. On 5 December 1941 it was forced on to the defensive, having reached 'the end of its strength'.[66] Soviet troops broke through its lines on several occasions. In this situation, the battalion was not incorporated into the front line but was used to secure a rear base. It had a

[61] Wagner, *Belgien*, 202 ff. See *DGFP* D xi, No. 204.
[62] Military commander in Belgium and Northern France, Chief of Military Administration No. 18/43, 27 Jan. 1943, on Léon Degrelle and his new political activity, BA-MA RW 4/v. 741.
[63] Degrelle, *Die verlorene Legion*, 8.
[64] Id., *La Cohue*, 517.
[65] Army Group South/Ia, war diary, 25 Sept. 1941, BA-MA RH 19 I/73.
[66] IV Army Corps/Ia, war diary, 9 Dec. 1941, ibid. RH 24-4/49.

strength of 23 officers and 649 NCOs and men.[67] Belgian documents reveal
that the winter temperature—on 6 December, for example, it reached
−24 °C—caused morale to deteriorate. There were also internal tensions. On
30 December 1941 the battalion commander was replaced by Captain Pauly.[68]
German records clearly indicate that conflicts were occurring within the
battalion over the political line to be taken. The divisional commander, Major-
General Maximilian Fretter-Pico, reported to IV Army Corps Command that
two groups had emerged, Rexists and 'a kind of National Socialists'.[69] He had
been asked to mediate between them. Fretter-Pico responded to this request
by asking the corps to deploy the battalion elsewhere. The corps shared
Fretter-Pico's view and judged the battalion to be 'worthless in military
terms'. For their part, the Walloon volunteers felt that they were being worse
treated by the German authorities than the Hungarians and Italians, and
complained directly to the Army High Command. The commander of Seventeenth Army wanted to avoid a row 'out of regard for subsequent foreign-
policy plans through these forces';[70] he therefore placed the Walloon 373rd
Infantry Battalion directly under the command of another corps. Tensions
none the less remained: 97th Light Infantry Division now complained that the
'very competent German liaison officer' had been 'reprimanded in an unpleasant manner in the presence of a corporal [Degrelle]' by the chief of staff
of LII Army Corps.[71] Once again the German leadership responded by changing the command structure. At the end of January 1942 the battalion was
placed under the command of 100th Light Infantry Division for 'locality and
railway protection'. One can only speculate about the group which was com-
peting with Degrelle's party. Might there have been members of the Flemish
Verdinaso among the Walloons? At any rate, the chief of the Militia,
Jef François, had given the name *De Nationaal-Socialist* to the newspaper he
had founded in June 1941.[72] In 1938 the Verdinaso, which also supported
ideas of a Greater Belgium, had described the Walloons as 'Romanized
Dietsche'.[73]

The Walloon 373rd Infantry Battalion was reorganized and given intensified training in tactics and discipline. At the beginning of January 1942
six officers and fifty men were sent back home on the grounds of incompetence or sickness. Degrelle, who had volunteered as an ordinary soldier,
was promoted to officer rank during 1942 for gallantry in action, and was
awarded the Iron Cross First and Second Class. In a major speech in January
1943 he repeated his claim for a say in the future shape of Belgium, now 'with

[67] 97th Lt. Inf. Div. Abt. IIa, activity report, 20 Dec. 1941, ibid., 97, Inf.Div., 18409/34.
[68] Documentation of Centre de Recherches et d'Études Historiques de la Seconde Guerre
Mondiale, Brussels. I am grateful to Mr Vanwelkenheuysen for kindly providing a photocopy.
[69] IV Army Corps/Ia, war diary, 20 Dec. 1941, BA-MA RH 24-4/54.
[70] Ibid., 21 Dec. 1941.
[71] Ibid., 25 Dec. 1941.
[72] Willequet, 'Fascismes belges', 85 ff.
[73] Wagner, *Belgien*, 26.

purely Germanic lineaments'.[74] Hitler noted the change: 'It is highly intere-
sting that the Walloons are suddenly considering themselves to be
Germanen.'[75] The way was now opening for Walloon volunteers to enter the
Waffen-SS.

Volunteers for Hitler's war in the east were found in south-eastern as well as
western Europe. Ante Pavelić, head of state of Croatia, responded to the
German attack on the Soviet Union by assuring Berlin of Croatia's 'complete
inner readiness to support this struggle by the Reich with its own forces also'.[76]
In a personal letter to Hitler, Pavelić offered Croatian volunteer formations
from the army, navy, and air force to fight 'shoulder to shoulder with their
German comrades against the Bolshevik enemy'.[77] The 'German general in
Agram [Zagreb]', Infantry General Edmund Glaise von Horstenau, regarded
the offer as a sincere and politically astute gesture.[78] It was part of an attempt
to establish such close relations with Germany that the Croats would be able
to resist further Italian territorial and political pressure. Though an 'independent state of Croatia' had been declared on 13 April 1941, it had been dominated by Rome since the Croatian–Italian treaty of 18 May 1941.[79] The
Croatian army leadership was permitted to create two infantry divisions and
three mountain divisions, each with six battalions and two artillery detachments.[80] In mid-June Croatia had joined the Tripartite Pact. On this occasion
the pro-German minister of defence and second most important man in the
state, Kvaternik, had told the German foreign minister that Croatian volunteer formations would be available for 'future operations'.[81] By providing
volunteers, the Croatian state leadership hoped to secure German help for the
armed forces it had begun to create; furthermore, Croatia might also be able
to evade the military agreements of the treaty of mid-May, which envisaged
the co-operation of Italy alone in the establishment of Croatian fighting forces.
Croat political calculations proved correct. Hitler accepted the offer of volunteers and ordered that issues of organization be settled by General Glaise von
Horstenau and the German minister in Zagreb, Siegfried Kasche. The Croat
offer was certainly governed by ideological considerations as well as domestic-
and foreign-policy motives. Both Pavelić and Kvaternik were convinced anti-
Communists and anti-Semites. Hitler was assured of a sympathetic audience

---

[74] See n. 62.

[75] Wagner, *Belgien*, 248. See Wegner, 'Pangermanische Armee', doc. 4.

[76] German legation Zagreb, telegram No. 544, 22 June 1941, PA, Büro St.S., Kroatien, vol. 1.

[77] Ibid., Büro RAM, Kroatien. See Gosztony, *Hitlers fremde Heere*, 130 ff.

[78] German legation Zagreb, IIa No. 165/41, 25 June 1941, BA-MA RH 31-III/1. See the
memoirs of Glaise von Horstenau, *General im Zwielicht.*

[79] See Olshausen, *Zwischenspiel auf dem Balkan*, 153 ff.

[80] Second Army Command Ic, war diary, 14 May 1941, BA-MA RH 20-2/1086; LI Army Corps/
Ia, No. 1550/41, 21 May 1941, ibid. E 432/2.

[81] German legation Zagreb, telegram No. 574, 24 June 1941, PA, Büro St.S., Kroatien, vol. 1.
Kvaternik had already made a similar offer on 12 Apr. 1941. Halder had described the idea of a
Croatian legion as a 'nonsense' on 15 Apr. 1941 (*Diaries*, 876).

when he gave free rein to his hatred of the Jews in a conversation with the Croatian minister of defence on 21 July 1941:

The Jews are the scourge of humanity . . . If the Jews had their way, as they have in the Soviet paradise, they would carry out the most lunatic plans. Thus Russia has become a plague-centre for humanity . . . If just one country tolerates a Jewish family in it for whatever reason, this would become the germ-centre for new corruption. If there were no longer any Jews in Europe, the unity of the states of Europe [under German rule!] would no longer be disturbed.[82]

Following this conversation, Marshal Kvaternik was unable to inspect Croatian troops on the eastern front, but he was permitted to visit Army Group South and Sixth Army. Thereafter he expressed great admiration 'for the greatness of the Reich', and for the indomitable courage, discipline, and organization of the German troops. Kvaternik also renewed his 'vow of loyalty to the Führer'.[83]

The Croatian leaders accepted German requests for self-contained volunteer formations by offering to second a regular infantry regiment to the Wehrmacht in addition to four air Staffeln and a larger number of marines. The heavy companies were to consist of volunteer reservists under the leadership of regular officers. Owing to the unconditional commitment of the political and military leadership, no major recruitment campaign was necessary. Pavelić, however, issued an appeal on 2 July. The Croatian army contingent assembled in Varazdin for transfer to the troop-training ground at Döllersheim in Lower Austria for training, while barely 300 'air-force volunteers' were sent to Germany. At the same time, the Croatian state leadership was placed under pressure to second a legion of battalion strength to the Italian army. Kvaternik described this idea as untenable in domestic politics. He received the personal support of Glaise von Horstenau in his endeavour to block this Italian request.[84] However, the German leadership officially adopted the role of neutral observer, with the result that the Croats were eventually forced to establish a Croatian Legion supervised by Italy. This was finally dispatched on 14 December 1941, and from 1942 was employed on the eastern front as part of the Italian expeditionary corps.

The Croatian volunteers in Döllersheim swore an oath of loyalty to Adolf Hitler on 31 July. From among their number, Military District XVII established the 'reinforced 369th Croatian Infantry Regiment'. After a short period of training in the camp, on 7 October it was placed under the command of 100th Light Infantry Division within Army Group South. The regiment con-

---

[82] *Staatsmänner*, ii. 556–7. See Hitler, *Monologe*, 99 (21 Oct. 1941), 130–1 (13 Nov. 1941).

[83] Telegrams to Ribbentrop, Göring, and Keitel, in telexes of the foreign ministry representative with Sixth Army Command, 24 July 1941, BA-MA, 6. Armee, 15623/2.

[84] German legation Zagreb, Ia Nos. 185/41 g.Kdos. and 192/41 g.Kdos., 10 July 1941, BA-MA RH 31-III/1. See also German legation Zagreb telegram No. 731, 12 July 1941; for the position of the foreign ministry on 15 July 1941 see PA, Büro St.S., Kroatien, vol. 1, and *Le operazioni al fronte russo*, 187–8. See also the memoirs of Edmund Glaise von Horstenau for 1941: *General im Zwielicht*, iii. 79 ff.

sisted of three battalions, each with four companies plus two heavy companies. It was reinforced by the 369th Light Artillery Detachment. The division was given the task of guaranteeing 'organization and discipline according to the German model' by providing further training.[85] Four weeks later the training of the regiment was transferred to the regimental commander, Colonel Ivan Markulj; responsibility for 369th Croatian Artillery Detachment under Lieutenant-Colonel Marko Mesić remained with German 83rd Artillery Regiment.[86] The reinforced 369th Infantry Regiment was an organic part of the 100th Light Infantry Division. On 21 November 1941 it had a strength of 104 officers, 5 officials, 496 NCOs and 3,195 men;[87] 60 per cent of the officer corps consisted of regular officers.[88]

As levels of training were still inadequate, the regiment was not initially employed as a self-contained unit. At the end of October, however, individual companies were assigned to German regiments and acquitted themselves 'quite well'. Nevertheless, the first report was highly critical of the officer corps. 'Though good will and consent to German instruction are found among the majority, a considerable section of the officers and NCOs, who do not meet requirements as leaders regarding character, personality, and intellectual ability ... must be replaced ... The leadership corps [of 369th Light Artillery Detachment] is altogether superior to that of the infantry regiment.'[89]

By 15 November 1941 the regiment had suffered 165 casualties (37 dead, 76 wounded, and 52 missing in action). The service of the Croatians was rewarded in mid-December with the award of 11 Iron Crosses Second Class. The reinforced Croatian regiment remained with 100th Light Infantry Division, later 100th Rifle Division, and took part in the German summer offensive. In the spring of 1942 the Croatian government offered to establish another regiment. Underlying this proposal was the desire to form a Croatian division. The Army High Command overrode the objections of Wehrmacht High Command by arguing that the urgent need for security forces demanded the acceptance of this 'stopgap'.

At the end of August 1942 Hitler finally ordered the extension of the Croatian troop units into an independent division.[90] He was also thereby accommodating the wishes of the Croatian leadership. However, the Croats took the decision to reinforce their contingent within the German army mainly for its effect in domestic politics. At the end of December 1941 Kvaternik had already offered to strengthen the 'Croatian Legion' serving with the Italian expeditionary corps by six battalions in order to prevent the planned extension

[85] 100th Lt. Inf. Div., Abt. IIa, activity report, 7 Oct. 1941, BA-MA, 100. Inf.Div., 15684/32.

[86] 100th Lt. Inf. Div./Ia No. 266/41, 10 Nov. 1941, ibid., 100. Inf.Div., 15684/21.

[87] Structure of Operations Dept., 21 Nov. 1941, ibid., 100. Inf.Div., 16370.

[88] This emerges from the officer posts as of 20 Nov. 1941, ibid., 100. Inf.Div., 15684/32.

[89] Report of Sixth Army Command, 27 Oct. 1941, BA-MA RH 19/I/75.

[90] GenStdH/Org.Abt., war diary, 6–12 May 1942, BA-MA RH 2/v. 821; OKW/WFSt/Qu (III) No. 02371/42, 21 Aug. 1942, PA, Büro Inland IIg, vol. 305.

of the security area of the Italian Second Army in Croatia. Both Kasche and Glaise von Horstenau had openly represented Croatian interests.[91]

3. Volunteers from Northern Europe at the Beginning of the War against the Soviet Union

Gerd. R. Ueberschär

One aim of National Socialist propaganda relating to the 'European crusade against Bolshevism' was to bring countries such as Finland and Sweden into the war against the Soviet Union on an official basis. However, the campaign was also designed to produce indirect support and military assistance from the countries of northern Europe. Accordingly, Berlin responded positively 'for political reasons' to the first registration of volunteers from Scandinavia.[92] On principle, the German government would welcome the registration of sufficient numbers of volunteers to enable them 'to take part as self-contained national formations in the European struggle against Bolshevism within the framework of the German armed forces'.[93]

After Finland entered the war, volunteers from Sweden quickly reported for service in the Finnish army. Although a volunteers' office was set up in Sweden in July, propaganda for the recruitment campaign was not permitted. At this stage Swedish military circles considered sending a self-contained air-force formation or an entire division to serve as a volunteer unit in Finland.[94] Berlin thought it appropriate not to object to such operations in Finland. However, the Germans hoped that 'a larger number of Swedish volunteers would also participate on the German side in the struggle against the Soviet Union, so that a Swedish volunteer corps can be established as well'.[95]

According to the guidelines issued by Hitler, these 'Germanic volunteers' were to enter the Waffen-SS. The 5th SS Division Germania (renamed the SS Division Viking from December 1940) had already been established in September 1940 as the volunteer formation of the 'Nordic' and 'west Germanic' peoples.[96] A small number of Swedes had joined the newly established SS Standarte Nordland within this division following Himmler's decision of 4 September 1940 to permit the recruitment of volunteers from Sweden.[97]

[91] German legation Zagreb, No. 416, 20 Dec. 1941, BA-MA RH 2/v. 428; German legation Agram, telegram No. 1634, 16 Dec. 1941, *ADAP* E i. No. 19; memorandum from Ambassador Ritter, 23 Dec. 1941, ibid., No. 54.

[92] 'Memorandum of the meeting in the foreign ministry on 30 June 1941 regarding volunteer registration in foreign countries for the struggle against the Soviet Union', Pol. I M 4796g, 2 July 1941, PA, Handakten Ritter, No. 55.

[93] Draft telegram von Weizsäcker, Pol. I M 4822g, July 1941, to legation in Lisbon, ibid.

[94] Telegram No. 739 to foreign ministry, 25 June 1941: see PA, Büro St.S., Schweden, vol. 2.

[95] Memorandum on meeting in foreign ministry, 30 June 1941 (see n. 92).

[96] On the history of the SS Viking Division see BA-MA RS 3-5/1–4, 8; also Stein, *Geschichte der Waffen-SS*, 86–7, 96–7; Straßner, *Freiwillige*; Steiner, *Die Freiwilligen*.

[97] As early as Aug. 1940 SS main office had made contact with Swedish private individuals with the aim of recruiting for the SS Standarte Nordland: see letter from SS Brigadeführer Berger,

New volunteer formations were now to be established for Operation Barbarossa. Recruitment for the Waffen-SS had previously appealed only to Fascist and anti-British sentiments and groups, but the launching of the war against the Soviet Union gave it an additional anti-Communist component which increased the political weight and appeal of the volunteer movement.

However, the Swedish government evaded the request of the German special emissary in Stockhom, Schnurre, for Swedish volunteers to serve within German formations in the war against the Soviet Union. For their own training purposes, the Swedes were prepared to release a group of regular officers from the Swedish army and permit them to take part in the fighting against the USSR within the German armed forces. It was planned that Swedish volunteers, however, would fight only in self-contained units in the Finnish army. Berlin was disappointed and irritated. Ribbentrop rejected such officer volunteers, who would 'not have any real sphere of activity'.[98] Furthermore, it is significant that Swedish officers had reacted extremely negatively to a questionnaire on the subject.

By the beginning of September 1941 approximately 2,000 Swedish volunteers had registered for service in Finland. Between 800 and 850 men had arrived in Finland and been sent into action at Hanko [Saarinaa] as the 'Hangöbataljonen'.[99] After the Soviet evacuation of Hanko, the Swedish volunteer unit was disbanded in December 1941. Some 200 Swedish volunteers stayed within Finnish units as officers and specialists at the front. In January 1942 more Swedes registered as volunteers, and a Swedish volunteer company was set up within the Finnish 13th Infantry Regiment ('Svirkompaniet') in Finland (Turku).[100]

Very few Swedish volunteers either reported individually to the German recruiting office of the Waffen-SS in Tornio, Finland, or travelled to Norway and directly to Germany to join the organization. Despite German consent,

---

chief of Waffen-SS training office, to Himmler on 29 Aug. 1940, Tgb. No. 131/40 g.Kdos.: recruitment in Sweden; also reply from Reichsführer SS, Personal Staff, to SS Brigadeführer Berger, 4 Sept. 1940, Tgb. No. 876/40 g.Kdos., reproduced in the documentary appendix of the unpublished work kindly provided to me by Lennart Westberg, Matfors, Sweden, 'Notizen zu der Rekrutierung von schwedischen Freiwilligen für die Waffen-SS 1940–1945'. The creation of the 'SS General Service Troops Standarte Nordland' had been ordered by Hitler on 20 Apr. 1940: see PA, Dept. Inland IIg, vol. 17a (also for Himmler's directive of 23 Apr. 1940 to the effect that the Standarte was to be composed 'half of volunteers from Denmark and Norway' and half 'of German SS men').

[98] Carlgren, *Svensk utrikespolitik*, 315–16; *DGFP* D xiii, No. 109 and n. 1, pp. 117–18; telegram Nos. 869 and 962, Schnurre to foreign ministry, 7 and 16 July 1941, PA, Büro St.S., Schweden, vol. 2.

[99] See the various figures in war diary of Naval Attaché, Helsingfors, vol. 2, 26 Aug. 1941, BA-MA PG 48, 779–84; Liaison Officer Col. Drews to OKW/WiRüAmt, Abt. I, 11 Sept. 1941, ibid., Wi/I E 3.30b; telegram No. 1354, German legation Stockholm to foreign ministry, 6 Sept. 1941, PA, Büro St.S., Schweden, vol. 3.

[100] Telegram No. 178, German legation Stockholm to foreign ministry, 23 Jan. 1942, PA, Büro St.S., Schweden, vol. 3. In May 1942 the 'Svirkompaniet' comprised around 160 men, according to information given to the author by Lennart Westberg, 7 Aug. 1981.

such volunteers were contravening the wishes of the Swedish government.[101] The practice was sharply criticized by the Swedish press and the general public. Entry by Swedish nationals into the war service of foreign powers without government permission was forbidden by law; in autumn 1941 the Swedish government officially repeated its opposition.[102] By this time volunteers had also begun to report for service with the Western powers. At the beginning of September, therefore, the government decided that no more Swedes would be permitted to volunteer for foreign service, other than with the Finnish army.[103] At the end of the month, in a discussion with the Swedish chargé d'àffaires in Berlin, Ribbentrop was bitterly critical of this indirect ban on the participation of Swedish volunteers in Germany's war on the Soviet Union. The German foreign minister declared that all Europe—even former enemies such as France—was providing volunteers in German uniform and thereby helping to 'defeat Bolshevism'.[104] Only Sweden and Switzerland 'had excluded themselves from participation in this struggle'. Ribbentrop recalled Molotov's visit to Berlin the year before, when he had expressed Soviet interest in Baltic Sea outlets 'along the Swedish coast', to argue that the Soviet Union had designs on Swedish territory. The Swedish attitude to the 'battle against Bolshevism', he declared, was 'totally incomprehensible'.

In February 1942 the Finnish–Swedish Colonel Ekström renewed efforts to bring Swedish volunteers to Norway for enrolment in the Waffen-SS.[105] This development received very little support in Sweden; the Swedish share in the contingent of European volunteers in the Waffen-SS remained relatively small at about forty men.

SS endeavours to recruit volunteers in Finland were considerably more successful. At the end of February 1941, at Himmler's request, Hitler gave his permission for the recruitment of Finnish volunteers to the Waffen-SS. This step had been planned since the beginning of that year by the head of the SS main office, SS Major-General Gottlob Berger, and his Finnish contact in Helsinki.[106] At the outset, it was decided that the volunteers were to be of

---

[101] See telegram No. 981 to foreign ministry, 18 July 1941, and copy Pol. I M 218g. Reichsführer SS-Chef des SS-Hauptamtes V.S. Tgb. No. 886/41 geh./VI Tgb. No. 146/geh., 30 July 1941, PA, Büro St.S., Schweden, vol. 2. The volunteer unit was to be set up at Kirkenes.

[102] Press report of 27 Aug. 1941, PA, Abt. Inland IIg, Akten betr. Waffen-SS, Schweden No. 321.

[103] Telegram No. 1318, Wied to foreign ministry, 1 Sept. 1941, PA, Büro St.S., Schweden, vol. 3, and *DGFP* D xiii, No. 270.

[104] *DGFP* D xiii, No. 364.

[105] See telegram No. 272, German legation Helsinki to foreign ministry, 5 Feb. 1942, PA, Büro St.S., Schweden, vol. 3.

[106] On the history of the Finnish volunteers for the Waffen-SS see extracts from war diaries Nos. 1 and 2 (1941–3) and No. 2 (1942–3) of the Finnish Volunteers' Battalion of the Waffen-SS, BA-MA RS 3-11/5, 6; also correspondence of the Chief of the SS main office, BA NS 19 alt/364; Stein and Krosby, 'Das finnische Freiwilligen-Bataillon der Waffen-SS'; Ueberschär, *Hitler und Finnland*, 304–7; on military operations see the Finnish account by Jokipii, *Panttipataljoona*; less satisfactory is Tieke, *Finnisches Freiwilligen-Bataillon*.

Swedish or Germanic descent where possible, and were to be recruited into the SS Standarte Nordland. An attempt was thereby made to accommodate the wishes of some military quarters in Finland, who wanted to revive a version of the old 'Royal Prussian 27th Rifle Battalion' which had served as a Finnish volunteer force in Germany during the First World War.[107] From mid-March, with the consent of the government in Helsinki, a private volunteers' committee was set up under the leadership of the former head of the Finnish criminal police, State Councillor Esto Riekki. This took on the task of organizing recruitment in co-operation with the German legation in Helsinki and the Waffen-SS recruiting board. The Finnish government initially wanted the volunteer formation to be incorporated into the German army.[108] However, it subsequently agreed to the creation of a self-contained formation within the Waffen-SS, thus preventing the Finns from serving with volunteers from occupied Norway and Denmark in the newly established SS Standarte Nordland.

At the end of April an agreement was reached between the German foreign ministry and the Finnish volunteers' committee about the position, use, supply, and accommodation of the volunteers, as well as the oath to be taken to the 'leader of the Greater Germanic community of destiny, Adolf Hitler'. Recruitment could now begin. The volunteers committed themselves to serve for a two-year period until June 1943. Out of regard for the sovereignty of Finland and its diplomatic and trade relations with Germany's enemies, the volunteers were described as workers for the 'Hermann Göring Werke at Fallersleben'. The first transport arrived in Germany at the beginning of May. By the launching of Operation Barbarossa, about 1,200 Finnish volunteers were already in Germany. In mid-June 1941 approximately 400 trained reservists and officers were distributed among individual units of the SS Division Viking and were thus already in place at the start of the invasion of the Soviet Union. Volunteers arriving subsequently were, as promised by Berlin, gathered in the 'SS Volunteer Battalion North-East', which was established as an independent formation on 13 June 1941. At the end of the month this special formation was approximately 1,000 strong; by the end of the year it contained around 1,180 men. The formation was renamed the 'Finnish Volunteer Battalion of the Waffen-SS' in September 1941. At the beginning of January 1942 it was sent into action with the SS Division Viking on the southern sector of the eastern front.

Significantly, only about 12 per cent of the Finnish volunteers were 'Finlanders' of Swedish descent; it was clear that the acceptance of the predominantly non-Germanic Finns had violated the original concept of the 'Germanic' SS. However, this fact did not affect the establishment and reten-

---

[107] In Aug. 1941, however, preservation of the traditions of the 'huntsmen's movement' was transferred by Army High Command to 92nd Inf. Reg., in order to prevent it being left to an SS formation. See report of the military attaché in Helsinki, 18 Aug. 1941, BA-MA RW 4/v. 325.

[108] See Halder, *Diaries*, 851 (3 Apr. 1941).

tion of the Finnish volunteer formation. The Finns did not swear an oath of loyalty to Hitler as 'leader of the Greater Germanic community of destiny', but took the oath of the European (non-Germanic) volunteers in the Waffen-SS.[109]

Field Marshal Mannerheim was informed about the affair only in retrospect. Along with the Finnish high command, he viewed the volunteer action with caution, if not outright rejection. It was noted with regret that the Finnish army was being deprived of virtually irrepleacable trained officers and NCOs on the eve of the country's own struggle against the Soviet Union.[110] After Finland entered the war against the USSR, no further major recruitment of volunteers for the Waffen-SS could be expected. Instead, appeals were made for the volunteer formation to be recalled prematurely, or at least for it to be sent into action in the Finnish theatre, for instance with SS Division North on the Salla front.[111] Contacts to that end through the German legation in Helsinki proved fruitless, however. SS main office in Berlin turned down the request on the grounds that this volunteer SS formation would deepen and consolidate German–Finnish relations more effectively than the normal foreign-ministry channels.

It is thus apparent that the Finnish volunteers had entered German service not after the beginning of the 'crusade against Bolshevism', but before it. The Finnish government had not consented to the sending of volunteers to Germany out of any real political and ideological affinity with National Socialist Germany. Instead, the Finnish aim was to create a sense of German obligation to Finland, thus persuading it to offer support if Finland were to be attacked by the Soviet Union. In the spring of 1941 Helsinki was eager to use the volunteer issue to consolidate German interest in Finland.

Norwegian volunteers had also been sworn into the Waffen-SS since the summer of 1940. In April 1940, only days after the occupation of Norway, the SS had set up its own supplementary office 'North' in Oslo in order to recruit volunteers for the newly established SS Standarte Nordland. Very few Norwegians had come forward by the end of the year. The leader of the Norwegian National Socialist Party (Nasjonal Samling), Vidkun Quisling, therefore made a radio appeal to 'nationally conscious' youth to volunteer for service in the Waffen-SS and its Volunteer Division Viking, formed in December 1940; their role would be to defend freedom and the independence of the homeland.[112]

[109] The oath ran: 'I swear to you, Adolf Hitler, as leader, loyalty and courage. I vow to you and the superiors appointed by you obedience until death, so help me God.' See Buss and Mollo, *Hitler's Germanic Legions*, 136; Tieke, *Finnisches Freiwilligen-Bataillon*, 76.

[110] On this subject see Jägerskiöld, *Marskalken av Finland*, 34 ff. German sources show a more positive attitude on the part of Mannerheim towards voluntary service in the Waffen-SS: see Ueberschär, *Hitler und Finnland*, 307.

[111] Jägerskiöld, *Marskalken av Finland*, 35.

[112] On Quisling's appeal of 13 Jan. 1941 see *Nordland-Echo*, 2/3 (19 Jan. 1941), and the section 'Quisling's Military Co-peration with Germany' in Andenæs *et al.*, *Norway and the Second World War*, 71 ff.

However, this vague slogan was unlikely to appeal to many volunteers. Until the summer of 1941 the results of this recruitment campaign were modest in the extreme. By the end of June 1941 294 Norwegians had joined the SS Standarte Nordland as volunteers—and SS main office was forced to withdraw its qualification regulations for the recruits. Nevertheless, the SS leadership in Berlin did not waver from its aim of meeting the growing need for personnel by recruitment in the 'Germanic' countries of northern Europe.[113]

The attack on the Soviet Union offered an opportunity for better results. Operation Barbarossa gave the recruitment campaign in Norway a broader base, thus making it possible for an appeal to be made to all anti-Communist groups within the population for the 'struggle against Bolshevism'. A considerable enlargement of the reservoir of potential volunteers was therefore to be expected.

On 29 June 1941, a few days after Finland entered the war, the 'Reich Commissioner for the occupied Norwegian territories', Gauleiter Terboven, issed a proclamation to the Norwegian population. He appealed with some skill to the sense of solidarity among the Scandinavian peoples by arguing that Soviet demands on Finland had been the cause of the war; Soviet power politics were described as an 'attack against the Nordic states and their culture'.[114] Terboven stressed that people had a duty to take an active part in fighting the threat from the east: 'What is true for the rest of Europe is true to an incomparably greater degree for the north and thus for Norway. From now on the issue is no longer first and foremost: England or Germany; but, above and beyond all domestic political variations of opinion and differences, it is simply, clearly, and imperiously: European Nordic culture or Asiatic Bolshevism.' To give the Norwegian population the opportunity 'to share in this conflict of unique historic significance', Hitler had acceded to the wishes of the Norwegian people and 'agreed to the immediate establishment of a "Norwegian Legion"'. This national formation would be 'equipped and employed according to Norwegian guidelines' as a self-contained unit under Norwegian leadership. In fact, this principle was not adopted immediately; the first 300 volunteers of the 'SS Volunteer Legion Norway', established by SS main office on 1 August 1941, came unambiguously within the framework of the Waffen-SS.[115] On 3 October 1941, in the presence of Quisling, the Norwegian 'legionaries' swore an oath to Hitler as 'supreme commander of the German armed forces' for the 'struggle against Bolshevism'.[116] At first the plan was to establish

---

[113] See the documentation in Wegner, 'Pangermanische Armee' (also for the following).

[114] Declaration of the Reich Commissioner for the Occupied Norwegian Territories, Terboven, on 29 June 1941, reproduced from DNB report in *Monatshefte für auswärtige Politik*, 8/7 (1941), 675–6.

[115] On the history of the 'SS Legion Norway' see Buss and Mollo, *Hitler's Germanic Legions*, 88–9; also the commemorative essary 'Der Schicksalsweg der norwegischen Freiwilligen-Division der Waffen SS'; from a Norwegian point of view see Blindheim, *Nordmenn*, 35 ff.

[116] The oath of the Norwegian legionaries on 3 Oct. 1941 was in line with the formula for 'foreign volunteers in the struggle against the Soviet Union': 'I swear by God this holy oath, that in the struggle against Bolshevism I offer unconditional obedience to the supreme commander of

the formations of the 'SS Volunteer Legion Norway' at regimental strength. However, it was soon apparent that far fewer volunteers had come forward then expected, forcing the SS leadership in Berlin to moderate its ambitious plans. The weak Norwegian response to the 'Norske Legion' (as the unit was known in Norway) may have been due in part to the refusal of the Norwegian clergy to call for volunteer participation in Hitler's war in the east. Most of the volunteers came from the ranks of Quisling's 'Nasjonal Samling'.[117] In consequence, the volunteer movement looked like a party-political manœuvre.

Nor was there any significant influx of volunteers to the SS Standarte Nordland after 22 June 1941. In September 1941, as before, some 300 Norwegians were serving in the SS Viking Division, for which Norwegian volunteers continued to be recruited. At the beginning of 1942 the 'SS Volunteer Legion Norway' consisted of approximately 1,200 men.[118] During the recruitment campaign there had been references to service in Finland, but in March 1942 the Legion was sent to the front at Leningrad. There it was placed under the command of Eighteenth Army within Army Group North. In July 1941 Colonel-General von Falkenhorst had refused to employ the Legion in his area of command in northern Finland. The staff of Army Command Norway argued that such employment was 'undesirable' on military and political grounds, since it might 'give impetus' to 'certain desires' in Norwegian circles for territory in northern Finland and northern Russia.[119] Furthermore, Colonel-General von Falkenhorst 'did not think much of the troops'.

Only a few weeks after the German occupation, from May 1940, volunteers in Denmark had also begun to come forward for the SS Standarte Nordland.[120] Most of them were members of the Dansk National Socialistik Arbejderparti (DNSAP: Danish National Socialist Workers' Party) and erstwhile volunteers for Finland's Winter War against the Soviet Union, who had returned to Denmark in June 1940. It was also hoped that former soldiers from the Danish army would be attracted after it was reduced in size at the end of April 1940.

the German Wehrmacht, Adolf Hitler, and as a brave soldier will be ready to stake my life for this oath at any time.' See decree of OKW/14g/w WFSt/Org(I)-19/42, 10 Jan. 1942, 'Guidelines for the employment of foreign volunteers in the struggle against the Soviet Union (revised version)', BA-MA RL 2 II/106; see Blindheim, *Nordmenn*, 21.

[117] According to Neulen, *Eurofaschismus*, 138, 60% of the volunteers were members of the 'Nasjonal Samling'.

[118] See also Halder, *Diaries*, 1405 (17 Feb. 1942), who gives the figure as 1,100 men. Buss and Mollo, *Hitler's Germanic Legions*, 92, and Neulen, *Eurofaschismus*, 107, give 1,218 men for the beginning of 1942. On 16 Mar. 1942 1,150 men were in action at Leningrad.

[119] The offer to send the 'Norwegian Legion' into action with Army Command Norway came from Reich Commissioner Terboven. On the refusal of Falkenhorst see telegram No. 4, German legation Helsinki to foreign ministry, 19 July 1941, PA, Büro St.S., Norwegen, No. 12/65.

[120] On the Danish volunteers' movement see Thomsen, *Besatzungspolitik*, 94 ff.; Buss and Mollo, *Hitler's Germanic Legions*, 76–87; on the dates see Tieke, *Tragödie*, 10–11; id., 'Geschichte des "Freikorps Danmark"'; and Schou, *Danske Østfront-frivillige*. On Hitler's order of 20 Apr. 1940 for the creation of the 'SS General Service Troops Standarte Nordland' see PA, Abt. Inland IIg, vol. 17a (also for the information given by Himmler to Ribbentrop).

In the view of the SS, the volunteers were preparing the way for a 'Greater Germanic empire'. The recruitment campaign was therefore extended to the ethnic Germans in northern Schleswig.[121] Though Danish law forbade the recruitment of volunteers on Danish soil for foreign military service, in September 1940 the SS opened a 'supplementary office of the Waffen-SS branch office North Sea' in Copenhagen. By June 1941, however, the Danish contingent in the SS Viking Division comprised only 216 men.[122]

After the war in the east began, the 'plenipotentiary of the German Reich' in Copenhagen, Minister von Renthe-Fink, told the Danish government that the Germans wanted Danish volunteers to participate in Operation Barbarossa. Their service should be organized 'mainly' on the German side and not in the Finnish army, for which Danes had begun to register immediately after the entry of Finland into the war.[123] At the begining of July 1941, with the official consent of Danish government authorities, a volunteer formation for the Waffen-SS, the 'Free Corps Denmark', was set up. The intention was to employ it as a self-contained Danish national formation with the Waffen-SS, and only in the struggle against the Soviet Union. The oath taken by the Danish volunteers to Hitler as the 'supreme commander of the German army' also referred explicity—like that of the Norwegians—to the 'struggle against Bolshevism'.[124] Throughout Denmark, recruitment offices began work under the leadership of the DNSAP. The government in Copenhagen even agreed that regular soldiers in the Danish army could volunteer for the new formation. Approximately 600 volunteers set off for training in Germany at the end of July. A major 'anti-Communist rally' was held in Copenhagen on 12 August 1941, at which the DNSAP warned that it was 'Denmark's duty to participate in the crusade against the Soviet Union'.[125] 'The military honour of the Danish people would be restored' by massive recruitment to the 'Free Corps Denmark' and active participation in the 'struggle against Bolshevism'. By the end of 1941 the 'Free Corps Denmark' comprised some 1,060 men; in May 1942 it was sent to Army Group North on the eastern front, as a reinforced infantry battalion with approximately 1,200 men.

After bitter fighting and heavy casualties, in September–October 1942 the 'Free Corps Denmark'—now 650 strong—was sent as a self-contained unit on leave to Denmark. Despite several propaganda rallies involving the 'Free

[121] See letter from German legation Copenhagen to foreign ministry, No. D Pol 3/624, 20 May 1940, PA, Abt. Inland IIg., Akten betr. Waffen-SS: Dänemark No. 300; here Minister von Renthe-Fink recommended turning only to the ethnic Germans in northern Schleswig, the Danish volunteers for Finland, and the members of the DNSAP.

[122] Neulen, *Eurofaschismus*, 100.

[123] Telegram No. 830, German legation Copenhagen to foreign ministry, 27 July 1941, PA, Büro St.S., Dänemark, vol. 2.

[124] The Danish volunteers were sworn to Hitler with the legionaries' oath. On its text see n. 116. See also Tieke, 'Geschichte des "Freikorps Danmark" ', 191.

[125] See report of the Plenipotentiary of the German Reich No. Inn. V 3 No. 355/41 to foreign ministry, 12 Aug. 1941, PA, Abt. Inland IIg., Akten betr. Waffen-SS: Dänemark No. 300 (also for the following quotations).

Corps', neither the German authorities nor the Danish National Socialists were able to achieve a significant increase in volunteer registration.[126] The 'Free Corps Denmark' was regarded as a creature of the Danish National Socialists, particularly as its recruitment offices were situated in DNSAP branch offices. Inevitably, the Danish public tended to regard the legion as a party body born out of internal dissension. The leader of the Danish National Socialists, Frits Clausen, complained in February 1942 that the German authorities had not adequately supported his efforts to counteract public hostility to the Danish volunteers.[127] Few sections of the population were impressed by the 'Free Corps Denmark', and very few Danes volunteered for military service against the Soviet Union either in German or in Finnish units.

Berlin revealed a particular interest in recruiting ethnic Germans from North Schleswig as volunteers. However, by the end of 1941 only about 530 volunteers had reported for service in the Waffen-SS, and approximately 100 for the Wehrmacht.[128] At the beginning of 1942 recruitment efforts were therefore intensified. The campaign, which was run from the end of February 1942, was notable for making volunteering 'the duty' of this ethnic group. By the end of April the Ethnic Group Agency in North Schleswig was able to report that over 1,400 volunteers had come forward for the 'final struggle against Bolshevism'.[129] At first the volunteers from North Schleswig were incorporated into the 'Free Corps Denmark'. However, the North Schleswig ethnic-group leader, Dr Jens Moeller, complained about this practice to the German plenipotentiary in Copenhagen and also directly to Himmler. Subsequently, the volunteers were assigned to the SS Death's Head Division.[130] Yet even after Himmler's decision, the Ethnic Group Agency and the National Socialist Workers' Party in North Schleswig made a number of complaints to SS departments that ethnic German volunteers from North Schleswig were being assigned against their will to the 'Free Corps Denmark'. In individual cases, volunteers also joined the Wehrmacht. Though the Party and SS leadership were unhappy about such cases, consent was given to them retrospectively.

Overall, the number of volunteers from Finland, Sweden, Norway, and Denmark—including the ethnic Germans from North Schleswig—reached 5,501

---

[126] On this 'propaganda holiday' see the files PA, Abt. Inland IIg., Akten betr. Waffen-SS: Dänemark No. 300.

[127] *ADAP* E i, No. 212, pp. 383–4 (6 Feb. 1942).

[128] Telegram Nos. 73, Ribbentrop to Copenhagen legation, 17 Jan. 1942, and 92, German legation Copenhagen to foreign ministry, 20 Jan. 1942, both in PA, Büro St.S., vol. 2; see also Noack, *Tyske mindretal*.

[129] Of these, 829 men were fit for service. See the numbers and telegrams in PA, Abt. Inland IIg., Akten betr. Waffen-SS: Dänemark No. 298.

[130] Decree of Himmler, Tgb. No. AK/1271/8-RF/V., 22 Apr. 1942, PA, Abt. Inland IIg., Akten betr. Waffen-SS: Dänemark No. 299. See also *ADAP* E ii, No. 176, pp. 294 ff. (29 Apr. 1942).

in the Waffen-SS at the beginning of 1942.[131] These men were to take part in the 'crusade against Bolshevism'. The total was a disappointment to the National Socialist leadership, which had expected more enthusiasm and greater numbers of volunteers from the 'north Germanic peoples'. Hitler had expressed this view in a proclamation on 2 October 1941, in which he emphasized that the nations of Europe had come together under his leadership 'for the first time' for 'joint action to save the most valuable continent of culture'.[132] Alongside this foreign-policy aspect, the SS leadership attempted to create as many volunteer formations as possible. At the same time, it was revealing a willingness to give up its claim to be an élite, or at least to redefine this claim to cover the whole of Europe. The creation of new legions in western and northern Europe can thus be regarded as a 'significant contribution to the transformation of the Waffen-SS into a supra-national mass army'.[133] There were even hopes that these legions, by being granted minor national concessions and limited autonomy in their relations with the rest of the Waffen-SS, might persuade the European peoples to adopt a more positive attitude towards the occupying power. In view of the minute numbers of recruits alone, these hopes were utterly unrealistic. The conduct of German authorities and liaison staffs towards the foreign volunteer formations also led to many justifiable complaints. Army High Command's deep mistrust of the employment of self-contained foreign volunteer formations was exemplified by its demand for specially 'increased' intelligence supervision and censorship of the volunteers' letters from the field.[134] At the end of 1941 Wehrmacht High Command was compelled to respond to the ill feeling and tension caused by the arrogance of the German authorities and the 'petty-minded criticism of the value of these formations', as well as to the lack of attention and care they had received. Field Marshal Keitel noted that it was 'the German Wehrmacht's obligation of honour to treat the foreign legions with particular respect and to extend to them all care, even if these formations do not always meet German military standards'.[135]

In view of the low number of volunteers in the months after 22 June 1941, the Germans stepped up their demands for the other European nations to take a greater part in operations planned for 1942. At the beginning of that year it was argued that they must help to 'guarantee the required superiority in forces for a rapid offensive operation' as part of the 'decisive

---

[131] A 'survey of the Germanic volunteers in the Waffen-SS' by SS main office, Dept. VI/2, 15 Jan. 1942, gives the following figures for the four nations: Finns, 1,180; Swedes, 39; Norwegians, 1,883; Danes (including men from northern Schleswig), 2,399. See IfZ MA 321, No. 3,910.

[132] Domarus, *Hitler*, ii. 1757; similarly Hitler's speech on 3 Oct. 1941, ibid. 1763.

[133] Wegner, 'Pangermanische Armee', 105.

[134] See letter from OKH/GenStdH/HWesAbt. (Abw) Az.Abw. III No. 88/10.41 geh. on foreign volunteers in action, 14 Nov. 1941, BA-MA RH 19 III/493.

[135] Chief of OKW WFSt/Abt. L (IV/Qn) No. 03203/41 geh. on foreign volunteer formations, 29 Dec. 1941, BA-MA RL 2 II/106.

struggle of all European nations' against the Soviet Union for 'existence or non-existence'.[136]

By now Wehrmacht High Command regarded the full utilization of the fighting power of all European countries as 'essential'. Ambitious demands were therefore addressed to allied or collaborating governments, politicians, and parties. In the light of these, it was inevitable that—especially in the occupied countries of Norway and Denmark—the existence of the volunteer formations became linked with certain political speculations and plans. The two leaders of the native Fascist parties in Denmark and Norway, Clausen and Quisling, thus saw the volunteer legions as the core or cadre for a national armed force. As this development concealed solid national interests, it was not welcome to the SS leadership in Berlin. The German authorities emphasized the special status of the legions as quasi 'semi-independent national units' simply in order to make entry into 'non-German formations' possible and attractive to foreigners.[137]

SS operations office, however, continued to regard the volunteer formations virtually as the contribution of various subordinate European peoples to Germany's struggle against Bolshevism. During 1942, when Berlin realized the 'national-state interpretation' of the formations, its response was to push through an increased concentration of the volunteere in major SS formations, and to 'out the cord' to the collaborating groups and Fascist parties in the occupied countries in order to achieve a 'reorientation in the Germanization policy of the SS'.[138] This SS Pan-Germanism, moreover, led to the removal of the previous limited autonomy of the legions by integrating and incorporating them completely into Waffen-SS divisions. There was a perceptible move away from any recognition of the unique national features of individual legions. The SS leadership now regarded the volunteers as the logical contributions of various Germanic Gaue to the 'Greater Germanic Reich' under Hitler and to his 'decisive struggle' against the Soviet Union.

[136] *ADAP* E i, No. 92, p. 171 (also for the following quotations). In this 'contribution of OKW to the discussion of the Reich foreign minister with Regent von Horthy', 4 Jan. 1942, the call was made directly to Hungary; however, it applied equally to the other countries of Europe.

[137] Neulen, *Eurofaschismus*, 108.

[138] See here Wegner, 'Pangermanische Armee', 108 ff.

VI. The Failure of the Economic 'Blitzkrieg Strategy'

ROLF-DIETER MÜLLER

1. ECONOMIC POLICY IN ANTICIPATION OF VICTORY

VOLUNTEERS from the occupied and dependent states of Europe were recruited largely because of the dilemma facing the German war economy—its inability to provide sufficient men either for the munitions industries or for the Wehrmacht. Even before the invasion of the Soviet Union, conscription to the Wehrmacht had left great gaps in the labour market, which could not be filled despite the increased reliance on French prisoners of war and other foreign workers. Another consequence was a significant rise among Germans in indiscipline and reluctance to work. According to the economic authorities in a report to the Reich Marshal, this was especially noticeable among young people and women, 'who are demanding excessively high wages without an appropriate return, as a result of their favourable situation *vis-à-vis* older skilled workers'.[1]

The increasing seriousness of the labour shortage was one important indicator of the excessive strains being placed on the German war economy. Another was the inadequate supply of raw materials, which was reaching a critical stage. The steep fall in iron and steel production was especially striking in this context. Its cause was a decline in the extraction of coal, as the result of the withdrawal of labour for the Wehrmacht and the priority given to military transports. The temporary obstruction of ore imports from Sweden and nickel imports from Norway, owing to the operations in the Baltic,[2] was of only minor significance in comparison. It is true that the region accounted for about a quarter of German iron-ore supplies, but transports across had declined by only 15 per cent in July 1941. Nevertheless, the German leadership regarded the potential danger to ore deliveries as so great that it warranted putting the navy on the offensive against the Soviet Baltic Fleet. Hitler repeatedly intervened in the direction of operations to press for the rapid occupation of Leningrad, which would safeguard the supply of iron ore from Sweden.

In the view of the political and military leadership at any rate, the bottlenecks in the German war economy had already reached dangerous proportions on the eve of the German invasion of the Soviet Union. From the outset,

[1] Reich Marshal of the Greater German Reich, Plenipotentiary for the Four-year Plan, VP 11594/41, g.Rs., survey on the overall economic situation, 23 July 1941, 8, BA R 26 I/44.
[2] See OKW/WiRüAmt/Stab Z-SR No. 2667/41 g.Kdos., war-economy situation report No. 23, July 1941, 11 Aug. 1941, BA-MA RW 19/177. For an assessment see also Wittmann, 'Deutsch-schwedische Wirtschaftsbeziehungen im Zweiten Weltkrieg', 202.

attempts were therefore made to eliminate or at least limit additional strains. The great hope was that the situation would be relieved by a quick end to the war in the east, thereby allowing the exploitation of Soviet resources. It appeared that the imminent decline in German war production, and the placing of extra burdens on the population, could be avoided only by making full use of Soviet raw materials and foodstuffs.

However, German economic preparations and economic war aims went beyond this short-term task.[3] Colossal armaments plans by the Wehrmacht for the period after Barbarossa, made with an eye to the expected conflict with the Anglo-Saxon bloc for world supremacy, demanded a ruthless exploitation of the projected Russian 'supplementary area' as a colonial economy to extend and complete the German supra-regional economy in Europe. Behind such plans lurked the traditional German goal of achieving world-power status. It was to be attained by the creation of an autarkic continental empire, which would stretch from the Atlantic to the Urals and be secure against blockade. In the preparatory phase of Operation Barbarossa, these economic ideas had become inextricably entwined both with Hitler's plans for racial and ideological annihilation, and with the apparent inherent necessities of the war economy.

These dimensions to the war in the east must be borne in mind during any attempt to show the historical significance of military events and to assess economic preconditions, accompanying developments, and consequences. There are three main requirements in such an analysis: first, to compare the economic approach and expectations of the German leadership with the actual course of the war; second, to examine specific armaments policies and their results in relation to the material demands of the war in the east; and third, to investigate the interaction between economic policy, operational leadership, and occupation policy.

For the economists and the men responsible for armaments production, the launching of the war against the Soviet Union had different implications from those confronting the soldiers engaged in fighting. The leaders of the economy were already debating and planning the period after Barbarossa. In the expectation of a short campaign, they believed that urgent measures to overcome bottlenecks in the war economy could be postponed. This anticipation of victory was partly due to the unwieldiness of the production process—the relatively long period which elapsed between the taking of an economic decision and the concrete results in production terms. However, it was also believed that Operation Barbarossa could be completed with only a limited armaments effort, which had already been largely completed. The shortage of reserves of production appeared to require immediate concentration on the tasks which were likely to arise after 'Barbarossa'.

The economic leadership thus relied totally on the success of Germany's

---

[3] See sect. I.III.2(*f*).

military planning for the war. They neglected to mobilize those reserves which were still available for the war in the east, and failed to combat frictions within the war economy which were often caused by sheer weaknesses of organization. Instead, the economists and armaments experts had begun to take the Russian 'booty' into their calculations even before it had been captured by the army. It was almost inevitable that the economy would adjust to the assumptions of the state leadership, especially in wartime, even though the consistency and success of war production were thus directly linked to the gamble being undertaken by the political leadership.

Such dependence was not one-sided. During the planning and preparation of the campaign against the Soviet Union, the political leadership had been forced to rely on the prognoses of the economic experts, and had guaranteed them a free hand both in establishing an Economic Organization East and in setting the economic goals. On 26 June 1941 Infantry General Thomas informed Göring of the results.[4] Göring described the preparatory work undertaken under the central control of the OKW as 'excellent', and declared 'that without the organization of the Ec[onomic] and Arm[aments] Department, it would not be possible to achieve success in the campaign in the east'. Göring submitted the material he had received from Thomas to Hitler, who signed a decree on the economy in the newly occupied eastern territories on 29 June 1941.[5] This gave Göring the authority to order all measures 'which are necessary for the greatest possible exploitation of the stocks and economic capacities that are found, and for the development of economic forces for the benefit of the German war economy'. Barely three weeks later, on 16 July, Hitler again explained his war aims to the leadership élite of the Reich.[6] The basic need was 'to break up the enormous cake into manageable slices, so that we can first rule, second administer, and third exploit it . . . We must make a Garden of Eden out of the newly won eastern territories; they are essential for us.'

Hitler left no doubt that other plans for the future, proposed on this occasion by Rosenberg, would have to take second place to the tasks of the war economy. As Reich Commissioner for the Ukraine he appointed Gauleiter Koch, who had a reputation for ruthlessness, despite the fact that Rosenberg had wanted to see Koch appointed to the Moscow area, where he could work to suppress racially and ideologically undesirable 'Russiandom'. In taking this step, Hitler was responding to the wishes of the economic authorities;[7]

[4] See memorandum Chief of War Economy and Armaments Department, report to Reich Marshal, 26 June 1941, BA-MA Wi/I A.84.

[5] Printed in *KTB OKW* i. 1019 (63).

[6] Bormann minute on the discussion on 16 July 1941, No. 221, *IMT* xxxviii. 86 ff.

[7] Two days before Hitler's decision, the leader of the Agriculture Group in Economic Staff East, Riecke, had held a conversation with Koch concerning his work in Russia: see Economic Staff East/Agriculture, War Diary notes, memorandum of 14 July 1941, BA-MA RW 31/42. The appointment of Koch nourished a conflict lasting years, especially with Rosenberg, whom Koch made the scapegoat for the failure of the political war effort. See the overall account in Dallin, *German Rule*.

these, anticipating rich economic gains in the Ukraine, were opposed to a more careful approach there of the sort advocated for political reasons by Rosenberg.

Under the impression that victory in the east was imminent, Hitler was devoting his attention to future armaments projects in the period after Barbarossa. At the forefront of his thinking was the expansion of the Luftwaffe. In Göring's view, the number of combat aircraft produced would have to be quadrupled.[8] At the same time, Hitler also demanded the implementation of Tank Programme 41. Each of these plans alone exceeded the current productive capacity of the German war economy; together—and with the navy's building plans—they could be put into effect only by exploiting Soviet economic potential.[9] The use of 8,400 machine-tools freed by the rupture of economic relations with Russia brought little relief.[10] Since Soviet raw materials and factories were not available at first, there was no prospect of getting the new programmes under way immediately, given the stagnation of German munitions production.

As a transitional solution, Hitler therefore ordered that the army share of total armaments should be further reduced. The capacity this released was to be concentrated on the production of tanks, submarines, and aircraft.[11] Once again the Chief of Army Armament Programmes was forced to reckon with the lowest conceivable production quota in his sphere.[12] He concluded that the resources saved would not be sufficient to allow the army to fulfil its new tasks. These involved an increase in the production of tanks, anti-aircraft guns, and anti-tank guns, and the establishment of a motorized expeditionary corps for operations after Barbarossa. In these circumstances, contributions from the army to support the expanded Luftwaffe programme could not be justified.[13]

For the time being, the Luftwaffe was forced to restrict itself to restoring its existing formations to full strength. In fact, a significant extension of capacity, and the employment of at least 200,000 extra workers, proved to be necessary even for this purpose. Clearly, appeals from the War Economy and Armaments Department for strict concentration on the most urgent tasks throughout the Wehrmacht[14] would not be sufficient to solve the armaments problem.

[8] See discussion with State Secretary Milch on 26 June 1941, in *KTB OKW* i. 1016–18 (60).

[9] See discussion between armaments chief and raw-materials chief with departmental head, 4 July 1941, KTB WiRüAmt/Stab 1941, 131–2, BA-MA RW 19/165.

[10] See presentation by armaments chief to departmental bead on 24 June 1941, ibid. 114, also urgent letter from Reich minister of economic affairs regarding guidelines on the restrictability of manufacturing—here: treatment of Russian orders, 26 June 1941, BA R7/4699.

[11] Hitler's guidelines of 14 July 1941 for future conduct of the war after the defeat of Russia, printed in Thomas, *Wehr- und Rüstungswirtschaft*, 452 ff. On this subject see *Das Deutsche Reich und der Zweite Weltkrieg*, v/1. 567 ff.

[12] Letter from Reich minister for armaments and ammunition to Wehrmacht branches regarding exchange of capacities, 11 July 1941, BA-MA Wi/I A. 84.

[13] Rü IIa No. 2418/41 g.Kdos., memorandum on discussion in WFSt/L of 17 July 1941 on Führer guidelines of 14 July 1941, KTB WiRüAmt/Stab 1941, 148–50, BA-MA RW 19/165.

[14] OKW/WiRüAmt/Rü (IIa) No. 2438/41 g.Kdos., letter on reorientation of armaments, 21 July 1941, BA-MA Wi/I A. 84.

For example, in a conversation with General Thomas, Major-General Adolf von Schell, General Plenipotentiary for Motor Transport, indicated that the new tank programme required large numbers of other motor-vehicles which could not be provided solely by restructuring the army.[15] Staff at Führer headquarters were obsessed with armoured cars, overlooking the numerous motor-vehicles that were essential to their support.

The Tank Committee, which was dominated by manufacturers, understandably welcomed Hitler's directive. It proposed to create a capacity of 900 armoured cars per month, i.e. more than double the current level.[16] Todt himself retracted this unrealistic projection shortly afterwards, and accepted that an increase to 650 armoured cars per month would be satisfactory[17] (production in June 1941 was 312). This kind of juggling with unrealistic figures and exaggerated expectations had been a damaging factor in the German armaments economy ever since the 1930s. Yet again the result was an organizational muddle, as even Todt was incapable of co-ordinating the mutually exclusive wishes and demands of the various branches of the Wehrmacht. Nevertheless, despite the opposition of Keitel, he reported to Hitler that things were functioning 'magnificently', and Hitler contented himself with the assertion that everything would be all right 'with more good will'.[18] In fact, the time when such problems could be solved by 'good will' alone was long past.

In this situation, leading German economic circles tightened their influence on war-aims planning and on the imminent distribution of the Soviet 'booty'. At a meeting of the Trade Committee of the Reich Chamber of Industry on 17 July 1941, the main issue was outlined by Hermann J. Abs, board member of the German Bank. Abs claimed that the

economy of Russia . . . will in considerable parts at least, be added to a future continental European economic sphere. In the current state of development it is not possible to estimate what increase will accrue to this area in productive strength and in consumer strength. In any case, it will be further consolidated, also from the point of view of being self-sufficient in important goods.[19]

Future prospects for expansion in the Russian territories were discussed in detail during an exchange of information with the state economic agencies.[20]

---

[15] Discussion of Gen. von Schell with departmental head, 24 July 1941, KTB WiRüAmt/Stab 1941, 159, BA-MA RW 19/165.

[16] Report by armaments chief to departmental head, 22 July 1941, ibid. 155.

[17] Discussion of departmental head with Minister Todt, 25 July 1941, ibid. 161.

[18] Report of armaments chief on a discussion with FM Milch, 2 Aug. 1941, ibid. 181.

[19] Lecture by H. J. Abs on 'Europe and USA in economic perspective', 17 July 1941, printed in *Anatomie des Krieges*, No. 173.

[20] Alongside numerous surveys for the military departments (BA-MA RW 19, appendix I), mention should be made of Gutachten des Instituts für Konjunkturforschung, 'Raw material balance of continental Europe with the inclusion of European Russia and North Africa', BA R 3/vorl. 1942. On the following see also Müller, 'Rolle der Industrie', and for the documentation Müller, 'Interessenpolitik'.

Interest was expressed in securing supplies of industrial raw materials, and in the continued operation of raw-material manufacturing industries, especially the extraction of coal and iron ore in the Donets region, of strategically important manganese ore in Nikopol, of Caucasian oil, and of significant phosphorus supplies on the Kola peninsula. For this to be achieved, Soviet power-stations had to be reopened and the transport network extended. In contrast, the industrial area of the Urals was regarded as unprofitable because of the unfavourable transport situation, and was virtually written off.[21] Detailed 'share-out plans' were also discussed.[22] Most vocal in this process was the industry of Upper Silesia, which laid claim to the 'eastern territories' as its domain with the same exclusiveness as had been demonstrated by the industry of Rhineland-Westphalia in western Europe.[23] The Reichswerke-Konzern thus made an immediate claim for the coal supplies of the Ukraine, first to pre-empt claims by Ruhr businesses dating back to the First World War, and second to seize the opportunity to extend the central and east European business empire to Russia, under the patronage of Göring.[24] For other industrial groups, this onslaught was an important aspect in restraining their own ambitions and in leading them to urge that the Russian 'spoils' should not be distributed until after the end of the war.[25] Overall, German heavy industry welcomed the extension of German steel capacity by the imminent conquest of Soviet foundries.[26] It had no serious reservations about taking over the installations, as the Soviet combines were largely self-supporting.[27] In the 'view of leading circles in the metallurgical industry', an 'improvement in work discipline' was the main requirement for a future increase in productivity from the Soviet blast furnaces.[28]

The light metal industry was of absolutely vital importance for armaments production. Developments here were typical of the way in which economic interests could sometimes conflict. Shortly after the German attack on the USSR began, interested companies had approached the ministry of economic affairs in order to obtain an agreement on the sharing out of Soviet

---

[21] See report from liaison officer War Economy and Armaments Department/Reich minister of economic affairs on Russia, 2 July 1941, BA-MA RW 45/15.

[22] Memorandum by Hans Hahl, owner of Rodingen ironworks, for Friedrich Flick, 26 June 1941, printed in *Anatomie des Krieges*, No. 166.

[23] Evidence in Eichholtz, *Kriegswirtschaft*, 204–5.

[24] For an overall view see Riedel, *Eisen*, 305 ff.; id., 'Bergbau', 245 ff. On the rivalries among the companies see Gibbons, 'Soviet Industry', 155 ff.

[25] See the retrospective account in the memorandum by the liaison officer in the War Economy and Armaments Department to the Main Trustee Office, 28 May 1942, BA-MA Wi/ID. 1600. A drive by the Gutehoffnung smelting-works and the Otto Wolff company, both of which had taken a leading role in German–Soviet trade and now wanted to establish themselves in the east, was rejected by Hitler; see report on the discussion between Lt.-Gen. von Hanneken and Ernst Poensgen on 25 July 1941, doc. NI-50, cited in Gibbons, 'Soviet Industry', 139.

[26] See the retrospective comments of the chief manager of the Economic Group Ferrous Industry, in Reichert, 'Europas Eisenerzeugung'.

[27] See e.g. 'Industrielle Entwicklung Sowjetrußlands'.

[28] See 'Die dringlichsten Aufgaben'.

firms.[29] However, this was opposed by the ministry of aviation, which considered that the installations could not be rebuilt until working and transport conditions, and the availability of raw materials, had been clarified.[30] The companies therefore concentrated their interest on the extraction of raw materials. Intense competition between them prevented the creation of a joint monopoly company,[31] of the kind founded in other branches of industry. The influential IG-Farben company thus chose to act on its own, and applied to take over factories making semi-finished goods with the aim of cannibalizing Soviet establishments rather than restarting them.[32]

However, the main interest of IG-Farben concerned the acquisition of the Soviet buna companies,[33] which were potentially very profitable in view of the bottlenecks in the German supply situation. An agreement was quickly reached with the ministry of economic affairs on the creation of the Russka Company Ltd. (Russka-Betrieb GmbH) to take over the Soviet installations.[34] However, deep differences with the ministerial bureaucracy came to the surface during the drafting of the company contract.[35] On the grounds that IG methods and patents would have to be applied to operate the firms, the company demanded a right of first refusal or appropriate compensation. This was refused by the ministry of economic affairs: the buna development had been subsidized before the war with considerable public funds, and the company's claims for compensation were therefore regarded as unsubstantiated. The decision led the company board to suspect that the Soviet buna firms might be intended for the German Labour Front, creating a state firm which might endanger the monopoly position enjoyed by IG-Farben.[36] However, its anxiety soon proved to be unfounded.

Such friction apart, close co-operation also rapidly developed between the state apparatus and the private economy in the chemical sector.[37] The critical petroleum problem had already been settled with the founding of the Continental Oil Corporation (Kontinentale Öl AG) in the spring of 1941. On 8 July

[29] See letter from Haeflinger, board member of IG-Farben, to Director Ziegler, Bitterfeld, 29 July 1941, doc. NI-14530, printed in *Trials*, viii, 269–70.

[30] Letter from Ziegler to Haeflinger, 8 Aug. 1941, doc. NI-14531, printed ibid. 271 ff.

[31] See Haeflinger to Ziegler, 9 Aug. 1941, doc. NT-14529, printed ibid. 270–1. On this issue see also the testimony of Haeflinger to the Nuremberg Tribunal, ibid. 299–300.

[32] Ziegler's letter of 8 Aug. 1941, doc. NI-6737, printed ibid. 271–2.

[33] See Circular No. 1 of the Buna agency, 1 July 1941, doc. NI-4969, printed ibid. 261–2. On this subject see Plumpe, 'Industrie'; on the role of the firm in Hitler's policy of expansion in general see Borkin, *Unheilige Allianz*.

[34] See Circular No. 2 of 14 July 1941, doc. NI-6737, printed ibid. 261–2.

[35] On the following see the account in the letter from August von Knieriem, board member of IG-Farben, to the Reich minister of economic affairs on the subject of the Synthesekautschuk-Ost GmbH, 17 Dec. 1941, doc. NI-6735, printed ibid. 274 ff.

[36] The conflict came to a head in the middle of 1942, when the Reich autborities demanded financial compensation from IG-Farben for the exploitation of looted Soviet patents: doc. NI-6735, printed ibid. 274 ff.

[37] On this subject in general see Gibbons, 'Soviet Industry', 199 ff.; Czollek, 'Estnische Phosphate'; Quiltzsch, 'Zur verbrecherischen Rolle', 157 ff.

Funk, the minister of economic affairs, invited the leading figures of the chemical industry to Berlin to discuss future action in Russia.[38] Funk assumed that the establishment and operation of a certain number of chemical firms in Russia was necessary, both for the supply of the occupied territories and to relieve pressures on the economy within Germany. His main concern here was the manufacture of medicines, fertilizers, and detergents. These would certainly be needed in the future German colonies in the east, and it would be more practical for firms in the east to supply them. It was decided to establish a consortium of eight companies under the leadership of IG-Farben, to reach agreement on the creation of a semi-nationalized Chemical East Company Ltd. (Chemie-Ost GmbH). It soon became apparent that IG-Farben was anxious to limit state influence and prevent the creation of binding business principles.[39] This, it was hoped, would protect the company against possible risks and losses which might result from the uncertain political conditions in the east.

Family firms, for example the textile sector, demonstrated rather less restraint than most other branches of industry. Thanks to his position as general representative for special duties within the ministry of economic affairs, its representative, the entrepreneur Hans Kehrl, was able to suppress plans for the foundation of a semi-nationalized monopoly company for textiles.[40] Instead, with the Ostfaser Company Ltd. (Ostfaser GmbH) he created an undertaking organized and directed exclusively by private industry. During the war years Kehrl built this company into the biggest textile concern in Europe, with around 300 Soviet factories. He worked closely with the German Bank, which had offered to act as investor. The bank, which had traditional business interests in Russia, attached great importance to 'taking a leading part in the new possibilities that offer themselves'. As the textile industry expected a turnover of several hundred million marks, the business 'would be a very comfortable one' for the bank.[41]

Kehrl got his way despite the opposition of State Secretary Backe, who refused to support him over the cultivation of flax and cotton in the east.

---

[38] See letter from Reich minister of economic affairs, 30 July 1941, printed in *Trials*, viii. 259–60. On the results of the various discussions see the report by Ilgner on 7 July 1941, doc. NI-1334, and the minutes of the 26th board meeting of IG-Farben on 10 July 1941, doc. NI-8077, both printed ibid. 262–3.

[39] On this subject see the memorandum of the legal department of IG-Farben, 23 July 1941, doc. NI-4962, ibid. 266 ff., and a corresponding letter from board member Georg von Schnitzler to the head of Economic Group Chemical Industry on 8 Aug. 1941, doc. NI-4961, ibid. 268–9. On 1 Nov. 1941 the Chemistry East Company was finally estabilshed. IG-Farben participated with an investment of RM1,000; see doc. NI-4964, printed ibid. 272–3.

[40] See the account in Kehrl, *Krisenmanager*, 222 ff., and specifically on the Baltic area Czollek, *Faschismus und Okkupation*, 137 ff.

[41] Memorandum by Gerhard Elkmann, deputy director of Deutsche Bank, of a discussion with the head of Economic Group Textile Industry, Hans Croon, on 9 July 1941, printed in *Anatomie des Krieges*, No. 169. On the foundation of Ostfaser GmbH, see also the position of the board member of Deutsche Bank, Karl Kimmich, on 19 Aug. 1941, also ibid., No. 175. On the role of Deutsche Bank overall see Radandt, 'Beziehungen', 9 ff.

Backe explained that he was much too preoccupied with the problem of food supply, and needed every acre of Russian soil within reach of transport. However, he also promised not to obstruct Kehrl if he chose to act on his own.[42] General Thomas, who had ordered that the textile-processing factories in the east should be neglected for the moment because of the needs of the armaments economy, responded in similar fashion. However, as German factories were only employed to 50 per cent of capacity, their owners were much more interested in finding favourable sources of raw materials and sales outlets than in obtaining additional processing capacity. When the textile industry explained that German cotton supplies would be exhausted the next winter, and that the situation would become 'very serious' without the implementation of detailed textile-manufacturing plans in Russia, Thomas promised his support.[43]

Overall, in its commitment to the east the main interest of the German private economy was in obtaining the use of Soviet raw materials. The desire of individual firms for expansion in the east took second place to a general endeavour to clarify the important issue of future ownership rights. The day after the German attack began, Göring attempted to accommodate these interests. During a discussion with leading representatives of industry, he announced his intention to reprivatize all state holdings in industry after the end of the war.[44] In the period that followed, the political leadership made it clear that the most efficient economy could be expected 'only on the proven foundation of (state-guided) private enterprise'. The collective economy in the east would be maintained only as long as was absolutely necessary 'to avoid disruption which could result from the sudden switch of economic systems', and which might damage the provision of supplies to the Wehrmacht or the development of the economy for German purposes.[45]

The Continental Oil Corporation offered a model for co-operation between the state and the private sector. This semi-nationalized company was to be established on a permanent basis, taking immediate and 'final' control of the Soviet petroleum economy. Similar solutions were envisaged for other raw materials, the 'permanent transfer of which to German hands [was] in the interests of the German economy as a whole'; the plan was to 'transfer the factories in question immediately into the possession of the German undertakings which would operate them in the long term'.[46] Generally, however, a

---

[42] See Kehrl, *Krisenmanager*, 223.

[43] See KTB WiRüAmt/Stab 1941, 188–9 (6 Aug. 1941), BA-MA 19/165.

[44] Minute of the meeting in the staff office on 23 June 1941, printed in Petrick, 'Schlüsseldokumente', No. 1.

[45] Reich Marshal of German Reich, Plenipotentiary for Four-year Plan, VP 12028, order of 27 July 1941 (copy), BA-MA RW 31/11; see also the memorandum of Odilo Burkhart, general plenipotentiary of the Flick concern, for Friedrich Flick on 13 Aug. 1941 (doc. NI-5262, printed in *Anatomie des Krieges*, No. 174), to the effect that Göring and Hitler were in agreement on the issue of reprivatization.

[46] Göring order of 27 July 1941, BA-MA RW 31/11.

transitional solution was chosen with the establishment of 'eastern companies' under the leadership of the ministry of economic affairs.[47] With effective participation from interested economic circles, these companies were to operate various sectors of the Soviet national economy as monopolies, and prepare the way for later privatization. This system offered the state apparatus sufficient opportunity to direct the companies according to the needs of the war economy, to skim off economic profits for the purpose of financing the war, and to avoid a 'great race by German industry for Russian plants'.[48] There was a price to be paid in the form of the further proliferation of the Economic Organization East. For the private sector itself, this settlement offered more advantages than an immediate transfer of ownership.

Through the use of trustees and temporary factory managers, firms were able to establish themselves in occupied Soviet territory without risks.[49] This procedure also secured them a legal claim for—though not a guarantee of—a subsequent transfer of ownership.[50] An acquisition would be carried out later only 'if the final shape of the political, legal, and economic conditions in the occupied Russian territory were taken into account' and if the German Reich intended to dispose of the factories.[51] Competition for the intended trustee posts was so fierce that the task of sorting out the applications monopolized the attention of the new section for the economic reorganization of the eastern territories within the ministry of economic affairs.[52] The applicants used every opportunity to exploit the chaos over authority in trusteeships for their own benefit, and to play off the various state offices against each other.[53]

The Economic Staff East operated at the junction of state and private-sector interests in the exploitation of the Soviet 'spoils'. Two days before the German attack on the Soviet Union, Göring's state secretary, Körner, had defined its main task as obtaining the greatest possible amount of vital goods from the

---

[47] See WiStabOst/Chefgruppe W/Allg.W/Gr. 1, No. 55256/42, survey of the tasks of the eastern companies, printed in Brown Folder, part A, Apr. 1942, appendix 9, BA-MA RW 31/134. For an account see Dallin, *German Rule*, 331 ff.; Czollek, *Faschismus und Okkupation*, 78 ff.; Czollek and Eichholtz, 'Konzeption', 161 ff.

[48] Memorandum of 13 Aug. 1941 (see n. 45); from the Marxist point of view, in the interpretation of these events the state apparatus is ascribed a 'unique' leading role: see Hass, 'Monopolkapital', 50 ff.

[49] See WiStabOst/Fü Ia No. 1361/41, special instructions No. 10: appointment of temporary administrators, 17 July 1941, printed in Brown Folder, part A, appendix 10, 65–6, BA-MA RW 31/134.

[50] Expectations along these lines on the part of industry are found, for example, in the memorandum by Kimmich dated 19 Aug. 1941, printed in *Anatomie des Krieges*, No. 175.

[51] Proposals from the Zeiss company for the Economic Group Precision Engineering and Optics, 18 Aug. 1941, printed in *Anatomie der Aggression*, No. 28. On the role of this company see also Schumann, 'Kriegsprogramm', 704 ff. and id., 'Zeiss-Konzern', 115 ff.

[52] See report of liaison officer War Economy and Armaments Dept./Reich ministry of economic affairs on economic reorganization of the occupied parts of Russia, 10 Sept. 1941, BA-MA RW 45/15.

[53] On this subject see the later report of the head of the Trustee Office East on the development of the trustee administration in the 'Ostland' for Göring, 16 Apr. 1942, BA-MA Wi/ID. 1600.

eastern territories which were occupied.[54] First and foremost, this meant petroleum and foodstuffs to supply the areas under German control.

In its attempt to accomplish this objective, the policy of the Economic Staff East was greatly affected both by the shortages facing the German war economy, and by the dominance of representatives of the civilian economic bureaucracy and the private sector in the organization. From the outset, the organization was always more concerned with economic 'reconstruction', and the cannibalization of existing installations for delivery to the Reich, than with providing direct military support for the army in the east.[55] Military influence on the creation of guidelines for action also declined steadily. After the distribution of the 'Green File', the War Economy and Armaments Department was immediately forced to begin work on a revised edition following numerous protests from civilian departments.[56] The strongest opposition came from Rosenberg's office. In response to the 'Green File', this office drafted different guidelines based on the following principle: 'The war against the Soviet Union is a political campaign, not an economic raid. The conquered territory as a whole must not be regarded as an object to be exploited, even though German food supply and the war economy must lay claim to larger areas.'[57]

OKW initially paid little attention to these differences. Like the ministry of economic affairs and the Four-year Plan authority, its members assumed that Rosenberg and his staff would not take over the administration of the occupied eastern territories until later in the war, and would not have any influence over economic policy. Proposals were thus made for a uniform network of economic agencies in the east, based on five economic inspectorates which would operate according to the directives of the Berlin Operations Staff. Since the authorities of the civilian administration would have to spend considerable time preparing for their practical work, the Economic Staff East also at first believed that its own political activities would be able to fill the vacuum. Its plan was therefore to extend the system of military administration by means of a 'dense network of commandants' offices (Kommandanturen) with economic advisers', and operate them for a considerable period against Hitler's express instructions. It also intended to create a 'halfway loyal' native leadership élite to support this structure.[58] An appropriate directive from Göring to the com-

---

[54] Reich Marshal of the Greater German Reich, Plenipotentiary for the Four-year Plan, VP 10103/1 g.Rs., 11th meeting of General Council, 24 June 1941, doc. NI-7474, Staatsarchiv Nürnberg.

[55] In his decree of 27 July 1941 on the aim of economic management in the east Göring had clearly laid down the postwar tasks: printed in *Deutsche Besatzungspolitik*, No. 76. Rosenberg dared to protest only against the system of eastern companies: see his letter to Göring of 2 Aug. 1941, BA R 6/23.

[56] Positions adopted in BA-MA RW 31/127. The second edition with appropriate supplements appeared in Nov. 1941: see BA-MA RW 31/130.

[57] Gibbons, 'Richtlinien', 259; see also Bräutigam, *So hat es sich zugetragen*, 315 ff.

[58] Chef WiStabOst No. 40046/41 g, fortnightly report start of campaign to 6 July 1941, dated 12 July 1941, BA-MA RW 31/11.

mander-in-chief of the army was expected to that end.[59] However, in a discussion between General Thomas and the quartermaster-general on 8 July
1941, it transpired that the army leadership had no particular interest in an
alliance of this kind with the economic agencies. Wagner was more concerned
to release the rear areas from his responsibility as soon as possible, despite the
fact that Rosenberg was nowhere near completing his own preparations.[60]
When Thomas suggested that they should jointly advocate that Rosenberg's
proposed administrative personnel should be attached either to the army or to
the Economic Staff East, Wagner was prepared to co-operate, but he left it to
Thomas to contact Göring on the subject.

On 16 July the Economic Staff East brought the political issue to the fore.
Its second report underlined the 'need for a larger number of district commander's offices with security and administrative tasks . . . The waves of German agricultural leaders now pouring in are the backbone of the future, but
will only obtain higher crop and livestock yields if they are given rapid backing
from these district commander's offices.'[61] On that day, however, Hitler reiterated his wish for the rapid installation of Rosenberg, and the restriction of
the military administration in the rear. Though confirming Göring's
autonomy in economic matters, Hitler left it to his vassals to agree among
themselves over the demarcation of authority.[62]

Rosenberg did not dare challenge Göring's position. He therefore abandoned the idea of establishing his own economic apparatus, and agreed that
the local economic commands should be turned into armaments commands
subordinate to OKW when territories were transferred to civilian administration. The various Agriculture, Labour, and Economy Groups would then
move step by step into civilian service, and be taken over by the Reich
Commissioners as the economic administration.[63]

These groups continued to receive their specialist directives via the Economic Operations Staff East. The departments of agriculture and of trade and
industry in the Economic Staff East were also taken over by the Ministry for
the East through personal union (the officials belonging to both bodies),
thereby maintaining the unity of economic leadership in principle at least. In
reality, however, the complicated regulations on the chain of command
opened the way for the administrative chaos in the east which was greatly
regretted later. Military responsibility was restricted to the area of operations

---

[59] See WiStabOst/La, War Diary notes, 9 July 1941, BA-MA RW 31/42.
[60] Minute on the discussion between Gen. Thomas and Gen. Wagner on 8 July, KTB
WiRüAmt/Stab 1941, 139–40 (11 July 1941), BA-MA RW 19/165.
[61] Chef WiStabOst No. 40063/41 g, 2nd situation report of 16 July 1941, BA-MA RW 31/11.
[62] See Führer conference of 16 July 1941, No. 221-L, *IMT* xxxviii, 86 ff., and First Decree of the
Führer on the Introduction of the Civilian Administration in the Newly Occupied Eastern
Territories, 17 July 1941, No. 1997-PS, ibid. xxix. 234 ff.
[63] See the Göring decrees of 18 July 1941 (VP 11064), 31 July 1941 (VP 12262), and the
appropriate implementation instructions from the War Economy and Armaments Department of
25 July and 22 Aug. 1941, printed in Green Folder, part ii, 2nd edn., Aug. 1942, BA-MA RW 31/
131.

from now on. The armaments inspectorates in the Reich Commissions could protect solely the armaments requirements of the Wehrmacht against the civilian economic agencies.[64]

On 17 July 1941 General Thomas met Göring to discuss administrative questions. By that time, the decision against a purely military solution—even for a specific transitional period—had already been taken.[65] For the time being, the chance for close co-operation between the economic organization and the machinery of the quartermaster-general, and for a unified direction and management of the economy to provide material support for the army in the east, had been lost.

Despite the official demarcation-lines *vis-à-vis* the civilian administration, the Economic Staff East remained mainly concerned with the 'rear', i.e. with the delivery of supplies to Germany and the preparation of the economic 'new order'. As long as the army in the east was operating near to the border and could make use of the relatively well-stocked supplies of the Reich, support for the troops was not necessarily compromised. However, the army's rapid advance into the Russian interior brought an increased need for material assistance, which was to be provided by Economic Staff East in line with the division of tasks between the Army High Command and OKW. The unsatis-factory fulfilment of this task, and the increasing recognition at the end of July 1941 that a rapid victory in the east was no longer possible, led to a serious crisis in both the operational and the economic leadership.

Alongside the issues of food supply and the labour force, the supply of fuel had become a serious problem for the army in the east, and indeed for the entire German war economy. While fuel consumption on the eastern front increased steadily, the amount of fuel seized as booty was declining; at the same time, Berlin expected to import at least 400,000 t. of mineral oil per month from Russia, beginning in October 1941, in order to meet the most urgent needs of the German war economy. Barely any reference was made to the enormous quantities required for the expanded aircraft programme.[66] In any case, on 16 July General Thomas had told Göring that the Caucasian mineral oilfields must be seized as quickly as possible.[67]

In the last three months of 1941, during preparations for a detailed memo-randum from the War Economy and Armaments Department on the fuel situation, it was finally decided that consumption in the areas under German control could not be cut back any further. No increases in productivity could be expected in the conquered oilfield at Drogobych, which had given Ger-

[64] See OKW/WiRüAmt/Stab I/O No. 3574/41, creation and operation of Armaments Inspector-ate Ostland, 27 Aug. 1941, BA-MA RW 31/11.

[65] See chief or War Economy and Armaments Department, result of talks with the Reich Marshal and with FM Keitel, 17 July 1941, BA-MA Wi/VIII. 138.

[66] Reports by chief of raw materials to departmental head, KTB WiRüAmt/Stab 1941, 136 (7 July 1941), BA-MA RW 19/165.

[67] Chief of War Economy and Armaments Department on occupation of the Caucasian oilfields, 16 July 1941, BA-MA Wi/I D. 82.

many control of 1 per cent of Soviet capacity, nor during the development of the Estonian shale-oil deposits. Under these circumstances, it was difficult to see how the needs of Russian agriculture, and of the winter building programme in the east, could be met.[68] In his aviation-fuel programme Krauch again called on OKW to demand annual imports of 9m. t. of petroleum from Russia, and the development of a new oilfield between Kiev and Kharkov.[69] However, Thomas preferred to base his plans on realistic foundations, and to prepare for the least favourable situation, i.e. for coping without major deliveries from Russia in 1941; this would eventually require further restrictions on German consumption.[70]

In its latest situation report, the Economic Staff East concluded that the raw materials already obtained in conquered Russian territory would not significantly improve the German supply situation.[71] It was still expected that the front would gradually advance from the mainly agrarian areas to 'get a grip on the industrial centres'. Nevertheless, the first signs of a failure of the economic strategy, which had aimed at a smooth 'take-over' of the Soviet economy, could not be overlooked. In particular, the increasing level of destruction and evacuation carried out by the Soviet side was taking its toll.

The leadership in Berlin was fully aware of the consequences of this development, which threatened to intensify as the war in the east was prolonged. During a discussion on 29 July 1941, the under-secretary of state, Lieutenant-General von Hanneken, told Thomas that he would have to curb the coal consumption of German industry by 40 per cent.[72] The 'time had been reached when the Führer himself must decide what is to happen in the raw-material sector in the winter'. Yet no one was prepared to bring 'the matter to the Führer for a decision finally'. Thomas and Hanneken both regarded the fuel supply as the biggest bottleneck. They agreed that, where supplies were running out, they must create a united front of all the economic agencies, allowing the Reich Marshal to give the Führer a clear picture of the situation and press for the most rapid possible conquest of the Caucasus.

Next day, it became apparent that the munitions companies were already drawing the appropriate conclusions from the confused situation. Ewald Loeser, a director of Krupp, asked General Thomas to release those members of the company's workforce who had been made available for service in Russia but had not yet been deployed.[73] In view of the constant decline in produtivity

[68] Report chief of raw materials to departmental head, KTB WiRüAmt/Stab 1941, 152 (21 July 1941), BA-MA RW 19/165.

[69] Discussion between Prof. Krauch and departmental head, ibid. (23 July 1941).

[70] See ibid. 159 (24 July 1941), 166 (28 July 1941).

[71] Chef WiRüAmt No. 40139/Id/41 g., fortnightly report WiStabOst (6–19 July 1941), 26 July 1941, BA-MA RW 31/11.

[72] Discussion between Lt.-Gen. von Hanneken and departmental head, KTB WiRüAmt/Stab 1941, pp. 169–70 (29 July 1941), BA-MA RW 19/165.

[73] Discussion between Director Loeser (Krupp) and departmental head, ibid. 171–2 (30 July 1941).

in German factories, the enormous demands on manpower for the reconstruction of the Soviet works could not be justified. It was more sensible to maintain the factories in the Reich at their current level of production, rather than keeping valuable workers ready for work in the Soviet installations.

A series of high-level meetings on the issue was held in Berlin on 31 July. These aimed to draw up an interim balance sheet, and to set the course for the imminent second phase of operations—the struggle for the vital economic centres in the European part of the Soviet Union. The problem of food supply came to the fore during a meeting of the Economic Operations Staff East under State Secretary Körner.[74] Like the subsequent discussions involving inspectors in the military Economic Staff East, this concluded that absolute priority must now be given to providing material support for the army in the east.[75] Previously, more attention had been devoted to economic considerations, on the assumption that military operations would be completed more swiftly. The report maintained: 'Now it is more correct not to be unnecessarily concerned with economic measures. The main duty of the organization is to solve short-term tasks.' Göring was only interested in oil and grain, while Rosenberg wanted to work according to the 'long view'. It was therefore better for the organization to show resraint in political measures; it should concentrate on supplying the troops, and only then on delivering material to the Reich. As regards the methods to be employed, the Russians were a 'stubborn pack and difficult to get to work'. More pressure would therefore have to be exerted on the population, with the economic organization being involved everywhere 'where there is something. All other areas must remain unworked. We cannot administer the whole country. The intelligentsia has been killed, the commissars are gone. Large areas will have to be left to themselves (to starve).'

In this context, General Thomas ordered that only industry in the Baltic was to be put back into operation for the time being. Industrial activity solely to assist employment policy would not be considered, since the workers could not be fed. It was essential to concentrate on factories which were important to the war effort, and leave everything else 'to go to the dogs'.

Apart from organizational changes to eliminate failings in the Economic Organization East, the leading economic agencies thus intended to maintain their previous course. The economic exploitation of the occupied Soviet territories was to be made more efficient mainly in order to help supply the troops. It was to be achieved not by making concessions or showing concern for the population, but by intensifying the policies of force and hunger which condemned countless civilians and prisoners of war to death. Behind it lay the belief that the economically vital regions in the European part of the Soviet

---

[74] Reich Marshal of the Greater German Reich, Plenipotentiary for Four-year Plan. VP 12295 g.Rs., minute of meeting of Economic Operations Staff East, 31 July 1941, BA-MA RW 31/11.

[75] See KTB WiRüAmt, 173–8 (31 July 1941), BA-MA RW 19/165, and Chef WiStabOst No. 40153/41 g., discussions in Berlin on 31 July 1941, BA-MA RW 31/11.

Union—the Caucasus (oil) and the lower Volga (grain)—would soon be in German hands. To supply the army in the east with the materials necessary to achieve this objective, while at the same time sending supplies of food to Germany, the economic leadership would stop at nothing. Only time would tell whether this determination would be sufficient to close the widening gap between the demands of the war in the east and the resources available to wage it.

2. FIRST MODIFICATIONS

The economic and armaments policy of the Third Reich had been based on the assumption of rapid military victory in the east. When the failure of the campaign plan became perceptible from July 1941, leading to the unexpected extension of the German–Soviet war, economic and armaments policy had to be adapted to the changed conditions. This process of adjustment, however, was sluggish and inconsistent. The political and military élites delayed making moves towards fundamental reorganization because they still hoped to achieve military victory over the following weeks. As a sense of reality was lost, refuge was taken in the art of improvisation. However, Hitler had begun to recognize that the war would probably last into 1942; he took this as additional support for his view that the capture of 'vital sources of raw materials' was more important than the achievement of operational advantages.[76] Hitler told his adjutant that he could not sleep at night,

as he was still not clear about many things. In his bosom two souls were struggling, the political-ideological and the economic. Politically he would say that the main abscesses must be removed: Leningrad and Moscow . . . Economically there were quite different objectives. Though Moscow was also a big industrial centre, the south was even more important, with oil, grain, absolutely everything that was necessary to secure living-space. A land flowing with milk and honey.[77]

Though this issue remained a matter of dispute between Hitler and the army leadership, some recognition of the logical consequences of unfavourable military developments could not be further delayed. Measures to reorganize and re-equip the army, originally planned for the autumn of 1941, had to be put off for the forseeable future.[78] However, this step was not accompanied by any abandonment of wildly unrealistic armaments plans.[79] During discussions between the responsible OKW departments in the middle of August, the Chief of Army Armament Programmes warned in vain of the need to emerge from 'cloud-cuckoo-land' and adjust military requirements to meet

[76] See Hitler's study on the continuation of the war in the east, 22 Aug. 1941, *KTB OKW* i. 1063 ff. (100).

[77] Engel, *Heeresadjutant bei Hitler*, 107 (28 July 1941).

[78] Führer conference of 19 Aug. 1941 with Brauchitsch and Fromm, *KTB OKW* i. 1059–60 (96).

[79] Chef OKW/WiRüAmt/Rü (IIa) No. 2600/41 g.Kdos., letter *re* reorientation of armaments, 10 Aug. 1941, BA-MA Wi/I A. 84.

the resources actually available.[80] Though the principle that existing plans must be scaled down to a feasible level was accepted, this did not produce any adjustment of armament production to help the army. Air-force armament remained the priority.[81] Past omissions had prevented the prompt deployment of a new wave of men and materials at the start of the second phase of the Russian campaign; now, the modification of strategic and armaments plans in July–August 1941 was unlikely to lead to a significant stepping up of the war effort.

As before, the biggest obstruction to armaments production was the man-power shortage.[82] Initially, it had been expected that rapid victory in the east would be followed by the release of around one million workers from the armed forces. These hopes, however, had been dashed. Some 1.5 million extra workers were required, a need which could not be fully met by the deployment of 500,000 French prisoners of war. One possible solution was to draw on the untapped reservoir of Soviet prisoners of war. However, there were political objections to this step.[83] In vain did the economic agencies argue that French prisoners of war, due to be transferred from agriculture to the armaments industry, should be replaced by Russians.[84]

The German coal-mining industry also demanded extra workers to meet the rapid increase in demands upon it. In September alone, for example, the industry was expected to supply 320,000 t. of locomotive coal to the east for operational purposes.[85] Since it was not practicable to release miners from the army in the current circumstances, the chairman of the Reich Coal Association, Paul Pleiger, eventually demanded the use of Soviet prisoners of war.[86] He also wanted to recruit Ukrainian miners for the Ruhr coalmines to replace Italian workers who had run off after the air raids. Himmler, in particular, objected to these measures on political grounds.[87] Only after the economic agencies had created a united front to support Pleiger did Hitler change his own mind; in October 1941 he gave permission for the employment of 10,000

---

[80] Minute of discussions with Chef OKW 14–16 Aug. 1941, KTB WiRüAmt/Stab 1941, 202–4, BA-MA RW 19/165, and OKW/WiRüAmt/Rü (IIa) No. 2747/41 g.Kdos., memorandum on the discussion Chef OKW with Wehrmacht branches, 16 Aug. 1941, printed in Thomas, *Wehr- und Rüstungswirtschaft*, 458 ff.; see also Reinhardt, *Moskau*, 38 ff.

[81] See Führer decree of 11 Sept. 1941 on armaments, BA-MA Wi/I F 5.208, part 2.

[82] On this subject see OKW/WiRüAmt/Stab Z/SR No. 3006/41 g.Kdos., situation report on the war economy No. 24, Aug. 1941, of 10 Sept. 1941, BA-MA RW 19/177. For an evaluation see Fanning, *German War Economy*, 153 ff.; and generally *Das Deutsche Reich und der Zweite Weltkrieg*, v/1. 928 ff.

[83] During the discussion of 16 Aug. 1941 (see n. 80) Keitel therefore urged restraint: see Thomas, *Wehr- und Rüstungswirtschaft*, 468.

[84] Report by armaments chief to departmental head, 25 Aug. 1941, KTB WiRüAmt/Stab 1941, 218, BA-MA RW 19/165.

[85] See letter from chairman of Reich Coal Association, Paul Pleiger, to Gen. Thomas, 26 Aug. 1941 (copy), BA-MA Rw 19/177.

[86] Discussion between Lt.-Gen. Hermann Reinecke (chief of General Wehrmacht Office), Director-General Pleiger, and others with departmental head, 17 Sept. 1941, KTB WiRüAmt/Stab 1941, 244, BA-MA RW 19/165.

[87] Talk between armaments chief and departmental head, 30 Sept. 1941, ibid. 254.

Ukrainian miners in the Reich.[88] Once this political and ideological taboo had been broken, Hitler also accepted that Soviet prisoners of war could be used. Yet no systematic solution to the manpower problem was found. With the exception of those men already in labour squads under the control of the quartermaster-general, most Russian prisoners of war were no longer fit for work because of the appalling living conditions in the camps. Their number was being decimated by hunger and epidemics.

Attempts to solve the raw-material problem were equally inconsistent. At the discussion of 16 August 1941 with the branches of the armed forces it was already apparent that the desired figures for armaments production would be completely out of reach without the capture of those parts of European Russia that were rich in raw materials. Hitler therefore decided to switch the main thrust of operations to the south, in order to obtain 'the high-grade iron-ore deposits and the large blast furnaces' by occupying Krivoy Rog.[89] This, of course, meant accepting the demands of the Thomas memorandum of February, which had been underpinned by the alarming decline in German iron and steel production. However, in his memorandum Thomas had predicted that the capture of the raw-material area would ease the situation only if the Germans managed to prevent large-scale destruction by Soviet forces, to solve the transport question, and to conquer the Caucasus in 1941.[90] Even in August 1941 it was obvious that these conditions could not be met.

In view of the destruction in Krivoy Rog, which made a resumption of iron-ore mining and the reopening of the smelting works impossible for some time to come, the Economic Staff East decided that it was more sensible to concentrate available workers, machines, and experts on the manganese-ore operations in Nikopol, which were vital for German steel manufacture.[91] Without the reconstruction and exploitation of the Ukrainian iron-smelting industry, it was virtually impossible to increase iron and steel production in German-dominated areas sufficiently to fulfil the gigantic armaments plans, and to keep pace with the war production of the enemy powers. Such plans would have to be abandoned for the time being, quite apart from the fact that the majority of German iron and steel industrialists were not inclined to help in such a task.

Despite these developments, on 26 August 1941 the Reich foreign minister issued a circular celebrating German victory in the east, and declaring that Germany would no longer face difficulties over food supplies and raw materials.[92] This claim was utterly unrealistic. On the contrary, OKW was forced to take far-reaching measures to obtain control even of the raw materials in the occupied territories, so that they could be exploited for the German war

[88] Talk between armaments chief and departmental head, 22 Oct. 1941, ibid. 289.
[89] Halder, *Diaries*, 1157 (6 Aug. 1941).
[90] See Thomas, *Wehr- und Rüstungswirtschaft*, 531.
[91] For further information see Riedel, 'Bergbau', 250 ff., and Eichholtz, 'Wirtschaftspolitik', 283.
[92] *DGFP* D xiii, No. 244.

economy as quickly as possible. In addition to the existing posts within the military and civilian economic agencies, Göring appointed Lieutenant-General Walter Witting as 'Inspector General for Registration and Utilization of Raw Materials in the Occupied Eastern Territories'.[93] Witting had a consultantys agreement with the Flick company, and on 22 August 1941 had written to its managing director Richard Bruh to tell him that he wanted to go as far east 'as our troops can manage, eventually by plane to Vladivostok and Turkestan, and [I] look forward with interest to receiving word of your wishes'.[94]

The raw-material question could not be solved by administrative measures alone. This was especially true of the supply of oil, the great long-term problem of the German war effort. Finding a solution to this problem was undoubtedly of vital importance for the operational and economic leadership alike, in the occupied eastern territories and in the whole area under German control. Despite temporary stopgaps, the chances of solving the problem ultimately depended on whether and when the armed forces managed to capture the oilfields of the Caucasus. This issue became even more important once it was clear that the war would not end quickly, and that fuel consumption by the army in the east could not be reduced. The reaction of the military élite was inconsistent. While Army High Command remained obsessed with Moscow, and therefore regarded the prospects for an operation against the Caucasus with scepticism, the Wehrmacht operations staff was more optimistic.[95] OKW drew up a new balance sheet relating to the need for mineral oil in the changed conditions; this starkly revealed the difficulties Germany would face until spring 1942 owing to inadequate oil supplies.[96] An overall balance was achieved, but only by severe curbs on consumption, especially in the civilian sphere. As a result, there would also be an acute danger of delays in production in the armaments factories, as well as other undesirable political, military, and economic repercussions. Only on these terms could the needs of the army in the east be secured until the end of 1941. It remained an open question what would happen thereafter, unless—against all expectations—consumption on the eastern front was drastically reduced.

In the context of the material conduct of the war, Hitler's decision to wage the battle for Kiev was thus a logical step, being designed to open the way to

[93] RK 13402 B: Reich Marshal of the Greater German Reich, Representative for Four-year Plan, Economic Operations Staff East, VP 11083/1, order of 6 Sept. 1941, BA R43/II 609.

[94] See Besymenski, *Generale ohne Maske*, 285–6. Through his earlier post as chief of the Central Raw Material Agency in the Reich air ministry, and then as War Economy Inspector IV (Dresden), Witting was predestined for his new role. His post was abolished by Göring ten months later, after the raw-materials economy had passed into the hands of the civilian administration; see Reich Marshal of the Greater German Reich, Plenipotentiary for the Four-year Plan, VP 10673/1/4/6/2, 14 July 1942, BA R 43/II 609.

[95] Report by raw-materials chief to departmental head, 5 Aug. 1941, KTB WiRüAmt/Stab 1941, 185, BA-MA RW 19/165; also Halder, *Diaries*, 1158–61 (7 Aug. 1941).

[96] WiRüAmt Az. 11 k 2209 (Ro Vs) No. 2873/41 g.Kdos., mineral-oil supply situation in second half of 1941 and first quarter of 1942, 26 Aug. 1941, BA-MA Wi/IF 5.2695.

the Soviet Union's industrial bases and raw-material deposits. The successful prosecution of the operation, and the advance into the Dnieper–Donets industrial region, did bring Hitler closer to achieving his main economic objectives. The price, however, was high. The consumption of fuel and ammunition, and the losses in men and material, were considerable. They significantly weakened the substance of the army in the east, since new production in the Reich was totally unable to compensate for the losses sustained.[97] Despite the inevitable erosion of the fighting power of the army in the east, the battle of Kiev was a success for Hitler's plans. However, it did not bring about an end to the conflict; nor was the success exploited to the full to boost the German war economy and to sustain further operations. The most important reason for this was the fact that the Red Army did not collapse, as the Germans had hoped. Instead, it continued the struggle with undiminished ferocity, and its measures of evacuation, paralysis, and destruction made it exceptionally difficult for the occupiers to exploit the land. The civilian population also played its part. Though its initial reception of the German troops had been friendly, the longer the war lasted, the more the population adopted a policy of passive—and in individual cases even active—resistance.[98]

Finally, the economic exploitation of military successes was also hampered by inefficiencies in economic management. The proliferation of high-level organizations, due to the multiplication of tasks and the increasing influence of civilian agencies, was only one cause of this process.[99] As before, the biggest problems arose over co-operation with Rosenberg's civilian administration. As a committee of the main economic functionaries, meeting only at irregular intervals, the Economic Operations Staff East could not provide the necessary central direction. Moreover, the civilian administration was not yet ready to take control; when Hitler established the Reich Commissariat Ukraine on 20 August 1941, it was still making its preparations.[100]

At this stage, Rosenberg appeared to be most interested in his power-struggle with Himmler and Göring for the dominant role in the east. Above all, he was anxious to prevent further expansion by the SS. Since Himmler was also trying to carve out a role in economic policy, Rosenberg found an important ally in Göring.[101] Yet agreement between them lasted only a short time; after they had successfully fended off Himmler's claims, rivalry and

[97] Figures from 'Survey of the army's armaments situation (weapons and equipment)' as of 1 Sept. 1941, BA-MA RH 8/v. 1090; graph showing losses of armoured fighting vehicles, ibid. RH 8/v. 1023, and the relevant 10-day reports, ibid. III W 805/5 and 6.

[98] Corresponding references in the USSR reports of the SS security service, BA R 58/214ff.

[99] By the end of 1941 there had also been established within the Economic Staff East a Main Group Labour and four special groups, e.g. for the professional associations and for forestry and wood; see business distribution plan, 1 Nov. 1941, BA-MA R 43/686a.

[100] Second Führer decree on the introduction of civilian administration in the newly occupied eastern territories, 20 Aug. 1941, printed in Green Folder, part ii, 2nd edn., BA-MA RW 31/131. On this subject see also sect. II.VII.3 at n. 260 (Förster).

[101] See the correspondence between Göring and Rosenberg in Aug. 1941, BA R6/23; also Müller, 'Interessenpolitik', 107ff.

disagreements between Göring and Rosenberg erupted again. Koch, the newly appointed Reich Commissioner for the Ukraine, was also trying to pursue an independent policy in carrying out his task of exploiting the region. His own strained relations with Rosenberg led him to turn first to the economic organization for support in building up an administrative apparatus in the Ukraine.[102] After a short time, however, Koch's activity also began to have a detrimental effect on economic management,[103] as the new agencies of the civilian administration sought to create their own sources of income. Koch encouraged the existing monopoly companies to demand that goods which were vital to the war effort be handed over by the military economic agencies for sale in the Reich, at least partly to swell the coffers of the Reich Commissariat.[104] He made this attempt even though, four weeks previously, Göring had decreed that the armed forces were to have first option on captured machinery, semi-finished goods, and raw materials in order to meet the needs of the troops. Only goods produced afterwards could be sold to improve the financial position of the Reich Commissioners.[105] Göring confirmed this guideline in a formal decree, thereby assuring the Wehrmacht of the decisive influence, at least in the armaments sector, even in areas controlled by the civilian administration.[106] The struggle for authority was officially settled.

Nevertheless, in individual cases the Wehrmacht commanders, and armaments agencies in the Reich Commissariats, became embroiled in conflict with the civilian administration. This was particularly the case over the appointment of provisional administrators in firms important for armaments production, the allocation of Wehrmacht orders, and the requisitioning of goods for the war effort.[107] Hosts of officials and officers were kept busy settling these disputes. In the city of Riga, for example, Supply District North had set up a fuel depot and an ammunition dump in the Meza Park and had organized the laying of railway tracks.[108] After Riga was removed from the army's area of operations, the newly appointed Area Commissioner protested against what he saw as an 'unjustified interference in the affairs of the city', and

[102] See Chief of Staff, memorandum on the discussion with State Secretary Körner on 4 Sept. 1941, BA-MA RW 19/177.

[103] On the role of Koch see also Dallin, *German Rule*, 133 ff.

[104] Report by raw-materials chief to departmental head, 14 Oct. 1941, KTB WiRüAmt/Stab 1941, 278, BA-MA RW 19/165; two months previously the suggestion that raw materials should be subjected to unified direction through the Reich Commissioner had been considered within the War Economy and Armaments Department itself, but had been rejected outright by Thomas: see Nagel memorandum, 11 Aug. 1941, BA-MA RW 31/127.

[105] Göring discussions of 15 and 16 Sept. 1941, No. 003-EC, *IMT* xxxvi. 105–6.

[106] See KTB WiRüAmt/Stab 1941, 279 (15 Oct. 1941), BA-MA RW 19/165, and decree of Reich Marshal of the Greater German Reich on the care to be provided for armaments firms and other commercial enterprises in the newly occupied eastern territories, 28 Oct. 1941, printed in Green Folder, part ii, 2nd edn., BA-MA RW 31/131.

[107] See e.g. Rosenberg's letter to Keitel, 29 Oct. 1941 (copy), BA-MA RW 41/9.

[108] For the following see letter from OKH/GenStdH/Außenstelle Gen.Qu./Versorgungsbezirk Nord/Abt. H. Vers. No. 274/41 to District Commissioner City of Riga, 18 Oct. 1941, BA-MA RH 3/v. 139.

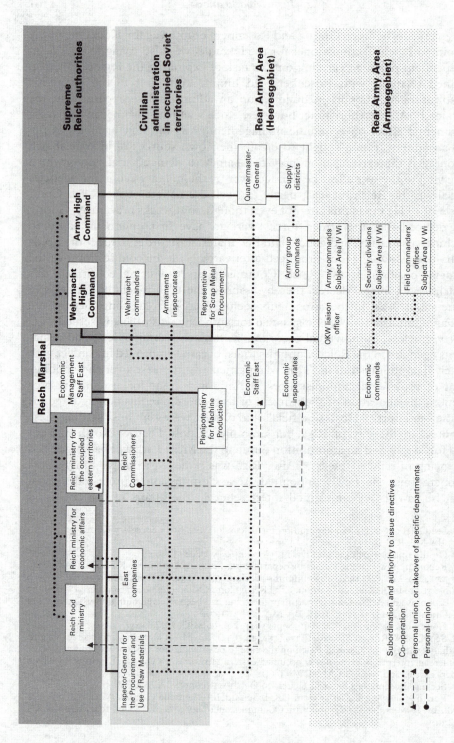

Supreme Reich authorities

Civilian administration in occupied Soviet territories

Rear Army Area (Heeresgebiet)

Rear Army Area (Armeegebiet)

Reich Marshal

Wehrmacht High Command

Army High Command

Economic Management Staff East

Wehrmacht commanders

Armaments inspectorates

Representive for Scrap Metal Procurement

Quartermaster-General

Supply districts

Army group commands

Army commands
Subject Area IV Wi

OKW liaison officer

Security divisions
Subject Area IV Wi

Field commanders' offices
Subject Area IV Wi

Economic Staff East

Economic inspectorates

Economic commands

Reich ministry for the occupied eastern territories

Reich Commissioners

Plenipotentiary for Machine Production

Reich ministry for economic affairs

East companies

Reich food ministry

Inspector-General for the Procurement and Use of Raw Materials

Subordination and authority to issue directives

Co-operation

Personal union, or takeover of specific departments

Personal union

DIAGRAM II.VI.I. The Ramifications of Economic Organization East from the Start of the Campaign to the End of 1941

demanded the transfer of the installation. At precisely this time—the middle of October 1941—the supply of the army in the east was in crisis owing to the unsatisfactory transport situation; the Wehrmacht departments were already at full stretch. In such circumstances, the damage done by these conflicts is clear.

The civilian administration's preoccupation with peacetime conditions sometimes even led to coalitions with the army departments against the economic apparatus. Rosenberg's new guidelines for the civilian administration,[109] completed in September 1941, again made it clear that the ministry for the east was concerned primarily with creating a racial and political 'New Order' in the east, and that it intended to use economic policy to that end.[110] The key issue involved the collective farms. Rosenberg wanted to press forward as quickly as possible with the reprivatization of agriculture, at least in the Baltic and the Ukraine, in order to win the co-operation of the native population. Here he was supported by some army offices, in the belief that such measures would help to pacify the hinterland.[111] The foreign ministry also advocated the immediate breaking up of the collective farms.[112]

However, the economic leadership maintained the view it had taken in the spring of that year, to the effect that hasty action would destroy any prospect of Germany gaining possession of the Russian harvest.[113] Backe refused to accept responsibility for anything more than the existing propaganda efforts—transformation of the collective farms into so-called communal farms.[114] For his part, Hitler avoided taking an unequivocal decision; after a discussion with Rosenberg, he advocated only a step-by-step and limited return of the collective farms to private ownership.[115]

The Economic Staff East pointed to Hitler's general directive to the effect that the Ukraine and the Caucasus were to be administered 'in a purely colonial manner', and that priority was to be given to exploiting them for the war effort.[116] Political considerations could not be taken into account. As

---

[109] Guidelines for the civilian administration in the occupied eastern territories, Sept. 1941, printed in part in *Weltherrschaft im Visier*, No. 128.

[110] See Rosenberg's letter to Göring, 28 Oct. 1941, BA R 6/23, in which he announced the creation of a planning department in his ministry in clear competition with the work of the SS leadership on a 'General Plan East'; see Müller, 'Interessenpolitik', 107.

[111] See e.g. Abwehr II/Army Group South, preconditions for the security of supplies and gaining the highest food surpluses in the Ukraine, 28 Oct. 1941, BA R6/69, and retrospectively the report of the military administration with the command of Army Group Centre, Aug. 1942, printed in part in Müller, 'Interessenpolitik', 132; also, offering the same assessment of the economic agencies, the memoirs of the head of the Grundsatzabteilung in the Ministry for the East, Otto Felix Bräutigam, *So hat es sich zugetragen*, 355, 385 ff.

[112] Letter from the Ministry for the East to Backe, 22 Aug. 1941, BA R6/23.

[113] Memorandum of Embassy Counsellor Hilger, *DGFP* D viii/1, doc. 237 (24 Aug. 1941).

[114] See commander of rear Army Area South No. 146/41, order Dept. VII No. 11, guidelines on the treatment of the collective question, 22 Aug. 1941, BA-MA RH 22/6.

[115] *DGFP* D xiii, No. 372 (1 Oct. 1941).

[116] Discussion between Min. Dir. Schlotterer and departmental head, 15 Oct. 1941, KTB WiRüAmt/Stab 1941, 279, BA-MA RW 19/165.

regards economic efficiency, there were diametrically opposing views, as was revealed in a meeting of the agricultural leaders of the Economic Inspectorates on 20 October 1941.[117] The Economic Inspectorate North opposed the proposal that the collective farming system should be at least partially dismantled. This was justified on the grounds of Hitler's decision to regard the Baltic as a German settlement area, which meant that no new property rights should be created for the native population. In contrast, the representative of Economic Inspectorate Centre claimed that the collective farming system could not be retained in his area if a further increase in damaging partisan activity were to be prevented. Agricultural production could only be maintained with the goodwill of the rural population. Finally, the Economic Inspectorate South argued that the collective system must be retained at all costs, since the area 'had to be ruled by force', and any relaxation might have unforeseen consequences. There should be an end to discussion; the policy should be carried out with full rigour.

As these discussions demonstrated, the economic leadership also faced a dilemma which increased inexorably as Germany's military position deteriorated. In such conditions, the original interplay between political-ideological and economic objectives could no longer function smoothly. On this occasion too, his preoccupation with the supply of the homeland and the troops led Backe to reject any alterations to the economic policy of exploitation.

However, this coalition between the civilian administration and the economic leadership was not successful, because the army leadership shrank from political conflicts. This attitude is demonstrated by a letter written by the quartermaster-general on 20 September, in which he announced his pleasure 'that this time we have nothing to do with any of the political business. In the west it worked, but here, where so many ideological questions play a part, I'm very glad.'[118] It also explains the general eagerness of the commander-in-chief of the army to hand over the occupied territories to the Reich Commissioners as quickly as possible, despite the fact that Koch, for example, wanted to wait until spring before taking over because there was not much he could do in the coming winter anyway.[119] And yet, despite these reservations, it remains true that in September 1941 the army began its efforts to bring about a modification of occupation policy. The objective was to pacify the hinterland by means of a more considerate treatment of the population, especially in economic matters.[120]

---

[117] WiStabOst, Chefgr. LA Ia No. 23443/41, report on the meeting of agricultural leaders on 20 Oct. 1941, BA-MA RW 31/42.

[118] Wagner *Generalquartiermeister*, 201.

[119] Discussion between Schlotterer and departmental head, 15 Oct. 1941, KTB WiRüAmt/Stab 1941, BA-MA RW 19/165.

[120] Thus, for example, Army High Command and the Ministry for the East together attempted to persuade the Economic Operations Staff East to make consumer goods available for the population in the conquered eastern territories, since these people could not be won over with 'paper money'; see letter from both agencies in BA R 6/287.

An important precondition for this approach was a closer integration of the Economic Organization East into the army apparatus, and greater concentration on satisfying the needs of the troops. Earlier agreements about the deployment of the economic agencies as near the front as possible, and close co-operation with the rear army authorities,[121] were not always observed because of the ponderous apparatus of the Economic Staff East. When the Economic Action Teams lagged behind, army agencies often had to take charge of the most urgent economic measures, such as bringing in the harvest. Most complaints about a lack of co-operation came from the sector covered by the Economic Inspectorate South, which was incapable of adjusting efficiently to the course of operations. According to the commander of Rear Army Area South, many specialists had little 'understanding for military matters'.[122] General Thomas took note of this criticism. Once again he instructed the economic agencies to seek greater co-operation with the army offices, and to put aside all political considerations in favour of the vital tasks of the war.[123]

The complaints did not stop, even though the quartermaster-general was ordered to rely more than before on the support of the economic agencies in implementing his new programme to create winter accommodation and equipment in the occupied eastern territories. There was no shortage of goodwill in the economic organization. However, it frequently lacked the ability to take an overall view, and the capacity to achieve its objectives. One specific example will serve to demonstrate the difficulties that arose. When Economic Inspectorate Centre ordered the subordinate economic commands, and specialists in the field commandant's offices and armies, to report details of possibilities for manufacturing consumer goods, building materials, and equipment for the winter accommodation programme, these failed to respond; they believed that their first duty was to help individual soldiers and local units rather than to supply the troops at the front.[124]

Similar events occurred in the sector covered by the quartermaster-general, as was revealed by a complaint from Armaments Inspectorate Ostland at the beginning of October 1941. During the preparation of winter quarters and efforts to meet the direct requirements of the troops, 'individual troop contingents, from the army down to the smallest units, were inclined to meet requirements by circumventing the official channels, sending details here directly to the armaments departments or even placing them directly with industry'.[125] Under these circumstances, it was scarcely possible for the eco-

---

[121] See KTB Befh. rückw. H.Geb. Süd, 74–5 (5 Aug. 1941), BA-MA RH 22/3, and War Diary Supply District North, 68 (7 Aug. 1941), BA-MA RH 19 III/615.

[122] KTB Befh. rückw. H.Geb. Süd, 77 ff. (9 Aug. 1941), BA-MA RH 22/3.

[123] Chef WiRüAmt/Stab Ia No. 2921/41 g., guidelines for the leadership and operation of the economic service agencies in the newly occupied eastern territories, 11 Aug. 1941, BA-MA Wi/VI. 227.

[124] KTB Außenstelle OKH/Gen Qu/Versorgungsbezirk Dnepr/Abt. IV Wi., entry 17 Oct. 1941, BA-MA Wi/ID. 1123.

[125] Armaments Inspectorate Ostland/Abt. Z/Ib No. 63/41 to Economic Staff East, 8 Oct. 1941, BA-MA H 17/85.

nomic agencies to obtain an overall view of capacity to complete Wehrmacht orders. Moreover, directly after the occupation of the country almost all important factories that were still in operation had been inundated with orders from Wehrmacht units, the Todt Organization, and other departments. Almost all of them would be working at full stretch for the foreseeable future.

The main problem was undoubtedly the independence of the economic organization; this hampered the co-ordination of policies. Thus, while Army Group South repeatedly demanded the deployment of German specialists to protect and reconstruct the industrial region of Krivoy Rog,[126] Economic Inspectorate South concentrated on starting manganese extraction at Nikopol, in accordance with instructions received from headquarters in Berlin.

General Thomas and the chief of Economic Staff East realized only gradually that it would have been preferable for the economic organization to be subordinate to the army from the outset.[127] Appropriate conclusions were drawn in November 1941: the economic inspectorates were attached to the army groups, and given the main task of securing supplies from the land for the troops.[128] Parallel to this, the quartermaster-general reorganized his field offices into Assistant Chief of Staff offices (Oberquartiermeister-Stäbe) with the army groups.[129] Now at last the army groups had control of their own economic apparatus, uniting responsibility both for the exploitation of the land and for the organization of supplies from Germany in the hands of the various senior commands.

The preparation of Operation Typhoon had revealed that these organizational changes were long overdue. After the battle of Kiev, Hitler had recognized that a further effort would be required to destroy the bulk of the Red Army before Moscow, enabling Germany to gain strategic supremacy in 1941 and favourable starting-positions for continued fighting in 1942. A study by the War Economy and Armaments Department, stressing the need to occupy the Moscow–Tula region in order to prevent the Russians from recovering during the winter, provided the basis for this decision.[130] The offensive was thus intended to bring the major fighting to an end, giving the army in the east the opportunity for rest and rehabilitation during the winter pause before finishing off the war in the following year.

However, the conditions for such a development were deteriorating rapidly. German armaments production was now unable to meet even the running requirements of the war. In these circumstances, it was inconceivable that the

[126] KTB Befh. rückw. H.Geb. Süd, 77 (9 Aug. 1941), BA-MA RH 22/3.

[127] Report by Lt.-Gen. Schubert, head of Economic Staff East, departmental head, 25 Oct. 1941, KTB WiRüAmt/Stab 1941, 298, BA-MA, RW 19/165.

[128] OKW/WiRüAmt/Stab I/O No. 5321/41, order to Economic Staff East, 3 Nov. 1941, BA-MA RW 31/12.

[129] See Befehlsstelle Süd OKH/Gen Qu No. 2955/41, suggestion for reorganization into a Q.Qu. staff, 31 Oct. 1941, BA-MA RH 3/Arb. No. 111.

[130] See report by Maj. Zinnemann to departmental head, 6 Sept. 1941, KTB WiRüAmt/Stab 1941, 230, BA-MA RW 19/165.

armaments programme for the period after Barbarossa could be fulfilled.[131] Though the effects of the growing, conscription-induced labour shortage were limited by internal reshuffles and the use of Soviet prisoners of war, the shortage of raw materials had become an insuperable obstacle to the implementation of the armaments project. Such manifest difficulties could not be eliminated by a reduction in the technical equipment of the armed forces, nor by other specific measures. New ammunition production, which had already been curbed, had to be dispatched directly to the front as replacement supplies, since stocks of ammunition had been exhausted. Owing to the shortage of labour and raw materials, prospects for increasing production were minimal. In the tank sector, despite rising production figures, new manufacture was insufficient to replace losses on the eastern front.

At the beginning of November 1941, after the offensive against Moscow had ground to a halt, Germany seemed in danger of losing the race against time. Hopes were pinned on a last, decisive battle to bring the 1941 campaign to such a triumphant conclusion that men could be released to increase war production during the winter pause. Whether the weakened and battered army in the east was remotely capable of such a victory would depend first and foremost on the efficiency of the supply leadership, which had the task of bringing to the front whatever supplies were obtained from the Reich or procured from the occupied territories.

3. THE SUPPLY OF THE ARMY IN THE EAST UNTIL THE FAILURE BEFORE MOSCOW

In the preparatory phase of operations, the quartermaster-general had made great efforts, and proposed numerous measures, to solve the problem of providing adequate supplies for the army in the east.[132] The supply task which had to be mastered outstripped all historical precedents. Over 3 million men, with approximately 600,000 motor-vehicles and around the same number of horses, had to be supplied with rations, fuel, ammunition, replacement parts, and other requirements of war. All this had to be achieved along a front stretching over 2,500 kilometres from the North Cape to the Black Sea; within a few weeks, moreover, this front was due to reach operational objectives lying 1,500 kilometres from the starting-positions. The territorial, climatic, and geographical conditions were all very different from those previously encountered by German armies during the Second World War. Until the last mo-

---

[131] See in detail in Reinhardt, *Moskau*, 102 ff.

[132] On this see sect. I.IV.7 (*g*) at n. 73 (Klink); for the following see also the account by Creveld, *Supplying War*, 143–80; Versorgungsführung [Supply management], MGFA T-8-6, Vorbereitungen und Grundlagen der Heeresversorgung [Preparations and foundations of army supply], MGFA T-8-1; also OKH/GenStdH/Gen.Qu/Abt. VersFührung/Qu 2 No. 1/17591/42 geh., Erfahrungen aus dem Ostfeldzug für die Versorgungsführung [Experiences from the eastern campaign for supply management], 24 Mar. 1942, BA-MA H 10-51/2. On the significance of the railway system see Schüler, *Logistik*.

ment, the country which the Wehrmacht was setting out to conquer in a lightning campaign had been supplying the German war economy with indispensable strategic commodities, ranging from grain to oil. This flow inevitably dried up when the attack was launched. It was the task of the economic leadership to survive on the meagre stocks available until imports—now obtained through the economic exploitation of the country—could be resumed.

The role of the Army High Command was to calculate and obtain in advance the outlay that would be necessary to achieve the envisaged goals of conquest. Some of the factors involved were almost impossible to predict. These included the speed of the advance (on which depended the consumption of fuel), the intensity of enemy resistance (which determined expenditure of ammunition), and—most of all—the duration of the campaign. Army High Command was too ready to rely on optimistic assumptions: that the expenditure of ammunition would be no greater than during the campaign against France; that much of the army's food could be obtained from the land; and that the Red Army could be completely destroyed in front of the Dnieper–Dvina line.

Even if these assumptions were correct, difficulties remained which overstretched the capacities of the Wehrmacht. For example, the problem of supplying tyres was almost impossible to solve because of the bottleneck in rubber supplies in Germany. From the outset, a high level of wastage had to be expected in the motorized columns, which had to negotiate the few and poor roads and the trackless terrain. Virtually no replacements were available. Armoured vehicles were also affected by the shortage because the development of a pure metal track was still not complete, and the rubber-padded tracks in use were not sufficiently durable.

Most serious of all was the fuel shortage. Although civilian and military consumption had been drastically reduced before the start of the campaign, and the motorization of the army was kept within extremely narrow limits, a reserve of three monthly consumption quotas was all that had been provided. Direct imports from Romania to the eastern front promised to provide some relief. On the other hand, captured stocks would be of little assistance, since Soviet fuels had a lower octane rating and could not be used in German engines without adaptation. The previous year there had been moves to assimilate German and Soviet fuel quality, but these had been thwarted by the breakdown of the negotiations involving IG-Farben in Moscow.[133] Overall, it had to be assumed that there would be a fuel shortage by July at the latest.

Another problem area was the enormous need for replacement parts by the army in the east. This was caused not only by the expected wear and tear on motor-vehicles, but also by the use of over 2,000 different types of vehicle[134] as a result of the use of captured material. More than a million different spare

---

[133] See sect. I.III at nn. 75–6.   [134] See Krumpelt, *Material*, 187.

parts were required in the area covered by Army Group Centre alone. Owing first to the multiplicity of types, and second to the inadequate production of replacement parts in Germany, it proved impossible to provide sufficient supplies to compensate for breakdowns and the poor state of many vehicles. The inevitable result was a steady decline in combat-readiness and levels of motorization.

In the ammunition sector, the Chief of Army Armament Programmes had initially demanded a reserve of twelve monthly consumption quotas, based on the highest levels of consumption during the French campaign. This could not be achieved because ammunition manufacture had to take second place to weapons production. Beyond the two to three basic issues, the army in the east had minimal reserves at its disposal.

Overall, the quartermaster-general had to assume that supplies from the Reich would be meagre. The ministry of food supply refused to provide rations, telling the Wehrmacht to live off the land. On the eve of the campaign, the manufacture of new weapons, equipment, and ammunition was restricted still further; the army's already small share of armaments was reduced in favour of the other services of the armed forces. Larger reserves of men and material were not available either in the training army or in other formations of the army in the field.

The problem of providing adequate supplies was overshadowed by the difficulty of transferring to the front such material as was available. Logistically, the sheer extent of the planned operations could be mastered only with the help of the railway system. The railway network in the Soviet Union, however, was inadequate. Apart from consisting of only a small number of lines, the Soviet network also used a wider gauge, which prevented a trouble-free takeover by the Germans.[135] It was no great technical problem to move the rails to the 8.9-cm. narrower German gauge, but this would still take more men and time than the Wehrmacht could afford if it hoped to prevent the Red Army from retreating into the vast Russian hinterland. Their intention to wage a lightning campaign forced the Germans to rely more than before on the use of motor-vehicle convoys, requiring increased costs (fuel, wear and tear, men) for smaller payloads. Some 1,600 lorries were needed to replace the capacity of a double-track stretch of railway.[136] Furthermore, there were not even enough motor-vehicles available to equip all the divisions of the army in the east with the planned motorized supply columns. Despite the use of large numbers of captured vehicles, 77 infantry divisions were equipped only with horse-drawn transport columns; each, in addition, received 200 wooden peasant carts.

By means of a systematic integration of motorized transport capacity, it proved possible to deploy 20,000 t. of haulage capacity with each army group.

---

[135] On this see Pottgießer, *Deutsche Reichsbahn*, 24 ff., and Die Bedeutung der Eisenbahn [The significance of the railway], MGFA T-8-27.

[136] Creveld, *Supplying War*, 143.

This consisted of heavy trailer lorries belonging to the Reich railway and civilian transport hauliers, which were called up with their drivers and amalgamated into three motor-vehicle regiments.[137] No further reserves wer available. The plan was for this system to cover the first 500 kilometres in one fell swoop, and then to establish a new supply-base for the second phase with the help of the railway. The Wehrmacht had no choice but to adopt this combination of road and rail. At most, the lorries could bring in about 10,000 t. of supplies per day to the front on their ever longer journeys, i.e. roughly 70 t. for each division; the estimated requirement of the mobile divisions, however, was 300 t. per day. In order to supply the armies over a distance of over 1,000 kilometres by motor convoys alone, transport capacity would have had to be increased tenfold. Germany lacked both the fuel and the vehicles to achieve this. A fully motorized supply-system would have been sensible for Operation Barbarossa, because of the intended rapidity of the operations and the problems of rail transport. During the Second World War, however, only the American army managed to achieve such a performance.

Army High Command attempted to find a new solution to cope with the two heterogeneous masses of the army in the east, one of which was advancing in front of the other. Its plan was to make the mobile assault troops independent of a supply-base in the first stages of the campaign, and to prevent the lorry convoys on their journey from the supply-depots to the most advanced units from becoming entangled with the marching infantry columns. This was to be achieved by equipping the motorized divisions with an extra 'suitcase' of supplies, consisting of 400–500 t. of transport capacity, integrated with the fighting troops. After supplies were consumed or unloaded, the lorries were to be taken back behind the front. There they would join the large-volume haulage vehicles in creating a 'necklace' of supply-bases. Starting from each army group's supply district, which was sited close to the border and was already partly stocked, bases were to be established at intervals of 100–200 kilometres to supply the various armies. As soon as motorized convoy capacity became available and the railways were made usable, the Army Group Supply District was to be moved further into captured territory, and then supplied from the rear by rail alone.

To direct and supervise this new system, the quartermaster-general established a field agency directly subordinate to him with each army group.[138] Its task was to direct the staffs of the assistant chiefs of staff in the separate armies. These would remain independent of the troop commanders, and would be able to set up priorities in the management of supplies. To this end, the haulage facilities and a range of supply-depots, field hospitals, equipment stores, and workshops were integrated into the supply district, and placed under the control of the field agencies. The separation of the army groups

---

[137] Windisch, *Nachschubtruppe*, 37 ff.
[138] For details see Fähndrich, Aufgaben und Arbeit der Außenstellen, MGFA T-8-2.

from the management of supplies enabled the quartermaster-general to set his own priorities and, if necessary, to establish a balance between the different sectors of the front. Yet the danger remained that the control of operations and the management of supplies were not always synchronized. At the beginning of 1942 the field agencies were therefore reorganized into Army Group Assistant Chief of Staff offices (Oberquartiermeisterstäbe der Heeresgruppen).

Other errors of organization occurred elsewhere. For example, the quartermaster-general had control over supplies from Army High Command stockpiles, and over the depots and haulage vehicles, but he had no authority over the railways which were operating between them. These were under the control of the Chief of Wehrmacht Transport, Lieutenant-General Rudolf Gercke.[139] This OKW department gathered individual requests for supplies, and decided on the final allocation of trains. The army's quartermaster-general could therefore bring supplies to the railway, and fetch them from the unloading-point, but he had little control over what quantities arrived at the destination, or when. The interests and approaches of the Army High Command and OKW did not always coincide. Furthermore, Gercke used his own troops, badly equipped and ill-prepared for their tasks in Russia, on this railway service. OKW's Authorized Transport Officer with each army group had authority over the Commander of Railway Engineers, with appropriate construction teams and a Field Railway Command of 22,000 men for the operation and development of the tracks prepared by the engineers. Though each army normally required its own stretch of line to supply it, the railway troops were seldom able to re-lay and operate more than one main line per army group. In the most favourable circumstances, four companies of railway engineers managed to re-lay 20 kilometres in 24 hours.[140]

In these conditions, it is surely very doubtful whether the ambitious operational objectives could have been achieved even if enemy resistance had collapsed rapidly, as the German leadership expected. In theory, the balance achieved between rail, wheel, and caterpillar track was the best that could be obtained. At the same time, however, there was no way of keeping the flow of supplies constant or distributing them evenly. As the Germans penetrated further eastwards, and formations sent increasing demands to the supply controllers, the supply of men and materials was bound to diminish. Difficulties were intensified because logistical issues had not been taken adequately into account during the planning and implementation of operations. Army High Command intended to achieve victory by means of rapid armoured spearheads—but not in the Ukrainian countryside, where conditions favoured tanks, nor with the support of fully motorized supplies—towards the vital

---

[139] Inf. Gen. from 1 Apr. 1942. On this subject in general see Rohde, *Wehrmachttransportwesen*, and Die Steuerung der Bahntransporte [The direction of railway transports], MGFA T-8-26.

[140] See Die Bedeutung der Eisenbahn [The significance of the railway], MGFA T-8-27.

oilfields of the Caucasus. Instead, victory was to be achieved in central Russia, which offered less favourable opportunities for movement, and obtained with a supply apparatus which became increasingly dependent on the railway and horse-drawn vehicles as the advance moved to the east. Nevertheless, the military élite had no doubt that the operation would be successful. Far from adjusting their operational objectives to the limited resources available, they considered that they might even have been too cautious in their calculations, and might reach their objectives even more quickly.[141]

In fact, the first few days of the campaign brought unpleasant surprises. Though the mobile divisions with their 'suitcases' advanced rapidly to the east and carried out the first encircling operations, the great bulk of the infantry divisions with their horse-drawn transport columns fell ever further behind. As the empty lorries travelled back from the armoured spearheads through the vast unsecured area between the two groups, the most advanced sections of the railway engineers began work repairing and re-laying the tracks. This was an unprecedented development in modern warfare: a section of the supply apparatus was advancing ahead of the bulk of the army instead of following in its wake. Inevitably, it resulted in heavy casualties.

Though Army High Command had been aware that the few roads were in poor condition, the sheer extent of the difficulties was greater than had been expected. The surfaced roads were not capable of bearing the heavy lorry traffic, and were often ruined after a few days. Unsurfaced roads were badly rutted by the horse-drawn vehicles; after heavy rainfall at the beginning of July 1941, these roads became little more than quagmires. The resulting breakdowns, including the losses caused by enemy action, amounted to 25 per cent of the haulage-vehicle capacity.[142] In Army Group Centre this figure rose to over 30 per cent by 20 July. A major problem was the fact that repair facilities, still sited far to the rear in the Government-General or the Reich itself, could not be brought to the front.

The rapid decline in available motorized transport capacity was accompanied by an unexpected increase in fuel consumption. Owing to poor road conditions and tactical detours, the daily requirement of the army in the east rose from the original estimate of 9,000 t. to 12,000.[143] In practice, fuel sufficient for 100 kilometres under normal conditions was enough for only 70 kilometres in the Russian countryside. As a result of periods of high temperatures during the day, the fuel was often unserviceable, and its use led to breakdowns. In Armoured Group 2, the spearhead of Army Group Centre, 30 Mark III and 4 Mark IV tanks broke down at the beginning of July 1941 because captured oil had been used.[144]

[141] Cecil, *Hitler's Decision*, 129.

[142] Halder, *Diaries*, 1026–9 (11 July 1941).

[143] Discussion between Thomas and Wagner on 11 July 1941. KTB WiRüAmt/Stab 1941, 140, BA-MA RW 19/165.

[144] KTB, Pz. AOK 2/O.Qu., 6 July 1941, BA-MA RH 21-2/v. 819.

Much of the damage sustained by the motor-vehicles could have been avoided if there had been enough time and fuel to prepare the drivers for the extraordinary conditions they would meet in Russia, and the special driving skills they would require.[145] A shortage of maps also necessitated travel in convoy, causing considerable loss of time in the event of a major breakdown. Many of the civilian vehicles used by the troops, especially the motor-cars, proved to be unserviceable because of their low ground clearance. In summer they bottomed out on sandy and sodden tracks, and in winter they were stuck in snowdrifts. As a result, these vehicles frequently suffered irreparable damage to their oil-sumps and transmission. During the advance, many breakdowns were also caused by broken suspensions. Stocks of spring steel in the replacement-part depots, provided on the basis of demand during the French campaign, were exhausted after a short period, compelling the armies to use their own lorries to fetch small amounts of spring steel from Königsberg and Elbing, or from Stuttgart and Ulm. Tyres proved unable to withstand the abrasion of the sandy tracks, but could be replaced only infrequently. On 10 July 1941, Army High Command informed the armies that no more tyres at all would be supplied.[146]

Difficulties and breakdowns plagued the numerous horse-drawn vehicles as well as the motor-vehicles. Their usual rubber tyres were rapidly worn to shreds, and had to be replaced with wooden wheels clad with iron hoops. Moreover, the German horses were not up to the demands made on them. The heavy columns and field howitzer detachments, in particular, were held fast by the deep, loose sandy ground. The number of horses lost through exhaustion rose inexorably, leaving some infantry divisions faced with the prospect of having to leave the heavy artillery behind. In some cases, radical temporary measures were adopted with the disbanding of the heavy convoys and the motorized baggage train. For example, 167th Infantry Division maintained its mobility and fighting strength by leaving its 'heavy baggage', vehicles, and equipment in a divisional camp at Slonim, together with 200 men who lived independently under military administration and did agricultural work.[147] The camp was disbanded only in the winter of 1942, when the division, inadequately clothed and equipped, was forced to end its advance 800 kilometres further east.

In the first phase of the campaign, when supplies had to be transported mainly by road, the numerous vehicle breakdowns inevitably reduced the movement of supplies. Very few replacement vehicles were available. Until the end of July, only about one in ten broken-down vehicles was replaced by a new one. Thereafter, Army High Command refused to provide more vehicles

[145] See Die Versorgung der 68. Infanterie-Division [The supply of 68th Inf. Div.], 18, MGFA T-8-13.
[146] See KTB AOK 9/O.Qu., activity report army motor transport officer, 14 July 1941, 2, BA-MA, 9. Armee, 13904/1.
[147] See Die Versorgung der 167. Infanterie-Division [The supply of 167th Inf. Div.], MGFA T-8-11.

because of the shortage of lorries, and because it planned to establish new formations.[148]

This reduction in motorized strength inevitably led to bottlenecks in supplies, because the railway network also performed below expectation. Army High Command had hoped that, in addition to the re-laying of tracks, extensive parts of the Soviet railway system could be taken over unaltered and operated with captured rolling-stock. However, the Red Army succeeded in evacuating most of its locomotives and wagons, partly because the most advanced German formations paid insufficient attention to this danger.[149] The only solution was to re-lay a major part of the railway network to the German gauge, and to operate it using German material. However, even this proved to be more difficult than expected. The bed of the Russian tracks was generally so weak, and the rails so lacking in load-carrying capacity, that the only German engines they could carry were light models dating from before the First World War. The railway system had also suffered serious damage: some rails had been torn up by the Russians with sleeper ploughs; many stations had been destroyed by the Luftwaffe; the German troops themselves had often inflicted excessive damage, such as the destruction of telephone lines, the burning of snow-fences and sleepers, the removal of serviceable railway material as scrap, etc. Moreover, since operations generally followed the roads, additional military operations were often necessary to clear the railway lines, further delaying efforts to put them back into operation.

Co-operation between the railway engineers and field railwaymen was seldom smooth. The engineers, who were expected to work quickly, frequently laid the track without regard to operational requirements. In many cases only one track was re-laid on two-track sections, so that important installations such as ramps and engine sheds were out of reach. The engineers' reports on the capacity of the lines proved to be too optimistic, since these took no account of the capacity of junction stations, or of the railways' own needs for coal and building material. In these conditions, Lieutenant-General Gercke's assessment of daily railway capacity was completely unrealistic.[150]

(a) Army Group North

The greatest problems of supply were undoubtedly to be found in the most northerly sector of the German–Soviet front, during the operation of German troops against Murmansk.[151] There were few transport networks and settlements in the subarctic tundra mountains, and the extreme climatic and geographical conditions made communications and supply very difficult to maintain. At the end of the year Mountain Corps Norway produced a devastating progress report complaining about the utter inadequacy of organiz-

[148] See activity report army motor transport officer (see n. 146), 3.
[149] Pottgießer, *Deutsche Reichsbahn*, 28.
[150] Rohde, *Wehrmachttransportwesen*. 173.
[151] See sect. II.III.1 (*b*) at n. 70 (Ueberschär).

ational and material conditions.[152] Supplies to this remote theatre were co-ordinated not by the quartermaster-general, but mainly by the OKW 'Home Staff Overseas'. This had to direct transports across the Baltic to Finland, and over the North Sea to Norway, and thence along the 500-km. long Arctic Sea route, or by sea to Kirkenes.

By comparison, Army Group North was relatively easy to supply. The distance from the jump-off base in East Prussia to Leningrad, its most important operational objective, was only about 750 km. At least in the former Baltic States, there was a relatively well-developed transport network. East of Lake Peipus, however, the countryside became more thickly wooded and trackless. Apart from the haulage vehicles, which were directly controlled by the quartermaster-general, the leader of Field Agency North, Major Alfred Toppe, was able to put to use about 50 lorry convoys and 10 motorized supply companies with bakeries, butchers, etc., plus the stocks of his supply district in East Prussia. With the capture of the Baltic ports, it was likely that some sea transport could be used to ease the strain on overland connections.

Toppe's greatest problem arose shortly after the beginning of the campaign, when Armoured Group 4 advanced with unexpected speed and left the infantry far behind. The tanks covered almost 350 km. within five days. When the armoured group's supply columns were held up on the advance roads by the following infantry during the day, serious temporary bottlenecks were created, which could be overcome only by air transport. In these circumstances, no further advance was possible until the supply-base was moved forward, thus condemning the tank formations to halt until 4 July. Thereafter, only limited new operations were possible. Even these required the entire haulage capacity of the army group to be concentrated behind Armoured Group 4, while 16th Army had to be held back. The delaying of the infantry advance had serious consequences on the approaches to Leningrad, when the armoured formations advanced into thickly wooded countryside which was unfavourable to tank operations. The armoured group was not deterred by the risk, and was eager to seize the opportunity for a rapid capture of Leningrad. It demanded that the entire transport capacity should be placed at its disposal to that end.[153] However, such a move would render Sixteenth and Eighteenth Armies immobile, while the armoured group itself would be dependent on long and vulnerable supply-lines. Field Marshal Ritter von Leeb could not be persuaded to take the risk; Armoured Group 4 was ordered to wait for the arrival of the infantry at the gates of Leningrad, where it faced a permanent supply crisis.

Meanwhile, though the railway troops had succeeded in making some

---

[152] Command Mountain Corps Norway/Ia No. 300/41 geh. Kdos., Erfahrungsbericht über den bisherigen Osteinsatz im Eismeergebiet [Experience of operations so far in the Arctic Ocean region], Dec. 1941, 16 ff., BA-MA. XIX. Geb.K., 76205.

[153] KTB Pz.Gr. 4/O.Qu., 63, 65 (9 and 10 July 1941), BA-MA RH 21-4/334.

500 km. of track usable,[154] only one train per day was arriving instead of the expected ten in Daugavpils, where Supply District North had been set up after its first move forward. The quartermaster-general had calculated that the tank formations could be provided with support from base as far as Leningrad.[155] However, his thinking would remain purely theoretical until the supply-base could be stocked with the necessary material, and until sufficient motorized convoys could be dispatched along supply-lines stretching several hundred kilometres to the front, and protected against the attacks of Soviet partisans. To have any hope of keeping pace with the rapid advance, it was necessary to make more use of captured rolling-stock on Russian tracks. However, the process of re-laying from German to Russian gauge soon became a bottleneck for the entire supply-system. The situation in Eydtkau and Siauliai became so catastrophic for a time that re-laying was taking up to eighty hours instead of the regulation three, and whole trains were being 'lost'. In these circumstances, only a small part of the network of track could be fully utilized. The army group, which demanded thirty-four trains per day to satisfy its needs, could count on receiving eighteen at most, and even this figure was reached only in exceptional cases.[156]

Though Field Agency North could argue that no unit had faced a dire emergency, complaints from the troops were increasing. In particular, Colonel-General Halder was very critical of the management of supplies.[157] Trains intended for his armoured group had been 'hijacked' by the infantry armies. The Luftwaffe was helping itself by claiming a larger share of the incoming trains than had been assigned to it, and guarding them with armed officer commandos. Neither Wagner nor Gercke was willing to take responsibility for the chaos, and there was very little improvement before the end of July despite the personal intervention of the commander-in-chief of the army.[158]

Railway capacity was inadequate to supply the front to the extent required, at the same time as laying in new stocks and moving the bases forward in line with the advance. The haulage vehicles therefore had to be used for this purpose. After their earlier losses, their capacity was only about 60 per cent of the original level. Heavy rainfall made the undulating roads of northern Russia impassable for lorries with trailers; on the other hand, unhitching the trailers virtually halved the transport capacity.[159] The use of the sea route to Riga, and the resumption of shipping traffic on Lake Peipus, brought some relief. In the second half of July the supply troops were fully engaged in advancing the supply-base from Daugavpils to Riga, and stocking up with supplies.

---

[154] For the schedule of supplies in Army Group North see the maps in the atlas of operations: 'Der Feldzug gegen die Sowjetunion, Kriegsjahr 1941' [The campaign against the Soviet Union, war year 1941), BA-MA RH 19/661 D.

[155] Halder, *Diaries*, 993–4 (1 July 1941), 996 (2 July 1941).

[156] See Creveld, *Supplying War*, 160–1.

[157] KTB Pz.Gr. 4/O.Qu., 77 (17 and 18 July 1941), BA-MA RH 21-4/334.

[158] See Creveld, *Supplying War*, 160.

[159] Versorgungsführung, 7, MGFA T-8-6.

There was some justice in the quartermaster-general's claim, in the face of complaints from Armoured Group 4, that the supply situation of Army Group North was much better than that of the rest of the eastern front.[160] Yet if the optimistic predictions of Wagner are compared with the actual results, it is clear that the unsatisfactory supply-system helped to prevent the rapid capture of Leningrad, which Hitler still regarded as one of the most important objectives of the campaign. The attack on Leningrad had to be postponed for supply reasons on seven occasions. Even Hoepner's desperate plan to attack the huge city with a single armoured corps was vetoed by Wagner, because he felt unable to guarantee the necessary supplies.[161]

When the offensive was eventually resumed on 8 August 1941, the defence of Leningrad was prepared. Heavy rainfall made the roads impassable, so that even the troops' urgent demands for ammunition could not be met. On 11 September Hitler withdrew Armoured Group 4 for the attack on Moscow. Leningrad was now to be destroyed by the Luftwaffe, and starved out.

(b) Army Group South

The operational objectives of Army Group South were even wider and more varied than those of Army Group North. The army group was intended to achieve the most important economic goals of the campaign, in the Ukraine, the Donets basin, and the Caucasus. The advance from Poland, south of the Pripet marshes, led into countryside which was favourable to tanks. However, this opportunity could not be fully exploited at first, because most of the mobile troops were deployed with Army Group Centre. Moreover, Army Group South encountered the bulk of the enemy forces in the Ukraine. The Soviet forces were well led, and offered vigorous resistance which slowed down the German advance. The bitter fighting led to an unexpectedly high ammunition requirement, which depended almost entirely on the achievements of the haulage vehicles, since only a few stretches of railway line were available. However, in the middle of July heavy rainfall turned the black Ukrainian soil into deep mud, forcing up the rate of breakdowns in the lorry convoys to 50 per cent. Supply-units were therefore forced to switch from motor-vehicles to peasant carts to a greater extent than had been anticipated.[162] This led to a significant fall in productivity, as incomparably more time and manpower had to be devoted to the horse-drawn convoys which were brought in to help the 'most modern army in the world' out of its supply difficulties. Added problems were caused by the delay in advancing the supply-base: supply-runs were often over 200 km. long, twice the distance considered acceptable.[163]

As in the other sectors of the front, by the end of July there was significant

---

[160] KTB Pz.Gr. 4/O.Qu., 95 (31 July 1941), BA-MA RH 21-4/334.

[161] Ibid. 99-100 (2 Aug. 1941).

[162] Halder, *Diaries*, 1061 (19 July 1941).

[163] Die Versorgung der 68. Infanterie-Divsion, 11, MGFA, T-8-13.

strain on the supply-system, there were increasing complaints from the troops, and reciprocal impounding of trains. In the operational planning of Barbarossa it had been envisaged that there would be a pause for rest and rehabilitation once the Dnieper–Dvina line was reached. During this period, following the destruction of most of the enemy's fighting strength, the formations would be restructured and fresh stocks provided for the second phase of the attack. In fact, this had not been achieved: in the sector of the front south of the Pripet marshes the encirclement of the strong Soviet formations had not been completed, while the German army had neither reached the course of the river nor established bridgeheads for the next move. Instead, Armoured Group 1 had to wait on the banks of the Dnieper for the infantry, while the enemy succeeded in establishing a new front. The Soviet Fifth Army held out in a gap between Army Group South and Army Group Centre, tying down significant parts of the inner flanking armies, preventing a concentration of forces for the advance across the Dnieper at Kiev, and hindering an orderly rehabilitation of the formations. In view of the continuing fighting, withdrawal of the armoured groups could not be contemplated. Meanwhile, the infantry was exhausted from fighting and marching to encircle the great pocket before becoming involved in repulsing the counter-offensive. It was no less in need of rest than the mobile formations.

In these circumstances, it was extremely important to advance the supply-base into the Dnieper bend. This was achieved only with considerable difficulties and delays, owing largely to the fact that the railway could provide only some of the necessary transports; the haulage vehicles that were required for the remainder had to make the entire journey as far as the former Polish border, 1,000 km. overall. When the offensive was continued across the Dnieper at the beginning of August, the supply-base had not been fully restocked, and bottlenecks inevitably intensified in the course of operations. For example, Armoured Group 1 had such low stocks of fuel and ammunition that incoming supply-trains had to be used to supply the immediate needs of the troops.[164] In the southern sector, it was hoped that the situation could be eased by exploiting the sea route to Nikolaev. An independent supply agency, the Assistant Chief of Staff Black Sea, was established for this purpose.[165] However, plans to use the Bug as a supply-route had to be abandoned because of the shortage of shipping capacity.

To prepare for the battle of Kiev, the quartermaster-general took personal charge of supply measures for Army Group South. Here the operation of motorized supply convoys played a bigger role than previously. For that reason, the haulage transport vehicles were withdrawn for rehabilitation at the end of August to be made ready for their forthcoming tasks. However, this measure met with little success, since the shortage of replacement parts prevented readiness for action from rising above the 70 per cent mark. Stocks

[164] KTB Pz.Gr. 1/O.Qu., 22, 23, 24 Aug. 1941, BA-MA RH 21-1/327.
[165] See Supply management, 6, 9, MGFA, T-8-6.

of spare parts were virtually exhausted. As the raw materials required for an increase in production were not available, the Army Ordnance Office argued that the critical question was whether the production of motor-vehicles should be reduced still further in favour of the manufacture of spare parts.[166] To maintain the current fleet of lorries, an annual production of 150,000 vehicles would have been necessary. In fact, only 39,000 lorries were built in 1941; a further weakening of this vital component of the transport system on the eastern front was inevitable. The allocation of an entire month's instalment of new lorries in August 1941 brought some relief, but covered only about half of the running loss (see Table II.vi.1).

There was thus little prospect of providing Army Group South with adequate stocks and guaranteeing further supplies, because the railway system was also overstretched. The most that was achieved was to supplement the first issue of the troops, and to cover regular consumption. Where no serious supply problems emerged in the course of the battle, this was due largely to favourable weather conditions, which made it easier to bring in motorized transports from the railhead at Pervomaysk. Overall, however, the two railway lines available to the army group were not sufficient to bring up adequate supplies. Instead of the 24 trains per day that were demanded, Rundstedt obtained 14.5 on average, or less than half as much as Army Group Centre.[167] In Supply Catchment Area South, where the trains were assembled, chaos ensued when one line was blocked by flooding. Trains frequently arrived at their destination only half loaded.

The greatest concern was how to get the railway traffic across the Dnieper. When the Germans failed to capture the Dnieper bridges intact, the process of re-laying the track came to a temporary halt. During the months of work to rebuild the bridges, a difficult ferry service had to be operated. In these circumstances, the army group considered that its operational objectives could not be achieved.[168] Nevertheless, after the liquidation of the Kiev pocket the advance was initially so rapid that Armoured Group 1 was cut off from its rear communications at the beginning of October, because the infantry columns were blocking the supply traffic. When the muddy season began on 6 October, the offensive generally came to a standstill. Many difficulties were caused by the policy of systematic, long-term destruction practised by the Soviets in the approaches to the Donets reagion. All convoys were brought to a halt on the unusable roads, and there were also significant delays in getting the railway into operation. Men and materials could no longer be brought up by road; instead, resort had to be made to time-consuming 'over-head' building.[169] On occasion a shuttle operation was maintained with the scant rolling-stock that

---

[166] Discussion between representatives of Army Ordnance Office and deparmental head, KTB WiRüAmt/Stab 1941, 219 (26 Aug. 1941), BA-MA RW 19/165.

[167] KTB Außenstelle OKH/GenQu/H.Gr. Süd, 16 Aug.–30 Sept. 1941, 4, BA-MA RH 3/Arb. No. 104.

[168] Ibid. 8.   [169] Die Bedeutung der Eisenbahn, 16, MGFA T-8-27.

TABLE II.vi.1. *Armoured Fighting Vehicles and Assault-guns on the Eastern Front between 22 June 1941 and 31 January 1942*[a]

	June 1941			July 1941			August 1941		
	Total losses	Allocation[b] (captured)	Manufacture (delivery)	Total losses	Allocation[b] (captured)	Manufacture[c] (planned)	Total losses	Allocation[b] (captured)	Manufacture (delivery)
Mark I tank	34	—	—	146	—	—	171	—	—
Mark II and F tank	11	—	15	112	—	20	104	1	36
Mark III tank	21	—	133	155	45	115	74	—	179
Mark 38(t) tank	33	—	65	182	27	65	183	8	64
Mark IV tank	15	—	38	109	15	41	68	—	44
Assault-gun	3	—	56	11	4	47	26	—	50
Armoured tractor	12	—	665	15	5	690	95	3	613
Unarmoured tractor	46	24		459	8(3)		473	118(8)	
Armoured command vehicle	1	—	5	17	—	15	12	2	—
Armoured scout car[d]	26	—	35	145	21	39	114	12	77
Truck	646	152	3,479	6,281	1,251(525)	1,383	7,655	3,733(1,538)	3,174
Other motor-vehicles	1,074	97	34	14,251	818(290)	92	18,066	1,454(406)	62
Light Field Howitzer 18 (horse-drawn)	12		89	66		100	124		130
Light Field Howitzer 18 (powered)	13			65			58		
Heavy Field Howitzer 18 (horse-drawn)	9		48	26		66	53		51
Heavy Field Howitzer 18 (powered)	10			64			48		
Heavy 10-cm. K 18	4		5	19		13	11		9
3.7-cm. anti-tank gun	135		183	837		100	817		135
5-cm. anti-tank gun 38	17		163	107		220	70		250
Light infantry gun 18	12		117	155		115	256		100
Heavy infantry gun 33	4		46	44		52	50		48

had been found locally, using railway personnel flown in by towed glider. Armoured Group 1 was able to continue its advance only by having the entire motorized capacity concentrated in its service until it too came to a standstill on 13 October. From then on, the supply situation deteriorated rapidly. On 17 October it was already being described as catastrophic.[170] Three days later, no supplies at all could be got to the front, forcing the armoured group to use its last stocks and live off the land. No fundamental change was to be expected before the onset of winter frosts, though a temporary improvement in the

[170] KTB Pz.Gr. 1/O.Qu., 17 and 20 Oct. 1941, BA-MA RH 21-1/327.

TABLE II.VI.I *(cont.)*

	September 1941			October 1941			November 1941		
	Total losses	Allocation[b] (captured)	Manufacture (delivery)	Total losses	Allocation[b] (captured)	Manufacture[c] (planned)	Total losses	Allocation[b] (captured)	Manufacture (delivery)
Mark I tank	7	—	—	18	—	—	33	12	—
Mark II and F tank	32	5	37	65	1	48	30	16	45
Mark III tank	104	6	178	77	187	179	116	39	206
Mark 38(t) tank	62	1	76	85	72	53	149	—	50
Mark IV tank	23	2	46	55	56	51	38	7	52
Assault-gun	12	—	38	23	7	71	10	—	46
Armoured tractor	21	1	872	23	—	650	77	19	688
Unarmoured tractor	337	34(1)		140	28(1)		521	32	
Armoured command vehicle	17	—	2	14	—	—	6	5	—
Armoured scout car[d]	99	22	28	72	3	16	79	48	30
Truck	4,943	2,018(917)	2,905	3,184	2,703(1,417)	3,741	5,996	1,348(378)	3,765
Other motor-vehicles	9,666	1,573(415)	62	5,401	927(323)	131	10,371	808(124)	100
Light Field Howitzer 18 (horse-drawn)	66		79	78		45	87		45
Light Field Howitzer 18 (powered)	35			19			28		
Heavy Field Howitzer 18 (horse-drawn)	20		32	26		39	27		10
Heavy Field Howitzer 18 (powered)	22			32			17		
Heavy 10-cm K 18	12		5	19		—	10		9
3.7-cm. anti-tank gun	391		95	299		39	146		3
5-cm. anti-tank gun 38	31		152	49		241	17		212
Light infantry gun 18	132		65	84		83	62		40
Heavy infantry gun 33	45		24	53		19	32		46

[continued over leaf]

weather at the end of October permitted a single corps to continue the advance on Rostov. By that time, almost all transport movements were made solely by peasant cart. Sixth Army also managed to avoid the destroyed Dnieper bridge at Kremenchug by using ferries; temporarily, it operated the stretch to Kharkov with some captured Soviet goods wagons drawn by rail lorries. These were heavy motorized tractors which were equipped with interchangeable road and rail wheels, the latter adjustable for wide and normal gauge.[171]

[171] Die Bedeutung der Eisenbahn, 15, MGFA T-8-27.

TABLE II.VI.I (*cont.*)

	December 1941			January 1942			Total 22 June 1941–31 Jan. 1942		
	Total losses	Allocation[b] (captured)	Manufacture (delivery)	Total losses	Allocation[b] (captured)	Manufacture[c] (planned)	Total losses	Allocation[b] (captured)	Manufacture (delivery)
Mark I tank	19	—	—	22	30	—	450	42	—
Mark II and F tank	70	15	50	68	31	38	492	69	289
Mark III tank	113	—	188	160	55	159	820	332	1,337
Mark 38(t) tank	102	—	50	27	—	59	823	108	482
Mark IV tank	40	—	56	48	22	59	396	102	387
Assault-gun	19	1	40	53	3	45	157	15	393
Armoured tractor	44	—	587	18	3	504	305	31	5,269
Unarmoured tractor	391	31		579	44		2,946	319(13)	
Armoured command vehicle	12	—	15	37	18	14	116	25	51
Armoured scout car[d]	72	1	11	38	48	10	645	155	246
Truck	5,189	855(128)	3,278	5,976	625(57)	3,210	39,870	12,685(4,960)	27,535
Other motor-vehicles	7,231	756(31)	139	8,734	331(22)	242	74,794	6,764(1,611)	862
Light Field Howitzer 18 (horse-drawn)	277		45	108		45	818		578
Light Field Howitzer 18 (powered)	175			89			482		
Heavy Field Howitzer 18 (horse-drawn)	71		9	69		26	301		281
Heavy Field Howitzer 18 (powered)	129			19			341		
Heavy 10-cm K 18	33		—	24		—	132		41
3.7-cm. anti-tank gun	651		—	438		4	3,714		559
5-cm. anti-tank gun 38	135		225	49		315	475		1,778
Light infantry gun 18	198		45	148		40	1,047		605
Heavy infantry gun 33	74		27	50		37	352		299

[a] The most important of the army's big equipment and weapons have been chosen. Figures of losses and allocation are taken from the 10-day reports of OKH/GenQu, BA-MA III W 805/5 ff. Obvious errors in addition have been corrected. These lead to minor divergences from the overall figures which appear in the GenQu reports from autumn 1941 and are frequently referred to in the literature; see e.g. the table in *KTB OKW* i. 115. Figures on manufacture were taken from Überblick über den Rüstungsstand des Heeres (Waffen und Gerät) Juni 1941–Januar 1942, BA-MA RH 8/v. 1090, 1091.

[b] Supply figures for artillery pieces are unavailable. Until Oct. 1941 losses were replaced on a running basis from the equipment depots of the GenQu or through deliveries from BdE and OQu West. Thereafter losses were not replaced because it was thought that divisions in the east would soon be recalled, leaving their heavy equipment and weapons to cover the losses sustained by the remaining units.

[c] As no evidence is available, the planned total from the survey of the preceding month has been used.

[d] Includes armoured radio vans, heavy and light armoured scout cars, observation cars, Panhard radio vans and Panhard scout cars, Somua and Hotchkiss tanks, and self-propelled mounts.

By means of similar stopgaps, also in the sector covered by Armoured Group 1, a first supply train was brought up in October via Mariupol to the Sea of Asov. But even after the railway bridges at Dnepropetrovsk were brought back into operation on 6 November 1941, and in winter, when rails were laid over the frozen Dnieper, the transport achievements of the railway could not begin to satisfy supply needs. Only about a third of the running supply requirements could be met, and that at the expense of bringing up the supplies necessary to restock.[172] This development was already perceptible in outline in the late autumn of 1941. During the whole of October, only 195 trains arrived at the Dnieper base instead of the expected 724.[173] The presence of German-allied troops proved to be another burden; almost immobile and badly equipped, these had to be additionally supplied by the German managers.

Army High Command was unwilling to accept the escalating supply crisis as a reason for Army Group South coming to a standstill.[174] However, Halder was forced to recognize that the army and corps commanders saw no possibility of continuing the advance to the Don, let alone to the Caucasus, in these circumstances. Further advances along the railway line to the east seemed possible only after winter restocking had been completed. The onset of the period of first on 14 November 1941 brought fresh unpleasant surprises: huge numbers of vehicle engines broke down in temperatures of $-20\,^{\circ}$C because of a lack of antifreeze; railway transport also deteriorated; the ice floes on the Dnieper hindered the passage of ferries with supplies. Field Agency South eventually reported that the troops could not be supplied even with essentials.[175] The success of Amoured Group 1 in reaching Rostov at all is remarkable. It paid a heavy price, including the deterioration of the army's vehicles to a state in which they were deemed 'no longer suitable for mobile warfare' owing to high losses, wear and tear, and the lack of repair facilities.[176]

The case of Army Group South proved the accuracy of the original assumption that the army in the east could be properly supplied only within an area 500 km. deep, i.e. as far as the Dnieper. Though the supply organization did its best to support the operation by means of improvisation, it too suffered from organizational weaknesses. The Army High Command, Hitler, and von Rundstedt all failed to take full account of the fact that the troops had reached the end of their tether. Instead, the Supreme Command assumed that the attack could be resumed before the end of 1941 through Rostov, although even this objective lay outside the range of the logistical apparatus. The successful

---

[172] See Pz.AOK 1/O.Qu. No. 2871/42 geh., Bericht über die Versorgungslage der 1. Panzerarmee im Winter 1941/42 [Report on the supply situation of First Arm. Army in winter 1941–2], 1 Apr. 1942, appendix 1, BA-MA RH 21-1/332.

[173] KTB Außenstelle OKH/O.Qu./H.Gr. Süd, Oct. 1941, 8, BA-MA RH 3/Arb. No. 104.

[174] See also sect. II.1.1(c) at n. 301 (Klink).

[175] Creveld, *Supplying War*, 166.

[176] See Pz.AOK 1/O.Qu., Comment on the reports on conditions of First Armd. Army, 30 Nov. 1941, 2, BA-MA RH 21-1/332.

Soviet counter-offensive, which led to the abandonment of Rostov, forced them to change their minds.

(c) Army Group Centre
(See the Annexe Volume, No. 26)

According to the plans of Army High Command, the outcome of the campaign was to be resolved in central Russia. For that reason, the biggest of the three army groups was deployed here with the bulk of the armoured formations, which were to destroy the enemy and advance on Moscow in rapid pincer operations. Yet despite these ambitious objectives, there was no genuine concentration of forces, which could have been achieved by integrating all the mobile troops and all the haulage transport. Not even for the thirty-one infantry divisions and sixteen mobile formations deployed was a fully motorized and efficient logistical apparatus established. The inadequate provision of motor-vehicles for the Wehrmacht was partly to blame for this situation. Other difficulties were created by the geographical and transport conditions of the region: owing to the inadequate road system, supplies had to be transferred to the railways as the advance moved further from the starting-point. Apart from the question of whether and how quickly the Soviet railway system could be got back into operation, the small number of serviceable tracks offered most cause for anxiety.

Though the terrain was less favourable to tanks than the Ukraine, it could be covered more easily than the countryside of northern Russia. Nevertheless, Army Group Centre did not advance as quickly as Army Group North. This was partly due to the fact that there were fewer roads in the sector covered by Bock's army group and the marching discipline of the formations was not sufficiently strict. Enormous masses of infantry blocked the Bug bridges in the first days, preventing the haulage vehicles intended for Guderian from crossing the river until the evening of 25 June; Armoured Group 2 had to be supplied with fuel by air.[177] Conditions in Ninth Army, where infantry and horse-drawn supply convoys struggled with Hoth's Armoured Group 3 for priority on the roads, were equally confused.[178] Frequent detours into the countryside dramatically increased the fuel consumption of the tank formations. However, this did not initially lead to difficulties, owing to the capture of a big Soviet fuel depot at Baranovichi; after appropriate technical processing, almost a third of the group's fuel consumption was for a time covered from captured stocks.

The spearheads of Guderian's armoured group reached the Dnieper, and thus the limits of assured supply, on 2 July 1941. Until that time no serious bottlenecks had occurred, although the dusty conditions and the shortage of spare parts led to breakdowns in the tank formations. With the advance so rapid, supply had to be concentrated on the fuel sector. Though supply stocks

---

[177] KTB Pz.Gr. 2/O.Qu., 2 July 1941, BA-MA RH 21-2/v. 819.
[178] KTB AOK 9/O.Qu., 22 June–6 July 1941, BA-MA, 9. Armee, 13904/1.

were full when the Dnieper was crossed, Guderian's assessment of his supply situation had been too optimistic.[179] There was a real danger that the offensive would be forced to a standstill sooner or later if serious enemy resistance was encountered. If that occurred, the overstretched supply-lines would be unable to respond to the dramatic increase in ammunition expenditure.

Following the deployment directive for Army Group Centre, Guderian attempted to reach the area Roslavl–Yelyna–Smolensk as quickly as possible. Yelyna was situated 750 km. from the supply-base, scarcely within reach of motorized supply. The transport problem thus became the dominant factor. Moreover, the important Warsaw–Minsk–Smolensk railway route was not brought into operation quickly enough. Large parts of the remaining railway network remained under Soviet control for longer than expected, and could not be used to ease the situation. At the beginning of July railway capacity was just sufficient to supply Armoured Group 3. Ninth Army was completely dependent on haulage transport, although the distance from the supply-base was now almost 400 km., and the roads were in poor condition.

Supply District Centre had been established in the area around Warsaw and Suwalki. In the first days of the invasion it had begun to set up supply-bases on the line Alitus–Voronovo–Lesna in order to shorten the supply-routes. Each supply-base included ammunition, fuel and foodstuffs depots, field hospitals, maintenace and repair workshops, bakers' and butchers' companies, a spare-parts detachment, and a supply battalion or else a detachment of the Reich Labour Service, as well as a Vehicle Transport Detachment, and public-order services. At the end of June 1941 preparations were made to create a new backbone of support for the supply-system, beginning on the line Molodechno–Minsk–Slutsk. However, the evacuation and movement of the workers and administrative personnel from the supply district in the deployment area took far too long.[180] For one thing, the supply district was still at full stretch, and was therefore reluctant to give up supply troops. In addition, there was insufficient transport available to stock the new bases. Railway capacity remained below requirements, so that motorized transport capacity was already at full stretch moving the necessary regular requirements from the supply district and from the bases along the advance roads to the troops. A great deal of time would have been saved if spare supply troops and motor-vehicle convoys not needed in the Warsaw area had been available for rebuilding work.

The new base, the Dnieper Supply District, was extended eastwards to the line Polotsk–Lepel–Borisov–Bobruysk by the middle of July. Restocking proceeded slowly once the track had been re-laid, and the railway was operating efficiently enough to bring increased supplies to the new bases. Halder and Wagner had intended that the Dnieper base would be ready by the end of July,

---

[179] See Krumpelt, *Material*, 165.

[180] On this see Fähndrich, Der Aufbau des Versorgungsbezirks Dnjepr [Structure of the Supply District Dnieper], MGFA T–8–4.

when it would be able to guarantee the tank formations an operational range as far as Moscow. Daily deliveries of 37,000 t. of supplies would have been necessary to achieve this objective. These conditions were not fulfilled: when Guderian crossed the Dnieper, the new base contained munitions sufficient for only five days' fighting, fuel for 40 km., and half a day's rations.[181] Yet the organizational structure of the base did keep pace with the advance. At the end of July the bases of Orsha and Smolensk were established along the army group's main line of advance.

At the same time, a serious ammunition crisis developed in the Yelnya salient.[182] When Soviet counter-attacks forced the German formations to mount a five-week defensive battle, the high level of ammunition expenditure could not be made good because of the long, overstretched communications with the rear. As long as the railway system was unable to transport regular daily supply requirements sufficiently close to the front, the troops would remain dependent on the efficiency of motorized transport capacity. Stocks at the advanced supply-bases were so low that the motorized convoys were compelled to travel back to the nearest working railhead—a distance of 750 km. Fundamentally, the crisis at Yelnya was no accident; the investigation ordered by Hitler found no evidence of a dereliction of duty. But only time would tell whether the right lessons were being learnt from the overstretching of supply management.

When priority was given to ammunition supply at the beginning of August, a drastic cut in the supply of fuel and rations was necessary. The armies which had been sent into action to liquidate the pocket at Smolensk were thus placed in a difficult situation. For some units, the distances were reduced by the advancing of the supply-bases—on the southern flank the Slutsk–Bobruysk–Mogilev axis, and on the northern flank, which was particularly difficult to reach due to the road and transport situation, the bases at Polotsk, Nevel, and Vitebsk. However, no decisive overall relief was possible as long as supplies from the Reich continued to be sluggish. Vital ammunition trains 'got lost' in the Warsaw supply catchment area, with days elapsing before they were located and sent further. The ammunition stocks of Army Group Centre declined even further, instead of increasing to the extent which would have been necessary to prepare a new offensive. The resistance of the Soviet troops in the Smolensk pocket also delayed the rest period which had been planned for the mobile formations. The Soviet forces held out for a month, although Guderian had originally calculated that only three or four days would be lost.

During August and September 1941 the Dnieper Supply District was moved forward to the area round Smolensk and expanded into a productive base. The rear bases had to be closed down step by step, and the supply troops moved

---

[181] Hofmann and Toppe, Verbrauchs- und Veschleißsätze [Consumption and wear-and-tear rates], 85, MGFA P-190, T. 2.
[182] On the following see Krumpelt, *Material*, 167–8.

forward in order to receive and distribute the supplies that were being moved up by train. In addition, the apparatus of the quartermaster-general was employed in order to obtain food, clothing, engineers' material, and other supplies, including captured weapons and ammunition, for the troops 'on the widest basis, by utilizing the institutions, supplies, and workers of the country'.[183] The rear services of divisions and armies endeavoured to live off the land as far as possible, in order to relieve the strain on supply. Under their supervision and with their co-operation, the harvests were brought in, and mills, dairies, bakeries, and craftsmen's businesses were set up. In the case of 167th Infantry Division, for example, these measures resulted in an improvement in rations, while captured tractors were repaired in the tractor station and used to motorize a heavy artillery battery and to establish a breakdown platoon with the workshop company.[184]

Army Group Centre's capacity to resume the offensive depended partly on the arrival of reinforcements, and partly on the restoration of its fighting strength by making good its losses and providing sufficient supplies. In September 1941 there was not enough time to achieve this. Though the advancing of the equipment store from the Warsaw area to Smolensk did shorten the supply-route, the losses of weapons and equipment could not be made good. Running losses alone exceeded the new production of the Reich in almost every sphere. Moreover, only part of this new material was available for the eastern front, because much of it was being held back for new formations. At first, Hitler had actually ordered a complete ban on supplies for the armoured force. If major losses were sustained, individual tank formations were to be amalgamated, and surplus support troops and occupation troops withdrawn.[185] With only minor exceptions, Hitler kept to this decision until the end of the year. By the end of August 1941 the army in the east had lost 1,488 armoured fighting vehicles, i.e. more than a third of the original supply; it was allocated 96 vehicles in replacement, from a new production of 815 during the period June–August 1941. The loss of tanks due to a shortage of spares was often greater than that caused by enemy fire.[186] Frequently the troops responded by obtaining spares from Germany independently, thus avoiding central direction by the quartermaster-general.[187] These material losses were even more damaging as there had been gaps in the equipment of the army in the east even before the campaign began.[188]

---

[183] OKH/GenQu/Abt. H. Vers. No. I/4385/41 g.Kdos., Reflections on supply for continuation of operations with far-reaching objectives, 6 July 1941, BA-MA, 17. Armee 14311/2.

[184] Die Versorgung der 167. Infanterie-Division [The Supply of 167th Inf. Div.], 17–8, MGFA T-8-11.

[185] See Führer order regarding tank programme within the framework of army re-equipment, 13 July 1941, BA-MA RH 2/v. 929.

[186] Discussion between Maj.-Gen. von Schell and departmental head, KTB WiRüAmt/Stab 1941, 159 (24 July 1941), BA-MA RW 19/165.

[187] For the reaction see ObdH/GenStdH/GenQu 3 IIb No. 34000/41, Anordnung betr. Nachschub von Kfz-Ersatzteilen [Instruction regarding supply of motor-vehicle replacement parts], 6 Oct. 1941, BA-MA RH 20-11/375.   [188] See sect. I.III.4 at n. 454.

At the beginning of September 1941 the tank position—compared with the starting-position—was as follows: total losses 30 per cent on average, under repair 23 per cent, ready for action 47 per cent.[189] Among the armoured divisions of Army Group Centre, however, only 34 per cent of tanks were ready for action. The repair units subordinate to the quartermaster-general's command posts were overstretched; as a result, damaged vehicles sometimes had to be transferred to the central repair facility in Germany, placing an additional burden on the inadequate railway system. Field repairs had to be carried out in unsatisfactory working conditions and with inadequate means, especially a shortage of tank engines, workshop installations, and fuel. Furthermore, the general condition of the repaired tanks had been so weakened by previous rough treatment that they were often unable to withstand new demands. It was calculated that when new operations were launched, between 20 and 30 per cent of the original and repaired tanks would break down again within 50 km.[190]

Under these conditions, it was extremely difficult to make a realistic assessment of the fighting power of the army in the east, particularly as the statistical declarations and reports available to Army High Command did not always appear to be reliable. Thus, for example, 157 captured light Czech 35-tonne tanks were sent into action with 6th Armoured Division, but these do not appear in any of the quartermaster–general's statistics, although the division still reported 41 total losses by the beginning of September 1941.[191] In view of the very different situations facing the individual armoured formations, overall figures and averages did not provide any reliable guide for the planning of combat tasks. Even a regular inventory was ineffective in the last analysis, because it gave no information about combat-worthiness. With increasing wear and tear, the shortage of spare parts, and the lack of repair facilities, the number of vehicles which were out of action inevitably rose steeply towards the end of the year. It should also be remembered that the figures for replacement vehicles dispatched did not mean an unconditional gain for the troops. Apart from the fact that a lengthy period might elapse between the allocation of the tanks and their arrival at the front, it was not unusual for armoured fighting vehicles to be delivered in an unsatisfactory condition. Brake fluid and accessories, which could not be supplied at the front, were often lacking. In addition, obsolescent models were delivered, and—during the winter—models with narrow tracks; these had to be kept back by the unit commanders until they could be made fit for service.[192]

It would certainly have been unrealistic to expect the front-line troops to

---

[189] OKH/GenStdH/Org.Abt. (I) No. 702/41 g.Kdos., on tank supply east, 15 Sept. 1941, appendix 1d, BA-MA RH 22/v. 1326.

[190] See OKH/GenStdH/GenQu/Abt. Heeresversorgung No. I/01017/41 g.K., memorandum on fuel and motor-vehicle situation in the new operations, 11 Sept. 1941, BA-MA RH 2/v. 1326.

[191] See Paul, *Brennpunkte*, 102, and OKH/GenStdH/Org.Abt. (I) on tank supply east (see n. 189).

[192] Winter 1941–2. 1 Apr. 1942, BA-MA RH 21-1/332.

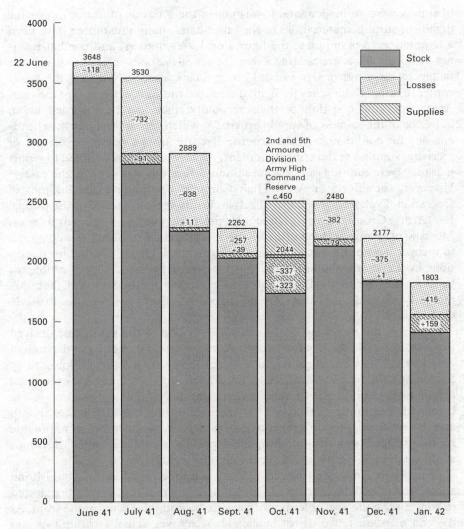

DIAGRAM II.vi.2. Effective Strength and Losses of Armoured Fighting Vehicles and Assault-guns, 22 June 1941–31 January 1942

(Marks I, II, IIF, III, 38(t), 35(t), IV, assault-guns, and armoured staff cars)

Source: See Table II.vi.1.

submit precise reports of losses and actions during the fighting. A tank which was initially regarded as a write-off might be repaired shortly after, and would then appear as a loss for the second time when it broke down again. It was also unlikely that accurate reports would be made of the many Soviet vehicles and weapons which were captured and used by the front-line troops; when levels of supply were so inadequate, it was not in the interests of a unit to provide details of surplus material.[193] On the other hand, there must often have been a temptation to manipulate the figures on losses, repairs, and combat-readiness, in order to secure as large a share of supplies as possible, or to justify the failure to carry out orders to hold on or attack, especially during the heavy winter fighting. Such 'cries for help' did indeed multiply at the end of the year. Apart from the question of their reliability, they can be regarded as an indicator of the success of supply provision, which was at least partly dependent on the confidence of the troops. If these troops could be certain of receiving supplies at the critical moment, they would be less tempted to report that they were running out of ammunition before this was actually the case.[194] However, the efforts of Army High Command to prepare the logistics of Operation Typhoon were hardly likely to justify the confidence of the troops. For Army Group Centre, Hitler's decision to postpone the advance on Moscow in favour of the battle of Kiev at least gave Armoured Group 2 time to recover before the forthcoming fighting in the Ukraine. During his operations in the south, Guderian did not face further serious supply problems, because the German railway transport had now reached Gomel, and Armoured Group 2 could therefore be supported effectively from the Roslavl–Gomel line.

However, the switching of the main supply-line to the south-east delayed the restocking of supplies for Second Army, whose supplies were dependent on a less efficient Soviet railway line from Gomel to Gorodnya. Not until 15 September did the army describe its supply situation as secure; and even then, the slow build-up of stocks made any resumption of the advance impossible before the beginning of October.[195] Moreover, in the northern sector, Ninth and Fourth Armies reported that transport capacity was insufficient to provide running supplies as well as stocking the depots to an extent at which the troops could totally rely on them during the coming fighting.[196]

Army High Command hoped that the advance on Moscow would bring about the last and decisive act of Operation Barbarossa. However, it neglected to concentrate the available supply capacity behind this sector of the front. At the end of August, 5,000 t. of haulage capacity was actually withdrawn and placed at the disposal of Army Group South in order to build up its supply-depots.[197] In order to cover running requirements, and at the same time to lay in sufficient stocks for the advance on Moscow, Field Marshal von Bock demanded 30 trains daily; Gercke could promise him only 24. In fact, in August Army Group Centre seldom received more than 18 trains per day.

---

[193] See Die Versorgung der 251. Infanterie-Division [The supply of 251st Inf. Div.], 14, MGFA T-8-10.

[194] Ibid. 32.

[195] AOK 2/O.Qu./Qu. 1 daily reports 3–15 Sept. 1941, BA-MA RH 20-2/1442.

[196] AOK 9/O.Qu. to OKH/GenQu, 14 Sept. 1941, BA-MA, 9. Armee, 13904/4, and AOK 4/O.Qu. No. 1859/41 g., Supply situation of army, 13 Sept. 1941, BA-MA RH 20-4/884.

[197] Halder, Diaries, 1198–9 (25 Aug. 1941).

Sufficient numbers were not dispatched even after the strategically important Orsha–Smolensk line had been re-laid.[198]

Despite these problems, the troops' supplies had been partially restocked by the end of September. The exception was Armoured Group 2, which had returned to Army Group Centre after the battle of Kiev and now had only small reserves of fuel available. On the other hand, the restocking of Dnieper Supply District was still in the early stages. It was clear that the offensive on Moscow and the encirclement of the city, plus the provision of cover against enemy relief attacks, would require vast quantities of ammunition. Moreover, the first supplies of winter equipment to the troops, which had still to be carried out, would make further demands on the supply system. Equally, the continuation of the fighting east of Moscow during the depths of winter would mean an extraordinary attrition of material of all kinds. At the beginning of the offensive Army Group Centre had no supply basis capable of meeting all these demands.

The establishment of supply-bases near to the front, in Gomel, Roslavl, Smolensk, and Vitebsk, could bring relief only until the stocks in store there were exhausted. Because of the inadequacies of the railway network and the damage inflicted upon it by partisan groups, the troops inevitably encountered increasing supply problems as they moved further away from the railheads. Given the scarcity of motorized transport capacity, these problems might easily develop into full-scale crises if weather conditions were to deteriorate.[199] The quartermaster-general's Army Supply Department warned that the position regarding tanks, motor-vehicles, and fuel was so precarious that the fighting strength and mobility of the army in the east might be 'insufficient to bring the eastern campaign to a conclusion in the autumn'.[200] 'A great reduction in the fighting power and mobility of the army, perhaps at the crucial moment', might occur unless drastic measures were adopted. These included a considerable increase in supplies to the eastern front, and the release of all new production to replace lost material.

This demand was partly fulfilled, at least as regards tanks, with the allocation of 316 armoured fighting vehicles—more than the total production for the month of September—and the dispatch of 2nd and 5th Armoured Divisions from Army High Command reserve with around 450 tanks. In addition, large numbers of captured French tanks were to be dispatched for deployment on security tasks in the rear area. In October 62 of these vehicles were already at the disposal of Army Group Centre (Army Group South had 21, Army Group North had 28).[201] Even then, the reinforcement of heavy equipment was not sufficient to restore the armoured formations in the central sector of the eastern front to full combat strength. In fact, Army High Command was not certain how the position should be assessed. The game of playing with

[198] Ibid. 1178–80, 1181 (15 and 16 Aug. 1941).　　　[199] Krumpelt, *Material*, 180.
[200] OKH/GenStdH/GenQu/Abt. HV, memorandum of 11 Sept. 1941 (see n. 190).
[201] Halder, *Diaries*, 1236–8, 1281–3 (15 Sept., 9 Oct. 1941).

percentages for combat-ready tanks, and the submission of widely differing situation reports, had become a serious problem. On the basis of the position taken by the army administration, Wagner reported to Halder that there was a deficiency of 40 per cent;[202] three days later, Army High Command Organization Department reported a deficiency of 53 per cent to OKW;[203] the two departments of Army High Command showed a difference of 543 tanks in the number of losses they reported. Such hair-raising errors in this order of magnitude were the result of different chains of reporting. Moreover, they were disregarded in the Army General Staff, which also used divergent figures on available new production. Only Hitler was irritated by the confusion. 'How was he to conduct a war, if he was counting on 1,000 additional tanks and then someone told him there were actually only 500? He had assumed that the people in the Ordnance Office could at least count.'[204]

Whatever the level of equipment available to Army Group Centre, it had been achieved at the expense of the supply of rations, replacement parts, and ammunition. The quartermaster-general estimated that the stockpile of one issue of ammunition was not sufficient to replace even two weeks' consumption in an attack.[205] Shortly before the launching of the attack, the arrival of fuel trains was considerably in arrears,[206] although the reinforced Army Group Centre now had three armoured groups and two infantry armies—eighty big formations—to keep moving. Fuel stocks would not support an advance of more than 300 km.—at most as far as the gates of Moscow. On the eve of the attack Wagner reported that supply for 'Typhoon' was 'satisfactory', and everything was 'ready for the jump-off'.[207] Though the last part of the report was accurate as far as it went, it was very doubtful whether the 'jump-off' would reach as far as Moscow and beyond. Wagner was still unshakeably optimistic in his conviction that he could get Army Group Centre to Moscow.[208] Further than that he dared not think, hoping that by then 'the winter [would be] here, and with luck the war would be at an end'. Wagner was playing a dangerous game with his readiness to take any risk in the conduct of operations, and his tendency always to give an optimistic answer to any question about the range of supply despite 'some nerves'.[209] Though all the signs indicated that Army Group Centre was not strong enough to achieve its operational goals, Halder was vociferous in advocating the advance on Mos-

---

[202] Ibid. 1225 (11 Sept. 1941).

[203] OKH/GenStdH/Org.Abt. (I) No. 702/41 g.Kdos. to OKW/WFSt/Abt. L, 15 Sept. 1941, BA-MA RH 2/v. 1326. Here, in contrast to the figures provided by the Dept. Army Administration, the losses of Mark I and Mark 35t were included. The differences are also explained by the fact that the Org. Dept. based its figures on the position on 5 Sept., and Dept. Army Supply on the position on 25 Aug. It is nevertheless remarkable that both reports were circulating in Army High Command at the same time without any adjustment.

[204] Engel, *Heeresadjutant bei Hitler*, 112 (4 Oct. 1941).

[205] Halder, *Diaries*, 1250–1 (22 Sept. 1941).   [206] Ibid. 1258 (26 Sept. 1941).

[207] Ibid. 1264 (29 Sept. 1941).   [208] Wagner, *Generalquartiermeister*, 203 (29 Sept. 1941).

[209] Ibid. 204, 206 (5 and 12 Oct. 1941); parallel to this see his attitude during the campaign against France, ibid. 180 (8 June 1940).

cow. Wagner was not the type of man to oppose him because of concern for the management of supply. Should a crisis arise, the railway was always a good scapegoat, particularly as it was not under the control of Army High Command.

The first problems of supply emerged at the beginning of October 1941, shortly after the launching of the new offensive. For example, after its operation with Army Group North, Armoured Group 4 had returned with only about 50 per cent of its combat-ready motorized transport capacity. It was therefore unable to make the supply trips to the depots which were necessary to cover its needs.[210] After great initial successes in the battles of encirclement at Vyazma and Bryansk, the army group encountered increasing difficulties during the pursuit, when heavy losses caused by enemy action were intensified by supply problems. The change in the weather between 9 and 11 October turned the few usable roads into deep mud. Tracked vehicles alone were able to tow individual vehicles and big guns to the front, a process which was extremely arduous and time-consuming. The armies were marooned in mud for almost three weeks, the divisions and their baggage-trains often hundreds of kilometres apart. An attempt was made to get essential material to the troops using tractors and peasant carts. Apart from local expedients of this kind, the movement of supplies came to a standstill almost everywhere. In the Smolensk–Vyazma sector the Minsk–Moscow highway was paved with cobblestones; this surface was quickly ruined by the heavy loads.[211] An entire infantry division eventually had to be employed to make this important route serviceable again. At a time when the fighting in the Mozhaysk defensive line would have demanded extensive supplies, there was a real collapse of supply management.[212]

Second Armoured Army had hoped to capture Bryansk quickly and establish a supply-base there. In fact, from the middle of October it faced a serious crisis in fuel supply. There were a number of reasons for this: Bryansk could not be stocked up by haulage vehicles as effectively as anticipated owing to the poor road conditions; the most important supply-route was barred by constant enemy incursions north of Glukhov; shortly afterwards, the number of fuel trains arriving in Orel fell sharply.[213] The army was forced to a standstill, even when the frost later made the roads passable again. This instance demonstrates that operations were not called off solely as the result of any single factor: not weather conditions, not the tactical situation, not even the permanent crisis of the railway system. Only in combination with the inadequate preparation of men and materials did they lead to failure.

Supply management was unable to provide adequate supplies and rehabilitation for Army Group Centre during its enforced standstill. Clearly, then, it

[210] Pz.Gr. 4/O.Qu., daily report, 30 Sept. 1941, BA-MA RH 21-4/358.
[211] Windisch, *Nachschubtruppe*, 32.   [212] Reinhardt, *Moskau*, 80–1.
[213] See KTB Pz.AOK2/O.Qu., entries of 3, 11 Oct, and 1 Nov. 1941, BA-MA RH 21-2/v. 819.

was in no position to lay in increased stocks for a new offensive, or to satisfy its running requirements. The supply-base was moved forward as far as the Rzhev–Vyazma–Bryansk line, with an advanced base in Orel, but there was insufficient transport capacity to stock it. Across almost 1,000 km. from the Reich border, through land that was almost empty from a logistical point of view, most supplies had to be moved along two railway lines (Warsaw–Minsk–Smolensk, and Brest–Gomel–Bryansk); these had only a limited capacity and were under attack by partisans. The ability of Dnieper Supply District to transport and distribute the supply goods brought in by train was dependent on available lorry capacity, i.e. on the number of serviceable vehicles, on the supply of fuel, and above all on the condition of the roads. Even when the supplies eventually arrived with the divisions, they still had to be taken to the front by peasant carts and a small number of motor-vehicles, often off the roads.

When the frost made the roads passable again at the beginning of October, the motor-vehicles—sometimes sunk to their axles in frozen mud—had to be dug out. In many cases they were damaged beyond repair. Though antifreeze had been sent to the army group from 11 October, many of the vehicles were not winterproof and broke down.

It is possible that Hitler had forbidden his commanders to refer to the problem of winter equipment. However, this had not prevented Halder from ordering appropriate measures from the beginning of July 1941.[214] Hundreds of regulations, orders, and circulars from the quartermaster-general had been issued during the autumn to deal with winter preparations.[215] These concerned three main problem areas. The first need was to define requirements for winter equipment and supplies. For this purpose the number and condition of the troops, their geographical distribution, and their form of service had all to be taken into account. In anticipation of a rapid victory, it was initially assumed that an occupying army of 56 divisions would be required,[216] to be provided with appropriate accommodation. Two-thirds of the army in the east would therefore be brought back home, leaving some of their material behind to provide stocks for the occupying troops. As early as the beginning of September 1941, the base figures for the winter programme had to be revised upwards by 50 per cent, to 750,000 men and 150,000 horses.[217]

When winter set in at the beginning of November, the entire army in the east was still in action. Army High Command was forced to adjust to the idea

[214] Halder, *Diaries*, 1016 (8 July 1941). On the problem of winter equipment see also Wagner, *Generalquartiermeister*, 313 ff.

[215] See Summary of the fundamental decrees of Army High Command on the securing of requirements for the winter, appendix 1 to Befehlsstelle Süd OKH/GenQu No. 1819/41 geh., 26 Oct. 1941, BA-MA RW 41/9.

[216] See memorandum on the occupation and securing of Russian territory and on the restructuring of the army after the completion of Barbarossa, 15 July 1941, *KTB OKW* i. 1022–5 (72).

[217] See OKH/GenStdH/GenQu/IVa No. 1010/41 (V) to Organization Todt headquarters, 31 Oct. 1941, BA-MA H 17/85.

that major operations on the eastern front would be necessary throughout the winter. Only in mid-December did its leaders recognize that it was no longer possible to bring divisions back to Germany, and that, on the contrary, considerable reinforcements would have to be brought into Russian territory. The bulk of the formations would have to be employed in the winter fighting, in areas which offered hardly any opportunities for them to live off the land, with exhausted troops, battered equipment, and without satisfactory stocks. The quartermaster-general was simply not prepared for the resulting demand for winter equipment and supplies.

The second need was to make the necessary material ready in good time. To this end, it was essential to consider productive capacities in the occupied eastern teritories as well as in the Reich. This option appeared particularly attractive, because the manufacture of accommodation and other winter equipment in the occupied areas would also reduce the need for transports from Germany. At any event, energy installations such as gas and electricity works in the occupied territories must be put into operation, and large repair workshops established for army equipment. In practice, moreover, given the strains facing the German war economy, extra orders to satisfy the needs of the Wehrmacht could not be accommodated within Germany. Production in the occupied territories was also sluggish, not least because of friction with the economic agencies and the civilian administration.[218]

Nevertheless, it was here that the only possibilities for improvement lay. In the middle of September Army High Command instructed the army forma-tions in the east to endeavour to lay in their own winter stocks,[219] despite the fact that the final accommodation areas and the composition of the occupying troops had not yet been defined. The overriding principle was 'to obtain and utilize the stocks and products of the country to the fullest possible extent, in order to relieve the homeland'.[220] The quartermaster-general therefore launched an extensive production programme in the area of operations. Alongside bathtubs, pokers, and other equipment, this included the manufac-ture of 252,000 handkerchiefs, 445,789 articles of knitted underclothing, and 30,000 snow-shirts.[221]

Third, such of the winter equipment as could not be produced in the occupied eastern territories had to be dispatched from the Reich and distrib-uted in good time. Decisions had to be taken according to operational con-

---

[218] On the quartermaster-general's production programme see the account in Kriegswirtschaft im Operationsgebiet des Ostens in den Jahren 1941–1943 [War economy in the area of operations in the east in the years 1941–1943], 220 ff., IfZ ED-2.

[219] See Befh. rückw. H.Geb. Mitte/Qu/IVa No. 415/41 geh., order regarding winter provision of potatoes and vegetables, 25 Sept. 1941, BA-MA RH 26-221/17.

[220] Befehlsstelle Süd OKH/GenQu No. 1819/41 geh., orders for supply in winter 1941/42, 26 Oct. 1941, BA-MA RH 3/Arb. No. 111.

[221] See OKH/GenStdH/GenQu I No. 913 a/41, order regarding supply with accommodation requirements and consumer goods in the east, 9 Oct. 1941, BA-MA RH 20-11/375, and the survey of production performances, WiRüAmt/Ro I/Ost, 22 June 1941, appendix 5, BA-MA, Wi/ID. 1185.

ditions and transport possibilities. Since rapid victory was anticipated in the east, it seemed reasonable to assume that the necessary winter goods could be dispatched to the troops after the conclusion of operations. Unexpected military developments, especially the preparation and implementation of Operation Typhoon, meant that consignments of ammunition and fuel were subsequently given priority.

In order to meet at least the most urgent needs of the troops, the quartermaster-general planned a transport movement—named 'Bow'—from 22 to 30 October 1941.[222] The 'Bow' trains were loaded in the Reich with clothing, accommodation material and equipment, motor-vehicle winter equipment, sledges, and skis. This plan, however, fell victim to the failures of railway transport. The trains were kept waiting in the Warsaw supply catchment area, and could only be brought to the front in isolated cases, slipped in between the ammunition and fuel trains which had priority.

As a result, it was left largely to the initiative of the individual armies to demand trains with winter equipment, if necessary at the expense of ammunition supplies. For example, Second Army, advancing through Bryansk to Tula, had decided on 16 October that the dispatch of winter clothing was urgently necessary to prevent frostbite; after the arrival of clothing at the Gomel supply-base, it applied for this to be brought to the front by air transport. A week later two army corps received a drop comprising 47,000 pairs of gloves and 68,000 Balaclava helmets. The situation had not greatly improved by the time the frost set in fourteen days later. Convoys containing light winter clothing were still on their way to XXXXVIII Armoured Corps; in the case of five divisions it was calculated that at least a week would be required in the absence of adequate supplies in the army area.[223]

When the need for winter equipment soared with the onset of winter, it would have been necessary for several hundred trains to be dispatched to meet the new demand.[224] Given the fact that the transport crisis was intensifying at this time, there was no possibility of an appropriate response. The situation was even worse because the winter clothing provided was inadequate to meet the demands of the Russian winter. Furthermore, even when the equipment had arrived with the armies, it could not easily be transferred to the front-line troops. With road and transport conditions so poor, it often took several days to get the clothing to the troops, while in the meantime the fighting units were decimated by frostbite. The situation in the individual formations varied considerably, even in Army Group Centre, which faced the worst conditions.

The onset of winter had its worst effect on the railway. German locomotives, unlike Russian ones, had their cooling-pipes on the outside; in icy conditions between 70 and 80 per cent of them froze and burst.[225] The ensuing

---

[222] See Headquarters South OKH/GenQu, orders for supply in winter (see n. 200), 3.

[223] AOK 2/O.Qu./Qu. 1, daily report of 16, 22 Oct. and 7 Nov. 1941, BA-MA RH 20-2/1442.

[224] See Wagner, *Generalquartiermeister*, 317.   [225] Pottgießer, *Deutsche Reichsbahn*, 35.

transport crisis exceeded all others. Between 12 November and 2 December no supply trains arrived at Second Army for days on end, necessitating serious reductions in consumption in all areas.[226] In the period from 9 to 23 November only one fuel-train came though to Ninth Army, and its contents could not be taken to the troops because there was only just enough fuel to fill the empty tanks of the lorry convoys.[227] At the same time, the railway tracks were continuing to carry 'Jew trains' from Germany. This led to an understandable protest from Bock, who feared that it 'would mean that a corresponding number of vital trains to supply the attack would have to be dropped'.

In this period the management of supplies depended almost exclusively on the effectiveness of the haulage vehicles. In fact, it was due to them that the army group survived at all at this time. From the beginning of the campaign until the end of the year 616th Lorry Transport Regiment employed with Army Group Centre carried 291,000 t. of supples, or the freight of 650 railway trains.[228] By mid-November half of the vehicles had already broken down. In response, Army High Command decided to amalgamate the serviceable units of the haulage fleet and to leave them in the area of operations, while vehicles in need of repair were sent back to Germany.[229]

A few days before this decision Halder had endeavoured, in Orsha, to convince the armies in the east that the offensive must be continued at all costs. Major (General Staff) Otto Eckstein, who was responsible for the supply of Army Group Centre, strongly opposed this view, with the assistant chief of staffs of the earmarked attacking armies also offering a pessimistic assessment of the situation.[230] However, Bock did not support his supply officer. He believed that it would be better to make one last major effort to take Moscow, rather than be forced to continue the fighting in winter. Though Halder too was aware that the operation could not be properly prepared, he agreed with Bock. In this situation even Wagner's optimism disappeared; he was now convinced that the army had reached the end of its strength.

In view of the heavy losses of material, Army High Command now estimated that the actual fighting strength of an armoured division was only 35 per cent of its normal strength. The situation facing Second Armoured Army was especially precarious. Guderian reported that he had begun the campaign with around 1,000 tanks, and had been assigned a further 150 during the course of operations, but that he now had only 150 tanks available.[231] Even more catastrophic was the condition of the unarmoured motor-vehicles; in the middle of November only 15 per cent of the fleet was fully ready for service. As a result, the motorized transport capacity of the armies had to be amalgamated, and the divisions were forced to resort to horse-drawn convoys.

[226] AOK 2/O.Qu./Qu. 1, daily reports 12 Nov.–2 Dec. 1941, BA-MA RH 20-2/1442.
[227] AOK 9/O.Qu., daily reports 9–23 Nov. 1941, BA-MA, 9. Armee 13904/5. On the following see Bock, Tagebuch, vol.ii, 12 Nov. 1941, MGFA P-210; BA-MA RH 19 II/121, 781.
[228] Windisch, *Nachschubtruppe*, 13.
[229] See Halder, *Diaries*, 1302 (18 Nov. 1941).   [230] See sect. II.1.1(*f*) at n. 528 (Klink).
[231] KTB Pz.AOK 2, 18 Nov. 1941, BA-MA, RH 21-2/v. 244.

Army Group Centre was thus sent into action for a last attack on Moscow. Its troops were exhausted and decimated; its motor-vehicles and tanks had sustained excessive damage; important sections of its armies were not ready for action because of the shortage of winter equipment; it lacked adequate stocks in the supply-base; and it had no prospect of receiving a smooth and sufficient flow of supply trains. The attack was based solely on the belief of the operational leadership that the enemy was in a much worse position. The initial successes of the attack could not be exploited because there was not enough fuel, and movements came to a temporary standstill.[232]

At the end of November the attack was finally called off altogether. Halder nevertheless remained full of confidence. During a discussion with the assistant chiefs of staff of the armies in the east, he painted a positive overall picture. In particular, the management of supplies had been a success up till that time.[233] Halder did concede that the weakness of the troops and the supply situation—in these weeks only 16 trains a day were arriving at Army Group Centre instead of the 31 demanded[234]—no longer permitted major co-ordinated operations in 1941. Nevertheless, Halder announced that the attack would be resumed before the end of the year, and urged the armies to accept 'the greatest risk in supply matters . . . for the sake of the operational concept'. At the same time, he submitted ideas for the rehabilitation of the army in the east during the winter months. Only a few days later these were shown to be already outdated.

When, at the beginning of December 1941, the supposedly defeated Red Army launched a surprising counter-attack, Army Group Centre was so shaken that the commander-in-chief of the army saw no way 'of saving the army from the difficult situation'.[235] Inadequate stocks with the armies and in the Dnieper Supply District meant that the army group found itself in extreme difficulty as soon as a few supply-trains failed to arrive. Soviet penetrations frequently forced the German formations into precipitate retreats because the troops had no confidence in the management of supplies. On the icy and congested roads the battered motor-vehicles were unable to withstand the renewed strains upon them. The constant shortage of fuel and replacement parts caused further problems, so that by the beginning of January 1942 more than 10,000 vehicles had had to be abandoned. Equally disastrous for the mobility and fighting power of the troops was the extraordinarily high loss of horses, particularly with the horse-drawn artillery. Guns either had to be blown up or allowed to fall into the hands of the enemy. Overall, the losses of weapons and equipment in December 1941 increased steeply. Replacements could not be brought up because of the lack of transport capacity, since the troop movements ordered by the army group served only to intensify the shortage of engines for the supply-trains.[236]

---

[232] Reinhardt, *Moskau*, 155.   [233] Halder, *Diaries*, 1312 (23 Nov. 1941).
[234] Ibid. 1303–5.   [235] Ibid. 1356–60 (15 Dec. 1941).
[236] See e.g. KTB Pz.AOK 2/O.Qu., 13 Dec. 1941 BA-MA RH 21-2/v. 819.

In the severe command crisis produced by the threat of defeat for the army in the east, Hitler urged the army leadership to adopt a ruthless approach to the civilian population. Villages were to be burnt down during retreats; all prisoners and civilians were to have their winter clothing confiscated in order to meet the needs of German soldiers.[237] Hitler also promised the immediate dispatch of reinforcements and supplies in order to support his orders to stand fast. From an operational point of view, it may appear sensible for him to have called on the troops not to yield an inch of ground. But in reality Army Group Centre faced a situation in which enormous losses of men and materials could be expected whether it held out in its existing positions or made withdrawal movements. At the Führer's headquarters, and in the Army High Command, the promised assistance may have looked impressive; but for the formations engaged in desperate defensive fighting the disastrous transport situation prevented the arrival of effective and immediate support.

In this situation the so-called 'elephants movement' was ordered as a replacement for the withdrawn haulage vehicles. Transport companies were hurriedly equipped with French lorries, totally untrained officers and drivers were selected from newly conscripted men, and the vehicles—some straight from the production line—were sent off in temperatures of $-20\,°C$ and without being run in.[238] Not surprisingly, an exceptionally high percentage of the vehicles had broken down by the time they were assembled in Warsaw. After a journey of almost 2,000 km. an insignificant number of serviceable vehicles reached Army Group Centre in January. Second Armoured Army, which had originally had six big lorry convoys of 60 t. at its disposal but at this stage was able to operate only one, received precisely 54 t. of additional transport capacity from the 'elephants movement'.[239]

Most of the remaining reinforcements did not arrive at the front until the Soviet offensive had already come to a standstill. To implement the movement from west to east, the quartermaster-general had established the 'Control Staff Centre'.[240] The idea was to continue using the railways as much as possible, but to become independent of them for a time and to supply the troops by road transport. Since the territory between the Reich border and the army fighting 1,000 km. to the east lacked any logistical installations, a supply relay would be created along the proposed supply-roads as far as the Smolensk area.

By 10 January 1942, 44 bases had been established to service the draft-conducting battalions, horse-moving detachments, and lorry convoys. The draft-conducting battalions were the first to be dispatched. A rest-day had to be included after every three marching days because of the exceptionally heavy falls of snow and snowdrifts, a persistent east wind reaching gale force, icy roads, and temperatures as low as $-45\,°C$. The lorry convoy set out at the end of January. Many of the vehicles had been brought straight from the factory

---

[237] Halder, *Diaries.* 1369–70 (20 Dec. 1941). [238] Windisch, *Nachschubtruppe*, 42.
[239] KTB Pz.AOK 2/O.Qu., daily report of 23 Jan. 1942, BA-MA RH 21-2/v. 819.
[240] See Braun, Der Leitstab Mitte, MGFA T-8-5.

to be loaded with winter equipment, replacement parts, lubricants, sledges, stoves, medicines, etc. These were followed by the divisions, and finally by the horse detachments. By the end of April, within 100 days, 5 infantry divisions with 60,000 men altogether, 26 draft-conducting battalions with 17,000 men, 6,500 horses, and 650 lorries with 3,000 t. of transport capacity had been brought to Army Group Centre.

During this period Dnieper Supply District near Smolensk, with its advanced bases of Roslavl, Vyazma, Bryansk, and Gomel, became the backbone of the winter fighting waged by Army Group Centre. The bases proved to be cornerstones of the defence. The troops withdrew to them at times of crisis, and used them as bases from which to launch counter-attacks to close gaps in the front and gain secure defensive positions in this sector of the eastern front. Supply troops frequently had to be sent into battle as a last resort. Of course, the concentration of the rear services in the few cities was liable to persuade the military commands that significant reserves for the front could be released by vigorous 'combing-out' operations. Apart from the questionable military value of these men, who were generally poorly armed and were often unsuitable for front-line service, such interventions had highly regrettable consequences.[241] They weakened rearward connections at a time when they were more valuable than ever, and when partisan attacks and appalling weather and transport conditions were placing them in increasing danger.

Though the combat strength of the infantry was declining, it was not feasible to enforce an equal reduction in the supply troops. The decline in fighting strength affected only the rations transports, which comprised only a small part of the supply load. Consumption of ammunition and fuel was unchanged. In fact, the need for ammunition actually tended to increase whenever an attempt was made to compensate for the weakened fighting power of the infantry by an increase in artillery firepower.[242] In addition, the demands on the personnel in workshops and salvage units rose as the aim was to get broken-down vehicles back to the front as quickly as possible, or to transport them to the rear during withdrawals.

Though the combing out of rear services was an obvious and popular emergency measure in the eyes of the combat troops, it could not resolve the contradiction between the demands of the war and the means available to wage it. With some justice, the supply leadership can be charged with mistakes in organization and some inefficiency, the quartermaster-general with a dangerous optimism, and the supply troops with a lack of discipline and poor preparation for action.[243] But even with the best will and the greatest dedication, the quartermaster-general's men could only bring to the front the ma-

[241] See e.g. the protest by XXXXVII Army Corps against the deployment of corps supply troops which had been ordered for the defence of Orel, KTB Pz.AOK 2/O.Qu., 23 Jan. 1942, BA RH 21-2/v. 819.

[242] Windisch, *Nachschubtruppe*, 11.

[243] See e.g. OB 4. Armee, O.Qu.III/IIa/Ic No. 2000/41 geh., special order for the maintenance of discipline, 11 Sept. 1941, BA-MA RH 20-/884.

terial provided by the war economy and the Economic Staff East—and that was simply not enough to satisfy the requirements of the army in the east. It may be that the principal reason for the failure of supply leadership lay in the fundamental errors of operational thinking, which was based on a belief that the bulk of the Red Army could be destroyed west of the Dnieper, and that relatively few forces would be required to occupy the remainder of European Russia. As far as the Dnieper–Dvina line, supplies proved to be secure and generally functioned satisfactorily. By contrast, the conditions for an adequate reconstruction of the supply-base on the far side of the Dnieper were wholly lacking.

Even in July 1941, it was obvious that the operations plan had failed. Despite this, no new war plan was developed to take account of economic and logistical possibilities. Hitler and the military leadership held to the strategic goal of the elimination of the Soviet Union as a military factor in 1941; they decided to continue operations despite the fact that increasing enemy resistance was producing an inexorable erosion of the strength of the troops. This improvised operational thinking was based on the assumption that the enemy was on the verge of collapse, and that guaranteed and secure supply services could be dispensed with. The quartermaster-general was not prepared to fetter the operational leadership by pointing out the realities of the supply situation. He accepted the risk of supplying the troops along diminishing supply-routes, even though it was clear that any interruption of the flow of supplies—whether due to organizational mishaps and bottlenecks in the war economy or to the effects of enemy action and the weather—would intensify local crises and could have unforeseen consequences. Wagner subordinated himself completely to the operational leadership, even when he knew that the army in the east had reached the limits of its strength in men and material. His conduct was partly a response to his position in the military hierarchy, and to the traditional failure to value the role of quartermaster-general in comparison with the art of operational leadership. But Wagner's position was also affected by his mediating role between the needs of the army and the civilian economic leadership, which was still waiting for a swift military victory in the east to free workers for war production. This interdependence between economic policy and the military conduct of the war can also be detected in the case of the food-supply issue. This, indeed, became the key problem of German occupation policy in the occupied eastern territories.

4. The Food-supply Issue: Starvation Strategy or Pragmatism

Obtaining foodstuffs from the occupied eastern territories was regarded from the outset as one of the most important economic objectives of the campaign. In the spring of 1941 the Reich Ministry of Food and OKW had agreed on a hunger strategy to be directed against the Soviet population. Its aim was to gain control of the surpluses and stocks of the country, and also to collect the largest possible quantity of foodstuffs for the Reich by enforcing a drastic reduction in overall consumption. For the military, the main incentive was that the army in the east could ease the strain on the supply-system by living off the land. For its part, the ministry of food hoped that the food-supply situation in Germany could be greatly improved, particularly if the entire Wehrmacht—more than five million men on the highest daily rations—could be removed from food-supply calculations. At the state secretaries' discussion of 2 May 1941 it was clearly understood that if the Wehrmacht were to live off the land this would mean death by starvation for millions of Russians. Clearly, the situation would be even more drastic if, in the long term, up to 10m. t. of grain were to be exported from the European part of the Soviet Union to cover the deficit in the Greater German economic area. This calculated catastrophic starvation went hand in hand with radical plans for deindustrialization, which would make millions of industrial workers, especially in the major cities, seem 'redundant'.

Two days after the beginning of the campaign, State Secretary Backe summarized his ideas in the General Council of the Four-year Plan.[244] He pointed out that 1.65m. t. of Soviet grain had been lost to Germany after the collapse of the trade treaty. At the same time, mass conscription to the Wehrmacht meant that many former recipients of standard rations were now receiving significantly higher Wehrmacht rations. In consequence, there would be a deficit of about 2.5m. t. in Germany's grain balance. Attempts by the army in the east to live off the land would be a relief measure worth approximately 1.9m. t. It was therefore necessary to transport at least 600,000 extra tonnes of grain into the Reich. Though it was no longer thought possible to meet the entire needs of the Wehrmacht in this way, the issue of how to calculate the procurement quota in the east remained open. In addition, Backe expected to obtain 1.5m. t. of oil-bearing seeds from the east in order to resolve Germany's shortage of fats. Several million cows and pigs would also have to be slaughtered in Russia, because the Führer was opposed to any further reduction of the meat ration in the Reich.

The food-supply question was therefore governed by an unequivocal political decision to avoid at all costs placing burdens on the German population. Instead, Germany's future eastern colonies were to be exploited ruthlessly. It cannot be argued that such an approach was unavoidable because of domestic constraints, since the German population had accepted the reduction in the meat ration in May 1941 'without undue excitement'. Hitler and the military leadership nevertheless remained extremely anxious, because the economic authorities reported that a further reduction would be necessary in the autumn 'unless very considerable surpluses are obtained from previously inaccessible

---

[244] Reich Marshal of the Greater German Reich, Plenipotentiary for the Four-year Plan, VP 10103/1, g.Rs., 11th meeting of General Council on 24 June 1941, doc. NI-7474, Staatsarchiv — Nürnberg.

sources'. There would 'certainly [be] greater repercussions' then.[245] A marked decline in the productivity and mood of the workers was already perceptible; if the critical harvest conditions in the occupied territories of west and south-east Europe were also taken into account, there seemed genuine reason for concern about internal security in the areas under German control.[246]

Hitler gave his full support to the plans of Backe and Thomas to implement a radical starvation strategy in Russia, particularly regarding their intentions of starving out the major cities. He informed Halder of his firm decision 'to raze Moscow and Leningrad to the ground, to prevent people remaining there whom we would then have to feed in winter'.[247] Conversely, the Economic Organization East also identified itself with the racial ideological component of this 'national catastrophe'. In the first phase of the campaign the Economic Staff East constantly pressed for 'harsh measures' against the Jewish section of the population, despite admitting in its first situation report that the Jews were 'economically at least temporarily necessary because of their large numbers'.[248] In its second situation report of 16 July 1941, after the mass murders carried out by the SS special-duty squads, the Economic Staff East referred to some initial successes in the 'solution of the Jewish question'. For example, the important petroleum refinery at Drogobych had needed its 'leading Jews' only a week ago, but was now operating 'completely Jew-free'. Further measures were urgently necessary for economic reasons, above all the rapid transfer of the remaining Jewish population into ghettos, 'so that the more reliable local non-Jews will get a chance and our economic work will not be endangered by Jewish counter-propaganda'. Production losses in the towns would also be avoided.[249]

Ten days later, attention was drawn once again to the 'Jewish danger'. Express approval was given to the shootings carried out by German police:

In this first period, the Jews, who form at least a third and often over half of the population in the towns, have in many cases openly expressed their hostility to and their hatred of Germany through whispering campaigns, and occasionally through illegal meetings. The reprisals taken by the native population against the Jews as henchmen of the Communist regime, and the shootings by the German police of numerous Jews suspected of sedition, have intimidated the Jews and to some extent made them willing to work.[250]

The economic agencies thus linked the security argument in favour of terror

---

[245] Reich Marshal of the Greater German Reich, Plenipotentiary for the Four-year Plan, VP 9499/41, g.Rs., survey of the overall economic situation, 21 June 1941, 5–6, BA R 26/44.

[246] See OKW/WiRüAmt/Rü Ie No. 2596/41 g.k., Significant points from the 28th situation report of the armaments inspectorates produced on 15 July, BA-MA RH 8/v. 1023. On food policy in the German sphere of power see Volkmann, 'Landwirtschaft'; *Das Deutsche Reich und der Zweite Weltkrieg*, v/1. 585 ff. (also for the subject of agriculture in general).

[247] Halder, *Diaries*, 1016 (8 July 1941).

[248] Chef WiStabOst, No. 40018/41 g., situation report 10 July 1941, BA-MA RW 31/11.

[249] Chef WiStabOst, No. 40063/41 g., situation report 16 July 1941, ibid.

[250] Chef WiStabOst, No. 40,139/Id/41 g., fortnightly report 26 July 1941, ibid.

and extermination with the argument of economic practicality. On one hand, mass liquidations eliminated 'useless mouths'. On the other, they seemed likely to have the deterrent effect which OKW believed to be necessary to 'remove any desire for insubordination from the population', and to prevent 'acts of despair and attacks' arising from the 'famine which can be expected in large parts of the conquered territories'.[251]

In the optimistic mood produced by the first military triumphs, the implementation by force of this hunger strategy appeared to pose few problems in Berlin. The army in the east had gone into action with 20 days' supply of rations; with the help of captured foodstuffs, this would probably be enough to feed the bulk of the Wehrmacht during the anticipated short campaign. The belief that a much smaller army of occupation could then live completely off the land—at the expense of the urban population—was not unrealistic. In the first phase of the campaign the economic agencies therefore concentrated on transporting to the Reich all obtainable foodstuffs which had not been claimed by the Wehrmacht. These would later be used to supply the Wehrmacht units which, it was thought, would soon be returning from the east, without breaking into the domestic balance. In addition, efforts were made to establish an agricultural organization in the occupied eastern territories, and to introduce effective measures of economic management in the longer term.[252]

With the economic agencies preoccupied with medium- and long-term planning, the immediate task of supplying the troops was regarded as much less important. In consequence, the quartermaster-general soon came into conflict with the Economic Staff East over the deduction of the foodstuffs obtained by the Wehrmacht in the occupied territory from the supplies brought in from the Reich, which the economic authorities wanted to curb as much as possible.[253] Army High Command considered that 'in contrast to opinion in Berlin, supplying the troops completely from the occupied territories had not yet been possible'. It demanded that further contributions of rations should be made available from the Reich; this was necessary if only to overcome local bottlenecks. The advance of the mobile formations often resulted in the establishment of vast, unsecured areas stretching over a hundred kilometres between them and the following infantry formations; in that area there was 'much stealing on the part of the population'.[254]

The most vigorous complaints about inadequate rations came from the GOC Armoured Group 4, Colonel-General Hoepner.[255] Some trains were not

[251] Letter from Keitel to Chief of Army Ordnance and Commander of Training Army, 5 July 1941, printed in *Deutsche Besatzungspolitik*, No. 32, p. 104. See also the supplement to Directive 33, 23 July 1941, *Hitler's Directives*, 89–90.

[252] See KTB 1 Außenstelle OKH/GenQu Versorgungsbezirk Dnepr/IV Wi, entry of 1 Aug. 1941, BA-MA Wi/ID. 1123.

[253] See WiStabOst/La, KTB entries, 5 July 1941, BA-MA RW 31/42.

[254] Chef WiStabOst No. 40063/41 g., second situation report, 16 July 1941, BA-MA RW 31/11.

[255] Der Befh. der Pz.Gr. 4/Abt. IVa, Az. 62 letter to Army Group North, 30 July 1941, on increased provision of supply, BA-MA RH 3/v. 138.

arriving at all, or only after being partially or completely plundered; the adjoining armies were better off simply because they were not operating, as the armoured group was, in a scanty, wooded area. With only three days' rations in stock, he could not properly prepare for the forthcoming operations. Hoepner saw no possibility of increasing the amount he obtained from the land, and demanded supplies from the Reich to bring stocks up to between six and ten days' rations.

At this stage, the army in the east was still being supplied relatively efficiently. Army High Command therefore saw no reason to take drastic action, even though Wagner reported that 50 per cent of overall supply requirements were having to be supplied from the Reich. The figures were on the increase, which meant that expectations of the ability of the troops to live off the land were not being fulfilled.[256] Anticipating rapid victory in the east, Army High Command regarded the emerging bottlenecks in supply as temporary, and was prepared to expose the troops to greater risks in pursuit of rapid victory. Since it was unable to put pressure on the economic authorities in the Reich to change their position, the army in the east was forced to resort to a more ruthless exploitation of the occupied territories. In this context, the army intendant rejected Hoepner's complaints and demands.[257] Even a reduction of stocks to one or two days' rations was not to be regarded as dangerous. The armoured group must simply 'try harder' to increase its exploitation of the occupied territory in order to overcome supply bottlenecks.

This instruction to try harder to live off the land was perhaps an indication that the troops had behaved with more restraint towards the civilian population than the supreme leadership had intended. In its first situation report of 10 July 1941 the Economic Staff East had noted the difficulty of imposing a unified policy concerning the issue of food supply. The basic position of the Berlin central authorities was that it was not the business of the German authorities to feed the native population:

However, with the territories so vast and the occupying forces along the army's rearward communications so slight, there is, on the one hand, a military interest in keeping the population quiet, but, on the other hand, an economic interest on the part of Wehrmacht and homeland in ensuring that not too much is consumed by the native population. Particularly as we do not yet know what we will find and harvest.[258]

These deliberations signalled the first tentative signs of a retreat from the radical hunger strategy. However, they remained insignificant because no

[256] See Halder, *Diaries*, 1137, 1040–4 (1, 2 Aug. 1941).

[257] Der Heeresintendant im OKH, Az. 803 (I, 1) letter to Intendant 4th Armd. Group on supply of bread and provisions, 2 Aug. 1941, BA-MA RH 3/v. 138.

[258] Chief WiStabOst No. 40018/41 g., 1st situation report, 10 July 1941, BA-MA RW 31/11. In the 1944 history of Economic Staff East mention is made of the fact that in 1941 it was believed that there were sufficient fighting forces in the east and that it was not necessary 'to be concerned with providing food, clothing, and accommodation for them'. This position was rapidly proved to be incorrect; see Kriegswirtschaft im Operationsgebiet des Ostens, 207 (see n. 218).

authority felt any responsibility for feeding the subject Soviet population. The task of the army's military administration was limited both in time and scope. From the military point of view, the issue was the responsibility of the economic authorities; for their part, the economic authorities were content to shift the responsibility to the civilian administration, which was not yet ready to begin its work.

For the time being, Army High Command still had to administer most of the occupied territory. Its ambivalence was clearly demonstrated in an instruction of 25 July. On the one hand, this demanded ruthless action against the native civilian population, and the prisoners of war, in order to secure the conquered territory and make its exploitation possible. On the other hand, however, it argued that efforts should be made to keep the inhabitants at work, because this was the quickest way to achieve pacification.[259] Although a wage was to be provided rather than rations in return for work, it was clear that the co-operation of the population could not be achieved without concessions in the supply of food. The economic leadership responded at once by declaring that German food supplies could only be ensured at the expense of the occupied territories, and that virtually nothng could be done for their inhabitants.[260] This was especially true in the central Russian area of deficiency, and in the big industrial cities; on the other hand, the help of the agricultural population was urgently needed by the German occupation authorities to bring in the harvest, and their support was to be gained by guarantees of adequate food.[261] In fact, the network of agricultural leaders was so thin, and the number of occupying troops so small, that they could not hope to to get complete control of the new harvest. In such circumstances, 'concessions' were easy to make. While the agricultural population could feed itself in an emergency, and the urban population managed to survive these early months by living on their stocks and making 'foraging trips', hundreds of thousands of Soviet prisoners of war became the helpless victims of German despotism.

Expecting a short war, the military élite saw no need to provide adequately for the masses of prisoners who fell into its hands.[262] Some attempts had been made during the planning stage of the campaign to argue that the prisoners of war were 'valuable' workers who should be fed according to the Geneva Convention. These came to nothing, because Army High Command had no authority over the economic apparatus in the occupied territory, and no agreement on food-supply guidelines for Soviet prisoners of war was made until August 1941. Until then it was left largely to the various army commands

[259] Printed in *Deutsche Besatzungspolitik*, No. 34, p. 104.
[260] Report by Chef Wito departmental bead, 26 July 1941, KTB WiRüAmt/Stab 1941, 164, BA-MA RW 19.165.
[261] See appeal of Army Inspectorate Centre, Main Group Agriculture, to farmers, 26 July 1941, BA-MA RH 26-221/19.
[262] See further in Streit, *Keine Kameraden*, 128 ff. Academically quite useless, on the other hand, is Roschmann, *Gutachten zur Behandlung und zu den Verlusten sowjetischer Kriegsgefangener*. Also against the above interpretation sect. I.IV.1(*h*) at n. 190 (Klink).

to decide what efforts should be made to feed the prisoners. Individual examples reveal that rations were usually fixed so low that the prisoners had little chance of surviving for long. The only exceptions were the prisoners of war who were taken along by the troops as indispensable workers. These were promised, and generally received, good provisions.[263]

It was the civilian economic authorities in the Reich which expressed most interest in preserving the work capacity of Soviet prisoners of war. In June 1941 these expected that the political directives forbidding Soviet prisoners from being put to work in the Reich would be withdrawn sooner or later; domestic political reservations about their use were unconvincing 'because of the many years of National Socialist indoctrination of the peasant circles, the great difference in culture, and ultimately also the lack of an adequate understanding of the language'.[264] Of course, such general interest on the part of the economic leadership in Soviet workers involved only a small section of the population or of the prisoners of war. It did not therefore give rise to any opposition to the extermination measures which were being planned and carried out in the east. After a few weeks, however, these practices had assumed such proportions that they ran counter to the growing interest among military and economic quarters in the utilization of Soviet manpower. This growing interest was due to the unfavourable military developments. The responsible military authorities were helpless and, in some cases, indifferent in the face of the consequences of famine and epidemics.

In the Minsk prison camp, for example, 100,000 prisoners of war and 40,000 civilian prisoners were herded together in an extremely small area.[265] They were guarded by a detail of active soldiers in company strength. The most brutal force was used against the prisoners, who received only small amounts of food from relatives in the neighbourhood. In these chaotic conditions, while prisoners 'killed each other for a piece of bread', the Organization Todt requested the selection of 10,000 'racially valuable skilled workers' for urgent road-building work. The appeal was rejected by Marshal von Kluge, because he wished to reserve any decison on the release of civilian prisoners to himself.

Catastrophic conditions were not confined to the area of operations in the east, but were to be found even more frequently in the camps of the Government-General and the Reich. This fact proves that the mass deaths of Soviet prisoners of war were not due solely to the ignorance of, and the extreme strains on, the military authorities. First and foremost, these developments were the consequence of a deliberate decision taken in Berlin: both the German population and the Wehrmacht were to be supplied with food

[263] WiStabOst A 1/41, order regarding labour employment of prisoners of war, 28 June 1941, BA-MA RW 31/11.
[264] Reich Marshal of the Greater German Reich, Plenipotentiary for the Four-year Plan, VP 11594/41, g.Rs., survey of overall economic situation, 23 July 1941, 8, BA R 26 I/44.
[265] See report by Min.Rat Xaver Dorsch, 10 July 1941, No. 022-PS, *IMT* xxv. 81 ff.

from the occupied eastern territories, without any consideration of the consequences for the enemy population which had come under German control. To that extent, it is justifiable to speak of a deliberate policy of extermination.[266]

When the Economic Operations Staff East drew up a first interim balance on 31 July 1941, State Secretary Backe offered impressive figures.[267] Beyond the partial supply of the Wehrmacht, around 500,000 t. of grain and 100,000 t. of meat had been obtained for the Reich. The short-term objectives of 24 June 1941 had almost been fulfilled. Prospects for the future were less favourable, however. In particular, the assumption that big reserves from earlier harvests would be found had proved to be incorrect. In view of the devastation and the lack of fuel, it was impossible to count on a regular autumn cultivation. With his eye on the imminent transfer of part of the occupied territory to the civilian administration, Backe explained that rations for the population must be 'the very smallest' from the outset. For the urban population, in particular, very little food was available 'because the main part of the produce requisitioned must be reserved to supply the troops and to be taken to the Reich'. Even if the civilian administration should eventually want to feed the inhabitants adequately, this would have 'invariably to take second place to the demands of the Greater German food economy'.

Backe's arguments were essentially a reaction to ideas circulating in the Ministry for the East. In a draft for the civilian administration, Rosenberg's political adviser, Minister Otto Bräutigam, rejected Backe's radical concept of exploitation. Bräutigam argued that it was an illusion to believe that large quantities of grain could already be obtained from this year's harvest. Expectations of quantities between 7 m. and 10 m.t. of grain were unrealistic. In fact, it might even be necessary to assist the population—except in the Russian areas—with German stocks. In any case, without the willing co-operation of the peasants, neither the political 'New Order' objectives nor the economic targets could be reached. Collection of grain must therefore 'depend exclusively on the size of surpluses which can be procured without *substantially* damaging the continuation of agriculture or the living standards of the population. It would be a sufficiently great achievement if the German army of millions could be fed from the land to a significant degree.'[268] Of course, German economic interests must not be neglected. 'However, procuring of stocks to an extent which drives the population of the occupied territory to desperation, and arouses hatred of Germany, may produce momentary relief at best, but cannot serve German interests in the long term.' Time would show

---

[266] See Streit, *Keine Komeraden*, 136.

[267] Reich Marshal of the Greater German Reich, Plenipotentiary for the Four-Year Plan, VP 1229 5/41 g.Rs., minutes of the meeting of the Economic Operations Staff East, 31 July 1941, BA-MA RW 31/11.

[268] Gibbons, 'Richtlinien', 261.

that Bräutigam's assessment of the practical difficulties of the policy of exploitation, and of its disastrous consequences, was correct. But in the summer of 1941 Hitler, Göring, and Backe were interested only in short-term gains. They believed that resistance in the occupied territory could be overcome by the use of the most brutal force. Once the anticipated rapid victory was achieved, there would be sufficient men available to apply it.

Despite sporadic attempts to adopt a more pragmatic approach, the German military leadership thus held to its radical policy of exploitation in the occupied Soviet territories, and permitting millions of people to die of starvation. Alongside State Secretary Backe, this concept was once again supported by General Thomas. He instructed his inspectors to exert strong pressure on the Soviet population, and to leave large areas to their own devices, i.e. expressly to let them 'starve to death'.[269]

The unexpected prolongation of the war in the east had two main consequences for occupation policy. First, it meant that more Russian workers had to be recruited to supply the most urgent needs of the troops and the homeland. Second, it became necessary to compensate for the growing shortage of security forces by introducing political and economic measures of pacification. This situation gave increasing weight to the pressure for a modification of the radical starvation strategy. Nevertheless, the economic leadership vehemently opposed all endeavours to change food policy, especially those encouraged by individual military quarters. When the Wehrmacht stated its growing demands and needs, Backe reminded it of its duty to exploit the occupied territory more fully.[270] At a meeting of the relevant departments on 16 September 1941, Göring supported Backe's approach, and essentially confirmed the existing guidelines. According to these, not only was a reduction in German rations to be avoided at all costs out of regard for the public mood at home, but if possible they were to be increased. Göring listed the order of priorities for the distribution of foodstuffs:

First come the *fighting* forces, then the remaining troops in *enemy countries*, and then the *troops at home*. The daily rations are fixed accordingly. Next the *German* non-military population is supplied. Only then comes the *population in the occupied territories*. Basically, in the occupied territories only those people who are working for us should be assured of appropriate food supplies. Even if one *wished* to feed all the rest of the inhabitants, one *could not* do so in the newly occupied eastern territory. As for issuing food to Bolshevik *prisoners*, we are, in contrast to the situation with other prisoners, not bound by any international obligations. Provisions for them can therefore only be determined according to the work they do for us.[271]

[269] See KTB WiRüAmt/Stab 1941, 173–8 (31 July 1941), BA-MA RW 19/165, and Chef WiStabOst No. 40153/41 g., discussions in Berlin on 31 July 1941, BA-MA RW 31/11.
[270] See chief of staff, memorandum on discussion with State Secretary Körner on 4 Sept. 1941, BA-MA RW 19/177.
[271] Memorandum of Maj.-Gen. Nagel, 16 Sept. 1941, No. 003-EC, *IMT* xxxvi. 107.

(a) Self-supply by the Wehrmacht

Although the Wehrmacht was granted the highest priority in the allocation of food, this did not relieve the situation confronting it on the eastern front. First, the Reich Ministry of Food remained anxious to remove the army in the east as much as possible from its calculations within the Reich, and to prevent supplies being sent to it from Reich stocks. Second, the ministry intended to continue transporting captured foodstuffs away from the occupied eastern territories.[272] The troops themselves were not always sufficiently frugal in their use of Russian supplies; accustomed to the regular supply of rations, they regarded Russian foodstuffs as mere supplements which could be consumed at will.[273] Despite many appeals for frugality, the soldiers were often responsible for wasteful exploitation which inflicted considerable damage. The GOC Fourth Army, Field Marshal von Kluge, issued a Draconian decree against looting and the vilest forms of crime, which he had found to be prevalent, especially in the hinterland. The occupied territory should be regarded as 'German economic land' and treated with due respect.[274] Looters were threatened with the death penalty, while superior officers who failed to stop their men running wild would face court martial.

Maintenance of discipline among the troops was also an essential precondition for organizing the large-scale exploitation of the country that Göring had demanded. In this context, Army High Command told the supply agencies 'that a ruthless and intensive exploitation of the country is an absolute necessity from the standpoint of the overall food situation'.[275] The entire food supply of the army in the east would have to be obtained from the land in the near future. Efforts to that end were to be intensified. For the army, the need was no longer simply to safeguard current supply, but also to lay in winter stocks for the occupying troops. According to directives from the quartermaster-general, self-supply in food was to be guaranteed through a close network of supply-depots situated near rail links, from which goods could be moved to the front when operations came to a stop. This would allow the army of occupation to survive the winter on a largely self-sufficient basis, by making itself independent of the difficult transport situation.[276] In fact, this objective was realized only to a slight degree. Individual units understandably showed little inclination to bring in the harvest or lay in stocks when it was likely that they would have to advance further east, or when they were due to return to Germany.

---

[272] As n. 270 and discussion between Min. Dir. Riecke and departmental head, 3 Sept. 1941, KTB WiRüAmt/Stab 1941, 226, BA-MA RW 19/165.

[273] WiStabOst, Chefgr. La, report on reconnaissace trip to territory of Economic Inspectorate South, 15 Sept. 1941, BA-MA RW 31/12.

[274] OB 4. Armee/O.Qu. III/IIa/Ic No. 2000/41 geh., special order on the maintenance of discipline, 11 Sept. 1941, BA-MA RH 20-4/884. See also AOK 17/Ia No. 0973/41 geh., conduct of German troops in the eastern territories, 17 Nov. 1941, BA-MA, 17. Armee, 14499/15.

[275] Der Heeresintendant im OKH/GenStdH/GenQu/Az. 830/41 (IV, 1) No. 2384/41 geh., letter on land use, 6 Oct. 1941, BA-MA RW 41/9.

[276] See Halder *Diaries*, 1247 (20 Sept. 1941).

In these conditions, there was little prospect of achieving the quotas laid down by the Economic Staff East at the end of September 1941.[277] Unreliable data—German and Russian units of area were sometimes confused during the calculations[278]—often led to the setting of exorbitantly high quotas. As a result, such supplies as could be obtained were transported to the Reich as soon as the immediate requirements of the troops had been met, thereby reducing the long-term prospects of survival for the troops. A brief examination of the relationship between the procurement quotas and the needs of the troops reveals that surpluses which could be taken to the Reich were to be expected only in the Ukraine; in central Russia, the procurement target fell far short of satisfying the needs of Army Group Centre (see Table II.VI.2).[279] The army group also calculated that, during Operation Typhoon, it would be advancing into a region which had already been harvested and stripped of food by the Red Army. The quartermaster-general therefore immediately demanded increased supplies from Germany to replenish stocks.[280] The economic authorities were unable to meet this demand: the desperate transport situation even ruled out an otherwise conceivable 'triangular transaction'—taking supplies from Reich stocks to Army Group Centre, and replenishing stockpiles with surpluses from the Ukraine.[281] Attempts to increase the exploitation of the area of operations for the needs of the troops also failed because the Economic Staff East had insufficient transport to get the food to the front, and the quartermaster-general could not provide any additional transport capacity.[282] Supplies could not be brought in when required owing to the priority accorded to ammunition and fuel convoys to support operations, at a time when the transport system was becoming less efficient. The troops just about managed to supply themselves in the Baltic and the Ukraine. However, Army Group Centre was forced to adopt a ruthless policy of 'eating the country bare', which made organized economic management for the winter more difficult from the outset.[283]

The overall food supply of the army in the east was under threat from the onset of the muddy season, particularly as it also brought agricultural operations to a halt. Even in Army Group South, cases of pillage and signs of

---

[277] See OKH/GenStdH/GenQu/IVa/Az. I/8300/41 (IV, 1) No. I/22893/41 geh., letter on securing troop requirements of supplies from the occupied eastern territories, 8 Oct. 1941, BA-MA RW 41/9.

[278] See Chefint. b. W.Befh. Ukraine, Sachgebiet E, No. 400/41 geh., situation report for OKH, 8 Nov. 1941, ibid.

[279] See memorandum on discussion with Main Group Agriculture of Economic Inspectorate Centre, KTB 1 Außenstelle OKH/GenQu Versorgungsbezirk Dnepr/IV Wi, entry 7 Oct. 1941, BA-WA Wi/ID. 1123.

[280] See minute of the discussion with the quartermaster-general on 8 Oct. 1941, BA-MA RW 31/12, and Economic Staff East/Agriculture, War Diary entries, 13 Oct. 1941, BA-MA RW 31/42.

[281] Report by Riecke to departmental head on 16 Oct. 1941, KTB WiRüAmt/Stab 1941, 281–2, BA-MA RW 19/165.

[282] Report by Lt.-Gen. Schubert to departmental head, 25 Oct. 1941, ibid. 298.

[283] See WiStabOst, half-monthly report 16–31 Oct. 1941, BA-MA RW 31/14.

TABLE II.VI.2. Deliveries of Agricultural Produce 1 September 1941–31 August 1942, as of 31 May 1942 (t.)

	Grain			Meat		
	Target	Actual	Expected shortfall	Target	Actual	Expected shortfall
Reich Commissariat Ostland/Econ. Insp. North	310,000	170,236	111,000	40,000	38,850	—
Gen. Comm. Belorussia/Econ. Insp. Centre	450,000	243,988	177,000	120,000	63,418	38,500
Reich Commissariat Ukraine/Econ. Insp. South	1,650,000	748,600	501,000	200,000	101,500	60,500
OCCUPIED EASTERN TERRITORIES OVERALL	2,410,000	1,162,224	789,000	360,000	203,768	99,000

	Fats			Potatoes		
	Target	Actual	Expected shortfall	Target	Actual	Expected shortfall
Reich Commissariat Ostland/Econ. Insp. North	30,000	17,098	7,000	240,000	172,747	65,000
Gen. Comm. Belorussia/Econ. Insp. Centre	10,000	735	9,000	360,000	343,814	16,000
Reich Commissariat Ukraine/Econ. Insp. South	10,000	7,100	—	360,000	140,000	200,000
OCCUPIED EASTERN TERRITORIES OVERALL	50,000	24,933	6,000	960,000	656,561	281,000

Source: WiStabOst, Landwirtschaftliche Auflagen 1914/42 (Handakte Dr. Baath), BA-MA Wi/ID. 1410.

disintegration among the troops were on the increase.[284] Although adequate food supplies were available in the hinterland, the front-line troops suffered hardship from time to time. Transport problems were not the only reason. The personal union of the agricultural leadership posts in the Economic Inspectorate South and in the Reich Commissariat did not always lead to a greater regard for military interests, as might have been expected, because the Chief Group Agriculture concentrated primarily on the demands of the home front to the detriment of food distribution in the area of operations. There was even deliberate deception of the agencies of the quartermaster-general over the purchase of foodstuffs in the territory of the Reich Commissariat.[285] Local agricultural leaders offered the army rations offices large quantities of grain, which had to be taken charge of immediately or be sent to the Reich. Owing to a lack of depot and transport capacity, the army offices were unable to accept these 'offers', giving the authorities of the Reich Commissariat the necessary justification to sell the stocks in the Reich. Only after an argument that dragged on for weeks was an agreement reached; this allowed the military offices to take over half of all the depots which were sited near railways, enabling them to buy up at least some of the produce offered them by the agricultural leaders.

The army group was in desperate need of this support. During its advance towards the Black Sea and the Donets industrial area, it was entering territories which had been largely denuded of male workers by the Red Army, so that it was extremely difficult to bring in the harvest. The ruthless plunder of valuable regions of agricultural surplus by Hungarian and Romanian troops further diminished food-supply prospects for the winter. The chief of staff of Sixth Army argued that the troops must therefore be spread out as widely as possible across the land to enable them to survive the winter.[286] He also warned against continuing the offensive to the Don, because this would mean reaching an area where nothing edible was likely to be found, and where poor rail communications made it impossible to bring up supplies.

However, the operational leadership took no account of these reservations. The army in the east was ordered to resume the battle after the end of the muddy season. Nevertheless, the quartermaster-general told the Reich Ministry of Food that a ration contribution must be made available from the Reich for the next six months, because full self-supply from the occupied territory would not be possible.[287] Moreover, since the next spring thaw would probably hamper the transport movements necessary to collect and distribute supplies

[284] See Ob.Kdo. H.Gr. Süd Ia/Ib No. 2987/41 geh., order on maintenance of discipline, 27 Oct. 1941, BA-MA RH 22/9.
[285] On the following see the letter from the Chefintendant beim Wehrmachtbefelshaber Ukraine to the Reich Commissioner, 25 Oct. 1941, and his situation report for OKH, 8 Nov. 1941, BA-MA RW 41/9.
[286] O.Qu., Assessment of Sixth Army food situation for the winter of 1941–2, 24 Oct. 1941, BA-MA RH 19 I/75.
[287] See KTB WiRüAmt/Stab 1941, 614 (21 Nov. 1941), BA-MA RW 19/166.

from the land, sufficient stocks must be laid down in the Reich to meet all the rations needs of the army in the east for at least two months. Backe agreed to these demands. However, these concessions were described merely as 'contributions' from Reich holdings, while the basic principle of self-supply from the land was maintained.

In view of the escalating transport crisis, and the priority given to fuel and ammunition transports needed to support operations, the front-line formations soon faced major difficulties in obtaining food supplies. With stocks as low as one or two days' rations, the troops were living virtually from hand to mouth. Any interruption in the transport of rations, whether due to the non-arrival of trains from Germany or to a fall in procurement levels, could lead to crises at least at local level. In this situation, the survival of the troops depended mainly on whether sufficient food could be found in the rear area and brought to the front. The greatest problem here was the continuing tug of war between the obligation to send deliveries back to the Reich and the supply needs of the Wehrmacht. In Army Groups North and Centre, the food collected locally by the German occupation authorities was almost all available for the Wehrmacht. On the other hand, the civilian administration in the 'Ukrainian bread basket' had to deliver high quotas for transport to the Reich.

The Chefintendant attached to the Wehrmacht Commander Ukraine, who was responsible for satisfying the needs of the troops, did not even have a precise idea of food-supply prospects or of amounts likely to be collected, because the Economic Inspectorate South and the agencies of the Reich Commissioner were unable to provide him with the necessary data.[288] Nevertheless, transports into the Reich were continued, though the civilian authorities themselves described this as a 'leap in the dark'. In November–December 1941, for example, five transport trains containing cattle were sent each day from the Ukraine to Germany, at a time when Army Group South was urgently calling for a supply of cattle from the rear area because it could no longer guarantee supplies of fresh meat.[289] Only after bitter protests from the Wehrmacht did the civilian administration declare itself willing to cut down on cattle transports to the Reich. From the beginning of 1942 it then dispatched twelve cattle-trains per week to the Field Agency South of the quartermaster-general. However, the quantities of processed meat products, likewise asked for, could not be prepared for dispatch because there were no nails for the crates.[290]

Similar friction also appeared over the supply of grain. Worst affected were the horses used by the army in the east, because State Secretary Backe refused

---

[288] Chefintendant beim W.Befh. Ukraine, situation report for Army High Command (see n. 278).

[289] See half-monthly report of Economic Staff East 1–15 Nov. 1941, BA-MA RW 31/14, and letter of Außenstelle Süd/OKH/GenQu/O.Qu. to Army Group South, authorized transport officer, 12 Nov. 1941, BA-MA RH3/Arb. No. 111.

[290] See Chefintendant beim W.Befh. Ukraine, Sachgebiet E, No. 194/42 secret, letter to OKH about fresh meat supply, 15 Jan. 1942, BA-MA RW 41/9.

to provide roughage and oats from the Reich, even after intervention by Brauchitsch.[291] In Army Group South the horses were eventually fed on grain; in Army Group Centre straw roofs in the villages were removed for use as fodder. With the onset of winter, the undernourished horses were unable to carry their increased burdens, and many perished. The supply of bread-grain was also uncertain.

The most likely solution to these problems was for the troops to rely increasingly on the grain that could be obtained from the land, and to enlarge the stocks under German control, i.e. to reduce the share remaining to the local people. To this end, the occupation authorities planned a large-scale threshing drive in November 1941.[292] In the course of the winter, troops were to be used to compel the peasants to bring in the remaining grain harvest, to thresh it, and to load it for the occupying power. The objective of the operation was outlined by the Wehrmacht Commander Ukraine: '*The utilization of the harvest of the occupied eastern territories is of vital significance for the further conduct of the war.* In particular, rapid procurement of the grain harvest is necessary to avoid spoilage, and to prevent access by the native population.'[293]

Though the Germans estimated the harvest in the Ukraine at 5.2 m. t., the collective farms had delivered only 1 m. t. of grain, almost all of which had already been distributed (Wehrmacht 250,000 t., transport to the Reich 50,000, Reich reserve in store 600,000).[294] Expectations of additional booty were therefore high—between 2 m. and 3 m. t. The men responsible—Göring, Koch, Thomas, and the Economic Staff East—realized that this target could be attained only if front-line troops were made available for the threshing drive. However, the quartermaster-general refused to make eight divisions available for this purpose, as that would doom the advance on Moscow to failure. Hitler declined to take an unambiguous decision on whether priority was to be given to the military operation or the economy.[295] The drive was set to begin on 15 December 1941. A few days before, however, all security formations which were at combat strength had to be withdrawn for front-line service in order to check the Red Army counter-offensive. In addition to the weakness of the military elements who were due to carry it out, the drive was also hindered by a shortage of fuel, threshing-machines, and means of transport. Almost half the harvest brought in was subsequently lost through damp and damage caused by mice.[296]

[291] See WiStabOst/La, War Diary entries, 28 Oct. 1941, BA-MA RW 31/42, and Halder, *Diaries*, 1306–7 (20 Nov. 1941).
[292] See KTB Befh. rückw. H.Geb. Süd 1941, 146 (5 Dec. 1941), BA-MA RH 22/3.
[293] W.Befh. Ukraine/O.Qu. No. 1780 (805)/41 geh., instruction on threshing drive, 2 Dec. 1941, BA-MA RW 41/9.
[294] See discussion of agriculture chiefs on 2–3 Mar. 1942, BA-MA RW 31/17.
[295] See WiRüAmt/Stab Z/SR, data for report to departmental head in Frankfurt am Main: food situation, Nov. 1941, 3, BA-MA Wi/ID. 112, *Das Deutsche Reich und der Zweite Weltkrieg*, v/ 1. 605–6.
[296] See discussion of agriculture chiefs (n. 294).

Despite the fact that the drive was carried out under military control, only part of the remaining harvest went to the Wehrmacht. Although there was an agreement with the civilian administration for 160,000 t. of grain to be handed over to the Wehrmacht, and although the Chefintendant attached to the Wehrmacht Commander Ukraine tried to get the purchasing districts of the army rations offices to operate according to the production levels of the harvest areas, the Agricultural Organization continued to refuse to provide actual collection figures, and moreover delayed the handing over of depot capacities as agreed.[297] Such conduct by the civilian authorities was not always due to an unwillingness to co-operate. They were often simply overstretched.

Thus, a disastrous shortage of sacks forced the closure of mills because the flour could neither be stored nor transported.[298] In Kirovo district, in the heart of the Ukraine, 600,000 t. of grain, pulses, etc. had to be moved from collective and state farm stores, where they were in danger of spoiling. Though goods in the region had previously been transported by rail, this became impossible because of the inadequacies of the German railway operation; the use of lorries was out of the question owing to the poor road conditions. With only 6,000 horse-drawn vehicles available, the necessary transports would take over 200 days. Army Rations Office 751 in Kirovo eventually demanded individual railway wagons to enable it to ensure at least the current supply for the troops.[299]

It is no exaggeration to claim that German endeavours to exploit the occupied territory to the full were condemned to failure. The root causes were the persistent inefficiency of an often chaotic administration, and the rivalry between military and civilian agencies. The self-supply of the Wehrmacht, the first priority of German food-supply policy in the east, was also affected by these conditions. Though in general the army in the east was relatively well supplied throughout the winter, the situation at the front varied considerably from sector to sector.[300] In the agriculturally poor region of northern Russia, Army Group North survived only because of a constant inflow of foodstuffs from the Baltic, which created considerable transport problems for Sixteenth Army in the Tikhvin area. Since the army area itself was 'an absolute wilderness without a hinterland', intermittent crises were inevitable. The situation facing Army Group Centre was more favourable. Apart from the case of Ninth

---

[297] See Chefintendant beim W.Befh. Ukraine, Sachgebiet E, No. 548/41 geh., situation report for OKH, 5 Dec. 1941, and instruction for creation of purchasing districts, 6 Dec. 1941, BA-MA RW 41/9.

[298] Chefintendant beim W.Befh. Ukraine, Sachgebiet E, No. 28/42 geh., situation report for Army High Command, 3 Jan. 1942, ibid.

[299] Supply Agency 751 Kirovo, report to Chefintendant beim W.Befh. Ukraine on transport, 12 Dec. 1941, ibid.

[300] For the following see WiRüAmt/Stab/Ia, discussion with liaison officers of armies in the east at War Economy and Armaments Department on 29 and 30 Dec. 1941, BA-MA Wi/ID. 1222, partially reproduced in *Deutsche Besatzungspolitik*, No. 84, pp. 205 ff.

Army in the Upper Volga region, there were stocks of cattle and grain in the rear area to allow the army to live off the land for extended periods. Some of these supplies, however, were lost during the precipitate retreats which marked the winter months.

Army Group South faced critical conditions. Sixth Army, in the Kharkov region, was operating in an area which had been 'eaten bare' for hundreds of kilometres. In the Donets industrial region Seventeenth Army encountered three major problems. First, transport conditions east of the Dnieper were so catastrophic that it was impossible to bring in enough supplies. Second, the slow rate of the German advance had given the Red Army time to destroy the region and denude it of stocks. Third, the position of the army was damaged by friction with the economic agencies. For example, the Economic Inspectorate South was transporting cattle from the Dnepropetrovsk area to Germany even as Seventeenth Army was being forced to bring in cattle from the western Ukraine for its own supplies. On the other hand, although First Armoured Army occupied an exposed position on the Don, it was helped by the fact that the supply leadership had established a base there which ensured adequate supplies. Despite the destruction of the war, the enormous agricultural wealth of the Don region allowed the army to live extensively off the land. In the Crimea, however, Eleventh Army faced a very different situation. Here the army would only be able to live off the land until the end of the year. Thereafter, it would be almost totally dependent on supplies being brought in.

(b) Selective Starvation Policy against the Soviet Civilian Population

The goal of food policy was to cover the food deficit in the Reich both by ensuring that the Wehrmacht was able to support itself completely from the occupied eastern territories and by exporting additional foodstuffs to Germany. This objective had been only partly achieved by the winter of 1941–2. Furthermore, so long as the German occupation authorities were unable to collect the quantities demanded for the troops and the homeland, they had no cause to worry about making food available to the civilian population. For conflicting ideological and economic reasons, the economic authorities were unprepared for such a task. Besides, the ruling élite in Berlin left no doubt of its desire to maintain the starvation strategy at all costs, a resolve strengthened by the arguments of State Secretary Backe that the policy was essential in order to maintain rations in the Reich. Nevertheless, there were repeated proposals for a change of direction from the occupation agencies directly concerned with implementing this policy.

At the heart of their reasoning lay practical considerations. Since unfavourable military developments were tying down all available military forces, the occupying power was unable to organize and exploit Soviet agriculture at the same time as maintaining control of the urban population whom it had effectively condemned to death by starvation. The growing demands of the front weakened the German presence in the hinterland, and increased the need for native workers who would have to be fed. Consequently, attempts to exempt larger sections of the civilian population from the starvation policy were inevitable. The first signs of this trend appeared in the military administration, next in Rosenberg's civilian administration, and last of all in the economic agencies.

Even in August 1941, when the military administration was earnestly endeavouring to bring in the harvest,[301] there was some flouting of the principle that the towns were not to be supplied with food and the population left to its own devices. The security police reported confidence among the population 'that the Germans would take every measure to avert this famine'.[302] In many places this confidence was apparently well founded. This is indicated, for example, by a progress report submitted by 213 Security Division, operating in the western Ukraine. The report, written at the end of August 1941[303]—before the area was handed over to the civilian administration—noted that the urban population could survive on its own stocks until the new harvest was brought in, with the Wehrmacht making some quantities available from captured stocks for the operation of community kitchens in an emergency. It concluded: 'Once the new harvest is brought in, the supply of the population ought not to cause any major difficulties.'

Such a procedure was covered by the immediate tasks assigned to local commandants' offices during the occupation of Soviet territories.[304] These included 'concern for the feeding of the civilian population, rationing if necessary in agreement with IV Wi of the field commandant's office', and the appeal to the peasants to supply the towns with food. The measures clearly contradicted Backe's guidelines of May 1941, because they allowed food to be consumed by the civilian population before German demands were met.

Conditions changed rapidly with the transfer of individual areas and towns to the civilian administration, and the development of the German Agricultural Organization. From the outset, Rosenberg's staff had shown disapproval of the starvation strategy advocated by the Four-year Plan Authority, but their views had little chance of being taken into account after the appointment of Koch as Reich Commissioner Ukraine. Koch committed the administrative machinery to meet war-economic objectives as its priority. Moreover, the agricultural organization directed by Backe had its main focus here. The state Zentralhandelsgesellschaft Ost (ZHO: Central Trade Company East) established a network of over 100 branches to procure, transport, and distribute the agricultural produce. This ensured that the food-policy guidelines could be

---

[301] See Befh. rückw. H.Geb. Mitte/Ia, instruction on harvest work, 15 Aug. 1941, BA-MA RH 26-221/17.

[302] Events report USSR No. 73, 4 Sept. 1941, 12, BA R 58/216.

[303] 213 Security Div./VII, Report on situation and lessons learnt, 27 Aug. 1941, BA-MA RH 22/204.

[304] See instruction sheet of 454 Security Div. on immediate tasks of local commandants' offices during the occupation of Soviet territories, 20 Aug. 1941, printed in *Deutsche Besatzungspolitik*, No. 10, pp. 57 ff.

ruthlessly enforced in the civilian administration. Even in ideal circumstances, it would have been difficult to create an effective system to procure and distribute food to the towns, owing to personnel deficiencies in the German administrative apparatus, and to the lack of transport. Nevertheless, if the German side had possessed the will, the urban population could still have been fed adequately. Enough food was available, at least in the Ukraine. About a million tonnes of grain were required to supply the population in the Ukrainian cities. However, the agricultural population quickly recognized that the occupying power was offering neither material nor political incentives for the delivery of surpluses. The inevitable result was that the collective farms often produced only enough to satisfy their own needs. The few German agricultural leaders, usually completely unqualified, were incapable of controlling and organizing agricultural production in the whole country outside individual points of concentration.

Ultimately, even the area of operations was affected by the attempt of the economic authorities to maintain the starvation strategy. Any pragmatic approach by the military quarters was therefore possible only within narrow limits. Nevertheless, some individual commanders did try to feed the civilian population under their control. Successes were most readily achieved by the implementation of emergency regulations. At the end of August 1941, for example, Army High Command responded to numerous requests by limiting an earlier decree from OKW, according to which members of former enemy states now working for the Wehrmacht were responsible for feeding themselves. Army High Command stipulated instead that Russian workers in mobile services—railway personnel, farm-cart drivers, and road-building columns of the Organization Todt—were to be fed from German stocks on the basis of the lowest daily rations in the Wehrmacht.[305] Another emergency regulation was issued shortly afterwards, to cover those engaged in non-mobile work for agencies of the army or of the army entourage in the territory under civilian administration. This laid down that provisions from Wehrmacht stocks could be supplied in return for wage reductions. Though the rations provided were only about half the Wehrmacht rations, and were accompanied by a big wage deduction (of 6 roubles per daily ration, compared with the hourly wage for an unskilled male worker of 1 rouble), they were much higher than those received by prisoners of war. These rations were also given to Jews, who, as a matter of principle, were to receive rations alone in place of wages.[306]

The Chief of the Economic Staff East in the area of operations, Lieutenant-General Schubert, went further. He supported a demand from the commander of Rear Army Area Centre that food should be provided for the whole

---

[305] Reproduced in Special instructions for Supply District South No. 112, 2 Sept. 1941, BA-MA RH 3/Arb. No. 105.

[306] Kdr. Vers.Bez. Süd/Qu., appendix to Special instructions to Supply District No. 121, 13 Sept. 1941, ibid.

civilian population.[307] The commander had pointed out that a deliberate 'guerrilla war' was being waged in his sector. The attitude of the population was crucial: the less able the Germans were 'to pacify them by guaranteeing minimal nourishment', the 'more effectively they were influenced' by the partisans. Schubert subsequently issued an order for the setting up of community kitchens for the urban population. Accepting that the 'complaints of our troops' would continue to increase, he asked General Thomas to urge Göring to change the guidelines covering food supply. So far as one can tell, he was not supported by Thomas or Backe.

On the contrary, Göring's directives of 16 September 1941, in which Backe appears to have had an important part, signalled a determination to maintain the previous course of feeding only those Soviet citizens who were working for the Germans.[308] According to Göring, because of the difficult food situation, larger towns were not to be occupied in future, but left to their own devices and starved out. Backe also obtained the support of Hitler for this course of action. After receiving information on the food supply of the Reich for the following winter, Hitler ordered that the capitulation of Leningrad and Moscow was not to be accepted, because the Germans could not justify feeding two cities' populations at the expense of Germany.[309]

These political guidelines were unequivocal. Nevertheless, even in the ensuing period some commanders continued to urge that the civilian population be left enough food 'for them to exist in makeshift fashion until the new harvest'.[310] If no food was available, native workers could not be found and put to work. At least in Army Group Centre, the need for manpower was so great that it could not be satisfied by the labour deployment offices of the economic inspectorate; Jewish skilled workers had 'perforce' to be used.[311]

The contradictions in economic policy were made manifest after the occupation of the big industrial cities of the Donets region. From the point of view of food policy, there might appear some justification for the notion that the administration and exploitation of the occupied territories in the east would be made easier by increased chaos, and by the 'increased flight of the population of the Soviet Russian cities to the interior of Russia'.[312] On the other hand, it was in the interests of the Economic Inspectorate South, and the troops

---

[307] On the following see letter from Head of Economic Staff East to Gen. Thomas, 26 Aug. 1941, BA-MA RW 31/11.

[308] See Nagel's report of 16 Sept. 1941, No. 003-EC, *IMT* xxxvi. 109.

[309] See WiStabOst/La, War Diary entries, 23 Sept. 1941, BA-MA RW 31/42; on Hitler's reaction see Jodl's letter to Army High Command, 7 Oct. 1941, No. C-123, *IMT* xxxiv. 425–6, and directive from GenStdH/Op.Abt. to H.Gr. Mitte, 12 Oct. 1941, *KTB OKW* i. 1070.

[310] See Kdt. rückw. Armee-Geb. 584/Gr. IV Wi, Guidelines for the securing of Wehrmacht requirements of foodstuffs and agricultural products, and of supplies for civilian population, 28 Sept. 1941, BA-MA RH 23/295.

[311] See WiStabOst/Fü/IL No. 40813/41 g., half-monthly report, 20 Oct. 1941, 8, BA-MA RW 31/13.

[312] AOK 17/Abt. Ia No. 0836/41 geh., telex of 21 Oct. 1941, BA-MA, 17. Armee, 14499/15, here adopting the formulation of the Führer decree of 7 Oct. 1941, No. C-123, *IMT* xxxiv. 326.

operating in the Donets region, to recruit as many workers as possible from those cities to reconstruct and operate the workshops, power-stations, railway lines, mines, and industrial plants. It was this attitude which led the anxious field commandants' offices to demand new directives for gaining the 'goodwill' of the Ukrainians, which was now also essential for the pacification and security of the hinterland.[313]

Rapidly emerging tensions between town and countryside aroused considerable interest on the part of the Germans. After all, the occupiers would be the obvious beneficiaries 'if the various parts of the population were to hold each other mutually responsible for the hunger that is inevitable in the future'.[314] On the other hand, passive resistance at the very least might be encouraged if, 'as reported by the representative of the Economic Inspectorate South, the delivery quotas are set five times as high for the collective farms as they were in Russian times', and if food-supply problems escalated. Sporadic initiatives from field commandants' offices, such as encouragement of a drift from the towns to the countryside while continuing municipal welfare, were bound to be ineffective so long as the economic agencies removed all the foodstuffs they could lay hands on without any concern for those sectors of the population left unprovided for.

Tensions increased with the onset of the muddy season, since Wehrmacht needs rose as supplies failed to arrive. The economic leadership, however, was not prepared to change course. In this situation, the army leadership at last began to support the efforts of local occupation authorities to achieve better treatment of the population. The commander-in-chief of the army, Field Marshal von Brauchitsch, now demanded a new order of priorities in the use of agricultural produce in the occupied territory: the troops should be supplied first, then the native population, and only then should any surpluses be sent to the Reich.[315] Backe rejected this request out of hand, on the grounds that if he accepted it, he would be unable to honour the meat coupon in the Reich[316] as Hitler and Göring had ordered. In the area of operations, the Economic Staff East, which had abandoned its push for independence and was seeking closer links with the command structure of the army, had reached a different conclusion. It considered that anxiety over growing resistance from the Soviet population was justified. The Germans were too weak to prevent those groups of the population who had been condemned to starve from joining the partisans and obtaining food by force of arms. Inadequate nourishment of the civilian population also reduced the 'enthusiasm for work' of men who were

---

[313] See 444, Sich.Div./Abt. VII/No. 239/41, situation report for Commander of Rear Army Area South, 20 Oct. 1941, BA-MA RH 22/202.

[314] Ibid. 4, also for the following.

[315] According to Riecke's report in his discussion with Gen. Thomas on 16 Oct. 1941, KTB WiRüAmt/Stab 1941, 281–2, BA-MA RW 19/165.

[316] Discussion between Economic Inspector South and departmental head on 18 Oct, 1941, KTB WiRüAmt/Stab 1941, 283–4, ibid., and WiStabOst/La, War Diary entries, 23 Oct. 1941, BA-MA RW 31/42.

urgently needed for German projects. All too often, workers simply failed to turn up because they were away bartering for food in the country. Increased emigration by the urban population also complicated the security problem, and made it more difficult to bring in big harvest yields. More food was being consumed by the population than the Germans had intended.[317]

On 6 November 1941 a discussion was held between the commander of Rear Army Area South, Infantry General Erich Friderici, and the head of Economic Inspectorate South, Lieutenant-General Hans Stieler von Heydekampf, in an attempt to reconcile these differing interests.[318] The economic leadership referred to a letter from GOC Army Group South, based on a suggestion by State Secretary Backe to the effect that the economic inspectorate was authorized to take drastic measures even against army units in order to fulfil the delivery quota. Stocks would suffice to cover the needs of homeland and troops, and possibly of the working part of the Ukrainian population, but not for their families or those without work.

In contrast, Friderici argued that the population must be guaranteed food 'to a certain degree'. 'A person working for us, in industry or trade, must not be allowed to starve totally. This is not a humanitarian matter, but a purely practical measure in the German interest.' This principle—that at least those people working for the Germans must be fed—was the lowest common denominator. It appeared that no more could be achieved. In any event, this seemed to be the conclusion drawn in a situation report written by the commander that same day. It stated:

The ruthless exploitation of the country to feed the homeland, which is the task laid upon the economic agencies, may lead to extensive hunger revolts and looting raids on the countryside by those sectors of the Russian population who are excluded from any provision. In addition to the military supply installations, protection against the starving urban proletariat will also have to be provided for those groups of urban workers who are working for us and are therefore still [sic] being fed, as well as for the rural population. The need for security forces will thereby be greatly increased.[319]

Hitler had already adjusted to this situation in July, and ordered the setting up of captured-tank units with the security divisions. Immediately upon the onset of winter, when the hunger crisis was reaching its peak, the first French armoured vehicles were allocated and the training of crews was begun.[320]

In his discussions of 7 and 8 November 1941 on the need for greater productivity in the German war economy, Göring emphasized that the food-supply guidelines must be maintained. The planned labour of large numbers

[317] See Economic Staff East, half-monthly report 16–31 Oct. 1941, BA-MA RW 31/14.

[318] KTB Bef. rückw. H.Geb. Süd 1941, 135 (6 Nov. 1941), BA-MA RH 22/3, partially reproduced in *Deutsche Besatzungspolitik*, No. 81, pp. 192 ff.

[319] Befh. rückw. H.Geb. Süd Abt. Ia/Ic 2270/41 g., letter to OKH/GenQu Abt. Kriegsverw., on assessment of the situation, 6 Nov. 1941, BA-MA RH 22/9.

[320] See letter from Chef OKW to Chef H Rüst, 5 July 1941, printed in *Deutsche Besatzungspolitik*, No. 32, pp. 104–5, and Befh. rückw. H.Geb. Süd/Abt. Ia No. 2344/41 geh., order on the establishment of armoured corps, 8 Nov. 1941, BA-MA RH 22/9.

of Soviet prisoners of war and civilian workers in Germany ought not to lead to a 'serious breach' of the food balance. He therefore ordered the 'establishment of their own diet (cats, horses, etc.)'.[321] Göring also made these remarks concerning food supplies for the Soviet population:

1. Provision for the rural population will create no especial difficulties. 2. The urban population can only receive very meagre quantities of foodstuffs. For the big cities (Moscow, Leningrad, Kiev) nothing at all can be done for the time being. The consequences of this are harsh, but unavoidable. 3. People working directly in the German interest are to be fed by direct distributions of food in the factories so that their ability to work is more or less sustained. 4. In the Ostland too, the food rations of the local population are to be set at a level well below the German, so that the greatest possible surpluses can also be obtained from there for the Reich.'[322]

Göring was well aware that the order to continue removing food to the Reich might bring about 'the greatest mortality since the Thirty Years War' in the occupied eastern territories.[323] He remained determined to maintain the ruthless policy of exploitation at all costs. Despite this, some occupation authorities did continue their efforts to achieve an improvement in the food supply for the Soviet population. The attitude of the civilian administration in Estonia, which refused to deliver bread cereals to the army at the expense of the native population,[324] was certainly an exception. The Economic Staff East applied itself to a 'policy of small steps' in these circumstances. It took advantage of the task of procuring food for the working section of the population in order to gain tighter control over the procurement and distribution of the foodstuffs available in the countryside as a whole.

On 4 November 1941 'maximum rations had been laid down for the supply of the towns' on condition that the needs of the Wehrmacht, the German authorities, and deliveries into the Reich were not affected.[325] The nutritional value of these rations was approximately 1,200 calories for inhabitants who were doing 'useful work', roughly 850 calories for those who were not working for German projects, and approximately 420 calories for children under the age of 14 and Jews. These were starvation rations which gave the population virtually no chance of survival in the long term. Additional rations above the maximum were forbidden, supposedly because they would inflict 'intolerable disadvantages for the feeding of the homeland'. Furthermore, the local econ-

---

[321] Rü IV, draft minute on comments by Göring at the meeting on 7 Nov. 1941, regarding employment of Russian workers in the war economy, 11 Nov. 1941, 1206-PS, *IMT* xxvii. 67.

[322] Memorandum of a discussion with Göring on economic policy and economic organization in the newly occupied eastern territories on 8 Nov. 1941, printed in *Deutsche Besatzungspolitik*, No. 82, p. 199.

[323] WiStabOst, Chef d.St., memorandum on the discussion with the Reich Marshal on 8 Nov. 1941, BA-MA Wi/ID. 1222.

[324] See half-monthly report of WiStabOst, 16–30 Nov. 1941, BA-MA RW 31/14.

[325] Special instruction of Economic Staff East on the care of the civilian population in the occupied eastern territories, 4 Nov. 1941, reproduced in Green Folder, part ii, 2nd edn., Aug. 1942, 196 ff., BA-MA RW 31/131.

omic agencies were instructed to delay until any stocks the population had managed to hoard were exhausted.

However, some efforts were made to introduce support measures which would improve the situation. The Economic Staff East made simple consumer goods available in order to offer the peasants an incentive to deliver surpluses.[326] The threshing drive was also designed to increase the procurement of foodstuffs. In addition, the economic agencies suggested that women should be regarded as particularly appropriate for work in the Reich, because they were least likely to be found work, and provided with food, in the east.[327] Special attention was paid to preventing a black market and flight from the towns.[328] The aim was 'to bind the workless urban population to the city, with the most productive possible exploitation of their work potential', in order to prevent the uncontrolled influx of foodstuffs from the land. To this end, orders were given for demolition and clearance work, the collection of material, road-building, and snow-clearing, all on condition that 'appropriate' provision could be supplied. The Economic Staff East hoped that this would achieve 'the regulation of food supplies in line with German interests', as well as 'relieving the countryside of unsafe elements from the politically more contaminated urban population'. Other measures were adopted alongside these work-creation projects: the larger towns were repeatedly sealed off, illegal imports of food were seized, and unauthorized markets were broken up by force.[329] Of course, such efforts to achieve a 'fair' distribution of available foodstuffs were extremely limited in scope. It should always be remembered that the 'maximum rations' were appallingly low, and that priority continued to be given to providing supplies for the Wehrmacht and the Reich.

The reaction of the military authorities remained inconsistent and indecisive. It fluctuated between resignation and a vain attempt at least to contain the starvation catastrophe which appeared to be inevitable. For example, in Orsha on 13 November 1941 the quartermaster-general reported that the food-supply question was 'catastrophic' for the civilian population, and that the army was virtually powerless to improve the situation.[330] At a ministry of food briefing on 20 November 1941 the commander-in-chief of the army again called for adequate rations to be given to the Russian civilian population.[331]

In the area of operations itself, reactions varied. The commander of Supply District South criticized the chaotic organization of economic matters, and demanded a 'modest but adequate supply of food' for Russian civilians.[332] On the other hand, some military quarters demanded the elimination of 'superflu-

---

[326] See WiStabOst, Chefgr. W, No. 38868/41, instruction of 15 Nov. 1941, BA R 7/1142.

[327] See half-monthly report of Economic Staff East, 8 Dec. 1941, BA-MA RW 31/14.

[328] For the following see WiStabOst, Gruppe Arbeit No. A 102/41 g. on prevention of emigration of unemployed urban population to the countryside, 20 Nov. 1941, RW 31/12.

[329] As n. 327.

[330] Quoted in Streit, *Keine Kameraden*, 157.

[331] Halder, *Diaries*, 1307 (20 Nov. 1941).

[332] Kdr. Vers.Bez. Süd/Iv Wi, economic situation report of 7 Nov. 1941, BA-MA RH 3/Arb. No. 111.

ous mouths' in the towns, especially inhabitants who were regarded as politically unreliable or racially inferior.[333] Some army commanders appealed to their soldiers to see the war as a racial and ideological war of extermination. 'Sympathy and softness towards the population' were therefore completely misplacd. 'The struggle against emerging difficulties of food supply is to be left to the self-administration of the enemy population.'[334] From the repeated prohibitions that had to be issued, it appears that ordinary soldiers often showed more humanity than their superiors, and fed Russians from their own field kitchens 'contrary to regulations'.[335] In any case, the quartermaster-general reported to Halder that German soldiers were often 'very considerate' towards the population.[336] Propaganda was therefore aimed at persuading the soldiers to remain 'hard in the face of starving women and children'. The German soldier would

be inclined to give some of his rations to the population. But he must say to himself: Every gram of bread or other food that I give to the population in the occupied territories out of the goodness of my heart, I am taking away from the German people and therefore from my family.'[337]

The Army High Command either could not or would not agree to more than a further, slight relaxation of the rations regulations for Russian workers in the service of the Wehrmacht.[338]

Ultimately, only marginal adjustments were made to the German starvation policy in the occupied eastern territories. The anticipated consequences were not long delayed. In the main Ukrainian cities of Kiev, Kharkov, Dnepropetrovsk, Zaporozhye, Poltava, and Taganrog the supply situation soon became critical.[339] As the local authorities were able to distribute only whatever small stocks were available, widely varying food quotas became the norm. In the newly occupied towns of the southern Ukraine, where the local people were still unaware of the real food situation, the military administration used propaganda in an attempt to keep them unsuspecting for as long as possible. In the long run, however, the food crisis in this region inevitably

[333] 339, Inf.Div./Ia No. 1466/41 of 5 Nov. 1941; see sect. II.vII.1 at n. 92 (Förster).

[334] AOK 17/Ia No. 0973/41 geh., conduct of German soldiers in the eastern territories, 17 Nov. 1941, BA-MA, 17. Armee, 14499/15. See also Streit, *Keine Kameraden*, 161–2, and sect. II.vII.1 at n. 110 (Förster).

[335] See Kdr. Vers.Bez. Süd/Qu., Instructions for Supply District No. 162, 10 Nov. 1941, BA-MA RH 3/Arb. No. 105. For the sector covered by Third Armd. Army, it was still being noted in spring 1942: 'Although no provisions may be handed over to the civilian population, for the most part the civilian population is being fed by the Wehrmacht' (KTB Pz.AOK 3/O.Qu., 11 May 1942, 176–7, BA-MA RH 21-3/v. 612).

[336] Halder, *Diaries*, 1317 (27 Nov. 1941).

[337] Appendix to OKH/GenStdH/HWes Abt. No. 221/10.41 geh., BA-MA RW 4/v. 253. For the context see Streit, *Keine Kameraden*, 162.

[338] OKH/GenStdH/GenQu/IVa No. I/43171/41, instruction regarding feeding of Russian manual and office workers, 25 Nov. 1941, reproduced in Green Folder, part ii, 2nd edn., 198 ff., BA-MA RW 31/131.

[339] See Befh. rückw. H.Geb. Süd/Abt. VII, activity report of 30 Nov. 1941, 3, BA-MA RH 22/203.

became acute, as everywhere else. Caught between the strict guidelines from Berlin and the growing pressure of problems on the spot, the occupation authorities searched in vain for a panacea. Their differing reactions, and the consequences, can be examined in the case of three cities which, according to express instructions, were to be starved out.

In line with orders from Hitler and Göring, Kiev, the capital of the Ukraine, was to receive the same treatment as Leningrad and Moscow by being cut off from all food supplies and starved out. Nevertheless, the military administration had initially tried to regulate the supply of food to the urban civilian population. Following Göring's directive of 16 September, the Economic Inspectorate South forbade any further importing of food into the city, but the field commandant's office continued to encourage at least the delivery of vegetables by the rural population.[340] When most of the military agencies had withdrawn from the city following the great fire, and had been replaced by the undermanned organs of the civilian administration, the 400,000 inhabitants of Kiev—about half the pre-war level—were left virtually to fend for themselves. In the middle of November 1941 conditions in the city were described by the Armaments Inspector Ukraine, Lieutenant-General Hans Leykauf:[341] not even the 25,000 workers on German projects could be fed adequately; the inhabitants were roaming the countryside in never-ending columns to barter for food, while the peasants travelled to the city with farm wagons to fetch the furniture they had been offered in return. Fourteen days later Leykauf wrote a vigorous letter to General Thomas demanding immediate measures to relieve the starvation, which he blamed on the thinking of the Wehrmacht:

'Skimming off the agricultural surpluses from the Ukraine for the food purposes [of the Reich] is . . . conceivable only if internal Ukrainian trade is suppressed to a minimum. Attempts are made to achieve this (1) by the elimination of superfluous mouths (Jews, population of the big Ukrainian cities which, like Kiev, receive no allocation of foodstuffs whatsoever); (2) by the most extreme reduction of the rations made available to the Ukrainians in the remaining towns; (3) by the reduction of the consumption of the peasant population.

However, the Germans must recognize that in the Ukraine 'in the last analysis, only the Ukrainians can produce objects of economic value through their work. If we shoot the Jews, let the prisoners of war die, allow much of the big city population to starve to death, we cannot answer the question: *Who will then produce economic assets here?*'[342]

After the fortunes of war changed, this question became more urgent. The vast distance of the front from the supply facilities back home, along with

---

[340] 454. Sich.Div./Abt. VII, memorandum on the visit to field commandant's office 195 in Kiev on 1 Oct. 1941, BA-MA RH 26-454/28.
[341] RüIn Ukraine, Z/A Id, No. 285/41 geh., situation report 16 Nov. 1941, BA-MA RW 41/9.
[342] Letter from armaments inspector, 2 Dec. 1941, No. 3257-PS, *IMT* xxxii. 74–5.

the difficult transport situation, strengthened the argument for building up the Ukraine as a supply-base for the fighting troops. In the search for unused industrial capacity, the attention of the Wehrmacht was inevitably drawn to big cities such as Kiev, where the basis already existed for the establishment of repair workshops and factories for accommodation needs and the requirements of the troops. This interest went hand in hand with efforts by the civilian administration to increase the economic benefits derived from the country by reviving the industrial economy.[343] Keeping the population alive and fit for work therefore came to be regarded as more important than before.

In December 1941 the starvation of Kiev was eased for the first time by the allocation of 200g. of bread per person per week, with an additional 600g. of bread for those at work. However, other vital foodstuffs such as fat, meat, etc. were not distributed; this resulted in a rapid increase in the number of people swollen with hunger.[344] Though the Wehrmacht was increasingly interested in the exploitation of the Ukraine for armaments purposes, its attitude thus had no lasting influence on the distribution of foodstuffs controlled by Backe. The approach taken by German heavy industry may also have helped to prevent a change in the course of German food-supply policy. After detailed enquiries into available industrial production capacities in the Ukraine, representatives of industry advocated the 'cannibalization' of the installations and their relocation to Germany.[345] The massive need for Soviet manpower in the German economy also suggested that moving people who were fit for work to Germany might be of greater benefit than leaving them in the occupied territory, where they could hardly be adequately fed and put to work under existing conditions.

This hesitation on the part of the German occupation regime left a large part of the population of Kiev to starve in the winter of 1942.[346] The shortage of food became so acute that there were not even enough rations for the 3,500 workers at the city's power-stations. Though the German authorities did not prevent a drift to the countryside, this often removed the most useful workers from the factories. The Armaments Inspector Ukraine reported on 11 March 1942: 'For many, work is almost a disadvantage, since those who work cannot concern themselves with obtaining food.'[347] The problem was exacerbated by the attempts of the civilian administration to prevent black-marketeering, on the grounds that it encouraged crime. This achieved the opposite effect to the one they had sought: the fixing of low market prices actually resulted in such food as had been freely on sale—and this was already in short supply—

---

[343] See RüIn Ukraine, Z/A Id, No. 113/42 geh., situation report 13 Feb. 1942, RW 30/104.
[344] Report of the mayor of Kiev, Dec. 1941, quoted in Sinicyna and Tomin, 'Proval agrarnoj politiki', 40.
[345] On this subject see Müller, 'Interessenpolitik', 110–11.
[346] As n. 343.
[347] RüIn Ukraine, Z. A. Id, No. 207/42 geh., situation report 11 Mar. 1942, BA-MA RW 30/104.

disappearing from the market altogether.[348] Stocks near to the city could not be used because of transport problems. The bitter cold and heavy snowfalls made things worse. Even the increase in the official allocation to 400g. of black bread per person per week, and the distribution of small amounts of barley, grits, flour, and occasionally a little meat, did not significantly ease the hardship.[349]

These attempts to provide emergency supplies for the urban population, but without challenging the priorities of German food-supply policy, could do very little to prevent starvation. A greater catastrophe, of the kind which the Germans had been prepared to see, was avoided largely by the efforts of the people of Kiev themselves. The fact that the city had a civilian administration made little difference. In fact, a second example demonstrates that the urban population fared no better under military administration.

Kharkov, the industrial metropolis of the Donets region, was conquered only in late autumn, and remained under military administration as a front-line city in the winter of 1941–42. The Red Army had succeeded in evacuating almost all food supplies; the remaining population—about half of the original 600,000 inhabitants—had no further chance of obtaining foodstuffs. Under these circumstances, the survival not only of the population, but also of Sixth Army, which was deployed in the city, was threatened during the coming winter.[350] The troops endeavoured to exploit the hinterland to find food for themselves, proceeding with some caution in order to prevent the area from being 'eaten bare' prematurely.

By the beginning of December 1941 food in the city was already so scarce that people were starving to death every day.[351] As there was not enough transport to bring sufficient food into the city, and stocks in the nearby areas had been exhausted, the military authorities advocated a partial evacuation of the population.[352] However, the local economic command feared that the inhabitants might consume more food out in the country than the quotas allowed them by the Germans. Instead, it proposed that a delivery quota be imposed on the surrounding villages in order to feed the city, thus keeping consumption under control.[353] Hitler made a personal intervention in the argument, to forbid evacuation into the hinterland. Keitel's compromise suggestion—that the population should be deported across the front into Soviet-held territory—was dismissed as impracticable by the GOC Sixth Army

---

[348] See events report USSR No. 187, 30 Mar. 1942, 12–13, BA R58/221.

[349] Events report USSR No. 191, 10 Apr. 1942, 30, ibid.

[350] See Gen.Kdo. LI. AK Qu/IVa, Order regarding securing of food for winter 1941–2, 19 Nov. 1941, BA-MA LI. AK, 15290/30.

[351] See activity report of Abt. VII/Befh. rückw. H.Geb. Süd, 15 Dec. 1941, 2, BA-MA RH 22/203.

[352] WiStabOst/Fü/IL No. 41330/41 g., half-monthly report 18 Dec. 1941, 23, BA-MA RW 31/41. See also sect. II.I.1(*g*) at n. 712 (Klink).

[353] Report of Economic Command Kharkov, 10 Dec. 1941, printed in *Deutsche Besatzungspolitik*, No. 83, pp. 204–5.

because the inhabitants refused to go voluntarily and the troops could not be expected to drive them out by force.

The conflict was quickly resolved by the decision that Sixth Army was not to be responsible for a forced evacuation. However, in January 1942, with a third of the inhabitants suffering from malnutrition, the city commandant decided to encourage people to leave. Following investigation by the security police, passes were handed out to individuals to allow them access to the hinterland.[354] Yet these people did not stay on the land for long, preferring to use the opportunity to barter for food and then return to the city. This black market was subsequently hampered by the appalling weather, and the food shortage reached catastrophic proportions in the spring of 1942. The Germans were now feeding only the workers employed by the Wehrmacht. The city commandant also ordered that units should make full use of their kitchen waste by distributing it to the starving population.[355]

The number of civilians who starved to death as a result of German food policy in the winter of 1941–2 cannot be assessed with any certainty. However, the greatest number of deaths undoubtedly occurred during the siege of Leningrad. Though the Wehrmacht lacked the strength to close the ring, so that limited food supplies could still be brought in and partial evacuations carried out, the death toll from starvation probably reached several hundred thousand during the 900–day siege. Admittedly, these people were only in-direct victims of the German starvation strategy, because they were on the other side of the German lines, but the connection is absolutely undeniable. In fact, the case of Leningrad sheds a particularly revealing light on the nature of the German starvation strategy. Owing to the successful defence of the city, German deliberations remained purely theoretical; the underlying approach of the various authorities towards the civilian population can therefore be seen with particular clarity, unaffected by practical considerations.

After the experiences at Kiev, Hitler and the Wehrmacht leadership re-solved to avoid battles for big cities whenever possible and not to occupy them permanently in future. Siege and starvation became the means by which military victory was to be achieved. In the case of Leningrad, however, the decision about the fate of the city had already been taken before the great fire in Kiev on 24 September 1941. Hitler had spoken to this effect at the beginning of July, and on 16 September, after Backe's report, Göring confirmed that the conquest and occupation of big cities were undesirable for 'economic reasons'. In the minutes of the discussions in the Wehrmacht operations staff of 21 September, a single reason is given for the decision not to occupy the city: 'because then we would be responsible for the food supply.'[356] This argument

[354] See events report USSR No. 156, 16 Jan. 1942, 44, BA R 58/220.

[355] Events report USSR No. 191, 10 Apr. 1942, 30–1, BA R 58/221.

[356] Landesverteidigung No. 02119/41 g.Kdos. (I Op), memorandum Leningrad, 21 Sept. 1941, BA-MA RW 4/v. 578. See sect. II.vi.4 at n. 245; also sect. II.i.1(c) at nn. 247 ff. (Klink) for a different interpretation of the facts, and sect. II.iii.2(b) at n. 155 (Ueberschär).

was to be repeated in all statements subsequently adopted by military command authorities.

The issue of food supply clearly also played a major role in later decisions taken by Hitler, and during the deliberations of the military concerning the fate of the city. This fact is important, because the capitulation of Leningrad was thought to be imminent. The idea of starving the city out had therefore lost its military utility and became merely an instrument of food policy. Political and ideological aspects were also involved: the city was regarded as the 'breeding-ground' of Bolshevism, and its depopulation and destruction were regarded as worthwhile objectives by the National Socialists. The military commands were determined to maintain the encirclement even if the city capitulated, to leave the population to fend for itself, to open fire on starving women and children if they tried to cross the German lines, and to leave open a corridor for evacuation to the east if necessary. This approach meant nothing less than the certain extinction of millions of human beings, in whose existence the occupying power had no political, ideological, or economic interest. The military commands produced scrupulously matter-of-fact reports on the practical possibilities open to the military authorities, revealing that they were fully aware of the consequences. The military made no attempt to examine in detail the assertion that Germany could take no responsibility for feeding the city at the expense of the Reich, even though vast quantities of food were being stored in the occupied territory for export to the Reich at a later date. During this period, the commanders expressed concern only for the morale of their troops. These facts in themselves cast significant light on the nature of the war being waged by Germany.

Despite original intentions, Army Group North did not manage to ignore the fate of the civilian population altogether. The long siege of Leningrad made it necessary to push large numbers of people from the area near the front into the hinterland, although this made it more difficult for the troops to live off the land.[357] In the winter of 1942 the remaining civilians close to the front at Leningrad were facing catastrophic conditions. Even those Russians who had been employed and fed by German units faced the threat of death by starvation in March, when several divisions were disbanded and their Russian auxiliaries left behind without work and practically without food. According to a report from Special Duty Squad A of the security police, in the period of three or four weeks before the new formations took on Russian workers 'a large section must try to evacuate or die'.[358]

The suffering of the population was so great that people could not be prevented even by threats of the most Draconian punishment from roaming near the front lines in search of food. To alleviate the worst suffering, the

---

[357] See minutes of discussion with the liaison officers of OKW War Economy and Armaments Department with the armies in the east on 29 and 30 Dec. 1941, quoted in *Deutsche Besatzungspolitik*, No. 84, P. 205.

[358] Events report USSR No. 190, 8 Apr. 1942, 6–7, BA R 58/221.

Wehrmacht agencies began to make more food and rations available to the civilian population. Nevertheless, the security police were mystified that 'mortality from starvation [was] not even higher'. Their only explanation was to suggest 'that the population is getting food by begging from Wehrmacht units; some have also preserved . . . stocks in especially well constructed hiding-places, [and the population also] appears to be accustomed to tolerating periods of hunger and surviving on inferior substitutes in a way undreamt of in German conditions'.[359] Even horses that had died and been buried the previous summer were being dug up and eaten. Uncounted thousands still died of starvation, and were piled up ready for burial when the thaw came. Special Duty Squad A reported: 'In Pushkin, for example, a squad was put together of members of the citizens' militia to search through the houses for bodies. About 400 bodies which had not been interred were found.'

Such reports inevitably give a more realistic picture of events than is provided in the positive account given by the Economic Staff East on 22 June 1942. This noted:

The experiences of the last winter have shown that the native population has an astonishing capacity to adjust. Despite all pessimistic predictions, it has proved possible to bring them through the winter without recognizable damage to health and with a minimum ration of food and heating material. But it has also been clear that without such a minimum ration, usually some form or other of feeding at work, the population simply does not come to work.'[360]

In the past winter almost every every urban household had possessed some reserves and objects which it could use to barter for food from the rural population. In future, the 'extent to which economic life in the occupied eastern territories can be maintained' would depend entirely on distributions to the inhabitants.

Fewer Soviet citizens starved to death during the first year of the German–soviet war than the millions which had been expected, consciously accepted, and even encouraged by the German leadership. It would certainly be misleading to attribute this to the assistance offered by the local occupation authorities, which began hesitantly and increased during the winter of 1942. First and foremost, it was the successes of the Red Army that forced the German occupation authorities to show more concern for the civilian population, and increased the need for native auxiliary workers. The GOC Ninth Army recognized this fact at the beginning of December: 'If the Russian campaign had been a lightning war, we would not have needed to take the civilian population into account. But no end can be seen . . . Under these circumstances it is unreasonable to follow a course which makes the civilian

[359] Ibid. 7.
[360] One year of the Russian campaign: Achievements of the war-economy formations of OKW/WiAmt. in the raw-material sector, compiled by OKW/WiAmt/Ro I Ost, 22 June 1942, 13, BA-MA Wi/ID. 1185.

population 100 per cent our enemy.'[361] The dependence of German food policy on considerations of power politics was revealed most clearly in the treatment of those Soviet citizens who were most vulnerable to German despotism: the prisoners of war.

(c) Mass Deaths among Soviet Prisoners of War

Though measures to enforce the starvation policy against the civilian population created a serious security problem, this was not true of the prisoners of war. Approximately 600,000 of them were to fall victim to the deliberate extermination measures of the SS during the war.[362] Another 700,000 were set to work as forced labourers by the Wehrmacht by the autumn of 1941,[363] and therefore had to be given at least some food. These men comprised the last and weakest link in the German food-chain, since even fewer rations were allocated to them than to Soviet civilian workers. On 6 August 1941 the feeding of the prisoners of war was made subject to uniform regulations in the entire military area for the first time.[364] On the grounds that Germany was under no obligation to feed the captured Soviet soldiers according to international law, a level of rations was fixed which—even had it been achieved in practice—would inevitably have led to malnutrition. The regulations were therefore unlikely to make any significant improvement to the catastrophic conditions in the camps.

At the beginning of September, when the Reich Labour Service units were withdrawn from the rear supply installations and deployed by the Wehrmacht as replacement manpower, there was a slight increase in the need for prisoners who were fit for work. In Supply District North, for example, six prisoners' battalions had to be established for skilled craft and loading work at the bases.[365] For the operation to run smoothly, it was essential to select capable, healthy prisoners of war, and to provide medical attention, clothing, and adequate food from army stocks.[366] This was only the first step: in the absence of German security forces, six 'escort companies' of Latvians and Lithuanians were set up to guard the prisoners of war; these too had to be fed by the

---

[361] Ninth Army Command to Army Group Centre, Proposal for immediate measures for the purpose of achieving positive co-operation from the Russian civilian population, 1 Dec. 1941, quoted in Dallin, *German Rule*, 331–2.

[362] This figure takes in the period until 1944, with the majority undoubtedly being killed in the second half of 1941; see Streit, *Keine Kameraden*, 105.

[363] See WiRüAmt/Rü IV f 2, memorandum on power rationing, 13 Nov. 1941, BA-MA Wi/ID. 112.

[364] See Streit, *Keine Kameraden*, 141–2.

[365] OKH/GenQu/Vers.Bez. Nord/Abt. HV, No. 210/41, Urgent letter to officer in charge of PoW camps attached to Commander of Rear Army Area North, 5 Sept. 1941, BA-MA RH 3/v. 139.

[366] See Vers.Bez. Nord/H. Vers. 229/41, report to Army High command/quartermaster-general on establishment of PoW labour battalions, 12 Sept. 1941, ibid.; parallel to this see special instruction No. 113 for Supply District South, 5 Sept. 1941, BA-MA RH 3/Arb. No. 105, ordering the provision of a hot midday meal for prisoners engaged in heavy work all day.

Wehrmacht.[367] In addition, from the autumn of 1941 increasing numbers of prisoners of war were released for use as 'volunteers' in anti-partisan operations and to reinforce the German security forces. They had to be fed as well as armed.

These men were the minority. Most of the prisoners of war, over three million men, were given no chance of survival. The steep rise in mortality, which reached approximately 1.4 million by December 1941, cannot be attributed to the conditions created by the war alone; the process began in the camps on Reich territory, and reached its peak in the area of operations only at the end of the year. The real cause of the deaths lay in the determination of the economic leadership to provide the least possible amount of foodstuffs both to the prisoners of war and to the Soviet urban population.

It was this objective which led the Economic Staff East to argue repeatedly that an increased use of Soviet prisoners of war as workers was unacceptable because of the food requirement.[368] Even the prisoners already being used in the rear army area could not be fed adequately, so that 'many would not survive this winter'. Göring confirmed the principles of German food policy once again on 16 September 1941. Thereafter, there was little chance that the efforts of some commanders on the eastern front to improve conditions in the camps, and to increase or at least honour daily ration levels,[369] would lead to a general change of policy. In no case were these fully supported by the military leadership.

Instead, the military leadership launched an unrestrained propaganda of hate, opposing humane treatment of the Soviet prisoners of war and 'false' sympathy with the starving.[370] It was in this spirit that the quartermaster-general also accepted the proposal of the Economic Staff East[371] for a drastic reduction in prisoners' rations. He instructed unit commanders to remember 'that every item of food that is granted to the prisoners either incorrectly or in excess must be taken from relatives at home or from German soldiers'. This order of 21 October 1941 can be explained by the assumptions of the previous spring, which remained largely intact. 'The decision was marked by the continued belief that many, at least, of the prisoners were expendable, and that deliberate efforts to sustain life were necessary only for those prisoners who could be of direct economic use to the German Reich.'[372] The quartermaster-

---

[367] Vers. Bez. Nord/Ia, No. 228/41, letter to Army High Command/quartermaster-general on escort companies, 26 Oct. 1941, BA-MA RH 3/v. 139. On the following see sect. II.VI.4(*c*) at n. 143 (Förster).

[368] See WiStabOst Fü Id No. 40609/41 g., half-monthly report of 29 Sept. 1941, 6, BA-MA RW 31/12.

[369] See e.g. AOK 16/O.Qu. (Qu. 2) IVb, instruction to Commandant of Army Rear Area (Armeegebiet) 584, 19 Oct. 1941, BA-MA RH 23/295.

[370] Order of FM von Reichenau, 10 Oct. 1941, No. D-411, *IMT* xxxv. 85. See also sect. II.VII.1 at nn. 110ff. (Förster).

[371] See WiStabOst/Chefgr. La/LaIII/411, proposal of 9 Oct. 1941, BA-MA RW 31/12: Streit, *Keine Kameraden*, 142.

[372] Streit, *Keine Kameraden*, 144.

general had allowed himself to be persuaded by the food-supply agencies that the food situation was 'dreadful', and that no adequate harvest—sufficient to satisfy the needs of the occupied eastern territories as well as cover the deficit faced by the Reich—could be expected until 1943.[373] From this point of view, a selective starvation policy appeared to be unavoidable.

However, Wagner's decision of 21 October 1941 appears in another light when set against the fact that the armaments economy had begun to achieve some success in its efforts to exploit the potential Russian labour force. In his function as chairman of the Reich Coal Association, Göring's industry manager, Pleiger, had been urging since the end of June 1941 that Soviet prisoners of war should be made available to him to cushion falling productivity in the German coal-mining industry.[374] After gaining the support of the War Economy and Armaments Office and the Reich Labour Ministry, Göring agreed to present the problem to Hitler. On 21 October Hitler decided that Pleiger should be allowed to recruit 10,000 Ukrainian miners to work in the Reich.[375]

The inflexible attitude of the German leadership had thus been changed for the first time. The decision also revived discussion about the exploitation of the Soviet prisoners of war, since the shortfall of workers in the German war economy was now almost two million. Besides, when operations came to a halt during the muddy season, all hope that the war could be concluded before the end of the year, and manpower thereby released to increase armaments production, was lost. According to a report from General Thomas, 'the commanding generals now approached the Führer . . . because of the situation of the Russian prisoners of war, owing to unfavourable repercussions on the mood of the troops. Führer has now given directive that the 3 mill. Russians are to be set to work in the economy and properly fed.'[376] The relevant Führer decree of 31 October 1941 was officially justified on the grounds that the manpower shortage was becoming 'an ever more threatening impediment to the future German war and armaments economy'. It was decided

that the labour of the Russian prisoners of war is also to be extensively utilized by making them work for the requirements of the war economy on a large scale. Precondition for their efficiency is an appropriate nutrition. Alongside this are envisaged very low pay for the most modest provision of some small luxuries of daily life, and bonuses should the occasion arise.[377]

However, State Secretary Backe felt unable to accept responsibility for feeding an extra three million recipients of rations in the Reich.[378] Hitler, on the other hand, refused to countenance a reduction in rations for the German

[373] See Wagner, *Generalquartiermeister*, 209 (21 Oct. 1941), and WiStabOst/La, War Diary entries, 24 Oct. 1941, BA-MA RW 31/42.
[374] On this see Streit, *Keine Kameraden*, 202 ff.
[375] Report by Chef Rü to departmental head, 22 Oct. 1941, KTB WiRüAmt/Stab 1941, 289, BA-MA RW 19/165.
[376] Report by Chef Rü to departmental head, 31 Oct. 1941, ibid. 310.
[377] Quoted from Streit, *Keine Kameraden*. 204.
[378] See KTB WiRüAmt/Stab 1941, 310 (31 Oct. 1941), BA-MA RW 19/165.

population. This conflict remained unresolved even as the collapse of the transport system, and widespread epidemics among the prisoners, prevented them being evacuated into the Reich. Mass mortality took its course, the more so as the Army High Command after nearly four weeks ordered no more than a paltry increase in rations (about 5 per cent more calories).[379] Once the harvest surpluses and the herds of cattle in the occupied eastern territories had been consumed or taken to depots, there was not enough food left for the urban population or the prisoners of war.

The military leadership was perfectly well aware of the consequences. At the discussions in Orsha on 13 November 1941 the quartermaster-general claimed that he was helpless, and explained that prisoners of war who were not working would simply have 'to starve to death'.[380] 'In individual cases, working prisoners of war could also be fed from army stocks. In view of the general food situation, however, even that cannot be ordered on a universal basis.' Yet not all military commanders were prepared to stand idly by while thousands starved. On 16 November, for example, the commander of Rear Army Area Centre ordered immediate action to organize the inhabitants of nearby villages to feed and clothe the prisoners in his sector.[381] To this end, a prisoners' spokesman was to be chosen in each camp in order to appeal to the local leaders for their charity. The aim was to organize a constant flow of horse-drawn vehicles from the villages to the prisoner-of-war camps.

As long as State Secretary Backe refused to provide food at the expense of the homeland and the troops,[382] there was little prospect that such stopgap measures would prevent catastrophe. At the end of November, after a discussion with the chiefs of staff of the army in the east, the quartermaster-general tried to accommodate the wishes of the troops. He moved to cancel the reduction of rations that had been introduced four weeks previously, and ordered daily rations—even for non-working prisoners[383]—which were higher than those of August. Supplements were also to be given to make the prisoners fit for work. The food for this purpose was to be obtained from the land.

This order not only came too late, but was also inadequate. Many camps were simply unable to obtain sufficient food from the surrounding land. Even in agricultural surplus regions of the Ukraine, attempts to provide food for the prisoners were fraught with problems. On 27 November 1941 the Economic Staff East reported:

On all the roads along which prisoners of war are taken, one sees leaves and discarded turnip-stalks being snatched from the fields in desperate hunger and devoured. These

[379] See Streit, *Keine Kameraden*, 138.

[380] Quoted ibid. 157.

[381] Befh. rückw. H.Geb. Mitte/Qu., special instructions for supplies No. 71, 16 Nov. 1941, BA-MA RH 26-221/18.

[382] See memorandum on a discussion in the Reich ministry for food, 24 Nov. 1941, No. 177-USSR, *IMT* xxxix. 446 ff.

[383] Telex OKH/GenQu Az. 960, 26 Nov. 1941 (copy), BA-MA RH 23/295.

columns of prisoners make a pitiable impression on the native population. In the villages, the inhabitants gather to throw turnips, potatoes, and slices of melon to the column. In the fields, the women near these prisoner transports throw turnips into their path, and these are hastily gathered up by the prisoners. The sight of these debilitated prisoners, with hunger staring from their eyes, must surely damage the feeling of the population towards the Germans.[384]

In central Russia it was not even possible to provide adequate quantities of grits and buckwheat. Worst fed of all, it seems, were the camps in the harsh countryside of northern Russia. For example, at the end of November the commandant of rear Armeegebiet 584 on Lake Ilmen in the sector of Sixteenth Army reported that there was hardly any food for the prisoners of war because of the great poverty of the country. Adequate nourishment was possible only by making distributions from the supply-depots at the front. In any case, the daily rations ordered by the Army High Command were not sufficient to save the prisoners of war, the majority of whom were already near starvation when they entered the camps. The prisoners, most of whom came from the territory occupied by the German troops, therefore asked to be released or to be put to work in the Reich.[385] The commandant of the SS-administered camp at Novgorod-Savaskiy, despite adequate food, classified almost half of the prisoners who were not put to work as 'candidates for death'.[386] Of the 2,800 men in the camp, between 50 and 60 were dying each day. In his monthly report for December 1941 the commandant of Prisoner of War District C in Rear Army Area North noted that there was no chance of finding enough food. As a result of the consequent high mortality rate, the number of prisoners able to work had already declined so much that it was impossible to meet even the most urgent demands for workers in the rear army area. He complained that though daily rations had been increased on paper, they were hardly ever available for distribution in full.[387]

In his report for General Thomas on 2 December 1941 the Armaments Inspector Ukraine also noted the economic absurdity of allowing hundreds of thousands of prisoners of war to starve to death in the coming winter, when they 'could profitably have been used for the economy in the Ukraine'.[388] Such warnings did not affect the appalling death rate of the Soviet prisoners of war, which continued until the spring of 1942. Of 3,350,000 prisoners taken in 1941, almost 60 per cent had died by 1 February 1942, including over 600,000 since the beginning of December 1941. Mortality was especially high in the Reich

---

[384] WiStabOst/Fü/IL No. 41159/41 g., half-monthly report 27 Nov. 1941, 22, BA-MA RW 31/14.

[385] Kdt. rückw. A.Geb. 584 No. 226/41 geh., report for Sixteenth Army Command on prisoner-of-war situation, 25 Nov. 1941, BA-MA RH 23/295.

[386] Kgf.-Bezirkskommandant J, report on the tour of inspection of 26 Nov.–10 Dec. 1941, 11 Dec. 1941, BA-MA RH 22/251.

[387] Kgf.-Bezirkskommandant C No. 1518/41, monthly report for OKH, 28 Dec. 1941, BA-MA RH 22/225.

[388] Letter of Armaments Inspector Ukraine to Gen. Thomas, 2 Dec. 1941, No. 3257-PS, IMT xxxii. 75.

(18.5 per cent as of December 1941), with about 47 per cent of Soviet prisoners of war there dying of starvation and typhus by the beginning of April 1942. This fact alone proves that the prisoners did not die as the result of an unavoidable 'emergency situation', but fell victim to a ruthless starvation policy.[389]

The leadership élite of the Third Reich accorded absolute priority to the nourishment of the homeland and the troops, because of an enduring anxiety about the stability of the system of government within Germany. This approach dictated the adoption of a policy that was directed not merely against the prisoners of war, but against the entire population of the conquered Soviet territories. In the spring of 1941 OKW and the Four-year Plan Authority had agreed on the objective of ruthless exploitation of the food capacity of the future colonies in the east on behalf of the German war effort. The death by starvation of 'umpteen million' Soviet citizens was consciously accepted. Certainly, the starvation policy also slotted seamlessly into a racial and ideological war of annihilation. Nevertheless, it seems clear that even Hitler regarded it less as a deliberate goal of occupation policy than as an apparently inevitable consequence of inherent economic necessities. This attitude made it difficult to change the course of food policy, even though Backe's measures were increasingly inconsistent with military interests and the requirements of armaments production after the autumn of 1941. The starvation strategy remained the official guiding principle of occupation policy until the spring of 1942.

Despite its retention, fewer Russians died from starvation than the Germans had expected. There are many reasons for this. First, the urban population had already fallen dramatically during the German invasion. The large-scale evacuation of munition workers, experts, administrative and Party officials by the Soviet government played a part, as did the mass liquidations carried out by the SS against the extensive Jewish section of the urban population. Second, the Germans had failed to achieve the expected rapid victory in the east. This greatly reduced the prospects of carrying out the starvation programme by force, because there were not enough security forces to seal off and starve out the big cities. From late summer 1941, some military quarters had tried to ensure an adequate supply of food for the Soviet population. The restrictive attitude of the economic agencies had prevented them from achieving results, even though the economic authorities recognized that the motives of the military were pragmatic, aimed at pacification of the hinterland and the recruitment of workers. By arguing that rations in the Reich could only be maintained by the ruthless exploitation of the occupied eastern territories, Backe could always rely on the support of Göring and Hitler for his policy. Interventions by military figures were bound to fail, because they were undertaken without the necessary vigour. Army leaders at the top and in the field

---

[389] On the figures see Streit, *Keine Kameraden*, 136.

could not agree on a decisive and unanimous approach. Hitler's concept of a racial and ideological war of annihilation was already so widely accepted by the command authorities of the Wehrmacht that it frequently determined their attitudes towards wartime difficulties. Like the administrative apparatus, the army in the east and the supporting Luftwaffe formations were forced to live largely off the land, i.e. at the expense of the native population. Because the military leadership still assumed that the war would end quickly, thereby easing the food situation, it was not inclined to provoke a conflict with the political and economic élites for the sake of a better treatment of the Soviet population.

The direct benefits of the troops and home front, as well as the opportunity to provide adequate food supplies for Soviet civilians and prisoners of war, were greatly reduced by the inefficiency of the German agricultural administration. A number of factors helped to keep results well below expectations: the number of qualified agricultural leaders was much too small: organizational conflicts and wrong decisions abounded; transport facilities and security forces were insufficient. Enough food was seized to feed the Wehrmacht tolerably well, and to create a substantial Reich reserve, though this had to be kept in the east owing to lack of transport capacity. (Of 600,000 t. of wheat, only around 50,000 t. were taken to the Reich by the spring of 1942.) Much of the reserve in the east was spoiled, as Bräutigam had foreseen. Almost nothing was left to feed the Soviet population. The occupying power was not even capable of providing enough food for the workers it employed.

The unintended result was to give the Soviet civilian population a better chance of survival by moving to the countryside and using the black market. Though many local occupation authorities were willing to tolerate or even to encourage such self-help, the fundamental approach of the political and military leaders did not change even after the experiences of the winter of 1941–42. Any slight improvement in the spring of 1942 was due mainly to the fact that the deaths of millions of prisoners of war and civilians had inevitably eased the demand for food in the occupied territories. The military élite continued to deny overall responsibility for feeding the enemy population. A progress report from the quartermaster-general on 24 March 1942 merely urged greater efficiency during future operations. It stated:

The selection and nourishment of native skilled workers among the prisoners and the civilian population must be undertaken as early as possible, even when these skilled workers cannot be set to work immediately on supply tasks or other labour duties. The workers will be required urgently by the troops or the Reich at a later date. Their labour must therefore be safeguarded as against the remaining civilian population, to prevent physical loss of strength as a result of inadequate accommodation and nourishment.[390]

---

[390] OKH/GenStdH/Abt. Vers.Führg./Qu 2 No. I/17591/42 geh., Lessons from the campaign in the east concerning supply management, 24 Mar. 1942, 12, BA-MA H 10-51/2.

These comments appeared to offer the opportunity to gain Hitler's consent to a change of direction in occupation policy. However, his decision at the end of October 1941 to use the Soviet prisoners of war as workers, and to feed them adequately, had no positive effect. Another step forward remained possible on the key issue of disbanding the collective farms, which the Wehrmacht and the civilian administration saw as the best way to win the support of the Soviet population. At the beginning of December 1941 Backe was outvoted in the Four-year Plan Authority.[391] Even Backe's own representative in the Economic Staff East had been convinced by the evidence of his own eyes that only a step-by-step reprivatization would lead to bigger yields. Surprisingly, on 15 Februay 1942 Hitler, despite protests from Backe and Koch, decided in favour of a draft along those lines from the Ministry for the East. Though the proclamation of the 'new agricultural order' brought the Russian peasants no substantial concessions—they would receive the land to be allocated to them only for their own use, not own it as their property—it was still the first step towards a 'more considerate' treatment of the Soviet population. The rescinding of the 'commissar order' was also a response to changed conditions at the front. When Albert Speer, the new Reich Minister for Armaments and Ammunition, attempted to get increased rations for Soviet prisoners of war, Hitler told him 'that he did not approve of the bad nourishment of the Russians. The Russians must receive an absolutely sufficient nourishment, and Sauckel had to see that this nourishment was secured from Backe.'[392]

At this stage Bormann and Backe intervened, and the reduction in rations for the German population and the Soviet prisoners of war went through asplanned. Clearly, a more drastic reduction of rations in the Reich would have been necessary in order to feed the prisoners adequately and leave the Soviet civilian population enough food to live on. Hitler was not prepared to make such a move. The starvation policy in the east was retained at a high price, because it inevitably led to an increase in passive and active resistance from the population. Equally, the destabilization of the hinterland further reduced the economic gains to be obtained from the occupied Soviet territory, and tied down military forces which could have been used elsewhere by the German operational leadership. This vicious circle arose as a result of the failure of Operation Barbarossa. It was also the direct consequence of yet another decision by the National Socialist leadership to postpone the total mobilization of the German population—at the expense of the occupied territories.

---

[391] On the following see Dallin, *German Rule*, 332 ff.

[392] Memorandum of Speer on the conference with Hitler on 22–3 Mar. 1942, in *Deutschlands Rüstung*, 86. On the background see also Streit, *Keine Kameraden*, 148; Fritz Sauckel, Gauleiter and Reich Governor in Thuringia, was appointed General Plenipotentiary for Manpower on 21 Mar. 1942.

5. Economic Causes and Consequences
of the Failed Blitzkrieg

At the beginning of November 1941, with the agreement of the military élite, Hitler had resolved to make one last effort to bring the offensive to a successful conclusion, and to win a breathing-space for the rest and rehabilitation of the army in the east.[393] The new offensive was designed partly to gain a great prestige victory, which was held to be necessary to improve the mood of the German population; above all, however, it was intended to destroy the remaining bulk of the Red Army, and to prevent the regeneration of Soviet fighting capability. Despite an inability to guarantee either adequate stocks and supplies or sufficient reinforcements for the troops, the German leadership still believed that the battle-weary divisions could achieve their ambitious operational objectives. The ability to make an accurate assessment of the enemy, and of the actual state of the German troops, had long been lost.

During the advance on Moscow, there were increasing signs that the Wehrmacht was reaching the limits of its strength in manpower and material. It had no prospect of regaining the level of armaments it had possessed at the start of the campaign.[394] Even the most urgent armaments orders of the Wehrmacht were not being fully completed because of the shortage of workers and raw materials. In fact, the chief of the army armaments programme was faced with such a serious decline in weapons and ammunition manufacture that he thought it advisable to make peace as soon as possible.[395]

His pessimism was shared by the Reich Minister for Armaments and Ammunition. After a tour of inspection by his tank commission to the eastern front, Todt became convinced that the war could no longer be won. On 29 November 1941 he advised Hitler to conclude a political peace.[396]

It was questionable whether the stopgaps contemplated by the Army High Command, especially the drastic reduction in army motorization,[397] would suffice to prepare at least some of the mobile formations for new offensive operations by the spring of 1942. Since October 1941 the supply of weapons to the eastern front had dried up, because Army High Command believed that large numbers of weapons would be accumulated by the planned disbanding of divisions in the east during the winter. This miscalculation bore bitter fruit in December, when it became clear that the divisions could not be disbanded, and when the high losses could not be replaced from the army groups'

---

[393] See Reinhardt, *Moskau*, 126 ff., and II.i.1(*f*) at n. 514 and ff. of the present volume.

[394] See Halder, *Diaries*, 1312, 1317 (23, 27 Nov. 1941).

[395] Ibid. 1314–15 (25 Nov. 1941). On the position of the German economy at the end of 1941 see also Milward, *German Economy*, 45 ff., and *Das Deutsche Reich und der Zweite Weltkrieg*, v/1. 610 ff.

[396] See Rohland, *Bewegte Zeiten*, 77–8.

[397] See Org.Abt. (III) No. 3356/41 geh.Kdos., memorandum on effects of PoW situation, 18 Nov. 1941, also Org.Abt.(I) No. 730/41 g.Kdos., letter on army reorganization 1941–2, 3 Nov. 1941, BA-MA RH 2/v. 428.

TABLE II.vi.3. *German Armaments Production before and during the Russian Campaign*

Type of weapon	Month of 1941 in in which maximum achieved	Relative decline in December 1941 (%)
Light infantry weapons	April	38
Heavy infantry weapons	August	49
Army artillery	April	67
Aircraft armament	August	36
Armoured fighting vehicle guns	December	—
Anti-aircraft artillery	July	17
Weapons overall	July	29

Source: Wagenführ, *Industrie*, 32.

equipment stocks. Five divisions of Army Group Centre reported the loss of more than half of their heavy weapons; many of the remaining artillery pieces would soon fail due to overuse and a shortage of replacement parts.[398] Two arms convoys were precipitately prepared for Army Group Centre, but the difficult transport conditions made it unlikely that the convoys would reach the front for several weeks. Selective stopgaps and emergency measures of this kind could not solve the overall problem. Army High Command was forced by exhausted stocks and the low level of new manufacture to maintain the principle of not replacing lost weapons, and of keeping back all available stocks for the rehabilitation of existing and the establishment of new formations for the east.

Overall, the balance sheet of Operation Barbarossa shows that the bulk of the armaments produced in 1941 was lost on the battlefields of the east. The German army was reduced in many areas to the level of armaments of 1940, and sometimes to the position of 1 September 1939 (the number of tanks capable of front-line service at the start of war was 3,506, as against 3,383 on 1 January 1942).[399] By 31 January 1942 losses of armoured fighting vehicles had reached 3,254 vehicles (the starting strength on 22 June 1941 was 3,648); losses of guns were 14,648, including 2,360 from the army artillery (the starting strength on 22 June 1941 was 7,184). Of approximately half a million motorvehicles, 121,529 had been lost, including 42,851 motor-cycles—a bloodletting from which the most mobile ground troops of the Wehrmacht, the

[398] See appendix 7 to OKH/GenStdH/GenQu/Abt. I/Qu 2 (III) No. I/6562/41 g.Kdos., evaluation of 10-day report, 25 Dec. 1941, BA-MA III W 805/7, T. 2.
[399] See summary in Müller-Hillebrand, *Heer*, iii. 274.

motor-cyclist riflemen, never recovered.[400] In addition, the supplies of fuel and ammunition were largely exhausted, and barely any trained reserves of personnel were left.

Fromm and Todt correctly foresaw that the Reich would find it very difficult to prevent a further decline in armaments production, or to mobilize those reserves that were still available. In any case, it could no longer compete with the hugely superior resources of Germany's enemies. Even if Hitler refused to accept the political consequences as Todt had outlined them, he could not change the fundamental balance of forces whatever he did. Despite the production records that Speer was to achieve later, the superiority of the anti-Hitler coalition increased steadily. The enormous losses sustained during Operation Barbarossa had already reduced the prospects for a successful resumption of the offensive in the summer of 1942. From now on, it was only a matter of time before the Allies' superiority in material and manpower brought about the defeat of the Third Reich.

After an exhausted Army Group Centre ground to a standstill before Moscow at the beginning of December 1941, Hitler ordered an increase in German armaments production.[401] He had apparently recognized that the period of Blitzkrieg was over, and that Germany faced a long war of attrition. Yet he was not prepared to take decisive action until the middle of that month, when the Soviet counter-offensive threatened to achieve an operational breakthrough which would shake the entire front, and when the entry of the United States brought another superior enemy into the ring. The immediate reorientation of armaments production in favour of the army required a fundamental reorganization of the German war economy. Hitler could no longer avoid introducing measures to centralize war production, and was forced to decide whether the war economy should be dominated by the military or civilian sector.

General Thomas submitted two memorandums in a vain attempt to advance the leadership claims of the military.[402] In his decree on 'Armaments 1942' of 10 January Hitler accepted the most important proposals made by Thomas. Nevertheless, it was Todt who made most of the running. Following an agreement with the most important armaments industrialists, Todt submitted his proposals for the rationalization of German armaments production at the end of January. These were accepted by Hitler. His system for the 'self-responsibility of industry' was later, after Todt's fatal accident, adopted by his

---

[400] See appendix 4 to OKH/GenStdH/GenQu/Abt. I/Qu 2 (III) No. I/720/42 g.Kdos., 5 Feb. 1942, BA-MA III W 805, T. 1; also Erb, *Kradschützen*, 162.

[401] Führer and Supreme Commander of the Wehrmacht/WiRüAmt/Rü (IIa) No. 3750/41 g.Kdos., 3 Dec. 1941, BA-MA W 01-8/28.

[402] See WiRüAmt/Arm, (IIa) No. 4010/41 g.Kdos., The demands on armaments allowing for the situation in Dec. 1941, 23 Dec. 1941, printed in Thomas, *Wehr- und Rüstungswirtschaft*, 470 ff.; also OKW/WFST/Org./WiRü No. 1/42 g.Kdos., memorandum on the armaments measures, 3 Jan. 1942, printed ibid. 478 ff. On the following see Führer and Supreme Commander of the Wehrmacht No. 1/42 g.Kdos., armaments 1942, 10 Jan. 1942, printed in *KTB OKW* ii. 1265 ff.

successor Speer. With its help, the industrialists finally ousted OKW and the ordnance departments from responsibility for the development and production of war material. From now on, only one other rival remained—partly with Hitler's support—to lay claim for the direction of war production. This was Heinrich Himmler, whose 'slave state' expanded dramatically after the beginning of 1942. In the autumn of 1941 attempts by the SS leadership to create its own economic and armaments concerns using Soviet prisoners of war had failed, because the extent of the executions and starvation measures had meant that hardly any prisoners were able to work.[403] However, the decline in German armaments production at the end of the year gave Himmler the chance to offer his concentration camps for armaments production and to build up the Goverment-General into a giant armaments workshop for the army. In January 1942 the Wannsee Conference created the organizational framework for the provision of the necessary labour force. Millions of European Jews, whose destruction had already been planned, were now to be channelled through the camps and factories of the SS. Those unable to work were to be murdered immediately as 'useless mouths', and the others subjected to 'destruction through labour'. The 'final solution of the Jewish question', which was motivated by racial and ideological considerations, was thus to be exploited to provide economic benefits in the armaments sector.

This development took concrete shape only in the summer of 1942, after Speer had finally eliminated the military from the direction of armaments production. Until this time, General Thomas had endeavoured to prevent the complete loss of his power, and to maintain military influence over the war economy. As in the spring of 1941, his attempt to gain Hitler's favour by making an excessively optimistic forecast about the prospects of success for the planned operations in the east[404] ended in failure. His earlier efforts to exaggerate the achievements of the military economic organization, which Thomas claimed as his greatest success so far, had been equally unsuccessful. In November 1941 the War Economy and Armaments Office had launched a major press campaign to publicize the work of the economic officers.[405] Thomas himself provided an introduction in which he praised the 'outstanding' achievements of his organization. Yet had the Economic Staff East really fulfilled the tasks entrusted to it?

Its most important objective, that of ensuring that the army in the east could be supplied from the land, had been achieved only partially and amid considerable organizational friction. Food requirements could not be fully met. The following goods, among others, had to be brought in from Germany:[406]

[403] Streit, *Keine Kameraden*, 217 ff., and for the following Speer, *Sklavenstaat*, 32 ff.

[404] WiRüAmt/Abt. Wi Chefs. No. 72/42 g.Kdos., The war-economy position of the USSR at the beginning of 1942, 31 Jan. 1942, BA-MA Wi/ID. 138; on the clashes over authority with Speer see also the account by Thomas, *Wehr- und Rüstungswirtschaft*, 307 ff.

[405] Documents and relevant press reports: BA-MA Wi/ID. 112.

[406] Following data from One year of the Russian campaign (see n. 360).

flour	14%
meat	32%
fat	50%
sugar	60%
fodder	50%

The exploitation of the occupied territory to meet the immediate requirements of the troops, mainly in the form of repair workshops and small factories to manufacture accommodation equipment, peasant carts, etc., achieved only modest success. In the area of operations some 57 factories were being supervised by the Wehrmacht on 1 March 1942. In the territories of the civilian administration the situation was scarcely more favourable. At the end of 1941, for example, the Armaments Inspector Ukraine considered that in view of the poor opportunities available, it would not be worth while to continue 'the activity of an armaments organization to the previous extent'.[407] Yet the Soviet government had managed to evacuate some 1,500 munitions factories from its lost territories; at precisely this time, most of them were being put back into operation, and were supplying the Red Army with increasing numbers of tanks, guns, aircraft, etc. The comparison demonstrates that the Economic Organization East was able to derive only minimal economic benefits from the occupied Soviet territories.

This relative failure can also be detected in another important objective of the campaign, the effort to obtain and utilize Soviet raw materials for the German war economy. Compared with the pre-war era, under German occupation the following production of raw materials was achieved up to the spring of 1942:[408]

brown coal	under 1%
cerium	—
mica	still under development
graphite	—
manganese	9%
oil	75%
oil shale	60%
phosphorite	still under development
quartz	still under development
mercury	—
salt	—
bituminous coal	under 1%
peat	still under development

---

[407] Retrospective account of armaments development for the period 12 Sept.–31 Dec. 1941, 23, BA-MA RW 30/91.

[408] Data taken from *One year of the Russian campaign* (see n. 360), appendix 3.

TABLE II.vi.4. *Performance of Economic Staff East over its First Twelve Months* (t.)

	Lost deliveries agreed by treaty	Produced or seized for homeland and troops	Difference
Grain	1,900,000	1,030,000	− 870,000
Fats	29,600	47,200	+ 17,600
Meat	9,200	213,500	+ 204,300
Mineral oil	700,000	750,000	+ 50,000
Skins/hides	1,000	15,000	+ 14,000
Manganese (concentrate)	255,000	105,000	− 150,000
Chromite	32,700	5,200	− 27,500
Phosphate	200,000	600	− 199,400

Source: Ergebnisse der Vierjahresplan-Arbeit, Ein Kurzbericht nach dem Stande vom Frühjahr 1942, bearb. von der Dienststelle des Beauftragten für den Vierjahresplan, 88, BA R 26/18.

Taking into account the fact that the short-term economic objective of the campaign had been at least to replace the commodities which had been promised by treaty but lost when war broke out, it is scarcely appropriate to talk of success.

In terms of the economic benefits derived, the 'economics of smash and grab' (Milward's phrase)[409] advocated mainly by OKW was barely more successful than the political war effort conducted by imperial Germany in the era of Brest-Litovsk. From the middle of 1917 to the end of 1918 some 1,249,950 t. of foodstuffs, cereals, and fodder had been obtained from the Russian area of occupation and the Ukraine (710,000 t. to the army of occupation, 539,950 t. exported to Germany).[410] Then political considerations regarding the native population had ensured a different order of priorities for the distribution of the agricultural produce: (1) local population, (2) occupying army, (3) Germany. Even so, the direct gain for Germany was scarcely less than in 1941, although it too had failed to meet original expectations. Assessed purely in economic terms, the policy of starvation and annihilation pursued by the National Socialists did not pay off.

The failure of the policy of economic exploitation (see Table II.vi.4) becomes even more explicit when actual developments are compared with the projections of the spring of 1941. At that time, grain acquisition was envisaged at between 8m. and 10m. t.; Thomas and Backe assured Hitler that the

[409] Milward, *German Economy at War*, 49.
[410] See activity report of WiStabOst, appendix: The utilization of the occupied territories to feed the front and homeland in the First World War 1914–1918, 30 (1944), BA-MA RW 31/78.

conquest of the European part of the Soviet Union would relieve him of all his economic worries.[411] These economic objectives could not be achieved in 1941, for much the same reasons as in 1918. First, the organization designed to secure them failed because of transport difficulties, organizational friction, and the passive and active resistance of the native population. Second, economic policy was unrealistic in that it concentrated more on the long-term tasks of reorganization of agriculture in the occupied territories than on the immediate measures needed to support home front and troops. Third, and most important, the war took a different course from that expected in Berlin. This was recognized too late.

In 1943 the representative for eastern questions in the Four-year Plan, Dr Friedrich Richter, wrote that Backe's 'colonial thesis' would have been a realistic possibility if the appropriate means of applying military force in the occupied territory had been available.[412] He continued:

I know from my own work in Berlin the immense pressure from the raw-material and food-supply side, which led to drastic measures and demands on the eastern territories . . . The short-term requirements of the war economy triumphed over the politically necessary line of a careful handling of the eastern peoples. This state of affairs was aggravated by the significant human inadequacy of many Germans in the eastern territories, which expressed itself in lack of financial moderation and the basest conduct. But the decisive factor [was] the inconstancy of the political line, owing to the arbitrary nature of many local and specialist rulers, and the wait-and-see attitude of many central authorities.

The dilemma facing the Economic Organization East is highlighted in a report from Chief Group Agriculture on 27 December 1941, concerning a tour of inspection to the Ukraine.[413] It noted that the same problems recurred constantly in all the discussions: not enough men and materials, critical shortage of fuel and means of communication and transport, lack of any tight concentration of forces, splits in the organization—all combining to prevent the more effective exploitation of the country. After the transfer of territories to the civilian administration, for example, the majority of agricultural leaders were employed in the administration, leaving practical work on the land in the hands of unqualified workers who revealed 'an alarming picture of rigidity, lack of knowledge, sometimes great lack of education as well'. The report also revealed continuing preoccupation on the part of the military economic staff with unrealistic tasks connected with the postwar period and the New Order. For example, there were detailed proposals for the division of the land. Zone I, containing between 2m. and 3m. hectares and sited directly round the markets of the larger towns and transport centres, would be the centre for the German specialist personnel and all available means of production. The base leaders, the future 'lords of the manor', would be joined by the first 10,000

[411] See sect. I.III.1(*f*) at n. 259.
[412] See extract from his army postal service letter of 26 May 1943, BA R 6/60a.
[413] See WiStabOst, Chefgr. La, Observations on Ukraine trip, 27 Dec. 1941, BA-MA RW 31/42.

German settlers, and would receive the 'best economic management and most secure foundation for staying the course and achieving prosperity'. This zone, which would receive preferential treatment, would have others attached to it. The other zones would be left to the natives to cultivate, and would be supported by the German colonial administration in varying degrees.

In general, these plans conformed to the deliberations of the SS leadership for a 'General Plan East'. However, the military Economic Staff East was preoccupied with them at a time when Operation Barbarossa had already failed, and the war threatened to assume unsuspected dimensions. Two main conclusions can be drawn. First, the claim that it worked almost exclusively for the material support of the troops[414] is only partly true. Not until the end of 1941 did a growing awareness of the real military demands of the war in the east lead to the greater integration of the economic apparatus into the army command structure, at least in the area of operations. However, this hesitant reorganization came too late to repair the inadequate level of support for the troops at the front, or to provide the conditions for the material superiority of the army in the east. Instead, organizational friction continued. For example, First Armoured Army later reported that it had tried in vain to strengthen the authority of the local economic command against the other, independent economic agencies.[415] After the occupation of the Donets industrial region, 'the Armeegebiet [was] flooded with a host of persons, commissions, special representatives, etc., some of them regular adventurers'. At first, organizations had sprung up 'like mushrooms'. However, after finding industrial opportunities less favourable than expected, 'some of these persons withdrew, mostly after dispatching long one-sided reports, which were often passed on, without the knowledge of the army, to the highest offices but which failed to correspond to the facts'. At the end of 1941 emissaries of the Berg- und Hüttenwerksgesellschaft Ost mbH (Mining and Smelting Works Company East Ltd.) appeared on the scene, hoping to take over those factories which had been put back into operation by First Armoured Army to assist in the repair of their motor-vehicles, tanks, and equipment,[416] and switch them to meet the needs of the German market.

Second, it is clear that the hugely ambitious plans of General Thomas—to build up an autonomous economic apparatus largely independent of the army leadership—significantly influenced the shape taken by Operation Barbarossa as a colonial war of exploitation. By giving the racial and ideological programme of annihilation an ostensible economic rationality, he helped to ensure that the Wehrmacht became even more entangled in this programme than before. The military élite never managed to disentangle itself. It remained

---

[414] See WiStabOst, Chefgr. W, Allg. Wirt., Gr. IV, contribution to War Diary Feb. 1942, BA-MA RW 31/331.

[415] Pz.AOK 1/O.Qu. No. 2871/42 geh., report on the supply situation of First Armd. Army in winter 1941–2. 1 Apr. 1942, 5, BA-MA RH 21-1/332.

[416] Memorandum of Abt. O.Qu., 30 Dec. 1941, BA-MA RH 21-1/332.

enmeshed even when the unfavourable course of the war forced its members to recognize that the unrestrained policy of annihilation and exploitation was against military interests; that, instead of mobilizing the maximum quantity of relief goods and additional workers for the eastern front, it was leading to the rapid destabilization of the hinterland and to additional military burdens.

VII. Securing 'Living-space'

JÜRGEN FÖRSTER

1. PACIFICATION OF THE CONQUERED TERRITORIES

IT is a little-known fact that large areas of the Soviet Union spent an extended period under German military administration in 1941.[1] This was not according to plan. Owing to the failure of Operation Barbarossa, only two of the four planned Reich Commissariats (Ostland and Ukraine) had been established, and of these the Ukraine was considerably smaller than originally envisaged. In the remaining occupied areas of the Soviet Union—that were still areas of operations—the military administration inevitably developed from a temporary into a permanent institution.

Hitler's declared intention had been to treat the military administration as only an interim stage leading to the political reorganization of the conquered 'living-space' in the east.[2] Military planning had been directed towards achieving a swift victory by the Wehrmacht over the Red Army, and ensuring the rapid collapse of the Bolshevik system. Both these objectives were to be assisted by the deliberate liquidation of the Communist functionaries, the 'Jewish-Bolshevik intelligentsia', inside and outside the Red Army. Their elimination, it was thought, would destroy not only the bases of Stalinist Bolshevism, but also the potential germ-cells for organized resistance to German rule.

The basis for military administration in the occupied Soviet territories was provided by OKW 'Guidelines on special territories to Directive No. 21' of 13 March 1941,[3] and by Army High Command's 'Special instructions for supply, part C' of 3 April 1941.[4] These orders were supplemented by oral explanations from the quartermaster-general. No detailed written working guidelines for the military administration, of the kind worked out before the war in the west in 1940,[5] were issued for Barbarossa.

---

[1] As yet there is no overall account of the German military administration in the east. The standard works by Rich, *War Aims*, ii, Dallin, *German Rule*, and Reitlinger, *Haus auf Sand gebaut*, largely neglect the issue; Simpson, 'Rear Area Security', is written predominantly from the standpoint of military security. For a Marxist view see Müller, *Wehrmacht und Okkupation*. In Vol. v/1 of this series (pp. 95 ff.) the various types of German occupation in Europe are examined systematically, and described for each of the countries affected, subject by subject (Umbreit). An overall account of German occupation policy in two army rear areas in the central sector has been provided by Schulte, *German Army*. For 1942–3 see Mulligan, *The Politics of Illusion*.

[2] See sect. I.VII.1 at nn. 6–13.   [3] *Hitlers Weisungen*, No. 21a (not in trans.).

[4] OKH/GenStdH/GenQu, Abt. Kriegsverwaltung No. II/0315/41 g.Kdos. Chefs., 3 Apr. 1941, BA-MA RH 22/12; *Deutsche Besatzungspolitik*, No. 4.

[5] OKH/GenStdH/GenQu No. 800/40 g., Sammelmappe 'Militärverwaltung', BA-MA RH 24-3/218. See Umbreit, *Militärbefehlshaber*, 3–4.

At the start of operations, Hitler formally transferred executive authority in the area of operations to the commander-in-chief of the army.[6] The area of operations was to consist of the army areas and three rear army areas under the control of the army groups. Each army area was subdivided into the combat area and army rear area (Armeegebiet).

Executive authority in the army area was in the hands of the army commander-in-chief, and in the rear army area was held by the commander of the rear army area, with both following the directives of the army group. *De jure* each of these commanders was the sole holder of disciplinary power and the right of decree, which he exercised via the various security divisions, field commanders' offices, and local commanders' offices under his control.[7] In the Reich commissariats executive authority was to lie with the Reich commissioner, while the Wehrmacht commander was to retain supreme military power.[8] However, the executive authority of the individual army commanders and commanders of the rear army areas *vis-à-vis* the civilian population was restricted from the outset: the special-duty squads of the security police and SD (the security service of the SS) were given special tasks 'outside the troops', and empowered to take 'executive measures' against the civilian population. These measures were to be carried out on their own responsibility, though in close co-operation with the appropriate intelligence officer[9] to ensure that they did not hamper military operations.

It was the task of the military command authorities in the rear area of operations to secure supply-bases, supply-routes, railway lines, lines of communication, vital airfields, and captured camps, as well to guard and evacuate the prisoners of war (see Diagram II.VII.1). Particular attention was paid to the protection of supply-bases.[10] The commanders of the rear army areas and the army rear areas had a variety of forces available to fulfil these tasks: security and order troops, security divisions and regiments, field and local commanders' agencies, units of the field gendarmerie and the secret field police, and staffs for prisoner assembly points and transit camps. Where necessary, the commanders were also authorized to call on units of the Waffen-SS and regular police which had been deployed in their areas and were subordinate to the local 'Higher SS and Police Leader' for security tasks.

[6] Chef OKW/WFSt/Abt. L (IV/Qu) No. 254/41, 26 June 1941, PA, Ust.S., Rußland I. On the general issue of 'executive power' see Umbreit, *Militärverwaltungen*, 13 ff.

[7] See Befh. rückw. H.Geb. Nord, VII just 1/41, 24 July 1941, BA-MA, Alliierte Prozesse 9, NOKW-1497.

[8] Hitler decree of 25 June 1941, PA, Dt. Ges. Helsinki, Schriftwechsel geheim, vol. ii; OKH/GenStdH/GenQu, Az.Abt. K.Verw. (Qu 4 B) No. II/4658/41 geh., 26 July 1941, on service regulations for Wehrmacht commanders, BA-MA RH 22/148.

[9] OKH/GenStdH/GenQu, Abt. Kriegsverwaltung No. II/2101/41 geh., 28 Apr. 1941, on regulation of operations of security police and SD within the army, BA-MA RH 22/155; Jacobsen, 'Kommissarbefehl', doc. 3.

[10] OKH/GenStdH/Ausb.Abt. (Ia) No. 700/41 g., 21 Mar. 1941, BA-MA RH 22/271; 285. Sich.Div./Ia No. 38/41 g.Kdos., 12 May 1941, on guidelines for the operation of the security division, ibid. RH 26-285/4.

The commanders were instructed to deploy the three security divisions under their command 'like a string of beads' along the major transport routes. Only in the Reich commissariats were 'considerations of space' to be the criterion for the security formations. As the representative of the quartermaster-general explained on 16 May 1941, away from the roads it was 'mainly' the security police and the SD who would be actively engaged in the army area (Heeresgebiet). The army could not be spread out.[11]

For the purposes of internal administration, i.e. the establishment and supervision of a native administration, the commanders, security divisions, and field commanders' agencies had at their disposal special departments (dept. VII) staffed with officials of the military administration. The creation of a systematic, closely integrated administrative apparatus, of the kind created in the west, was not planned in Russia. There were two main reasons for this decision. It was considered that 'primitive conditions in Russia',[12] and the plan to establish a civil administration very swiftly, made such a step unnecessary. Ordered conditions were to be established only to the extent that was deemed essential to secure the rear areas and exploit the land for the benefit of the troops by relieving the burden on supply.[13] The existence of a civil administrative apparatus was not generally envisaged.

Political decisions by the Reich commissioners were not to be anticipated under any circumstances. As a result, mayors were installed in the municipalities and towns, and superintendents in the *Rayons* (districts). Anti-Bolshevik inhabitants of non-Russian stock—Lithuanians, Latvians, Estonians, Poles, Ukrainians—tended to be appointed to these posts in the Baltic States, Belorussia, and the Ukraine. They were investigated for political reliability and technical suitability by means of close co-operation between the intelligence officer and the security police and SD. The district administration was usually dealt with by the field commanders' agencies. It was the task of the mayors, under German supervision, to re-establish and maintain law and order by creating an organization to keep public order, registering the population, and distributing identity papers.[14] For example, Sixth Army Command defined the tasks of the Ukrainian public-order service as 'picking up of the activist young men, supervision of important military installations, discovery of Bolshevik suspect elements, and the search for escaped Red Army members'.[15]

[11] 285. Sich.Div., Ia, 19 May 1941, memoranda on discussion with Army High Command/ quartermaster-general on 15 and 16 May 1941, BA-MA RH 26-285/4; AOK 9, O.Qu., discussion with quartermaster-general 15–16 May 1941, ibid., 9. Armee, 13904/3b. See sect. I.vii.2(*a*) at n. 41.

[12] OKH/GenStdH/GenQu, Qu 1/IIa No. I/050/41 g.Kdos., Feb. 1941, app. 15, BA-MA RH 3/ v. 132.

[13] 221. Sich.Div., Abt. Ia, 20 July 1941, on orders for operation of local and field commandants' offices, Dulags [transit camps], and range of duties of Dept. VII and the economic service agencies with Div. HQ, BA-MA RH 26-221/12.

[14] Befh. rückw. H.Geb. 103 [South], Abt. VII/No. 1/41, 10 July 1941, on special instructions regarding duties of Abt. Verwaltung [Administration] (VII), BA-MA RH 22/5.

[15] Order for the creation of Ukrainian auxiliary committees in former Polish Volhynia, in German and Ukrainian, 26 July 1941, BA-MA, 6. Armee, 15623/2.

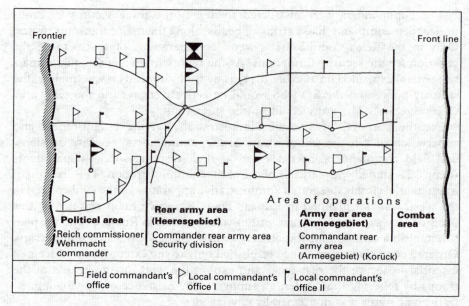

DIAGRAM II.VII.1. Structure of the Occupied Territories

Source: BA-MA, 9. Armee 13904/3b. See HDv (1938 and 1945).

Fourteen days after the start of the invasion, the German army had advanced so far east that it was possible to establish rear army areas for the three army groups, on 2, 3, and 9 July 1941. The commanders were Infantry Generals Franz von Roques (North), Max von Schenckendorff (Centre), and Karl von roques (South). The staff of the commander of Rear Army Area South noted that they faced an exceptionally difficult task. The army areas were extended eastwards as operations progressed; to the west, large parts of the occupied land were taken over by the Reich commissioners, or transferred to the Government-General or East Prussia. The first piece of territory to be detached from the army area of operations was the city of Brest-Litovsk, which was transferred to the military commander in the Government-General on 18 July 1941.[16] Reich Commissariat Ostland was established a few days later (25 July), though at first its territory covered Lithuania alone.[17] On 1 August 1941

---

[16] 221. Sich.Div., Abt. Ia, 18 July 1941, on handing over of city of Brest and surrounding area . . . , BA-MA RH 26-221/12. Executive authority in civilian matters appears not to have passed to the governor-general, since the incident was not mentioned either in Frank, *Diensttagebuch*, 386 ff., or in *Generalgouvernement*, 59 ff. The 'Security Sector Brest' belonged to the Reich Commissariat Ukraine from 1 Sept. 1941: OKH/GenStdH/GenQu, Abt. K.Verw. (Qu 4), No. II/5458/41 geh., 21 Aug. 1941, BA-MA RH 22/271.

[17] Befh. rückw. H.Geb. Nord, Abt. Ia No. 749/41 geh., 21 July 1941, BA-MA RH 22/271. See Myllyniemi, *Neuordnung*, 78 ff., and the different times given by Müller, *Wehrmacht und Okkupation*, 76, and *Deutschland im zweiten Weltkrieg*, ii. 123. See the Annexe Volume, No. 27, and *Das Deutche Reich und der Zweite Weltkrieg*, v/1. 87 ff.

the district of Białystok was placed under the administration of the president of East Prussia, Gauleiter Koch;[18] Galicia and Lemberg (Lvov) were taken over by Governor-General Dr Hans Frank,[19] and Reich Commissariat Ostland was extended by adding the district of Vilna (Vilnius).

When the military administration began its activity, the political objectives of the supreme leadership for the shaping of 'living-space' existed only in outline. Moreover, the Reich Minister for the Occupied Eastern Territories, Rosenberg, had yet to be officially appointed. Commanders at various levels were forced to apply the general guidelines they had received according to their own assessment of the situation. In the Baltic States and the Ukraine, in particular, they encountered political endeavours which they had been ordered not to accommodate. Though most officers and civil servants regarded it as their duty to follow orders and to give them, it is clear that the German conduct towards the Soviet population combined elements of 'uncertainty, racial arrogance, a national-political programme, and an unreflecting faith in the methods of force'.[20] Conduct of this kind had not been embarked upon in the countries of western and northern Europe occupied by the Wehrmacht, though it had appeared in Poland. From the outset, the guidelines issued by OKW and Army High Command to secure the conquered territories were harsh. Active and passive resistance was to be nipped in the bud through the impositition of Draconian punishments. Army High Command regarded a deliberate and ruthless approach to 'anti-German elements' as an effective preventive measure, though it failed to define these elements more closely.[21] On the other hand, the OKW guidelines of 19 May 1941 were more specific.[22] These demanded 'ruthless and energetic action against Bolshevik agitators, guerrillas, saboteurs, Jews'. Though the military administration in the west had stipulated that 'special measures' could not be taken 'solely on the basis that the inhabitant is a *Jew*',[23] this restriction was dropped in the struggle against 'Jewish Bolshevism', the 'deadly enemy of the National Socialist German people'. It was not the supreme leadership alone which regarded the Jews in the occupied Soviet territories, along with the Communists, as 'anti-German elements'; even before the start of operations, Army Command Norway had issued a leaflet attacking the treacherous Soviet conduct of the

[18] 221. Sich.Div., Abt. Ia, 29 July 1941, BA-MA RH 26-221/12.

[19] Befh. rückw. H.Geb. Süd, Abt. Ia No. 1145/41 g., 29 July 1941, and the 'Order for the ceremonial transfer of Old Galicia to the Government-General', 30 July 1941, BA-MA RH 22/5; Frank, *Diensttagebuch*, 391–2; OKW/WFSt/Abt. L (IV/Qu) No. 495/41, 23 Aug. 1941, BA-MA RH 26-221/13.

[20] Umbreit, *Militärverwaltungen*, 137. On the conduct of the occupying power towards the ethnic Germans in the Soviet Union see Pinkus and Fleischhauer, *Die Deutschen in der Sowietunion*, 232 ff.

[21] See sect. II.vii.1 n. 4.

[22] OKW/WFSt/Abt. L (IV/Qu) No. 44560/41 g.Kdos. Chefs., 19 May 1941, special instructions No. 1 to Directive No. 21, app. 3: Guidelines for the conduct of the troops in Russia, BA-MA RW 4/v. 524; *Deutsche Besatzungspolitik*, No. 7.

[23] Folder 'Militärverwaltung' [Military administration], point 6, BA-MA RH 24-3/218 (emphasis added). See sect II.vii.1 n. 5.

war, and urging the troops to pay 'particular attention' to Jews as well as priests and commissars.[24] Seventeenth Army Command informed its soldiers that the Soviet conduct of the war was 'treacherous and sadistic' because the peoples of the Soviet union were partly Asiatic, and were 'under Bolshevik-Jewish leadership'.[25] At the beginning of July 1942, III (Motorized) Army Corps HQ informed its troops that in the Ukrainian towns they must pay particular attention to 'Jews, Russians, Poles'.[26] It also demanded from Armoured Group 1 the production and distribution of more effective leaflets among the Red Army. Among other things, these should call on Red Army soldiers to 'dispose of political commissars and Jews'.[27] The occupying power removed from their public posts all Jews who had not fled, set them to work as forced labour before involving other groups, and ordered that they be registered and made to wear distinguishing marks. That was only the beginning. The first moves were also made to evacuate the Jews and confine them to ghettos.[28] The way was thus prepared not only for the exploitation of Jews for forced labour, but also for their subsequent systematic annihilation by the special-duty squads of the security police and the SD.

The first declarations and appeals of the German troops in the conquered territories announced that the Wehrmacht had marched in to liberate the 'working people, workers, and farmers' from the Bolshevik yoke. The protection of the German army would be available to all those who behaved 'quietly, peacefully, and obediently', continued to work hard, and followed the directives issued.[29] Espionage, sabotage, guerrilla activity, and assisting escaped Red Army soldiers would be punishable by death. After a maximum of three days, the life of any person found in possession of weapons, ammunition, fixed knives, radios, transmitters, and Communist literature would be forfeit. Similar decrees had also been worked out before the war in the west, and covered by the usages of war.[30] In the occupied Soviet territories, however, as in Poland, the military administration quickly demonstrated 'the little value it accorded human life'.[31] In so doing, it was merely following the guidelines that had been issued, foremost among them the order concerning the exercise of martial jurisdiction of 13 May 1941, its supplements and explanations.[32] The term 'guerrilla' was interpreted very widely. The logical consequence of this

[24] Point II, g., BA-MA RW 39/20. See sect. I.VII.4 at n. 115.
[25] AOK 17, Ic/AO No. 354/41 g.Kdos., 16 June 1941, BA-MA, 17. Armee, 14499/51.
[26] Gen.Kdo. (mot.) III. AK, Abt. Ic, 7 July 1941, BA-MA RH 24-3/134.
[27] Telephone-call No. 135 to 1st Armd. Group, 5 July 1941, ibid. Apparently the impetus came from Sixth Army, which had informed its subordinate formations that west of Minsk 20,000 Soviet officers and men had deserted after shooting their political commissars.
[28] Befh. rückw. H.Geb. Süd, Abt. VII, No. 3/41 of 12 July, No. 17 of 21 July 1941 (BA-MA RH 22/5); instruction Abt. VII No. 12 of 28 Aug. 1941 (ibid. RH 22/6); Deutsche Besatzungspolitik, No. 16; 221. Sich.Div., Abt. Ia of 8 July 1941, daily report, BA-MA RH 26-221/19.
[29] Undated proclamation, BA-MA, 6. Armee, 15623/1; undated announcement, ibid. RH 20-2/1096; undated announcement, Deutsche Besatzungspolitik, No. 9.
[30] Folder 'Militärverwaltung'. See sect. II.VII.1 n. 5, and Umbreit, Militärbefehlshaber, 118 ff.
[31] Umbreit, Militärverwaltungen, 144.   [32] See sect. I.VII.2(b) at n. 75.

approach was revealed in an order by VII Army Corps HQ on 29 June 1941, to the effect that 'civilians who are encountered armed, even when they only have razors in their boots', were to be regarded as guerrillas and executed.[33] Ninth Army HQ also ordered that persons in civilian or semi-civilian dress were to be regarded as guerrillas if they were armed.[34]

Further radicalization in the conduct of the war in the army area of operations was encouraged by two factors: the shootings and/or terrible mutilation of German prisoners of war by Soviet troops, and Stalin's call for a 'patriotic war against German Fascism' and the 'unleashing of partisan warfare everywhere'. At first Army High Command tried to counteract this development, stressing pragmatic arguments for its approach rather than humanitarian concerns. When Sixth Army HQ proposed on 2 July that captured Red Army soldiers should be shot in reprisal for the illegal treatment of German soldiers in Soviet captivity, the commander-in-chief of the army at first hoped that such measures could be avoided. Brauchitsch believed that in fighting 'the *Russians*—unlike the Western powers'—the shooting of large numbers of Soviet prisoners of war would be counter-productive. It would achieve only an 'increasing bitterness in the fighting'.[35] At the beginning of July 1941 he regarded this as undesirable, since it would delay the signs of disintegration that he was expecting to see in the Red Army. However, shortly before he received the guidelines from Army High Command, the commander of Sixth Army, Field Marshal von Reichenau, had ordered a number of officers from the Soviet 124th Rifle Division to be shot in reprisal for 'atrocities' committed by their subordinates.[36] A month later, in line with the approach taken by Brauchitsch, the commander of Seventeenth Army, Infantry General Carl Heinrich von Stülpnagel, rejected the suggestion of XXXXIX (Mountain) Army Corps HQ that Soviet generals should be shot in reprisal for the murder of German prisoners, and that this should be publicized by means of leaflets. He argued that German reprisals would only intensify Soviet resistance.[37] Though this attitude by the commander-in-chief of the army and individual officers prevented official reprisals on a major scale, it was unable to stop acts

[33] Gen.Kdo. VII. AK, Ia, special instructions on corps order for 30 June 1941, dated 29 June 1941, BA-MA RH 26-221/12. See the warning by 225th Inf. Div. on 27 June 1941, BA-MA RH 20-4/682.

[34] AOK 9, Ic/AO No. 2058/41 g., 3 July 1941; quoted from compilation of Korück 582, 11 Oct. 1941, BA-MA RH 23/227.

[35] OKH, Gen. z.b.V.b. ObdH/Az. 454 Gr. R.Wes. No. 1215/41 geh., 9 July 1941, on illegal treatment of German soldiers in Soviet Russian captivity, BA-MA RH 20-2/1090. In this context see the report by the commander of 25th (mot.) Inf. Div., Lt.-Gen. Heinrich Clössner, of 5 July 1941, on the discovery of 153 dead soldiers (ibid. RH 24-3/134), the announcement of the murder of 209 soldiers by the general commanding III (mot.) Army Corps on 3 July 1941 (ibid. RH 27-13/111); see sect. II.II.12 at n. 342 (Hoffmann), and Zayas, *Die Wehrmacht-Untersuchungsstelle.*

[36] See the substance of the sentence against the commander of 781st Rifle Reg., Maj. Piotr Matvijevitch, 5 July 1941, BA-MA, 6. Armee, 15623/1. The grounds for the sentence and the handwritten insertion of the name into the printed text make it likely that M. was not the only one to be shot.

[37] AOK 17, Ic/AO, telephone-call of 12 Aug. 1941, BA-MA, 17. Armee, 14499/51.

of revenge committed by German soldiers after the discovery of mutilated comrades.[38] The conduct of some Soviet units was clearly in violation of international law. It gave added impact to the propaganda campaign begun by the German side even before the launching of operations, stressing the treachery and brutality of Soviet warfare and the bestiality of the commissars and political leaders. Further impetus was provided by the destructive operations of NKVD troops against political prisoners and thousands of people suspected of spying, whose bodies were found by the advancing German units. Lvov stands as a symbol for many other incidents.[39]

The development of the German–Soviet war into a war of ideologies and annihilation was not due solely to the measures taken by the German side before 22 June 1941. Its roots also lay in the Soviet reaction to the German invasion. On 3 July 1941 Stalin delivered a broadcast in which he argued that the war against 'Fascist Germany' was no 'ordinary war' between two armies. 'It is also the great war of the entire Soviet people against the Fascist German troops.'[40] The Soviet people should understand that the struggle against 'German Fascism' was a matter of life and death, and should 'have no pity for the enemy'. Stalin called for 'the unleashing of partisan war'. The aims of this 'patriotic people's war against the Fascist oppressors' were 'to crush the enemy', and to liberate the peoples of Europe who had been subjugated by the Germans. Stalin called on the 'workers, collective farmers, and intellectual workers' in the occupied territories of the Soviet Union to create intolerable conditions for the Wehrmacht by blowing up bridges and roads, destroying lines of communication, and setting fire to woods and camps. The enemy must be ceaselessly pursued and annihilated. Soviet leaflets were produced in German to make the occupying soldiers aware of this appeal. In Hitler's view, 'the totally indoctrinated Bolshevik population' would ensure that the vast expanses of occupied territory continued to pose great dangers for communications with the rear, despite the ruthless action being taken. Furthermore, measures of pacification using infantry methods alone would be time-consuming, involve heavy casualties, and fail to have the necessary deterrent effect. On 5 July 1941, following Hitler's instructions, Keitel therefore instructed the Chief of Army Armament Programmes and commander of the replacement army to equip the security divisions, local defence formations, and police formations with captured French tanks.[41] Hitler regarded Stalin's appeal as the 'chance' to present his war of annihilation as an act of armed conflict. Ten days later he declared openly that the partisan war behind the front offered the

---

[38] See Bock, Tagebuch, vol. ii (30 June 1941), MGFA P-210. See also the order by Sixth Army of 29 June 1941 that, in response to the barbaric methods of fighting adopted by the Red Army, no prisoners should be taken during mopping-up operations in the rear area (BA-MA, LI. AK, 15290/1).

[39] See sect. II.II.12 at n. 321 (Hoffmann).

[40] BA-MA RH 24-3/134; Jacobsen, *1939–1945*, doc. 71 (extract). See the resolutions of the Central Committee of the CPSU(B) on 29 June and of the Politburo on 18 July 1941 (*Deutschland im zweiten Weltkrieg*, ii. 193–4, and sect. II.II.7 at n. 173 (Hoffmann)).

[41] OKW/WFSt/Abt. L No. 441158/41 g.Kdos. Chefs., 5 July 1941, BA-MA RW 4/v. 578.

opportunity 'to eliminate anything that opposes us'. In order to pacify this immense area as quickly as possible, it was best 'to shoot dead anyone who even looks at us askance'.[42] At this discussion, on 16 July 1942, Keitel also advocated Draconian measures against acts of resistance. Civilians must realize 'that anyone who did not function would be shot', and that they would be held collectively liable for conduct which contravened German orders. To ensure that the troop leaders also adopted this attitude, on 23 July 1941 OKW supplemented Directive No. 33 by stipulating that the occupying power would break resistance in the occupied eastern territories 'not by the legal punishment of the guilty, but by striking such terror into the population that it loses all will to resist'.[43] At the same time, Hitler ordered that the native inhabitants were to be disarmed immediately 'as a special measure, using the most drastic means'.[44]

In mid-July, in the belief that the Red Army was already defeated, the operations department of the Army General Staff had begun to work on plans for the structure and subsequent distribution of the formations which would be required 'to occupy and secure the Russian space'.[45] The intention was to keep the number of occupation formations as low as possible, and to concentrate them on the most important industrial areas and transport points. In addition to their occupation duties, these formations must also be capable of destroying any potential revival of resistance by advancing mobile formations deep into the areas not occupied by troops. Underlying these plans was an over-optimistic assessment of the situation, which was soon overtaken by the development of operations. In this context, the radical conduct demanded by Hitler and Keitel was designed to compensate for the fact that the number of security forces was inadequate to pacify the ever expanding area of operations, particularly as they had to be reinforced by combat formations withdrawn from the front.

In contrast, the Army High Command and some troop leaders wished to adopt a different policy. They argued that the troops in the western areas of the Soviet Union had been regarded as 'liberators from Bolshevism' by the population, and frequently greeted with bread and salt. These officers wanted to forbid arbitrary requisitions and the seizure of goods without payment by soldiers 'in this impoverished and plundered land'.[46] In addition, they wished to treat the population 'reasonably', and not to institute collective reprisals

[42] Bormann memorandum on conference of 16 July 1941, *IMT* xxxviii. 88.

[43] *Hitler's Directives*, No. 33a, p. 90.

[44] OKH/Gen. z.b.V.b. ObdH/Az. 453 Gr. R.Wes. No. 1332/41 g., 23 July 1941. Palpable in an order from commander of Rear Army Area South, 23 Aug. 1941, BA-MA, Alliierte Prozesse 9, NOKW-2590.

[45] Memorandum of 15 July 1941, g.Kdos., *KTB OKW* i. 1022 ff. See Abt. Landesverteidigung (I Op) No. 441208/41 g.Kdos. Chefs., 18 July 1941, a division of forces approved by Hitler 'after the interim conclusion of the campaign in the east', BA-MA RH 2/v. 427.

[46] Gen.Kdo. (mot.) III. AK, Abt. Qu/Ic, 27 July 1941, on conduct towards the civilian population, BA-MA RH 24-3/134. See the orders from the commander of Seventeenth Army on 19 July and 24 Aug. 1941 on the treatment of the population and the maintenance of discipline, BA-MA, 17. Armee, 14499/51.

against the population in punishment for acts of sabotage, which remained relatively infrequent. Instead, such acts should be blamed predominantly on Communists, Russians, and Jews.

Advocates of these measures regarded the taking of hostages, and the shooting of selected people considered to be 'anti-German', as a sure method of driving the 'loyal population' back into the 'Bolshevik camp'. On 12 July 1941 Army High Command issued appropriate guidelines.[47] Some days before, LI Army Corps HQ had already ordered that Ukrainians were not to be regarded as generally sympathetic to the Germans. Instead, it was necessary to distinguish between Communists and non-Communists. For that reason hostages should be taken in every billet by the highest-ranking officer: '(*a*) from the Russian and Jewish population, (*b*) from Communist circles considered to be responsible for attacks on Germans.'[48] On 20 July 1941 III (Motorized) Army Corps HQ ordered three Jews to be shot, on the grounds that their 'authorship or complicity' in the murder of a German soldier was regarded as proven because of 'the known hostile attitude of the Jews, especially in the Red Army'. The actual culprit had managed to escape.[49] The commander of 44th Infantry Division, Lieutenant-General Friedrich Siebert, ordered collective measures to be taken after unsolved cases of sabotage. These could consist of the shooting of local Jews or Russians, and the burning down of Jewish or Russian houses.[50] Second Army HQ also instructed the troops in the former Polish and Belorussian territories to distinguish between 'activist Party men and Jews' on one hand, and the mass of the population on the other. Since the latter regarded the Wehrmacht as its liberator from the 'political and economic terror of the Soviet rulers', hostages should be taken 'only from Party men' belonging to the previous system.[51] This measure clearly demonstrated an affinity between the ideological outlook of senior and top-ranking officers and the National Socialist concept of 'Jewish Bolshevism'. However, it also contained pragmatic elements: 'Though the troops must appear as masters, especially in the eastern territory, they must also avoid everything that is likely to shake the population's trust in the German armed forces.'[52]

On 25 July 1941 the commander-in-chief of the army responded to information about Soviet instructions for the creation of partisan detachments by political cadres. In addition, it was claimed that 'the required harshness [had] not been employed at all points' by the German side. The guidelines laid down before the start of operations were expanded by the issuing of a special order

[47] OKH/GenStdH/HWes. Abt. (Abw.), Az.Abw. III No. 2111/41, 12 July 1941, BA-MA RH 27-7/156.

[48] Gen.Kdo. LI. AK, Abt. Ia No. 1882/41, 8 July 1941, appendix to corps order No. 8: Special instructions for conduct towards the civilian population.

[49] Gen.Kdo. (mot.) III. AK, Abt. Ic, 19 July 1941, BA-MA RH 24-3/134.

[50] 44. Inf.Div., Abt. Ia op No. 63/41, 21 July 1941, BA-MA RH 26-44/33.

[51] AOK 2, Ic/AO No. 1388/41 geh., 17 July 1941, BA-MA RH 20-2/1090.

[52] Ibid. The commander of 221st Security Div., Lt.-Gen. Pflugbeil, also ordered a raid on Białystok on 18 July 1941 to take 'hostages (especially Jews)', to be shot in the event of the slightest unrest, BA-MA RH 26-221/12.

on the 'treatment of enemy civilians and Russian prisoners of war in the rear army area'.[53] This order was typical in combining preventive and punitive elements, and in justifying them on military and ideological grounds. It was emphasized that the main priority was 'absolute safety for the German soldier'. The army leadership judged this safety to be endangered, particularly in 'purely Russian areas', by the massive size of the area of operations and the 'perfidy and peculiarity of the Bolshevik enemy'. Rapid pacification was necessary 'to rule the territory gained and to exploint the land'; this could only be achieved if every 'threat from the enemy civilian population' was ruthlessly suppressed. Russians had long been accustomed to hard and merciless action from the authorities. Any from of leniency and softness on the part of the Germans would be regarded as weakness, and would endanger the troops. Soviet plans to organize partisan detachments, their call for young people to form bands, and 'the inflammatory effect of the carriers of the Jewish-Bolshevik system' made it likely that guerrilla warfare would recur even in areas which had previously been quiet. On behalf of Braucbitsch, Lieutenant-General Müller again urged that collective drastic measures be used against passive resistance, or in cases of sabotage where the culprits were not immediately identified. The troops were expressly instructed that it was not necessary to have taken hostages beforehand as a guarantee against '*future* wrongdoing'. *Ad hoc* 'punishment measures', i.e. summary executions and the destruction of whole localities, became the rule.

Soviet soldiers who had been cut off from their units during the fighting, whether in uniform or civillian dress, were also regarded by the army leadership as a potential threat to the pacification of the conquered territory. Public announcements were to be made ordering them to report to Wehrmacht posts by a certain date in each area. Once the date had expired, these stragglers were to be regarded as guerrillas and shot, whether or not they had actually taken part in acts of sabotage. Any support and help for partisans and stragglers from the civilian population was to be punished by death. In addition, the army leadership ordered that all 'suspicious elements' who appeared 'dangerous as regards character and attitude', even if they had not committed any known offence, were to be handed over to the special-duty squads or commandos of the security police and SD.

To implement the Army High Command directive of 25 July 1941, the commander of Rear Army Area South ordered that all stragglers captured

---

[53] OKH/Gen. z.b.V.b. ObdH/Az. 453 Gr. R.Wes. No. 1332/41 geh., 25 July 1941, BA-MA RH 22/271; *Deutsche Besatzungspolitik*, No. 34. The fighting formations were instructed at the same time 'to treat as *guerrillas* members of Soviet "partisan" detachments appearing in front of or behind our front and, as regards observance of the rules of war, clothing, equipment, or *identifiability*, not unquestionably meeting the conditions set for a body of fighting men, a militia, or a volunteer corps. It is irrelevant whether they were previously soldiers, still describe themselves as soldiers, or are non-soldiers. Civilians who give any kind of help to such partisan detachments are thereby supporting irregular action and are likewise to be regarded as guerrillas according to the usage of war' (OKH/Gen. z.b.V.b. ObdH/Az. 454 Gr. R.Wes. No. 1260/41 g., 18 July 1941, BA-MA RH 19 I/124; *Deutsche Besatzungspolitik*, No. 33).

after 8 August were to be treated as guerrillas.[54] A similar order for Rear Army Area Centre stipulated that all 'soldiers who were stragglers and still roaming about' west of the Berezina after 15 August should be treated as guerrillas.[55] However, the expiry date was extended by fourteen days because hundreds of Red Army men were coming forward to surrender.[56] At the end of August 1941 Schenckendorff ordered that any Red Army man encountered between the Dnieper and Berezina after 15 September 1941 was to be shot as a partisan.[57]

Army High Command's guidelines for the treatment of enemy civilians in the rear army areas were adopted by Seventeenth Army HQ in its sector at the end of July 1941. The troops must 'take more action that before against any kind of guerrilla activity, sabotage, and passive resistance, and even crush the first signs of these'. As soon as such activity was attributed to them, guerrillas were to be shot on the order of an officer. 'Suspicious elements' were to be handed over to the special-duty squads of the security police and SD 'if possible'. At that time there were two such squads (6 and 4a) in the army area. As a separate measure from the Army High Command guidelines, Stülpnagel gave details of the conduct to be adopted in cases of passive resistance or acts of sabotage where the culprits were not captured immediately. 'Collective measures *not* to be taken *indiscriminately*. Where the initial act cannot be attributed to the *Ukrainian* local inhabitants, the local superintendents are to be instructed to name Jewish and Communist inhabitants in the first instance. By means of such pressure, the population is to be forced to inform the police.' Since most of the active older Communists had fled, the younger ones should be seized where necessary. 'The Jewish Komsomol [Communist Youth Organization] members in paticular are to be regarded as supporters of sabotage and the organization of gangs.'[58] These scapegoating methods were designed to convince the bulk of the population that the Wehrmacht was behaving firmly but justly towards pro-German loyal inhabitants in cases of sabotage. In this context, the commander of Seventeenth Army was convinced that there was 'in many cases an inflamed sentiment against the *Jews*' among the Ukrainian population. However, Stülpnagel also reported that the 'Draconian measures against the Jews [had aroused] pity and sympathy among some circles of the population'. In his letter to Army Group South on the 'position and influence of Bolshevism' he therefore argued that a 'determined *enlightenment*' of the Ukrainian population regarding Jewry was 'necessary at the outset in order to obtain a resolute and more

[54] Befh. rückw. H.Geb. Süd, Abt. Ic No. 1125/41 g., 29 July 1941, BA-MA RH 22/170.
[55] Befh. rückw. H.Geb. Mitte, Ia, corps order No. 39, 11 Aug. 1941, BA-MA RH 26-221/13.
[56] Refh. rückw. H.Geb. Mitte, Ia, corps order No. 40, 16 Aug. 1941, ibid.
[57] Befh. rückw. H.Geb. Mitte, Ic No. 20/41, 28 Aug. 1941, BA-MA RH 20-2/1092.
[58] AOK 17, Gruppe Ic/AO Br.B. No. 2784/41 geh., 30 July 1941, BA-MA, Alliierte Prozesse 9, NOKW-1693. The commander of Rear Army Area South also ordered that reprisals should be taken against Jews and Russians, and not against Ukrainians (Befh. rückw. H.Geb. Süd, Abt. VII/ No. 103/41, 16 Aug. 1941, BA-MA RH 22/6).

uniform rejection' of Jews. Stülpnagel also wanted to prevent the Jews from becoming 'active as centres of a resistance movement'. He therefore made detailed proposals to Army Group South for Wehrmacht propaganda, and argued that it should be independent of 'the goals being pursued by German policy'.[59]

The harshness of collective measures against members of specific population groups and non-participants cannot be explained solely by the need of the troops for security in the rear area, nor by pragmatic considerations. In truth, the ideological background to these measures is beyond question. The reprisals went far beyond what was necessary, as is demonstrated by an order from Army Group Centre on 7 August 1941.[60] It opposed such measures. Though there was understandable anger among the troops as a result of attacks by armed guerrillas, reprisals should not be inflicted on communities simply because they were 'close to' the location of the attack. Inhabitants should be shot only when there was irrefutable proof that they were the culprits, or had been connected with them. Second Army HQ passed on this instruction to the corps commands, noting that experience had shown that the partisan groups in the rear of the troops 'were being supported less by the mass of the people than by the remaining political functionaries and other activist-minded Communists'.[61] Second Army therefore applied to the army group for larger SD units to be sent forward into the army area from the rear army area.

Second Army HQ supported this request by claiming that experienced specialists were needed to expose Bolshevik elements. Reservations about the increased use of the SD in the army area had to take second place to the security requirements of the troops, 'particularly as the troops also urgently [desired] such measures'.[62] The activities of Special Commando 7b (SS Major Günther Rausch), which had advanced with the army but had insufficient men, had 'always been gratefully welcomed by the troops'. If the troops could be certain that organizations sent in for the purpose were working to defeat the 'dangerous elements' at their rear, they would stop imposing the excessive collective measures which had been criticized by the army group. Army Group Centre appears to have submitted the request from Second Army to Army High Command. On 14 August Army High Command ordered that operations in the rear army areas by the SS, or by police units subordinate to the higher SS and police leaders, would not be 'considered under any circumstances'.[63] However, seven days before, in Eleventh Army sector, Special Duty

[59] Commander Seventeenth Army, 12 Aug. 1941, BA-MA, 17. Armee, 14499/52.

[60] H.Gr. Mitte, Ic/AO/AO III No. 103/41 g.Kdos., 7 Aug. 1941, BA-MA RH 20-2/1091. An analagous order was issued by the commander of Rear Army Area Centre on 12 Aug. 1941: ibid. RH 26-221/13.

[61] AOK 2, Ic/AO No. 206/41 g.Kdos., 11 Aug. 1941, BA-MA RH 20-2/1091.

[62] AOK 2, Ic/AO No. 1662/41 g.Kdos., 10 Aug. 1941, on combating guerrillas, ibid.

[63] OKH/GenStdH/GenQu, Abt. Kriegsverwaltung (Qu 4), No. II/5271/41 geh., 14 Aug. 1941, BA-MA RH 22/91.

Squad D had already been instructed to take over responsibility for 'the defensive security of the combat area behind the fighting troops, alongside its previous tasks'.[64] Together with the secret field police, it was to hunt for escaped Red Army men in uniform or civilian dress. In contrast to Second Army, which had only one special commando assigned to it, Eleventh Army had two special commandos and three special-duty squads at its disposal.

From autumn 1941 the German–Soviet war of annihilation took on another dimension in the rear areas. There were several reasons for this: the growing activity of well-organized, trained Soviet 'partisan detachments and diversionary groups' under the leadership of local administrative and Party agencies; the ever widening gap between the tasks of the German security formations and the resources available to them, especially as some units had to be withdrawn and employed in battle duties; and the increasing disillusionment of the civilian population over the retention of the collective economy and the inadequate supply of food. The rural population in particular found itself wedged between the Soviet hammer and the National Socialist anvil (A. Dallin's expression). While the partisan groups demanded support in men and material, and moved ruthlessly against collaborators, the occupying power expected the population to behave loyally and provide help in anti-partisan activities.[65]

The commanders and commandants reported that Stalin's appeal for a 'patriotic people's war' was not being obeyed by the bulk of the population. As a result, the Germans were not being opposed by an armed popular movement. They dismissed Communist leaflets which maintained the contrary as 'typical Jewish insolence and Communist distortion'.[66] However, the treatment of actual or supposed 'partisans', 'guerrillas', 'bandits', 'go-betweens' and their sympathizers and helpers was to be even more severe. The starting-point was intelligence regarding Soviet instructions for the 'organization and activity of the partisan detachments and diversionary groups'. This led the Germans to assume that it was the political and state officers of the NKVD and NKGB, and not the Red Army, who were the 'exponents' of the partisan

---

[64] Quoted in Krausnick and Wilhelm, *Die Truppe des Weltanschauungskrieges*, 199, 216. The relevant documents are missing from BA-MA.

[65] III (mot.) Army Corps HQ notified Armd. Group 1 on 13 Aug. 1941 that it was to treat as guerrillas even those civilians who had been forced into resistance. 'If a Ukrainian, for fear of being shot by the commissar, allows himself to be forced to participate in the struggle, he must know that the German Wehrmacht will condemn him to death and shoot him according to international law': BA-MA RH 24-3/135. Armd. Group 1 responded with an order on the 'treatment of fighting civilians' (Pz.Gr. 1, Abt. Ic/AO No. 3441/41 g., 19 Aug. 1941, BA-MA RH 27-13/111). On the other hand, any person who, by his information, made it easier to combat partisans, to clear up acts of sabotage, to discover arms caches, or to capture Communist functionaries, was promised a reward of up to 1,000 roubles: appeal to the population of 10 Oct. 1941, BA-MA RH 27-7/158.

[66] AOK 2 Ic/AO/Abw. III No. 2075/41 g., 2 Oct. 1941, on combating Soviet partisans (guerrillas), BA-MA RH 20-2/1093.

movement.[67] Consequently, Second Army regarded the 'elimination of the leaders of such agencies' as the key to successful action against the partisans.[68] For its part, Army Group Centre devised proposals for the creation of mobile 'hunt commandos' with heavy weapons and pioneers to operate alongside commandos of the secret field police and SD.[69] At the same time, in response to a query from Sixth Army, Army High Command dispatched an ambiguous instruction from the commander-in-chief of the army.[70] This stated that uniformed Soviet fighting troops led by responsible officers had a claim to be treated as prisoners of war even when fighting behind the front; on the other hand, Soviet soldiers or groups which disrupted German rear communications 'incoherently on their own initiative' after fighting had ended were to be regarded as guerrillas. It was the duty of the troop commanders to make the decision in individual cases, according to the tactical situation. Second Army concluded that the 'Bolshevik rabble' in the rear of the troops could not be separated into Red Army men, uniformed or civilians, but was to be regarded as one 'organic *special* entity' and shot as guerrillas.[71] In the interests of Wehrmacht security, Seventeenth Army advocated that harsh measures against the civilian population must be taken wherever necessary; the Soviet leadership had exploited lenient German behaviour to supervise civilian traffic and 'to bring partisans, saboteurs, and spies through the advanced line into the army and into the hinterland'. Various 'suspicious elements' were listed: outsiders of both sexes in the locality, disguised NKVD militiamen (partisans), escaped military and civilian political commissars, and Jews of both sexes and all ages. The commander of 285th Security Division, Lieutenant-General Wolfgang Baron von Plotho, requested an order from Rear Army Area North for all Red Army men still roaming the land to be treated as partisans and shot.[72] Presumably with Roques's approval, Plotho then issued an order to that effect. Exceptions were to be made only for Red Army men who had undoubtedly deserted, or for escaped prisoners of war who had had no contact with other Soviet soldiers. 'In cases of doubt, every partisan and Red Army man is to be shot.'[73]

In its guidelines on anti-partisan activity, Second Army ruled that the

[67] OKH/GenStdH/OQu IV/Abt. Fremde Heere Ost II No. 1600/41, contained in AOK, Ic/Abw. III No. 1202/41, 13 Sept. 1941, BA-MA RH 20-2/1092.

[68] Ibid.

[69] H.Gr. Mitte, Ic/AO, leaflet on organization and combating of partisans, 14 Sept. 1941, BA-MA RH 20-2/1093. Not until 25 Oct. 1941 did Brauchitsch issue 'Guidelines for combating partisans' (ObdH/GenStdH/Ausb. Abt. (Ia) No. 1900/41, BA-MA 100. Jäg.Div., 44657/1). See Cooper, *Phantom War*, 49–50.

[70] OKH/Gen. z.b.V.b. ObdH/Az. 454 Gr. R.Wes. No. 1678/41 geh., 13 Sept. 1941, BA-MA RH 23/295.

[71] AOK 2, Ic/AO/Abw. III No. 2075/41 g., 2 Oct. 1941, BA-MA RH 20-2/1093. For the following: AOK 17, Gr. Ic/AO, 7 Sept. 1941, on surveillance of civilian traffic, BA-MA, 17. Armee, 14499/51.

[72] 285. Sich.Div., Ia No. 2206/41 geh., 23 Nov. 1941, BA-MA RH 26-285/5.

[73] 285. Inf.Div., Ia No. 2270/41 geh., 28 Nov. 1941, ibid.

population should be dealt with tactfully to persuade them to provide information about partisans. 'Collective measures against villages and their inhabitants must be the exception and are only to be taken where the mass of the population makes such a measure, the success of which is always doubtful, unavoidable.'[74]

In his order of 25 July 1941 regarding the 'treatment of enemy civilians and Russian prisoners of war in the rear army area', the commander-in-chief of the army had referred to the 'inflammatory activity of the exponents of the Jewish-Bolshevik system' in opposition to German efforts at pacification. Some individual army commanders had then adopted this order within their own sectors. From the outset, the army regarded the Jews, as well as the political cadres of the Red Army and the Communist functionaries, as 'exponents of the enemy attitude' and 'Bolshevik driving forces', and therefore as suspected partisans. During the capture of Daugavpils and Rezekne at the beginning of July 1941, the deliberate hunting down and arresting of Jews was justified on the grounds that they had been guilty of acts of sabotage against the troops 'directly or *indirectly*'.[75] At the same time, the commander of Rear Army Area Centre enlisted the regular police and SD to carry out the evacuation of all male Jews in whose neighbourhood there were suspected Red Army stragglers.[76] When, on 3 September 1941 in a report on the 'pacification of the Pripet marshes', 1st SS Cavalry Brigade (SS Colonel Hermann Fegelein) reported to Command Centre that links between the partisan groups were being maintained 'above all by Jews', and that 'Jew-free' villages had never been partisan bases, this ludicrous assertion was accepted without question.[77] The customary approach taken by the SS brigade was recommended to the army security troops some days later. Schenckendorff thought that the 'multi-faceted partisan struggle' had to be opposed by 'equally multifaceted ways of fighting' on the part of the security divisions. Anti-partisan operations were described as a 'rich field of soldierly activity' for intellectually alert and inventive divisional and troop commanders.[78] To promote the pacification of the army area, Schenckendorff inaugurated an 'exchange of experience' between the army and SS regarding the struggle against the partisans. Participating officers were selected according to 'their achievements and experience' in

---

[74] AOK 2 Ic/AO/Abw. II No. 2075/41 g., 2 Oct. 1941, BA-MA RH 20-2/1093. Similarly the commander of Seventeenth Army on 19 July 1941, ibid., 17. Armee, 14499/51.

[75] Activity report of Ic/04, 22 June 1941, BA-MA, LVI. AK, 17956/32 (emphasis added).

[76] Refh. rückw. H.Geb. Mitte, ten-day report to OKH/GenQu, Abt. Kriegsverwaltung, 9 July 1941 geh., BA-MA RH 22/227. See also the daily report of 221st security. Div. on 8 July 1941, ibid. RH 26-221/19.

[77] BA-MA RH 22/224. Ic of 50th Inf. Div. was similarly convinced that Jews and Party members in particular were maintaining an intelligence service across the fronts: Activity report, entry of 6 Sept. 1941, ibid. RH 26-50/85. 52nd Inf. Div. ordered on 16 Sept. 1941 (Abt. Ic No. 401/41 geh.) that the Bolshevik functionaries were to be executed discreetly, since all political and Party organs were undoubtedly engaged in raising partisan units: ibid. RH 26-52/61. On the procedure of 1st SS Cavalry Brg. see Krausnick and Wilhelm, *Die Truppe des Weltanschauungskrieges*, 222–3, and Büchler, 'Kommandostab Reichsführer-SS', 15 ff.

[78] Befh. rückw. H.Geb. Mitte, Ia, corps order No. 52, 14 Sept. 1941, BA-MA RH 26-221/13.

operations alredy undertaken.[79] The course included lectures from the higher SS and police leader, SS Major-General Erich von dem Bach-Zelewski, on the 'seizure of commissars and partisans', and from the chief of Special Duty Squad B, Major-General Arthur Nebe, on the 'co-operation of troops and SD in fighting the partisans'. There were also realistic demonstrations of systematic searches of a locality.[80] Not surprisingly, participants in the course used their experiences as the basis for future pacification practices in their units: 'Where the partisan is, the Jew is, and where the Jew is, there is the partisan.'[81] The chief of staff with the commander of Rear Army Area Centre, Lieutenant-Colonel Rübesamen, informed the quartermaster-general that the experiences of the course had fully confirmed the need for discussions. The participants, who included representatives of the Army High Command and Army Group Centre, had gained new ideas which would have a 'fruitful' effect on the struggle against the partisans.[82]

Many officers accepted the idea that the resistance came mainly from Jews and Communists. As a result, the special-duty squads of the security police and SD were able to report an 'excellent understanding' with the military leadership, and a 'pleasingly good attitude' on the part of the officer corps with regard to the Jews.[83] In their reports, the units of the army's secret field police repeatedly referred to their positive and smooth co-operation with the special-duty commandos and special squads.[84] The attitude of the troops towards the extermination policy of the security police and SD varied. While some remained aloof and closed their eyes to what was happening, others were sympathetic to the measures being taken. In 1941 the destruction of east European Jewry was marked by co-operation between the army and the SS. Here, of course, it is necessary to make a distinction between two kinds of conduct: one involved co-operation with the measures to establish distinguishing marks for Jews, to hunt and evacuate Jews and force them into ghettos, and to help the special-duty squads to carry out mass executions; the other relates to joint action between the Wehrmacht and the SS to pacify the rear areas. One major reason for co-operation was the acceptance by many officers and men of the propaganda image of 'Jewish Bolshevism'. Another was the fact that the differences between military tasks and security policing measures had deliberately been blurred, as Hitler had desired. Before Barbarossa there had still been a gap between the various tasks, but numerous orders from army and

---

[79] Befh. rückw. H.Geb. Mitte, Ia, corps order No. 53 *re* struggle against the partisans, exchange of information, ibid.

[80] Befh. rückw. H.Geb. Mitte, Ia, 23 Sept. 1941, order of the day for the course on 'combating partisans' 24–6 Sept. 1941, BA-MA RH 22/225.

[81] Quoted from Krausnick and Wilhelm, *Die Truppe des Weltanschauungskrieges*, 248.

[82] Befh. rückw. H.Geb. Mitte, Ia, Br.B. No. 1006/41 geh., 13 Oct. 1941, monthly reports for Sept., BA-MA RH 19 II/123.

[83] Events report No. 128, 3 Nov. 1941 g.Rs., Special Duty Squad C (BA R 58/218, pp. 344 ff.), and events report No. 14, 6 July 1941 g.Rs., Special Detachment 4b (BA R 58/214, p. 86).

[84] See as a typical instance Gruppe GFP (secret field police) 721, Tgb. No. II/176/42 geh., 26 Jan. 1942, BA-MA RH 22/199.

field commanders since June 1941 had helped to bridge it. For example, the army carried out summary executions of Jews, Communists, and Russians as 'collective drastic measures' in punishment for unsolved acts of resistance; these merged with the ideological policy of extermination being undertaken by the special-duty squads for the 'final elimination of Bolshevism'.[85] Was there an attitude which can be regarded as typical or representative of the approach of senior officers towards the activities of the security police and SD in the occupied Soviet territories? Since this survey cannot provide a quantitative assessment of German occupation policy, it must suffice to note a number of cases as examples of conduct. When the commander of Rear Army Area North, Infantry General Franz von Roques, complained about the mass murder of Lithuanian Jews in Kaunas to Ritter von Leeb, the commander-in-chief of Army Group North, Leeb noted in his diary: 'We have no influence on these measures. The only thing to do is to keep clear of them. Roques is certainly right to think that the Jewish question cannot be solved in this way. The most reliable course would be to solve it by sterilizing all male Jews.'[86] The fact that Leeb and Roques discussed the mass sterilization of Jews as an alternative to mass murder reveals how deeply the 'poison of anti-Semitism' had 'corroded' the mentality of senior conservative officers.[87] When the shootings of several hundred Jews and Communists aroused 'some unrest' among men of 281st Security Division (Army Group North), the commander consulted with General von Roques. He then declared himself satisfied that the actions were legal, and forbade any criticism.[88] The commander of 444th Security Division (Army Group South) merely noted in his situation report at the end of August that 'the Jewish question [was being] settled by the SD', but that the division had no clear idea of the individual measures taken.[89] No resistance was possible from officers who were prepared to close their eyes in the face of the extermination of the Jews, which was described by Hitler's adjutant as a 'necessary cleansing of the land'.[90] It was even less likely from those others who expressly consented to the actions of the security police and SD, or saw them as helping their own pacification policy. The 3rd Staff Officer of 221st Security Division (Army Area Centre) considered

[85] This is how SS Standartenführer Nockemann described the task of the special-duty squads to the Ic of the army groups and armies on 6 June 1941, BA-MA RH 19 III/688. See Cooper, *Phantom War*, 37 ff.

[86] Leeb, *Tagebuchaufzeichnungen*, 288 (8 July 1941). By coincidence, at the same time a leaflet by Theodore N. Kaufman, *Germany Must Perish* (Newark, 1941), had appeared in the USA, demanding the sterilization of all German men under 60 and all German women under 45. Needless to say, the Reich government from the end of July 1941 used these ideas of an insignificant fanatic to launch a wide-ranging propaganda campaign against Roosevelt and his policy. After the war Kaufman was portrayed by radical right-wing circles as the intellectual founder of the National Socialist programme of annihilation. See Benz, 'Judenvernichtung', 623 ff.

[87] So a doctor employed in the east wrote in retrospect; quoted in Krausnick and Wilhelm, *Die Truppe des Weltanschauungskrieges*, 255.

[88] Ibid. 227.   [89] 444. Sich.Div., Abt. VII No. 125, 28 Aug. 1941, BA-MA RH 22/202.

[90] KTB H.Gr. Nord, entry of 3 July 1941, NA T 311, Roll 53. I am grateful to Academic Director Dr Meyer for this reference. See Leeb, *Tagebuchaufzeichnungen*, 62 ff.

that 'superior control of this old national struggle' (between Poles and Belorussians) 'with the simultaneous eradication of Jewry . . . [was] the key to total political and economic pacification' of the Białystok region.[91] The commander of 213th Security Division (Army Area South) noted that the 'harsh measures' carried out by the special-duty squads against the Jews had met with 'complete understanding' from the Ukrainian population and had weakened the Jewish will to resist. 707th Infantry Division (Commissariat-General Belorussia) also believed that the 'complete eradication of this alien element [would] best advance the pacification of the country'.[92] The commander of 339th Infantry Division (Army Area Centre), Lieutenant-General Georg Hewelcke, reported that the population felt more free after its 'liberation from Jews and politically damaging elements'. In areas 'where a removal of Jews by the SD' had not yet occurred, the population was less actively involved in the pacification of the area.[93] In another situation report, Hewelcke had suggested 'eliminating all harmful persons and useless eaters (escaped and recaptured prisoners of war, tramps, Jews, and gypsies)'. This would be better than making big cuts in the rations of the Ukrainian auxiliary guard units.[94] 62nd Infantry Division considered it appropriate for 'SD or police units to remove' the 120 Jews in the town of Gadyach, particularly as bandits were operating in the area. This suggestion was noted by the staff of the commander of Rear Army Area South, and passed on by the 3rd staff officer to the higher SS and police leader.[95]

The gorge of Babiy Yar near Kiev, where 33,771 human beings were murdered, is a symbol not only of the atrocities of the special-duty squads, but also of the support they received from the army.[96] SS Special Detachment 4a, under the command of SS Colonel Paul Blobel, took up its 'security police' work in Kiev on 26 September 1941. It reported to Berlin that it envisaged the execution of at least 50,000 Jews. Blobel used explosions in the city, which damaged people and property, as a welcome excuse for 'appropriate measures of punishment'.[97] The city commandant of Kiev and Field Commandant 195, Major-General Kurt Eberhard, welcomed these measures and asked Blobel

[91] 221. Sich.Div., Abt. Ic, 28 July 1941, transfer report, BA-MA RH 26-221/70.

[92] Der Kdt. in Weißruthenien [Belorussia] des WB Ostland, Abt. Ia, monthly reports of 11 Oct.–10 Nov. 1941, 1–30 Nov. 1941 geh., BA-MA RH 26-707/1.

[93] 339. Inf.Div., Ia, 3 Dec. 1941, activity report for Nov. 1941, BA-MA, 339. Inf.Div., 13914/6.

[94] 339. Inf.Div., Ia No. 1466/41, 5 Nov. 1941, Evaluation of the situation, BA-MA, 339. Inf.Div., 13914/4.

[95] 62. Inf.Div., Abt. VII, 25 Nov. 1941, situation report, BA-MA RH 22/203.

[96] Here I am following the account of Krausnick and Wilhelm, *Die Truppe des Weltanschauungskrieges*, 188–9, 235. However, it is based solely on the operational reports of the participating special-duty squad and disregards the documents of Field Commandant's Office 195 (454th Security Div.), stationed in Kiev. On the suppression of public memory of the systematic extermination of the Jews in the Soviet Union see Goldjagen, 'Der Holocaust', 503–4.

[97] Thus Field Commandant's Office 195 lost 3 men killed and 7 wounded on 24 Sept. 1941 through time bomb or remote-controlled bomb. The resulting fire reduced about 1 sq. km. of the city to ashes and made around 10,000 inhabitants homeless. See War Diary of the quartermaster of 454th Security Div., entry of 25 Sept. 1941 (BA-MA RH 26-454/25), and the report by Dept. VII of the same division, 2 Oct. 1941, on visit to Field Commandant's Office 195, Kiev (BA-MA RH 26-454/28).

for 'radical action'. At a discussion between Eberhard, Blobel, and the chief of
Special Duty Squad C, Dr Otto Rasch, plans to shoot the Jews were discussed
quite openly. Subsequently, with the support of 637th Propaganda Company
in Sixth Army, Major-General Eberhard issued an appeal to the Jews of Kiev
to report for 'resettlement' on 29 September. Special Detachment 4a boasted
after this action that the Jews had believed that they were being resettled until
immediately before they were killed 'as a result of thoroughly skilful organization'. It was proud that, in co-operation with other SS units, it had murdered
almost 34,000 human beings within two days.

Of course, there were some commanders who advocated a clear distinction
between the tasks of the security police and those of the troops. 'Incidents' in
which these distinctions had been blurred led the commander of 207th Security Division (Army Area North), Lieutenant-General Karl von Tiedemann, to
issue an order on 22 July 1941.[98] After repeating verbatim the regulations in the
order of 28 April 1941, Tiedemann specifically forbade 'members of the
division from taking part in tasks of the SD, and superior officers from giving
permission for such activity or employing their troops in tasks of the SD'. A
few days later, the commander of Rear Army Area South, Infantry General
Karl von Roques, felt compelled to forbid the 'participation of Wehrmacht
members in excesses'.[99] 'The German soldier who participates in pogroms
against Jews etc. seriously damages the reputation of the Wehrmacht, and
displays an unsoldierly mentality.' Though the 'Führer decree' of 13 May 1941
allowed the troops to use the harshest measures against a hostile civilian
population 'in the course of fighting', 'unauthorized acts of violence' in the
pacified territory were nothing other than arbitrary acts. It was the duty of all
superior officers to punish such acts.

It would not be true to say that a resistance had arisen within the army to
'constant close co-operation' between it and the SS as demanded by the army
leadership in the ideological war against 'Jewish Bolshevism'. However, the
troop leaders were concerned that individual soldiers were involving themselves 'in an unpleasant manner' in the tasks of the security police and the SD.
At the beginning of August 1941, for example, the commanding general of
XXX Army Corps, Infantry General Hans von Salmuth, ordered that 'only
such soldiers who are specifically ordered to do so' could participate in special
commando actions against Party members and Jews in the army rear area: 'I
also forbid any participation as onlookers . . . Where troops are ordered to
[take part in] actions of this kind, they must stand under the leadership of
officers. These officers are responsible for ensuring that no unpleasant excesses on the part of the troops take place.'[100] A few days later, the commander

---

[98] 207. Sich.Div., Abt. Ia Az. 16 No. 809/41 geh., 22 July 1941, regulating the operation of the
security police and SS security service within the army, BA-MA RH 22/271.

[99] Befh. rückw. H.Geb. Süd, Abt. Ic No. 1125/41 g., 29 July 1941, on pacification measures,
point 1, BA-MA, RH 22/170.

[100] Gen.Kdo. XXX. AK, Abt. Ic No. 628/41 geh., 2 Aug. 1941, Intelligence Decree No. 4, point
2, BA-MA, Alliierte Prozesse 9, NOKW-2963.

of Sixth Army, Field Marshal von Reichenau, also forbade 'any participation by soldiers of the army as onlookers or performers in executions [by the SD] which are *not ordered* by a military superior'.[101] His order was issued after off-duty soldiers had volunteered to assist the SD in carrying out executions, had been present as onlookers, and had taken photographs. However, in this order Reichenau also spoke of the need for these 'executions of criminal, Bolshevik, mostly Jewish elements', and allowed local commandants to provide cordons against onlookers if requested by the SD. On 20 August 1941 the 1st staff officer of 295th Infantry Division, Lieutenant-Colonel Helmuth Groscurth, protested to the chief of staff of Army Group South about the shooting of ninety Jewish children and a number of women in Belaya Tserkov. Yet Groscurth was aware that the underlying orders were irrevocable. He therefore based his arguments almost exclusively on the need to maintain discipline, and demanded that 'similar measures take place away from the troops'. Groscurth was certainly aware of the order issued by the commander-in-chief of the army on 7 February 1940, when Brauchitsch had informed the field commanders that Hitler's order for the 'solution of national political tasks . . . [would] inevitably lead to unusual, harsh measures' against the Polish population. Subsequently, Himmler had promised 'to keep events and actions that are damaging to the spirit and discipline of the army away from the troops'.[102] After the field commandant, Lieutenant-Colonel Riedl, had repeatedly explained that 'this scum must be exterminated', and the commander of Sixth Army had given his consent to the execution, Groscurth, who in earlier years had played an important part in the military opposition to the regime, resigned himself to the apparently inevitable.

Roques's order of 29 July 1941 did not have the desired effect. He was growing increasingly concerned that the troops were moving beyond the control of their officers and might become little more than a 'mob'. On 1 September 1941 Roques issued a further order because 'cases [have] occurred recently in which soldiers and also officers have carried out shootings of Jews independently or have participated in them'. The tasks of the Wehrmacht in the army rear area were clearly defined. 'Any independent overstepping of these tasks undermines the discipline and reputation of the Wehrmacht and leads to the degeneration of the troops.' It was the duty of every superior officer to intervene immediately and resolutely in all these cases. '*Executive measures* against specific sections of the population (especially Jews)' were the sole responsibility of the forces of the higher SS and police leader, particularly in areas that had already been pacified. Roques continued: 'Any *unauthorized* shooting of native inhabitants, even of Jews, by *individual* soldiers, and any

[101] AOK 6, O.Qu/Qu. 1, Special instructions for supplies and for supply troops No. 50, 10 Aug. 1941, appendix 1, on executions by the SD, Nbg. Dok. NOKW-1654; quoted from Krausnick and Wilhelm, *Die Truppe des Weltanschauungskrieges*, 230–1.

[102] Groscurth, *Tagebücher*, appendix IV, 534 ff., and army C.-in-C. No. 231/40 geh., 7 Feb. 1940, regarding army and SS, Nbg. Dok. NOKW-1799; quoted from Krausnick and Wilhelm, *Die Truppe des Weltanschauungskrieges*, 104.

participation in executive measures of the SS and police forces [was] to be punished as disobedience in disciplinary terms at least, in cases where legal intervention [was] not necessary'.[103] The orders of Generals von Tiedemann, von Roques, von Salmuth, and von Reichenau were wholly in accordance with the distinctions made by the commander-in-chief of the army in his 'disciplinary decree' of 24 May 1941; Roques even reminded the officers of the content of Article 16a of the decree on martial jurisdiction. Brauchitsch had indeed sanctioned the temporary replacement of martial jurisdiction by 'ruthless action' of the troops in the event of punishable offences by the Soviet civilian population. At the same time, however, he had exhorted all officers 'to prevent arbitrary excesses by *individual* army members, and to prevent degeneration of the troops by timely intervention'.[104]

To the fury of Special Duty Squad 5 under SS Brigadier Erwin Schulz, a major action against the Jews in Uman was 'damaged extraordinarily' by the 'premature' and 'unplanned excesses' of Ukrainian militia members and Wehrmacht members. Army Group Command South was informed, and Rundstedt felt compelled to intervene. Like Salmuth, Roques, and Reichenau before him, he pointed out that 'the search for and combating of activities and elements hostile to the Reich in the occupied territories [was] solely the task of the special commandos of the security police and SD'. These were to carry out the 'necessary measures', particularly against Communists and Jews, on their own responsibility. '*Unauthorized* action by individual Wehrmacht members, or participation by Wehrmacht members in excesses by the Ukrainian population against the Jews, is forbidden, as are watching or taking of photographs during the implementation of the measures of the special squads.'[105] The Wehrmacht Commander Ukraine extended the ban on off-duty photography: 'If anyone photographs the sick, the suffering, those writhing in pain, the dead, and the dying, then he is demonstrating that he has a base character and is not fit to be called a German soldier.'[106] In October 1941 and March 1942 the commanders of Rear Army Areas Centre and South felt it necessary to repeat the ban on off-duty participation in shootings carried out by SS and police forces. This fact must be regarded as confirmation that such incidents were taking place.[107] As in Poland before, many incidents had taken place which persuaded the commanders to forbid lynch law against Jews, and acts of terror against other Soviet citizens. Evidence for this is provided by 'Special Corps Order No. 25', issued by the commander of Rear Army Area

[103] Befh. rückw. H.Geb. Süd, Az. III, Tgb. No. 3/41 geh., 1 Sept. 1941, appendix 2, BA-MA, Alliierte Prozesses 9, NOKW-2594.
[104] See sect. I.VII.2(*b*) at n. 69.
[105] Ob.Kdo. H.Gr. Süd, Abt. Ic/AO (Abw. III), 24 Sept. 1941, on combating elements hostile to the Reich, BA-MA RH 24-3/136 (emphasis added).
[106] OKH/GenQu/Außenstelle Süd, Kdr. Vers.Bezirk, Abt. II, order of the day No. 45, 6 Oct. 1941, appendices 2 and 3, subsection b, BA-MA, GenQu, Arb. No. 108.
[107] Befh, rückw. H.Geb. Mitte, 28 Oct. 1941 (BA-MA RH 22/9) and 21 Mar. 1942 (RB 22/230); also Befh. rückw. H.Geb. Süd, 20 Mar. 1942 (RH 22/24).

Centre on 5 September 1941. On the basis of a rumour against them, four Russian civilian prisoners, 'after being whipped for hours on end, had petrol poured over them by . . . a crowd of soldiers and were burnt alive. The local commandant, a captain, [had] watched this outrageous activity to the end without intervening.' Schenckendorff had the culprits court-martialled, with the most severe punishment meted out to the officer who had tolerated this 'bestial brutality'.[108]

The commander of Fourth Army, Field Marshal von Kluge, also felt it necessary to issue a 'special order' to maintain discipline.[109] It was 'high time to *put a complete end* to the unjustified methods of obtaining supplies, the raids, the plundering trips over vast distances, all the senseless and criminal activity'. The honour of the German soldier demanded a decent approach to the population in the conquered territories. Criminal conduct could turn the opinion of the 'basically harmless population' into hatred. The result would be more participation in acts of sabotage, and higher casualties for the Wehrmacht. Kluge threatened severe punishment not only for plunderers and criminals, but also for superior officers who tolerated such conduct.

A high point in the blurring of military tasks and security-police measures during Operation Barbarossa was reached on 10 October 1941. On that date the commander of Sixth Army, Field Marshal von Reichenau, issued an order covering the conduct of the troops 'towards the Bolshevik system'.[110] A number of explanations can be given for this order, though none is sufficient in itself. They include the deterioration in the army's operational position since the start of the campaign, the increased activity of organized partisan groups, the lack of concern for civilians displayed by many soldiers, and friction between troops and security police in the rear army area. Yet the decisive factor was widespread acceptance within the army of the concept of 'Jewish Bolshevism'. This enabled the physical destruction of east European Jewry to be explained purely as an act of retribution. In this context, the supposed links between Jewry and the partisan movement appeared simply as an additional justification. Only days before, in his order of the day for Operation Typhoon, Hitler had again branded the Jews as the instigators of the Bolshevik and the capitalist systems.[111] Reichenau argued that the most important goal of the campaign against 'the Jewish-Bolshevik system'

---

[108] Along with a term of imprisonment, a loss of rank was imposed: Befh. rückw. H.Geb. Mitte, Br.B No. 322/41 geh., 5 Sept. 1941, special corps order of the day (No. 25), BA-MA RH 26-221/17.

[109] Commander of Fourth Army, Ia/III/Ic No. 2000/41 geh., 11 Sept. 1941, BA-MA RH 20-4/884. At the end of Sept. 1941 the C.-in-C. of the army charged three generals with the task of maintaining discipline in the army group sectors, especially in the rear army areas (OKH/GenStdH/Org.Abt. II/No. 8280/41 geh., 29 Sept. 1941, ibid. RH 22/255). See also the order of Army Group South, Ia/Ib No. 2987/41 geh., 27 Oct. 1941, on maintenance of discipline, ibid. RH 22/9.

[110] AOK 6, Abt. Ia, Az. 7 geh., BA-MA RH 20-6/493; *Ursachen und Folgen*, xvii, doc. 3166. See also AOK 6, KTB (9 Oct. 1941), BA-MA RH 20-6/131.

[111] Domarus, *Hitler*, ii. 1757 (2 Oct. 1941).

was the 'complete destruction of the means of power, and the elimination of the Asiatic influence in the European sphere of culture'. This objective also led to

stasks for the troops which [went beyond] conventional one-sided soldiering. The soldier in the east is not just a fighter according to the rules of the art of war, but also the bearer of an implacable national idea, and the avenger of all the bestialities inflicted on the German and related peoples. For that reason, the soldier must have full understanding of the need for a harsh but just punishment of Jewish subhumanity.

Some of these arguments were based on the second part of the decree on martial jurisdiction; the last, however, clearly exceeded it, and offered a justification of the actions of Special Duty Squad C.[112] This 'punishment' had 'the further aim of stifling revolts to the rear of the Wehrmacht, which experience shows [are] always instigated by Jews'.

Reichenau also demanded Draconian measures against the 'enemy behind the front', which he considered was not taken seriously enough by the troops. The demand was based on an assessment of captured Soviet orders by the Department Foreign Armies East in the Army General Staff, and on the depositions of captured partisans. These indicated that German military quarters had consistently offered only reluctant support for anti-partisan activity.[113] 'Caring for local inhabitants and prisoners of war at troop kitchens if they are not in the service of the Wehrmacht is misunderstood humanity just as much as the handing out of cigarettes and bread.' If the civilian population refused to take an active part in the struggle against Bolshevism, its members could not complain about 'being judged and treated as adherents of the Soviet system'. On the basis of the supplement to 'Directive No. 33' of 23 July 1941, but with a characteristic individual slant, the army order of 10 October 1941 stipulated:

Fear of German countermeasures must be greater than the threat posed by the Bolshevik remnants roaming about. Irrespective of any political considerations of the future, the German soldier must achieve two things:

(1) the complete annihilation of the Bolshevik heresy, the Soviet state, and its armed forces;
(2) the merciless elimination of alien perfidy and atrocity,

thereby securing the life of the German Wehrmacht in Russia. Only in this way can we fulfil our historic task of liberating the German people from the Asiatic-Jewish danger once and for all.

Reichenau's attitude was not unique. This is demonstrated by the fact that other senior officers in the east declared themselves 'completely in agreement' with his order, and distributed it in their own areas of authority. The com-

---

[112] The extent of the mass killings—about 80,000 people—is revealed by events report No. 128 of 4 Nov. 1941 g.Rs., fo. 341, BA R 58/218.
[113] OKH/GenStdH/OQu IV, Abt. Fr.H. Ost (IIc) No. 3703/41 g., 3 Oct. 1941, BA-MA RH 24-3/136.

mander of Army Group South, Field Marshal von Rundstedt, did so on 12 October,[114] and the Wehrmacht Commander Ukraine, Air Force General Karl Kitzinger, on 17 October 1941.[115] The commander of Rear Army Area South described it as a 'binding principle'.[116] Four weeks later, the commanding general of LI Army Corps, Infantry General Hans Wolfgang Reinhard, ordered that every soldier 'must be *inoculated*' with the ideas of the order of 10 October.[117] Hitler described the initiative of Sixth Army HQ as 'excellent'. At the end of October 1941 Army High Command informed all army groups, armies, and commanders of Reichenau's order, and requested them 'to issue appropriate instructions along the same lines'.[118]

At the beginning of November 1941 Reichenau's visits to the troops convinced him that his order regarding 'the conduct of the troops in the east' had not yet been made sufficiently clear to the men. He instructed his officers to ensure 'that every last man knows what it is about, and why measures are being taken in the east that are not applicable in civilized countries.'[119] Historians are thus entirely justified in drawing attention to the striking differences between the conduct of the war in the west and that of the war in the east.[120]

However, OKW attempted to reduce this inequality of treatment from autumn 1941, following orders from Hitler. After the beginning of the war against the Soviet Union, there was a significant increase in acts of sabotage in the occupied countries of western, northern, and south-east Europe. Keitel instructed the various commanders that any case of opposition to the occupying power there—irrespective of the individual circumstances—should be attributed 'to Communist intrigues', since it was 'nothing but a *mass movement led consistently* by Moscow'.[121] The commanders were to use harsh measures at the first provocation. Suitable deterrence could be achieved only by 'unusual harshness' (which, of course, was already the rule in the east). The execution

---

[114] Ob.Kdo. H.Gr. Süd, Ia No. 2682/41 geh., 12 Oct. 1941, BA-MA, Alliierte Prozesse 9, NOKW-309. With regard to the imminent wintering, and the small number of forces in the rear areas, the carelessess and softness which were still frequently encountered were not tolerable after the fighting.

[115] Wehrmacht Commander Ukraine, Abt. Ia, No. 1032 (516) geh., 17 Oct. 1941, BA-MA RW 41/31.

[116] Befh. rückw. H.Geb. Süd, Abt. Ic No. 2252/41, 2 Nov. 1941 g., BA-MA RH 22/171.

[117] Gen.Kdo. LI. AK, Ic No. 2677/41 geh., 12 Nov. 1941, corps command's implementing instructions to army order on combating partisans of 9 Nov. 1941, point 4a, BA-MA, LI. AK, 15290/26.

[118] OKH/GenStdH/GenQu, Abt. K.Verw. (Qu 4/b) No. II/7498/41 g., 28 Oct. 1941, BA-MA RH 22/271; *Deutsche Besatzungspolitik*, No. 39.

[119] AOK 6, Abt. Ia Az. 7, 1 Nov. 1941, on conduct of the troops in the eastern territories, BA-MA, 100. le. Inf.Div., 15684/21.

[120] Nolte, *Faschismus*, 463, contrasts the 'normal European war' in the west with the war against the Soviet Union, which he rightly refers to as the 'most monstrous war of conquest, enslavement, and annihilation' in modern times.

[121] Der Chef OKW/WFSt/Abt. L (IV/Qu) No. 002060/41 g.Kdos., 16 Sept. 1941, *Ursachen und Folgen*, xvii, doc. 3163a. For France, see Umbreit, *Militärbefehlshaber*, 126 ff.; for Serbia, Browning, 'Wehrmacht Reprisal Policy'.

of 'from 50 to 100 Communists' should be regarded as 'appropriate punishment for a German soldier's life'. Action according to martial jurisdiction was to be the exception, though the most severe punishment was also demanded in these cases. This summary order for the imposition of collective punishments, and for the restriction of the operation of military courts, can be regarded as an attempt to apply the thinking behind the decrees of 13 May and 25 July 1941 to the other occupied territories. A more radical pacification policy was the result.

The commander-in-chief of Seventeenth Army (from 5 October 1941), Colonel-General Hoth, was convinced that the '*campaign in the east . . .* [must] be brought to an end in a different way from e.g. the war against the French'. In the east '*two inwardly unbridgeable outlooks* are fighting each other . . . German honourable and racial feeling, centuries of old German military tradition, against Asiatic ways of thinking with their primitive instincts, whipped up by a small number of mainly Jewish intellectuals'.[122] His order for the 'conduct of the German soldiers in the east' was issued on 17 November 1941. Hoth was not content merely to follow the suggestions made by the commander-in-chief of the army. Nor was he motivated solely by a concern for the lack of a uniform view of the tasks of the German soldier in the Soviet Union. He also believed that he was passing on the unequivocal views of Hitler, which ought to be the sole guiding principle for the Wehrmacht.

Hoth's definition of the meaning of the war clearly reflected his own sense of mission:

More strongly than ever, we carry in us the belief that this is the turning-point of an era, in which the leadership of Europe is transferred to the German people by virtue of the superiority of its race and its achievements. We clearly recognize our mission to save European culture from the advance of Asiatic barbarism. We now know that we have to fight against an embittered and tenacious opponent. This struggle can only end with the annihilation of one or the other; there can be no settlement.

Hoth listed the following war aims:

- (a) to defeat the Red armed forces so that it is impossible for them to be re-created;
- (b) to instil in the Russian population an awareness of the impotence of its former masters, and of the implacable will of the Germans to exterminate these holders of power as bearers of Bolshevik thinking;
- (c) to exploit the conquered territory to the utmost in order to relieve the provisioning of the homeland.

He believed that the military objective of the campaign had been achieved. However, the war against Bolshevism was still unfinished. To win it, Hoth demanded a sense of unconditional superiority, a conscious hostility to the enemy world outlook, the strictest discipline, implacable resolution, and tireless watchfulness. '*We are the masters of this land* which we have conquered.'

---

[122] AOK 17, Ia, No. 0973/41 geh., 17 Nov. 1941, BA-MA, 17. Armee, 14499/15,

Since Red Army men had 'bestially murdered' German soldiers, 'sympathy and leniency towards the population are completely misplaced'. Any trace of active or passive resistance, and 'any form of machination by Bolshevik-Jewish rabble-rousers, is to be wiped out'. The soldiers especially must understand the '*necessity of harsh measures against racially and nationally alien elements*'. More resolutely than Reichenau, Hoth justified the exterminations being carried out by Special Duty Squad C by directing his subordinates to look at German history, at the supposed guilt of the Jews for domestic political events after the First World War. The extermination of the 'same Jewish class of people', which Hoth described as the 'intellectual supports of Bolshevism, the exponents of its murder organization, the helpers of partisans', was a 'require-ment of self-preservation'.

After commenting on the nature of the exploitation of the land, the com-mander of Seventeenth Army referred to the attitude of the officers and NCOs. This would determine the conduct of the troops. The simple soldier's healthy feeling of hatred should not be suppressed, but must be strengthened. Officers had never

occupied a heavier and more responsible post in history than in this war . . . Russia is not a European state, but an Asiatic state. Every step further into this bleak, enslaved land teaches us the difference. Europe, and especially Germany, must be freed from this pressure, and from the destructive forces of Bolshevism, for all time. It is for this we are fighting and working.

Since 'potentially successful' anti-partisan activity was not solely the concern of Ic, the Intelligence III troops, the SD, or the secret field police, Seventeenth Army HQ was establishing a bigger organization for the whole army sector to track down and combat partisans.[123]

In November 1941 the commander of Eleventh Army, Infantry General von Manstein, also felt it necessary to explain the aim of the war against the Soviet Union, and to state his attitude towards the annihilation of east European Jewry. Acording to his army order of 20 November 1941,[124] the German people were engaged in a life-and-death struggle against the Bolshevik system. This struggle was not being waged against the Red Army by European rules of war; the fighting was also continuing behind the front line. Manstein depicted Jewry as the 'intermediary' between the two. 'More than in Europe, it holds all the key points of political leadership and administration, of trade and crafts, and also forms the cells of all unrest and possible revolts.' He described the aim of the war: 'The Jewish-Bolshevik system must be wiped out once and for all. Never again must it interfere in our European living-space.' Like Reichenau and Hoth before him, Manstein saw the task of the German soldier as twofold. First, the Red Army must be defeated. Second, however, each German soldier must conduct himself as the 'bearer of a national idea, and

---

[123] AOK 17, Ia/Ic/AO No. 4020/41 geh., 20 Nov. 1941, ibid. 14499/51.
[124] AOK 11, Abt. Ic/AO No. 2379/41 geh., 20 Nov. 1941, *IMT* xxxiv. 129 ff.

avenger of all the atrocities inflicted on him and the German people'. Once again, the relevant sections of the decree on martial jurisdiction appear to have provided the principles underlying this order. Manstein criticized the careless-ness and thoughtlessness of the troops towards the 'Bolshevik struggle behind the front', and attacked the distribution of foodstuffs to Soviet citizens who were not serving the Wehrmacht. Like Reichenau and Hoth, Manstein urged the soldiers to understand 'the need for the harsh punishment of Jewry, the intellectual carrier of Bolshevik terror'. In the army area remarks of this kind could only be a reference to the activities of Special Duty Squad D. These were justified partly as reprisal for past atrocities against the German people and German soldiers, but also as a preventive measure 'to stifle all revolts, which [were] mostly instigated by Jews'. In conclusion, Manstein appealed to the traditional soldier's ethos to demand proper treatment of the population, but only the non-Bolshevik parts. Where these did not decide voluntarily in favour of 'active co-operation against Bolshevism', appropriate means must be used to compel them.

However, other voices were also heard. The commanding general of III (Motorized) Army Corps, Cavalry General von Mackensen, issued an order regarding 'conduct towards the population' on 24 November 1941. This was significantly different from those issued by Reichenau, Hoth, and Manstein.[125] Of course, Mackensen also demanded 'ruthless action against and extermi-nation of enemy elements'. Nevertheless, he indicated that not everyone who looked 'Bolshevistic'—ragged, uncared for, unhygienic—was to be regarded as an enemy. The decision was to be made quickly and correctly, if possible by an officer, who was to be suitably cautious in dealing with denunciations. This was only one point among ten; the others were marked by the traditional view of proper conduct in occupied territories. In addition to the unavoidable consequences of war, Mackensen thought that unjust or psychologically mis-taken behaviour by the troops and agencies in the rear area had contributed to the perceptible decline in positive pro-German feeling among the population after a few weeks of occupation. Hatred of Bolshevism must not be transferred to the population. Both they and the prisoners of war should be treated justly and dispassionately. This principle was not undermined by 'the harshness appropriate to eastern people'. Though extensive supplies from the land for the Wehrmacht, the Reich, and Europe would be crucial over the following years, the population must not be regarded as an 'object of exploitation'. Instead it was a 'necessary member of the European economy'. German soldiers should behave as they themselves would wish to be treated in an emergency. A thoroughly good attitude would best convince 'a population that is accustomed to the bad attitude of the Red Army of the strength of the army and of our people . . . It is up to every soldier!'

The crucial question is how far this order was representative of the conduct

---

[125] Gen.Kdo. (mot.) III. AK, Abt. Ic No. 531/41 geh., 24 Nov. 1941, BA-MA RH 24-3/136.

of the German army in the Soviet Union. Since no quantitative investigation has yet been made, it can only be answered indirectly. In the reports of the fighting formations and security forces there are frequent references to the selection of specific population groups as 'hostages', and to summary executions after unsolved acts of sabotage ('drastic collective measures'). These measures were based on the decree on martial jurisdiction of 13 May and the Army High Command decree of 25 July 1941. The reports reveal a vast discrepancy between the number of 'guerrillas', 'partisans', and 'Red Army men' killed and the number of German casualties. Equally, they show only minimal differences between the number of people arrested and the number shot. The statistics tell their own story. They cannot be justified solely by the regular references to the security requirements of the troops. In fact, the ideological background is absolutely unmistakable.[126] To all intents and purposes, mere suspicion of actual or potential anti-German activities was sufficient to cause the shooting of civilians and Red Army stragglers who were found moving about the countryside. The fatal legal basis for such conduct had been created by the decrees of the Wehrmacht and army leaderships, and by their oral interpretation by the various commanders, commandants, officers, and soldiers, each acting according to his own cast of mind and under the impact of military developments and the Soviet response. In May 1941 the theory was that only military measures were to be taken, and that there was to be no punishment of local inhabitants. Eight months later these restraints had disappeared. Measures taken by officers in retribution for punishable acts by the Russian population were now regarded purely as administrative decrees, and were to be presented as such.

When the shooting of civilians is to be carried out, it is to be assumed that these cover administrative decisions which have been transferred to the officers by virtue of martial jurisdiction for the safety of the troops . . . These decisions may not be clothed in legal form. The content of the decisions is rather to be subject to summary assessment according to the security need of the troops.[127]

Security was to be provided by the ruthless pursuit and annihilation of the partisans and their 'accomplices'. It was accepted that 'innocent people [would] also be affected on occasion'.[128] Only a few days after the start of operations, an individual officer proposed that the orders regarding the treatment of Russian guerrillas should be altered because innocent civilians had

---

[126] See Cooper, *Phantom War*, 56.

[127] 281. Sich.Div. Ia/VII-28/42 geh., 12 Jan. 1942, on execution of power of punishment in the occupied Old Russian territories, BA-MA, Alliierte Prozesse 9, NOKW-2095. See also the order from XXVI Army Corps, Dept. Ia/U (Ic, III) No. 21/41 geh., 26 Dec. 1941, ibid., NOKW-2512.

[128] Gen.Kdo. LI. AK, Ic No. 2677/41 geh., 12 Nov. 1941, corps command's implementing instructions to army order on combating partisans of 9 Nov. 1941, Allgemeines (*a*), BA-MA, LI. AK, 15290/26. Timothy P. Mulligan has attemptd a first quantitative analysis of the partisan struggle, 'Reckoning'; see Schulte, *German Army*, 117 ff.; Bartov, *Eastern Front*, 119 ff.; Bonwetsch, 'Sowjetische Partisanen'; and Wilenchik, 'Partisanenbewegung in Weißrußland'.

been shot; the 3rd staff officer in III (Motorized) Army Corps HQ refused to support him on the grounds that the Soviet population ought to stay indoors at night and 'above all, not wear items of Russian army clothing'.[129] However, security needs were not met if punishment measures led 'to a general massacre and burning of villages by individual soldiers'.[130] Such conduct endangered the discipline of the troops. Drastic measures of this kind were associated with decisions by a commander. A few examples can be cited to demonstrate the situation. As successes in anti-partisan activity, Second Army thus reported that, in the period between August and October 1941, 1,836 persons had been arrested, of whom 1,179 were shot.[131] After a 'cleaning-up operation' in Rear Army Area South, 62nd Infantry Division shot 45 partisans, plus the 'entire Jewish population in Mirgorod (168 persons) because of links with partisans'.[132] In its provisional final report on anti-partisan activities in the forest region of Novomoskovsk (Army Area South), 444th Security Division reported that it had shot 305 bandits, 6 gunwomen, 39 prisoners of war, and 136 Jews.[133] According to 285th Infantry Division, between 22 June and 31 December 1941 almost 1,500 'partisans, civilians, Red Army men' had been either killed in battle or subsequently shot. Its own casualties were 7 dead and 11 wounded.[134] 707th Infantry Division, under the command of Wehrmacht Commander Ostland, shot 10,431 out of 10,940 'prisoners' in a single month while carrying out security duties in Belorussia. In fighting with partisans it had sustained only 7 casualties: 2 dead and 5 wounded.[135] The head of the secret field police attached to the Commander of Rear Army Area South, Stephainski, reported the results of three months of anti-partisan activity: just under 2,400 'guerrillas, saboteurs, parachutists treated according to the law of war', compared to its own casualties of 7 dead and 5 wounded.[136] The commandant of Local Headquarters II/930, Major Graf Yrsch, reported that between 18 July and 31 December 1941 627 partisans had been shot at a cost

---

[129] Gen.Kdo. (mot.) III. AK, Ic, KTB (26 June 1941), BA-MA RH 24-3/133.

[130] Gen.Kdo. LI. AK, Ic No. 2677/41 geh., 12 Nov. 1941, BA-MA, LI. AK, 15290/26.

[131] AOK 2, Ic/intelligence officer/intell. III No. 2377/41 g., 17 Nov. 1941, report on the struggle against partisans for the period 1 Aug.–31 Oct. 1941, BA-MA RH 20-2/1094. The commander of Rear Army Area North reported (Ic Tgb. No. 620) that 1952 'Red Army men and partisans, etc.' had been shot out of 32,392 prisoners (ibid. RH 22/271). By the end of Mar. 1942 these figures increased to 6,635 partisans killed and 8,329 taken prisoner, who 'for the most part [had been] executed later' (ibid. RH 22/261).

[132] Befh. rückw. H.Geb. Süd, Ia, KTB (3 Nov. 1941), BA-MA RH 22/3.

[133] Befh. rückw. H.Geb. Süd, Ia, appendices to activity report (6 Jan. 1942), BA-MA RH 22/19. Its own casualties were 9 dead and 17 wounded.

[134] 285. Sich.Div., Ic, 2 Jan. 1942, BA-MA RH 26-285/17.

[135] Kdt. in Weißruthenien des OB Ostland, Abt. Ia, monthly reports, 11 Oct.–10 Nov. 1941 geh., BA-MA RH 26-707/v. 1. This involved both former Red Army men and escaped POWs, as well as 'prisoners' taken during mopping-up operations, i.e. actual or suspected enemies. See daily report of 707th Inf. Div. of 10 Oct. 1941: out of 74 prisoners, 49 were shot (ibid. RH 26-221/14). See Förster, 'New Wine in Old Skins?', 317.

[136] Senior field police director with commander Rear Army Area 103 [South], Tgb. No. 62/42 geh., 15 Jan. 1942, BA-MA RH 22/19. See also the report of the army field police chief on the development of the partisan movement in the first half of 1942, 31 July 1942, ibid. RH 19 III/458.

of only 2 casualties sustained by the Russian Public Order Service. In the view of Graf Yrsch, this success was due to the 'enlistment of decent Russian informers, the most decent treatment of the decent part of the Russian population, and the systematic establishment of a civilian administration urged to do clean work'.[137] He also claimed that it was virtually impossible 'to behave more cleanly and worthily as soldiers during the executions [of partisans] than was insisted upon by Local Headquarters II/930'.[138]

Two examples will serve to reveal the role played by the outlook of individual officers in the fighting against partisans. The head of the advance party of 350th Infantry Regiment criticized the 'softness' of his soldiers on the grounds that it was unacceptable for officers to have to do the shooting while their men looked on.[139] On the other hand, a platoon leader in 3 Company, 50th Cycle Guard Battalion, complained that the adjutant of the above-mentioned Local Headquarters II/930 had personally shot three partisans.[140] The commandant of Rear Army Area 582, Lieutenant-General Oskar Schellbach, defended the conduct of the adjutant in a report to Ninth Army HQ, but instructed him 'that the active participation of an officer in the shooting of partisans [was] inappropriate and unworthy of an officer'.[141] Membership of the CPSU was certainly a cause for suspicion of anti-German conduct in every case, but it should not automatically lead to the shooting of suspects. The order of 25 July 1941 from the commander-in-chief of the army was thus interpreted in at least two different ways. For example, Field Headquarters (V) 376 informed the commander of Rear Army Area South that two Romanian officer patrols, reinforced by two German field gendarmes, had *cautioned* 55 'former Communists'.[142] Secret Field Police Group 721 (Army Area South) reported that it had handed over 28 Jews and 20 Communists to the SD.[143]

Autumn 1941 was a turning-point in the German military administration—not only with regard to pacification policy, but also for practical military reasons. Owing to a lack of manpower for security tasks, armed units composed of members of the varied ethnic groups of the Soviet Union were established in the army area of operations. On the assumption that the campaign would be won within a few weeks, the armies and commanders of the rear army areas had been provided with very few public-order and security forces. These found themselves in a precarious situation when the expected rapid victory over the Red Army did not materialize, and when their strength

---

[137] OK II/930, 1 Jan. 1942, on combating partisans, BA-MA RH 23/237.
[138] OK II/930, 5 Oct. 1941, on shooting of partisans, BA-MA RH 23/238.
[139] Advance detachment 350th Inf. Reg., 14 Oct. 1941. Report . . . , BA-MA RH 26-221/22.
[140] Report of 24 Sept. 1941, on shooting of partisans, BA-MA RH 23/228; printed with further documents in Schulte, *German Army*, 335 ff.
[141] Kdt. d. rückw. A.Geb. 582, Qu, 7 Oct. 1941, ibid.
[142] Feldkdtr. (V) 376, Abt. Ia, 20 Jan. 1942, on patrols to comb out the field command rear area, BA-MA RH 22/19.
[143] GFP Gruppe 721, activity report for Feb., 26 Feb. 1942 geh., BA-MA RH 22/199.

was further reduced to support military operations. All this occurred at a time when partisan activities, and the size of the army areas (Heeresgebiete) and Armeegebiete to be patrolled, were on the increase. There were not enough security forces available to enforce law and order in the occupied territories, particularly in areas which had not been 'combed through' beforehand by fighting units. Moreover, the divisions had begun to complain about their inadequate levels of equipment and manpower. At the beginning of November 1941, in answer to a query from the quartermaster-general and the commander of Army Area Centre,[144] the commander of 221st Security Division, Lieutenant-General Johann Pflugbeil, reported that the division in its 'current composition' was inadequate. It was unable to fulfil the demands made upon it by the Army High Command. The premisses of the 'principles laid down in the order of 21 March 1941' had 'not proved accurate'.[145] In order to achieve the objectives he had been set, the commander of 339th Infantry Division in Army Area Centre, Lieutenant-General Hewelcke, demanded the assigning of secret field police, the creation of a military administration section in the divisional staff, and the employment of the SD in his sector.[146]

At that time, the rear army area covered approximately 145,000 sq. km.,[147] or roughly the area of the current German states of Bavaria, Baden-Württemberg, Rhineland Palatinate, and Hesse combined. The security area of 221st Security Division at the end of July 1941 covered 35,000 sq. km., almost the size of Baden-Württemberg.[148] At the end of September 1941 the rear area of Ninth Army extended over 17,600 sq. km., a larger area than Schleswig-Holstein.[149] The area covered by Field Headquarters (Feldkommandantur) 198 (Army Area South) was 9,600 sq. km.[150] From the outset, there were not enough public-order forces to provide an individual police service in the municipalities, towns, and districts. By the end of July 1941 the commanders of the rear army areas were already being permitted, in co-operation with the appropriate higher SS and police leader, to set up a 'native auxiliary police' made up of released prisoners of war.[151] At the start

---

[144] OKH/GenStdH/GenQu, Abt. K.Verw. (Qu 4) No. II/7562/41 g., 29 Oct. 1941, BA-MA RH 22/225. See Befh. rückw. H.Geb. Süd, Abt. Ia/Ic No. 2270/41 g., 6 Nov. 1941, on evaluation of situation, ibid. RH 22/9.

[145] 221. Sich.Div., Abt. Ia No. 640/41 geh., 4 Nov. 1941, BA-MA RH 26-221/15.

[146] 339. Inf.Div., Ia No. 1466/41 geh., 5 Nov. 1941, BA-MA, 339. Inf.Div., 13914/4.

[147] Situation map, position 31 Oct. 1941, BA-MA RH 22/225. From 1942 to 1944 the territory occupied by Army Group Centre comprised 200,000 sq. km. and 9m. people: report of 10 Aug. 1944, ibid. RH 19 II/334.

[148] 221. Sich.Div., KTB (22 July 1941), BA-MA RH 26-221/10. Three months later the subsistence strength of the division was approximately 9,500 men.

[149] Kdt. d. rückw. A.Geb. 582, Qu/Ic, 22 Sept. 1941, BA-MA RH 23/227. For the struggle against partisans and for patrols, only some 350 men were available to Korück 582.

[150] Activity report of 6 Jan. 1942, BA-MA RH 22/19. In terms of public-order forces, 341 men were available to the field commandant's office.

[151] OKH/GenStdH/GenQu, Az. Abt. K.Verw. (Qu 4 B Kgf.) No. II/4590/41 geh., II. Ang., 25 July 1941, BA-MA RH 23/219. See Befh. rückw. H.Geb. Nord, Ia, Tgb. No. 1077/41 geh., 29 Aug. 1941 (ibid. RH 22/271), Tgb. No. 991/41, 22 Oct. 1941 (ibid. RH 22/255), and report on Estonian

of operations, these units were composed mainly of Lithuanians, Latvians, Estonians, Belorussians, and Ukrainians. The German military command authorities were helped in their recruitment efforts by the deep anti-Communist sentiments of the population in the areas which Moscow had annexed in 1939–40 following the Hitler–Stalin pact. In the middle of August 1941, for example, the Latvian 'police escort' in Riga comprised almost 3,000 men.[152] At the same time, it was ordered that the security forces could be further reinforced by 'auxiliary guards' recruited from freed prisoners of war of non-Russian nationality.[153]

In the unfavourable conditions of the autumn of 1941, Army High Command also agreed to a proposal from Eighteenth Army HQ for the establishment of a Cossack 'special troop to subdue Soviet partisans'. On 6 October 1941 the quartermaster-general gave permission for the commanders of Rear Army Areas North, Centre, and South to create initially one experimental 'Cossack squadron' each, comprised of prisoners of war 'in agreement' with the higher SS and police leaders, and to employ them against partisans.[154] This was the first time that permission had been given for the establishment of auxiliary formations consisting of members of the *Russian* people, as the Cossacks had to be regarded as Russians. Infantry General von Schenckendorff wanted to go even further. He hoped to allow the security divisions to set up cavalry squadrons from released prisoners of war of Ukrainian and Belorussian nationality.[155] According to the commander of Rear Army Area Centre, the anti-partisan course of 24–6 September 1941 had proved that the cavalry platoons in the infantry regiments of the security divisions must be reinforced to enable them to fulfil their reconnaissance and operational tasks. Army High Command agreed to this proposal in the middle of November 1941.[156] A month before, the quartermaster-general had also empowered the army groups to set up 'auxiliary guards' for security tasks and surveillance purposes; these were to be made up of freely recruited native inhabitants.[157] The SD was to be involved in the security screening.

Both the circle of those eligible for recruitment and the tasks given to the auxiliary formations were quickly extended. In order to free the troops from

escort squads, 3 Dec. 1941 (ibid.); Befh. rückw. H.Geb. Mitte, Abt. VII Az. 20/41, 27 Nov. 1941, service regulations for the public-order service, ibid. RH 23/228.

[152] Higher SS and Police Leader Ostland No. 175/41 geh., 21 Aug. 1941, BA-MA RH 22/271.

[153] OKH/GenStdH/GenQu, Abt. K.Verw. (Qu 4/Kgf.) No. II/4590/41 geh., IV. Ang., 18 Aug. 1941, palpable in the instruction of 22 Oct. 1941, BA-MA RH 23/219.

[154] OKH/GenStdH/GenQu, Abt. K.Verw. (Qu 4) No. II/6878/41 g., 6 Oct. 1941, BA-MA RH 22/32. Hoffmann, *Ostlegionen*, 21, describes this date as the 'birthday of the eastern troops'.

[155] Extract from corps order No. 61 of 12 Oct. 1941, BA-MA RH 19 III/492.

[156] OKH/GenStdH/Org. Abt. (II) No. 9639/41, 16 Nov. 1941, BA-MA RH 19 III/492.

[157] OKH/GenStdH/GenQu, Abt. K.Verw. (Qu 4/Kgf.) No. II/7344/41 geh., 22 Oct. 1941, BA-MA RH 23/219. See 339. Inf.Div., Abt. Ic No. 1460/41 geh., 2 Nov. 1941, instruction leaflet on jurisdiction, subordination, and duties of . . . , subsection II, ibid., 339. Inf.Div., 13914/4; AOK 9, O. Qu./Qu 2 No. 2881/41 geh., 29 Nov. 1941, ibid. RH 23/219. On the feeding of these units see Befh. rückw. H.Geb. Mitte, Qu., 1 Nov. 1941, special instructions for supplies No. 64, ibid. RH 26-221/18.

guard duties of all kinds, the security formations increasingly drew even on the Russian population as 'public-order police'.[158] In the middle of November 1941 the commander of Rear Army Area South was authorized to set up two separate squadrons of released prisoners of war of 'Turkestani and Caucasian nationality'.[159] The reservoir of native manpower was used for military and political reasons: to top up the security divisions and fighting formations, for guard and security duties, and for anti-partisan work. At the end of November 221st Security Division applied for the establishment of sapper companies for each infantry regiment, to be made up of trained 'Russian pioneers—Ukrainians, Volga Germans' released from captivity. It had already formed sapper platoons with the local defence battalions by enlisting released prisoners of war.[160] The commander of Rear Army Area South recognized the significance of the proposal. However, there were objections 'at higher level' to 'establishing and arming new formations made up of Russian prisoners'. The division was allowed to set up a sapper company, but the prisoners of war were 'neither to be dressed in field grey nor to be armed in any way'.[161] At the same time, the commander of Ninth Army, Colonel-General Strauss, asked for 'the labour potential of the great mass of prisoners to be placed at the service of the Wehrmacht even more than had apparently been envisaged'.[162] Combat strengths had been so reduced that it was essential to 'fill them up'. For that reason much of the 'fetching and carrying behind the front' should be done by released prisoners of war under German leadership and supervision. Soldiers would then be released for service at the front. Strauss thought that the prisoners, who were 'completely worn out and near starvation', would think themselves fortunate if they were allocated two-thirds of the rations available to German soldiers. Of course, it was understood 'that the Asiatic subhumanity would have to remain in the prison camps'. Ninth Army also tried to dispel any fear on the part of higher authorities 'that the German soldier might be unfavourably influenced by living alongside Russians, which could not be avoided entirely'. The 'inherent feeling of superiority' among the Germans would rule this out. Moreover, Ninth Army considered that this enlistment of Soviet prisoners of war would provide benefits for the Germans '*after the war*', because 'the Russian' would have learnt discipline and the rudiments of the German language and methods.

Army Group Centre passed on the request from Ninth Army to all the armies and armoured groups under its command, as well as to the commanders of the rear areas, and asked for their views.[163] Based on personal

---

[158] 221. Sich.Div., Abt. Ia, 27 Oct. 1941, on employment of public-order police established from the Russian population, BA-MA RH 22/9.

[159] OKH/GenStdH/GenQu, Abt. K.Verw. (Qu 4) No. II/18795/41, 15 Nov. 1941, BA-MA RH 22/32. See Befh. rückw. H.Geb. Süd, KTB (6 Dec. 1941), ibid. RH 22/3, and Hoffmann, *Ostlegionen*, 25 ff.

[160] 221. Sich.Div., Abt. Ia, 25 Nov. 1941, BA-MA RH 26-221/15.

[161] Befh. rückw. H.Geb. Mitte, Ia, 28 Nov. 1941, ibid.

[162] AOK 9, Ia No. 4346/41, 23 Nov. 1941, BA-MA RH 23/219.

[163] Befh. rückw. H.Geb. Mitte, Qu. No. 684/41 geheim, 2 Dec. 1941, BA-MA RH 26-221/15.

experience, the commandant of Army Rear Area (Korück) 582 (Ninth Army) opposed the deployment of released prisoners on labour service or with the baggage train, and advocated using them as auxiliary guards and in the fight against partisans.[164] The numbers involved should reach perhaps 30 per cent of the strength of the German squadrons, but certainly not more at the outset. Korück 582 also argued that it was unwise to place too much emphasis on the nationality of the prisoners of war. Discontent with Bolshevism was just as widespread among the Russians as among the Ukrainians, but so was unreliability. 'No prisoners at all would make their way to service in the German Wehrmacht for intellectual reasons. The reason why they will be ready is terror of the prison camps, and the prospect of a better life with the German troops.'

In contrast to Korück 582, 221st Security Division made a positive assessment of the work of freed prisoners of war,[165] which had released German units for the struggle against the partisans. It considered that prisoners of war could be permitted to make up 25 per cent at most of the authorized strength of the supply services. Though reorganization would be necessary, its disadvantages would 'be of considerably less weight than the advantage of obtaining detachments for the front'.

Military utilitarianism and positive experiences in the army areas also lay behind an Army High Command order at the beginning of January 1942, authorizing each army to establish a squad of reliable released prisoners of war and local inhabitants for deployment in the security service and in the struggle against the partisans.[166] The shortage of security forces compelled the army 'to exploit for security purposes all the native elements of the occupied territories who are hostile to the Soviet system'. Those local inhabitants who were to be armed for the 'struggle against Bolshevism' would be placed under German military jurisdiction. As a result, they would not be affected by the decree on martial jurisdiction.[167]

At the end of December 1941 Hitler authorized Army Group South to create four legions: Turkestani, Georgian, Caucasian-Muslim, and Armenian.[168] A few days later he also permitted the recruitment and engagement of volunteer Tartars as 'fighters in the German troops'.[169] Approximately 3,000 Tartars came forward in the Crimea within four weeks. The liaison officer of the War Economy and Armaments Department with Second Army HQ reported at the end of January 1942: 'Since outwardly they are not

---

[164] Kdt. d. rückw. A.Geb. 582, Qu., 7 Dec. 1941, on increased involvement of prisoners of war, BA-MA RH 23/219.

[165] 221. Sich.Div., Abt. Ia No. 678/41 geh., 12 Dec. 1941, BA-MA RH 26-221/15.

[166] OKH/GenStdH/Org. Abt. (II) No. 213/42 geh., 9 Jan. 1942 (BA-MA RH 19 III/492), and KTB, entry of 1 Jan.–5 Jan. 1942 (BA-MA RH 2/v. 821). On the situation in Army Group North in Apr. 1942 see sect. II.11(*g*) n. 696 (Klink).

[167] OKH/Gen. z.b.V.b. ObdH/Az. 500 Gr. R.Wes. No. 99/42 g. Kdos., 17 Apr. 1942, BA-MA RH 19 III/492.

[168] Memorandum by Kramarz, 30 Dec. 1941, PA, Handakten Ritter, Rußland (No. 29). See Hoffmann, *Ostlegionen*, 25 ff., and Zur Mühlen, *Zwischen Hakenkreuz und Sowjetstern*, 57 ff.

[169] OKW/WFSt/Qu (2) No. 0061/42 g.Kdos., 6 Jan. 1942, BA-MA Wi/I. 345.

distinguishable in any way from German soldiers, one may sometimes speak to a soldier on the street who does not understand a word of German.'[170] It is therefore inaccurate to claim that there was 'no social or political basis for collaboration' in the Soviet territories lying further east, on the grounds that—in contrast to Lithuania, Latvia, Estonia, western Belorussia, and the Ukraine—socialist organization and socialist education had strengthened 'the political and moral unity of the Soviet people' there. The Soviet state was by no means as monolithic as Marxist historiography has described it.[171] There were many Soviet citizens—prisoners of war and civilians—who preferred the swastika to the Soviet star. In addition to rejection of the Soviet system, of course, the sheer desire to survive played a vital part in persuading them.

The Soviet counter-offensive round Moscow had considerable repercussions on German pacification policy. Army and Waffen-SS units as well as police battalions had to be withdrawn from Rear Army Area Centre and employed at the front. In consequence, Soviet partisans controlled large parts of the region; Infantry General von Schenckendorff judged that he was 'no longer master of the situation' in spring 1942. Though assessments of the situation in the other two army areas were much more positive,[172] the 'commanding general of the security troops and commander in Army Area Centre' reported at the end of May 1942 that 'the great reconstruction work of the last months' had been undone.[173] Some 25 local defence battalions remained to him, of which more than 50 per cent were inadequately trained, badly armed, and generally led by over-age officers. In the opinion of Schenckendorff, these were insufficient for active anti-partisan work. Though he managed to keep open the railway line for troops and supply transports through his area of command, the intervening territory had been 'completely removed from his influence'. There the partisans were in almost total control. The units at his disposal were totally incapable of offensive operations against the 'greatly increased, well-trained, and well-equipped enemy groups amalgamated under military leadership'. Consequently, the commander demanded the return of the strike forces which—though theoretically assigned to him—had been seconded to various armies.

Schenckendorff did not suggest any increase in the recruitment of Soviet citizens for fighting and security tasks in the rear army area, because Hitler had forbidden new formations in the area of operations at the end of March

[170] AOK II, IV (Wi), report for the period 1 Dec. 1941–31 Jan. 1942, BA-MA RH 20-11/415. See also his report from Mar. 1942, ibid. Overall, 9,255 Tartars from 203 localities and 5 prisoner-of-war transit camps had made themselves available.

[171] *Deutschland im zweiten Weltkrieg*, ii. 123.

[172] See memorandum from chief of staff with general commanding the security troops and commander of Rear Army Area South, 27 Apr. 1942 (BA-MA RH 22/27), and Befh. rückw. H.Geb. Nord, Abt. Ic/AO, survey of partisan activity since 15 Dec. 1941 (ibid. RH 22/259).

[173] General commanding the security troops and commander of Rear Army Area Centre, Ia, Br.B. unnumbered/42 geh., 31 May 1942, evaluation of situation in Army Area Centre, BA-MA RH 22/231.

1942.[174] This decision had been obtained by the organization department in the Army General Staff after some of the armies had exceeded the order of 9 January and either established, or planned to establish, several 'foreign squads'. Hitler was prepared to accept only what seemed absolutely essential, 'otherwise he fears [it would cause] political effects which would pre-empt a subsequent decision on the question of the treatment of the occupied eastern territories'.[175] The SS alone was now permitted to establish units made up of minority peoples in the Reich commissariats, 'in the form of local police organizations'.[176] At this stage there were already more than twice as many 'auxiliary police' units, made up of politically reliable local inhabitants, as there were German regular police units deployed in the east (60,421 to 29,230).[177] Once before, in the autumn of 1941, Hitler had accepted the pragmatic arguments of the field commanders and allowed military co-operation between the Wehrmacht and local people, thus departing from an earlier dogma.[178] Subsequently, in February 1942, in an attempt to deal with the changed military situation, he was also prepared to change his guidelines for the treatment of the political leaders in the Red Army, which had been based on ideological assumptions.

2. IMPLEMENTATION OF THE 'COMMISSAR ORDER'

In postwar discussion of the two unlawful decrees—the restriction of martial jurisdiction and the treatment of the commissars—more attention has been devoted to the 'commissar order' of 6 June 1941 than to the 'Führer decree' of 13 May. More people were actually killed as a result of the 'special measures' taken by the troops against the civilian population under the decree on martial jurisdiction. However, the violation of international law was more blatant in the case of the shooting of commissars. In the case of the commissar order, the shooting of a specific group in the Red Army was no longer justified even by the mere suspicion of resistance to the Wehrmacht, but simply by their position and function within the enemy system. After the war, all the field commanders at the OKW trials vigorously denied that Soviet commissars had been shot in their areas of command. This assertion has been maintained by senior officers in their own memoirs and books on the campaign in the east.[179] They have argued that it would have violated all soldierly sentiment

---

[174] OKH/GenStdH/GenQu-Org. Abt. (II) No. 1349/42 g.Kdos., 24 Mar. 1942, BA-MA RH 19 III/492.

[175] GenStdH/Org. Abt., war diary, entry of 6–10 Feb. 1942, BA-MA RH 2/v. 821.

[176] H.Gr. Süd, Ia No. 266/42 g.Kdos., 11 Feb. 1942, BA-MA RH 22/23.

[177] OKH/WFST/Org. No. 22230/52 g.Kdos. Chefs., 6 June 1942, on combat strength 1942 [as of Mar. 1942], BA-MA RM 7/395.

[178] On 16 July 1941 Hitler had declared that west of the Urals no one but a German could ever be allowed to bear arms, 'not the Slav, not the Czech, not the Cossack, nor the Ukrainian!': *IMT* xxxviii. 88.

[179] See Manstein, *Lost Victories*, 179–80, and Helmdach, *Überfall?*, 72–3. In 1941 Helmdach was a major on the general staff, and 3rd general staff officer in Fourth Army Command.

simply to have shot the commissars after they were taken prisoner; German soldiers had never demonstrated an unsoldierly attitude, and had not abandoned decent conduct even in the face of repeated Soviet breaches of interational law.

In the absence of any quantitative assessment, it is difficult 'to obtain an accurate overall view of the practical implementation of the "commissar order" by the troops'.[180] However, the numerous official reports of executions tell their own story. It would be profoundly mistaken to underestimate the significance of the commissar order, or to believe that only a few units had carried it out while the rest had sabotaged it.[181] After the war, doubts were expressed about the factual accuracy of the surviving reports. Even so, these cannot disguise the fact that it was carried out. The argument that many commissars were actually shot in the prisoner-of-war camps, and that this proves that the soldiers did not carry out the order, is also invalid.[182] Until the beginning of October 1941, when Army High Command entrusted the task of picking out and executing the commissars in the POW camps in the army's area of operations to the security police and SD, the camp commandants followed the Army High Command's 'special instructions'—by obeying the spirit of the commissar order and the decree on martial jurisdiction.

There was no uniform method of reporting on the subject of political commissars in the army. Some divisions and corps included the shootings of commissars in their routine reports on the situation of the enemy,[183] covering them in the returns submitted by the 3rd staff officer,[184] or noted them in the listing of prisoners.[185] Other commands demanded fortnightly overall reports.[186] This did not mean that false reports were sent in; often they were covered by 'reporting error'.[187] The phrasing of the reports also varied. References were made to shooting, disposing of, dealing with, collecting, deporting. To date, the *non*-implementation of the order has been recorded only in the case of 17th Armoured Division under Lieutenant-General von Arnim.[188] The

---

[180] Jacobsen, 'Kommissarbefehl', 153. See Schulte, *German Army*, 215 ff.

[181] As Nolte, *Faschismus*, 437, assumes.

[182] As assumed by Jacobsen, 'Kommissarbefehl', 153, and Streim, *Die Behandlung sowjetischer Kriegsgefangener*, 52–3, 94–5.

[183] 99th Mountain Inf. Reg., morning report of 27 June 1941, BA-MA RH 28-1/v. 128; 99th Lgt. Inf.Div., Ic, special instructions No. 2 on the Ic area, 5 July 1941, BA-MA, 99. le. Inf.Div., 21400/17; Armd. Group 3, Dept. Ic, morning report of 19 July 1941, ibid. RH 21-3/v. 430.

[184] Gen.Kdo. (mot.) III. AK (22 June 1941), BA-MA RH 24-3/133.

[185] 221. Sich.Div., Abt. Ic, 16 July 1941, Prisoners-of-war, BA-MA RH 26-221/21. Here it was also noted that 23 civilian political commissars had been handed over to the police. The same division reported on 23 July 1941 that it had handed over 14 political functionaries to the secret field police: ibid. RH 26-221/19.

[186] H.Gr. Mitte, Ic/AO No. 2123/41 geh., 6 July 9141, BA-MA RH 20-2/1091; AOK 6, Ic/AO No. 2390/41, 8 July 1941, ibid., 6. Armee, 15623/2; AOK 2, Ic/AO No. 1661/41, 12 Aug. 1941, ibid. RH 20-2/1092.

[187] L. AK, Ic, evening report of 23 July 1941, and XXVIII. AK, Ic, morning report of 30 Aug. 1941, BA-MA, 16. Armee, 22745/38. By 23 July 1941 the last-named corps had reported 14 commissars as having been shot.

[188] Halder, *Diaries*, 1248 (21 Sept. 1941). However, the division's reports on commissars shot in Aug.–Sept. 1941 tell a different story.

3rd staff officer of Armoured Group 3 noted, in his progress report in mid-August 1941, that the 'implementation of the special treatment of the political commissars' had not been a problem for the troops.[189] Even before the commissar guidelines were issued, the commander of Armoured Group 4, Colonel-General Hoepner, had demanded: 'In particular, no mercy must be shown to the exponents of the present Russian-Bolshevik system'.[190] In the German view this included the commissars, who were seen as the executors of the will of the Communist Party in the Red Army, and as 'exponents of the Jewish-Bolshevik world outlook'.[191] The 3rd staff officer with the commander of Rear Army Area South summarized his views in mid-July 1941: 'In the type of the political commissar, we are confronted by the Asiatic grimace of the entire Red system. He has ensured that this conflict is no longer a struggle between soldiers of two states. The Red political commissar gives the Red Army its character, his destruction is the precondition for our victory.'[192] In fact, this conviction must be regarded as a self-fulfilling prophecy. The officer had been informed of the instructions of Army High Command before the start of operations, referring to the German concept of a war of annihilation. He also cited Hitler in support of his view: 'The Führer was well aware of these matters when he coined the phrase in an order: "These Asiatic methods cannot be countered with west European means."' The officer concluded his situation report as follows:

We have all come to know these Asiatic methods, every town, every village in the Ukraine harbours its unfortunate victims.[193] We must have the gravest fears for the fate of all our comrades, including those of the allied nations, who have the misfortune to fall alive into the hands of these Red devils. Our duty and our right to free the world from the Red plague are all the greater. Yet haughty England, in association with America, took it upon herself to fight in loyal brotherhood-in-arms with Moscow for the victory of world revolution.

It is not surprising that large numbers of commissars were reported shot at the beginning of operations. At this stage they were still recognizable by special badges on their uniforms. For example, Amoured Group A reported '172 disposed of' by 19 July 1941,[194] Second Army '177' by 24 July,[195] Armoured

[189] P2.Gr. 3, Ic, activity report No. 2 of 19 Aug. 1941, pp. 25, 30, BA-MA RH 21-3/v. 423. This assessment is missing in Jacobsen, 'Kommissarbefehl', doc. 19.

[190] Kdr. Pz. Gr. 4, Ia, No. 20/41 g.Kdos. Chefs., 2 May 1941, deployment and battle instruction 'Barbarossa' (study), appendix 2: operations, BA-MA, LVI. Pz.Korps, 17956/7a.

[191] See sect. I.vii.2(*c*).

[192] Befh. rückw. H.Geb. Süd, Abt. Ic, situation report of 19 July 1941, BA-MA RH 22/170.

[193] Here he was presumably alluding to the events in Lvov after the start of the war. See sect. II.ii.12 at n. 316 (Hoffmann). Also interesting in this context is the entry in the War Diary of 1st Mountain Div. on 1 July 1941: 'During the commanders' conference shooting was heard in the GPU prison of Lvov, where Jews were forced to bury the Ukrainians (several thousand) murdered here in recent weeks by the Russians after Jewish denunciations. At the urging of the Ukrainian population there was a real pogrom of Jews and Russians in Lvov on 1 July' (BA-MA RH 28-1/v. 20).

[194] P2.Gr. 4, Ic, report of 27 July 1941, BA-MA RH 21-4/271.

[195] AOK 2, Ic/AO, reports of 9, 12, and 26 July 1941, BA-MA RH 20-2/1090, 1091.

Group 3 'about 170 got rid of separately',[196] and 44th Infantry Division '122 commissars disposed of' by the beginning of October.[197] On 17 July Armoured Group 3 reported that 'two commissars in civilian clothing' had been captured and shot by the *staff*.[198] After hearing about the measures against them, the commissars and political leaders of the Red Army disguised themselves as officers or ordinary soldiers and removed their insignia.[199] Thereafter, the German offices were instructed to rely on interrogations and denunciations by fellow prisoners. The army leadership urged the troops to keep combing the prison camps for commissars.[200] The commander of Rear Army Area Centre, Infantry General von Schenckendorff, also emphasized the importance of discovering commissars both in the camps and in 'search operations'.[201] He publicly offered a reward of 100 roubles to every captured Red Army man or civilian whose information led to the discovery of a commissar.[202] 52nd Infantry Division praised the special leader seconded to it, Vlasov, for removing 'commissars or Communist functionaries' from the camps on several occasions.[203] As regards the treatment of prisoners, 1st Cavalry Division ordered that only officers and commissars from divisional formations upwards were to be handed over to it for interrogation; civilians who were described as 'Communists or commissars' by other local inhabitants were 'to be dealt with according to the prescribed regulations after detailed investigation of the situation by an officer'.[204] On 24 July 1941 the quartermaster-general ordered that 'politically intolerable and suspicious elements, commissars, and agitators' were to be picked out 'immediately' in POW camps in the area of operations.[205] The camp commandants were to deal with them according to

[196] P2. Gr. 3, Ic, activity report No. 2 of 19 Aug. 1941, p. 30, BA-MA RH 21-3/v. 423; Jacobsen, 'Kommissarbefehl', doc. 19.

[197] 44. Inf.Div., Ic, activity report (4 Oct. 1941), BA-MA RH 26-44/32.

[198] P2. Gr. 3, Abt. Ic, evening report of 17 July 1941, (D) Various, BA-MA RH 20-3/v. 430. By 25 July 1941 Armd. Group 2 reported 82 commissars (ibid. RH 21-2/v. 637); in a later list the figure was revised upwards by 10 (RH 21-2/v. 638).

[199] Attention was drawn to this by, for example, Armd. Group 4 on 16 Aug. 1941 (BA-MA RH 21-4/270), and by Second Army on 9 Sept. 1941 (ibid. RH 20-2/1092); Jacobsen, 'Kommissarbefehl', doc. 20.

[200] AOK 18, Ic, No. 2034/41, 14 July 1941, memorandum of a conversation between Lt.-Gen. Müller and Gen. Staff Maj. Jessel (Ic Army Group North) on 10 July 1941, Jacobsen, 'Kommissarbefehl', doc. 17. See Halder, *Diaries*, 1137 (1 Aug. 1941).

[201] Befh. rückw. H.Geb. Mitte, Ic, activity report (July 1941), BA-MA RH 22/228.

[202] Announcement in German and Russian, 7 Aug. 1941, BA-MA RH 26-221/17.

[203] 52. Inf.Div., Ic, 12 July 1941 on guerrilla activity, BA-MA RH 26-52/60. LIII Army Corps HQ reported to Second Army that Vlasov had 'finished off' 6 commissars: BA-MA, Alliierte Prozesse 9, NOKW-2062.

[204] 1. Kav.Div., Abt. Ic, 11 July 1941, on treatment of prisoners, BA-MA RH 29-1/5. See Kdt. rückw. A.Geb. 582 No. 82/41, 6 Sept. 1941, Basic instructions for establishment and management of army prisoner collecting-points, ibid. RH 23/234.

[205] OKH/GenStdH/Gen. z.b.V.b. ObdH/GenQu/Abt. K. Verw. No. II/4590/41 geh., 24 July 1941, BA-MA, Alliierte Prozesse 9, NOKW-2423. See Streit, *Keine Kameraden*, 85, 99–100, 109. That the quartermaster-general was also thinking of leaving to the SD the separation of suspected or actual opponents in the transit camps of the area of operations is proved by an enquiry from the chief of the War Administration Dept., Maj. (Gen. Staff) Schmidt von Altenstadt, of the chief

the 'special directives' laid down—that is, have them shot by guards on the basis either of the decree on martial jurisdiction or of the commissar order. The deployment of special-duty squads of the security police and SD was 'not appropriate here'. 'Asiatics (by race), Jews, German-speaking Russians' were also to be segregated, but were to be kept away from Germany rather than being executed. This order from the quartermaster-general restricted the applicability, in territory and content, of the 'Guidelines for the segregation of civilians and suspicious prisoners of war in prisoner-of-war camps in the occupied territory, in the area of operations, in the Government-General, and in the camps of the Reich'.[206] These guidelines, agreed a few days previously between Wehrmacht and SS, had authorized the commandos of the security police and SD to pick out 'politically intolerable elements' among the civilian prisoners and prisoners of war, and to shoot them. However, these 'elements' included not only the Soviet political cadres inside and outside the Red Army, but also all Jews. The state police office in Tilsit thus shot at least 700 commissars in July and August 1941.[207]

The commanders in charge of the prisoners of war in Military District I (East Prussia) and in occupied Poland, as well as the camp commandants, were informed that the 'intention' underlying these guidelines was for the Wehrmacht to 'free itself from all those elements among the POWs' who were regarded as 'Bolshevik driving forces'. 'The special situation of the campaign in the east thus requires *special measures*, which must be implemented in a responsible manner free from bureaucratic and administrative influences.' Previous orders for the treatment of prisoners of war had been based on 'exclusively *military* considerations', but now the 'political aim must be achieved of protecting the German people from Bolshevik agitators, and of taking firm charge of the occupied territory'.

The limiting order of 24 July 1941 from the quartermaster-general does not appear always to have been strictly applied.[208] Nevertheless, the main aim of the selection procedures in prison camps in the area of operations was to hunt out commissars. The commandant of Transit Camp 155 in Lida, Major von Treuenfels, reported that by 21 August his men had successfully 'seized at least 125 commissars and dealt with them appropriately'.[209] The informer

of staff of the commander of Rear Army Area South, Col. (Gen. Staff) von Krosigk, at the beginning of Aug. 1941 (handwritten note on the conference of 5–6 Aug. 1941, BA-MA RH 22/5).

[206] Chief of security police and SD, IV A Ic No. 21 B/41 g.Rs., 17 July 1941, operational order No. 8, app. 1; Streim, *Die Behandlung sowjetischer Kriegsgefangener*, doc. I.1.

[207] Streim, *Die Behandlung sowjetischer Kriegsgefangener*, 233.

[208] See the report of the orderly officer of POW District Commandant J, 23 July 1941 (BA-MA RH 22/251), the instruction from commander of Rear Army Area South, 24 Aug. 1941 (Krausnick and Wilhelm, *Die Truppe des Weltanschauungskrieges*, 241–2), and events report No. 47 of 9 Aug. 1941, g.Rs., fo. 288 (BA R 58/215), events report No. 58 of 20 Aug. 1941 g.Rs., fo. 100 (ibid. R 58/216), and events report No. 71 of 2 Sept. 1941 g.Rs., fo. 270 (ibid.).

[209] POW District Commandant J, memorandum on conference at Dulag 155 on 21 Aug. 1941, BA-MA RH 22/251.

system had 'proved useful'. However, the 'Prisoner of War District Commandant J' with the commander of Rear Army Area Centre, Colonel Marschall, did not receive unanimous reports of 'intelligence' successes during his inspection of the camps. The commandant of Transit Camp 126 in Minsk was reprimanded on 25 August 1941 because intelligence had 'utterly failed': 'very few' commissars had been discovered.[210] In his progress report for the month of August the responsible chief of staff in Rear Army Area Centre claimed that the capture of commissars had sometimes proved very difficult. It was certain that they had not been 'completely rounded up'. Nevertheless, the use of informers (Tsarist officers, Ukrainians, Latvians, Lithuanians) had been successful.[211] A month later he merely noted: 'Commissars detected by informers were dealt with according to the regulations.'[212] However, this did not happen in every camp. For example, the commandant of Transit Camp 100 in Porchov (Army Area North) reported the transfer of 898 officers, 16,394 NCOs and men, and 2 commissars to organizations at home, or to other camps.[213]

On 7 October 1941 Army High Command allowed the security police and SD squads access to the transit camps in the rear army areas. In so doing, they extended to the army area of operations those practices which had been ordered in the OKW sector since the middle of July, and renewed there at the beginning of September.[214] The 'separation of intolerable elements' and their execution was now undertaken by special units of the special-duty squads 'on their own responsibility'. These had a duty to co-operate closely with the camp commandants and intelligence officers. The handing over of selected Soviet prisoners to the special units was officially regarded as a release from prisoner-of-war captivity.[215] When the commander in chief of Army Group Centre, Field Marshal von Bock, was informed, he raised objections with Brauchitsch, and referred to the indivisible responsibility of the army for the 'life and safety of its prisoners of war'. However, Bock continued that if the 'separation of specific persons [was] necessary . . . for political reasons, outside the army area they [can] be treated as the political needs and security of the Reich demand'.[216]

The quartermaster-general's order of October 1941 naturally brought consequences in its wake. For example, the intelligence officer of Transit Camp 230 in Vyazma, Captain Bernstein, reported that '200 Jews and 50–60 *politruk*s had been handed over to the SD' during the lifetime of the camp. His own activity had accounted for approximately 40 Jews and 6–8 *politruk*s.[217] In

---

[210] Ibid.   [211] BA-MA RH 22/247.   [212] Activity report of 1–30 Sept. 1941, ibid.
[213] Dulag 100, Abt. Ia Az. 1120/41, 29 Aug. 1941, BA-MA 23/295.
[214] OKH/GenStdH/GenQu, Az. Abt. K.Verw. No. II/unnumbered/41 g.Kdos., 7 Oct. 1941, app. 2 to operational order No. 14 form chief of security police and SD, 29 Oct. 1941; Streim, *Die Behandlung sowjetischer Kriegsgefangener*, doc. I.3. See Streit, *Keine Kameraden*, 103–4; Krausnick and Wilhelm, *Die Truppe des Weltanschauungskrieges*, 253–4.
[215] Streim, *Die Behandlung sowjetischer Kriegsgefangener*, 55 n. 116, draws attention to this.
[216] Bock, Tagebuch, vol. ii (9 Nov. 1941), MGFA p-210.
[217] POW District Commandant J, report on inspection of Dulags Vyazma and Gzhatsk on 17 and 18 Jan. 1942, BA-MA RH 22/251.

contrast, the commandant of Transit Camp 185 in Mogilev, Major Wittmer, is on record as having refused to hand over a number of Jewish prisoners 'for special treatment', since he had received no order from the responsible Wehrmacht authority, which alone he recognized.[218] As a result of the systematic conduct of the security police and SD special commandos, it is probable 'that most of the Soviet commissars, functionaries, holders of power etc. were not [shot] at the front, but in the various prison camps'[219] in the army area of operations, in the Reich commissariats, in occupied Poland, in the Reich, or in concentration camps. It has been calculated that by May 1944 *at least* 580,000–600,000 Soviet prisoners of war must have been handed over to the security police and SD and shot.[220]

After the start of operations, direct and indirect proposals for an extension of the commissar guidelines were also made by the troops. For example, at the end of July Second Army criticized the German propaganda being carried out in the Red Army. Second Army considered it 'particularly important' to present the commissars as 'the representatives of the system which is to blame for this war', and as the originators of the terror practised by the Red Army.[221] The Soviet soldiers should be urged not to believe the lies of the commissars, and to eliminate them. There were also proposals from the troops for a wider definition of the term 'commissar'. Even in July 1941 the commander of Rear Army Area Centre had asked Army Group Command to clarify 'whether the Russian army officers [were] political commissars at the same time'.[222] In response to a query from an unnamed army group, the legal affairs group with the 'General for Special Duty' Centre applied to the national defence department in the Wehrmacht operations staff to clarify 'whether political helpers with the companies (*politruk*s) are to be regarded as political commissars in the sense of the "Guidelines for the treatment of political commissars", and treated accordingly'.[223] On the basis of information received from the Foreign Armies East Department in the Army General Staff, OKW answered in the affirmative.[224] An order to that effect was sent out to the troops from Army

---

[218] See Streit, *Keine Kameraden*, 102–3; Streim, *Die Behandlung sowjetischer Kriegsgefangener*, 295.

[219] Krausnick, 'Kommissarbefehl', 736.

[220] Thus Streit, *Keine Kameraden*, 105. By contrast, Streim, *Die Behandlung sowjetischer Kriegsgefangener*, 244, gives only a figure of at least 140,000. The actual number of Soviet prisoners of war executed may, however, be '*considerably* higher' in Streim's view also, since no exact figures are available for the sectors of Wehrmacht Commanders Ukraine and Ostland (p. 235). What is certain is that the handing over of Soviet prisoners of war to the SD did not invariably mean they were shot. Many of them were also enlisted for police service.

[221] AOK 2, Ic/AO, 25 July 1941, on success of leaflet drop and 'red–white projectiles', BA-MA RH 20-2/1091. The Wehrmacht propaganda department adopted this proposal in its 'supplementary directives for the handling of propaganda against the Soviet Union', 21 Aug. 1941, ibid. RW 4/v. 578. See Buchbender, *Das tönende Erz*, 88 ff. As early as 16 July 1941, the commander of Sixth Army had personally drafted an appropriate leaflet, though conscious that 'the Führer alone can find the right moment and the right words': BA-MA, 6. Armee, 15623/2.

[222] Befh. rückw. H.Geb. Mitte, Ic, activity report (July 1941), BA-MA RH 22/228.

[223] OKH/Gen. z.b.V.b. ObdH/Az. 500 Gr. R.Wes. No. 412/41 g.Kdos., 16 Aug. 1941, signed Dr Lattmann, BA-MA RW 4/v. 578.

[224] OKH/WFSt/Abt. L (IV/Qu) No. 001797/41 g.Kdos., 18 Aug. 1941, ibid.

High Command at the end of August 1941.[225] Even before this, some divisions had already treated *politruk*s as 'representatives of the political system', and had liquidated them.[226] 221st Infantry Division had attempted to counteract the shortage of knowledge about political workers in the Red Army. It informed officers that *politruk*s and commissars often tried to disguise their political activity by arguing that they had been responsible only 'for the morale' or 'for the attitude' of the troops. This claim could easily be refuted, because 'those affected [could] demonstrate none of the knowledge appropriate to their military rank'. They were *politruk*s and commissars, and were 'to be treated as such'.[227]

From the middle of August, as knowledge of the implementation of the commissar guidelines spread, there were increased claims from the troops that the 'harsh orders on the treatment of the commissars and *politruk*s [were] one of the causes of the tough enemy resistance'.[228] The political cadres of the Red Army would continue to fight, and exert 'terror' over their troops, because they were convinced that they would be shot after being taken prisoner. In the middle of September 1941 the commanding general of XXXIX (Motorized) Army Corps, Armoured Troop General Schmidt, therefore produced a 'memorandum on the possibility of shattering Bolshevik resistance from within'. In it he demanded as an 'immediate measure' that the 'shooting decree for political commissars' should be rescinded, and 'the Russian people shown a positive future . . . in the long term'.[229] Army High Command was sufficiently sympathetic to the initiatives of the field commanders to pass a corresponding request to OKW. Lieutenant-General Müller did not support the request with humanitarian arguments, but by referring to military necessities:

In the current battle situation, where the heavy casualties, the decrease in the supply of men and materials, the mixing up of formations, and the uncertainty of leadership are causing signs of slackening to appear here and there on the Russian side, a paralysis of the general will to fight by breaking the resistance of the commissars could produce not inconsiderable successes and save much blood.[230]

---

[225] See AOK 2, Ic/AO No. 215/41, 30 Aug. 1941, on treatment of political assistants with the companies, BA-MA RH 20-2/1092.

[226] See the commanders' conference of 454th Security Div. on 20 June 1941, BA-MA RH 26-454/6; 24. Inf.Div., Ic, 9 July 1941: interim report on prisoner interrogation (BA-MA RH 26-14/72), and AOK 16, Ic, evening report of 11 Aug. 1941 (BA-MA, 16. Armee, 22745/38).

[227] 221. Sich.Div., Ic, 6 Sept. 1941, BA-MA RH 26-221/17.

[228] AOK 2, Ic/AO No. 218/41 g.Kdos., 9 Sept. 1941, BA-MA RH 20-2/1092; Jacobsen, 'Kommissarbefehl', doc. 20. On the ferocious resistance of the Red Army as a result of the commissar order see the evaluation of the enemy situation by LI Army Corps, Ic, 26 Sept. 1941 (BA-MA, LI. AK, 15290/26), and report No. 10 by the foreign ministry representative/AOK 2, 13 Aug. 1941 (ibid. RH 20-2/1092).

[229] Memorandum of 18 Sept. 1941, BA-MA, Alliierte Prozesse 9, NOKW-2413; extracts in Jacobsen, 'Kommissarbefehl', doc. 21.

[230] OKH/Gen. z.b.V.b. ObdH/Az. 501 No. 516/41 g.Kdos., 23 Sept. 1941, BA-MA Rw 4/v. 578; Jacobsen, 'Kommissarbefehl', doc. 22.

Jodl submitted the request of Army High Command to Hitler, who refused to make any alteration to the orders that had been issued. The army groups were informed of this decision at the beginning of October.[231] Not until spring 1942 did the appeals of the field commanders bear fruit. The commissar decree was then abandoned in the area of operations,[232] with the aim of encouraging Soviet soldiers to desert, and entire units to surrender. The 'special treatment' of the commissars and *politruk*s in the prison camps was also stopped.[233] The HQs were to determine whether they were dealing with commissars and *politruk*s who had deserted, or whether they had been taken prisoner in battle. While the latter were to be executed immediately, deserters were to be sent to Mauthausen concentration camp. For 'Jews, criminals, etc.', the prevailing treatment remained in force—they were shot.

The commissar decree was implemented by the army to a greater extent than field commanders were prepared to admit after the war.[234] Yet it was not only the army leadership which, profoundly affected by the image of 'Jewish Bolshevism', accepted Hitler's view that the commissars were not genuine soldiers. The orders, directives, and reports cited here lead to the conclusion that a large part of the line officer corps also accepted this view; many either conducted themselves according to it, or at the very least were unwilling to risk trouble by opposing it. An order by the commanding general of XXXXVII (Motorized) Army Corps on 30 June 1941 can be regarded as typical: 'The decree of the Führer orders a ruthless action against Bolshevism (pol. commissars) and any kind of guerrilla activity! Persons irrefutably shown to be among them are to be taken away and shot, exclusively on the order of an officer.' However, Armoured Troop General Lemelsen also felt compelled to oppose the numerous shootings by members of his army corps of prisoners, defectors, and deserters from the Red Army. These he described as murder: 'The Russian soldier who has been encountered on the battlefield and has fought courageously is no guerrilla, but has the right to honourable, good treatment and care as a wounded man . . . It is this lie about the shooting of prisoners, however, that the enemy is using to keep his soldiers in line . . . The German army would be saved much blood by harsh measures against guerrillas and fighting civilians, and equally so by the good treatment of prisoners and deserters in accordance with orders.'[235] Lemelsen thus made a clear distinction between the treatment of

[231] OKH/Gen. z.b.V.b. ObdH/Az. 500 Gr. R.Wes. No. 527/41 g.Kdos., 2 Oct. 1941, BA-MA RH 19 II/123. This decision was to be transmitted further by word of mouth alone.

[232] On 6 May 1942; see Warlimont, *Hauptquartier*, 185–6.

[233] See Streit, *Keine Kameraden*, 253–4, and Streim, *Die Behandlung sowjetischer Kriegsgefangener*, 140 ff.

[234] In this context see two contemporary books which express the anti-Jewish and anti-Communist sentiments then prevailing among the troops: Slesina, *Soldaten*, and Haussleiter, *Ostfront*; also the portrayal by a war reporter on 12 Aug. 1941, 'Der Zug der Zehntausend', about the discovery and shooting of a commissar: BA-MA, Alliierte Prozesse 9, NOKW-2241.

[235] Quoted from Buchbender, *Das tönende Erz*, 104–5.

commissars and guerrillas on one hand, and the soldiers of the Red Army on the other.

Significantly, protests from the field commanders against the commissar order increased when the impetus of the German operations had already weakened and the resistance of the Red Army had stiffened. For example, the 3rd staff officer in Army Group Centre, Major Rudolf-Christoph Baron von Gersdorff, visited the front in Fourth Army area of operations at the beginning of December 1941. Subsequently he reported:

During every extended conversation with officers, without having referred to it myself, I was asked about the shootings of Jews. I gained the impression that the shooting of the Jews, the prisoners, and the commissars was almost universally rejected in the officer corps, especially the shooting of commissars, because it served to strengthen enemy resistance. The shootings are regarded as a violation of the honour of the German army, specifically the German officer corps. The question of the responsibility for this was raised in more or less sharp form, according to the temperament and disposition of those concerned.[236]

This report was not accepted in Army Group Centre, as the wavy lines in the margin reveal. Significantly, though, such criticism was being expressed in the sector of an army whose command had passed on the commissar decree, and had noted that it was being carried out.[237]

In July 1941 the 3rd staff officer of Fourth Army, Major Helmdach, had already pointed out to the commander-in-chief of the army, Field Marshal von Kluge, how important it was to solve 'the military-political problem of the east'. He had produced a memorandum, which Kluge signed and submitted both to the commander-in-chief of the army and to Hitler's adjutant.[238] In mid-September the commanding general of XXXIX (Motorized) Army Corps, Armoured Troop General Schmidt, had demanded that 'the Russian people be shown a positive future'; in the long term, he regarded this as much more important than dropping the 'shooting decree for political commissars'.[239] Though accepting that it was undesirable to give the Russians 'an ideal, to say nothing of National Socialism', he thought it was vital 'to draw up clear rules, at least in everyday things'. Schmidt wanted to encourage the Soviet population to turn away from Bolshevism and put its hopes in Germany. 'Such measures', including the regulation of private property, would also have an effect 'in as yet unconquered Russia, and thus weaken the strength of resistance there'. However, apart from his murderous programme of annihilating 'Jewish Bolshevism', Hitler could not come to a decision about

---

[236] KTB H.Gr. Mitte, app. to p. 943 (9 Dec. 1941), IfZ Fd 600/1.

[237] AOK 4, Ic, evening report of 27 June 1941, in which 6 political commissars were reported to have been executed: BA-MA, 4. Armee, 17170/2.

[238] AOK 4, Ic, KTB (21, 26 July 1941), BA-MA, 4. Armee, 17170/1. This memorandum is mentioned in the war diary but could not be traced.

[239] Memorandum to Sixteenth Army Command with request for passing on to Hitler, BA-MA, Alliierte Prozesse 9, NOKW-2413; extracts published in Jacobsen, 'Kommissarbefehl', doc. 21.

the future development of the occupied Soviet territories during Operation Barbarossa.

3. THE ORGANIZATION OF 'LIVING-SPACE'

For Hitler, the conquest of the European part of the Soviet Union would ensure the existence of the German people in the long term. At the same time, it was the essential foundation which would allow the Third Reich to achieve undisputed world-power status (or world supremacy): 'The struggle for hegemony in the world will be decided in favour of Europe by the possession of the Russian space: it will make Europe into an impregnable fortress, the most blockade-proof place on earth.'[240] America could then 'get lost, as far as we are concerned'.[241] However, Hitler had devoted less thought to the question of how to organize the 'living-space' thus gained. For him, the overriding requirement was to defeat the Soviet Union in a rapid campaign. Everything was concentrated on achieving the rapid collapse of the Red Army and the Stalinist system. Four 'representatives' were envisaged for this task: '*Wehrmacht*: defeat of the enemy; *Reich Leader SS*: political-police activity against the enemy; *Reich Marshal*: economy; *Rosenberg*: political reconstruction.'[242] In terms of content and organization, the first three of these aims had been integrated even before the start of operations; co-operation between the last two 'representatives', however, was given concrete form only after 22 June 1941. But what notions did the Germans have regarding the organization of 'living-space' in the summer and autumn of 1941? When, how, and where were the military authorities replaced by civilian authorities? What parts of the occupied Soviet territories were assigned to the German Reich or to the Government-General?[243]

The 'representative for the central shaping of the east European space', Alfred Rosenberg, had been working on proposals for the future of the Russian territories for some time. However, before 22 June 1941 his ideas received Hitler's approval only to the extent that the occupied territories were to be divided into four Reich commissariats: Baltland, Ukraine, Russia, and Caucasia.[244] In the middle of July 1941, when the German leaders thought

[240] Hitler, *Monologe*, 62 (17–18 Sept. 1941); cf. pp. 69–70 (25 Sept. 1941) and 110 (26–7 Oct. 1941).

[241] Thus Hitler to Ambassador Abetz on 16 Sept. 1941, *DGFP* D xiii, No. 372. Similar words were used by the quartermaster-general in a letter to his wife on 20 Sept. 1941: 'A space, which cannot be ruled with men, the idea of a German India comes to mind, I believe: Europe autarkic, so that America can get lost for all we care' (Wagner, *Generalquartiermeister*, 202). See *Das Deutsche Reich und der Zweite Weltkrieg*, v/1. 133–4.

[242] Thus Maj. (Gen. Staff) Schmidt von Altenstadt on 6 June 1941, BA-MA RH 19 III/722. See sect. I.vii.2 (*a*) at n. 44.

[243] See the Annexe Volume, No. 27. The economic exploitation has been described in another chapter, and a systematic analysis of the civilian administration in the Reich Commissariats Ostland and Ukraine will be undertaken elsewhere in this series.

[244] See sect. I.vii.1 at n. 23.

victory over the Red Army had already been won, Hitler reduced his programme in the east to the bare formula: 'First dominate, second administer, third exploit.'[245] The fundamental need was 'to cut the giant cake into manageable pieces'. Germany was to be the sole beneficiary of this process, with only a couple of pieces on the periphery conceded to his main allies, Finland and Romania. A 'Garden of Eden' was to be created for the Germans in the east, 'our India'.[246] Hitler intended to annex only the Crimea, the Baltic States, and former Austrian Galicia. The rest of the space he regarded as 'colonial land', which was to be ruled, administered, and exploited by a handful of men, supposed members of the master race, under four 'viceroys',[247] the Reich commissioners. The Slavs were by nature a 'slave mass crying out for a master'.[248] Hitler thought it important to keep his objectives hidden from world opinion. 'We will simply act as though we wanted to exert a mandate. But it must be clear to *us* that we are never leaving these territories again.' All the measures necessary for a 'final settlement . . . shooting, resettlement, etc.—we can and will carry out nevertheless'.[249]

The boundary of the 'Greater Germanic empire' was to be the Urals. To the west of them, only Germans would be able to carry weapons, 'not the Slav, not the Czech, not the Cossack, nor the Ukrainian!'.[250] In Hitler's view, an 'east wall' of living people of Germanic race offered the best protection against the 'mass of nations of Asia' behind the Urals. Constant border fighting would prevent them becoming slack, and racial selection would 'preserve the species'.[251] Peace, on the other hand, would only result in *playing* at soldiers. After the conclusion of Operation Barbarossa, it was envisaged that the following troops would be required to provide security for the eastern territories, including the Government-General, and for planned operations in the Middle East: 37 infantry divisions, including 10 for tasks of economic security, 3 mountain, 6 motorized infantry, and 12 armoured divisions.[252] The occupied territories were to be Europeanized, or rather Germanized. On the best soil, Danes, Dutchmen, Norwegians, and Swedes would be settled as peasant farmers alongside long-serving German NCOs, while the Slav population would be 'sifted' and the 'destructive Jew' completely 'kicked out'.[253] Trans-

[245] Discussion of 16 July 1941 with Rosenberg, Lammers, Keitel, Göring, and Bormann, *IMT* xxxviii. 87 ff.

[246] Thus Hitler to Abetz, 16 Sept. 1941, *DGFP* D xiii, No. 372.

[247] Hitler, *Monologe*, 50–1 (1–2 Aug. 1941).   [248] Ibid. 62 (17–18 Sept. 1941).

[249] *IMT* xxxviii. 88. Goebbels too had stated on 5 Apr. 1940, to the editors-in-chief of the Berlin press and the chief representatives of the foreign press in Berlin, that although National Socialism was carrying out in Europe the same revolution that it had achieved on a smaller scale in Germany, these plans would not be exposed to public criticism, in order to avoid increasing resistance. 'Today we say "living-space". Everyone can imagine what he wants. What we want we will know when the time is right': Jacobsen, *Der Zweite Weltkrieg*, No. 60. See *Kriegspropaganda*, 313–14 (5 Apr. 1940).

[250] *IMT* xxxviii. 88.   [251] Hitler, *Monologe*, 55 (8–11 Aug. 1941), 68 (25 Sept. 1941).

[252] Chef OKW/WFSt/Abt. L (II Org.) No. 441349/41 g.Kdos. Chefs., 8 Aug. 1941, BA-MA RW 4/v. 513. In addition, there were the troops of Germany's allies.

[253] Hitler, *Monologe*, 90 (17 Oct. 1941). A few days later he explained: 'When we eliminate this

port routes, motorways, and railway lines would run across the 'cleansed' land on which German towns and settlements would be built 'as on a string of beads'.[254] In this land 'the lowliest stable lad must rank higher than one of the natives'.[255] Hitler reminded his listeners at the end of July 1941 that he had 'always thought that the soil in the east was necessary'; he saw no reason to change his mind now.[256]

In outlining this programme, Hitler regarded himself as the architect and executor of a historical will, with the task of making Germany into an undisputed world power.[257] He wanted to rewrite history on a racial basis: Hitler was convinced that genuine world domination could be founded only on German blood. This blood had therefore to be protected from possible 'corruption'. 'Jewish Bolshevism' must be wiped out for that reason. Significantly, it was at precisely this time that anti-Semitic measures were intensified. On 31 July 1941, on Hitler's instructions, Göring ordered Heydrich to 'make all necessary preparations in organizational, technical, and material matters for an overall solution of the Jewish question in the German sphere of influence in Europe'.[258] The annihilation of European Jewry was to be followed by that of the Jews of northern, central, south-eastern, and western Europe. Closely linked with this objective, both chronologically and in terms of its subject, was SS Major Alfred Meyer's submission of the first 'General Plan East' on the orders of Himmler.[259] After mass deportations and measures of destruction on a large scale, this envisaged the settlement of Germans in eastern Europe over a period of thirty years.

With victory over the Red Army apparently won, Hitler and other leading figures of the Third Reich went beyond this consideration of racial criteria for the organization of the conquered 'living-space'. Hitler was also contemplating the strategic possibilities which would be opened up by the defeat of the Soviet Union: a global war by Germany and Japan against the Anglo-Saxon naval powers.[260] This was to be preceded by joint military action by Berlin and Tokyo against the Red Army, in order to ensure the rapid collapse of the Stalinist system. Hitler was realistic enough to recognize 'that one cannot

---

pestilence we shall perform a deed for humanity whose significance our men out there cannot even imagine' (ibid. 99).

[254] Ibid.   [255] Ibid. 63 (17–18 Sept. 1941).   [256] Ibid. 49 (27–28 July 1941).

[257] Ibid. 91 (17 Oct. 1941), 101–2 (21–2 Oct. 1941).

[258] Krausnick, 'Judenverfolgung', 306, and *IMT* xxvi. 266–7; as photocopy in *Deutschland im zweiten Weltkrieg*, ii. 117. See Browning, 'Zur Genesis der "Endlösung" ', and *Das Deutsche Reich und der Zweite Weltkrieg*, v/1. 289.

[259] As photocopy in *Deutschland im zweiten Weltkrieg*, ii. 119. See Eisenblätter, *Grundlinien*, 206–7, 213 ff.

[260] See sect. II.IV.2(*b*) at n. 150. On 17 July 1941 Ribbentrop continued in the same vein to the German mission chiefs in Königsberg: 'If after the defeat of Russia the USA continues to provoke us, it shall have its war. We do not fear a British–US front. We shall attack with submarines and aircraft and defend ourselves with gigantic anti-aircraft fire such as the world has never seen. However, we shall not escape unscathed' (PA, Handakten Etzdorf, Vertrauliche Aufzeichnungen, Frame No. 337690).

conquer Russia'.[261] Against the background of Germany's strategic situation *vis-à-vis* the United States, he asked himself 'with alarm: How much time do I still have to overcome Russia, and how much time do I still need?'[262] A rapid intervention by the Japanese in Siberia would thus be very useful to him as a means of accelerating the collapse of the Bolshevik regime.

In discussions at his headquarters, Hitler took concrete decisions as well as day-dreaming about the future. For example, he appointed Alfred Rosenberg as 'Reich minister for the occupied eastern territories'.[263] In theory, the prospective Reich commissioners would be subordinate to him. In practice, however, Rosenberg's responsibility for the civilian administration in the east was limited by the authority vested by Hitler in Göring (29 July 1941) for the economic exploitation of the occupied territories, and in Himmler (17 July 1941) for political security measures there. As regards the future co-operation between the Four-year Plan Authority, the SS, and the Ministry for the East, Hitler thought that 'practice would decide'.[264] Believing that an official announcement of his appointment was imminent, the leader of the 'chaos ministry' [*Chaostministerium*: a pun on 'east'] wrote an address for the German newsreel. In it he referred to the historic mission of the German people, and to the beginning of the 'final struggle' against its 'deadly enemy'—'Marxism as a whole, especially in its extreme Jewish-Bolshevik manifestation'. Roseberg described this struggle, and the establishment of 'welfare and public order for the peoples of the east coming under German administration', as a 'gigantic task'.[265] In fact, his appointment was not made public until 18 November 1941.

The Gauleiter of Schleswig-Holstein, Hinrich Lohse, was appointed as Reich commissioner for 'Ostland' on 17 July 1941. His territory was to consist of the former Baltic States—Lithuania, Latvia, and Estonia—and Belorussia.[266] The timing of his assumption of office, of course, would depend on the progress of operations. Because the army found it convenient 'to get out of' the rear area 'as quickly as possible',[267] Lohse was able to take control over Lithuania on 25 July 1941. In mid-July it was also decreed that the civilian administration in Białystok district would be taken over by the president of the province of East Prussia, Gauleiter Erich Koch,[268] and the civilian administration in former Austrian 'then until 1939 Polish' Galicia by the governor-

---

[261] Thus Keitel on 25 July 1941 passed on Hitler's opinion (Bock, *Tagebuch*, vol. ii, MGFA P-210). 'Russia' is used here as a synonym for 'Soviet Union'.

[262] Ibid.   [263] Decree of 17 July 1941, *KTB OKW* i. 1027–8.

[264] PA, Handakten Etzdorf, Vertrauliche Aufzeichnungen (17 July 1941). See the memorandum by Thomas on 18 July 1941 on his reports to Göring and Keitel, BA-MA RW 19/185.

[265] 2 July 1941, BA NS 8/71.

[266] Decree of 17 July 1941, PA, Dt. Ges. Helsinki, Schriftwechsel geheim, vol. ii. See Myllyniemi, *Neuordnung*, 60 ff., and Rich, *War Aims*, ii. 357 ff.

[267] Thus the quartermaster-general to the head of the War Economy and Armaments Department on 8 July 1941, BA-MA RW 19/165.

[268] See sect. II.VII.1 at n. 15, and OKW/WFSt/Abt. L (IV/Qu) No. 495/41, 23 Aug. 1941, Hitler decree of 15 July 1941, BA-MA RH 26-221/13.

general in Cracow, Hans Frank. Both decrees came into effect on 1 August 1941. On the same day, the Reich commissioner for Ostland took over the civilian administration of the district around Vilna (Vilnius).[269] The separation of Galicia from the Ukraine severely damaged not only the Ukrainian endeavour to achieve autonomy,[270] but also Rosenberg's ideas for the future development of the Ukraine. More regions were removed from the army's area of operations on 1 September. Reich Commissariat Ostland was enlarged by adding Latvia and the area round Minsk, and Reich Commissariat Ukraine was established.[271] The new Reich commissioner, Erich Koch, was 'very reluctant' about his new task. He was prepared to do the job 'only for as long' as was helpful to the Four-year Plan Authority, because 'he was interested only in East Prussia'.[272] However, since the autumn of 1939 East Prussia had been extended by the addition of large areas taken from Poland, to which Białystok and the Grodno region were added in the middle of September 1941.[273] This region was regarded as possessing military significance as a bridgehead on the far bank of the Memel (Niemen).

Even when his Reich commissariat was extended to the Dnieper line on 20 October 1941,[274] Koch showed no great interest in the tasks entrusted to him. He wanted 'to leave his territory under military administration until spring, as there was not much to be done in winter anyway'.[275] For that reason, there could be no ceremonial transfer of executive power from the military to the civilian administration, as had been the case when Galicia was transferred to Frank and Belorussia to Commissioner-General Wilhelm Kube. Koch failed to put in an appearance, and the new territories were handed over informally to his plenipotentiary, District Administrator Wuttke.[276] When Koch's area of authority was extended yet again in November 1941, the commander of Rear Army Area South was forced to hand over military jurisdiction for the Bug–Dnieper area to the Wehrmacht Commander Ukraine,[277] since Koch had neither appeared himself nor sent a representative. Nevertheless, the com-

---

[269] OKW/WFSt/Abt. L (IV/Qu) No. 001543/41 g.Kdos., 1 Aug. 1941; Hitler decree of 22 July 1941, BA-MA RW 4/v. 578.

[270] See *DGFP* D xvi, No. 184 (6 Aug. 1941).

[271] Hitler decree of 20 Aug. 1941, OKH/GenStdH/GenQu, Abt. K. Verw. (Qu 4) No. II/5458/41 geh., 21 Aug. 1941, BA-MA RH 22/271. See Rich, *War Aims*, ii. 372 ff.

[272] PA, Handakten Etzdorf, Vertrauliche Aufzeichnungen, Frame No. 337727, information from Consul-General Bräutigam, 12 Aug. 1941.

[273] OKH/GenStdH/GenQu, Abt. K. Verw. (V) No. II/6778/41 geh., 4 Oct. 1941, Hitler decree of 18 Sept. 1941, BA-MA RH 22/9. As a result the previously established borders in the south and south-east of the Białystok area were altered.

[274] OKW/WFSt. L (IV) No. 684/41, 11 Oct. 1941 (BA-MA RH 22/8), and Wehrmacht Commander Ukraine, Dept. Ia No. 1056/41 geh., 19 Oct. 1941 (ibid.).

[275] KTB WiRüAmt/Stab (15 Oct. 1941) g.Kdos., BA-MA RW 19/165.

[276] Befh. rückw. H.Geb. Süd, Abt. VII, activity report of 1–30 Oct. 1941, BA-MA RH 22/203.

[277] OKW/WFSt/Abt. L (IV) No. 764/41 g., 4 Nov. 1941, and Wehrmacht Commander Ukraine, Dept. Ia, unnumbered, geh., 15 Nov. 1941, BA-MA RH 22/9. To fulfil the tasks assigned him, the Wehrmacht Commander Ukraine, Air Force Gen. Kitzinger, had at his disposal some 22,500 men, in addition to the Slovak Security Div., the Hungarian occupation troops, and the Romanian VI Army Corps (report of 4 Dec. 1941, ibid. RW 41/31).

mander of Rear Army Area South refused to accept any further responsibility for administrative matters in the Bug–Dnieper area.[278]

Reich Commissariat Ostland was not extended to the Nevel–Vitebsk–Mogilev line, as had originally been planned.[279] A new attempt to include Estonia in the civilian administration also ended in failure. The commander of Rear Army Area North had already refused to accept this development previously, in mid-October.[280] Infantry General Franz von Roques had justified his attitude by arguing that the supply of the troops in winter would be threatened, and the civilian administration in Estonia could not 'work through' as intensively as the military agencies. His protests met with some response: when Estonia finally became part of Reich Commissariat Ostland on 5 December 1941, with Commissioner-General Karl-Sigmund Litzmann taking control of the administration, Estonia nevertheless remained part of the army's area of operations.[281] Furthermore, the commander of Rear Army Area North was also responsible for ensuring military security of Estonia within and without, and for the supply of the troops off the land.

Up to the autumn of 1941, the organization of 'living-space' had taken more or less the form described by State Secretary in the Reich Ministry of the Interior Wilhelm Stuckart in mid-September. In his memorandum on 'the German eastern border' he had argued that it was an important war aim 'to reduce the great Slav state structure in the east to the narrower Great Russian people, to remove from Russian influence all territories lying westward of it containing non-Great Russian population, and to link them organically to the central European space'.[282] Stuckart had suggested moving 'the borders of the narrower German space, including the Government-General' to the east. East Prussia should acquire 10,000 sq. km. of Lithuanian and 25,000 sq. km. of Belorussian territory, as well as receiving 1,200 sq. km. from the Government-General. The Government-General should be enlarged by the addition of eastern Galicia, the bridgehead of Brest, and small parts of the area round Białystok. Stuckart's thinking had been motivated not only by racial, economic, and military considerations, but also by political ones. He regarded it as highly desirable to insert a German barrier separating Hungary from the Ukraine, while obtaining a common border and direct transport links between Germany and Romania. Such thinking had tallied with Romanian ideas.[283]

Though Hitler wanted to keep his plans regarding the conquered 'living-space' secret from those affected and from world opinion, the military expected a clear political programme for the reorganization of the occupied territories. In their view, this should offer a positive future to the Soviet population after its 'liberation from Bolshevism'. For example, 444th Security

---

[278] Report of 15 Nov. 1941, BA-MA RH 22/9.

[279] OKW/WFSt/Abt. L (IV) No. 764/41 g., 4 Nov. 1941, map, ibid.

[280] Befh. rückw. H.Geb. Nord, Ia, No. 1355/41 geh., 16 Oct. 1941, BA-MA RH 22/255. See Myllyniemi, *Neuordnung*, 80.

[281] Befh. rückw. H.Geb. Nord, Ia, No. 1577/41 geh., 6 Dec. 1941, BA-MA RH 22/255.

[282] Foreign ministry, Pol. XII 5111 g., 11 Sept. 1941, PA, Pol. XII, vol. xii.

[283] See sect. II.IV.1(a) at n. 6.

Division regretted the fact that the 'German Wehrmacht comes, conquers, and stays silent'.[284] The rural population expected the breaking up of the collective economy, the restoration of personal property, and a uniform price policy. It was quite unsatisfactory for military and economic authorities in Rear Army Area South to fix very different maximum prices. 213th Security Division made the same point.[285] Though the population remained favourably disposed to the Germans, and was unwilling to support the partisans, this could change in a moment, 'as soon as the peasant realizes that the new situation is no better for him, and that there might be some truth in the assertion that the Germans have come as exploiters'. In any case, the problem of agricultural prices had a military aspect. It offered the perfect seedbed for every kind of anti-German propaganda. The commander, Lieutenant-General René de l'Homme de Courbière, informed the commander of Rear Army Area South that the sector could be pacified 'with the completely inadequate forces available' only if the partisans received no support from the population.

However, the supreme leadership was still thinking in the global categories of German territorial, racial, and food-supply policy. In Hitler's opinion, the collectivization so brutally introduced by Stalin, especially the big state farms, offered the 'best, probably the only, possibility of intensive cultivation' of the conquered territory. This was particularly the case 'since the actual Russian intelligentsia [should] be regarded as annihilated, and the people were mostly accustomed to living and being treated like animals. In any case, there was a mile-wide difference between the Russian peoples of today and the German people as regards intellectual maturity.'[286] It was this approach which determined the treatment of the population in the east. Its consequences soon came to be felt by the troops. However, their own conduct also helped to ensure that the original sympathy of the Soviet population was lost. The intelligence officer in Seventeenth Army, First Lieutenant Theodor Oberländer, made this complaint at the end of October 1941: 'Not merely out of bitterness at the fighting methods of the Bolsheviks, we show an inner aversion towards, indeed a hatred of, this country, and an arrogance towards this people, which exclude any positive co-operation.'[287] He demanded an element of self-criticism from

[284] 444. Sich.Div., Abt. VII, No. 125/41, 28 Aug. 1941, BA-MA RH 22/202.

[285] 213. Sich.Div., Abt. Ia, 27 Aug. 1941, BA-MA RH 22/204. See also the situation and experience report of Dept. VII that same day, which the commander evaluated as 'very clear and vivid', ibid.

[286] Report by Commissioner-Gerneral Fritz Schmidt on the visit made by himself and Reich Commissioner (for the occupied Netherlands) Seyss-Inquart to Hitler on 26 Sept. 1941, *DGFP* D xiii, No. 377. See also the memorandum by Lammers on Rosenberg's report and Hitler's comments on 29 Sept. 1941, ibid., No. 372.

[287] Memorandum by Oberländer on 'Preconditions for the security of supplies and the gaining of the greatest food surpluses in the Ukraine' of 28 Nov. 1941 geheim, BA R 6/69. In autumn 1941 Oberländer became leader of a formation of Caucasian volunteers (Hoffmann, *Ostlegionen*, 28 ff., 66–7). On similar memoranda see Buchbender, *Das tönende Erz*, 129 ff., and Dallin, *German Rule in Russia*, 511 ff. Others considered the question 'How can and how will Russia wage war in 1942?' See the work of the 3rd general staff officer of 44th Inf. Div., 18 Nov. 1941 (BA-MA RH 26-44/32), and the identically entitled memorandum by Gustav Hilger of 8 Dec. 1941 (PA, Handakten Ritter, Rußland, No. 29). A further 'memorandum battle' set in during autumn 1942.

the troops, and investigation of the measures which had been taken. Moreover, Oberländer also indicated that passive and active resistance could pose a serious danger to the security of German supplies, if the population continued to be treated as an 'object of exploitation'. He considered passive resistance to be much more dangerous than partisan activity in this respect. As a necessary measure, he urged that every German in the occupied territories should be instructed that the population did not consist solely of Bolsheviks. As a result of Bolshevism they were poor and therefore badly dressed; they did not work as well as the Germans because they had always worked for others; they were not independent or active, because they had always been suppressed. Since the 'three most certain factors of order—work, bread, and consumer goods—would not be sufficiently available in the immediate future', small measures of assistance should be offered to ease the burdens facing the population. Oberländer made a series of suggestions covering propaganda as well as economic and security issues. He concluded by arguing that the honour and decency of the German people demanded 'that a people which is in no way hostile towards us is treated in a manner that enables it to work with us out of conviction, and inwardly to overcome the past'.

However, the guidelines issued by Rosenberg in mid-November to the Reich commissioner for the Ukraine, the 'old National Socialist fighter' Erich Koch, pointed in a different direction.[288] These described the vital aim of 'eastern work' as 'to create new land for Germany, to reduce Muscovy (Russia) to its own living-space'. This was 'a struggle to secure life for the German people as well as for the whole of the new Europe, a struggle of an ideological nature, a political war which involves a new conception of our continent and advances Europe decisively to the east'. Rosenberg distanced himself from his original concept of treating the various peoples of the USSR differently. He was thereby adopting Hitler's maxim that the administration of the Ukraine should be 'purely colonial'. Its exploitation to meet German war requirements was to take first place.[289] On 19 November Rosenberg stated his views: 'The extent of the shedding of German blood, the need to expand the space of central Europe, and the will to ward off the consequences of a British continental blockade for all time force the adoption of a self-contained major plan. This can only be ensured by an *authoritarian German administration*.' The idea mooted *before* the war, of building up 'Ukrainedom' as a political power against Moscow, had therefore been abandoned. 'In the *current* situation the German Reich can no longer assume an increased solicitude for an alien nationality which has not reached the difficult situation it faces today through any fault of Germany.'

For these political and economic reasons, the supreme German leadership

[288] First general political directive of 19 Nov. 1941 No. 530/41 g.Rs., BA R 6/69. See also OKW/WFSt/Abt. L (IV/Qu) No. 02410/41 g.Rs., 17 Nov. 1941, Guidelines for conduct towards the Ukrainian population, BA-MA Wi/I. 345.

[289] KTB WiRüAmt/Stab (15 Oct. 1941), g.Kdos., BA-MA RW 19/165.

was not prepared to change occupation policy in the east, despite the fact that such a step was increasingly being advocated on practical military grounds. Thus the commander-in-chief of the army urged that the Soviet population should be better fed, at the expense of transports to Germany, 'in the interests of maintaining law and order'.[290] Previous priorities—troops, homeland, local population—remained intact. Hitler claimed in mid-October 1941 that he could not assume responsibility for feeding the Soviet population at the expense of the German homeland. 'The chaos in Russia will get even greater, our administration and exploitation of the occupied eastern territories even easier, the more the population of the Soviet Russian cities flees to the interior of Russia.'[291] Hitler's wishes, OKW informed Army High Command, must be brought to the attention of all commanders. When the Red Army offensive forced the German army to evacuate Soviet cities, Hitler considered forcing the Soviet population through their own lines to the east so that neither the troops nor Germany would be deprived of foodstuffs. In the case of Kharkov, the commander of Army Group South, Field Marshal von Rundstedt, advocated on military grounds that the population should be evacuated to the west into territories 'in which the stocks available cannot be collected in any case due to the lack of means of recovering them'.[292] In the view of the responsible military quarters, Soviet powers of resistance would best be 'undermined' by ensuring an improved food supply, the solution of the land question, and the exploitation of the suppressed national strivings of the non-Russian peoples, leading to the establishment of 'sham governments'. In addition, greater use of indigenous formations would be particularly helpful. The 'final struggle against Bolshevism in the depths of Asiatic space' should be fought out by Russian forces.[293] To some degree, the failure of Operation Barbarossa had made Hitler ready to take account of pragmatic arguments from the military and economic experts, e.g. on the question of Soviet workers, the commissars, native formations, and the abolition of the collective economy.[294] He was not prepared, however, to give a whole new meaning to the war against the Soviet Union. Nevertheless, the new political and military situation facing the

---

[290] Ibid. (16 Oct. 1941).

[291] H.Gr. Nord, Ia, KTB, 12 Oct. 1941, BA-MA RH 19 III/168. This directive, relating to Leningrad, was also to be applied 'analogously' to Kharkov (KTB H.Gr. Süd, BA-MA RH 19 I/74, entry of 20 Oct. 1941).

[292] H.Gr. Süd, KTB, 18 Dec. 1941, BA-MA RH 19 I/88. See conversation between Hitler and Budak on 14 Feb. 1942, *Staatsmänner*, ii, doc. 4, p. 62.

[293] Proposals from Maj. (Gen. Staff) Schmidt von Altenstadt and Capt. Bleicken, 24 Feb. 1942, PA, Handakten Etzdorf, Vertrauliche Aufzeichnungen, Frame No. 337851. See H.Gr. Süd, KTB, 17 Jan. 1942, BA-MA RH 19/89.

[294] See sect. II.vi.4 at n. 389 (Müller), and Buchbender, *Das tönende Erz*, 133 ff. As early as 3 Nov. 1941, the Chief Group Agriculture in the Economic Staff East had laid down 'the reasons for the proclamation of a new agrarian order'. But this should be proclaimed only for the time being; during 1942 it would 'only be introduced to a very modest extent of about 10% in North and Centre and 1% in South'; PA, Pol. XIII (6). For the propaganda treatment of the issue see OKW/WFSt/WPr No. 1140/42, 18 Feb. 1942: Propaganda directive for the reorganization of the agrarian order in the eastern territories, BA-MA RH 19 III/483.

German Reich forced him to emphasize the 'defensive' character of his war aim: the establishment of a Germanic empire from the Atlantic to the Urals. He told the chief of the operations department in the Naval War Staff, Captain Gerhard Wagner, that 'German living-space' must be secured by a strong west wall in France, a strong north wall in Norway, and an equivalent east wall stretching roughly from Lake Ladoga or east of it to the Don or Volga bend. 'Then Germany would be *unassailable*. What relations we wanted to have with the rest of the world from this space could be considered later.'[295] However, the German troops in the Soviet Union were still west of the line envisaged by Hitler.

---

[295] *Lagevorträge*, 351–2 (7 Feb. 1942) [not in trans.] (emphasis added). On Hitler's strategy in 1941–2 *Das Deutsche Reich und der Zweite Weltkrieg*, vi. 101 ff.

Operation Barbarossa in Historical Perspective

Jürgen Förster

The various contributions to this volume do not present a 'uniform' picture of the war against Russia. Consequently, though it is based on their work, the following summary will make no attempt to disguise the fact that these authors have offered opinions which are sometimes very divergent. Nevertheless, an attempt will be made here to place the German–Soviet war in 'historical perspective', even though some of the contributors do not share the present author's conclusions.

Operation Barbarossa was not a campaign like those that preceded it, but a carefully prepared war of annihilation. Of course, National Socialist propaganda attempted to depict the war as a necessary operation to ward off an imminent Soviet attack; on the basis of the participation of some European states and volunteer formations, it was also described as a 'crusade of Europe against Bolshevism', and the beginning of the new 'European solidarity'. The unique character of the German–Soviet war was partly a result of the close connection between the 'conquest of new living-space in the east' and the 'final solution of the Jewish question'. German public opinion, however, tends to concentrate on the 'German catastrophe' at the expense of the 'Jewish' and the 'Russian'.

Academic controversy over the problems of the German–Soviet war has also endured. However, all historians agree that the consequences of that war are still perceptible in political affairs today. One result of the massive efforts forced upon it by Hitler between 1941 and 1945 was the rise of the Soviet Union to the status of a world power equal to the United States. The defeat of the Third Reich simultaneously marked the beginning of the long East–West conflict, which had as its direct consequence the creation of two German states. Yet this is only one important aspect arising from the discussion of Hitler's war in the east. Another approach regards it as an integral part of German war policy. This perspective permits the historian to assess continuity and discontinuity in German great-power politics since 1871, culminating in Hitler's bid for world-power status—or world supremacy—for the Third Reich.

The starting-point for an analysis of the causes of the attack on the Soviet Union must be the world-view and political goals of the man who dominated German politics between 1933 and 1945. Hitler took the decision to wage war as a consequence of his 'living-space' programme, in which expansion in the east, the destruction of Bolshevism, and the extermination of the Jews were inextricably intertwined. Each goal, indeed, was the precondition for achieving the others. This does not mean that the 'programme' was pursued without regard for the course of events. Nevertheless, Hitler's doctrinaire concepts of war, living-space, race, economic autarky, and world-power status must be regarded as forming the basis of his political conduct, despite all the tactical improvisations he made. It is therefore pointless to impose a sequence of priorities, choosing between ideological fixations and political or economic motives, to explain the turn to the east. Hitler's core goal in foreign policy, the great war for living-space at the expense of the Soviet Union, was a symbiosis of dogma and calculation, ideology and the will to power, racial policy and world politics. His vision of a continental empire of the 'Nordic race' stretching to the Urals went beyond the traditional goals of German great-power and world-power politics. Nevertheless, his 'living-space' programme had some affinity with ideas common to the traditional leadership élites in the armed forces, industry, and the diplomatic service; these had found expression in the war-aims discussions of the First World War, especially in the supplementary treaties of Brest-Litovsk. Hitler's programme achieved its catastrophic effects precisely because the 'constants of his world view', including the radical foe images of Jewry and Bolshevism, did not run totally counter to prevailing opinion. The extent to which military men, economists, and diplomats agreed with Hitler's views on the winning of the 'Russian space', its exploitation, and the treatment of the Slav population varied considerably. The spectrum of agreement ranged from a partial identity of interests to a genuine fusion of traditional and National Socialist ideas. In this ideological climate, fundamental military values such as loyalty, obedience, and fulfilment of duty were exploited and deliberately abused. The effects of this process on society as a whole can scarcely be exaggerated.

A further starting-point for the analysis of the attack on the Soviet Union must be the rapid victory over France, which had a profound psychological, political, military, and strategic significance for Hitler and the Germans. The conclusive defeat of the 'traditional enemy' was seen to expunge the 'humiliation of November 1918'. Overwhelming victory in the west not only undermined the opposition to Hitler's war policy, but achieved a high degree of unanimity between regime and population. Hitler's unlimited authority in political and military questions was assured. In the ensuing triumphalist atmosphere, work was begun on the establishment of a polical 'New Order' in western Europe, and plans for a continental European greater economic area were outlined; in this the Soviet Union was initially envisaged as playing a supplementary role.

Notwithstanding the triumphalism which accompanied victory over Germany's two enemies from the First World War, German hegemony in Europe was by no means secure. It remained dependent on the willingness of the two flanking powers, Britain and the Soviet Union, to come to an agreement with Germany. This open strategic situation virtually forced actions and decisions:

'Wait and see' was not an appropriate slogan for the political and military leadership of the Third Reich if it intended to retain the initiative. Hitler considered that he had now freed his rear for an attack to the east—and overcome the 'reversed' front position of 1939–40. For a short time it seemed certain that London would 'climb down'. As in the 1930s, wishful thinking and ideological assumptions prevented a more realistic assessment of fundamental British interests, and led to renewed hopes of a global agreement with Britain.

By July 1940 this hope, based on Hitler's dogmatic image of Britain, had disappeared. Only when his plans for a 'division of the world' with Britain had proved to be an illusion did Hitler order the commander-in-chief of the army to plan for an attack on the Soviet Union. The discussions of the army leadership regarding a 'military strike against Russia', which had begun much earlier, thus came to the fore. This fact should not mislead us into regarding Hitler as only one of several factors of equal significance in the process. He was the dominating figure in the German leadership in the summer of 1940. It was his decision of 31 July 1940 to plan for a war against the Soviet Union in the spring of 1941 that set in motion the subsequent political, military, and armaments measures to that end. Equally, it was his directives of March 1941 that turned Operation Barbarossa into a war of annihilation against Bolshevism and Jewry. Investigation of the military leadership's role in preparing and implementing this war made it possible to give a a more comprehensive answer to the question of who were the pillars of German war policy in 1940–1. The military leadership produced operational plans on its own initiative, at first for a limited offensive war against the Soviet Union, and worked to turn ideological intentions into functioning decrees. This cannot be regarded as purely technical or specialist military conduct. It was at the same time a form of co-operation and collaboration marked by political agreement on fundamental issues.

Hitler's turn to the east at the end of July 1940 can justly be interpreted as a sign that, in his view, living-space policy was linked with the strategic need to safeguard the areas under German control against the threat of intervention by the Anglo-Saxon naval powers. However, it is also necessary to evaluate the individual elements in his motivation. Hitler thought that it was both necessary and possible to conclude Operation Barbarossa before an intervention by the United States. It can therefore be said that the operation was planned and carried out *despite*, not *because of*, Britain's decision to continue the war. Against the background of his political alternatives of 'all or nothing', Hitler put his trust in the 'advantage of the moment' against the emerging alliance against him. He did not wish to leave the responsibility for 'securing living-space', for the 'existence or non-existence' of the German people, to a later generation. In his view, Germany's flanks and rear were still clear for the conquest of the 'Russian space' in 1941. Only the acquisition of that territory would enable the Reich to pursue world policy, and 'even to wage the struggle against continents in future'.

Hitler's decision of 31 July 1940 changed the previous thrust of operational discussions by the army leadership, led the naval leadership to make its 'observations on Russia', and required a reorientation in the armaments industry. At the same time, it also produced a re-evaluation of the states and peoples of south-east and northern Europe. From the summer of 1940, Hitler was determined to exploit Germany's political weight in order to secure strategic, operational, and economic objectives in Romania and Finland. He thereby reclaimed from the Soviet Union an influence on states in which, only a year before, the Third Reich had declared no interest. The *rapprochement* of Romania and Finland with Germany led these countries to participate in Hitler's war on the Soviet Union. However, it was due less to German pressure than to a combination and interaction of historical, political, ideological, and economic factors, which were given added significance by Soviet policy and military interventions after autumn 1939. While Hitler believed that he could dispense with Italy and Japan, Romania and Finland were welcome co-belligerents. They became his main allies.

Hitler left the military planning of the war against the Soviet Union largely to the general staffs. Not until the end of 1940 did he have the operational intentions of Army High Command submitted to him. These plans received his overall consent, even though they deviated from his directives on significant points. It was characteristic of the relationship between Hitler and Halder that their obvious differences of opinion concerning the start of the second phase of operations were not clarified. While Hitler assumed that his directive would be followed, Halder believed that Hitler would yield to his judgement if operational developments proved it to be correct. For Hitler, the capture of important economic bases in the north and south was always a major priority, first to make it easier for the Germans to live off the land, and second to prevent the enemy from recovering his strength in men and materials. In contrast, Halder hoped to win the war by making a concentrated attack on Moscow. Conflict over the priority of Moscow as an operational objective—as against Leningrad and the possession of the economic potential of the Ukraine and the Caucasus—was thus inevitable from the outset. Halder decided to follow *his* plan of operations. As he had during his autonomous planning in the summer of 1940, he considered that the far-reaching tasks of the Army General Staff gave him the position of supreme military strategist.

After counter-proposals, and in the expectation of a short war, the Luftwaffe leadership also accepted Hitler's plans for attack in the east. Following the disappointments of the strategic air war against Britain, the chief of the general staff was eager for another opportunity to achieve military success in a 'regular war', this time by mounting a co-operative air campaign in support of the army. In addition, the Luftwaffe leadership considered that Communism must be kept away from Europe. Soon after the start of the war, it was clear that the Luftwaffe was not strong enough to contain the enemy air forces and support German troops at the same time as attacking transport routes and industrial sites.

The military image of the Soviet enemy was linked to the Germans' expectation of a rapid collapse of the Stalinist system. In the judgement of the German general staff, the Red Army in 1940 was a 'giant instrument of war' which was on the point of developing into a modern army but would as yet pose no acute danger in 1941. If quality were ever added to quantity, however, Germany would have to deal with a Red Army that was capable of an offensive war. Despite the political agreement between Hitler and Stalin, the latent threat to German hegemony over Europe would then be manifest. It was essential to eliminate it while the Wehrmacht was still superior and able to move east with all its forces. Hitler and the military leadership judged Soviet intentions to be defensive, describing a Red Army attack as 'not likely'. In fact, Hitler's greatest fear was that Stalin might make a gesture of concession at the eleventh hour, thereby ruining his plans.

In March 1941 Hitler rejected draft guidelines from OKW for a military administration of the eastern territories. He did not regard Operation Barbarossa as a simple 'conflict of arms', but as the decisive struggle between two opposing world-views. For Hitler, military operations to conquer 'living-space', its ruthless exploitation for the war economy, and political-policing measures to eliminate 'Jewish Bolshevism' were only different aspects of a single great war in which the SS as well as the Wehrmacht would play a significant role. The special-duty squads of the security police and SD were to hunt down 'enemies of the state and Reich' even in the army's area of operations; the troops—not the courts—were to deal brutally with actual and supposed 'bearers of the Jewish-Bolshevik world-view', the Red Army commissars. During Operation Barbarossa, Hitler was able to amalgamate SS actions and military operations into a whole which it was almost impossible to disentangle. This could be achieved because officers and legal experts in the high commands of the Wehrmacht, army, and Luftwaffe were also convinced that there was a racial and ideological gulf between National Socialist Germany and the Bolshevik Soviet Union. They were therefore willing to suspend international law, and to restrict martial jurisdiction, for the duration of what was expected to be a short campaign. Conduct of this kind also had a practical aspect. Hitler and his military and legal advisers saw the cadres of the Communist Party and the political functionaries of the Red Army, the commissars, as the germ-cells of an organized resistance against German occupation. The rapid elimination of actual and potential opponents in the area of operations, whether by the special-duty squads or by the troops, would help to 'save German blood'. Attempts to 'enlighten' German soldiers on the eastern front about the meaning of the war were begun on the first day of the invasion. This trend towards a war of annihiliation was reflected in an appeal by Hitler, in OKW guidelines for German conduct, and in army leaflets about the 'treacherous' war being waged by the Red Army.

Economic factors played an important role in Hitler's concept of living-space. In 1940–1, however, this long-term motive for expansion in the east was inextricably interwoven with the needs of the moment. Soviet supplies of raw materials, previously guaranteed by German–Soviet commercial agreements, were vitally important for the German war economy. However, the ensuing German dependence on Soviet sources, and the Soviet demands for arma-ments-related return payments, were increasingly perceived as incompatible with ideological and economic objectives which were fundamentally hostile to Russia. The solution of the 'Russian problem' by force, which Hitler had planned from the summer of 1940, thus appeared to offer an acceptable way out of the situation in economic terms. Hitler also provided the impetus for the formulation of principles covering the economic exploitation of the terri-tories to be occupied. This move was greeted with enthusiasm rather than objections from the functionaries, who were content to produce plans without scruple, and allowed themselves to be guided by ideological assumptions. Their aim was to relieve the German war economy by seizing raw-material and food supplies, and to feed the 'whole Wehrmacht from Russia in the third year of the war'. The resulting starvation of 'umpteen million people' was con-sciously accepted. These economic war aims were laid down independently by the military and the economic bureaucrats in agreement with leading repre-sentatives of the economy, and ran counter to Rosenberg's idea of the primacy of eastern *politics*. Hitler's decision to create an economic apparatus indepen-dent of the civil and military administration, and under the auspices of Göring, led to chaos in occupation policy.

In 1929 the Soviet Union had launched an immense rearmament process which inevitably developed its own dynamic. The Soviet planned economy was transformed into an armaments economy in which all the important economic measures were placed either directly or indirectly at the service of rearmament. By 1941 the Soviet fighting forces had acquired a multiple superiority over the German army in the east in tanks, ordnance, and aircraft. Just as Stalin's foreign policy was built on the ideological axiom that the Soviet Union was surrounded by a ring of fundamentally hostile states, and that a military conflict was unavoidable in the long term, so Soviet military teaching emphasized offensive theory and neglected the art of defensive warfare. Both the leadership and the morale of the fighting forces were massively weakened by the 'purges' set in motion by Stalin. Yet by making an alliance of self-interest with its ideological enemy in August 1939, the Soviet Union was able to push its strategic glacis far to the west and south. Following setbacks in its campaigns against Poland and Finland, and in the light of German military successes, the Soviet leadership made energetic attempts after May 1940 to turn the Red Army into a serviceable instrument of war. From the spring of 1941 its formations moved closer to the border, creating 'operational configurations' in the areas around Białystok and Lvov. Nevertheless, the Soviet armed forces were not ready for war. Moscow did not nurse any offensive designs in 1941, and made every effort to avoid giving Berlin a reason to attack, though Stalin did not rule out the possibility of a war with Germany in 1942.

On 22 June 1941 Hitler launched his war between two opposing world-views. Stalin responded to the onslaught in a way which added lurid touches to German propaganda claims of 'Asiatic' conduct. The excesses against German prisoners of war, and the mass shooting of political prisoners by NKVD special troops, demonstrate that the Soviet side too resorted to methods that violated international law. These methods also enabled the Germans to present the murderous activities of the security police and the SD as a form of reprisal. Of course, these facts cannot be used to justify, or to diminish the horror of, what occurred. This is true of the excesses of both sides. Historical investigation has also proved that German conduct cannot be explained simply as a reaction to Soviet atrocities, though it was certainly exacerbated by them. In this context, it is a caricature of the truth to claim that the SS was solely responsible for attacking the phantom of 'Jewish Bolshevism', while the Wehrmacht restricted itself to conducting military operations. The army leadership must share the responsibility for blurring the differences between military tasks and security policing measures. The effects of this process can be seen in the shooting of troop commissars, and in the summary executions of Jews, Communists, and Russians by army units in punishment for unsolved acts of resistance. As in Poland, the real nature of the occupying power was revealed by the minimal value it accorded to human life. Stalin accommodated Hitler's concept of a war of annihilation between two world-views by appealing for a merciless patriotic war against 'German Fascism'. The call for partisan warfare behind the front gave Hitler the opportunity to portray his programme of annihilation as an act of war; it also encouraged the 'special measures' of the German troops, ordered before the war began, against the vaguest threat to its security. Such conduct, in violation of international law, gave free rein to irrational emotions and the thirst for revenge on both sides, despite the attempts of military leaders in the Wehrmacht and the Red Army to forbid arbitrary action by their soldiers and to maintain discipline. Unrestrained conduct was *one* characteristic aspect of the German–Soviet war in 1941.

On 22 June 1941 neither Hitler nor his military leaders doubted that they had enough time and means to destroy the Soviet forces, thereby also striking a decisive blow against Britain. The huge successes of the early days confirmed these expectations. German military confidence and self-esteem rose to unprecedented heights. After only two weeks, Halder and Hitler regarded the campaign as won. Yet only a few days later it became apparent that the first operational objectives had been achieved only geographically, not militarily: the 'mass of the Russian army' west of the Dnieper–Dvina line had not been destroyed. The situation reports had to be amended to conform with realities.

Within the German leadership in July and August 1941, Hitler and Halder advocated different objectives for the second stage of operations, and supported different methods of achieving them. The main debate was whether the two armoured groups of Army Group Centre should wheel round towards one of the two flanks (Leningrad or the Sea of Asov), or whether Army Groups North and South could fulfil their objectives without such reinforcement, leaving all the forces in the centre to be concentrated for the defeat of the Soviet forces massing before Moscow. This debate in the summer of 1941 also reflects the growing awareness of the German leadership that Operation Barbarossa had failed; 'the Russian colossus' had been underestimated in terms of its military and economic strength and its ability to organize. Insufficient time and men were available to defeat the Soviet Union in a 'mobile campaign' before the onset of winter. The Soviet regime had been able to organize an effective defence, and to withdraw combat-ready units of the Red Army over the 'magic' Dnieper–Dvina line to the east. German encirclement operations designed to prevent this had not been fully successful because of the different rates of advance of the armoured and infantry forces. The 'vastness of the Russian space' provided the Wehrmacht with problems which became ever more difficult to solve as German attacking strength declined.

It seems that Hitler was a more realistic judge of the situation than Halder in the summer of 1941. The chief of the Army General Staff still believed he could achieve victory by launching a wide-ranging operation against Moscow. By the end of August 1941, on the other hand, Hitler considered that the war against the Soviet Union could no longer be completed in that year. He therefore hoped to destroy the fighting force of the Red Army in narrow encirclements, to capture the sources of Soviet power, and to establish good starting-positions for 1942. At the same time, the army groups and armies were making assessments of their own and the enemy's combat efficiency; these were increasingly at odds with those of Army High Command. Nevertheless, in November 1941 Halder and the command of Army Group Centre decided on a new—frontal—attack on Moscow. This 'final effort' would enable the Germans to occupy the Soviet capital and thereby bring about the end of the war. The superior leadership skills, 'harder will', and proven resilience of the German soldiers, it was considered, were more important than the other vital factors in a situation report: German personnel and material situation, enemy, terrain, and climate.

The unexpected counter-attack of the Red Army before Moscow struck hard at the German formations, which had reached a low point physically and psychologically. Equally severe were its effects on the German leadership, which was divided about the causes of the 'current crisis' and the measures necessary to overcome it, because at first it refused to accept that the initiative had passed to the enemy. With the co-operation of the Army High Command, and against the views of the army commands, Hitler ordered that the front should be held at all costs. The aim was to eliminate the risk of the collapse of

Army Group Centre by offering 'fanatical resistance', assisted by the immediate dispatch of 'gun-carriers' to the burnt-out divisions and the preparation of defensible positions. The operational crisis developed into a leadership crisis between Hitler, the Army High Command, and the commanders at the front. On 19 December 1941 Brauchitsch was replaced. Hitler placed himself in supreme command of the army. In agreement with the army groups, he responded to contraventions of his form of operational leadership by reshuffling senior positions. No account of previous achievements was taken during this process, even in the case of Guderian. Halder was proud that the 'Führer' was now the head of the army, and expected the army groups and armies to carry out his will.

The big Red Army offensive of 5 December 1941 inflicted heavy casualties on the Wehrmacht. Nevertheless, it did not achieve its strategic objectives of encircling and destroying Army Groups North and Centre and recovering the Crimea. This was due both to an over-assessment of the attacking capability and leadership of the Soviet forces and to the stubborn German resistance encountered. Nevertheless, the perceptible successes of the Soviet forces raised the military and political prestige of the Soviet Union. Stalin was able to bring this factor into play in dealing with his British ally.

On the German side, the winter crisis had apparently been overcome by the middle of February 1942. Operational prospects were assessed more realistically after the immense losses in men and material during Operation Barbarossa. In autumn 1941 the leadership was already aware that it would no longer be able to field an army such as had existed before the attack. In 1942 the entire attacking force of the army in the east was therefore to be concentrated on the southern flank of the front, in order to attack the Caucasus and Stalingrad. The objective was to gain control of the oilfields, to eliminate the munitions centre on the Volga, and to cut Moscow off from one of its two supply-lines to the British and Americans.

Both German and Soviet historians have referred to these developments as the great 'turning-point before Moscow'. If the campaign plans of the Army General Staff are taken as the basis for assessment, Operation Barbarossa had failed even before the attacks on Moscow, Leningrad, and Rostov were called off. This turning-point in the war against the Soviet Union produced many repercussions: political, strategic, economic, and ideological. They affected the Third Reich and its allies as well as the states occupied by it. In autumn 1941 Hitler recognized that his strategy had failed: the Soviet Union had not been defeated; British will to resist had been strengthened; and direct American intervention in the war was to be expected in 1942. Hitler's realization that the alliances of the First World War were re-forming did not persuade him to try for a negotiated peace. This was not the result of a realistic judgement that the enemy coalition would refuse to negotiate with him, but of Hitler's abiding commitment to the social-Darwinist alternatives of 'all or nothing'. If the German people proved insufficiently strong to come through its life-and-death struggle, it deserved to go under. At the same time, however, the course of the 'life-and-death struggle' against the racial enemy, Jewry, was finally determined at the Wannsee Conference in January 1942. It had already been decided at the end of July 1941 that this struggle was to be extended to the entire German sphere of influence in Europe. The war against the Soviet Union offered Hitler the ideal medium for 'charging' (M. Broszat's term) his paranoid, aggressive anti-Semitism, and thus realizing the threat he had made on 30 January 1939. On that occasion he had publicly proclaimed that in the event of another world war the result would be the destruction of the 'Jewish race' in Europe. Victories and defeats alike caused the radicalization of the dogmatic racial policy of National Socialism in 1941–2. Yet this radical decision for the future conduct of the war has often obscured the fact that, after the failure to achieve quick victory, Hitler was also ready to deviate from his axioms where this would bring military or economic advantages, weaken Soviet powers of resistance, and thus advance his strategy. He therefore accepted the recruitment of Russian civilians and prisoners of war in response to an acute shortage of workers in the Reich and of security forces in the occupied Soviet territories. Hitler also agreed to a revision of the guidelines covering the treatment of commissars and the future of the Soviet collective economy.

Overall, the economic objectives associated with Barbarossa were not achieved. Lost Soviet supplies could not be replaced. The priorities fixed for the distribution of agricultural produce, laid down under the trauma of the First World War, could not even satisfy the needs of the army in the east. However, the inadequacy of the economic organization did improve the prospects for survival of the population in the occupied territories. While the Soviet Union was waging a 'total war' from the summer of 1941, the Third Reich did not dare to impose similar burdens on the Germans.

It was typical of the 'Hitler coalition' against the Soviet Union that there was no formal alliance with jointly formulated political objectives. Of course, Germany, Italy, Finland, Romania, Hungary, and Slovakia were allied with each other through the anti-Comintern pact and the Tripartite Pact (except Finland). Yet despite their near identical declarations regarding the war against Bolshevism, they pursued separate interests based on a variety of motives; in the case of Hungary and Romania, these were directed more against each other than against the Soviet Union. The British declaration of war on Finland, Hungary, and Romania, forced on it by Moscow, demonstrated to these German allies that their participation in Hitler's war in the east had dragged them into a world war. The anti-Soviet partners of the Third Reich differed not only in their assessment of German military defeats, but also in their view of American entry into the war. Romania and Hungary acceded to German demands by declaring war on the United States and providing significant forces for the German summer offensive against the Red Army. In contrast, Finland announced that its support for German operations in 1942 was dependent on the fall of Leningrad. It would not allow itself to be drawn into the world war, and took account of Washington's wishes in its conduct of the war itself.

Against the background of the 'blank cheque' given to Japan in April 1941, and confirmed in December of that year to cover the eventuality of war against the United States, the German declaration of war on the United States appears more as a calculated decision than as a forced reaction or 'flight forwards'. Yet Hitler did not know how the United States could be defeated. The declaration of war was intended as a demonstration of strength to disguise the fact that, with the failure of Barbarossa and the extension of the European war into a world war, Germany's bid for world-power status, or world supremacy, had failed. Though the defeat of the Third Reich was to be expected, it could hold out longer in alliance with Japan, so long as the United States was compelled to divide its forces between Europe and East Asia. Hitler was therefore anxious to eliminate the possibility of a separate peace between the United States, Britain, and Japan. But it was Germany which was the first to lay down arms, thereby allowing the victors to assume 'supreme authority' with regard to Germany.

The volume has provided a survey of the development of Operation Barbarossa from the victory over France in June 1940 until the Soviet counter-attack in December 1941 and its aftermath. It has revealed that here, as in no other operation, ideological and political objectives were directly associated with the social-Darwinist values of the Third Reich. These produced a self-destructive tendency which found expression in victory and defeat, in the alternation of far-sighted clarity and crass opportunism, and in the futility of all the sacrifices made. Above all, this impulse led from European to world war, thereby sealing the fate of the Reich as well as the regime. Its death-agony, however, was to last for several destructive years.

Bibliography

Only sources quoted have been included. The major part of the documentary material of military origin originates from the files deposited in the Bundesarchiv-Militärarchiv (Federal Archives/Military Archives) in Freiburg. The researchers, however, were unable to use a complete collection of documents of the three Wehrmacht services. The papers of the senior command authorities of the Luftwaffe, for instance, were almost completely destroyed at the end of the war. Moreover, as the former Wehrmacht documents are not yet available in the Military Archives in their totality, it was necessary in some instances to resort to copies appended to the largely unpublished studies compiled after the war, on instruction by the US Army's Historical Division, under the direction of Colonel-General (retd.) Franz Halder within the 'Military Studies' research programme. Processing of the documents which have meanwhile come into the Military Archives is not yet complete, and as a result old labels (e.g. those of the Army Archives in Potsdam) or provisional auxiliary labels had to be used. In other archives too occasional relabelling has taken place. The newest labels have only partly been substituted. To facilitate location of individual documents, a systematic arrangement of the groups of documents and of document titles from all archives has been effected, though this does not invariably represent an accurate organization chart of the civilian authorities, ministries, or military command authorities. Reasons of space have also necessitated the amalgamation of certain groups and titles of documents.

I. UNPUBLISHED SOURCES

1. Bundesarchiv Koblenz [Federal Archive, Koblenz]

Reichsfinanzministerium [Reich Ministry of Finance]

R 2/24243	Innen- und außenpolitische Angelegenheiten der Reichsregierung während des 2. Weltkrieges (Handakten des Reichsfinanzministers Graf Schwerin v. Krosigk) 1939–1943
R 2/30921	Wirtschaftliche Erschließung des Ostraumes (Handakten des Ministerialrates Dr Breyhan) 1941

Reichsministerium für Rüstung und Kriegsproduktion [Reich Ministry for Armaments and War Production]

R 3/v. 1942	Institut für Konjunkturforschung, Rohstoffbilanz Kontinentaleuropa unter Einschluß des europäischen Rußland und Nordafrikas

Reichsministerium für die besetzten Ostgebiete [Reich Ministry for the Occupied Eastern Territories]

R 6/23	Ministerbüro
R 6/52	Handakten des SA-Brigadeführers Major O. W. Müller als Beauftragter RMfbO, Bd 2, 1943–1944

R 6/60a   Hauptabteilung Politik, Gedanken zur deutschen
Politik in den besetzten Ostgebieten

R 6/69   Handakten Bräutigam über Reichskommissariat
Ukraine, Bd 1

R 6/77   Berichte über die politische Lage im
Reichskommissariat Ukraine 1941–1944

R 6/287   Handakten Gewerbliche Wirtschaft, Aufbau der
Wirtschaftsverwaltung, Bd 1

R 6/408   Hauptabteilung Wirtschaft

Reichsministerium für Wirtschaft [Reich Ministry of Economic Affairs]

R 7/1142   Osterlasse über Richtlinien für die Ausnutzung der besetzten
Ostgebiete für die deutsche Kriegswirtschaft (Verwaltung,
Rüstungsbetriebe, Arbeitseinsatz, Tätigkeit des Wirtschaftsstabes Ost, Verzeichnis und Tätigkeit der Ostgesells-
chaften etc.)

R 7/3413   August 1940. Zahlen zur Entwicklung des deutschen
Außenhandels seit Kriegsbeginn

R 7/4699   Ländererlasse, Bd 37

Statistisches Reichsamt [Reich Statistical Office]

R 24/24   Rohstoffversorgung des großdeutschen Wirtschaftsraumes,
1940

Reichsamt für Wirtschaftsausbau [Reich Office for Economic Development]

R 25/14   Berichterstattung: Durchführung der wehrwirtschaftlichen
Ausbau- und Erzeugungspläne für die Sachgebiete
Mineralöl, Kautschuk, Leichtmetalle, Pulver, Sprengstoffe,
Kampfstoffe, Energiewirtschaft usw., April 1939

R 25/40   Die Rohstoffversorgung Europas bei voller Ausnutzung der
Gewinnungsmöglichkeiten in Europa und Afrika

R 25/53   Rohstoffversorgung: Möglichkeiten einer Großraumwehrwirtschaft unter deutscher Führung, Teil 1 (August
1939)

R 25/94   Wehrwirtschaftliche Planung und Durchführung versch.
Produktionsprogramme auf dem Chemiegebiet (1941)

Beauftragter für den Vierjahresplan [Plenipotentiary for the Four-year Plan]

R 26 I/18   Ergebnisse der Vierjahresplan-Arbeit, 1942

R 26 I/44   Übersicht über die wirtschaftliche Gesamtlage, Jan. 1940–
Aug. 1941

Reichskanzlei [Reich Chancellery]

R 43 II/332   Betreffsakten Handel und Wirtschaft: Außenhandel, Bd 10:
1935–1942

R 43 II/609   Betreffsakten Krieg: Kriegswirtschaft (ohne Ernährungs-
wirtschaft), Bd 3: 1940–1943

R 43 II/686a   Betreffsakten Krieg: Wirtschaftsmaßnahmen, Währungs-
fragen und Einsatz der Technik in den besetzten
Ostgebieten, Bd 1: 1941–1943

Reichssicherheitshauptamt [Reich Central Security Office]

R 58/214–221   Der Chef der Sicherheitspolizei und des SD, Ereignismeldungen UdSSR, Nr. 1-195, 23.6.1941–24.4.1942

Kanzlei Rosenberg [Rosenberg's chancellery]

NS 8/71   Manuskripte und Vorträge als Reichsminister für die besetzten Ostgebiete, 1941–1944

Parteiamtliche Prüfungskommission zum Schutze des NS-Schrifttums [Party Supervision Commission for the Protection of NS Literature]

NS 11/28   Rede Hitlers vor den Truppenkommandeuren des Heeres am 10.2.1939

Persönlicher Stab Reichsführer SS [Personal staff of Reich Leader SS]

NS 19 alt/364   German. Freiwilligenwerbung, Schriftverkehr Chef des SS-Hauptamtes

Reichsorganisationsleiter der NSDAP [Reich Leader of Party Organization]

NS 22/1026   Streng vertrauliche und vertrauliche Informationsberichte über einzelne Länder (Hrsg.: Hauptschulungsamt der NSDAP, Amt Lehrwesen), Bd 5: UdSSR 1940–1941

Außenpolitisches Amt der NSDAP [Foreign Policy Department of the NSDAP]

NS 43/3   Aktennotizen von Amtsleiter Leibbrandt
NS 43/37   Sowjetunion, Bd 3

2. Bundesarchiv-Militärarchiv Freiburg [Federal Archive/Military Archive, Freiburg]

(a) Oberkommando der Wehrmacht (OKW) [Wehrmacht High Command]

OKW/Chef Wehrmachtführungsstab (WFSt) [OKW Chief of Operations Staff]

RW 4/v. 35   Abschriftensammlung 1938–1945 (Gen. Oberst Jodl)

OKW/WFSt/Abteilung Landesverteidigung (L) [OKW Operations Staff, Department for Defence]

RW 4/v. 522   Vorbereitung 'Barbarossa' Dez. 1940–März 1941
RW 4/v. 524 and 525   Besondere Anordnungen Nr. 1 zu Weisung Nr. 21 (Fall 'Barbarossa') mit Anl. 1 und Anl. 3 vom 19.5.1941
RW 4/575   Chefsachen 'Barbarossa', Februar–Mai 1941
RW 4/v. 577   Chefsachen 'Barbarossa' Mai 1941
RW 4/v. 578   Chefsachen 'Barbarossa', Vorbereitung und Durchführung, Mai–Dez. 1941

OKW/WFSt/Abteilung Wehrmacht-Propaganda (WPr) [OKW Operations Staff/Wehrmacht Propaganda Department]

RW 4/v. 145   Geheimakten über Organisation, Wehrpflicht vom 2.12.1939–4.11.1940

RW 4/v. 251	Geheimakten über Propaganda für die Wehrmacht, Mai–Juli 1941
RW 4/v. 253	Geheimakten Propaganda für die Wehrmacht, Bd 16: Sept.–Nov. 1941
RW 4/v. 308	Industrie-, Wirtschafts- und Rohstoff-Fragen (Geheimsache; Az. 65/66)
RW 4/v. 325	Geheimakten über fremde Staaten—Finnland—(Berichte d. Mil.Att. in Helsinki) 1939–1943
RW 4/v. 325 D	Fremde Staaten—Finnland 1940–1944
RW 4/v. 328 and 329	Sowjetrußland (Sammlung von Unterlagen), geheim, Bd 1: 1940–Juni 1941; Bd 2: Juli–Dez. 1941
RW 4/v. 330 (W 01-6/5781	Fremde Staaten, Rußland, Anlagen, Januar–Juli 1942
RW 4/v. 334	Ungarn: Berichte des Mil.Att. in Budapest; V-Mann-Berichte u.a. (geheim)

OKW/WFSt/Heimatstab Übersee [OKW Operations Staff/Base Staff Overseas]

RW 4/v. 769	Heimatstab Nord d. WB Norwegen, Sept. 1940–Mai 1942

OKW/WFSt/Qu [OKW Operations Staff/Quartermaster]

RW 4/v. 513	Führerweisungen und andere Befehle
RW 4/v. 581	Chefsachen, Sammelmappe 'Gelb'
RW 4/v. 639	Chefsachen Skandinavien (Norwegen, Finnland, Dänemark), 1941–1944
RW 4/v. 741	Belgien, Sept. 1942–Nov. 1943
RW 4/v. 759	Chefsachen 'Rosenberg' (Verwaltung und Wirtschaft in den neubesetzten Ostgebieten; Aufgaben der WB)

OKW/Amt Ausland/Abwehr [OKW Department Foreign Intelligence]

RW 5/v. 443 and 445	Slowakei, Bd 5 U. Bd 7
RW 5/v. 461 and 462	Reichswehrministerium/Abteilung Ausland, Rußland, 1934–1935, Bd 1 u. Bd 2
RW 5/v. 506	Kriegsgefangene und Internierte August 1940–Juli 1943
RW 49/82	Dienststellen und Einheiten der Abwehr, Abwehrleitstelle Frankreich, Verschiedenes

OKW/Allgemeines Wehrmachtamt (AWA) [OKW Wehrmacht General Department]

RW 6/v. 98	Polen Bd 2: Sept. 1939–Mai 1940
RW 6/v. 279	Angebl. Kriegsgefangenenlage in der UdSSR, September 1941

OKW/Wehrwirtschafts- und Rüstungsamt (WiRüAmt) [OKW War Economy and Armaments Department]

OKW/WiRüAmt/Stab [OKW War Economy and Armaments Department/Staff]

RW 19/99	Kriegswirtschaftliche Lageberichte, Januar 1941–Oktober 1942
RW 19/164 to 166	KTB der Stabsabt., H. 2-4, 29.11.1939–31.3.1942

RW 19/176, 177 (Wi/VI. 227) and 178 (W 01-8/28)
Anlagen zum KTB der Stabsabt., 1939–1943, H. 6–8: 5.10.1940–31.12.1941

RW 19/185
Chef WiRüAmt, 4.12.1939–9.9.1942, Fotokopien einzelner Besprechungsprotokolle aus dem KTB der Stabsabt.; Niederschriften von Besprechungen bei Gen. Thomas als Amtschef des Wehrwirtschaftsamtes bzw. als General z.b.V. 1

III W 803
10-Tagesmeldungen

III W 805/2, Teil 2
10-Tagesmeldungen, April–Okt. 1940

III W 805/5 to 8, Teil 1
10-Tagesmeldungen, Juni 1941–März 1942

Wi/I D. 82
Vorträge beim Reichsmarschall (1941–2) durch Chef WiRü

Wi/I D. 112
Osteuropa, Stabsbefehle April–August 1942

Wi/I D. 1716
Auswirkungen eines Angriffs auf Rußland (Aktennotiz über Vortrag beim Reichsmarschall) (1941)

Wi/I F 5.2151
Chef des OKW, Schriftwechsel

Wi/I F 5.2232
Aktenverzeichnis 1935, 1938, 1939, 1940, 1941, 1942 [und Thomas-Memorandum vom 19.11.1939]

Wi/I F 5.2294
Quittungen für Geheimschreiben, Ic

Wi/I F 5.2695
Anlagen (Originale) für Ausarbeitung 'Mineralöl-Wirtschaft', Oberst Sadewasser

Wi/I F 5.2748
Verschiedene Verfügungen des OKW vom 1.2.1940–22.4.1942

Wi/I F 5.3172
Verschiedene Ausgaben von 'Meldungen aus dem Reich', hrsg. vom Chef der Sicherheitspolizei und des SD, Juli–August 1940

Wi/I F 5.3662
Nachrichten des Reichsministers für Rüstung und Kriegsproduktion

Wi/VIII. 138
Allg. und Verwaltungs-Unterlagen, Organisation, Schrift-wechsel Gen. Thomas u. a.

Wi/VIII. 323
betr. Pläne für Wirtschaftsverwaltung der besetzten Ostgebiete, April 1941

OKW/WiRüAmt/Wehrwirtschaftliche Abteilung [OKW War Economy and Armaments Department/War Economy Section]

RW 19/244
Wochenberichte der wehrwirtschaftlichen Abteilung, H. 4: 1940 (= KTB WiRüAmt/Wi 1940)

W 01-8/296
Die Wehrwirtschaft der Union der Sozialistischen Sowjet-Republiken (UdSSR), Teil I. Kurze Charakteristik und Gesamtbeurteilung der wehrwirtschaftlichen Lage, Stand März 1941

Wi/I. 37
Die Mineralölversorgung Deutschlands im Kriege, Teil I und II

Wi/I. 262
Transporte Ausland, 1939–40

Wi/I. 345
Verschiedene Verfügungen des OKW vom 1.6.1940–6.9.1944

Wi/I C 4.2a	Berichte, 16.6.1941–27.5.1942
Wi/I C 4.34	Rumänien 2–5, 1939 Rohstoffe; Ernährung und Landwirtschaft; Wehrmacht (Rüstung); Haushalt und Finanzen
Wi/I C 4.58	12–13, 1940. Militär-Attaché Rumänien, Berichte
Wi/I C 4.64	1940–1941. Deutsche Wehrwirtschaftsmission Rumänien (Tätigkeitsberichte; Organisation; Dienstanweisungen; Verhandlungen etc.); Wehrwirtschaftsstab Rumänien
Wi/I D. 19	WStb: Wehrwirtschaft UdSSR
Wi/I D. 38	WiRüAmt/Ausarb. Varain: Die landw. Produktion der Ukraine vor und im Weltkrieg 1914/18 (1941)
Wi/I D. 45	WiRüAmt: Unternehmen Barbarossa, wehrwirt. Vorbereitungen (1941)
Wi/I D. 138	Osteuropa, Die wehrwirtschaftliche Lage der UdSSR zu Beginn des Jahres 1942 (Ausarb.)
Wi/I D. 1123	Osteuropa, KTB 1 Abt. IV WiAußenstelle OKH/GenQu. Versorgungsbezirk Dnepr
Wi/I D. 1185	Osteuropa, WiRüAmt Ausarb.: Ein Jahr Rußlandfeldzug (Leistungen wehrwirtschaftlicher Formationen des WiAmtes auf dem Rohstoffgebiet) (1942)
Wi/I D. 1222	Osteuropa, Sitzungsberichte betr. Ostwirtschaft (1942)
Wi/I D. 1410	Osteuropa, Landwirtschaftliche Auflagen 1941/42 (Handakte Dr Baath)
Wi/I D. 1645	Erzeugung und Verbrauch von Nahrungs- u. Futtermitteln in der UdSSR, bearb. im Stabsamt des Reichsbauernführers, 28.3.1941
Wi/I D. 1658	Die Lebensmittellieferungen der Ukraine 1918 (zusammenfass. Bericht)
Wi/I D. 1740	Karten: 1. Europ. Rußland mit eingezeichneten Bereichen und Standorten der vorgesehenen WiIn und WiKdos. 2. Schwergewichtsgebiete der Wehrwirtschaft des europ. Teils der UdSSR (1.3.1941)
Wi/I E 3.30b	Schweden, geheim
Wi/I E 4/1	Die Wehrwirtschaft Finnlands, Teil I: Kurze Charakteristik und Gesamtbeurteilung der Wehrwirtschaft Finnlands, Stand: März 1941
Wi/I F 3.130	Slowakei Sept.–Dez. 1941 und älter
Wi/I F 3.143	Sitzung über Fragen im Zusammenhang mit dem deutsch-slowakischen Wehrwirtschaftsvertrag am 21.5.1940. Aktenvermerk über die Bespr. bei Generaloberst Keitel am 21. Juli 1939
Wi/I F 5.655	Ausarbeitungen für Ernährung und Bekleidung, Bd II, 1939–1942
Wi/I F 5.662	Ausarbeitungen und Berichte, 1939–1942
Wi/I F 5.2199	Die deutsche Roh- und Treibstofflage, 1939–1940, Dr F. Friedensburg
Wi/VI. 13b	Mappe Erdöl '66D 34,30', '1935–41'
Wi/VI. 119	Geschichte der Wehrwirtschaft

| Wi/VI. 160 | Auslandsberichte, Bd 1 |
| Wi/VI. 397 | Die Erkundung der materiellen Wehrkraft der großen europäischen und außereuropäischen Staaten und die sich daraus ergebenden Vorbereitungen für den Wirtschaftskrieg |

OKW/WiRüAmt/Rüstungswirtschaftliche Abteilung [OKW War Economy and Armaments Department/Armaments Section]

RW 19/257	KTB der Rüstungswirtschaftlichen Abteilung, H. 5: Okt.–Dez. 1940
Wi/I A. 13	Anlagen zur 'Umsteuerung der Wirtschaft'
Wi/I F 5.120	Steigerung der Rüstung, IIw, Bd I und II
Wi/I F 5.208	Deutschland, Binnen- und Kriegswirtschaft, Bd II u. IV, Rüstungsprogramme, Waffen- und Munitionserzeugung August–November 1941
Wi/I F 5.366	'Dekaden-Übersichten', 1939–1941

OKW/WiRüAmt/Geheimarchiv [OKW War Economy and Armaments Department/Secret Archive]

RW 19 Anhang I/176	Die Lage und die Ausrüstungen der Eisenindustrie der Sowjetunion, März 1941
RW 19 Anhang I/700	Materialanhang zum Rußland-Bericht, bearb. vom Institut für Weltwirtschaft
RW 19 Anhang I/702	Institut für Weltwirtschaft: Das russische Wirtschaftspotential und die Möglichkeit einer Intensivierung der deutsch-russischen Handelsbeziehungen, September 1939
RW 19 Anhang I/1147	Institut für Konjunkturforschung: Die Wirtschaft der UdSSR in Einzeldarstellungen, H. 2: Die Textilwirtschaft der Sowjetunion, März 1941
RW 19 Anhang I/1135	Schriften des Instituts für Konjunkturforschung: Die Wirtschaft der UdSSR in Einzeldarstellungen, H. 1: Ausfuhrmöglichkeiten für die Erzeugnisse des sowjetrussischen Bergbaus, Sept. 1940
RW 19 Anhang I/1147	Institut für Konjunkturforschung: Die Selbstversorgungsmöglichkeiten des mitteleuropäischen Wirtschaftsblocks mit Lebensmitteln, Juni 1940
RW 19 Anhang I/1229	Stickstoff-Syndikat, Wiss.Abt.: Ukraine, Mai 1941
RW 19 Anhang I/1510	Wirtschaftsgruppe Chemische Industrie: Die Chemische Industrie der Sowjet-Union. 2. erw. Fassung, Juni 1941
RW 19 Anhang I/1515	Materialsammlung über Lagerstätten, eisenschaffende und eisenverarbeitende Industrie im europäischen Gebiet der ehem. UdSSR, Bericht Nr. 3, Juli 1941 (Reichswerke A. G. Hermann Göring)
RW 19 Anhang I/1550	W. v. Poletika: Naturverhältnis und Agrargeographie der Sowjetunion
Wi/I A. 84	Wehrwirtschaftliches Archiv, Sonderakten, 1941–42
Wi/I F 5.378	Wehrwirtschafts-Archiv, Sonderakten 1940

OKW/WiRüAmt/Lehrstab [OKW War Economy and Armaments Department/ Training Staff]

Wi/I. 216   Wehrwirtschaft des Auslands

OKW/WiRüAmt/Außenstellen [OKW War Economy and Armaments Department/ External Agencies]

RW 30/91   Rüstungsdienststellen in den Reichskommissariaten Ostland und Ukraine, KTB Nr. 2, Der RÜIn Ukraine, 1.10.–31.12.1941

RW 30/104   Rüstungsdienststellen in den Reichskommissariaten Ostland und Ukraine, Lagebericht der RÜIn Ukraine vom 13.2.1941–14.5.1942

OKW/WiRüAmt/Wirtschaftsstab Ost [OKW War Economy and Armaments Department/Economic Staff East]

RW 31/11 to 14	KTB 1941, Anlagen Nr. 1 bis 4
RW 31/17	KTB I/1942
RW 31/41	Anlagen zum KTB, 2. Vj. 1944
RW 31/42	Wirtschaftsstab Ost/La. KTB-Beiträge
RW 31/78	TB 1944
RW 31/80	'Geschichte des WiStabOst, Gliederung der Materialsammlung'
RW 31/127	Vorarbeiten Grüne Mappe Teil II
RW 31/128 D	'Richtlinien für die Führung der Wirtschaft', 'Grüne Mappe', Teil I, Juni 1941
RW 31/130	Wirtschafts-Führungsstab Ost (OKW/WiRüAmt/Stab I/O Nr. 5561 geh.), Richtlinien für die Führung der Wirtschaft in den neubesetzten Ostgebieten (Grüne Mappe), Teil II (2. Auflage), Ergänzungsmaterial zu Teil I, Berlin, November 1941
RW 31/131	Richtlinien für die Führung der Wirtschaft 'Grüne Mappe', Teil II, Aug. 1942
RW 31/134	Stab/Ia, Verfügungen des Reichsministeriums f. d. bes. Ostgebiete
RW 31/135	'Kreislandwirtschaftsführer-Mappe'
RW 31/162	Aufstellung der Wi.Org. z.b.V. 'Oldenburg'
RW 31/195	Verb.St.d. OKW/WiRüAmt b. RM; Stellenbesetzung und Organisation der WiIn z.b.V. Westfalen; Einsatzvorschläge in Südrußland
RW 31/331	Aufgaben und Arbeitsergebnisse der Chefgruppe W (Ausarbeitung)
Wi/I D. 1600	Verb.Offz. des WiRüAmtes zur HTO, 1941–1942
Wi/VIII. 335	Deutschland und besetztes Europa, allg. und Verwaltungs-Unterlagen, Varia WiStab Ost
Wi/VIII. 347	Betr. Wirtschaftsorganisation z.b.V. Oldenburg (Wirtschaftsstab Ost), 1941

Wi/VIII. 411   ZI/II Oldenburg III betr. Wehrwirtschaftsorganisation Ost, Arbeitsstab Oldenburg, 1940–1941

OKW/WiRüAmt/Verbindungsoffiziere [OKW War Economy and Armaments Department/Liaison Officers]

RW 45/15 and 16   Berichte des Verb.Offz. (Oberst Drews) zum RWM,
(Wi/VI. 326)   20.5.1941–29.6.1942

Nachgeordnete, dem Chef OKW unterstellte Dienststellen (*Wehrmachtbefehlshaber*) [Agencies subordinated to the OKW Chief: Wehrmacht commanders]

RW 39/20   WB in Norwegen, TB Abt. Ia, Ic, IIa, für Juni 1941 mit
(13386/1), 26, 30   Anlagen, für Dezember 1941 und für Februar 1942
RW 41/4   WB Ukraine, Schriftwechsel, Weisungen, Ausarbeitungen, 'Hinweise zur Ukrainischen Frage' usw., Juni 1941–Januar 1942
RW 41/9   WB Ukraine/Chefintendant, Versorgungsangelegenheiten
RW 41/31   WB Ukraine, Geheimanlage 'B', 23.6.1941–7.11.1942
W 02-24/1   Dokumentation von Oberst a.D. Kitschmann 'Als Militärattaché in Helsinki' vom Dez. 1962

OKW/Wehrmachtuntersuchungsstelle für Verletzungen des Völkerrechts [OKW Wehrmacht Investigation Agency for Violations of International Law]

RW 2/v. 158   Russische Befehle über die Behandlung der Gefangenen

(*b*) *Oberkommando des Heeres* (*OKH*) [Army High Command]

OKH/Generalstab des Heeres (*GenStdH*)*/Zentralabteilung* [OKH Army General Staff/Central Department]

RH 2/v. 154–157   Anlagenbände 1–4 zu: Die personelle Entwicklung des Generalstabes des Heeres während des Krieges 1939–1942
RH 2/195   Verfügungen, Jan. 1934–Dez. 1935
RH 2/v. 238   Die personelle Entwicklung des Generalstabes des Heeres während des Krieges 1939–1942, Textband

OKH/GenStdH/Operations-Abteilung (*Op.Abt.*) [OKH/Army General Staff/Operations Department]

RH 2/v. 325   Lage Ost, April 1942, M: 1:1 000 000
RH 2/v. 390   Op.Abt. (III), Chefs., Hauptakte, Gruppe Landes-befestigungen vom 16.10.1939–7.7.1940
RH 2/v. 427 and 428   Op.Abt. (III), Chefsachen 1941, Bd 1 u. 2, Jan. 1941–1.1.1942
RH 2/v. 522   Op.Abt. (III), Allgemein—V, Bd 2, 27.7.1940–29.4.1943
RH 2/v. 1325, 1326,   Barbarossa, Bd 1, 7.1.–8.5.1941, Bd 2, 12.8.–26.9.1941, Bd
1327   3, 25.9.1941–12.1.1942

RH 2/v. 1328	Aufmarsch 'Barbarossa' 1941
H 28/25	Entwurf zur Aufmarschanweisung 'Barbarossa'

OKH/GenStdH/Organisation-Abteilung (Org.Abt.) [OKH Army General Staff/
Organization Department]

RH 2/v. 821	KTB vom. 1.1.–31.7.1942
RH 2/v. 929	Chefsachen Bd 13, 8.5.1941–28.2.1942

OKH/GenStdH/Oberquartiermeister IV (OQu IV) [OKH Army General Staff/Chief
Quartermaster IV]

RH 2/v. 1478 and 1479	K. v. Tippelskirch, Tagesnotizen 1939–1940, 30.10.1939–2.12.1940
III H 1001/6	Schriftwechsel OQu IV mit Mil.Att. Budapest 1937–1939
III H 1001/7	Schriftwechsel OQu IV mit Mil.Att. Bukarest 1939–1941
III H 1001/8	Schriftwechsel OQu IV mit Mil.Att. Helsinki 9.11.1937–23.1.1942
III H 1001/9	Schriftwechsel OQu IV mit Mil.Att. Kowno vom 16.2.1937–11.6.1940
III H 1001/13	Schriftwechsel OQu IV mit Mil.Att. Moskau vom 21.6.1937–18.6.1941
III H 1001/19	Schriftwechsel OQu IV mit Mil.Att. Stockholm vom 4.4.1939–29.9.1942
III H 1001/20	Schriftwechsel OQu IV mit Mil.Att. Tokyo vom 7.11.1936–4.6.1941

OKH/GenStdH/OQu IV/Abt. Fremde Heere Ost [OKH Army General Staff/Chief
Quartermaster IV/Dept. Foreign Armies East]

RH 2/v. 1923	Studie über das Pripjet-Gebiet vom 12.2.1941
RH 2/v. 1928	Chefsachen, Bd 1a, April 1939–Mai 1941
RH 2/v. 2623	II a, Anlagen zum KTB vom 1.11.1944–28.3.1945
H 3/1	Chefsachen, Bd I, 24.4.1939–2.9.1941
H3/152	1941–1942, Führerstellenbesetzung der Roten Armee
H 3/482	Chefsachen, Kräfteverteilung der Roten Armee (u.a.) vom 6.2.–21.6.1941
H 3/484	Lageberichte Ost, 1941
H 3/485	Lageberichte Ost u.a. 1941
H 3/673, 1 + 2 (RH 2/v. 2732–40, 2772, 2760–2)	Lageberichte, Meldungen über die Rote Armee
H 3/675 (RH 2/2731, 2788, 2790)	Ausrüstung der Roten Armee 1940
H 3/1726 (RH 2/v. 2048, 2087, 2106)	Werturteil über die Rote Armee vom 19.12.1939, Lageberichte u.ä.

OKH/GenStdH/OQu IV/Attaché-Abteilung [OKW Army General Staff/Chief Quartermaster IV/Attaché Department]

H 27/9	Entwürfe und Unterlagen 'Bildung Militär-Mission Rumänien', Sept. 1940
H 27/43	Chefsachen 1941

OKH/GenStdH/Chef des Transportwesens [OKH Army General Staff/Chief of Transport]

H 12/135	1939–1940; Verbindungsstab Moskau

OKH/GenStdH/Generalquartiermeister (Gen.Qu.) [OKH Army General Staff/Quartermaster-General]

RH 3/ArbNr. 104	KTB 2 Vers.Bez.Süd, 6.9.–31.12.1941
RH 3/ArbNr. 105	KTB 2 Vers.Bez.Süd, Bes. Anordnungen für den Vers.Bez., 16.8.–17.11.1941
RH 3/ArbNr. 108	Bes. Anlagen Nr. 4 zum KTB Nr. 2 des Vers.Bez.Süd, Tagesbefehle 29.8.–9.11.1941
RH 3/ArbNr. 111	KTB 2 Vers.Bez.Süd, Bes. Anlagen Nr. 7, Einzelanlagen
RH 3/v. 132	Versorgung der in Rußland eingesetzten Truppen, Aufbau einer Kriegsverwaltung u. dgl. 1940/41
RH 3/v. 136	Umgliederung der Dienststelle 'Generalquartiermeister' mit Wirkung vom 1.10.1940
RH 3/v. 138 and 139	Vers.Bez.Nord, Tagebuch offen ausgehender Schreiben ab 12.7.1941 und ab 18.8.1941
H 10-51/2	Erfahrungen aus dem Ostfeldzug über die Versorgungsführung (Gen.Qu.Abt. Versorgungsführung—Qu 2), 24.3.1942
H 17/28	Qu 3/III, Befehl über die Erfassung der Beute bei Operationen 1941
H 17/85	Winterunterkunftsprogramm 21.8.–31.10.1941
H 17/191	Akten 'Kalender Barbarossa' 1941

Chef der Heeresrüstung und Befehlshaber des Ersatzheeres (Chef HRüst u. BdE)/Heereswaffenamt [Chief of Army Armaments and Director-General of Training]

RH 8/v. 1022 and 1023	Rüstungsstand (Verlust- und Verbrauchszahlen, Fertigung), Bd 1 u. 2: Sept. 1938–Aug. 1941
RH 8/v. 1068	Vortragsnotizen zur Rüstungslage (Entwürfe 1939–1943)
RH 8/v. 1071	Überblick über den Rüstungsstand des Heeres (Munition), hrsg. vom Chef HRüst u. BdE, Stab II (Rüst), Bd 3: Dez. 1940, Febr.–Mai 1941
Rh 8/v. 1090 and 1091	Überblick über den Rüstungsstand des Heeres (Waffen und Gerät), Bd 3: Juni–Dezember 1941; Januar–März 1942
RH 8/v. 1130	Die Schwerpunktprogramme des Heeres: Panzerprogramm 41, Heeresflakprogramm (unter besonderer Berücksichtigung der Werkzeugmaschinenlage, Denkschrift des WaA), Mai 1941

Chef der Heeresrüstung und Befehlshaber des Ersatzheeres, Truppenteile [Chief of Army Armaments and Director-General of Training, Troop Formations]

RH 54/101	Inf.Pz.Abw.Ers.Kp. 27: Personalangelegenheiten (allg.), 1940

(*c*) *Kommandobehörden und Divisionen des Heeres, sonstige Heeresdienststellen* (*Verbindungsstäbe, Heeresmissionen etc.*) [Command agencies and divisions of the army: liaison staffs, army missions, etc.]

Heeresgruppe Süd [Army Group South]

RH 19 I/50	OKH-Befehle und -Lagemeldungen sowie Lagemeldungen der H.Gr. an OKH 1.–25.6.1940
RH 19 I/66	KTB Nr. 1, 2.2.–21.6.1941
RH 19 I/67, 67a,b, 68	Anlagen zum KTB Nr. 1, Operationsunterlagen, Bd 1: Januar–Mai 1941; Bd 2: 30.1.–6.5.1941; Bd 4: 4.6.–18.6.1941
RH 19 I/69	Anlagen zum KTB Nr. 1, Tagesmeldungen vom 22.4.–21.6.1941
RH 19 I/70	Anlagen zum KTB Nr. 1, Planspiel 'Otto', Februar 1941
RH 19 I/71, 72 to 74	KTB Nr. 2, Bd 1: 22.6.–15.7.1941; Bd 3 bis 5: 16.8.–31.10.1941
RH 19 I/75	Anlagen zum KTB Nr. 2, Operationsunterlagen, Bd 7: 20.10.–31.10.1941
RH 19 I/87 to 90	KTB Nr. 3 vom 1.11.1941–30.4.1942, Bd 1 bis 4: 1.11.1941–28.2.1942
RH 19 I/119 and 121	Ic, Lageberichte Ost, OKH/GenStdH/Fr.H.Ost, Bd 1: August 1940–Mai 1941; Bd 3: 15.7.–15.8.1941
RH 19 I/122 to 124	Ic, Truppenfeststellungen, Nachrichten über die Rote Armee, die wirtschaftliche und politische Lage in der Sowjetunion u.ä., Nov. 1939–Jan. 1941; Mai–17.6.1941; 19.6.–22.8.1941 (mit Karten und Skizzen)
RH 19 I/125	Ic, Feststellung russischer Truppen I, 1.4.–19.8.1941
RH 19 I/130 to 135	Luftaufklärungsmeldungen u. dgl., Bd 1 bis 7: 21.4.–18.10.1941
RH 19 I/136	Luftaufklärungsmeldungen Lfl 4 22.6.–12.7.1941
RH 19 I/161 17664/46	OQu, 'Fall Weiß'—Anlagen zur Aufmarschanweisung vom Juni 1939 Ic (Aug. 41)

Heeresgruppe Mitte [Army Group Centre]

RH 19 II/15	Anlagen zum KTB (Polenfeldzug), Feindnachrichten sowie Berichte über Zusammentreffen mit russischen Truppen 28.8.–7.10.1939
RH 19 II/119, 121 and 122	KTB Nr. 1, Bd 2: 1.–31.8.1941, Bd 5 u. 6: 31.10.–31.12.1941
RH 19 II/123 and 124	Anlagen zum KTB Nr. 1, Bd 1 und 2: (Aug.) 30.9.–3.11.1941

RH 19 II/125   Anlagen zum KTB Nr. 1: Tagebuch des Majors der N.K.W.D. Schabalin, Leiter der Besonderen Abteilung des N.K.W.D. bei der 50. Armee, 12.8.–19.10.1941

RH 19 II/126   Anlagen zum KTB Nr. 1, OKH Lageberichte Ost, . . . Einsatzmeldungen d. Luftflotte 2 . . . 1941

RH 19 II/127   Anlagen zum KTB Nr. 1, OKH Lageberichte Ost . . . Einsatzmeldungen VIII. Fliegerkorps usw. 30.11.–15.12.1941

RH 19 II/132   Anlagen zum KTB Nr. 1, Tagesmeldungen, Bd 5: 16.9.–7.10.1941

RH 19 II/334   OQu VII, Erfahrungsbericht der Militärverwaltung beim Ob.Kdo. d. H.Gr. Mitte 22.6.1941 bis August 1944

Heeresgruppe Nord [Army Group North]

RH 19 III/141   Ia, Anlagen zu den KTB 4 und 5, Umgliederung des Heeres im Westen, Neuverteilung der Heerestruppen und dergl., 26.6.–2.8.1940 (mit Karten)

RH 19 III/144   Ia, Anlagen zum TB, Gliederung des Heeresgruppenkommandos C, Bd 4: 21.2.–26.3.1941

RH 19 III/146 and 147   Anlagen zum TB, Organisationsangelegenheiten, Bd 1: (Jan. 1939–Juli 1940), 1.10.1940–20.2.1941; Bd 2: 18.7.–26.11.1940

RH 19 III/148   Anlagen zum TB, Zustandsberichte, 25.11.1940–20.3.1941

RH 19 III/149   Anlagen zum TB, Zustandsberichte und Reiseberichte, 10.11.1940–27.2.1941

RH 19 III/152   Anlagen zum TB, Ausbildungsangelegenheiten, 5.7.1940–23.5.1941

RH 19 III/153 and 154   Anlagen zum TB, Ausbildungsangelegenheiten, Schulung von GenSt.-Offizieren, insbes. für den Quartiermeister- und Ic-Dienst, Bd 1: Okt. 1940–Jan. 1941; Bd 2: Jan.–April 1941 (mit Karte und Skizze)

RH 19 III/167 and 168   Ia, KTB Nr. 3 und 4: 1.9.–31.10.1941

RH 19 III/171   Anlagen zum KTB Nr. 1-6, Operationen gegen die Baltischen Inseln—Planung 'Beowulf I' und 'Beowulf II', 29.4.–7.7.1941

RH 19 III/178 and 179, 181 and 182   Ia, KTB Nr. 7 u. 8: 1.1.–28.2.1942, Nr. 10 u. 11: 1.4.–31.5.1942

RH 19 III/271   Ia, KTB Nr. 32, 1.2.–29.2.1944, Bd 2: 15.2.–29.2.1944

RH 19 III/380 and 381   Ic, Lage Sowjetunion sowie Finnland, Lageberichte Fr.H.Ost, Bd 1 u. 2: Okt. 1939–Mai 1940

RH 19 III/388   Ic, Verschiedene Ic-Angelegenheiten, OKH-Erlasse, Einsatz der Sicherheitspolizei und des SD im Verbande des Heeres, u.ä., 1941, 1943

RH 19 III/458   Ic, Bd 1: 3.8.–24.8.1942

RH 19 III/483   Ic, Grundlegende Verfügungen von OKW und OKH betr. Propagandaführung u. dergl., Januar 1940–Oktober 1942

RH 19 III/492	Ic/AO, TB mit Anlagen, Anwerbung, Aufstellung, Betreuung u. dergl. von Verbänden aus Landeseinwohnern, August 1941–18.10.1943
RH 19 III/493	Ic/A.O., Span. Division, 14.11.1941–16.3.1944
RH 19 III/615	KTB Versorgungsbezirk Nord, Bd 1: 22.6.1941–31.1.1942
RH 19 III/661 D	Der Feldzug gegen die Sowjetunion. Operationsatlas der Heeresgruppe Nord für das Kriegsjahr 1941: Kartenband 22.4.–11.12.1941
RH 19 III/663	Operationsatlas der H.Gr. Nord, Der Feldzug gegen die Sowjetunion der H.Gr. Nord, Kriegsjahr 1942
RH 19 III/671 and 672 Teil 1, 676	Handakten des Oberbefehlshabers der H.Gr. Nord, Bd 4: 1.–12.8.1941 (mit Feindlageskizzen); Bd 5: 13.–25.8.1941; Bd 9: 7.–22.10.1941
RH 19 III/688	Ia, KTB März 1942
RH 19 III/707	Ia, KTB-Anlagen, Jan.–Sept. 1942
RH 19 III/722	Ic, Anlagen 6.2.–21.6.1941

2. *Armee* [Second Army]

RH 20-2/31 (41181/94)	Ia, Abwehr gegen Flieger mit sämtlichen Waffen, 1.10.1939–1.7.1943
RH 20-2/139	Ia, Persönliche Notizen Oberstlt. i.G. Feyerabend (Ia), 15.9.1939–5.11.1940
RH 20-2/164a	Anlagen zum KTB Teil 1, Bd 4: 11.–13.7.1941
RH 20-2/165b	Anlagen zum KTB Teil 1 (Operationsakten), Bd 7: 19.–20.7.1941
RH 20-2/168a to 181	Anlagen zum KTB Teil 1, Bd 11-29: 29.7.–18.9.1941
RH 20-2/208 to 218	Anlagen zum KTB (Rußland) Teil 2 (Operationsakten), Bd 1-11: 19.9.–17.10.1941
RH 20-2/1086	Ic/AO, TB vom 25.4.–20.6.1941
RH 20-2/1090 to 1094	Ic/AO, Anlagen zum KTB, 26.6.–17.11.1941
RH 20-2/1096	Ic/AO, Meldungen Rußland, 22.6.–8.7.1941
RH 20-2/1442	Anlagen zum KTB/OQu./Qu. 1, Tagesmeldungen an Gen.Qu. vom 22.6.–31.12.1941

4. *Armee* [Fourth Army]

RH 20-4/216 and 218	Anlagen A zum KTB Nr. 9, Bd 4: 24.9.–1.10.1941, Bd 6: 10.–19.10.1941
RH 20-4/228, 232, 234 to 236, 239	Anlagen B zum KTB Nr. 9 (Tagesmeldungen, Fernsprüche, Berichte und Tagesnotizen); Bd 2: 28.8.–2.9.1941; Bd 6: 27.9.–1.10.1941; Bd 8-10: 6.–14.10.1941; Bd 13: 23.–26.10.1941
RH 20-4/252	Armeebefehle 'T' Nr. 1 u. 2, Besondere Hinweise u.a. vom 20.9.–3.10.1941
RH 20-4/279	Ia, KTB Nr. 11, Teil 1 vom 3.1.–10.2.1942
RH 20-4/281 (III H/373/11)	Ia, KTB Nr. 11, 3.1.–10.2.1942
RH 20-4/285	Ia, Anl. z. KTB Nr. 11, Bd 3: 3.1.–31.3.1942

RH 20-4/287	Ic/AO, Anlagenband A zum KTB Nr. 11, Bd 3 und 4
(17380/4) and 288	
RH 20-4/296	Ia, Anl. A zum KTB Nr. 11, Bd 12, 28.–31.3.1942
RH 20-4/302	Ia, Anl. B zum KTB Nr. 11, Bd 6, 10.–18.2.1942
RH 20-4/671	TB der Abt. Ic, 25.5.–28.11.1941
RH 20-4/672	Ic-Meldungen an H.Gr. und AOK 4, Ia, 22.6.–1.10.1941
RH 20-4/682	Ic, Anlage 2 zum TB 22.6.–1.7.1941
RH 20-4/884	AOK 4, Anlagen zum KTB OQu. Bd 3, vom 8.–18.9.1941

6. Armee [Sixth Army]

RH 20-6/131	Fü.Abt., KTB Nr. 9, 30.9.–9.11.1941 (Zweitschrift)
(30155/23)	
RH 20-6/133	Fü.Abt., Anl. Bd 9 zum KTB Nr. 9
RH 20-6/490	Ic/AO, TB mit Anlagen, 16.7.–5.8.1941
(15623/2)	
15623/1	Anlagen zum TB, Ic, Rußland Fü.Abt., 21.6.–23.7.1941.
RH 20-6/493	Ic/AO, KTB-Anlagen vom 1.–25.10.1941
(15623/5)	

9. Armee [Ninth Army]

13904/4	OQu, KTB und TB (Rußland)
13904/3b	OQu, Notizen Oberstleutnant Windisch 9.10.1940–10.8.1941
13904/4 and 5	Meldungen an Gen.Qu. 23.6.1941–2.1.1942
14008/15	Anlagen zum KTB Nr. 3, Bd X: Beiträge der Armee, Chefsachen, 28.6.–14.10.1941
21520/1 (III H/374/4)	KTB, 1.1.–31.3.1942

11. Armee [Eleventh Army]

RH 20-11/4aK	Ia, Anlagen z. KTB 'Barbarossa' vom 28.5.–19.6.1941
RH 20-11/11	KTB Ia, Operationsakten, 21.4.–22.6.1941
RH 20-11/91	Anlagen zum KTB, Ic—sowie Ia-Lagemeldungen usw., Bd 55, 15.8.1941
RH 20-11/179	Anlagen zum KTB, Bd 143, 3.–4.12.1941
RH 20-11/271	Ia, Anlagen z. KTB Nr. 2, Bd 5, vom 9.–10.4.1942
RH 20-11/334	Ic/AO, Einsätze, Berichte, 15.6.–28.12.1941
RH 20-11/335	Ic/AO, Abwehr III, Anl. Bd 3, TB Abwehrtrupps V und VI, Einsätze—Berichte
RH 20-11/337	Ic/AO, Anlagenband 6 zum TB vom 11.4.1941–16.12.1942
RH 20-11/338	Ic/AO, Anlagenband 8 zum TB—Fallschirmspringer—Juli–Oktober 1941
RH 20-11/375	Anlagen zum KTB OQu. Nr. 1-3, Bes. Anordnungen f.d. Versorgung und die Versorgungstruppen, Bd 2, vom 26.8.–26.10.1941
RH 20-11/381	TB Abt. Qu 2 mit Anlagen, 23.6.–10.10.1941
RH 20-11/386	TB IVd/ev., 22.5.–31.10.1941, und TB III, 5.–31.10.1941
RH 20-11/415	Anlage M zum KTB Nr. 4 und 5, TB IV Wi, 24.10.1941–31.3.1942

RH 20-11/455   Ia, Anlagenband zum KTB vom 21.12.1941–10.1.1942
RH 20-11/456   Ia, Anlagenband zum KTB vom 12.–31.1.1942
RH 20-11/458   Ia, Anlagenband zum KTB vom 1.–21.3.1942
RH 20-11/485   Ic/AO, Anlagenband 2 zum TB vom Juni 1941–Januar 1943

14. Armee [Fourteenth Army]

P 200, d   Ic, Meldungen der Korps, 23.8.–7.10.1939

16. Armee [Sixteenth Army]

22745/7	Anlagen A zum KTB, Eingehende Befehle, 21.6.–21.12.1941
22745/10	Anlagen B zum KTB, Ausgehende Befehle, 21.6.–21.12.1941
22745/38	Ic, Nebenakte 8, Abendmeldungen der A.K., 10.8.–31.10.1941
22745/79 to 81	Anlagen zum KTB Nr. 5, Teil 3, O.Qu., Qu 1, Luftversorgung, 8.1.–1.4.1942
23468/3	Ia, KTB Nr. 5 (3. Teil), Bd II, 1.–28.2.1942
23468/5	Ia, Anlagen zum KTB, Eingehende Befehle
23468/6	KTB Nr. 5, Teil III, Anl. Bd BI, Ausgehende Befehle, 22.12.1941–28.2.1942
23468/8	Anlagen zum KTB, c. Führerbefehle
23468/11	KTB/Ia, Nr. 5, Teil III, Anl. Bd F, Eingehende Fernschreiben
23468/19	KTB Nr. 5, Teil III, Anlagen, Beurteilungen der Lage

17. Armee [Seventeenth Army]

14311/2	KTB OQu/Qu. 1, 15.5.–12.2.1941
14499/5	Ia, Anlage 2 zum KTB Nr. 1, 'Barbarossa', Operationsakten vom 4.5.–31.8.1941
14499/15	Abt.Ia, KTB Nr. 1 (Rußland), 15.4.–12.12.1941
14499/51	Fü.Abt. TB Ic/AO, Anlagen, Erlassene Befehle, Grundsätzlicher Schriftverkehr vom 16.3.–12.12.1941
14499/52	Ic/AO, KTB, Ic, Meldungen an H.Gr. 4.4.–10.9.1941

18. Armee [Eighteenth Army]

13767/20	OQu, KTB 8, Anl. Bd 11a, Ordnungsdienste, Allgemeines vom 3.6.–8.10.1941
17562/1	Ia, KTB vom 4.7.–31.12.1940
17562/2	Ia, KTB 3a, Chefsachen, vom 26.6.–17.12.1940
17562/3	Ia, KTB 3a, Befehle, Meldungen usw., vom 4.7.–20.12.1940
17562/8	Ia, KTB 3a, 3b, vom 5.8.–19.11.1940
17562/9	Ia, Akte Vorbereitungen 'Aufmarsch Ost', Bd II, 10.9.–3.10.1940
17562/17	Ia, KTB vom 1.1.–21.6.1941
17562/19	Ia, KTB 3b, Chefsachen, Bd 1, vom 14.2.–21.6.1941
17562/91, 111, 128, 134, 152, 159, 163, 207, 208, 233, 234	Tagesmappen (als Anlagen zum KTB Ia, 1941)
19601/2	Ia, KTB 3b, Besprechungen März–Juni 1941

| 36061/212 | Einsatzkarten (als Anlagen zum KTB Ia) 1.1.–31.3.1942 |
| 44911/4 | Erfahrungsberichte als Anlagen zum KTB Ia 1.4.–30.6.1942 |

20. Armee [Twentieth Army]

RH 20-20/124	Fr.H.Ost, Feindlagebeurteilungen 1941, Grenzschutz-verbände, 1940/41
RH 20-20/133 (25353/2)	AOK Norwegen-Befehlsstelle Finnland, Ic-Anlagen zum KTB Nr. 2, Juni–Dez. 1941
12564/1, 3, and 6	TB d.Abt. Ia, Ic, IIa für November 1940, Januar und April 1941
13386/1	TB Ia, Ic, IIa, Chefsache f.d. Monat Juni 1941
19070/1-14	KTB, 3.6.1941–13.1.1942 mit Anlagenbänden
20844/1-6	Anlagen zum KTB, Ia, Chef, 'Silberfuchs' und 'Renntier', 16.8.1941–10.1.1942
23861	KTB des finn. Batl. Ivalo, 22.6.1941–31.3.1942, Anlagenband 21 zum KTB Rußland 2 des Gen.Kdo. Geb.-Korps Norwegen
25353/1-8	Ic, Anlagen zum KTB Nr. I–VI, 14.6.–31.12.1941
35198/1-7	KTB, 3.6.1941–13.1.1942, mit Anlagen zum KTB
35641	Chefs., Ia, Allgemein, Bd 1, 21.9.1940–1.5.1942
58628/1	Vermischtes, 2.6.–31.12.1941 (Anl. 1 zu Geb. AOK 20, Ia Nr. 290/44 vom 21.7.1944)
58628/2	Vermischtes, 19.7.–21.11.1941 (Anl. 3 zu AOK 20, Ia Nr. 290/44 vom 21.7.1944)
75430	Ia, Anlageband Juni 1941–Dez. 1944
E 280/2	Gruppe XXI, Anlageband 2 zum KTB Nr. 4, 21.9.–31.10.1940

Panzergruppe 1/1. Panzerarmee [Armoured Group 1/First Armoured Army]

RH 21-2/55	Ia, KTB Nr. 6, Anlagen-Bd 1, 15.2.–4.6.1941
RH 21-1/327	KTB der O.Qu.Abt. vom 2.5.–31.10.1941
RH 21-1/332	Anlagenband A zum KTB

Panzergruppe 2/2. Panzerarmee [Armoured Group 2/Second Armoured Army]

RH 21-2/v. 100	Ia, KTB Akte Ausbildung 1941, vom 28.12.1940–5.6.1941
RH 21-2/v. 224 (III H 375/2)	KTB, 1.11.–5.12.1941
RH 21-2/v. 257	Ia, Anlagen zum KTB vom 25. und 26.11.1941
RH 21-2/v. 277 (III H 375/3)	Ia, KTB 6.–26.12.1941
RH 21-2/637	Ic, Anlagen zum TB, Bd 5: 22.6.–31.8.1941
RH 21-2/638	Ic, Anlagen zum TB, Bd 6: Nov. 1941–März 1942
RH 21-2/v. 819	KTB der O.Qu.-Abt. vom 21.6.1941–31.3.1942
RH 21-2/v. 876 and 877	KTB vom 6.12.1941–31.3.1942, Abschnitt b: Die Abwehrkämpfe im Raum nordostwärts Orel (27.12.1941–31.3.1942)
RH 21-2/v. 879	Anl.Bd. Nr. 17a zum KTB Nr. 1, Chefsachen vom 9.10.1941–20.1.1942

Panzergruppe 3/3. Panzerarmee [Armoured Group 3/Third Armoured Army]

RH 21-3/v. 138	Die Winterschlacht bei Rshew (21.1.–20.2.1942), Gefechtsbericht des 3. Pz.AOK—Abschrift
RH 21-3/423	Abt. Ic, TB Nr. 2 vom 1.1.–11.8.1941
RH 21-3/v. 430	Ic, Anlage D, Teil I zum TB Nr. 2, 22.6.–11.8.1941
RH 21-3/v. 612	OQu, KTB vom 1.1.–30.6.1942, Rußland

Panzergruppe 4/4. Panzerarmee [Armoured Group 4/Fourth Armoured Army]

RH 21-4/15 (18738/2)	Anlagen zum KTB Nr. 5, Bd 1: 22.6.–16.9.1941, Befehle von oben
RH 21-4/24 (18738/11)	Anlagen zum KTB Nr. 5, Bd 10: 19.6.–15.9.1941, Nachbarn, Koluft, Meldungen, Gefechts- und Verpflegungsstärken
RH 21-4/50 (III/H/376/3, 22457/35)	KTB, 'Rußlandfeldzug' III. Teil, 6.12.1941–9.1.1942
RH 21-4/265	Ic, Nachrichten über Rußland, Mai–Juni 1941
RH 21-4/270	Morgen- und Abendmeldungen, 22.6.–17.9.1941
RH 21-4/271	Ic, Abgegangene Meldungen, 1.7.–15.9.1941
RH 21-4/334	KTB 1 der Quartiermeisterabteilung, 22.4.–21.9.1941
RH 21-4/337 (22392/40)	Qu, 'Barbarossa' (Studie) I vom 18.3.–15.12.1941
RH 21-4/358	Versorgungsmeldungen, Anlage 5 zum KTB 1, 18.9.–30.11.1941
18738/1	Ia, KTB Nr. 5, Rußlandfeldzug, 22.6.–19.9.1941
22392/41	Qu, Durchführungsbestimmungen für die Versorgung 'Barbarossa', (Studie) II

Befehlshaber rückwärtiger Heeresgebiete [Commanders of Rear Army Areas]

RH 22/2	Befh. rückw. H.Geb.Süd, Ia, TB 13.3.–21.6.1941
RH 22/3	Befh. rückw. H.Geb.Süd, KTB Nr. 1, 22.6.–31.12.1941
RH 22/4 to 9	Befh. rückw. H.Geb.Süd, Ia, Anlagen 1 zum KTB Nr. 1, Bd 1 bis 6, vom 21.6.–20.11.1941
RH 22/12	Befh. rückw. H.Geb.Süd, Ia, Anlagen zum KTB Nr. 1, Bd 9, vom 3.4.–25.10.1941
RH 22/19	Befh. rückw. H.Geb.Süd, Anlage zum TB vom Januar 1942, H. 1
RH 22/23	Befh. rückw. H.Geb.Süd, Anlagen zum TB vom Februar 1942, H. 2
RH 22/27	Befh. rückw. H.Geb.Süd, Anlagen zum TB vom April 1942, H. 2
RH 22/32	Befh. rückw. H.Geb.Süd, Sammelakte, Anlagen Ia, Okt. 1941–Sept. 1943
RH 22/91	Befh. rückw. H.Geb.Süd, Anlagen zum KTB, Mappe VII (Angegliederte Stellen etc.), vom Juli 1941 bis Dezember 1942
RH 22/v. 132 (RH 22/111)	Befh. H.Geb.Süd/Ia, Anlagen zum KTB: Sondermappe 'Geheime Kommandosachen', Bd 2, Teil 2 (1943)

RH 22/148, 155, and 156 — Befh. rückw. H.Geb.Süd, Komm.Gen. der Sich.Tr.Süd, Ia, Anlagen zum KTB, Bd 41: 15.4.1941–21.11.1942, Bd 50: 18.4.1941–23.6.1942, Bd 51: 9.6.1942–23.4.1943

RH 22/170 and 171 — Befh. rückw. H.Geb.Süd, Ia/Ic, TB vom 21.6.–31.12.1941, mit Anlagen, Teil 2 und 3

RH 22/182 — Auszug aus dem Operationstagebuch der 105. Honvéd-Infanterie-Brigade, 23.10.1941–Mai 1942, mit Anlagen

RH 22/183 — Komm.Gen. der Sich.Tr. und Befh. im H.Geb.Süd/III; Justizangelegenheiten: Unterlagen und Bestimmungen über die Militärgerichtsbarkeit und das Disziplinarwesen gegen Soldaten und Kriegsgefangene, März 1941–Dezember 1943

RH 22/199 — Befh. rückw. H.Geb.Süd, TB der GFP-Gruppen, Jan.–Aug. 1942

RH 22/202 — Befh. rückw. H.Geb.Süd/Abt. VII (Mil. Verwaltung): Monatsberichte der FK 248, 249, 538, 607, 676, 753, 756, 774 sowie der 444. Sich.Div. zum Sachgebiet VII (Militärverwaltung), Oktober 1941–August 1942

RH 22/203 — Befh. rückw. H.Geb.Süd/Abt. VII (Mil. Verwaltung): Monatsberichte des Befh. rückw. H.Geb.Süd sowie der FK 194, 239, 248, 538 und 679 zum Sachgebiet VII (Militärverwaltung), Oktober 1941 bis August 1942

RH 22/204 — Befh. rückw. H.Geb.Süd/Abt. VII (Mil. Verwaltung): Monatsberichte der Sich.Div. 213 und 403 sowie der FK 197, 198, 503, 679, 754 und der Standortkommandantur Charkow, November 1941–August 1942

RH 22/224 and 225 — Befh. rückw. H.Geb. Mitte/Ia, Anlagen zum KTB, 21.3.–31.12.1941

RH 22/227 — Befh. rückw. H.Geb.Nord, Anlagen zum KTB, 10-Tagesmeldungen, Juli–Dezember 1941

RH 22/228 — Befh. rückw. H.Geb. Mitte, Anlagen zum KTB, Gefechts- und Verpflegungsstärken, Kriegsrangliste, Verlustliste, Ic-Tätigkeitsber. April–Dezember 1941

RH 22/230 and 231 — Befh. rückw. H.Geb. Mitte, Anlagen z. KTB Nr. 2, 1.1.–29.6.1942

RH 22/247 — Befh. rückw. H.Geb. Mitte/Qu, KTB Nr. 1, 15.5.–31.12.1941, mit Anlagen

RH 22/251 — Befh. rückw. H.Geb. Mitte/Leitender Kriegsgefangenen-Bezirkskommandant, Anlagen zum KTB Nr. 1, Juli 1941–März 1942

RH 22/253 — Befh. rückw. H.Geb. Nord/Ia, KTB Nr. 1, 22.6–31.12.1941 mit Anlagen vom 22.6.–7.8.1941

RH 22/255 — Befh. rückw. H.Geb. Nord, Anl. zum KTB Nr. 1, Sept. 1941–Januar 1942

RH 22/259 — Befh. rückw. H.Geb. Nord, Anlagen zum KTB, 1.1.–31.3.1942

RH 22/261 — Komm.Gen. der Sich.Tr. u. Befh. im H.Geb. Nord. Ia, KTB mit Anlagen 1.4.–30.6.1942

RH 22/271   Befh. rückw. H.Geb. Nord/Ic, Anlagen zum KTB Nr. 1, 21.3.–19.10. 1941

Kommandanten rückwärtiger Armeegebiete (*Korück*) [Commanders of Rear Army Areas]

RH 22/219   Korück 582, Anlagen zum KTB, 24.2.–13.12.1941

RH 22/227   Korück 582, Partisanentätigkeit im Gebiet Witebsk-Smolensk, 18.7.–6.11.1941

RH 22/228   Korück 582, Anlagen zum KTB, Einzelbefehle zum Einsatz in Rußland, 9.5.–31.12.1941

RH 22/234   Korück 582, Kommandanturbefehle, 30.4.–30.9.1941

RH 22/237   Korück 582, Anlagen zum KTB Nr. 4

RH 22/295   Korück 584, Anlagen zum KTB Nr. 2, 15.7.–24.12.1941

III. Panzerkorps [III Armoured Corps]

RH 24-3/51   Anl. zum KTB Nr. 6, Der Weg des III. Pz.K. vom 22.6.1941–21.11.1942 (Bericht)

RH 24-3/52   Ia, KTB Nr. 7 vom 24.7.–15.12.1941

RH 24-3/56 and 57   Ia, Anl. z. KTB Nr. 7, Bd 4 und 5: 6.10.–14.11.1941

RH 24-3/133   Ic, TB Nr. 1, 15.5.–15.12.1941

RH 24-3/134 to 136   Ic, Anlagen zum TB Nr. 1, Bd 1–3: 11.6.–12.12.1941

RH 24-3/218   Anlagen zum KTB vom 25.8.1939–1.7.1940. Militärverwaltung

IV. Armeekorps (*Gruppe v. Schwedler, Korps Mieth*) [IV Army Corps: Group von Schwedler, Corps Mieth]

RH 24-4/34   IV. A.K., Anlagen zum KTB Nr. 9: Anlagen vom 26.2.–21.6.1941 (Nr. 1-198; mit Karte und Planpausen)

RH 24-4/49 and 54   IV. A.K. (Gruppe v. Schwedler), KTB Nr. 12, Bd 2: 16.11.–12.12.1941; Nr. 13: 13.12.1941–31.1.1942

VIII. Armeekorps (*Gruppe Höhne*) [VIII Army Corps: Group Höhne]

RH 24-8/44   Anlagen zum KTB Nr. 1 vom 10.5.–30.6.1941 (Nr. 1-355)

X. Armeekorps [X Army Corps]

RH 24-10/116   Anlagen zum KTB Nr. 3, Meldungen von Divisionen u. anderen unterstellten Verbänden, Bd 2: 11.3.–25.4.1942 (Nr. 256-486)

XII. Armeekorps [XII Army Corps]

RH 24-12/13   Anlagen zum KTB, Bd I: 29.3.–1.9.1940

XIV. Armeekorps [XIV Army Corps]

RH 24-14/58 (16616/26)   Anlagen 1–206 zum KTB, H. 1, Spalte 5, 23.4.–27.8.1941

XIX. Armeekorps (*Gebirgskorps Norwegen*) [XIX Army Corps: Mountain Corps Norway]

RH 24-19/9 D (23450)   Ia, KTB, Nr. 1, Tagebuchberichte, 15.11.1940–15.3.1941

9269/3	KTB Nr. 2, 15.8.–3.12.1940
9269/4	Anlagen zum KTB Nr. 2, 14.8.–31.10.1940
15085/1–32	Ia, KTB Rußland I, 19.6.–31.12.1941, Textband mit Anlagenbänden 1–29
15085/33	Anlagenband 30 zum KTB I, Sondertätigkeitsbericht: Vorbereitung des Feldzuges gegen Rußland, 16.4.–19.6.1941
26373/1	Ia, Chefsache Bd I: 19.5.–23.12.1941
26373/2	Chefsache Ia 'Renntier', 29.8.1940–29.4.1941
76205	Erfahrungsbericht über den bisherigen Osteinsatz im Eismeergebiet, 12.12.1941

XXIX. Armeekorps [XXIX Army Corps]

| 15147/3 | Qu, KTB-Anl. vom 1.7.–30.9.1941 |
| 15192/7 | Ia, KTB-Anl. vom 20.9.–9.11.1941, Meldungen Rußland |

XXXVI. Armeekorps (Höheres Kommando XXXVI) [XXXVI Army Corps: Higher Command XXXVI]

22102/3 to 24	Ia, KTB Nr. 3, Textband, 'Einsatz in Nordfinnland' 9.5.–2.9.1941, mit Anlagebänden A–U
23305	KTB, Einsatz in Nordfinnland 3.9.–17.9.1941
24307/1 to 10	KTB Nr. 3 mit Anlagebänden und TB Ia, Ic, IIa, 18.9.–31.12.1941

XXXX. Armeekorps [XXXX Army Corps]

| 76043/4 | Ia, KTB-Anlagen, Sept. 1940 |

XXXXII. Armeekorps [XXXXII Army Corps]

| RH 24-42/12 | Anlagen zum KTB Ia, Nr. 3, Bd 7: 22.6–17.8.1941 |

LI. Armeekorps [LI Army Corps]

15290/1	Ia, KTB, 18.6.–17.8.1941
15290/23	Ic, TB, Mappe 1, 19.6.–31.7.1941
15290/26	TB der Abt. Ic, 19.9.–31.12.1941
15290/30	Abt. Qu, KTB Nr. 3, 19.6.–31.12.1941
E 432,2	Ia, Korpsbefehle vom 31.3.–17.12.1941

LII. Armeekorps [LII Army Corps]

| 16041/9 | Ia, Anl. z. KTB, H. 1 (operative Unterlagen), 10.5.–4.6.1941 |

LVI. Armeekorps [LVI Army Corps]

| 17956/32 | Abt. Ic, TB über das Absetzen vom Moskwa-Wolga-Kanal bis zum Übergang in die Verteidigung in der 'Königsberg-Linie', 1.12.1941–21.1.1942 |
| 17956/7a | Ia, Anlage: Kommandeur der Panzergruppe 4/Abt. Ia Nr. 20/41 g.Kdos. Chefs. vom 2.5.1941 (= LVI. A.K. 5/41 g.Kdos.) |

Finnisches III. Armeekorps [Finnish III Army Corps]

19654/1 and 2	KTB, 10.6.–31.12.1941 mit Anlagen
19654/3	KTB der finn. Div. 'I', 11.6.–31.12.1941
19654/4	KTB der 3. finn. Div. 20.6.–31.12.1941

7. Infanteriedivision [7th Infantry Division]

RH 26-7/19   Ia, Anlagenband 7 zum KTB Nr. 4 'Rußland', 17.11.1941–7.1.1942

22. Infanteriedivision [22nd Infantry Division]

RH 26-22/66   Anlage TB Ic, Bd I: 12.4.–11.12.1942

RH 26-22/67   Ic, Anlagenheft zum TB vom 16.6.–6.10.1941

24. Infanteriedivision [24th Infantry Division]

RH 26-24/72   Ic, Anlagen zum TB, Einsatz 'Ost', 22.6–Ende Sept. 1941

44. Infanteriedivision [44th Infantry Division]

RH 26-44/32   Ic, TB II, 21.6.–31.12.1941

45. Infanteriedivision [45th Infantry Division]

RH 26-45/16   Ia, KTB 1.4.–20.6.1941

50. Infanteriedivision [50th Infantry Division]

RH 26-50/85   Feldzug Rußland, TB Ic und Anlagen zum TB der Abt. Ic vom 16.6.–31.12.1941 zum KTB Nr. 5 der Fü.Abt.

52. Infanteriedivision [52nd Infantry Division]

RH 26-52/60   Ic, Anlagen zum TB, 20.6.–19.8.1941

RH 26-52/61   Ic, TB 20.8.–30.9.1941 mit Anlagen

97. leichte Infanteriedivision [97th Light Infantry Division]

18409/34   IIa, Tätigkeitsbericht

99. leichte Infanteriedivision [99th Light Infantry Division]

RH 26-99/7   Ia, Anlagenband Nr. 2b zum KTB, Führungsanordnungen vorges. Dienststellen vom 21.6.–23.9.1941

RH 26-99/16   Ia, Anlagenband Nr. 5 zum KTB, Gefechts- und Erfahrungsberichte vom 27.6.–29.9.1941

21400/17   Ia, Anlagenband 8 zum KTB, TB der Abt. Ic mit Anlagen vom 20.12.1940–1.10.1941

100. leichte Infanteriedivision [100th Light Infantry Division]

15684/21   Fü.Abt., KTB, 11.–21.11.1941

15684/32   Abt. IIa, TB Rußland, 22.6.–15.12.1941

16370   Fü.Abt., Übersichtsband, 22.6.–15.12.1941

44657/1   Ia, Sonderanlagenband zum KTB, 30.9.1941–4.8.1942

163. Infanteriedivision [163rd Infantry Division]

16260/16-24   Ia, KTB Nr. 3 mit Anlagebänden 1–7, 10.6.–31.12.1941

169. Infanteriedivision [169th Infantry Division]

17664/11 to 52   Anlagebände z. KTB Nr. 2 und TB Ic, 29.5.–31.12.1941

20291/1 and 2   KTB Nr. 2 Fü.Abt., T. 1 und 2: 1.6.–31.12.1941

20291/4 and 5   Ic, Tätigkeitsberichte, 25.6.1940–31.12.1941

221. Sicherungsdivision [221st Security Division]

RH 26-221/10	Ia, KTB Nr. 2, 6.5.–13.12.1941
RH 26-221/12 to 15	Ia, Anl. zum KTB, Bd Ib, Ic, Id, Ie, vom 20.6.–13.12.1941
RH 26-221/17, 18 and 19	Ia, Anlagen zum KTB Nr. 2, Bd 7: 30.7.–20.10.1941; Bd 8: 21.10.–13.12.1941; Bd 9: Tagesmeldungen, 6.5.–12.12.1941
RH 26-221/21 and 22	Ia, Anlagen zum KTB Nr. 2, Bd IVb: 7.7.–31.10.1941: Bd 4c: 4.10.–20.12.1941
RH 26-221/70	Ic, TB, 1.11.1940–14.12.1941

285. Sicherungsdivision [285th Security Division]

RH 26-285/4	Ia, KTB-Anlagen vom 22.4.–5.8.1941
RH 26-285/5	Ia, Erschießung von versprengten Rotarmisten, Anl. zum KTB 2, 7.8.–31.12.1941
RH 26-285/17	Ia, Anlagen z. KTB Nr. 1, TB Ic-d, IIa, 23.4.–31.12.1941

339. Infanteriedivision [339th Infantry Division]

13914/4	Ia, Anlage zum KTB Nr. 2, 26.8.–5.11.1941
13914/6	Ia, Anlagen zum KTB Nr. 3, 8.11.–18.12.1941

454. Sicherungsdivision [454th Security Division]

RH 26-454/6	Ia, KTB-Anlagen vom 12.5.–17.8.1941
RH 26-454/25	Qu-Abt., KTB Nr. 1, 15.5–31.12.1941
RH 26-454/28	Qu-Abt., Anlagenband 3 zum KTB Nr. 1, TB vom 1.9.–31.12.1941

707. Infanteriedivision [707th Infantry Division]

RH 26-707/v. 1, v. 1 D	[Monatsberichte November 1941–Mai 1942]

1. Panzerdivision [1st Armoured Division]

RH 27-1/48 to 51	Anlagen zum KTB Nr. 6, Bd XIX–XXII: Befehle, Meldungen (Durchbruch durch äußeren Ring Leningrad), 9.–18.9.1941

6. Panzerdivision [6th Armoured Division]

RH 27-6/30 to 40, 46	Anlagen zum KTB, Bd 8-18: 8.7.–18.9.1941, Bd 46: 1.–4.10.1941

7. Panzerdivision [7th Armoured Division]

RH 27-7/156 and 158	Abt. Ic, Anlagen zum TB, Bd I: 1.6.–7.8.1941; Bd III: 1.10.–28.11.1941

8. Panzerdivision [8th Armoured Division]

RH 27-8/18, 26 to 34, 37 to 39, 44 to 47	Anl. zum KTB (Pz.Gr.-, Korps- u. Divisionsbefehlee Berichte, Sprüche, Meldungen, Bd VII: 5.–6.7.1941; Bd XV–XXIII: 17.7.–19.8.1941; Bd XXVI–XXVIII: 28.8.–10.9.1941; Bd XXXIII–XXXVI: 2.–22.10.1941

11. Panzerdivision [11th Armoured Division]

RH 27-11/21	Anlagen zum KTB Nr. 2, Teil I, Bd V: Befehle, Meldungen, Sprüche, Übergang über die Desna, Angriff auf Spas-Demansk, 11.9.–2.10.1941

13. Panzerdivision [13th Armoured Division]

RH 27-13/2	Ia, Anlagen zum KTB Nr. 4, Bd I: Chefsachen, Geheimbefehle, 24.9.1940–10.5.1941
RH 27-13/11	Ia, Anlagen zum KTB Nr. 4: Paraden, gr. Übungen, Berichte, Besprechungen, 7.10.1940–20.4.1941
RH 27-13/111	Ia, KTB Nr. 5, TB Abt. Ic mit Anlagen 20.5.–15.12.1941

1. Gebirgsdivision [1st Mountain Division]

RH 28-1/v. 20	Ia, KTB Nr. 1, 19.4.–10.8.1941
RH 28-1/v. 128	Abt. Ic, Einsatz Rußland, Bd 1 zum TB (Anlagen), 22.6.–10.7.1941

2. Gebirgsdivision [2nd Mountain Division]

RH 28-2/v. 8	Abt. Ia, TB, 1.3.–18.6.1941
RH 28-2/v. 11	KTB Nr. 1-5, 19.6.–3.11.1941
RH 28-2/v. 16	Anlageheft zum KTB Nr. 1-3
RH 28-2/v. 17 and 18	Anlageheft zum KTB, 1.8.–3.11.1941
RH 28-2/v. 19	Gefechtsbericht zum KTB, 22.6.–31.10.1941
RH 28-2/v. 20	Lagekarten zum KTB, 22.6.–31.10.1941
RH 28-2/v. 21	KTB, 14.11.1941–10.1.1942
RH 28-2/v. 26	Anlageheft zum KTB, 4.11.1941–4.1.1942
RH 28-2/v. 29 K	Kartenmaterial zum KTB, 9.11.1941–31.5.1942
RH 28-2/v. 30	Gefechtsstärken zum KTB, 1.11.1941–1.6.1942
RH 28-2/v. 48 to 50	TB Ic, 18.6.–3.11.1941
RH 28-2/v. 51	Anlagen zum TB Ic, 2.6.–12.9.1941
RH 28-2/v. 52	Anlagen zum TB Ic, Mai–Okt. 1941
RH 28-2/v. 53	Sonst. Anlagen zum TB Ic, 16.6.–17.10.1941
RH 28-2/v. 54	Ic, Gefangenenvernehmungen, 30.6.–24.10.1941
RH 28-2/v. 55	4. TB Ic, 4.11.1941–2.4.1942
RH 28-2/v. 73 and 74	TB IIa, 18.6.1941–2.4.1942

3. Gebirgsdivision [3rd Mountain Division]

RH 28-3/v. 5 and 6	Abt. Ia, TB mit TB der Abt. Ic und IIa und KTB Nr. 4: 1.3.–31.12.1941
RH 28-3/v. 7	Ia, Anlagen zum KTB Nr. 4, Bd I, Meldungen an vorges. Dienststellen, 21.6.–30.12.1941
RH 28-3/v. 8	Ia, Anlagen zum KTB Nr. 4, Bd II, Befehle vorgesetzter Dienststellen, 19.6.–26.12.1941
RH 28-3/v. 9	Ia, Anlagen zum KTB Nr. 4, Bd III, Befehle an unterstellte Dienststellen, 19.6.–30.12.1941
RH 28-3/v. 10 to 16	Ia, Anlagen zum KTB Nr. 4, Bd IV, Teil 1-7, Meldungen unterstellter Truppenteile, 7.6.–17.11.1941

RH 28-3/v. 17 — Ia, Anlagen zum KTB Nr. 4, Bd V, Wintermarsch vom Eismeer z. Bottnischen Meerbusen, 15.10.–27.11.1941

RH 28-3/v. 18 — Ia, Anlagen zum KTB Nr. 4, Bd VI, Erfahrungsbericht über Osteinsatz, 19.6.–30.11.1941

RH 28-3/v. 23 to 26 — Ic, TB mit Anlagen, 19.6.–28.12.1941

RH 28-3/v. 32 — IIa, TB, 21.6.–21.12.1941

1. Kavalleriedivision [1st Cavalry Division]

RH 29-1/5 — Ia, Anlagen zum KTB, Bd I, Befehle, Meldungen, Gliederung, Kriegsrangliste, Gefechts- u. Verpflegungsstärken und TB der Abt. Ic und IIa, 1.4.–23.7.1941

Deutsche Heeresmission in Rumänien [German Army Mission in Romania]

RH 31-I/v. 15 — Ia, Akte 'W'; Weisungen für Sicherung und Verteidigung der Grenzen Rumäniens gegen Rußland vom 10.6.1941, mit Karten

RH 31-I/v. 16 — Ia, Akte Aufmarsch 'R', 16.11.1940–15.3.1941

RH 31-I/v. 23 — Ia, Anlagen zum KTB 'Marita', 8.12.1940–5.4.1941

RH 31-I/v. 24, 26, 29 — KTB-Anlagen, Bd I: 17.9.–15.11.1940; Bd III: 1.1.–15.2.1941; Bd VI: 2.5.–3.6.1941

RH 31-I/v. 39 — Ia, Akte 'München', 12.6.–4.7.1941

RH 31-I/v. 40 — Ia, Akte 'Barbarossa', 25.2.–20.6.1941

RH 31-I/v. 41 — Sonderakte 'Barbarossa', 30.5.–21.6.1941

RH 31-I/v. 93 and 94 — Chefsachen, Bd I u. II, 1941–1942

RH 31-I/v. 98 — Aufbau und Einsatz des rumänischen Heeres seit Bestehen der DHM. Gliederung und Zustand des Heeres, 1942

Deutscher Bevollmächtigter General in Kroatien [German General with Full Powers in Croatia]

RH 31-III/1 — Deutscher Bevollmächtigter General in Agram, April–Dezember 1941

Deutsche Heeresmission in der Slowakei [German Army Mission in Slovakia]

RH 31-IV/v. 15 — Anlagenband II zum KTB, 18.7.–8.8.1941

Bevollmächtigter General der Deutschen Wehrmacht in Ungarn [German General with Full Powers in Hungary]

RH 31-V/1 — Der Deutsche General beim Oberkommando der Kgl. ungarischen Wehrmacht, KTB, 30.3.–29.7.1941

Deutscher General beim ital. AOK 8 [German General with the Italian Eighth Army Command]

RH 31-IX/22 — Gliederungen IV, 2.9.1942–2.2.1943

Militärbefehlshaber [Military Commanders]

RH 53-23/49 — Mil.Befh. im Generalgouvernement, KTB des Ausbildungsstabes 22.8.1941–31.3.1942

RH 53-23/v. 95   Mil.Befh. im Generalgouvernement, Anlage vom 17.9.1941.–11.1.1944

(d) Der Reichsminister der Luftfahrt und Oberbefehlshaber der Luftwaffe (R.d.L. u. Ob.d.L.) [The Reich Minister of Aviation and Commander-in-Chief of the Luftwaffe]

R.d.L. u. Ob.d.L./Generalstab der Luftwaffe [Luftwaffe General Staff]

RL 2/v.3058a   8. (Kriegsw.) Abt., Teil 1: KTB-Unterlagen vom 19.5.1943–9.4.1945

RL 2 I/1   Generalstab der Luftwaffe—Chef des Generalstabes, Vorbereitung Einsatz aller Fronten, 10.1.1941

R.d.L. u. Ob.d.L./Generalstab d. Lw/Luftwaffenführungsstab [Luftwaffe General Staff/ Luftwaffe Operations Staff]

RL 2 II/21   1. Abt.; Luftwaffe (Flakartillerie, Fliegertruppe); Luftverteidigung Reich (Organisatorische Maßnahmen): Luftverteidigung von Groß-Berlin; Luftschutz: Luftwarndienst Groß-Berlin (Befehle, Stellungnahmen, Vorschläge), 1940–1942

RL 2 II/89   1. Abt.; Luftwaffe (Fliegertruppe: Kommandobehörden); Organisation: Aufstellung Stab Fliegerführer Ostsee

RL 2 II/106   1. Abt., Verschiedene Sachgebiete der Lw. (Sammelakte mit Befehlen, Meldungen, Berichten, Stellungnahmen, Vorschlägen), 1941–1942

RL 2 II/214–269   Luftwaffenführungsstab, 5. Abt., Einsatz alle Fronten, tgl. Lageberichte, 15.9.1940–9.11.1941

RL 2 II/446 (RL 2   Luftwaffenführungsstab, 5. Abt., Luftlage in Europa,
II/v. 535)   Frühjahr 1939

R.d.L. u. Ob.d.L./Generalstab d. Lw/Generalquartiermeister [Luftwaffe General Staff/ Quartermaster-General]

RL 2 III/702, 707,   6. Abt., Pers. u. mat. Einsatzbereitschaft, flieg. Verbände,
708, 713 to 717   8.6.–23.9.1939, 4.5.–29.6.1940, 6.7.–7.9.1940, 7.6.–21.2.1942

R.d.L. u. Ob.d.L./Generalstab d. Lw/8. Abteilung [Luftwaffe General Staff, 8th Department]

RL 2 IV/33   Luftkrieg gegen England, Aug. 1940–Juni 1941

RL 2 IV/34   Studie: Einsatz der Luftwaffe bei der Besetzung der Baltischen Inseln 1941

RL 2 IV/42   Studie: Auswirkungen u. Folgen d. unmittelbaren Heeresunterstützung, 1943

RL 2 IV/170 (RL 2   Die luftstrategische Lage in Mitteleuropa 1944
II/v. 3163)

R.d.L. u. Ob.d.L./Generalluftzeugmeister [Inspector-General of Air Force Equipment]

RL 3/34	Wortberichte der Entwicklungskonferenzen des R.L.M., 3.7.–12.12.1942
RL 3/51	Versch. Berichte u. Korrespondenzen, Juni 1937–Dez. 1944
RL 3/60 and 61	Konferenzen mit Göring, 8.1.1942–8.10.1943 und 27.6.–5.11.1943
RL 3/63	Kurzberichte von Treffen und Konferenzen mit Göring, versch. Korrespondenzen, 1936–1943
RL 3/192	Taktische Forderungen 1930–1937
RL 3/352	Beschaffung, allg. 1941
RL 3/859	Organisatorische Angelegenheiten
RL 3/864	'Göring-Programm', Steigerung d. Flugzeugfertigung ab Sommer 1941
RL 3/865	Planungen 1942–1944
RL 3/887	Beschaffungsprogramme für Luftfahrtgeräte bis 1944 vom 5.6.1941
RL 3/990	C-Amts-Programme
RL 3/991	C-Amts-Programme, LP 18/3, 1.11.1940
RL 3/993	C-Amts-Programme, LP 19/1, 1.2.1941
RL 3/994	C-Amts-Programm 19/2, März–Juli 1941
RL 3/1010	Lieferplan gemäß 'Elch'-Programm
RL 3/1015	Flugzeugbeschaffungsprogramme, C-Amts-Programme Nr. 18 u. 19, 1940–1941
RL 3/1016	LC 2/IA, Ausbringungskurven nach LP 19, 1. Entwurf, 20.11.1940
RL 3/1086	Industrie-Vorplanung (Denkschrift) bis 1.4.1945
RL 3/1104	Programmentwicklung Me 110 u. 210, Denkschrift, 5.2.1942
RL 3/1411	Programmentwürfe, Planungen 1941–1943
RL 3/1833	Luftrüstungsvergleich Deutschland/Italien–Großbritannien/USA, Stand 1.7.1941
RL 3/2102	Techn. Amt: Aufstellungs- u. Ausrüstungsunterlagen 1940/41
RL 3/2142	Nachschub, Zahlenmaterial, 12.10.1939–1942
RL 3/2245	Bericht Industriebesichtigungsreise vom 28.3.–17.4.1941 in Rußland

R.d.L. u. Ob.d.L./Luftwaffeninspektionen, -inspekteure, Waffengenerale [Luftwaffe Inspectorates and Inspectors, Armament Generals]

RL 4 II/77	General der Luftwaffe beim Oberbefehlshaber des Heeres u. Befh. der Heeresfliegerverbände, Anlage 1 zur Planstudie 1939, H. 1

Truppenführungsstäbe der Lw [Luftwaffe Ground Forces Operations Staffs]

RL 7/8	Lfl. 1, Einsatz Feldzug gegen Rußland, 1.1.–31.12.1942
RL 7/11	Organisation der Lfl. 1, 1940
RL 7/12	Organisation Lfl. 1, Feldzug gegen Rußland, 1941

RL 7/16	Lfl. 1, Nachschub, Kraftfahrwesen, Feldzug gegen Rußland, 31.3.–4.7.1941
RL 7/466	Lfl.Kdo 4, Einsatz Rußland—Südabschnitt (Weisungen für die Fortführung der Operationen 'Barbarossa', Fü.Abt. Ia op), 1941
RL 7/467 to 470	Lfl.Kdo 4, Einsatz Rußland—Südabschnitt (Befehle zur Kampfführung, Absichten, Auszüge aus Abendmeldungen, Einsatzmeldungen—Sammelbände Verb.Stab Lfl. 4, Oberst Bassenge), Bd 1-4: 22.8–Nov. 1941
RL 7/471	Lfl.Kdo 4, Einsatz Rußland—Südabschnitt, Juni–Oktober 1941, Feindnachrichtenblätter Lfl.Kdo 4, Fü.Abt. Ic
RL 7/472 to 474	Lfl.Kdo 4, Einsatz Rußland—Südabschnitt, Feindlage, Eigene Lage: Luftlage, Erdlage, Seelage (Feindnachrichtenblätter Lfl.Kdo 4 Fü.Abt.Ic), Bd 1-3, Nr. 60-134, vom 17.8.–30.10.1941
RL 7/479	Lfl.Kdo 4, Einsatz der rum. Lw, Rußland—Südabschnitt; Zusammenarbeit rum. Lw dt. Lw, Juni–August 1941
RL 7/577	Luftwaffenbefehlshaber Mitte, Reichsluftverteidigung 1941

Truppenführungsstäbe Fliegertruppe [Operations Staffs Flying Forces]

RL 8/26	IV.Fl.K., Vorbereitung u. Einsatz, Feldzug gegen Rußland, Juni 1941
RL 8/27 and 28	IV.Fl.K., Einsatz Rußland—Südabschnitt.—Aufklärungsergebnisse, Bd 1: Juni 1941; Bd 2: Sept.–Dez. 1941
RL 8/31 and 32	IV.Fl.K., Auswertung Einsatz Rußland—Südabschnitt Feind- und eigene Lage (Lageberichte Ic), Bd 1 u. 2, 22.2.–29.10.1941
RL 8/33 and 34	IV.Fl.K., Einsatz Rußland—Südabschnitt—Einsatz, Dislozierung der fliegenden Verbände, Bd 1 u. 2, Sept. u. Okt. 1941
RL 8/35	IV.Fl.K., Einsatz Rußland—Südabschnitt, 21.8.–20.10.1941
RL 8/37	IV.Fl.K., Nachrichten über fremde Streitkräfte Ost u. West, 1941
RL 8/47	VIII.Fl.K., Einsatz Rußland—Mittelabschnitt, 19.6.–2.8.1941, tägl. Aufzeichnungen etc.
RL 8/48	VIII.Fl.K., Einsatz Rußland—Nordabschnitt—Tätigkeit bei der Unterstützung des Durchbruchs des I.A.K. bis zur Eisenbahnlinie Leningrad-Breslau vom 10.4.–21.8. 1941
RL 8/49	VIII.Fl.K., Einsatz Rußland—Mittelabschnitt, Unterstützung der Verbände der Pz.Gr. 3, dann H.Gr. Mitte, während der deutschen Herbstoffensive 1941 und der russischen Winteroffensive 1941/42 (Zusammenstellung des Kampfverlaufes in Tagebuchform durch H.W. Deichmann, Oberst a.D., damaliger Adjutant des VIII.Fl.K., an Hand von Aufzeichnungen, Umfragen und des Tagebuches des Gen.Feldm. Dr. Ing. Frhr. v. Richthofen—Maschinenschrift), 28.9.1941–12.4.1942

RL 8/50   VIII.Fl.K., Einsatz Rußland—Mittel- u. Südabschnitt—Menschenführung: Anerkennung der Leistung der Truppe, 1941, 1942

RL 8/239   VIII.Fl.K., Einsatz Unternehmen Kreta, 1.5.–4.6.1941

Komm. General der Luftwaffe in befreundeten und besetzten Gebieten [GOC in Friendly and Occupied Territories]

RL 9/39 (RL9/91)   Komm.Gen.d.dt. Lw in Rumänien, Organisation der rum. Luftwaffe, Januar 1942

RL 9/53   Komm.Gen.d.dt.Lw. in Rumänien; Einsatz im Feldzug gegen Rußland; Vorbereitung des Aufmarsches 'Barbarossa'

RL 9/54   Komm.Gen.d.dt.Lw. in Rumänien; Tätigkeit der DLM in Rumänien; verschiedene Sachgebiete, Juni–Okt. 1941

RL 9/62   Komm.d.dt.Lw. in Rumänien, Luftverteidigung, Ölgebiet Rumänien, Dez. 1941

RL 9/85   Komm.Gen.d.dt.Lw. in Rumänien; Dienstbetrieb; Unterrichtung der Kommandeure über die allgemeine Lage und Lage Rumäniens, Dez. 1940–Juni 1941

Verbände der Fliegertruppe [Air Formations]

RL 10/476 and 477   JG 54, Einsatz im Feldzug gegen Rußland, 22.6.1941–30.4.1942

Luftwaffenverbindungsstäbe zum Heer [Luftwaffe Liaison Staff with Army]

RL 18/9   Kommandeure der Luftwaffe bei Kommandobehörden des Heeres, Koluft Pz.Gr. 4, Ic-Angel. Fliegertruppe, UdSSR

Kommandos Flughafenbereiche [Air Field Area Commands]

RL 20/48 and 51   Kdo. Flughafenbereich 2/I Jesau, Anlagen zum KTB, 1941 und April–Dezember 1941

RL 20/69   Kdo. Flughafenbereich 3/I Neuhausen, KTB Nr. 2, 7.6.1941–20.3.1942

RL 20/272   Kdo. Flughafenbereich 4/II Siedlce, KTB 2 mit Anlagen, März 1941–Februar 1942

RL 20/281 and 282   Kdo. Flughafenbereich 1/VIII Breslau, Zamosc, Reichshof, Lemberg, Einsatz Osten, Anl. 1 zu KTB 3 u. 4, Febr. 1941–Mai 1943, u. Anl. 2 zu den KTB 5–7, Sept. 1941–Mai 1942

Luftwaffen-Akten, Verschiedenes [Luftwaffe Documents, Various]

RL 200/17   General Hoffmann v. Waldau, Persönl. Tagebuch, auszugsweise Abschrift

(e) Oberkommando der Kriegsmarine (OKM) [High Command of the Navy]

OKM/Oberbefehlshaber der Kriegsmarine (ObdM) [Commander-in-Chief of the Navy]

RL 6/66   Handmaterial ObdM, Rußland, 3.9.1938–29.7.1940

Case 527 (PG 32601)   ObdM, Handakte 'Barbarossa', Bd I: Januar 1941–Januar 1942

RM 6/139   Gen.d.Lw. b. ObdM, KTB Nr. 19, Nov. 1941

OKM/Stab/Marineattachés [Staff/Naval Attachés]

PG 48779-784   Marine-Attaché Helsingfors, KTB, Bd 2, 1.4.1941–30.6.1942

OKM/Seekriegsleitung (Skl) [Naval War Staff]

PG 32087c   Mar.Verb.Offz. der Skl. zum ObdH/GenStdH, Chefsachen, 1.1.–30.6.1941

RM 7/812 to 814   Kampfanweisungen für die Kriegsmarine (Ausgabe Mai 1939), 3 Bde

RM 7/985 (PG 31025)   'Barbarossa', Weisungen des OKW und Zeittafel, Bd I, vom 11.12.1940–20.6.1941

Case 599 (PG 33687)   Völkerrecht, Handhabung der Neutralität: Finnland, Januar 1939–Dezember 1940

OKM/Seekriegsleitung/Operationsabteilung (1. Skl) [Naval War Staff/Operations Department]

RM 7/14 to 16   1. Skl, KTB, Teil A, Bd 11–13, 1.7.–30.9.1940

RM 7/22, 23, 25 (III M 1000/20 to 22)   1. Skl, KTB, Teil A, Bd 19–22, 1.3.–30.6.1941

RM 7/29   1. Skl, KTB, Teil A, Bd 26, 1.–31.10.1941

RM 7/46 and 47   1. Skl, KTB, Teil A, Bd 43, 1.3.–30.4.1943

RM 7/159   1. Skl, KTB, Teil C III (Ostsee), Bd 1, Sept. 1939–Dez. 1942

RM 7/170   1. Skl, KTB, Teil C V, Luftkrieg, Bd 2, 4.1.–22.12.1941

RM 7/395   1. Skl, OKW/Wehrkraft der Wehrmacht im Frühjahr 1942

RM 7/521 and 522   1. Skl, KTB, Teil D 3, Fernschreib- und Funkspruchsammlung, Bd 39 u. 40, vom 9.–23.9.1941

RM 7/771 and 772   1. Skl, KTB, Teil D 8g, Lage Kriegsmarine für GenStdH/Fr.H.Ost, Bd 4 u. 5, 3.9.–31.12.1941

Case GE 958 (PG 32957)   1. Skl II-2, Gedankenaustausch Führungsstab, Bd 1, Mai–Dez. 1941

Case GE968 to 972 (PG 32968 to 32972)   1. Skl IL, Kriegsakte Skl-GenStdLw/GendLwbObdM, Anfragen, Ersuchen, Weisungen Befehle, H. 6–10; OKt. 1940–April 1941

OKM/Seekriegsleitung/Kriegswissenschaftliche Abteilung der Marine [Naval War Staff/Naval Strategy Department]

RM 8/K 10-2/10   Betrachtungen über Rußland 1940

OKM/Marinegruppenkommando Nord [Naval Group North Command]

M/127/34835   KTB 1.6.–31.7.1941

OKM/Admiral Südost (später Marinegruppenkommando Süd in Sofia) [Admiral South-east-(later Naval Group Command South in Sofia)]

RM 35 III/5   KTB (Bd 5), 1.–15.6.1941, mit Stellungnahme 1. Skl zur Frage der Erstellung von Siebelfähren

OKM/*Deutsche Marinemission in Rumänien* [German Naval Mission in Romania]

RM 45/v.	KTB, 1.5.–15.6.1941
M/698/45605	

(*f*) *Waffen-SS* [Armed SS]

RS 3-5/1 to 4	5. SS-Div. 'Wiking', Aufstellungsunterlagen und diverse Meldungen
RS 3-5/8	5. SS-Div. 'Wiking', ungeordneter Aktenbestand
RS 3-6/2	6. SS-Geb.Div. Nord, Ia, KTB Nr. 1, Teil 1 u. 2, 8.6.–31.12.1941
RS 3-6/3 to 9	6. SS-Geb.Div. Nord, Anlagenband 1-6 z. KTB Nr. 1
RS 3-6/23 D	6. SS-Geb.Div. Nord, Anlagenband 1 z. KTB Nr. 1, Abt. Ib, 18.3.–20.9.1941
RS 3-6/24	6. SS-Geb. Div. Nord, Anlagenband 2 z. KTB Nr. 1, Abt. Ib, 1.4.–31.12.1941
RS 3-11/5	Finn. Freiwilligen-Bataillon der Waffen-SS, KTB Nr. 1 und 2 (1941–1943)
RS 3-11/6	Finn. Freiwilligen-Bataillon der Waffen-SS, KTB Nr. 2 (1942–1943)

(*g*) *Bestand Nachlässe* [Posthumous Papers]

N 22/9 and 13	Nachlaß Gen.Feldm. Fedor v. Bock, Tagebuchnotizen Osten I (22.6.1941–5.1.1942), u. Osten II (16.1.–15.7.1942)
N 63/53	Nachlaß Gen. Oberst Zeitzler
N 67/1	Nachlaß Hans Felber, Kriegserinnerungen. Handschriftliche Tagebuchaufzeichnungen des Generals der Infanterie Hans Felber v. 1.1.1939–12.5.1945 sowie vom 2.10.–24.12.1941: Militärische Ereignisse
N 67/2	Kriegserinnerungen. Handschriftliche Tagebuchaufzeichnungen des Generals der Infanterie Hans Felber über die Ereignisse vom 16.4.1939–3.9.1940: Vorbereitung der Einsätze im Polenfeldzug 1939 und Westfeldzug 1940
N 122/9	Nachlaß Oskar Ritter v. Niedermayer, Publizistische Tätigkeit: Ausarbeitungen, November 1939–März 1941
N 220/42	Nachlaß Gen. Oberst Halder, Das persönliche Kriegs-Tagebuch des Generalobersten Franz Halder, Chef des Generalstabes des Heeres (OKH), Bd IV
N 257/1	Nachlaß General Erfurth, Pers. Tagebuch 'Im Hauptquartier Mannerheims', Bd 1, 12.6.1941–1.1.1942
N 300/2	Nachlaß Generaloberst v. Falkenhorst, H. 2: Prozeßnotizen und Zeugenaussagen
N 300/4	Nachlaß Generaloberst v. Falkenhorst, 'Kriegserinnerungen 1939–1945'

(*h*) *Militärgeschichtliche Sammlungen* (*MSg*) [Military History Collections]

MSg 2/2558	Stellungnahme von Wilhelm Schubert betr. Dokumentation über WiStabOst 1941/42, vom 20. Juli 1965
MSg 149/11	Sammlung Vladimir Pozdnjakoff (Vlasov-Bewegung), Verschiedene Artikel Pozdnjakovs und anderer. Korrespondenz Pozdnjakov-Köstring (Druckschriften, Zeitungsausschnitte und Briefe)
MSg 149/14	Sammlung Vladimir Pozdnjakoff, Brief des Generalmajors Meandrov, Jan. 1946
MSg 149/46	Sammlung Vladimir Pozdnjakoff, Tagebuch des Gen.Maj. Borodin
MSg 149/48	Sammlung Vladimir Pozdnjakoff, A.A. Vlasov
MSg 149/52	Sammlung Vladimir Pozdnjakoff, Generale der ROA

(*i*) *Bestand 'Historical Division'* [Collection 'Historical Division']

Historical Division/Materialsammlung der Studiengruppe Geschichte des Luftkrieges (*Lw*) [Documents of the Study Group for Air War History]

Lw 101/3 Teil 2	Organisation, Aufbau, 30.8.1993: Organisation der Lw
Lw 103/5	Technik, Rüstungsberichte
Lw 103/25	Technik, Organisation der Luftrüstung
Lw 103/84	Technik, Flugzeugproduktion 1942
Lw 106/5	Einsatz, Planstudien
Lw 106/6	Einsatz, Tabellen des Ob.d.L., Verteilung der Verbände, 27.10.1940–20.12.1941
Lw 106/9	Einsatz, Leistungstabellen (Flugzeuge)
Lw 106/13	Einsatz, Strategisch-operativer Luftkrieg
Lw 107/67	Feldzüge, Einsatzvorbereitungen Osten
Lw 107/68	Feldzüge, Osten 1941–1945
Lw 107/74	Feldzüge, Osten 1941–1943
Lw 107/78	Feldzüge, Osten 1941–1943
Lw 107/79	Feldzüge, Einsatz 1941
Lw 107/80	Feldzüge, Einsatz 1941, Luftflotte 1 u. 2
Lw 107/81	Feldzüge, Einsatz 1941, Luftflotte 4 u. 5
Lw 107/82	Feldzüge, Einsatz 1941, Korpsbefehle II. Flakkorps
Lw 107/84	Feldzüge, Rußland 1941
Lw 107/85	Feldzüge, II. Flakkorps, Lagebericht Ostfront, 1941–42
Lw 107/170	Feldzüge, Luftkrieg 1939–1945, Beurteilung der Lage
Lw 108/16	Deutsche Unterlagen, Berichte und Studien (2)
Lw 112/6	Einsatz, Mittelmeer
Lw 118/5	Ouellen 1941 (3): Bericht über den Einsatz des I. Fliegerkorps, 22.6.–1.11.1941 (o. Verf.)
Lw 127/1	Versch. Ausarbeitungen, ohne Gesamttitel
Lw 133/1	Heeresunterstützung durch die Luftwaffe (1) III
Lw 135	Ic-Dienst; Geheimdienst

(*j*) *Bestand 'Alliierte Prozesse'* [Collection 'Allied Trials']

Alliierte Prozesse 9, NOKW-Material

(*k*) *Bestand 'Dt. Dienststellen zur Vorbereitung der Europäischen*
Verteidigungsgemeinschaft' [Collection 'German Agencies for the Preparation
of the European Defence Community']

Bw 9/138	Dipl.Ing. Erich Schneider, Gen.Lt. a.D.: Einige Erfahrungen des Heereswaffenamtes mit der Industrie, besonders in der Entwicklung und Prüfung von Waffen, Munition und Gerät, vom 25.6.1952

3. Führungsakademie der Bundeswehr
[Leadership Academy of the Bundeswehr]

Luftwaffenarchiv

4. Archiv des Instituts für Zeitgeschichte, München [Archive
of the Institut für Zeitgeschichte, Munich]

ED 2	Kriegswirtschaft im Operationsgebiet des Ostens in den Jahren 1941–1943; Beitrag zur Geschichte des Wirtschafts-Stabes-Ost (WiStab Ost). Nach Unterlagen der Fachgruppen bearbeitet von Generalmajor Hans Nagel (1944). 2 Bde
ED 83/2	Tagebuch Josef Goebbels
ED 84	Hammerstein, Christian Frhr. v.: Mein Leben (Privatdruck ohne Ort und Datum)
ED 100	Tagebuch Walther Hewel
Fd 600/1	Heeresgruppe Mitte, Kriegstagebuch Nr. 1 (Bd Dezember 1941)
MA 321	Mikrofilm: Pers.Stab Reichsführer SS, Schriftgutverwaltung
ZS 97	Briefe Gen.Major a.D. v. Loßberg an W. E. Paulus

5. Militärgeschichtliches Forschungsamt, Potsdam
[Research Institute for Military History, Potsdam]

(*a*) *Unveröffentlichte Manuskripte und Studien* [Unpublished Manuscripts
and Essays]

A-83	Brauchitsch, Bernd v., Oberst i.G. a.D., Aufgabe und Stellung der Luftwaffe im Rahmen der Gesamt-kriegsführung. Angefertigt Juli 1945. Mit Stellungnahme des

	letzten Generalstabschefs der Luftwaffe, General der Flieger Koller
Lw 4/1–24	Plocher, Hermann, Generalleutnant a.D., Der Krieg im Osten
Lw 10	Deichmann, Paul, General der Flieger a.D., Die Unterstützung des Heeres durch die deutsche Luftwaffe im Zweiten Weltkrieg
Lw 11b	Grabmann, Walter, Generalmajor a.D., Geschichte der deutschen Luftverteidigung 1933–1945
Lw 15	Kreipe, Werner, und Oberst a.D. Köster, Die fliegerische Ausbildung in der deutschen Luftwaffe. Überarbeitet und zusammengestellt von Karl Gundelach
Lw 17	Nielsen, Andreas, Generalleutnant a.D., Nachrichtenbeschaffung und Auswertung für die deutsche Luftwaffenführung
Lw 21/3	Suchenwirth, Richard, Hermann Göring, der Oberbefehlshaber der deutschen Luftwaffe
Lw 21/4	Suchenwirth, Richard, Der Staatssekretär Milch. Lebenslauf und Werdegang
Lw 21/5	Suchenwirth, Richard, Hans Jeschonnek. Ein Versuch über Wesen, Wirken und Schicksal des vierten Generalstabschefs der deutschen Luftwaffe
Lw 21/6	Suchenwirth, Richard, Ernst Udet. Generalluftzeugmeister der deutschen Luftwaffe 1939–1941
Lw 22/1	Schwabedissen, Walter, Generalleutnant a.D., Die russische Luftwaffe mit den Augen deutscher Kommandeure gesehen
Lw 25	Schwabedissen, Walter, Generalleutnant a.D., Mehrfrontenkrieg. Probleme der deutschen Luftwaffe während des Zweiten Weltkrieges
Lw 35	Suchenwirth, Richard, Historische Wendepunkte im Kriegseinsatz der deutschen Luftwaffe
P-030	Müller-Hillebrand, Burkhart, Die Improvisierung einer Operation
P-31a, Bd 26, Teil I	Speidel, Wilhelm, General der Flieger a.D., Gedanken über den deutschen Generalstab, Landsberg am Lech, 20.1.1949
P-108/II	Müller-Hillebrand, Burkhart, Generalmajor a.D., Die militärische Zusammenarbeit Deutschlands und seiner Verbündeten während des Zweiten Weltkrieges, Bd II
P-114a	Müller-Hillebrand, Burkhart, Der Feldzug gegen die Sowjetunion im Nordabschnitt der Ostfront 1941–1945. I. Teil: Die Offensive des Jahres 1941 bis zum Ladoga-See, mit Anhängen A–H; II. Teil: Das Ringen um die Behauptung des gewonnenen Raumes (Dezember 1941–Dezember 1942)
P-114b	Hofmann, Rudolf, Der Feldzug gegen die Sowjetunion im Mittelabschnitt der Ostfront. Teil I: Vorbereitungszeit vor Beginn der Operation; Teil II: Die Offensive bis zum Festlaufen vor Moskau

P-114c   Hauck, Friedrich Wilhelm, Die Operationen der deutschen Heeresgruppen an der Ostfront 1941–1945. Südliches Gebiet. I. Teil: Die deutsche Offensive bis zur Mius-Donets-Stellung. 22. Juni bis November 1941; II. Teil: Die Abwehrkämpfe am Donets und auf der Krim und das Wiedergewinnen der Initiative. Dezember 1941 bis Juni 1942

P-190, T. 2   Hofmann, R. und A. Toppe, Verbrauchs- und Verschleißsätze während der Operationen der deutschen Heeresgruppe Mitte vom 22.6.1941–31.12.1941

P-210   Generalfeldmarschall v. Bock, Tagebuchnotizen (Abschrift). Bd 1: Zum Polen-Feldzug, Mai/Juni 1939–3.10.1939; Westen, Vorbereitungszeit, 8.10.1939–9.5.1940; Westen, Offensive und Besatzungszeit, 10.5.–11.9.1940. Bd 2: Osten, 20.9.1940–22.6.1941, Vorbereitungszeit; Osten I, 22.6.1941–5.1.1942

T-6b   Heusinger, Adolf, und Gotthard Heinrici, Der Feldzug in Rußland. Überblick über die Jahre 1941/42

T-8-1   Vorbereitungen und Grundlagen der Heeresversorgung für den Ostfeldzug seitens des OKH/GenQu.

T-8-2   Fähndrich, Ernst, Aufgaben und Arbeit der Außenstellen des OKH/GenQu. während der Aufmarschvorbereitungen im Osten im Frühjahr 1941 und beim Antreten zum Angriff

T-8-4   Fähndrich, Ernst, Der Aufbau des Versorgungsbezirks Dnjepr als Vorschwingen der Versorgungsbasis der Heeres-Gruppe Mitte nach Erreichen des Dnjepr für den weiteren Vormarsch auf Moskau (Juli bis Oktober 1941)

T-8-5   Braun, Der Leitstab Mitte. Das vorübergehende Einstellen der Angriffsoperationen im Winter 1941/42 an der Ostfront

T-8-6   Die Versorgungsführung während des Vormarsches in Rußland bis zum Winter 1941

T-8-11   Die Versorgung der 167. Infanterie-Division beim Vormarsch durch Rußland

T-8-13   Die Vorbereitungen der Versorgung der 68. Infanterie-Division im Frühjahr und Sommer 1941 und die Versorgung in Rußland vom 22.6.1941–1.2.1942

T-8-26   Die Steuerung der Bahntransporte vom OKH zu den Heerestruppen

T-8-27   Die Bedeutung der Eisenbahnen als Nachschubträger bei weitreichenden Operationen, dargestellt am Feldzug der 17. Armee in der Ukraine 1941

T-17   Brennecke, Kurt, u.a., Die Operationen der Heeresgruppe Nord vor Leningrad 1941

(b) *Befragungen* [Interviews]

Befragungsprotokoll Oberst a.D. v. Below vom 25.7.1973

Befragung General a.D. Kammhuber vom 30.10.1968

Befragung Oberst i.G. a.D. Wodarg vom 31.3.1972
Befragungsprotokoll Oberst i.G. a.D. Wolter vom 6.6.1972

(c) *Sonstiges* [Other]

Sammlung Grabmann R 849: Die Leistungen der deutschen Frontflugzeuge am 1.9.1939 und am 1.9.44 (Gegenüberstellung). Zusammengestellt aus Unterlagen des Chefs TLR von der 8. Abt./ChefdGenStdLw. 1944

Bieneck, Helmuth, General der Flieger a.D.: Geschichte der Luftgaukommandos II, Posen, im zweiten Weltkrieg. Handschriftliche Ausarbeitung, o.D. (Nachkriegsausarbeitung vor Oktober 1967)

Darnóy, Pal: Organisation der königlich ungarischen Honved-Armee 1941–1944 (M 2/1–2 und Anhänge)

Harten, Direktor Dip.Ing.: Vortrag vor den Rüstungskommandeuren vom Januar 1943 über 'Leistungssteigerung in der Luftwaffenfertigung'. Geheim! Nr. 185 Industrierat des Reichsmarschalls für die Fertigung von Luftwaffengerät.

Milch, Erhard, Generalfeldmarschall: Erinnerungen. Nürnberg 1947. Masch.Ms. (Abschrift)

6. National Archives, Washington

T 311, Roll 53 KTB der H.Gr.Nord (22.6.–31.10.1941)

7. Politisches Archiv des Auswärtigen Amtes, Bonn [Political Archive of the German Foreign Ministry, Bonn]

Dienststelle Ribbentrop
Akten betr. UdSSR

Büro Reichsaußenminister (*RAM*) [Reich Foreign Minister's Cabinet]

Büro RAM Akten betr. Kroatien

Büro Staatssekretär (*St.S.*) [State Secretary's Office]

Akten betr. Bulgarien, Bd 5
Akten betr. Dänemark, Bd 2
Akten betr. Finnland, Bde 2–4
Akten betr. Frankreich, Bd 9
Akten betr. Jugoslawien, Bd 2
Akten betr. Kroatien, Bd 1
Akten betr. Norwegen, Nr. 12/65
Akten betr. Rumänien, Bd 7
Akten betr. Rußland, Bde 2 und 5

Akten betr. Schweden, Bde 2–4
Akten betr. Slowakei, Bd 1 und 2
Akten betr. Ungarn, Bde 1–5

Büro Unterstaatssekretär (U.St.S) [Under-Secretary of State's Office]

Rußland I (29): Organisation, Personalfragen und Rußlandkomitee 1941
Rußland, Bd 42
Stromkommission (Oktober bis Dezember 1936); Militärmission in Rumänien
   (September 1940–Januar 1941); Bled (Februar–Juli 1939)

Politische Abteilung (Pol.Abt.) [Political Department]

Pol.Abt. XII Nr. 12: Der geplante Verlauf [der deutschen Ostgrenze]
Pol.Abt. XIII Nr. 6: Die Agrarordnung in den Ostgebieten Aug. 1941–April 1942
Pol.Abt. XIII Nr. 17: Allgemeine Akten betr. Lage in den besetzten Ostgebieten,
   Januar–Februar 1942
Pol.Abt. XIII Nr. 25: Berichte der VAA bei den AOK

Deutsche Botschaften und Gesandtschaften sowie Konsulate [German
Embassies, Legations, and Consulates]

Deutsche Botschaft Rom, 2281, Geheimakten
Deutsche Gesandtschaft Bukarest, Akten politisch geheim
Deutsche Gesandtschaft Helsinki, Berichte Nr. 1-250 von 1941 (6/1) und Nr. 251-500
   von 1941 (6/2); Drahtberichte Nr. 1-200 von 1941 (7/2 und 7/5); Erlasse Nr. 501-813
   von 1940 (1/4); Akten betr. Schriftwechsel geheim, Bde 1–4
Deutscher Konsul Ploesti, 1/5

Handelspolitische Abteilung (Ha.Pol.) [Trade Policy Department]

Handakten Wiehl, Rußland, Bd 13; Schweden, Bd 6
IV a: Handel 13, Ungarn
Va, Ostgebiete, Wirtschaft 6: Beteiligung des Auslandes am wirtschaftlichen Aufbau
   der besetzten Gebiete
VI: Schweden, Wirtschaft, 6/2: Großraumwirtschaft (Nr. 23/4) 1941–1943
Rumänien, betr. Kriegsgerät, Bd 4

Handakten Ritter [Personal File Ritter]

Betr. deutsche Kriegswirtschaft
Betr. Rumänien 1940–1941 (Nr. 26)
Betr. Rußland (Nr. 29)
Betr. Dienststelle Gesandter Altenburg und Freiwillige (Nr. 55)
Betr. OKW 1941–1944 (Nr. 56)

Handakten Etzdorf [Personal File Etzdorf]

Akten betr. Frankreich, Bd 2
Akten betr. Nordeuropa
Akten betr. Rußland 1940–1942
Vertrauliche Aufzeichnungen des Vertreters des Auswärtigen Amts beim OKH, Nr.
  1-3

Handakten, Vertreter des AA beim Reichskommissar Ukraine [Personal Files, Foreign Ministry Representative with the Reich Commissioner Ukraine]

Runderlasse Wirtschaft

Nachlaß Renthe-Fink [Posthumous Papers Renthe-Fink]

Nachlaß Renthe-Fink, Nr. 2/6: 1.4.1940–3.9.1942

Abteilung Inland II geheim [Department Inland II, secret]

Akten betr. Waffen SS, Werbeaktion und Einberufung Volksdeutscher: Dänemark,
  Nr. 298–300; Finnland, Nr. 303; Kroatien, Nr. 305; Schweden, Nr. 321; Nr. 366:
  Berichte und Meldungen zur Lage in und über Frankreich.
Akten betr. geheime Reichssachen (Bd 17a)

8. Public Record Office, London

Premier 3: Prime Minister's Private Office, Operational Papers

Premier 3/170/1 Finland, 1941 Sep–Dec.
Premier 3/170/4 Finland, 1941 July-1943 Dec., Various

War Cabinet, Chiefs of Staff Committee

Cab 79/1 Minutes of Meetings, September 1939

Foreign Office Documents

Vol. 24844 (1940)

9. Salzgitter A.G. Konzern-Archiv [Salzgitter AG, Firm's Archives]

14/9/2 Berichte des Hauptabwehrbeauftragten

10. Staatsarchiv Nürnberg [State Archive Nuremberg]

Bestand Kriegsverbrecher-Anklage Dokumente (Collection Indictment of War Criminals)

Ps-1456 Aktennotizen Chef WiRüAmt
NI-7474 Sitzungen des Generalrats
NID-13844 Der Vierjahresplan. Vortrag vor der Verwaltungsakademie Berlin am 29. April 1941, gehalten von St.S. Neumann

11. Privatbesitz [Privately Owned]

Campus, Eliza: Anglo-Rumanian Relations 1913–1919. Referat auf der britisch-rumänischen Historikertagung im Mai 1978 in London; unveröff. Manuskript (Privatbesitz Förster)
Herwarth v. Bittenfeld, Hans: Russian Volunteers in the German Army, 22 S., ungedruckt. Manuskript (Privatbesitz Hoffmann)
Hewel, Walther, Botschafter: Tagebuch 1941 (eingesehene Photokopie aus Privatbesitz Irving)
Pintér, István: Oppositionelle und illegale Propaganda der Linken in Ungarn während des zweiten Weltkrieges. Referat auf der internationalen Tagung über 'Die Kriegspropaganda und die illegale Presse in Südosteuropa während des zweiten Weltkrieges' (Budapest, 1978), unveröff. Manuskript (Privatbesitz Förster)
Richthofen, Generalfeldmarschall Dr. Ing. Wolfram Frhr. v.: Persönliches Tagebuch (Privatbesitz Gundelach, Freiburg)
Tóth, Sándor: Kriegspropaganda und Erziehung in der Ungarischen Armee 1941–1944. Referat auf der internationalen Tagung über 'Die Kriegspropaganda und die illegale Presse in Südosteuropa während des zweiten Weltkrieges' (Budapest, 1978); unveröff. Manuskript (Privatbesitz Förster)

II. SERVICE REGULATIONS

1. Heeresdruckvorschriften (H.Dv.) [Army Regulations]

H.Dv. 3/1 I. Militärstrafgesetzbuch (MStGB) vom 10.10.1940; II. Kriegssonderstrafrechtsverordnung (KSSVO) vom 17.8.1939
H.Dv. 3/13 I. Verordnung über das Sonderstrafrecht im Kriege und bei besonderem Einsatz (Kriegsstrafrechtsverordnung—KSSVO) mit den Änderungen und Ergänzungen der 1. und 2. Ergänzungsverordnung vom 1.1.1938 und 27.2.1940 und der Verordnung zur Änderung vom 10.10.1940; II. Verordnung über das Strafverfahren im Kriege und bei besonderem Einsatz (Kriegsstrafverfahrensordnung, KStVO) mit den Anordnungen und Ergänzungen der 2.–7. Durchführungsverordnung 1938; Nachdruck mit eingearbeiteten Deckblättern 1–18 und sonstigen Berichtigungen 1942

H.Dv. g. 11 a/2 Erfahrungen aus dem Ostfeldzug für die Versorgungsführung 1943 (OKH/GenStdH/GenQu/Abt. I/Qu 2 Nr. I/17591/42)

H.Dv. 38/2 Vorschriften für das Kriegsgefangenenwesen: I. Abkommen über die Behandlung der Kriegsgefangenen vom 27.7.1929, Berlin 1940

H.Dv. g. 89 OKH/Chef GenStdH, Entwurf der Vorschrift 'Feindnachrichtendienst' (F.N.D.) Berlin 1941

H.Dv. g. 90 Versorgung des Feldheeres, OKH/GenStdH/GenQu, 1938

H.Dv. g. 92 OKH/Chef GenStdH, Handbuch für den Generalstabsdienst im Kriege, Berlin 1939

H.Dv. g. 150 Dienstvorschrift für die Geheime Feldpolizei vom 24.7.1939

H.Dv. 231/I Kriegsvölkerrecht, Sammlung zwischenstaatlicher Abkommen für die höhere Führung, 1939

H.Dv. 231/II Völkerrecht, Sammlung zwischenstaatlicher Abkommen für die höhere Führung, 1939

2. Marinedruckvorschriften (M.Dv.) [Naval Regulations]

M.Dv. Nr. 601 Operationen und Taktik. Auswertung wichtiger Ereignisse des Seekrieges, H. 12: Der Ostseekrieg gegen Rußland im Jahr 1941, OKM (Kriegswiss. Abt.), Berlin, Januar 1944

3. Merkblätter und Druckvorschriften der Abt. Fremde Heere Ost/GenStdH sowie sonstige Druckschriften [Memoranda and Regulations of Department Foreign Armies East/Army General Staff, and Other Pamphlets]

Merkblatt 19/1 OKH/GenStdH/OQu IV/Abt. Fremde Heere Ost, Taschenbuch Russisches Heer

Merkblatt 19/2 OKH/GenStdH/OQu IV/Abt. Fremde Heere Ost, Merkblatt über die Eigenarten der russischen Kriegführung, 1941

Merkblatt 19/9 OKH/GenStdH/OQu IV/Abt. Fremde Heere Ost, Vorläufige Felddienstordnung der Roten Arbeiter- und Bauernarmee (RKKA) 1936, Übersetzung Berlin 1937

OKH/GenStdH/OQu IV/Abt. Fremde Heere Ost, Die Landesbefestigungen der Union der Sozialistischen Sowjetrepubliken (UdSSR), Stand: 15.3.1941, Teil I, III

OKH/OQu IV/Abt. Fremde Heere Ost, Die Landesbefestigungen der UdSSR, Stand: 6. und 22.6.1941

OKH/GenStdH/OQu IV/Abt. Fremde Heere Ost, Die Kriegswehrmacht der Union der Sozialistischen Sowjetrepubliken (UdSSR), Stand: 1.1.1941, Teil I und II

OKH/GenStdH/OQu IV/Abt. Fremde Heere Ost, Die Kriegswehrmacht der Union der Sozialistischen Sowjetrepubliken (UdSSR), Stand: Dezember 1941, Teil I, II

OKH/GenStdH/Abt. für Kriegskarten und Vermessungswesen (IV.Mil.Geo.). Erster Entwurf zu einer militärgeographischen Beschreibung über das europäische Rußland, abgeschlossen am 10. August 1940, Berlin 1940

III. PUBLISHED SOURCES

ABSALJAMOV, M., and ANDRIANOV, V., 'Organizacija partizanskich sil i formy rukovodstva ich boevoj dejatel'nost'ju v Otečestvennoj vojne' [Organization of partisan forces and forms of direction of their combat activity in the Fatherland War], *VIŽ* 1966, No. 9, pp. 18–26.

—— 'Taktika sovetskich partizan' [The tactics of Soviet partisans], *VIŽ* 1968, No. 1, pp. 42–55.

—— 'Durchbruchs-Operation der Baltischen Rotbanner-Flotte von Reval auf Kronstadt', *MR* 64 (1967), 26–45.

AČKASOV, V. I., 'Operacija po proryvu Krasnoznamennogo Baltijskogo flota iz Tallina v Kronštadt' [Breakthrough operations of the Red Banner Baltic Fleet from Tallinn to Kronshtadt], *VIŽ* 1966, No. 10, pp. 19–31.

—— 'Protivodesantnaja oborona ostrovov Moonzundskogo archipelaga v 1941 godu' [Defence of the Muhu archipelago islands against a landing in 1941], *VIŽ* 1969, No. 5, pp. 28–39.

—— and PAVLOVIČ, N. B., *Soviet Naval Operations in the Great Patriotic War, 1941–1945* (Annapolis, Md., 1981).

ADAP: see *Akten zur deutschen auswärtigen Politik.*

Agriculture and Food-supply in the Second World War. Landwirtschaft und Versorgung im Zweiten Weltkrieg, ed. Bernd Martin and Alan S. Milward (Ostfildern, 1985).

Akademija imeni Frunze: Istorija voennoj ordena Lenina, Krasnoznamennoj, ordena Suvorova akademii [The Frunze Academy: History of the Military Academy decorated with the Order of Lenin, the Red Banner, and the Suvorov Order] (Moscow, 1973).

ÅKERRÉN, BENGT, 'Schweden als Schutzmacht', in *Schwedische und schweizerische Neutralität* (q.v.), 111–19.

Akten zur deutschen auswärtigen Politik 1918–1945, Series B: *1925–1933* (Göttingen, 1966–78); Series C, *1933–1937* (Göttingen: 1971–5); Series D (i–xiii): *1937–1945* (Baden-Baden, 1951–7); Series E (i–viii): *1941–1945* (Göttingen, Baden-Baden, and Frankfurt a.M., 1969–79). [For trans. see *Documents on German Foreign Policy*, but note that Series E does not exist in trans.]

ALLARD, SVEN, *Stalin und Hitler: Die sowjetrussische Außenpolitik 1930–1941* (Berne and Munich, 1974).

Allianz Hitler-Horthy-Mussolini: Dokumente zur ungarischen Außenpolitik, 1933–1944, ed. M. Adam (Budapest, 1966).

Anatomie der Aggression: Neue Dokumente zu den Kriegszielen des faschistischen deutschen Imperialismus im zweiten Weltkrieg, ed. with intro. by Gerhart Hass and Wolfgang Schumann (Berlin, 1972).

Anatomie des Krieges: Neue Dokumente über die Rolle des deutschen Monopolkapitals bei der Vorbereitung und Durchführung des zweiten Weltkrieges, ed. with intro. by Dietrich Eichholtz and Wolfgang Schumann (Berlin, 1969).

Anatomie des SS-Staates, ed. Hans Buchheim [*et al.*], 2 vols. (Olten and Freiburg, 1965) [sections by Hoffmann, Klink]; (Munich, 1967) [section by Förster].

ANDENÆS, JOHANNES, RISTE, OLAV, and SKODVIN, MAGNE, *Norway and the Second World War* (Oslo, 1966).

'Andere Deutschland' im Zweiten Weltkrieg, Das: Emigration und Widerstand in

internationaler Perspektive, ed. Lothar Kettenacker (Veröffentlichungen des Deutschen Historischen Instituts London, 2; Stuttgart, 1977).

ANDERSSON, INGVAR, *Schwedische Geschichte: Von den Anfängen bis zur Gegenwart* (Munich, 1950).

ANDREEN, PER G., *Finland i Brännpunkten: Mars 1940–Juni 1941* (Stockholm, 1980).

ANDREEV, G., and BOBKOV, N., 'O znakach različija v Krasnoj Armii, 1918–1943' [Badges of rank in the Red Army, 1918–1943], *VIŽ* 1968, No. 2, pp. 108–14.

Anfänge der Ära Seeckt, Die Militär und Innenpolitik 1920–1922, ed. Heinz Hürten (Quellen zur Geschichte des Parlamentarismus und der politischen Parteien, 2nd ser.: Militär und Politik, 3; Düsseldorf, 1979).

ANFILOV, V. A., *Načalo Velikoj Otečestvennoj vojny, 22 ijunja–seredina ijulja 1941 goda: Voenno istoričeskij o čerk* [The beginning of the Great Fatherland War, 22 June–mid-July 1941: A military-history survey] (Moscow, 1962).

ANISIMOV, N., 'Komandarm 18-j A. K. Smirnov' [GOC Eighteenth Army A. K. Smirnov], *VIŽ* 1968, No. 8, pp. 115–17.

ANTONOV, B. I., 'Der Marsch nach Polen im September 1939, von sowjetischer Seite aus gesehen', in *Die Rote Armee* (q.v.), 80–5.

Archiv der Gegenwart, vols. 9–12 (Vienna, 1939–42).

ARENZ, WILHELM, 'Die deutschen Luftangriffe auf Moskau 1941: Einleitung zu Oberst N. Svjetlišin, "Die Abwehr des ersten massierten Angriffs der deutsch-faschistischen Luftwaffe auf Moskau" ', *WWR* 20 (1970), 98–110.

ARUŠANJAN, B., 'Boevye dejstvija 12-j armii v načal'nyj period vojny' [Operations of Twelfth Army in the initial period of the war], *VIŽ* 1973, No. 6, pp. 60–5.

ARUTJUNJAN, Ju. V., *Sovetskoe krest'janstvo v gody Velikoj Otečestvennoj vojny* [Soviet peasantry during the years of the Great Fatherland War] (Moscow, 1963).

ASENDORF, MANFRED, 'Ulrich von Hassells Europakonzeption und der Mittel-europäische Wirtschaftstag', *Jahrbuch des Instituts für Deutsche Geschichte der Universität Tel-Aviv*, 7 (1978), 387–419.

ASSMANN, KURT, *Deutsche Schicksalsjahre: Historische Bilder aus dem Zweiten Weltkrieg und seiner Vorgeschichte* (Wiesbaden, 1950).

AUER, VÄINÖ, JUTIKKALA, EINO, and VILKUNA, KUSTAA, *Finnlands Lebensraum: Das geographische und geschichtliche Finnland* (Helsinki, 1941).

Auf antisowjetischem Kriegskurs: Studien zur militärischen Vorbereitung des deutschen Imperialismus auf die Aggression gegen die UdSSR, 1933–1941 (Berlin, 1970).

BACHARACH, WALTER ZWI, 'Die Ideologie des deutschen Rassenantisemitismus und seine praktischen Folgerungen', *Jahrbuch des Instituts für Deutsche Geschichte der Universität Tel-Aviv*, 4 (1975), 369–86.

BACKE, HERBERT, *Die russische Getreidewirtschaft als Grundlage der Land- und Volkswirtschaft Russlands* (Berlin, 1941).

BAGRAMJAN, I. CH., *Tak načinalas' vojna* [Thus began the war] (Moscow, 1971).

—— 'Èto bylo pod El'com' [This was near Yelets], *VIŽ* 1970, No. 3, pp. 53–62; No. 4, pp. 59–67.

BAGRAMJAN, I. CH., 'Geroičeskaja oborona stolicy Sovetskoj Ukrainy: K 20-letiju osvoboždenija Kieva' [The heroic defence of the capital of the Soviet Ukraine On the 20th anniversary of the liberation of Kiev], *VIŽ* 1963, No. 10, pp. 53–66.

—— 'Razgrom 1-j tankovoj armii generala Klejsta' [The smashing of Gen. Kleist's First Armoured Army], *VIŽ* 1969, No. 11, pp. 60–9; No. 12, pp. 65–75.

BAILEY, THOMAS A., and RYAN, PAUL B., *Hitler vs. Roosevelt: The Undeclared Naval War* (New York and London, 1979).

BALFOUR, MICHAEL, *Propaganda in War 1939–1945: Organization, Policies and Publics in Britain and Germany* (London, 1979).

BANSE, EWALD, *Wehrwissenschaft: Einführung in eine neue nationale Wissenschaft* (Leipzig, 1933).

Barbarossa: The Axis and the Allies, ed. John Erickson and David Qilks (Edinburgh, 1994).

BARKER, ELISABETH, *British Policy in South-east Europe in the Second World War* (London, 1976).

BARTOV, OMER, *The Eastern Front, 1941–1945: German Troops and the Barbarization of Warfare* (Basingstoke and London, 1985).

BASSIN, ALEXANDRE, 'Les Juifs en Finlande pendant la deuxième guerre mondiale', *Le Monde juif*, 28/68 (1972), 43–7.

BAUMBACH, WERNER, *Zu spät? Aufstieg und Untergang der deutschen Luftwaffe* (Munich, 1949). [Trans. Frederick Holt, *Broken Swastika, The Defeat of the Luftwaffe* (London, 1960).]

BAUMGART, WINFRIED, *Deutsche Ostpolitik 1918: Von Brest-Litowsk bis zum Ende des Ersten Weltkrieges* (Munich and Vienna, 1966).

—— 'General Groener und die deutsche Besatzungspolitik in der Ukraine 1918', *Geschichte in Wissenschaft und Unterricht*, 21 (1970), 325–40.

BECKMANN, ODA, 'Katyn: Moskaus Kampf gegen die historische Wahrheit. Die Verschleierung eines Kriegsverbrechens', *Beiträge zur Konfliktforschung*, 10/4 (1980), 137–63.

Befreiungsmission der Sowjetstreitkräfte im zweiten Weltkrieg, Die, ed. A. Grečko (Berlin, 1973).

BEKKER, CAJUS, *Angriffshöhe 4000: Ein Kriegstagebuch der deutschen Luftwaffe* (Oldenburg and Hamburg, 1964).

BELIKOV, A. M., 'Tjaželuju promyšlenost '—v glubokij tyl' [Heavy industry into the deep hinterland], in *Ešelony idut na vostok: Iz istorii perebazirovanija proizvoditel'nych sil SSSR v 1941–1942 gg.* [Trains are moving east: From the history of the transfer of the productive potential of the USSR during the years 1941–1942] (Moscow, 1966), 31–53.

—— 'Gosudarstvennyj Komitet Oborony i problemy sozdanija složennoj voennoj ėkonomiki' [The State Defence Committee and the problems connected with the creation of a well-organized war economy], in *Sovetskij tyl* (q.v.), i. 70–9.

BELOUSOV, M. A., *Ob ètom ne soobščalos' Zapiski armejskogo čekista* [This was not reported . . . Notes of an Army Cheka man] (Moscow, 1978).

BELOW, NICOLAUS VON, *Als Hitlers Adjutant 1937–45* (Mainz, 1980).

BENZ, WIGBERT, *Der Rußlandfeldzug des Dritten Reiches: Ursachen, Ziele, Wirkungen. Zur Bewältigung eines Völkermordes unter Berücksichtigung des Geschichtsunterrichts*[2] (Frankfurt a.M., 1988).

—— 'Präventiver Völkermord? Zur Kontroverse um den Charakter des deutschen Vernichtungskrieges gegen die Sowjetunion', *Blätter für deutsche und internationale Politik*, 33 (1988), 1215–27.

BENZ, WOLFGANG, 'Judenvernichtung aus Notwehr? Die Legenden um Theodore N. Kaufmann', *VfZG* 29 (1981), 615–30.

BERCHIN, I. B., *Voennaja reforma v SSSR, 1924–1925 gg.* [Military reform in the USSR

1924–1925] (Moscow, 1958).

BEREŠKOV (Bereshkow), VALENTIN MICHAJLOVIČ, *In diplomatischer Mission bei Hitler in Berlin 1940–1941* (Frankfurt a.M., 1967).

—— *Jahre im diplomatischen Dienst* (Berlin, 1975).

Berichte des Oberkommandos der Wehrmacht vom 1. Januar 1941 bis 31. Dezember 1941 ([Berlin, 1942]).

Besprimernyj podvig: Materialy naučnoj konferencii, posvjaščennoj 25-letiju razgroma nemecko-fašistskich vojsk pod Moskvoj [Unparalleled heroism: Documents for a scholarly conference on the occasion of the 25th anniversary of the defeat of the German–Fascist troops at Moscow] (Moscow, 1968).

BESSEL-LORCK, *Kampf an der Liza: Bericht aus dem Einsatz einer Gebirgsdivision [3. Geb. Div.] 22. 6.–20. 12. 1941* (Reval, [1942]).

BESYMENSKI, L. A. *see* BEZYMENSKIJ, LEV ALEKSANDROVIČ.

BETZ, HERMANN DIETER, *Das OKW und seine Haltung zum Landkriegsvölkerrecht im Zweiten Weltkrieg* (diss. Würzburg, 1970).

BEZYMENSKIJ, LEV ALEKSANDROVIČ , *Generale ohne Maske* (Berlin, 1963).

—— *Sonderakte 'Barbarossa': Dokumente, Darstellung, Deutung* (Stuttgart, 1968).

—— *Sonderakte Barbarossa: Dokumentarbericht zur Vorgeschichte des deutschen Überfalls auf die Sowjetunion, aus sowjetischer Sicht* (Reinbek, 1973).

—— 'Kogda polupravda chuže lži: Po povodu odnoj zapadnogermanskoj publikacii [When half-truth is worse than a lie: On the occasion of a West German publication], *Novoe Vremja*, 1985, No. 9, pp. 18–21.

—— 'Byt' li vtoromu Njurnbergu?' [Will there be a second Nuremberg?], *Novoe Vremja*, 1986, No. 48, pp. 9–10.

BIDLINGMAIER, GERHARD, *Seegeltung in der deutschen Geschichte: Ein seekriegsgeschichtliches Handbuch* (Darmstadt, 1967).

BILENKO, S. V., *Istrebitel'nye batal'ony v Velikoj Otečestvennoj vojne* [Annihilation battalions in the Great Fatherland War] (Moscow, 1969).

BINION, RUDOLPH, *Hitler among the Germans* (New York and Oxford, 1976).

BIRKENFELD, WOLFGANG, 'Stalin als Wirtschaftspartner Hitlers, 1939–1941', *Vierteljahrsschrift für Sozial- und Wirtschaftsgeschichte*, 53 (1966), 477–510.

BIRN, RUTH BETTINA, *Die Höheren SS- und Polizeiführer: Himmlers Vertreter im Reich und in den besetzten Gebieten* (Düsseldorf, 1986).

BJÖRKMAN, LEIF, *Sverige inför Operation Barbarossa: Svensk neutralitetspolitik 1940–1941* (Stockholm, 1971).

Blauweiß-Buch der finnischen Regierung, ii. *Die Einstellung der Sowjetunion zu Finnland nach dem Moskauer Frieden* (Publications of the Ministry of Foreign Affairs; Helsinki, 1941).

BLEYER, WOLFGANG, and CZOLLEK, ROSWITHA, 'Die Vereitelung der Aggressionspläne des faschistischen deutschen Imperialismus gegenüber den baltischen Staaten durch die Sowjetunion im Sommer/Herbst 1939', *Militärgeschichte*, 19 (1980), 422–33.

BLINDHEIM, SVEIN, *Nordmenn under Hitlers fane: Dei norske frontkjemparane* (Oslo, 1977).

BLÜCHER, WIPERT VON, *Gesandter zwischen Diktatur und Demokratie: Erinnerungen aus den Jahren 1935–1944* (Wiesbaden, 1951).

BLUMHOFF, ONNO, *Der Einfluß der deutschen Besetzung auf Geld- und Bankwesen in den während des Zweiten Weltkrieges besetzten Gebieten* (Cologne, 1961).

BOBKOV, N., 'K istorii voinskich zvanij v Sovetskich vooružennych silach' [On the history of service ranks in the Soviet armed forces], *VIŽ* 1970, No. 9, pp. 86–90.

BOELCKE, WILLI A., 'Kriegsfinanzierung im internationalen Vergleich', in *Kriegswirtschaft und Rüstung* (q.v.), 14–72.

BOETTICHER, MANFRED VON, *Industrialisierungspolitik und Verteidigungskonzeption der UdSSR 1926–1930: Herausbildung des Stalinismus und äußere Bedrohung* (Düsseldorf, 1979).

Boevoj put' sovetskich vooružennych sil [The battle road of the Soviet armed forces] (Moscow, 1960).

Boevoj put' sovetskogo voenno-morskogo flota [The battle road of the Soviet navy] (Moscow, 1967).

BOLGARI, P., *et al.*, *Černomorskij flot*: see *Černomorskij flot*.

BOND, BRIAN, 'Brauchitsch: Field-Marshal Walter von Brauchitsch', in *Hitler's Generals*, ed. Correlli Barnett, (London, 1989), 75–99.

BONWETSCH, BERND, 'Sowjetische Partisanen 1941–1944: Legende und Wirklichkeit des "allgemeinen Volkskrieges" ', in *Partisanen und Volkskrieg: Zur Revolutionierung des Krieges im 20. Jahrhundert*, ed. Gerhard Schulz (Göttingen, 1985), 92–124.

BOOG, HORST, 'Ernst Udet: Der Pakt mit dem Teufel', *Luftwaffe*, 17/4 (1976), 11–14.

—— 'Generalstabsausbildung und Führungsdenken in der deutschen Luftwaffe', *WWR* 29 (1980), 23–32.

—— *Die deutsche Luftwaffenführung 1935–1945: Führungsprobleme, Spitzengliederung, Generalstabsausbildung* (Beiträge zur Militär- und Kriegsgeschichte, 21; Stuttgart, 1981).

—— 'Das Offizierkorps der Luftwaffe 1935–1945', in *Das deutsche Offizierkorps 1860–1960: Büdinger Vorträge 1977*, in conjunction with MGFA, ed. Hanns Hubert Hofmann (Deutsche Führungsschichten der Neuzeit, 11; Boppard, 1990), 269–325.

—— *Die Luftwaffe im Balkanfeldzug, dem letzten erfolgreichen 'Blitzkrieg' der Wehrmacht, und 'Barbarossa'* (Athens, 1992) [annexe to Acta of the International Congress for the 50th anniversary of the battle of Crete].

BOR, PETER, *Gespräche mit Halder* (Wiesbaden, 1950).

Bor'ba za sovetskuju Pribaltiku v Velikoj Otečestvennoj vojne 1941–1943, T. 1. *Pervye gody* [The battle for the Soviet Baltic in the Great Fatherland War 1941–1943, i. The first years] (Riga, 1966).

BORKIN, JOSEPH, *Die unheilige Allianz der I.G. Farben: Eine Interessengemeinschaft im 3. Reich* (Frankfurt a.M. and New York, 1979). [Trans. *The Crime and Punishment of IG Farben* (Amsterdam and Oxford, 1979).]

BOROWSKY, PETER, *Deutsche Ukrainepolitik 1918 unter besonderer Berücksichtigung der Wirtschaftsfragen* (Historische Studien, 416; Lübeck, 1970).

BORSÁNYI, JULIÁN, *Das Rätsel des Bombenangriffs auf Kaschau 26. Juni 1941: Wie wurde Ungarn in den Zweiten Weltkrieg hineingerissen? Ein dokumentarischer Bericht* (Studia Hungarica, 16; Munich, 1978).

BRACHER, KARL DIETRICH, *Die Krise Europas 1917–1975* (Propyläen-Geschichte Europas, 6; Frankfurt a.M., Berlin and Vienna, 1976).

BRANDELL, ULF, 'Die Transitfrage in der schwedischen Außenpolitik während des Zweiten Weltkrieges', in *Schwedische und schweizerische Neutralität* (q.v.), 82–96.

BRANDT, WILLY, *Der Zweite Weltkrieg: Ein kurzer Überblick*, ed. Komitee für Demokratischen Wiederaufbau (SDU) (Stockholm, 1945).

BRÄUTIGAM, OTTO, *So hat es sich zugetragen: Ein Leben als Soldat und Diplomat* (Würzburg, 1968).

BRINKMANN, CARL, 'Die wirtschaftliche Gestaltung des europäischen Großraums', *Bank-Archiv*, 41/2 (1941), 29–31.

BROCKDORFF, WERNER, *Geheimkommandos des Zweiten Weltkrieges: Geschichte und Einsätze der Brandenburger, der englischen Commands und SAS-Einheiten, der amerikanischen Rangers und sowjetischer Geheimdienste* (Munich, 1967).

—— *Kollaboration oder Widerstand: Die Zusammenarbeit mit den Deutschen in den besetzten Ländern während des Zweiten Weltkrieges und deren schreckliche Folgen* (Munich, 1968).

BROSS, WERNER, *Gespräche mit Göring während des Nürnberger Prozesses* (Flensburg and Hamburg, 1950).

BROSZAT, MARTIN, 'Die Eiserne Garde und das Dritte Reich', *Politische Studien*, 9 (1958), 628–36.

—— 'Deutschland—Ungarn—Rumänien', *HZ* 206 (1968), 45–96.

—— 'Soziale Motivation und Führer-Bindung im Nationalsozialismus', *VfZG* 18 (1970), 392–409.

BROWNING, CHRISTOPHER R., 'Zur Genesis der "Endlösung": Eine Antwort an Martin Broszat', *VfZG* 29 (1981), 97–108.

—— 'Wehrmacht Reprisal Policy and the Mass Murder of Jews in Serbia', *MGM* 33 (1983), 31–47.

BRÜGEL, JOHANN WOLFGANG, 'Das sowjetische Ultimatum an Rumänien im Juni 1940', *VfZG* 11 (1963), 403–17.

BUCHBENDER, ORTWIN, *Das tönende Erz: Deutsche Propaganda gegen die Rote Armee im Zweiten Weltkrieg* (Militärpolitische Schriftenreihe, 14; Stuttgart, 1978).

BÜCHELER, HEINRICH, *Hoepner: Ein deutsches Soldatenschicksal des 20. Jahrhunderts* (Herford, 1980).

BUCHHEIT, GERT, *Der deutsche Geheimdienst: Geschichte der militärischen Abwehr* (Munich, 1966).

BÜCHLER, YEHOSHUA, 'Kommandostab Reichsführer-SS: Himmler's Personal Murder Brigades in 1941', *Holocaust and Genocide Studies*, 1 (1986), 11–25.

BUCHNER, ALEX, *Gebirgsjäger an allen Fronten: Berichte von den Kämpfen der deutschen und österreichischen Gebirgsdivisionen* (Hanover, 1954).

—— *Die deutsche Gebirgstruppe 1939–45: Bilddokumentation* (Dorheim/H., 1971).

BURCKHARDT, CARL J., *Meine Danziger Mission 1937–1939* (Munich, 1960).

BUSS, PHILIP H., and MOLLO, ANDREW, *Hitler's Germanic Legions: An Illustrated History of the Western European Legions with the SS, 1941–1943* (London, 1978).

BUTLER, Sir JAMES RAMSAY MONTAGU, *et al.*, *Grand Strategy* (6 vols.; History of the Second World War, United Kingdom Military Series; London, 1956–76); vol. ii: September 1939–June 1941 (1957); vol. iii (with J. M. A. Gwyer): June 1941–August 1942 (1964).

BYČEVSKIJ, B., 'V načale vojny pod Leningradom' [At the beginning of the war at Leningrad], *VIŽ* 1963, No. 2, pp. 60–70.

BYČKOV, L. N., *Partizanskoe dviženie v gody Velikoj Otečestvennoj vojny 1941–1945: Kratkij ŏcerk* [The partisan movement in the Great Fatherland War 1941–1945: A brief study] (Moscow, 1965).

BYČKOV, SERGEJ, 'Blutiges Jahr: Lenins Krieg gegen die russisch-orthodoxe Kirche erreichte 1922 seinen Höhepunkt', *Moskau News*, 1990, No. 9.

ČADAEV, JA. E., *Èkonomika SSSR v period Velikoj Otečestvennoj vojny, 1941–1945 gg.* [Soviet economy during the Great Fatherland War, 1941–1945] (Moscow, 1965).

CADOGAN, Sir ALEXANDER, *The Diaries of Sir Alexander Cadogan O.M., 1938–1945*, ed. David Dilks (London, 1971).

CARLGREN, WILHELM M., *Svensk utrikespolitik 1939–1945* (Aktstycken utgivna Utrikes Departementet, NS II. 26; Stockholm, 1973).

—— *Swedish Foreign Policy during the Second World War* (London, 1977).

—— *Mellan Hitler och Stalin: Förslag och försök till försvars- och utrikespolitisk samverkan mellan Sverige och Finland under krigsåren* (Stockholm, 1981).

—— 'Sweden and the Great Powers 1941–1945', *Revue internationale d'histoire militaire*, 53 (1982), 71–84.

——, 'Die Mediationstätigkeit in der Außenpolitik Schwedens während des Zweiten Weltkrieges', in *Schwedische und schweizerische Neutralität* (q.v.), 97–110.

—— *Svensk underrättelsetjänst 1939–1945* (Stockholm, 1985).

CARLSSON, STEN, 'Die schwedische Neutralität: Eine historische Übersicht', in *Schwedische und schweizerische Neutralität* (q.v.), 17–29.

CARNES, JAMES DONALD, *General zwischen Hitler und Stalin: Das Schicksal des Walther v. Seydlitz* (Düsseldorf, 1980).

CARR, WILLIAM, *Poland to Pearl Harbor: The Making of the Second World War* (London, 1985).

CARSTEN, FRANCIS L., *Reichswehr und Politik 1918–1933*[3] (Cologne and Berlin, 1966).

CASSIDY, HENRY C., *Moscow Dateline* (London, 1943).

CAVALLERO, UGO, *Comando Supremo: Diario 1940–43 del Capo di S.M.G.* (Bologna, 1948).

CECIL, ROBERT, *Hitler's Decision to Invade Russia 1941* (London, 1975).

ČEREDNIČENKO, M., 'O načal'nom periode Velikoj Otečestvennoj vojny' [The initial phase of the Great Fatherland War], *VIŽ* 1961, No. 4, pp. 28–35.

ČEREMUCHIN, K., 'Ob odnoj fal'šivoj versii' [About a false version], *VIŽ* 1961, No. 9, pp. 119–22.

—— 'Na smolensko-moskovskom strategičeskom napravlenii letom 1941 goda' [On the Smolensk–Moscow Strategic Direction in the summer of 1941], *VIŽ* 1966, No. 10, pp. 3–18.

ČERNECKIJ, V., 'O nekotorych voprosach operativnogo iskusstva VVS nakanune Velikoj Otečestvennoj vojny' [On some questions of the operational skill of the air forces on the eve of the Great Fatherland War], *VIŽ* 1973, No. 8, pp. 88–93.

Černomorskij flot: Istoričeskij očerk [The Black Sea Fleet: A historical outline], ed. P. Bolgari (Moscow, 1967).

CHALES DE BEAULIEU, WALTER, *Der Vorstoß der Panzergruppe 4 auf Leningrad 1941* (Die Wehrmacht im Kampf, 29; Neckargemünd, 1961).

—— *Generaloberst Erich Hoepner: Militärisches Porträt eines Panzer-Führers* (Die Wehrmacht im Kampf, 45; Neckargemünd, 1969).

CHAR'KOV, A., 'Ukreprajony nakanune vojny' [Fortified districts on the eve of the war], *VIŽ* 1976, No. 5, pp. 88–92.

CHOL'MSTON-SMYSLOVSKIJ, B. A., *Izbrannye stat'i i reči* [Selected articles and speeches] (Buenos Aires, 1953).

CHOR'KOV, A., 'Meroprijatija po povyšeniju boevoj gotovnosti vojsk zapadnych voennych okrugov nakanune vojny' [Measures to increase the combat-readiness of the troops in the western military districts on the eve of the war], *VIŽ* 1978, No. 4, pp. 85–90.

CHOROŠILOV, G., and BAŽENOV, A., 'El'ninskaja nastupatel'naja operacija 1941 goda' [The offensive operation at Yelnya in 1941], *VIŽ* 1974, No. 9, pp. 75–81.

CHRENOV, A., and AGANIČEV, A., 'Ėvakuacija vojsk s primorskogo placdarma. Po opytu evakuacii Odessy v oktjabre 1941 goda' [Evacuation of the troops from a bridgehead by the sea. The lessons of the evacuation of Odessa in October 1941], *VIŽ* 1964, No. 3, pp. 17–31.

CHRULEV, A., 'Stanovlenie strategičeskogo tyla v Velikoj Otečestvennoj vojne [The creation of a strategic hinterland in the Great Fatherland War], *VIŽ* 1961, No. 6, pp. 64–86.

—— 'V bor'be za Leningrad' [In the struggle for Leningrad], *VIŽ* 1962, No. 11, pp. 27–36.

CHURCHILL, WINSTON S., *The Aftermath* [vol. v of *The World Crisis*] (London, 1929).

—— *The Second World War*, iii. *The Grand Alliance*, pt. 1. *Germany Drives East*; pt. 2. *War Comes To America*; iv. *The Hinge of Fate*, pt. 1. *The Onslaught of Japan*; pt. 2. *Africa Redeemed* (London and Boston, Mass., 1948–52).

CIANO, GALEAZZO, *Diario 1937–1943*, ed. Renzo De Felice (Milan, 1980). [Trans. Andreas Mayor, *Ciano's Diary 1937–1938* (London, 1952); anon., *Ciano's Diary 1939–1943* (London, 1947); both with intro. by Malcolm Muggeridge.]

COLLIER, BASIL, *The Defence of the United Kingdom* (History of the Second World War, United Kingdom Military Series; London, 1957).

COLLOTTI, ENZO, 'L'alleanza italo-tedesca 1941–1943', in *Gli italiani sul Fronte Russo*, ed. Istituto Storico della Resistenza in Cuneo e Provincia (Bari 1982), 3–61.

COLVILLE, JOHN, *The Fringes of Power: Downing Street Diaries, 1939–1955* (London, 1985).

'Common Graves The', *Soviet War News* (publ. by the Press Department of the Soviet Embassy in London), 177 (5 Feb. 1942); 41.

COMPTON, JAMES V., *The Swastika and the Eagle: Hitler, the United States and the Origins of the Second World War* (London, 1968).

CONQUEST, ROBERT, *The Great Terror: Stalin's Purge in the Thirties* (London 1969).

—— *Harvest of Sorrow* (London, 1986).

CONZE, WERNER, *Die Geschichte der 291. Infanterie-Division 1940–1945* (Bad Nauheim, 1953).

COOPER, MATTHEW, *The Phantom War: The German Struggle against Soviet Partisans, 1941–1944* (London 1979).

CREVELD, MARTIN LEVI VAN, *Supplying War: Logistics from Wallenstein to Patton* (London and Cambridge, 1977).

CRUCCU, RINALDO, 'Le operazioni italiane in Russia 1941–1943', in *Gli italiani sul fronte russo* (Bari, 1982), 209–27.

CSIMA, JÁNOS, 'Magyarország Katonai részvétele a második vilagárborútan [Hungary's military role in the Second World War], *Hadtórténehni Közleméych*, 3 (1966), 635–65.

CSNADI, NORBERT, NAGYVÁRADI, SÁNDOR, and WINKLER, LÁSZLÓ, *A Magyar Repülés Története*[2] [History of Hungarian flying] (Budapest, 1977).

CVETKOV, A., 'Vojna v tylu vraga' [The war behind the enemy's lines], *VIŽ* 1975, No. 10, pp. 108–12.

CYKIN, A., 'Taktika dal'nej bombardirovočnoj aviacii v letne-osennej kompanii (1941 god)' [The tactics of the long-range bomber forces in the summer and autumn of 1941], *VIŽ* 1971, No. 12, pp. 64–9.

CZOLLEK, ROSWITHA, 'Estnische Phosphate im Griff der IG Farbenindustrie AG', *JWG* 1966, No. 4, pp. 201–14.

—— *Faschismus und Okkupation: Wirtschaftspolitische Zielsetzung und Praxis des faschistischen deutschen Besatzungsregimes in den baltischen Sowjetrepubliken während des 2. Weltkrieges* (Schriften des Zentralinstituts für Geschichte, 39; Berlin, 1974).

—— and EICHHOLTZ, DIETRICH, 'Die deutschen Monopole und der 22. Juni 1941: Dokumente zu Kriegszielen und Kriegsplanung führender Konzerne beim Überfall auf die Sowjetunion' *ZfG* 15 (1967), 64–76.

—— —— 'Zur wirtschaftspolitischen Konzeption des deutschen Imperialismus beim Überfall auf die Sowjetunion: Aufbau und Zielsetzung des staatsmonopolistischen Apparats für den faschistischen Beute- und Vernichtungskrieg', *JWG* 1968, No. 1, pp. 141–81.

DALLEK, ROBERT, *Franklin D. Roosevelt and American Foreign Policy, 1932–1945* (New York, 1979).

DALLIN, ALEXANDER, *German Rule in Russia 1941–1945: A Study of Occupation Policies* (London, 1957).

DAŠIČEV, VJAČESLAV, 'Der Pakt der beiden Banditen', *Rheinischer Merkur/Christ und Welt* (21 Apr. 1989).

—— 'Stalin hat den Krieg gewollt', *Rheinischer Merkur/Christ und Welt* (28 Apr. 1989).

DAVEY, OWEN ANTHONY, *La Légion des Volontaires Français contre le Bolchevisme: A Study in the Military Aspects of French Collaboration, 1941–1942* (diss. Univ. of New Brunswick, 1969).

—— 'The Origins of the Légion des Volontaires Français contre le Bolchevisme', *JCH* 6/4 (1971), 29–45.

DAVIES, JOSEPH E., *Mission to Moscow: A Record of Confidential Dispatches to the State Department . . . up to October 1941* (London, 1942).

DEAKIN, FREDERICK WILLIAM, *The Brutal Friendship: Mussolini, Hitler, and the Fall of Italian Fascism* (Cologne and Berlin, 1964).

—— and STORRY GEORGE R., *The Case of Richard Sorge* (London, 1962).

DEANE, JOHN R., *The Strange Alliance: The Story of American Efforts at Wartime Co-operation with Russia* (London, 1947).

Defeat of the German Air Force, The[2] (European Report No. 59, Jan. 1947), in *The United States Strategic Bombing Survey*, iii. [1–44].

DEGRELLE, LÉON, *La Cohue de 1940* (Lausanne 1949).

—— *Die verlorene Legion* (Preuss. Oldendorf, 1972).

DEKER, NIKOLAI K., 'The Meaning of Genocide (Aims and Methods of Group Destruction)', in *Genocide in the USSR* (q.v.), 1–2.

DENZEL, EUGEN, *Die Luftwaffen-Felddivisionen 1942–1945 sowie die Sonderverbände der Luftwaffe im Kriege 1939/45* (Neckargemünd, 1963).

DERRY, THOMAS KINGSTON, *A History of Modern Norway 1814–1972* (Oxford, 1973).

Deutsche Besatzungspolitik in der UdSSR 1941–1944: Dokumente, ed. Norbert Müller (Kleine Bibliothek, 194; Cologne, 1980).

Deutsche Reich und der Zweite Weltkrieg, Das, 6 vols. so far published by MGFA:

i. *Ursachen und Voraussetzungen der deutschen Kriegspolitik,* by Wilhelm Deist, Manfred Messerschmidt, Hans-Erich Volkmann, und Wolfram Wette (Stuttgart, 1979). [Trans. P. S. Falla, Ewald Osers, and Dean S. McMurry, *Germany and the Second World War,* i. *The Build-up of German Aggression* (Oxford, 1990).]

ii. *Die Errichtung der Hegemonie auf dem europäischen Kontinent,* by Klaus A. Maier, Horst Rohde, Bernd Stegemann, and Hans Umbreit (Stuttgart 1979). [Trans. P. S. Falla, Dean S. McMurry, and Ewald Osers, *Germany's Initial Conquests in Europe* (Oxford, 1991).]

iii. *Der Mittelmeerraum und Südosteuropa: Von der 'non belligeranza' Italiens bis zum Kriegseintritt der Vereinigten Staaten,* by Gerhard Schreiber, Bernd Stegemann, and Detlev Vogel (Stuttgart, 1984). [Trans. P. F. Falla, Ewald Osers, Dean S. McMurry, and Louise Willmot, *The Mediterranean, South-east Europe, and North Africa: From Italy's Declaration of Non-belligerence to the Entry of the United States into the War* (Oxford, 1994).]

iv. *Der Angriff auf die Sowjetunion,* by Horst Boog, Jürgen Förster, Joachim Hoffmann, Ernst Klink, Rolf-Dieter Müller, and Gerd R. Ueberschär (Stuttgart, 1983). [Original of the present vol.]

v. *Organisation und Mobilisierung des deutschen Machtbereichs,* pt. 1. *Kriegsverwaltung, Wirtschaft und personelle Resourcen 1939–1941,* by Bernhard R. Kroener, Rolf-Dieter Müller, and Hans Umbreit (Stuttgart, 1988).

vi. *Der globale Krieg: Die Ausweitung zum Weltkrieg und der Wechsel der Initiative 1941–1943,* by Horst Boog, Werner Rahn, Reinhard Stumpf, and Bernd Wegner (Stuttgart, 1990).

Deutsche Wirtschaftspolitik in den besetzten sowjetischen Gebieten 1941–1943, Die: Der Abschlußbericht des Wirtschaftsstabes Ost und Aufzeichnungen eines Angehörigen des Wirtschaftskommandos Kiew, ed. with intro. by Rolf-Dieter Müller (Deutsche Geschichtsquellen des 19. und 20. Jahrhunderts, 57; Boppard, 1991).

Deutschland im zweiten Weltkrieg, i. *Vorbereitung, Entfesselung und Verlauf des Krieges bis zum 22. Juni 1941,* by a group of authors under the direction of Gerhart Haas (Cologne, 1974); ii. *Vom Überfall auf die Sowjetunion bis zur sowjetischen Gegenoffensive bei Stalingrad, Juni 1941 bis November 1942,* by a group of authors under the direction of Karl Drechsler (Cologne, 1975).

Deutschlands Rüstung im Zweiten Weltkrieg: Hitlers Konferenzen mit Albert Speer 1942–1945, ed. with intro. by Willi A. Boelcke (Frankfurt a.M., 1969).

DGFP: see Documents on German Foreign Policy.

Diktierte Option: Die Umsiedlung der Deutsch-Balten aus Estland und Lettland 1939–1941, documentation compiled and with intro. by A. Loeber (Neumünster, 1972).

'Direktivnoe pis'mo Stavki Verchovnogo Glavnokomandovanija ot 10 janvarja 1942 goda' [Letter with directive from Soviet Supreme Command HQ of 10 January 1942], *VIŽ* 1974, No. 1, pp. 70–4.

DITTMAR, KURT, 'Der "Flüstermarsch" der Kampfgruppe Behle', *ASMZ* 118 (1952), 808–19.

—— 'Die Schlacht um Salla, 1–8. Juli 1941', *ASMZ* 120 (1954), 110–20.

—— 'Die Schlacht um die Gora Lyssaja im September 1941', *ASMZ* 121 (1955), 514–24.

D'JAČAN, G., 'Boevye dejstvija sovetskich vojsk na Kerčenskom poluostrove, dekabr' 1941 g.–maj 1942 g.' [Operations of Soviet troops on the Crimean peninsula, December 1941–May 1942], in *Krym v Velikoj Otečestvennoj vojne Sovetskogo Sojuza 1941–1945 gg.* [The Crimea in the Great Fatherland War of the Soviet Union 1941–1945] (Simferopol' 1963), 94–119.

DŁUGOBORSKI, WACŁAW, and MADAJCZYK, CZESŁAW, 'Ausbeutungssysteme in den besetzten Gebieten Polens und der UdSSR', in *Kriegswirtschaft und Rüstung* (q.v.), 375–416.

Documents on German Foreign Policy, Series D (i–xiii): *1937–1945* (US Government Printing Office, Washington, DC [vols. i and ii], and HM Stationery Office, London [vols. iii–xiii], 1949–64) [trans. of *Akten zur deutschen auswärtigen Politik* (q.v.)].

Documents on Polish–Soviet Relations 1939–1945, ed. General Sikorski Historical Institute, London, i. *1939–1943* (London, Melbourne, and Toronto, 1961).

DOKUČAEV, G. A., *Sibirskij tyl v Velikoj Otečestvennoj vojne* [The Siberian hinterland in the Great Fatherland War] (Novosobirsk, 1968).

DOMARUS, MAX, *Hitler: Reden und Proklamationen 1932–1945. Kommentiert von einem deutschen Zeitgenossen*, 2 vols. (Wiesbaden 1973).

DOMBROVSKIJ, T., 'Pol'sko-sovetskoe bratstvo po oružiju na boevom puti ot Lenino do Berlina, 12 oktjabrja 1943 g.–9 maja 1945 g.' [Polish–Soviet brotherhood-in-arms on the fighting road from Lenino to Berlin, 12 October 1943–9 May 1945], in *Očerki istorii sovetsko-pol'skich otnošenij (12 oktyabrya 1943 g.–9 maja 1945 g.)* (q.v.), 293–324.

DOROFEEV, M., 'O nekotorych pričinach neudačnych dejstvij mechanizirovannych korpusov v načal'nom periode Velikoj Otečestvennoj vojny' [Some reasons for the unsuccessful military operations by mechanized corps in the initial phase of the Great Fatherland War], *VIŽ* 1964, No. 3, pp. 32–44.

DRESS, HANS, *Slowakei und faschistische Neuordnung Europas 1939–1941* (Berlin, 1972).

'Dringlichsten Aufgaben zur Steigerung der Leistungen der sowjetischen Hochöfen und Stahlwerke, Die', *Der Ostexpreß: Vertraulicher Wochendienst*, 28 (17 July 1941).

DUBINSKIJ, I., 'Obraz komandarma' [The portrait of an army commander], *VIŽ* 1963, No. 12, pp. 78–81.

DUDIN, LEO, and MILLER, MICHAEL, 'The Russians (Partial Destruction of National Groups as Groups)', in *Genocide in the USSR* (q.v.), 111–26.

DÜLFFER, JOST, 'The Tripartite Pact of 27th September 1940: Fascist Alliance or Propaganda Trick?', *International Studies*, 3 (1984), 1–24.

DWOROK, ECKEHARD, *Konventionelle Kriegsführung und kriegswirtschaftliche Zwänge: Eine Analyse ökonomischer Aspekte der deutschen Kriegsführung im Zweiten Weltkrieg, insbesondere gegen die Sowjetunion* (diss. Kassel, 1986).

DZERŽINSKIJ: *Feliks Ėdmundovič Dzeržinskij: Biografija* , ed. S. K. Cvigun and S. S. Chromov (Moscow, 1977).

ECKSTEIN, OTTO, 'Die Tätigkeit des Generalquartiermeisters Eduard Wagner', in Wagner, *Generalquartiermeister* (q.v.), 272–301.

EHRENBURG, ILJA, *Russia at War*, with an introduction by J. B. Priestley (London, 1943).

—— *People and Life, Memoirs of 1891–1917*, trans. A. Bostock and Yvonne Kapp (5 vols.; London, 1961–6).

EICHHOLTZ, DIETRICH, *Geschichte der deutschen Kriegswirtschaft 1939–1945*, i. *1939–1941* (Berlin, 1969).

—— 'Die Norwegen-Denkschrift des IG-Farben-Konzerns von 1941', *Bulletin des Arbeitskreises Zweiter Weltkrieg*, 1974, Nos. 1–2, pp. 4–66.

EICHHOLTZ, DIETRICH, 'Expansionsrichtung Nordeuropa: Der "Europäische Großwirtschaftsraum" und die nordischen Länder nach dem faschistischen Überfall auf die UdSSR', *ZfG* 27 (1979), 17–31.

—— 'Wirtschaftspolitik und Strategie des faschistischen deutschen Imperialismus im Dnepr-Donez-Industriegebiet', *Militärgeschichte*, 18 (1979), 281–96.

—— 'The "European Greater Economic Sphere" and the Nordic Countries after June 22, 1941', *Revue internationale d'histoire militaire*, 53 (1982), 55–69.

EICHLER, GERHARD, *Die deutsch-sowjetischen Wirtschaftsbeziehungen vom August 1939 bis zum faschistischen Überfall im Juni 1941* (diss. Halle, 1965).

EINBECK, EBERHARD, *Das Exempel Graf Sponeck: Ein Beitrag zum Thema Hitler und die Generale* (Bremen, 1970).

EINZIG, PAUL, *Economic Problems of the Next War* (London, 1939).

EISENBLÄTTER, GERHARD, *Grundlinien der Politik des Reichs gegenüber dem Generalgouvernement, 1939–1945*, (diss. Frankfurt a.M., 1969).

EKMAN, PER-OLOF, 'Untergang des finnischen Panzerschiffes "Ilmarinen"', *MR* 59 (1962), 301–5.

ELISEEV, I., 'Pervye dni oborony Sevastopolja' [The first days of the defence of Sevastopol], *VIŽ* 1968, No. 8, pp. 51–60.

ENDRES, ROBERT, 'Zum Verbleib der Luftwaffenakten beim Zusammenbruch 1945 und danach', in *Fünfzig Jahre Luftwaffen- und Luftkrieggeschichtsschreibung*, ed. MGFA (Freiburg i.Br., 1970), 25–31.

ENGEL, GERHARD, *Heeresadjutant bei Hitler 1938–1943: Aufzeichnungen des Majors Engel*, ed. and with a commentary by Hildegard von Kotze (Schriftenreihe der Vierteljahrshefte für Zeitgeschichte, 29; Stuttgart, 1974).

ENGELMANN, JOACHIM, and SCHEIBERT, HORST, *Deutsche Artillerie 1934–1945: Eine Dokumentation in Text, Skizzen und Bildern* (Limburg, 1974).

ENGELS, FRIEDRICH, introduction to Karl Marx, *The Class Struggles in France 1848 to 1850* (London, 1924).

ERB, HASSO, *Kradschützen: Die Geschichte der schnellsten Truppe des Heeres* (Stuttgart, 1981).

ERDMANN, KARL DIETRICH, *Die Zeit der Weltkriege*, 2 part-vols., 9th rev. edn. (Handbuch der deutschen Geschichte, 4; Stuttgart, 1973–6).

EREMENKO, A. I., *Na zapadnom napravlenii: Vospominanija o boevych dejstvijach vojsk Zapadnogo, Brjanskogo frontov i 4-j udarnoj armii v pervom periode Velikoj Otečestvennoj vojny* [In a westerly direction: Recollections of operations by the troops of the Western and Bryansk Fronts and the Fourth Assault Army in the first phase of the Great Fatherland War] (Moscow, 1959).

—— 'Na jugo-zapadnych podstupach k stolice' [On the south-western approaches to the capital], in *Besprimernyj podvig* (q.v.), 76–97.

—— 'Nastuplenie v lesach Valdaja' [Attack in the Valday forests], *VIŽ* 1971, No. 7, pp. 67–70.

ERFURTH, S., 'Finnland und seine Probleme für deutsche Transportdienststellen, Juni 1941 bis Ende 1941', *Der Freiwillige*, 15/3 (1969), 13–16; 15/4, 17–19.

ERFURTH, WALDEMAR, 'Das Problem der Murman-Bahn', *WWR* 2 (1952), 281–96, 342–9.

—— *Die Geschichte des deutschen Generalstabes von 1918 bis 1945*[2] (Studien und Dokumente zur Geschichte des Zweiten Weltkrieges, 1; Göttingen, Berlin, and Frankfurt a.M., 1960).

—— *Der Finnische Krieg 1941–1944*[2] (Wiesbaden, 1977).

ERICKSON, JOHN, *The Soviet High Command: A Military-Political History 1918–1941* (London and New York, 1962).

—— *Stalin's War with Germany*, i. *The Road to Stalingrad* (London, 1975).

Èstonskij narod v bor'be za svobodu i nezavisimost' sovetskoj rodiny v 1941–1943 godach [The Estonian people in the struggle for the freedom and independence of the Soviet motherland 1941–1943] (Tallinn, 1973).

EYERMANN, KARL-HEINZ, *Luftspionage*, 2 vols. (Berlin, 1963).

FABRY, PHILIPP WALTER, *Der Hitler-Stalin-Pakt 1939–1941: Ein Beitrag zur Methode sowjetischer Außenpolitik* (Darmstadt, 1962).

—— 'Die sowjetische Außenpolitik 1939–1941', in *Weltpolitik* II (q.v.), 53–73.

Fall Barbarossa: Dokumente zur Vorbereitung der faschistischen Wehrmacht auf die Aggression gegen die Sowjetunion, 1940/1941, selected and with an intro. by Erhard Moritz (Berlin, 1970).

Fall 6: Ausgewählte Dokumente und Urteil des IG-Farben-Prozesses, ed. Hans Radant (Berlin, 1970).

FANNING, WILLIAM JEFFRESS, *The German War Economy in 1941: A Study of Germany's Material and Manpower Problems in Relation to the Overall Military Effort* (diss. Texas Christian Univ., 1983).

FĂTU, MIHAI, and SPĂLĂŢELU, ION, *Die Eiserne Garde: Terrororganisation faschistischen Typs* (Bucharest, 1975).

FEDOROV, A. G., *Aviacija v bitve pod Moskvoj* [The air force in the battle outside Moscow] (Moscow, 1971).

FENYO, MARIO D., *Hitler, Horthy, and Hungary: German–Hungarian Relations, 1914–1944* (Yale Russian and East European Studies, 11; New Haven, Conn., and London, 1972).

FEST, JOACHIM, *Hitler: Eine Biographie*[7] (Frankfurt a.M., 1974). [Trans. Richard and Clara Winston, *Hitler* (New York, 1974).]

FEUCHTER, GEORG W., *Der Luftkrieg*[3] (Frankfurt a.M. and Bonn, 1964).

FISCHER, ALEXANDER, 'Die Anfänge der Roten Armee 1917/18: Zur Theorie und Praxis revolutionärer Militärpolitik im bolschewistischen Rußland', *MGM* 14 (1973), 63–73.

FISCHER, KURT, *Deutsche Truppen und Entente-Intervention in Südrußland 1918/19* (Wehrwissenschaftliche Forschungen, Abt. Militärgeschichtliche Studien, 16; Boppard, 1973).

FLEISCHHAUER, INGEBORG, '"Unternehmen Barbarossa" und die Zwangsumsiedlung der Deutschen in der UdSSR', *VfZG* 30 (1982), 299–321.

Foreign Relations of the United States 1935–1940 (Washington, 1952).

FÖRSTER, JÜRGEN, '"Croisade de l'Europe contre le Bolchevisme": La participation d'unités de volontaires européens à l'opération "Barberousse", en 1941', *Revue d'histoire de la deuxième guerre mondiale*, 30/118 (1980), 1–26.

—— 'The Dynamics of Volksgemeinschaft: The Effectiveness of the German Military Establishment in the Second World War', in *Military Effectiveness*, ed. Allan Reed Millett and Williamson Murray, iii. *The Second World War* (Boston, London, and Sydney, 1988), 180–220.

—— 'The German Army and the Ideological War against the Soviet Union', in *The Policies of Genocide: Jews and Soviet Prisoners of War in Nazi Germany*, ed. Gerhard Hirschfeld (London, Boston, and Sydney, 1986), 15–29.

—— 'New Wine in Old Skins? The Wehrmacht and the War of "Weltanschauungen"', 1941', in *The German Military* (q.v.), 304–22.

—— 'Rumäniens Weg in die deutsche Abhängigkeit: Zur Rolle der deutschen Militärmission 1940/41', *MGM* 25 (1979), 47–77.

—— *Stalingrad: Risse im Bündnis 1942/43* (Einzelschriften zur militärischen Geschichte des Zweiten Weltkrieges, 16; Freiburg, 1975).

—— 'Zur Bündnispolitik Rumäniens vor und während des Zweiten Weltkrieges', in *Militärgeschichte. Probleme, Thesen, Wege* (q.v.), 294–310.

—— 'Zur Rolle der Wehrmacht im Krieg gegen die Sowjetunion', *Aus Politik und Zeitgeschichte*, 45 (1980), 3–15.

FORSTMEIER, FRIEDRICH, *Odessa 1941: Der Kampf um Stadt und Hafen und die Räumung der Seefestung 15. August bis 16. Oktober 1941* (Einzelschriften zur militärischen Geschichte des Zweiten Weltkrieges, 1; Freiburg, 1967).

FRANK, HANS, *Das Diensttagebuch des deutschen Generalgouverneurs (Hans Frank) in Polen 1939–1945*, ed. Werner Präg and Wolfgang Jacobmeyer (Quellen und Darstellungen zur Zeitgeschichte, 20; Stuttgart, 1975).

FRANTZ, G., 'Die Rückführung des deutschen Besatzungsheeres aus der Ukraine 1918/19', *Wissen und Wehr*, 15 (1934), 445–64.

FRANZ-WILLING, GEORG, *Der Zweite Weltkrieg: Ursachen und Anlaß*³ (Leoni, 1980).

FREYMOND, JEAN F., *Le IIIᵉ Reich et la réorganisation économique de l'Europe 1940–1942: Origines et projets* (Collection de Relations Internationales, 3; Leiden and Geneva, 1974).

FRICKE, KARL WILHELM, *Politik und Justiz in der DDR: Zur Geschichte der politischen Verfolgung 1945–1968. Bericht und Dokumentation* (Cologne, 1979).

Frieden mit der Sowjetunion, eine unerledigte Aufgabe: Ein Memorandum ed. Dietrich Goldschmidt (Gütersloh, 1989).

FRIEDENSBURG, FERDINAND, 'Die sowjetischen Kriegslieferungen an das Hitlerreich', *Vierteljahrshefte zur Wirtschaftsforschung* 1962, pp. 331–8.

FRITZ, MARTIN, *German Steel and Swedish Iron Ore, 1939–1945* (Publications of the Institute of Economic History of Gothenburg University, 29; Göteborg, 1974).

—— 'A Question of Practical Politics: Economic Neutrality during the Second World War', *Revue internationale d'histoire militaire*, 57 (1984), 95–118.

—— 'Wirtschaftliche Neutralität während des Zweiten Weltkrieges', in *Schwedische und schweizerische Neutralität* (q.v.), 48–81.

FRUS: see *Foreign Relations of the United States 1935–1940*.

FUGATE, BRYAN I., *Operation Barbarossa: Strategy and Tactics on the Eastern Front 1941* (Novato, Calif., 1984).

'Führer Conferences on Naval Affairs': see *Lagevorträge*.

FUNK, WALTHER, 'Europas neue Wirtschaftsordnung', *Südost-Echo*, 30 (26 July 1940), 1–2.

FUNKE, MANFRED, 'Die deutsch-italienischen Beziehungen: Antibolschewismus und außenpolitische Interessenkonkurrenz als Strukturprinzip der "Achse"', in *Hitler, Deutschland und die Mächte* (q.v.), 823–46.

FURLANI, SILVIO, 'Pripjet-Problem und Barbarossa-Planung', in *Beiträge zur Zeitgeschichte: Festschrift Ludwig Jedlicka zum 60. Geburtstag*, ed. Rudolf Neck and Adam Wandruszka (St Pölten, 1976), 281–97.

GAFENCU, GRIGORE, *Vorspiel zum Krieg im Osten: Vom Moskauer Abkommen (21.8.1939) bis zum Ausbruch der Feindseligkeiten in Rußland (22.6.1941)* (Zurich, 1944).

GALAI, NIKOLAI, 'Die Partisanen', in *Die Rote Armee* (q.v.), 167–85.

—— 'Political Groups (Attempted Destruction of Political and Social Groups and the Cossacks as a Group)', in *Genocide in the USSR* (q.v.), 217–29.

GALICKIJ, K. N., *Gody surovych ispytanij 1941–1944: Zapiski komandarma* [Years of tough trials, 1941–1944: Notes of an army commander] (Moscow, 1973).

GALLAND, ADOLF, *Die Ersten und die Letzten: Die Jagdflieger im Zweiten Weltkrieg* (Darmstadt, 1953). [Trans. Mervyn Savill, *The First and the Last: Rise and Fall of the German Fighter Force* (London, 1970).]

GAPIČ, N., 'Nekotorye mysli po voprosam upravlenija i svjazi' [Some reflections on issues of leadership and communications], *VIŽ* 1965, No. 7, pp. 47–55.

GARTHOFF, RAYMOND L., *Soviet Military Doctrine* (Santa Monica, Calif., 1953).

—— *Die Sowjetarmee: Wesen und Lehre* (Cologne, 1955).

GAUSE, FRITZ, *Die Russen in Ostpreußen 1914/15* (Königsberg, 1931).

General Dietl: Das Leben eines Soldaten, ed. Gerda-Luise Dietl and Kurt Herrmann (Munich, 1951).

General Ernst Köstring: Der militärische Mittler zwischen dem Deutschen Reich und der Sowjetunion, 1921–1941, ed. Hermann Teske (Profile bedeutender Soldaten, 1; Frankfurt a.M., 1965).

Generalgouvernement, Das: Seine Verwaltung und seine Wirtschaft. Sammlung von Vorträgen . . . , ed. Josef Bühler (Cracow, 1943).

Genocide in the USSR: Studies in Group Destruction (Institute for the Study of the USSR, Munich, Series I, No. 40; Munich and New York, 1958).

GERHARDT, MARTIN, *Norwegische Geschichte²*, re-ed. Walther Hubatsch (Bonn, 1963).

German Military in the Age of Total War, The, ed. Wilhelm Deist (Leamington Spa, 1985).

Geroi graždanskoj vojny [Heroes of the civil war] (Moscow, 1963).

GERSDORFF, RUDOLF-CHRISTOPH Frhr. VON, *Soldat im Untergang* (Frankfurt a.M., Berlin, and Vienna, 1977).

Geschichte der internationalen Beziehungen, ed. W. G. Truchanovskij. i. *1917–1939*; ii. *1939–1945* (Berlin, 1963–5).

Geschichte des Großen Vaterländischen Krieges der Sowjetunion, ed. Institute for Marxism-Leninism under the Central Committee of the Soviet Communist Party, 6 vols. (East Berlin, 1962–8).

Geschichte des zweiten Weltkrieges 1939–1945 in zwölf Bänden: Von einem Redaktionskollegium, i. *Die Entstehung des Krieges* (Berlin, 1975); ii. *Am Vorabend des Krieges* (Berlin, 1975); iii. *Der Beginn des Krieges* (Berlin, 1977); iv. *Die faschistische Aggression gegen die UdSSR* (Berlin, 1977).

Geschichtswende? Entsorgungsversuche zur deutschen Geschichte, with an intro. by Walter Dirks, ed. Gernot Erler [*et al.*] (Freiburg, 1987).

'Gesprengter Blockadering', in *Die deutsche Volkswirtschaft*, 9/6 (1940), 154–5.

GESSNER, KLAUS, 'Zur Organisation und Funktion der Geheimen Feldpolizei im Zweiten Weltkrieg', *Revue internationale d'histoire militaire*, 43 (1979), 154–67.

—— *Geheime Feldpolizei: Zur Funktion und Organisation des geheimpolizeilichen Exekutivorgans der faschistischen Wehrmacht* (Militärhistorische Studien, 24; Berlin, 1986).

GEYER, HERMANN, *Das IX. Armeekorps im Ostfeldzug 1941*, ed. Wilhelm Meyer-Detring (Die Wehrmacht im Kampf, 46; Neckargemünd, 1969).

GIBBONS, ROBERT JOSEPH, 'Soviet Industry and the German War Effort, 1939–1945' (diss. Yale University, 1972).

—— 'Opposition gegen "Barbarossa" im Herbst 1940: Eine Denkschrift aus der deutschen Botschaft in Moskau', *VfZG* 23 (1975), 332–40.

—— 'Allgemeine Richtlinien für die politische und wirtschaftliche Verwaltung der besetzten Ostgebiete', *VfZG* 25 (1977), 252–61.

GILLESSEN, GÜNTHER, 'Der Krieg der Diktatoren: Wollte Stalin im Sommer 1941 das Deutsche Reich angreifen?', *Frankfurter Allgemeine Zeitungs* (20 Aug. 1986).

—— 'Der Krieg der Diktatoren: Ein erstes Resümee der Debatte über Hitlers Angriff im Osten', *Frankfurter Allgemeine Zeitung* (25 Feb. 1987).

—— 'Der Krieg zweier Aggressoren: Was plante Stalin vor dem Angriff Hitlers auf die Sowjetunion?', *Frankfurter Allgemeine Zeitung* (27 Apr. 1989).

GIRBIG, WERNER, *Jagdgeschwader 5 "Eismeerjäger": Eine Chronik aus Dokumenten und Berichten 1941–1945* (Stuttgart, 1975).

GLADKOV, TEODOR, 'Robert Ejdeman', in *Geroi graždanskoj vojny* (q.v.), 221–50.

GLAISE VON HORSTENAU, EDMUND, *Ein General im Zwielicht: Die Erinnerungen Edmund Glaises von Horstenau*. ed. with intro. by Peter Broucek, 3 vols. (Vienna, Cologne, and Graz, 1980–8).

GLOWINSKYI, EUGEN, 'The Western Ukrainians (Partial Destruction of National Groups as Groups)', in *Genocide in the USSR* (q.v.), 147–54.

GOEBBELS, JOSEPH, *Diaries*: see next entry.

—— *Tagebücher aus den Jahren 1942–1943: Mit anderen Dokumenten*, ed. Louis P. Lochner (Zurich, 1948). [Trans. and ed. Louis Lochner, *The Goebbels Diartes* (London, 1948); trans. and ed. F. Taylor, *The Goebbels Diaries 1939–1941* (London, 1982); references are to Lochner unless otherwise stated.]

—— *Die Tagebücher: Sämtliche Fragmente*, ed. Elke Fröhlich for Institut für Zeitgeschichte and in collaboration with the Bundesarchiv. pt. 1. *Aufzeichnungen 1924–1941*, 4 vols. (Munich and London, 1987).

GOLDHAGEN, ERICH, 'Der Holocaust in der sowjetischen Propaganda und Geschichtsschreibung', *VfZG* 28 (1980), 502–8.

GOLIKOV, F., 'Rezervnaja armija gotovitsja k zaščite stolicy' [The reserve army prepares for the defence of the capital], *VIŽ* 1966, No. 5, pp. 65–76.

—— 'Rezervnaja armija vstupaet v sraženie južnee Moskvy' [The reserve army goes into battle south of Moscow] *VIŽ* 1966, No. 11, pp. 56–68.

GOLUBEV, A., 'Vydajuščijsja sovetskij voennyj teoretik' [An outstanding Soviet military theoretician], *VIŽ* 1968, No. 3, pp. 107–14.

GOLUŠKO, I., 'Tyl Sovetskich vooružennych sil v pervom periode Velikoj Otečestvennoj vojny' [The rear of the Soviet fighting forces in the first phase of the Great Fatherland War], *VIŽ* 1973, No. 10, pp. 31–8.

GORDON, GERD STRAY, *The Norwegian Resistance during the German Occupation 1940–1945: Repression, Terror and Resistance. The West Country of Norway* (diss. University of Pittsburgh, 1978).

GORODETSKY, GABRIEL, *Stafford Cripps' Mission to Moscow, 1940–1942* (Cambridge, 1984).

—— 'Stalin und Hitlers Angriff auf die Sowjetunion: Eine Auseinandersetzung mit der Legende vom deutschen Präventivschlag', *VfZG* 37 (1989), 645–72.

GOSZTONY, PETER, *Hitlers fremde Heere: Das Schicksal der nichtdeutschen Armeen im Ostfeldzug* (Düsseldorf and Vienna, 1976).

—— 'Ungarns militärische Rolle im Zweiten Weltkrieg', pts. 1–2, *WWR* 26 (1977), 158–65; 30 (1981), 152–60.

'Gott mit uns': Der deutsche Vernichtungskrieg im Osten 1939–1945, ed. Ernst Klee (Frankfurt a.M., 1989).

GRÄVELL, WALTER, 'Richtungswechsel im Außenhandel?', *Die Deutsche Volkswirtschaft*, 9 (1940), 616–17.

GREČKO, A., '25 let tomu nazad: K godovščine napadenija fašistskoj Germanii na Sovetskij Sojuz' [25 years ago. On the anniversary of Fascist Germany's attack on the Soviet Union], *VIŽ* 1966, No. 6, pp. 3–15.

GREENWOOD, JOHN T., 'The Great Patriotic War, 1941–1945', in *Soviet Aviation and Air Power: A Historical View*, ed. Robin Higham (Boulder, Colo., and London, 1978), 69–136.

GREINER, HELMUTH, *Die oberste Wehrmachtführung 1939–1943* (Wiesbaden, 1951).

GRIGORENKO, PETR GRIGOR′EVIČ, *Erinnerungen* (Munich, 1981).

GRIGOROVIČ, D. F., 'Geroičeskaja stranica: K 20-j godovščine oborony Kieva v 1941 godu' [A heroic page: On the 20th anniversary of the defence of Kiev, 1941], *VIŽ* 1961, No. 6, pp. 15–26.

—— *Kiev—gorod-geroj* [Kiev, the heroic city], (Moscow, 1978).

—— 'Die sowjetischen Luftstreitkräfte in der Gegenoffensive bei Moskau, 5. Dezember–Ende Dezember 1941', *Militärwesen* (B), 18/11 (1974), 122–6.

GROEHLER, OLAF, 'Die faschistische Luftwaffe vor dem Überfall auf die UdSSR', *Militärwesen* (B), 16/7 (1972), 120–4.

—— 'Der Beginn des faschistischen Überfalls auf die UdSSR', *Militärwesen* (B), 17/1 (1973), 123–6.

—— 'Die faschistische Luftwaffe in den Grenzschlachten des Großen Vaterländischen Krieges der Sowjetunion, 22. Juni 1941–10. Juli 1941', *Militärwesen* (B), 17/3 (1973), 122–5.

—— 'Die sowjetischen Luftstreitkräfte in der Anfangsperiode des Großen Vaterländischen Krieges', *Militärwesen* (B), 17/5 (1973), 120–3.

—— 'Die Luftverteidigung Moskaus im Juli 1941', *Militärwesen* (B), 17/7 (1973), 117–21.

—— 'Die Abwehr der ersten faschistischen Luftoffensive gegen Moskau, Juli bis August 1941', *Militärwesen* (B), 17/10 (1973), 119–22.

—— 'Die sowjetischen Luftstreitkräfte während der Verteidigungsschlacht vor Moskau', *Militärwesen* (B), 18/7 (1974), 120–4.

—— 'Das Ende der Blitzkriegsstrategie der faschistischen Luftwaffe vor Moskau, November–Dezember 1941', *Militärwesen* (B), 18/9 (1974), 123–7.

—— 'Die faschistische Luftwaffe in der Schlacht bei Moskau, September bis November 1941', *Militärwesen* (B), 18/5 (1974), 122–6.

—— *Geschichte des Luftkrieges 1910–1970* (Berlin, 1975).

—— 'Die Auswirkungen der Niederlage vor Moskau auf die faschistische Luftwaffe', *Militärwesen* (B), 19/1 (1975), 121–4.

—— 'Stärke, Verteilung und Verluste der deutschen Luftwaffe im Zweiten Weltkrieg', *Militärgeschichte*, 17 (1978), 316–36.

—— *Bombenkrieg gegen Deutschland 1940–1945* (Berlin (East), 1990).

—— and SCHUMANN, WOLFGANG, 'Zu den Bündnisbeziehungen des faschistischen Deutschlands im zweiten Weltkrieg', *ZfG* 28 (1980), 624–39.

GROPMAN, ALAN L., 'The Battle of Britain and the Principles of War', *Aerospace*

Historian, 18/3 (1971), 138–44.

GROSCURTH, HELMUTH, *Tagebücher eines Abwehroffiziers 1938–1940*, ed. H. Krausnick and H. C. Deutsch in collaboration with H. von Kotze (Quellen und Darstellungen zur Zeitgeschichte, 19; Stuttgart, 1970).

Große Weltbrand des 20. Jahrhunderts, Der: Der Zweite Weltkrieg, by Gheorghe Cazan *et al.* (Bucharest, 1975).

GROSSMANN, HORST, *Rshew: Eckpfeiler der Ostfront* (Friedberg, 1980).

GRUCHMANN, LOTHAR, 'Schweden im Zweiten Weltkrieg: Ergebnisse eines Stockholmer Forschungsprojekts', *VfZG* 25 (1977), 591–657.

GUDERIAN, HEINZ, *Erinnerungen eines Soldaten*[4] (Heidelberg, 1951). [Trans. C. FitzGibbon with a foreword by Capt. B. H. Liddell Hart, *Panzer Leader* (London 1952).]

GUNDELACH, KARL, *Die deutsche Luftwaffe im Mittelmeer 1940–1945*, 2 part-vols. (Europäische Hochschulschriften, series 3, vol. 136; Frankfurt a.M., Berne, and Cirencester, 1981).

GUNST, PETER, 'Politisches System und Agrarstruktur in Ungarn 1900–1945', *VfZG* 29 (1981), 397–419.

GUNZENHÄUSER, MAX, *Geschichte des geheimen Nachrichtendienstes: Spionage, Sabotage und Abwehr. Literaturbericht und Bibliographie* (Schriften der Bibliothek für Zeitgeschichte, 7; Frankfurt a.M., 1968).

GUSTMANN, KURT, *Die schwedische Tagespresse zur Neutralitätsfrage im Zweiten Weltkrieg* (diss. Münster, 1958).

GWYER, J. M. A., *Grand Strategy*, iii/1. *June 1941–August 1942* (History of the Second World War; United Kingdom Military Series; London, 1964).

HAFFNER, SEBASTIAN, *Anmerkungen zu Hitler*[2] (Munich, 1978). [Trans. Ewald Osers, *The Meaning of Hitler* (London 1979).]

HÄGGLÖF, GUNAR, *Svensk krigshandelspolitik under andra världskriget* (Stockholm, 1958).

HALDER, FRANZ, *Hitler als Feldherr: Der ehemalige Chef des Generalstabes berichtet die Wahrheit* (Munich, 1949). [Trans. Paul Findlay, *Hitler as War Lord* (London, 1950).]
—— *Kriegstagebuch: Tägliche Aufzeichnungen des Chefs des Generalstabes des Heeres 1939–1942*, pub. by Arbeitskreis für Wehrforschung Stuttgart, ed. Hans-Adolf Jacobsen and A. Philippi, ii. *Von der geplanten Landung in England bis zum Beginn des Ostfeldzuges (1.7.1940–21.6.1941)*; iii. *Der Rußlandfeldzug bis zum Marsch auf Stalingrad (22.6.1941–24.9.1942)* (Stuttgart, 1962–4). [Trans. and ed. Trevor N. Dupoy, *The Halder Diaries, 1939–1942*, 2 vols. (Boulder, Colo., 1975). German edn. cited as Halder, *KTB*.]

HAMPE, ERICH, and BRADLEY, DERMOT, *Die unbekannte Armee: Die technischen Truppen im Zweiten Weltkrieg*, with intro. by Karl Hollidt (Studien zur Militärgeschichte, Militärwissenschaft und Konfliktforschung, 21; Osnabrück, 1979).

Handbuch der europäischen Geschichte, vii. *Europa im Zeitalter der Weltmächte*, ed. Theodor Schieder (Stuttgart, 1979).

Handbuch der neuzeitlichen Wehrwissenschaften, ed. for Deutsche Gesellschaft für Wehrpolitik und Wehrwissenschaften by Hermann Franke, iii/2. *Die Luftwaffe* (Berlin and Leipzig, 1939).

Handlingar rörande Sveriges politik under andra världskriget: Frågor i samband med norska regeringens vistelse utanför Norge 1940–1943, ed. Erik Sjöborg [*et al.*] (Aktstycken utgivna av Kungl. Utrikesdepartementet; Stockholm, 1948).

Handlingar rörande Sveriges politik under andra världskriget: Transiteringsfrågor och därmed sammanhängande spörsmål, april–juni 1940, ed. Sture Bolin [*et al.*] (Aktstycken utgivna av Kungl. Utrikesdepartementet; Stockholm, 1947).

HARDESTY, VON, *Red Phoenix: The Rise of Soviet Air Power, 1941–1945* (Washington, DC, 1982).

HART, B. H. LIDDELL, *History of the Second World War* (London, 1970).

HARTMANN, CHRISTIAN, *Generalstabschef Halder und Hitler 1938–1941* (diss. Cologne, 1989).

HASS, GERHART, 'Das deutsche Monopolkapital und der Überfall auf die UdSSR am 22. Juni 1941', *Bulletin des Arbeitskreises Zweiter Weltkrieg*, 1972, No. 1/2, pp. 50–60.

HASSELL, ULRICH VON, *Vom andern Deutschland: Aus den nachgelassenen Tagebüchern 1938–1944* (Zurich and Freiburg, 1946).

HAUNER, MILAN, 'Did Hitler Want a World Dominion?', *JCH* 13/1 (1978), 15–32.

HAUPT, WERNER, *Demjansk 1942: Ein Bollwerk im Osten* (Bad Nauheim, 1961).

——*Baltikum 1941: Die Geschichte eines ungelösten Problems* (Die Wehrmacht im Kampf, 37; Neckargemünd, 1963).

——*Kiew: Die größte Kesselschlacht der Geschichte* (Bad Nauheim, 1964).

HAUSSLEITER, AUGUST, *An der mittleren Ostfront: Ein deutsches Korps im Kampf gegen die Sowjets*, pub. by the XIII Army Corps Command for a Franconian army corps (Nuremberg, 1942).

HAYES, PAUL M., 'Quislings politische Ideen', in *Internationaler Faschismus 1920–1945*, ed. Walter Laqueur and George L. Mosse (Munich, 1968), 201–17.

HEARDEN, PATRICK J., *Roosevelt Confronts Hitler: America's Entry into World War II* (Dekalb, Ill., 1987).

HEGEMANN, MARGOT, 'Einige Dokumente zur "Deutschen Heeresmission in Rumänien", 1940/41', *Jahrbuch für Geschichte der UdSSR und der volksdemokratischen Länder Europas*, 5 (1961), 315–46.

HEINEN, ARNIM, *Die Legion "Erzengel Michael" in Rumänien: Soziale Bewegung und politische Organisation. Ein Beitrag zum Problem des internationalen Faschismus* (Südosteuropäische Arbeiten, 83; Munich, 1986).

HEINKEL, ERNST, *Stürmisches Leben*[4], ed. Jürgen Thorwald (Stuttgart, 1953).

HEINRICHS, ERIK, *Mannerheimgestalten*, i. *Den vite generalen 1918–1919* (Helsingfors, 1958); ii. *Marskalken av Finland* (Helsingfors, 1959).

HEINSIUS, PAUL, 'Der "deutsch-sowjetische Nichtangriffspakt" im Rahmen sowjetischer Seestrategie', *WWR* 28 (1979), 188–90.

HELD, WALTER, *Verbände und Truppen der deutschen Wehrmacht und Waffen-SS im Zweiten Weltkrieg: Eine Bibliographie der deutschsprachigen Nachkriegsliteratur* (Osnabrück, 1978).

HELLER, MICHAIL, and NEKRIČ ALEKSANDR, *Geschichte der Sowjetunion*, i. *1914–1939* (Königstein, 1981).

HELLMER, HEINRICH, 'Neue deutsche Ölpolitik', *Wirtschafts-Illustrierte Arbeit und Wehr*, 11/15 (1941).

HELMDACH, ERICH, *Überfall? Der sowjetisch-deutsche Aufmarsch 1941*[2] (Neckargemünd, 1976).

HENKE, JOSEF, 'Hitlers England-Konzeption, Formulierung und Realisierungsversuch', in *Hitler, Deutschland und die Mächte* (q.v.), 584–603.

HERBERT, ULRICH, *Fremdarbeiter: Politik und Praxis des "Ausländer-Einsatzes" in der Kriegswirtschaft des Dritten Reiches* (Berlin and Bonn, 1985).

HERDE, PETER, *Pearl Harbor, 7. Dezember 1941: Der Ausbruch des Krieges zwischen Japan und den Vereinigten Staaten und die Ausweitung des europäischen Krieges zum Zweiten Weltkrieg* (Impulse der Forschung, 33; Darmstadt, 1980).

HERHUDT VON ROHDEN, HANS-DETLEF, 'Letzter Großeinsatz deutscher Bomber im Osten', *Europäische Sicherheit*, 1/1 (1951), 21–7.

HERLIN, HANS, *Udet: Eines Mannes Leben und die Geschichte seiner Zeit* (Hamburg, 1958).

HERWARTH VON BITTENFELD, HANS-HEINRICH, *Against Two Evils: Memoirs of a Diplomat* (New York and London, 1981).

——*Zwischen Hitler und Stalin: Erlebte Zeitgeschichte 1931–1945* (Frankfurt a.M., Berlin, and Vienna, 1982).

HESS, WILHELM, *Eismeerfront 1941: Aufmarsch und Kämpfe des Gebirgskorps Norwegen in den Tundren vor Murmansk* (Die Wehrmacht im Kampf, 9; Heidelberg, 1956).

HESSE, ERICH, *Der sowjetrussische Partisanenkrieg 1941 bis 1944 im Spiegel deutscher Kampfanweisungen und Befehle* (Studien und Dokumente zur Geschichte des Zweiten Weltkrieges, 9; Göttingen, Zurich, and Frankfurt a.M., 1969).

HEWINS, RALPH, *Quisling: Verräter oder Patriot? Porträt eines Norwegers* (Leoni, 1972).

HILDEBRAND, KLAUS, *Vom Reich zum Weltreich: Hitler, NSDAP und koloniale Frage 1919–1945* (Veröffentlichungen des Historischen Instituts der Universität Mannheim, 1; Munich 1969).

——'Hitler: Rassen- contra Weltpolitik. Ergebnisse und Desiderate der Forschung', *MGM* 19 (1976), 207–24.

——'Hitlers "Programm" und seine Realisierung 1939–1942', in *Hitler, Deutschland und die Mächte* (q.v.), 63–93.

——*Das Dritte Reich* (Oldenbourgs Grundriß der Geschichte, 17; Munich and Vienna, 1979).

——*Deutsche Außenpolitik 1933–1945: Kalkül oder Dogma?*[24] With an epilogue: *Die Geschichte der deutschen Außenpolitik (1933–45) im Urteil der neueren Forschung* (Stuttgart, Berlin, Cologne, and Mainz, 1980). [Trans. Anthony Fothergill, *The Foreign Policy of the Third Reich* (London, 1973).]

——'Der Hitler-Stalin-Pakt als ideologisches Problem', in Hillgruber and Hildebrand, *Kalkül* (q.v.), 35–61.

——'Krieg im Frieden und Frieden im Krieg: Über das Problem der Legitimität in der Geschichte der Staatengesellschaft 1931–1941', *HZ* 244 (1987), 1–28.

HILGER, GUSTAV, *Wir und der Kreml: Deutsch-sowjetische Beziehungen 1918–1941. Erinnerungen eines deutschen Diplomaten*[2] (Frankfurt a.M., Berlin, 1956).

HILLGRUBER, ANDREAS, 'Deutschland und Ungarn 1933–1944: Ein Überblick über die politischen und militärischen Beziehungen im Rahmen der europäischen Politik', *WWR* 9 (1959), 651–76.

——'Der Einbau der verbündeten Armeen in die deutsche Ostfront 1941–1944', *WWR* 10 (1960), 659–82.

——*Hitler, König Carol und Marschall Antonescu: Die deutsch-rumänischen Beziehungen 1938–1944*[2] (Veröffentlichungen des Instituts für Europäische Geschichte Mainz, 5; Wiesbaden, 1965).

——*Hitlers Strategie: Politik und Kriegführung 1940–41* (Frankfurt a.M., 1965).

——*Deutschlands Rolle in der Vorgeschichte der beiden Weltkriege* (Die deutsche Frage in der Welt, 7; Göttingen 1967). [Trans. William C. Kirby, *Germany and the Two World Wars* (Cambridge, Mass., 1981).]

—— 'Japan und der Fall "Barbarossa": Japanische Dokumente zu den Gesprächen Hitlers und Ribbentrops mit Botschafter Oshima vom Februar bis Juni 1941', *WWR* 18 (1968), 312–36.

—— *Kontinuität und Diskontinuität in der deutschen Außenpolitik von Bismarck bis Hitler* (Düsseldorf, 1969).

—— 'Die "Endlösung" und das deutsche Ostimperium als Kernstück des rassenideologischen Programms des Nationalsozialismus', *VfZG* 20 (1972), 133–53.

—— 'Die weltpolitische Lage 1936–1939: Deutschland', in *Weltpolitik 1933–1939*, 13 lectures for Ranke-Gesellschaft—Vereinigung für Geschichte im öffentlichen Leben, ed. Oswald Hauser (Göttingen, 1973), 270–92.

—— *Der Zenit des Zweiten Weltkrieges Juli 1941* (Institut für Europäische Geschichte Mainz, Vorträge, 65; Wiesbaden, 1977).

—— 'Die "Hitler-Koalition": Eine Skizze zur Geschichte und Struktur des "Weltpolitischen Dreiecks" Berlin–Rom–Tokio 1933–1945', in *Vom Staat des Ancien Régime zum modernen Parteienstaat: Festschrift für Theodor Schieder zu seinem 70. Geburtstag*, ed. Helmut Berding (Munich and Vienna, 1978), 467–83.

—— 'Das Rußland-Bild der führenden deutschen Militärs vor Beginn des Angriffs auf die Sowjetunion', in *Rußland–Deutschland–Amerika. Russia–Germany–America: Festschrift für Fritz T. Epstein zum 80. Geburtstag* (Frankfurter historische Abhandlungen, 17; Wiesbaden, 1978), 296–310.

—— 'Tendenzen, Ergebnisse und Perspektiven der gegenwärtigen Hitler-Forschung', *HZ* 226 (1978), 600–21.

—— 'Die ideologisch-dogmatische Grundlage der nationalsozialistischen Politik der Ausrottung der Juden in den besetzten Gebieten der Sowjetunion und ihre Durchführung 1941–1944', in *German Studies Review* 2 (1979), 263–96.

—— *Sowjetische Außenpolitik im Zweiten Weltkrieg* (Königstein and Düsseldorf, 1979).

—— 'Der Hitler-Stalin-Pakt und die Entfesselung des Zweiten Weltkrieges', in Hillgruber and Hildebrand, *Kalkül* (q.v.), 7–34.

—— *Zur Entstehung des Zweiten Weltkrieges: Forschungsstand und Literatur. Mit einer Chronik der Ereignisse Sept. bis Dez. 1939* (Düsseldorf, 1980).

—— and HILDEBRAND, KLAUS, *Kalkül zwischen Macht und Ideologie: Der Hitler-Stalin-Pakt, Parallelen bis heute?* (Texte und Thesen, 125, Sachgebiet Politik; Zurich and Osnabrück, 1980).

HIMMLER, HEINRICH, *Geheimreden 1933 bis 1945 und andere Ansprachen*, ed. Bradley F. Smith and Agnes F. Peterson with intro. by Joachim C. Fest (Frankfurt a.M., Berlin, and Vienna, 1974).

HINSLEY, FRANCIS HARRY, *British Intelligence in the Second World War: Its Influence on Strategy and Operations*, i (History of the Second World War, United Kingdom Military Series; London, 1979).

HITLER, ADOLF, *Mein Kampf*, i. *Eine Abrechnung*[42] (Munich, 1936); ii. *Die nationalsozialistische Bewegung*[39] (Munich, 1937). [Trans. and annotated by James Murphy (London, 1939).]

—— *Monologe im Führerhauptquartier 1941–1944: Die Aufzeichnungen Heinrich Heims*, ed. Werner Jochmann (Hamburg, 1980).

—— *Sämtliche Aufzeichnungen 1905–1924*, ed. Eberhard Jäckel and Axel Kuhn (Quellen und Darstellungen zur Zeitgeschichte, 21; Stuttgart, 1980).

Hitler, Deutschland und die Mächte: Materialien zur Außenpolitik des Dritten Reiches, ed.

Manfred Funke (Bonner Schriften zur Politik und Zeitgeschichte, 12; Düsseldorf, 1976).

Hitlers Lagebesprechungen: Die Protokollfragmente seiner militärischen Konferenzen 1942–1945, ed. Helmut Heiber (Quellen und Darstellungen zur Zeitgeschichte, 10; Stuttgart, 1962).

Hitler's Secret Book: see *Hitlers zweites Buch.*

Hitlers Städte: Baupolitik im Dritten Reich. Eine Dokumentation, ed. Jost Dülffer (Cologne and Vienna, 1978).

Hitler's War Directives: see next entry.

Hitlers Weisungen für die Kriegführung 1939–1945: Dokumente des Oberkommandos der Wehrmacht, ed. Walther Hubatsch (Frankfurt a.M., 1962). [Trans. with comment by H. R. Trevor-Roper, *Hitler's War Directives 1939–1945* (London, 1964).]

Hitlers zweites Buch: Ein Dokument aus dem Jahre 1928, with intro. and commentary by Gerhard L. Weinberg (Quellen und Darstellungen zur Zeitgeschichte, 7; Stuttgart 1961). [Trans. Salvator Attanasio, *Hitler's Secret Book* (New York, 1962).]

HOENSCH, JÖRG KONRAD, 'Die Slowakische Republik 1939–1945', in *Geschichte der Tschechoslowakischen Republik 1918–1948*, ed. V. S. Mamatey and R. Zuza (Forschungen zur Geschichte des Donauraumes, 3; Vienna, Cologne, and Graz, 1980), 292–313.

—— *Geschichte Ungarns 1867–1983* (Stuttgart, Berlin, Cologne, and Mainz, 1984).

HOFFMANN, JOACHIM, 'Der Volkskrieg in Frankreich in der Sicht von Karl Marx und Friedrich Engels', in *Entscheidung 1870: Der deutsch-französische Krieg*, publ. by MGFA, ed. Wolfgang von Groote and Ursula von Gersdorff (Stuttgart, 1970), 204–55.

—— *Deutsche und Kalmyken 1942–1945* (Einzelschriften zur militärischen Geschichte des Zweiten Weltkrieges, 14; Freiburg, 1974).

—— *Die Ostlegionen 1941–1943: Turkotataren, Kaukasier und Wolgafinnen im deutschen Heer* (Einzelschriften zur militärischen Geschichte des Zweiten Weltkrieges, 19; Freiburg, 1981).

—— *Die Geschichte der Wlassow-Armee*[2] (Einzelschriften zur militärischen Geschichte des Zweiten Weltkrieges, 27; Freiburg, 1986).

—— 'Stalin wollte den Krieg', *Frankfurter Allgemeine Zeitung* (16 Oct. 1986).

—— *Istorija Vlasovskoj Armii* [The history of the Vlasov Army] (Issledovanija Novejšej Russkoj Istorii [Recent Russian history research], 8; Paris, 1990).

—— 'Die Angriffsvorbereitungen der Sowjetunion 1941', in *Zwei Wege nach Moskau: Vom Hitler-Stalin-Pakt bis zum 'Unternehmen Barbarossa'*, publ. for MGFA, ed. Bernd Wegner (Munich and Zurich, 1991), 367–88.

HOFFMANN, MAX, 'Ist eine militärische Intervention in Rußland notwendig?' *Nationalzeitung*, Berlin (11 Jan. 1922).

—— *Die Aufzeichnungen des Generalmajors Max Hoffmann*, ed. Karl Friedrich Nowak, 2 vols. (Berlin, 1929).

HÖHNE, HEINZ, *Canaris: Patriot im Zwielicht* (Munich, 1976). [Trans. J. Maxwell Brownjohn, *Canaris* (London, 1979).]

HOIDAL, ODDVAR, *Quisling: En studie i landssvik* (Oslo, 1988).

HOLLEY, IRVING BRINTON, *Buying Aircraft: Matériel Procurement for the Army Air Forces* (United States Army in World War II, Special Studies; Washington, DC, 1964).

HÖLTER, HERMANN, 'Die Probleme des deutsch-finnischen Koalitionskampfes', *Wehrkunde* 2/8 (1953), 16–18.

—— *Armee in der Arktis: Die Operationen der deutschen Lappland-Armee²* (Munich, 1977).

HOMZE, EDWARD L., *Arming the Luftwaffe: The Reich Air Ministry and the German Aircraft Industry, 1919–1939* (Lincoln, Nebr., 1976).

HOPPE, HANS-JOACHIM, 'Die Balkanstaaten Rumänien, Jugoslawien, Bulgarien: Nationale Gegensätze und NS-Großraumpolitik', in *Innen- und Außenpolitik unter nationalsozialistischer Bedrohung: Determinanten internationaler Beziehungen in historischen Fallstudien*, ed. Erhard Forndran, Franz Golczewski, and Dieter Riesenberger (Opladen, 1977), 161–75.

—— *Bulgarien, Hitlers eigenwilliger Verbündeter: Eine Fallstudie zur nationalsozialistischen Südosteuropapolitik* (Studien zur Zeitgeschichte, 15; Stuttgart 1979).

HOPPER, BRUCE, 'How Much Can and Will Russia Aid Germany?', *Foreign Affairs* (New York), 18 (1939–40), 229–43.

HORTHY, MIKLÓS, *The Confidential Papers of Admiral Horthy* (Budapest, 1965).

HOSOYA CHIHIRO, 'The Japanese–Soviet Neutrality Pact', in *The Fateful Choice: Japan's Advance into Southeast Asia 1939–1941*, ed. James William Morley (Japan's Road to the Pacific War; New York, 1980), 13–114.

HOTH, HERMANN, *Panzer-Operationen: Die Panzergruppe 3 und der operative Gedanke der deutschen Führung Sommer 1941* (Die Wehrmacht im Kampf, 11; Heidelberg, 1956).

HUAN, CLAUDE, 'La marine soviétique en guerre, 1941–1945', *La Revue maritime*, 345 (1979), 268–78; 346 (1979), 390–410.

Hubatsch, Walther, *61. Infanterie-Division: Kampf und Opfer ostpreußischer Soldaten²* (Bad Nauheim, 1961).

HULL, CORDELL, *The Memoirs of Cordell Hull*, 2 vols. (New York, 1948).

Hümmelchen, Gerhard, 'Die Luftstreitkräfte der UdSSR am 22. Juni 1941 im Spiegel der sowjetischen Kriegsliteratur', *WWR* 20 (1970), 325–31.

—— *Die deutschen Seeflieger 1935–1945* (Wehrwissenschaftliche Berichte, 9; Munich, 1976).

IMT (International Military Tribunal): see *Trial*.

'Industrielle Entwicklung Sowjetrußlands', *Wirtschaftsdienst*, 26 (1941), 70–2.

IRVING, DAVID, *The Rise and Fall of the Luftwaffe* (London, 1973).

—— *Hitler's War* (New York, 1977).

ISHOVEN, ARMAND van, *Udet: Biographie* (Vienna and Berlin, 1977).

ISRAËLJAN, V. L., *Antigitlerovskaja koalicija: Diplomatičeskoe sotrudničestvo SSSR, SŠA i Anglii v gody vtoroj mirovoj vojny* [The anti-Hitlerite coalition: Diplomatic collaboration between the USSR, the USA, and Great Britain during the Second World War] (Moscow, 1964).

ISSERSON, G., 'Razvitie teorii sovetskogo operativnogo iskusstva v 30-e gody' [The development of the theory of Soviet operational skill in the 1930s], *VIŽ* 1965, No. 1, pp. 36–46; No. 3, pp. 48–61.

Istorija diplomatii, iii. *Diplomatija v period podgotovki vtoroj mirovoj vojny, 1919–1939 gg.* [History of diplomacy, iii: Diplomacy during the preparatory period for the Second World War, 1919–1939] (Moscow, 1945).

Istorija Kommunističeskoj Partii Sovetskogo Sojuza v šesti tomach, v. *Kommunističeskaja partija nakanune i v gody Velikoj Otečestvennoj vojny, v period upročenija i razvitija socialističeskogo obščestva 1938–1958 gg.*, pt. 1. *1938–1945 gg.* [History of the CPSU in 6 vols., v. The CP on the eve and during the years of the Great Fatherland War, in the period of the consolidation and development of the socialist society, 1938–1958, pt. 1. 1938–1945] (Moscow, 1970).

Istorija ordena Lenina Leningradskogo Voennogo okruga [History of the Leningrad military district, awarded the Order of Lenin] (Moscow, 1974).

Istorija Velikoj Otečestvennoj vojny Sovetskogo Sojuza 1941–1945 v šesti tomach [History of the Great Fatherland War 1941–1945 in 6 vols.] (Moscow, 1960–5).

IVANOV, V., and ČEREMUCHIN, K., 'O knige "V načale vojny"' [About the book 'At the Beginning of War'], *VIŽ* 1965, No. 6, pp. 72–80.

'Iz dnevnika Mironovoj Aleksandry Nikolaevny' [From the diary of Aleksandra Nikolaevna Mironovaya], in *Oborona Leningrada* (q.v.), 754–61.

JAAKKOLA, JALMARI, *Die Ostfrage Finnlands* (Helsinki, 1941).

JÄCKEL, EBERHARD, *Frankreich in Hitlers Europa: Die deutsche Frankreichpolitik im Zweiten Weltkrieg* (Quellen und Darstellungen zur Zeitgeschichte, 14; Stuttgart, 1966).

—— *Hitlers Weltanschauung: Entwurf einer Herrschaft*, new enlarged and revised edn. (Stuttgart, 1981). [Trans. Herbert Arnold, *Hitler's Weltanschauung: A Blueprint for Power* (Middleton, Conn., 1972).]

JACOBSEN, HANS-ADOLF, *Dokumente zur Vorgeschichte des Westfeldzuges 1939–1940* (Studien und Dokumente zur Geschichte des Zweiten Weltkrieges, 2a; Göttingen, 1956).

—— *Dünkirchen: Ein Beitrag zur Geschichte des Westfeldzuges 1940* (Die Wehrmacht im Kampf, 19; Neckargemünd, 1958).

—— *1939–1945: Der Zweite Weltkrieg in Chronik und Dokumenten*[5] (Darmstadt, 1959).

—— *Zur Konzeption einer Geschichte des Zweiten Weltkrieges 1939–1945: Disposition und ausgewähltes Schrifttum*, ed. with the co-operation of Joachim Röseler (Schriften der Bibliothek für Zeitgeschichte, 2; Frankfurt a.M., 1964).

—— 'Kommissarbefehl und Massenexekutionen sowjetischer Kriegsgefangener', in *Anatomie des SS-Staates*, ii (Olten and Freiburg, 1965), 161–278.

—— *Der Zweite Weltkrieg: Grundzüge der Politik und Strategie in Dokumenten* (Fischer Bücherei, 645/646; Frankfurt a.M., 1965).

—— 'Primat der Sicherheit 1928–1938', in *Osteuropa-Handbuch: Sowjetunion. Außenpolitik*, i. *1917–1955*, ed. Dietrich Geyer (Cologne and Vienna, 1972), 213–69.

JACOBSEN, OTTO, *Erich Marcks: Soldat und Gelehrter* (Göttingen, 1971).

JÄGER, JÖRG-JOHANNES, *Die wirtschaftliche Abhängigkeit des Dritten Reiches vom Ausland: Dargestellt am Beispiel der Stahlindustrie* (Berlin, 1969).

JÄGERSKIÖLD, STIG, *Fältmarskalken Gustaf Mannerheim 1939–1941* (Helsingfors, 1975).

—— *Marskalken av Finland Gustaf Mannerheim 1941–1944* (Keuruu, 1979).

Jahr 1941 in der europäischen Politik, Das, ed. Karl Bosl (Munich and Vienna, 1972).

Jahrbuch der deutschen Luftwaffe 1939, ed. Hans Eichelbaum (Leipzig, 1938).

JELINEK, YESHAYAHU, *The Parish Republic: Hlinka's Slovak People's Party 1939–1945* (New York and London, 1976).

JODL, ALFRED, 'Dienstliches Tagebuch' [Service Diary], 4.1.1937–25.8.1939 (Dok. 1780-PS), in *IMT* xxviii. 345–90.

JOHANSSON, ALF W., *Per Albin och kriget: Samlingsregeringen och utrikespolitiken under andra världskriget*[2] (Stockholm, 1988).

JOKIPII, MAUNO, *Panttipataljoona: Suomalaisen SS-pataljoonan historia* [The loan battalion: The history of the Finnish SS battalion] (Helsinki, 1968).

—— 'Ein Strohhalm für Finnland: Die Hintergründe, die zur Aufstellung des finnischen SS-Bataillons im Winter 1940/41 führten', in Tieke, *Finnisches Freiwilligen-Bataillon* (q.v.), 50–63.

—— *Saksan ja suomen laivasto-yhteistyö 1941 jatkosodan Syyttymisen asti* [German–Finnish fleet co-operation 1941 to the outbreak of the continuation war], *Sotahistoriallinen aikauskirja*, 1 (1980), 25–100.

—— 'Finland's Entrance into the Continuation War', in *Revue internationale d'histoire militaire*, 53 (1982), 85–103.

—— *Jatkosodan synty: Tutkimuksia Saksan ja Suomen sotilaallisesta yhteistyöstä 1940–41* [The origin of the continuation war: Investigations of German–Finnish military co-operation 1940–41] (Keuruu, 1987).

JONAS, HANS, 'Ostpreußen und Königsberg im neuen Wirtschaftsaufbau Osteuropas', *Weltwirtschaft*, 29 (1941), 38–9.

JORDAN, RUDOLF, *Erlebt und Erlitten: Weg eines Gauleiters von München nach Moskau* (Leoni, 1971).

JUHÁSZ, GYULA, *Hungarian Foreign Policy 1919–1945* (Budapest, 1979).

JUNKER, DETLEF, 'Nationalstaat und Weltmacht: Die USA 1938–1941', in *Weltpolitik II* (q.v.), 17–36.

—— 'Deutschland im politischen Kalkül der Vereinigten Staaten 1933–1945', in *Der Zweite Weltkrieg: Analysen, Grundzüge, Forschungsbilanz* (q.v.), 57–73.

JURASOV, I. V., 'Iz istorii sovetskogo tankostroenija' [From the history of Soviet tank construction], in *Sovetskij tyl* (q.v.), ii. 107–15.

JUR'EV, A., 'Fakty protiv fal'sifikatorov' [Facts against falsifiers], *VIŽ* 1971, No. 7, pp. 92–5.

JUUTILAINEN, ANTTI, 'Operational Decisions by the Defence Forces 1941–1944', *Revue internationale d'histoire militaire*, 62 (1985), 153–75.

KABANOV, S. I., *Na dal'nych podstupach* [On distant approaches] (Moscow, 1971).

KABYSH, SIMON, 'The Belorussians (Partial Destruction of National Groups as Groups)', in *Genocide in the USSR* (q.v.), 77–88.

KAELAS, A., *Human Rights and Genocide in the Baltic States: A Statement, Submitted to the Delegations to the United Nations General Assembly, September 1950* (Stockholm, 1950).

KAHLE, GÜNTER, 'Britische Infiltrationsbemühungen in Transkaukasien 1939/40', *MGM* 16 (1974), 97–110.

KAHN, DAVID, *Hitler's Spies: German Military Intelligence in World War II* (London, Sydney, Auckland, and Toronto, 1978).

KALELA, JORMA, 'Right-wing Radicalism in Finland during the Interwar Period: Perspectives from and an Appraisal of Recent Literature', *Scandinavian Journal of History*, 1 (1976), 105–24.

KALININ, P., 'Učastie sovetskich vojnov v partizanskom dviženii Belorussii' [Participation of Soviet servicemen in the partisan movement of Belorussia], *VIŽ* 1962, No. 10, pp. 24–40.

KANAPIN, ERICH, *Die deutsche Feldpost: Organisation und Lokalisation 1939–1945* (Osnabrück, 1979).

'Kann Europa ausgehungert werden?', *Die deutsche Volkswirtschaft*, 9/19 (1940), 579.

KAUFMAN, THEODORE N., *Germany Must Perish* (Newark, NJ, 1941).

KAZAKOV, M., *Sozdanie i ispol'zovanie strategičeskich rezervov: Po opytu pervogo i vtorogo periodov Velikoj Otečestvennoj vojny* [Raising and use of strategic reserves: Experience of the first and second period of the Great Fatherland War], *VIŽ* 1972, No. 12, pp. 45–53.

KAZASOV, DIMO, *Burni godini 1918–1944* [Tempestuous years, 1918–1944] (Sofia, 1949).

KEHRL, HANS, *Die Aufgaben der Wirtschaft nach dem Kriege: Vortrag, gehalten vor Wiener Wirtschaftsführern im Rahmen der Wirtschaftskammer Wien am 2. April 1941* (Vienna, 1941).

——*Krisenmanager im Dritten Reich: 6 Jahre Frieden, 6 Jahre Krieg. Erinnerungen* (Düsseldorf, 1973).

[KEITEL], *Generalfeldmarschall Keitel: Verbrecher oder Offizier? Erinnerungen, Briefe, Dokumente des Chefs OKW*, ed. Walter Görlitz (Göttingen, Berlin, and Frankfurt a.M., 1961). [Trans. David Irving, *The Memoirs of Field Marshal Keitel*, ed. with intro. and epilogue by Walter Görlitz (London, 1965).]

KENNEDY, PAUL, *The Realities behind Diplomacy: Background Influences on British External Policy, 1865–1980* (Glasgow, 1981).

KENS, KARLHEINZ, and NOWARRA, HANS JOACHIM, *Die deutschen Flugzeuge 1933–1945: Deutschlands Luftfahrt-Entwicklungen bis zum Ende des Zweiten Weltkrieges*[4] (Munich, 1972).

KERSTEN, FELIX, *Totenkopf und Treue* (Hamburg, 1952).

KESSELRING, ALBERT, *Soldat bis zum letzten Tag* (Bonn, 1953). [Trans. Lynton Hudson, *The Memoirs of Field Marshal Kesselring* (London, 1965).]

KETTENACKER, LOTHAR, 'Die britische Haltung zum deutschen Widerstand während des Zweiten Weltkrieges', in *Das 'Andere Deutschland'* (q.v.), 49–76.

——'Die Diplomatie der Ohnmacht: Die gescheiterte Friedensstrategie der britischen Regierung vor Ausbruch des Zweiten Weltkrieges', in *Sommer 1939* (q.v.), 223–79.

KIESEWETTER, BRUNO, 'Europäische Rohstoffprobleme', in *Probleme des europäischen Großwirtschaftsraumes*, ed. Anton Reithinger (Veröffentlichungen des Deutschen Auslandswissenschaftlichen Instituts, 11; Berlin, 1942), 33–58.

KIRCHHOFF, HANS, *Kamp eller tilpasning: Politikerne og modstanden 1940–5* (Copenhagen, 1987).

KIRIMAL, EDIGE, 'The Crimean Turks (Complete Destruction of National Groups as Groups)', in *Genocide in the USSR* (q.v.), 20–9.

KIRSANOV, N., Review of S. V. Bilenko, *Istrebitel'nye batal'ony* [Destroyer battalions], in *VIŽ* (1970), No. 12, 94–5.

KITCHEN, MARTIN, 'Winston Churchill and the Soviet Union during the Second World War', *Historical Journal*, 30 (1987), 415–36.

KLATT, PAUL, *Die 3. Gebirgs-Division 1939–1945* (Bad Nauheim, 1958).

KLEE, KARL, *Das Unternehmen 'Seelöwe': Die geplante deutsche Landung in England 1940* (Studien und Dokumente zur Geschichte des Zweiten Weltkrieges, 4a; Göttingen 1958).

——*Dokumente zum Unternehmen 'Seelöwe': Die geplante deutsche Landung in England 1940* (Studien und Dokumente zur Geschichte des Zweiten Weltkrieges, 4b; Göttingen, 1959).

——'Der Entwurf zur Führer-Weisung Nr. 32 vom 11. Juni 1941: Eine quellenkritische Untersuchung', *WWR* 6 (1959), 127–41.

KLEINFELD, GERALD R., and TAMBS, LEWIS A., *Hitler's Spanish Legion: The Blue Division in Russia* (London and Amsterdam, 1979).

KLINK, ERNST, 'Deutsch-finnische Waffenbrüderschaft 1941–1944', *WWR* 8 (1958), 389–412.

—— 'The Organization of the German Military High Command in World War II', *Revue internationale d'histoire militaire*, 47 (1980), 129–57.

KLOKOV, V. I., *Vsenarodnaja bor'ba v tylu nemecko-fašistskich okkupantov na Ukraine 1941–1944: Istoriografičeskij očerk* [The people's struggle behind the lines of the German–Fascist occupiers in the Ukraine 1941–1944: A historiographic study] (Kiev, 1978).

KLUKE, PAUL, 'Nationalsozialistische Europaideologie', *VfZG* 3 (1955), 240–75.

KNABE, KONRAD, *Das Auge Dietls: Fernaufklärung am Polarkreis* (Leoni, 1978).

KOCH, HANNSJOACHIM WOLFGANG, 'Hitler's "Programme" and the Genesis of Operation "Barbarossa"', *Historical Journal* 26 (1983), 891–920.

KODOLA, D., 'Vnezapnost' v morskich desantnych operacijach' [Surprise in sea landing operations], *VIŽ* 1970, No. 3, pp. 15–24.

'Komandarm 2 ranga A. I. Kork: K 80-letiju so dnja rozdenija' [Army Commander 2nd Rank A. I. Kork: On the 80th anniversary of his birth], *VIŽ* 1967, No. 7, pp. 124–8.

'Komandarm pervogo ranga' [An Army Commander 1st Rank], *VIŽ* 1961, No. 12, pp. 121–2.

KONEV, I. S., 'Načalo Moskovskoj bitvy' [The beginning of the battle of Moscow], *VIŽ* 1966, No. 10, pp. 56–67.

—— 'Na Kalininskom fronte' [On the Kalinin font], in *Besprimernyj podvig* (q.v.), 63–75.

KORDT, ERICH, *Wahn und Wirklichkeit* (Stuttgart, 1947).

KORHONEN, ARVI, *Barbarossaplanen och Finland* (Tammerfors, 1963) [Finn. edn.: *Barbarossa suunnitelma ja Suomen Jatkosodansynty* (Porvoo, 1961).]

KOSTYLEV, V., 'Stanovlenie i razvitie vozdušno-desantnych vojsk' [The establishment and development of the airborne troops], *VIŽ* 1975, No. 9, pp. 80–5.

KOŽEVNIKOV, M. N., 'Razvitie operativnogo iskusstva VVS' [Development of the operational skill of the air forces], *VIŽ* 1969, No. 11, pp. 15–25.

—— *Komandovanie i štab VVS Sovetskoj Armii v Velikoj Otečestvennoj Vojne 1941–1945 gg.* [Command and staff of the air forces of the Soviet army in the Great Fatherland War 1941–1945] (Moscow, 1978).

KOZLOV, I. A., and SLONIM, V. S., *Severnyj flot* [The Northern Fleet] (Moscow, 1966).

KOZLOV, S. N., *et al.*, *O sovetskoj voennoj nauke*[2] [On Soviet military science] (Moscow, 1964).

KRAJNJUKOV, K., 'V bojach za Rostov v 1941 godu' [In the fighting for Rostov in 1941], *VIŽ* 1961, No. 1, pp. 70–84.

KRAUSNICK, HELMUT, 'Judenverfolgung', in *Anatomie des SS-Staates*, ii (Munich, 1967), 235–366. [Trans. Dorothy Long, 'The Persecution of the Jews', in *Anatomy of the SS State* (London, 1968), 1–124.]

—— 'Kommissarbefehl und "Gerichtsbarkeitserlaß Barbarossa" in neuer Sicht', *VfZG* 25 (1977), 682–738.

—— and WILHELM, HANS-HEINRICH, *Die Truppe des Weltanschauungskrieges: Die Einsatzgruppen der Sicherheitspolizei und des SD 1938–1942* (Quellen und Darstellungen zur Zeitgeschichte, 22; Stuttgart, 1981).

KRÄUTLER, MATHIAS, and SPRINGENSCHMIDT, KARL, *Es war ein Edelweiß: Schicksal und Weg der zweiten Gebirgsdivision* (Graz and Stuttgart, 1962).

KRAVČENKO, G. S., *Voennaja èkonomika SSSR 1941–1945* [The Soviet war economy 1941–1945] (Moscow, 1963).

—— 'Ėkonomičeskaja pobeda sovetskogo naroda nad fašistskoj Germaniej' [The Soviet people's economic victory over Fascist Germany], in *Sovetskij tyl* (q.v.), i. 39–48.

KRAVCOV, V., 'Krach nemecko-fašistskogo plana "Barbarossa": Okončatel'nyj proval plana "Barbarossa"' [The failure of the German Fascist 'Barbarossa' plan: The final collapse of Operation 'Barbarossa'], *VIŽ* 1968, No. 12, pp. 36–45.

KREBS, GERHARD, *Japans Deutschlandpolitik 1935–1941: Eine Studie zur Vorgeschichte des Pazifischen Krieges*, 2 vols. (Mitteilungen der Gesellschaft für Natur- und Völkerkunde Ostasiens, 91; Hamburg, 1984).

KRIEGSHEIM, HERBERT, *Getarnt—getäuscht und doch getreu! Die geheimnisvollen 'Brandenburger'* (Berlin, 1958).

Kriegspropaganda 1939–1941: Geheime Ministerkonferenzen im Reichspropagandaministerium, ed. and with intro. by Willi A. Boelcke (Stuttgart, 1966). [Trans. (in parts) Ewald Osers, *The Secret Conferences of Dr. Goebbels, October 1939–March 1943* (London, 1977).]

Kriegstagebuch der Seekriegsleitung 1939–1945, for MGFA in collaboration with Bundesarchiv-Militärarchiv und Marine-Offizier-Vereinigung, ed. Werner Rahn and Gerhard Schreiber; facsimile edn. pt. A, vols. 1–26 (Herford and Bonn, 1988–91); being continued.

Kriegstagebuch des Oberkommandos der Wehrmacht (Wehrmachtführungsstab) 1940–1945: Geführt von Helmuth Greiner und Percy Ernst Schramm, for Arbeitskreis für Wehrforschung, ed. P. E. Schramm, 4 vols. [incl. addendum], i–ii (Frankfurt a.M., 1961–79).

Kriegswirtschaft und Rüstung 1939–1945, publ. for MGFA, ed. Friedrich Forstmeier and Hans-Erich Volkmann (Düsseldorf, 1977).

KRIKUNOV, V. P., 'Frontoviki otvetili tak! Pjat' voprosov General'nogo staba' [This was the answer of the front-liners: Five questions by the General Staff], *VIŽ* 1989, No. 3, pp. 62–9.

KRINICYN, F., 'Oborona Moonzundskich ostrovov v 1941 godu' [The defence of the Muhu Sound islands, 1941], *VIŽ* 1966, No. 9, pp. 119–24.

KROENER, BERNHARD R., 'Squaring the Circle: Blitzkrieg Strategy and Manpower Shortage, 1939–1942', in *The German Military* (q.v.), 282–303.

KROSBY, HANS PETER, 'Petsamo in the Spotlight: A Study in Finnish–German Relations, 1940–1941' (diss. Columbia Univ., 1967).

—— *Finland, Germany and the Soviet Union, 1940–1941: The Petsamo Dispute* (Madison, Wisc., and London, 1968).

KRÜGER, PETER, 'Das Jahr 1941 in der deutschen Kriegs- und Außenpolitik', in *Das Jahr 1941* (q.v.), 7–38.

—— 'Zu Hitlers "nationalsozialistischen Wirtschaftserkenntnissen"', *Geschichte und Gesellschaft*, 6 (1980), 263–82.

KRUMMACHER, FRIEDRICH ARNOLD, and LANGE, HELMUT, *Krieg und Frieden: Von Brest-Litowsk zum Unternehmen Barbarossa* (Munich and Esslingen, 1970).

KRUMPELT, IHNO, *Das Material und die Kriegführung* (Frankfurt a.M., 1968).

KRUPČENKO, I., 'Razvitie tankovych vojsk v period meždu pervoj i vtoroj mirovymi vojnami' [The development of armoured forces between the two World Wars], *VIŽ* 1968, No. 5, pp. 31–45.

KRYLOV, N., 'Slovo o zaščitnikach Odessy' [About the defenders of Odessa], *VIŽ* 1966, No. 11, pp. 69–77.

KTB OKW: see *Kriegstagebuch des Oberkommandos der Wehrmacht.*

KUHN, AXEL, *Hitlers außenpolitisches Programm: Entstehung und Entwicklung 1919–1933* (Stuttgarter Beiträge zur Geschichte und Politik, 5; Stuttgart, 1970).

KÜHNRICH, HEINZ, *Der Partisanenkrieg in Europa 1939–1945* (Berlin, 1965).

KULIKOV, V., 'Strategičeskoe rukovodstvo vooružennymi silami' [The strategic leadership of the armed forces], *VIŽ* 1975, No. 6, pp. 12–24.

KUM'A N'DUMBE III, ALEXANDRE, *Hitler voulait l'Afrique: Le Projet du 3ᵉ Reich sur le continent africain* (Paris, 1980).

KUMANEV, G., 'Perebazirovanie proizvoditel'nych sil na Vostok SSSR v 1941–1942 godach' [The relocation of productive forces to the east of the USSR during 1941–1942], *VIŽ* 1963, No. 2, pp. 114–17.

KUROČKIN, P. A., 'Sorok pjat' let Voennoj akademii imeni M. V. Frunze' [45 years of the M. V. Frunze Military Academy], *VIŽ* 1963, No. 12, pp. 111–15.

—— 'My sražalis' na Severo-Zapadnom fronte' [We fought on the north-west front], in *Na Severo-Zapadnom fronte* (q.v.), 13–51.

KUROWSKI, FRANZ, *Seekrieg aus der Luft: Die deutsche Seeluftwaffe im Zweiten Weltkrieg* (Herford, 1979).

—— *Balkenkreuz und Roter Stern: Der Luftkrieg über Rußland 1941–1944* (Friedberg, 1984).

KUSNEZOWA, OLGA, and SELESNJOW, KONSTANTIN, 'Der politisch-moralische Zustand der faschistischen deutschen Truppen an der sowjetisch-deutschen Front in den Jahren 1941–1945: Überblick über sowjetische Quellen und Literatur', *Zeitschrift für Militärgeschichte*, 9 (1970), 598–608.

KUUSSAARI, EERO, and NIITEMAA, VILHO, *Finlands Krig 1941–1945* (Helsingfors, 1949).

KUZNECOV, J. J., 'Generaly 1940 goda' [The generals of the year 1940], *VIŽ* 1988, No. 10, pp. 29–37.

KUZNECOV, N. G., *Narodnyj komissar (ministr) Voenno-Morskogo Flota* [People's Commissar (Minister) for the Navy], in *Oborona Leningrada* (q.v.), 222–46.

—— *Am Vorabend* (Berlin, 1973).

LAEUEN, HARALD, *Marschall Antonescu* (Essen, 1943).

Lagevorträge des Oberbefehlshabers der Kriegsmarine vor Hitler 1939–1945, ed. Gerhard Wagner (Munich, 1972). [Trans. (with some omissions) as 'Führer Conferences on Naval Affairs, 1939–1945', in *Brassey's Naval Annual* (Portsmouth, 1948).]

LAGUNOV, F., J. LOMAN, and SOT, R., 'O nekotorych netočnostjach v rabotach po istorii bitvy za Leningrad' [A few inaccuracies in studies on the history of the battle for Leningrad], *VIŽ* 1964, No. 12, pp. 93–7.

LANG, JOCHEN VON, *Der Sekretär: Martin Bormann. Der Mann, der Hitler beherrschte*, in collaboration with C. Sibyll (Stuttgart, 1977).

LANGER, WILLIAM L., and GLEASON, S. EVERETT, *The Undeclared War 1940–1941* (New York, 1953).

LAQUEUR, WALTER, *The Terrible Secret: An Investigation into the Suppression of Information about Hitler's Final Solution* (London, 1980).

—— and BREITMAN, RICHARD, *Breaking the Silence: The Secret Mission of Eduard Schulte, Who Brought the World News of the Final Solution* (London, 1986).

LAUN, RUDOLF, *Die Haager Landkriegsordnung: Das Übereinkommen über die Gesetze und Gebräuche des Landkrieges³* (Wolfenbüttel and Hanover, 1947).

LEACH, BARRY A., *German Strategy against Russia 1939–1941* (Oxford, 1973).

LEE, ASHER, *The Soviet Air Force* (London, 1952).

LEEB, GENERALFELDMARSCHALL WILHELM RITTER VON, *Tagebuchaufzeichnungen und Lagebeurteilungen aus zwei Weltkriegen*, ed. from posthumous papers with biographical notes by Georg Meyer (Beiträge zur Militär- und Kriegsgeschichte, 16; Stuttgart, 1976).

LEHMANN, HANS GEORG, 'Leitmotive nationalsozialistischer und großjapanischer Wirtschaftspolitik: Funks Unterredung mit Matsuoka am 28. März 1941 in Berlin', *Zeitschrift für Politik*, 21 (1974), 158–63.

LEHMANN, JOACHIM, 'Faschistische Agrarpolitik im zweiten Weltkrieg: Zur Konzeption von Herbert Backe', *ZfG* 28 (1980), 948–56.

LEHMANN, RUDOLF, *Die Leibstandarte*, 4 vols. (Osnabrück, 1978–86).

LELJUŠENKO, D. D., *Moskva, Stalingrad, Berlin, Praga: Zapiski komandarma²* [Moscow, Stalingrad, Berlin, Prague: Notes of an army commander] (Moscow, 1973).

LENIN, VLADIMIR IL'IČ, *Clausewitz' Werk 'Vom Kriege': Auszüge und Randglossen* (Berlin, 1957).

—— *Über Krieg, Armee und Militärwissenschaft: Eine Auswahl aus Lenins Schriften*, 2 vols. (Berlin, 1958–9).

—— *Polnoe sobranie sočinenij*, t. 23. *Mart–sentjabr' 1913 g.* [Collected works, 23: March–September 1913] (Moscow, 1961).

LEONHARD, WOLFGANG, *Die Revolution entläßt ihre Kinder* (Cologne, 1955). [Trans. C. M. Woodhouse, *Child of the Revolution* (London, 1957).]

LESNJAK, T., 'Nekotorye voprosy organizacii i vedenija partizanskoj bor'by v pervye mesjacy vojny' [A few questions on the organization and leadership of the partisan struggle during the first months of the war], *VIŽ* 1963, No. 9, pp. 30–8.

LEVERKÜHN, PAUL, *Der geheime Nachrichtendienst der deutschen Wehrmacht im Kriege* (Frankfurt a.M., 1957). [Trans. R. H. Stevens and C. FitzGibbon, *German Military Intelligence* (London, 1954).]

LEWYTZKYJ, BORYS, *Die rote Inquisition: Die Geschichte der sowjetischen Sicherheitsdienste* (Frankfurt a.M., 1967).

LIBAL, MICHAEL, *Japans Weg in den Krieg: Die Außenpolitik der Kabinette Konoye 1940/41* (Düsseldorf, 1971).

LICHOMANOV, M. I., *Organizatorskaja rabota partii v promyšlennosti v pervyj period Velikoj Otečestvennoj vojny, 1941–1942 gg.* [The Party's organizational work in industry during the first phase of the Great Fatherland War, 1941–1942] (Leningrad, 1969).

LIDDELL HART: *see* HART.

LIPSCHER, LADISLAW, 'Die Verwirklichung der antijüdischen Maßnahmen in den vom Dritten Reich beeinflußten Staaten', in *Das Jahr 1941* (q.v.), 121–41.

LISICYN, F. Ja., '1-ja Udarnaja nastupaet' [The First Assault Army attacks], in *Na Severo-Zapadnom fronte* (q.v.), 76–110.

LISS, ULRICH, *Westfront 1939/40: Erinnerungen des Feindbearbeiters im OKH* (Die Wehrmacht im Kampf, 23; Neckargemünd, 1959).

LOBAČEV, A. A., *Trudnymi dorogami* [By difficult roads] (Moscow, 1960).

LOOCK, HANS-DIETRICH, 'Zeitgeschichte Norwegens: Forschungsbericht', *VfZG* 13 (1965), 83–111.

—— *Quisling, Rosenberg und Terboven: Zur Vorgeschichte und Geschichte der nationalsozialistischen Revolution in Norwegen* (Quellen und Darstellungen zur Zeitgeschichte, 18; Stuttgart, 1970).

LORBEER, HANS-JOACHIM, *Westmächte gegen die Sowjetunion* (Einzelschriften zur militärischen Geschichte des Zweiten Weltkrieges, 18; Freiburg, 1975).

LORENZ, HERMANN, 'Die Ostsee-Kriegführung der Roten Flotte im Zweiten Weltkrieg. Darstellung und Urteil nach deutschen Unterlagen', in *Das deutsche Bild der russischen und sowjetischen Marine: Vorträge der 5. historisch-taktischen Tagung der Flotte 6.-7. Dez. 1961* (Marine-Rundschau, suppl. 7/8; Berlin and Frankfurt a.M., 1962), 95–108.

LOSSBERG, BERNHARD VON, *Im Wehrmachtführungsstab: Bericht eines Generalstabsoffiziers* (Hamburg, 1950).

LUDENDORFF, ERICH, *Der totale Krieg* (Munich, 1935). [Trans. A. S. Rappoport, *The Nation at War* (London, 1936).]

LUDLOW, PETER W., 'The Unwinding of Appeasement', in *Das 'Andere Deutschland'* (q.v.), 9–48.

LUDWIG, KARL-HEINZ, *Technik und Ingenieure im Dritten Reich* (Düsseldorf, 1974).

LUKAS, RICHARD C., *Eagles East: The Army Air Forces and the Soviet Union, 1941–1945* (Tallahassee, Fla., 1970).

LUNDIN, CHARLES LEONARD, *Finland in the Second World War* (Bloomington, Ind., 1957).

LUNGU, DOV B., *Romania and the Great Powers 1933–1940* (Durham, NC, 1989).

LUPKE, HUBERTUS, *Japans Rußlandpolitik von 1939 bis 1941* (Schriften des Instituts für Asienkunde, 10; Frankfurt a.M. and Berlin, 1962).

LUSAR, RUDOLF, *Die deutschen Waffen und Geheimwaffen des Zweiten Weltkrieges und ihre Weiterentwicklung* (Munich, 1971). [Trans. R. P. Heller and M. Schindler, *German Secret Weapons of the Second World War* (London, 1959).]

LUTZHÖFT, HANS-JÜRGEN, 'Deutschland und Schweden während des Norwegenfeldzuges, 5. April–10. Juni 1940', *VfZG* 22 (1974), 382–416.

—— 'Schwedische Reaktionen auf die deutsche Politik im Osten 1939–1943', *Zeitschrift für Ostforschung*, 29/1 (1980), 71–83.

MACHT [Oberstleutnant], 'Engpässe der russischen Wehrwirtschaft', *Die Luftwaffe*, 3/1 (1938), 53–76.

MACKINTOSH, JOHN MALCOLM, 'Die Rote Armee 1920–1926', in *Die Rote Armee* (q.v.), 59–70.

MAGENHEIMER, HEINZ, 'Die Sowjetunion und der Ausbruch des Zweiten Weltkrieges: Sowjetische Positionen zum Zeitabschnitt 1938/39–1941', *Österreichische militärische Zeitschrift*, 27 (1989), 385–96.

MAJSKIJ, I. M., *Vospominanija Sovetskogo posla* v 2 t. T. 2. *Mir ili vojna?* [Memoirs of a Soviet ambassador, 2 vols., ii. Peace or War?] (Moscow, 1964).

—— *Memoiren eines sowjetischen Botschafters* (Berlin, 1967).

MÄKELÄ, JUKKA L., *Im Rücken des Feindes: Der finnische Nachrichtendienst im Krieg* (Frauenfeld and Stuttgart, 1967).

MAKSIMOV, S. N., *Oborona Sevastopolja 1941–1942* [Defence of Sevastopol 1941–1942] (Moscow, 1959).

MALAN'IN, K., 'Razvitie organizacionnych form Suchoputnych vojsk v Velikoj Otečestvennoj vojne' [Development of the organizational forms of the land forces in the Great Fatherland War], *VIŽ* 1967, No. 8, pp. 28–39.

MALINOVSKIJ, R., 'Dvadcatiletie načala Velikoj Otečestvennoj vojny' [The 20th anniversary of the beginning of the Great Fatherland War], *VIŽ* 1961, No. 6, pp. 3–14.

MANNERHEIM, CARL GUSTAV, *Erinnerungen* (Zurich and Freiburg, 1952). [Trans. Count Eric Lewenhaupt, *The Memoirs of Marshal Mannerheim* (London, 1953).]

MANNINEN, OHTO, 'Syväri vai Kannas-Suomen: Hyökkäyssuunnan ratkaisu Kesäkuussa 1941' [Svir or Karelian Isthmus: The decision on the Finnish operational objective, June 1941], *Sotahistoriallinen seura ja Sotamuseo, Vuosikirja* [Yearbook of the War-Historical Society and War Museum], 10 (1978), 5–43.

—— 'Die Beziehungen zwischen den finnischen und deutschen Militärbehörden in der Ausarbeitungsphase des Barbarossaplanes', *MGM* 26 (1979), 79–95.

—— 'Political Expedients for Security during the "Interim Peace" and at the Start of the Continuation War, 1940–1941', *Revue international d'histoire militaire'*, 62 (1985), 97–132.

MANSTEIN, ERICH VON, *Verlorene Siege* (Bonn, 1955). [Trans. A. G. Powell, *Lost Victories* (London, 1958).]

MARANDI, REIN, *Med grannens ögon: Finlands fortsättningskrig 1941–1944 i svensk pressdiskussion* (Ekenäs, 1970).

MARGUERAT, PHILIPPE, *Le IIIᵉ Reich et le pétrol roumain 1938–1940: Contribution à l'étude de la pénétration économique allemande dans les Balkans à la veille et au début de la Seconde Guerre mondiale* (Institut Universitaire de Hautes Études Internationales, Collection de Relations Internationales, 6; Geneva and Leiden, 1977).

MARKOV, I., 'Kerčensko-Feodosijskaja desantnaja operacija' [The landing operation at Kerch-Feodosiya], *VIŽ* 1967, No. 1, pp. 121–4.

MARTIN, BERND, *Deutschland und Japan im Zweiten Weltkrieg: Vom Angriff auf Pearl Harbor bis zur deutschen Kapitulation* (Studien und Dokumente zur Geschichte des Zweiten Weltkrieges, 11; Göttingen and Zurich, 1969).

—— 'Britisch-deutsche Friedenskontakte in den ersten Monaten des Zweiten Weltkrieges: Eine Dokumentation über die Vermittlungsversuche von Birger Dahlerus', *Zeitschrift für Politik*, 19 (1972), 206–21.

—— *Friedensinitiativen und Machtpolitik im Zweiten Weltkrieg 1939–1942* (Geschichtliche Studien zur Politik und Gesellschaft, 6; Düsseldorf, 1974).

—— 'Japans Weg in den Krieg: Bemerkungen über Forschungsstand und Literatur zur japanischen Zeitgeschichte', *MGM* 23 (1978), pp. 183–209.

—— 'Amerikas Durchbruch zur politischen Weltmacht: Die interventionistische Globalstrategie der Regierung Roosevelt 1933–1941', *MGM* 30 (1981), 57–98.

MARX, KARL, *Der Bürgerkrieg in Frankreich: Adresse des Generalrats der Internationalen Arbeiterassoziation vermehrt durch die beiden Adressen des Generalrats über den Deutsch-Französischen Krieg und durch eine Einleitung von Friedrich Engels³* (Berlin, 1963). [Trans. *The Civil War in France: Address to the General Council of the Working-men's Association, 1871* (London, 1941).]

MASER, WERNER, *Nürnberg, Tribunal der Sieger* (Düsseldorf and Vienna, 1977).

MASTNÝ, VOJTĚCH, 'The Beneš–Stalin–Molotov Conversations in December 1943: New Documents', *Jahrbücher für Geschichte Osteuropas*, 20 (1972), 367–402.

MATLOFF, MAURICE, and SNELL, EDWIN M., *Strategic Planning for Coalition Warfare 1941–1942* (United States Army in World War II, the War Department; Washington, DC, 1953).

MATVEEV, P., and SELJANICEV, A., 'Krasnoznamennyj Baltijskij Flot v načale Velikoj Otečestvennoj vojny' [The Red Banner Baltic Fleet at the beginning of the Great Fatherland War], *VIŽ* 1962, No. 4, pp. 33–51.

MAYER, ARNO J., *Why Did the Heavens Not Darken? The 'Final Solution' in History* (New York, 1988).

—— *Der Krieg als Kreuzzug: Das Deutsche Reich, Hitlers Wehrmacht und die 'Endlösung'* (Reinbek, 1989).

MAZUNIN, N., 'Kerčensko-Feodosijskaja desantnaja operacija' [The landing operation at Kerch-Feodosiya], *VIŽ* 1976, No. 12, pp. 99–103.

MEDLICOTT, WILLIAM NORTON, *The Economic Blockade*, i (History of the Second World War, United Kingdom Military Series; London, 1952).

MEHRING, FRANZ, 'Die Pariser Commune 1871', *Preußische Jahrbücher*, 44 (1879), 59–105.

MEIER-DÖRNBERG, WILHELM, *Die Ölversorgung der Kriegsmarine 1935–1945* (Einzelschriften zur militärischen Geschichte des Zweiten Weltkrieges, 11; Freiburg, 1973).

MEIER-WELCKER, HANS, *Aufzeichnungen eines Generalstabsoffiziers 1939–1942* (Einzelschriften zur militärischen Geschichte des Zweiten Weltkrieges, 26; Freiburg, 1982).

MEISSNER, BORIS, 'Die kommunistische Machtübernahme in den baltischen Staaten', *VfZG* 2 (1954), 95–114.

MEISTER, JÜRG, *Der Seekrieg in den osteuropäischen Gewässern 1941–1945* (Munich, 1958).

Meldungen aus dem Reich: Auswahl aus den geheimen Lageberichten des Sicherheitsdienstes der SS 1939–1944, ed. Heinz Boberach (Neuwied and Berlin, 1965).

MELZER, WALTHER, *Kampf um die Baltischen Inseln 1917, 1941, 1944: Eine Studie zur triphibischen Kampfführung* (Die Wehrmacht im Kampf, 24; Neckargemünd, 1960).

MENGER, MANFRED, *Deutschland und Finnland im zweiten Weltkrieg: Genesis und Scheitern einer Militärallianz* (Militärhistorische Studien, new series 26; Berlin, 1988).

MERECKOV, K. A., 'Na jugo-vostočnych podstupach k Leningradu' [On the south-eastern approaches to Leningrad], *VIŽ* 1962, No. 1, pp. 65–79.

—— [contribution], in *Oborona Leningrada* (q.v.), 186–98.

—— *Na službe narodu: Stranicy vospominanija* [In the service of the nation: Memoirs] (Moscow, 1970).

MERGLEN, ALBERT, 'Soldats français sous uniforms allemands 1941–1945: LVF et "Waffen-SS" français', *Revue d'histoire de la deuxième guerre mondiale*, 27/108 (1977), 71–84.

MESSE, GIOVANNI, *Krieg im Osten* (Zurich, 1948).

MESSERSCHMIDT, MANFRED, *Die Wehrmacht im NS-Staat: Zeit der Indoktrination* (Hamburg, 1969).

—— 'Politische Erziehung der Wehrmacht: Scheitern einer Strategie', in *Erziehung und Schulung im Dritten Reich*, ed. Manfred Heinemann, pt. 2 (Veröffentlichungen der Historischen Kommission der Deutschen Gesellschaft für Erziehungswissenschaften, 4/2; Stuttgart, 1980), 261–84.

—— 'Deutsche Militärgerichtsbarkeit im Zweiten Weltkrieg', in *Die Freiheit des Anderen: Festschrift für Martin Hirsch*, ed. Hans-Jochen Vogel, Helmut Simon, and Adalbert Podlech (Baden-Baden, 1981), 111–42.

—— 'Das Verhältnis von Wehrmacht und NS-Staat und die Frage der Traditionsbildung', *Aus Politik und Zeitgeschichte*, 17 (1981), 11–23.

—— and WÜLLNER FRITZ, *Die Wehrmachtjustiz im Dienst des Nationalsozialismus: Zerstörung einer Legende* (Baden-Baden, 1987).

MICHALKA, WOLFGANG, 'Vom Antikominternpakt zum euro-asiatischen Kontinentalblock: Ribbentrops Alternativkonzeption zu Hitlers außenpolitischem "Programm"', in *Nationalsozialistische Außenpolitik*, ed. Wolfgang Michalka (Wege der Forschung, 297; Darmstadt, 1978), 471–92.

—— *Ribbentrop und die deutsche Weltpolitik 1933–1940: Außenpolitische Konzeptionen und Entscheidungsprozesse im Dritten Reich* (Munich, 1980).

MIKOLA, K. J., *Finland's Wars during World War II, 1939–1945* (Mikkeli, 1973).

Militärgeschichte: Probleme, Thesen, Wege, for MGFA on its 25th anniversary, selected and compiled by Manfred Messerschmidt, Klaus A. Maier, Werner Rahn, and Bruno Thoß (Beiträge zur Militär- und Kriegsgeschichte, 25; Stuttgart, 1982).

MILLER, MARSHALL LEE, *Bulgaria during the Second World War* (Stanford, Calif., 1975).

MILWARD, ALAN S., *The German Economy at War* (London, 1965).

—— 'Could Sweden Have Stopped the Second World War?', *Scandinavian Economic History Review*, 11 (1967), 127–38.

—— *The Fascist Economy in Norway* (Oxford, 1972).

—— 'Arbeitspolitik und Produktivität in der deutschen Kriegswirtschaft unter vergleichendem Aspekt', in *Kriegswirtschaft und Rüstung* (q.v.), 73–91.

—— *Der Zweite Weltkrieg: Krieg, Wirtschaft und Gesellschaft 1939–1945* (Geschichte der Weltwirtschaft im 20. Jahrhundert, 5; Munich, 1977).

MINASJAN, N. M., *Meždunarodnye prestuplenija tret'ego rejcha* [International crimes of the Third Reich] (Saratov, 1977).

MIRONOV, N. M., 'Rol' Moskovskoj zony oborony v razgrome nemcev pod Moskvoj [The role of the Moscow defence zone in the smashing of the Germans outside Moscow], in *Besprimernyj podvig* (q.v.), 114–30.

Mißtrauische Nachbarn: Deutsche Ostpolitik 1919/1970. Dokumentation und Analyse, ed. Hans-Adolf Jacobsen in collaboration with Wilfried von Bredow (Düsseldorf, 1970).

MIYAKE MASAKI, 'Die Lage Japans beim Ausbruch des Zweiten Weltkrieges', in *Sommer 1939* (q.v.), 195–222.

MOLODYCH, S., 'O načal'nike štaba JuZF, generalmajore V. I. Tupikov' [About the chief of staff of the south-west front, Major-General V. I. Tupikov], *VIŽ* 1972, No. 2, pp. 124–5.

MOLOTOV, V. M., *28-ja godovščina Velikoj Oktjabr'skoj socialističeskoj revoljucii* [28th anniversary of the great October socialist revolution] (Moscow, 1945).

MONIN, M., 'K istorii "Katynskogo dela"' [On the history of the 'Katyn Affair'], *VIŽ* 1982, No. 2, pp. 67–73.

MONTFORT, HENRI DE, *Le Massacre de Katyn: Crime russe ou crime allemand?* (Paris, 1969).

Mord an den Juden im Zweiten Weltkrieg, Der: Entschlußbildung und Verwirklichung, ed. Eberhard Jäckel (Stuttgart, 1985).

MORITZ, ERHARD, 'Zur Fehleinschätzung des sowjetischen Kriegspotentials durch die faschistische Wehrmacht in den Jahren 1935–1941', in *Auf antisowjetischem Kriegskurs* (q.v.), 150–84.

MORZIK, FRITZ, *Die deutschen Transportflieger im Zweiten Weltkrieg: Die Geschichte des 'Fußvolkes der Luft',* ed. for Arbeitskreis für Wehrforschung by Gerhard Hümmelchen (Frankfurt a.M., 1966).

MOSKALENKO, K. S., *Na Jugo-Zapadnom napravlenii: Vospominanija komandarma* [In a south-westerly direction: Recollections of an army commander] (Moscow, 1969).

'Moskovskaja bitva v cifrach: Period kontrnastuplenija' [The battle of Moscow in figures: The period of the counter-offensive', *VIŽ* 1967, No. 1, pp. 89–101.

'Moskovskaja bitva v cifrach: Period oborony' [The battle of Moscow in figures: The period of defence], *VIŽ* 1967, No. 3, pp. 69–79.

Moskva—frontu 1941–1945: Sbornik dokumentov i materialov [Moscow for the front 1941–1945: Collection of documents and materials] (Moscow, 1966).

MOTTER, THOMAS HUBBARD VAIL, *The Persian Corridor and Aid to Russia* (United States Army in World War II, The Middle East Theater; Washington, DC, 1952).

MÜHLEN, PATRIK VON ZUR: *see* ZUR MÜHLEN.

MÜLLER, KLAUS-JÜRGEN, *Das Heer und Hitler: Armee und nationalsozialistisches Regime 1933–1940* (Beiträge zur Militär- und Kriegsgeschichte, 10; Stuttgart, 1969).

—— 'Armee und Drittes Reich: Versuch einer historischen Interpretation', in *Armee, Politik und Gesellschaft in Deutschland 1933–1945: Studien zum Verhältnis von Armee und NS-System* (Paderborn, 1979), 11–50.

—— *General Ludwig Beck: Studien und Dokumente zur Tätigkeit und Vorstellungswelt des Generalstabchefs des deutschen Heeres 1933–1938* (Schriften des Bundesarchivs, 30; Boppard, 1980).

MÜLLER, NORBERT, *Wehrmacht und Okkupation 1941–1944: Zur Rolle der Wehrmacht und ihrer Führungsorgane im Okkupationsregime des faschistischen deutschen Imperialismus auf sowjetischem Territorium* (Berlin, 1971).

MÜLLER, ROLF-DIETER, 'Industrielle Interessenpolitik im Rahmen des "Generalplans Ost": Dokumente zum Einfluß von Wehrmacht, Industrie und SS auf die wirtschaftspolitische Zielsetzung für Hitlers Ostimperium', *MGM* 29 (1981), 101–41.

—— *Die Sowjetunion im wirtschaftspolitischen Kalkül des Deutschen Reiches von Compiègne bis zum Hitler-Stalin-Pakt, 1919–1939* (diss. Mainz, 1981).

—— 'Die Rolle der Industrie in Hitlers Ostimperium', in *Militärgeschichte: Probleme, Thesen, Wege* (q.v.), 383–406.

—— *Das Tor zur Weltmachts: Die Bedeutung der Sowjetunion für die deutsche Wirtschafts- und Rüstungspolitik zwischen den Weltkriegen* (Wehrwissenschaftliche Forschungen, Abt. Militärgeschichtliche Studien, 32; Boppard, 1984).

—— 'Das "Unternehmen Barbarossa" als wirtschaftlicher Raubkrieg', in *'Unternehmen Barbarossa'* (q.v.), 173–96.

—— 'Kriegsrecht oder Willkür? Helmuth James Graf v. Moltke und die Auffassungen im Generalstab des Heeres über die Aufgaben der Militärverwaltung vor Beginn des Rußlandkrieges', *MGM* 42 (1987), 125–51.

—— '"Gen Ostland wollen wir reiten": Zur Partnerschaft von Industrie und Nationalsozialismus beim Griff nach der Weltherrschaft', *Salzgitter Forum 1988*, No. 15, pp. 11–19.

—— *Hitlers Ostkrieg und die deutsche Siedlungspolitik* (Fischer Taschenbuch, 10573; Frankfurt a.M., 1991).

MÜLLER-HILLEBRAND, BURKHART, *Das Heer 1933–1945: Entwicklung des organisatorischen Aufbaues*, i. *Das Heer bis zum Kriegsbeginn* (Darmstadt, 1954); ii. *Die Blitzfeldzüge 1939–1941* (Frankfurt a.M., 1956); iii. *Der Zweifrontenkrieg: Das Heer vom Beginn des Feldzuges gegen die Sowjetunion bis zum Kriegsende* (Darmstadt and Frankfurt a.M., 1969).

MULLIGAN, TIMOTHY PATRICK, 'Reckoning the Cost of People's War: The German Experience in the Central USSR', *Russian History*, 9 (1982), 27–48.

—— *The Politics of Illusion and Empire: German Occupation Policy in the Soviet Union, 1942–1943* (New York, Westport, Conn., and London, 1988).

MURAWSKI, ERICH, *Der deutsche Wehrmachtbericht 1939–1945: Ein Beitrag zur Untersuchung der geistigen Kriegführung. Mit einer Dokumentation der Wehrmachtberichte vom 1.7.1944 bis zum 9.5.1945*[2] (Schriften des Bundesarchivs, 9; Boppard, 1962).

MURRAY, WILLIAMSON, *Strategy for Defeat: The Luftwaffe 1933–1945* (Washington, DC, 1983).

MYLLYNIEMI, SEPPO, *Die Neuordnung der Baltischen Länder 1941–1944: Zum nationalsozialistischen Inhalt der deutschen Besatzungspolitik* (Historiallisia Tutkimutesia, 90; Helsinki, 1973).

—— *Die baltische Krise 1938–1941* (Schriftenreihe der Vierteljahrshefte für Zeitgeschichte, 38; Stuttgart, 1979).

NAGY-TALAVERA, NICHOLAS M., *The Green Shirts and the Others: A History of Fascism in Hungary and Rumania* (Hoover Institution Publications, 85; Stanford, Calif., 1970).

Na Severo-Zapadnom fronte 1941–1943 [On the north-west front 1941–1943] (Moscow, 1969).

NAUMOV, D., 'Taktika belorusskich partizan' [Tactics of the Belorussian partisans], *VIŽ* 1970, No. 11, pp. 40–50.

NAZAREVIČ, R., 'Rol' PPR v upročnenii pol'sko-sovetskoj družby v gody vtoroj mirovoj vojny' [The PPR's role in the consolidation of Polish–Soviet friendship during the Second World War], in *Očerki istorii sovetsko-pol'skich otnošenij* (q.v.), 250–76.

NEBELIN, MANFRED, *Die deutsche Ungarnpolitik 1939–1941* (Opladen, 1989).

NEKRIČ (Nekritsch), ALEKSANDR, and GRIGORENKO, PETR, *Genickschuß: Die Rote Armee am 22. Juni 1941*, ed. with intro. by Georges Haupt (Vienna and Frankfurt a.M., 1969).

Neotvratimoe vozmezdie: Po materialam sudebnych processov nad izmennikami Rodiny, fašistskimi palačami i agentami imperialističeskich razvedok [Inevitable retribution: According to evidence in legal proceedings against traitors, Fascist hangmen and agents of imperialist intelligence services] (Moscow, 1973).

NEULEN, HANS WERNER, *Eurofaschismus und der Zweite Weltkrieg: Europas verratene Söhne* (Munich, 1980).

NEWMAN, SIMON, *March 1939: The British Guarantee to Poland. A Study in the Continuity of British Foreign Policy* (Oxford, 1976).

NIEDERMAYER, OSKAR RITTER VON, 'Sowjetrußland: Ein wehrpolitisches Bild', *Militärwissenschaftliche Rundschau*, 4 (1939), 704–23.

NIEDHART, GOTTFRIED, 'Weltherrschaft versus World Appeasement: Konkurrierende Friedensmodelle und außenpolitisches Konfliktverhalten europäischer Großmächte im 20. Jahrhundert', *Neue politische Literatur*, 23 (1978), 281–91.

NIKITIN, A., 'Perestrojka raboty voennoj promyšlennosti SSSR v pervom periode Velikoj Otečestvennoj vojny' [Reorganization of the work of the Soviet war industry in the first phase of the Great Fatherland War], *VIŽ* 1964, No. 2, pp. 11–20.

NILSSON, GÖRAN B., 'Midsommarkrisen 1941', *Historisk tidskrift* (Stockholm), 91/4 (1971), 477–532.

NISH, IAN H., *Japanese Foreign Policy, 1869–1942* (London, 1977).

NOACK, JOHAN PETER, *Det tyske mindretal i Nordslesvig under besættelsen* (Dansk Udenrigspolitisk Instituts Skrifter, 6; Copenhagen, 1974).

NOLTE, ERNST, *Die faschistischen Bewegungen: Die Krise des liberalen Systems und die Entwicklung der Faschismen*[5] (dtv Weltgeschichte des 20. Jahrhunderts, 4; Munich, 1977).

—— *Der Faschismus in seiner Epoche: Die Action française. Der italienische Faschismus. Der Nationalsozialismus* (Munich and Zurich, 1979).

Norge i Krig, ed. Magne Skodvin, 8 vols. (Oslo, 1984–7).

NOVIKOV, A. A., [contribution], in *Oborona Leningrada* (q.v.), 75–101.

Oborona Leningrada 1941–1944: Vospominanija i dnevniki učastnikov [The defence of Leningrad 1941–1944: Recollections and diaries of participants] (Leningrad, 1968).

Obščevojskovaja armija v nastuplenii: Po opytu Velikoj Otečestvennoj vojny 1941–1945 gg. [The army on the attack: Experiences of the Great Fatherland War 1941–1945] (Moscow, 1966).

Očerki istorii sovetsko-pol'skich otnošenij 1917–1977 [Notes on the history of Soviet–Polish relations 1917–1977] (Moscow, 1979).

ODINCOV, G. F., [contribution], in *Oborona Leningrada* (q.v.), 102–39.

OERTEL, MANFRED, 'Zur Beteiligung der Deutschen Reichsbank an der faschistischen Aggression gegen die Sowjetunion', *Militärgeschichte*, 20 (1981), 579–86.

OFFNER, ARNOLD A., *American Appeasement: United States Foreign Policy and Germany, 1933–1938* (Cambridge, Mass., 1969).

OLSHAUSEN, KLAUS, *Zwischenspiel auf dem Balkan: Die deutsche Politik gegenüber Jugoslawien und Griechenland vom März bis Juli 1941* (Beiträge zur Militär- und Kriegsgeschichte, 14; Stuttgart, 1973).

' "Operationsentwurf Ost" des Generalmajors Marcks vom 5. August 1940, Der', ed. with an intro. by Ingo Lachnit and Friedhelm Klein, *Wehrforschung*, 1 (1972), 114–23.

Operazioni delle unità italiane al fronte russo, 1941–1943, Le, ed. Ufficio Storico dello Stato Maggiore dell'Esercito (Rome, 1977).

Oružie pobedy 1941–1945 [Weapons of victory 1941–1945], illustr. by V. Ivanov (Moscow, 1975).

OVERY, RICHARD JAMES, *The Air War 1939–1945* (London, 1980).

PAASIKIVI, JUHO KUSTI, *Am Rande der Supermacht: Behauptung durch Diplomatie*, ed. with intro. by Gösta von Uexküll (Hamburg, 1972).

PAGET, REGINALD T., *Manstein: His Campaigns and his Trial*, with a foreword by Lord Hankey (London, 1951).

PANKOV, D., 'Komandarm 1 ranga I. E. Jakir: K 80-letiju so dnja roždenija' [Army Commander 1st rank I. E. Yakir: On his 80th birthday], *VIŽ* 1976, No. 7, pp. 125–7.

PANOV, B., and NAUMOV, N., 'Vosstanovlenie strategičeskogo fronta na Zapadnom napravlenii, ijul' 1941 g.' [Establishment of a strategic front in a westerly direction, July 1941], *VIŽ* 1976, No. 8, pp. 15–23.

PANTELEEV, J. A., [contribution], in *Oborona Leningrada* (q.v.), 140–78.

PAUL, WOLFGANG, *Brennpunkte: Die Geschichte der 6. Pz.Div. (1. leichte) 1937–1945* (Krefeld, 1977).

PAULUS, FRIEDRICH, *'Ich stehe hier auf Befehl!' Lebensweg des Generalfeldmarschalls Friedrich Paulus. Mit Aufzeichnungen aus dem Nachlaß, Briefen und Dokumenten*, ed.

Walter Görlitz (Frankfurt a.M., 1960). [Trans. Col. R. H. Stevens, *Paulus and Stalingrad*, with a preface by Ernst Alexander Paulus (London, 1963).]

PAULUS, WILHELM-ERNST, *Die Entwicklung der Planung des Rußlandfeldzuges 1940/41* (diss. Bonn, 1957).

PAVLENKO, NIKOLAJ, 'Stalins Krieg gegen die Rote Armee', *Moscow News* 1989, No. 6.

Perepiska Predsedatelja Soveta Ministrov SSSR s prezidentami SŠA i prem'erministrami Velikobritanii vo vremja Velikoj Otečestvennoj vojny 1941–1945 gg. [Correspondence of the Chairman of the USSR Council of Ministers with the Presidents of the USA and the Prime Ministers of Great Britain during the Great Fatherland War 1941–1945], 2 vols. (Moscow, 1957).

PERESYPKIN, I., 'Vojska svjazi v pervyj period Velikoj Otečestvennoj vojny' [The signals troops during the first phase of the Great Fatherland War], *VIŽ* 1968, No. 4, pp. 36–43.

—— 'Svjaz' General'nogo štaba' [The communications system of the General Staf f], *VIŽ* 1971, No. 4, pp. 19–25.

PETRICK, FRITZ, 'Zwei Schlüsseldokumente zur faschistischen "Aufteilung der Europäischen Aluminiumindustrie"', *JWG* 1977, No. 1, pp. 249–68.

—— 'Das Okkupationsregime des faschistischen deutschen Imperialismus in Norwegen 1940–1945', *ZfG* 31 (1983), 397–413.

PETROV, JU. P., *Stroitel'stvo politorganov, partijnych i komsomol'skich organizacij armii i flota, 1918–1968* [Establishment of political organs and Komsomol organizations in the army and navy, 1918–1968] (Moscow, 1968).

PETZINA, DIETER, 'Die Mobilisierung deutscher Arbeitskräfte vor und während des Zweiten Weltkrieges', *VfZG* 18 (1970), 443–55.

PFLANZ, HANS-JOACHIM, *Geschichte der 258. Infanterie-Division, i. 1939 und 1940: Aufstellung und Frankreichfeldzug* (Hamburg, [1975]).

PHILIPPI, ALFRED, *Das Pripjetproblem: Eine Studie über die operative Bedeutung des Pripjetgebietes für den Feldzug des Jahres 1941* (Wehrwissenschaftliche Rundschau, suppl. 2; Darmstadt, 1956).

—— and HEIM, FERDINAND, *Der Feldzug gegen Sowjetrußland 1941–1945: Ein operativer Überblick*, ed. by Arbeitskreis für Wehrforschung (Stuttgart, 1962).

PICKER, HENRY, *Hitlers Tischgespräche im Führerhauptquartier 1941–1942*, for Deutsches Institut für Geschichte der nationalsozialistischen Zeit, arranged, introduced, and published by Gerhard Ritter (Bonn, 1951). [Trans. N. Cameron and R. H. Stevens, *Hitler's Table Talk*, with an introductory essay by H. R. Trevor-Roper on The Mind of Adolf Hitler (London, 1953).]

PIETROW-ENNKER, BIANKA, *Stalinismus, Sicherheit, Offensive: Das 'Dritte Reich' in der Konzeption der sowjetischen Außenpolitik 1933–1941* (Kasseler Forschungen zur Zeitgeschichte, 2; Melsungen, 1983).

—— 'Deutschland im Juni 1941, ein Opfer sowjetischer Aggression? Zur Kontroverse über die Präventivkriegsthese', *Geschichte und Gesellschaft*, 14 (1988), 116–35.

—— 'Die Sowjetunion in der Propaganda des Dritten Reiches: Das Beispiel der Wochenschau', *MGM* 46 (1989), 79–120.

PINKUS, BENJAMIN, and FLEISCHHAUER, INGEBORG, *Die Deutschen in der Sowjetunion: Geschichte einer nationalen Minderheit im 20. Jahrhundert*, ed. Karl-Heinz Ruffmann (Osteuropa und der internationale Kommunismus, 17; Baden-Baden, 1987).

PITERSKIJ, N. A., *Die Sowjet-Flotte im Zweiten Weltkrieg*, for Arbeitskreis für

Wehrforschung, ed. with a commentary by Jürgen Rohwer (Oldenburg and Hamburg, 1966).

50 [pjat' desjat] let vooružennych sil SSSR [50 years of Soviet armed forces], (Moscow, 1968).

PLJAČENKO, P., 'Trudy po teorii boevogo primenenija Sovetskich VVS, 1918–1940 gg.' [Studies on the theory of operational engagement of the Soviet air forces, 1918–1940], *VIŽ* 1970, No. 8, pp. 82–8.

PLOCHER, HERMANN, *The German Air Force versus Russia, 1941* (USAF Historical Studies, 153; New York, 1968).

PLOETZ, *Geschichte des Zweiten Weltkrieges*, ii. *Die Kriegsmittel* (Würzburg, 1960).

PLUMPE, GOTTFRIED, 'Industrie, technischer Fortschritt und Staat: Die Kautschuksynthese in Deutschland 1906–1944/45', *Geschichte und Gesellschaft*, 9 (1983), 564–97.

Pograničnye vojska v gody Velikoj Otečestvennoj vojny 1941–1945: Sbornik dokumentov [The frontier troops during the Great Fatherland War 1941–1945: Documents] (Moscow, 1968).

POKROVSKIJ, A., 'Na Jugo-Zapadnom napravlenii, ijul'–sentjabr' 1941 g.' [In a southwesterly direction, July–September 1941], in *VIŽ* 1978, No. 4, pp. 64–72.

'Polen erinnert Moskau an Völkermord', *Frankfurter Allgemeine Zeitung*, 218 (19 Sept. 1979), 1.

Polnisch-sowjetrussische Krieg 1918–1920, Der, publ. by the Army General Staff, i (Berlin, 1940).

POLUBOJAROV, P. P., 'Krepče broni' [Stronger than armour], in *Na Severo-Zapadnom fronte* (q.v.), 111–32.

POLVINEN, TUOMO, *Finland i stormaktspolitiken 1941–1944: Bakgrunden till fortsättningskriget* (Stockholm, 1969).

—— 'The Great Powers and Finland 1941–1944', in *Revue internationale d'histoire militaire*, 62 (1985), 133–52.

PONOMARENKO, P., 'Bor'ba sovetskogo naroda v tylu vraga' [The struggle of the Soviet people behind the enemy lines], *VIŽ* 1965, No. 4, pp. 26–36.

Popel', N. K., *Tanki povernuli na zapad* [The tanks turned west] (Moscow, 1960).

POPOV, M. M., [contribution], in *Oborona Leningrada* (q.v.), 29–74.

POSTAN, MICHAEL M., *British War Production* (History of the Second World War, United Kingdom Civil Series; London, 1952).

POTTGIESSER, HANS, *Die Deutsche Reichsbahn im Ostfeldzug 1939–1944* (Die Wehrmacht im Kampf, 26; , 1960).

POULSEN, HENNING, *Besættelsesmagten og de danske nazister: Det politiske forhold mellem tyske myndigheder og nazistiske kredse i Danmark 1940–43* (Copenhagen, 1970).

POZDNJAKOV, V. V., 'Sovetskaja agentura v lagerjach voennoplennych v Germanii, 1941–1945 gg.' [The Soviet Secret Service in the POW camps in Germany, 1941–1945], *Novyj žurnal* , 101 (1970), 156–71.

—— 'Novoe o Katyni' [New information on Katyn], *Novyj žurnal* , 107 (1971), 262–80.

—— *Roždenie ROA: Propagandisty Vul'chaide, Ljukenval'de, Dabendorfa, Rigi* [The creation of the Russian liberation army: The propagandists of Wuhlheide, Luckenwalde, Dabendorf, and Riga] (Syracuse, NY, 1972).

—— *Andrej Andreevič Vlasov* (Syracuse, NY, and Buenos Aires, 1973).

'Pravda o gibeli generala M. P. Kirponosa' [The truth about Gen. M. P. Kirponos's death], *VIŽ* 1964, No. 9, pp. 61–9.

Probleme des europäischen Großwirtschaftsraumes, contributions by Anton Reithinger [*et al.*] (Veröffentlichungen des Deutschen Auslandswissenschaftlichen Instituts, 11; Berlin, 1943).

PROCHOROVA, M. P., [contribution], in *Oborona Leningrada* (q.v.), 445–52.

PROCOPÉ, HJALMAR JOHAN, *Sowjetjustiz über Finnland: Prozeßakten aus dem Verfahren gegen die Kriegsverantwortlichen in Finnland* (Zurich, 1947).

PROCTOR, RAYMOND, *Agonía de un Neutral: Las relaciones hispanoalemanas durante la segunda guerra mundial y la División Azul* (Madrid, 1972).

PROÈKTOR, D. M., *Vojna v Evrope 1939–1941 gg.* [The war in Europe 1939–1941] (Moscow, 1963).

QUILITZSCH, SIEGMAR, 'Zur verbrecherischen Rolle der IG-Farben während der faschistischen Aggression gegen die Sowjetunion: Dargestellt am Beispiel der Filmfabrik Agfa Wolfen', in *Juni 1941: Beiträge zur Geschichte des hitlerfaschistischen Überfalls auf die Sowjetunion*, ed. Alfred Anderle and Werner Bader (Veröffentlichungen des Instituts für Geschichte der Völker der UdSSR an der Martin-Luther-Universität, Halle-Wittenberg, series B, 2; Berlin, 1961), 157–87.

QUISLING, VIDKUN, *Quisling ruft Norwegen! Reden und Aufsätze* (Munich, 1942).

RADANDT, HANS, 'Zu den Beziehungen zwischen dem Konzern der Deutschen Bank und dem Staatsapparat bei der Vorbereitung und Durchführung des zweiten Weltkrieges', in *Der deutsche Imperialismus und der zweite Weltkrieg*, publ. by Kommission der Historiker der DDR und der UdSSR, ii. *Beiträge zum Thema: Die Vorbereitung des zweiten Weltkrieges durch den deutschen Imperialismus* (Berlin, 1961), 9–40.

RADZIEVSKIJ, A., 'Proryv oborony v pervom periode vojny' [Penetration of the defences in the first phase of the war], *VIŽ* 1972, No. 3, pp. 11–21.

RAGIONIERI, ERNESTO, 'Italien und der Überfall auf die UdSSR', *ZfG* 9 (1961), 761–808.

RAKICKIJ, A., and PRESNJAKOV, M., 'Boevye dejstvija v rajone Kalinina v oktjabre 1941 goda' [Operations in the Kalinin area in October 1941], *VIŽ* 1976, No. 11, pp. 81–9.

Rapport du Comité International de la Croix-Rouge sur son activité pendant la seconde guerre mondiale, 1 septembre 1939–30 juin 1947, i. *Activités de caractère général* (Geneva, 1948).

RASCHHOFER, HERMANN, *Der Fall Oberländer: Eine vergleichende Rechtsanalyse der Verfahren in Pankow und Bonn* (Tübingen, 1962).

RAUCH, GEORG VON, *Geschichte des bolschewistischen Rußland* (Wiesbaden, 1956).

—— 'Der deutsch-sowjetische Nichtangriffspakt vom August 1939 und die sowjetische Geschichtsforschung', in *Kriegsbeginn 1939: Entfesselung oder Ausbruch des Zweiten Weltkrieges?*, ed. Gottfried Niedhart (Wege der Forschung, 374; Darmstadt, 1976), 349–66.

RAUSCHNING, HERMANN, *Gespräche mit Hitler* (repr. Vienna 1973). [Trans. E. W. Dickes, *Hitler Speaks* (London, 1939).]

READ, ANTHONY, and FISHER, DAVID, *The Deadly Embrace: Hitler, Stalin and the Nazi-Soviet Pact 1939–1941* (London, 1988).

REICHERT, JACOB WILHELM, 'Europas Eisenerzeugung', *Weltwirtschaft*, 30 (1942), 10–15.

REILE, OSCAR, *Geheime Ostfront: Die deutsche Abwehr im Osten 1921–1945* (Munich, 1963).

REINHARDT, HELLMUTH, 'Die russischen Luftlandungen im Bereich der deutschen

Heeresgruppe Mitte in den ersten Monaten des Jahres 1942', *WWR* 8 (1958), 372–88.

REINHARDT, KLAUS, *Die Wende vor Moskau: Das Scheitern der Strategie Hitlers im Winter 1941/42* (Beiträge zur Militär- und Kriegsgeschichte, 13; Stuttgart, 1972).

REITENBACH, GEORG, *UdSSR: Staatssystem, Parteiaufbau, Komintern*² (Berlin, 1941).

REITLINGER, GERALD, *Ein Haus auf Sand gebaut: Hitlers Gewaltpolitik in Rußland 1941–1944* (Hamburg, 1962).

REYNOLDS, NICHOLAS, 'Der Fritsch-Brief vom 11. Dezember 1938: Dokumentation', *VfZG* 28 (1980), 358–71.

RHODE, GOTTHOLD, 'Polen von der Wiederherstellung der Unabhängigkeit bis zur Ära der Volksrepublik 1918–1970', in *Handbuch der europäischen Geschichte*, vii (q.v.), 978–1061.

—— 'Die südosteuropäischen Staaten von der Neuordnung nach dem 1. Weltkrieg bis zur Ära der Volksdemokratien, i. Rumänien 1918–1968', in *Handbuch der europäischen Geschichte*, vii (q.v.), 1134–82.

—— 'Die Tschechoslowakei von der Unabhängigkeitserklärung bis zum "Prager Frühling" 1918–1968', in *Handbuch der europäischen Geschichte*, vii (q.v.), 920–77.

—— 'Ende des Schweigens? Perestrojka und die Tabus sowjetischer Geschichtsschreibung', *Frankfurter Allgemeine Zeitung* (21 Sept. 1988).

RIBBENTROP, JOACHIM von, *Der Freiheitskampf Europas: Rede, gehalten am 26. November 1941 in Berlin* (Schriften des deutschen Instituts für außenpolitische Forschung, 96; Berlin, 1942).

RICH, NORMAN, *Hitler's War Aims*, i. *Ideology, the Nazi State, and the Course of Expansion* (New York, 1973); ii. *The Establishment of the New Order* (London, 1974).

RIECKHOFF, HERBERT JOACHIM, *Trumpf oder Bluff? 12 Jahre deutsche Luftwaffe* (Geneva, 1945).

RIEDEL, MATTHIAS, 'Die Eisenerzversorgung der deutschen Hüttenindustrie zu Beginn des Zweiten Weltkrieges', *Vierteljahrschrift für Sozial- und Wirtschaftsgeschichte*, 58 (1971), 482–96.

—— 'Bergbau und Eisenhüttenindustrie in der Ukraine unter deutscher Besetzung', *VfZG* 21 (1973), 245–84.

—— *Eisen und Kohle für das Dritte Reich: Paul Pleigers Stellung in der NS-Wirtschaft* (Göttingen, Frankfurt a.M., and Zurich, 1973).

RIEMENSCHNEIDER, MICHAEL, *Die deutsche Wirtschaftspolitik gegenüber Ungarn 1933–1944* (Europäische Hochschulschriften, 3rd series, 316; Frankfurt a.M., Berne, New York, and Paris, 1987).

RINGS, WERNER, *Leben mit dem Feind: Anpassung und Widerstand in Hitlers Europa 1939–1945* (Munich, 1979).

RINTALA, MARVIN, *Three Generations: The Extreme Right Wing in Finnish Politics* (Bloomington, Ind., 1962).

Rise and Fall of the German Air Force, 1933–1945, The, ed. W. H. Tantum IV and E. J. Hoffschmidt (Old Greenwich, Conn., 1969).

RITTER, GERHARD, *Das Kommunemodell und die Begründung der Roten Armee im Jahre 1918* (Osteuropa-Institut an der Freien Universität Berlin, Philosophische und soziologische Veröffentlichungen, 6; Berlin and Wiesbaden, 1965).

ROBERTSON, ESMONDE M., 'Hitler Turns from the West to Russia, May–December

1940', in *Paths to War: New Essays on the Origins of the Second World War*, ed. Robert Boyse (London, 1989), 367–82.

ROCKBERGER, NICOLAUS, *Göteborgstrafiken, Svensk lejdtrafik under andra världskriget* (Stockholm, 1973).

ROHDE, HORST, *Das deutsche Wehrmachttransportwesen im Zweiten Weltkrieg: Entstehung, Organisation, Aufgaben* (Beiträge zur Militär- und Kriegsgeschichte, 12; Stuttgart, 1971).

ROHLAND, WALTER, *Bewegte Zeiten: Erinnerungen eines Eisenhüttenmannes* (Stuttgart, 1978).

RÖHRICHT, EDGAR, *Probleme der Kesselschlacht: Dargestellt an Einkreisungs-Operationen im Zweiten Weltkrieg* (Karlsruhe, 1958).

ROHWER, JÜRGEN, 'Sowjetische Kriegsschiff-Verluste während des Zweiten Weltkrieges', in *Das deutsche Bild der russischen und sowjetischen Marine: Vorträge der 5. historisch-taktischen Tagung der Flotte, 6.–7. Dez. 1961* (Marine-Rundschau, suppl. 7/8; Berlin and Frankfurt a.M., 1962), 125–38.

—— 'Der Minenkrieg im Finnischen Meerbusen, 1. Juni–August 1941; 2. September–November 1941', *MR* 64 (1967), 16–25, 94–102.

—— 'Der Seekrieg im Nordmeer 1941–1945', in *Seemacht* (q.v.), 642–97.

—— 'Die deutsch-finnischen Minensperren im Finnischen Meerbusen vom 22.6. bis 28.8.1941', *MR* 64 (1967), 42–3.

—— 'Die Verluste der Baltischen Rotbanner-Flotte bei der Evakuierung von Reval', *MR* 64 (1967), 44–6.

—— 'Die sowjetischen U-Boot-Erfolge in der Ostsee im Zweiten Weltkrieg', *MR* 65 (1968), 427–39.

—— and HÜMMELCHEN, GERHARD, *Chronik des Seekrieges 1939–1945* (Oldenburg and Hamburg, 1968). [Rev. Eng. edn., ed. A. J. Watts, trans. D. Masters, *Chronology of the War at Sea, 1939–1945* (2 vols., London, 1972).]

ROKOSSOVSKIJ, K. K., 'Na severnych podstupach' [On northern approaches], in *VIŽ* 1966, No. 12, pp. 50–62.

—— 'Na volokolamskom napravlenii' [In direction Volokolamsk], *VIŽ* 1966, No. 11, pp. 46–55.

—— *Soldatskij dolg* [A soldier's duty] (Moscow, 1968).

ROMAN, VIOREL S., *Rumänien im Spannungsfeld der Großmächte*, [ii.] *1878–1947: Von der okzidentalischen Peripherie zum orientalischen Sozialismus* (Offenbach, 1989).

Roosevelt, Franklin Delano: His Personal Letters, ed. Elliott Roosevelt, i. *Early Years 1905–1928*; ii. *1928–1945* (New York, 1947–50).

ROSCHMANN, HANS, *Gutachten zur Behandlung und zu den Verlusten sowjetischer Kriegsgefangener in deutscher Hand von 1941–1945 und zur Bewertung der Beweiskraft des sogenannten 'Documents NOKW 2125'* (*Nachweisung des Verbleibs der sowjetischen Kriegsgefangenen nach dem Stande vom 1.5.1944*) (Veröffentlichungen der Zeitgeschichtlichen Forschungsstelle Ingolstadt, 1; Ingolstadt, 1982).

ROSENBERG, MICHAEL, *Die Schwerindustrie in Russisch-Asien: Eine Studie über das Ural-Kusnezker-Kombinat* (Berlin, 1938).

ROSENGREEN, BJORN, *Dr. Werner Best og tysk besættelsespolitik i Danmark 1943–1945* (Odense University Studies in History and Social Sciences, 75; Odense, 1982).

ROSINSKI, HERBERT, *The German Army*, ed. with intro. by Gordon A. Craig (London, 1966).

ROSSI, ANDRÉ [i.e. ANGELO TASCA], *Physiologie du Parti Communiste Français* (Paris, 1948).

—— *Zwei Jahre deutsch-sowjetisches Bündnis* (Cologne and Berlin, 1954).

Rote Armee, Die, ed. Basil H. Liddell Hart (Bonn, 1956).

RÜCKER, WILHELM VON, 'Die Vorbereitungen für den Feldzug gegen Rußland', in Wagner, *Generalquartiermeister* (q.v.), 313–18.

Rückführung des Ostheeres, Die, for the Reich War Ministry, ed. and publ. by Forschungsanstalt für Kriegs- und Heeresgeschichte (Darstellungen aus den Nachkriegskämpfen deutscher Truppen und Freikorps, 1; Berlin, 1936).

RUDAKOV, M., 'Rol′ voennych sovetov frontov i armij v rukovodstve boevymi dejstvijami partizan v gody Velikoj Otečestvennoj vojny' [The role of war councils of fronts and armies in the conduct of operations of partisans during the Great Fatherland War], *VIŽ* 1962, No. 7, pp. 3–14.

RUDEL, HANS-ULRICH, *Trotzdem* (Gmunden and Bad Ischl, 1953).

RUEF, KARL, *Gebirgsjäger zwischen Kreta und Murmansk: Die Schicksale der 6. Gebirgsdivision* (Graz and Stuttgart, 1970).

—— *Odyssee einer Gebirgsdivision: Die 3. Gebirgsdivision im Einsatz* (Graz and Stuttgart, 1976).

—— *Winterschlacht im Mai: Die Zerreißprobe des Gebirgskorps Norwegen (XIX. Geb.A.K.) vor Murmansk* (Graz and Stuttgart, 1984).

RÜF, HANS, *Gebirgsjäger vor Murmansk: Der Kampf des Gebirgskorps 'Norwegen' an der Eismeerfront 1941/42* (Innsbruck, 1957).

RUGE, FRIEDRICH, *Der Seekrieg 1939–1945*[2] (Stuttgart, 1956). [Trans. M. G. Saunders, *Sea Warfare 1939–1945: A German Viewpoint* (London, 1957).]

RUHL, KLAUS-JÖRG, *Spanien im Zweiten Weltkrieg: Franco, die Falange und das 'Dritte Reich'* (Historische Perspektiven, 2; Hamburg, 1975).

RUMJANCEV, N. M., *Razgrom vraga v Zapoljar′e, 1941–1944 gg. Voenno-istoričeskij očerk* [The smashing of the enemy in the Arctic region, 1941–1944: A military-historical study] (Moscow, 1963).

'Rüstungspotential der Sowjets, Das', *Militärwochenblatt*, 126 (1941), 470–2.

RYTI, RISTO, *Stunden der Entscheidung: Reden des finnischen Staatspräsidenten Risto Ryti* (Leipzig and Berlin, 1943).

RYŽAKOV, A., 'K voprosu o stroitel′stve bronetankovych vojsk Krasnoj Armii v 30-e gody' [On the question of the creation of the Red Army's armoured forces in the 1930s], *VIŽ* 1968, No. 8, pp. 105–11.

RYŽI, N. K., 'Na Sevastopol′skich rubežach' [On the outskirts of Sevastopol], in *U černomorskich tverdyn′* (q.v.), 139–78.

RŽEŠEVSKIJ, O., 'Iz istorii odnogo predatel′stva' [History of a case of treason], *VIŽ* 1969, No. 9, pp. 26–34.

—— and G. Ivanickij, 'Pravda i lož′ o žizni nemeckich voenno-plennych v SSSR' [Truth and falsehood about the life of German POWs in the USSR], *VIŽ* 1978, No. 10, pp. 76–82.

ŠACHURIN, A. I., 'Aviacionnaja promyšlennost′ nakanune i v gody Velikoj Otečestvennoj vojny' [The aircraft industry on the eve of and during the Great Fatherland War], in *Sovetskij tyl* (q.v.), ii. 67–106.

SALEWSKI, MICHAEL, *Die deutsche Seekriegsleitung 1935–1945*, 3 vols. (Frankfurt a.M. and Munich, 1970–5).

—— 'Basis Nord: Eine fast vergessene Episode aus dem zweiten Weltkrieg', *Schiff und*

Zeit, 3 (1976), 11–17.

SALISBURY, HARRISON E., *The Siege of Leningrad* (London 1969).

SAMSONOV, A. M., 'Moskvu zaščiščala vsja strana' [Moscow was defended by the whole country], in *Besprimernyj podvig* (q.v.), 51–62.

SANDALOV, L., 'Oboronitel'naja operacija 4-j armii v načal'nyj period vojny' [The defensive operation of Fourth Army in the initial phase of the war], *VIŽ* 1971, No. 7, pp. 18–28.

ŠAPOŠNIKOV, B. M., *Vospominanija: Voenno-naučnye trudy* [Reminiscences: Military studies] (Moscow, 1974).

ŠAVORONKOV, GENADIJ, 'Charkow, ein zweites Katyn', *Moscow News*, 1990, No. 7.

SAVOST'JANOV, V., 'Eronim Uborevič', in *Geroi graždanskoj vojny* (q.v.), 66–120.

SAVU, Al. Gh., 'The Type of Defensive War Envisaged by the Romanian Inter-war Military Policy', in *The Army and the Romanian Society*, ed. Al. Gh. Savu (Bucharest, 1980), 124–40.

SAZONOV, I., 'Nastupaet 1-ja gvardejskaja . . .' [The First Guards Army on the attack], *VIŽ* 1969, No. 12, pp. 60–4.

ŠČELOKOV, A., and KOMAROV, N., 'Oborona Leningrada v ložnom svete mistra Solsberi' [The defence of Leningrad in the mendacious light of Mr Salisbury], *VIŽ* 1970, No. 6, pp. 85–91.

SCHALL-RIAUCOUR, HEIDEMARIE GRÄFIN, *Aufstand und Gehorsam: Offiziertum und Generalstab im Umbruch. Leben und Wirken von Generaloberst Halder, Generalstabschef 1938–1942* (Wiesbaden, 1972).

SCHAPIRO, LEONHARD, 'Die Geburt der Roten Armee', in *Die Rote Armee* (q.v.), 31–9.

—— 'Die große Säuberung', in *Die Rote Armee* (q.v.), 71–9.

SCHICKEL, ALFRED, 'Polen 1939, gesehen mit britischen Augen: Englische Diplomaten beschreiben Stimmungen und Pläne der Polen vor Ausbruch des Krieges', *Frankfurter Allgemeine Zeitung*, 202 (31 Aug. 1979), 5–6.

—— 'Ein vergessenes Kapitel Zeitgeschichte: Gefangene Polen in deutschen Offizierslagern', *WWR* 30 (1981), pp. 28–32.

'Schicksalsweg der norwegischen Freiwilligen-Division der Waffen-SS, Der', *Der Freiwillige*, 12/4 (1966), 11–14.

'Schlafende Aggressoren', *Der Spiegel*, 44/22 (1990), 170–2.

SCHMIDT, PAUL, *Statist auf diplomatischer Bühne 1923–1945: Erlebnisse des Chefdolmetschers im Auswärtigen Amt mit den Staatsmännern Europas* (Bonn, 1954). [Trans. (abridged) R. H. C. Steed, *Hitler's Interpreter* (London, 1951).]

SCHMOKEL, WOLFE W., *Der Traum vom Reich: Der deutsche Kolonialismus zwischen 1919 und 1945* (Gütersloh, 1967).

SCHNEIDER, 'Der Kampf der Giganten', in *Wirtschafts-Illustrierte Arbeit und Wehr*, 11/6 (1941), 162.

SCHNEIDER, MICHAEL, *Das 'Unternehmen Barbarossa': Die verdrängte Erblast von 1941 und die Folgen für das deutsch-sowjetische Verhältnis* (Frankfurt a.M., 1989).

SCHOFIELD, BRIAN BETHAN, *The Russian Convoys* (London, 1944).

SCHOU, SOREN, *De danske Østfront-frivillige* (Copenhagen, 1981).

SCHREIBER, FRANZ, *Kampf unter dem Nordlicht: Deutsch-finnische Waffenbruderschaft am Polarkreis. Die Geschichte der 6. SS-Gebirgs-Division Nord* (Osnabrück, 1969).

SCHREIBER, GERHARD, 'Zur Kontinuität des Groß- und Weltmachtstrebens der deutschen Marineführung', *MGM* 26 (1979), 101–71.

—— 'Der Mittelmeerraum in Hitlers Strategie 1940: "Programm" und militärische Planung', *MGM* 28 (1980), 69–99.

SCHRÖDER, HANS-JÜRGEN, 'Deutsche Südosteuropapolitik 1929–1936: Zur Kontinuität deutscher Außenpolitik in der Weltwirtschaftskrise', *Geschichte und Gesellschaft*, 2 (1976), 5–32.

SCHUKOW, GEORGI, K.: *see* Žukov, G. K.

SCHÜLER, KLAUS A. FRIEDRICH, *Logistik im Rußlandfeldzug: Die Rolle der Eisenbahn bei Planung, Vorbereitung und Durchführung des deutschen Angriffs auf die Sowjetunion bis zur Krise vor Moskau im Winter 1941/42* (Europäische Hochschulschriften, 3rd series, 331; Frankfurt a.M. [etc.], 1987).

SCHULTE, THEO, J., *The German Army and Nazi Policies in Occupied Russia* (Oxford, New York, and Munich, 1989).

SCHUMANN, WOLFGANG, 'Der Zeiss-Konzern im System des staatsmonopolistischen Kapitalismus während des Faschismus', *JWG* 1962, No. 4, pp. 115–38.

—— 'Das Kriegsprogramm des Zeiss-Konzerns: Ein Beitrag zum Problem des staatsmonopolistischen Kapitalismus und der faschistischen Politik der "Neuordnung" Europas und Ostasiens während des zweiten Weltkrieges', *ZfG* 11 (1963), 704–28.

—— 'Die faschistische "Neuordnung" Europas nach den Plänen des deutschen Monopolkapitals. Programme der Metallindustrie, des Metallerz- und Kohlenbergbaus im Jahre 1940', *ZfG* 19 (1971), 224–41.

SCHUSTEREIT, HARTMUT, 'Die Mineralöllieferungen der Sowjetunion an das Deutsche Reich 1940/41', *Vierteljahrsschrift für Sozial- und Wirtschaftsgeschichte*, 67 (1980), 334–53.

—— *Vabanque: Hitlers Angriff auf die Sowjetunion 1941 als Versuch, durch den Sieg im Osten den Westen zu bezwingen* (Herford and Bonn, 1988).

SCHWARTZ, ANDREW, J., *America and the Russo-Finnish War* (Washington, DC, 1960).

Schwedische und schweizerische Neutralität im Zweiten Weltkrieg, ed. Rudolf L. Bindschedler [*et al.*] (Basle and Frankfurt a.M., 1985).

SCHWERDTFEGER, BERNHARD, *Deutschland und Rußland im Wandel der europäischen Bündnisse* (Hanover, 1939).

SCHWERIN VON KROSIGK, LUTZ GRAF, *Persönliche Erinnerungen*, pts. 1–3 (Essen, [1973–5]).

SEATON, ALBERT, *Der russisch-deutsche Krieg 1941–1945*, ed. Andreas Hillgruber (Frankfurt a.M., 1973).

ŠECHOVCOV, N., 'Sovetskoe strategičeskoe rukovodstvo i izmyšlenija fal'sifikatorov' [Soviet strategic leadership and the inventions of the falsifiers], *VIŽ* 1974, No. 3, pp. 45–52.

Secret Conferences of Dr. Goebbels: see *Wollt Ihr den totalen Krieg?*

Seemacht: Eine Seekriegsgeschichte von der Antike bis zur Gegenwart, ed. Elmer B. Potter and Chester W. Nimitz, German rev. edn. by Jürgen Rohwer (Munich, 1974).

ŠELACHOV, G., and GELLER, C. Ju., 'O polkovodčeskoj i voenno-organizatorskoj dejatel'nosti I. E. Jakira' [On I. E. Yakir's work as a military leader and organizer], *VIŽ* 1962, No. 5, pp. 25–43.

SEMENOV, G., 'Iz opyta organizacii i vedenija nastupitel'noj operacii 3-j udarnoj armiej zimoj 1942 goda' [Organization and leadership of the offensive operations mounted by the Third Assault Army in the winter of 1942], *VIŽ* 1977, No. 1, pp. 85–92.

SEMENOV, V. A., *Kratkij očerk razvitija sovetskogo operativnogo iskusstva* [Short outline of the development of Soviet operational skill] (Moscow, 1960).

SENGER UND ETTERLIN, FERDINAND MARIA VON, *Die deutschen Panzer 1926–1945*[2] (Munich, 1965).

ŠIKIN, I., 'Podvigu žit' v vekach!' [That heroism will live for ever!], *VIŽ* 1971, No. 12, pp. 52–63.

SILAGI, DENIS, 'Ungarn seit 1918: Vom Ende des 1. Weltkrieges bis zur Ära Kádár', in *Handbuch der europäischen Geschichte*, vii (q.v.), 883–919.

SIMPSON, KEITH, 'The German Experience of Rear Area Security on the Eastern Front, 1941–45', *Journal of the Royal United Services Institute for Defence Studies*, 121 (1976), 39–46.

SINICYNA, N. I., and TOMIN, V. P., 'Proval agrarnoj politiki gitlerovcev na okkupirovannoj territorii SSSR, 1941–1944 gg.' [The failure of Hitlerite agrarian policy in the occupied territories of the USSR, 1941–1944], *Voprosy istorii*, 1965, No. 6, pp. 32–44.

SIPOLS, V. Ja., *Diplomatičeskaja bor'ba nakanune vtoroj mirovoj vojny* [The diplomatic struggle on the eve of the Second World War] (Moscow, 1979).

—— *Die Vorgeschichte des deutsch-sowjetischen Nichtangriffsvertrags* (Cologne, 1981).

SJOQVIST, VIGGO, *Eric Scavenius: Danmarks udenrigsminister under to verdenskrige. Statsminister 1942–1945*, 2 vols. (Copenhagen, 1973).

SKŠIPEK, A., 'Pol'sko-sovetskie diplomatičeskie otnošenija 1933–1939 gg.' [Polish–Soviet diplomatic relations 1933–1939], in *Očerki istorii sovetsko-pol'skich otnošenij* (q.v.), 155–76.

SLESINA, HORST, *Soldaten gegen Tod und Teufel: Unser Kampf in der Sowjetunion. Eine soldatische Deutung* (Düsseldorf, 1942).

SMIRNOV, N., 'Delo ob ubijstve bakinskich komissarov' [The case of the murder of the Baku Commissars], in *Neotvratimoe vozmezdie* (q.v.), 73–89.

SOFRONOV, G. P., 'Odesskij placdarm' [The Odessa bridgehead], in *U černomorskich tverdyn'* (q.v.), 5–29.

SOIKA, GÜNTHER, *Der Außenhandel Rußlands* (diss. Vienna, 1941).

SOKOLOVSKIJ, V. D., 'Velikaja bitva pod Moskvoj i ee istoričeskoe značenie' [The great battle at Moscow and its historic significance], in *Besprimernyj podvig* (q.v.), 18–37.

SOLDATOV, N., and KOROL'ČENKO, A., 'Znamenskij desant' [The Znamenka landing], *VIŽ* 1972, No. 12, pp. 71–4.

SOLŽENIZYN, ALEKSANDR, *The Gulag Archipelago*, trans. T. P. Whitney (London, 1974).

SOMMER, THEO, *Deutschland und Japan zwischen den Mächten 1935–1940: Vom Antikominternpakt bis zum Dreimächtepakt. Eine Studie zur diplomatischen Vorgeschichte des Zweiten Weltkriegs* (Tübinger Studien zur Geschichte und Politik, 15; Tübingen, 1962).

Sommer 1939: Die Großmächte und der europäische Krieg, ed. Wolfgang Benz and Hermann Graml (Schriftenreihe der Vierteljahrshefte für Zeitgeschichte, special issue; Stuttgart, 1979).

Sovetskaja èkonomika v period Velikoj Otečestvennoj vojny 1941–1945 gg. [The Soviet economy during the Great Fatherland War 1941–1945] (Moscow, 1970).

Sovetskie tankovye vojska 1941–1945: Voenno-istoričeskij očerk [The Soviet armoured forces: A military-historical study] (Moscow, 1973).

Sovetskij tyl v Velikoj Otečestvennoj vojne, i. *Obščie problemy*; ii. *Trudovoj podvig naroda*

[The Soviet hinterland in the Great Fatherland War, i. General problems; ii. The labour heroism of the people] (Moscow, 1974).

Soviet Air Force in World War II, The: The Official History, originally publ. by the Ministry of Defence of the USSR, ed. Ray Wagner (London, 1974).

Soviet Army, The [by various authors], ed. B. H. Liddell Hart (London, 1956).

'Sowjetunion gesteht das Massaker von Katyn ein, Die', *Frankfurter Allgemeine Zeitung* (14 Apr 1990).

SPEER, ALBERT, *Erinnerungen* (Frankfurt a.M., 1969). [Trans. Richard and Clara Winston, *Inside the Third Reich* (London, 1975).]

—— *Der Sklavenstaat: Meine Auseinandersetzung mit der SS* (Stuttgart, 1981).

SPEIDEL, HELM, 'Reichswehr und Rote Armee', *VfZG*, 1 (1953), 9–45.

SPETZLER, EBERHARD, *Luftkrieg und Menschlichkeit: Die völkerrechtliche Stellung der Zivilpersonen im Luftkrieg* (Göttinger Beiträge zu Gegenwartsfragen des Völkerrechts und der internationalen Beziehungen, 12; Göttingen, 1956).

Staatsmänner und Diplomaten bei Hitler: Vertrauliche Aufzeichnungen über Unterredungen mit Vertretern des Auslandes 1939–1941, ed. Andreas Hillgruber, 2 vols. (Frankfurt a.M., 1967).

STALIN, JOSIF VISSARIONOVIČ , *Über den Großen Vaterländischen Krieg der Sowjetunion*[3] (Moscow, 1946).

—— *Werke*, 13 vols. (Berlin, 1951–5).

Stalin's Correspondence with Churchill, Attlee, Roosevelt and Truman 1941–1945, pts. 1–2 (London, 1958).

Stalin und Hitler: Pakt gegen Europa, ed. with intro. Johann Wolfgang Brügel (Vienna, 1973).

STARINOV, I., 'Ėto bylo tajnoj' [That was a secret], *VIŽ* 1964, No. 4, pp. 76–91.

STECKEVIČ, S. M., 'Sovetsko-pol'skie dogovory o družbe, sotrudničestve i vzaimnoj pomošči 1945 i 1965 gg. i ich istoričeskoe značenie' [The Soviet–Polish treaties of friendship, co-operation, and mutual aid 1945 and 1965, and their historic significance], in *Očerki istorii sovetsko-pol'skich otnošenij* (q.v.), 383–96.

STEGEMANN, BERND, 'Hitlers Ziele im ersten Kriegsjahr 1939/40: Ein Beitrag zur Quellenkritik', *MGM* 27 (1980), 93–105.

—— 'Geschichte und Politik: Zur Diskussion über den deutschen Angriff auf die Sowjetunion 1941', *Beiträge zur Konfliktforschung*, 17/1 (1987), 73–97.

STEIGLEDER, H., 'Bedeutung und Auswirkung des Kampfes der Baltischen Rotbannerflotte auf die Seeverbindungen des Gegners im Jahre 1941', *Militärwesen* (C), 16/8 (1972), 117–23.

—— 'Operation "Eisstoß": Ein letzter Versuch der faschistischen deutschen Führung zur Vernichtung der Baltischen Rotbannerflotte', *Militärwesen* (C), 16/10 (1972), 120–6.

STEIN, GEORGE, H., *Geschichte der Waffen-SS* (Düsseldorf, 1978).

—— and KROSBY, HANS PETER, 'Das finnische Freiwilligen-Bataillon der Waffen-SS: Eine Studie zur SS-Diplomatie und zur ausländischen Freiwilligen-Bewegung', *VfZG* 14 (1966), 413–53.

STEINER, FELIX, *Die Freiwilligen: Idee und Opfergang* (Göttingen, 1958).

STEINERT, MARLIS G., *Hitlers Krieg und die Deutschen: Stimmung und Haltung der deutschen Bevölkerung im Zweiten Weltkrieg* (Düsseldorf and Vienna, 1970).

ŠTEMENKO, S. M., *General'nyj štab v gody vojny*, i [The General Staff during the war years] (Moscow, 1968).

Stökl, Günther, *Russische Geschichte: Von den Anfängen bis zur Gegenwart* (Stuttgart, 1962).

Stoler, Mark, A., *The Politics of the Second Front: American Military Planning and Diplomacy in Coalition Warfare, 1941–1943* (Westport, Conn., and London, 1977).

Strassner, Peter, *Europäische Freiwillige: Die Geschichte der 5. SS-Panzerdivision Wiking* (Osnabrück, 1968).

Streim, Alfred, *Die Behandlung sowjetischer Kriegsgefangener im 'Fall Barbarossa': Eine Dokumentation. Unter Berücksichtigung der Unterlagen deutscher Strafvollzugsbehörden und der Materialien der Zentralen Stelle der Landesjustizverwaltungen zur Aufklärung von NS-Verbrechen* (Motive, Texte, Materialien, 139; Heidelberg and Karlsruhe, 1981).

Streit, Christian, *Keine Kameraden: Die Wehrmacht und die sowjetischen Kriegsgefangenen 1941–1945* (Studien zur Zeitgeschichte, 13; Stuttgart, 1978).

—— 'Sowjetische Kriegsgefangene, Massendeportationen, Zwangsarbeiter', in *Frieden mit der Sowjetunion* (q.v.), 102–16.

Stumpf, Reinhard, 'Die Luftwaffe als drittes Heer: Die Luftwaffen-Erdkampfverbände und das Problem der Sonderheere 1933–1945', in *Soziale Bewegung und politische Verfassung: Beiträge zur Geschichte der modernen Welt*, ed. Ulrich Engelhardt [*et al.*] (Stuttgart, 1976), 87–894.

Sundhaussen, Holm, 'Die Weltwirtschaftskrise im Donau-Balkan-Raum und ihre Bedeutung für den Wandel der deutschen Außenpolitik unter Brüning', in *Aspekte deutscher Außenpolitik im 20. Jahrhundert: Aufsätze Hans Rothfels zum Gedächtnis*, ed. W. Benz and H. Graml (Stuttgart, 1976), 121–64.

Suomen Sota 1941–1945 [Finland's War 1941–1945], ed. Sotahistoriallinen Tutkimuslaitos [War-Historical Research Institute], 10 vols. (Helsinki, 1952–65).

Surčenko, A., 'Likvidacija proryva v rajone Naro-Fominska' [Liquidation of the penetration in the Naro-Fominsk area], *VIŽ* 1962, No. 12, pp. 49–57.

Suvorov, Viktor, *Der Eisbrecher: Hitler in Stalins Kalkül* (Stuttgart, 1989).

Sveriges förhållande till Danmark och Norge under krigsåren: Redogörelser avgivna till utrikesnämnden av ministern för utrikes ärendena 1941–1945 (Stockholm, 1945).

Svetlišin, N., 'Ot soldata do maršala: K 70-letiju G. K. Žukova' [From private to marshal: On the 70th birthday of G. K. Zhukov]; *VIŽ* 1966, No. 11, pp. 31–40.

Szöllösi-Janze, Margit, *Die Pfeilkreuzlerbewegung in Ungarn: Historischer Kontext, Entwicklung und Herrschaft* (Studien zur Zeitgeschichte, 35; Munich, 1989).

Talvela, Paavo, *Muistelmat: Sotilaan elämä* [Reminiscences: A soldier's life], 2 vols. (Jyväskylä, 1976–7).

Tasca, Angelo: *see* Rossi, André.

Tel'puchovskij (Telpuchowski), B. S., *Die sowjetische Geschichte des Großen Vaterländischen Krieges 1941–1945*, for Arbeitskreis für Wehrforschung, Stuttgart, publ. and critically elucidated by A. Hillgruber and H.-A. Jacobsen (Frankfurt a.M., 1961).

—— 'Dejatel'nost' KPSS po ukrepleniju oboronnoj mošči SSR v 1939–1941 gg.' [CPSU activity to strengthen the defensive power of the USSR in 1939–1941], *VIŽ* 1973, No. 10, pp. 61–5.

Tervasmäki, Vilho, *Mannerheim: Valtiomies ja sotapäällikkö talvi- ja jatkosotien käännekohdissa* [Mannerheim: Statesman and general at the turning-points of the Winter War and the Continuation War] (Hämeenlinna, 1987).

Tessin, Georg, *Verbände und Truppen der deutschen Wehrmacht und Waffen-SS im Zweiten Weltkrieg 1939–1945*, 14 vols. (Osnabrück, 1977–80).

THAMER, HANS-ULRICH, and WIPPERMANN, WOLFGANG, *Faschistische und neofaschistische Bewegungen: Probleme empirischer Faschismusforschung* (Erträge der Forschung, 72; Darmstadt, 1977).

THIES, JOCHEN, *Architekt der Weltherrschaft: Die 'Endziele' Hitlers*[2] (Düsseldorf, 1976).

THOMAS, GEORG, 'Gedanken und Ereignisse', *Schweizer Monatshefte*, 25 (1945), 538–59.

——— *Geschichte der deutschen Wehr- und Rüstungswirtschaft, 1918–1943/45*, ed. Wolfgang Birkenfeld (Schriften des Bundesarchivs, 14; Boppard, 1966).

THOMSEN, ERICH, *Deutsche Besatzungspolitik in Dänemark 1940–1945* (Studien zur modernen Geschichte, 4, Düsseldorf, 1971).

THULSTRUP, ÅKE, 'Gustav V's roll under midsommarkrisen 1941', *Historisk tidskrift* (Stockholm), 92/1 (1972), 72–9.

——— 'Die schwedische Pressepolitik im Zweiten Weltkrieg', in *Schwedische und schweizerische Neutralität* (q.v.), 128–43.

TIEKE, WILHELM, *Tragödie um die Treue: Kampf und Untergang des III. (germ.) SS-Panzerkorps* (Osnabrück, 1968).

——— *Im Lufttransport an Brennpunkte der Ostfront* (Osnabrück, 1971).

——— 'Geschichte des "Freikorps Danmark"', in Tieke, *Im Lufttransport* (q.v.), 149–290.

——— *Das Finnische Freiwilligen-Bataillon der Waffen-SS: III. (finn.) 'Nordland'* (Osnabrück, 1979).

TILKOVSZKY, L., 'Die Werbeaktionen der Waffen-SS in Ungarn', *Acta Historica Academiae Scientiarum Hungaricae*, 20 (1974), 137–80.

TIPPELSKIRCH, KURT VON, *Geschichte des Zweiten Weltkrieges*[2] (Bonn, 1956).

TITOV, F., 'Kljatvoprestupniki' [They broke their oaths], in *Neotvratimoe vozmezdie* (q.v.), 214–34.

TJULENEV, I. V., *Čerez tri vojny* [Through three wars] (Moscow, 1960).

TODORSKIJ, A. I., *Maršal Tuchačevskij* [Marshal Tukhachevsky] (Moscow, 1964).

TOLSTOY, NIKOLAI, *Victims of Yalta* (London, Sydney, Auckland, and Toronto, 1977).

TOPITSCH, ERNST, *Stalin's War: A Radical New Theory of the Origins of the Second World War* (New York, 1987).

——— *Stalins Krieg: Die sowjetische Langzeitstrategie gegen den Westen als rationale Machtpolitik*[3] (Herford, 1990).

TÓTH, SÁNDOR, 'Ungarns militärische Rolle im zweiten Weltkrieg: Historiographischer Überblick', in *Ostmitteleuropa im zweiten Weltkrieg*, ed. F. Glatz (Budapest, 1978), 79–99.

TOYAMA SABURO, 'Die japanischen Planungen für den Großostasienkrieg 1941', in *Kriegswende Dezember 1941: Referate und Diskussionsbeiträge des internationalen historischen Symposiums in Stuttgart vom 17.–19. September 1981*, ed. Jürgen Rohwer (Koblenz, 1984), 17–34.

Trial of Major War Criminals by the International Military Tribunal Sitting at Nuremberg, Germany, 42 vols. (London, 1947–9). (Vols. i–xxii are cited according to the English version; the remaining vols. according to the German text, which was not translated: *Der Prozeß gegen die Hauptkriegsverbrecher vor dem Internationalen Militärgerichtshof, Nürnberg, 14. November 1945 bis 1. Oktober 1946* (42 vols.; Nuremberg, 1947–9)).

Trials of War Criminals before the Nuernberg Military Tribunals under Control Council Law No. 10, Nuernberg October 1946–April 1949, viii. *The I.G. Farben Case* (Washington, DC, 1952).

TRIBUC, V. F., 'Ėvakuacija garnizona Chanko' [The evacuation of the Hangö garrison], *Voprosy istorii* 1966, No. 11, pp. 103–16.

—— 'Die Räumung der Garnison von Hangö', *MR* 64 (1967), 103–10, 158–79.

TROCKIJ, LEV DAVIDOVIČ, *Geschichte der Russischen Revolution*, ii. *Oktoberrevolution* (Berlin, 1933). [Trans. Max Eastman, *History of the Russian Revolution* (London, 1932).]

TROTSKY: *see* preceding entry.

Truth about Katyn, The: Report of the Extraordinary State Commission for Ascertaining and Investigating Crimes Committed by the German-Fascist Invaders and their Associates (privately owned by Dr Hoffmann).

TSCHUNKE, FRITZ, 'Große deutsch-sowjetische Wirtschaftsplanung: Neue Aufgaben für den Rußland-Ausschuß der Deutschen Wirtschaft', *Die Ostwirtschaft*, 28/10–11 (1939), 125–6.

TUCHAČEVSKIJ, M. N., *Izbrannye proizvedenija* [Selected works], i. *1919–1927 gg.*; ii. *1928–1937 gg.* (Moscow, 1964).

TUIDER, OTHMAR, LEGLER, ANTON, and WITTAS, HANS-EGON, *Bibliographie zur Geschichte der Felddivisionen der Deutschen Wehrmacht und Waffen-SS 1939–1945*, ed. Heeresgeschichtliches Museum, Militärwiss. Institut, Militärwiss. Abteilung (Vienna, 1976) [duplicated typescript.]

TURTOLA, MARTTI, *Erik Heinrichs: Mannerheimin ja Paasikiven kenraali* [Erik Heinrichs: Mannerheim's and Paasikivi's general] (Keuruu, 1988).

Tyl sovetskich vooružennych sil v Velikoj Otečestvennoj vojne 1941–1945 gg. [The rear area of the Soviet fighting forces in the Great Fatherland War 1941–1945] (Moscow, 1977).

Učernomorskich tverdyn': Otdel'naja Primorskaja armija v oborone Odessy i Sevastopolja [At Black Sea fortresses: The Independent Coastal Army in the defence of Odessa and Sevastopol] (Moscow, 1967).

UEBERSCHÄR, GERD, R., *Hitler und Finnland 1939–1941: Die deutsch-finnischen Beziehungen während des Hitler-Stalin-Paktes* (Frankfurter Historische Abhandlungen, 16; Wiesbaden, 1978).

—— 'Guerre de coalition ou guerre séparée: Conception et structures de la stratégie germano-finlandaise dans la guerre contre l'URSS, 1941–1944', *Revue d'histoire de la deuxième guerre mondiale*, 30/118 (1980), 27–68.

—— 'Koalitionskriegführung im Zweiten Weltkrieg: Probleme der deutsch-finnischen Waffenbrüderschaft im Kampf gegen die Sowjetunion', in *Militärgeschichte: Probleme, Thesen, Wege* (q.v.), 355–82.

—— 'Hitlers Entschluß zum "Lebensraum"-Krieg im Osten: Programmatisches Ziel oder militärstrategisches Kalkül?', in *'Unternehmen Barbarossa'* (q.v.), 83–110.

—— '"Historikerstreit" und "Präventivkriegsthese": Zu den Rechtfertigungsversuchen des deutschen Überfalls auf die Sowjetunion 1941', *Tribüne*, 26 (1987), 108–16.

—— 'Zur Wiederbelebung der "Präventivkriegsthese": Die neuen Rechtfertigungsversuche des deutschen Überfalls auf die UdSSR 1941 im Dienste "psychopolitischer Aspekte" und "psychologischer Kriegführung"', *Geschichtsdidaktik*, 12 (1987), 331–42.

—— 'Die Haltung deutscher Widerstandskreise zu Hitlers Rußlandpolitik und Ostkrieg', in *Frieden mit der Sowjetunion* (q.v.), 117–34.

—— '"Der Pakt mit dem Satan, um den Teufel auszutreiben": Der deutsch-sowjetische Nichtangriffsvertrag und Hitlers Kriegsabsicht gegen die UdSSR', in *Der Zweite Weltkrieg: Analysen, Grundzüge, Forschungsbilanz* (q.v.), 568–85.

UHLICH, WERNER, 'Decknamen deutscher Unternehmen und Vorhaben im Zweiten Weltkrieg', *Jahresbibliographie: Bibliothek für Zeitgeschichte*, 44 (1972), 490–534.

UHLIG, HEINRICH, 'Das Einwirken Hitlers auf Planung und Führung des Ostfeldzuges', in *Vollmacht des Gewissens* (q.v.), ii. 147–286.

—— 'Der verbrecherische Befehl: Eine Diskussion und ihre historisch-dokumentarischen Grundlagen', in *Vollmacht des Gewissens* (q.v.), ii. 287–410.

UHLIN, ÅKE, *Februarkrisen 1942: Svensk säkerhetspolitik och militärplanering 1941–1942* (Stockholm, 1972).

UMBREIT, HANS, *Der Militärbefehlshaber in Frankreich 1940–1944* (Wehrwissenschaftliche Forschungen, Abt. Militärgeschichtliche Studien, 7; Boppard, 1968).

—— *Deutsche Militärverwaltungen 1938/39: Die militärische Besetzung der Tschechoslowakei und Polens* (Beiträge zur Militär- und Kriegsgeschichte, 18; Stuttgart, 1977).

Undersøkelseskommisjonen av 1945: Instilling, 3 vols. plus 3 suppl. vols., publ. by the Storting (Oslo, 1946–7).

United States Strategic Bombing Survey, The, with intro. by David MacIsaac, 10 vols. (New York, London, 1976).

'Unternehmen Barbarossa': Der deutsche Überfall auf die Sowjetunion 1941. Berichte, Analysen, Dokumente, ed. Gerd R. Ueberschär and Wolfram Wette (Paderborn, 1984).

UPTON, ANTHONY, F., *Finland in Crisis 1940–1941: A Study in Small-power Politics* (London, 1964).

Ursachen und Folgen: Vom deutschen Zusammenbruch 1918 und 1945 bis zur staatlichen Neuordnung Deutschlands in der Gegenwart. Eine Urkunden- und Dokumentensammlung zur Zeitgeschichte, ed. Herbert Michaelis and Ernst Schraepler, xvii. *Das Dritte Reich* (Berlin, 1972).

USSBS: see *United States Strategic Bombing Survey*.

VAIL MOTTER, THOMAS HUBBARD: *see* Motter.

VAINU, HERBERT, 'Zu militärischen Aspekten der Einbeziehung Finnlands in die faschistische Aggression gegen die UdSSR', *Nordeuropa-Studien* (Greifswald), 7 (1974), 59–68.

VANNIKOV, B., 'Iz zapisok Narkoma vooruženija' [From the notes of the People's Commissar for Armaments], *VIŽ* 1962, No. 2, pp. 78–88.

VASILEVSKIJ, A., 'Soldat, polkovodec: K 80-letiju so dnja roždenija maršala A. I. Egorova' [Soldier and army leader: On the 80th birthday of Marshal A. I. Yegorov], *VIŽ* 1973, No. 10, pp. 39–43.

—— *Delo vsej žizni*² [A task for life] (Moscow, 1975).

VEHVILÄINEN, OLLI, 'Zur Frage der finnischen Kriegsziele', *Bulletin des Arbeitskreises Zweiter Weltkrieg*, 1976, Nos. 2–3, pp. 34–7.

VENOHR, WOLFGANG, *Aufstand in der Tatra: Der Kampf um die Slowakei 1939–1944* (Königstein, 1979).

VOGT, MARTIN, 'Selbstbespiegelung in Erwartung des Sieges: Bemerkungen zu den Tischgesprächen Hitlers im Herbst 1941', in *Der Zweite Weltkrieg: Analysen, Grundzüge, Forschungsbilanz* (q.v.), 641–51.

Vojna v tylu vraga: O nekotorych problemach istorii sovetskogo partizanskogo dviženija v gody Velikoj Otečestvennoj vojny [War behind the enemy lines: Some problems in the history in the Soviet partisan movement during the Great Fatherland War] (Moscow, 1974).

VÖLKER, KARL-HEINZ, *Die Entwicklung der militärischen Luftfahrt in Deutschland 1920–1933: Planung und Maßnahmen zur Schaffung einer Fliegertruppe in der Reichswehr* (Beiträge zur Militär- und Kriegsgeschichte, 3; Stuttgart, 1962), 121–292.

—— *Die deutsche Luftwaffe 1933–1939: Aufbau, Führung und Rüstung der Luftwaffe sowie die Entwicklung der deutschen Luftkriegstheorie* (Beiträge zur Militär- und Kriegsgeschichte, 8; Stuttgart, 1967).

VOLKMANN, HANS-ERICH, 'Außenhandel und Aufrüstung 1933–1939', in *Wirtschaft und Rüstung am Vorabend des Zweiten Weltkrieges*, ed. Friedrich Forstmeier and Hans-Erich Volkmann (Düsseldorf, 1975), 81–131.

—— 'Autarkie, Großraumwirtschaft und Aggression: Zur ökonomischen Motivation der Besetzung Luxemburgs, Belgiens und der Niederlande 1940', *MGM* 19 (1976), 51–76.

—— 'Ökonomie und Machtpolitik: Lettland und Estland im politisch-ökonomischen Kalkül des Dritten Reiches, 1933–1940', *Geschichte und Gesellschaft*, 2 (1976), 471–500.

—— 'NS-Außenhandel im "geschlossenen" Kriegswirtschaftsraum, 1939–1941', in *Kriegswirtschaft und Rüstung* (q.v.), 92–133.

—— 'Zum Verhältnis von Großwirtschaft und NS-Regime im Zweiten Weltkrieg', in *Zweiter Weltkrieg und sozialer Wandel: Achsenmächte und besetzte Länder*, ed. Wacław Długoborski (Kritische Studien zur Geschichtswissenschaft, 47; Göttingen, 1981), 87–116.

—— 'Landwirtschaft und Ernährung in Hitlers Europa 1939–45', *MGM* 35 (1984), 9–74.

VOLKOGONOV, DMITRIJ ANTONOVIČ, *Triumf i tragedija: Političeskij portret I. V. Stalina* , 2 vols. [Triumph and tragedy: A political portrait of I. V. Stalin] (Moscow, 1989). [German edn.: *Stalin: Triumph und Tragödie. Ein politisches Porträt* (Düsseldorf, 1989).

Vollmacht des Gewissens (2 vols.; Frankfurt a.M. and Berlin, 1960–5).

Voprosy strategii i operativnogo iskusstva v sovetskich voennych trudach, 1917–1940 gg. [Questions of strategy and operational skill in Soviet military writings, 1917–1940] (Moscow, 1965).

VORONOV, N. N., [contribution], in *Oborona Leningrada* (q.v.), 199–221.

V sraženijach za Pobedu: Boevoj put' 38-j armii v gody Velikoj Otečestvennoj vojny 1941–1945 [Battles for victory: The combat road of Thirty-eighth Army in the Great Fatherland War 1941–1945] (Moscow, 1974).

VVEDENSKY, GEORGE, 'The Volga Germans and Other German Groups (Complete Destruction of National Groups as Groups)', in *Genocide in the USSR* (q.v.), 49–57.

WAGENFÜHR, ROLF, *Die deutsche Industrie im Kriege 1939–1945*[2] (Berlin, 1963).

WAGNER, EDUARD, *Der Generalquartiermeister: Briefe und Tagebuchaufzeichnungen des Generalquartiermeisters des Heeres General der Artillerie Eduard Wagner*, ed. Elisabeth Wagner (Munich and Vienna, 1963).

WAGNER, RAIMUND, 'Die kriegsökonomische Vorbereitung des Überfalls auf die Sowjetunion und die Rolle der militärischen Wirtschaftsorganisation des Oberkommandos der faschistischen Wehrmacht', in *Auf antisowjetischem Kriegskurs* (q.v.), 260–303.

WAGNER, WILFRIED, *Belgien in der deutschen Politik während des Zweiten Weltkrieges* (Wehrwissenschaftliche Forschungen, Abt. Militärgeschichtliche Studien, 18; Boppard, 1974).

WALDE, KARL J., *Guderian* (Frankfurt a.M., 1976).

WANGEL, CARL-AXEL, 'Verteidigung gegen den Krieg', in *Schwedische und schweizerische Neutralität* (q.v.), 30–47.

WARLIMONT, WALTER, *Im Hauptquartier der deutschen Wehrmacht 1939–1945: Grundlagen, Formen, Gestalten* (Frankfurt a.M. and Bonn, 1962).

WÄSSTRÖM, SVEN, 'Schweden als Arena der Nachrichtendienste', in *Schwedische und schweizerische Neutralität* (q.v.), 120–7.

WATZDORF, BERNHARD, 'Lehren aus der Geschichte: Zum 30. Jahrestag des Überfalls auf die UdSSR', *Mitteilungsblatt der Arbeitsgemeinschaft ehemaliger Offiziere*, 14/6 (1971), 13–15.

WEBER, REINHOLD, R., *Die Entstehungsgeschichte des Hitler-Stalin-Paktes 1939* (Europäische Hochschulschriften, 3rd series, 141; Frankfurt a.M. and Berne, 1990).

WEBER, THEO, *Die Luftschlacht um England* (Wiesbaden, 1956).

WEBER, WOLFRAM, *Die innere Sicherheit im besetzten Belgien und Nordfrankreich 1940–1944: Ein Beitrag zur Geschichte der Besatzungsverwaltungen* (Düsseldorf, 1978).

WEGNER, BERND, 'Die Garde des "Führers" und die "Feuerwehr" der Ostfront: Zur neueren Literatur über die WAFFEN-SS', *MGM* 23 (1978), 210–36.

—— 'Auf dem Weg zur pangermanischen Armee: Dokumente zur Entstehungsgeschichte des III. ("germanischen") SS-Panzerkorps', *MGM* 28 (1980), 101–36.

—— *Hitlers Politische Soldaten: Die Waffen-SS 1933–1945. Studien zu Leitbild, Struktur und Funktion einer nationalsozialistischen Elite*[4] (Paderborn, 1990).

Wehrgeographischer Atlas der Union der Sozialistischen Sowjetrepubliken, ed. Oskar Ritter von Niedermayer (Berlin, 1941).

WEINBERG, GERHARD L., 'Der deutsche Entschluß zum Angriff auf die Sowjetunion', *VfZG* 1 (1953), 301–18.

—— 'Deutschlands Wille zum Krieg: Die internationalen Beziehungen 1937–1939', in *Sommer 1939* (q.v.), 15–32.

WEINKNECHT, FRIEDRICH, 'Der Generalquartiermeister des Heeres: Amt und Mensch', in E. Wagner, *Generalquartiermeister* (q.v.), 247–60.

—— 'Der Ostfeldzug', in Wagner, *Generalquartiermeister*, 261–71.

'Weiterer Ausbau der deutsch-russischen Zusammenarbeit', *Deutsche Wirtschaftszeitung*, 38/2 (1941), 24.

WEIZSÄCKER, ERNST VON, *Erinnerungen: Mein Leben*, ed. Richard von Weizsäcker (Munich, Leipzig, and Freiburg, 1950).

—— *Die Weizsäcker-Papiere*, ed. Leonidas E. Hill, 2 vols. (Frankfurt a.M., Berlin, and Vienna, 1974–82).

Weltherrschaft im Visier: Dokumente zu den Europa- und Weltherrschaftsplänen des deutschen Imperialismus von der Jahrhundertwende bis Mai 1945, ed. with intro. by Wolfgang Schumann and Ludwig Nestler (Berlin, 1975).

Weltkrieg 1914 bis 1918, Der: Die militärischen Operationen zu Lande, ii. *Die Befreiung Ostpreußens*, ed. at the Reichsarchiv (Berlin, 1925); iv. *Der Marne-Feldzug: Die Schlacht*, ed. at the Reichsarchiv (Berlin, 1926); xiii. *Die Kriegführung im Sommer und*

Herbst 1917: Die Ereignisse außerhalb der Westfront bis November 1918, for the Army High Command, ed. Kriegsgeschichtliche Forschungsanstalt des Heeres (Berlin, 1942).

Weltpolitik II: 14 Vorträge. Für die Ranke-Gesellschaft—Vereinigung für Geschichte im öffentlichen Leben, ed. Oswald Hauser (Göttingen, Frankfurt a.M., and Zurich, 1975).

'Weltwirtschaft im Kriegszustand', *Der Vierjahresplan*, 3 (1939), 1196.

WENDT, BERND-JÜRGEN, 'Südosteuropa in der nationalsozialistischen Großraumwirtschaft: Eine Antwort auf Alan S. Milward', in *Der 'Führerstaat': Mythos und Realität. Studien zur Struktur der Politik des Dritten Reiches*, ed. G. Hirschfeld and L. Kettenacker (Veröffentlichungen des Deutschen Historischen Instituts London, 8; Stuttgart, 1981), 414–27.

Wer ist der Imperialist? Deutsche Ausgabe einer Veröffentlichung des amerikanischen Gewerkschaftsbundes AFL-CIO (Stuttgart, 1973).

WERTH, ALEXANDER, *Russia at War 1941–1945* (London, 1964).

WEST, JOHN MILLER, 'German–Swedish Relations, 1939–1942' (diss. Univ. of Denver, 1976).

WETTE, WOLFRAM, 'Hitlerfaschismus, Kriegspropaganda und öffentliche Meinung', *MGM* 12 (1972), 173–90.

——'Über die Wiederbelebung des Antibolschewismus mit historischen Mitteln. Oder: Was steckt hinter der Präventivkriegsthese?', in *Geschichtswende* (q.v.), 86–115.

WETZLER, PETER, 'Kaiser Hirohito und der Krieg im Pazifik: Zur politischen Verantwortung des Tennô in der modernen japanischen Geschichte', *VfZG* 37 (1989), 611–44.

WHITING, KENNETH R., 'Soviet Aviation and Air Power under Stalin, 1928–1941', in *Soviet Aviation and Air Power: A Historical View*, ed. Robin Higham (Boulder, Colo., and London, 1978), 47–67.

WIESBAUER, TONI, *In Eis und Tundra: Drei Jahre an der Lapplandfront* (Im Blick zurück, 17; Neckargemünd, 1963).

Wilenchik, Witalij, 'Die Partisanenbewegung in Weißrußland 1941–1944', *Forschungen zur osteuropäischen Geschichte*, 34 (Wiesbaden, 1984), 129–297.

WILHELMUS, WOLFGANG, 'Schweden und das faschistische Deutschland im Zweiten Weltkrieg', *ZfG* 21 (1973), 791–809.

——'Die Bedeutung des schwedischen Eisenerzes für die faschistische Kriegswirtschaft', *JWG* 1973-4, 37–56.

——'Das faschistische Deutschland und Schweden während des Kampfes in Norwegen 1940', *Bulletin des Arbeitskreises Zweiter Weltkrieg*, 1974, Nos. 1–2, pp. 83–124.

——'Das schwedische Echo auf die faschistischen "Neuordnungs"-Pläne im zweiten Weltkrieg', *JWG* 1975, No. 1, pp. 35–46.

——'Vorbereitungen der faschistischen Wehrmacht zur Besetzung Schwedens', *ZfG* 23 (1975), 1032–40.

——'Zu den Beziehungen zwischen dem faschistischen Deutschland und Schweden nach dem Überfall auf die Sowjetunion, Juni bis September 1941', *ZfG* 26 (1978), 687–99.

WILLEQUET, JACQUES, 'Les fascismes belges et la seconde guerre mondiale', *Revue d'histoire de la deuxième guerre mondiale*, 17/66 (1967), 85–109.

WINDISCH, JOSEF, *Die Deutsche Nachschubtruppe im Zweiten Weltkrieg* (Rosenheim, 1953).

WINTERSTEIN, ERNST MARTIN, and JACOBS, HANS, *General Meindl und seine Fallschirmjäger: Vom Sturmregiment zum II. Fallschirmjägerkorps 1940–1945. Eine Dokumentation in Wort und Bild* (Hamburg, 1969).

WITTMANN, KLAUS, *Schweden in der Außenwirtschaftspolitik des Dritten Reiches 1933–1945* (diss. Hamburg, 1976).

—— 'Deutsch-schwedische Wirtschaftsbeziehungen im Zweiten Weltkrieg', in *Kriegswirtschaft und Rüstung* (q.v.), 182–218.

—— *Schwedens Wirtschaftsbeziehungen zum Dritten Reich 1933–1945* (Studien zur modernen Geschichte, 23; Munich and Vienna, 1978).

WOLF, DIETER, *Die Doriot-Bewegung: Ein Beitrag zur Geschichte des französischen Faschismus* (Quellen und Darstellungen zur Zeitgeschichte, 15; Stuttgart, 1967).

WOLF, FRIEDA, *Die deutsch-russischen Handelsbeziehungen seit dem Weltkriege* (diss. Vienna, 1941).

Wollt Ihr den totalen Krieg? Die geheimen Goebbels-Konferenzen 1939–1943, ed. Willi A. Boelcke (Stuttgart, 1967). [Trans. Ewald Osers, *The Secret Conferences of Dr. Goebbels, October 1939–March 1943* (London 1977).]

WOODWARD, Sir LLEWELLYN, *British Foreign Policy in the Second World War*, 5 vols. (History of the Second World War, United Kingdom Civil Series; London, 1970–6).

WUORINEN, JOHN H., *A History of Finland* (New York and London, 1965).

YURCHENKO, ALEXANDER V., 'The Ukrainians (Partial Destruction of National Groups as Groups)', in *Genocide in the USSR* (q.v.), 138–48.

ZACHAROV, M., 'Načal'nyj period Velikoj Otečestvennoj vojny i ego uroki' [The initial phase of the Great Fatherland War and its lessons], *VIŽ* 1961, No. 7, pp. 3–14.

—— 'Predislovie' [preface], in *Oborona Leningrada* (q.v.), 5–16.

—— 'O teorii glubokoj operacii' [On the theory of in-depth operation], *VIŽ* 1970, No. 10, pp. 10–20.

—— 'Kommunističeskaja partija i techničeskoe perevooruženie armii i flota v gody predvoennych pjatiletok' [The Communist Party and technical rearmament of the army and navy during the pre-war five-year plans], *VIŽ* 1971, No. 2, pp. 3–12.

ZAMERCEV, I., 'V bojach za Dnepropetrovsk' [In the fighting for Dnepropetrovsk], *VIŽ* 1964, No. 11, pp. 74–84.

Zaroždenie i razvitie partizanskogo dviženija v pervyj period vojny, ijun' 1941-nojabr' 1942 [Origin and development of the partisan movement in the first phase of the war, june 1941–Nov. 1942] (*Vsenarodnoe partizanskoe dviženie v Belorussii v gody Velikoj Otečestvennoj vojny, ijun' 1941-ijul' 1944: Dokumenty i materialy* [The all-people partisan movement in Belorussia during the Great Fatherland War, June 1941–July 1944: Documents and materials], 3 vols., vol. i; Minsk, 1967).

ŽAVORONKOV, S. F., 'Avgust–sentjabr' 1941 goda: Počemu my stali bombit' Berlin' [August–September 1941: Why we began to bomb Berlin], *VIŽ* 1969, No. 4, pp. 65–71.

ZAWODNY, JANUSZ K., *Zum Beispiel Katyn: Klärung eines Kriegsverbrechens* (Munich, 1971).

ZAYAS, ALFRED MAURICE DE, *Die Wehrmacht-Untersuchungsstelle: Deutsche Ermittlungen über alliierte Völkerrechtsverletzungen im Zweiten Weltkrieg*[3] (Munich, 1980).

ZEMSKOV, V., 'Nekotorye voprosy sozdanija i ispol'zovanija strategičeskich rezervov' [Some questions on the creation and use of strategic reserves], *VIŽ* 1971, No. 10, pp. 12–19.

ZETTERBERG, KENT, 'Marskrisen 1941, en alternativ tolkning', *Historisk tidskrift* (Stockholm), 94/1 (1974), 59–81.

—— 'Le transit allemand par la Suède de 1940 à 1943', *Revue d'histoire de la deuxième guerre mondiale*, 28/109 (1978), 59–80.

ZHUKOV, FOGMI, 'The Origins of the Second World War', *Social Sciences*, 11/3 (1980), 22 ff.

ZHUKOV, G. K.: *see* ŽUKOV.

ZIEMKE, EARL, F., *The German Northern Theater of Operations, 1940–1945* (Department of the Army Pamphlet, 20-271; Washington, DC, 1959).

—— and BAUER, MAGNA E., *Moscow to Stalingrad: Decision in the East* (Army Historical Series; Washington, DC, 1987).

ŽILIN, P. A., 'Kak A. Solženicyn vospel predatel'stvo vlasovcev' [How Alexander Solzhenitsyn sang a paean for the treason of the Vlasov followers], *Istvestija* (29 Jan. 1974), 5.

—— *Problemy voennoj istorii* [Problems of military history] (Moscow, 1975).

ZITELMANN, RAINER, *Hitler: Selbstverständnis eines Revolutionärs* (Hamburg, Leamington Spa, and New York, 1987).

—— 'Zur Begründung des "Lebensraum"-Motivs in Hitlers Weltanschauung', in *Der Zweite Weltkrieg: Analysen, Grundzüge, Forschungsbilanz* (q.v.), 551–67.

ZLEPKO, DMYTRO, *Der ukrainische Hunger-Holocaust: Stalins verschwiegener Völkermord 1932/33 an 7 Millionen ukrainischen Bauern im Spiegel geheimgehaltener Akten des deutschen Auswärtigen Amtes* (Sonnenbühl, 1988).

ZUBAKOV, V., 'Kniga-dokument o geroičeskoj epopee Leningrada' [A documentary book of the heroic epic of Leningrad], *VIŽ* 1969, No. 1, pp. 75–82.

ŽUKOV, G. K., 'V bitve za stolicu' [In battle for the capital], *VIŽ* 1966, No. 8, pp. 53–63; No. 9, pp. 55–65.

—— 'Kontrnastuplenie pod Moskvoj' [Counter-attack at Moscow], *VIŽ* 1966, No. 10, pp. 68–85.

—— 'Voenačal'niki vspominajut' [Army leaders remember], *VIŽ* 1970, No. 5, pp. 52–60.

—— 'Bitva pod Moskvoj' [The battle of Moscow], 1. 'Oboronitel'nye operacii' [Defensive operations]; 2. 'Kontrnastuplenie sovetskich vojsk' [Counter-offensive by Soviet troops], *VIŽ* 1971, No. 10, pp. 58–68; No. 12, pp. 43–52.

—— *Vospominanija i razmyšlenija* (Moscow, 1969). [Trans. APN, *Reminiscences and Reflections* (London, 1971).]

ZUR MÜHLEN, PATRIK VON, *Zwischen Hakenkreuz und Sowjetstern: Der Nationalsozialismus der sowjetischen Orientvölker im Zweiten Weltkrieg* (Bonner Schriften zur Politik und Zeitgeschichte, 5; Düsseldorf, 1971).

Zweite Weltkrieg, Der: Analysen, Grundzüge, Forschungsbilanz², publ. for MGFA by Wolfgang Michalka (Serie Piper, 811; Munich and Zurich, 1990).

Zwei Wege nach Moskau: Vom Hitler-Stalin-Pakt zum Unternehmen 'Barbarossa', for MGFA, ed. Bernd Wegner (Serie Piper, 1346; Munich, 1991).

Index of Persons

(Hitler is not listed)

Abetz, Otto III, 1058–60, 1064, 1235
Abramov, N.O. 83
Abs, Hermann J. 167, 1085
Adam, Wilhelm 69
Adelmann von und zu Adelmannsfelden,
  Rüdiger Count 1027
Airo, Aksel F. 445, 450, 465, 971
Akimov, S.D. 860
Aksenov, A.M. 73
Alekseev (Alexeew), Soviet Maj.-Gen. 915
Alexianu, Georg 1025
Alfieri, Dino 280, 1040
Alksnis, Jakov Ivanovič 65, 69
Alt, Erich 363
Ambros, Otto 169
Amelin, Michail Petrovič 66
Anders, Władysław 933
Anisimov, N. 883
Antonescu, Ion 395, 398–401, 405–8, 416,
  428, 457, 548, 604, 606, 1021–8, 1032, 1034,
  1040
Antonescu, Mihai 1021, 1023, 1027, 1028
Antonyuk, M.A. 860
Arnim, Hans-Jürgen von 1226
Aschenbrenner, Heinrich 104, 339, 341
Aschmann, Frank 23
Assmann, Kurt 454
Astakhov, Georgy 98
Attlee, Clement 17
Axthelm, Walther von 363, 366

Bach-Zelewski, Erich von dem 1205
Backe, Herbert 124, 151, 154, 160, 169, 171,
  173, 175–7, 180, 186, 189, 488, 1088, 1089,
  1103, 1143, 1148, 1149, 1154, 1157, 1158,
  1160–2, 1169, 1174, 1175, 1177, 1179, 1185,
  1186
Baentsch, Alfred 615
Bagramyan, Ivan Christoforovič 71, 95, 874,
  875, 884, 885
Bajczy-Zsilinszky, Endre 1030, 1051
Baranov, Pëtr Ionovič 69
Bárdossy, László von 417, 420–3, 1030, 1031,
  1033, 1034
Bartha von Dalnokfalva, Károly 421, 1033
Bartholdi, Gottfried 989
Bassenge, Gerhard 363
Batov, Pavel Ivanovič 72, 884
Baudrillart, Alfred 1061
Baumbach, Norbert von 171, 379
Baun, Major 917

Bayerlein, Fritz von 249
Bazilevič, Georgij Dmitrievič 66
Beck, Ludwig 19, 72, 128, 228, 229, 243, 410,
  411, 413
Becker, Heinrich 427
Beckmann, Theodor 363
Belov, Ivan Panfilovič 65
Belov, Pavel Alekseevič 896, 898, 924
Below, Nicolaus von 333, 518
Beneš, Eduard 70, 99
Berdnikov, Soviet Col. 104
Berezhkov, Valentin Michajlovič 166
Berger, Gottlob 1070–2
Beriya, Lavrentij Pavlovič 340, 867, 909, 912,
  920, 939
Berlioz III
Bernardis, Robert 37
Bernstein, Capt. 1230
Bernuth, Julius von 733
Berzarin, Nikolaj Erastovič 858, 922
Bethlen, István Count 409
Bieneck, Hellmuth 363
Billewicz, Polish Gen. 103
Birman, Soviet Col. 971
Bleicken, Capt. 1243
Blick, Aarne 465, 971
Blobel, Paul 1207, 1208
Blomberg, Werner von 69, 513
Blücher, Wipert von 430, 439, 441, 445, 478,
  976, 984–5
Blumentritt, Günther 733
Blyukher, Vasilij Konstantinovič (Visilij
  Gurov) 62, 64, 65, 69
Bock, Fedor von 48, 256, 284, 497, 506, 525,
  530, 531, 533–6, 576, 577, 581, 583, 584,
  589, 593, 595, 598, 601, 664, 666, 670, 675–
  8, 680, 682, 688–92, 694–7, 701–3, 706–16,
  718, 719, 755, 757, 762, 1046, 1055, 1062,
  1130, 1137–8, 1230
Bodenberger, Wolf 363
Bodenschatz, Karl 334
Bodin, Pavel Ivanovič 884
Boehm, Hermann 465, 945, 966, 967, 971
Boehme, Franz 952
Boehmer, Kurt 465
Boenicke, Walter 363
Bogatsch, Rudolf 255, 332, 356
Bogdanov, I.A. 866
Bohatyrewicz, Polish Gen. 103
Boissel, Jean 1059
Bojarsky, Vladimir Il'ič 88

Boldin, Ivan Vasil'evič 112, 886–9, 891, 896, 898, 901, 924
Bonch-Bruevich, Michail Dmitrievič 56
Bonin, Reimar von 464
Boris III, King of Bulgaria 1042
Borisenko, Anton Nikolaevič 66
Bormann, Martin 41, 986, 1018, 1050, 1083, 1179, 1197, 1236
Borodin, S.N. 91
Borus, Josef 409, 1031
Boskanov, Gaspar Karapetovič 66
Bossi-Fedrigotti, Anton Count von 851
Bothmer, Karl Frhr von 482
Bouillon, Godfrey de 1061
Bräutigam, Otto Felix 196, 489, 1103, 1148, 1178, 1239
Brand, Albrecht 104
Brand, Fritz 104, 784
Brandt, Georg 967
Brătianu, C.I.C. 1028
Brauchitsch, Walther von 13, 18, 22, 26, 28, 225, 227, 240, 242, 244, 247, 251, 253, 256, 270, 283, 284, 301, 302, 305–9, 334, 378, 396, 403, 419, 427, 433, 453, 457, 485, 486, 493, 494, 498, 503, 504, 507, 510, 514, 526, 530, 541, 545, 558, 563–5, 573, 574, 576, 584, 590–3, 598, 601, 618, 619, 621, 634, 664, 671, 674, 683–5, 693, 706, 710–13, 715–19, 721, 723, 1062, 1091–2, 1096, 1104, 1116, 1155, 1161, 1190, 1195, 1199, 1203, 1204, 1209–11, 1214, 1219, 1230, 1234, 1243, 1247, 1253
Breguet, Louis 349
Brennecke, Kurt 537, 633, 638, 642, 738
Brezhnev, Leonid Il'ič 52
Brinon, Comte Fernand de 1060, 1061, 1062
Brockdorff-Ahlefeldt, Walter Count von 739, 740, 747, 748
Broz-Tito, Josip 932
Bruch, Hermann 363, 955, 971
Brüning, Heinrich 388
Bruhn, Richard 1099
Brunn, Joachim von 287
Bucard, Marcel 1059
Budak, Mile 1050, 1051, 1243
Budennyy (Budënny), Semen Michajlovič 56, 62, 556, 774, 783, 836, 837, 843, 846, 848, 871–3, 885, 889, 912
Bukharin, Nikolaj Ivanovič 66
Bürkner, Leopold 459
Bütow, Hans 465
Buhl, Vilhelm 1012
Buhle, Walter 275
Bulganin, Nikolaj Aleksandrovič 891, 917
Bulin, Anton Stepanovič 66
Bullitt, William C. 936
Burckhardt, Carl J. 151
Burkhart, Odilo 1089
Burmistenko, Michail Alekseevič 844, 870,

874, 875
Burylin, Soviet Battalion Commissar 915
Busch, Ernst 538, 546, 650, 653, 737–9, 741, 747, 749, 777
Buschenhagen, Erich 279, 446, 447, 450, 452, 459, 460, 463, 465, 476, 951, 963, 967
Bushmanov, N.S. 892
Busse, Theodor 404
Bychkovskiy, A.F. 926

Cadogan, Sir Alexander 16
Calinescu, Armand 390
Canaris, Wilhelm 141, 280, 339, 412
Carls, Rolf 382, 460, 465, 955, 956
Carol II, King of Romania 388–93, 395, 399, 414
Čatloš, Ferdinand 426–8, 1034–7
Cavallero, Ugo 1038, 1039
Černák, Matúš 427
Chachan'jan, Grigorij Davidovič 66
Chales de Beaulieu, Walter 542, 726
Chamberlain, Neville 34, 108
Chapaev, Vasilij Ivanovič 56
Chappuis, Friedrich-Wilhelm von 1056
Cherepanov, Soviet Gen. 971
Cherevichenko, Jakov Timofeevič 83, 112, 883, 902, 927
Christian X, King of Denmark 1006, 1012
Churchill, Winston S. 14–17, 27, 33, 46, 115, 454, 850, 929, 930, 932, 934, 935, 937–9, 984
Ciano, Galeazzo Count 439, 1040, 1041
Ciuperca, Nicolae 407
Clausen, Frits 1004, 1006, 1012, 1078, 1080
Clausewitz, Carl von 26, 49
Clémenti, Pierre 1059
Clodius, Carl August 129, 398, 1022, 1023
Clössner, Heinrich 1195
Codreanu, Corneliu Zelea 387, 388
Coelln, von, Maj. 37
Constantini, Pierre 1059, 1060
Criegern, Dietrich Georg von 363
Cripps, Sir Richard Stafford 17, 18, 98, 112, 937, 938
Crome, Hans 1059
Croon, Hans 1088
Csáky, Graf István 414
Cvetkovič, Dragiša 415
Czernicki, Polish Admiral 103

Daladier, Édouard 108
Dallin, Alexander 850
Darányi, Kalman 411
Daskalov, Teodosi 1042
Davies, Joseph E. 99, 929
Déat, Marcel 1058–60, 1064
Degrelle, Léon 1064–6
Degtyarev, Vasilij Alekseevič 81
Deichmann, Paul 363

Dekanosov, Vladimir Georgevič 50, 112
Deloncle, Eugène 1058–60
Demelhuber, Karl 465, 946, 952, 953, 971
Denikin, Anton Ivanovič 58
Dessloch, Otto 362, 363, 783
Deyhle, Willy 281
Dieckhoff, Hans Heinrich 17
Dietl, Eduard 432, 445, 446, 455, 458, 465,
    941–3, 945, 956, 964, 970, 971
Dietrich, Col. 165
Dimitrov, Georgij Michajlovič 106, 107
Dirksen, Herbert von 70
Dittmar, Kurt 465, 946
Dolmatov, V.N. 888
Dönitz, Karl 170, 955
Donskoy, Dmitriy 853
Doriot, Jacques 1061–3
Dorsch, Xaver 1147
Dostler, Anton 757
Dovator, Lev Michajlovič 894
Drews, Col. 996
Dubovoy, Ivan Naumovič 65
Duclos, Jacques 110
Dukhonin, Nikolaj Nicolaevič 54
Dumitrescu, Petre 407
Ďurčanký, Ferdinand 425
Dushenov, Konstantin Ivanovič 66
Dybenko, Pavel Efimovič 65
Dzerzhinsky, Feliks Édmundovič 58

Eberhard, Kurt 1207, 1208
Eckstein, Otto 679, 690, 1137
Eden, Anthony 50, 98, 935–8, 985
Efimov, Nikolaj Alekseevič 66
Efremov, Michail Grigor'evič 891, 896, 898,
    903
Ehrenburg, Ilja 912, 916, 917
Ehrenrooth, Gustav 465
Eicke (Group E.) 741, 744, 747, 749, 750
Eisenlohr, Ernst 172, 1058
Ekström, Swedish Col. 1072
Elkmann, Gerhard 1088
Engel, Gerhard 561, 717, 1096
Engelbrecht, Erwin 465, 479, 971, 974, 975,
    987
Engels, Friedrich 54, 877, 879
Enkiö, S.L. 465
Erdmannsdorff, Otto von 390
Eremenko, Andrej Ivanovič 849, 867–9, 875,
    885, 887, 888, 923
Erfurth, Waldemar 463, 466, 468, 479, 949,
    951, 960, 964, 965, 970, 971, 972–6, 978–82
Etzdorf, Hasso von 14, 44, 231, 238, 256,
    275, 440, 1047, 1051
Eulenburg, Jonas Count zu 740
Eydeman, Robert Petrovič 63, 66, 69

Fabricius, Wilhelm 390
Fagernäs, Frans Uno 465, 950

Falkenhorst, Nikolaus von 432, 444, 446,
    453, 456, 459, 463, 465, 471, 475, 941, 943,
    947, 949, 951, 960, 962, 965, 966, 970, 993,
    1018, 1076
Fedyuninskiy, Ivan Ivanovič 861, 882, 903,
    921
Fedko, Ivan Fedorovič 65
Fedorov, Aleksej Grigor'evič 888
Fegelein, Hermann 1204
Feige, Hans 465, 945, 947
Feklenko, N.V. 872, 873
Felber, Hans 512
Fel'dman, Soviet Corps Commander 66
Feuerstein, Valentin 967
Feyerabend, Gerhard 243, 245, 255, 259, 262,
    265, 275, 314
Fiebig, Martin 769, 784
Filatov, P.M. 865
Filov, Bogdan 1042
Fischer, Veit 363
Fleischer, Friedrich-Wilhelm 398, 404
Flick, Friedrich 1086, 1089
Förster, Helmuth 363, 367
Franco y Bahamonde, Francisco 41, 280,
    1053, 1054, 1057
François, Jef 1066
Frank, Hans 163, 513, 1193, 1239
Fretter-Pico, Maximilian 1066
Fricke, Kurt 24, 37, 134, 135, 170, 283, 378,
    379
Friedensburg, F. 130
Friderici, Erich 1162
Friedrich, Rudolf 756
Fritsch, Werner Frhr von 36, 250
Frolov, Valerian Aleksandrovič 465, 860, 971
Fromm, Fritz 195, 200, 207, 209, 216, 317,
    713, 760, 1084, 1096, 1182, 1196
Frunze, Michail Vasil'evič 59, 60, 63, 71, 75,
    90
Funk, Walther 115, 131, 135, 157, 184, 1088

Gablenz, Eccard Frhr von 729
Gafencu, Gregor 97
Gailani, Raschid Ali al 115
Gaj, Gaja Dmitrievič (Gajk Bžiškjan) 66
Gajlit, Jan Petrovič 66
Galaktionov, Soviet Maj.-Gen. 847
Galanin, Ivan Vasil'evič 904, 921
Gamarnik, Jan Borisovič 66
Gapich, N.J. 86
Gaulle, Charles de 932
Gavrilov, Petr Michajlovič 841
Gavrilović, Milan 87, 114
Gehlen, Reinhard 240, 536, 537
Gekker, Anatolij Il'ič 66
Gerasimenko, Vasilij Filippovič 865
Gercke, Rudolf 713, 723, 1111, 1114, 1116,
    1130
German, Soviet Col. 919

Germanovič, Markian Jakovlevič 66
Gersdorff, Rudolf-Christoph Frhr von 584, 1234
Gerstenberg, Alfred 395
Getman, Andrej Lavrent'evič 896
Gilsa, Werner Frhr von und zu 730
Glaise von Horstenau, Edmund 1067, 1068, 1070
Gnamm, Walther 362
Goebbels, Joseph 376, 817, 851, 1002, 1003, 1018, 1062, 1236
Goldmann, Nahum 96
Golikov, Filipp Ivanovič 834, 896–8, 901, 924
Golovko, Arsenij Grigor'evič 83, 465, 971
Golubev, Konstantin Dmitrievič 867, 898, 903, 924
Gömbös, Gyula 440
Gorbačev, Boris Sergeevič 66
Gordov, Vasilij Nikolaevič 914
Gorelenko, Filipp Danilovič 465, 859, 971
Göring, Hermann 20, 115, 119, 126–9, 135, 142, 144, 145, 150, 153–7, 159, 161, 165–7, 169, 171, 172, 174, 175, 185, 186, 192–5, 207, 208, 211–15, 326, 329–35, 341, 355, 359, 363, 389, 404, 433, 434, 441, 443, 445, 446, 474, 480, 489, 494, 592, 713, 765, 771, 776, 778, 804, 811, 816, 821, 825, 827–9, 831, 992, 1018, 1027, 1028, 1068, 1073, 1083, 1084, 1086, 1089–93, 1095, 1099–1101, 1103, 1149, 1150, 1155, 1160–3, 1166, 1169, 1173, 1174, 1177, 1236–8
Gorjačev, Elisej Ivanovič 66
Gorodetskiy, Soviet Col. 971
Gorodnyanskiy, A.M. 887, 896, 898, 902, 926
Gorshkov, Sergej Georgievič 905
Gottwald, Klement 114
Govorov, Leonid Aleksandrovič 896, 898, 901, 924
Graevenitz, von, Maj. 586
Grandell, Leonhard 443, 992
Grävell, Walter 131
Grechko, Andrej Antonovič 833, 836, 926
Greiffenberg, Hans von 20, 244, 251, 253, 525, 535, 576, 583, 677, 678, 680, 690, 698, 703, 712
Greim, Robert Ritter von 362, 363, 815
Gren, I.I. 882
Gribov, Sergej Efimovič 66
Grigorenko, Petr Grigorevich 846, 873, 876, 909
Grigoryev, Soviet Gen. 847
Grjaznov, Ivan Kensorinovič 66
Grolman, Helmuth von 677
Gröpler, Erich 363
Grosch, Walther 363
Groscurth, Helmuth 1209
Grosskopf, Georg Wilhelm 165, 183, 186
Grote, Otto von 493

Grundherr, Werner von 1005, 1006, 1008, 1011
Gryaznov, A.S. 922
Grzybowski, Wacław 100
Guderian, Heinz 72, 85, 244, 245, 249, 291, 307, 308, 310, 311, 526, 530, 532–6, 570, 572, 573, 577, 578, 583, 585, 587, 590–3, 595, 596, 598–600, 664, 671–3, 693–6, 698–701, 706, 710–12, 714, 715, 718–23, 725, 726, 729, 739, 762, 770, 773, 907, 1124–6, 1130, 1137, 1253
Günther, Christian 473, 477–9, 998
Gustav V Adolf, King of Sweden 473, 479, 996, 1002

Haakon VII, King of Norway 1013
Haefliger, Paul 1087
Hägglöf, Gunnar 476
Hägglund, Woldemar 465, 971, 973
Hahl, Hans 1086
Hakkila, Väinö 988
Halder, Franz 20–2, 26, 28, 48, 51, 52, 138, 141, 147, 149, 165, 167, 195, 200, 225–9, 231, 232, 239–45, 249–59, 262, 263, 265, 266, 269, 270, 273, 275–82, 284–8, 291–4, 300, 301, 305, 307, 308, 310–12, 315–20, 322, 332, 335, 358, 383, 401, 402, 413, 419–22, 427, 433, 440, 444, 445, 446, 448–50, 453, 457–9, 461, 475–6, 485, 491–4, 497, 499, 500, 502, 508, 510, 520, 525–7, 530–7, 540–4, 547, 549, 556, 557, 559–64, 566–71, 573–81, 583–6, 588–95, 597–601, 604–7, 613, 616–18, 620–2, 625–7, 632–4, 636, 638, 641, 642, 648, 649, 653, 664–7, 670–5, 679, 680, 682–98, 700, 702–5, 707, 709–15, 717–19, 721–30, 733, 736–42, 745–50, 752, 754, 759, 760, 762, 763, 765, 767, 947, 974, 978, 1028, 1031, 1064, 1067, 1123, 1125, 1132, 1134, 1143, 1165, 1248, 1251–3
Halifax, Viscount, Baron Irvin (Edward F.L. Wood) 15, 929, 936
Haller, S. 103
Halm, Hans 1061
Hammerschmidt, Maj. 1060
Hammerstein-Equord, Kurt Frhr von 69
Hanell, Edvard Fritjof 465, 976
Hankey, Sir Maurice, Lord 389
Hanneken, Hermann von 189, 1086, 1094
Hannuksela, Hannu Esa 465
Hansen, Christian 742, 747
Hansen, Erik 397, 399, 402–5, 407
Hansson, Per Albin 472, 473, 478, 996
Hasse, Wilhelm 738, 740, 743, 744, 750
Hassell, Ulrich von 173, 519
Hauffe, Arthur 401, 402, 404, 405, 407, 1021, 1022, 1025, 1026
Hedin, Sven 475
Heigl, Heinrich 363
Heinemann, Lothar von 359

Heinrichs, Erik 448, 450, 458, 459, 461, 465, 970, 971, 972, 973, 975, 982

Heinrici, Gotthard 732, 733

Heising, Fritz 363

Heiskanen, Kaarlo 465

Helmdach, Erich 507, 729, 1225, 1234

Hengl, Georg Ritter von 971

Hennig, Werner 363

Henrichs, Paul 168

Herhudt von Rohden, Hans-Detlef 363

Hersalo, Niilo 465

Herwarth von Bittenfeld, Hans-Heinrich 96, 238, 850

Hess, Rudolf 50

Heusinger, Adolf 146, 307, 402, 403, 427, 485, 537, 605, 608, 616, 624, 625, 627, 629, 635, 682, 686, 712, 740, 744, 750, 752

Hewel, Walther 1039

Hewelcke, Georg 1207, 1220

Heydrich, Reinhard 491–3, 496, 1237

Heye, Wilhelm 69

Heyna, Max 363

Hildebrand, Karl 477

Hilger, Gustav 88, 90, 1103, 1241

Himer, Kurt 416, 420–3

Himmler, Heinrich 34, 153, 156, 483, 484, 492, 495, 817, 946, 1052, 1066, 1070–2, 1078, 1097, 1100, 1183, 1209, 1237, 1238

Hirohito, Emperor of Japan 1045, 1048

Hirschauer, Friedrich 363

Hlinka, Andrej 425

Hoepner, Erich 520, 538, 543, 546, 570, 633, 634, 696, 701, 708, 715, 726, 729, 739, 1116, 1117, 1144, 1145, 1227

Hoffmann, Max 141

Hoffmann von Waldau, Otto 326, 327, 332, 333, 335, 338, 766, 767, 788, 789, 794, 797, 814, 816, 822, 831

Holle, Alexander 955, 958, 971

Hollidt, Karl Adolf 229, 230

Hölter, Hermann 465

Homburg, Erich 363

l'Homme de Courbière, René de 1241

Hopkins, Harry Lloyd 78, 930

Horthy von Nagybánya, Miklós 409, 410, 413, 415, 417, 419, 420, 422, 423, 1028–34, 1040, 1053, 1080

Hösen, Hans 908

Hoth, Hermann 526, 527, 532, 534, 535, 583, 608, 755, 1066, 1124, 1214–16

Hoyningen-Huene, Oswald Frhr von 1057

Hube, Hans Valentin 397

Hull, Cordell 1026

Iacobici, Iosif 407, 1028

Ilgner, Max 169, 1088

Imrédy, Béla 411, 1034

Isakov, Ivan Stepanovič 862

Isserson, Georgij Samojlovič 63, 64, 74

Ivanchenko, Soviet Brigade Commissar 915, 916

Ivanov, P.A. 904

Jacobs, Capt. 1065

Jansen, Col. 143, 148

Jebb, Gladwyn 99

Jebens, Claus 363

Jenghiz Khan 929

Jeschonnek, Hans 253, 335, 336, 339, 353, 355, 363, 500, 501, 744, 815, 816, 822, 828, 830, 832

Jessel, Karl-Friedrich 1228

Joațiu, A. 407

Jodl, Alfred 20, 22, 47, 150, 199, 209, 210, 247, 250, 251, 253, 254, 270, 271, 280–2, 288, 303, 333, 355, 422, 443, 458, 459, 463, 482, 483, 500, 507, 509, 513, 541, 573, 577, 578, 585, 588, 593, 605, 635, 675, 688, 701, 712, 714, 717, 719, 943, 948, 962, 964, 976, 978, 1031, 1050, 1053, 1160, 1233

Jodl, Ferdinand 971

Jonas, Hans 197

Jordan, Rudolf 341

Juncker, Danish economic director 1009

Junkers, Hugo 67

Just, Emil 399

Kabanov, S.I. 864

Kachalov, Vladimir Jakovlevič 848, 866

Kachanov, K.M. 860

Kaganovich, Lazar' Moiseevič 95, 855

Kahl, Siegfried 363

Kahlden, von, Lt.-Col. 694

Kalchenko, E.A. 915

Kalinin, S.A. 866

Kallio, Kyösti 441

Kalmykov, Michail Vasil'evič 66

Kamenev (Rosenfeld), Leo B. 66

Kamenev, Sergej Sergeevič 63

Kammhuber, Josef 334

Kasche, Siegfried 1067, 1070

Kashirin, Nikolaj Dmitrievič 66

Kathmann, Walter 363

Kaufman, Theodore N. 1206

Kayser, Horst 363

Kazalapov, Soviet official 881

Kehrl, Hans 169, 1088, 1089

Keitel, Wilhelm 29, 143, 148, 150–2, 160, 187, 195, 202, 203, 205, 209, 210, 215, 254, 271, 281, 394, 399, 414, 443, 452, 458, 463, 484, 501, 514, 573, 584, 622, 624, 634, 642, 646, 653, 664, 717–19, 737, 738, 741, 753, 822, 959, 975, 977, 978, 980–2, 993, 1033, 1034, 1037, 1042, 1046, 1053, 1068, 1079, 1085, 1093, 1097, 1101, 1144, 1168, 1196, 1197, 1213, 1236, 1238

Keller, Alfred 335, 363, 367, 821

Kennedy, Joseph P. 936

Kersten, Charles J. 909
Kesselring, Albert 335, 359, 363, 366, 664,
  765, 770, 774, 783, 811, 822
Keune, Capt. 511
Khalepsky, Innokentij Andreevič 66
Kharitonov, Fëdor Michajlovič 883, 884, 926
Khokhlov, J.S. 918
Khomenko, Vasilij Afanas'evič 866, 888, 890,
  894
Khozin, Michail Semënovič 90, 861, 863,
  904, 971
Khrulev, Andrej Vasil'evič 838, 914
Khrushchev, Nikita Sergeevič 52, 71, 92, 93,
  833
Kienitz, Werner 561, 562
Killinger, Manfred Frhr von 404, 425, 1026
Kimmich, Karl 1088, 1090
Kinzel, Eberhard 137, 266, 268, 269, 321,
  397, 460
Kireev, Grigorij Petrovič 66
Kirillov, Soviet Maj.-Gen. 848, 871
Kirov, Sergij Mironovič (Kostrikov) 66
Kirponos, Michail Petrovič 83, 844, 870,
  872–5
Kitsa, Soviet Battalion Commissar 918
Kitschmann, Horst 984
Kitzinger, Karl 363, 1210, 1213, 1239
Kivimäki, Toivo M. 991
Klagges, Dietrich 488
Kleinrath, Kurt 363
Kleist, Ewald von 311, 548, 605, 625–6, 755,
  757, 885
Klich, N.A. 847
Klimov, I.D. 891
Klimovskikh, V.E. 847
Kluge, Günther von 527, 532–5, 537, 678,
  692, 698, 700, 708–12, 715, 716, 719–22,
  725, 726, 729, 730, 732, 733, 1055, 1147,
  1150, 1211, 1234
Klykov, Nikolaj Kuz'mič 860, 882, 904, 921
Knieriem, August von 1087
Knoth, Capt. 892
Knox, Frank 53
Koch, Erich 197, 488, 1083, 1101, 1104,
  1155, 1179, 1193, 1238, 1239, 1242
Koch, Henry 992
Kolchak, Aleksandr Vasil'evič 58
Kolpakchi, Vladimir Jakovlevič 885
Konev, Ivan Stepanovič 865, 885, 886, 888,
  889, 891, 899, 900, 923
Kononov, Ivan Nikitovič 845, 891
Konoye, Fumimaro 41, 1045, 1047
Konrad, Lt. 849
Koppelow, Hans von 363
Kork, Avgust Ivanovič 63, 66
Körner, Paul 155, 156, 334, 989, 1090, 1095,
  1101, 1149
Korobkov, A.A. 85, 847
Korte, Hans 363

Korten, Günther 335, 363
Koskimies, Eino Rafael 465
Kosmodem'janskaja, Zoja Anatol'evna 908
Kosobutskiy, Soviet Maj.-Gen. 847
Kostenko, Fëdor Jakovlevič 844, 870, 873,
  895, 898, 900, 902, 926
Köstring, Ernst August 65, 69, 75, 103, 112,
  198, 231–3, 238, 239, 259, 265, 337, 379, 454
Kot, Stanisław 933
Kotik, Soviet Maj. 918
Kovalevsky, Michail Prokof'evič 102
Kovtjuch, Epifan Jovič 66
Kowalewski, Polish Gen. 103
Koževnikov, Sergej Nikolaevič 65
Kozhanov, Ivan Kuz'mič 66
Kozlov, Dmitrij Timofeevič 905, 927, 928
Kozlov, Evgenij 881
Kramarz, Hans 1038
Krappe, Günther 420
Krasin, Leonid 69
Krauch, Carl 119, 143, 161, 169, 170, 1094
Krebs, Hans 50, 104, 239, 322
Krestinsky, Nikolaj Nikolaevič 69
Kreysing, Hans 465, 942
Kreyzer, Jakov Grigor'evič 887, 890, 896, 902
Kristóffy, József 422
Krosigk, Ernst-Anton von 1031, 1229
Kruglov, S.N. 867
Krupp von Bohlen und Halbach, Gustav 68,
  193
Krutikov, Soviet Maj.-Gen. 971
Krutikov, Alexej D. 116
Krylenko, Nikolaj Vasil'evič 54
Kube, Wilhelm 1239
Kübler, Ludwig 719, 722
Küchler, Georg von 37, 245, 249, 251, 318,
  519, 520, 538, 651, 737–42, 745–50
Kujbyšev, Nikolaj Vladimirovič 66
Kulik, Viktor Georgievič 72, 860, 861
Kun, Béla 410
Kuntzen, Adolf 507
Kurochkin, Pavel Alekseevič 865, 921
Kusserow, Ernst 763
Kutjakov, Ivan Semënovič 66
Kuttig (Stab K) 358
Kutuzov (Goleniščev-Kutuzov), Michail
  Illarionovič 853
Kutuzov, Soviet Senior Political Guide 918
Kuznetsov, A.A. 859, 862, 863
Kuznetsov, Fëdor Isidorovic 83, 858, 867,
  897, 902
Kuznetsov, Nikolaj Gerasimovič 109, 836
Kuznetsov, Vasilij Ivanovič 873, 895, 897,
  898, 901, 913
Kvaternik, Slavko 1050, 1067–9

Laatikainen, Taavetti 465, 971, 973, 977
Labonne, Roger 1060–4
Lagus, Ruben 465

Lammers, Hans Heinrich 41, 488, 489, 1236, 1241

Landfried, Friedrich 150, 191, 192

Langemak, Georgij Èrichovič 66

Lapin, Albert Janovič (Lapiu'š) 66

Larsen, Gunnar 1008, 1009

László, Dezsö 422, 1030, 1031

Laternser, Hans 907

Lattmann, Erich 504, 505, 508, 1231

Laval, Pierre 1060

Lazarev, I.G. 861

Lebedev, Pavel Pavlovič 67, 69

Leeb, Wilhelm Ritter von 256, 497, 498, 536, 542–6, 633–6, 638–42, 647, 648, 650–2, 664, 675, 684, 735–41, 743, 744, 979, 1115, 1206

Lehmann, Rudolf 496, 497, 499–501

Leibbrandt, Georg 166, 186, 196

Lelyushenko, Dmitrij Danilovič 890, 894, 898, 901

Lemelsen, Joachim 1233

Lengerke, von, Maj. 1036

Lenin (Ul'janov), Vladimir Il'ič 49, 53–5, 58, 66, 67, 92, 94, 237, 520, 845, 858, 876, 877, 882, 907, 929

Levandovsky, Michail Karlovič 66

Levchenko, Gordej Ivanovič 884

Lewinski gen. von Manstein, Erich von 243, 538, 539, 543, 544, 577, 607, 611–13, 627–31, 633, 759, 786, 918, 1215, 1216

Ley, Robert 122

Leykauf, Hans 1166

Liebe (German Embassy, Paris) 1059

Liebenstein, Kurt Frhr von 689, 692

Lieth-Thomsen, Hermann von der 68

Lindemann, Georg 738, 747

Litvinov, Maksim Maksimovič (Wallach or Finkelstein) 95, 96, 931

Litzmann, Karl-Sigmund 1240

Loerzer, Bruno 363, 366, 795

Loeser, Ewald 1094

Löhr, Alexander 335, 362, 363, 780, 786

Lohse, Hinrich 488, 1008, 1009, 1238

Loktionov, Aleksandr Dmitrievič 66

Longva, Roman Vojcechovič 66, 73

Lopatin, Anton Ivanovič 885, 926

Lorentzen, Lt.-Col. 363

Lorenz, Walter 464

Lossberg, Bernhard von 238, 255, 257, 270–4, 280, 281, 396, 397, 418, 441, 481, 675

Loycke, Otto 383

Ludendorff, Erich 243

Ludin, Hans 426, 427

Ludwig, Max 68

Lukin, Michail Fëdorovič 845, 856, 865, 888, 889, 891, 892

Łukowski, Polish Gen. 103

Lundqvist, Jarl 465

Lützow, Günther 765, 782

Lvov, Vladimir Nikolaevič 905

Mackensen, Eberhard von 604, 617, 620, 625, 757, 1216

Mäkinen, Einar 971, 973

Malar, Slovak Col. 1036

Malenkov, Georgij Maksimilianovič 889, 920

Malinovsky, Rodion Jakovlevič 72, 834, 872, 883, 926

Malitskiy (Malitzkij), Soviet Col. 915

Maljuk, Soviet Intendant 2nd Rank 917

Malleson, British Maj.-Gen. 43

Malyshkin, Vasilij Fedorovič 892

Mamay, Chief of the Tartars 853

Maniu, Juliu 395, 1028

Mannerheim, Carl Gustav Frhr 75, 319, 395, 430, 434, 438, 445, 450, 453, 460, 463–6, 645, 812, 947–9, 951–3, 959, 960, 965, 966, 970, 971, 972–83, 986–90, 1040, 1074

Manstein, Erich von, *see* Lewinski gen. von Manstein

Marcks, Erich 22, 28, 48, 137, 245, 249–51, 257–9, 261–75, 279, 396, 418, 444, 481, 581, 763

Maria Theresa, Empress 1036

Markulj, Ivan 1069

Marras, Efisio 1038

Marschall, Col. 1230

Marshall, George C. 53

Marty, André 110

Marx, Karl 54, 55, 97

Maslennikov, Ivan Ivanovič 860, 889, 898, 900, 923

Maslov, A.G. 926

Matsuoka, Yosuke 50, 114, 1044, 1045

Mattenklott, Franz 630

Matvijevich, Piot 1195

Matzky, Gerhard 420, 478, 963

Maxim, Sir Hiram 81

Mayskiy (Maisky), Ivan Michajlovič 50, 108, 109, 929, 934, 938, 985

Meandrov, Michail Alekseevič 91

Mehring, Franz 54

Meister, Rudolf 363

Mekhlis, Lev Zacharovič 582, 843, 846, 854

Mensch, Fritz 363

Mensching, Karl-Albrecht 363

Meretskov, Kirill Afanasevich 49, 72, 883, 903, 904, 920

Mesič, Marko 1069

Messe, Giovanni 1040, 1041

Messerschmidt, Willy 353

Meyer, Alfred 1237

Meyer-Heydenhagen, Maximilian 124

Mezits, Avgust Ivanovič 65

Michael I, King of Romania 395, 1024

Mihaylovich, Draža 932

Miklós, Béla von 1029

Mikoyan, Anastas Ivanovič 889

Mikoyan, Artem Ivanovič 341
Milch, Erhard 216, 334, 335, 814, 827–31, 1084, 1085
Minin (Suchoruk), Kuz'ma 853
Minkiewicz, Polish Gen. 103
Model, Walter 729
Moeller, Jens 1078
Mohr, Otto Carl 1007
Mölders, Werner 612, 778, 786
Molotov, Vjačeslav Michajlovič 18, 43–6, 50, 95, 96, 100, 101, 104–7, 109–11, 113, 114, 117, 122, 145, 165, 194, 195, 198, 209, 232, 239, 277, 326, 333, 358, 380, 416, 422, 437–41, 446, 454, 458, 836, 848, 889, 929, 938, 985, 1072
Moltke, Helmuth James Count von 141, 519
Morozov, Vasilii Ivanovič 858, 921
Morzik, Fritz 798
Moskalenko, Kirill Semënovič 926
Moskvin, Soviet Maj.-Gen. 919
Mössel, Wilhelm 335, 805, 826
Müller, Eugen 292, 299, 314, 499, 500, 502, 505, 508, 511, 1199, 1228, 1232
Müller, O.W. 910
Muklevich, Romual'd Adamovič 66, 69
Muñoz Grandes, Augustín 1054–6
Münster, Frhr von Oër, Eberhard Count zu 586
Mussolini, Benito 29, 41, 122, 186, 392, 411, 413, 439, 1037–41
Muzyčenko, I.N. 845, 870, 871, 892

Nadolny, Rudolf 70
Nagel, Hans 165, 1101, 1149, 1160
Nagy, Emmerich von 941, 967
Napoleon Bonaparte 853, 877
Nebe, Arthur 584, 1205
Nejman, Konstantin Avgustovič 66
Neryanin (Aldan), Andrej Georgievič 879
Neubacher, Hermann Theo 391, 1026, 1027
Neuhausen, Franz 157
Neumann, Erich 189
Nevskiy, Alexander 853
Niedermayer, Oskar Ritter von 69, 121, 172, 259
Nielsen, Andreas 363, 464, 465, 971
Nikishev, M.S. 465
Nikishev, Soviet Divisional Commissar 915
Nikišin, H.H. 971
Nikitin, Soviet Divisional Commissar 112
Nikolaev, Ivan Fëdorovič 861
Nikolaev, Soviet Regimental Commissar 844
Nitti, Francesco 94
Nockemann, SS-Standartenführer 495
Novikov, Aleksandr Aleksandrovič 859
Nygaardsvold, Johann 1013

Oberländer, Theodor 1241, 1242
Oberländer 204

Oehquist, Harald 466, 971, 975, 978
Oesch, Karl Lennart 465, 971, 974
Oinonen, Woldemar 465, 973, 976, 977
Oktyabrsky, Filipp Sergeevič 83, 884, 905
Okunev, Grigorij Sergeevič 66
Olszyna-Wilczynski, Polish Gen. 103
Orlov, Vladimir Mitrofanovič 66, 69
Osepjan, Gajk Aleksandrovič 66
Oshima, Hiroshi 1043, 1046
Ott, Eugen 1044, 1045
Otto, Paul 425, 427, 1036–7

Paalu, Paavo 465
Paasikivi, Juho K. 438
Paget, Reginald T. 918
Pajari, Aaro O. 465
Palgunov, Chief of Press Dept. of Soviet Foreign Commissariat 111
Palojärvi, Finnish Col. 971
Panin, R.I. 465, 971
Pankratov, Soviet Col. 918
Pantserzhansky, Eduard Samuilovič 66
Parisius, Maj. 363
Paulus, Friedrich 275, 276, 577–9, 633, 649, 694, 733, 755, 967
Pauly, Capt. 1066
Pavelić, Ante 1067, 1068
Pavlov, Dmitrij Grigor'evič 72, 83, 526, 836, 847, 873
Peresypkin, Ivan Terent'evič 838
Pervushin, A.N. 905
Pétain, Henri Philippe 41, 1059, 1062
Petin, Nikolaj Nikolaevič 66
Petri, Major 119, 139
Petrov, Ivan Efimovič 884
Petrov, M.P. 867, 887
Pflugbeil, Johann 362, 363
Pflugbeil, Kurt 1198, 1220
Philipp, Christian 971
Philippi, Alfred 559
Piekenbrock, Hans 324
Pilfousek, Rudolf 1035
Pittler, Maj. 363
Pleiger, Paul 169, 1097, 1174
Pliev, Issa Aleksandrovič 924
Plisowski, Polish Gen. 103
Plocher, Hermann 359, 363, 815
Plotho, Wolfgang Edler Herr und Frhr von 1203
Pochhammer, Wilhelm von 388
Podlas, Kuz'ma Petrovič 873
Poensgen, Ernst 1086
Pogodin, Soviet Brigade Commissar 914
Pokrovskiy, Aleksandr Petrovič 871, 875
Poletika, Waldemar von 176
Poluboyarov, Pavel Pavlovič 80
Ponedelin, P.G. 848, 870, 871, 892
Ponomarenko, Pantelejmon Kondrat'evič 879
Popkov, P.S. 859

Popov, Ivan Vladimir 1042
Popov, Markian Michajlovič 83, 85, 465, 858, 860, 902, 924
Popov, Vasilij Stepanovič 902
Post, Erik von 998
Potapov, M.I. 870, 873, 915
Potez, Henry 349
Potocki, Józef 96
Pozdnjakov, Vladimir Vasil'evič 91
Pozharskiy, Dmitrij Michajlovič 853
Preobrazhenskiy, Evgenij Nikolaevič 864
Primakov, Vitalij Markovič 66
Pshennikov, Pëtr Stepanovič 465, 859, 896, 902
Pugačev, Semën Andreevič 66
Pulanich, Anton 1036
Purkaev, Maksim Alekseevič 870, 922, 923
Putna, Vitovt Kazimirovič 66
Putzier, Richard 363
Pyadyshev, K.P. 859

Quisling, Vidkun 461, 1013–15, 1017–19, 1074–6, 1080

Raappana, Erkki J. 465, 971
Racovita, A. 407
Raczyński, Edward 938
Radek, Karl (Sobelssohn) 67, 68, 95
Radke, Lt.-Col. 494
Raeder, Erich 19, 21, 23, 24, 39, 46, 109, 121, 253, 377–81, 420, 455, 474, 659, 957, 969
Rahola, Eero A. 465
Raithel, Johann 789
Rakutin, K.I. 885, 889
Rangell, Jukka W. 441, 442, 468, 990
Rasch, Otto 1208
Rausch, Günther 1201
Rechberg, Arnold 161
Reichard, Hans 168
Reichenau, Walter von 548, 562, 565, 581, 595, 603, 618, 620, 621, 624–6, 628–31, 671, 698, 699, 752–5, 759, 1173, 1195, 1209–13, 1215, 1216
Reichert, Jakob Wilhelm 130
Reinecke, Hermann 1097
Reinhard, Hans Wolfgang 1213
Reinhardt, Georg-Hans 538, 539, 543, 708
Reitz, Erwin 433
Remezov, Fëdor Nikitič 884
Renthe-Fink, Cecil von 1004, 1005, 1008–13, 1077
Ribbentrop, Joachim 38–46, 48, 98–101, 105, 107, 112, 115, 116, 122, 195, 283, 398, 414, 421, 422, 427, 435–40, 480, 513, 980, 984, 985, 989, 990, 994–6, 998, 1002, 1003, 1005–9, 1013, 1019, 1028, 1033, 1037, 1040, 1042–6, 1053, 1058, 1068, 1071, 1072, 1078, 1080, 1098, 1237
Richter, Friedrich 175, 1186

Richthofen, Wolfram Frhr von 38, 363, 366, 766, 767, 771, 777, 794, 797, 798, 815–17, 820, 1048
Riecke, Hans Joachim 157, 1083, 1150, 1151, 1161
Riedl, Lt.-Col. 1209
Riekki, Esko 1073
Ritter, Karl 115, 116, 123, 124, 127, 128, 191, 195, 398, 1042, 1051, 1058, 1070
Röchling, Hermann 161
Rogachev, Dmitrij Dmitrievič 83
Rohland, Walter 204
Rokossovskiy, Konstantin Konstantinovič 866, 889, 890, 893, 894, 898, 901, 924
Romanenko, Prokofij Logvinovič 76
Romanov, Michail Timofeevič 843
Roosevelt, Franklin Delano 15–17, 27, 41, 46, 47, 99, 930, 934, 937–9, 1047, 1206
Roques, Franz von 1056, 1192, 1203, 1206, 1218, 1240
Roques, Karl von 507, 604, 606, 1035, 1192, 1199, 1208–10, 1218–19, 1229, 1239, 1241
Rosenberg, Alfred 153, 156, 160, 181–6, 196, 472, 488, 489, 494, 509, 514, 986, 1001, 1008, 1010, 1014, 1050, 1083, 1091, 1095, 1100, 1101, 1103, 1148, 1158, 1193, 1235, 1236, 1241, 1242, 1250
Rossi, André (Angelo Tasca) 97
Rössing, Horst 438, 444, 445, 455, 460, 466
Rosso, Augusto 98
Rothkirch und Panthen, Friedrich-Wilhelm von 397
Rowehl, Theodor 337, 339, 340
Rozengolts, A.P. 68, 69
Rübesamen, Lt.-Col. 1205
Rundstedt, Gerd von 256, 419, 537, 546, 549, 552, 557, 558, 562, 564, 584, 618, 621, 622, 624–6, 699, 717, 718, 729, 786, 1119, 1210, 1213, 1243
Ruoff, Richard 726
Ryabyshev, Dmitrij Ivanovič 872, 926
Rychagov, P.V. 847
Rykov, Aleksej Ivanovič 66, 69
Ryti, Risto 430, 434, 441, 442, 458, 463, 467, 468, 980, 981, 983, 986, 987

Sabiani, Simon 1059
Salazar, Antonio Oliveira 1057
Salmuth, Hans von 1208, 1210
Sandler, Rickard 472
Sato, Naotake 40
Sauckel, Fritz 1179
Savelin, Soviet Maj. 913
Sazontov, Andrej Jakovlevič 66
Sbytov, N.A. 888
Scavenius, Erik (von) 1004, 1006, 1007, 1011
Schall, Col. 1031
Schell, Adolf von 669, 1085, 1127

Schellbach, Oskar 1219, 1223
Schenckendorff, Max 733, 1192, 1200, 1204,
    1211, 1220, 1221, 1224, 1228, 1231
Schenk, Otto 465, 971
Scherer, Theodor 739, 745
Schickedanz, Arno 488
Schimpf, Richard 363
Schlemmer, Ernst 455, 465, 942
Schlotterer, Gustav 157, 184, 1103, 1104
Schmid (Donau-Flugzeugbau A.G.) 831
Schmid, Josef (Beppo) 335, 336, 340, 376,
    823, 827
Schmidt, Fritz 1241
Schmidt, Rudolf 637, 708, 709, 711, 712, 721,
    722, 730, 731, 755, 1232, 1243
Schmidt von Altenstadt, Hans Georg 494,
    495, 1190, 1228, 1235, 1243
Schmundt, Hubert 465, 958, 966, 971
Schmundt, Rudolf 544, 557, 711, 713–15,
    717, 721, 809, 942
Schneider, Erich 163
Schniewind, Otto 383, 445
Schnitzler, Georg von 1088
Schnurre, Karl 98, 115, 116, 128, 131, 192,
    194, 197, 458, 478, 992, 996, 1001, 1071
Schobert, Eugen Ritter von 403, 405, 547,
    1021, 1024
Schönborn-Wiesentheid, Klemens Count
    von 782
Schoenfeld, Fredrick 467, 468, 986
Schörner, Ferdinand 943, 963, 970, 971
Schubert, Wilhelm 155, 1106, 1150, 1159, 1160
Schulenburg, Friedrich Werner Count von
    der 48, 50, 98–101, 104, 107, 109–17, 198
Schulz, Erwin 1210
Schulz, Horst 908
Schuster, Karlgeorg 383
Schwarzhaupt, Lt.-Col. 1036
Schwedler, Viktor von 511, 562, 595, 781
Schwencke, Dietrich 341
Schwerin von Krosigk, Lutz Count 172
Sedyakin, Aleksandr Ignat'evič 66
Seidel, Hans-Georg von 335, 358, 363, 450,
    452, 814, 818, 829
Seidemann, Hans 363
Seidlitz und Gohlau, Hans-Heinrich Frhr
    von 603
Selikhov, Soviet Maj.-Gen. 847
Semenev, Soviet Gen. 847
Serdič, Danilo Fedorovič 66
Serrano Suñer, Ramón 1053–5, 1057
Seydlitz-Kurzbach, Walter von 747, 749
Seyss-Inquart, Arthur 1241
Shabalin (Schabalin), Soviet Maj. 849, 850,
    888, 889
Shaposhnikov, Boris Michajlovič 57, 63, 69,
    70, 103, 837, 842, 848, 867–9, 873, 874,
    876, 885, 887, 894, 898–900, 904, 906, 914,
    920, 922, 928

Shaumyan, Stepan Georgievič (Suren,
    Surenin Ajaks) 57
Shavyrin, Boris Ivanovič 66
Shcherbakov, Vladimir Ivanovič 860
Shevchenko, Soviet Maj.-Gen. 971
Shifres, Aleksandr L'vovič 66
Shilovsky, Evgenij Aleksandrovič 63
Shpagin, Georgij Semënovič 81
Shtemenko, Sergej Matveevič 71
Shtykov, T.F. 859
Shulikov, Soviet Brigade Commissar 915
Shvernik, N.M. 855
Shvetsov, Vasilij Ivanovič 900, 923
Siebel, Fritz 827, 830
Siebert, Friedrich 1198
Sihvo, Aarne 465
Siilasvuo, Hjalmar 445, 465, 950–2, 971
Sikorski, F. 103
Sikorski, Władysław 932, 933, 937–9
Sima, Horia 393, 395, 399, 400
Simonev, Sergej Gavrilovič 80
Sivkov, A.K. 66
Skierski, Polish Gen. 103
Skuratowicz, Polish Gen. 103
Skvirsky, Soviet Col. 971
Slavin, Josif Eremeevič 66
Smirnov, Andrej Kirillovič 883
Smirnov, Soviet Divisional Medical
    Officer 914
Smorawinski, Mieczysław 103
Snellman, Aarne 465
Sobennikov, P.P. 858, 885, 887, 888
Sodenstern, Georg von 274, 554, 559, 563,
    564, 576, 594, 600, 604, 605, 616–18, 621,
    624, 626–30, 752, 754, 755, 759, 786
Sofronov, G.P. 871, 884
Sokolov, G.G. 904
Sokolov, S.V. 923
Sokolov, Soviet Col. 844
Sokolov, Soviet Lt.-Gen. (NKVD) 84
Sokolovskiy, Vasilij Danilovič 901
Solovyev, N.V. 859
Sommé, Walter 363
Sorge, Helmut-Günther 352
Sotenskiy, V.I. 851, 875
Spang, Karl 631
Speer, Albert 831, 1179, 1182, 1183
Speidel, Hans 1059
Speidel, Wilhelm 362, 363, 397, 399, 403, 404
Sponeck, Hans Count von 629–31, 729, 759
Stalin (Džugašvili), Josif Vissarionovič 18, 19,
    29, 42, 43, 49–51, 52, 61, 65, 70, 71, 73–5,
    88–91, 95–9, 104, 105, 107, 108, 110, 114–
    16, 123, 128, 190, 196, 198, 228, 237, 239,
    252, 283, 340, 380, 391, 394, 429, 434, 438,
    440, 454, 466, 520, 582, 601, 660, 833, 834,
    836–8, 842, 843, 846–54, 861, 863, 865,
    867–9, 871, 873, 876–8, 886, 887, 892, 894,
    895, 899, 900, 903, 904, 906, 909, 911, 912,

916–20, 922–4, 926, 928, 930–3, 935, 939, 1061, 1196, 1202, 1241, 1249–51
Stauning, Thorvald 1004, 1008, 1012
Steinhardt, Laurence A. 96, 105, 106, 454, 936
Stephainski (GFP) 1218
Stieler von Heydekampf, Hans 1162
Stimson, Henry Lewis 53
Stohrer, Eberhard von 1053
Strang, William 99
Strauss, Adolf 526, 725, 726, 728, 777, 1222
Stresemann, Gustav 1049
Stuckart, Wilhelm 1240
Stud, Erich 144, 146, 148, 165, 208
Stülpnagel, Carl Heinrich von 548, 608, 1195, 1200, 1201, 1204
Stülpnagel, Joachim von 36
Stülpnagel, Otto von 1059
Stumme, Georg 581
Stumpff, Jürgen 363, 464, 465, 971
Sundman, Finnish Col. 465, 955
Sundman, S.A. 465
Suvorov, Aleksandr Vasil'evič 853
Svensson, Antero 465
Sviridov, Vladimir Petrovič 882
Szálasi, Ferenc 410, 415, 1034
Szombathelyi, Ferenc 1029–31, 1033, 1034
Sztójay, Döme 415, 416, 421–4, 1051

Talvela, Paavo 445, 465, 475, 973
Tamerlane 929
Tamm, Fabian 473
Tanner, Väinö 430, 988, 989, 992
Tapola, Kustaa 465
Tarasov, G.F. 923
Tataranu, Nicolae 407, 1025
Teleki, Graf Pál 411, 412, 414, 415, 417
Terboven, Josef 452, 970, 1013, 1014, 1016–18, 1075, 1076
Ter-Nedden, Wilhelm 157
Thörnell, Olof 477, 995
Thomas, Georg 41, 126, 143–8, 150–7, 159–61, 166, 167, 171, 173, 175, 177, 179, 181, 182, 185, 187, 189, 191–3, 195, 197, 199, 202, 203, 281, 394, 414, 434, 443, 482, 760, 830, 989, 992, 1085, 1089, 1092–5, 1100, 1101, 1105, 1106, 1112, 1143, 1149, 1155, 1160, 1161, 1166, 1174, 1176, 1182, 1183, 1185, 1187, 1238
Thomsen, Hans 985
Thorez, Maurice 110
Tiedemann, Karl von 1208, 1210
Timoshenko (Timoschenko), Semen Konstantinovič 75, 76, 102, 234, 665, 666, 671, 755, 785, 834, 836, 837, 848, 865, 866, 873, 874, 883–5, 895, 902, 920, 926
Tippelskirch, Kurt von 228, 242, 243, 256, 266, 268, 270, 392–6, 399, 412, 413
Tippelskirch, Werner von 501

Tiso, Josef 425–8, 1037
Tittel, Hermann 971
Titulescu, Nicolae 388
Todt, Fritz 143, 148, 150, 187, 195, 200–2, 204–6, 210, 215, 306, 513, 703, 959, 960, 1085, 1106, 1159, 1180, 1182
Tokarev, Fëdor Vasil'evič 80
Tolstoy, Lev Nikolaevič 907
Tolstoy, Nikolai 841
Tomberg, Willi 143, 187
Toppe, Alfred 1115
Toussaint, Rudolf 1029
Tresckow, Henning von 520
Treuenfels, von, Maj. 1229
Triandafillov, Kiriakovič Vladimir 63–5
Tributs, Vladimir Filippovič 83, 465, 861
Trotsky (Leib Bronstein), Lev Dadidovič 55–7, 66, 67, 877
Tschersich, engineer 341, 354
Tschunke, Fritz 122
Tsyganov, Viktor Viktorovič 883
Tuka, Vojtěch 426, 427, 1037
Tukhachevsky, Michail Nikolaevič 57, 62–5, 67, 69, 75, 259, 260, 840
Tupikov, V.J. 843, 844, 870, 873, 875
Tupolev, Andrej Nikolaevič 66
Turanec, Slovak Col. 1036
Turtola, J. 950
Twardowski, Fritz von 70
Tyulenev, Ivan Vladimirovič 102, 871
Tyurin, A.A. 887

Uborevich, Ieronim Petrovič 63, 64, 66, 68, 69
Uckermann, Horst Frhr von 747
Udet, Ernst 211, 353, 354, 828–31
Ujszászy, István 412, 420, 421
Umanskiy, K.A. 930
Unshlikht, Iosif Stanislavovič 69
Urickij, Semen Petrovič 66
Uronov, Chief of Fifth Army political propaganda 87, 88
Uthmann, Bruno von 478, 963
Utkin, Soviet Maj.-Gen. 914

Vajner, Leonid Jakovlevič 66
Valera Iglesias, José Enrique 1055
Valve, Väinö 465
Vanyushin, A.F. 892
Varain, Rittmeister 148, 149
Varfolomeev, Nikolaj Efimovič 64
Vartejeanu, Eugen 407
Vasilevskiy, Aleksandr Michajlovič 867, 873, 889, 891, 899, 900, 904, 906
Vasilyev, Soviet Brigade Commissar 917
Veltjens, Joseph 433, 434, 436, 437, 444
Vierling, Albert 363
Vihma, Einar 465, 971
Viikla, V.A. 465, 947, 950

Viktorov, Michail Vladimirovič 66
Viljanen, Kaarlo 465
Vishnevskiy, S.V. 888, 889, 891
Vlasov, Andrej Andreevič 88, 851, 868, 872, 873–5, 892, 895, 897, 898, 901, 911, 921, 924
Vlasov, special leader 1228, 1229
Vogel, Capt. 363
Vörnle, János 421
Voronov, Nikolaj Nikolaevič 72, 882
Voroshilov, Kliment Efremovič 59, 60, 62, 68–70, 78, 101, 103, 243, 544, 834, 836, 837, 848, 860, 861, 889
Vostrukhov, Vladimir Ivanovič 889, 900, 923
Voznesenskiy, Nikolaj Alekseevič 920
Vrangel, Pëtr Nikolaevič 58
Vyshinsky, Andrej Januar'evič 87, 112

Waber, Bernhard 363
Wagner, Eduard 120, 126, 140, 147, 158, 159, 164, 170, 174, 255, 292, 293, 299, 301, 303, 305, 481, 482, 485, 491–4, 689, 696, 723, 851, 914, 1092, 1104, 1105, 1109–11, 1112, 1116, 1118, 1125, 1127, 1132, 1133, 1137, 1140, 1141, 1144, 1145, 1150, 1151, 1164, 1165, 1173, 1174, 1189, 1191, 1205, 1221, 1228–30
Wagner, Gerhard 1244
Wahle, Carl 392, 393
Walden, Rudolf 430, 434
Walther, Gebhardt von 48, 138, 151, 238, 485
Wang Tsching-wei 1045
Warlimont, Walter 215, 247, 281, 432, 499, 500, 508, 509, 591, 605, 675, 943, 951, 965, 967, 970, 980
Weber, Max 28
Weber, Oberkriegsgerichtsrat 506, 511
Wedel, Hasso von 507, 515
Weichs, Maximilian Frhr von 527, 727, 730
Weisenberger, Karl 971
Weizsäcker, Ernst Frhr von 14, 21, 48, 123, 171, 198, 231, 251, 427, 440, 477, 985, 990, 1006, 1008–10, 1019, 1038, 1047, 1050, 1051, 1058, 1070
Welles, Sumner 17, 99, 930, 939
Werth, Alexander 90, 91
Werth, Henrik 412, 414, 419–23, 1029–30
Westrick, Ludger 1059
Wied, Viktor Prince zu 1072
Wiehl, Emil Karl Josef 124
Wietersheim, Gustav von 552
Wild, Wolfgang von 363, 367, 800, 801

Winell, Claës Bertel 465
Winneberger, Capt. 1062
Wirth, Josef 67
Witting, Rolf 430, 434, 477, 980, 984, 986, 987, 990, 1052
Witting, Walter 1099
Wittmer, Berthold 1231
Wodarg, Rudolf 358, 826
Woermann, Ernst 109, 1023, 1042
Wolter, Hans 827
Wrede, Theodor Frhr von 412
Wühlisch, Heinz von 363, 801
Wuttke, Landrat 1239

Yakir, Iona Ėmmanuilovič 63–5, 69
Yakovlev, Vsevolod Fëdorovič 883
Yegorov, Aleksandr Ivanovič 57, 62, 63, 65, 69
Yeliseev, A.B. 864
Yeremin (Jeremin), Soviet Col. 915
Yermakov, A.N. 885–7, 890
Yershakov, F.A. 865, 889, 891
Yeshov, Nikolaj Ivanovič 67
Yonai, Mitsumasa 40
Yrsch, Count, Maj. 1218, 1219
Yudenich, Nikolaj Nikolaevič 58
Yushkevich, Vasilij Aleksandrovič 890, 898

Zakharkin, Ivan Grigor'evič 891, 894, 896, 898, 901, 903, 924
Zakharov, Matvej Vasil'evič 71, 74
Zaleski, August 936
Zaytsev, Soviet Regimental Commissar 919
Zeitzler, Kurt 359, 627
Zerbel, Alfred 559
Zhdanov, Andrej Aleksandrovič 112, 859, 860, 862, 863, 882, 904
Zhilenkov, Georgij Nikolaevič 892
Zhmachenko, F.F. 91
Zhukov, Gavriil Vasil'evič 871, 884
Zhukov, Georgij Konstantinovič 71, 86, 87, 699, 834, 837, 847, 848, 854, 861–4, 867, 873, 886, 889–91, 894–6, 917–19, 924–6, 928
Ziegler, industrialist 1087
Zingales, Francesco 1038, 1040
Zinnemann, Maj. 1106
Zinovyev (Hirsch Apfelbaum), Grigorij 66
Zlobin, V.M. 867
Zof, Vjačeslav Ivanovič 68, 69
Zonberg, Žan Fricevič 66
Zorn, Hans 747
Zorya, Soviet Gen. 984